PALMER'S COMPANY LAW

VOLUME I

AUSTRALIA

The Law Book Company Ltd.
Sydney : Melbourne : Brisbane

CANADA AND U.S.A.

The Carswell Company Ltd.
Agincourt, Ontario

INDIA

N. M. Tripathi Private Ltd.
Bombay
and
Eastern Law House Private Ltd.
Calcutta and Delhi
M.P.P. House
Bangalore

ISRAEL

Steimatzky's Agency Ltd.
Jerusalem : Tel Aviv : Haifa

MALAYSIA : SINGAPORE : BRUNEI

Malayan Law Journal (Pte.) Ltd.
Singapore

NEW ZEALAND

Sweet & Maxwell (N.Z.) Ltd.
Auckland

PAKISTAN

Pakistan Law House
Karachi

All rights reserved.
No part of this publication may be reproduced or transmitted in any form or by any means, electronic, mechanical, photocopying, recording or otherwise, or stored in any retrieval system of any nature, without the written permission of the copyright holder and the publisher, application for which shall be made to the publisher.

PALMER'S COMPANY LAW

by

CLIVE M. SCHMITTHOFF

LL.M., LL.D. (London), DR.JUR. (Berlin), DRES.h.c., Hon.F.I.Ex.;
of Gray's Inn, Barrister;
Visiting Professor in International Business Law at the City University;
Hon. Professor of Law at the University of Kent at Canterbury;
Hon. Professor of Law at the Ruhr-Universität Bochum

in collaboration with

PAUL L. DAVIES, M.A., LL.M.
Fellow of Balliol College, Oxford;
Lecturer in Law at the University of Oxford

JOHN H. FARRAR, LL.M., PH.D.
Solicitor; Barrister (N.Z.);
Professor of Law at University College Cardiff

MAURICE KAY, LL.B., PH.D.(Sheffield)
of Gray's Inn, Barrister;
Visiting Professor of Law at the University of Keele

and

GEOFFREY K. MORSE, LL.B.(Newcastle)
of Lincoln's Inn, Barrister;
Reader in Law at the University of Liverpool

VOLUME I
THE TREATISE

LONDON • STEVENS & SONS
EDINBURGH • W. GREEN & SON
1982

First Edition	(1898)	By Sir Francis Beaufort Palmer
Second Edition	(1898)	
Third Edition	(1901)	
Fourth Edition	(1902)	
Fifth Edition	(1905)	
Second Impression	(1907)	
Sixth Edition	(1909)	
Seventh Edition	(1909)	
Eighth Edition	(1910)	
Ninth Edition	(1911)	
Second Impression	(1912)	
Tenth Edition	(1916)	By A. F. Topham
Eleventh Edition	(1921)	
Twelfth Edition	(1924)	
Thirteenth Edition	(1929)	
Fourteenth Edition	(1930)	By A. F. Topham and A. M. R. Topham
Fifteenth Edition	(1933)	
Second Impression	(1934)	
Third Impression	(1935)	
Sixteenth Edition	(1938)	
Seventeenth Edition	(1942)	By His Honour Judge Topham
Second Impression	(1943)	
Third Impression	(1944)	
Fourth Impression	(1948)	
Eighteenth Edition	(1948)	
Nineteenth Edition	(1949)	By His Honour A. F. Topham
Twentieth Edition	(1959)	By Clive M. Schmitthoff and T. P. E. Curry
Second Impression	(1960)	
Twenty-First Edition	(1968)	By Clive M. Schmitthoff and James H. Thompson
Second Impression	(1970)	
Third Impression	(1972)	
Twenty-Second Edition	(1976)	By Clive M. Schmitthoff (with Maurice Kay and Geoffrey K. Morse)
Twenty-Third Edition	(1982)	By Clive M. Schmitthoff (with Paul L. Davies, John H. Farrar, Maurice Kay and Geoffrey K. Morse)

Published in 1982 by
Stevens & Sons Ltd. of
11 New Fetter Lane London
and W. Green & Son Ltd.
of St. Giles' Street, Edinburgh
Computerset by Promenade Graphics Ltd., Cheltenham
and printed in Scotland

Palmer Complete Service: ISBN 0 420 44660 5
This Volume Only: ISBN 0 420 45760 7 (Special Edition)

Stevens & Sons Ltd., London

1982

EDITORS

CLIVE M. SCHMITTHOFF

LL.M., LL.D. (London), DR.JUR. (Berlin), DRES.h.c., Hon.F.I.Ex.;
of Gray's Inn, Barrister;
Visiting Professor in International Business Law at the City University;
Hon. Professor of Law at the University of Kent at Canterbury;
Hon. Professor of Law at the Ruhr-Universität Bochum

in collaboration with

PAUL L. DAVIES, M.A., LL.M.
Fellow of Balliol College, Oxford;
Lecturer in Law at the University of Oxford

JOHN H. FARRAR, LL.M., PH.D.
Solicitor; Barrister (N.Z.);
Professor of Law at University College Cardiff

MAURICE KAY, LL.B., PH.D.(Sheffield)
of Gray's Inn, Barrister;
Visiting Professor of Law at the University of Keele

and

GEOFFREY K. MORSE, LL.B.(Newcastle)
of Lincoln's Inn, Barrister;
Reader in Law at the University of Liverpool

Specialist Editors

Scots Law
DAVID A. BENNETT, M.A. LL.B.(Edinburgh), W.S.
Solicitor (Edinburgh)

Accounting
PETER A. BIRD, B.SC.(ECON.)(London), F.C.A.
Professor of Accounting at the University of Kent, Canterbury

Practice Notes
S. J. S. ELEY, F.C.I.S.

Tax Law
GEOFFREY K. MORSE

PREFACE

Sir Francis Palmer indicated the object of this work in a passage which appeared in the Preface to all nine Editions prepared by the author himself and which, it is suggested, should always introduce this work. These are his words:

"The author has laboured to make the work practically useful not only to lawyers and to students of law, but generally to businessmen; for nowadays, looking to the vast number of persons interested as directors, shareholders, officials, customers, creditors or otherwise in companies, there are but few businessmen who can escape the task of acquiring some knowledge of company law."

The Editors of this—the twenty-third—Edition have attempted to bring up to date Sir Francis Palmer's work in the spirit expressed in that passage, although the fundamental changes which have taken place in company law and practice since the work was first published have made it necessary to present it in an entirely new form.

These changes are, indeed, fundamental. In the more than 84 years which have passed since Sir Francis gave the famous lectures on which the work was originally founded, company law has become the law of business organisation and management in Great Britain. In the wider context of business law, company law has become a discipline of its own, with its own characteristics and its own atmosphere. The mechanics of that discipline appear to be complex and technical but the intricate legal pattern at once assumes life and significance if considered against its extra-legal background. Many tendencies have shaped that background, foremost amongst them the influence of the professional element on company affairs, the effect of taxation on company operations, and the acceptance of the principle of social responsibility in the conduct of company affairs. Today Sir Francis Palmer's aim to make this work practically useful to the lawyer and businessman can only be achieved if these tendencies are duly taken into account when the legal framework of companies is considered.

Company law has acquired a new dimension. The recognition of the principle of social responsibility implies that the function of the company in the economic life of the nation has changed. This principle has now found statutory expression in section 46 of the Companies Act 1980. The company is no longer regarded—as in the liberal age—as an instrument for extracting the highest profits for the financial benefit of the shareholders. It has ceased to be the sole concern of directors, shareholders and creditors. The employees of the enterprise and the community as a whole have likewise a legitimate interest in its well-being. It is therefore necessary in this work, which attempts to give a complete account of company practice in the United Kingdom, to treat the legal aspects of the company in their financial, industrial and social setting. This approach will enable the practitioner, the businessman and the student to appreciate the present structure of company law.

Further, the law of the European Economic Communities has made a considerable impact on the company law of the United Kingdom. The EEC has set itself the ambitious task of harmonising the company laws of its members because without the creation of a "common market of companies" the economic aims of the EEC cannot be attained. The harmonisation of company law in the EEC is one of the major legal developments of the twentieth century. It is mainly carried out by Directives adopted by the Council of Ministers. The Member States are obliged to give effect to these Directives in their national jurisdictions. After its accession to the EEC the United Kingdom enacted the European Communities Act 1972; section 9 of this enactment seeks to give effect in Great Britain to the First EEC Directive on Company Law Harmonisation, which had been adopted by the Council of Ministers in 1968. The Companies Acts 1980 and 1981 are designed to introduce into the law of Great Britain the provisions of the Second and Fourth EEC Directives of 1976 and 1978 respectively. The United Kingdom was one of the first Member States to give effect to these two EEC Directives in the national jurisdiction. The process of company law harmonisation in the EEC is not concluded yet. Further Harmonisation Directives are already adopted by the Council of Ministers and others are planned. On the whole, the influence of EEC law has been beneficial. It has stimulated early reform and contributed to a highly necessary modernisation of British company law.

The recent reform of British company law has advanced in a piecemeal fashion. At present the statutory provisions on this subject are contained in not less than six enactments, the Companies Acts 1948 (still the main Act), 1967, 1976, 1980 and 1981, and the European Communities Act 1972, s. 9. Some of these Acts, notably those of 1980 and 1981, are very complicated; perhaps they are unnecessarily complex. The present statutory regulation is highly unsatisfactory. But it should not be overlooked that the present state of affairs can only be provisional. In the end Parliament will have to pass consolidating legislation. It will probably take the form of several Companies Acts, arranged according to subject-matter, similar to the law of property reform of 1925.

The changes introduced by the 1980 and 1981 Acts are radical. The private company has become the residual form of the company and the public company the exception, different from the legal regulation before but more in accordance with economic reality. A minimum capital is prescribed for the public company but not for the private company. Certain shareholders are given statutory pre-emption rights on the issue of specified shares, subject to exceptions. Insider dealing is made a criminal offence and the net of insiders is cast wide. The responsibility of adopting an admissible name for the company rests now on those who wish to register the name and the former requirement of the approval of the name by the Department of Trade is abolished. The company is permitted, subject to certain conditions, to purchase or redeem its own equity shares, and a private company may do so even out of capital. A remedy available in case of unfairly prejudicial treatment is substituted for the former largely ineffective alternative remedy. Many other new features are introduced by the new legislation.

The main change which has occurred in British company law is not, however, in the introduction of new statutory provisions and the reversal of old almost sacrosanct doctrines. It is in the transformation of the character of this subject. Company law has become one of the most complicated branches of law. In complexity it is second only to tax law. This change in the character of company law required the adoption of new methods of presentation. For this reason *Palmer*, as the first of the major reference works on company law, added in 1976, when the 22nd edition was published, a looseleaf service to the treatise which has retained its traditional bound form. The looseleaf service covers comprehensively the whole field of company regulation. In addition to Companies Legislation, it covers Investor Protection, The Stock Exchange, the Take-Over Panel, Merger Control, Accounting Practice, Financial Control, Winding Up, Insurance and Banking Companies, Scots Law, Taxation and miscellaneous other topics. Regular releases published during the year bring the Treatise and the looseleaf volumes up-to-date. In 1982 a monthly publication, *Palmer's Company Law Reporter*, was added. The *Reporter* is designed to inform the company law practitioner as quickly as possible of the latest developments in this volatile subject. In spite of these alterations, the main objectives of *Palmer* remain the same as before, namely to present the living law, as it is today, to the company practitioner, whether he is a lawyer, accountant, company secretary or other professional man, and to present it fully and comprehensively. This approach will enable the practitioner, the businessman and the student to appreciate the present structure of company law and practice.

It has also become necessary to extend the treatment of Scots law further, without in any way reducing or affecting the established usefulness of this work to the English practitioner. The Companies Acts are common to England and Wales and to Scotland and the case law interpreting their provisions is of equal importance to the English and Scottish lawyer. But in three areas divergencies exist: as far as the rules of company law have to be gathered from the common law which, as is well known, is different in the two legal systems, in the law relating to debentures, and in winding-up procedure. These divergencies are fully treated in this work. It is hoped that the new edition will be as useful to the Scottish lawyer and accountant as it has been for a long time to the English practitioner.

A work of such magnitude as the preparation of the present edition could not be undertaken by me alone, in view of the heavy demands of my academic duties and of my practice. I had the good fortune of having been supported very ably by a team of outstanding company lawyers. There were Mr. Paul L. Davies, of Oxford University; Professor John H. Farrar, of University College, Cardiff; Professor Maurice Kay, of the University of Keele; and Mr. Geoffrey K. Morse, Reader in the University of Liverpool. We worked together as a very happy team and were in complete agreement on the aims which we wanted to achieve and the methods which we wanted to apply. My collaborators had already proved their ability, scholarship and skill before. Professor Kay and Mr. Morse were my valued collaborators on the previous edition of *Palmer*. Mr. Davies is the editor of the general section on Companies in the *Journal of Business Law,* Professor Farrar is one of the editors of the section on Insolvency in that Journal, and Mr. Morse is its editor of the section on Securities Regulations. I should like to express sincere thanks to these friends and scholars for their unfailing support, care and devotion to work.

My further thanks are due to Mr. David A. Bennett, Solicitor and Writer to the Signet, Edinburgh, the Editor on Scots Law, on whom fell the heavy burden of enlarging the notes on Scots Law; to Professor Peter A. Bird, Professor of Accounting at the University of Kent at Canterbury, who revised the chapters on Accounting in the light of the new statutory regulations and modern thinking on this subject; to Mr. S. J. S. Eley, F.C.I.S., who brought the Practice Notes up to date in the light of his great experience as a practising company secretary; to Mr. Geoffrey K. Morse who revised the chapters on Taxation, and to the Editorial Staff of the Publishers, who assembled the material in the looseleaf volume with competence and patience. My thanks are also due to Mr. John W. Tinnion, of the University of Leeds, who provided a full and detailed index, which has long been required.

The following gave valuable information and allowed the inclusion of copyright matter: H.M. Stationery Office, The Department of Trade, the Registrar of Companies, the Bank of England, the Stock Exchange, the City Panel on Take-overs and Mergers, the Issuing Houses Association, the Institute of Chartered Secretaries and Administrators and the Institute of Chartered Accountants.

The law is stated as on August 1, 1982, except in Part X on Tax Law, in which the law is stated as on February 1, 1982, but, as far as possible, later decisions and other developments have been noted throughout this volume. The work is kept up to date by *Palmer's Company Law Reporter* and the regular releases to the Treatise and the looseleaf volumes. Further, the latest information on company law and practice is contained in articles and notes of the *Journal of Business Law,* published bimonthly by Stevens and Sons, London.

CLIVE M. SCHMITTHOFF

10 South Square,
Gray's Inn,
London WC1R 5EU.

ADDENDA

Chapter 25—The Prevention of Fraud (Investments) Act 1958
Para. 25–04, note 16, on p. 296.

On September 6, 1982 the Department of Trade published a document entitled "Licensed Dealers in Securities—Draft Rules and Regulations proposed to be made under the Prevention of Fraud (Investments) Act 1958." This document contains the texts of two proposed statutory instruments and three draft general permissions. The object of this publication is to enable persons to make representation on the proposed delegated legislation. The Department intends after the expiration of the time fixed for objections to lay the draft statutory instruments before Parliament and hopes that they will come into operation before the end of 1982. The new measures deal with the authorisation of licensed dealers and their conduct of business. They will impose much more stringent requirements than are in force at present. If approved by Parliament, the new measures will be included in *Palmer,* Vol. II, Part B.

CLIVE M. SCHMITTHOFF

Chapter 46—Remedies of Debenture Holders
Para 46–09, p. 635.

THE TRANSFER OF UNDERTAKINGS REGULATIONS AND THE RECEIVER. The Transfer of Undertakings (Protection of Employment) Regulations 1981, which were made by statutory instrument[1] under section 2 (2) of the European Communities Act 1972, purport to implement EEC Council Directive 187 of February 14, 1977. They introduce automatic transfer of contracts of employment, collective agreements and trade union recognition in the case of certain transfers of commercial undertakings or part thereof to another person. (Regulations 5, 6 and 9.) They also render a dismissal which is connected with such a transfer and is effected for a reason which is not an economic, technical, or organisational reason, automatically unfair. (Regulation 8.) A duty is imposed to inform and consult representatives of recognised trade unions. (Regulation 10.) A complaint may be made to an Industrial Tribunal that these duties have not been performed and the tribunal may award compensation.

Regulation 4 (1) creates an exemption for a hiving down operation by a receiver.[2] In essence, the automatic transfer only operates when control of the new enterprise passes outside the group. This is achieved by providing

[1] S.I. 1981 No. 1794. Regulations 1 to 3 and 10 to 13 came into operation on February 1, 1982 and Regulations 4 to 9 and 14 on May 1, 1982.
[2] The Regulations also apply to a liquidator in a creditors' voluntary winding up.

that the transfer shall be deemed not to have been effective for the purposes of the regulations until immediately before (a) the transferee company ceases to be a wholly owned subsidiary of the transferor company (otherwise than by reason of its being wound up) or (b) the relevant undertaking is transferred by the transferee company to another person, whichever dealing occurs first. At this point, the transfer is to be taken to have been effected immediately before that date by one transaction only. The effect of this is that employees who are in the employment of the parent company at the date of the hiving down are then automatically transferred to the subsidiary. This changes the law and practice in this area in that the regulations will make this happen automatically unless something is done, which is the reverse of the former position. Where employees are dismissed wholly or principally for economic, technical, or organisational reasons, their dismissal will not automatically be unfair (Regulation 8 (2)). Where employees are not transferred, they have only claims against the insolvent company whose assets have been hived down. This is arguably incompatible with article 3 (1) of the Directive and with the obligation of the United Kingdom to implement the EEC Directive of October 20, 1980 on the protection of employees in the event of insolvency.[3] Whether these give rise to legal rights of individuals is uncertain and may need to be referred to the European Court under article 177 of the Treaty of Rome.

JOHN H. FARRAR

[3] See B. Hepple [1982] 11 I.L.J. 29, 34.

Sir Francis Beaufort Palmer
A Biographical Note

FRANCIS BEAUFORT PALMER, the author of this work, was born in June 1845. His father, the Rev. William Palmer of Oxford, was a friend of Cardinal Newman and Mr. Gladstone. Francis Palmer was educated at Eton and University College, Oxford. He joined the Inner Temple and was called to the Bar in 1873. He never took silk but was elected a Bencher of his Inn in 1907. He helped to draft the Companies Acts of 1900 and 1907 and the Companies (Consolidation) Act 1908. In 1907 he was knighted. He was married and had three children. He died on June 15, 1917, aged 72 years.

Francis Palmer was a remarkable man. He began his career at the Chancery Bar without any special advantages, such as connection with leading solicitors or big commercial firms. He was a man of great quickness of perception and exceptional power of work, coupled with a courteous manner and remarkably placid temper. In his young years he went to court. He appeared in *Allcard* v. *Skinner* (1887) 36 Ch.D. 145, a *cause célèbre* of its time. Palmer, who represented the plaintiff, Miss Allcard, was led by Sir Charles Russell, the later Lord Russell of Killowen, and Sir Robert Finlay, the later Lord Finlay L.C. Miss Allcard had joined an Anglican sisterhood, the Sisters of the Poor, and had transferred part of her considerable property to the sisterhood for the benefit of the poor. She then left the sisterhood and was received into the Roman Catholic faith. Some six years after she left the sisterhood, she commenced proceedings for the return of the property, claiming that she had been induced by undue influence to transfer it to the sisterhood. Her claim was dismissed by Kekewich J. and the Court of Appeal on the ground of laches and acquiescence. In the early nineties Palmer found it impossible to attend court regularly and began to devote himself wholly to his prosperous practice in chambers and the writing of his books. No doubt his deafness and his shy and sensitive nature had something to do with that decision.

Palmer's most important work was undoubtedly his *Company Law,* published in 1898. It originated in six lectures which he gave in January and February 1897 in the Inner Temple Hall upon the request of the Council of Legal Education. His other major work was the *Company Precedents.* He also published two small works, one of which was a handy book for solicitors and liquidators; the other related to the formation of private companies. Among his other works was the "Shareholders' and Directors' Legal Companion," which by the time of his death had reached the 24th edition. He also published a book on Peerage Law in 1907.

In his writings on company law, Palmer aimed at a wider public than the professional lawyer. He aimed at making the intricate topic of company law accessible to the educated layman who may find himself in the position of a company director or may hold shares in a company. The fact that his

Company Law was written for lawyers and laymen alike and that it originated in a set of lectures, accounts for some of its unique features. Although the list of cases quoted in the first edition covers not less than 29 pages, the presentation of his subject-matter is lively and easy to understand. The original arrangement of the work was rather casual and a more systematic order had to be adopted in later editions. The last chapter of the first edition consisted of a summary of leading cases, with references to the pages on which they were treated in the text; that chapter must have been heaven-sent to students preparing for examinations. Amusing is Palmer's attitude to *Salomon* v. *Salomon & Co. Ltd.* [1897] A.C. 22. He treated the decision of the Court of Appeal, which had lifted the veil of corporateness, at length and then continued: "This decision caused great anxiety, as well it might, but it was unanimously reversed by the House of Lords." He evidently heaved a sigh of relief at the decision of the House of Lords.

Sir Francis Palmer was a man of refined taste. He collected works of art, including old tapestry and Tanagra ware. In their house in Bryanston Square he and Lady Palmer entertained their friends with thoughtfulness and care.

C.M.S.

VOLUME I

CONTENTS

PART SEVEN—ARRANGEMENTS AND RECONSTRUCTIONS

PART EIGHT—WINDING UP OF THE COMPANY

PART NINE—SPECIAL KINDS OF COMPANIES AND OTHER FORMS OF BUSINESS ORGANISATION

PART TEN—TAX LAW

G. K. Morse

TABLE OF CASES TO VOLUME 1

Customs and Excise Officers' Mutual Guarantee Fund, *Re* [1917] 2 Ch. 18; 86 L.J.Ch. 457; 117 L.T. 86; 36 T.L.R. 311 85–04
Cuthbert Cooper & Sons Ltd., *Re* [1937] Ch. 392.......... 85–10, 85–16
Cutts, *Re* (a Bankrupt) [1956] 1 W.L.R. 728; 100 S.J. 449; [1956] 2 All E.R. 537 85–80
Cyclists' Touring Club *v.* Hopkinson [1910] 1 Ch. 179; 79 L.J.Ch. 82; 101 L.T. 848; 26 T.L.R. 117; 54 S.J. 134 .... 9–15, 9–44, 61–02
Cyona Distributors Ltd., *Re* [1967] Ch. 889; [1967] 2 W.L.R. 369; 110 S.J. 943; [1967] 1 All E.R. 281; reversing [1966] 2 W.L.R. 761; 110 S.J. 329 [1966] 1 All E.R. 825.......... 18–21, 85–84, 87–72

D. & L. Caterers & Jackson *v.* D'Anjou [1945] K.B. 364; 114 L.J.K.B. 386; 173 L.T. 21; 61 T.L.R. 343; [1945] 1 All E.R. 563 18–14
D.H.N. Distributors Ltd. *v.* Tower Hamlets London Borough Council; Bronze Investments *v.* Same; D.H.N. Food Transport *v.* Same [1976] 1 W.L.R. 852; 120 S.J. 215; [1976] J.P.L. 363; 74 L.G.R. 506; *sub nom.* D.H.N. Food Distributors (in liquidation) *v.* Tower Hamlets London B.C.; Bronze Investments (in liquidation) *v.* Same; D.H.N. Food Transport (in liquidation) *v.* Same (1976) 32 P. & C.R. 240; reversing *sub nom.* D.H.N. Food Distributors, Bronze Investments and DHN Food Transport *v.* London Borough of Tower Hamlets (Ref. Nos. 36, 37 and 38/1974); (1975) 30 P. & C.R. 251, Lands Tribunal 18–04, 18–23
Dad's Cookie Co. (B.C.) Ltd., *Re* (1969) 7 D.L.R. (3d) 243 81–11
Dafen Tinplate Co. *v.* Llanelly Steel Co. (1907) Ltd. [1920] 2 Ch. 124; 89 L.J.Ch. 346; 123 L.T. 225; 36 T.L.R. 428; 64 S.J. 446 .... 4–12, 14–22, 37–18, 58–14, 58–16
Dailuaine Talisker Distillery *v.* Mackenzie 1910 S.C. 913; 47 Sc.L.R. 717 79–09
Daimler Co. Ltd. *v.* Continental Tyre and Rubber (G.B.) Ltd. [1916] 2 A.C. 307; 85 L.J.K.B. 1333; 114 L.T. 1049; 32 T.L.R. 624; 22 Com.Cas. 32; 60 S.J. 602 8–13
Dale and Plant, *Re* (1889) 43 Ch.D. 255; 61 L.T. 206; 5 T.L.R. 585; 1 Meg 61–33
Dale (Charles) Ltd. 1927 S.C. 130 87–33
Dalling *v.* Browning (1944) 60 *Sheriff Court Reports* 143 9–08
Danby *v.* Coutts & Co. (1885) 29 Ch.D. 500; 54 L.J.Ch. 577; 52 L.T. 401; 1 T.L.R. 313; 33 W.R. 559 27–19
Daniels *v.* Daniels [1978] Ch. 406; [1978] 2 W.L.R. 73; [1978] 2 All E.R. 89; (1977) 121 S.J. 605 58–14
Daponte *v.* Schubert [1939] Ch. 958; 108 L.J.Ch. 423; 161 L.T. 268; 55 T.L.R. 940 39–41
Davey & Co. *v.* Williamson & Sons [1898] 2 Q.B. 194; 67 L.J.Q.B. 699; 78 L.T. 755; 46 W.R. 571.......... 43–25, 44–10, 44–16
David Alester Ltd., *Re* [1922] 2 Ch. 211 45–06
David and Adlard, *Re*, *ex p.* Whinney [1914] 2 K.B. 694; *sub nom. Re* David & Johnson, *ex p.* Whinney, 83 L.J.K.B. 1173; 110 L.T. 942; 30 T.L.R. 366; 58 S.J. 340; 21 Mans. 148 85–86
Davideson (R. & W.) Ltd., 1937 S.N. 108.......... 32–01
Davidson *v.* Hamilton 1904 12 S.L.T. 353 .... 21–32, 21–56
Davidson & Syme (W.S.) *v.* Kaye and Others 1970 S.L.T. (Notes) 65.......... 18–04
Davies *v.* Elsby Brothers Ltd. [1961] 1 W.L.R. 170; 105 S.J. 107; [1960] 3 All E.R. 672; leave to appeal to H.L. dismissed [1961] 1 W.L.R. 519 18–17
Davies Investments (East Ham) Ltd., *Re* [1961] 1 W.L.R. 1396; [1961] 3 All E.R. 926 *sub nom.* Davis Investments (East Ham), *Re* 105 S.J. 966.......... 60–02, 85–25
Davis (S.) & Co., *Re* [1945] Ch. 402; 114 L.J.Ch. 253; 173 L.T. 40; 61 T.L.R. 403; 89 S.J. 269 86–24
Davis *v.* Bank of England (1824) 2 Bing. 393; 9 Moo. 747 39–29
Davis *v.* Bowsher (1794) 5 Term. Rep 488 42–09
—— *v.* Gas Light & Coke Co. [1909] 1 Ch. 708; 78 L.J.Ch. 445; 100 L.T. 553; 25 L.T.R. 428; 53 S.J. 399; 16 Mans. 147; affirming [1909] 1 Ch. 248 50–11
Davis & Collett Ltd., *Re* [1935] Ch. 693; 153 L.T. 329; 104 L.J.Ch. 340 85–08
Davis (S.I.) & Co., *Re* [1945] Ch. 402 87–98
Davison *v.* King [1927] N.I. 1 76–26
Dawes' Case, *Re* China Steamship Co. (1868) L.R. 6 Eq. 232; 37 L.J.Ch. 901; 16 W.R. 995.......... 41–07, 49–12
Dawkins *v.* Antrobus (1881) 17 Ch.D. 615; 44 L.T. 557; 29 W.R. 511 41–01

TABLE OF STATUTES TO VOLUME I

TABLE OF STATUTORY INSTRUMENTS TO VOLUME I

RULES OF THE SUPREME COURT

RULES OF THE COURT OF SESSION 1965

SHERIFF COURT RULES

Part One

INTRODUCTION

The Organisation of Business in Great Britain

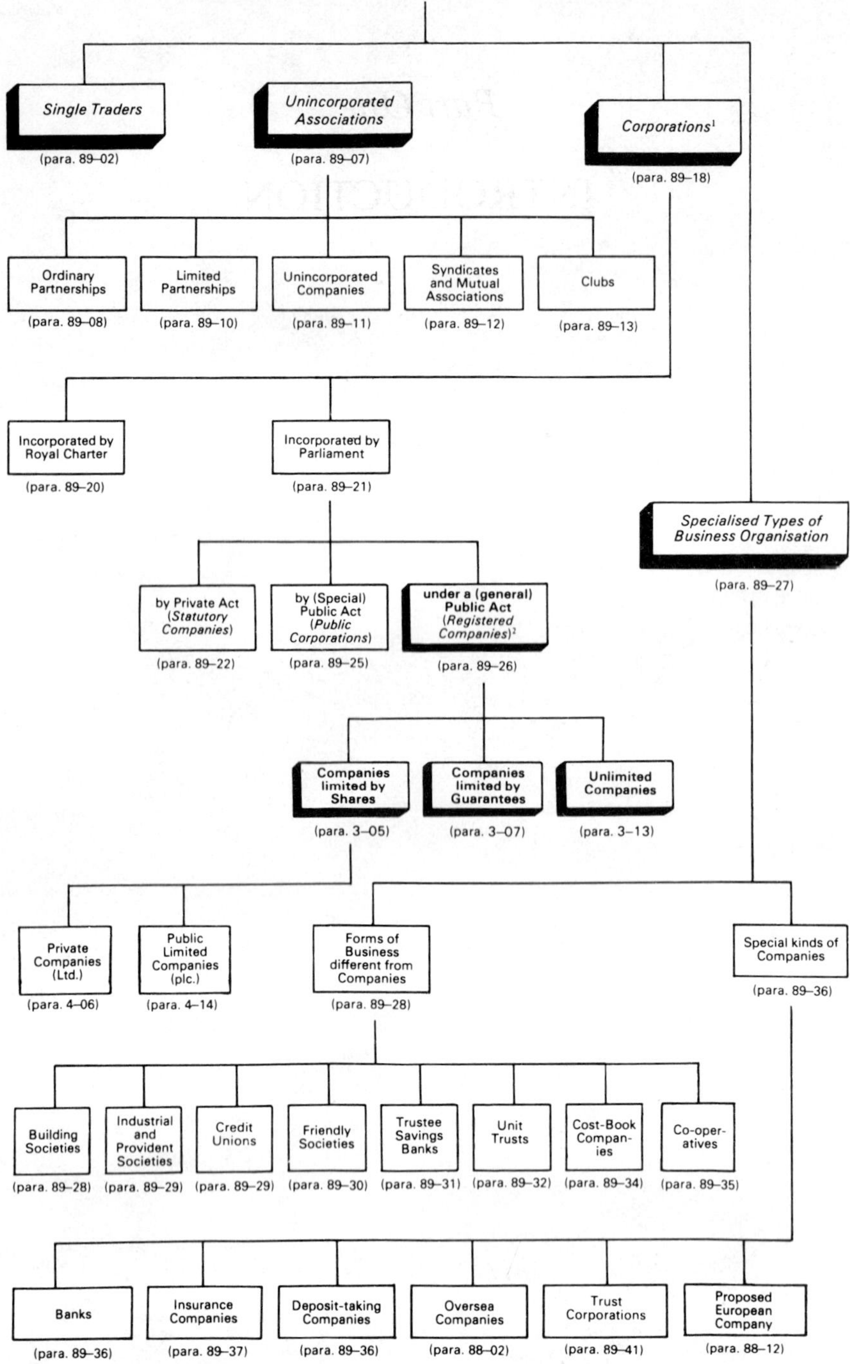

[1] The distinction between corporations sole and corporations aggregate is treated at para. 89–19, *post*.
[2] The distinction between public and private companies is treated at paras. 4–01 *et seq.*, *post*.

CHAPTER 1

THE PLACE OF THE COMPANY IN THE ORGANISATION OF BUSINESS

1–01 THIS work treats almost exclusively of companies regulated by the Companies Acts of 1948[1] to 1981[2] and by section 9 of the European Communities Act 1972. The company limited by shares, one of the types of companies registrable under the Acts,[3] is undoubtedly the most important legal form of business organisation in Great Britain; in its various forms[4] it is adopted by all kinds of business, large and small.

However, important as the company is for modern business, it is not the only form which the law places at the disposal of the businessman. According to their legal characteristics, the forms of business organisation in use in Great Britain today can be arranged as shown on the preceding page.

While it is appropriate to proceed at once to the subject-matter of this treatise, a brief review of the various legal forms of business organisation will be given in a later chapter.[5] There it will be explained that the four major categories into which the organisation of business in Great Britain is divided are:

single traders;
partnerships and other unincorporated associations;
corporations; and
specialised types of business organisation.

Companies incorporated under the Companies Acts fall within the third of those categories, *viz.* corporations. The status of the company as a corporation, *i.e.* as a legal person distinct from its members, is the outstanding legal characteristic which distinguishes the company from other forms of business organisation.[6]

1–02 The Companies Acts 1948 to 1981 deal mainly with the organisation of the company, its creation, constitution, relationship to members and

---

[1] In this work all references to sections are to those of the Companies Act 1948, unless stated otherwise. References to the Companies Acts 1967, 1976, 1980 and 1981 are introduced by reference to the amending Act in question, *e.g.* "1981 Act." References to articles are to those of Table A of the Act of 1948. For convenience and where it is obvious from the context "the Acts" refer to the 1948 Act and the amending Acts, and to section 9 of the European Communities Act 1972.
References to sections 106A and 106K of the 1948 Act are to the sections inserted in that Act as "Part III A" by the Schedule to and section 6 of the Companies (Floating Charges and Receivers) (Scotland) Act 1972.

[2] On the earlier Companies Acts, see paras. 2–09 *et seq*.

[3] On the types of companies registrable under the Acts, see paras. 3–01 *et seq., post*.

[4] On the forms of companies admitted by the Acts, see paras. 4–01 *et seq., post*.

[5] See para. 89–01, *post*.

[6] On the corporate existence of the company, see para. 18–01, *post*; on the power to create corporations generally, see para. 89–18, *post*. It should be noted, however, that a Scottish partnership has legal personality distinct from its members (Partnership Act 1890, s. 4 (2)).

creditors, its management and winding up and dissolution. However, the position of the company in modern business is not determined by those factors alone. To appreciate it properly, other aspects, some of them outside the confines of company law in the traditional sense, have to be taken into account and are reflected in the treatment of the subject in the following pages. They are:

1–03 1. The administration of the affairs of companies is now widely entrusted to persons of professional standing. In the case of public companies this, or at least proven experience, is, indeed, required by section 79 of the 1980 Act.

Their recognised practice is summarised in the Practice Notes appended to various chapters of this work.

2. The requirement of public accountability, which is a prominent feature of the Companies Acts,[7] makes it necessary to pay due attention to the generally recognised principles of accountancy, particularly as they have been given statutory force in Schedules 8 and 8A of the 1948 Act, as amended by subsequent Acts.[8] Further, principles of accounting practice are contained in the Statements of Standard Accounting Practice, issued by the Institute of Chartered Accountants, which are applied almost universally.[9] The industrial aspect of the requirement of public accountability is indicated in the provisions on disclosure of information in the Employment Protection Act 1975 and the Industry Act 1975.[10]

3. The law relating to company finance extends far beyond the provisions of the Companies Acts. Those desirous of providing the company with funds have to take into account the requirements for Admission of Securities to Listing of The Stock Exchange and the Statements of the Council for the Securities Industry. These documents are frequently referred to in this work and are reproduced in Volume 2, Part C. These persons must also comply with the provisions of the Prevention of Fraud (Investments) Act 1958,[11] the Borrowing (Control and Guarantees) Act 1946, and the regulations made thereunder[12] and other enactments.[13]

4. In the case of take-over bids and mergers of companies the provisions of the City Code on Take-overs and Mergers and the relevant provisions issued by The Stock Exchange have to be taken into account.[14] Further, on the level of public law, the regulation contained in the Fair Trading Act 1973 and in other statutes and statutory instruments has to be observed.[15] A survey of these topics is included in this work.

5. Employees' share schemes and pension schemes for the employees of

---

[7] See para. 2–12, *post*.
[8] See para. 69–01, *post*.
[9] See para. 70–05, *post*.
[10] See para. 74–01, *post*.
[11] See paras. 25–01, *et seq., post*.
[12] See paras. 26–01 *et seq., post*.
[13] *e.g.* the Exchange Control Act 1947; see para. 26–24, *post*.
[14] See para. 82–01, *post*.
[15] See para. 83–01, *post*.

the company, with their considerable social and industrial implications, cannot be ignored.[16]

6. Last but not least, the position of the company in Great Britain today cannot be properly understood if the tax aspects of the company are ignored.

It has, therefore, been necessary to include in this work a short survey of the law of taxation relating to the company.[17]

---

[16] See para. 94–01, *post*.
[17] See para. 90–01, *post*.

Chapter 2

HISTORY OF THE COMPANIES ACTS. INTERPRETATION OF THE PRESENT ACTS

History of the Companies Acts

The Bubble Act 1720 and its repeal (1825)

2–01 The history of modern company law[1] begins in 1825 when the Bubble Act was repealed.[2]

The Bubble Act had been passed by a "panic-stricken"[3] Parliament in order to stop the flood of speculative and often fraudulent schemes of company flotations which were characteristic of the first two decades of the eighteenth century and of which the notorious scheme of the South Sea Company[4] is the best-known example. By the Bubble Act the legislator, confusing the fraudulent substance of the flotations with the innocent form of the company, prohibited generally the use of corporations unless the corporation was authorised to act as such by Act of Parliament or Royal Charter, but exempted from this prohibition all undertakings established before June 24, 1718.

However, the Bubble Act did not lead to a suppression of the form of company. Apart from the types of companies expressly admitted by the Act, unincorporated associations were formed which, in law, were large partnerships but which, particularly from the beginning of the nineteenth century onwards, by ingenious legal devices[5] were approximated to the form of companies having transferable shares. The constitution of these unincorporated associations was contained in deeds of settlement and much use was made in their formation of the trust.

2–02 MAIN TYPES OF COMPANIES USED IN 1825. In the result, in 1825 when the Bubble Act was repealed, three main types of companies were known—

(1) companies incorporated by Royal Charter;

---

[1] For the history of company law, see in particular: L. C. B. Gower, *Modern Company Law* (4th ed., 1979), Chaps. 2, 3 (a brilliant and well-documented summary); Holdsworth, *History of English Law*, Vol. 8, pp. 192–222; Sir Cecil Carr, "Early Forms of Corporateness," in *Select Essays in Anglo-American Legal History*, Vol. 3, pp. 161–255; W. R. Scott, *Joint Stock Companies to 1720*; Sir Cecil Carr, *Select Charters of Trading Corporations* (Selden Society, Vol. 28, 1913); A. B. DuBois, *The English Business Company after the Bubble Act, 1720–1800*; B. C. Hunt, *The Development of the Business Corporation in England, 1800–1867*; C. M. Schmitthoff, "The Origin of the Joint Stock Company" (1939) 3 Toronto L.J. 74–96.

[2] By the Bubble Companies, etc., Act 1825.

[3] F. W. Maitland in 3 *Collected Papers* (1911), p. 390.

[4] An unknown pamphleteer wrote in 1740: "The South Sea Company upon the whole has seemed to be a Company calculated for Scheming rather than trading." *A Description of Trades*, Goldsmiths' Library Pamphlet Collection XVIII–40–4.

[5] See A. B. DuBois, *loc. cit.*, Chap. 3, pp. 215. *et seq.*

(2) companies incorporated by special Act of Parliament; and
(3) deed of settlement companies.

Of these, the former two types have survived to the present day and are discussed later.[6] The deed of settlement company, which is no longer in use, calls for comment here.

2–03 THE DEED OF SETTLEMENT COMPANY. In the eighteenth and the beginning of the nineteenth centuries this form of association became increasingly popular, despite the difficulties which the Bubble Act, as long as it was on the statute-book, placed in its way. As the Industrial Revolution advanced, men of business began again to recognise the advantages derived from co-operation in commercial enterprise, *viz.* the advantage of raising funds for the purposes of large undertakings by means of contributions from a number of small capitalists ready and willing to co-operate, and that of minimising the risk by spreading the liability. The difficulty was how to secure these advantages. A charter or private Act of Parliament was often too costly or impracticable. Businessmen had to devise for themselves a new form of partnership which would possess the advantages as nearly as might be of a chartered corporation, and in particular would have shares of a fixed amount freely transferable by the holders. The outcome of these commercial needs was the unincorporated company, the lineal ancestor of the ordinary company under the Companies Act.

The deed of settlement by which such an unincorporated company was formed was made between the various shareholders and a trustee or trustees with whom the shareholders covenanted to observe the provisions of the deed. The deed commonly declared that the several persons for the time being holding shares in the capital of the company should constitute and be a company with a specified name, and with a specified capital, and subject to specified regulations (set out in the deed) until dissolved in a specified manner. The deed usually also made the shares transferable. To secure the continuity of the concern, notwithstanding the death or bankruptcy of members, the management of the enterprise was transferred to a select body of directors, often known as the committee of directors, to the exclusion of the members generally, and the property of the company was vested in all or some directors as trustees.

What the founders of these associations aimed at was, in fact, to make them as nearly as possible a corporation with continuous existence, and with transferable and transmissible stock, but without any individual right in any associate to bind the other associated members or to deal with the assets of the association. In some cases they even obtained a private Act of Parliament enabling them to sue and be sued in the name of some specified officer.[7]

---

[6] See paras. 89–20 and 89–21, *post*.
[7] The Friendly Societies Act 1793 generally permitted actions to be brought in the names of the treasurer or trustees of such societies.

Such associations being in the contemplation of law nothing but large partnerships with some special features, the members were always held liable for the debts and liabilities to the full extent of their means.

Since 1844 the formation of unincorporated companies, at least of some size, has not been possible: the Joint Stock Companies Act of that year and all subsequent Joint Stock Companies Acts and Companies Acts prohibited the formation of unregistered companies, associations or partnerships for gain where the members exceeded a certain small number.[8] The Companies Act 1948 retained this prohibition and prohibits such associations if the number of members exceeded, in the case of banking enterprises, 10 (s. 429), and in that of other enterprises, 20 (s. 434); but these limits have been relaxed by sections 119 to 122 of the 1967 Act in the case of certain professional partnerships, and the Department of Trade is empowered to grant further exemptions.[9]

The Joint Stock Companies Acts

2–04 In the decade following 1825 the commercial need for general admission of joint stock enterprise became pressing, and it became clear that if the legislator did not act the future development of companies would be an evolution of the unincorporated company, with its cumbrous constitution, its confused legal status and the great disadvantage of merely contractual limitation of liability of members. "If the State had not given way," said Maitland,[10] "we should have had in England joint stock companies, unincorporated, but contracting with limited liability."

During that period the legislator was hesitant to admit generally the incorporated joint stock company and experimented with the form of the chartered company, by authorising the Crown by the Chartered Companies Act 1837 to provide in the charter that the members of the company should be liable to a limited extent for the liabilities of the company. The chartered company did not, however, become a general form of business corporation because the costs to obtain a Royal Charter were considerable and such a charter was not easily granted.

2–05 INCORPORATION BY REGISTRATION. In 1844, as the result of Gladstone's initiative as President of the Board of Trade,[11] Parliament passed the Joint Stock Companies Act 1844,[12] which prohibited large unincorporated

---

[8] The Act of 1844 fixed 25 as the maximum number; this was reduced to 20 by the Act of 1856.

[9] See para. 89–09, *post*.

[10] F. W. Maitland, "Trust and Corporation," *Selected Essays*, 1936, pp. 141, 210.

[11] Gladstone's administration likewise prepared the measure which was later enacted as the Companies Clauses Consolidation Act 1845, by which the clauses adopted by companies created by private Acts of Parliament were standardised; see para. 89–23, *post*.

[12] Some of the circumstances which made the intervention of the legislature necessary are pointed out by Lord Cranworth in *Oakes* v. *Turquand* (1867) L.R. 2 H.L. 325, 358.

companies[13] and for the first time admitted the creation of joint stock companies by registration—an imaginative and bold innovation. The Act created an anomalous situation: on the one hand, it incorporated the companies registered under it, and thus endowed them with faculties, privileges and powers denied to an unincorporated company; in particular it facilitated legal proceedings and the holding of property. On the other hand, it still withheld from them one of the most important incidents of an incorporated company—the immunity of the members from direct liability. Indeed, it expressly imposed on the members liability for the debts of the company just as if they were partners.[14]

Although it was a great advance that corporate status could now be obtained by registration and no longer only by Royal Charter or a private Act of Parliament, it was not easy to comply with the registration procedure, which, judged by modern standards, was cumbersome: a provisional registration for a few preliminary purposes was followed by a complete registration, and only when the latter was completed did the company acquire corporate status. The office of Registrar of Companies was created and full publicity was provided for the documents registered with him, which included the deed of settlement and annual returns. A separate enactment[15] of the same year dealt with the winding up of companies.[16]

2–06 ADMISSION OF LIMITED LIABILITY. The Act of 1844 withheld, as has been seen, the privilege of limited liability from the members of the companies registered under that Act. It took more than 10 years before the time was ripe for the introduction of that feature of the modern company.

By the Limited Liability Act 1855, a company could secure the limited liability of its members to the nominal amount of the shares held by them respectively upon certain conditions, the most important of which were:

(1) that the company should have at least 25 members holding at least three-fourths of the nominal capital, each member having paid up to at least 20 per cent.[17];

(2) that the word "Limited" was the last component of the company's name[18]; and

---

[13] See note 8, *supra*.

[14] Notwithstanding this provision, an effort was in some cases made to obtain limited liability for a company registered under the Act. It was thought that the insertion in the deed of settlement of a clause limiting the liability of the members to the amount of their shares would or might be effective, as the deed of settlement was filed with the Registrar and was open for public inspection, but it was ultimately held by the court that this attempt to limit was, as regards outsiders, ineffectual (see *Greenwood's Case* (1854) 3 De G.M. & G. 459).

[15] 7 & 8 Vict. c. 111.

[16] The history of winding-up jurisdiction, the transfer of that jurisdictioin from the Court of Bankruptcy to the Court of Chancery and the ensuing conflict between these jurisdictions is treated by Gower, *loc. cit.*, pp. 42–43.

[17] These requirements were repealed by the Joint Stock Companies Act 1856.

[18] The suggestion that "Limited" should be the last word of the company's name was made by Lord Bramwell. On the centenary of the passing of the Act of 1855, *The Times* (December 8, 1955) wrote: "It was his idea that the word 'limited' should be the last word of a company's name, that it should appear on their notepaper and documents, and should be painted on their premises and engraved on their brass plates. He was an enthusiast for his word. 'Write it on my tombstone,' he said after the Bill had been passed."

(3) that the auditor of the company should be approved by the Board of Trade.[19]

2–07 THE JOINT STOCK COMPANIES ACT 1856. The Limited Liability Act 1855 remained in operation for less than a year; it was superseded by the Joint Stock Companies Act 1856, which consolidated it in a revised form with the Joint Stock Companies Act 1844 and another enactment.

The Act of 1856 marks the beginning of a new era in company law. The main object of the Act which reflected the then prevailing doctrine of economic liberalism and *laissez-faire* was to throw open to all the coveted privilege of carrying on business with limited liability. The principle of the Act was to allow the greatest freedom both in the formation and working of a limited liability company, and at the same time to ensure that those who dealt with such concerns should be informed that the liability of the members was limited.

Abandoning the old cumbersome system introduced by the Act of 1844 of provisional and complete registration, the Act made the formation of a company a simple and inexpensive process—all that was required for the formation of a company was seven signatures to a written or printed document called a memorandum of association; there was no longer a deed of settlement, but, in addition to the memorandum, the company could register articles or adopt the model articles attached to the Act.[20] These constitutional documents, on payment of a fee, were to be registered and a certificate of incorporation to be given, and thereupon the company was at liberty at once to commence business. It was not bound before starting business to have any capital paid up or subscribed beyond the seven shares to be taken by the signatories of the memorandum; it might start on its commercial career without any further subscription, might at once enter into contracts, borrow money, if it could, and carry on business.[21] As in the Act of 1855, the great boon of limited liability was secured by the insertion in the memorandum, as part of the name of the company, of the magic word "Limited," together with a clause stating that the liability of the members was to be limited.

Companies in Scotland

2–08 The early history of companies legislation in Scotland parallels that of England. Joint stock companies, in effect large partnerships with transferable equity stock, were recognised and do not appear to have been inhibited by the Bubble Act of 1720. Companies incorporated by Royal Charter (such as the Scottish Banks) or special Act of Parliament also

---

[19] These requirements were repealed by the Joint Stock Companies Act 1856.

[20] In Table B of the Schedule to the Act of 1856.

[21] The requirement in the 1855 Act that the company should have at least 25 members holding £10 each which were paid up to at least 20 per cent. was repealed; so was the requirement that the auditors be approved by the Board of Trade; see para. 2–06, *ante*.

appeared, and for the benefit of the latter (mainly in the field of large public undertakings) a series of Companies Clauses Acts for Scotland were passed in 1845, 1863 and 1869, which contained a constitution and code of management available for adoption by special Act Companies. The position of members and creditors of such companies may differ from that of companies incorporated under the Companies Acts, with which this work is mainly concerned.

The legislation passed before 1856 which is discussed in the foregoing paragraphs of this chapter did not always apply to Scotland. The Limited Liability Act 1855 did not, so that the introduction of limited liability as a facility generally available to the business community of Scotland dates from 1856. The Joint Stock Companies Act 1856, and all subsequent general legislation in the field of company law, applies to Scotland as well as to England, although there remain parts of the statutory code which apply exclusively to one jurisdiction or the other.

The earlier Companies Acts

2–09 THE COMPANIES ACT 1862. The first enactment to bear the short title "Companies Act" was the Companies Act 1862, described by Sir Francis Palmer as the "magna carta of co-operative enterprise."

This Act consolidated the Joint Stock Companies Act 1856 with a considerable number of other Acts, amongst them five Acts passed between 1856 and 1862.[22] This first great consolidation Act concerning companies was a masterpiece of draftsmanship and arrangement and, apart therefrom, introduced a number of amendments. For the first time the model set of articles which a company could adopt instead of registering its own articles appeared in Table A of the First Schedule,[23] where it has remained in all subsequent companies' consolidation enactments, companies limited by guarantee and unlimited companies were admitted, and the provisions relating to winding up were elaborated.

2–10 THE COMPANIES (CONSOLIDATION) ACT 1908. Although the Act of 1862 marked considerable progress, the modern company was still in its experimental stage and between 1862 and 1908, when the next great consolidation Act was passed, no less than 18 amending statutes had to be passed.

In the last years of the nineteenth century the weakest part of company law was that dealing with the liability for misleading statements in prospectuses, as was demonstrated by *Derry* v. *Peek*,[24] in which it was held that directors who in a prospectus carelessly made a statement which they knew to be true were not liable in damages if they acted honestly, and not

---

[22] Notable amongst them were the Joint Stock Banking Companies Acts 1857 and 1858, which made it possible to form banks as companies limited by shares.
[23] In the 1856 Act it had been Table B of the Schedule to the Act.
[24] (1889) 14 App.Cas. 337.

fraudulently.[25] This unfortunate decision was modified by the Directors' Liability Act 1890, which, with the Companies Act 1900, did much to stop prospectus frauds.

Following the recommendations of the Loreburn Committee, which were published in 1906,[26] Parliament passed the Companies Act 1907, which incorporated many important alterations of the law. The Act of 1907 was then consolidated with that of 1862, the Companies Acts passed between 1862 and 1908, and other relevant enactments, in the Companies (Consolidation) Act 1908, the second great companies' consolidation enactment.

The outstanding feature of the company reform culminating in the Act of 1908 was the introduction of the private company[27] which was not required to file its balance sheet with its annual return because, in the words of the Loreburn Report, "as they do not appeal to the public for subscriptions, there is no need for publishing their private affairs, and . . . the disclosure involved in the filing of the documents would, or might, seriously prejudice their interests."[28] Apart therefrom, the general tendency of the 1908 reform was greatly to strengthen the requirements relating to prospectuses, the publication of accounts and the registration of charges and mortgages.

The reform of 1908 set the pattern for the company law reforms of 1929 and 1948; the President of the Board of Trade constituted a committee of eminent practitioners to report on the desirability or necessity of amending the Companies Act; the committee reported; Parliament adopted such of the recommendations of the committee as it deemed fit in a new Companies Act containing those amendments of the old Act; and in the following year the old and the new Acts were consolidated in an Act which repealed all previous enactments.[29] This convenient method has enabled the practitioner to find practically the whole statute law relating to companies in one enactment. This benefit has now been lost, as the statutory regulation of company law is provided in six enactments, viz. the Companies Acts of 1948, 1967, 1976, 1980 and 1981 and the European Communities Act 1972, s.9, but the consolidation of these enactments is already under consideration. The Department of Trade published in November 1981 a consultative document entitled "Consolidation of the Companies Acts" (see para. 2–63, *post*).

2–11 THE COMPANIES ACT 1929. This Act was founded upon the recommendations of the Greene Committee, which reported in 1926.[30] Parliament

---

[25] How far the law has travelled since then may be seen by contrasting it with *R.* v. *Kylsant* [1932] 1 K.B. 442.
[26] Cmd. 3052 (1906).
[27] It was defined for the first time in s. 37(1) of the Act of 1907.
[28] Cmd. 3056 (1906), para. 46.
[29] Except as expressly saved; see para. 2–19, *post*.
[30] Cmd. 2657 (1926). This was the first general review of the operation of the Companies Acts since the Loreburn Committee was appointed in 1905. The Report of the Wrenbury Committee in 1918 dealt only with matters limited in scope and was not acted upon.

adopted most of these suggestions in the amending Companies Act 1928, which was consolidated with the previous Acts[31] in the Companies Act 1929.

The approach of the Greene Committee to the reform of company law was cautious, as is demonstrated by the numerous topics which the Committee considered and which it recommended not to change but which had to be altered subsequently, *e.g.* group accounts, private companies as subsidiaries of public companies and share hawking. Nevertheless, the contribution of the reform of 1929 to the modernisation of company law was considerable. The outstanding alteration was the recognition of the special relationship which exists in a group of companies between the holding company and its subsidiaries: the Act required the former to annex to its balance sheet particulars showing how the profits and losses of the subsidiaries were dealt with in the accounts of the holding company. Another important alteration was the admission of redeemable preference shares. Further major amendments concerned the accounts of the company, offers for sale, the protection of the minority in the case of alteration of rights of a class of shares, a simplification of the procedure for passing a special resolution and the winding up of the company.

The Companies Acts 1948 to 1981

2–12 The reference to the "Companies Acts 1948 to 1981" includes the following enactments (1981 Act, s. 119 (2)):

The Companies Act 1948;
the Companies Act 1967, Parts I and III;
the Companies (Floating Charges and Receivers)(Scotland) Act 1972;
the European Communities Act 1972, s. 9;
the Stock Exchange (Completion of Bargains) Act 1976, ss. 1 to 4;
the Insolvency Act 1976, s. 9;
the Companies Act 1976;
the Companies Act 1980; and
the Companies Act 1981, except sections 28 and 29.

THE COMPANIES ACT 1948. This Act, which is still the principal Act in operation, was the next great consolidation Act. It was founded on the report of the Cohen Committee which was published in 1945.[32] The great majority of the recommendations of that Committee was enacted by Parliament in the Companies Act 1947, which was consolidated with the Companies Act 1929 and other relevant enactments[33] in the Companies Act 1948.

The reforms suggested by the Cohen Committee were resolute and

[31] The Companies Acts 1908 and 1917.
[32] Cmd. 6659 (1945).
[33] See s. 459 (1) and Sched. VII.

far-reaching. In the words of the Report[34] the aim of the reform was twofold:

> *first,* without "placing unreasonable fetters upon business which is conducted in an efficient and honest manner, . . . to ensure that as much information as is reasonably required shall be made available both to shareholders and creditors of the companies concerned and to the general public"; and
>
> *secondly,* "to find means of making it easier for shareholders to exercise a more effective general control over the management of their companies."

The outstanding feature of the 1948 reform was its emphasis on the public accountability of the company. The valued privilege of balance sheet secrecy was made available only to exempt private companies, while other private companies, in particular those the shares in which were held by public companies, had to publish their balance sheets (s. 129). Generally recognised principles of accountancy were given statutory force and had to be applied in the preparation of the balance sheet and profit and loss account (Sched. 8). Group accounts were required for inter-connected companies (ss. 150–154), and, on principle, professional standing was demanded of the auditor (ss. 161), whose independence *vis-à-vis* the directors was strengthened (ss. 160, 162). Further, the 1948 legislation extended the protection of the minority (s. 210) and the powers of the Board of Trade to order an investigation of the company's affairs (ss. 164–175); and for the first time the shareholders in general meeting were given power to remove a director before the expiration of his period of office, although such removal might constitute a breach of the contract of service of the company with him or be contrary to the articles, but his right to compensation for loss of office or to damages for breach of contract was preserved (s. 184).

The Companies (Floating Charges) (Scotland) Act 1961 introduced to Scotland the facility of securing loans by floating charge and made provision for registering most charges granted by companies. These provisions were amended by the Companies (Floating Charges and Receivers) (Scotland) Act 1972, which also permitted, for the first time, the appointment of a receiver in Scotland, restricted to the holder of a floating charge.[35]

2–13 THE COMPANIES ACT 1967. This Act was the first stage in the implementation of the recommendations of the Jenkins Committee, which presented its report in 1962.[36] The Committee took the view that, on the whole, the existing law worked well, and consequently few of its recommendations involved major changes in the law, except in relation to the disclosure of information by companies. The Companies Act 1967 adopted and con-

---

[34] Para. 5.
[35] See para. 47–05, *post*.
[36] Cmnd. 1749 (1962).

siderably extended in some respects, the recommendations of the Committee as to disclosure. The Act abolished the exempt private company (s. 2), and required *all* limited companies to file accounts (s. 47), but empowered certain limited companies to re-register as unlimited to avoid this requirement (s. 43). Further information was required in the accounts (ss. 3–12, and Scheds. 1 and 2), and the directors' report became a document of prime importance (ss. 15–24). More stringent provisions were imposed in relation to directors' interests in the company and disclosure thereof (ss. 25–32), and disclosure of certain substantial shareholdings was required (ss. 33–34). The powers of the Department of Trade to investigate the affairs of a company were extended (ss. 35–42, 109–118), and, in order to discourage the irresponsible formation of new companies, the fees on registration were substantially increased (s. 48 and Sched. 3). A large proportion of the Act was devoted to special provisions relating to insurance companies, now consolidated with subsequent legislation in the Insurance Companies Acts 1974 to 1981, to partnerships (ss. 119–122), and to moneylenders, now contained in the Consumer Credit Act 1974.

THE COMPANIES ACT 1976. This Act attempted to remedy a variety of defects which had become evident in the application of the Acts of 1948 and 1967. The 1976 Act strengthened the requirements of public accountability and those relating to the disclosure of interests in the shares of the company. As regards the latter, it reduced severely the time limits and the amounts of notifiable transactions. Notable were, in particular, three innovations introduced by the Act. First, it was made a criminal offence for a director of the company knowingly or recklessly to make a false statement to the auditor. Secondly, a company with shares listed at the Stock Exchange was given the right to compel the registered holders of its voting shares to disclose the beneficial interests in those shares; by the 1981 Act this power of the company was extended to *all* public companies. Thirdly, the court was given power to disqualify a person, who was persistently in default in relation to the requirements of the Companies Acts, from being connected with the management of a company for a period not exceeding five years; here again, the 1981 Act extended the provisions of the 1976 Act and the court was given power in certain circumstances to issue a disqualification order for 15 years.

In addition, companies with registered offices in Wales were authorised to use the Welsh language in their names and company documents.

THE COMPANIES ACT 1980. This was a major measure of company law reform. It gave effect to the Second EEC Directive on Company Law Harmonisation of December 13, 1976[37] in the United Kingdom and introduced other reforms.

The 1980 Act changed fundamentally the structure of company law.

---

[37] O.J. 1977, L26/1.

Before this Act the public company was the residual form of the company and the private company was a variation of that form. The 1980 Act reversed this position. The private company became the residual form and a company was a public company only if it satisfied the specified requirements provided by the Act. The most important of them was that the public company must have a fixed minimum capital and its shares must be paid up to at least one-quarter of its nominal account and the whole premium.

Insider dealing was made a criminal offence. The shareholders were given a right of pre-emption in the case of new issues of shares in specified circumstances. Dealings between the directors and their companies became greatly restricted and financial maximum limits have been introduced for such dealings. The directors became obliged in the performance of their functions to bear in mind the general interests of the employees of the company. The protection of the minority shareholders was extended by enabling them to petition the court for relief if their position was unfairly prejudiced.

THE COMPANIES ACT 1981. This Act gave effect in the United Kingdom to the provisions of the Fourth EEC Directive on Company Law Harmonisation of July 25, 1978[37a] and introduced other important changes. For the purposes of accounting and disclosure, companies were divided into small, medium-sized and other companies and their disclosure requirements were differentiated accordingly.[37b] The law relating to the names of companies was simplified by the abolition, in principle, of the approval of the name by the Department of Trade. The company was authorised, subject to certain conditions, to issue redeemable equity shares and to purchase its own shares. The provisions relating to the disclosure of interest in shares and investigations into shareholdings and the affairs of the company were strengthened. The criminal liability of persons concerned in fraudulent trading was extended to cases in which the company was not in the course of winding up.

The 1981 Act further abolished the register of business names which had to be kept under the Registration of Business Names Act 1916.[37c]

CONSOLIDATION OF COMPANIES ACTS. Active steps have been taken to prepare consolidating measures relating to the Companies Acts 1948 to 1981 which, in their present form, provide an extremely complicated statutory regulation. The Companies Act 1981 provides in section 116 that these enactments may be amended by order in council if the amendments are jointly recommended by the Law Commission and the Scottish Law Commission as desirable to enable a satisfactory consolidation of the whole or the greater part of the Companies Acts to be produced. Such order in council shall not be made unless a draft is approved by a resolution of each

---

[37a] O.J. 1978 L 222/11.

[37b] See para. 70–10, *post*.

[37c] See para. 89–03, *post*.

House of Parliament. In November 1981 the Department of Trade published a consultative document entitled "Consolidation of the Companies Acts." In this document the various methods of consolidation and their relative advantages for the practice are discussed.

The European Communities Act 1972, s. 9

2–14 The EEC is at present engaged in the major work of harmonisation of the national company laws of the member states. This effort has a considerable influence on the reform of company law in the United Kingdom.[38]

When the United Kingdom joined the EEC, it had to give effect to the First Council Directive on Harmonisation of Company Law which had already been approved by the Council of Ministers on March 9, 1968.[39] This was attempted by section 9 of the European Communities Act 1972.[40]

Section 9 (8) provides that "this section shall be construed as one with the Companies Act 1948." It follows that the definitions of the 1948 Act, such as "companies" (s. 455), or "default fine" (s. 440), apply to section 9.

Section 9 is expressly extended to unregistered companies, as far as the provisions of the 1948 Act are applicable to them (s. 9 (8) of the 1972 Act).

The main provisions of section 9 are:

1. The *ultra vires* doctrine is restricted (s. 9 (1))[41];
2. the law relating to the powers of the directors to act for the company is affected (s. 9 (1))[42];
3. pre–registration contracts are regulated (s. 9 (2))[43];
4. official notification of the issue or receipt of specified documents is introduced (s. 9 (3) and (4))[44];
5. the latest version of the memorandum and articles must be made available to the public in an easily accessible form (s. 9 (5) and (6))[45];
6. certain particulars must be stated on business letters and order forms (s. 9 (7)).[46]

The Act applies to all companies as defined in section 455 of the Companies Act 1948 (s. 9 (8)). It does not apply to oversea companies (Part X of the 1948 Act). Provisions similar to section 9 are enacted for companies incorporated in Northern Ireland under section 4 (3) of the 1972 Act; as to subordinate legislation affecting Northern Ireland, see Schedule 2, paragraph 3 of the 1972 Act.

---

[38] See para. 2–15, *post*.
[39] 68/151 EEC, published in J.O. 1968, L65/8–9. The First Directive is reproduced, in English, in Vol. II, Part L, of this work.
[40] s. 9 is reproduced in Vol. II, Part A, of this work.
[41] See paras. 9–24 and 9–25, *post*.
[42] See para. 28–1, *post*.
[43] See para. 27–3, *post*.
[44] See para. 17–01, *post*.
[45] See paras. 8–05 and 13–05, *post*.
[46] See para. 8–05, *post*.

The harmonisation of national company laws by the EEC

2–15 The EEC aims at establishing "a common market of companies" in the Community in order to carry out the economic integration of its members. The most important mechanism to carry out this intention is the use of Directives issued by the Council of Ministers. These Directives are issued by virtue of Article 54 (3) (*g*) of the EEC Treaty. The national legislatures are obliged to give effect to them in their jurisdictions. So far the Council has approved the First, Second, Third, Fourth and Sixth Directives. The other Directives exist in draft form or are in an early stage of preparation.

THE FIRST DIRECTIVE.[47] The full title of the First Directive is "First Directive of the Council on co-ordination of the safeguards which, for the protection of the interests of members and others are required by member states of companies or firms with a view to making such safeguards equivalent throughout the Community." As already observed, effect was given to the First Directive by the Companies Act 1972, s. 9.

The aims of the First Directive are threefold: to afford protection to third parties dealing with the company and its directors, to provide for publicity of essential information regarding the company in a manner easily accessible throughout the Community, and to restrict the declaration of nullity of the company after its incorporation. The third of these aims is irrelevant in the company law of the United Kingdom, in view of the conclusive character attributed to the certificate of incorporation by sections 3(4), 5(9), 8(10) and 10(5) of the Companies Act 1980, and is, therefore, not dealt with in section 9 of the 1972 Act.

It is doubtful whether section 9 gives effect to the First Directive in all respects. By virtue of article 189 (3) of the EEC Treaty, a Directive is binding upon the member states, while leaving to national authorities the choice of form and methods. It follows that only section 9, but not the First Directive, has become part of the municipal law of the United Kingdom. Reference to the provisions of the First Directive may, however, be made in order to clarify any ambiguities in section 9.

THE SECOND DIRECTIVE. This Directive was adopted by the Council of Ministers on December 13, 1976.[48] It deals with the formation of public companies and the maintenance and alteration of its capital. Effect was given to its provisions in the United Kingdom by the Companies Act 1980.

THE THIRD DIRECTIVE. It was adopted by the Council on October 9, 1978.[49] It deals with national mergers of public companies. It has not been given effect in the United Kingdom yet.

---

[47] See note 39.
[48] 77/91 EEC, published in O.J. 1977, L26/1.
[49] 78/855 EEC, published in O.J. 1978, L295/36.

THE FOURTH DIRECTIVE. It was accepted by the Council on July 25, 1978.[50] It deals with the presentation and content of the annual accounts and the valuation of assets and liabilities. The Directive was given effect in the United Kingdom by the Companies Act 1981.[51]

THE FIFTH DIRECTIVE. It exists so far only in draft form which was submitted by the Commission to the Council on October 9, 1972.[52] It proposed that the boards of public companies shall have a two-tier structure and that in companies having 500 or more employees there should be employee participation on the supervisory board. These proposals met with serious opposition in several member states, including the United Kingdom. The Commission then published in 1975 a discussion paper under the title "Employee Participation and Company Structure." In this paper the Commission made more flexible proposals and suggested, in particular, a transitional period. The consideration of the Fifth Draft Directive by the EEC authorities is not concluded yet.

THE SIXTH DIRECTIVE. It was adopted by the Council in 1980.[54] It attempts to co-ordinate the requirements for the drawing up, scrutiny and distribution of listing particulars of securities admitted to official stock exchange listing.

THE SEVENTH DIRECTIVE. The draft of this Directive has not been submitted to the Council yet. The Directive will deal with the requirements of group accounts.

THE EIGHTH DIRECTIVE. This has likewise not reached the Council of Ministers yet. This Directive will attempt to harmonise the requirements for the qualifications of auditors of companies.

THE NINTH DIRECTIVE. This Directive is likewise still in the stage of preparation by the Commission. It will deal with groups of companies, the relationship of controlling and controlled companies and the protection of minority interests in groups of companies.

THE TENTH DIRECTIVE. This is still in the preparatory stage. It will deal with the winding up of companies.

Other legislation affecting companies

2–16 The procedure for transfer of fully paid shares and debentures of companies was simplified by the Stock Transfer Act 1963; and in the same year

---

[50] 78/660 EEC, published in O.J. 1978, L222/11.
[51] See para. 2–13, *ante*.
[52] J.O. 1972, C 131/49.
[53] Bull. Supp. 8/75.
[54] 80/390 EEC, published in O.J. 1980, L100/1.

special provision was made for the protection of investors in deposit-taking companies by the Protection of Depositors Act 1963, but the latter Act has been superseded and repealed by the Banking Act 1979.

Apart from the Companies Act and the Acts above mentioned, the affairs of the company are affected by a number of other Acts which, though regulating more general aspects of business law than companies, have a special bearing on company administration. Prominent among them are the Prevention of Fraud (Investments) Act 1958, which, inter alia, deals with share hawking and other invitations to acquire securities or to invest or lend money,[55] the Borrowing (Control and Guarantees) Act 1946,[56] which requires the consent of the Treasury for the issue of shares or debentures or for other forms of borrowing by the company—at present of little practical consequence owing to the General Consent of the Treasury of August 4, 1961—and the Exchange Control Act 1947, which although exchange control was abolished, except with effect to Rhodesia on October 23, 1979, and with effect to Rhodesia on December 13, 1979, is still on the statute-book.[57]

The Fair Trading Act 1973 and other enactments contain provisions relating to the public control of monopolies and mergers.[58]

The Stock Exchange (Completion of Bargains) Act 1976 introduced changes intended to enable The Stock Exchange to carry out a computerised settlement and stock transfer system (TALISMAN) and to establish a central shareholding nominee company, known as Sepon Limited (an abbreviation of Stock Exchange Pool Nominees). The Act exempts companies from the obligation imposed by the Companies Act 1948, s. 80 (1), to issue share or debenture certificates if the securities are held by a Stock Exchange nominee recognised by the Department of Trade.

The Insolvency Act 1976 has considerably affected the law relating to the winding up of companies by, inter alia, increasing the monetary units relating to winding up; enabling the Secretary of State to have audited any accounts sent to him; establishing the Insolvency Services Account; and providing for the disqualification of directors of insolvent companies.

The Charging Act 1976, s. 5, has affected the law relating to stop orders and notices.[59]

Banking companies are governed by the Banking Act 1979 and insurance companies by the Insurance Companies Acts 1974–1981. The Credit Unions Act 1979 enables the registration of credit unions under the Industrial and Provident Societies Act 1965.

Finally, the taxation of companies was put on a different basis from the taxation of individuals and partnerships by the Finance Act 1965, which introduced corporation tax and the concept of the "close company"; the

---

[55] See para. 25–01, *post*.
[56] And the statutory instruments made thereunder; see para. 26–01, *post*.
[57] See para. 26–24, *post*.
[58] See para. 83–01, *post*.
[59] See para. 39–41, *post*.

law relating to corporation tax was substantially amended by the Finance Act 1972 which introduced the "imputation system" designed to avoid the double taxation of distributed profits for the basic rate taxpayer.[60]

The Board of Trade and the Department of Trade

2–17 On the creation of the Department of Trade and Industry in 1970, the Board of Trade was left in existence, for legal reasons.[61] The Secretary of State for Trade and Industry was concurrently the President of the Board of Trade. In 1974 the Department of Trade and Industry was divided into four Departments, the newly created Department of Trade dealing with company matters.

While it would, thus, be correct to refer to the Board of Trade, and this expression is still used in the relevant legislation, in the narrative text of this work the more colloquial phrase "Department of Trade" has been preferred.

Conclusions

2–18 From this historical survey the following conclusions emerge: in the first half of the nineteenth century the legislator adopted an attitude of cautious reserve to the company limited by shares and, after some futile experiments with the chartered corporation, granted the incidents of incorporation by registration to the company with limited liability reluctantly and one by one. In 1856 the pendulum swung to the other side and utmost liberty in the formation of the company and the conduct of its affairs became the policy of the legislator. From that time onwards, the Companies Acts have become progressively stricter, in particular with respect to prospectuses and public accountability. From 1844 onwards every successive Act has left its mark on the organisation of the modern company, though many provisions of the earlier Acts have not survived. There can be no doubt that the Companies Acts have largely stimulated and developed British trade and co-operative enterprise in all parts of the world. In the Companies Acts 1948 to 1981 we thus find gathered together the experience of over 100 years of company legislation.

At the present time the reform of company law has become a volatile subject. This is due to two causes. It is necessary to adjust company legislation to the rapidly changing economic, financial and social circumstances, and in particular to the concept of social responsibility which is now accepted as the foundation of the English legal order. Secondly, the implementation of the grandiose project of harmonisation of the national company laws of the member states of the EEC requires frequent changes in the legislation. It was therefore necessary to abandon the relatively simple scheme of traditional company law reform which led to the consolidating Companies Acts of 1862, 1908, 1929 and 1948. Instead, frequent

[60] See para. 90–01, *post*.
[61] The Secretary of State for Trade and Industry Order 1970 (S.I. 1970 No. 1537).

enactments were required which amended the main Act of 1948. The result was a statutory regulation of great complexity. A consolidation of the 1948 Act and the amending Act is contemplated but it is doubtful whether the whole statutory law relating to companies will be consolidated again in a single enactment.

Repeal and savings of previous Acts

2–19 It is in the nature of a consolidating Act to repeal its predecessors and to contain within one enactment the whole statute law relating to the subject in hand. The Companies Act 1948 made no exception to that rule and, apart from certain savings, the most important of which will be considered later, repealed[62] the whole of the 1929 Act and all sections of the 1947 Act, except those which affected other enactments, such as the Registration of Business Names Act 1916 (now repealed by the Companies Act 1981), the Bankruptcy Act 1914, and the Act which has now become the Prevention of Fraud (Investments) Act 1958.[63]

In the result, the Act of 1948 applies to all companies incorporated under it and to those existing at the date when the Act came into operation (July 1, 1948; see s. 462 (2)) and formed under the Joint Stock Companies Act 1856 or a later Act. Section 455, which is the definition section of the Act, makes this clear. It defines as a "company" within the meaning of the Act of 1948 "a company formed and registered under this Act or an existing company"; it then proceeds to define as "an existing company" a company formed and registered under the "Joint Stock Companies Acts" or the Acts of 1862, 1908 or 1929,[64] and it goes on to explain that "Joint Stock Companies Acts" includes the Joint Stock Companies Act 1856 and the Acts passed between 1856 and 1862.[65] The provisions of Part 1 of the Act of 1967 (which amend the law with respect to companies generally) likewise apply to all such companies (1967 Act, s. 53).

The Act of 1948, in the provision repealing the previous enactments (s. 459), saves Table B of the Joint Stock Companies Act 1856 and the Tables A of the Companies Acts 1862, 1908 and 1929, so far as applying to companies registered under any one of those Acts (s. 459 (14); and see the definition of "articles" in s. 455).

This saving applies to companies which have adopted Table A.[66] It means that a company incorporated under one of the earlier Acts and having adopted Table A[67] continues to have as its articles the Table appended to the Act under which it is incorporated and not Table A of the

---

[62] s. 459 and Scheds. XVII and XVIII.
[63] See para. 24–01. *post*.
[64] Exclusive of Northern Irish companies (s. 455, under "Existing companies"). The Act does not extend to Northern Ireland (s. 461).
[65] An important difference exists, however, between "existing companies" formed between 1856 and 1862 and those formed under or after the 1862 Act: the former can be registered under Part VIII but the latter cannot be so registered (see s. 382 (1), proviso (i)).
[66] See para. 14–01, *post*.
[67] Or in the case of the Act of 1856,Table B.

Act of 1948; *e.g.* a company incorporated in 1933 which had adopted Table A of the Act of 1929—the Act then in force—continues to have as its articles Table A of that Act, and not Table A of the Act of 1948. Only if an article in a former Table A cannot be reconciled with an imperative provision in the 1948 Act, or one of the amending Acts, *i.e.* a provision that cannot be abrogated, does the article no longer apply.

Interpretation of present Companies Acts

2–20 The Act of 1948 was, as has been explained earlier,[68] a consolidation Act; it was not a codifying enactment. The rule applying to the latter type of legislation as laid down by Lord Herschell in *Bank of England* v. *Vagliano Brothers*[69] does not apply with equal force to the interpretation of a consolidating enactment. In that case Lord Herschell said:

> "I think the proper course is in the first instance to examine the language of the statute and to ask what is its natural meaning, uninfluenced by any considerations derived from the previous state of the law, and not to start with inquiring how the law previously stood, and then, assuming that it was probably intended to leave it unaltered, to see if the words of the enactment will bear an interpretation in conformity with this view."

The rule for the interpretation of consolidating and amending Acts such as the Companies Acts 1948 to 1981 was laid down by Chitty L.J. in *Thames Conservators* v. *Smeed, Dean & Co.*[70] In reference to the Thames Conservancy Act 1894 said:

> "The Act which we have to construe is a consolidating and amending Act; the general object of such Acts is to present the whole body of the statutory law on the subject in a complete form, repealing the former statutes. The principle of interpretation of a codifying Act is laid down by Lord Herschell in *Bank of England* v. *Vagliano*[71]: a statute codifying the law is to be interpretated as it stands, and recourse is not to be had to the former law, except upon some special ground, such, for instance, as an ambiguous provision. The same principle applies to such an Act as that which is now before us, but in a less stringent degree. In this Act clauses of the repealed Acts are found repeated, but often in altered form, and with amendments, whereby the sense may be in great measure changed. Speaking generally, I think that the enactments must be dealt with as they now stand, and that a minute critical examination of repealed clauses ought not to be entered upon for the purpose of interpretation, except upon special grounds."

---

68 See para. 2–12, *ante*.

69 [1891] A.C. 107, 144. Lord Herschell's observations refer to the Bills of Exchange Act 1882; see also Cozens-Hardy M.R. in *Bristol Tramways Co.* v. *Fiat Motors Ltd.* [1910] 2 K.B. 831, 836; Scrutton L.J. in *Laurie & Morewood* v. *Dudin & Sons* [1926] 1 K.B. 223, 235; and the judgments of the House of Lords in *Beswick* v. *Beswick* [1968] A.C. 58, *passim*. There is also a very full statement of the effects and limitations of consolidating Acts in the 6th Report of the Joint Committee on Consolidation Bills 1966–67 reporting on the Capital Allowances Bill [H.L.] with proceedings (H.L. 18–VI, 196–I and H.C. 341–I).

70 [1897] 2 Q.B. 334, 346, C.A.

71 See note 69, *supra*.

In cases where the present Acts have adopted the wording of the Act of 1929 or the earlier Acts, there is however, ample scope for reference to the decisions on those Acts.

Thus, in *Mersey Dock and Harbour Board Trustees* v. *Cameron,*[72] Blackburn J., in delivering the opinion of the majority of the judges, said:

> "Where an Act of Parliament has received a judicial construction putting a certain meaning on its words, and the legislature in a subsequent Act *in pari materia* uses the same words, there is a presumption that the legislature uses these words intending to express the meaning which it knew has been put upon the same words before; and unless there is something to rebut that presumption, the Act should be so construed, even if the words were such that they might originally have been construed otherwise."

Hence it may be taken that where the provisions of the Companies Acts 1862 to 1929 have been re-enacted without alteration, the legislature has not disturbed the decided cases, and that those decided cases are still to be treated as relevant and available for the interpretation of the present Acts. The application of a decision may, however, be excluded by a change in the language of the later Act.[73]

Interpretation of the European Community Act, s. 9

2–21 Section 9 (8) provides that that section "shall be construed as one with the Companies Act 1948," and then contains special provisions for the applicability of its provisions to unregistered companies.[74]

While thus, in principle, the provisions and definitions of the 1948 to 1981 Acts may be referred to for the interpretation of section 9, some caution is apposite. The object of that section and its purpose within the framework of the international instruments of Accession and of European Community law should not be ignored. It will, *e.g.* be seen that, in spite of the definition of a "company" in section 455, section 9 of the 1972 Act is unlikely to apply to unlimited companies.[75]

Where the provisions of section 9 are ambiguous—and unfortunately these ambiguities are not infrequent—reference may be made to the Council Directive of March 9, 1968, which that section attempts to implement, in order to ascertain the true meaning of the words used in section 9. Such ambiguity exists, *e.g.* with respect to the phrase "in good faith" used in subsection (1).[76] The Council Directive does not use that phrase but refers, in article 9 (1), to a "third party [who] knew that the act was outside [the objects of the company] or could not in view of the circumstances have

---

[72] (1864) 11 H.L.Cas. 443, 480.
[73] *Thomas* v. *United Butter Cos. of France* [1909] 2 Ch. 484, subject also to the limitations referred to in the Report cited in note 69, *supra.*
[74] See para. 3–21, *post.*
[75] See para. 3–18, *post.*
[76] See para. 9–24, *post.*

been unaware of it; disclosure of the statutes[77] shall not of itself be sufficient proof thereof"; it is, thus, clear from article 9 (1) of the Directive that a person is not in "good faith" if, by virtue of the surrounding circumstances he is put on inquiry.[78] In some instances, however, the Directive is as unenlightening as section 9, *e.g.* it does not contain a definition of "order form" in the provision which is reproduced in subsection (7) of section 9[79]; the French text of the Directive uses here the phrase *notes de commande.* [80]

[77] That this is the constitutional document or documents of the company.
[78] This view is supported by the decision of Lawson J. in *International Sales & Agencies Ltd.* v. *Marcus* [1982] 2 C.M.L.R. 46.
[79] See para. 8–06, *post.*
[80] In art. 4.

Part Two

FORMATION OF THE COMPANY

A. KINDS OF COMPANIES REGISTRABLE UNDER THE COMPANIES ACTS

CHAPTER 3

COMPANIES LIMITED BY SHARES, COMPANIES LIMITED BY GUARANTEE, UNLIMITED COMPANIES

The various kinds of companies

3–01 The Companies Acts place a very great variety of forms of companies at the disposal of businessmen. The requirements of business vary greatly: some people wish to limit their liability; others, while trading as a corporation, wish to be liable without limitation for the obligations which they have undertaken or the money entrusted to them; some businesses are large, others small; in some instances the capital required for the business is provided by the promoters; in others it is contemplated inviting the public to contribute to the capital of the company; and in others again no initial capital is required; in some cases the owners of the business wish to manage it themselves; in others ownership and management are in different hands and the management is practically self–perpetuating. The aim of the Companies Acts is to make available the form of corporate organisation to company promoters pursuing these different purposes.

With this aim in view, the Act of 1948 provides three basic types of companies, *viz.* companies limited by shares, companies limited by guarantee, and unlimited companies (s. 1 (2)), and two forms of companies, *viz.*, private and public companies. Since hybrids of the three basic types are admitted and, on principle, each of the basic types may be formed as a private or as a public company. It is convenient to set out the kinds of companies recognised by the Acts in tabular form.

3–02 One division of companies is into:

Types of Companies

(1) Companies limited by shares (s. 1 (2) (*a*)).
(2) Companies limited by quarantee (s. 1 (2) (*b*)).
Guarantee companies are subdivided into:
  (a) Companies limited by guarantee and not having a share capital (see s. 11 (*b*)); and
  (b) Companies limited by guarantee and having a share capital (see s. 11 (*c*)). But after December 22, 1980[1] it is no longer

[1] The Companies Act (Commencement No. 2) Order 1980 (S. I. 1980 No. 1785)

possible to form or to become a company limited by guarantee and having a share capital (1980 Act, s. 1 (2)). The then existing companies of this type are not affected by this regulation.

(3) Unlimited companies (s. 1 (2) (*c*)).
They may be:
(a) Unlimited companies not having a share capital; or
(b) Unlimited companies having a share capital.

3–03 Another division of companies is into:

Forms of Companies

(1) Private companies [2];
(2) Public companies.

Since the arrangement in the preceding sections may overlap, the following picture emerges:

Kinds of Companies recognised by the Act

(1) Private companies limited by shares;
(2) Public companies limited by shares;
(3) Private companies limited by guarantee and not having a share capital[3];
(4) Public companies limited by guarantee and not having a share capital*;
(5) Private companies limited by guarantee and having a share capital*;
(6) Public companies limited by guarantee and having a share capital*;
(7) Private unlimited companies not having a share capital;
(8) Public unlimited companies not having a share capital*;
(9) Private unlimited companies having a share capital;
(10) Public unlimited companies having a share capital;
* *These companies can not be formed after December 22, 1980*

3–04 Apart therefrom, the following three additional types of companies may be registered:
(11) Oversea companies (ss. 406–415);
(12) Companies incorporated in the Channel Islands or the Isle of Man and having a place of business in England or Scotland (s. 416);
(13) Certain companies formed before November 2, 1862,[4] or created by

---

[2] Under the 1948 Act private companies were divided into ordinary private companies and exempt private companies (s. 129); exempt private companies were abolished by s. 2 of the 1967 Act as from January 27, 1968. The present provisions relating to private companies are to be found in the 1980 Act, particularly in s. 15.
[3] This is the only type of guarantee company which can now be formed.
[4] On this day the 1862 Act came into operation.

Act of Parliament (other than a Companies Act), or by letters patent, or within the stannaries, or otherwise duly constituted according to the law and having two or more members (s. 382 (1)).[5]

Further,

(14) a company already registered as a limited company may be re-registered as unlimited, and an unlimited company re–registered as limited (1967 Act, ss. 43–45).[6]

This work treats almost exclusively of companies limited by shares, but in order to understand the arrangements of the Acts it is also necessary to consider shortly in the following paragraphs of this chapter companies limited by guarantee and unlimited companies. These types of companies and, indeed, all companies registrable under the Companies Acts have one feature in common: they all have legal personality.[7]

Companies limited by shares

3–05 A company limited by shares is defined as "a company having the liability of its members limited by the memorandum to the amount, if any, unpaid on the shares respectively held by them" (s. 1 (2) (*a*)). Accordingly the memorandum of the company, and more specifically its capital clause, has to provide, *inter alia*, that the share capital is divided into "shares of a fixed amount" (s. 2 (4) (*a*)); it is this amount which, *vis-à-vis* the company, on principle[8] determines the maximum liability of the shareholder.

A share is a thing in action[9] of proprietary character. A shareholder is a co-owner of the company—not of its assets which, in view of the nature of the company as a legal person, are vested in the company[10]—and the extent of his rights and duties as co-owner is measured by the amount of his shareholding, so that all the shareholders of the company constitute its proprietors and the amount due from all of them to the company is equal to the issued capital of the company.

---

[5] See para. 3–20, *post*.

[6] These sections replace s. 16 (1) of the 1948 Act which allowed conversion from unlimited to limited but not from limited to unlimited: see paras. 5–17 and 5–20, *post*.

[7] On legal personality, see para. 18–01, *post*.

[8] For exceptional cases, see para. 10–04, *post*.

[9] In English law property is classified into real property ("land, tenements and hereditaments") and personal property. The latter is divided into chattels real (interests in land, *e.g.* a lease) and chattels personal (all property other than real property and chattels real). Chattels personal are subdivided into things (or "choses") in possession (which can be recovered by reduction into possession) and things (or "choses") in action (which can only be recovered by action in the courts). The former includes tangible movable property, the latter intangible personal property such as rights and debts. Shares are "property" within R.S.C. 1965, Ord. 86: *Woodlands* v. *Hinds* [1955] 1 W.L.R. 688, 690. They are personal property (s. 73); see para. 33–05, *post*.

In Scots law land, buildings and permanent fixtures are classed as "heritable," other property as "moveable" ("corporeal" or "incorporeal"). Although Scottish property law is quite different, there is a rough correspondence between these and the English classifications of "real property;" "things in possession" and "things in action." Shares in Scots law are incorporeal moveables.

[10] See para. 18–09, *post*.

A company limited by shares obtains its working funds by the issue of shares[11] which may be subscribed by the signatories to the memorandum of association or allotted to applicants for cash or for consideration in kind, *e.g.* the transfer of a business. Typical in this respect is the example given by the legislator in Part 1 of Schedule 1 to the 1980 Act[12]: the company named therein, *viz.* "The Western Steam Packet Public Limited Company," is formed with the object of conveying passengers and goods in ships and boats. In view of this object, the statutory illustration is unrealistic because it is obvious that a steamship company requires some initial capital but that is not provided in the statutory illustration. It is stated therein that the capital of the company shall be £50,000 which represents the "authorised minimum" that every public limited company shall have (1980 Act, ss. 3 (2) and 85 (1)) and that each of the two subscribers[13] shall subscribe to one share of £1 each; as he has to pay up the subscribed share to one-quarter (1980 Act, s. 6 (1) (*b*)) but this amount has to be paid in cash (1980 Act, s. 29), the initial assets at the disposal of the company would be the derisive sum of 50p. If the directors wish to issue the remaining 49,998 shares, they may do so if authorised by the articles; otherwise an ordinary resolution of the general meeting is required (1980 Act, s. 14 (1)). If the company wishes to increase the capital to a realistic amount, an ordinary resolution of the general meeting is necessary for this measure, provided that authority to that effect is contained in the articles (s. 61 (1) (*a*)).

3–06 In the company limited by shares the shareholder need not pay the whole nominal amount of his share to the company at once when acquiring the share. Here the distinction between the private and the public limited company is relevant. Further, a distinction has to be drawn between the subscription to the original memorandum and the subsequent allotment of shares.

As regards the subscription to the original memorandum, in a private company the subscribers need pay nothing on the shares subscribed and may wait until the directors—or the liquidator—make calls on them. In a public limited company the subscribers have to pay on the shares subscribed at least one-quarter of the nominal value and the whole of any premium (1980 Act, s. 6 (1) (*b*)) and shall make this payment, and all other payments on the shares subscribed, in cash (1980 Act, s. 29).

As regards the subsequent allotment of shares, the position is the same as on subscription, except that in a public limited company the allottees have to pay at least one-quarter of the nominal amount of the shares plus

---

[11] Unless it obtains it as loan capital which would be economically unsound.

[12] Parts I and II of Schedule 1 to the 1980 Act have superseded Tables B and D in Schedule 1 to the 1948 Act (1980 Act, s. 2 (4)). These forms and those contained in Tables C and E of Schedule 1 to the 1948 Act which are mentioned later on, may be altered by the Department of Trade by statutory instrument in the manner set out in s. 454.

[13] By virtue of the 1980 Act, s. 2 (1), the minimum number of shareholders in a public limited company is two, and no longer seven, as was required by the 1948 Act, s. 1 (1).

the whole of the premium at which the shares are issued (1980 Act, s. 6 (1) (*b*)) but they need not make this payment in cash. It is characteristic of the company limited by shares that, subject to the provisions of the articles, the directors may call upon the shareholders at any time to pay up the unpaid portion of the nominal amount of their shares. Such calls may be made during the active life of the company or during the winding up; it will be noted that the statutory definition of the company limited by shares in section 1 (2) (*a*) does not contain any qualification or restriction on the power of the company to make calls. The intention of the legislator is that, once the initial working funds which were provided by the initial payments of the shareholders on their shares are exhausted, the directors may make further calls if and when the financial position of the company demands; no maximum or minimum amount of the call is prescribed by the statutes.[14] In the contemplation of the legislator, the call imports an element of uncertainty both as regards time and amount.

In practice, as will be seen later,[15] the procedure for paying up shares is very different. First, it would be unusual for subscribers or allottees in a private company to pay nothing or in a public limited company only the relatively small statutory amount required by the law. Secondly, in modern practice a system of payment of the nominal amount of shares by fixed instalments is almost invariably adopted. The advantage of fixed instalments is that certainty as regards time and amount of the payments is substituted for uncertainty, and further that the newly issued shares are fully paid up within a relatively short time. The modern system of fixed instalments is usually linked up with the old system of calls by a provision in the articles similar to article 19 of Table A, which states that a fixed instalment shall be deemed to be a call duly made and payable on the date on which by the terms of issue the fixed instalment becomes payable.

The modern practice of fixed instalments and the older practice of calls on shares when required have one point in common: the unpaid portion of the nominal amount of the share may be made payable at any time during the existence of the company, *i.e.* during the active life as well as during the winding up. This point is of the essence of the company limited by shares.

Companies limited by guarantee

Definition and nature

3–07 The 1948 Act defines a company limited by guarantee as "a company having the liability of its members limited by the memorandum to such amount as the members may respectively thereby undertake to contribute to the assets of the company in the event of its being wound up" (s. 1 (2) (*b*)).

---

[14] The articles may provide such limits; see art. 15.
[15] See para. 35–02, *post*.

The guarantee company has two features in common with the share company: in both cases:

(1) the company has legal personality; and
(2) the liability of the members is limited, in the case of the share company by the nominal amount of shares held by each member, and in the case of the guarantee company by the amount of the guarantee undertaken by the member. Accordingly, both types of companies have to embody into their memorandum a statement to the effect that the liability of their members is limited (s. 2 (2)).

In law, the distinction between these two types of companies is that in the share company the liability of the member may have to be implemented at any time during the existence of the company, *i.e.* during its active life as well as during the winding up, whereas in the guarantee company that liability need only be implemented after the commencement of the winding up[16] of the company, and even then only subject to certain conditions (s. 2 (3)).

It follows from the statutory definition that a guarantee company[17] does not obtain its initial working funds from its members. This type of company is, therefore, only suitable if no initial funds are required or those funds are obtained from other sources, *e.g.* from endowments, fees, charges, donations or subscriptions. In the example of a memorandum of a company limited by guarantee and not having a share capital in Table C[18] of the 1948 Act this feature of the guarantee company is evident: the legislator refers to the Kent School Association Limited, the objects of which are the carrying on of a school for boys in the county of Kent. The seven—now there need be only two (1980 Act, s. 2 (1))—promoters, who have subscribed the memorandum, state that they are schoolmasters by profession. If one of them uses his house as school premises and they all teach at the school, initial funds are hardly required and the expenses of the enterprise can be recovered from the fees which the pupils have to pay.

3–08 The guarantee company, in its pure form,[19] is always a private company; as it has no share capital, it cannot satisfy the requirements of a public limited company. The guarantee company not having a share capital is obviously unsuitable as a form of organisation for ordinary business purposes, but a considerable number of associations pursuing other purposes have availed themselves of this type of corporate organisation, *e.g.* professional associations, trade associations, research associations set up by companies working in a particular field of business, associations for mutual

---

[16] For the meaning of the term "commencement of winding up," see ss. 229, 280 and paras. 85–27, 86–03 and 87–23, *post.*

[17] The observations in the text refer to the guarantee company in its pure form, *i.e.*, the guarantee company not having a share capital. The hybrid form of the guarantee company having a share capital is treated in para. 3–10, *post*. For an example of a guarantee company in the pure form, see *Re N.F.U. Development Trust Ltd.* [1972] 1 W.L.R. 1548.

[18] See note 12 to para. 3–05, *ante*.

[19] See note 17, *supra*.

information, for pooling and realising produce of various kinds, or for mutual insurance, *e.g.* for insuring against marine risks. In many instances guarantee companies, which satisfy the requirements of section 25 of the 1981 Act, do not add the word "Limited" to their names, but where this is not the case, a company limited by guarantee, like a company limited by shares, has to incorporate the word "Limited"[20] as the last word of its name (s. 2 (1) (*a*)).

A company limited by guarantee may distribute its profits to its members unless its memorandum or articles otherwise provide, as invariably is the case where the company is exempt from the requirement of adding "Limited" as the last word in its name (1981 Act, s. 25 (2) (*b*)).

The guarantee

3–09 The memorandum of a guarantee company has to contain a clause stating that each member undertakes to contribute to the assets of the company in the event of its being wound up while he is a member, or within one year after he ceases to be a member, in the events stated in section 2 (3), a sum not exceeding a specified amount.

The amount of the guarantee has to be stated in the memorandum; the Act does not provide minimum or maximum limits. The Act further does not prohibit the creation of several classes of guarantees of different amount: it would, *e.g.* be possible to provide that the guarantee of one class of members shall be £2 and that of another shall be £1. Nevertheless a provision in the memorandum or articles purporting to give a person a right to partake in the profits, otherwise than as a member, is void in the case of a guarantee company not having a share capital and registered after January 1, 1901 (s. 21 (1)).[21] It is, however, submitted that it is lawful for the articles to give members the right to participate in the profits in accordance with the amount of their guarantee, so that in the preceding example members who have undertaken a guarantee of £2 will receive twice the dividend as those who have undertaken a guarantee of £1. Section 21 (1) does not, it is submitted, apply to this case because the members partake in the profits still "as members"; the section merely prohibits the creation of rights to profits in favour of persons who are not "members," or in a manner which is disproportionate to their membership guarantee. Similarly, it is believed that, if there are various classes of guarantees notwithstanding article 20 of the articles in Table C, the right of members to vote can by the articles be made proportionate to the amount of their guarantee.

---

[20] See para. 7–01, *post*.

[21] This provision was introduced into company law by the Companies Act 1900, s. 27, in order to prohibit the registration of companies limited by guarantee and not having a share capital with articles dividing the undertaking into shares of no par value—a form of association described by Sir Francis Palmer as "most convenient."

Since the guarantee materialises only in the event of winding up,[22] the persons liable under it are:

(1) the members of the company at the commencement of the winding up[23]; and

(2) past members who ceased to be members within a year prior to that date (s. 2 (3)).

The guarantee becomes effective with respect to:

(a) the debts and liabilities of the company;

(b) the costs of winding up:

but, in the case of past members, subject to the important qualification that each past member is only liable for the debts and liabilities of the company contracted before he ceased to be a member; and

(c) the adjustment of the rights of the members amongst themselves (s. 2 (3)).

The liability of the members of a guarantee company under their guarantee thus corresponds closely to that of present and past members as contributories in the winding up of a share company (s. 212); in particular, past members of a guarantee company—like those on the B list of a share company (s. 212 (1) (*c*))[24]—are not liable unless the existing members are unable to satisfy the contributions required from them.[25] Directors who are *ex officio* members of the company are not as such liable on the guarantee.[26]

Types of guarantee companies

3–10 The Company Acts recognise two types of guarantee companies, *viz.*—

(1) The company limited by guarantee and not having a share capital (s. 11 (*b*) and Table C); and

(2) The company limited by guarantee and having a share capital (s. 11 (*c*) and Part II of Schedule 1 of the 1980 Act[27]).

The former is the guarantee company in its pure form, the latter is a hybrid form combining elements of the guarantee and the share company.

However, the guarantee company having a share capital is discontinued in future. The 1980 Act, s. 1 (2) provides that on or after the appointed day, *viz.* on December 22, 1980,[28]

> "no company may be formed as, or become, a company limited by guarantee with a share capital."

Guarantee companies with a share capital which exist on the appointed day are not affected by this prohibition.

When admitting the guarantee company having a share capital the

---

22 *Robertson* v. *British Linen Co.* (1891) 18 R. (Ct. of Sess.) 1225.

23 For the meaning of the term "commencement of winding up," see ss. 229, 280 and paras. 85–27, 86–03 and 87-23, *post*.

24 See paras. 85–45, 86–27 and 87–38, *post*.

25 *Re Premier Underwriting Association (No. 1)* [1913] 2 Ch. 29.

26 *Re Premier Underwriting Association (No. 2)* [1913] 2 Ch. 81.

27 This form has superseded Table D of Schedule 1 of the 1948 Act (1980 Act, s. 20 (4)).

28 See note 1 to para. 3–02.

legislator apparently thought of cases in which the company required some initial capital which was to be contributed by the shareholders, *e.g.* in order to buy its business premises, while the normal working funds would be provided from other sources, such as fees, charges, subscriptions, etc. In these cases the guarantee is intended to reinforce the financial position of the company, similarly to the case of a share company which has created a reserve liability (s. 60). In practice, the guarantee company having a share capital is not frequently used and this justifies its abolition, for the future, by the 1980 Act. Normally, where the situation is as envisaged by the legislator, a company limited by shares is registered.

The memorandum of a guarantee company having a share capital provides for the liability of the members in two clauses, *viz.* in the guarantee clause and in the capital clause (see cls. 6 and 7 of the memorandum in Part II of Schedule 1 of the 1980 Act). On principle, every member of such a company is subject to a twofold liability, *viz.* to the guarantee which may become effective in the winding up of the company, and to the liability to pay up the nominal amount of his share which may be effective before that event. In normal cases in which there are not several classes of guarantees, the liability of the members on the guarantee is equal, whereas their liability on the shares varies in accordance with the amount of their shareholding. The voting power in a guarantee company having a share capital is determined by the shareholding, not by the guarantee. Apart from an article stating the number of members in compliance with section 7 (2), the articles of the guarantee company having a share capital may be indentical with those of a share company.

Members

3–11 As is evident from the preceding observations, the number of members in a guarantee company need not be constant.

The articles must state that the number of members with which the company proposes to be registered (s. 7 (2)), and any increase has to be notified to the Registrar of Companies within fifteen days and has to be registered by him (s. 7 (3)). This information, together with the amount of the guarantee stated in the guarantee clause of the memorandum (s. 2 (3)), enables members of the public to ascertain the total amount of the guarantee which the members have to provide in the event of the winding up of the company.

The increase in the number of members in a guarantee company can be left to the decision of the directors, who may likewise be given power to admit applicants to membership (see arts. 2 and 3 of the articles in Table C).

Unless the articles otherwise provide, a member who wishes to discontinue his membership in the company may do so by giving the company notice, and on receipt of the notice the cesser of membership becomes effective. As has been observed earlier, the former member remains liable on his guarantee, subject to qualifications, for one year after he ceased to be a member.[29] A guarantee company, like every other company, must keep a register of members (s. 110) which may be inspected by members of the public (s. 113). If the guarantee company has no share capital, its annual return (s. 125) need not give the particulars as to members required in the case of a company having a share capital (s. 124).

In a guarantee company having a share capital a member combines, as has been pointed out earlier,[30] the position of guarantor and of shareholder. The annual return, which has to be filed in this case, has to give the usual particulars as to members (s. 124).

Formation and application of Companies Acts

3–12 In order to form a company limited by guarantee, a memorandum and articles of association must be filed. In particular, the registration of articles is compulsory in this case (s. 6); the Act does not provide that a model set of articles, such as Table A in the case of a share company, shall apply unless excluded.

The memorandum and articles of a guarantee company not having a share capital must be in accordance with the forms set out in Table C, or as near thereto as the circumstances permit, and similarly the constitutional documents of a guarantee company having a share capital must correspond with the memorandum in Part II of Schedule 1 of the 1980 Act and the articles in Table D of the 1948 Act (s. 11 (*b*) and (*c*), as amended by the 1980 Act, s. 2 (4)). Section 11 is, however concerned only with the form, not the content, of the articles, and it is admissible to add, subtract or vary as circumstances require, so long as the general form of the relevant Table is followed; the words of the section are merely directory in their effect.[31]

The provisions of the Companies Act 1948 to 1981 apply to guarantee companies, unless otherwise stated in a particular section.

Registration fees and stamp duty

Upon the registration of a company limited by guarantee, the registration fee must be paid, as provided by the Schedule to the Companies (Fees) Regulations 1980,[32] issued by virtue of section 37 (1) of the 1976 Act. The amount of the fee for registration is at present[33] £50.[34]

Unlimited companies

3–13 An unlimited company is defined as "a company not having any limit on the liability of its members" (s. 1 (2) (*c*)).

---

[29] See para. 3–09, *ante*.
[30] See para. 3–10, *ante*.
[31] *Gaiman* v. *National Association for Mental Health* [1971] Ch. 317.
[32] S.I. 1980 No. 1749.
[33] Position: August 1, 1982.
[34] As regards guarantee companies having a share capital, stamp duties on statements relating to the capital were abolished by s. 49 of the Finance Act 1973.

The 1948 Act had to admit this type of company because it prohibits the formation of partnerships and unincorporated business associations consisting of more than 20 persons (s. 434) or, if formed for the purpose of carrying on the business of banking, consisting of more than ten persons (s. 429); but these restrictions have now been relaxed in certain cases by sections 119–122 of the 1967 Act.[35] Except as provided by the 1967 Act, if persons in excess of these numbers wish to associate for the stated purposes in a manner rendering themselves liable without limitation for the debts of their business, they have to choose the form of an unlimited company.

Effect of the 1976 Act[36]

3–14 By section 1 (8) of the 1976 Act,[37] unlimited companies are in general exempted from the obligation imposed by section 1 (7) of that Act to deliver to the Registrar a copy of every document required to be comprised in the accounts of the company in respect of the relevant accounting reference period. This exemption does not, however, apply if at any time during that period the company has been—

(a) to its knowledge, the subsidiary of a limited company, or would have been a subsidiary if shares or powers held by two or more companies had been held by a single company; or
(b) the holding company of a limited company; or
(c) carrying on business as the promoter of a trading stamp scheme within the meaning of the Trading Stamps Act 1964.

The reference to holding and subsidiary companies in this provision includes foreign limited companies (1976 Act, s. 1 (8), end).

This exemption is attractive to companies which do not wish to publish their annual accounts. The 1967 Act, which provided that *all* private companies, like public companies, had to publish their accounts admitted, for the first time, provisions for the re-registration of a limited company as unlimited. In view of the increased liability of the members resulting from such re-registration, these provisions are very strict. They are considered, together with the converse provisions for re-registration of an unlimited company as limited in paragraphs 5–17 and 5–20, *post*.

Liability of members

3–15 Although the liability of the members of an unlimited company, like that of the partners of a partnership, is unlimited, the position of those members differs fundamentally from that of partners. The unlimited company is a legal person but the partnership in England has no corporate existence. Consequently, the partners are liable directly to the creditors of the partnership, but the members of the unlimited company are not liable to the

---

[35] See para. 89–09, *post*.

[36] The regulation of section 1 (8) of the 1976 Act was preceeded by section 47 of the 1967 Act but that provision was repealed by the 1976 Act. For the position before the 1967 Act, see 21st ed., pp. 27–28.

[37] s. 47 of the 1967 Act was repealed by the Companies Act 1976, Sched. 3 with effect from October 1, 1977 (the Companies Act 1976 (Commencement No. 5) Order 1977 (S.I. 1977/1348)).

company's creditors who, if they sued the members for a debt incurred by this company, would be unsuccessful since the members could plead *res inter alios acta*. Although a Scottish partnership has independent legal personality, this distinction still holds good, because creditors of the firm can recover directly from the partners.[38]

If the creditors of the unlimited company cannot obtain payment from the company, they may petition the court for a winding-up order; the liquidator will then ask the members to contribute to the payment of the debts of the company and the costs of winding up, and the members are liable to do so without limitation of their liability. But a policy issued by the company or another contract made by it may contain a provision whereby the liability of individual members on the policy or contract is restricted or whereby the funds of the company are alone made liable in respect of the policy or contract, and a defence arising from such a contractual term may validly be taken against the creditor (s. 212 (1) (*f*)).

Memorandum and articles

3–16 In the case of an unlimited company the clause in the memorandum that the liability of the members is limited is omitted, and the name of the company need not incorporate "Limited" or "public limited company" at the end. The company must register articles (s. 6) which have to state the number of members with which the company proposes to register (s. 7 (1)), and any increase in members has to be notified to the Registrar of Companies within 15 days (s. 7 (3)). The memorandum and articles of association of an unlimited company have to be in the form of Table E[39] or as near thereto as circumstances admit (s. 11 (*d*)).

An unlimited company may have a capital divided into shares, or no such capital.

Application of Companies Acts

3–17 The provisions of the Companies Acts 1948 to 1981 apply to unlimited companies unless a particular section otherwise provides. These companies appear to be bound by the provisions of section 53 regulating underwriting commissions, and also by sections 42 to 44 of the 1981 Act, which, subject to wide exceptions, prohibit the company from giving financial assistance for the acquisition of its own shares; but an unlimited company, apparently even if having a share capital, can freely reduce its capital without leave of the court, since section 66 does not apply, and the form of articles in Table E gives power to reduce capital in any way. A member can retire and cease to be a member in the manner provided by the memorandum or articles (subject, of course, to his liability as a past member under section 212).[40] It would also appear that the company might purchase the shares of members.[41] The fees for the registration on an unlimited company are

---

[38] Partnership Act 1890, s. 4 (2).
[39] See note 12 to para. 3–05, *ante*.
[40] *Re Borough Commercial Society* [1893] 2 Ch. 242.
[41] *Ibid*.

those fixed under the Companies Act 1976, s. 37, according to which the registration fee is £50.[42]

Application of European Communities Act 1972, section 9

3–18 It is thought that this section does not apply to unlimited companies. The Act concerning the Conditions of Accession and the Adjustments to the Treaties,[42] annexed to the Treaty of Accession of January 22, 1972, provides in Annex I, III, H, that the Council Directive of March 9, 1968, which section 9 seeks to implement, shall apply in the United Kingdom to "companies incorporated with limited liability."

It is realised that subsection (8) of section 9 provides that that section shall be construed as one with the Companies Act 1948 and that the definition of a company in section 455 includes an unlimited company but it is submitted that it is justified to interpret the wording of subsection (8) with reference to the Council Directive of March 9, 1968, as amended by the Act of Accession.

Companies not formed under the 1948 Act

3–19 The 1948 Act, s. 382, as amended by the 1980 Act, Sched. 3, para. 29, authorises the registration of certain companies not formed under it. The ambit of this provision is narrow because the companies formed and registered under the earlier Companies Acts are automatically governed by the Act of 1948 and do not require re-registration under that Act.

The arrangement of the Act of 1948 is the following: in section 455 the Act defines a "company" as "a company formed and registered under this Act as an existing company," and it then proceeds to define an "existing company" as a company formed and registered under the Joint Stock Companies Acts[43] or the Companies Acts of 1862, 1908 or 1929, except companies registered in Northern Ireland and Eire. By section 377 the Act is made applicable to "existing companies," and by sections 378 and 379 to companies registered or re-registered under the Joint Stock Companies Acts or the earlier Companies Acts, except companies registered in Northern Ireland or Eire (s. 381). In the result, the Acts of 1948 to 1981[44] apply automatically to all companies formed and registered under the 1948 Act or registered under the Joint Stock Companies Acts or under the Companies Acts of 1862, 1908 and 1929, but they do not apply to companies registered in Northern Ireland and the Irish Republic (to which territories the Act of 1948 does not extend); the only qualification which has to be added is that if any of these earlier companies has adopted what is now Table A, the Table of the Act under which the company was formed

---

[42] S.I. 1980 No. 1749.

[42] Briefly called "The Act of Accession." This, of course, is an international instrument and not an Act of Parliament of the United Kingdom.

[43] Which are likewise defined in s. 455.

[44] 1967 Act, s. 53; 1976 Act, s. 40; 1980 Act, s. 86 and Sched. 3 para. 29; 1981 Act, s. 114.

continues to apply, and Table A of the 1948 Act does not apply (s. 459 (14)).

3–20 Certain companies to which the Act of 1948 does not automatically apply are authorised to register under the Act (s. 382, as amended by the 1980 Land 1981 Acts). A company desirous of so doing must have at least two members and further, subject to certain exceptions,[45]

(1) must either have been in existence on November 2, 1862[46];

(2) or, if formed after that date (whether before or after the commencement of the Act of 1948[47]), must have been formed in pursuance of an Act of Parliament (other than the Companies Act 1948), or of letters patent, or being a company within the stannaries,[48] or otherwise duly constituted by the law.[49]

These provisions re-enact similar provisions in earlier Companies Acts[50]; their purpose is mainly to enable old companies to which the Act does not apply automatically to obtain registration, even if this is only done with a view to the company's being wound up; the Act provides expressly that a registration for that purpose shall not be invalid (s. 382 (1)), but a registration cannot be obtained after a petition to wind up an unregistered company has been presented,[51] nor can it be obtained by a foreign company.[52] An unregistered company can obtain registration as an unlimited company, for the sole purpose of being wound up voluntarily and transferring, in the winding up, its business for shares in another company, in exercise of the power now given by section 287.[53] The certificate of incorporation given by the Registrar by virtue of section 390 (2) is conclusive evidence that the company was authorised to be so registered.[54]

If the company is a joint stock company, it can register as a company limited by shares, otherwise it must register as a company limited by guarantee or an unlimited company (s. 382 (1), proviso (iv)).

A majority of members present in person or by proxy has to assent to the registration in the manner set out in section 382 (1), provisos (v)–(vii). Where a company the constitution of which was contained in a deed of settlement is registered, a memorandum and articles of association may be substituted for the deed of settlement (s. 395 (1)); the objects may be stated in the memorandum wider than they were stated in the deed of settlement,[55] but the members are entitled to object in the manner pro-

---

45 s. 382 (1), provisos (i)–(iv).

46 When the 1862 Act came into operation.

47 The Act of 1948 came into operation on July 19, 1948 (s. 462 (2)).

48 For definition, see s. 455. On stannaries, see para. 89–34, *post*.

49 This latter class has been held to be restricted to companies constituted in some manner analogous to the three former classes in this group: *R.* v. *Joint Stock Companies Registrar* [1891] 2 Q.B. 598, *Re Cusson's Ltd.* (1904) 73 L.J.Ch. 296.

50 Part VII of the 1862 Act authorised the registration of companies existing before it came into operation.

51 *Re Hercules Insurance Co.* (1871) L.R. 11 Eq. 321.

52 *Bulkeley* v. *Schutz* (1871) L.R. 3 P.C. 764; and *Bateman* v. *Service* (1881) 6 App.Cas. 386.

53 *Southall* v. *British Mutual Life Assurance Society* (1871) 6 Ch.App. 614.

54 *Hammond* v. *Prentice Brothers Ltd.* [1920] 1 Ch. 201.

55 *Re Hewitt Bros. Ltd.* [1931] W.N. 213.

vided in section 5 for the alteration of the objects of the company (s. 395 (2)). Before registration joint stock companies and other companies have to produce certain documents to the Registrar (ss. 384 and 385). Upon registration the company is placed in virtually the same position as if it had originally been formed under the Act.

On registration the property of the company vests in the company as incorporated under the Act (s. 391), and registration does not affect the rights or liabilities of the company in respect of obligations incurred or contracts entered into before that event (s. 392). Part VIII contains in sections 393 and 394 further detailed provisions as to the effect of registration of a company under that Part.

Application of 1967, 1976, 1980 and 1981 Acts

3–21 The provisions of Part I of the 1967 Act apply, to the same extent as the provisions of the 1948 Act, to companies formed or registered under earlier Acts[56] and to companies not formed under the 1948 Act but registered thereunder (1967 Act, s. 53 (1)).[57] The 1976 Act is made applicable to these companies by section 40, the 1980 Act by section 86, and the 1981 Act by section 114.

Application of Acts to unregistered companies

Certain provisions of the Acts relating to prospectuses, allotments, annual return, accounts and audit are made applicable[58] to unregistered companies incorporated in and having a place of business in Great Britain, other than companies incorporated by or registered under a public general Act, companies not formed for the purpose of gain, and companies exempted by the Department of Trade.

Some provisions of section 9 of the European Communities Act 1972 can be made applicable to unregistered companies, but only in so far as may be specified; such regulations may refer to the registered office (s. 107) and service of documents (s. 437).[59]

---

56 See para. 3–19, *ante*.
57 See above in text.
58 By s. 435 of and Sched. 14 to the 1948 Act, as amended by s. 54 of the 1967 Act, and the Companies (Unregistered Companies) Regulations 1975 (S.I. 1975 No. 597, replacing S.I. 1967 No. 1876). The 1975 Regulations are amended by the Companies (Unregistered Companies) (Amendment) Regulations 1980 (S.I. 1980 No. 1784).
59 European Communities Act 1972, s. 9 (8), S.I. 1975 No. 597.

CHAPTER 4

PRIVATE AND PUBLIC COMPANIES. SMALL, MEDIUM-SIZED AND OTHER COMPANIES. DORMANT COMPANIES

History

4–01 A company having a share capital may be formed as a private or as a public company.[1]

The introduction of the private company by the Companies Acts 1907/1908

Before the Companies Act 1907, which was combined with the earlier Companies Acts as the Companies (Consolidation) Act 1908, the private company was not recognised by the legislature as a form of corporate organisation, although the term "private company" was already known in practice[2] and was used in much the same descriptive manner as is the term "close corporation" in the United States of America nowadays, *viz.* as denoting a company the shares in which are intended to be held by a restricted group of persons and cannot be acquired freely by members of the public.[3] The Act of 1907[4] provided for the first time a statutory definition of the private company which was amended by subsequent legislation. The 1980 Act does not provide a definition of a private company but describes it in section 15; it states, however, in section 1 (1) that " 'private company,' unless the context otherwise requires, means a company that is not a public company."

When according statutory recognition to the private company, the legislator intended to make available the advantages of corporate trading to the small trader. With this object in view, he required the minimum number of members for this form of company to be two, and not seven as was required before the 1980 Act of the public company, and granted it balance-sheet secrecy by providing that a balance-sheet need not be attached to the annual return which the private company—like every other company—had to file with the Registrar, in order to protect it against competition from financially stronger rivals.

---

[1] See para. 3–03, *ante*.

[2] The term was already in use in 1877 when Sir Francis Palmer published his *Private Companies and Syndicates*. The Companies Act 1900 drew a distinction between companies offering their shares for subscription to the public and others. Early judicial references to "private companies" occur in *Re British Seamless Paper Box* (1881) 17 Ch.D. 467 (*per* Cotton L.J.); *Re George Newman & Co.* [1895] 1 Ch. 674, 685 (*per* Lindley L.J.); and *Salomon* v. *Salomon & Co.* [1897] A.C. 22 (*per* Lord Macnaghten).

[3] See Professor F. Hodge O'Neal, "The American Equivalent of the Private Company" [1956] B.L.R. 304. The term "close company" is used by the Income and Corporation Taxes Act 1970, s. 282 (1) to describe closely controlled companies to which special fiscal provisions are applicable: see para. 91–01, *post*.

[4] s. 37 (1).

The admission of the private company by the 1907/1908 legislation followed the German example which for a long time distinguished between the public company (*Aktiengesellschaft*, A.G.) and private company (*Gesellschaft mit beschränkter Haftung*, GmbH). This distinction was adopted in 1925 by France where the public company is known as *société anonyme* (S.A.) and the private company as *société à responsabilité limitée* (S.a.r.l.). But while on the continent these two types of company were conceived as fundamentally different legal structures, the position was different in the law of the United Kingdom. Here the private company was admitted as a variation of the normal type of the public company. Consequently, the principle was until 1980 that every company was a public company unless it satisfied the requirements of a private company. The public company was thus until 1980 the residual form of the company in the United Kingdom. There was a—rebuttable—presumption that every company was a public company unless stated otherwise in its constitution. All provisions of the Companies Acts applied to private companies as well as to public companies unless the Acts provided differently.

The regulation of the Companies Act 1948

4–02 The Companies Act 1948 retained this conceptual structure of British company law. The Act did not impose a statutory requirement on private companies. A private company was defined by section 28 as a company which by its articles—regulations—introduced three restrictions. These restrictions were known as regulatory restrictions. Section 28 provided:

> "(1) For the purposes of this Act, the expression 'private company' means a company which by its articles—
> (a) restricts the right to transfer its shares; and
> (b) limits the number of its members to 50, not including persons who are in the employment of the company and persons who, having been formerly in the employment of the company, were while in that employment, and have continued after the determination of that employment to be, members of the company; and
> (c) prohibits any invitation to the public to subscribe for any shares or debentures of the company.
> (2) Where two or more persons hold one or more shares in a company jointly, they shall, for the purposes of this section, be treated as a single member."

Of these three restrictions, the most important was the third because it prevented the securities of the private company from being listed at The Stock Exchange.

However, the Cohen Committee, when preparing the Companies Act 1947, which was later combined with the earlier Acts into the Companies Act 1948, found that the form of the private company, and in particular the privilege of balance-sheet secrecy, had been abused. The private company was not only used by small business for which it was originally devised. It was also used by some public companies which withheld information from their shareholders by the simple device of carrying on business activities, which they did not wish to disclose in their accounts, through private companies, with the result that the shareholders in the parent company were unable to ascertain whether the subsidiaries which were private companies made a profit, and, if so, what that profit was.

By the Companies Act 1947, the legislator divided private companies into two categories, *viz*. ordinary and exempt. He required the former to file a balance-sheet with their annual accounts but, although in that respect placing them on the same footing as public companies, allowed them to retain most other privileges of the private company. He further provided that only private companies which satisfied a number of requirements additional to those which all private companies had to satisfy were exempt—hence the name "exempt private company"—from the obligation to file a balance-sheet with the annual return. The additional requirements for exempt private companies were essentially that the shares or debentures of the company were not held by a body corporate other than an exempt private company and that they were not held by a nominee, but exemptions were admitted to these rules. These provisions were re-enacted by the Act of 1948 (s. 129).

The 1948 Act introduced a further important innovation. It provided in Table A, the model set of articles, a Part II which applied to private companies that had not adopted their own articles and had not excluded the application of Table A.

The regulation of the Companies Act 1967

4–03 This Act adopted a new company law philosophy. Following the suggestions first made by the Jenkins Committee[5] in 1962, that balance-sheet disclosure and public accountability should be correlated to the privilege of using the corporate form, it enacted that every limited company should publish its accounts, and abolished, as from January 27, 1968, the form of the exempt private company (1967 Act, s. 2).

The reform introduced by the Companies Act 1980

4–04 This Act introduced an entirely new company classification which constituted a complete break with the traditional relationship between the public and private company in the United Kingdom.

This was due to two causes. First, the Act had to give effect in the United Kingdom to the Second EEC Directive on Company Law Harmonisation and that Directive demanded a clearer distinction between the two types of company than prevailed in the United Kingdom hitherto. Secondly, in the United Kingdom small and medium-sized business is normally promoted in the form of the private company, with the result that the number of private companies in the United Kingdom is much greater than in any other country in the EEC; on the continent these businesses widely use the form

[5] Cmnd. 1749 (1962), paras. 55–63.

of partnerships or single traders. According to the Annual Report of the Department of Trade on Companies in 1980, on December 31, 1980 there were 828,496 companies on the register, of which 818,171 were private companies and 10,325 public companies. This preponderance of private companies had to be given effect in the 1980 Act.

The 1980 Act therefore reversed the traditional structure of company law. The private company is made the residual form of company. Every company is a private company unless it satisfies the special requirements of the public company.

4–05 One of the requirements of the public company is that it must have a statutory minimum capital, the "authorised minimum," which at present is fixed in the rather low sum of £50,000. For the private company, on the other hand, a minimum capital is not prescribed. Further, the shares of the public company have to be paid up to one-quarter plus the whole premium, but the shares of the private company need not be paid up. The two types of company are given different designations. The name of the public company ends in the phrase "public limited company" (plc), and that of the private company in the word "Limited" (Ltd.). The indicated abbreviations and also, if the company has its registered office in Wales, the Welsh equivalents, may be used and there is no obligation to add an English translation to the Welsh adjunct (1980 Act, s. 78 (3) and (4)).

The legal requirements of the private and the public company will be discussed fully in the further sections of this chapter. Two points may, however, be mentioned already in this historical introduction. As far as the private company is concerned, the 1980 Act abolished the three regulatory requirements of section 28 of the 1948 Act and adopted a single statutory requirement: the private company shall not offer any shares or debentures to the public.[6] It is thus made clear that the securities of the private company cannot be dealt with at The Stock Exchange. Secondly, Part II of Table A in Schedule 1 to the 1948 Act has been repealed[7] and Part I is amended to be applicable to the private as well as the public company.

Private companies

Their functions

4–06 The modern private company serves two purposes: first, to enable those carrying on a family business to avail themselves of the advantages of corporate trading, and, secondly, where used as a subsidiary in a group of companies, to avoid, with respect to that part of the group, the strict requirements obligatory for public companies. Although these purposes differ intrinsically, one feature is common to all private companies, a feature which, at the same time, limits the economic use of that form of company: according to its constitution, members of the investing public cannot acquire shares in the private company at will, and where it is

[6] 1980 Act, s. 15.
[7] 1980 Act, s. 88 and Sched. 3, para. 36 (1).

intended that the company should be able to invite members of the public to acquire a proprietary interest in it without participating in the management, the private company is not the appropriate form and the company has to be formed as, or more frequently converted into, a public company. In many private companies, particularly those carrying on family businesses, the ownership in the company and its management will be in the same hands.

The company to have two members

Every private company must have at least two members (s. 1 (1)). A company having only one member is not admitted in English company law. If the number of members falls below two, section 31 of the 1948 Act, as amended by the 1980 Act,[8] applies. That section provides that after a period of grace of six months the one member who knowingly allows the company to carry on business with only one member shall, jointly and severally with the company, be liable for the debts of the company contracted during that period or, as the case may be, any part of it.

A single member may hold the shares in a private company with his nominee. The nominee is treated by the company as a full member,[9] and consequently the legal requirement that there must be at least two members is satisfied.

There is no maximum limitation on the number of members in a private company.

Every company to be private unless public

The 1980 Act makes it clear that the private company is the residual form of the company. It provides in section 1 (1): " 'private company,' unless the context otherwise requires, means a company that is not a public company."

This provision raises a problem. A public company may state in its memorandum that it shall be a public company but it may fail to satisfy the factual requirements of a public company, *e.g.* it may have reduced its capital below the statutory minimum without first being re-registered as a private company, as required by section 12 of the 1980 Act, unless the court directs otherwise. Such a company continues to be a public company because the certificate of the Registrar that the company is a public company is conclusive evidence (1980 Act, s. 5 (9) (*b*)) until it is rescinded.

The statutory requirement

4–07 A private company must satisfy only one statutory requirement: it must not offer any shares or debentures to the public, either by way of a direct prospectus, or by means of an offer for sale, or in any other manner, nor must it allot or agree to allot such securities to the public (1980 Act, s. 15 (1)).

---

[8] 1980 Act, s. 88 and Sched. 3.

[9] See s. 117, para. 50–06, *post*.

The 1980 Act expresses this prohibition in the following manner. It makes it a criminal offence for a private company (except a company limited by guarantee and not having a share capital) to make such offer (1980 Act, s. 15 (1)). The company and any of its officers in default are liable on conviction to a fine not exceeding the statutory maximum (1980 Act, s. 15 (3)).

The provisions of the 1948 Act relating to offers to the public apply likewise to offers contemplated by section 15 of the 1980 Act. In particular, the following provisions of the 1948 Act apply: section 45 (2) which establishes a presumption in the cases in which an offer is made to the public, and section 55 which defines the "public."[10] The latter reference brings into operation subsection (2) of section 55, according to which shares or debentures are not offered to the public, *inter alia*, if the offer is the "domestic concern" of the persons making or receiving it. Consequently, although by virtue of section 55 (1) an offer to the members of the company is regarded as an offer to a section of the public, a small private company which makes a rights issue to its members by way of non-renounceable letters of allotment would not make an issue to the public. Further, if the bankers of a small private company offer shares in it for sale to a select number of customers in a manner making the acceptance of the offer personal to the offerees, the offer is likewise not made to the public, but on the authority of *Hudson* v. *Bishop Cavenagh (Commodities) Ltd.*[10a] which deals with the definition of a circular within section 14 of the Prevention of Fraud (Investments) Act 1958 it can be argued, that a letter addressed in a standard form to 60 named recipients is an offer to the public.

The validity of an allotment or offer for sale of securities in a private company is not affected by the fact that it may contravene section 15 of the 1980 Act (s. 15 (4)).

These provisions do not apply to an "old public company"[11] during the transitional period[12] but after the expiration of that period they apply to such a company as if it were a private company (1980 Act s. 15 (5)).

Restrictions on transfer of shares

4–08 Although the 1980 Act no longer so requires as a regulatory condition, clauses are generally inserted in the articles with a view to preserving, as far as practicable, the private character of the concern. These provisions will be considered in detail later.[13] Their general purpose is to prohibit a member or his executors or administrators from transferring his shares to any outsider, unless and until the shares have first been offered to the continuing members, either at par or at a fair value to be fixed by the auditor, or ascertained by arbitration, or by some sliding scale, or at the

---

[10] See para. 21–17, *post*.
[10a] (1981) N.L.J. 1238; see para. 25–16, *post*.
[11] See para. 4–17, *post*.
[12] Which ended on June 22, 1981.
[13] See para. 39–13, *post*.

"current price" fixed half-yearly by a general meeting, or at, say, 10 times the average yearly dividend, or at the amount paid up with an addition proportioned to the average profits during, say, the last three years past, or otherwise; the clauses usually go on to provide that if none of the continuing members desires to purchase the shares, they may be transferred to an outsider, but even in that case the directors are usually given a very wide discretion as to approving of the admission of an outsider. The validity of such provisions is clear.[14]

4–09 A private company has many advantages over the public company.[15] The main of these advantages are:

(1) no "authorised minimum," *i.e.* minimum subscribed capital, is prescribed (1980 Act, s. 6 (1) (*a*));
(2) it is not necessary for the allotted shares to be paid up to at least one-quarter of their nominal amount plus the whole premium (1980 Act, s. 6 (1) (*b*));
(3) the memorandum need not contain a clause indicating the nature of the company (1980 Act, s. 1 (1));
(4) it may commence business on the grant of a certificate of incorporation; the trading certificate required by section 4 of the 1980 Act need not be obtained by the private company;
(5) it need have only one director (1948 Act, s. 176);
(6) no individual resolution of the general meeting for the separate appointment of each director is required (1948 Act, s. 183 (1));
(7) the provisions relating to the retirement of directors on reaching the age limit do not apply unless the company is the subsidiary of a public company (s. 185 (8))[16];
(8) at the general meeting proxies may not only attend and vote but also address the meeting (s. 136);
(9) the provisions regulating insider dealing which, apart from off-market dealings, apply only to stock exchange dealings do not apply to private companies (1980 Act, s. 68 *et seq.*);
(10) the right of pre-emption which the 1980 Act gives certain shareholders may in the case of a private company be excluded by the memorandum or the articles (1980 Act, s. 17 (9));
(11) the stringent provisions of the 1980 Act regulating dealings of the directors with their companies and aimed at the avoidance of a conflict of interest apply in many instances only to public companies and to private companies which form part of a group including a public company (1980 Act, ss. 46–67; see the definition of "relevant company" in s. 65 (1));
(12) an expert's valuation report is not required if a private company

[14] Borland's Trustee v. *Steel Brothers & Co.* [1901] 1 Ch. 279; *Att.-Gen.* v. *Jameson* [1904] 2 Ir.R. 644; *Stewart* v. *James Keiller & Sons* 1902, 4 F. 657.
[15] *Cf.* para. 4–15, *post*.
[16] Or its equivalent in Northern Ireland (s. 185 (8)).

wishes to acquire certain non-cash assets during two years from a subscriber or member (1980 Act, s. 26);

(13) a private company which has lost half or more of its called-up capital need not hold an extraordinary general meeting to consider what measures should be taken to deal with the serious loss of capital (1980 Act, s. 34);

(14) only a private company limited by guarantee shall henceforth be exempt by virtue of section 25 of the 1981 Act from ending its name in the word "Limited".

(15) a private company, which is not a member of a group including a public company, may give financial assistance for the acquisition of its own shares, if the net assets of the company are not reduced thereby or, to the extent that they are reduced, if the financial assistance is provided out of distributable profits (1981 Act, s. 43).

(16) a private, but not a public, company may redeem or purchase its own shares out of capital (1981 Act, s. 54).

(17) only a private company can satisfy the qualifying conditions for small and medium-sized companies which may in certain circumstances enjoy exemption from the obligation to file full accounts (1981 Act, ss. 5–10).

On the other hand, a private company has the following disadvantages:

(1) it shall not make an offer to the public (whether for cash or otherwise) of any of its shares in or debentures of the company and shall not allot, or agree to allot, any of its shares in or debentures of the company with a view to them being offered for sale to the public (1980 Act, s. 15 (1));

(2) its shares or debentures cannot be listed at The Stock Exchange[16a];

(3) a member must not appoint more than one proxy to attend a general meeting on the same occasion (1948 Act, s. 136 (1) (*b*)).

Further considerations applicable to private companies

4–10 OBLIGATIONS OF PRIVATE COMPANY. It must be borne in mind that a private company, though it has many advantages, has also obligations under the Acts. This was pointed out by Lord Macnaghten in *Trevor* v. *Whitworth*[17]:

> "It is said that the company was a family company. But a family company, whatever the expression means, does not limit its trading to the family circle. If it takes the benefit of the Act, it is bound by the Act as much as any other company. It can have no special privilege or immunity."

Directors, too, of a private company will be equally liable for a misapplication of the company's funds or for other misfeasance. Thus, in *Re*

[16a] This would prima facie infringe s. 15 (1). If an old public company, which was listed, re-registers as a private company, its equity share capital can no longer be listed but The Stock Exchange raises no objection to its other capital and debentures to continue to be listed (Stock Exchange Circular of February 1981, No. 1).

[17] (1887) 12 App.Cas. 409.

Geo. Newman & Co.,[18] one Newman had converted his business into a "private" company, and had applied funds of the company, with the privity and consent of the other members, to *ultra vires* purposes. It was held that he was guilty of misfeasance, and that the fact that it was a private company did not in any way exempt or protect him.

A private company is subject to the restrictions of section 53 of the 1948 Act as to underwriting commissions.[19] Where it pays underwriting commission a statement in the prescribed form[20] must be filed for the purpose of disclosing the amount of rate of commission (s. 53 (1) (*c*) (ii)).

4–11 GOVERNING, PERMANENT OR LIFE DIRECTORS. The articles of a private company sometimes vest the management in a small number of directors, or in a "governing" or "permanent" or "life" director. In the latter case it is a common course to insert provisions enabling such governing or permanent director to appoint, if and when he thinks fit, other persons to be ordinary directors to act under him, and to determine their powers, duties and remuneration; also to remove any ordinary director from office. A permanent or governing director is generally given very wide powers in regard to the management of the business of the company. Sometimes two or more persons are appointed joint governing or permanent directors with like powers. Usually, the powers of a governing or permanent director are limited to the time during which he holds a certain large proportion of the capital—*e.g.* one-half or one-third of the issued capital—and sometimes his powers are made transmissible, in case of his death, to his executors or their nominee, but so long only as the shares or a large proportion of them remain part of his estate.

In modern company law a governing, permanent or life director, even of a private company, has no security of office but can be removed by the general meeting at any time before the expiration of his period of office (1948 Act, s. 184 (1))[21]; this is done by ordinary resolution requiring special notice (s. 184 (1) and (2)). This statutory provision, which renders such phrases as "permanent" or "life" director misleading, cannot be excluded by the articles or by agreement between the company and the director (s. 184 (1)).[22]

A governing, permanent or life director who wishes to protect himself against removal can do so in several ways: he can retain the majority of shares carrying voting rights, thereby making it impossible for the general meeting to pass a resolution removing him; he can insist that the articles shall provide that, in the event of a resolution being proposed to remove

---

[18] [1895] 1 Ch. 674, 685.

[19] *Dominion of Canada, etc., Syndicate* v. *Brigstocke* [1911] 2 K.B. 648.

[20] Prescribed by the Companies (Forms) Order 1979 (No. 1547), Form 58. The form is reproduced in Vol. II, para A–3133, of this work.

[21] On the removal of directors, see para. 61–27, *post*.

[22] On the position of a life director who held office on July 18, 1945, see s. 184 (1), proviso, and para. 61–27, *post*; further *Bersel Manufacturing Co. Ltd.* v. *Berry* [1968] 2 All E.R. 552 (H.L.).

him from office, the shares held by him shall carry additional voting rights sufficient to command a majority,[23] or he can arrange in his contract with the company that the latter shall pay him adequate compensation in the case of his removal from office. The right to such compensation is not affected by the removal (1948 Act, s. 184 (6)).

Governing, permanent or life directors are usually expressly excluded from the retirement by rotation where provisions for retirement in such manner are adopted by the articles.[24]

4–12 COMPULSORY RETIREMENT OF MEMBERS. Provision for the compulsory retirement of members in certain contingencies is occasionally found in the articles of private companies. It is sometimes provided that a large proportion in value of the shareholders, *e.g.* nine-tenths, shall be at liberty to buy out any small shareholder by paying him the fair value of his shares.[25] Such an article, which does not oblige the majority to assign a reason to its action, is very convenient where a minority shareholder is objectionable, ceases to be employed by the company or takes an interest in a rival business. Sometimes the power to requisition the transfer of shares at their fair value is vested in the founder. The exercise of a power to require a compulsory sale of shares by a minority shareholder can be restrained by the court if carried out in an obviously unfair way,[26] and in appropriate cases the minority shareholder may petition the court if in consequence of the exercise of the compulsory acquisition power he is unfairly prejudiced by the conduct of the majority (1980 Act, s. 75).[27] A company may alter its articles by introducing a provision authorising the compulsory sale of shares at a fair price if the proposed alteration can be justified as in the bona fide opinion of the majority being for the benefit of the company; thus in one case[28] the adoption of an article whereby a person carrying on "any business which is in direct competition with the business of the company" could be compelled to sell out was held to be good. If, in the judgment of the court, the proposed alteration of the articles does not satisfy this test, *e.g* if it is for the benefit of the majority and not for that of the company, the court will restrain the company from carrying out the resolution for alteration.[29] Further, the expropriation of a member, even if authorised by the articles, may constitute a ground for the winding up of the company by the court under the "just and equitable" clause (1948 Act, s. 222 (*f*)).[30]

---

[23] *Bushell* v. *Faith* [1970] A.C. 1099 (H.L.); see para. 61–28, *post*.
[24] On retirement by rotation, see para. 61–24, *post*.
[25] For a specimen article, see *Precedents*, (17th ed., 1956), No. 244, p. 726.
[26] *Phillips* v. *The Manufacturers' Securities Ltd.* (1917) 86 L.J.Ch. 305.
[27] See para. 60–01, *post*.
[28] *Sidebottom* v. *Kershaw, Leese & Co. Ltd.* [1920] 1 Ch. 154 (C.A.). See further *Shuttleworth* v. *Cox Bros. & Co. (Maidenhead) Ltd.* [1927] 2 K.B. 9.
[29] *Brown* v. *British Abrasive Wheel Co.* [1919] 1 Ch. 290; *Dafen Tinplate Co.* v. *Llanelly Steel Co.* [1920] 2 Ch. 124.
[30] See paras. 85–08 and 87–11, *post*.

The articles of private companies frequently contain clauses providing for the compulsory retirement of members in case of bankruptcy or for an option in favour of surviving members to buy the shares of a deceased member,[31] but an article providing that on the death of a member his shares shall be deemed to have passed to his widow, if surviving, is invalid because it is contrary to section 75 of the 1948 Act, which provides that no transfer of shares shall be registered without an instrument of transfer, nor is it a transmission of the shares of the deceased by operation of law.[32]

"Private company" may be included in reference to "public company"

4–13 Some enactments other than the Companies Acts, particularly older enactments, use the term "public company" as including private companies within the meaning of company law. The Larceny Act 1916, s. 20 (1) (ii), which was repealed by the Theft Act 1968,[33] used the expression "public company" and it was held[34] that that expression included a private company; the Theft Act 1968 no longer uses the expression "public company." Further, the expression "public company" in the Apportionment Act 1870 includes a private company.[35]

Public companies

Minimum numbers

4–14 The minimum number of members in a public company is two, and no longer seven as was required before the 1980 Act (1980 Act, s. 2 (1)).

The observations made earlier on the minimum number of members in a private company[36] likewise apply to public companies.

Statutory requirements

A public company, whether limited by shares or limited by guarantee and having a share capital, has to satisfy the following statutory requirements:

(1) The memorandum of the company must state that the company shall be a public company (1980 Act, s. 1 (1)). This will be clause 2 of the memorandum (1980 Act, Sched. 1, Pt. I).

(2) The name of the company shall end with the words "public limited company" or, if the company has its registered office in Wales, those words or their equivalent in Welsh, but these words, whether in English or Welsh, shall not be preceded by the word "Limited" (1980 Act, s. 2 (1)). It is also admissible to use the abbreviation plc,

---

31 See *Precedents*, 17th ed., 1956, Form No. 248, p. 728.
32 *Re Greene, Greene* v. *Greene* [1949] Ch. 333.
33 The Theft Act 1968, like the Larceny Act 1916 which it replaces, does not apply to Scotland.
34 *R.* v. *Davies* [1955] 1 Q.B. 71.
35 *Re Lysaght* [1898] 1 Ch. 115, 122; *Re White* [1913] 1 Ch. 231, 238.
36 Para. 4–06, *ante*.

or, in appropriate cases, the Welsh equivalent (1980 Act, s. 78). Where the designation in Welsh is used, the English equivalent need not be added.[37]

(3) The allotted capital shall not be less than the amount of the "authorised minimum" (1980 Act, ss. 3 (2) and 6 (1) (*a*)). That amount is fixed at present at £50,000 but that sum may be altered by statutory instrument (1980 Act, s. 85 (1)).

(4) Each of the allotted shares must be paid up at least as to one-quarter of the nominal value and the whole premium (1980 Act, ss. 22 (1) and 6 (1) (*b*)).

The shares may be allotted and any premium payable on them may be paid up in.money (cash) or money's worth (kind) (1980 Act, s. 20 (1)). It should be noted that "payment" in this connection, contrary to normal linguistic usage, includes also consideration provided in kind. But the shares taken by the subscribers to the memorandum of a public company must be paid in cash (1980 Act, s. 29). It is thought that that applies not only to one-quarter of the nominal amount but to the whole nominal amount.

The allotment of shares in a public company, other than on subscription to the memorandum, is subject to special provisions which will be considered later.[38]

(5) The company must be registered or re-registered as a public company (s. (1) (*b*)).

Nature of public companies

4–15 Only shares and debentures of public companies are capable of being dealt in on The Stock Exchange. This does not mean that the shares and debentures of *all* public companies are admitted to Stock Exchange dealings. A number of public companies exist the shares and debentures of which are not listed at The Stock Exchange and it is possible for a public company to have some classes of its shares and debentures listed on The Stock Exchange and others not. A company which wishes its shares or debentures to be dealt in and listed[39] on The Stock Exchange has to obtain permission from the Council of The Stock Exchange[40] which will only be given if the rules of The Stock Exchange on *Admission of Securities to Listing* have been complied with.[41] In the interest of the investing public these rules contain strict requirements which go beyond the statutory

[37] See para. 7–01, *post*.
[38] See para. 22–23, *post*.
[39] Listed securities are those listed in the Official List. In the case of an introduction of an equity security in which no market already exists, listing will normally become effective to enable dealings to begin on the second business day following that on which listing is granted. The object of this delay is to enable a realistic price for the securities to be established (*Stock Exchange Admission of Securities for Listing*, Ch. 1, para. 20).
[40] For a specimen form of Application for Admission to the Official List, see *Stock Exchange Admission of Securities for Listing*, p. 128.
[41] The rules for listing and leave to deal on the Scottish Stock Exchange are the same, *mutatis mutandis*, as those for the Stock Exchange in London.

requirements; in particular, a company applying for listing has to embody into its articles certain specified provisions[42] and further to enter into a Listing Agreement whereby it promises to give certain information and to take certain other measures, particularly with respect to the issue of share certificates, allotment letters and balance certificates.

The provisions applying only to public companies are too numerous to be catalogued here. Some of them, in a negative form, have been mentioned in paragraph 4–09, above, which deals with the advantages of a private company.

Listed companies

4–16 The Companies Acts contain provisions which deal specifically with companies listed at The Stock Exchange. Some of these provisions are:

(1) directors of the company and of associated companies are prohibited from dealing in options to buy or sell any listed shares or debentures of the company (1976 Act, s. 25);

(2) the provisions making insider dealing a criminal offence apply to dealings on a recognised stock exchange but also to off-market deals (1980 Act, ss. 68–73).

(3) the auditor must be qualified under section 161 (1) of the 1948 Act; the—minor—qualification under section 13 (1) of the 1967 Act is not sufficient. This requirement also applies to companies which have offered shares or debentures to the public although no stock exchange listing has been obtained (1967 Act, s. 13 (1));

Listed companies must, as already observed,[43] comply with the rules of The Stock Exchange for *Admission of Securities to Listing*.

Transitional provisions

The principles of transitional regulation

4–17 The transition to the new classification of companies introduced by the 1980 Act was not easy to effect although the Act attempted to introduce a simple procedure of re-registration.

The transitional regulation was founded on two principles:

(1) A private company continued as such *ipso jure*. It might, of course, if it was so minded, remove the three regulatory restrictions required by the then repealed section 28 of the 1948 Act,[44] by altering its articles by special resolution (1948 Act, s.10).

(2) A public company[45] had to re-register as such during the re-registration period.

---

[42] The rules of the Stock Exchange on *Admission of Securities for Listing* are reproduced in Vol. II, Part C.

[43] See para. 4–15, *ante*.

[44] See para. 4–02, *ante*.

[45] This includes a public company limited by shares and a public company limited by guarantee and having a share capital.

A public company existing on the appointed day, i.e. December 22, 1980, or incorporated pursuant to an application made before that day, was technically known as an "old public company" (1980 Act, s. 8).

Transitional and re-registration periods

4–18 The 1980 Act admitted a generous period for the transition. The "transitional period" was fixed for 18 months from the appointed day (1980 Act, s. 87 (1)) which was December 22, 1980. The transitional period thus expired on June 22, 1981.

The "re-registration period," during which the old public company had to re-register, was shorter. It was only 15 months from the appointed day (1980 Act, ss. 9 (1) and 87 (1)). It thus expired on March 22, 1981.

Formalities of transitional regulation

4–19 Since the transitional period admitted by the 1980 Act has now expired and no legal problems relating to the transitional provisions appear to be extant, it is thought that it is unnecessary to adumbrate on this subject. The formalities of the transitional regulation are discussed in the books dealing with the 1980 Act, notably Clive M. Schmitthoff, *The Companies Act 1980*, published by the London Chamber of Commerce; Victor Joffe, *The Companies Act 1980, a practical Guide,* published by Oyez Publishing Ltd.; Mary Arden and George W. Eccles, *Tolley's Companies Act 1980,* published by Tolley Publishing Col Ltd.; and Nigel Savage, *The Companies Act 1980,* published by McGraw-Hill Book Co. (U.K.) Ltd.

Certificates by the Registrar of Companies

4–20 Where an old public company satisfying the requirements of a new public limited company had re-registered as a new one or where an old public company not satisfying those requirements became a private company, the Registrar issued certificates showing the new character of the company (1980 Act, ss. 8 (9) and 5 (6) (*b*)).

But the Registrar was not to issue a certificate that an old public company had become a new one if it appeared to him that the court had made an order confirming a reduction of the company's capital which would bring the allotted capital below the authorised minimum (1980 Act, s. 5 (7)).

The certificates of the Registrar are conclusive evidence of the status of the company (ss. 5 (9) and 8 (10)).

Fines

4–21 If an old public company has failed to re-register at the end of the re-registration period, the company and any officer of it in default are liable to criminal prosecution, unless—

(1) the company has so applied and the application has not been refused or withdrawn, or

(2) the company has passed a special resolution to become a private company and that resolution has not been cancelled (1980 Act, s. 9).

An officer is "in default" only if he has *mens rea*. This follows from section 440 (2) of the 1948 Act, where "an officer in default" is defined as "any officer of the company who knowingly and wilfully authorises or permits the default, refusal or contravention mentioned in the Act." If the offence is continued after the officer has been summarily convicted of it, the penalty is increased on a second summary conviction (1980 Act, s. 80 (2)).

Small, medium-sized and other companies

4–22 The 1981 Act has added a further classification of companies, but only in connection with company accounting and disclosure.[46] Companies are divided into small, medium-sized and other companies. Small and medium-sized companies enjoy certain exemptions for individual accounts (1981 Act, s. 8). They have to file with the Registrar only modified accounts, *i.e.* accounts omitting certain specified items from the full accounts prescribed by the 1948 to 1981 Acts. But they have to present full accounts to their shareholders. The 1981 Act thus introduces a discretionary double standard of accounting, one for the shareholders and another for the Registrar and the public. This regulation is a retreat from the philosophy of the 1967 Act which required all companies, small, medium-sized and other, in principle to file full accounts with the Registrar.

Small companies

4–23 A small company has to satisfy at least two of the following conditions (1981 Act, s. 8 (2)):

(a) the amount of its turnover must not exceed £1,400,000;
(b) its balance sheet total must not exceed £700,000; and
(c) the average number employed by the company in the financial year in question (determined on a weekly basis) must not exceed 50.

A small company need not file a profit and loss account with its accounts, nor does it need to file a directors' report (1981 Act, s. 6 (2) (*b*) and (6)) and has to file only a modified balance sheet (1981 Act, s. 6 (2) (*a*)).

Medium-sized companies

4–24 A company falling within this category has to satisfy at least two of the following conditions (1981 Act, s. 8 (3)):

(a) the amount of the turnover must not exceed £5,750,000;
(b) its balance sheet total must not exceed £2,800,000; and
(c) the average number of persons employed by the company in the financial year in question (determined on a weekly basis) must not exceed 250.

---

[46] See para. 70–10, *post*.

A medium-sized company shall file with its accounts a modified profit and loss account but it has to file a directors' report (1981 Act, s. 6 (7) and (8)).

Other companies

4–25 They include obviously any company which does not satisfy the qualifying conditions of small and medium-sized companies.

In addition, they include the following categories of companies, even if they satisfy those qualifying conditions (s. 5 (3) and (4)):

(a) a public company;

(b) a banking company, insurance company or shipping company, as defined in Schedule 2, para. 8 of the 1981 Act;

(c) a member of what the Act styles inelegantly an "ineligible group." This is essentially a group which includes a company of the type specified under (a) and (b), above, or a body corporate (other than a company) which may offer its shares or debentures to the public, or a body corporate (other than a company) which is a bank or deposit-taking institution or an insurance company, as defined in the relevant Acts.

"Other companies" have to file full accounts with the Registrar.

Dormant companies

4–26 The 1981 Act, in a singularly complex section, exempts dormant companies from the obligation to appoint auditors. This exemption implies that such a company need not file audited accounts with the Registrar (1981 Act, s. 12).

A company is dormant during any period during which no significant accounting transaction occurs (1981 Act, s. 12 (6)).

However, in order to avail itself of this exemption, the company must satisfy two conditions, viz.

(1) the company must be a small company, as defined above; and

(2) it has been dormant since the end of the last financial year (1981 Act, s. 12 (4)).

Moreover, it cannot avail itself of the benefit of section 12 of the 1981 Act, if it is under an obligation to prepare group accounts, *i.e.* if it is a holding company (1981 Act, s. 12 (3).[49] In order to qualify as a dormant company, the general meeting must resolve by special resolution that the company shall be exempt from its obligation to appoint auditors (1981 Act, s. 12 (5)).

The exemption of a dormant company to file accounts during the period, during which it is dormant, relieves the company, the accounting profession and the Registrar of an unnecessary formality. Of course, if during an accounting reference period the company ceases to be dormant, the appropriate accounts have to be filed.

[47] See the 1976 Act, s. 1 (taken with s. 150 of the 1948 Act).

CHAPTER 5

CHANGES IN THE FORM OF AN EXISTING BUSINESS

5–01 In this chapter it is intended to deal with changes in the form of an existing business. In the first part the advantages of the conversion of the business of a single trader or a partnership into a company limited by shares are considered, and in the second part the possibilities of transforming an existing company into another type of company recognised by the Acts are discussed.

Conversion of business of single trader or partnership into company limited by shares

5–02 The inducements to such conversion are[1]:

(1) The protection of limited liability which the members obtain. This alone is of great value to the businessman. The ordinary law does not allow a single trader to separate his private means from those used in his business and to render immune the former from liability for business debts although modern tax law has no difficulty in recognising for purposes of income tax valuation "part of a taxpayer's activities . . . as a self-contained trade."[2] Consequently, the position of a single trader in ordinary law is fraught with danger: a misfortune in his business affairs which may be due to an event beyond his control or a miscalculation may jeopardise his home and savings and expose him and those depending on him to penury. The prudent businessman will avoid this risk by carrying on his business as a private company.

Even worse is the position of a partner,[3] for partnership is based on mutual confidence, and if one partner abuses that confidence he may commit his co-partner to ruinous liabilities by reason of the doctrine of English law that each partner, so far as the outside world is concerned, is the unlimited agent of the other partner or partners in all matters within the scope of the partnership business. This risk is eliminated by conversion of the partnership business into a private company. For not only the amount at stake is limited, but the agency of the directors is restricted by articles of which all the world has notice.

The Limited Partnerships Act 1907 allows a member of a firm to acquire the privilege of limited liability, but the limited partnership is at a great disadvantage as compared with the private company: the limited partner must not take part in the management of the business, and the privilege of

---

[1] The remarks in this section, although couched in terms of English law, hold good in general terms in Scotland; the law of bankruptcy in Scotland is, however, different from the law of England.

[2] *Per* Lord Radcliffe in *Sharkey (Inspector of Taxes)* v. *Wernher* [1956] A.C. 58, 84.

[3] On the distinction between a company and a partnership; see para. 18–24, *post*.

limited liability is qualified by other statutory provisions. This explains why the private company limited by shares is much more popular than the limited partnership.

(2) The advantages incident to incorporation, particularly in respect of the holding of property and the continuance of the concern notwithstanding deaths, bankruptcy, transfer of shares, or other change of interest or title. In the case of a partner dying, for instance, the learned editors of *Lindley on Partnership* say[4]:

> "The position of the executors of a deceased partner is, in fact, often one of considerable hardship and difficulty; if they insist on an immediate winding up of the firm, they may ruin those whom the deceased may have been most anxious to benefit; whilst if for their advantage the partnership is allowed to go on, the executors may run the risk of being ruined themselves."

With incorporation these difficulties disappear. The shares of the deceased partner form part of his estate and are bequeathed in trust or otherwise dealt with as may be convenient, and if the necessity arises the estate can be represented on the board of directors by his trustees or their nominees, who being mere agents of the company can act without incurring personal liability. Again, the bankruptcy of a partner dislocates a partnership. With a company the trustee in bankruptcy sells the shares of the bankrupt, or if they are worthless, disclaims them; the company on its part proves for the estimated value of future calls, and there is an end of it. So, too, in the matter of contracts, in the admission of new members and the retirement of old members, in the sale, mortgage and settlement of shares, the company enjoys a striking superiority. The property, again, in the case of partnership, has constantly to be conveyed with the admission, retirement, death or bankruptcy of a partner; with a company the property is vested in it as a body corporate. Shareholders may come and go, but no changes of individual membership affect the title.[5]

5–03 (3) The simplification of arrangements between the members and the concern, which, in the case of an ordinary partnership, would be extremely complicated. Thus, if a shareholder is indebted to a company for money lent or in respect of a call made in his shares, the company can sue for the loan or call without difficulty. Conversely, if a shareholder lends money to the company, he can sue for it and enforce any security given him by the company, just as if he were not a shareholder, and, should the company fail, he can prove for the money lent in competition with the outside creditors. In the case of partnership one partner cannot sue another except for an account,[6] and great inconvenience arises in seeking to enforce contracts between the members of a partnership; while, should the firm

---

[4] 14th ed., 1979, p. 659.

[5] The last two sentences of this paragraph apply only in England. In Scotland the property of a partnership is normally vested in the partners as trustees for the firm and a transfer of title is not essential on every change of membership, although it may often be desirable.

[6] *Green* v. *Hertzog* [1954] 1 W.L.R. 1309.

become insolvent, a member of it is disentitled to prove in competition with the outside creditors of the firm.[7]

(4) The possibility of issuing shares to the public. In most cases the business of a single trader or a partnership will be converted into a private company which, as has been stated earlier,[8] has to prohibit an invitation to the public to subscribe for its shares or debentures (1980 Act, s. 15 (1)). However, if circumstances require, a private company can be converted into a public company in the manner discussed later.[9]

The conversion into a private company opens the prospect for a successful enterprise to expand further by converting, at a later propitious date, into a public company, *i.e.* in stock exchange language, "to go public." When this is done, the public can be interested in the business, the capital resources can be greatly strengthened and eventually listing for the securities of the public company on a stock exchange can be applied for. Many successful public companies have been developed from private companies which, in turn, originated in businesses owned by single traders or partnerships.

(5) The borrowing facilities, especially on debentures and debenture stock, particularly as these debentures can be secured by floating charges. The floating charge, as we shall see,[10] is a convenient means of securing indebtedness,[11] but a floating charge can only be issued by a company, whether it is a private or public company, and not by a single trader or partnership.

By means of a debenture issue a public company can raise a large sum on easy terms by the contributions of a number of small lenders on the same co-operative principle on which a company's capital is subscribed. Such debentures are securities with which the public is familiar, are easily enforced and readily transferable. If issued by a public company of good repute they are a very marketable security. So advantageous, indeed, is this mode of raising money that it is not uncommon for a business to be converted into a company solely for the purpose of raising a loan by the issue of debentures or debenture stock, secured or unsecured. Sometimes a debenture secured by a fixed or floating charge or by both is issued to a bank in order to secure a loan facility, and this is also often done by private companies.

(6) The scheme of company taxation, under the imputation system of corporation tax now in operation may offer advantages from the point of view of taxation to the individual trader or partner in the higher tax

---

[7] The problems described here do not arise in Scots law, except that, as in England, a partner cannot claim a ranking on the estate of his insolvent firm.

[8] See para. 4–07, *ante*.

[9] See para. 5–05, *post*.

[10] See paras. 44–03 (England) and 47–03 (Scotland).

[11] Admitted in Scotland by the Companies (Floating Charges and Receivers) (Scotland) Act 1972, which replaced the Companies (Floating Charges) (Scotland) Act 1961 (except s. 7 (*b*), (*c*) and (*d*) thereof).

brackets. Such a company will, almost inevitably, be a "close company" for tax purposes and may qualify for the lower "small companies rate" of corporation tax.[12]

Speaking generally, on conversion into a company four aspects of the law of taxation have to be considered: corporation tax, income tax at the basic and higher rates and the investment income surcharge, the tax treatment of capital gains and capital transfer tax.

A trading company whose trading income is above a certain level and which has a good prospect of rapid expansion will probably pay less tax than a private trader or a partnership in a similar position. Conversely, the formation of a family investment company should not normally be overlooked.

Transformation of companies

5–04 The transformation of a company into another form of company is carried out by re-registration of the new status of the company. The law lays down strict requirements for re-registration. These requirements are discussed in the following paragraphs.

On re-registration the Registrar grants the company a new certificate of incorporation showing its new status and such certificate is conclusive evidence that all requirements antecedent to the re-registration have been satisfied and the company has acquired the new status.

Despite the requirement of re-registration and the issue of a new certificate of incorporation, the legal personality of the old company is continued in the new form. It is not the law that the old persona of the company is extinguished and a new one has come into existence. Consequently, no transfer of property is required from the old to the new company and legal proceedings by or against the company may be continued.

Private company into public company

5–05 A private company can apply for re-registration as a public company (1980 Act, ss. 5 and 6). This happens often in practice. In some cases a concern which is owned by a family or another closely connected group of persons and is carried on in the form of a private company, may have operated so successfully that those in control wish "to go public," *i.e.* to invite the public to contribute to the company's funds. In other cases promoters who from the beginning intend to form a public company will first incorporate the enterprise as a private company and then re-register it as a public company. This procedure, which is nowadays the normal method of forming a public company, enables the company to commence business on incorporation at once without first obtaining a trading

[12] See paras. 91–01 and 90–51, *post*.

certificate (1980 Act, s. 4).[13] This restriction, which is required of a company formed from the beginning as a public company, is regarded by the practice as inconvenient.

5–06 THE REQUIREMENTS FOR RE-REGISTRATION. The requirements for the re-registration of a private company as a public company are (1980 Act, s. 5 (1)):

(a) a special resolution of the general meeting is necessary to alter the company's memorandum, by stating as clause 2, that the company shall be a public company. This resolution must also make incidental alterations in the memorandum and articles (1980 Act, s. 5 (2)).

(b) an application must be delivered to the Registrar in the prescribed form. It has to be signed by a director or secretary. It has to be accompanied by the documents specified in the 1980 Act, s. 5 (3). The most important of them have to be prepared by the auditor of the company (1980 Act, s. 5 (3) (*b*) to (*d*)); they will be discussed in the next paragraph. A printed copy of the memorandum and articles, as altered, has to be attached to the application for re-registration (1980 Act, s. 5 (3) (*a*)).

5–07 THE ACCOUNTING REQUIREMENTS. These requirements, already referred to in paragraph 5–06 (b), have taken the place of the statement in lieu of prospectus that was required by section 30 of the 1948 Act; this section is repealed by the 1980 Act (s. 88 (2) and Sched. 4).

The auditor must issue a written statement that in his opinion the company's balance-sheet, which must be prepared to a date not more than seven weeks before the company's application for re-registration, shows that the amount of the company's net assets was not less than the aggregate of its called-up share capital and the undistributable reserves (1980 Act, s. 5 (3) (*b*) and (10)). If shares have been allotted between the balance-sheet date and the passing of the special resolution, the auditor has to add a valuation report relating to the consideration (1980 Act, s. 5 (5)). Copies of the balance-sheet, the auditor's report and, where applicable, the auditor's valuation report have to be appended to the application to the Registrar for re-registration.

5–08 GRANT OF CERTIFICATE OF INCORPORATION. If the Registrar is satisfied on the application for re-registration, he will issue a certificate of incorporation stating that the company is a public company (1980 Act, s. 5 (6) (*b*)). Of course, if the Registrar notices that the court has made an order confirming the reduction of the company's capital below the authorised minimum, he will not issue such certificate of incorporation (1980 Act, s. 5 (7)). On the issue of the certificate, the company becomes a public company and the certificate is conclusive evidence that the requirements of the

[13] See para. 19–02, *post*.

Act in respect of re-registration have been complied with and that the company is a public company (1980 Act, s. 5 (8)).

Public company into private company

5–09 A public company having a share capital[14] may be converted into a private company. This is done in the following manner.

(a) A special resolution of the general meeting is required. It shall alter the memorandum, by deleting the clause that the company is a public company and shall make the necessary incidental alterations to the memorandum and articles (1980 Act, s. 10 (1) (*a*) and (2)).

(b) An application for re-registration as a private company shall be made to the Registrar of Companies in the prescribed form which has to be signed by a director or secretary. Printed copies of the altered memorandum and articles have to be attached (1980 Act, s. 10 (1) (*b*)).

(c) The time for the minority objection treated in the next paragraph has expired without such an objection having been lodged or the objection having been withdrawn or rejected by the court (1980 Act, ss. 10 (1) (*d*) and 11).

5–10 THE MINORITY OBJECTION. When a special resolution for re-registration of a public company as a private company is passed, a minority of shareholders may apply to the court for cancellation of the resolution (1980 Act, s. 11). The minority which may make such application shall consist of—

(a) the holders of not less in the aggregate than 5 per cent. of the company's issued capital, or

(b) not less than 50 members, or

(c) if the company is not limited by shares, not less than 5 per cent. of its members (1980 Act, s. 11 (3)).

The objection shall be lodged within 28 days after the passing of the resolution and may be done by way of a representative application, *i.e.* any one or more of the objectors may apply on behalf of all of them (1980 Act, s. 11 (4)). Notice of the application has to be given to the Registrar in the prescribed form *forthwith* (1980 Act, s. 11 (5) (*a*)).

On the hearing of the application the court may make an order cancelling or confirming the resolution and may do so subject to such terms and conditions as it thinks fit. In particular, the court may adjourn the proceedings in order that an arrangement may be made to its satisfaction for the purchase of the shares of the dissentient members. It may also issue directions or orders facilitating or carrying out such arrangement (1980 Act, s. 11 (6)). The court may even order, if it thinks fit, that the company shall acquire the shares of any member and the capital of the company be reduced accordingly (1980 Act, s. 11 (7)). An office copy of the court order cancelling or confirming the special resolution for re-registration shall be

[14] And also, it seems, a company limited by guarantee and not having a share capital, and an unlimited company not have a share capital; see para. 3–03, *ante*.

delivered to the Registrar within 15 days or such longer time as the court may direct (1980 Act, s. 11 (5) (*b*)).

5–11 GRANT OF CERTIFICATE OF INCORPORATION. If the Registrar is satisfied that all formalities have been complied with, he issues a certificate of incorporation appropriate to a company that is not a public company (1980 Act, s. 10 (3) (*b*)). By virtue of this certificate the company becomes a private company and the certificate is conclusive evidence that the company has acquired that status (1980 Act, s. 10 (4) and (5)).

5–12 AN OLD PUBLIC COMPANY SATISFYING THE REQUIREMENTS OF A PUBLIC COMPANY WISHING TO RE-REGISTER AS A PRIVATE COMPANY. This was one of the possibilities existing with respect to an old public company,[15] during the re-registration period under the transitional provisions of the 1980 Act.[16] If the old public company wished to avail itself of this possibility, it had to apply the procedure just described for the conversion of a public into a private company (1980 Act, s. 8 (8)).

When a public company must convert into a private company

5–13 In two cases a public company is required to apply for re-registration as a private company.

5–14 (a) When the court makes an order confirming a reduction of capital (1948 Act, s. 66) and the effect of carrying out the reduction would be to bring the allotted capital below the authorised minimum,[17] the Registrar shall not register the court order (1948 Act, s. 69 (1)) unless the company first re-registers as a private company or the court otherwise directs (1980 Act, s. 12 (1)). The court, when making the order, may authorise the company to be re-registered without having passed a special resolution (1980 Act, s. 12 (2)). This provision dispenses with the right of the minority to object but any one member may do so in the proceedings for confirmation of the special resolution for reduction of the capital by the court. The court, if authorising the company, shall specify the appropriate alterations of the memorandum and articles (1980 Act, s. 12 (2) and (3)).

5–15 (b) Section 37 (1) of the 1980 Act deals with four cases in which shares are held by or on behalf of a public company. They are:

(1) the forfeiture or surrender of shares which are not fully paid up, if there is a failure to pay them up;

(2) the acquisition, by the company, of its own shares and the company has a beneficial interest in them, otherwise than by any of the methods for redemption or purchase of its own

---

[15] For definition see para. 4–17, *ante*.
[16] On the re-registration period see para. 4–18, *ante*.
[17] On the authorised minimum, see para. 4–14, *ante*.

shares admitted by Part III of the 1981 Act. This may happen if the company acquires its own fully paid shares otherwise than for valuable consideration, *e.g.* by way of a gift or a bequest (1980 Act, s. 35 (2) and (4), as amended by the 1981 Act, Sched. 3, para. 43).

(3) the acquisition, by a nominee of the company, of shares in the company without financial assistance by the company and the company has a beneficial interest in them;

(4) the acquisition, by any person, of shares in the company with its financial assistance and the company has a beneficial interest in them.

The company is bound, after the expiration of a period of grace,[18] to cancel the shares and, if the effect of the cancellation is that the allotted capital falls below the authorised minimum, it shall appply for re-registration as a private company (1980 Act, s. 37 (2)). The application must be preceded by a special resolution of the general meeting altering the memorandum and articles (1980 Act, s. 37 (2) and (4)) but the capital reduction procedure laid down in sections 66 and 67 of the 1948 Act, which requires the confirmation by the court, need not be followed.

The application for re-registration as a private company shall be made in the prescribed form and signed by a director or secretary and must be accompanied by a printed copy of the altered memorandum and articles (1980 Act, s. 37 (5)). The certificate of incorporation as a private company is conclusive evidence (1980 Act, s. 37 (7) and (8)).

If a public company required by section 37 of the 1980 Act to re-register as a private company fails to apply for re-registration within the prescribed period of grace, it is prohibited, subject to a penalty, from making a public issue of its shares or debentures but in all other respects it continues to be treated as a public company until it is re-registered as a private company (1980 Act, s. 37 (6)).

5–16 The 1980 Act does not provide that, if in the course of a compromise or amalgamation by virtue of section 206 of the 1948 Act affecting a public company the allotted capital is reduced below the authorised minimum, the company shall re-register as a private company. Such a measure, like the reduction of capital by virtue of section 66 of the 1948 Act, requires the approval of the court. It is, therefore, thought that in this case the provisions of section 12 of the 1980 Act apply by way of analogy.

Unlimited company into company limited shares or by guarantee

5–17 The 1967 Act provides by section 44 procedure for such a change.[19]

The proposal to re-register must be approved by the members by a special resolution, which must

[18] In cases (1) to (3) three years; in case (4) one year (s. 37 (11)).

[19] s. 44 of the 1967 Act has replaced s. 16 (1) of the 1948 Act which, by virtue of s. 45 of the 1967 Act, has ceased to apply. The alteration became effective on October 27, 1967 (s. 57 (1) (*a*) of the 1967 Act).

(1) specify whether the company is to be limited by shares or by guarantee;
(2) if the company is to have a share capital, specify the amount of that capital; and
(3) provide for the requisite alterations of the company's memorandum and articles.

Application for re-registration must then be made to the Registrar of Companies in the prescribed from,[20] signed by a director or the secretary, accompanied by printed copies of the memorandum and articles, as altered.

The Registrar will then issue a certificate of incorporation appropriate to the new status of the company, and upon the issue of that certificate the company's status is changed from unlimited to limited (1967 Act, s. 44 (4)). The Registrar's certificate of incorporation is conclusive evidence that the requirements of re-registration have been complied with (*ibid*. s. 44 (5)).

On re-registration the Registrar closes the former registration of the company. The re-registration has the same effect as if it were the first registration of the company under the Act of 1948, but the Registrar may dispense with the delivery of copies of documents with which he was furnished on the original registration of the company (1948 Act, s. 16 (2)).

If the company originally was registered under a previous Companies Act, such Act shall be treated as a "different" Act "from that under which the company is registered as a limited company" (s. 16 (2)); the object of this obscure provision is apparently to bring into operation, with respect to the re-registered company, the provisions of sections 382 to 397 of the 1948 Act and to nullify proviso (i) to subsection (1) of section 382.

If it is intended to re-register an unlimited company as a public company, the provisions for the re-registration of a private company as a public company are applicable and the requirements laid down for that case have to be complied with (1980 Act, s. 7).

5–18 On re-registration as a limited company the unlimited company, if having a share capital, may form a reserve liability which can only be called up in the event and for the purposes of winding up (s. 64). The reserve liability may be formed

(1) by increasing the nominal amount of the shares (which leads to an increase of the nominal capital); or
(2) by transferring part of the existing issued but uncalled capital to reserve; or
(3) by carrying out both measures at the same time.

Provision is made for the continuance of the unlimited liability of past or present members, who would have been liable as contributors at the date of re-registration, for debts and liabilities of the company contracted

---

[20] See Form No. R3, as prescribed by the Companies (Forms) Regulations 1979 (S.I. 1979 No. 1547), reproduced in Vol. II, para. A–3144.

before the date of re-registration if the company goes into liquidation within three years thereafter (1967 Act, s. 44 (7)).[21]

An unlimited company which was formerly limited and which has been re-registered as unlimited under section 43 of the 1967 Act[22] cannot revert to its former status by further re-registration under section 44.[23]

Company limited by shares into company limited by guarantee, and vice versa.

5–19 The Companies Acts do not authorise changes of this kind.

Company limited by shares or by guarantee into unlimited company

5–20 The Act of 1967 admits the re-registration of a limited company as an unlimited company (s. 43), mainly in order to enable former exempt private companies which were abolished by that Act to retain the privilege of balance-sheet secrecy, which is now available only to unlimited companies.[24] A company registered as a limited company at the coming into operation of the 1967 Act or thereafter can apply for re-registration as an unlimited company (s. 43 (1)). Such an application requires the assent of *all* the members of the company (s. 43 (3) (*a*)).

The procedure is this: an application for re-registration in the prescribed form,[25] signed by a director or secretary of the company, must be lodged with the Registrar (s. 43 (1)). The application must set out—

(a) such alterations in the company's memorandum as are required of an unlimited company (s. 43 (2) (*a*)); and

(b) the necessary alterations of the articles (s. 43 (2) (*b*)).

The application must be accompanied by the following documents:

(a) the prescribed form of assent of all members (s. 43 (3) (*a*));

(b) a statutory declaration of the directors that all members of the company have assented and, if that is not the case, that the directors have taken all reasonable steps to satisfy themselves that each person who has subscribed the assent was duly empowered by a member to do so (s. 43 (3) (*b*));

(c) a printed copy of the altered memorandum (s. 43 (3) (*c*)); and

(d) a printed copy of the altered articles (s. 43 (3) (*d*)). In spite of the wording of section 43 (3) (*d*), it is believed that the unlimited company must register articles, since section 6 of the 1948 Act is not repealed by the 1967 Act.

5–21 The Registrar will issue a new certificate of incorporation and upon its issue the status of the company is changed from limited to unlimited

---

[21] See further, as to the liability of past and present members as contributories, paras. 85–45, 86–27 and 87–37, *post*.
[22] See *infra*.
[23] See s. 44 (1) of the 1967 Act.
[24] See para. 3–14, *ante*.
[25] Form R1 of the Companies (Forms) Regulations 1967 (S.I. 1979 No. 1547). See Form R2 of the same Regulations; see Vol. II, paras. A–3142/1 and A–3143.

(s. 43 (4) (*a*)), and this certificate is conclusive evidence that the requirements of re-registration have been complied with (s. 43 (5)).

Past members are protected from any increase in their liability resulting from re-registration of the company as unlimited, if they were past members at the time of re-registration and have not again become members (s. 43 (6)).

A limited company which was formerly unlimited and which has been re-registered as limited under section 44 of the 1967 Act cannot revert to its former status by further re-registration under section 43.[26]

[26] See s. 43 (1) of the 1967 Act.

B. THE CONSTITUTION OF THE COMPANY

CHAPTER 6

THE MEMORANDUM AND ARTICLES OF ASSOCIATION

The formation of the company

6–01 The mode of forming a company is very simple. After having decided on the kind of company most suitable for their purposes, the promoters will prepare, or ask their advisers to prepare, the constitutional documents of the company, viz. the memorandum of association (1948 Act, s. 2) and the articles of association (if there are to be any[1]) (1948 Act, s. 6). Registration stamps are not required.[2]

These documents, together with certain other documents,[3] are then taken to the Registrar of Companies, who, on payment of the requisite registration fee and capital duty, registers and retains the documents (1948 Act, s. 12).[3] The "Registrar of Companies" for companies, whose registered office is intended to be situate in England or Wales, is the Registrar for England, and, if the registered office is intended to be situate in Scotland, the Registrar for Scotland (s. 12). The address of the office of the Registrar for England is:

Companies Registration Office,
Crown Way,
Maindy,
Cardiff CF4 3UZ
(tel.: Cardiff 388588).

He maintains facilities for inspecting company records in London at the following address:

Companies House,
55–71 City Road,
London E.C.1.

The address of the Registrar for Scotland is:

Exchequer Chambers,
102 George Street,
Edinburgh 2.

Companies which have their registered offices in Wales may use the Welsh language for their names and company documents. This is explained in paragraph 6–07, *post*.

When the required documents have been filed with the Registrar, he will issue a certificate of incorporation[4] (1948 Act, s. 13 (1)), and from the date mentioned therein the company comes into existence as a legal person

---

[1] See para. 14–01 *post*.
[2] See the Act of 1967, s. 48 and Sched. 3.
[3] See para. 15–01, *post*.
[4] See para. 16–01, *post*.

(s. 13 (2)).[5] If the company is formed as a private company it may commence business at once, but if it is formed as a public company it has to satisfy further requirements before it is granted a trading certificate authorising it to commence business (1980 Act, s. 4).[6]

The requirements of the memorandum, with its various clauses, and of the articles, as well as the registration of the company and the commencement of business, will be discussed in detail in the following chapters of this Part. In this chapter a few further preliminary observations have to be made.

Division of constitutional documents into memorandum and articles of association

6–02 It should be noted that the constitution of the company is contained in two documents, the memorandum of association and the articles of association.[7] This division of the constitutional documents was first adopted by the Joint Stock Companies Act 1856. Before that Act the constitution of the English company was contained in one document, *viz.* the deed of settlement. The system of a single constitutional document is in use in many continental company laws,[8] whereas the state legislatures in the United States of America provide for the division of the constitutional documents similar to that applying to companies in the United Kingdom.[9]

When introducing the division of the constitutional documents into the memorandum and the articles, the legislator contemplated that the former should contain the fundamental law of the company and should be unalterable in the interest of the shareholders, particularly those of the minority, and the public, especially the creditors of the company, while the latter should be freely alterable by the shareholders in general meeting.[10] Accordingly, the Act of 1856 did not authorise the alteration of the memorandum, except in case of an increase of capital,[11] but expressly admitted the alteration of the articles by special resolution.[12] The Companies Act 1862 explicitly prohibited the alteration of the memorandum, except in the cases expressly authorised by the Act, which were extended and then covered the change of name with the consent of the Board of Trade, and further the increase of capital, the consolidation of shares into shares of larger de-

---

[5] See para. 18–01, *post*.
[6] See para. 19–02, *post*.
[7] *Humbold Redwood Co.* v. *Coats,* 1908 S.C. 751, 753.
[8] See, *e.g.* the *statut* of the French *société anonyme,* the *acte constitutif* of the Belgian and Luxembourg *société anonyme*, the *Satzung* of the German *Aktiengesellschaft*, or the *statuten* of the Netherlands *naamloze vennootschap*. In Italy two documents are, or may be, required for the formation of a *società per azioni, viz*. an *atto costitutivo* and a *statuto*.
[9] The United Kingdom memorandum of association corresponds to the "articles of incorporation," or "certificate of incorporation" or "charter contract" in the American states. The United Kingdom articles of association correspond to the "by-laws" of American companies.
[10] *Cf.* Lord Cairns L.C. in *Ashbury Railway Carriage and Iron Co.* v. *Riche* (1875) L.R. 7 H.L. 653, 671.
[11] See art. 20 of Table B of the Act of 1856.
[12] In s. 33.

nomination and the conversion of fully paid-up shares into stock,[13] but the Act did not authorise the alteration of the objects of the company which remained absolutely prohibited[14] until 1890 when it was authorised[15] for certain specified purposes. To the present day, the memorandum is, on principle, unalterable unless alterations are authorised by the Companies Acts which, however, have admitted such alternatives in many circumstances (1948 Act, s. 4).[16] The principle that the articles are freely alterable by the shareholders by a special resolution of the general meeting still applies (s. 10); indeed, it has been held that a clause in the articles excluding any article from liability to alteration is invalid.[17]

The memorandum of association

6–03 It is obvious from the preceding observations that the memorandum is a document of great importance in relation to the proposed company. In the case of a company limited by shares it has to be in accordance with the form set out in Table B of the First Schedule of the 1948 Act (as regards private companies), or as near thereto as circumstances admit (s. 11 (*a*)), and Part I of Schedule 1 of the Companies Act 1980 (as regards public companies).[18] Accordingly, it has to contain the following six or, in the case of a public company, seven clauses, the first five or six respectively being numbered and the last being unnumbered:

(1) the Name Clause[19];
(2) in the case of a public company, a clause defining the status of the company (1980 Act, Sched. 1);
(3) the Registered Office Clause[20];
(4) the Objects Clause[21];
(5) the Limited Liability Clause[22];
(6) the Capital Clause[23]; and
(7) the Association Clause.[24]

These clauses are the *obligatory* clauses of the memorandum; apart therefrom, it may contain *additional* clauses which could likewise have been contained in the articles.[25]

In previous editions it was stated that the memorandum may be wholly in writing, or it may be printed (save as regards the signatures), or it may

[13] s. 12 of the Act of 1862.
[14] Lord Cairns' famous statement in *Ashbury* v. *Riche, supra,* should be read in the light of this fact.
[15] By the Companies (Memorandum of Association) Act 1890.
[16] *Cf.* Wynn-Parry J. in *Re Paringa Mining and Exploration Co. Ltd.* [1957] 1 W.L.R. 1143, 1145.
[17] *Walker* v. *London Tramways Co.* (1879) 12 Ch.D. 705; *Malleson* v. *National Insurance, etc., Corporation* [1894] 1 Ch. 200; see para. 14–17, *post*.
[18] In the case of other kinds of companies it has to correspond with the appropriate form in Tables C and E of the First Schedule of the 1948 Act. The form of a memorandum of a public company limited by guarantee and bearing a share capital must satisfy the requirements of Part II of Sched. 1 of the 1980 Act (s. 11 (*b*)–(*d*)).
[19] See para. 7–01, *post*.
[20] See para. 8–01, *post*.
[21] See para. 9–01, *post*.
[22] See para. 10–01, *post*.
[23] See para. 11–01, *post*.
[24] See para. 12–01, *post*.
[25] See para. 13–03, *post*.

be partly printed and partly in writing. It is, however, thought that, at least since the coming into operation of the European Communities Act 1972, s. 9 (January 1, 1973), the memorandum must be in a form accepted by the Registrar of Companies as "printed" (save as regards the signatures).[26] This appears to follow from section 9 (5) of that Act, which requires an altered memorandum to be printed. It would be odd if the memorandum in its original form could be in writing but required printing when altered. The 1980 Act likewise refers throughout to the "printed" form of the memorandum and articles.

The document has to be subscribed by at least two persons (s. 1 (1), as amended by the 1980 Act, s. 2 (1)). Before the coming into operation of this provision of the 1980 Act (December 22, 1980), the number of subscribers of the memorandum of a public company had to be seven. The signature of each subscriber must be attested by at least one witness which is declared to be sufficient in England as well as in Scotland (1948 Act, s. 3).[27]

The articles of association

6–04 These contain the internal regulations for the management of the affairs of the company and the conduct of its business (s. 6).

In the case of a company limited by shares there is no obligation to register articles of association, and if it is registered without articles, the regulations in Table A in the First Schedule to the 1948 Act are deemed to be the articles of the company; that table applies in all cases in which its provisions are not excluded or modified by registered articles (s. 8).[28] There is a third alternative: a short set of articles, supplementing or modifying Table A but otherwise leaving Table A to operate, may be registered; in such a case Table A, together with the supplementary or modifying provisions, will constitute the regulations of the company.[28]

The articles (if any) must be divided into numbered paragraphs and printed (s. 9 (*a*) and (*b*)). They must further be signed by the subscribers of the memorandum whose signatures have to be duly attested (s. 9 (*d*)).[29]

Relation of the articles to the memorandum

6–05 The articles of a company are subordinate to and controlled by the memorandum of association, which is the dominant instrument.[30] The memorandum contains the conditions upon which alone the company is granted incorporation—conditions which are fundamental, but some of which are alterable by the correct procedure. The articles are the internal

---

[26] See para. 8–07, *post*.
[27] As far as Scotland is concerned, this is an exception to the general rule which requires the attestation of a deed by at least two witnesses.
[28] See para. 14–01, *post*.
[29] See para. 14–04, *post*.
[30] Liquidator of *Humbold Redwood Co. Ltd.* v. *Coats* 1908 S.C. 751, 753.

regulations of the company, and over these the members have full control, and may alter them from time to time as they think fit by pursuing the course pointed out in sections 10 and 141 of the 1948 Act; subject only to this, that they keep within the limits marked out by the memorandum of association and the Act itself. As was said by Lord Cairns L.C.[31]:

> "The memorandum is, as it were, the area beyond which the action of the company cannot go; inside that area the shareholders may make such regulations for their own government as they think fit."

Hence, any articles that go beyond the company's sphere of action are inoperative, and anything done under the authority of such articles is void and incapable of ratification.

If, e.g. before the coming into operation of the 1981 Act the articles purported to confer on the company a power to buy its own shares,[32] or if they purport to authorise the company to pay dividends out of capital,[33] or to issue shares at a discount,[34] or prohibit the members from exercising the statutory rights of applying for a winding-up order,[35] or provide for the application of the profits in a manner which is inconsistent with some provision in the memorandum of association,[36] or purport to deprive shareholders who dissent from a scheme of reconstruction under section 287[37] of their statutory right to be paid out in cash,[38] they are to that extent invalid and ineffectual.

6–06 But though the articles cannot alter or control the memorandum, yet, if there is an ambiguity in the memorandum, the articles registered at the same time may be used to explain it, but not so as to extend the objects. Thus, Jessel M.R., in *Anderson's* case,[39] said: "Where there are two contemporaneous documents executed and assented to by the same persons at the same time . . . it appears to me that the ordinary rule applies, according to which contemporaneous documents are to be read together, so that if there is an ambiguity in one it may be explained by the other." But these words must be read as qualified by the words which had just gone before: "I am not now speaking," said the learned judge, "of those portions of the memorandum of association which the Act of Parliament requires to be stated in the memorandum." This distinction was further emphasised by Bowen L.J. in *Guinness* v. *Land Corporation of Ireland*,[40] where he pointed out that

> "The memorandum contains the fundamental conditions upon which alone the company is allowed to be incorporated. They are

---

31 In *Ashbury Ry. Carriage Co.* v. *Riche* (1875) L.R. 7 H.L. 653, 671.
32 *Trevor* v. *Whitworth* (1887) 12 App.Cas. 409.
33 *Guinness* v. *Land Corporation of Ireland* (1882) 22 Ch.D. 349.
34 *Welton* v. *Saffery* [1897] A.C. 299.
35 *Re Peveril Gold Mines* [1898] 1 Ch. 122.
36 *Ashbury* v. *Watson* (1885) 30 Ch.D. 376.
37 Substituted for s. 192 of the Act of 1908.
38 *Baring-Gould* v. *Sharpington, etc., Synd.* [1899] 2 Ch. 80; *Payne* v. *Cork Co.* [1900] 1 Ch. 308.
39 *Re Wedgwood Coal and Iron Co., Anderson's Case* (1877) 7 Ch.D. 75, 99.
40 (1882) 22 Ch.D. 349, 381.

conditions introduced for the benefit of the creditors, and the outside public, as well as of the shareholders. The articles of association are the internal regulations of the company. How can it be said that in all cases the fundamental conditions of the charter of incorporation, and the internal regulations of the company are to be construed together. . . . In any case it is, as it seems to me, certain that for anything which the Act of Parliament says shall be in the memorandum you must look to the memorandum alone. If the legislature has said one instrument is to be dominant you cannot turn to another instrument and read it in order to modify the provisions of the dominant instrument."

Where the memorandum clearly establishes the rights of shareholders, a reference in the memorandum to the articles and an ambiguity said to arise from the construction of the articles should not be used to depart from the clear meaning of the memorandum so as to diminish those rights.[41]

Companies with registered offices in Wales

6–07 The following provisions apply to a company which states in the registered office clause of its memorandum (s. 2 (1) (*b*)) that its registered office will be situated in Wales (1976 Act, s. 30 (1)). Such a company may express its memorandum and articles, if any, in the Welsh language but has to add a certified translation into English. Any alterations in the memorandum and articles shall be in the same language as the original document. It further may deliver any document required by the Companies Acts to be delivered to the Registrar of Companies in Welsh, with a certified English translation attached (1976 Act, s. 30 (6) and (7)).

If such a company has registered its memorandum and articles in English, it may deliver to the Registrar a certified translation into Welsh (1976 Act, s. 30 (6)).

The use of the Welsh language for the private "Limited" or "Public Limited Company" is treated in paragraph 7–02, *post*.

Public inspection of memorandum and articles

6–08 The memorandum and articles of association (if any) of a company are registered in a public register and are open for public inspection on payment of a small fee (s. 426). They are public documents.

The effect of this publication of the constitutional documents of the company will be considered later. In particular, it will have to be examined whether a shareholder or an outsider, who has no actual notice of these documents, can be deemed to have constructive notice of them.[42]

---

[41] *Scottish National Trust Co. Ltd.* 1928 S.C. 499; 1928 S.L.T. 352.
[42] See paras. 9–25 and 28–01, *post*.

C. MEMORANDUM OF ASSOCIATION

CHAPTER 7

THE NAME CLAUSE

"Limited" or "Public Limited Company" as last words of name

7–01 The name clause of the memorandum states the company's name. In a private company, the last word of the name must be the word "Limited" (s. 2 (1) (*a*)[1] and in a public company the phrase "Public Limited Company" but that phrase must not be preceded by the word "Limited" (1980 Act, s. 2 (3)). This applies to companies limited by shares as well as to companies limited by guarantee. The certificate of incorporation, when given, will then incorporate the company by its name (s. 13 (2)). To this name the company must adhere.[2] The customary abbreviations which companies may use in their business communications are "Ltd." for "Limited" and "plc" for "Public Limited Companies."

Companies with registered offices in Wales

7–02 A limited company which states in the registered office clause of its memorandum that its registered office shall be situate in Wales may use "Cyfyngedig" as the last word of its name, instead of "Limited" (1976 Act, s. 30 (3). After April 18, 1977, when section 30 of the 1976 Act came into operation, the name of such a company can be altered by changing the last word from "Limited" to "Cyfyngedig" and vice versa, without the Department of Trade's approval, which before the coming into operation of the 1981 Act was required for the change of name of a company[3] (1976 Act, s. 30 (4)). If the company is a public company, the Welsh equivalent for public limited company may be used (1980 Act, s. 2 (2)).

A Welsh company which uses the Welsh equivalent as the last designation of its name must state in English and in legible letters that the company is a limited, or public limited, company respectively

(a) in all prospectuses, bill-heads, letter paper, notices and other official publications of the company; and

(b) in a notice conspicuously displayed in every place in which the company's business is carried out (1976 Act, s. 30 (5)).

Contravention of this provision is punishable (*ibid.*). This provision should satisfy the requirements of the First EEC Directive on Company

---

[1] Unless dispensation with this requirement is granted under s. 25 of the 1981 Act; see para. 7–07, *post*.

[2] But the omission of the word "Limited" in a legal document is not necessarily fatal; it may be simply a case of misnomer (*Whittam* v. *W. J. Daniel & Co. Ltd.* [1962] 1 Q.B. 271); on the question whether the addition of "Limited" constitutes a misnomer or the substitution of a new party in pleadings, see para. 18–17, *post*.

[3] See para. 8–02, *post*.

Law and the European Communities Act 1972, s. 9 (see para. 2–14), having regard to the fact that Welsh is not one of the official languages of the EEC.

Object of legislature

It has been seen earlier[4] that, in the view of Sir Francis Palmer, the twin principles on which the Joint Stock Companies Act 1856 rested were to allow the greatest freedom in the formation and working of a limited liability company, and, at the same time, to ensure that those dealing with the company knew that the liability of its members was limited. The latter principle is carried out by the provision that, apart from exceptional cases,[5] the company must have "Limited" or "Public Limited Company" as the last component of its name. It is not necessary that the company should include the word "company" in its name; many modern instances exist of companies the names of which omit that word.

In view of the fundamental importance which the Act attributes to the "magic word 'Limited,' "[6] or "Public Limited Company" it is not surprising that it

(1) compels companies limited by shares or by guarantee continuously to bring the fact that they are "limited" to the notice of those who are dealing or might deal with them; and
(2) prohibits persons other than limited liability companies from using one of the protected words as the last component of their name.

Publication of name

7–03 By section 108 of the 1948 Act, the name must be painted up or affixed to the outside of every office or place in which the business of the company is carried on in a conspicuous position in letters easily legible and must be engraved in legible characters on its seal. It must also be mentioned (at the risk of heavy penalties for neglect to the company and the directors) in legible characters in all business letters of the company and in all notices, and other official publications of the company, in all bills of exchange, promissory notes, indorsements, cheques,[7] and orders for money or goods, purporting to be signed by or on behalf of the company, and in all bills of parcels, invoices, receipts and letters of credit of the company.

Further, a company[8] shall not state, in any form, the name of any of its directors on any business letter on which the company's name appears unless it states on the letter in legible characters the Christian name, or the

---

[4] See para. 2–07, *ante*.
[5] See note 1, *supra*.
[6] See note 18 to para. 2–06.
[7] It is at least arguable that a cheque made out "Cash or Order" (which is not a cheque within the meaning of the Bills of Exchange Act 1882, as amended) is not a "cheque" under s. 108 (4): *Gader* v. *Flower* (1979) C.A.T. 286.
[8] The companies to which this provision applies are defined in section 201 (2) of the 1948 Act, as amended.

initials thereof, and surname of every director of the company who is an individual and the corporate name of every corporate director.[9]

Personal liability of directors and others if incorrect company name used

7–04 It is dangerous for the directors to neglect compliance with the injunctions of section 108, for, in addition to pecuniary penalties, any director or other officer of a limited company, or any person on its behalf, who signs or authorises to be signed on behalf of the company any bill of exchange, promissory note, indorsement, cheque, order for money or goods, etc.,[9a] wherein the name of the company is not mentioned in manner specified, is personally liable to the holder of such bill of exchange, etc., for the amount thereof unless the same is duly paid by the company (s. 108 (4)). Thus, in *Atkins & Co.* v. *Wardle and Others*,[10] the South Shields Salt Water Baths Co. Ltd. was misdescribed in a bill as the Salt Water Baths Co. Ltd., and it was held that the directors were personally liable on the bill.[11] Further, in *Hendon* v. *Adelman and Others*,[12] the directors of L. & R. Agencies Ltd. purported to sign a cheque for the company by writing "L.R. Agencies Ltd."; MacKenna J. held that they were personally liable under section 108 (4) (*b*) because, by omitting the connecting ampersand, they had not used the correct name of the company. It makes no difference that the holder of those instruments has not been misled by the misdescription.[13] On the other hand, the use of "Ltd." instead of "Limited" or "plc" for "public limited company," or "Co." for "Company" or similar abbreviations does not make the name of the company incorrect and does not render the directors or other officers liable.[14] These persons, if liable, are in the position of sureties[15]: they have only to pay if the company fails to do so. That, however, does not mean that all the rules relating to the purely contractual liability of a surety apply to the signatory's statutory liability under section 108 (4). In particular, the rule does not apply that a non-consenting surety is not liable if the creditor has granted the debtor time; on the contrary, in such a case the signatory continues to be personally liable under section 108 (4) unless the debt is duly paid by the company.[16] Where the holder has expressly or impliedly indicated that he will accept an incorrect form of signature, *e.g.* where he has himself

---

[9] Section 201 (1) of the 1948 Act, as amended by the 1981 Act, Sched. 3, para. 11.

[9a] "Services" are not included in s. 108 (4). Electricity is not "goods": *East Midlands Electricity Board* v. *Grantham* [1980] C.L.Y. 271. The Supply of Goods and Services Act 1982 does not apply to s. 108 (4).

[10] (1889) 61 L.T. 23. affd. by C.A. in (1888) 5 T.L.R. 734; see also *Maxform SpA* v. *B. Mariani & Goodville Ltd.* [1981] 2 Lloyd's Rep. 54 (C.A.).

[11] See also *Dermatine Co.* v. *Ashworth* (1905) 21 T.L.R. 510; *Nassau Steam Press* v. *Tyler* (1894) 70 L.T. 376; *Civil Service Co-operative Society* v. *Chapman* (1914) 30 T.L.R. 679.

[12] (1973) 117 S.J. 631.

[13] *Durham Fancy Goods Ltd.* v. *Michael Jackson (Fancy Goods) Ltd.* [1968] 2 Q.B. 839, 846.

[14] *F. Stacey & Co.* v. *Wallis* (1912) 106 L.T. 544. *Banque de l'Indochine et de Suez S.A.* v. *Euroseas Group Finance Co.* [1981] 3 All E.R. 198.

[15] See note 13, *supra*.

[16] *British Airways Board* v. *Parish* [1979] 2 Lloyd's Rep. 361.

inserted the incorrect words, he will be estopped from enforcing the personal liability arising under the section.[17]

In *Maxform SpA* v. *Mariani and Goodville Ltd.*[17a] Goodville Ltd., a company registered in England (the second defendants), traded under the name "Italdesign" registered as a business name under the Registration of Business Names Act 1916, extended to companies by section 58 of the Companies Act 1947 (both enactments were repealed by the 1981 Act). The plaintiffs drew three bills of exchange on "Italdesign." They were accepted by Mr. Mariani, the first defendant, who signed them without any addition to his name. Mocatta J. held that the "name" in section 108 meant the name under which the company was registered in the Companies Register and not its registered business name. Both the learned judge and the Court of Appeal held Mr. Mariani liable by virtue of section 108 (4).

It is respectfully submitted that section 108 (4) is interpreted in some of the cases, notably in *Hendon* v. *Adelman and Others*[17b] too strictly. The ratio of that section is to avoid confusion. Where there is no danger of confusion and the variation from the registered name of the company is only trivial, the officer who signed on behalf of the company should not be held to be personally liable.

There can be little doubt that the name of the company can be marked upon goods manufactured or supplied by the company in a shortened form without the word "Limited," such goods not being "official publications" within secton 108.

On the obligation of the company to publish certain particulars on its business letters and order forms, in compliance with the European Communities Act 1972, s. 9 (7), see paras. 8–05 and 8–06, *post*.

Prohibition of the use of 'Limited" by others

7–05 The Act further provides that if any person or persons trade or carry on business under any name or title of which the word "Limited" or "Cyfyngedig" or any contraction or limitation of those words are the last word, that person or persons shall, unless duly incorporated with limited liability, be liable to a fine not exceeding £5 for every day upon which that name or title has been used (s. 439, as amended by the 1976 Act, Sched. 2). There does not appear to be a similar prohibition with respect to the use of the phrase "public limited company" in the 1980 Act; the prohibition of section 439 of the 1948 Act which provides a criminal sanction, cannot be applied analogously.

The effect of the 1981 Act on the name law

7–06 Before the coming into operation of the relevant provisions of the 1981 Act on February 26, 1982,[17c] the name of the company was under the strict control of the Department of Trade. The Department had to approve the

[17] But see *Scottish & Newcastle Breweries Ltd.* v. *Blair,* 1967 S.L.T. 72; see para. 27–23, *post.*
[17a] [1981] 2 Lloyd's Rep. 54.
[17b] (1973) 117 S.J. 631.
[17c] Companies Act 1981 (Commencement No. 3) Order 1982 (S.I. 1982 No. 103).

name before it could be registered or changed (1948 Act, ss. 17 and 18) and to grant a licence if the company—and it could only be a private company—wished to obtain dispensation with the requirement of "Limited" as the last word of its name (1948 Act, s. 19).

The 1981 Act has altered this position fundamentally. It abolished the requirement of approval of the Department of Trade for the adoption or change of the company's name and placed the burden of choosing a legally admissible name on the incorporators and the company (1981 Act, ss. 22–24). It also abolished the licence of the Department for the dispensation with the word "Limited" and placed the responsibility of complying with the statutory requirements for such exemption on those who sought to obtain it (1981 Act, s. 25).

Exemption from the requirement of "Limited"

Advantages of such companies

7–07 The advantages of incorporation for associations which may be exempted from using "Limited" as the last word of their name are great. The association gains in stability, public estimation and credit. It becomes a body corporate with perpetual succession, just as if it were incorporated by Royal Charter or special Act of Parliament. It can adopt in lieu of "company" a more suitable name, such as chamber, club, college, guild, association. It can have a common seal; it can hold property in its own name without the intervention of trustees; it can contract and take and defend legal proceedings in its own name; its affairs can be conducted much more efficiently, and—finally—its officers and members are freed from personal liability.

It enjoys all the privileges of a private company and is subject to all its obligations, except the use of the word "Limited" in its name and sending lists of members to the Registrar but, as mentioned in the next section, it must indicate on its business letters and order forms that it is a limited company.

Associations obtaining dispensation with "Limited" registered in the past in a great number of cases as companies limited by guarantee. Since the 1981 Act they are obliged to do so. Generally, membership is constituted by election or by application in writing accepted by the governing body. Sometimes (*e.g.* in charitable associations) a candidate for election must make a donation. The governing body is not infrequently called the committee or the council. When, as is often the case, the association is formed to absorb and continue some existing association of the same name, the members of this all join the registered association, and the property, if any, is transferred to it, and the incorporated association thus silently takes the place of predecessor.

Requirements of European Communities Act

7–08 The European Communities Act 1972, s. 9 (7) (*c*), requires a limited company which is exempt from the use of the word "Limited" to state in all business letters and order forms of the company that it is, in fact, a limited company; see para. 8–05, *post*. The name of a company which is exempt does not show "Limited" as part of it but on the stationery specified in section 9 (7) the company must include a statement that it is a limited company.

Only private companies limited by guarantee can obtain exemption from the requirement of "Limited"

7–09 The 1980 Act, Sched. 3, para. 5 provided already that no licence dispensing with the requirement of "Limited" as the last component of the company's name should be granted to a public company after that provision came into operation on December 22, 1980.

The 1981 Act has gone further than that. Section 25 (1) (*a*) provides that in future only a private company limited by guarantee can be exempt from the requirement to include the word "Limited" as the finite of its name. The provisions of the 1980 Act mentioned in the preceding paragraph have been repealed by the 1981 Act, Sched. 4.

The present position is, then, that in future only a private company limited by guarantee can obtain exemption from including the word "Limited" as the finite of its name, provided that it satisfies the requirements of section 25 of the 1981 Act, which are explained in the following paragraphs.

However, the position existing before section 25 came into operation on February 26, 1982 is not affected. There are, therefore, still in existence private and (until June 22, 1982[17d]) public companies which obtained a licence from the Department of Trade under section 19 of the 1948 Act, as amended by the 1980 Act, to dispense with the requirement of "Limited" as the last word of their name.

Application of section 25

7–10 This section applies to any company which

(a) on or after February 26, 1982 is or is about to be registered as a private company limited by guarantee, and

(b) immediately before that date is a private company limited by shares which had been granted a licence by the Department of Trade under section 19 of the 1948 Act, as amended.

(1981 Act, s. 25 (1)).

As regards public companies having obtained such a licence before December 22, 1980, see below under "Transitional provisions."[17d]

The requirements for exemption

7–11 They are (1981 Act, s. 25 (2)):

"(a) that the objects of the company are, or, in the case of a company about to be registered, are to be the promotion of commerce, art, science, education, religion, charity or any profession and anything incidental or conducive to any of those objects; and

[17d] See para. 7–17, *post*.

(b) that the memorandum or articles of association of the company—

(i) require the profits, if any, or other income to be applied in promoting its objects;

(ii) prohibit the payment of dividend to its members; and

(iii) require all the assets which would otherwise be available to its members generally to be transferred on its winding up either to another body with objects similar to its own or to another body the objects of which are the promotion of charity and anything incidental or conducive thereto (whether or not the body is a member of the company)."

The application to the Registrar

7–12 In order to obtain exemption from the requirement of "Limited," there shall be delivered to the Registrar a statutory declaration in the prescribed form—

(a) in the case of a company to be formed, made by a solicitor engaged in the formation of the company or by a person named as a director or secretary of the company in the statement delivered under section 21 of the 1976 Act (statement of first directors and secretary);

(b) in the case of a company about to be registered in pursuance of Part VIII of the 1948 Act, by two or more directors or other principal officers of the company;

(c) in the case of a company which is proposing to change its name so that it ceases to have as part of its name "Limited," by a director or secretary of the company.

(1981 Act, s. 25 (4).)

No alteration of the memorandum and articles

7–13 A company whose name does not include "Limited" as the last word, shall not alter its memorandum or articles so that it ceases to be a company qualifying for the exemption (1981 Act, s. 25 (5)).

No lists of members to be sent to the Registrar

7–14 A company which satisfies the requirements for exemption from the obligation to include "Limited," need not send lists of members to the Registrar (1981 Act, s. 25 (3)).

Direction by the Secretary of State

7–15 If it appears to the Secretary of State for Trade that a company which has obtained dispensation with the requirement to include "Limited" does not satisfy the requirements for that exemption, he may issue a direction in writing to the company that it shall change its name by a resolution of the directors within a specified time so that its name ends in "Limited" (1981 Act, s. 25 (6)). This resolution has to be registered with the Registrar (*ibid.*). A company which has received such a direction shall not thereafter be registered by a name which does not end in "Limited" without the approval of the Secretary of State (1981 Act, s. 25 (7)).

Criminal sanctions

7–16 The Act contains criminal sanctions in case of contravention of these provisions (1981 Act, s. 25 (9) and (10)).

Transitional provisions

7–17 Some old public companies (para. 4–17, above) may have obtained dispensation with "Limited" before this facility was withdrawn from public companies by the 1980 Act. Their position is safeguarded by the 1981 Act until the expiration of the transitional period under the 1980 Act on June 22, 1982 (1981 Act, s. 35 (1)).

A company which by virtue of the repeal of section 19 of the 1948 Act ceases to be exempt from the requirement that its name should end in "Limited," may change its name by resolution of the directors, so as to add this finite. This resolution shall be passed within 12 months of the repeal of section 19 of the 1948 Act (1981 Act, s. 35 (2)). A company which contravenes this provision is liable to criminal sanction (1981 Act, s. 35 (3)).

Admissibility of names

History

7–18 Before the coming into operation of sections 22 to 27 of the 1981 Act on February 26, 1982, the powers of the Department of Trade relating to the use of names by a company were very wide. These powers were exercised in three stages:

(1) The Department of Trade could refuse the registration of any name which in its opinion was undesirable (1948 Act, s. 17);

(2) within six months after the registration the Department could compel the company to change its name if the name was too like that by which an existing company had already been registered (1948 Act, s. 18 (2)); and

(3) at any time the Department could direct a change of name if the name by which the company was registered was so misleading as to be likely to cause harm to the public (1967 Act, s. 46).

The 1981 Act has altered this position. It abolished the pre-examination of admissibility of the company's name by the Department of Trade and placed the duty to avoid a name which is the same as that of an already registered company or is otherwise prohibited or requires approval by the Secretary of State on the persons or company seeking the registration of a name, but some control by the Department of Trade has been retained. In order to enable interested parties to ascertain whether the name which they wish to choose is still available, the Registrar of Companies maintains an index of names of registered companies.

It is possible that this change may lead to an increase of common law actions aimed at restraining companies from using misleading names.

The index of names

7–19 The Registrar shall keep an index of registered names. The use of a name which is the same as a name appearing on the index is prohibited (1981 Act, s. 23 and s. 22 (1) (*c*)).

The index comprises the names of the following companies (1981 Act, s. 23 (1)):

(a) companies within the meaning of the 1948 Act;

(b) oversea companies;

(c) incorporated and unincorporated bodies to which any provision of the 1948 Act applies by virtue of section 435 of that Act;

(d) limited partnerships registered under the Limited Partnerships Act 1907;

(e) companies within the meaning of the Companies (Northern Ireland) Act 1960; and

(f) societies registered under the Industrial and Provident Societies Act 1965.

For the purposes of the index, an oversea company is defined as a company which has complied with section 407 of the 1948 Act and which appears to the Registrar to have a place of business in Great Britain (1981 Act, s. 23 (2)).

The Secretary of State for Trade has power to alter the list of companies whose names are to be included into the index by statutory instrument (1981 Act, s. 23 (3)).

"The same name"

7–20 It has been observed that the registration of a name which is "the same name" as a name appearing on the index is prohibited. When determining whether the name which is intended to be registered is "the same name," trifling variations do not constitute a differentiation in the identity of the name. The 1981 Act gives the following list of such trifling variations which have to be disregarded when determining whether a name is "the same name" as that on the index (1981 Act, s. 22 (3)):

(a) the definite article where it is the first word of the name;

(b) the following words and expressions where they appear at the end of the name, *i.e.* "company," "and company," "company limited," "and company limited," "limited," "unlimited," "public limited company" or their Welsh equivalents;

(c) abbreviations of any of those words and expressions where they appear at the end of the name;

(d) type and case of letters, spaces between letters, accents and punctuation marks; and

(e) "and" and "&" shall be taken to be the same.

Absolutely prohibited names

7–21 The following names are absolutely prohibited (1981 Act, s. 22 (1)):

(a) a name which includes otherwise than at the end of the name any of the following words and expressions, *i.e.* "limited," "unlimited," or "public limited company" or their Welsh equivalents;

(b) a name which includes otherwise than at the end of the name abbreviations of any of these words or expressions;

(c) a name which is the same as a name appearing in the index of names kept by the Registrar;

(d) a name the use of which by the company would in the opinion of the Secretary of State constitute a criminal offence; or

(e) a name which in the opinion of the Secretary of State is offensive.

Conditionally prohibited names

The following names are conditionally prohibited, *i.e.* they are prohibited except if approved by the Secretary of State (1981 Act, s. 22 (2)):

(a) a name which in the opinion of the Secretary of State would be likely to give the impression that the company is connected in any way with Her Majesty's Government or any local authority; or

(b) a name which includes any word or expression specified by regulation made by the Secretary of Trade (1981 Act, ss. 22 (2) (*b*) and 31).

Specified names requiring approval of the Secretary of State

7–22 The Secretary of State has specified the names and expressions which require his approval by virtue of section 22 (2) (*b*) of the 1981 Act, quoted above, in the Companies and Business Names Regulations 1981 (S.I. 1981 No. 1685), which came into operation on February 26, 1982. According to these Regulations the words and expressions stated in column (1) of the following require his approval prior to the registration of the name. This approval is given by the body stated in column (2). Where two bodies are specified in the alternative in column (2), it depends on whether the company has, or is to have, its registered office or principal or only place of business in England and Wales or in Scotland; in the former case approval of the English body, and in the latter case that of the Scottish body, has to be obtained. It should, however, be noted that the Secretary of State has power to designate further specified words and expressions as requiring his prior approval; this will likewise be done by statutory instruments which will be included into Part A of Volume II of this work.

Where no body is stated in column (2), the approval of the Secretary of State for Trade should be sought.

SPECIFICATION OF WORDS, EXPRESSIONS AND RELEVANT BODIES

Column (1)	Column (2)
Word or expression	Relevant body
Abortion	Department of Health and Social Security

Column (1)	Column (2)
Word or expression	Relevant body
Apothecary	Worshipful Company of Apothecaries or Pharmaceutical Society of Great Britain
Association	
Assurance	
Assurer	
Authority	
Benevolent	
Board	
Breed Breeder Breeding	Ministry of Agriculture, Fisheries and Food
British	
Building Society	
Chamber of Commerce	
Chamber of Industry	
Chamber of Trade	
Charitable Charity	Charity Commission or Scottish Home and Health Department
Charter	
Chartered	
Contact Lens	General Optical Council
Co-operative	
Council	
Dental Dentistry	General Dental Council
District Nurse	Panel of Assessors in District Nurse Training
Duke	Home Office or Scottish Home and Health Department
England	
English	
European	
Federation	
Friendly Society	
Foundation	
Fund	
Giro	
Great Britain	
Group	
Health Centre Health Service	Department of Health and Social Security
Health Visitor	Council for the Education and Training of Health Visitors
Her Majesty His Majesty	Home Office or Scottish Home and Health Department
Holding	
Industrial and Provident Society	
Institute	
Institution	
Insurance	
Insurer	
International	
Ireland	
Irish	

Column (1)	Column (2)
Word or expression	Relevant body
King	Home Office or Scottish Home and Health Department
Midwife	Central Midwives Board or Central Midwives Board for Scotland
Midwifery	
National	
Nurse	General Nursing Council for England and Wales or General Nursing Council for Scotland
Nursing	
Nursing Home	Department of Health and Social Security
Patent	
Patentee	
Police	Home Office or Scottish Home and Health Department
Post Office	
Pregnancy Termination	Department of Health and Social Security
Prince	
Princess	Home Office or Scottish Home and Health Department
Queen	
Reassurance	
Reassurer	
Register	
Registered	
Reinsurance	
Reinsurer	
Royal	
Royale	Home Office or Scottish Home and Health Department
Royalty	
Scotland	
Scottish	
Sheffield	
Society	
Special School	Department of Education and Science
Stock Exchange	
Trade Union	
Trust	
United Kingdom	
Wales	
Welsh	
Windsor	Home Office or Scottish Home and

Secretary of State may direct change of too similar name

7–23 If a company is registered by a name which, in the opinion of the Secretary of State, is the same or too like a name which at the time of registration is, or should have been, on the index of names, the Secretary of State may direct the company with the later registration to change its name (1981 Act, s. 24 (2)). In the event of such a direction being given within 12 months of its being registered the new company is bound to change its name within the time specified in the direction or such longer period as the Department may allow, and in default is liable to a default fine. This criminal sanction is on summary conviction a fine not exceeding one-fifth of the statutory maximum, as defined in section 87 of the 1980 Act, or, on conviction after continued contravention, a default fine not exceeding one-fiftieth of the statutory maximum (1981 Act, s. 24 (5)).[18]

Secretary of State may direct change of name if misleading information is supplied

7–24 Where it appears to the Secretary of State that a company has provided misleading information for the purpose of its registration by a particular name or has given undertakings or assurances for that purpose which have not been fulfilled, he may direct a change of name of that company (1981 Act, s. 24 (3)). This provision obviously applies only to names conditionally prohibited by the 1981 Act. The direction must be issued within five years of the date of registration of the offending name. The company must comply within such period as the direction specifies. Here again, the Secretary has power to extend the period of compliance. The penalties for non-compliance are the same as in the preceding case (s. 24 (4) and (5)).

Department of Trade may direct change of misleading name

7–25 The Department of Trade has further power, by virtue of section 46 of the 1967 Act, to direct a company to change its name at any time if, in the opinion of the Department, the name gives so misleading an indication of the nature of the company's activities as to be likely to cause harm to the public. However, a direction under this provision is different from the cases in which a direction may be given under section 24 of the 1981 Act. In the latter cases, which were discussed in the preceding two paragraphs, the ruling of the Secretary of State is final. In the case of a direction under section 46 of the 1967 Act the company to which the direction is addressed has a right of appeal to the court. The appeal must be lodged within three weeks from the date of the direction. If no appeal is lodged, the company must comply with the direction within six weeks from its date or such longer time as the Department allows. In case of non-compliance a default fine may be imposed.

Oversea companies

7–26 The names of oversea companies[19] are included in the index of names kept by the Registrar (see para. 7–19, *ante*).

The 1976 Act contained already a regulation of names of oversea companies in section 31. This section has been amended by section 27 of the

[18] It is thought that the company has to carry out the change by special resolution although—unlike subs. (1)—this is not expressly stated in subs. (2). That subsection does not purport to deal with the procedure for change of name—a topic dealt with in subs. (1).

[19] For definition of an oversea company see s. 406 of the 1948 Act and para. 88–02, *post*.

1981 Act and these amendments came into operation on February 26, 1982. In the following, reference is made to the amended version of section 31 and the position is stated as it is at present.

The Secretary of State may serve on the oversea company a notice of objection to its corporate name, if he is of opinion

(1) that the name of the company would have been either a prohibited name or a specified name requiring approval of the Secretary of State and he would not have approved it (s. 31 (1)); or
(2) that the name of the company is too like a name on the index of names kept by the Registrar (s. 31 (1A)).

The notice of the Secretary of State must be served within 12 months after the "relevant date," or if that date is before the day when section 27 of the 1981 Act came into operation, six months after that date (s. 31 (2)). The "relevant date" is defined as the date on which the company has complied with

(a) section 407 of the 1948 Act (Delivery to the Registrar of certain documents); or
(b) section 409 (2) of the 1948 Act, if there has been a change in the corporate name (Return to the Registrar of altered documents) (s. 31 (2)).

The oversea company has to comply with the notice of the Secretary of State within two months or such longer period as may be specified in the notice (s. 31 (5)). Within this period the company may submit to the Registrar a name approved by the Secretary of State (other than its corporate name) under which it wishes to carry on business in Great Britain (s. 31 (3)) or it must cease carrying on business in Great Britain at the end of this period. If it contravenes this provision, the company and every officer or agent of the company who knowingly and wilfully authorises or permits the contravention is liable to a fine. During this period the Secretary of State may withdraw the notice (s. 31 (5)).

Common law actions restraining use of misleading names

7–27 The registration of a name under company law does not provide efficient protection against an action at common law for an injunction at the suit of anyone prejudiced by the adoption of the name.

A common law action aiming at a restraint upon the company to use the name under which it is registered and claiming, as against the company, the removal of that name from the register is normally founded on

(1) contract; or
(2) the tort of passing off.

A company, or individual controlling a company, may contract not to use a particular name. If this undertaking is broken and the company is registered under that name, an injunction restraining the company from using that name may be claimed.

As regards passing off, the principle on which the court interferes in such cases is that a person is not to be permitted to represent the business which is carried on by another as carried on by himself.[20] On this principle the court will even prevent the use of the name of a world-wide organisation although that organisation is not at present represented in England.[21] The basis of the action for passing off is a proprietary right not so much in the name itself but in the goodwill established through the use of the name in connection with the plaintiff's business.[22]

The inadvertent omission by a limited company to publish its corporate name will not disentitle it to have the use of its trade name protected by injunction.[23]

A company finding out that another company has been or is about to be registered under the same name as itself may have a common law right to restrain the newcomer from the use of that name. It will certainly have the right if the name has been used with the intention of misleading third parties, or for some fraudulent purpose.[24] It will also be able to restrain a company from using a name with which it has been registered if, owing to the fact that its name is the same as or closely similar to[25] that of a company already exisitng (even if not a company regulated by the Companies Acts, *e.g.* a firm or an unregistered company[26]), the original company can show that confusion has existed, or that persons have dealt with the second company believing it to be the old one; in that respect, the sound as well as the spelling of the name is material.[27] In some cases the court may make the restraint purely local,[28] and if the locality of operation, or intended operation, or of the type of business, is such that there is no real danger of confusion, the court will not grant an injunction.

But the court does not require to be convinced either that there is fraud, or a deliberate intention to confuse, or that the public has been misled. It will suffice to show that the name with which a company proposes to be registered is "calculated" to mislead, the word "calculated" carrying no

---

[20] *Tussaud* v. *Tussaud* (1890) 44 Ch.D. 678; *North Cheshire and Manchester Brewery Co.* v. *Manchester Brewery Co.* [1899] A.C. 83; *La Société Anonyme, etc., Panhard et Levassor* v. *Panhard Levassor, etc., Co.* [1901] 2 Ch. 513; *Ewing* v. *Buttercup Margarine Co.* [1917] 2 Ch. 1; *Harrods* v. *R. Harrod* (1924) 40 T.L.R. 195; *Standard Bank of South Africa* v. *Standard Bank* (1909) 25 T.L.T. 420; *Legal and General Assurance Society Ltd.* v. *Daniel* (1967) 111 S.J. 808; *Maxim's Ltd.* v. *Dye* [1977] 1 W.L.R. 1155; *Warnink* v. *Townsend & Sons (Hull)* [1979] A.C. 731; *Cadbury-Schweppes Pty. Ltd.* v. *Pub Squash Co. Pty. Ltd.* [1981] 1 W.L.R. 193.

[21] *Sheraton Corpn. of America* v. *Sheraton Motels Ltd., The Times*, July 13, 1963.

[22] *Ad-Lib Club Ltd.* v. *Granville* [1971] 2 All E.R. 300.

[23] *Randall Ltd.* v. *British and American Shoe Co.* [1902] 2 Ch. 354.

[24] *Turton* v. *Turton* (1889) 42 Ch.D. 128; *Reddaway* v. *Banham* [1896] A.C. 199.

[25] *Hendriks* v. *Montagu* (1881) 17 Ch.D 638; *North Cheshire and Manchester Brewery Co.* v. *Manchester Brewery Co.* [1899] A.C. 83.

[26] *Hendriks* v. *Montagu* (1881) 17 Ch.D. 638; *Hoby* v. *Grosvenor Library Co. Ltd.* (1880) 28 W.R. 386.

[27] *Ouvah Ceylon Estates* v. *Uva Ceylon Rubber Estates* (1910) 27 T.L.R. 24.

[28] *Lee* v. *Haley* (1869) L.R. 5 Ch. 155.

hint of intention but meaning, in effect, little more than "morally certain."[29]

Change of name by company

Voluntary change

7–28 In harmony with the general scheme of the 1981 Act, the approval of the Department of Trade to the change of name, formerly required by section 18 (1) of the 1948 Act, has been abolished.

The only requirement for the change in name is a special resolution of the general meeting (1981 Act, s. 24 (1)).

Care has to be taken in the choice of the new name. It must not be an absolutely or conditionally prohibited name (para. 7 21, *ante*) or a specified name requiring approval of the Secretary of State unless the approval of the competent body has been obtained (para. 7–22, *ante*).

Directions of the Secretary of State

7–29 The Secretary of State has also power to issue directions requiring the change of an objectionable name, where a new name has been adopted by the company.

These directions may be issued in three cases:

(1) where the chosen name is the same or too like a name on the index of names (1981 Act, s. 24 (2); para. 7–23, *ante*);
(2) where the choice of the name is founded on misleading information or an unfulfilled undertaking (1981 Act, s. 24 (3); para. 7–24, *ante*);
(3) where the name is likely to be harmful to the public, having regard to the activities of the company (1967 Act, s. 46; para. 7–25, *ante*).

Issue of new certificate of incorporation

When a company has changed its name, the Registrar enters the new name in the register and in the index, in the place of the former name, and issues a new certificate of incorporation, showing the new name of the company (1981 Act, s. 24 (6)).

A change in name does not affect any rights or obligations of the company or renders defective any legal proceedings, and legal proceedings commenced in the old name can be continued under the new name (1981 Act, s. 24 (7)).[29a]

Use of business names by a company

7–30 A company may carry on business under a name other than its corporate name. Such a name is known as the business name. Formerly the company

[29] See *per* James L.J. in *Hendriks* v. *Montagu* (1881) 17 Ch.D. 638, 645, 646; *North Cheshire and Manchester Brewery Co.* v. *Manchester Brewery Co.* [1899] A.C. 83. See also *Dunlop Pneumatic Tyre Co.* v. *Dunlop Motor Co.* 1907 S.C. (H.L.) 15; *Scottish Union and National Insurance Co.* v. *Scottish National Insurance Co.* 1909 S.C. 318; *Williamson* v. *Meikle* 1909 S.C. 1272.

[29a] *Cf. Richards & Wallington (Earthmoving) Ltd.* v. *Whatlings Ltd.* 1982 S.L.T. 66.

could register its business name in the register of business names constituted under the Registration of Business Names Act 1916; this Act was extended to companies by the Companies Act 1947, s. 58. Both enactments are repealed by the 1981 Act, Sched. 4. The law applicable at present is contained in sections 28 to 35 of the 1981 Act which came into operation on February 26, 1982.

Control of business names

7–31 The 1981 Act preserves the right of a company to use a business name (s. 28 (1) (*c*)) but subjects such use, as the use of business names in general,[30] to the control of the Secretary of State. The company shall not, without the written approval of the Secretary of State, use a name which—

(a) would be likely to give the impression that the business is connected with Her Majesty's Government or any local authority; or
(b) includes any word or expression specified in regulations as requiring the approval of the Secretary of State. These words and expressions are the same as are specified for company names and set out in para. 7–22, *ante*.

(1981 Act, s. 28(2)).

The approval of the Secretary of State is not required if the company carried on the business under a name lawfully registered under the Registration of Business Names Act 1916 immediately before the appointed day (1981 Act, s. 28 (5) and (6)). Where such a business is transferred, the transferee likewise does not require the approval of the Department of Trade (1981 Act, s. 28 (4)). Where the business of the company is carried on under a business name which required the approval of the Secretary of State but that approval was not obtained, the company has committed a criminal offence (1981 Act, s. 28 (7)). A director, manager, secretary or other similar person, or a person who was purporting to act in such capacity, is likewise punishable if the offence was committed with his consent or connivance (1981 Act, s. 28 (8)). Where the affairs of the company are managed by its members, they are in the same position as the directors of the company and can be punished if the requirements of subsection 7 of section 28 are satisfied (1981 Act, s. 28 (9)).

Disclosure of corporate name

7–32 A company which uses a business name shall give disclosure of its corporate name in the following manner.

The company has to state its corporate name in legible characters on all business letters, invoices and receipts issued in the course of the business and in written demands for payment of debts arising in the course of the business. It has also to state in the like manner on these communications an address in Great Britain at which service of any document can be effected (1981 Act, s. 29 (1) (*a*)).

Further, the company has to state its corporate name and the address at

[30] Single traders and partnerships may likewise use business names, see para. 89–03, *post*.

which service can be effected in any premises where business is carried on and to which the customers of the business or suppliers of goods or services have access. The statement must be displayed in a prominent position, so that it can be easily read by such customers or suppliers (1981 Act, s. 29 (1) (*b*)).

Where a company using a business name negotiates anything in the course of its business and is asked to disclose its corporate name and the address, at which service can be effected, the company has to comply with this request (1981 Act, s. 29 (2)).

The Secretary of State may require by statutory instrument that the notices to be displayed in the business premises and to be given in the course of the negotiations should be in a specified form (1981 Act, s. 29 (5)).

A company which fails to comply with these provisions without reasonable excuse, is liable to a fine. The same liability extends to directors, managers, secretaries, other similar officers, persons purporting to act in any of these capacities, shareholders who manage the affairs of the company, if the offence is committed with their consent or connivance (1981 Act, s. 29 (6) and (8)).

Dismissal of civil proceedings in case of non-compliance with section 29

7–33 The 1981 Act, following the regulation of the repealed Registration of Business Names Act 1916, provides a statutory remedy in case of non-compliance with the disclosure provision (s. 30).

If a company using a business name but having failed to comply with the disclosure provisions of section 29 (1) and (2) of the 1981 Act brings legal proceedings against a defendant to enforce any right arising out of a contract made in the course of business, the proceedings shall be dismissed if the defendant shows

(a) that he has a claim against the plaintiff arising out of the contract which he has been unable to pursue by reason of the plaintiff's breach of section 29 (1) or (2); or
(b) that he has suffered some financial loss in connection with the contract by reason of the plaintiff's breach of section 29 (1) or (2).

This is a heavy burden of proof which the defendant has to discharge. Moreover, the court has power not to grant the statutory remedy if satisfied that it is just and equitable to permit the proceedings to continue.[31]

The statutory remedy is without prejudice to the right of any person to enforce his rights against another person in any proceedings brought by that person.

---

[31] *Cf. Thomas Montgomery & Sons* v. *W.B. Anderson & Sons Ltd.* 1979 S.L.T. 101.

PRACTICE NOTES

Choice of name

7–34 Care should be taken in registering the name of a company to avoid the possibility of a passing off action being taken by an existing company (see para. 7–27, *ante*). This can best be done by employing one of the specialist company registration agents to undertake a search of the index kept under section 23 of the 1981 Act prior to registering or changing the name of a company.

Procedure on change of name by company

7–35 A copy of the memorandum, altered to show the new name, must accompany the copy of the resolution and the fee sent to the Registrar.[32] A company with listed securities must also send a copy of the memorandum, as altered, to The Stock Exchange, together with four copies of the resolution. A copy of the special resolution must be inserted in every copy of the memorandum and articles in stock (1948 Act, s. 143) and should be sent to every person known to be in possession of a copy of the memorandum and articles, *e.g.* directors, auditors, bankers, solicitors, Inland Revenue, etc. From the date of the certificate of incorporation on change of name, the new name must appear on all letters, share certificates and other business documents issued by the company and all premises in which the company operates. A common seal engraven with the new name will have been obtained in advance and will be formally adopted by the directors as soon as the certificate on change of name has been issued by the Registrar.

In cases where, for commercial or other reasons, it is essential that the name is formally changed on a given date, the Registrar should be consulted in advance to ensure that his certificate of incorporation on change of name bears the required date.

Where the name of a company is changed after the institution of legal proceedings by or against the company, the new name must be substituted and the former name mentioned in brackets in all future proceedings therein.[33]

---

[32] Change of name necessitates reprinting of the memorandum and articles under the European Communities Act 1972, s. 9 (5). But see para. 56–12, *post*.
[33] *Practice Direction* [1965] 1 W.L.R. 120. This practice does not apply in Scotland.

CHAPTER 8

THE REGISTERED OFFICE CLAUSE

Situation of registered office

8–01 This clause states in which part of the United Kingdom the registered office of the company is to be situate, *viz.* whether it is to be situate in England (which, for this purpose, includes Wales[1]) or in Scotland (1948 Act, s. 2 (1) (*b*)). The clause may also state that the registered office shall be situate in England and Wales, or in Wales. But a clause stating that the registered office shall be situate in the United Kingdom is inadmissible because it does not identify the register in which the company is registered.

The statement as to the situation of the registered office is material for various reasons, and, in particular, because on the situation of the registered office depends the place where the company is to be registered and which is to be the country having jurisdiction over it.[2] Thus, if the registered office is to be in England, the company must be registered with the Registrar for England in Cardiff,[3] unless the memorandum states that the object is to work mines in the counties of Devon or Cornwall; in that case it must be registered in Truro. If the memorandum states that the company's registered office shall be situate in Wales, the company may avail itself of the linguistic privileges admitted for Welsh companies (see next paragraph). If the registered office is to be in Scotland, the company must be registered with the Registrar for Scotland in Edinburgh.[3]

Situation of registered office in Wales

8–02 A company which states in the registered office clause of the memorandum that its registered office shall be situate in Wales, may use the Welsh language in its name and in the company documents.[4] Such a company is bound by that clause to have a registered office at all times at an address in Wales. If, however, the memorandum states that the registered office shall be situate in England, or in England and Wales, the office may be situate at an address in England or Wales and may be changed from an address in England to an address in Wales or vice versa, but the linguistic privileges of Welsh companies are not available to such companies.

Every company must have a registered office

8–03 A company shall at all times have a registered office to which communications and notices can be addressed (1976 Act, s. 23 (1)).

---

[1] See the Wales and Berwick Act 1746, s. 3.
[2] *Cf. R.* v. *Industrial Disputes Tribunal, ex p. Kigass Ltd.* [1953] 1 W.L.R. 411, 414.
[3] For the addresses of the Registrars for England and Scotland, see para. 6–01, *ante*.
[4] See para. 7–02, *ante*.

The first—intended—situation of the registered office has to be indicated in the statement filed with the Registrar of Companies prior to the incorporation of the company.[5]

Change of registered office

8–04 If the company wishes to change its registered office, it must give the Registrar notice in the prescribed from within 14 days of the change, and the Registrar will record the new situation (1976 Act, s. 23 (3)).[6] Any notice of a change in the situation of the registered office must be officially notified by the Registrar in the *London* or *Edinburgh Gazette*. Until the notification of the new registration takes effect in accordance with the provisions of section 9 (4) of the European Communities Act 1972,[7] the address of the registered office of the company is its old address and communications and notices may be sent to that address.

The company can change the situation of its registered office only in the part of the United Kingdom in which it is registered. Consequently, an English company cannot change its registered office to an address in Scotland nor vice versa, but such change has been carried out by Private Act of Parliament.

If default is made in complying with subsections (1) or (3) of section 23 of the 1976 Act, the company and every officer of the company who is in default is liable for a default fine which is specified in Schedule 2 to the 1980 Act.

The company may have its principal—as distinguished from its registered—office anywhere, even outside the part of the United Kingdom in which it is registered.

Publication of particulars of registration on company stationery

Section 9 (7) of the European Communities Act 1972

8–05 Subsection (7) requires the company to state on all business letters and order forms of the company the following particulars:

"(a) the place of registration of the company, and the number with which it is registered;

(b) the address of the registered office; and

(bb) in the case of an investment company certified as such under section 41 (3) of the Companies Act 1980, the fact that it is such an investment company; and[8]

---

[5] See para. 15–01, *post*.

[6] s. 23 of the 1976 Act has superseded s. 107 of the 1948 Act which has been repealed (Sched. 3 to the 1976 Act).

[7] See para. 17–04, *post*. See also *Ross* v. *Invergordon Distillers Ltd.* 1961 S.L.T. 358.

[8] Para. (bb) is added by the Companies Act 1980, Sched. 3 with effect from December 22, 1980.

(c) in the case of a limited company exempt from the obligation to use the word "Limited" as part of its name, the fact that it is a limited company."

Further, if in the case of a company having a share capital there is on the stationery a reference to the amount of the share capital, the reference shall be to the paid-up capital.

Companies affected by subsection (7)

Subsection (7) applies to all companies incorporated in Great Britain under the Companies Acts, including unregistered companies within the meaning of section 435 of the 1948 Act, but, it is submitted, it does not apply to unlimited companies. It is true that subsection (8) states that section 9 of the 1972 Act "shall be construed as one with the Companies Act 1948" and the definition of a "company" in section 455 of the 1948 Act includes unlimited companies. But section 9 must be construed by reference to the First Council Directive on Company Law Harmonisation of March 9, 1968[9] since the section is intended to give effect to that Directive. The Act of Accession provides expressly in Annex I, III (*h*) (1)[10] that the Council Directive shall apply in the United Kingdom to "companies incorporated with limited liability." As unlimited companies are outside the ambit of the First Council Directive, they may be assumed also to be outside the ambit of section 9.

A problem arises further with respect to limited companies which are exempt from the requirement to use "Limited" under the 1981 Act, s. 25. Such companies, whether they are limited by shares or by guarantee, must show the particulars required by subsection (7) on their stationery, including the special detail required by paragraph (*c*) of that subsection and mentioned above, but they need not add the word "Limited" or an abbreviation of this word to their name. The requirement of subsection (7) (*c*) is surprising because section 25 companies are not "profit-making companies" within the meaning of Article 58 (2) of the EEC Treaty which provides:

> "The term 'companies or firms' shall be understood to mean companies or firms constituted under civil or commercial law, including co-operative societies, and other legal persons under public or private law, save for non-profit-making companies or firms"

Section 25 companies have, of course, to comply with the requirements of section 9 (7) (*c*) of the European Communities Act 1972, as long as this provision is not repealed, but it should be emphasised that they are not subject to the Directives relating to companies issued by the EEC and future legislation giving effect of these Directives in the United Kingdom should exempt them from their application.

---

[9] No. 68/151 (J.O. 1968, L65/8).

[10] Encyclopedia of European Community Law, Vol. BI, para. B9–263.

Requirements of subsection (7) additional to section 108 of 1948 Act

The requirements of this subsection are additional to those of section 108 (1) (*c*) of the Companies Act 1948, as far as business letters and order forms are concerned. The duty to publish the registration number and other particulars mentioned in this subsection does not extend to the other documents listed in section 108 (1) (*c*).

Business letters and order forms; statement of capital

8–06 It is not clear what the reference to "order forms of the company" in subsection (7) includes. The natural meaning of that phrase is a reference to order forms by which the company orders goods or services, if it uses standardised forms for that purpose; such an interpretation makes sense because a supplier might wish to consult the register of the company with a view to ascertaining its creditworthiness and it would be of assistance to him to know the locality of the register, particularly as the registration number has likewise to be shown. However, the Department of Trade and Industry, in the notice published below, gives the phrase another interpretation; it states that "order form in this context means a document which a company makes available to other people to enable them to order goods or services from the company. The term includes, for example, order coupons printed in newspaper advertisements." The Department does not state whether this somewhat artificial interpretation is exclusive of or additional to what is described here as the natural meaning of the phrase. It is believed that the phrase covers order forms on a standardised form both to the company's suppliers and customers. On the other hand, it is thought that the Department's view on newspaper advertisements requires qualification; if the advertisement only invites the sending of catalogues or literature containing order forms, the particulars required by subsection (7) need not be added to the advertisement. But if the advertisement itself constitutes the order form, the view of the Department may well be right.

There is no obligation under subsection (7) of the Companies Acts for a company to state its capital on its stationery. If a company having a share capital does so voluntarily, it is obliged by subsection (7) to refer on its business letters and order forms to its paid-up capital.

Change of registered office

In case of change of the address of the registered office the subsection does not allow a period of grace *expressis verbis* but it is thought that the period of 14 days admitted by section 23 (3) of the Companies Act 1976 applies by analogy.

Criminal sanctions

Non-compliance with the provisions of subsection (7) may have criminal consequences.[11]

---

[11] Subs. (7), second para.

Notice of the Department of Trade

8–07 The Department of Trade has published the following notice relating to the company law provisions of the European Communities Act 1972. The notice refers not only to information on company stationery required by subsection (7), but also to other company matters affected by the Act.

"COMPANY LAW PROVISIONS OF THE EUROPEAN COMMUNITIES ACT

Changes in British company law which will bring it more into line with EEC practice and which comes into effect when Britain joins the Community are included in section 9 of the European Communities Act.

Information on company stationery. From January 1, 1973, companies will have to show on business letters and order forms their place of registration, registered number and the address of their registered office. The place of registration may be indicated by the words: 'registered in England' or 'registered in Scotland,' as appropriate; 'registered in London' or 'registered in Edinburgh' would also be acceptable. If the only address shown on the stationery is that of the registered office, an indication should be given that it is the registered office address. A reference to capital is not obligatory, but where such is made, it must be to the amount of paid-up share capital.

A company authorised under section [25 of the Companies Act 1981] to dispense with the word 'limited' in its name must indicate on its stationery that it is a limited company. But this does not alter the right to omit the word 'limited' from its name. The existing requirement for names of directors to be included on business letters is unaltered by the new Act; so too are the circumstances in which this requirement may be waived.

The Act makes no stipulation as to the exact location on the stationery of the required new information; nor is it essential for it to be printed, as stamping or typing will be acceptable.

An order form in this context means a document which a company makes available to other people to enable them to order goods or services from the company. The term includes, for example, order coupons printed in newspaper advertisements.

What is a printed document? Section 9 of the Act requires certain printed documents to be sent to the Registrar of Companies in addition to those already stipulated by the Companies Acts. For all these purposes, the Registrar will accept as printed documents produced by the following processes:

Letterpress, gravure, lithography;
'Office' type-set, offset lithography;
Electrostatic photocopying;
'Photostat' or similar processes properly processed and washed;
Stencil duplicating, using wax stencils and black ink.

No document will be acceptable if in general appearance, format or durability it is unsuitable for publication and use on the company's file. Experience has shown that documents produced by dye-line copying, spirit duplicating or thermo-copying are unsatisfactory.

Memorandum and articles. Companies may need to comply with the requirement that an up-to-date copy of the memorandum or articles of association must be delivered to the registrar where any alteration has been made. Section 9 requires these documents as altered to be printed. This is already a requirement where the memorandum has been altered by special resolution in accordance with section 5 of the Companies Act 1948. It is a new requirement where the memorandum has been altered in accordance with some other provision or where the articles have been altered.

The registrar will accept copies of the memorandum and articles amended in accordance with the following rules. Where the amendment is small in extent, such as a change of name or a change in the nominal capital, a copy of the original document may be amended by rubber stamping, typing or in some other permanent manner (but not a manuscript amendment). An alteration of a few lines or a complete short paragraph may be similarly dealt with if the new version is permanently affixed to a copy of the original in such a way as to obscure the amended words. Where more substantial amendments are involved, the pages amended may be removed from a copy of the original, the amended text inserted and the pages securely collated. The inserted material must be 'printed' as defined above but need not be produced by the same process as the original. In all cases the alterations must be validated by the seal or an official stamp of the company. The registrar reserves the right to change these arrangements if experience should show them to be unsatisfactory.

Amended copies are required to be delivered to the registrar within one month of the entry date (January 1, 1973).

Which companies are affected? All companies incorporated in Great Britain under the Companies Acts must comply with these new provisions. They do not apply to branches of companies incorporated outside Great Britain which have an established place of business here. Similar provisions will be enacted under section 4 (3) of the new Act for companies incorporated in Northern Ireland."

Information on company stationery

8–08 The Companies Registration Office has indicated that it will also accept the following statements:

Registered in England and Wales.
Registered in Cardiff.
Registered in Wales.

This is additional to the statements indicated in the Notice of the Department of Trade reproduced in the preceding paragraph.

Official notification

8–09 Official notification is required of a change in the situation of the company's registered office.[12] On official notification see paragraph 17–01, *post*.

Nationality, domicile and residence of company

8–10 The situation of the registered office determines the nationality and domicile of the company but it does not determine its residence.[13] Where

[12] European Communities Act 1932, s. 9 (3) (*e*), as amended by the 1976 Act, s. 23 (6).

[13] The following observations are founded on Clive M. Schmitthoff, *The English Conflict of Laws* (3rd ed., 1954), pp. 371–372 and 379 *et seq*. Scots law does not differ from English law in these matters.

legal rules use these criteria and it is obvious that the rules have to be applied to legal persons, it becomes necessary to apply these criteria by way of analogy from the case of natural persons. "It is obvious that a corporation can no more have a domicile or residence than it can marry or have children. On the other hand, effect must be given to the legal prescript, which is clearly intended to cover the case of the artificial person as well as that of the natural person. Here the task of the courts is to interpret the enactment in question in relation to the artificial person."[14] Sir Raymond Evershed M.R. said[15]:

> "The sense of the words must, therefore, as respects a body corporate, be derived, as Lord Loreburn L.C. observed in his much quoted opinion in *De Beers Consolidated Mines Ltd.* v. *Howe*,[16] from analogy. But the analogy involves no mere technicality, no great mystery or mental strain; it leaves, we should have thought, room for common sense."

Nationality

The nationality of a company is determined by the law of the country in which it is incorporated and from which it derives its personality.[17]

In English law, nationality is rarely adopted as a legal test.

Domicile

The place of registration is likewise the domicile of a company, and this domicile clings to it throughout its existence.[18] It is, however, possible that by operation of the law of the company's domicile, another system of law may be substituted for the law of the place of registration.[19]

Unlike an individual, a company cannot have a domicile of choice.

Residence

8–11 The residence of a company is not as easily established as its nationality or its domicile. The test of residence is mainly used if questions pertaining to taxation, the character of the company as an overseas trading corporation, service of process on the company and attribution of enemy character to the company arise. In these cases, the residence of the company is not determined by the application of a uniform test but a different meaning is given to those words in each of them. Moreover, a company—like an individual—may have several residences at the same time, whereas it can have one domicile and one nationality only.

---

14 Schmitthoff, *loc. cit.*, p. 372.

15 In *Union Corporation* v. *I.R.C.* [1952] 1 All E.R. 646, 654; affd. [1953] A.C. 482.

16 [1906] A.C. 455, 458.

17 *Janson* v. *Driefontein Consolidated Mines Ltd.* [1902] A.C. 484, 505; *Gasque* v. *I.R.C.* [1940] 2 K.B. 80; *Kuenigl* v. *Donnersmarck* [1955] 1 Q.B. 515, 535. The law of the country of incorporation may be relevant not only in questions of status of the company but also in a dispute over the control of the company: *Bailey (Malta) Ltd.* v. *Bailey* [1963] 1 Lloyd's Rep. 595 (C.A.).

18 *Gasque* v. *I.R.C., supra*; *Kuenigl* v. *Donnersmarck, supra*.

19 *Per* Buckley J. in *Carl Zeiss Stiftung* v. *Rayner & Keeler Ltd.* (*No. 3*) [1970] Ch. 506, 544.

8–12 TAX LAW. In tax law a company is ordinarily resident where the actual management of the company is carried on,[20] even though it ought to be managed elsewhere according to its constitution.[21] If this is done at several places, the company has a dual residence[22] (or possibly even more residences), but in that case at *least* some part of the superior and directing authority of the company must be present in the country in which it is sought to establish the residence of the company.[23] A company incorporated under one of the British Companies Acts and having its registered office in England may not be resident in England at all although, of course, it has British nationality, and is domiciled here. Thus, it was held in *Egyptian Delta Land and Investment Co. Ltd.* v. *Todd*[24] that the company, which was incorporated in England and had its registered office in this country, but was entirely controlled and managed from Cairo, where the director and the secretary permanently resided, was not resident in England but was solely resident in Egypt.

8–13 SERVICE OF PROCESS ON COMPANIES. A British company incorporated under one of the Companies Acts can always be served with legal process at its registered office (1948 Act, s. 437)[25] whether or not it carries on business in this country or is "resident" here. An English company can be served with process of a foreign court in a manner recognised by English law only if it is "resident" in the foreign jurisdiction, and that is the case if it carries on business there "at a definite and, to some reasonable extent, permanent place."[26] Where in an action or other legal proceeding in the English courts the writ, petition or other document cannot be served by reason of there being no registered office, it is believed that the court will make an order for substituted service.[27]

Service of a document is effected "by leaving it at or sending it by post to the registered office of the company" (1948 Act, s. 437 (1)). If the docu-

---

[20] *De Beers Consolidated Mines Ltd.* v. *Howe* [1906] A.C. 455; *Mitchell* v. *Egyptian Hotels Ltd.* [1915] A.C. 1022; *American Thread Co.* v. *Joyce* (1913) 29 T.L.R. 266; *New Zealand Shipping Co. Ltd.* v. *Thew* (1922) 8 Tax Cas. 208; *Union Corporation Ltd.* v. *I.R.C.* [1953] A.C. 482; *Koitaki Para Rubber Estates Ltd.* v. *Federal Commissioner of Taxes* (1940) 64 C.L.R. (Australian) 15, 19.

[21] *Unit Construction Co. Ltd.* v. *Bullock* [1960] A.C. 351.

[22] *Swedish Central Ry.* v. *Thompson* [1925] A.C. 495; also *Goerz & Co.* v. *Bell* [1904] 2 K.B. 136.

[23] Union Corporation Ltd. v. *I.R.C.* [1953] A.C. 482.

[24] [1929] A.C. 1.

[25] R.S.C. 1965, Ord. 65, r. 3, although considerably shorter than the former Ord. 9, r. 8, which it replaces, has not changed the existing rules: *Addis Ltd.* v. *Berkeley Supplies Ltd.* [1964] 1 W.L.R. 943. The Scottish Rules of Court allow postal citation of a company in England or Northern Ireland providing there is also edictal citation and without prejudice to pleas as to the jurisdiction of the Court of Session (Rules of Court 1965 Nos. 74–75A).

[26] *Littauer Glove Corpn.* v. *F. W. Millington (1920) Ltd.* (1928) 44 T.L.R. 746.

[27] Under R.S.C., Ord. 65, r. 4. See *Sloman* v. *Govt. of New Zealand* (1875) 1 C.P.D. 563; *Hillyard* v. *Smyth* (1888) 36 W.R. 7; *O'Connor* v. *The Star Newspaper Co.* (1908) 30 L.R.Ir. 1.

ment is sent by post, section 7 of the Interpretation Act 1978 applies, which provides:

"Where an Act authorises or requires any document to be served by post (whether the expression 'serve,' or the expression 'give' or 'send,' or any other expression is used) then, unless the contrary intention appears, the service shall be deemed to be effected by properly addressing, prepaying, and posting a letter containing the document, and unless the contrary is proved to have been effected at the time at which the letter would be delivered in the ordinary course of post."

Where the company has changed its registered address without notifying the Registrar (as required by the 1976 Act, s. 23) and a writ is served at the old address, a judgment in default will not be set aside as of right although the company has no knowledge of the proceedings but it may be set aside on an affidavit of merits (and payment of the costs).[28]

These considerations apply with particular force after January 1, 1973, when on principle the situation of the registered office is regarded as changed only when the official notification becomes effective, except if any of the conditions qualifying the effect of official notification are present (European Communities Act 1972, s. 9 (4), see paragraph 17–04, *post*).

8–14 Bearing in mind that the European Communities Act 1972, s. 9, does not apply to oversea or other foreign companies,[29] foreign companies can be served with process of the English courts in three sets of circumstances:

(a) *The company may have registered as an oversea company*.[30] In that case the company has to register the names and addresses of one or more persons resident in Great Britain and authorised to accept service on behalf of the company (s. 407 (1) (*c*)). Service on that person or those persons is sufficient (s. 412), but service can likewise be effected at the office—not a former, and at the date of the service vacated, office[31]—or upon any of the officers of the company if they are in the jurisdiction. Registration under Part X is regarded as voluntary submission, on the part of the company, to the jurisdiction of the English courts.[32]

An injunction may be issued by an English court against an oversea company which has registered the name of a person authorised to accept service on its behalf.[33]

---

[28] *A/S Catherineholm* v. *Norequipment Trading Ltd.* [1972] 2 Q.B. 314. (C.A.), following *Saga of Bond Street Ltd.* v. *Avalon Promotions Ltd.* [1972] 2 Q.B. 325 and disapproving *Thomas Bishop Ltd.* v. *Helmville Ltd.* [1972] 1 Q.B. 464. It has been held in Scotland that a person taking proceedings against a company is entitled to proceed on the basis of the registered office as disclosed by the official file: *Ross* v. *Invergordon Distillers Ltd.* 1961 S.L.T. 358.

[29] See para. 2–14, *ante*.

[30] Part X, s. 406; see para. 88–03, *post*.

[31] *Deverall* v. *Grant Advertising Inc.* [1955] Ch. 111; see para. 88–04, *post*.

[32] *Employers' Liability Assurance Corp.* v. *Sedgwick, Collins & Co.* [1927] A.C. 95, 115; *The Madrid* [1937] P. 40, 45.

[33] *Acrow (Automation Ltd.* v. *Rex Chainbelt Inc.* [1971] 1 W.L.R. 1676; see para. 88–04, *post*.

(b) *The company has not registered as an oversea company but carries on business within the jurisdiction*. In this case it may be possible to serve proceedings under R.S.C. 1965, Ord. 65, r. 3, if the company is here by its chairman, president, secretary, "similar officer," or other person who carries on business for the company in this country.[34]

R.S.C. 1965, Ord. 65, r. 3 replaced the former R.S.C. 1883, Ord. 9, r. 8, which admitted service on a company that was here by, *inter alia*, a "head officer." Not every agent who on behalf of the company transacted business within the jurisdiction was regarded as a "head officer."[35] If the authority of the agent was limited to transmitting orders to his principal and to waiting for his decision, the agent did not qualify in that respect and no service was possible.[36] It is thought that a similar interpretation applies to the term "similar officer" in R.S.C. 1965, Ord. 65, r. 3.

Here, as in the case under (a) above, it is insufficient to serve proceedings by leaving the documents at a former, and at the date of the service vacated, office of the company.[37]

(c) *The company is not within the jurisdiction and has not submitted to the jurisdiction of the English courts*. Here the question is whether the facts of the case can be brought under one of the cases under R.S.C., Ord. 11,[38] which is likewise applicable to companies[39]; if these conditions are satisfied, the court may grant leave to serve process out of the jurisdiction.

A company whose registered office is in Scotland or which has a place of business in Scotland may be cited at that address. An oversea company with an address registered in Scotland under section 407 of the 1948 Act may be cited there. If the company cannot be cited in Scotland but is nevertheless subject to the jurisdiction of the Scottish courts, edictal citation is required.

8–15 ATTRIBUTION OF ENEMY CHARACTER.[40] The question whether a company is an enemy arises either under statute or at common law.

(a) The Trading with the Enemy Act 1939 provides in section 2 (1) that,

---

[34] See Buckley L.J. in *Okura & Co. Ltd.* v. *Forsbacka Jernverks Aktiebolag* [1914] 1 K.B. 715, 718.

[35] See on this question Schmitthoff, *op. cit.*, pp. 386 *et seq*. and the cases quoted there.

[36] *Dunlop Pneumatic Tyre Co.* v. *A/G für Motor und Motorfahrzeugbau* [1902] 1 K.B. 342, 347; *Re Tovarishestvo Manufactur Liudvig-Rabenek* [1944] Ch. 404; *Okura & Co. Ltd.* v. *Forsbacka Jernverks Aktiebolag* [1914] 1 K.B. 715.

[37] *Deverall* v. *Grant Advertising Inc.* [1955] Ch. 111.

[38] See Schmitthoff, *op. cit.*, pp. 430 *et seq.*

[39] "Ordinarily resident" in the meaning of Ord. 11, r. 1 (*c*), refers to the place where the chief office or registered office of the company is situate (*Jones* v. *Scottish Accident Insurance Co.* (1866) 17 Q.B.D. 421, 422; *Watkins* v. *Scottish, etc., Co.* (1889) 23 Q.B.D. 285).

[40] The remarks in this section, derived from English law, are thought to be equally applicable in Scotland.

subject to the provisions of that section, the expression "enemy" for the purposes of this Act means—

". . . . . . .

(c) any body of persons (whether corporate or unincorporate) carrying on business in any place, if and so long as the body is controlled by a person who, under this section, is an enemy,
(d) any body of persons constituted or incorporated in, or under the laws of, a State at war with His Majesty, and
(e) as respects any business carried on in enemy territory, any individual or body of persons (whether corporate or unincorporate) carrying on that business;

but does not include any individual by reason only that he is an enemy subject."

It follows from these provisions that a company is an enemy under the Act if it is enemy-controlled (whether a British or foreign company); if it is incorporated in the enemy state; or if it carries on business in enemy territory.

(b) At common law a person is an alien enemy if he resides voluntarily in enemy territory.[41] In the case of companies, the courts have adopted the test of control as analogous to voluntary residence among the Queen's enemies. Lord Parker said in *Daimler Co. Ltd.* v. *Continental Tyre and Rubber Ltd.*[42]: "I think that the analogy is to be found in control, an idea which, if not familiar in law,[43] is of capital importance and is very well understood in commerce and finance." English common law has thus adopted as the test of alien enemy corporations a rule similar to the *siège social* rule prevailing in most continental countries, and the United States of America have adopted a similar test.[44]

Consequently, a company registered in England may be an "alien enemy" if its agents or the persons in *de facto* control of its affairs, whether authorised or not, are alien enemies, and in determining whether alien enemies have such control, the number of alien enemy shareholders is material.[45] But a company registered in England and carrying on business in an enemy country is not necessarily an enemy alien. In *Re Hilckes, ex p. Muhesa Rubber Plantations,*[46] the directors and the majority of the shareholders were English, and the only evidence of enemy character was

---

[41] Schmitthoff, *op. cit.,* pp. 445 *et seq*. The following paragraphs apply equally to a Scottish company.
[42] [1916] 2 A.C. 307, 339; *Kuenigl* v. *Donnersmarck* [1955] 1 Q.B. 515.
[43] These words were spoken in 1916. The law is now familiar with the concept of control as a legal criterion; see s. 154 of the Act of 1948 (the test of control as the test of holding companies was first adopted by s. 127 of the Act of 1929).
[44] Schmitthoff, *op. cit.*, p. 389.
[45] *Daimler Co.* v. *Continental Tyre, etc., Co.* [1916] 2 A.C. 307; as to the sixth proposition of Lord Parker in this case (at p. 346), see *Re Hilckes, ex p. Muhesa Rubber Plantations* [1917] 1 K.B. 48.
[46] [1917] 1 K.B. 48.

that the company owned a rubber estate in enemy territory on which it kept a manager when war broke out. It was held that merely doing business in an enemy country through an agent did not constitute the company an "alien enemy."

It should be noted that the definition of an enemy under the Trading with the Enemy Act 1939 is wider than that at common law.

8–16 A company incorporated under the laws of England and registered in England does not cease by English law to be an English company subject to English law by reason of the fact that it is under enemy control and, consequently, has assumed enemy character.[47] Such a company remains subject to all its obligations under the Companies Acts as an English company,[48] and is further subject to all the prohibitions imposed by the Trading with the Enemy Act 1939.[49] Thus in *Kuenigl* v. *Donnersmarck*[47] an English company had become an enemy in the Second World War; its directors who resided in enemy territory purported to conclude there a contract with another enemy. McNair J. held that the authority of the directors and other agents in enemy territory was automatically terminated on the outbreak of war and that, consequently, the contract could not be taken to be the contract of the company.

Situs of shares

8–17 Since it is at the registered office that registered shares in a company can effectively be dealt with,[50] and that "for the contributory's title to his shares, his status as a shareholder, and the enforcement of his rights, recourse must be had to the statutory register, which remains localised at the registered office, and to the court with which alone . . . abides the power to rectify the register,"[51] it is there that such shares are situate, in the eyes of the English courts.[52] Thus in *Baelz* v. *Public Trustee*[53] shares were held by a German domiciled in Germany, in a company registered in England, the directors of which were domiciled in Holland, where, moreover, all administrative work was carried out and where all meetings, whether of the directors or members, were required by the articles to be held, and the company being resident for tax purposes in Holland; but the shares were held to be situate within His Majesty's dominions.[54] If the register of members is kept at a place other than the registered office of the company (1948 Act, s. 110 (2), proviso), the *situs* of the registered shares

---

[47] *Kuenigl* v. *Donnersmarck* [1955] 1 Q.B. 515.
[48] *Ibid.* at p. 535.
[49] *Ibid.* at p. 539.
[50] *Brassard* v. *Smith* [1925] A.C. 371, 376.
[51] *Per* Eve J. in *Baelz* v. *Public Trustee* [1926] Ch. 863, 869.
[52] Scots law is in agreement with the principles of English law here described.
[53] [1926] Ch. 863.
[54] Following *Att.-Gen.* v. *Higgins* (1857) 2 H. & N. 339 and *Brassard* v. *Smith* [1925] A.C. 371.

would appear to be the place at which the register is kept in accordance with the law.

The *situs* of bearer shares is the place at which those shares are held because they are negotiable instruments which are transferred by delivery.

Documents to be kept at the registered office

8–18 The following documents have to be kept at the registered office of the company unless stated otherwise:

(1) The register of members (1948 Act, s. 110 (2)).

[Upon certain conditions this register may be kept elsewhere but not outside the part of the United Kingdom in which the company is registered: s. 110 (2), proviso.]

(2) The register of debenture holders (if the company keeps such a register) (1948 Act, s. 86 (1) and (2)).

[Upon certain conditions this register may be kept elsewhere but not outside the part of the United Kingdom in which the company is registered: s. 86 (1) and (2).]

(3) The register of directors and secretaries (1948 Act, s. 200 (1) as amended by the 1981 Act, s. 95). It is now required to register directorships held during the preceding five years.

(4) The register of directors' interests in shares or debentures (1967 Act, s. 29).[55]

[This register may be kept at the registered office or at any other place where the register of members is kept: 1967 Act, s. 29 (7).]

(5) The register of interests in shares required to be kept by public companies (1981 Act, s. 73).[56]

[This register must be kept at the same place as the register of directors' interests: (1981 Act, s. 73 (8) (*a*)).

(6) The register of charges (1948 Act, s. 104 (1) or s. 106 I).

[Copies of the instruments creating charges have likewise to be kept there: s. 103 or s. 106 H.]

(7) The books containing the minutes of general meetings (s. 146).

(8) Accounting records (1976 Act, s. 12).

[These books may alternatively be kept at such other place as the directors think fit.]

(9) Copies of directors' contracts of service, or written memoranda thereof setting out the terms (1967 Act, s. 26).

[These documents must be kept at an "appropriate place," *viz.* either the registered office, or any other place where the register of members is kept, or the company's principal

---

[55] This register replaces the former register of directors' shareholdings which was required to be kept under s. 195 of the 1948 Act: see para. 66–11, *post*.

[56] See para. 51–01, *post*.

place of business, but not outside the part of the United Kingdom in which the company is registered: 1967 Act, s. 26 (2).]

(10) A recognised bank shall make available at its registered office the register containing certain transactions relating to its directors and other relevant persons 15 days before the date of the annual general meeting (1980 Act, s. 57 (1)).

(11) Further, in the case of companies which are limited insurance companies or deposit, provident or benefit societies, financial statements in the form of Schedule XIII (1948 Act, s. 433).[57]

[These statements have likewise to be exhibited at every branch office or other place of business; they have to be exhibited before the company commences business and on every first Monday in February and first Tuesday in August in every year: s. 433 (1) and (2).]

[57] See para. 89–37 *et seq., post.*

CHAPTER 9

THE OBJECTS CLAUSE

Function of the objects clause

9–01 Every memorandum of association must state the objects of the proposed company (1948 Act, s. 2 (1) (*c*)). This statement has a twofold function:

(1) It affirmatively determines the purposes for which the company is created; for the stated objects confer on the company the capacity reasonably requisite to the attainment of those purposes.

(2) It limits and restricts the capacity of the company to act, save so far as its capacity is extended by statute.

Hence, as it rests with the subscribers to declare the objects, it follows that the subscribers are by the Acts furnished with the means, not merely to initiate the creation of a corporation authorised by statute—it comes into existence when the Registrar issues the certificate of incorporation (s. 13 (1))—but to form that body for such purposes as they think fit, provided that those purposes are not illegal.

Accordingly the following rules are applicable:

(a) The objects must not include anything in contravention of the Acts themselves. For example, it is not a lawful object to exclude the provisions of the 1980 Act on insider dealing.[1]

(b) The objects stated must not include anything in contravention of the general law. For example, it would not be legal to include in the objects a clause requiring the company to practise racial discrimination, contrary to the Race Relations Act 1976. Further, objects in unreasonable restraint of trade are illegal[2]; so also are blasphemous objects, but objects involving a denial of Christianity are not necessarily blasphemous.[3]

(c) The objects must not include any which would render the company a trade union.[4] The registration of a trade union as a company is void by virtue of the Trade Union and Labour Relations Acts 1974 and 1976 (1974 Act, s. 2 (2).[5]

The objects must be stated with particularity

9–02 The law does not admit a general statement of the object, such as that the company may transact any lawful business. The objects must be de-

---

[1] 1980 Act, ss 68–73.
[2] *Joseph Evans & Co.* v. *Heathcote* [1918] 1 K.B. 418; *McEllistrim* v. *Ballymacelligott, etc., Society* [1919] A.C. 548.
[3] *Bowman* v. *Secular Society* [1917] A.C. 406; see para. 16–07, *post*.
[4] See also s. 459 (9) (*b*) of the Companies Act 1948.
[5] A trade union is defined in the Trade Unions and Labour Relations Act 1974, s. 28 (1).

fined with some degree of particularity. An illustration is provided in the Companies Acts[6]: "The conveyance of passengers and goods in ships or boats between such places as the company may from time to time determine, and the doing of all such things as are incidental or conducive to the attainment of the above object." But it is sufficient to particularise the object in more general terms, such as "to carry on business as financiers, capitalists, concessionaires, bankers, commercial agents, mortgage brokers, financial agents and advisers, exporters and importers of goods and merchandise of all kinds and merchants generally."[7] The incorporation by reference to the terms of another document stating the objects is not admissible.[8]

The reason for the requirement of particularity, even if defined in fairly wide terms, is the application of the *ultra vires* doctrine, one of the tenets of the common law, which would become unworkable if a general objects clause were admitted.[9]

The insistence on particularity in the objects clause is regarded, in practice, as an inconvenient limitation on the expansion of an enterprise. This has given rise to the use of the inflated objects clause and the independent objects clause which will be considered later on.[10]

Legality of objects

9–03 The purposes stated in the objects clause must be lawful (s. 1 (1)).

An employers' association may be formed as a body corporate, such as a company, or as an unincorporated association.[11] An association to protect copyright is not a trade union.[12]

Objects clause and ultra vires doctrine

9–04 The function of the objects clause in defining the capacity of the company is of great importance because a company incorporated by registration under one of the Companies Acts, like any other corporation created by Act of Parliament, has no existence, and cannot act as a legal person, outside the purposes (*ultra vires*) defined in the objects clause of the memorandum (or given to it by statute[13]). A company incorporated under the Companies Acts does not enjoy full legal personality, as, *e.g.* a chartered company does,[14] but its legal personality exists only for the particular purposes of its incorporation as defined in the objects clause.[15] An act

[6] Private companies: 1948 Act, Sched. 1, Table B; public companies: 1980 Act, Sched. 1, Pt. 1.
[7] *Re New Finance and Mortgage Co. Ltd. (in liquidation)* [1975] Ch. 420.
[8] *Proprietors of Royal Exchange Buildings, Glasgow* 1911 S.C. 1337; 1911 2 S.L.T. 197.
[9] See para. 9–07.
[10] See para. 9–11.
[11] s. 3 of the Trade Union and Labour Relations Act 1974.
[12] *Performing Right Society* v. *London Theatre of Varieties* [1922] 2 K.B. 433.
[13] See para. 9–50, *post*.
[14] Sutton's Hospital Case (1613) 10 Co.Rep. 1a, 23a. See para. 89–20, *post*.
[15] Lord Cranworth L.C. in *Eastern Counties Ry.* v. *Hawkes* (1855) 5 H.L.C. 331, 346; Lord Selborne in *Ashbury Ry. Carriage Co.* v. *Riche* (1875) L.R. 7 H.L. 653, 694.

which is *ultra vires* the company is null and void in the same manner as an act done by a local authority outside its statutory authority.[16] Such an act cannot be ratified by the general meeting but the general meeting may alter the objects in the prescribed manner (paras. 9–38 *et seq.*) and thus extend the objects of the company. Such alteration of the objects has no retrospective effect. In common law, if the company concludes a contract which is *ultra vires*, neither the company nor the other contracting party can sue on it.[17] Where a company has gone into liquidation, the court has no power under section 307 of the 1948 Act to authorise the liquidator to carry out *ultra vires* transactions.[18]

There are two reasons why the *ultra vires* doctrine has been developed by the courts[19]: first, as a matter of constitutional law, Parliament, as the sovereign power in the country, does not grant more power to delegated bodies than it has authorised, and, secondly, as a practical consideration, it was thought that the rule would protect investors in the company and creditors of it against the unauthorised use of the company's funds.

Although, when the registered company was a comparatively new institution, the *ultra vires* doctrine was useful for checking those abuses, in modern law its disadvantages clearly outweighed its benefits and, as will be seen later,[20] it sometimes caused hardship to third parties who transacted business with the company in good faith. It was, therefore, welcome that the European Communities Act 1972, s. 9 (1), restricted the ambit of that doctrine; these restrictions and the present ambit of the doctrine will have to be explained later on.[21]

9–05 Acts which are *ultra vires* the company have to be distinguished from acts *intra vires* the company but *outside the authority* if its directors. The former the company is incapable of doing, the latter it is capable of transacting, but in this type of case the directors have no authority to act on behalf of the company, often because, according to the articles, they require the consent of the general meeting, or the board of directors has not delegated power to the directors purporting to act for the company. It is evident that different considerations apply to these two types of situation: a person contracting with a company has notice, actual or constructive, of its capacity, since the memorandum which sets out the objects is registered and can be inspected by the public; but a member of the public cannot normally ascertain from the public documents whether the directors have the consent or authority or the delegated powers, which, according to the articles, they require in order to act on behalf of the company, since

[16] *Prescott* v. *Birmingham Corporation* [1955] Ch. 210; also *Thompson* v. *J. Barke & Co. (Caterers) Ltd.* 1975 S.L.T. 67.

[17] But see *Bell Houses Ltd.* v. *City Wall Properties Ltd.* [1966] 2 Q.B. 656, 694, where Salmon L.J., *obiter*, queried whether in an executed contract the company was barred by the *ultra vires* doctrine from suing the other contracting party.

[18] *Re Salisbury Railway and Market House Co. Ltd.* [1969] 1 Ch. 349.

[19] See the analysis of the history of the *ultra vires* doctrine in L. C. B. Gower, *Modern Company Law*, (4th ed., 1979), pp. 162 *et seq.*

[20] See para. 9–23, *post*.

[21] See para. 9–25, *post*.

these authorities, consents or delegations are normally matters of the "indoor management" of the company's affairs. Consequently, where acts which are *intra vires* the company but *outside the authority* of the directors are in question, different considerations apply and the party contracting with the company might be protected by the provisions of the European Communities Act 1972, s. 9 (1) and under the rule in *Royal British Bank* v. *Turquand,*[22] which both will be considered later.[23]

Objects and powers of the company

Objects and powers distinguished

9–06 In logic, the objects (or purposes) for which a company is created should be distinguished from the powers which it can exercise. Strictly speaking, the objects clause should only set out the former but should not contain the latter. The former, the real objects of the company, are sometimes referred to as "substantive objects."[24] The substantive objects of a company may be the carriage of passengers and goods by air, sea and land, but its powers may include the power to hold land, to acquire shares in other companies, to borrow money, and so forth.

In practice, it is customary in the United Kingdom[25] to provide in the objects clause also a catalogue of powers which the company may exercise. Lord Wrenbury in *Cotman* v. *Brougham*[24] deprecated this practice but grudgingly conceded that it was too late to alter it.

The reason for this practice is that companies find that limiting the clause strictly to the objects raised, on occasion, the difficulty of defining whether a proposed transaction is within or outside the objects of the company.

Even if the powers of the company are not expressed in the objects clause, the company has such implied powers as are reasonably incidental to the attainment or pursuit of its substantive objects. Buckley L.J. said in *In re Horsley & Weight Ltd.*[26]:

> "A company has no capacity to pursue objects outside those stated. It does not follow, however, that any act which is not expressly authorised by the memorandum is ultra vires the company. Anything reasonably incidental to the attainment or pursuit of any of the express objects of the company will, unless expressly prohibited, be within the implied powers of the company."

---

[22] (1856) 6 El. & Bl. 327.
[23] See paras. 28–07 and 28–10, *post.*
[24] Buckley L. J. in *In re Horsley* v. *Weight Ltd.* [1982] 3 W.L.R. 431, 437.
[25] *Ibid.* p. 523. In some Commonwealth countries a separation of the objects from the incidental and ancillary powers of the company is carried out in recent companies statutes. These powers are contained in the statute itself or a schedule thereto, and thus need not be set out explicitly in the objects clause. This arrangement is adopted, *e.g.* by the Canada Corporations Act 1970, s. 16, and by Australian and New Zealand statutes. Whilst it would be desirable if a future companies statute in the United Kingdom adopted a similar arrangement, it is necessary here to deal with the existing practice.
[26] [1982] 3 W.L.R. 431, 436–437.

The learned judge stated, with the concurrence of Cumming-Bruce L.J., that the difference between the pursuit of a substantive object and the exercise of a power (whether expressed in the memorandum or implied) was that a power can only be exercised for the benefit of the company or the promotion of its prosperity but that no such limitation exists with respect to an act done within the terms of an express substantive object, unless such limitation is expressly or impliedly contained in the memorandum. However, this rule has to be applied with caution. It is submitted that even the pursuit of a substantive object is *ultra vires* the company if it cannot be justified by any stretch of imagination as being in the interest of the company.

The ultra vires doctrine

History

9–07 That the powers of a registered company were dependent on and governed by the objects as defined in the objects clause was recognised in an early case decided on the Joint Stock Companies Act 1856, the immediate forerunner of the Companies Act 1862, and which contained provisions as to formation almost identical with those subsequently adopted in the Act of 1862. In particular, the Act required that the memorandum should state the objects of the proposed company, and it prohibited any alteration of the conditions contained in the memorandum of association. It was in relation to a company formed under this Act that *Simpson* v. *Westminster Palace Hotel*[27] was decided in 1860. In that case the memorandum stated that "the objects for which the company is established are the purchase of leasehold lands in the City of Westminster, the erection, furnishing and maintenance of an hotel thereon, and the carrying on the usual business of an hotel and tavern therein, and the doing all such things as are incidental or otherwise conducive to the attainment of these objects." The directors, whilst the hotel was in course of being built, agreed to let off for a stipulated period—a few years—a large portion of the building to the head of a government department for the business of his office, and evidence was given that such a letting was calculated to be productive of advantage to the company in its intended business. The case went to the House of Lords, and it was decided that the letting was not *ultra vires*, on the ground that it was temporary and preliminary, and conducive to the ultimate object of the whole being devoted to the proper purpose of the hotel.

Ashbury Railway Carriage Co. v. *Riche*

9–08 After the Act of 1862 came in operation, this decision was treated as applicable to companies registered under that Act. The true position with

[27] (1860) 8 H.L.C. 721.

respect to the *ultra vires* doctrine was finally settled by the House of Lords in the celebrated case of *Ashbury Railway Carriage and Iron Co.* v. *Riche*,[28] decided in 1875. In that case the objects of the company were "to make, and sell, or lend on hire, railway carriages and waggons, and all kinds of railway plant, fittings, machinery, and rolling stock; and to carry on the business of mechanical engineers and general contractors; to purchase, lease, work, and sell mines, minerals, land, and buildings; to purchase and sell, as merchants, timber, coal, metals, or other materials, and to buy and sell any such materials on commission or as agents; to acquire; purchase, hire, construct or erect works or buildings for the purposes of the company; and to do all such other things as are necessary, contingent, incidental or conducive to all or any of such objects."

The company, with this memorandum defining its objects, had entered into a contract with the plaintiff for the financing of the construction of a railway line in Belgium, and the question raised in the action was whether that contract was valid.

The House of Lords held that the contract was *ultra vires* the company and therefore altogether void. Lord Cairns L.C., after stating[29] that the subscribers "are to state the objects for which the proposed company is to be established, and the existence, the coming into existence, of the company is to be an existence and to be a coming into existence for those objects and for those objects alone," and after referring to the words at the end of section 12 (re-enacted in an amended form in section 4 of the Act of 1948) to the effect that "no alteration shall be made by any company in the conditions contained in its memorandum of association," proceeded as follows:

> " . . . if that is the purpose for which the corporation is established—it is a mode of incorporation which contains in it both that which is affirmative and that which is negative. It states affirmatively the ambit and extent of vitality and power which by law are given to the corporation, and it states, if it is necessary so to state, negatively, that nothing shall be done beyond that ambit, and that no attempt shall be made to use the corporate life for any other purpose than that which is so specified."[30]

The House of Lords further held, as a corollary from the above, that the contract, being *ultra vires*, and therefore void in its inception, was incapable of ratification even by the unanimous consent of all the shareholders.

9–09 Subsequently in *Att.-Gen.* v. *Great Eastern Ry.*[31] the principle laid down in *Ashbury Railway Carriage Co.* v. *Riche*[32] was again affirmed by the House of Lords, but it was in some degree qualified by the rule there laid

---

28 (1875) L.R. 7 H.L. 653.
29 At p. 669.
30 At p. 670. See also *Dalling* v. *Browning* (1944) 60 *Sheriff Court Reports* 143.
31 (1880) 5 App.Cas. 473. See also *Life Association of Scotland* v. *Caledonian Heritable Security Co.* 1886 13 R. 750.
32 (1875) L.R. 7 H.L. 653.

down that the principle was one to be reasonably, and not unreasonably, understood and applied, and that whatever may fairly be regarded as incidental or consequential upon those things which the legislature had authorised (that is, those things specified in the memorandum as objects) ought not, unless expressly prohibited, to be held by judicial construction to be *ultra vires*.

In *London County Council* v. *Att.-Gen.*,[33] Lord Halsbury L.C., referring to *Ashbury Railway Carriage Co.* v. *Riche*[34] and *Att.-Gen.* v. *Great Eastern Ry.*,[35] said: "I think now it cannot be doubted that those two cases do constitute the law upon the subject."

It is thought that today *Ashbury Railway Carriage Co.* v. *Riche* would be decided differently. In any event, the doctrine enunciated in this case is today greatly reduced by the European Communities Act 1972, s. 9 (1). The effect of this Act will be considered later.[36]

The implied powers

9–10 The ambit of the implied powers of the company has already been discussed.[36a]

Thus, a company formed "to buy, sell and deal in coal," may, *for the purpose of carrying out these objects,* do the following things which can be said to be fairly incidental to and consequential on its substantive objects.

(1) purchase or take on lease stores;
(2) open shops and agencies;
(3) buy and hire lorries, trucks, carts and horses;
(4) enter into service agreements with employees[36b];
(5) draw and accept bills of exchange;
(6) borrow and give security[37];
(7) incur debts;
(8) make contracts for purchase supply;
(9) have a banking account;
(10) bring actions and take proceedings;
(11) compromise actions and disputes[38];
(12) employ agents;
(13) pay bonuses and, subject to certain conditions, pensions[39] to employees.

Such a company may also pay all the expenses incurred in setting up and registering as a company, and it may pay dividends out of profits, and may provide for payment, even out of capital, of interest on capital paid up in

---

33 [1902] A.C. 165.
34 (1875) L.R. 7 H.L. 653.
35 (1880) 5 App.Cas, 473.
36 See para. 9–25.
36a See para. 9–06, *ante*.
36b *Taupa Totara Timber Co. Ltd.* v. *Darcy Kevin Rowe* [1978] A.C. 537 (P.C.).
37 See para. 42–01, *post*.
38 *Bath's Case* (1878) 8 Ch.D. 334.
39 See 1980 Act, s. 74.

advance of calls, for article 21 treats such outgoings and expenses as properly dealt with by the articles, and what Table A authorises is not to be treated as *ultra vires*.[40]

These ancillary powers are not to be treated as separate objects, complete in themselves, but only as incidental to the company's specified objects and able to be used only for the purpose of carrying out those objects.

The inflated objects clause and the "independent objects" clause

9–11 The result of these cases, and in particular of *Ashbury Railway Carriage Co.* v. *Riche*,[41] was that the only method by which a company could extend its objects was by altering them in accordance with the Act, a measure which before the 1947–48 legislation invariable required confirmation by the court.[42] In order to avoid this cumbersome procedure, it has become the practice, as already observed,[43] for companies to inflate the objects clause by adding to its principal objects a large number of objects and powers (many of the latter would in any case be implied), many of which are in fact never needed by the company.

Added to this catalogue of possible or conceivable objects and powers is normally a clause which provides that each of the objects specified in the clause shall be regarded as independent objects, and shall not be limited or restricted (except where otherwise expressed) by reference to any other paragraph of the objects clause. The House of Lords in *Cotman* v. *Brougham*,[44] though severely criticising this practice, held that it was to be effective and that it excluded the "main objects" rule of construction.[45]

This development was carried further by *Bell Houses Ltd.* v. *City Wall Properties Ltd.*,[46] In that case the Court of Appeal did not raise an objection to a clause which provided that the company may "carry on any other trade or business whatsoever which can, in the opinion of the board of directors, be advantageously carried on by the company in connection with or ancillary to any of the above businesses or the present business of the company." This is a subjective test. The discretion of the board of directors, or of the director to whom authority to act on behalf of the board is given, must be exercised honestly.

It should, however, be noted that clauses empowering a company to carry out administrative acts, such as borrowing money, granting security, drawing cheques, etc., must be read as if qualified by the words "for the

---

40 *Lock* v. *Queensland, etc., Mortgage Co.* [1896] A.C. 461.
41 (1875) L.R. 7 H.L. 653.
42 s. 5 (2) of the Act of 1929.
43 See para. 9–02, *ante*.
44 [1918] A.C. 514. See also Vaisey J. in *Re E. K. Cole Ltd.* [1945] 1 All E.R. 521n. and Buckley J. in *Re Introductions Ltd.* [1968] 2 All E.R. 1221; affd. *sub. nom. Introductions Ltd.* v. *National Provincial Bank Ltd.* [1970] Ch. 199 (C.D.). In Scotland also the court has been critical of such a provision, see *North of Scotland, etc., Steam Navigation Co.* 1920 S.C. 633; 1920 2 S.L.T. 176.
45 See para. 9–30, *post*.
46 [1966] 2 Q.B. 656.

purposes of the company." Where a company is carrying on a single business which is not authorised by its memorandum any such administrative act is necessarily *ultra vires*. In other circumstances it is the nature of the transaction and not its means of execution which determines its validity. A cheque drawn for a purpose which is *ultra vires* is itself invalid notwithstanding a general power to draw bills of exchange.[47]

In the result, in modern practice the objects clause has become a much more lengthy document than the comparatively simple clause set out in Table B of the 1948 Act and Schedule 1 to the 1980 Act and this practice is not likely to cease until the legislature completely abolishes the *ultra vires* doctrine for dealings of the company with third parties.[48]

Specimen clauses

9–12 The following are paragraphs commonly found in objects clauses; many of them are inserted because of old decisions and although it is doubtful whether the courts would today exclude such implications, the only safe course is to provide the specific object since the results of *ultra vires* transactions are so sweeping.

1. A clause authorising the company to carry on the particular business which it is proposed to carry on, and also to carry on various other businesses which it may probably or possibly be desirable to carry on.
2. A clause empowering the company to acquire any other business similar to its own.[49]
3. A clause empowering the company to enter into any agreement for sharing profits, joint ventures or other arrangements of a like nature with other persons or companies carrying on any similar business.[50]
4. A clause empowering the company to take shares in other companies having similar objects, etc. Such a power is commonly wanted, and not easily implied,[51] but may be implied, *e.g.* from a clause allowing amalgamation.[52]
5. A clause empowering the company to promote other companies for any purpose calculated to benefit the company.[53]
6. A power generally to acquire property and rights which the company may think necessary or convenient for the purpose of its business. In dealing with outsiders, it is found useful to have an express power like this, and so preclude any question of capacity.
7. A power to lend money and guarantee the performance of contracts by customers and others.
8. A power to borrow or raise money by the issue of debentures, debenture stock, or otherwise.[54]

---

[47] *Thompson* v. *J. Barke & Co. (Caterers) Ltd.* 1975 S.L.T. 67.
[48] See para. 9–28, *post*.
[49] *Ernest* v. *Nicholls* (1857) 6 H.L.C. 401.
[50] *Re European Society Arbitration Acts, ex p. British Nation, etc., Association* (1878) 8 Ch.D. 679, 704.
[51] *Re Barned's Banking Co.* (1867) L.R. 3 Ch. 105; *Re Lands Allotment Co.* [1894] 1 Ch. 616, 630.
[52] *Re William Thomas & Co.* [1915] 1 Ch. 325.
[53] See *Joint Stock Discount Co.* v. *Brown* (1869) L.R. 8 Eq. 381.
[54] See para. 42–01, *post*.

9. A power to draw, make, accept, indorse, discount and issue promissory notes, bills of exchange, debentures and other negotiable or transferable instruments.

This is very desirable; for, although a trading company has implied power to make and accept promissory notes and bills of exchange for the purpose of its business,[55] the fact that various kinds of companies have been held not to possess any such implied power clouds the implication with a most inconvenient uncertainty.

9–13 10. A power to sell and dispose of the undertaking of the company for shares, debentures or securities of any other company having objects altogether, or in part, similar to those of this company.[56]

In the absence of an express power like this, a company cannot sell or dispose of its whole business.[57] According, however, to *Bisgood* v. *Henderson's Transvaal Estates*,[58] if winding up and distribution among the shareholders of the proceeds of sale is in contemplation, a company cannot, under a power in its memorandum, sell its undertaking for shares or debentures and, as an essential part of the agreement for sale, provide for the distribution of the shares in a particular manner.[59]

11. A power to apply for an Act of Parliament for any purpose which may seem expedient.

Without such an express power a company cannot apply its funds in promoting a Bill to effect any modification in its constitution or for any other purpose.[60]

12. A power to sell, improve, manage, develop, exchange, lease, mortgage, dispose of, turn to account, or otherwise deal with, all or any part of the property and rights of the company.[61]

13. A power to carry on any other trade or business whatsoever which can, in the opinion of the board of directors, be advantageously carried on by the company in connection with or ancillary to any of the businesses specified in the objects clause or the general business of the company.[62]

14. A declaration that the objects specified in the sub-clauses of the clause shall be regarded as independent objects, and shall be construed independently of the other sub-clauses of it and that none of the objects mentioned in any sub-clause shall be deemed to be merely subsidiary to the objects in any other sub-clause (except where otherwise expressed in such sub-clause).

This is an illustration of the "independent objects" clause discussed earlier.[63]

---

[55] *Re Peruvian Rys.* (1867) L.R. 2 Ch. 617, 623.

[56] *Cotton* v. *Imperial, etc., Corporation* [1892] 3 Ch. 454; *Grant* v. *United Kingdom Switchback Rys.* (1888) 40 Ch.D. 135 (a sale of the undertaking or any part was one of the objects); *New Zealand, etc., Co.* v. *Peacock* [1894] 1 Q.B. 622 (a sale under the power in the memorandum valid); *Foster* v. *Borax Co.* [1901] 1 Ch. 326; *Re Vivian & Co.* [1900] 2 Ch. 654.

[57] *Simpson* v. *Westminster Palace Hotel Co.* (1860) 8 H.L.C. 712.

[58] [1908] 1 Ch. 743.

[59] See para. 80–14, *post*.

[60] *Munt* v. *Shrewsbury, etc., Ry.* (1850) 13 Beav. 1; *Simpson* v. *Denison* (1852) 10 Hare 51; *Vance* v. *East Lancashire Ry.* (1856) 3 K. & J. 50; see also *Re Salisbury Railway and Market House Co. Ltd.* [1967] 3 W.L.R. 651.

[61] See *Re Patent File Co.* (1870) L.R. 6 Ch. 83; *Bell Houses Ltd.* v. *City Wall Properties Ltd.* [1966] 2 Q.B. 656.

[62] *Bell Houses Ltd.* v. *City Wall Properties Ltd.* [1966] 2 Q.B. 656.

[63] See para. 9–11, *ante; Re Kingsbury Collieries and Moore's Contract* [1907] 2 Ch. 259.

Intra vires and ultra vires transactions

9–14 It is a corollary from the rule in *Ashbury Railway Carriage Co.* v. *Riche*[64] that a company's objects circumscribe its powers—that the funds of a company under the Act can only be applied in carrying out its authorised objects. Lord Herschell said in *Trevor* v. *Whitworth*[65]:

> "It cannot be questioned, since the case of *Ashbury, etc., Co.* v. *Riche*,[66] that a company cannot employ its funds for the purpose of any transactions which do not come within the objects specified in the memorandum. . . . The capital may, no doubt, be diminished by expenditure upon and reasonably incidental to all the objects specified. A part of it may be lost in carrying on the business operations authorised. Of this all persons trusting the company are aware, and take the risk. But I think they have a right to rely, and were intended by the legislature to have a right to rely, on the capital remaining undiminished by any expenditure outside those limits, or by the return of any part of it to the shareholders."

Here again, reference may be made to the restriction of the effect of the doctrine in *Ashbury Railway Carriage Co.* v. *Riche*[66] introduced by the European Communities Act 1972, s. 9 (1).[67]

Illustrations of intra vires transactions

9–15 The following are some of the cases in which the expenditure of the company's funds, or the employment of its property, has been held a legitimate expenditure or employment on the objects of the company and therefore *intra vires*, though not expressly provided for:

where a company, formed to work a patent, expended its funds in purchasing such patent[68];

where a company, formed to work mines of which it had acquired a lease, spent money in buying the freehold, including the surface[69];

where a company, being second mortgagee of land in England, paid off the first mortgagee in order to prevent foreclosure[70];

where a company, bound to supply boats for a ferry, employed the boats, when not wanted for the ferry, in excursions[71];

where an hotel company let off temporarily part of its premises not wanted for the purposes of its business[72];

where a colliery company sold land from time to time when the sale was reasonably necessary[73];

where a company, formed to acquire and work a mine, paid fees to

64 (1875) L.R. 7 H.L. 653.
65 (1887) 12 App.Cas. 409, 414, 415.
66 (1875) L.R. 7 H.L. 653.
67 See para. 9–25, *post*.
68 Leifchild's Case (1865) L.R. 1 Eq. 231.
69 *Johns* v. *Balfour* (1889) 5 T.L.R. 389.
70 *Sheffield, etc., Society* v. *Aizlewood* (1889) 44 Ch.D. 412.
71 *Forrest* v. *Manchester, etc., Ry.* (1861) 30 Beav. 40.
72 *Simpson* v. *Westminster Palace Hotel Co.* (1860) 8 H.L.C. 712.
73 *Re Kingsbury Collieries and Moore's Contract* [1907] 2 Ch. 259.

a mining expert for a report on the mine to its solicitors and brokers, and for advertisements and printing[74];

where a company paid its workmen a gratuity,[75] or granted a pension to an ex-officer or his widow,[76] provided that the company continued as a going concern[77];

9–16 where a company compromised a bona fide dispute[78];

where a company paid to a broker a reasonable brokerage for issue of its capital[79];

where a company incurred expenses on printing, stamping and sending out proxy papers and circulars to secure the defeat of a resolution which the directors considered adverse to the company's interest[80];

where a company, with wide powers of lending, lent money to a servant of the company[81];

where a company expended money on scientific research, where the main object of the company was the business of chemical maufacturers[82];

where a company guaranteed debentures of another company under a power to "subsidise or assist"[83];

where a gas company, having power to convert and manufacture residual products, manufactured other substances for the purpose of dealing more effectively with its residual products[84];

where a property development company, having knowledge of a particular source of finance, made that knowledge available to another company in consideration of a procuration fee[85];

where a company formed, *inter alia*, for the purpose of carrying on the business of "merchants generally," carried on the business of a petrol filling and car service station.[86]

All these have been held *intra vires*. So it is *intra vires* for a trading company to borrow, raise money and give security on its property.[87]

---

[74] *Lydney, etc., Co.* v. *Bird* (1886) 33 Ch.D. 85.
[75] *Hampson* v. *Price's Patent Candle Co.* (1876) 24 W.R. 754.
[76] *Henderson* v. *Bank of Australasia* (1888) 40 Ch.D. 170; *Cyclists' Touring Club* v. *Hopkinson* [1910] 1 Ch. 179.
[77] *Hutton* v. *West Cork Ry.* (1883) 23 Ch.D. 654, 672: for the requirements to ensure the effectiveness of such a payment, see *Re Lee, Behrens & Co.* [1932] 2 Ch. 46 (as explained in *Charterbridge Corpn.* v. *Lloyds Bank Ltd.* [1970] Ch. 62 and *In re Horsley* v. *Weight Ltd.* [1982] 3 W.L.R. 431); *Parke* v. *Daily News Ltd.* [1962] Ch. 927; and *Re W. & M. Roith Ltd.* [1967] 1 W.L.R. 432. See also Companies Act 1980, s. 74, para. 9–21, *post*.
[78] *Bath's Case* (1878) 8 Ch.D. 334.
[79] *Metropolitan Coal, etc., Association* v. *Scrimgeour* [1895] 2 Q.B. 604.
[80] *Peel* v. *L. & N.W. Ry.* [1907] 1 Ch. 5; *Campbell* v. *Australian Mutual, etc., Society* (1908) 99 L.T. 3.
[81] *Rainford* v. *James Keith and Blackman Co.* [1905] 2 Ch. 147.
[82] *Evans* v. *Brunner, Mond & Co.* [1921] 1 Ch. 359.
[83] *Re Friary, Holroyd and Healey's Breweries* [1922] W.N. 293; *Cape Insulation Ltd.* v. *Braid Investments Ltd.* 1979 S.L.T. 66.
[84] *Deuchar* v. *Gas Light and Coke Co.* [1925] A.C. 691.
[85] *Bell Houses Ltd.* v. *City Wall Properties Ltd.* [1966] 2 Q.B. 656.
[86] *Re New Finance & Mortgage Co. Ltd. (in liquidation)* [1975] Ch. 420.
[87] *General Auction, etc., Co.* v. *Smith* [1891] 3 Ch. 432, 436.

Illustrations of ultra vires transactions

9–17 Before section 9 (1) of the European Communities Act 1972 became effective (on January 1, 1973), the following transactions were held to be *ultra vires*[88]:

where the prosperity of a railway company depended materially on the navigation of a river being improved, and accordingly they proposed to apply to Parliament for the requisite powers, an application of the funds of the company towards the promotion of the Bill was *ultra vires*[89];

where a railway company proposed to secure the capital and guarantee the profits of another company about to run steamboats in connection with the line[90];

where a railway company was working coal mines and dealing in coal for profit[91];

where the capital of a company was about to be applied, or had been applied, to the payment of dividends[92];

where, before the coming into operation of section 46 of the Companies Act 1981 (which authorises the company, subject to certain conditions, to acquire its own shares), the capital of a company had been applied to the purchase of its own shares, or a contract had been made so to do[93]; even though expressly authorised by its memorandum[94];

9–18 where the articles of a company provided that a dismissed employee should surrender his shares[95];

where the company had issued shares at a discount[96]; even though expressly authorised by its memorandum or articles[97];

where the company had issued bonus shares pursuant to an agreement, but without consideration[98];

where a company offered debentures at a discount with an option, at once exercisable, to exchange them for shares, fully paid, equal in nominal value to the face value of the debentures[99];

---

[88] Today, these transactions would have to be examined in the light of the provisions of s. 9 (1) of the European Communities Act 1972.

[89] *Munt* v. *Shrewsbury, etc., Ry.* (1850) 13 Beav. 1; and see *East Anglian Ry.* v. *E.C. Ry.* (1851) 11 C.B. 775.

[90] *Colman* v. *E.C. Ry.* (1846) 10 Beav. 1.

[91] *Att.-Gen.* v. *G.N. Ry.* (1860) 1 Dr. & Sm. 154.

[92] See paras. 76–02 *et seq., post.*

[93] See para. 38–02, *post.*

[94] *Raine's Case* (1887) 4 T.L.R. 302; *Mersina and Adana Construction Co.* (1888) 5 T.L.R. 680; *General Property Investment Co.* v. *Matheson's Trustees* (1888) 16 R.(Ct. of Sess.) 282; *British and American, etc., Corpn.* v. *Couper* [1894] A.C. 399.

[95] *Re Walker and Hacking Ltd.* (1887) 57 L.T. 763. It is doubtful that this decision would be followed today.

[96] See para. 24–11, *post.*

[97] *Welton* v. *Saffery* [1897] A.C. 299.

[98] *Re Eddystone, etc., Co.* [1893] 3 Ch. 9.

[99] *Moseley* v. *Koffyfontein Mines* [1904] 2 Ch. 108; and see *Trustees Corpn. Ltd.* v. *Commissioners of Income Tax, Bombay* (1930) I.L.R. 54 (Bom.) 437 (P.C.).

9–19 where a company borrowed money for an *ultra vires* purpose under an express borrowing power in the memorandum, notwithstanding a provision that the objects set out in each sub-clause, should be treated as independent objects[1];

where a company, formed to make and sell railway carriages and wagons and to carry on the business of mechanical engineers and general contractors and other specified objects, had engaged in the financing of a railway line in Belgium,[2] it was held in that case that the words "general contractors" must be read as referring to such contracts, and to such contracts only, as were incidental to the business of a mechanical engineer[3];

where the funds of the company had been applied in paying the costs of a prosecution against a person who had libelled the company's directors, the libel not applying to the company itself[4];

9–20 where directors were issuing new shares without the sanction of a resolution of the company in general meeting[5];

where the company's net profits were applied in buying off opposition to a parliamentary Bill, or getting a public body to exercise powers in its favour which were for the public benefit[6];

where, in the winding up of a company, a resolution was passed for the distribution of a large sum among its officers[7];

9–21 where a company issued debentures with bonus certificates for payment of an additional sum out of profits, it could not afterwards, by arrangement, issue fully paid shares in satisfaction of the certificates[8];

where a marine insurance company, whose memorandum excluded fire insurance, granted a policy to cover risks which were almost exclusively fire risks[9];

where a private company, five years after the death of the managing director, covenanted to pay an annuity to his widow, there being no evidence that this was intended to be for the benefit of the company, and the court being of opinion that the predominant motive was to make provision for the widow.[10] Similarly, where a company had

---

1 *Introductions Ltd.* v. *National Provincial Bank Ltd.* [1970] Ch. 199 (C.A.).

2 *Ashbury Ry. Carriage, etc., Co.* v. *Riche* (1875) L.R. 7 H.L. 653.

3 There was no "independent objects" clause in the memorandum; see now para. 9–16, *ante* on the meaning of "merchants generally"; see *Re New Finance & Mortgage Co. Ltd. (in liquidation)* [1975] 3 W.L.R. 443.

4 *Studdert* v. *Grosvenor* (1886) 33 Ch.D. 528.

5 *Moseley* v. *Koffyfontein Mines Ltd.* [1911] A.C. 409.

6 *Greenwich Pier Co.* v. *Thames Conservators* (1905) 21 T.L.R. 669.

7 *Stroud* v. *Royal Aquarium, etc., Soc.* [1903] W.N. 146; 19 T.L.R. 656; and see *Hutton* v. *West Cork Ry.* (1883) 23 Ch.D. 654.

8 *Famatina Development Corpn.* v. *Bury* [1910] A.C. 439; *Re Railway Time Tables Publishing Co.* (1893) 68 L.T. 649; *Moseley* v. *Koffyfontein Mines Ltd.* [1904] 2 Ch. 108.

9 *Re Argonaut Marine Insurance Co.* [1932] 2 Ch. 34.

10 *Re Lee, Behrens & Co. Ltd.* [1932] 2 Ch. 46 (for an explanation of this case see *Charterbridge Corpn.* v. *Lloyds Bank Ltd.* [1970] Ch. 62 and *In re Horsley* v. *Weight Ltd.* [1982] 3 W.L.R. 431). See also *Kerr* v. *Walker* 1933 S.C. 453; 1933 S.L.T. 354.

contracted to pay a pension to the wife of the controlling shareholder after his death, in consideration of his agreeing to act as general manager for the remainder of his life, the court held that the agreement was a "sham"[11];

Before the coming into operation of section 74 of the Companies Act 1980 (December 22, 1980), where after cessation of the major part of the business of the company and the continuation of its other business the company proposed to make large *ex gratia* payments to its former employees[12]; section 74 of the 1980 Act provides that the powers of a company shall include power to make provision for the benefit of employees or former employees of the company or any of its subsidiaries, in connection with the cessation or the transfer of the whole or part of its undertaking, but this power can only be exercised subject to certain conditions.[13] This provision effectively overrules *Parke* v. *Daily News Ltd.*[14] The payment of gratuities to employees has always been held to be *intra vires* if it can be said to be in the interest of the company as a going concern[15];

where assets are taken out of the company by way of voluntary disposition, other than by way of dividend or duly authorised reduction of capital or in a winding up[16];

where company funds were used to repay personal borrowings by a director[17];

where a public utility company, incorporated by a private Act of Parliament and subsequently registered under Part VIII of the 1948 Act, altered its objects to enable it to abandon its main undertaking, and contracted to transfer its assets to a municipal corporation.[18]

Effect of ultra vires acts before the coming into operation of the European Communities Act 1972

9–22 The practical effect of the *ultra vires* doctrine is today determined by two factors: the law, as it existed before the European Communities Act 1972 which came into operation on January 1, 1973, and the provisions of section 9 (1) of that Act. The *ultra vires* doctrine is not abolished by section 9 (1) but the doctrine, in its traditional form, still applies in certain circumstances.

As the ambit of the *ultra vires* doctrine is in certain situations determined by the old law and in others by the 1972 Act, both regulations have to be

---

11 *Re W. & M. Roith Ltd.* [1967] 1 W.L.R. 432; doubted in *In re Horsley* v. *Weight Ltd.* [1982] 3 W.L.R. 431.

12 *Parke* v. *Daily News Ltd.* [1962] Ch. 927.

13 These conditions include a resolution of the general meeting or an authority in the memorandum or articles.

14 [1962] Ch. 927.

15 The payments must satisfy the test laid down by Eve J. in *Re Lee, Behrens & Co., supra*, as explained in *In re Horsley* v. *Weight Ltd.* [1982] 3 W.L.R. 431.

16 *Ridge Securities Ltd.* v. *I.R.C.* [1964] 1 W.L.R. 479.

17 *Thompson* v. *J. Barke & Co. (Caterers) Ltd.* 1975 S.L.T. 67.

18 *Re Salisbury Railways and Market House Co. Ltd.* [1969] 1 Ch. 349.

considered here. It is appropriate to deal first with the old law because the effect of the 1972 enactment can best be understood by indicating in what respects the 1972 Act has modified the old law. But the cases in which the old law still applies constitute today the exception to the new regulation. These exceptional cases are listed later.

9–23 Under the old law, where a company does an act which is *ultra vires*, no legal relationship or effect ensues from it. Such an act is absolutely void and cannot be ratified even if all the shareholders agree.[19] Whether it is possible to recover money paid or property transferred under such a void transaction, will be discussed later.[20]

The effect of an *ultra vires* transaction under the old law is, thus, that it might cause considerable hardship to a third party who acted in good faith, namely to a party who did not read the memorandum, and was, therefore, unaware of the incapacity of the company. Today section 9 (1) here provides some—but not complete—relief. The section establishes the principle that the company cannot plead that it has acted *ultra vires* against a third party who has contracted with it in good faith.[21]

9–24 The hardship which the unmodified *ultra vires* doctrine can cause to third parties who have contracted with the company in good faith is demonstrated in *Re Jon Beauforte (London) Ltd.*[22] In that case the objects of the company were to carry on the business of costumiers and gown makers and similar business; after the Second World War the company decided to manufacture veneer panels, an activity which, as the court held, was *ultra vires* the company. For the purpose of making veneers, it built a factory in a different part of the country, purchased veneers from suppliers, and obtained coke from a fuel merchant for use at the factory. The builders who constructed the factory and the veneer suppliers signed judgment against the company. In the compulsory winding up of the company their claims and that of the fuel merchant were rejected by the liquidator and that rejection was upheld by Roxburgh J. As regards the fuel merchant the learned judge held that as the merchant had clear notice that the coke was to be used in the veneer factory and had constructive notice of the memorandum, he was sufficiently aware that the transaction was *ultra vires* the company; as regards the builders and the veneer suppliers, the *ultra vires* character of the original contracts was clear but the question arose whether the fact that their claims had merged into judgments made a difference. The learned judge answered this question in the negative; he said:

> " . . . in the case of an *ultra vires* contract no judgment founded upon it is inviolable, unless it embodies a decision of a court upon the issue of *ultra vires* or a compromise of that issue . . . "

---

[19] See para. 9–04, *ante; Re Birkbeck Building Soc.* [1912] 2 Ch. 183.
[20] See para. 9–35, *post.*
[21] See para. 9–25, *post.*
[22] [1953] Ch. 131.

Effect of the European Communities Act 1972 on the ultra vires doctrine

9–25 Section 9 (1) of the 1972 Act restricts the application of the *ultra vires* doctrine but does not abolish it. The doctrine can no longer be relied upon by the company against a third party if two cumulative conditions are satisfied:

1. The third party must have acted in good faith; and
2. The transaction in question must have been decided on by the directors.

GOOD FAITH. This term is nowhere defined in the European Communities Act 1972 or the Companies Acts 1948 to 1981. The third party is certainly not in good faith if he had *actual notice* that the transaction in question is *ultra vires* the company. It is, however, doubtful whether mere *constructive notice* is sufficient to destroy the good faith; it is submitted that that is not the case because otherwise the objective of the provision would be defeated.

Between these two extremes are the cases in which the circumstances are so unusual or suspicious that the third party could not have been unaware that the transaction was *ultra vires*. If he is thus put on *inquiry* and neglects to pursue it, he has not acted in good faith. This view is supported by *International Sales & Agencies Ltd.* v. *Marcus*,[22a] where Lawson J. said[22b]:

> ". . . the test of lack of good faith in somebody entering into obligations with a company will be found either in proof of his actual knowledge that the transaction was *ultra vires* the company or where it can be shown that such a person could not in view of all the circumstances, have been unaware that he was a party to a transaction *ultra vires*."

THE DIRECTORS. Section 9 (1) provides that the transaction in question must have been decided on by the "directors." The use of the plural is not accidental. It is an attempt at rendering in English the word "organs" which is used in article 9 of the First Council Directive on Company Law Harmonisation of March 9, 1968. Consequently, the argument that by virtue of section 6 (*c*) of the Interpretation Act 1978 the plural includes the singular, is untenable and does not support the view that section 9 (1) applies if a single member of a multi-member board of directors has acted.

Where a single member of the board has acted, three cases have to be distinguished. First, the member has actual or ostensible[23] authority of the board to act on its behalf; in that case section 9 (1) applies. Secondly, the board consists only of one member; this may be the case legitimately in a private company[24] or *de facto* in a public company; here the section applies

---

[22a] [1982] 2 C.M.L.R. 46.
[22b] *Ibid.*, para. 21.
[23] *Freeman and Lockyer* v. *Buckhurst Park Properties (Mangal) Ltd.* [1964] 2 Q.B. 480; *Kreditbank Cassel G.m.b.H.* v. *Schenkers* [1927] 1 K.B. 826; *Panorama Development (Guildford) Ltd.* v. *Fidelis Furnishing Fabrics Ltd.* [1971] 2 Q.B. 711.
[24] s. 176.

again. Thirdly, where the company has a multi-member board, the single director who has acted is not authorised but acts "on a frolic of his own"; here section 9 (1) does not apply.

9–26 EFFECT OF SECTION 9 (1) ON THE PREVIOUS DECISIONS. The effect of this provision is that *Ashbury Railway Carriage Co* v. *Riche*[25] and *Re Jon Beauforte (London) Ltd.*,[26] have ceased to be applicable. *Introductions Ltd.* v. *National Provincial Bank Ltd.*,[27] on the other hand, is still good law because in that case the Court of Appeal held that the bank had *actual* notice that the company acted *ultra vires*.

Continued applicability of the ultra vires doctrine

9–27 In the following exceptional cases the *ultra vires* doctrine can still be invoked and the old law still applies:

(i) the company can plead it against a third party if the company can prove that he has not acted in good faith;
(ii) if the transaction has not been approved by the directors (see *supra*);
(iii) internally, *i.e.* in the relationship between the directors and the shareholders or the directors and the company, the operation of the *ultra vires* doctrine is not affected by section 9 (1). *Parke* v. *Daily News Ltd.*,[28] was, it is thought, not affected by this provision but, as has been mentioned,[29] has been virtually overruled by section 74 of the 1980 Act;
(iv) a third party can still claim as against the company that the latter has acted *ultra vires*. It can be argued that equity will view with disfavour such an unequal position and disallow the plea of a third party that the company has acted *ultra vires* but it is thought that this argument is untenable because, apart from its wording, the object of subsection (1) is to provide protection for the third party and not to qualify or reduce his common law rights; and
(v) a shareholder can obtain an injunction against the company with a view to preventing it from acting *ultra vires*.

The future of the ultra vires doctrine

9–28 It is to be regretted that the legislature of 1947–48 did not deem fit to accept the suggestion of the Cohen Committee[30] that the doctrine should be limited so as to define the powers of the company as between the directors and shareholders, thus enabling a shareholder to feel reasonably confident that the company in which he holds shares will not carry on a

---

[25] (1873) L.R. 7 H.L. 653.
[26] [1953] Ch. 131.
[27] [1970] Ch. 199.
[28] [1962] Ch. 927; see also *Gibson's Executors* v. *Gibson* 1980 S.L.T. 2.
[29] See para. 9–21, *ante*.
[30] Cmd. 6659 (1954), para. 12, pp. 9–10.

business completely foreign to its memorandum, but that as regards outsiders the company should have the full powers of an individual, so that the position would be regained which existed before the decision in *Sutton's Hospital* case in 1612[31] and the coming into operation of the company legislation of the nineteenth century. The Companies Bill 1973, which lapsed with the dissolution of Parliament in 1974, following the suggestions of the Jenkins Committee,[32] provided in clause 5 for the virtual abolition of the doctrine of *ultra vires*, except if the third party had actual notice of the fact that the company had acted in that manner; it was also provided that the third party should be protected if he did not understand the provisions indicating that the company had acted *ultra vires* and that his failure was in all the circumstances reasonable. Clause 5 went far beyond section 9 (1) of the European Communities Act 1972 and provided for the repeal of the latter.

The 1980 Act has not adopted the regulation proposed in the—lapsed—Companies Bill 1973 and, in spite of the amelioration achieved by section 9 (1) of the European Communities Act 1972, the position with respect to the *ultra vires* doctrine remains unsatisfactory.

Construction of interpretation of objects

General rules of construction

9–29 Whether any given transaction is or is not within the capacity of a company is a question of law depending on the construction to be placed on the objects clause of the memorandum of association.[33] In *Ashbury Railway Carriage, etc., Co.* v. *Riche*,[34] the whole case turned, as appears from the opinions of the Lords, on the construction to be placed on the objects clause of the memorandum of association. Accordingly, if a question arises as to whether a transaction is or is not within the powers of a company to be inferred from its objects, one must scrutinise the objects clause and ascertain its meaning, and in doing this the rules which are to be applied to its interpretation or construction must be borne in mind. To construe a document is, as Lord Chelmsford said in *Scott* v. *Corporation of Liverpool*,[35] nothing more than this: to arrive at the meaning of the parties. For this purpose there are certain well-recognised rules which apply to a memorandum and articles of association, just as much as to any other document. Thus—

(1) The whole document must be read and considered.

(2) The expressed intention is to have effect; we are not to speculate as to what the parties intended, but to ascertain it from the words

[31] (1612) 10 Co.Rep. 1a, 23a, see para. 89–20, *post*.
[32] Cmnd. 1749 (1962), paras. 35–42.
[33] *Simpson* v. *Westminster Palace Hotel Co.* (1860) 8 H.L.C. 712.
[34] (1875) L.R. 7 H.L. 653.
[35] (1858) 3 De G. & J. 334, 360.

used, for the expressed meaning is to be taken to indicate the intention.

(3) The "golden rule" must be observed, namely, that the grammatical and ordinary sense of the words is to be adhered to, unless that would lead to absurdity, or some repugnance or inconsistency with the rest of the instrument, in which case the grammatical and ordinary sense of the words may be modified so as to avoid that absurdity, repugnance or inconsistency, but no further.[36] Where the language is clear and unambiguous it must have effect, even though in the result it may operate in a capricious and unreasonable manner; if it is ambiguous, the more reasonable construction should be adopted.

(4) Popular words are to be taken prima facie to be used in their popular sense, and technical words in their technical sense; but in each case the prima facie sense may be displayed or qualified by the context.

(5) The words used must be read with reference to the subject-matter.

(6) The *ejusdem generis* rule and the maxim *expressio unius est exclusio alterius* are also, at times, applicable.

A memorandum of association, like any other document, must be read fairly and its import derived from a reasonable interpretation of the language which it employs.[37]

Further, an object which is unequivocally expressed in the memorandum should not be interpreted as being impliedly limited by reference to the state of mind of the parties concerned, as, *e.g.* whether a transaction is thought by the directors to be for the benefit of the company; "the state of mind of the directors . . . is irrelevant upon [the] issue of *ultra vires*"[38] *per* Pennycuick J. at p. 132. But the position is different if the objects clause expressly introduces a subjective test, *e.g.* by empowering the company to do anything which "in the opinion of the board of directors" can be carried on advantageously in connection with the other objects.[39]

To sum up, in modern law the courts are unlikely to hold a contract to be *ultra vires* the company unless, on a reasonable construction of the objects clause and the other clauses of the memorandum and articles, there are compelling grounds to arrive at that result.[40]

"Main objects" rule of construction

9–30 A special rule of construction is applied where the objects of a company are expressed in a series of paragraphs, and one paragraph (commonly the first) appears to embody the main or dominant object of the company. In

[36] *Grey* v. *Pearson* (1857) H.L.C. 61, 106.
[37] *Egyptian Salt and Soda Co.* v. *Port Said Salt Association Ltd.* [1931] A.C. at p. 682.
[38] *Charterbridge Corpn.* v. *Lloyds Bank Ltd.* [1970] Ch. 62.
[39] See *Bell Houses Ltd.* v. *City Wall Properties Ltd.* [1966] 2 Q.B. 656 and para. 9–10, *ante*.
[40] *Bell Houses Ltd.* v. *City Wall Properties Ltd.* [1966] 2 Q.B. 656; *Re New Finance & Mortgage Co. Ltd. (in liquidation)* [1975] Ch. 420; *In re Horsley* v. *Weight Ltd.* [1982] 3 W.L.R. 431.

such a case all the other paragraphs are to be treated as merely ancillary to this main object, and as limited and controlled thereby.[41] The "main objects" rule was expressed by Lindley L.J. in *Re German Date Coffee Co.*[42] as follows:

> "In construing . . . any . . . memorandum of association in which there are general words, care must be taken to construe those general words so as not to make them a trap for unwary people. General words . . . must be taken in connection with what are shown by the context to be the dominant or main objects of the company. It will not do, under general words, to turn a company for manufacturing one thing into a company for importing something else, however general the words are."

9–31 Sometimes the memorandum declares the intention to be that the objects specified in each paragraph of the clause shall, except where otherwise expressed in such paragraph, be in nowise limited or restricted by reference to or inference from the terms of any other paragraph or the name of the company. These words are obviously intended to exclude the application of the "main objects" rule of construction, and the court is bound to give effect to the intention thus indicated.[43] This applies whether the question is as to *ultra vires* acts, or as to the substratum having gone.[44] In *Stephens* v. *Mysore Reefs*,[45] general words in a later paragraph were held to be cut down by reference to the "main object" where the question was one of *ultra vires*, notwithstanding the presence of words intended to exclude any such rule. This decision, though not expressly overruled in *Cotman* v. *Brougham*,[46] appears to be quite inconsistent with the principle there laid down, and has now been stated no longer to represent the law.[47]

An "independent objects" clause must, however, be read as subject to a qualification where the context otherwise requires: it cannot render independent a provision which by its nature is dependent on other parts of the projects clause. Thus, an express power to borrow money is meaningless in isolation and can only be exercised for the purpose of furthering the company's legitimate objects.[48]

The existence of words which give a power to do anything are ineffective except in so far as incidental to the main object.[49] But an object showing the intention to operate in one place may not exclude the object of

---

41 *Re Haven Gold Mining Co.* (1882) 20 Ch.D. 151; *Re German Date Coffee Co.* (1882) 20 Ch.D. 169; *Re Crown Bank* (1890) 44 Ch.D. 634; *Re Amalgamated Syndicate* [1897] 2 Ch. 600.

42 (1882) 20 Ch.D. 169, 188.

43 *Cotman* v. *Brougham* [1918] A.C. 514; *Anglo-Overseas Agencies Ltd.* v. *Green* [1961] 1 Q.B. 1; see also *Re E. K. Cole Ltd.* [1945] 1 All E.R. 521n.; *cf. Introductions Ltd.* v. *National Provincial Bank Ltd.* [1970] Ch. 199 (C.A.). *London and Edinburgh Shipping Co.* 1909 S.C. 1; 16 S.L.T. 386.

44 *Re Kitson & Co. Ltd.* (1946) 175 L.T. 25; *Re Taldua Rubber Co. Ltd.* [1946] 2 All E.R. 763.

45 [1902] 1 Ch. 745.

46 [1918] A.C. 514.

47 In *Anglo-Overseas Agencies Ltd.* v. *Green* [1961] 1 Q.B. 1, *per* Salmon J.

48 *Introductions Ltd.* v. *National Provincial Bank Ltd.* [1970] Ch. 199 (C.A.).

49 See, further, as to interpretation, Palmer, *Company Precedents,* Part I (17th ed.), Chap. 8, p. 369.

operating elsewhere; so that such words as "in or out of the colony"[50] or "in Mysore and elsewhere"[51] have been held not to be restricted by the context, but to be world-wide. This can be of importance not only where the question is as to whether acts are *ultra vires* but also where it is a question whether or not the company's substratum has gone.[52]

General concluding words

9–32 The objects clause commonly concludes with the words "To do all such other things as are incidental or conducive to the attainment of the above objects or any of them,"[53] but it seems very doubtful whether such words really add anything to what the law already implies as incidental to the specifically enumerated objects.[54]

The operation of such general words should, it seems, be considered to be limited to such things as are naturally conducive to the objects specified, *i.e.* doing something bona fide connected with the objects to be attained and in the ordinary course of business adapted to their attainment.[55]

Where, however, the objects clause also incorporates a provision empowering the company to do anything which "in the opinion of the board of directors" can be carried on advantageously in connection with its other objects, or incidentally thereto, the above test is replaced by a subjective one. It has been held[56] that, where such words appear, any act is within the company's power if the directors honestly form the view that it can be advantageously combined with the other objects, even though the directors are mistaken, and in fact the buiness in question cannot be carried on as the directors believe. Such a clause will not, however, justify the adoption of a new activity, which is not expressly authorised, after the existing business of the company has been completely discontinued, as there is then no other business to which the new business can be related.[57]

Reference to other documents

9–33 While, as has already been observed,[58] the objects of the company cannot be stated by reference to another—outside—document, it is pos-

---

[50] Campbell v. *Australian Mutual, etc., Society* (1908) 99 L.T. 3.
[51] *Pedlar* v. *Road Block Gold Mines* [1905] 2 Ch. at p. 435.
[52] See para. 85–08, *post*.
[53] See *Evans* v. *Brunner, Mond & Co.* [1921] 1 Ch. 359.
[54] *Re Baglan Hall Colliery Co.* (1870) L.R. 5 Ch. 346; *Simpson* v. *Westminster Palace Hotel Co.* (1860) 8 H.L.C. 712; *Taunton* v. *Royal Insur. Co.* (1864) 2 H. & M. 135.
[55] *Joint Stock Discount Co.* v. *Brown* (1866) L.R. 3 Eq. at p. 150; same case, L.R. 8 Eq. at p. 395; *Ashbury Ry., etc., Co.* v. *Riche* (1875) L.R. 7 H.L. 653; *British and Foreign, etc., Co.* v. *Ashbury Carriage, etc., Co.* (1869) 20 L.T. 360; *Deuchar* v. *Gas Light and Coke Co.* [1925] A.C. 691.
[56] In *Bell Houses Ltd.* v. *City Wall Properties Ltd.* [1966] 2 Q.B. 656, following *Keren Kayemeth Le Jisroel Ltd.* v. *I.R.C.* [1931] 2 K.B. 465; *Oxford Group* v. *I.R.C.* [1949] 2 All E.R. 537; and *Associated Artists Ltd.* v. *I.R.C.* [1956] 2 All E.R. 583 (all of which were concerned with the completely different question of whether the companies were entitled to exemption from income tax as companies formed exclusively for charitable purposes); see also *Peruvian Railways* v. *Thames, etc., Co.* (1867) L.R. 2 Ch. 617; *London Financial Assn.* v. *Kelk* (1884) 26 Ch.D. 107.
[57] *Introductions Ltd.* v. *National Provincial Bank Ltd.* [1970] Ch. 199 (C.A.).
[58] See para. 9–02, *ante*.

sible, if the objects are defined in the objects clause with sufficient certainty, to refer in that clause in their supplementation to another document. But such reference to an outside document should be interpreted restrictively. Thus, in *Mitton Butler Priest and Co. Ltd. (in liquidation)* v. *Ross and Others*[59] the objects clause provided that the company should carry on the business of stockbrokers "in accordance with the rules and regulations [of The Stock Exchange] for the time being in force and as a limited corporate member thereof," The Rules of The Stock Exchange stipulated for personal unlimited liability of stockbrokers. The directors of the company were held not to be personally liable to the outside creditors of the company, *i.e.* creditors having claims other than arising from stock exchange transactions.

Indefinite objects

9–34 Sometimes it is contended that when the objects are very widely stated in general terms there is no sufficient "statement" or particularity[60] of the objects within the requirements of the Act, but any objection of this kind is precluded if the Registrar has granted his certificate of incorporation because the Acts make such certificate conclusive evidence of compliance with the preliminary conditions, one of which is a statement of the objects.[61] However, where the objects are ambiguous, a construction should be preferred which brings them within reasonable limits.

Recovery under ultra vires contracts

9–35 It has already been stated[62] that a contract which is *ultra vires* the company is absolutely void, except if the party with whom the company has contracted can invoke section 9 (1) of the European Communities Act 1972. The question arises whether, if the *ultra vires* contract has been wholly or partially executed, recovery can be made of moneys paid or property transferred thereunder. This question arises in two sets of circumstances: whether the company can make recovery against the party with whom it has contracted, and whether that party can make recovery against the company.

On principle, these two questions should be answered in the same way. However, it would appear that the courts enforce the consequences of *ultra vires* more strictly if the company seeks to recover its money or property from the other party; in other words, they are more friendly disposed to a claim by the company than against it. The reason for this discrepancy is that the courts consider it important to protect the company's creditors and shareholders against *ultra vires* dispositions of its assets.

---

59 *The Times,* December 22, 1976.
60 See para. 9–02, *ante*.
61 *Cotman* v. *Brougham* [1918] A.C. 514.
62 See para. 9–23.

RECOVERY BY THE COMPANY. If the company has made an *ultra vires* loan, it cannot sue in debt because the contract is void. But it is thought that an action in quasi-contract for money had and received is admissible if it can be established that the other party is unjustifiably enriched at the expense of the company because in this action the company need not rely on the void contract.[63] If the requirements of an action in quasi-contract are satisfied, the company need not fall back on secondary remedies, such as tracing in law or equity.

As regards the transfer of the company's property, title does not pass to the purchaser under an *ultra vires* contract and an action for recovery of the company's property or in conversion by the company or its liquidator should be successful unless the purchaser is protected by section 9 (1) of the European Communities Act 1972 or has acquired a prescriptive title.[64] The purchaser who has restored the company's property is entitled to recover the purchase price from the company as there has been total failure of consideration.

RECOVERY BY THE CONTRACTING PARTY. If this party is not protected by section 9 (1) of the European Communities Act 1972, very difficult questions arise which have not been resolved fully by the courts. They concern mainly loans obtained by the company *ultra vires* its borrowing powers; these questions are considered more fully in paragraph 42–11, *post*. Only this may be said here. Although in the case of unjustifiable enrichment on the part of the company to the detriment of the *ultra vires* lender an action of quasi-contract appears to be a perfectly good remedy, the House of Lords in *Sinclair* v. *Brougham*[65] has expressly ruled out the admission of such a remedy as this would be an indirect means of enforcing the *ultra vires* loan. The lender is thus compelled to have recourse to the secondary remedies of subrogation and tracing in law or equity. If his loan has been used to satisfy *intra vires* creditors of the company, he is subrogated to their rights against the company but he does not appear to be subrogated to securities held by them.[66] The *ultra vires* lender may also trace his loan in law or equity into the assets of the company.[67]

If the other party has transferred property to the company in an *ultra vires* transaction, in the present state of the authorities it is wholly unclear whether title passes to the company. There is slight authority for the view that title does pass, at least if the transfer of property is subsequent to the

---

63 *Brougham* v. *Dwyer* (1913) 108 L.T. 504; 29 T.L.R. 234 (D.C.); Mocatta J. in *Bell Houses Ltd.* v. *City Wall Properties Ltd.* [1965] 3 W.L.R. 1065, 1073.

64 *Per* Lord Parker of Waddington in *Sinclair* v. *Brougham* [1914] A.C. 398, 440; *Re Working UDC (Basingstoke Canal) Act 1911* [1914] 1 Ch. 300, 309.

65 [1914] A.C. 398, 440.

66 *Re Wrexham Mold and Connah's Quay Ry. Co.* [1899] 1 Ch. 440.

67 *Sinclair* v. *Brougham* [1914] A.C. 398, as considered in *Re Diplock* [1948] Ch. 465, 526. *In Re Airdale Co-operative Worsted Manufacturing Society* [1953] Ch. 639, and the cases referred to in para. 42–11, *post*.

conclusion of the void contract.[68] This view can be founded on the ground that the other party is estopped from claiming that the contract is void. This, however, is a weak argument and a better solution would be in *ultra vires* transactions to treat the transfer of property to the company in exactly the same manner as the transfer of property by the company.

Liability of directors acting ultra vires the company

9–36 Here two cases have to be considered, *viz.* the liability of the director to the company and that to third parties, including the contracting party.

LIABILITY TO THE COMPANY. If a director, on behalf of the company, enters into a transaction which is *ultra vires* the company, he is guilty of grave dereliction of duty. It is his duty to acquaint himself fully with the memorandum and articles of his company and to ensure that the company has capacity to enter into the contemplated transaction. It is irrelevant whether the director ignores this duty deliberately or whether he has done so negligently or without fault of his own. If, in consequence of such an act or omission, the company suffers a loss, the director who acted on behalf of the company is fully liable to the company.

The director cannot rely on section 9 (1) of the European Communities Act 1972 because that Act does not apply to the internal affairs of the company. Nor is it likely, in view of the gravity of his misconduct, that the court, in the exercise of its discretion, will grant him relief under section 448, even if the requirements of that section are satisfied.

LIABILITY TO THIRD PARTIES. Such liability is governed by the general principles of law. Company law does not contain special provisions dealing with this situation.

If the director misrepresented to the third party that the contemplated transaction was within the capacity of the company, there are two sets of circumstances in which he is liable for the misrepresentation. First, if it is deliberate and fraudulent, he can be sued in tort for deceit. Secondly, if the misrepresentation is negligent, the director may well be liable under the *Hedley Byrne* principle.[69] This principle is stated by Lord Denning M.R. in *Esso Petroleum Co. Ltd.* v. *Mardon*[70] in these terms:

> "If a man, who has or professes to have special knowledge or skill, makes a representation by virtue thereof to another—be it advice, information or opinion—with the intention of inducing him to enter into a contract with him, he is under a duty to use reasonable care to see that the representation is correct, and that the advice, information or opinion is reliable. If he negligently gives unsound advice or mis-

[68] See *Ayers* v. *South Australian Banking Co.* (1871) L.R. 3 P.C. 548; *National Telephone Co.* v. *Constables of St. Peter Port* [1900] A.C. 317; *Great Eastern Rail Co.* v. *Turner* (1872) 8 Ch. App. 149.

[69] *Hedley Byrne & Co. Ltd.* v. *Heller Partners Ltd.* [1964] A.C. 465. But see *J. E. B. Fasteners Ltd.* v. *Marks Bloom Co., The Times,* July 28, 1982.

[70] [1976] Q.B. 801.

leading information or expresses an erroneous opinion, and thereby induces the other side to enter into a contract with him, he is liable."

A director is a person professing to have special knowledge or skill, and the words "contract with him" cover the case in which the wrongdoer purports to contract as an agent.

The Misrepresentation Act 1967 is inapplicable because a misrepresentation relating to the capacity of the company to contract is one of law, and not one of fact.

The possibility of a third party, who acts in good faith, being injured by a misrepresentation by a director relating to the capacity of his company to enter into the contemplated contract is diminished by section 9 (1) of the European Communities Act 1972, according to which the company is unable to rely on the defence of *ultra vires* if the requirements of that provision are satisfied.

Company's responsibility for acts of its agents

9–37 An ingenious perversion of the doctrine of *ultra vires* has sometimes led to its being contended that, inasmuch as the funds of a company can be applied only to the promotion of its objects, they cannot be applied in making good damage caused by the fraud, or negligence, or misconduct, of its agents and servants.

This is a fallacy. There is nothing in the rule of *ultra vires* which in any way protects a company acting within its legitimate sphere from liability, to the extent of its assets, for the consequences of the acts of its agents, done by them on behalf of the company and in the course of the company's business. This liability is derived from the ordinary law of principal and agent, and it makes no difference whether the agent's wrongful act or default takes the form of malice, negligence, nuisance or fraud. ". . . these objects [of the company]," as Lord Cranworth said in *Ranger* v. *G.W. Ry.*[71]

> "can only be accomplished by the agency of individuals; and there can be no doubt that if the agents employed conduct themselves fraudulently, so that if they had been acting for private employers, the persons for whom they were acting would have been affected by their fraud, the same principles must prevail when the principal under whom the agent acts is a corporation."

See also *Barwick* v. *English Joint Stock Bank*[72] and *Houldsworth* v. *City of Glasgow Bank*,[73] where Lord Selborne, quoting with approval the observations of Willes J. in *Barwick* v. *English Joint Stock Bank*, said: "With respect to the question whether a principal is answerable for the act of his agent in the course of his master's business, no sensible distinction can be drawn between the case of fraud and the case of any other wrong."

---

71 (1854) 5 H.L.C. 72, 86.
72 (1867) L.R. 2 Ex. 259.
73 (1880) 5 App.Cas. 317, 326.

Hence a corporation may be held liable for negligence[74]; for trespass[75]; for malicious prosecution[76]; for libel[77]; for assault and battery[78]; for nuisance[79]; for fraud[80]; for conspiracy.[81] It may be indicted or fined for breach of duty imposed by the law.[82] It may be estopped by the acts of its agents.[83] It may form an "intention" within the meaning of the Landlord and Tenant Act 1954, s. 30.[84] Finally, it may be held guilty of laches, and bound by acquiescence.[85] For although it may not have eyes and see what is going on, it has agents who can see.[86]

The extent of the company's liability is not limited because its constitution limits the amount of its expenditure.[87]

A company can ratify an act which has been done on its behalf without authority, provided that the act is not *ultra vires*.[88]

Alteration of objects

Alteration procedure in general

9–38 The Act of 1862 contained no provision for altering the objects of a company as defined in its memorandum of association. It was, however, always possible to alter the objects by special Act of Parliament, and in many cases this was done; but obtaining a private Act was an expensive and dilatory process. The only other alternative was to reconstruct—a course, again, involving inconvenience and dislocation. This hindrance to the legitimate expansion of a company's business the legislature recognised in the Companies (Memorandum of Association) Act 1890, which provided that a company might, for certain purposes, by special resolution alter its memorandum with respect to its objects, but subject to confirmation by the court.

---

[74] *Mersey Dock and Harbour Board Trustees* v. *Gibbs* (1866) L.R. 1 H.L. 93.
[75] *Maund* v. *Monmouthshire Canal Co.* (1842) 4 Man. & Gr. 452.
[76] *Abrath* v. *N.E. Ry.* (1886) 11 App.Cas. 247; *Edwards* v. *Midland Ry.* (1880) 6 Q.B.D. 287; *Cornford* v. *Carlton Bank* [1900] 1 Q.B. 22.
[77] *Whitfield* v. *S.E. Ry.* (1858) E.B. & E. 115, 122; *Finburgh* v. *Moss's Empires* 1908 S.C. 928; 16 S.L.T. 116.
[78] *Butler* v. *Manchester, etc., Ry.* (1888) 21 Q.B.D. 207.
[79] *Rapier* v. *London Tramways Co.* [1893] 2 Ch. 588.
[80] *Barwick* v. *English Joint Stock Bank* (1867) L.R. 2 Ex. 259; *Houldsworth* v. *City of Glasgow Bank* (1880) 5 App.Cas. 317.
[81] *British Steel Corpn.* v. *Granada Television* [1980] 3 W.L.R. 774, 817.
[82] *R.* v. *Birmingham, etc., Ry.* (1842) 3 Q.B. 223; *R.* v. *Tyler and the International, etc., Co.* [1891] 2 Q.B. 588; see further para. 18–16, *post*.
[83] *Burkinshaw* v. *Nicolls* (1878) 3 App.Cas. 1004; *Robinson* v. *Montgomeryshire Brewery Co.* [1896] 2 Ch. 841; *Bloomenthal* v. *Ford* [1897] A.C. 156; *Panchaud Frères S.A.* v. *Etablissements General Grain Co.* [1970] 1 Lloyd's Rep. 530; see para. 27–08, *post*.
[84] *H. L. Bolton (Engineering) Co. Ltd.* v. *T. J. Graham & Sons Ltd.* [1957] 1 Q.B. 159.
[85] *Erlanger* v. *New Sombrero, etc., Co.* (1878) 3 App.Cas. 1218; *Nicol's Case* (1885) 29 Ch.D. 421, 429.
[86] *Crook* v. *Corporation of Seaford* (1871) L.R. 6 Ch. 551.
[87] *Gallsworthy* v. *Selby Dam Drainage Commissioners* [1892] 1 Q.B. 348; *Re United Service Co.* (1870–71) L.R. 6 Ch. 212.
[88] *Grant* v. *United Kingdom Switchback, etc.* (1888) 40 Ch.D. 135; *Wilson* v. *West Hartlepool Ry.* (1865) 2 De G.J. & S. 475; *Libertas-Kommerz G.m.b.H.* 1978 S.L.T. 222; 1977 S.C. 191.

These purposes were extended from time to time, and the Act of 1947 dispensed with the necessity for confirmation by the court, but subject to the right of a specified minority to apply for cancellation. The present law is stated in section 5 of the 1948 Act,[89] under which the objects of a company may be altered by special resolution, so far as may be required to enable the company to do one or more of seven specified things (s. 5 (1)), but application may be made by a specified minority of shareholders or of certain debenture holders to the court to cancel the alteration (s. 5 (1) proviso).

The seven specified purposes

9–39 The Act lays down seven purposes[90] for which the objects of the company may be altered (s. 5 (1)). They permit the company to extend or restrict its business activities.

The statutory authority to alter the objects is not limited to business *ejusdem generis* but the alteration may extend to quite different business if it can be conveniently or advantageously combined with the existing business of the company (s. 5 (1) (*d*)).[91]

It can be argued that subsection (1) of section 5 does not admit the substitution of an entirely new set of objects for the existing ones. Indeed, in *Re Consett Iron Co.*,[92] Cozens-Hardy J. expressed doubts whether the court had jurisdiction under the Act then in operation to sanction an alteration which amounted to an improvement in the language of the memorandum by rewriting the objects in modern form, and accordingly in that case the old objects were left, whilst clauses setting out new objects in modern form were added. The court has, however, frequently sanctioned alterations which introduced a series of new objects in modern form instead of the old objects, and Kekewich J. in 1901, in *Re Carlisle and Cumberland Banking Co. Ltd.*,[93] sanctioned an alteration which substituted a complete new set of objects in modern form for the old concise and imperfect objects. The view that section 5 admits such rewriting of the objects clause in a modern form is supported by the wording of the section itself, which empowers a company to "alter" its objects and not merely to "extend," or "add to," them.[94]

The legislative facilities thus offered to companies for enlarging the scope of their business objects have been often made use of. Thus a

[89] The Act applies to companies formed under the Joint Stock Companies Act 1856 or any of the subsequent Companies Acts; *Re Copiapo Mining Co.* [1889] W.N. 25; 6 Mans. 320; *Re Euphrates and Tigris Steam Navigation Co.* [1904] 1 Ch. 360.

[90] The present heads were introduced as to (*a*) to (*e*) inclusive in 1890, and as to (*f*) and (*g*) in 1928.

[91] See *Re Parent Tyre Co.* [1923] 2 Ch. 222 (tyre company authorised to carry on financial operations).

[92] [1901] 1 Ch. 236.

[93] Unreported.

[94] In some cases general powers expressed in such terms were adopted (*Re New Westminster Brewery* [1911] W.N. 247; *Re Anglo-American Telegraph Co.* [1911] W.N. 248), but it often required evidence to show that these powers were really necessary.

considerable number of companies have obtained power to raise money by debentures and perpetual debenture stock.[95]

9–40 The area of a company's operations has been enlarged in several cases; several banks have largely extended their objects; other companies have been enabled to acquire other business concerns of a like nature, or enter into arrangements for joint working, or to take power to sell their undertaking; investment companies have been allowed to enlarge the scope of their investments; insurance companies to extend their objects so as to take in cognate businesses; guarantee companies to extend their business to indemnity, burglary, etc.; shipping companies or other companies engaged in transport or forwarding to extend to air transport or groupage of air and other cargo. In some cases objects have been so extended as to allow the promotion of foreign companies and holding shares in them. Many companies whose business was completely altered by the Second World War have altered their memoranda to meet the changed circumstances. An unlimited company having neither shares nor capital has been allowed to alter its memorandum.

The above instances, which are only a few of the many alterations sanctioned by the court under the earlier Acts, show how wide is the scope of the seven heads of section 5 (1). It is extremely unusual to find an alteration of objects which cannot be brought within one head or another. Since the 1948 Act there appears to be only one case[96] recorded where an objection to a proposed alteration has been upheld by the court. Here a *cy-près* provision in the company's objects clause providing for the distribution of surplus assets in the winding up of the company was altered to raise a secondary beneficiary to the position of sole and primary beneficiary. It was held that this was not an alteration enabling the company to "restrict or abandon" any of its objects or otherwise falling within section 5 (1), and accordingly the alteration was cancelled.[97]

The objecting minority

9–41 The minority entitled to object to the alteration of objects is:

(1) 15 per cent. of the issued capital of the company (s. 5 (2) (*a*)); or
(2) 15 per cent. of any class thereof (s. 5 (2) (*a*)); or
(3) 15 per cent. of any debentures issued before December 1, 1947, and secured by a floating charge (s. 5 (2) (*b*) and (5)).

If the minority wishes to object, it must, within 21 days after the resolution was passed, apply to the court for the alteration to be cancelled; the application—which is by petition[98]—may be made on behalf of the persons entitled to make it by such one or more of their number as they may appoint in writing (s. 5 (3)).

---

95 *Re Reversionary Interest Society* [1892] 1 Ch. 615.
96 *Re Hampstead Garden Suburb Trust Ltd.* [1962] Ch. 806.
97 See para. 9–42, *post*.
98 This para. refers to England. In Scotland the minority would petition the Court of Session, or sheriff court if the issued capital did not exceed £120,000.

Persons who voted in favour of, or consented to, the alteration may not join the objecting minority which must consist of those who voted against the resolution, abstained or were not present at the meeting (s. 5 (2), proviso).

If an application is made by the objecting minority in accordance with section 5, the effect of the alteration is suspended; it will only have effect in so far as confirmed by the court (s. 5 (1), proviso).

If no application is made to the court within 21 days, the validity of an alteration cannot subsequently be questioned on the ground that it was not authorised by section 5 (1) (s. 5 (9)). Thus, it appears that if the consent of all the members and debenture holders is obtained, the company has unlimited power to alter its objects, and in such a case is not restricted to the seven heads specified in section 5 (1).

Petition to court by objecting minority

9–42 The procedure to obtain cancellation of the alteration is by petition.[99]

The jurisdiction under the Act of 1929 was, by section 164, vested in the judges of the Chancery Division, including the judge to whom winding up is assigned. Section 96 of the Companies Act 1947 repealed section 164 of the Act of 1929 and substituted the provisions of the Judicature Act 1925, which makes the distribution of business subject to Rules of Court.[1]

Court orders on petition of minority

9–43 On the petition of the objecting minority, the court may make any of the following orders:

(1) it may confirm the alteration, thereby dismissing the petition; or
(2) it may cancel the alteration, thereby deciding in favour of the petitioners; or
(3) it may make a confirmation of the alteration dependent on conditions; or
(4) it may adjourn the proceedings in order that an arrangement may be made for the purchase of the interests of the dissentient members to the satisfaction of the court, and may give orders or directions for facilitating that aim (1948 Act, s. 5 (4)).
(5) it may order the purchase by the company of the shares of any member and the reduction accordingly of the company's capital and such alterations in the memorandum and articles as may be required in consequence of such order (1948 Act, s. 5 (4A) added by the 1980 Act, Sched. 3).

Although in view of the alteration of the procedure by the 1947–48 legislation (under which the confirmation by the court is no longer obligatory but is only required on application of an objecting minority) the cases decided before that legislation have only illustrative character, it is of

[99] R.S.C. 1965, Ord. 102, r. 5 (*a*).
[1] See Judicature Act 1925, s. 55 and R.S.C. 1965, Ord. 102, r. 6; *Re Mining Shares, etc. Co.* [1893] 2 Ch. 660.

practical value to note in what cases before that date the court refused confirmation and in what circumstances it imposed conditions.

9–44 CONFIRMATION REFUSED. In *Re Jewish Colonial Trust (Juedische (1) Colonialbank)*,[2] the court refused to sanction an alteration involving the abandonment of objects of the company of a fundamental character, and confining them (from a world-wide) to a limited local area. In *Re Cyclists' Touring Club*,[3] the court refused to sanction an alteration extending the objects of a company formed to cater for, protect and assist cyclists so as to include the catering for and assistance of motorists, the latter being one of the dangers against which cyclists needed protection. The court further refused its confirmation where the alteration was unconnected with and opposed to the existing objects[4]; or where the change would alter the basis of the company.[5] The Scottish courts were at one time reluctant to sanction an unqualified power to sell the whole undertaking of the company,[6] except in the case of an investment company,[7] but the most recent case[8] appears to accept that such power is legitimate in principle, at any rate on the eve of liquidation. Power to procure incorporation abroad has also been refused.[9]

9–45 CONDITIONS IMPOSED. The court may also impose some qualification or condition before sanctioning the proposed alteration. Thus, in one case where the company proposed to adopt new powers of unlimited extent the alteration was only permitted subject to modification.[10]

In other cases the power contained in section 395 (2) of the 1948 Act, enabling a company regulated by deed of settlement to adopt a memorandum and articles, has been exercised.[11]

If the alterations of the objects sanctioned were such as to render the name of the company misleading, the court often required the company's name to be changed so as to express the alteration in its aims or sphere of

---

[2] [1908] 2 Ch. 287.
[3] [1907] 1 Ch. 269.
[4] *Re Bolsom Bros. (1928) Ltd.* [1935] W.N. 9 (varied with consent [1935] W.N. 50); sanctioned on appeal on further evidence [1935] Ch. 413; see also *Strathspey Public Assembly and Agricultural Hall Co. Ltd.* v. *Anderson's Trustees*, 1934 S.C. 385. See para. 9–39, *ante*.
[5] *Re North of England, etc., Association* (1929) 45 T.L.R. 296; but see *Re Scientific Poultry Breeders' Association Ltd.* [1933] Ch. 227. *Scottish Veterans Garden City Assn.*, 1946 S.C. 417; *Glasgow Tramway, etc., Co.* v. *Magistrates of Glasgow* 1891, 18 R. 675; *Western Ranches* v. *Nelson's Trs* 1899, 1 F 812, 6 S.L.T. 396; *Kirkcaldy Cafe Co.* 1921 S.C. 861, 1921, 1 S.L.T. 286.
[6] *John Walker & Sons*, 1914 S.C. 280, 1914 1 S.L.T. 107; *Macfarlane Strang & Co.*, 1915 S.C. 196, 1914, 2 S.L.T. 414; *Aberdeen Steam Navigation Co.*, 1919 S.C. 464, 1919, 1 S.L.T. 249; *Tayside Floorcloth Co.*, 1923 S.C. 590, 1923 S.L.T. 324.
[7] *Metropolitan Reversions Ltd.*—1928 S.C. 480, 1928 S.L.T. 299.
[8] *Waverley Hydropathic Co.*, 1948 S.C. 59, 1948 S.L.T. 152.
[9] *Tayside Floorcloth, supra, Leith and Flensburg Shipping Co.*, 1925 S.N. 111.
[10] *Re John Brown Ltd.* [1914] W.N. 434; *Macfarlane, Strang & Co.*, 1915 S.C. 196; *North of Scotland, etc., Steam Navigation Co.*, 1920 S.C. 633, 1920 2 S.L.T. 176; *Union Bank of Scotland*, 1918 S.C. 21; *Edinburgh Southern Cemetery Co.*, 1923 S.C. 867, 1923 S.L.T. 514.
[11] See *Re Braintree and Bocking Gas Co. Ltd.* [1920] 2 Ch. 12.

operations.[12] The court also sometimes added words to the resolution so as to limit the extended objects.[13] These salutary powers of the court are now only available if an objecting minority applies to the court for cancellation of the alteration.

Where an order made by the court under section 5 requires the company not to make any, or any specified, alterations in the memorandum and articles, the company has no power to make any alterations in breach of the court order, except by leave of the court (s. 5 (4B) and (4C), added by the 1980 Act, Sched. 3).

Notices to Registrar

9–46 (1) Within 15 days after its passing, the special resolution of the general meeting for alteration of the objects has to be registered in pursuance of section 143 of the 1948 Act.

Registration is required in any case, whether the minority does, or does not, object.

(2) If there is no objecting minority,[14] the company may, it is submitted, at once deliver to the Registrar a printed copy of the memorandum, as altered, in compliance with section 5 (7) (*a*).

(3) If the minority is sufficiently strong to object but does not apply to the court for cancellation of the alteration within the 21 days allowed for it, the company, within 15 days from the end of that time, has to deliver to the Registrar a printed copy of the memorandum, as altered (s. 5 (7) (*a*)). Consequently, in this case the Registrar should receive the newly printed memorandum, as altered, within 36 days.

(4) If the minority has properly objected,[15] the company has

(a) at once to give notice of that fact in the prescribed form to the Registrar (s. 5 (7) (*b*) (i));

(b) within 15 days from the date of the court order confirming or cancelling the alteration

(i) to deliver to the Registrar an office copy of the order; and

(ii) if the court confirms the alteration, to deliver a printed copy of the memorandum, as altered (s. 5 (7) (*b*)).

The times for the delivery of these documents may be extended by the court (s. 5 (7), end). The Registrar cannot refuse to register the

---

[12] *Re Governments Stock Investment Co.* [1892] 1 Ch. 597; *Re Alliance Marine Assurance Co.* [1892] 1 Ch. 300; *Re National Boiler Insurance Co.* [1892] 1 Ch. 306; *Scottish Accident Insurance Co.*, 1896, 23 R. (Ct. of Sn.) 586; *Scottish Employers' Liability, etc., Assurance Co.*, 1896, 23 R. 1016; *Mutual Property Insurance Co.*, 1934 S.C. 61. A change of name was not required in, *e.g. Scottish American Investment Co.*, 1891 28 S.L.R. 421; *Northern Accident Insurance Co.*, 1893, 30 S.L.R. 834; *King Line Ltd.*, 1902, 4 F. (Ct. of Sn.) 504; *Kirkcaldy Steam Laundry Co.*, 1904, 6 F. 778; *Australian Mutual Provident Co.*, 1908, 46 S.L.R. 683.

[13] *Re Spiers and Pond* [1895] W.N. 135; *Re Fleetwood Estate Co.* [1897] W.N. 20.

[14] See para. 9–41, *ante*.

[15] See para. 9–42, *ante*.

court's order on the ground that the procedure was, in his view, irregular.[16]

Failure to give these notices or to deliver these documents renders the company and every officer in default liable to a default fine, as defined in Sched. 2 to the 1980 Act (s. 5 (8)).

Notice of special resolution for alteration of objects

9–47 The same notice of intention to move a special resolution for alteration of objects as must be given to the members has to be given to those debenture holders who are entitled to object (s. 5 (5)).[17] Notice to the trustees alone is not sufficient.[18]

No one other than the persons specified by the section may object to any alteration even if they have some interest in the company.[19]

Official notification of alteration

9–48 The Registrar must give official notification of any alteration of the memorandum in the *London Gazette*, if the company is incorporated in England and Wales, and in the *Edinburgh Gazette*, if it is registered in Scotland.

The procedure of official notification and the consequence of giving it are discussed later.[20]

Objects contained in other clauses of memorandum

9–49 If the objects of the company are contained not solely in the objects clause but likewise in other clauses of the memorandum, as may occasionally be the case, the procedure for alteration of objects appears to apply likewise to those additional clauses.[21] The company cannot, however, alter clauses in the memorandum which have to be contained in it but do not relate to the objects, *e.g.* it cannot remove unlimited liability in certain cases.[22] Clauses of the memorandum which could lawfully have been contained in the articles may, within the limits of section 23,[23] be altered by procedure similar to that provided by section 5 for the alteration of objects.[23] But where a company expresses something as an object in its memorandum, it is precluded from arguing that what is so expressed is not an object but merely a condition which could have been contained in the articles and could be altered as provided by section 23.[24]

---

16 *Proprietors of Royal Exchange Buildings, Glasgow*, 1919, 1 S.L.T. 88.
17 See para. 9–41, *ante*.
18 *Re Hampstead Garden Suburb Trust Ltd.* [1962] Ch. 806.
19 *Re Hearts of Oak Life, etc., Co. Ltd. and Reduced* [1920] 1 Ch. 544.
20 See para. 17–01, *post*.
21 *Incorporated Glasgow Dental Hospital* v. *The Lord Advocate*, 1927 S.C. 400.
22 *Re Society for Promoting Employment of Women* [1927] W.N. 145; *Scottish Special Housing Association*, 1947 S.C. 17.
23 See para. 13–03, *post*.
24 *Re Hampstead Garden Suburb Trust Ltd.* [1962] Ch. 806; for the significance of this point, see n. 2 to para. 13–03, *post*.

Statutory powers and duties independent of memorandum

Statutory powers

9–50 Besides the powers given to a company by its memorandum of association, it has numerous other supplemental powers expressly given to it by the Companies Acts 1948 to 1981. Of these the following may be mentioned, but those indicated by an asterisk (*) can only be exercised if the articles of the company so authorise:

1. Power to change its name in manner specified (1981 Act, s. 24).
2. Power to alter its articles (1948 Act, s. 10).
3. Power to have a common seal (1948 Act, s. 13 (2)).
4. Power to keep a register of members (1948 Act, s. 110).
5. Power to keep a dominion register (1948 Act, s. 119).
6. *Power to issue share warrants to bearer (1948 Act, s. 83).
7. *Power to increase its capital, consolidate its shares, convert shares into stock, and to reconvert stock into shares (1948 Act, s. 61).
8. *Power to subdivide its shares (1948 Act, s. 61).
9. *Power to reduce its capital in various ways (1948 Act, s. 66).
10. Power to make part of its uncalled capital incapable of being called up, except in a winding up (1948 Act, s. 60).
11. Power to contract without seal (1948 Act, s. 32)
12. Power to appoint an attorney to execute deeds, etc., abroad (1948 Act, s. 34).
13. Power to pay, in certain cases, commissions for taking up, underwriting or placing shares (1948 Act, s. 53).
14. *Power to issue redeemable shares (1981 Act, s. 45).
15. Power to acquire its own fully paid shares otherwise than for valuable consideration, *e.g.* by gift or bequest (1980 Act, s.35 (2)).
16. *Power to acquire its own shares in other cases (1981 Act, s. 46).

The repeal of section 14 by section 38 (1) of and Schedule VII, Part II to the Charities Act 1960 means that there is no longer an express statutory power to hold lands, but it is thought that such a power will be implied in so far as it is reasonably incidental to the company's substantive objects.[25]

Statutory duties

9–51 Together with these powers the Acts impose on a company a number of duties and obligations of which the following may be mentioned. The company must:

1. Supply to members on demand printed copies of its memorandum and articles, and of any special resolutions (1948 Act, s. 24 and 143).
2. Keep a register of members (1948 Act, s. 110) to be open for inspection (1948 Act, s. 113).

[25] As to the law prior to the repeal of s. 14, see Palmer's *Company Law* (20th ed.), pp. 132–133; bearing in mind that, since the Mortmain and Charitable Uses Acts 1888 and 1891 did not apply to Scotland, the problems caused by them did not arise in that country.

3. Prepare, lay and deliver annual returns to the Registrar, in respect of each accounting reference period, in the form prescribed by section 124 and the Sixth Schedule, as required by the 1976 Act, ss. 1 to 11.
4. Give to the Registrar notices of increase of capital and consolidation of shares, etc. (1948 Act, ss. 62 and 63).
5. Have a registered office, and notify to the Registrar its situation and any change of situation (1976 Act, s. 23).
6. Put up the name of the company outside its office or place of business, and insert it in all its business publications, etc. (s. 108). Further, insert on its business letters and order forms the place of registration, the number of registration, the address of the registered office, and where applicable, the fact that it is a limited company and the amount of its paid-up capital (European Communities Act 1972, s. 9 (7)).
7. Hold its annual general meeting every year (1948 Act, s. 131).

9–52 8. A recognised bank shall make available at its registered office the register containing certain transactions relating to its directors and other relevant persons 15 days before the date of the annual meeting (1980 Act, s. 57 (1)).
9. Register special and extraordinary resolutions (1948 Act, s. 143).
10. Keep at its registered office a register of its directors or managers and its secretary, and send a copy to the Registrar and notify changes (1948 Act, s. 200).
11. Deliver its prospectus (if any) to the Registrar for registration (1948 Act, s. 41).
12. In issuing a prospectus, comply with section 38 of the 1948 Act.
13. Where section 47 of the 1948 Act applies, refrain from allotting shares or commencing business until the requirements of those sections have been satisfied.
14. Make returns of allotments to the Registrar within one month (1948 Act, s. 52).
15. Deliver for registration contracts and make returns where shares are allotted for a consideration other than cash (1948 Act, s. 52).
16. Prepare annual accounts as prescribed in Schedules 8 or 8A to the 1948 Act (Schedule 8 is contained in Schedule 1 to the 1981 Act and Schedule 8A in Schedule 2 to the 1967 Act).
17. Comply with the requirements as to audit (1948 Act, ss. 159–161, and s. 14 of the 1967 Act).
18. Have certificates of shares ready for delivery within two months (1948 Act, s. 80).
19. Register with the Registrar of Companies all mortgages and charges to which section 95 or 106A of the 1948 Act applies.
20. Keep a register of mortgages and charges open for inspection by shareholders, creditors and the public (1948 Act, ss. 104, 105, 106I and 106J).
21. Maintain the number of the members at two (1948 Act, s. 31).

22. Keep a register of directors' interests in its shares or debentures to be open for inspection (1967 Act, s. 29).
23. If the company is a public company to keep a register of interests in shares (1981 Act, s. 73), an interest in voting shares equal to the notifiable percentage (at present 5 per cent.) has to be registered.
24. Make copies of directors' contracts of service or written memoranda thereof available for inspection by members (1967 Act, s. 26).

PRACTICE NOTE

Alteration of objects

9–53 In addition to sending to the Registrar (and to The Stock Exchange in the case of a listed company) a copy of the memorandum as altered, a copy of every special resolution must be inserted in every copy of the memorandum and articles in stock (1948 Act, s. 143) and should be sent to every person known to be in possession of a copy of the memorandum and articles (see Practice Note at para 7–35, *ante*).

CHAPTER 10

THE LIMITED LIABILITY CLAUSE

Purpose of the clause

10–01 The 1948 Act requires the memorandum of a company limited by shares or of a company limited by guarantee to state that the liability of the members is limited (1948 Act, s. 2 (2)). In compliance with this requirement, clause 4, or in a public company clause 5, of the memorandum states: "The liability of the members is limited."

Although the words notifying the limited liability of the members are the same in the memorandum of a company limited by shares as in that of a company limited by guarantee,[1] the character of limited liability varies considerably according to the nature of the company in question. This clause of the memorandum serves merely as a general notice to those dealing with the company that the liability of the members is limited but does not purport to inform third parties in what respects it is limited.

10–02 The true character of the limited liability of the members is only ascertained when the clause is read in conjunction with the provisions of the Act, in particular with those applying to the winding up of the type of company in question. The following is the result:

(1) in the case of a company limited by shares, no contribution is required from a member exceeding the amount (if any) unpaid on the shares in respect of which he is liable as a present or past member (1948 Act, s. 212 (1) (*d*));

(2) in the case of a company limited by guarantee and having no share capital, no contribution is required from a member exceeding the amount of his guarantee (1948 Act, s. 212 (1) (*e*));

(3) in the case of a guarantee company having a share capital, no contribution is required from a member exceeding the amount of his guarantee and further the amount (if any) unpaid on the shares held by him (1948 Act, s. 212 (3)). But on and after December 22, 1980 a company limited by guarantee and having a share capital can no longer be formed (1980 Act, s. 1 (2)).

Limited liability of members

10–03 The provisions of the Act limiting the liability of the members of companies limited by shares (or by guarantee) are of the utmost importance; they concern a fundamental right of the member who normally is only willing to become a member because he is aware that this right cannot be abrogated by the company or a majority of members. Accordingly, no

[1] *Cf.* Tables B, C and D.

alteration in the memorandum or the articles can, in principle, compel a member to take up more shares than the number which he held at the date when the alteration was made, or increase his liability to contribute money; any provision to the contrary in the memorandum or articles would be null and void (1948 Act, s. 22).[2] Likewise, a limited company cannot re–register as unlimited without the written assent of every member (1967 Act, s. 43).

The right of a member not to be compelled to contribute beyond the limits of the liability which he undertook when he became a member is one of the rights described by Jenkins L.J. in *Edwards* v. *Halliwell*[3] as "individual rights of membership."[4] It is, indeed, an individual membership right of the highest order because, as has been seen, it cannot be overruled by a majority of even all the members other than the opposing one.[5]

A member can, of course, by contract with another member or a third party undertake to subscribe to or acquire more shares in the company but this obligation is a contractual obligation and not an obligation flowing from his status as a member of the company.

Increased liability of members

10–04 In the following exceptional cases a member may be liable in excess of the limited liability which he undertook when he became a member:

(1) If the member agrees in writing, either before or after the alteration is made, to be bound by the alteration requiring him to take more shares or increasing his liability (1948 Act, s. 22, proviso).

It is believed that the agreement to which the proviso refers must be signed under the hand of the member or his duly authorised agent. The ordinary authority of a proxy does not imply authority to sign such a statement but merely covers the right to attend a general meeting and to vote at it (1948 Act, s. 136).

The proviso deals only with the undertaking of a member to the company and his liability *qua* member. A member can verbally agree with another member[6] or a third party to acquire further shares or to accept a higher liability than he has at the date of the agreement. Such an agreement is governed by the general principles of the law of contract.

(2) If every member agrees in writing to the re-registration of the company as unlimited, and the company is re-registered as such in accordance with the provisions of section 43 of the 1967 Act.[7]

---

[2] *McKewan's Case* (1877) 6 Ch.D. 447 and *Biddulph and District Society* v. *Agricultural Wholesale Society* [1927] A.C. 76. But see now *Hole* v. *Garnsey* [1930] A.C. 472, where it was held that the decision in the *Biddulph* case depended on the assent of the objecting member, and that an alteration in the rules imposing additional liability was not binding.
[3] [1950] 2 All E.R. 1064, 1067.
[4] See para. 58–04, *post*.
[5] On so-called expropriation clauses in articles, see para. 58–16, *post*.
[6] See *Rayfield* v. *Hands* [1960] Ch. 1.
[7] See para. 5–20, *ante*.

10–05 (3) If, to the knowledge of a member, the number of shareholders has fallen below the legal minimum, which is two members, and the company has carried on business for more than six months while the number is reduced, the remaining member is personally liable for all debts contracted by the company after the six months (1948 Act, s. 31, as substituted by the 1980 Act, Sched. 3, para. 7).

The member is in this case liable to creditors of the company directly, not to the company. Presumably a creditor can sue him jointly and severally with the company.

This increased liability hardly causes hardship to the member because it attaches only if the member is cognisant of the reduction of membership below the legal minimum. The member can avoid the extension of his liability by transferring some shares to nominees and thereby restoring the legal minimum or by petitioning for the winding up of the company (1948 Act, s. 222 (*d*), as amended by Sched. 4 of the 1980 Act).

(4) If one of the subscribers of the memorandum is a nominee of the company and fails to pay up his shares within 21 days from being called on to do so, the other subscribers are jointly and severally liable for that amount (1980 Act, s. 36 (2)). This provision is subject to exceptions which will be discussed later on.[8]

(5) Where the company has made an unlawful distribution to its members, *e.g.* has paid dividend otherwise than out of profits available for distribution, any member who, at the time of the distribution, knew or had reasonable grounds for believing that the distribution was unlawful is liable to repay what he has received or, if the distribution was otherwise than in cash, has to refund its value (1980 Act, s. 44).[9]

---

[8] See para. 12–09, *post*.

[9] *Moxham* v. *Grant* [1899] 1 Q.B. 480; affd. [1900] 1 Q.B. 88. In these cases the company sometimes sues the directors for the return of the wrongly paid dividend and the directors claim to be indemnified by such shareholders as received the money with notice of the relevant facts: see the orders of the court in *Re National Funds Assurance Co.* (1878) 10 Ch.D. 118 and *Re Alexandra Palace Co.* (1882) 21 Ch.D. 149.

CHAPTER 11

THE CAPITAL CLAUSE

Its contents

11–01 In the memorandum of a company limited by shares,[1] the capital clause must state the amount of the nominal capital, the number of shares into which it is divided, and the amount of each share (s. 2 (4) (*a*)). The "amount" must be expressed in a monetary value. This makes it impossible to issue no par value shares.[2]

The capital clause need not state anything else, and it is usually better that it should not do so.

Amount of capital

11–02 What is to be the amount of the capital is a matter left to the discretion of the promoters. It can be as small or as large as they choose. Companies have been registered as private companies with a capital of £2 or less, and others—numerous now—public or private companies, with a capital of £5,000,000 and upwards. The material consideration in fixing the amount of capital is: what funds will the company want, and how much in the shape of paid-up shares are the vendors, if any, to get? Suppose the company is to be formed to acquire a going concern, and that the price to be paid therefore is £50,000 in paid-up shares, and £50,000 in cash, and the company besides that will want a working capital of £200,000. This makes a total of £300,000. Then, in addition to this, it may be desirable to have some shares in reserve, which can be issued as and when the company wants further capital, so that, in such case, the capital may properly be fixed at, say, £400,000. Or, to take another case, the purchase consideration may be £300,000 to be paid as to £200,000 in cash and as to £100,000 in paid-up ordinary shares, and the company may determine to raise the cash part of the consideration by the issue of £100,000 of debentures and £100,000 of preference shares. In such a case the capital will be, say, £200,000, or, with an addition for working capital, £400,000. In a case where the company is not proposing to buy any existing concern or property, but to start a fresh business, the question will simply be: what sum will it cost to start the new concern and to provide sufficient working capital? The nominal capital will then be fixed accordingly.

---

[1] In the memorandum of a company limited by guarantee the capital clause states the guarantee which every member undertakes in the event of the company in winding up being unable to pay its debts (s. 2 (3) and Table C). The memorandum of a guarantee company having a share capital has two capital clauses, one relating to the guarantee and the other relating to the share capital (see Table D) but this type of company can no longer be formed as from December 22, 1980 (1980 Act, s. 1 (2)).

[2] See para. 33–3, *post*.

The authorised minimum

If it is intended that the company shall be a public company, the authorised capital must be not less than £50,000 and that amount would have to be fully subscribed. This is necessary in order to satisfy the requirements of the 1980 Act relating to the "authorised minimum" (s. 6 (1) (*a*)), which at present is fixed at £50,000 (s. 85 (1)) but the Secretary of State has power to alter this sum by statutory investment (s. 85 (1)). This applies whether the public company is formed as such or whether, as is the normal course, a private company is formed first and then re-registered as a public company, but in the latter case the requirements relating to the authorised minimum need only be satisfied on re-registration.

Amount of shares

11–03 As regards the amount of the shares, this is again for the promoters to determine. £1 shares are very common, as are shares as low as 5p each. Shares have on occasion been fixed as high as £1,000, or even £5,000 each. When the original capital is divided into several classes of shares, the amount of the different classes often varies. Some may be £1 each and others 5p each. All these are matters which have to be thought out, with reference to the special requirements of the company, by those concerned with its formation.

Classes of shares

11–04 It is not unusual to divide the shares in the original capital into two or more classes, *e.g.* preference shares and ordinary shares, or preference shares and *A* ordinary shares and *B* ordinary shares, or ordinary shares and deferred shares, or preference shares, ordinary shares, and founders' shares, and to attach various special rights, privileges and conditions to such shares. As regards preference shares and founders' shares, it is not usual to find these rights, privileges and conditions declared expressly in the memorandum of association, although extra protection is thereby secured to the holders of such entrenched shares against any alteration of their status.[3] It is not essential to specify these rights in the memorandum or, indeed, to disclose the fact that it is intended to divide the capital into different classes of shares, and in modern practice provisions relating to preference shares and founders' shares are usually found in the articles of association of the company. Thus, the memorandum may state that the capital is £100,000 divided into £1 shares, and the articles may state that of the shares in the capital 50,000 shall be preference, with specified rights attached, and 50,000 shall be ordinary shares.

Alteration of capital clause

11–05 The articles normally authorise the alteration of the capital which, when duly carried out, leads to an alteration of the capital clause.

---

[3] See further as to classes of share capital, para. 33–06, *post*.

The various respects in which the capital can be altered are treated later. It will be seen that, even where the articles authorise an alteration, a resolution of the general meeting is invariably required: the increase or diminution of capital, or the consolidation or subdivision of shares, requires an ordinary resolution (1948 Act, s. 61),[4] the reduction of capital, which normally but not necessarily, leads to an alteration of the capital clause, requires a special resolution and confirmation by the court (1948 Act, s. 66).[5]

Decimalisation of share amounts

11–06 On February 15, 1971, the Decimal Currency Act 1969 came into operation. It did not affect the amount of shares if expressed in whole pounds or multiples thereof. In that case the company could re-label the value of its shares in its memorandum in decimal currency without passing a resolution to that effect. Such an alteration involved only a change of label and not a change of substance and could therefore be effected without any formalities.[6]

Different was the position where the amount of shares was expressed in shillings and pence. In that case resolutions altering the memorandum and the articles were necessary. If the conversion could not be effected without altering the previous amount of the shares, a consolidation or subdivision of the shares had to be carried out.

[4] See para. 31–01, *post*.
[5] See para. 32–01, *post*.
[6] *Re Harris & Sheldon Group Ltd.* [1971] 1 W.L.R. 899.

CHAPTER 12

THE ASSOCIATION CLAUSE. SUBSCRIPTION OF MEMORANDUM

Association clause

12–01 The memorandum of association of a company limited by shares concludes with what is commonly referred to as the association clause,[1] whereby the subscribers declare that they desire to be formed into a company, and agree to take shares, and the clause is followed by a tabular form in which the names, addresses and descriptions of the subscribers, and the number of shares taken by each, appear.

Subscription of memorandum

Statutory requirements

12–02 These are:

(1) the memorandum has to be signed by each subscriber in the presence of at least one witness, who must attest the signature;

(2) each subscriber must write opposite to his name the number of shares which he agrees to take (1948 Act, s. 2 (4) (*c*));

(3) no subscriber may take less than one share (1948 Act, s. 2 (4) (*b*)). In practice the subscribers usually each subscribe one share; but sometimes they subscribe for a larger number.

Who may be a subscriber

12–03 Anyone may be a subscriber. A married woman may be a subscriber: so may a bankrupt, an alien,[2] or a minor,[3] but not where the objects indicate that minors are not to be members.[4] An incorporated company with the requisite power may be a subscriber, and several persons may jointly be subscribers. An English partnership cannot subscribe since it is not a legal person, and its partners must do so individually; a Scottish firm, however, may subscribe by the firm name since it is a separate legal person.

---

[1] *Cf.* for private companies: Sched. 1 of Table B of 1948 Act; for public companies: Sched. 1, Pt. I of 1980 Act; similar clauses are used in the cases of guarantee and unlimited companies: see Tables C, D and E.

[2] *Princess of Reuss* v. *Bos* (1871) L.R. 5 H.L. 176.

[3] *Re Laxon & Co. (No. 2)* [1892] 3 Ch. 555. *Hill* v. *City of Glasgow Bank* (1880) 7 R. (Ct. of Sn.) 68. In England and Wales the age of majority was reduced from 21 to 18 by the Family Law Reform Act 1969, s. 1. In Scots law a minor is a boy aged 14 but under 18 or a girl aged 12 but under 18; a child below the age of minority is a pupil and cannot subscribe. (The status of pupillage is unknown in England and Wales.) The age of majority was reduced in Scotland from 21 to 18 by the Age of Majority (Scotland) Act 1969.

[4] *Seymour* v. *Royal Naval School* [1910] 1 Ch. 806, 811.

Number of subscribers

12–04 In a private and a public company the minimum number of subscribers is two (s. 1 (1) and 1980 Act, s. 2 (1)).

How to subscribe

12–05 A subscriber usually subscribes the memorandum in his own hand; but he can subscribe by the hand of an agent duly authorised by him.[5] The Registrar does not call for evidence of authenticity if the subscriber subscribes in his own hand.

In subscribing the memorandum of association care must be taken to write clearly. The number of shares subscribed for may be in words or figures, but if more than one share is subscribed the words or figures must be written by each subscriber. The signature should set out the full name of the subscriber, and should be followed by the subscriber's county or address, clearly written, and sufficiently explicit, and also by words denoting his occupation, or, if he has none, stating the fact. Thus the term "broker" should be qualified by stating what sort of broker. "Clerk" should also be qualified; but it is not necessary to state to whom the subscriber is clerk. It is sufficient to say, for example, "clerk to a public company." It is thought that the description "company director" is sufficient, but this is not free from doubt and the view is sometimes expressed that the subscriber has to add the name of the company, other than the one whose memorandum is being subscribed.

Attention to such details as these is necessary, otherwise, when the document comes before the Registrar of Companies, he may refer it back, on the ground that he cannot read the signatures, or that some of the requisite particulars are not clearly expressed. It is his duty to see that the statutory requirements are complied with, and that the documents are in order.[6]

Witnesses

12–06 As regards the witnesses to the signatures of the subscribers, one witness for all the signatures will suffice, and, in that case, the words "Witness to the above signatures" will be used; but sometimes the same witness cannot attest all the signatures, and in that case the attestation clause must be altered. It may run thus:

Witness to the above signatures other than that of A,

or,

Witness to the signatures of the above B,

The witness or witnesses must in each case give his or their address and occupation. This also should be clearly written and sufficiently explicit for identification. One of the subscribers cannot witness and attest the signature of the other subscriber or subscribers.

---

[5] *Re Whitley Partners* (1886) 32 Ch.D. 337.
[6] *Peel's Case* (1867) L.R. 2 Ch. 674, 682.

A subscriber to the memorandum cannot, after the issue of the certificate of registration, repudiate his subscription on the ground that he was induced to sign by misrepresentation.[7]

Subscribers as members

12–07 The subscribers of the memorandum are deemed to have agreed to become members of the company, and on its registration shall be entered as members in its register of members (1948 Act, s. 26 (1)).[8]

Liability of subscribers

12–08 The subscribers of the memorandum of a private or public company need pay nothing to the company on subscription; their undertaking to pay when called upon is sufficient.

As will be seen later in the chapter on Commencement of Business (Chapter 19), a private company can commence business at once on the grant of the certificate of incorporation irrespective of the amount subscribed and although nothing has been paid by the subscribers, but in the case of a public company the position is different.

Each subscriber is liable to pay to the company the full amount of the shares for which he has subscribed, when a call to pay up is made on him by the directors or on the date or dates fixed for payment. In a private company such payment may be in cash or kind as arranged, but the subscribers to the memorandum of a public company must always pay cash (1980 Act, s. 29).

The obligation to pay for the shares subscribed applies even if the subscriber is the nominee of another person (s. 117). Logically, a subscriber to the memorandum cannot act as the nominee of the company itself because, when he subscribes, the company has not come into existence yet, but it is clear from section 36 (2) (*a*) of the 1980 Act that the legislator envisages even this possibility; such a nominee is also personally liable for the amount subscribed (s. 36 (1)).

Joint and several liability of subscribers

12–09 If one of the subscribers to the memorandum has acted as a nominee of the company and he fails to pay up his shares within 21 days from being called on to do so, the other subscribers are jointly and severally liable for that amount (1980 Act, s. 36 (2)).

The other subscribers are not so liable if the company does not have a beneficial interest in the shares held by the nominee (1980 Act, s. 36 (6) (*a*)) or the court has granted them relief (1980 Act, s. 36 (3) and (4)).

---

[7] *Re Metal Constituents Ltd., Lord Lurgan's Case* [1902] 1 Ch. 707. See para. 16–04 *post.*
[8] See para. 49–03, *post.*

Acquisition of assets from the subscribers

2–10 A public company shall not acquire from the subscribers to the memorandum assets equal in value to at least one-tenth of the issued capital during two years from the issue of the certificate of incorporation unless a valuation report of an independent valuer is provided and the general meeting, with notice of that report, has approved the acquisition by ordinary resolution (1980 Act, s. 26).

Similar provisions apply, *mutatis mutandis*, on the re-registration of a private company as a public company (*ibid.*).

Irregular subscriptions

2–11 If an irregularity occurs in connection with the subscription to a memorandum, the question is whether relief is sought before or after the grant of the certificate of incorporation.

Before the grant of that certificate the usual remedies are available, *e.g.* for misrepresentation, fraud, etc.

After the grant of the certificate of incorporation the position is different: the certificate is conclusive evidence that all matters precedent to the incorporation have been complied with and that the company was registered under the Act. In view of this character of the certificate of incorporation,[9] irregularities relating to the subscription, such as the signature by less than the prescribed number of subscribers or the forgery of the signature of a subscriber, would not affect the status and existence of the company as a legal person although such irregularities might give rise to claims between the subscribers.

---

[9] See para. 16–05, *post*.

Chapter 13

EFFECT AND ALTERATION OF MEMORANDUM

Effect of memorandum

13–01 Speaking generally, the memorandum has the same effect as if it had been a deed duly signed and sealed by each member and as if it contained covenants on the part of each member to observe all the provisions of the memorandum (1948 Act, s. 20).

The same effect is accorded by section 20 to the articles, and since the judicial interpretation of the section relates mainly to that aspect of it, it is convenient to consider the section later on in the chapter dealing with the articles of association.[1] What is said there applies to the effect of the memorandum as a deed *mutatis mutandis*.

Alteration of memorandum

Alteration of obligatory clauses

13–02 The Act does not provide a uniform procedure for the alteration of the six or, in the case of a public company, seven obligatory clauses of the memorandum. On the contrary, it authorises their alteration only in the mode and to the extent for which express provision is made in the Act, and, apart from these cases, prohibits the alteration of the conditions of the memorandum (1948 Act, s. 4).

Consequently, the only obligatory clauses of the memorandum which can be altered in the manner described earlier are:

(1) the name clause (see para. 7–28, *ante*);
(2) in the case of a public company, the clause that the company has this status (see para. 5–09, on re-registration of the public company as a private company);
(3) the objects clause (see para. 9–38, *ante*);
(4) the limited liability clause (see paras. 5–17 and 5–20, on re-registration of an unlimited as a limited company and vice versa); and
(5) the capital clause (see para. 11–05, *ante,* and paras 31–01 and 32–01, *post*).

Alteration of additional clauses

13–03 Occasionally additional provisions are inserted into the memorandum, clauses, for example, defining rights attached to different classes of shares, rights as regards dividend, voting and participation in assets on a winding up, and various other matters. There is nothing illegal in the insertion in

---

[1] See para. 14–07, *post*.

the memorandum of such additional provisions, which likewise could have been contained in the articles, but it must be borne in mind that, if inserted without qualification, they become conditions contained in the company's memorandum within the meaning of section 4 of the 1948 Act.

The provisions applying to the alteration of these additional clauses of the memorandum are as follows:

(1) On principle, these additional clauses can be altered in the same manner as the objects of the company, *viz.* by special resolution of the general meeting, subject to the right of a minority of 15 per cent. of the issued share capital or any class thereof[2] to object to the alteration within 21 days from the date of the resolution by applying to the court for the alteration to be cancelled (1948 Act, s. 23 (1) and (3)), as amended by the 1980 Act, Sched. 3, para 6).

(2) This principle does not, however, apply

  (a) if the memorandum itself prohibits the alteration. In this case the rights of the shareholders stated in the memorandum become entrenched rights, *i.e.* they are unalterable;

  (b) if the memorandum provides procedure for the alteration (which procedure has precedence over the statutory rule); and

  (c) to a variation or abrogation of class rights of any class of members (1948 Act, s. 23 (2)).[3]

(3) Further, if a provision is contained in the objects clause, the appropriate procedure for alteration is that of section 5, and not that of section 23.[4] The difference between these two procedures is indicated above.[5]

Alteration to be embodied into memorandum

13–04 Any alteration of the memorandum, whether of the obligatory or of the additional clauses, has to be embodied into the memorandum, and the issue of a copy of the memorandum which does not contain the alteration renders the company and its officers in default liable to a fine (1948 Act, s. 25) which is defined in Schedule 2 to the 1980 Act.

The members of the company are entitled to a copy of the memorandum and of the articles, in their latest form, on payment of a sum not exceeding 5p (s. 24).[6]

Reprinting of memorandum in case of alterations

13–05 All alterations of the memorandum must be notified to the Registrar. The alterations of the name clause, the objects clause and the non-

---

[2] A minority of debenture holders is not entitled to apply under this section (see s. 23 (3) and s. 5 (2) (*b*)).

[3] See para. 33–07, *post*.

[4] *Re Hampstead Garden Suburb Trust Ltd.* [1962] Ch. 806; see para. 9–49, *ante*.

[5] See note 2, *supra*.

[6] The conversion from the pre-decimal reference to the shilling in s. 24 to new pence was carried out by the Decimal Currency Act 1969, s. 10.

obligatory clauses of the memorandum, if alterable, require special resolutions, and the obligation to notify follows in these cases from section 143 (4) (*a*) of the 1948 Act. The increase of capital requires only an ordinary resolution but here the duty to notify is provided for in section 63, and the reduction of capital again requires a special resolution and section 143 (4) (*a*) applies.

The duty to notify the Registrar of any alteration of the memorandum brings into operation section 9 (5) of the European Communities Act 1972. That section provides that the company shall send with the notice of alteration "a printed copy of the memorandum . . . as altered." The only exception thereto is the alteration of the objects of the company by virtue of section 5 of the 1948 Act, but that exception is only apparent because section 5 (7) (*a*) already stipulates the sending of a printed copy of the memorandum to the Registrar.[7]

What constitutes a "printed copy of the memorandum" is explained in the notice of the Department of Trade reproduced earlier (see para. 8–07, *ante*).

Failure to comply with section 9 (5) of the European Communities Act 1972 exposes the company and any officer in default to a default fine as defined in Schedule 2 to the Companies Act 1980.

Official notification of alteration

13–06 Official notification of any document making or evidencing an alteration of the memorandum has to be given by virtue of the European Communities Act 1972, s. 9 (3) (*b*), and the effect of the alteration depends on the proper publication of the official notification (s. 9 (4) (*b*)).

These topics are treated in para. 17–01, *post*.

[7] Although the time for sending the printed memorandum is calculated differently.

D. ARTICLES OF ASSOCIATION

CHAPTER 14

THE ARTICLES OF ASSOCIATION

Form and subscription: Table A

14–01 As already mentioned, the memorandum of association, when submitted to the Registrar for registration, may be accompanied by articles of association, containing regulations[1] for the management of the affairs of the company, and in some cases articles must be so registered (s. 6).[2]

If no articles[3] are registered, the articles contained in Table A of the 1948 Act under which the company is incorporated are to apply to the company.[4] Thus, any company registered under that Act automatically adopts the regulations in Table A of the Act except in so far as it has excluded them (1948 Act, s. 8 (2)).

There are three alternative forms in which a company may adopt articles:

(1) it may adopt Table A in full[5];

(2) it may wholly exclude Table A and set out its own regulations in full;

(3) it may set out its own articles and adopt part of Table A, by not expressly excluding the application of Table A.

Both courses (2) and (3) are of common occurrence. The partial adoption of Table A has particular advantages for small companies, first because of economy of printing, and secondly because any provision of Table A is legal beyond any doubt.[6]

Completion of lacunae in the articles

14–02 It happens sometimes that articles adopted by the company do not provide a comprehensive regulation of the internal affairs of the company. The question then arises how these *lacunae* have to be filled. Here two cases have to be distinguished.

(a) The company has expressly excluded the application of Table A. The *lacuna* can only be filled by reference to the general law.

---

[1] The expression "regulations" was used in a similar sense in the Companies Acts 1862 to 1929.

[2] Namely, in the case of a company limited by guarantee or an unlimited company.

[3] As defined in s. 455.

[4] See s. 459 (14) (*b*)–(*e*) of the Act of 1948, and see also s. 455 defining the word "articles."

[5] Formerly, under the 1948 Act, Table A was divided into two Parts. Part I was suitable for public companies and Part II for private companies. The 1980 Act, Sched. 4, repealed Part II, and Table A now consists only of Part I which applies, unless excluded, to private and public companies.

[6] See *per* Kay L.J. in *Lock* v. *Queensland Investment and Land Mortgage Co.* [1896] 1 Ch. 397, 406–407.

(b) The company has not expressly excluded the application of Table A, *i.e.* it has partially adopted that regulation. The *lacuna* is filled by reference to Table A.

The Interpretation Act 1978 applies to Table A and to articles which adopt Table A in part.[7]

Table A is applicable to private and public companies

14–03 Table A of the 1948 Act was divided into two Parts. Part I applied to the management of public companies and Part II to that of private companies.

The 1980 Act abolished this division. It repealed the regulations contained in Part II (Sched. 4) and also amended some of the regulations contained in Part I (Sched. 3, para. 36). The abolition of the division of Table A became necessary to give effect to the new classification of companies under which the normal and residual form of companies is that of the private company.

Form of articles

14–04 If articles are registered, they must be expressed in separate paragraphs numbered consecutively. Moreover, they must be printed and must be signed by the subscribers to the memorandum of association. Each subscriber must sign in the presence of a witness, who must attest the signature (1948 Act, s. 9). As in the case of the memorandum, the signature may be under the signatory's own hand or that of his duly authorised agent.[8] A subscriber cannot attest the signature of another.

Copies

14–05 Each member of the company is entitled to a copy of the memorandum and articles (1948 Act, s. 24) on payment of a sum not exceeding 5p.

Where articles have been registered, a copy of every special resolution or other resolution listed in section 143 (4) of the 1948 Act, as amended, for the time being in force is to be annexed to or embodied in every copy of the articles of association that may be issued after the passing of such resolution; where no articles have been registered, a copy of any such resolution is to be forwarded[9] to any member requesting the same on payment of 5p or such less sum as the company may direct (s. 143 (3)). There is a penalty for default, as defined in Schedule 2 of the 1980 Act.

Relation of the articles to the memorandum

14–06 This topic has been discussed at para. 6–05, *ante*. There it has been stated, *inter alia*, that though the articles cannot alter or control the

[7] *Fell* v. *Derby Leather Co.* [1931] 2 Ch. 252.
[8] See para. 12–05, *ante*.
[9] On a literal interpretation, it appears that copies of resolutions to be forwarded to members are still required to be printed, although this requirement no longer applies to copies forwarded to the Registrar (see s. 143 (3) and *cf*. s. 51 (2) of the 1967 Act.) This interpretation, however, would be highly unsatisfactory.

memorandum; they can be used to explain an ambiguity in its terms but not so as to extend the objects of the company.

Interpretation of articles

4–07 Articles of association are commercial documents. They should not be interpreted as meticulously as, *e.g.* conveyances. In interpreting them, the maxim *ut res magis valeat quam pereat* should be applied[10] which, in the words of Vaisey J.,[11] "directs us to 'validate if possible.' " Thus Jenkins L.J. said in *Holmes* v. *Keyes*[12]:

> "I think that the articles of association of the company should be regarded as a business document and should be construed so as to give them reasonable business efficacy, where a construction tending to that result is admissible on the language of the articles, in preference to a result which would or might prove unworkable. In my view, the (view) for which the plaintiffs contend would produce a wholly unreasonable result, and I decline to adopt it unless constrained to do so by the terms of the Act and the articles."

4–08 Thus, in *Rayfield* v. *Hands*,[13] the articles of a private company provided:

> "11. Every member who intends to transfer shares shall inform the directors who will take the said shares equally between them at a fair value but subject to the above no person shall hold more than 1,000 shares in the capital of the company."

The plaintiff, a shareholder, informed the defendants as directors of the company of his intention to transfer his shares to them as provided by article 11 but they were unwilling to accept the transfer and contended that the article did not impose an enforceable liability upon them. They founded their objection mainly on the construction of article 11, arguing that the words "the directors who will take the said shares" did not create an obligation but imported merely an option on the part of the directors and that article 11 was unworkable if, *e.g.* the offering member himself was a director.

Vaisey J. rejected both arguments and held that, on its proper construction, article 11 imposed an obligation on the defendants to purchase the plaintiff's shares at a fair price. In this connection the learned judge observed that the articles as a commercial document should not be construed too meticulously, that the language of article 11 was that of a mutual obligation between the offering shareholder and the directors who had to accept the shares offered for purchase, and there was no reason to invalidate the article in the case before him (in which effect could be given to it), on the ground that it might be difficult to enforce the article in other, hypothetical, circumstances.

---

10 *Per* Wynn-Parry J. in *Re Hartley Baird Ltd.* [1955] Ch. 143, 146.
11 In *Rayfield* v. *Hands* [1960] Ch. 1, 4.
12 [1959] Ch. 199, 215.
13 [1960] Ch. 1.

Vaisey J. then considered "the most difficult" point whether the obligation imposed by article 11 on the directors was a corporate obligation which could only be enforced by the company or whether it was a personal contractual obligation which could be enforced by the plaintiff without joining the company (see para. 14–13, *post*). He decided in favour of the latter view and gave judgment for the plaintiff.

Subject-matter of articles

14–09 The matters with which a company's articles usually deal are—

(1) the exclusion, wholly or in part, of Table A;
(2) the execution or adoption of a preliminary agreement, if any, subject to the provisions of the 1980 Act (s. 26);
(3) power of the directors to issue "relevant securities" (see 1980 Act, s. 14 (1) and (10));
(4) in a private company, the exclusion of the pre-emption rights of the shareholders in respect to the issue of equity securities for cash (1980 Act, s. 17 (9));
(5) calls and forfeiture for non-payment of calls;
(6) transfer and transmission of shares;
(7) increase of capital;
(8) reduction of capital;
(9) borrowing;
(10) general meetings;
(11) directors;
(12) dividends and reserve fund;
(13) accounts and audit;
(14) notices;
(15) special provisions for winding up.

These various matters will be found dealt with under their respective headings.

Binding force of articles

14–10 Articles when registered bind the company and its members to the same extent as if they had been signed and sealed by each member, and contained covenants on the part of each member to observe all the provisions of the articles (1948 Act, s. 20 (1)). The same, as has been seen, is true of the memorandum. If no articles are registered Table A has the same effect, and if articles adopt Table A in part, that part of Table A which is adopted has likewise the same effect. Any alteration to the articles is, for this purpose, treated as if it were part of the original articles and will bind the company and its members accordingly.[14]

---

[14] s. 10 (2) and s. 455.

The members bound to the company by implied covenant

14–11 The members are thus all bound to the company by the implied covenant. Where, *e.g.* the articles gave the company a lien on the shares of a member, it was held that the plaintiff, being a member, was to be treated as having covenanted with the company to give it such lien.[15] Lord Blackburn said[16]: "This property in the shares was, by virtue of the sixteenth section of the Act already quoted [the corresponding section of the 1862 Act], bound to the company as much as if he had (at the time he became holder of these shares) executed a covenant to the company in the same terms as article 103." Again, Lord Herschell observed[17]: "It is quite true that the articles constitute a contract between each member and the company." Similarly, Lord Kilbrandon observed[18] with reference to an article which was similar in content to regulation 80 of Table A: "This is a term of the contract between the shareholders and the company." And Bowen L.J. said[19]: "We must consider what are the rights of the directors and shareholders, for the articles of association by section 16[20] are to bind all the company and all the shareholders as much as if they had all put their seals to them." That this is the true construction follows from the many decisions in which it has been held that the company is entitled to sue its members for the enforcement, and to restrain the breach by them of its articles, and to treat as irregular anything which is done in contravention thereof.[21] Where, however, the terms of the articles are contrary to public policy, the courts will not enforce them.[22]

How far binding between members

14–12 In *Wood* v. *Odessa Waterworks Co.*[23] Stirling J. said[24]:

> "The articles of association constitute a contract not merely between the shareholders and the company, but between each individual shareholder and every other."

If this statement is taken literally—although it cannot be argued on the strength of it that a shareholder can enforce a duty owed by another shareholder[25] or by a director[26] to the company—it can be contended that it means that one shareholder can enforce the articles, or any covenant in

---

15 *Bradford Banking Co.* v. *Briggs, Son & Co.* (1886) 12 App.Cas. 29.
16 At p. 33.
17 *Welton* v. *Saffery* [1897] A.C. 299, 315.
18 *Alexander Ward & Co. Ltd.* v. *Samyang Navigation Co. Ltd.* [1975] 1 W.L.R. 673, 683 (P.C.); 1975 S.L.T. (H.L.) 126; 1975 S.C. (H.L.) 26.
19 *Imperial Hydropathic, etc., Co., Blackpool* v. *Hampson* (1882) 23 Ch.D. 1, 13.
20 Of the Act of 1862, which corresponds to s. 20 of the Act of 1948.
21 *Imperial Hydropathic, etc., Co., Blackpool* v. *Hampson* (1882) 23 Ch.D. 1; *Macdougall* v. *Gardiner* (1875) 1 Ch.D. 13; *Pender* v. *Lushington* (1877) 6 Ch.D. 70; *Harben* v. *Phillips* (1883) 23 Ch.D. 14.
22 *St. Johnstone F.C. Ltd.* v. *Scottish Football Association Ltd.* 1965 S.L.T. 171.
23 (1889) 42 Ch.D. 636.
24 At p. 642.
25 *Foss* v. *Harbottle* (1843) 2 Hare 461; *Burland* v. *Earle* [1902] A.C. 83, 93 (for the rule in *Foss* v. *Harbottle* and the exceptions to it, see paras. 58–09 *et seq., post*).
26 *Macdougall* v. *Gardiner* (1875) 1 Ch.D. 13.

them, against another shareholder, at any rate in the capacity of shareholder.[27] It is submitted that this contention is not entirely correct. Lord Herschell said in *Welton* v. *Saffery*,[28] and this has never been dissented from:

> "It is quite true that the articles constitute a contract between each member and the company, and that there is no contract in terms between the individual members of the company; but the articles do not any the less, in my opinion, regulate their rights inter se."

The result seems to be that the articles constitute the agreement between the members, but that normally they can only enforce such agreement through the medium of the company.

Exceptionally, however, a stipulation in the articles has to be interpreted as a personal undertaking by a member and in such a case the other members may sue him, not *qua* member, but on the personal contractual undertaking in the articles, without joining the company as a party.[29]

How far binding on the company

14–13 IN RELATION TO MEMBERS AS MEMBERS. The company is bound to its members in the same way as the members are bound to the company, and just as the liabilities imposed upon a member are limited to liabilities incurred by him in this capacity,[30] so are the rights which he has against the company limited to rights *qua* member. Consequently, a right purported to be conferred upon him by the articles as a director or as an outsider cannot normally be enforced by him by virtue of the articles.[31]

The wording of section 20, "the articles shall bind the company," makes it clear that the company is to be deemed to have covenanted with the members as such. This construction is supported by numerous decisions showing that the company is bound. Thus, in *Johnson* v. *Lyttle's Iron Agency*,[32] an irregular forfeiture of shares was impeached by a member, and set aside by the Court of Appeal on the ground, as James L.J. said, that the notice prior to forfeiture "did not comply strictly with the provisions of the contract between the company and the shareholders which is contained in the regulations." In *Oakbank Oil Co.* v. *Crum*,[33] it was held that the plaintiff, a member, was entitled, as against the company, to insist on the observance of the articles as to dividends so long as they stood unaltered. Further, in *Wood* v. *Odessa Waterworks Co.*,[34] Stirling J. granted an injunction, at the instance of a member, to restrain the defen-

---

[27] See *supra*.
[28] [1897] A.C. 299, 315.
[29] *Borland's Trustees* v. *Steel Bros. & Co. Ltd.* [1901] 1 Ch. 279; *Rayfield* v. *Hands* [1960] Ch. 1. See the analogous case of the company being bound to a shareholder on a personal undertaking, para. 14–14, *post*.
[30] See para. 10–03, *ante*.
[31] See below.
[32] (1877) 5 Ch.D. 687.
[33] (1882) 8 App.Cas. 65.
[34] (1889) 42 Ch.D. 636.

dant company from contravening the articles. In *Burdett* v. *Standard Exploration Co.*,[35] Cozens-Hardy J. held that a member was entitled to enforce compliance by the company with a clause in the articles giving him a right to a share certificate.

14–14 IN RELATION TO MEMBERS IN SOME OTHER CAPACITY. The decisions discussed in the preceding paragraph all deal with cases in which members claimed and sought to enforce or protect rights given them as members of the company. Where rights are by the articles given to members not as such, but in some other capacity (*e.g.* as directors, policy holders, or otherwise), a member claiming to enforce them cannot, it seems, sue on the articles—treating them as a contract by the company with him—he must make out a contract outside the articles.

Thus, in *Eley* v. *Positive, etc., Co.*,[36] the articles contained a clause providing that A should be employed for life as solicitor for the company, and should not be removed except for misconduct; he took office and was so employed for some time, and, whilst so employed, he became a shareholder; later on the company discontinued his employment; he, still being a shareholder, sued for breach of contract, and it was held that no action lay, for the right which he attempted to enforce was conferred upon him in a capacity other than that of a shareholder. The matter was disposed of rather summarily in the Court of Appeal; Lord Cairns L.C. delivered the judgment of the court, and refused the plaintiff relief. After saying that the articles "are an agreement *inter socios*," he continued: "Now, so far as that is concerned, it is *res inter alios acta*; the plaintiff is no party to it. . . .[37] This article is either a stipulation which would bind the members, or else a mandate to the directors. In either case it is a matter between the directors and shareholders, and not between them and the plaintiff."

This case was followed in *Browne* v. *La Trinidad*,[38] where the articles contained a provision that a contract with the plaintiff, made before incorporation, should be adopted by the company, and that it was thereby confirmed, and that the provisions thereof, so far as applicable to the company, should be construed as part of the regulations. Yet it was held that the plaintiff, though a member of the company, had no cause of action against the company on this clause. Lindley L.J. said[39]:

> "Having regard to the construction put upon section 16 [of 1862][40] in the case of *Eley* v. *Positive, etc., Co.*, and subsequent cases,[41] it must be taken as settled that the contract upon which he (the plaintiff) relies is not a contract upon which he can maintain any action, either on the common law side or the equity side. There might have been

---

35 (1899) 16 T.L.R. 112.
36 (1876) 1 Ex.D. 20, 88.
37 Although he was a member (*the Editor*).
38 (1887) 37 Ch.D. 1.
39 At p. 14.
40 Corresponding to s. 20 of the Act of 1948.
41 None to be found (*the Editor*).

some difficulty in arriving at that conclusion if it had not been for the authorities, because it happens that this gentleman has had shares allotted to him and is therefore a member."

A provision in the articles providing for arbitration in case of disputes between the members and the company has been held not to be a written agreement for submission to arbitration of a dispute between the company and a director.[42]

14–15 It is not easy to reconcile the rule laid down in these decisions with section 20, which expressly provides that the regulations "shall bind the company and the members thereof," but they must be taken to have settled the law in this respect. The effect of these decisions is that the implied covenant only binds the members to observe such of the provisions of the articles as concern their rights, privileges, powers and obligations as members.

Finding a difficulty in applying the above rule consistently with justice the courts have in some cases acted on the footing that a clause in the articles, not dealing with the rights of a member as such, but apparently intended to operate as a contract with him, is to be regarded as the basis of a contract, *i.e.* as indicating the terms on which the company proposes to contract with him, and that, if the parties enter into the relations contemplated by the clause, they are to be treated as having made a contract in the terms of the clause and are bound accordingly. This is illustrated by *Swabey* v. *Port Darwin Gold Mining Co.*[43] In that case the articles provided for the payment to each director by way of remuneration of a specified sum per annum. By a special resolution, in July, the company reduced this as from the end of the preceding year. The plaintiff thereupon resigned, and sued the company for three months' remuneration for services prior to the date of his resignation; and the court held that he was entitled to recover on the footing of an implied contract in the terms of the clause. "The articles," said Lord Esher, "do not themselves form a contract, but from them you get the terms upon which the director is serving." This proposition was adopted by Stirling J. in *Re International Cable Co.*,[44] and by Wright J. in *Ex p. Beckwith*.[45] Moreover, the principle involved is not confined to members; it extends also to outsiders, *e.g.* to persons who take office as directors.[46] If a contract is implied in this way a person who has acted in accordance with it cannot be deprived, by an alteration of the articles, of rights accrued thereunder.[47] But a change of articles would in

42 *Beattie* v. *Beattie* [1938] Ch. 708; *Hickman* v. *Kent, etc., Assn.* [1915] 1 Ch. 881.
43 (1889) 1 Meg. 385.
44 (1892) 66 L.T. 253.
45 [1898] 1 Ch. 324.
46 *Isaacs' Case* [1892] 2 Ch. 158; *Salisbury-Jones and Dale's Case* [1894] 3 Ch. 356; *Pritchard's Case* (1873) L.R. 8 Ch. 956.
47 *Re European Assurance Society Arbitration Acts, Doman's Case* (1876) 3 Ch.D. 21; *Re Argus Life Assurance Co.* (1888) 39 Ch.D. 571; *Swabey* v. *Port Darwin Gold Mining Co.* (1889) 1 Meg. 385.

many instances, it is submitted, be valid to alter the terms of the implied contract[48] for the future, at least after a period of reasonable notice.[49]

The line of cases from *Eley* v. *Positive, etc., Co.* may not be valid in Scotland. In Scots law two contracting parties may confer rights upon a third party which that third party is entitled to enforce, provided that the contract shows that this was the parties' intention (*jus quaesitum tertio*).[50] It is therefore conceivable that, if the point arose, a Scottish court would reach a different conclusion from these English authorities.

14–16 BINDING UPON DIRECTORS. The directors of a company are bound by the articles. Their powers are to be derived from the articles and they must observe any restrictions imposed upon them by the latter. If they act otherwise than in accordance with the provisions of the articles two separate effects have to be considered: the first is the effect of such acts *vis-à-vis* third parties, and, secondly, the effect within the company. The former is dealt with later when the rule in *Royal British Bank* v. *Turquand*[51] is considered. As regards the latter, the directors render themselves liable to an action at the instance of the members. If as a result of the breach of duty any loss has resulted to the company the directors are liable to refund to the company any damage so suffered.

Alteration of articles

The power to alter

14–17 Section 10 (1) of the 1948 Act gives to a company power by special resolution, but "subject to the provisions of the Companies Acts 1948 to 1981 and to the conditions contained in its memorandum," to alter its articles, and it expressly provides that "any alteration so made . . . shall . . . be as valid as if originally contained therein, and be subject in like manner to alteration by special resolution." Nothing could be wider than the terms of this section. It does not say that the articles for the management or administration of the business may be altered, or that the articles, other than those which form part of the constitution of the company, may be altered; there is no limitation, except that the power is to be subject to the Acts and the memorandum. Subject to this, therefore, all or any of the articles may be altered, and a company cannot by a clause in its articles exempt any article from liability to alteration under the section.[52]

---

[48] As to express contracts, see *Nelson* v. *James Nelson & Sons Ltd.* [1914] 2 K.B. 770; and see *Punt* v. *Symons & Co.* [1903] 2 Ch. 506; *Baily* v. *British Equitable Assurance Co.* [1904] 1 Ch. 374 (reversed by the House of Lords [1906] A.C. 35, on the ground that there was in fact no contract); and *British Murac Rubber Syndicate Ltd.* v. *Alperton Rubber Co.* [1915] 2 Ch. 186.

[49] *Cf. Martin-Baker Aircraft Co.* v. *Canadian Flight Equipment Ltd.*; *Same* v. *Murison* [1955] 2 Q.B. 556.

[50] See further Walker, *Contracts* (Butterworths, 1979), paras. 29–11 to 29–16.

[51] (1856) 6 E. & B. 327; see para. 28–10, *post*.

[52] *Walker* v. *London Tramways Co.* (1879) 12 Ch.D. 705; *Malleson* v. *National Insurance, etc., Corporation* [1894] 1 Ch. 200.

This applies not only as between the company itself and its shareholders,[53] but likewise as between the company and an outsider.[54]

At an early period, however, in the history of the Act of 1862, a construction was placed on the corresponding section in the Companies Act 1856 which for many years had the effect of fettering to a large extent the freedom of companies under the Act of 1862. The case was *Hutton* v. *Scarborough Cliff Hotel Co.* (*No. 2*).[55] The company there was desirous of issuing some of the shares in the original capital as preference shares, but there being no power in its memorandum or articles to do so, the court held that[56] it could not be done. It was then proposed to alter the articles of association so as to enable new shares to be created and issued with a preference attached to them; but it was held that this again could not be done, as it amounted to an alteration of the constitution of the company and was, therefore, *ultra vires* and invalid.

This decision was for many years recognised as authoritative but in *British and American Corporation* v. *Couper*[57] Lord Macnaghten dissented from it and it was finally overruled by the Court of Appeal in *Andrews* v. *Gas Meter Co.*[58] In that case the original articles contained no power to issue preference shares, but the company, by special resolution, had altered its articles so as to take power, and had issued preference shares accordingly. The court overruled *Hutton* v. *Scarborough Cliff Hotel Co.* (*No. 2*),[59] and held the alteration to be effective.

Consents to alteration

14–18 A provision in the articles that any specific article may only be altered with the consent of a named person is valid, and without such consent any attempted alteration would be ineffective. But the article which provides for such consent to be given can itself be altered and the person named cannot prevent this or have any rights in default.

If it is desired to ensure in company law that a particular article shall not be altered except with the agreement of a specific person, this can be achieved in one of two ways: either the person to be protected can be issued with shares of a separate class, whose class rights (alterable only with the consent of the class) include the right to veto any alteration of the article concerned; or alternatively, if the company is a private company, the article concerned may include a term that, upon any resolution proposed to alter it, the shares held by the person to be protected shall carry

---

53 *Allen* v. *Gold Reefs of West Africa* [1900] 1 Ch. 656; *Oban etc. Distilleries*, 1904 5 F. (Ct. of Sn.) 1141.

54 *Punt* v. *Symons & Co.* [1903] 2 Ch. 506; but see, on breach of contract, para. 14–22, *post*.

55 (1865) 2 Dr. & Sm. 521. Similar problems arose in Scotland, see *Ramsbottom* v. *Scottish American Investment Co.* 1891, 18 R. 558; *Liquidator of the Milford Haven Fishing Co.* v. *James* 1895, 22 R. 577.

56 4 De G.J. & S. 672.

57 [1894] A.C. 399, 417.

58 [1897] 1 Ch. 361 (C.A.).

59 See note 55, *supra*.

a plural vote large enough to prevent the passing of a special resolution altering the articles.[60] In contract this result cannot be achieved effectively because the company can always break the contract.[61]

It is legitimate to purchase the consent, *e.g.* from shareholders whose rights are being altered.[61a]

A special resolution altering the articles is not required if all shareholders, acting unanimously, agree to alter the company's articles and if the alteration is *intra vires* the company.[61b]

Retrospective alterations and alterations affecting existing rights

14–19 In *Allen* v. *Gold Reefs of West Africa*[62] it was argued that the power to alter the articles conferred by what is now section 10 did not justify a retrospective alteration, *e.g.* the insertion of a lien clause[63] intended to give the company a lien on the shares of members for debts incurred before as well as after the insertion of the clause. The Court of Appeal rejected this argument and held that the power of altering the articles was not thus to be limited and that the introduction of such a clause was valid and effective, though in some senses it operated retrospectively.

In that case Lindley M.R. said[64]:

> "The power thus conferred on companies to alter the regulations contained in their articles is limited only by the provisions contained in the statute and the conditions contained in the company's memorandum of association. . . . It must be exercised, not only in the manner required by law, but also bona fide for the benefit of the company as a whole, and it must not be exceeded. These conditions are always implied, and are seldom, if ever, expressed. But if they are complied with I can discover no ground for judicially putting any other restrictions on the power conferred by the section than those contained in it."

In *Sidebottom* v. *Kershaw, Leese & Co.*[65] a similar alteration which gave rights of expropriation of the shares held by any member who was in business in competition with the company was likewise held to be valid, although at that time a particular member was within the ambit of the alteration.

In short, if the shareholders have acted honestly in what they believe to be the interests of the company, the court will not be disposed to disallow the alteration, unless there are no grounds upon which reasonable men could have come to the same decision.

---

[60] *Cf. Bushell* v. *Faith* [1970] A.C. 1099.
[61] See para. 14–22, *post*.
[61a] *Caledonian Insurance Co.* v. *Scottish American Investment Co.* 1951 S.L.T. 23.
[61b] *Cane* v. *Jones* [1980] 1 W.L.R. 1451. See also paras. 56–05 and 56–06, *post*.
[62] [1900] 1 Ch. 656.
[63] See para. 40–01, *post*.
[64] At p. 671. In that case the alteration did not amount to oppression because it affected equally all members of the company and it was irrelevant that at the same time it applied, in fact, to one member only.
[65] [1920] 1 Ch. 154 (C.A.).

"The absence of any reasonable ground for deciding that a certain course of action is conducive to the benefit of the company may be a ground for finding lack of good faith or for finding that the shareholders with the best motives, have not considered the matters which they ought to have considered. On either of these findings their decision might be set aside."[66]

14–20 The foregoing decisions are in accordance with the decision in *Pepe* v. *City and Suburban Permanent Building Society*.[67] In that case the plaintiff, a holder of fully paid-up shares, had under the rules given notice of withdrawal; afterwards, and before repayment, the society altered the rules by giving the directors power to pay off in priority members holding less than £50 in the society. It was held that the alteration was valid though in some sense it took away the vested right of the plaintiff.[68] But in a company limited by shares, when, after a transfer is presented for registration, the company alters its articles by restricting the right to transfer the shares, with a view to preventing the registration of the particular transfer, the alteration does not deprive the applicant of his right to have the transfer registered in accordance with the articles before alteration.[69]

The members of a company may alter the voting rights of shareholders, or a class thereof, conferred by the articles, provided that the alteration is sanctioned by the members in accordance with the constitution of the company or the provisions of section 32 of the 1980 Act, in good faith and for the benefit of the company as a whole.[70]

Limits to alteration

14–21 Nevertheless, a limit must be placed on the general words contained in section 10; and the limit is this, that the section cannot be used to oppress or defraud a minority of shareholders, or to violate any statutory provision or principle of law,[71] which includes the provision that the interests of some of the members must not be unfairly prejudiced (1980 Act, s. 75). The power, in other words, like other powers, must be exercised fairly and according to law. It is clear from the authorities that any abuse of the statutory power will be restrained; a majority, for instance, will not be permitted by the court, under colour of the section, to commit a fraud on the minority.[72]

---

[66] *Per* Scrutton L.J. in *Shuttleworth* v. *Cox Bros. & Co.* [1927] 2 K.B. 9, 23.

[67] [1893] 2 Ch. 311.

[68] See also *Doman's Case* (1876) 3 Ch.D. 21; *British Equitable Assurance Co.* v. *Baily* [1906] A.C. 35; *Rosenberg* v. *Northumberland Building Soc.* (1889) 22 Q.B.D. 373; *Re Barrow Haematite Steel Co.* (1888) 39 Ch.D. 582.

[69] *McArthur* v. *Gulf Line*, 1909 S.C. 732. See also *Moir* v. *Duff & Co.* 1900, 2 F. 1265.

[70] *Rights and Issues Investment Trust Ltd.* v. *Stylo Shoes Ltd.* [1965] Ch. 250; *Re James Colmer Ltd.* [1897] 1 Ch. 524.

[71] *Re Peveril Gold Mines* [1898] 1 Ch. 122; *Payne* v. *The Cork Co.* [1900] 1 Ch. 308; *St. Johnstone F.C. Ltd.* v. *Scottish Football Association Ltd.* 1965 S.L.T. 171.

[72] *Menier* v. *Hooper's Telegraph Co.* (1874) L.R. 9 Ch. 350; *Gray* v. *Lewis* (1873) L.R. 8 Ch. 1035; *Atwool* v. *Merryweather* (1868) L.R. 5 Eq. 464n.; *Mason* v. *Harris* (1879) 11 Ch.D. 97; *Macdougall* v. *Gardiner* (*No. 2*) (1875) 1 Ch.D. 13; *Burland* v. *Earle* [1902] A.C. 83; *Normandy* v. *Ind Coope & Co.* [1908] 1 Ch. 84.

Breach of contract

14–22 It was held by Sargant J. in *British Murac Rubber Syndicate* v. *Alperton Rubber Co.*[73] that a company will not be allowed to alter its articles in breach of contract with an outsider, but in *Punt* v. *Symons & Co.*[74] it was held that a company cannot by contract preclude itself from altering its articles.[75] This conflict in the lower courts was settled by the House of Lords, which decided in *Southern Foundries (1926) Ltd.* v. *Shirlaw*[76] that a company is not prevented from altering its articles by the fact that such an alteration would be a breach of contract, but that an action for damages may lie for the breach. In that case a director was by contract appointed to be a managing director for 10 years, and the articles provided that, "subject to the provisions of any contract," the managing director should cease to be managing director if he ceased to be a director. The articles were altered in such a way as to authorise another company to remove any director. The House of Lords held that there was an implied undertaking by the company not to remove the managing director and not to alter its articles so as to create a right to do so. Consequently, the managing director was held entitled to damages for breach of contract. Lord Porter said[77]:

> "A company cannot be precluded from altering its articles, thereby giving itself power to act upon the provisions of the altered articles—but so to act may nevertheless be a breach of contract if it is contrary to a stipulation in a contract validly made before the alteration."

In short, the position is similar to that under section 184 of the 1948 Act, which in subsection (1) gives the company a right—which cannot be abrogated by the articles or by contract—to remove a director but which by subsection (6) preserves any right for compensation or damages which he might have.[78]

It has also been held that a company cannot take power to expropriate individual shareholders,[79] unless clearly for the benefit of the company as a whole.[80]

Reprinting of altered articles and official notification

14–23 The European Communities Act 1972, s. 9, requires that the articles, as altered, should be printed and sent to the Registrar (s. 9 (5) and (6)) and that official notification of any document altering them should be published (s. 9 (3) (*b*) and (4) (*b*)).

---

[73] [1915] 2 Ch. 186.
[74] [1903] 2 Ch. 506.
[75] In *Baily* v. *British Equitable Assurance Co.* [1904] 1 Ch. 374 it was held that certain by-laws fixing the rights of the policy holders must not be altered so as to prejudice their contractual rights, but this case did not decide that the deed of settlement could not be altered.
[76] [1940] A.C. 701.
[77] At p. 740.
[78] See para. 61–27, *post*.
[79] *Brown* v. *British Abrasive Wheel Co.* [1919] 1 Ch. 290.
[80] *Sidebottom* v. *Kershaw, Leese & Co.* [1920] 1 Ch. 154. See also *Dafen Tinplate Co.* v. *Llanelly Steel Co.* [1920] 2 Ch. 124. Dicta of Peterson J. in this case disapproved in *Shuttleworth* v. *Cox Bros. & Co.* [1927] 2 K.B. 9. See para. 58–16, *post*.

The requirements of the European Communities Act have been discussed when the alteration of the memorandum was treated.[81] They apply to the alteration of the articles *mutatis mutandis*.

Rectification of articles by court

14–24 The articles of association have statutory operation,[82] and the court has no power to rectify them under its equitable jurisdiction even if it is proved that they do not give effect to the intention of the parties.[83]

PRACTICE NOTE

Alteration of articles

14–25 In addition to sending to the Registrar (and to The Stock Exchange in the case of a listed company) a copy of the articles, as altered, a copy of the special resolution must be inserted in every copy of the memorandum and articles in stock (1948 Act, s. 143) and should be sent to every person known to be in possession of a copy of the articles.[84]

[81] See para. 13–05, *ante*.
[82] *Evans* v. *Chapman* (1902) 86 L.T. 381.
[83] *Scott* v. *Frank F. Scott (London) Ltd.* [1940] Ch. 794.
[84] See Practice Note at para. 7–35.

E. INCORPORATION AND COMMENCEMENT OF BUSINESS

CHAPTER 15

REGISTRATION OF THE COMPANY

Documents to be submitted to the Registrar

15–01 The following documents have to be submitted to the Registrar of Companies when application is made for the registration of a company, whether it is a private or public company:

(1) The memorandum of association; this must be duly signed by the subscribers[1] (s. 12, as amended by the 1976 Act, Sched. 2);

(2) The articles of association (unless it is intended to adopt Table A *in toto*); this document has likewise to be signed[2] (s. 12, as amended by the 1976 Act, Sched. 2);

(3) A statement of the directors and secretary (1976 Act, s. 21). This statement has to be submitted on Form 42.[3]

  (a) The statement has to show the first director or directors of the company, and

  (b) The first secretary or joint secretaries of the company.

  (c) The statement has to contain the particulars required by section 200 (2) and (3) of the 1948 Act, as amended by section 95 of the 1981 Act, with respect to those persons. These are the particulars which have to be entered into the register of directors and secretaries. They include directorships held during the past five years. The statement has to be signed by the subscribers and shall contain the consent signed by the persons named as directors and secretaries (1976 Act, s. 21 (2) and (3)).

  (d) Where the memorandum is delivered by a person acting as agent for the subscribers, the statement shall specify that fact and give the name and address of the agent (1976 Act, s. 21 (4)).

  (e) An appointment as first director or secretary in the articles is void unless the person in question is named in the statement (1976 Act, s. 21 (5)).

(4) A statement of the situation of the registered office (1976 Act, s. 23(2)).

(5) A statutory declaration in the prescribed form (Form No. 41[3a]) by a solicitor engaged in the formation of the company or by a person

---

[1] See para. 12–02, *ante*.
[2] See para. 14–04, *ante*.
[3] See Companies (Forms) Order 1979; Vol. II, para. A–3117 of this work.
[3a] Vol. II, para. A–3116.

named in the statement mentioned under (3) hereof that the requirements relating to the registration and all matters precedent and incidental thereto have been complied with (1980 Act, s. 3 (5)).

The purpose of this declaration is to secure care in the preparation of the documents and in the matters preliminary to the registration;

(6) A statement relating to the payment of capital duty in compliance with the Finance Act 1973, Part V, s. 47 (3). This statement should be made on Form PUC1 which can be obtained in England[4] from the Controller of Stamps (Special Section), Bush House, Aldwych, London W.C.2. The calculation of capital duty is discussed below.

Calculation of capital duty

15–02 The capital duty has taken the place of the stamp duties payable on the nominal capital of the company, which was abolished with effect from August 1, 1973.[5] This was done in compliance with EEC Directive 69/335 on the raising of capital, published on pp. 29–37 of Part II (Taxation) of the H.M.S.O. volumes of European Communities Secondary Legislation.

The capital duty is charged on, broadly, the value of contributions to share capital, at the rate of 1 per cent. per £100 or part of £100. On formation of the company, as already observed, Form PUC1 must be delivered to the Registrar when applying for incorporation of the company.

In the case of a private company with a small capital intending to have two members only, it is advantageous for all the shares to be taken and paid for by the prospective members as subscribers to the memorandum in order to avoid the completion of a later return of allotments and a further payment of capital duty.

Useful information connected with Part V of the Finance Act 1973, which provides for the imposition of capital duty, is contained in the booklet "Capital Duty," issued by the Controller of Stamps (Special Section), Bush House, Aldwych, London W.C.2; this booklet is reproduced in volume III of this work, para. K–070.

Registration and payment of fees

15–03 The applicants will deliver the documents listed in the preceding paragraph to the English or Scottish Registrar of Companies for registration.

The addresses of these two Registrars are stated in para. 6–01, *ante*.

After an official examination of the documents the applicants will pay the registration fee and the (additional) capital duty. At present the registration fee is £50.[6]

---

[4] In Scotland: 16–22 Picardy Place, Edinburgh.
[5] Finance Act 1973, s. 49.
[6] The Companies (Fees) Regulations 1980 (S.I. 1980 No. 1749).

Registered number of the company

15–04 The Registrar shall allocate a number to every company and, in addition, he may allocate a letter to it. The number and letter are known as the company's "registered number." (1981 Act, s. 97(1)).

Registered numbers are likewise allocated to oversea companies and incorporated or unincorporated bodies to which any provision of the 1948 Act applies by virtue of section 435 of that Act (*ibid.*, s. 97 (2)).

Grant of certificate of incorporation

15–05 After the official examination the Registrar, if satisfied that the statutory requirements and of the law generally are complied with and that the objects of the proposed company are not illegal,[7] will issue the certificate of incorporation and from the date stated therein the company comes into existence as a legal person (1948 Act, s. 13 (2)).

The certificate, and its effect, will be considered in the following two chapters.

Contracts concluded on behalf of the company before incorporation

15–06 This subject is treated in para. 27–01, *post.*

Admissibility of Registrar's file in evidence

15–07 The Companies Acts make certain matters admissible in evidence. The certificate of incorporation is made "conclusive evidence" that all the requirements of registration and of matters precedent and incidental thereto have been complied with.[8] Section 118 of the 1948 Act provides that the register of members shall be "prima facie evidence" of any matters by the Act directed or authorised to be inserted therein. Section 145 (2) states that the minutes of proceedings of general meetings and of meetings of the directors or managers, if purporting to be signed by the chairman of the meeting or the next successive meeting, shall be "evidence" of the proceedings.

As regards the annual return and other documents of the company which have to be filed with the Registrar of Companies and are not made expressly evidence by the Act, the common law rules on the admission of public documents apply.[9] Four conditions have here to be satisfied: first, the document must be brought into existence and preserved for public use on a public matter. Secondly, it must be open to public inspection. Thirdly, the entry must be made promptly after the events which it purports to record. Fourthly, the entry must be made by a person having a duty to inquire and satisfy himself as to the truth of the recorded facts.

---

[7] See para. 9–03, *ante,* and para. 16–09, *post.*
[8] This is provided for in the 1980 Act ss. 3 (4), 4 (6), 5 (9), 7 (3) (*b*), 8 (10) and 10 (5). On the meaning of conclusive evidence see para. 16–06, *post.*
[9] *R.* v. *Halpin* [1975] 3 W.L.R. 260, 263.

With respect to the annual return, the Court of Appeal held in *R.* v. *Halpin*[10] that the first two conditions were clearly satisfied and the third affected the weight of the evidence and not its admissibility. In the fourth condition the function which originally was performed by one person was now shared by several: the first—the directors (1948 Act, s. 155)—having the knowledge and the statutory duty to record that knowledge and forward it to the Registrar of Companies, the second—the Registrar—having the duty to preserve that document and to show it to members of the public. The Court held that the annual balance sheet filed with the Registrar was admissible in evidence as prima facie showing the identity of the directors.

Form of notices and company documents

15–08 The 1976 Act provides that prescribed forms of notices and other communications shall be used by companies (s. 34 (2)), that the Department of Trade by statutory instrument may lay down certain standards with respect to size, durability and legibility of company documents (s. 35), and that the Registrar of Companies may accept information or microfilm or material other than documents (s. 36).

The prescribed forms in use at present are contained in Companies (Forms) Regulations which are reproduced in Part A of Volume II of this work.

[10] [1975] 3 W.L.R. 260.

CHAPTER 16

THE CERTIFICATE OF INCORPORATION

Nature and form of the certificate

16–01 The issue of the certificate of incorporation by the Registrar of Companies, whether issued on registration or re-registration of the company, is an act of delegated legislation: from the date mentioned in the certificate as the date of incorporation the company comes into existence as a legal person—a "body corporate" (1948 Act, s. 13 (2))—a status which it continues to enjoy until it is dissolved.[1] The Registrar, when issuing the certificate of incorporation, thus, by virtue of his powers under the Companies Acts, does what—apart from the prerogative of the Crown to create a corporation by royal charter[2]—only Parliament itself can do: he creates a corporation. The doctrine of free covenant, according to which corporateness can be created by free association of men, is unknown to English or Scots law.[3]

The certificate may be authenticated by a seal of the Registrar prepared under section 424 (5) of the 1948 Act (s. 13 (1) as amended by the 1976 Act, s. 38(2) and the 1981 Act, s. 99). According to present practice,[4] the date stated in the certificate as date of incorporation is the date at which the Registrar actually issues the certificate, but if the certificate states an earlier date to be the date of incorporation that date, and not the date of issue, is decisive.[5] Official notification is required of the certificate of incorporation.[6]

16–02 Members of the public are entitled to inspect a copy of the certificate of incorporation of any company at the Registrar's office[7] (s. 426 (1) (*a*), as amended by the 1981 Act, s. 98) and further to obtain a certificate on payment of the prescribed fee[8] (s. 426 (1) (*b*)); copies of any other document may likewise be obtained on payment of a lower fee[9] and no

---

[1] It should be noted that in the stage of winding up the company continues to have legal *persona*; only at the end of the winding up when the company is dissolved (see 1948 Acts ss. 274, 290 and 300) does it cease to be a legal person; exceptionally, *i.e.* if it is a "defunct" company, the company may be dissolved without going through the winding-up procedure (s. 353).

[2] See para. 89–20 *post*.

[3] See Shaw Livermore, *Early American Land Companies*, New York, 1939, pp. xii and xix.

[4] Before August 18, 1924, it was the practice to state as date of incorporation the date on which the fees and duty were paid.

[5] Lord Sumner in *Jubilee Cotton Mills Ltd.* v. *Lewis* [1924] A.C. 958, 972.

[6] See para. 17–01, *post*.

[7] On payment of the inspection fee which is £1 for each inspection (Companies (Fees) Regulations 1980 (S.I. 1980 No. 1749); see loose leaf Vol. III, Pt. L).

[8] £3.50 for each certificate.

[9] 30p for each page.

stamp duty is payable on the certification of the copies of other documents by the Registrar[10] (s. 426 (1) (*b*)).

Where a certificate is required for use abroad it may be necessary to have the signature of the Registrar authenticated by a notary public and in some instances even to have the document legalised by the consul of the country where it is intended to be used, or in another manner.

The company is not required by law to exhibit its certificate of incorporation at the registered office or anywhere else. The certificate will normally be in the custody of the secretary of the company, who should arrange for it to be kept in a safe place with the other statutory records of the company. It is unwise to have the certificate framed, since it will need to be produced to third parties from time to time, *e.g.* in connection with the opening of a bank account, some property transactions and any application made to the court under the Companies Acts.

Turning now to the effect of the certificate of incorporation, two questions have to be examined: first, the conclusiveness of the certificate, and, secondly, the corporate existence of the company which is the direct result of the issue of the certificate. The former will be considered in this, and the latter in one of the next chapters (Ch.18).

Conclusiveness of certificate

Historical background

16–03 The Companies Act 1862 provided in section 18 that "the certificate of incorporation of any company given by the Registrar shall be conclusive evidence that all the requisitions of this Act in respect of registration have been complied with." Soon after the passing of the Act it was held that the words "the requisitions of this Act in respect of registration" meant "the requisitions and conditions precedent and incidental to registration," and, accordingly, that once the certificate of incorporation was given, the company named therein as incorporated was to be taken to be duly and effectually incorporated, and all reference to prior matters was precluded.

Thus, in *Peel's Case*,[11] the memorandum of association had, after signature and before registration, been altered without the privity of the signatories so materially that, in the words of Lord Cairns, "the alteration entirely neutralised and annihilated the original execution and registration of the document." The company was, however, registered, and the Registrar gave his certificate of incorporation; subsequently the question arose whether this certificate was conclusive, since according to the section as then in force, the memorandum before registration had to be subscribed "by seven or more persons associated for any lawful purpose," whereas here the signatures had been entirely annihilated. Nevertheless, it was held

[10] The duty was repealed by the Finance Act 1949, s. 35.
[11] (1867) L.R. 2 Ch. 674.

that the Registrar's certificate of incorporation *was* conclusive. Lord Cairns said[12]:

> "The certificate of incorporation . . . is not merely a prima facie answer, but a conclusive answer to any such objection . . . when once the certificate of incorporation is given, nothing is to be inquired into as the regularity of the prior proceedings."

Shortly afterwards, Lord Chelmsford L.C., dealing with the same point in *Oakes* v. *Turquand*,[13] said:

> "I think that the certificate prevents all recurrence to prior matters essential to registration, amongst which is the subscription of a memorandum of association by seven persons, and that it is conclusive in this case that all previous requisitions have been complied with."

This view was, however, departed from in *Re National Debenture, etc., Corporation*,[14] where Kekewich J. refused to treat a certificate of incorporation as conclusive when he found as a fact that the memorandum of association had been subscribed by six persons only instead of seven. This decision was reversed on appeal on the ground that the evidence did not establish the fact so found; but the judges of the Court of Appeal let fall some dicta to the effect that if the judge below had been right as to the facts, his decision would have been correct in point of law, and the existence of these dicta cast a shadow of uncertainty on the conclusiveness of the certificate. It was also doubtful, from the remarks of Turner L.J. in *Re Northumberland, etc., Banking Co.*,[15] whether the certificate was conclusive if the company was one not authorised to be registered under the Act then in force.

16–04 To remove these doubts section 1 (1) of the Companies Act 1900 was passed and dealt with both points in a form which, apart from trifling and verbal alterations, has been adopted by subsequent Companies Acts and which was enacted in section 15 (1) of the Act of 1948, which provided:

> "A certificate of incorporation given by the registrar in respect of any association shall be conclusive evidence that all the requirements of this Act in respect of registration and of matters precedent and incidental thereto have been complied with, and that the association is a company authorised to be registered and duly registered under this Act."

The present law

16–05 Section 15 of the 1948 Act was repealed by the 1980 Act (Sched. 4). This Act contains not less than five references to the conclusive nature of the certificate of incorporation. They are listed below. The first of these

---

[12] At p. 681.
[13] (1867) L.R. 2 H.L. 325, 354.
[14] [1891] 2 Ch. 505.
[15] (1858) 2 De G. & J. 357.

references is to the certificate issued on registration of the company and the other four cases concern certificates issued on occasion of various cases of re-registration. The references to the conclusiveness of the certificate of incorporation in the 1980 Act occur on:

(1) registration of a company (s. 3 (4))[16];
(2) re-registration of a private company as a public company (s. 5 (9));
(3) re-registration of an unlimited company as a public company (s. 7 (3) (*b*));
(4) re-registration of an old public company as a private company (s. 8 (10)); and
(5) re-registraton of a public company as a private company (s. 10 (5) and 12 (3)).

As regards the certificate issued on the registration of the company ((1), above), the 1980 Act first enjoins the Registrar in subsection (1) of section 3 not to register the memorandum "unless he is satisfied that all the requirements of the Companies Acts in respect of registration and the matters precedent and incidental thereto have been complied with," and then states in subsection (4) of that section:

> "A certificate of incorporation given under that section in respect of any association shall be conclusive evidence—
> (a) that the requirements mentioned in subsection (1) above have been complied with, and that the association is a company authorised to be registered and is duly registered under the 1948 Act; and
> (b) if the certificate contains a statement that the company is a public company, that the company is such a company."

It follows that under the 1980 Act the conclusive effect of the certificate of incorporation is the same as it was under section 15 of the 1948 Act, except that the regulation provided by the 1980 Act is more complicated in consequence of the necessity to extend that effect to the various cases of re-registration.

16–06 The present effect of the conclusiveness of the certificate of incorporation leaves little room for doubt: it prevents the reopening of matters prior and contemporaneous to the registration and essential to it,[17] and it places the existence of the company as a legal person beyond doubt. Consequently, even if the two signatures to a memorandum were written by one person, or were forged, the certificate would be conclusive that the company was duly incorporated. So, too, if the signatories were all minors, the certificate would still be conclusive.[18] Further, a subscriber cannot, after

[16] The trading certificate issued when a public company is formed as such (see para. 19–02, *post*) is likewise conclusive evidence that the company is entitled to do business and exercise its borrowing powers (1980 Act, s. 4 (6)).
[17] Thus, after the grant of the certificate the original articles cannot be rectified: *Scott* v. *Frank F. Scott (London) Ltd.* [1940] Ch. 794; see para. 14–24, *ante*.
[18] It is submitted that this is correct even if the decision in *Re Laxon & Co.* (*No. 2*) [1892] 3 Ch. 555 that a minor is a "person" within the section cannot be supported; see also *Hammond* v. *Prentice Bros.* [1920] 1 Ch. 201 and *Bowman* v. *Secular Society Ltd.* [1917] A.C. 406, 438.

the issue of the certificate of registration repudiate his subscription on the ground of misrepresentation,[19] mistake or fraud, although he retains any claims for damages against the person who misled him.

The certificate is also conclusive that the company came into existence on the date of the certificate, and it must be taken to have been in existence during the whole of that day.[20]

The certificate is conclusive but not exclusive evidence. A fact to which the certificate refers can also be proved by evidence other than the production of the certificate.

16–07 In view of the conclusive character of the certificate of incorporation it was unnecessary for section 9 of the European Communities Act 1972 to introduce into the law of the United Kingdom the provision of Section III of the First Council Directive on Company Law Harmonisation of the European Communities of March 9, 1968 (No. 68/151/EEC).[21] That section deals with the nullity of the company in certain circumstances and the procedure which the member states are required to provide in actions for a declaration that the company is a nullity in law. In the law of the United Kingdom, the question whether the formation of the company is null and void cannot arise, once the certificate of incorporation is issued.

Compliance with the Acts

16–08 The certificate of incorporation is conclusive evidence that the requirements of the Companies Acts have been complied with.[22] "All that the courts can do is to construe the memorandum as it stands."[23] Thus, in *Cotman* v. *Brougham*[24] Lord Wrenbury said quite definitely that a memorandum containing an inflated objects clause[25] was not in compliance with the Act, but he added that as the Registrar had granted the certificate of incorporation the court had to confine itself to the construction of the document; since the objects clause contained at the end the common "independent and separate objects" clause,[25] the construction of it did not admit of reasonable doubt and the court had to hold that the transaction in question—the underwriting of shares in another company—was *intra vires* one of the sub-clauses of the objects clause of the underwriting company's memorandum. It follows that a company which has, but ought not to have, been registered because it was a trade union or the registration contravened another statute is a legal person, but its registration can probably be impeached in the manner indicated below.[26]

---

[19] *Re Metal Constituents Ltd., Lord Lurgan's Case* [1902] 1 Ch. 707.
[20] *Jubilee Cotton Mills Ltd.* v. *Lewis* [1924] A.C. 958.
[21] See Vol. III, para. L–601.
[22] *Cotman* v. *Brougham* [1918] A.C. 514.
[23] *Per* Lord Finlay L.C., *ibid.* at p. 518.
[24] [1918] A.C. 514.
[25] See para. 9–11, *ante*.
[26] See para. 16–10, *post*.

The conclusiveness of the certificate does not, however, extend to being conclusive evidence that the company was not a trade union—a trade union must not be registered under the Companies Acts[27]—and, consequently, that it was *capable* of registration.[28] The Trade Union and Labour Relations Acts 1974, s. 2 (2), states expressly that the registration of a trade union incapable of registration shall be void.

Illegality of objects

16–09 The certificate, in the words of Lord Dunedin in *Bowman* v. *Secular Society Ltd.*,[29] "prevents anyone alleging that the company does not exist," but as Lord Sumner[30] observed, it "does not prove that all the memorandum powers are lawfully exercisable." In the same case Lord Finlay L.C. said[31]:

> "It was argued before us that the society could not have been properly incorporated if its objects were illegal, and that, as the certificate is conclusive to show that the company is one authorised to be registered and duly registered, it follows that it cannot for any purpose be contended that the objects are illegal. In my opinion this argument is an attempt to extend the effect of these enactments beyond their fair meaning and manifest object. What the legislature was dealing with was the validity of the incorporation, and it is for the purpose of incorporation, and for this purpose only, that the certificate is made conclusive."

It follows that even if all or some of the objects of the company are illegal but it has obtained registration, the certificate of incorporation prevents any doubt from being raised as to the legal persona of the company but it does not validate the illegal objects.

A company pursuing illegal objects should not be registered, and the Registrar is entitled to refuse an application for registration as was decided in a case[32] in which the objects of the company were the sale of tickets of an Irish Hospitals' sweepstake authorised in the Irish Republic but illegal as a lottery in England. His refusal to register is subject to examination by the Queen's Bench Division on application for a mandamus ordering him to register the company.[33]

---

[27] Trade Union and Labour Relations Act 1974, s. 2 (2), and Companies Act 1948, s. 459 (9) (*b*).

[28] *British Association of Glass Bottle Manufacturers Ltd.* v. *Nettlefold* (1911) 27 T.L.R. 527; *cf. Edinburgh and District Aerated Water Manufacturers' Defence Association* v. *Jenkinson* (1903) 5 F. 1159. See also *Blythe* v. *Birtley* [1910] 1 Ch. 228 (conversion of friendly society into company).

[29] [1917] A.C. 406, 435.

[30] At p. 452.

[31] At p. 421.

[32] *R.* v. *Registrar of Joint Stock Companies* [1931] 2 K.B. 197.

[33] *R.* v. *Registrar of Companies, ex p. Bowen* [1914] 3 K.B. 1161.

Impeaching incorporation

16–10 The further question whether a company, once incorporated by registration under the Companies Acts, can be removed from the register and disincorporated was considered by the House of Lords in *Princess of Reuss* v. *Bos.*[34] In that case the question arose as to the regularity of the constitution of a company called: "The General Company for the Promotion of Land Credit Limd." All the subscribers to the memorandum of this company were foreigners, and there was no intention to carry on business in England. The company was ordered to be wound up. Neither of these circumstances affected its validity, but the articles of association contained provisions contrary to the Act of 1862, under which the company was incorporated, and Lord Hatherley L.C. said[35]:

> "All we have to ask ourselves is this, my Lords. Has this company come into existence—has it been born? If it has been born, I think . . . it ought to be, as speedily as possible, extinguished. . . . The question is therefore simply whether it has been created. If created, there is no power given in this Act of Parliament, nor in any other Act of Parliament that I am aware of, by which, through any result of a formal application, like an application for *scire facias* to repeal a charter, the company can be got rid of, unless by winding up."

But the statute does not bind the Crown, and, accordingly, where a company has been registered for an illegal object, proceedings could be instituted by the Attorney-General (in Scotland, the Lord Advocate) to have the registration cancelled.[36]

34 (1871) L.R. 5 H.L. 176.
35 At p. 193.
36 *Bowman* v. *Secular Society* [1917] A.C. 406, 439, 440.

Chapter 17

OFFICIAL NOTIFICATION

Meaning of official notification and duty to notify

17–01 The European Communities Act 1972, s. 9, introduced a new notion into company law, *viz.* that of official notification. The provisions dealing with that subject are contained in subsections (3) (as amended by the 1976, 1980 and 1981 Acts) and (4) of section 9. The object of this measure is to give persons in the United Kingdom and the other member states of the EEC official intimation that an important change in the constitution of the company has occurred. Official notification is not intended to be a substitute for the perusal of the documents relating to the company at the register of companies or for obtaining copies of such documents.

"Official notification" means that the issue or receipt of certain documents relating to the company is published in the official *Gazette*, *viz.* according to the place of registration of the company, the *London Gazette* or the *Edinburgh Gazette*.[1] The documents themselves to which the notification refers are not published in the *Gazette*. The notice merely states that the documents have been issued or received by the Registrar.

17–02 The duty to notify officially the issue or receipt of those documents falls on the Registrar of Companies; it does not fall on the company. It presupposes that the company will promptly perform its duty, imposed by various provisions of the Companies Acts, to file the relevant documents with the Registrar. Indeed, as will be seen, the performance of this duty is of enhanced importance to the company, apart from the avoidance of fines. It is also in the interest of the company, after having filed the requisite documents, to examine the *Gazette* and to ascertain that the Registrar has published the official notices relating to them because the effect of some of the measures in question, such as the removal of a director or the change of a provision in the memorandum or the articles, may depend on the official notification in the *Gazette*. The only case in which the duty officially to notify does not fall on the Registrar, is that of section 305 of the Companies Act 1948; here the duty to publish his appointment in the *Gazette* falls on the liquidator in the voluntary winding up and this announcement is treated as official notification.

17–03 Official notification is required by subsection (3) of section 9, as amended by the 1976, 1980 and 1981 Acts, of the issue or receipt of the following documents:

(a) a certificate of incorporation of a company;

---

[1] In the *London Gazette* official notification particulars are published in special *Company Law Official Notification Supplements*.

(b) a document making or evidencing an alteration in the memorandum or articles of association;
(c) any notification of a change among the directors of a company;
(d) any documents delivered by a company in pursuance of section 1 (7) of the Companies Act 1976;
(da) any statutory declaration delivered in pursuance of section 4 (2) of the Companies Act 1980;
(db) any report as to the value of a non-cash asset under section 24 or 26 of the Companies Act 1980;
(dc) any copy of a resolution of a public company which gives, varies, revokes or renews an authority for the purposes of section 14 of the Companies Act 1980;
(dd) any copy of a special resolution of a public company passed under section 18 (1), (2) or (3) of the Companies Act 1980;
(de) any statement or notice delivered by a public company under section 33 of the Companies Act 1980;
(df) a copy of any resolution or agreement to which section 148 of the Companies Act 1948 applies and which—
  (i) states the rights attached to any shares in a public company, other than shares which are, in all respects, uniform (for the purposes of section 33 (1) of the Companies Act 1980) with shares previously allotted;
  (ii) varies rights attached to any shares in a public company; or
  (iii) assigns a name or other designation, or a new name or other designation, to any class of shares in a public company;
(dg) any return of allotments of a public company;
(dh) any notification of the redemption of shares under section 62 of the Companies Act 1948 by a public company;
(e) any notice of a change in the situation of a company's registered office;
(f) a copy of a winding-up order. As regards voluntary winding up, section 305 of the Companies Act 1948 requires already the publication of the appointment of the liquidator in the *Gazette*, and that publication is treated as "official notification";
(g) an order for dissolution of a company on a winding up;
(h) a return by a liquidator of the final meeting of a company on winding up.

The reason why no official notification is required for the dissolution of a defunct company without winding up is presumably that section 353 of the Companies Act 1948 requires the insertion of notices into the *Gazette* in any case.

Effect of official notification

17–04 Only when the official notification has become fully effective, can the company absolutely rely on any of the events listed in subsection (4) of section 9 and set out below and is a third party treated as having constructive notice of the event in question. Before the official notification becomes fully effective, the company can rely on any of those events only if certain conditions are satisfied. Official notification becomes fully effective after the expiration of a period of grace which is 15 days but is extended if the last day is a "non-business day" (see below).

The events listed in subsection (4) are:

(a) the making of a winding-up order in respect of the company, or the appointment of a liquidator in a voluntary winding up of the company; or

(b) an alteration of the company's memorandum or articles of association; or

(c) any change among the company's directors; or

(d) (as regards service of any document on the company) any change in the situation of the company's registered office.

The effect of subsection (4) of section 9 of the European Communities Act 1972 appears to be this:

(1) If the event listed in subsection (4) is not officially notified, the company can rely on it as against a third party only if it can prove that he had actual notice of it. That applies even if the official notification later becomes effective; it does not have retroactive effect.

A director would not appear to be a "third party" within the meaning of this subsection.

(2) If the event has been officially notified but the period of grace of 15 days has not expired, the company can rely on the event in question unless the third party shows that he was unavoidably prevented from knowing the event at the time when he contracted with the company, *e.g.* because he was incapacitated by illness.

(3) After the expiration of 15 days from the date of the official notification the company can absolutely rely on the event in question.

17–05 These provisions are of particular importance as far as service of a document on the company at its registered office is concerned.[2] They mean, in effect, that until the official notification of a change in the situation of the registered office has become fully effective, service at the old address may operate against the company in the circumstances set out in (1) and (2) above.

Subsection (4) contains detailed provisions for the calculation of the period of grace of 15 days. If the 15th day is a "non-business day," the period ends on the next day which is not so qualified. A "non-business day" means a Saturday or Sunday, Christmas Day, Good Friday and any

[2] See para. 8–13, *ante*.

other day which, in the part of Great Britain in which the company is registered, is a bank holiday under the Banking and Financial Dealings Act 1971.

It was held in *Re Peek Winch & Todd Ltd.*,[3] that, as against a party who had no actual notice of a winding-up order, the company and the receiver appointed by the holders of debentures issued by the company could not rely on the winding-up order until it was gazetted, *i.e.* until official notification became effective. This decision was affirmed by the Court of Appeal.[4]

[3] (1979) 129 N.L.J. 494.
[4] (1980) 130 N.L.J. 116.

CHAPTER 18

CORPORATE EXISTENCE

The company as legal person

18–01 Upon the issue of the certificate of incorporation, the company becomes a body corporate or, in other words, a corporation (1948 Act, s. 13 (2), as amended by the 1980 Act). Prior to the date of the certificate the company has no legal existence.[1]

A corporation is not, like a partnership in English law or a family, a mere collection or aggregation of individuals.[2] In the eyes of the law it is a person distinct from its members or shareholders, a metaphysical entity or a fiction of law, with legal but no physical existence. It is, as Lord Selborne said,[3] "a mere abstraction of law," and, as Lord Macnaghten observed,[4] "at law a different person altogether from the subscribers to the memorandum of association."[5]

The company's persona and the ultra vires doctrine

18–02 The legal personality of a company, like that of every corporation created by, or by authority of, Parliament, is, on principle, restricted in so far as the company cannot act *ultra vires, i.e.* beyond the objects for which it is incorporated,[6] but, as has been seen,[7] this inherent limitation of the legal personality of the company is considerably modified by section 9 (1) of the European Communities Act 1972.

The principle in Salomon v. *Salomon & Co. Ltd.*

18–03 The principle of the independent corporate existence of a company was explained and emphasised by the House of Lords in the case of *Salomon* v. *Salomon Co. Ltd.*[8] In that case Aron Salomon, a leather merchant and wholesale boot manufacturer, was the owner of a profitable business, and in order to obtain the advantages of limited liability, he, being perfectly solvent at the time, converted his business into a company. The nominal capital of the company was £40,000, divided into £1 shares. Of that amount

---

1 *F. J. Neale (Glasgow) Ltd.* v. *Vickery*, 1973 S.L.T. (Sh.Ct.) 88.
2 On the common law rules relating to the power to create a corporation, see para. 89–18 *post*.
3 *G. E. Ry.* v. *Turner* (1872) L.R. 8 Ch. 149, 152; see further Cotton L.J. in *Flitcroft's Case* (1882) 21 Ch.D. 519, 536; Cave J. in *Re Sheffield, etc., Society* (1889) 22 Q.B.D. 470, 476.
4 In *Salomon* v. *Salomon & Co.* [1897] A.C. 22, 51.
5 But the formation of a company will not protect individuals from liability for wrongful acts authorised by them: *Belvedere Fish Guano Co.* v. *Rainham Chemical Works* [1920] 2 K.B. 487; [1921] 2 A.C. 465.
6 See 9–07, *ante*.
7 See para. 9–25. *ante*.
8 [1897] A.C. 22.

he, his wife and his five children had subscribed one share each and a further 20,000 shares were issued to Aron Salomon. No other shares were issued. Salomon received also mortgage debentures to the amount of £10,000 in part-payment by the company for the business.

Later, the company was in financial difficulties; the then holder of the debentures appointed a receiver and the company went into liquidation.

The courts were asked to decide whether the debentures originally issued to Salomon were valid and entitled to priority over the unsecured creditors who denied them priority on the ground that the company was a "one-man company" and a sham, and so Vaughan Williams J. held, being of opinion that A. Salomon & Co. Ltd. was a mere alias or agent for Aron Salomon, and, therefore, that Salomon was bound to pay the unsecured creditors of the company out of his own pocket notwithstanding that his shares had all been fully paid up. The decision of the learned judge was affirmed by the Court of Appeal on the somewhat different ground that the whole scheme was a fraud on the policy of the Act, and that it was never intended by the legislature that a company should consist of one substantial person and six mere dummies devoid of any real interest.

This decision was unanimously reversed by the House of Lords[9] on the ground that the only mode of ascertaining the intent and meaning of the Act was to examine its provisions and find what regulations it had imposed as a condition of trading with limited liability.

Lord Halsbury L.C. said[10]:

> " . . . the statute enacts nothing as to the extent or degree of interest which may be held by each of the seven, or as to the proportion of interest or influence possessed by one or the majority of the shareholders over the others."

Lord Macnaghten said[11]:

> "There is nothing in the Act requiring that the subscribers to the memorandum should be independent or unconnected, or that they or any of them should take a substantial interest in the undertaking, or that they should have a mind and will of their own, as one of the learned Lords Justices seems to think, or that there should be anything like a balance of power in the constitution of the company."

Further illustrations

18–04 Further illustrations of the fundamental principle that the company is an independent legal person distinct from its members are found in numerous

[9] *Salomon* v. *Salomon & Co.* [1897] A.C. 22.
[10] At p. 30.
[11] At p. 50.

cases, old and modern.[12] Already before *Salomon's* case, in *Farrar* v. *Farrars Ltd.*,[13] Lindley L.J. had said[14]:

> "A sale by a person to a corporation of which he is a member is not, either in form or in substance, a sale by a person to himself. To hold that it is, would be to ignore the principle which lies at the root of the legal idea of a corporate body, and that idea is that the corporate body is distinct from the persons composing it. A sale by a member of a corporation to the corporation itself is in every sense a sale valid in equity as well as at law."

Further, in *North West Transportation Co.* v. *Beatty*[15] it was held that a sale of property of the company to one of its members, which had been sanctioned by a general meeting, could not be invalidated on the ground that it was carried by the votes of the purchaser[16]; and a person who holds shares in or even controls a company can vote in favour of its winding up notwithstanding that such a resolution will lead to a claim for damages by him against the company for breach of a service contract.[17]

18–05 A more modern illustration of the principle under review is found in *Ebbw Vale U.D.C.* v. *South Wales Traffic Area Licensing Authority*,[18] in which the facts were as follows: the shares of an omnibus company which provided passenger road services in a district in South Wales were, by virtue of a power contained in the Transport Act 1947, s. 2 (2) (*f*), acquired by the British Transport Commission which held all, save two, shares in it. The omnibus company applied to the licensing authority for permission to increase the fares but the Ebbw Vale U.D.C. objected on the ground that as the services provided by the company were, in fact, provided by the British Transport Commission the licensing authority had no jurisdiction to hear the application[19] The Court of Appeal held that the omnibus company had retained its character as a separate legal entity and did not act as agent of the Commission; that, consequently, the services were provided

---

[12] In addition to the cases mentioned in the text, see also *Henry Browne & Son Ltd.* v. *Smith* [1964] 2 Lloyd's Rep. 476; *Littlewoods Mail Order Stores Ltd.* v. *I.R.C.* [1969] 1 W.L.R. 1241, 1254; *Lep Air Services Ltd.* v. *Rollowswin Investments Ltd.* [1971] 1 W.L.R. 934. Also *Sarna* v. *Adair*, 1945 J.C. (Ct. of Sn.) 141, 145; *Davidson & Syme, W.S.* v. *Kaye and Others,* 1970 S.L.T. (Notes) 65; *D.H.N. Distributors Ltd.* v. *Tower Hamlets London Borough Council* [1976] 1 W.L.R. 852; *In re Brauch* [1977] 3 W.L.R. 354 for the purposes of bankruptcy jurisdiction, a debtor, who managed the business of his company in England, was held not to be "carrying on business" in England within s. 4 (1) (*d*) of the Bankruptcy Act 1914 even though he was in complete control, but on the facts of the case he was held to carry on business in England independently of that of the company. See further *Woolfson* v. *Strathclyde Regional Council*, 1977 S.L.T. 60 affd. 1978 S.L.T. 159, para. 18–23, *post; The Busiris* [1980] 1 Lloyd's Rep. 569, 589, 597; *Bluebell Apparel Ltd.* v. *Dickinson* 1980 S.L.T. 157.

[13] (1888) 40 Ch.D. 395.

[14] At p. 409. *Cf. In re Hellenic & General Trust Ltd.* [1976] 1 W.L.R. 123, 126.

[15] (1887) 12 App.Cas. 589.

[16] And see *Burland* v. *Earle* [1902] A.C. 83.

[17] *Fowler* v. *Commercial Timber Co.* [1930] 2 K.B. 1 (C.A.)

[18] [1951] 2 K.B. 366; see also *British Thomson-Houston Co.* v. *Sterling Accessories Ltd.*; *Same* v. *Crowther & Osborn Ltd.* [1924] 2 Ch. 33. *Cf. Merchandise Transport Ltd.* v. *British Transport Commission* [1962] 2 Q.B. 173.

[19] In consequence of ss. 72 *et seq.* of the Transport Act 1947, under which the charges schemes had to be approved by the Transport Tribunal.

by the company and not by the Commission; and that the licensing authority and not the Transport Tribunal had to consider the charges scheme. Cohen L.J. observed[20]:

> ". . . it is quite plain that Parliament when it passed this Act had in mind the general rule of law to which I have referred as laid down in *Salomon* v. *Salomon & Co.*,[21] and many other cases, that a subsidiary company is not the agent of the parent company, but is an entirely separate entity. Its acts are not the acts of the parent company, and the parent company is not responsible for its acts or defaults, in the absence of special provisions in some contract between the parties."

8–06 Again, in *Lee* v. *Lee's Air Farming Ltd.*[22] the defendant company was formed for the purpose of carrying on the business of aerial top-dressing. Lee, a qualified pilot, held all but one of the shares in the company and by the articles was appointed governing director of the company and chief pilot. Lee was killed while piloting the company's aircraft, and his widow claimed compensation for his death under the New Zealand Workers' Compensation Act 1922. This statute required an employer to pay compensation on the death or injury of a "worker," defined by the Act as "any person who has entered into or worked under a contract of service . . . with an employer . . . whether remunerated by wages, salary or otherwise." The company opposed the claim (on the instructions of its insurers) on the ground that Lee was not a "worker" within the statutory definition, as the same person could not be both employer and employee. The Judicial Committee, reversing the New Zealand Court of Appeal, held that there was a valid contract of service between Lee and the company, and Lee was therefore a "worker" within the meaning of the Act. It was a logical consequence of the decision in *Salomon's* case[21] that one person may function in the dual capacity both as director and employee of the same company.

Reduction of number of members below legal minimum

8–07 Even if the number of members falls below two,[22a] the company continues to have a separate corporate existence. This fact can be a source of considerable embarrassment, particularly in a private company, for it may happen that all the directors die and only one shareholder remains, so that it is impossible, under the company's articles, for the company to continue to function, since there are no directors to act on behalf of the company or to convene a general meeting. On occasion a company may even be left

---

[20] At pp. 373–374.
[21] [1897] A.C. 22.
[22] [1961] A.C. 12, a decision of the Judicial Committee of the Privy Council on appeal from the Court of Appeal of New Zealand; this decision was followed in *Road Transport Industry Training Board* v. *Readers Garage* [1969] K.I.R. 137. See also *Boulting* v. *Assn. of Cinematograph, etc., Technicians* [1963] 2 Q.B. 606.
[22a] Two are the legal minimum in the case of a private or public company. On the consequences of the number of members falling below the legal minimum, see s. 31 as amended by the 1980 Act, and para. 10–05 *ante*.

with no directors or shareholders alive, but the company does not thereby cease to exist. In these cases sections 131 (2) or 135 (1) of the 1948 Act may sometimes provide procedure to break the deadlock. Under the former provision, if at least one member applies, the Department of Trade may call or direct the holding of a general meeting if default is made in holding the annual general meeting, and under the latter provision the court, of its own motion or on the application of any director or member having a vote, may order a general meeting to be called if it is impracticable to call a meeting in the manner prescribed by the articles or the Act. Further, if there are no directors, even an unauthorised person may act on behalf of the company and his act may later be ratified by subsequently appointed directors or the general meeting; if the company is in winding up, even the liquidator may ratify; the ratification has retroactive effect.[22b]

Private companies

18–08 The fact that a company has a separate persona is sometimes overlooked in the management of private companies. Thus, in *Re Strathblaine Estates Ltd.*,[23] in the voluntary winding up of a private company, it was resolved to divide the surplus assets—freehold properties—in equal shares between the shareholders and, after the discharge of its liabilities, the company was dissolved, but the legal estate in the properties was not conveyed to the shareholders who were merely given the title deeds. In this case the consequences, which could be rectified by a vesting order under the Trustee Act 1925, s. 44 (ii) (*c*), were not serious because the failure to treat the company as a separate person affected only the members. But in some cases the consequences are that assets are withdrawn from the company to the detriment of creditors, and this may mean not only that the creditors are prejudiced but also that directors may in due course find themselves liable in misfeasance proceedings,[24] although they may not themselves have profited by the distribution of the assets; in such a case their right of indemnity against the members will only be of value if the members were aware of all the facts and if, in fact, they have assets on which the directors can execute a judgment.

Further, if the company is a "one man" company and its principal shareholder and managing director meets with an accident, there is a high probability that serious injuries sustained by him will have a damaging effect upon the business of the company controlled by him, but if he wants to recover damages for loss of profitability of the business he must be able to quantify this loss and he will fail to do so if his books of account are largely unreliable.[25]

22b *Alexander Ward & Co. Ltd.* v. *Samyang Navigation Co. Ltd.* [1975] 1 W.L.R. 673; 1975 S.L.T. (H.L.) 126 1975 S.C. (H.L.) 26.
23 [1948] Ch. 228.
24 s. 333; see para. 85–88, *post*.
25 *Ashcroft* v. *Curtin* [1971] 1 W.L.R. 1731.

Position of company as legal person

18–09 The legal fiction that the company is, as Cave J. put it,[26] "a legal persona just as much as an individual" is subject to obvious natural limitations which were pointed out poignantly by counsel[27] in the days of James II when asking: "Can you hang its common seal?" In the following pages the application of the principle that the company is a separate legal entity to some legal relations will be considered. It will be seen that though the principle is still firmly established in English and Scots law as, in the words of Lindley L.J.,[28] lying "at the root of the legal idea of a corporate body," modern practice, in deference to the reality of economic facts, has frequently admitted exceptions to it in which the veil of corporateness is lifted.[29]

Nationality, domicile and residence of company

18–10 The application of these qualities of an individual to a company has been considered earlier.[30]

Capacity to contract

18–11 The contractual capacity of a company incorporated under the Companies Acts or one of their predecessors is the same as that of a natural person, provided that the company is not acting *ultra vires*. Similarly, the company's contracts may be made in the same form as those of a natural person (1948 Act, ss. 32 *et seq.*).[31] Where a question of knowledge or intention arises, as, *e.g.* in connection with misrepresentation, the company's "knowledge or ignorance must be found in the minds of its agents."[32]

Capacity to form companies and partnerships

18–12 A company may be a subscriber to the memorandum of, or shareholder in, another company, subject to certain statutory restrictions applying to the holding of shares of a subsidiary in its holding company.[33] Further, a company may be a director, a secretary, or a manager of another company or a trustee for debenture holders of another company but it cannot be an auditor (s. 161 (2) (*c*)), liquidator (s. 335), receiver or receiver and manager (England: s. 366; Scotland: Companies (Floating Charges and Receivers) (Scotland) Act 1972, s. 11 (3) (*a*)).

A company may be a partner in a partnership, indeed all the partners in a partnership may be companies. These companies, like all partners (ex-

---

[26] *Re Sheffield, etc., Society* (1889) 22 Q.B.D. 470, 476.
[27] In *R.* v. *City of London* (1632) 8 St.Tr. 1087, 1138.
[28] In *Farrar* v. *Farrars Ltd.* (1888) 40 Ch.D. 395, 409.
[29] See para. 18–22, *post.*
[30] See para. 8–10, *ante.*
[31] See para. 27–09, *post.*
[32] *Per* Pearson J. in *Regina Fur Co. Ltd.* v. *Bossom* [1958] 2 Lloyd's Rep. 466, 484.
[33] s. 27; see para. 49–09, *post.* A company can purchase its own shares subject to the conditions stated in the 1981 Act, s. 46; see para. 38–02 *post.*

cept limited partners of a limited partnership), are liable for the debts of the partnership without limitation; that the liability of the incorporators, *i.e.* the members of those partners, is limited is irrelevant.

Capacity to commit torts[34]

18–13 It is well established in modern common law that a company—which as a *persona ficta*, can only act through its agents or servants—is vicariously liable for torts committed by those agents or servants in the course of their employment or business on behalf of the company in the same manner in which any other principal or employer would be vicariously liable.

It has been pointed out earlier[35] that, on this basis, a company is fully responsible for torts committed by its agents and servants. This applies, in particular, to torts requiring an element of intention or some other subjective test for its commission, such as malicious prosecution, malicious libel, fraudulent misrepresentation or negligence.[36]

It is a matter of controversy whether a company is only liable for torts done by its agents or servants *intra vires* the objects of the company—whether those torts have or have not a subjective element[37]—or whether, in appropriate circumstances, the company might even be liable for *ultra vires* torts purported to have been done by its agents or servants in the course of their employment or business on behalf of the company.[38] This question can only arise if the company expressly authorises the commission of the *ultra vires* tort because the implied authority of agents or servants undoubtedly does not extend to the commission of such acts.[39] Although does not extend to the commission of such acts.[39] It is believed that in these circumstances the company is liable for the torts of its agents or servants, even though these torts are *ultra vires* its objects.[40] *Obiter dicta* in American decisions[41] and eminent writers[42] can be quoted in support of this view. It is thought that this view is in harmony with the scanty modern indications of English judicial opinion on this issue.[43]

---

[34] The terminology in this section is that of English law, but the principles so far as relating to companies are similar, *mutatis mutandis*, in the Scots law of delict.
[35] See para. 9–37, *ante*.
[36] *Citizens' Life Assurance Co.* v. *Brown* [1904] A.C. 423; *Barwick* v. *English Joint Stock Bank* (1867) L.R. 2 Ex. 259; and para. 9–37, *ante*.
[37] See para. 9–37, *ante*.
[38] See Salmond and Heuston, *The Law of Torts,* 18th ed., 1981, pp. 404 *et seq*.
[39] *Poulton* v. *London & S.W. Ry.* (1867) L.R. 2 Q.B. 534; *Campbell* v. *Paddington Corpn.* [1911] 1 K.B. 869, 878; *Mill* v. *Hawker* (1874) L.R. 9 Ex. 309, 324.
[40] In the previous editions of this work, the opposite view was taken; see *Palmer's Company Law,* 22nd ed., 1976, para. 18–13.
[41] *The National Bank* v. *Graham* (1879) 100 U.S. 702; *Salt Lake City* v. *Hollister* (1885) U.S. 260; *Nims* v. *Mount Hermon Boys' School* (1893) 39 Am. State Rep. 467; *Central Railroad and Banking Co.* v. *Smith* (1889) 52 Am.Rep. 333.
[42] Clark & Lindsell *on Torts,* 15th ed., 1982, para. 2–46; Salmond and Heuston, *ibid.*
[43] *Campbell* v. *Paddington Corpn.* [1911] 1 K.B.869. But see *Poulton* v. *London & S.W.Ry.* (1867) L.R. 2 Q.B.534, Pigott and Cleasby BB. in *Mill* v. *Hawker* (1874) L.R. 9 Ex. 309, 324.

A company can sue for libel or slander affecting its business reputation without proof of special damage.[44]

18–14 The shareholders are personally liable for a fraudulent misrepresentation by a director as regards the sale of the company's business if—and only if—they have authorised him as their agent to negotiate the sale of their shares; such authority may be given by a resolution of the general meeting at which the director reports that a take-over bid has been received[45]; the shareholders are vicariously liable in such a case even though they did not authorise the fraudulent misrepresentation of the director and were, in fact, unaware of it because, as Bramwell L.J. observed[46]:

> " . . . every person who authorises another to act for him in the making of any contract, undertakes for the absence of fraud in that person in the execution of the authority given, as much as he undertakes for its absence in himself when he makes the contract."

Capacity to hold land

18–15 A company has the same capacity to hold land as a natural person, provided that this is not inconsistent with its objects. The former restrictions imposed in certain cases by sections 14 and 408 of the 1948 Act were removed by section 38 (1) of and Schedule VII, Part II, to the Charities Act 1960.[47]

Capacity to commit crimes[48]

18–16 A company, like any other entity recognised by the law, can as a general rule be indicted for its criminal acts which from the very necessity of the case must be performed by human agency and which in given circumstances become the acts of the company, and for this purpose there is no distinction between an intention or other function of the mind and any other activity.

The offences for which a limited company cannot be indicted are exceptions to the general rule arising from the limitations which must inevitably attach to an artificial entity such as a company. Included in these exceptions are the cases in which, from its very nature, the offence cannot be committed by a corporation, as, for example, perjury, an offence which cannot be vicariously committed, or bigamy. A further exception comprises

---

44 *South Hetton Coal Co.* v. *North-Eastern News Assn.* [1894] 1 Q.B. 133; *D. & L. Caterers Ltd.* v. *D'Ajou* [1945] K.B. 364; *Bognor Regis U.D.C.* v. *Campion* [1972] 2 Q.B. 169 (local government authority which is a statutory corporation may sue for defamation affecting its "governing" reputation).

45 *Briess* v. *Woolley* [1954] A.C. 333.

46 *Weir* v. *Bell* (1878) 3 Ex.D. 238, 245.

47 For the former law, see Palmer's *Company Law* (20th ed.), pp. 132–133. The problems of the law prior to 1960 did not affect Scottish companies, to which the repealed provisions did not apply.

48 The procedural aspects of this section apply to England only. The Rules of the Supreme Court and the Criminal Justice Acts and amending Acts do not apply to Scotland. For the Scottish position, see G. H. Gordon, *The Criminal Law of Scotland* (2nd ed., 1978), paras. 8–84 to 8–93. The principles of the applicability of Scottish Criminal Law to companies are broadly similar to those enunciated in this section (see Gordon, *loc. cit.*).

offences for which the only punishment the court can impose is imprisonment.[49] The Sunday Observance Act 1677, s. 1, does not apply to companies, since a company cannot engage in public or private worship, and consequently a contract concluded on behalf of a company on a Sunday is not illegal.[50]

Upon these principles a company can be charged with conspiracy to defraud[51]; and may be convicted of making use of a document false in a material particular with intent to deceive.[52] It may be guilty of aiding and abetting if those managing the company know that an offence is being committed by a servant of the company; but in this case the knowledge of the servant himself is insufficient to render the company liable.[53]

A company can "use" a motor vehicle on a road contrary to section 134 of the Road Traffic Act 1960[54] and may be guilty of "counselling and procuring" the commission of an offence, contrary to section 1 of that Act.[55]

For the purposes of the Trade Descriptions Act 1968, s. 24 (1), the shop manager of a supermarket was "another person" than the company owning the supermarket, because no managerial function, giving him full discretion to act independently, was delegated to him; he was only a cog in the machinery and not within the "brain area" of the company.[56] To make a company criminally responsible under that Act it must be established that the natural persons concerned had the status and authority to make their acts those of the company.[57] A Scottish partnership is a "body corporate" for the purposes of the Trade Descriptions Act 1968.[58]

Where a company has committed an offence under the Unsolicited Goods and Services Act 1971, any director, manager, secretary or similar

---

[49] This and the preceding paragraph are based on the judgment of the Court of Criminal Appeal read by Stable J. in *R.* v. *I.C.R. Haulage Ltd. and Others* [1944] K.B. 551, 554. This decision virtually overruled *R.* v. *Cory Bros.* [1927] 1 K.B. 810, in which it was held that a company could not be indicted for manslaughter and personal violence. The modern rule was first indicated in *Director of Public Prosecutions* v. *Kent & Sussex Contractors Ltd.* [1944] K.B. 146; see also *Chuter* v. *Freeth & Pocock Ltd.* [1911] 2 K.B. 832. See Insurance Companies Act 1974, s. 79 (1) which provides that where an offence under that Act is committed by a body corporate and it is proved that it was committed with the consent or connivance of, or is attributable to any neglect on the part of, any director, chief executive, manager, secretary or other similar officer, he, as well as the body corporate, shall be guilty of the offence. See also *Dean* v. *John Menzies (Holdings) Ltd.* 1981 S.L.T. 51 (in which a majority of the Scottish Court of Appeal held that a company could not be charged with the offence of "shamelessly indecent" conduct).

[50] *Rolloswin Investments Ltd.* v. *Chromolit Portugal Cutelarias e Produtos Metalicos S.A.R.L.* [1970] 1 W.L.R. 912.

[51] *R.* v. *I.C.R. Haulage Ltd.* [1944] K.B. 551. The crime of conspiracy requires two independent minds and accordingly a charge against the proprietor of a "one-man" company of conspiring with the company cannot be sustained: *R.* v. *McDonnell* [1966] 1 Q.B. 233. On the circumstances in which a company can be charged with conspiracy, see *British Steel Corporation* v. *Granada Television Ltd.* [1980] 3 W.L.R. 774, 817.

[52] *Director of Public Prosecutions* v. *Kent and Sussex Contractors Ltd.* [1944] K.B. 146.

[53] *John Henshall (Quarries) Ltd.* v. *Harvey* [1965] 2 Q.B. 233.

[54] *Brown* v. *Grange Tours Ltd.* (1968) 112 S.J. 1010.

[55] *R.* v. *Robert Millar (Contractors) Ltd.* [1970] 2 Q.B. 54.

[56] *Tesco Supermarkets Ltd.* v. *Nattrass* [1970] 2 Q.B. 133, see also *British Steel Corporation* v. *Granada Television Ltd.* [1980] 3 W.L.R. 774, 817.

[57] *R.* v. *Andrews-Weatherfoil Ltd.* [1972] 1 W.L.R. 118.

[58] *Douglas* v. *Phoenix Motors*, 1970 S.L.T. 57 (Sh.Ct.).

officer or any person purporting to act in such a capacity is likewise liable to be prosecuted if the offence was committed by the company with the knowledge or connivance of such a person or is attributable to his neglect, and if the members of the company manage the affairs of the company they are treated, for the purposes of this provision, as if they were the directors of the company (s. 5 of the 1971 Act). The Banking and Financial Dealings Act 1971, s. 2 (5), contains similar provisions.

A company cannot be committed or attached for contempt of court; but a fine can be imposed on a company under the Contempt of Court Act 1981 and an order against a company may be enforced by sequestration of its property or by attachment against the directors, if they have been guilty of contempt.[59] Further, an order for committal may be made against any director or other officer of the company, even though he did not actively aid or abet the contempt but played only a passive role; for the purposes of contempt proceedings it is irrelevant whether an injunction was made against the company or an undertaking was given to the court on behalf of the company.[60] An order may be properly served if addressed to the directors and left at the registered office; but a writ of attachment cannot issue against the directors unless the memorandum indorsed on the order is addressed to the company.[61] A company is not vicariously liable for contempt if its agent does not know that the act constitutes contempt.[61a]

While at common law a company cannot be committed for trial,[62] modern statutes have remedied this position.[63]

Practice and procedure affecting companies

18–17 A company cannot appear in person in court. It must appear by counsel, or, in the county courts (in England) and sheriff courts (in Scotland), by a solicitor or other person specially authorised by the judge.[64]

A company cannot give oral evidence by a "proper officer." The evidence of such an officer is his own, not that of the company, although an admission made by him may bind the company. The company, may, however, be compelled to produce documents required by discovery or interrogatories (England)[65] or specification of documents (Scotland); but it was held in *Lonrho Ltd.* v. *Shell Petroleum Ltd.*[66] that an English company did not have the documents of a foreign subsidiary in its "power," within

---

59 R.S.C. 1965, Ord. 45, r. 5. See *Phonographic Performance Ltd.* v. *Amusement Caterers (Peckham) Ltd.* [1964] Ch. 195; *Re Garage Equipment Assn.'s Agreement* (1964) L.R. 4 R.P. 491.
60 *Biba Ltd.* v. *Stratford Investments Ltd.* [1973] Ch. 281.
61 *Benabo* v. *Jay and Partners Ltd.* [1941] Ch. 52.
61a *Z Ltd.* v. *A–Z and AA–LL,* [1982] 2 W.L.R. 288, 303.
62 *R.* v. *Daily Mirror Newspapers Ltd.* [1922] 2 K.B. 530.
63 Criminal Justice Act 1925, s. 33, as amended by the Administration of Justice (Miscellaneous Provisions) Act 1933; see *R.* v. *H. Sherman Ltd.* [1949] 2 K.B. 674; *R.* v. *Wolverhampton Deputy Recorder* [1951] 1 All E.R. 627n. Further, Criminal Justice Act 1948, s. 13.
64 *Tritonia Ltd.* v. *Equity and Law Life Assurance Society* [1943] A.C. 584.
65 *Penn-Texas Corpn.* v. *Murat Anstalt and Others* [1964] 1 Q.B. 40.
66 [1980] Q.B. 358 (C.A.); [1980] 1 W.L.R. 627 (H.L.).

the meaning of the Rules of the Supreme Court 1965, Ord. 24, rr. 2 and 3, and could, therefore, not be compelled to give discovery of documents held by the foreign subsidiary.

If in pleadings the word "Limited" or the words "public limited company" in the name of a company are omitted and the company is described as "a firm," the question arises whether this is a mere misnomer which can be amended by leave of the court, or whether the amendment would mean the substitution of a new defendant. If it is clear who is meant from the document as a whole, this is a mere misnomer, but if the misdescription necessitates further inquiries, the position may be different.[67] On service upon the company, see para. 8–13, *ante*.

Where a foreign corporation is the plaintiff in English proceedings but it ceases to exist after the institution of the proceedings owing to a merger with another foreign corporation, and judgment is entered in the English court against the original plaintiff corporation, the English court may, even after judgment and even though the judgment is a nullity, under its own inherent jurisdiction and R.S.C., Ord. 15, rr. 6 and 7 substitute the foreign corporation with which the original plaintiff has merged for the latter.[67a]

Business tenancies and rent restriction[68]

18–18 A company can form an intention within the meaning of the Landlord and Tenant Act 1954, s. 30,[69] under which an application by a tenant of business premises for a new lease could be opposed by the landlord on the ground that he intended to occupy the premises for a business to be carried on by him personally. In the words of Denning L.J.,[70] "the state of mind of [the] managers is the state of mind of the company and is treated by the law as such." Such an intention can be formed without being resolved at a formal board meeting, provided that the directors discussed the matter on other occasions and agreed on it.[70] By section 6 of the Law of Property Act 1969, where the landlord has a controlling interest in a company, any business to be carried on by the company shall be treated for the purposes of section 30 (1) (*g*) of the Landlord and Tenant Act 1954 as a business to be carried on by him. A controlling interest for this purpose means either the power to appoint or remove a majority of the directors, or the beneficial ownership of more than half the company's equity share capital.[71]

---

[67] *Per* Devlin L.J. in *Davies* v. *Elsby Brothers Ltd.* [1961] 1 W.L.R. 170, 176; *cf. Whittam* v. *W. J. Daniel & Co. Ltd.* [1962] 1 Q.B. 271. (This cannot be taken as valid in Scotland.)

[67a] *Mercer Alloys Corporation* v. *Rolls Royce Ltd.* [1971] 1 W.L.R. 1520.

[68] In Scotland the enactments referred to in this section do not apply and there is no equivalent protection of business tenancies other than shops, see generally Campbell and Paton, *Landlord and Tenant* (W. Green & Sons. Edinburgh, 1967), pp. 628 *et seq*.

[69] *H. L. Bolton (Engineering) Co. Ltd.* v. *T. J. Graham & Sons Ltd.* [1957] 1 Q.B. 159; *Betty's Cafés Ltd.* v. *Phillips Furnishing Stores Ltd.* [1959] A.C. 20. The intention must be stated honestly and truthfully in the notice and must be proved as existing at the date of the hearing at the court of first instance, *i.e.* before judgment is given in that court.

[70] *H. L. Bolton (Engineering) Co. Ltd.* v. *T. J. Graham & Sons Ltd.* [1957] 1 Q.B. 159, 172.

[71] The principle laid down in *Tunstall* v. *Steigman* [1962] 2 Q.B. 593 presumably still applies where the landlord has no controlling interest.

The fact that the company is an artificial entity can be a disadvantage in gaining the benefit of statutory provisions; thus, a company cannot be in personal residence within the meaning of the Rent Acts.[72]

Unintentional act of company in patent law

18–19 The Patent Acts provide that in some cases a patent that has been allowed to lapse, through failure to pay a renewal fee in time, may be restored to life, provided the patentee can show that the failure to pay was 'unintentional." If the patent is owned by a company, the company cannot claim that the non-payment was "unintentional" if some individual occupying a position of responsibility in the company made a deliberate decision to allow the patent to lapse unless it is clear that he had no right to exercise his judgment and that his decision was contrary to the intention, at the time, of the person with whom the decision more properly lay.[73]

Loss of privilege of shareholder's limited liability

18–20 That in certain exceptional cases a shareholder may lose the privilege of limited liability has, in principle, nothing to do with the status of the company as a separate legal entity because that privilege is a privilege of the shareholder, and not of the company. Two cases have to be distinguished here which, strictly speaking, are not *in pari materia:* the legislator may provide that the shareholder shall be liable, beyond the amount which he has agreed to pay on his shares, to the creditors of the company directly; this is a true instance of the modern tendency to disregard, in exceptional circumstances, the principle of legal persona of the company. Or the legislator may provide that the shareholder shall be liable to the company in excess of what he has to pay on his shares; in that case the corporate status of the company is fully respected and the position is similar to that of an unlimited company.

18–21 The cases in which a shareholder may lose the privilege of limited liability are:

1. Where the number of shareholders is reduced below the legal minimum and the company carries on business for more than six months while the number is so reduced.

In this case the sole remaining shareholder who is aware of these facts is liable directly to the creditors for the debts of the company contracted during that time (1948 Act, s. 31),[74] the creditors being permitted to look behind the company to the owner of the shares for their satisfaction.

---

[72] *Lee* v. *K. Carter Ltd.* [1949] 1 K.B. 85 (C.A.). Further, it cannot have the benefit of the protection granted to an occupier under the Leasehold Property (Temporary Provisions) Act 1951 if the lease is in the name of a shareholder: *Pegler* v. *Craven* [1952] 2 Q.B. 69 C.A. On notice by a director for the company, see *Harmond Properties Ltd.* v. *Gajdzis* [1968] 1 W.L.R. 1858 (C.A.).

[73] *Witton Engineering Co.'s Application* [1959] R.P.C. 53.

[74] See para. 10–05, *ante*.

2. Where in the course of winding up it appears that any business of the company has been carried on with intent to defraud creditors.

In this case the court may declare any persons who were knowingly parties to the transaction personally responsible without limitation of liability for all or any of the debts or other liabilities[75] of the company (1948 Act, s. 332).

It will be observed that under this section the court may make a shareholder, director or any other person liable but that section 31 deals only with the liability of shareholders.

Where the court makes an order under section 332 in favour of the company,[76] the money becomes part of the general assets of the company available for all creditors, not only for those whose debts were contracted while the business was carried on fraudulently.[77] In this case the creditors have no direct claim against a shareholder against whom an order is made, and the legal persona of the company is fully respected.

"Fraud," for the purposes of this section, is, in the words of Maugham J.,[78] "actual dishonesty involving, according to current notions of fair trading among commercial men, real moral blame." The court has power in its declaration to state that a person shall be personally liable (without any limitation of liability) in respect of a certain sum, being part of the debts or other liabilities of the company.[79]

3. In another case, which is different in character from the two preceding cases, a person other than the registered shareholder may be liable for what is due on the shares. If the shares are issued to a person who acts as a nominee of the company or if they have been acquired by him in this capacity, and he fails to pay the amount due on the shares within 21 days from being called on to do so, then—

(a) if the shares were issued to him as a subscriber to the memorandum, the other subscribers; or

(b) if the shares were otherwise issued to or acquired by him, the directors of the company at the time of the acquisition,

are jointly and severally liable with the nominee, as far as the liability to the company is concerned (1980 Act, s. 36 (2)). This provision is subject to certain exceptions (1980 Act, s. 36 (6)).

---

75 s. 332 refers to "debts or other liabilities" while s. 31 refers only to "debts." Prima facie the latter term means liquidated contractual liabilities and not liabilities sounding in damages: *Re Collbran* [1956] Ch. 250. But see *In re Berkeley Securities (Property) Ltd.* [1980] 1 W.L.R. 1589.

76 The court has also a discretion to make an order under this section in favour of a particular creditor or class of creditors, in which case the money does not become payable to the company, but to the persons in whose favour the order is made: *Re Cyona Distributors Ltd.* [1967] Ch. 889 (C.A.).

77 *Re W. C. Leitch Bros. Ltd.* (*No. 2*) [1933] Ch. 261.

78 *Re Patrick & Lyon Ltd.* [1933] Ch. 786, 790.

79 *Re W. C. Leitch Bros. Ltd.* [1932] 2 Ch. 71, 80; see further paras. 85–84 and 87–73, *post*.

Looking behind the company as legal persona. Lifting the veil

18–22 It may be convenient to list briefly the main instances in which modern company law disregards the principle that the company is an independent legal entity.[80] Generally speaking, the courts are more inclined, in appropriate circumstances, to "lift the veil" of corporateness where questions of control are in issue than where a question of ownership arises. The veil of corporateness is lifted in the following cases:

1. Where companies are in the relationship of holding and subsidiary (or sub-subsidiary) companies, the Companies Acts require, on principle, group accounts.[81]

2. Where a shareholder has lost the privilege of limited liability and has become directly liable to certain creditors of the company on the ground that, with his knowledge, the company continued to carry on business six months after the number of its members was reduced below the legal minimum (1948 Act, s. 31; see para. 18–21, *ante*).

3. In certain matters pertaining to the law of taxation, particularly where the question of the "controlling interest" is in issue.[82]

These topics are dealt with, as to corporation tax, in Chapter 90 (para. 90–40, *post*); as to capital transfer tax, in Chapter 92 (para. 92–05, *post*); and, as to stamps in Chapter 43 (para. 43–42, *post*).

4. In the law relating to trading with the enemy where the test of control is adopted (see para. 8–15, *ante*).

5. In the law of merger control in the United Kingdom. The Fair Trading Act 1973 adopts the test of "distinct enterprises." Cessation of being "distinct enterprises," irrespective of the legal form of those enterprises, constitutes, subject to certain conditions, a merger situation (see para. 83–02, *post*).

18–23 6. In the competition law of the European Economic Community, as contained in articles 85 and 86 of the EEC Treaty and in secondary legislation on that subject, a holding company and a subsidiary, which does not determine its behaviour on the market in an autonomous manner, are treated as forming an economic unit. An arrangement between a holding company and its non-autonomous subsidiary does not fall under article 85[83] and a holding company incorporated in a country which is not a member of the EEC is regarded as being

---

[80] The list in the text does not include cases in which the members would ordinarily be liable for acts or omissions of the company at common law, *e.g.* under the law of agency or the law of torts: an instance of such liability is *Briess* v. *Woolley* [1954] A.C. 333; para. 64–03, *post*. The company was treated as agent of the incorporator in *Smith, Stone & Knight* v. *Birmingham Corporation* [1939] 4 All E.R. 116; and *Re F. G. (Films) Ltd.* [1953] 1 All E.R. 615. See also *Camilla Cotton Oil Co.* v. *Granadax S.A.* [1975] 1 Lloyd's Rep. 470.

[81] See para. 71–03, *post*.

[82] *S. Berendsen Ltd.* v. *I.R.C.* [1958] 1 Ch. 1 (C.A.). On "control" for the purposes of the former estate duty, see *Barclays Bank Ltd.* v. *I.R.C.* [1961] A.C. 509. On "group treatment" under VAT, see *In re Nadler Enterprises Ltd.* [1981] 1 W.L.R. 23.

[83] *Re Christiani and Nielsen* [1970] C.M.L.R. D19.

present in the EEC if it has a non-autonomous subsidiary in EEC territory.[84]

7. The court will not allow an abuse of section 209 by the formation of a new company by members holding nine-tenths of the shares in an existing company, if the new company is formed solely for the purpose of expropriating the shares of the minority shareholders in the existing company.[85]

8. The courts have further shown themselves willing to "lift the veil" where the device of incorporation is used for some illegal or improper purpose. So, where a transport company sought to obtain licences for its vehicles, which it was unlikely to obtain if it made application on its own behalf, by causing the application to be made by a subsidiary company to which the vehicles were to be transferred, the court refused to treat parent and subsidiary as independent bodies, and decided the application on the basis that they were one commercial unit.[86] Similarly, where a vendor of land sought to avoid an action for specific performance by transferring the land in breach of contract to a company he had formed for the purpose, the court treated the company as a mere "sham" and made the order applied for by the purchaser.[87] Further, where three companies were controlled by one person, it was held that the companies were so "mixed up" that the person controlling them must be regarded as having actual or ostensible authority to act for any of them.[88] Where a bankrupt obtained credit for himself through the "charade" of a company, he committed an offence under section 155(*a*) of the Bankruptcy Act 1914, although normally the offence is not committed if the credit is obtained for another person.[88a]

9. Where a private company is founded on a personal relationship between the members, the court is prepared to order the winding up of the company under the "just and equitable" clause (1948 Act, s. 222 (*f*)), if a member commits a breach of good faith which the members owe each other as the result of the personal relationship and thereby acts inequitably.[89] Such a relationship exists also where the

---

[84] *I.C.I. and Others* v. *EEC Commission* [1972] C.M.L.R. 557; *Commercial Solvents Corpn.* v. *EEC Commission* [1973] C.M.L.R. 309 (the *Zoja* case).

[85] *Re Bugle Press Ltd.* [1961] Ch. 270; see para. 81–12, *post*.

[86] *Merchandise Transport Ltd.* v. *British Transport Commission* [1962] 2 Q.B. 173; see also the observations of Lord Denning M.R. in *Littlewood's Mail Order Stores* v. *I.R.C.* [1969] 1 W.L.R. 1241, 1254.

[87] *Jones* v. *Lipman* [1962] 1 W.L.R. 832. For further cases on this subject, see Samuels, "Lifting the Veil" [1964] J.B.L. 107; Schmitthoff, "Salomon in the Shadow," [1978] J.B.L. 218. See also *Malyon* v. *Plummer* [1964] 1 Q.B. 330 (damages to wife for cessation of company's activities caused by death of husband) and *Freddie Goodwin Ltd.* v. *Birmingham City Football Club* (1980) 130 N.L.J. 471 (company failed reasonably to mitigate damages; it would be unreasonable if the corporator and the company received a double benefit).

[88] *Ford Motor Credit Co. Ltd.* v. *Harmack, The Times,* July, 7, 1972; [1972] J.B.L. 225.

[88a] *R.* v. *Godwin* (1980) 71 Cr.App.R. 97 (C.A.).

[89] *Ebrahimi* v. *Westbourne Galleries Ltd.* [1973] A.C. 360.

members of the private company have entered into a management participation agreement,[90] according to which each group of members shall appoint one director and one group refuses to allow the other group to exercise this right. That these quasi-partnership companies may be wound up by the court by virtue of section 222 (*f*) in appropriate circumstances constitutes a lifting of the veil of corporateness, because here the substance of the association prevails over its legal form. In *Ebrahimi* v. *Westbourne Galleries Ltd.* Lord Wilberforce, when commenting on the words "just and equitable" in section 222 (*f*), said that "the words are a recognition of the fact that a limited company is more than a mere judicial entity, with a personality in law of its own: that there is room in company law for recognition of the fact that behind it, or amongst it, there are individuals, with rights, expectations and obligations *inter se* which are not necessarily submerged in the company structure."[91]

10. In industrial relations, several companies promoted by the same controlling shareholder may constitute a single "undertaking" for the purposes of section 27 (1) (*a*) of the Industrial Relations Act 1971 (re-enacted by the Trade Union and Labour Relations Act 1974, Sched. 1, Pt. II), which deals with unfair dismissal.[92]

11. In other exceptional cases, in which the facts or equitable considerations justify an exemption from the strict rule in *Salomon* v. *Salomon & Co. Ltd.*[93] the courts are prepared to "lift the veil" of corporateness. Thus, in *D.H.N. Food Distributors Ltd.* v. *Tower Hamlets London Borough Council,*[94] land which was registered in the name of a subsidiary was compulsorily acquired by the Borough Council. The subsidiary did not carry on business on the land but the parent company did, and as the result of the compulsory acquisition the parent lost the opportunity of carrying on its trade on the land. The Borough Council pleaded that only the subsidiary was entitled to compensation for the disturbance of business, but not the parent and, as the subsidiary did not carry on business on the land, it had not suffered any loss. The Court of Appeal rejected this defence and held that the parent company was entitled to compensation for disturbance of business. The ratio of this decision was that the parent was the equitable owner of the land and it would have been impossible for the subsidiary to terminate the occupation of the land by the parent and to prevent the latter from carrying on its trade on the land.

The *D.H.N. Food Distributors* case was distinguished on its facts in the Scottish case of *Woolfson* v. *Strathclyde Regional Council.*[95] In this

---

[90] *In re A. & B.C. Chewing Gum Ltd.* [1975] 1 W.L.R. 579.
[91] *Supra*, at p. 379.
[92] *Kapur* v. *Shields* [1976] 1 W.L.R. 131, 139.
[93] [1897] A.C. 22.
[94] [1976] 1 W.L.R. 852.
[95] 1977 S.L.T. 60; 1977 S.C. 84; affd. 1978 S.L.T. 159 (H.L.); (1979) 38 P. & C.R. 521; 1978 S.C. (H.L.) 90.

case a property partly owned by Woolfson and partly by a family company (Solfred Holdings Ltd.) was compulsorily acquired by the local authority. The occupants were a further company (M. & L. Campbell (Glasgow) Ltd.—"Campbell") which had carried on business in the premises for a number of years prior to the compulsory purchase. Campbell had 1,000 issued shares, 999 held by Woolfson and the remaining share held by his wife. Campbell operated in every respect as a normal trading company, Mr. and Mrs. Woolfson being directors and full-time employees. There was no formal lease between Campbell and the owners and the arrangements for payment of rent were changed from time to time, apparently to suit Mr. Woolfson's tax position and his wish to transfer funds to Solfred Holdings Ltd. The owners of the property (Woolfson and Solfred Holdings Ltd.) sought compensation for disturbance under the Land Compensation (Scotland) Act 1963, s. 12 (6) which restricted such a claim to an owner-occupier (this has since been amended by the Land Compensation (Scotland) Act 1973). The claimants invited the court to look behind the legal position and proceed on the basis of the alleged "reality" of an "economic unit" comprising Woolfson and the two companies, thus entitling it to regard Woolfson and Campbell as a single "owner-occupier." The House of Lords held, however, that the "reality" in this case was the independent existence of Campbell, and there was no basis for departing from the principle of separate legal personality established by *Salomon*.

12. In *Lonrho Ltd.* v. *Shell Petroleum Co. Ltd.*[96] the question arose whether English holding companies could be compelled by an English court to give discovery of documents held by their Rhodesian and South African subsidiaries under the Rules of the Supreme Court 1965, Ord. 24, rr. 2 and 3, which required the disclosure of all documents (except privileged ones) in the "possession, custody or power" of a party. It was clear that the Rhodesian and South African documents were not in the "possession or custody" of the English holding companies but the question was whether they were in their "power." The Court of Appeal held that much depended on the facts of the individual case and that in the present case the documents were not in the "power" of the holding companies, as the subsidiaries enjoyed a great deal of autonomy and compliance with a request for disclosure would have exposed the directors of the subsidiaries to criminal prosecution in the countries in which they carried on business. The House of Lords affirmed this decision of the Court of Appeal.[97]

13. In a trade mark case, *Revlon Inc.* v. *Cripps & Lee*[98] the Court of Appeal held that, as far as the use of the trade mark "*Revlon Flex*"

[96] [1980] 2 W.L.R. 367.
[97] [1980] 1 W.L.R. 627.
[98] [1980] F.S.R. 85.

was concerned, the Revlon Group of companies should be treated as a whole and the trade mark as belonging to all companies of the group. Consequently, an action by some companies of the group against importers of the product manufactured in the United States of America and marked with the mark "Revlon Flex," and sold in the United Kingdom under that mark was dismissed because, on the facts of the case, all companies in the Revlon group had to be treated as having consented to the use of that trade mark in the United Kingdom. The House of Lords refused leave to appeal.

14. In *Amalgamated Investment & Property Co. Ltd. (in liquidation)* v. *Texas Commerce International Bank Ltd.*[98a] the plaintiffs undertook a guarantee for loans advanced by the defendant bank to one of the plaintiffs' subsidiaries. Some of these loans were given, for exchange control reasons, through a wholly-owned subsidiary of the bank in the Bahamas named Portsoken, but the guarantee was never expressly extended to the Portsoken loans. The Court of Appeal held that the plaintiffs' guarantee covered the Portsoken loans. Lord Denning M.R. said that Portsoken had to be regarded as the alter ego of its parent, the bank, but the other judges (Eveleigh and Brandon L.JJ.) preferred to found their judgments in favour of the bank on an estoppel created by the course of dealing between the parties.

15. It was held in *Canada Enterprises Corpn. Ltd.* v. *MacNab Distilleries Ltd.*[98b] and *Orri* v. *Moundreas*[98c] that, in exercising its power to grant a stay of execution under R.S.C. 1965, Ord. 47, the court would look behind the corporate structure of one or both parties to ascertain the persons truly interested; if there were several actions in which different parties were involved but the parties were controlled by identical persons. The powers of the court under Ord. 47 were wide enough to enable the court to order a stay of execution of one or more of the several actions.

Liability of holding company for the debts of a subsidiary

This problem is increasingly discussed in modern company law. The legal principle is clear: On principle, "the separate legal existence of the consitutent companies of the group has to be respected"; *per* Lord Wilberforce in *Ford & Carter Ltd.,* v. *Midland Bank Ltd.*[99] The rule in *Salomon* v. *Salomon & Co. Ltd.* thus prevails; see also Pennycuick J. in *Charterbridge Corporation* v. *Lloyds Bank Ltd.*[1] That is particularly so when the creditors of the holding company are different from those of the subsidiary, as will normally be the case. However, the holding company is liable for a debt of the subsidiary if it has guaranteed

---

[98a] [1981] 3 W.L.R. 365 (C.A.).
[98b] [1981] Com.L.R. 167 (C.A.).
[98c] [1981] Com.L.R. 168 (Musthill.J.)
[99] (1979) 129 N.L.J. 543, 544.
[1] [1970] Ch. 62.

that debt or if it can be established, as a matter of fact, that the subsidiary has acted in a particular transaction as an agent of the holding company or that there has been an abuse of the corporate form. In *Ford & Carter Ltd.* v. *Midland Bank Ltd.*, above, companies in a group gave guarantees to a bank. Ford & Carter Ltd. joined the group later. Mr. Rust, who was director of some of the subsidiaries, but not of Ford & Carter Ltd., was invested with authority from the group or from the parent company to commit the subsidiary companies to guarantee the accounts of those companies with the bank. But apparently no document was signed by which Ford & Carter Ltd. undertook a guarantee for the group liability to the bank. Whitford J. held that Ford & Carter Ltd. were not bound by the group guarantee to the bank, but the Court of Appeal, on the construction of the guarantee, reversed that decision. The House of Lords reversed the decision of the Court of Appeal and restored the decision of Whitford J. Lord Wilberforce observed: "In the absence of some contractual act or document, they [the companies which joined the group subsequently] cannot be bound to the bank. So far as the companies themselves are concerned, it is undisputable that no such contractual act or document exists. Were they then committed through the agency of Mr. Rust? I can find no evidence to support such a contention." It is respectfully observed that, while the legal reasoning of this decision is unimpeachable, one could have taken the view that, as a matter of fact, there was sufficient evidence before the court to find that Mr. Rust had sufficient authority to bind the companies which subsequently joined the group; see also the observations of Templeman L.J. in *Re Southard & Co. Ltd.*[2]

Distinction from partnership

18–24 The principle that, apart from exceptional cases, the company is a body corporate, distinct from its members, lies at the root of many of the most perplexing questions that beset company law. It is a fundamental or cardinal distinction—a distinction which must be firmly grasped. The principle is thrown into clear relief by contrasting an incorporated company with a partnership, for under English law (though not under Scottish law or that of most Continental systems) a firm or partnership is not a separate entity from its members.

The principal distinctions between a company and an English partnership are as follows:

1. In the case of a partnership the property of the firm belongs to the individual members. They are collectively entitled to it, whereas, in the case of a company, it belongs to the company, and not to the members.[3]

---

[2] [1979] 1 W.L.R. 1198, 1208, Clive M. Schmitthoff, "The Wholly Owned and the Controlled Subsidiary" in [1978] J.B.L. 218.

[3] *R.* v. *Arnaud* (1846) 9 Q.B. 806; *Re George Newman & Co.* [1895] 1 Ch. 674, 685.

2. Creditors of a firm are creditors of the members of the firm, and on obtaining judgment against the firm can levy execution on the property of the partners in the firm, whereas, in the case of a company, "the creditor has no debtor but that impalpable thing, the corporation,"[4] and judgment against the company normally gives no right to levy execution against the members.

3. A member of a firm can on behalf of the firm dispose of property and incur liabilities, within the scope of the business, to any extent (unless this authority is expressly excluded), whereas a member of a company, as such, has no such power.

4. A partner cannot contract with the firm, whereas a member of the company can contract with the company.

18–25 So far as Scottish partnerships are concerned, the position in the above matters is as follows:

1. The partnership property belongs to the firm. Generally title is taken in name of the partners in trust for the firm and its partners present and future.

2. As in England.

3. As in England.

4. A contract between a partner and his firm is possible.[5]

---

[4] Jessel M.R. in *Flitcroft's Case* (1882) 21 ChD. 519, 533.

[5] See *Dove* v. *Young* 1868, 7 M. 304.

Chapter 19

COMMENCEMENT OF BUSINESS

Private companies

19–01 A private company may commence business immediately on the issue of the certificate of incorporation. It may, as from that date, forthwith exercise all the functions of an incorporated company, including its borrowing powers.

This principle applies to all types of private companies, whether limited by shares, limited by guarantee, or unlimited.

Public companies formed as such

19–02 Such a company is not entitled to commence business or to exercise its borrowing powers on the issue of the certificate of incorporation, unless the Registrar has issued it with a further certificate or it is re-registered as a private company (1980 Act, s. 4 (1)). This further certificate is commonly known as the trading certificate or the section 4 certificate.

The Registrar will issue the trading certificate only if:

1. he is satisfied that the nominal value of the allotted capital of the company is not less than the authorised minimum (1980 Act, s. 4 (2)),[1] and

2. a statutory declaration in the prescribed form and signed by a director or secretary is delivered to the Registrar. It has to state (1980 Act, s. 4 (3)):–

   (a) the amount of the allotted share capital (which must not be less than the authorised minimum);

   (b) the amount paid up, at the time of the appliation, on the allotted share capital. The shares allotted must be paid up at least as to one quarter of their nominal value and the whole of any premium (1980 Act, s. 22 (1)). The shares taken by the subscribers shall be paid in cash, and not in consideration other than cash (1980 Act, s. 29).

   (c) the preliminary expenses and the persons liable for them; and

   (d) any benefit given or intended to be given to any promoter of the company and the consideration for it.

19–03 When calculating the allotted capital of the company, as required under (1) and (2) (*a*) of the preceding paragraph, shares allotted under any employees' share scheme[2] shall not be taken into account unless they are

---

[1] On the authorised minimum, see para. 11–02, *ante*.
[2] On employees' share schemes, see para. 94–01, *ante*.

paid up at least as to one-quarter of their nominal value and the whole of any premium (1980 Act, s. 4 (4)).

Effect of doing business before the issue of the trading certificate

19–04 A third party with whom the public company enters into a transaction before the grant of the trading certificate is protected and the transaction is valid as against the company. If the company fails to comply with its obligations under such a transaction within 21 days after being called upon to do so, the directors jointly and severally are liable to indemnify the third party for any loss or damage which he has suffered in consequence of the company's failure to comply with its obligations (1980 Act, s. 4 (8)).

The company and any of its officers who are in default are liable to criminal sanctions if the public company engages in business before the grant of the trading certificate (1980 Act, s. 4 (7)).

If the company has not been issued with a trading certificate within one year of its original registration, it may be wound up by order of the court (1948 Act, s. 222 (*b*), as amended by the 1980 Act, Sched. 3, para. 27).

Statutory meeting

19–05 The holding of a statutory meeting prior to the grant of the trading certificate and the presentation of a statutory report to this meeting are no longer necessary. Section 130 of the 1948 Act which contained these requirements is repealed by the 1980 Act (Sched. 4).

Public companies re-registered after having been private companies

19–06 Such a company may commence business and exercise its borrowing powers on being registered as a private company and being granted a certificate of incorporation as such a company. A trading certificate is not required on re-registration as a public company. Re-registration is carried out as described in para. 5–05, *ante*.

As regards such a company, the position is the same, before and after re-registration, as described earlier for private companies (para.19–01, *ante*).

Unpopularity of restrictions on commencement of business

19–07 The inability of the public company to commence business before the grant of the trading certificate is in practice regarded as being extremely inconvenient, particularly in the normal cases in which arrangements for the financing of the company are made before it is formed. This requirement is the main reason why in modern practice, when it is intended to form a public company, the company is first registered as a private company which is later re-registered as a public company in accordance with section 5 of the 1980 Act.

F. ISSUE OF SHARES

CHAPTER 20

PROMOTERS

Who are promoters?

20–01 The word "promoter" conveys to the layman a picture of a person whose activities are directed specifically and deliberately towards the bringing into being of a company or companies: but just as, for the purpose of the Companies Acts, the word "director" covers a wider field than that pictured by the layman, so, in company law, does the name "promoter"[1]: in each case it is a question of fact whether or not a person is a promoter. Any person who undertakes to take part in forming a company, or who, with regard to a proposed or newly formed company, takes part in raising capital for it, is prima facie a promoter of the company, for he has taken part in setting going a company formed with reference to a given object.[2] Thus a person may be a promoter though he has taken a comparatively minor part in the promotion proceedings.[3] Anyone who assists in the promotion, *e.g.* by obtaining a director, or agreeing to place shares, or negotiating an agreement, or merely by putting a vendor in touch with persons who may form a company to exploit or purchase his goods, may find himself a promoter of any company which is consequently formed.

20–02 A person who merely acts in a professional capacity on behalf of a promoter, such as a solicitor who draws up an agreement or articles of association or an accountant or valuer who prepares figures or a valuation on behalf of a promoter, and who is paid by the person for whom he acts whether or not a company comes into being as a result, will not find himself to be a promoter.[4] If, however, he goes further than this as, for instance, by putting his client in touch with a person who may be interested in taking shares in the new company, he is liable to find himself regarded as a promoter. In section 43, which deals with prospectuses, a promoter for the purposes of that section specifically excludes "any person by reason of his acting in a professional capacity for persons engaged in procuring the formation of the company" (s. 43 (5) (*a*)). In the same category are clerks

---

[1] The 1948 Act contains a general definition of "director" in s. 455 and the 1980 Act, s. 63, a definition of "shadow director" for the purposes of Pt. IV of that Act, but none of the Companies Acts contains a general definition of "promoter." The 1948 Act contains, in s. 43 (5) (*a*), a definition for the purposes of that section which deals with prospectuses only and is not of general purport.

[2] See Cockburn C.J. in *Twycross* v. *Grant* (1877) 2 C.P.D. 469, 541; *Emma Silver Mining Co.* v. *Lewis* (1879) 4 C.P.D. 396, 407.

[3] See Viscount Finlay in *Jubilee Cotton Mills Ltd.* v. *Lewis* [1924] A.C. 958, 965.

[4] *Re Great Wheal Polgooth Co. Ltd.* (1883) 53 L.J. Ch. 42.

and employees of a person engaged in the promotion. They are not thereby themselves promoters, but if they in fact take part, outside their duties as clerks or employees, in the promotion, they will themselves be promoters. A person who acts in a professional capacity and does not qualify as a promoter in the legal sense, may, nevertheless, in appropriate circumstances be liable under the principle established in *Hedley Byrne & Co. Ltd.* v. *Heller and Partners Ltd.*[5]

20–03 Persons who intend to form a private company and before its incorporation work together but do not intend to carry on business in common with a view to profit, are not partners within the meaning of section 1 (1) of the Partnership Act 1890.[6]

Purchase of property as trustee for company

20–04 It will be seen from the above that a person who purchases property expressly as trustee for an intended company is himself a promoter of the company.[7] But the law looks not merely to the words but to the substance of any transaction, so that even if he does not state that he is acquiring the property as trustee for the intended company, if in fact he purchases property with a view to getting the company formed to take it over, he is, in the eyes of the law, in the position of a promoter. So in *Gluckstein* v. *Barnes*[8] certain persons bought some property with an express view of either having a company formed to purchase it or of exploiting it themselves; the court found on the facts that the real intention was the former, and that the latter intention was never really in their contemplation; accordingly they were, from the moment that they proposed to purchase the property with a view to such resale, promoters of the company which was in due course formed.

Acquisition of non-cash assets by the company

20–05 If a public company (other than an old public company[9]) wishes to acquire non-cash assets for a consideration of at least one-tenth of the issued capital from a subscriber to the memorandum during two years from the issue of the trading certificate, an expert's valuation report is required (1980 Act, s. 26).[10] The same applies on the re-registration of a private company as a public company, but in this case the persons disposing of the non-cash assets are the members at the date of re-registration and the two-years' period begins to run from the date of re-registration (1980 Act, s. 26).

---

[5] [1964] A.C. 465; *Esso Petroleum Co. Ltd.* v. *Mardon* [1976] Q.B. 801; *Box* v. *Midland Bank Ltd.* [1979] 2 Lloyd's Rep. 391. But there is no liability if there is no "reliance" by the plaintiff on the defendant's statement: *J.E.B. Fasteners Ltd.* v. *Marks, The Times,* July 24, 1982 (C.A.).

[6] *Spicer (Keith) Ltd.* v. *Mansell* [1970] 1 W.L.R. 333.

[7] *Bagnall* v. *Carlton* (1877) 6 Ch.D. 371, 407.

[8] [1900] A.C. 240.

[9] On the definition of "old public company" see para. 4–17, *ante*.

[10] See para. 12–10, *ante*.

Date from which a person becomes a promoter

20–06 It will thus be seen that not only does the question arise of who are the promoters of a company, but, secondly, from what date did each become a promoter. The answer to the second question follows from that of the first, namely, that a person is a promoter of a company from the moment that he takes part in forming it or setting it going. Thus the members of the syndicate in *Gluckstein* v. *Barnes*,[11] which agreed to combine to purchase the property with a view to selling it later to a company to be formed by them, were promoters from the moment that they took the first step to carry out this object. On the other hand, a person who purchases property with a view to working it himself, and who at a later date decides to have a company formed with a view to purchasing the property from him, is not, at the date when he acquired the property, a promoter of the subsequently formed company, but from the moment that he takes steps to have the company formed he becomes a promoter. Finally, there is the third case of this nature where an owner of property sells it to a newly formed company, or to persons who purchase it on behalf of a proposed company, or to persons who purchase it with a view to forming a company to take the property from them: in none of these cases is the original owner, by virtue of his ownership of the property, a promoter of the company which is eventually formed, for he has taken no steps in forming it or setting it going.

The date upon which a person becomes a promoter can be a matter of great importance to him and to the company, because once the relationship has arisen the promoter is in a fiduciary relationship towards the company, and once the company has come into existence it will be able to take the necessary measures to secure its position *vis-à-vis* the promoter.

Fiduciary position of promoters

20–07 The promoters of a company, as Lord Cairns said in *Erlanger* v. *New Sombrero Phosphate Co.*,[12] "stand undoubtedly in a fiduciary position. They have in their hands the creation and moulding of the company. They have the power of defining how, and when, and in what shape, and under what supervision, it shall start into existence and begin to act as a trading corporation."

The importance of the rule, which thus creates a fiduciary relationship[13] between the promoter and the company he brings into existence, will be at once seen when we consider its consequences—the corollary which the law deduces from it—namely, that a promoter, being in a fiduciary position, may not make, either directly or indirectly, any profit at the expense of the

[11] [1900] A.C. 240.
[12] (1878) 3 App.Cas. 1218, 1236.
[13] On the fiduciary position of directors and their duty to account for profits to their company, see *Regal (Hastings) Ltd.* v. *Gulliver* [1942] 1 All E.R. 378; and Chapter 64, *post*.

company he promotes, without the knowledge and consent of the company, and that, if he does make a secret profit in disregard of this rule, the company can compel him to account for it.[14] Thus promoters will be compelled to surrender secret profits; and the fact that the promoter is acting as agent for the vendors, or for other promoters, will not exonerate him from accounting to the company, when formed, for any secret profit made by him.[15] The same principle applies where a promoter desires to sell his own property to the company. He is quite entitled to so, subject to the valuation referred to in para. 20–05, *ante*, if the conditions mentioned therein are applicable; but he is bound to protect the company he has created by furnishing it with an independent and competent board of directors, and by disclosing his interest in the property to such directors, so that they can exercise an intelligent judgment on the transaction.[16] or by ensuring that "the real truth is disclosed to those who are induced by the promoters to join the company."[17] Thus, if a syndicate of joint owners of property sell the property to a company formed by them for that purpose and in which they are the sole shareholders, any profit made by them as a result of such sale cannot be impeached by the company, for all the members at the time were aware of it.[18]

20–08 The company can claim any profit made by the promoter, and there need be no "necessary imputation of evil purpose or conscious fraud."[19] Lord Blackburn said[20]:

> "I think, however, that under such circumstances the burden of proof lies on the fiduciary agents, agents selling to those to whom they owed a duty to prove, if not that insufficient protection had been afforded, at least that they had sufficient reasons for *bona fide* believing that sufficient protection had been afforded to their purchasers."

A promoter-vendor cannot evade this liability of disclosure by putting in a nominee-vendor to sell to the company,[21] or by making disclosures merely to a board of directors who are under his influence or in his pay. Lord Halsbury L.C in *Gluckstein* v. *Barnes*[22] observed:

> "It is too absurd to suggest that a disclosure to the parties to this transaction is a disclosure to the company of which these directors

---

[14] *Emma Silver Mining Co.* v. *Grant* (1879) 11 Ch.D. 918; *Bagnall* v. *Carlton* (1877) 6 Ch.D. 371; *Gluckstein* v. *Barnes* [1900] A.C. 240; *Whaley Bridge Co.* v. *Green* (1879) 5 Q.B.D. 109; *Mann* v. *Edinburgh Northern Trams Co.* [1893] A.C. 69; *Re Leeds and Hanley Theatre of Varieties Ltd. (No. 1)* [1902] 2 Ch. 809; *Henderson* v. *The Huntington Copper and Sulphate Co.* 1877, 5 R. (H.L.) 1.

[15] *Lydney and Wigpool Iron Ore Co.* v. *Bird* (1886) 33 Ch.D. 85.

[16] *Per* Lord Cairns in *Erlanger* v. *New Sombrero Phosphate Co.* (1878) 3 App.Cas. 1218, 1236.

[17] *Per* Lindley M.R. in *Lagunas Nitrate Co.* v. *Lagunas Nitrate Syndicate* [1899] 2 Ch. 392, 422.

[18] See *Salomon* v. *Salomon & Co. Ltd.* [1897] A.C. 22; *Re British Seamless Paper Box Co.* (1881) 17 Ch.D. 467; *Lagunas Nitrate Co.* v. *Lagunas Nitrate Syndicate* [1899] 2 Ch. 392; *Re Sale Hotel and Botanical Gardens* (1898) 78 L.T. 368.

[19] *Per* Lord O'Hagan in *Erlanger* v. *New Sombrero Phosphate Co.* (1878) 3 App.Cas. 1218, 1256.

[20] *Ibid.* at p. 1277.

[21] *Glasier* v. *Rolls* (1889) 42 Ch.D. 436.

[22] [1900] A.C. 240, 247.

were the proper guardians and trustees. They were there by the terms of the agreement to do the work of the syndicate, that is to say, to cheat the shareholders; and this, forsooth, is to be treated as a disclosure to the company, when they were really there to hoodwink the shareholders . . . ."

Lord Macnaghten said[23]:

" 'Disclosure' is not the most appropriate word to use when a person who plays many parts announces to himself in one character what he has done and is doing in another. To talk of disclosure to the thing called the company, when as yet there were no shareholders, is a mere farce."

Where a promoter in selling his property to the company does not comply with his obligations as regards disclosure and otherwise, the sale may be set aside at the instance of the company.[24] And if for any reason rescission has become impossible, the company is entitled to damages against the promoter, the measure of such damages being the profit made by the promoters upon the purchase and resale of the property.[25]

When a promoter acquires property after he has commenced to promote and sells it to the company, a question of fact is raised as to whether or not he acquired it as trustee for the company, and there is no presumption of law that he did. Thus, in *Omnium Electric Palaces Ltd.* v. *Baines*[26] a company agreed to purchase from its promoters what was described as a lease "agreed to be granted" to the promoters: in fact there was at the time no such agreement for the lease as could have been enforced by the promoters, but subsequently they acquired the agreement for the lease and assigned it to the company, thereby making a profit. The Court of Appeal held that there was no secret profit here, nor did the promoter acquire the agreement for the lease as trustees for the company.

20–09 In relation to disclosure it must be borne in mind that a half-disclosure is sometimes worse than none; for example, if the prospectus states that the promoters' profit was £30,000, whereas it really was £50,000, the partial concealment falsifies the statement made. Thus in *Gluckstein* v. *Barnes*[27] the promoters disclosed to the company that they had purchased for £140,000 the property which the company was now to purchase for £180,000. But apart from the profit which they thus disclosed, the promoters had in addition made a profit which they had not disclosed, in that shortly before they purchased the property, they had bought, at a figure well below par, debentures in the company which at that time owned the property, knowing that such debentures would be repaid at par if the sale materialised: in effect, therefore, the purchase price payable by them for the property was reduced accordingly, and the House of Lords had no

---

23 *Ibid.* at p. 249.
24 See *Erlanger* v. *New Sombrero Co., supra.*
25 *Re Leeds and Hanley Theatre of Varieties* [1902] 2 Ch. 809 (C.A.).
26 [1914] 1 Ch. 332.
27 [1900] A.C. 240.

difficulty in holding that these profits should also have been disclosed. Moreover, it was held that a reference in the prospectus to "intermediate transactions," which might have led a reader to investigate further, was not adequate disclosure, that is, a promoter of a company whose duty it is to disclose what profits he has made does not perform that duty by making a statement, not disclosing the facts, but containing something which, if followed up by further investigation, will enable the inquirer to ascertain that profits have been made, and what they amounted to. Consequently an authorisation by the company for the promoters to retain such intermediate profits was, in the circumstances, inoperative.

20–10 In *Jubilee Cotton Mills* v. *Lewis*,[28] it was held that a promoter who received, by way of a secret reward for his part in promoting a company, an allotment of shares which had been allotted before a statement in lieu of prospectus, which was then required by law, had been filed was liable to account for the profit made on the resale of the shares.[29]

A partner of a person who makes a secret profit which is paid into the partnership account is himself liable for it.[30] All the promoters who have shared a secret profit are severally liable for the whole but with a right of contribution from their co-promoters,[31] though promoters are not, as such, co-partners. Expenses properly incurred may be deducted.[32]

Remuneration of promoters

20–11 Having seen how varied are the types of persons who are classified as promoters, it will be readily realised that the modes in which promoters obtain their remuneration vary considerably.

Sometimes the promoters agree with the owner of a going business or some other property that they will form and float a company to acquire the same, and the vendor, in consideration of their doing so, agrees to pay them a commission or part of the consideration for the sale when received. Sometimes the plan resorted to is for the promoters to purchase the business, concession, patent or other property which the proposed company is formed to acquire, and then to resell it to the company at a profit.

In other cases the promoters form the company with part of its share capital in founders' shares, or deferred shares, and then take these founders' or deferred shares credited as paid up, in consideration of their paying the expenses of forming and floating the company. In such cases, that is, of shares allotted as fully paid but not for cash, a contract or particulars must still be registered under section 52 (1) (*b*), and the shares must be entered as fully paid in the return of allotments required by the same section.

---

[28] [1924] A.C. 958.
[29] On the duty of the directors to account to their company for a profit made by an undisclosed subscription of shares in a subsidiary, see para. 64–23, *post*.
[30] *Bagnall* v. *Carlton* (1877) 6 Ch.D. 371.
[31] *Gluckstein* v. *Barnes* [1900] A.C. 240; Law Reform (Married Women and Joint Tortfeasors) Act 1935. (This Act does not apply to Scotland where the common law would achieve a similar result.)
[32] *Gluckstein* v. *Barnes* [1900] A.C. 240.

In other cases the promoters are content to accept as their remuneration the privilege of subscribing for a certain number of shares of small amount carrying valuable rights, *e.g.* founders' or deferred shares, and paying for these in cash, relying for their profit on the likelihood of the shares substantially increasing in value in the near future.

Sometimes promoters take an option to subscribe within a year for a certain portion of the company's unissued shares at par. If the shares in the company are likely to go to a premium, such an option may be of considerable value. Such an option is valid,[33] and may be given as the consideration for subscribing for, underwriting or placing shares.[34]

Sometimes the articles of association provide that the directors will pay a specified sum to the promoters in respect of their services in promoting the company; but a clause of this kind gives, it must be remembered, merely an authority to the directors to pay such expenses, and does not constitute a contract on which the promoter can sue the company.[35] Nor will the presence of such a clause justify the directors in paying out money without due inquiry.[36]

Whatever be the nature of the remuneration or benefit, it must be disclosed in the prospectus if paid within the preceding[37] two years or intended to be paid at any time (see s. 38 (1) and Sched. IV, Pt. I, para. 13).

A promoter can only recover from the company what he has paid in preliminary expenses where he proves a contract by the company to pay.[38]

A promoter who has abused his fiduciary position is generally held liable as a constructive trustee. A claim against him will be barred by a delay of six years after the company has discovered, or could with reasonable diligence have discovered, the abuse of the fiduciary position, except if fraud can be established, in which case no time limit applies (Limitation Act 1980, s. 21).[39] In case of bankruptcy of a promoter, an order of discharge does not release him from any liability incurred by fraud or fraudulent breach of trust.[40]

Liability of promoters in respect of propectuses

20–12 Promoters who take part in the issue of prospectuses offering shares, debentures or debenture stock for subscription may incur serious liabilities

---

[33] *Re South African Trust Co., ex p. Hirsch* (1896) 74 L.T. 769.
[34] *Hilder* v. *Dexter* [1902] A.C. 474.
[35] *Re Rotherham Alum, etc., Co.* (1883) 25 Ch.D. 103.
[36] *Re Englefield Colliery Co.* (1878) 8 Ch.D. 388; *Marzetti's Case* (1880) 28 W.R. 541; *Mason's Trustees* v. *Poole and Robinson* 1903 5 F. 789, 11 S.L.T. 52.
[37] From the date of the prospectus (s. 37); see para. 21–20, *post*.
[38] *Re English and Colonial Produce Co.* [1906] 2 Ch. 435; the decision in this case that the promoter can, without proving a contract, recover the registration fees was overruled in *Re National Motor Mail-Coach Co.* [1908] 2 Ch. 515; *Edinburgh Northern Tramways Co.* v. *Mann* 1896, 23 R. 1056, 4 S.L.T. 90.
[39] The Limitation Act 1980 does not apply to Scotland where such a claim would be barred only by the operation of the negative prescription, or on principles of personal bar.
[40] *Emma Silver Mining Co.* v. *Grant* (1880) 17 Ch.D. 122; Bankruptcy Act 1914, s. 28 (1) (not applicable to Scotland). See also, as to bankruptcy, *Re Kent County Gas Co.* [1913] 1 Ch. 92.

in regard thereto. They may, if the prospectus omits to give the information required by section 38 and Schedule IV, or makes any untrue statement, be held liable to compensate subscribers for any damage sustained by them.[41]

[41] See further, para. 21–36, *post*.

CHAPTER 21

THE PROSPECTUS

Methods of public offers of shares or debentures

21–01 A public company[1] desirous of raising money by the issue of shares or debentures may do so in various ways. The following are the principal methods:

Direct invitations by the company

21–02 This is the most obvious method by which a company will seek to raise capital: it will do so by inviting members of the public to subscribe for its shares or debentures and, by setting out the prospects of the company and the purposes for which the capital is required, will attempt to attract investors directly.

Financial men, when referring to an issue by way of prospectus, will normally think of this procedure. It will, however, be seen[2] that a prospectus in the legal sense has a much wider connotation and includes many instances in which the invitation to the public does not emanate from the company directly.

Offers for sale

21–03 An offer for sale occurs where a company allots shares or debentures to allottees, normally an issuing house, which will publish an invitation to the public offering them the shares or debentures for sale. On an application by a member of the public the issuing house renounces the allotment, as far as relating to the securities to which the application refers, in favour of the purchaser who becomes a direct allottee of the shares or debentures. This procedure has the advantage of saving stamp duty which would be payable on a transfer of the shares or debentures from the issuing house to the purchaser but which is not payable on direct allotment.

As far as the company is concerned, this procedure, which today is much more common than direct invitations to the public, has much to recommend it. The issuing house agrees to underwrite[3] the issue and thus bears the risk of its success or failure if the public does not take up the whole issue. In this event, the issuing house is allotted the balance of the shares and debentures and attempts to "place" them with investors later on.

An offer for sale is a prospectus within the meaning of the 1948 Act (s. 45).

---

[1] The methods by which a private company may raise money by the issue of shares or debentures are different and outside the purview of this chapter, unless stated otherwise; see further s. 55 (2) (*a*), para. 21–17, *post*.

[2] See paras. 21–15 *et seq.*, *post*.

[3] On underwriting, see para. 23–01, *post*.

Placings

21–04 In this case the issuing house (or firm of stockbrokers) to whom the shares or debentures are allotted sells and transfers them to its clients and associates, usually in fairly substantial blocks.

The procedure of placings differs from the preceding two types of issue procedure in several respects: first, no invitation, direct or indirect, is addressed to the public; and, secondly, many forms of placings are in use, and although in many instances renounceable letters of allotment are issued, *e.g.* where the issuing house or firm of stockbrokers has placed some blocks of the newly issued shares or debentures privately beforehand with institutional investors, sometimes the securities are allotted to the issuing house or stockbrokers, and are sold and transferred by them to their institutional or individual customers.

Whether the procedure of placings requires a prospectus in the legal sense cannot be answered generally. The definition of an offer of shares or debentures to the public in section 55 (1) of the 1948 Act is sufficiently wide to include this procedure: the subsection refers expressly to "any section of the public, whether selected . . . as clients of the person issuing the prospectus or in any other manner." The answer depends on the facts surrounding the placings: if the placings are to a small closely restricted circle of select investors, they will fall within section 55 (2) and no prospectus is required, but if the placings are to a wide clientele of the allottees who by way of a circular letter or a similar general communication draw the attention of their clients to the availability of the shares or debentures as an investment, this is no longer the "domestic concern of the persons making and receiving" the invitation (s. 55 (2)), and the placings would have to satisfy the requirements of a prospectus.

Offers by tender

21–05 In this case the minimum price of the shares is fixed and the promoters are prepared to accept offers at this or a higher price. The promoters normally reserve the right to refuse any application. The shares will be allotted to the highest bidder, unless, for one reason or another, his bid is unacceptable. In their invitation for tenders the promoters reserve the right to accept bids in part if the issue is oversubscribed.

The aim of this procedure is to make available any excess above the issue price to the company rather than to speculators "stagging" the issue.[4]

Pre-emption rights of existing members or debenture holders. Rights issues and bonus issues, and scrip dividend

21–06 By virtue of the 1980 Act, certain shareholders and holders of other equity securities in private and public companies have a pre-emption right, if the issue of new shares or other equity securities is for cash and that right is not excluded in a manner admitted by the Act (1980 Act, ss. 17–19).[5]

---

[4] As to the "stagging" of new issues, see para. 22–05, *post*.
[5] On the pre-emption right in detail, see para. 24–03, *post*.

Where the statutory provisions relating to the pre-emption right apply, the shareholders or other beneficiaries are entitled to a proportionate allotment of a new issue, and that option has to be kept open for 21 days.[6] Further, under the Stock Exchange Regulations, a public company listed at the Stock Exchange has to agree to give the holders of equity shares and certain other equity securities a pre-emption right if there is a new issue for cash, unless the general meeting otherwise decides or a special Stock Exchange dispensation is obtained.[7] Sometimes, particularly in private companies, the articles provide a pre-emption right in favour of the other shareholders, if a shareholder is desirous of transferring his shares.[8]

In practice issues to the existing shareholders are frequently made. They are either rights issues or bonus issues.[9] The 1948 Act recognises this position by drawing, in a few instances,[10] a distinction between prospectuses issued generally, *i.e.* to persons who are not existing members or debenture holders of the company (s. 39 (1) (*a*)), and other prospectuses.

In the case of a rights issue the existing shareholders are given the right to apply for the new shares or debentures in a fixed proportion, *e.g.* three new shares for every £10 of old shares. Often the price at which the new shares are offered is below the market quotation of the old shares, even taking into account the falling market value which will result by reason of the enlarged issued capital. The price thus contains an element of "bonus."

21–07 The normal method of making a rights issue is for the company to send an explanatory letter to each member, accompanied by a provisional allotment letter in respect of the shares for which each member is entitled to apply. The directors, in allotting the shares, resolve that they be allotted to the parties named on the allotment sheets or on the provisional allotment letters or to their nominees, provided that the provisional allotment is accepted on or before a certain date. The provisional allotment letter has attached a form of acceptance and a form of renunciation, so that the member is in a position to exercise his right to the shares, or he can renounce his right to the shares in favour of some other person. Where a company's shares are dealt in on a stock exchange and there is some "bonus" element in the price at which the company is offering the shares, the stockjobbers will arrange a market in the "rights." In due course and on or before a given date, the original member, or, if he has renounced his

---

[6] In the U.S.A. the courts have worked out a broad principle giving shareholders that right; see Elvin R. Latty, "Minority Shareholder Protection in American Corporation Law" [1957] J.B.L. 111.

[7] Stock Exchange Regulations on Admission of Securities to Listing, Chap. 2, "Listing Agreement—Companies," rule 13.

[8] *Lyle & Scott* v. *Scott's Trustee* [1959] A.C. 763; *Safeguard Industrial Investments Ltd.* v. *National Westminster Bank Ltd.* [1982] 1 W.L.R. 589.

[9] In financial terminology, bonus issues are sometimes called "scrip issues." This term has no definite technical meaning, and its use varies. "Scrip certificates" were formerly issued by companies; they were often bearer certificates entitling the holder to a further specified number of shares on a future allotment on payment of certain instalments. In modern practice renounceable letters of allotment have taken the place of scrip certificates.

[10] ss. 39 (1) (*a*), 41 (1) (*b*).

shares, the renouncee, will complete the form of acceptance and application and lodge it with the company or its bankers, together with a cheque covering the amount payable on application for the shares. Failure to return the document duly completed by the given date will mean that the right to apply for the shares in question lapses. When payment has been made of what is due on the shares the company will, in exchange for the completed application form, issue the share certificates.

The treatment of fractions of a new share varies. Often the terms of issue provide that fractions shall be disregarded. Further, the old shareholders are sometimes given the right of applying for additional shares, which have not been taken up, at the same favourable price as that at which the proportionate new shares are provisionally allotted. If, with respect to the additional shares, the issue is oversubscribed, the allotment of these shares is correspondingly reduced.

In the case of bonus shares,[11] the bonus is provided out of the credit balance of the profit and loss account, out of reserves, or out of one of the quasi-capital funds,[12] so that the shareholders to whom the shares are allotted have to pay nothing. A bonus issue cannot be used for the purpose of raising new capital; its purpose is to capitalise profits which may be available for distribution, or to utilise quasi-capital funds. Here again, it is usual to carry out the issue by means of circular and fully paid letters of allotment[13] or fully paid renounceable share certificates, and, if the shares are quoted on The Stock Exchange, these "rights" to bonus shares are likewise traded there. Again, on a bonus issue fractions of a new share might arise, but normally in this case a cash payment at an agreed rate per share is made to the shareholder entitled to the fraction.

Rights issues to existing members or debenture holders have to satisfy the statutory requirements of a prospectus, but the prospectus may be made in an abridged form; it need not contain the matters specified in the Fourth Schedule (1948 Act, s. 38 (5) (*a*)). Bonus shares are not issued "for subscription or purchase" and consequently an issue of bonus shares need not satisfy the statutory requirements of a prospectus.

21–08 Sometimes, on the annual distribution of profits, a company offers its shareholders a right of election; they may take their dividend in form of either cash or bonus shares. The latter alternative is called a scrip dividend.[14] In that case the resolution for the distribution of profits provides that a bonus share may be taken in lieu of the cash dividend for a fixed number of shares; *e.g.* each holding of 10 ordinary shares entitles the holder to one bonus share. The option of scrip is not open to a shareholder who holds less than the fixed minimum number of shares or who, after

[11] These shares are sometimes called "capitalisation shares." The circumstances in which bonus shares may be issued and the procedure on issuing them is discussed in para. 76–23, *post*.

[12] See para. 29–09, *post*.

[13] For a form of a renounceable letter of allotment of bonus shares, see Form 484 in Palmer's *Company Precedents*, Part I (17th ed., 1956), p. 927.

[14] The nature and requirements of the scrip dividend are discussed at para. 75–17, *post*.

taking scrip, holds a fraction not entitled to scrip; here the shareholder must take cash for the amount which cannot be expressed in scrip. If, *e.g.* a shareholder may take one bonus share on every 10 shares and he holds 52 shares, and he then elects to take scrip, he would receive five bonus shares and a cash dividend on the remaining two shares.

Introductions

21–09 This procedure does not denote the issue of shares or debentures in the legal sense, but means the introduction to The Stock Exchange of already existing—*i.e.* already issued—securities not identical with securities already listed. This operation requires an advertisement in the form prescribed by the Stock Exchange. The advertisement is not a prospectus within section 455 of the 1948 Act because in the case of an introduction no invitation or offer is made to the public, but the Regulations of The Stock Exchange on Admission of Securities to Listing require the directors to accept responsibility for the accuracy of the information given.[15] The following is the statement which the Regulations require to be included:

> "This document includes particulars given in compliance with the Regulations of the Council of the Stock Exchange for the purpose of giving information with regard to the company. The directors have taken all reasonable care to ensure that the facts stated herein are true and accurate in all material respects and that there are no other material facts the omission of which would make misleading any statement herein whether of fact or of opinion. All the directors accept responsibility accordingly."

Prospectuses of companies incorporated abroad

21–10 Prospectuses—and here again the word has the wide connotation given to it by section 455[16]—offering shares in or debentures of companies incorporated (or to be incorporated) outside Great Britain are subject to similar requirements to those applying to prospectuses issued by United Kingdom companies (ss. 417–423).

It should be noted that these statutory provisions apply not only to prospectuses issued by oversea companies as defined in section 406, *i.e.* companies incorporated outside Great Britain which have established a place of business within Great Britain, but also to companies incorporated abroad which have not established a place of business in this country (s.417 (1)).

Stock Exchange requirements[17]

21–11 The Rules and Regulations of the Stock Exchange, as revised in April, 1979,[17a] contain, in Appendix 34, detailed Requirements for Admission to

[15] Stock Exchange Regulations on Admission of Securities to Listing, Sched. II, Part B, para. 2. The stock exchange in Scotland is fully integrated with The Stock Exchange and the Stock Exchange Regulations for Admission of Securities to Listing apply also to the Scottish unit of The Stock Exchange.

[16] See s. 423 (3). The requirements of s. 455 are discussed at paras. 21–15 *et seq., post.*

[17] For Scotland see n. 15, *ante.*

[17a] And amended from time to time.

the Official List with respect to shares and debentures. These are arranged in Section A under two headings:

Part I. Companies no part of whose capital is already listed.

Part II. Companies part of whose capital is already listed.

The Stock Exchange Requirements for issues of shares and debentures are reproduced in Volume II, Part C. In particular, when a company seeks an initial quotation it must satisfy the following requirements:

(1) the company must have a minimum market value of £500,000;

(2) there must be a minimum market value of £200,000 for any one security.

Various statutory regulations

1–12 When the issue of shares or debentures by way of a prospectus or by other methods is contemplated, the provisions of enactments other than the Companies Acts have also to be complied with.

Under the Banking and Financial Dealings Act 1971, s. 2, the Treasury is authorised to suspend certain financial dealings if this appears to it to be necessary or expedient in the national interest. In particular, the Treasury may direct that no member of a stock exchange shall, on the day or days specified in the order of the Treasury, effect any transaction on that exchange (s. 2 (1) (*g*)).

Under the Borrowing (Control and Guarantees) Act 1946, and the orders made thereunder,[18] an issue of shares or debentures requires the consent of the Treasury given on application to the Capital Issues Committee; but the provisions of this legislation have been progressively relaxed and are, from the practical point of view, of insignificant effect.[19]

Under the Prevention of Fraud (Investments) Act 1958, s. 14, restrictions are imposed on the distribution of documents and circulars relating to investments but, speaking generally, these restrictions do not apply to issues for which prospectuses are required under the Companies Act.[20]

These enactments provide heavy penalties where persons are found guilty of contravening their provisions.

What is a prospectus?

1–13 It is obvious from the preceding observations that when an issue of shares or debentures of a public company is contemplated, the first question is whether the circular, advertisement or other announcement relating to it constitutes a prospectus within the meaning of the 1948 Act, as amended.

Prohibition of application forms for shares or debentures unless accompanied by a prospectus

1–14 The importance of this question is enhanced by the prohibition, except in the cases in which a certificate of exemption has been obtained from a

[18] See para. 26–01, *post*.
[19] See para. 26–04, *post*.
[20] See para. 25–09, *post*.

stock exchange (s. 39), of the issue of application forms for shares or debentures to the public unless the forms are accompanied by a prospectus complying with the statutory requirements (s. 38 (3)).

In *Government Stock and Other Securities Investment Co. Ltd.* v. *Christopher*[21] company A offered to acquire the shares of companies B and C in exchange for shares to be allotted in company A. An opposing shareholder sought to persuade the court that the "form of acceptance and transfer" issued by company A with its offer to the shareholders of companies B and C was "a form of application" within the meaning of section 38 (3) and should have been accompanied by a prospectus. Wynn Parry J. rejected this suggestion and held that the "form of acceptance and transfer" was not a "form of application for shares" within the meaning of section 38 (3), but was an acceptance of the offer of company A and of the shares therein, and a transfer to company A of the existing holdings of the shares in companies B and C.

Definition of prospectus

21–15 Section 455 of the 1948 Act defines a prospectus as

> "any prospectus, notice, circular, advertisement, or other invitation, offering to the public for subscription or purchase any shares or debentures of a company."

The meaning of the term "prospectus" in section 38 is no more extended than this definition.[22]

The definition of a prospectus in section 455 requires closer examination.

21–16 "ANY . . . INVITATION, OFFERING . . . ANY SHARES OR DEBENTURES." In this context, the words "invitation" and "offer" are not used in the strict meaning attributed to them in the law of contract. Indeed, it is irrelevant whether in contract law the communication offering shares or debentures is an invitation or an offer because, in any event, if the other requirements are satisfied, it qualifies as a prospectus within the meaning of the Act.[23] If, *e.g.* the company issues a direct prospectus to the public offering shares for subscription and attaches application forms to it, the prospectus is clearly an invitation, the application is an offer and the allotment by the company is an acceptance.[24] On the other hand, if in a rights issue the company attaches to the circular non-renounceable provisional allotment letters, these are offers by the company which may be accepted by the addressees. In this case the contract between the company and the allottees may contain various special conditions, *e.g.* that if payment is to be made by instalments a failure to pay the final instalment when due will render any

---

21 [1956] 1 W.L.R. 237.
22 *Per* Wynn-Parry J. in *Governments Stock and Other Securities Investment Co. Ltd.* v. *Christopher* [1956] 1 W.L.R. 237, 243.
23 *Cf.* the words "offer or invitation" in s. 55 (2).
24 *Cf.* s. 50 (5), and *Ramsgate Hotel Co.* v. *Montefiore* (1866) L.R. 1 Ex. 109.

amount previously paid liable to forfeiture and the allotment to cancellation.

A prospectus is to be treated as addressed exclusively to those who subscribe for shares in response to it, and they alone can sue in respect of any misrepresentation in it. Other persons who may read it and buy shares in the market on the strength of it acquire no such right.[25] However, where it is shown that a prospectus was intended to be used and was, in fact, used to induce persons to buy shares, and that it contained a statement known to be false, the purchasers on the market are able to sue the persons responsible for the issue for damages.[26]

An allotment to persons who are acting as agents or nominees for an undisclosed principal cannot be rescinded by them on the ground that the principal was misled by misrepresentation in the prospectus: nor is he in any better position by virtue of having the shares renounced in his favour.[27]

21–17 "TO THE PUBLIC." Section 55 provides an aid for the construction of the phrase offering shares or debentures "to the public," but that aid is flexible and enables the courts to deal with each case according to its surrounding circumstances. The section provides in subsection (1) that any reference to the public in the Act or in the articles of the company shall be construed as including—

> "reference to . . . any section of the public, whether selected as members or debenture holders of the company concerned or as clients of the person issuing the prospectus or in any other manner. . . ."

This provision places it beyond doubt that a circular addressed by the company to its members or debenture holders in the case of a rights issue is, on principle, a prospectus and that the same applies to placings by issuing houses or stockbrokers. Subsection (1) of section 55 thus extends the meaning of an offer "to the public" beyond the popular meaning of that phrase.

While subsection (1) thus extends the area of operation of the prospectus provisions of the Act, subsection (2) excludes from it offers which are essentially the domestic concern of the persons making and receiving them. Subsection (2), as amended by the 1980 Act, provides:

> "The foregoing subsection shall not be taken as requiring any offer or invitation to be treated as made to the public if it can properly be regarded, in all the circumstances, as not being calculated to result, directly or indirectly, in the shares or debentures becoming available for subscription or purchase by persons other than those receiving the offer or invitation, or otherwise as being a domestic concern of the persons making and receiving it, and in particular—
>
> (*a*) a provision in a company's articles prohibiting invitations to

25 *Peek* v. *Gurney* (1873) L.R. 6 H.L. 377, 403; *Nicol's Case* (1858–59) 3 De G. & J. 387.
26 *Andrews* v. *Mockford* [1896] 1 Q.B. 372.
27 *Collins* v. *Associated Greyhound Racecourses Ltd.* [1930] 1 Ch. 1.

the public to subscribe for shares or debentures shall not be taken as prohibiting the making to members or debenture holders of an invitation which can properly be regarded as aforesaid[28];

(*b*) [repealed by the 1980 Act, Sched. 4.]

The last part of the subsection, beginning with the words "and in particular," safeguards the position of the private company: it places it beyond doubt that in such a company a pre-emptive offer of a new issue of shares or debentures to the existing holders is not caught by subsection (1) of section 55.

Of greater importance is the first half of subsection (2). These provisions make it clear that the issue is not to the public if

(a) it is directed to specified persons; and

(b) it is not "calculated to result" in the shares or debentures becoming available to other persons;

or, as the subsection phrases it happily, if the issue is the "domestic concern" of the persons making and receiving the offer or invitation.

Consequently, where an issuing house places the whole or part of a new issue privately with a few institutional investors, *e.g.* pension funds, which have agreed to hold the securities as long-term investments, the issue would not appear to be made to the public. Further, where a business is converted into a company and shares are offered by the vendors to a small circle of friends, relations, or to select customers or suppliers, the offer is not made to the public; "in such cases it is common to announce publicly that 'none of the shares will be offered to the public, the whole having been taken up by the vendors and their friends and customers.' "[28] Similarly, an offer by a promoter to a few of his friends, relations or customers has been held not to be an offer to the public.[29] On the other hand, a distribution of 3,000 copies of a prospectus to all the members of certain gas companies has been held to be an offer to the public.[30]

21–18 In *Governments Stock and Other Securities Investment Co. Ltd.* v. *Christopher*,[31] Wynn-Parry J. considered, amongst other issues, whether an offer was made to the public in circumstances where the offer was made to all the shareholders of two companies who alone were entitled to accept the offer. Those who accepted the offer received non-renounceable letters of allotment. Wynn-Parry J. accepted the proposition put forward by counsel:

> " . . . that the test is not who receives the circular, but who can accept the offer put forward. In this case it can only be persons legally or equitably interested as shareholders in the shares of Union-Castle or

---

28 Palmer's *Company Precedents* (17th ed.), Part I, 1956, p. 58.

29 *Sleigh* v. *Glasgow and Transvaal Options* (1904) 6 F. 420 (Ct. of Sess.); *Sherwell* v. *Combined Incandescent Mantles Syndicate* [1907] W.N. 110.

30 *Re South of England Natural Gas and Petroleum Co.* [1911] 1 Ch. 573.

31 [1956] 1 W.L.R. 237.

Clan. In the case of those who accept non-renounceable letters of allotment will be issued. In these circumstances the case appears to me to fall within section 55 (2) of the Companies Act, 1948."

Where the issue is made to existing holders of shares or debentures, much will depend on whether the letters of allotment which the company issues are renounceable or non-renounceable. In the latter case it cannot normally be said that the offer is "calculated to result, directly or indirectly, in the shares or debentures becoming available for subscription or purchase by persons other than those receiving" the offer, and, consequently, the offer is not to the public. Where the company issues renounceable letters of allotment the circle of original allottees can easily be broken by renunciation of those rights and complete strangers may become the allottees; here the offer will normally be held to be made to the public.

"FOR SUBSCRIPTION OR PURCHASE." These words in the definition of a prospectus were judicially interpreted in *Governments Stock and Other Securities Investment Co. Ltd.* v. *Christopher*[32]; following *Re V.G.M. Holdings Ltd.*,[33] Wynn-Parry J. held that the offer in question did not constitute an offer for the purchase of shares, the shares being still unissued, nor was it an offer for the subscription of shares, which expression meant taking or agreeing to take shares for cash.[34]

Bonus shares are not issued "for subscription or purchase" and consequently an issue of bonus shares need not satisfy the statutory requirements of a prospectus.

Prospectus admitting partial subscription

21–19 Special restrictions apply to prospectuses, when it is intended that, even if the capital offered in the prospectus is not subscribed in full, the shares subscribed will be allotted in any event or subject to conditions (1980 Act, s. 16). The prospectus is required to contain a statement to that effect. The topic is treated in para. 22–27, *post*.

Form of prospectus

21–20 A prospectus has to satisfy a number of formalities required by the 1948 Act, as amended.

Date and registration of prospectus

Every prospectus must be dated and that date shall, unless the contrary is proved, be taken as the date of its publication (s. 37). It may not be issued unless, on or before the date of publication, a copy has been delivered to the Registrar of Companies for registration (s. 41 (1)). On the

---

32 [1956] 1 W.L.R. 237; see para. 21–14, *ante*.
33 [1942] Ch. 235.
34 But see *Akerhielm* v. *De Mare* [1959] A.C. 789 (P.C.) (para. 21–30, *post*).

face of the prospectus there must be a statement that it has been so delivered, and the statement must further specify, or refer to, all documents which are required to be indorsed on or attached to the copy of the prospectus delivered to the Registrar (s. 41 (2)). These documents are:

(*a*) *in the case of every prospectus*

(i) any consent to the issue of the prospectus required to be given by an expert (s. 41 (1) (*a*)), *i.e.* in respect of every statement in the prospectus purported to be made by an expert, a consent by him to the issue of the prospectus with the statement included in the context and form in which it is included (s. 40).

The prospectus must also state that the consents of such experts have not been withdrawn (s. 40 (1) (*b*));

(*b*) *in the case of a prospectus issued generally*[35]

(ii) a copy of, or memorandum of particulars of, all material contracts referred to in the prospectus (s. 41 (1) (*b*) (i))[36];

(iii) a statement signed by any persons who have made a report which is incorporated in the prospectus, setting out any adjustments which they have made in that report (s. 41 (1) (*b*) (ii)).

Signature of directors

Every person who is named in the prospectus as a director or proposed director must, himself or by his agent authorised in writing, sign the copy which is delivered to the Registrar (s. 41 (1)).

Contents of prospectus

Full prospectus

21–21 The requirements of the 1948 Act as to disclosures in a full, *i.e.* unabridged,[37] prospectus are contained in section 38 and the Fourth Schedule. This section and Schedule have been developed from the provisions of earlier Acts, bringing in such additions as litigation or practical experience has shown to be needed. Much of the experience has been gained from The Stock Exchange, and the requirements of The Stock Exchange are still in advance of those of the Act.

Section 38 itself requires, in principle,[37] that all matters specified in the Fourth Schedule must be stated in the prospectus (subs. (1)) and renders void any attempted condition requiring an applicant for shares or debentures to waive compliance with the section, or purporting to affect him with

[35] *i.e.* a prospectus issued to persons who are not existing members or debenture holders of the company (s. 39 (1) (*a*)).

[36] See para. 21–31, *post*. If the contract is in a foreign language a copy translation is required (s. 41 (1)) in the form prescribed by the Department of Trade (see s. 455, under "prescribed").

[37] On abridged prospectuses, see paras. 21–24 *et seq.*, *post*.

notice of any contract, document or matter not specifically referred to in the prospectus (subs. (2)). Thus, any matter required by the Fourth Schedule to be specifically referred to cannot be evaded by an attempt to make the applicant waive specific notice.

The Fourth Schedule sets out at considerable length the matters to be stated in the prospectus, which, in its unabridged form, under the present legislation has become a document of considerable complexity. Thus, where shares are offered to the public for subscription the amount payable on application and allotment on each share, including the amount of any premium, has to be shown (Fourth Schedule, para. 6, and amended by the Companies Act 1976, s. 33). The Schedule is reproduced in the second volume of this work but certain of those matters must be commented upon here.

21–22 THE MINIMUM SUBSCRIPTION.[38] The first—and only the first[39]—prospectus which is issued with respect to the shares of the company[40] has to state the minimum subscription (s. 47 (1) and (2)). This is the amount which, in the opinion of the directors, must be raised by the issue in order to provide for

(1) the purchase price of any property purchased or to be purchased out of the proceeds of the issue;
(2) any preliminary expenses, including underwriting commission (and so-called overriding commission which is payable to the principal underwriter who has procured sub-underwriters);
(3) the repayment of moneys borrowed by the company in respect of any of the foregoing matters;
(4) the working capital of the company (Sched. IV, para. 4 (*a*)).

The Act does not require the minimum subscription to be a percentage of the issue or in any other way to be a fixed amount. It leaves its quantification to the discretion of the directors (s. 47 (1)). An unreasonable error in judgment by them constitutes a material misstatement in the prospectus and may have civil and criminal consequences.

If the minimum subscription has not been subscribed within 40 days after the first issue of the prospectus, the issue has failed and all application moneys received by the company must be returned (s. 47 (4)). The consequences of the failure of applications to reach the minimum subscription are described later.[41]

21–23 REPORTS TO BE SET OUT IN PROSPECTUS. Part II of the Fourth Schedule requires reports to be set out in the prospectus. These are: a report by the auditors of the company with respect to the profits or losses of the company in respect of each of the five financial years immediately preceding the

---

[38] See further, paras. 22–23, *et seq., post.*
[39] See s. 47 (6).
[40] It is immaterial whether this prospectus is issued on the occasion of a direct issue by the company, an offer for sale, placing, or other method of issue requiring a prospectus.
[41] See para. 22–25, *post.*

issue of the prospectus, and with respect to the rates of dividends, if any, paid by the company in respect of each class of shares in the company in respect of each of the said five years, giving particulars of each such class of shares on which such dividends have been paid and particulars of the cases in which no dividends have been paid in respect of any class of shares in respect of any of those years, and, if no accounts have been made up in respect of any part of the period of five years ending on a date three months before the issue of the prospectus, containing a statement of that fact. The report must relate to the assets and liabilities of the company as shown in the last balance sheet, and where the company has subsidiaries, the auditors' report, besides dealing with the company's profits or losses, must deal with the profits or losses of its subsidiaries and must deal as a whole with the assets and liabilities of the company and its subsidiaries.

If the proceeds, or any part of the proceeds, of the issue of the shares or debentures are or is to be applied directly or indirectly in the purchase of any business, a report by accountants, who must be named in the prospectus, has to set out the profits or losses of the business in respect of each of the five financial years immediately preceding the issue of the prospectus, and the assets and liabilities of the business at the last date to which the accounts of the business were made up. If any of the proceeds of the issue are to be applied in acquiring shares of another company which will become a subsidiary, further special reports must be made.

All necessary adjustments must be made in a report (para. 29) and reports must be made by properly qualified accountants (para. 30).

The effect of inaccurate statements in reports referred to in a prospectus is discussed later.[42]

Abridged prospectuses

21–24 The requirements of the Fourth Schedule are—as is proper—detailed and strict and compliance with them entails much labour. In cases in which the circumstances of the issue do not demand such strictness, the Act reduces its requirements and admits abridged prospectuses which need not comply with the requirements of section 38 and of the Fourth Schedule.

Abridged prospectuses are admitted in two cases:

(1) Without consent of a stock exchange, if the issue is restricted with respect to those to whom it is made or to the shares or debentures offered (s. 38 (5)).

(2) Upon grant of a certificate of exemption by a prescribed stock exchange (s. 39).

21–25 WITHOUT CONSENT OF A STOCK EXCHANGE. Abridged prospectuses (or forms of application) may be issued automatically, *i.e.* without consent[43] by a stock exchange, where the issue of shares or debentures

---

[42] See para. 21–36, *post*.

[43] Any consent of the Treasury or other government departments or agencies under the statutory regulations set out in para. 21–12, *ante*, would still be required.

(1) is to existing holders of shares or debentures, whether the allotment letters are renounceable or non-renounceable (s. 38 (5) (*a*)).

This exception admits abridged prospectuses in the case of rights issues[44] and bonus issues,[44] unless these issues do not require prospectuses at all, *e.g.* because they are not treated as being made to the public[45]; or

(2) relates to shares or debentures which are in all respects uniform with shares or debentures previously issued and for the time being dealt in or quoted on a prescribed[46] stock exchange (s. 38 (5) (*b*)).

In these cases the requirements of the Fourth Schedule need not be complied with at all. A full prospectus is obviously unnecessary as the persons to whom the prospectus is addressed have already sufficient information about the company.

21–26 UPON A CERTIFICATE OF EXEMPTION. Where it is proposed to offer any shares or debentures to the public by a prospectus issued generally (*i.e.* to persons who are not existing members or debenture holders of the company: s. 39 (1) (*a*)), and application is made to The Stock Exchange[46] for permission for those shares or debentures to be dealt in or quoted on The Stock Exchange, The Stock Exchange may give a certificate of exemption to the effect that having regard to the proposals, the size and other circumstances of the issue and the number and class of persons to whom the offer is made, compliance with the requirements of the Fourth Schedule would be unduly burdensome (s. 39).

A prospectus containing abridged particulars under section 39 is not as favourable as an abridged prospectus under section 38 (5) (*a*) or (*b*) because in the latter case the requirements of the Fourth Schedule are completely dispensed with, while in the former case The Stock Exchange may—and in practice does—require particulars to be published to a considerable extent, and it is merely provided that a prospectus complying with the requirements of The Stock Exchange shall be seemed to comply with the requirements of the Fourth Schedule.

The conditions upon which The Stock Exchange will grant a certificate of exemption vary from case to case, but normally The Stock Exchange will require a statement of profits and dividends for the last 10 years, whereas the Fourth Schedule requires such a statement only for the past five years.

A further feature of an abridged prospectus issued under section 39 is that the provisions of section 50 do not apply to it, in particular subsection (5), according to which applications for shares or debentures are irrevocable for three days after the opening of the subscription lists (s. 50 (7)).

---

[44] See para. 21–06, *ante*.
[45] See para. 21–17, *ante*.
[46] The stock exchanges are prescribed by the Department of Trade (under s. 455) by statutory instrument: the prescribed stock exchange is The Stock Exchange (Companies (Stock Exchange) Order; S.I. 1973 No. 484).

An abridged prospectus under section 39 must be registered with the Registrar of Companies in the same way as a full prospectus. In addition, where, in connection with the application to The Stock Exchange, such exemption is granted and a copy or memorandum of any contract is required to be available for inspection, such copy or memorandum must be indorsed on or attached to the prospectus so registered.[47]

Statements in prospectuses

The principle

21–27 A prospectus is required to give to the persons to whom it is addressed a full, accurate and fair picture of the state and prospects of the company.

In framing the prospectus the following rules must be borne in mind:

(1) The prospectus should not contain any misrepresentation of any material fact, or any deceptive or misleading statement, or any ambiguous statement which is not true in every sense in which it might be reasonably understood.

(2) It should disclose every material fact and contract, subject to the qualifications below mentioned.

(3) The prospectus should comply with the requirements of s. 38 of the 1948 Act[48] and s. 16 (1) (*b*) of the 1980 Act.[48a]

(4) The provisions of section 43 (compensation for untrue statements) should also be borne in mind, and all due precautions taken accordingly.[49]

Neglect of these precautions may give the allottee

(*a*) the right to rescind the contract and repudiate the allotment[50];

(*b*) the right to sue for damages or compensation those who have issued the prospectus, and others who are, by statute or common law, responsible.[51]

The "golden rule" as to framing prospectuses

21–28 The obligation of those who issue prospectuses inviting application for shares was long ago laid down by Kindersley V.-C. in *New Brunswick, etc., Co.* v. *Muggeridge*[52] in words which Page-Wood V.-C., in *Henderson* v. *Lacon*,[53] described as a "golden legacy":

> "Those who issue a prospectus, holding out to the public the great advantages which will accrue to persons who will take shares in a proposed undertaking, and inviting them to take shares on the faith of the representations therein contained, are bound to state everything with strict and scrupulous accuracy, and not only to abstain from

[47] See Sched. IV, para. 14, and para. 21–20, *ante*.
[48] See para. 21–21, *ante*.
[48a] See para. 21–19, *ante*.
[49] See paras. 21–53 *et seq.*, *post*.
[50] See para. 21–42, *post*.
[51] See paras. 21–51 *et seq.*, *post*.
[52] (1860) 1 Dr. & Sm. 363, 383.
[53] (1867) L.R. 5 Eq. 249, 262.

stating as fact that which is not so, but to omit no one fact within their knowledge, the existence of which might in any degree affect the nature, or extent, or quality, of the privileges and advantages which the prospectus holds out as inducements to take shares."

In *Central Railway of Venezuela* v. *Kisch*,[54] Lord Chelmsford said that no misstatement or concealment of any material facts or circumstances ought to be permitted; that the public who were invited by a prospectus to join in any new venture ought to have the same opportunity of judging of everything which had a material bearing on the true character of the adventure as the promoters themselves possessed, and that the utmost candour ought to characterise their public statements; and his lordship referred with approval to the rule laid down by Kindersley V.-C. as above mentioned.

21–29 This "golden rule" is, perhaps, somewhat of a "counsel of perfection"; at all events, it has been qualified by subsequent decisions, not, indeed, as regards any active misstatements in the prospectus, but as to the effect of mere non-disclosure. Thus, in *Peek* v. *Gurney*,[55] it was held that, to support an action for deceit, there must be some active misstatement of fact, or, at all events, such a partial or fragmentary statement of fact as that the withholding of that which is not stated makes that which is stated absolutely false. This, it will be observed, was said in regard to an action for deceit, in which fraud is of the essence of the action, and which differs essentially from one brought to obtain rescission on the ground of misrepresentation of a material fact[56]; but Romer J. in *McKeown* v. *Boudard, Peveril Gear Co.*[57] held that, even in an action for rescission, proof of mere non-disclosure of material facts is not enough to entitle the plaintiff to relief; for the duty of disclosure in the case of a prospectus inviting share subscriptions, as Lord Watson said in *Aaron's Reefs* v. *Twiss*,[58] is not the same as in the case of a proposal for marine insurance. Thus, a prospectus not stating that the directors have been presented with their qualification by the company's contractor will not entitle a person who has taken shares on the faith of the prospectus to rescind his contract.[59] The *suppressio veri* must be such as to falsify the prospectus. A half-truth, for instance, represented as a whole truth may be tantamount to a false statement.[60] Lord Halsbury L.C. said, in *Aaron's Reefs* v. *Twiss*[61]:

> "I do not care by what means it is conveyed—by what trick or device or ambiguous language: all those are expedients by which fraudulent people seem to think they can escape from the real substance of the transaction. If by a number of statements you intentionally give a false impression and induce a person to act upon it, it is not the

---

[54] (1867) L.R. 2 H.L. 99, 123.
[55] (1873) L.R. 6 H.L. 377, 403; see also *Honeyman* v. *Dickson* 1896, 4 S.L.T. 130.
[56] *Per* Lord Herschell L.C. in *Derry* v. *Peek* (1889) 14 App.Cas. 359.
[57] (1896) 74 L.T. 310; 74 L.T. 712 (C.A.).
[58] [1896] A.C. 273.
[59] *Heymann* v. *European Central Ry.* (1868) L.R. 7 Eq. 154.
[60] *Aaron's Reefs* v. *Twiss* [1896] A.C. 273.
[61] At p. 281.

less false although if one takes each statement by itself there may be a difficulty in shewing that any specific statement is untrue."[62]

Misleading statements

21–30 Section 46 gives statutory effect to the principle laid down in the cases mentioned above. This section provides that a statement included in a prospectus is to be deemed to be untrue if it is misleading in the form and context in which it is included. The principle had already been applied in *R.* v. *Kylsant*,[63] where it was held in a prosecution under the Larceny Act 1861, s. 84, now the Theft Act 1968, s. 19,[64] that a prospectus in which all statements were literally true but which failed to disclose that the dividend stated in it as paid was not paid out of trading profits but was, in fact, paid out of realised capital profits was false in a material particular.

The following false statements have, in their respective contexts, been held to be material statements of fact: that more than one-half of the first issue of shares had already been subscribed for[65]; that the surplus assets as shown in the last balance sheet amounted to upwards of £10,000[66]; that a particular mine was in full operation and making large daily returns[67]; that patented articles were a commercial success and beyond the experimental stage[68]; that a promoter who was to get part of the purchase money was one of the vendors[69]; that the vendor was to pay all the preliminary expenses[70]; that the company was the sole manufacturer of asbestos in France and had a practical monopoly[71]; that the company's process was a commercial success[72]; that no promotion money was to be paid[73]; that the vendors in nitrate grounds had obtained a supply of water brought to them in pipes, and that the company would have the right of using a certain part of the water.[74]

A statement in a prospectus as to the persons who are to be directors is a material statement, and, if it is untrue, a person subscribing on the faith of it is prima facie entitled to rescind.[75] A shareholder who has agreed to

---

[62] Note also the observations of Lord Watson in that case (at p. 287); and see *Greenwood* v. *Leather Shod Wheel Co.* [1900] 1 Ch. 421 (C.A.), where the same principle was acted on.
[63] [1932] 1 K.B. 442; see para. 21–62.
[64] The Acts mentioned in the text do not apply to Scotland.
[65] *Ross* v. *Estates Investment Co.* (1868) L.R. 3 Ch. 682; *Kent* v. *Freehold Land Co.* (1868) L.R. 3 Ch. 493; *Henderson* v. *Lacon* (1867) L.R. 5 Eq. 249. As to the meaning of "subscribed," see *infra*.
[66] *Re London and Staffordshire Fire Insurance Co.* (1883) 24 Ch.D. 149.
[67] *Reese River, etc., Co.* v. *Smith* (1869) L.R. 4 H.L. 64.
[68] *Greenwood* v. *Leather Shod Wheel Co.* [1900] 1 Ch. 421.
[69] *Capel & Co.* v. *Sim's, etc., Co.* (1888) 58 L.T. 807.
[70] *Re Liberian Government Concessions, etc., Co.* (1892) 9 T.L.R. 136.
[71] *Hyde* v. *New Asbestos Co.* (1891) 8 T.L.R. 121.
[72] *Stirling* v. *Passburg Grains, etc., Ltd.* (1891) 8 T.L.R. 71.
[73] *Lodwick* v. *Earl of Perth* (1884) 1 T.L.R. 76.
[74] *Lagunas Nitrate Co.* v. *Lagunas Nitrate Syndicate* [1899] 2 Ch. 392, 397, 429.
[75] *Re Scottish Petroleum Co.* (1883) 23 Ch.D. 413; *Anderson's Case* (1881) 17 Ch.D. 373; *Smith* v. *Chadwick* (1882) 20 Ch.D. 27; *Ex. p. Wainwright* (1890) 62 L.T. 30; *Re Kent County Gas, etc., Co.* (1906) 95 L.T. 756; *Blakiston* v. *London and Scottish Banking and Discount Corporation* 1894, 21 R. 417; 1 S.L.T. 462.

subscribe in the knowledge that directors named in the prospectus have withdrawn is not entitled to rescind the contract.[76]

Where a company was formed to buy a mine, and extracts from the report of an expert were set out which gave a misleading impression of that report and induced the belief that the mine was similar to a rich adjacent mine, it was held that a subscriber was entitled to relief.[77]

The statement in a prospectus that share capital has been "subscribed" does not necessarily mean that it has been "subscribed in cash"; it is sufficient if shares have been allotted for a valuable consideration, *i.e.* a consideration which is money's worth. Thus, such a statement is no misrepresentation if formation expenses of the company and the acquisition of patent rights to the company have been met out of the share capital by allotment of fully paid shares.[78] On the other hand, it would be a misrepresentation in a prospectus to state that the company has contracted for the purchase of a property when, in fact, there is only negotiation.[79] It is not a misrepresentation if the prospectus states that the capital is £x and the memorandum and articles contain the usual powers to increase or reduce the capital.[80]

Normally the applicant has no relief where the misrepresentation is an innocent omission of information which should have been given in the prospectus and concerned merely unimportant matters.[81] Grandiloquent statements which are substantially true are not misrepresentations.[82]

Material contracts

21–31 In displaying the utmost candour that is required of those issuing the prospectus, every material contract must be specified. This requirement is the result of much litigation and difference of judicial opinion as to what must be specified, and only in the circumstances of any given case can it be decided what is a material contract.[83] Every contract should be specified "the knowledge of which might have an effect upon a reasonable subscriber for shares in determining him to give or withhold faith in the promoter, director or trustee issuing the prospectus."[84] If in doubt it is wise to disclose a contract.

If a contract is material, it makes no difference whether the contract not disclosed is executed or executory.[85] A verbal contract is as much within

---

[76] *Chambers* v. *Edinburgh and Glasgow Aerated Bread Co.* 1881, 18 R. 1039.
[77] *Re Mount Morgan, etc., Ltd.* (1887) 56 L.T. 622.
[78] *Akerhielm* v. *De Mare* [1959] A.C. 789 (P.C.), disapproving *Arnison* v. *Smith* (1889) 41 Ch.D. 348 and, *impliciter, Governments Stock and Other Securities Investment Co. Ltd.* v. *Christopher* [1956] 1 W.L.R. 237, 242.
[79] *Ross* v. *Estates Investment Co.* (1868) L.R. 3 Ch. 682.
[80] *City of Edinburgh Brewery Co.* v. *Gibson's Trustees* 1869 7 M. 886.
[81] See para. 21–40, *post*.
[82] *City of Edinburgh Brewery Co.* v. *Gibson's Trustees supra*.
[83] See *Sullivan* v. *Mitcalfe* (1880) 5 C.P.D. 455; *Gover's Case* (1875) 1 Ch.D. 182; *Twycross* v. *Grant* (1877) 2 C.P.D. 469, 485.
[84] *Gover's Case* (1875) 1 Ch.D. 182, 200, *per* Brett J.; *Cackett* v. *Keswick* [1902] 2 Ch. 456.
[85] *Broome* v. *Speak* [1903] 1 Ch. 586 (C.A.).

the rule as a contract in writing.[86] Where a contract has been rescinded by another contract, the latter and perhaps both might require to be specified.[87]

It is to be remembered, however, that in order to obtain relief the plaintiff must show that but for the omission to disclose the contract he would not have subscribed.[88]

Effect of references to reports in prospectuses

21–32 If the company takes it upon itself to assume the authenticity of the reports referred to in the prospectus and represents as facts the matters stated in those reports, it must take the consequences should they prove false.[89] If the company does not intend to issue the shares on the basis of the facts stated in the report, it must dissociate itself from the report in clear and unambiguous terms. Calculations of profits based on statements in the report may amount to a misrepresentation.[90] But if the persons issuing a prospectus merely refer to the report, *e.g.* of a mine, as telling all they know, and propose to send out someone to test it, they will not be treated as guaranteeing its truth.[91] Directors, promoters and others who authorise the issue of a prospectus are not liable to pay compensation for loss or damage to subscribers if they made untrue statements in a prospectus, purporting to be extracts from reports or valuations by engineers, valuers, accountants or other experts, provided that they can prove that they had reasonable ground to believe, and did up to the time of the issue of the prospectus believe, that the person making the statement was competent to make it (s. 43 (2) (*d*) (ii)).[92] A material misrepresentation as to the source of an expert report would give rise to liability.[93]

Statement only of belief or opinion

21–33 The statement that something *will* be done is not a statement of an existing fact so much as a contract or promise. It may, however, imply the existence of facts which are non-existent, or it may be a material term in the contract[94]; and a representation of belief, expectation or intention may be a representation of fact, for "the state of a man's mind is as much a matter of fact as the state of his digestion."[95]

---

86 *Capel* v. *Sim's Composition Co.* (1888) 36 W.R. 689; *Arkwright* v. *Newbold* (1881) 17 Ch.D. 301.
87 *Re London and Northern Bank, Haddock's Case* [1902] 2 Ch. 73.
88 *Nash* v. *Calthorpe* [1905] 2 Ch. 237; *Macleay* v. *Tait* [1906] A.C. 24.
89 *Re Reese River Silver Mining Co., Smith's Case* (1867) L.R. 2 Ch. 604, 611; *Rawlins* v. *Wickham* (1858) 3 De G. & J. 304; *Mair* v. *Rio Grande Rubber Estates* [1913] A.C. 853.
90 *Re Pacaya Rubber Co.* [1914] 1 Ch. 542.
91 *Re British Burmah Lead Co.* (1887) 56 L.T. 815.
92 See para. 21–52, *post*; see also *Gray* v. *Central Finance Corp.* 1903, 11 S.L.T. 309.
93 *Davidson* v. *Hamilton* 1904, 12 S.L.T. 353.
94 *Karberg's Case* [1892] 3 Ch. 1; *Beattie* v. *Ebury* (1874) L.R. 7 Ch. 777, 804; *Alderson* v. *Maddison* (1883) 8 App.Cas. 467; *Bellairs* v. *Tucker* (1884) 13 Q.B.D. 562.
95 *Per* Bowen L.J. in *Edgington* v. *Fitzmaurice* (1885) 29 Ch.D. 459, 483.

Ambiguous statements

21–34 There is no safety in ambiguous statements, which, in one sense, are true, though in another, not true, "which keep the word of promise to the ear and break it to the hope"; for the rule is that the applicant is entitled to put any reasonable construction on such a statement, and if, according to that construction, it is untrue, he is entitled to relief.[96]

Reliance of applicant on statement of fact without trying to verify

21–35 Another rule, which on the authorities is clear, is that if a prospectus contains statements of fact, the recipient is entitled to rely upon them. He is not bound to verify them. Thus, if the prospectus states the effect or terms of a document, or purports so to do, and offers it for inspection, he is not bound to inspect it. He is entitled to assume in either case that the prospectus is true:

> "One of the most familiar instances . . . is where men issue a prospectus in which they make false statements of the contracts made before the formation of the company, and then say that the contracts themselves may be inspected at the offices of the solicitors. It has always been held that those who accepted those false statements as true were not deprived of their remedy merely because they neglected to go and look at the contracts."[97]

The answer is: "You put me off my guard"[98]; see also *Aaron's Reefs* v. *Twiss*,[99] in which Lord Watson said:

> "It was argued for the company that, inasmuch as its contracts for the purchase of the concession are generally referred to towards the end of the prospectus, the respondent must be held to have had notice of their contents. This appears to me to be one of the most audacious pleas that ever was put forward in answer to a charge of fraudulent misrepresentation. When analysed it means simply that a person who has induced another to act upon a statement made with intent to deceive must be relieved from the consequences of his deceit if he has given his victim constructive notice of a document, the perusal of which would expose the fraud."

Civil liability for misstatements in prospectuses

21–36 Under this head must be considered the claims of an allottee who by a misstatement in the prospectus was induced to apply for the shares or debentures offered therein or to accept the company's offer of allotment.

---

96 *R.* v. *Kylsant* [1932] 1 K.B. 442; *Hallows* v. *Fernie* (1868) L.R. 3 Ch. 467, 476; *Arkwright* v. *Newbold* (1881) 17 Ch.D. 301, 322; *Smith* v. *Chadwick* (1884) 9 App.Cas. 187.

97 *Per* Jessel M.R. in *Redgrave* v. *Hurd* (1881) 20 Ch.D. 1, 14; *Smith* v. *Chadwick* (1882) 20 Ch.D. 27, 57; (1884) 9 App.Cas. 187; *Re Mount Morgan West Gold Mine Co.* (1887) 56 L.T. 622.

98 This is a short summary by Sir Francis Palmer of Lord Chelmsford's judgment in *Venezuela Co.* v. *Kisch* (1867) L.R. 2 H.L. 99, as explained by Lord Halsbury L.C. in *Aaron's Reefs Ltd.* v. *Twiss* [1896] A.C. 273.

99 [1896] A.C. 273.

The allottee may have claims

(1) against the company;

(2) against the directors, promoters or persons who have authorised the issue of the prospectus;

(3) against experts.

First, however, some preliminary conditions of civil liability for misstatements in prospectuses have to be considered.

Preliminary conditions of liability

21–37 "ISSUE" OF PROSPECTUS. Liability under a prospectus can only arise where the prospectus has been issued, and only in favour of persons who subscribe for shares in response to it. The Act does not define the word "issue" and it may depend on the circumstances of any given case whether or not the prospectus has been issued. Thus, where a document, which was found by the jury to be an offer of shares to the public, was "sent to [the respondent] to give him a general idea of the position of the company in case he might think it afforded a suitable opening in which he could find employment upon the terms of investing a small amount of his capital," this was held by the House of Lords not to amount to the "issue" of a prospectus.[1] It has not yet been decided whether there can be an "issue" to one person only.[2]

21–38 WHERE ALLOTTEE HAS NOTICE OF FACT NOT STATED. Where an allottee has notice of a fact not stated, *e.g.* in the case of a contract not referred to, if he had notice not merely of its existence but also of its content,[3] he acquires no rights against the company or any person responsible in respect of such omission.

Rights against the company

21–39 DOCUMENTS FOR WHICH COMPANY IS RESPONSIBLE. A company is not responsible for the statements in a prospectus unless it is shown that the prospectus was issued by the company or by someone with the authority of the company—by the board of directors, for instance. If it was so issued, the company is responsible, and cannot keep a contract for shares obtained by it if the statements contained in it were false or misleading.[4] The company is also responsible if, though the prospectus is issued by the promoters, the board ratify and adopt the issue, for the prospectus is the

---

[1] *Nash* v. *Lynde* [1929] A.C. 158; the words quoted are from the judgment of Lord Hailsham L.C. at p. 165: for a similar case, see *Baty* v. *Keswick* [1901] W.N. 167.

[2] See the judgments of Lord Hailsham L.C. and Lord Sumner in *Nash* v. *Lynde, supra*, and of Eve J., Scrutton L.J. and Atkin L.J. in the same case in the courts below. See also *Sleigh* v. *Glasgow and Transvaal Options* (1904) 6 F. (Ct. of Sess.) 420; *Sherwell* v. *Combined Incandescent Mantles Syndicate* [1907] W.N. 110; *Re South of England Natural Gas and Petroleum Co.* [1911] 1 Ch. 573.

[3] *Watts* v. *Bucknall* [1903] 1 Ch. 766.

[4] *National Exchange Co. of Glasgow* v. *Drew* (1855) 2 Macq. 103, 124; *Houldsworth* v. *City of Glasgow Bank* (1880) 5 App.Cas. 317.

basis of the contract for shares.[5] Hence, if the company, acting by the board of directors, allot shares knowing that they have been subscribed on a particular prospectus or statement of facts, the company is responsible.[6] Where a company publishes an abridged prospectus abroad, a foreigner who subscribes on the faith of it may be entitled to relief.[7]

The terms of a prospectus may form part of the contract made with the subscribers for shares.[8]

21–40 When the non-compliance involves the misstatement of a material fact, there is, as will be explained presently, a right of rescission under the general law; in this connection it must be borne in mind that the statement of a half-truth may amount to a misstatement.[9] Where, however, the non-compliance consists in the mere omission to state some fact which under section 38 and the provisions of the Fourth Schedule ought to be stated, and the omission to make that statement does not falsify that which is stated, it has been held that the section gives no right of rescission.[10] Neville J. said in *Re Wimbledon Olympia Ltd.*[11]:

> " . . . I cannot attribute to the legislature the intention that the mere fact of the omission of any of the facts required by this section to be stated should give the shareholders this right to get rid of their shares."

This was approved and adopted in relation to "unimportant matters" by Swinfen-Eady J. in *Re South of England Natural Gas and Petroleum Co. Ltd.*[12] It is thought that the same considerations apply to the omission of the statement required by section 16 (1) (*b*) of the 1980 Act.

21–41 ONLY ALLOTTEE ENTITLED TO RELIEF. Only an allottee is entitled to rescind his contract. A person who has bought shares on the market on the basis of the prospectus,[13] or in whose favour shares have been renounced,[14] has no rights against the company.

21–42 WHEN RIGHT TO RESCIND EXISTS. Although mere non-compliance with section 38 does not give rise to a claim for rescission, where shares or debentures are subscribed for on the faith of a prospectus containing a misrepresentation, the allottee is, on principle, entitled to avoid the contract of allotment and to claim his money back, for it is a general rule that a contract induced by a material misrepresentation is voidable, and may, at

---

[5] *Pulsford* v. *Richards* (1853) 17 Beav. 87; *Jennings* v. *Broughton* (1854) 17 Beav. 234.
[6] *Henderson* v. *Lacon* (1867) L.R. 5 Eq. 249; *Ross* v. *Estates Investment Co.* (1868) L.R. 3 Ch. 682; *Lynde* v. *Anglo-Italian, etc., Co.* [1896] 1 Ch. 178; *Karberg's Case* [1892] 3 Ch. 1.
[7] *Roussell* v. *Burnham* [1909] 1 Ch. 127.
[8] *Jacobs* v. *Batavia, etc., Trust* [1924] 2 Ch. 329.
[9] See para. 21–34, *ante*.
[10] *Re Wimbledon Olympia Ltd.* [1910] 1 Ch. 630, followed by Swinfen-Eady J. in *Re South of England Natural Gas, etc., Co.* [1911] 1 Ch. 573.
[11] [1910] 1 Ch. 630, 632.
[12] [1911] 1 Ch. 573.
[13] *Peek* v. *Gurney* (1873) L.R. 6 H.L. 377; *Nicol's Case* (1858–59) 3 De G. & J. 387; but see *Andrews* v. *Mockford* [1896] 1 Q.B. 372; *Duranty's Case* (1858) 26 Beav. 268.
[14] *Collins* v. *Associated Greyhound Racecourses Ltd.* [1930] 1 Ch. 1.

the option of the party deceived, be rescinded, and it makes no difference that the misrepresentation was merely an innocent one.[15] The same principle applies to misrepresentations made by agents of the company and *not contained in a prospectus.*[16]

21–43 WHEN RIGHT TO RESCIND IS LOST. Though voidable, the contract is valid until rescinded, and a consequence of this principle is that an allottee of shares who discovers that he has been deceived is bound to elect forthwith whether he will rescind his contract or not, for, his name being on the register, he is being held out as a member and a contributor to the assets.[17]

"It is difficult," as Lord Cairns said in *Re Cachar Co.*,[18] "to disembarrass these cases of the effect which a man's name being on the register has in inducing other persons to alter their position."

Hence, a very short delay after discovery may deprive him of the right to rescind.[19] This principle may also apply where, although he has no actual knowledge, he has good reason to suspect that there has been a misrepresentation, but stands by inactive and takes no steps to look into the matter.[20] If so, it is doubtful whether he can rely on other misrepresentations discovered during the trial of the action.[21]

He may also lose his right to rescind by an implied ratification, *e.g.* if after discovering that he has a right to rescind, he treats the contract as subsisting, by endeavouring to sell the shares,[22] or by executing a transfer,[23] or by paying calls or receiving dividends,[24] by attending and voting at a general meeting in person or by proxy,[25] or in any other manner. He is allowed a reasonable time to obtain evidence before taking action.[26] Acting as a member is not a bar when the shareholder has previously issued a writ claiming rescission, for that may be regarded as a

---

[15] *Smith's Case* (1867) L.R. 2 Ch. 604, 615; *Reese River, etc., Co.* v. *Smith* (1869) L.R. 4 H.L. 64; *Re London and Staffordshire Co.* (1883) 24 Ch.D. 149. In the case of an innocent misrepresentation, however, the court may order the payment of damages instead of rescission (Misrepresentation Act 1967, s. 2 (2)): see para. 21–50, *post*. The Misrepresentation Act 1967 does not apply to Scotland. The statement in the text is valid in Scots law, with the qualification that *restitutio in integrum* must be possible before a voidable contract is rescinded; damages may be claimed in Scots law for fraudulent, but not for innocent, misrepresentation.

[16] *Hilo Manufacturing Co.* v. *Williamson* (1911) 28 T.L.R. 164.

[17] See para. 49–05, *post*.

[18] (1867) L.R. 2 Ch. 412, 417.

[19] *Re Scottish Petroleum* (1883) 23 Ch.D. 413; *Tatie's Case* (1867) L.R. 3 Eq. 795; *Peel's Case* (1867) L.R. 2 Ch. 674; *Skelton's Case* (1893) 68 L.T. 210; *Caledonian Debenture Co.* v. *Bernard* 1898, 5 S.L.T. 392.

[20] *Ashley's Case* (1870) L.R. 9 Eq. 269; *Scholey* v. *Central Ry. of Venezuela* (1868) L.R. 9 Eq. 266n.; *Cargill* v. *Bower* (1878) 10 Ch.D. 502; *cf. Leaf* v. *International Art Galleries* [1950] 2 K.B. 86.

[21] *Re Christineville Rubber Estates* [1911] W.N. 216.

[22] *Ex p. Briggs* (1866) L.R. 1 Eq. 483.

[23] *Crawley's Case* (1869) L.R. 4 Ch. 322.

[24] *Scholey* v. *Central Ry.* (1868) L.R. 9 Eq. 266n.; *Re Dunlop-Truffault Cycle Co., ex. p. Shearman* (1896) 66 L.J.Ch. 25.

[25] *Sharpley* v. *Louth, etc., Co.* (1876) 2 Ch.D. 663.

[26] *Central Ry., etc.* v. *Kisch* (1867) L.R. 2 H.L. 99.

definite election to rescind.[27] Negotiations may also excuse delay.[28] A transfer of part of the shares before discovery does not preclude relief as to the rest.[29]

21–44 WINDING UP A BAR TO RESCISSION. A winding up is a bar to rescission, for, on winding up, the rights of the whole body of the company's creditors have intervened, and after the commencement of the winding up, the right to rescind is gone.[30] The allottee of shares cannot escape liability in the winding up as a contributory if he is placed on the register of members before the commencement of the winding up, though under a voidable contract, unless he has commenced legal proceedings to enforce rescission before the date of that event.[31]

An allottee is in a different position where the allotment is irregular under section 47 (relating to the minimum subscription). It is enough that he gives notice of avoidance, within the month allowed, without taking legal proceedings.[32]

21–45 RESCISSION RETROSPECTIVE. Where a contract is avoided for misrepresentation, it is rescinded *ab initio*, and accordingly the shareholder cannot, in a winding up, be placed on the list of contributories even as a past member.[33]

21–46 INJUNCTION. Where the shareholder sues for rescission of the allotment, the court can on terms restrain a forfeiture of the shares pending the hearing.[34]

21–47 WHAT THE ALLOTTEE MUST PROVE. Before an allottee can claim relief for misrepresentation he must establish

(1) that the misrepresentation was one of fact[35];
(2) that it was material; and
(3) that he acted upon it.

It need not, and normally cannot, be shown that it was the sole fact relied upon, but it must have been one of the facts relied upon.[36] The principles upon which the court decides what is a material representation of fact were discussed earlier.[37]

---

[27] *Tomlin's Case* [1898] 1 Ch. 104; *Palmer's Company Precedents,* Part I (17th ed.), p. 92. But *cf. Clarkson Booker Ltd.* v. *Andjel* [1964] 2 Q.B. 775.
[28] *Tibbatts* v. *Boulter* (1895) 73 L.T. 534.
[29] *Re Mount Morgan, etc., Ltd.* (1887) 56 L.T. 622.
[30] *Oakes* v. *Turquand* (1867) L.R. 2 H.L. 325.
[31] *Oakes* v. *Turquand, supra*; *Burgess's Case* (1880) 15 Ch.D. 507; *Reese River, etc., Co.* v. *Smith* (1869) L.R. 4 H.L. 64.
[32] *Re National Motor Mail-Coach Co.* [1908] 2 Ch. 228.
[33] *Wright's Case* (1871) L.R. 7 Ch. 55.
[34] *Lamb* v. *Sambas Rubber* [1908] 1 Ch. 845.
[35] *Eaglesfield* v. *Marquis of Londonderry* (1877) 4 Ch.D. 702.
[36] *McMorland's Trustees* v. *Fraser* 1896, 24 R. 65; 4 S.L.T. 128.
[37] See para. 21–30, *ante*.

21–48 RECTIFICATION OF REGISTER. Where the name of the allottee has been placed on the register of members or debenture holders, as the case may be, and the allottee has rescinded the allotment for a valid reason, he can claim rectification of the register if the company refuses to remove his name therefrom.

If the company removes his name voluntarily, no court order for rectification or removal of his name from the register is necessary,[38] for the company is not bound to contest every claim.

21–49 ACTION FOR DECEIT.[39] The allottee can recover damages from the company for any loss which he has suffered if the invitation or offer to subscribe to the shares or debentures emanates from the company and those making it on behalf of the company have fraudulently misrepresented material facts. This action is founded on the tort of deceit. That in appropriate cases the company is vicariously liable for torts committed by its agents or servants in the course of their employment has been explained earlier.[40]

In order to succeed in an action for deceit against the company, the allottee has to prove, in addition to the three facts mentioned above,

(4) that those acting on behalf of the company acted fraudulently[41];
(5) that those purporting to act on behalf of the company were authorised to act in its behalf; and
(6) that he suffered a loss or damage.

21–50 ACTION FOR DAMAGES FOR MISREPRESENTATION. Under section 2 (1) of the Misrepresentation Act 1967 the allottee can likewise recover damages for any loss he has suffered in consequence of an innocent misrepresentation made by or on behalf of the company; but it is a defence for those acting on behalf of the company to prove that they had reasonable ground to believe and did believe up to the time of allotment that the facts represented were true.

In practice, actions for damages against the company have rarely been brought. The usual claim against the company has been for rescission of the contract of allotment. When damages have been claimed, the action has usually been directed against the directors, promoters or others who authorised the issue of the prospectus personally, or against experts who signed reports referred to in the prospectus, since in such an action it has not been necessary to prove fraud. It is possible that this practice will change in the future, in consequence of the Misrepresentation Act 1967, under which an action for damages against the company will lie without proof of fraud.[42]

---

[38] *Wright's Case* (1871) L.R. 7 Ch. 55.
[39] Although this section expresses English law, Scots law does not differ in principle.
[40] See para. 9–37, *ante*.
[41] The onus of proving fraud is discussed in paras. 21–51 *et seq. post*.
[42] The Misrepresentation Act 1967 does not apply to Scotland. In Scots law a claim for damages of misrepresentation will only lie in a case of fraud.

Rights against directors or promoters[43]

21–51 ACTION FOR DECEIT. At common law an allottee may have an action for deceit against the directors. If directors have been fraudulent in misrepresenting facts stated in the prospectus, they will be liable for damages at the suit of any allottee thereby deceived.

A person who buys shares in the market on the strength of a prospectus, however, has no rights against the directors if the prospectus contained a misrepresentation,[44] unless the directors intended by issuing the prospectus to induce purchases in the market.[45]

In order to obtain any personal remedy in damages against directors who have issued a prospectus containing untrue statements it is necessary for the plaintiff to prove affirmatively that the statements were made fraudulently, that is to say, either with knowledge that they were false, or recklessly,[46] *i.e.* not caring whether they were true or false, or not believing them to be true. It is not enough to prove that the director sued had been guilty of gross negligence,[46] or that he made the statement without any reasonable grounds for believing it to be true. The test is a subjective one, as is shown in the following passage from the judgment in *Akerhielm* v. *De Mare*[47]:

> "The question is not whether the defendant in any given case honestly believed the representation to be true in the sense assigned to it by the court on an objective consideration of its truth or falsity, but whether he honestly believed the representation to be true in the sense in which he understood it albeit erroneously when it was made. This general proposition is no doubt subject to limitations. For instance, the meaning placed by the defendant on the representation made may be so far removed from the sense in which it would be understood by any reasonable person as to make it impossible to hold that the defendant honestly understood the representation to bear the meaning claimed by him and honestly believed it in that sense to be true."

21–52 The defendant in an action for deceit has various defences, though some once open are now closed to him under section 43. Thus, he may escape if he can prove that he did believe the fact stated, even though his belief was not based on reasonable grounds, for, if he believed the statement, fraud is negatived[48]; or, again, he may escape if he can prove that the plaintiff was not, in fact, misled,[48a] *e.g.* that he knew the statement to be false when he

---

[43] What is stated in this section applies equally to an action in delict in Scotland.

[44] *Peek* v. *Gurney* (1873) L.R. 6 H.L. 377.

[45] *Andrews* v. *Mockford* [1896] 1 Q.B. 372.

[46] The Prevention of Fraud (Investments) Act 1958, s. 13 (1), as amended by the Protection of Depositors Act 1963, s. 21 (1) (*a*), refers to "the reckless making (dishonestly or otherwise) . . . " with reference to misleading statements. (The Protection of Depositors Act 1963 was repealed by the Banking Act 1979 but this amendment of the Prevention of Frauds (Investments) Act 1958 remains in force.) The provision of the 1958 Act is in harmony with the interpretation of "reckless" in the earlier Act of 1939 as meaning "a high degree of negligence without dishonesty": *per* Donovan J. in *R.* v. *Bates* [1952] 2 All E.R. 842, 846; affirmed *sub nom. R.* v. *Russell* [1953] 1 W.L.R. 77 (C.C.A.); see further *R.* v. *Grunwald* [1963] 1 Q.B. 935, and para. 25–06, *post*.

[47] [1959] A.C. 789, 805 (P.C.).

[48] *Derry* v. *Peek* (1889) 14 App.Cas. 337; *Akerhielm* v. *De Mare, supra*.

[48a] *Cf. JEB Fasteners Ltd.* v *Marks, The Times,* July 24, 1982 (C.A.).

applied for the shares, but he cannot avail himself, as we have seen above,[49] of the "audacious plea"[50] that the plaintiff might easily, by inquiry or otherwise, have ascertained that the statement was untrue.[51]

No action will lie against a director under the Misrepresentation Act 1967, since this Act admits a remedy only against the other contracting party.[52] The question whether the directors can be held liable in negligence for an untrue statement in the prospectus, outside their statutory liability, under the principle in *Hedley Byrne & Co. Ltd.* v. *Heller & Partners Ltd.*[53] is unlikely to arise in practice, since the burden of proof under section 43 is more easily discharged than that required to establish the tort of negligence at common law.

21–53 COMPENSATION UNDER THE 1948 ACT, S. 43. As a result of the inadequacy of the law disclosed by *Derry* v. *Peek*,[54] statutory provisions have shifted the onus of proof, so that an allottee, once he proves that a material statement in the prospectus is untrue, and that he took shares on the faith of the prospectus and sustained damage, is entitled to sue every director, promoter or person who has authorised the issue of the prospectus,[55] and to compel them to pay compensation for his loss. Once the statement is proved to be untrue the director (or other person) must prove affirmatively that he had reasonable grounds to believe the statement to be true, and that he did, in fact, believe it to be true.[56] In addition, if the statement was made or purports to be made by an expert or is contained in a public official document, other defences are open to the director (or other person), *viz.* in the former case that the expert was competent to make it and had given his consent in the proper form and not withdrawn it,[57] and in the latter case that it was a correct and fair representation of an official statement.[58]

A director makes a statement which is untrue within the meaning of section 43 if he states in a prospectus that the company has acquired a specified property when in fact it has not at the time acquired it, though the director honestly believes that it has been acquired. The uncorroborated statements of a vendor afford no reasonable grounds for believing that his statements are true, still less those of a vendor-promoter.[59]

A director cannot escape liability for non-disclosure of a material con-

---

[49] See para. 21–35, *ante*.
[50] *Per* Lord Watson in *Aaron's Reefs* v. *Twiss* (1896) A.C. 273.
[51] See para. 21–35, *ante*.
[52] The Act does not apply in Scotland.
[53] [1964] A.C. 465; see further *Mutual Life and Citizens' Assurance Co. Ltd.* v. *Evatt* [1971] A.C. 793; *Esso Petroleum Co. Ltd.* v. *Mardon* [1975] 2 W.L.R. 147; *Box* v. *Midland Bank Ltd.* [1979] 2 Lloyd's Rep. 391; *JEB Fasteners Ltd.* v. *Marks, The Times,* July 24, 1982 (C.A.); and para. 65–05, *post*.
[54] (1889) 14 App.Cas. 337.
[55] The persons liable under s. 43 are listed in subs. (1) (*a*)–(*d*) of that section.
[56] s. 43 (2) (*d*) (i); *Smith* v. *Moncrieff, etc.* 1894, 2 S.L.T. 140.
[57] s. 43 (2) (*d*) (ii).
[58] s. 43 (2) (*d*) (iii).
[59] *Adams* v. *Thrift* [1915] 2 Ch. 21 (C.A.).

tract of the existence of which he was aware by professing ignorance of the contents or materiality of the contract, or by alleging that he left the matter to his legal advisers.[60] To exonerate himself he must show that he was not responsible for the prospectus; in other words, that he was defrauded or deceived into giving his sanction to it.[61]

21–54 ISSUE WITHOUT DIRECTOR'S CONSENT. If a prospectus has been issued without the knowledge or consent of a director (or other person to whom section 43 (1) (*a*)–(*d*) refers), he will escape liability if, on becoming aware of its issue, he forthwith gives reasonable public notice that it was issued without his knowledge or consent (s. 43 (2) (*b*)). This will not, however, protect a director who, knowing that a prospectus is to be issued, abstains from asking to see it until after an action is brought on account of misrepresentation therein.[62]

A person will also be protected if he can show that, having consented to become a director of the company, he withdrew his consent before the issue of the prospectus, and that it was issued without his authority or consent (s. 43 (2) (*a*)). So, too, if, after the issue of the prospectus and before allotment as a result of it, he discovers an untrue statement and both withdraws his consent and gives reasonable public notice of his withdrawal and the reason, he will be exonerated (s. 43 (2) (*c*)).

21–55 PERIOD OF LIMITATION. In England, the period of limitation on an action for compensation under this section is six years, under section 9 of the Limitation Act 1980. The cause of action first arises for the purposes of that Act when the shares are allotted to the plaintiff[63]: but in the case of fraud the period begins to run from the time when the fraud was, or might with reasonable diligence, have been, discovered.[64] In Scotland (where the Limitation Act 1980 has no application), a claim under section 43 would be cut off by the negative prescription.

Under the Prescription and Limitation (Scotland) Act 1973, s. 6 and Sched. 1, in Scotland this is the period of five years from the date the loss occurred (which may be taken to be the date of allotment), subject to an extension if the shareholder was not aware and could not with reasonable diligence have become aware that loss had occurred at that time (s. 11).

21–56 DEATH OF DIRECTOR. In England, it was held in *Geipel* v. *Peach*[65] that the action, founded on what is now section 43, was an action in tort, and if the

---

[60] *Watts* v. *Bucknall* [1903] 1 Ch. 766; *Tait* v. *Macleay* [1904] 2 Ch. 631; *Shepheard* v. *Broome* [1904] A.C. 342.
[61] *Watts* v. *Bucknall* [1902] 2 Ch. 628; [1903] 1 Ch. 766; *Hoole* v. *Speak* [1904] 2 Ch. 732.
[62] *Drincqbier* v. *Wood* [1899] 1 Ch. 393; *cf. Cargill* v. *Bower* (1878) 10 Ch.D. 502.
[63] *Cf. Thomson* v. *Lord Clanmorris* [1900] 1 Ch. 718.
[64] *Gibbs* v. *Guild* (1882) 9 Q.B.D. 59; *Thorne* v. *Heard* [1895] A.C. 495; *Bulli Coal Mining Co.* v. *Osborne* [1899] A.C. 351; *Oelkers* v. *Ellis* [1914] 2 K.B. 139.
[65] [1917] 2 Ch. 108.

director died, it would not lie against his executor unless by the tortious act property or the proceeds or value of property belonging to the person injured had been added to the director's estate; but now, by the Law Reform (Miscellaneous Provisions) Act 1934, s. 1, all causes of action survive against the estate of a deceased person, provided that proceedings were pending at the date of his death, or the cause of action arose not more than six months before his death and proceedings are commenced not later than six months after his personal representatives take out representation. In Scotland, where the ratio of *Geipel* v. *Peach* and the Act of 1934 are both inapplicable, an action in delict would lie against the estate of a deceased director within the five-year negative prescription (subject to pleas of personal bar).[66]

Claims under section 43 are provable in bankruptcy.[67]

In an action under this section the measure of damages is the loss suffered by reason of the false statement, *i.e.* the difference between the value which the shares would have had if the company had possessed the advantages stated in the prospectus (but not exceeding the price paid) and the true value of the shares at the time of allotment in the circumstances which in fact existed.[68]

Rights against experts

21–57 An expert who has given his consent to a statement in a prospectus may be liable as a person who has authorised the prospectus, within section 43 (1) (*d*), but only in respect of an untrue statement purporting to be made by him as an expert (see the proviso to subs. (1))[69] In that case the provisions of the section, which were discussed in the preceding paragraphs,[70] apply to him *mutatis mutandis*.

If an action lies against the expert under section 43, the defences available under subsection (2) are likewise open to him. In particular, he escapes liability if he can prove that he withdrew his consent in writing before delivery of a copy of the prospectus for registration or before allotment, in the latter case giving also reasonable public notice of his withdrawal, or that he was competent to make the statement and had reasonable ground to believe and did believe down to the date of allotment that the statement was true (s. 43 (3)).

---

66 See Walker on *Delict* (2nd, ed., 1981), p. 408.

67 Bankruptcy Act 1914, s. 30; *Greenwood* v. *Humber & Co.* [1898] W.N. 162. Such claims are also provable in Scotland.

68 *McConnell* v. *Wright* [1903] 1 Ch. 546; *Clark* v. *Urquhart* [1930] A.C. 28; *Davidson* v. *Hamilton* 1904, 12 S.L.T. 353.

69 It may also be possible to bring an action against an "expert" for negligence on the principle in *Hedley Byrne & Co. Ltd.* v. *Heller & Partners Ltd.* [1964] A.C. 465; see n. 53 to para. 21–52, *ante*. Normally, however, it will be easier to satisfy the requirements of s. 43.

70 See paras. 21–51 *et seq.*, *ante*.

Criminal liability in connection with prospectus

For misstatements in prospectus

21–58 Apart from general offences such as obtaining money by false pretences, persons responsible for misstatements in prospectuses may be prosecuted for one or several of the following offences:

21–59 UNDER THE 1948 ACT, S. 44. Under this provision the fact that a statement in a prospectus is untrue constitutes prima facie an offence and any person who authorised the issue[71] of the prospectus is prima facie guilty of this offence, whether he is a director or auditor of the company, or an expert whose report is referred to in the prospectus, or a solicitor, managerial official of an issuing house or—if he has approved the issue of the prospectus—the banker to the issue, or any other person. The requirements of liability are, thus, reduced to a minimum and the class of persons potentially liable is very wide.

In criminal proceedings, the extensive interpretation given to a prospectus and to statements made therein which applies to civil matters likewise applies. Thus, a "prospectus" within the meaning of section 44 has the wide connotation discussed earlier,[72] and, in particular, includes offers for sale and, in appropriate cases, placings.[73] Further, an "untrue statement" includes a statement literally true and correct but misleading in the form and context in which it appears (s. 46 (*a*)),[74] and statements in reports or memoranda included in, or referred to by, the prospectus are deemed to be statements in the prospectus and issued therewith (s. 46 (*b*)).

The accused may, however, plead one or more of the defences expressly admitted by section 44. Contrary to the normal principles of English and Scots criminal law that section places the onus of proof of innocence upon the accused: he has to satisfy the court that the conditions of the defence upon which he wishes to rely are present. The admitted defences are:

(1) that the statement was immaterial. This defence is open to the accused even if it is alleged that the statement was fraudulent (s. 44 (1)); or

(2) that he had reasonable ground to believe and, up to the time of the issue of the prospectus, did believe that the statement was true (s. 44 (1)).

The Act applies an objective standard here. It is not sufficient that the accused believed at all times the statement to be true; he has to establish in evidence that he had "reasonable ground" to believe it to be true. Consequently, the accused is liable under

---

[71] On the meaning of the term "issue of the prospectus," see para. 21–37, *ante*.
[72] See paras. 21–13 *et seq.*, *ante*.
[73] Although s. 45, which deals with these topics, follows the section dealing with criminal liability (s. 44).
[74] See para. 21–30, *ante*.

section 44 for an untrue statement if he negligently failed to ascertain that it was not correct.

21–60 An expert is not criminally liable for an untrue statement in a prospectus only on the ground that he consented in writing to the inclusion therein of his expert report[75]: section 44 (2) provides that such consent shall not be deemed to be the expert's authority to the issue of a prospectus. But if the untrue statement is contained in his report, the criminal liability of the expert is the same as that of other persons to whom the section applies.

The punishment provided under the section is: on conviction on indictment, imprisonment not exceeding two years, or a fine, or both; and on summary conviction, imprisonment not exceeding six months or a fine not exceeding the statutory maximum, or both s. 44 (1) as amended by the 1980 Act, Sched. 2).

21–61 UNDER THE THEFT ACT 1968, S. 19.[76] This section provides:

(1) Where an officer of a body corporate or unincorporated association (or person purporting to act as such), with intent to deceive members or creditors of the body corporate or association about its affairs, publishes or concurs in publishing a written statement or account which to his knowledge is or may be misleading, false or deceptive in a material particular, he shall on conviction on indictment be liable to imprisonment for a term not exceeding seven years.

(2) For purposes of this section a person who has entered into a security for the benefit of a body corporate or association is to be treated as a creditor of it.

(3) Where the affairs of a body corporate or association are managed by its members, this section shall apply to any statement which a member publishes or concurs in publishing in connection with his functions of management as if he were an officer of the body corporate or association.

The maximum punishment which the court may impose under this provision is seven years' imprisonment.

The conditions of this offence are much more limited than those of section 44. The accused is not guilty if he acted merely negligently, and the prosecution has the onus of proving that the accused knew that the untrue statement, which was made, was false, and that he had the intent to deceive or defraud any of the persons mentioned in the section.

21–62 In *R.* v. *Kylsant*[77] it was held that a statement is false within the meaning of section 84 of the Larceny Act 1861—which preceded the Theft Act 1968, s. 19—if in its context it conveys a misleading impression although it is

---

[75] Such consent is required under s. 40; see para. 21–20, *ante*.
[76] This Act does not apply to Scotland.
[77] [1932] 1 K.B. 442 (C.C.A.); see, further, *R.* v. *Bishirgian* [1936] 1 All E.R. 586 (C.C.A.).

literally correct—a principle which is now given statutory effect by section 46 (*a*).

There appears, therefore, to be no distinction between an "untrue" statement within section 44 and a "false" statement within section 19 of the Theft Act 1968. In *R.* v. *Kylsant*[77] Lord Kylsant, the chairman of the Royal Mail Steam Packet Company, had signed a prospectus of that company relating to an issue of £2,000,000 5 per cent. debenture stock. The prospectus showed a table of dividend paid between 1911 and 1927 and varying between 4 to 8 per cent. and contained the following statement:

> "The interest on the present issue of debenture stock will amount to £100,000. Although this company in common with other shipping companies has suffered from the depression in the shipping industry, the audited accounts of the company show that during the past 10 years the average annual balance available has been sufficient to pay the interest on the present issue more than five times over."

In actual fact from 1921 onwards the company had operated at a loss and maintained its dividend distribution only out of the successful recovery of taxes and other claims on the Treasury, the use of reserves, capitalised profits and similar transactions, but not out of trading profits—a fact which was not disclosed in the prospectus. Lord Kylsant was found guilty under section 84 of the Larceny Act 1861, and convicted. In the Court of Criminal Appeal, Avory J. said[78]:

> "The falsehood in this case consisted in putting before intending investors, as material on which they could exercise their judgment as to the position of the company, figures which apparently disclosed the existing position, but in fact hid it. In other words, the prospectus implied that the company was in a sound financial position and that the prudent investor could safely invest his money in its debentures . . . a statement which was utterly misleading when the fact that those dividends had been paid, not out of current earnings, but out of funds which had been earned during the abnormal period of the war, was omitted."

Under section 84 of the Larceny Act 1861, it was doubtful whether the phrase "public company" which occurred in that provision included a private company, as formerly defined by the Companies Act 1948, s. 28 (1). This question had to be answered in the affirmative, on the analogy of *R.* v. *Davies*,[79] decided on section 20 (1) (ii) of the Larceny Act 1916 (now repealed), and the other cases discussed earlier.[80] Section 19 of the Theft Act 1968, avoids this ambiguity by omitting the reference to a "public company."

21–63 UNDER THE PREVENTION OF FRAUD (INVESTMENT) ACT 1958, S. 13. This provision which is worded very widely is discussed in detail later.[81] Criminal

---

78 At p. 448.
79 [1955] 1 Q.B. 72.
80 See para. 4–13, *ante*.
81 See para. 25–05, *post*.

liability attaches not only for fraudulent or dishonest statements or concealments of material statements but likewise for any statement, promise or forecast which, being misleading, false or deceptive, is made recklessly. "Reckless" in section 13 (1) of the Act of 1958 includes also the case where there is a high degree of negligence without dishonesty.[81]

A person is guilty of an offence under section 13[82] if by a false or deceptive statement or concealment of material facts made fraudulently, dishonestly or recklessly he induces, attempts or conspires to induce another person to enter into or offer to enter into various types of agreements, particularly to acquire, dispose of, subscribe for or underwrite securities.[83]

The maximum punishment under the section is seven years' imprisonment (s. 13 (2) of the Act of 1958).

For non-compliance with statutory requirements

21–64 The Companies Acts contain penalties for the contravention of many of its provisions dealing with prospectuses. The most important of them is section 38 (3), which (apart from underwriting agreements and offers of shares or debentures otherwise than to the public) declares to be unlawful the issue of forms of application for shares or debentures unless the forms are accompanied by a prospectus, and imposes a fine on a person contravening this provision.[84]

Debenture prospectuses

21–65 The rules stated above apply for the most part to prospectuses offering debentures, debenture stock, and other securities for subscription but subject to the following qualifications:

(1) Mere delay after discovering misrepresentation is not so dangerous as in the case of shares, for there is no holding out to the creditors of the company as a member and potential contributory, as in the case of shares[85]; nevertheless, any act showing an election to affirm the contract destroys the right of rescission. Thus, if a debenture holder, entitled to repudiate, after discovering the facts giving such right acts as a debenture holder, *e.g.* by voting at a meeting or otherwise, he thereby disentitles himself to relief.

(2) Section 43 (compensation for untrue statements) is applicable to debenture prospectuses.

(3) An action for deceit is available where there is a fraudulent misrepresentation.

---

[82] For the exact wording of this section, see Volume II, Part B. This section is discussed in paras. 25–05 *et seq.*, *post.*

[83] s. 13 (1) (*a*). The definition of "securities" includes "share or debentures, or rights or interests (described whether as units or otherwise) in any shares or debentures" (s. 26 (1)).

[84] Other penalties are provided by ss. 40 (2), 41 (4).

[85] See para. 21–43, *ante*.

(4) In England, but not in Scotland, an action for damages is available against the company under the Misrepresentation Act 1967 for a misrepresentation which is not fraudulent.

(5) Sections 37 and 38 and the Fourth Schedule (general requirements as to prospectuses) are also applicable.

A prospectus offering debentures or debenture stock is headed with the name of the company, states the nominal and issued capital of the company, the number and description of the debentures or debenture stock offered, the nature of the security, the terms of issue, the names of the directors, bankers, solicitors, brokers, auditors, and secretary, the objects and prospects of the company, the facts required by section 38 and the Fourth Schedule to be stated, how applications are to be made, and where copies of the memorandum and articles of association, and of the debentures and debenture stock deed, may be inspected.

Statements in lieu of prospectus

21–66 Statements in lieu of prospectus, which were required by the 1948 Act, ss. 30 (1) and 48, are abolished by the 1980 Act, which has repealed those two sections and Sched. 5 to the 1948 Act. (1980 Act, s. 88 and Sched. 4).

CHAPTER 22

APPLICATION FOR AND ALLOTMENT OF SHARES

Application for shares

The application as offer

22–01 An application for shares in a company may be made in a formal or informal manner. It is usually made in writing signed by the applicant but an application by word of mouth would likewise be effective.[1]

An application is an offer by the applicant and, like any other offer to make a simple contract, may, subject to what is said below[2] in connection with an application pursuant to a prospectus issued generally, be revoked at any time before acceptance. The revocation, where admissible, may be by word of mouth[3] or by post but in the latter case it is not effective unless it is received by the company before the allotment of the shares.[4]

The application must clearly evince an intention to subscribe, and be more than an expression of willingness to do so on a future occasion.[5] Mere concurrence in the company's suggestion that a name remain on the register and the shares be transferred, to correct the company's initial error in making the entry, does not imply agreement to be a shareholder.[6]

Application by agent

22–02 The general rule *qui facit per alium facit per se* applies to a contract to take shares, and, accordingly, A can authorise B to apply for shares on his, A's, behalf, and, if shares are allotted to A, he becomes a member.[7] Nor is it essential that the agent should have actual authority: it is sufficient if he is held out as having authority. Thus, where A gives B an open letter authorising him to apply for shares but gives him private instructions limiting the authority and B applies showing his authority but concealing the private instructions, A is bound, though the application is in contravention of the private instructions,[8] unless the seller has actual notice of the private instructions; the principles developed by the courts on ostensible, as distinguished from actual, authority would apply in this case. If the

---

1 *Bloxam's Case* (1864) 33 Beav. 529; *Levita's Case* (1867) L.R. 3 Ch. 36; *Goldie* v. *Torrance* 1882, 10 R. 174.
2 See para. 22–05, *post*.
3 *Truman's Case* [1894] 3 Ch. 272.
4 *Byrne* v. *Van Tienhoven* (1880) 5 C.P.D. 344.
5 *Mason* v. *Benhar Coal Co.* 1882 9 R. 883; *Jackson* v. *Liquidator of Star Fire and Burglary Insurance Co.* 1902, 10 S.L.T. 279; *Liquidator of Miller & Sommerville* v. *Miller* 1910 S.C. 868; 1910, 2 S.L.T. 33; *The Kingsburgh Motor Construction Co.* v. *Scott* 1902, 10 S.L.T. 424; *Curror's Trustee* v. *Caledonian Heritable Security Co.* 1880 17 R. 479.
6 *Liquidator of the Florida Mortgage & Investment Co.* 1890, 7 R. 525.
7 *Barrett's Case* (1864) 4 De G.J. & S. 416; *Re Hannan's Empress, etc., Co.* [1896] 2 Ch. 643; *Hindley's Case* [1896] 2 Ch. 121.
8 *Re Henry Bentley & Co.* (1893) 69 L.T. 204; *Premier Briquette Co.* v. *Gray* 1922 S.C. 329; 1922 S.L.T. 230.

purported agent had no authority, his acts may later be ratified by the principal.[9]

If A applies for shares in a fictitious name and is allotted some, he will be held liable as a member in respect of them and his real name may be entered on the register.[10] In English law, where an application is sent in the name of another person who is not *sui juris* (*e.g.* a minor), it has been held that the position is the same as if the application were sent in in a false or fictitious name, and the applicant himself may be put on the list of contributories[11] but there must, to constitute liability in such a case, be a contract, and there can be no contract where there is no intention of contracting.[12] It must be noted that Scots law differs from English law on legal capacity, and, in particular, there is no objection in Scotland in principle to a minor (*i.e.* a boy of 14 or older or a girl of 12) being registered as a shareholder.[13]

Conditional applications

2–03 Sometimes an application for shares is made subject to a condition precedent, *e.g.* A writes to an hotel company saying, if you will give me an order for furniture, I will take up 50 shares in your capital, which please allot. In such case an allotment disregarding the condition may be repudiated by the allottee; for where there is a conditional application for shares and an unconditional allotment there is no contract constituted. The parties are not *ad idem*.[14] The condition need not be contained in the letter of application. It is sufficient if the letter containing the condition reaches the directors before allotment.[15] But in such cases if, after note of allotment before the condition is complied with, the allottee abstains from repudiating, he will be taken to have waived the condition and be bound.[16]

A distinction of a very material kind exists between an application subject to a condition precedent and an application with a collateral agreement or a condition subsequent. In the latter case the applicant has agreed absolutely to become a member, with only a right to enforce (if valid) the collateral agreement or condition subsequent against the company.[17] The distinction may be important if the company is insolvent. Thus in *Elkington's Case*[18] a person applied for shares by signing an

---

9 *G. H. Levita's Case* (1870) L.R. 5 Ch. 489.
10 *Pugh and Sharman's Case* (1872) L.R. 13 Eq. 566.
11 *Pugh and Sharman's Case* (1872) L.R. 13 Eq. 566; *Richardson's Case* (1875) L.R. 19 Eq. 588.
12 *Coventry's Case, Re Britannia Fire Association* [1891] 1 Ch. 202 (C.A.).
13 See, *e.g.* I.R.C. v. *Wilson* 1927 S.C. 733, affd. 1928 S.C. 42 (H.L.).
14 *Roger's Case and Harrison's Case* (1868) L.R. 3 Ch. 633; *Wood's Case* (1858) 3 De G. & J. 85; *Shaw's Case* (1876) 34 L.T. 715; *Wood's Case* (1873) L.R. 15 Eq. 236.
15 *Roger's Case, Harrison's Case, supra.*
16 *Wheatcroft's Case* (1873) 29 L.T. 324.
17 *Elkington's Case* (1867) L.R. 2 Ch. 511; *Fisher's Case and Sherrington's Case* (1885) 31 Ch.D. 120; *Bridger's Case* (1870) L.R. 5 Ch. 305; and *Thomson's Case* (1865) 4 De G.J. & S. 749 are good illustrations of the distinction; see also *Miln* v. *North British Fresh Fish Supply Co.* 1887, 15 R. 21; *National House Property Investment Co.* v. *Watson* 1908 S.C. 888; 16 S.L.T. 96.
18 (1867) L.R. 2 Ch. 511.

application form in which he agreed to pay 30s. upon allotment, and calls when made, and to sign the articles of association when required to do so. He was allotted the shares, paid the 30s., received and retained the certificates, and received circulars and notice of a further call. He refused to pay this call on the ground that the shares were taken on the distinct understanding that until goods to the amount of £3,000 had been actually taken and paid for by the company from him no further call was to be paid on the shares. The court found that the applicant had agreed to become a member and was bound by his application, and that the agreement as to the purchase of goods from him was not a condition precedent to his becoming a member but a collateral agreement. The applicant was therefore a member of the company and rightly put on the list of contributories.

Mistake as to company

22–04 Where a person applies for and takes an allotment of shares in company A believing it to be company B, he may in exceptional cases be entitled to repudiate membership if he acts promptly on discovering his mistake.[19]

Application pursuant to prospectus

Statutory restriction on revocability of application

22–05 It has been seen earlier[20] that an application for shares, as an offer to conclude a simple contract, can at common law be revoked by the applicant until the company has allotted the shares.

A statutory exception to this rule is admitted in the case of an application pursuant to a prospectus issued generally,[21] *i.e.* issued to persons who are not existing members or debenture holders of the company. Such an application is not freely revocable by the applicant: he may not normally revoke the application until after the expiration of the third day after the time of opening the subscription lists (s. 50 (5)).

This statutory limitation of the applicant's common law right does not, however, apply:

(1) to an abridged prospectus issued under a certificate of exemption by a stock exchange (ss. 50 (7), 39)[22];

(2) where a promoter, director or a person who has authorised the issue of the prospectus before the expiration of the third day has given public notice having the effect of excluding his responsibility (s. 50 (5)).

In these cases the applicant is free to make use of his common law right to revoke.

The object of limiting the power to revoke is to prevent speculators who

---

[19] Normally the principle applied in *Harrison & Jones Ltd.* v. *Bunton & Lancaster Ltd.* [1953] 1 Q.B. 646 and *Neuchatel Asphalte Co. Ltd.* v. *Barnett* [1957] 1 W.L.R. 356, 359 will prevent him from setting aside the transaction on the ground of mistake.

[20] See para. 22–01, *ante*.

[21] s. 39 (1) (*a*); see para. 21–26, *ante*.

[22] See para. 21–26, *ante*.

"stag" the issue, by applying for more shares than they intend to take up with a view to selling them on the market at a profit or from revoking their applications if the issue appears to be unsuccessful. Otherwise the directors would not know whether the issue was genuinely successful because revocations might at any time alter the position. Stagging, as such, is not illegal, but if the only funds out of which the greater part of the stag's application money could be paid were funds which were not in existence when the application was made and that money could only be paid out of return cheques which the issuing houses were expected to send for much larger applications for shares than were allotted, the jury could find that the stags acted deliberately dishonestly and the stags were convicted for obtaining property by deception, contrary to section 15 (1) of the Theft Act 1968.[23]

Exchange of shares for shares

2–06 Where a company offers to acquire the shares of another company in exchange for its own shares, as may be the case in amalgamations and take-over bids, a form of acceptance often accompanies that offer; this form is not a form of application,[24] but, if completed by the shareholder and duly returned, is an acceptance of the company's offer, and concludes the agreement whereby the acceptor agrees to become a member of the company.

Form of application

2–07 No form of application may be sent out in respect of any shares or debentures unless it is accompanied by a prospectus (s. 38 (3)), except where

(1) the form is issued in connection with an invitation to a person to underwrite the shares (s. 38 (3) (*a*)); or

(2) the shares or debentures are not offered to the public (s. 38 (3) (*b*)).

Where a prospectus is required to accompany an application form, it must comply with the provisions of section 38 and of the Fourth Schedule of the 1948 Act and section 16 (1) (b) of the 1980 Act, which relates to partial allotments.

The above mentioned requirements of the 1948 Act need not be complied with if

(1) the form of application is issued to existing members or debenture holders, whether the allotment letter is intended to be renounceable or not (s. 38 (5) (*a*)); or

(2) the form of application relates to shares or debentures which are to be in all respects uniform with shares or debentures previously issued and dealt in or listed on a prescribed[25] stock exchange (s. 38 (5) (*b*)); or

---

[23] *R.* v. *Greenstein* [1975] 1 W.L.R. 1353.

[24] *Government Stock and Other Securities Investment Co. Ltd.* v. *Christopher* [1956] 1 W.L.R. 237; see para. 21–14, *ante*.

[25] See para. 21–26, *ante*.

(3) a certificate of exemption of a stock exchange has been granted in respect of the issue (s. 39).[26]

Application forms are normally worded so that the offer contained therein is to take a certain number of shares or such lesser number as may be allotted to the applicant. Otherwise the allotment of a smaller number of shares by the company than that applied for by the applicant would constitute a refusal of his original offer combined with a counter-offer by the company, and the allotment would not be final.

Allotment of shares

The allotment as acceptance

22–08 While the application for shares is normally an offer to take the shares, acceptance is achieved by allotment notified to the applicant. The allotment itself does not constitute acceptance; it must be notified to the applicant[27] in the manner discussed later.[28]

To be effective, an acceptance of an application for shares must be unconditional. If it introduces a new term it is not an effective acceptance and amounts to a new offer by the company which will not result in a contract unless accepted by the applicant.[29]

The position that arises where a new term is introduced when a company purports to accept an application, or where shares are allotted although no formal application has been made, is discussed with reference to decided cases at para. 49–05, *post*.

Specific performance of contract for the allotment of shares

22–09 The court has jurisdiction to decree specific performance of an undertaking by a person to take, or by a company to allot, shares or debentures.[30]

Application must be accepted within reasonable time

22–10 It is an implied term in an application for shares that the offer must be accepted within a reasonable time; if this is not done, the applicant is entitled to repudiate the allotment.[31] What is a reasonable time depends on circumstances; but an allottee who receives notice of allotment after a reasonable time has expired must exercise his right of repudiation promptly. If he fails to do so, he will be bound; the same applies *a fortiori* if the rights of the creditors have intervened by the appointment of a receiver or a winding up.[31a]

---

[26] See para. 21–26, *ante*.
[27] *Re Scottish Petroleum Co.* (1883) 23 Ch.D. 413, 430.
[28] See para. 22–11, *post*.
[29] *Re Leeds Banking Co., Addinell's Case* (1865) L.R. 1 Eq. 225; *Jackson* v. *Turquand* (1869) L.R. 4 H.L. 305; *Liquidator of the Consolidated Copper Co. of Canada* v. *Peddie* 1877 5 R. 393.
[30] See para. 49–06, *post*.
[31] See *Crawley's Case* (1869) L.R. 4 Ch. 322 and *Ramsgate Victoria Hotel* v. *Montefiore* (1866) L.R. 1 Ex. 109.
[31a] *Boyle's Case* (1885) 33 W.R. 450; *Crawley's Case* (1869) L.R. 4 Ch. 322.

Notice of allotment

22–11 "I think," said Lord Cairns in *Pellatt's Case*,[32] "that where an individual applies for shares in a company, there being no obligation to let him have any, there must be a response by the company, otherwise there is no contract," and this statement of the law has always been accepted. The communication of the acceptance need not necessarily be in writing, but it must be communicated in some way, whether by writing or verbally, or by conduct.[33] A letter demanding payment may be a sufficient notification of acceptance.[34] Prima facie notice of allotment must be given to the applicant or to his agent duly authorised to receive notice of allotment.[35] It depends on the facts of each case whether an agent to apply for shares has implied authority to receive notice of allotment.[36] Thus, if A, in applying, says: "Give notice of allotment to B" and notice is so given, that is sufficient.[37] An applicant may waive notice of allotment, and there are other cases in which notice of allotment is not necessary to complete the contract, *e.g.* where, by virtue of some agreement upon reconstruction or amalgamation, the company is under an obligation to allot the shares, and a person entitled to an allotment in response to a circular calling on him to come in claims allotment of his shares. In such a case notice of allotment is not necessary,[38] unless the circular shows that the offer is intended to invite application, not acceptance,[39] in which case the company could refuse to allot. In any case in which the company, by letter or otherwise, in effect offers a specified number of shares to a person and he writes back accepting them, no further notice of allotment is necessary.

Allotment and notice after incorporation, in response to an application before incorporation, is sufficient to constitute a complete contract,[40] for in such a case the application operates as a continuing offer and matures, on acceptance by the company after incorporation, into a contract.

Instantaneous acceptance

22–12 If the acceptance is verbal, by telephone, telex,[41] or by conduct it is, in accordance with the general rules of the law of contract, effective when it is received by the applicant, unless there is a different intention of the parties.

---

32 (1867) L.R. 2 Ch. 527, 535.
33 *Gunn's Case* (1867) L.R. 3 Ch. 40; *Chapman* v. *Sulphite Pulp Co.* 1892, 19 R. 837; *Nelson* v. *Fraser* 1906, 14 S.L.T. 513.
34 *Forget* v. *Cement Products Co. of Canada* [1961] W.N. 259.
35 *Levita's Case* (1870) L.R. 5 Ch. 489; *De Rosaz's Case* (1869) 21 L.T. 10.
36 *Robinson's Case* (1869) L.R. 4 Ch. 330; *Wallis's Case* (1868) L.R. 4 Ch. 325n.
37 *De Rosaz's Case* (1869) 21 L.T. 10.
38 *Gunn's Case* (1867) L.R. 3 Ch. 40.
39 *Wallace's Case* [1900] 2 Ch. 671.
40 *Downes* v. *Ship* (1868) L.R. 3 H.L. 343; *Lawrence's Case* (1867) L.R. 2 Ch. 412.
41 *Entores Ltd.* v. *Miles Far East Corporation* [1955] 2 Q.B. 327; *Brinkibon Ltd.* v. *Stahag* [1980] 2 Lloyd's Rep. 556 (effect of repudiation by telex); affd. by H.L. [1982] 2 W.L.R. 264.

Acceptance by post

22–13 As a general rule, notice of allotment may be given by post.[42] The old rule, at least in England, was that in such a case the contract was complete when the letter was posted,[43] even though it was never received.[44] The Post Office was deemed to be the common agent of both parties.[45] Handing to a postman in the street who is clearing a pillar box was regarded as not enough, since in accordance with Post Office regulations the letter was not posted until it was proved to be in the custody of the Post Office.[46] In modern law[47] a wide exception is admitted to the old rule. The rule does not apply if "having regard to all the circumstances, including the nature of the subject matter under consideration, the negotiating parties cannot have intended that there should be a binding agreement until the party accepting an offer or exercising an option had in fact communicated the acceptance or exercise to the other."[48] As in normal circumstances the parties will intend that the acceptance shall be communicated, the effect of this qualification is—and that is good law—that an acceptance by posting must normally be communicated to complete the contract, and only in exceptional cases, in which it is clear that the parties so intended, is the posting sufficient to make the acceptance effective. As far as the allotment of shares is concerned which, as we have seen, is normally an acceptance in the eyes of the law, the parties clearly intend that the allotment should be communicated to the applicant, and there is no contract if the company has failed to do so.

In Scots law it has always been at least doubtful whether mere posting of an acceptance concludes a contract. It has been suggested that no contract can exist if the offeror proves he did not receive the acceptance.[49]

Proof of notice

22–14 If notice of allotment is disputed, the onus is on the company to prove the notice[50]; but this onus it may discharge by proving acts on the part of the alleged member going to show that he was aware of the allotment and assented to it.[51] The effect is the same whether notice of the allotment reaches the allottee from the company or otherwise, and will bind him,[52]

---

[42] *Household Fire, etc., Insurance Co.* v. *Grant* (1879) 4 Ex.D. 216; *Henthorn* v. *Fraser* [1892] 2 Ch. 27.
[43] *Harris's Case* (1872) L.R. 7 Ch. 587.
[44] See n. 42, *supra*.
[45] *Household Fire Insurance Co.* v. *Grant* (1879) 4 Ex.D. 216.
[46] *Re London and Northern Bank, ex p. Jones* [1900] 1 Ch. 220.
[47] *Holwell Securities Ltd.* v. *Hughes* [1974] 1 W.L.R. 155.
[48] *Per* Lawton L.J., *ibid.* at p. 161.
[49] *Mason* v. *Benhar Coal Co.* 1882, 9 R. 883, 890; Walker, *The Law of Contracts, etc., in Scotland* (1979), para. 7.63; Gloag and Henderson, *Introduction to the Law of Scotland* (8th ed., 1980), p. 54.
[50] *Reidpath's Case* (1870) L.R. 11 Eq. 86.
[51] *Crawley's Case* (1869) L.R. 4 Ch. 322; *Re Richards and Home Assurance Association* (1871) L.R. 6 C.P. 591; *Chapman* v. *Sulphite Pulp Co.* 1892, 19 R. 837.
[52] *Wallis's Case* (1868) L.R. 4 Ch. 325n.

e.g. if the allottee is present at a board meeting at which the allotment is resolved on.[53]

In *Crawley's Case*,[54] C had applied for shares that were not allotted to him for 14 months, and accordingly he might have refused the allotment on the ground that it was not made within a reasonable time.[55] No notice of the allotment was given to him, but some months afterwards, he, at the request of B, signed a blank transfer of the shares, and that was held sufficient to show that he must have known of, and assented to, the allotment. "I think that after that act," said Selwyn L.J.,[56] "he cannot be heard to say that he did not know of the allotment, or that it had not been communicated to him."

Stamp duty

22–15 Letters of allotment or of renunciation are exempted from stamp duty.[57]

Allotment by irregularly constituted board of directors

22–16 To constitute a valid allotment there must, as a general rule, be a duly constituted board of directors,[58] but the rule in *Royal British Bank* v. *Turquand*[59] may sometimes render an allotment by an irregular board effective.[60] Further, an allotment may be effective even if the board is not duly constituted in cases where an article is found similar to article 105 of Table A, which validates, *inter alia*, the acts of a meeting of the directors notwithstanding that it be afterwards discovered that there was some defect in the appointment of any of the directors.

An allotment by a board irregularly constituted may be subsequently ratified by a regular board.[61] A director who has joined in an allotment to himself will be estopped from alleging the invalidity of the allotment.[62]

The rules on official notification[63] under the European Communities Act 1972, s. 9 (3) and (4), may, on occassion, cure an allotment which is defective on the ground that the board was irregularly constituted.

Ultra vires allotment

22–17 An allotment of shares which is *ultra vires*, on the ground that no authority to issue shares of the class in question exists in the memorandum and articles, is void and any subscription money is returnable to the allottee.[64] On the other hand, if a member is admitted who is not duly qualified in terms of the articles, only the company, and not the member, can plead that his

---

[53] *Re Saloon Steam Packet Co.* [1867] W̄.N. 259.
[54] (1869) L.R. 4 Ch. 322.
[55] *Ramsgate Victoria Hotel* v. *Montefiore* (1866) L.R. 1 Ex. 109.
[56] At p. 328.
[57] Finance Act 1949, Sched. VIII, Pt. I, para. 17.
[58] *Re Homer District Consol. Gold Mines* (1888) 39 Ch.D. 546.
[59] (1856) 6 E. & B. 327; see para. 28–10, *post*.
[60] See *Owen and Ashworth's Claim* [1900] 2 Ch. 272.
[61] *Re Portuguese Consolidated Copper Mines* (1889) 42 Ch.D. 160; see para. 62–03, *post*.
[62] *York Tramways Co.* v. *Willows* (1882) 8 Q.B.D. 685.
[63] On official notification, see para. 17–01, *ante*.
[64] *Waverly Hydropathic Co.* v. *Barrowman* 1895, 23 R. 136; 3 S.L.T. 161.

admission was *ultra vires*,[65] subject to the provisions of the European Communities Act 1972, s. 9 (1).

Directors' duty as to allotment

22–18 The duty of the directors as to allotment, as in all matters, is that they are bound to act in good faith in the best interests of the company.[66] This does not imply that they may not properly offer the shares to the existing shareholders at par or over, even though the shares stand at a higher price in the market: there is no duty to the company to hold out for the highest price.[67] Apart from other considerations, the directors, when offering the shares to the existing shareholders below the market price (but above par), may wish such "rights" issue to carry an element of bonus for the shareholders—an entirely legitimate intention.

Effect of irregular allotment

This subject is discussed fully later.[68]

Renounceable and non-renounceable letters of allotment

22–19 The distinction between these two types of allotment letters is of considerable importance when the question arises whether an offer of shares or debentures is issued to the public and, consequently, is a prospectus (s. 55). This question has already been considered.[69]

Combined renounceable share certificates and allotment letters

22–20 In modern practice, in the case of bonus issues, renounceable share certificates are sometimes issued. Thereby two stages in the procedure, *viz.* the issue of letters of allotment and the subsequent issue of share certificates, are combined into one stage. The notification of the company accompanying these renounceable share certificates and addressed to the shareholders will contain the following, or a similar, statement:

> "A renounceable share certificate is enclosed in respect of the new shares allotted to you.
>
> "If you decide to retain all your new shares the document will serve as a permanent share certificate which should be kept in a safe place.
>
> "Should you wish to dispose of all or some of your new shares, the document will enable you to do so in the same way as if it were a renounceable allotment letter in the usual form. The instructions on the reverse side of the share certificate explain the procedure to be followed, but in case of difficulty, you should consult your Banker, Stockbroker or Solicitor."

---

65 *Aberdeen Master Masons Incorporation* v. *Smith* 1908 S.C. 669; 15 S.L.T. 953.

66 *Re London and Colonial Finance Corporation* (1897) 13 T.L.R. 576 (C.A.); *Shaw* v. *Holland* [1900] 2 Ch. 305; *Percival* v. *Wright* [1902] 2 Ch. 421; *Gething* v. *Kilner* [1972] 1 W.L.R. 337.

67 *Hilder* v. *Dexter* [1902] A.C. 474.

68 See para. 22–33, *post*.

69 See para. 21–17, *ante*.

Statutory restrictions on allotment

Restrictions on first allotment

22–21 PRIVATE COMPANIES. The Companies Acts do not contain restrictions on the allotment of shares or debentures by a private company. Such a company may proceed to allotment as soon as it is incorporated.

22–22 PUBLIC COMPANIES WHICH DO NOT INVITE PUBLIC SUBSCRIPTION. A public company, after having been formed, is not required by the Acts to obtain its working capital by inviting the public[70] to subscribe for its shares or debentures. It may allot those securities to allottees, as it were, as their domestic concern,[71] without issuing a prospectus.[72]

The public company must, of course, comply with the requirements of the 1980 Act relating to the subscription of the authorised minimum and the payment of one-quarter of the nominal amount of the issued shares and the whole premium, before allowed to commence business or exercise its borrowing powers; these requirements were discussed earlier.[73]

If a company obtains its initial capital by domestic allotments of shares but later decides to make a further issue of shares[74] by inviting the public to apply for them, this invitation—the first share prospectus of the company—has to comply with the requirements relating to the minimum subscription which are discussed in the following paragraphs.

22–23 PUBLIC COMPANIES WHICH INVITE PUBLIC SUBSCRIPTION; THE MINIMUM SUBSCRIPTION. Where a public company for the first time invites the public to subscribe for its shares, the statutory provisions relating to the minimum subscription have to be complied with, and no allotment of shares must take place unless the minimum subscription has been taken up by applicants and the sums payable by them for the shares constituting the minimum subscription have been paid (s. 47 (1)). The "minimum subscription" discussed here should not be confused with the "statutory minimum" required of public companies and at present amounting to £50,000. The "minimum subscription" is an entirely different and disassociated concept from the "authorised minimum."

The statutory requirements relating to the minimum subscription have to be complied with whether the first prospectus inviting the public to subscribe for its shares is issued by the company immediately upon its formation or much later in its life. However, they apply only to the first share prospectus. They need not be satisfied for the second and any subsequent invitation to the public to subscribe for shares, nor do they apply to

[70] "Public" includes any section of the public, subject to certain exceptions (s. 55); see para. 21–17, *ante*.
[71] This phrase is taken from s. 55.
[72] For the meaning of "prospectus," see s. 455 and paras. 21–13 *et seq.*, *ante*.
[73] See paras. 15–02 *et seq*, *ante*.
[74] Not debentures.

any—the first or any later—invitation to subscribe for the debentures of the company.

What, then, is the minimum subscription? It is not a sum fixed by the articles or calculated as a percentage of the shares issued under the prospectus. It is the minimum amount stated in the prospectus[75] which in the opinion of the directors must be raised in order to provide for:

(1) the price of any property purchased or to be purchased out of the proceeds of the issue;
(2) any preliminary expenses,[76] and any underwriting commission (including so-called overriding commission, *i.e.* commission retained by the principal underwriter, *e.g.* an issuing house, who has arranged for subscription of the issue by sub-underwriters);
(3) the repayment of moneys borrowed by the company in respect of any of the foregoing matters; and
(4) the working capital (Sched. IV, para. 4 (*a*)).

If any of items (1) to (3) have been paid for out of borrowed money which is to be repaid out of the issue, the borrowed money must itself be covered; but where money is borrowed to provide for any of them and is not to be repaid out of the issue, the minimum subscription is only required to cover the balance.

22–24 The prospectus will normally state the proportion of the capital to be paid for each share upon application, and in such a case this proportion of the minimum subscription must have been paid prior to allotment (s. 47 (1)). The words "has been paid to and received by the company" were not formerly satisfied by a cheque until the cheque was honoured,[77] but section 47 (1) now provides that a cheque satisfies this requirement if it has been received in good faith by the company and the directors have no reason for suspecting that it will not be paid. Where shares are not payable in full on application, provided that a sufficient number of shares are subscribed for, which, when paid in full, will amount to the minimum subscription, the requirements of the Act are satisfied. In other words, if a company issues 10,000 ordinary shares at £1 each payable as to 25p on allotment and the minimum subscription is £7,500, provided that applications are received for 7,500 shares the minimum subscription has been subscribed although, at the time of allotment, the company has only received £1,875, *i.e.* 7,500 x 25p.

The minimum subscription must be reckoned exclusive of any amount payable otherwise than in cash (s. 47 (2)). The provisions relating to the minimum subscription cannot be contracted out, *i.e.* a condition whereby the applicant waives compliance with them is void (s. 47 (5)).

---

[75] *i.e.* the prospectus upon which the applicant subscribed: *Roussel* v. *Burnham* [1909] 1 Ch. 127.

[76] This means expenses incurred in connection with the formation of the company.

[77] *Mears* v. *Western Canada Pulp and Paper Co.* [1905] 2 Ch. 353; *Re National Motor Mail-Coach Co., Anstis and McClean's Claims* [1908] 2 Ch. 228; *Burton* v. *Bevan* [1908] 2 Ch. 240.

22–25 MINIMUM SUBSCRIPTION NOT RECEIVED. If the minimum subscription has not been received within 40 days of the first issue of the prospectus all money received from applicants for shares must be repaid to them forthwith, without interest. If any such money is not repaid within the next eight days, every director then becomes personally liable to repay it with interest, unless he proves that the default in repayment was not due to any misconduct or negligence on his part (s. 47 (4)).

MINIMUM SUBSCRIPTION RECEIVED SUBSEQUENTLY. The crucial date for ascertaining whether an allotment is valid is the date of allotment. If at that date the minimum subscription has not been received, the allotment is invalid, and the fact that it is later received does not validate any such allotment.[78]

22–26 WHERE PROSPECTUS ISSUED, BUT NO SHARES ALLOTTED PURSUANT THERETO. Where a company issues a prospectus but does not proceed to allot any of the shares offered to the public, *e.g.* because the minimum subscription is not reached, it may not make a first allotment of any of its shares or debentures.[79]

Restrictions on partial allotments

22–27 Where a partial, and not a full, subscription is intended to be sufficient, the prospectus must state so, and the same is the case if the partial allotment is made conditional (1980 Act, s. 16 (1)). The prospectus must state that, even if the capital offered in the prospectus is not subscribed for in full, the shares subscribed for will be allotted in any event or in the event of certain conditions, which must be specified in the prospectus.

No allotment of shares is allowed unless the conditions specified in the prospectus are satisfied (1980 Act, s. 16 (2)), and the provisions of the 1948 Act, ss. 47 (4) (repayment of money paid by the applicants) and 49 (effect of irregular allotment) apply to the case of shares prohibited from being allotted by section 16 (1).

These provisions are made applicable to shares offered as wholly or partly payable otherwise than in cash (1980 Act, s. 16 (3)).

Restrictions applicable to all allotments

22–28 The following restrictions apply to all allotments, the first one as well as the subsequent ones.

22–29 NO ALLOTMENT UNTIL THIRD DAY AFTER ISSUE OF PROSPECTUS. No allotment may be made pursuant to a prospectus issued generally, *i.e.* to persons who

---

[78] This follows from *Mears* v. *Western Canada Pulp and Paper Co. Ltd.* [1905] 2 Ch. 353; *Glasgow Pavilion Ltd.* v. *Motherwell* (1903) 6 F. (Ct. of Sess.) 116.

[79] The provisions of s. 48 of the 1948 Act (statement in lieu of prospectus) were repealed by the 1980 Act s. 82(*a*) and Sched. 4.

are not existing members or debenture holders of the company (s. 39 (1) (*a*)), until the beginning of the third day after that on which the prospectus is first issued (s. 50 (1)). A prospectus is first issued generally on the day when it is first issued as a newspaper advertisement, but if it is first issued in another manner more than two days before the advertisement is published the date of the earlier issue is the relevant day (s. 50 (2)). Saturdays, Sundays and bank holidays in any part of Great Britain are excluded in reckoning the period: *e.g.* a day which is a bank holiday in Scotland would be excluded in computing the period after the issue of a prospectus in Scotland as well as in England (s. 50 (6)).

The restriction of section 50 does not apply to a prospectus issued in the abridged form under a certificate of exemption obtained from a stock exchange (ss. 39, 50 (7)).

An allotment contravening this restriction is valid but may lead to criminal prosecution of the company and the officers in default (s. 50 (3)).

22–30 REFUSAL OF APPLICATION TO DEAL. Where a prospectus states that application has been or will be made for the shares or debentures to be dealt with on the Stock Exchange, any allotment made on an application under the prospectus shall be void

(1) if permission has not been applied for before the third day after the first issue of the prospectus; or

(2) if permission is refused before the expiration of three weeks (subject to the extension by the Stock Exchange to six weeks) from the date of the closing of the subscription lists (s. 51 (1)).

It should be noted that under case (2), above, the allotment is not void if the Stock Exchange merely defers the decision on permission to deal, or does not arrive at a decision within the stated time.

During the periods stated in cases (1) and (2), above, the application money received by the company from shareholders who applied for shares has to be kept on a separate account (s. 51 (3))[80]; 'that appears," as Harman J. observed in *Re Nanwa Gold Mines Ltd.*,[81] "to be an attempt to erect, so to speak, by statute a kind of trust for applicants"; consequently, the application money thus kept on separate account does not form part of the general assets of the company which are charged by a debenture secured by a floating charge. The relationship between the applicants and the company which holds the application moneys on separate account is that of bailors and bailee, and not of creditors and debtor.[81]

Where permission has not been applied for as required under case (1), above, or has been refused within the time stated in case (2), above, the application moneys for the shares have to be returned forthwith, and if the moneys are not repaid within eight days the directors are jointly and

---

[80] Default in complying with this provision renders the company and every one of its officers who is in default liable to a default fine (s. 51 (3)).

[81] [1955] 1 W.L.R. 1080, 1085.

severally liable to repay them with interest at the rate of 5 per cent. per annum. Only a director who can prove that the default in the repayment was not due to his misconduct is exempt from this liability (s. 51 (2)).

The same provisions apply to shares or debentures agreed to be taken by underwriters of an issue; the latter are treated as if they were applicants for those shares or debentures (s. 51 (6) (*a*)).

Where the prospectus is in the form of an offer for sale, the provisions of section 51 apply *mutatis mutandis* (s. 51 (6) (*b*)).

22–31 ISSUE OF SHARES AT A PREMIUM OR AT A DISCOUNT. The issue of shares at a premium or at a discount is considered in Chapter 24.[82]

22–32 STATUTORY REGULATIONS OUTSIDE THE COMPANIES ACTS. On the issue of shares statutory regulations outside the Companies Acts may have to be considered. The most important of them are:

(1) those contained in the Prevention of Fraud (Investments) Act 1958[83]; and
(2) those relating to the control of borrowing, under the Borrowing (Controls and Guarantees) Act 1946, and the statutory instruments made thereunder.[84]

Irregular allotments

22–33 It should not be thought that a defect in the allotment renders the allotment automatically void. Three cases have to be distinguished:

1. Where the allotment is defective because it is made before the lapse of the third day after the publication of a prospectus issued generally, the allotment is valid, but the company and its officers in default are liable to a fine (s. 50 (3)).
2. Where the allotment is defective because no application to the Stock Exchange for permission to deal is made or such application is refused, the allotment is void (s. 51 (1)).
3. Where the provisions relating to the minimum subscription or the application money have not been complied with (s. 47), the allotment is voidable at the instance of the allottee (s. 49).[85]

This case requires further consideration in the following paragraphs.

Voidability of irregular allotment

22–34 THE TIME LIMIT. If an allotment is made by a company in contravention of the restrictions upon allotment set out in section 47, the allotment, though

---

[82] See paras. 24–08 *et seq.*, *post*.
[83] See para. 25–01, *post*.
[84] See para. 26–01, *post*.
[85] Except where an attempt is made by a condition in the terms of issue to contract out of the statutory provisions relating to the minimum subscription. Such a condition is void (s. 47 (5)).

irregular, is nonetheless an allotment.[86] Such an allotment is, however, voidable (s. 49 (1)). An applicant may avoid the allotment provided that he does so within one month after the date of the allotment.

22–35 There can be no avoidance outside the time limit, but the right to avoid the contract does not lapse if, within the time limits, the company goes into liquidation.

The allottee must, within the period named, inform the company that he avoids the allotment. If legal proceedings have to be taken these need not be within the month, provided that the notice of avoidance was within that time, but they should be reasonably prompt thereafter if they are required to be brought.[87]

22–36 IRREGULAR ALLOTMENT VOIDABLE, NOT VOID. An allotment which is irregular because it does not comply with section 47 is only voidable at the option of the shareholder. The company cannot insist on paying back the application moneys, for the shareholder may prefer to keep the shares. Thus, where an allotment was made and subsequently the directors discovered that the minimum subscription had not been reached, and the directors therefore circulated allottees giving them the option of avoiding or accepting the shares allotted to them, this option was valid, and an allottee could not restrain the directors from so acting.[88] The right to avoid the allotment is given as a protection to applicants in the appropriate circumstances, and if an allottee chooses to accept the shares notwithstanding these facts, there is no reason why he should not be allowed to do so. He may, however, as is explained later,[89] still bring his action against the directors who have "knowingly contravened" the section to compel them to make good the loss occasioned to him by the irregular allotment.

22–37 APPLICATION MONEYS ON VOIDABLE ALLOTMENT. An injunction may be obtained to restrain directors from parting with or otherwise dealing with application moneys received from an applicant who repudiates in time.[90]

Rights against directors

22–38 BY ALLOTTEE. Any director who knowingly contravenes or permits or authorises the contravention of section 47 is liable to compensate an allottee who has sustained a loss or damage or has incurred costs, but the allottee must have commenced proceedings for compensation not later than two years from the date of the allotment (s. 49 (2)).

"Knowingly contravening" in this provision means contravening it with

---

86 *Ellet* v. *Steinberg* (1910) 27 T.L.R. 127.
87 *Re National Motor Mail-Coach Co.* [1908] 2 Ch. 228.
88 *Burton* v. *Bevan* [1908] 2 Ch. 240.
89 See below in text.
90 *Mears* v. *Western Canada Pulp and Paper Co. Ltd.* [1905] 2 Ch. 353.

knowledge of the facts upon which the contravention depends.[91] It is immaterial whether the directors were aware that the facts of which they had knowledge constituted a contravention of the section or were unlawful. A director who was not present at a meeting at which a resolution for the irregular allotment was passed will not be fixed with knowledge so as to become liable under the section because those minutes are confirmed at a subsequent meeting at which he is present.

22–39 BY COMPANY. The company has likewise a claim for compensation against every director who knowingly contravenes or permits or authorises the contravention of section 47; here, again, proceedings must be commenced within two years from the date of the allotment (s. 49 (2)).

Consideration for the allotment

Who is liable

22–40 In the case of an issue of shares for cash the allottee is liable to pay to the company the full amount of the shares allotted to him. He and any subsequent transferee who is registered as a member are liable to pay to the company any amount that remains unpaid upon the shares which he holds.[92]

In English law it is the registered holder of a share who is liable in respect of anything unpaid on the share, and it makes no difference whether he is the beneficial owner of the share or a mere trustee, nor, in the latter case, whether the company is or is not cognisant of the trust, because in the case of companies registered in England, by virtue of section 117 of the 1948 Act, no notice of any trust shall be entered on the register, or is receivable by the Registrar. This provision is usually extended by the articles by regulations in the terms of, or similar to, article 7 of Table A.[93] The beneficial owner cannot be made liable either as shareholder or as a contributory,[94] for there is not privity of contract between him and the company. Section 117 does not apply in Scotland; a Scottish company may recognise a trust holding, if not precluded by its articles, such as article 7 of Table A in the case of companies adopting the 1948 version of Table A; a claim against the trust funds rather than against the trustees personally may be raised by the company in such circumstances.

A nominee may also hold shares for the company itself.[95] He is likewise treated as holding the shares on his own account and the company is regarded as having no beneficial interest in the shares (1980 Act, s. 36 (1)).

[91] *Burton* v. *Bevan* [1908] 2 Ch. 240.
[92] *Ooregum Gold Mining Co. of India* v. *Roper*; *Wallroth* v. *Roper* [1892] A.C. 125, 145.
[93] *Chapman and Barker's Case* (1867) L.R. 3 Eq. 361; see para. 50–06, *post*.
[94] *Bunn's Case* (1860) 2 De G.F. & J. 275, 300; *Somervail* v. *Cree* (1879) 4 App.Cas. 648.
[95] *Re Castiglione's W.T.s* [1958] Ch. 549.

If a nominee holding shares for the company fails to pay what is due on them within 21 days from being called on to do so, then—

(a) if the shares were issued to him as a subscriber to the memorandum, the other subscribers; or

(b) if they were otherwise issued or acquired by him, the directors of the company at the time of the issue or acquisition,

are jointly and severally liable with the nominee to pay the amount due on the shares (1980 Act, s. 36 (2)). But such a person may be relieved of his liability by the court if it thinks that he has acted honestly and reasonably and that, having regard to all the circumstances of the case, he ought fairly be excused from his liability (1980 Act, s. 36 (3) and (4)). Section 36 (1) and (2) does not apply to cases in which the company truly has no beneficial interest in the shares held by the nominee, *e.g.* where the company has acted as a trustee only (1980 Act, s. 36 (6)). The 1980 Act further contains detailed provisions dealing with the treatment of shares held by or on behalf of a public company (s. 37); such a company must cancel these shares or dispose of them within a certain time and cannot exercise their voting power. By virtue of the Companies Act 1981, ss. 46 *et seq.*, a company may also purchase its own shares but it follows from the reference to section 45 of the 1981 Act in section 46(2) that the shares must be fully paid up; it is thought that the company cannot purchase unpaid or only partly paid shares in itself (see Chapter 37, *post*).

The liability of the registered holder to pay arises in most cases from section 20 (2), which provides that "all money payable by any member to the company under the memorandum or articles, shall be a debt due from him to the company." Further, the articles generally provide that each member shall pay to the company the amounts called on his shares or the instalments due on them (arts. 15 and 19).[96] Sometimes, however, the articles are defective in this respect, and in such cases it is necessary to resort to the contract under which the shares were issued, and to rely on the promise therein to pay the whole or part by specified instalments.

In a winding up the liability to pay whatever may be called for arises under section 212. Where the member dies, his estate remains liable in respect of his share until some other person is registered as the holder thereof. When the holder transfers the shares and the transferee is registered, the transferee becomes liable to pay all moneys subsequently becoming payable in respect of the share. But though a person has by transfer, redemption, purchase by the company, forfeiture, or surrender, ceased to be a member, he still remains secondarily liable in the event of a winding up commencing within one year after he ceased to be a member, if the requirements for the liability of a contributory on the B list are satisfied (s. 212).[97]

---

[96] See paras. 35–02 *et. seq.*, *post.*
[97] See paras. 85–45 and 87–39, *post.*

Consideration may be cash or kind

22–41 The consideration for the allotment may be money or, with the consent of the company, money's worth, *e.g.* the transfer to the company of property or the rendering to it of services.[98]

If the consideration for the allotted shares is not cash, it is necessary within one month after allotment to deliver to the Registrar for registration the contract constituting the title of the allottee to the shares or a memorandum of the contract (s. 52 (1) (*b*) and (2)). The court may grant relief in case of accidental or inadvertent omission (s. 52 (3), proviso) and thereby the time for registration of these contracts may be extended. In *Re Wilkinson Sword Co. Ltd.*,[99] a contract was allowed to be filed 24 years after the formation of the company in respect of shares for which the memorandum had been subscribed. If it is desired to found proceedings on such a contract, it may be necessary to obtain the court's sanction to allow late registration, even where particulars (on Form 52) have already been filed[1]; the usual Scottish practice is to remit the petition for relief to a reporter.[2]

If a valid contract is made for the acceptance by the company of specified property or services of substantial value in payment or part-payment of shares, the court will not, whilst the contract stands, inquire into the value of the consideration even at the instance of the liquidator.[3] A contract to pay for shares can therefore be discharged by accord and satisfaction, but it is not open to a company to agree with the holder or proposed holder of its shares to replace the statutory liability by a special contract sounding in damages only, *e.g.* for future services.[4]

Where a company owes a creditor a debt presently due, that debt may be used as consideration against an allotment of shares to the creditor and such arrangement is proof of payment for the shares (the allotment being treated as for cash),[5] but if shares are allotted to a creditor by way of accord and satisfaction, the allotment is not for cash and a contract has to be filed under section 52 (2).[6]

Shares issued for a past consideration or by way of a gift cannot be treated as paid up and the allottees can be made liable to pay for them.[7] The position is different where bonus shares are issued, because in that

---

98 *Re Baglan Hall Colliery Co.* (1870) L.R. 5 Ch. 346; *Cameron* v. *Glenmorganie Distillery Co.* 1896, 23 R. 1092; 4 S.L.T. 93.

99 [1913] W.N. 27.

1 *Anderson & Munro Ltd.* 1924 S.C. 222; 1924 S.L.T. 151.

2 *Brownlie* v. *Liquidator of Scottish Heritage Co.* 1898 6 S.L.T. 249; *Anderson & Munro Ltd., supra.*

3 *Pell's Case* (1869) L.R. 5 Ch. 11; *Re Baglan Hall Colliery Co.* (1870) L.R. 5 Ch. 346; *Re Wragg Ltd.* [1897] 1 Ch. 796; *Re Theatrical Trust* [1895] 1 Ch. 771; *Re Innes & Co.* [1903] 2 Ch. 254.

4 See *Pellatt's Case* (1867) L.R. 2 Ch. 527; *Gardner* v. *Iredale* [1912] 1 Ch. 700; *National House Property Investment Co.* v. *Watson* 1908 S.C. 888; 16 S.L.T. 96.

5 *Spargo's Case* (1873) L.R. 8 Ch. 407; *White's Case* (1879) 12 Ch.D. 511; but see *Re Johannesburg Hotel Co.* [1891] 1 Ch. 119, 129, and *cf. Larocque* v. *Beauchemin* [1897] A.C. 358; *North Sydney Investment, etc., Co.* v. *Higgins* [1899] A.C. 263.

6 *Re Johannesburg Hotel Co.* [1891] 1 Ch. 119.

7 *Ooregum Gold Mining Co. of India* v. *Roper* [1892] A.C. 125; *Re Eddystone Marine Insurance Co.* [1893] 3 Ch. 9.

case the shares are fully paid up out of profits of the company available for distribution by way of dividend or out of quasi-capital funds.[8]

Where the contract is fraudulent or shows on the face of it that the consideration given to the company is illusory, or is clearly not equivalent to the nominal value of the shares, the shares cannot to this extent be treated as fully paid,[9] and the shareholder may be held liable to pay for them in full.[10]

In the case of an allotment for cash, calls must be paid in cash. Where under a scheme of arrangement the company agreed to accept "deferred creditors' certificates" of another company in payment of calls, the shares were held not to be fully paid for the purposes of the liquidation of the first-mentioned company.[11]

Return of allotments

22–42 Within one month of any allotment of shares the company has to make a return to the Registrar stating the number and nominal amount of the shares allotted; the names, addresses and descriptions of the allottees; the amount paid or due and payable on each share; and, where the shares are allotted for a consideration other than cash, the contract in writing under which they were issued, or if no such contract was in writing, prescribed particulars of the contract. The contract, or prescribed particulars, must be duly stamped (s. 52 (1)–(3)).

In the event of default in making the return every officer who is in default is liable on conviction on indictment to a fine, or on summary conviction a fine not exceeding the statutory maximum or, after continued contravention, a default fine not exceeding one-tenth of the statutory maximum (s. 52 (3), as amended by the 1980 Act, Sched. 2), but the time for delivery of any document under the section may be extended by the court if it is satisfied that the omission was accidental or due to inadvertence or that it is just and equitable to grant relief (s. 52 (3), proviso).

In practice, where renunciation rights are given, and the last day for renunciation is more than one month after allotment, the Registrar will accept a return of allotments made up with reference to the renunciation, provided that it is filed within a reasonable time after the last day for renouncing.

If a rights issue is made on renounceable provisional letters of allotment, capital duty under the Finance Act 1973, Part V, is payable within one month of receipt of acceptances; in other cases where renounceable letters of allotment are issued, duty is payable within one month of allotment. In

---

[8] Out of the share premium account (s. 56 (2)) or the capital redemption reserve (s. 53 (3) of the 1981 Act).

[9] *Re Wragg Ltd.* [1897] 1 Ch. 796, 836; *Hong Kong & China Gas Co.* v. *Glen* [1914] 1 Ch. 527 (an agreement to allot as fully paid a certain proportion of all future increases of capital).

[10] *Re James Pitkin & Co.* [1916] W.N. 112.

[11] *Re White Star Line* [1938] Ch. 458.

order to avoid incurring a fine under the Finance Act 1973, s. 47 (7) companies may deliver to the Registrar within the foregoing periods a return of allotments (PUC2 or PUC3) with the appropriate amount of duty, noting on the reverse that details of allottees would be filed after expiry of the renunciation period. Such later notification on form PUC2 or PUC3 should be cross-referenced to the previous return.

Statement in notes to the accounts

22–43 If, in the financial year, the company has allotted any shares or issued debentures, there must be stated, by way of notes to the accounts (if not given in the accounts)

(1) the reason for making the allotment/or issue;
(2) the classes of shares allotted or debentures issued;
(3) as regards each class, the number of shares allotted or amount of debentures issued; and
(4) the consideration received by the company for the allotment/or issue (1981 Act, Sched. 8, paras. 39 and 41).

Capital duty on return of allotments

22–44 Some public companies have in issue two classes of ordinary shares, *e.g.* ordinary and convertible ordinary, which rank *pari passu* in all respects except that the convertible ordinary shares are not entitled to dividends. On the exercise of the conversion rights attaching to the convertible shares, the number of ordinary shares allotted will invariably be greater than the number of convertible shares converted, *e.g.* 120 ordinary shares for every 100 convertible ordinary shares held.[12] There is accordingly an effective increase in the issued share capital, but as this does not involve a contribution to the assets of the company, no capital duty is payable. In such cases, the Controller of Stamps, on application, will issue a letter confirming that no duty is payable and the letter should be attached to the return of allotments on Form PUC3 lodged with the Registrar, which should also be accompanied by Form 52 to constitute the title of the allottees, in the absence of a written contract, to fully paid shares allotted for a consideration other than cash.

Conversely, the conversion of debenture stock or unsecured loan stock into shares gives rise to a liability to pay capital duty, since the cancellation of the debt represented by the debenture or loan stock effectively makes a contribution to the assets of the company.

---

[12] Convertible ordinary shares are possibly caught by s. 34 and Sched. 8 of the Finance (No. 2) Act 1975.

CHAPTER 23

UNDERWRITING

The purpose of underwriting

23–01 Where a company wishes to offer shares or debentures to the public it almost invariably makes arrangements for the issue to be underwritten. Underwriting in its simplest form consists of an undertaking by some person or persons that if the public fails to take up the issue, he or they will do so. In return for this undertaking the company agrees to pay the underwriters a commission on all shares or debentures, whether taken by the public or by the underwriters, or to remunerate them in kind, *e.g.* by giving them an option on a specified number of shares or debentures.

At one time underwriting was frequently carried out by individuals engaged in general banking business or *ad hoc* syndicates, but with the development of the modern issuing business it has become important to have underwriters with considerable financial resources, and underwriting has now become a specialised financial activity which, for the most part, is in the hands of a small group of merchant banks, known as issuing houses, which are professional underwriters. Many of these companies and partnerships are members of the Issuing Houses Association. In addition, stockbroking firms, trust companies, other banks and insurance companies sometimes act as underwriters.

The underwriters themselves will usually choose to spread their risk by using sub-underwriters who agree to take a certain number of the shares for which they accept responsibility and for which they receive a commission; in that case the difference between the commission paid by the company to the principal underwriters and the commission paid by them to the sub-underwriters is known as overriding commission[1]

In the result, if an issue to the public is a success, the underwriters receive their commission without having to take up any of the shares or debentures, but if it is a failure the underwriters and sub-underwriters are "landed" with the issue and have to take up a large proportion of it.

An agreement to take shares must be distinguished from an agreement to place shares.[2] One who merely agrees to place does not underwrite, and the restrictions on underwriting do not apply to an agreement to place shares. On the other hand, placings may be governed by the provisions applying to prospectuses.[3]

---

[1] See the words "procuring or agreeing to procure subscriptions" in s. 53 (1) and in Sched. IV, para. 4 (*a*) (ii).
[2] *Gorrissen's Case* (1873) L.R. 8 Ch. 507.
[3] See para. 21–04, *ante*.

Company's power to pay commission

23–02 At one time it was uncertain whether a company had power to pay underwriting commission.[4] It was decided in *Metropolitan Coal Consumers' Association* v. *Scrimgeour*[5] that a commission of 2½ per cent. paid to brokers for their services as such was not *ultra vires*, but this decision did not remove all doubts. It is now provided by section 53 of the 1948 Act that underwriting commission is lawful, subject to the following conditions:

(1) It must be authorised by the articles, and must not exceed 10 per cent. of the price at which the shares are issued or the amount or rate authorised by the articles, whichever is the lower (s. 53 (1) (*a*) and (*b*)).

If the articles authorise commission at a certain rate per cent. this does not authorise payment of a lump sum.[6]

(2) The prospectus, or statement to be delivered to the Registrar, prescribed by section 53 (1) (*c*) (ii), as amended by the 1980 Act, Sched. 3, para. 9, or circular or notice must disclose the amount or rate per cent. and the number of shares which the underwriters have agreed to subscribe absolutely. Where the document is in the form of a prescribed statement, it must be filed with the Registrar of Companies before the allotment of the shares and the payment of the commission; otherwise the commission is unlawful.[7]

If the above conditions are fulfilled, the company may apply any of its shares or capital money in payment of commission. If they are not fulfilled, it may not do so.

Commission is only payable upon a person subscribing or agreeing to subscribe, not on a purchase of shares; but where a person agreed to buy shares of an old company which gave him the right to subscribe for shares in a new company, and he agreed with the new company to exercise that right, he was agreeing to subscribe for shares in the new company and commission paid to him by the company was validly paid.[8]

Commission paid otherwise than out of newly issued shares

23–03 There is nothing in section 53 to prevent commission, or some other consideration, being paid otherwise than out of newly issued shares or capital money received for them. It is, *e.g.* quite legitimate and not unusual to give underwriters by way of consideration an option to subscribe for a

---

4 *Re Faure Electric Accumulator Co.* (1888) 40 Ch.D. 141; and *Ooregum Co.* v. *Roper* [1892] A.C. 125.
5 [1895] 2 Q.B. 604.
6 *Booth* v. *New Africander Gold Mining Co.* [1903] 1 Ch. 295.
7 *Andreae* v. *Zinc Mines of Great Britain* [1918] 2 K.B. 454.
8 *Barrow* v. *Paringa Mines (1909) Ltd.* [1909] 2 Ch. 658. As to the meaning of "subscribe" in relation to an exchange of shares for shares, see *Government Stock and Other Securities Investment Co.* v. *Christopher* [1956] 1 W.L.R. 237; paras. 21–14 and 21–18, *ante*.

specified number of shares of the company at a specified price within a specified time.[9]

Moreover, section 56 (2) (*b*) expressly authorises the application of a company's share premium account in writing off commission paid on any issue of shares or debentures.[10]

While it is clear that, within the limits authorised by section 53 (1) (*b*), a company may apply

(a) its newly issued shares or the moneys received for them, or

(b) its share premium account

to the payment of underwriting commission, a slight doubt exists whether a company, within those limits, may pay commission out of its profits. This depends on the interpretation of the words in subsection (2) of section 53: "save as aforesaid, no company shall apply any of its shares or capital money . . . in payment of any commission." If these words are intended to restrict subsection (1), so as to make it only lawful to pay commission out of the newly issued shares or capital money received for them, the payment of commission out of profits would appear to be prohibited by section 42 of the 1981 Act, which, in principle, prohibits a company from giving any financial assistance in connection with, *inter alia*, the subscription of its own shares. If, on the other hand, subsection (2) is not intended to restrict subsection (1) but contains a separate and independent provision, the application of profits of the company within the limits of subsection (1) (*b*) of section 53 would be permissible. It is thought that the latter interpretation is correct and that the words in subsection (2) of section 53 are intended to make it clear that the former practice may be continued under which a company could use its profits for the payment of commission within the permitted limits.[11] But it is thought that the company may use for that purpose only profits which do not constitute "capital money." By that phrase are meant assets of the company representing its paid-up capital.

The restrictions laid down in section 53 (1) (*b*) apply to a private company as well as a public company.[12]

If commission is paid without the disclosure required by section 53 (1) (*c*), any director responsible will be liable to refund it to the company.[13]

Restrictions on commission not limited to public issues

23–04 Section 53 of the Act of 1948 applies to all kinds of issues, and, consequently, the shares or debentures of private companies may likewise be underwritten, subject to the conditions laid down in that section.

---

[9] *Hilder* v. *Dexter* [1902] A.C. 474.

[10] The share premium account, of course, represents capital money. See *Short* v. *Colwill* [1909] W.N. 218, 219.

[11] *Hilder* v. *Dexter* [1902] A.C. 474.

[12] *Dominion of Canada, etc., Syndicate* v. *Brigstocke* [1911] 2 K.B. 648.

[13] *South African Territories* v. *Wallington* [1898] A.C. 309.

Underwriting debentures

23–05 It is not necessary under section 53 to disclose a commission on underwriting debentures, but, it is thought, the commission must be disclosed in any prospectus under Schedule IV. It must also be disclosed in the annual return and balance sheet and, if the debentures are secured by any of the charges mentioned in section 95 (2), must be registered under subsection (9) of that section.

Formerly the court had no jurisdiction in the case of a contract underwriting debentures or debenture stock to compel specific performance of the contract by the underwriter. The company's remedy—and it was a very inadequate one—was to sue the underwriter for damages.[13] Now, however, specific performance may be ordered (1948 Act, s. 92).

Disclosure in annual return and balance-sheet

23–06 Section 124 and paragraph 3 (*f*) of the Sixth Schedule to the 1948 Act require that the annual return shall state, *inter alia*, "(*f*) the total amount of the sums (if any) paid by way of commission in respect of any shares or debentures" and the Second Schedule, para. 3 (*b*) to the 1967 Act, provides that there shall be stated under separate headings, so far as they are not written off, "any expenses incurred in connection with any issue of share capital or debentures."

Form of underwriting agreement

23–07 The underwriting agreement is generally formed by the acceptance by the company of an offer by the proposing underwriter.[14] The latter will normally offer to underwrite, and even if the words which he uses may appear to be an acceptance, as "I agree to underwrite," they will in law only operate as an offer if, upon the facts, they are so intended. The same is equally true of contracts for sub-underwriting. Consequently the following remarks and the decisions of the cases apply both to underwriting and to sub-underwriting.

To become binding the offer must be accepted by the company, and notice of such acceptance given to the underwriter.[15] The acceptance may be in writing or oral,[16] and it is prima facie no objection that the notice of acceptance is not given until after the lists are closed,[17] for the court is not disposed to import into underwriting contracts implied conditions in derogation of the express terms of the contract.[18] Where the agreement is to underwrite on the terms of a specified prospectus, a serious variation of the

---

[14] For forms of underwriting and sub-underwriting applications, contracts, etc., see Palmer's *Precedents* (17th ed.), Pt. I, 1956, Nos. 42–50, pp. 175 *et seq.*
[15] *Re Consort Deep, etc., Co.* [1897] 1 Ch. 575 (C.A.).
[16] *Re North Charterland, etc., Co.* (1896) 13 T.L.R. 80.
[17] *Re Hemp, Yarn and Cordage Co.* [1896] 2 Ch. 121 (C.A.).
[18] *Re Crown Lease Proprietary Co.* (1897) 14 T.L.R. 47.

terms of the prospectus may vitiate the contract, even though the agreement expressly allows for variations in the prospectus.[19]

The agreement may be in the form that the underwriter will only be bound to take up his rateable proportion of what the public does not take up—a particularly useful form where there are two or more underwriters. If the agreement constitutes an application for shares, in response to a prospectus issued generally,[20] it cannot (like any other application for shares) be withdrawn until after three days after the opening of the subscription list (1948 Act, s. 50 (5)).[21]

Firm underwriting

23–08 It sometimes happens that one or more of the underwriters desires to take "firm" the whole or a proportion of their underwriting. The effect of this is that the underwriter will be allotted the number of shares taken "firm" irrespective of whether the issue is over- or under-subscribed. The underwriter who takes "firm" part of the shares he has underwritten stands in the same position as other underwriters in respect of the balance of the shares he has not taken "firm."

Authority to apply for shares in underwriter's name

Unconditional authority

23–09 Where the underwriting is concluded with a person other than the company, *e.g.* with a promoter or—in the case of sub-underwriting—with the principal underwriter, the underwriting contract usually provides that if the underwriter makes default in applying, the other party to the underwriting agreement may apply for the shares on his behalf. This authority, if properly framed, is effective and irrevocable where there is a complete contract; for in such cases it is one of the terms of the contract that the authority shall subsist, and it is not open to one party to a contract by notice to the other to revoke what is a term of the contract.[22] The executors of a deceased underwriter are liable on the underwriting contract.[23]

Conditional authority

23–10 It happens sometimes, however, that such an authority is expressed in contingent terms, as, for instance, "I will, if called on by you, subscribe, etc." Where this is the case, the authority does not arise until after the condition is performed, that is, after the underwriter has been called on to

---

19 *Warner International Co. Ltd.* v. *Kilburn, Brown, etc., Co.* [1914] W.N. 61.
20 On prospectuses issued generally, see para. 21–26, *ante*.
21 See para. 22–05, *ante*.
22 *Carter* v. *White* (1883) 25 Ch.D. 666; *Re Hannan's Empress Mining Co., Carmichael's Case* [1896] 2 Ch. 643 (C.A.); *Pole's Case* [1920] 2 Ch. 341.
23 *Warner Engineering Co.* v. *Brennan* (1913) 30 T.L.R. 191; *Ex p. Pathé Frères* [1914] 2 K.B. 299.

subscribe; and, accordingly, if the other party exercises the authority before this has been done, the allotment will be ineffective.[24]

If the condition precedent is not expressed in the offer, the offeror may be estopped from denying the existence of an agreement where the condition precedent has not been fulfilled. Where a proposing underwriter signed an application form, which he handed to a promoter B, together with a letter saying that the application was subject to a condition precedent, namely, acceptance within a specified time, he was nevertheless bound by the agreement which appeared to have been made free from the condition precedent (which was not fulfilled), in circumstances where the company never knew of the condition: the authority apparently given to B to apply for the shares in the proposing underwriter's name was good to bind the latter.[25] So, too, a sub-underwriter cannot withdraw where he has authorised an application to be made on his behalf, even though he repudiates before notice of acceptance of his application has been received by the company.[26]

The principle of this is that the applicant has an *apparent* authority from the underwriter to apply, and the underwriter is therefore, as against the company accepting the application in good faith and without notice of any qualification or condition affecting the authority, estopped from denying the validity of the authority.

The principle would not, of course, apply if the company knew from the form of the letter or *aliunde* that the authority was qualified or conditional.

Misrepresentation in prospectus

23–11 An underwriter who takes up shares on the faith of a prospectus containing untrue statements has, on principle, the same right to repudiate these shares as any other subscriber for shares.[27] However, in fact, his position may not be as good as that of another subscriber; where, *e.g.* an underwriter sought relief from an agreement with promoters of a company, he could not obtain the benefit of the statutory provisions requiring disclosure of a material contract[28] because he could not prove that they had entered into the agreement on the strength of the non-existence of the contract in question.[29] This case should be contrasted with a similar, successful, action by a subscriber who was not an underwriter,[30] reported immediately prior to the report of the underwriter's case.

---

[24] *Ormerod's Case* [1894] 2 Ch. 474; *Brussels Palace of Varieties* v. *Prockter* (1893) 10 T.L.R. 72; *Sangster* v. *Netter* (1893) 9 T.L.R. 441.

[25] *Re Henry Bentley & Co., etc., ex. p. Harrison* (1893) 69 L.T. 204; *Re Bultfontein Sun Diamond Mine* (1896) 12 T.L.R. 461; *Premier Briquette Co.* v. *Gray* 1922 S.C. 329; 1922 S.L.T. 230.

[26] *Re Olympic Fire and General Co., Pole's Case* [1920] 1 Ch. 582.

[27] *Karberg's Case* [1892] 3 Ch. 1 (C.A.), where the company did not exist when the application was made.

[28] See para. 21–30, *ante*.

[29] *Baty* v. *Keswick* (1901) 85 L.T. 18.

[30] *Cackett* v. *Keswick* (1901) 85 L.T. 15.

The underwriter has, however, the remedies provided by the general law, such as the common law remedies in the case of misrepresentation and the remedies provided by the Misrepresentation Act 1967.[31]

Stamping of underwriting agreements

23–12 In England, an underwriting contract, if under hand, does not require a stamp.[32] If the contract is under seal, a 50p stamp is required. The fact that the contract contains an authority to apply for shares on the underwriter's behalf does not render a power of attorney stamp requisite.[33] In Scotland, if the agreement contains a consent to registration, it is liable to the 50p deed stamp.

---

[31] This Act does not apply to Scotland.
[32] The 6d. stamp previously necessary was abolished by the Finance Act 1970, Sched. 7.
[33] *Walker* v. *Remmett* (1846) 15 L.J. (N.S.) C.P. 174.

CHAPTER 24

AUTHORITY TO ISSUE SHARES. PRE-EMPTION RIGHTS. ISSUES AT A PREMIUM OR DISCOUNT

Authority to issue shares

24–01 The shares of the company, apart from those taken by the subscribers of the memorandum, are issued by the board of directors who, however, cannot issue shares beyond the amount fixed as the authorised capital of the company. The directors may issue shares only for a proper purpose, *i.e.* in the best interest of the company, and an issue for an ulterior motive, such as altering the voting power in the company[1] or for serving only the self-interest of the directors,[2] would be void.

The law before the coming into operation of the 1980 Act (December 22, 1980) did not impose any further restrictions on the powers of the directors to issue shares. They were entitled to do so under their general powers of management (Table A, reg. 80, see also reg. 2), and no special authority in the articles or by a resolution of the general meeting was required.

Restrictions introduced by the 1980 Act

The 1980 Act imposes statutory restrictions on the powers of the directors to issue shares within the limits of the authorised capital (s. 14).[3] Indeed, these restrictions relate not only to shares, they relate to "relevant securities."

Relevant securities

"Relevant securities" are defined in section 14 (10) as—

"(a) shares in the company other than shares shown in the memorandum to have been taken by the subscribers thereto or shares allotted in pursuance of an employees' share scheme; and

(b) any right to subscribe for, or to convert any security into, shares in the company other than shares so allotted."

There are no restrictions on the powers of the directors to issue debentures, except convertible debentures which are covered by section 14 (10) (*b*); the amendment to regulation 79 of Table A, introduced by the 1980 Act, does not go further than that and, besides, it would not apply to companies which have not adopted Table A. It is doubtful whether an

---

[1] *Fraser* v. *Whalley* (1864) 2 Hem. & M. 10; *Punt* v. *Symons & Co. Ltd.* [1903] 2 Ch. 506; *Piercy* v. *S. Mills & Co. Ltd.* [1920] 1 Ch. 77; *Hogg* v. *Cramphorn Ltd.* [1967] Ch. 254; *Howard Smith Ltd.* v. *Ampol Ltd.* [1974] A.C. 821.

[2] The cases referred to in n. 1 and *Ngurli Ltd.* v. *McCann* (1953) 90 C.L.R. 425.

[3] References in this section (Authority to issue shares) and the next section (The pre-emption rights) are to the 1980 Act unless stated otherwise.

option to take up relevant securities, as contrasted with a right to do so, is covered by section 14; it is thought that this question has to be answered in the affirmative because the option, when exercised, results in a right; this view is supported by section 25 of the 1967 Act.

The required authority

The authority which the directors require for the issue of relevant securities has to be given—

(a) by an ordinary resolution of the general meeting; or
(b) in the articles (s. 14 (1)).

It may be given for a particular issue or generally, and it may be unconditional or subject to conditions (s. 14 (2)).The authority must state the maximum amount of the relevant securities which may be allotted thereunder, and the date on which it shall expire, but any authority, including one given in the articles, may be previously revoked or varied by the general meeting at any time (s. 14 (3)).

It may be expected that articles adopted by companies will give the directors normally an unconditional general power to issue relevant securities which, in the case of a share issue, must not exceed the amount of the authorised but unissued capital. Table A does not contain a general or particular authority.

Authority limited to five years. Renewal of authority

24–02 The 1980 Act further provides that the authority of the directors to issue relevant securities is limited to five years, *i.e.* must not exceed this time, whether the authority is contained in the articles or in a resolution of the general meeting. The time begins to run—

(a) if the authority is contained in the articles adopted at the time of the original incorporation, from the date of incorporation; and
(b) if the authority is contained in a resolution of the general meeting, from the date of the resolution (s. 14 (3)).

The authority may be renewed from time to time by an ordinary resolution of the general meeting for further periods not exceeding five years. The renewal resolution must state, or restate, the amount of the relevant securities and must specify the date on which the renewed authority will expire (s. 14 (4)). It has also to state whether it relates to all relevant securities not yet issued, or to which relevant securities, and whether it is general or conditional.

Resolution authorising issue of shares

As already stated, the general meeting may give the directors authority to issue relevant securities by ordinary resolution and may renew it in the like manner.

A copy of such resolution has to be registered with the Registrar under section 143 of the 1948 Act (s. 14 (6)) and has to be notified in the *Gazette* by virtue of section 9 (3) (*dc*) of the European Communities Act 1972.

Issues without authority

If an authority has been given and an offer or agreement to take up the relevant securities has been made before the expiry of the authority, the directors may allot the securities, although the allotment takes place after the authority has expired (s. 14 (5)).

The validity of any allotment is not affected by the lack of, or a defect in, the authority (s. 14 (7)).

Criminal sanctions

A director who knowingly and wilfully contravenes, or permits or authorises, a contravention of section 14, is liable to a fine (s. 14 (7)).

Transitional provisions

The strict application of section 14 is relaxed during the transitional period which ends 18 months after the coming into operation of that provision, *i.e.* on June 22, 1982.[4] During the transitional period the following rules apply:

(a) an authority to issue relevant securities is not required if an allotment takes place in pursuance of an offer made or agreement entered into before the holding of the first general meeting following—
   (i) the registration of the company, if it is registered as a private company; or
   (ii) the registration of the company, if it was originally registered in another form (s. 14 (9)).[5]

(b) But any resolution of the general meeting to give, vary or revoke an authority is effective, if it is passed at any time after the passing of the 1980 Act, which received the Royal Assent on May 1, 1980 (s. 14 (9)).

(c) If the company is originally registered as a public company, section 14 always applies (s. 14 (9)).

(d) After the end of the transitional period the relaxation stated under (a) above is no longer available and section 14 always applies.

The pre-emption rights

24–03 A pre-emption right is the entitlement of an existing shareholder to have allotted to him a proportionate part of a new issue of shares. The pre-emption right, if exercised by the existing shareholder, protects him against a dilution of his present holding in the company as the result of a new share issue.

---

[4] 1980 Act, s. 87; Companies Act 1980 (Commencement No. 2) Order 1980 (S.I. 1980 No. 1785) which came into operation on December 22, 1980.

[5] *e.g.* an old public company is re-registered as a new public company, or a private company is re-registered as a public company, or a public company is re-registered as a private company (see paras. 5–04 *et seq.*, *ante*).

The pre-emption right occurs in three sets of circumstances. First, the 1980 Act provides statutory pre-emption rights. These rights are circumscribed strictly and subject to many safeguards making them inapplicable in some cases and admitting their exclusion in others. These statutory pre-emption rights will be considered in this chapter. Secondly, in private companies the articles often provide a—non-statutory—pre-emption right in favour of the remaining shareholders if a shareholder is desirous of disposing of and transferring his shares. The object of this non-statutory pre-emption right is to preserve the character of the private company as a "close corporation" and to prevent an unwelcome outsider from buying himself into the company and taking it over. This type of pre-emption right is treated in paragraph 39–13, *post*, but it will be seen from the observations in this chapter that the statutory pre-emption rights, while generally giving way to the non-statutory pre-emption right in the memorandum or articles, have restricted the non-statutory pre-emption right in some respects. Thirdly, the Stock Exchange Regulations for Admission of Securities to Listing require in the Listing Agreement, paragraph 13, a pre-emption right in favour of equity shareholders of listed companies in the case of new issues for cash. This requirement is subject to exemption in certain specified cases.

The statutory pre-emption rights

These rights are regulated in sections 17 to 19 of the 1980 Act.

The shares entitled to pre-emption

The shares entitled to pre-emption rights are—

(a) "relevant shares," and
(b) "relevant employee shares"(s. 17 (1)).

The offer for pre-emption has to be made to the persons who are holders of these shares at the date of the new issue.

"Relevant shares" are all shares, except—

"(a) shares which as respects dividend and capital carry a right to participate only up to a specified amount in a distribution; and
(b) shares held, or to be held, under an employees' share scheme" (s. 17 (11)).

In other words, all equity shares and those preference shares which participate either as to dividend or as to capital carry pre-emption rights, but preference shares which are non-participating both as to dividend and capital are excluded.

"Relevant employee shares" are "shares which would be relevant shares in the company but for the fact that they are held under an employees' share scheme" (s. 17 (11)).

The securities which have to be offered for pre-emption

24–04 The shares mentioned in the preceding paragraph are entitled, by virtue of their pre-emption rights, to have offered to them all "equity securities" newly issued (s. 17 (1)).

An "equity security" is defined in section 17 (11) as—

> "a relevant share in the company (other than a share shown in the memorandum to have been taken by a subscriber thereto to a bonus share) or a right to subscribe for, or convert any securities into, relevant shares in the company, and references to the allotment of equity securities or of equity securities consisting of relevant shares of a particular class shall include references to the grant of a right to subscribe for, or to convert any securities into, relevant shares in the company or, as the case may be, relevant shares of a particular class, but shall not include references to the allotment of any relevant shares pursuant to such right."

It should be noted that convertible debentures fall under the definition of "equity securities." Here again, it is doubtful whether an option to have allotted equity securities falls under the definition of "a right to subscribe for or convert"; the better view, as explained,[6] is to answer this question in the affirmative.

Time and terms of pre-emption offer

The pre-emption offer must state the period during which it can be accepted by the holders of relevant shares and relevant employee shares. That period must not be less than 21 days. The offer shall not be withdrawn before the end of that period (s. 17 (7)). The Act does not state the time from which the offer period begins to run but it is obvious that that is the time when the offer has been served on the registered holder of the shares entitled to pre-emption or, in the case of share warrants to bearer, the date of publication in the *Gazette* (s. 17 (6)). The offer period may be shortened if the company has received within that period notice of the acceptance or refusal of every offer which has been made. Otherwise the company must not proceed to allotment before the offer period is at an end (s. 17 (1) (*b*)).

The terms, on which the pre-emption offer has to be made, must be the same or more favourable terms as are proposed to the outside offerees. The offer must be made in a proportion which is, as nearly as practicable, equal to the nominal value held by the offeree of the aggregate of relevant shares and relevant employee shares (s. 17 (1)). The reference to aggregation means that all shares entitled to the pre-emption and held by the member have to be counted together, even if they pertain to different classes. But the Act does not contain provisions regulating fractions of the allotment. Thus, if the issue is on the basis of one new share for five old shares and a shareholder holds only four shares in the aggregate, he is not entitled to exercise his pre-emption right, nor is he entitled to the allotment

[6] See para. 24–01, *ante*.

of the fractions which, in a listed company, he may be able to sell at the Stock Exchange, nor is he entitled to be paid the value of the fractions in cash. The Act likewise does not state in general terms what shall be done with the shares not taken up by some of the entitled members; after all, some members may refuse to exercise their right of pre-emption which in law is merely an option; there is no provision that these shares must be offered to the existing members proportionately. It is thought that the directors are at liberty to dispose of the shares which, owing to fractionalising or refusal, are not taken up by the shareholders entitled to the pre-emption, and may offer these shares to outsiders.

The pre-emption offer may be made by way of renunceable allotment letters, enabling the shareholder entitled to the pre-emption to sell the new equity securities and to renounce the allotment in favour of the purchaser,[7] a procedure which saves stamp duties that would become payable on a transfer of the securities.[8]

The pre-emption offer must be served on every shareholder entitled thereto in the manner specified in regulations 131 to 133 of Table A. If he is the holder of a share warrant to bearer or if the company has adopted regulation 134 of Table A without modification, he would not be entitled to receive a personal notice; the offer may then be made by publication in the *Gazette* (s. 17 (6)).

Non-application of pre-emption rights

24–05 In the following cases the pre-emption rights are not available.

1. The particular offer of new equity securities is made for a consideration other than cash (s. 17 (4)).
2. The equity securities, apart from a renunciation or allotment, would be held under an employees' share scheme (s. 17 (5)).[9]
3. If the memorandum or the articles of a company, whether private or public, contain provisions requiring the company, when proposing the allotment of new relevant shares of any particular class, to allot these shares proportionately to the holders of old relevant shares or relevant employee shares of that class (s. 17 (2) and (3)). In this case the non-statutory pre-emption right in favour of the class overrides the statutory pre-emption rights. But it is thought that, if the members of the class do not take up the relevant shares, the pre-emption right of *all* holders of relevant shares and relevant employee shares arises with respect to the shares not taken up; that appears to follow from the last sentence of section 17 (3). It should also be noted that here the securities, to which the offer extends, are not all forms of "equity securities," but only "equity securities consisting of relevant shares of a particular class" (s. 17 (2)).

---

[7] See the reference to renunciation in s. 17 (4) and (5).
[8] See para. 22–15, *ante*.
[9] On employees' share schemes, see para. 94–01, *post*.

4. The pre-emption rights do not arise if they would contravene an enactment which prohibits, generally or in specified circumstances, the company from offering or allotting equity securities to any person (1980) Act, s. 17 (12)). This provision was intended to cover prohibitions imposed by virtue of the Exchange Control Act 1947 but this contingency no longer applies as exchange control has been abolished. The prohibition is, however, expressed in general terms and would, *e.g.* appear to cover the case of section 174 (2) (*c*) of the 1948 Act.

Exclusion of pre-emption rights

4–06 In the following cases the pre-emption rights of holders of relevant shares or relevant employee shares can be excluded.

1. In a private company, the pre-emption rights can be excluded by the memorandum or the articles (s. 17 (9)). If the memorandum or the articles of a private company provide for a—non-statutory—pre-emption right, these provisions override the statutory pre-emption rights, as far as the statutory provisions are inconsistent with the non-statutory provisions, save that the statutory pre-emption rights in favour of *all* holders of relevant shares and relevant employee shares would appear to remain intact with respect to equity securities which the offerees have failed to take up (s. 17 (9), last sentence).
2. If the directors are authorised to make an issue of new "relevant securities" under section 14 of the 1980 Act,[10] they may be given power to dispense with or modify the pre-emption rights. This applies to private as well as to public companies (s. 18). But this power of dispensation and modification is limited to the time of the authority to make the new issue—not more than five years—and can be renewed with that authority for a period not exceeding that of the authority (s. 18 (3)).

   Two procedures are provided here.

   (a) If the authority is a general authority, the dispensatory or modifying power may be given—
      (i) by the articles; or
      (ii) by a special resolution of the general meeting (s. 18 (1)).
   (b) If the authority if for a particular issue, the dispensatory or modifying power may be given by a special resolution of the general meeting (s. 18 (2)). But this special resolution must be recommended by the directors who have to state:
      (i) the reasons for making the recommendation;
      (ii) the amount to be paid to the company in respect of the equity securities to be allotted; and

[10] See para. 24–01 *ante*.

(iii) the directors' justification of that amount.

Written notice of this recommendation of the directors has to be given with the notice of the meeting (s. 18 (5)).

It should be noted that the resolution of the general meeting giving the directors dispensatory or modifying powers with respect to the pre-emption rights must be a special resolution, while the resolution giving them authority to issue new "relevant securities" under section 14 may be an ordinary resolution. It is thought that, if it is intended to give the authority and the powers at the same time by one measure, this can be done by a special resolution, but if the authority is for a particular issue, the statement of the directors described under (b) above has to be circulated.

Civil sanctions

A person to whom a pre-emption offer should have been made but, in contravention of section 17 (1), (6) or (7) or a provision to which (3) applies, has not been made, has a claim for compensation for any loss, damage, costs or expenses sustained or incurred by reason of the contravention, and this claim is against the company and every of its officers who knowingly authorised or permitted the contravention. The company and such officers are liable jointly and severally (s. 17 (10)).

Criminal sanctions

Section 17 (10) contains criminal sanctions applicable to officers of the company who knowingly authorise or permit a contravention of the provisions relating to the pre-emption rights.

Section 18 (6) provides criminal sanctions for persons who knowingly or recklessly authorise or permit the inclusion in the directors' statement required under section 18 (5) of any matter which is misleading, false or deceptive in a material particular.

Transitional provisions

24–07 Section 19 contains transitional provisions relating to the statutory pre-emption rights. They can be summed up as follows:

(a) The provisions relating to the pre-emption rights (ss. 17 and 18) do not apply to an issue and allotment of equity securities made by a public company (other than a company originally registered as a public company) before the company holds its first general meeting after having been re-registered or before the end of the transitional period on June 22, 1982, whichever is the earlier date (s. 19(1)(*a*)).

(b) If the company was originally registered as a public company, the exemption stated under (a) does not apply (s. 19 (1) (*a*)).

(c) In the case of a public company (other than one originally registered as such), which, by the terms of its memorandum or articles or otherwise (*e.g.* under an agreement) is obliged, when making an allotment of new equity securities, to give existing holders a pre-emption right, the provisions relating to the statutory pre-emption rights (ss. 17 and 18) do not apply, as far as inconsistent with the non-statutory pre-emption rights. But they do not apply only to an issue and allotment of equity securities made in the period stated in (a) above (s. 19 (1) (*b*) and (2)).

(d) In the case of a private company, if before the "relevant time" a pre-emption right is given otherwise than by the memorandum or the articles, *e.g.* in an agreement, and such non-statutory pre-emption right, according to section 17 (9), would have the effect of excluding the statutory pre-emption rights, such non-statutory pre-emption right is equated to a non-statutory pre-emption right in the memorandum or articles and likewise overrides the statutory pre-emption rights (s. 19 (14)).

The "relevant time" is defined as follows:

"(*a*) except in a case falling within paragraph (*b*) below, the end of the transitional period; and

(*b*) in the case of a company which is re-registered or registered as a public company in pursuance of an application made before the end of that period, the time at which the application is made" (s. 19 (5)).

Issue of shares at a premium

24–08 A company issues shares at a premium if the consideration which it receives for them exceeds in value the nominal amount of the issued shares. The company may so issue shares freely; the Acts do not impose any restriction on it. They impose, however, restrictions on the application of the premiums received by the company (s. 56 of the 1948 Act, as amended by ss. 36–41 of the 1981 Act).

Formation of a share premium account

Such premiums are not a trading profit and sound business practice demands that they should be set aside as reserve. Before the coming into operation of the 1947 legislation, premiums received on the issue of shares could be treated as profits and distributed by way of dividend even if the company made a trading loss.[11] Section 56 of the 1948 Act, as amended, prevents in principle this undesirable course and provides that, subject to exceptions, the premium has to be transferred to a quasi-capital fund, the "share premium account," which may be used for purposes specified by the Companies Acts and, apart from these exceptional cases which will be treated later, can be distributed by way of dividend only in accordance with the provisions relating to the reduction of capital, *viz.* by special resolution and confirmation of the court (s. 66).

[11] *Drown* v. *Gaumont-British Picture Corporation Ltd.* [1937] Ch. 402.

Application of the share premium account

24–09 The share premium account may be applied for the following purposes:

(1) the paying up of fully paid bonus shares to be issued by the company to its members;

(2) the writing off of preliminary expenses of the company;

(3) the writing off of the expenses of, or underwriting commission on, any issue of shares or debentures of the company.

It should be noted that this applies not only to the issue of the shares on which the premium is paid but likewise to other issues of shares or debentures;

(4) the providing of a premium payable by the company on redemption of debentures of the company (s. 56 (2)) and 1981 Act, Sched. 4); or

(5) the providing of a premium of redeemable shares issued at a premium and redeemable at a premium (1981 Act, s. 45 (6) (*b*)).

It has already been observed that, if it is intended to apply the share premium account for any other than one (or several) of the five purposes stated above, the procedure for reduction of share capital set out in sections 66 *et seq.* has to be applied (s. 56 (1))[12]; this is *e.g.* the case where it is intended to write down or to write off the share premium account because the assets representing it have been lost,[13] or to distribute the share premium account to the members by way of dividend.

Relief from the obligation to form a share premium account

24–10 The consideration which a company issuing shares at a premium receives, may consist of cash or kind. Section 56 (1) states this expressly and, moreover, requires a sum equal to the aggregate "amount or value" to be transferred to the share premium account. The word "amount" refers to a cash premium, and the word "value" to a premium other than cash. According to the judgment of Harman J. in *Henry Head & Co.* v. *Ropner Holdings Ltd.*[14] the provisions of section 56 applied even in take-over situations where the issuing company was a newly formed company which had no assets at all other than those which it would acquire as consideration for the issue of its own shares. This case was followed by Walton J. in *Shearer* v. *Bercain Ltd.*[15]

These two cases created considerable disquiet because the ratio of section 56, to avoid the distribution of a capital profit, was absent. Their effect was that a pre-acquisition profit in companies which were taken over by the issuing company became non-distributable after the acquisition because it had to be placed into the share premium account of the issuing company.

12 Transitional provisions are contained in s. 56 (3).

13 No reference to the share premium account has to be made in the minute of reduction approved by the court under s. 69: *Re Paringa Mining and Exploration Co.* [1957] 1 W.L.R. 1143.

14 [1952] Ch. 124.

15 [1980] 3 All E.R. 295.

For this reason the 1981 Act has alleviated the position in the case of mergers and group reconstructions. In these cases the 1981 Act grants relief from the obligation to form a share premium account, subject to strict statutory requirements (1981 Act, ss. 36 to 41). These provisions of the 1981 Act have abolished the rule in *Henry Head* and *Bercain*.

The abolition of the obligation to form a share premium account in these cases has retrospective effect for share acquisitions prior to February 4, 1981. This relief is subject to certain conditions (s. 39). These conditions are:

(a) that the company whose shares are acquired was or as the result of the merger or reconstruction has become a subsidiary of the company which issued the shares at a premium, and

(b) the premium has not been transferred to a share premium account or it does not form part of the issuing company's identifiable reserves. (s. 39 (2) and (3)).

The Secretary of State has authority to add other cases to the relief from the obligation to form a share premium account, in addition to the relief in the cases of merger and reconstruction; he has also power to restrict or modify the relief in those two cases (s. 41).

Merger relief is provided in the following circumstances (1981 Act, s. 37). Assume that company A holds at least 90 per cent. of the equity shares in company B. If A now issues equity shares of a nominal value of £1 to the shareholders in B in exchange of their equity shares, which have the same nominal value but a market value of £3, A has issued its shares at a premium of £2 per share because this is the value it has received, in excess of the nominal value of its (A's) shares. In this situation the 1981 Act provides that section 56 of the 1948 Act (which would compel A to form a share premium account of £2 per value of each share received) shall not apply to the premium at which A's shares are issued (s. 37 (2)). This means in practice that if the excess value of £2 was distributable as a profit in the hands of B before the take-over, it remains distributable in the hands of A after the take-over and does not become part of a quasi-capital fund. The same applies if A, in addition to equity shares in B, acquires non-equity shares in exchange for its (A's) own shares (s. 37 (3)).

Group relief from the obligation to form a share premium account under section 56 of the 1948 Act is available in the following circumstances. If company A (the issuing company) is a wholly-owned subsidiary of company B and allots shares to B or another wholly-owned company (C) of B in consideration of the transfer to it of shares in another company in the group (whether wholly-owned or not) (C or D), then, if the shares of A are issued at a premium, A need not form a share premium account in excess of the "minimum premium value." This is the "base value" of the shares transferred by A. The "base value" shall be taken as:

(a) the cost of the shares in A issued to the shareholders in B, C or D, or

(b) the amount at which the issued shares are stated in the accounting records immediately before the transfer,

whichever is less (s. 38).

The amount of the shares for which relief is available from the obligation to form a share premium account need not be shown in the balance sheet (s. 40 (1)).

Issue of shares at a discount

In principle inadmissible

24–11 A company issues shares at a discount if the cash consideration[16] which it receives for them, *i.e.* the price, is less than the nominal amount of the issued shares. The issue of shares at a lower price than the market price—but a price equal to or higher than their nominal amount—which is often done in modern practice in the case of a "rights" issue carrying an element of bonus, does not constitute an issue of shares at a discount.

The issue of shares at a discount was, in principle, inadmissible in common law because it constituted a reduction of capital without confirmation by the court, as required by section 66 of the 1948 Act.[17] The issue of shares at a discount is now expressly prohibited by the 1980 Act, s. 21.

Before the coming into operation of this prohibition on December 22, 1980, neither the memorandum nor the articles nor the contract between the company and the shareholder to whom the shares were issued could authorise such issue, and any provision in them purporting to authorise it was ultra vires the company[18]; the issue itself, as long as executory, *i.e.* as the allottees were not registered as members, was invalid. Lord Macnaghten, in one case,[19] quoted with approval the following words from *Buckley's Companies Acts*: "The dominant and cardinal principle of these Acts is that the investor shall purchase immunity from liability beyond a certain limit, on the terms that there shall be and remain a liability up to that limit," and continued:

> "It is plain that [this principle] is one which cannot be dispensed with by anything in the articles of association, or by any resolution of the company, or by any contract between the company and outsiders who have been invited to become members of the company and who do come in on the faith of such a contract."

The 1948 Act prohibited by implication, the issue of shares at a discount, as Lord Macnaghten pointed out in the case just referred to[19]: the Act provided (s. 1 (2) (*a*)) that the liability of members in a company limited by

---

[16] As to consideration other than cash, see para. 24–12, *post.* It should be noted that the position does not entirely correspond to the issue of shares at a premium: see para. 24–10, *ante.*

[17] *Trevor* v. *Whitworth* (1887) 12 App.Cas. 409.

[18] *Ooregum Gold Mining Co. of India* v. *Roper* [1892] A.C. 125; *Welton* v. *Saffery* [1897] A.C. 299; *Klenk* v. *East India Co. for Exploration and Mining* 1888, 16 R. 271; *Newburgh and North Fife Ry. Co.* v. *North British Ry. Co.* 1913, S.C. 1166; 1913, 2 S.L.T. 212.

[19] *Ooregum, etc.* v. *Roper, supra,* at p. 145.

shares is limited "to the amount, if any, unpaid on the shares respectively held by them," and that in the winding up "no contribution shall be required from any member exceeding the amount, if any, unpaid on the shares" in question (s. 212 (1) (*d*)).

It followed—and it has been so held by the House of Lords[20]—that if shares were issued at a discount (in cases other than those in which exceptionally such issues were admitted by the 1948 Act, s. 57[20a]) and the allottees allowed themselves to be registered as members, they were nevertheless liable to the full nominal amount of the shares. Nothing but payment, and payment in full, could put an end to the liability.

4–12 If the consideration received by the company is other than cash—kind—but has been undervalued, the question arises whether this constitutes, in effect, an issue of shares at a discount. Since the 1980 Act, this question is of diminished importance because the non-cash consideration has to be valued by an independent person, *i.e.* a person qualified to act as auditor of the company, before the shares are allotted (1980 Act, s. 24). But the rules developed by the courts in earlier decisions are still of interest. Accordingly, if a valid contract is made by the company for the allotment of shares in consideration of specific property, or of services of substantial value, the court will not, as long as the contract stands, examine whether the consideration is adequate.[21] On the other hand, if the consideration is clearly not equivalent to the nominal value of the shares, or, on the face of it, is illusory or colourable, the shares have to be treated as issued at a discount and the shareholders may be held liable to pay for them in full.[22] In the result, in the case of consideration other than cash, while a margin is left for honest undervaluation of the consideration and sometimes, in effect, an issue at a discount cannot practically be upset, nevertheless, if the undervaluation of the consideration is not a matter of honest opinion, the shares cannot to that extent be treated as fully paid.

Before the 1980 Act

4–13 Before the 1980 Act, the issue of shares at a discount was admissible and lawful in two cases:

1. where the issue complied with the conditions of section 57 of the 1948 Act; and
2. where the allottees were entitled to deduct or to be paid underwriting commission (s. 53 of the 1948 Act).

---

[20] See note 18, above.

[20a] Repealed by the 1980 Act, s. 88 and Sched. 4.

[21] *Pell's Case* (1869) L.R. 5 Ch. 11; *Re Baglan Hall Colliery Co.* (1870) L.R. 5 Ch. 346; *Re Wragg Ltd.* [1897] 1 Ch. 796; *Re Theatrical Trust* [1895] 1 Ch. 771; *Re Innes & Co.* [1903] 2 Ch. 254; *Pellatt's Case* (1867) L.R. 2 Ch. 527.

[22] *Gardner* v. *Iredale* [1912] 1 Ch. 700; *Re Wragg Ltd.* [1897] 1 Ch. 796, 836; *Hong Kong & China Gas Co.* v. *Glen* [1914] 1 Ch. 527 (an agreement to allot as fully paid a certain proportion of all future increases of capital); *Re James Pitkin & Co.* [1916] W.N. 112.

After the 1980 Act

24–14 Section 57 of the 1948 Act was repealed by the 1980 Act and the issue of shares at a discount is now expressly prohibited (1980 Act, s. 21 (1)).

If shares are allotted in contravention of this prohibition, the allottees are liable to pay the company the discount and interest thereon (1980 Act, s. 21 (2)). Any person other than the allottees, who were concerned in the transaction, is likewise so liable unless he proves that at the time of the allotment he did not have actual notice of the contravention, or unless he derived title to the shares (directly or indirectly) from a person who became a holder of them after the contravention and was not so liable (1980 Act, s. 21 (3)).

Section 21 contains transitional provisions validating transactions which, before the coming into operation of that section (December 22, 1980) were valid and lawful by virtue of the now repealed section 57 of the 1948 Act, (s. 21 (4)).

Underwriting commission

24–15 Section 53 of the 1948 Act admits the payment of underwriting commission not exceeding 10 per cent. of the price at which the shares are issued. This section is generally regarded as permitting the payment of commission only for underwriting or similar services, but its wording is wide enough to cover the payment of commission for merely subscribing for shares.[23] Such a payment will, however, be viewed with suspicion by the court, which will require to be satisfied that the payment is not intended to be an—illegal—issue of shares at a discount.

[23] *Keatinge* v. *Paringa Consolidated Mines Ltd.* (1902) 18 T.L.R. 266.

CHAPTER 25

THE PREVENTION OF FRAUD (INVESTMENTS) ACT 1958

The purpose of the 1958 Act

25–01 Two sections of the Prevention of Fraud (Investments) Act 1958—referred to in this chapter as "the 1958 Act"—relate closely to company law: sections 13 and 14. Before their effect is considered it will be convenient to deal shortly with other provisions of the Act which provide the background to these two sections.

The main purpose of the 1958 Act is to prevent dealings in securities except by persons licensed to deal in them or exempt from the requirement of a licence. General provisions relating to the prevention of fraud in connection with investments were first introduced by the Prevention of Fraud (Investments) Act 1939. Before the passing of the Act the sole provisions for this purpose were contained in the Companies Act 1929, particularly section 356, but these provisions did not prove adequate for preventing share-hawking and other practices harmful to the investing public and were not re-enacted in the Companies Act 1948. The Act of 1939[1] was repealed and re-enacted by the 1958 Act, as amended.[2]

"Securities" within the Act

25–02 For the purposes of the 1958 Act, the term "securities"[3] is widely defined (s. 26 (1)) as meaning:

> "(*a*) shares or debentures, or rights or interests (described whether as units or otherwise) in any shares or debentures, or
>
> (*b*) securities of the Government of the United Kingdom or of Northern Ireland or the Government of any country or territory outside the United Kingdom, or
>
> (*c*) rights (whether actual or contingent) in respect of money lent to, or deposited with, any industrial and provident society or building society,
>
> and includes rights or interests (described whether as units or otherwise) which may be acquired under any unit trust scheme under which all property for the time being subject to any trust created in pursuance of the scheme consists of such securities as are mentioned in paragraph (*a*), paragraph (*b*) or paragraph (*c*) of this definition."

---

[1] As amended by the Companies Act 1947, s. 117 (likewise repealed). The Prevention of Fraud (Investments) Act 1958, like its predecessor, does not apply to Northern Ireland. The Act of 1958 came into operation on October 23, 1958.

[2] By the Building Societies Act 1960, s. 7 (5), and the Building Societies Act 1962, s. 133 (6); and further by the Banking Act 1979, Sched. 6, para. 5.

[3] On the meaning of "securities," see *R.* v. *Findlater* [1939] 1 K.B. 594. (The case arose under s. 356 of the Companies Act 1929, but is of use for the interpretation of "securities" in the 1958 Act.)

Shares and debentures are likewise defined by the Act. The definition of both includes stock,[4] and that of debentures includes bonds of a corporation and states that it shall make no difference whether the debentures or bonds are secured by a charge or not.

A prosecution under the Act is possible with respect to proposed securities of a company not yet incorporated, and not merely with respect to securities of companies already in existence.[5]

"Dealing in securities"

25–03 The 1958 Act defines in section 26 (1) "dealing in securities" as doing any of the following, whether as a principal or as an agent:

> "making or offering to make with any person, or inducing or attempting to induce any person to enter into or offer to enter into—
> (*a*) any agreement for, or with a view to acquiring, disposing of, subscribing for or underwriting securities or lending or depositing money to or with any industrial and provident society or building society, or
> (*b*) any agreement the purpose or pretended purpose of which is to secure a profit to any of the parties from the yield of securities or by reference to fluctuations in the value of securities."

Restrictions imposed by the Act

25–04 The 1958 Act restricts any person from carrying on the business of dealing in securities unless he is exempt under the Act or has obtained a licence.

A. There are two principal classes of exempt persons:

(1) *Bodies specifically exempted by the Act.*

Hereunder fall the Bank of England, any statutory corporation[6] or municipal corporation, industrial and provident society or building society (s. 2 (1) (*b*)).

(2) *Persons or bodies exempt by order of the Department of Trade under the Act.*

Hereunder fall:

(a) members of a recognised stock exchange (s. 2 (1) (*a*) and s. 15). The following stock exchange is recognised at present[7]:

---

[4] The definition of "shares" further includes shares in an unincorporated building society such as is mentioned in s. 7 of the Building Societies Act 1874; as to these shares, see now s. 125 of the Building Societies Act 1962. Building societies registered under the 1962 Act are incorporated (s. 3).

[5] *R.* v. *Hamid* [1945] K.B. 540 (C.C.A.). This follows from the definition of "dealing in securities" in s. 26 (1) of the Act.

[6] The term "statutory corporation" does not include a company (see s. 26 (1)).

[7] See s. 26 (1), under "recognised stock exchange."

The Stock Exchange[8];

(b) member of a recognised association of dealers in securities (s. 2 (1) (*a*) and s. 15)[9];

(c) any exempted dealer (s. 2 (1) (*b*) and s. 16).[10] The Department must be satisfied that the requirements of section 16 are satisfied before they may make an exemption order;

(d) any authorised unit trust scheme (s. 2 (1) (*c*) and s. 17 and Sched. I).[11]

In the case of a unit trust scheme the Department of Trade have to be satisfied as to the substance of the various matters which the trust deed is required by the Schedule to contain and may refuse to authorise the unit trust scheme even though all matters referred to in the Schedule are set out in the deed, if the Department do not approve of them, *e.g.* because the initial service charge is too high.[12] Moreover, it was said, *obiter*, by Danckwerts J.[12]—as is thought, rightly—that the Department of Trade have a general discretion under what is now section 17 (1) (*c*) to refuse a scheme whether the conditions of the First Schedule to the Act of 1958 are fulfilled or not.

The exemptions may be revoked by the Department of Trade, in cases (a) and (b) unqualifiedly, and in cases (c) and (d) subject to certain qualifications.

B. Licensed persons are granted either a principal's licence (s. 3 (1) (*a*) and s. 4) or a representative's licence (s. 3 (1) (*b*)).[13]

There is a fundamental difference between any exemption and a licence under the 1958 Act: while the exemption is purely discretionary, the provisions relating to licences are "imperative . . . requiring the Department of Trade to issue a licence if the conditions are satisfied."[14] A licence can only be refused or revoked after proceedings before a quasi-judicial tribunal constituted under section 6 of the Act.[15]

---

8 The Department of Trade has not declared the Stock Exchange to be the "recognised stock exchange" by statutory instrument but has published notices to that effect under what is now s. 15 (3); for details, see "Particulars of Dealers in Securities and of Unit Trusts under the Prevention of Fraud (Investments) Act 1958," published annually by the Department of Trade.

9 At present the following associations are recognised: the Association of Canadian Investment Dealers and members of the Toronto and Montreal Stock Exchanges in Great Britain, the United Kingdom Association of New York Stock Exchange Members, the Association of Stock and Share Dealers, the Law Society of Scotland, and the London Discount Market Association. Solicitors in Scotland who benefit from the general exemption as members of the Law Society of Scotland, require to observe the Solicitors (Scotland) Prevention of Fraud (Investment) Rules 1961, which are reproduced in Vol. III, Part J.

10 Lists of exempted dealers are published by the Department of Trade under s. 16 (4) in the pamphlet mentioned in note 8, *ante*.

11 Lists are likewise published in the pamphlet mentioned in note 8, *ante*.

12 *Allied Investors' Trusts Ltd.* v. *Board of Trade* [1956] Ch. 232. The restrictions on charges of the managers are now removed (1981).

13 For licensing procedure, see the Prevention of Fraud (Investments) Act Licensing Regulations 1944 (S.R. & O. 1944 No. 119).

14 *Per* Danckwerts J. in *Allied Investors' Trusts Ltd.* v. *Board of Trade* [1956] Ch. 232, 242.

15 See the Licensed Dealers (Tribunal of Inquiry) Rules 1965 (S.I. 1965 No. 373); Vol. II, Pt. B, para. B–046 of this work.

The Department of Trade have powers to regulate the conduct of business by holders of licences (s. 7).[16]

Section 13

Comparison between sections 13 and 14

25–05 The two main sections of the 1958 Act which supplement the provisions of the Companies Acts are, as has been observed earlier,[17] sections 13 and 14. The former section attempts to prevent people from fraudulently or recklessly inducing persons to invest money, the latter one attempts to restrict the distribution of circulars (other than prospectuses within the Companies Acts) relating to the investments of funds. Both sections provide a criminal sanction for persons guilty of contravening them. There is however, a fundamental difference between them: while *mens rea*—"a guilty mind"—is required of an offender against section 13, whether that guilty intention is dishonesty or mere recklessness, section 14 can be infringed unintentionally by a person who unwillingly and unwittingly contravenes its provisions. The offences under section 14 may be described as technical in character though they are grave, but a conviction under section 13 carries invariably a high degree of blame, if not moral turpitude. This is reflected in the punishments provided by these sections: the maximum penalty under section 13 is seven years' imprisonment—no fine is admitted—and conspiracy to commit an offence under section 13 is punishable (s. 13 (2)), whereas the maximum penalty under section 14 is two years' imprisonment or a fine not exceeding £500, or both, and prosecution under section 14 is only possible with the consent of the Board of Trade or the Director of Public Prosecutions (s. 14 (6) and (7)).

The practical effect of section 14 is far-reaching and honest persons seeking investors can easily become entangled in its prohibitions.

Personal conditions of liability

25–06 A person can be convicted under section 13 only if he

(1) knows the statement, promise or forecast which he has made to be misleading, false or deceptive; or
(2) dishonestly conceals material facts; or
(3) recklessly (dishonestly or otherwise)[18] makes a statement which is misleading, false or deceptive (s. 13 (1)).

---

[16] The following regulations were made under the 1958 Act: The Licensed Dealers (Conduct of Business) Rules 1960 (S.I. 1960 No. 1216). On January 19, 1981 the Department of Trade published a memorandum proposing a revision of these Rules. It is intended to make these Rules much stricter and to prescribe, in particular, that customers' moneys shall be held by the dealers in separate trust accounts. The Licensed Dealer Rules and other S.I.s made under the 1958 Act are listed in Vol. II, Part B.

[17] See para. 25–01, *ante*.

[18] The words in brackets were added by s. 21 (1) of the Protection of Depositors Act 1963. After the repeal of that Act by the Banking Act 1979 these words were retained by the latter Act, Sched. 6, para. 5 (1). The object of the alteration was to make clear that a person can act "recklessly" without being dishonest, thus overruling *R.* v. *Mackinnon* [1959] 1 Q.B. 150.

In order to be reckless the "statement or promise must be a rash statement or promise and must be made heedless of whether the person making it has any real facts on which to base the statement or promise."[19] In *R.* v. *Grunwald*[19] a banker who had made a false statement was held not to have acted recklessly because, before making the statement, he made inquiries and was assured by a responsible solicitor who, as he was aware, knew all the circumstances that it was a proper statement to make. But a forecast made recklessly which was misleading, false or deceptive would be within the prohibition.[20]

Offences under section 13

5–07 As far as the investment in shares or debentures of a company is concerned, a person who satisfies any of the three personal conditions set out in the preceding paragraph is guilty of an offence under section 13 (1)[21] if he induces or attempts to induce another person

"(*a*) to enter into or offer to enter into—
  (i) any agreement for, or with a view to, acquiring, disposing of, subscribing for or underwriting securities . . . , or
  (ii) any agreement the purpose or pretended purpose of which is to secure a profit to any of the parties from the yield of securities or by reference to fluctuations in the value of securities, or

(*b*) to take part or offer to take part in any arrangements with respect to property other than securities, being arrangements the purpose or effect, or pretended purpose or effect, of which is to enable persons taking part in the arrangements (whether by becoming owners of the property or any part of the property or otherwise) to participate in or receive profits or income alleged to arise or to be likely to arise from the acquisition, holding, management or disposal of such property, or sums to be paid or alleged to be likely to be paid out of such profits or income, or

(*c*) to enter into or offer to enter into an agreement the purpose or pretended purpose of which is to secure a profit to any of the parties by reference to fluctuations in the value of any property other than securities."

Conspiracy to commit any of these acts is likewise punishable (s. 13 (2)).

It would appear that, if the personal conditions set out earlier are satisfied, the speculation in differences is caught by section 13 (1) (*a*) (ii), *e.g.* where, instead of agreeing to acquire securities, a person speculates upon the rise or fall in their value.[22]

---

[19] *Per* Paull J. in *R.* v. *Grunwald* [1963] 1 Q.B. 935, 939.

[20] See *R.* v. *Bates* [1952] 2 All E.R. 842; *R.* v. *Russell* [1953] 1 W.L.R. 77.

[21] As amended by the Protection of Depositors Act 1963, s. 21 (1) (*b*). After the repeal of that Act by the Banking Act 1979, the amendments were retained by the latter Act, Sched. 6, para. 5.

[22] The same applies, again subject to the personal conditions of liability, to the speculation in differences in the value of property other than securities, *e.g.* a commodity: see s. 13 (1) (*c*).

The effect of the section is generally to prevent any person, whether or not a director or other officer of a company, from attempting to induce other people to make almost any form of investment, whether in securities or other property, by means of any fraudulent statement or omission or by any statement made recklessly.

Offences committed in England and abroad

25–08 In *Reg.* v. *Markus*[23] the House of Lords had to consider the criminal liability under section 13 (1) (*b*) of a defendant who, in the words of Lord Diplock,[24] "played a leading part in running a gigantic international swindle known as 'Agri-fund'." The essential facts were that the fund was alleged to be a trust established in Panama to invest its capital in food-producing industries. The organisation charged with selling units in the Fund to the public was run from offices in London by an English company, Agri-International (U.K.) Ltd., of which the defendant was a director and which he managed. The units were marketed on the continent, mainly in West Germany, by a team of salesmen who obtained offers for the purchase of the units from members of the public. These offers, together with powers of attorney of the victims, and their cheques for the whole or part of the price, were sent to the London office, where they were "processed," *i.e.* the cheques were cashed in a circuitous manner and eventually credited to the account of the London company in a Swiss bank. (There was an alternative procedure under which securities in another fund, so-called I.O.S. shares, could be sold by the victims and the proceeds of sale be invested in the purchase of Agri-Fund units.) When the money was credited to the London company, it sent the victim's acceptances and eventually worthless certificates for the appropriate number of units in the Agri-Fund.

The House of Lords held that section 13 (1) (*b*) referred to two clearly separate and distinct offences, *viz.* that of inducing (or attempting to induce) a person "to take part" in any arrangement mentioned in that provision, and that of inducing (or attempting to induce) a person "to offer to take part" in such arrangement, and that these two offences were not mutually exclusive but to have committed the one did not preclude the possibility of subsequently committing the other. In the present case, the offence of inducing a person "to offer to take part" in an arrangement within section 13 (1) (*b*) was committed in Germany where the victims were induced to make offers to buy the units and that was outside the criminal jurisdiction of the English courts, but the offence of inducing a person "to take part" in such arrangement was committed in England when, by virtue of the power of attorney of the victim, his cheques or I.O.S. certificates were cashed and other steps in the processing of his application were taken; anything that the victim did to enable him to

23 [1976] A.C. 35.
24 *Ibid.* at p. 714.

receive profits or income alleged to arise from the acquisition of the property constituted taking part in "any arrangements" and could be done through persons acting on his behalf.

The appeal of the accused who had been sentenced to a total of seven years' imprisonment was dismissed by the House of Lords.

Section 14

Offences under section 14

25–09 Subsection (1) of this section makes it an offence for a person, subject to the provisions of the other subsections, to

> "(*a*) distribute or cause to be distributed any documents which, to his knowledge, are circulars containing—
> (i) any invitation to persons to do any of the acts mentioned in paragraphs (*a*) to (*c*) of subsection (1) of [section 13[25]], or
> (ii) any information calculated to lead directly or indirectly to the doing of any of those acts by the recipient of the information, or
> (*b*) have in his possession for the purpose of distribution any documents which, to his knowledge, are such circulars as aforesaid, being documents of such a nature as to show that the object or principal object of distributing them would be to communicate such an invitation or such information as aforesaid."

Conspiracy to commit any of those acts is not made an offence.

It will be noted that section 14, in subsection (1) (*a*), adopts only the *acts*, but not the *personal conditions* of liability of section 13. Unlike the latter, an offence under section 14 can be committed without *mens rea*.[26]

Section 14 is supplemental to the prospectus provisions of the Companies Act 1948, and does not apply where such provisions govern (see below). The restrictions of this section do not penalise a person who is ignorant of the fact that the document

(a) is a circular, or

(b) contains such an invitation or information.

Apart, however, from this excuse the section is worded in very wide terms, and the words "calculated . . . directly or indirectly" in section 14 (1) (*a*) (ii) cover a very wide field.

Particular difficulty is caused by the meaning of the word "circulars" in this section. This point will be considered later[27]; first it is intended to deal with the closely defined exceptional cases in which section 14 (1) does not apply.

---

[25] See para. 25–07, *ante*.
[26] See para. 25–05, *ante*.
[27] See para. 25–18, *post*.

Exemptions

25–10 PROSPECTUSES AND OTHER DOCUMENTS AUTHORISED BY ACT OF PARLIAMENT. The Act contains in section 14 (2) detailed provisions exempting from the prohibition of subsection (1) prospectuses issued in pursuance of section 38[28] or 417[29] of the Companies Act 1948; forms of application for shares or debentures together with a circular complying with section 38; application forms if issued with a bona fide invitation to enter into an underwriting agreement; or documents the distribution of which is required or authorised by an Act other than the 1958 Act, *e.g.* by the Companies Acts. Thus, a report of the directors would fall under this exemption (s. 14 (2) (*c*)).

Subsection (2), by (*a*) (i) and (*b*) (ii), further exempts the distribution of documents by a company incorporated in Great Britain but not registered, if the documents would have qualified as exempted prospectuses or circulars had the company been registered under the Companies Act 1948.

25–11 DOCUMENTS PERMITTED BY DEPARTMENT OF TRADE. This exemption is permitted by section 14 (2), end. In practice such permission can normally be obtained at very short notice.

Application for such permission should be made to:

The Assistant Secretary,
Insurance and Companies Department,
Department of Trade,
1 Victoria Street,
London, SW1H 0ET.

A General Permission has been granted by the Department of Trade allowing the distribution by and on behalf of certain specified persons[30] of any circular containing an invitation or information with respect to securities created in pursuance of any unit trust scheme which is not an authorised unit trust scheme if—

(1) the scheme relates solely to one class of securities in a single corporation incorporated outside Great Britain; and either
(2) the circular is distributed in compliance with The Stock Exchange requirements for Admission of Securities to the Official List, Section A, Part I, para. III (a) and Part II, para. III, for the purpose of obtaining a listing of the securities created in pursuance of that scheme (whether described as units or otherwise); or
(3) the securities created in pursuance of that scheme are listed on The Stock Exchange.[31]

---

[28] The exemption likewise applies if no prospectus is required or an abridged prospectus is admitted under ss. 38 (5) and 39.

[29] This exemption likewise applies if no prospectus is required or an abridged prospectus is admitted under s. 417 (5).

[30] These persons are (1) a member of any recognised stock exchange, *i.e.* The Stock Exchange; (2) a member of any recognised association of dealers in securities; (3) an exempted dealer; (4) the holder of a principal's licence.

[31] The General Permission came into operation on July 3, 1961 (published by the then Board of Trade on June 13, 1961, and obtainable from H.M.S.O., Ref. 51–9999); see Vol. II, Pt. B, para. B–049.

25–12 CIRCULARS BY COMPANY TO CREDITORS OR MEMBERS.[32] A circular by a company addressed exclusively to holders of securities in, or employees or creditors of, the company or any subsidiary thereof is exempt (subs. (3) (*a*) (iii)).

25–13 LICENSED OR EXEMPT PERSONS.[32] The prohibition of section 14 (1) does not apply to the distribution or possession of documents which contain an invitation or information relating to securities, if the invitation is made or the information given

(1) by a licensed person holding a principal's licence[33] (s. 14 (3) (*a*) (i));
(2) an exempt person[34] (s. 14 (3) (*a*) (i) (ii) and (iv));
(3) an industrial and provident society or building society, with respect to shares of the society, or loans or deposits to, or with, it (s. 14 (3) (*a*) (vi)).

25–14 TRUSTEES.[35] Circulars by, or on behalf of, a trustee to beneficiaries under the trust are likewise exempt if sent by the trustee in his character of trustee (s. 14 (3) (*a*) (vii)).

25–15 AUCTION SALES.[35] Exemption is further granted for circulars issued in connection with a sale or proposed sale of securities by auction (s. 14 (3) (*a*) (viii)).

25–16 DEALERS IN PROPERTY. Since section 14 (1) applies to circulars relating to all investments specified in section 14 (1), including those in property other than securities (s. 13 (1) (*b*) and (*c*)), it would be impossible for a dealer in any property other than securities, *e.g.* real estate or commodities, to make any invitation or to issue any information with regard to such property unless he were granted exemption. Subsection (3) (*b*), therefore, exempts likewise any person whose ordinary business is to buy and sell any property other than securities (whether as a principal or as an agent) in so far as any invitation is made or information given in the ordinary course of such business.

Circulars providing facilities for the participation in profits or income of such property are not exempt and fall within the general prohibition of section 14 (1) (s. 14 (3), proviso). In view of this proviso the prohibition of section 14 (1) applies even to many circulars relating to real property and other transactions not concerning securities. A document may be a "circular" within section 14 (1) if it is one of 60 letters addressed in a standard form to recipients named in the letter: *Hudson* v. *Bishop Cavenagh (Commodities) Ltd.*[35a]

---

[32] This exemption does not apply to an unauthorised unit trust scheme (proviso to subs. (3) of s. 14); but see the General Permission referred to above in the text.
[33] See para. 25–04, *ante*.
[34] See para. 25–04, *ante*.
[35] See note 32, *supra*.
[35a] (1981) N.L.J. 1238.

25–17 DISTRIBUTION OF DOCUMENTS TO DEALERS IN SECURITIES. Subsection (5) provides exemption for a person distributing documents to persons whose business involves the question of disposal, or the holding of securities (whether as principal or as agent), or causes documents to be distributed to such persons, or has in his possession documents for the purpose of such distribution.

What is a circular?

25–18 Subsection (4) might be described as a draftsman's nightmare: it provides that documents shall not be deemed *not* to be circulars by reason only that they are in the form of a newspaper or other periodical publication. The effect of this would appear to be that a person cannot avoid the provisions of the section by publishing his invitation or information in any such newspaper or periodical instead of by distributing or sending out documents to individual persons. What is not clear from the subsection is

(1) whether or not any such newspaper or periodical is itself the circular, or

(2) whether an invitation or information which appears in a newspaper or periodical (together with such other news, gossip and advertisements as may appear in such a newspaper) can be said to be "in the form of a newspaper or periodical," for the invitation or information will not in such case be itself "in the form of a newspaper or periodical" but will be in the form of a printed notice appearing in such a newspaper or periodical.

Nevertheless, the only possible safe course is to treat any such invitation or information appearing in a newspaper or periodical as if it were a circular caught by section 14, and Department of Trade permission to the distribution thereof should be obtained.

Persons who insert the prohibited invitation or information in a newspaper or other periodical are punishable under section 14 (1) whether they themselves distribute the periodical or whether the distribution is done by those owning or managing it. They are guilty, in the former case, of "distributing" the circular, and, in the latter case, of "causing [it] to be distributed" (s. 14 (1) (*a*)). The view expressed elsewhere[36] that those inserting such an invitation or information into a periodical are not guilty under the section unless they distribute copies of the publication themselves cannot be accepted. First, it fails to give effect to the offence of causing the distribution of prohibited circulars, and, secondly, it unduly restricts the meaning of section 14 (4), contrary to the intention of the legislator. As pointed out earlier, the safe course is to ask the Board of Trade for permission to circulate, under section 14 (2), end.

Newspaper vendors or similar persons who have in their possession the offending newspaper or periodical only by reason that they distribute it are

---

[36] Gore-Brown, *Handbook of Joint Stock Companies*, 43rd ed., 1977, para. 12–30.

expressly protected by section 14 (4) and do not commit an offence under that section by doing so or by having the newspaper or periodical in their possession.

Penalties

25–19 The only persons who are liable under the section are persons who have knowledge that the documents are circulars containing an invitation or information of the kind specified. Upon summary conviction any such person is liable to imprisonment for six months and/or a fine of £100, or on indictment to two years' imprisonment and/or a fine of £500 (s. 14 (6)).

No proceedings under the section may be instituted in England without the consent of the Department of Trade or the Director of Public Prosecutions (subs. (7)). Nevertheless a person may be arrested and remanded before such consent has been obtained, and a justice of the peace is empowered to issue a warrant under which premises may be searched for such documents, wherever there is reasonable ground for suspecting their existence (subs. (8)), and any documents seized as a result of such a search may be retained for one month or, if proceedings are started within one month, until the close of such proceedings (subs. (9)). Upon any such proceedings the court may order the disposal of any such documents (subss. (10) and (11)).

Offences by a company against section 13 or 14 of the 1958 Act

25–20 Where any offence committed by a company under any section of the 1958 Act is proved to have been committed with the consent or connivance of any director, manager, secretary or other officer of the company, such person shall also be deemed to have committed the offence, as well as the company itself, and shall be liable accordingly under the 1958 Act (s. 19).[37]

Civil liability

25–21 No civil liability is imposed by the 1958 Act, so that a breach of any of its provisions will not, for that reason, give rise to any civil rights or liabilities. These will be governed by the general law. If, *e.g* a person, by an untrue statement, induces another to acquire securities, he may be liable to that person under the common law relating to misrepresentation, or under the Misrepresentation Act 1967.[38]

---

[37] *Reg.* v. *Markus* [1976] A.C. 35.
[38] This Act does not apply to Scotland.

CHAPTER 26

CONTROL OF BORROWING. EXCHANGE CONTROL

Control of borrowing

Aims of borrowing control

26–01 By the Borrowing (Control and Guarantees) Act 1946[1] the Treasury is given power to control public and private investment. The aim of the Act[2] is by the control of investment to assure priority for those projects of capital development which are of the greatest importance in the national interest and, at the same time, by a regulation of the flow of capital to investment to alleviate the transition from conditions of economic buoyancy to depression; that cyclical movement was very marked before the Second World War and caused much individual hardship. The control provided by this Act is purely monetary.

The fundamental scheme of the Borrowing (Control and Guarantees) Act 1946 is simple: the Treasury is authorised to regulate by orders certain specified investment transactions (s. 1); this power is particularly important if money seeking investment is abundant. Further, the Treasury is given power to guarantee any loan "if satisfied that it is expedient so to do for the purpose of facilitating the reconstruction or development of any industry"[3] in Great Britain but the aggregate of these loans must not exceed a specified sum (s. 2); this power will be exercised if it is necessary to stimulate the flow of money to capital investment. The control exercised under the Act by the Treasury over investment has been progressively relaxed and is now insignificant for issues of sterling securities by companies in Great Britain.

In this work we are solely concerned with the power of the Treasury to exercise investment control; the authority of the Treasury to guarantee loans need not be considered.

Ambit of borrowing control

26–02 Theoretically the ambit of Treasury control of investments is very wide and extends far beyond borrowing in the ordinary sense of the term.[4]

---

[1] The Act applies only to Great Britain; Northern Ireland is not covered by the Act (s. 6). As regards the latter the Borrowing (Control and Guarantees) (Northern Ireland) Act 1946 applies.

[2] The aims of this legislation are explained in Cmnd. 6726.

[3] "Industry" includes any undertaking engaged in the provision of supplies or services in question (s. 2 (5)). Under these provisions, the Treasury has power to guarantee debentures issued by any company.

[4] See para. 26–06, *post*.

The regulations authorised by the Act and contained in the orders made thereunder state:

(1) the transactions which are prohibited except with consent of the Treasury (this consent can be obtained by application to the Bank of England[5]); and

(2) the transactions which do not require the consent of the Treasury, either because the control of borrowing does not apply to them or because they are exempt therefrom.

The Act provides heavy penalties[6] for those contravening it but states expressly that the legal rights of the parties under any prohibited transaction are not affected by it (s. 1 (3)).[7]

26–03 It is convenient here to indicate the transactions pertaining to company law which the Treasury is authorised by section 1 (1) of the Act of 1946 to regulate by orders. They are:

> "(*a*) the borrowing[8] of money in Great Britain where the aggregate of the amount of money borrowed under the transaction and of any other amounts so borrowed by the same person in the previous twelve months . . . exceeds ten thousand pounds;
>
> (*b*) the raising of money in Great Britain by the issue, whether in Great Britain or elsewhere, by any body corporate, of any shares in that body corporate;
>
> (*c*) the issue for any purposes—
>
> (i) by any body corporate of any shares in or debentures or other securities of that body corporate, if either the body corporate is incorporated under the law of England or Scotland or the shares, debentures or other securities are or are to be registered in England or Scotland; or
>
> (ii) . . . ;
>
> (*d*) the circulation in Great Britain of any offer for subscription, sale or exchange of—
>
> (i) any shares in or debentures or other securities of any body corporate not incorporated under the law of England or Scotland; or
>
> (ii) . . . "

These provisions are qualified by a proviso according to which the subsection shall not apply to the borrowing of money by any person (other than a local authority) in the ordinary course of his business[9] from a person carrying on a banking undertaking. Consequently ordinary banking transactions, such as the arrangement of an overdraft or a borrowing on short term notes, do not require the consent of the Treasury, irrespective of the amount in question. They are further qualified by a number of specified exceptions which are considered later.[10]

---

[5] See para. 26–22, *post*.
[6] See para. 26–23, *post*.
[7] See para. 26–23, *post*.
[8] The extended meaning of "borrowing" is discussed at para. 26–06, *post*.
[9] On the meaning of "in the ordinary course of business," see para. 26–13, *post*.
[10] See para. 26–11, *post*.

26–04 It will be noted that the Treasury's power with regard to the raising of money by the issue of shares and debentures is unlimited, whereas its power with regard to borrowing is limited by the Act to sums in excess of £10,000 in any period of 12 months. This means that the Treasury cannot by order provide that their consent shall be necessary for borrowings below that sum: borrowings of £10,000 or less are, by virtue of Act of Parliament, completely exempt from control. As regards borrowing in excess of £10,000, the free limit is in the discretion of the Treasury.

By articles 8 and 8A of the Control of Borrowing Order 1958,[11] as amended,[12] the Treasury have admitted an *overall exemption* from investment control for all types of transactions, borrowings as well as the raising of money by issue of shares and debentures, unless:

(a) the transaction is effected by or on behalf of a person resident outside the United Kingdom, and is not a transaction consisting of or including the issue of non-sterling securities; or

(b) the transaction is effected by or on behalf of an investment trust company which is resident in the scheduled territories but outside the United Kingdom; or

(c) the transaction is effected by a local authority.

Further, some degree of Treasury control is maintained in the following cases:

(i) the issue of certain narrower-range investments requiring advice under the Trustee Investments Act 1961,[13] unless the terms on which the securities are to be issued have, before the making of the issue, been approved by the Bank of England on behalf of the Treasury;

(ii) the issue of any sterling securities where the amount of the money to be raised by the issue is not less than £3 million,[14] unless the time at which the securities are to be issued has, before the making of the issue, been approved by the Bank of England on behalf of the Treasury.

26–05 It follows from the preceding observations that Treasury control extends at present to these classes of transactions:

1. transactions effected by or on behalf of non-residents if the transaction concerns the issue of sterling securities;
2. transactions effected by local authority;
3. Bank of England approval is required for—
   (a) the terms on which the stated investments under the Trustee Investments Act 1961 are issued; and
   (b) the timing of issues of £3 million or more.

---

[11] S.I. 1958 No. 1208.

[12] By the Control of Borrowing (Amendment) Order 1970 (S.I. 1970 No. 708), and the Control of Borrowing (Amendment) Order 1979 (S.I. 1979 No. 794).

[13] The investments referred to in paras. 1 to 5 of Part II of Schedule 1 to the Trustee Investments Act 1961.

[14] Raised from £1 million to £3 million by the Control of Borrowing (Amendment) Order 1972 (S.I. 1972 No. 1218).

Since the Act of 1946 is merely an enabling Act, the practitioner who has to ascertain whether a particular transaction that prima facie is within the ambit of the Act requires Treasury consent has to examine the regulations made under section 1. They are contained in the Control of Borrowing Order 1958, as amended. This Order is reproduced in Volume III, Part G, but some of its provisions have to be discussed here.

Borrowing

26–06 This term which, as already noted, in the context of this legislation has a much more extensive meaning than it has in ordinary language,[15] is defined in article 2 of the Order of 1958.[16] According to this definition references to "borrowing of money" include:

> "2—(1). . .
> (*a*) references to the making of any arrangement to provide any guarantee or to mortgage or charge any property to secure the payment of any sum which is already due when the arrangement is made or is payable not later than six months after the arrangement is made; and
> (*b*) references to the making of any arrangement by which the price of any property, except the price of goods sold by a person in the ordinary course of his business, is allowed to remain unpaid either for a fixed period or indefinitely but charged on any property,[17]
>
> but do not include references to the making of any other arrangement by which a sum which would otherwise be payable at any date is payable at a later date; and references to loans shall be construed accordingly."

"Borrowing," as is evident from article 2 (1) (*b*), thus includes the deferment of the payment of the price of goods for a fixed period or, in certain circumstances, indefinitely, but the extended meaning of "borrowing" applies only to transactions which are contracts of sale and purchase, and not to contracts in which the consideration consists of the issue of shares and debentures and the money or cash is allowed to remain unpaid. This was decided by Upjohn J. in *London and Country Commercial Properties Investments Ltd.* v. *Att.-Gen.*[18] In the course of his judgment the learned judge observed[18a]:

> "I have to find a contract of sale and purchase for cash, and arrangement by which that cash is to remain unpaid . . .
>
> "There is, in fact, no cash consideration here at all. No money is being allowed to remain unpaid. This is quite a different transaction. This is a transaction in consideration of the issue of a series of debenture stock secured by a debenture trust deed. Under the terms of that trust deed, moneys, of course, become payable from time to time to

---

[15] See para. 26–02, *ante*.
[16] This definition is more elaborate than that in s. 4 (2) of the Act of 1946.
[17] This situation may arise where land is purchased and the price is not fully paid.
[18] [1953] 1 W.L.R. 312.
[18a] *Ibid*, 320–321.

the holders from time to time of the stock certificates. How that can be said to be 'allowing money to remain unpaid,' when in effect all that is being considered is a section and regulation which extends the meaning of the 'borrowing,' I do not understand."

It should, however, be noted that Upjohn J. found as fact that "this [was] a genuine transaction; there [was] nothing colourable about it." If the issue of shares and, in particular, of debentures merely disguises the payment of a price which remains unpaid the position may well be different.

26–07 The Order further provides that where money is payable on demand or a fixed period after demand, it shall be deemed to be payable at the time when the arrangement of borrowing is made (art. 2 (2); this is important for the calculation of the six months' period under article 2 (1) (*a*).

Where money is borrowed in instalments it is thought that the money is actually borrowed on the date when the individual instalment in question is paid and not on the date when the agreement is made.

Money is deemed to be borrowed (or raised) in Great Britain, if it is made available in Great Britain or borrowed on the security of property in Great Britain (Act of 1946, s. 4 (3)).

Raising money by issue of shares or debentures

26–08 TRANSACTIONS COVERED BY ARTICLES 3 AND 4. Subject to the exemptions contained in the Order, and, in particular, the overall exemption in favour of all transactions, Treasury consent is required for the following transactions of a body corporate:

1. the raising of money in Great Britain by the issue, whether in Great Britain or elsewhere, of any shares in that body corporate (art. 3 (1));
2. the issue of partly paid shares, if either the body corporate is incorporated under the law of England or Scotland or the shares are or are to be registered in England or Scotland (art. 4 (1));
3. the issue of any securities by a body corporate under English or Scots law, if the purposes or effects of the transaction consist of or include:

"(*a*) the raising or borrowing of money outside Great Britain,[19] unless the borrowing is in the ordinary course of its business and is from a person carrying on a banking undertaking, and the money is made available in the scheduled territories[20]; or

(*b*) the exchanging or substituting of new securities for redeemable securities already issued by the body corporate, unless such new securities are not redeemable or are redeemable not earlier than the earliest date on which the securities already issued are redeemable." (Art. 4 (3).)

---

[19] Such a transaction may also require consent under the Exchange Control Act 1947; para. 26–24, *post*.

[20] As defined in the Exchange Control Act 1947, s. 1 (3). The scheduled territories are set out in note 35, *post*.

4. the issue of any securities by a body corporate not incorporated under English or Scots law which securities are or are to be registered in England or Scotland if the purposes or effects of the transaction consist of or include:

"(*a*) the raising or borrowing of money outside Great Britain; or
(*b*) the exchanging or substituting of new securities for redeemable securities already issued by the body corporate, unless such new securities are not redeemable or are redeemable not earlier than the earliest date on which the securities already issued are redeemable." (Art. 4 (4).)

26–09 RELATIONSHIP OF ARTICLES 3 AND 4. Articles 3 and 4 are separate provisions. A transaction may appear to be permissible without Treasury consent, by virtue of an exemption under article 3,[21] but may, nonetheless, be subject to restriction under article 4. Article 3 is primarily concerned with the raising of money by the issue of shares, and article 4 with the issue of shares or other securities, whether or not any money is to be raised: but although in any specific case the raising of the money may not give rise to the application of the restrictions imposed by the Order, the issue of the shares may, and vice versa.

26–10 UNIT TRUSTS. Subject to the exemptions contained in the Order, again including the overall exemption,[22] the consent of the Treasury is required for the raising of money in Great Britain for the purposes of a unit trust scheme by the issue of any unit (art. 7 (1) (*a*)), and further for the issue of units under a scheme providing for the raising of money abroad if either the scheme is governed by English or Scots law or the units are to be registered in England or Scotland (art. 7 (1) (*b*)).

Exemptions

26–11 It is intended to treat the exemptions admitted by the Order under four headings, *viz.*:

1. as regards borrowing;
2. as regards the raising of money by the issue of shares or debentures;
3. miscellaneous exemptions; and
4. the overall exemption.

26–12 AS REGARDS BORROWING. *From bankers.* Article 1 (which deals with borrowing[23]) provides in paragraph (2) that it shall not apply to:

"(*a*) borrowing by any person, other than a local authority, if the borrowing is in the ordinary course of his business and is from a person carrying on a banking undertaking."(Art. 1. (2) (*a*).)

---

[21] These exemptions are treated at paras. 26–17 and 26–18, *post*.
[22] See para. 26–21, *post*.
[23] See para. 26–06, *ante*.

26–13 Borrowing in the ordinary course of business will as a rule be comparatively simple to interpret, but occasions may arise when a company may borrow money for the purposes permitted by its memorandum of association which are not perhaps usual transactions carried on by the company. It will then be necessary to consider whether or not the business for which the money is borrowed can be said to be part of the ordinary business of the company.

For these purposes it must be remembered that a company may carry on a number of different businesses, which will all comprise its undertaking. For instance, a company which manages a rubber estate but which also uses its surplus cash for carrying on an investment business, will, it is thought, be able to borrow money for the latter purpose.

Where the borrowing is from a banker, it is irrelevant whether it is secured or unsecured or whether or not it is guaranteed.

26–14 *Unsecured loans not exceeding six months after demand.* Article 1 further states in paragraph (2) that it shall not apply to:

> "(*b*) borrowing by any person, other than a local authority, where the money borrowed is repayable on demand or not more than six months after demand and the loan is wholly unsecured of is secured only by a bill of exchange payable on demand or at a fixed period not exceeding six months after the date of the borrowing or after sight or by a promissory note payable not more than six months after the date of the borrowing." (Art. 1 (2) (*b*).)

A loan which is guaranteed, is for the purpose of this provision not an unsecured loan (art. 1 (3)). This would, *e.g.* apply where a director guarantees a loan granted to his company.

Consequently if the company borrows in excess of the overall exemption from a person who is not a banker, or if it borrows from a banker otherwise than in the ordinary course of its business, the exemption depends on two cumulative conditions, *viz.*:

1. that the loan is payable not later than six months after demand; and
2. that it is unsecured.

If either of these conditions is absent, Treasury consent is required.

26–15 *Moneys received by bankers.* They are exempt, whether or not any security is given, under the following provision:

> "(*d*) acceptance by a person carrying on a banking undertaking or a member of the London Discount Houses Committee of moneys to be placed to the credit of a current deposit account, whether or not any security is given." (Art. 1 (2) (*d*).)

26–16 *Borrowing by personal representative.* This, if done for the purpose of paying death duties, is likewise exempt:

> "(*e*) borrowing by the personal representative of a deceased person in his capacity as such for the purpose of paying death

duties payable by reason of the death of the deceased." (Art. 1 (2) (*e*).)

26–17 AS REGARDS THE RAISING OF MONEY BY THE ISSUE OF SHARES OR DEBENTURES

Subscription to the memorandum of association. The prohibition contained in article 3 against raising money by the issue of shares without consent of the Treasury does not apply to the subscription of a memorandum of association if the total amount of shares subscribed does not exceed £500. This is provided in paragraph 2 of that article which states:

"(2) This Article shall not apply to money raised by the issue of shares to the subscriber of a memorandum of association where the total consideration for the issue of all those shares issued to the said subscribers does not exceed five hundred pounds."

The purpose of this provision is to safeguard subscribers if the Treasury makes use of the enabling power in the Act and requires Treasury consent for the raising of any amount by the issue of shares. Since article 3 is subject to the overall exemption,[24] the special exemption in article 3 (2) is inoperative.

26–18 *Cash involved in purchase of an undertaking*. Treasury consent is further not required if a company, whether private or public, purchases an undertaking in a manner involving cash[25] and issues fully paid shares to the vendors of their nominees. The exemption is contained in article 3 (3):

"(3) This article shall not apply to money raised by the issue by a private company of shares to the vendors or the nominees of the vendors of any undertaking sold to the company if

(*a*) the shares are all fully paid; and

(*b*) the money raised is cash forming part of the assets of the undertaking or cash which has been paid to the vendors as, or as part of, the purchase price of the undertaking."

This exemption covers three cases:

1. where the company purchased for fully paid shares an undertaking the assets of which comprise cash[26];
2. *a fortiori*, where the company does so but the assets of the undertaking do not comprise cash; or
3. where the procedure adopted is for the vendors of the undertaking (or their nominees) to sell the undertaking to the company for cash and to apply that cash in acquiring the shares of the company. This is a common practice which avoids the necessity of filing a contract for

---

[24] See para. 26–21, *post*.

[25] If the purchase is not on a cash basis the transaction might fall under "borrowing"; see para. 26–06, *ante*.

[26] If the acquired undertaking is itself a company, the restrictions of ss. 42 to 44 of the Companies Act 1981 have to be borne in mind.

the allotment of shares (which contract would be subject to stamp duty) under section 52 (1) (*b*) of the 1948 Act.[27]

It should be noted that this exemption applies only if the purchaser is a private company. The vendor, or his nominee, may be a private or public company.

26–19 *Profit-sharing schemes*. Where under a profit sharing scheme shares are issued by means of a capitalisation of profits to the employees of the company who are entitled to participate in such a scheme, such an issue of shares does not require the consent of the Treasury, provided

(1) that the shares to be issued are fully paid;
(2) that not less than three-quarters of the total number of employees are entitled to participate in the scheme; and
(3) that the bonus shares are additional to the payment to the employees of wages at the standard rates in that industry.

This exemption is absolute and need not be aggregated with other conditional exemptions (art 10).

26–20 MISCELLANEOUS EXEMPTIONS. *Building societies and industrial and provident societies*. The Order of 1958 exempts from its operations these societies and any borrowing, raising of money or issue of securities by them (art. 9).

Transactions sanctioned in Northern Ireland. Transactions sanctioned by the Minister of Finance, Northern Ireland, under regulations made under the Borrowing (Control and Guarantees) (Northern Ireland) Act 1946, do not require the consent of the Treasury (art. 11).

26–21 THE OVERALL EXEMPTION. The overall exemption contained in articles 8 and 8A of the Order of 1958, as amended, has already been discussed.[28] It has further been explained in which cases the overall exemption does not apply or applies only in a qualified manner.[28]

Treasury consent

26–22 Where consent of the Treasury is still required, the application should be addressed in the first instance to the Bank of England, Threadneedle Street, London, E.C.2.

Effect of non-compliance

26–23 Non-compliance with the Act makes the offender liable to prosecution.[29] The transaction in question, and any security given under it, remains valid and the rights of the persons concerned in the transaction are not affected.[30]

---

[27] See *Spargo's Case* (1873) L.R. 8 Ch. 407. *Cf.* further *Escoigne Properties Ltd.* v. *I.R.C.* [1958] A.C. 549.
[28] See para. 26–04, *ante*.
[29] See Act of 1946, s. 1 (3) and Schedule.
[30] *Ibid.* s. 1 (3).

The Act is "highly penal,"[31] in so far as if the offence is committed by a company every person, who at the time of the commission of the offence was a director, secretary or similar officer of the company, is deemed to be guilty unless he proves that the offence was committed without his consent or connivance and that he exercised due diligence.[32] The traditional rule of English and Scots law that a man is innocent until proved guilty is thereby reversed.

Exchange control

26–24 Exchange control was abolished in the United Kingdom on October 24, 1979, except for transactions affecting Southern Rhodesia, and on December 13, 1979 with respect to Southern Rhodesia. This was done by statutory instruments[33] which were consolidated on December 6, 1979 into an instrument granting general exemption.[34] But the Exchange Control Act 1947 has been retained on the statute book and the Exchange Control (Scheduled Territories) Orders have not been revoked.[35]

In view of the complete abolition of exchange control in the United Kingdom, a treatment of this subject is not called for in this work.[36]

---

[31] *Per* Upjohn J. in *London & Country Commercial Properties Investments Ltd.* v. *Att.-Gen.* [1953] 1 W.L.R. 312, 319; and see *Re H. P. C. Productions Ltd.* [1962] Ch. 466.

[32] Act of 1946, Sched., para. 3 (4).

[33] Exchange Control (Revocation) Directions 1979 (S.I. 1979, No. 1339); Exchange Control (Revocation) (No. 2) Directions 1979 (S.I. 1979, No. 1662).

[34] Exchange Control (General Exemption) Order 1979 (S.I. 1979, No. 1660).

[35] The scheduled territories are: (1) the U.K., (2) the Channel Islands, (3) the Isle of Man, (4) the Republic of Ireland, and (5) Gibraltar (Exchange Control Act 1947, s. 1 (3) (*b*) and Sched. 1; Exchange Control (Scheduled Territories) (No. 2) Order 1972 (S.I. 1972, No. 930, amended by S.I. 1972, No. 2040)).

[36] For the exchange control regulation affecting securities before the abolition of exchange control in the U.K., see the 22nd edition of this work, Chap. 26.

Part Three

ACTIVITIES OF THE COMPANY

CHAPTER 27

CONTRACTS

Pre-incorporation contracts and provisional contracts

27–01 Although this chapter deals primarily with contracts made by a company which has full powers to contract, it is convenient to consider here also pre-incorporation and provisional contracts.

Pre-incorporation contracts are contracts purported to be made on behalf of an unformed company before its incorporation. Provisional contracts are contracts made by a public company between the grant of the certificate of incorporation and the grant of the trading certificate. In the former case a contract is attempted to be made for a company which is non-existent; in the latter case the contract is made by a company which does not have full capacity to contract.

Pre-incorporation contracts

27–02 IN COMMOM LAW. Before its incorporation a company has no capacity to contract. Consequently, in common law[1] nobody can contract for it as agent because an act which cannot be done by the principal himself cannot be done by him through an agent, nor can a pre-incorporation contract be ratified by the company after its incorporation.[2] There is, however, nothing to prevent the company when incorporated from entering into a new contract to put into effect the terms of the pre-incorporation contract.[3] This would be an act of novation. But the mere acting after incorporation on the preliminary contract does not in itself constitute sufficient evidence of the creation of a new contract.[4]

If a pre-incorporation contract is purported to be made by a company which does not exist, the contract is a nullity, and neither the company, when formed, nor the promoter whose signature is added can sue or be sued on the contract.[5] If, however, the promoter has contracted ostensibly as agent for the non-existent company, he may be made personally liable on the contract: in such a case the party with whom he has contracted can show that, though having contracted as agent, he is in fact the principal, for

---

[1] On the position under the European Communities Act 1972, s. 9 (2), see next section.
[2] *Kelner* v. *Baxter* (1867) L.R. 2 C.P. 174; *Natal Land and Colonisation Co.* v. *Pauline Syndicate* [1904] A.C. 120.
[3] *Touche* v. *Metropolitan Railway Warehousing Co.* (1871) 6 Ch.App. 671; *Howard* v. *Patent Ivory Manufacturing Co.* (1888) 38 Ch.D. 156; *James Young & Sons Ltd., etc.*, 1902, 10 S.L.T. 85.
[4] *Re Northumberland Avenue Hotel Co.* (1886) 33 Ch.D. 16; *Natal Land and Colonisation Co.* v. *Pauline Syndicate, supra.*
[5] *Newborne* v. *Sensolid (Great Britain) Ltd.* [1954] 1 Q.B. 45; *Tinnevelly Sugar Refining Co.* v. *Mirrlees, Watson & Yaryan Co.* 1894, 21 R. 1009, 2 S.L.T. 149; *Cummings and Ors.* v. *Quartzag Ltd.* 1981 S.L.T. 205.

it is only by holding him personally liable that any effect can be given to the contract.[6] Thus, Parker J. said in *Newborne's*[7] case on *Kelner* v. *Baxter*[8]:

> " . . . it is plain that this principle, that the agent is liable, is not based on breach of warranty of authority, because, as I have said, the principal is not in existence; it is not based on any question of estoppel; but it is based on this principle, that it is only by holding him personally liable that any effect can be given to the contract. In other words, it is permissible for the plaintiff seeking to hold the agent liable to show that that agent, though he has contracted as agent, is himself in fact the principal."

The common law position does not depend on the way in which the contract on behalf of the unformed company is made. It depends on the real intent, as revealed in the contract. Did the actor intend to make himself personally liable or was the intention that the unformed company should be the only person liable, in which case there was no contract? Oliver L.J. made this position clear in *Phonogram Ltd.* v. *Lane*,[8] when he said[9]:

> "The question I think in each case is what is the real intent as revealed in the contract? Does the contract purport to be one which is directly between the supposed principal and the other party, or does it purport to be one between the agent himself—albeit acting for the supposed principal—and the other party? In other words, what you have to look at is whether the agent intended himself to be a party to the contract."

27–03 EUROPEAN COMMUNITIES ACT, S. 9 (2). This provision deals with pre-incorporation contracts. It provides that such a contract, whether purported to be made by the company or on its behalf, shall, "subject to any agreement to the contrary . . . have effect as a contract entered into by the person purporting to act for the company or as agent for it, and he shall be personally liable on the contract accordingly."

This provision has swept away the subtle distinctions—wrongly—thought to exist in the common law and thought to depend on the form of signature by the purported agent, when acting for the unformed company. These distinctions were founded, in particular, on *Kelner* v. *Baxter*[10] and *Newborne* v. *Sensolid (Great Britain) Ltd*,[11] decisions which can now be regarded as overruled by section 9 (2), as interpreted in *Phonogram Ltd.* v. *Lane*.[8] In this case negotiations took place for the financing of a new pop group which was to be managed by a company to be called Fragile Management Ltd. Before the formation of this company, the plaintiffs Phonogram

---

[6] *Kelner* v. *Baxter* (1867) L.R. 2 C.P. 174; for an explanation of this case see *Newborne* v. *Sensolid (Great Britain) Ltd.* [1954] 1 Q.B. 45, 47. See further para. 27–03, *post*.
[7] [1954] 1 Q.B. 45, 51.
[8] [1981] 3 W.L.R. 736.
[9] *Ibid.*, p. 741.
[10] (1867) L.R. 2 C.P. 174.
[11] [1954] 1 Q.B. 45.

Ltd. paid £6,000 as initial payment for records to be produced by the pop group. The defendant Lane signed the contract in the following manner: "Signed by [Brian Lane] for and on behalf of Fragile Management Ltd." When the contract was made, all parties concerned were aware that that company was still unformed. In fact, Fragile Management Ltd. was never formed and the pop group never performed under it. Phonogram Ltd. sued Mr. Lane personally for the £6,000. The trial judge, Phillips J., found as a fact that the intention of the contracting parties was that Mr. Lane should not be personally liable under the contract. The Court of Appeal, which had to accept this finding of fact, unanimously held that Mr. Lane was personally liable by virtue of section 9 (2) of the 1972 Act. In the words of Lord Denning M.R., this provision "means that in all cases such as the present, where a person purports to contract on behalf of a company not yet formed, then however he expresses his signature, he himself is personally liable on the contract."

The meaning of the phrase "subject to any agreement to the contrary" in subsection (2) is apparently that the agent who purports to act for the unformed company and the other party may agree that the former shall not be personally liable. It is thought that in view of the wording of section 9 (2) such agreement must either be made expressly or must be capable of being clearly and unambiguously inferred from the other terms of the contract. The onus is on the agent who claims that he is not personally liable, and it is not an easy onus to discharge.

It is doubtful whether the phrase "subject to any agreement to the contrary" admits a change in the present law suggested by the Jenkins Report of 1962 (Cmnd. 1749, paras. 44 and 54 (*b*)), according to which the parties to a pre-incorporation contract may agree that the company, after its formation, may ratify the contract. The English courts would probably answer this question in the negative. It is regrettable that the U.K. legislature has not yet seen fit to introduce this change. Other common law jurisdictions admit the ratification of a pre-incorporation contract by the company after its formation. Thus, the Singapore Companies Act 1967, s. 35 (1), as amended, states:

> "Any contract or other transaction purporting to be entered into by a company prior to its formation or by any person on behalf of a company prior to its formation may be ratified by the company after its formation and thereupon the company shall become bound by and entitled to the benefit thereof as if it had been in existence at the date of the contract or other transaction had been party thereto."

This provision was applied by the Privy Council on appeal from Singapore in *Cosmic Insurance Corporation Ltd.* v. *Khoo Chiang Poh*, July 10, 1980, [1981], N.L.J., 286.

27–04 HOW TO MAKE PRE-INCORPORATION CONTRACTS BINDING. Promoters who wish to make a pre-incorporation contract immediately binding on the other party would therefore have to assume personal responsibility on the contract, but they may restrict this liability in a number of ways. First, as already observed, they may exclude their personal liability by agreement with the other party. Further, the promoter may obtain an option on the terms that the rights contained therein may be assigned to the future company and that the option shall lapse on a specified date if not exercised; or the promoters may enter into the contract as trustees for the future company subject to their being released from liability upon the company's entering into a new contract on similar terms. If it is not considered necessary to make the contract immediately binding, it may be prepared in draft form only, for execution by the company after its incorporation. It is usual to make express provision in the company's objects clause for the company to enter into an agreement in the terms of the preliminary contract.[12]

Provisional contracts

27–05 The 1948 Act provided that any contract made by a public company between its incorporation and the grant of its trading certificate "shall be provisional only, and shall not be binding on the company until [the] date [of the grant of the trading certificate], and on that date it shall become binding" (s. 109 (4)). This provision did not apply to private companies which were—and still are—entitled to commence business on incorporation and do not require a trading certificate. Consequently, the provision had no application where the normal procedure was followed whereby, if it is intended to form a public company, the company is first incorporated as a private company, and subsequently converted into a public company.[13] If the company never became entitled to commence business, provisional contracts never became binding on it and no one could sue in respect of them.[14]

27–06 The 1980 Act altered this position. Section 109 of the 1948 Act was repealed.[15] Under section 4 of the 1980 Act a company registered as a public company on its original incorporation will not be permitted to do business or exercise borrowing powers until the Registrar has issued it with a certificate to the effect that the new provisions on minimum capital have been complied with.[16] Criminal sanctions are imposed on companies and their officers for contravention of this provision,[17] but section 4 is stated to be "without prejudice to the validity of any transaction entered into by" the company.[18] If the company has entered into a transaction in breach of section 4 and fails to comply with its obligations thereunder, the directors are jointly and severally liable to indemnify the other party.[19]

---

[12] See Palmer's *Precedents* (17th ed.), Part 1, pp. 38, 205 *et seq*.
[13] See para. 19–07, *ante*.
[14] *Re "Otto" Electrical Manufacturing Co., Jenkins's Case* [1906] 2 Ch. 390; *Clinton's Claim* [1908] 2 Ch. 515.
[15] 1980 Act, s. 88 and Sched. 4.
[16] See para. 4–14, *ante*.
[17] s. 4 (7).
[18] s. 4 (8).
[19] *Ibid*.

It appears, therefore, that the 1980 Act has reversed the position as it was under the 1948 Act and that provisional contracts are now valid *ab initio*, provided that a trading certificate is never granted, the position is doubtful but it is thought that even in this case the provisional contract is valid.

Contracts made by a company having full capacity to contract

Power of company to contract

27–07 A company can, on principle, only do such acts as by its memorandum it is expressly or impliedly authorised to do. Any purported act which is not authorised is *ultra vires* the company. This rule is dealt with fully in an earlier chapter of this work.[20] For the purpose of this chapter it is sufficient to summarise the law briefly, at the risk of inacuracy,[21] by stating that any *ultra vires* contract which a company purports to enter into is wholly void and cannot be enforced,[21] subject always to the overriding provisions of the European Communities Act 1972, s. 9 (1), which have restricted the operation of the *ultra vires* doctrine.[22]

Authority to act on behalf of the company

27–08 The main question that is likely to arise is: who has authority to act as the agent of the company?[23] In many cases express authority will be found in the articles, as, for instance, authority given to the board of directors: but the articles may further empower the delegation of the directors' powers to committees, managers, managing directors, or other persons, and such delegation may be made either expressly, as where a manager is given specific powers by resolutions of the board, or by implication, as where an agent is permitted to exercise certain powers; or the agent may have ostensible authority to exercise such powers.[24] If the person dealing with the officer can show that the officer had ostensible authority, *e.g.* because the company held out that officer as having such authority, or that such authority was within the ordinary scope of his duties, the company will be bound even if the officer had been expressly forbidden to do such acts.[25] Moreover, an act by the directors or an officer in excess of their or his authority may be ratified by the competent body.[26]

According to the European Communities Act 1972, s. 9 (1), it is deemed in favour of a person dealing with the company in good faith that the powers of the directors shall be free of any limitation under the memorandum

---

[20] See para. 9–07, *ante*.
[21] For the full effect of such a purported contract see paras. 9–23 and 9–35, *ante*.
[22] See para. 9–25, *ante*.
[23] This question is discussed fully in Chap. 28, *post*.
[24] See para. 28–12, *post*.
[25] See *Freeman and Lockyer* v. *Buckhurst Park Properties (Mangal) Ltd.* [1964] 2 Q.B. 480 (C.A.) and cases discussed therein.
[26] *Bamford* v. *Bamford* [1970] Ch. 212 (C.A.). See also *Re Land Credit Company of Ireland* (1869) L.R. 4 Ch. 460, 469.

or articles or, it is submitted, under a resolution of the board of directors. The section likewise provides that the third party who deals with the company is not bound to inquire as to any limitation on the powers of the directors and shall be presumed to have acted in good faith unless the contrary is proved. This does not mean that every director is deemed, *virtute officii*, to be authorised to act on behalf of the company. The protection of section 9 (1) is only available if the director who purported to act for the company has actual or ostensible authority to act on behalf of the company[27] but his authority was limited. Further, the third party must have acted in good faith; it is thought that that means that he did not have actual notice of the limitation of authority; constructive notice is not sufficient. There may, however, be exceptional circumstances which are so unusual that the third party is put on inquiry and if he fails to inquire he cannot be said to have acted in good faith.

Form of contracts

27–09 Provided that the proposed contract is *intra vires*, a company can, in general, contract in the same form as an individual. Where, according to English law, the contract has to be under seal, the company's common seal has to be affixed (s. 32 (1) (*a*)). Where writing is required of an individual, the company by its agents may make the contract in writing signed by a person acting under its authority (s. 32 (1) (*b*)); and where an individual is capable of contracting orally, the company, acting by its duly authorised agents, may likewise do so (s. 32 (1) (*c*)).[28]

The 1948 Act provides further that "a contract made according to this section[29] may be varied or discharged in the same manner in which it is authorised by this section to be made" (s. 32 (3)).[30] This provision is permissive and not compulsory: it does not provide that the permitted mode of a variation or discharge is the only one admitted by the law. In equity a contract under seal can be varied or discharged by a simple contract and the rule of equity now prevails[31] over the old common law rule according to which a contract under seal could only be varied or discharged by another contract under seal. This likewise applies, it is thought, to contracts executed under the common seal of a company;

---

[27] See, as to manager, *Cartmell's Case* (1874) L.R. 9 Ch. 691; as to managing directors *Harold Holdsworth Ltd.* v. *Caddies* [1955] 1 W.L.R. 352, and para. 62–07, *post*; as to secretary, para. 67–06, *post*, and cases there cited.

[28] This provision took companies governed by the Act outside the former common law rule that unsealed contracts by corporations were unenforceable. The Corporate Bodies Contracts Act 1960 abrogated this rule and introduced a provision similar to s. 32 which applies to all other bodies corporate. The Corporate Bodies Contracts Act 1960 does not apply to Scotland, where no such common law rule applied. s. 31 (1) (*b*) and (*c*) applies to Scottish companies.

[29] This is a reference to s. 32 (1).

[30] s. 32 (3) applies to Scotland. The rest of this paragraph, however, refers to English law and has no relevance to Scots law. The general rule of Scots law is that any variation or discharge must be at least as formal as the original contract, and this subsection appears to be an exception to that rule.

[31] Judicature Act 1925, s. 44; *Steeds* v. *Steeds* (1889) 22 Q.B.D. 537; *Berry* v. *Berry* [1929] 2 K.B. 316.

section 32 (3) does not abrogate from these general principles of law and, consequently, a contract by a company made under its seal can be varied or discharged by a simple contract made by the duly authorised agents of the company.

Contracts under seal

27–10 REQUIREMENT AND USE OF SEAL. Every company incorporated under the Companies Acts has a seal,[32] upon which its name is engraven in legible letters (1948 Act, s. 108 (1) (*b*)).

The right to use the seal of the company for the purposes of its business is usually vested in the directors. Occasionally the power is vested in them by express words, but more usually their power arises from the terms of a general clause in the articles of the company enabling them to exercise all the powers of the company (see art. 80).[33]

IN ENGLAND. A company is not (as has already been pointed out) required to contract under seal in all circumstances, but where in the case of an individual a seal is requisite, it is requisite in the case of a company.

Thus, to convey freehold property, and to assign or surrender leasehold property, or to give a power of attorney, a seal is necessary. A seal is further required for some instruments in order to obtain certain statutory advantages, *e.g.* in the case of a certificate of title to shares (s. 81, amended, by section 2 of the Stock Exhange (Completion of Bargains) Act 1976; in the case of a share warrant (s. 83 (1)); and in the Law of Property Act 1925 various statutory incidents require the execution of a deed.

IN SCOTLAND. The concept of a "contract under seal" has no application in Scotland (although s. 81 and the amending provision apply). In Scots law the seal is the "signature" of the company[34] and must accordingly appear on all deeds, *i.e.* probative writings, executed by it. Deeds are required, *inter alia*, for the conveyance of land and other heritable property.

Section 32 (4), which appplies only to Scotland, provides:

> "A deed to which a company is a party shall be held to be validly executed according to the law of Scotland on behalf of the company if it is executed in accordance with the provisions of this Act or is sealed with the common seal of the company and subscribed on behalf of the company by two of the directors or by a director and the secretary of the company, and such subscription on behalf of the company shall be binding whether attested by witnesses or not."

It is clear that a deed which is sealed and signed by two directors, or one director and the secretary, is validly executed, notwithstanding any more

---

[32] To have a common seal is incidental to a corporation: *Sutton's Hospital Case* (1612) 10 Co.Rep. 1a, 23a, 30b. However, the requirement for a common seal in s. 13 (2) of the 1948 Act was repealed by the 1980 Act (s. 88 and Sched. 4).

[33] *Re Barned's Banking Co.* (1867) L.R. 3 Ch. 105, 116; see para. 27–12, *post*.

[34] *Clydeside Bank (Moore Place) Nominees Ltd.* v. *Snodgrass*, 1940 S.L.T. 46, 49.

elaborate formalities laid down in the articles or the normal requirement of Scots law that a deed must have two witnesses. The difficulty is, however, that the effect of the words "in accordance with the provisions of this Act" is obscure. It cannot refer to section 32 (1) since by definition that subsection refers to contracts where a deed is not called for. Possibly it may refer to sections 34 and 35 (execution of deeds abroad).

Section 34 (4) does not exclude other modes of execution, such as a seal and single signature. If these are employed, however, the protection of the Act is lost and there must be two witnesses. The party accepting a less formal manner of execution should also satisfy himself that the articles authorise it and, if a delegate of the directors signs, that proper authority has been given. If the company is in liquidation, only the liquidator may be presumed to have authority to act for the company, and his signature with two witnesses and the seal will constitute valid execution.[35] The same principle applies to a receiver in respect of the property under his control.[36]

Under the Conveyancing and Feudal Reform (Scotland) Act 1970, s. 44, after November 29, 1970, a deed requires to be executed only on the last page, and on the last page of any inventory, appendix, schedule or plan annexed.

27–11 REGULATIONS AS TO USE OF SEAL. Where the articles contain special provisions as to the affixing of the seal, *e.g.* that the instrument must also be signed by two directors, those who deal with the company are bound to see that the document on the face of it accords with the articles.

27–12 PRESUMPTION OF VALIDITY. If the instrument is on the face of it regular, persons dealing with the company have a right to presume that the seal so affixed has been duly affixed, that the directors were duly appointed and their signatures duly made,[37] and the burden of proving the contrary rests with those who allege it.[38] This is a corollary from the rule in *Royal British Bank* v. *Turquand*[39] and the European Communities Act 1972, s. 9 (1).

In *County of Gloucester Bank* v. *Rudry, etc., Co.*,[40] the seal had been irregularly affixed to an instrument, but the company was held bound by it, for the instrument appeared to be in accordance with the articles and the irregularity was only in regard to the "indoor" management, with which an outsider could not be acquainted.

---

35 *Liquidators of Style & Mantle Ltd.* v. *Prices' Tailors Ltd.*, 1934 S.C. 548.
36 Companies (Floating Charges and Receivers) (Scotland) Act 1972, s. 15 (1) (*i*).
37 *Re County Life Assurance Co.* (1870) L.R. 5 Ch. 288; *Mahony* v. *East Holyford Mining Co.* (1875) L.R. 7 H.L. 869.
38 *Clarke* v. *Imperial Gas, etc., Co.* (1832) 4 B. & Ad. 315; *Hill* v. *Manchester, etc., Co.* (1833) 5 B. & Ad. 866.
39 (1856) 6 E. & B. 327; see para. 28–10, *post*.
40 [1895] 1 Ch. 629.

In *Re Barned's Banking Co.*,[41] a company's regulations provided no formalities for the use of the seal but in practice it appeared that no resolution of the director was formally passed before the seal was applied. Accordingly, when it was attempted to show that the seal had been improperly affixed to a contract, in the absence of a formal authorisation, the court rejected this argument upon the finding that the persons in the position of directors had in fact approved the application of the company's seal.

On the other hand, it has been held in *Ruben* v. *Great Fingall Consolidated*[42] that if the seal is affixed fraudulently by the secretary for his own private ends, the company is not estopped. The court refused to accept the argument that the secretary was authorised, merely by the fact that in the course of his employment he handed out the share certificate concerned upon which the seal was affixed, to represent or warrant that the certificate was genuine. A stockbroker who requests the registration of a share transfer which a company is under a duty to effect, thereby impliedly warrants to the company that the transfer deeds are genuine, even if, without the knowledge of the stockbroker who throughout acted in good faith, the share certificates were stolen.[42a]

Where the presumption of validity does not apply, as in the case of a non-trading corporation, an investment to which the seal was affixed, to represent or warrant that the certificate was genuine. In this case an instrument to which the seal has been irregularly affixed is inoperative.[43]

27–13 VALIDITY OF SEAL ON DEED. The Law of Property Act 1925, s. 74,[44] contains a further provision for the validity of the seal of a company affixed to a deed.[45] It provides that in favour of a purchaser a deed shall be deemed to have been duly executed by a company if its seal is affixed thereto in the presence of and attested by its clerk, secretary or other permanent officer or his deputy, and a member of the board of directors, council or other governing body. This provision overrides any provision in the articles that the seal must be affixed, *e.g.* in the presence of two directors: it only applies in favour of the purchaser, so that the company itself cannot invoke the doctrine against such a person. The section further provides that where a seal purporting to be the company's seal has been affixed to a deed and attested by persons purporting to hold any of the above-named offices, the deed shall be deemed to have been executed in

---

[41] (1867) L.R. 3 Ch. 105.
[42] [1906] A.C. 439; see para. 37–08, *post*.
[42a] *Yeung* v. *Hong Kong and Shanghai Banking Corp.* [1980] 2 All E.R. 599 (P.C.).
[43] *Bank of Ireland* v. *Evans's Trustees* (1855) 5 H.L.C. 389; *Mayor of the Staple* v. *Bank of England* (1887) 21 Q.B.D. 160; and see *London Freehold Land Co.* v. *Suffield* [1897] 2 Ch. 608.
[44] The Law of Property Act 1925 does not apply to Scotland, and this paragraph is relevant to England only. For the Scottish position, see s. 32 (4) and para. 27–10, *ante*.
[45] A share certificate is not a deed: *South London Greyhound Racecourses Ltd.* v. *Wake* [1931] 1 Ch. 496.

accordance with the requirements of the section and to have taken effect accordingly.

27–14 DELIVERY OF DEED: PRESUMED IN THE CASE OF A CORPORATION.[46] A deed to be effective must be sealed and delivered; but, in the case of a corporation, the affixing of the seal imports delivery.[47] Accordingly, whilst in the case of a private individual it is usual to add an attestation clause to the effect that the instrument was "signed, sealed and delivered" in the presence of the witness, in the case of a company the clause merely states that "the common seal was affixed hereto in the presence of —— and ——."

Prima facie, therefore, if the common seal is duly affixed to a deed it becomes operative.[48] This, however, is merely a presumption, and those who allege that the affixing of the seal does not import delivery of the deed are at liberty to establish that fact.

27–15 ESCROWS.[49] Although normally delivery is not required of a deed executed by a corporation, the corporation can execute a deed in escrow, *i.e.* can seal it subject to a condition suspending its efficacy. In *Xenos* v. *Wickham*[50] Lord Cranworth said:

> "The efficacy of a deed depends on its being sealed and delivered by the maker of it, not on his ceasing to retain possession of it. This, as a general proposition of law, cannot be controverted. It is not affected by the circumstances that the maker may so deliver it as to suspend or qualify its binding effect. He may declare that it shall have no affect until a certain time has arrived, or until some condition has been performed; but when the time has arrived, or the condition has been performed, the delivery becomes absolute, and the maker of the deed is absolutely bound by it, whether he has parted with the possession or not. Until the specified time has arrived, or the condition has been performed, the instrument is not a deed. It is a mere escrow. . . . I know of nothing intermediate between a deed and an escrow."

Whether a document sealed by a company is or is not intended to operate as a complete and operative instrument, or as an escrow, depends on the intention of the parties as expressed or implied, when the document is executed. In *Derby Canal Co.* v. *Wilmot*,[51] where the company's seal was affixed to a conveyance, but the clerk was directed to retain it until certain accounts were adjusted, the court held[52] that,

> "in order to give effect, the affixing of the seal must be done with intent to pass the estate; otherwise it operates no more than a

[46] This section has no application in Scotland. Delivery is normally required to make a contract effective, but is provable by facts and circumstances and is not presumed merely by the fact of sealing.
[47] Rol.Abr.Faits. 23 (I) 50; Comyns' *Digest*, Fact A (3).
[48] *London Freehold, etc., Co.* v. *Suffield* [1897] 2 Ch. 608.
[49] Escrows do not exist in Scots law, and this section does not apply to Scotland.
[50] (1866–67) L.R. 2 H.L. 296, 323, 324.
[51] (1808) 9 East 360.
[52] At p. 361.

feoffment would do without livery of seisin; whereas here, though the seal was directed to be and was affixed to the instrument for form, yet it was with a reservation of any present effect to pass the title out of the company, as they do not choose to deliver over the possession of the conveyance till the accounts were settled between them and the purchaser."

So, too, in *Mowatt* v. *Castle Steel, etc., Co.*,[53] the court found as a fact that debentures to bearer sealed by the company had not in fact been delivered, and held them void in consequence.

The onus of proving that a deed duly sealed was only executed in escrow rests with those who so assert.[54]

27–16 WHETHER SEALED DOCUMENT A DEED.[55] A document to which the seal is affixed is not necessarily a deed; thus a certificate of title to shares is not a deed[56]; but it would seem that every *contract* under the seal is a deed, save only that, by the Bills of Exchange Act 1882, s. 91, a corporation is empowered to seal, instead of signing, acceptances, indorsements and the like.[57]

27–17 SEAL FOR USE ABROAD. Besides its common seal, a company may under section 35 obtain power to have an official seal for use abroad and under section 34 it can authorise any person as the attorney of the company to execute under his seal deeds outside the United Kingdom.

27–18 POWERS OF ATTORNEY

Appointment of attorneys. Articles sometimes give the directors express power to appoint attorneys (see art. 81). Even if no such express power is given the directors may appoint attorneys for the purposes of the company's business under the article which delegates to them the general management of the company (see art. 80), but an express power is desirable in the articles in order to avoid any doubts which might arise by reason of the principle expressed by the maxim *delegatus non potest delegare*. Powers of attorney are governed by the Powers of Attorney Act 1971[58] with respect to their execution and effect.

Section 34 of the 1948 Act expressly authorises a company to appoint attorneys to execute deeds on its behalf outside the United Kingdom. The appointment has to be made under the company's common seal and may

---

[53] (1886) 34 Ch.D. 58.

[54] *Roberts* v. *Security Co.* [1897] 1 Q.B. 111, and *London Freehold, etc., Co.* v. *Suffield* [1897] 2 Ch. 608.

[55] The Bills of Exchange Act 1882, s. 91, applies to Scotland, but the rest of this paragraph is English law. However, a document sealed and executed under s. 32 (4) (see para 27–10, *ante*), will be a deed or probative writing in Scots law.

[56] *Reg.* v. *Morton* (1873) L.R. 2 C.C.R. 22; *South London Greyhound Racecourses Ltd.* v. *Wake* [1931] 1 Ch. 496, 503.

[57] See para. 27–22, *post*.

[58] The Powers of Attorney Act 1971 does not apply to Scotland, except s. 3 (proof of instruments creating powers of attorney) which does apply to Scotland.

be a general or special power of attorney (s. 34 (1)). A deed signed by such attorney on behalf of the company and under his seal shall bind the company and have the same effect as if it were under the company's own seal (s. 34 (2)).

Section 7 of the Powers of Attorney Act 1971 provides that the donee of a power of attorney may execute and do any assurance, instrument or thing in and with his own name and signature, and under his own seal where sealing is required, in the name of the donor of the power. Sections 5 and 6 of that Act contain provisions protecting persons acting thereunder. Before the commencement of the 1971 Act (October 1, 1971) a power of attorney could be deposited in the Central Office of the Supreme Court of Judicature under section 219 of the Judicature Act 1925; after the commencement of the 1971 Act it is no longer possible to deposit powers of attorney at the Central Office.

27–19 *Strict construction*. Powers of attorney are strictly construed, so that where, *e.g.* a power of attorney is given to act prior to the happening of some contingency it may be necessary to prove that the contingency has not happened[59]; and the operation of a power of attorney may be cut down with reference to what appears to have been the purpose for which it was executed.[60]

27–20 *Third parties on inquiry*. Prima facie, those who deal with a person acting under, or purporting to act under, a power of attorney are bound to inquire into the authenticity of the power unless the power is a general power of attorney made in the form set out in the 1971 Act or expressed to be made under that Act; in that case the donee of the power has, by virtue of section 10 (1) of the Act, power to do on behalf of the donor anything which the donor himself can lawfully do by an attorney.[61] Where the agent is acting under a written authority, and what he does comes within the terms of that authority, the principal cannot repudiate on the ground that the agent acted in his own interests and not in those of the principal, unless the other party was aware of the facts.[62] Where the agent has powers exercisable in special circumstances, a person dealing with him need not inquire whether those special circumstances have arisen, provided that that person acted bona fide and had no notice of any matter which would put him on inquiry.[63]

Stamp. A power of attorney requires a 50p stamp,[64] except in certain cases for the receipt of money.

---

[59] *Danby* v. *Coutts & Co.* (1885) 29 Ch.D. 500.

[60] *Attwood* v. *Munnings* (1827) 7 B. & C. 278; *Jonmenjoy Coondoo* v. *Watson* (1884) 9 App.Cas. 561; *Jacobs* v. *Morris* [1902] 1 Ch. 816; *Hambro* v. *Burnand* [1904] 2 K.B. 10.

[61] *De Bouchout* v. *Goldsmid* (1800) 5 Ves. 210; *Earl of Sheffield* v. *London Joint Stock Bank Ltd.* (1888) 13 App.Cas. 333; *Bryant, Powis and Bryant* v. *La Banque de Peuple* [1893] A.C. 170.

[62] *Hambro* v. *Burnand* [1904] 2 K.B. 10.

[63] *Montaignac* v. *Shitta* (1890) 15 App.Cas 357.

[64] Stamp Act 1891, Sched. I.

Contracts in writing

27–21 IN GENERAL. A company, being an artificial person, can contract in writing only through its agents. The normal form is for the company to be made a party by its corporate name, the contract being signed by the agents on behalf of the company. No personal liability under the contract attaches in principle to the agents where they sign "on behalf" of the company.[65]

Care must be taken to show on the face of the contract that the person who signs it is acting for, or on account or on behalf of, the company by inserting words to that effect in the description of the parties, or in the body of the agreement, or in connection with the signature. Any of these places will do.[66] If the words "for the —— Company Ltd." are written or printed immediately above or below or opposite the signature that is sufficient.

Where, however, the words showing that the person who signs is signing for or on behalf of the company are omitted, it will nevertheless be the company and not the person so signing who can sue and be sued on the contract if the intention is clear that the signature shall only be that of the company.[67]

For the purposes of the Moneylenders Act 1927, repealed by the Consumer Credit Act 1974, it was held that a memorandum signed by a director and secretary "for and on behalf of" the company was "signed personally by the borrower."[68]

27–22 BILLS OF EXCHANGE, CHEQUES AND PROMISSORY NOTES.[69] Particulary important examples of contracts in writing are the contracts contained in bills of exchange, cheques and promissory notes, although, as we shall see, these may be under the seal of the company.

Whether a company can make, accept, indorse, or issue bills of exchange, promissory notes, and other negotiable instruments depends on its objects; it cannot issue such instruments unless it has an express or implied power given to it by its memorandum. In the case of a trading company there is an implied power to accept and issue bills and notes as there is to borrow—business convenience requires it—and there are other commercial concerns which may also have implied power.[70] But usually the memorandum of association contains express power. The following are instances in which it has been held that companies had no such implied power, and illustrate the inconvenience of relying on an implied power: a

---

[65] *Gadd* v. *Houghton* (1876) 1 Ex.D. 357; and see paras. 65–01 *et seq., post*; see also *Newborne* v. *Sensolid (Great Britain) Ltd.* [1954] 1 Q.B. 45.

[66] See *Gadd* v. *Houghton* (1876) 1 Ex.D. 357.

[67] See the judgments in *Chapman* v. *Smethurst* [1909] 1 K.B. 927, and *Newborne* v. *Sensolid (Great Britain) Ltd.* [1954] 1 Q.B. 45. *Cf. The Swan* [1968] 1 Lloyd's Rep. 5, 13.

[68] *Re British Games* [1938] Ch. 240.

[69] This section applies equally to Scotland.

[70] *Re Peruvian Ry.* (1867) L.R. 2 Ch. 617, 623.

gas company[71]; a mining company[72]; a cemetery company[73]; a railway company.[74]

Section 33 of the 1948 Act enacts that a bill of exchange[75] or promissory note shall be deemed to have been made, accepted, or indorsed on behalf of a company if made, accepted, or indorsed in the name or by or on behalf or on account of the company, by any person acting under its authority. Alternatively, section 91 (2) of the Bills of Exchange Act 1882, provides that "in the case of a corporation where . . . any instrument in writing is required to be signed, it is sufficient if the instrument in writing be sealed with the corporate seal." Accordingly, if preferred, a bill may be in that form.

27–23 *Danger of omitting the word "Limited," or not stating the name correctly.* In relation to bills of exchange and promissory notes the provisions of section 108 (1) (*c*) of the 1948 Act must be borne in mind. The true name of the company must appear, and, in particular, the word "Limited" must not be omitted. Any breach of this enactment involves heavy penalties, and, what is more, may impose personal liability on the directors. The personal liability of the directors may arise under subsection 4 (*b*) of section 108. The numerous cases decided under section 108 (4) are considered in para. 7–04 *ante.* It is only necessary to add that the word "Public" should not be omitted in relation to the public limited company after Part I of the 1980 Act was brought into operation on December 22, 1980.

In Scotland it appears that the personal liability of an officer who signs a bill which does not correctly state the name of the company is strict. In *Scottish & Newcastle Breweries Ltd.* v. *Blair*,[76] the court rejected an attempt to put forward a defence of personal bar on the grounds that (a) the holder of the bill was not in fact misled by the incorrect name, or (b) the holder had sent the bill for acceptance in circumstances which suggested that he would treat it as properly signed on behalf of the company notwithstanding the wrong name, or (c) the holder had himself inscribed the incorrect name. This contrasts unfavourably with the English court's view that in such circumstances a plea of estoppel would be available.[77]

27–24 *Danger of signing without addition of "for the company."* It has already been indicated[78] that care has to be taken to indicate that the person who signs a document does so "for," "on account of," or "on behalf of" the company. The importance of adding to the signature an indication that the signatory signs as agent or representative of the company is particularly great in the case of negotiable instruments because, as far as persons who

---

[71] *Bramah* v. *Roberts* (1837) 3 Bing.N.C. 963.
[72] *Dickinson* v. *Valpy* (1829) 10 B. & C. 128.
[73] *Steele* v. *Harmer* (1845) 14 M. & W. 831.
[74] *Bateman* v. *Mid-Wales Ry.* (1866) L.R. 1 C.P. 499.
[75] This term includes cheques. A cheque is a bill of exchange drawn on a banker and payable on demand (Bills of Exchange Act 1882, s. 73).
[76] 1967 S.L.T. 72.
[77] *Durham Fancy Goods Ltd.* v. *Michael Jackson (Fancy Goods) Ltd.* [1968] 2 Q.B. 839.
[78] See para. 27–21, *ante*.

do not know of his representative character are concerned, the agent or representative is only free from personal liability if his intention to sign as such is stated on the instrument or otherwise is necessarily implied, *e.g.* as a matter of construction from the context in which the signature appears. In this connection section 26 of the Bills of Exchange Act 1882 provides:

> "(1) Where a person signs a bill as drawer, indorser, or acceptor, and adds words to his signature, indicating that he signs for or on behalf of a principal, or in a representative character, he is not personally liable thereon; but the mere addition to his signature of words describing him as agent, or as filling a representative character, does not exempt him from personal liability.
>
> "(2) In determining whether a signature on a bill is that of the principal or that of the agent by whose hand it is written, the construction most favourable to the validity of the instrument shall be adopted."

A note in the form "We, the directors of the A Company Limited, promise to pay," etc., signed by the chairman and three other directors, with the seal of the company in the corner, was held to bind the directors personally.[79] A bill accepted in the form "H. I. and R. M., Directors, Fashions Fair Exhibition Ltd.," and indorsed at the request of the plaintiff by the directors, "Fashions Fair Exhibition Ltd.: H. I. and R. M. Directors," was held in the circumstances to render the directors liable as indorsers.[80] In *Maxform S.p.A.* v. *Mariani and Goodville Ltd.*[81] it was held that where the drawee company was described by its trade name and not by its registered company name and the sole director accepted the bill without addition to his signature, he was personally liable by virtue of section 108 (4) of the 1948 Act. But where a promissory note was framed: "I, —, promise to pay to Mr. C. the sum of £300, J. H. S., etc., Ltd., J. H. S., Managing Director," it was held that J. H. S. was not personally liable,[82] notwithstanding the use of the word "I."

Where a managing director signed a bill on behalf of the company without any authority to do so, it was held that the company was bound to a person taking the bill in due course,[83] because the power might properly have been delegated to him.[84]

27–25 REGULATED AGREEMENTS UNDER THE CONSUMER CREDIT ACT 1974. If a company is the creditor under a consumer credit agreement, where the total purchase price does not exceed £5,000, the agreement must be in

---

79 *Dutton* v. *Marsh* (1871) L.R. 6 Q.B. 361.

80 *Elliott* v. *Bax Ironside* [1925] 2 K.B. 301; *Brebner* v. *Henderson* 1925 S.C. 643; *The Swan* [1968] 1 Lloyd's Rep. 5, 13.

81 [1981] 2 Lloyd's Rep. 54.

82 *Chapman* v. *Smethurst* [1909] 1 K.B. 927 (C.A.), reversing [1909] 1 K.B. 73; see also *Newborne* v. *Sensolid (Great Britain) Ltd.* [1954] 1 Q.B. 45.

83 *Dey* v. *Pullinger Engineering Co.* [1921] 1 K.B. 77; dissenting from *Premier Industrial Bank* v. *Carlton Co.* [1909] 1 K.B. 106.

84 See para. 28–10, *post*, where this principle is discussed.

writing and the company will only be able to enforce the agreement if the provisions of the Consumer Credit Act 1974 as to its form are complied with. This Act does not apply if a body corporate is the debtor, and in such a case the agreement need not be in any particular form, although in practice the terms will be reduced to writing for the sake of convenience.[85]

Oral contracts

27–26 IN GENERAL. Where it is desired to make an oral agreement, the person who is to make it on behalf of the company must have an express or implied authority, and then a contract made by word of mouth between him and the other party will bind the company.

27–27 EVIDENCE BY A NOTE OR MEMORANDUM IN WRITING.[86] The statutory provisions under which an agreement is not enforceable by action unless it can be proved by a note or memorandum in writing signed by the party to be charged likewise apply to companies. Such evidence is required for action brought upon:

(1) guarantees (under the Statute of Frauds 1677, s. 4, as amended by the Law Reform (Enforcement of Contracts) Act 1954, s. 1); and,
(2) contracts for the sale or other disposition of land or any interest in land (Law of Property Act 1925, s. 40).

A proposal in writing accepted orally may be a sufficient memorandum for this purpose as against the proposer.[87] The same applies to a letter from the company to its own solicitor mentioning the terms of the contract made,[88] or a letter by an agent of the person sought to be charged.[89] A record of the terms of the contract in the minutes signed by the chairman may also suffice,[90] or part performance unequivocally referable to the contract.[91] "The court," as Bowen L.J. said,[92] "is not in quest of the intention of the parties, but only of evidence under the hand of one of the parties to the contract that he has entered into it."

If in the memorandum evidencing the contract the name of the company is incorrectly stated, but the company can clearly be identified by reference to characteristics other than its name, the company can properly be regarded as a party to the contract and can enforce it accordingly.[93]

---

[85] Consumer Credit Act 1974, s. 8 (1).
[86] The Acts of 1677, 1925 and 1954 referred to in this section and the case law deriving from them do not apply to Scotland. Only the provisions of the Moneylenders Act 1927 are relevant in Scots law.
[87] *Reuss* v. *Picksley* (1866) L.R. 1 Ex. 342.
[88] See *Gibson* v. *Holland* (1865) L.R. 1 C.P. 1.
[89] *Bailey* v. *Sweeting* (1861) 9 C.B.(N.S.) 843.
[90] See *Jones* v. *Victoria Graving Dock* (1877) 2 Q.B.D. 314; *Re Queensland, etc., Co.* [1894] 3 Ch. 181.
[91] *Wilson* v. *West Hartlepool Ry.* (1865) 2 De G.J. & S. 475, 492; *Howard* v. *Patent Ivory Co.* (1888) 38 Ch.D. 156, 163.
[92] *Hoyle* v. *Hoyle*[1893] 1 Ch. 99.
[93] *F. Goldsmith (Sicklesmere) Ltd.* v. *Baxter* [1970] Ch. 85.

Chapter 28

THE DOCTRINE OF NOTICE. UNAUTHORISED ACTIVITIES OF THE COMPANY'S AGENTS

Constructive notice

The doctrine of constructive notice

28–01 This doctrine was once of considerable significance in company law. Its essence was that, since the memorandum and articles are public documents and open to public inspection on payment of a small fee (1948 Act, s. 426), anyone, whether a shareholder or an outsider, who had dealings with the company, had to be taken to have notice of the contents of those documents, whether he had read them or not. If applied to its logical conclusion, the doctrine would have been unworkable and would have led to patently unjust results. It was, therefore, mitigated by the rule in *Royal British Bank* v. *Turquand*[1] which provided that third parties who had dealings with the company need not inquire into the regularity of the indoor management but could assume that its requirements had been complied with. The rule in *Turquand's* case was again subject to exceptions. Even this solution would have been unacceptable in modern circumstances, had the courts not established the principle that a director or other officer could bind the company if he had ostensible or apparent authority, even though the board of directors had not endowed him with actual authority. By this circuitous route English and Scottish company law developed a pattern of legal rules which were acceptable to modern practice and worked, on the whole, satisfactorily.

The introduction of the European Communities Act 1972 has altered this situation. As far as the powers of the board of directors to bind the company are concerned, the doctrine of constructive notice has been practically abolished by section 9 (1) of that Act. This change in the theoretical basis has not, however, resulted in a fundamental change in practice. It has only confirmed and extended the rule in *Turquand's* case. But section 9 (1) deals only with the problem of primary delegation, *viz.* the authority given by the company to the board of directors to act on its behalf; it does not deal with the problem of secondary delegation, *viz.* the delegation of authority from the board of directors to the individual director or secretary, who acts *viz-à-viz* the third party. Here the principles of actual and ostensible authority developed by the courts still apply and provide a considerable degree of protection for the third party.

In order to understand the situation as it exists today, it is necessary to explain the operation of the doctrine of constructive notice, as it existed

[1] (1856) 6 E. & B. 327; see para. 28–10, *post.*

before the commencement of the European Communities Act 1972 (January 1, 1973), and to treat the provisions of section 9 (1) against that background.

Companies registered under the Companies Acts

28–02 The doctrine of constructive notice of the memorandum and articles as public documents was explained by Lord Hatherley in *Mahony* v. *East Holyford Mining Co.*[2] as follows:

> 'Every joint stock company has its memorandum and articles of association . . . open to all who are minded to have any dealings whatsoever with the company, and those who so deal with them must be affected with notice of all that is contained in those two documents."

Persons dealing with the company must be taken not only to have read those documents but to have understood them according to their proper meaning.[3]

Special resolutions, if duly registered in accordance with section 143, likewise become public documents, so that an outsider is on notice of their contents in the same way as he is of the articles of association.[4] The same would appear to apply to other resolutions required to be registered under section 143 of the 1948 Act.

It would further appear that charges on the undertaking of the company or on specific property belonging to it, if registered according to section 95, are likewise public documents, but this applies only to the registered particulars and not to "special provisions contained in that charge restricting the company from dealing with their property in the usual manner when the subsisting charge is a floating security."[5]

Beyond this no guidance can be obtained from decided cases on what are public documents of registered companies for the purposes of the doctrine of constructive notice. It is thought that not all documents which a company has to register fall within that category. A distinction has to be drawn between documents affecting the powers of the company and its agents and other documents. Only documents which fall into the former category are public documents, *e.g.* the other resolutions—other than special resolu-

---

[2] (1875) L.R. 7 H.L. 869, 893. This principle was already recognised in regard to registered companies before the Companies Act 1862: see *Ernest* v. *Nicholls* (1857) 6 H.L.Cas. 401.

[3] *Griffith* v. *Paget (No. 2)* (1877) 6 Ch.D. 517; *Oakbank Oil Co.* v. *Crum* (1882) 8 App.Cas. 65, 71; *Marshall* v. *Glamorgan Iron and Coal Co.* (1868) L.R. 7 Eq. 129; *Re Barrow Haematite Steel Co.* (1888) 39 Ch.D. 582; *Re Argus Life Assurance Co.* (1888) 39 Ch.D. 571; *County of Gloucester Bank* v. *Rudry, etc., Co.* [1895] 1 Ch. 629; *Owen and Ashworth's Claim* [1901] 1 Ch. 115.

[4] *Irvine* v. *Union Bank of Australia* (1877) 2 App. Cas. 366.

[5] *Per* Eve J., *obiter*, in *Wilson* v. *Kelland* [1910] 2 Ch. 306, 313; and see Kekewich J. in *Re Standard Rotary Machine Co.* (1906) 95 L.T. 829, 834. These comments are presumably equally true of charges registered by Scottish companies under s. 106A. The degree of reliance which the public might place on the Register maintained by the Registrar of Companies in Scotland is qualified by the extent to which it may be out of date or fail to disclose such information as a change of creditor—see para. 47–17, *post*.

tions—requiring registration under section 143 and particulars relating to the directors (see s. 200), but documents falling within the second category, such as balance-sheets or entries in the register of directors' interests (see s. 29 of the 1967 Act), are not, it is thought, "public documents" for the purposes of the doctrine of constructive notice, because their purpose is merely to provide information of the financial position of the company or the interest of its managers in the company.

Statutory and chartered companies

28–03 In the case of a statutory company the special Act of Parliament under which the company is incorporated, and in that of a chartered company the Royal Charter creating it, are public documents because these documents which define the powers of those companies are publicly obtainable.

More difficult is the position with respect to the by-laws of these companies. It was held by the Judicial Committee of the Privy Council in *Montreal & St. Lawrence Light & Power Co.* v. *Robert*[6] that the by-laws of a statutory company were not "public property." This decision, however, it is thought, does not go further than to lay down that if the by-laws of such companies are not made public they are not public documents. Where such by-laws are made public, as, *e.g.* the by-laws of public corporations carrying on nationalised undertakings, there is no reason to deny them the quality of public documents. The test, it is believed, is whether the by-laws are made public or not.

Effect of constructive notice

Acts ultra vires the company

28–04 The powers of a company are, as has already been pointed out,[7] limited to those derived expressly or impliedly from its memorandum of association. Under the law as it stood before the coming into operation of section 9 (1) of the European Communities Act 1972, by the operation of the doctrine of constructive notice every person dealing with the company was treated as having knowledge of the contents of the memorandum. Section 9 (1) of that Act provides, as has been seen,[8] that the company cannot plead that it has acted *ultra vires* against a person who dealt with it in good faith, provided that the transaction was decided upon by the board of directors.

Acts outside the authority of the directors

28–05 A company, being an artificial person, can only act through agents. The agents will normally be the directors or executive employees of the company, and their powers are conferred either directly by the company's

6 [1906] A.C. 196, 203.
7 See para. 9–04, *ante*.
8 See para. 9–25, *ante*.

articles of association or by an authority under the articles. An example of the former is found in the normal provision of the articles whereby the directors are empowered to borrow money upon the security of the company's assets, subject, perhaps, to certain limits (see art. 79). An example of the latter occurs in the usual article empowering the directors to appoint a managing director and delegate certain powers to him (see art. 107).

28–06 BEFORE THE EUROPEAN COMMUNITIES ACT 1972. Where an act was *intra vires* the company but outside the authority of the directors (or other agents) two possibilities existed before the coming into operation of the European Communities Act 1972. The lack of authority might have been evident from the public documents of the company, in which case the doctrine of constructive notice applied without mitigation. The person dealing with the directors was fixed with notice of the directors' powers and of any limitations and restrictions thereon imposed by the articles or other regulations, and could not hold the company bound by the directors' act. This was, for example, the case if the directors gave security on a loan in excess of their specified borrowing powers, or a single director signed a bill of exchange which, by the articles, required the signature of two directors. So, too, if the articles provided that the seal of the company was to be affixed in the presence of two directors, who were to sign their names, a person dealing with the company must see that this was done.[9]

On the other hand, there might have been cases in which the lack of authority of the directors was not evident from the public documents, *e.g.* where the articles required the directors to obtain the consent of the members by ordinary resolution before exercising their specified borrowing powers or where the powers of the board of directors might be delegated by a resolution of the board to a managing director or a committee. In these cases a person dealing with the company could not gather from the public documents that a director had exceeded his authority. If such a person honestly and without reason for suspicion thought that the director with whom he negotiated was authorised to act for the company, the company was normally bound by the director's act under the rule in *Royal British Bank* v. *Turquand*,[10] which is considered in detail below.

AFTER THE EUROPEAN COMMUNITIES ACT 1972. After the coming into operation of this Act of January 1, 1973, the position is simplified. The doctrine of constructive notice, which required the adoption of the dichotomy in the old law no longer applies if the third party has acted in good faith. This will be explained in the next section.

[9] In the case of a deed this obligation is to some extent lightened by s. 74 of the Law of Property Act 1925: see para. 27–13, *ante*. The 1975 Act, however, does not apply to Scotland.

[10] (1856) 6 E. & B. 327: see para. 28–10, *post*.

Constructive notice does not operate against a person acting in good faith

28–07 The European Communities Act 1972, s. 9 (1), provides in favour of a person dealing with the company in good faith that "the power of the directors to bind the company shall be deemed to be free of any limitation under the memorandum or articles of association; and a party to a transaction [decided on by the directors] shall not be bound to enquire as to . . . any such limitation on the powers of the directors and shall be presumed to have acted in good faith unless the contrary is proved."

This provision makes it clear that the rule in *Royal British Bank* v. *Turquand*[10] is not inapplicable on the ground that the third party must be deemed to have constructive notice of any defect in the powers of the directors, *e.g.* because a restriction of these powers was contained in the articles. If the third party was in good faith and did not have actual notice of such a restriction he is protected. The onus of proving that he did not act in good faith falls on the company.[11] It is thought that if a director has dealings with the company *qua* third party, he will normally be put on inquiry and the onus of proving that he did not act in good faith may be relatively easy for the company to discharge.

The subsection protects the third party only if the board of directors, as such, has acted beyond its powers[12] but, if read in conjunction with the words of the subsection restricting the *ultra vires* doctrine,[13] it may protect him even if the unauthorised act of the board is *ultra vires* the company. The argument that the subsection also applies if one of the directors, but not the board, has acted beyond his powers, on the ground that by virtue of section 6 of the Interpretation Act 1978 the plural includes the singular, is untenable in view of the intent and object of the subsection, which are to give effect to the expression "organs of the company" in article 9 (1) of the First Directive of March 9, 1968.[14] Of course, the "board of directors" may consist of a single director, *e.g.* in the case of a private company (see s. 176), and then section 9 (1) would apply. Moreover, section 9 (1) has no application where the directors have been superseded by a liquidator or a receiver and manager who purports to contract on matters *ultra vires* the company.

It follows that the subsection does not provide an answer to the important question whether the third party is protected if a director (or the secretary) who purports to act for the company is not duly authorised by the board of directors.[15] Here the principles relating to ostensible authority of these agents and to acts within their usual authority continue to apply.[16]

---

[11] The reference to "good faith" has introduced an element of uncertainty. It is not easy to define "good faith" in this context, but an attempt has been made at para. 9–25, *ante*.

[12] This was called, in para. 28–01, *ante*, the problem of primary delegation.

[13] See para. 9–25, *ante*.

[14] See para. 9–25, *ante*.

[15] This is the case of secondary delegation; see para. 28–01, *ante*.

[16] See *Freeman and Lockyer* v. *Buckhurst Park Properties (Mangal) Ltd.* [1964] 2 Q.B. 480; *Kreditbank Cassel G.m.b.H.* v. *Schenkers* [1927] 1 K.B. 826; *Panorama Developments (Guildford) Ltd.* v. *Fidelis Furnishing Fabrics Ltd.* [1971] 2 Q.B. 711; see further, para. 28–12, *post*.

Ratification

28–08 While an act which is *ultra vires* the company is incapable of ratification,[17] an act which is *intra vires* the company but outside the authority of the directors may be ratified by the company in proper form. For example, if directors have without a quorum purported to act in a manner which is authorised for the directors, a proper meeting of the directors can ratify the act. Likewise, if directors purport to act in a manner for which authority has not been delegated to them (*i.e.* where the power is retained by the company in general meeting) the company in general meeting may ratify it. This does not amount to an alteration of the articles, but an exercise by the general meeting of its powers, so that an ordinary resolution suffices.[18]

Inconsistent agreements

28–09 No agreement can be made by a company with a third party which purports to override any rights created by the articles. Thus, in a case dealing with the rights of a managing director, Harman J. said[19]:

> "So, everybody who becomes a managing director of this company which has adopted Table 'A' knows that he has certain rights, and that the board cannot alter them."

The rule in Royal British Bank v. Turquand

Statement of the rule

28–10 According to this rule, while persons dealing with a company are assumed to have read the public documents of the company[20] and to have ascertained that the proposed transaction is not inconsistent therewith, they are not required to do more; they need not inquire into the regularity of the internal proceedings—what Lord Hatherley called[21] "the indoor management"—and may assume that all is being done regularly (*omnia praesumuntur rite ac solemniter esse acta*).[22]

This rule, which is based on a general presumption of law, is eminently practical, for business could not be carried on if a person dealing with the apparent agents of a company was compelled to call for evidence that all internal regulations had been duly observed. Thus, where the articles give

---

[17] See para. 9–04, *ante*.

[18] *Bamford* v. *Bamford* [1970] Ch. 212 (C.A.). See also *Grant* v. *United Kingdom Switchback Rys.* (1888) 40 Ch.D. 135. As to the question of ratification when a company has no directors, see *Alexander Ward & Co. Ltd.* v. *Samyang Navigation Co. Ltd.* [1975] 1 W.L.R. 673; 1975 S.C. (H.L.) 26 1975 S.L.T. 126.

[19] *Read* v. *Astoria Garage (Streatham) Ltd.* [1952] 1 All E.R. 922, 924; affd. [1952] Ch. 637 (C.A.).

[20] See para. 28–02 *ante*.

[21] In *Mahony* v. *East Holyford Mining Co.* (1875) L.R. 7 H.L. 869, 898.

[22] *Mahony* v. *East Holyford Mining Co.* (1875) L.R. 7 H.L. 869; *Bargate* v. *Shortridge (1855) 5 H.L.C. 297, 318; Re Land Credit Co. of Ireland* (1869) L.R. 4 Ch. 460, 469; *Re County Life Assurance Co.* (1870) L.R. 5 Ch. 288; *Duck* v. *Tower Galvanizing Co.* [1901] 2 K.B. 314; *Heiton* v. *Waverley Hydropathic Co.* 1877, 4 R. 830; *Gillies* v. *Craigton Garage Co. Ltd.* 1935 S.C. 423.

power to borrow with the sanction of an ordinary resolution of the general meeting, a lender who relies on this power need not inquire whether such sanction has in fact been obtained.[23] He may assume that it has, and if he is acting bona fide he will, even though the sanction has not been obtained, stand in as good a position as if it had been obtained.

The same applies in the case of a mortgagee taking from a company a mortgage which, as far as he can tell, has been duly executed. In *County of Gloucester Bank* v. *Rudry, etc., Co.*[24] a person dealing with a company in due course obtained from the company a mortgage under seal signed by two directors and the secretary. The articles contained no special provision as to the execution of such a document, but the mortgage had been sealed at a meeting at which no quorum was present. It was held, notwithstanding, that the mortgage was good, for the mortgagee had no means of knowing of this internal irregularity in the management. So, too, in a similar case,[25] debentures issued under the seal of the company were held to be valid, though there had been no meetings or resolutions of the company or the board.

The rule in *Turquand's* case may even apply in circumstances where, although power to borrow is delegated by the articles to the directors, the company itself has retained the power to borrow and thence the power to borrow through agents. In such circumstances borrowing by agents may effectively bind the company, even if the agents borrow in excess of the actual powers delegated to them.[26]

While the rule is normally relied upon by a third party to uphold a transaction which the company seeks to repudiate, the company may also found upon it to prevent a third party from escaping liability on the ground of an alleged irregularity in the internal proceedings of the company.[27]

Application of the rule

28–11 ACTS WITHIN THE "USUAL" AUTHORITY OF THE COMPANY'S AGENT. The authority of an agent may be an actual authority or an ostensible or apparent authority.[28] The former arises from the express or implied[29]

---

[23] *Royal British Bank* v. *Turquand* (1856) 6 E. & B. 327. The position would be different if the articles required a special—as opposed to an ordinary—resolution because special resolutions are public documents: *Irvine* v. *Union Bank of Australia* (1877) 2 App. Cas. 366, but here s. 9 (1) of the European Communities Act 1972 may protect the third party; see para. 28–07, *ante*. Also *Patersons Trustees* v. *Caledonian Heritable Society Co. (in liquidation)* 1885, 13 R. 369.

[24] [1895] 1 Ch. 629.

[25] *Duck* v. *Tower Galvanizing Co.* [1901] 2 K.B. 314; and see *Re Fireproof Doors Ltd.* [1916] 2 Ch. 142.

[26] *Mercantile Bank of India* v. *Chartered Bank of India* [1937] 1 All E.R. 231.

[27] *Muirhead* v. *Forth, etc., Mutual Insurance Association* 1893, 21 R. (H.L.) 1; *Alexander Ward & Co.* v. *Sanyang Navigation Co.* 1975 S.C. (H.L.) 26; 1975 S.L.T. 126; (1975) 1 W.L.R. 673.

[28] On the distinction between "actual" and "ostensible" authority, see Diplock L.J. in *Freeman and Lockyer* v. *Buckhurst Park Properties (Mangal) Ltd.* [1964] 2 Q.B. 480, 502–505, and *Hely-Hutchinson* v. *Brayhead Ltd.* [1968] 1 Q.B. 549, 583, 593 (C.A.); *Sorrell* v. *Finch, The Times*, June 13, 1975 (C.A.). See also *Ford Motor Credit Co.* v. *Harmack, The Times*, July 7, 1972; [1972] J.B.L. 225.

[29] See *Hely-Hutchinson* v. *Brayhead Ltd.* [1968] 1 Q.B. 549 (C.A.).

appointment of the agent by the principal; the latter by a representation by the principal to a third party that the agent has authority to act on his behalf. In either case if the agent is appointed, or is held out as having been appointed, to a particular office, persons dealing with him are entitled to assume that he has the authority usually conferred on a person in that position, and are not bound by any limitation imposed by the principal upon the agent inconsistent with his "usual"[30] authority of which they have no knowledge.

These general principles of agency apply to agents of companies subject to the qualification that the agent's powers are in any event limited by the powers of the company itself, subject always to the effect of section 9 (1) of the European Communities Act 1972. Subject to this, any person who has been expressly appointed agent may bind the company by any act which is within the usual authority of such an agent. The rule in *Turquand's* case, in combination with section 9 (1), will operate in such case to relieve the third party from any obligation to ascertain whether authority was given to carry out the particular transaction. So, where a person has been appointed managing director under a power in the articles, the third party need not concern himself as to what powers have actually been delegated to the managing director: he can safely assume that the person he is dealing with has the usual powers of a person in that position. This rule was expressed by Atkin L.J. in *Kreditbank Cassel G.m.b.H.* v. *Schenkers*[31] as follows:

> "If you are dealing with a director in a matter in which normally a director would have power to act for the company you are not obliged to inquire whether or not the formalities required by the articles have been complied with before he exercises that power."

28–12 OSTENSIBLE AUTHORITY. Where there is no actual appointment, or the agent is acting outside his usual authority, the third party can only enforce the contract against the company if the following four conditions are satisfied.[32] He must show:

(1) that a representation was made to him that the agent had authority to enter on behalf of the company into a contract of the kind sought to be enforced;
(2) that such representation was made by a person or persons who themselves had actual authority to manage the business of the company either generally or in respect of those matters to which the contract relates;
(3) that he was induced by that representation to enter into the contract, that is, that he in fact relied upon it; and
(4) that under its memorandum or articles of association the company

[30] As to what constitutes the "usual" authority of the various officials of a company, see para. 27–08, *ante*.
[31] [1927] 1 K.B. 826, 844.
[32] *Per* Diplock L.J. in *Freeman and Lockyer* v. *Buckhurst Park Properties (Mangal) Ltd.* [1964] 2 Q.B. 480, 506; see also Slade J. in *Rama Corporation Ltd.* v. *Proved Tin and General Investments Ltd.* [1952] 2 K.B. 147.

was not deprived of the capacity either to enter into a contract of the kind sought to be enforced or to delegate authority to enter into a contract of that kind to the agent.

Where the agent has actual authority, express or implied, the ostensible authority coincides with the actual authority.[33] Where he has no actual authority but a representation of the kind just described has been made, the agent has ostensible authority although actual authority is lacking. In most cases the person dealing with the agent has no means of knowing whether the agent has any actual authority, and relies on some representation of the members or board of directors which confers ostensible authority upon the agent. Such a representation may take the form of a positive statement that the agent is authorised, or it may arise out of the conduct of the members or directors in allowing the agent to act as such. So, where the members of a company allowed certain persons to act as directors, although no directors had in fact been appointed, their acts were binding upon the company, as they had apparent authority to act in that capacity; their conduct was perfectly consistent with the company's articles, and the failure to make the appointment was an irregularity in the internal management of the company with which, under the rule in *Turquand's* case, outsiders were not concerned.[34]

More usually, the representation is made by the existing directors. In *Freeman and Lockyer* v. *Buckhurst Park Properties (Mangal) Ltd.*[35] the articles of the company authorised the appointment of a managing director, but no such appointment was made. The board of directors nevertheless allowed one of the directors to act as managing director in carrying on the business of the company. It was held that the directors had by their conduct held out their colleague as managing director, and, since the acts he had undertaken on behalf of the company were within the ordinary ambit of the authority of a managing director, the company was bound.[36] Further, it was held in *Panorama Developments (Guildford) Ltd.* v. *Fidelis Furnishing Fabrics Ltd.*[37] that the secretary of the company, as its chief administrative officer, has ostensible authority, by virtue of his office, to

---

33 *Sorrell* v. *Finch*, [1977] A.C. 728.

34 *Mahony* v. *East Holyford Mining Co.* (1875) L.R. 7 H.L. 869.

35 [1964] 2 Q.B. 480 (C.A.); see also *Biggerstaff* v. *Rowatt's Wharf Ltd.* [1896] 2 Ch. 93; *Clay Hill Brick and Tile Co. Ltd.* v. *Rawlings* [1938] 4 All E.R. 100; and *British Thomson-Houston Co. Ltd.* v. *Federated European Bank Ltd.* [1932] 2 K.B. 176 (where the company was held bound by a guarantee given by the chairman of the board, the articles containing a power of delegation of the directors' powers to any one or more of their number). *Ford Motor Credit Co. Ltd.* v. *Harmack, The Times*, July 7, 1972; [1972] J.B.L. 225 (where a person controlling three companies was held to have actual or ostensible authority to act for any of them). Further, *Cleveland Manufacturing Co. Ltd.* v. *Muslim Commercial Bank Ltd.* [1981] Com. L.R. 247.

36 It is respectfully thought that a representation arising from the conduct of the board of directors cannot be relied on where the person dealing with the company is himself a director, notwithstanding the decision of Roskill J. in *Hely-Hutchinson* v. *Brayhead Ltd.* [1968] 1 Q.B. 549, affd. on other grounds, *ibid.* at p. 573: see the discussion in [1967] J.B.L. 225 *et seq*.

37 [1971] 2 Q.B. 711.

enter on behalf of the company into contracts connected with the administrative side of the company's affairs, such as employing staff and hiring cars. In that case the secretary of the defendant company hired cars on behalf of the company without being authorised and used them for his own purposes; it was held that he had ostensible authority to act for the company and that the company was liable for the hire.

A statement in the articles might in itself be sufficient to constitute a representation that a person is authorised to act on behalf of the company. Under the rule in *Turquand's* case, the third party is not required to ensure that the powers which could be conferred upon the agent under the articles have in fact been conferred, provided that the act is one which is ordinarily within the power of a person in the position of the particular agent.[38]

28–13 ACTS OUTSIDE THE "USUAL" AUTHORITY OF THE COMPANY'S AGENT. If the agent who purports to act on behalf of the company purports to make a contract which is not within the ordinary ambit of the powers of such an agent, the outsider is not protected by the rule in *Turquand's* case.[39] Whether in such a case the outsider can rely on section 9 (1) of the European Communities Act 1972, depends on whether it can be said that he has acted in good faith and whether the transaction was decided upon by the directors. That will be a question of fact. If the divergence of the agent's act from what is the "usual" authority in the circumstances of the company is relatively small, section 9 (1) will protect the outsider. On the other hand, if it is quite obvious to a reasonable person that the agent could not have had authority, the third party has not acted in good faith and is not protected by section 9 (1).

Subject to this qualification, the cases decided before the coming into force of the European Communities Act, s. 9 (1), still hold good. In *Houghton & Co.* v. *Nothard, Lowe and Wills*, Sargant L.J. said[40]:

> "But, in my opinion, this is to carry the doctrine of presumed power far beyond anything that has hitherto been decided, and to place limited companies, without any sufficient reason for so doing, at the mercy of any servant or agent who should purport to contract on their behalf. On this view, not only a director of a limited company with articles founded on Table A, but a secretary or any subordinate officer might be treated by a third party acting in good faith as capable of binding the company by any sort of contract, however exceptional, on

---

[38] See Willmer L.J. in *Freeman and Lockyer* v. *Buckhurst Park Properties (Mangal) Ltd.* [1964] 2 Q.B. 480, 496, and cases there cited.

[39] This rule emerges from the following cases in which, however, the outsider had no actual knowledge of the public documents of the company; *Houghton & Co.* v. *Nothard, Lowe and Wills* [1927] 1 K.B. 246; in H.L. on another point [1928] A.C. 1; *Kreditbank Cassel G.m.b.H.* v. *Schenkers Ltd.* [1927] 1 K.B. 826; *Rama Corporation Ltd.* v. *Proved Tin & General Investments Ltd.* [1952] 2 K.B. 147. Further: *Premier Industrial Bank* v. *Carlton Manufacturing Co. [1909] 1 K.B. 106 (dissented from in Dey* v. *Pullinger Engineering Co.* [1921] 1 K.B. 77, *sed quaere*). See the discussion of these cases in *Freeman and Lockyer* v. *Buckhurst Park Properties (Mangal) Ltd.* [1964] 2 Q.B. 480. See also *Cook* v. *North British Rly. Co.* 1872, 10 M. 513, where an employee was unable to rely upon an agreement with certain directors which was clearly beyond their authority.

[40] [1927] 1 K.B. 246, 266.

the ground that a power of making such a contract might conceivably have been entrusted to him."

In this case a director purported to make on behalf of his company an agreement with the plaintiffs whereby the plaintiffs were to sell on commission goods imported by the defendant company on terms that the plaintiffs should retain the proceeds of sale as security for a debt due from another company. In *Kreditbank Cassel G.m.b.H* v. *Schenkers*[41] a branch manager of a company carrying on business as forwarding agents purported to draw bills of exchange on behalf of the company, which he subsequently indorsed on its behalf. In *Rama Corporations Ltd.* v. *Proved Tin and General Investments Ltd.*[42] a director of the defendant company purported to make an agreement with a director of the plaintiff company whereby the two companies were to join in subscribing to a fund to be used for financing the sale of goods produced by a third company, the defendant company being responsible for administering the fund and accounting to the plaintiffs.[43] All these cases involved transactions which were outside the scope of the usual authority of persons in the position of those acting for the company, and in each of them the plaintiffs were forced to rely on the fact that, under the articles, the requisite powers might have been delegated to the persons with whom they contracted. The plaintiffs had not, in fact, inspected the articles, but even if they had, this might not in itself have been sufficient, for "if the articles merely empower the directors to delegate to an officer authority to do the act, and the officer purports to do the act, then, if the act is one which would ordinarily be beyond the powers of such an officer, the plaintiff cannot assume that the directors have delegated to the officer power to do the act; and if they have not done so, the plaintiff cannot recover."[44]

In such a case the purported agent's own knowledge of the irregularity cannot be imputed to the company, and consequently the company is not estopped on the ground that it acquiesced in the unauthorised act.[45]

Exceptions to the rule in Turquand's case

Persons having knowledge of irregularity

28–14 A person who deals with a company and who is on notice of an irregularity in its internal management in connection with the subject-matter of his dealings cannot claim the benefit of the rule in *Turquand's* case.[46]

---

41 [1927] 1 K.B. 826.
42 [1952] 2 K.B. 147.
43 The summaries of these cases are taken from the judgment of Willmer L.J. in *Freeman and Lockyer* v. *Buckhurst Park Properties (Mangal) Ltd.* [1964] 2 Q.B. 480, 494.
44 *Ibid.* at p. 496, where Willmer L.J. expressly approved the note in the above terms appended by the reporter to the report of *British Thomson-Houston Co. Ltd.* v. *Federated European Bank Ltd.* [1932] 2 K.B. 176, 184.
45 *Houghton & Co.* v. *Nothard, Lowe & Wills* [1928] A.C. 1, 14.
46 *Morris* v. *Kanssen [1946] A.C. 459, 476.*

Thus, a director of the company cannot normally claim such a benefit, at least where he is also acting for the company in the transaction.[47] Where directors were empowered to borrow up to £1,000 and such further sums as the company in general meeting might authorise, and to secure such borrowings, debentures were issued to them for sums in excess of £1,000 borrowed without the authority of the general meeting, the debentures were invalid.[48]

WHAT CONSTITUTES KNOWLEDGE OF AN OUTSIDER COMPANY. A company is not automatically on notice of irregularity in the internal management of another company with which it is dealing, where it has a common officer with that other company, *e.g.* a common director or secretary.[49] At all events the outsider company will not be upon such notice unless "the common officer had some duty imposed upon him to communicate that knowledge to the other company, and had some duty imposed upon him by the company which is alleged to be affected by the notice to receive the notice.[50]

Persons on inquiry

28–15 If a person is put upon inquiry he cannot claim the benefit to the rule in *Turquand's* case in circumstances under which he would have discovered the irregularity if he had made the proper inquiries.

Thus, where a sole director and principal shareholder of a company paid into his own account cheques drawn in favour of the company, the bank into which such payment was made was held to be put upon inquiry, and the bank was accordingly disentitled to rely upon the ostensible authority of the director.[51] Similarly a bank was put upon inquiry where directors of a company secured their own indebtedness by a charge upon the company's property and was not entitled to the benefit of the charge which had not in fact been authorised.[52] A person dealing with a company may be upon inquiry by reason of the unusual magnitude of the transaction, having

---

[47] *Howard* v. *Patent Ivory Co.* (1888) 38 Ch.D. 156; *Morris* v. *Kanssen* [1946] A.C. 459; *cf. Hely-Hutchinson* v. *Brayhead Ltd.* [1968] 1 Q.B. 549, *per* Roskill J. at pp. 564–568; and see note 36, *supra*, and see *John* v. *Rees* [1970] Ch. 345, 386.

[48] *Howard* v. *Patent Ivory Co* (1888) 38 Ch.D. 156, 170; and see *Tyne Mutual Association* v. *Brown (1896) 74 L.T. 283.*

[49] *As to cases involving common directors, see Re Marseilles Extension Ry.* (1871) L.R. 7 Ch. 161; *Re Hampshire Land Co.* [1896] 2 Ch. 743; *Young* v. *David Payne & Co.* [1904] 2 Ch. 608 (C.A.). As to a common secretary, see *Re Fenwick Stobart & Co.* [1902] 1 Ch. 507. The position is analogous to partnerships having a partner in common, where facts communicated to him as partner of one firm are not presumed to be within the knowledge of the other firm, see *Campbell* v. *McCreath*, 1975 S.C. 81; 1975 S.L.T. (notes) 5.

[50] *Per* Vaughan Williams J. in *Re Hampshire Land Co.* [1896] 2 Ch. 743; approved by himself in *Young* v. *David Payne & Co.* [1904] 2 Ch. 608 (C.A.). In the latter case the irregularity consisted of the intention to use the money for an unauthorised purpose.

[51] *A. L. Underwood* v. *Bank of Liverpool* [1924] 1 K.B. 775. Selangor United Rubber Estates Ltd. v. *Cradock (No. 3)* [1968] 1 W.L.R. 1555; *Karak Rubber Company Ltd.* v. *Burden* [1972] 1 W.L.R. 602; *Groves-Ruffin Construction Ltd.* v. *Bank of Nova Scotia* [1976] 1 Lloyd's Rep. 373 (Can); *Rowlandson* v. *National Westminster Bank Ltd.* [1978] 1 W.L.R. 798.

[52] *E. B. M. Co.* v. *Dominion Bank* [1937] 3 All E.R. 555. *Thompson* v. *J. Barke (Caterers) Ltd.* 1975 S.L.T. 67.

regard to the position of the agent who is acting for the company.[53] Further, an individual who has lent money to another individual, and is repaid by cheques drawn upon the account of a company of which the borrower is a director and shareholder, is put on his inquiry by the unusual nature of the transaction.[54]

Forgery

28–16 The rule in *Turquand's* case does not apply if a document is forged so as to purport to be the company's document. In *Ruben* v. *Great Fingall Consolidated*,[55] a share certificate was forged by the secretary who then purported to issue it on behalf of the company, in return for money advanced. The appellants claimed to be entitled to be registered as holders of the shares. The House of Lords held that the company was not estopped from disputing the appellants' claim. As regards the rule in *Turquand's* case, Lord Loreburn L.C. said[56]:

> "It is quite true that persons dealing with limited liability companies are not bound to inquire into their indoor management, and will not be affected by irregularities of which they had no notice. But this doctrine, which is well established, applies only to irregularities that otherwise might affect a genuine transaction. It cannot apply to a forgery."

Subrogation

28–17 Where directors, acting in excess of their powers, purport to borrow money on behalf of the company, and the lender is unable to obtain the benefit of the rule in *Turquand's* case, he may nevertheless stand in the shoes of any creditor of the company whom the company has paid off out of the money lent. This principle has been applied in a number of cases,[57] even where the lender knew that the company had no power to borrow.[58]

The principle is sometimes referred to as "subrogation." This, however, is not its true nature, as Wright J. observed in *B. Liggett (Liverpool)* v. *Barclays Bank*[59]:

---

[53] See para. 28–13, *ante*.
[54] *Thompson* v. *J. Barke (Caterers) Ltd.* 1975 S.L.T. 67.
[55] [1906] A.C. 439; and see Scrutton C.J. in *Kreditbank Cassel G.m.b.H.* v. *Schenkers* [1927] 1 K.B. 826, 838, 839 and *South London Greyhound Racecourses Ltd.* v. *Wake* [1931] 1 Ch. 496, where it was held that a share certificate sealed without the necessary authority of the board of directors was a forgery, notwithstanding that the signatures on the certificate were genuine. It is submitted that the test is not whether the document can properly be described as a "forgery," but whether the person putting it forward as genuine was acting within his usual authority or was held out as having authority to do so by the company. On either of these tests, it is respectfully thought that *Wake's* case was wrongly decided.
[56] [1906] A.C. 439, 443; see also Stirling L.J. in [1904] 2 K.B. 712, 729 (C.A.).
[57] See, *e.g.*, *Blackburn Building Society* v. *Cunliffe, Brooks & Co.* (1883) 22 Ch.D. 61; *Re Cork and Youghal Ry. (1869) L.R. 4 Ch. 748; see also A. L. Underwood Ltd.* v. *Bank of Liverpool* [1924] 1 K.B. 775, 794.
[58] *Reversion Fund and Insurance Co.* v. *Maison Cosway Ltd.* [1913] 1 K.B. 364.
[59] [1928] 1 K.B. 48, 61.

"The ground is sometimes put in this way, that the lender or the quasi-lender is subrogated to the rights of the creditor who has been paid off. That, obviously, is not precisely true, because no question of subrogation to securities can arise in such a case."

The principle is founded upon an implied contractual undertaking by the company to repay the sum in question to the lender.[60] It follows that the right of the lender to be refunded can only arise

(1) if the company can be regarded as having knowledge of the loan; and

(2) if it has taken the benefit of the loan or, at least, acquiesced in the position.

28–18 If these conditions are absent it cannot be said that the company has impliedly undertaken to repay the loan, and that is the case if, *e.g.* it has no board of directors competent to act[61]; or if it stands by, neither accepting nor rejecting the position, because it has no knowledge of it or is paralysed. As to be knowledge of a company of the position in such a case Viscount Sumner observed[62]:

"Has knowledge then been brought home to the respondent company on which to found the alleged standing by? In the case of a natural person, if information is intelligibly conveyed to and received by him, its source, whether a servant or a stranger, whether he is high or low, matters little, if at all. With an artificial incorporated person it must necessarily be otherwise, for an impersonal corporation cannot read or hear except by the eyes and ears of others. Who are to be the organs, by which it receives knowledge so as to affect its rights, may be specially determined by the articles of its constitution, but otherwise, in a matter where knowledge may lead to a modification of the company's rights according as it is or is not followed by action, the knowledge, which is relevant, is that of directors themselves, since it is their board that deals with the company's rights. The mind, so to speak, of a company is not reached or affected by information merely possessed by its clerks, nor is it deemed automatically to know everything that appears in its ledgers. What a director knows or ought in the course of his duty to know may be the knowledge of the company, for it may be deemed to have been duly used so as to lead to the action, which a fully informed corporation would proceed to take on the strength of it."

---

[60] *Re Cleadon Trust Ltd.* [1939] Ch. 286.
[61] See Scott L.J., *ibid.*, p. 311.
[62] In *Houghton & Co.* v. *Nothard, Lowe & Wills* [1928] A.C. 1, 18; see also the dissenting judgment of Sir Wilfrid Greene M.R. in *Re Cleadon Trust Ltd.* [1939] Ch. 286, 299.

Part Four

SHARE CAPITAL AND DEBENTURES

A. CAPITAL

CHAPTER 29

TYPES OF CAPITAL

29–01 THE word "capital" is used in company law in various senses. It is properly used to denote the share capital of a company and in this context it is necessary to distinguish between

(a) the nominal (also called authorised) capital;
(b) the issued capital;
(c) the allotted share capital;
(d) the paid-up capital;
(e) the authorised minimum capital.

In connection with this subject it is convenient to refer further to the meaning of

(f) reserve liability (sometimes called reserve capital);
(g) three statutory funds which have a quasi-capital nature, *viz.* the share premium account, the capital redemption reserve, and a reserve fund in certain cases of nominee shares, etc.,

and also to mention the terms sometimes used in business and accounting circles, *viz.*—

(h) equity share capital;
(i) loan capital;
(j) fixed and current (circulating) capital.

Nominal capital

29–02 Every company limited by shares is required to have nominal capital with which it is registered.[1] This is one of the essential features of the company's constitution and must be stated in the memorandum of association.[2] It is equal to the nominal value of the shares[3] which the directors are authorised to issue (hence the term "authorised capital"). For public companies such figure must not be less than the authorised minimum.[4] The nominal capital may be increased above, or reduced below, the figure stated in the memorandum.[5] A reduction below the authorised minimum for public companies will cause that company to be re-registered as a private company.[6]

---

[1] Companies limited by guarantee and having a share capital are also subject to these rules. Such companies may no longer be formed: 1980 Act, s. 1 (2).
[2] s. 2 (4) (*a*).
[3] See para. 33–03, *post*.
[4] 1980 Act, s. 3 (2). See below.
[5] *i.e.* in the capital clause: see paras. 32–02, and 32–01, *post*.
[6] 1980 Act, s. 12. See below and paras. 5–14, *ante* and 32–14, *post*.

Issued capital

29–03 The nominal capital in its original or altered form sets the limit of capital available for issue, and accordingly the *issued capital* of a company can never exceed its nominal capital. The nominal capital is, strictly speaking, not "capital" at all since, as we have seen, it is only an authority by the shareholders to the directors to create new capital by the issue of shares. The issued capital, on the other hand, represents the shares which have actually been taken up by shareholders who have agreed to give consideration in cash or kind for the shares issued to them unless those shares are fully paid bonus shares; the issued capital is thus a reality and not merely an authority.

Capital is issued by the directors of the company. They must be duly authorised to make such an issue and, subject to certain conditions, equity shareholders or holders of other equity securities, such as convertible debentures, may have a pre-emption right entitling them, if they so desire, to subscribe newly issued shares, if the issue is for cash, proportionally in the ratio of their present holdings. These topics are treated in an earlier chapter.[7]

29–04 The fact that the actual, as contrasted with the nominal, value of the shares so issued may subsequently alter does not affect the amount of the issued capital. This applies to the whole concept of share capital in whatever sense that term is used. "The capital of a company may remain wholly unchanged while estimates of the value of the company's assets or its undertaking or its shares fluctuate greatly on the Stock Exchange and elswhere," *per* Megarry J. in *Canada Safeway Ltd.* v. *I.R.C.*[8] In that case the learned judge held that the words "issued share capital" in the Finance Act 1930, s. 42 (2), as amended by the Finance Act 1967, s. 27—a stamp-duty enactment—had to be construed in a manner consonant with the Companies Act 1948 and signified the nominal value of the issued capital and not the actual value of the shares represented by it. In practice, however, the full amount agreed to be paid for the issued shares is regarded as the issued capital. Insofar as this exceeds its nominal value it is known as a share premium.[9] This is, however, different from the actual value of the share at any given time.

While an increase or a reduction of the nominal capital cannot be effected without a resolution of the company in general meeting[10] the issue of shares up to that amount may be decided upon by the board of directors without recourse to a general meeting,[11] provided that the articles of association so provide.[12]

---

[7] See para. 24–01, *ante*.
[8] [1973] Ch. 374, 380.
[9] See below and para. 24–03, *ante*.
[10] s. 61 (2), para. 31–02; s. 66 (1), para. 32–01, *post*.
[11] Provided that they are not in breach of their fiduciary duties, see para. 63–02, *post*.
[12] 1980 Act, s. 14. See para. 24–01, *ante*.

The difference between the nominal and the issued capital is known as the *unissued capital*.

Allotted share capital

29–05 Many of the provisions relating to the capital of a company introduced or codified by the 1980 Act are concerned not with the issue but the allotment of shares.[13] Thus the rules as to payment for shares[14] and the limits on public company directors' powers noted above[15] are defined by reference to the allotment of shares. In particular the authorised minimum capital required of a public company refers to the nominal value of the company's allotted share capital.[16] For the purposes of the Acts shares are allotted when a person acquires the unconditional right to be included in the company's register of members in respect of those shares,[17] and allotted share capital should be construed accordingly.

Whether there is any difference in practice between the issued and allotted share capital figures seems doubtful. The former may perhaps be regarded as a term of art by way of contrast to the nominal capital whereas the latter is a specific term used for specific provisions and their consequences.

Paid-up capital

29–06 When the nominal capital is issued in whole or in part, each of the persons to whom it is issued becomes liable to pay to the company the nominal value of the shares taken.[18] The 1980 Act envisages that the obligation of the shareholder shall be payable either on the company making a call on him or by way of instalment fixed on the issue of the shares or by the articles. Calls are in practice very rare. The articles normally provide that sums payable by way of instalments on such fixed dates shall be treated as if they were payable on a call.[19] The money received on each share as a result of calls is said to be paid up and the total amount that has been paid up on the company's shares is the *paid-up capital*, which can, of course, never exceed the issued capital. Public companies may not, however, in general allot any share unless it has been paid up as to at least one-quarter of its nominal value and the whole of any

---

[13] In certain cases the word "issue" in the 1948 Act was amended to "allot" by the 1980 Act, Sched. 3. See, *e.g.* Sched. 3, paras. 12 and 14 amending ss. 56 (2) and 58 (5) of the 1948 Act.
[14] 1980 Act, ss. 20–31. See para. 24–03, *ante*.
[15] 1980 Act, s. 14.
[16] 1980 Act, s. 4 (3) (*a*). See below and para. 4–14, *ante*.
[17] 1980 Act, s. 87 (2). See para. 24–01, *ante*.
[18] See Chap. 24, *ante*.
[19] See Table A, art. 19. This is now contained in a statutory definition of called-up share capital: 1980 Act, s. 87 (1).

premium.[20] If any reference to a company's capital is made in its business letters or order forms such reference must be paid to the paid-up capital.[21]

As long as anything remains *uncalled* on an issued share, there is an unpaid liability[22] for the balance, and the total amount of these liabilities will be regarded in the books of the company as the *uncalled capital*. There may be an amount of the issued capital which has been called but has not been paid by the shareholders, due to *calls in arrear*.[23]

Authorised minimum capital

29–07 Following the 1980 Act no public company may be registered as such unless its authorised nominal capital is at least equal to the *authorised minimum*.[24] Equally no such company may commence business or exercise any borrowing powers unless the nominal value of its allotted share capital is equal to or exceeds that figure.[25] This new concept is quantified in section 85 of the 1980 Act at £50,000 but the Secretary of State may vary that amount by an order approved by a resolution of each House of Parliament.[26] If the figure is increased public companies with an allotted share capital of which the nominal value is less than the new amount will be required to increase its allotted capital or re-register as a private company.[27] Appropriate changes to the authorised capital figure may also be necessary.

Reserve liability

29–08 A company may resolve by special resolution that part or the whole of the uncalled capital shall not be called up except in the event of a winding up (s. 60). This amount resolved by the company to meet a contingency in the winding up is sometimes called the *reserve capital*, although the Act uses a more accurate term—*reserve liability*.

A company which has created a reserve liability resembles, from the business point of view, a company limited by guarantee and having a share capital. There is, however, this essential difference between a reserve liability and a guarantee: the former attaches according to the shareholding of every member, so that the bigger the shareholding, the greater the reserve liability, whereas the guarantee attaches *per capita* and is the same for each member, or, if the amount of the guarantee varies according to

---

[20] 1980 Act, s. 22. See Chap. 24 *ante; c.f.* the definition of "paid up in cash": 1980 Act, s. 87 (3) (*a*).
[21] European Communities Act 1972, s. 9 (7), see para. 8–05, *ante*.
[22] The liability might be contingent, *viz*. if the whole or part of the uncalled capital has been made a "reserve liability," it cannot be called up except in certain events and for certain purposes (s. 60 and next paragraph in text).
[23] For the consequences of non-payment of calls, see Chap. 36, *post*.
[24] 1980 Act, s. 3 (2). See para. 4–14, *ante*.
[25] *Ibid*. s. 4 (3). See para. 19–02, *ante*.
[26] *Ibid*. s. 85 (3).
[27] *Ibid*. s. 85 (2).

classes of members, for each member of the class in question.[28] Thus the creation of a reserve liability is still allowed whereas companies limited by guarantee and having a share capital may no longer be formed.[29]

Quasi-capital funds

29–09 The Act requires in certain circumstances the constitution of two funds which, although not forming part of the capital of the company, "can be distributed in the same restricted way and with the same leave of the court as if paid-up share capital was being returned to the shareholders"[30] unless the funds are used for certain limited purposes expressly authorised by the Act. The two funds are the share premium account and the capital redemption reserve fund.

The share premium account

29–10 The consideration which a shareholder has to provide in cash or kind for the shares issued to him by the company may not be equal to the nominal value of those shares. Where the consideration exceeds the nominal value of the share the issue is at a premium and where it is below the nominal value the issue is at a discount. Where shares are issued at a premium it would be commercially unwise to allow the distribution of the premium as dividend to the shareholders because it could hardly be considered as a profit. For that reason section 56 provides that a figure equivalent to this premium shall be placed to an account to be called the *share premium account*; the section specifies certain purposes for which this account may be used, including the allotment of bonus shares. The rules as to preservation and maintenance of capital apply, however,[31] and if it is intended to use it for other purposes the capital reduction procedure must be used.[32]

The obligation imposed by section 56 is in general mandatory whenever shares are issued for more than their nominal value. This is true where the shares are issued for cash but the position is more complex where the shares are issued for assets other than cash, in particular for other shares. Case law established that when a company issued shares in return for other shares which the parties knew represented a premium on the issued shares the directors were obliged to transfer the excess to the share premium account—it was an obligation "imposed by law" for the purposes of corporation tax.[33] In that case there was no stated premium but one clearly existed and it was held that any attempt to distinguish between cash and non-cash premiums would defeat the object of section 56 which was that

---

[28] A reserve liability created before the constitution of a floating charge is exempt therefrom: see para. 42–04, *post*.
[29] 1980 Act, s. 1 (2).
[30] *Per* Harman J. in *Henry Head & Co. Ltd.* v. *Ropner Holdings* [1952] Ch. 124, 127.
[31] See Chap. 30, *post*.
[32] See Chap. 24, *ante*. On capital reduction procedure, see Chap. 32, *post*. But see ss. 45 (6) and 54 (5) of the 1981 Act.
[33] *Shearer* v. *Bercain Ltd.* [1980] S.T.C. 359.

whatever was purchased with capital in the shape of shares, or an equivalent amount, was itself to be treated as capital. The section itself refers to the "amount or value" of a premium and this clearly envisages such a situation.

The obligation however no longer applies to certain cases under sections 36–41 of the 1981 Act, where an issuing company either acquires a 90 per cent. holding in a subsidiary or acquires a shareholding in a fellow subsidiary, being a wholly owned subsidiary itself. Retrospective relief was also given on a wider basis for share for share acquisitions prior to February 4, 1981. These rules are dealt with fully in Chapter 24, *ante*. If they do not apply the general principle remains valid.

The capital redemption reserve

When shares are redeemed or purchased out of profits under sections 45 and 46 of the 1981 Act[34] there would at that time be available a book profit equivalent to the amount of the redeemed or purchased capital. In order to prevent the distribution of that profit section 53 of the 1981 Act requires the company to form a *capital redemption reserve* which thenceforth has to appear on the liabilities side of the balance-sheet. This fund can be capitalised by the allotment of bonus shares or used to purchase or redeem such shares out of capital under section 54 of the 1981 Act.[35] If any other use is intended, here, as in the case of the share premium account, the rules as to preservation and maintenance of capital apply and the capital reduction procedure applies. The former requirements in section 58 of the 1948 Act relating to the *capital redemption reserve fund*, established on the redemption of redeemable preference shares, have been repealed. Any such fund will now be regarded as a capital redemption reserve for all purposes, including any provisions in the company's articles.[35a]

Reserve fund when public company's own shares shown as assets

29–11 When either a public company acquires its own shares,[36] otherwise than by purchase, or a nominee for that company acquires such shares so that the company has an interest in those shares[37] and either those shares or that interest is shown in the company's balance-sheet as an asset, the 1980 Act requires the transfer to a statutory reserve fund from profits available for dividend,[38] an amount equal to those shares or that interest.[39] Such a sum is not to be available for distribution as dividends.[40] Companies may acquire their own shares by way of purchase, redemption, gift, surrender

---

[34] See para. 33–13 and Chap. 37, *post*.
[35] *Ibid.*
[35a] 1981 Act, s. 62 (5).
[36] 1980 Act, s. 35.
[37] 1980 Act, s. 36.
[38] See Chap. 76, *post*.
[39] 1980 Act, s. 37 (10).
[40] Distribution is defined in s. 45 (2), but for that part of the Act only. *Quaere* whether it will apply to s. 37 (10)?

or forfeiture. All shares purchased or redeemed must be cancelled[41] and public companies must subsequently dispose of or cancel any of their shares acquired by gift, forfeiture or surrender.[41a] It can be assumed that the fund created by this provision will be regarded as a quasi-capital fund.

Equity share capital

29–12 This phrase, whatever its meaning in the business world,[42] has a legal connotation. The term includes the issued share capital except shares limited to a specified amount as regards dividend and capital.[43] The equity share capital of a company thus consists of the whole of its issued ordinary, deferred and preference capital carrying participating rights (except where the participating rights are limited in amount); only non-participating preference shares and other shares have limited rights as to capital and dividend do not fall within the term.

The Acts use the term "equity share capital" when defining holding and subsidiary companies and the term will be treated in that connection.[44]

Loan capital

29–13 This phrase, though frequently used in business circles, is, in the eyes of a lawyer, a contradiction in terms. The term denotes the debentures and debenture stock issued by the company. The holders of these securities are creditors of the company and have not, as such, a proprietary interest in the company in the way that a member has. Loan capital, being a debt and not risk capital is not subject to the rules as to raising and maintenance of capital.[45]

Fixed and current capital

29–14 The substituted Eighth Schedule,[46] refers to fixed assets, current assets, and assets that are neither fixed nor current. In addition the statutory rules as to distributable profits make reference to "fixed" and "current" assets.[47] There are no definitions, however, and as a general rule a "fixed" asset is any asset which is not a "current" asset.[48] In general, however, those rules do not rely heavily on the distinction. Fixed and current assets are frequently referred to in commerce and accountancy as *fixed and circulating capital* although some disagreement exists in those circles on the delimitation of those terms. In addition a company which makes a profit on the realisation of a capital asset will often put a sum equal to such profit to a *capital reserve*.

---

41 1981 Act, s. 45 (8). See para. 33–13, *post*.
41a 1980 Act, s. 37 (2). See Chap. 37, *post*.
42 The term is used in the City Code on Take-overs and Mergers but is nowhere defined.
43 s. 154 (5).
44 See para. 71–01, *post*.
45 See Chap. 30, *post*. For debentures generally see Chap. 43, *post*.
46 Sched. 1 to the 1981 Act.
47 1980 Act, ss. 39 (5) (8).
48 *Ibid*. s. 39 (8).

CHAPTER 30

THE RAISING AND MAINTENANCE OF CAPITAL SERIOUS LOSS OF CAPITAL

30–01 THE *issued*[1] share capital of a company (whether *paid-up*[2] or *uncalled*[3]) is regarded by the courts as constituting at least in principle a permanent fund available to creditors of the company if necessary. This principle has also been strongly adopted by the legislature with regard to the *allotted* share capital[4] as a result of the 1980 Act. This is required for the protection of creditors since the liability of the shareholder is in general limited to the nominal amount of the shares taken up by him. Thus the only fund of last resort available to a creditor is the issued capital of the company. "The capital is fixed and certain, and every creditor of the company is entitled to look to that capital as his security," *per* Lord Halsbury L.C. in *Ooregum Gold Mining Company of India* v. *Roper*.[5]

It has therefore been necessary for the courts and the legislature to provide: (a) That the full value of that capital is raised; and (b) that it is maintained as a fund so far as the ordinary risks of business will allow.

> "Paid up capital may be diminished or lost in the course of the company's trading; that is a result which no legislation can prevent; but persons who deal with, and give credit to a limited company, naturally rely upon the fact that the company is trading with a certain amount of capital already paid, as well as upon the responsibility of its members for the capital remaining at all; and they are entitled to assume that no part of the capital which has been paid into the coffers of the company has been subsequently paid out, except in the legitimate course of its business." *Per* Lord Watson in *Trevor* v. *Whitworth*.[6]

Disclosure of these figures enables creditors to judge the creditworthiness of the company.[7] The 1981 Act does allow for the outflow of capital from private companies for the redemption or purchase of shares but only under strictly controlled conditions.[7a] The detailed rules evolved to meet these general requirements can be found elsewhere in this book but it is thought desirable to collate them as follows:

Raising of Capital

30–02 (*a*) The issue of shares at a discount is, on principle, prohibited because

---

[1] See para. 29–03, *ante*.
[2] See para. 29–06, *ante*.
[3] *Ibid.*
[4] See para. 29–05, *ante*.
[5] [1892] A.C. 125, 133.
[6] (1887) 12 App.Cas. 409, 423. See also *per* Lord Herschell, *ibid.* p. 415.
[7] See Chap. 24, *ante*.
[7a] See Chap. 37 and para. 33–13, *post*.

it would mislead persons dealing with the company into thinking that the full value of the issued capital has been received by the company at sometime during its existence.[8]

(*b*) The premium obtained on the issue of shares has in general to be transferred to a share premium account and cannot be distributed by way of dividend. The share premium account is a quasi-capital fund, *i.e.* it is, on principle, treated as if it were issued capital and can only be applied in accordance with the law.[9]

(*c*) Payment for shares must be in money or money's worth, and for public companies must not consist of an undertaking to do work or perform services.[10]

(*d*) A public company may not allot any share unless it is paid up at least to one-quarter of its nominal value and the whole of any premium.[11]

(*e*) A public company may not allot any share in return for non-cash consideration without a valuation report on such consideration.[12]

(*f*) A public company may not allot any share in return for an undertaking to provide non-cash consideration more than five years from the date of the allotment.

(*g*) A public company may not acquire assets, whether in return for shares or otherwise, from the subscribers to its memorandum within two years of being able to commence business without a valuation report. A similar prohibition applies to assets acquired from members of a private company within two years of its re-registration as a public company.[14]

(*h*) Any shares taken by the subscribers to the memorandum of a public company as a result of such subscription must be paid up in cash.[15]

(*i*) A public company may not commence business unless it has an allotted share capital of at least the authorised minimum.[16]

(*j*) A public company must hold an extraordinary general meeting in the event of a serious loss of capital.[17]

(*k*) The powers of directors of companies to issue shares without reference to the general meeting are restricted.[18]

---

[8] See Chap. 24, *ante*.
[9] See Chap. 24, and para. 29–10, *ante*. This includes the reduction of capital provisions: *Re Moorgate Mercantile Holdings Ltd.* [1980] 1 All E.R. 40, 56.
[10] See Chap. 24, *ante*.
[11] *Ibid*.
[12] *Ibid*.
[13] *Ibid*.
[14] See para. 12–10, *ante*.
[15] *Ibid*.
[16] See para. 19–02, *ante*.
[17] See para. 30–04, *post*.
[18] See para. 24–01, *ante*.

Maintenance of Capital

30–03 (i) The reduction of the issued capital must comply with strict legal requirements, including the confirmation by the court.[19]

(ii) A company may only purchase or redeem shares out of distributable profits or the proceeds of a special issue for that purpose. Exceptionally private companies may use other funds subject to investor and creditor protection, and all companies may use the share premium account to fund redemption or purchase of shares originally issued at a premium.[20]

(iii) A company may not issue shares to a nominee.[21]

(iv) A public company must dispose of or cancel any of its shares acquired by itself or by a nominee by forfeiture, surrender or gift. All companies must cancel any of their own shares acquired by redemption or purchase.[22]

(v) In such circumstances if such shares are shown as assets in the company's balance-sheet an amount equal to that value must be transferred to a capital reserve from profits.[23]

(vi) A public company may not, on principle, finance the acquisition of its own shares. A private company may do so if properly authorised but no so as to reduce that company's net assets.[24]

(vii) The rules laid down by the courts and the 1980 Act for the distribution of dividend aim at the maintenance of the paid-up capital.[25]

Serious Loss of Capital

Obligation to convene extraordinary general meeting

30–04 Under a completely new provision of the Companies Act 1980 the directors of a public company are under a duty to convene an extraordinary general meeting of the company in the event of a serious loss of capital.

By virtue of section 34 (1) of the 1980 Act this obligation arises when two factors are present:

(i) where the net assets of a public company are half or less of the amount of the company's called-up share capital; and

(ii) where that fact is known to a director of the company.

Fall in net assets

30–05 The net assets of a public company are defined in the 1980 Act as "the

---

[19] See Chap. 32, *post*.
[20] See para. 33–13 and Chap. 37, *post*.
[21] *Ibid*.
[22] *Ibid*.
[23] *Ibid*.
[24] *Ibid*.
[25] See Chap. 76, *post*.

aggregate of its assets less the aggregate of its liabilities."[1] No attempt is made to distinguish between fixed and current assets or liabilities but clearly reference to the balance-sheet will usually indicate a debit balance from the profit and loss account if a serious loss of capital has occurred. A further definition provides that "liabilities" for this purpose include those in the substituted Eighth Schedule to the 1948 Act except to the extent that they are taken into account in calculating the value of any asset of the company.[2]

The qualification must be made by reference to the company's called-up share capital. This too has a statutory definition: it means so much of the company's share capital as equals the aggregate amount of the calls made on its shares, whether or not they have been paid, together with any capital paid up without being called and any share capital to be paid on a specified future date under the articles, the terms of allotment of the relevant shares or any other arrangements for payment of those shares.[3] In general terms therefore it is the amount of consideration received or payable without further call, *e.g.* by instalments.[4] It remains to be seen whether the inclusion of unpaid but payable amounts will affect the operation of this section. No provision appears to have been made for the writing off of any of this amount *vis-à-vis* the obligation.

Knowledge of a director

30–06 The fact that the net assets of the company have fallen to half or less of its called-up share capital need only be known to a director of the company for the obligation to call the meeting to arise.[5] Any director will presumably suffice for this purpose and the standard definition of a director for the Companies Acts will apply,[6] *i.e.* any person occupying the position of director by whatever name he is called. The more complex definition of a "shadow director" set out in the 1980 Act[7] does not, however, apply.[8] It is important therefore that the strength of this new provision is brought to the attention of all public company directors, executive or non-executive.

No guidance is given in the section as to how this information is to be known to a director, nor as to whether constructive or actual notice will suffice. The language suggests comprehension of the fact, so that the obligation may depend both upon the nature of the information given and the understanding of the recipient. Wilful blindness to the fact may also cause problems of interpretation. It is to be hoped that the courts if called upon will interpret this provision so as to include both "honest fools" and "clever rogues," since only public companies are involved.

---

[1] 1980 Act, s. 87 (4) (*c*).
[2] *Ibid.*
[3] 1980 Act, s. 87 (1).
[4] See para. 29–06, *ante* for a discussion of called and paid-up capital.
[5] 1980 Act, s. 34 (1).
[6] 1948 Act, s. 455 (1).
[7] 1980 Act, s. 63.
[8] That definition applies only to ss. 46–67 of the 1980 Act.

Timing of the meeting

30–07 Two time limits are involved once the obligation to convene the meeting has arisen. The first relates to the actual process of calling the meeting[9] and it requires the directors to so act within 28 days from the earliest day on which the relevant fact was known to a director,[10] *i.e.* from when the obligation arose. As indicated above this may be subject to some difficulty of proof.

The second time limit relates to the actual date of the meeting itself. This must be fixed for a date not more that 56 days from the obligation arising.[11] At least four weeks' notice of the meeting must actually be given therefore but no longer than eight weeks are allowed in total.

Business of the meeting

30–08 The meeting is to be called "for the purpose of considering whether any, and if so what, measures should be taken to deal with the situation."[12]

This provision is very wide and clearly contemplates decisions as to whether to reduce the company's capital under section 66[13] and as to the general conduct of the company's trading or business ventures which have produced this situaton. More difficult is the question as to whether consequential matters may be discussed, *e.g.* a reduction in salary of the directors deemed to be responsible for the situation.[14] The Act itself is not particularly helpful on this matter. Section 34 (3) provides that nothing in the section shall be taken as authorising the consideration at such a meeting "of any matter which could not have been considered at the meeting apart from this section."

This is capable of two interpretations. First, that only business properly dealt with at an extraordinary general meeting may be so considered[15] and therefore that specific items must be included in the notice, or, secondly, that it allows, by reference back to the general wording of subsection (1), discussion of any matter which appertains to "dealing with the situation," however wide. Since it is the directors who are to convene the meeting, the latter construction is clearly preferable.

Failure to convene

30–09 If there is a failure to convene a meeting required by section 34 of the 1980 Act, a criminal offence is committed by each director who either "knowingly and wilfully" authorises or permits the failure, or after the

---

[9] For this procedure see para. 54–01, *post*.
[10] 1980 Act, s. 34 (1).
[11] *Ibid.*
[12] *Ibid.*
[13] See Chap. 32, *post*.
[14] The dismissal of a director would require "special notice" under s. 184 of the 1948 Act.
[15] See para. 53–05, *post*.

56-day period has elapsed "knowingly and wilfully authorises or permits that failure to continue."[16]

[16] 1980 Act, s. 34 (2).

Chapter 31

ALTERATION OF CAPITAL (OTHER THAN REDUCTION)

In general

31–01 The 1948 Act authorises on certain conditions the following modes of alteration of the capital of the company—

Under Section 61

1. The increase of share capital (s. 61 (1) (*a*)).
2. The consolidation of shares (s. 61 (1) (*b*)).
3. The subdivision of shares (s. 61 (1) (*d*)).
4. The conversion of shares into stock and vice versa (s. 61 (1) (*c*)).
5. The diminution of the capital (s. 61 (1) (*e*)).

Under Section 66

6. The reduction of share capital.

This chapter deals with the first five modes of alteration, *i.e.* the alterations authorised by section 61, while the capital reduction procedure authorised by section 66 is dealt with in the following chapter.[1]

Three principles are common to all modes of alteration of capital authorised by section 61—

(a) the articles must authorise such alterations;
(b) these alterations must be made by the company in general meeting and cannot be delegated by the articles or otherwise to the board of directors or anybody else[2] (s. 61 (2)); and
(c) the modes of alteration provided for in sections 61 and 66 must be clearly distinguished. A cancellation of shares in consequence of a resolution authorised by section 61, *e.g.* of a subdivision of shares or diminution of the share capital, does not constitute a reduction within the meaning of section 66 (s. 61 (3)). A cancellation of shares which have actually been issued and not replaced is, however, a reduction of capital although a different procedure may be adopted than that under section 66.[3]

---

[1] See para. 32–01, *post*. These sections apply only to limited companies. Unlimited companies need only comply with the requirements of their own Memorandum and Articles of Association.

[2] The Act of 1908 did not say how the company might exercise the authority. The Act of 1929 provided in s. 50 (2) the same provision as has been re-enacted in s. 61 (2) of the Act of 1948.

[3] For example on a redemption or purchase by a company of its own shares; see Chap. 37, *post*.

The modes of alteration authorised in sections 61 and 66 extend to companies limited by guarantee and having a share capital (s. 61 (1), s. 66 (1)).

Increase of share capital

Procedure

31–02 To increase the nominal capital of a company limited by shares[4] involves an alteration of one of the conditions of its memorandum, but section 61 (1) (*a*) empowers a company limited by shares "if so authorised by its articles" to alter that condition of its memorandum so as to "increase its share capital by new shares of such amount as it thinks expedient." Article 44 of Table A is a specimen of such an authorisation by the articles. If this provision of Table A is excluded and the articles give no authority, the articles must be altered before the resolution to increase is passed,[5] but if the company passes a special resolution authorising the creation and issue of the desired new shares, that will in effect not only give the authority to increase required by section 61 but *uno flatu* enable the directors to exercise it.[6] The power to increase can be exercised from time to time. An increase of capital does not of itself imply a further issue of shares, it merely increases the *nominal* and not the *issued* capital. The *issue* of shares is done by the directors but they require authority to do so by an ordinary resolution of the general meeting or the articles[7] and their authority is limited to five years.[8] The power to increase the capital must, as stated earlier in general terms,[9] be exercised by the company in general meeting, and the directors have no power to exercise it. Subject to this, the power must be exercised in the manner indicated in its articles. The 1948 Act admits provisions in the articles authorising the increase of capital by ordinary resolution (s. 61 (1) (*a*)) and this is the method expressly authorised by article 44 as regards companies to which Table A applies. There is no objection to a company in its registered articles prescribing additional, and stricter, requirements, *e.g.* that the capital may be increased by extraordinary or by special resolution, but such provisions are uncommon in modern company practice.

Notice of general meeting

The notice convening the meeting should specify the proposed increase.[10]

---

[4] This power also applies to companies limited by guarantee and having a share capital.
[5] *Metropolitan Cemetery Co.*, 1934 S.C. 65.
[6] *Campbell's Case* (1873) L.R. 9 Ch. 1, 21.
[7] See para. 24–01, *ante.*
[8] See para. 24–02, *ante.*
[9] *Ibid.*
[10] *MacConnell* v. *E. Prill & Co. Ltd.* [1916] 2 Ch. 57.

Notice to Registrar

31–03 Where the capital has been increased, notice thereof must be given to the Registrar, together with particulars of the conditions on which the new shares are issued and a printed copy of the resolution, within 15 days after the passing of the resolution authorising the increase; in default the company and every director and manager, secretary or other officer knowingly permitting the default will be liable to a penalty of £200 or on conviction after continued contravention an alternative penalty of £20 per day (s. 63 (3),[11] as amended).

Capital duty and fees

Capital duty,[12] at the rate of 1 per cent., is levied not on the increase of the *nominal* capital but, *inter alia*, on the increase of the issued capital.[13] The European Court has ruled that to comply with the EEC Directive imposing this charge member states must levy the duty on the actual value of the assets received on such increase.[14] The Court decided that a potential tax liability attaching to the assets was not to be deductible from the basis of charge.

Consolidation of shares

31–04 Consolidation is the process of combining a specified number of shares into one new share, the new share having a nominal value equal to the aggregate of the shares so consolidated. Like the power to increase the capital the power to consolidate is exercised by the general meeting in the manner authorised by the articles, which will specify the resolution required for such exercise. Table A, art. 45, prescribes an ordinary resolution. Even where there is no power in the articles, the power may be exercised by a special resolution without first altering the articles, since the special resolution constitutes an *ad hoc* alteration of the articles.[15]

Notice of consolidation has to be given to the Registrar of Companies within one month (s. 62 (1) (*a*)). There are penalties of £200 or £20 per day in default (s. 62 (2), as amended).

The consolidation of classes of shares is treated later.[16]

Subdivision of shares

31–05 The subdivision of shares is also provided for in section 61. A power to subdivide must be contained in the articles and must be exercised by a resolution of the company in general meeting. Before the Act of 1929 a

---

[11] These sums may be amended under s. 28 of the Criminal Law Act 1977.

[12] Introduced by sections 47–49 of the Finance Act 1973 in compliance with Directive 335 of 1969 of the EEC (J.O.L. 249/25 O.J. (Special Edition) 1969 (II) 412).

[13] This is a "chargeable transaction" under Finance Act 1973, Sched. 19, Pt. I, para. 1.

[14] *P. Conradsen A/S* v. *Ministeriet for Sketter ög Afgiter* (Case 161/78) [1978] 1 C.M.L.R. 121.

[15] This would appear to follow from the reasoning in *Campbell's Case* (1873) L.R. 9 Ch. 1, 22, 23.

[16] See para. 33–26, *post*.

special resolution was necessary but this is no longer required, and Table A, art. 45, provides for the exercise of this power by ordinary resolution. Within one month notice of a resolution to subdivide shares must be given to the Registrar (s. 62 (1) (*d*)). Similar penalties to those relating to the notice of consolidation may be imposed (s. 62 (2), as amended). The articles sometimes contain power on subdivision to attach a preference to some of the shares resulting from the subdivision as against the other shares; and, having regard to the decision in *Andrews* v. *Gas Meter Co.*,[17] such a power is valid, whether inserted in the articles originally or at a later date, provided that no provision in the memorandum is thereby contravened. Implicit in that decision is the fact that such a subdivision is not a variation of class rights. If this is still the position no special procedures need be adopted to comply with section 32 of the 1980 Act.[18] In the event of a contrary interpretation, however, the new procedures will have to be followed and since variation is in effect achieved by an ordinary resolution a notice of the variation will have to be made to the Registrar within one month of the resolution within section 33 (3) of that Act. Even if no variation is involved particulars of the new shares may have to be sent to the Registrar under section 33 (1) if the subdivision amounts to an allotment within the meaning of that Act,[19] an argument which appears to be quite tenable.

Where the shares are not fully paid up, the proportion between the amount paid and the amount unpaid on each reduced share must be the same as it was before subdivision (s. 61 (1) (*d*)).[20]

Conversion of shares into stock and vice versa

31–06 The conversion of paid-up shares into stock may likewise be effected by resolution of the company in general meeting. Such a conversion can only be made where the shares are fully paid up. Notice of conversion must, as in the case of consolidation and subdivision, be given to the Registrar (s. 62 (1) (*b*) and (*c*)).

Stock differs, in principle, from shares in the following respects[21]:

(1) stock need not be numbered while shares may have to be numbered (see s. 74)[22]; and

(2) stock need not be divided into equal parts but may be divided into fractions, *e.g.* assuming that the stock arises from shares of £1 each a stockholder may hold £1.60p worth of stock.

Before the company law reform culminating in the Act of 1948 a considerable number of companies availed themselves of this power, and

---

[17] [1897] 1 Ch. 361.

[18] See para. 33–26, *post.*

[19] 1980 Act, s. 87 (2). See para. 29–05, *ante*.

[20] See also para. 33–06, *post,* as to subdivision of classes of shares. It would be consistent if the same rule applies to the consolidation of partly paid shares but no such express wording is to be found in s. 61 (1) (*b*) as in s. 61 (1) (*d*).

[21] *Morrice* v. *Aylmer* (1874) L.R. 10 Ch. 148.

[22] As to the cases in which shares need not be numbered, see below in text.

converted their shares into stock in order to obtain the benefit of the first of these characteristics, *viz*. the absence of numbers. This is convenient in company practice because it becomes no longer necessary in a transfer to specify all the numbers of the various shares comprised in the transfer. A transfer is merely of so much stock. The inducement for the conversion of fully paid shares into stock has, however, greatly receded, since the Act of 1948 provides that the company may dispense with distinguishing numbers of shares if those shares are fully paid up and rank *pari passu* (s. 74, proviso).

31–07 By the articles the directors may be authorised to fix a minimum amount of stock transferable (art. 41 of Table A), *e.g*. assuming that the stock arises from shares of a nominal amount of £1 the directors may fix the minimum amount of transferable stock at whatever figure they choose, whether £1 or less; these units are known as *stock units*.[23] Table A, art. 41, states that where a company creates stock units, their amount must not exceed that of the nominal amount of the share. This restriction may well be because this would in fact amount to a consolidation of the shares without the approval of the company in general meeting as required by section 61 (1) (*b*).

Under section 61 stock can be reconverted into shares in the same way. Stock cannot be issued direct by the company. But where a company properly converted its preference and ordinary shares into preference and ordinary stock, additional stock issued directly in return for cash was held to be valid, the "irregularity" of omitting the intermediate formality of issuing the shares and then converting them being treated as waived by lapse of time. But direct issues of bonus stock and partly paid stock were held to be entirely void, the holders having no rights, and calls could not be made on them. No agreement to take notionally converted shares could be implied.[24]

A company is empowered by the 1948 Act to issue stock warrants to bearer[25] but under the Exchange Control Act that power was subject to Treasury consent and therefore little used. All restrictions of this nature were lifted, apart from Southern Rhodesia, with effect from October 24, 1979 and for all purposes with effect from December 13, 1979[26] so that the power is now fully operative again.

Diminution of capital

31–08 This term is used in this work to denote a cancellation of the authorised but not issued capital, or, as section 61 (1) (*e*) expresses it, the cancellation

---

[23] If the stock was created before the introduction of decimal currency in 1971 and was transferable in units of less than 1p it may now only be transferred in units of 1p or multiples of 1p: Decimal Currency Act 1969, s. 8 (1).

[24] *Re Home and Foreign Investment, etc., Co.* [1912] 1 Ch. 72.

[25] *Pilkington* v. *United Rys., etc.* [1930] 2 Ch. 108.

[26] Exchange Control (General Exemption) Order 1979. (S.I. 1979, No. 1660); see para. 26–24, *ante*.

of "shares which at the date of the passing of the resolution in that behalf have not been taken or agreed to be taken by any person."

The diminution of capital should be distinguished from the reduction of capital; the Act provides expressly that diminution does not constitute a reduction within the meaning of that Act (s. 61 (3)). Diminution is carried out, if this procedure is authorised by the articles (s. 61 (1) (*e*)), by an ordinary resolution. A reduction (which must also be authorised by the articles) is required by the Act to be effected by a special resolution and to be confirmed by the court (s. 66 (1)).

The cancellation of issued shares is therefore usually part of a reduction scheme under section 66[27] but section 37 of the 1980 Act requires public companies to either dispose of or cancel shares which have been issued and subsequently forfeited or surrendered in lieu of forfeiture for non-payment of calls or instalments within three years of this happening.[28] Similar rules apply to shares which the company acquires, otherwise than by purchase or redemption, and has a beneficial interest in,[29] shares acquired without financial assistance from the company by a nominee of that company in which it has a beneficial interest[30] and shares acquired by anyone with financial assistance from such a company provided that the company has a beneficial interest therein.[31] If such a cancellation occurs and the effect will be to reduce the company's allotted share capital below the authorised minimum[32] the directors may re-register the company as a private company, as they must do, without complying with the reduction of capital provisions in section 66 of the 1948 Act.[33] Any of its own shares acquired by any company either by purchase or redemption under sections 45 and 46 of the 1981 Act must be cancelled.[33a] This would be a diminution of the issued share capital but has no effect on the authorised capital[33b] and no relationship with section 61.

The diminution of capital, as such, is a measure rarely adopted by companies; if the authorised capital figure was created partly or wholly before August 1, 1973 it would result in loss of the capital duty paid on the authorised capital[34] and, apart from this, would have hardly any practical effect. It is, however, sometimes applied in connection with a reduction of capital or other cases in which the capital structure of the company is altered, *e.g.* a reconstruction or amalgamation. Where the capital is diminished in connection with a reduction of capital, "it is usual and convenient

[27] See note 35 below.
[28] 1980 Act, s. 37 (1) (*a*), (2) (11). See para. 41–04, *post*.
[29] *Ibid*. s. 37 (1) (*b*).
[30] *Ibid*. s. 37 (1) (*c*).
[31] *Ibid*. s. 37 (1) (*d*). The time limit is one year in this case.
[32] See para. 4–14, *ante*.
[33] *Ibid*. s. 37 (2).
[33a] *Ibid*. s. 37 (2).
[33b] *Ibid*.
[34] This will not apply to diminutions of authorised capital figures created wholly after July 31, 1973. See para. 31–03 *ante*.

not to treat [the diminution] as a separate matter being dealt with under section 61 but as part of the general scheme of reduction"[35] to which section 66 applies.

Notice of diminution must be sent to the Registrar within one month (s. 62 (1) (*f*)). Default penalties of £200 or £20 per day apply in the event of failure (s. 62 (2)).

Decimalisation

31–09 If any of these alterations of capital involve a change to decimal currency no additional resolution of the company is required. Nor is it necessary to invoke section 61 to effect a straight change in the description of a share from the old currency to the new.

PRACTICE NOTE

Consolidation and subdivision of shares

31–10 In addition to amending the holdings in the register of members, the Registrar must be informed of the consolidation or subdivision on Form 28. A copy of the relevant resolution is not required to be filed if the change is effected by ordinary resolution. Fractions of shares (if any) arising on consolidation should be sold and the proceeds distributed to the shareholders entitled thereto. Share certificates should be recalled for replacement or amendment by means of a rubber stamp or gummed slip. Alternatively, gummed slips could be issued to shareholders to be affixed to their certificates.

In the case of subdivision, it is not the usual practice to recall share certificates for replacement or amendment (unless the shares bear distinguishing numbers) but gummed slips may be issued for affixing to the certificates.

[35] *Per* Roxburgh J. in *Re Castiglione, Erskine & Co. Ltd.* [1958] 1 W.L.R. 688, 692. See also *Ormiston Coal Co.*, 1949 S.C. 516.

CHAPTER 32

REDUCTION OF CAPITAL

Power to reduce

32–01 Section 66 of the 1948 Act provides for the reduction of capital. In order to effect this, the articles of the company must contain power to reduce; it is not sufficient to provide for reduction in the memorandum.[1]

If there is no such empowering clause in the articles, they must be altered by special resolution, and subsequently a further special resolution must be passed to reduce the capital in the manner proposed.[2] The resolutions may be passed successively at the same meeting.[3] The resolution for reduction, though it need not purport in terms to alter the memorandum of association,[4] must state with sufficient clearness what is to be done in the way of reduction.[5] It seems, however, following the decision in *Re Moorgate Mercantile Holdings Ltd.*[6] that the notice of the resolution, required by section 141 of the 1948 Act must specify the exact amount of the proposed reduction. Any change in that amount, however small, in the resolution which is actually passed from that specified in the notice will render the resolution void and the court will have no jurisdiction to confirm the reduction.

Reduction of capital may involve a reduction in the nominal capital. It may, at the same time, involve a reduction of the issued capital: so, too, it may involve a reduction in the paid-up capital or in capital that is issued but not paid up, as where an uncalled liability is cancelled.

The reduction of capital, in its technical meaning, has to be distinguished from the diminution of capital (s. 61 (1) (*e*)). That measure, which refers to the cancellation of the authorised but not issued capital, has been considered in the preceding chapter.[7]

Modes of reduction

32–02 A reduction of capital, if authorised by the articles, is carried out by special resolution but is not effective unless and until it has been confirmed by the court and the order and minute in terms prescribed by section 69 (1) have been registered with the Registrar of Companies (s. 69 (2)). Repay-

---

1 *Re Dexine Patent Packing and Rubber Co.* (1903) 88 L.T. 791; *John Avery & Co.* 1890, 17 R. 1101.

2 *Re Patent Invert Sugar Co.* (1885) 31 Ch.D. 166; *Re Oregon Mortgage Co.*, 1910 S.C. 1904.

3 *Fraserburgh Commercial Co.*, 1946 S.C. 444.

4 *Campbell's Case* (1873) L.R. 9 Ch. 1, 21.

5 *Scottish Manitoba Co.*, 1893, 20 R (Ct. of Sess.) 31; *W. Morrison & Co. Ltd.* 1892, 19 R. 1049; *Walker Steam Trawl Fishing Co.* 1908 S.C. 123, 15 S.L.T. 470; *R. & W. Davidson Ltd.* 1937 S.N. 108.

6 [1980] 1 All E.R. 40.

7 See para. 31–08, *ante*.

ment of capital without the sanction of the court is *ultra vires* and the court will not grant retrospective approval.[8] The court thereby is able to safeguard the interests of the creditors of the company, who have dealt with the company on the footing of its issued capital being a reality, of the registered shareholders being liable for the unpaid portions of their shares, and of the company having received the paid-up capital which appears in its register and in the returns to the Registrar of Companies. If this liability to pay up were realised, or the paid-up capital returned to shareholders, or the creditors' security in any other manner given away or tampered with, it would seriously alter their position.[8] The discretion of the court to refuse to sanction a reduction of capital also acts as a safeguard against unfair prejudice to shareholders, not only the current members of the company but also those who may later buy its shares as an investment.[9]

Section 66 (1) gives a company the power to reduce its share capital *in any way*. The words in italics appeared for the first time in the 1908 Act. Section 66 (1) specifically mentions certain ways in which the reduction of capital may be effected, but expressly states that this is to be without prejudice to the generality of the power of the company to reduce its capital.[9a] Provided that its procedure is correct, the motives of the company are irrelevant.[10] Section 66 (1) covers, *inter alia*, the following contingencies[11]:

A. Where the company is overcapitalised

32–03 A company may wish to repay capital either because it is in excess of its needs[12] or because it may wish to obtain fresh capital more cheaply elsewhere.[13] It may do this by:

(a) Extinguishing or reducing the liability of shareholders in respect of uncalled or unpaid capital, *e.g.* where the shares are £10 each with £5 paid up, reducing them to £5 fully paid-up shares, and thus relieving the shareholders from liability on the uncalled capital (s. 66 (1) (*a*)).

(b) Paying off or returning paid-up capital not wanted for the purposes

---

[8] *Alexander Henderson Ltd.*, 1967 S.L.T. (Notes) 17.

[9] *Westburn Sugar Refineries Ltd.* 1951 S.C. (H.L.) 57; 1951 S.L.T. 261; [1951] A.C. 625; *Wilsons and Clyde Coal Co. Ltd.* v. *Scottish Insurance Corpn. Ltd.* 1949 S.C. (H.L.) 90; 1949 S.L.T. 230; [1949] A.C. 462; *Prudential Assurance Co. Ltd.* v. *Chatterly-Whitfield Collieries Co. Ltd.* [1949] A.C. 512.

[9a] *Re Hoare & Co. Ltd.* [1904] 2 Ch. 208 was decided before the modern wording; in that case the court required that there should be a rateable reduction in a reserve account in the company's balance-sheet but it is thought that the basis of this decision has been destroyed as the result of the modern wording of what is now s. 66 (1).

[10] *Westburn Sugar Refineries*, *supra*; *David Bell Ltd.* 1954 S.C. 33 (overruling *A. & D. Fraser* 1951 S.C. 394; 1951 S.L.T. 273). See also *Scottish Queensland Mortgage Co.* 1908, 16 S.L.T. 394; *Alloa Coal Co.* 1947 S.C. 651; 1948 S.L.T. 78.

[11] These may, of course, be combined, *e.g. West End Cafe Co.* 1894, 21 R. 381, 1 S.L.T. 450.

[12] *Wilsons & Clyde Coal Co. Ltd.* [1949] A.C. 462; *Prudential Assurance Co. Ltd.* v. *Chatterley-Whitfield Collieries Co. Ltd.* [1949] A.C. 512; *Alloa Coal Co.* 1947 S.C. 651; 1948 S.L.T. 38.

[13] On a fluctuation of interest rates or fiscal considerations: *e.g. Lawrie & Symington Ltd., Petitioners*, 1969 S.L.T. 221; *David Bell Ltd.* 1954 S.C. 33.

of the company, *e.g.* where the shares are £10 fully paid up, reducing them to £5, and paying back £5 per share[14] (s. 66 (1) (*c*)).

(c) Paying off paid-up capital on the footing that it may be called up again. Thus, if the shares are £10 fully paid up, paying off £2 per share on the footing that when desired the company may call it up again, the uncalled liability not being extinguished[15] (s. 66 (1) (*c*)). This liability may immediately be extinguished by a capitalisation of reserves, this being part of the original reduction scheme.[16]

(d) A combination of the preceding methods.

A company need not necessarily return cash to the shareholders. It may return capital in kind and such assets may be in excess of the amount by which the paid-up value of the shares is reduced, provided that the company does not thereby render itself insolvent.[17] If a company acquires its own shares on a reduction of capital this is a permitted method of such acquisition.[18]

B. Where the company has suffered a loss of capital

32–04 (e) Cancelling capital which has been lost or is unrepresented by available assets (s. 66 (1) (*b*)).

This is one of the most common modes of reduction, and is a very useful means of reintroducing reality into the balance-sheet position of the company. Where a company has lost a large part of its capital so that its profit and loss account is heavily in debit, the effect is, *inter alia*, that the assets side of the balance-sheet will show an item (the profit and loss account debit balance) which will prevent the distribution of dividends until the loss has been eradicated by subsequent profits. As far back as 1877 it was realised that it is desirable for the company to be able to write off the loss and put itself with a clear balance-sheet in a position to resume payment of dividends out of subsequent profits.

The provisions empowering a company to cancel any lost capital, or any capital unrepresented by available assets, are alternative provisions, and the latter is not explanatory of the former.

---

[14] *Re Lees Brook Spinning Co.* [1906] 2 Ch. 394; *Re Artizans' Land and Mortgage Corpn.* [1904] 1 Ch. 796; *Re Piercy* [1907] 1 Ch. 289.

[15] *Re Fore-Street Warehouse Company Ltd.* (1888) 59 L.T. 214. See also *Scottish Vulcanite Co.*, 1894, 21 R. (Ct. of Sess.) 752; *William Brown, Sons & Co.*, 1931 S.C. 701; *Stevenson, Anderson & Co. Ltd.*, 1951 S.C. 346.

[16] *Doloi Tea Co., Petitioners*, 1961 S.L.T. 168.

[17] *Ex p. Westburn Sugar Refineries Ltd.* [1951] A.C. 625. In a South African case it was held that the grant to shareholders of a permanent right to occupy flats belonging to the company was not a return of capital in kind. *Rosslare (Pty) Ltd.* v. *Registrar of Companies* [1972] S.A.L.R. (2) 524 (S.A.).

[18] 1980 Act, s. 35 (4) (i) (*aa*). See Chap. 37, *post*.

If the company seeks to reduce capital on this ground the court must be provided with at least prima facie evidence of actual loss of capital.[19]

In practice a resolution for the reduction of authorised and issued capital is often followed by an increase of the authorised capital to the former amount, thus enabling the general meeting or the directors to issue further shares to the authorised amount if required. Although such an issue will be a "chargeable transaction" for the purposes of capital duty, relief is available if less than four years elapse between the reduction and issue of shares.[20]

C. Where an order for purchase has been made by the court

32–05 (f) Under section 75 of the 1980 Act a member or members of the company may petition the court on the basis of unfairly prejudicial conduct of the affairs against him.[21] If the court is satisfied that the petition is well founded it may make such order as it thinks fit for giving relief[22] and in particular it may, *inter alia*, provide for the purchase by the company of the shares of any member and in such an event it may provide for the reduction of the company's capital accordingly.[23]

The court has a similar power under section 11 of the 1980 Act on a minority petition to cancel a resolution to re-register a public company as a private company[24]; under section 44 of the 1981 Act on a minority petition to cancel a resolution authorising a private company to give financial assistance for the purchase of its own shares[24a]; and, under section 57 of the 1981 Act on a similar petition to cancel a resolution authorising a private company to redeem or purchase its own shares out of capital.[24b]

All-round reduction

32–06 Prima facie, where the reduction of capital is because of loss of capital, it should be an all-round one; that is to say, where capital is to be paid off or to be cancelled as lost or unrepresented by available assets, or where the liability for uncalled capital is to be reduced the same percentage should be paid off or cancelled or reduced in respect of each share; and this *pari passu* mode of reduction has been held to be the proper mode where there

---

19 *City Property Investment Trust Corpn.* v. *Thorburn* 1896, 23 R. 400; *Caldwell* v. *Caldwell* 1916 S.C. (H.L.) 120; (1916) W.N. 70.
20 Finance Act 1973, Sched. 19, Pt. II, paras. 9 (2), and (5).
21 See Chap. 60, *post*.
22 1980 Act, s. 75 (3).
23 *Ibid.* s. 75 (4) (*d*).
24 *Ibid.* s. 11 (7).
24a 1981 Act s. 44 (3).
24b *Ibid.* s. 57 (6).

are several classes of shares, *e.g.* ordinary and preference shares.[25] Where, however, the preference shares have priority as regards capital in winding up,[26] the loss should be thrown first on the ordinary shares.[27]

Where preference shareholders have no priority as to capital, but are merely entitled to a fixed cumulative preferential dividend on the nominal capital from time to time paid up on their shares, a rateable reduction on all the shares, both preference and ordinary, is not an alteration of the rights of the preference shares notwithstanding that their dividend will thereafter be reduced as being payable on a smaller amount of capital.[28]

No unfair discrimination

32–07 Conversely, where the reduction is on the ground of overcapitalisation, the court will normally sanction a reduction where the rights of different classes are correctly adhered to, and it will do this even if a class of shareholders thereby loses a possibility of some additional benefit outside their rights in the company.[29] So in *Prudential Assurance Co. Ltd.* v. *Chatterley-Whitfield Collieries Co. Ltd.*,[30] the House of Lords confirmed a reduction under which preference shares were paid off in accordance with their rights, notwithstanding that it precluded them from the opportunity of some additional advantage as a result of the Coal Industry Nationalisation Act 1946. This depreciation did not make the reduction one which was not fair and equitable, so as to persuade the court in its discretion to refuse to confirm the reduction.[31] Further, preference shares which have priority as regards capital in winding up may be paid off first, and this will not be regarded as unfair discrimination against them, even though, if they are participating as to dividend, this may deny them a share in undrawn or future profits.[32] This would also normally be denied them on a liquidation, and this dual vulnerability is now accepted as a characteristic of preference shares unless the terms of issue otherwise provide.[33] In one case,[34] a reduction was sanctioned even though the preference shareholders were entitled to participate in the surplus assets on a liquidation. In the light of these decisions it is unlikely that any variation of class rights will be involved so as to invoke section 32 of the 1980 Act.[35]

---

[25] *Bannatyne* v. *Direct Spanish Telegraph Co.* (1886) 34 Ch.D. 287; *Re Direct Spanish Telegraph Co.* (1886) 34 Ch.D. 307; *Re Barrow Haematite Steel Co.* (1888) 39 Ch.D. 582; *Re Credit Assurance and Guarantee Corporation* [1902] 2 Ch. 601.

[26] *Re American Pastoral Co.* (1890) 62 L.T. 625.

[27] *Re Floating Dock Co. of St. Thomas* [1895] 1 Ch. 691; *Re London and New York, etc., Co.* [1895] 2 Ch. 860; *Re Thomas de la Rue & Co.* [1911] 2 Ch. 361.

[28] *Re Mackenzie & Co.* [1916] 2 Ch. 450.

[29] The court will refuse a reduction which is unfair to some class or minority of shareholders; see para. 32–09, *post.*

[30] [1969] A.C. 512. See further *Re Saltdean Estate Ltd.* [1968] 1 W.L.R. 1844.

[31] See also *Scottish Insurance Corporation Ltd.* v. *Wilsons and Clyde Coal Co. Ltd.* [1949] A.C. 462; 1949 S.C. (H.L.) 90; 1949 S.L.T. 230.

[32] *Re Chatterley-Whitfield Collieries Co. Ltd.* [1948] 2 All E.R. 593, 596 (C.A.).

[33] *Re Saltdean Estate Ltd.* [1968] 1 W.L.R. 1844.

[34] *Re William Jones & Sons Ltd.* [1969] 1 W.L.R. 146. But, in this case no objections were raised by the preference shareholders.

[35] See para. 33–26, *post.*

Other reduction practices

32–08 But it is open to a company to pass a special resolution reducing the capital otherwise than in accordance with the legal rights of the shareholders, *e.g.* by paying off wholly or in part *some* of the shareholders, although all are entitled to rank *pari passu*,[36] or by cancelling part of the capital paid up on one class, although both classes rank evenly as regards capital.[37] If only the reduction of a class of preference shares is contemplated and the majority holds a large number of both preference and ordinary shares but the minority holds only preference shares, the majority, when voting at the separate class meeting, must take account of the interests of the preference shareholders as a class: if the majority is only guided by its own interests there is no effective sanction of the reduction by the class meeting.[38] It is further settled that the court has jurisdiction to confirm any kind of reduction, notwithstanding that it involves a departure from the legal rights of the classes[39]; for the court's power to confirm a reduction is perfectly general. In Scotland it has been held that a reduction will be sanctioned even if its sole purpose is the avoidance of tax.[40]

In *British and American Corporation* v. *Couper*[41] Lord Herschell L.C. said:

> "It will be observed that neither of these statutes [1867 and 1877, for which sections 67–71 are now substituted] prescribes the manner in which the reduction of capital is to be effected. Nor is there any limitation of the power of the court to confirm the reduction, except that it must first be satisfied that all the creditors entitled to object to the reduction have either consented or been paid or secured. . . . I think it was the policy of the Legislature to entrust the prescribed majority of the shareholders with the decision whether there should be a reduction of capital, and if so, how it should be carried into effect. The interests of the dissenting minority of the shareholders (if there be

---

[36] *Banknock Coal Co.* (1897) 24 R. (Ct. of Sess.) 476; *William Dixon Ltd.*, 1948 S.C. 511; *Fife Coal Co.*, 1948 S.C. 505.

[37] But where it is proposed to pay off part of the equity shares, and all the shareholders have not consented, the reduction should be made by means of a scheme of arrangement under s. 206 (see para. 79–04, *post*): *Re Robert Stephen Holdings Ltd.* [1968] 1 W.L.R. 522; the court has no jurisdiction to approve such a scheme if it proposes to expropriate some shareholders without compensation: In *Re N.F.U. Development Trust Ltd.* [1972] 1 W.L.R. 1548. The rule in *Robert Stephen Holdings Ltd. supra*, would seem to supplement the decision in *Neale* v. *City of Birmingham Tramways Co.* [1910] 2 Ch. 464, where it was held that more capital could be repaid on some shares of the same class than on others.

[38] *Re Holders Investment Trust Ltd.* [1971] 1 W.L.R. 583.

[39] *British and American, etc., Corpn.* v. *Couper* [1894] A.C. 399; *Re Credit Assurance and Guarantee Corporation* [1902] 2 Ch. 601; *Re Allsopp & Sons* (1903) 51 W.R. 644; *Re Welsbach Incandescent Gas Light Co.* [1904] 1 Ch. 87; *Re National Dwellings Society* (1898) 78 L.T. 144; *Re Louisiana and Southern States Real Estate, etc., Co.* [1909] 2 Ch. 552; *Re Thomas de la Rue & Co.* [1911] 2 Ch. 361; *Fraser Bros., Petitioners*, 1963 S.C. 139 (where it was held that a resolution of a separate class meeting was required; *sed quaere*); *Re William Jones & Sons Ltd.* [1969] 1 W.L.R. 146 (where it was held that a resolution of a separate class meeting was *not* required); *Donaldson Line Ltd.* 1945 S.C. 162; 1945 S.L.T. 46; *D. M. Stevenson & Co.* 1947 S.C. 646; 1948 S.L.T. 81; *Fife Coal Co.* 1948 S.C. 505; 1948 S.L.T. 421; *Arniston Coal Co.* 1948 S.C. 505; 1948 S.L.T. 421.

[40] *David Bell Ltd.* 1954 S.C. 33.

[41] [1894] A.C. 399, 403–406. See also *Balmenach-Glenlivet Distillery* v. *Croall* 1906 8 F. (Ct. of Sess.) 1135.

such) are properly safeguarded by this: that the decision of the majority can only prevail if it be confirmed by the court."

Lord Macnaghten in *Poole* v. *Nat. Bank of China* said[42]:

> "The condition that gives jurisdiction [to confirm a reduction of capital] is not proof of loss of capital or proof that capital is unrepresented by available assets, or that capital is in excess of the wants of the company. The jurisdiction arises whenever the company seeking reduction has duly passed a special resolution to that effect."

In exceptional circumstances the court has even sanctioned an *ultra vires* reduction of capital. Thus in *Re Liverpool Cotton Association Ltd.*[43] the company had purported to purchase some of its own shares[44] at various dates before 1889. The invalidity of this purchase, at that time, was not discovered until a take-over bid was made for the shares many years later. The court approved a proposal to reduce the capital by cancelling the shares purchased by the company and thereby to regularise the position. On the other hand, in *Alexander Henderson Ltd., Petitioners*,[45] the court refused to make an order for reduction where a repayment of capital had inadvertently been made before presentation of the petition, on the ground that it could not condone an illegal proceeding of this kind.

Modes of reduction not sanctioned

32–09 The court has refused to sanction the cancellation of a class of shares on the footing that in lieu thereof the company was to issue to the holders a larger amount of paid-up shares of another class.[46] Such a course would amount to an allotment of shares at a discount.[47]

The court will likewise refuse to confirm a reduction which is unfair to some class or minority of shares.[48] If the reduction of a class of preference shares is resolved and the majority, when voting at the separate class meeting, was guided by its own interests and did not take into account the interests of the preference shareholders as a class, the onus of proving that the reduction is fair falls on the majority; prima facie the reduction of capital by cancellation of redeemable preference shares having a fixed date of redemption in exchange of unsecured loan stock redeemable at a much later date is unfair.[49] The objecting shareholders must show prejudice to their interests.[50] The court cannot confirm a conditional reduction.[51]

---

42 [1907] A.C. 229, 239.
43 (1963) 107 S.J. 195.
44 This was an *ultra vires* activity prior to the 1980 and 1981 Acts. See Chap. 37, *post*.
45 1967 S.L.T. (Notes) 17.
46 *Re Development Co. of Central and West Africa* [1902] 1 Ch. 547.
47 1980 Act, s. 21.
48 See *British and American, etc., Corpn.* v. *Couper* [1894] A.C. 399, 406, 413; *Scottish Insurance Corporation Ltd.* v. *Wilsons and Clyde Coal Co. Ltd.* [1949] A.C. 462, 486, 499; 1949 S.C. (H.L.) 90; 1949 S.L.T. 230. On unfair discrimination against preference shareholders see also, Chap. 34, *post*.
49 *Re Holders Investment Trust Ltd.* [1971] 1 W.L.R. 583.
50 *Hoggan* v. *Tharsis Sulphur and Copper Co.* 1882, 9 R. 1191.
51 *Re Castiglione, Erskine & Co. Ltd.* [1958] 1 W.L.R. 688, 690.

If circumstances have so changed since the proceedings commenced that the basis on which shareholders agreed to the scheme no longer obtains, the court will not sanction the reduction until they have had an opportunity to reconsider it.[52]

Procedure for obtaining consent of creditors

32–10 Reduction of capital which involves the repayment of capital or the diminution of unpaid liability on shares requires the consent of creditors (s. 67 (2)) unless the court is satisfied that it may dispense with such consent (s. 67 (3)).[53] The issue of debentures in place of shares is a repayment of capital.[54] The procedure under section 67 (2) involves an inquiry at the sight of the court to settle a list of creditors, followed by the payment of their claims, or their consent to the reduction. The court may dispense with the consent of particular creditors on satisfactory security being provided. Although a creditor has a theoretical right to object to a cancellation of paid-up capital which has been lost, it is unlikely that he could show sufficient interest for his objections to be entertained.[55]

In modern practice the procedure of section 67 (2) is unlikely to be invoked. The company will rely on being able to obtain dispensation under section 67 (3). This may be granted if there is in fact no diminution of capital, as where one class of shares is repaid and the proceeds applied in subscription for new shares.[56] In other circumstances the court has to be satisfied that, so far as can be reasonably foreseen, the relevant creditors, *i.e.* those who would be entitled to the benefit of s. 67 (2), would not be adversely affected by the reduction of capital.[57] The company may be able to show that it has already secured the payment of such claims satisfactorily or obtained the consent of all its creditors.[58]

In most reductions, however, dispensation is sought on the basis that the company's readily realisable assets exceed the total of its liabilities (existing and contingent) and the amount of any proposed repayment, with sufficient fixed and current assets in addition to cover its remaining paid-up capital.[59] In addition to cash and gilt-edged securities, trade debts may be regarded as readily realisable if the company can satisfy the court that it has made adequate provision for bad and doubtful debts, and that it has in the past paid its own trade debts promptly and received prompt payment from its trade debtors.[60] The court may in the exercise of its discretion

---

52 *Halley & Sons* 1948 S.C. 612; 1948 S.L.T. 500 (contrast *Gardiner & Sons* 1948 S.C. 34; 1948 S.L.T. 136).
53 The power to dispense with consent was introduced by the Companies Act 1928, s. 19 (2).
54 *Lawrie & Symington Ltd.* 1969 S.L.T. 221.
55 *Re Meux's Brewery* [1919] 1 Ch. 28.
56 *New Duff House Sanatorium Ltd.* 1931 S.L.T 337.
57 *Re Luciania Temperance Billiard Halls (London) Ltd.* [1966] Ch. 98.
58 *Cadzow Coal Co. Ltd.* 1931 S.C. 272; 1931 S.L.T. 272; *Re Luciania Temperance Billiard Halls (London) Ltd., supra.*
59 *Re Luciania Temperance Billiard Halls (London) Ltd.* [1966] Ch. 98.
60 *Anderson Brown & Co. Ltd.* 1965 S.C. 81.

relax these conditions. A company whose assets were not readily realisable (ships) obtained dispensation where the court was satisfied that in practice its creditors would be paid promptly.[61] In that case there was the additional factor that it would have been impossible to apply s. 67 (2) since the company could not reasonably have been expected to ascertain the full list of its creditors.

Proceedings to obtain confirmation of court in England

32–11 The first step is to pass the requisite special resolution reducing the capital. The next is to apply to the court to confirm the resolution (s. 67 (1)). The application is made by petition.[62]

The petition states the incorporation and nature of the company, its subsequent history, the passing of the special resolution for reduction, and the facts requisite to show that it is a proper case for reduction, and prays for a confirmation order.[63] Where there is more than one class of shares the petition should state specifically whether there is or is not any priority as to capital.[64] The petition is not required to state that the company is carrying on business.[65]

Reduction in case of lost capital[66]

32–12 Where the reduction does not involve either the diminution of liability or the payment off of any paid-up capital, the procedure is short and simple. A summons in chambers is taken out, and on it directions are given fixing a day for hearing the petition and ordering meanwhile advertisements to be inserted in the *London Gazette* and other newspapers. The petition then comes on and the order can be made at once without setting in motion any of the complicated machinery provided by the legislature where the rights of creditors are involved. Creditors have no right to objection in these cases except in very special circumstances.[67] Where the reduction is based upon an assertion that capital has been lost or is not represented by assets, the court requires prima facie proof of this assertion.[68] The exact extent of the evidence required is, however, uncertain. In *Re Moorgate Mercantile Holdings Ltd.*,[69] Slade J. raised but did not decide the question as to whether the court should in practice always insist on evidence as to the current net value of the company's assets where a reduction is sought on

---

[61] *Unifruitco Steamship Co.* 1930 S.C. 1104; 1930 S.L.T. 735.
[62] See R.S.C. 1965, Ord. 102, r. 5 (*f*). For applications in the long vacation see Practice Directions of March 3, 1977 [1977] 1 W.L.R. 317, and February 23, 1978 [1978] 1 All E.R. 820. A judge will be available to sit on an early Wednesday in August and each Wednesday in September; see Vol II, paras. A–5001 and A–5002.
[63] See *Company Precedents* (17th ed.), Part I, pp. 1003 and 1031.
[64] *Re Mackenzie & Co.* [1916] 2 Ch. 450.
[65] *Re Great Universal Stores Ltd.* [1960] 1 W.L.R. 78.
[66] See para. 32–04, *ante*.
[67] *Re Meux's Brewery Ltd.* [1919] 1 Ch. 28.
[68] *Re Barrow Haematite Steel Co.* [1901] 2 Ch. 746; *Caldwell* v. *Caldwell & Co.* 1916 S.C. (H.L.) 120; [1916] W.N. 70.
[69] [1980] 1 All E.R. 40.

the basis of lost capital and the creditors are not otherwise provided for. In that case the company sought a reduction on the basis of a severe decline in the value of its shareholdings in other companies four years before the petition was brought.[70]

Reduction in cases of overcapitalisation[71]

In cases which involve a diminution of liability or a return of paid-up capital, the procedure is more elaborate.[72] The replacement of preference shares by loan stock in a reduction involves payment to a shareholder of paid-up share capital within the meaning of section 67 (2) of the 1948 Act. Although no immediate payment will fall due, the company is assuming a liability to repay at a later date when the loan stock matures.[73] An inquiry has to be made as to the debts and liabilities, advertisements have to be issued and the consent of creditors has to be obtained (s. 67 (2)). Such creditors as do not consent must be paid off or provision must be made for paying their debts into court. The court may dispense with these requirements (s. 67 (3)), but will only do so if the creditors would be no worse off than they would be if they were permitted to attend and to object.[74] Such dispensation is likely to be given if the company gives adequate security for the payment of all debts existing and contingent in respect of which the dispensation is sought, or if the debts are guaranteed by a bank. In special circumstances it may even be sufficient to satisfy the court that the company holds sufficient cash and gilt-edged securities to cover the return of capital (if any), and any creditors or contingent creditors of the company, with an adequate surplus. In due course the petition comes before the judge dealing with company matters and the order sought is made, provided that the judge is satisfied that the reduction is fair and complies with the statutory conditions. The order directs how the reduction is to be advertised. If the judge is of the opinion that the reduction should not be confirmed he has an absolute discretion to refuse it.[75]

Words "and reduced." Publication of reasons for reduction

32–13 The court may attach conditions to its sanctions of the reduction (s. 68 (1)) and, if for any special reason it thinks fit to do so, order that the words "and reduced" be added to the company's name and used for a longer or shorter period (s. 68 (2) (*a*)), but in practice this power has not been used by the court for many years. Occasionally the court directs the publication of the reasons for the reduction (s. 68 (2) (*b*)).[76]

---

[70] *Ibid.* at pp. 56–57.
[71] See para. 32–03, *ante*.
[72] See R.S.C. 1965, Ord. 102, rr. 8–15.
[73] *Lawrie & Symington Ltd., Petitioners*, 1969 S.L.T. 221.
[74] *Re Luciania Temperance Billiard Halls (London) Ltd.* [1966] Ch. 98.
[75] *Prudential Assurance Co. Ltd.* v. *Chatterley-Whitfield Collieries Co. Ltd.* [1949] A.C. 512; *Scottish Insurance Corporation Ltd.* v. *Wilsons and Clyde Coal Co. Ltd.* [1949] A.C. 462; 1949 S.C. (H.L.) 90.
[76] *Re Truman, Hanbury & Co.* [1910] 2 Ch. 498.

Court minute and certificate

In making the order the court approves a minute[77] expressing the new capital structure of the company (s. 69 (1)). The following may serve as an example of such an order[78]:

> "The capital of —— Limited was by virtue of a special resolution and with the sanction of an Order of the High Court of Justice dated the —— reduced from £100,000 divided into 50,000 preference shares of £1 each and 500,000 ordinary shares of 10p. each to £75,000 divided into 50,000 preference shares of £1 each and 500,000 ordinary shares of 5p. each. At the date of the registration of this minute all the said preference shares of £1 each and all the ordinary shares of 5p. each have been issued and are deemed to have been fully paid up."

If the capital is re-increased contingently on the reduction the minute should state the re-increased capital.[78a]

This minute, together with a copy of the order, has to be delivered to the Registrar, who gives a certificate under his hand (s. 69 (4)). The reduction takes effect from the grant of this certificate (s. 69 (2))[79] and the certificate is conclusive of the reduction (s. 69 (4)). Even if it is shown afterwards that the company had not by its articles any power to reduce,[80] or that the special resolution for reduction was invalid,[81] the reduction cannot be upset. The minute is conclusive of the capital of the company from the date of its registration. If and so far as is necessary the resolution for the reduction may alter the company's memorandum by reducing the amount of its share capital and shares accordingly (s. 66 (1)).

Since the court minute is deemed to form part of the company's memorandum (s. 69 (5)) and to be an alteration thereof (s. 69 (6)), it requires official certification under the European Communities Act 1972, s. 9 (3).[82]

Reduction below authorised minimum of allotted share capital of a public company

32–14 Where the court order has the effect of bringing the nominal value of a public company's allotted share capital[83] below the authorised minimum,[84] the Registrar will not register the order under section 69 (1) unless either the court directs him to or the company is first re-registered as a private company.[85]

Proceedings to obtain confirmation of court in Scotland

32–15 After the resolution has been passed, a petition is presented to the Court

---

[77] This "minute" should not be confused with the minutes of the general meeting passing the special resolution for the reduction. The two are quite unconnected.
[78] See further Palmer, *Company Precedents* (17th ed.), Part I, pp. 1023 *et seq*.
[78a] *Simpson (D) Ltd.* 1929 S.C. 65; 1928 S.L.T. 675; *Doloi Tea Co. Ltd.* 1961 S.L.T. 168.
[79] *Re Castiglione, Erskine & Co. Ltd.* [1958] 1 W.L.R. 688, 690.
[80] *Re Walker and Smith Ltd.* (1903) 72 L.J.Ch. 572.
[81] *Ladies' Press Association* v. *Pulbrook* [1900] 2 Q.B. 376.
[82] See para. 17–03, *ante*.
[83] See para. 29–05, *ante*.
[84] See para. 4–14, *ante*.
[85] 1980 Act, s. 12. See para. 5–14, *ante*.

of Session[86] or, if the company's capital before reduction does not exceed £120,000, to the Sheriff Court where its registered office is situated.[87] The petition states that the company is one to which the Act and the court's jurisdiction apply, its main objects and date of incorporation, the fact that power to reduce is contained in its articles, and its capital structure, and narrates the procedure up to and including the registration of the resolution with the Registrar of Companies. The grounds for the reduction in terms of one or more of the options permitted by section 66 are to be given. Any consents by classes or groups of shareholders which are necessary are averred, along with the procedure by which they were obtained. The assets and liabilities are stated in accordance with the latest audited balance-sheet, together with any subsequent changes (or a statement that there have been none). A draft of the minute to be registered is provided. All the documents necessary to vouch these matters are produced with the petition.

The first order craved, which is granted automatically, is for intimation on the walls of court and advertisement in the *Edinburgh Gazette* and local newspapers. When the *induciae* have expired copies of the papers and a certificate of intimation, etc., are lodged. Assuming there have been no answers lodged by objecting shareholders or creditors the petitioners will seek a remit to a practising solicitor to enquire into the matters set forth in the petition and the regularity of the proceedings, and report to the court.[88]

In addition to verifying the regularity of the procedure undertaken by the company leading up to the petition, the facts stated therein and the productions referred to, and the petition procedure itself, the reporter will be concerned to advise the court whether it should dispense with the procedure of section 67 (2), and whether there is any reason such as unfair prejudice to shareholders which would justify the court in withholding or delaying sanction, or granting conditional sanction. Unless the irregularity is fundamental, such as repayment of capital without court sanction,[89] defects can usually be cured by amendment to the petition, or if need be by further meetings of shareholders or class meetings. The reporter will satisfy himself that the assets and liabilities are as stated, and will require a certificate from the auditors as to the up-to-date position, to advise the court whether the criteria for dispensing with section 67 (2) have been met. He will also approve the proposed minute. If such defects as remain are unimportant, he may recommend the court to disregard them.

---

[86] Rules of the Court of Session, rr. 190–195 apply. See further McBryde and Dowie *Petition Procedure in the Court of Session*, W. Green & Son, Edinburgh, 1980, Chap. 2.

[87] s. 455 (1) ("the Court") and ss. 220 (1) and (3) as amended by the Insolvency Act 1976, s. 1 and Sched. 1. The limit of £120,000 may be amended by statutory instrument. The initial step in the Sheriff Court is by initial writ. The procedure described in the text is as in the Court of Session, which is normally followed, *mutatis mutandis,* in the Sheriff Court.

[88] This is now the invariable practice—*Clyde Structural Iron Co.* 1930 S.C. 785; 1930 S.L.T. 513; *Unifruitco Steamship Co.* 1930 S.C. 1104; 1930 S.L.T. 735.

[89] *Alexander Henderson Ltd.* 1967 S.L.T. (Notes) 17.

32–16 When the report has been lodged the company will seek the final order sanctioning the reduction, approving the minute, and directing registration thereof with the Registrar of Companies and further advertisement of the reduction.

The procedure outlined has to be modified if it is necessary to combine the application for sanction of a reduction of capital with approval of a scheme of arrangement under section 206.[90]

The observations made in paragraphs 32–13 and 32–14 equally apply to Scotland.

Application of reduction procedure to share premium account and capital redemption reserve

32–17 These quasi-capital funds are closely akin to the paid-up capital of the company: as was pointed out earlier,[91] the company is entitled under section 56 of the 1948 Act and sections 45 (6), 53 (3) and 54 (5) of the 1981 Act to use them for certain specified purposes; if it wishes to use them for other purposes the procedure for reduction of capital has to be applied; *e.g.* where a company wishes to make a distribution of dividend out of the share premium account or wishes to cancel that account to the amount lost or unrepresented by assets, a special resolution and confirmation by the court—as prescribed by section 66—is required.[91a] The minute of such a reduction should not refer to the share premium account.[92]

Exceptional cases in which reduction procedure is not required

32–18 The reduction of capital without the need for confirmation by the court is permitted in the following cases:

(a) Where a company has issued redeemable shares[93] they may be redeemed in accordance with the terms of the articles provided section 45 of the 1981 Act is complied with.[94]

(b) A company may forfeit shares for non-payment of calls or instalments pursuant to its articles. Under section 37 of the Companies Act 1980 a public company must either dispose of such shares, they may for example be reissued,[95] or cancel them and diminish the amount of the share capital by their nominal value within three years. These provisions have no application to private companies. In either case, however, if the shares are reissued the transferee will become liable for any amount unpaid on the shares at the time of

---

[90] *Wilson Bros.* v. *D. G. Howat & Co.* 1939 S.L.T. 68.
[91] Para. 29–09, *ante*. See, *e.g. Re Moorgate, Mercantile Holdings Ltd.* [1980] 1 All E.R. 40.
[91a] See 1981 Act, s. 53 (3).
[92] *Re Paringa Mining and Exploration Co. Ltd.* [1957] 1 W.L.R. 1143. The same rule was applied to the capital redemption reserve fund in *Re Knap Hill Nurseries Ltd.* (February 29, 1960, unreported).
[93] See para. 33–13, *post*.
[94] *Ibid.*
[95] *Re Exchange Banking Co. Ltd., Ramwell's Case* (1881) 50 L.J.Ch. 827.

the sale[96] and the 1948 Act clearly contemplates such an action as an allowable proceeding (arts. 33 to 39 of Table A).

If, however, the forfeited shares of a public company are cancelled and the share capital figure diminished it is thought that this will amount to a reduction of capital which will require the sanction of the court.[97] By way of exception to this, if the effect of cancelling the shares will be to lower the company's allotted share capital figure below the authorised minimum[98] the company must apply for re-registration as a private company and the directors may take such steps as are necessary to achieve this without complying with sections 66 and 67.[99]

No such obligation is imposed on a private company if the shares are not reissued and there is some doubt as to whether any reduction of capital is involved. In view of the 1980 legislation being limited to public companies the doubt must remain although clearly cancellation, etc., is the better course.

(c) A company may in certain cases accept a surrender of shares, *viz.* as a short cut to forfeiture[1]; but if a company proposes to take back shares which are repudiated on the ground of misrepresentation, it seems doubtful whether the power to accept a surrender can safely be exercised, unless it is sanctioned by the court, or unless the company is in a position to forfeit the shares and bona fide arranges a surrender as a short cut to the same end. The validity of each case of surrender of shares must be decided upon its own merits.[2]

In general such a course is not allowed, so that in *Bellerby* v. *Rowland and Marwood's S.S. Co.*[3] a surrender of partly paid shares, though made in good faith, was held to be invalid. Cozens-Hardy L.J. said[4]: "Every surrender of shares, whether fully paid up or not, involves a reduction of capital, which is unlawful, except when sanctioned by the court under the Companies Acts. . . . Forfeiture is a statutory exception, and is the only exception." Further, in *Trevor* v. *Whitworth*,[5] Lord Macnaghten said: "A surrender of shares in return for money paid by the company is a sale, and open to the same objection as a sale. . . . "

(d) A company may acquire its own shares if they are fully paid and are either purchased[6] or acquired otherwise than for valuable

---

96 See para. 41–04, *post*.
97 See para. 31–08, *ante*.
98 See para. 4–14, *ante*.
99 1980 Act, s. 37 (2). See para. 5–14, *ante*.
1 This is covered by the 1980 Act, s. 37 in the same way as forfeited shares, see the previous paragraph of the text.
2 See para. 41–08, *post*.
3 [1902] 2 Ch. 14.
4 At p. 32.
5 (1887) 12 App.Cas. 409, 438; *British and American Corporation* v. *Couper* [1894] A.C. 399; *Bellerby* v. *Rowland and Marwood's S.S. Co.* [1902] 2 Ch. 14.
6 1981 Act, s. 46; see Chap. 37 *post*

consideration.[6a] If the shares are purchased they must be cancelled.[6b] In other cases if the acquiring company is a public company and the company has a beneficial interest in them, section 37 of the Companies Act 1980 applies in the same way as to forfeited shares.[7] There is no guidance in the 1980 Act as to whether in other circumstances a reduction of capital petition need follow.

Liability of members in respect of reduced shares

32–19 After the reduction the members cease to be liable for calls or other contributions as regards the amount by which the nominal amount of their shares has been reduced (s. 70 (1)); but, exceptionally, if the company becomes unable to pay its debts within one year after the reduction, creditors who by reason of their ignorance of the reduction were not entered on the register of creditors can claim the reduced amount against persons who at the date of the reduction were members of the company (s. 70 (1), proviso).

Penalty for concealing name of creditor, etc.

32–20 Any officer of the company who either:

(i) wilfully conceals the name of any creditor entitled to object to the reduction; or

(ii) wilfully misrepresents the nature or amount of the debt or claim of any creditor; or

(iii) aids, abets or is privy to any such concealment or misrepresentation,

is liable on conviction on indictment to a fine, and on summary conviction to a fine not exceeding £1,000 (s. 71, as amended).

PRACTICE NOTE

Office procedure

32–21 An officer of the company (usually the secretary) should keep a detailed record of each stage of the procedure, as he will be called upon to make an affidavit evidencing the due calling of the general meeting approving the reduction, including the number of notices despatched and the time, date and place of posting. He and the chairman will be required to provide evidence by affidavit on other matters in support of the company's petition to the court, depending upon the nature of the reduction.

[6a] 1980 Act, s. 35 (2); see Chap. 37, *post*.
[6b] 1981 Act, s. 46 (2).
[7] See para. (b) in the text above.

B. SHARES

CHAPTER 33

NATURE AND CLASSES OF SHARES

Nature of a share

Proprietary character of share

33–01 A share in a company is the expression of a proprietary relationship: the shareholder is the proportionate owner of the company but he does not own the company's assets which belong to the company as a separate and independent legal entity.

Rights and duties carried by a share

33–02 Although the rights and duties carried by a share are, on principle, indivisible, it is often convenient to regard a share as a bundle of several rights and liabilities and to consider these separately.

The principal rights[1] which a share may carry are

(1) the right to *dividend* if, while the company is a going concern, a dividend is duly declared[2];

(2) the right to *vote* at the meetings of members[3]; and

(3) the right, in the winding up of the company, after the payment of the debts to receive a proportionate part of the *capital* or otherwise to participate in the distribution of assets of the company.[4]

The principal duty of a shareholder, as far as the company is concerned, is

> *to pay* what is due on the share, *i.e.* disregarding any premium or discount,[5] *the nominal amount* of the shares.
>
> The moneys payable on the share have to be paid by the shareholder when a *call* for payment is made upon him by the company, or at the dates fixed for payment by the terms of issue (art. 19). In the case of a public company at least one-quarter of the nominal value of the share and the whole premium must be paid up before the share is allotted.[6]

Apart from these principal rights and duties, others of ancillary character are carried by a share, *e.g.* the following rights of the shareholder:

---

[1] See art. 2: "dividend, voting, return of capital or otherwise."
[2] For the rules relating to the declaration of dividends see Chap. 76, *post*.
[3] This right may be abrogated by law: 1980 Act, s. 37 (3). See para. 41–04, *post*.
[4] The right to such payment may be deferred to certain payments to employees made under 1980 Act, s. 74. See para. 9–21, *ante*.
[5] On the issue of shares at a premium and at a discount, see Chap. 24 *ante*.
[6] 1980 Act, s. 22 (1). See para. 4–14, *ante*.

(a) to receive notice of general meetings unless the articles otherwise provide (1948 Act, s. 134 (*a*));
(b) to receive a copy of every balance-sheet (and of the documents annexed thereto) which is to be laid before the general meeting (1948 Act, s. 158);
(c) to receive a copy of the memorandum and the articles (1948 Act, s. 24);
(d) to inspect and obtain copies of the minutes of general meetings (1948 Act, s. 146);
(e) to inspect copies of directors' service contracts (1967 Act, s. 26);
(f) to inspect the various registers to be maintained by the company without charge;
(g) to subscribe for new shares of the same class unless the directors are duly authorised to the contrary (1980 Act, s. 17);
(h) to have his shares redeemed or purchased by initial or subsequent agreement (1981 Act, ss. 45 and 46).

Apart from those principal and ancillary rights which a share carries, the shareholder is further entitled to the numerous corporate and individual membership rights which the constitution of the company or the Acts themselves give him; examples of these rights are:

(a) to petition the court for the winding up of the company (1948 Act, ss. 222, 224);
(b) to petition for the remedy available in case of unfairly prejudicial conduct (1980 Act, s. 75).

Examples of ancillary liabilities of the shareholder are:

(a) in the winding up of the company, to be placed, upon certain conditions, as a past member on List B of the Contributories (1948 Act, s. 212[6a]);
(b) to be personally and severally liable, in the conditions of section 31, for certain debts of the company, if the number of shareholders is reduced below the minimum (1948 Act, s. 31);
(c) to repay any dividend received which he knew or ought to have known was made in contravention of the rules as to distributable profits (1980 Act, s. 44).

To sum up: The holding of a share in a company limited by shares generally carries the right to receive a proportion of the profits of the company and of its assets in the winding up, and all other benefits of membership, combined with an obligation to contribute to its liabilities, all measured by a certain sum of money[7] which is the nominal value of the share, and all subject to the memorandum and articles of the company.[8]

[6a] See also 1981 Act, s. 58. See para. 33–23, *post*.
[7] Except for the liability to contribute, which may include an agreed premium; see paras. 29–03, *et seq.*, *ante*.
[8] See Farwell J. in *Borland's Trustee* v. *Steel Bros. & Co.* [1901] 1 Ch. 279, 288 and Romer L.J. in *Re Paulin (Sir William Thomas)* [1935] 1 K.B. 26, 56–57.

Shares to have a nominal amount

33–03 The Act postulates that in the case of a company having a share capital[9] the memorandum, in its capital clause, must state, apart from the authorised capital, "the division thereof into *shares of a fixed amount*" (1948 Act, s. 2 (4) (*a*)). This provision requires the issue of shares having a nominal amount, and makes it impossible to issue shares of no par value. Accordingly by the law, as in operation at present,[10] the nominal value of the share, expressed, as it is, in the currency of the realm, *e.g.* £10, £1, 50p, etc., is the measuring-rod determining the proportionate rights and liabilities of the shareholder.

All shares issued since February 15, 1971, will be expressed in decimal currency. The Decimal Currency Act 1969 makes no specific mention of shares still expressed in pre-decimal currency values. Any alteration to decimal currency values needs no resolution under section 61[11] and will presumably involve no alteration of capital if the conversion table provided in the Act is followed.[12]

Numbering of shares

33–04 Shares must bear distinguishing numbers (1948 Act, s. 74), but if the following cumulative conditions are satisfied, the directors may dispense with the requirement of numbering, *viz*. if the shares

(a) are fully paid up;
(b) rank *pari passu*; and
(c) are *all* the issued shares of the company or *all* the issued shares of a particular class (s. 74, proviso).

In practice numbers are frequently dispensed with.

Shares as personal estate in England

33–05 Shares, which are choses in action, *i.e.* intangible movables, are, according to section 73 of the 1948 Act, personal estate. This applies even to shares of companies incorporated with the object of holding land for the purposes of management or investment.

The distinction between real and personal estate has, as far as the substantive law is concerned, lost today its practical importance, apart from a few exceptional cases,[13] but in connection with capital transfer tax

[9] This applies to companies limited by shares, and companies limited by guarantee and having a share capital. Unlimited companies having a share capital are expressly exempted from this provision (s. 2 (4) (*a*)).

[10] The suggestion of the Gedge Committee (Cmd. 6639 (1945), paras. 17–18) and the Jenkins Committee (Cmnd. 1749 (1962), paras. 32–34) that the issue of no par value shares should be allowed was not followed in the 1967 Act. The Conservative Government's White Paper, Company Law Reform (Cmnd. 5391 (1973), para. 49) also rejected the earlier committees' suggestions.

[11] *Re Harris & Sheldon Group Ltd.* [1971] 1 W.L.R. 899. See para. 31–01, *ante*.

[12] Decimal Currency Act 1969, Sched. 1.

[13] The Administration of Estates Act 1925, s. 1, provides that in the case of intestate succession the estate shall vest in the next-of-kin and no longer in the heir-at-law (except where the estate is connected with an honour of dignity).

the distinction, though not normally affecting the liability for duty, affects the incidence of the tax on particular beneficiaries under a will.[14]

Shares as moveable property in Scotland

In Scots law shares are incorporeal moveables (whatever the nature of the company's business) and are subject to the law of succession to moveable property. The distinction between moveables and heritage is still important in rights of succession despite the passing of the Succession (Scotland) Act 1964.

Classes of shares

33–06 Prima facie the rights carried by the shares rank *pari passu, i.e.* the shareholders participate in the benefits of membership equally.[15] It is only when a company divides its share capital into different classes with different rights attached to them that the prima facie presumption of equality of shares may be displaced.

Speaking generally, a separate class of shares is constituted when the principal rights[16] carried by the shares differ from those carried by other shares; *e.g.* some shares carry preferential or deferred rights as to dividend or capital, or more votes than other shares. But differentiation between other rights may suffice to create a different class of shares, *e.g.* differences as to freedom of transferability, or redeemability under the 1981 Act.[17]

Where a company has divided its capital into different classes, these classes have usually distinguishing descriptions and a company is at liberty to attach to them such descriptions as appear appropriate. Often the classes of shares are described as "ordinary shares," "preference shares," "employees' shares" and "deferred shares." Sometimes, however, a company may use a more complicated terminology and, *e.g.* refer to them as "first preference shares," "ordinary preference shares," etc. The law does not attach a rigid, uniformly applicable meaning to these descriptions. The rights carried by the shares have, in every case, to be gathered from the *terms of issue* which normally reproduce the relevant provisions of the memorandum and articles.

A company may divide its shares into different classes only if so authorised by its articles, as originally framed or as altered by special resolution; this applies both to the issue of newly created shares carrying rights different from those of other shares and to the alteration of rights of some part of the shares already issued.[18] A typical provision in articles authorising the issue of shares of a particular class is article 2 of Table A.

---

14 F.A. 1975, Sched. 4, para. 20.

15 See *Birch* v. *Cropper* (1889) 14 App.Cas. 525, *per* Lord Macnaghten at p. 543.

16 As defined in para. 33–02, *ante*. Exceptionally there may be different classes of shares although the shares carry the same rights, *e.g.* where "co-partnership" shares are issued to, or for the benefit of, employees; see para. 33–12, *post*.

17 See *I.R.C.* v. *Beveridge* [1979] S.T.C. 592.

18 On the requirement of consent of shareholders to such alteration, see para. 33–26, *post*.

While it is essential that the articles should contain authority for the division of shares into various classes, it was held as early as 1897[19] that no such authority need be provided in the memorandum. On the other hand, if the memorandum expressly[20] enjoins equality among the shareholders these provisions cannot be altered by the articles. The position is, it is believed, correctly summarised in *Campbell* v. *Rofe*[21] as follows:

> "While the memorandum must state the amount of capital, divided into shares of a certain fixed amount, provision as to the character of the shares and rights to be attached to them is more properly made by the articles of association, which may be altered from time to time by special resolution of the company. If equality of the shareholders is expressly provided in the memorandum, that cannot be modified by the articles of association. If nothing is said in the memorandum, the articles of association may provide for the issue of the authorised capital in the form of preference shares; if the articles do not so provide, or do provide for equality *inter socios*, the power to issue preference shares may be obtained by alteration of the articles."

33–07 On the other hand, the clause in the memorandum itself may be altered under section 23 of the 1948 Act, by a special resolution provided that this does not authorise any variation or abrogation of the special rights of any class of members (s. 23 (2)). It is submitted that an alteration which creates a new class of shares as distinct from altering the rights of existing shareholders does not infringe section 23. The 1980 Act seems to support this view as it only applies to "rights attached to a class of shares by the memorandum," in the context of a variation of those existing rights.[22]

The modern practice is to keep the capital clause of the memorandum as simple as possible and to define the rights of the different classes of shares in the articles.[23] The company's register of members must also show the class of shares (if there is more than one) of each member.[23a]

Questions arising in connection with the variation of special rights of classes of shareholders are discussed later.[24]

It was held by Roxburgh J. in *Re Powell-Cotton's Resettlement*[25] that there may be sub-classes within a class of shares; *e.g.* ordinary shares may be divided into preferred ordinary shares and deferred ordinary shares, the former taking precedence over the latter. This view, however, was expressed only in connection with the construction of a particular settlement and not in connection with a point arising in company law. It is thought that in

---

[19] *Andrews* v. *Gas Meter Co.* [1897] 1 Ch. 361; see also *Sidebottom* v. *Kershaw, Leese & Co.* [1920] 1 Ch. 154, 170.

[20] The inference that such a term is an implied condition of the memorandum must be very strong and can be drawn in practice only in rare instances. See *Re Marshall, Fleming & Co. Ltd.* 1938 S.C. 873, 878.

[21] [1933] A.C. 91, 98 (a Privy Council case). This would appear to be still correct after the changes introduced by the 1980 Act.

[22] 1980 Act, s. 32 (4). See para. 33–26, *post.*

[23] See, *e.g.* Table B in the First Schedule to the Act.

[23a] 1981 Act, s. 101. See para. 50–02, *post.*

[24] See para. 33–26, *post.*

[25] [1957] Ch. 159.

company law a "sub-class" constitutes a separate class of shareholders, *e.g.* for the variation of special rights of classes of shareholders.

Ordinary shares

33–08 Ordinary shares, in financial terminology sometimes referred to as the "equity"[26] or "risk" capital, normally confer on their holders the residue of rights of the company which have not been conferred on other classes. The ordinary shares usually carry the main financial risk if the company is unsuccessful, but they carry the greatest prospects of financial reward if the venture of the company is successful. Indeed, subject to the rights of other classes (which are normally, though not always, limited in extent) the ordinary shares are unlimited in their possibilities: after dealing with the distributable profits as required by the articles, *e.g.* after providing for any dividend which is preferentially conferred upon other classes of shares, the whole of the profits distributable as dividend can be made available to them (unless preference shareholders or others have participating rights). If—as is frequently the case—the ordinary shareholders constitute the only class of shares carrying votes, they can have the whole of these available profits distributed to themselves by way of dividend, if they so wish, or can have them capitalised and distributed as bonus shares or debentures.[27]

This description of the position of ordinary shares (as against other classes) may, however, be departed from, as where ordinary share capital is repaid before the whole of the preference share capital.[28]

In a winding up the ordinary shares are entitled to the entire surplus of assets remaining after payment of the liabilities of the company[29] and after the return of the capital of all classes of shares, unless preference shares are given the right to participate in the distribution of those surplus assets.

Non-voting shares

33–09 It is permissible for companies to issue ordinary shares not carrying voting rights. Such shares are sometimes referred to as "A" shares. This practice has proved to be controversial[30] and is intended, in a time of inflationary tendencies, to give investors an opportunity of acquiring "equity capital," in the sense in which the term is used earlier, without exercising control. The practice is not, however, widespread[31] and is disapproved by The Stock Exchange.[32] Non-voting ordinary shares are a separate class of shares.

---

[26] This term must not be confused with the term "equity share capital," which is a legal and not merely a financial term (see s. 154 (5) and para. 29–12, *ante*).

[27] See art. 128.

[28] *William Dixon Ltd.* 1948 S.C. 511; 1948 S.L.T. 423.

[29] Including any payments to employees under 1980 Act, s. 74. See para. 9–21, *ante*.

[30] See the Report of the Jenkins Committee (Cmnd. 1749 (1962), paras. 123–140, and the Note of Dissent on pp. 207–210 of the Report. See also the White Paper on Company Law Reform (Cmnd. 5391 (1973), para. 48).

[31] Cmnd. 5391 (1973), para. 48.

[32] For The Stock Exchange rules relating to non-voting shares see Admission of Securities to Listing, Sched. VII, P.A. para. K.

Preference shares

33–10 One of the most important classes of shares which a company may issue is preference shares. This class of shares will be considered in detail in the following chapter.[33]

Founders' or deferred shares

33–11 Besides ordinary and preference shares, it was at one time not uncommon to issue shares known as founders' or deferred shares.[34] Where these shares are issued, they are usually mentioned in the capital clause of the memorandum, *e.g.*:

> The capital of the company is £110,000 divided into 100,000 shares of £1 each and 200,000 deferred shares of 5p. each.

When this is the case, the memorandum generally defines the rights attached to the deferred shares, *e.g.* that they shall confer on the holders the right to 10 per cent. of the surplus profits of the company for each year, which remain after paying a cumulative dividend at the rate of 10 per cent. on the capital paid up on all the other shares for the time being issued. This example is merely given by way of illustration; other clauses are in use and the rights attached to such shares vary considerably.

Founders' shares are mostly subscribed for by the vendors and promoters.

Deferred shares, as their name suggests, are usually deferred in priority to the ordinary shares.[35] The 1948 Act recognises such types of shares, and a prospectus must, under section 38 (except in the cases specified in section 38 (5)[36]), state the number of founders' or management or deferred shares, if any, and their rights and interests in the property and profits, and their voting rights.

Employees' shares

33–12 Many companies have in recent years issued shares to their employees under one of many varying employee share schemes.[37] Their importance has been increased by recent tax incentives afforded to certain types of scheme. The various types of scheme and their fiscal aspects are dealt with in a later part of this book.[38] In general, however, the shares issued under the various schemes have few common characteristics and may or may not constitute a separate class of shares from other ordinary or preferred

---

33 See Chap. 34, *post*.
34 See Palmer, *Company Precedents* (17th ed.), Part I, p. 815.
35 Art. 2; Sched. IV, para. 1.
36 See para. 21–24, *ante*.
37 See generally G. K. Morse and D. W. Williams, *Profit Sharing—Legal Aspects of Employee Share Schemes* (Sweet & Maxwell, 1979).
38 See Chap. 94, *post*.

shares.[39] Some restrictions on transfer in the early years of ownership are common and frequently voting rights are restricted.

The 1980 Act defines employee share schemes for the purpose of that Act as any scheme for encouraging or facilitating the holding of shares or debentures in a company by or for the benefit of[40] the company's bona fide employees or former employees or those of the company's group, or their spouses, widows, widowers or infant children or step-children.[41] Shares held under such schemes are accorded special rights or exemptions under the 1980 Act[42] and new issues under such schemes are regarded generally as being domestic concerns of the company making them and thus not an issue to the public either for the purposes of the private company classification or for prospectus liability.[43]

Redeemable shares

Power to issue redeemable shares

33–13 Section 45 of the 1981 Act authorises both private and public companies to issue redeemable shares, *i.e.* those specifically redeemable under the terms of their issue. This replaces the earlier, narrower, authority given to companies by section 58 of the 1948 Act to issue redeemable preference shares.[44] This new power must be seen in the context of sections 46–51 of the 1981 Act which allow companies, subject to certain procedures, to purchase their own shares.[45] Thus all shares are now potentially redeemable either by initial agreement on issue or by subsequent agreement to purchase. The rules for the funding of a redemption or purchase are the same.[46] The appearance of the new general powers of redemption and purchase in the 1981 Act reflects current thinking that there is a demand for this facility particularly to encourage outside investors to take a minority interest in private companies.

The power to issue redeemable shares must be contained in the articles but, subject to that, such shares may be issued as redeemable either at a set date or event, or at the option either of the company or the shareholder.[47] For obvious reasons no redeemable shares may be issued if there are no issued non-redeemable shares at that time.[48] One non-redeemable issued share will however suffice. For similar reasons a company may not purchase

---

39 Approved schemes under the 1978 Finance Act and share option schemes under the 1980 Finance Act must expressly not create a separate class.
40 *e.g.* held by trustees.
41 1980 Act, s. 87 (1).
42 *e.g.* 1980 Act, s. 22 as to the requirement of paying up a quarter of the nominal value of a public company's share on allotment does not apply to such shares.
43 1948 Act, s. 55 (3) (4) as amended.
44 s. 58 was repealed by Sched. 4 to the 1981 Act. For a discussion of such shares see the 22nd edition of the work, paras. 35–18 *et seq*. For the transitional provisions see para. 33–25 below.
45 See Chap. 37, *post*.
46 See below and Chap. 37, *post*.
47 1981, s. 45 (1).
48 *Ibid*. s. 45 (2).

its own shares under section 46 of the 1981 Act if that would leave only redeemable shares in existence.[49]

Terms and effect of redemption

33–14 The redemption of redeemable shares may be "effected on such terms and in such manner as may be provided by the articles of the company."[50] In fact, however, all shares which are redeemed must be fully paid[51] and the terms in the articles must provide for payment on redemption.[52]

On redemption the shares must be cancelled and the issued share capital diminished by that amount.[53] This has no effect on the authorised share capital figure and should be distinguished from a diminution of capital under section 61 or the 1948 Act.[54]

Replacement issues

33–15 Where shares are redeemed under section 45 of the 1981 Act they may be replaced by a subsequent issue of shares under the general rules relating to such issues.[55] In addition, however, where a company "is about to redeem" such shares it may before redemption make a fresh issue of shares without any increase, if that would otherwise be necessary, in the authorised share capital figure under section 61 of the 1948 Act.[56] There are no time limits specified for the use of this power but if the stamp duty concessions outlined below are sought the redemption must follow within one month of the fresh issue.[57]

STAMP DUTIES. No stamp duty under section 47 of the Finance Act 1973 will be payable on an issue of replacement shares unless the actual value of the shares so issued exceeds the value of the shares redeemed at the date of redemption. If there is such an excess, duty is payable on the difference between the chargeable amount which would have been payable if the shares had not been replacement shares and the value of the redeemed shares at the date of redemption.[58] Shares are replacement shares for this purpose if they are issued either within one month prior to the redemption[59] or subsequently, up to the nominal value of the redeemed shares.[60]

---

[49] *Ibid.* s. 46 (3). See para. 37–08, *post.*
[50] *Ibid.* s. 45 (7); *cf.* 1948 Act, s. 58 (2), now repealed.
[51] *Ibid.* s. 45 (3); *cf.* 1948 Act, s. 58 (1) (*b*). This prevents any incidental reduction of capital.
[52] *Ibid.* s. 45 (4). There was no equivalent requirement in s. 58 of the 1948 Act.
[53] *Ibid.* s. 45 (8); *cf.* 1948 Act, s. 58 (3). For the effects on the balance sheet, see below. This is a different treatment from forfeited shares under s. 37 of the 1980 Act.
[54] See para. 31–08, *ante.*
[55] See Chap. 24, *ante.*
[56] 1981 Act, s. 45 (9).
[57] *Ibid.* s. 45 (12).
[58] *Ibid.* s. 45 (10).
[59] *Ibid.* s. 45 (11) (*b*), (12).
[60] *Ibid.* s. 45 (11) (*a*).

Funding of the redemption—all companies

33–16 Section 45 (5) provides that redeemable shares may only be redeemable out of distributable profits[61] or the proceeds of a fresh issue of shares made for the purposes of redemption. It further provides that any premium payable on redemption must be paid solely out of distributable profits. Under the former provisions of section 58 of the 1948 Act such premiums could be paid out of the share premium account.[62]

By way of exception, however, when the redeemable shares were themselves issued at a premium, any premium payable on redemption may be paid out of the proceeds of a fresh issue of shares made for that purpose up to the amount of that original premium or the amount of the share premium account at the time of the redemption, whichever is the smaller.[63] The principle is to balance capital going out against capital coming in and to affect the share premium account insofar as it reflects the amount credited to it on the original issue unless that amount has been taken out of that account, *e.g.* by an issue of bonus shares.

CAPITAL REDEMPTION RESERVE. Where the shares are redeemed wholly out of distributable profits,[64] the amount by which the issued share capital is diminished on the cancellation of the shares under section 45 (8) of the 1981 Act is to be transferred to a quasi-capital reserve known as the capital redemption reserve.[65] When the proceeds of a fresh issue of shares are used and those proceeds do not cover the aggregate nominal value of the redeemed shares the amount of the difference, which must represent distributable profits, must be transferred to the capital redemption reserve.[66] The function of this reserve is exactly the same as the capital redemption reserve fund formerly required by section 58 of the 1948 Act on the redemption of redeemable preference shares, *i.e.* it is a balancing item in the accounts. The capital redemption reserve is a quasi-capital fund subject to the rules relating to the reduction of capital[67] although it may be capitalised by an issue of fully paid bonus shares[68] or, in certain circumstances, used to fund the purchase or redemption of shares by private companies.[69]

Redemption out of capital—private companies

33–17 Section 54 of the 1981 Act authorises *private* companies to redeem shares out of funds other than distributable profits or the proceeds of a fresh issue of shares,[70] provided that a strict timetable is adhered to and it

---

61 *Ibid.* s. 62 (1). See Chap. 75, *post*.
62 See para. 29–10, *ante*. s. 56 of the 1948 Act has been amended accordingly.
63 1981 Act, s. 45 (6). This may be amended by subsequent regulations: 1981 Act s. 61 (2) (1).
64 *Ibid.* s. 62 (1). See Chap. 75, *post*.
65 *Ibid.* s. 53 (1).
66 *Ibid.* s. 53 (2).
67 See Chap. 32, *ante*.
68 1981 Act, s. 53 (3).
69 *Ibid.* s. 54 (5).
70 Those are the funds generally authorised for redemption by s. 45 (5). See para. 33–16 *ante*.

has authority to do so in the articles. Payment otherwise than out of those two funds is referred to in the legislation as a payment out of capital, although it may not strictly be so, as undistributable profits such as the revaluation reserve may be used. The essential concept, however, is that such additional funding is only allowed if the *available profits* of the company, together with any proceeds of a fresh issue of shares, are insufficient to meet the redemption price.[71] There must be a shortfall of generally authorised funds. The amount of the shortfall and thus the amount of capital authorised to be used is known as the *permissible capital payment*.[72]

To ascertain this permissible capital payment the company must deduct from the redemption price any relevant issue proceeds (there is no compulsion to make such an issue) and its *available profits*. This latter concept is defined as the company's profits which are available for distribution under Part III of the 1980 Act,[73] but by reference to such accounts as are drawn up within three months prior to the directors' statutory declaration (which is the first step in the authorisation procedure)[74] as are necessary to enable a reasonable judgment to be made as to the amounts contained in the relevant items[75] of those accounts.[76] These accounts need not necessarily be the same as those used for the purposes of distributing a dividend under the 1980 Act.[77]

The available profits, so ascertained, may be reduced by any distribution lawfully made between the date of the accounts and the statutory declaration.[78] These include not only the payment of dividends but the properly authorised use of such profits to give financial assistance for the purchase of its own shares,[79] to purchase such shares,[80] and either to acquire an option to purchase such shares[81] or to obtain the variation[82] or release from a contract to purchase such shares.[83]

33–18 ACCOUNTING REQUIREMENTS. If the permissible capital payment together with the proceeds of any fresh issue of shares made for the purpose of redemption is less than the nominal amount of the redeemed shares (so that profits are being used), the amount of the difference is to be transferred to the capital redemption reserve.[84] On the other hand if the combined total of those amounts exceeds the nominal value of the redeemed shares

---

71 1981 Act, s. 54 (2).
72 *Ibid.* s. 54 (3).
73 See Chap. 75, *post.*
74 1981 Act, s. 55 (3). See below.
75 1980 Act. s. 43. See Chap. 75, *post.*
76 *Ibid.* s. 54 (7), (8), (10).
77 *Ibid.* s. 54 (7). See Chap. 75, *post.*
78 *Ibid.* s. 54 (9).
79 Within 1981 Act, s. 42 (7) or 43 (2). See Chap. 37, *post.*
80 Within 1981 Act. s. 46. See Chap. 37, *post.*
81 Within s. 48 of the 1981 Act. See Chap. 37, *post.*
82 Within ss. 47 or 48 of the 1981 Act. See Chap. 37, *post.*
83 Within ss. 47, 48 or 49 of the 1981 Act. See Chap. 37, *post.*
84 1981 Act, s. 54 (9). These rules may be amended by subsequent regulations: 1981 Act, s. 61 (2) (*a*).

(so that a premium is in fact being repaid) any or all of the share capital figure, the share premium account, the capital redemption reserve or the revaluation reserve may be reduced by the excess.[85]

33–19 REQUIREMENTS FOR REDEMPTION OUT OF CAPITAL. Unless the procedure set out in sections 55 to 57 of the 1981 Act are followed it is unlawful for a private company to redeem shares out of capital under section 54 of that Act.[86] Provided it has the requisite authority in the articles[87] the company must approve the payment out of capital by a special resolution.[88] This resolution must however be preceded by a *statutory declaration of solvency* by the directors in the prescribed form[89] stating both the amount of the permissible capital payment for the shares in question and the immediate and prospective solvency of the company.[90]

The directors must specifically state that having made full inquiry into the affairs and profits of the company they have formed the opinion that immediately after the payment there will be no ground upon which the company will be unable to pay its debts (initial solvency),[91] and that for the year following the payment the company will be able to continue to carry on business as a going concern and pay its debts as they fall due (potential solvency).[92] In forming their opinion of the company's initial solvency they must take into account all the liabilities relevant to a winding up petition on the grounds of insolvency.[93] In forming their latter opinion of potential solvency they must have regard to their management intentions and the amount and character of the financial resources which will, in their view, become available to the company during that year.[94]

The statutory declaration must have annexed to it an *auditor's report* to the effect that the permissible capital payment has, in their view, been properly ascertained[95] and that they are not aware of anything which makes the declaration unreasonable.[96]

33–20 IMPLEMENTATION OF THE PROCEDURE. The statutory declaration must be followed on the same day or within one week by the passing of the requisite

---

85 *Ibid.* s. 54 (4), (6). This obligation supersedes any which may arise under s. 53 of the 1981 Act—see para. 33–16, *ante*.
86 *Ibid.* s. 54 (5), (6).
87 *Ibid.* s. 55 (1). This is the same wording as in s. 42 of the 1981 Act and formerly in s. 54 of the 1948 Act relating to financial assistance and it presumably incorporates similar civil liability. See Chap. 38, *post*. For criminal sanctions see s. 55 (9).
88 *Ibid.* s. 55 (2).
89 *Ibid.* s. 55 (5).
90 *Ibid.* s. 55 (3).
91 *Ibid.* s. 55 (3) (*a*).
92 *Ibid.* s. 55 (3) (*b*).
93 *Ibid.* s. 55 (4). See 1948 Act, s. 223 (*d*), para. 85–05, *post*.
94 *Ibid.* s. 55 (3) (*b*). These are penalties for unreasonable declarations by directors—see s. 55 (9).
95 In accordance with s. 54 of the 1981 Act. See para. 33–17, *ante*.
96 *Ibid.* s. 55 (5). The requirements as to the statutory declaration and the annexed report may be subsequently amended by regulations: 1981 Act, s. 61 (1) (*d*), (*e*).

special resolution.[97] For five weeks following the passing of that resolution the company may not implement it, thus allowing time for any dissentient minority shareholder or creditor to petition the court to have the resolution set aside.[98] Since the resolution ceases to have any effect after seven weeks, two further weeks are thus allowed for implementation.[99]

The holder of the shares to be redeemed must not vote with shares, whether on a poll or not, if the resolution would not have been passed without such votes. If he does the resolution will be ineffective. Any member may demand a poll as of right on this matter, irrespective of the articles.[1] He has no duty under this section to abstain from voting with any other shares he may have.[2] Nor need he vote against the resolution with the relevant shares.[3]

The resolution will also be ineffective unless the statutory declaration and auditors' report are available for inspection at the meeting.[4]

33–21 PUBLICITY FOR THE PROPOSED PAYMENT. The requirement of a special resolution will put the members on notice but a proposed payment out of capital is inevitably of concern to the company's creditors.[5] Accordingly section 56 of the 1981 Act is intended to provide a method of informing creditors of the proposed payment. Publicity must take two forms. First the company must put a notice in the appropriate Gazette within a week of the resolution stating that the resolution has been passed and specifying both the amount of the permissible capital payment and the date of the resolution. The notice must also state that the statutory declaration and auditors' report are available for inspection at the company's registered office and that any creditor may petition the court to have the payment set aside, within five weeks of the date of the resolution.[6] The appropriate Gazette is the one relating to the place of the company's incorporation and not necessarily where it does business. Secondly it must, also within one week of the resolution, either place a similar notice in "an appropriate national newspaper" or give notice in writing to each of its creditors. The newspaper must in fact be in circulation throughout the relevant jurisdiction.[7]

Further disclosure of the declaration and report is required by registration of a copy of each with the Registrar by the date of the first appearance of either of the notices (the *first notice date*).[8]

By the *first notice date* the company must have the declaration and report

---

[97] Twenty-one days notice of such resolution will usually be required. See para. 56–07, *post*.
[98] See para. 33–22, *post*.
[99] 1981 Act, s. 55 (6).
[1] *Ibid.* s. 55 (7). Proxies are included: s. 55 (10).
[2] *Quaere* whether he has any fiduciary duty in this respect?
[3] *Cf. Re Gee* [1948] Ch. 284 as to the use of votes by trustees.
[4] 1981 Act, s. 55 (8).
[5] See Chap. 32, *ante*.
[6] 1981 Act, s. 56 (1). This is the interim period required by s. 55 (6). See above in the text.
[7] 1981 Act, s. 56 (2). England and Wales or Scotland, according to where the company is registered. The writing to all creditors option is unlikely to prove viable.
[8] *Ibid.* s. 56 (3), (4).

available for inspection at its registered office by creditors or members during business hours. In default the court may order an immediate inspection[9] and impose default fines.[10] The obligation ceases five weeks after the date of the resolution (*i.e.* when an objection petition can no longer be made).[11]

33–22 CANCELLATION OF THE RESOLUTION. Under section 57 of the 1981 Act a single dissentient[12] member of any creditor[13] of the company may petition the court within five weeks of the resolution to have the resolution cancelled.[14] The petition may be in representation form. It should be remembered that the resolution may not be implemented during that time.[15] On such a petition the court has wide powers to cancel or confirm the resolution and to make ancillary orders, *e.g.* as to the time limits of the resolution. In particular it has the power to order a purchase by the majority of a minority shareholder's shares.[16]

If an application is made under this section the company must inform the Registrar "forthwith," and on the making of any order by the court, file an office copy of that order with him, normally within 15 days.[17] There is however no automatic suspension of the right to implement the resolution on the bringing of a petition.[18]

33–23 PAYMENT OUT OF CAPITAL FOLLOWED BY LIQUIDATION OF THE COMPANY. Section 58 applies where a private company has made a payment out of capital to redeem its shares and the company goes into liquidation within one year of that payment and it cannot pay all its debts and expenses, etc. In such a case the recipient of the payment of capital together with any director who signed the statutory declaration of solvency are liable jointly and severally to repay the amount paid up to the amount needed to cover the insolvency.[19] Any person so required to make a payment to the liquidator may apply to the court to order others liable with him to make a contribution to him.[20]

Anyone who is a potential contributor only by virtue of this section and not under the general rules relating to a liquidation[21] is not subject to the rules relating to contributors in sections 212 and 224 or the 1948 Act nor,

---

9 *Ibid.* s. 56 (6).
10 *Ibid.* s. 56 (7).
11 *Ibid.* s. 56 (5).
12 *i.e.* one who did not vote for or consent to the resolution.
13 There are no financial limits.
14 The time limit for creditors may in fact be only four weeks since the company has one week to publish the newspaper and Gazette notices under s. 56.
15 *Ibid.* s. 55 (6).
16 *Ibid.* s. 57 (4)–(6).
17 *Ibid.* s. 57 (3). There are penalties in default—see s. 57 (7).
18 *Cf. ibid.* s. 43 (9) (*b*). See Chap. 38, *post.*
19 A director may be excused if he can show that he had reasonable grounds for forming the opinion set out in the declaration: 1981 Act, s. 58 (2) (*b*).
20 *Ibid.* s. 58 (4).
21 1948 Act, s. 212. See para. 85–45, *post.*

unless expressly specified, by any such rules in the company's articles.[22] On the other hand such a person may bring a petition for a winding up under sections 222 (*e*) and (*f*) of the 1948 Act but does not *qua*. such a potential contributor has the right to petition on other grounds.[23]

Failure by company to redeem shares

33–24 If the company fails to honour its obligation to redeem redeemable shares it will clearly be in breach of contract. If the company is still a going concern the shareholder may exercise any rights relating to that contract except that by virtue of section 59 (2) of the 1981 Act he may not sue for damages in respect of the breach of contract.[24] It is further provided by that subsection that he cannot obtain specific performance of the contract to redeem if the company can show that it could not fulfil its obligation to redeem out of distributable profits.[25]

If the company is being wound up and the date for redemption occurred prior to the commencement of the winding up the terms of the redemption may be enforced in the liquidation.[26] This right will, however, be lost if between the date of redemption and the commencement of the winding up the company could not have fulfilled its obligation out of distributable profits.[27] In any event the amount so claimed is a deferred debt in the liquidation, both beyond all other debts (except for debts due to a member as such) and any amounts due to the holders of preference shares[28] who have any rights as to capital or income in priority to the redeemable shares in question.[29] The amount claimed is to be deferred even beyond interest on another debt.[30]

The section has no effect on redeemable shares where the date for redemption has not accrued at the commencement of a winding up.

Transitional provisions—redeemable preference shares

33–25 Many companies have redeemable preference shares issued under section 58 of the 1948 Act,[31] and a consequent capital redemption reserve fund. Section 62 of the 1981 repealed section 58 of the 1948 Act,[32] but provides for those transitional provisions covering such shares. In addition the rules as to recovery of damages etc. on a breach of the obligation to redeem do not apply to such shares.[33]

---

22 1981 Act, s. 58 (6).
23 *Ibid*. s. 58 (7).
24 This was doubtful anyway if he retained any other shares in the company by virtue of *Houldsworth* v. *City of Glasgow Bank* (1880) 5 App. Cas. 317 and *Re Addlestone Linoleum Ltd*. (1887) 37 Ch.D. 191.
25 As defined in 1981 Act. s. 62 (1).
26 *Ibid*. s. 59 (4), 5 (*a*). The shares will be cancelled in such a case: s. 59 (4).
27 *Ibid*. s. 59 (5) (*b*).
28 See Chap. 34, *post*.
29 1981 Act, s. 59 (6).
30 *Ibid*. s. 59 (7).
31 See 22nd edition of this work, para. 35–18.
32 1981 Act. s. 62 (2).
33 *Ibid*. s. 59 (1) only applies to shares issued under the 1981 Act See para. 33–24, *ante*.

The three transitional provisions are as follows:

(1) Existing redeemable preferences shares which could have been redeemed under section 58 of the 1948 Act may be redeemed in accordance with the new procedure (*i.e.* out of distributable profits,[34] a fresh issue of shares,[35] or, if appropriate, capital.[36, 37]

(2) If those shares are being redeemed otherwise than out of capital,[38] any premium payable on redemption may be paid out of the share premium account.[39] In other words, the repeal of that part of section 56 of the 1948 Act,[40] is not to have effect for those shares. They will only be subject to the new rules as to funding insofar as distributable profits are used.[41]

(3) Any capital redemption reserve fund established under section 58 of the 1948 Act is to be known as the capital redemption reserve.[42] All references in legislation or the company's articles or any other instrument to the capital redemption reserve redemption reserve fund are to be construed accordingly[43]

Variation of special rights of classes of shareholders

33–26 When preferential or other special rights are attached to a class of shares, it is of great practical importance to ascertain whether these rights can be varied, and, if so, by what procedure.[44] In particular, the question may arise whether a class of shares carrying special rights but being a minority of the total issued capital can be deprived of their special rights wholly or in part by the majority of all shareholders of the company. Here a problem of protection of minority rights arises which is often complicated by a conflict between the personal interest of a group of shareholders with that of the company as a going concern.[45] A power to vary class rights has been held in Scotland not to include a power to extinguish them.[46] Although the 1980 Act, s. 32 (9) now provides that, as a general rule, variation includes abrogation of class rights, this does not apply where the context requires otherwise. It is competent for a company to make a payment to a class of shareholders in consideration for clarifying their rights, in the interests of the company.[47]

Special rights of a class of shares do not mean rights which are different

---

34 *Ibid.* s. 62 (1).
35 *Ibid.* s. 45 (3).
36 *Ibid.* s. 53.
37 *Ibid.* s. 62 (2).
38 *Ibid.* s. 53.
39 *Ibid.* s. 62 (3).
40 By Sched. 4 to the 1981 Act. See para. 33–16, *ante*.
41 *Ibid.* s. 62 (1).
42 *Ibid.* s. 62 (4). See para. 33–16, *ante*.
43 *Ibid.*
44 See D. G. Rice, "Class Rights and their Variation in Company Law" [1958] J.B.L. 29.
45 *Cf.* Evershed M.R. in *Greenhalgh* v. *Arderne Cinemas Ltd.* [1951] Ch. 286, 291. For a classic example of a conflict arising between the majority holding ordinary and preference shares and the minority holding preference shares only see *Re Holders Investment Trust Ltd.* [1971] 1 W.L.R. 583; para. 32–08, *ante*.
46 *Gill* v. *Arizona Copper Co.*, 1901, 2 F. (Ct. of Sess.) 843.
47 *Caledonian Insurance Co.* v. *Scottish American Investment Co. Ltd.* 1951 S.L.T. 23.

from "normal" rights of shares; it would be difficult to define what "normal" rights are, in view of the great variety of rights which shares may carry.[48] The term "special rights" of a class of shares, which is used in the 1948 Act, section 23 (2) and article 2, refers to rights especially given to shares of that class by the terms of the memorandum or the articles. Special class rights may likewise be created by the terms of issue or by a special resolution,[49] in which cases they are to be treated in the same manner as those defined in the articles (1948 Act, s. 10). These special class rights relate normally—but not invariably[49]—to dividend, voting or the distribution of assets in the winding up of the company.

A cancellation of shares carrying special rights as to prior repayment of capital is not a variation of those rights. Unless the reduction can be shown to be unfair on other grounds, it is in accordance with the right and liability to prior repayment of capital attached to the shares.[50] Shares carrying special rights as to voting may, it is submitted, be similarly cancelled without reference to the variation rules. Cancellation is not a variation in the technical sense.[51] Class rights may be varied as part of a reduction of capital.[52]

When a question of variation of special rights of a class of shareholders arises, it is first necessary to ascertain whether those rights are defined in the memorandum or in the articles. The definition of special rights in the memorandum may give members of a class of shareholders a higher degree of protection than their definition in the articles, but it is more usual to define special class rights, *e.g.* the rights of preference shareholders, in the articles than in the memorandum (see art. 4). If the definition of rights is difficult to interpret, a scheme of arrangement under section 206 may be necessary to clarify them.[53]

Definition of special class rights in the memorandum

33–27 If the special rights of a class of shares are attached by the memorandum[54]—three possibilities exist. In none of them can those rights be altered by virtue of section 23 of the 1948 Act, although the provisions

---

[48] Gower, *Modern Company Law,* (4th ed., 1979), p. 562.

[49] See *Re Old Silkstone Collieries Ltd.* [1954] Ch. 169, where the assets of a colliery were vested in the National Coal Board under the Coal Industry Nationalisation Act 1946. By resolutions of the general meeting the right to adjustment under s. 25 of the Act of 1946 was expressly reserved in favour of the preference stockholders but later it was resolved to repay the stock without regard to the preference stockholders' right under s. 25. The Court of Appeal held that the resolutions of the general meeting created "special rights" in favour of the preference stockholders and—the company having in its articles a provision similar to art. 4—that these special class rights could only be varied by consent of a qualified majority of the preference stockholders.

[50] *Re Saltdean Estate Co. Ltd.* [1968] 1 W.L.R. 1844.

[51] See note 68 to para. 33–29, *post.*

[52] *Belmenach-Glenlivet Distillery* v. *Croall* 1906, 8 F. 1135, 14 S.L.T. 261.

[53] *Edinburgh Rly., etc., Co.* v. *Scottish Metropolitan Assurance Co.* 1932 S.C. 2, 1932 S.L.T. 49.

[54] Presumably this includes class rights defined in the memorandum by reference to the articles: see *Dimbula Valley (Ceylon) Tea Co. Ltd.* v. *Laurie* [1961] Ch. 353.

relating to them could lawfully have been contained in the articles instead of the memorandum, because that section states expressly that it does not authorise "any variation or abrogation of the special rights of any class of members" (s. 23 (2)). The position has been altered with respect to the variation of class rights by section 32 of the 1980 Act. Variation is defined as to include abrogation of those rights.[55]

The three possibilities are:

(1) THE MEMORANDUM PROVIDES A VARIATION PROCEDURE. In this case, subject to one reservation, the special class rights can be varied by observance of the stated procedure.[56] The 1980 Act nowhere states this as a positive fact but it presupposes such a situation in section 32 (3) which in fact relates to a compulsory minimum form of variation procedure for the variation of certain rights even if the procedure is contained in the memorandum. Since any additional requirements in the stated procedure must also be complied with such a procedure must otherwise be valid.[57]

If the variation procedure requires the consent of a specified proportion of the class or the sanction of a separate class meeting, the minority right of section 72 of the 1948 Act is brought into operation: under this section holders of not less than 15 per cent. of the class may, in certain conditions, apply to the court to have the variation cancelled, and the court has discretion to do so if satisfied that the variation would unfairly prejudice the shareholders (s. 72 (1) and (3)).[58]

(2) THE MEMORANDUM PROHIBITS A VARIATION. In this case, which, in view of section 23 (2) of the 1948 Act and the wording of the 1980 Act, appears to be admitted by the law, the variation of special class rights is, on principle, excluded. Nothing in the 1980 Act provisions relates to a prohibition in the memorandum. Exceptionally, however, such variation may be possible under a scheme of arrangement or reconstruction as sanctioned by the court under section 206 of the 1948 Act.[59]

(3) THE MEMORANDUM DOES NOT CONTAIN PROVISIONS RELATING TO VARIATION. Prior to the 1980 Act the wording of section 23 (2) precluded any variation other than under section 206, since to allow an alteration of the memorandum under section 23 (1) would authorise a "variation or abrogation of the special rights of any class of members."[59a]

Under the 1980 Act, however, two additional possible modes of varia-

---

[55] 1980 Act, s. 32 (9). See para. 34–19, *post.*

[56] *Re Welsbach Incandescent Gas Light Co.* [1904] 1 Ch. 87, 97 (in that case the memorandum provided that the rights attached to the various classes of shares might be modified in the manner mentioned in the articles).

[57] For this compulsory minimum procedure see para. 33–31, *post.*

[58] See para. 33–29, *post.*

[59] See Chap. 79, *post.*

[59a] *City Property Investment Trust Corporation Ltd.* 1951 S.C. 570; 1951 S.L.T. 371.

tion are provided. First, if the articles contain a variation procedure which was included in the articles at the time of the company's original incorporation then such a procedure must be followed (1980 Act, s. 32 (4) (*a*)). This is subject to the reservation as to the variation of certain rights under section 32 (3).[60]

Secondly, if neither the memorandum nor articles contain a variation procedure the special class rights may be varied if all the members of the company (not just the class) agree to the variation (1980 Act, s. 32 (5)).

If neither of these possibilities exist then any variation must be achieved within the framework of a scheme of arrangement under section 206 or a minority protection order made by the court under section 75 of the 1980 Act[61] (1980 Act, s. 32 (10)).

Definition of special class rights in the articles

33–28 If the rights are attached by the articles only, the position is altogether different, and there is greater scope for alteration. This is a matter of great importance, for after issuing preference shares it is not uncommon to find it desirable to alter the rights attached thereto, *e.g.* by sanctioning the creation of pre-preference shares, or of further preference shares ranking *pari passu* with the original issue, or by reducing the rate of the preferential dividend.

In modern company law[62] two possibilities exist here:

33–29 (1) THE ARTICLES PROVIDE A VARIATION PROCEDURE. The articles commonly contain a clause, known as the modification of rights article, providing for the alteration of special class rights by an extraordinary resolution passed at a separate meeting of the class or by consent in writing of three-fourths of the issued shares of that class (art. 4). Under the 1980 Act any variation must comply with such an express procedure whenever it was included in the articles subject to the reservation as to the variation of certain rights under section 32 (3)[63] (1980 Act, s. 32 (4) (*b*)).

Any meeting required by such an express procedure must be governed by the provisions of the articles relating to general meetings so far as applicable, subject to any necessary modifications, provided that the necessary quorum at any such meeting other than an adjourned meeting is two persons holding or representing by proxy at least one-third in nominal value of the issued shares of that particular class and at an adjourned meeting one person holding shares of that class or his proxy (1980 Act, s. 32 (6)). That section further provides that any member of the class or his

---

[60] See para. 33–31.
[61] See Chap. 60, *post*.
[62] Formerly it was thought that the rights of shareholders could only be altered if the articles authorising the alteration were in force when the shares were issued (see, as regards preference shares, *Ashbury* v. *Watson* (1885) 30 Ch.D. 376). This general view was rejected in *Andrews* v. *Gas Meter Co.* [1897] 1 Ch. 361 (C.A.). See also *Ramsbotham* v. *Scottish American Investment Co.* 1891, 18 R. 558; *Liquidator of Milford Haven Fishing Co:* v. *Jones* 1895, 22 R. 577; 2 S.L.T. 562.
[63] See para. 33–31, *post*.

proxy may demand a poll[64] and that sections 133,[65] 134,[66] and 140[67] of the 1948 Act relating to the length of notice, votes and circulation of resolutions respectively shall also apply to class meetings.

This article does not apparently prevent the issue of preference shares ranking *pari passu* with, or even in priority to, existing preference shares, if otherwise authorised by the memorandum or articles. But where the articles state expressly—as, *e.g.* article 5 does—that preferential or other special class rights shall not, unless the terms of issue of the shares of that class otherwise expressly provide, "be deemed to be varied by the creation or issue of further shares ranking *pari passu* therewith," it is believed that the company has no power to issue shares carrying rights *in priority* of those preference shares, although, of course, it has power to create shares carrying the same preferential or special rights as those already issued.

Whenever the articles authorise the variation of rights of a class of shares subject to the consent of a specified proportion of the issued shares of that class, *e.g.* by adopting a modification of rights article similar to article 4 of Table A, section 72 of the 1948 Act is brought into operation.[68] This section provides that the holders of 15 per cent. of the issued shares of the class who did not consent to the variation may apply to the court within 21 days to have the variation cancelled, and it will not then become effective unless sanctioned by the court. The application may be made by one or more of those who did not assent, on behalf of all of them; but the holders of at least 15 per cent. of the shares of the class affected must not have assented and notice of their support must have reached the petitioner before the petition is presented. The application must be made within 21 days after the consent by the majority of the class was given or the extraordinary resolution at the class meeting was passed (s. 72 (2)). The sole ground on which the court can disallow the variation is that "it is satisfied, having regard to all the circumstances of the case, that the variation would unfairly prejudice the shareholders of the class represented by the applicant.[69]" If it is not so satisfied, the court must allow the variation.[70]

The modification of rights clause itself, being part of the articles, would be subject to alteration under section 10 by the company generally and not just by the class it is intended to protect. The 1980 Act, however, resolving any previous dispute,[71] provides that any such alterations, or even the insertion of such a clause, is itself to be regarded as a variation of the rights

---

64 See para. 55–10, *post*.
65 See para. 54–01, *post*.
66 See para. 55–03, *post*.
67 See para. 54–05, *post*.
68 This section has no application on the cancellation of a class of shares, *Re Saltdean Estate Co. Ltd.* [1968] 1 W.L.R. 1844.
69 *Re Suburban and Provincial Stores* [1943] Ch. 156; *Re Sound City (Films) Ltd.* [1947] Ch. 169.
70 *Cf. Last* v. *Buller & Co.* (1919) 36 T.L.R. 35.
71 See the 22nd edition of this work, para. 34–15.

themselves, and therefore subject to the existing variation procedure (1980 Act, s. 32 (7)).

33–30 (2) THE ARTICLES DO NOT PROVIDE A VARIATION PROCEDURE. Prior to the 1980 Act the position where there were no modification of rights articles was open to doubt.[72] Now there is a statutory variation procedure which must be complied with on any variation. This is in effect that provided in article 4 of Table A, *i.e.* a variation requires an extraordinary resolution passed at a separate general meeting of the class approving it or the consent in writing of three-quarters in nominal value of the holders of the issued shares of that class (1980 Act, s. 32 (2)).

Section 72 of the 1948 Act,[73] the minority protection section, applies to this statutory procedure as it does to an express modification of rights article (1980 Act, s. 32 (8)) and the provisions as to meetings, quorum, etc., similarly apply (1980 Act, s. 32 (6)).

Variation of certain class rights

33–31 The above rules as to the variation of class rights are subject to one reservation. Where there is an express procedure for variation either in the memorandum or articles which the 1980 Act otherwise requires compliance with, this is subject to a reservation if the particular rights being varied are connected either with

(i) the giving, variation, revocation or renewal of an authority to the directors for the purposes of allotting new shares under section 14 of the 1980 Act[74]; or

(ii) a reduction of capital under section 66 of the 1948 Act.[75]

In either of those cases the variation must be agreed to either by an extraordinary resolution of that class at a separate meeting or the written consent of three-quarters (in value) of that class, in addition to any extra conditions laid down in the express variation procedure (1980 Act, s. 32 (3)). In practice this will not affect those companies which have adopted Table A.

Construction of modification of rights clauses

33–32 A variation or alteration of the rights of one class of shares is bound to affect consequentially the rights of the other classes of shares in the company. The question whether such consequential effect makes it necessary, if the articles contain the usual modification of rights provision,[76] to obtain the separate consent of each of the classes not directly affected by the proposed alteration is a question of construction of the relevant article.

---

[72] See *ibid.* para. 34–16.
[73] See para. 33–29, *ante.*
[74] See para. 24–01, *ante.*
[75] See Chap. 32, *ante.*
[76] See para. 33–29, *ante.*

The courts have shown a disinclination to construe a modification of rights article as requiring the separate consent of the classes not directly affected; they are inclined to hold that the article does not apply where the consequential effect is merely of commercial, and not of legal, character. This has led to unfortunate constructions being applied to words commonly used in such clauses. Only an express and unambiguous wording of that article—which it is possible to devise—would compel the courts to construe the articles as requiring the separate consent of each class which is consequentially affected.

33–33 These propositions may be illustrated by some recent decisions of the courts. In *Greenhalgh* v. *Arderne Cinemas Ltd. (No. 1)*[77] the modification of rights article was in the form of what is now article 4 of Table A[78]; it provided, as far as relevant here:

> "If at any time the share capital is divided into different classes of shares, the rights attached to any class (unless otherwise provided by the terms of issue of the shares of that class) may be *varied*[79] with the . . . sanction of an extraordinary resolution passed at a separate general meeting of the holders of the shares of the class."

Vaisey J. held that a subdivision of a class of ordinary shares of 10s. each into shares of 2s. each did not *vary* the rights of a holder of another class of ordinary shares of 2s. each, though the value of his voting power was affected to such an extent as to change the control of the company. The Court of Appeal affirmed the decision of Vaisey J., and Lord Greene M.R. observed[80]:

> "As a matter of law, I am quite unable to hold that, as a result of the transaction, the rights are varied; they remain what they always were—a right to have one vote per share *pari passu* with the ordinary shares for the time being issued which include the new 2s. ordinary shares resulting from the subdivision."

In *White* v. *Bristol Aeroplane Co. Ltd.*[81] and in *Re John Smith's Tadcaster Brewery Co. Ltd.*[82] the companies had registered articles which provided that

> "all or any rights or privileges attached to any class of shares . . . may be *affected*,[83] modified, dealt with or abrogated in any manner with the sanction of an extraordinary resolution passed at a separate meeting of the members of that class."

---

77 [1945] 2 All E.R. 719; affd. [1946] 1 All E.R. 512 (C.A.). See also *Re Stewart Precision Carburettors* (1912) 28 T.L.R. 335; *Dimbula Valley (Ceylon) Tea Co. Ltd.* v. *Laurie* [1961] Ch. 353.

78 The case concerned actually art. 3 of Table A of the Companies Act 1929, which, apart from minor and irrelevant modifications, is identical in wording with art. 4 of Table A of the Act of 1948.

79 Italics ours (*the Editors*).

80 [1946] 1 All E.R. 512, 518.

81 [1953] Ch. 65; see also *Re Schweppes Ltd.* [1914] 1 Ch. 322.

82 [1953] Ch. 308.

83 Italics ours (*the Editors*).

The Court of Appeal held in both cases that the proposed issue of new capital did not "affect" the rights or privileges of the existing preference stockholders; they might be affected as a matter of business by reason of the new preference stock which would be in the possession of the ordinary shareholders and have a majority over the existing preference stock. This, however, would affect the enjoyment of the rights, and not the rights themselves. Evershed M.R. observed in *White* v. *Bristol Aeroplane Co. Ltd.*[84]:

> "I agree that Lord Greene[85] used the word 'affected,' but I draw attention to the fact that the distinction was not between 'affected' and 'varied,' but between 'affected as a matter of business' and 'varied as a matter of law.' "

Some doubt may respectfully be expressed as to the correctness of the decision in these two cases as it does not appear to conform with the intention of the parties, when using the word "affected" nor with the normal meaning of that word.

Registration of particulars of special rights

33–34 In many cases the creation or variation of special class rights will be notified to the Registrar automatically either because they are contained in the memorandum or articles of the company and so filed in the Companies Registry, or because they are the subject of a special or extraordinary resolution or the written consent of a sufficient number of that class and then forwarded to the Registrar under the provisions of section 143 of the 1948 Act.[86]

Exceptionally, however, special rights may be created or varied by other means, *e.g.* by the terms of the issue or by an ordinary resolution if the articles so provide and in such cases section 33 of the 1980 Act requires their separate registration. Three specific acts may give rise to this obligation:

33–35 (1) CREATION OF SPECIAL RIGHTS NOT OTHERWISE REGISTERABLE. Where shares are allotted with rights which are not registerable under section 143 and are not contained in the memorandum or articles, the company must register particulars of those rights within one month of the allotment.[87] This obligation does not apply, however, if the shares are in all respects uniform with shares previously allotted (1980 Act, s. 33 (1)). For this purpose the new shares are not to be regarded as different from existing shares if the only difference is that they do not carry the same rights as to

---

[84] [1953] Ch. 65, 80.
[85] In the *Greenhalgh* case; see note 77, *supra*.
[86] See para. 56–10, *post*. This is in addition to their disclosure in the register of members. 1981 Act, s. 101. See para. 50–02 *post*.
[87] *Quaere* whether a subdivision of shares amounts to an allotment for this purpose? See para. 31–05, *ante*.

dividends as the existing shares during the 12 months immediately following their allotment (1980 Act, s. 33 (2)).

33–36 (2) VARIATION OF SPECIAL RIGHTS NOT OTHERWISE REGISTERABLE. Where the special rights attached to shares are varied otherwise than by a resolution within section 143 or by an amendment of the memorandum or articles, the company must register particulars of the variations within one month from the date of such variation (1980 Act, s. 33 (3)).

33–37 (3) DESIGNATION OR VARIATION OF THE NAME OF A CLASS OF SHARES NOT OTHERWISE REGISTERABLE. If a company assigns a name or designation to a class of shares or varies the existing name or designation of such a class otherwise than by its inclusion in the memorandum or articles or by a resolution within section 143, it must register the relevant particulars within one month from such designation or variation (1980 Act, s. 33 (4)).

Penalties for default

33–38 In the event of non-compliance with any of these obligations the company and every officer who is in default will be liable to a fine of £200 initially or after continued contravention to a fine of £20 per day until the relevant particulars are registered (1980 Act, s. 33 (6)).

33–39 CLASS RIGHTS OF MEMBERS IN COMPANIES WITHOUT A SHARE CAPITAL. Section 102 of the 1981 Act requires any company without a share capital (guarantee companies) to register the rights of different classes of members if those are not stated in the memorandum or articles. Registration is required of any existing class rights; alterations to those rights; creation of any new class of members; and the re-designation of any class; together with particulars of the rights attached to each class.

Practice Note

Dispensation with distinguishing numbers on shares

33–40 It is possible to dispense with the numbers on shares already in issue provided that the conditions mentioned in para. 33–04, *ante* are complied with. A resolution of the directors will usually be sufficient to achieve this object unless the memorandum or articles contain provision to the contrary or either of those documents specifically require the shares to be numbered, in which event a special resolution to alter them or either of them must first be passed.

When the shares of a company are listed, the distinguishing numbers attached to them cannot be dispensed with until a new listing for unnumbered shares has been granted by The Stock Exchange, to which application must be made by the company through its stockbrokers.

Since shares must be issued before they can become unnumbered shares, it is necessary in a resolution of allotment of any new shares, *e.g.* a rights issue or an issue by way of capitalisation of reserves, to state the distinguishing numbers to be attached to the shares and immediately (provided that the other conditions in para. 33–04, *ante* are satisfied) for a further resolution to be passed dispensing with the numbers.

CHAPTER 34

PREFERENCE SHARES

Preferential rights

34–01 As their name implies, preference shares carry some preferential rights in relation to other classes of shares, particularly in relation to the ordinary shares.[1] These preferential rights are of great variety but refer normally to one or two of the principal rights carried by shares,[2] *viz.* the right to *dividend* and the right, on winding up, to receive a proportionate part of the *capital* or otherwise to participate in the distribution of assets of the company.

There may be more than one class of preference share, *e.g.* first preference and second preference shares, as well as ordinary shares; or there may be preference shares, ordinary shares and deferred shares, in which case the ordinary shares may, in fact, themselves be preferential in relation to the deferred shares. The name of the shares is not itself decisive: what matters is their relation to the other classes of shares of the company.

Preferential, cumulative and participating rights

34–02 In considering the rights of holders of preference shares four questions arise:

1. *As to preferential rights.* The shares will invariably carry preferential rights as to dividend, but do they likewise carry preferential rights as to capital?[3]
2. *As to cumulative rights.* Are the rights of the preference shares cumulative as to dividend? This is the case where the shareholders are entitled, if the company has failed to declare the preference dividend in any one year, to claim the missed dividend in the subsequent year and so forth, so that an accumulation of preference dividend takes place. On the other hand, they are non-cumulative where it is intended that the shareholders, if not receiving preference dividend in any one year, shall not be entitled to the missed dividend in any subsequent year.

   The question whether the preference shareholders are entitled to cumulative dividend arises only during the active life of the company,[4] but such accumulation may further raise a problem in the winding up, *viz.* if there are so-called arrears of cumulative preference

---

[1] *Cf.* Roxburgh J. in *Re Powell-Cotton's Resettlement* [1957] Ch. 159, 162.
[2] See para. 33–02, *ante.*
[3] See para. 34–13, *post.*
[4] See para. 34–07, *post.*

dividend outstanding at the commencement of winding up, can they be recovered in the winding-up proceedings?[5]

3. *As to participating rights*. The question here is whether the preference shares carry the right to participate in the distribution of dividend in excess and beyond their right to preferential—and possibly cumulative—dividend,[6] and, further, whether they are entitled to participate in the distribution of the surplus assets of the company remaining after the payment of the company's liabilities and the return of the capital to the shareholders.[7]
4. *As to frustration of those rights*. In recent years it has become necessary to ask whether all or any of these rights may be frustrated by a reduction of capital under section 66 of the 1948 Act.[8]

Financial and legal aspects of preference shares

34–03 Before the rights carried by preference shares are examined in detail it is necessary to note the different approach to preference shares by the businessman and the lawyer.

From the financial point of view a difference is drawn between "risk capital," sometimes called "the equity of the company," and "loan capital." Preference shares which do not carry participating rights are not regarded in financial circles as representing part of the equity of a company.

From the legal point of view preference shares, whether carrying participating rights or not, are undoubtedly shares and are treated as such; in particular, when it is intended to pay them off, the capital reduction procedure (s. 66) has to be complied with,[9] and in the winding up they rank as shares, *i.e.* a distribution on them can only take place after the creditors of the company have been satisfied.

In more recent years the financial and legal points of view have drawn closer together: first, the Acts themselves have adopted the test of the "equity share capital"[10] when defining the holding company in relation to its subsidiaries; the statutory definition of "equity share capital" includes participating preference shares but excludes non-participating preference shares. Secondly, important dicta from the Bench, in particular from Lord Simonds[11] and Sir Raymond Evershed,[12] have recognised that the position of the preference shareholder has become more approximated to that of the debenture holder than was the case some 60 years ago, and that

---

[5] See para. 34–08, *post*.
[6] See para. 34–11, *post*.
[7] See para. 34–15, *post*.
[8] See paras. 34–12, 34–17, *post*.
[9] Except if the shares are issued as redeemable shares; see para. 33–13, *ante*.
[10] s. 154 (5), and 1967 Act, s. 4 (1) and (8).
[11] In *Scottish Insurance Corporation Ltd.* v. *Wilsons and Clyde Coal Co. Ltd.* [1949] A.C. 462, 487; 1949 S.C. (H.L.) 90; 1949 S.L.T. 230.
[12] In *Re Isle of Thanet Electricity Supply Co.* [1950] Ch. 161, 175.

recognition is reflected in recent decisions.[13] However, the fundamental legal concept that a preference share is a share has never been qualified by the courts or by statute and obviously cannot be qualified.

Express regulation of preferential rights

34–04 The rights of the preference shares may be stated in the memorandum, articles or terms of issue of the shares[14]; in modern practice they are normally set out in detail in the articles.[15]

Where the provisions dealing with the preference shares in the memorandum or the articles or both state clearly the rights of the preference shares to accumulation and participation as regards the dividend, those rights are prima facie exhaustive.[16] The effect of this is that no further rights can be implied. This proposition is, however, only prima facie, and if the memorandum sets out rights which are prima facie exhaustive (for instance, giving a right to dividend and a right in a winding up) but the articles give a further right (for instance, the right to a premium in a winding up), such further right is effective. Where two classes of preference shares entitled to dividend at different rates are stated to rank *pari passu*, this means that their preferential ranking *inter se* is proportional to their dividend rights.[17]

It is desirable that the rights of the preference shareholders should be stated in the articles or, if desired, in the memorandum as precisely and exhaustively as possible. This will exclude any doubt as to the nature and ambit of those rights.

Where preferential rights not exhaustively stated

34–05 Where the rights of the preference shares are not exhaustively stated in the memorandum and articles, the difficult question may arise as to what rights those shares carry. This question is in every case a question of construction of the relevant provisions in the articles, memorandum or terms of issue, and thus depends entirely on the words used in those provisions, in the light of the surrounding circumstances. In the following pages the rules of construction relating to the rights carried by preference shares are treated, but it should be borne in mind that these rules are not absolute and that the courts, in a particular case, may apply a different construction if the provisions defining the rights of the preference shares require a different construction.

---

13 Notably in *Scottish Insurance Corporation Ltd.* v. *Wilsons and Clyde Coal Co. Ltd.* [1949] A.C. 462 (H.L.); *Prudential Assurance Co. Ltd.* v. *Chatterley-Whitfield Collieries Co. Ltd.* [1949] A.C. 512 (H.L.); *Re Isle of Thanet Electricity Supply Co.* [1950] Ch. 161 (C.A.); *Re Saltdean Estate Co. Ltd.* [1968] 1 W.L.R. 1844; *Re William Jones & Sons Ltd.* [1969] 1 W.L.R. 146; See para. 34–15, *post*.

14 See para. 33–06, *ante*.

15 See para. 33–07, *ante; cf.* also *Re Old Silkstone Collieries Ltd.* [1954] Ch. 169.

16 *Scottish Insurance Corporation Ltd.* v. *Wilsons and Clyde Coal Co. Ltd.* [1949] A.C. 462; see para. 34–15, *post*.

17 *Beaumont* v. *Great North of Scotland Rly. Co.* 1868, 6 M. 1027.

Preferential rights as to dividend

No absolute right to dividend

34–06 Preference shares invariably carry a preferential right as to dividend which is expressed as a percentage of the nominal amount of the share, *e.g.* "7 per cent. preference shares."

This does not mean that the preference shareholder is invariably entitled to 7 per cent. per annum. Unlike the debenture holder, the preference shareholder who, after all, is a shareholder, is only entitled to income from his investment if a distributable profit within the meaning of the law[18] is available. His right is not to dividend but to preferential treatment if and when a dividend is distributed.

Moreover, this right will, in normal cases, not automatically become effective when distributable profit is available; normally, according to the terms defining the rights of the preference shares, the preference shareholders are only entitled to claim preferential treatment when a dividend is declared. However, while the existence of distributable profit is a *sine qua non* for their right to preference dividend, the position is different with respect to the declaration of dividend. The terms defining the rights of the preference shares—usually to be found in the articles—may provide that whenever distributable profit is available or exceeds a certain sum, it shall be distributed by way of preference dividend to the amount to which the preference shareholders are entitled to such dividend. Further, it is sometimes provided that preference dividend shall be declared by the directors and not—as is usual with respect to other final dividend—by the company in general meeting; even such a provision, however, does not dispense with the declaration of dividend, albeit by the directors,[19] and introduces an element of discretion on their part.

Cumulative dividend rights

34–07 Prima facie where the clause defining the preferential rights declares that the preference shares are to be entitled to a preferential dividend at a specified rate per cent., the dividend is cumulative,[20] but for clearness the word "cumulative" is sometimes inserted in the definition of rights, *e.g.* "a fixed cumulative preferential dividend of 7 per cent. per annum."

If the dividend is to be non-cumulative, the clause must clearly show this intention. In this case the clause has to be framed carefully. It must state the funds to which the holders of the preference shares are to be entitled to look for the payment of their dividend, *e.g.* "out of the profits made by the company in each year."[21] If it is plain that a preferential dividend is to

---

[18] See Chap. 76, *post*; see also *Monkland Iron & Coal Co.* v. *Henderson, etc.* 1883, 10 R. 494.

[19] Farwell J. in *Bond* v. *Barrow Haematite Steel Co.* [1902] 1 Ch. 353, 362; Romer J. in *Re Buenos Ayres Great Southern Ry.* [1947] 1 All E.R. 729, 741.

[20] *Henry* v. *Great Northern Ry.* (1857) 1 De G. & J. 606; *Webb* v. *Earle* (1875) L.R. 20 Eq. 556; *Foster* v. *Coles* (1906) 22 T.L.R. 555; *Miln* v. *Arizona Copper Co. Ltd.* 1899, 1 F. 935, 7 S.L.T. 57; *Ferguson & Forrester Ltd.* v. *Buchanan, etc.* 1920 S.C. 154; 1920 1 S.L.T. 84.

[21] On the meaning of "profits," see para. 76–01, *post*.

come only out of the profits of a particular year, the court will give effect to the intention though imperfectly expressed.[22]

THE FUND OUT OF WHICH PREFERENCE DIVIDEND IS PAYABLE. The fund out of which a preference dividend is payable may be still further restricted, particularly in the case of non-cumulative dividend. It is then necessary to discover from the memorandum or articles of association what comprises that fund. This is a matter of construction in each case. In *Evling* v. *Israel & Oppenheimer Ltd.*[23] clause 6 of the memorandum of association provided that "the profits of the company" in each year should be applied in an order of priorities, in which the placing of sums to reserve was expressed to be subsequent to the payment of preference dividend. Moreover, the clause used the words "the profits of the company" in one part, contrasting them with the words "the moneys of the company available for dividend" in another part of the clause. Eve J. held that the "profits" in this context consisted of the credit balance of the profit and loss account for each year *before* putting sums to reserve. Preference shares having the right to rank for dividend from a particular date have no claim in respect of the period before that date.[24]

On the other hand, where it was necessary to put aside a sum for restoring the company's fixed assets to an efficient condition, a preference dividend payable out of the profits of a particular year was held to be payable out of the profits *after* setting aside such sum: but the dividend took priority over the setting aside of further sums which should have been applied in earlier years in such maintenance but were in fact applied in paying dividends to the ordinary shareholders.[25] Further, where directors were authorised by the articles to set aside sums to reserve before recommending any dividend, and the preference dividend was payable out of "profits available for dividend," any sums transferred by the directors to reserve had to be deducted before the "profits available for dividend" could be ascertained.[26]

ARREARS OF CUMULATIVE PREFERENCE DIVIDEND IN WINDING UP. This term, stigmatised by Parker J.[27] as inaccurate but nevertheless generally used as conveniently brief, calls for explanation: the term does not mean declared dividend which has not been paid,[28] either because, after declaration, the

---

22 *Staples* v. *Eastman Photographic Materials Co.* [1896] 2 Ch. 303; *Thornycroft & Co.* v. *Thornycroft* (1927) 44 T.L.R. 9; *Niddrie & Benhar Coal Co.* v. *Hurll* 1891, 18 R. 805.
23 [1918] 1 Ch. 101.
24 *Macindoe's Trs.* v. *J.P. Coats Ltd., etc.* 1902, 9 S.L.T. 341.
25 *Dent* v. *London Tramways Co.* (1880) 16 Ch.D. 344.
26 *Fisher* v. *Black and White Publishing Co.* [1901] 1 Ch. 174; *Long Acre Press Ltd.* v. *Odhams Press Ltd.* [1930] 2 Ch. 196; *Re Buenos Ayres Great Southern Ry.* [1947] Ch. 384, 400; *Wemyss Collieries Trust* v. *Melville* 1905, 8 F. 143, 13 S.L.T. 551.
27 In *Weymouth Waterworks Co.* v. *Coode and Hasell* [1911] 2 Ch. 520, 529.
28 Such dividend is a debt of the company, para. 76–08, *post,* but the shareholders (including former shareholders: *Re Consolidated Goldfields of New Zealand* [1953] Ch. 689) are deferred to the creditors of the company (s. 212 (1) (*g*)).

company is unable to pay it or because it has not been claimed, but it means undeclared cumulative dividend which the company has failed to declare and to pay one year and with which it is "in arrear" the next year and the following years.

34–08 *Express provisions in articles, etc.* Here again, it is desirable that it should be stated expressly in the articles or the memorandum whether, in the event of winding up, the preference shareholders shall be entitled to those arrears.

A provision entitling the preference shareholders to "arrears of dividend due on their shares" does not entitle them to arrears except with regard to dividends that have been declared, since dividends are not "due" until then.[29]

34–09 *Where articles, etc., are silent.* If the term specifying the rights of the preference shares are silent, the question whether they are entitled to claim arrears of cumulative preference dividend is, again, one of construction of those terms.

In *Re Walter Symons Ltd.*[30] the memorandum of association conferred upon the holders of the preference shares "the right to a fixed cumulative preferential dividend at the rate of 12 per cent. per annum" and, after setting out other rights in the distributable profits, provided that these shares were to

> "rank both as regards dividends and capital in priority to the ordinary shares, but shall not confer the right to any further participation in profits or assets. . . ."

Maugham J. held that on the true construction of these provisions the preference shareholders were entitled in the winding up to be paid arrears of preference dividend in priority to any payment on the ordinary shares. The *ratio* of his decision was that this construction alone could give any meaning to the words "rank . . . as regards dividend . . . in priority to the ordinary shares," because these words, in their context, could only apply to a winding up, and "dividend" must mean here "arrears of dividend."

In *Re Wood, Skinner & Co. Ltd.*[31]—which should be contrasted with *Re Walter Symons Ltd.*[32]—the relevant provision was:

> "Such preference shares shall confer the right to a fixed cumulative dividend of £6 per cent. per annum on the capital paid up thereon and shall rank both as regards dividend and capital in priority to the ordinary shares."

In this context the provision for ranking was not confined to a winding up; as regards capital it would refer to a winding up, but as regards dividend it had to be taken as applying when the company was a going concern, as there was otherwise no indication that the dividend provided

29 *Re Roberts and Cooper Ltd.* [1929] 2 Ch. 383.
30 [1934] Ch. 308.
31 [1944] Ch. 323.
32 [1934] Ch. 308.

for was to be preferential. Consequently, Cohen J.[33] distinguished the case from *Re Walter Symons Ltd.*[34] and held that the reference to dividend did not include arrears of the cumulative preference dividend in the winding up.

The Court of Appeal found a right to arrears of cumulative preference dividend in the winding up before the distribution of capital in *Re de Jong (F.) & Co. Ltd.*,[35] where the provision was similar to that in *Re Walter Symons Ltd.*,[36] *viz.*:

> "The said preference shares shall carry the right to a fixed cumulative preferential dividend at the rate of 6 per cent. per annum on the capital for the time being paid up thereon, and shall have priority as to dividend and capital over the other shares in the capital for the time being, but shall not carry any further rights to participate in the profits or assets."

Morton L.J. analysed these provisions, and the grounds for the finding by the court were the following:

(1) the priority of the preference shares for dividend was given by the word "preferential";

(2) one would expect to find provisions for winding up, and the words "shall have priority as to dividend and capital over the other shares" supplied this: the priority as to capital was, the court held, clearly referable to a winding up, and as regards "dividend," this provision would not be required for the company as a going concern since it added nothing to the earlier word "preferential": to make sense of it the provision must refer to arrears of dividend in a winding up.

These decisions were carried one stage further in *Re E. W. Savory Ltd.*,[37–39] which can now be considered as the leading authority on the subject. The articles provided here that

> "The preference shares . . . shall confer on the holders the right to a fixed cumulative preferential dividend at the rate of £6 per cent. per annum on the capital paid up thereon and shall rank both as regards dividend and capital in priority to all other shares. . . . "

Wynn-Parry J. held that, following the decision in *Scottish Insurance Corporation Ltd.* v. *Wilsons and Clyde Coal Co. Ltd.*,[40] it was implied that further participation was excluded: the provision was therefore in line with *Re Walter Symons Ltd.*[41] and *Re de Jong*,[42] and the preference shares were entitled to arrears of dividend.

---

33 It should be noted that at that date *Re William Metcalfe & Son Ltd.* [1933] Ch. 142 was still considered to be good law: see *per* Wynn-Parry J. in *Re E. W. Savory Ltd.* [1951] 2 All E.R. 1036.
34 [1934] Ch. 308.
35 [1946] Ch. 211 (C.A.).
36 [1934] Ch. 308.
37–39 [1951] 2 All E.R. 1036.
40 [1949] A.C. 462; and see para. 35–15, *post*.
41 [1934] Ch. 308.
42 [1946] Ch. 211.

The earlier case of *Re Foster & Son Ltd.*,[43] which held that a similar article did not give the preference shareholders a right to arrears of cumulative preferential dividend on a winding up, must now be regarded as no longer authoritative, as it was decided before the House of Lords decision in *Scottish Insurance Corporation Ltd.* v. *Wilsons and Clyde Coal Co. Ltd.*[44]

Arrears of dividend are payable down to the date of the commencement of the winding up, not to the date of repayment.[45]

34–10 *Assets liable for payment of arrears*. If arrears of dividend are found to be payable in a winding up, they are payable out of the company's assets which remain after payment of the company's liabilities due to the creditors, and—unless the articles or other provisions setting out the rights of the preference shares compel another construction—in priority to any repayment of capital.[46]

Moreover, the arrears are payable out of the remaining assets whether or not these originated in profits earned before the winding up and, before that event, would have been available for distribution by way of dividend.[47] Wynn-Parry J. in *Re Wharfedale Brewery Co. Ltd.*[48] expressed this principle as follows:

> "The surplus divisible assets represent no doubt a mixed fund, but a fund which for all purposes in a winding up must be treated as assets and not as partly assets and partly profits."

But the articles may be so framed as to upset this rule.[49]

Tax treatment of arrears. When arrears of dividend are paid in a winding up they are payable gross, and not subject to deduction of advance corporation tax.[50] However, it is a common practice to provide in modern articles that in a winding up the preference shareholders shall be entitled to all arrears or accruals of dividend less a sum equal to the income tax at the basic rate in force at such date which would be deductible on an equivalent income payment. This rate will usually be the equivalent of advance corporation tax.

Arrears of non-cumulative preference dividend in winding up. The question whether arrears of non-cumulative preference dividend can be claimed in the winding up can only arise in very exceptional circumstances. Such claim can arise only for arrears of one year, and no arrears can be claimed if no profits have been made.[51]

---

[43] (1942) 111 L.J.Ch. 221.
[44] [1949] A.C. 462.
[45] *Re E. W. Savory Ltd.* [1951] 2 All E.R. 1036, 1040.
[46] *Re E. W. Savory Ltd.* [1951] 2 All E.R. 1036.
[47] *Re Springbok Agricultural Estates Ltd.* [1920] 1 Ch. 563; *Re Wharfedale Brewery Co. Ltd.* [1952] Ch. 913; *Re Hall (W. J.) & Co. Ltd.* [1909] 1 Ch. 521 has been repeatedly disapproved (but see note 49).
[48] [1952] Ch. 913, 916.
[49] This is the possible explanation of *Re Hall (W. J.) & Co. Ltd.* [1909] 1 Ch. 521.
[50] I.C.T.A. 1970, s. 233 (1). See Bramwell, *Taxation of Companies* (2nd ed., 1979), para. 7.01 n. 2.
[51] *Coulson* v. *Austin Motor Co.* (1927) 43 T.L.R. 493.

Participating dividend rights

34–11 It is not uncommon to find that, in addition to their preferential dividend, preference shares carry a right to participate in the distribution of further dividend, *e.g.* it may be provided that the preference shares shall be entitled to participate *pari passu* with the ordinary shares after a dividend of a fixed percentage has been paid on the ordinary shares.[52] Various arrangements are possible here, as is indicated by a comparison of *Re Isle of Thanet Electricity Supply Co. Ltd.*[53] where the preference shares participated further in any year where a dividend of 6 per cent. had been paid on the ordinary shares, with *Steel Company of Canada Ltd.* v. *Ramsay*,[54] where further participation only arose after the ordinary shares had received dividends which gave them 7 per cent. per annum since the incorporation of the company. Furthermore, the extent of the preference shareholders' participation may be limited, *e.g.* when the dividend paid on the ordinary shares exceeds 7 per cent. the preference shareholders shall become entitled to a further participating dividend of 1 per cent.

The right of the preference shares to participate further in the distribution of the available profits must be given them in the memorandum or articles of association or in the terms of issue. If it is not so set out, the preference shares do not carry participating rights.

In the case of preference shares which carry participating rights, the rule in *Birch* v. *Cropper*,[55] according to which prima facie all shares share equally in profits, does not apply. This was decided by the House of Lords in *Will* v. *United Lankat Plantations Co.*[56] on the ground that a preference shareholder who finds rights attached to his shares by the memorandum, articles or terms of issue expects to find there all the rights. Lord Haldane L.C. said[57]:

> ". . . when you turn to the terms on which the shares are issued you expect to find all the rights as regards dividends specified in the terms of the issue. And when you do find these things prescribed it certainly appears to me unnatural to go beyond them, . . ."

Frustration of rights as to dividend

34–12 Certain changes in the fiscal and economic climate have prompted many companies to repay their preference shares by a reduction of capital under section 66. In *Re Saltdean Estate Co. Ltd.*[58] it was held that such a risk was an integral part of the bundle of rights which make up a preferred share.

---

[52] The priority as to dividend out of distributable profit in this example would be: *first*, the fixed preference dividend, *then* the dividend on the ordinary shares to the fixed amount, and *finally* the surplus would be divided between ordinary and preference shareholders *pari passu*.
[53] [1950] Ch. 161.
[54] [1931] A.C. 270 (P.C.).
[55] (1889) 14 App.Cas. 525; see para. 33–06, *ante*.
[56] [1914] A.C. 11.
[57] At p. 17.
[58] [1968] 1 W.L.R. 1844. See para. 32–05, *ante*.

The petition was approved even though under the articles the preference shareholders were entitled to participating dividend rights (on an equal footing with the ordinary shareholders) and further large distributions of profits could be expected.

Advance corporation tax and preferential dividends

34–13 With the introduction of the imputation system of corporation tax by the Finance Act 1972 a company became obliged to pay an amount of advance corporation tax equal to a prescribed fraction of the dividends paid. The shareholder is then liable to income tax on the amount of the dividend received together with the appropriate amount of advance corporation tax. The advance corporation tax paid is, however, available to the shareholder as a tax credit and is intended to cancel out any liability to basic rate of income tax on the grossed-up dividend. Thus as the basic rate of income tax varies so does the fraction of advance corporation tax. This has certain consequences for preferential dividends expressed as a fixed percentage.

In *Sime Darby London Ltd.* v. *Sime Darby Holdings Ltd.*[59] the preference shareholders were entitled to a fixed cumulative dividend of 7½ per cent. Before 1973 the shareholders received £75 gross for each £1,000 shares owned and then paid income tax on the £75. For the tax year 1973–74 the new system required that the 7½ per cent. figure be a gross figure to be divided into the net dividend payable and the appropriate fraction of advance corporation tax (and therefore tax credit). The appropriate fraction for that year was three-sevenths and the Finance Act 1972, Sched. 23, para. 18 (1) provided by way of transition that for preference shares in existence before April 6, 1973 the gross percentage was to be divided between the net dividend and an amount of advance corporation tax calculated at the rate in force "on that date." Accordingly, on the same figures, the preference shareholder would receive £52.50 net together with a tax credit of £22.50. But for the year 1974–75 the fraction was altered to thirty-three-sixty-sevenths and the dispute was whether the fixed percentage should be divided again so that the amount received together with the tax credit amounted to 7½ per cent. or whether the words "on that date" indicated that the net amount of dividend was fixed once and for all at 5 ¼ per cent. (*i.e.* the net amount received in 1973–74) and the tax credit alone would vary. Brightman J. applied the first interpretation, since only that would leave the preference shareholders' rights unaltered—*i.e.* at a gross figure of 7½ per cent. The alternative view would let the gross amount of the dividend vary with the rates of advance corporation tax and only rarely coincide with the figure in the articles. For example, with a rate of thirty-three-sixty-sevenths on a fixed net dividend of 5¼ per cent. the approximate tax credit would be 2⅗per cent. giving a gross dividend of 7 9/10 per cent. If the rate of advance corporation tax was to fall the gross dividend could be less than that allowed in the article.

---

59 [1976] 1 W.L.R. 59. See Bramwell, *op. cit.* in n. 50, *ante*, para. 8–04.

This decision was, however, overruled by section 46 of the Finance Act 1976 which firmly establishes the view rejected by Brightman J. Power was given for companies which had underpaid any preference shareholders by adopting the "alternative view" to make up the difference where the preference shares were not cumulative (when the underpayment can be automatically adjusted). But there was no obligation to do this and the section protected all persons who acted in good faith from any liability (s. 46 (5)). It seems therefore that the fixed percentages of preference dividend expressed in the articles are no longer an accurate picture of the gross dividend received for tax purposes.

Preferential rights as to capital

Priority as to capital in winding up

It cannot be presumed that because a class of shares carries a preference as to dividend, it likewise carries a right to preferential treatment as to capital in the winding up.[60] Prima facie shares rank *pari passu* both as regards dividend and capital.[61] If shares are given preference as to dividend—as is the case with preference shares—the prima facie rule is displaced to that extent, but the prima facie rule of equal treatment of shares in the winding up remains.[62] That rule is only displaced if the articles, the memorandum or the terms of issue contain an indication of a different intention.

Similarly, the fact that certain shares have been issued at a premium does not entitle the holders to any additional rights in a winding up over shares issued at par.[60]

Although, thus, in the absence of special provisions, a preference shareholder is not entitled on a winding up to have his capital paid off in priority to the other shareholders, the articles, memorandum or terms of issue usually give him expressly a preference as to capital in the winding up.[63] In Scotland it has been held that interest may be due from the date the liquidator ascertained that funds would permit repayment, at the rate the funds had earned in his hands.[64]

Participating rights as to capital

34–14 EXPRESS PROVISION FOR PARTICIPATION. Where the provisions defining the rights of the preference shares state expressly that the shares shall be entitled to participate in the distribution of any surplus assets after all shares have been repaid in full, the preference shareholders are entitled to participate in the distribution of *all* assets which remain after paying

---

[60] *Re Driffield Gas Light Co.* [1898] 1 Ch. 451.
[61] *Birch* v. *Cropper* (1889) 14 App.Cas. 525.
[62] *Re Driffield Gas Light Co.* [1898] 1 Ch. 451; *Re Syston and Thurmaston Gas, Light and Coke Co. Ltd.* [1937] 2 All E.R. 322.
[63] *Cf. Re Bangor and Portmadoc Slate and Slab Co. Ltd.* (1875) L.R. 20 Eq. 59.
[64] *Scottish Acid and Alkali Co.* 1950 S.L.T. (Notes) 53.

creditors, costs and arrears of the preference dividend and after repaying all paid-up capital. It is irrelevant that part of these distributable assets orginated in accumulated profits which, before the winding up, the ordinary shareholders could have secured to themselves for their exclusive enjoyment by passing the appropriate resolutions. The fact that the ordinary shareholders might have been able to defeat the expectations of the preference shareholders to participate in the winding up in the undistributed assets by distributing them before the winding up is not necessarily inconsistent with the preference shareholders having such a right in the winding up.[64a]

Such a distribution to the ordinary shareholders before winding up may possibly be opposed, in appropriate circumstances, by the participating preference shareholders as a fraud on the minority[64b] or as oppressive conduct under section 75 of the 1980 Act,[65] but in view of the precarious nature of the preference shareholders' rights, as stated in *Re Saltdean Estate Co. Ltd.*,[66] it is probable that some further evidence of fraud or oppression will be necessary in addition to the mere act of distribution.

34–15 NO PROVISION FOR PARTICIPATION. Where the provisions defining the rights of the preference shares do not state expressly whether those shares shall be entitled to participate in the distribution of any surplus assets after all shares have been repaid in full, it is, again, a matter of construction of the relevant provisions, in the light of all surrounding circumstances, whether the preference shares are intended to carry participating rights as to capital. Here, as in the case of dividend rights, three basic prima facie rules apply:

first, if no rights are specified in those provisions all shares have to be treated *pari passu*[67];

secondly, if the rights attached to a class are specified, and in particular the class is given preferential rights as to dividend and capital, the rights set out in the relevant provisions are in each case exhaustive[68]; and

thirdly, the onus of proving that the specified rights are not exhaus-

---

[64a] *Dimbula Valley (Ceylon) Tea Co. Ltd.* v. *Laurie* [1961] Ch. 353; see also *Re Bridgewater Navigation Co.* [1891] 2 Ch. 317; *Scottish Insurance Corporation Ltd.* v. *Wilsons and Clyde Coal Co. Ltd.* [1949] A.C. 462.

[64b] See Chap. 58, *post.*

[65] See Chap. 60, *post.*

[66] [1968] 1 W.L.R. 1844, 1852.

[67] *Birch* v. *Cropper* (1889) 14 App.Cas. 525; see *Will* v. *United Lankat Plantations Co.* [1914] A.C. 11.

[68] *Scottish Insurance Corporation* v. *Wilsons and Clyde Coal Co.* [1949] A.C. 462; *Prudential Assurance Co. Ltd.* v. *Chatterley-Whitfield Collieries Co. Ltd.* [1949] A.C. 512; *Re Isle of Thanet Electricity Supply Co.* [1950] Ch. 161. The first two cases also raised points under s. 25 of the Coal Industry Nationalisation Act 1946; for a discussion of these points, see Palmer's *Company Law* (20th ed.), p. 303.

tive is upon the preference shareholders who allege that they have further and better rights.[69] This onus is not easy to discharge.

The position as regards the preference shareholders' right to participate in the distribution of the surplus assets in winding up is thus analogous to that regarding their right to participate in the distribution of surplus profits: they are entitled to participating rights only if these rights are set out in the provisions defining the preference shareholders' rights. This was finally established in two decisions of the House of Lords,[70] *Scottish Insurance Corpn.* v. *Wilsons and Clyde Coal Co.*[71] and *Prudential Assurance Co.* v. *Chatterley-Whitfield Collieries Co. Ltd.*,[72] and in a decision of the Court of Appeal, *Re Isle of Thanet Electricity Supply Co. Ltd.*[73] Wynn-Parry J., giving the judgment of the Court of Appeal in the last-mentioned case, summed up the legal position as follows.[74]

> " . . . the effect of the authorities as now in force is to establish . . . two principles . . .
>
> *first*, that, in construing an article which deals with rights to share in profits, that is, dividend rights, and rights to share in the company's property in a liquidation, the same principle is applicable; and
>
> *second*, that that principle is that, where the article sets out the rights attached to a class of shares to participate in profits while the company is a going concern or to share in the property of the company in liquidation, prima facie, the rights so set out are in each case exhaustive."

34–16 It should be noted that the presumption that the preference shares do not carry participating rights as to capital unless they are set out in the relevant provisions is not even displaced where the preference shareholders are entitled, while the company is a going concern, to participate in excess of their preference dividend in the distribution of profits. The argument that such a right would imply that all undistributed profits should be shared by the preference shareholders with the ordinary shareholders in a winding up is fallacious because on a winding up the undistributable profits lose their character as such and are merely assets of the company.[75] Indeed, the contrast with participation whilst a going concern, with no specific provision in the event of winding up, raises the presumption that *inclusio unius est exclusio alterius*. Sargant J. observed in one case[76]:

---

[69] *Re Isle of Thanet Electricity Supply Co.* [1950] Ch. 161, 168, 172.
[70] Overruling the decision of the Court of Appeal in *Re William Metcalfe Ltd.* [1933] Ch. 142, and, by implication, the Court of Session decisions in *Williamson-Buchanan Steamers Ltd.* 1936 S.L.T. 106, and *Town and Gown Assn. Ltd.* 1948 S.L.T. (Notes) 71.
[71] [1949] A.C. 462; 1949 S.C. (H.L.) 90, 1949 S.L.T. 230.
[72] [1949] A.C. 512.
[73] [1950] Ch. 161.
[74] At p. 171.
[75] *Re Wharfdale Brewery Co. Ltd.* [1952] Ch. 913; see para. 34–10, *ante*. See also *Re Saltdean Estate Co. Ltd.* [1968] 1 W.L.R. 1844.
[76] *Re National Telephone Co.* [1914] 1 Ch. 755, 774.

"... it appears to me that the weight of authority is in favour of the view that, either with regard to dividend or with regard to the rights in a winding-up, the express gift or attachment of preferential rights to preference shares, on their creation, is, prima facie, a definition of the whole of their rights in that respect, and negatives any further or other right to which, but for the specified rights, they would have been entitled."

That the modern rule, as established in *Scottish Insurance Corpn. Ltd.* v. *Wilsons and Clyde Coal Co. Ltd.*[77] and the related cases, is in harmony with the concept which businessmen have of the preference share[78] was expressed by Lord Simonds[79]:

"Reading these articles as a whole with such familiarity with the topic as the years have brought, I would not hesitate to say ... that the last thing a preference stockholder would expect to get (I do not speak here of the legal rights) would be a share of surplus assets, and that such a share would be a windfall beyond his reasonable expectations. ..."

Frustration of rights as to capital

34–17 In view of the limited rights ordinarily accorded to preference shares on a winding up, it has been held that preference shares may be repaid on a reduction of capital under section 66 what they would be entitled to on a winding up.[80] In *Re William Jones & Sons Ltd.*[81] it was further held that if a winding up was not in prospect preference shareholders could be repaid at a lower value than that obtaining on a winding up.

Redeemable preference shares

34–18 As has been stated earlier all shares may now be issued as redeemable.[82] Prior to the 1981 Act only redeemable preference shares were admitted, and those existing at the date of implementation of the 1981 Act have been assimilated into the new procedure.[83] Section 58 of the 1948 Act has accordingly been repealed.[84]

---

[77] [1949] A.C. 462. The preference shares in the two House of Lords decisions did not carry participatory rights as to dividend but the preference shares in the *Isle of Thanet Electricity Supply* case carried such rights.

[78] See para. 34–03, *ante*.

[79] [1949] A.C. 462, 487. *Cf.* also the observations of Lord Loreburn in *Will* v. *United Lankat Plantations Co.* [1914] A.C. 11, 19.

[80] *Scottish Insurance Corporation* v. *Wilsons & Clyde Coal Co. Ltd.* [1949] A.C. 462; *Prudential Assurance Co.* v. *Chatterley-Whitfield Collieries Co. Ltd.* [1949] A.C. 512.

[81] [1969] 1 W.L.R. 146. See para. 32–05, *ante;* see also *William Dixon Ltd.* 1948 S.C. 511; 1948 S.L.T. 423.

[82] See para. 33–13, *ante*.

[83] See para. 33–25, *ante*.

[84] 1981 Act, Sched. 4.

CHAPTER 35

CALLS AND INSTALMENTS ON SHARES

Liability of member

35–01 A member is under a liability to pay up in accordance with the articles the amount for the time being unpaid on his shares. If his shares have been issued as paid up or partly paid up, whether for cash or otherwise, or if he or some prior holder has paid them up wholly or in part, he would be wholly or *pro tanto* exempt from calls; but prima facie his liability is to pay the full amount in money[1] or, subject to the rules relating to the payment for shares, in money's worth.[1]

The nature of this liability is defined by section 20 of the 1948 Act. A shareholder is bound to pay the full amount unpaid on his shares, but, unless the terms of issue so provide, he is not bound to pay up at once.[2] A public company's shares cannot, however, be allotted unless at least one-quarter of its nominal value and any premium are paid up in full.[3] He is only bound to pay in accordance with the articles, *e.g.* by fixed instalments, according to the terms of issue, or in response to calls.[4] When the liability to pay has thus matured into a debt, this indebtedness on the shareholder's part to the company is in England "of the nature of a specialty debt" (s. 20 (2)); consequently, the period of limitation is 12 years (Limitation Act 1939, s. 2 (3)).[5] The reasoning of Slade J. in *Re Compania de Electricidad de la Provincia de Buenos Aires Ltd.*[6] does not apply here. Section 20 provides that the contract is regarded as sealed by each member, which in this case is the debtor, whereas in that case the company was the debtor.[7]

Instalments and calls

35–02 In modern company practice the arrangement envisaged by the legislator, *viz*. that the liability of the shareholder shall be contingent upon a call being made upon him, is rarely adopted as far as public companies are concerned.[8] Where these companies issue shares, the terms of issue nor-

---

[1] See para. 22–40, *ante*.
[2] If he applies for shares in response to a prospectus issued by the company, he has to pay on application at least 5 per cent. of the nominal amount of the shares (s. 47 (3) and (6)).
[3] See para. 4–14, *ante*.
[4] *Whittaker* v. *Kershaw* (1890) 45 Ch.D. 320; *Re Russian Spratts Ltd.* [1898] 2 Ch. 149; *Alexander* v. *Automatic Telephone Co.* [1900] 2 Ch. 56.
[5] In Scotland, where the Limitation Act is inapplicable, the debt is subject to negative prescription which will normally be the period of five years from the date of the call (Prescription and Limitation (Scotland) Act 1973, s. 6 and Sched. 1).
[6] [1978] 3 All E.R. 668.
[7] See para. 75–09, *post*.
[8] The Council of the Stock Exchange are not normally prepared to admit to listing shares which remain partly paid subsequent to registration; see *Admission of Securities to Listing*, Chap. 1, para. 5.

mally provide that what is due on the shares shall be paid by fixed instalments, so that within a relativey short time after the issue the shares are fully paid. Apart from financial considerations this method has the additional convenience to the company that the shares may be converted into stock (1948 Act, s. 61 (1) (*c*)) or that the numbering of the shares may be dispensed with, provided that the other conditions laid down in section 74, proviso, of the 1948 Act are complied with. Although, strictly speaking, an instalment payable by the terms of issue at a fixed date is not a call,[9] the articles usually provide that any sum payable at a fixed day shall be deemed to be a call duly made and payable on the date on which it became due, and in a case of non-payment the provisions of the articles dealing with the consequences of non-payment of a call shall apply (art. 19). Apart from the conditions upon which the liability of the shareholder depends, there appears in such cases, therefore, to be no practical difference between the method of payment by fixed instalments and that of payment upon calls in the technical sense.

Call-making power a trust

35–03 The power to make calls is a power in the nature of a trust, and it must be exercised for the general benefit of the company.[10] If it is exercised mala fide, *e.g.* for the directors' own ends or some other indirect purpose, this is an abuse of their power, and an injunction may be obtained restraining the call.[11] But the court does not readily accede to such an application. The onus of proving mala fides in such a case is on the shareholder.[12] In the absence of proof of mala fides it is a well-established principle that the court will not interfere with the discretion of the directors in making a call.[12]

Making of calls

35–04 A call is made by the directors of the company pursuant to the provisions of the company's articles.

These generally provide (arts. 15–20) that the directors may from time to time make such calls as they think fit upon the members in respect of all moneys unpaid on the shares held by them and not by the conditions of allotment thereof made payable at fixed times, and that each member shall pay the amount of every call so made on him to the persons and at the times and places fixed by the directors. Usually the notice of a call is 14 or

---

[9] *Croskey* v. *Bank of Wales* (1863) 4 Giff. 314; *Alexander* v. *Automatic Telephone Co.* [1900] 2 Ch. 56.

[10] *Gilbert's Case* (1870) L.R. 5 Ch. 559; *Alexander* v. *Automatic Telephone Co.* [1900] 2 Ch. 56. See generally Chap. 63, *post*.

[11] See para. 35–15, *post*.

[12] *Odessa Tramways Co.* v. *Mendel* (1878) 8 Ch.D. 235.

21 days. The terms thus defined by the articles are the terms on which, and on which only, the shareholder has agreed to pay, and in making a call care must, therefore, be taken that the directors making it are:

(1) duly appointed[13]; and
(2) duly qualified[14];
(3) that the meeting of the directors has been duly convened[15];
(4) that the proper quorum is present[16]; and
(5) that the resolution making the call is duly passed and specifies the amount of the call, the time and place of payment—for these are of its essence—and to whom the call is to be paid.[17]

A proper entry must also be made in the minutes.[18] Unless these matters are attended to the call may be invalid, and when the company comes to sue for the amount or seeks to enforce payment by forfeiture, it may be embarrassed by finding that all the proceedings are vitiated by an initial irregularity.[19]

Sometimes the articles limit the amount of a call; they provide, *e.g.* that the amount shall not exceed one-fourth of the nominal amount of the share, and sometimes that a specified interval must elapse between the times fixed for payment of two successive calls (art. 15). Any conditions of this kind must be observed in making a call. More than one call may be made on one day each being for the maximum permitted amount, provided that the dates for payment differ by the required interval.[20]

35–05 Calls should be made *pari passu* unless the articles otherwise provide. Article 20 authorises the directors, on the issue of shares, to differentiate between the holders as to the amount of calls to be paid and the times of payment. It is believed that if a company alters its articles subsequent to the allotment of shares by introducing the power to discriminate, the directors cannot exercise it with respect to shares previously allotted because such a retrospective use of that power would be an attempt to alter the terms of the contract between the shareholder and the company unilaterally. Directors can only justify a call made on certain selected members (even where the articles permit this) on very special grounds.[21]

It may sometimes be proper for directors to make a call in order to restrain threatened transfers[22]: and where a company is about to sell its

---

13 *Howbeach Coal Co.* v. *Teague* (1860) 5 H. & N. 151.

14 *Iron Ship, etc., Co.* v. *Blunt* (1868) L.R. 3 C.P. 484; *Sharp* v. *Dawes* (1876) 2 Q.B.D. 26; *The Galloway Saloon Steam Packet Co.* v. *Wallace* 1891, 19 R. 330.

15 *Garden Gully United Quartz Mining Co.* v. *McLister* (1875) 1 App.Cas. 39; *Faure Electric Accumulator Co.* v. *Phillipart* (1888) 58 L.T. 525.

16 *Austin's Case* (1871) 24 L.T. 932; *The Galloway Saloon Steam Packet Co.* v. *Wallace, supra; The Universal Corporation Ltd.* v. *Simson* 1908, 6 S.L.T. 618.

17 See *Re Cawley & Co.* (1889) 42 Ch.D. 209; *cf. Johnson* v. *Lyttle's Iron Agency* (1877) 5 Ch.D. 687.

18 *Cornwall, etc., Mining Co.* v. *Bennett* (1860) 5 H. & N. 423.

19 See, however, as to such irregularities, Chap. 62–04, *post*.

20 *The Universal Corpn. Ltd.* v. *Hughes* 1909 S.C. 1434; 1909, 2 S.L.T. 37.

21 *Galloway* v. *Hallé Concerts Society* [1915] 2 Ch. 233.

22 *Gilbert's Case* (1870) L.R. 5 Ch. 559.

undertaking, there is no objection to a call being made with a view to increasing the saleable assets by the amount thereof.[23]

A call may be made payable in instalments without any express authority in the articles[24];

Directors may make calls after a voluntary winding up has commenced with the sanction of a general meeting or of the liquidator.[25]

Interest on calls

35–06 The articles usually contain a provision to the effect that, if any call is not paid at the time fixed, the holder for the time being of the share is to be liable to pay interest at a specified rate (art. 18). Such a clause is binding and will be given effect to.[26] It does not, however, apply in the case of calls made by the liquidator of a company.[27] As to liability to pay interest on calls after forfeiture of the shares, see *Stocken's Case*,[28] and *Faure Electric Accumulator Co.* v. *Phillipart*.[29]

Payment of dividend on partly paid shares

35–07 The articles usually provide that, subject to the rights of shares with special rights as to dividends, all dividends are declared and paid according to the amounts paid or credited as paid on the shares (art. 118). Where the articles registered by the company do not contain such a provision and the application of Table A is excluded, dividend has to be declared and paid on all shares—except those carrying preferential or deferred rights as to dividend—equally, and it is irrelevant whether they are fully paid or partly paid; this follows from the principle that the shareholders have to be treated *pari passu* unless the articles otherwise provide.

Past member

35–08 The liability of a member does not always cease when he ceases to be a member; in the winding up of the company he may be placed, as a past member, on the B list of contributories (s. 212)[30]; and after the reduction of capital a person who, at the date of the registration of the order for reduction and minute, was a member may likewise be liable to contribute in the case of inability of the company to pay its debts on the conditions laid down in section 70 of the 1948 Act.[31]

---

[23] *New Zealand, etc., Co.* v. *Peacock* [1894] 1 Q.B. 622.
[24] *Ambergate, etc., Ry.* v. *Norcliffe* (1851) 6 Ex.Reps. 629; *Lawrence* v. *Wynn* (1839) 5 M. & W. 355.
[25] *Re Fairbairn Engineering Co., Ladd's Case* [1893] 3 Ch. 450.
[26] *London & North West American Mortgage Co.* v. *Stewart* 1900, 8 S.L.T. 98.
[27] *Re Welsh Flannel and Tweed Co.* (1875) L.R. 20 Eq. 360, 367. For the position in Scotland see s. 275 of the 1948 Act and para. 87–41, *post*.
[28] (1868) L.R. 3 Ch. 412.
[29] (1888) 58 L.T. 525.
[30] See para. 85–45 and para. 87–39, *post*.
[31] See para. 32–16, *ante*.

Deceased member

35–09 Although the articles generally provide that calls are to be made on the "members," a deceased member, whilst his name remains on the register, is to be treated as a continuing member so far as may be necessary to make his estate liable.[32]

In the administration of the insolvent estate of a deceased person the amount due for calls which may be made in respect of shares in a company held by him should be estimated and proved for, both when the company is a going concern and also when it is being wound up.[33]

Bankrupt member

35–10 If a shareholder becomes bankrupt and the company proves in the bankruptcy for the uncalled liability on the shares and receives a dividend, these facts, as such, do not make the shares fully paid shares. The shares are only paid-up shares to the amount that they have, in fact, been paid up.[34]

Calls on forfeited shares

35–11 If shares are forfeited for non-payment of calls[35] and subsequently transferred rather than cancelled, the transferee is liable for any amount unpaid on the shares at the time of the transfer.[36]

Enforcing payment

35–12 The duty of the directors of a company when a call is made is to compel every shareholder to pay to the company the amount due from him in respect of the call, and they are guilty of a breach of their duty if they do not take all reasonable means for enforcing payment.[37]

It is a breach of trust for them to favour any director in such a matter.[38]

It is now common to sue for a call on a specially indorsed writ.[39] After judgment has been obtained against the defaulting shareholder the company can, if needs be, proceed against him in bankruptcy[40] or, if it has these powers in its articles, declare his shares as forfeit.[41]

35–13 In English law whilst the company is a going concern the shareholder can plead a set-off,[42] but no set-off is allowed against a call once the company is

---

32 *New Zealand, etc., Co.* v. *Peacock* [1894] 1 Q.B. 622.
33 *Re McMahon, Fuller* v. *McMahon* [1900] 1 Ch. 173.
34 *Re West Coast Goldfields* [1906] 1 Ch. 1; *The Cresswell Ranche & Cattle Co. Ltd.* v. *Balfour Melville* 1902, 9 S.L.T. 356.
35 See paras. 41–01 *et seq., post.*
36 See para. 41–07, *post.*
37 *Spackman* v. *Evans* (1868) L.R. 3 H.L. 171.
38 *Alexander* v. *Automatic Telephone Co.* [1900] 2 Ch. 56.
39 R.S.C. 1965, Ord. 6, r. 1, and Appendix A, Form 3. In Scotland an action of payment would be appropriate.
40 *Re Winterbottom* (1886) 18 Q.B.D. 446.
41 See para. 41–01, *post.*
42 *Re Hiram Maxim Lamp Co.* [1903] 1 Ch. 70.

in liquidation.[43] This rule even extends to the case where the call is made before winding up and an action is commenced to establish a set-off against the call, but before judgment the company goes into liquidation: thenceforth no right of set-off can exist.[44]

35–14 In Scots law compensation (*i.e* set-off) is available in all cases where both claims are liquid and provided that both parties are debtor and creditor in the same personal capacity. The claim may arise out of different situations.[45] Thus a shareholder having a debt due by a company can set this off against a call[46] but not if, for example, the debt was due to him personally and the call was on him as a trustee holding shares. If the company goes into liquidation calls made beforehand may be subject to compensation even if the shareholder's claim is illiquid, but calls made after winding up has commenced, at least in an insolvent winding up cannot be set off against pre-liquidation debts until all creditors have been satisfied.[47]

Misrepresentation is no defence to an action for calls unless the defendant has promptly applied for rectification of the register either by counterclaim in the action or by separate proceedings.[48]

Injunction to restrain enforcement of call

35–15 If a call is improperly made, the shareholder can obtain an injunction to restrain the directors from enforcing the call by forfeiture pending the trial of the question; but usually only on the terms that the amount of the call should be paid into court.[49]

An injunction cannot be granted to restrain the enforcement of a call by action at law.[50]

Payment in advance of calls

35–16 The articles of a company usually contain a clause similar to article 21, empowering the directors to receive from any member money in advance of calls, on the footing that interest is to be paid thereon whilst in advance. This is an extremely important power. It is in the nature of a trust to be faithfully exercised for the benefit of the company, and accordingly the directors should only receive money in advance when, in their judgment, the same can be advantageously used for the purposes of the company, and

---

[43] *Re Vulcan Ironworks Co.* [1885] W.N. 120.

[44] As to the method of enforcing calls due to an English company from contributories in Ireland, see *Re Bank of Egypt Ltd.* [1913] 1 Ir.R. 502.

[45] Compensation Act 1592 (of the Scottish Parliament).

[46] *Liquidators of Coustonholm Paper Mills Co.* v. *Law* (1891) 18 R. (Ct. of Sess.) 1076, 1092.

[47] *Asphaltic Limestone* v. *Corporation of Glasgow* 1907, S.C. 463; see para. 87–46, *post.*

[48] *First National Re-insurance Co.* v. *Greenfield* [1921] 2 K.B. 260.

[49] *Lamb* v. *Sambas Rubber, etc., Co.* [1908] 1 Ch. 845; *Jones* v. *Pacaya Rubber, etc., Co.* [1911] 1 K.B. 455.

[50] Judicature Act 1925, s. 41; *Galloway* v. *Hallé Concerts Society* [1915] 2 Ch. 233. This point does not arise in Scotland where the Judicature Act 1925 does not apply.

the rate of interest should not be excessive.[51] Hence, where directors under a power of this kind paid up in advance their own shares, and the same day appropriated the amount in payment of their fees, the company being insolvent, it was held that the transaction, not being bona fide, was ineffectual, and that the directors remained liable on their shares.[52]

The articles further usually state that advance payments (which carry interest) are not regarded, for the purposes of dividend, as sums paid on the shares and, under the normal regulations, do not qualify for dividend (art. 118). It would be iniquitous if the same sum paid on shares carried interest and dividend at the same time.

35–17 It is well established that where money is paid up in advance under such a clause on the footing that it is to carry interest, such interest is to be paid whether there are or are not profits for the payment thereof. If there are no profits, or the profits are insufficient, then the company must pay out of capital, and there is nothing *ultra vires* in this.[53]

Where capital has been paid up in advance, it ranks for repayment in a winding up prima facie before capital not paid up in advance.[54] The company is not entitled to repay the amount advanced at any time against the wish of the shareholder in the absence of a duly sanctioned reduction of capital.[55]

---

[51] *Poole, Jackson and Whyte's Case* (1878) 9 Ch.D. 322; *Re Pyle Works* (1890) 44 Ch.D. 534, 586.

[52] *Sykes's Case* (1872) L.R. 13 Eq. 255. See, however, *Mason's, etc., Case, Re Liverpool, etc., Insurance Co.* (1882) 30 W.R. 378; *Re A. M. Woods, Ship's Woodite Protection Co.* (1890) 2 Meg.C.R. 164; also *Re Washington Diamond Mining Co.* [1893] 3 Ch. 95.

[53] *Lock* v. *Queensland, etc., Mortgage Co.* [1896] A.C. 461, 467.

[54] *Ex p. Maude* (1870) L.R. 6 Ch. 51; *Re Wakefield, etc., Co.* [1892] 3 Ch. 165; *Re Exchange Drapery Co.* (1888) 38 Ch.D. 171.

[55] *London and Northern S.S. Co.* v. *Farmer* [1914] W.N. 200; 111 L.T. 204.

CHAPTER 36

SHARE CERTIFICATES AND SHARE WARRANTS

Nature and form of share certificate

Issue of share certificates

36–01 The Act provides that certificates must be completed and ready for delivery within two months after allotment or after a transfer is lodged (1948 Act, s. 80).[1] This obligation does not, however, extend to transfers to a Stock Exchange nominee (SEPON) where it has been dispensed with to facilitate the new system of transfers on the Stock Exchange.[2] In case of refusal to register, notice of refusal must be given to the transferee within two months (s. 78), and the court may order the company to make good the default, and may order any officer of the company to pay the costs (s. 80 (3)). There are other penalties in default (s. 80 (2)).

A share certificate is meant to facilitate dealings by shareholders with their shares in the market by enabling them, on any such dealing, whether it is one of sale, mortgage or pledge, to show on the spot a good prima facie marketable title to the shares[3] " . . . the certificates," said Lord Selborne in *Société Générale de Paris* v. *Walker,*[4] "are the proper (and indeed the only) documentary evidence of title in the possession of a shareholder . . . "

Right to share certificate

The articles usually give the member the right to receive a share certificate and that such certificate be available free of charge (art. 8). In addition the Rules of the Stock Exchange provide that a new certificate shall be issued free of charge if either it is to replace one that has worn out or been lost or destroyed, or if it is a certificate for the balance where the holder has sold part of his holding.[5]

The right to a certificate can be enforced by action against the company.[6]

Split certificates

36–02 The articles usually give the member the right to receive a share certificate and that such certificate be available free of charge (art. 8). In

---

[1] Unless the terms of issue otherwise provide (s. 80 (1)).

[2] Stock Exchange (Completion of Bargains) Act 1976, s. 1. See para. 39–30, *post*.

[3] Accordingly in Canada it has been held that an agent employed to purchase shares under a contract expressly contemplating acquisition of the share certificate is in breach of his fiduciary duty in obtaining a substitute document: *Laskin* v. *Beche & Co. Inc.* (1971) 23 D.L.R. (3d) 385.

[4] (1885) 11 App.Cas. 20, 29. See further Cockburn C.J. in *Re Bahia, etc., Ry.* (1868) L.R. 3 Q.B. 584, 594.

[5] *Admission of Securities to Listing*, issued by the Stock Exchange, Sched. VII, Part A, para. 132, Part B, para. 168.

[6] *Burdett* v. *Standard Exploration Co.* (1899) 16 T.L.R. 112.

small fee for every certificate after the first or such less sum as the directors may determine from time to time (art. 8). The issue of such "split certificates" is useful where the shareholder is a trustee under several unconnected trusts, *e.g.* a trustee department of a bank which holds shares in the same public company for different trust funds; if several certificates are issued, they can be kept by the bank on the several trust securities accounts. Often the same result is achieved by placing the various shares into "designated accounts" of the same registered shareholder.[7]

Where articles provide that a shareholder shall be entitled to one certificate free or to several certificates on payment of a small fee for every subsequent certificate, the shareholder is entitled to have any number of certificates for one or more shares making together the total number of shares held.[8]

The issue of a great number of split certificates to the same shareholder may considerably inconvenience the company, and for that reason articles sometimes provide that the issue of several certificates relating to the same holding shall be in the discretion of the directors.

Form of share certificate

THE USUAL FORM

36–03 A share certificate relating to ordinary shares where there are two classes of fully paid shares would be in the following form:

ORDINARY SHARES

Certificate No. *Number of Shares*

THE "A" PUBLIC LIMITED COMPANY[9]

(*Incorporated under the Companies Act 1948.*)

THIS IS TO CERTIFY *that* ....

....

is/are the Registered Holder(s) of ....

Ordinary Shares of Fifty Pence each, fully paid, in THE "A" PUBLIC LIMITED COMPANY, *subject to the Memorandum and Articles of Association of the Company.*

GIVEN *under the (Common) Seal of the Company on* ....

.... *Director*

.... *Secretary*

Exd...................

T. No...................

NOTE.—No transfer of the above Shares or any of them will be registered without the production and surrender of a Certificate relating thereto.

Registrars: "X" & Co., London Wall, London, E.C.2.

---

[7] See para. 50–08, *post*.
[8] *Sharpe* v. *Tophams* [1939] Ch. 373.
[9] A private company would of course use the words COMPANY LIMITED.

Share certificates relating to preference shares normally state the conditions as to capital, dividends and redemption (if any) under which they are issued; this is in accordance with the Stock Exchange requirements discussed below.[10]

STATUTORY AND REGULATORY REQUIREMENTS

36–04 The Act does not postulate any requirements as regards the form of the share certificate except that it has to be a "certificate," *i.e.* a document, but it makes the important provision[11] that a share certificate is prima facie evidence of the title of the member to the share dependent upon the certificate being issued "under the common seal of the company, specifying any shares held by the member" (1948 Act, s. 81). The articles usually provide that every certificate shall be under the seal of the company and shall specify the shares to which it relates and the amount paid up thereon (art. 8).

The Stock Exchange (Completion of Bargains) Act 1976 authorises companies to use an official seal for sealing documents creating or evidencing issued securities. This must be a facsimile of the common seal with the addition of the word "securities" (s. 2 (1)). The use of the word "seal" in section 81 and article 8 of Table A of the Companies Act 1948 is appropriately extended (s. 2 (3)). The Stock Exchange (Completion of Bargains) Act 1976 came into force on February 12, 1979, by virtue of the Stock Exchange (Completion of Bargains) Act 1976 (Commencement) Order 1979.

It will be noted that the usual share certificate, a specimen of which is reproduced above, bears at the foot a note to the effect that before any transfer is registered the certificate must be produced. This note, it seems, is only a warning to the shareholder to take care of the certificate. It is not addressed to outsiders, and therefore does not create a contract or estoppel against the company on which they can rely.[12]

A share certificate is not a deed so as to be subject to the provisions of section 74 of the Law of Property Act 1925, which deals with the signing of deeds by corporations.[13] As it is not a deed, although it is sealed by the company it does not require a stamp.[14] Likewise, a scrip certificate or other document entitling any person to become the proprietor of any share of any company or proposed company does not require a stamp.[15]

---

[10] See para. 36–05, *post.*
[11] See para. 36–07, *post.*
[12] *Rainford* v. *James Keith and Blackman Co. [1905] 1 Ch. 296; Guy* v. *Waterlow Bros.* (1909) 25 T.L.R. 515. See dicta to the contrary in *Société Générale de Paris* v. *Walker* (1885) 11 App.Cas. 20.
[13] *South London Greyhound Racecourses* v. *Wake* [1931] 1 Ch. 496, 503. See also *Re Compania de Electricidad de la Provincia de Buenos Aires Ltd.* [1978] 3 All E.R. 668, *per* Slade J. The Law of Property Act 1925 does not apply to Scotland, but share certificates are not treated as deeds for stamp duty purposes in Scotland.
[14] See Sergeant, *Stamp Duties* (6th Edition), p. 127.
[15] Finance Act 1949, s. 35, Sched. 8, Pt. 1.

STOCK EXCHANGE REQUIREMENTS

36–05 Of particular importance are the requirements of the Stock Exchange relating to the issue of share certificates. These are contained in Schedule IV, A, of the Stock Exchange Rules, and require[16] that share certificates:

(1) state the authority under which the company is constituted;
(2) state, preferably in the top right-hand corner, the number of shares or amount of stock the certificate represents and, if applicable, the number and denomination of units;
(3) bear a footnote stating that no transfer of the security or any portion thereof represented by the certificate can be registered without production of the certificate;
(4) state, if applicable, the minimum amount and multiples thereof in which the security is transferable;
(5) if there is more than one class of share in issue, bear (preferably on the face) a statement of the conditions conferred thereon as to capital and dividends;
(6) be dated and (in the absence of statutory authority for issue under signature of appropriate officials) be issued under seal;
(7) should be on an overall size no larger than 9 inches × 8 inches (22.5 cm. × 20 cm.). (It is the policy of the Committee of the Stock Exchange that certificates should be of the uniform size 9 inches × 8 inches and companies are expected to take the earliest opportunity to make the appropriate arrangements to adopt this size.)

It will be noted that the ordinary share certificate reproduced at para. 36–03 satisfies the requirements of the Stock Exchange as far as applicable.

Stock certificates

36–06 These are certificates issued with respect to registered stock. The observations as to share certificates apply to them *mutatis mutandis*.

Lost or defaced share certificates

The articles very commonly contain provision for the issue of a fresh certificate in the place of any certificate which has been lost or defaced (art. 9).

Certificate prima facie evidence of title

36–07 By section 81 of the 1948 Act a certificate under the common seal, or the official seal authorised for this purpose,[17] of the company, specifying any shares (or stock) held by any member, is to be prima facie evidence of the title of the member to the shares (or stock).

> "Now a certificate of the shares or stock of a railway company is merely a solemn affirmation under the seal of the company that a

[16] The Rules do not now require the share certificate to state the unauthorised capital of the company and the nominal amount and denomination of each class of shares.
[17] Stock Exchange (Completion of Bargains) Act 1976, s. 2.

certain amount of shares or stock stands in the name of the individual mentioned in the certificate."[18]

The certificates "in companies of this kind, are the proper (and, indeed, the only) documentary evidences of title in the possession of a shareholder. . . ."[19]

"Now, the statute and the articles of association must be taken together. The former shews that the certificates are to be prima facie evidence of the title to the shares; and the latter that the certificates are the only instruments and evidence of title which the member is entitled to have delivered to him."[20]

Estoppel

36–08 A share certificate "is a declaration by the company to all the world that the person in whose name the certificate is made out, and to whom it is given, is a shareholder in the company, and it is given by the company with the intention that it shall be so used by the person to whom it is given, and acted upon in the sale and transfer of shares."[21] Being thus addressed to the world, and all persons being invited to rely upon it, the directors of a company are bound to use the utmost care in issuing certificates; for the general rule is that a person making a representation of fact with the intention that it shall be acted on is estopped from denying its truth as against any person acting on it bona fide.[22] Hence if, by inadvertence or negligence, an incorrect certificate is issued, the company incurs serious liabilities in respect thereof. But the case is different where the secretary of a company, for his private ends, has fraudulently affixed the seal of the company to a certificate and forged the names of two of the directors. A certificate so issued is a mere forgery and raises no estoppel against the company in favour even of a mortgagee without notice.[23] In *Re South London Greyhound Racecourses Ltd.* v. *Wake*,[24] a certificate in fact signed by a director and the secretary, but without proper authority, was held to be a forgery.[25] On the other hand, even if the authority of the directors is fraudulently obtained by the secretary, a certificate issued under the board's authority will estop the company.[26] The cases on estoppel by certificate fall into two classes—representations raising an estoppel as to title, and representations raising an estoppel as to the amount paid up on the shares. The principle in both is the same.

---

[18] *Per* Lord Cairns L.C. in *Shropshire Union, etc., Co.* v. *The Queen* (1875) L.R. 7 H.L. 496, 509.

[19] *Per* Lord Selborne, *Société Générale de Paris* v. *Walker* (1885) 11 App.Cas. 20, 29.

[20] *Per* Lord Fitzgerald, *ibid.* at p. 44. See also *Woodhouse & Rawson* v. *Hosack* 1894, 2 S.L.T. 279 (holding that it is inappropriate in Scottish procedure to bring an action of reduction of a share certificate as a preliminary step to a claim for payment of a call which the shareholder seeks to oppose by reference to the terms of the certificate).

[21] *Per* Cockburn C.J. in *Re Bahia, etc., Ry.* (1868) L.R. 3 Q.B. 584, 595. And see *per* Lord Cairns L.C. in *Shropshire Union, etc., Co.* v. *The Queen* (1875) L.R. 7 H.L. 496, 509, and *Burkinshaw* v. *Nicolls* (1878) 3 App.Cas. 1004, 1017.

[22] *Pickard* v. *Sears* (1836) 6 Ad. & El. 469; *Freeman* v. *Cooke* (1848) 2 Ex.Reps. 654.

[23] *Ruben* v. *Great Fingall Consolidated Co.* [1906] A.C. 439.

[24] [1931] 1 Ch. 496. See also *Mahony* v. *East Holyford Mining Co.* (1875) L.R. 7 H.L. 869.

[25] *Sed quaere*; see para. 28–16, *ante*.

[26] *Dixon* v. *Kennaway & Co.* [1900] 1 Ch. 833.

Estoppel as to title to shares

6–09 In *Re Bahia and San Francisco Ry.*,[27] the company, acting upon a forged transfer, purporting to be a transfer by A, a shareholder, to B, issued to B a certificate representing him to be the owner of the shares. C, in reliance on this certificate and in good faith, purchased and paid for the shares specified in it, and was duly registered as owner thereof. The forgery was subsequently discovered, and the company was compelled to restore the name of A to the register in respect of the shares in question: his title, of course, no forgery could displace[28]; but the company was also held liable, in an action by C, to pay him damages for wrongfully removing his name; for though the shares were not really his, the company was estopped, by its conduct, from setting up this defence.

In *Re Ottos Kopje Diamond Mines*,[29] A bought shares on the faith of a certificate representing B as the holder, and took a transfer from B accordingly. The company had, in fact, issued the certificate to B in pursuance of a forged transfer, and refused to register the transfer to A. The court held that A was, under the circumstances, entitled to damages, and that the measure of such damages was the value of the shares at the time of the refusal to register.

6–10 The company is not, however, estopped as against a transferee who obtains his share certificate by depositing a forged transfer with the company—although the transferee may himself have acted in good faith in the belief that the transfer is genuine.[30] By filing the transfer the transferee impliedly warrants that it is genuine, and he cannot set up an estoppel which involves a denial of that warranty. Indeed he may be liable to indemnify the company against any loss incurred by the company to a third party.[31] A transferee for this purpose may include the stock broker presenting the shares for transfer as an agent.[32] The indemnity might, however, be limited if the company is considered to be partly responsible for the damage within section 2 (1) of the Civil Liability (Contribution) Act 1978.[33]

But a third party who subsequently buys the shares, relying on the certificate issued by the company, is unaffected by the circumstances inducing the issue of that certificate, and can claim to be indemnified by the company if his title is displaced by that of the true owner.[34] So, too, where a person is fraudulently induced to accept a duly executed transfer from a transferor who has in fact no title to the shares he is purporting to sell, the

---

27 (1868) L.R. 3 Q.B. 584.
28 *Barton* v. *L. & N.W. Ry.* (1888) 38 Ch.D. 144.
29 [1893] 1 Ch. 618.
30 *Simm* v. *Anglo-American Telegraph Co.* (1879) 5 Q.B.D. 188; *Coates* v. *L. & S.W. Ry.* (1879) 41 L.T. 553; *Re Vulcan Ironworks Co.* [1885] W.N. 120.
31 *Sheffield Corporation* v. *Barclay* [1905] A.C. 392, 403; see further, para. 39–29, *post*.
32 *Yeung* v. *Hong Kong & Shanghai Bank* [1980] 2 All E.R. 599 (P.C.).
33 *Ibid. per* Lord Scarman at p. 607.
34 *Re Bahia, etc., Ry., supra*; *Re Ottos Kopje Diamond Mines, supra*.

transferee may himself raise an estoppel against the company if, after issuing a share certificate to him, the company subsequently refuses to register him,[35] or a purchaser of shares from him,[36] as a member.

Estoppel as to payment on shares

36–11 If a company issues a certificate describing a share as fully paid up, when in fact it is not fully paid up, the company is liable to be estopped from denying that the share is paid up against a person who acts on the faith of the certificate. In *Burkinshaw* v. *Nicolls*[37] a purchaser in these circumstances was able to hold the shares as fully paid. In *Parbury's* case[38] an original allottee was in the same position. Even if the certificate does not state the amount paid up, but refers to another document where this information is to be found, a transferee is not put on inquiry and can plead estoppel (personal bar) against the company.[39] In *Bloomenthal* v. *Ford*[40] the principle of estoppel was extended in favour of a mortgagee of shares in the company. Here A lent the company £1,000 on the terms that he was to have fully paid shares as security, and the company issued to him a certificate stating that he was the registered holder of 10,000 fully paid-up shares. The shares were, in truth, not paid up, but of this fact the lender had no knowledge, and it was held, in a winding up, that the company was estopped from saying that the shares were not paid up, and that A, who honestly believed the representation made in the certificate to be true was not bound to make any inquiry, or to ascertain how it was that the company was in a position thus to register him as the holder of paid-up shares for which he had not in fact paid. The company, in such a case, has no right to say, in the words of Lord Halsbury L.C. in the *Bloomenthal* case[41]: "I told you so-and-so; but you ought not to have believed me. You were too great a fool. I had a right to mislead you because you were too great a fool."

The estoppel will arise in favour of a firm, though one of the directors signing the certificate is a member of the firm.[42]

36–12 A transferee with knowledge or notice that the representation is not correct cannot, however, invoke the doctrine of estoppel in his favour[43] but the onus of proving notice rests on the person setting up the case of

---

[35] *Dixon* v. *Kennaway & Co.* [1900] 1 Ch. 833.
[36] *Balkis Consolidated Co.* v. *Tomkinson* [1893] A.C. 396.
[37] (1878) 3 App.Cas. 1004. See also *Rowland's Case* [1880] W.N. 80; and *Markham and Darter's Case* [1899] 1 Ch. 414.
[38] *Re Building Estates Brickfields Co., Parbury's Case* [1896] 1 Ch. 100. See also *Penang Foundry Co. Ltd.* v. *Gardiner* 1913 S.C. 1203.
[39] *Liquidator of Scottish Heritages Co. Ltd.* 1898, 5 S.L.T. 336.
[40] [1897] A.C. 156.
[41] At p. 162.
[42] *Re Coasters Ltd.* [1911] 1 Ch. 86.
[43] *Crickmer's Case* (1875) L.R. 10 Ch. 614.

notice.[44] But this rule is subject to that established in *Barrow's Case*,[45] where a transferee of such shares acquired a good title to the shares as fully paid which the company was estopped from denying, and was able to give the same title to any transferee from him, whether or not the new transferee had notice.

Directors who issue certificates for shares or stock which do not exist may be held personally liable in damages upon an implied warranty of authority.[46]

Certification of transfer

36–13 This topic is considered in Chapter 39, which deals with the transfer and transmission of shares.[47]

Share warrants

36–14 Share warrants to bearer can be issued only if the articles so authorise and the shares are fully paid up (s. 83 (1)).[48] There is a valid mercantile custom to treat them as negotiable instruments, and this is effective.[49] Private companies could not issue share warrants to bearer prior to the 1980 Act owing to the definition requirement of restricted transfer. Such issues are now possible.[50]

Until 1979 share warrants required Treasury consent for issue. Under the Exchange Control legislation no such restrictions now apply. A company may also issue stock warrants to bearer.[51] In this case, however, the Rules on *Admission of Securities to Listing* issued by the Stock Exchange provide that no new share warrant shall be issued to replace one that has been lost, unless the company is satisfied beyond reasonable doubt that the original has been destroyed.[52] It was not usual for companies incorporated in the United Kingdom to issue share or stock warrants prior to the abolition of Exchange Control.

The Act provides in section 124 and the Sixth Schedule, para. 3 (*j*), for the particulars to be contained in the annual return where share warrants have been issued.

Penalties for personation in connection with share warrants are provided

---

[44] *Re A. W. Hall & Co.* (1887) 37 Ch.D. 712; *Liquidator of Scottish Heritages Co. Ltd.* 1898, 5 S.L.T. 336.

[45] (1880) 14 Ch.D. 432: doubted in *Re London Celluloid Co.* (1888) 39 Ch.D. 190, 197. But *Barrow's Case* remains the law, and a salutary one if the freedom of transfer inherent in a share is to be retained. *Cf.* the analogous doctrine regarding a bona fide purchaser for value without notice of real property subject to an equity (this analogy has no force in Scotland, where different rules of property law apply).

[46] *Firbank's Executors* v. *Humphreys* (1886) 18 Q.B.D. 54.

[47] See para. 39–26, *post*.

[48] For the provisions of the Stock Exchange relating to share warrants, see *Admission of Securities to Listing*, issued by the Stock Exchange, Sched. IV, Part B. See Vol. II, Part C.

[49] *Webb, Hale & Co.* v. *Alexandria Water Co.* (1905) 93 L.T. 339.

[50] See para. 4–08, *ante*.

[51] *Pilkington* v. *United Railways of Havana* [1930] 2 Ch. 108.

[52] *Admission of Securities to Listing*, issued by the Stock Exchange, Sched. VII, Part A, para. 133.

by sections 15 and 20 of the Theft Act 1968,[53] and for forgery in connection with share warrants in Scotland by section 85, and in England by the general provisions of the Forgery Act 1913.

A form of share warrant, and of the detailed conditions indorsed thereon, will be found in the *Precedents*.[54] One of the most important of these conditions is the following which enables the warrant holder to vote at general meetings and which prevents personation on these occasions:

> No person shall as bearer of a share warrant be entitled to attend, or vote, or exercise in respect thereof any of the rights of a member, at any general meeting of the company, or sign any requisition for or aid in calling any general meeting, unless three days at least before the day appointed for the meeting, in the first case, and unless before the requisition is left at the office, in the second case, he shall have deposited the share warrant at the registered office, or such other place as the directors appoint, together with a statement in writing of his name and address, and unless the share warrant shall remain so deposited until after the general meeting, or any adjournment thereof shall have been held. The names of more than one as joint holders of a share warrant shall not be received.

36–15 A share warrant to bearer is liable upon issue to stamp duty which is normally three times the *ad valorem* duty on a transfer for a consideration of the nominal value of the share or stock[55]; the duty may be commuted under section 115 of the Stamp Act 1891. Duties are further imposed on certain other bearer instruments.[56]

Penalties are provided for issuing warrants which are not duly stamped.[57]

PRACTICE NOTES

Share certificates

36–16 Because of the requirement of The Stock Exchange that certificates shall be issued within 14 days of the date of lodgement of a transfer, most public listed companies take power in their articles to dispense with signatures on share certificates, if the directors so resolve. It is particularly important that such power be taken where the share registration work is done by professional registrars, otherwise it may be found impossible to comply with the requirement.

A company which has an official seal for sealing securities (see para. 36–04, *ante*) may seal share certificates with the official seal instead of the common seal. In practice, it is more likely that the company would authorise the registrars to use the official seal on its behalf, provided that

---

[53] This does not apply to Scotland.
[54] (17th ed., 1956), Vol. 1, Forms 289 and 290, pp. 762 *et seq*.
[55] Stamp Act 1891, Sched. I, as amended by Finance Act 1963, ss. 59–61. As to the duty on a transfer, see para. 39–24, *post*.
[56] Finance Act 1963, s. 59.
[57] Stamp Act 1891, s. 107.

adequate precautions are taken and that the registrars make a report on all certificates sealed by them.

In the case of a company which was incorporated before February 12, 1979 (the date of the coming into operation of the Stock Exchange (Completion of Bargains) Act 1976), an official seal may be used to seal share certitifactes notwithstanding anything contained in the articles and any provision in the articles requiring the certificates to be signed will not apply when the official seal is used. It should be noted, however, that if a company which has an official securities seal chooses to use the common seal on a share certificate, it is still bound by the provisions of its articles in regard to share certificates sealed with the common seal (see para. 43–44, *post* in regard to certificates for debentures or debenture stock).

Duplicate certificates

36–17 The articles will set out the procedure to be followed when a share certificate becomes worn out or defaced or is lost or destroyed. In the case of a certificate reported lost, the shareholder should first be asked to cause a further search to be made for the missing document and to report the result of that search. If the certificate still cannot be found, a duplicate may be issued, subject to the articles, on receipt of an indemnity acceptable to the company. The standard form of indemnity in use[58] requires a bank, insurance company or guarantee society to join in the indemnity given by the shareholder, but some companies are prepared to waive the guarantee in the case of very small holdings of shares. If a certificate is lost in transit between the company and an agent of the shareholder or between an agent and the shareholder, most companies are prepared to accept the agent's indemnity supported, if necessary, by a guarantee.

[58] See para. EE 16, The Chartered Secretaries Manual of Company Secretarial Practice.

CHAPTER 37

ACQUISITION BY A COMPANY OF ITS OWN SHARES

37–01 ANY company limited by shares has the potential to buy, sell or assist the purchase of property. Special problems arise, however, if that property consists of its own shares. In this and the following chapter these problems are considered. There are four basic situations:

There are four basic situations:

(i) A company acquires its own shares otherwise than by purchase;

(ii) A company purchases its own shares;

(iii) A nominee acquires shares in a company on behalf of that company, with or without financial assistance from the company;

(iv) A person acquires shares in his own right in a company with financial assistance from that company.

The acquisition may be by way of surrender or by transfer from a third party. The problems which arise are as to what extent such acquisitions should be permitted, what civil and criminal consequences attach to a breach of any such restrictions and how such acquired shares, if permitted, should be regarded? A related topic is the acquisition by a company of shares in its holding company.

A company may not acquire its own shares; the exceptions

The general rule

37–02 It was established in 1887 by the House of Lords that a limited company may not acquire its own shares by purchase unless—exceptionally—authorised by statute to hold its own shares, and even express authority in the memorandum to the contrary was unavailing.[1] The main reasons for this prohibition were that such a purchase could either amount to "trafficking" in its own shares, thereby enabling the company in an unhealthy manner to influence the price of its own shares on the market, or it would operate as a reduction of capital which can only be effected with the sanction of the court and in the manner laid down in section 66.[2]

37–03 This general prohibition received a statutory restatement in section 35 of the 1980 Act. Subject to the exceptions discussed below no company limited by shares, or limited by guarantee and having a share capital, may acquire its own shares in any manner.[3] In breach of this general rule the

---

[1] *Trevor* v. *Whitworth* (1887) 12 App.Cas. 409. And see *Re Liverpool Cotton Association Ltd.* (1963) 107 S.J. 195, where, exceptionally, the court sanctioned a reduction of capital to cancel shares illegally bought by the company many years before, in order to regularise the position. Different considerations would now apply.

[2] *British and American, etc., Corpn.* v. *Couper* [1894] A.C. 399. See generally Chap. 32, *ante*.

[3] 1980 Act, s. 35 (1). The prohibition applies whether the acquisition is by "purchase, subscription or otherwise."

acquisition is void.[4] This restatement was necessary as a result of the Second Directive on Company Law[5] which nevertheless permitted, but did not require, member States to relax the general rule. In fact the 1981 Act provides for a very wide exception to the rule, so that it will operate only in rare cases where the correct procedure is not followed.[6]

The exceptions

37–04 There are six exceptions to the general prohibition in section 35 of the 1980 Act.

(i) ACQUISITION OTHER THAN FOR VALUABLE CONSIDERATION. A company may acquire its own shares provided that they are fully paid up and that no valuable consideration is paid for them (1980 Act, s. 35 (2)). This involves no reduction of capital but it may still lead to "trafficking" so that such shares are then subject to restrictions.[7] Such an acquisition may be by way of a trust for the company since the rules in section 36 of the 1980 Act relating to the acquisition by a nominee for the company do not apply to the acquisition of fully paid shares.[8] This follows the pre-Act case-law.[9]

(ii) PURCHASES UNDER THE COMPANIES ACT 1981. The 1981 Companies Act allows companies to purchase their own shares subject to following the prescribed procedures.[9a]

(iii) ACQUISITION ON AN AUTHORISED REDUCTION OF CAPITAL. The 1980 Act preserves the existing position *vis-à-vis* section 66 as to an order for the reduction of capital which involves the repurchase or reacquisition of shares (1980 Act, s. 35 (4)(*aa*)).

(iv) REDEEMING REDEEMABLE SHARES. The redemption of redeemable shares under section 45 of the 1981 Act[10] is not an acquisition for the purpose of section 35 of the 1980 Act (1980 Act, s. 35 (4) (*a*)).

(v) PURCHASE UNDER A COURT ORDER. Exceptionally the court may order a company to purchase its own shares, usually as an instance of minority relief. Thus there is no acquisition of shares for the purposes of section 35 of the 1980 Act on a purchase as a result of order under section 5 of the 1948 Act,[11] or sections 11[12] or 75[13] of the 1980 Act (1980 Act, s. 35 (4) (*b*)).

---

[4] *Ibid.* s. 35 (3).
[5] O.J. 1977 L26/1, arts. 19–42.
[6] 1981 Act, ss. 46–62; Sched. 3, para. 43.
[7] See para. 37–06, *post*.
[8] 1980 Act, s. 36 (1). See para. 37–20, *post*.
[9] *Kirby* v. *Wilkins* [1929] 2 Ch. 444; *Re Castiglione's W.T.* [1958] Ch. 549. See also *Re Buckingham* (1944) 170 L.T. 53.
[9a] See para. 37–08, *post*.
[10] See para. 33–13, *ante*.
[11] See para. 9–43, *ante*.
[12] See para. 5–10, *ante*.
[13] See para. 60–08, *post*.

(vi) PERMITTED FORFEITURE OR SURRENDER OF SHARES. Where a company forfeits its own shares, or accepts a surrender, for non-payment of calls or instalments[14] there is no acquisition for the purposes of section 35 (1980 Act, s. 35 (4) (*c*)).

Consequences of a breach

37–05 Any acquisition apart from these exceptions is void (1980 Act, s. 35 (3)). In addition the company and any officer in default in purporting to make such a prohibited acquisition commits a criminal offence which may be tried summarily or on indictment and, in the case of an officer, may involve a term of imprisonment on conviction (1980 Act, s. 35 (3)).

Treatment of permitted acquired shares

37–06 Where a company acquires its own shares under one of the six exceptions noted above the question arises as to how they are to be regarded. Shares acquired on the redemption of redeemable shares are dealt with by section 45 of the 1981 Act,[15] as are shares purchased under the 1981 Act procedure[15a]; forfeited shares are similarly subject to specific rules for public companies.[16] Where the shares are purchased under a court order a reduction of capital will be ordered.[17] It must be remembered that in none of those cases is there an acquisition in breach of section 35 of the 1980 Act. Shares acquired under the other exceptions are, however, subject to section 37 of the 1980 Act insofar as the company is a public company. There are no rules for shares legally acquired, *e.g.* by gift or trust, by private companies unless and until they re-register as public companies.[18] Private companies apparently may hold, cancel, or resell such shares at will.

37–07 PUBLIC COMPANIES. Where shares in a public company are legitimately acquired by that company, otherwise than by purchase or redemption, or on a reduction of capital, and it has a beneficial interest[19] in such shares the provisions of section 37 of the 1980 Act apply.[20] Under this section the company must either dispose of the acquired shares or cancel them and diminish the share capital figure by their nominal value (1980 Act, s. 37 (2) (*a*)). This must be done within three years of the acquisition.[21] A fine or

---

[14] See para. 41–01, *post*.
[15] See para. 33–13, *ante*.
[15a] See para. 37–08, *post*.
[16] See para. 41–04, *post*.
[17] See 1948 Act, s. 5 (4A), added by 1980 Act, Sched. 3, para. 4; 1980 Act, ss. 11 (7) and 75 (5).
[18] 1980 Act, s. 37 (9). The procedure is the same as applied to forfeited shares of private companies. See para. 41–04, *post*.
[19] This does not include any right by the company as a trustee of its own shares to recover its expenses or to be remunerated out of the trust property: 1980 Act, s. 37 (1). Is this a possible loophole?
[20] This can only apply where the 1980 Act, s. 35 permits an exception—otherwise the acquisition is void by virtue of s. 35 (3).
[21] 1980 Act, s. 37 (11) (*a*).

default fine may be imposed on the company or any officer in default (1980 Act, s. 37 (7)).

If the company opts for cancellation that will amount to a reduction of capital[22] and if the effect will be to reduce the company's allotted share capital below the authorised minimum[23] the company must apply to be re-registered as a private company (1980 Act, s. 37 (2) (*b*)). The directors may take such steps as are necessary to achieve this, including passing a resolution making the necessary alterations to the memorandum without complying with the procedure under section 66[24] (1980 Act, s. 37 (4)). An application for re-registration in due form must be delivered to the Registrar (1980 Act, s. 37 (5)) who will then act as if it was an application by a public company under section 10 of the 1980 Act[25] (1980 Act, s. 37 (8)). In default fines may be levied on the responsible officers and the company will be regarded as a private company after the three-year period for re-registration has expired for the purposes of section 15 of the 1980 Act—*i.e.* it will not be able to ask the public to subscribe for its shares[26] (1980 Act, s. 37 (6)).

Whilst the acquired shares remain in the company's hands it may not validly exercise any votes in respect of them (1980 Act, s. 37 (3)). In addition, if it shows them as assets in its balance-sheet a compensating quasi-capital fund must be created[27] (1980 Act, s. 37 (10)).

A company may purchase its own shares

Power to purchase its own shares

37–08 Section 46 of the 1981 Act authorises both public and private companies to purchase their own shares, provided that the appropriate procedure is followed. This is by way of exception to the general rule against such acquisitions in section 35 of the 1980 Act,[28] and reverses the actual decision of the House of Lords in *Trevor* v. *Whitworth*.[29] This power is closely linked to the power to issue redeemable shares[30] and many of the rules relating to purchase are identical to those relating to redemption. The provisions of the 1981 Act as to the authority required for a purchase by a company of its own shares may be amended by subsequent regulations.[31]

The power to purchase its own shares must be contained in the company's articles[32] but they need not specify the terms and manner of the

---

22 See para. 31–08, *ante*.
23 See para. 4–14, *ante*.
24 See para. 32–01, *ante*.
25 See para. 5–09, *ante*.
26 See para. 4–07, *ante*.
27 See para. 29–11, *ante*.
28 s. 35 (4) of the 1980 Act was amended appropriately by Sched. 3, para. 43, to the 1981 Act.
29 (1887) 12 App.Cas. 409.
30 1981 Act. s. 45. See para. 33–13, *ante*.
31 *Ibid*. s. 61 (1) (*a*).
32 *Ibid*. s. 46 (1); *cf*. s. 45 (1), para. 33–13, *ante*.

purchase.[33] A company may even purchase redeemable shares[34] if, for some reason, the parties wish to anticipate the date of redemption, although no purchase may be made if as a consequence only redeemable shares would remain in existence.[35] Since no redeemable shares may be issued at any time when there are no issued non-redeemable shares,[36] the intention of the legislation seems clear, *i.e.* to prevent a company from purchasing or redeeming itself out of existence. One gap appears to be the redemption of all existing redeemable shares followed by the purchase of the remainder.

The appropriate procedure to be followed on a purchase depends upon whether it is a *market* or *off-market* purchase, or the purchase of a right to purchase, referred to in the legislation as a *contingent purchase contract.* These various procedures are detailed below in the text. Shares, once purchased, must be cancelled and the issued share capital diminished by that amount.[37]

Replacement issues

37–09 When shares have been, or are about to be, purchased under section 46 of the 1981 Act they may be replaced by a fresh issue of shares in exactly the same way as a replacement issue on a redemption of shares. The stamp duty consequences of such an issue are also identical to the position *vis-à-vis* redemption.[38]

Funding of the purchase; all companies

37–10 Shares may be purchased out of the same funds as are available for the redemption of redeemable shares, *viz.* distributable profits or the proceeds of a fresh issue of shares.[39] When distributable profits are used there must be a compensating transfer to the *Capital Redemption Reserve* in exactly the same way as on a redemption of redeemable shares.[40]

When the purchase is of a contingent purchase contract, or money is spent on obtaining either any variation of the contract of purchase of an off-market purchase or a contingent purchase contract[41] or the release from any contract for purchase or contingent purchase contract, the payment must be funded solely out of distributable profits.[42] In breach of this requirement the consequent purchase of shares (if the payment was used for a contingent purchase contract or a variation of a contract) or release (if the payment was used to obtain that) will be unlawful.[43]

---

33 *Ibid.* s. 46 (2); *cf.* s. 45 (7), para. 33–14, *ante.*
34 *Ibid.* s. 46 (1).
35 *Ibid.* s. 46 (3); *cf.* s. 45 (2); para. 33–13, *ante.*
36 *Ibid.* s. 45 (2).
37 *Ibid.* s. 46 (2) incorporating the relevant provisions of s. 45; see para. 33–13, *ante.*
38 *Ibid.* see para. 33–15, *ante.*
39 *Ibid.* see para. 33–16, *ante.*
40 *Ibid.* s. 53. See para. 33–16, *ante.*
41 Market purchases cannot be varied under Stock Exchange practice.
42 1981 Act, s. 51 (1). Distributable profits are defined in s. 62 (1) of the 1981 Act.
43 *Ibid.* s. 51 (2). For the consequences of an unlawful payment see para. 37–24, *post.*

Purchase out of capital; private companies

37–11 Funds other than distributable profits and the proceeds of a fresh issue of shares may be used for the purchase of its own shares by a private company, by virtue of section 54 of the 1981 Act. These provisions apply equally to the redemption of redeemable shares by private companies and are detailed in paras. 33–13—33–19 above, to which reference should be made. It is thought that this power will not apply to the purchase of a contingent purchase contract or the variation or release of any contract to purchase shares required by section 51 of the 1981 Act to be made out of distributable profits.[44]

Off-market purchases

37–12 Off-market purchases of shares must be made in pursuance either of a contract approved under section 47 of the 1981 Act or a contingent purchase contract[45] approved under section 48 of the Act.[46] Market purchases require authorisation under section 49 of the Act.[47] A market purchase is a purchase of shares on a recognised stock exchange[48] provided they are subject to a marketing agreement on that stock exchange.[49] A marketing agreement in this case includes only those shares which are listed, or dealt with in the unlisted securities market.[50] Shares purchased in either way would be impossible to fit into the individual authorisation procedure of section 47. Any other purchase is an off-market purchase and subject to sections 47 and 48 of the 1981 Act. Thus over-the-counter market purchases and those on secondary markets run by large unquoted companies will require authorisation under sections 47 or 48.

If a company wishes to make an off-market purchase of its own shares it must be made pursuant to a contract of purchase approved by a special resolution of the company.[51] The essence of the procedure is therefore prior individual approval of each contract of purchase, rather than the purchase itself. Public companies must specify a time limit in the resolution to the authority thereby conferred to enter into a contract of purchase.[52] This must not exceed 18 months from the date of the resolution.[53] After such date the authority will expire and must be renewed by another special resolution. No such time limits apply to private companies who may specify one only if it wishes. In any event provided the contract is made during the relevant time the actual purchase may take place later.

The holder of the shares in question will invalidate the resolution if he

---

44 See para. 37–10, *ante*.
45 See para. 37–13, *post*.
46 1981 Act, s. 47 (4).
47 *Ibid*. s. 49 (3). See para. 37–14, *post*.
48 1948 Act, s. 455 (1).
49 1981 Act, s. 47 (2).
50 *Ibid*. s. 47 (3).
51 *Ibid*. s. 47 (5).
52 *Ibid*. s. 47 (7).
53 *Ibid*. s. 47 (8).

votes,[54] either on a show of hands or a poll, with the voting rights attached to those shares and the resolution would not have been passed if he had not so voted.[55] Any member may demand a poll on such a resolution irrespective of the company's articles.[56] On the other hand the prospective vendor is not bound to vote against the resolution with the relevant shares[57] and he may vote on a poll in respect of any other shares he may hold.[58]

The resolution will also be void unless a copy of the proposed contract, or a memorandum of its terms,[59] is available for inspection at the company's registered office for 15 days ending with the date of the meeting,[60] and at the meeting itself.[61] This fact need not however be drawn to the members' attention. The names of all the prospective vendors must be stated either in the contract or a memorandum so that it is clear who may not vote freely on the resolution.[62]

The original *authority* conferred by the resolution may be varied, revoked or renewed by a special resolution of the company subject to the same procedural and voting restrictions imposed on the original resolution.[63] Any proposed variation of an *authorised contract to purchase* once it has been concluded must be authorised in the same way as the original contract except that copies or memoranda of both the original contract and the varied contract must be available for inspection prior to and at the meeting.[64]

Contingent purchase contract

37–13 A similar procedure to the authorisation of a contract to make an off-market purchase[65] is applied to the authorisation of an option taken by a company to purchase its own shares. Section 48 of the 1981 Act applies to the approval of such contingent purchase contracts. These are contracts by which the company is not bound to purchase some of its own shares but may become[66] entitled or obliged to purchase them.[67] Each such contingent purchase contract thus requires prior disclosure and approval by a special resolution of the company in the same way as an off-market

---

[54] Either in person or by proxy, *ibid.* s. 47 (12). For the power to appoint a proxy see 1948 Act, s. 136.
[55] *Ibid.* s. 47 (9).
[56] *Ibid.* This includes a demand by a proxy, s. 47 (12). This right is by way of exception to the general rules as to polls: 1948 Act, s. 137 (1) (*b*).
[57] *Cf. Re Gee* [1948] Ch. 284.
[58] *Cf. Clemens* v. *Clemens Bros. Ltd.* [1976] 2 All E.R. 268.
[59] If the contract itself is not in writing.
[60] Twenty-one days' notice will usually be necessary for a special resolution but it may be waived in special circumstances: 1948 Act, s. 143 (2).
[61] 1981 Act, s. 47 (10).
[62] *Ibid.*
[63] *Ibid.* s. 47 (6).
[64] *Ibid.* s. 47 (11). Payment for such variation may only be out of distributable profits: s. 51. See para. 37–10, *ante*.
[65] See para. 37–12, *ante*.
[66] Subject to any conditions.
[67] 1981 Act, s. 48 (1). Payment for the acquisition or variation of such contracts must be out of distributable profits: s. 51. See para. 37–10, *ante*.

purchase contract.[68] The regulation as to time limits for implementation of the authority, voting rights and procedures, prior disclosure of the contract and proposed possible vendors, variations, renewals or revocations of the authority to contract and variations of the contract itself, once concluded, are the same as those for off-market purchase contracts.[69]

One effect of applying this procedure to options to purchase will be to prevent the purchase of an option or traded option of the Stock Exchange. Public companies will not be able to speculate against their own share price. A suggested use for this section is to allow private companies to negotiate with individual shareholders the right or obligation to acquire their shares at a certain time in the future without the need to create a separate class of redeemable shares.[70]

Market purchases

7–14 A market purchase by a company of its own shares is one of listed securities or of those traded on the unlisted securities market.[71] Purchases of such shares by a company contains the danger of market-rigging not present in off-market deals but if companies are to be allowed to purchase their own listed shares they cannot, by the nature of the market, be restricted to prior approval of each contract of purchase as applied to off-market purchases. Section 49 of the 1981 Act accordingly provides that such purchases must be made pursuant to an authority conferred by an ordinary resolution of the company.[72] The authority so conferred may be general or specific to a class or description of shares, and conditional or unconditional,[73] but it must specify the maximum number of shares authorised to be acquired,[74] the maximum and minimum prices to be paid for the shares[75] and a time limit on which it is to expire.[76] Purchases entered into within the time limit of the authority but concluded afterwards are only valid if the original authority so provides.[77] Any variation, revocation or renewal of the authority must be approved in the same way.[78]

The difficulties of market transactions explain much of this considerably laxer system of authorisation when compared with off-market purchases, but it is difficult to see why such difficulties require the approval of an ordinary resolution in the former and a special resolution in the latter. On

[68] *Ibid*. s. 48 (2), (3). This may be altered by subsequent regulations: s. 61 (1) (*b*).
[69] *Ibid*. s. 48 (3). See para. 37–12, *ante*.
[70] See para. 33–13, *ante*.
[71] 1981 Act, s. 49 (2). See para. 37–12, *ante*.
[72] *Ibid*. s. 49 (3); *cf*. ss. 47 (5), 48 (3); paras. 37–12 and 37–13, *ante*. Although an ordinary resolution is required it must be registered with the Registrar under s. 143 of the 1948 Act: 1981 Act, s. 49 (10).
[73] *Ibid*. s. 49 (4).
[74] *Ibid*. s. 49 (5) (*a*).
[75] *Ibid*. s. 49 (5) (*b*). These maxima and minima may be fixed either by a specific price or by reference to a formula which does not depend upon any person's discretion or opinion: 1981 Act, s. 45 (9).
[76] *Ibid*. s. 49 (5) (*c*). This must not exceed 18 months from the date of the resoltuion: 1981 Act, s. 49 (7); *cf*. s. 47 (7), (8).
[77] *Ibid*. s. 49 (8).
[78] *Ibid*. s. 49 (6).

the other hand since Part V of the 1980 Act on insider dealing will apply to such purchases, any company wishing to make a purchase of its own shares which was likely to affect the price of such shares would be advised to give prior publicity of its intentions to avoid any criminal liability. In addition both the Stock Exchange and the Council for the Securities Industry will produce self-regulating procedures to supplement this section.

Assignment and release of contractual rights to purchase

37–15 A company may not assign its rights under either an authorised or approved contract to purchase its own shares whether by a market or an off-market purchase, or an approved contingent purchase contract.[79] A company may not speculate against its own share price by buying and selling rights to purchase them. For similar reasons all purchased shares must be cancelled.[80]

The *release* of any such rights is however allowed if the contract was approved by the off-market procedure or as a contingent purchase contract,[81] provided it has the prior approval of a special resolution of the company.[82] Such releases will be registered in the same way as the variation of such contracts.[83]

Release from a company's *obligations* under any approved or authorised contract within these provisions is permitted but it must be funded out of distributable profits only.[84]

Disclosure of authorised purchases and contracts

37–16 All companies must deliver a return to the registrar of its own shares purchased under a contract approved under sections 47 or 48 or authorised under section 49.[85] Registration must take place within 28 days of the delivery to the company of any such shares. Delivery may be by way of surrender of shares to the company thus avoiding an instrument of transfer and stamp duty. The information required relates to the number and nominal value of each class of shares as acquired and the date of delivery. In addition public companies must state the aggregate amount paid for the shares and the maximum and minimum amount paid for each class of shares.[86] Such returns may be composite, *i.e.* including several purchases on different dates, provided the 28 day period is not infringed.[87] There are fines and default fines for failure to deliver the return as required.[88]

In addition to the disclosure to the registrar a copy[89] of each contract for

---

[79] *Ibid*. s. 50 (1).
[80] *Ibid*. s. 46. See para. 37–08, *ante*.
[81] *Ibid*. s. 50 (2).
[82] *Ibid*. s. 50 (3).
[83] *Ibid*. s. 50 (3). See s. 47 (11), para. 37–12, *ante*.
[84] *Ibid*. s. 51 (1) (*c*).
[85] *Ibid*. s. 52 (1). This provision may be amended by subsequent regulation: s. 61 (1) (*c*).
[86] *Ibid*. s. 52 (2). The latter requirement is particularly relevant to market purchases.
[87] *Ibid*. s. 52 (3).
[88] *Ibid*. s. 52 (6).
[89] Or memorandum if the contract is not in writing.

an off-market purchase approved under section 47, each contingent purchase contract approved under section 48 or for a market purchase authorised under section 49 of the 1981 Act must be kept at the company's registered office from the date of the conclusion of the contract (not necessarily the actual delivery of the shares) until 10 years from the conclusion of the purchase(s) under it, or the expiry of the contract, *e.g.* when an option to purchase runs out.[90] The period will then usually be greater than 10 years in total. Contingent purchase contracts must therefore be kept at the registered office but they will not be declared to the registrar unless activated. Details of any variation of the contract must be kept in a similar fashion.[91]

Public companies must allow public inspection of such contracts during business hours without charge. Private companies need only allow such inspection by its members. In either case the general meeting of the company may place reasonable restrictions on access provided that not less than two hours per day[92] are allowed for inspection.[93] There are fines in default of these obligations of record and inspection[94] and a court may order an immediate inspection of the contract if one is refused.[95]

Failure by company to purchase its own shares

37–17 If a company fails to implement an agreement to purchase its own shares section 59 of the 1981 Act applies. The position is exactly the same as a failure by a company to redeem its redeemable shares and reference should be made to para. 33–24 above.

Compulsory purchases

37–18 There is nothing in the Act[96] as to whether a private company may now by its articles give itself the power to compulsorily purchase its own shares. Existing case law suggests that a majority of the shareholders may not take such blanket powers for themselves,[97] but it is far from clear that this would necessarily apply to the company itself. In any event it is unlikely that anyone purchasing a share after the company included such a power in its articles could object. The problems would arise in relation to existing shareholders subjected to an alteration of the articles under section 10 of the 1948 Act.

---

90 *Ibid.* s. 52 (4). This obligation applies to both public and private companies.
91 *Ibid.* s. 52 (9).
92 Presumably business days.
93 *Ibid.* s. 52 (5).
94 *Ibid.* s. 52 (7).
95 *Ibid.* s. 52 (8).
96 The Bill contained a clause on this point but it was dropped during the final stages of its Parliamentary career.
97 *Brown* v. *British Abrasive Wheel Co. Ltd.* [1919] 1 Ch. 290; *Dafen Tinplate Co. Ltd.* v. *Llanelly Steel Co.* [1920] 2 Ch. 124; *cf. Sidebotham* v. *Kershaw Leese & Co.* [1920] Ch. 154, (C.A.).

A company may not acquire its own shares through a nominee

The general rule; full ownership by the nominee

37–19 The restrictions on acquisition and purchase in section 35 of the 1980 Act and section 46 of the 1981 Act could easily be circumvented by a company holding its own shares beneficially behind a trust. In general therefore this device is prevented by the operation of section 36 of the 1980 Act. Where shares are issued to a nominee of the company or where they are acquired partly paid by such a nominee from a third party, then "for all purposes" the nominee is to be regarded as holding the shares on his own account and the company is to have no beneficial interest in them (1980 Act, s. 36 (1)). A nominee may therefore acquire fully paid shares for his company, just as the company itself may acquire such shares without giving any consideration for them.

The exceptions

37–20 The general rule of treating the nominee as full legal and beneficial owner does not apply in two cases.

(i) PUBLIC COMPANY GIVING FINANCIAL ASSISTANCE FOR THE ACQUISITION. Section 36 has no application where any person acquires shares in a public company with financial assistance given to him directly or indirectly by that company "for the purpose of or in connection with" that acquisition and the company has a beneficial interest[98] in those shares (1980 Act, s. 36 (5)). In such cases the company retains its beneficial title to the shares insofar as section 36 is concerned but the whole transaction may prove to be void under section 42 of the 1981 Act.[99] It is not clear, however, whether the concept of "financial assistance" has the same meaning as in that section.[1] The new definition of financial assistance in section 42 (8) of the 1981 Act applies only for the purposes of that section; whereas the definition in force when the 1980 Act was implemented, in section 54 of the 1948 Act, had no such limits. The relationship between these sections is far from clear. Section 36 of the 1980 Act applies to private companies in these circumstances although under sections 43 and 44 of the 1981 Act the general rules for financial assistance are relaxed for such companies.

(ii) WHERE THE COMPANY HAS NO BENEFICIAL INTEREST. Where the shares are acquired by a nominee for a company which is itself a trustee for a third party,[2] section 36 does not apply (1980 Act, s. 36 (6) (*a*)); the full legal and

---

[98] In this case a beneficial interest may arise by virtue of the company acting as a trustee (in equity) and recovering its expenses or remuneration out of the trust property: 1980 Act, s. 36 (5), 377 (1) (*d*).

[99] See para. 38–02, *post*.

[1] See para. 38–02, *post*.

[2] The company has no beneficial interest as such trustee by recovering its expenses or remuneration out of the trust property: 1980 Act, s. 36 (6) (*a*).

beneficial consequences of the arrangement will stand, subject to exception (i) above.

Consequences of a breach

37–21 Where shares are acquired by a nominee in circumstances where he is regarded as being the absolute owner of the shares by virtue of section 36 (1) of the 1980 Act, he will be liable to pay for the shares, either the amount still unpaid or the full issue price as appropriate. In such circumstances if the nominee fails to pay any such amount within 21 days of being called upon to do so, the directors of the company at the time of issue or acquisition of the shares are jointly and severally liable with him to pay that amount (1980 Act, s. 36 (2) (*b*)). If the shares were issued to him as a result of his subscribing to the memorandum[3] that liability falls upon the other subscribers (1980 Act, s. 36 (2) (*a*)). Any director or subscriber who is liable under this section may be excused by the court if he has acted honestly and reasonably and in the circumstances he ought fairly to be excused from liability (1980 Act, s. 36 (3)). He may also apply to the court for such relief in advance of proceedings against him if he has reason to apprehend such proceedings (1980 Act, s. 36 (4)).

37–22 This additional liability on directors and subscribers applies equally to a situation where the nominee has acquired a public company's shares with financial assistance from the company even though he is not then regarded as being the absolute owner of those shares.[4] On the other hand, since the transaction may well be void under section 42 of the 1981 Act the liability may not often arise in such circumstances.[5]

Treatment of shares held by a nominee

37–23 Where shares in that company are acquired from a third party by a nominee of a public company without financial assistance from the company and that company has a beneficial interest in them,[6] section 37 of the 1980 Act applies to those shares in exactly the same way as it applies to such shares acquired by a public company itself (1980 Act, s. 37 (1) (*c*)).[7] Thus the company must either cancel or resell the shares within three years of the acquisition. Private company shares are not so caught unless it subsequently becomes a public company.[8]

If the shares were acquired by a nominee from a third party, only partly paid up, by virtue of section 36 (1) of the 1980 Act the company is to be regarded as having no beneficial interest in the shares so that section 37 cannot apply. The latter section is limited to the acquisition of fully paid-up shares by a nominee, which is allowed by section 36.

---

3 See para. 12–02, *ante*.
4 The exception to s. 36 (1) in such circumstances provided by s. 36 (5) does not extend to s. 36 (2).
5 See para. 38–02, *post*.
6 See note 19, *supra*.
7 See para. 37–06, *ante*.
8 1980 Act, s. 37 (9). See para. 41–05, *post*.

Further when any person acquires shares in a public company with financial assistance from that company and the company has a beneficial interest in those shares[9] section 37 will apply to those shares as to shares acquired, otherwise than by purchase under section 46 of the 1981 Act, by the company itself[10] with one modification (1980 Act, s. 37 (1) (*d*)). The only difference being that the cancellation or disposal must take place within one rather than three years of the acquisition.[11]

In such cases the nominee is not regarded as the absolute owner and section 36 does not apply.[12] If the transaction is void by virtue of section 42 of the 1981 Act[13] then there will, presumably, be no acquisition for the purposes of section 37.

A company cannot hold shares in its own holding company

37–24 Subject to certain exceptions, a company cannot be a member of its own holding company and any allotment or transfer of shares in a company to its subsidiary or a nominee for its subsidiary is void (s. 27 (1) and (4)).[14] The terms "holding company" and "subsidiary" have, in this connection, the same meaning as in section 154. The reason for the prohibition in section 27, which was first introduced into company law by the legislation culminating in the Act of 1948, is to prevent the "trafficking" in its own shares by the company by indirect means, but this purpose has been achieved only partially since the company is still not barred from holding its own shares through nominees.

The prohibitions of section 27 (1) and (4) do not apply where the subsidiary (or its nominee) is concerned as personal representative or trustee unless the holding company or its subsidiary is beneficially interested in the trust, except by way of security issued in the ordinary way of business which includes the lending of money (s. 27 (2)).

A subsidiary which was a member of its holding company at the commencement of the Act[15] may continue to be a member, but with no power to vote at the meetings of the shareholders, or of any class thereof, of the holding company (s. 27 (3)).

Section 27 contains a notable gap: it does not provide what is to happen if company A, on becoming the subsidiary of company B *after the commencement of the Act*, already holds shares in B. The section does not provide that the subsidiary is obliged to sell the "pre-acquired" shares in its holding company, nor is the continued holding of those shares declared to be unlawful or made subject to criminal sanction. On the other hand, the

---

[9] See note 28, *supra*.
[10] See para. 37–06, *ante*.
[11] 1980 Act, s. 37 (11) (*b*).
[12] 1980 Act, s. 36 (5). See para. 37–19, *ante*.
[13] See para. 38–02, *post*.
[14] The same provision applies to guarantee companies and unlimited companies, *mutatis mutandis* (s. 27 (5)).
[15] July 1, 1948 (see s. 462 (2)).

section provides categorically that the subsidiary "*cannot*"[16] be a member of its holding company. It is believed that the prohibitions of section 27 apply only after the relationship of holding and subsidiary companies has been constituted between the two companies in question. It follows that the section does not apply to pre-acquired shares, and that the subsidiary can even vote with these shares at the meetings of the holding company. On the other hand, if the holding company, after acquiring this status *vis-à-vis* the other company, issues bonus shares to its shareholders, the other company is prevented by section 27 from accepting such allotment.

In the practice of the take-over panel, when company B makes company A a subsidiary by acquiring its shares, any shares which company A already owns in company B are regarded as assets acquired by company B and company B will be treated as acquiring its own shares.[17]

In Scotland a defender may be subjected to the jurisdiction of the Scottish courts by arrestment *ad fundandam jursidictionem* of incorporeal moveables within the jurisdiction, such as shares in a Scottish company registered in the name of the defender. It the pursuer is successful in the principal action he may ultimately arrest in execution and obtain a decree of furthcoming which would entitle him, *inter alia*, to take possession of the subjects arrested. A held shares in H, the parent company of L. Both H and L were registered in Scotland and A was resident in England. L raised an action for payment against A in the Court of Session and arrested A's shares in H *ad fundandam jursidictionem*. A contended that the arrestment was ineffective because section 27 (1) prevented L from taking possession of the subjects arrested. It was held that although section 27 (1) would prevent L from having the shares in H adjudged to it, the arrestment was effective because L could use the alternative procedure of having them sold to satisfy L's claim.[18] It may be inferred that, had the shares been not marketable, A would have succeeded.

---

[16] Contrast this with the wording of s. 42 (1) of the 1981 Act.

[17] *Cf.* the City Panel report on the *P.R. Grimshawe & Co./Grimshawe-Windsor Merger* [1973] J.B.L. 46.

[18] *Stenhouse London Ltd.* v. *Allwright* 1972 S.L.T. 255.

CHAPTER 38

FINANCIAL ASSISTANCE BY A COMPANY FOR THE ACQUISITION OF ITS OWN SHARES

The general rule before the 1981 Act

38–01 Prior to the 1981 Act it was not lawful for a company to give a person financial assistance for the purchase of,[1] or subscription for, its own shares (s. 54 (1)). This prohibition was expressed in wide terms: it encompasses financial assistance, whether given "directly or indirectly, and whether by means of a loan, guarantee, the provision of security or otherwise"; it likewise prohibited such assistance by a subsidiary company to anybody desirous of acquiring, or subscribing for, the shares in its holding company (s. 54 (1)).[2] The section, however, gave rise to some problems of interpretation, principally as to the meaning of "financial assistance,"[3] and the civil consequences of a breach *vis-à-vis* both the validity of the transaction itself[4] and the liability of those involved.[5]

The section itself created a criminal offence for the company and any officer in default (s. 54 (2)). The penalty, formerly a £100 fine and thus of limited effect, became under the 1980 Act either a term of imprisonment or a fine or both.[6] The section was criticised as being too wide but the reforms suggested by the Jenkins Committee[7] could not be applied to public companies in view of the Second Directive on Company Law.[8] The abuses that stem from the practice of giving financial assistance have been demonstrated over the years by many Inspectors' Reports, but nevertheless section 54 was repealed by the 1981 Act and replaced by sections 42 to 44 of that Act.

The general rule under the 1981 Act

38–02 Section 54 was repealed by section 42 (13) of the 1981 Act and replaced by sections 42 to 44 of the 1981 Act. Section 42 re-enacts the basic prohibition of section 54 in a much modified form and applies to all companies. Private companies are, however, to be permitted to give such

---

[1] Loans by a company on the security of its own shares, and financial assistance by a company to a person to enable him to subscribe and pay for shares were prohibited by s. 45 of the 1929 Act and were of doubtful validity before that Act (see *R.* v. *Lorang* (1930) 22 Cr. App.R.167). The 1947–48 legislation extended the prohibition to the *subscription* for shares and thereby overruled *Re V. G. M. Holdings* [1942] Ch. 235 on that point.

[2] For the definition of "holding company" and "subsidiary" see s. 154.

[3] See *Belmont Finance Corpn.* v. *Williams Furniture Ltd. (No. 2)* [1980] 1 All E.R. 393 (C.A.).

[4] See para. 38–11, *post*.

[5] See para. 38–13, *post*.

[6] 1980 Act, Sched. 2 amending s. 54 (2). On indictment the maximum term of imprisonment was two years, on summary conviction, six months.

[7] Cmnd. 1749 (1962), paras. 170–186.

[8] Art. 23.

financial assistance, except for shares in any public holding company, subject to safeguards for creditors and minority shareholders,[9] under sections 43 and 44. Thus the Jenkins Committee Report has been applied to private companies; the Second Directive preventing its application to all companies. The special rules for private companies are dealt with later in the text.

The basic prohibition under section 42 on the giving of financial assistance applies in two ways depending upon whether the assistance precedes or follows the acquisition.

(1) WHERE THE ASSISTANCE PRECEDES OR IS CONTEMPORANEOUS WITH THE ACQUISITION. It is unlawful for a company[10] to give financial assistance directly or indirectly for the purpose of an acquisition, or proposed acquisition, by any person of its own shares or those of its holding company, either before or at the same time as the acquisition took place.[11] Financial assistance is defined below.[12] The similarities to the repealed section 54 are that such financial assistance is an unlawful act[13] and the assistance may be "direct" or "indirect." By way of contrast to the former rule the prohibition now applies to the *acquisition* of shares rather than purchase or subscription so that it clearly includes transfers of shares otherwise than for cash.[14] Further, the ban now only applies to financial assistance given *for the purpose of* an acquisition and no longer *in connection with*, as in section 54. This is an attempt to narrow the scope of the prohibition and should be read in connection with the new wide exceptions based on the purpose for which the assistance was given.[15]

(2) WHERE THE ASSISTANCE IS SUBSEQUENT TO THE ACQUISITION. By an entirely new provision[16] it is unlawful for a company[17] to give financial assistance directly or indirectly for the purpose of reducing or discharging any liability incurred by any person for the purpose of an acquisition of that company's own shares or those of its holding company. This only applies however when the acquisition took place prior to the assistance being given. The emphasis is again on purpose,[18] both in relation to the incurring of the liability (for the purpose of the acquisition) and the subsequent giving of financial assistance (for the purpose of the reduction or discharge of that liability). The prohibition applies whether the liability was by the acquiror of the shares or any other person.

The question as to what amounts to financial assistance is set out below

---

[9] But see 1981 Act, s. 43 (3).
[10] Subject, in the case of private companies, to sections 43 and 44 of the 1981 Act, and in the case of all companies to the various exceptions set out below in the text.
[11] *Ibid*. s. 42 (1).
[12] See para. 38–03, *post*.
[13] Thus the detailed case law on the civil consequences of a breach of section 54 remains valid. See para. 38–10, *post*.
[14] As a consequence bonus shares are now specifically exempted: *ibid*. s. 42 (5) (*b*).
[15] See para. 38–06, *post*.
[16] 1981 Act, s. 42 (2); added on Report in the House of Commons.
[17] See note 52, *ante*.
[18] See para. 38–06, *post*.

and is the same as for antecedent assistance.[19] But for the purpose of this prohibition a person incurs a liability (*inter alia*) if he changes his financial position by making any agreement (enforceable or unenforceable) either on his own account or with any other person, or by any other means.[20] Similary a company reduces or discharges such a liability by the giving of financial assistance if it is given wholly or partly for the purpose of restoring that person's financial position to what it was before the acquisition took place.[21] It must still be *financial assistance* as defined below but the 1981 Act is clear that in deciding whether such assistance has been given after an acquisition it is necessary to examine the overall financial position of the people involved.

One effect of a breach of *either* of these new prohibitions will be the committing of criminal offence by the company and any officer who is in default[22] with a maximum penalty of two years' imprisonment for conviction on indictment and six months on summary conviction plus a fine.[23] For the civil consequences see para. 38–09 below.

Meaning of "financial assistance"

38–03 The definition of financial assistance in section 42 (8) of the 1981 Act is very wide. It clearly includes direct financing by the company and the more common indirect financing whereby a take-over bidder purchases the shares of a cash company by means of a loan and then using the assets of the company to repay the loan.[24] It also includes guarantees, the provision of security, gifts and indemnities.[25] Indemnities in respect of the indemnifier's own neglect or default are not included so that a company may, *e.g.* indemnify an underwriter of a new issue of the company's shares against neglect or default on the company's part.[26] The definition also applies to the provision of any form of credit[27] and any form of financial assistance which reduces the net assets[28] of the company to a material extent, or, if it has no assets, any form of financial assistance at all.[29]

The purpose exceptions

38–04 One of the questions which arose under section 54 was where the company entered into a commercial transaction at the same time as the purchase, as a result of which it parted with money or money's worth,

---

[19] See para. 38–03, *post*.
[20] 1981 Act, s. 42 (9).
[21] *Ibid*. s. 42 (10).
[22] See 1948 Act, s. 440 (2).
[23] 1981 Act, s. 42 (12). This re-enacts the 1980 Act penalties for section 54 of the 1948 Act.
[24] See, *e.g. Selangor United Rubber Estates Ltd.* v. *Cradock (No. 3)* [1968] 1 W.L.R. 1555; *Karak Rubber Co.* v. *Burden (No. 2)* [1972] 1 W.L.R. 602; *Wallersteiner* v. *Moir* [1974] 1 W.L.R. 991 (C.A.) [1975] 1 W.L.R. 1093 (H.L.). 1981 Act, s. 42 (8) (*c*).
[25] 1981 Act, s. 42 (8) (*a*), (*b*).
[26] *Ibid*. s. 42 (8) (*b*).
[27] *Ibid*. s. 42 (8) (*c*).
[28] Net assets for this purpose are defined by reference to their actual and not their book value: 1980 Act, s. 87 (4) (*c*); *cf*. the definition for the purposes of s. 42 (7) of this Act.
[29] *Ibid*. s. 42 (8) (*d*).

which in turn was used to finance the purchase of its own shares. This was the situation in *Belmont Finance Corporation* v. *Williams Furniture Ltd. (No. 2)*.[30] It was accepted that unless the transaction involving the company was bona fide section 54 would apply. The dispute centred as to what is a bona fide commercial transaction in these circumstances? The Court of Appeal, disagreeing with the judge at first instance, held that if the transaction was merely part of a scheme to enable the purchaser to acquire the shares it would offend section 54 even if it was at a fair price. The transaction must be capable of being justified commercially in the company's own interests irrespective of the wider scheme.[31] Even in that case, however, the Court of Appeal left open the point as to whether a breach of section 54 could occur if in fact the money was used for the purchase of shares.

Buckley L.J. spelt out the possibilities by way of examples:

> "If A Ltd buys from B a chattel or a commodity, like a ship or merchandise, which A Ltd genuinely wants to acquire for its own purposes, and does so having no other purpose in view, the fact that B thereafter employs the proceeds of the sale in buying shares in A Ltd should not, I would suppose, be held to offend against the section; but the position may be different if A Ltd makes the purchase in order to put B in funds to buy shares in A Ltd. If A Ltd buys something from B without regard to its own commercial interests, the sole purpose of the transaction being to put B in funds to acquire shares in A Ltd, this would, in my opinion, clearly contravene the section, even if the price paid was a fair price for what is bought, and a fortiori that would be so if the sale to A Ltd was at an inflated price. The sole purpose would be to enable (i.e. to assist) B to pay for the shares. If A Ltd buys something from B at a fair price, which A Ltd could readily realise on a resale if it wished to do so, but the purpose or one of the purposes, of the transaction is to put B in funds to acquire shares of A Ltd, the fact that the price was fair might not, I think, prevent the transaction from contravening the section, if it would otherwise do so, though A Ltd could very probably recover no damages in civil proceedings, for it would have suffered no damage. If the transaction is of a kind which A Ltd could in its own commercial interests legitimately enter into, and the transaction is genuinely entered into by A Ltd in its own commercial interests and not merely as a means of assisting B financially to buy shares of A Ltd, the circumstance that A Ltd enters into the transaction with B, partly with the object of putting B in funds to acquire its own shares or with the knowledge of B's intended use of the proceeds of sale, might, I think, involve no contravention of the section, but I do not wish to express a concluded opinion on that point."[32]

It was also held that financial assistance could be given in breach of that section if it was made to the vendor of the shares, *e.g.* if the company made

---

[30] [1980] 1 All E.R. 393 (C.A.); reversing [1979] 1 All E.R. 118 on this point.
[31] Extending the reasoning in the South African case of *Gradwell (Pty) Ltd.* v. *Rostra Printers Ltd.* 1959, 4 (S.A.) 419.
[32] [1980] 1 All E.R. 393, 402.

a payment to the owner of some of its shares which facilitated a sale by him to a purchaser, even where the purchaser bought the shares in a perfectly normal manner. This was the situation in *Armour Hick Northern Ltd.* v. *Whitehouse*[33] where a subsidiary company paid off its parent company's debts to a third party which the third party required before it was prepared to sell its shares to the directors of that company. The judge decided that assistance was given on the basis that the sale would not have proceeded without it and that such assistance was financial since it involved the transfer of money. This, he said, was giving the words of section 54 "their plain ordinary meaning."

38–05 As a result of these, and earlier cases, the parameters of the prohibition on financial assistance were redrawn in the 1981 Act by the inclusion of a new exception to the general rules on financial assistance set out above based on the concepts of *purpose*, *principal purpose*, *larger purpose* and *good faith*. Not one of these concepts is defined in the 1981 Act. These exceptions can be found in section 42 (3), in relation to financial assistance given before or at the same time as an acquisition, and section 42 (4) for such assistance given subsequent to an acquisition. Both these subsections however contain the same two exceptions as follows:

38–06 (1) WHERE THE PRINCIPAL PURPOSE OF GIVING THE FINANCIAL ASSISTANCE WAS NOT FOR THE PURPOSE OF THE ACQUISITION OR REDUCING[34] ANY RELEVANT LIABILITY,[35] AND WAS GIVEN IN GOOD FAITH IN THE INTERESTS OF THE COMPANY. It has already been noted[36] that the new prohibitions only apply if the purpose of giving the financial assistance was to enable someone to *acquire* that company's shares[37] or to reduce a liability incurred for such a purpose.[38] This exception narrows the prohibitions even further in that it is only if the principal purpose of giving such assistance was to enable the acquisition or reduction, as appropriate, to take place. It is an attempt to limit the possibilities explored by Buckley L.J. in the *Belmont* case set out in para. 38–04, above. It will no longer be enough that assisting the relevant acquisition or reduction of liability was *one of the purposes*, it must be the *principal purpose*. It is probable however that the criteria of legitimate commercial interests of the company, applied at the end of the passage of the judgment of Buckley L.J. set out in para. 38–04, above, would in fact amount to a similar test. On the other hand the Lord Justice was there at pains to stress the genuineness of the transaction. In the new statutory test the criteria of *good faith* is required. This is a vague criteria

---

[33] [1980] 3 All E.R. 833. Following *E. H. Dey Pty Ltd.* v. *Dey* [1966] V.R. 464 concerning the Victorian equivalent of section 54.
[34] Or discharging.
[35] *i.e.* one incurred prior to the acquisition for the purpose of the acquisition of 1981 Act, s. 42 (2). See also *ibid*. s. 42 (9), (10)—para. 38–02, *ante*.
[36] See para. 38–02, *ante*.
[37] 1981 Act, s. 42 (1).
[38] *Ibid*. s. 42 (2). Reduction is used in the text to include discharge of the liability.

used elsewhere in the companies legislation without definition.[39] Even the case law on the subject is prohibitive of any settled definition.[40] In addition to this element of vagueness the *principal purpose* of the company must be ascertained. Ascertaining the purpose or intention of a company is usually divine from the intention of the controllers or directors of the company.[41] If there is a dominant group in control the possibilities of abuse clearly exist.

One of the reasons why the 1981 Act divides ante- and post-acquisition assistance was that this new principal purpose exception has a particular relevance for post-acquisition assistance in group manoeuvres. One example would be where following the acquisition of a new subsidiary company the acquiring company has to charge the assets of that subsidiary to secure a pre-existing debenture which requires all the assets of group to be charged to secure it. In such a case the security would not be given for the principal purpose of reducing a liability incurred for the purpose of acquiring the subsidiary. It is even arguable that it was not even one of the purposes—it is merely a consequence of the acquisition.

38–07 (2) WHERE EVEN IF THE PRINCIPAL PURPOSE OF THE GIVING OF THE FINANCIAL ASSISTANCE WAS FOR THE ACQUISITION OF SHARES, OR THE REDUCTION[42] OF A RELEVANT LIABILITY,[43] IT WAS AN INCIDENTAL PART OF SOME LARGER PURPOSE, AND WAS GIVEN IN GOOD FAITH IN THE INTERESTS OF THE COMPANY. If the principal purpose exeption is not available, sections 42 (3) and (4) have an alternative, incidental to a larger purpose, exemption. The element of good faith is again required. The concept of a *larger purpose* is no clearer than *principal purpose* and similar comments to those made in the preceding paragraph could apply.

The exception is more readily applicable to post-acquisition financial assistance within a group of companies. For example where a subsidiary company provides funds to its parent company some years after its acquisition to effect a more efficient deployment of assets within the group or to improve its financial position. The provision of such funds may relieve the parent company of indebtedness incurred for the purpose of acquiring the subsidiary but if the larger purpose can be established it will be excluded.

Authorised transaction exceptions

38–08 Section 42 (5) of the 1981 Act sets out nine specific transactions, all of which are permitted under company law, and which, for the avoidance of doubt, are not subject to the prohibitions in that section. These are new to

---

[39] European Communities Act 1972, s. 9 (1). See para. 9–25, *ante*.
[40] See para. 58–14, *post*.
[41] See paras. 18–09 *et seq.*, *post*.
[42] Or discharge.
[43] See note 35, *ante*.

the 1981 Act in the sense that they were never expressly stated as such in the now repealed section 54. The exceptions are:

(i) any distribution of a company's assets by way of dividend lawfully made.[44] One of the abuses prior to section 54 of the 1948 Act, was the extraction from a company, by way of unusually large dividends, of funds to repay a loan used by the borrower to gain control of the company. Such payments are now excluded from the prohibition if they are *lawfully made*, *i.e.* they fulfil the criteria laid down in Part III of the 1980 Act,[45] and the relevant articles of association, which should protect creditors and minority shareholders respectively. This is the most important of the nine exceptions; and should facilitate the extraction of liquid funds from companies;

(ii) any distribution made in the course of a winding up of a company[46];

(iii) the allotment of bonus shares.[47] This is because the use of the word "acquisition" in sections 42 (1) and (2) could conceivably apply to them whereas they are neither purchased nor subscribed for;

(iv) anything done in pursuance of an order of the court under section 206 of the 1948 Act[48];

(v) anything done under an arrangement made between a company and its creditors which is binding on the creditors by virtue of section 306 of the 1948 Act[49];

(vi) anything done under an arrangement made in pursuance of section 287 of the 1948 Act[50];

(vii) any reduction of capital confirmed by an order of the court under section 68 of the 1948 Act[51];

(viii) a redemption of shares under section 45 of the 1981 Act[52];

(ix) a purchase of its own shares by a company under sections 46–62 of the 1981 Act.[53]

Loans and employee share scheme exceptions

38–09 Section 54 of the 1948 Act contained three exceptions which have been generally re-enacted in section 42 (6) of the 1981 Act, incorporating the 1980 Act amendments.[54] There are two important and one minor

[44] 1981 Act, s. 42 (5) (*a*).
[45] See Chap. 76, *post*.
[46] 1981 Act, s. 42 (5) (*a*). See Chap. 85. *post*.
[47] *Ibid*. s. 42 (5) (*b*).
[48] *Ibid*. s. 42 (5) (*c*). See Chap. 79, *post*.
[49] *Ibid*. s. 42 (5) (*d*).
[50] *Ibid*. s. 42 (5) (*e*). See Chap. 80, *post*.
[51] *Ibid*. s. 42 (5) (*f*). See Chap. 32, *ante*.
[52] *Ibid*. s. 42 (5) (*g*). See para. 33–13, *ante*.
[53] *Ibid*. s. 42 (5) (*h*). See para. 37–08, *ante*.
[54] 1948 Act, s. 54 (1), (1A) (1B). See 1980 Act, Sched. 3., para. 10.

difference in the 1981 Act exceptions to those in the amended version of section 54.

In all three cases, however, a public company may not take advantage of them unless it has net assets which are either not thereby reduced or, if they are, the assistance is provided out of profits which are available for dividend.[55] Net assets for this purpose means the aggregate of its assets less the aggregate of its liabilities[56] but unlike the former requirement under section 54 (1) (A) of the 1948 Act this formula is to be calculated by reference to book values and not actual value.[57] The requirement that a public company has net assets to begin with was also a new provision in the 1981 Act.

(i) LENDING AS PART OF THE ORDINARY COURSE OF BUSINESS. If the lending of the money is in the ordinary course of business of the company *and* the loan itself is within the ordinary course of that business section 42 of the 1981 Act does not apply (s. 42 (6) (*a*)). This applies to banks and other finance houses, but it must be stressed that both parts of the proviso must be complied with so that an unusual loan by such an institution would not be exempt.[58]

(ii) EMPLOYEE SHARE SCHEMES. The provision of money for the acquisition of fully paid shares in the company or its holding company in accordance with an employee's share scheme is valid (s. 42 (6) (*b*)). Employee share schemes for this purpose are those defined by section 87 (1) of the 1980 Act.[59] A new facet of this exemption is that the finance need no longer take the form of a loan to trustees administering the scheme. This was always required by section 54 (1) of the 1948 Act and shaped the tax provisions on approved profit sharing schemes.[60] Directors will be included if they are also employees. This exception has been used by them to fight take-over bids but such action will usually be a breach of their fiduciary duties.[61]

(iii) LOANS TO EMPLOYEES TO PURCHASE SHARES. A company may lend money to those employed in good faith by the company with a view to their purchasing shares in that company or its holding company for their own benefits (s. 42 (6) (*c*)). This exception does not apply to directors.[62] The change from section 54 (1) (*c*) of the 1948 Act is that *bona fide in the employment* has become *employed*

[55] 1981 Act, s. 42 (7). For distributable profits see Chap. 76, *post*. See also s. 60 of the 1981 Act.
[56] *Ibid*. s. 42 (11) (*b*).
[57] *Ibid*. s. 42 (11) (*a*); *cf*. s. 54 (1A) of the 1948 Act and s. 87 (*b*), (*c*) of the 1980 Act.
[58] *Steen* v. *Law* [1964] A.C. 287 (P.C.)—thus a loan deliberately made by such a company with the purpose of an acquaintance in mind is unlikely to be regarded as a usual loan.
[59] See para. 33–12, *ante*.
[60] See Chap. 94, *post*. See also Morse and Williams, *Profit Sharing—Employee Shares Schemes* (Sweet & Maxwell, 1979).
[61] See para. 64–09, *post*.
[62] The wording may preclude directors both of the company and its holding company, or even of any company at all.

in good faith by. The intention of both is to ensure that the employment is genuine.

Validity of the transaction

38–10 The actual wording of section 42 of the 1981 Act, as in section 54 of the 1948 Act, merely renders the giving of financial assistance "unlawful" and creates a criminal offence. It says nothing as to the consequences of a breach on the transaction as whole or even as to whether any security given by the company which assists the purchase of its shares is void. It seems clear, however, that the courts have provided an answer on the identical wording of the former section to the latter question whereas the former has rarely been before the courts. There is no reason to suppose that the following cases are not equally applicable to section 42 of the 1981 Act.

38–11 VALIDITY OF ANY SECURITY. Roxburgh J. in *Victor Battery Co. Ltd.* v. *Curry's Ltd.*[63] held that such a security was valid despite the section[64] but Ungoed-Thomas J. in *Selangor United Rubber Estates Ltd.* v. *Cradock and Others (No. 3)*[65] considered that this was incorrect. The argument used by Roxburgh J. was that financial assistance could only be given under section 54 so as to constitute the criminal offence if the security was valid, an invalid security could give no assistance. Ungoed-Thomas J., however, pointed out that a security could never give financial assistance in the narrow sense of payment, it was security for repayment. If a wider meaning of financial assistance was therefore adopted "its being the means of giving financial assistance does not depend on its being valid, at any rate, when the financial assistance is in fact given. Indeed the greater the invalidity the greater the assistance, because the less the liability to repay."[66] This view was followed by Fisher J. in *Heald* v. *O'Connor*[67] where a security was held to be invalid if given in contravention of section 54; the section was even held to be infringed if the provision of the security was *ultra vires* the company because it was sufficient that the lender believed that the security was valid. A guarantee supporting an agreement invalid under section 54 has likewise been held to be void.[67]

38–12 VALIDITY OF THE AGREEMENT. In most of the cases the action simply sought to enforce a security which was held void as a result of a breach of section 54. In two cases, however, the judges have discussed the wider effects of such a breach on the agreement to purchase the shares as a whole. In *South Western Mineral Water Co.* v. *Ashmore*[68] Cross J. suggested that an agreement to purchase shares which is supported by a security invalid under

---

63 [1946] Ch. 242.
64 See also *Curtis's Furnishing Stores Ltd.* v. *Freeman* [1966] 1 W.L.R. 1219.
65 [1968] 1 W.L.R. 1555.
66 *Ibid.* at p. 2055.
67 [1971] 1 W.L.R. 497.
68 [1967] 1 W.L.R. 1110.

section 54 may be saved if the parties proceed with the purchase of the shares in a manner dissociating the purchase from the invalid security, either by the seller waiving the rights arising therefrom or by the buyer paying the purchase price forthwith; if the parties fail thus to sever the invalid security from the purchase agreement, the agreement itself becomes unenforceable and the parties should be restored, as far as possible, to their original position. In such circumstances the provisions of sections 36 and 37 of the 1980 Act cannot apply since there would be no acquisition by the purchaser.

On the other hand, the Court of Appeal decided in *Lawlor* v. *Gray*[69] that where an agreement between a vendor-controller of shares in a company and a purchaser for the sale of the vendor's shares could have been achieved in a number of lawful ways the fact that the vendor operated in breach of section 54 did not prevent the purchaser from enforcing the agreement. The Court of Appeal in so deciding held that a vendor in such a position owed both a contractual duty to the purchaser and a statutory duty to the company to achieve the terms of the agreement without any breach of the section. The distinction between the cases would seem one of construction of the agreement.

Liability of those participating in the breach

38–13 Directors owe a fiduciary duty to their company.[70] It follows that every director who is a party to a breach of section 42 of the 1981 Act is guilty of a breach of that duty or, where the company is wound up, of misfeasance and an action will lie against them for the company to recover its loss.[71] It has been held that section 54 was passed to protect the company from having its assets misused and not merely to protect its creditors,[72] and this would seem to apply to section 42 of the 1981 Act. If, however, the person against whom the claim for compensation is made is himself a shareholder, he will not be required to pay that part of the compensation awarded to the company which would come to him on a distribution of assets in the liquidation of the company.[73]

In addition anyone who receives the funds of the company so misapplied by the directors with either actual or constructive notice of the breach will be liable to the company as a constructive trustee.[74] An alternative basis

---

[69] (1980) 130 N.L.J. 317 (C.A.).

[70] See Chap. 64, *post*.

[71] *Belmont Finance Corpn.* v. *Williams Furniture Ltd. (No. 2)* [1980] 1 All E.R. 393; *Wallersteiner* v. *Moir* [1974] 1 W.L.R. 991; *Selangor United Rubber Estates Ltd.* v. *Cradock (No. 3)* [1968] 1 W.L.R. 1555; *Karak Rubber Co.* v. *Burden (No. 2)* [1972] 1 W.L.R. 602; *Curtis's Furnishing Store Ltd.* v. *Freedman* [1966] 1 W.L.R. 1219. For relief see s. 333.

[72] *Wallersteiner* v. *Moir* [1974] 1 W.L.R. 991, 1014, *per* Lord Denning M.R.; *Heald* v. *O'Connor* [1971] 1 W.L.R. 497. See *contra per*. Harman L.J. in *Essen Aero Ltd.* v. *Cross* (November 17, 1961) unreported, noted in *Selangor United Rubber Estates* v. *Cradock (No. 3) ante*.

[73] *Re V. G. M. Holdings Ltd.* [1942] Ch. 235, applied in *Selangor United Rubber Estates* v. *Cradock (No. 4)* [1969] 1 W.L.R. 1773.

[74] *Belmont Finance Corpn.* v. *Williams Furniture (No. 2)* [1980] 1 All E.R. 393; *Selangor United Rubber Estates* v. *Cradock (No. 3)* [1968] 1 W.L.R. 1555; *Karak Rubber Co.* v. *Burden (No. 2)* [1972] 1 W.L.R. 602.

for holding a party to the scheme liable as a constructive trustee is that he has assisted the directors with knowledge of the facts in a dishonest design on the part of the directors to misapply the company's funds.[75] It appears, however, that in such cases of "knowing assistance" only actual notice or wilful blindness on the part of the alleged constructive trustee will make him liable as such.[76] Constructive notice is only satisfactory for "knowing receipt" cases.

An alternative remedy for the company may lie in the tort of conspiracy. For this remedy it must proved: (i) that the conspirators combined to participate into a common agreement with a common purpose; (ii) that the combination was to effect an unlawful purpose, *i.e.* the provision of financial assistance contrary to section 54; (iii) that the company suffered damage as a consequence.[77] It is no defence to say that the company is a conspirator even if it is a party to the agreement if that is due to the acts of its misfeasant directors. An action in tort does, however, require proof of damage—an action for breach of constructive trust does not.

Provision of financial assistance, private company exemption

38–14 Sections 43 and 44 of the 1981 Act provide a general exemption for private companies from the prohibition on the giving of financial assistance for the purpose of an acquisition of their own shares contained in section 42 of that Act. There were no equivalent provisions in the earlier legislation. Exemption is obtained by compliance with a set procedure and timetable, and provision is made for the protection of creditors[78] and minority shareholders.[79] Private companies therefore have a choice of relying on the various exceptions available to all companies under section 42 or implementing, if they are able to, the procedure of sections 43 and 44. The general exemption conferred by use of this procedure is available for the acquisition of shares in the company itself or of its holding company if that is also a private company.[80] It is thus not available for shares in a public company. It is further provided that a private company may not use the general exemption for the acquisition of shares in its private holding company, if it is also the subsidiary of a public company which is itself a subsidiary of that holding company.[81]

The other general restriction on the use of this exemption is that the company must have net assets which are either not thereby reduced, or, if they are, the payment is made out of distributable profits.[82] This is intended to protect creditors by preventing the use of funds other than those

---

75 *Belmont Finance Corpn.* v. *Williams Furniture (No. 2)* [1980] 1 All E.R. 393, 405, 412, 417.
76 *Ibid.* at pp. 406, 413, 417.
77 *Belmont Finance Corpn.* v. *Williams Furniture (No. 2) ante.*
78 See 1981 Act, s. 43 (2) (6).
79 *Ibid.* ss. 43 (4), 44 (2).
80 *Ibid.* s. 43 (1).
81 *Ibid.* s. 43 (3).
82 *Ibid.* s. 43 (2). For the effect on dividends see Chap. 76, *post* and s. 60 of the 1981 Act.

profits available for distribution under Part III of the 1980 Act.[83] Those rules, however, do not require private companies to make provision for unrealised losses and thus this is an additional requirement that the directors make a statutory declaration of solvency.[84] Net assets for this purpose are the same as those applicable for public companies using the loans and employee share scheme exception,[85] *i.e.* by reference to book and not actual values.

38–15 DECLARATION OF SOLVENCY. In all cases the directors of the company proposing to give the assistance must make a statutory declaration of solvency prior to giving the assistance.[86] This obligation extends to the directors of the assisting company's holding company if its shares are to be acquired with the assistance and any intermediary company between them in the group.[87]

The declaration must be in the prescribed form complying with section 43 (7) of the 1981 Act. It must first detail the assistance to be given, the business of the company of which they are the directors and identify the recipient of the assistance.[88] Secondly the directors must state that *in their opinion* the company will be able to pay its debts, both immediately after giving the assistance, and as they fall due during the year immediately following the giving of the assistance.[89] The latter requirement is different if it is intended to wind up the company within 12 months of giving the assistance. In that case the directors must state that in their opinion the company will be able to pay its debts in full within 12 months of the commencement of the winding up.[90] The directors are required when making the statutory declaration to take into account both the contingent and prospective liabilities of the company as in the case of a liquidation petition for insolvency.[91]

The declaration of solvency must have annexed to it an auditors' report to the effect that they have inquired into the affairs of the company and are not aware of anything to indicate that the opinion of the directors as to the company's immediate and medium term solvency is unreasonable.[92]

It is a criminal offence for any director to make the statutory declaration without having reasonable grounds for the opinion expressed in the declaration.[93] There are no equivalent provisions relating to the auditors.

---

[83] See Chap. 76, *post*.
[84] See para. 38–15, *post*.
[85] 1981 Act, s. 44 (8). See para. 38–09, *ante*.
[86] *Ibid*. s. 44 (6). For the timing of the declaration see para. 38–16, *post*.
[87] No public company must be insolvent see s. 43 (1), (3).
[88] 1981 Act, s. 44 (7) (*a*).
[89] *Ibid*. s. 43 (7) (*b*) (ii).
[90] *Ibid*. s. 43 (7) (*b*) (i).
[91] *Ibid*. s. 43 (7). The criteria are applied by reference to s. 223 (*d*) of the 1948 Act; see para. 85–05, *post*.
[92] *Ibid*. s. 43 (8).
[93] *Ibid*. s. 44 (7).

38–16 SPECIAL RESOLUTION. Shareholder control, as distinct from creditor protection, is provided by the requirement that the financial assistance must be approved by a special resolution of the company.[94] Wholly owned subsidiaries are by their nature exempt from the requirement. When the assisting company is giving assistance for the acquisition of shares in its holding company a special resolution of approval is required both of the holding company and any intermediate company between them in the group, wholly owned subsidiary accepted.[95] The timetable for implementing the authority required by section 43 of the 1981 Act can only be discovered from reading sections 43 (9) and 44 (1), (4) and (5) together. The steps are as follows:

(i) Making of statutory declaration of solvency and auditors' report;
(ii) Availability of such declaration and report at the meeting to pass the requisite special resolution (s. 44 (4) (*a*));
(iii) Passing of the requisite special resolution on the same day as or within one week of the making of the declaration (s. 44 (1));
(iv) Registration of the declaration, auditors' report and resolution (if necessary) within 15 days of the passing of the resolution[96–97] (s. 44 (5) (*a*));
(v) A waiting period of four weeks from the date of the resolution during which time the company may not implement the authority to give the assistance unless all the members who may do so write in favour of the resolution. This enables a dissentient minority to activate the minority protective procedure.[98] Where more than one company has to pass a resolution[99] the four week period runs from the date of the last one to be passed (s. 43 (9) (*a*));
(vi) If the minority protection procedure is not activated the authority conferred by the declaration of solvency and special resolution must be implemented within eight weeks of the making of the first declaration of solvency (s. 43 (*a*) (*c*)). In general therefore companies will have between three and four weeks to implement the authority depending upon the time gap between the declaration and the resolution. It shoud be noted that if more than one resolution and declaration is required these should be synchronised as much as possible since the four week delay under (v) begins after the *last* resolution has been passed whereas the eight week maximum period for implementation begins on the making

---

[94] *Ibid.* s. 43 (4). For the timing of the resolution see para. 38–20D, *post*.
[95] *Ibid.* s. 43 (5).
[96–97] If no such resolution is required because the company is a wholly owned subsidiary registration must be within 15 days of making the declaration: 1981 Act, s. 44 (5) (*b*). For defaults in registration see s. 44 (6).
[98] See para. 38–17, *post*.
[99] *i.e.* where a holding company is involved.

of the *first* declaration of solvency, so that the time for actual implementation may be very short.

38–17 MINORITY PROTECTION. After the passing of any of the requisite special resolutions a dissentient minority may apply to the court to have the resolution set aside (s. 44 (2)). A dissentient minority for this purpose are the holders of at least 10 per cent. of the nominal visual capital or any class thereof[1] who did not consent to or vote for the resolution (abstention will suffice).[2] This application must be made within 28 days of the passing of the resolution, during which time the company cannot act upon it.[3]

The court has wide powers on such an application which is subject to the same procedure as on a petition to prevent a public company becoming a private company under section 11 of the 1980 Act[4] (s. 44 (3)). One of these powers is to order that the minority be bought out. If the court does cancel the resolution it ceases to be effective for the purpose of section 43.[5] Whilst the petition is being considered the resolution cannot be implemented unless the court orders otherwise.[6] If the court confirms the resolution it may extend the eight weeks' time limit for its effectiveness.[7]

[1] If the company is not limited by shares the number is 10 per cent. of the members.
[2] 1981 Act, s. 44 (2) (*a*).
[3] *Ibid*. s. 43 (9) (*a*).
[4] See para. 5–10, *ante*.
[5] 1981 Act, s. 44 (4) (*b*).
[6] *Ibid*. s. 43 (9) (*b*).
[7] *Ibid*. s. 43 (9) (*c*).

CHAPTER 39

TRANSFER AND TRANSMISSION OF SHARES. MORTGAGING OF SHARES

39–01 THREE topics are treated in this chapter:

(1) *The transfer of shares*

This is the voluntary conveyance of the rights and, possibly, the duties of a member, as represented in a share in the company,[1] from a shareholder who wishes to cease to be a member to a person desirous of becoming a member.

(2) *The transmission of shares*

This is the passing of a share by operation of law from a shareholder to another person or body. Transmission occurs, *e.g.* on the death or bankruptcy of a shareholder. It may also take place under legislation providing for the nationalisation of particular industries.[2] Further, in time of war, by virtue of delegated legislation made under the Trading with the Enemy Act 1939, s. 7, the Department of Trade can make a vesting order transferring shares which are enemy property to the Custodian of Enemy Property.[3]

(3) *The mortgaging of shares*

This occurs where a shareholder uses his shares as security on which to borrow money.

Transfer of shares

Right to transfer

39–02 "When joint stock companies were established," said Lord Blackburn,[4] "the great object was that the shares should be capable of being easily transferred." In pursuance of this object, section 73 of the 1948 Act provides that shares in a company shall be capable of being transferred in manner provided by the articles of the company; and it is well settled that, unless the articles otherwise provide, the shareholder has a free right to transfer to whom he will.[5]

It is not necessary to seek in the articles for a power to transfer, for the Act itself gives such a power; it is only necessary to look to the articles to ascertain the restrictions, if any, upon it.[6] Thus a member has a right to transfer his shares to another person unless this right is clearly taken away

---

[1] See para. 33–01, *ante*.
[2] *e.g.* Cable and Wireless Act 1946, s. 1; Iron and Steel Act 1949, s. 11; Iron and Steel Act 1953, s. 1 (1) (*b*).
[3] See Trading with the Enemy (Custodian) Order 1939 (No. 1198) (as amended), rr. 2 and 6.
[4] *Re Bahia, etc., Ry.* (1868) L.R. 3 Q.B. 584, 595.
[5] *Weston's Case* (1868) L.R. 4 Ch. 20.
[6] *Gilbert's Case* (1870) L.R. 5 Ch. 559, 565.

by the articles.[7] The provisions restricting the transfer of shares which were sometimes found in the articles of public companies[8] and until the 1980 Act had to be contained in the articles of private companies are considered later.[9]

A transferee under a valid transfer has an absolute right to be registered unless the company has a power to refuse to register and has effectively so refused[10]; thus, where, under the articles, the directors had power "to decline" to register a transfer and owing to a deadlock on the board they were unable either to pass the transfer or to decline it, the court held that the power to decline had not been exercised and that the transferee was entitled to be registered. The directors must exercise any right to decline to register a transfer within a reasonable time, and four months delay is certainly "unreasonable,"[11] but the consequences of their failure to do so may not yet be absolutely clear. The leading English authority[12] suggests that delay beyond the period of two months specified in section 78[13] extinguishes the right of refusal, but this case was decided without consideration of the only other (Scottish) case directly in point,[14] which suggests that the applicant must show prejudice beyond mere delay. In *Swaledale Cleaners* the refusal to register had no merit, since the applicant was one of two directors and already held shares, and the only other shareholder and director was clearly protecting his own position. In *Property Investment Co. of Scotland* the transfer was of partly paid shares to a person whose ability to meet calls was in doubt and there was no suggestion that refusal to register was not in good faith. The English court clearly thought that section 78 altered the position by making failure to send notice of refusal within two months an offence, but, with respect, there is no general rule that an act cannot be done out of time merely because penalties attach to late performance. In any event, at least one of the judges in *Swaledale Cleaners*[15] cautiously indicated that delay beyond two months was unreasonable only "other things being equal." So absolute, prima facie, is the right of the transferee to be registered that a transfer by a shareholder, if out and out, cannot be impeached on the ground that it was made to a pauper and with the avowed object of escaping liability.[16]

---

[7] *Delavenne* v. *Broadhurst* [1931] 1 Ch. 234; *Greenhalgh* v. *Mallard* [1943] 2 All E.R. 234.
[8] The Rules on *Admission of Securities for Listing*, issued by the Stock Exchange require that all fully paid shares shall be free from any restriction on the right of transfer. Rules of the Stock Exchange, Sched. VII, Part A. See Vol II, para. C–274.
[9] See para. 39–11, *post*.
[10] *Re Hackney Pavilion* [1924] 1 Ch. 276; approved in *Moodie* v. *Shepherd (Bookbinders) Ltd.* [1949] 2 All E.R. 1044 (H.L.); 1950 S.C. (H.L.) 60; 1950 S.L.T. 90.
[11] *Property Investment Co. of Scotland* v. *Duncan* 1887, 14 R. 299; *Re Swaledale Cleaners Ltd.* [1968] 3 All E.R. 619.
[12] *Re Swaledale Cleaners Ltd., supra.*
[13] Introduced first as s. 66 of the 1929 Act.
[14] *Property Investment Co. of Scotland* v. *Duncan, supra.*
[15] Harman L.J., at p. 623A.
[16] *De Pass's Case* (1859) 4 De G. & J. 544. See also *Furness & Co.* v. *Liquidators of "Cynthiana" Steamship Co.* 1893, 21 R. 239, 1 S.L.R. 365.

Contract to transfer

39–03 The contract by which a shareholder undertakes to transfer his shares is usually a contract of sale whereby the proposed transferor agrees to sell, and the proposed transferee agrees to buy, the shares; this contract may be concluded on the Stock Exchange if the shares in question are those of a public company and are quoted or dealt in on the Stock Exchange, or it may be concluded otherwise. The obligation to transfer shares may further arise from other contracts or agreements: thus, a settlor may undertake in the trust instrument to transfer specified shares to the trustees.

Where the obligation to transfer shares arises from a contract of sale of those shares the following are implied terms:

(1) that the transferee will pay the price and that the transferor will hand over to him genuine instruments of transfer and share certificates[17];

(2) that the certificate carries the rights and interests which it purports to convey[17];

(3) that there is no undertaking by the transferor that the transferee will be registered[18];

(4) that the transferor will do nothing to prevent the transferee from having the transfer registered or to delay that event[19];

(5) that the transferee will indemnify the transferor from any calls or liability which may arise in respect of the shares subsequently to the transfer.[20]

39–04 Once the contract has been entered into the transferee has an equitable title to the shares and the transferor holds them, until registration, as trustee for the transferee.[21] However, until the purchase price is fully paid the seller remaining on the register is entitled, *vis-à-vis* the purchaser, to vote in respect of the shares without reference to the wishes of the purchaser.[22]

If the company, under its powers properly exercised, refuses to register the transfer, the transferee has no right against the transferor for breach of any implied warranty to have the transfer registered, or for the recovery of the purchase price and rescission of the contract.[23] Any such term must be expressly provided for. Otherwise the seller's duty is performed when he hands over to the buyer a duly executed instrument of transfer, together

[17] *Stray* v. *Russell* (1859) 1 E. & E. 888, 900.

[18] *London Founders' Association Ltd. and Palmer* v. *Clarke* (1888) 20 Q.B.D. 576.

[19] *Hooper* v. *Herts* [1906] 1 Ch. 549.

[20] *Kellock* v. *Enthoven* (1874) L.R. 9 Q.B. 241; *Loring* v. *Davis* (1886) 32 Ch.D. 625; *Levi* v. *Ayers* (1878) 3 App.Cas. 842; *Hardoon* v. *Belilios* [1901] A.C. 118. The rule applies in the case of a blank transfer: *Spencer* v. *Ashworth, Partington & Co.* [1925] 1 K.B. 589.

[21] *Loring* v. *Davis* (1886) 32 Ch.D. 625; *Hardoon* v. *Belilios* [1901] A.C. 118; *Stevenson* v. *Wilson* 1907, S.C. 445.

[22] *Musselwhite* v. *C. H. Musselwhite & Son Ltd.* [1962] Ch. 964.

[23] *London Founders' Association Ltd. and Palmer* v. *Clarke* (1888) 20 Q.B.D. 576.

with the certificate or its equivalent.[24] If the buyer wishes to protect himself he must buy "with registration guaranteed."

Upon a breach of a contract to transfer shares, the measure of damages is the difference between the contract price and the market price at the date of the breach.[25]

Capacity to transfer

39–05 In general any person who has properly[26] become a member of the company has the capacity to transfer his shares. Thus an infant[27] who is a member has, it is submitted, capacity to transfer his shares.[28] So in *Gooch's Case*[29] shares had been transferred by an adult to an infant who transferred to another infant who transferred to an adult: later the company was wound up. Lord Selborne L.C. said[30]:

> "From the time when [the company] had a good shareholder upon their register, with respect to whom they were bound, and who was bound with respect to them, they ceased to have any interest in the voidable character of the intermediate transfer."

The effect of this decision was that the transfers were effective, through the different stages, to transfer the shares from the first adult to the second. Further, in *Mann's Case*,[31] where an infant transferee of 200 shares transferred 180 of them, and later repudiated the contract in respect of the remaining 20 shares, the transferor was placed on the list of contributories in respect of the 20 shares but the transfer by the infant of the 180 shares was not, so far as appears, disputed. The same was true of the transactions before the court in *Curtis's Case*.[32]

Shares held by a member of unsound mind or by joint holders, one of whom is of unsound mind, can only be transferred pursuant to an order of the Court of Protection and by the person named in the order.

There is no restriction on the right of a married woman to transfer.

39–06 A member can transfer his shares by attorney. The power of attorney must be produced to the company with the instrument of transfer and duly authenticated. If the power is either revocable under section 126 of the Law of Property Act 1925, or where the power has been revoked (*e.g.* by the death of the appointor) then in favour of a transferee who dealt with the donee of the power without knowledge of the revocation, the transfer

[24] *Skinner* v. *City of London, etc., Corporation* (1885) 14 Q.B.D. 882; *London Founders' Association* v. *Clarke* (1888) 20 Q.B.D. 576.

[25] *Jamal* v. *Moolla Dawood & Co.* [1916] 1 A.C. 175.

[26] *i.e.* he must have the capacity of becoming a member; see para. 49–07, *post*.

[27] In Scotland capacity of pupils and minors to transfer is regulated by the law governing their ability or disability to contract.

[28] The learned author of the 19th edition thought otherwise; so, too, did the author of *Simpson on Infants*. Both these learned authors stated that an order of the Chancery Division was necessary.

[29] (1872) 8 Ch.App. 266.

[30] At p. 268.

[31] (1867) 3 Ch.App. 459n.

[32] (1868) L.R. 6 Eq. 455.

will be deemed to be valid.[33] There are prescribed circumstances in which the transferee will be conclusively presumed not to have such knowledge.[34] An innocent donee of the power is similarly protected on the transaction.[35] In addition if the transfer is a "stock exchange transaction"[36] a statutory declaration by the donee of the power that the power had not been revoked, made within three months of the transfer, will fully protect the transferee.[37]

Transfers prior to registration in England

39–07 A transfer is incomplete until registered.[38] Pending registration, the transferee has only an equitable right to the shares transferred to him. He does not become the legal owner until his name is entered on the register in respect of these shares. But delay in registration involves danger to him, for some already existing prior equity may come to light, as in *Ireland* v. *Hart*,[39] where a husband had mortgaged shares of which he was trustee for his wife and, before the mortgagee had become the registered holder of the shares, the wife took proceedings claiming that her equitable title prevailed over that of the mortgagee, a claim which the court upheld; or a second transfer may be passed and registered, and thus the first transfer may be defeated.

> "[The rule on this point is that,] as between two persons claiming title to shares in a company like this, which are registered in the name of a third party, priority of title [*i.e.* equitable title] prevails, unless the claimant second in point of time can show that as between himself and the company, before the company received notice of the claim of the first claimant, he, the second claimant, has acquired the full *status* of a shareholder; or at any rate that all formalities have been complied with, and that nothing more than some purely ministerial act remains to be done by the company, which as between the company and the second claimant the company could not have refused to do forthwith; so that as between himself and the company he may be said to have acquired, in the words of Lord Selborne,[40] 'a present, absolute, unconditional right to have the transfer registered, before the company was informed of the existence of a better title.' "[41]

---

[33] Powers of Attorney Act 1971, s. 5 (2); this does not apply to Scotland. Further, the Law of Property Act 1925 does not apply to Scotland; in Scots law a power of attorney remains valid and effectual as regards third parties until they have actual notice of its cancellation, or of facts showing its invalidity.

[34] *Ibid.* s. 5 (4).

[35] *Ibid.* s. 5 (1).

[36] As defined in the Stock Transfer Act 1963, s. 4.

[37] Powers of Attorney Act 1971, s. 6.

[38] *Société Générale* v. *Walker* (1885) 11 App.Cas. 20; *Shropshire Union, etc., Co.* v. *The Queen* (1875) L.R. 7 H.L. 496; *Roots* v. *Williamson* (1888) 38 Ch.D. 485; *Powell* v. *London and Provincial Bank* [1893] 2 Ch. 555.

[39] [1902] 1 Ch. 522.

[40] *Société Générale* v. *Walker* (1885) 11 App.Cas. 20, 29.

[41] *Per* Romer J. in *Moore* v. *N.W. Bank* [1891] 2 Ch. 599, 602; *Peat* v. *Clayton* [1906] 1 Ch. 659; *Guy* v. *Waterlow Bros.* (1909) 25 T.L.R. 515; *Coleman* v. *London County and Westminster Bank Ltd.* [1916] 2 Ch. 353.

39–08 It has never been clearly decided in what circumstances the "present, absolute, unconditional right to have the transfer registered" to which Lord Selborne refers[42] arises. It is thought that in many instances the test is that indicated by Jenkins J. in *Re Rose*[43]:

> "I was referred on that to the well known case of *Milroy* v. *Lord*[44] and also to the recent case of *Re Fry, Chase National Executors & Trustee Corpn.* v. *Fry*.[45] Those cases, as I understand them, turn on the fact that the deceased donor had not done all in his power, according to the nature of the property given, to vest the legal interest in the property in the donee. In such circumstances it is, of course, well settled that there is no equity to complete the imperfect gift. If any act remained to be done by the donor to complete the gift at the date of the donor's death the court will not compel his personal representatives to do that act and the gift remains incomplete and fails.
>
> In *Milroy* v. *Lord*[46] the imperfection was due to the fact that the wrong form of transfer was used for the purpose of transferring certain bank shares. The document was not the appropriate document to pass any interest in the property at all. In *Re Fry*[47] the flaw in the transaction, which was a transfer or transfers of shares in a certain company, was failure to obtain the consent of the Treasury which in the circumstances surrounding the transfers in question was necessary under the Defence (Finance Regulations) Act 1939, and, as appears from the headnote, what was held was that the donor's executors ought not to execute confirmatory transfers. . . . In this case, as I understand it, the testator had done everything in his power to divest himself of the shares in question to Mr. Hook. He had executed a transfer. It is not suggested that the transfer was not in accordance with the company's regulations. He had handed that transfer together with the certificates to Mr. Hook. There was nothing else the testator could do. . . . Therefore it seems to me that the present case is not *in pari materia* with the two cases to which I have been referred. The real position, in my judgment, is that the question here is one of construction of the will. The testator says 'if such preference shares have not been transferred to him previously to my death.' The position was that, so far as the testator was concerned, they had been so transfered."

Even if the principle in *Re Rose*[48] is inapplicable the equitable rights of the transferee may protect him against later equities. Thus, in *Hawks* v. *McArthur*[49] a purported transfer which could not have been effective since the company's articles gave pre-emptive rights to other members preceded a valid charging order on the shares by a judgment creditor against the transferor. Notwithstanding the serious imperfection of the transfer it was

---

42 *Société Générale* v. *Walker* (1885) 11 App.Cas. 20, 29.
43 [1949] Ch. 78, 89. The C.A. approved this decision in *Re Rose* [1952] Ch. 499, a case involving different parties and concerning different though not dissimilar facts.
44 (1862) 4 De G.F. & J. 264.
45 [1946] Ch. 312.
46 (1862) 4 De G.F. & J. 264.
47 [1946] Ch. 312.
48 [1949] Ch. 78.
49 [1951] 1 All E.R. 22.

held, on the facts of the case, that the transferees (who had paid in full the consideration for the shares) had acquired equitable rights in them in priority over the charging order.

Transfers prior to registration in Scotland

39–09 As in English law, an unregistered transfer is incomplete, although the seller has contractual obligations towards the purchaser.[50] As between two applicants for membership, priority of registration determines the question of who is a member.[51] In a question between a registered member as transferor and a third party, such as a creditor seeking to arrest his shares, however, as soon as the transfer has been lodged for registration the transferee will be preferred, on the ground that the transferor has effectively parted with his rights before the inchoate arrestment has been completed by furthcoming.[52]

Liability of transferor and transferee

39–10 Delay in registration may prejudice the transferor as well as the transferee, for in the case of shares which are only in part paid up, the transferor, whilst the transfer is unregistered, continues to be liable to the company to pay all calls in respect of the shares comprised therein that may be made by the company and remains on the B list of contributories until a correspondingly later date.[53] Hence the transferor is given by law a right to enforce registration of the transfer (1948 Act, s. 77).

It is not clear that the registration of the transfer terminates the liability of the transferor for calls in arrear.[54] Where the transfer is in the usual form, it seems that the company may sue the transferee in respect of such calls,[55] and it is equally clear that the transferee takes the shares on the footing that the call has not been paid, and cannot vote in respect thereof if the articles provide that no member shall be entitled to vote at all if any calls or other sums of money shall be due and payable to the company in respect of the shares of such members.[56] In a winding up the transferee can certainly be called on to pay up whatever is then unpaid on his shares (1948 Act, s. 222 (1)), and it would seem that, even while the company is a going concern, it could make a fresh call on him for the amount of the outstanding call, and that he would be liable to pay it.[57]

Where there is a liability in respect of uncalled capital on the transferred shares, the transferor, upon registration of the transfer, is free from this liability, subject to the qualification that, if a winding up commences within one year[58] after he ceased to be a member, he may be placed on the B list

---

[50] *Stevenson* v. *Wilson* 1907, S.C. 445.
[51] *Morrison* v. *Harrison* 1876, 3 R. 406.
[52] *National Bank of Scotland Glasgow Nominees Ltd.* v. *Adamson* 1932 S.L.T. 492.
[53] See paras. 85–45, 86–27 and 87–39, *post*.
[54] *Re Hoylake Ry.* (1874) L.R. 9 Ch. 257.
[55] *Herbert Gold Ltd.* v. *Haycraft* (C.A.), March 27, 1901.
[56] *Randt Gold Mining Co.* v. *Wainwright* [1901] 1 Ch. 184.
[57] *Randt Gold Mining Co.* v. *New Balkis Eersteling* [1904] A.C. 165.
[58] See s. 229; paras. 85–45, 86–27 and 87–39, *post*.

of contributories as a past member and if the present member on the A list appears to be unable to contribute what is due on the shares in question, he—the transferor on the B list—is liable for certain debts of the company (s. 212 (1) (*a*) (*b*) (*c*)).

Restrictions on transfer by the articles

39–11 IN GENERAL. Provisions in articles whereby the right of the shareholders to transfer their shares is restricted used to be obligatory in the case of private companies before the coming into operation of the 1980 Act which repealed this requirement,[59] and are not uncommon in the case of public companies, but if the shares of the latter are dealt in or listed on the Stock Exchange, fully paid shares have to be free from any restriction on the right to transfer.[60]

There is nothing to limit the restrictions which a company's articles may place on the right of transfer.[61] The articles may give the directors power to refuse to register a transfer in any specified cases, for instance, where calls are in arrear, or where the company has a lien on the shares—and some such provisions are usually inserted. Thus article 24 provides that the directors may decline to register any transfer of a share (not being a fully paid share) to a person of whom they do not approve, and may also decline to register any transfer of shares on which the company has a lien. But the articles in many cases go far beyond this. They may prohibit, for example, the transfer of a share to any person who is not a member of a specified class, or provide, as they often do in private companies, that before transferring to an outsider the intending transferor must first offer the shares to the other members, and give them a right of pre-emption.[62] Such provisions, though permanent, do not contravene the English law against perpetuities.[63]

39–12 It has already been observed that even in public companies restrictions on the right of transfer are not uncommon; for instance, most shipping companies provide restrictions on the transfers of their equity shares or stock to foreigners or their nominees. An extreme example of restrictions in a public company was found in the articles of Mann, Crossman & Paulin Ltd., which were discussed in the House of Lords in connection with estate duty in *I.R.C* v. *Crossman*.[64] The effect of these restrictions[65] was to enable a male holder to transfer his shares or appoint them by will to sons

[59] See para. 4–08, *ante*.
[60] Admission of Securities to Listing, Sched. VII, Part A, A. See Vol II, Part C, para. C–274. The Stock Exchange Council has power to grant exemption from this provision and may, in exceptional cases, exercise its discretion, particularly in the case of deferred or founders' shares which have a controlling interest in the company and are not quoted on the Stock Exchange.
[61] *Re Crawley & Co.* (1889) 42 Ch.D. 209, 231; *Re Stockton Malleable Iron Co.* (1875) 2 Ch.D. 101.
[62] *Borland's Trustee* v. *Steel Brothers & Co.* [1901] 1 Ch. 279; *Rayfield* v. *Hands* [1960] Ch. 1.
[63] See on restrictions on transfer in a private company, para. 39–13, *post*.
[64] [1937] A.C. 26.
[65] Which are set out in full on pp. 32–36 of the report in [1937] A.C. 26.

or brothers or sons of sons or of brothers subject to the transferees or appointees attaining the age of 25 years and being in other respects duly qualified in the opinion of the directors; subject thereto, the article gave the other holders of ordinary shares a right of pre-emption over the shares of living members and an option to purchase the shares of deceased members at a price calculated in a manner therein specified; the article had an overriding provision that the directors might, without assigning any reason for their opinion, refuse to register any transferee whom it was not, in their opinion, desirable to admit to membership.[66]

Where a shareholder, in accordance with the provisions of the articles, offers to sell the whole of his shareholding at a certain price and the offer, on the true construction of the articles, cannot be regarded as a separate offer in respect of each of the shares, another shareholder cannot accept the offer in respect of part only of the shares[67]; for this reason articles often expressly give the right to accept part only of the shares offered. Prima facie an offer to sell shares may be withdrawn.[68]

Where bonus shares are issued upon renounceable allotment letters, and an allottee renounces in favour of another person, this does not amount to a transfer and accordingly is not subject to restrictions on transfer that may be contained in the articles.[69]

39–13 RESTRICTIONS ON TRANSFER IN PRIVATE COMPANIES. A private company is normally what the Americans call a "close corporation"[70]; this means that its members are connected by bonds of kinship, friendship or similar close ties and that the intrusion of a stranger as shareholder would be felt to be undesirable unless his admission is accepted by those for the time being interested in the company. Some private companies are in fact so constructed as to amount in economic terms to incorporated partnerships with the attendant close connection between the members.[71] For this reason in private companies the regulation dealing with the restriction of the right to transfer shares, even though no longer required by law,[72] remains of particular practical importance.

The restrictions which a private company may choose to impose by its articles may be wide in character and easy to satisfy or they may be the opposite. Thus, the articles may provide that the shareholders must be adult persons, or British or EEC nationals or of male sex.[73]

---

66 This summary of the effect of the restrictions is in part taken from the report on the case in [1937] A.C. 26.

67 *The Ocean Coal Co.* v. *The Powell Duffryn Steam Coal Co.* [1932] 1 Ch. 654.

68 *Smith* v. *Wilson* 1909, 9 S.L.T. 137.

69 *Re Pool Shipping Co.* [1920] 1 Ch. 251.

70 The expression "close company" is now used in the Income and Corporation Taxes Act 1970, ss. 282–303; see further para. 91–03, *post*.

71 See para. 85–08, *post*. See *Re Westbourne Galleries Ltd.* [1973] A.C. 360, 373 (*per* Lord Wilberforce); and G. K. Morse and R. H. Tedd, "Partnership Companies" [1971] J.B.L. 261.

72 Section 28 (1) (*a*) of the 1948 Act was repealed by the 1980 Act.

73 Neither the Sex Discrimination Act 1975 nor the Race Relations Act 1976 appear to cover such restrictions.

It is admissible that the articles provide restrictions for the transfer of some, but not of all, shares.

The following is a common clause[74] often to be found in the articles:

> "the directors may, in their absolute discretion and without assigning any reason therefor, decline to register any transfer of any share, whether or not it is a fully paid share, ..."

but usually the restriction clauses in registered articles of private companies supplement that clause by more elaborate provisions.

In particular, various types of pre-emption clauses, sometimes of very detailed character, are found in the articles of private companies.[75] Sometimes it is provided that the proposing transferor shall offer the shares first to all other shareholders rateably; sometimes he is entitled to select the shareholder to whom he wants to sell; sometimes the first offer has to be made to certain shareholders, *e.g.* those holding founders' shares; sometimes holders of those shares or of deferred shares need not offer their shares first to other shareholders but are only subject to the general restriction clause giving the directors discretion to decline the registration of a transfer; sometimes the first offer has to be made to the directors and the second offer to other members; sometimes to larger holders and then to other members; and sometimes the articles provide that in certain circumstances, *e.g.* in the case of death of a member, the surviving members or directors are obliged to acquire the deceased member's shares.[76] It is usual to supplement these pre-emption clauses with the general restriction clause by providing, for example, that, after the failure of those entitled to pre-emptive rights to acquire the shares and after their subsequent offer to another person, the directors may decline the transfer. The pre-emption clause is brought into operation where shareholders agree to sell the shares, receive the purchase price and retain it[77]; *i.e.* where a court can draw the inference that the parties intended that the transaction should take effect as a contract for the sale of the shares and that the owner had sufficiently evinced a desire to transfer the legal interest in them.[77a]

39–14 Where the pre-emption clause provides—as is normally the case—that a share may be transferred to any member but shall not be transferred to a person who is not a member so long as any member is willing to purchase the same at the fair value, the transfer between members is completely unrestricted and such transfer does not bring into operation the provisions of the pre-emption clause.[78] "Member" in this case means, it is thought, a person registered as such in the register of members; it is irrelevant—at

---

[74] This clause was contained in the 1948 Act, Table A, Pt. II, art. 3, but the whole Pt. II of Table A was repealed by the 1980 Act, s. 88 and Sched. 4.

[75] Palmer, *Company Precedents*, Part I (17th ed., 1956), Forms 232–240.

[76] *Dean* v. *Prince* [1954] Ch. 409; *Rayfield* v. *Hands* [1960] Ch. 1.

[77] *Lyle & Scott Ltd.* v. *Scott's Trustee* [1959] A.C. 763; 1959 S.C. (H.L.) 64; 1959 S.L.T. 198.

[77a] *Safeguard Industrial Investments Ltd.* v. *National Westminster Bank Ltd.* [1980] 3 All E.R. 849, affmd. [1982] 1 All E.R. 449 (C.A.).

[78] *Greenhalgh* v. *Mallard* [1943] 2 All E.R. 234.

least in England—whether the registered person holds the shares as a beneficiary or as a nominee, in view of section 117 of the 1948 Act.[79] So, in *Roberts* v. *Letter "T" Estates Ltd.*,[80] where a pre-emption clause provided that "any person (not a member . . .) becoming entitled to shares in consequence of the death of a member" should within three months offer the shares to certain members at the fair value, an executor who was himself already a member of the company was not bound to offer the shares; the fact that he was only a nominee made no difference. If the executor is not a member, such a clause is binding upon him, even where there is only one surviving member to whom the shares can be offered.[81]

There is some doubt as to whether the provisions of a pre-emption clause apply to the transfer of a beneficial interest in the share to an outsider. In *Lyle & Scott Ltd.* v. *Scott's Trustees*[82] the articles of the company provided that no transfer of ordinary shares by a shareholder should take place for an onerous consideration so long as any other ordinary shareholders were willing to acquire the shares; and that

> "Any such ordinary shareholder who is desirous of transferring his ordinary shares shall inform the secretary in writing of the number of ordinary shares which he desires to transfer."

A take-over bid for the shares was accepted by the majority of shareholders, and the purchase price was paid to them. The company then drew the attention of the shareholders who had accepted the offer to the provisions of the above article and, when the shareholders ignored the company's letter, brought proceedings for a declaration that the defendants were bound to comply with the provisions of the article. The defendants contended that they were not "desirous" of transferring their shares: they did not deny that they had received and intended to keep the price for the shares but they said that "at present" neither they nor the offeror intended transfers to be executed. The shareholders further contended that they were no longer "desirous" to transfer their shares because their task was done and their desire was satisfied. The House of Lords rejected these contentions. Viscount Simmonds said (at p. 774):

> "It is not open to a shareholder who has agreed to do a certain thing and is bound to do it, to deny that he is desirous of doing it. I wish to make it quite clear, for it goes to the root of the matter, that I regard Scott's trustees as desirous of transferring their ordinary shares unless and until their agreement with [the offeror] is abrogated. Of this at least one acid test would be the return by them of the price they have received."

---

79 See para. 50–06, *post*.
80 [1961] A.C. 795.
81 *Jarvis Motors (Harrow) Ltd.* v. *Carabott* [1964] 1 W.L.R. 1101. It has been held in Canada that an executor of the will of a majority shareholder may alter the pre-emption articles to give effect to the will's requirements to transfer the deceased's shares to non-members. *Re Rudderham* (1969) 9 D.L.R. (3d) 492.
82 [1959] A.C. 763; 1959 S.C. (H.L.) 64; 1959 S.L.T. 198.

In *Safeguard Industrial Investments Ltd.* v. *National Westminster Bank Ltd.*,[82a] Vinelott J. considered that the *Lyle & Scott Ltd.* case did not establish a general proposition that the word "transfer" in a pre-emption clause included transfers of the beneficial interest. In his judgment the completion of the administration of the estate of a deceased shareholder whereby his personal representative[82b] held his shares on trust for two other members of the company did not amount to a transfer for the purposes of a pre-emption clause. A declaration of trust by a shareholder could not be regarded as a transfer, unless possibly the legal owner handed over an irrevocable proxy to vote to the beneficial owner. Nor did the wishes of the testator expressed in his will, and taking effect on completion of the administration, take effect as a transfer by him.

This decision is difficult to reconcile with the *Lyle & Scott Ltd.* case. The rule that a member has not transferred his shares if he has disposed only of an equitable interest in it will leave wide avenues open for avoidance of pre-emption clauses. Vinelott J. reached his decision with "some regret" but it was confirmed by the Court of Appeal[82c] and so appropriate pre-emption clauses should be altered accordingly to cover equitable transfers.

Liability of valuer

39–15 Most pre-emption clauses contain provisions for the ascertainment of the "fair value" of the shares; they often provide that, in the absence of agreement between the transferor and the transferee, that value has to be ascertained by the auditor. The auditor who, in the words of Denning L.J.,[83] acts in this respect as an expert and not as an arbitrator need not state reasons for his valuation and the burden of proving that it was an improper valuation is on the person objecting to it.[84] It was decided by the House of Lords in *Arenson* v. *Cassen, Beckman, Rutley & Co.*[85] that if auditors had acted as valuers, and not as arbitrators, and if it were proved that they had acted negligently (which was not established in evidence in that case), a claim in negligence may lie against them. Lord Simon followed the decision of the House of Lords in *Sutcliffe* v. *Thackrah*[86] where an architect was sued for negligence in issuing certificates of the value of work executed for the purpose of instalment payments to a builder. He was held to be merely deciding on a sum by the application of his care and skill and could not be said to be exercising a quasi-judicial function. Consequently, if the auditor merely puts a value on the shares and does so negligently, he has acted as valuer and is liable for the negligent valuation. If, on the other hand, a dispute has arisen between the parties about the

[82a] [1980] 3 All E.R. 849.
[82b] The P.R. had a right to registration free of the pre-emption clause and so could be regarded as the original owner.
[82c] [1982] 1 All E.R. 449.
[83] *Dean* v. *Prince* [1954] Ch. 409, 426.
[84] *Bruce* v. *James Keiller & Son Ltd.* 1901, S.L.T. 184.
[85] [1977] A.C. 405.
[86] [1974] 2 W.L.R. 295.

value of the shares, each placing a different value on them for different reasons, and the auditor is called upon to decide that dispute, he acts as an arbitrator and would appear[87] to be immune from liability for negligence.

There may be some dispute as to whether an auditor is acting as an expert valuer or as an arbitrator. In *Leigh* v. *English Property Corporation*[88] Brightman J. suggested that an agreement for valuation is not, prima facie, an agreement for an arbitration. The function of the valuer is usually to settle a price so that no difference arises between the parties. His function is not to make an award after a difference has already arisen. But this distinction can be blurred and where a reference to the auditors was to be made only on a failure to agree a price it was held to be arguable that in the absence of contrary wording the auditors were acting as arbitrators. This view was endorsed by the Court of Appeal.

In view of the development in the tort of negligence in relation to an auditor acting as an expert and not an arbitrator, the right to have a valuation set aside simply for an alleged negligent mistake in valuing the shares no longer applies in the absence of fraud or collusion. This was the decision of the Court of Appeal in *Baber* v. *Kenwood Manufacturing Co. Ltd.*[89] The plaintiff had agreed to sell his shares to the defendants at a price "which the auditors for the time being of the company shall certify in writing to be in their opinion the fair selling value thereof." The auditors were to be considered to be acting as experts and not as arbitrators. The plaintiff challenged the valuation as being vitiated by fundamental errors of principle and not binding on them. The Court of Appeal decided that even if the plaintiff's allegations were correct the valuation was binding on both parties and any remedy lay against the auditors for damages in tort. The Court followed *Campbell* v. *Edwards*[90] and upheld the decision of Goulding J. in the present case. Two factors were considered relevant. First, the agreement to treat the auditors as experts and not as arbitrators indicated that the parties desired a degree of certainty. A reference to arbitration might suggest that a case should be stated by either side because of some error in the award. Secondly, the relationship between an action to set aside the valuation and an action for negligence against the auditors had to be reviewed. Earlier cases relating to grants of specific performance had expressed the view that a mistake could vitiate the valuation.[91] This view was now out of date since a remedy was available against the valuer. If the valuation could be set aside the damages available to the plaintiff in an action against the valuer would be minimal as he would have suffered no direct loss.

The position is different if the expert's certificate is a "speaking certi-

---

[87] But see the speech of Lord Kilbrandon, who inclined to the view, *obiter*, that even an arbitrator may be liable in negligence.

[88] [1976] 2 Lloyd's Rep. 298.

[89] [1978] 1 Lloyd's Rep. 175.

[90] [1976] 1 W.L.R. 403.

[91] See, *e.g.* *Collier* v. *Mason* (1858) 25 Beav. 200, 204; *Emery* v. *Wise* (1801) 5 Ves. Jr. 846; (1803) 8 Ves. Jr. 504. *Cf.* *Dean* v. *Prince* [1953] 1 Ch. 590.

ficate," *i.e.* if it gives reasons or shows the method of valuation used and those reasons or the method can be shown to be wrong. For example, where the parties have agreed on a valuation of assets on a going concern basis, the total capitalisation method or the super profits method of valuation may be used, but a valuation at break-up value contravenes the agreement of the parties: *Jones (M.)* v. *Jones (R.)*.[92] In that case the valuation was held to be vitiated and there was no need to show that a valuation conducted on the correct basis would have produced a different result. In this context in the absence of any contrary agreement the phrase "fair value" must be given its ordinary meaning.[93] Whether a valuation can also be set aside if the alleged mistake is innocent and no action will then lie for negligence against the valuers was left open in the *Baber* case but it is suggested that such an action will not be well founded in contract. If, however, the valuation relates to the wrong number or wrong type of shares then there is no valuation at all in accordance with the express terms of the contract and clearly neither party is bound by it. If the auditors are acting as arbitrators different considerations may apply.[94]

A provision in the articles that upon the death of a director leaving a wife him surviving the director's shares shall be deemed to have passed upon his death to his wife is invalid because it contravenes section 75.[95]

39–16 DISCRETION OF DIRECTORS AS TO REGISTRATION OF TRANSFERS. Where a discretion as to registering transfers is given by the articles to the directors, the court will not control the exercise of this discretion, unless it is proved that the directors are not exercising it bona fide[96]; in other words, that they are acting oppressively, capriciously, or corruptly or in some way mala fide.[97] In *Re Smith & Fawcett Ltd.*,[98] the court would not find mala fides where, on the death of a member who held half the company's shares, the surviving director, who held the other half of the shares, refused to register the executors except in respect of part of the holding and upon condition that the balance be transferred to himself.

It is common for articles to provide that the directors shall have the power of declining to register a transfer without assigning any reason therefor; or in their absolute and uncontrolled discretion; or in some equally sweeping terms; in such a case the court will not draw unfavourable inferences against directors because they do not give their reasons for refusing to pass a particular transfer, for they are under no obligation to disclose their reasons either in court or out of court; it is enough that they

---

92 [1971] 1 W.L.R. 840.
93 *Smith* v. *Gale* [1974] 1 W.L.R. 9. See also *Wright* v. *Frodoor* [1967] 1 W.L.R. 506; *Dean* v. *Prince, supra*.
94 See *Leigh* v. *English Property Corporation* [1976] 2 Lloyd's Rep. 298.
95 *Re Greene* [1949] Ch. 333.
96 *Re Gresham, etc., Society* (1872) L.R. 8 Ch. 446; *Re Coalport China Co.* [1895] 2 Ch. 404; *Re Smith and Fawcett Ltd.* [1942] Ch. 304; *Kennedy* v. *North British Wireless Schools Ltd.* 1916, 1 S.L.T. 407.
97 *Re Bell Bros.* (1891) 65 L.T. 245; *Stewart* v. *James Keiller & Sons Ltd.* 1902, 4 F. 657.
98 [1942] Ch. 304.

have in fact considered the transfer, and that in the exercise of the discretion given to them by the articles they have not passed it.[99] If the directors choose to give their reasons, the court will then consider whether they are legitimate or not.[1] Interrogatories have been allowed as to the grounds upon which the directors refused, where the articles provided that the directors might "without assigning any reason" decline to register a transfer upon certain alternative specified grounds[2]: the interrogatories were allowed in order to discover the actual ground upon which the directors had declined, but no further.[3] Where the articles provided that the directors should "not be bound to specify the grounds" upon which registration was declined, interrogatories were not allowed.[4] Where the discretion is to refuse to register transfers to persons of whom they do not approve, the refusal must be on grounds personal to the proposed transferee: so that the directors had no power to refuse to register individuals against whom they had no personal objection but who were nominees of a person of whom they did not approve.[5] In the absence of a wider power to refuse to register a transfer, the directors cannot refuse on the ground that the title will on the registration vest in the trustee in bankruptcy of the transferee.[6]

This power to refuse to register must be exercised in order to be effective: if for some reason the board do not positively refuse, the power has not been exercised and the transferee has a statutory right to be registered. So, where directors had power to refuse to register a transfer and the board was equally divided, there being no casting vote, the court held that the power to decline had not been exercised and the transfer must be registered.[7] Further, where one of two directors (the quorum being two) refused to attend a meeting to consider the transfers which were executed by the other, the court ordered the register to be rectified by registering the transfers.[8] The power of refusal must be exercised within a reasonable time, which, by analogy to the period allowed by section 78 of the 1948 Act for refusal to be notified to the transferee, must normally not exceed two months.[9] If the power of refusal is not exercised within that time, then it is lost.[10] The existence of a condition attached to the directors' right to refuse

---

[99] See *Re Coalport China Co., supra*; *Re Smith and Fawcett Ltd., supra*; *Re Bell Bros., supra.*

[1] *Re Bell Bros., supra.*

[2] *Duke of Sutherland* v. *British Dominions, etc., Corporation* [1926] Ch. 746.

[3] As to the exercise of a discretion on a wrong basis, see *Dean* v. *Prince* [1954] Ch. 409.

[4] *Berry and Stewart* v. *Tottenham Hotspur Football, etc., Co.* [1935] Ch. 718. The references to "interrogatories" arise from English court procedure. Similar principles would apply in Scotland, where a proof would be allowed limited to averments of corruption, etc., but not a general inquiry into the reasons for refusal where the directors were given absolute discretion; see *Stewart* v. *James Keiller & Sons Ltd. supra.*

[5] *Re Bede S.S. Co.* [1917] 1 Ch. 123.

[6] *Sutton* v. *English and Colonial Produce Co.* [1902] 2 Ch. 502.

[7] *Re Hackney Pavilion* [1924] 1 Ch. 276; approved in *Moodie* v. *Shepherd (Bookbinders) Ltd.* [1949] 2 All E.R. 1044 (H.L.); 1950 S.C. (H.L.) 60; 1950 S.L.T. 90.

[8] *Re Copal Varnish Co.* [1917] 2 Ch. 349.

[9] *Re Swaledale Cleaners Ltd.* [1968] 1 W.L.R. 1710. (In this case the power to refuse the transfer was held to have been lost by unreasonable delay, which extended over four months); *Property Investment Co. of Scotland* v. *Duncan* 1887, 14 R. 299.

[10] *Ibid.* See para. 39–02, *ante*; *sed quaere Property Investment Co. of Scotland* v. *Duncan, supra*, discussed in para. 39–02, *ante*.

registration which is illegal and unenforceable (that the company must purchase any shares whose transfer is refused), does not deprive the directors of that right.[11]

39–17 POWER TO REPUDIATE REGISTERED TRANSFER. Where the articles contain a clause empowering the directors to reject a transferee of whom they do not approve, and a holder of partly paid-up shares has improperly induced the directors to pass and register a transfer which but for his conduct they would have refused to register, the company on discovering the facts may repudiate the registration,[12] and where the directors have a discretion as to registering transfers and the consideration is misstated, the company, on discovering the facts, may repudiate the transfer and restore the transferor's name to the register.[13] But where the articles contain no clause authorising the directors to reject a transferee, a shareholder may at the last moment before liquidation, and for the express purpose of escaping liability, transfer his partly paid shares to a transferee even though he be impecunious, and may compel the directors to register that transfer, provided that it is an out-and-out transfer, reserving to the transferor no beneficial right to the shares, direct or indirect.[14] Whether the transfer is of that character is a question of fact.[15]

Where the directors refuse to register a transfer, the company must inform the transferee within two months of the deposit of the transfer[16]: but it is not required to inform the transferor.[17]

Restrictions on the right of transfer may restrict a mortgagee's power of sale over the shares since he can have no right of transfer that is forbidden to members.[18] Registration by the secretary without the authority of the directors can be repudiated by them.[19]

One of several transferors revoking his signature on mere suspicion of a breach of trust does not justify an absolute refusal to register. The court stated that in such circumstances it was the duty of the company to require the transferor who purported to revoke his signature within a reasonable time to take proceedings to prevent the registration: and if he failed to do so, the company should register the transfer.[20]

A party aggrieved by a refusal to register a transfer should proceed by motion or summons to rectify the register.[21] A winding-up petition is not

---

[11] *Moir* v. *Duff & Co.* 1900, 2 F. 1265.
[12] *De Pass's Case* (1859) 4 De G. & J. 544; *Lindlar's Case* [1910] 1 Ch. 312, 321–322.
[13] *Snow's Case* (1871) 19 W.R. 1057; *sub nom. Rogers' Case*, 25 L.T. 406; *cf. Weston's Case* (1868) L.R. 4 Ch. 20, 27, where there was no misrepresentation.
[14] He will not, however, thereby escape liability as a B List contributory: paras. 85–45, 86–27 and 87–39, *post*.
[15] *Hyam's Case* [1859] 1 De G.F. & J. 75; *Costello's Case* (1860) 2 De G.F. & J. 302; *De Pass's Case* (1859) 4 De G. & J. 544; *Lindlar's Case* [1910] 1 Ch. 312.
[16] s. 78. See also *Re Swaledale Cleaners Ltd.* [1968] 1 W.L.R. 1710; para. 39–02, *ante*.
[17] *Gustard's Case* (1869) L.R. 8 Eq. 438.
[18] *Hunter* v. *Hunter* [1936] A.C. 222.
[19] *Chida Mines* v. *Anderson* (1905) 22 T.L.R. 27.
[20] *Grundy* v. *Briggs* [1901] 1 Ch. 444.
[21] See para. 50–14, *post*.

the appropriate remedy, and the presentation of such a petition will be restrained as an abuse of the process of the court.[22]

As to forged transfers, see paragraph 39–29, *post*.

Form of transfer

39–18 Section 75 of the 1948 Act requires a "proper instrument of transfer" to be delivered to the company before a transfer of shares can be registered. In the case of a transfer of fully paid shares this may be either in the form set out in the Stock Transfer Act 1963 or in the form specified in the articles, so long as this form satisfies the requirements of the 1963 Act, or in the special forms for transfers within the Stock Exchange.[23] In the case of partly paid shares, the requirements of the articles must be observed, otherwise the company is entitled to refuse to register the transfer. If the company registers the transfer it need not comply with the formalities prescribed by the articles, provided that it is an instrument which will attract stamp duty.[24]

39–19 FULLY PAID SHARES. Under section 1 of the Stock Transfer Act 1963, fully paid registered securities issued by a company incorporated under the Companies Acts, other than a company limited by guarantee or an unlimited company, may be transferred by an instrument under hand in the form set out in Schedule 1 to the Act.[25] This *stock transfer form* need be executed only by the transferor and need not be attested. It must show particulars of the consideration, the description and number or amount of the securities, the full name(s) of the registered holder(s), and the full name and address of the transferee.

Where securities are sold on a prescribed stock exchange[26] to a number of different transferees, the transferor need prepare only one stock transfer form from which he will omit the particulars of the consideration and the names and addresses of the transferees. These particulars will then be supplied by the selling broker, who will prepare *brokers' transfers*, in the form set out in Schedule 2 to the Act,[27] in favour of each transferee, identifying the stock transfer and specifying the securities to which each instrument relates and the consideration paid for those securities. Where this procedure is followed, any person to whom the blank stock transfer form is delivered pursuant to the transfer must not part with possession of it, or allow it to leave Great Britain, before the name of the transferee has been inserted.[28]

---

22 *Charles Forte Investments Ltd.* v. *Amanda* [1964] Ch. 240.
23 See para. 39–30, *post*.
24 *Re Paradise Motor Company Ltd.* [1968] 1 W.L.R. 1125.
25 See Vol. II, Part A.
26 The prescribed stock exchange is now the Stock Exchange; Stock Transfer (Recognised Stock Exchanges) Order 1973 (S.I. 1973/536).
27 See Vol. II, Part A.
28 Finance Act 1963, s. 67; Registered Securities (Completion of Blank Transfers) Order 1963 (S.I. 1963 No. 1743).

The procedure for transfer laid down by the Stock Transfer Act 1963 may be followed notwithstanding any additional requirements prescribed by the articles of a company, but an instrument executed in the form specified in the articles is still perfectly valid, provided that it complies with the requirements as to execution and contents of a stock transfer under the Act (ss. 1 (3), 2 (1)). As to the validity of such transfers in Scotland, see section 2 (4) of the Act.[29]

39–20 PARTLY PAID SHARES. The Stock Transfer Act 1963 has no application to the transfer of partly paid shares, and these remain subject to the form specified in the articles. These often require the transfer to be made "in the usual or common form" (art. 28). It is thought that this requirement may now be satisfied by a transfer in the form set out in Schedule 1 to the Stock Transfer Act.[30] The obligation to prepare the transfer is, as a general rule, on the purchaser.[31]

Where the regulations require a transfer to be under hand, the fact that it is under seal does not make it the less effective on the principle that the greater includes the lesser.[32]

If a deed is required, it must in English law be duly signed, sealed and delivered.[33] A printed circle with the words "place for seal" is not equivalent to a seal.[34] Where a transferor leaves any portion blank, it will not be a valid deed if the blanks are later filled in unless he redelivers the deed.[35] In Scots law the equivalent requirement would be for a probative deed duly delivered, since sealing (by individuals) has no part in the Scots law of execution of deeds.[36]

39–21 IRREGULARITIES OF FORM. The directors may refuse to register if the prescribed form is not substantially followed, but they may waive any irregularity and should not be too technical. Thus, where the articles required a transfer to be "in the usual common form," according to which the address of the transferor and the distinctive number of the shares should appear, and the transfer tendered omitted these particulars, but was accompanied by the transferor's share certificate giving the omitted particulars, it was held that the transfer should be registered.[37] A party to a transfer (or a successor to his interest) cannot, apart from exceptional circumstances, seek to object to the transfer on the ground that it was irregular in form, if he has in fact signed it.[38]

---

[29] Vol. II, Part A.
[30] Vol. II, Part A. As to the form of transfer commonly in use prior to the 1963 Act, see Palmer's *Company Law* (20th ed.), p. 345.
[31] *Birkett* v. *Cowper-Coles* (1919) 35 T.L.R. 298.
[32] *Ortigosa* v. *Brown, Janson & Co.* (1878) 38 L.T. 145.
[33] *Powell* v. *London and Provincial Bank* [1893] 2 Ch. 555.
[34] *Re Balkis Consolidated Co.* (1888) 36 W.R. 392.
[35] *Société Générale de Paris* v. *Walker* (1885) 11 App.Cas. 20, 30.
[36] *Clydesdale Bank (Moore Place) Nominees Ltd.* v. *Snodgrass* 1939, S.C. 805; 1940 S.L.T. 46.
[37] *Re Letheby and Christopher Ltd., Jones's Case* [1904] 1 Ch. 815.
[38] *Smellie's Trs.* v. *Smellie* 1953, S.L.T. (Notes) 21.

Where there are joint holders, a transfer, to be effective, must be executed by all. If the signature of anyone be forged, the transfer will be void.[39]

By section 75 of the 1948 Act it is illegal for a company to register a transfer of shares unless a proper instrument of transfer has been delivered. The object of this is to prevent the evasion of stamp duty, and the directors may refuse to register a transfer which is not duly stamped, since an unstamped transfer is of no validity at law (s. 80 (1), second paragraph). This view of section 75 prompted the decision in *Re Paradise Motor Company Ltd.*[40] that a "proper instrument of transfer" within the meaning of that section is any instrument which will attract stamp duty. The directors may go behind the consideration shown on the transfer to the true consideration if they have reason to suspect that the true consideration has not been shown.[41] Any officer who registers a transfer which has not been duly stamped is liable to a fine of £10.[42]

NO INSTRUMENT OF TRANSFER IN CASE OF TRANSMISSION. Section 75 further provides that no transfer shall be required in respect of shares to which any person has become entitled by operation of law.[43] But where a company's articles provided that the widow of a deceased member should be entitled to the shares of the deceased, this did not enable the company to register her without a proper transfer, since the persons entitled by operation of law were the personal representatives and not the widow.[44]

Practice observed on transfer

39–22 The instrument of transfer, when executed by the transferor, is handed to the tranferee or his broker, together with the share certificates, and is then deposited with the company for registration (but see paras. 39–30, *post*). It will not be necessary for the transferee to execute the transfer, unless the transfer is of partly paid shares and the company's articles expressly require such execution.

Delivery of certificates

A seller of shares is bound, if the contract fixes no date, to deliver the certificates within a reasonable time, and the reasonableness of the time cannot depend upon circumstances which are unknown to the buyer and are not disclosed to him by the seller.[45]

---

39 *Barton* v. *L. & N.W. Ry.* (1889) 24 Q.B.D. 77.
40 [1968] 1 W.L.R. 1125.
41 *Maynard* v. *Consolidated Kent Collieries Corporation* [1903] 2 K.B. 121; *Conybear* v. *British Briquettes* [1937]) 4 All E.R. 191.
42 Stamp Act 1891, s. 17.
43 See Transmission, para. 39–34, *post*.
44 *Re Greene* [1949] Ch. 333.
45 *De Waal* v. *Adler* (1886) 12 App.Cas. 141.

Investigation by company before registration

A company is not bound to register a transfer at once. It may inquire, *e.g.* as to the authenticity of the transfer.[46] Where a transfer purports to be executed or signed by the agent of the transferor, the directors are entitled to call for evidence of authority.

Requirements as to time

39–23 The company shall, within two months after the date on which the transfer is lodged with it,[47] complete and have ready for delivery the share certificate unless the conditions of issue of the shares otherwise provide (1948 Act, s. 80 (1)) or the transfer is to a stock exchange nominee, Sepon Ltd.[48] If the company refuses the registration, notice of the refusal has to be sent likewise within two months (1948 Act, s. 78).[49] Non-compliance with these provisions renders the company and every officer in default liable to an initial fine or after continued contravention a default fine.

Under the Stock Exchange Rules the share certificate has to be issued within 14 days, instead of two months.[50]

Stamp duties

39–24 A transfer of shares must, on principle, be duly impressed with *ad valorem* stamp duty at the rate of £2 per cent. (Finance Act 1974) but certain non-residents and charities continue to pay at the lower rate of £1 per cent.[51] There are two sets of circumstances in which, although no consideration passes, *ad valorem* duty is payable, *viz*.

(1) Transfer by way of gift *inter vivos*.[52]

(2) Transfer from an executor to a beneficiary in satisfaction of a pecuniary bequest.

Such transfers must be distinguished from those for which the revenue will permit a rate of stamp duty at less than the full *ad valorem* duty. Such transfers can be classified under four main headings, *viz*.

(a) Transfers for a nominal consideration. These are transfers which do not actually constitute a sale, *e.g.* transfers to or from a mere nominee of the transferor where no beneficial interest in the shares passes. The stamp duty payable on transfers for a nominal consideration is at the fixed rate of 50 pence.

---

[46] *Société Générale de Paris* v. *Walker* (1885) 11 App.Cas. 20, 41; *Ireland* v. *Hart* [1902] 1 Ch. 522; *Re Ottos Kopje Diamond Mines* [1893] 1 Ch. 618.

[47] Where the shares have been transferred by means of a stock transfer and a brokers' transfer, the date to be taken is that on which the later of these documents is lodged with the company: Stock Transfer Act 1963, s. 2 (3) (*b*).

[48] Stock Exchange (Completion of Bargains) Act 1976. See para. 39–30, *post*.

[49] *Cf.* the time limit on the exercise of the power to refuse a transfer; *Re Swaledale Cleaners Ltd.* [1968] 1 W.L.R. 1125, para. 39–02, *ante*.

[50] *Admission of Securities to Listing*, Chap. 2, para. 17.

[51] Stamp Act 1891, Sched. I (conveyance or transfer on sale); Finance Act 1963, s. 55 and Sched. 11; see also Finance Act 1965, s. 90, which was introduced to nullify the decision in *Wm. Cory & Son Ltd.* v. *I.R.C.* [1965] A.C. 1088. See B. J. Sims and E. M. E. Sims, *Sergeant on Stamp Duties* (6th ed., 1972), pp. 62 *et seq*.

[52] Finance (1909–10) Act 1910, s. 74.

(b) Transfers under section 42 of the Finance Act 1920. Circumstances often arise in dealings on the Stock Exchange where a jobber who has purchased shares from a broker may not have resold the shares. If the selling broker wishes to complete the transaction on behalf of his client, the shares will be transferred to the jobber or his nominee (but see para. 39–30, *post*). As it is the intention of the jobber to sell the shares to a bona fide purchaser, section 42 of the Finance Act 1920 provides that the transfer of the shares into the jobber's own name need only be stamped at the fixed rate of 50 pence, provided that the jobber transfers the shares to the bona fide purchaser within two months.[53] If the jobber fails to dispose of the shares within two months, then he must pay the full *ad valorem* stamp duty on the value of the shares. Such transfers bear the Inland Revenue "Supplementary Stamp" containing the words "Finance Act 1920, s. 42" in addition to the 50 pence duty stamp.[54]

With effect from 1980–81 section 42 has been extended to certain dealers in unlisted securities of United Kingdom companies in the same way as it applies to jobbers.[55] These persons include stock exchange brokers and exempted dealers under the Prevention of Fraud (Investments) Act 1958.[56]

(c) Domestic transfers. Where the transferor retains an interest in the securities and no consideration passes, the stamp duty should be adjudicated and is based on the value of the interest transferred, thus it may be on one-half of the market value of the shares concerned, *e.g.* where a man transfers shares out of his name into the joint names of himself and his wife.[57]

(d) Transfer between associated companies. Under section 42 of the Finance Act 1930, as amended by the Finance Act 1967, s. 27, particularly subsection (2), stamp duty is not charged on any instrument if the Commissioners are satisfied that the effect thereof is to convey or transfer a beneficial interest in property from one body corporate to another, and that the bodies in question are associated, that is to say, one is beneficial owner of not less than 90 per cent. of the issued share capital of the other, or a third such body is beneficial owner of not less than 90 per cent. of the issued share capital of each. Such beneficial ownership may be either direct or through another body corporate or other bodies corporate or partly the one and partly the other. When the share capital is divided into two or

---

[53] A transfer by a jobber or his nominee to a stock exchange nominee is to be regarded, as a transfer to a bona fide purchaser for the purposes of s. 42: F.A. 1976, s. 127 (3). See para. 39–30, *post*.

[54] See Finance Act 1920, s. 42.

[55] F.A. 1920, s. 42, as amended by F.A. 1980, s. 100.

[56] F.A. 1920, s. 42 (3), as amended by F.A. 1980, s. 100 (4).

[57] Revocable settlements were formerly not liable to *ad valorem* duty though the right to revoke could later be relinquished. Finance Act 1965, s. 90 (5), nullifies this device though the duty paid can be reclaimed if revocation takes place within two years.

more classes of shares, the words of the statute "90 per cent. of the issued share capital" refer to the nominal value of the share capital and not to the actual value of the shares as attributed to them at the Stock Exchange or elsewhere, because the concept of share capital in the Companies Act 1948 is wholly removed from the fluctuating valuation of the shares.[58]

39–25 It is the responsibility of the company to ensure that the consideration stated in the transfer is reasonable, having regard to the current market price of the shares at the time the transfer is lodged for registration or, in cases where the shares are not quoted, on other information.[59] On being satisfied that the consideration stated is reasonable, then the registering authority must see that the proper stamp duty has been paid in respect of the consideration stated. Registering authorities are liable to account to the Inland Revenue for any loss of tax arising by reason of an instrument of transfer being improperly stamped.

Where securities are transferred by means of a stock transfer and a brokers' transfer, the brokers' transfer is deemed to be the conveyance or transfer for the purposes of stamp duty.[60]

To facilitate the new stock exchange system of transfers[61] section 127 (1) of the Finance Act 1976 provides that no stamp duty shall be payable on any transfer to a stock exchange nominee (as designated) which is executed for the purpose of a stock exchange transaction (see Stock Transfer Act 1963, s. 4). A transfer from the nominee to a jobber or his nominee is to be stamped as a sale at market value (s. 27 (2)). Sepon Ltd. has been designated as a stock exchange nominee for this purpose by the Stock Exchange (Designation of Nominees) Stamp Duty Order 1979 (S.I. 1979 No. 370).

Apart from revenue considerations, directors cannot safely register a transfer not duly stamped, for the transfer in such a case not being available as evidence for any purpose in a court of justice,[62] the directors could not use it to justify the register.[63] It makes no difference that the stamp is sufficient on the face consideration, if the directors know that such consideration is less than the real consideration.[64]

Certification of transfers

39–26 When the holder of shares executes a transfer of them, it is for the transferee, as the party mainly concerned, to get the transfer registered, and in order to do this he must be prepared to hand over, or to procure

[58] *Canada Safeway Ltd.* v. *I.R.C.* [1973] Ch. 374.
[59] *e.g.* in the case of a private company, the value of the shares may be calculated on the break-up value of the company, but no "rule of thumb or accountancy principle [limits] the possible basis of calculation to be adopted": *Dean* v. *Prince* [1954] Ch. 409, 419 (C.A.).
[60] Stock Transfer Act 1963, s. 2 (3) (*c*).
[61] See para. 39–30, *post*.
[62] Stamp Act 1891, s. 14 (*a*).
[63] *Maynard* v. *Consolidated Kent Collieries Corporation Ltd.* [1903] 2 K.B. 121.
[64] *Ibid.*

someone else to hand over, to the company the tranferor's share certificate. If the certificate comprises the shares transferred and no more, it is handed over with the transfer to the transferee, and can then be delivered by him to the company. If the certificate includes other shares which are not transferred by the instrument of transfer or if the certificate is in respect of shares sold to more than one transferee, the transferor lodges his certificate with the company, and the company's secretary, at the request of the transferor or his broker, certificates the transfer with a statement to the effect that a certificate in respect of the shares in the transfer has been lodged with the company. This process is known as "certification."[65]

The Stock Transfer Act 1963 has not affected the need for certification, and the two forms of transfer provided for by the Act[66] include a space for certification in the top right hand corner.[67] However, it is now more usual for the certification to be effected by The Stock Exchange under its computerised settlement system (see para. 39–30, *post*).

The *ratio* of the certification procedure is commercial caution: the transferor is not willing to deliver to the transferee a share certificate referring to more shares than the latter has bought, and the transferee is not prepared to part with the price unless he knows that the transferor no longer has the certificate and can defeat his title by a fraudulent transfer to and registration of a third party acquiring the shares in good faith.

Section 79 of the 1980 Act enacts that certification shall be taken as a representation by the company to any person acting on the faith of it that there have been produced to the company such documents as on the face of them show a prima facie title to the shares. It is not, however, a representation that the transferor has any title to the shares.

39–27 Where any person acts on the faith of a false certification made fraudulently or negligently the company will be liable for the false certification. But this only applies where the person certificating is authorised by the company to do so.[68] If there is no such authority the company will not be liable and the transferee cannot rely on the doctrine *omnia praesumuntur rite esse acta* to establish liability. The transferee is, however, assisted by a statutory presumption which applies when the certification is signed: in this case it is presumed that it was signed by a duly authorised person, and the onus of proving that the person who signed the certification was not authorised is on the company (s. 79 (3) (*c*)).[69]

---

[65] For the rules of the Stock Exchange, see *Admission of Securities to Listing*, Chap. 2, para. 11. [66] See para. 39–18, *ante*.

[67] For these forms, see Vol II, Part A.

[68] Or where he is so authorised on behalf of a company authorised to certificate, *e.g.* the company's registrars or secretaries if they happen to be a company themselves (s. 79 (3) (*b*) (ii)). It should, however, be noted that the secretary (or registrar) of a company is not, *virtute officii*, authorised to certificate; *cf. Bishop* v. *Balkis Consolidated Co.* (1890) 25 Q.B.D. 512; *quaere* whether this is still good law after the decision in *Panorama Developments (Guildford)* v. *Fidelis Furnishing Fabrics Ltd.* [1971] 2 Q.B. 711; see Chap. 67, *post*.

[69] The provisions of this section which were introduced by the Companies Act 1947 largely reverse the decisions of the House of Lords in *George Whitechurch Ltd.* v. *Cavanagh* [1902] A.C. 117 and *Kleinwort Sons & Co.* v. *Associated Automatic Corporation* (1934) 151 L.T. 1.

These provisions apply equally to certification on the transfer of debentures.

If the company, after certificating, returns the certificate by mistake to the transferor, and the transferor pledges it in fraud of the transferee, this, it seems, gives the pledgee no ground of action against the company.[69a]

A transfer certificated as above is, by the rules of the Stock Exchange, accepted as good delivery of the shares to a purchaser without delivery of the certificate.[70] But, irrespective of these rules, by general practice a transferee requires the share certificate or a certificated transfer in order to comply with the articles of the company, which usually provide for the production of the certificate before a transfer will be registered.

The Stock Exchange will certificate transfers relating to any quoted security, thus obviating the necessity for brokers taking or posting the transfers to the offices of the respective companies. In certificating transfers The Stock Exchange is not an agent of the company. Therefore no liability can attach to the company by reason of such certification.

Transfers during winding up

39–28 Where the winding up is compulsory or under supervision, transfers of shares (but not of debentures) during the winding up are avoided by section 227 of the 1948 Act unless sanctioned by the court, and the court will not, if a transfer is incomplete by reason of want of registration at the commencement of the winding up, put the buyer on the register.[71]

A voluntary liquidator has power, under section 282, to register a transfer after winding up,[72] and the transfer, if registered, has full effect. The transferee in such a case ought to be placed on the A list of contributories, the transferor on the B list. But registration is no longer a right of the transferee: the liquidator can refuse to register and the transferee cannot compel registration. The liquidator may sanction the transfer upon conditions, and if he does so he can refuse to register the transfer until those conditions are complied with.

It is doubtful whether a voluntary liquidator can rectify *nunc pro tunc*, although the court can.[73]

Forged transfers

39–29 If a forged transfer is presented for registration and the company acts upon it, it may incur serious liability, for the registration of the transfer

[69a] *Longman* v. *Bath Electric Tramways* [1905] 1 Ch. 646.
[70] *Admission of Securities to Listing*, Chap. 2, para. 11.
[71] *Emmerson's Case* (1866) 1 Ch.App. 433; *Re Onward Building Society* [1891] 2 Q.B. 463; *Sullivan* v. *Henderson* (1972) 116 S.J. 969 (the court may even refuse specific performance as between a seller and a buyer of the shares, but may admit an action for damages for non-delivery). See also *Nelson Mitchell* v. *City of Glasgow Bank* 1879, 6 R. (H.L.) 66.
[72] *Re National Bank of Wales* [1897] 1 Ch. 298 (C.A.).
[73] *Re Sussex Brick Co.* [1904] 1 Ch. 598.

does not defeat the title of the true owner, and he has a right to require the company to restore his name to the register.[74] The company may, on discovering the forgery, remove the name of the transferee from the register; it is not estopped by the registration.[75] But, if it has issued to the transferee a share certificate, and a bona fide buyer from him has acted thereon, the company may be liable in damages.[76]

Where, however, the certificate has been issued and sealed by the secretary fraudulently, without the authority of the directors and for his own purposes, it has been held that the company is not estopped.[77]

A person, claiming under a forged transfer, who sends in and procures registration of the transfer and the issue of a fresh certificate is bound, though acting in good faith, to indemnify the company.[78] On the same principle, where a stockbroker, acting innocently under a forged power of attorney from one of two trustees of stock, had induced the Bank of England to transfer the stock, he was held liable to indemnify the Bank as having impliedly warranted his authority to the Bank.[79] Similarly where a firm of stockbrokers presented a forged transfer for registration in innocence they were held liable to indemnify the company—the principle is not limited to a person acting on his own behalf.[80] Under the Civil Liability (Contribution) Act 1978, s. 2 (1), however, the company may not be able to recover in full if it fails to check the signatures on the transfer against any specimen ones it may possess, or otherwise can be said to be partly responsible for the loss.[81]

In order to minimise the danger incident to the registration of transfers, some companies, upon the deposit of a transfer, write to the transferor a letter informing him of the deposit of the transfer, and stating that it will be registered unless, by return of post, he objects. This course of procedure operates as a practical safeguard, but, in adopting it, a company does not relieve itself of its obligation to ascertain the authenticity of the deposited transfer. The transferor may not receive the notice, and, even if he does receive it, he is not bound to reply; by not replying, he does not estop himself from asserting his rights at some subsequent period.[82] However, notification to the transferor is not a legal requirement, and many companies do not give such notice.

Companies can, in some cases, pay compensation under the Forged

---

[74] *Davis* v. *Bank of England* (1824) 2 Bing. 393; *Sloman* v. *Bank of England* (1845) 14 Sim. 475; *Barton* v. *L. & N.W. Ry.* (1888) 38 Ch.D. 144, 149.
[75] *Simm* v. *Anglo-American, etc., Co.* (1879) 5 Q.B.D. 188, 214.
[76] *Re Bahia and San Francisco Ry.* (1868) L.R. 3 Q.B. 584, 595; *Balkis Consolidated Co.* v. *Tomkinson* [1893] A.C. 396; *Bloomenthal* v. *Ford* [1897] A.C. 156; see para. 37–09, *ante*.
[77] *Ruben* v. *Great Fingall Consolidated* [1906] A.C. 439, overruling *Shaw* v. *Port Philip, etc., Mining Co.* (1884) 13 Q.B.D. 103.
[78] *Sheffield Corporation* v. *Barclay* [1905] A.C. 392 (H.L.); *Welch* v. *Bank of England* [1955] Ch. 508.
[79] *Starkey* v. *Bank of England* [1903] A.C. 114; *Oliver* v. *Bank of England* [1902] 1 Ch. 610; *Welch* v. *Bank of England* [1955] Ch. 508.
[80] *Yeung* v. *Hong Kong and Shanghai Banking Corpn.* [1980] 2 All E.R. 599.
[81] *Ibid.* at pp. 607–608, *per* Lord Scarman.
[82] *Barton* v. *L. & N.W. Ry.* (1889) 24 Q.B.D. 77.

Transfer Acts 1891 and 1892. These Acts, however, do not give any *right* to compensation; they merely give the company power to pay.[83]

Transfers of shares within The Stock Exchange

39–30 The Stock Exchange has replaced its traditional method of transaction between jobbers and brokers with a new computerised system. This involves the transfer of all shares bought and sold on the market to a nominee company, Sepon Ltd., to hold the legal title until the transfer to the ultimate purchaser. It is hoped thereby to avoid the present peak of work centred on account days. To facilitate this change the Stock Exchange (Completion of Bargains) Act 1976 provided for three changes to the general law. By the Stock Transfer Act 1982, the transfer by a computerised system has been extended to specified other securities, including securities issued by H.M. Government in the United Kingdom and by public authorities, nationalised industries and local authorities in the United Kingdom.

First, if a share is allotted or transferred to Sepon Ltd., which has been designated as a stock exchange nominee for this purpose by the Secretary of State, under section 7 of the Act, by virtue of the Stock Exchange (Designation of Nominees) Order 1979[84] there is no obligation on the company to issue it with a share certificate within two months required by section 80 of the 1948 Act (s. 1).

Secondly, the Stock Transfer Act 1963 is extended to allow the Treasury to designate new approved forms of transfer to allow for the nominee company (s. 6). This power has been exercised by the Stock Exchange (Addition of Forms) Order 1979.[85]

Thirdly, trustees and personal representatives are exempted from any action for breach of trust arising out of paying for shares from a stock exchange nominee before a transfer to them is effected or from transferring shares to such a nominee before the price is paid to them, provided that the sale is otherwise authorised (s. 5). The Stock Exchange (Completion of Bargains) Act 1976 came into force on February 12, 1979, by virtue of the Stock Exchange (Completion of Bargains) Act 1976 (Commencement) Order 1979.[86]

Share warrants to bearer

39–31 IN GENERAL. Under section 83[87] a company is empowered, if so authorised by its articles, to issue, with respect to any share which is fully paid

---

[83] Few companies have adopted the facilities under these Acts. Most companies cover the risk of forged share transfers by insurance, either at Lloyd's or with the larger insurance companies.

[84] S.I. 1979 No. 238.

[85] S.I. 1979 No. 277.

[86] ss. 1 and 2 of the 1976 Act were extended to certain unregistered companies by the Companies (Unregistered Companies) (Completion of Stock Exchange Bargains) Regulations 1980 (S.I. 1980 No. 926).

[87] The Act of 1862 made no provision for the creation of shares to bearer. Shares of this description were first permitted by the Companies Act 1867, and the provisions there relating to them are re-enacted in s. 83 of the 1948 Act.

up, or with respect to stock, a warrant under the common seal stating that the bearer of the warrant is entitled to the share or shares or stock therein specified. The section also empowers the company to provide, by coupons or otherwise, for the payment of future dividends.

A share warrant entitles the bearer of the warrant to the shares or stock specified in it, and such shares or stock may be transferred by delivery of the share warrant. Share warrants to bearer are always treated as negotiable instruments. Whether they are so or not under the Act is not quite clear, but there is a valid mercantile custom to treat them as negotiable which is as effective as a statutory provision.[88]

When a share warrant is issued, the name of the prior holder of the share is struck out of the register of members and particulars entered of the issue of the warrant, the shares included in the warrant, distinguishing each share by its number, if it has a number,[89] and the date of the issue of the warrant (1948 Act, s. 112). Hence, whilst the share warrant is outstanding there will be no registered holder, but if the articles so provide, the bearer of a share warrant may be deemed to be a member of the company within the meaning of the Act, either to the full extent or for any purposes defined in the articles.[90]

The 1948 Act provides in section 124 and the Sixth Schedule, para. 3 (*j*), for the particulars to be contained in the annual summary where share warrants have been issued, and sections 15 and 20 of the Theft Act 1968[91] provide penalties for forgery and personation.

Holding a share warrant will not qualify a director where a share qualification is required (1948 Act, s. 182 (2)).

The right to vote in respect of bearer shares is usually qualified by providing for the deposit beforehand of the warrant.

Dividends payable on bearer shares are provided for by means of numbered coupons attached to the share warrant; and one of these is given up to the company for each dividend declared.

39–32 STAMP DUTIES. No stamp duty is payable on the transfer of share warrants, but they are liable to duty when they are issued.[92]

Penalties are provided for issuing warrants which are not duly stamped (Stamp Act 1891, s. 107).

EXCHANGE CONTROL ACT 1947. The former restrictions imposed by this Act[93] were lifted with effect from October 24, 1979.[94] Treasury permission

---

88 *Webb, Hale & Co.* v. *Alexandria Water Co.* (1905) 21 T.L.R. 572.
89 Subject to s. 74, proviso; see para. 33–04, *ante*.
90 s. 112 (5).
91 The penal section in Scotland is s. 85 of the Companies Act 1948.
92 See para. 39–24, *ante*.
93 Exchange Control Act 1947, s. 10. It should be noted that the restriction applied not only to the United Kingdom but likewise to the issue of bearer certificates or coupons outside the United Kingdom by a person resident in the United Kingdom. The section likewise prohibited, without Treasury consent, the alteration of an existing document into a bearer certificate or coupon.
94 Exchange Control (General Exemption) Order 1979 (S.I. 1979 No. 1660).

is no longer required for share warrants—which become fully negotiable again.

Transfers contrary to existing contractual interests[95]

39–33 If the shares have been acquired by means of a loan which requires payment of the debt out of specific property including those shares, such a contract is enforceable by a grant of specific performance and creates an equitable interest in the shares in favour of the lender. A subsequent equitable mortgagee of the shares, who proposes to deal with the shares in such a way as to cause a breach of that contract will be restrained by injunction if he acquired them with actual knowledge of the contract. Constructive notice will not, however, suffice: *Swiss Bank Corporation* v. *Lloyds Bank Ltd.*[96] In that case the plaintiff bank made a loan in Swiss francs to I.F.T. to enable them to purchase foreign securities. The Bank of England insisted on stringent exchange control restrictions, including a provision that the securities were to be held in a separate account and if they were sold the loan was to be repaid out of the proceeds. In the event I.F.T. transferred the securities to the defendant bank in pursuance of a charge and they were later sold for dollars which in turn were sold for sterling. On the facts both the House of Lords and the Court of Appeal held that no binding equitable charge had arisen but reaffirmed the general rule.

Transmission of shares

Personal representatives

39–34 IN GENERAL. Where a member of a company dies, his shares vest in his executors or administrators, and the estate is liable for calls if the shares are not fully paid.[97] The executors or administrators, in whom shares have so become vested, are entitled to be registered as the holders of the shares, in the absence of provisions in the articles to the contrary[98]; but the executors or administrators do not *ipso facto* become members of the company, nor is the company entitled, without their consent, to register them as members.[99] Such registration (as members) may involve them in personal liability,[1] and to justify it there must be a distinct request for registration on their part.[2] If executors accept new shares offered to them in that capacity they will be personally liable.[3] Where registered as mem-

[95] This paragraph is not applicable in Scots law.
[96] [1980] 2 All E.R. 419 (C.A.); affd. [1981] 2 All E.R. (H.L.); reversing [1978] 2 All E.R. 853. See [1978] J.B.L. 369.
[97] *Baird's Case* (1870) 5 Ch.App. 725.
[98] *Scott* v. *Scott (London) Ltd.* [1940] Ch. 794; *Safeguard Industrial Investments Ltd.* v. *National Westminster Bank Ltd.* [1980] 3 All E.R. 849.
[99] *Stewart* v. *James Keiller & Sons* 1902, 4 F. 657.
[1] *Re Cheshire Banking Co., Duff's Executor's Case* (1886) 32 Ch.D. 301.
[2] *Buchan's Case* (1879) 4 App.Cas. 549, 588; see also *Re Jermyn Street Turkish Baths Ltd.* [1970] 1 W.L.R. 1194, 1205, where Pennycuick J. observed that no particular form is required by statute for the registration of personal representatives, and, unless provided otherwise by the articles, all that is needed is a "distinct and intelligent request" to that effect.
[3] *Re Leeds Banking Co., Fearnside and Dean's Case, Dobson's Case* (1865) L.R. 1 Ch. 231.

bers, there should be a clean registration, without any reference to their representative capacity. They may choose the order in which their names are to stand.[4] Such a registration is not a transfer, and no instrument of transfer is necessary (1948 Act, s. 75). The company is bound to accept the production of probate, letters of administration or confirmation of executors, etc., as sufficient evidence of their title (1948 Act, s. 82).

Section 76 of the 1948 Act enables the personal representatives of a deceased member, without themselves becoming registered, to transfer the shares of the deceased, and the provision is commonly repeated in the articles.[5] This power is frequently exercised by the personal representatives, particularly when the shares are not fully paid up.

One of two executors registered as shareholders cannot transfer: all must concur.[6] Executors can transfer to one of themselves.[7]

39–35 The articles usually provide that the personal representatives may elect (art. 30), or may be required by the directors to elect (art. 32, proviso), to be registered themselves as members or to transfer the shares of the deceased. If they decide in favour of the former alternative, they have to give the company notice in writing signed by them stating that they so elect; if they adopt the latter alternative, they have to execute a transfer. Any restrictions on the transfer of shares laid down in the articles are usually declared to be applicable to such notice or transfer (art. 31), but these restrictions must be so construed as not unreasonably to prevent shareholders from fairly and reasonably exercising their powers as members of the company.[8] Any such restrictions may only be exercised by a properly constituted board of directors.[9] If the personal representatives do not comply within 90 days with the request of the directors to elect, the directors are often empowered to withhold the payment of all dividends and other moneys payable on the shares until the request is complied with (art. 32, proviso).

In *Re Hackney Pavilion Ltd.*,[10] where the articles provided that a person becoming entitled on the death of a member should have the right to be registered, but the directors should have the right to decline registration, and the board were equally divided, it was held that the right to be registered was absolute.

A provision in the articles that on the death of a director (who leaves a wife him surviving) his shares shall be "deemed to have passed" to the wife

---

[4] *Re Saunders & Co.* [1908] 1 Ch. 415.
[5] See arts. 29–32.
[6] *Barton* v. *North Staffordshire Ry.* (1888) 38 Ch.D. 458; *Barton* v. *L. & N.W. Ry.* (1889) 24 Q.B.D. 77.
[7] *Grundy* v. *Briggs* [1910] 1 Ch. 444.
[8] *Re Hobson, Houghton & Co.* [1929] 1 Ch. 300. As to restrictions on transfer upon the death of a member, see para. 39–14, *ante*, and cases there cited. For the dangers of not including articles 30–32 see *Safeguard Industrial Investments Ltd.* v. *National Westminster Bank Ltd.* [1980] 3 All E.R. 849, affmd. [1982] 1 All E.R. 449 (C.A.).
[9] *Re Cedar Engineering Co. Ltd.* (1976) 120 S.J. 146.
[10] [1924] 1 Ch. 276. This decision was approved by the House of Lords in *Moodie* v. *Shepherd (Bookbinders) Ltd.* [1949] 2 All E.R. 1044, 1950 S.C. (H.L.) 60; 1950 S.L.T. 90.

and her title to the shares shall forthwith be registered is invalid because it requires the company to register a transfer without delivery of a proper instrument of transfer, and the widow is not entitled by operation of law (see s. 75).[11]

The articles usually give power to the personal representatives to vote[12] at meetings on proof of transmission. Such a provision is fairly construed in favour of the representatives.[13]

If a shareholder is domiciled abroad, the company may not recognise the overseas executor or administrator until an ancillary grant is obtained in England or Scotland as appropriate.[14]

39–36 DEATH OF PERSONAL REPRESENTATIVE. Where the personal representative of the deceased shareholder dies, two cases have to be distinguished: if the shares were registered in the name of the personal representative, no problem arises and his own personal representative, whether an executor or administrator, can deal with the shares (which originally were registered in the name of the deceased shareholder) in the ordinary manner in which a personal representative can deal with them (see *supra*).

If, on the other hand, the shares were not so registered, the position is more difficult: if the personal representative was an executor and he died testate, there is an unbroken *chain of personal representation* through executors, and the second executor can be registered by the company as holder of the shares of the original shareholder. If the original shareholder dies intestate and his administrator dies, this ends the authority of the latter, and a new administrator has to be appointed. If a deceased administrator's executor obtains a grant of letters of administration *de bonis non* this will suffice.[15] If the original shareholder dies testate and his executor dies intestate (without having been registered as holder of the shares), the chain of personal representation is broken and a new personal representative of the original shareholder has to be appointed by the court; the administrator of the deceased executor cannot be registered as the holder of the shares standing in the name of the original shareholder.

Trustee in bankruptcy[16]

39–37 The trustee of a bankrupt member generally has a right under the articles to be registered as a member in respect of the bankrupt's shares (art. 32).[17] In *Re W. Key & Son Ltd.*[18] there was a lien clause, and the

---

[11] *Re Greene* [1949] Ch. 333.
[12] See *Re Rudderham* (1969) 9 D.L.R. (3d) 492.
[13] *Marks* v. *Financial News* [1919] W.N. 237.
[14] See, J. H. C. Morris, *Dicey and Morris, The Conflict of Laws* (9th ed., 1973), pp. 579 *et seq.*; and Clive M. Schmitthoff, *The English Conflict of Laws* (3rd ed., 1954), pp. 224 *et seq*.
[15] *Re New Cedar Engineering Co. Ltd.* (1976) 120 S.J. 146.
[16] For Scotland, see *infra*.
[17] *Re Bentham Mills Spinning Co.* (1879) 11 Ch.D. 900; *Re W. Key & Son Ltd.* [1902] 1 Ch. 467.
[18] [1902] 1 Ch. 467.

company claimed to enter the trustee's name with a memorandum stating the lien, and to indorse a similar memorandum, but the court disallowed the entry and held the trustee entitled to a "clean" certificate. Such a certificate would be subject to the articles, and the company would not thereby be estopped from claiming the lien if it showed that under the articles it was entitled to one. The equitable title vests in the trustee, and he has also, under section 48 (3) of the Bankruptcy Act 1914, a statutory power to transfer the shares subject to the same conditions as those to which the bankrupt is subject.

If the shares are onerous, the trustee may by writing, within 12 months of his appointment, disclaim the shares, leaving the company to prove for the loss caused by the disclaimer (Bankruptcy Act 1914, s. 54),[19] the measure of which is the amount which could have been called up on the shares.[20] A bankrupt's equity of redemption in shares which are not fully paid and which he has mortgaged can likewise be disclaimed.[21]

On the bankruptcy of a trustee of shares, the shares will not pass to his trustee in bankruptcy.[22]

A company cannot refuse to register a transfer of shares to a bankrupt director on the ground that if registered the shares will pass to the trustee in bankruptcy.[23]

A provision in articles for the compulsory transfer of shares of a bankrupt shareholder at a prearranged valuation is not a fraud on the bankruptcy law, and can be enforced by the company.[24]

An article, entitling a company to refuse to register any *transfer* made by a member who is indebted to it, has no application to a person claiming by *transmission*, such a trustee in bankruptcy or an executor[25]; but articles can be, and in practice are usually, so framed as to include cases of transmission.

A bankrupt shareholder whose name remains on the register does not cease to be a member and does not lose his right to vote in person or by proxy at the meetings of the company,[26] provided that the company is not in liquidation,[27] although he has no longer a beneficial interest in the shares and the company is entitled to pay any dividends to his trustee in bankruptcy.[28]

If the bankrupt shareholder is still registered as the holder of the shares,

---

[19] *Re West of England Bank, ex p. Budden and Roberts* (1879) 12 Ch.D. 288; *Levi* v. *Ayers* (1878) 3 App.Cas. 842.
[20] *Re Hallett* [1894] W.N. 156; *Re Hooley* [1899] 2 Q.B. 579.
[21] *Wise* v. *Lansdell* [1921] 1 Ch. 420.
[22] Bankruptcy Act 1914, s. 38 (1); *Colonial Bank* v. *Whinney* (1886) 11 App.Cas. 426.
[23] *Sutton* v. *English and Colonial Produce Co.* [1902] 2 Ch. 502.
[24] *Borland's Trustee* v. *Steel Brothers* [1901] 1 Ch. 279.
[25] *Re Bentham Mills Spinning Co.* (1879) 11 Ch.D. 900; see, however, *Ex p. Harrison* (1884) 26 Ch.D. 522.
[26] *Morgan* v. *Gray* [1953] Ch. 83.
[27] If the company is in liquidation, the bankrupt shareholder, although remaining on the list of contributories, has no longer a beneficial interest in the company and has no standing in the liquidation: *Re Cape Breton Co.* (1881) 19 Ch.D. 77.
[28] *Morgan* v. *Gray* [1953] Ch. 83.

his trustee in bankruptcy has no *locus standi* to petition for a compulsory winding up of the company.[29]

Trustee in sequestration in Scotland

The position of the trustee in Scotland under the Bankruptcy (Scotland) Act 1913 is comparable. His title is the court's Act and Warrant[30] which vests the bankrupt's estate in him *ipso jure* on behalf of the creditors absolutely. Article 32 governs his registration as a shareholder. Onerous shares may be disclaimed, the company then being entitled to rank in the sequestration for unpaid calls.[31]

Mortgaging of shares in English companies

39–38 A shareholder might wish to borrow on the security of his shares. In this case he may mortgage his shares by granting

(1) a legal mortgage, or
(2) an equitable mortgage on them.

Legal mortgage of shares

39–39 This is done by the transfer of the shares from the borrowing shareholder to the lender who is registered in the register of members as a fully entitled shareholder of the company. On redemption of the loan the shares are retransferred from the lender to the borrower. In view of section 117, the lender cannot be registered in England merely as a mortgagee because this would reveal notice of a trust, in particular of the equity of redemption of the borrower. During the time that the lender is registered as a shareholder, the company will pay to him all dividends and other moneys with respect to the shares, and he is entitled to vote.[32]

A legal mortgage on shares provides the best security which the lender can obtain when a loan or advance is secured on shares. When registered, the lender can be certain that his security cannot be defeated by any fraud on the part of the borrower. This method has, however, two disadvantages: stamp duties are payable twice, *viz.* on transfer and retransfer, and it is obviously unsuitable for shares which are not fully paid up.

This method is sometimes used where a shareholder wishes to obtain an advance from a bank: he transfers the shares to the bank or its nominee which continues to be registered as his nominee even after the repayment of the advance; if a further advance is then required, the shares would again be available as security.

---

[29] *Re H. L. Bolton Engineering Co. Ltd.* [1956] Ch. 577. But the trustee may require the bankrupt himself to present a winding-up petition: see *Re K/9 Meat Supplies (Guildford) Ltd.* [1966] 1 W.L.R. 1112.
[30] Bankruptcy (Scotland) Act 1913, s. 70.
[31] *Myles* v. *City of Glasgow Bank* (1879) 6 R. (Ct. of Sn.) 718.
[32] See para. 50–06, *post*.

Equitable mortgage of shares

39–40 CREATION. An equitable mortgage of shares is normally created by a deposit of the share certificate relating thereto,[33] with or without delivery of a blank transfer to the lender. The borrower remains on the register and retains all the rights of a member unless other arrangements are made as between himself and the lender.

It is common practice, on an equitable mortgage of shares, for the transferor to sign and hand over a blank transfer (*i.e.* a transfer signed by the transferor, but with a blank for the name of the transferee), the intention being that the purchaser or mortgagee shall be at liberty later on to fill up the blank and perfect his security by getting himself registered: if the transfer may be under hand, the authority to fill up the blank may be oral and may be implied from the nature of the transaction,[34] and the same would now appear to apply to cases which fall within the Stock Transfer Act 1963[35]; whereas if the articles require the transfer to be by deed, and the Stock Transfer Act 1963 does not apply, the transferee cannot effectively fill up the blank and deliver the deed unless authorised so to do by power of attorney under seal.

SALE OR FORECLOSURE. A person taking a blank transfer and certificate by way of security is an equitable mortgagee, not a pledgee, and can sell after reasonable notice.[36] Alternatively he has the usual right of a mortgagee to foreclose.[37]

There is nothing to prevent a mortgagee from selling the shares mortgaged to him, and agreeing to repurchase at the sale price if called upon: and he can allow the purchase-money to be left on mortgage.[38]

Where a shareholder executes blank transfers to enable another to deal with the shares, he is bound not to do anything to prevent registration of the transfer; and if he improperly intervenes, he is liable in damages.[39] The measure of damages in such a case is the difference between the value of the shares (*i.e.* the price which could have been realised on a sale of the shares) at the time when the transfer ought to have been registered and the value at the time when the transfer was in fact registered.[40]

If the mortgagee sells the shares to a purchaser who fills in his own name, the purchaser can only hold them as security for the amount due under the mortgage to the mortgagee[41]; the purchaser cannot get a better title than

---

[33] *Fuller* v. *Glyn Mills, Currie & Co.* [1914] 2 K.B. 168; *Harrold* v. *Plenty* [1901] 2 Ch. 314.

[34] *Hibblewhite* v. *McMorine* (1840) 6 M. & W. 200; *Powell* v. *London and Provincial Bank* [1893] 2 Ch. 555; *France* v. *Clark* (1884) 26 Ch.D. 257; *Re Tahiti Cotton Co.* (1874) L.R. 17 Eq. 273; *Re Tees Bottle Co.* (1876) 33 L.T. 834. In Scotland such transfers may be void under the Act of 1696 (c. 25); *Shaw* v. *Caledonian Rly.* (1890) 17 R. 466, 478.

[35] *i.e.* in any case where the shares in question are fully paid; see para. 39–19, *ante*.

[36] *Stubbs* v. *Slater* [1910] 1 Ch. 632.

[37] *Harrold* v. *Plenty* [1901] 2 Ch. 314.

[38] *Belton* v. *Bass, Ratcliffe & Gretton* [1922] 2 Ch. 449.

[39] *Hooper* v. *Herts* [1906] 1 Ch. 549.

[40] *Ibid.*

[41] *France* v. *Clark* (1884) 26 Ch.D. 257.

the vendor because the fact that the transfer is in blank puts him on notice of third party's rights.

A person who gives an agent a blank transfer of shares with authority to borrow on the security of the shares may be bound by a pledge of those shares by the agent, even if it was not in accordance with the authority given.[42]

Priorities as between persons taking such blank transfers depend upon the date upon which the blank transfer was given, and not the date when the purported transferee sent the transfers to the company for registration.[43]

39–41 CHARGING ORDERS. A judgment creditor of a shareholder may apply to the court for an order charging the shares registered in the name of the debtor; the purpose of such an order is the subsequent sale of the shares. First a charging order nisi is made, which prevents the company from registering any transfer of the debtor's shares, and later the order is made absolute. The charging order is made in accordance with the Charging Orders Act 1979 and RSC 1965, O.50; these provisions do not extend to Scotland.

A charging order has no operation except upon shares standing in the name of a debtor in his own right or in the name of some person in trust for him[44]; and the effect is that it entitles the judgment creditor to all such remedies as he would have been entitled to if a charge had been made in his favour by the judgment debtor himself.[45] Hence a mortgage by way of deposit of certificates with blank transfer has priority over a charging order subsequent in date.[46] A charging order on shares of an undischarged bankrupt is not a transaction for value within the rule in *Cohen* v. *Mitchell*,[47] and is therefore invalid against the trustee.[48]

The remedy of the holder of a charging order on shares is sale, not foreclosure.[49]

The Limitation Act 1980 fixes the period of limitation in respect of mortgages of shares and other personalty at 12 years.

Debentures cannot be attached by way of a charging order.

STOP NOTICE.[50] An equitable mortgage of shares is defeated if the transferor obtains a second share certificate from the company under the pretence that he has lost the original certificate—he will normally be asked to give the company an indemnity—and then sells the shares to a bona fide

---

[42] *Fry* v. *Smellie* [1912] 3 K.B. 282.
[43] *Société Générale de Paris* v. *Walker* (1885) 11 App.Cas. 20.
[44] *Cooper* v. *Griffin* [1892] 1 Q.B. 740; *Howard* v. *Sadler* [1893] 1 Q.B. 1.
[45] *Scott* v. *Lord Hastings* (1858) 4 K. & J. 633, 636.
[46] *Gill* v. *Continental Union Gas Co.* (1872) L.R. 7 Ex. 332; *Re General Horticultural Co.* (1886) 32 Ch.D. 512.
[47] (1890) 25 Q.B.D. 262; see now Bankruptcy Act 1914, s. 47 (1).
[48] *Hosack* v. *Robins (No. 2)* [1918] 2 Ch. 339.
[49] *Daponte* v. *Schubert* [1939] Ch. 958.
[50] This was formerly referred to as a notice in lieu of distringas. On the history of this notice, see Palmer's *Company Law* (20th ed.), p. 359, n. 2.

purchaser; if he delivers to the latter an instrument of transfer and the second share certificate and the bona fide purchaser is registered in the register of members, the latter acquires a legal title to the shares which defects the equitable interest of the lender who holds the first certificate by way of equitable mortgage.

This result, which has particularly unfortunate consequences for the lender if the original shareholder (the borrower) is insolvent, can be avoided if the lender serves a stop notice upon the company.[51] The object of such a notice is to prevent the company from registering a transfer without giving the issuer of the notice an opportunity of asserting his claim. If, whilst the notice continues in force, the company receives from the person in whose name the shares specified in the notice are standing a request to transfer the shares or to pay a dividend on them, the company has to inform the issuer of the notice and must not register the transfer or pay the dividend within eight days after the date of the request, but thereafter it cannot refuse the request, without an order of the court to the contrary.[52] The effect of the notice is thus temporary only: it enables the issuer of the notice within those eight days to obtain an injunction restraining the company from registering the transfer or paying the dividend.

The notice is obtained in the following manner: The applicant files the notice, together with a supporting affidavit by him or his solicitor, in the Central Office of the High Court or in any district registry, and after it has been sealed and certain copies have been procured, it is served on the company.[53] The notice has to set out the shares to which it refers and has to be signed by the deponent to the affidavit. There has to be appended to the affidavit a note stating the person on whose behalf it is filed, and to what address notices (if any) for that person are to be sent.[54]

Mortgaging of shares in Scottish companies

39–42 In Scots law a fixed security over shares can only be effected by a duly registered transfer to the creditor.[55] "Legal" and "equitable" mortgages are foreign to Scots law. A mere deposit of a share certificate creates no security. Deposit of certificate with transfer (unregistered) is an unreliable alternative. If the transfer is blank it may be void under the Blank Bonds and Trusts Act 1696.[56] The holder may find his "security" defeated by the debtor's fraudulent transfer, or by an arrestment laid by another creditor. While it has been held competent to present such a transfer for registration at any time before the debtor's trustee in sequestration has sought to be

---

[51] Charging Orders Act 1979, s. 5 and R.S.C. 1965, Ord. 50, rr. 11–15; for form of affidavit and notice, see Appendix A, Form 80.
[52] R.S.C. 1965, Ord. 50, r. 12.
[53] *Ibid.* r. 11 (2).
[54] *Ibid.* r. 11 (3) (4).
[55] *The National Commercial Bank of Scotland Glasgow Nominees* v. *Adamson* 1932, S.L.T. 492.
[56] Of the Scottish Parliament.

registered,[57] a transfer executed within 60 days of bankruptcy has been reduced.[58]

PRACTICE NOTES

Stamp duty on transfers

39–43 Purchases of shares for full consideration by persons resident outside the scheduled territories (see para. 26–24, n. 35, *ante*) are relieved from the increase in stamp duty imposed by the Finance Act 1974 and continue to be liable to *ad valorem* duty at 1 per cent. All transfers in respect of which the conditions for relief from the increased duty are satisfied must have indorsed on them the following certificate signed by an authorised depositary "Certified within para. 21, Schedule 11, Finance Act 1974."

Purchases by and gifts to charities are also relieved from the increased rate of *ad valorem* duty but transfers evidencing such purchases or gifts stamped at the lower rate will not be registered unless they bear the adjudication stamp of the Inland Revenue.

Forms of transfer

39–44 The forms of transfer designated by the Treasury (see para. 39–30, *ante*) consist of a sold transfer and a bought transfer. The former, which is exempt from stamp duty, contains a request to transfer the security to Sepon Ltd. (see para. 2–16, *ante*) and is signed by the seller of the security. The latter states that Sepon Ltd. transfers the security to the person(s) named as transferee(s) and requests that the necessary entries be made in the register. The amount of stamp duty payable is noted on the transfer, but is accounted for by Sepon Ltd. to the Inland Revenue under the terms of a composition agreement, so that no impressed stamp duty appears on the transfer. These forms are used only in connection with the purchase and sale of securities through The Stock Exchange. Other transactions in securities continue to be evidenced by an instrument of transfer in common form or otherwise as required by the articles of association of the company.

Transmission; small estates

39–45 Although the title to shares registered in the name of a deceased holder can only be established by the production to a company of a grant of probate or administration, public listed companies are sometimes prepared to consider recognising as the person entitled to deal with the shares of a deceased holder a widow, widower or other next-of-kin where the total value of the estate is so small that the cost of obtaining a grant of representation would not be justified. In such a case, the company would require

[57] *Morrison* v. *Harrison* (1867) 3 R.(Ct. of Sn.) 406.
[58] *Gourlay* v. *Mackie* (1887) 14 R. 403.

production of the share certificate, the death certificate, a statutory declaration of the facts and an indemnity from the claimant.

This procedure could also be adopted when the chain of personal representation (see para. 39–36, *ante*) has been broken and the value of the unadministered estate is small.

Chapter 40

LIEN ON SHARES

How created

40–01 In English law a company has, prima facie, no lien on the share of a member[1]; but the articles may, and usually do, provide that the company shall have a first and paramount lien on the shares of each member for his debts and liabilities to the company, whether matured or not (art. 11).[2] Such a provision is fully effective for private companies[3] but is of limited effect for public companies as a result of the 1980 Act.[4] A lien clause may be adopted by special resolution.[5]

In England any lien thus created takes effect as an equitable charge[6] created in favour of the company by covenant of the shareholder, the covenant being implied by virtue of section 20. In Scots law a right of retention (lien) exists at common law in favour of a company in respect of all indebtedness by the registered shareholder to the company whether his shares are fully paid or partly paid.[7] This right is additional to any express right of lien in the articles, but may be limited by their terms.

A right of lien may be discharged by a clear arrangement between the shareholder and the company.[8]

Liens available to public companies

40–02 A private company may enforce any lien so created by its articles but public companies may only validly enforce three particular liens against their own shares. By virtue of section 38 (1) of the 1980 Act any other lien or charge taken by a public company on its own shares, whether expressly or implicitly, is void. This clearly restricts the wider ambit of an article such as article 11.

The three liens which a public company may now take on its own shares are:

(1) Liens for unpaid calls or instalments

40–03 All public companies may take a lien on their own shares, other than fully paid up shares, for any amount payable in respect of the shares (1980

---

[1] *Pinkett* v. *Wright* (1842) 2 Ha. 120; on appeal, *sub nom. Murrary* v. *Pinkett* (1846) 12 Cl. & Fin. 764.

[2] See *Precedents* (17th ed., 1956), Pt. I, p. 428.

[3] *New London, etc., Bank* v. *Brocklebank* (1882) 21 Ch.D. 302; *Bradford Banking Co.* v. *Briggs* (1886) 12 App.Cas. 29.

[4] See the next paragraph in the text.

[5] *Allen* v. *Gold Reefs of West Africa* [1900] 1 Ch. 656; *Bell's Trustee* v. *Coatbridge Tinplate Co.* (1886) 14 R. (Ct. of Sess.) 246.

[6] *Re General Exchange Bank* (1871) 6 Ch.App. 818.

[7] *Bell's Trustees* v. *Coatbridge Tinplate Co. Ltd.* 1886, 14 R. 246.

[8] *Bank of Africa* v. *Salisbury Gold Mining Co.* [1892] A.C. 281.

Act, s. 38 (2) (*a*)). This is in practice the most common lien created by all companies.

(2) Liens of lending or credit companies arising in the ordinary course of business

40–04 This lien is only available to a public company if its ordinary business includes the lending of money or consists of the provision of credit or the bailment (or, in Scotland, the hiring) of goods under a hire-purchase agreement, or both. This is clearly a question of fact although it should be noted that such business need not be its sole or major business but simply a part of the ordinary business.

Such companies may validly enforce any lien on their own shares, whether fully paid or not, if it arises in connection with a transaction entered into by the company in the ordinary course of its business (1980 Act, s. 38 (2) (*b*)). Again this in the end resolves itself into a question of fact in each case. Much may depend upon who has the burden of proof. Clearly both the debt and the security must be usual in that company's dealings.[9]

(3) Liens created by private companies prior to re-registration as public companies

40–05 A public company may enforce any lien on its own shares which was "in existence" immediately before its application to re-register as a public company under section 5 of the 1980 Act,[10] *i.e.* while it was still a private company (1980 Act, s. 38 (2) (*c*)).

Two problems exist with this part of the 1980 Act. First when is a lien "in existence" for this purpose? It is submitted that the most sensible answer is that it exists as soon as it becomes enforceable by the company, *i.e.* when the debt or liability giving rise to the lien is created. An alternative answer is that it exists whenever the possibility of an enforceable lien in the future arises, *e.g.* for non-payment of a debt after a certain time or on the happening of certain contingencies, but that would seem open to abuse.

Second when does a company make an application for re-registration under section 5 of the 1980 Act?[11] This is the cut-off date for the validity of such liens. Section 5 itself requires delivery of the application to the Registrar[12]—can this be equated with the making of an application by the company? It would seem more logical and certain than any other date.

Moneys secured by the lien

40–06 The lien clause may be worded very differently in the articles, and it depends entirely on the words of the lien clause in the articles which claims of the company against the shareholder are secured by the lien.[12a]

[9] *Cf.* the definition in s. 42 of the 1981 Act, para. 38–09, *ante*.
[10] See para. 5–05, *ante*.
[11] This section also applies to joint stock companies registering under s. 13 of the 1980 Act. See Chap. 89, *post*.
[12] C.A. 1980 s. 5 (1) (b).
[12a] In Scots law the company's lien at common law may be wider; see para. 40–01, *ante*.

Article 11 gives the company, in fact, two first and paramount liens[13]: one to secure "all moneys (whether presently payable or not) called or payable at a fixed time in respect of that share," and the other for "all moneys presently payable by [the shareholder] or his estate to the company." Whilst the former lien is intended to secure calls or fixed instalments due with respect to the share, the latter is of much wider ambit; it covers trading debts and other liabilities of the shareholder to the company, provided that they are payable "presently," *i.e.* at the relevant date. As such it is now much restricted by section 38 of the 1980 Act for public companies (see above). It is possible to word this article even wider, *e.g.* "all moneys or liabilities whether presently due or due at a future date or due subject to a condition or contingency," but the use of such wide liens is not general. It is important, however, to realise that, if the articles so provide, the company's lien may secure claims of the company other than those for calls on shares insofar as allowed by section 38 of the 1980 Act.[13a] The lien is limited to moneys owed by the shareholders to the company and does not secure, for example, a guarantee by the shareholder in favour of preference shareholders to meet their dividends.[14]

Lien on partly paid and on fully paid shares

40–07 While the lien set out in article 11 attaches only to partly paid shares of the company, lien clauses may be so worded as to give a company a lien on its fully paid shares, usually in addition to that on the partly paid shares.[15] In *Allen* v. *Gold Reefs of West Africa*[16] it was held that a company, the articles of which gave the company only a lien on its partly paid shares, could by special resolution alter its articles and extend the lien to its fully paid shares and that such extension would even be effective as against the shareholders holding fully paid shares acquired before the resolution was passed. This will not, however, operate so as to justify refusal to register a transfer of fully paid shares which has already been presented, and which could not be refused in the absence of a lien.[17]

A lien on fully paid shares is not admitted by the Rules of the Stock Exchange for shares quoted or dealt in.[18] Section 38 of the 1980 Act only allows liens for non-payment of calls against partly paid shares for public companies, although the other liens so allowed may be enforceable against any shares.[19]

---

[13] They are both called "first and paramount" in order to define their position in a dispute on priorities with a third claimant; the words do not, of course, refer to the priority *inter se*.

[13a] See e.g. *Champagne Perrier-Jouet S.A.* v. *H.H. Finch Ltd.*, *The Times* April 29, 1982.

[14] *Stark* v. *Fife & Kinross Coal Co.* 1899, 1 F. 1173; 7 S.L.T. 130.

[15] In Scotland, a lien over fully paid shares exists at common law, para. 40–01, *ante*.

[16] [1900] 1 Ch. 656.

[17] *McArthur* v. *Gulf Line* 1909 S.C. 732.

[18] Rules of the Stock Exchange, Sched. VII, Pt. A, para. 128.

[19] See para. 40–04, *ante*.

Validity of lien against third persons in English law. Priorities

40–08 A lien clause in the articles not infrequently gives rise to questions of priority between the company asserting the lien and persons claiming under the shareholder. For example, the company may receive notice that the shareholder has mortgaged or sold the shares, and the question then arises whether, if the shareholder subsequently becomes indebted to the company, the company's lien, if otherwise valid, will rank in priority to the mortgagee or purchaser.

Where articles contain exemption clause

40–09 The articles sometimes contain a clause (referred to below as an exemption clause) relieving the company from the obligation to take notice of equities in relation to its shares. The terms of exemption clauses vary considerably. In *New London and Brazilian Bank* v. *Brocklebank*[20] the clause ran—

> "The company shall not be bound by or recognise any agreement to transfer or charge any share,or any equitable, contingent, future or partial interest, or other right in, to, or in respect of such share, except an absolute right thereto in the person from time to time registered as the holder thereof."

Another provision very commonly found in articles is that

> "[Save as herein otherwise provided] the company shall be entitled to treat the registered holder of any share as the absolute owner thereof, and, accordingly, shall not [except as ordered by a court of competent jurisdiction or as by statute required] be bound to recognise any equitable or other claim to, or interest in, such shares on the part of ay other person."

Such a clause is framed with a view to enabling the company, whether in relation to a lien clause or otherwise, to deal with the registered holder of a share as the absolute owner, and to relieve the company altogether from any obligation to take notice of any claims or assertions of equitable interests that may come to it.

40–10 It is doubtful, having regard to the decisions of the courts, whether these exemption clauses add much, if anything, for this purpose to the effect of section 117 of the 1948 Act[21]; but it will be convenient to consider, in the first place, cases where an exemption clause was adopted.

In *New London and Brazilian Bank* v. *Brocklebank*[22] there was a paramount lien clause and also an exemption clause. The shares were acquired with trust money. One of the holders became indebted to the bank, and upon the bank seeking to enforce its charge the prior equity of the beneficiaries was set up. The Court of Appeal held that the bank had a lien on the shares which must prevail over the title of the beneficiaries.

---

20 (1882) 21 Ch.D. 302; *cf.* Table A, art.7.
21 See para. 50–06, *post.*
22 (1882) 21 Ch.D. 302; *cf.* Table A, art. 7.

Jessel M.R. considered that, as the lien was given by the articles, it took effect from the time the member was admitted, and, further, that the beneficiaries were not entitled to repudiate the lien and exemption clauses; and Lindley L.J. said that he failed to see upon what ground the equitable owner could claim title to the shares and yet "repudiate the terms upon which the trustees have acquired the shares." It was not alleged in this case that the company had notice of the trust before the obligation of the company was incurred. The principle of this decision appears to be that a shareholder cannot both approbate and reprobate, and that those who claim under him cannot repudiate either the lien clause or the exemption clause.[23]

In *Mackereth* v. *Wigan Coal and Iron Co.*,[24] Peterson J. held that a company could not, after specific notice that three persons held certain shares as executors, make advances to one of them and then claim a lien on the shares as against the beneficiaries. This decision appears to establish the proposition put forward in the argument for the plaintiffs that, notwithstanding the exemption clause, *in disputes between the company and other persons* the company is subject to the ordinary rules of law and equity. "Where the company in which shares are held sees fit to deal with the shares for its own benefit, then that company is liable to be affected with notice of the interest of a third party."[25]

Where articles do not contain exemption clause

40–11 Where the articles contain a lien clause but do not contain a clause exempting the company from taking notice of trusts and equities, the company has to rely exclusively on section 117, which provides that "no notice of any trust, expressed, implied or constructive, shall be entered on the register, or be receivable by the registrar, in the case of companies registered in England."[26]

In *Bradford Banking Co.* v. *Briggs*[27] the articles contained a clause giving the company a first and paramount lien, and there was no exemption clause. The company received notice of a mortgage by the shareholder; afterwards it advanced money to him and claimed priority for its advance, contending (1) that on the true construction of the lien clause in its articles (which gave the company "a first and paramount lien") the shareholder had agreed that the company should have a lien ranking in priority to all other charges with or without notice and that the second mortgagee with notice of this bargain could not establish any claim in violation of it; and (2) that the company, under what is now section 117, was entitled to disregard the notice as notice of a trust, and, on that ground, was entitled to priority.

[23] *Borland's Trustee* v. *Steel Brothers & Co.* [1901] 1 Ch. 279.
[24] [1916] 2 Ch. 293.
[25] *Per* Peterson J. quoting Stirling J. in *Rainford* v. *James Keith, etc., Co.* [1905] 2 Ch. 147, 161.
[26] See para. 50–06, *post*.
[27] (1886) 12 App.Cas. 29. This case must be taken as overruling the contrary decision of the Court of Appeal in *Miles* v. *New Zealand, Alford, etc., Co.* (1886) 32 Ch.D. 266.

The House of Lords, applying the principle of *Hopkinson* v. *Rolt*,[28] held that there being nothing in the articles to the contrary, the company was not entitled to disregard notices of the mortgage and to insist upon priority for its subsequent advances.

40–12 It is material to note that this case was decided on the construction of the articles and of what is now section 117.[29] It did not decide that there was any inexorable rule of equity making it impossible, by the articles, to exclude the application of the rule in *Hopkinson* v. *Rolt*.[30] The provisions of the articles were carefully considered, and it was held that they did not import any intention to exclude the rule, for they in no way attempted to relieve the company from noticing equities. As regards the predecessor of section 117, the case decided that, in so far as the company claimed a beneficial interest in the shares, which conflicted with that of the mortgagee, notice of the mortgage was not notice of a trust but only notice to the company in its capacity as a trader. *Bradford Banking Co.* v. *Briggs*,[31] therefore, in no way derogates from the authority of *New London and Brazilian Bank* v. *Brocklebank*[32] and *Borland's Trustee* v. *Steel Brothers & Co.*,[33] but it is submitted that this decision, together with the later decision in *Mackereth* v. *Wigan Coal and Iron Co.*,[34] makes it clear that, whether or not there is an exemption clause in the articles, notice to the company of an equitable interest in shares will operate to protect that interest against any subsequent claim made by the company itself in respect of those shares.

Validity of lien against third parties in Scots Law

40–13 The company's lien (whether at common law or under the articles) will be effective against the claims of any third party, including the trustee in bankruptcy of the member, subject only to whatever limitations may be contained in the articles of Association.[35]

Enforcement of lien by sale in England

40–14 The articles generally give power to the company to enforce a lien by sale after default (art. 12), and if need be, to transfer the shares into the purchasers' names. In the absence of some such provision, it may be necessary to apply to the court.[36] On the other hand, in England, the charge which a lien creates being a mortgage within the meaning of section 205 (1) (xvi) of the Law of Property Act 1925, the shareholder or his transferee is entitled, by section 95 (1) of that Act, to require the company,

---

28 (1861) 9 H.L.C. 514; see now Law of Property Act 1925, s. 94 (1) (*b*).
29 Then s. 30 of the Act of 1862.
30 (1861) 9 H.L.C. 514.
31 See note 27, *supra*.
32 (1882) 21 Ch.D. 302; see para. 39–39, *ante*.
33 [1901] 1 Ch. 279, 288.
34 [1916] 2 Ch. 293.
35 *Bell's Trustees* v. *Coatbridge Tinplate Co. Ltd.* 1886, 14 R. 246.
36 *New London, etc., Bank* v. *Brocklebank* (1882) 21 Ch.D. 302.

on payment of the sum due, to assign the debt and the lien on the shares to his nominee.[37]

This being so, it may be that the power of sale given by section 101 of the same Act to mortgagees is applicable. Section 101, no doubt, only gives the power to a mortgagee to sell where the mortgage is "by deed," but, by virtue of section 20 of the 1948 Act, the lien clause binds the shareholder as if it were his deed of covenant with the company.[38] If the company has a power of sale it is subject to any restrictions on the transfer of its shares in the articles, e.g. the shares must be offered first to the existing shareholders.[38a]

The clause conferring a lien extends not only to the shares, but to the dividends thereon (art. 11, last sentence),[39] and also to any assets which, in a winding up, may come to the shareholders in respect thereof.[40]

When the holder of shares subject to a lien by the company sells some of them, the purchaser is entitled to marshal as against an execution creditor of the vendor, and to throw the lien in the first instance upon the shares remaining unsold.[41]

The lien can be claimed against the estate of a deceased shareholder if it is so worded in the articles (see art. 11).

Lien not enforceable by forfeiture in England

40–15 Occasionally the articles provide that a lien may be enforced by forfeiture, but such a provision is not effective in England; for the lien is an equitable mortgage, and a clause for forfeiture in a mortgage is, in equity, inoperative. The rule is that "once a mortgage, always a mortgage"[42] and any attempt to clog the equity of redemption is futile. Further, in *Hopkinson* v. *Mortimer, Harley & Co.*,[43] it was held that a forfeiture of shares by directors for non-payment of an ordinary debt would be invalid as an unauthorised reduction of capital.

Enforcement of lien in Scotland

40–16 In principle, a lien is no more than the right to retain the shares until the debt is satisfied, and there is no power of sale unless this is contained in the articles.[44] Such power can, however, be adopted by alteration of the

---

[37] *Everitt* v. *Automatic, etc., Co.* [1892] 3 Ch. 506; but see *Re Magneta Time Co.* [1915] W.N. 318 as to the necessity of concurrence of a subsequent encumbrancer.
[38] *Bradford Banking Co.* v. *Briggs* (1886) 12 App.Cas. 29.
[38a] *Champagne Perrier-Jouet S.A.* v. *H.H. Finch Ltd., The Times* April 29, 1982.
[39] *Re General Exchange Bank* (1871) 6 Ch.App. 818; *Hague* v. *Dandeson* (1848) 2 Ex.Reps. 741.
[40] *Re General Exchange Bank, supra.*
[41] *Gray* v. *Stone & Funnell* [1893] W.N. 133; 69 L.T. 282.
[42] *Salt* v. *Marquis of Northampton* [1892] A.C. 1.
[43] [1917] 1 Ch. 646.
[44] *e.g.* Table A, arts. 12–14.

articles.[45] Forfeiture (other than for non-payment of calls) in a limited company would be invalid as an unauthorised reduction of capital.[46]

Loss of lien

40–17 A company may lose its lien on its shares by allowing a registered transfer of those shares.[47] The shares of an indebted member may be sold but that "cannot mean subject to a set-off against him"—otherwise the shares of A might be sold, and then rights refused to B because A was still indebted to the company.[48]

---

[45] See para. 14–17, *ante*.
[46] See para. 32–18, *post*.
[47] *Higgs* v. *Assam Tea Co.* (1869) L.R. 4 Exch. 387; *Re Northern Assam Tea Co. ex parte Universal Life Assurance Co.* (1870) L.R. 10 Eq. 458. Both these cases concerned liens on debentures but the articles in question were equally applicable to shares. *Paul's Trustee* v. *Thomas Justice & Sons* 1912 S.C. 1303; 1912, 2 S.L.T. 141. *O'Meara* v. *The El Palmer Rubber Estates* 1913, 1 S.L.T. 383. (These two cases concerned liens on shares.)
[48] (1869) L.R. 4 Exch. 387, 395.

CHAPTER 41

FORFEITURE AND SURRENDER OF SHARES

Forfeiture for non-payment of calls

41–01 The articles of a company generally contain provisions for the forfeiture of shares for non-payment of calls or instalments (arts. 33–39). Such a power to forfeit is not inherent in a company.[1] It only exists where it is given by the articles or introduced into them, as it may be, by special resolution.[2] When given, it is, like other powers of directors, fiduciary, *i.e.* it is to be exercised for the benefit of the company.[3]

A power to forfeit shares for non-payment of debts other than calls or instalments is invalid as an unauthorised reduction of capital.[4] This is not so in forfeiture for non-payment of calls.[5]

Effect of forfeiture on the shareholder

41–02 From the date on which the forfeiture becomes effective, the shareholder whose shares are forfeited ceases to be a member of the company (art. 37). Theoretically that means that he loses not only the privileges and rights of membership but likewise is no longer bound by the obligations resulting from membership, particularly the duty to pay the outstanding calls, although he can be placed, as a past member, on the B list of contributories in a winding up.

It will be seen later, however, that these conclusions are merely theoretical; the articles commonly provide that the shareholder whose shares are forfeited shall remain liable to pay to the company all moneys which, at the date of the forfeiture, were payable by him in respect of the shares (art. 37). This continued liability is *qua* debtor, and no longer *qua* member.

Collusion. Irregularity

A collusive forfeiture made for the purpose of enabling a member favoured by the directors to escape from his liabilities is an abuse of the power and a fraud on the other shareholders.[6] This must, however, be distinguished from a bona fide compromise.[7] Forfeiture is treated very

---

1 *Clarke* v. *Hart* (1858) H.L.C. 633.
2 *Dawkins* v. *Antrobus* (1881) 17 Ch.D. 615, 634; *Allen* v. *Gold Reefs of West Africa* [1900] 1 Ch. 656.
3 See Chap. 64, *post*.
4 *Hopkinson* v. *Mortimer, Harley & Co.* [1917] 1 Ch. 646. Nor does a company acquire its own shares in infringement of s. 35 of the 1980 Act by such forfeiture: 1980 Act, s. 35 (4) (*c*).
5 See para. 32–18, *ante*.
6 *Re Esparto Trading Co.* (1879) 12 Ch.D. 191; *Spackman* v. *Evans* (1868) L.R. 3 H.L. 171, 186; *Lord Wallscourt's Case* [1899] W.N. 258.
7 *Liquidator of General Property Investment Co.* v. *Craig* 1891, 18 R. 389.

strictly by the courts, and directors seeking to enforce it must pursue exactly the course of procedure marked out by the articles.[8] A slight irregularity is as fatal as the greatest.[9] Thus, if the call in respect of which the forfeiture is made is not validly made,[10] or if the notice on which the forfeiture is founded is inaccurate in requiring payment of interest from a wrong date, *e.g.* the date of the call instead of the date appointed for payment, the forfeiture may be held invalid.[11] Where a shareholder is seeking to rescind his contract the court can restrain a forfeiture.[12]

Where a shareholder is bankrupt, the notice of forfeiture may still be given to him[13]; but it is advisable to give notice to the trustee also. So where the shareholder is dead, as was the case in *Allen* v. *Gold Reefs of West Africa*,[14] the notice may be sent to his registered address. In that case the notice in fact reached the executors, but the statement of the law by Lindley M.R.[15] is probably sufficient to override the doubt expressed in *James* v. *Buena Ventura Nitrate, etc., Syndicate*.[16]

The exercise of a power of forfeiture is a question of expedience as to which the directors must use their discretion.[17] On forfeiture the shares become the property of the company and may be sold by the company (art. 36).

Directors do not lose the power of forfeiture because the company charges all its uncalled capital in favour of trustees for debenture holders.[18]

Sale of shares

41–03 The articles generally give power to the directors to sell forfeited shares (art. 36). In such a case the directors can sell for less than the amount paid up prior to the forfeiture,[19] but the transferee will remain liable to pay any amount remaining unapid on the shares at the time of sale.[20] In such a case the transferee will be a holder of shares in respect of which money is due, and may therefore by a clause in the regulations be debarred from voting.[21] He should be credited with any subsequent payments made by the ex-owner.[22]

---

[8] *Clarke* v. *Hart, supra.*

[9] *Garden Gully, etc., Mining Co.* v. *McLister* (1875) 1 App.Cas. 39; *Johnson* v. *Lyttle's Iron Agency* (1877) 5 Ch.D. 687.

[10] *Garden Gully United Quartz Mining Co.* v. *McLister, supra.*

[11] *Johnson* v. *Lyttle's Iron Agency, supra*; *Watson* v. *Eales* (1856) 23 Beav. 294; *Faure Electric Accumulator Co.* v. *Phillipart* (1888) 58 L.T. 525.

[12] *Lamb* v. *Sambas Rubber, etc., Co.* [1908] 1 Ch. 845; *Jones* v. *Pacaya Rubber and Produce Co.* [1911]) 1 K.B. 455.

[13] *Graham* v. *Van Diemen's Land Co.* (1856) 26 L.J. Ex. 73.

[14] [1900] 1 Ch. 656.

[15] At p. 670.

[16] [1896] 1 Ch. 456, 465.

[17] *Bigg's Case* (1865) L.R. 1 Eq. 309.

[18] *Re Agency Land and Finance Co. of Australia* (1903) 20 T.L.R. 41.

[19] *Morrison* v. *Trustees, Executors, etc., Corpn.* (1898) 68 L.J.Ch. 11 (C.A.).

[20] *Ibid.*; *New Balkis Eersteling* v. *Randt Gold Mining Co.* [1904] A.C. 165; and see also para. 32–18, *ante.*

[21] *Randt Gold Mining Co.* v. *Wainwright* [1901] 1 Ch. 184.

[22] *Re Randt Gold Mining Co.* [1904] 2 Ch. 468.

Power to annul

The articles very commonly give power to the directors, so long as they have not sold the forfeited shares, to annul the forfeiture on such terms as they think proper (art. 36). This power cannot be exercised without the consent of the late holder.[23]

Forfeiture after winding up

In a voluntary winding up the directors can exercise the power of forfeiture if they officiate by sanction of the liquidator or the company in general meeting in case of a members' voluntary winding up (s. 285 (2)), or by sanction of the committee of inspection or the creditors in the case of a creditors' voluntary winding up (s. 296 (2)).[24]

Treatment of forfeited shares

Public companies

41–04 Where shares in a public company are forfeited under the articles for non-payment of calls or instalments, section 37 of the 1980 Act requires the company either to dispose of the forfeited shares (*e.g.* under a power of sale[25] or annulment[26]) or to cancel them and diminish the share capital figure by their nominal value (1980 Act s. 37 (2) (*a*)). This must be done within three years of the forfeiture.[27] A fine or default fine may be imposed on the company or any officer in default of that obligation (1980 Act, s. 37 (7)).

Such a cancellation is in effect a reduction of capital and where the effect will be to reduce the company's allotted share capital below the authorised minimum[28] the company must apply to be re-registered as a private company (1980 Act s. 37 (2) (*b*)). The directors may take such steps as are necessary to achieve this, including passing a resolution making the necessary alterations to the memorandum without complying with the procedure under section 66 of 1948 Act[29] (1980 Act, s. 37 (4)). An application for re-registration in due form must be delivered to the Registrar (1980 Act, s. 37 (5)). The Registrar will then operate as if the application was one made by a public company under section 10 of the 1980 Act[30] (1980 Act, s. 37 (8)). Fines may be levied on those officers in default; in addition the company will be regarded as a private company at the end of the three year period without re-registration for the purposes of section 15 of the 1980

---

[23] *Re Exchange Trust Ltd., Larkworthy's Case* [1903] 1 Ch. 711.
[24] *Re Fairbairn Engineering Co.* [1893] 3 Ch. 450.
[25] See para. 41–03, *ante*.
[26] 1980 Act, s. 37 (11).
[27] See para. 37–06, *ante*.
[28] £50,000. See para. 4–14, *ante*.
[29] See para. 32–01, *ante*. This resolution must be registered under s. 143 of the 1948 Act.
[30] See para. 5–09, *ante*.

Act—*i.e.* it will not be able to ask the public to subscribe for its shares[31] (1980 Act s. 37 (6)).

Whilst the forfeited shares remain in the company's hands it may not validly exercise any votes in respect of them (1980 Act, s. 37 (3)). In addition if it shows them as assets in its balance sheet a compensating quasi-capital fund must be created[32] (1980 Act, s. 37 (10)).

Private companies

41–05 No such obligations are placed on private companies. The directors have freedom of choice within the articles. However, if the company subsequently re-registers as a public company the provisions of section 37 of the 1980 Act, noted above, will apply to shares forfeited even before such re-registration. The three year period for disposal or cancellation and possible re-registration as a private company runs from the date of re-registration as a public company (1980 Act, s. 37 (9)).

Relief against forfeiture

41–06 Where a forfeiture has been duly and bona fide effected, equity will not relieve against it.[33] A shareholder who desires to challenge a forfeiture as invalid may bring an action to set it aside[34]; and may obtain an injunction to restrain the forfeiture pending the trial, usually on the terms of payment of the amount called up into court.[35]

Mere laches will not disentitle a legal owner of shares to such relief if the forfeiture is invalid[36]; but it is different where years have elapsed and the shareholder claiming relief was a trustee for a director who was himself a party, as director, to the forfeiture.[37]

In Scots law it is thought that proceedings for declarator of invalidity or interdict would be appropriate. Damages may be claimed as an alternative or in addition.

Damages for irregular forfeiture

A shareholder whose shares have been irregularly forfeited (*e.g.* without proper notice) can sue the company or, in a winding up, prove for damages against the company.[38]

A clause in a company's articles forfeiting the shares of any shareholder who should commence or threaten an action against the company or the

---

[31] See para. 4–07, *ante*.
[32] See para. 29–11, *ante*.
[33] *Sparks* v. *Liverpool Waterworks* (1807) 13 Ves. 428
[34] *Sweny* v. *Smith* (1869) L.R. 7 Eq. 324; *Johnson* v. *Lyttle's, etc., Agency* (1877) 5 Ch.D. 687; *Re New Chili, etc., Co.* (1890) 45 Ch.D. 598.
[35] See *Lamb* v. *Sambas Rubber, etc., Co.* [1908] 1 Ch. 845 and *Jones* v. *Pacaya Rubber, etc., Co.* [1911] 1 K.B. 455 (where the forfeiture was restrained pending the trial of an action claiming rescission of the contract to take the shares).
[36] *Garden Gully, etc., Co.* v. *McLister* (1875) 1 App.Cas. 39.
[37] *Jones* v. *North Vancouver Land, etc., Co.* [1910] A.C. 317.
[38] *Re New Chili, etc., Co.* (1890) 45 Ch.D. 598.

directors on payment to the shareholder of the full market value of his shares is invalid, as an infringement of a shareholder's legal rights.[39]

Liability after forfeiture

41–07 Forfeiture of shares prevents prima facie any action by the company for past calls[40] But the articles commonly provide that where a share has been forfeited the member shall be liable for payment of the call with interest, and this creates a new obligation,[40] which can be enforced, as against every debtor of the company, by action at law, but not by placing the holder on the list of contributories (art. 37).[41]

A call may be "owing" within the meaning of such a clause, though it has not become payable when the forfeiture takes place.[42] But the company cannot recover more than the difference between the amount payable on the shares and the amount received from subsequent holders of the forfeited shares.[43]

When a person has been induced by misrepresentation to become a member, and is sued by the company after forfeiture of his shares, he can set up the misrepresentation by way of defence, even in a winding up.[44]

The forfeiture of a share does not relieve the forfeiting member from liability to be placed on the B list if the company should be wound up within a year after the forfeiture.[45] Thus, a shareholder who has transferred his shares within a year of a winding up is liable as a past member, though the shares have been forfeited in the hands of a transferee.[46]

A liquidator has no power to cancel a forfeiture of shares duly made by the directors before the commencement of the winding up.[47]

When shares forfeited for non-payment of calls are sold, the purchaser is liable to a fresh call in respect of the amounts comprised in such prior calls,[48] for the company cannot sell free from that liability. But subsequent payments by the former holder, on account of the prior calls, should be credited to the purchaser in due course.[49]

Sureties released

Where a surety has guaranteed the repayment of calls on shares, he will be released if the company forfeits the shares and thus alters the liability of the principal debtor and deprives the surety of the lien which he would otherwise have had if called upon to pay.[50]

---

39 *Hope* v. *International Financial Society* (1876) 4 Ch.D. 327.
40 *Stocken's Case* (1868) L.R. 3 Ch. 412, 415.
41 *Ladies' Dress Association* v. *Pulbrook* [1900] 2 Q.B. 376.
42 *Faure, etc., Co.* v. *Phillipart* (1888) 58 L.T. 525.
43 *Re Bolton* [1930] 2 Ch. 48.
44 *Aaron's Reefs* v. *Twiss* [1896] A.C. 273; *Liquidator of Mount Morgan (West) Gold Mine* v. *McMahon* 1891, 18 R. 772.
45 *Creyke's Case* (1869) L.R. 5 Ch. 63.
46 *Bridger's and Neill's Cases* (1869) L.R. 4 Ch. 266.
47 *Dawes' Case* (1868) L.R. 6 Eq. 232.
48 *New Balkis Eersteling* v. *Randt Gold Mining Co.* [1904] A.C. 165.
49 *Re Randt Gold Mining Co.* [1904] 2 Ch. 468.
50 *Re Darwen and Pearce* [1927] 1 Ch. 176.

Surrender

41–08 Where a company's articles give the directors power to accept a surrender of shares,[51] this power will be recognised as valid if it is used merely to avoid the formalities of forfeiture.[52] But it is *ultra vires* if the shares are not liable to forfeiture, so that such a surrender of partly paid shares would not relieve the shareholder from his uncalled liability: such a surrender would amount to a purchase by the company of its own shares, or a reduction of capital without the court's sanction, and is invalid.[53] It is, however, valid to accept the surrender of partly paid shares from an insolvent member and discharge liability for future calls thereon, if this represents a bona fide compromise of the company's claim on him.[54]

The effect of a valid surrender is the same as forfeiture, *viz.* provided the articles authorise it, the shares can be reissued. Shares surrendered in lieu of forfeiture are also subject to the requirements of section 37 of the 1980 Act, *i.e.* public companies must either dispose of or cancel them within three years.[55]

Surrender also occurs where shares are exchanged, new shares of the same nominal value being taken in place of those surrendered.[56] But a voluntary transfer of shares to a trustee foı the company does not amount to a surrender.[57]

PRACTICE NOTE

Procedure on forfeiture

41–09 Care must be taken to ensure that the resolution of the directors forfeiting the shares is properly passed at a validly constituted meeting and that there is strict compliance with the articles of association.

Under most articles, including Table A, it is not necessary to advise a shareholder that his shares have been forfeited, but it is advisable to inform him of the forfeiture by letter despatched by the recorded delivery service. At the same time, he should be asked to surrender for cancellation the share certificate in his possession. It is unlikely that the shareholder will comply with this request, with the result that when the company sells the forfeited shares and issues a new certificate to the purchaser, two documents of title will be in existence for the same shares. For this reason, regulation 38 of Table A provides that a statutory declaration in writing by a director or the secretary that a share has been forfeited shall be conclusive evidence as against all persons claiming to be entitled to the share.

---

51 Table A does not give power to accept a surrender; it contains no regulations on this subject.

52 *Trevor* v. *Whitworth* (1887) 12 App.Cas. 409, 429. This is given statutory recognition in the 1980 Act, s. 35 (4) (*c*).

53 *Bellerby* v. *Rowland and Marwood's Steamship Co.* [1902] 2 Ch. 14.

54 *Liquidator of General Property Investment Co.* v. *Craig* 1891, 18 R. 389.

55 See para. 41–04, *ante*.

56 *Rowell* v. *John Rowell & Sons Ltd.* [1912] 2 Ch. 609.

57 *Kirby* v. *Wilkins* [1929] 2 Ch. 444.

C. BORROWING POWERS AND DEBENTURES IN GENERAL

Chapter 42

BORROWING POWERS

Borrowing powers in trading and non-trading companies

42–01 Most companies, like individuals, require to borrow from time to time for the exigencies of their business. To entitle a company to borrow it must have power to borrow given to it by its constitution. Whether a company under the Act has or has not such a power will depend on the objects and powers specified in clause 3 of its memorandum. If these objects comprise, as they usually do, an express power to borrow, there is of course no question[1]; but it is not always necessary to find an express power. It is sufficient if there is an implied power.

An implied power arises whenever the objects are such that a power to borrow may fairly be regarded as incidental to the company's objects. This is the case with a *trading* company. It has—it must have—as incidental to carrying on its business, an implied power to borrow up to a reasonable amount[2]: but in regard to *non-trading* companies, there must be something in the memorandum or articles to show expressly or inferentially that the company is to have power to borrow; for a company registered under this Act is, as we have seen,[3] a statutory creation with limited powers. In the case of *The Queen* v. *Sir Charles Reed*,[4] Cotton L.J. observed[5]:

> " . . . it was said that every corporation, unless restricted by its act of incorporation, has the same power as an individual to enter into contracts, including that of borrowing money. In our opinion this contention . . . cannot be maintained . . . the power of a corporation established for certain specified purposes must depend on what those purposes are, and except so far as it has express powers given to it, it will have such powers only as are necessary for the purpose of enabling it in a reasonable and proper way to discharge the duties or fulfil the purposes for which it was constituted . . . A trading corporation stands, as regards an implied power of borrowing, in a very different position . . . ."[6]

---

[1] Provided that the power is exercised in relation to one of the authorised objects of the company. *Re Introductions Ltd.* [1968] 2 All E.R. 1221; affd. *sub nom. Introductions Ltd.* v. *National Provincial Bank Ltd.* [1970] Ch. 199 (C.A.). *Cf.*, however, *Re Tivoli Freeholds Ltd.* [1972] V.R. 445 where *Re Introductions Ltd.* was said to be inconsistent with *Cotman* v. *Brougham* [1918] A.C. 514 and the High Court of Australia case of *H. A. Stephenson & Son Ltd.* v. *Gillanders Arbuthnot & Co.* (1931) 45 C.L.R. 476. See para. 42–10, *post*.

[2] *Bryon* v. *Metropolitan, etc., Co.* (1858) 3 De G. & J. 123; *Ex p. City Bank* (1868) L.R. 3 Ch. 758; *General Auction, etc., Co.* v. *Smith* [1891] 3 Ch. 432.

[3] See para. 9–04, *ante*.

[4] (1880) 5 Q.B.D. 483.

[5] At pp. 488, 489.

[6] See also *Baroness Wenlock* v. *River Dee* (1885) 10 App.Cas. 354.

If a company has no power by its memorandum to borrow, it can remedy the defect by taking such a power, or extending it if its existing power is unduly limited, by altering its objects in the manner provided by section 5 of the 1948 Act.[7]

A company registered as a public company on its original incorporation must not exercise any borrowing powers unless the Registrar of Companies has issued it with a certificate under s. 4 of the Companies Act 1980 or the company is re-registered as a private company. Section 4 replaces section 109 of the Companies Act 1948. To obtain a certificate under section 4 the company must satisfy the registrar that the nominal value of its allotted share capital is not less than the authorised minimum and deliver a statutory declaration complying with section 4 (3). Section 4 (3) requires the statutory declaration to be in the prescribed form and signed by a director or secretary of the company. It must state that the nominal value of the company's allotted share capital complies with the authorised minimum and give details of the paid up share capital, preliminary expenses and payments or benefits to promoters. A certificate issued under the section is conclusive evidence that the company is entitled to do business and exercise any borrowing powers (s. 4 (6)).

If a company exercises its borrowing powers in contravention of this section the company and any officer who is in default are liable on conviction on indictment to a fine and on summary conviction to a fine not exceeding the statutory maximum (s. 4 (7)). The provisions of the section are without prejudice to the validity of any transaction entered into by the company. However, if a company enters into a transaction in contravention of section 4 and fails to comply within 21 days from being called upon to do so, the directors of the company shall be jointly and severally liable to indemnify the other party to the transaction in respect of any loss or damage suffered by him by reason of the failure to comply with those obligations (s. 4 (8)). The wording of section 4 (8) is infelicitous. Section 4 (1) contains a prohibition backed by criminal sanction (s. 4 (7)). Section 4 (8) nevertheless appears to suggest that the borrowing is not illegal and void. If the borrowing is not illegal and void it is difficult to see what loss the lender will suffer. The new wording is different from section 109 of the 1948 Act. The latter expressly provided that any such contract was provisional and only became binding when the company was entitled to commence business, and did not contain any indemnity provision. A lender could thus lose interest. The directors, however, could be liable for breach of warranty of authority if their conduct implied a warranty on their part that the contracts were immediately binding on the company.[8]

Presumably the new wording has been adopted to comply with article 4 of the Second Directive which provides that where the laws of Member States prescribe that a company may not commence business without

---

[7] See para. 9–38, *ante*.
[8] *Brownett* v. *Newton* (1941) 64 C.L.R. 439.

authorisation they shall also make provision for responsibility for liabilities incurred by or on behalf of the company during the period before such authorisation is granted or refused. This was not to apply to liabilities concluded under contracts made by the company conditionally upon it being granted authorisation to commence business. The new wording is unfortunate and the directive would have been adequately complied with by adding the case law rule to a modified version of section 109.

Limits of borrowing powers

42–02 Sometimes, though rarely, the memorandum limits the borrowing powers to a specific sum, or to a sum not exceeding the paid-up capital; but in the vast majority of cases no limit is imposed by the memorandum, and there is nothing in the Acts to limit borrowing powers. If, therefore, the company has express or implied power to borrow, it may from time to time borrow as much as it wants, subject to any restrictions in its articles.

Powers incidental to borrowing powers

Power to give security

42–03 Where a company has power to borrow, it has, as incidental thereto, power to secure the repayment of borrowed money by mortgage or charge of all or any of its property, real or personal, present or future.[9]

Power to mortgage uncalled capital in England

It is now settled[10] that a power to borrow, if there is nothing to the contrary in the memorandum or articles, includes the power to charge the uncalled capital of the company. But "if the memorandum when authorising certain charges has omitted to authorise a charge upon uncalled capital, the omission may imply a prohibition."[11]

It is not essential that a power to mortgage uncalled capital or future calls should be given in terms by the articles; something less may be sufficient; thus a power in the memorandum to mortgage the property *and rights* of the company is sufficient.[12] So, too, a power to mortgage the company's "assets" appears to be sufficient[13]; or to raise money "in various modes," or "in such manner as the company may determine"[14]; or to raise money on "any security of the company."[15] But a power to borrow on the *property* of the company will not authorise a

---

[9] *Australian, etc., Co.* v. *Mounsey* (1858) 4 K. & J. 733; *Re Patent File Co.* (1870) L.R. 6 Ch. 83. On charges securing debentures, see paras. 44–01 *et seq., post.*
[10] *Re Phoenix Bessemer Co.* (1875) 44 L.J.Ch. 683; 32 L.T. 403; *Re Pyle Works* (1890) 44 Ch.D. 534; *Newton* v. *Debenture Holders of Anglo-Australian, etc., Co.* [1895] A.C. 244. For the history of the rule, see Palmer, *Company Law*, (19th ed.), p. 259.
[11] *Per* Lord Macnaghten in *Newton* v. *Debenture Holders of Anglo-Australian, etc., Co.* [1895] A.C. 244, 249.
[12] *Howard* v. *Patent Ivory Co.* (1888) 38 Ch.D. 156.
[13] *Page* v. *International, etc., Co.* (1893) 68 L.T. 435.
[14] *Jackson* v. *Rainford* [1896] 2 Ch. 340.
[15] *Newton* v. *Debenture Holders of Anglo-Australian, etc., Co., ante.*

charge on the company's uncalled capital, for uncalled capital is only "property" potentially, that is to say, when called up[16]; and even the words "property both present and future" are insufficient.[17]

A mortgage of uncalled capital does not prevent the company from forfeiting the shares for non-payment of calls.[18]

A receiver cannot make calls, unless

(1) the articles authorise the directors to delegate their power of making calls to a receiver, or
(2) the court orders him to make calls. The court may also order the directors, or (in a winding up) the liquidator, to make calls and hand them over to the receiver.[19]

Power to mortgage uncalled capital in Scotland

42–04 A company may, if so authorised by its memorandum and articles, create a fixed security over its uncalled capital, and this power is subject to the same qualifications as apply in England. To make the security effective, however, there must be intimation of the assignation to each shareholder.[20] A company limited by guarantee cannot grant a fixed security over its guarantee fund, since this is available only to meet claims in its liquidation.[21]

A company may by statute grant a floating charge over its uncalled capital, and if it is so charged it will be within the powers of a receiver appointed by virtue of that charge to call it up.[22]

As to mortgaging reserve liability[23]

42–05 The Court of Appeal, in *Re Mayfair Property Co., Bartlett* v. *Mayfair Property Co.*,[24] held that a reserve liability created under sections corresponding to section 60 (or section 64) cannot be charged by the company under a power in its memorandum or articles to charge its uncalled capital. In that case the reserve liability was created *before* the creation of the floating charge; it is believed that if the sequence is reversed, *viz.* if the reserve liability is created *after* the creation of the floating charge, the part of the uncalled capital already charged by way of the floating charge remains so charged.

Borrowing on the security of property situate abroad

42–06 A company holding property abroad may have to consider how such property can best be made available as security. The leading principle to be

---

16 *Irvine* v. *Union Bank of Australia* (1877) 2 App.Cas. 366.
17 *Re Streatham Estates Co.* [1897] 1 Ch. 15; *Re Russian Spratts Ltd.* [1898] 2 Ch. 149.
18 *Re Agency Land and Finance Co.* (1903) 20 T.L.R. 41.
19 See *Re Phoenix Bessemer Co., supra; Company Precedents*, Part III (15th ed.), p. 698.
20 *Liquidator of the Union Club Ltd.* v. *The Edinburgh Life Assurance Co.* 1906, 8 F. 1143; 14 S.L.T. 314; *Liquidator of Ballachulish Slate Quarries Co. Ltd.* v. *Malcolm, etc.* 1908, 15 S.L.T. 963; 1908, 16 S.L.T. 48.
21 *Robertson* v. *British Linen Bank* 1890, 18 R. 1225.
22 Companies (Floating Charges and Receivers) (Scotland) Act, 1972, ss. 1 and 15.
23 On reserve liability generally, see para. 29–08, *ante*.
24 [1898] 2 Ch. 28; and see *Re Irish Club Co. Ltd.* [1906] W.N. 127.

borne in mind with regard to this is that immovable property is generally governed by the *lex situs*, and therefore to perfect the title of the mortgagee or chargee upon property situate abroad the local law must be complied with.[25] Unless it is, the title of the mortgagee or chargee may be defective or may have to give way to a local mortgage, charge, lien or execution. It would be impossible here to consider the various peculiar conditions of the *lex situs* in different countries: sometimes the local law does not permit land to be vested in aliens, or in a foreign corporation: sometimes it does not recognise trusts or a floating charge: sometimes it does not allow concessions to be charged or chattels to be mortgaged unless possession is at once taken by the mortgagee. In cases like these the company should perfect as far as possible the security it offers according to the requirements of the local law. If it is unable to do this, it may yet through its articles give constructive notice to all persons dealing with it of the charge. These persons would then, at least, according to English law, be unable to claim that they had no notice of the charge.

Even without complying with the formalities required by the *lex situs* in relation to legal mortgages or transfers, it is still competent to an English company to create an effective equitable charge on property belonging to it in a foreign country; for the English courts, exercising their equitable jurisdiction *in personam*, enforce equities in regard to foreign land where the mortgagor company is within the jurisdiction[26]; and in determining whether there is an equity the court applies English, not foreign, law, and if according to English law there is an equity, *e.g.* if for valuable consideration a company agrees to give a charge on foreign property, the court will enforce it, although the equity may be one not recognised by the *lex situs*[27]; but—and this is the danger of the situation—it will only enforce it subject to any rights which may in the meanwhile have been rightfully acquired under the local law of the foreign country. This is illustrated in *Maudslay* v. *Maudslay, Sons & Field*.[28] There the debenture holders of an English company had a floating charge on its assets which included a French debt due to the company. A creditor of the company in France attached this debt by legal process in France, and the court in England held that the title

---

[25] See Clive M. Schmitthoff, *The English Conflict of Laws*, (3rd ed., 1954), pp. 171 *et seq.*; Dicey and Morris, *The Conflict of Laws*, (10th ed., by Dr. J. H. C. Morris and others), Vol. 2, Part Four. For a discussion of the Extra-territoriality of Floating Charges and of Receiverships see *Kerr on Receivers*, (15th ed., by R. Walton), Chap. 18 and App. VI (Securities Comparable to Floating Charges in other Jurisdictions). See also Lawrence Collins "Floating Charges, Receivers and Managers and the Conflict of Laws" (1978) 27 I.C.L.Q. 691. The difficult questions of security over movables and choses in action and priorities are not discussed here and the reader should consult the above works.

[26] *Penn* v. *Lord Baltimore* (1750) Ves.Sen. 444; W. & T.L.C., (9th ed.), p. 638; *Cranstown* v. *Johnston* (1796) 3 Ves. 170; *Mercantile, etc., Co.* v. *River Plate, etc., Co.* [1892] 2 Ch. 303; *Duder* v. *Amsterdamsch Trustees Kantoor* [1902] 2 Ch. 132; *British South Africa Co.* v. *De Beers* [1912] A.C. 52; *Re Anchor Line Henderson Brothers) Ltd.* [1937] Ch. 483. See para. 44–06, *post*.

[27] *Ex p. Pollard* (1838–40) 4 Deac. 27; *Coote* v. *Jecks* (1872) L.R. 13 Eq. 597; *Hicks* v. *Powell* (1869) L.R. 4 Ch. 741; *Ex p. Holthausen* (1874) L.R. 9 Ch. 722.

[28] [1900] 1 Ch. 602.

of the French creditor must prevail against a receiver for the debenture holders subsequently appointed.[29]

Exercise of borrowing powers

42–07 Usually the articles authorise the directors to exercise the company's borrowing powers. This authority may be given in two ways: either *generally* by a clause empowering the directors to exercise all such powers as may be exercised by the company, and are not, by the articles or by statute, expressly directed or required to be exercised or done by the company in general meeting (art. 80),[30] or by a *special* clause empowering the directors to borrow or raise money; but it is not uncommon for articles to provide that the directors shall not borrow more than a specified sum without the sanction of a general meeting (art. 79).[31]

The Rules of the Stock Exchange require,[32] as regards companies the shares or debentures of which are quoted or dealt in on the Stock Exchange, that the borrowing power of directors be limited so that

> "the aggregate amount for the time being remaining undischarged of all moneys borrowed by the group (exclusive of inter-group borrowings) shall not, except with the consent of the company in general meeting, exceed an ascertainable amount."

For the purpose of this limit the issue of loan capital is deemed to constitute borrowing notwithstanding that it has been issued in whole or part for a consideration other than cash.

Borrowing for a specific purpose[33]

42–08 A company may by the terms of a contract of loan from a third party bind itself to use the money for one specific purpose only, *e.g.* the payment of particular creditors.[33a] This gives rise to a primary trust in favour of those creditors. In the event of the money not being used for that purpose a secondary trust will arise in favour of the lender and the money will not become part of the general assets of the company.[34] Knowledge or notice of this trust is, however, necessary to bind the company's bank but notice received after receipt of the money may be effective.[35]

If the company receives money, not by way of a loan, but as purchase price for its goods paid in advance of delivery by members of the public, a trust for the purchasers may be constituted by transferring the advance payments to a separate "customers' trust deposit account."[36]

---

[29] These principles do not apply to Scottish companies.
[30] *Re Patent File Co.* (1870) L.R. 6 Ch. 83; *Re Anglo-Danubian Co.* (1875) L.R. 20 Eq. 339.
[31] See further Palmer's *Company Precedents*, Part I, (17th ed.), pp. 538 *et seq.*.
[32] Rules of the Stock Exchange, Sched. VII, Pt. A, D (1), para. 136.
[33] This paragraph refers to English law and is not applicable in Scotland.
[33a] *Cf. Re Rogers, ex p. Holland & Hannen* (1891) 8 Morr. 243 (C.A.).
[34] *Barclays Bank Ltd.* v. *Quistclose Investment Ltd.* [1970] AC 567. See also *Swiss Bank Corpn.* v. *Lloyds Bank Ltd.*, [1981] 2 All E.R. 449 (H.L.).
[35] [1970] AC at p. 582 *per* Lord Wilberforce; *cf.* p. 578 *per* Lord Reid.
[36] *Re Kayford Ltd.* [1975] 1 W.L.R. 279. See also *Re Chelsea Cloisters Ltd.* (1981) 131 N.L.J. 482 (C.A.).

Mode of borrowing

42–09 A company which has power to borrow may borrow in such manner as it thinks fit. It can therefore raise money on a legal mortgage of any specific portions of its property, or by equitable charge, *e.g.* deposit of title deeds, or by a floating charge on the whole undertaking of the company,[37] or by bonds, or by promissory notes, or by debentures or debenture stock.[38]

Bank overdrafts

Incurring a bank overdraft is a form of borrowing and, as such, counts for the purpose of calculating whether a company has exceeded any limit on its borrowing.[39] A bank has a lien to secure its overdraft on securities belonging to the company which are deposited with it[40] unless; (a) the terms of the deposit expressly exclude it[41] or (b) the securities are deposited for a specific purpose.[42] Securities deposited for safe keeping are not subject to the bank's lien,[43] probably because receipt for such purposes involves an implied contract inconsistent with a lien.[44]

Negotiable instruments

Negotiable instruments are often used for the purposes of incurring credit. Trade bills—drawn against produce or goods—are extremely common. Increasingly common now are commercial bills whereby financial institutions effectively lend a company their credit by accepting them and enabling it to discount the bills through a broker or discount house. Holders of the company's bills and notes are unsecured creditors and in a winding up rank as ordinary creditors.[45] Under the older authorities it was held that a company could only make use of this form of credit if it was expressly empowered or if its business made it necessary.[46] It is thought that a more lenient view would be taken today at least as regards payment by cheque and in any event section 9 of the European Communities Act 1972 would generally protect the holder.[47]

---

37 See further paras. 44–01 *et seq., post.*
38 See as to these, paras. 43–04 *et seq., post.*
39 *Looker* v. *Wrigley* (1880) 9 Q.B.D. 397; *Brooks* v. *Blackburn Building Society* (1885) 9 App. Cas. 857, 865, 868.
40 *Davis* v. *Bowsher* (1794) 5 Term. Rep. 488; *Bock* v. *Gorrisen* (1860) 2 De G.F. & J. 434; *London Chartered Bank* v. *White* (1879) 4 App. Cas. 413, 422 (P.C.).
41 *Wilde* v. *Radford* (1864) 33 L.J. Ch. 51; *Re Bowes, Earl of Strathmore* v. *Vane* (1887) 33 Ch.D. 586.
42 *Brandao* v. *Barnett* (1846) 12 Cl. & F. 787; *Leese* v. *Martin* (1873) L.R. 17 Eq. 224. Such an arrangement may give rise to an equitable charge or interest which is prior in time to the lien—*Swiss Bank Corpn.* v. *Lloyds Bank Ltd.* [1981] 2 All E.R. 449 (H.L.).
43 *Brandao* v. *Barnett* (*supra*); *Hamilton* v. *Bank of New South Wales* (1894) 15 L.R. (N.S.W.) 100.
44 For a more detailed discussion see Paget's *Law of Banking*, by Megrah and Ryder (8th ed.), pp. 498 *et seq.*.
45 For a useful detailed discussion see *Byles on Bills of Exchange* (24th ed.; by M. Megrah Q.C. and F. R. Ryder), Chap. 34.
46 *Re Peruvian Railways Co.* (1867) L.R. 2 Ch. App. 617, 622. *Bateman* v. *Mid-Wales Ry. Co.* (1886) L.R. 1 C.P. 499.
47 See para. 9–25 *et seq., ante.* See also Bills of Exchange Act 1882, s. 22 (2) which preserves the liability of other parties.

Where the company holds the bills or notes of a third party it may use them as a form of collateral security.

Consumer credit

By virtue of sections 8, 16 and 189 of the Consumer Credit Act 1974 borrowing by a company is not a regulated personal credit agreement but a company may be a "joint debtor" with an individual and thus become subject to the Act (s. 185 (5)). A joint and several obligation would not be caught. A guarantee by an individual of a loan to the company would also not be caught.[48]

Ultra vires borrowing

Borrowing ultra vires the company

42–10 Where a company has no borrowing power or where the memorandum of association fixes a limit to the borrowing powers of the company—a very rare thing—any borrowing in the one case and any borrowing in excess of such limit in the other case is potentially[49] *ultra vires* the company. Even if the company has such a power, a loan made in pursuance of an *ultra vires* object is also potentially[49] *ultra vires* if the lender knows both of the purpose of the loan and that the purpose is an *ultra vires* one, or has not otherwise acted in good faith in that respect.[50] This is because a power to borrow can never be a separate object of the company, even if the memorandum expressly states so, but must always be incidental to one of the objects.[51] If the lender could not have ascertained the purpose of the loan he is entitled to assume that it is being applied for an authorised purpose.[52]

Borrowing outside the powers of the directors

If the company has unlimited powers of borrowing but the directors, having only limited powers, exceed them, the borrowing is irregular for want of authority. This is not, however, a question of *ultra vires* and the act may be ratified by the shareholders.[53] In addition, the lender may be protected by the rule in *Royal British Bank* v. *Turquand*[54] and section 9 (1) of the European Communities Act 1972.[55]

The articles of companies listed at the Stock Exchange must contain

---

[48] See *Gore-Browne on Companies*, (43rd ed., by Boyle and Sykes), para. 17–2.

[49] Subject to s. 9 (1) of the European Communities Act 1972. See below, and para. 9–25, *ante*.

[50] The phrase "good faith" is used in s. 9 (1) of the European Communities Act 1972; on its meaning, see para. 9–25, *ante*.

[51] *Re Introductions Ltd.* [1968] 2 All E.R. 1221; affd. *sub nom. Introductions Ltd.* v. *National Provincial Bank Ltd.* [1970] Ch. 199 (C.A.) but see footnote 1, *ante*.

[52] *Re David Payne & Co. Ltd.* [1904] 2 Ch. 608; *Charterbridge Corporation Ltd.* v. *Lloyds Bank Ltd.* [1970] Ch. 62.

[53] *Irvine* v. *Union Bank of Australia* (1877) 2 App. Cas. 366.

[54] (1857) 6 El.. & Bl. 327, see para. 28–10, *ante*. See also *Gillies* v. *Craighton Garage Co. Ltd.* 1935 S.C. 423 and, for England, Law of Property Act 1925, s. 74.

[55] See para. 9–25, *ante*.

certain restrictions on the borrowing powers of the directors; in particular, it must be provided that the aggregate amount for the time being remaining undischarged of all moneys borrowed by the group (exclusive of inter-group borrowings) shall not, except with the consent of the company in general meeting, exceed an ascertainable amount.[56]

Effect of an ultra vires borrowing

42–11 Before January 1, 1973, any borrowing *ultra vires* the company rendered the contract void and incapable of ratification.[57] The effect of section 9 (1) of the European Communities Act 1972, which operates as from January 1, 1973, is substantially to amend that rule.[58] Provided that the transaction has been decided on by the directors[59] and the lender is acting in good faith[60] then the transaction will be valid in favour of the lender. He is protected as to (a) the existence of any borrowing power; (b) any limitations on the borrowing power; and (c) the purpose for which the money is to be borrowed.[61]

If the loan is *ultra vires* the company and the lender cannot avail himself of the protection of section 9 (1) because the requirements of the section are not satisfied, he may still have certain rights against the company in respect of the moneys received by the company though not under the contract of loan nor in an action for moneys had and received.[62]

If the lender intervenes before the money has been spent, he has a right to trace his money and to obtain an injunction restraining the company from parting with it. Even if the company has spent it but it has been applied in paying off *intra vires* debts owing to creditors of the company, he may be allowed by an equitable right akin to subrogation, to stand in the place of and to enjoy the rights of those creditors as simple contract creditors,[63] but not any securities for their debts held by such creditors.[64] The rights of a depositor in a bank where the whole banking business was *ultra vires* were decided in *Sinclair* v. *Brougham*[65] where it was held that the surplus assets after payment of valid debts must be distributed *pari passu* among the depositors and the shareholders in proportion to the amounts paid or subscribed by them.

---

[56] Rules on *Admission of Securities to Listing* issued by the Stock Exchange, Sched. VII, Part A, D (1), para. 136. See Vol II.
[57] For the position prior to 1973, see Palmer's *Company Law*, (21st ed.), pp. 361–363.
[58] See para. 9–25, *ante*.
[59] *Ibid.*
[60] *Ibid.*
[61] *Cf. Re David Payne & Co. Ltd.* [1904] 2 Ch. 608.
[62] *Sinclair* v. *Brougham* [1914] A.C. 398.
[63] *Blackburn Building Society* v. *Cunliffe, Brooks* (1883) 22 Ch.D. 61; 9 App.Cas. 357; *Re Cork and Youghal Ry.* (1869) L.R. 4 Ch. 748; *Re German Mining Co.* (1853) 4 De G.M. & G. 19; *Baroness Wenlock* v. *River Dee (No. 2)* (1887) 19 Q.B.D. 155; *Neath Building Society* v. *Luce* (1889) 43 Ch.D. 158; *Re Harris Calculating Machine Co.* [1914] 1 Ch. 920; *Sinclair* v. *Brougham* [1914] A.C. 398; and *Re Airedale Co-operative Society* [1933] Ch. 639.
[64] *Re Wrexham Mold and Connah's Quay Ry.* [1899] 1 Ch. 440 (C.A.)
[65] [1914] A.C. 398.

Joint debentures

Where several companies issued a joint debenture and each of them had power to borrow but no power to borrow jointly on debentures, each company was held chargeable for what it received.[66]

Personal liability of directors

42–12 The lender of money borrowed *ultra vires* the company has in some cases a right against the directors personally for breach by them of their implied warranty of authority, if their acts amount to an implied representation of fact[67] and it makes no difference as to the liability of the directors in such a case that they did not know that they were exceeding their powers.[68] But the directors are not liable if their acts amount only to a misrepresentation of law[69] except, perhaps, where the misrepresentation is fraudulent[70] or gives rise to an action for damages under the Misrepresentation Act 1967.[71] For example, a statement by the directors that they, the directors, had the necessary borrowing powers would be a statement of law; but a statement that the proposed borrowing would make the total sum borrowed by the company, say, £10,000, would be a statement of fact.

In *West London Commercial Bank* v. *Kitson*[72] the directors were held liable on a warranty of authority, though the private Acts by which the bank was constituted gave no power to accept bills. Since in this case the company was formed under two private Acts "the terms of which," in the words of Brett M.R.[73] "no one knew or was bound to know but they [the directors] themselves," this decision did not appear to be at variance with the old rule that a person dealing with the company must be taken to have notice of the contents of its memorandum of association or other documents by which it was constituted.[74]

It is doubtful as to the extent to which this liability is of any practical consequence since section 9 (1) of the European Communities Act 1972 became law. Only a lender induced by a misrepresentation may bring an action and such a person will be in "good faith" for the purpose of that section and so may regard the whole transaction as valid. It is only if the transaction is not "decided on by the directors" or if the company is insolvent that a lender misled by that director will have to seek a remedy under breach of warranty of authority.

Where directors personally guarantee repayment by a company of a loan which is secured by an *ultra vires* arrangement with the company, the

---

66 *Re Johnston Foreign Patents* [1904] 2 Ch. 234.
67 *Firbank* v. *Humphreys* (1886) 18 Q.B.D. 54; *Weeks* v. *Propert* (1873) L.R. 8 C.P. 427.
68 *Weeks* v. *Propert, supra.*
69 *Rashdall* v. *Ford* (1886) L.R. 2 Eq. 750 (where the company has no power at law to borrow on Lloyd's Bonds); *Beattie* v. *Ebury (Lord)* (1874) L.R. 7 Ch. 777.
70 *West London Commercial Bank* v. *Kitson* (1884) 13 Q.B.D. 360.
71 This would not arise in Scotland where the 1967 Act does not apply.
72 (1884) 13 Q.B.D. 360.
73 At p. 361.
74 See Chap. 28, *ante*.

guarantors are not necessarily relieved from liability by the claim being unenforceable against the company.[75] The matter is ultimately one of construction of the guarantee. If the guarantors undertake only to pay those sums which the principal debtor could lawfully be called on to pay but has not duly paid they will not be liable. If, on the other hand, the guarantors promise to pay those sums which the principal debtor has promised to pay but has not paid, whether the principal debtor could lawfully be called on to pay them or not, they will be liable.[76]

Control of borrowing

42–13 The powers of the Treasury to control borrowing in Great Britain, which were discussed earlier,[77] limit the exercise of the general borrowing powers which a company may possess under its constitution.

As the result of the General Consent of April 3, 1961, issued by the Treasury under the Control of Borrowing Order 1958,[78] it is not at present necessary for a company to obtain Treasury consent before exercising its borrowing powers, except in the circumstances specified at para. 26–06, *ante*.

---

[75] *Garrard* v. *James* [1925] Ch. 616.
[76] *Heald* v. *O'Connor* [1971] 2 All E.R. 1105, 1113, *per* Fisher J.
[77] See para. 26–01, *ante*.
[78] S.I. 1958 No. 1208. The order is made under the Borrowing (Control and Guarantees) Act 1946.

CHAPTER 43

DEBENTURES

Meaning of "debenture"

Not a technical term

43–01 The term debenture is not a technical term.[1] Lindley J. observed in one[2] case:

> ". . . what the correct meaning of 'debenture' is I do not know. I do not find anywhere any precise definition of it. We know that there are various kinds of instruments commonly called debentures. You may have mortgage debentures, which are charges of some kind on property. You may have debentures which are bonds; . . . You may have a debenture which is nothing more than an acknowledgment of indebtedness. And you may have a thing like this, which is something more; it is a statement by two directors that the company will pay a certain sum of money on a given day, and will also pay interest half-yearly at certain times and at a certain place, upon production of certain coupons by the holder of the instrument."

Chitty J. expressed a similar view[3]:

> "I cannot find any precise legal definition of the term, it is not either in law or commerce a strictly technical term, or what is called a term of art."

In another case[4] the same learned judge described the meaning of the term "debenture" as follows:

> "The term itself imports a debt—an acknowledgment of a debt—and speaking of the numerous and various forms of instruments which have been called debentures without anyone being able to say the term is incorrectly used, I find that generally, if not always, the instrument imports an obligation or covenant to pay. This obligation or covenant is in most cases at the present day accompanied by some charge or security."

43–02 In modern commercial usage a debenture denotes an instrument issued by the company, normally—but not necessarily—called on the face of it a debenture and providing for the payment of, or acknowledging the indebtedness[5] in, a specified sum—say, £100—at a fixed date, with interest thereon. It usually—but not necessarily—gives a charge by way of security,

---

[1] Only the modern meaning of "debenture" is considered in the text. On the historical meaning of that term, see Palmer, *Company Precedents*, Pt. III (16th ed.), pp. 1 *et seq*.

[2] *British India, etc., Co.* v. *I.R.C.* (1881) 7 Q.B.D. 165, 172, 173. See further *Knightsbridge Estates Trust* v. *Byrne*; [1940] A.C. 613, 621, 628, and Stroud, *Judicial Dictionary*, 4th ed., 1972, Vol. 2, tit. "Debenture."

[3] In *Levy* v. *Abercorris Co.* (1887) 37 Ch.D. 260, 264.

[4] *Edmonds* v. *Blaina Co.* (1887) 36 Ch.D. 215, 219.

[5] See *British India, etc., Co.* v. *I.R.C.* (1881) 7 Q.B.D. 165.

and is often—though not invariably—expressed to be one of a series of like debentures.

But the term, as used in modern commercial parlance, is of extremely elastic character, for

(1) it is sometimes used, both by lawyers and businessmen, to describe an instrument which is not called, on the face of it, a debenture, *e.g.* a bond[6];
(2) it is used of an instrument which is not one of a series.[7] A single debenture may be issued to one man[8];
(3) it is not the less a debenture because
  (a) it is not under seal[9]; or
  (b) it does not contain a charge[10]; or
  (c) it does not provide for payment at any fixed date but only in the event of winding up, or on some contingency[11]; or
  (d) there is no personal liability on the company to pay but the company charges its property as security for the debt of another person;
  (e) the debt is not quantified at the date of its creation.[11a]

Although the modern meaning of the term "debenture" is thus very wide, it would go too far to assert that every document creating or acknowledging an indebtedness of the company is a debenture. Commercial men and lawyers would certainly not use this term when referring to bills of exchange or other negotiable instruments, deeds of covenant and many other documents in which a company stipulates to pay a sum of money.

Statutory definition

43–03 The 1948 Act provides that "debenture" includes debenture stock, bonds and any other securities of a company, whether constituting a charge on the assets of the company or not (s. 455). This definition, introduced into company law by the reforms of 1928–29, extended the statutory meaning of debenture so as to include a mortgage by a company issued to a single mortgagee. Thus in *Knightsbridge Estates Trust Ltd.* v. *Byrne,*[12] the company mortgaged freehold land to the trustee of a friendly society to secure £310,000, and the mortgage provided that this sum, with interest, should be repayable by eighty half-yearly instalments. The company

---

6 *Gardner* v. *London, Chatham & Dover Ry.* (1867) L.R. 2 Ch. 201.
7 *Levy* v. *Abercorris Co.* (1887) 37 Ch.D. 260, 264.
8 *Robson* v. *Smith* [1895] 2 Ch. 118.
9 *British India, etc., Co.* v. *I.R.C.* (1881) 7 Q.B.D. 165, where a debenture was merely signed by two directors.
10 *Ibid.*; and *Speyer Bros.* v. *I.R.C.* [1907] 1 K.B. 246; [1908] A.C. 92; *Lemon* v. *Austin Friars Investment Trust* [1926] Ch. 1 (income stock entitling holder to portion of profits, but containing no charge).
11 On perpetual debentures, see para. 43–06, *post*.
11a *N.V. Slavenburg's Bank* v. *Intercontinental Resources Ltd.* [1980] 1 All E.R. 955, 976. *Cf.* however, *Re White & Shannon Ltd.* [1965] N.I. 15, 20 which was not cited.
12 [1940] A.C. 613.

claimed to be entitled to redeem the mortgage on the ground that the postponement of the date of redemption for forty years was a clog on the equity of redemption. This contention was rejected by the House of Lords, which held that the mortgage was a debenture, and that the doctrine of clogging the equity did not apply to a debenture, since, by what is now section[89] of the 1948 Act a debenture may be made irredeemable.[13]

"Securities" is apparently used in section 455 in a sense slightly in excess of its strict legal meaning; but it can hardly be intended to bear the wider or commercial meaning, which it is given, *e.g.* in the Exchange Control Act 1947, s. 42, and the Stock Transfer Act 1963, which includes shares.[14]

Apart from the Companies Acts, the term "debenture" is used in other Acts of Parliament, *e.g.* in the Stamp Act 1891.

Debenture stock

Debentures and debenture stock

43–04 The main difference between the position of a debenture holder and a debenture stockholder corresponds to that between a shareholder and a stockholder[15]: it is in the divisibility of stock.

A debenture is always for a fixed or ascertainable sum, *e.g.* for £100, and this sum is only transferable as an entirety, whereas debenture stock, unless the articles otherwise provide, can be transferred in fractional amounts, *e.g.* £550, or £71 or £13, and several small holdings can be consolidated into one larger holding, a single certificate being obtained for the aggregate amount. In order to prevent inconvenience to the company the articles commonly make the stock transferable in debenture stock units, *e.g.* of £5 or multiples of it, in the same manner in which they usually provide that, if shares are converted into stock, stock units may be issued (art. 41).

Two further differences between debentures and debenture stock should be noted: *first*, a terminological difference, *viz.* a "debenture" is the description of an instrument, whereas "debenture stock" is the description of a debt or sum secured by an instrument. It is borrowed capital consolidated into one mass for the sake of convenience.

Secondly, debenture stock is generally created by a trust deed which varies in its provisions from that securing debentures; this point merits further examination later.[16]

In the matter of security, of payment of interest, and of transfer, debenture stock hardly differs from debentures. Debenture stock is much used in modern practice; if the issue is "perpetual,"[17] it is very often in the form of debenture stock.

---

[13] See para. 43–06, *post*.
[14] *Cf. Re Rayner* [1904] 1 Ch. 176.
[15] See para. 32–06, *ante*.
[16] See below in the text.
[17] See para. 43–06, *post*.

Constitution of stock by trust deed

Debenture stock, as mentioned above, is generally constituted by a trust deed. The deed contains a covenant for the payment, either at a fixed date or in certain events (*e.g.* a winding up), of a specified capital sum—say, £100,000—which is to be called the stock, and for the payment of interest, and gives to the trustees security, by way of mortgage or charge, as in a debenture trust deed.[18] It contains also provisions for the keeping of a register, of the beneficial owners of the stock, and for transfers and transmissions thereof, and for the issue to such owners of certificates of title, and for meetings of the stockholders, etc., and it usually reserves to the company power to redeem at a premium before maturity.

Under the terms of the deed, there is not usually any direct contract by the company with the stockholder; but he is a beneficiary, and, as such, the court will recognise and protect his title.[19]

Debenture stock of a company under the Companies Act 1948 is essentially different from debenture stock issued by statutory companies under the Companies Clauses Act 1863.

Secured and unsecured debentures

43–05 Since a debenture need not, of necessity, contain a charge,[20] debentures are sometimes classified into secured and unsecured debentures.

According to the Rules of the Stock Exchange,[21] it is essential, in the case of debentures or debenture stock which constitute an unsecured liability of the company, that the same should be entitled "unsecured."

The charges by which debentures can be secured are considered in Chapters 44 to 46 for England and Chapter 47 for Scotland.

Perpetual debentures[22]

43–06 For many years it was common to issue debentures or debenture stock described as "perpetual" or "irredeemable," meaning that such debentures were made payable only in the event of a winding up or some serious default by the company. Sometimes, also, debentures and debenture stock were made payable at a remote period, such as 50 or 100 years after issue. In cases like these, doubts often arose whether the securities were effective, or whether the indefinite or prolonged postponement of the right of redemption was not in effect a "clog on the equity," and, as such, void. To remove these doubts, and to bring the law into accord with what it has

---

[18] In this respect, the provisions of the trust deed are the same as those of a trust deed securing an issue of debentures; see para. 44–18, *post*.

[19] *Re Empress Engineering Co.* (1880) 16 Ch.D. 125; *Gandy* v. *Gandy* (1885) 30 Ch.D. 57. It is not easy to reconcile with this *Re Dunderland Iron Ore Co.* [1909] 1 Ch. 446.

[20] See para. 42–02, *ante*.

[21] Rules of the Stock Exchange, Sched. VII, Pt. B, F (1), para. 170; see Vol. II hereof, Part C—316.

[22] The references to the doctrine of clogging the equity do not apply to Scots law. s. 89 applies in Scotland; see also the Redemption of Standard Securities (Scotland) Act 1971, s.2.

commonly been taken to be, the Act provides[23] that, notwithstanding any rule of equity to the contrary, no condition in a debenture or in a deed securing debentures shall be invalid by reason only that the debentures are thereby made irredeemable or redeemable on a contingency or after the expiration of a remote period (1948 Act, s. 89).

A mortgage of land by a company to a single mortgagee is a debenture within this section, and is not invalid by reason of the date of redemption being postponed to a remote period.[24]

For the wording of a perpetual debenture, see para. 43–10, *post*.

Section 89 does not, of course, validate the debenture if terms other than those relating to the date of its maturity constitute a clogging of the equity of redemption. These cases are considered later.[25]

Convertible debentures

43–07 The company may further issue so-called convertible debentures which are a hybrid form between debentures proper and shares.[26] A convertible debenture which may be issued secured or unsecured contains an option entitling the holder to convert his debt, at times stated in the debenture, into ordinary or preference shares of the company at stated rates of exchange. The rates for the exchange of the debentures into shares must not be lower than par unless the requirements of the Act as to the issue of shares at a discount are complied with.

Convertible debentures may be issued as debentures or debenture stock.

The Rules on *Admission of Securities to Listing* issued by the Stock Exchange[27] contain detailed provisions as regards convertible debentures; in particular, the debentures must be designated "convertible" and the company must maintain at all times sufficient unissued capital to cover all outstanding conversion rights.

The existence of potential shares from the conversion of convertible loan stock may cause problems in a take-over to which section 209 applies.[28]

Registered debentures and debentures to bearer

43–08 Debentures may be issued as

(1) debentures payable to registered holder;
(2) debentures payable to bearer;
(3) hybrid combinations of (1) and (2), being
   (a) either debentures payable to registered holder, but with interest coupons payable to bearer;

---

[23] A provision to that effect was first enacted by s. 14 of the Act of 1907.
[24] *Knightsbridge Estates Trust Ltd.* v. *Byrne* [1940] A.C. 613; see para. 43–03, *ante*.
[25] See para. 44–11, *post*.
[26] A specimen form will be found in Palmer's *Company Precedents*, Pt. III (16th ed.), pp. 247 *et seq*.
[27] Rules on *Admission of Securities to Listing* issued by the Stock Exchange, Sched. VII, Pt. B, B, paras. 157-159; see Vol. II, Part C.
[28] See *Re Simo Securities Trust Ltd.* [1971] 1 W.L.R. 1455, para. 81–07, *post*.

(b) or debentures payable to bearer, but with power for bearer to have them placed on a register and to have them at any time withdrawn therefrom.

The issue of debentures payable to bearer or of any of the hybrid combinations has been relatively rare in the United Kingdom since until recently it required the consent of the Treasury under the Exchange Control Act 1947, s. 10.[29]

In each case the debentures are usually secured by a specific or floating charge or by both.[30] These charges may be contained in the debenture itself, or in the trust deed (if any), or possibly in both documents.

A debenture, though one document, consists usually of two parts,

(1) the body of the instrument containing the bond or covenant and charge, and

(2) the indorsed conditions.

Debentures to registered holder

43–09 The object of the form of debenture[31] is to meet the requirements of the money market, and to facilitate and simplify dealings. It may be convenient to go through the various provisions of the usual form, and explain briefly their object and operation.

FORM OF REGISTERED DEBENTURE

Title ——.

The —— Company Limited

Issue of £100,000 *of debentures of* £100 *each, carrying interest at x per cent. per annum*

DEBENTURE

43–10 1. *The —— Company Limited (hereinafter called "the company") will, on the —— day of ——, or on such earlier day as the principal moneys hereby secured become payable in accordance with the conditions indorsed hereon, pay to A B of —— or other the registered holder for the time being hereof, the sum of* £100.

The registered debenture has many advantages:

1. The title of the debenture holder is recorded in the books of the company, and is consequently not exposed to the risks of loss or damage incident to a debenture to bearer passing from hand to hand.

2. The registered holder is the only person recognised by the company as entitled to the debentures. This simplifies dealings with the security.

---

[29] See para. 26–24, *ante*.
[30] See para. 44–01, *post*.
[31] The form of debenture discussed in the text is couched in terms of English law, and would require modification for use by a Scottish company, or if Scottish property is used as security.

3. The company having the names and addresses of the registered holders can more easily communicate with them where it wishes to do so for purposes of redemption, compromise or reconstruction.

4. The registered debenture is a species of security well understood on stock exchanges and favoured by investors.

CONSIDERATION. It will be observed that clause 1 does not express the consideration. In the case of a deed there is no need to do so; but if the instrument be under hand only, then the consideration should be stated, and even in the case of a debenture by deed, there is, perhaps, some advantage in showing, on the face of it, that it was, in fact, issued for valuable consideration.[32] In such a case, where it is desired to be more explicit, the clause can begin with the words "For valuable consideration already received," or, if desired, "In consideration of the sum of £—— already received."

"WILL PAY." The clause uses the term "will pay." This is a perfectly simple, intelligible and effective expression, and it is more suitable for an ordinary business document than the expression "covenants." But there is no magic in the term, and occasionally the words "undertakes," "promises," "covenants" or "binds itself" are substituted.[33]

TIME FOR PAYMENT. A debenture usually fixes a date for payment as above, *e.g.* at the end of five, 10, 20, 30 years, but sometimes it is framed as a perpetual debenture,[34] and in that case the clause runs "will, as and when the principal moneys hereby secured become payable in accordance with the conditions indorsed hereon," the intention being that the principal shall only become payable in the events specified in clauses 8, 9 and 9A of these conditions.[35]

Occasionally, where there is a temporary loan on debentures, they are made payable on demand, and then the clause runs "will, on demand in writing," or "will, at the expiration of seven days after demand in writing, etc." Such debentures are often issued to a company's bankers as security for an overdraft.

Where the money is payable on demand the debenture holder need only give the company time to get the money from some convenient place. He is not bound to give the company time to negotiate a deal which might produce the money.[36] If, therefore, the company has neither the money

---

[32] This point is not material in Scottish companies, since the doctrine of "consideration" has no application in Scots law.
[33] See *Ex p. City Bank* (1868) L.R. 3 Ch. 758; *Norton* v. *Florence Land Co.* (1877) 7 Ch.D. 332.
[34] See para. 43–06, *ante*.
[35] See paras. 43–24, 43–25, *post*.
[36] *Brighty* v. *Norton* (1862) 3 B. & S. 305, 312.

nor any convenient place to go to get it, the interval between the demand and the appointment of the receiver may be as short as one hour.[37]

PAYMENT TO REGISTERED HOLDER. The object of making the debenture payable to the registered holder is to simplify the title, and enable the company to look to some specified person as the holder to whom it can make payments, and whose receipt will be a sufficient discharge to the company.

In the absence of provisions as to register and ancillary clauses, the company would have to take notice of any number of assignments, charges and claims that might be brought to its notice.

Payment of interest

43–11 2. *The company will, during the continuance of this security, pay to such registered holder interest thereon at the rate of —— per cent, per annum by half-yearly payments on the —— day of —— and —— day of —— in each year, the first of such half-yearly payments or a proportionate part thereof, calculated from the date of issue of this Debenture, to be made on the —— day of —— next.*

CURRENCY OF INTEREST. A debenture almost always provides for payment of interest as in clause 2; but sometimes the interest is made payable quarterly. Very commonly the expression used is "will in the meantime pay," but there is some ambiguity in this expression. It may mean "until the date fixed for payment" or "until the date of actual payment." The latter construction would seem to accord best with the intention; and, as the words are ambiguous, should be preferred. Should the former construction prevail, however, subsequent interest would only be recoverable by way of damages.[38]

A provision in the debenture according to which interest shall be paid "free of income tax" is void as infringing the Taxes Management Act 1970, s. 106 (2).

HOW JUDGMENT AFFECTS INTEREST. Moreover, if the holder should obtain judgment on the debenture the interest would henceforth cease to be payable under the debenture, for the contract would merge in the judgment, which carries interest at 14 per cent. only.[39] However, by using the words "during the continuance of this security" both these difficulties are

[37] *R. A. Cripps & Son Ltd.* v. *Wickenden* [1973] 1 W.L.R. 944, 955 but *cf.* the Canadian cases of *West City Motors Ltd.* v. *Delta Acceptance Corp. Ltd.* [1963] 40 D.L.R. (2d) 818 and *Ronald Elwyn Lister Ltd.* v. *Dunlop Canada Ltd.* [1978] 85 D.L.R. (3d) 321 which represent a more realistic and humane approach.

[38] *Goodchap* v. *Roberts* (1880) 14 Ch.D. 49; *Cook* v. *Fowler* (1874) L.R. 7 H.L. 27; *Gordillo* v. *Weguelin* (1877) 5 Ch.D. 287, 303.

[39] Judgments Act 1838, s. 17. Administration & Justice Act 1970, s. 44 (1); Judgment Debts (Rates of Interest) Order 1982 (S.I. 1982 No. 696). See *Re European, etc., Ry.* (1876) 4 Ch.D. 33; *Ex p. Fewings* (1883) 25 Ch.D. 338.

avoided. Sometimes interest is made payable only out of profits,[40] and if the profits are insufficient or no profits are earned, the interest on the debenture is reduced accordingly; such debentures are known as "income" debentures.

A debenture holder who has neglected to cash cheques for interest before winding up does not lose his right to be paid arrears of interest.[41]

Charges[42]

43–12 3. *The company hereby charges with such payments its undertaking, and all its property, present and future, including its uncalled capital for the time being.*

A mortgage debenture generally contains a charge as in clause 3. Sometimes, however, the charge is effected by a trust deed[43]; but even where there is a trust deed, a floating charge[44] as above is very commonly inserted in the debenture. The word "charge" creates a good equitable mortgage; but equity is not particular as to the terms used, and the word "bind" or "mortgage" is equally effective. So, too, if it is stated that the property shall stand as a security, or shall be a security for payment, etc., that is sufficient. All that equity requires is a sufficient indication of the intention to charge.[45]

The words "including the uncalled capital" are very commonly inserted into the floating charge where the company has power to charge its uncalled capital.[46]

The inclusion of uncalled capital adds additional security, and, at the same time, does not prevent the company from calling up and dealing with its capital as and when required.

Reference to indorsed conditions

43–13 4. *This debenture is issued subject to, and with the benefit of, the conditions indorsed hereon, which shall be deemed to be incorporated herewith.*

The effect of these words in clause 4 is to import the indorsed conditions into the contract, and make them part of it.

Sometimes the above clause is omitted and the conditions are set out on the face of the debenture. This is an alteration merely in form, not in substance.

---

[40] See *Company Precedents*, Part III (16th ed.), p. 258; *Heslop* v. *Paraguay Central* (1910) 54 S.J. 234; *Popple* v. *Sylvester* (1882) 22 Ch.D. 98, and the observations thereon in the last-mentioned case.
[41] *Re Defries & Sons* [1909] 2 Ch. 423.
[42] On charges generally, see para. 44–01 and, for Scotland, para. 47–01, *et seq, post*.
[43] See para. 44–18, *post*.
[44] See para. 44–03, *post*.
[45] *Re Strand Music Hall Co.* (1865) 3 De G.J. & S. 147; *Re New Durham Salt Co.* (1890) 7 T.L.R. 13. The position is similar in Scotland under the Companies (Floating Charges and Receivers) (Scotland) Act 1972, s. 2.
[46] See para. 42–03, *ante*.

Sometimes the debenture, if secured by a trust deed, refers to the deed and its provisions.

Sealing

43–14 *Given under the common seal of the company this —— day of ——.*
Affixed in the presence of —— (L.S.)

In England a debenture is almost always under seal, but it need not be so; it may be under hand, and occasionally is.[47]

If the articles contain any special provisions as to affixing the seal, they must, of course, be observed.

Indorsed Conditions

43–15 On the back a series of conditions are usually indorsed as follows:

The conditions within referred to

"Pari passu" clause

43–16 1. *This debenture is one of a series of* 1,000 *debentures, each for securing the principal sum of* £100 *and interest. The debentures of the said series are all to rank pari passu in point of charge without any preference or priority one over another, and such charge [save as regards the hereditaments comprised in the trust deed below mentioned] is to be a floating security, but so that the company is not to be at liberty to create any mortgage or charge upon its property or assets or any part thereof so as to rank pari passu with or in priority to the debentures of this series except specific charges for securing temporary loans or overdrafts in the ordinary course of business.*

In many modern instances the prohibition to create prior or equal charges or mortgages is not absolute but is made subject to the consent of three-fourths in value of the outstanding debentures.

This condition does not prevent the company from reissuing the debenture after its redemption, provided that the requirements of section 90 are satisfied.[48]

EXPRESS "PARI PASSU" PROVISION.[49] The object of the *pari passu* provision is to place all the debentures on the same level as to security; so that, if the security is to be enforced, whatever is realised from it shall be divided amongst them rateably, in proportion to the amounts paid up on each

[47] See *British India, etc., Co.* v. *I.R.C.* (1881) 7 Q.B.D. 165, where the debentures were merely signed by two directors on behalf of the company, and *Re Fireproof Doors Ltd.* [1916] 2 Ch. 142, 150.
In Scots law a loan must be proved by writing signed by a duly authorised officer of the company, but it need not be a probative writ, or sealed; the position is thus equivalent to that in England.

[48] See para. 44–11, *post*.

[49] In Scots law the question of whether debenture holders rank *pari passu* is to be determined by the terms of the security document.

debenture[50]; and if more interest is in arrear on some of the debentures than on others, in proportion to the total amount due to each debenture holder for capital and interest.[51] But for some such provision the debentures would rank in point of security according to their dates of issue; and accordingly, the first issued would rank as a first charge, and the next issued as a second charge, and so on.[52] This would be entirely destructive of the marketable character of the security. Where there is a *pari passu* clause, a debenture holder who seeks to enforce the security must sue on behalf of himself and the other debenture holders. The presence of a *pari passu* clause does not, however, prevent a debenture holder whose debt is due from getting judgment and obtaining payment from the company if he can, and so, too, if, without judgment, he can obtain payment from the company, he cannot be called on to hand back what he has received for the benefit of the other debenture holders.

EFFECT AS TO SET-OFF.[53] Where a holder of debentures of a series containing a *pari passu* clause owes money to the company, he cannot, on a distribution of the proceeds of sale of the company's assets, set off his debt against the amount due to him on his debentures. The principle to be applied is that where a person entitled to participate in a fund (*viz.* the proceeds of sale) is also bound to make a contribution (*viz.* his debt) in aid of that fund, he cannot be allowed to participate unless and until he has fulfilled his duty to contribute,[54] and since this duty to pay his debt is enforceable by the company, he cannot, merely by refusing to pay it, obtain the effect of a set-off. This is not contracting out of set-off since the matter is one of equitable principle.

FLOATING CHARGE. "Such charge is to be a floating security."[55] It is, and has been for many years, usual to state expressly that the charge is a "floating security," or a "floating charge," although the presence of the word "undertaking" in the debentures imports this. And even where the word "undertaking" is not used, the fact that the charge is a general charge on all the property of the company as a going concern is regarded by the court as a sufficient indication of intention that the charge is to be a floating security merely; for, otherwise, the business of the company would be paralysed.[56]

---

[50] *Re Smelting Corporation* [1915] 1 Ch. 472; see also *Elders Trustee & Executor Co. Ltd.* v. *Beneficial Finance Corporation Ltd.* [1979] 21 S.A.L.R. 216.
[51] *Re Midland Express Ltd.* [1914] 1 Ch. 41.
[52] *Re New Clydach, etc., Co.* (1868) L.R. 6 Eq. 514.
[53] This paragraph does not apply in Scotland but a similar result would normally be obtained because the debenture holder is not debtor and creditor in the same capacity, being debtor as an individual but creditor jointly with others.
[54] *Cherry* v. *Boultbee* (1839) 4 My. & Cr. 442; *Re Goy & Co.* [1900] 2 Ch. 149, 153 *Re Brown & Gregory Ltd.* [1904] 1 Ch. 627; *Re Rhodesia Goldfields Ltd.* [1910] 1 Ch. 239 and *cf. Re Peruvian Ry.* [1915] 2 Ch. 144; *Wilkins & Elkington Ltd.* v. *Milton* (1916) 32 T.L.R. 618.
[55] See further as to this, para. 44–03, and, for Scotland, chapter 47 *post*.
[56] *Re Florence Land Co.* (1878) 10 Ch.D. 530; *Re Colonial Trusts* (1879) 15 Ch.D. 465, 473.

43–17 LATER SPECIFIC CHARGES. In condition 1 above, the floating character of the charge is largely qualified; for one of the most important features of such a charge is that it leaves the company at liberty to create specific mortgages or charges ranking in priority thereto. The condition, as above framed, restricts this power. Occasionally the prohibition is not confined to the freehold and leasehold land, but is general. Such a general prohibition, however, is often found extremely inconvenient.

LATER LEGAL MORTGAGE.[57] The prohibition, though good, is not absolutely protective; for, if the company, disregarding it, creates a legal mortgage or charge on the property in favour of a person who takes for value without notice of the prohibition in the debenture holders' charge, such person, in accordance with the ordinary rules, obtains priority by virtue of the legal estate.[58] And it has been held that an equitable mortgagee who obtains the title deeds and takes without notice of the prohibition obtains priority.[59] Where the clause expressly allows the company to mortgage its property, this does not, prima facie, authorise the company to create a further floating charge *pari passu* with the existing charge[60]; but an unlimited power to create charges over certain property may be sufficient to authorise a floating charge.[61] The practice of banks and others of inserting details of the prohibition in the registered particulars cannot give rise to constructive notice since it is not a required particular in England and Wales.[62] The position is different in Scotland.[63] However, even in England and Wales there is the possibility of actual knowledge which we shall discuss later. A practice is developing of inserting automatic crystallisation clauses in floating charges which provide *inter alia* that on breach of such a prohibition the charge shall attach and become fixed. These are common in Australia and New Zealand. The effect of such clauses is not free from doubt and we shall discuss them later.[64]

Register to be kept

43–18 2. ***A register of the debentures will be kept at the company's registered office wherein there will be entered the names, addresses and descriptions of the registered holders and particulars of the debentures held by them respectively, and such register will at all reasonable times during***

---

[57] This paragraph does not apply to Scotland, legal mortgages being invalid in Scots law.
[58] *English and Scottish, etc., Co. Ltd.* v. *Brunton* [1892] 2 Q.B. 700 (C.A.); see para. 44–08 *post*.
[59] *Re Castell & Brown Ltd.* [1898] 1 Ch. 315. See, as to a solicitor's lien, *Brunton* v. *Electrical Engineering Corpn.* [1892] 1 Ch. 434.
[60] *Re Benjamin Cope & Sons* [1914] 1 Ch. 800.
[61] *Re Automatic Bottle Makers Ltd.* [1926] Ch. 412.
[62] See Company (Forms) Regulations 1979 (S.I. 1547), Form 47. See J. H. Farrar [1974] 38 Conv. (N.S.) 315, 325 *et seq*.
[63] See Farrar, *op. cit.*
[64] See paras. 43–25, 44–10, *post*.

business hours be open to the inspection of the registered holder hereof, and his legal personal representatives and any person authorised in writing by him or them.

The original purpose of this provision, which predates compulsory registration of the charges with the company and the Registrar of Companies, was to simplify the title, and afford both to the company and the debenture holder, and those who may deal with the latter, a simple mode of ascertaining who is for the time being the proprietor of the debenture. Coupled with the next condition it has greatly facilitated dealings with debentures. Registration of the charges with the company is now prescribed by section 104 and registration with the Registrar of Companies by section 95 of the Companies Act 1948 (*vide post*, Chap. 45).[64a] There is still no obligation to keep a register of debenture holders but if one is kept the 1948 Act as amended imposes certain obligations.

Every registered holder of debentures or shareholder is entitled to inspect the register of debenture holders free of charge and to acquire a copy at a charge of not more than ten pence for every 100 words; and every other person has the same right, but may be called upon to pay an inspection fee not exceeding five pence (1948 Act, s. 87, as amended by s. 52 of the 1967 Act and the Decimal Currency Act 1969, s. 10 (1)). However the Companies (Registers and other Records) Regulations 1979 (S.I. 1979 No. 53), para. 4 allows such a register to be kept in a non-legible form.

The provisions of section 110 (2) as to the place where the register of members may be kept[65] also apply to the register of debenture holders (1948 Act, s. 86).

Registered holder only recognised

43–19 3. *The registered holder, or his legal personal representatives, will be regarded as exclusively entitled to the benefit of this debenture, and all persons may act accordingly; and the company shall not be bound to enter in the register notice of any trust, or, save as herein provided, and except as by some court of competent jurisdiction ordered, to recognise any trust or equity affecting the title to the debenture or the moneys thereby secured, save [as herein provided or] as ordered by a court of competent jurisdiction.*

The object of condition 3 is to fortify the title of the registered holder by making the company agree to recognise him exclusively. The latter part of the condition is intended to relieve the company, as far as is practicable, from the obligation to take notice of trusts or equities. Such a provision cannot, of course, relieve the company from its duty to recognise an order of the court[66]; but it is apprehended that, where there is such a condition, a mere notice of an equity may be disregarded; for one who claims under a

---

[64a] For Scotland, the equivalent sections are ss. 106A and 106D; see chapter 47, *post*.

[65] See para. 50–03, *post*.

[66] *Binney* v. *Ince Hall, etc., Co.* (1866) 35 L.J.Ch. 363.

debenture must be bound by the terms of the contract, and cannot be allowed both to approbate and reprobate.[67]

Transfer

43–20 4. *Every transfer of this debenture must be in writing under the hand of the registered holder or his legal personal representatives. The transfer must be delivered at the registered office of the company [with a fee of 15p] and such evidence of title or identity as the company may reasonably require, and thereupon [if this debenture remains registered in the name of the transferor the transferee will be recognised as having become entitled to the benefit of this debenture free from any equities, set-off or cross-claims which, but for this provision, the company would be entitled to set up against the transferor and] the transfer will be registered and a note of such registration will be indorsed hereon. The company shall be entitled to retain the transfer.*

The principal object of this clause likewise is to simplify the title to the debenture, by providing for the delivery of every instrument of transfer to the company, so that if any question as to the title arises the company will have the requisite documents in its possession. In the absence of some such provision, the company would only receive a notice of the transfer which might or might not be authentic. In practice the condition is found extremely useful. The clause says nothing about a debenture holder's trustee in bankruptcy. He has power to transfer under section 48 of the Bankruptcy Act 1914.[68] Debentures which are listed on a Stock Exchange must be transferable without fee.[69]

A company is bound to exercise considerable care in regard to the registration of transfers. If it registers a forged transfer, it may incur serious liability.[70] No transfer must be registered unless an instrument of transfer is produced (see 1948 Act, s. 75), and the company (even in liquidation) is bound by the conditions.[71]

The company has, within two months from the date when the transfer is lodged with the company, to have complete and ready for delivery the debenture or certificate of debenture stock, unless the conditions of issue of the debentures or debenture stock otherwise provide (1948 Act, s, 80); if the company refuses to register the transfer, it has to inform the transferee within two months after the transfer of the debenture was lodged with it (s. 78).[72] The obligation under section 80 does not apply on a transfer to a Stock Exchange nominee. (Stock Exchange (Completion of Bargains) Act 1976, s. 1. See para. 39–30, *ante*. s. 5 of that Act also applies to debentures.)

---

[67] See, however, *Mackereth* v. *Wigan Coal and Iron Co.* [1916] 2 Ch. 293, and other cases discussed at para. 40–10, *ante*.
[68] Or in a Scottish sequestration under the Bankruptcy (Scotland) Act 1913, s. 97.
[69] Rules of the Stock Exchange Sched. VII Part B. D. 11.
[70] See para. 39–29, *ante*.
[71] *Farmer* v. *Goy & Co.* [1900] 2 Ch. 149; see further para. 43–39, *post*.
[72] See para. 39–23, *ante*.

On the death of a holder of debentures on which are indorsed conditions similar to 3 and 4 above, the company is bound to register the executor as a holder in his own name on production of probate, and cannot insist on a transfer being executed.[73]

As to the words in square brackets, see note to condition 7, *infra*.

Joint holder

43–21 5. *In the case of joint registered holders, the principal moneys and interest hereby secured shall be deemed to be owing to them on a joint account.*

Condition 5 is commonly inserted, but, having regard to section 111 of the Law of Property Act 1925, it is probably unnecessary.[74]

Closing of register

43–22 6. *No transfer shall be registered during the fourteen days immediately preceding the day by this debenture fixed for payment of interest.*

Condition 6 is inserted in order to prevent the great inconvenience that may arise if transfers come in just when the half-year's interest is being calculated. As companies are obliged to send out the interest on the day it becomes due, it is practically impossible to do this if a number of transfers come in during the calculations.

Exclusion of equities

43–23 7. *The principal moneys and interest hereby secured will be paid [and such moneys are to be transferable free from and] without regard to any equities between the company and the original or any intermediate holder hereof, or any set-off or cross-claim, and the receipt of the registered holder for such principal moneys and interest shall be a good discharge to the company for the same.*

Condition 7 is one of the most important conditions in the debenture. Prima facie a debenture, being a chose in action, is only assignable subject to all equities between the company and the original subscribers.[75] Thus, in *Athenaeum, etc., Soc.* v. *Pooley*,[76] debentures had been issued to A as part of the consideration for property sold by him to the company. The price was excessive, and A had bribed the company's manager, who arranged the sale. A afterwards transferred the debentures to B, who sold in the market to C, who bought without any notice of the circumstances relating to their issue. C subsequently sought to enforce them as against the company. Held, that though C was a bona fide purchaser without notice,

---

73 *Edwards* v. *Ransomes & Rapier Ltd.* [1930] W.N. 180.

74 It is of more value in Scotland where the 1925 Act does not apply.

75 *Mangles* v. *Dixon* (1852) 3 H.L.C. 702; *Re Natal Investment Co.* (1868) L.R. 3 Ch. 355. Law of Property Act 1925, s. 136 (1), replacing s. 25 (6) of the Judicature Act 1873. These Acts do not apply to Scotland, but under Scots law the assignee of a debenture could not at common law assert any better right than the assignor. This condition is therefore of equal value in Scottish law.

76 (1858) 3 De G. & J. 294.

yet, being only a purchaser of a chose in action, he could stand in no better position than A, and therefore that his claim failed. Knight-Bruce L.J observed[77]:

> "Mr. —— appears to have bought these debentures innocently, but very imprudently, in the belief, probably, that they were good securities, and without notice of anything to the contrary. Unfortunately, however, he bought what the English law calls a chose in action, and it is too clearly settled to admit of question or argument that a person buying a chose in action, which can only be put in suit in the name of the original holder, cannot in general stand in a better position than the original holder."

But this "is a rule which must yield when it appears from the nature or terms of the contract that it [the chose in action] must have been intended to have been assignable free from and unaffected by such equities,"[78] and it is now a matter of course to insert such a provision in a debenture unless the circumstances are very special; for investors long since discovered the extreme inconvenience of dealing with a security which was liable to be defeated or depreciated by the unexpected intervention of some latent equity.

The efficacy of the condition is exemplified by the decision of Stirling J. in *Farmer* v. *Goy & Co.*,[79] which may be contrasted with *Re Taunton, Delmard & Co.*[80] and *Re Rhodesia Goldfields Ltd.*[81]

In the absence of the bracketed words in this condition and the wording of condition 3, the company can set up equities against an unregistered transferee of the debenture.[82] The bracketed words go far to nullify this power. In the light of *National Westminster Bank Ltd.* v. *Halesowen Presswork & Assemblies Ltd.*,[83] however, it would seem no longer possible to contract out of a right of set-off on a winding up but compare with such a right the application of the rule in *Cherry* v. *Boultbee*, discussed in para. 43–19, *ante*.

The latter part of the condition is useful as relieving the company from going into the question of title.

Notice by company to pay off

3–24 8. *The company may at any time give notice in writing to the registered holder hereof, his executors or administrators, of its intention to pay off this debenture, and, upon the expiration of six months from*

---

[77] *Ibid.* at pp. 298, 299.

[78] *Per* Lord Cairns L.J., *Re Agra etc. Bank* (1865) 2 Ch.App. 391, 397; *Crouch* v. *Crédit Foncier* (1873) L.R. 8 Q.B. 374, 385; *Re Blakely Ordnance Co.* (1867) L.R. 3 Ch. 154; *Higgs* v. *Northern Assam Tea Co.* (1869) L.R. 4 Ex. 387; *Re Northern Assam Tea Co.* (1870) L.R. 10 Eq. 458.

[79] [1900] 2 Ch. 149.

[80] [1893] 2 Ch. 175.

[81] [1910] 1 Ch. 239.

[82] *Re Palmer's Decoration and Furnishing Co.* [1904] 2 Ch. 743; *Andrews* v. *Brown and Gregory* [1904] 2 Ch. 448.

[83] [1972] A.C. 785.

such notice being given, the principal moneys hereby secured shall become payable.

Sometimes the words "after the —— day of —— next" are inserted before the words "give notice," so that the holder may have, at any rate, a term of five or ten or sometimes twenty years' quiet enjoyment of the security; but in large numbers of cases the clause is left as it stands above.

In instruments which came into operation after the commencement of the Law of Property Act 1925, "month" means "calendar month."[84]

As to the mode of giving notice, see clause 13.[85]

Immediate payment where default as to interest or winding up

43–25 9. *The principal moneys hereby secured shall immediately become payable:*

(a) *If the company makes default for a period of six months in the payment of any interest hereby secured, and the registered holder hereof, before such interest is paid, by notice in writing to the company, calls in such principal moneys; or*

(b) *If an order is made or an effective resolution is passed for the winding up of the company; or*

(c) *If a distress or execution is levied or enforced upon or against any of the chattels or property of the company, and is not paid or discharged within five days; or*

(d) *If a receiver is appointed of the undertaking of the company or of any of its property or assets; or*

(e) *If the company ceases or threatens to cease to carry on its business.*

REPAYMENT IF DEFAULT IN INTEREST. As to paragraph (a), it is more satisfactory to the investor to know that if his interest gets largely into arrear he can call up his principal, as in the case of an ordinary mortgage, and such a provision is valid. It is not regarded as a penalty against which equity can relieve.[86]

REPAYMENT ON WINDING UP. As to paragraph (b), it was long since settled that where a winding up ensues, the debenture holder is entitled to enforce his charge and obtain immediate payment, even though his debenture has not matured,[87] and even though winding up for the purposes of reconstruction is not one of the specified causes on the happening of which the security becomes enforceable.[88] Accordingly, the clause does not pre-

[84] See Law of Property Act 1925, s. 61 (*a*). The Interpretation Act 1978, s. 5 and Sched. 1. would apply a similar interpretation in Scotland.

[85] See para. 43–32, *post*.

[86] *Thompson* v. *Hudson* (1869) L.R. 4 H.L. 1; *Wallingford* v. *Mutual Society* (1880) 5 App.Cas. 685.

[87] *Hodson* v. *Tea Co.* (1880) 14 Ch.D. 859; *Wallace* v. *Universal, etc., Co.* [1894] 2 Ch. 547 (C.A.).

[88] *Re Crompton & Co.* [1914] 1 Ch. 954.

judice the position of the company, while, at the same time, it serves to make clear the position of the debenture holder—a position which otherwise would have to be ascertained from a study of the authorities. A clause such as 9 above enables the company to insist on paying off debenture holders in the event of the winding up of the company.[89] But the company cannot require trustees for debenture holders to release their security without satisfying them that all the debentures are paid off.[90] A clause restraining a debenture holder from taking proceedings on his debenture without the consent of the majority of the debenture holders is valid.[91]

The word "effective" is sometimes omitted. It may be very inconvenient for the debenture holder to have to wait to see whether a disputed or opposed resolution will become effective.

REPAYMENT IN THE EVENT OF DISTRESS, APPOINTMENT OF RECEIVER, ETC. Paragraphs (c) and (d) are necessary for the debenture holders' protection, as any of these events is evidence of an unsatisfactory, perhaps precarious, state of the company's affairs.

REPAYMENT ON CEASING BUSINESS. Where the company ceases to carry on business, it is clearly desirable for the debenture holders' right of repayment to arise. But it may be difficult to say whether in fact the company has so ceased, and even more difficult to show a threat to cease.

As an alternative to clause 9 the following clause is sometimes used:

Automatic Crystallisation where Default

9A. *The principal moneys hereby secured shall immediately become due and payable and the charge hereby created shall immediately attach and become affixed:*

(a)–(e) *as in 9 above*

(f) *If the company mortgages charges or encumbers or attempts to mortgage charge or encumber any of its property or assets contrary to the provisions of clause 1 hereof without the prior written consent of the registered holder.*

The practice of inserting such clauses has not been expressly tested in the English courts although there is some limited authority in their favour.[92]

In New Zealand Speight J. in *Re Manurewa Transport Limited*[93] upheld such a clause in 1971 but recently in British Columbia Berger J. rejected automatic crystallisation in *The Queen* v. *Consolidated Churchill Copper*

---

[89] *Consolidated Goldfields* v. *Simmer and Jack East* [1913] W.N. 41; 108 L.T. 488.

[90] *Re General Motor Cab. Co.* [1913] 1 Ch. 377, as explained in *Consolidated Goldfields* v. *Simmer and Jack East, supra.*

[91] *Pethybridge* v. *Unibifocal Co.* [1918] W.N. 278.

[92] *Re Horne and Hellard* (1885) 29 Ch.D. 736, *Davey & Co.* v. *Williamson & Sons* [1898] 2 Q.B. 194 and dicta in *Illingworth* v. *Houldsworth* [1904] A.C. 355, 358 and *Evans* v. *Rival Granite Quarries Ltd* [1910] 2 K.B. 979, 994.

[93] [1971] N.Z.L.R. 909. *Cf.* also *Stein* v. *Saywell* [1969] A.L.R. 481; 121 C.L.R. 529 (H.Ct. of Australia).

Corporation Ltd.[94] Since this raises important issues of principle and practice in relation to floating charges, we shall consider it in detail in the next chapter.

Warrant for interest

43–26 10. *In respect of each half-year's interest on this debenture a warrant on the company's bankers payable to the order of the registered holder hereof, or, in the case of joint holders, to the order of that one whose name stands first in the register as one of such joint holders, will be sent by post to the registered address of such registered holder, and the company shall not be responsible for any loss in transmission. The payment of the warrant, if purporting to be duly indorsed, shall be a good discharge to the company.*

Until payment of the warrant, the debt is not satisfied.[95]

If the debenture is under seal, the debt is a specialty debt, and the period of limitation is twelve years under the Limitation Act 1980.[96]

A statement of the amount of a debenture debt and accrued interest in the company's balance sheets, if duly signed by the directors, is capable of being an effective acknowledgment of the state of indebtedness as at the date of the balance sheet.[97] In most cases the signature of the directors will be made after the date of the balance sheet but it is not usually necessary under English law to prove that the debt was still in existence at the date of the signature.[98] The cause of action will be deemed to have accrued at the date of the balance sheet being the date to which the signatures relate, so that even if the date of the signatures is outside the period, it will suffice if the date of the balance sheet is within it.[99] It is doubtful whether such a statement can ever be relied on as an acknowledgment if a copy of the balance sheet is not produced to the creditor by the company.[1]

A director who signed the balance sheet cannot, in principle, rely on

---

[94] [1978] 5 W.W.R. 652.

[95] *Re Defries & Son* [1909] 2 Ch. 423.

[96] ss. 8 and 20. See also Rules of the Stock Exchange, Sched. VII, Parts B–G as regards forfeiture of unclaimed interest. In Scots law unpaid instalment of interest prescribe after five years unless the period of prescription is interrupted by a "relevant" claim or acknowledgment: Prescription and Limitation (Scotland) Act 1973, s. 6, etc.

[97] *Re Atlantic and Pacific, etc., Co.* [1928] Ch. 836; *Jones* v. *Bellgrove Properties Ltd.* [1949] 2 K.B. 700; *Consolidated Agencies Ltd.* v. *Bertram Ltd.* [1965] A.C. 470; *Re Gee & Co. (Woolwich) Ltd.* [1974] 2 W.L.R. 515; *Re Compania de Electricidad de la Provincia de Buenos Aires Ltd.* [1978] 3 All E.R. 668. In the last case Slade J. held that proof of receipt of the accounts by a shareholder was necessary for an acknowledgment to him of a debt of unclaimed dividends; see below, *post.* See also *Re Overmark Smith Warden, The Times,* March 22, 1982 (statement of affairs).

[98] *Re Gee & Co. (Woolwich) Ltd., supra*, where Brightman J. refused to accept the Privy Council decision in *Consolidated Agencies Ltd.* v. *Bertram Ltd., supra.*

[99] *Re Gee & Co. (Woolwich) Ltd., supra.*

[1] *Consolidated Agencies Ltd.* v. *Bertram Ltd., supra*, where the Privy Council distinguished *Jones* v. *Bellgrove Properties Ltd., supra*, on the grounds that there the balance sheet had been produced to the creditor and no question was raised as to the precise date to which the acknowledgment related. *Re Atlantic and Pacific, etc., Co., supra*, was decided under an earlier enactment, now repealed, where the requirements as to acknowledgment were less stringent than under the present Act. See also *Miller* v. *Belmill Products Ltd.* [1976] 1 N.Z.L.R. 311 and *Re Compania, etc. supra.*

such an acknowledgment[2] because, in view of his confidential position, he cannot profit from the exercise of his powers for his own benefit unless so permitted by the articles. Exceptionally, however, a director may rely on the balance sheet signed by himself as an acknowledgment of a debt owed to him by the company, *viz.* if such acknowledgment is sanctioned by every member of the company.[3] In that case it cannot be said that the director was acting in breach of his fiduciary duty.

Power to appoint receiver[4]

43–27 11. *At any time after the principal moneys hereby secured become payable [or after the security constituted by the trust deed below mentioned becomes enforceable] the registered holder of this debenture may from time to time, with the consent in writing of the holders of the majority in value of the outstanding debentures of the same series, appoint by writing any person or persons [approved by the trustees of the said trust deed] to be a receiver or receivers of the property charged by the debentures [and not comprised in such trust deed], and may with the like consent remove any such receiver, and every such appointment or removal shall be as effective as if all the holders of debentures of the same series had concurred therein, and a receiver so appointed shall have power*

(1) *to take possession of, collect and get in the property charged by the debentures, and for that purpose to take all proceedings in the name of the company or otherwise as may seem expedient;*
(2) *to carry on or concur in carrying on the business of the company, and for that purpose to raise money on the premises charged in priority to the debentures or otherwise;*
(3) *to sell or concur in selling all or any of the property charged by the debentures after giving to the company at least seven days' notice of his intention to sell, and to carry any such sale into effect by conveying in the name and on behalf of the company or otherwise;*
(4) *to make any arrangement or compromise which he or they shall think expedient in the interest of the debenture holders.*

A receiver so appointed shall be deemed to be the agent of the company and the company shall be solely reponsible for his acts or defaults and for his remuneration. The provisions of sections 101 (1) *and* (2), 104, 106, 107 *and section* 109 (3) (4) (6) (7) *and* (8) *of the Law of Property Act* 1925 *and the powers thereby conferred on a mortgagee or receiver shall, so far as applicable, apply to the receiver so appointed*

---

[2] *Re Coliseum (Barrow) Ltd.* [1930] 2 Ch. 44; *Re Transplanters (Holding Company) Ltd.* [1958] 1 W.L.R. 822.
[3] *Re Gee & Co. (Woolwich) Ltd., supra,* at p. 527.
[4] For the position in Scotland, see Chap. 48, *post.*

as if such provisions were incorporated herein save that all moneys received by such receiver after providing for the matters specified in clauses (i) to (iii) of section 109 (8) *aforesaid and for all costs, charges and expenses of or incidental to the exercise of any of the powers of such receiver shall be applied in or towards satisfaction pari passu of the debentures.*

43–28 When a receiver[5] has been appointed, every invoice, order for goods or business letter must contain a statement to that effect (s. 370). The power to appoint a receiver may be vested in a third party, but in such a case is in the nature of a trust.[6] In the absence of a clause such as that set out above, the provisions of the Law of Property Act 1925 as to the appointment of receivers do not apply, at any rate to a debenture which is one of a series, charging the undertaking of the company.[7] A corporation or an undischarged bankrupt cannot be appointed receiver.[8]

Where the appointment is to be made "by writing," the instrument of appointment may be drawn up before it is intended to take effect, and dated and delivered at a subsequent date, although such an appointment, if by deed, would be invalid.[9]

The appointment in writing takes effect when the document of appointment is handed to the receiver by a person having authority to do so and the receiver accepts the proffered appointment.[10]

Unless the conditions of issue of the debenture expressly provide that the receiver shall be the agent of the company,[11] it might be held that he is the agent of the debenture holders; this applies even if the conditions expressly embody the sections of the Law of Property Act 1925 referred to in clause 11.[12]

The question of the receiver's agency is now perhaps of less importance, since section 369 (2) of the Act of 1948 provides that the receiver is to be personally liable on any contract entered into by him in the performance of his functions to the same extent as if he had been appointed by order of the court, except in so far as the contract otherwise provides, and is entitled to indemnity out of the assets. Thus, in *Re Mack Trucks (Britain) Ltd.*[13] the receiver was held personally liable in damages to employees expressly employed by himself for failing to give the requisite period of notice of termination of employment as prescribed by the Contracts of Employment

---

[5] On receivers (England) see para. 46–05, *post*, and on receivers (Scotland) see para. 48–01, *post*.

[6] *Re Maskelyne British Typewriter* [1898] 1 Ch. 133.

[7] *Blaker* v. *Herts, etc., Waterworks Co.* (1889) 41 Ch.D. 399.

[8] See para. 46–10, *post*.

[9] *Windsor Refrigerator Co. Ltd.* v. *Branch Nominees Ltd.* [1961] Ch. 375.

[10] *R. A. Cripps & Son Ltd.* v. *Wickenden* [1973] 1 W.L.R. 944, 953.

[11] See Palmer, *Company Precedents* (16th ed.), Vol. III, p. 239; *Cully* v. *Parsons* [1923] 2 Ch. 512.

[12] *Deyes* v. *Wood* [1911] 1 K.B. 806.

[13] [1967] 1 W.L.R. 780. The question whether the receiver would have been so liable if he had merely continued to employ servants under their existing contracts was expressly left open. As to the effect of the receiver's appointment on such contracts, see para. 46–07, *post*.

Act 1963. The effect of this section was also considered in *Lawson (Inspector of Taxes)* v. *Hosemaster Machine Co. Ltd.*,[14] where the Court of Appeal, reversing the decision of Cross J.,[15] held that the section did not preclude a subsequent receiver from ratifying an unauthorised act of the agent of a previous receiver, and, in the event of such ratification, did not impose any liability on the previous receiver, as he had never been a party to the contract.

43–29 Although the receiver may be the agent of the company, he cannot be compelled to perform existing contracts entered into by the company, nor can he be restrained by injunction from repudiating such contracts, provided that the repudiation will not adversely affect the realisation of the assets or the company's trading prospects; in this respect the receiver is in a better position than the company.[16] When exercising the power to sell contained in the debenture, the receiver is not the trustee of the company, even if he is its agent. He is not even its trustee in the general sense in which a director is sometimes described as such. The receiver is entitled to exercise the power to sell in the best interests of the debenture holders. It does not matter that the moment of sale may be unpropitious and that he might obtain a higher price by postponing the sale but he cannot choose the worst possible time. He must exercise reasonable care.[16a] The receiver is liable to the company if, when carrying out the sale, he acts in bad faith or omits to take reasonable care, *e.g.* if he negligently fails to make public important particulars of the property to be sold, and consequently the price obtained for it is lower than it would otherwise have been.[17] The duty is also owed to a guarantor of the company's indebtedness.[18] For the purposes of calculating redundancy payment, no transfer of business takes place from the company to the receiver and the company's employees continue to be employed by the company, and not by the receiver in his personal capacity.[19]

The receiver ceases to be the agent of the company if a winding-up order is made or a resolution for voluntary winding up is passed[20]; but he does not thereupon become the agent of the debenture holders, and the trustees for the debenture holders do not become personally liable upon contracts made by the receiver.[21] It should also be noted that although a receiver's authority to bind the company is determined by a winding up, his powers

---

[14] [1966] 1 W.L.R. 1384.

[15] [1965] 1 W.L.R. 1399. It is respectfully submitted that the view expressed by Cross J. at p. 1411 that s. 369 (2) has the effect of imposing upon the receiver the character of principal is not justified by the wording of that section.

[16] *Airlines Airspares Ltd.* v. *Handley Page Ltd.* [1970] Ch. 193.

[16a] *Standard Chartered Bank* v. *Walker, The Times,* June 21, 1982 (C.A.).

[17] *Cuckmere Brick Co. Ltd.* v. *Mutual Finance Ltd.* [1971] Ch. 949 (C.A.); *Standard Chartered Bank* v. *Walker, supra.*

[18] *Standard Chartered Bank* v. *Walker, supra.*

[19] *Deaway Trading Ltd.* v. *Calverley* [1973] I.C.R. 546 (N.I.R.C.).

[20] *Gosling* v. *Gaskell* [1897] A.C. 575.

[21] *Thomas* v. *Todd* [1926] 2 K.B. 511.

with regard to the property comprised in the charge are not affected[22] and an important advantage may be thereby gained in winding up by the insertion of a clause for the appointment of a receiver.[23] Where a receiver carries on an action brought by the company before his appointment and continues it after the company goes into winding up he may be ordered to pay the costs provided he has a right of recourse against the debenture holders.[24]

By section 369 (1) the receiver may apply to the court for directions.

A power to get in the property includes power to bring actions in the name of the company for that purpose.[25] A receiver appointed under the law of any part of the United Kingdom may exercise his powers in any other part of the United Kingdom, so far as their exercise is not inconsistent with the law applicable there.[26]

As to the receiver's duty to file his accounts, see section 374.[27] The court may fix the remuneration of the receiver on the application of the liquidator.[27]

If the appointment of the receiver is irregular or the charge under which he is appointed is invalid, *e.g.* for non-registration, he may be liable to the company as a trespasser. Likewise, if he takes possession of assets included in the charge but not belonging to the company, he will be liable to the true owner thereof.[28] But, in either case, he may be entitled to an indemnity against the assets or against the persons appointing him, provided he has himself acted in good faith.

The question of receivers is more fully discussed in Chap. 46, *post*.

Trust deed referred to

43–30 [11A. *The holders of the debentures of this issue are and will be entitled pari passu to the benefit of, and subject to the provisions contained in, a trust deed dated the —— day of ——, and made between the company of the one part and —— and —— of the other part, whereby [certain property] was charged in favour of trustees for securing the payment of the principal moneys and interest payable in respect of the said debentures.*]

This condition should be inserted where there is to be a trust deed.

It imports into the debenture the provisions of the trust deed, and renders the security subject to the obligations of the trust deed, and entitled to the benefit of it.[29]

Under section 87 (3) of the 1948 Act (as amended by section 52 (1) (*b*) of

---

22 *Gough's Garages* v. *Pugsley* [1930] 1 K.B. 615.
23 *Re Henry Pound, Son and Hutchings* (1889) 42 Ch.D. 402.
24 *Bacal Contracting Ltd.* v. *Modern Engineering (Bristol) Ltd.* [1980] 2 All E.R 655 and S&M Hotels Ltd. v. *Family Housing Association* [1979] Court of Appeal Transcript 132 (March 19, 1979).
25 *Wheeler (M.) & Co. Ltd.* v. *Warren* [1928] Ch. 840.
26 Administration of Justice Act 1977, s. 7; see Vol. III, para. L-734.
27 See para. 46–13, *post*.
28 *Re Goldburg* [1912] 1 K.B. 606; *Re Simms* [1934] Ch. 1.
29 See para. 44–18, *post*.

the 1967 Act) a copy of any trust deed must be forwarded to the holders of the debentures at their request on payment of a nominal sum.

Place of payment

43–31 12. *The principal moneys and interest hereby secured will be paid at —— Bank Limited, No. —, —— Street, London, or at the registered office of the company.*

In the absence of some such provision, the ordinary rule prevails, and the company is bound to search out its creditor and pay him, and interest runs until such tender is made.[30] Where a clause is framed in the alternative as above, it rests with the debenture holder to elect at which place payment shall be made, and he must communicate his election to the company.[31]

CURRENCY OF PAYMENT. The currency in which the debt has to be paid is determined by the proper law of the contract of loan.[32] In the case of an Australian company the debenture holders had an option to require payment in London and it was held that debentures which became payable in London were payable in English pounds sterling.[33]

A provision that the debentures should be repayable in gold of a certain weight and fineness was held to be valid in *Feist* v. *Société Intercommunale Belge*.[34]

If, according to the proper law of the contract, the loan is payable in a foreign currency, the English courts have jurisdiction, on application of the creditor, to give judgment in the foreign currency of the contract.[35] The foreign currency judgment can be executed in England only in pound sterling, and the rate of exchange will be the rate ruling at the date of the application for leave to enforce the judgment.

---

30 *Fowler* v. *Midland Electric Corporation* [1917] 1 Ch. 527, 532.

31 *Saunderson* v. *Bowes* (1811) 14 East 500, 508; *Thorn* v. *City Rice Mills* (1889) 40 Ch.D. 357.

32 See A. V. Dicey & J. H. C. Morris, *The Conflict of Laws* (10th ed., 1980), pp. 887 *et seq.*; P. M. North, *Cheshire's Private International Law*, (9th ed., 1974), pp. 247 *et seq.*; Clive M. Schmitthoff, *English Conflict of Laws*, (3rd ed., 1954), pp. 126 *et seq.*; F. A. Mann, *The Legal Aspect of Money* (4th ed., 1982), Chap. IX. (on International Monetary Obligations).

33 *Adelaide Electric Co.* v. *Prudential Assurance Co.* [1934] A.C. 122, overruling *Broken Hill Proprietary Co.* v. *Latham* [1933] Ch. 373. See further *Bonython* v. *Commonwealth of Australia* [1951] A.C. 201, and the cases quoted in Schmitthoff, *op. cit.*, p. 126, n. 97; further *The River Loddon* [1955] 1 Lloyd's Rep. 503 (Australian case).

34 [1934] A.C. 161. On gold clauses, see Schmitthoff, *op. cit.*, p. 127; Mann, *op. cit.* Chap. VIII; Andrew G. Lang, *Inflation as it affects Legal and Commercial Transactions* (1974), pp. 67–68 and E. Hirschberg [1970] 5 Israel L.R. 155. In *Treseder-Griffin* v. *Co-operative Insurance Society* [1956] 2 Q.B. 127 Denning L.J. in what appears to have been an *obiter dictum* suggested that a gold clause in a domestic contract was unlawful, but in *Multiservice Bookbinding Ltd.* v. *Marden* [1978] 2 All E.R. 489 Browne-Wilkinson J. refused to follow the dictum and held that an index linked money obligation in a domestic contract was not void as being contrary to public policy. See [1978] J.B.L. 118.

35 *Schorsch Meier GmbH* v. *Hennine* [1975] Q.B. 416; *Miliangos* v. *George Frank (Textiles) Ltd.* [1976] A.C. 443 (H.L.).

Service of notices on holder

43–32 13. *A notice may be served by the company upon the holder of this debenture by sending it through the post in a prepaid letter addressed to such person at his registered address. Any notice served by post shall be deemed to have been served at the expiration of twenty-four hours after it is posted, and in proving such service it shall be sufficient to prove that the letter containing the notice was properly addressed and put into the post office.*

It is a matter of great convenience to the company to have some special mode like this of serving notices provided by the debenture. In the absence of such a provision, it is for the company, if it desires to give notice, *e.g.* for the purpose of redemption, to find out the address of the debenture holder, and to take care that notice is effectually served on him. The above clauses relieve the company from this difficulty, or, at any rate, simplify the position very much.

Debentures to bearer

43–33 In framing a debenture to bearer the object is to endow it with the characteristics of a negotiable instrument, and in particular

(1) to make it transferable by delivery;
(2) to make it transferable free from equities;
(3) to render the delivery of the debenture and any interest coupon a good discharge to the company;
(4) to enable the bearer to sue the company in his own name, if necessary; and
(5) to insure a good title to any person who acquires the debenture bona fide for valuable consideration, notwithstanding any defect in the title of the person from whom he acquires it.

Negotiability of bearer debentures

In making the instrument payable to bearer the object is to make the security negotiable.[36] There is no objection in point of law to making the instrument payable to bearer without the production of any assignment.[37]

It was long doubtful whether debentures to bearer were negotiable instruments, but the time when it could be argued that they did not possess this quality has long passed, and it is now clearly established that bearer debentures are negotiable.[38] Bigham J. expressed this view in *Edelstein* v. *Schuler & Co.*[39] as follows:

---

[36] See para. 37–14, *ante*.

[37] *Per* Rolt L.J. in *Re Blakeley Ordnance Co.* (1867) L.R. 3 Ch. 154, 159; *Re Natal Investment Co.* (1868) L.R. 3 Ch. 355. In Scots law, bearer debentures are valid, by virtue of section 93, notwithstanding the Blank Bonds and Trusts Act 1696.

[38] *Goodwin* v. *Robarts* (1875) L.R. 10 Ex. 337; affd. (1876) 1 App.Cas. 476 (overruling *Crouch* v. *Crédit Foncier* (1873) L.R. 8 Q.B. 374). See further *Bechuanaland Exploration Co.* v. *London Trading Bank* [1898] 2 Q.B. 658; *Edelstein* v. *Schuler & Co.* [1902] 2 K.B. 144. For the historical development of the recognition of negotiability of bearer debentures, see Palmer, *Company Law* (19th ed.), pp. 292-295.

[39] [1902] 2 K.B. 144, 155.

"In my opinion the time has passed when the negotiability of bearer bonds, whether Government bonds or trading bonds, foreign or English, can be called in question in our courts. The existence of the usage has been so often proved and its convenience is so obvious that it must be taken now to be part of the law . . . ."

Care should, however, be taken that no condition or stipulation repugnant to or inconsistent with the nature of a negotiable instrument appears in the body of the debenture or in the indorsed conditions because that might deprive the debenture of its negotiability.

Payment of interest

In the case of a debenture to bearer it is necessary to provide for payment of interest in accordance with coupons annexed, for otherwise it would be necessary to insist on production of the debenture for payment of interest, and make some indorsement thereon of the payment. Where the payment is not to be made till a distant date, or the debenture is what is known as a perpetual one,[40] it is usual in the first instance to issue with the debenture only a limited number of coupons providing for the payment of interest, say, for 10 or 20 years. In such a case provision is made for the issue of further coupons when the original coupons are exhausted.

Exchange control regulations relating to bearer debentures or coupons

According to the Exchange Control Act 1947, s. 10, except with the permission of the Treasury, no bearer certificate or coupon must be issued, or a document must not be so altered that it becomes a bearer certificate or coupon.[41] This prohibition has, to some extent, extraterritorial effect: it applies to any issue or alteration—

(1) in the United Kingdom; and
(2) outside the United Kingdom if the issue or alteration is done by a person resident in the United Kingdom.

However, the Exchange Control (General Exemption) Order 1979 (S.I. 1979, No. 1660) removes the necessity for such permission. Bearer debentures and coupons are, therefore, possible.

Hybrid forms of debentures

43–34 A few observations have to be added with respect to the two types of hybrid debentures noted earlier.[42] The exchange control restrictions explained in the preceding paragraph apply to both of them.

Debentures to registered holder with coupons to bearer

These are framed on the basis of the registered debentures set out above,[43] but the conditions relating to the payment of interest (Condition 10)[44] are modified so as to provide for interest coupons.

---

[40] See para. 43–06, *ante*.
[41] See para. 26–24, *ante*.
[42] See para. 43–08, *ante*.
[43] See para. 43–09, *ante*.
[44] See para. 43–26, *ante*.

Debentures to bearer capable of being registered

This form of security may be said to combine the advantages of the registered debenture and the debenture to bearer. Those investors who prefer a debenture to bearer get it, and those who—like trustees—wish to avoid the risk incidental to the possession of an instrument to bearer can safeguard themselves by registering.

The form adopted for this convertible debenture usually provides for payment "to the bearer, or, when registered, to the registered holder of the debenture," and the conditions empower the bearer at any time to take it in to be registered in his name, and provide that thenceforth, whilst registered, the registered holder is to be regarded as the owner, and shall alone be entitled to give receipts for the principal moneys, and to transfer; and a further provision enables the registered holder at any time to have the registration cancelled and the instrument liberated and made again "to bearer."

Issue of debentures

Statutory and other provisions

43–35 IN COMPANY LAW. The provisions of the Act relating to prospectuses apply likewise to the offering of debentures, unless it is stated that they shall apply to shares only. The definition of a prospectus in section 455 and that of "offering shares or debentures to the public" in section 55 apply to both types of securities alike.

PREVENTION OF FRAUD. The regulations of the Prevention of Fraud (Investments) Act 1958, in particular the prohibitions and restrictions of sections 13 and 14, apply to debentures in the same manner as to shares.[45] The definition of "securities" in section 26 of the Act expressly includes debentures.

GOVERNMENT REGULATIONS. Apart from the special regulations formerly applying to bearer debentures and coupons,[46] the issue of every type of debenture, whether registered, to bearer or hybrid, has to comply with two sets of Government regulations, *viz.*—

(1) those applying to the issue and transfer of securities to persons resident outside the scheduled territories. These regulations are contained in the Exchange Control Act 1947[47]; and

(2) those governing the control of borrowing, as laid down by the Borrowing (Control and Guarantees) Act 1946, and delegated legislation made thereunder.[48]

---

[45] See para. 25–01, *ante*.
[46] See para. 26–24, *ante*.
[47] See para. 26–24, *ante*.
[48] See paras. 26–01 *et seq.*, *ante*.

Exchange control has now been suspended but the Bank of England must approve the timing of issues of £3 million or more.

STOCK EXCHANGE REQUIREMENTS. Where it is intended that the debentures should be quoted or dealt in on the Stock Exchange, the requirements of the Stock Exchange Rules, Sched. VII, Part B, have to be complied with. The most important of these regulations are noted in the text of this work, and Schedule VII itself is set out in Volume II.

Issue at a discount

43–36 Debentures may be issued at a discount where the directors have the general powers of the company, and there is nothing in the articles or memorandum to prevent issue at a discount.[49] The considerations which render the issue of the shares of a limited company at a discount illegal have no application to debentures or debenture stock. But where a debenture issued at a discount contains a clause enabling the holder to call for the allotment in satisfaction of fully paid-up shares equal to the full nominal amount of the debenture, that clause, it has been held, is objectionable,[50] since this would enable the company to issue shares, indirectly, at a discount.

In *Famatina Development Corpn.* v. *Bury*[51] bonus certificates payable out of profits were issued with debentures, and it was held that to satisfy such certificates by the issue of paid-up shares before profits had been earned was *ultra vires*.

But debentures may be issued as the consideration for the release of a right to share in profits, if the transaction is bona fide.[52]

Agreement to issue[53]

43–37 Where money is advanced to a company upon the terms that debentures charged upon the undertaking, or upon any specified property of the company, shall be issued by way of security, the lender at once obtains a charge in equity; for equity treats that as done which ought to be done.[54] The deposit by way of security of debentures containing a blank for the payee's name affords evidence of an agreement to give security by complete debentures in the form of those so deposited.[55]

Thus, where a prospectus offered for subscription £20,000 worth of mortgage debentures "to be secured on the entire property of the com-

---

[49] *Re Anglo-Danubian, etc., Co.* (1875) L.R. 20 Eq. 339; *Re Regent's Canal, etc., Co.* (1876) 3 Ch.D. 43.
[50] *Moseley* v. *Koffyfontein Mines Ltd.* [1904] 2 Ch. 108.
[51] [1910] A.C. 439.
[52] *Investment Trust Corpn.* v. *Singapore Traction Co.* [1935] Ch. 615
[53] This section has no application in Scots law.
[54] *Levy* v. *Abercorris Slate Co.* (1887) 37 Ch.D. 260, 264; *Tailby* v. *Official Receiver* (1888) 13 App.Cas. 523.
[55] *Re Strand Music Hall* (1865) 3 De G.J. & S. 147; *Re Queensland Land and Coal Co.* [1894] 3 Ch. 181; *Re Hampshire Land Co.* [1896] 2 Ch. 743; *Pegge* v. *Neath District, etc., Co.* [1898] 1 Ch. 183; *Simultaneous Colour Printing Syndicate* v. *Foweraker* [1901] 1 K.B. 771.

pany," and S. applied for debentures "upon the terms of the company's prospectus," and a resolution to allot was passed by the directors and notified to S., but no allotment took place, and afterwards a trust deed was executed charging certain property specified "in the schedule" in favour of the debenture holders, but no schedule was annexed, the court in the winding up held S. entitled to a charge on the entire property of the company.[56]

The operation of these cases is, however, to some extent modified by section 95, which requires particulars of every mortgage or charge for securing debentures or debenture stock to be registered "within twenty-one days after the date of its creation," and in default avoiding the charge as against the liquidator and the creditors.[57] Hence where there is an agreement for a charge, as in the case last mentioned, the equitable charge must be registered; even where, as in the case of debentures executed in blank and deposited by way of security, there is no accompanying memorandum of deposit. But although the court would be unable to treat an unregistered agreement in writing to give a mortgage or charge as a subsisting charge,[58] it would in some cases be able to compel the company to perform the agreement by creating the requisite securities,[59] and might in such a case, if the company was solvent, allow an extension of the time for registration (s. 101),[60] In brief, if no equitable charge is created at the time of the agreement, there would appear to be no obligation to register until the charge comes into existence.[61]

Scrip certificates for debentures or debenture stock, where the debentures or trust deed are not to be issued or executed for some time, are occasionally registered so as to afford interim protection. But where there is an agreement to issue debentures in the event of certain contingencies, there is no charge, even if the agreement is registered, until the contingency arises.[62]

Irregular issues

43–38 Irregular issues may be ratified and debentures irregularly issued may be enforced as agreements to issue debentures.[63]

Transfer of debentures

Form and effect of transfer

43–39 A debenture to bearer is transferable by delivery, and so is a debenture stock certificate to bearer. A debenture to registered holder is transferable

[56] *Re New Durham Salt Co.* (1890) 2 Meg. 360; 7 T.L.R. 13.
[57] See para. 45–03, *post*.
[58] *Ex p. MacKay* (1873) L.R. 8 Ch. 643.
[59] *Ex p. Homan, Re Broadbent* (1871) L.R. 12 Eq. 598; *Ex p. Hauxwell* (1883) 23 Ch.D. 627.
[60] See para. 45–10, *post*.
[61] *Re Jackson & Bassford Ltd.* [1906] 2 Ch. 467, 477; *Re Eric Holmes (Property) Ltd.* [1965] Ch. 1052.
[62] *Re Gregory, Love & Co.* [1916] 1 Ch. 203.
[63] *Re Fireproof Doors* [1916] 2 Ch. 142; *cf. Re Anchor Line (Henderson Brothers) Ltd.* [1937] Ch. 483.

in the manner specified therein, subject to the provisions of section 75 of the 1948 Act which require an instrument of transfer to be delivered to the company. This makes it necessary to have an instrument in writing. In the case of fully paid registered debentures a transfer in the form prescribed by the Stock Transfer Act 1963[64] may be used. The transfer is taken or sent to the office of the company to be registered and a note of registration is then indorsed on the transfer. The provisions of section 79 relating to the certification of transfers[65] apply to the transfer of registered debentures. As to the Talisman system of transfers of securities listed on the Stock Exchange see paragraph 39–30, *ante*.

After notice to the company of a transfer, the transferee can sue in his own name. Prima facie a transferee of a debenture not to bearer takes subject to all equities.[66] But, as appears above, the instrument usually excludes equities. As to forged transfers, see paragraph 39–29, *ante*. After a resolution to wind up voluntarily, a debenture of the company in the hands of a shareholder can only be assigned subject to future calls that may be made upon the shares held by the transferor.[67] It is otherwise where the debenture is by its terms to be transferable free from equities.[67] But even there the terms of the debenture may be such that the transferee cannot, until registration, maintain his title to the benefit of the provision.

It was held in *Driver* v. *Broad*[68] that debentures creating a floating charge on the undertaking of a company, which included land, created an interest in land, and that a contract for the sale of such a debenture was a contract for the sale of an interest in land within what is now section 40 of the Law of Property Act 1925, and therefore not enforceable unless in writing signed by the vendor or his agent. This would seem to apply to debentures to bearer charged on land as well as to registered debentures; but the solution of the difficulty is that, once delivery of a debenture to bearer is effected pursuant to the contract, the bearer is brought into direct privity with the company under whose seal the debenture is given, and his title is evidenced by writing.

Deposit of debentures or certificates[69]

43–40 Sometimes money is raised by the deposit by the directors of debenture or certificates of debenture stock which they have power to issue. There is no objection prima facie to such a mode of raising money. If the instrument deposited is negotiable, the depositee gets the legal title, and if the instrument is to registered holder, the depositee obtains a good equitable title,

---

64 See para. 39–18, *ante*.
65 See para. 39–26, *ante*.
66 See para. 43–23, *ante*.
67 *Re China Steamship Co.* (1869) L.R. 7 Eq. 240; *Re Taunton, Delmard, Lane & Co.* [1893] 2 Ch. 175; *Partridge* v. *Rhodesia Goldfields* [1910] 1 Ch. 239.
68 [1963] 1 Q.B. 744. This paragraph is not relevant to Scottish companies.
69 Mere deposit, except in the case of a negotiable debenture, is ineffective to create a security over the debentures of a Scottish company.

even though the debentures deposited are only in blank.[70] If the company is insolvent, the person with whom the debentures are deposited can claim a dividend on the deposited debentures *pari passu* with the other debentures of the series, until the whole of the debt as security for which the debentures were deposited has been paid.[71]

Specific performance[72]

43–41 Before 1908 specific performance of a contract to take or to subscribe for debentures could not be enforced. Thus, if A agreed to take up debentures of the company, and failed to pay, he could not be forced to do so, the theory of law being that the company could get the loan elsewhere and did not need to invoke the special jurisdiction of equity to aid it. All that the company could do was to sue the defaulter for the damages (if any) it had sustained.[73] But section 92 of the 1948 Act[74] expressly provides that a contract with a company to take up and pay for any debentures of the company may be enforced by an order for specific performance.

Where debentures are issued payable by instalments, and the company has declared the debentures forfeited, the company cannot recover calls made before the forfeiture under this section.[75]

Stamp duties

No duty on issue of non bearer debentures

43–42 In compliance with the law of the European Economic Community[76] the Finance Act 1973, s. 49 (2) abolished loan capital duty[77] on the issue of debentures from January 1, 1973, unless the obligation to deliver the required statement of the amount of the issue arose before then.[78] In addition all stamp duty on marketable securities apart from that imposed on bearer debentures or stock certificates to bearer was abolished as from that date.[79] The result is that for debentures not transferable by delivery there is now no stamp duty payable on issue.[80]

Duty payable on issue of debentures to bearer

A debenture to bearer was formerly stamped on issue[81] at a rate equal to three times the duty which would be payable in respect of an instrument in

---

70 *Re Regent's Canal Ironworks Co.* (1876) 3 Ch.D. 43; *Re Strand Music Hall* (1865) 3 De G.J. & S. 147; *Re Hampshire Land Co.* [1896] 2 Ch. 743.
71 *Re Regent's Canal Ironworks* (1876) 3 Ch.D. 43.
72 A contract to take up a debenture can be enforced in Scotland by action of specific implement.
73 *South African Territories Ltd.* v. *Wallington* [1898] A.C. 309.
74 This provision was first introduced in the Act of 1908.
75 *Kuala Pahi Estate* v. *Mowbray* (1914) 111 L.T. 1072.
76 Directive 335 of 1969 of the EEC (J.O. L249/25; O.J. (Special Edition) 1969 (II) 412).
77 *i.e.*, under the Finance Act 1899, s. 8.
78 This was required by the Finance Act 1849, s. 8.
79 Finance Act 1973, s. 49 (3).
80 For the new provisions on Capital Duty see para. 3-12, *ante*. For the provision applicable before January 1, 1973 see Palmer's *Company Law* (21st ed.) pp. 389-392.
81 Stamp Act 1891, Sched. 1; Finance Act 1963, s. 59 (1); Finance Act 1973, Sched. 22, Part V.

writing transferring the security constituted by the bearer instrument in question for a consideration equal to the market value of that security.[82] Stamp duty is now no longer payable unless the debentures fall within the two categories discussed below.[83]

Duty payable on transfer of debentures

Formerly *ad valorem* stamp duty was payable on transfers of non-bearer debentures at the same rate as a transfer of shares. No duty was payable on the transfer (as opposed to the issue) of bearer debentures. Now duty has been abolished by section 126 of the Finance Act 1976 with effect from May 17, 1976, in respect of any transfer of loan capital as defined in section 126 (5). This covers non-bearer and bearer debentures and debenture stock which are borrowed capital or which have "the character of borrowed money." This seems to cover all normal loan capital whether issued for cash or for a consideration other than cash. Certain categories are, however, excluded by section 126 (2) and (3). These are: (a) convertible debentures which are given a wide definition capable of covering rights of conversion into or subscriptions for loan capital of the same description; and (b) certain non fixed interest debentures which are given a wide and in parts rather vague definition. The latter covers loan capital with (a) a right to interest which (i) exceeds a reasonable commercial return on the nominal amount of the capital or (ii) falls or has fallen to be determined to any extent by reference to the results of or of any part of a business or to the value of any property or (b) a right on repayment to an amount exceeding the nominal amount of the capital and which is not reasonably comparable in that respect to loan capital listed on the Stock Exchange. Stamp duty, therefore, continues to be payable on the transfer of loan capital falling within section 126 (2) and (3) at the same rate as corresponding share transfers.

PRACTICE NOTES

Redemption of debentures or debenture stock

3–43 The principal methods by which debentures or debenture stock can be redeemed[84] are:

(1) Out of the proceeds of a fresh issue of share or loan capital. It is not safe to rely on this method, as the redemption date may not be a propitious time for raising new capital.

(2) By setting aside a predetermined annual sum by way of a sinking fund, such sum being calculated in a manner which ensures that the amount required on final redemption is available at the redemption date. Subject to the terms of issue, the sinking fund may be used for

---

82 Finance Act 1963, s.59 (3).
83 Finance Act 1976 s. 126.
84 See further Rules of the Stock Exchange, Sched. VII, Part B, para. A1-3.

partial redemptions before the final redemption date as explained below.

(3) By purchase in the market, by tender or private treaty. The terms of issue of debentures or debenture stock usually authorise a company, at its option, to redeem a part of the issue at any time by purchase in the market or by tender available to all holders and to utilise the sinking fund payments for this purpose. The maximum price payable for debentures so redeemed is normally restricted to their nominal value. When the market price is lower than par, most companies will take advantage of purchasing stock for redemption on these favourable terms. Purchases by tender or private treaty are rarely resorted to by companies with listed debenture stock, but may be used by others when there is an opportunity of acquiring debentures for redemption at less than their nominal value.

(4) By annual drawings, which will usually involve paying the nominal value and sometimes a premium in addition. Subject to the terms of issue, this method would only be used when the market price is at or above par or when, for other reasons, it may be impossible to redeem by purchase or tender. The conditions attaching to the debentures or debenture stock will provide for the length of notice of a drawing to be given to the holders, the units or batches into which the whole of the issue is to be divided, *e.g.* into lots of £100, and the procedure for the drawing of the lots, which will invariably be conducted under the supervision of a notary.

Certificates for debentures and debenture stock

43–44 The conditions for the use of an official securities seal are similar to those applying to certificates for shares (see para. 36–04, *ante*). Thus, in the case of a trust deed securing or constituting an issue of debenture stock (which includes unsecured loan stock) made before February 12, 1979, any provision of the deed which requires certificates to be signed will not apply if they are sealed with the official securities seal.

D. CHARGES AND REMEDIES RELATING TO DEBENTURES IN ENGLAND AND WALES

CHAPTER 44

CHARGES SECURING DEBENTURES

44–01 DEBENTURES, as was explained in the preceding chapter,[1] may be issued either unsecured or secured by a charge on property of the company. In this chapter it is proposed to examine the charges by which debentures may be secured. This is a matter of great practical importance, as debentures are normally of the secured type.

Debentures may be secured:

(1) by way of a specific charge or mortgage on particular property of the company; or

(2) by way of a floating charge; or

(3) by both a specific and a floating charge. It is usual when specifically secured debentures are issued to add, by way of a further security, a floating charge.

Specific charges securing debentures

44–02 A specific or fixed charge, or mortgage, securing a debenture does not raise problems peculiar to company law. Such a charge is granted on particular property of the company, normally land, interests in land or ships, in the same manner in which a physical person owning property would grant such a charge or mortgage. If the charge is on "fixed" assets of the company a New Zealand case has decided that those are assets which are normally expected to be available to a company and remain "permanently" with the company for the purpose of carrying out its business. Fixed assets are to be contrasted with circulating or current assets which are traded to bring in revenue and it does not simply mean those assets physically attached to the premises.[2] In the winding up of the company a debenture holder secured by a specific charge is in the highest ranking class of creditors, *viz.* in that of secured creditors.[3] The priority of several specific charges on the same property is determined by the general rules relating to the priority of charges[4] as affected by the system of registration discussed in Chapter 45.

It is impossible to create a charge on future book debts which operates in

---

[1] See para. 43–05, *ante*.
[2] *Tudor Heights Ltd.* v. *United Dominions Corporation Finance Ltd.* [1977] 1 N.Z.L.R. 532.
[3] See para. 85–63, *post*.
[4] See Megarry & Wade *The Law of Real Property* (4th ed., 1975), pp. 958 *et seq*.

equity as a specific charge on the proceeds of such debts as soon as they are received.[4a]

Where particular property of the company is specifically charged in favour of debenture holders, the company cannot dispose of it unencumbered by the charge without having obtained the consent of the holders of the charge. It will be seen presently that in the case of a debenture secured solely by a floating charge the position is different: in this case the company may dispose of the property on which the charge exists unencumbered without consulting the holders of the charge until an event happens on which the floating charge, according to its terms, "crystallises," *i.e.* becomes a fixed charge.

Where a company makes an issue of a series of debentures carrying the same rights, and these debentures are secured by way of a fixed charge, it is a practical necessity to appoint trustees for the debenture holders and to vest the fixed charge in them; otherwise the transfer of a single debenture would invariably require a transfer of the security by all debenture holders jointly. Trust deeds for securing an issue of debentures are governed by strict provisions of the Act (ss. 87–88), particularly as regards the liability of the trustees.[5]

The Rules on *Admission of Securities to Listing* issued by the Stock Exchange provide[6] that debentures described as "Mortgage Debentures" have to be secured to a substantial extent by a specific mortgage or charge.

An English company wishing to create a specific charge over Scottish heritable property must employ the form of fixed security laid down by Scots law which, since November 29, 1970, has for all practical purposes been restricted to a standard security under the Conveyancing and Feudal Reform (Scotland) Act 1970.[7]

A charge on a particular asset is void if it is illegal, *e.g.* as being in contravention of the Exchange Control Act.[8]

Floating charges

Nature of floating charge

44–03 GENERAL DESCRIPTION. The floating charge, as a type of equitable security, is peculiar to companies as borrowers. The best general description of a floating charge is contained in the following observations of Lord Macnaghten in *Government Stock Co.* v. *Manila Ry.*[9]

[4a] *Siebe Gorman & Co. Ltd.* v. *Barclays Bank Ltd.* [1979] 2 Lloyd's Rep. 142, 159. See also *Evans Coleman & Evans Ltd.* v. *R. A. Nelson Construction Ltd.* 16 D.L.R. 123 but *cf.* the unreported Northern Irish case of *Re Armagh Shoes Ltd. (in liquidation).* December 4, 1981 where Hutton J. held that the description of such a charge as a fixed charge did not prevent it from being a floating charge. The charge in question, unlike that in *Siebe Gorman*, did not contain any provision restricting the company from dealing with the assets charged.

[5] See para. 44–21, *post.*

[6] In Sched. VII, Pt. B, F (2), para. 171.

[7] For fuller comment see Chap. 47, *post.*

[8] *Swiss Bank Corporation* v. *Lloyds Bank Ltd.* [1981] 2 All E.R. 449 (H.L.).

[9] [1897] A.C. 81, 86.

> "A floating security is an equitable charge on the assets for the time being of a going concern. It attaches to the subject charged in the varying condition in which it happens to be from time to time. It is of the essence of such a charge that it remains dormant until the undertaking charged ceases to be a going concern, or until the person in whose favour the charge is created intervenes. His right to intervene may of course be suspended by agreement. But if there is no agreement for suspension, he may exercise his right whenever he pleases after default."

The same learned judge observed in *Illingworth* v. *Houldsworth*[10]:

> "I should have thought there was not much difficulty in defining what a floating charge is in contrast to what is called a specific charge. A specific charge, I think, is one that without more fastens on ascertained and definite property or property capable of being ascertained and defined; a floating charge, on the other hand, is ambulatory and shifting in its nature, hovering over and so to speak floating with the property which it is intended to affect until some event occurs or some act is done which causes it to settle and fasten on the subject of the charge within its reach and grasp."

44–04 RECOGNITION OF FLOATING CHARGE IN ENGLISH LAW. The validity and effect of a "floating charge" on the property, both present and future, of a company was first recognised in *Re Panama, New Zealand, etc., Co.*[11] by Giffard L.J. In that case the company had issued debentures, and thereby charged its "undertaking" with the payment thereof. It was held that the word "undertaking" meant all the property, present and future, of the company, and that the charge thereon was effective and was to operate by way of floating security. Giffard L.J. said:

> ". . . I take the object and meaning of the debenture to be this, that the word 'undertaking' necessarily infers that the company will go on, and that the debenture holder could not interfere until either the interest which was due was unpaid, or until the period had arrived for the payment of his principal, and that principal was unpaid. I think the meaning and object of the security was this, that the company might go on during that interval, and, furthermore, that during the interval the debenture holder would not be entitled to any account of mesne profits, or of any dealing with the property of the company in the ordinary course of carrying on their business . . . I see no difficulty or inconvenience in giving that effect to this instrument. But the moment the company comes to be wound up, and the property has to be realised, that moment the rights of these parties, beyond all question, attach. My opinion is, that even if the company had not stopped the debenture holders might have filed a bill to realise their security. I hold that under these debentures they have a charge upon all property of the company, past and future, by the term 'undertaking,' and that they stand in a position superior to that of the general creditors, who can touch nothing until they are paid."

---

[10] [1904] A.C. 355, 358.

[11] (1870) L.R. 5 Ch. 318. For contrasting discussions of the evolution of the floating charge see R. R. Pennington (1960) 23 M.L.R. 630 and W. J. Gough, *Company Charges*, pp.77–83.

In the words of Sir Francis Palmer,[12] "this decision was of the utmost importance, not merely because it put this construction on the word 'undertaking'—a word which had been largely used in debentures—but because it recognised clearly what many other nations do not recognise—the legal validity of a general charge on all the property of a company, both present and future, by way of floating security."

INTRODUCTION OF FLOATING CHARGE INTO SCOTS LAW. While the floating charge has thus been recognised in England since 1870, it was not admitted in Scots law until 1961, when it was introduced there by the Companies (Floating Charges) (Scotland) Act 1961. The present law is contained in the Companies (Floating Charges and Receivers) (Scotland) Act 1972[13]

44–05 THE TEST. Romer L.J. said in *Re Yorkshire Woolcombers' Assn.*[14] that if a charge had the following three characteristics, it was a floating charge, *viz.*:

> "(1) If it is a charge on a class of assets of a company present and future;
> "(2) if that class is one which in the ordinary course of the business of the company, would be changing from time to time; and
> "(3) if you find that by the charge it is contemplated that, until some future step is taken by or on behalf of those interested in the charge, the company may carry on its business in the ordinary way as far as concerns the particular class of assets I am dealing with."

The learned judge added, however, that he did not exclude the possibility that there might be a floating charge which did not contain those three characteristics.

It is evident from the above observations that a floating charge is an equitable charge which does not fasten upon any specific or definite property, but is a charge upon property which may be constantly varying: it will normally be upon the whole of the company's property, including any which is subject to a fixed charge, but it can be restricted to a limited class of property, and the property which is subject to the floating charge can be dealt with by the company without consulting the holder of the charge, and may be sold, exchanged or otherwise dealt with in any way that the directors may think fit provided that it is in the ordinary course of business. Upon the happening of certain events, which are usually set out in the charging deed, the floating charge becomes fixed or, in technical terminology, it "crystallises,"[15] and thereafter the assets comprised in the charge are subject to the same restrictions as those under a specific charge. Unless otherwise agreed, a floating charge will also crystallise on the appointment

[12] Palmer, *Company Law*, (9th ed., 1911), p. 307.
[13] See Chap. 47, *post*.
[14] [1903] 2 Ch. 284, 295.
[15] *Re Griffin Hotel Co., Ltd.* [1941] Ch. 129, 135; see para. 46–12, *post*.

of a receiver (either by the court or by a debenture holder under a power contained in the debenture) or on the commencement of winding up.[16] Crystallisation will take place on a winding up even though the debentures are not expressed to be repayable in that event.[17] Crystallisation is considered in greater depth at para. 44–10, *post*.

A fundamental question remains, granted that a floating charge is a present security and charge before crystallisation, does it transfer any equitable interest before crystallisation? The authorities are not completely clear but it would appear that while a floating charge does not transfer a fixed proprietary interest it does transfer a species of equitable interest which is defeasible.[18] Defeasibility is not necessarily inconsistent with the idea of an equitable interest since the debtor company has only a limited right to dispose of the assets subject to the charge—its transactions must be in the ordinary course of business which normally necessitates *quid pro quo* and a turnover of assets.[19] The utility of a floating charge is that it removes the need for an endless series of deeds of substitution and release.

Property comprised in the floating charge

44–06 A GENERAL CHARGE. Convenient though it is as a typical term, it must not be supposed that the word "undertaking" has any magic in it, or that an effective floating charge on the property, both present and future, of a company cannot be created by any other forms of words. A charge on all the property, both present and future, will create a floating security. So will a charge upon all the property now belonging or hereafter acquired by the company.[20] Indeed, the court is strongly disposed so to construe a general charge on all the company's property, present and future, the *ratio decidendi* in such cases being that the charge contemplates the continuance of the company as a going concern, and such a state of things as would be rendered impossible if the charge were to be construed as fixed and not floating. Thus, where a company issued bonds binding itself and its estate,

---

[16] *Re Florence Land Co.* (1878) 10 Ch.D. 530, 541; *Government Stock, etc., Co.* v. *Manila Ry.* [1897] A.C. 81; *Foster* v. *Borax Co.* [1901] 1 Ch. 326; *Nelson & Co.* v. *Faber & Co.* [1903] 2 K.B. 367; *Evans* v. *Rival Granite Quarries* [1910] 2 K.B. 979, 1001.

[17] *Re Crompton & Co. Ltd.* [1914] 1 Ch. 954.

[18] *Driver* v. *Broad* [1893] 1 Q.B. 744 (C.A.); *Wallace* v. *Evershed* [1899] 1 Ch. 891; *Re Dawson, Pattison* v. *Bathurst* [1915] 1 Ch. 626 (C.A); *Dempsey* v. *Traders' Finance Corporation Ltd.* [1933] N.Z.L.R. 1258, 1286; *Re Manurewa Transport Ltd.* [1971] N.Z.L.R. 909, 915 1.1 36 *et seq*. and *Landall Holdings Ltd.* v. *Caratti* [1979] W.A.R. 97 (W. Australian S. Ct. Full Court); see generally on this question J. H. Farrar [1980] 1 Co. Law 83. Dr. W. J. Gough in his learned work *Company Charges* takes the view that before crystallisation a floating charge gives rise to no proprietary or equitable interest. He is therefore obliged to regard some of the above cases as wrongly decided. His view on this question conditions his view of restrictive clauses—see para. 44–08, *post*. *Cf*. E. I Sykes, *The Law of Securities* (3rd ed.). pp. 785–786 and see *Cretanor Maritime Co. Ltd.* v. *Irish Marine Management Ltd.* [1978] 3 All E.R. 164, 173, *per* Buckley L.J.

[19] Note that the requirement that the transaction be in the ordinary course of business is similar to, but not identical with, the notion of a bona fide purchase for value without notice. Bona fides and value are probably required but the fact that there is actual or constructive notice of the existence of the floating charge does not invalidate the transaction. It may be otherwise if there is notice of a restrictive clause. *Vide post*.

[20] Wheatley v. *Silkstone, etc., Co.* (1885) 29 Ch.D. 715.

property and effects.[21] or binding itself and its real and personal estate,[22] the court held that the charge was intended to operate as a floating security and, therefore, to charge both present and future property. Although a floating charge embraces a debt due to the company the debtor retains his right of set-off against the holder of the floating charge. The holder on crystallisation of his charge is an equitable assignee of the company and cannot assert a better right than the assignor.[23]

CHARGE ON PART OF COMPANY'S PROPERTY. It is not essential that the charge should be on all the assets of the company.[24] It may be made to operate on a class of assets of the company, *e.g.* all its present and future book and other debts, with the benefit of the securities for the same[25]; or "the furniture and effects which now are or may from time to time be placed on" certain specified premises[26] or one-fourth of the profits of certain schemes for developing lands.[27]

This concept has recently been extended to include rights under a retention of title clause in a contract of sale of goods. In *Re Bond Worth Ltd.*[28] such a clause, which passed the property in the goods, raw fibre, to the buyer company, but purported to retain "equitable and beneficial ownership" in the sellers pending payment in full, was construed by Slade J. as a grant of the full legal and equitable ownership with a grant back of equitable ownership by way of charge. The purported bare trust therefore amounted, in the circumstances in essence to a floating charge as it fulfilled the criteria laid down by Romer L.J. in *Re Yorkshire Woolcombers' Association Ltd.*[29] The facts that enforcement may in practice have been difficult and that the drafting was misleading, did not render the security void *ab initio*. This basis was used by Slade J. to distinguish the retention of title clause from those in *Romalpa Aluminium Ltd.* v. *Aluminium Industrie Vaassen BV*,[30] where property did not pass to the buyer until payment, thus giving rise to a bailment and a fiduciary relationship. No such possibility existed in the *Bond Worth* case and the only proprietary rights attaching to the sellers were those under a floating charge. If the decision is correct it is hard to see how the sellers could enforce the charge in any practical way. In *Borden (U.K.) Ltd.* v. *Scottish Timber Products Ltd.*[31] it was held that the purchasers did not receive the goods as bailees or in a fiduciary capacity but for themselves as purchasers subject to the reservation of property clause. However, the title of the sellers to the goods was extinguished

---

21 *Re Florence Land Co.* (1878) 10 Ch.D. 530.
22 *Re Colonial Trusts Corpn.* (1879) 15 Ch.D. 465.
23 *Rother Iron Works Ltd.* v. *Canterbury Precision Engineers Ltd.* [1974] Q.B. 1.
24 *Re Colonial Trusts Corpn.* (1879) 15 Ch.D. 465.
25 *Re Yorkshire Woolcombers' Assn.* [1903] 2 Ch. 284; affirmed as *Illingworth* v. *Houldsworth* [1904] A.C. 355.
26 *National Provincial Bank* v. *United Electric Theatres Ltd.* [1916] 1 Ch. 132.
27 *Hoare* v. *British Columbia Assn.* (1912) 107 L.T. 602.
28 [1979] 3 W.L.R. 629.
29 [1903] 2 Ch. 284, 295; see para. 44–05, *ante*.
30 [1976] 1 W.L.R. 676.
31 [1979] 3 W.L.R. 672; [1979] 3 All E.R. 961 (C.A.).

because, as a result of a manufacturing process, the goods had ceased to exist. Had the title to the goods not been extinguished the clause would have constituted an unregistered equitable charge. This decision considerably restricts the effect of a clause such as was in issue in the *Romalpa* case. Leave to appeal to the House of Lords was refused.[32]

CHARGE ON FOREIGN ASSETS. An English company which owns land or other property in a country the laws of which do not recognise the creation of a floating charge[33] can grant such a charge on the property situate in the other country in a manner valid in English law.[34] Luxmoore J. said in *Re Anchor Line (Henderson Brothers) Ltd.*[35]:

> "When an English company possesses land abroad and purports to charge it by way of floating charge, the charge, putting it at its lowest, amounts to an agreement to charge that land, and is a valid equitable security according to English law."

Floating charges created over Scottish property by companies incorporated outside Scotland have been recognised since 1961.[36] Charges created by English companies do not require registration in Scotland, but a charge of any kind created by a company incorporated outside Great Britain has to be registered in Scotland if it affects Scottish property.[37]

RESERVE LIABILITY. A floating charge does not extend to a reserve liability validly constituted before the floating charge was created.[38]

BOOKS OF THE COMPANY. The words "all the property of the company" in a floating charge have been held not to extend to the ordinary books of the company,[39] and, on a winding up, the liquidator is accordingly entitled to claim possession of the minute book and share register and other books which relate to the management of the company as distinct from documents in the nature of title deeds, which may be retained by the debenture holders or their receiver.[40] There are books which, by the provisions of the

---

[32] Templeman L.J. thought that the clause might have created a corporate bill of sale or floating charge whereas Buckley L.J. thought is was only capable of being a corporate bill of sale [1979] 3 All E.R. 973, 974. For comment see M. Burke [1979] 129 New L.J. 1183 and Farrar [1980] 1 Co. Law 83.

[33] A legal mortgage has to comply with the *lex situs*; see para. 42–06, *ante*. As to foreign securities akin to a floating charge see *Kerr on Receivers* (15th ed., by R. Walton), Appendix VI (Muir Hunter).

[34] See *British South Africa Co.* v. *De Beers Consolidated Mines Ltd.* [1910] 1 Ch. 354; [1910] 2 Ch. 502; [1912] A.C. 52; *Re Anchor Line (Henderson Brothers) Ltd.* [1937] Ch. 483.

[35] [1937] Ch. 483, 487. Whether the Scottish courts would have assisted in the enforcement of the charge against assets in Scotland was never tested and is doubtful. The problem cannot now arise; see text, *ante*, and note 37, *post*.

[36] See now Companies (Floating Charges and Receivers) (Scotland) Act 1972.

[37] s. 106K as amended by the Companies (Floating Charges and Receivers) (Scotland) Act 1972.

[38] *Re Mayfair Property Co., Bartlett* v. *Mayfair Property Co.* [1898] 2 Ch. 28; *Re Irish Club Co. Ltd.* [1906] W.N. 127; see para. 42–05, *ante*.

[39] *Re Clyne Tin Plate Co.* (1882) 47 L.T. 439.

[40] *Engel* v. *South Metropolitan, etc., Co.* [1892] 1 Ch. 442; *Re Capital Fire Insurance Association* (1883) 24 Ch.D. 408.

Companies Acts, are to be kept at the office of the company, such as the register of members and the register of mortgages; and for the directors to mortgage or charge these would, as Cotton L.J. pointed out,[41] be to deal with the property of the company in a way inconsistent with its objects and constitution; and the same principle applies to books which, by the articles of the company, are to be kept at its office.

Dealings with charged property before crystallisation

44–07 Although a floating charge operates as an *immediate* and continuing charge on the property charged, nevertheless, before it crystallises the company has a licence to deal with and dispose of the property charged in the ordinary course of its business.[42] It may do so by way of sale, lease, exchange, specific mortgage, or otherwise, as it deems most expedient. Thus, an assignment by the company of arrears of rent made before the appointment of a receiver gives the assignees a good title as against debenture holders having only a floating charge; but if the land is specifically charged by the debentures, the debenture holders can claim the rents.[43] As to the effect of a prior mortgage of a lease on the debenture holders' interest in fixtures, it was held in *Re Rogerstone Brick Co.*[44] that the mortgagee by assignment was entitled to the proceeds of sale of the fixed plant as against the debenture holders. By dealing with its debtors during the currency of the floating charge, the company may give them a right of set-off,[45] but there is no mutuality, and therefore no right of set-off, where the debts arise after the floating charge has crystallised.[46]

It should, in particular, be noted that before crystallisation of the floating charge the company has power to create legal mortgages[47] and equitable charges[48] in priority to the floating charge, and such priority is not affected by notice of the floating charge.[49] In *Wheatley* v. *Silkstone Co.*[50] where the company, after creating a floating charge on its undertaking, had created a subsequent equitable charge in favour of its bankers by deposit of title deeds, North J., after referring to the authorities, said:

> " . . . those authorities furnish a very clear and intelligible principle to be followed. In this case I find that the debenture is intended to be a general floating security over all the property of the company, as it

---

[41] *Re Capital Fire Insurance Assn.* (1883) 24 Ch.D. 408, 418.
[42] *Re Florence Land Co.* (1878) 10 Ch.D. 530, 541; *Re Standard Manufacturing Co.* [1891] 1 Ch. 627; *Hubbuck* v. *Helms* (1887) 56 L.T. 232; *Foster* v. *Borax Co.* [1901] 1 Ch. 326; *Nelson & Co.* v. *Faber & Co.* [1903] 2 K.B. 367; *Hamer* v. *London City and Midland Bank (1918) 118 L.T. 571; Cretanor Maritime Co. Ltd.* v. *Irish Marine Management Ltd.* [1978] 1 W.L.R. 966 (C.A.).
[43] *Re Ind, Coope & Co.* [1911] 2 Ch. 223.
[44] [1919] 1 Ch. 110.
[45] *Biggerstaff* v. *Rowatt's Wharf* [1896] 2 Ch. 93; *Nelson & Co.* v. *Faber & Co.* [1903] 2 K.B. 367.
[46] N. W. Robbie & Co. Ltd. v. *Witney Warehouse Co. Ltd.* [1963] 1 W.L.R. 1324.
[47] *Re Florence Land Co.* (1878) 10 Ch.D. 530; *Re Colonial Trusts* (1879) 15 Ch.D. 465.
[48] *Wheatley* v. *Silkstone Co.* (1885) 29 Ch.D. 715; *Re Castell & Brown Ltd.* [1898] 1 Ch. 315.
[49] *Re Hamilton's Windsor Ironworks* (1879) 12 Ch.D. 707, 712.
[50] (1885) 29 Ch.D. 715.

exists at the time when it is to be put in force; but it is not intended to prevent and has not the effect of in any way preventing the carrying on of the business in all or any of the ways in which it is carried on in the ordinary course; and, inasmuch as I find that in the ordinary course of business and for the purpose of the business this mortgage was made, it is a good mortgage upon and a good charge upon the property comprised in it, and is not subject to the claim created by the debentures."

This decision is a specially strong one, because the debentures in question were expressed to be by way of *first charge* on the undertaking; but in regard to this the learned judge said:

"I find also that the first charge referred to in the debentures is fully satisfied by being the first charge against the general property of the company at the time when the claim under the debentures arises and can have effect given to it. There will be a declaration, therefore, that the charge of the plaintiff is prior to the debentures."[51]

The company may not, however, create a further floating charge *on the same assets* to rank in priority to the existing charge,[52] unless such a power is reserved in the debenture first issued.[53]

Prohibition of prior charges

44–08 The extreme elasticity of a floating charge, and the wide powers which it thus allows to the company of dealing with property that is subject to the debenture holders' charge, are in some cases considered excessive, and, accordingly, it is not uncommon to insert in the instrument creating the charge a restrictive clause containing words to the effect that the floating charge is *not* to authorise the company to create any mortgage or charge ranking in priority to or *pari passu* with the debentures, and this qualification is for the most part effective. Thus, if the company creates a mortgage in favour of any person who has notice[54] of the floating charge *and the restrictive clause*, such person ranks after the floating charge. But a person who obtains a legal mortgage, and can show either

(1) that he was not aware of the existence of the floating charge; or
(2) that though he was aware of the charge he was not aware of the restrictive clause,

is entitled to priority by virtue of the legal estate.[55]

Such a clause in a floating charge is to be strictly construed. In *Brunton* v. *Electrical, etc., Corporation*,[56] the qualification did not prevent the company's solicitor from acquiring a lien in priority to the debentures.[57]

---

[51] See also *Ward* v. *Royal Exchange Shipping Co.* (1887) 58 L.T. 174.
[52] *Re Benjamin Cope & Sons* [1914] 1 Ch. 800; *Re Automatic Bottle Makers Ltd.* [1926] Ch. 412, see para. 44–06, *post*.
[53] See para. 43–17, *ante*.
[54] As to what constitutes notice, see Chap. 28, *ante*.
[55] *English and Scottish, etc., Co.* v. *Brunton* [1892] 2 Q.B. 700; *Coveney* v. *Persse* [1910] 1 Ir.R. 194; *Welch* v. *Bowmaker (Ireland) Ltd.* [1980] I.R. 251.
[56] [1892] 1 Ch. 434.
[57] And see *Robson* v. *Smith* [1895] 2 Ch. 118.

Nor will the prohibition operate against a subsequent equitable mortgagee who obtains the title deeds of property comprised in the debenture holder's security and takes without notice from obtaining priority.[58] Nor will it prevent a mortgage to a vendor of after-acquired property to secure purchase money,[59] or a mortgage to secure an advance of part of the purchase money by a third party.[60] The reason for the latter is that the equitable rights under the contract make the mortgage attach to the property before the company acquires the legal ownership on completion and thus the mortgage has priority over the equity created by the restriction.[61] It would be different if the mortgage was created out of an interest unfettered by any such prior agreement since the charge would bite on the unencumbered fee simple; by analogy with *Church of England Building Society* v. *Piskor*.[62] Where a specific charge was made expressly subject to a floating charge, the specific charge was postponed when the floating charge crystallised by the appointment of a receiver.[63]

The practice has been adopted by banks and others of inserting details of such restrictive clauses in the registered particulars of the charge.[64] It is sometimes stated that this gives rise to constructive notice.[65] This is not so since the details are not required in the prescribed form in England and Wales. The position is different in Scotland.[66] However, constructive notice of the charge itself, the common practice of inserting such clauses and the entitlement of an existing creditor under section 105 of the Companies Act 1948 to inspect a copy of the charge at the company's registered office may possibly give rise to an inference of actual knowledge[67] on the basis of wilful blindness. This is an evidential presumption of fact which can be rebutted. It would be odd for a subsequent chargee not to seek sight of a copy of the floating charge in any event. In one case there was the

---

58 *Re Castell & Brown Ltd.* [1898] 1 Ch. 315; *Re Standard Rotary Machine Co.* (1906) 95 L.T. 829.

59 *Wilson* v. *Kelland* [1910] 2 Ch. 306.

60 *Re Connolly Bros. Ltd.* [1912] 2 Ch. 25.

61 *Security Trust Co.* v. *Royal Bank of Canada* [1976] A.C. 503 (A.C.).

62 [1954] 2 W.L.R. 952.

63 *Re Robert Stephenson & Co. Ltd.* [1913] 2 Ch. 201 (C.A.). See also *Re Camden Brewery Ltd.* (1912) 106 L.T. 598 (C.A.). In both cases the floating charge in question had crystallised. *Quaere* the effect of a subordination provision before crystallisation and its relationship to the priority rules. It would seem that under the latter rules a subordination clause necessarily involves notice of the restriction and always gives rise to postponement without crystallisation.

64 See J. H. Farrar, (1974) 38 Conv. (N.S.) 315, 325.

65 See L. C. B. Gower, *Principles of Modern Company Law* (3rd ed.), pp. 422–423. The learned author has now changed his mind; see 4th ed., p. 475.

66 See Farrar, *op. cit.*, p. 325.

67 Ibid. p. 329 citing Lord Esher M.R. in *English & Scottish Mercantile Investment Co.* v. *Brunton* [1892] 2 Q.B. 700, 707–708. Dr. Gough thinks otherwise, *op. cit. p. 357*. He points to *Re Standard Rotary Machine Co. Ltd.* (1906) 95 L.T. 829 where such an argument was impliedly rejected. The important point here is that such clauses were still relatively uncommon at that date. He also points to the fact that a potential subsequent chargee has no right to inspect the copy instrument. This is so if he is not an existing creditor but it is unlikely that the company will refuse to supply his solicitors with a copy in practice. After all, he can refuse to make his advance. *Cf.* however, *Welch* v. *Bowmaker (Ireland) Ltd.* [1980] I.R. 251, 256, 262 noted by D.M. Hare & D. Milman (1982) 126 S.J. 74.

suggestion that this might be tantamount to equitable fraud.[68] Whether the matter is analysed in terms of knowledge, equitable fraud or estoppel, it would seem that the subsequent charge in such circumstances may be postponed.

Invalidity of floating charges

44–09 A floating charge created within 12 months of the commencement of a winding up is invalid unless it is proved that the company was solvent immediately after the creation of the charge, except to the amount of any cash paid to the company at the time of or after the creation of, and in consideration for, the charge, with interest at 5 per cent. (or such other rate as may be ordered by the Treasury) (s. 322).

The section only invalidates the floating charge; the debt remains, but is an unsecured debt.[69] Money is paid "at the time of" the creation of the charge although it is paid some days before the charge is created, if the payment was made in reliance upon a promise to issue the charge.[70] The test for the requirement of "cash paid to the company" is whether, looking at the matter from a practical point of view, it can be said that, in substance and not merely in form, the money was paid to the company; the mere fact that it was paid into the company's account is not conclusive: the payment must have been intended to benefit the company and not some other person.[71] "Cash" may include cheques paid by a bank on behalf of the company out of money advanced to the company.[72] The words "in consideration for the charge" do not bear the technical meaning of consideration in the law of contract, but mean merely "in consideration of the fact that the charge exists."[73] Where a floating charge is issued to a bank to secure an existing overdraft and further advances are then made by the bank, the rule in *Clayton's* case[74] applies, and money subsequently paid into the account by the company may be set off against the pre-charge indebtedness.[73]

A floating charge may also be invalid if it constitutes a fraudulent preference under section 320,[75] or if it is not duly registered under section 95.[76]

Crystallisation

44–10 It is well settled that a floating charge crystallises (1) when a company

[68] *Williams* v. *Quebrada Railway Co.* [1895] 2 Ch. 751, 755.
[69] *Re Parkes Garage (Swadlincote) Ltd.* [1929] 1 Ch. 139.
[70] *Re Columbian Fireproofing Co.* [1910] 2 Ch. 120; *Re F. & E. Stanton Ltd.* [1929] 1 Ch. 180; *Re Olderfleet Shipbuilding Co.* [1922] 1 Ir.R. 26.
[71] *Re Matthew Ellis Ltd.* [1933] Ch. 458; *Transport & General Credit Corporation* v. *Morgan* [1939] Ch. 531; *Re Destone Fabrics Ltd.* [1941] Ch. 319; *Re Ambassadors (Bournemouth) Ltd.* (1961) 105 S.J. 969.
[72] *Re Yeovil Glove Co. Ltd.* [1965] Ch. 148 (C.A.).
[73] *Re Yeovil Glove Co. Ltd., supra; Re Thomas Mortimer Ltd.* [1965] Ch. 186 (Note).
[74] (1816) 1 Mer. 572.
[75] See para. 85–80, *post*.
[76] See Chap. 45, *post*.

goes into liquidation[77]; and (2) where a receiver is appointed.[78] In addition there are suggestions in a number of cases that crystallisation occurs when the company ceases to carry on business or ceases to be a going concern.[79] The two situations are similar but not identical.[80] A company may cease to be a going concern without actually ceasing to carry on business. Crystallisation may also occur where a creditor takes possession of assets subject to the charge through seizure under power or licence but this is probably limited to the situation where this causes the company to cease to carry on business or be a going concern.[81]

A more difficult question is whether it is possible to insert in a floating charge an express crystallisation clause which provides for automatic and self-generating crystallisation in certain events.[82] The possibility of such clauses was recognised by Sir Francis Palmer[83] but the practice of inserting them has only begun to develop in recent years. As it is, they are more common in Australia and New Zealand than in England and Wales and New Zealand practitioners are beginning to develop two-tier clauses—one tier providing for automatic crystallisation and the other providing for crystallisation on notice by the debenture-holder. Conceptually automatic crystallisation is not possible in Scotland where the floating charge has only a statutory form.

In *Re Horne and Hellard*[84] in 1885, there is recognition of the validity of such clauses by Pearson J. when he held that a purchaser was entitled to reasonable evidence that there had been no default which under the terms of the particular debentures would have crystallised the floating charge. The wording of the clause which provided that the charge should be a floating charge until default was " . . . to the intent that the same charge shall, until default in the payment of the principal or interest to accrue due and become payable in respect of the said sum of £500,000, or some part thereof, be a floating security upon the undertaking, works, and property of the company, not hindering sales or leases of, or other dealings with, any of the property or assets of the company in the course of its business as a going concern . . . " As can be seen, it was a reasonably explicit auto-

---

[77] *Re Panama, etc. Royal Mail Co.* (1870) 5 Ch. App. 318, 322–323; *Re Colonial Trusts Corporation* (1879) 15 Ch.D. 465, 472–473; *Wheatley & Silkstone & Haigh Moor Coal Co.* (1885) 29 Ch.D. 715, 718; *Wallace* v. *Universal Automatic Machines Co.* [1894] 2 Ch. 547; *Re Crompton & Co. Ltd.* [1914] 1 Ch. 954 (a case of voluntary winding up for the purposes of reconstruction).

[78] *Re Florence Land Co.* (1878) 10 Ch.D. 530, 541; *Taunton* v. *Sheriff of Warwickshire* [1895] 2 Ch. 319, *Re Carshalton Park Estate* [1908] 2 Ch. 62, 66. It is not sufficient merely to commence proceedings: *Re Hubbard & Co.* (1898) 68 L.J. Ch.34.

[79] *Hubbock* v. *Helms* (1887) 56 L.J Ch. 536, 538; *Robson* v. *Smith* [1895] 2 Ch. 118, 124–125; *Government Stock, etc., Co.* v. *Manila Railway Co.* [1897] A.C. 81, 86; *Edward Nelson & Co.* v. *Faber & Co.* [1903] 2 K.B. 367, 376–377. See further J. H. Farrar, (1976) 40 Conv. (N.S.) 397, 399, and Gough, *op. cit.*, 85–86.

[80] Farrar, *op. cit.*, p. 399.

[81] *Re Hamilton's Windsor Ironworks Co.* (1879) 12 Ch.D. 707, 710; *Biggerstaff* v. *Rowatt's Wharf Ltd.* [1896] 2 Ch. 93, 105–106, *Mercantile Bank of India* v. *Chartered Bank of India* [1937] 1 All E.R. 231.

[82] See J. H. Farrar, (1976) 40 Conv. (N.S.) 397, 400 *et seq.* and [1980] 1 Co. Law 83; Gough, *op. cit.*, pp. 96 *et seq.*; A. J. Boyle [1979] J.B.L. 231.

[83] See Farrar, *op. cit.*, 402, 414–5.

[84] (1885) 29 Ch.D. 736.

matic crystallisation clause. In addition to this case there is *Davey & Co.* v. *Williamson & Sons*[85] and dicta in *Illingworth* v. *Houldsworth*,[86] *Evans* v. *Rival Granite Quarries Ltd.*[87] and *Re Bond Worth Ltd.*[87a] *Davey & Co.* v. *Williamson & Sons* was an appeal from a county court to the Divisional Court of the Queen's Bench Division. It involved a claim by a debenture holder for goods which had been seized by the sheriff under a writ of *fi.fa*. The goods were not sold and the sheriff interpleaded. The due date of the debentures had not arrived; there was no winding up and no receiver had been appointed. There was, however, a provision in the trust deed that the floating charge became "enforceable" in certain events. The full wording from the report was " . . . the principal money and interest owing- . . . shall be a floating charge . . . and, subject as aforesaid, the trustee shall hold the premises upon trust to permit the company and its assigns to hold and enjoy the premises, and to carry on the business and any business authorised by the memorandum of association of the company until the happening of one or more of the events upon which the security thereby constituted became enforceable." The events contemplated were 12 in number but the only important one for the purposes of the case was as follows: "If any execution, sequestration, extent or other process of any Court or authority is sued out against the property of the company for any sum whatsoever." Lord Russell C.J. and Mathew J. held that "The company as a going concern had come to an end, and although the due date of the debentures had not arrived, the holders were entitled to intervene to protect their security."[88] They were not bound to apply for a receiver or proceed with a view to winding up.

Davey's case is not a clear authority and is flawed by some obscure remarks about crystallisation taken from the judgment of the county court judge and the last paragraph of the Divisional Court's judgment which cites two earlier cases[89] in support and erroneously states that the rights of the debenture holders in at least one of those cases had not crystallised.[90] It is possible to interpret the *Davey* case as Fletcher Moulton L.J. did obiter in *Evans* v. *Rival Granite Quarries Ltd.*[91] as an example of crystallisation by cesser of business. (Fletcher Moulton L.J. uses that term although the Divisional Court itself as we have seen referred to ceasing to be a going

---

85 [1898] 2 Q.B. 194.
86 [1904] A.C. 355.
87 [1910] 2 K.B. 979.
87a [1979] 3 W.L.R. 676.
88 [1898] 2 Q.B. 200, 201. It appears that the company was insolvent (*ibid.* p. 197).
89 *Re Standard Manufacturing Co.* [1891] 1 Ch. 627 and *Re Opera Ltd.* [1891] 3 Ch. 260.
90 At [1898] 2 Q.B. 200 the court seems to equate crystallisation with the moneys becoming payable. At p. 201 the court says "It seems to us that this reasoning is fully supported by the authorities: see *In re Standard Manufacturing Co.* in which case the rights of the debenture holders had not 'crystallised'. See also *In re Opera Limited.*" The error is referred to in the judgment of Fletcher Moulton L.J. in the *Evans* case [1910] 2 K.B. 979, 997.
91 [1910] 2 K.B. 979, 997.

concern.) On the other hand Buckley L.J. in the Evans case in his obiter dicta equated enforceability and crystallisation and appeared to treat Davey's case as one of the happenings of an express crystallisation event.[92]

The dictum of Lord Macnaghten in *Government Stock, etc., Investment Co.* v. *Manila Railway Co.*[93] cited earlier mentioned both ceasing to be a going concern and intervention but as we have seen in his later dictum in *Illingworth* v. *Houldsworth*[94] he said that a floating charge floats "until some event occurs or some act is done which causes it to settle." The reference to the occurrence of an event lends some apparent support to the express crystallisation event idea. It is suggested that this apparent support is probably real support. Lord Macnaghten as an experienced Chancery lawyer with a clear appreciation of business[95] would almost certainly have been aware that the *Government Stock* case had been litigated because the draftsman of the charge had followed the precedent in the first edition in 1877 of Palmer's *Company Precedents* but, either by accident or design, had omitted the clause which provided that on the happening of certain events the company's authority to deal with assets should cease. The *Government Stock* case was really about whether such a clause could be implied into the existing wording. The House of Lords held it could not. The comment of the seventh (1898) edition of Palmer's *Company Precedents* was "If the omitted clause had been inserted the decision would have been different."[96] This comment is still repeated in the current edition. It is, therefore, a reasonable assumption to make that Lord Macnaghten probably had this in mind when he uttered his dictum in the *Illingworth* case, although the actual wording of the precedent in the first edition of Palmer's *Company Precedents* is not a particularly explicit automatic crystallisation clause.

Evans v. *Rival Granite Quarry Co.*[97] concerned a floating charge which was only to crystallise on the appointment of a receiver. The Court of Appeal held that mere demand for the repayment of the loan or a notice to the company's bankers claiming the balance which had been attached by a creditor were not sufficient to crystallise the charge. Although there are passages in the judgments of Vaughan Williams[98] and Fletcher Moulton

---

[92] [1910] 2 K.B. 979, 1000–1001. The wording in *Davey's Case* seems to be closer to *Re Horne and Hellard* than the *Government Stock* case.

[93] [1897] A.C. 81, 86.

[94] [1904] A.C. 355, 358. The italics are supplied.

[95] See his biography in D.N.B. 1912–21, pp. 361–362, by Lord Sumner. His eldest son, Charles Macnaghten, who became a leader of the Chancery Bar, assisted Palmer with his *Company Precedents* in the 5th (1891), 6th (1896), 7th (1898) and 10th (1910) eds. Palmer's *Company Precedents* was very much the company practitioners' *vade-mecum* at this time.

[96] *Op. cit.* 7th ed., p. 777; 16th ed., Pt. III, pp. 57–58. Lord Macnaghten's son, Charles, was assisting Palmer in the 7th ed., which was the first after the full report of the case appeared. In the 7th ed. a number of changes were made. The words "unless otherwise agreed" appear (p. 773) and a reference to a floating charge not "finally" attaching until winding up, appointment of a receiver or stoppage of business in the 6th ed. is altered to "generally" (p. 777). See also Palmer's *Company Law*, 1st ed. (1898), p. 213.

[97] [1910] 2 K.B. 979.

[98] [1910] 2 K.B. 979, 986.

L.J.J.[99] to the effect that the debenture holder must intervene, these must be read in the light of the facts of the case and the express wording of the charge, and Fletcher Moulton L.J. did in fact cite Lord Macnaghten's dictum in the *Illingworth* case.[1] Buckley L.J. recognised the possibility of an express crystallisation event when he referred to "any event may happen which is defined as bringing to an end the licence to the company to carry on business."[2]

In *Re Bond Worth Ltd.*[2a] discussed in paragraph 44–06 Slade J. referred to winding up, the appointment of a receiver "or the happening of some other agreed event."

In the New Zealand case of *Re Manurewa Transport Limited*[3] the matter was expressly considered at first instance. Here the facts were that the company operated a carrying business and had created a floating charge which contained the usual form of restrictive clause forbidding the creation of further mortgages without consent. There was also an express automatic crystallisation clause which provided that the charge should "attach and become affixed" on the happening of a number of events, one of which was breach of the restrictive clause. After delay by the company in the payment of its garage bills a garage firm seized a truck and refused to release it until they were given security for their account. A chattel security was created over the truck and registered. The consent of the debenture holder was never obtained and the matter fell for decision on the company's insolvency. Speight J. decided in favour of the debenture holder. He held that under the New Zealand legislation there was constructive notice not only of the existence of a floating charge but also of its contents including a restrictive clause, as far as it related to chattels.[4] The floating charge, therefore, had priority. Secondly he expressly upheld the view that crystallisation can take place without intervention on the happening of an automatic crystallisation event. He relied on the *Davey* case, Buckley L.J. in the *Evans* case and a New Zealand case of *Paintin & Nottingham Ltd* v. *Miller Gale & Winter*[5] where North P. had paraphrased Lord Macnaghten's dictum in the *Illingworth* case.[6] Speight J. continued: "After all, a floating charge is not a term of art, it is a description for a type of security contained in a document which may provide a variety of circumstances whereupon crystallisation takes place."[7] A view contrary to *Re Manurewa*

[99] *Ibid*. p. 993.
[1] *Ibid*. p. 994. [2] *Ibid*., p. 1000.
[2a] [1979] 3 W.L.R. 676. See also *Siebe Gorman & Co. Ltd.* v. *Barclays Bank Ltd.* [1979] 2 Lloyd's Rep. 142, 159.
[3] [1971] N.Z.L.R. 909. See D. W. McLauchlan, "Automatic Crystallisation of a Floating Charge" (1972) N.Z.L.J. 330, *C.f.* also *Stein* v. *Saywell* [1969] A.L.R. 481; 12 C.L.R. 529.
[4] See s. 102 (12) of the Companies Act 1955 and s. 4 (2) of the Chattels Transfer Act 1924. See also *Dempsey* v. *Traders Financial Association Corpn*. [1933] N.Z.L.R. 1258. This is also the case in Scotland but not in England and Wales.
[5] [1971] N.Z.L.R. 164.
[6] Speight J.'s decision can also be supported by the New Zealand Court of Appeal's decision in *Geoghegan* v. *The Greymouth-Point Elizabeth Railway & Coal Co*. [1898] 16 N.Z.L.R. 749, 768, 771 which was not cited and is not referred to in the New Zealand textbooks.
[7] [1971] N.Z.L.R. 909, 917.

Transport Ltd. was recently expressed by Berger J. in the British Columbia case of *The Queen* v. *Consolidated Churchill Copper Corporation Ltd.*[8] This involved a claim by the Province of British Columbia that its statutory lien had priority over a floating charge. This depended on the charge not having crystallised. Berger J. held that the charge had not crystallised: (1) because the appointment of a manager under a management contract did not make the manager a receiver particularly where he did not file particulars of his appointment with the Registrar; (2) a notice served pursuant to a clause in the charge was defective; and (3) the concept of self-generating crystallisation was not to be recognised and in any event there was conduct by the debenture holder inconsistent with the assertion of its claim for such crystallisation. The British Columbia case was a poor set of facts on which to argue automatic crystallisation but the judgment of Berger J. is interesting for his analysis of the English authorities and *Re Manurewa Transport Ltd.* He regarded the English cases as providing no clear support and proceeded to consider the policy issues. A parlous state of affairs would result if automatic crystallisation clauses were recognised. The requirement for filing by a receiver under the Companies Acts would be a dead letter. The company would not know where it stood; neither would its creditors. Automatic crystallisation would enable a debenture holder to render the company immune from executions. The debenture holder would have all the advantages of allowing the company to continue in business and all of the advantages of intervening at one and the same time, to the prejudice of all other creditors. In Berger J.'s view, neither in the older cases nor in the recent cases nor in the exigencies of policy was there any justification for the adoption of automatic crystallisation.

In conclusion, therefore, it is submitted that there is some limited support in the authorities for automatic crystallisation and floating charges are a species of contract which can be adapted by the parties to suit their needs. The authorities are not clear cut and there are disadvantages and anomalies for the company and its other creditors which can result. The use of such clauses represents perhaps a development of the floating charge towards the notion of a springing fixed charge.[9]

Clogging the equity of redemption

44–11 Where by the terms of redemption the security still remains charged, after the principal moneys and interest have been paid off, to secure to the debenture holder some collateral advantage, such a provision may be bad as a clog on the equity of redemption; *e.g.* a clause securing to the holders of debentures a bonus of 100 per cent. payable out of profits, and providing that after the principal had been paid off the security should still remain

[8] [1978] 5 W.W.R. 652.

[9] See Gough, *op. cit.* p. 199 and App. IV for precedents. This has not found favour with the Committee to Review Insolvency Law and Practice (Cmnd. 8558 (1982)) which recommended in para. 1580 a statutory definition of crystallisation which would not include automatic crystallisation.

charged with the payment of such a bonus.[10] But where the collateral advantage obtained by the debenture holder is not part of the mortgage transaction, it is not a clog on the equity of redemption.[11] And, even where the collateral advantage is contained in the same document, it is valid, provided it is not unfair or in the nature of a penalty clogging the equity of redemption or inconsistent with the legal or equitable right to redeem.[12] Where debentures have been issued, the date of redemption of which is postponed for many years, the doctrine of clogging the equity does not apply (1948 Act, s. 89).[13]

Priorities of debenture holders

44–12 The priorities of debentures depend on various considerations: on the true construction of the instrument or instruments creating them, on the rule that the legal estate prima facie gives priority, or the rule that prima facie he who is first in time has the better equity, and on the registration or non-registration under section 95 of the 1948 Act.[14] In the next chapter we shall set out some detailed general rules but here we shall discuss some specific points affecting priorities.

Presumption of equality of debenture holders of same issue

44–13 As a general, almost invariable, rule, debenture holders of the same series are made to rank *pari passu inter se*; and even if it is not so expressed, the court will, from slight indications, infer equality. Where such equality exists, no individual debenture holder is allowed to get an advantage for himself. If he gets judgment, the judgment enures for the benefit of all the debenture holders[15]; if he obtains a collateral security he holds it as trustee for all.[16] As to obtaining judgment in a separate action, in *Cleary* v. *Brazil Ry.*[17] the plaintiff, despite the pendency of a debenture holder's action, obtained judgment for arrears of interest. The series constitutes, in fact, one great contributory mortgage.

The issue of part of a series of debentures which are all to rank *pari passu* does not by implication restrict the company's power as regards the terms on which the rest of the issue may be dealt with.[18] The company may even issue the balance of such debentures although a debenture holders' action has been commenced, at any time before a receiver has been appointed in the action.[19]

---

10 *Re Rainbow Syndicate* [1916] W.N. 178.
11 *De Beers Consolidated Mines Ltd.* v. *British S. Africa Co.* [1912] A.C. 52.
12 *G. & C. Kreglinger* v. *New Patagonia Meat Co.* [1914] A.C. 25; *Re Cuban Land and Development Co.* [1921] 2 Ch. 147, where debenture stock secured to the holder a share of the surplus assets on a winding up.
13 See para. 43–06, *ante*.
14 See para. 45–03, *post*.
15 *Bowen* v. *Brecon Ry.* (1867) L.R. 3 Eq. 541.
16 *Small* v. *Smith* (1884) 10 App.Cas. 119, 131; *Landowners* v. *Ashford* (1880) 16 Ch.D. 411.
17 [1915] W.N. 178.
18 *Re Regent's Canal Ironworks* (1876) 3 Ch.D. 43.
19 *Hubbard* v. *Hubbard* (1898) 68 L.J.Ch. 54; *Geisse* v. *Taylor* [1905] 2 K.B. 658.

Reissue of redeemed debentures

44–14 Whether a company can redeem some of the debentures of a series and reissue them to rank *pari passu* with those left unredeemed is a difficult question, which must be determined on the construction of the language of the debenture and the terms of section 90 of the 1948 Act. The object of this section is to override the principle laid down by the court,[20] according to which a debenture once paid off was extinguished and could not be reissued.[21] Section 90 confers power to reissue debentures unless the company has manifested an intention to cancel them. This enables the company to reissue debentures where, as often happens, the question of reissue was not considered on their redemption. If section 90 can be read as an implied condition of the original issue of the debentures, then presumably any that are redeemed may be reissued to rank *pari passu* with the unredeemed ones.

Debentures repayable on a fixed date cannot be reissued as perpetual debentures or as repayable at some date other than the original date.[22]

Where a debenture is deposited, *e.g.* with a bank, to secure advances from time to time on current account or otherwise, the debenture is not deemed to be redeemed on the ground only that the company is no longer in debit whilst the debenture is deposited with the lender (s. 90 (3)).

Several series of debentures

44–15 Where two or more series of debentures are issued giving a floating charge, they will rank according to the date of issue, in the absence of anything to show that they are to rank *pari passu*.[23] Hence, where mortgage debentures of a specific series are to rank *pari passu*, the company cannot issue debentures of some further series to rank *pari passu* with the original series, unless the terms of the last-mentioned series have reserved such a power to the company, either expressly or impliedly.[24] The reservation of a power to create mortgages is not sufficient for this purpose.[25]

Current account

The rule in *Clayton's* case[26] applies where a company, after giving a charge to secure an overdraft on current account, creates a second charge on the same property, and, accordingly, unless some other arrangement has been made, the payments into the credit of the account must be taken as satisfying the amounts debited to the account in the order of date.[27]

---

[20] *Re Routledge (George) & Sons Ltd.* [1904] 2 Ch. 474; *Re Tasker (W.) & Sons* [1905] 1 Ch. 283; *Re Perth Electric Tramways* [1906] 2 Ch 216; *Re Russian Petroleum Co.* [1907] 2 Ch. 540.

[21] *Fitzgerald* v. *Persse* [1908] 1 Ir.R. 279.

[22] *Re Antofagasta (Chili) and Bolivia Ry.'s Trust Deed* [1939] Ch. 732.

[23] *James* v. *Boythorpe Colliery Co.* (1890) 2 Meg. 55; *Gartside* v. *Silkstone Coal Co.* (1882) 21 Ch.D. 762; *Lister* v. *Henry Lister & Son* (1893) 41 W.R. 330.

[24] *Ibid.*

[25] *Re Benjamin Cope & Sons* [1914] 1 Ch. 800; see para. 43–17, *ante*.

[26] (1816) 1 Mer. 572.

[27] See *Deeley* v. *Lloyds Bank* [1912] A.C. 756; and see para. 44–09, *ante*.

Specific property charged

Where a company issues a series of debentures charging (but not by way of legal mortgage) *specific* property of the company, such a charge ranks prima facie in priority to any subsequent charge on the same property by the company on the principle *qui prior est tempore potior est jure*; but this rule yields to that reverence with which the law always regards the legal estate and the bona fide purchaser for value, and if, consequently, the company creates a subsequent charge, whether in favour of debenture holders, or otherwise, and the persons in whose favour such charge is created advance their money in good faith, without notice (actual or constructive) of the prior debenture charge and get the legal estate, then, by virtue of such legal estate, they take priority over the prior charge of the debenture holders. It is to prevent this danger that a legal estate is usually vested in trustees.

Floating charge

44–16 SUBSEQUENT MORTGAGEES. As to property comprised in a floating charge, we have already seen that debenture holders having a charge thereon may be postponed to subsequent specific mortgages,[28] and this, in some cases, even though the conditions of the charge prohibit the creation of prior mortgages.[29] If there is no such prohibition, the subsequent specific mortgage takes priority, by virtue of the fact that the floating charge is a floating security, and, by its very nature, therefore, permits the company, in carrying on its business, to create charges in priority to it. If there is such a prohibition, then the subsequent mortgagee takes priority—in cases where he does so—by virtue of his good faith and the legal estate or a better equity.[30] If a subsequent mortgagee has actual knowledge or notice of a restrictive clause he will be postponed. There is no constructive notice of such a clause by insertion of details in the registered particulars since the statutory form does not require them in England and Wales. The position is otherwise in Scotland. It may be, however, that constructive notice of the floating charge itself, the fact that such clauses are very common and the entitlement of an existing creditor to inspect a copy may give rise to inferred knowledge at common law. This is an evidential presumption of actual knowledge where a subsequent mortgagee has been wilfully blind and has failed to make further enquiry which he knows will prejudice him. It is rebuttable. If it is established the subsequent mortgagee may be postponed on the basis of knowledge, estoppel or equitable fraud.[31]

---

[28] See para. 44–08, *ante*.

[29] See para. 43–17, *ante*.

[30] *Bower* v. *Foreign Gas Co.* [1877] W.N. 222; *Brunton* v. *Electrical Engineering Corpn.* [1892] 1 Ch.434; *Re Castell & Brown* [1898] 1 Ch. 315; *Re Valletort Sanitary Steam Laundry* [1903] 2 Ch. 654; and see Palmer, *Company Precedents*, Part III, 16th ed., p. 55.

[31] In any event it is up to a subsequent chargee to establish that he is a bona fide purchaser for value without notice—see *Union Bank of Halifax* v. *The Indian and General Investment Trust* [1908] 40 S.C.R. 510. *Cf.*, however, *Cox* v. *Dublin City Distillery Co.* [1906] 1 I.R. 466. See para. 44–08, *ante*, for a discussion of restrictive clauses and para. 45–07, *post*, for a discussion of priorities.

EXECUTION CREDITORS. A floating charge is valid as against execution creditors,[32] save that if the execution creditor takes property in execution, and completes the execution, *e.g.* by seizure and sale by the sheriff, or obtains a garnishee order absolute (but not a garnishee order nisi)[33] before the charge crystallises, he obtains priority.[34] So, also, if money is paid to the sheriff whilst the charge is a floating charge to induce him to refrain from selling property in his hands.[35]

DISTRESS BY LANDLORD. A landlord can distrain for rent before the appointment of a receiver. Afterwards he can still distrain at common law, but where a receiver has been appointed by the court he must apply for leave of the court.[36] He cannot distrain on lands not comprised in the lease.[37]

44–17 HIRE-PURCHASE AGREEMENTS. Where chattels are in the company's possession under a hire-purchase agreement, under which the goods are to remain the property of the supplier, thc rights of the owner prevail over a floating charge created by the company, even if the chattels become fixtures. This was decided in a case[38] in which the hire-purchase agreement was made before the debentures were issued; but it is submitted that, even if the hire-purchase agreement were later in date than the floating charge, the debenture holders would only obtain a charge on the company's interest, which is subject to the rights of the owner of the chattel.[39] A mortgagee who obtains a fixed legal mortgage, without notice of the terms of the hire-purchase agreement, would have a prior right to fixtures on taking possession.[40] But this principle does not apply to an equitable charge.[41]

PREFERENTIAL DEBTS. Preferential creditors, as defined in section 319, are entitled[42] to priority over a debenture holder secured by a floating charge.

---

32 *Re Opera* [1891] 3 Ch. 260 (C.A.); *Taunton* v. *Sheriff of Warwickshire* [1895] 2 Ch. 319; *Re Standard Manufacturing Co.* [1891] 1 Ch. 627; *Davey & Co.* v. *Williamson & Sons* [1898] 2 Q.B. 194; *Simultaneous Colour Printing Syndicate* v. *Foweraker* [1901] 1 K.B. 771; *Duck* v. *Tower Galvanizing Co.* [1901] 2 K.B. 314; *Re London Pressed Hinge Co.* [1905] 1 Ch. 576.

33 *Norton* v. *Yates* [1906] 1 K.B. 112.

34 *Evans* v. *Rival Granite Quarries* [1910] 2 K.B. 979.

35 *Heaton & Dugard Ltd.* v. *Cutting Bros.* [1925] 1 K.B. 655.

36 *General Share and Trust Co.* v. *Wetley, etc., Co.* (1882) 20 Ch.D. 260; *Re New City Constitutional Club* (1887) 34 Ch.D. 646.

37 *Re Roundwood Colliery Co.* [1897] 1 Ch. 373.

38 *Re Morrison, Jones and Taylor Ltd.* [1914] 1 Ch. 50.

39 *Re Morrison, Jones and Taylor, supra, per* Eve J. at p. 55; *cf. Wilson* v. *Kelland* [1910] 2 Ch. 306; *Re Connolly Bros. (No. 2)* [1912] 2 Ch. 25; *Hamer* v. *London City and Midland Bank* (1918) 87 L.J.K.B. 973; *Security Trust Co.* v. *The Royal Bank of Canada* [1976] 2 W.L.R. 437 (P.C.).

40 *Hobson* v. *Gorringe* [1897] 1 Ch. 182; *Ellis* v. *Glover and Hobson Ltd.* [1908] 1 K.B. 388; *Reynolds* v. *Ashby & Son* [1904] A.C. 466.

41 *Re Samuel Allen & Sons Ltd.* [1907] 1 Ch. 575.

42 The receiver is under a duty to pay the preferential creditors and not merely under a negative duty not to pay the debenture holders before having paid the preferential creditors: *Westminster City Council* v. *Haste* [1950] Ch. 442.

This applies equally in the case where a receiver is appointed for the debenture holders when the company is actively pursuing its objects and is not in winding up (s. 94,[43] and when the company is being wound up (s. 319).[44] A debenture holder secured by a validly created floating charge has, however, priority over the unsecured creditors, whether in a winding up or otherwise.[45]

GENERAL LIEN. If the goods on which a bailee claims a contractual general lien have come into his possession *before* the appointment of the receiver becomes effective, the general lien prevails over the floating charge. If they have come into his possession *after* the appointment of the receiver *but* the contract by virtue of which the general lien is claimed was concluded before that date, the result is the same because the debenture holder's rights which arose when the floating charge crystallised on the appointment of the receiver took effect subject to the contractual rights acquired by the bailee before the appointment of the receiver.[46]

STATUTORY RIGHT OF DETENTION. If the goods subject to the floating charge are subject to a statutory right of detention for non-payment of money, then that statutory right will prevail even if the holder of that right had notice of the charge and the appointment of a receiver under it.[47] A statutory right of detention must therefore be carefully distinguished from a lien.[48]

MAREVA INJUNCTION. If the property charged has become subject to a *Mareva* injunction restraining the company from removing it from the jurisdiction it is not subject to a pre-trial attachment order but simply to an order in personam to prohibit the company from doing certain things in relation to the asset. On the subsequent crystallisation of the floating charge the debenture holder may apply for a discharge of the injunction if necessary and this will be granted if the holders of the injunction are unsecured creditors and there appears to be no prospect of any surplus becoming available for such creditors on a liquidation. The injunction is designed to retain the property in the jurisdiction so that if the unsecured creditor should be awarded judgment he may seek to levy execution on the property. If such events occur the unsecured creditor would still be subject to the rights of the chargee.[49] The jurisdiction is now the subject of express provision in the Supreme Court Act 1981, s. 37 (1) and (3).

---

[43] See para. 46–12, *post*.
[44] See para. 85–60, *post*.
[45] *Re General South American Co.* (1876) 2 Ch.D. 337.
[46] *George Baker (Transport) Ltd.* v. *Eynon* [1974] 1 W.L.R. 462 (C.A.). *Cf.* a common law lien which depends on possession.
[47] *Channel Airways Ltd.* v. *Manchester Corporation* [1974] 1 Lloyd's Rep. 456; *Emilie Millon* [1905] 2 K.B. 817.
[48] See *Channel Airways Ltd.* v. *Manchester Corporation, supra.*
[49] *Cretanor Maritime Co. Ltd.* v. *Irish Marine Management Ltd.* [1978] 1 W.L.R. 966 (C.A.). For the origin of this type of injunction see: *Nippon Yusen Kaisha* v. *Karageorgis* [1975] 1 W.L.R. 1093; *Mareva Compania Naviera S.A.* v. *International Bulkcarriers S.A.* [1975] 2

Trust deeds

44–18 Debentures and debenture stock are often secured by a trust or covering deed, conveying property of the company to trustees in favour of the debenture holders, charging other property and containing a number of ancillary provisions regulating the respective rights of the company and the debenture holders. Whether there should be a trust deed or not must depend on the circumstances; where the debentures are issued only for a temporary purpose, *e.g.* to bankers as security for an overdraft or to other persons for a short term, or are to be taken up by the directors, a deed may be dispensed with; but where the transaction is of some magnitude, in particular where large-scale borrowing by companies from the public is in question, a trust deed is commonly used.

Advantages of trust deed

The advantages of a trust deed may be briefly summarised as follows:

1. It constitutes trustees charged with the duty of looking after the rights and interests of the debenture holders. Thus they may vote as they consider best in respect of any shares which may be vested in them as trustees.[50]
2. The debenture holders can by these trustees enter and sell the property comprised in the security.
3. A legal estate is sometimes vested in the trustees with the protection which is conferred thereby.

Contents of trust deed

44–19 A trust deed usually contains a legal mortgage of the freehold and leasehold properties, *e.g.* in the case of a brewery, the brewery and tied houses, and a general charge by way of floating security on the rest of the assets and undertaking. Under the Law of Property Act 1925, s. 87, the legal mortgage takes the form of a demise to the trustees for a term of years or a charge by way of legal mortgage.

Following on the charge comes a clause specifying the various events on the happening of which the security is to become enforceable. These usually are:

1. default in payment of principal or interest;
2. winding up;
3. breach of covenant; or
4. appointment of a receiver.

Other events are sometimes added.

Lloyd's Rep. 509; *Rasu Maritime S.A.* v. *Pertamina* [1977] 3 W.L.R. 518; *Siskina* v. *Distos S.A.* [1977] 1 W.L.R. 532; *Third Chandris Shipping Corporation* v. *Unimarine S.A.* [1979] 2 All E.R. 972 (C.A.); *Chartered Bank* v. *Daklouche* [1980] 1 All E.R. 205; *Iraqi Minister of Defence* v. *Arcepey Shipping Co.* [1980] 1 All E.R. 480. For useful comment see D. G. Powles [1978] J.B.L. 11, [1980] J.B.L. 59, [1981] J.B.L. 415 and F. Meisel [1980] Lloyds Maritime & Comm. L.Q. 38.

[50] *Burns* v. *Siemens Bros.* [1918] 2 Ch. 324.

The trust deed then provides that, when the security becomes enforceable, the trustees may at their discretion and shall, at the request of a specified proportion of the debenture or debenture stockholders, sell the mortgaged premises, and apply the net proceeds in paying off the debentures or debenture stock and hand the balance to the company.

The deed also empowers the trustees to appoint receivers or managers to carry on the business, provides for the trustees' indemnity, for meetings of the debenture holders, giving large powers to majorities, and imposes on the company certain obligations as regards insurance, repairs, furnishing information, further assurance, etc. In the case of debenture stock, the trust deed, in addition to the above provisions, usually constitutes the stock by a covenant therein contained—on the part of the company—to pay the amount of the stock, and the interest, or by any acknowledgment of indebtedness to the trustees for the amount thereof.

Trust deeds constituting debenture stock contain, in addition to the provisions found in ordinary trust deeds securing debentures, special provisions relating to the payment of the capital sum and interest.[51]

Majority clauses

4–20 Debenture trust deeds commonly, and debentures sometimes, contain provisions enabling a majority—say, three-fourths—of the holders of the debentures or debenture stock at a meeting to assent to modifications of the rights of the holders as a class. The object of such a power is, of course, to prevent a perverse or unreasonable minority from obstructing a beneficial arrangement, *e.g.* where it may be necessary to give the company time for payment of interest or to allow reduction of the rate, or enable it to raise further funds by a fresh issue of debentures to rank *pari passu*. The operation of such a clause has been discussed in a number of cases,[52] and the result of these cases may be summed up by saying that the powers of the meeting depend entirely on the true construction of the provisions in question. Each class of persons may vote in accordance with their own interests, provided that the whole scheme is fair,[53] but not where there is a secret bargain to secure the vote of persons controlling the majority.[54] Persons entitled to an immediate allotment of debentures (under a scheme) are entitled to vote.[55] In several cases, the provisions of the clause were held sufficient to enable the majority to bind the class to accept shares or debentures[56] of a new company in satisfaction of the securities of the existing company, but they have been held not to enable the company to

---

[51] See para. 43–04, *ante*.
[52] *Follit* v. *Eddystone, etc., Co.* [1892] 3 Ch. 75; *Mercantile Co.* v. *International Co. of Mexico.* [1893] 1 Ch. 484n. (C.A.); *Mercantile Investment, etc., Trust Co.* v. *River Plate, etc., Co.* [1894] 1 Ch. 578; *Sneath* v. *Valley Gold Co.* [1893] 1 Ch. 477 (C.A.); *Cox Moore* v. *Peruvian Corporation* [1908] 1 Ch. 604; *Shaw* v. *Royce Ltd.* [1911] 1 Ch. 138; *Northern Assurance Ltd.* v. *Farnham United Breweries* [1912] 2 Ch. 125.
[53] *Goodfellow* v. *Nelson Line Ltd.* [1912] 2 Ch. 324.
[54] *British America Nickel Corporation* v. *O'Brien* [1927] A.C. 369.
[55] *Dey* v. *Rubber, etc., Corporation* [1923] 2 Ch. 528.
[56] *Re Hutchinson (W. H.) & Sons Ltd.* (1915) 31 T.L.R. 324.

sell its assets and distribute them among those of the debenture holders who were willing to accept the lowest price for their debentures.[57] Where there is no such majority clause, the court can sanction an arrangement or compromise under section 206 of the 1948 Act.[58]

Remuneration of trustees

44–21 The trustees are commonly given remuneration by the deed, but, unless otherwise provided, this ranks after the debenture or debenture stockholders.[59] The deed usually provides otherwise, and gives the trustees a lien, which is effective.[60] Whether the trustees are entitled to remuneration after the appointment of a receiver depends on the construction of the trust deed. Remuneration was not allowed in *Re Locke & Smith Ltd.*,[61] where remuneration was payable "during the continuance of this security" and "as and by way of remuneration for their services as trustees," on the ground that in the ordinary course, where a receiver is appointed, the services of the trustees are terminated. But it was allowed in *Re Anglo-Canadian Lands*,[62] where the deed provided for remuneration until the mortgaged property was reconveyed or realised, and in *Re British Consolidated Oil Corporation*[63] when the deed provided for remuneration at a fixed rate.

Liability of trustees

The 1948 Act contains strict provisions nullifying clauses whereby a trustee is exempted from, or indemnified against, liability for negligent breach of trust (s. 88). These provisions, which were first introduced into company law by the reform culminating in the Act of 1948,[64] are modelled on the provisions of section 205 which avoid clauses exempting directors and other officers of the company and auditors from liability for negligence.[65]

According to section 88 (1), any provision in a trust deed securing debentures or in a contract with debenture holders is void so far as it could have the effect of exempting a trustee from, or indemnifying him against, liability for breach of trust where he fails to show the degree of care and diligence required of him as trustee.

This, however, does not prevent a release given after the event or a provision in the trust deed enabling a release to be given by agreement of a majority of not less than three-fourths in value of the debenture holders

---

57 *Re New York Taxicab Co.* [1913] 1 Ch. 1.
58 See paras. 79–04 *et seq., post.*
59 *Hodgson* v. *Accles* (1902) 51 W.R. 57.
60 *Re Piccadilly Hotel Ltd.* [1911] 2 Ch. 534.
61 [1914] 1 Ch. 687.
62 [1918] 2 Ch. 287.
63 [1919] 2 Ch. 81, not following *Re Locke & Smith Ltd., supra.* See, further, *Company Precedents*, Part III.
64 s. 75 of the Act of 1947 was re-enacted as s. 88 of the Act of 1948.
65 See para. 64–32, *post.*

present at a meeting summoned for that purpose and in respect of specific acts or omissions or on the trustee dying or ceasing to act (s. 88 (2)). Further, a person who was a trustee at the commencement of the Act[66] may still be protected by provisions of the deed then in force (s. 88 (3)). Moreover, the debenture holders may resolve by a resolution passed by a three-quarters majority in value of those present or by proxy[67] that the same protection may be extended to other, and even to future, trustees while there is at least one trustee entitled to the protection of a pre-Act exemption clause (s. 88 (4)).

While in the case of a director, other officer of the company and auditor the Act empowers the court, if of opinion that such person, although liable acted honestly and reasonably and, having regard to all the circumstances of the case, ought fairly to be excused of his liability, to relieve him of it (1948 Act, s. 448), the Act does not contain provision enabling the court to relieve a trustee from his liability. Such provision, however, would be redundant because the court has already this power in the case of a trustee for debenture holders under the Trustee Act 1925, s. 61.

Stock Exchange requirements relating to trust deeds

44–22 The Rules of the Stock Exchange require trust deeds to contain a number of provisions designed to protect the interests of the debenture holders.[68] The most important of these requirements are:

(1) *as regards trustees*: that if there is a sole trustee, it must be a trust corporation, and, if there are several trustees, one at least of them must be a trust corporation; that the trust corporation must have no interest in or relation to the company which might conflict with the position of trustee; and that a new trustee must prior to his appointment be approved by an extraordinary resolution of the relevant class of debenture holders[69];

(2) *as regards debenture holders' meetings and voting rights*: that machinery is laid down for the requisitioning of a meeting of debenture holders on the requisition of the holders of at least one-tenth of the nominal amount of the debentures for the time outstanding; that provision is made for the passing of an extraordinary resolution of debenture holders, for the quorum at their meetings, the demand for a poll, and related matters.[70]

Group debentures

44–23 It is possible to grant a floating charge on the assets of companies forming a group. Where a holding company wishes to issue debentures, the

---

66 July 1, 1948 (s. 462 (2)).

67 If the trust deed makes no provision for summoning meetings, the court may summon a meeting for that purpose (s. 88 (4)).

68 Rules of the Stock Exchange, Sched. VII, Pt. B; see Vol. II, Part C hereof.

69 *Ibid*. Sched. VII, Pt. B. para. 153.

70 *Ibid*. Sched. VII, Pt. B, C, paras. 160–165.

security of a floating charge is not very effective, since the assets charged will consist mainly of shares in subsidiary companies, and the claims of the debenture holders against those assets will be postponed to the rights of the creditors of the subsidiaries. For this reason the trust deed may comprise, in addition to the charge on the assets of the holding company, floating charges on the assets of some or all of the subsidiary companies.[71] Such a scheme would not, however, be extended to include foreign subsidiaries incorporated in countries which do not recognise the concept of the floating charge, and other subsidiaries may have to be excluded where there are minority shareholdings held by other persons.

---

[71] For problems which can arise see *Charterbridge Corporation Ltd.* v. *Lloyds Bank Ltd.* [1970] Ch. 62. This must now be read in the light of s. 9 of the European Communities Act 1972.

CHAPTER 45

REGISTRATION OF CHARGES

45–01 THE 1948 Act contains two sets of provisions dealing with the registration of mortgages and charges on the assets of the company: sections 103–105, which provide that all charges affecting the property of the company, including floating charges, shall be registered in a register of charges to be kept, together with copies of all instruments creating such charges, at the registered office of the company; and sections 95–102, which provide for the registration of certain charges with the Registrar of Companies.

These two sets of provisions are not co-extensive but they overlap: section 95 applies only to specified classes of mortgages or charges[1] while section 104 is general in nature and ambit.[2] Consequently, while every charge registered under sections 95–102 is likewise registrable under sections 103–105, certain charges are only registrable under the latter sections but not under the former; *e.g.* mortgages or charges on a concession or mortgages by deposit of dock warrants, bills of exchange or other mercantile documents are not registrable under the former statutory provisions while they would appear to be registrable under the latter. It follows that, from the point of view of the creditors or other interested persons, the register of charges kept at the registered office of the company is more informative than are the records kept with respect to charges by the Registrar.

The provisions of the Act, as far as they deal with the registration of charges, extend to oversea companies[3] with respect to charges on property situate in England, whether that property is immovable or movable property (s. 106).[4]

It is intended to examine first the registration of mortgages and charges under sections 103–105 and then to deal with the registration of charges under sections 95–102.

Registration at the registered office of the company

Requirements of registration

45–02 Every limited company is required to keep at its registered office a register of all charges specifically affecting property of the company and all floating charges on the undertaking or any property of the company, and to enter in it a short description of the property charged, the amount of the

---

[1] See s. 95 (2); para. 45–03, *post*.
[2] See s. 104 (1); see below in the text.
[3] For the definition of an oversea company, see s. 406; oversea companies are treated in Chap. 88, *post*.
[4] On the *situs* of movables, see Dicey and Morris, *The Conflict of Laws,* (10th ed, by Dr. J. H. C. Morris and others), Pt. Four.

charge, and the names of the persons entitled to it (s. 104). The register may be kept in non-legible form, *e.g.* on a computer (Companies (Registers and other Records) Regulations (S.I. 1979 No. 53)).

A member or an existing creditor[5] of the company may inspect the register of charges or the instruments creating such charges without fee. A member of the public may inspect the register (but not the copy of the instruments creating the charges) on payment of a fee not exceeding 5p (s. 105 (1)[6]).

Effect of non-registration

Under section 104 (2), as amended by the Companies Act 1980, s. 80, and Schedule 2, the sanction for non-registration is on conviction on indictment a fine and on summary conviction a fine not exceeding the statutory maximum. Non-registration does not vitiate the security[6a] and an error on the register does not affect priorities.[6b]

Registration with the Registrar of Companies

Registration of charges created by the company

45–03 The Act provides for the registration in a public register of prescribed particulars of the following mortgages and charges of a company together with the instrument creating or evidencing them (s. 95 (2)):

(a) a charge for the purpose of securing any issue of debentures;
(b) a charge on uncalled share capital of the company;
(c) a charge created or evidenced by an instrument which, if executed by an individual, would require registration as a bill of sale;
(d) a charge on land, wherever situate, or any interest therein, but not including a charge for any rent or other periodical sum issuing out of land;
(e) a charge on book debts of the company;
(f) a floating charge on the undertaking or property of the company;
(g) a charge on calls made but not paid;
(h) a charge on a ship or any share in a ship;
(i) a charge on goodwill, on a patent or a licence or a licence under a patent, on a trade mark or on a copyright or a licence under a copyright.[7]

Charges on aircraft are also now registrable, see para. 45–06, *post*.

The section ignores the distinction between legal and equitable securities in its legislative categories but does not expressly provide for remedies or lay down a comprehensive scheme of priorities. The legal or equitable

---

[5] *Wright* v. *Horton* (1887) 12 App.Cas. 371 (H.L.).
[6] As amended by the Decimal Currency Act 1969, s. 10 (1).
[6a] *Wright* v. *Horton* (1887) 12 App.Cas. 371 (H.L.).
[6b] *Re General South American Co.* (1876) 2 Ch.D. 337 (C.A.).
[7] The section applies to charges (a) to (f) created after July 1, 1908, and (g) to (i) if created after November 1, 1929 (s. 95 (10) (*b*)).

character of the security, is, therefore, still important although not conclusive.

THE OBJECT OF THE LEGISLATION. The object of the legislation is to enable those who deal with limited companies to search the register to find whether the company has encumbered its property or not.[8] Hence where a mortgagee has done everything which he is required to do by the Act to register his charge, registration is effective in his favour notwithstanding that the Registrar may have failed to note the charge properly.[9]

CREATION OF A CHARGE. The charge in question must be created by the company. Charges arising by operation of law are not registrable. A mortgage or a charge is created when the trust deed or agreement is executed or entered into, even though the advance is made subsequently.[10] In the case of a series of debentures unsecured by a trust deed it has been held that the charge is created when the first of the series are issued.[11]

45–04 WHAT CONSTITUTES A REGISTRABLE CHARGE. For the purpose of these sections the word "charge" is defined as including a mortgage (s. 95 (10) (*a*)). It also includes a lien or equitable charge. In this context it is immaterial whether the charge is created or evidenced by deed or instrument in writing or created by oral communication express or implied, *e.g.* by deposit of title deeds or by an agreement to deposit.[12] But a lien which is not created by the company but which arises by operation of law, *e.g.* a solicitor's lien or a unpaid vendor's lien when a person sells land to the company need not be registered,[13] since registration is only required in the case of charges "*created* after the fixed date" (s. 95 (1)). If a purported retention of ownership clause is construed as a corporate bill of sale or floating charge, this is registrable as such.[14]

An agreement which creates a *present* equitable interest in the security should be registered.[15] An agreement to give a security at some *future* time or on some *future* event occurring need not be registered,[16] but a charge

---

8 *Re Jackson and Bassford Ltd.* [1906] 2 Ch. 467, 476; *Esberger & Son Ltd.* v. *Capital and Counties Bank* [1913] 2 Ch. 366, 374.

9 *Re Inglis Bros. & Co. Ltd. (in liquidation)* [1932] N.Z.L.R. 874, 878 but *cf.* W. J. Gough, *Company Charges*, p. 303.

10 *Watson & Co.* v. *Spiral Globe Co.* [1902] 2 Ch. 209; *Re Harrogate Estates Ltd.* [1903] 1 Ch. 498; *Appleyard* v. *New London and Suburban Co.* [1908] 1 Ch. 621; *Esberger & Son Ltd.* v. *Capital and Counties Bank* [1913] 2 Ch. 366; *Dublin City Distillery Co.* v. *Doherty* [1914] A.C. 823.

11 *Watson & Co.* v. *Spiral Globe Co.* [1902] 2 Ch. 209.

12 *Dublin City Distillery Co.* v. *Doherty* [1914] A.C. 823; and see *Re F.L.E. Holdings Ltd.* [1967] 1 W.L.R. 1409, and *Capital Finance Co. Ltd.* v. *Stokes* [1969] 1 Ch. 261.

13 *London and Cheshire Insurance Co. Ltd.* v. *Laplagrene Property Co. Ltd.* [1971] Ch. 499; *Capital Finance Co. Ltd.* v. *Stokes* [1969] 1 Ch. 261 (C.A.); *Re Bernstein* [1925] Ch. 12. The point was, however, left open in *Burston Finance* v. *Speirway Ltd.* [1974] 3 All E.R. 735.

14 *Re Bond Worth Ltd.* [1979] 3 W.L.R. 629; *Borden (U.K.) Ltd.* v. *Scottish Timber Products Ltd.* [1979] 3 W.L.R. 672 (C.A.).

15 *Re Jackson & Bassford* [1906] 2 Ch. 467.

16 *Re Gregory Love & Co., Francis* v. *Gregory Love & Co.* [1916] 1 Ch. 203.

later executed pursuant to such an agreement will be registrable and may in certain circumstances be a fraudulent preference within the meaning of section 320 and, accordingly, be invalid.[17]

A separate charge on profits securing a bonus to debenture holders should be registered.[18]

A charge of substituted property made pursuant to an unregistered trust deed should be registered[19] unless the trustees of the deed merely carry into effect a sale and reinvestment without the company being made party to the conveyance.[20] When, however, particulars of an issue of debentures or debenture stock are registered under section 95 (8) there is no need to register a charge of substituted property notwithstanding that it was created by the company.[21] For in such a case "A particular description sufficient to identify each item or particular property is not required by the statute."[22]

A charging order on land belonging to the company obtained by a judgment creditor need not be registered under this section, although it must be registered under the Land Registration Act 1925.[23]

It should be emphasised that the sections only apply to the specified categories of mortgages and charges. A simple mortgage or charge which does not fall into any of these categories need not be registered.

45–05 CHARGES FOR THE PURPOSE OF SECURING ANY ISSUE OF DEBENTURES. This category is potentially very wide. The phrase "issue of debentures" is not defined in the 1948 Act. If it is regarded as covering the issue of a single debenture then it is wide enough to cover all the others. The New Zealand Court of Appeal has held that it is not to be so regarded.[24] The category only refers in a collective sense to the aggregate of a number of individual debentures issued by the company,[25] usually a series, although not necessarily a public issue. Section 95 (8) provides for an alternative mode of registration when a series of debentures, whose holders are entitled *pari passu* to the benefit of a charge, is issued. Instead of registering the individual instrument, it is sufficient to deliver the following particulars:

(a) the total amount secured by the whole series;
(b) the dates of the resolutions authorising the issue of the series and the date of the covering deed, if any, by which the security is created or defined;
(c) a general description of the property charged; and

---

17 *Re Eric Holmes (Property) Ltd.* [1965] Ch. 1052.
18 *Hoare* v. *British Columbia Association* [1912] W.N. 235; 107 L.T. 602.
19 *Cornbrook, etc., Co.* v. *Law Debenture Corporation* [1904] 1 Ch. 103.
20 *Bristol United Breweries* v. *Abbott* [1908] 1 Ch. 279.
21 *Cunard Steamship Co.* v. *Hopwood* [1908] 2 Ch. 564.
22 *Ibid. per* Swinfen-Eady J. at p. 579.
23 *Re Overseas Aviation Engineering (G.B.) Ltd.* [1963] Ch. 24 (C.A.).
24 *Automobile Association (Canterbury) Inc.* v. *Australasian Secured Deposits Ltd.* [1973] 1 N.Z.L.R. 417.
25 *Per* Richmond J. at [1973] 1 N.Z.L.R. 425 1.20.

(d) the names of the trustees, if any, for the debenture holders; together with the deed containing the charge, or, if there is no such deed, one of the debentures of the series.

CHARGES ON UNCALLED SHARE CAPITAL. This is a charge on the company's own capital not that of its subsidiaries. A charge on shares held in another company is not a species of registrable charge.[26]

45–06 CHARGES CREATED OR EVIDENCED BY AN INSTRUMENT WHICH IF BY AN INDIVIDUAL WOULD BE REGISTRABLE AS A BILL OF SALE.[27] No mortgage or charge of chattels (whether securing debentures or not) made by a company incorporated under the Companies Acts need be registered as a bill of sale.[28] Accordingly, no debenture, mortgage or charge by such a company will be invalidated against the execution creditors[29] or liquidator[30] of a company for want of registration under the Bills of Sale Acts 1878 and 1882, and the fact that the debenture holder's chattel property remains at the date of winding up in the possession of the company, as reputed owner, makes no difference; for section 317 of the 1948 Act, when making applicable to winding up certain bankruptcy rules, does not introduce the provisions relating to reputed ownership.[31]

Any charge which would have been registrable as a bill of sale by an individual must in the case of companies be registered with the Registrar of Companies (1948 Act, s. 95 (2) (*c*)).

A bill of sale as defined by section 4 of the Bills of Sale Act 1878 includes all assurances of personal chattels with certain exceptions. A pledge of goods accompanied by delivery of possession to the pledgee is not a bill of sale,[32] and this is not affected by the addition of a letter of trust[33]; nor is an oral agreement giving security followed by possession[34]; nor prima facie are inventories of goods with receipt attached[35] nor sale and hiring agreements.[36] Consequently, these transactions, if effected by a company, do not require registration under section 95 (2) (*c*). Section 1 of the Bills of

---

[26] The Jenkins Report (Cmnd. 1749), paras. 301, 306 (f) recommended that it should be registrable.

[27] The Bills of Sale Act 1878 does not apply to Scotland or Ireland.

[28] *Re Standard Manufacturing Co.* [1891] 1 Ch. 627. See further *Clark* v. *Balm, Hill & Co.* [1908] 1 K.B. 667 and *NV Slavenburg's Bank* v. *Intercontinental Natural Resources Ltd.* [1980] 1 All E.R. 955.

[29] *Re Standard Manufacturing Co., supra; Taunton* v. *Sheriff of Warwickshire* [1895] 2 Ch. 319; *Robson* v. *Smith* [1895] 2 Ch. 118; *Re Opera Co.* [1891] 3 Ch. 260.

[30] *Re Marine Mansions Co.* (1867) L.R. 4 Eq. 601, 607; *Re Asphaltic Wood, etc., Co.* (1883) 49 L.T. 159.

[31] *Re Crumlin Viaduct Works Co.* (1879) 11 Ch.D. 755; *Gorringe* v. *Irwell, etc., Works* (1886) 34 Ch.D. 128; see Bankruptcy Act 1914, s. 38 (*c*).

[32] *Ex p. Hubbard* (1886) 17 Q.B.D. 690. See also *R. A. Barrett & Co. Ltd.* v. *Livesey* [1980] C.A.T. 805; (1981) 131 N.L.J. 1213 (C.A.) where it was held that the asset pledged could be used.

[33] *Re David Allester Ltd.* [1922] 2 Ch. 211; and see *Wrightson* v. *McArthur and Hutchinson (1919) Ltd.* [1921] 2 K.B. 807.

[34] *Charlesworth* v. *Mills* [1892] A.C. 231; *Ramsay* v. *Margrett* [1894] 2 Q.B. 18.

[35] *Ramsay* v. *Margrett, supra.*

[36] *Manchester Ry.* v. *North Central Wagon Co.* (1888) 13 App.Cas. 554.

Sale Act 1890 as amended exempts an instrument creating any security on imported goods given prior to their deposit in a warehouse, factory or store. It has been held that this does not cover a document which creates a general charge on all future goods but it does cover a consignment of goods which are not specific goods provided it is sufficiently identified. A general charge is, therefore, registrable under s. 95 (2) (*c*).[37]

Not all documents registrable as bills of sale fall within section 95 (2) (*c*): to do so the transaction must be a charge to secure the repayment of money.[38] But the court will look to the true nature of the transaction and not merely at its form, and will not allow the section to be evaded by making what is in fact a charge in form an absolute assignment.[39]

The Industrial and Provident Societies Act 1967 makes similar provisions for registration with the Registrar of Friendly Societies of charges created by a registered society, and expressly provides by section 1 (1) that instruments creating or evidencing a fixed or floating charge which are executed after July 14, 1967, are not to be treated as bills of sale if application for registration is duly made under the Act.[40]

Where a company incorporated under a foreign legal system owns chattels in England, it need not register a charge on them as a bill of sale although neither English law nor the foreign law of corporations provides machinery for the registration of such charges.[41]

CHARGES ON LAND. This covers legal and equitable mortgages or charges of land even where the land is situated abroad. A charge on the land for rent or other periodic payment is excluded from the category. So if the company has entered into a lease or agreed to pay a rent charge payable out of its land these are not registrable but a mortgage over the company's own leasehold interests or rent charges would be.

Specific charges on unregistered land after 1st January 1970 must be registered under the Land Charges Act 1972 as well as at the Companies Registry.[42] All specific charges on registered land must be registered at the Land Registry and the Companies Registry. A floating charge over unregistered land need only be registered at the Companies Registry. A floating charge over registered land can only be protected at the Land Registry by a notice if the land certificate can be produced and by a caution against

---

[37] *NV Slavenburg's Bank* v. *Intercontinental Natural Resources Ltd.* [1980] 1 All E.R. 955, 977, Lloyd J.

[38] *Stoneleigh Finance Ltd.* v. *Phillips* [1965] 2 Q.B. 537.

[39] [1965] 2 Q.B. 537, 574, *per* Russell L.J.

[40] Prior to this Act charges created by such societies were void unless registered as bills of sale: see *Great Northern Ry.* v. *Coal Co-operative Society* [1896] 1 Ch. 187; *Re North Wales Produce and Supply Society* [1922] 2 Ch. 340. For the position in Scotland see paras. 47–17 *et seq., post.*

[41] *Clark* v. *Balm, Hill & Co.* [1908] 1 K.B. 667.

[42] ss. 3 (7) and (8) Land Charges Act 1972. See *Property Discount Corporation Ltd.* v. *Lyon Group Ltd.* [1981] 1 All E.R. 379 (C.A.)—registration of a charge on an equitable interest under s. 95 effective for the purposes of s. 3 (7) of the 1972 Act even though it was registered against the company which created the charge and not against the estate owner. See the useful notes by D. J. Hayton (1980) 1 Co. Law 144 and (1981) 2 Co. Law. 127.

dealings if it cannot.[43] Generally unless this is done a purchaser under a registered disposition is not concerned, whether or not he has notice "express, implied or constructive."[44] When an instrument creates both a fixed and floating charge it will normally be registered as a charge under sections 25 and 26 of the Land Registration Act 1925 as to the fixed provisions so that a copy of the deed would either be bound up in the charge certificate or be issued as part of it. So far as registered land was affected by the floating provisions it could be protected by notice under section 40 of the Act. When debentures or trust deeds which create floating charges are noted on the register under section 49 and they contain a restrictive clause, the entry on the register will refer to the clause and be to the following effect: "By a Trust Deed dated . . . of . . . Limited, the land is charged as security for the monies therein mentioned. The charge is expressed to be by way of floating security but not so as to permit the creation of charges in priority thereto or *pari passu* therewith." If the floating charge is protected by a caution under section 54 of the Act the Registry will neither see nor possess a copy but anyone interested in the land learning of the caution will need to go to the deed itself for full information about it.

An agreement to create a mortgage or charge over land amounts to an equitable mortgage[45] and is registrable. Any mortgage or charge subsequently created is also registrable and its validity is unaffected by non-registration of the agreement.[46]

An equitable charge arising by presumption of law by deposit of title deeds is nevertheless contractual and does not arise by operation of law.[47] The presumption reads into the contract the charge which is implied. The charge is, therefore, registrable. This applies even where the debt secured is owed by a third party. If the charge is avoided everything ancillary to it is also void. Accordingly no separate lien on the deeds and documents will be recognised.[48]

A lien arising by operation of law such as a solicitor's lien is not registrable.[49] An unpaid vendor's lien is thus not registrable.[50] Neither is a right of subrogation to an unpaid vendor's lien.[51] However, it is not

---

[43] ss. 49 (1) (*f*), 54, 60, 64 of the Land Registration Act 1925 and s. 26 of the Administration of Justice Act 1977 (abolition of mortgage caution). See Ruoff and Roper *Law and Practice of Registered Conveyancing* (4th ed.), p. 502, J. H. Farrar (1974) 38 Conv. (N.S.) 315, 324–5. See also Practice Direction dated January 17, 1977, noted (1977) 121 S.J. 72.

[44] ss. 59 (6) and 110 (7) of the Land Registration Act 1925.

[45] *Eyre* v. *McDowell* (1861) 9 H.L. Cas. 619 (H.L.) but *cf. Williams* v. *Burlington Investments Ltd.* (1977) 121 S.J. 424 (H.L.) where a contract to create a legal charge on a particular event was held not to be registrable as it did not create a present equitable right to a security but was merely an agreement that in some future circumstances a security would be created.

[46] *Re Columbian Fireproofing Co. Ltd.* [1910] 2 Ch. 120 (C.A.).

[47] *Re Wallis & Simmonds (Builders) Ltd.* [1974] 1 All E.R. 561.

[48] *Re Molton Finance Ltd.* [1968] Ch. 325 (C.A.).

[49] *Brunton* v. *Electrical Engineering Corp.* [1892] Ch. 434.

[50] *London & Cheshire Insurance Co. Ltd.* v. *Laplagrene Property Co. Ltd.* [1971] Ch. 499; *Bank of Ireland Finance Ltd.* v. *D. J. Daly Ltd. (in liquidation)* [1978] I.R. 79.

[51] *Burston Finance Ltd* v. *Speirway Ltd.* [1974] 3 All E.R. 735. *Cf. Coptic Ltd.* v. *Bailey Finance Ltd.* [1972] 1 All E.R. 1242 which was not followed.

normally possible to allege an unpaid vendor's lien if a valid but unenforceable charge is obtained as security.[52] It is otherwise if the latter charge is void from inception; in this case one can rely on the unpaid vendor's lien.[53] The unpaid vendor's lien will be excluded if the intention was simply the creation of an unsecured loan.[54] Where an equitable charge is duly registered and under a term thereof a legal mortgage is later executed the latter need not be registered.[55]

Under section 95 (7), the holding of debentures entitling the holder to a charge on land shall not be deemed to be an interest in land for the purposes of the section. A charging order over land by way of execution is not registrable under the section[56] but must be registered under the Land Registration Act 1925.

CHARGES ON BOOK DEBTS. "Book debts" for this purpose are debts owing to the company connected with and arising out of the company's trade or business, which are entered, or commonly would be entered in the ordinary course of business, in well kept books of such a trade or business.[57] Any assignment of a book debt is within the section if it is intended to be a security for a debt,[58] whether or not the debt is in fact entered in the books of the company.[59] A charge on future book debts is likewise registrable.[59] A document purporting to be a sale of hire-purchase agreements was construed by Eve J. as a charge on book debts, but was held by the Court of Appeal to be a sale.[60] A block discounting agreement whereby the bank made advances to the company in return for the assignment to the bank of blocks of credit sale agreements due to the company was construed as an absolute assignment of the customers' debts and not as a charge upon them, even though in fact only 80 per cent. of the debts were actually taken by the bank in return for the advances. The transactions were not a "sham" nor had the parties any intention of creating a charge over book debts or

---

52 *Re Beirnstein* [1925] Ch. 12; *Capital Finance Co. Ltd.* v. *Stokes* [1969] 1 Ch. 261 (C.A.); *London & Cheshire Insurance Co.* v. *Laplagrene Property Co. Ltd.* [1971] Ch. 499. *Cf. Sunnucks* (1970) 33 M.L.R. 131.

53 *Thurstan* v. *Nottingham Permanent Benefit Building Society* [1902] 1 Ch. 1 (C.A.); [1903] A.C. 6 (H.L.); *Ghana Commercial Bank* v. *Chandiram* [1960] A.C. 732 (P.C.); *Congresbury Motors Ltd.* v. *Anglo-Belge Finance Co. Ltd.* [1971] Ch. 81; *Greendon Investments* v. *Mills* (1973) 226 *Estates Gazette* 1957; *Burston Finance Ltd.* v. Speirway Ltd. [1974] 3 All E.R. 735.

54 *Paul* v. *Speirway Ltd.* [1976] Ch. 220.

55 *Cunard S.S. Co.* v. *Hopwood* [1908] 2 Ch. 564; *Re William Hall Contractors Ltd.* [1967] 1 W.L.R. 948.

56 *Re Overseas Aviation Engineering (G.B.) Ltd.* [1963] Ch. 24 (C.A.).

57 See *Shipley* v. *Marshall* (1863) 14 C.B.(N.S.) 566; *Tailby* v. *Official Receiver* (1888) 13 App.Cas. 523; *Dawson* v. *Isle* [1906] 1 Ch. 633; *Re Law Car, etc., Corporation* [1911] W.N. 91; *Independent Automatic Sales Ltd.* v. *Knowles & Foster* [1962] 1 W.L.R. 974; *Paul & Frank Ltd.* v. *Discount Bank (Overseas) Ltd.* [1967] Ch. 348.

58 *Saunderson & Co.* v. *Clark* (1913) 29 T.L.R. 579; and see *Ladenburg & Co.* v. *Goodwin, Ferreira & Co.* [1912] 3 K.B. 275.

59 *Independent Automatic Sales Ltd.* v. *Knowles & Foster* [1962] 1 W.L.R. 974.

60 *Re George Inglefield Ltd.* [1933] Ch. 1 *Lloyds and Scottish Finance Ltd.* v. *Prentice* (1977) S.J. 847; *cf. Independent Automatic Sales Ltd.* v. *Knowles & Foster, ante.*

merely making a series of loans.[61] Cash at the bank has been held in New Zealand not to be a book debt although entered in the books of the company and although the relationship of bank and customer is that of debtor and creditor.[62] On the other hand a letter directing moneys payable under a contract to be remitted to the company's bankers with whom the company had an overdraft containing the words, these instructions "to be regarded as irrevocable," unless the bank should consent to their cancellation, has been held to be a charge on book debts.[63] A charge on an insurance policy issued by the Export Credits Guarantee Department of the Department of Trade is not registrable, as the policy is not a book debt.[64] An assignment of a part of a book debt is not a charge on the book debt[65] but an assignment of so much of a debt as may be necessary to indemnify the assignees in consideration of an advance is registrable[66] The court will look at the substance as well as the form. Where a bill of exchange has actually been entered in the books of the company it is a book debt[67] but s. 95 (6) provides that the deposit of a negotiable instrument in payment of book debts for the purpose of securing an advance shall not be treated as a charge on those book debts.

Where a company is supplied goods subject to a reservation of property by the supplier under a contract which constitutes the company the supplier's agent in respect of subsales until the price under the supply contract is paid, the contract is not registrable as a charge on book debts.[68] However where an attempt is made to reserve beneficial ownership in the goods the clause may be construed as a floating charge and any provision for transfer of ownership in new goods made by using the original goods may be construed as an equitable charge over future goods. In both cases the clause is registrable.[68]

FLOATING CHARGES. Floating charges have already been discussed in Chapter 44, *ante*. The legislative category refers to floating charges on the undertaking or property of the company. This is clearly disjunctive so that a floating charge on any part of the property is covered.[69] Floating charges must always be registered even if they only relate to property over which a fixed charge would not need to be registered, *e.g.* shares in another company or debts which are not book debts.

---

[61] *Lloyds and Scottish Finance Ltd.* v. *Prentice* (1977) S.J. 847; see also *Lloyds & Scottish Finance Ltd.* v. *Cyril Lord Carpets Sales Ltd.* (1979) (unreported) (H.L.).
[62] *Watson* v. *Parapara Coal Co. Ltd.* [1915] 17 G.L.R 791. This seems illogical.
[63] *Re Kent and Sussex Sawmills Ltd.* [1947] Ch. 177.
[64] *Paul & Frank* v. *Discount Bank (Overseas) Ltd., ante.*
[65] *Ashby Warner & Co.* v. *Simmons* (1936) L.J.K.B. 127.
[66] *Saunderson & Co.* v. *Clark* (1913) 29 T.L.R. 579.
[67] *Dawson* v. *Isle* [1906] 1 Ch. 633.
[68] *Aluminium Industries Vaassan BV* v. *Romalpa Aluminimum Ltd.* [1976] 2 All E.R. 552 (C.A.); *Borden (U.K.) Ltd.* v. *Scottish Timber Products Ltd.* [1979] 3 W.L.R. 672 (C.A.), *Re Interview Ltd.* [1975] I.R. 382 and *Re Bond Worth Ltd.* [1979] 3 W.L.R. 629, and see further para. 46–09, *post.*
[69] *Mercantile Bank of India Ltd.* v. *Chartered Bank of India, Australia & China* [1937] 1 All E.R 231, 241.

CHARGES ON CALLS. We have referred to charges on uncalled capital above. This category consists of the calls themselves made but not yet paid. They are a species of debt but are not regarded as book debts.

CHARGES ON SHIPS. This covers mortgages of ships or a share in a ship. Legal mortgages are effected in accordance with the form laid down in the Merchant Shipping Act 1894 and registered at the ship's port of registry. Equitable mortgages need not comply with these formalities.

CHARGES ON GOODWILL, PATENTS, TRADEMARKS, AND COPYRIGHT. This covers charges on goodwill, patents, patent licences, registered trademarks, copyright or copyright licences but not registered designs. Charges over patents,[70] registered trademarks[71] and registered designs[72] must be notified to the Patents Office.

CHARGES ON AIRCRAFT. This was not originally covered by s. 95 (2). However by a statutory instrument made under section 16 of the Civil Aviation Act 1968[73] there is now provision for a Register of Aircraft Mortgages to be kept by the Civil Aviation Authority and for registration at the Companies Registry.[74]

CHARGES BY OVERSEA COMPANIES. Section 106 extends the provisions of Part III to charges created and property subject to charges acquired by a company (whether a company within the meaning of the Act or not) incorporated outside England which has an established place of business in England. This section applies to all oversea companies, not merely those incorporated in Scotland and Northern Ireland. The practice of the Registrar of Companies of requiring registration of the oversea company under section 407 prior to registration of the charge under section 95 has no legal foundation and does not affect the outcome between the parties. Liquidators abroad may plead section 95 since section 106 is to be taken as extending the scope of section 95 provided that the winding up is similar in character to an English winding up. Even if the liquidator was not entitled to plead section 95 the court would allow joinder of an English creditor on a representative basis under R.S.C. Ord. 15, r. 6 (1), to plead the liquidator's case. Section 95 as extended by s. 106 applies to floating charges created overseas and is not confined to property in England when the charge is created. Once having fallen within section 95 by virtue of section 106 property remains within section 95 even though the company has

---

[70] Patents Act 1977, s. 32 (2).
[71] Trade Marks Act 1938, s. 25 (1).
[72] Registered Designs Act 1949, s. 19 (1).
[73] The Mortgaging of Aircraft Order 1972 (No. 1268) *operative* since 1st October 1972.
[74] *Ibid.*, Art. 16 (2).

ceased to have a place of business in England before the commencement of the winding up.[75] This section as interpreted produces chaos and should be reformed. At present it would seem advisable to safeguard the lender to deliver particulars of such charge to the Registrar even where there is no reason to suspect that the company has an established place of business here. That the particulars will not then appear on a public file only heightens the absurdity of this particular provision.[75a]

45–07 EFFECT OF NON-REGISTRATION. Failure to register within twenty-one days of the creation of the charge has the effect of making the charge void as against the creditors and liquidator, but against them only; it is good as against the company.[76] Accordingly, until liquidation the person seeking to enforce such a charge has available to him all the remedies of a mortgagee and the company may give a subsequent valid mortgage to secure the same debt. But if a subsequent creditor even with notice of the first charge takes a registered charge before the first charge is registered, he obtains priority.[77] During liquidation the sum purporting to be secured by the void charge ranks as an unsecured debt. In this connection it should be noted that when a charge becomes void for want of registration the money secured thereby becomes immediately payable (s. 95 (1)).

An equitable chargee whose charge is void on the ground of non-registration, has no lien on the title deeds or documents deposited with him, as the deposit is only ancillary to the—void—charge.[78]

REGISTRATION AND PRIORITIES. As we have seen, section 95 does not distinguish between legal and equitable mortgages and charges. Nevertheless, such securities retain their legal or equitable character. Furthermore although the system of registration affects the validity of charges it does not entirely replace the legal and equitable priority rules. The result is a peculiar hybrid system of priorities.

The legal and equitable rules when read together produce a system where a legal mortgage ranks before an earlier equitable mortgage unless the legal mortgage had notice. As between legal or equitable mortgages *inter se* the first in time prevails. Registration affects this system by (1) avoiding charges not duly registered as against the liquidator and other creditors and (2) by virtue of the doctrine of constructive notice attendant on it. Registration affects validity but subject thereto priorities are still normally determined by the date of creation, not registration. The latter point is reinforced to some extent by the new practice of the Registrar of

[75] *NV Slavenburg's Bank* v. *Intercontinental Natural Resources Ltd.* [1980] 1 All E.R. 955, Lloyd J.

[75a] For telling criticisms see the Memorandum by the Law Society's Standing Committee on Company Law on the *Slavenburg* case. See also D. Milman (1981) 125 S.J. 294.

[76] The company cannot therefore itself apply for a declaration that the charge is void for non-registration; if the company is in liquidation such proceedings should be brought by the liquidator in his own name: *Independent Automatic Sales Ltd.* v. *Knowles & Foster, ante.*

[77] *Re Monolithic Co.* [1915] 1 Ch. 643.

[78] *Re Molton Finance Ltd.* [1968] Ch. 325 (C.A.).

entering special warning fiches[79] directing searchers to the Special Enquiry Counter for documents which have been received subsequently relating to mortgages, charges or the appointment of receivers or liquidators. The new practice gives rise to the possibility of actual knowledge of such documents or inferred knowledge if a search is made but the documents are not inspected. It is difficult to say whether it gives rise to constructive notice. On balance the better view would appear to be that it does not since (1) the practice seems to be an administrative act of the Registrar without express legal duty and (2) the information given is unspecific.

The resulting detailed rules can be stated as follows.[80]

Specific charges

1. A registered charge ("A") takes priority over an unregistered charge ("B"), whether prior or subsequent, except that where B has been created within 21 days before A and is subsequently duly registered B will achieve priority.[81] B will lose such priority if (i) displaced by estoppel or in equity or (ii) A constitutes a legal charge without actual or constructive notice or has a better equity. Actual or inferred knowledge of B may arise if it has been lodged and a special warning fiche has been entered on the company's file by the Registrar but there is probably no constructive notice of B until it is registered.

2. A subsequent purchaser of the mortgaged property takes subject to the registered charge because of the doctrine of constructive notice.[82]

3. Where registration under another system is also required this must be carried out to achieve priority.[83]

4. Registered charges depend for priority on registration but take priority from the date of their creation unless displaced by (i) estoppel or in equity, or (ii) the later charge is a legal charge without actual or constructive notice or has a better equity.[84] Knowledge of an unregistered charge lodged with the Registrar may arise if a special warning fiche is entered on the company's file by the Registrar and a search is made but there is probably no constructive notice until registration.

5. An unregistered charge may effectively achieve priority over a

---

79 See further J. H. Farrar (1976) 40 Conv. (N.S.) 397, 413.

80 This scheme of priorities is based on Dr. W. J. Gough, *Company Charges*, pp.401–402. It differs, however in the following three respects: (1) although it recognises that validity of charges depends on registration it proceeds on the basis that, once registered, charges basically rank in order of creation not registration; (2) it recognises the possibility of inferred knowledge of a restrictive clause in a floating charge and (3) it deals with the new practice of special warning fiches.

81 This was raised but unanswered by Buckley J. in the course of argument in *Re Anglo-Oriental Carpet Co.*, [1903] 1 Ch. 914, 917. Dr. Gough, *op. cit.* p. 336 states that the priority rules of the general law apply since s. 95 cannot apply in favour of either registered secured creditor against the other.

82 *Wilson* v. *Kelland* [1910] 2 Ch. 306.

83 This is necessary since both systems of registration are capable of invalidating or postponing the charge for non-registration. See further Gough, *op. cit.* pp. 387, 393, 395.

84 s. 95 (1) and the general law.

subsequent registered charge if it has been discharged before its validity has been called in question.[85]

Floating charges

1. A registered floating charge without a restrictive clause ranks after a prior or subsequent specific charge which is duly registered.[86]

2. A subsequent registered floating charge over the undertaking purporting to rank prior to or *pari passu* will (unless otherwise agreed) rank after the first registered floating charge in such circumstances.[87]

3. A subsequent registered floating charge over part of the company's property made under a power expressly reserved to create security over part ranking prior to the earlier charge will obtain priority in such circumstances.[88]

4. A registered floating charge with a restrictive clause ranks before a subsequent registered specific charge where the specific chargee has knowledge or notice of the clause.[89] Constructive notice of the floating charge is not constructive notice of the restrictive clause[90] but there may be circumstances of wilful blindness which give rise to an inference of knowledge.[91]

5. A crystallised registered floating charge takes priority over a subsequent registered specific charge or an assignment unless the mortgagee or assignee had no notice of the crystallisation. There will be constructive notice of the appointment of a receiver or a winding up although there is a time-lag problem tempered to some extent by the system of special warning fiches.[92]

6.The preferred creditors mentioned in section 319 take priority over the holder of a floating charge by virtue of section 94.

5–08 CHARGES EXISTING ON PROPERTY ACQUIRED BY THE COMPANY. Companies acquiring property subject to one of the charges specified in section 95 (2) are required to register them within twenty-one days after the date on which the acquisition is completed (s. 97 (1)).[93] It is submitted that this date is the date of the conveyance or transfer of the proprietary interest in question. In the case of property situate abroad the twenty-one days begin

[85] The charge but not the debt is invalidated against the liquidator and creditors. See *Mercantile Bank of India* v. *Chartered Bank of India* [1937] 1 All E.R. 231. Once the debt has been discharged the priority question is no longer relevant.
[86] *Re Hamilton's Windsor Ironworks* (1879) 12 Ch.D. 707.
[87] *Re Benjamin Cope & Sons Ltd.* [1914] 1 Ch. 800.
[88] *Re Automatic Bottle Makers Ltd.* [1926] Ch. 412.
[89] *English and Scottish Mercantile Investment Co. Ltd.* v. *Brunton* [1892] 2 Q.B. 700.
[90] *Wilson* v. *Kelland* [1910] 2 Ch. 306.
[91] See Farrar (1974) 38 Conv. (N.S.) 315, 325 and [1980] 1 Co. Law 83. *Cf.* also *Union Bank of Halifax* v. *The Indian & General Investment Trust* [1908] 40 S.C.R. 510 as to proof of title.
[92] See Farrar (1976) 40 Conv. (N.S.) 397, 406 *et seq.*
[93] As to the relationship between ss. 95 and 97, see *Capital Finance Co. Ltd.* v. *Stokes* [1968] 1 All E.R. 573, affd. by C.A. [1969] 1 Ch. 261.

to run from the receipt in Great Britain of a copy of the instrument relating to the charge (1948 Act, s. 97 (1), proviso).

CHARGES ON SUBSTITUTED PROPERTY. Property subject to a specific charge is sometimes released and replaced by other property. Where this is done a mortgage or charge on the substituted property requires registration unless there is a trust deed which has been registered under section 95 (8). Having regard to section 97 (1) the mere fact that the charge was not created by the company would not affect the necessity for registration. The case of *Bristol United Breweries* v. *Abbott*[94] which suggests the contrary was decided before section 97 (1) was adopted and must be taken to be overruled by section 97.

In the case of a charge securing an issue of debentures registered under section 95 (8), however, no registration is needed of any substituted security since registration under that subsection protects the substituted property without further registration.[95] Such a case falls within section 98 (1) (*a*), and under section 98 (2) the Registrar's certificate is conclusive evidence that the registration requirements have been complied with.

EFFECT OF NON-REGISTRATION. Unlike s. 95 (1) failure to register charges required to be registered under section 97 (1) does not invalidate the charge in any way but exposes the officers of the company to penalties (1948 Act, s. 97 (2) as amended by the Companies Act 1980 s. 80 and Schedule 2).

45–09 WHO SHOULD EFFECT REGISTRATION. The duty to effect registration under section 95 is imposed on the company by section 96, but anybody interested is at liberty to do it and recover from the company the cost properly incurred thereby. If neither the company nor any other person interested registered the prescribed particulars, every officer in default is liable to pay a fine. (1948 Act, s. 96 (3) as amended by s. 80 and Sched. 2 to the Companies Act 1980).

PARTICULARS TO BE REGISTERED. Section 98 (1) of the 1948 Act requires the Registrar to keep for each company a register in the prescribed form of all charges required to be registered and to enter the following particulars:

(a) in the case of a charge to the benefit of which the holders of a series of debentures are entitled, such particulars as are specified in section 95 (8), *i.e.*

(i) the total amount secured by the whole series;

(ii) the dates of the resolutions authorising the issue of the

---

[94] [1908] 1 Ch. 279.

[95] *Cunard S. S. Co.* v. *Hopwood* [1908] 2 Ch. 564. See further Palmer's *Company Precedents* (16th ed.), Part 3 by A. F. Topham K.C. and R. Buchanan-Dunlop, p. 157 and Gough *op. cit.* p. 300.

series and the date of the covering deed, if any, by which the security is created or defined;

(iii) a general description of the property charged;

(iv) the names of the trustees, if any, for the debenture holders.

(b) in the case of any other charge

(i) if the charge is a charge created by the company, the date of its creation, and if the charge was a charge existing on property acquired by the company, the date of the acquisition of the property; and

(ii) the amount secured by the charge; and

(iii) short particulars of the property charged; and

(iv) the persons entitled to the charge.

By virtue of Schedule 3 to the Companies Act 1976 no fees are payable for inspection of the register.

When debentures are issued at a discount, this fact should also be included amongst the particulars required to be registered but omission to do so will not affect the validity of the debentures (s. 95 (9)). The deposit of debentures to secure a debt of the company is not treated as an issue of debentures at a discount for this purpose (s. 95 (9), proviso).

When the prescribed particulars are registered, the Registrar gives a certificate of registration of the charge which should be indorsed on every debenture or certificate of debenture stock which is issued by the company (s. 98 (2) as amended by s. 38 (2) of the Companies Act 1976). The certificate of registration is conclusive evidence that the prescribed particulars have been presented to the Registrar and entered in the register of charges,[96] even though the particulars supplied are incomplete or partially incorrect, as where part of the property charged is omitted,[97] or the amount secured is incorrectly stated,[98] or the charges are incorrectly dated.[99] It has been suggested, however, that if a chargee fraudulently deceives the Registrar, a creditor personally damaged by the fraud can take proceedings in personam.[1] The certificate is not evidence of the *accuracy* of the particulars: in order to ascertain the terms and effect of the charge it is necessary to look at the document creating the charge and not at the register.[2]

RELEASE OF CHARGE. The Registrar may, on proof that the debt has been paid in whole or in part or that part of the property has been released from the charge, enter a memorandum of satisfaction in whole or in part, or of the fact that part of the property or undertaking has been released from the

---

[96] *Re Yolland, Husson and Birkett* [1908] 1 Ch. 152; *Re Mechanisations (Eaglescliffe) Ltd.* [1966] Ch. 20; *Re C. L. Nye Ltd.* [1971] Ch. 442 (C.A.), overruling the decision of Plowman J. in [1969] 2 All E.R. 587.

[97] *National Provincial Bank* v. *Charnley* [1924] 1 K.B. 431.

[98] *Re Mechanisations (Eaglescliffe) Ltd., supra.*

[99] *Re Eric Holmes (Property) Ltd.* [1965] Ch. 1052.

[1] *National Provincial Bank* v. *Charnley* [1924] 1 K.B. 431; *Re C. L. Nye Ltd.* [1971] Ch. 442, 474, *per* Russell L.J.

[2] *Re Mechanisations (Eaglescliffe) Ltd., ante, per* Buckley J. at p. 31.

charge or has ceased to form part of the company's property or undertaking, as the case may be (1948 Act, s. 100). This is not, however, conclusive as to release of the charge since the memorandum of satisfaction may be fraudulent. In this case those making it will be guilty of perjury but a subsequent chargee relying on it will be postponed. Section 100 should be amended to require the memorandum to be filed by the holder of the charge.

Extension of time. Rectification of mistakes

45–10 As has been stated,[3] registration has normally to be effected within 21 days after the creation of the charge or the acquisition of the charged property. The time may, however, be extended under section 101. The same section provides for the rectification of mistakes. A judge of the High Court may grant extension of time or rectification on being satisfied that the omission to register a mortgage or charge within the time required (by s. 95 (1)), or that the omission or misstatement of any particular with respect to such mortgage or charge, "was accidental or due to inadvertence or to some other sufficient cause, or is not of a nature to prejudice the position of creditors or shareholders of the company, or that, on other grounds, it is just and equitable to grant relief."[4] The wording is not, however, wide enough to empower the court to order the deletion of the whole entry from the register.[5] Nor will the section apply if the charge has actually been registered out of time by virtue of a mistake as to the date of creation.[6] The court may extend the time for registration on such terms and conditions as seem to the judge just and expedient. The court is not precluded from exercising this power by the fact that the validity of the charge is being challenged in other proceedings but there is no power to grant interim relief.[7] The words "accidental or due to inadvertence" have a very wide meaning.[8] In exercising this discretionary power[9] of granting relief on terms, it became the practice to insert in the order the following words: "This order to be without prejudice to the rights of parties acquired prior to the time when such debentures shall be actually registered."[10]

This proviso, as the Court of Appeal explained in *Re Ehrmann Bros.*

[3] See para. 45–07, *ante*.

[4] The court has no power to grant interim relief under this section: *Re Heathstar Properties Ltd.* [1966] 1 W.L.R. 993.

[5] *Re C. L. Nye Ltd.* [1971] Ch. 442, 474, 476.

[6] *Ibid.* at p. 474, *per* Russell L.J.

[7] *Re Heathstar Properties Ltd. (No. 2)* [1966] 1 W.L.R. 993.

[8] *Re Jackson & Co.* [1899] 1 Ch. 348.

[9] As to the evidence required to satisfy the court, see *Re Abrahams & Sons Ltd.* [1902] 1 Ch. 695 and *Re Kris Cruisers Ltd.* [1949] Ch. 138. Twenty months after the creation of the charge is far too late especially if a winding up is imminent. *Re Resinoid and Mica Products Ltd.* (1967) 111 S.J. 654.

[10] *Re Joplin Brewery Co.* [1902] 1 Ch. 79; *Re Spiral Globe Co.* [1902] 1 Ch. 396; *Re Abrahams & Sons* [1902] 1 Ch. 695; *Re Ehrmann Bros.* [1906] 2 Ch. 697; *Re Cardiff Workmen's Cottage Co.* [1906] 2 Ch. 627; *Re Kris Cruisers Ltd.* [1949] Ch. 138. Whenever an extension order is made it should contain words saving rights acquired prior to registration: *Re Resinoid and Mica Products Ltd.* (1967) 111 S.J. 654, *per* Lord Denning M.R. For a constructive criticism of the wording of the proviso see M. R. Bennett (1974) 118 S.J. 286.

Ltd.,[11] was merely designed to protect rights acquired against the property of the company in the interval between the expiration of the 21 days for registering and the extended time allowed by the order. If the rights were acquired *before* the expiration of the original 21 day period then the proviso did not of itself elevate those rights over an earlier debenture to which the order applies[12] Only if a second debenture was *created* within the period between the 21 days and the extended time was it protected by the proviso. Mere registration within that period did not suffice.[13] Rights were not acquired for this purpose merely by the appointment of a receiver.[14] The above form of wording of the proviso was used until the decision of Templeman J. in *Watson* v. *Duff Morgan and Vermont (Holdings) Ltd.*[15] in 1974. As a result of that decision Mr. Registrar Berkeley reconsidered the wording and, after consultation with the Companies Court judges, the following new wording was substituted:

> "That the time for registering the charge be extended until the —— day of —— 19 ——; and this order is to be without prejudice to the rights of the parties acquired during the period between the date of creation of the said charge and the date of its actual registration."

The rationale of the new form of wording appears to be that if the charge is not registered within the 21 day period it becomes void *ab initio* for the purposes of section 95 of the 1948 Act and remains so unless and until registered pursuant to an order under section 101 of that Act. The old form of wording as interpreted in the cases was based on the assumption that registration pursuant to section 101 validated the charge *ab initio* and the old form of wording was thus capable of producing injustice since the degree of protection afforded to holders of other charges depended quite fortuitously upon how long after the charge the subject of the order the other charges were created.[16] If they were created within the 21 day period they were unprotected whereas if they were created after that period they were protected. This anomaly is now removed by the explicit terms of the new form of wording. As the matter is one of judicial discretion and court practice this method of amendment would seem to be in order. The proviso does not protect the existing unsecured creditors who have not obtained any security or charge upon the property subject to the debentures.[17] Where

---

[11] [1906] 2 Ch. 697.

[12] *Watson* v. *Duff Morgan and Vermont (Holdings) Ltd.* [1974] 1 W.L.R. 450; *Ram Narain* v. *Radha Kishen Moti Lal Chamaria Firm* (1929) L.R. 57 Ind.App. 76 (P.C.).

[13] *Re Monolithic Co.* [1915] 1 Ch. 643 as explained in *Watson* v. *Duff Morgan and Vermont (Holdings) Ltd., ante.*

[14] *Watson* v. *Duff Morgan and Vermont (Holdings) Ltd., ante.*

[15] [1974] 1 W.L.R. 450.

[16] See M. Bennett (1974) 118 S.J. 286, 287.

[17] See *Re Johnson (I. C.) & Co.* [1902] 2 Ch. 101 (C.A.) and *Company Precedents*, Part III, (15th ed.,), pp. 193–195. As to the possibility of inserting wording protecting them see *Re Cardiff Workmen's Cottage Co. Ltd.* [1906] 2 Ch. 627, 630. See also *Re Herts & Essex Waterworks Co. Ltd.* [1909] W.N. 48. *Re Cardiff Workmen's Cottage Co. Ltd.* was disapproved in this respect by the Court of Appeal in *Re MIG Trust Ltd.* [1933] Ch. 542 but *c.f.* the Australasian authorities cited in Paterson and Ednie, *Australian Company Law*, (2nd ed.), para. 106–11.

an order extending the time is made, and these words appear in it, and before actual registration a winding up commences, the mortgage or charge, if subsequently registered, is not effective as against the general body of the creditors.[18]

The application should be made by summons[19] and may be made by the company and any person interested.

An order for extension will not be made after a winding up commences, unless the circumstances are very exceptional.[20] Where a meeting has been convened to consider a winding up, the order ought to provide an opportunity for the liquidator, if a winding up occurs, to apply to discharge the order.[21] Similar principles apply where the winding up is only imminent.[21a]

Sometimes, in cases where an extension of time is not obtainable, the company, in lieu thereof, may call in and cancel the debentures and issue new debentures, to be registered in due course.[22]

Where the directors of a company, knowing that the company was bound to go into liquidation, did not oppose the extension of time for registration of a charge, and did not inform the court of the circumstances, the proceedings were held by Eve J. to be a fraudulent preference[23] and the registration was declared void; but the Court of Appeal and the House of Lords held that there was not sufficient evidence of an intention to prefer.[24] An order under section 353 (*b*) of the 1948 Act to restore the company to the register has been held to operate to activate retrospectively a charge created after the company has been struck off for failure to file annual returns and the charge will be treated as if particulars had been duly registered under section 95 of that Act. It should be noted, however, (1) that the company was solvent and no subsequent charges had been created and (2) particulars had been lodged but refused registration.[25]

Fees

45–11 By the Companies (Fees) Regulations 1967,[26] and the Third Schedule to the Companies Act 1976 fees are no longer payable for entries in the register of charges kept by the Registrar or for inspecting the register of charges.

---

18 So held by Buckley J. in *Re Anglo-Oriental Carpet Co.* [1903] 1 Ch. 914.

19 R.S.C. 1965, Ord. 102, r. 2. The court has power to extend the time even where the default was made before January 1, 1909: see Interpretation Act 1889, s. 38 now replaced by s. 17 (2) of the Interpretation Act 1978; *Re Herts and Essex Waterworks Co.* [1909] W.N. 48; *Re Lush & Co.* [1913] W.N. 39; 108 L.T. 450.

20 *Re Abrahams & Sons, supra; Re Mechanisations (Eaglescliffe) Ltd.* [1966] Ch. 20.

21 *Re Charles (L.H.) & Co. Ltd.* [1935] W.N. 15.

21a In *re Ashpurton Estates Ltd, The Times,* May 18, 1982.

22 *Bowen* v. *Defries & Co.* [1904] 1 Ch. 37.

23 See para. 85–80, *post*.

24 *Re M.I.G. Trust* [1933] Ch. 542; affirmed *sub nom. Peat* v. *Gresham Trust* [1934] A.C. 252; *Re Kris Cruisers* [1949] Ch. 138.

25 *Re Boxco Ltd.* [1970] Ch. 442.

26 S.I. 1967 No. 1557; replacing the Companies (Fees) No. 1 Order 1929 and the Companies (Fees) (Scotland) Regulations 1961. The fees for the inspection of the register of charges are set out in the Companies (Fees) Regulations 1980 (S.I. 1980 no. 1749), amended by S.I. 1982 no. 105.

PRACTICE NOTES

The register of charges

45–12 The register of charges mentioned in para. 45–02, *ante,* should be kept by every limited company whether or not any entries fall to be made in the register. The right of inspection given by section 105 relates to the register itself and a person inspecting it is entitled to ascertain that there are no charges affecting the property of the company, if that is the case.

Time limit for registration of a charge

45–13 Since under Section 95 (i) a charge is void if not registered within 21 days of its creation (see para. 45–07, *ante*), it is wise to avoid possible postal delays by delivering the necessary documents to the Registrar by hand. This may be done at Companies House, City Road, London as an alternative to delivery by hand or by post at Cardiff. The Registrar has warned that no allowance for postal delay can be made in the event that documents do not reach his office within 21 days of the creation of a charge.

45–14 **Early warning fiches**

COMPANY NUMBER	REFERENCE			

IMPORTANT—DOCUMENT NOT YET READY FOR FILMING

The document referred to above has been received but has not yet been accepted by CRO. A copy is available for inspection on application to the General Counter under the reference shown. The letter(s) immediately following the company number indicates the subject of the document, namely:–

M = Mortgage
MS = Memorandum of Satisfaction
R = Receivership
L = Liquidation

A new system of warning fiches of which the above is an example has been introduced by the Registrar of Companies to replace the former practice of attaching coloured tags to the relevant company file to warn a searcher that further documents are in the hands of the Registrar but not included in those immediately available for public inspection.

The purpose of the warning fiche is primarily to refer a searcher to the Search Room Enquiry Counter. The fiche contains an indication of the type of document within the allocated code *i.e.* "M" for Mortgage, "L" for Liquidation or "R" for Receivership.

Lists are transmitted between London and Cardiff every hour of the codes allocated to documents in the respective categories received since the last list was transmitted. When the list has been sent copies are used in both libraries for the preparation of warning fiches which are then placed within the appropriate company records. In other words, in normal circumstances there will be a gap of no more than an hour-and-a-half between receipt of the document either at the Special Counter in London or in the Mortgage Section in Cardiff and the insertion of the warning fiche in the record in each library.

The warning fiche is an administrative act of the Registrar to assist searchers and the warning is merely an indication of receipt and not of acceptance for registration.

It is the intention of the Companies Registry to include any warning fiche in a company record sent as a result of a postal enquiry. People using such a system will be advised, however, that if such a fiche is included and the document concerned is relevant to the issue in which they are interested, a copy can be made available by post in response to a specific request.

The question of whether this practice gives rise to constructive notice is discussed in paragraph 45–07, *ante*.

CHAPTER 46

REMEDIES OF DEBENTURE HOLDERS

Remedies available

46–01 The question of the availability of remedies is determined by (1) the terms of the debenture or trust deed and (2) the general law. The debentures or trust deed must always be the starting point since they will usually contain express provisions which define default and indicate the remedies.[1] Some remedies will be available without recourse to the courts but others will require application to the courts. The conditions laid down must be strictly complied with. For instance where the consent of a certain proportion of debenture holders is necessary it must be obtained before action can be started.[2]

We shall now consider the remedies generally available in the case of (a) unsecured debentures (b) secured debentures.

In case of unsecured debentures

Where the debenture is not secured by any mortgage or charge,[3] the remedy of the holder is either to bring an action to enforce the debenture and obtain judgment and then levy execution on the property of the company; or he may, either before or after judgment, present a petition for the winding up of the company. If there is a winding up in progress, he can prove in the winding up for the amount due to him, but, not having any security, he has no priority either in the winding up or otherwise; he ranks merely with the ordinary creditors although he will usually be a specialty creditor which has advantages as regards limitation of actions.

Where there is a debenture stock trust deed the covenants are normally made with the trustee and the debenture stockholder is not a creditor of the company. The fact that there is a covenant between the company and the trustees that the company will pay the principal and interest to the stockholders does not entitle them to sue the company as direct creditors and does not make them creditors entitled to present a winding-up petition.[4] It may be that if the interest on the stock had been duly paid the receipt of the stockholders would be a good discharge for the money[5] but

---

[1] *Thorn* v. *City Rice Mills* (1889) 40 Ch.D. 357; *Re Escalera Silver Co.* (1908) 25 T.L.R. 87. For a detailed discussion of the effect of particular clauses see Palmer's *Company Precedents* Part III (16th ed.), by A. E. Topham KC and R. Buchanan-Dunlop, Chap. 28.

[2] *Pettybridge* v. *Unibifocal Co.* [1918] W.N. 278. See further Palmer's *Company Precedents, op. cit.*, Chap. 14.

[3] On secured and unsecured debentures, see para. 43–05, *ante*; on the various types of secured debentures, see Chap. 44, *ante*.

[4] *Re Dunderland Ore Co.* [1909] 1 Ch. 446. This decision of Swinfen Eady J. may, however, have been *per incuriam Gandy* v. *Gandy* (1885) 30 Ch.D. 57 and *Re Empress Engineering Co.* (1880) 16 Ch.D. 125. See Palmer's *Company Precedents, op. cit.* 10–11, 412.

[5] *Re Empress Engineering Co.* (1880) 16 Ch.D. 125.

that is a different matter. In such a case the trustee must bring the proceedings to enforce the covenant. If the trustee refuses, a debenture stockholder may institute proceedings to enforce the trusts. Where, however, the trust deed requires the request of a certain proportion of the debenture stockholders the court will not grant the remedies against the wishes of the trustees and the majority of stockholders.[6] Some trust deeds require a majority in number as well as value of the stockholders.[7] The court will not normally appoint a receiver unless the debentures are secured by a charge.[8]

In case of secured debentures

46–02 The holder of a secured debenture is in a much stronger position than that of an unsecured debenture holder.

Usually the terms of the deed creating the charge, *i.e.* the debenture or the trust deed, contain provisions relating to the enforcement of the security without the aid of the court. It is commonly provided in these documents that the debenture holders,[9] or the trustee,[9] may appoint a receiver; the far-reaching powers which such a receiver is normally given may be gathered from clause 11 of the Indorsed Conditions discussed earlier,[10] which include the power to sell the property of the company.

Apart from the exercise of the rights provided for in the charging deed, the debenture holder may bring a debenture holders' action on behalf of himself and the other members of the class; by this action he demands payment and the enforcement of his security. His rights to do so may, however, be the subject of express provision which requires the prior consent of a certain proportion of the debenture holders as we have seen above. Further if he is the holder of debenture stock he is not usually a creditor of the company but a beneficiary under the trust deed.

In rare cases a debenture holder may apply to the court for foreclosure.

The debenture holder is a creditor of the company and, as such, entitled to petition the court for a winding-up order of the company under section 222. If the company makes default he can found his petition on the ground that the company is unable to pay its debts. (1948 Act, s. 222 (*e*)). Where there is a debenture stock trust deed the stockholder is not usually a creditor of the company and winding-up proceedings must be brought in the name of the trustee.

It is proposed to consider these remedies in the following order:

(1) debenture holders' action;
(2) receivers;
(3) foreclosure;
(4) winding-up petition.

---

[6] *Mercantile, etc., Co.* v. *River Plate Trust* [1892] 2 Ch. 303; *Kempe* v. *Jones* [1884] W.N. 214.
[7] *Kempe* v. *Jones* (*supra*).
[8] *Harris* v. *Beauchamp Bros.* [1896] 1 Q.B. 801 (C.A.); *Wylie* v. *Carlyon* [1922] 1 Ch. 51.
[9] See para. 44–19, *ante*; as regards the power of the trustee to appoint a receiver, see para. 43–27, *ante*.
[10] See para. 43–27, *ante*.

Debenture holders' action

Who may bring the action

46–03 The ordinary remedy of a debenture holder, when the company is in default as regards principal or interest, is to bring an action against the company to obtain payment and to enforce his security. Where a debenture holder is required to give notice to the company prior to action he must do so.[11] Similarly he must obtain any necessary approval of a majority of the debenture holders required by the debenture. The form of such majority clauses varies considerably but where the terms are clear the court must give effect to them.[12] Where, however, the majority have some interest adverse to the general interests of the class, the court will not allow them to benefit at the expense of the minority.[13]

Where it is necessary to bring an action, any holder of debentures may do so subject to any contrary provision in the debenture on trust deed. He brings the action in a representative capacity, *e.g.* he sues on behalf of himself and the other debenture holders of the same class.[14] After a winding up has commenced, the debenture holder must first apply to the court for liberty to commence the action; but the court will give liberty to bring or proceed with the action as a matter of course.[15]

Conduct of the action

A debenture holder, though suing on behalf of himself and others, is *dominus litis*, and accordingly can as a rule stop the action when he chooses, *e.g.* on his claim being satisfied,[16] but where the plaintiff has interests conflicting with those of the other debenture holders, the court may give the conduct of the proceedings to an independent debenture holder.[17]

If the plaintiff does not proceed properly with the action or has a conflicting interest,[18] or in other appropriate cases, the court may require any person to be made a party to the action, and may give the conduct of the action to him, as it thinks fit.[19] The question of conduct is within the discretion of the court; the Court of Appeal will normally not interfere with the exercise of that discretion,[20] except in special circumstances.[21]

---

[11] *Rogers & Co.* v. *British, etc., Association* (1899) 68 L.J.Q.B. 14.
[12] *Wallis* v. *Smith* (1882) 21 Ch.D. 243, 266; *Samuel* v. *Jarrah Timber Corp.* [1904] AC 323.
[13] *Mercantile Investment Co.* v. *River Plate Co.* [1894] 1 Ch. 578, 596. See further Palmer's *Company Precedents, op. cit.*, Chap. 14 especially pp. 141–142.
[14] See R.S.C. 1965, Ord. 15, r. 12. If some of the debenture holders reside outside the scheduled territories, as defined by the Exchange Control Act 1947, the indorsement of the writ shall so state and shall state the residence of such person (Ord. 6, r. 3 (2)).
[15] *Lloyd* v. *David Lloyd & Co.* (1877) 6 Ch.D. 339 (C.A.); *Re Joshua Stubbs Ltd.* [1891] 1 Ch. 475; *Strong* v. *Carlyle Press* [1898] 1 Ch. 268.
[16] *Ward* v. *Alpha Co.* [1903] 1 Ch. 203.
[17] *Re Services Club Estate Syndicate Ltd.* [1930] 1 Ch. 78.
[18] *Re Rhodesia Goldfields Ltd.* [1910] 1 Ch. 239.
[19] R.S.C. 1965, Ord. 15, r. 12 (2).
[20] *Dowbiggin* v. *Trotter* (1872) 20 W.R. 1024.
[21] *Re Swire* (1882) 21 Ch.D. 647.

Where several debenture holders commence separate actions, the court has power to consolidate them.[22]

The plaintiff has no authority to make any arrangement binding the others without their consent.[23]

Appointment of receiver

46–04 In a debenture holders' action the court usually appoints a receiver (if necessary a receiver and manager), and by its judgment declares the debentures to be a charge on the property, directs inquiries as to who are the holders, and the amount due, and either orders a sale of the property or gives liberty to apply for a sale.[24] Where a receiver and manager has been appointed it is for the court to say what court proceedings the receiver is to be allowed to take or continue at the cost of the company's assets.[25]

Where trust deed exists

Where there is a trust deed, whether for securing debentures or debenture stock, the trustees can be plaintiffs in an action for enforcing the charge; but, commonly, the action is brought by a holder of the debentures or debenture stock, and the company and the trustees are made defendants. In such an action, similar relief is usually granted.[26]

Exclusion of debenture holders from division

The court has jurisdiction to order that debenture holders who do not claim within a certain time shall be excluded from a scheme of division.[27]

Costs of action

In a representative debenture holders' action the plaintiff is entitled to solicitor and client costs out of the fund.[28] Where, however, the assets are sufficient to pay this series in full, but insufficient to pay any subsequent series in full, the plaintiff can only get party and party costs out of the assets.[29]

The company and the subsequent encumbrancers, though necessary parties,[30] must, where sued by the first debenture holders, look to the surplus for their costs.[31] They are, however, sometimes allowed costs where their presence has been beneficial to the realisation of the assets.

---

[22] R.S.C. 1965, Ord. 4, r. 10.
[23] *Securities & Properties Investment Corp.* v. *Brighton Alhambra* (1893) 62 L.J. Ch. 655; *Re Calgary and Medicine Hat Co.* [1908] 2 Ch. 652, 659. R.S.C., 1965, Ord. 15, r. 12.
[24] See *Company Precedents*, Part III, pp. 619 *et seq*. See R.S.C. 1965, Ord. 31, r. 1.
[25] *Viola* v. *Anglo-American Cold Storage Co.* [1912] 2 Ch. 305.
[26] See *Company Precedents*, Part III, p. 620.
[27] *Saragossa and Mediterranean Ry.* v. *Collingham* [1904] A.C. 159.
[28] *Re New Zealand Midland Ry., Smith* v. *Lubbock* [1901] 2 Ch. 357; *Re Clayton Engineering and Electrical Construction Co.* (1904) 90 L.T. 283.
[29] See also *Re W. C. Horne & Sons Ltd.* [1906] 1 Ch. 271; and, as to trustees' costs, *Mortgage Insurance Corp.* v. *Canadian Agricultural Coal Co.* [1901] 2 Ch. 377.
[30] *Re Wilcox & Co.* [1903] W.N. 64.
[31] *Re Clayton Engineering Co., ante*.

The trustees will usually be allowed their full costs in priority to the debenture holders.[32] Where they appear by the same solicitor the company will not be allowed separate costs.[33]

Receivers

Appointment of receivers and managers

46–05 Receivers and managers can be appointed either by the court or under the express powers of the debentures or trust deed.[34] We shall deal with each in turn.

The appointment of a receiver as distinguished from a receiver and manager does not confer any power to carry on the business of the company. The duty of a receiver is merely to take possession and protect the property over which he is appointed. If there is a business comprised in the security it is more usual for a receiver and manager to be appointed. Receivers appointed out of court are invariably appointed receivers and managers. In the discussion which follows the term receiver refers to a receiver and manager unless otherwise indicated.

Appointment by the court

46–06 PROCEDURE. The court has power to appoint a receiver in a debenture holders' action[35] to enforce the security and is usually asked to exercise it. Apart therefrom, a receiver, or receiver and manager, may be appointed in proceedings commenced by originating summons,[36] and this, being a short cut to the enforcement of the security, is nowadays the normal procedure.

The appointment of a receiver by the debenture holders under their debenture does not necessarily prevent the court from appointing a receiver.[37] The fact that a liquidator appointed by the shareholders is also receiver for the debenture holders is a reasonable ground for the unsecured creditors desiring his removal as liquidator.[38]

Where the company is registered in this country, it is no objection to the appointment of a receiver that the property is abroad.[39]

On the recognition of the title of a foreign receiver to assets situate in the United Kingdom and the appointment of an auxiliary receiver by the English court, see paragraph 46–15, *post*.[40]

---

[32] The question of costs is discussed in more detail in Palmer's *Company Precedents, op. cit.* pp. 725–727.
[33] *Mortgage Insurance Corp.* v. *Canadian Agricultural Co.* [1901] 2 Ch. 377.
[34] See para. 46–02, *ante*.
[35] See para. 46–04, *ante*.
[36] *Re Francke* (1887) 57 L.J.Ch. 437; *Gee* v. *Bell* (1887) 35 Ch.D. 160; *Supreme Court Practice*, notes to Ord. 102, rr. 2–8 and Vol. 2, Part 7 G.
[37] *Re "Slogger" Automatic Co.* [1915] 1 Ch. 478.
[38] *Re Karamelli & Barnett Ltd.* [1917] 1 Ch. 203.
[39] *Ex p. Pollard.* (1838–40) 4 Deac. 27; *Coote* v. *Jecks* (1872) L.R. 13 Eq. 597.
[40] *Schemmer* v. *Property Resources Ltd.* [1974] 3 W.L.R. 406, 414.

GROUNDS FOR APPOINTMENT. The power of the court to appoint a receiver is not confined to cases in which the principal or interest is in arrear although this is the most usual case.[41] The court may also appoint a receiver in the following circumstances—(a) where the security is in jeopardy; (b) where the company threatens to dispose of its whole undertaking in violation of the rights of the debenture holders; (c) where a winding up of the company is taking place or is imminent; (d) where disputes between the directors have led to a neglect by the management of the company's affairs; (e) where the company is in a state of suspended animation.

JEOPARDY. The courts are inclined to extend the jeopardy category to embrace the others. Instances of jeopardy are where the company has become insolvent and closed its works[42]; where the company proposed to distribute amongst its members a reserve fund created out of profits which was practically its only asset[43]; and the fact that creditors have levied or are threatening to levy execution against the company.[44]

DISPOSAL OF UNDERTAKING. Where the company threatens to dispose of the whole of its undertaking in violation of the rights of the debenture holders a receiver will be appointed.[45] A receiver will not be appointed where a company is only selling one of several businesses which it carries on.[46]

WINDING UP.[47] Where a petition has been presented to wind up the company a receiver will be appointed. This will also be done where the winding up is merely a voluntary winding up for the purpose of reconstruction.[48]

DISPUTES BETWEEN DIRECTORS. A receiver was appointed for a limited time on an application by contributories and the company where disputes between directors had led to a dereliction of their duties. A receiver who had previously been appointed in a mortgagee's foreclosure action was appointed.[49]

---

41 *Bissill* v. *Bradford Tramways* [1891] W.N. 51.
42 *McMahon* v. *North Kent Ironworks* [1891] 2 Ch. 148.
43 *Re Tilt Cove Copper Co.* [1913] 2 Ch. 588.
44 *Re Braunstein & Marjolaine Ltd.* [1914] W.N. 335; *Edwards* v. *Standing Rolling Stock Syndicate* [1893] 1 Ch. 574.
45 *Hubbuck* v. *Helms* (1887) 56 L.T. 232.
46 *Re Borax Co.* [1901] 1 Ch. 326.
47 *Hodson* v. *Tea Co.* (1880) 14 Ch.D. 859; *Wallace* v. *Universal, etc., Co.* [1894] 2 Ch. 547; *Re Victoria Steamboats Co.* [1897] 1 Ch. 158.
48 *Re Crompton & Co. Ltd.* [1914] 1 Ch. 954.
49 *Stanfield* v. *Gibbon* [1925] W.N. 11. See also *Featherstone* v. *Cooke* (1873) L.R. 16 Eq. 298 and *Trade Auxiliary Co.* v. *Vickers* (1873) L.R. 16 Eq. 303. Normally, however, a meeting will be directed under s. 135 of the Companies Act 1948 in lieu of an appointment.

SUSPENDED ANIMATION. The only case under this head[50] concerns a German club which was necessarily in this state during the First World War.

It has been held that the power to appoint a receiver includes, also, power to appoint a manager[51]; and that the court, after appointing a receiver, can enforce the security.[52]

Whilst the court will be prepared to appoint a receiver whenever the debenture holders' security is in danger, it will refuse to do so merely because, without the company being in default, the assets of the company, if realised, would be insufficient to pay the debenture holders in full.[53]

SECURITY. The order usually provides for security to be given by the receiver. If a receiver is appointed "upon his giving security," he is not entitled to take possession until he has given security, and until then he is not to be deemed to be in possession as against third parties.[54] But if the order appoints the receiver out-and-out, and orders him to give security, the appointment takes effect at once, and he is entitled to take possession before security is given, and as against third parties is to be deemed to be in possession as from the time the order is perfected.[55] So a landlord who distrains after the making of a receivership order, but before it is drawn up, will not be disturbed.[56] If the receiver does not give security within the time limited, his appointment lapses unless the time is extended.[57]

As to the practice on receiver's security see the detailed discussion in Palmer's *Company Precedents*[58] and *Kerr on Receivers*.[59]

LEGAL STATUS OF RECEIVER APPOINTED BY COURT. A receiver appointed by the court: (1) is an officer of the court; (2) is neither agent of the debenture holders nor the company[60]; (3) entirely supersedes the powers of the company and the authority of its directors in the conduct of its business which remain in abeyance during his appointment[61]; (4) is a fiduciary[62];

---

[50] *Higginson* v. *The German Athenaeum Ltd.* (1916) 32 T.L.R. 277.
[51] *Re Victoria Steamboats Co., Smith* v. *Wilkinson* [1897] 1 Ch. 158.
[52] *Re Carshalton Park Estate* [1908] 2 Ch. 62.
[53] *Re New York Taxicab Co.* [1913] 1 Ch. 1; *Lawrence* v. *West Somerset Ry.* [1918] 2 Ch. 250. But see *Re Braunstein and Marjolaine Ltd.* [1914] W.N. 335; 58 S.J. 755, where part of the business had been closed down.
[54] *Edwards* v. *Edwards* (1876) 2 Ch.D. 291.
[55] *Morrison* v. *Skerne Ironworks Co.* (1889) 60 L.T. 588, in which case the appointment was held good as against execution creditors; *Ex p. Evans* (1879) 11 Ch.D. 691; 13 Ch.D. 252.
[56] *Lee* v. *Roundwood Colliery Co.* [1897] 1 Ch. 373.
[57] *Re Sims & Woods Ltd.* [1916] W.N. 223 (Practice Note).
[58] *Op. cit.* Chap. 48.
[59] 15th ed. by R. Walton, pp. 118 *et seq.*
[60] *Parsons* v. *Sovereign Bank of Canada* [1913] A.C. 160, 167 (P.C.).
[61] *Moss Steamship Co.* v. *Whinney* [1912] A.C. 254 (H.L.).
[62] Re Gent, Gent-Davis v. *Harris* (1880) 40 Ch.D. 190; *Re Magadi Soda Company Ltd.* (1925) 41 T.L.R. 297; *Visbord* v. *F.C.T.* (1943) 68 C.L.R. 354, 384 (H.Ct. of Australia) and see below.

and (5) is, *qua* receiver, not an occupier of property so as to be liable for rates.[63]

OFFICER OF THE COURT. When the court appoints a receiver of property, it in effect takes the custody of the property into its own hands—for the receiver is an officer of the court—and thus assumes the protection and safe keeping of it for the benefit of the parties interested in it. The receiver being an officer of the court, any interference with him, whether by a party to the action or by a stranger, is a contempt of court and punishable accordingly. Thus, proceedings for recovery of possession cannot be commenced by a first mortgagee without leave of the court.[63a] See, however, as to independent actions by debenture holders, *Cleary* v. *Brazil Ry*.[64] This decision may be supported on the ground that there was no interference with the company's assets until execution.

By leave of the court, an action may be brought against a receiver appointed by the court by the person at whose instance the receiver was appointed.[65]

NO AGENCY. It follows from the fact that a receiver appointed by the court is an officer of the court, that he is not an agent for the debenture holders, whose credit he cannot pledge, or of the company, which cannot control him.[66] He pledges his own credit and is personally liable on the contracts which he makes.[67] He does, however, have the right to be indemnified out of the assets of the company for the liabilities which he properly incurs.[68] If the liabilities are incurred improperly, for instance by entering into contracts not necessary for the carrying on of the business, he may be refused an indemnity.[68] Entering into contracts as "receiver and manager" will not absolve him from personal liability.[69] Section 369 of the Companies Act 1948, which expressly allows contracting out of personal liability in the case of a receiver appointed out of court, does not apply to a receiver appointed by the court but it has been held in the case of the latter that where the liability was negatived by agreement the creditor was not entitled to claim payment out of the assets by a summons in the debenture action.[70]

APPOINTMENT SUPERSEDES COMPANY'S POWERS. The appointment of a receiver by the court "practically removes the conduct and guidance from the

---

63 *Gyton* v. *Palmour* [1945] K.B. 426. See also *Re Mayfair and General Property Trust* [1945] 2 All E.R. 523.
63a *Re Metropolitan Amalgamated Estates Ltd.* [1912] 2 Ch. 497.
64 (1915) 85 L.J.K.B. 32.
65 *L. P. Arthur (Insurance) Ltd.* v. *Sisson* [1966] 1 W.L.R. 1384.
66 *Parsons* v. *Sovereign Bank of Canada* [1913] A.C. 160, 167; *Moss Steamship Co.* v. *Whinney* [1912] A.C. 254, 266, 271.
67 *Burt* v. *Bull* [1895] 1 Q.B. 276.
68 *Moss Steamship Co.* v. *Whinney* [1912] A.C. 254, 271.
69 *Burt* v. *Bull* [1895] 1 Q.B. 276.
70 *Re Ernest Hawkins & Co.* (1914) 31 T.L.R. 247.

directors appointed by the company, and places it in the hands of" the receiver and manager, "who thereupon absolutely supersedes the company itself, so that the company becomes incapable of making any contract on behalf of the company or exercising any control over any part of any property or assets of the company."[71] The company is not thereby dissolved or annihilated any more than the taking of possession by a mortgagee of land annihilates the mortgagor. Its powers in these respects are thereby in abeyance.[72] Thus no question of *ultra vires* arises.[73]

It should be noted, however, that the company's powers and the directors' authority are only in abeyance in respect of assets within the scope of the charge. For those which are not and possibly for those where the receiver has refused to act, the company and directors retain power and authority to act.[74] Thus they may sue in the company's name, challenge the receiver's appointment and oppose a winding-up petition. If the case is one of refusal to act, it would appear that the sanction of the court should be obtained in the case of a receiver appointed by the court.

RECEIVER A FIDUCIARY.[75] In *Re Magadi Soda Company Ltd.*[76] in 1925 Eve J. held that a receiver appointed by the court "not only fills a fiduciary position towards all the debenture holders, but his appointment to an office of such responsibility presupposes that he will discharge his duties with punctilious rectitude."[77] He is, by his office, disqualified from purchasing the interests of anyone towards whom he stands in a fiduciary position. This case was apparently not cited to it but a similar view was taken by the Court of Appeal in *Re B. Johnson & Co. (Builders) Ltd.*[78] in 1955 when it held that a receiver and manager appointed by a debenture holder was not an officer of the company and was outside section 333 of the Companies Act 1948. In the *Johnson* case all three members of the court, while not referring expressly to fiduciary obligations, recognised that a person appointed as receiver and manager is concerned not for the benefit of the company but for the benefit of the debenture holders in realising the security. That is the whole purpose of the appointment and all the powers which are conferred on him are really ancillary to that purpose. An

---

71 *Moss Steamship Co.* v. *Whinney* [1912] A.C. 254, *per* the Earl of Halsbury, at p. 260.
72 *Ibid. per* Lord Atkinson, at p. 263.
73 *Ibid. per* Lord Mersey, at p. 271.
74 *Newhart Developments Ltd.* v. *Co-operative Commercial Bank Ltd.* [1978] 2 W.L.R. 636 and the *Reprographic Exports (Euromat) Ltd.* (1978) 122 S.J. 400. See also *Hawkesbury Development Co. Ltd.* v. *Landmark Finance Pty. Ltd.* (1970) 92 W.N. (N.S.W.) 99, 210 and *Toronto Dominion Bank* v. *Fortin* [1978] 85 D.L.R. (3d) 111. *Cf. Re Emmadart Ltd.* [1979] 1 All E.R. 599.
75 The text which follows is based on J. H. Farrar [1975] J.B.L. 23.
76 (1925) 41 T.L.R. 297. See also *Boddington* v. *Langford* (1845) 15 Ir. Ch. Rep. 558n; *Alven* v. *Bond* (1841) Fl. & K. 196; *Watkins* v. *Lestrange* (1863) 2 S.C.R. (Eq.) 85 (N.S.W); *Re Gent, Gent-Davis* v. *Harris* (1888) 40 Ch.D. 190; and *Nugent* v. *Nugent* [1908] 1 Ch. 546 (C.A.).
77 (1925) 41 T.L.R. 300.
78 [1955] 1 Ch. 634. *Cf. R.* v. *Board of Trade, ex p. St. Martins Preserving Co.* [1965] 1 Q.B. 603, which held that a receiver's activities could fall within s. 165 (*a*) of the Companies Act 1948 and be the subject of investigation.

argument based on the fact that often (indeed usually) the receiver is agent for the company was brushed aside by Evershed M.R. His attitude seems to be justified on the basis of the dissenting judgment of Rigby L.J. in *Gosling* v. *Gaskell*[79] where the latter said that for valuable consideration a mortgagor in such circumstances has committed the management of his property to an attorney whose appointment he cannot interfere with. Rigby L.J.'s judgment was approved by the House of Lords on appeal.[80]

Now this seems to indicate that a receiver is fiduciary for the debenture holder and not for the company despite the fact that he may be expressed in the debenture to be agent for the company.[81] Where there is such a provision it is in fact usual in any event to provide expressly that the company is responsible for his acts and defaults. This, of course, only deals with the liability *inter se* of the company and debenture holder towards third parties. Such a clause does not exonerate *the receiver* from whatever duties he owes to the company. It seems from the *Johnson* case that he owes at least the duty of a mortgagee in such circumstances, *i.e.* basically a duty of good faith.[82] He must not exceed or abuse the special powers and discretions vested in him by the debenture for the special purpose of enabling the assets comprised in the security to be preserved and realised.

The principles laid down above were redefined and their scope amplified in two later Australian cases, *Re Neon Signs (Australia) Ltd.*[83] and *Duffy* v. *Super Centre Development Corporation Ltd.*[84] In the first case Adam J. held that the court would interfere where there is an *abuse of power* but in the absence of evidence of dishonest or reckless[85] exercise of power it would not interfere. The mere fact that unsecured creditors or shareholders suffer a prejudice is irrelevant. Street J. in *Duffy's* case went further. The court, he said, will entertain an application if there is evidence of want of good faith or "some erroneous approach in law or in principle." It is not clear what "in principle" means in contradistinction to law and good faith. His Honour went on to say[86] that where the challenge is that there has been an absence of prudence or wisdom in the receiver's decisions, "a far heavier onus rests upon the party who seeks to challenge the decision in question." It must be shown that "there is a decision of real significance in the affairs of the company and as to which there are real and substantial grounds for questioning its correctness." This too is rather vague.

It has recently been established, that a receiver can be liable in certain circumstances for negligence as well as fraud or recklessness. In *Cuckmere*

---

[79] [1896] 1 Q.B. 669, 692.

[80] [1897] A.C. 575. See also *Lawson (Inspector of Taxes)* v. *Hosemaster Machine Co. Ltd.* [1966] 2 All E.R. 944 (C.A.), at p. 951 I. See Winn J. in *R.* v. *Board of Trade, ex p. St. Martins Preserving Co.* [1965] 1 Q.B. 603, 617, where he says: "his agency . . . is special and limited in its character."

[81] Farrar *op. cit.*

[82] See Jenkins L.J. in *Re B. Johnson, supra*, at p. 662.

[83] [1965] V.R. 125.

[84] [1967] 1 N.S.W.R. 382.

[85] Following the mortgagee cases. Recklessness is of course a notoriously ambiguous concept capable of comprehending gross negligence.

[86] [1967] 1 N.S.W.R. 383.

Brick Co. Ltd. v. *Mutual Finance Ltd.*[87] the Court of Appeal, faced with conflicting dicta, held that a mortgagee exercising his power of sale owed a duty to the mortgagor to take reasonable care to obtain a proper price or, according to Salmon L.J., "the true market value." In *Bank of Cyprus (London) Ltd.* v. *Gill*[87a] Lloyd J. held that a mortgagee in possession was entitled to sell at any time and was not obliged to wait on a rising market or for a market to recover but he could not sell without taking proper steps to secure the best available price at the time in question. This was upheld by the Court of Appeal. This liability extends to a receiver exercising a power of sale. In the recent case of *Standard Chartered Bank* v. *Walker*[88] the Court of Appeal held that a receiver owed such a duty not only to the company but also to a guarantor of the company's indebtedness. Statements in *Re B. Johnson* which suggest that the *only* duty of a receiver is one of good faith would appear to be merely *obiter.* The *Johnson* case does not appear to have been cited in the *Cuckmere* case. Liability might also extend to negligence in carrying on the business with a view to sale. It is arguable that if a receiver is to be held liable for negligence in respect of this his duty of care should be no higher than that of the directors, whose powers he has assumed.[89] It would appear that the duty of care is in addition to, and not a part of, the obligation of good faith.[90] It is, however, an equitable as well as common law duty.[90a]

The above principles were usefully reconsidered and restated in the Australian case of *Expo International Pty. Ltd.* v. *Chant*[91] where Needham J. held:

---

[87] [1971] Ch. 949. See the notes in (1971) 87 L.Q.R. 303 and (1971) 35 Conv. (N.S.) 281. See also *Palmer* v. *Barclays Bank Ltd.* (1971) 23 P. & C.R. 30; *Duke* v. *Robson* [1973] 1 All E.R. 481, 488 *Johnson* v. *Robbins* (1975) 235 E.G. 757, *Bank of Cyprus (London) Ltd.* v. *Gill* [1980] 2 Lloyd's Rep. 51 (C.A.) and *cf. Barclays Bank Ltd.* v. *Thienel* (1978) 122 S.J. 472; *Latchford* v. *Beirne* [1981] 3 All E.R. 705. For a useful analysis of Commonwealth cases see P. Butt (1979) 53 A.L.J. 172. The earlier New Zealand case of *Nelson Bros Ltd.* v. *Nagle* [1940] G.L.R. 507 contains *obiter* remarks by Myers C.J. to the effect that a receiver *qua* agent for the company can be liable for negligence in such circumstances—see p. 508. However, the mere fact that he has acted unwisely and failed to keep proper accounts does not mean that he is guilty of negligence in not getting a better price. Such circumstances may, however, be relevant on the issue of costs—see p. 510.

[87a] [1980] 2 Lloyd's re 51. (C.A.).

[88] *Standard Chartered Bank* v. *Walker, The Times,* June 21, 1982.

[89] In *Re B. Johnson, supra*, at p. 662, Jenkins L.J. said "the whole purpose of the receiver and manager's appointment would obviously be stultified if the company could claim that a receiver and manager owes it any duty comparable to the duty owed to a company by its own directors or managers." It would appear, however, from the context of the remarks that Jenkins L.J. really meant that a receiver did not owe *all* the duties of a director or manager. He recognised the duty of good faith. (*Ibid.*) *Cf.* the higher standard of care required of a liquidator (*vide post*).

[90] See Salmon L.J. [1971] Ch. at p. 966D. Cross and Cairns L.JJ. seem to agree but are less explicit.

[90a] The earlier cases of *Barclays Bank Ltd.* v. *Thienel, supra* and *Latchford* v. *Beirne, supra*, held that there was no duty owed to a guarantor were erroneous. On the other hand, the position of other unsuccessful creditors was left open. It is arguable that there is insufficient proximity in such cases. *Fennell* v. *Gardner* (1884) 1 T.L.R. 397 (C.A.). Cf. however, *Standard Chartered Bank* v. *Walker (supra)* where it was regarded as only a particular application of the 'neighbour' principle.

[91] (1980) A.C.L.C. 34, 43.

(1) that a receiver owes a duty both to the debenture holder and the company;
(2) the duty to the company includes:
  (a) an obligation to exercise his powers in good faith (including an obligation not to sacrifice the company's interests recklessly);
  (b) an obligation to act strictly within and in accordance with the conditions of his appointment;
  (c) an obligation to account after the debenture holder's security has been discharged not only for surplus assets but also for the conduct of the receivership;
(3) the duty to the company does not extend to negligence provided that the loss arose out of a bona fide act.

This case contains an analysis of the English cases but must be read with caution on (3) since the authority of *Cuckmere Brick Co. Ltd.* v. *Mutual Finance Ltd.*[92] in Australia is in some doubt. In England the duty to the company extends at least to liability for negligence in exercising the power of sale.

In the recent case of *Smiths Ltd.* v. *Middleton*[93] Blackett Ord V.C. held that a receiver owed an equitable duty to the company to account which went beyond section 372 (2) of the Companies Act 1948. This decision is consistent with the statement of principles by Needham J in the *Expo* case.

Can the duty of good faith be excluded or the receiver be released from liability for breach of the duty of care by prior arrangement? The first and obvious point to make there is that in normal circumstances there will be no initial contract to which the receiver is a party. He will not be a party to the debenture which will at the most merely refer to *a* receiver. Secondly, a strong argument can be made on the grounds of public policy that one should never be allowed in advance to contract out of a duty of good faith. Whether these points apply to the concomitant duty of care is debatable. In principle it would seem possible to exclude liability in tort by suitable wording provided that it is reasonable (Unfair Contract Terms Act 1977, s. 2). It is likely, however, that a document containing a clause benefiting a receiver will be outside the Act and, therefore, not subject to the statutory requirement of reasonableness. (Sched. 1, paras. (*b*) and (*e*).)[93a]

In Australia where there is no equivalent of the Unfair Contract Terms Act 1977 Needham J. in *Expo International Pty. Ltd.* v. *Chant*[94] held that the receiver could not rely on an exemption clause exonerating "any receiver" on two grounds. First, he held that although such clauses are construed against the party benefiting thereby the question of their application to a particular circumstance is one of interpretation of the clause in its context. The particular clause only exempted the receiver from liabilities

[92] [1971] Ch. 949.
[93] [1979] 3 All E.R. 842.
[93a] Cf. however, Lord Denning M.R. in *Standard Chartered Bank* v. *Walker, The Times*. June 21, 1982. This seems to be *per incuriam*.
[94] *Supra*.

arising "by reason of entering into possession." This was to be narrowly construed and did not cover the major fiduciary obligations stated above. Secondly, and in the alternative, he held, following *Midland Silicones Ltd.* v. *Scruttons Ltd.*,[95] *New Zealand Shipping Co. Ltd.*v. *A.M. Satterthwaite & Co. Ltd.*[96] and *Port Jackson Stevedoring Pty. Ltd.* v. *Salmond & Spraggon (Australia) Pty. Ltd.*[97] that at the date of mortgage the identity of any receiver was unknown. Therefore there was no actual authority for the mortgagee to contract on behalf of the receiver and it was not possible for the receiver to ratify. Needham J. did not feel it necessary to consider the public policy argument. This case shows the difficulties involved in excluding the receiver's liability in the debenture.

PURE RECEIVER NOT OCCUPIER. It has been held that a receiver is not an occupier so as to be liable for rates.[98] Similarly where rents include an element of rates he is not liable for the rate element in the rent.[99] It is otherwise where he is receiver and manager and enters into possession,[1] and in any event the general rates are preferred debts which he must pay out of the assets of the company by virtue of sections 94 and 319 of the Companies Act 1948.

APPOINTMENT BY THE DEBENTURE HOLDER OUT OF COURT. The power of the debenture holder or trustee to appoint a receiver depends on the terms of the debenture or trust deed. The power will either be; (a) express, or (b) by reference to the Law of Property Act 1925, the latter being unusual. The power must be strictly complied with.

GROUNDS FOR APPOINTMENT. These will be set out in the debenture or trust deed. For an example of such a clause see Clause 11 set out in para. 43–27, *ante* which must be read with Clause 9 which deals with default. Only if the facts fall within one of the specified situations can an appointment be made.

SECURITY. Usually no security will be necessary but the terms of the receiver's liabilities will be determined by the debenture in question and his appointment. It is common practice for a receiver appointed out of court to seek a comprehensive indemnity from the appointor on his appointment.

LEGAL STATUS OF RECEIVER APPOINTED OUT OF COURT. The receiver (1) is not an officer of the court; (2) is agent of the appointor although this is

---

[95] [1960] A.C. 446, 474.
[96] [1975] A.C. 154, 166.
[97] (1978) 18 A.L.R. 333, 341.
[98] *Gyton* v. *Palmour* [1945] K.B. 426.
[99] *Re Mayfair and General Property Trust* [1945] 2 All E.R. 523.
[1] *Meigh* v. *Wickenden* [1942] 2 K.B. 160 (a case on the Factories Act 1937 but presumably the same principle applies for rating purposes).

commonly varied by agreement; (3) entirely supersedes the powers of the company and the authority of its directors; (4) is a fiduciary; (5) is not, *qua* receiver, an occupier of land for rating purposes. In respect of (3), (4) and (5) his position appears the same as a receiver appointed by the court.

NOT AN OFFICER OF THE COURT. Since he is not appointed by the court he is not an officer of the court. The rights and duties discussed in para. 46–06 do not, therefore, apply to him.

AGENCY. Whereas a receiver appointed by the court is not an agent for the company or the debenture holder, debentures usually provide that a receiver appointed thereunder is to be agent for the company. Where this is not done it may be inferred that the receiver is agent for the debenture holders where he is given powers to carry on the business or in excess of those conferred by statute.[2] The question is one of construction in each case. The agency for the company is an artificial one with odd consequences since the company cannot dismiss him and his duties are merely those of a mortgagee in possession. Also when he is in possession he really represents the mortgagee. His agency is terminated by the winding up of the company but not his receivership powers.[3]

A practice has developed in recent years of giving a power of attorney under the debenture to the debenture holder or receiver to counteract the termination of the latter's agency on a winding up. Questions arise both under the general law of agency and the Powers of Attorney Act 1971 as to the revocability of such powers. In *Sowman* v. *David Samuel Trust Ltd.*,[4] Goulding J. held that the power given to the debenture holders had not been revoked by the winding up. His reasons were twofold. First, they had an authority coupled with an interest and, secondly, the case fell within section 4 of the Powers of Attorney Act 1971. The debenture holders had in fact at the request of the receiver used their power as mortgagees to execute a conveyance in the name of the company. The receiver had also been a party to the conveyance. Goulding J. held that this was valid. He also referred to the arguments in favour of the irrevocability of a power given to a receiver. In addition to possible arguments on the lines of power coupled with an interest at common law and as a substitute for the debenture holder under section 4 (2) of the Powers of Attorney Act 1971, he mentioned sections 101 and 104 of the Law of Property Act 1925. At the end of the day, however, he refused to express a view on the matter. In

[2] s. 109 (2) of the Law of Property Act 1925; *Re Vimbos Ltd.* [1900] 1 Ch. 470; *Robinson Printing Co.* v. *Chic Ltd.* [1905] 2 Ch. 123; *Deyes* v. *Wood* [1911] 1 K.B. 806. See also J. H. Farrar [1980] J.B.L. 280; D.Milman [1981] 44 M.L.R. 658 and R.M. Goode [1981] J.B.L. 312.

[3] *Gosling* v. *Gaskell* [1897] A.C. 575; *Thomas* v. *Todd* [1926] 2 K.B. 511; *Gough's Garages Ltd.* v. *Pugsley* [1930] 1 K.B. 615; *Bacal Contracting Ltd.* v. *Modern Engineering (Bristol) Ltd.* [1980] 2 All E.R. 655. *Cf. Re KVE Homes Pty. Ltd. and the Companies Act* [1979] 4 A.C.L.R. 47—appointment of a provisional liquidator does not have the same effect.

[4] [1978] 1 All E.R. 616.

Barrows v. *Chief Land Registrar*,[5] which has not been fully reported, Whitford J. held that notwithstanding the determination of the receiver's agency for the company on liquidation the receiver is entitled to exercise his receivership powers in the name of the company. A receiver could, for the purposes of disposal of the assets secured, be considered as being the *alter ego* of the debenture holder. A disposition by the receiver was not within section 227 of the Companies Act 1948, which avoids dispositions of property made after the commencement of a winding up by the court unless the court otherwise orders, because the rights and powers given by the debenture are themselves property belonging to the debenture holder not the company. A power of attorney granted to a receiver, however, can only be made irrevocable if it is granted to secure a proprietary interest of the receiver or performance of an obligation owing to him. Neither of these conditions were satisfied in *Barrows'* case nor will they be satisfied in the usual forms of debenture.[6]

H.M. Land Registry now takes the view that a disposition executed by a receiver in the name and on behalf of the borrower company can properly be accepted for registration, even though that company is in liquidation, provided that an express power to effect dispositions of the relevant type is given to the receiver by the mortgage or debenture pursuant to which he is appointed.

As a matter of practice, it requires the deed by which the disposition is effected to be executed in a form which makes the position clear. The execution should show clearly that the receiver is acting as receiver in the name and on behalf of the company pursuant to the powers given to him for that purpose by the mortgage and it should follow the statutory procedure laid down in section 74 (3) of the Law of Property Act 1925. For example, the following form of execution would be acceptable in appropriate circumstances:

Signed sealed and delivered by A.B. Co. Ltd. [in liquidation] by C.D. its Receiver pursuant to powers granted to him in clause . . . of a debenture dated . . . in favour of E.F. Bank Ltd., in the presence of:–	A.B. Co. Ltd. by its Receiver C.D. (S).

46–07 EFFECT OF APPOINTMENT OF RECEIVER BY THE COURT. The following are the main legal effects of the appointment of a receiver by the court:

(1) Floating charges crystallise and become fixed. This prevents the

[5] *The Times*, October 20, 1977. Noted in *Ruoff and Roper on the Law of Registered Conveyancing* (4th ed., 1979), p. 540. We are greatly obliged to the Chief Land Registrar for supplying us with a copy of the judgment and advising us as to the current practice at the Registry.

[6] *Cf. Gore-Brown on Companies,* (43rd ed. by A.J. Boyle and R. Sykes), para. 32-21. The argument there put forward seems no longer tenable in the light of *Barrows* v. *Chief Land Registrar*. *Cf.* also Peter Millett Q.C. [1977] 41 Conv. (N.S.) 83.

company from dealing with the assets subject to the charge without the receiver's consent.[7]

(2) The company's powers and the directors' authority is suspended in relation to the assets covered by the receivership. The directors cannot claim remuneration from the receiver unless he employs them but they can still make a claim for remuneration against the company for any remuneration to which they are entitled.[8]

(3) The company's employees are automatically dismissed and may claim damages for breach of contract even when they are employed by the receiver.[9]

(4) Existing contracts remain binding upon the company and the receiver should carry them out if they affect the goodwill of the business[10] but in other cases he may be authorised to disregard them.[11] If he carries them out he is not personally liable on them unless there is an express novation.[12] If he fails to complete the contract the other contracting party is entitled to set-off a claim for damages for breach of the contract against any claims the company may have against him.[13]

As regards new contracts entered into by the receiver and manager, the company is not liable on such contracts, but the receiver is personally liable, subject to his right of indemnity.[14] He may, however, contract on terms excluding personal liability, leaving the other contracting party to look to the assets for payment.[15]

46–08 EFFECT OF APPOINTMENT OF RECEIVER OUT OF COURT. The main legal effects are the same as in the case of a receiver appointed by the court (on which see para. 46–07, *ante*) except in relation to employees. The appointment by the debenture holders of a receiver and manager as agent of the company, not being an appointment under an order of the court, does not of itself automatically terminate contracts of employment previously made and subsisting between the company and all its employees.[16] In three exceptional circumstances, however, such an appointment will result in termination of employment contracts, *viz.*:

(1) where the appointment of a receiver is accompanied by a sale of the business of the company[17];

---

[7] *R. A. Cripps & Son Ltd.* v. *Wickenden* [1973] 1 W.L.R. 944.
[8] *Re South Western of Venezuela Railway* [1902] 1 Ch. 701.
[9] *Reid* v. *Explosives Co. Ltd.* (1887) 19 Q.B.D. 264 (C.A.).
[10] *Re Newdigate Colliery Ltd.* [1912] 1 Ch. 468. (C.A).
[11] *Airlines Airspares Ltd.* v. *Handley Page Ltd.* [1970] Ch. 193.
[12] *Parsons* v. *Sovereign Bank of Canada* [1913] A.C. 160 (P.C.).
[13] *Parsons* v. *Sovereign Bank of Canada* (*supra*): *cf. N. W. Robbie & Co. Ltd.* v. *Witney Warehouse Co. Ltd.* [1963] 1 W.L.R 1324.
[14] *Moss Steamship Co.* v. *Whinney* [1912] A.C. 254.
[15] *Re British Power Traction Co., supra; Re Ernest Hawkins & Co.* (1915) 31 T.L.R. 247.
[16] *Re Foster Clark Ltd.'s Indenture Trusts* [1966] 1 W.L.R. 125; *Re Mack Trucks (Britain) Ltd.* [1967] 1 W.L.R. 780; *Griffiths* v. *Secretary of State for Social Services* [1974] Q.B. 468. As regards the entitlement of employees to redundancy payments, see *Deaway Trading Ltd.* v. *Calverley* [1973] I.C.R. 546.
[17] *Re Foster Clark Ltd.'s Indenture Trusts, supra.*

(2) where the receiver enters into a new agreement with a particular employee that may be inconsistent with the old contracts[18];

(3) where the continuation of the employment of a particular employee is inconsistent with the role and function of a receiver and manager.[19] That an employee is described as "managing director" does not, in itself, establish such inconsistency[20] where he has been under stringent control by the board and the receiver has not been appointed to work full time on the conduct of the company's business but merely to exercise supervision and control over the way in which the business was run with particular regard to finance.

If the receiver closes down the company's business then all subsisting contracts of employment are brought to an end and the employees may be entitled to redundancy payments. If, however, a change occurs in the ownership of a business and the new owner renews the employees' contracts or re engages them on new contracts there is continuity of employment for redundancy purposes. (ss. 94 and 84 of the Employment Protection (Consolidation) Act 1978). In considering the legislation the courts appear to adopt a purposive approach and to be prepared to side step awkward refinements of receivership law and the effect of an insolvent liquidation. Thus where a company under receivership had dismissed its employees who had been re-engaged by the receiver, the company had then gone into voluntary liquidation and the business had been transferred to another company with whom new contracts were entered into, the court held that there was no change in the ownership of the business prior to the sale to the second company. Therefore there was continuity of employment and the employees were eligible for redundancy payments based on the continuous employment.[21] The transfer of an undertaking or part thereof is governed by S.I. 1981 No. 1794.[21a]

The position of directors is not affected, although their powers to deal with the property charged are suspended during the currency of the receivership. A director appointed receiver and manager is not thereby disentitled to be paid his fees as director.[22]

Moreover, the appointment of a receiver under a debenture does not preclude the director of the company from pursuing a right of action provided that the interests of the debenture holders *qua* debenture holders are not threatened.[23] The appointment of a receiver out of court does not automatically terminate the actual or ostensible authority of the company's solicitor. Even after a winding-up order has been made, the company may be estopped from denying that the solicitor has authority at least until the

---

[18] *Re Mack Trucks (Britain) Ltd., supra; Griffiths* v. *Secretary of State for Social Services, supra.*
[19] *Griffiths* v. *Secretary of State for Social Services, supra,* at p. 854.
[20] See Lawson J. in *Griffiths* v. *Secretary of State for Social Services, supra,* at pp. 844–845, referring to Pennycuick J. in *Re Mack Trucks (Britain) Ltd., supra,* at p. 786.
[21] *Deaway Trading Ltd.* v. *Calverley* [1973] I.C.R. 546. See also *Teesside Times Ltd* v. *Drury,*
[21a] See Addendum following Preface.
[22] *Re South Western of Venezuela Ry.* [1902] 1 Ch. 701.
[23] *Newhart Developments* v. *Co-operative Commercial Bank* [1978] 2 W.L.R. 636 (C.A.).

other party has actual or constructive notice of the winding-up order and the order has been gazetted under section 9 (4) of the European Communities Act 1972.[24]

46–09 RENT. COVENANT IN LEASE. A receiver in a debenture holders' action will not, at the instance of a landlord, be ordered to pay the rent of leasehold premises mortgaged by sub-demise to the trustees for the debenture holders, there being no privity in such a case between the lessor and sub-lessees[25]; and the same rule apparently applies where a receiver is appointed for an equitable mortgagee.[26] A receiver who by agreement paid rent for the period after his appointment was held to be entitled to deduct income tax in respect of rent paid before his appointment.[27]

The same rule would appear to apply to the liability of a receiver on the covenants in a lease.

RIGHTS AS LESSEE. Where the security comprises leasehold property and fixtures, and the company by passing a voluntary resolution to wind up forfeits the lease, the receiver may remove the fixtures within a reasonable time.[28] A receiver for holders of debentures containing a floating charge can exercise in the name of the company the statutory rights of a tenant of business premises.[29]

LEAVE TO BORROW. In debenture holders' actions the business of the company is commonly the most valuable asset, and in order to protect and preserve it as a going concern, and for this or other pressing exigencies, the court has jurisdiction—which it frequently exercises—to authorise the receiver to borrow money in priority to the debentures or debenture stock.[30] The receiver should keep within the limits allowed.[31]

The jurisdiction to raise a salvage loan of this kind is beneficial to all persons interested, and has saved many companies from destruction.[32]

The expenses of realisation rank before securities given by the receiver and manager.[33]

---

24 *Re Peek Winch & Tod Ltd.* (1979) 129 N.L.J. 494.
25 *Hand* v. *Blow* [1901] 2 Ch. 721. See R. M. Goode [1981] J.B.L. 396.
26 *Hay* v. *Swedish and Norwegian Ry.* (1892) 8 T.L.R. 775; see also *Justice* v. *James* (1899) 15 T.L.R. 181 (where the receiver had paid rent for a time); *Re J. W. Abbott & Co.* [1913] W.N. 284 (where the receiver was in possession); *Re Westminster Garage Co.* (1914) 84 L.J.Ch. 753 (where the lessor had recovered judgment for possession).
27 *Re Hayman, Christy and Lilly Ltd.* [1917] 1 Ch. 545.
28 *Re Glasdir Copper Mines, English Electro-Metallurgical Co.* v. *Glasdir Copper Mines* [1904] 1 Ch. 819.
29 *Gough's Garages* v. *Pugsley* [1930] 1 K.B. 615. As to these rights, see the Landlord and Tenant Acts 1927 and 1954.
30 *Greenwood* v. *Algeciras (Gibraltar) Ry.* [1894] 2 Ch. 205; *Lathom* v. *Greenwich Ferry* (1895) 72 L.T. 790.
31 *Re Glasdir Copper Mines* [1906] 1 Ch. 365; *Re British Power Traction Co.* [1906] 1 Ch. 497.
32 *Securities and Properties Investment Corp.* v. *Brighton Alhambra* (1893) 68 L.T. 249; *Re Glasdir Copper Mines* [1906] 1 Ch. 365; *Robinson Printing Co.* v. *Chic Ltd.* [1905] 2 Ch. 123.
33 *Strapp* v. *Bull* [1895] 2 Ch. 1; *Re Glasdir Copper Mines* [1906] 1 Ch. 365; *Re London United Breweries* [1907] 2 Ch. 511.

MAREVA INJUNCTION. A *Mareva* injunction does not prevail as against the debenture holder where the floating charge created *before* the grant of the injunction crystallised *after* the injunction had been granted as the rights of the debenture holder over the deposited fund stemmed from the creation of the debenture, and not from the appointment of the receiver which merely crystallised the existing equitable charge and removed the right of the company to deal with its assets in the course of its business. The injunction thus had to give way to the prior rights of the debenture holders secured by a floating charge. Although the receiver, as agent of the company, cannot obtain the discharge of the injunction, the debenture holders, if equitable assignees, can do so. In the circumstances of the case, the application of the receiver should be treated as if made by the debenture holders and the certificate relating to the deposit of the money under the *Mareva* injunction should be released to the receiver.[34]

RECEIVER'S LIABILITY. A receiver appointed out of court, like a receiver appointed by the court, is personally liable on any contract entered into by him in the performance of his functions (s. 369 (2)). The subsection then goes on to allow contracting out of such liability and to grant him an indemnity out of the assets. The practice has developed of inserting clauses in receiver's contracts excluding personal liability but whether the other contracting party will accept such a clause depends on his bargaining position. Section 369 (2) does not cut down any express indemnity which the receiver has obtained or limit his liability on contracts entered into without authority.

SET-OFF AND LIENS. The rights of set-off and lien[35] are analogous; the effect of both of them is to prevent circuity of action.[36] Both confer advantages akin to security[37] in a receivership. The position regarding set-off is complicated but can perhaps be reduced to the following rules[38]:

(1) The appointment of a receiver causes a floating charge to crystallise. The crystallisation operates as an equitable assignment of debts owing to the company, subject to rights of legal set-off and equities subsisting at that date. Debts arising after crystallisation are automatically assigned as they come into existence if the charge extends to after acquired property.[39]

(2) Where before the appointment of a receiver there is a contract

---

[34] *Cretanor Maritime Co. Ltd.* v. *Irish Marine Management Ltd.* [1978] 1 W.L.R. 966.

[35] There are similar, but not identical, principles of compensation and lien in Scotland, see Professor D. M. Walker's *Principles of Scottish Private Law* (2nd ed.), pp. 668 and 1583 *et seq.*

[36] See J. Cross, *A Treatise on the Law of Lien and Stoppage in Transitu*, p. 7.

[37] It is, of course, arguable that a lien is a species of security. It is not a mortgage but an equitable lien creates a charge and both legal and equitable liens are encumbrances. See Romer J. (*obiter*) in *Jones* v. *Barnett* [1899] 1 Ch. 620.

[38] The following analysis is based to some extent on J. O'Donovan (1978) 52 A.L.J. 562.

[39] *Biggerstaff* v. *Rowatts Wharf Ltd.* [1896] 2 Ch. 93 (C.A.); *N. W. Robbie & Co. Ltd.* v. *Witney Warehouse Co. Ltd.* [1963] 1 W.L.R. 1324 (C.A.); *Lynch* v. *Ardmore Studios (Ireland) Ltd.* [1966] I.R. 133; *Ferrier* v. *Bottomer* (1971–1972) 126 C.L.R. 597 (H.Ct. of Australia).

between the company and a third party, set-off will generally be allowed in respect of competing claims thereunder provided that they: (a) accrued due before notice of the assignment (whether or not payable before that date); or (b) arose out of the same contract; or (c) are closely connected with that contract. A debt which is neither accrued nor connected in this way may not be set-off even though it arises from a contract made before the assignment[40] unless there is some equitable ground for protection.[41]

(3) Where the claim by the company arises under a pre-receivership contract and the claim by the third party arises out of a separate and unconnected contract after the appointment it seems that set-off will not be allowed[42] unless the third party can show some equitable ground for being protected.[43] This might be satisfied if the debenture holder is the person for whose ultimate benefit and at whose direction the later debt is incurred.[44]

(4) Where the claim by the third party arises under a pre-receivership contract and the company has a claim against the third party arising out of a separate and unconnected contract after the appointment set-off will not be allowed since there is no mutuality in the absence of some ground for equitable set-off.[45]

(5) Where there are competing claims whether arising out of the same contract or not entered into after the appointment of a receiver set-off will usually be allowed.[46] If the debt by the company to the third party is incurred first this is a case of legal set-off to which the debenture holder takes subject on the automatic assignment of the third party's debt to it. If the debt by the third party to the company is incurred first this will be assigned to the debenture holder subject to equities arising under the contract. The debt owing to the third party may also be a receivership expense if the receiver does not exclude personal liability and even if he does so an equitable set-off may be allowed.[47]

---

[40] *Business Computers Ltd.* v. *Anglo-African Leasing Ltd.* [1977] 2 All E.R. 741 where the earlier cases are reviewed; see also *Government of Newfoundland* v. *Newfoundland Railway Co.* (1888) 13 App.Cas. 199 (P.C.) and *Rother Iron Works Ltd.* v. *Canterbury Precision Engineers Ltd.* [1974] Q.B. 1 (C.A.). *Cf.* O'Donovan, *op. cit.* p. 562.

[41] See note 43 *infra*.

[42] *Biggerstaff* v. *Rowatts Wharf Ltd.* [1896] 2 Ch. 93 (C.A.); *Business Computers Ltd.* v. *Anglo-African Leasing Ltd.* [1977] 2 All E.R. 741; *Lynch* v. *Ardmore Studio (Ireland) Ltd.* [1966] I.R. 133.

[43] *Rawson* v. *Samuel* (1841) Cr. & Ph. 161; I. C. Spry, "Equitable Set-Offs" (1969) 43 A.L.J. 265; *Handley Page Ltd.* v. *Commissioners of Customs & Excise* [1970] 2 Lloyd's Rep. 459; *West St. Properties Pty. Ltd.* v. *Jamieson* [1974] 2 N.S.W.L.R. 435.

[44] *West St. Properties Pty. Ltd.* v. *Jamieson* [1974] 2 N.S.W.L.R. 435. See also *Re B. Johnson & Co. (Builders) Ltd.* [1955] 1 Ch. 634 (C.A.).

[45] *N. W. Robbie & Co. Ltd.* v. *Witney Warehouse Co. Ltd.* [1963] 1 W.L.R. 1324 (C.A.); *Felt & Textiles of New Zealand Ltd.* v. *R. Hubrich Ltd.* [1968] N.Z.L.R. 716; *Rendell* v. *Doors & Doors Ltd.* [1975] 2 N.Z.L.R. 191, 201. See, however, the critical discussion of Robbie's case in R. P. Meagher Q.C., W. M. C. Gummow and J. R. F. Lehane, *Equity: Doctrines and Remedies*, pp. 575–576. (Mr. Meagher was counsel in the West St. Properties case, *supra*.) See also O'Donovan, *op. cit.* p. 565.

[46] *Parsons* v. *Sovereign Bank of Canada* [1913] A.C. 160 and see also the other cases cited in *Kerr on Receivers* (15th ed. by R. Walton), pp. 327–8.

[47] *Handley Page Ltd.* v. *Commissioner of Customs & Excise* [1970] 2 Lloyd's Rep. 459; *West St. Properties Pty. Ltd.* v. *Jamieson* [1974] 1 N.S.W.L.R. 435.

(6) In general equitable set-off will be allowed where there is an equity in the sense that one claim impeaches the title to the other.[48] There is an increasing tendency in the English cases to a liberal interpretation of this requirement although the mere facts that there are cross claims or even cross claims arising out of the same contract are not *per se* sufficient.[49] Given such an equity it is possible to set-off in Equity claims which are not mutual[50] or liquidated.[51]

(7) Where the receiver enters into a contract in his own right and assumes personal liability it would appear that there can be no set-off of a pre-receivership debt unless there is some ground for equitable set-off.[52]

(8) Where the debenture holders are paid in full out of other assets their beneficial interests cease, mutuality is restored and a right of set-off between the company and the third party can be exercised either under the general law or, if the company is then in liquidation for reasons of insolvency, under section 31 of the Bankruptcy Act 1914 as applied by section 317 of the Companies Act 1948.[53]

Since the equitable assignment on crystallisation is subject to pre-existing equities it is subject to subsisting liens and also to pre-assignment contractual rights which can now include a contractual lien. This last point was decided by the Court of Appeal in the recent case of *George Barker (Transport) Ltd.* v. *Eynon*[54] in a carrier's lien situation. On this basis a general lien created by contract in a lien by operation of law situation was given effect to even though there was not possession at the time of the receiver's appointment.

This seems to create new law. Formerly it was regarded as axiomatic that possession was essential to constitute a legal lien.[55] The *Barker* case seems to distinguish between a legal lien and a contractual lien in a legal lien type of situation, possession being essential to the existence of the first but merely "a preliminary to the exercise of the right claimed" in the case of the second.[56] Possession is of course not essential for an equitable lien and the present decision thus seems to put the contractual lien into an intermediate position, at least in this respect.

To obtain full advantage of this new principle it would appear that the carrier should obtain possession of the goods and, depending on the terms

---

48 *Rawson* v. *Samuel* (1841) Cr. & Ph. 161 and see the other cases cited by Dr. I. C. Spry in "Equitable Set-Offs" (1969) 43 A.L.J. 265.

49 See *Federal Commerce Ltd.* v. *Molena Alpha Inc.* [1978] 3 W.L.R. 309 (C.A.). See also *Hanak* v. *Green* [1958] 2 Q.B. 9. *Cf.* the stricter Australian approach discussed by Dr. Spry, *op. cit.*

50 See, *e.g. Ex p. Stephens* (1805) 11 Ves. 24.

51 See, *e.g. Pigott* v. *Williams* (1821) 6 Madd. 95.

52 *Cf. Parsons* v. *The Sovereign Bank of Canada* [1913] A.C. 160, 167 (P.C.).

53 *Rendell* v. *Doors and Doors Ltd.* [1975] 2 N.Z.L.R. 191, 202–203. This seems sound in principle although the authority relied on by Chilwell J. does not support it.

54 [1974] 1 W.L.R. 462.

55 See, *e.g. Hammonds* v. *Barclay*, 2 East. 277, 235, *per* Grose J., *Pollock and Wright on Possession*, p. 213, and *Paton on Bailment*, p. 184.

56 See Stamp L.J. at [1974] 1 All E.R. 910.

of the particular clause, perform his part of the contract or obtain the agreement of the receiver that he can claim his lien before he might otherwise be entitled.[57]

From the receiver's point of view such a contract will often be an onerous one which he will wish to repudiate. If he wishes to do so and escape the lien altogether then it appears that he should not only notify the carrier of this but also refuse the carrier the opportunity of performing his obligations under the contract. In other words, he must, if he can, physically prevent the carrier from obtaining possession.

EFFECT OF ROMALPA CLAUSES ON FLOATING CHARGES AND RECEIVERSHIPS. In the scramble for payment on an insolvency, trade creditors tend to lose to commercial finance and investment creditors. If the transaction is one of sale of goods they have the limited proprietorial remedies conferred by the Sale of Goods Act 1979, s. 39, namely lien, stoppage in transit and a limited right of resale, and possibly a right of set-off but otherwise they have no security or other rights akin thereto. Trade creditors have recently begun to feel that these limited rights were not enough and this has led to the growth of so-called *Romalpa* clauses.[58] Under the Sale of Goods Act 1979, ss. 17 and 19 where there is a contract for the sale of specific goods or goods are subsequently appropriated to the contract, the seller may by the terms of the contract or appropriation reserve the property or a right of disposal of the goods until certain conditions are fulfilled. Surprisingly, until recently this type of provision does not appear to have been common in the United Kingdom except in relation to export sales.

Now, as a result of publicity given to the Court of Appeal's decision in *Aluminium Industries Vaassen BV* v. *Romalpa Aluminium Ltd.*[59] in 1976 it is more common. In that case the court had to construe a literal translation of a Dutch form of contract which purported to reserve ownership until payment and to follow the goods into sale proceeds or mixed goods. The use of such clauses is very common in civilian jurisdictions. The Court of Appeal applying English law upheld the provision and held that there was an equitable tracing remedy. This creates a new security device for suppliers which may not need registration and consequently prejudices secured creditors by depleting the assets falling within a floating charge and

---

[57] See the useful article "Receiver Contractor Relationships—Businessmen should be wary of inducements," by Michael Tugendhat (counsel for *Barkers*) in [1974] *Lloyd's Maritime and Commercial Law Quarterly* 30, 41.

[58] See H. C. Rumbelow (1976) 73 L.S. Gaz. 837; R. M. Goode (1976) 92 L.Q.R. 360, 528, 548; J. H. Farrar and N. Furey [1977] C.L.J. 27; R. Prior (1976) 39 M.L.R. 585; O. P. Wylie (1978) Conv. 37. J.H. Farrar [1980] 1 Co.Law. 83, 88 *et seq.*; A.M. Tettenborn [1981] J.B.L. 173 and W.G. Gough, *Company Charges*, pp. 185–6. The discussion which follows is based on J. H. Farrar [1980] 1 Co. Law 83, 88 *et seq*.

[59] [1976] 1 W.L.R. 677. For an interesting criticism of the decision by a Dutch insolvency practitioner see R. de Ruuk in *Proceedings of the Symposium of the International Bar Association on Consequences and Experiences concerning Competition between Floating Charges and Reservation of Title,* p. 28. He shows that the reference to "fiduciary" ownership is standard Dutch security terminology and that the Court of Appeal came to a different decision from that which a Dutch court would have made in bankruptcy.

creating havoc in a receivership. Complex legal problems can arise from the use of such clauses, some of which have been adumbrated by subsequent cases.

First, the wording of the clause in question was somewhat eccentric as far as English law is concerned and the exact nature of the legal relationships created by the clause in question was not clearly analysed in the *Romalpa* case. It was conceded that the purchaser was a bailee of goods in its possession until all moneys had been paid. Also there is some suggestion by Roskill L.J.[60] that there was no principal and agent relationship *vis-à-vis* sub-purchasers, but that the purchaser nevertheless held the proceeds of the subsale as agent for the supplier. This removed any liability of the supplier to the sub-purchaser for defects in the goods and is questionable[61] because *ex p. White, Foley* v. *Hill*, *South Australian Insurance* v. *Randell* and *Henry* v. *Hammond*[62] do not appear to have been cited to the court. These cases establish that it is incompatible with a presently subsisting fiduciary relationship that the alleged fiduciary has the right to mix tangible assets or moneys with his own assets or moneys. Also, it is questionable because agency necessarily involves the power to alter the legal relations between the agent's principal and a third party. One cannot have one's cake and eat it by attempting to make a person an agent and not an agent at the same time. A better interpretation of the clause would seem to be that up to the time of the subsale the purchaser was a buyer in possession but, should he decide not to keep the goods, he sold as agent for the original supplier. If this is the case then the supplier may be liable to sub-purchasers as an undisclosed principal.

The second set of problems arise out of the right to trace the original goods. This appears to be lost, either because the original purchaser is an agent with authority to resell or is a buyer in possession under the Sale of Goods Act 1979, s. 25 (2).[63] It has been suggested[64] that if the goods are sold and a book debt arises this can only be the subject of an equitable tracing claim which may be defeated if a factor of the original purchaser's book debts or a receiver gets in the legal title to the debt by absolute statutory assignment. It would seem, however, that if the original purchaser resold as agent then the supplier may be able to sue the third party on the debt[65] direct as undisclosed principal, and does not need to rely on an equitable right to trace.

The third set of problems arise out of the drafting of the clause and the

---

[60] [1976] 1 W.L.R. 677, 690 C-E *per* Roskill L.J.

[61] *Cf.* Gough, *op. cit.* p. 186.

[62] (1870) 6 Ch.App. 397; (1848) 2 H.L.C. 28; (1869) L.R. 3 P.C. 10; [1913] 2 K.B. 515 respectively.

[63] *Re Interview Ltd.* [1975] I.R. 382; see also *Fueur Leather Corporation* v. *Frank Johnstone & Sons* (1981) 131 N.L.J. 1112 where an attempt was made to argue constructive trusteeship.

[64] R. M. Goode (1976) 92 L.Q.R. 528, 556–557.

[65] See *Halsbury's Laws of England* (4th ed., Butterworths), Vol 1, "Agency," para. 821, and F. M. B. Reynolds and B. J. Davenport, *Bowstead on Agency* (14th ed.), pp. 256 *et seq.*

nature of the interest reserved. In *Re Bond Worth Limited*[66] the supplier of raw fibre to be used in the manufacture of carpets, instead of reserving the legal property, purported to reserve "equitable and beneficial ownership" and allowed the buyers liberty to dispose of the goods on any terms they thought fit. Although the equitable and beneficial ownership was then expressed to attach to the proceeds of sale, the company was left free to deal with the book debts for its own purposes and benefit. Slade J. in a marathon judgment held as follows:

(1) that the reservation of equitable ownership was intended by way of security;
(2) that where the legal and beneficial ownership were combined it was not possible to reserve equitable ownership out of the title and transfer the bare legal title so that the attempted reservation of equitable ownership in effect was to be construed as a grant of the full legal and equitable ownership with a grant back of equitable ownership by way of charge;
(3) the purported bare trust in the circumstances, therefore, amounted in essence to a floating charge and was void for non-registration under the Companies Act 1948, s. 95.

Slade J. left open the important further question of whether it is ever open to an alleged beneficiary to seek remedies by way of declaration of equitable charge on a mixed fund of assets, where he cannot affirmatively prove that his particular fund contains or represents any of the assets affected by the trust and when his claim is not founded on any alleged breach of trust which is said to have caused the assets in which his interest originally subsisted to lose their identity. The *Bond Worth* case highlights the necessity for very careful drafting of such clauses as the court will look to the substance as well as the form. The clause must generally reserve legal property in the goods; clearly identify the legal relationship between the parties, and so far as possible, earmark the property and proceeds to be subject to the right to trace.

A fourth set of problems arises out of the physical alteration of the goods and mixing. The clause must contain express provision dealing with this, otherwise where chattels are affixed to land there is a strong presumption that they become part of the land and the right to trace is lost. (An express reservation in such circumstances creates an equitable interest[67] binding on a receiver under a floating charge.) The right to trace is also lost if the goods are no longer severable.[68] In Roman law there are subtle distinctions drawn between *commixtio, confusio, accessio* and *specificatio*.[69] The first is

---

[66] [1979] 3 All E.R. 919. Noted by M. Burke (1979) 129 N.L.J. 651; J.W.A. Thornely [1980] C.L.J. 48.

[67] *Re Samuel Allen & Sons Ltd.* [1907] 1 Ch. 575; *Re Morrison Jones & Taylor Ltd.* [1914] 1 Ch. 50.

[68] *Appleby* v. *Myers* (1867) L.R. 2 C.P. 651, 659, 660; *Bain* v. *Brand* [1876] 1 A.C. 762 (H.L. (S.C.)); *Gough* v. *Wood & Co.* [1894] 1 Q.B. 713 (C.A.); *Reynolds* v. *Ashby & Son* [1904] A.C. 466 (H.L.). See O. P. Wylie [1978] Conv. 37.

[69] See J. A. C. Thomas, *Textbook of Roman Law*, pp. 169 *et seq.*

the mixing of separables, the second the mixing of inseparables, the third the incorporation of one thing into another and the fourth the creation of a new object. The common law is less rich in detail and subtlety. At common law it is recognised that accidental and consensual mixing result in a tenancy in common in proportion to the original share of the ingredients.[70] If the amount of the original contributions cannot be ascertained then there is a presumption of equality.[71] However, the terms of the particular contract may indicate that property passes at the time of mixing—especially if the risk has passed[72]—and express provision should be inserted to clarify the parties' intention. In the *Romalpa* case itself the parties dealt with the matter by providing for automatic transfer of the property in the mixed goods. There are two drawbacks with such a provision. First, it can lead to complications if each supplier separately stipulates that this is to be the case. Secondly, it probably amounts to an equitable mortgage of future goods and will be void against the liquidator and the creditors if not registered under the Companies Act 1948, s. 95.[73] An apparently contrary view was taken by Judge Rubin sitting as an additional judge of the High Court in *Borden (U.K.) Ltd.* v. *Scottish Timber Products Ltd.*[74] where he held that resin used in the manufacture of chipboard did not result in a tenancy in common of the chipboard but that there was nevertheless a right to trace which was not registrable. This decision, which extended the scope of the *Romalpa* remedy to cover mixed goods, has recently been reversed on appeal on the tracing point.[75] The Court of Appeal held that the liberty which the supplier gave to the purchaser to use the resin in the manufacturing process for the purchaser's benefit producing its own chipboard destroyed the very existence of the resin and therefore all possibility of property in it.

Last, where property has not been expressly reserved in the original contract and is purportedly reserved by a later supplementary contract, this may be regarded as an attempt to contract out of the *pari passu* principle if the company goes into liquidation.[76] As such it is contrary to public policy. It may also constitute a fraudulent preference under the Companies Act 1948, s. 320. An analogous situation applies where there is a contract of

[70] 2 B. Comm 405 citing Inst. 2 1 27, 28 and 1 Vern. 217. The latter does not clearly support the text. See, however, *Spence* v. *Union Marine Insurance Co.* (1868) L.R. 3 C.P. 427; *Smurthwaite* v. *Hannay* [1894] A.C. 494, 505 (H.L.) and *Farnworth* v. *F.C.T.* (1949) 78 C.L.R. 504, 510.

[71] *Jones* v. *Moore* (1841) 4 Y. & C. Ex. 350; *Buckley* v. *Gross* (1863) 2 B. & S. 566, 575; *Sandeman & Sons* v. *Tyzack & Branfoot Steamship Co.* [1913] A.C. 680, 694–69 (H.L. (S.C.)).

[72] A. G. Guest, *Benjamin's Sale of Goods* (2nd ed.), para. 297. See also *South Australian Insurance Co.* v. *Randell* (1869) L.R. 3 P.C. 101.

[73] *Borden (U.K.) Ltd.* v. *Scottish Timber Products Ltd.* [1979] 3 All E.R. 961, 973, 974. See Farrar and Furey [1977] C.L.J. 31. *Cf.* Tettenborn [1981] J.B.L. 173, 174–175.

[74] (1978) 122 S.J. 8.

[75] [1979] 3 All E.R. 961. Noted by M. Dyer [1980] 1 Co. Law. 34; J. W. A. Thornely [1980] C.L.J. 48.

[76] *British Eagle International Airlines Ltd.* v. *Compagnie Nationale Air France* [1975] 2 All E.R. 390. See further Farrar and Furey [1977] C.L.J. 31.

sale by, as opposed to sale to, a company on the brink of insolvency and there is an attempt made to expedite the passing of property by a supplementary agreement.

As can be seen, the use of *Romalpa* clauses can create complex legal and practical problems. The *Bond Worth* and *Borden* cases indicate that the courts are beginning to "lean against" such clauses and construe them restrictively. The matter has recently been reviewed by the Committee on Insolvency Law Reviews which has made important recommendations.[76a] The matter is also under consideration by the E.E.C. Commission and the Council of Europe.

THE USE OF THE TRUST DEVICE. Apart from the reservation of property, the trust device has recently been adopted to protect consumers successfully in one case and unsuccessfully in another. The trust was successfully used in *Re Kayford Ltd.*[77] where an express trust was declared on mail order subscriptions by a company in difficulties on the advice of accountants. A separate trust account was opened. Sir Robert Megarry VC had no difficulty in holding that there was a valid trust which in the result meant that the consumers could recover their money which fell outside the assets of the company on its winding up. In *Re London Wine (Shippers) Ltd.*,[78] however, sold but unappropriated wine held in a warehouse was held not to be sufficiently certain subject-matter for a trust by Oliver J. His Lordship's principal reasons appear to be as follows:

(1) it was not clear at the various dates, when the beneficial interests in the wine were supposed to take effect, what the composition of the consignments were in respect of which the purchaser's proportionate shares were to take effect;

(2) there was not sufficient appropriation of the wine to the various contracts because there could not be appropriation by exhaustion where there was nothing to stop the vendors meeting their commitments from other consignments.

Oliver J. also held that there was no interest by estoppel since estoppel did not confer a proprietary interest. It is a pity that the case has not been fully reported.

SALE BY HIVING DOWN.[79] Instead of the receiver selling the undertaking and assets to a purchaser immediately he often enters into a contract as receiver binding the company to sell them down to a "clean" subsidiary directly or indirectly[79a] in exchange for shares. He then sells the shares in

76a "Insolvency Law and Practice", Cmnd. 8558 (1982), paras. 1639 and 1650.

77 [1975] 1 All E.R. 604. See C. M. Schmitthoff [1975] J.B.L. 83 and J. H. Farrar [1976] J.B.L. 214, 229–230. See also *Re Chelsea Cloisters Ltd.* [1981] 131 N.L.J. 482 (C.A.).

78 (1976) 126 N.L.J. 977.

79 On hiving down see the useful discussion in *S. Samwell, Corporate Receiverships* pp. 82 *et seq.*

79a By which is meant sale is either for shares or for cash to be satisfied by the issue of shares. The latter technique is used because it can provide a useful figure for capital gains purposes.

the subsidiary to the purchaser. The advantages of such an operation are that it is a useful method of separating off the viable from the unviable parts of the business; it passes the assets without the liabilities; and it provides clear continuity of employment minimising the risk of compensation for loss of office and redundancy payments. The main disadvantages are the formalities which must be carefully carried out and certain fiscal consequences.[80] Clearly ordinary unsecured creditors will lose out in the arrangement[81] and in *Airline Airspares Ltd.* v. *Handley Page Ltd.*[82] in 1970 one such creditor sought an injunction to restrain the sale of shares. Although prepared to grant an *ex parte* injunction, Graham J. discharged it after a full hearing. He recognised that a receiver is in a better position than the company in regard to current contracts and can disregard them in circumstances where the company itself could not. The only limits are that repudiation of the contract must not adversely affect the realisation of the assets or seriously affect the trading prospects of the company in question, if it is able to trade in the future.

TRANSFER OF UNDERTAKINGS AND THE RECEIVER. See Addendum following Preface.

APPLICATION TO THE COURT FOR DIRECTIONS. Doubts often arise as to the powers enjoyed by receivers and the manner in which they should be exercised. Prior to the Companies Act 1948 a receiver appointed out of court had no means of obtaining the court's directions and the practice was to try to persuade the other party to apply. Now as a result of the recommendations of the Cohen Committee[83] section 369 (1) enables him to make an application. A receiver so appointed may apply to the court for directions in respect of any matter arising in connection with the performance of his functions and on any such application the court may give such directions or make any such order declaring the rights of persons before the court or otherwise as the court thinks just. The company, or a representative of the debenture holders and the trustees (if any) should be made respondents to such an application.

Statutory provisions applying to all receivers

46–10 DISQUALIFICATIONS FOR APPOINTMENTS. A body corporate is not qualified for appointment as receiver of the property of a company. Contravention is subject to criminal sanction (1948 Act, s. 366).

If an undischarged bankrupt acts as receiver, he becomes liable to a fine

---

[80] When the subsidiary leaves the group there will be corporation tax on capital gains arising on a reopening of the previous transaction. The purchaser will seek an indemnity which the receiver will be reluctant to give. In the end the matter is often settled by a reduction of the purchase price. This is a distinct disadvantage of this method of sale. Another disadvantage is that relief for prior tax losses may be lost. See Samwell, *op. cit.* pp. 83, 84.

[81] Unless they have a right of lien or set-off or can assert commercial pressure.

[82] [1970] Ch. 193. The case seems to leave open the question aired but not decided in *Re Botibol, decd.* [1947] 1 All E.R. 26 that a receiver might be liable in tort for inducing a breach of contract. The effect of Graham J.'s judgment would seem to negate such a right in normal circumstances.

[83] Report of the Committee on Company Law Amendment, Cmd. 6659 (1945), para. 67.

or imprisonment, or both (1948 Act, s. 367 (1)), but this does not apply where the appointment and the bankruptcy both took place before the commencement of the Act or where he was appointed by the court (s. 367 (2)).

Where the company is compulsorily wound up in England, and an application is made to the court to appoint a receiver on behalf of the debenture holders or other creditors, the official receiver may be appointed receiver of the company (1948 Act, s. 368).

DISQUALIFICATION ORDERS. Under the provisions of section 93 of the 1981 Act the court may make disqualification orders in the following circumstances:

(a) Where a person is convicted of an indictable offence in connection with a receivership or management;
(b) Where a person has been persistently in default with filing documents with the Registrar of Companies;
(c) Where in the course of the winding up of a company it appears that a person has been guilty of fraud in relation to the company or breach of his duty as receiver or manager.

REGISTRATION OF APPOINTMENT. The appointment of a receiver must be registered in the register of charges kept by the Registrar of Companies. Application for registration has to be made within seven days from the date of the court order or of the appointment under a power in an instrument (1948 Act, s. 102).

NOTICE OF APPOINTMENT ON INVOICES, ETC. Where a receiver or manager of the property of a company has been appointed, every invoice, order for goods or business letter issued by or on behalf of the company or the receiver or manager or the liquidator of the company, being a document on or in which the name of the company appears, shall contain a statement that a receiver or manager has been appointed (1948 Act, s. 370).

46–11 NOTICE OF APPOINTMENT TO COMPANY. STATEMENT OF AFFAIRS. FILING OF ACCOUNTS. Where a receiver or manager of all or substantially all the property of the company is appointed on behalf of the holders of debentures secured by a floating charge he must send to the company notice of his appointment forthwith and the company must within (usually) 14 days make out and submit to the receiver a statement as to the affairs of the company (1948 Act, s. 372). The statement must show the date of the receiver's appointment, particulars of the company's assets and liabilities and particulars as to the creditors, and the securities held by them. The statement must be verified by affidavit (or a statutory declaration where the receiver was appointed out of court) of a director and the secretary, and past directors, employees and officers of the company, and persons who have taken part in the formation of the company may in certain cases be required by the receiver to submit and verify the statement (1948 Act, s. 373).

Within two months after receiving this statement the receiver must send to the Registrar (and to the court if he was appointed by the court) a copy of the statement and any comments he sees fit to make, and must send to the Registrar a summary of the statement and of his comments and must send to the company a copy of his comments and to the trustees and all the debenture holders a copy of the summary (s. 372 (1) (*c*)).

The receiver must also within two months after the end of each year, and within two months after he ceases to act as receiver or manager, send to the Registrar, to the trustees, to the company and the debenture holders an abstract of his receipts and payments during the relevant period (s. 372 (2)).

Penalties are imposed in case of default (ss. 372 (7) and 373 (5)) and the court may order the receiver to make good his default (1948 Act, s. 375).

Where section 372 (2) is not applicable, a receiver or manager appointed by debenture holders must deliver to the Registrar an abstract of his receipts and payments at six-monthly intervals, and within one month after he ceases to act as receiver (1948 Act, s. 374).

46–12 PREFERENTIAL PAYMENTS. A receiver appointed on behalf of the holders of debentures secured by a floating charge is bound to pay out of the first assets coming to his hands creditors who would be entitled to preferential payments in a winding up (1948 Act, ss. 94, 319[84]) in priority to any claim for principal or interest in respect of the debentures. There are some modifications to adjust the rules as to preferential payments to the fact that they are being dealt with by a receiver (s. 94 (2)). If he distributes the assets or uses them up in carrying on the business without providing for these preferential payments, he renders himself liable.[85] In *I.R.C.* v. *Goldblatt*[86] a debenture holder revoked the appointment of a receiver and agreed that in consideration of the receiver delivering to the company all assets held by him as receiver, the debenture holder would indemnify him against all liabilities incurred by him in the performance of his office. Assets then passed from the receiver to the company and thence to the debenture holder, no account being taken of the plaintiffs' entitlement to preferential payment. It was held that the receiver was not entitled to account to the company and that since payment to the debenture holder would have been a breach of statutory duty under section 94, it followed that payment to the company by the direction and on the indemnity of the debenture holder would not be anything less. Moreover, the debenture holder himself was also liable for breach of statutory duty and as a con-

---

[84] See para. 85–60, *post*.

[85] *Woods* v. *Winskill* [1913] 2 Ch. 303; *Westminster City Council* v. *Haste* [1950] Ch. 442; *I.R.C.* v. *Goldblatt* [1972] Ch. 498.

[86] *Supra*.

structive trustee. In the event of a winding up, the costs of the winding up are payable before the preferential debts, but if the general assets after payment of such costs are insufficient to pay the preferential debts, then the amount of the deficiency must be made up by the debenture holder out of the property subject to his floating charge.[87] The costs and expenses of the receiver and his remuneration also come before the preferential creditors.[88] These preferential payments have no priority over property comprised in a fixed charge, even though the debenture contains also a floating charge.[89]

Where a receiver is appointed of part of the property of the company which is comprised in a floating charge, debts incurred in connection with other property of the company after the appointment of the receiver will not rank as preferential debts against the property in the hands of the receiver, since the floating charge over that property crystallises upon the appointment of the receiver.[90]

As to rates, the liability of the receiver depends upon the question whether there has been a change of possession.[91]

Additional rights under the Employment Protection (Consolidation) Act 1978

46–13 Under the Employment Protection Act 1975, ss. 63–69, certain entitlements of employees under the provisions of the Act (*e.g.* statutory guarantee and maternity payments) were assimilated to wages for the purposes of section 319 of the Companies Act 1948. Also, employees of an insolvent company (defined so as to include both receivership and liquidation situations) were given the right to be paid by the Secretary of State for Employment out of the Redundancy Fund in respect of certain amounts owed to them by the company—to a maximum of £135 per week per debt. The amounts include arrears of pay for a period not exceeding eight weeks; pay in lieu of notice; holiday pay (not exceeding six weeks); a basic award of compensation for unfair dismissal; certain other entitlements created by the Employment Protection Act itself (including statutory guarantee payments and maternity pay); and payments into an occupational pension fund. The provisions are now consolidated in the Employment Protection (Consolidation) Act 1978, Pt. VII as amended by the Employment Act 1980 and S.I. 1982 No. 77 and are discussed in greater detail at para. 85–60, *post.* When the Secretary of State has paid employees or made any contribution to an occupational pension scheme under these provisions, he

[87] *Westminster Corporation* v. *Chapman* [1916] 1 Ch. 161; *Re Barleycorn Enterprises Ltd.* [1970] Ch. 465.

[88] *Re Glyncorrwg Colliery Co.* [1926] Ch. 951. The word "forthwith," which appeared in the corresponding s. 107 of the Act of 1908, and was commented upon in this case, has now been omitted.

[89] *Re Lewis Merthyr Consolidated Collieries* [1929] 1 Ch. 498.

[90] *Re Griffin Hotel Co. Ltd.* [1941] Ch. 129.

[91] *National Provincial Bank* v. *United Electric Theatres* [1916] 1 Ch. 132. [1946] Ch. 269.

is subrogated to their rights, including any preferential rights, as against the company.

ORDER OF PAYMENT. The basic order of payment of debts and distribution is as follows:

(1) costs of realisation;
(2) costs including remuneration of receiver;
(3) expenses of the debenture or debenture stock trust deed including the trustee's remuneration where this is to be paid before the debenture;
(4) the costs of the debenture holder's action (if any);
(5) preferential creditors if the debentures are secured by a floating charge and the company is not being wound up;
(6) subject to prior debentures, the debenture holders' debt with interest;
(7) any subsequent debenture holder;
(8) ordinary creditors.

REMUNERATION. The remuneration of a receiver appointed by the court is fixed by the court, and that of a receiver appointed under a power in the debentures, by agreement with the debenture holders. In either case, on an application made by the liquidator of a company which is being wound up, the court may fix the remuneration of a receiver or manager (1948 Act, s. 371 (1)). This power is extended in section 371 (2) (*a*) of the Act of 1948 to fixing the remuneration for any period before the making of the order or the application to the court, thereby overruling *Re Greycaine Ltd.*,[92] and is exercisable notwithstanding that the receiver has died or ceased to act before the application. Where he has received more than the rate fixed, he may be ordered to refund the excess.

In the case last mentioned, it was held that the power might be exercised although the receiver had been receiving remuneration at a rate fixed by the trustees for debenture holders by agreement with the receiver.[93]

Scope and extent of powers of receivers and managers

46–14 Where a company has an article in the form of article 80 of Table A, a receiver has no power to present a petition for the winding up of the company as the company's agent. However, he may have such a power under the express provisions of the debenture under which he was appointed. In *Re Emmadart Ltd.*[94] Brightman J. also took the opportunity to say that the practice of directors presenting petitions to wind up insolvent companies in the name of the company itself but without reference to

[92] See further Palmer, *Company Precedents*, Part III (16th ed.), pp. 693 *et seq.*, and, as to correction of the order, where remuneration has been omitted, *Re City Housing Trust Ltd.*
[93] [1942] 1 All E.R. 369.
[94] [1979] 1 All E.R. 599.

the shareholders or any specific power in the articles should be discontinued.

A receiver appointed under the law of any part of the United Kingdom in respect of the whole or part of any property or undertaking of a company and in consequence of a floating charge may exercise his powers in any other part of the United Kingdom so far as their exercise is not inconsistent with the law applicable there. (The Administration of Justice Act 1977, s. 7 (1)). Receiver for this purpose includes a manager and a receiver and manager (s. 7 (2)).

Recognition of foreign receiver in the English jurisdiction

46–15 Before an English court will recognise the title of a foreign receiver to assets located in the United Kingdom or direct the setting up of an auxiliary receivership, the court has to be satisfied of a sufficient connection between the foreign company and the foreign jurisdiction in which the receiver was appointed to justify recognition of the foreign court's order as having effect outside the foreign jurisdiction. Thus, where a company was incorporated under the laws of the Bahamas but the receiver was appointed by a court in New York, the English court held that his title to assets in England could not be recognised in the English jurisdiction. Moreover, the appointment of the American receiver arose in proceedings under the United States Securities Exchange Act 1934 and that Act was a penal statute unenforceable in the United Kingdom.[95]

Foreclosure

46–16 This is a remedy which is occasionally available in debenture holders' actions,[96] but not where the property has been conveyed to the trustees of a debenture trust deed on trust for sale.[97] All the debenture holders as well as the company are necessary parties to a foreclosure action.[97] If the others refuse to join as plaintiffs they can be joined as co-defendants.[98] All the debenture holders subsequent to the mortgagee should be parties to a foreclosure action by a legal mortgagee even where their security constitutes only a floating charge.[99] Foreclosure in consequence is often impracticable and in such cases nearly the same result can be obtained by an order for sale with liberty for the debenture holders to bid.[1]

Winding-up petition

46–17 A debenture holder to whom the company is indebted in a sum presently payable can demand payment, and, if default is made, can petition for the

[95] *Schemmer* v. *Property Resources Ltd.* [1974] 3 W.L.R. 406.
[96] *Sadler* v. *Worley* [1894] 2 Ch. 170; *Elias* v. *Continental, etc., Co.* [1897] 1 Ch. 511.
[97] *Schweitzer* v. *Mayhew* (1862) 31 Beav. 37.
[98] *Wallace* v. *Evershed* [1899] 1 Ch. 891; *Elias* v. *Continental, etc., Co., supra.*
[99] *Luke* v. *South Kensington Hotel Co.* (1879) 11 Ch.D. 121.
[1] *Wallace* v. *Evershed* [1899] 1 Ch. 891; *Westminster Bank Ltd.* v. *Residential Properties Ltd.* [1938] Ch. 639.

winding up of the company, and this whether he is the registered holder of the security, or the holder of a security to bearer.[3] The mere fact that he has obtained the appointment of a receiver does not preclude him from applying for a winding-up order.[4] The holder of a mortgage debenture who applies for a winding-up order is not bound to give up his security.[5]

Where there is nothing presently due to the debenture holder, he may still be able to petition as a contingent or prospective creditor under section 224 (1)(*c*) of the 1948 Act.[6]

Where there is a debenture stock trust deed the covenants are usually with the trustee and the holder of debenture stock may not be regarded as a creditor for this purpose.[7]

Proof by debenture holders in winding up

46–18 In the case of a solvent company a debenture or debenture stockholder can prove for his principal and interest,[8] and is not bound to value his security before proving.[9] But if the company is insolvent,[10] section 317 of the Companies Act 1948 applies, and the holders of secured debentures who want to prove must value their securities or must realise them and then prove for the balance; and for the purpose of ascertaining the balance for which he can prove, the debenture holder can only apply the proceeds of his security in payment of interest accrued up to winding up. He may then prove as an unsecured creditor for the balance of the principal and interest due at the commencement of the winding up after deducting the amount arising from realisation of his security.[11]

It has been held that, by virtue of section 317, section 66 of the Bankruptcy Act 1914 applies in the case of an insolvent company.[12] This section provides that, for the purposes of dividend, interest is not to exceed 5 per cent. per annum in the first instance, and that any higher rate of interest may only be recovered after all the debts proved have been paid in full.

Where a debenture is not payable when a winding up commences, the holder can nevertheless prove for the full amount of the principal subject to a rebate of interest and also value and prove the liability to pay future

---

2 See further Palmer's *Company Precedents*, Part 3, p. 738.

3 *Re Olathe Silver Co.* (1884) 27 Ch.D. 278; *Re Uruguay Central Ry.* (1879) 11 Ch.D. 372.

4 *Re Borough of Portsmouth Tramways* [1892] 2 Ch. 362.

5 *Moor* v. *Anglo-Italian Bank* (1879) 10 Ch.D. 681.

6 See para. 85–15, *post*.

7 *Re Dunderland Ore Co.* [1909] 1 Ch. 446. This decision of Swinfen Eady J. appears to have been *per incuriam*. See para. 46–01 and note 4, *ante*.

8 *Re Colonial Trusts Corporation* (1879) 15 Ch.D. 465, 473.

9 *Kellock's Case* (1868) L.R. 3 Ch. 769.

10 "Until it is shown that the assets are sufficient to pay its debts in full" a company in winding up must be treated as subject to the bankruptcy rules: *per* Lord Selborne L.C. in *Re Milan Tramways Co.* (1884) 25 Ch.D. 587, 596. The declaration of solvency would, subject to the provisions of s. 288, exclude that presumption.

11 *Quartermaine's Case* [1892] 1 Ch. 639.

12 *Re Theo Garvin Ltd.* [1969] 1 Ch. 624; following *Re Leng* [1895] 1 Ch. 652 (C.A.); *Re Whitaker* [1901] 1 Ch. 9 (C.A.); and *Re Bush* [1930] 2 Ch. 202; not following *Re Agricultural Wholesale Society* [1929] 2 Ch. 261 and *Re Wells* [1929] 2 Ch. 269; see para. 85–69, *post*.

interest to maturity where, by the terms of the instrument, the principal carries such interest to maturity.[13]

Debenture holders and debenture stockholders are entitled as against their securities, whether the company be solvent or insolvent, to take principal, interest up to date of payment, and costs.[14]

Interest after judgment is limited to 14 per cent. per annum[15] unless there is a separate covenant to pay interest at a higher rate during the continuance of the security.[16] If there is no covenant to pay "during the continuance of this security"[16a] interest under the debenture merges in the judgment and ceases. For the position in relation to an insolvent company see above.

Calls made before winding up and other debts can be set off against money due on debentures, if there are no effective provisions in the debentures to the contrary.[17]

Where a debenture is guaranteed by a guarantee company, both companies being insolvent, the holder can prove in the winding up of the guarantee company for the balance remaining after realising his security; but he is not directly entitled to the benefit of any reinsurance effected by the guarantee company.[18]

---

[13] *Re Browne and Wingrove, ex p. Ador* [1891] 2 Q.B. 574 (C.A.); *Re Theo Garvin Ltd.*, *supra*.
[14] *Cotterell* v. *Stratton* (1872) L.R. 8 Ch. 302; *Re Talbott* (1888) 39 Ch.D. 567.
[15] Judgment Act 1838, s. 17; Administration of Justice Act 1970, s. 44 (1); Judgment Debts (Rates of Interest) Order 1982 (S.I. 1982 No. 696). *Re. European Central Ry.* (1876) 4 Ch.D. 33; *Re Sneyd* (1883) 25 Ch.D. 338. The 1838 Act does not apply to the county court—see further para. 85–69, *post*.
[16] *Popple* v. *Sylvester* (1882) 22 Ch.D. 98.
[16a] *Re European Central Ry.* (1876) 4 Ch. D 33.
[17] *Re Taunton, Delmard, Lane & Co.* [1893] 2 Ch. 175; *Re Richard Smith & Co.* [1901] 1 Ir.R. 73; and *Partridge* v. *Rhodesia Goldfields* [1910] 1 Ch. 239.
[18] *Re Law Guarantee Trust, etc., Society* [1915] 1 Ch. 340.

E. CHARGES AND REMEDIES RELATING TO DEBENTURES IN SCOTLAND

CHAPTER 47

CHARGES SECURING DEBENTURES. REGISTRATION OF CHARGES

47–01 CHAPTERS 42 and 43, dealing with borrowing powers and the form of debentures, may be treated as valid in regard to Scotland with the variations noted in those chapters. While the normal form of debenture, especially the registered debenture, follows the pattern described in Chapter 43 and usually includes a trust deed for debenture holders, this is not essential.

Securing debentures in Scotland

47–02 In Scots law "debenture" is not a term of art and in law a debenture is indistinguishable from any other form of deed acknowledging a loan. Loan must be proved by writ or oath of the debtor, but in practice debentures are invariably constituted by probative deed under the company's seal. The manner of securing debentures is distinctive in Scotland since it derives from Scots property law. To be effective at common law, a right in security must (in general) be constituted a real right in favour of the creditor according to the nature of the property over which it subsists, as follows:

(a) Heritable property—by recording an appropriate deed (now in almost every case a Standard Security) in the Register of Sasines or Land Register[1];
(b) Corporeal Moveables—by physical or constructive delivery (but there are limited exceptions such as the mortgaging of a ship—*Tyne Dock Engineering Co. Ltd.* v. *Royal Bank of Scotland Ltd.*[1a] and the common law rights of hypothec whose details are beyond the scope of this work).
(c) Incorporeal Moveable Rights—by assignation to the creditor (or equivalent, *e.g.* share transfer) coupled with intimation to the "debtor" whose obligation is assigned (*e.g.* the company).

So far as securities by companies are concerned, the foregoing is still valid in respect of fixed securities. The powers of realisation, etc., possessed by the creditor derive from the general law and are the same as arise in the case of securities granted by individuals. The creditor is entitled to

---

[1] See para. 47–32, *post*.
[1a] 1974 S.L.T. 57.

enter upon possession of the security subjects and sell or otherwise deal with the same, subject to safeguards for the debtor's reversionary rights. The details of this are beyond the scope of this work, but some note is taken (*infra*) of securities over heritage since this is the most important fixed security granted by companies.

In *Tyne Dock Engineering Co.* v. *Royal Bank of Scotland*[2] a firm of ship repairers failed to establish the (somewhat improbable) proposition that a company instructing necessary repairs to a ship mortgaged by it to their bank was acting as the bank's agent and pledging the bank's credit in respect of the repair costs.

47–03 Few companies have sufficient heritable property to provide adequate security for all their borrowings. In England this had long been overcome by the "floating charge" which "crystallises" on the happening of a specified event, such as the commencement of winding up or the appointment of a receiver, or other event specified in the relevant deed. The essential feature is that assets can be removed from or added to the security by the company at will prior to crystallisation. This was, of course, in direct conflict with the general law of Scotland on the constitution of rights in security, and the absence of the "floating charge" was a serious inhibition on the power of Scottish companies to borrow for their normal requirements. As will be seen, this disability was removed by statute in 1961.

Although normally discussed in the context of borrowing (and guarantees for loans) it should be remembered that securities may also be granted for non-monetary obligations to do particular acts (obligations *ad factum praestandum*). This is true of both fixed and floating charges.

From the manner of constituting rights in security at common law it will be seen that in all cases there is objective evidence of the creditor's position. In the case of heritage his right is recorded in the property register; in the case of corporeal moveables the subjects are in his physical or constructive possession (with limited but well-defined exceptions); in the case of incorporeal moveable rights the person whose obligation is assigned in security has received intimation. In the case of a floating charge, however, it was necessary to create a register, maintained by the Registrar of Companies, so that members of the public might be aware of all floating charges granted by companies. This was also established in 1961, and at the same time the obligation to register was extended to certain fixed securities granted by companies in Scotland.

47–04 A number of criticisms were made of the 1961 legislation and the Companies (Floating Charges and Receivers) (Scotland) Act 1972, which is the current statute, made modifications to the law on the creation of floating charges and the procedure for registration. Some features, however, remain unsatisfactory.

Under the 1961 Act the holder of a floating charge was in a difficult position when it came to enforcing his security. Assuming he could make

---

[2] 1974 S.L.T. 57.

an immediate claim, he could of course sue for payment like any other creditor, but that did not give him the advantage implicit in a "right in security." The only other remedy accorded him by the 1961 Act was to petition for winding up on the ground that his security was "in jeopardy" (as defined). This was, however, not necessarily to his advantage since such action might prejudice the viability of the company's trading position, and devalue his security.

The improvement obtained in 1972 was the power to appoint a receiver on the assets comprised within the floating charge. This power, unlike the English situation, is exclusive to the holder of a floating charge.

It is important for anyone familiar with English company law to appreciate that Scots law is entirely statutory in the matter of floating charges, registration of charges and receivers. There are, of course, similarities, especially in registration, but close analogy drawn from English common law would be dangerous.

The floating charge in Scotland

The Companies (Floating Charges and Receivers) (Scotland) Act 1972

47–05 The Companies (Floating Charges) (Scotland) Act 1961, which came into force on October 27, 1961, introduced the floating charge into Scots law. It also contained, in the Second Schedule (adding sections 106A to 106K to the Companies Act 1948), procedure for registration of charges, fixed and floating, granted by Scottish companies (and certain floating charges granted by companies incorporated outside Scotland).

The 1961 Act was repealed, except for s. 7 (*b*), (*c*) and (*d*), by the Companies (Floating Charges and Receivers) (Scotland) Act 1972, which came into force on November 17, 1972; s. 7(*d*) was repealed by the Companies Act 1980, (Sched. 4).

The 1972 Act substantially amended the 1961 code in the light of criticism and difficulties which had been experienced. It also introduced to Scots law the facility of appointing a receiver, but this is only available to the holder of a floating charge (including such a charge created under the 1961 Act). The position of a receiver in Scotland is discussed in Chapter 48, *post*.

In this chapter, unless otherwise indicated, references are to the 1972 Act and sections 106A,[2a] to 106K of the Companies Act 1948 as contained in the Schedule to the 1972 Act.

Power to create floating charges

47–06 Any incorporated company in Scotland (whether registered under the 1948 Act or not) can now grant a floating charge, and Scots law will recognise floating charges granted by English companies over assets

---

[2a] S. 106A (7) was amended by the Companies Act 1980, Sched. 3, para. 15.

situated in Scotland.[3] Such a charge may be used to secure any debt or other obligation of the company, including a cautionary obligation (guarantee), incurred or to be incurred by the company or any other person (s. 1 (1)).

The charge may "float" over all or any part of the property which may from time to time be comprised in the company's property and undertaking, including uncalled capital (s. 1 (1)); the reference to uncalled capital was added in 1972. Uncalled capital, which has been constituted a reserve liability under sections 60 or 64 of the 1948 Act, may not be capable of being charged.[4] Heritable property may be subject to a floating charge, notwithstanding that the instrument is not recorded in the Register of Sasines (s.3) or Land Register.[4a]

The 1961 Act (s. 2 and First Schedule) laid down a form of words for a floating charge which proved cumbersome in practice. The 1972 Act (s. 2) abandons the 1961 form and requires merely the execution under seal of an instrument or bond or other written acknowledgement of debt or obligation which purports to create a floating charge. This may be in the same instrument as the bond, or a separate document, and it is also competent to have the charge executed by the company's attorney duly authorised in writing under seal (s. 2 (2)). The latter facility, also introduced in 1972, will greatly simplify the practical aspects of the creation of several charges simultaneously, *e.g.* by a group of companies. The instrument will define the property comprised within the charge as circumstances require.

The abandonment of a statutory form of floating charge raises the question of whether the particular words employed are sufficient to constitute a floating charge. In English law the words "floating charge" need not appear so long as there is a charge over a class of assets of the company which the company is free to release from or bring within the charge until crystallisation.[5] It has been held in England[6] that title reservation clauses in contracts for the supply of goods (so-called "Romalpa"[7] clauses) may constitute registrable charges if their effect is to pass ownership to the purchaser subject to a trust in favour of the seller until payment. In Scots law, however, the requirement of a deed executed under the seal of the company (or by its duly appointed attorney) would prevent a floating charge from arising merely from the terms of a supplier's contract conditions. There remains, however, the problem of whether a deed which does not expressly refer to a "floating charge" may nevertheless contain its essential features and so "purport to create a floating charge."

---

[3] For the law prior to 1961 see *Carse* v. *Coppin*, 1951 S.L.T. 145, and *Re Anchor Line (Henderson Bros.) Ltd.* [1937] Ch. 483.

[4] See para. 42–05, *ante.*

[4a] Land Registration (Scotland) Act 1979, s. 29 (2).

[5] *Re Yorkshire Woolcombers Association Ltd.* [1903] 2 Ch. 284, 295. See para. 44–05, *supra.*

[6] *Re Bond Worth Ltd.* [1979] 3 W.L.R. 629.

[7] *Aluminium Industries Vaassen B.V.* v. *Romalpa Aluminium Co. Ltd.* [1976] 1 W.L.R. 676; [1976] 2 All E.R. 552. Such clauses are of doubtful effect on Scots law; see *Clark Taylor & Co. Ltd.* v. *Quality Site Development (Edinburgh) Ltd.* 1981 S.L.T. 308.

Crystallisation of floating charges

47–07 Until the commencement of winding up (s. 1 (2)) or the appointment of a receiver (ss. 1 (3), 13 (7) and 14 (7)) the company is free (unless the terms of the loan document provide otherwise) to dispose of property which is the subject of a floating charge, and to acquire property which may become subject to the charge. On the occurrence of such an event, however, the charge crystallises and attaches to the charged property then comprised in the company's property and undertaking as if it were a fixed security for the debt or obligation to which it relates and any interest due thereon (s. 1 (2)). Crystallisation cannot occur except on either of the events specified.

The interest secured includes interest accruing after the commencement of the winding up, or the appointment of a receiver, until payment of the sum due under the charge (s. 1 (4)).[8]

The security obtained on crystallisation of a floating charge is postponed to the rights of any person who:

(a) has effectually executed diligence[9] on the property, or
(b) holds a fixed security or floating charge having a prior ranking (s. 1 (2)). Rules for ranking of floating charges are contained in section 5 (see below).

In so far as the assets available for payment of general creditors are sufficient to pay the prior debts specified in the 1948 Act, s. 319 (1) to (4), such debts are to be paid out of the property which is subject to a floating charge in priority to the claims of the holder of the charge (s. 1 (2) and 1948 s. 319 (5).

Enforcement of a floating charge

47–08 Prior to the 1972 Act, the only method whereby the holder of a floating charge could enforce his security was to obtain a winding-up order. The 1972 Act has provided the additional remedy of appointing a receiver (s. 11).[10] If the company goes into liquidation, however, the holder of a floating charge will enforce his rights by lodging a claim with the liquidator[11] unless a receiver is appointed by him or by the court on his application.

Extension of power to wind up

47–09 The circumstances in which the court has power to wind up a company under sections 222 and 399 (5) of the 1948 Act are extended for the advantage of a creditor entitled to the benefit of a floating charge (s. 4). The court must be satisfied that the creditor's security is in jeopardy. The

[8] *Cf. National Commercial Bank of Scotland Ltd.* v. *Liquidator of Telford Grier Mackay & Co. Ltd.*, 1969 S.L.T. 306, 1969 S.C. 181 where a similar result was held to follow under the 1961 Act; also *Royal Bank of Scotland* v. *Williamson*, 1972 S.L.T. (Sh. Ct.) 45. Section 1 (4) of the 1972 Act was introduced "for the avoidance of doubt."

[9] As to the meaning of this phrase see *Lord Advocate* v. *Royal Bank of Scotland, etc.* 1976 S.L.T. 130; 1978 S.L.T. 38; 1977 S.C. 155 and para. 48–08, *infra*.

[10] See para. 48–03, *post*.

[11] *National Commercial Bank of Scotland Ltd.* v. *Liquidator of Telford Grier Mackay & Co. Ltd, supra*; *Libertas-Kommerz GmbH* 1978 S.L.T. 222, 225.

security is deemed to be in jeopardy if the court is satisfied that events have occurred, or are about to occur, which render it unreasonable in the interests of the creditor that the company should retain power to dispose of the property which is subject to the floating charge. The holder of a floating charge may, of course, also rely on the grounds available generally in seeking a winding-up order.

Ranking of floating and other charges

47–10 The provisions of the 1961 Act (s. 5) regulating the ranking of floating and other charges have been substantially amended by the 1972 Act (s. 5). The rules are now as follows (subject always to the priorities preserved by section 1 (2), above):

(1) A fixed security arising by operation of law ranks in priority to a floating charge, and it is not competent to provide otherwise (s. 5 (2));

(2) Subject to rule (1), the instrument creating the floating charge, or any instrument of alteration under section 7 (*infra*), but not, apparently, any collateral deed such as the bond or acknowledgement of the debt secured, may contain provisions—

   (a) restricting or prohibiting the creation of fixed or floating charges ranking prior to or *pari passu* with the charge; or

   (b) regulating the order in which the floating charge shall rank with any other subsisting or future fixed or floating charges (s. 5 (1)); and

(3) In the absence of any conventional ranking clause under section 5 (1), a fixed security which has been constituted a real right before crystallisation of a floating charge has priority over the floating charge; floating charges rank *inter se* in order of registration with the Registrar of Companies, charges received by the same postal delivery ranking equally (s. 5 (4)).

Restriction of security

47–11 The holder of a floating charge having a postponed ranking may restrict the preference of a prior ranking floating charge by giving written intimation of the registration of his charge to the holder of the prior charge (s. 5 (5)). "Holder" is not defined, and this may create difficulty in the event of an assignation of the creditor's interests. In that event the Register of Charges maintained by the Registrar of Companies will show the "holder" to be the original creditor, but the register to be maintained by the company should disclose the true position.[12] Thus, a creditor giving notice under section 5 (5) should inspect the company's own register of charges to ascertain the identity of the true "holder" of the existing charge. Nevertheless the 1972 Act makes no reference to assignation of floating charges and it is open to debate whether section 5 (5) is intended to refer to the original

[12] See *Libertas-Kommerz GmbH* 1978 S.L.T. 222, 224 and para. 47–16, *infra*.

holder or to the assignee. Logic suggests the latter, but prudence may suggest intimation to both.

On receipt of such intimation, the preference in ranking of the prior floating charge is restricted to present advances, future advances the holder is required to make in terms of the instrument creating the charge or any "ancillary document," interest due or to become due on all such advances and any expenses which the holder may reasonably incur (s. 5 (5)). It appears that this restriction applies generally, and not merely in a question with the holder of the postponed charge. "Ancillary document" is defined (s. 31 (1)) as a document relating to the floating charge executed by debtor or creditor therein prior to registration of the charge with the Registrar of Companies, or an instrument of alteration under section 7.

Alteration of charges

47–12 There was no express provision for the alteration of floating charges in the 1961 Act. The 1972 Act (s. 7) contains provisions for the execution and registration of an "instrument of alteration."

The instrument of alteration may alter the instrument "creating a floating charge under section 2 of this Act" or any "ancillary document" (s. 7 (1)). The use of the words "creating a floating charge under section 2 of *this* Act" would appear to exclude the execution of an instrument of alteration of a floating charge created under the 1961 Act. Nevertheless, the definition of "ancillary document" (s. 31 (1) (see above)) is apt to include a document "relating to" a floating charge under the 1961 Act, and it may be arguable that on this basis an instrument of alteration of such a charge would be competent.

The instrument of alteration must be executed by the company, the holder of the charge and the holder of any charge (fixed or floating) which would be adversely affected by the alteration (s. 7 (1)).

The Act (s. 7 (2)) makes provision for the execution of the instrument by the company and by or on behalf of debenture holders. The company must execute under seal, or by its attorney duly authorised in writing under seal (s. 7 (2) (*a*)). If trustees are acting for debenture holders the trustees execute the instrument (s. 7 (2) (*b*)). If no trustees are acting the instrument may be validly executed on behalf of a series of debenture holders by a specified proportion of them (s. 7 (2) (*c*)). The instrument of alteration may also be executed in such manner as may be provided for in the instrument of charge or any ancillary document (s. 7 (2) (*d*)). These provisions do not bear to exhaust the means by which an instrument of alteration may be validly executed.

Registration under section 106A (1) of the 1948 Act (Form 48a (Scot)) is required if the instrument of alteration affects ranking, releases property or increases the amount secured (s. 7 (3)). An instrument adding to the property affected by the charge would (to that extent) be a fresh charge, registrable accordingly. The time limit is 21 days from the date of the instrument (s. 7 (4)).

Floating charges as fraudulent preferences

47–13 At common law a preference may be challenged as fraudulent if the grantor was insolvent at the time it was created, no matter how great the interval between its creation and the challenge.[13] Under section 322 of the 1948 Act a floating charge could only be challenged if created within 12 months prior to the commencement of the winding up. This provision only applied to England. The 1961 Act extended it to Scotland without making it clear that it was to supplant the common law rule. The 1972 Act (s. 8) has removed all grounds for such a challenge other than section 322.[14]

Validation of doubtful provisions in floating charges created prior to the 1972 Act

47–14 The 1972 Act (s. 30) retrospectively validates *ab initio* certain provisions in floating charges created prior to, and subsisting on November 17, 1972, which might otherwise have been open to challenge. These are—

(1) floating charges which might have been invalid because they were not in the form prescribed in the First Schedule to the 1961 Act (s. 30 (2)); and
(2) ranking clauses contained in an instrument of charge or ancillary document (s. 30 (3)).

The document in question must have been executed prior to, and the charge must still be subsisting, on November 17, 1972. The floating charge or ranking clause must be such as would have been valid if created under the 1972 Act. These provisions (s. 30 (2) and (3)) do not in terms refer to charges created under the 1961 Act but to floating charges purporting to subsist at the commencement of the 1972 Act. *Quaere* whether this might validate a purported floating charge created *before* the commencement of the 1961 Act.

Fixed securities in Scotland

The standard security

47–15 The Conveyancing and Feudal Reform (Scotland) Act 1970 has radically altered the procedure for creating fixed securities over Scottish heritable property. With the exceptions specified in section 9 (7) (securities under the Small Dwellings Acquisition (Scotland) Acts, and over entailed land) the existing forms of heritable security ceased to be competent after November 29, 1970. With these minor exceptions the only competent method of creating a fixed security over Scottish heritage after that date is in the form of a standard security prescribed in Schedule 2 to the Act, recorded in the appropriate Register of Sasines or Land Register.[15]

Certain clauses in the statutory form of standard security cannot be varied by the parties (s. 11 (3) of the 1970 Act). These originally included

---

[13] See para. 87–67, *infra*.
[14] See para. 87–70, *infra*.
[15] Land Registration (Scotland) Act 1979. References herein to the "Register of Sasines " or "Property Register" may be taken to refer to the Land Register, where applicable; see paras. 47–32, *infra*.

the debtor's power to redeem at any time on two months' notice, which inhibited the "time bargain" necessary to long-term finance. By the Redemption of Standard Securities (Scotland) Act 1971, s. 1, parties may now by agreement vary the statutory form so as to restrict the debtor's power of redemption. A similar variation may be made in respect of standard securities granted before the 1971 Act came into force (s. 3 of the 1971 Act).

The standard security can specify the amount secured or the maximum amount, or be in respect of "all sums due and that may become due." The rule in the Bankruptcy Act 1696 (of the Scots Parliament) that a heritable security is not valid in respect of debts contracted after it has been recorded in the Register of Sasines is abolished in relation to a standard security (1970 Act, s. 9 (6)).

A standard security may also be used to secure a non-monetary obligation, in which case (if granted by a company) there is doubt whether it constitutes a registrable charge.[16]

Change of creditor or debtor

47–16 In Scots law it is always open to the creditor in a security right to assign his interest. The form of assignation of a fixed security over land is laid down by statute, principally the Conveyancing and Feudal Reform (Scotland) Act 1970, Sched. 4; such an assignation must be recorded in the Property Register. There is no statutory form for assigning a fixed security over incorporeal moveables. Neither the 1961 Act nor the 1972 Act mention the assignation of the benefit of a floating charge, but it has been established that a floating charge is assignable by the creditor. The assignation must be intimated to the company in writing. The company must enter the change of creditor in its own register of charges, even though there is no provision for recording a change of creditor in the register of charges kept by the registrar of companies.[17]

A change of debtor is also competent in principle, subject to agreement by the creditor. In the case of a fixed security, the new debtor will acquire the property affected subject to the charge and will also assume the personal obligations secured thereby. Registration is required in this case.[18] It is not possible to assign the debtor's interest in a floating charge since by its nature it is a security created by a particular company and does not attach to any specific property until crystallisation.

Registration of charges in Scotland

Registration of floating and other charges

47–17 Section 6 of and the Schedule to the Companies (Floating Charges and Receivers) (Scotland) Act 1972 provide for the registration of all floating

---

[16] See para. 47–18, *post.*
[17] *Libertas-Kommerz GmbH* 1978 S.L.T. 222. See para. 47–24, *post.*
[18] See para. 47–24, *post.*

charges and certain fixed charges created after October 27, 1961 (when the 1961 Act came into force), by Scottish companies, and (in certain circumstances) charges created by companies incorporated outside Great Britain. This is done by amending the Act of 1948 so as to add a new Part III A (ss. 106A to 106K). References in this section are to sections 106A to 106K as contained in the Schedule to the 1972 Act. The operation of these sections has been criticised by the Scottish Law Commission (Memorandum No. 33, December 1, 1976). The information available from the official Register of Charges and that kept by the company may be inaccurate, and a creditor suffering loss as a result if relying upon it may find this loss difficult to recover.[18a]

Effect of non-registration

The purpose of registration is to publish the existence of the charge on the file maintained by the Registrar of Companies in Edinburgh and available for public inspection. Accordingly, if a charge is one to which section 106A applies, any security thereby created is void against the liquidator and any creditor unless the prescribed particulars together with a duly certified copy of the instrument "if any" are "delivered to or received by" the registrar within 21 days after the date of its creation. The court may extend the time for registration under section 106G. Two observations may be added: first, it seems inconceivable that a valid charge to which section 106A applies can be constituted without writing. The "prescribed particulars" are contained on official Form 47 (Scot) and the copy instrument has to bear a signed docket "certified a true copy." Secondly, delivery of the particulars and copy within the time limit is sufficient compliance, even if the Registrar subsequently refuses registration, *e.g.* on the (erroneous) view that the charge is not registrable.[19] If a charge becomes void by reason of non-registration the money secured thereby becomes immediately payable, and avoidance of the charge does not prejudice any personal obligation for repayment (s. 106A (1)). Once the charge has been satisfied (*e.g.* by payment) it can no longer be challenged for want of registration.[19]

Charges which are registrable

47–18 Section 106A (2) defines the charges which are registrable,[19a] if created by a company incorporated in Scotland (s. 106A (10)). These are:

(a) a charge on land, wherever situated, or any interest therein, excluding a charge for rent, ground annual or other periodical sum payable in respect of the land and excluding also a charge on debentures which entitle the holder to a charge on land[20]; but including a heritable security within the meaning of section 9 (8) of the Conveyancing and Feudal Reform (Scotland) Act 1970;

[18a] See McBryde and Allan; "*The Registration of Charges*" 1982 S.L.T. (News) 177.
[19] *NV Slavenburg's* v. *Intercontinental Natural Resources Ltd., etc.* [1980] 1 All E.R. 955
[19a] For a comment on this list and its origins see McBryde and Allan, *op. cit.*
[20] See s. 106A (6).

(b) a security over uncalled share capital;

(c) a security over incorporeal moveable property of any of the following categories:

(i) book debts of the company;

(ii) calls made but not paid;

(iii) goodwill;

(iv) a patent or a licence under a patent;

(v) a trademark;

(vi) a copyright or a licence under a copyright;

(d) a security over a ship (or aircraft[21] or any share in a ship; and

(e) a floating charge[22]

Registration in Scotland is necessary wherever the property charged is situated.[23] As a result of an amendment to s. 106 by the 1981 Act, however, a Scottish company charging property in England no longer requires to register the charge in England.[23a] Since 1972 an English company charging property in Scotland has not required to register in Scotland (s. 106K, amending in this respect the equivalent 1961 provisions). It should be noted that the charges specified as registrable include charges other than floating charges, and in this respect the titles of both the 1961 Act and that of 1972 are misleading.

Not every charge created by a Scottish company will be registrable. The list of incorporeal moveable property in section 106A (2) is not exhaustive. It does not, for example, include a fixed security over shares in another company.[24]

It is also possible that certain forms of heritable security are outside the scope of section 106A (2), even though it now refers to "charges" secured by standard security under the Conveyancing and Feudal Reform (Scotland) Act 1970. Because of an extended definition of "debt" (1970 Act, s. 9 (8) (*c*)), in addition to securing the repayment of indebtedness a standard security may be used to secure any obligation to pay an annuity or an obligation *ad factum praestandum, i.e.* to perform a specific non-monetary obligation. While a standard security is clearly a "charge" if granted in respect of a money debt, a standard security in respect of an obligation *ad factum praestandum* (and perhaps also an annuity) may not be; in Scotland "charge" is neither a term of art nor has it been defined by statute or judicial authority.

The deposit of a negotiable instrument to secure payment of book debts for the purpose of securing an advance to the company is not, for the purposes of section 106A, to be treated as a charge on those book debts (s. 106A (5)).

---

21 Added by Mortgaging of Aircraft Order 1972 (S.I. 1972, No. 1268), art. 16 (2).

22 As to the meaning of "floating charge," see para. 47–06, *supra*.

23 *Amalgamated Securities Ltd.*, 1967 S.L.T. 273; 1967 S.C. 56.

23a Companies Act 1981 Schedule 3 para. 3 (effective December 22, 1981).

24 *Scottish Homes Investment Co.*, 1968 S.C. 244.

Further advances

47–19 A fixed charge created by a heritable security such as a standard security can be expressed to secure advances of capital to be made after the date of its original creation. A similar situation obtained under an *ex facie* absolute disposition, which never specified the amount secured thereby. Where a further advance of capital was made on such a security to a company, there was difficulty over the registration requirements of the 1961 Act since more than 21 days would have elapsed since the creation of the charge.[25] The 1972 Act has removed these difficulties by providing that the further advance shall be treated as a fresh charge created on the date of the back letter or other agreement increasing the amount secured, which must be registered within 21 days thereafter (s. 106A (9)).

In the case of a charge created by standard security (or *ex facie* absolute disposition) qualified by a back letter or agreement (which regulates the terms of the advance secured), publication in the register of charges is not of itself sufficient to render the charge unavailable as security for future indebtedness (s. 106A (9)). This renders inapplicable the common law rule that publication of the terms of the advance prevents the security being used to secure advances after the date of publication.

Procedure for registration

47–20 The duty to register a charge or the issue of a series of debentures requiring registration (see s. 106A (7))[25a] is imposed on the company creating the charge, but any other interested person may register it, the expense being recoverable from the company (s. 106B). In practice, because non-registration invalidates his security, charges are normally registered by the creditor.

The normal time limit for registration is "within 21 days after" the date of creation of the charge (s. 106A (1)). That is to say, if the charge was created on January 1, the last day for registration is January 22. Where more than one charge is created, the precise time of registration may be critical (s. 5 (4)).[26]

The court may, conditionally if it thinks fit, extend the time to permit late registration on being satisfied that the omission was "accidental, or due to inadvertence or to some other sufficient cause," and that late registration will not prejudice shareholders or creditors. The court may also do so on other grounds if it is "just and equitable" to allow it (s. 106G).[26a]

The official form (47 (Scot)) giving the prescribed particulars of the charge requires to be signed by an officer of the company, or by the solicitor for either the company or the person effecting registration. The

---

[25] See *Archibald Campbell, Hope & King Ltd., Petitioners*, 1967 S.L.T. 83 and *Scottish and Newcastle Breweries Ltd.* v. *Liquidator of Rathburne Hotel Co. Ltd.*, 1970 S.L.T. 313.
[25a] s. 106A (7) was amended by the Companies Act 1980, Sched. 3, para. 15.
[26] See para. 47–10, *ante*.
[26a] See para. 47–27, *infra*.

copy instrument creating the charge which should accompany the form requires to be certified a true copy by such an officer or a solicitor.

In addition (by s. 106A (8)), particulars must be given as to the amount or rate of any commission, allowance or discount paid or made (directly or indirectly) by the company to any person for subscribing or procuring subscriptions for debentures secured by the charge. Failure to do so, however, does not invalidate the debentures. A deposit of debentures in security by the company is not to be treated, for the purpose of this provision, as an issue of debentures at a discount.

Charges created over foreign properties

47–21 Section 106A (3) extends the time for registration in the case of "a charge created out of the United Kingdom comprising property situated outside the United Kingdom." The period of 21 days for registration is to be computed from the date "on which the copy of the instrument creating it could, in due course of post, and if despatched with due diligence, have been received in the United Kingdom." This apparently simple provision contains a number of potential difficulties.

In the first place, having regard to the variable efficiency of the world's postal systems, there is bound to be room for argument as to the length of delay which may legitimately be claimed in a particular case.

Secondly, at what point does the duty to post the copy instrument arise? This seems to be the time of creation of the charge, as defined in section 106A (10). In the case of a floating charge executed abroad, the charge is created when executed by the company. This is in itself not always self-evident (see para. 47–23, *infra*). In the case of a fixed charge, the date of creation is the date on which the right of the holder of the charge is constituted a real right. Since section 106A (3) is exclusively concerned with charges on property situated outwith the United Kingdom, the date of creation of a fixed charge, and thus the date on which the obligation to post a copy of the instrument of charge will arise, will depend on the relevant *lex situs* of the property in question, and perhaps on several different foreign legal systems if property located in several countries is involved.

Section 106A (4) applies to a charge which is created in the United Kingdom but comprises property outside the United Kingdom. Section 106A (3) does not apply, therefore no extension of the time for registration is permitted, and such a charge has to be registered in the usual way within 21 days of its creation. It may, nevertheless, not be fully effective until some further formality of the *lex situs* has been complied with. In such circumstances section 106A (4) permits, but does not oblige, registration to proceed before such formalities have been completed, presumably to avoid the charge passing out of time while they are attended to. Section 106A (4) is, however, inconsistent with section 106A (10), under which a fixed charge is not "created" until such steps as may be required to complete the holder's real right have been carried out. It is therefore incorrect to refer to a charge over foreign property executed in the United Kingdom but not yet constituted as a real right under foreign law as having been "created." A company creating such a charge ought to be able to register it within 21 days of the charge being constituted a real right in the foreign system, not the date of its execution in the United Kingdom.

Registration of a series of debentures

47–22 It is customary for a company to issue a series of debentures secured *pari passu* by a single charge. In these circumstances, registration of each debenture separately is unnecessary (s. 106A (7)). Registration is effected by forwarding a copy—the Act does not prescribe a certified copy—of the deed containing the charge for registration within 21 days after its date of execution (*not* the date of creation of the charge) together with the following particulars (Form 47a (Scot))[27]:

(a) the total amount secured by the whole series of debentures;
(b) the date of the resolutions authorising the issue of the series and the date of the deed, if any, creating or defining the security;
(c) a general description of the property charged;
(d) the names of the trustees, if any, for the debenture holders; and
(e) if the security is by way of floating charge, details of any provisions governing the company's power to grant prior or *pari passu* securities or which regulate the order of its ranking in relation to subsisting securities.

If there is no separate instrument containing the charge, the prescribed particulars (Form 47a (Scot)), together with a copy of one of the debentures must be forwarded for registration within 21 days of the date of execution of any debenture in the series. Where there are subsequent issues of debentures in the same series there must be sent to the Registrar for entry in the register, particulars[27] of the date and amount of each issue, but there is no time limit on the provision of this information and failure to do so does not invalidate the debentures issued (s. 106A (7), as amended by the Companies Act 1980, Sched. 3 para. 15).

The provisions of section 106A (7) are alternative to the registration provisions of section 106A.

Date of creation of charges

47–23 The date of creation of charges, by reference to which, *inter alia*, the time for registration is normally calculated, is defined in section 106A (10). In the case of a fixed security, it is the date on which the right of the person entitled to the benefit thereof was constituted a real right, *i.e.* (in the case of Scottish property) the date of recording or registration in the Property Register in the case of a heritable security, or the effective date of intimation in the case of a security over an incorporeal moveable right.

In the case of a floating charge, the date of creation is the date of execution by the company creating the charge. There are areas of possible difficulty arising out of the conflict between this provision and the normal

[27] Form 48 (Scot).

Scottish practice whereby the date of execution by each party to a deed is given, but the deed is effective only when fully executed (and, in some cases, not until it is subsequently delivered to the obligee). If this practice is adhered to, an instrument might pass out of time for registration before it has become legally binding on execution by all parties. Further, the definition in section 106A (10) is expressed to be for the purposes of "this Part of the Act" (*i.e.* ss. 106A–K of the 1948 Act). The effective date of creation of a floating charge for other purposes (*e.g.* s. 322) is nowhere defined; *quaere* would one then have to apply the general rule previously described.

Registration on change of creditor and on acquisition of charged property

47–24 It has already been observed[28] that a creditor can, in principle, assign the benefit of a charge held by him, whether fixed or floating. The 1972 Act makes no provision for such a change of creditor to be intimated to the Registrar of Companies, and accordingly the public register of charges kept by him is likely to contain erroneous information in this respect. The company itself, however, would require to enter such a change in its register, kept under section 106I (see below).[29] If property subject to a fixed charge (but not, of course, a floating charge) is acquired by a company, it must forward the prescribed particulars for registration by the Registrar of Companies (Form 47b (Scot)), together with a certified copy of the instrument creating the charge, under section 106C. The charge must be one which, if it had been created by the company after the acquisition, would have been registrable under section 106A. Assuming it is of a kind which is otherwise registrable, a charge to which section 106C applies might have been created by an individual and not a company, or it might have been created before October 27, 1961.

The prescribed particulars and the manner of certification of the copy instrument are similar to the requirements under section 106A.

The time limit for forwarding particulars for registration under section 106C is 21 days after the transaction by which the property in question was acquired was "settled." There is an extension for the case of property and charge situated outside the United Kingdom, similar to section 106A (3), allowing additional time for postal delays.

There is considerable doubt as to what the section means by "settlement" of a transaction; although this phrase has a customary significance in the purchase of heritage, it is conceivable that it may be difficult to establish a precise date of "settlement" in some cases.

Failure to register under section 106C carries no disadvantage to the company or creditor except liability to a nominal default fine (s. 106C (2)). The value of this provision to the public is therefore doubtful.

---

[28] See para. 47–16, *ante*.
[29] *Libertas-Kommerz GmbH* 1978 S.L.T. 222.

Registration of alterations of floating charges

47–25 The 1972 Act, s. 7, introduced the facility of executing an instrument altering a subsisting floating charge.[30] Under section 7 (3) any such instrument is registrable if it:

(a) prohibits or restricts the creation of any fixed security or any other floating charges ranking prior to or *pari passu* with the floating charge;
(b) varies or otherwise regulates the position of the charge in its ranking with other charges;
(c) releases property from the floating charge; or
(d) increases the amount secured by the floating charge.

Section 7 (3) and (4) give effect to these requirements by applying section 106A (1) to any such instrument of alteration with the following modifications:

(a) references in section 106A (1) to a "charge" are to be read as references to an "alteration to a floating charg";
(b) the time for registration (normally 21 days) is to be calculated from the date of execution of the alteration; the reference is not to execution by the company (*cf.* s. 106A (10) (*a*)), but to execution of the instrument, which has at least one other party (see s. 7 (1)), and therefore, presumably, to the date on which it has been fully executed, regardless of when the company executed it; and
(c) it is the alteration, not the charge itself, which is to be void against the liquidator in the event of failure to register timeously.

The adapted wording of section 106A (1) reads:

> "Every alteration to a Floating Charge created by a company shall, so far as any security on the company's property or any part thereof is conferred thereby, be void against the Liquidator and any creditor of the company unless (the prescribed form and certified copy are registered) within 21 days after the date of its execution, etc."

This does not mean that an unregistered instrument of alteration which has one or more of the effects listed in section 7 (3) is always void, except in the case of an instrument increasing the amount secured, and even in that case (as with an unregistered charge) the company's obligation to repay the sum secured remains and is immediately enforceable. An instrument of alteration which prohibits the creation of prior or *pari passu* charges, or which releases property from the charge, does not confer any security and so cannot be affected by section 106A (1) (as adapted). The same is true, it is suggested, of an instrument which merely alters the order of ranking of charges, and in such a case all those affected thereby will be parties to the instrument and may be personally barred from founding on non-registration.

There is, nevertheless, the curious anomaly that the release of property

---

[30] See para. 47–12, *ante*.

from a floating charge may be registrable under two different statutory provisions, section 106A (1) as applied by section 7, and section 106F.

As with a charge, registration is effected by forwarding to the Registrar of Companies the prescribed particulars together with a certified copy of the instrument. The official form 48a (Scot) calls for particulars of both the original charge and the instrument of alteration, the property originally charged and the alteration so far as within each category of section 7 (3).

There is no provision for registering any alteration to a floating charge other than one falling within the limits indicated above, nor is there any provision for registering any similar alteration, *e.g.* as to ranking, of a fixed charge.

The requirements imposed on the company by sections 106H to J to keep copies of every instrument creating a charge open for inspection (see below) do not appear to extend to instruments of alteration unless a strained construction of section 7 (5) is intended to have this effect.

Section 106G (*infra*), which gives the court power to extend the time for registration and to rectify the register of charges kept by the Registrar, is extended to give similar powers in respect of instruments of alteration (s. 7 (3) and (4)).

Official register of charges

47–26 The Registrar of Companies maintains an official register of charges which is available for inspection by the public (s. 106D, as amended by the 1976 Act, Sched. 3). The particulars in the register are those which the company is required to register under sections 106A and 106C (above), together with the optional memoranda of satisfaction and release, etc., under section 106F (*infra*). Copy instruments are not filed.

The official register of charges will also show the appointment of a receiver under Part II of the 1972 Act.[30a]

The Registrar is required to issue a certificate of registration of any charge duly registered, stating the name of the company, the person entitled to the benefit of the charge and the amount secured. If there is more than one person entitled to the charge the first-named only is shown, and if the registration is of a series of debentures, the holder of the first such debenture to be issued will appear (s. 106E). The Registrar's certificate is conclusive evidence that the requirements of Part IIIA of the 1948 Act as to registration have been complied with. The certificate is not, however, conclusive in any other respect, such as the validity of the charge registered.[31] The requirement of the 1961 Act (s. 106E) that the company send a copy of the Registrar's certificate to every debenture holder no longer applies.

[30a] See ss. 13 (5) and 14 (5); as to receivers see Chap. 48, *post*.

[31] *Scottish and Newcastle Breweries Ltd.* v. *Liquidator of Rathburne Hotel Co. Ltd.*, 1970 S.L.T. 313.

Complete or partial satisfaction of the debt for which a charge was given, or the release of any property from the charge, or the fact that it has ceased to form part of the company's undertaking, may be registered under section 106F; as to the apparent conflict of this section and section 7 (3) of the 1972 Act, see above. Registration under this section is entirely voluntary (Forms 49 (Scot), 49a (Scot), and 49b (Scot)).

Before registering a memorandum of satisfaction or release, in the case of a floating charge (s. 106F (2) (*a*); the restriction of this safeguard to floating charges is surely an error) the Registrar must be furnished with a certificate by or on behalf of the creditor entitled to the benefit of the charge that the particulars are correct (s. 106F (2)). The court has power to direct registration if satisfied such certification cannot readily be obtained (s. 106F (2) (*b*)).

The declaration by the company is under seal and must be signed by the secretary and at least one director.

If the Registrar enters a memorandum under section 106F on the register he is obliged, if required, to furnish the company with a copy (s. 106F (1)).

The copies of instruments creating charges, and of instruments of alteration, which are called for by the Act are not retained by the Registrar but are returned to the person presenting them for registration.

Rectification of the official register

47–27 The court's power to extend the time for registration of a charge or an instrument of alteration (under s. 106G) has already been mentioned. The same section empowers the court to rectify an omission or mis-statement of particulars on the official register. It covers memoranda of satisfaction (under s. 106F) but not, apparently, memoranda of release of property.

The court must be satisfied that the failure to register timeously or the omission or mis-statement, was "accidental, or due to inadvertence or to some other sufficient cause, or is not of a nature to prejudice the position of creditors or shareholders of the company, or that on other grounds it is just and equitable to grant relief." These words, although apparently very wide, do not unfortunately warrant the court granting an application where the register is erroneous by reason of defects in the registration requirements of the Act.[32] The court's order may be conditional.[32a]

It is a defect in section 106G that there is no explicit requirement that the court must inquire into the possibility of prejudice to creditors before granting an order. It is also unsatisfactory that a court order extending the time for registration preserves the date of creation of the charge for ranking purposes, so that a search in the register of charges for 21 days

[32] *Archibald Campbell, Hope & King Ltd.*, 1967 S.L.T. 83.

[32a] Petitions under s. 106G, although relatively frequent, are not often reported (*M. Milne Ltd.* [1963] C.L.Y. 3727; *Amalgamated Securities Ltd. supra*; *Archibald Campbell, Hope and King Ltd. supra* appear to be the only examples). See further McBryde "Company Petitions in the Inner House" 1978 S.L.T. (Notes) 81 and for the procedure in the Court of Session McBryde and Dowie "Petition Procedure in the Court of Session" (W. Green & Son, Edinburgh, 1980), p. 18.

after a particular date will not necessarily disclose all charges in existence at that date.

If a charge has not been timeously registered, it appears to be an alternative to presenting a petition under section 106G that the money secured be instantly repaid and, the unregistered charge being void under section 106A (1), a fresh charge be granted.

Register of charges to be kept by the company

47–28 The company must maintain at its registered office a register of charges created by it, whether registrable under section 106A or not (s. 106I (1)) and copies of every instrument creating a charge which requires registration (or a copy of one of a series of uniform debentures) (s. 106H). The register must show all fixed and floating charges, describing briefly the property charged, and showing the amount secured and (except in the case of bearer securities) the names of the persons entitled thereto. Any creditor or member may inspect the register and copy instruments during normal hours (minimum two hours per day) on payment of a maximum fee of 5p (s. 106J (1)). The court may order the company to make the register or copies available (s. 106J (3)).

The register kept by the company should contain information which may not be correct on the official register, *e.g.* as to the release of property from the charge or the assignment of the creditor's interest,[32b] and will also disclose charges which do not require registration on the official register.

There is no express requirement that the company shall keep available for inspection a copy of an instrument of alteration of a floating charge executed under section 7 of the 1972 Act.

Registration of charges by foreign companies

47–29 Under section 106K the provisions as to registration of charges are applied to charges on property in Scotland which are created, and to charges on property which is acquired, by a company incorporated outside Great Britain which has a place of business in Scotland.[33] Companies incorporated in England or Wales are not affected. The equivalent English provision (s. 106) no longer requires a Scottish company to register a charge over English property in England.[34]

An overseas company which has not been registered in Great Britain under Part X of the 1948 Act must still comply with the registration requirements of section 106A. Section 106K will continue to apply, so as to

[32b] *Libertas-Kommerz GmbH, supra.*

[33] This is the current (1972) version. Under the 1961 Act, section 106K applied to floating charges only, and to companies incorporated outside Scotland which had an "established" place of business in Scotland, or where heritable property in Scotland was subject to the charge. The 1972 Act applies to all kinds of registrable charge, does not apply to companies registered in England or Wales (but does apply to Northern Ireland) and does not require the company's place of business to be "established"; the alternative qualification that a floating charge was registrable if it included heritable property in Scotland has been abandoned. A series of "F" forms is prescribed for use under section 106K.

[34] See para. 47–19 note 23a, *supra.*

render an unregistered charge over Scottish property open to challenge, even after the company has ceased to have a place of business in Scotland; on the other hand, if a foreign company with no place of business in Scotland charges Scottish property that charge does not appear to be registrable even if the company subsequently acquires a place of business here. A "liquidator" entitled to challenge the validity of a charge on the grounds of failure to register includes a person appointed under foreign law to a position similar to that of a liquidator in Great Britain.[35]

Penalties

47–30 Failure to comply with sections 106B (duty of the company to register charges), 106C (duty of the company to register charges existing on property acquired), 106I (maintenance of the company's register of charges) or 106J (duty to make the register and copy instruments available for inspection) may result in a default fine being incurred. The maximum penalties have been substantially increased by the Companies Act 1980, Schedule 2.

PRACTICE NOTES

Sasine registration

47–31 A fixed security over Scottish heritable property is invalid unless it has been recorded in the division of the Register of Sasines (property register) for the county where the property is located.[35a] Since the Conveyancing and Feudal Reform (Scotland) Act 1970 the normal method of constituting such a security will be by way of standard security. Recording in the Register of Sasines constitutes the creditor's real right. The process of recording, however, takes several weeks from the date the deed is received and recorded in the presentment book of the Sasines Register, during which time deeds are checked by the officials in order of presentment, the date of presentment being the date of recording if the deed is acceptable. The Keeper of the Register of Sasines will, on request, expedite this process and issue confirmation of recording within a few days of presentment where registration of a charge is to follow.

In the case of a heritable security by a company, confirmation of recording should always be obtained as this will be the "date of creation" of the charge under section 106A (10) (*b*). This will enable the correct date to be inserted in the form for registration under section 106A (1) within the time limit of 21 days.

Under the 1961 Act, s. 5 (2), where the heritable security was intended to rank in priority to a floating charge, it was essential to ensure that the heritable security has been recorded in the Sasines Register before the

---

35 See (on the points in this paragraph) *NV Slavenburg's* v. *Intercontinental Natural Resources Ltd.* (1980) 1 All E.R. 955.

35a If the Land Registration (Scotland) Act 1979 has been applied to that county, see para. 47–32 of the text.

floating charge was registered.[36] This is no longer so vital because the effect of section 5 of the 1972 Act is to rank a fixed security in priority to any floating charge, except a prior floating charge which prohibits such a ranking, provided that the fixed security has been created a real right before crystallisation of the floating charge.

Land Registration (Scotland) Act 1979

47–32 The procedure for constituting real rights in heritable property and heritable securities in Scotland by way of registration in the Register of Sasines is being replaced by registration in the Land Register of Scotland, under the Land Registration (Scotland) Act 1979. In respect of any interest in land which is not a heritable security a real right is constituted by registration, the evidence for which is a "Land Certificate" issued by the Keeper of the Register. In the case of a heritable security the real right of the creditor is also constituted by registration and evidenced by a "Charge Certificate" issued by the Keeper. The new procedure commenced with the County of Renfrew on 6th April 1981, and will gradually be extended to cover the rest of the country.

Where a company creates a fixed charge by way of heritable security within an area to which the Land Registration Act applies, or in respect of which a voluntary registration has occurred, the creditor will apply to the Keeper of the Register for a Charge Certificate, and the date of registration will normally be the date of his application. Registration in the Register of Charges will have to be effected within 21 days of that date. Since the process of issuing a Charge Certificate will normally exceed this period, the Keeper of the Registers of Scotland has established a procedure to issue confirmation of the date of registration of securities granted by a company within a few days of application, to enable registration in the Register of Charges to be effected. Application should be made to the Keeper when the Standard Security is submitted for registration.

[36] See Palmer's *Company Law* (20th ed.), pp. 421, 422.

CHAPTER 48

REMEDIES OF DEBENTURE HOLDERS OR HOLDERS OF CHARGES

In general

48–01 The holder of a debenture or a charge created by a Scottish company has the ordinary remedies available to any creditor, *viz.* to sue for payment in the courts and/or to petition for a winding up. Where the interests of the holders are represented by trustees for debenture holders, the trustees' duties to the holders are those of trustees generally to the beneficiaries of a trust. A reconveyance of property held in security by the trustees to the company may be reduced if void *ab initio* on the grounds that the trustees acted *ultra vires*.[1]

If a receiver is appointed by the holder of a floating charge, it is suggested that the latter is barred from raising an action for payment of the amount secured by the charge, since the receiver's appointment would prevent the company answering such an action by payment. There is, however, nothing to suggest that the appointment of a receiver in Scotland will bar the holder of the charge from petitioning for a winding up.

Receivers (Scotland)

Appointment

48–02 The Companies (Floating Charges and Receivers) (Scotland) Act 1972 introduced, as from November 17, 1972, the facility of appointing a receiver of property belonging to a Scottish company. The office of receiver in Scotland is, however, different in many respects from its English counterpart and precedents of English law on the subject must be treated with caution. The principal differences are as follows:

(a) only the "holder" of a floating charge may appoint or secure the appointment of a receiver;
(b) while it is possible for the instrument creating the floating charge to add to or limit his powers, the powers of a Scottish receiver under statute are extensive and will generally be sufficient;
(c) express power to appoint a receiver need not be taken in the instrument; and
(d) the law referring to receivers in Scotland is wholly statutory, with no origins in common law, being contained in Part II of the 1972 Act.

The introduction of receivership into Scots law is to be welcomed in respect that it removed a basic weakness in the remedies available to the holder of a floating charge. Under the Companies (Floating Charges) (Scotland) Act 1961, the holder of a floating charge could enforce his

[1] *Kidd and Others* v. *Patons Trustees* 1912, S.L.T. 363.

security only by obtaining a winding-up order, to the detriment of the value of the undertaking held as security, apart from being unnecessarily harmful to other interests. This remedy is still available where the appointment of a receiver would be or has proved to be inadequate.[2] If the company is already in liquidation, the holder of a floating charge may, instead of appointing a receiver, claim a preferential ranking in the liquidation.[3]

References in this Chapter, unless otherwise indicated, are to the Act of 1972.

Part VI of the 1948 Act ("Receivers and Managers") does not apply to receivers in Scotland under the 1972 Act (s. 31 (5)).

It may be assumed that references to a floating charge in this Chapter include references to a charge as altered under section 7 (s. 28 (3)).

Circumstances in which receivers may be appointed

48–03 The holder of a floating charge created by a company which the Court of Session has jurisdiction to wind up (whether a company within the meaning of the 1948 Act or not) has power to appoint a receiver (s. 11 (1)), or to apply to the court for such an appointment (s. 11 (2)).

The 1972 Act grants this power not only to holders of floating charges created after its commencement, but also in respect of subsisting floating charges created under the 1961 Act (s. 11 (1)).

The circumstances in which the power may be exercised are as follows (s. 12 (1) and (2)):

(1) the instrument creating the charge (or an instrument of alteration under s. 7) may specify the circumstances in which the holder may either appoint a receiver or apply to the court for such an appointment;

(2) in so far as such instrument does not otherwise provide, the holder may appoint a receiver directly on the occurrence of any of the following events (s. 12 (1)):

(a) the expiry of 21 days after the making of a demand for payment of the whole or any part of the principal sum secured by the charge, without payment having been made;

(b) the expiry of a period of two months during the whole of which interest due and payable under the charge has been in arrears;

(c) the making of an order or the passing of a resolution to wind up the company; or

(d) the appointment of a receiver by virtue of any other floating charge created by the company.

(3) In so far as such instrument does not otherwise provide, the court may appoint a receiver (s. 12 (2)):

(a) on the occurrence of any of the events (a) to (c) above; or

(b) if it is satisfied on the application of the holder that his position is likely to be prejudiced if no such appointment is made.

---

[2] See para, 47–08, *ante*.

[3] *Libertas-Kommerz GmbH* 1978 S.L.T. 222, 225.

It will be observed that it is unnecessary to stipulate for power to appoint a receiver in the relevant instrument. This is obviously essential to make it applicable to charges created under the 1961 Act. The wording of both section 12 (1) and (2), "in so far as not otherwise provided for therein," suggests that restriction on the power of appointment is competent (and essential in respect of section 12 (1) (*a*) in cases where the creditor's power to demand repayment before a stated date is to be restricted). If the charge empowers the holder to appoint a receiver in circumstances which are more beneficial to him than s. 12 (2) the procedure laid down in the deed must be strictly adhered to; where the holder is entitled to appoint a receiver immediately on the issue of a notice of indebtedness (without waiting 21 days as under s. 12 (2) (*a*) signed by one of a group of specified officials, a notice signed by or on behalf of another official (even one senior to those named), or on behalf of one of those named, would not be a valid basis for appointing a receiver.[3a]

Persons who may be appointed as receiver

48–04 Any individual except an undischarged bankrupt[3b] may be appointed as a receiver (s. 11 (3)). One can only deplore the failure to require at least some recognised professional qualification for the exercise of the wide and onerous powers the Act confers.

Joint receivers are competent (s. 11 (5)), but not bodies corporate or a firm under the law of Scotland (s. 11 (3)). Penal sanctions attach to the appointment of a disqualified person or body (s. 11 (4)). Joint receivers must act jointly unless otherwise provided in their instruments of appointment (s. 16 (3)).

One individual may be appointed receiver by virtue of several floating charges (s. 16 (7)).

Mode of appointment

48–05 BY THE HOLDER OF THE CHARGE. Where the holder of a floating charge may appoint a receiver directly by virtue of powers in the charge or under section 12 (1), the power is exercised by means of a validly executed instrument of appointment (s. 13 (1)). The instrument of appointment may be executed either by the holder or by any person duly authorised in writing to execute it on his behalf (s. 13 (4) (*a*)). If the appointment is by the holders of a series of secured debentures, a resolution of the debenture holders is required to authorise a person to execute the instrument on their behalf (s. 13 (4) (*b*)).

If executed by a company the instrument must be executed in accordance with the provisions of section 32 of the Act of 1948 as if it were a contract.[4] Section 32 of the 1948 Act, however, refers to two classes of

---

[3a] *Elwick Bay Shipping Co. Ltd.* v. *Royal Bank of Scotland Ltd.* 1982 S.L.T. 62.

[3b] Or a person disqualified by the court under the Insolvency Act 1976 s. 9 as amended by the Companies Act 1981 s. 94.

[4] s. 13 (3) (*a*).

written contract, *viz.* contracts which under English law require to be executed under seal (s. 32 (1) (*a*)), and all other kinds of written contracts (s. 32 (1) (*b*)). These latter require simply to be signed by any person acting under the authority of the company, express or implied. Presumably the 1972 Act did not intend to introduce to Scotland the exclusively English law concept of a contract under seal, so that an instrument of appointment of a receiver by a company requires to be executed simply by any person expressly or impliedly authorised to act on its behalf. In view of the requirements for execution by an individual (s. 13 (3) (*b*), below) this seems extraordinarily informal. The 1972 Act may have intended to refer to section 32 (4) of the 1948 Act and to require sealing and signature by two officers (or possibly one officer and witnesses), but section 32 (4) refers to *deeds,* not contracts. This ambiguity is most unfortunate. In these circumstances the instrument should be sealed and signed by two officers, as a deed, to avoid any question as to its validity.

If executed by any person other than a company, the instrument of appointment must be executed in the manner required or permitted by the law of Scotland in the case of an attested deed (s. 13 (3) (*b*)). An attested deed in Scots law is a deed signed by the grantor in the presence of two witnesses who also sign, and whose designations, *i.e.* addresses and (usually) occupations, appear on the deed. The words "or permitted by" may refer to the relaxation, in most cases, introduced by the Conveyancing and Feudal Reform (Scotland) Act 1970, s. 44, whereby the grantor need sign on the last page of the deed only; it may also cover notarial execution where the grantor of the deed is blind or unable to write, but the precise scope of this phrase is not clear.

The appointment of a receiver must be notified to the Registrar of Companies and to the company (see paras. 48–06 and 48–17 *infra*).

BY THE COURT. If the holder of a floating charge requires to apply to the court for the appointment of a receiver, the procedure is by petition, served on the company (s. 14 (1)). The court has discretion to make or refuse the appointment, and may require caution (*i.e.* an insurance bond) to be found (s. 14 (2)). The court's interlocutor is equivalent to the instrument of appointment.

Intimation of the appointment to the Registrar and to the company is again necessary (see paras. 48–06 and 48–17 *infra*).

The Court of Session is required to frame Rules of Court to include special provision for cases of urgency (s. 14 (8)); these Rules[5] became effective on March 31, 1973, but do not appear to contain any such "special provision."

Registration of appointments

48–06 The appointment of a receiver requires to be intimated to the Registrar

[5] Rule 218 A of the Rules of the Court of Session. See further McBryde and Dowie "Petition Procedure in the Court of Session" (W. Green & Son Ltd. Edinburgh 1980) p. 15.

of Companies, who enters the particulars in the Register of Charges (ss. 13 (5) and 14 (5)). The Registrar must, however, be satisfied that the appropriate formalities have been complied with.

REGISTRATION OF INSTRUMENT OF APPOINTMENT. When the holder of a floating charge executes an instrument of appointment he must deliver to the Registrar, within seven days of its date, an appropriately certified copy of the instrument, together with a notice (Form 53a (Scot)) giving details of the appointment, including a statement of the circumstances justifying it. The form requires reference to the floating charge and the name of the person entitled to the benefit thereof (or the first-named of several). This may give rise to difficulties where the benefit has been assigned, since the Registrar has no means of checking the assignee's identity, assignations not being recorded in the official register of charges.[6]

REGISTRATION OF APPOINTMENT BY THE COURT. A copy, certified by the clerk of court, of the interlocutor appointing the receiver must be delivered to the Registrar within seven days of its date or such longer period as the court may allow, together with a notice (Form 53b (Scot)) giving particulars (s. 14 (3)). The difficulty as to assignations may not arise, simply because the Registrar is unlikely to question the correctness of the court's order.

If the court has required caution to be found, the Registrar must withhold registration until he receives a certificate by the appropriate officer of the court (*e.g.* the accountant of court) that caution has been found (s. 14 (5)).

Effect of non-registration

Non-registration of the appointment of a receiver carries no sanction other than a possible default fine of £5 per day (ss. 13 (2) and 14 (4)). The failure of the Act to provide adequate sanctions against non-registration or delay is most unfortunate, since inspection of the official register of charges may not yet disclose the fact that a receiver has been appointed.

Date of appointment

48–07 The effective date of appointment of a receiver is the date of execution of the instrument of appointment (s. 13 (6)) or the court's interlocutor (s. 14 (6)).

Effect of appointment of a receiver

The appointment is in respect of such part of the property of the company (including uncalled capital) as is subject to the floating charge (s. 11 (1) and (2)). The directors cease to have power to deal with the property comprised in the receivership.[7] They must keep accounting records under the Companies Act 1976, s. 12.[8]

---

[6] See para. 47–24, *ante*.
[7] *Imperial Hotel (Aberdeen) Ltd.* v. *Vaux Breweries Ltd.* 1978 S.L.T. 113.
[8] *Smiths Ltd.* v. *Middleton* [1979] 3 All E.R. 842.

On appointment the charge crystallises and attaches to the property then subject to it as if it were a fixed security (ss. 13 (7) and 14 (7)). The position is identical to crystallisation on the commencement of winding up.[9] The notice to the Registrar (Forms 53a or b (Scot)) of the appointment requires to state whether the receiver is of the whole or substantially the whole of the company's property or merely of part of its property.

It appears from the terms of section 11 (1) and (2) that the holder of the floating charge cannot restrict the scope of the appointment to a part only of the property subject to the charge.

The appointment of a receiver by instrument of appointment is subject to sections 106A and 322 of the 1948 Act (s. 13 (7)). The holder of a floating charge which is invalid through want of registration under section 106A cannot, therefore, appoint a receiver under section 13. Section 322 provides that a floating charge granted within 12 months of the commencement of winding up is invalid except in respect of actual advances and interest thereon, unless it is proved that the company was solvent.[9a]

For reasons which are not immediately apparent, an appointment by the court under section 14 is not expressed to be subject to either sections 106A or 322. It is, however, inconceivable that an appointment by the court could be valid if the charge on which it proceeds is invalidated by either section.

Powers of receiver

48–08 The receiver's powers may be defined in the floating charge and, in addition, he has the following statutory powers in relation to the property attached by the charge in so far as they are not inconsistent with any provision in that instrument (s. 15 (1)):

(a) to take possession of, collect and get in the property from the company, or any person including a liquidator of the company, and to take any proceedings he thinks expedient for that purpose;
(b) to sell, feu, hire out or otherwise dispose of the property by public roup or private bargain, with or without advertisement;
(c) to borrow money and grant security therefor over the property;
(d) to appoint a solicitor, accountant, or other professionally qualified person to assist him;
(e) to apply to the court for directions;
(f) to bring or defend legal proceedings in the company's name[10];
(g) to refer questions to arbitration;
(h) to effect and maintain insurances;
(i) to use the company's seal;
(j) to act and to execute deeds, receipts and other documents in name of the company;
(k) to draw, accept, etc., bills of exchange or promissory notes in name of the company;
(l) to appoint agents and to employ and discharge servants;

---

[9] See s. 1 (2), para. 47–07, *ante*.
[9a] See para. 87–70, *post*.
[10] *e.g.* to oppose a winding-up petition *(Foxhall & Gyle (Nurseries) Ltd., Ptns.* 1978 S.L.T. (Notes) 29).

(m) to carry out work on the company's property and do anything necessary for its realisation;
(n) to make payments necessary or incidental to his functions;
(o) to carry on the company's business;
(p) to grant and take leases, input and output tenants;
(q) to rank and claim in bankruptcy or liquidation, receive dividends and accede to trust deeds for creditors;
(r) to present or defend a petition for the winding up of the company; and
(s) to do all things incidental to the exercise of his powers.

In terms of section 15 (2) the receiver's powers are subject to the rights of any person who has effectually exercised prior diligence, and to the rights of the holder of a charge ranking prior to or *pari passu* with the floating charge by virtue of which he was appointed. "Effectually executed diligence" in section 15 (2) should be construed as similar in meaning to the provisions of section 327, arising on liquidation. If this were not so, a receiver might be obliged to put the company into liquidation in order to cut down on arrestment under section 327, and this would defeat one of the main purposes of his appointment, namely his power to carry on the business. An arrestment which has not been completed by a decree of furthcoming is not an "effectual diligence." The failure of the 1972 Act to give the holder of an ineffectual diligence preference for his expenses (which he has under s. 327) is presumably an oversight, not an indication of a distinction of principle between the two provisions.[11]

A receiver or manager appointed under the law of any part of the United Kingdom in respect of a floating charge may exercise his powers (*i.e.* the powers given by the jurisdiction in which he has been appointed) in any other part of the United Kingdom so far as their exercise is not inconsistent with the law applicable there (Administration of Justice Act 1977, s. 7, replacing 1972 Act, s. 15 (4)). This would apply to the receiver or manager of an English company with property in Scotland and vice versa. The appointment of a receiver or manager of the English company causes the charge to crystallise over the Scottish property in the same way as a charge by a Scottish company crystallises on the appointment of a receiver. Its effect on prior diligence is also the same.[12]

The statutory powers of a receiver are extensive, and he is accorded wide discretion as to whether he should exercise them and in what manner. The powers expressed in section 15 (1) are capable of being construed as duties, but the nature and extent of the receiver's duties to the various interested parties (company, holder of the charge, other creditors) is not made clear in the Act. It is not indicated whether he must realise the property with all possible speed, or balance the preservation of the company's undertaking against the desire of the holder of the charge to realise his security. Since he is to some extent protected against removal by

[11] *Lord Advocate* v. *Royal Bank of Scotland, etc.*, 1976 S.L.T. 130; 1977 S.C. 155; 1978 S.L.T. 38.
[12] *Gordon Anderson (Plant) Ltd.* v. *Campsie Construction Ltd., etc.*, 1977 S.L.T.7.

the holder of the charge (s. 22 (3), *infra*), it may be assumed he will be regarded as in a fiduciary position similar to a liquidator, and thus be required to act in the interests of all parties so far as they can be reconciled, but his primary duty must be to the holder of the charge.

It has been held[12a] that a receiver can elect whether to take proceedings in his own name under (a) or in name of the company under (f), and if he sues for a debt due to the company in his own name, a plea of compensation which would have been a defence to proceedings in name of the company cannot be raised. This view was disapproved in a later decision [12b] which held that power (a) cannot be used to sue for a debt due to the company, and that a plea of compensation available against the company was available against the receiver suing under power (f), in name of the company even if the debtor acquired the compensating claim after the receiver's appointment, there being no warrant for applying liquidation rules (which would have barred compensation in such circumstances) to receivership. It has also been suggested [12c] that compensation in the latter case should not have been allowed on the basis that the appointment of a receiver operates as a fixed charge over the property concerned (ss. 13(7) and 14 (7)); in the case of book debts this would imply an assignation to the charge holder which would terminate the *concursus debiti et crediti* essential for compensation to operate.

Precedence of and among receivers

48–09 A duly appointed receiver takes precedence over a liquidator, from whom he has power to recover the property charged (s. 15 (1) (*a*)). Since there may be several floating charges created by one company, the Act provides for rules of precedence among the receivers who may be appointed by each holder (s. 16).

As between the holders of floating charges, the receiver appointed in respect of the charge having prior ranking takes precedence and exercises his powers to the exclusion of any other receiver (s. 16 (1)). Receivers appointed in respect of charges having equal ranking are deemed to be joint receivers (s. 16 (2)). Joint receivers may also be appointed by the holder of a single charge (s. 11 (5)). Unless otherwise provided in the instrument or instruments of appointment, joint receivers must act jointly (s. 16 (3)).

The powers of a receiver are suspended as from the date of appointment of a receiver having precedence over him, to such extent as may be necessary to enable the receiver having precedence to exercise his powers (s. 16 (4)). The postponed receiver can, therefore, continue to exercise his powers in so far as they do not conflict with those of the prior receiver, for example over property excluded from the prior charge. If, for any reason (including failure by the prior receiver to act under section 22 (6), *infra*),

---

[12a] *McPhail* v. *Lothian Regional Council* 1981 S.L.T. 173;
[12b] *Taylor Petnr*, 1982 S.L.T. 172;
[12c] "*The Receiver* and Book Debts" 1982 S.L.T. (News) 129.

the prior charge ceases to attach to the property, and is either extinguished or re-floats, the suspended powers of the postponed receiver revive. The suspended receiver is, however, entitled to retain property and papers of the company under his control until he receives a valid indemnity from the prior receiver in respect of expenses, charges and liabilities incurred before suspension, limited to the value of that part of the company's property subject to the charge by virtue of which he was appointed (s. 16 (5)).

Suspension of the receiver's powers does not re-float the charge (s. 16 (7)).

Agency and liability of receivers

48–10 A receiver is the agent of the company in relation to the property attached by the charge (s. 17 (1)). His liability and that of the company are therefore to be ascertained on the normal principles of agency, subject to the provisions of the 1972 Act. He is personally liable on contracts entered into by him unless he contracts as agent under section 17 (1), or unless the contract otherwise provides (s. 17 (2)), but subject to a right of relief recoverable from the property subject to the charge (s. 17 (3)). Suspension of his powers does not relieve him of personal liability, if incurred (s. 17 (2)). Subject to section 23 (2), *infra* a receiver appointed on an invalid charge incurs personal liability.

A receiver whose powers are, or are liable to be, suspended by the appointment of a prior receiver, is in danger of losing the effective benefit of his right of indemnity in respect of personal liability under section 17. The prior receiver may exercise his powers in such a way as to remove or diminish the property of the company from which the postponed receiver hopes to be indemnified. He has, admittedly, his rights of retention or lien under section 16 (5) (*supra*), but these may not be enough to afford complete protection.

A receiver does not incur personal liability on contracts entered into before his appointment which continue in force thereafter (s. 17 (4)).

Effect of appointment or suspension on contracts

48–11 Unless otherwise provided in the contract, a contract entered into by the company before the appointment of a receiver, or a contract entered into by a receiver before suspension of his powers, continues in force thereafter (s. 17 (4) and (5)). The court will not, however, ordain a receiver to perform a contract (entered into by the company before his appointment) where he has no means at his disposal of doing so; in such circumstances the remedy is in damages only.[13]

Remuneration of receivers

48–12 The receiver's remuneration is, in the first instance, for agreement between himself and the holder of the charge by virtue of which he was appointed (s. 18 (1)).

---

[13] *Macleod* v. *Alexander Sutherland Ltd.* 1977 S.L.T. (Notes) 44.

The receiver's remuneration will appear in the regular annual abstracts circulated under section 25 (2) (below), and if agreement cannot be reached, or the amount is disputed, the auditor of the Court of Session may fix his remuneration. Application to the auditor of court must be in writing within one month of receipt of the abstract (s. 18 (3)), and can be made by the receiver, the holder of any charge, the company or its liquidator (s. 18 (2)). The receiver must account for any excess if the auditor fixes his remuneration at less than the sum agreed or retained (s. 18 (4)).

Payments and distributions

48–13 When a receiver is appointed and the company is not at the time of his appointment being wound up, he must pay out of any assets in his hands, in priority to the claims of the holder of the floating charge, claims which would have ranked as preferential debts in a winding up,[14] provided that they have come to his notice within six months after he has advertised for claims in the *Edinburgh Gazette* and a local newspaper (s. 19 (1) and (2)). It follows that the receiver will arrange for such advertisement early in his period of office, and cannot safely make payments to the holder of the floating charge for at least six months thereafter.

In construing the relevant provisions of the 1948 Act, the date of appointment of the receiver is substituted for the date of commencement of the winding up (s. 19 (3) and (4)).

The receiver has a right of relief in respect of any payments made under section 19 out of the assets available for payment of ordinary creditors (s. 19 (5)).

In addition to the preferential creditors protected under section 19, the claims of the holder of the floating charge are postponed to certain other creditors (s. 20 (1)), *viz.*:

(a) Holders of prior or *pari passu* fixed securities over the property subject to the floating charge;

(b) Persons who have effectually executed diligence over such property[15];

(c) Creditors in respect of liabilities incurred by the receiver; and

(d) The receiver in respect of his remuneration, expenses and liabilities.

Subject to the foregoing, the receiver is to pay moneys received by him to the holder of the floating charge on account of the debt secured (s. 20 (2)). Any surplus is to be paid in accordance with their respective rights and interests to any other receiver, the holder of a fixed security over the property subject to the floating charge, or the company or its liquidator (s. 20 (3)). If any dispute arises, or if the receiver cannot get a proper receipt or discharge, he must consign the amount in question in a Scottish bank in the name of the accountant of court for behoof of the person or persons entitled thereto (s. 20 (3)).

---

[14] Companies Act 1948, s. 319. See para. 87–49, *post.*

[15] See para. 48–08, *supra.*

If the receiver wishes to dispose of property which is subject to any charge or encumbrance, or to effectual diligence, held by another creditor, he will normally require that creditor's consent. If consent cannot be obtained he may apply to the court for authority to sell free from such encumbrance or diligence (s. 21 (1)). The court's power to grant authority is discretionary and it may impose conditions; consent cannot be given, however, if there is a prior fixed charge on the property which has not been met or provided for in full (s. 21 (2)). For the procedure in the Court of Session see Rules of the Court of Session para. 218A.

If the court authorises a sale under section 21, the receiver will grant an appropriate document of transfer or conveyance and, on the purchaser completing his title in the appropriate way, the property is freed from the encumbrance or diligence in question (s. 21 (3)).

The procedure under section 21 for dispensing with his consent does not prejudice the creditor's right to rank for the debt in a winding up (s. 21 (4)).

Resignation and removal of a receiver, re-floating

48–14 A receiver appointed by instrument of appointment is at liberty to resign, but he must give one month's written notice to (a) the holders of *all* floating charges; (b) the company or its liquidator, and (c) the holders of any fixed security affecting the property subject to the charge by virtue of which he was appointed (s. 22 (1)).

A receiver appointed by the court may resign only with the authority of the court and on such conditions as it may impose (s. 22 (2)).

A receiver can only be removed by the court on cause shown, whether he was appointed by the court or directly by the holder of the charge. In terms of the Act (s. 22 (3)) only the holder of the charge by virtue of which he was appointed may apply to the court for his removal. It is suggested, however, that there may be circumstances in which the Court of Session might, in the exercise of its *nobile officium*, entertain a petition for removal by the company or another creditor.

On his appointment ceasing, the receiver has a right of indemnity in respect of his expenses, charges and liabilities out of the property subject to the charge (s. 22 (4)).

If he ceases to act otherwise than by death, the receiver must notify the Registrar within seven days (Form 57A (Scot)). On his removal by the court, the holder of the charge must give similar notice. The Registrar enters the notice in the register of charges. A default fine may be incurred if notice is not timeously given (s. 22 (5)). It is not clear whether in the event of removal by the court, both the receiver and the holder of the charge have to give notice, but presumably notice by the holder of the charge alone will suffice in practice. If the receiver dies, there is no provision for notifying the Registrar or any other party of this fact.

Whereas resignation involves notice to interested parties (above), the Act does not stipulate intimation to the company or to the holders of other charges of any petition for removal but this may be inferred from the general Rules of Court applicable to petitions. When the receiver has completed his duties and discharged the claims of the holder of the charge by virtue of which he was appointed, it appears he must formally resign, applying to the court for permission if he was appointed by it.

If one month after the receiver has been removed or has ceased to act, no other receiver has been appointed by the holder of the same charge, the floating charge re-floats (s. 22 (6)). Re-floating is automatic on expiry of the time limit, and the property ceases to be attached by the charge.

Powers of the court

48–15 In addition to its powers as to the appointment and removal of receivers, the court is given further powers under section 23:

(1) The holder of a floating charge by virtue of which a receiver has been appointed, may apply for directions on any matter connected with the receiver's functions. By inference from section 15 (1) (*e*) the receiver may also apply for directions.

(2) If a receiver is appointed by virtue of a floating charge which is found to be invalid, he may apply to the court for relief from personal liability for any act or omission which would have been proper, but for the invalidity. The court has discretion as to granting relief, and may impose conditions. The court may transfer liability to the person making the invalid appointment. For the procedure in the Court of Session see Rules of the Court of Session para. 218A.

Publication and notification of appointment of a receiver

48–16 Where a receiver has been appointed, every invoice, order for goods or business letter issued by or on behalf of the company or the receiver or the company's liquidator, on which the company's name appears, must contain a statement that a receiver has been appointed (s. 24 (1)). Failure may incur a default fine of £20 (s. 24 (2)).

In addition to notification to the Registrar of Companies under sections 13 (1) or 14 (3) (*supra*), the receiver must send notice of his appointment to the company forthwith (s. 25 (1); Form 108 (Scot)), but the only consequence of his failure to do so is a possible fine of £5 per day.

These provisions are similar to those applicable in England.[16]

Statements and returns to be made to and by a receiver

48–17 The provisions of sections 25 and 26 of the 1972 Act are similar to the equivalent provisions applicable to receivers and managers in England.[17] The Scottish provisions, however, apply to every receiver and not merely to a receiver of "the whole or substantially the whole of the property of the company," and they also differ in some details. The provisions of English

---

[16] Companies Act 1948, ss. 370 and 372.
[17] Companies Act 1948, ss. 372 and 373.

law which apply to receivers not subject to section 372[18] consequently have no equivalent in Scotland.

The first step after appointment is for the receiver to give notice of his appointment to the company (s. 25 (1) (*a*) Form 108 (Scot)). The company must submit to him a statement of its affairs in the prescribed form (Forms 109 (Scot) and 109A (Scot)), within 14 days of receipt of the notice of appointment or such longer period as the court or the receiver in writing, may permit (s. 25 (1) (*b*)).

The statement under section 25 must show as at the date of the receiver's appointment, particulars of the company's assets and liabilities, and of the creditors and the securities held by them (s. 26 (1)). The statement must be verified by a statutory declaration by at least one director and the secretary of the company. Alternatively, certain past officers, promoters or employees may be required to submit and verify the statement, subject to the direction of the court (if the receiver was appointed by the court) or the Secretary of State (if the appointment is by instrument) (s. 26 (2) and (4)). The reasonable expenses of preparing the statement and statutory declaration are to be paid by the receiver (s. 26 (3)).

Within two months after receiving this statement, the receiver must send to the Registrar, and to the court, if he was appointed by the court, a copy of the statement and of any comment he sees fit to make. Within the same period he must also send to the Registrar a summary of the statement and of his comments, to the company a copy of his comments (or a notice that he has none) and to the holder of the floating charge or any trustee for debenture holders on whose behalf he was appointed and (so far as traceable) to all such debenture holders, a copy of the summary of statement and comments (s. 25 (1) (*c*)).

The appointment of a receiver to act along with an existing receiver, or in place of one who has died or ceased to act, does not of itself bring the provisions as to initial statement and comments into effect (s. 25 (4)).

The receiver must also within two months after the end of each year, and within two months after he ceases to act as receiver, send to the Registrar, to the company, to the holders of *all* charges, to any trustees for debenture holders on whose behalf he was appointed, and (so far as traceable) to all such debenture holders, an abstract of his receipts and payments during the relevant period and the aggregate amount of receipts and payments during preceding periods (s. 25 (2); Form 57 (Scot)). The court, if he was appointed by the court, or the Secretary of State, may extend the period beyond two months.

The receiver remains liable to account for his intromissions to the persons entitled to require an accounting from him on general principles of

---

[18] Companies Act 1948, s. 374.

law (s. 25 (6)). This includes the company itself, and the receiver must provide its directors with sufficient information to enable them to prepare statutory accounts.[19]

Penalties may be imposed in case of default by the receiver or the company (ss. 25 (7) and 26 (5)) and application may be made to the court to enforce compliance by the receiver (s. 27; Rules of the Court of Session para. 218A).

Appointment of a receiver and other acts on behalf of a series of debenture holders

48–18 A floating charge securing a debenture or series of debentures may have no one holder entitled to appoint a receiver and to perform other functions assigned to the holder. If the relevant document provides for a receiver to be appointed by a specified person or body, he or it is to be treated as the holder of the charge in Part II of the 1972 Act. In the absence of any such nomination and in the case of a series of debentures, the trustees are to be regarded as the holder. If there are no trustees, the holder is a specified majority of debenture holders (s. 28 (2)).

Fixed securities; power of sale

48–19 The holder of a fixed security over Scottish property will require to reserve power in his security deed to sell or otherwise realise the property.[20] He has no power to appoint a receiver.

In the case of a fixed security over heritable property, the remedies of the creditor are now governed by the Conveyancing and Feudal Reform (Scotland) Act 1970. This Act provides for a statutory power of sale in every such security and other remedies. The purchaser is protected against reduction of his title, any remedy being restricted to a claim for damages by the debtor against the seller.[21]

---

[19] *Cf. Smiths Ltd.* v. *Middleton* [1979] 3 All E.R. 842 (decided on the equivalent English provisions).

[20] *United Dominions Trust* v. *Site Preparations Ltd. (No.1)* 1978 S.L.T. (Sh. Ct.) 14.

[21] *Imperial Hotel (Aberdeen) Ltd.*, v. *Vaux Breweries Ltd.* 1978 S.L.T. 113.

[72] [illegible]

Part Five

MEMBERSHIP OF THE COMPANY

A. POSITION OF MEMBERS

Chapter 49

THE STATUS OF MEMBERSHIP

The meaning of membership; "members" and "shareholders"

49–01 Every company is composed of members, though in the contemplation of law it is an entity distinct from its constituent members. In the case of a company limited by shares, a member is a person holding shares in the company; there can be no membership, *i.e.* proprietary relationship to a company, otherwise than through the medium of shareholding. Consequently the terms "member" and "shareholder" are synonymous, apart from the now exceptional case of the bearer of a share warrant who is a shareholder but is not a member because he is not registered in the register of members.[1]

It is in his capacity of member that the shareholder exercises the rights, enjoys the benefits and is subject to the obligations which the holding of shares carries. Although the rights of a member do not necessarily depend on the number of shares he holds,[2] normally the quantum of membership in a company limited by shares is determined by the number of shares which the member holds, in conjunction with the provisions in the memorandum and articles defining the rights and duties carried by the shares. Assuming that a company has only one class of shares, a member holding 10 shares has, on principle, 10 times the rights of a member holding one share, and at the same time is liable to contribute 10 times the amount which the latter has to contribute.

What constitutes membership

49–02 We have now to consider what it is which constitutes membership in a company. This is a point of first importance in the law of companies, and to answer it we must turn to section 26 of the 1948 Act,[3] which provides that the members of a company are:

(1) the subscribers to the memorandum of the company (they become

---

[1] See s. 26 (2). The articles may provide that, in certain aspects or all, the bearer of a warrant may *be deemed* to be a member (1948 Act, s. 112 (5)); see also para. 39–31, *ante*.

[2] *e.g.* the right to vote on a show of hands; the right to receive a copy of the memorandum and articles (1948 Act, s. 24); the right to receive copies of the balance sheet and auditors' report (1948 Act, s. 158 (1)); the right to petition for the alternative remedy (1980 Act, s. 75) or for a compulsory winding up (1948 Act, ss. 222, 224). See further on individual and corporate membership rights, paras. 58–02 *et seq.*, *post*.

[3] The section applies also to guarantee companies and unlimited companies.

members of the company upon its incorporation even though they are not registered in the register of members) (s. 26 (1))[4];

(2) other persons who have agreed to become members (they become members upon registration in the register of members) (s. 26 (2)).

These, and only these, can strictly be called members in the sense of having acquired the full status of membership.[5]

A person may, therefore, become a member in any of the following ways:

(1) By subscribing the memorandum of association, *upon the registration of the company*.[6]

(2) By agreeing with the company to take a share *and being placed on the register of members*.

(3) By taking a transfer of a share *and being placed on the register of members*.

(4) By succeeding to the estate of a deceased or bankrupt member *and being placed on the register of members*.

(5) By allowing his name to be on the register of members or otherwise holding himself out or allowing himself to be held out as a member.[7]

Subscribers to the memorandum

49–03 Every subscriber to the memorandum of association becomes a member *ipso facto* on the incorporation of the company, and liable as the holder of whatever number of shares he has subscribed for. "It is plain," said Lord Cairns in *Evans' Case*,[8] "that the original subscribers are, by the Act of Parliament, deemed to have taken the shares set opposite their names," the object being that the public might rely with confidence on the subscribers of the memorandum becoming members of the company.[9] In the case of the subscribers of the memorandum, therefore, no allotment is required,[10] and no entry on the register of members is necessary in order to constitute membership.[11] The subscriber is bound to take the shares from the company, and to pay for them on calls duly made like any other shareholder.[12] He cannot in satisfaction of this obligation take a transfer of fully paid shares from another member; the only way he can possibly escape liability is by showing that all the shares have been allotted to

---

4 In a company formed as a public company persons being appointed directors who have signed an undertaking to take and pay for their qualification shares are in the same position as the subscribers of the memorandum (1948 Act, s. 181 (2)).

5 *Nicol's Case* (1885) 29 Ch.D. 421.

6 See para 12–02, *ante*.

7 See paras. 49–05, 50–13, *post*.

8 (1867) L.R. 2 Ch. 427, 430.

9 And see *Migotti's Case* (1867) L.R. 4 Eq. 238.

10 *Re London and Provincial, etc., Co*. (1877) 5 Ch.D. 525.

11 *Nicol's Case* (1885) 29 Ch.D. 421; *Alexander* v. *Automatic Telephone Co*. [1900] 2 Ch. 56, 63.

12 *Alexander* v. *Automatic, etc., Co., supra*.

others.[13] In *Re Esparto Trading Co.*[14] a subscriber who had not been placed on the register was nevertheless held liable after a lapse of nine years for the shares for which he had subscribed.

But where the subscriber showed that his subscription was intended to be on behalf of his firm, and the shares were allotted to the firm, it was held that, on the facts of the case, there was only one agreement to take shares, and that the subscriber's obligation was accordingly discharged when his firm took the shares for which he had subscribed the memorandum.[15]

After the incorporation of the company a subscriber cannot repudiate on the ground of misrepresentation,[16] nor, it is believed, has the court jurisdiction to order the rectification of the list of subscribers.[17]

While in the case of subscribers the entry in the register of members is not an essential condition of membership, such entry is mandatory, since section 26 (1) requires the company on registration to enter the names of the subscribers in its register of members; this section does not, however, contain a criminal sanction, such as a default fine, if the company fails to comply with its provisions.[18]

Other members

49–04 In the case of members other than the subscribers to the memorandum two essential conditions have to be satisfied to constitute a person a member:

(1) an agreement to become a member; and
(2) entry on the register.

These two conditions are cumulative: unless they are both satisfied, the person in question has not acquired the status of member.

Thus, an agreement to become a member alone does not create the status of membership; it is a condition precedent to the acquisition of such status that the shareholder's name should be entered on the register.[19] Conversely, the company is not entitled to place a person's name on the register without his having agreed to become a member; a person improperly registered without his assent is not bound thereby and may have his name removed from the register.[20]

---

[13] *Mackley's Case* (1875) 1 Ch.D. 247; *Evans' Case, ante.*
[14] (1879) 12 Ch.D. 191.
[15] *Dunster's Case* [1894] 3 Ch. 473.
[16] *Re Metal Constituents Co.* [1902] 1 Ch. 707; this decision is based on the doctrine that the right is lost when third parties are affected (*i.e.* by reliance on the memorandum). It follows that, if no third party has yet been affected, the right to repudiate should not be lost even after incorporation but the existence of the company as a legal person would not be affected thereby (s. 15 (1)).
[17] On the analogy of *Scott* v. *Frank F. Scott (London)* [1940] Ch. 794, which dealt with the rectification of the articles.
[18] Contrast this with s. 110 (1) and (4).
[19] *Nicol's Case* (1885) 29 Ch.D. 421; *Musselwhite* v. *C. H. Musselwhite & Son Ltd.* [1962] Ch. 964; see para. 39–04, *ante*.
[20] As to rectification of the register, see para. 50–14, *post*.

The agreement to take shares in the case of allotment and of transfer

A person desirous of acquiring shares may express his agreement to do so in one of two forms. He may apply to the company for shares and may have them allotted to him,[21] or he may have the shares transferred[22] to him in pursuance of a contract of sale or other transaction. There is no difference, as Chitty J. said in *Nicol's Case*,[23] between a contract to take shares and any other contract. A formal contract is not necessary. If, in substance, an agreement is made, the form is not material.[24]

The agreement to take shares in the case of transmission

Here again the company is not entitled without his consent to place the name of the person who may become the shareholder in consequence or by reason of the death or bankruptcy of a member, or any other event constituting transmission[25] on the register of members.

The articles often provide that such a person is put to an election, *viz*. to be registered himself as holder of the share or to have some other person so registered as his nominee or as transferee. In the former case, the agreement to be registered has normally to be signified in writing; in the latter case it has to be effected by the execution of a transfer to that other person. The articles further often authorise the directors upon certain conditions to withhold the payment of dividends, bonuses or other moneys payable in respect of the share until these requirements have been complied with.[26]

Examples of agreements to take shares

49–05 (a) A applies to the company for an allotment of a specified number of shares, and agrees to accept the same or any less number that may be allotted to him. In response to this application, the directors resolve that a specified number of shares be allotted to him, and notice of such allotment is given to him. This constitutes the agreement, and his name should at once be entered on the register.

(b) The company allots or offers to A a specified number of shares, and A notifies to the company his acceptance of the shares so offered. The agreement is complete, and A's name should be entered on the register.

(c) A authorises some agent to apply for shares on his behalf, and the agent applies accordingly. The shares are allotted to A, and notice is given to him as above, and he is duly registered.

(d) A, being the holder of shares, transfers them by an instrument complying with the articles of the company to B; B takes the transfer to the company, and the company passes it and places B's name on the register.

---

21 See para. 22–01, *ante*.
22 See para. 39–02, *ante*.
23 (1885) 29 Ch.D. 421.
24 *Ritso's Case* (1877) 4 Ch.D. 782. The same is true in Scots law: *Jackson, etc*. 1902, 10 S.L.T. 279, 281.
25 *e.g.* a vesting order under the Trading with the Enemy Act 1939.
26 See arts. 30–32.

In this case, B becomes a member in respect of the shares comprised in the transfer.

(e) A accepts office as a director of the company. The regulations of the company state that the qualification of a director is so many shares, and that, unless he acquires such qualification within (say) a month after the incorporation of the company, he is to be deemed to have agreed to take the shares from the company, and is to be registered accordingly. A does not take up the shares within the month, and shortly afterwards he is placed on the register by the officers of the company as the holder of shares. He thereby becomes a member in respect of those shares. If by accepting the office he can be regarded as in effect agreeing to become a director on the terms that he takes up the shares, it can be assumed that by accepting the office he has applied for the shares and by placing his name on the register the company has accepted his offer.[27]

(f) A, who has not applied for shares, is informed that he has been registered as a holder of a specified number of shares in a company. He signs a proxy paper in respect of the shares, or otherwise acts as the owner of them. He is estopped from denying that he is the holder of those shares.[28]

(g) A applies for shares on the footing that he is not to be liable thereon for the full amount, and the company allots shares which involve the full liability. A nevertheless exercises acts of ownership, *e.g.* by selling some and appointing proxies. A is a member and is bound to pay the full amount for the shares.[29]

The cases under the last two heads come to this: that a person is to be regarded as a member if his name is on the register of members with his consent, or if he is estopped from denying that he is registered with his consent.[30] He may not have applied for the shares. They may have been placed there without his consent and contrary to his wishes, but if he assents to his name being on the register, he is to be considered a member of the company.

Mere entry of a person's name on the company's register, however, without agreement or assent is not enough. Thus, if a director resigns before the time for taking up his qualification shares has expired, and the company has, notwithstanding, entered his name on the register, without his assent, as the holder of the qualification shares, he may compel the company to take his name off the register.[31] So, too, if a person's name is put on the register upon the application of some person professing to act as his agent, but without any authority in fact, the company can be compelled to remove his name.[32] Or, again, where a person applies for shares, but

---

27 *The Kingsburgh Motor Construction Co.* v. *Scott*, 1902, 10 S.L.T. 424.
28 *Crawley's Case* (1869) L.R. 4 Ch. 322.
29 *Re Railway Time Tables, etc., Co.* (1889) 42 Ch.D. 98.
30 See para. 50–13, *post*.
31 *Salisbury-Jones and Dale's Case* [1894] 3 Ch. 356.
32 *Ormerod's Case* [1894] 2 Ch. 474.

withdraws his application before acceptance, if, nevertheless, the company allots shares and puts his name on the register, he may have it taken off.[33]

A person improperly registered as a transferee of a share is not bound and may have his name taken off the register.[34]

Specific performance[35]

49–06 The court has jurisdiction to decree specific performance of a contract by a person to take, or by a company to allot, shares[36] but the matter is one of judicial discretion, and if, before the action is brought, all the shares have been allotted to other persons, the only remedy of a plaintiff claiming an allottment is an action for damages for breach of contract.[37] A company may, by delay, disentitle itself from obtaining specific performance.[38] The company cannot, however, compel performance of an agreement to take shares to which it is not a party.[39]

Who may be a member

English law

49–07 A foreigner may take shares,[40] but in time of war the power of voting of a person who is an enemy,[41] and his right to receive notices, is suspended,[42] and he may cease for the time being to be a member altogether.[43]

A person who is not *sui juris*, such as a minor or person of unsound mind, can become a member, but subject to the ordinary rules of contract, so that the contract is voidable,[44] *i.e.* until it is disaffirmed, the contract remains valid.

Consequently, a transfer to a minor is good provided that the company registers the transfer, which it has a power to refuse. Even if the registration takes place and the company later learns that the transferee is a minor, it may repudiate the registration and retain the name of the transferor. A

---

[33] *Hebb's Case* (1867) L.R. 4 Eq. 9; *Truman's Case* [1894] 3 Ch. 272.
[34] *Heritage's Case* (1869) L.R. 9 Eq. 5; *Cartmell's Case* (1874) L.R. 9 Ch. 691.
[35] The following paragraph would also hold for the equivalent Scottish remedy of specific implement.
[36] *New Brunswick, etc., Land Co.* v. *Muggeridge* (1860) 1 Dr. & Sm. 363; *Oriental Inland Steam Co.* v. *Briggs* (1861) 31 L.J.Ch. 241; *Odessa Tramways Co.* v. *Mendel* (1878) 8 Ch.D. 235.
[37] *Ferguson* v. *Wilson* (1866) L.R. 2 Ch. 77.
[38] *Nicol's Case* (1885) 29 Ch.D. 421.
[39] *Myles* v. *City of Glasgow Bank*, 1879 6R. 718.
[40] *Princess of Reuss* v. *Bos* (1871) L.R. 5 H.L. 176, 193.
[41] Speaking generally, an alien enemy is at common law a person voluntarily residing in enemy territory. See Clive M. Schmitthoff, *The English Conflict of Laws* (3rd ed., 1954), pp. 445 *et seq.*, where the definiton of an alien enemy at common law and of an enemy under the Trading with the Enemy Act 1939 is discussed.
[42] *Robson* v. *Premier Oil and Pipe Line Co. Ltd.* [1915] 2 Ch. 124 (C.A.); *Re Anglo-International Bank Ltd.* [1943] Ch. 233.
[43] See Trading with the Enemy Act 1939, s. 7; *Re Pharaon et Fils* [1916] 1 Ch. 1.
[44] *Hamilton* v. *Vaughan-Sherrin, etc., Co.* [1894] 3 Ch. 589; *Steinberg* v. *Scala (Leeds) Ltd.* [1923] 2 Ch. 452.

minor has a like power to repudiate a contract to take shares at any time during his minority or within a reasonable time after attaining his majority.[45] What constitutes a reasonable time depends on the circumstances of each case and any act after attaining majority affirming the contract or the acceptance of any benefit will preclude the right to repudiate. This power to repudiate is lost when the company is wound up unless the liquidator consents. Upon any such repudiation a minor can recover sums he has paid the company in respect of the shares provided that there was a total failure of consideration. If the shares were of any value he cannot recover money which he has paid although he can resist any further calls.[46]

Until repudiation either by the company or the minor, a minor has the full powers of membership.[47] A transferor to a minor remains liable for all future calls on such shares so long as they are held by the minor even though the transferor may have been ignorant of the minority. A transfer by the minor to another person will relieve the original transferor of liability on the shares thus transferred and he will cease to be on the "B" list one year after his original transfer of those shares.[48]

If a purchaser procures shares to be transferred into the name of a minor he will liable himself to indemnify the transferor against any calls that may be made upon such transferor, but the true purchaser will not be able to obtain a transfer of the shares into his own name unless the name of the minor was used as a mere alias. A director who procures an allotment to a minor may be liable for future calls to the company and may be put on the list of contributories.[49] As to whether such an allotment is an advancement, see *Re Shephard, Cartwright* v. *Shephard.*[50]

A bankrupt may be a member of a company; as long as he is on the register of members, he is entitled to vote[51] and to make use of the rights of a minority shareholder.[52]

Scots law

49–08 The position of foreigners, enemy aliens, persons of unsound mind and bankrupt persons is as stated above in English law.

In Scots law, with the foregoing exceptions, a person attains full contractual capacity at age 18.[53] Under that age he is a pupil to age 12 (in the case

---

45 *Cork & Bandon Ry.* v. *Cazenove* (1847) 10 Q.B. 935; *Birkenhead, etc., Ry.* v. *Pilcher* (1850) 5 Exch. 114; and the cases quoted in the preceding note.

46 *Lumsden's Case* (1868) L.R. 4 Ch. 31, 34; *Ebbett's Case* (1870) L.R. 5 Ch. 302; *Capper's Case* (1868) L.R. 3 Ch. 458; *Re Yeoland Consols (No. 2)* (1888) 58 L.T. 922; *Symons' Case* (1870) L.R. 5 Ch. 298; *Steinberg* v. *Scale (Leeds) Ltd.* [1923] 2 Ch. 452.

47 *Capper's Case* (1868) L.R. 3 Ch. 458; *Pugh and Sharman's Case* (1872) L.R. 13 Eq. 566.

48 *Gooch's Case* (1872) 8 Ch.App. 266.

49 *Re Crenver and Wheal Abraham United Mining Co., ex p. Wilson* (1872) 8 Ch.App. 45; *Richardson's Case* (1875) L.R. 19 Eq. 588; *Manley's Case* (1890) 2 Meg. 74.

50 [1953] Ch. 728.

51 *Morgan* v. *Gray* [1953] Ch. 83; see para. 39–37, *ante*.

52 *Birch* v. *Sullivan* [1957] 1 W.L.R. 1247; see para. 58–23, *post*.

53 Age of Majority (Scotland) Act 1969.

of a girl) or 14 (in the case of a boy) then a minor to age 18. Pupils have no contractual capacity sufficient to contract for the subscription or acquisition of shares, but such contracts may be entered into on their behalf by their legal guardian (called a *tutor*), normally father or mother.

Minors are in a different position. If a minor is living independently (*i.e.* is *forisfamiliated*), or if he holds himself out as of full age, he has full capacity. The same applies if he is in business and the contract relates to the business. If, however, he has a legal guardian (now called a *curator*) he will normally contract with the curator's consent.

A pupil or minor who contracts validly to subscribe for or acquire shares has the benefit of being able to reduce the contract on the ground of *minority and enorm lesion* not only during pupillarity or minority but also during the *quadriennium utile*, *i.e.* until age 22. This right is, however, lost in the case of business contracts, holding out as full age, or if, on attaining majority, he ratifies the contract knowing of his right of reduction. *Enorm lesion* does not simply mean loss, the minor has to show that the contract was not a reasonable one at the time. He will be able to satisfy the court on this more easily if he had no curator.

It will be appreciated that in principle a pupil or a minor can acquire shares by subscription or purchase,[54] but there are risks for the other party (company or transferor) if the investment proves to be unwise.

Companies as members of companies

49–09 A COMPANY MAY BE A MEMBER OF ANOTHER COMPANY. On principle and subject to the qualifications stated later, a company, if so authorised by its memorandum of association,[55] can be a member of another company.

A COMPANY HOLDING ITS OWN SHARES. This topic is treated in Chapter 37, *ante*, which is entitled "Acquisition by a company of its own shares."

A COMPANY CANNOT HOLD SHARES IN ITS OWN HOLDING COMPANY. Further, subject to certain exceptions, a company cannot be a member of its own holding company and any allotment or transfer of shares in a company to its subsidiary or a nominee for its subsidiary is void (1948 Act, s. 27 (1) and (4)).[56] The terms "holding company" and "subsidiary" have, in this connection, the same meaning as in section 154 of the 1948 Act. The reason for the prohibition in section 27, which was first introduced into company law by the legislation culminating in the Act of 1948, is to prevent the "trafficking" in its own shares by the company by indirect means, but this purpose

[54] See, *e.g. Inland Revenue* v. *Wilson* 1927 S.C. 733; 1927 S.L.T. 463 (affd. 1928 S.C. (H.W.) 42; 1928 S.L.T. 374).

[55] *Re Barned's Banking Co.* (1867) L.R. 3 Ch. 105, 112.

[56] The provision applies to guarantee companies and unlimited companies, *mutatis mutandis* (s. 27 (5)).

has been achieved only partially since the company is still not barred from holding its own shares through nominees.

The prohibitions of section 27 (1) and (4) do not apply where the subsidiary (or its nominee) is concerned as personal representative or trustee unless the holding company or its subsidiary is beneficially interested in the trust, except by way of security issued in the ordinary way of business which includes the lending of money (s. 27 (2)).

A subsidiary which was a member of its holding company at the commencement of the Act[57] may continue to be a member, but with no power to vote at the meetings of the shareholders, or of any class thereof, of the holding company (s. 27 (3)).

49–10 Section 27 contains a notable gap: it does not provide what is to happen if company A, on becoming the subsidiary of company B *after the commencement of the Act*, already holds shares in B. The section does not provide that the subsidiary is obliged to sell the "pre-acquired" shares in its holding company, nor is the continued holding of those shares declared to be unlawful or made subject to criminal sanction. On the other hand, the section provides categorically that the subsidiary "*cannot*" be a member of its holding company. It is believed that the prohibitions of section 27 apply only after the relationship of holding and subsidiary companies has been constituted between the two companies in question. It follows that the section does not apply to pre-acquired shares, and that the subsidiary can even vote with these shares at the meetings of the holding company. On the other hand, if the holding company, after acquiring this status *vis-à-vis* the other company, issues bonus shares to its shareholders, the company is prevented by section 27 from accepting such allotment.

In the practice of the take-over panel, when company B makes company A a subsidiary by acquiring its shares, any shares which company A already owns in company B are regarded as assets acquired by company B and company B will be treated as acquiring its own shares.[58]

In Scotland a defender may be subjected to the jurisdiction of the Scottish courts by arrestment *ad fundandam jurisdictionem* of incorporeal moveables within the jurisdiction, such as shares in a Scottish company registered in the name of the defender. If the pursuer is successful in the principal action he may ultimately arrest in execution and obtain a decree of forthcoming which would entitle him, *inter alia*, to take possession of the subjects arrested. A held shares in H, the parent company of L. Both H and L were registered in Scotland and A was resident in England. L raised an action for payment against A in the Court of Session and arrested A's shares in H *ad fundandam jurisdictionem*. A contended that the arrestment was ineffective because section 27 (1) prevented L from taking possession of the subjects arrested. It was held that although section 27 (1) would

---

[57] July 1, 1948 (see s. 462 (2)).

[58] *Cf.* the City Panel report on the *P. R. Grimshawe & Co., Grimshawe-Windsor Merger* [1973] J.B.L. 46.

prevent L from having the shares in H adjudged to it, the arrestment was effective because L could use the alternative procedure of having them sold to satisfy L's claim. The fact that the shares arrested were readily marketable assisted the pursuer, but the opinions suggest that even had this not been the case, procedure would have been available to prevent section 27 (1) being an obstacle.[59]

Convertible debentures

49–11 Holders of convertible debentures are not members until their debentures have been converted into shares and they are duly registered as shareholders. Where the terms of issue give the debenture holders an absolute right to conversion in the case of a take-over offer, the "scheme or contract involving the transfer of shares" within the meaning of section 209 (1) of the 1948 Act involves not only the shares then existing but also the conversion shares, *i.e.* the shares which result from the exercise, by the debenture holders, of their right of conversion. Conversion shares are only shares with respect to which the debenture holders have, in fact, exercised their right of conversion. In determining who is an assenting or a dissenting shareholder under section 209, the conversion shares have to be taken into account but a debenture holder who has not exercised his right of conversion and remained a creditor falls into neither of these categories.[60]

Cesser of membership

49–12 A person may cease to be a member of a company—

(1) by transferring his shares to another person. In such a case, the transferor ceases to be a member so soon as the transferee is registered, but not before. After registration the transferor is still liable to be placed on the B list of contributories as a past member, if the company is wound up within a year[61];
(2) by his shares being forfeited[62];
(3) by his shares being sold by the company under some provision in its articles (*e.g.* for enforcing a lien), and by the purchaser being registered as holder in his place;
(4) by death; but in such a case the deceased member's estate remains liable until the registration of some person entitled under a transfer from his executors or administrators[63];
(5) by a valid surrender[64];

---

59 *Stenhouse London Ltd.* v. *Allwright* 1972 S.L.T. 255; S.C. 209; 1972 S.L.T. 255.
60 *In Re Sims Securities Trust Ltd.* [1971] 1 W.L.R. 1455.
61 *Stanhope's Case* (1866) 1 Ch.App. 161; *Heritage's Case* (1869) L.R. 9 Eq. 5; and see paras. 85–45 and 87–39, *post.*
62 *Dawes' Case* (1868) L.R. 6 Eq. 232; and see para. 41–02, *ante.*
63 *Heward* v. *Wheatley* (1853) 3 De G.M. & G. 628; *Baird's Case* (1870) 5 Ch.App. 725.
64 *Trevor* v. *Whitworth* (1887) 12 App. Cas. 409; and see para. 41–08, *ante.*

(6) by the trustee in bankruptcy of an insolvent member disclaiming his shares[65];

(7) by rescission of the contract of membership on the ground of misrepresentation[66] or mistake.[67] This, however, does not apply to shares subscribed for in the memorandum of association.

---

65 See Bankruptcy Act 1914, s. 54. This does not apply to Scotland, where there is no right of disclaimer on bankruptcy.

66 See para. 50–14, *post.*

67 See para. 49–05, *ante.*

CHAPTER 50

THE REGISTER OF MEMBERS

50–01 EVERY company is required by the 1948 Act to keep a register of its members (s. 110). The register may be in one or more bound books or it may be kept in any other manner, *e.g.* in loose-leaf form, provided that adequate precautions are taken against falsification, and facilitating its discovery (s. 436).

Contents of register

50–02 The register must contain:

(1) The names and addresses of the members,[1] and in the case of a company having a share capital a statement of the shares or amount of stock held by each member, distinguishing each share by its number (if any),[2] and of the amount paid or agreed to be considered as paid on the shares of each member.

(2) The date at which each person was entered in the register as a member.

(3) The date at which any person ceased to be a member.

Although the obligation in (1) does not expressly require the register to specify the class of shares held by each member, Brightman J. in *Re Performing Right Society Ltd.*[3] expressed the view that companies having a share capital must specify the particular class of shares held by each member. He applied this idea to the case before him which concerned a guarantee company having no share capital but with three distinct classes of members, only one of which enjoyed voting rights. This decision was reversed by the Court of Appeal[4] on the grounds that whatever the obligations arising in respect of companies having a share capital the only part of section 110 (1) applicable to companies without a share capital is the first phrase and the details as to such matters as members and amounts paid have no relevance. Accordingly only the names and addresses of the members used be disclosed. However, the Court of Appeal did not decide on the merits of Brightman J.'s dicta relating to companies having a share capital.

Location of register

50–03 The register must be kept at the registered office (s. 110 (2)). Exceptionally, if the work of making it up is done at another office of the

---

[1] It is not now necessary, as was the case under s. 95 (1) (*a*) of the Act of 1929, to state the occupations of members.

[2] See para. 34–04, *ante*.

[3] [1978] 2 All E.R. 712.

[4] [1978] 1 W.L.R. 1197.

company or by another person, *e.g.* a solicitor, practising company secretary or accountant, it may be kept at that other office of the company or at the office of that other person, as the case may be, but so that the register of a company incorporated in England must not be kept at a place outside England, nor that of a Scottish company outside Scotland (s. 110 (2), proviso).

The company must send notice to the Registrar of Companies of the place where its register of members is kept and any change in that place (s. 110 (3)). But where the register has always been kept at the registered office throughout its existence, or in the case of a register in existence at the commencement of the Act,[5] no notice need be sent until there is a change (s. 110 (3), proviso).

In default the company and every officer in default are liable to a default fine (s. 110 (4)).

Changes in the registered particulars

50–04 All changes in the registered particulars of which the company has notice have to be registered, because otherwise the register would become as untrue as if false particulars had been registered initially. Thus, when a change occurs in the ownership of shares, as, for example, upon transfer or transmission, the register will require to be altered. Further, joint holders of shares may request the company to enter their names on the register in a certain order, or execute transfers to have the holding split, with the result that part of the holding is entered on the register showing the name of one holder and part showing the name of another. Alternatively, joint holders may split their holding into a number of smaller holdings so that their names appear in a different order in each split account. Thus, if A and B hold 200 shares on joint account they may execute a transfer for 100 shares in favour of B and A. The reason for this operation is that the articles of most companies provide that, in the case of joint holders, the vote of the senior who tenders a vote shall be accepted to the exclusion of the other joint holders, and for this purpose seniority shall be determined by the order in which the names stand in the register of members (art. 63).[6]

Notice of any change of name or of address is to be entered on the register.

All such alterations are carried out by the secretary or person appointed to keep the register, after the board of directors has approved them. The secretary has no power to alter the register without authority by the board of directors,[7] but it is possible that such authority may readily be inferred by the courts in the light of modern practice.[8]

---

[5] July 1, 1948 (see s. 462 (2)).

[6] *Burns* v. *Siemens Bros.' Dynamo Works* [1919] 1 Ch. 225; *Re Bell Bros., ex p. Hodgson* (1891) 65 L.T. 245.

[7] *Wheatcroft's Case* (1873) 29 L.T. 324, 326; *Chida Mines Ltd.* v. *Anderson* (1905) 22 T.L.R. 27.

[8] See para. 67–06, *post*, for the legal recognition of these wider powers.

In a voluntary winding up the liquidator may alter the register on sanctioning transfers of shares made after the commencement of the winding up (s. 282).[9]

Who may be registered as members: see para. 44–07, *ante*.

Registration of partnership

50–05 A firm can be registered in England under its partnership name[10] although it is not a legal entity.[11] That a Scottish partnership, which is regarded as a legal entity,[11] can be registered under its firm name is not remarkable.

Registration of trustee or nominee

50–06 In the case of companies registered in England,[12] no notice of any trust is to be entered on the register or is receivable by the company (s. 117). This is one of the key sections of the 1948 Act. Its effect is twofold: first, the registered holder is liable to the company for the calls; and secondly, a beneficiary who is not registered as a holder of shares has no connection with, or rights in, a company in which shares are held on trust for him. He cannot, for instance, except by taking legal proceedings to seek the protection of the court for his interests, interfere with the normal transfer procedure. In *Re Perkins, ex p. Mexican Santa Barbara Mining Co.*[13] Lord Coleridge C.J. said:

> "It seems to me extremely important not to throw any doubt on the principle that companies have nothing whatever to do with the relation between trustees and their *cestuis que trust* in respect of the shares of the company. If a trustee is on the company's register as the holder of shares, the relations which he may have with some other person in respect of the shares are matters with which the company have nothing whatever to do; they can look only to the man whose name is on the register."

The actual point decided in this case was that, as the company was not bound to recognise trusts, it had no lien upon the shares for a debt due to it by the *cestui que trust* of the shareholder.

In *Re Key & Son*[14] the court refused to allow a memorandum of lien to be entered on the register by the company.

Section 117 should be read in conjunction with the articles of the company which usually go beyond the statutory provisions by stating that the company shall not be bound to recognise any equitable interest or any other right in a share except an absolute right in the registered holder. This

---

[9] *Taylor, Phillips and Rickard's Case* [1897] 1 Ch. 298.
[10] *Weikerheim's Case* (1873) 8 Ch.App. 831.
[11] Partnership Act 1890, s. 4.
[12] England, for this purpose, includes Wales.
[13] (1890) 24 Q.B.D. 613.
[14] [1902] 1 Ch. 467.

goes beyond section 117 in so far as it relates not merely to the question of registration of the membership right but generally to the recognition of trusts in connection with shares. A typical example of such a regulation is provided by article 7 of Table A, which states:

> "Except as required by law, no person shall be recognised by the company as holding any share upon any trust, and the company shall not be bound by or be compelled in any way to recognise (even when having notice thereof) any equitable, contingent, future or partial interest in any share or any interest in any fractional part of a share or (except only as by these regulations or by law otherwise provided) any other rights in respect of any share except an absolute right to the entirety thereof in the registered holder."

It should be noted that such a provision in the articles would not prevent an English company, if it so desired, from recognising an equitable interest in a share although, in view of section 117, it must not enter it on the register; the article merely provides that the company is not *bound and cannot be compelled* to recognise such interests.[15]

As the result of section 117, if the registered holder is a nominee for some other person who really controls the share, this fact does not, in the case of a company incorporated in England, appear on the register. This enables the persons who are really in control of a company to conceal their position from the shareholders and from the public.

Section 117 does not apply in Scotland. Although in Scottish practice notice is taken of the fact that a holding is registered in the name of trustees, and the company will amend the register of members in accordance with a deed of assumption or similar document on a change of trustees, this does not affect the relationship between the company and the registered member as holder of the shares.[16] The terms and purposes of the trust are no concern of the company.[17]

50–07 In order to prevent any abuse of this provision, three limitations of section 117 should be noted, the first two being genuine qualifications, the third an administration safeguard. These limitations apply to companies registered in England and in Scotland alike. These limitations are:

(1) The register of directors' interests has to show, in addition to the shares registered in the name of the directors, shares held in trust for them or shares in which they have any interest, however remote (1967 Act, ss. 27–29).[18] Such information must also be disclosed by the company to the Stock Exchange if the shares are listed on a recognised stock exchange.[19]

---

[15] Although s. 117 does not apply in Scotland, the adoption of such an article by a Scottish company puts it in the same position as an English company.

[16] *Muir* v. *City of Glasgow Bank* 1878, 6 R. 392 (affd. 6 R. (H.L.) 21; 4 A.H. Cases 337); *Trotter* v. *British Linen Bank* 1898, 6 S.L.T. 213.

[17] *B. Elliot* v. *Mackie & Sons Ltd.* 1935 S.C. 81.

[18] See para. 66–03, *post*.

[19] Companies Act 1976, s. 24. The Stock Exchange Listing Agreement, para. 5 (*c*), note 27 (see Vol. II, para. C–034 requires an immediate announcement of any matter notified pursuant to sections 27 or 31 of the 1967 Act.

(2) The register of substantial individual interests in share capital carrying restricted voting rights, which must be maintained if any part of the company's share capital is quoted on a stock exchange, has to show the interest of any person in shares of a nominal value equal to one-fifth or more of the voting capital or any change in that interest (1967 Act, ss. 33–34, as amended by the 1976 Act, s. 26).[20]

(3) The Department of Trade has power, where it appears to the Department that there is good reason so to do, to appoint an inspector to investigate and report on the membership of the company, and in certain circumstances, i.e. where a qualified minority applies to the Department of Trade, the latter is bound to appoint such an inspector (1948 Act, s. 172 (1) and (3)). The purpose of the investigation is to determine "the true persons who are or have been financially interested in the success or failure (real or apparent) of the company or able to control or materially to influence the policy of the company" (s. 172 (1)), and the inspector may, if so authorised, require information for that purpose from the persons interested in the shares. If in the opinion of the Department of Trade, there is good reason for an investigation into the ownership of the shares but the appointment of an inspector is unnecessary, the Department may directly obtain the disclosure of the persons beneficially interested in the shares (1948 Act, s. 173).[21]

(4) If a listed company exercises its power to require the disclosure of any nominee or trust holdings of shares, the beneficial interests therein and any agreements transferring control of the voting power of shares must be entered in a separate part of the register of interests in voting shares.[22]

Designated accounts

50–08 Companies are sometimes asked to split an account appearing in the register of members into several separately designated accounts in the same name, each designated account bearing some reference, *e.g.* "A A/c." Care must be taken in this connection as no designation reference must be capable of being construed as the entry on the register of a notice of trust, expressed, implied or constructive, contrary to the provisions of section 117. A reference which merely facilitates the disposal of documents received by the registered holder from the company cannot, it is submitted, in any way be construed as the recognition of a trust.

The company is not bound to accede to a request for a particular account to be split into a number of "designated" accounts, unless the articles make express provision for this to be done, but if it does so, no formal instrument of transfer is required if shares are taken from one designated account to

---

[20] See para. 51–01, *post*.
[21] See para. 78–17, *post*.
[22] Companies Act 1976, s. 27; see Chap. 66, *infra*.

another of the same member, as a transfer implies a change of ownership, *i.e.* a transferor and a transferee. Consequently a change in the designation of an account or accounts of the same person cannot be deemed a "transfer" of shares.[23]

Index to the register of members

50–09 A company having more than 50 members must keep an index of the names of its members unless the register is in the form of an index, and all alterations in the register must be carried to the index within 14 days (1948 Act, s. 111). The index must be kept at the same place as the register. The register or index may be in loose-leaf ledgers, provided that adequate precautions are taken to safeguard against falsification (1948 Act, s. 436).

Where a company maintains its registers on the mandate system (see para. 75–24, *post*), it is permissible for separate registers to be kept for shareholders banking at a particular bank. Thus shareholders whose mandates authorise payment to Barclays Bank Ltd. are recorded in alphabetical order in one register, those authorising payment to the Midland Bank Ltd. are recorded in alphabetical order in another register, and so on. This subdivision of the register of members must be clearly indicated to anyone inspecting the register. The Registrar of Companies will accept an annual return made up in the separate alphabetical sections arising from such subdivision of the register, provided that this fact is clearly indicated in the return. In addition, the company may now keep its register or records in a non-legible form provided that it is capable of being reproduced in a legible form (*e.g.* computer print-out), even if the articles of association say otherwise.[24]

Register prima facie evidence

50–10 The register of members is to be prima facie evidence of any matter by the Act directed or authorised to be inserted therein (1948 Act, s. 118).

The register is not conclusive evidence of those matters.[25] Consequently, the reliance to be placed on the register is qualified to this extent, that anyone dealing with the company must be taken to know—

(1) That shares may be transferred in accordance with the articles, and thus an insolvent shareholder may be substituted for a solvent one.
(2) That a member who has been induced to take shares by misrepresentation or mistake, even though on the register for years, may, while the company is a going concern, repudiate his shares and have his name removed from the register.[26]
(3) That there may be persons on the register placed there without their

---

[23] See further, para. 50–19, *post.*
[24] Stock Exchange (Completion of Bargains) Act 1976, s. 3 (1) (2).
[25] *Reese River, etc., Co.* v. *Smith* (1869) L.R. 4 H.L. 64, 80.
[26] See para. 50–14, *post.*

consent who may subsequently enforce the removal of their names.[27]

(4) That a person whose name has been improperly entered on the register under an allotment in contravention of sections 47 and 48 may claim under section 49 of the 1948 Act to be removed.[28]

(5) Where the entry on the register is there stated to be subject to some condition, membership is not complete.[29]

Inspection of register

50–11 The register of members commencing from the date of the registration of the company and the index of members are to be open for not less than two hours daily for inspection by members without charge, and for inspection by any other person on payment of five pence or such less sum as the company may prescribe for each inspection (1948 Act, s. 113 (1)).[30] Where the register is kept in a non-legible form, *e.g.* in a computer as allowed by section 3 (1) of the Stock Exchange (Completion of Bargains) Act 1976, the right of inspection is construed as a right to inspect a reproduction of the recording, or the relevant part of it, in legible form.[31] Copies may not be taken,[32] but a right is given to require a copy of the register and index or any part thereof, which must be sent within 10 days (s. 113 (2)). The obligation to supply a part of the register means an obligation to supply a part as identified by the applicant without reference to anything other than that which is on the register. Accordingly, in the case of a company not having a share capital which does not have to disclose the class of membership of each member on the register, an applicant cannot ask for the names of those members of a particular class. He would have to ask, *e.g.* for particulars of members already identified by him.[33] A penalty is imposed in case of default of either of these provisions. In addition to this penalty a judge sitting in chambers[34] may by order compel an immediate inspection of the register, or direct that the copies required shall be sent to the persons requiring them, and disobedience of that order, being a contempt of court, may be punished by imprisonment (s. 113 (3) and (4)).

Where copies are required, a charge not exceeding 10 pence per 100 words must be paid (s. 113 (2), as amended by s. 52 (2) of the 1967 Act).

The right terminates on a winding up.[35] Refusal in this section means a distinct and definite refusal.[36] A creditor or member may inspect by his

---

[27] *Reese River, etc., Co.* v. *Smith* (1869) L.R. 4 H.L. 64, 80; *Baillie's Case* [1898] 1 Ch. 110.
[28] See para. 78–17, *post*.
[29] *Spitzel* v. *Chinese Corporation* (1899) 80 L.T. 347.
[30] *Cf.* inspection of a register of debenture holders (s. 87), para. 43–18, *ante*.
[31] *Ibid*. s. 3 (3).
[32] *Re Balaghat Gold, etc., Co.* [1901] 2 K.B. 665, overruling *Boord* v. *African, etc., Co.* [1898] 1 Ch. 596.
[33] *Re Performing Right Society Ltd.* [1978] 1 W.L.R. 1197 (C.A.).
[34] This refers to English court procedure only.
[35] *Re Kent Coalfields Syndicate* [1898] 1 Q.B. 754.
[36] *R.* v. *Wilts and Berks Canal Navigation* (1835) 3 Ad. & El. 477. See also *R.* v. *Thames Navigation Commissioners* (1839) 8 Ad. & El. 901.

solicitor or agent.[37] The court will compel production, irrespective of motive.[38]

Closing of register

50–12 The company is empowered to close the register upon giving notice by advertisement in a newspaper circulating in the area of the company's registered office, but not for more than 30 days in each year (1948 Act, s. 115).

Advantage of this section is sometimes taken during the period prior to the payment of a dividend or issue of new shares, or on other occasions when a company's registration office is hard-pressed. It should be noted, however, that even if the register of members is closed, action must be taken in regard to the registration of probates and letters of administration, notices of change of name or address and court orders, such as charging orders, etc. Thus, the advantage of closing the register is somewhat negatived and to avoid the necessity for this, many companies, when paying dividends or offering shares to existing holders, fix a date on which shareholders must be registered in order to qualify for the dividend or right to apply for new shares, *e.g.* the directors may recommend at a board meeting held on September 16 that a dividend be paid on October 20 to all shareholders whose names appear on the register of members on September 30.

These arrangements apply only as between the company and the registered shareholder. Where shares quoted on the Stock Exchange have been sold, the rights as to dividend and other benefits between the seller of the shares and the buyer are governed by the contract of the parties; if the contract is silent, all benefits accruing after the date of the sale have to be made available to the buyer (Rules and Regulations of the Stock Exchange, rr. 111, 114).[39]

Publicity of register

50–13 It is important to note that the register of members is to be open to the public. Lord Cranworth observed[40]:

> "When the legislature enabled shareholders to limit their liability, not merely to the amount of their shares but to so much of that amount as should remain unpaid, it is obvious that no creditor could safely trust the company without having the means of ascertaining, first, who the shareholders might be, and, secondly, to what extent they would be liable. . . . The legislature took care to provide the register as the means of enabling persons dealing with the company to know to whom and to what they might trust."

[37] *Bevan* v. *Webb* [1901] 2 Ch. 59, 75.
[38] *Davies* v. *Gas Light & Coke Co.* [1909] 1 Ch. 248.
[39] See further, para. 75–11, *post*.
[40] In *Oakes* v. *Turquand* (1867) L.R. 2 H.L. 325, 366.

Doctrine of holding out

On the same principle, in *Sewell's Case,*[41] where a registered shareholder wishes to disclaim the ownership of certain shares, Lord Cairns, while assuming in the shareholder's favour that he might have had a right to disclaim, was of opinion that "not having done so, and being aware that he was held out to the public as the holder of twenty-three shares, it is too late for him months or years afterwards to enter into that question." "It is difficult," the same learned judge remarked on another occasion during the argument, "to disembarrass these cases of the effect which a man's name being on the register has in inducing other persons to alter their position."[42]

Delay

The result of this doctrine of holding out is that if a person's name is on the register with his consent, and he claims a right to have it removed on some ground or other, he must exercise the right promptly, otherwise he forfeits it.[43] Even where pursuant to a *void* contract a name is placed on the register, delay after knowledge may be fatal.[44] Where an allottee under a void allotment sold the shares and transferred them to a purchaser who was registered, the allottee was held not to be entitled to sue the company for the money subscribed as paid for a consideration which had failed.[45]

Rectification of register

50–14 It is a corollary from the principle that the register of members is to be the creditors' guarantee, showing them to whom and to what they have to trust, that the register should be properly kept and that the names appearing therein should be the names of the persons really for the time being liable to the creditors. But if there is an error in the register this cannot be rectified by the company without applying to the court.[46] Accordingly, section 116 of the 1948 Act provides a summary mode of rectifying the register from time to time by application to the court in two classes of cases:

(1) Where the name of any person is without sufficient cause entered in or omitted from the register of members.

(2) Where default is made or unnecessary delay takes place in entering on the register the fact of any person having ceased to be a member.

This jurisdiction is exercisable after as well as before winding up,[47] and is frequently exercised. It may be invoked by the company,[48] or by the

---

41 (1868) 3 Ch.App. 131, 138.
42 *Lawrence's Case* (1867) L.R. 2 Ch. 412, 417.
43 *Re Scottish Petroleum Co.* (1883) 23 Ch.D. 413, 434.
44 *Re Railway Time Tables Publishing Co.* (1889) 42 Ch.D. 98, 107; see para. 49–05, *ante*.
45 *Linz* v. *Electric Wire Co. of Palestine* [1948] A.C. 371.
46 *Gardiner* v. *Victoria Estates Co. Ltd.* 1885, 12 R. 1356.
47 *Re Sussex Brick Co.* [1904] 1 Ch. 598; *Stocker* v. *Liquidators of Coustonolm Paper Mills Co.*, 1891, 19 R. 17; *Jackson, etc, Ptnrs.* 1902, 10 S.L.T. 279.
48 *Re Indo-China Steam Navigation Co.* [1917] 2 Ch. 100.

person aggrieved (whether a member or not), or by any member. The following are a few illustrative cases in which orders have been made: where the applicant was induced to take shares by misrepresentation[49]; where the company improperly neglected to register a transfer[50]; where shares had been issued to the applicant as paid up without filling a contract in compliance with what is now section 52 of the Act of 1948[51]; where shares were improperly forfeited[52]; where the company, acting on a forged transfer, had removed the name of the applicant, the real owner[53]; where there was a dispute between the vendor and purchaser of shares[54]; where shares had been irregularly allotted to an applicant[55]; where the signatory of an underwriting letter not constituting a contract had been placed on the register[56]; where a shareholder, who had made an *ultra vires* surrender of his shares to the company, claimed to have his name reinstated.[57]

Procedure in England

50–15 The court has rarely declined, as between a member and the company, to exercise its jurisdiction under the section[58]; but the court had and has a discretion, although the words "if satisfied of the justice of the case" in section 35 of the Act of 1862 were not used in section 32 of the Act of 1908, and are likewise not used in section 116 (3) of the Act of 1948. See *per* Lord Macnaghten in *Trevor* v. *Whitworth*[59] as to the materiality of these words. Where justice requires it, the order to rectify will be made *nunc pro tunc*.[60] In *Re Transatlantic Life Assurance Co. Ltd.*[61] the company had inadvertently issued shares in contravention of the Exchange Control Act 1947. When the error was discovered, the company itself applied to the court under section 116 (1) for rectification of the register by striking out the name of the holder. Slade J. held that the holder's name had been entered on the register "without sufficient cause" within the meaning of section 116 (1) (*a*) and that the court had jurisdiction under section 116 (2) to order rectification of the register by deleting the holder's name in relation to the wrongly issued shares. An application under section 116 may be by motion

---

49 *Stewart's Case* (1866) 1 Ch.App. 574; *Anderson's Case* (1881) 17 Ch.D. 373.
50 *Re Stranton Iron and Steel Co.* (1873) L.R. 16 Eq. 559.
51 *Re New Zealand Kapanga, etc., Co.* (1873) 18 L.R. Eq. 17n. (the case arose under s. 25 of the Companies Act 1867).
52 *Re Ystalyfera Gas Co.* [1887] W.N. 30.
53 *Re Bahia, etc., Co.* (1868) L.R. 3 Q.B. 584.
54 *Ex p. Shaw* (1877) 2 Q.B.D. 463.
55 *Re Portuguese Consolidated, etc., Mines* (1889) 42 Ch.D. 160; *Re Homer District Consolidated Gold Mines* (1888) 39 Ch.D. 546.
56 *Re Consort, etc., Mines* [1897] 1 Ch. 575.
57 *Bellerby* v. *Rowland and Marwood's Steamship Co.* [1902] 2 Ch. 14 (C.A.).
58 *Ex p. Parker* (1867) L.R. 2 Ch. 685.
59 (1887) 12 App.Cas. 409, 440. See also *Elliot* v. *Mackie & Sons*, 1935 S.C. 81, where the court declined to intervene on averments that a transfer was in breach of trust.
60 *Re Sussex Brick Co.* [1904] 1 Ch. 598. (It is doubtful whether a voluntary liquidator can rectify *nunc pro tunc*.)
61 [1980] 1 W.L.R. 79.

or summons,[62] but should normally be by motion.[63] Even if there is no winding up pending, the application is normally made to the Companies Court, but it may be made to any judge of the Chancery Division, preferably not, in such case, to the winding-up judge.[64] Directors are not proper parties as respondents,[65] and cannot be made to pay the costs of the motion,[65] except where added at their own request.[66] There is jurisdiction to rectify the register not only upon motion under section 116, but in an action against the company,[67] and this course should invariably be adopted in complicated cases.

Under a winding up by the court, the liquidator can now only rectify the register with the special leave of the court (1948 Act, s. 273).[68]

Upon making an order for rectification the court has power, for instance, where there are no directors and no secretary, to appoint the applicant or some other person to rectify the register.[69] But there must be a register to rectify, so that if, for example, the register has been destroyed a new one must be prepared on whatever information is available, such as the latest annual return, before there can be rectification.

Procedure in Scotland

Section 116 is regarded as a summary procedure available as an alternative to the ordinary jurisdiction of the courts. It is normally invoked by petition at the instance of the company, a registered member or a person claiming to be registered. It is always a matter for the court to determine, in the exercise of its discretion, whether it would be more convenient to dispose of the issues raised in the petition process or by ordinary action. A petition under section 116 is, however, appropriate where the issues raised are simple and do not require complex investigation of the facts.[70]

Dominion or branch registers

50–16 A company is given power, in certain circumstances, to cause to be kept in any part of the H.M. dominions outside Great Britain, the Channel

[62] See R.S.C. 1965, Ord. 102, r. 3.
[63] *Duffin* v. *Mexican Gold and Silver Ore Reduction Co.* [1890] W.N. 116; *Precedents* (17th ed.), Pt. I, p. 1086; for forms of notice of motion and orders to rectify, see *Precedents*, pp. 1088 *et seq*.
[64] The practice was formerly otherwise: see *Re British Columbian Exploitation and Gold Estates* [1899] W.N. 32. In Scotland, application is made to the court of competent jurisdiction, as defined by s. 220. s. 220 has been amended by the Insolvency Act 1976, s. 1 and Sched. 1.
[65] *Re Keith, Prowse & Co.* [1918] 1 Ch. 487.
[66] *Re Copal Varnish Co.* [1917] 2 Ch. 349.
[67] *Reese River, etc., Co.* v. *Smith* (1869) L.R. 4 H.L. 64, 80.
[68] On the power of the liquidator in the voluntary winding up to alter the register on sanctioning a transfer, see s. 282 and para. 39–28, *ante*.
[69] R.S.C. 1965, Ord. 45, r. 8; *Re Manihot Rubber Plantations* (1919) 63 S.J. 827.
[70] *Scottish Amalgamated Silks Limited* v. *Macalister* 1930 S.L.T. 593; *National Bank of Scotland Glasgow Nominees Ltd.* v. *Adamson* 1932 S.L.T. 492; see also *Blackie* v. *Coats* 1893, 21 R. 150; 1 S.L.T. 320; *The Anglo-American Land, etc., Co.* 1896, 4 S.L.T. 37; *Colquhoun's Tr.* v. *British Linen Co.* 1900, 2 F. 945; 8 S.L.T. 45; *Aikman* v. *James Young* 1900, 7 S.L.T. 301; *Sleigh* v. *Glasgow & Transvaal Options* 1904, 6 F. 420; 11 S.L.T. 593; *Gowans* v. *Dundee Steam Navigation Co.* 1904, 6 F. 613; 11 S.L.T. 819; *Kinghorn* v. *The Glasgow Fireclay Co.* 1907, 14 S.L.T. 683.

Islands or the Isle of Man, in which it transacts business, a branch register or registers of the members resident in that part (1948 Act, s. 119). Such a register is called by the Act a "dominion register" (s. 119 (1)); in company practice it is often referred to as a "branch register." A company which maintains a dominion register is required to give to the Registrar of Companies notice of the situation of the office where it is kept and the fact of its discontinuance within 14 days of the opening of the office or of any change or discontinuance. The dominion register, which may be rectified by any competent court in the dominion, becomes part of the register of the company. Shares entered in the dominion register must not be dealt with in the main or "principal register." The company must transmit to its registered office a copy of every entry in its dominion register as soon as may be, and keep at the place where the company's principal register is kept a duplicate of its dominion register (1948 Act, s. 120 (3)). Dominion registers and duplicates thereof are deemed to be part of the principal register and are required to be kept in the same manner as the principal register.

Branch registers of dominion companies may also be kept in Great Britain so far as authorised by Order in Council (1948 Act, s. 123).

Companies registered in Great Britain may be authorised by statute to keep dominion registers in former dominions which have become independent. Such statutory provisions have been made in respect of Malaysia,[71] the Republic of South Africa,[72] and Pakistan.[73]

Duplicate registers

50–17 Where a company has an office abroad, the *complete* register may be kept in two places, *viz.* at the registered office (or other admitted locality[74]) in this country, and at the "branch" transfer office abroad. In this case the latter register is referred to as the "duplicate register." This type of register, which has no statutory foundation, must not be confused with the duplicate of the dominion register required by section 120 (3) of the 1948 Act. Where a "duplicate register" is kept, the two offices communicate changes continuously and thereby keep the original register and the duplicate register up to date. For convenience the registers are sometimes divided into two sections, *e.g.* the "London" register and the "Johannesburg" register.

In law only one authentic register exists in this case, *viz.* the original register, the other register being, as the name implies, ancillary and merely a duplicate. Companies incorporated in South Africa and having transfer offices in England often keep duplicate registers in England.

---

[71] Companies Registers (Malaysia) Order 1964 (S.I. 1964 No. 911), made under the Malaysia Act 1963, s. 4 (1), and the Federation of Malaya Independence Act 1957, s. 2 (1) (*b*).

[72] South Africa Act 1962, s. 2 and Sched. II, para. 4.

[73] Pakistan Act 1973, s. 4 (1) and Sched. III, para. (3) (1). See also Bangladesh Act 1973, s. 1 (3) and Sched., para. 10 (1).

[74] See para. 50–03, *ante*.

PRACTICE NOTES

Inspection and copies of register

50–18 The maintenance of the register of members by computer (which is permitted by the Stock Exchange (Completion of Bargains) Act 1976) is further governed by regulations relating to the inspection of the visible record of the register and to the notification of the place of inspection prescribed by the Companies (Registers and other Records) Regulations 1979.[75]

Problems arise when applications are received for copies of a part only of the register. Most computer programmes will provide for listing shareholders with given holdings, *e.g.* those holding 19,000 shares or more, and some may be able to cope with selective lists of different types of shareholder, *e.g.* private individuals, bodies corporate, nominee companies, etc. In cases where it is possible to provide a copy of a part of the register only at considerable expense to the company (and this would apply whether or not a computer is used), *e.g.* a request for a list of shareholders having John as their first forename, it is suggested that a copy of the complete register should be offered on payment of the statutory fee, on the grounds that it is not the responsibility of the company to finance the research necessary to comply with the request. Since any such unusual request for a copy of a part of the register would normally be made for commercial purposes and not for reasons connected with the Companies Acts, it seems unlikely that the applicant would find sympathy in the court if he applied for an order under s. 113 (4) of the 1948 Act.

Designated accounts

50–19 A company the securities of which are listed on The Stock Exchange is obliged to arrange for designated accounts if requested by holders of securities (Listing Agreement, para. 18). A standard form of designation/re-designation for completion by holders desiring this facility is reproduced as para. EE26 of *The Chartered Secretaries Manual of Company Secretarial Practice* (Jordan & Sons Ltd., London). The relative share or stock certificate should be lodged with the form for amendment or substitution and a fee is normally charged for the service.

---

[75] S.I. 1979 No. 53.

Chapter 51

DISCLOSURE OF INTERESTS IN SHARES

51–01 The Companies Acts 1967 and 1976 contained provisions the purpose of which was to secure a degree of disclosure of sizeable shareholdings in public companies. With the passage of time a variety of techniques enabled shareholders to operate beyond the purview of the legislation and led to a proliferation of "concert parties" and "dawn raids" which provoked adverse publicity. Part IV of the Companies Act 1981, has now repealed sections 33 and 34 of the 1967 Act and sections 26 and 27 of the 1976 Act.[1] Sections 63 to 72 of the 1981 Act, which are treated in this chapter, are headed "Disclosure of Interests in Voting Shares in Public Companies."

The obligation to notify

51–02 The basic obligation is to notify a public company of an interest in voting shares in certain circumstances. This basic obligation applies to a person who either:

(a) to his knowledge acquires any interest in shares comprised in the relevant share capital of a public company or ceases to be interested in any shares so comprised (whether or not he retains any interest in other shares so comprised); or

(b) becomes aware that he has acquired any interest in shares so comprised or that he has ceased to be interested in any shares so comprised in which he was previously interested (1981 Act, s.63(1)).

Such a person is under an obligation to notify the company where:

(a) he has an interest subject to the notification requirement immediately after the relevant time[2] but did not have such an interest immediately before that time; or

(b) he had an interest subject to the notification requirement immediately before the relevant time[2] but does not have such an interest immediately after that time; or

(c) he has such an interest both immediately before and immediately after the relevant time[2] but the percentage levels of his interest immediately before and immediately after are not the same. (s.63(2)).

---

[1] 1981 Act, s.83(1) and Sched. 4.

[2] "Relevant time" refers to the time of the event or change in circumstances relevant for the purposes of s.63(1)(*a*) or (4)(*a*) or the time when he acquires the knowledge relevant for the purposes of s.63(1)(*b*) or (4)(*b*): s.63(9).

Left to themselves, these provisions would not extend to circumstances where notification might be appropriate by reason of factors outside the personal position of the individual shareholders. For example, a company may change from being a private company to a public company or the amount of its nominal capital may alter. In such circumstances, provision is made for an extension of the obligation to notify (s.63(4)).

For the time being the notifiable percentage for the purposes of section 63 is five per cent.[3] but provision is made for the alteration of the prescribed percentage by statutory instrument (s.64(1)).

The only share capital to which Part IV of the 1981 Act applies is such of the issued share capital of a public company of a class carrying rights to vote in all circumstances at general meetings of the company. Moreover, the temporary suspension of voting rights does not affect the application of Part IV in relation to interests in those or any other shares comprised in that class (s.63(10)).

Contents and timing of notification

51–03 The obligation to notify must be performed within the period of five days next following the day upon which the obligation arises (s.63(6)). The notification must be in writing and must specify the share capital to which it relates. It must also either:

(a) state the number of shares comprised in that share capital in which the person making the notification knows he was interested immediately after the time when the obligation to notify arose; or

(b) in any case where the person making the notification no longer has an interest subject to the notification requirement, state that he no longer has such an interest (s.63(5)).

The meaning of "interests" to be notified

51–04 The 1981 Act goes much further than its predecessors in defining when a person is and is not possessed of a notifiable "interest" in shares and also in the extent to which it brings a variety of family, corporate and concerted interests within the obligation to notify.

The basic definition of an "interest in shares" for the purposes of section 63 is "an interest of any kind whatsoever in the shares," disregarding "any restraints or restrictions to which the exercise of any right attached to the interest is or may be subject" (s.70(2)). To this general definition, the following particular provisions are added:

(i) Where any property is held on trust and any interest in shares is comprised in that property, any beneficiary of that trust who otherwise does not have an interest in the shares is to be taken as having such an interest (s.70(3)).

[3] s.63(8).

(ii) A person is taken to have an interest in shares if he enters into a contract for their purchase by him (whether for cash or other consideration) or, not being the registered holder, he is entitled to exercise any right conferred by the holding of the shares or is entitled to control the exercise of any such right (s.70(4)).

(iii) A person is also taken to have an interest in shares if, otherwise than under a trust, he has a right to call for delivery of the shares to himself or to his order or he has a right to acquire an interest in shares or is under an obligation to take such an interest. It matters not whether the right or obligation is conditional or absolute (s.70(5)).

(iv) Persons having a joint interest shall be taken each of them to have that interest (s.70(7)).

(v) It is immaterial that shares in which a person has an interest are unidentifiable (s.70(8)).

51–05 The Act then goes on to provide that the following interests in shares are to be disregarded for present purposes:

(a) an interest in reversion or remainder or of a bare trustee or custodian trustee and any discretionary interest under an English trust;
(b) an interest in fee or of a simple trustee and any discretionary interest under a Scottish trust;
(c) various interests in relation to unit trusts, charities, trustee investments and other matters of statutory definition[4];
(d) interest held by or on behalf of the Church of Scotland;
(e) certain life interests arising under settlements which are irrevocable and in which the settlor has no interest;
(f) an exempt interest held by a recognised jobber as defined in section 71(4);
(g) an exempt security interest as defined in section 71(5)[5];
(h) an interest of the President of the Family Division pursuant to section 9 of the Administration of Estates Act 1925;
(i) an interest of the Accountant General of the Supreme Court; and
(j) any other interest prescribed by the Secretary of State by statutory instruments (s.71(1)).

Recognising that a notifiable "interest in shares" may involve notification by a person who is not the registered holder of the shares, section 65 provides that a notification must include particulars of the identity of each registered holder of any shares to which the notification relates, together

[4] The statutory provisions referred to are Prevention of Fraud (Investments) Act 1958; Charities Act 1960, s.22; Trustee Investment Act 1961, s.11; Administration of Justice Act 1965, s.1; and Church Funds Investment Measure 1958 (Schedule).

[5] An interest is an exempt security interest if it is held by a bank or insurance company, a trustee savings bank or a member of the Stock Exchange *and* it is held by way of security only for the purposes of a transaction entered into in the ordinary course of business; similarly, if it is held by way of security by the Bank of England or the Post Office in its banking capacity (*ibid*).

with particulars of the number of those held by each such registered holder, so far as these matters are known to the notifier at the date of notification.

Family and corporate interests

51–06 For purposes of the obligation to notify, a person is taken to be interested in any shares in which his spouse, infant child or step-child is interested (s.66(1)). A person is also taken to be interested in shares if a body corporate is interested in them and:

(a) that body corporate or its directors are accustomed to act in accordance with his directions or instructions; or
(b) he is entitled to exercise or control the exercise of one-third or more of the voting power at general meetings of that body corporate. (s.66(2)).[6]

Group interests of persons acting together: "concert parties"

51–07 Hitherto, one of the avoidance devices used to circumvent notification requirements under the 1967 and 1976 Acts has been the "concert party" whereby persons acting in concert have together amassed a 5 per cent. holding or more without any individual person, human or corporate, becoming obliged to notify his interest or changes therein. Part IV of the 1981 Act has now introduced stringent anti-avoidance measures, designed to bring such concerted action out into the open. Section 67 concerns agreements between two or more persons which include provision for the acquisition by one or more of the parties of interests in shares in a particular company known as "the target company." For the section to apply, the agreement must—

(a) include provisions imposing obligations or restrictions on one or more of the parties with respect to their use, retention or disposal of interests in the target company's shares acquired in pursuance of the agreement; and
(b) result in one or more of the parties acquiring an interest in that company's shares (s.67(1)).

The expression "use" of interests means the exercise of any rights or of any control or influence arising from those interests (including the right to enter into any agreement for the exercise, or for control of the exercise, of any of those rights by any other person) (s.67(2)).

The provisions of section 67 to 69 are complicated provisions dealing with sophisticated arrangements. It was essential to cast the net more widely than "agreements" in the formal sense. Thus, "agreement" is defined so as to include "any agreement *or arrangement*" and "provisions of an agreement" include "undertakings, expectations or understandings

[6] These concepts of corporate control are elaborated in s.66(3) and (4).

operative under any agreement . . . and . . . any provisions, whether express or implied and whether absolute or not" (s.67(4)). Agreements which are not legally binding are not included unless they involve "mutuality in the undertakings, expectations or understanding of the parties" (s.67(5)).

Once the parties in concert are identified they are each assumed to own the interests of all the others and the obligation to notify applies to the aggregate (s.76(6)). The obligation to notify then includes the obligation to disclose the agreement and the parties to it (s.67(8)). Agreements to underwrite and sub-underwrite offers of shares are expressly excluded from section 67 (s.67(10)).

Having defined the kinds of arrangement now brought within the catchment of notification, the 1981 Act goes on to make detailed provision for the obligatory exchange of information between the parties to the arrangement (s.68). It then applies the section 63 obligation to notify to section 66 arrangements (s.69).

Agents

51–08 A shareholder who authorises an agent to acquire or dipose of relevant interests in shares on his behalf is obliged to secure that the agent notifies him immediately of acquisitions or disposals of such interestes which may give rise to an obligation to notify (s. 72(1)).

Criminal penalties

51–09 The obligation to notify is reinforced by the following criminal offences:

(a) failure to fulfil, within the proper period, an obligation to make any notification required by section 63;

(b) in purported fulfilment of such an obligation, making to a company a statement which the maker knows to be false or which is false and is made recklessly;

(c) failure to notify the other members of the "concert party" under section 68; and

(d) failure to secure in accordance with section 72(1) (s.72(3)).

A person who is guilty of any of these offences is liable on conviction on indictment to a term of imprisonment for a term not exceeding two years, or a fine, or both. On summary conviction the maximum penalties are six months' imprisonment, a fine not exceeding the statutory maximum, or both. (s.72(4)). There are various ancillary provisions relating to criminal sanctions and it is expressly provided that proceedings shall not be instituted except by, or with the consent of, the Secretary of State or the Director of Public Prosecutions (s.72(9)).

CHAPTER 52

THE REGISTER OF INTERESTS IN SHARES

52–01 EVERY public company is obliged to keep a register for the purposes of recording the information notified under the 1981 Act, sections 63 and 65.[1] Whenever the company receives information from a person pursuant to his obligations under those sections, the company must inscribe in the register, against the name of that person, the information and the date of inscription. (1981 Act, s.73(1)). If a notification includes a statement that the person making it has ceased to be a party to a section 67 agreement,[2] the company must record such information against the name of that person in every place where his name appears in the register as a party to the agreement (s.73(2)).

The obligation to record information in the register must be fulfilled within the period of three days next following the day on which the obligation arises (s.73(3)). Entries must be in chronological order in respect of each name and the register must be kept in index-form or else have a separate index (s.73(4) and (5)). The register and any associated index must be kept in the same place as the register of directors' interests[3] and be available for inspection (s.73(8)).

If default is made in complying with the duties imposed by section 73, the company and every officer who is in default is liable on summary conviction to a fine not exceeding one-fifth of the statutory maximum or, on conviction after continued contravention, a default fine not exceeding one-fiftieth of the statutory maximum.

Removal of entries from register

52–02 A company may remove an entry against any person's name from its register of interests in shares where more than six years have elapsed since the date of its inscription and either (a) the entry recorded the fact that the person in question had ceased to have an interest subject to the notification requirement or (b) it has been superseded by a later entry inscribed under section 73 (*ante*) (s.78(1)). Provision is also made for the removal of registered information which has been incorrectly recorded and of other out-of-date or misleading information. If the company fails to remove information, application can be made to the court for an order directing the company to remove the information from the register (s.78(5)). Defaulting companies and officers may be fined (s.78(8)).

---

[1] See Chapter 51, *ante*.
[2] See para. 51–07.
[3] *Cf.* 1967 Act, s.29, para. 66–10, *infra*.

Entries in a company's register of interests in shares must not be deleted otherwise than in accordance with section 78. An entry wrongly deleted must be restored to the register as soon as is reasonably practicable. Unauthorised deletions and failures to restore are punishable by default fines (s.79).

Investigation by a company of interests in its shares

52–03 Any public company may issue a notice in writing to any person whom it believes or has reasonable cause to believe to be, or to have been in the three years prior to the notice, interested in shares comprised in relevant share capital of that company. Such a notice may require the person involved to indicate whether or not he is or was so interested. It may further require him: (a) to give particulars of his own past or present interest in shares comprised in relevant share capital in the company held by him at any time during the preceding three years; (b) to give particulars of any other interests subsisting in the shares; and (c) in relation to past interests, to provide particulars and the identity of any person who held the interest immediately upon the addressee ceasing to hold it (s.74(2)). Particulars may also be required of any section 67 agreements (s.74(3)). Information sought by the company under section 74 must be sought and given in written form.

Whenever information is gathered under section 74, the company is bound to record it in a separate part of the register of interests in shares. (s.75).

52–04 A company may be required to exercise its powers under section 74 on the requisition of members holding not less than one-tenth of such of the paid up capital of the company as then carries the right to vote at general meetings (s.76(1)). Provision is made as to the form and the procedure in relation to requisitions under section 76. An important control is that those making a requisition must not only specify the manner in which they require the powers to be exercised but must also give reasonable grounds for requiring the company to exercise the powers in the manner specified.[4] Moreover, on the conclusion of an investigation carried out by the company in pursuance of a requisition, it is the duty of the company to prepare a report of the information received in pursuance of the investigation. The report must be available at the registered office within a reasonable time after the conclusion of the investigation (s.76(5)).

Section 76 contains further provisions relating to the time scale for investigations and reports, interim reports and other matters. Again there is a default fine for non-compliance, criminal proceedings being either summary or on indictment (s.76(12)).

[4] s.76(2).

If, as a result of a section 74 inquiry, the company receives information relating to the present interests held by any persons in relevant shares, it must inscribe against the name of the registered holder of those shares in a separate part of its register of interests in shares—

(a) the fact that the requirement was imposed and the date on which it was imposed; and

(b) any information in respect of present interests received in pursuance of the requirement (s.75).

Penalties for failure to provide information under section 74

52–05 The obligation to provide information under section 74 is backed by two forms of sanction. First, failure to supply information within the time specified in a section 74 notice entitles the company to apply to the court for an order directing that the shares in question shall be subject to the restrictions imposed by section 174 of the 1948 Act.[5] Secondly, there are criminal penalties in respect of (a) failure to comply with a section 74 notice and (b) the making of statements known to be false in a material particular or recklessly. On conviction on indictment the maximum punishment is two years' imprisonment, a fine or both. On summary conviction, it is six months' imprisonment, a fine not exceeding the statutory maximum or both (s.77(5)). A defendant is provided with a statutory defence if he proves that the requirement to give the information was frivolous or vexatious (s.77(6)). Provision is made for exemption of persons from the obligation to provide information, the exemption being granted by the Secretary of State (s.77(7)).

Inspection of register and reports

52–06 A register and any report which is required by section 76 to be available for inspection must, during business hours (but subject to reasonable restrictions), be open to inspection by any member of the company or any other person without charge (s.80(1)). Provision is made for the supply of copies, default fines and mandatory enforcement orders.

Transitional provisions

52–07 Section 83 contains transitional provisions in respect of the relationship between notifications under the sections of the 1967 Act which are now repealed and notification under the 1981 Act.

[5] As to s.174, see para. 78–23. The company or any person aggrieved by the order may apply to the court for an order directing that the shares shall cease to be subject thereto: 1981 Act, 2.77(3).

B. GENERAL MEETINGS

Chapter 53

KINDS OF GENERAL MEETINGS

53–01 The members of the company normally express their will at general meetings by passing resolutions. In exceptional circumstances the will of the members may be ascertained without the passing of a formal resolution.[1] The meetings have to be properly convened[2] and due notice of them has to be given.[3] The procedure at the meetings must not be irregular[4]; the resolutions have to be carried by the majorities required by statute or the articles, and, in some cases, have to be confirmed by the court.[5] Further, some resolutions have to be notified to the Registrar of Companies in the time and manner laid down by the Act,[6] and all have to be duly recorded in the minutes of the meetings.[7]

There are three types of meetings of members of a company[8]:

(1) annual general meetings;
(2) extraordinary general meetings;
(3) separate meetings of classes of shareholders.

Annual general meeting

Date of the annual general meeting

53–02 The date on which the annual general meeting is to be held is—apart from the first meeting which is subject to different rules—determined by two factors of time (1948 Act, s. 131 (1)):

(1) The meeting must be held in each year[9]; and
(2) It must not be held later than 15 months from the date of the previous annual meeting.

These two requirements are cumulative and separate: failure to comply with either constitutes an offence for which the company and every officer in default is liable to a fine not exceeding £50 (s. 131 (5)). There are thus

---

[1] See para. 53–12, *post*.
[2] See para. 53–07, *post*.
[3] See para. 54–01, *post*.
[4] See para. 55–01, *post*.
[5] See para. 32–02, *post*.
[6] See para. 56–10, *post*.
[7] See para. 57–02, *post*.
[8] Before the coming into operation of the 1980 Act, a fourth type of general meeting existed, *viz*. the statutory meeting. It was abolished by the 1980 Act, s. 82 (*d*) and Sched. 4. For the pre-1980 law, see Palmer's *Company Law* (22nd ed.), paras 51–02 to 51–03.
[9] Year means calendar year; *Park* v. *Lawton* [1911] 1 K.B. 588. Failure to hold the meeting may result in the directors automatically ceasing to hold office: *Alexander Ward & Co. Ltd.* v. *Samyang Navigation Co. Ltd.* [1975] 1 W.L.R. 673; 1975 S.L.T. 126 (H.L.).

two separate offences, and an offence is committed if default is made as regards one requirement, though the other requirement is satisfied; further, the offence of failing to comply with one requirement may be committed earlier than that of failing to comply with the other.[10]

The first annual general meeting is not required to be held in any given year provided that it takes place within 18 months of the incorporation of the company (s. 131 (1), proviso).[11] For example, a company formed on July 31, 1980 need not hold an annual general meeting during 1980 or 1981; its first annual general meeting must take place by January 31, 1982. This enables a company which is incorporated other than on the first day of what it wishes to be its financial year to draw up its first set of accounts for a longer period than one year and still produce them in time for the first annual general meeting.

The notice convening the annual general meeting must specify the meeting as such (s. 131 (1)); consequently, it is not sufficient to refer to it as an ordinary meeting even if the articles so designate it.

Power of Department of Trade to call annual general meeting in case of default

53–03 If default is made in holding the annual general meeting, a member may apply to the Department of Trade to call or direct the calling of such a meeting, and on any such application the Department has power to call the meeting and to give such directions as appear to it expedient in relation to the calling, holding and convening of the meeting; these directions may even modify the articles of the company (s. 131 (2)).[12] A meeting convened under this provision is deemed to be an annual general meeting of the company, subject to the directions of the Department of Trade (s. 131 (3)).

If the meeting is held in the year in which the default is made, it obviously is the annual meeting of that particular year. If, however, it is held in the following year, at a date when the next annual meeting is already due, a difficulty might arise which will be evident from the following example: assuming that the last date for holding the annual meeting of 1981 was April 1, 1981, and the Department of Trade directs an annual meeting to be held on August 1, 1982, is the latter meeting the annual meeting for 1981, or for 1982 or for both years? The company may resolve at the meeting—and presumably due notices of the resolution are required—that the meeting shall be treated as the annual general meeting for both years but unless it so resolves, the meeting will be treated as the

[10] *Smedley* v. *Registrar of Companies* [1919] 1 K.B. 97.

[11] Here, again, default in complying with the provision constitutes an offence (s. 131 (5)).

[12] The provision goes so far as to "declare"—in order to leave unaffected the position at common law (see para. 55–02, *post*)—that *one* member present in person or by proxy shall be deemed to constitute a meeting.

annual general meeting for 1981 only, with the effect that a second annual meeting, *viz*. that for 1982, has to be held in 1982 (s. 131 (3)).[13]

Default in holding a meeting convened by the Department of Trade renders the company and its officers who are in default liable to a fine of £50; such default may be not holding the meeting at all, or holding it in disregard of the directions of the Department (s. 131 (5)).

Ordinary business of annual general meeting

53–04 The business of the annual general meeting depends upon the articles. Table A provides that the ordinary business of such a meeting shall be the declaration of a dividend, the consideration of the accounts, balance sheets, and the reports of the directors and auditors, the election of directors in the place of those retiring and the appointment of, and the fixing of the remuneration of, the auditors (art. 52). Any business which is not by the articles defined as "ordinary business of an annual general meeting" is known as "special business."

The directors must lay before the company in general meeting, usually the annual general meeting, a profit and loss account and balance sheet in respect of each accounting reference period, within a specified time after the end of that period (1976 Act, s. 1 (6)). The accounts are to be made up to a date no more than seven days before or seven days after the end of the period (s. 1 (2)) and must be laid before the company within 10 months of the close of the period which they cover if it is a private company and seven months for any other company (s. 6 (2)). The relevant time is extended by three months for any company which carries on business or has interests overseas (s.6(3)).[13a] If the company's first accounting reference period after incorporation is in excess of 12 months the relevant time is reduced by the excess over 12 months but with a minimum period allowed of three months (s. 6 (4) and (5)). The reports of the company's auditors on the accounts must be attached to the balance sheet (1948 Act, s. 156 (1), 1976 Act, s. 1 (5)) together with a report by the directors (1948 Act, s. 157 (1), 1976 Act, s. 1 (5)). The auditors' report must be read at the general meeting and be open to inspection by any member (1967 Act, s. 14 (2)).

The proceedings at the meeting are of a formal nature. The chairman of the company will normally propose the adoption of the accounts and will first make a statement on the company's affairs and any other circumstances of interest to the company and will answer questions from members. The chairman's statement is frequently printed and circulated in advance with the reports and accounts.

There is no obligation on the company to adopt or approve the accounts; thus article 52 merely requires that they should be considered. Resolutions

---

[13] A copy of the resolution that the meeting shall be treated as the annual meeting of the year in which it is held has to be forwarded to the Registrar and to be recorded by him (s. 131 (4)).

[13a] But only if notice is given on the prescribed form for each separate accounting period (s. 6 (3)).

are required for declaring dividends and normally these are included in a resolution to receive the accounts.

Motions for the election or re-election of directors in public companies have to be dealt with separately. If a single resolution is passed for the election or re-election of more than one director, the resolution is invalid unless previously a resolution has been passed and agreed to, *nemine contradicente*,[14] that such election should be dealt with in a composite resolution (1948 Act, s. 183).[15]

Auditors hold office from one general meeting at which the accounts are laid before the meeting to the next. This does not have to be an annual general meeting but will usually be so. Under the 1976 Act auditors are no longer automatically reappointed without a resolution to that effect but must be appointed each year (s. 14 (1)). The Secretary of State may appoint an auditor in default of such appointment (s. 14 (2)). The meeting must also deal with the auditor's remuneration including expenses (s. 14 (8)). The resolution for this will either fix the amount to which the auditors shall be entitled or will empower the directors to fix the amount.

Extraordinary general meetings

53–05 General meetings other than annual general meetings and the statutory meetings are called "extraordinary general meetings" (art. 48). The articles usually provide that the directors *may* call an extraordinary general meeting at any time they think fit (art. 49), and further that they *shall* call an extraordinary meeting whenever they are required to do so by a requisition signed by a specified proportion of the members[16] (art. 49).

At a requisitioned extraordinary general meeting resolutions may be moved—

(1) by the requisitionists; or
(2) by the directors if they have power under the articles to call such meetings[17] (see art. 49).

Individual shareholders are not entitled to move resolutions not covered by the terms of the requisition.[17] Section 132 of the 1948 Act provides powers which are additional to, and independent of, any power in the articles. Under the section, which lays down one of the most important minority rights, the directors must call an extraordinary general meeting on the requisition of the holders of not less than one-tenth of such of the paid-up capital of the company as carries the right of voting at general meetings, and if the directors do not, pursuant to any such requisition, convene a meeting within 21 days the requisitionists, or any of them representing more than one-half of their total voting rights, may them-

[14] *i.e.* without anyone voting against it.
[15] See para. 61–04, *post*.
[16] *Macdougall* v. *Gardiner* (1875) 10 Ch.App. 606.
[17] *Ball* v. *Metal Industries Ltd.*, 1957 S.L.T. 124; 1957 S.C. 315.

selves convene such a meeting; the rights of the requisitionists are discussed later in detail.[18]

The directors are also obliged to convene an extraordinary general meeting if the net assets of a public company are half or less of the amount of the company's called-up share capital.[19]

An auditor who has resigned may requisition an extraordinary general meeting under the 1976 Act.[20]

Meetings of classes of shareholders

When required

53–06 Meetings of classes of shareholders are obviously only possible if the shares of the company are divided into various classes.[21] Class meetings have to be held when the Acts or the articles or the terms of issue so require.

The most frequent case in which class meetings are required arises when it is proposed to alter, vary or affect the rights of a particular class of shares.[22] The articles normally provide in this case that the holders of shares of that class shall sanction the variation by a resolution passed at a separate meeting of holders of those shares or shall otherwise consent in writing. Thus Table A provides that the rights of a particular class of shares can only be varied with the consent in writing of the holders of three-fourths of the shares of the class or with the sanction of an extraordinary resolution passed at a separate general meeting of the holders of the shares of that class (art. 4), unless otherwise provided by the terms of issue; this provision of article 4 applies whether or not the company is being wound up. If the articles require for the variation of class rights the consent of a specified proportion of a class of shareholders by means of a resolution of a class meeting or in another form, the minority of that particular class of shares has a valuable right to object (1948 Act, s. 72)[23]: the holders of 15 per cent. of the issued shares of that class being persons who did not consent to the resolution—*i.e.* who either voted against it, or abstained, or did not attend the meeting either in person or by proxy—may object within 21 days to the alteration approved by the majority of the class and may apply to the court to have the variation cancelled. The court will disallow the variation[24] if satisfied that it would unfairly prejudice the shareholders of the class (s. 72 (2) and (3)). The decision of the court on such an application is final (s. 72 (4)) and the company has to file with the Registrar

---

[18] See para. 53–08, *post*.
[19] 1980 Act, s. 34. See Chap. 31.
[20] 1976 Act, s. 16.
[21] See para. 34–06, *ante*. However, it appears that for the purpose of s. 206 of the 1948 Act heterogeneous groups within a single class may have to meet separately: *Re Hellenic & General Trust Ltd.* [1976] 1 W.L.R. 123. See Chap. 79, *infra*.
[22] See para. 34–13, *ante*.
[23] See also para. 34–16, *ante*.
[24] Variation, in this connection, includes abrogation (s. 72 (6)).

of Companies a copy of the court order within 15 days after it is made under penalty of a default fine (s. 72 (5)). It should be noted that section 72 only comes into operation and can only be invoked if the articles contain provisions similar to those of article 4 with respect to the class of shares in question, *viz.* that the consent of a specified proportion of shareholders of the particular class of shares at a separate class meeting or in another form is required. Similar provisions apply where the articles do not contain a variation procedure.[25]

Sometimes the articles provide—and, in certain circumstances, this may be a salutary provision—that, if the rights of one class of shares are altered, varied or affected, separate meetings not only of that class but likewise of another class, or all other classes, of shares in the company shall be held which have to approve the proposed alteration in the manner specified by the articles.

The Act provides that the court may convene meetings of classes of shareholders in the case of reconstruction (1948 Act, s. 206).[26]

Class meetings and meetings of all shareholders

Where the Acts or the articles require separate meetings of a class of shareholders, two general meetings have to be held, *viz.* a meeting of all the shareholders and a meeting of the class in question. The requirements as to notices, quorum, procedure and resolutions have to be satisfied with respect to each of these meetings independently and separately.

Procedure at class meetings

The procedure at class meetings is the same as that at meetings of all shareholders, *mutatis mutandis*, unless the articles contain other provisions. The former provisions of Table A that at class meetings two persons at least holding or representing by proxy one-third of the issued shares of the class shall constitute the necessary quorum and that any holder of shares of the class being present in person or by proxy may demand a poll (art. 4, last sentence) were repealed by the 1980 Act, s. 88 and Sched. 4.

Who may convene general meetings

Meetings convened by the directors

53–07 When the directors wish or are bound to call a general meeting, they will normally do so by resolution passed at a duly convened and constituted meeting of the board,[27] but if the articles provide that a resolution in writing signed by the directors without meeting is as effective as a resolution passed at a board meeting, as is normally the case (art. 106), a general

[25] See 1980 Act, s. 32 and para. 34–17, *ante*.
[26] See para. 79–08, *post*, and note 2, *ante*.
[27] *Re Haycraft Gold Reduction, etc., Co.* [1900] 2 Ch. 230; *Harben* v. *Phillips* (1883) 23 Ch.D. 14.

meeting may be convened on a resolution so signed. Notice of a general meeting given by the secretary without the sanction of the directors or other proper authority is invalid,[28] but such a notice may be ratified by the directors before the meeting.[29]

Moreover, a resolution passed by a meeting which has the appearance of being regularly convened will not be invalidated because some of the directors who joined in convening the meeting were not duly appointed.[30] A meeting convened as a meeting of directors may be valid as a meeting of the company if all the members are present.[31]

Directors, in calling meetings, as in other matters, must consider the general interest of the company.

Meetings convened by the shareholders

53–08 It has already been observed earlier that a specified minority of shareholders is entitled to demand, or—as it is usually called—to requisition, an extraordinary general meeting.[32] This right may be given to the shareholders by the articles of the company, or the shareholders may rely on their statutory right which is laid down in section 132 of the 1948 Act. Where the right in the articles is independent of the statutory right, the shareholders can proceed under either provision, as may seem the more convenient, but whereas the articles may provide wider powers for this purpose, they cannot abridge the statutory right. Shareholders have been held to have forfeited their right to requisition a meeting if, in their capacity as directors, they have prevented the board from carrying out its duty to convene a meeting under section 132 by absenting themselves from directors' meetings, when the result of their absence was (in terms of the particular company's articles) to secure a voting advantage for themselves.[33]

The minority which by virtue of section 132 may requisition an extraordinary general meeting must consist of not less than one-tenth of the paid-up capital of the company carrying voting rights at the date of the deposit of the requisition (s. 132 (1)).[34]

If the directors fail to call the meeting within 21 days from the date of deposit of the requisition, the requisitionists themselves, or those holding more than one-half of their voting rights, are entitled to do so; they have to convene the meeting as the directors would be required to do it, or as nearly as possible, and if the meeting so convened is not held within three

---

[28] *Ibid.*; and see *Re State of Wyoming Syndicate* [1901] 2 Ch. 431.
[29] *Hooper* v. *Kerr Stuart & Co.* (1900) 83 L.T. 729.
[30] *Browne* v. *La Trinidad* (1887) 37 Ch.D. 1; *British Asbestos Co.* v. *Boyd* [1903] 2 Ch. 439. See also *Boschoek Proprietary Co.* v. *Fuke* [1906] 1 Ch. 148, where the object was to confirm past proceedings. But see *Morris* v. *Kanssen* [1946] A.C. 459 (H.L.).
[31] *Re Express Engineering Works* [1920] 1 Ch. 466.
[32] See para. 53–05, *ante*.
[33] *Thyme* v. *Lauder* 1925 S.N. 123.
[34] The provision applies likewise to guarantee companies and unlimited companies but in the case of companies not having a share capital the minority must consist of members holding not less than one-tenth of the total voting rights (s. 132 (1)).

months from the date of the deposit of the requisition, the requisition is exhausted; the requisitionists have lost the right to convene a meeting and if they still wish to do so, they would have to serve a new requisition (s.132 (3) and (4)).

If the requisitionists convene a meeting by reason of the failure of the directors to do so, they may recover from the company their reasonable expenses incurred in the convening of the meeting, and the company may retain such sums out of moneys which become due to the defaulting directors by way of fee or other remuneration for their services (s. 132 (5)). The company is not entitled to retain the sums out of dividend due to the directors as shareholders of the company, nor can it apparently sue the directors for those sums, though a set-off against a claim by the directors for fees or remuneration would be within the provision.

The requisition which the minority shareholders have to deposit at the registered office of the company must state the objects of the requisitioned meeting (s. 132 (2)). All the requisitioning members must sign the requisition, but the requisition may comprise a number of documents in like form signed separately by the several requisitionists, and slight differences of language in the documents so signed will not invalidate the effect of the requisition.[35] Nor will the mere fact that some of the resolutions referred to in the requisition could not be put to the meeting relieve the directors from an obligation to call the meeting.[36]

It is thought that the shareholders can demand the convening of a general meeting under section 132 where the requirements of that section are satisfied, even though the articles enable the requisitionists themselves to call the meeting.[37] In an urgent case a mandatory injunction may be granted directing the directors to call a meeting "forthwith" under that section.[38] Where the directors had declined to call a meeting, but convened it immediately after the issue of a writ by the requisitionists, the latter were given the costs of the action.[39]

The 1948 Act further states that if the articles do not make other provision, two or more members holding not less than one-tenth of the issued capital may call a meeting (s. 134 (*b*)). This section is of very limited application, since the articles almost invariably empower the directors to convene meetings (arts. 47–49). Under article 49, if there are insufficient directors available to form a quorum, any director or any two members may call an extraordinary general meeting; in the absence of such an article, a meeting may be convened under section 134 (*b*) if there are no directors available for this purpose.[40]

---

[35] *Fruit and Vegetable Growers' Association* v. *Kekewich* [1912] 2 Ch. 52.
[36] *Isle of Wight Ry.* v. *Tahourdin* (1883) 25 Ch.D. 320.
[37] The view expressed in the text is not in harmony with *Macdougall* v. *Gardiner* (1875) 10 Ch.App. 606, but is, it is submitted, supported by the wording of s. 132.
[38] s. 66 (1) of the Act of 1908; *Rutherford* v. *Farmery* (1915, R. No. 1524), Astbury J., November 12, 1915. And in *Maxwell* v. *Mitchell* (1921, M. No. 2633).
[39] By P. O. Lawrence J. (June 27, 1922).
[40] *Re Brick and Stone Co.* [1878] W.N. 140.

Meeting convened by the court

53–09 If it is impracticable to call a meeting or to conduct it in the manner prescribed by the articles, the court may, either on its own motion or on the application of a director or any member entitled to vote, order a meeting to be called, held and conducted in such manner as the court thinks fit, and may direct a "meeting" of one member (1948 Act, s. 135).[41] The court may exercise its jurisdiction even where the application is opposed by other shareholders,[42] for a minority may not utilise the quorum provisions as a right to frustrate the wishes of the majority.[43]

The court has further power to order a meeting of the shareholders or of any class thereof to be summoned during the reconstruction of the company (1948 Act, s. 206 (1)).[44]

It is thought that in exercise of the very wide power contained in section 75 of the 1980 Act the court has power, if the requirements of that section are satisfied, to convene a general meeting of the members of the company or of any class thereof.

Meetings convened by the Department of Trade

53–10 The Department of Trade has power to call or to direct the calling of the annual general meeting of the company if default has been made in holding such a meeting (1948 Act, s. 131 (2) and (3)). This power of the Department of Trade been discussed earlier.[45]

Meetings convened by an auditor who has resigned

If an auditor has resigned his office under section 16 of the 1976 Act and has included in his resignation a statement of the circumstances connected with his resignation which he considers should be brought to the attention of the shareholders or creditors he may require the directors to call an extraordinary general meeting to consider whatever relevant matters he may wish to put before that meeting (1976 Act, s. 17 (1)).

If the directors fail to call the meeting within 21 days from the date of deposit of the requisition, for a day not more than 28 days after the date on which the notice convening the meeting is given they are liable to prosecution for a criminal offence (1976 Act, s. 17 (3)).

Restraining a company from holding a general meeting

53–11 A strong case is required before the court will restrain a general meeting of the company.[46] In *Harben* v. *Phillips*,[47] directors prima facie improperly

---

[41] The provision as to a meeting of one member was first introduced by s. 6 of the Act of 1947. The court under the formal legislation could (and of course still can) reduce the quorum. *Edinburgh Workmen's Houses Improvement Co.* 1935 S.C. 56; 1934 S.L.T. 513.

[42] *Re El Sombrero Ltd.* [1958] Ch. 900 (where the meaning of the word "impracticable" is considered).

[43] *Re H. R. Paul & Son Ltd.* (1973) 118 S.J. 166.

[44] See para. 79–08, *post*.

[45] See para. 53–03, *ante*.

[46] *Isle of Wight Ry.* v. *Tahourdin* (1883) 25 Ch.D. 320.

[47] (1883) 23 Ch.D. 14.

appointed were restrained from holding a meeting called by them as an extraordinary general meeting or from representing it as such. In case of a deadlock the court will sometimes appoint a receiver.[48]

Approval of members without holding general meeting

53–12 If it can be shown that all the shareholders who have a right to attend and vote at a general meeting of the company assent to some matter which a general meeting of the company could carry into effect, then that assent is as binding as a resolution in general meeting would be.[49] The assent may take the form of signing the balance sheet[50] or the adoption of a resolution of which inadequate notice has been given.[51] In exceptional circumstances members are treated as having assented if, with knowledge of the assent of the others, they stood by without protesting and by their conduct created the impression that they did not intend to object; their attitude constitutes an estoppel by conduct.[52] Shareholders who have no right to attend and vote need neither approve nor be consulted.[53]

---

48 *Stanfield* v. *Gibbon* [1925] W.N. 11. This would not be possible in Scotland where, however, a judicial factor might be appointed. See *Patrick Fraser, Petitioner* 1971 S.L.T. 146.
49 *Re Duomatic Ltd.* [1969] 2 Ch. 365; *Re Express Engineering Works Ltd.* [1920] 1 Ch. 466; *Parker and Cooper Ltd.* v. *Reading* [1926] Ch. 975; *Re Bailey, Hay & Co. Ltd.* [1971] 1 W.L.R. 1357; *Re Gee & Co. Ltd.* [1974] 2 W.L.R. 515.
50 *Re Duomatic Ltd., ante; Re Gee & Co. Ltd., ante.*
51 *Re Bailey, Hay & Co. Ltd.* [1971] 1 W.L.R. 1357.
52 *Ibid.*
53 *Re Duomatic Ltd., ante.*

CHAPTER 54

NOTICE OF GENERAL MEETINGS

Length of notice

54–01 The length of notice required by the 1948 Act for convening a general meeting is not less than 21 days for the annual general meeting and not less than 14 days for other meetings (s. 133). This requirement overrides any provision in the articles for a shorter period: but articles can validly provide for longer notice than the statutory minimum periods (s. 133 (1)).

If any resolution is to be proposed at a meeting as a special resolution, not less than 21 days' notice must be given whether or not the meeting is an annual general meeting (s. 141 (2)), except where condition (a) or (b) below—as appropriate—is complied with.

A meeting may, however, be called by shorter notice and is to be deemed to be duly called if it is so agreed

(a) in the case of the annual general meeting, by all members entitled to attend and vote;

(b) in the case of any other meeting, by a majority in the number of the members having a right to attend and vote at the meeting and holding not less than 95 per cent. in nominal value of the shares giving a right to attend and vote at the meeting, or, if there is no share capital, representing not less than 95 per cent. of the total voting rights at the meeting of all the members (s. 133 (3)).

Calculation of period of notice

54–02 The articles usually provide that the period of notice shall be "clear" days, *i.e.* excluding both the day of service and that of the meeting (*e.g.* art. 50).[1] Where the articles fail to specify "clear" days of notice a different interpretation of the words "not less than 21 days" in section 141 appears to have arisen in England and Scotland. In England this provision is interpreted as implying "clear" days[2] but this was considered to be erroneous in the more recent Scottish case of *Neil McLeod & Sons Ltd., Petitioners*.[3] It is evident from that case that in Scotland the provisions as to notice will be satisfied if the meeting is held on the last day of the specified number after the day the notice is deemed to have been served. In reckoning the period of notice the day of service is excluded, but the day of the meeting may be counted. It is submitted that this is a more satisfying interpretation of the statutory provision.

---

[1] See also *Re Bailey, Hay & Co. Ltd.* [1971] 1 W.L.R. 1357.
[2] *Re Hector Whaling Ltd.* [1936] Ch. 208.
[3] 1967 S.L.T. 46; 1967 S.C. 16, see also *Aberdeen Comb Works Co. Ltd.* 1902, 10 S.L.T. 210.

To whom notice is to be given

54–03 Notice of meetings must be given to all those persons who, under the articles, are entitled to receive notice[4]: in addition to the members, the auditors are entitled to notice of all general meetings (1967 Act, s. 14 (7)). An auditor who has been removed or has resigned before the expiration of his term of office is entitled to notice either of the general meeting at which his term of office would have expired or of any general meeting at which it is proposed to fill the vacancy created by his removal or resignation (1976 Act, ss. 15 (6) and 17 (5)). If an auditor who has resigned has requisitioned a meeting under section 17 (1) of the 1976 Act[5] he is also entitled to notice of that meeting (s. 17 (5)). In the absence of any provision in the articles, only those persons who are entitled to attend and vote at a meeting are entitled to receive notice of it. An omission to give due notice to any person entitled to it invalidates a meeting[6]; but a clause in the articles commonly relaxes this rule as regards an accidental omission[7] or non-receipt (art. 51); and as to members who are abroad, see *infra*. The failure to give notice to one member of a committee has been held to invalidate the meeting even though that member had given general notice of inability to attend.[8] To convene a meeting of the subscribers of the memorandum a reasonable notice is sufficient. Two days was held sufficient in *John Morley Building Co.* v. *Barras*.[9] Apart from any express provision to the contrary, Sunday counts as a day for the purpose of notice.[10]

Personal representatives and trustees in bankruptcy

Where the articles provide for notice to "members," the executors or administrators of a deceased member, until registered, are not entitled to notice, nor is the company bound to send notice to the deceased's address, after official notification of the death has been received.[11] Sometimes, however, the articles provide that notice must be given to the personal representative or trustee in bankruptcy—even if unregistered—of a shareholder (art. 134 (*b*)).

---

[4] For the requirement of notice to a Sheriff on an execution order see *Hellyer* v. *Sheriff of Yorkshire* [1975] Ch. 16; para 85–72, *post*.

[5] See para. 73–03, *supra*.

[6] *Smyth* v. *Darley* (1849) 2 H.L.C. 789. But the right of the shareholder to claim that the meeting was invalid because the notice was defective might be lost by acquiescence or, in England, by operation of the equitable doctrine of laches: *Re Bailey, Hay & Co. Ltd.* [1971] 1 W.L.R. 1357.

[7] As to what may constitute an accidental omission, see *Re West Canadian Collieries Ltd.* [1962] Ch. 370. A mistake of law is not "accidental": *Musselwhite* v. *C. H. Musselwhite & Son Ltd.* [1962] Ch. 964.

[8] *Young* v. *Ladies Imperial Club* [1920] 2 K.B. 523; *John* v. *Rees* [1970] Ch. 345, 402.

[9] [1891] 2 Ch. 386.

[10] *Child* v. *Edwards* [1909] 2 K.B. 753.

[11] *Allen* v. *Gold Reefs of West Africa* [1900] 1 Ch. 656, 670, *per* Lindley M.R.

Shareholders resident abroad

Where a shareholder is resident abroad beyond calling distance, no notice need be given[12]; the articles usually go further and dispense with notice to members having no registered address in the United Kingdom (art. 134 (*a*)).

Dispensation with notice

In one case the requirements as to notice may be altogether dispensed with. In *Re Express Engineering Works*[13] Younger L.J. said: "If you have all the shareholders present, then all the requirements in connection with a meeting of the company are observed." In *Parker and Cooper Ltd.* v. *Reading*,[14] Astbury J. said: "Where a transaction is *intra vires* the company and honest the sanction of all the members of the company, however expressed, is sufficient to validate it," and Brightman J. said in *Re Bailey, Hay & Co. Ltd.*[15]: "It is established law that a company is bound in a matter, *intra vires* the company, by the unanimous agreement of all its corporators." Further, in *Re Oxted Motor Co.*[16] it was held that the requirements of the Companies Act then in force for notice of an extraordinary resolution did not invalidate a resolution of all the members, who thereby waived the requirement.

Contents of notice. Special or ordinary business

54–04 Every notice calling a general meeting shall show, with reasonable prominence, a statement that a member entitled to attend and vote may appoint a proxy; failure to comply with this provision may render every officer of the company who is in default liable to a fine (s. 136 (2)). On proxies generally, see paras. 55–11 to 55–13, *post*.

The notice of meeting must be given in accordance with the articles. The notice must specify the date, place and hour of meeting, and, in the case of special business, the general nature thereof. Where the articles are thus framed, it is necessary to define what is special business, and this is usually done by saying that, at the annual general meeting, the consideration of the accounts and reports, the election of directors and other officers in the place of those retiring by rotation and the declaration of a dividend shall be considered ordinary business; but that any *other* business transacted at an annual general meeting and *all* business transacted at an extraordinary meeting shall be considered *special* business. An annual general meeting may deal with special business, if the notice specifies it.[17] The noticc

[12] *Re Union Hill Silver Co.* (1870) 22 L.T. 400; *Smyth* v. *Darley* (1849) 2 H.L.Cas. 789; *Young* v. *Ladies' Imperial Club* [1920] 2 K.B. 523.

[13] [1920] 1 Ch. 466. See also para. 53–12, *ante*, as to the dispensation with the necessity of holding a meeting.

[14] [1926] Ch. 975, 982.

[15] [1971] 1 W.L.R. 1357, 1366.

[16] [1921] 3 K.B. 32.

[17] *Graham* v. *Van Diemen's Land Co.* (1856) 26 L.J.Ex.73.

convening a meeting at which any special business is to be transacted must state the nature thereof, otherwise the notice is irregular and the special business cannot be dealt with.[18] An injunction was granted restraining the directors from acting on a resolution passed at an extraordinary general meeting where the notice had given insufficient particulars of the proposals for the members to exercise their judgment thereon.[18]

Where the court orders the directors to use their "best endeavours" to procure a certain state of affairs which necessitates the passing of a resolution the directors must issue a circular which invites a favourable response from the shareholders.[19]

Circulation of intended resolutions and statements

54–05 By section 140 of the 1948 Act, members representing

(1) not less than one-twentieth of the total voting rights of all the members having a right to vote at the meeting which the requisition relates, or

(2) not less than 100 members holding shares on which there has been paid up an average sum per member of not less than £100.

can claim by requisition at their own expense that the company shall circulate the members entitled to have notice of any resolution which is intended to be moved, and which may properly be moved, at the annual general meeting, or any statement of not more than 1,000 words with respect to the business to be dealt with at any meeting. A copy of the requisition signed by the requisitionists must be deposited at the registered office not less than six weeks before the meeting, where it requires notice of a resolution, and in other cases one week before the meeting. A reasonable sum for expenses must also be deposited. The court may disallow the circulation if needless publicity is given to defamatory matter.

The requirements of this section cannot be avoided by giving special notice under section 142 where that is relevant.[20]

Special notice

54–06 Certain ordinary resolutions require "special notice" to be given *to*, not *by*, the company. The resolutions requiring special notice are for

(1) the removal of a director (1948 Act, s. 184 (2));

(2) the appointment of a director over 70 years of age (1948 Act, s. 185 (5));

(3) the appointment as auditor of a person other than the retiring auditor (1976 Act, s. 15);

---

[18] *Lawe's Case* (1852) 1 De G.M. & G. 421; *Re Hampshire Land Co.* [1896] 2 Ch. 743; *Kaye* v. *Croydon Tramways Co.* [1898] 1 Ch. 358 (C.A.); *Pacific Coast Coal Mines Ltd.* v. *Arbuthnot* [1917] A.C. 607.

[19] *Northern Counties Securities Ltd.* v. *Jackson & Steeple Ltd.* [1974] 1 W.L.R. 1133.

[20] *Pedley* v. *Inland Waterways Association Ltd.* [1977] 1 All E.R. 209.

(4) the filling of a casual vacancy in the office of auditor;
(5) the reappointment as auditor of a retiring auditor who was appointed by the directors to fill a casual vacancy; or
(6) the removal of an auditor before the expiration of his term of office (1976 Act, s. 15 (1) (*a*)–(*d*)).

The requirement of special notice means that not less than 28 days before the meeting at which the resolution is to be moved, notice of the intention to move it must be given to the company. The company must then give its members notice of the resolution at the same time and in the same manner as it gives notice of the meeting. If that is not practicable it must give them notice of the resolution either by advertisement in a newspaper having an appropriate circulation, or in any other mode allowed by the articles, not less than 21 days before the meeting (s. 142). This provision covers bearer shares.

The requirement on the company under section 142 of the 1948 Act to give notice of a resolution to the members has been held not to confer on any individual member of a company who gives the requisite notice the right to have any resolution of which special notice is required placed by the company on the agenda for the relevant meeting, irrespective of any rights conferred on the member by virtue of section 140; see para. 54–05, *ante*. It is merely intended to confer on the members of a company the right to receive notice of any resolution of which special notice is required, and which has been duly given and which is to form part of the agenda to be dealt with at the relevant meeting. In *Pedley* v. *Inland Waterways Association Ltd.*[21] the plaintiff gave the requisite notice under section 142 and requested inclusion of his resolution on the agenda. He had no rights under the articles to require such an inclusion and he could not comply with the conditions of section 140 to compel inclusion. Slade J. stated that the requirement in section 142 could admit of two interpretations, but for reasons of practicality and considering the type of resolutions for which special notice is required he regarded the section as a protective rather than an enabling one. Any right of inclusion on the agenda must derive from the articles or section 140. Any other decision would have produced an anomaly in that rights more extensive than those under section 140 would have been acquired simply because the resolution was one of those specified in the Companies Acts as requiring special notice.

The requirement of special notice is relaxed if a meeting is called within 28 days of the notice being given (s. 142, proviso): this proviso prevents the directors from calling a meeting at shorter notice than 28 days without including the proposed resolution in the convening notice on the ground that the statutory requirement of 28 days' notice has not been complied with.

---

[21] [1977] 1 All E.R. 209.

Terms of notices not strictly construed; but must be reasonably sufficient

54–07 Except in cases of a special or extraordinary resolution it is not necessary that the resolution as passed at the meeting should be in the identical terms of the resolution specified in the notice of meeting, provided that the resolution is, in substance, covered by the notice.[22]

Notices are not construed with excessive strictness.[23] Substantial compliance with the articles is sufficient,[24] and in construing a notice, the rule is that the shareholders, to whom it is addressed, are to be presumed to know the Acts of Parliament, and also the terms of the memorandum and articles; and they must therefore read the notice in the light of these documents.[25]

Section 141 (1) and (2) of the 1948 Act state that the notice of an extraordinary or special resolution must specify the intention to propose the resolution "as an extraordinary (or special) resolution." It is normal practice to make specific reference to the nature of the resolution in the notice accordingly, and it has been held in England that failure to do so invalidates the proceedings[26]; in Scotland, however, the opposite view has been taken.[27] Copies of special resolutions, extraordinary resolutions and certain other resolutions must be registered with the Registrar of Companies (s. 143). Notices are to be construed as a businessman would construe them, and to be understood in the ordinary sense[28]; but it is not enough in a notice of an extraordinary meeting merely to say "special business."[29] Nor is it enough to state that remuneration is to be allowed to the directors, without stating the amount, if the amount is large.[30] Nor is it enough, at any rate in the case of an extraordinary or special resolution, to say that the capital will be increased without stating the amount.[31]

54–08 A notice of a resolution to adopt a particular course of action will not justify the adoption of only a part thereof, for it is impossible for the court to know how many shareholders abstained from attending the meeting, being satisfied that the arrangement as it was proposed was advantageous to them, and being quite content to exercise no voice about it.[32] Thus, where a meeting was convened to consider resolutions for reconstruction and for winding up as incidental thereto, and at the meeting a naked resolution for winding up was passed, it was held to be invalid as not in

---

[22] *Torbock* v. *Lord Westbury* [1902] 2 Ch. 871.

[23] *Grant* v. *United Kingdom Switchback, etc., Co.* (1888) 40 Ch.D. 135, 137; *Henderson* v. *Bank of Australasia* (1890) 45 Ch.D. 330.

[24] *Re British Sugar Refining Co.* (1857) 3 K. & J. 408; *Young* v. *South African, etc., Syndicate* [1896] 2 Ch. 268.

[25] *Re Espuela Land and Cattle Co.* (1900) 48 W.R. 684.

[26] *MacConnell* v. *E. Prill & Co. Ltd.* [1916] 2 Ch. 57 (approved in *Re Moorgate Mercantile Holdings Ltd.* [1980] 1 All E.R. 40).

[27] *North of Scotland, etc., Co.* 1920 S.C. 94; 1920, 1 S.L.T. 21.

[28] *Alexander* v. *Simpson* (1889) 43 Ch.D. 139.

[29] *Wills* v. *Murray* (1850) 4 Ex.Reps. 843, 869. See para. 54–04, *ante*.

[30] *Baillie* v. *Oriental Telephone, etc., Co.* [1915] 1 Ch. 503.

[31] *MacConnell* v. *E. Prill & Co.* [1916] 2 Ch. 57.

[32] *Clinch* v. *Financial Corporation* (1868) L.R. 5 Eq. 450, 478.

accordance with the notice.[33] Where, however, the notice specified several separate resolutions, one of these being to wind up the company, and the others (which were *ultra vires*) being concerned with the sale of the undertaking and consequent reorganisation, the winding-up resolution was effective and the others void.[34] It is, therefore, clear that if one resolution is only to be effective if other proposed resolutions become effective, either they must be worded accordingly or they must be set out as a single resolution: and the notice must be drafted accordingly.

If the articles or the Acts give a general power to deal with certain business at a general meeting without notice of such business, the fact that the notice convening the meeting specifies a particular resolution for dealing with such business does not limit the powers of the meeting: *Bethell* v. *Trench Tubeless Tyre Co.*[35] In this case it was held that at a meeting to confirm a special resolution for winding up voluntarily, the company, having a general power under the Act to appoint a liquidator without notice, might appoint B though the notice stated that A would be proposed. In *Betts & Co.* v. *Macnaghten*[36] the notice showed a proposal to elect A, B and C as directors for the ensuing year. At the meeting D and E were also elected and Eve J. held that this was within the terms of the notice since the articles provided that the appointment of directors was part of the business of an ordinary meeting (which this was) and required not specific notice.

54–09 Where a contract is to be submitted to a meeting for confirmation, and directors of the company are interested therein, it has been held that the notice convening the meeting should give particulars as to that interest.[37]

Where a meeting is convened to pass a special resolution adopting a new set of articles in lieu of the existing articles, the learned editor of the nineteenth edition considered that if the notice stated the terms of the proposed resolution, that was a sufficient compliance with section 141 of the Act, without the notice specifying the details of alterations involved. This approach is not, however, in accordance with the only reported case on the point, in which the Court of Session (Inner House) held that if the text of the new articles was not sent with the notice, and no reference was made to where their text could be inspected, the notice was insufficient.[38] If there is any substantial alteration of rights, certainly short particulars should be set out of these alterations and inspection of the proposed new articles should be offered at the registered office or elsewhere. In the

[33] *Re Teede & Bishop* (1901) 70 L.J.Ch. 409.
[34] *Thomson* v. *Henderson's Transvaal Estates Co.* [1908] 1 Ch. 765: and see *Clinch* v. *Financial Corporation* (1868) 4 Ch.App. 117 and Lord Selborne in *Ashbury Ry., etc., Co.* v. Riche (1875) L.R. 7 H.L. 653, 693.
[35] [1900] 1 Ch. 408.
[36] [1910] 1 Ch. 430.
[37] *Kaye* v. *Croydon Tramways Co.* [1898] 1 Ch. 358 (C.A.); *Tiessen* v. *Henderson* [1899] 1 Ch. 861; *Normandy* v. *Ind, Coope & Co.* [1908] 1 Ch. 84. See *contra, Southall* v. *British Mutual, etc., Soc.* (1871) 6 Ch.App. 614 (C.A.) and *Grant* v. *United Kingdom Switchback Ry.* (1888) 40 Ch.D. 135 (C.A.).
[38] *North of Scotland, etc., Co.* 1920 S.C. 94; 1920 1 S.L.T. 21.

course of considering what information as to the proposals to be made should be given in a notice convening a meeting Kekewich J. said[39]: "Every case must be looked at with regard to its particular circumstances, and those directors will be best advised who take the shareholders into their confidence and tell them that they propose . . . to affect the position of the members in important particulars which can be easily specified." This is the modern practice.[40]

A notice that a meeting will be held in a certain contingency is not a good notice,[41] but a notice which is certain is valid though the business to which it refers is contingent.[42]

PRACTICE NOTES

Issue of notice

54–10 The issue of a notice of a meeting to a shareholder resident overseas (see para. 54–03) cannot be avoided by a company the shares in which are listed on the Stock Exchange because of the requirement to send to all persons entitled to vote at a meeting proxy forms with provision for two-way voting (Listing Agreement, para. 12).

Contents of notice

54–11 If a notice of an annual general meeting of a listed company includes special business (see para. 54–04 *ante*), proof prints of the notice must be submitted in advance to The Stock Exchange, together with proof prints of the form of proxt (Listing Agreement, para. 6).

The notice convening the annual general meeting of a listed company must include a note stating the place and time at which copies of the service contracts of directors will be available for inspection or, if there are no such contracts, a statement to that effect (Listing Agreement, para. 11 (*c*)).

---

[39] In *Normandy* v. *Ind, Coope & Co.* [1908] 1 Ch. 84, 102.
[40] See, too, *Grant* v. *United Kingdom Switchback Ry.* (1888) 40 Ch.D. 135; *Southall* v. *British Mutual, etc., Soc.* (1871) 6 Ch.App. 614.
[41] *Alexander* v. *Simpson* (1889) 43 Ch.D. 139; *North of Scotland, etc., Co., supra.*
[42] *Tiessen* v. *Henderson* [1899] 1 Ch. 861; *Re Jenner Institute of Preventive Medicine* (1899) 15 T.L.R. 394; *Re North of England Steamship Co.* [1905] 2 Ch. 15.

CHAPTER 55

PROCEEDINGS AT GENERAL MEETINGS

What constitutes a "meeting"

On principle a meeting comprises more than one person

55–01 The word "meeting" prima facie means a coming together of more than one person. So that where a single shareholder purported to hold a meeting of a company incorporated under the Stannaries Act 1869 for the purpose of making a call, the Court of Appeal held that no meeting was constituted and accordingly its proceedings were invalid and ineffectual. Lord Coleridge C.J. accepted that it is possible to show that the word "meeting" has a meaning different from the ordinary meaning, but there was nothing there to show that to be the case.[1] Even where the single member held proxies for the only other three members, no meeting was constituted.[2] Where two members initially constituted a meeting and one subsequently withdrew then there ceased to be a meeting.[3] This must be distinguished from the case where a meeting initially is constituted by several members forming the required quorum, but subsequently is depleted below the quorum figure although still comprising two or more members. In that event the proceedings after the depletion are valid.[4] In *Re London Flats Ltd.*[5] the question was "meeting or no meeting," not "quorum or no quorum." Any hardship caused by this decision may be rectified under section 135 of the 1948 Act.[6]

Meeting consisting of one person

55–02 In *East* v. *Bennett Brothers Ltd.*[7] Warrington J., whilst recognising that in an ordinary case it is quite clear that a meeting must consist of more than one person, found that the special circumstances of the case took it out of the ordinary rule. The "meeting" in dispute was a meeting of a separate class of shareholders: all the shares of the class were held by one person, which was permitted under the constitution. This shareholder attended a "meeting" of the class and signed a resolution purported to be passed thereat. The "meeting" was held to be valid and the resolution validly passed.

In modern company law, statutory provisions state occasionally that

---

[1] *Sharp* v. *Dawes* (1876) 2 Q.B.D. 26; *Re Sanitary Carbon Co.* [1877] W.N. 223; *Prain & Sons*, 1947 S.C. 325; 1947 S.L.T. 289.
[2] *Re Sanitary Carbon Co.* [1877] W.N. 223.
[3] *Re London Flats Ltd.* [1969] 1 W.L.R. 711.
[4] *Re Hartley Baird Ltd.* [1955] Ch. 143.
[5] [1969] 1 W.L.R. 711.
[6] See para. 53–09, *ante*.
[7] [1911] 1 Ch. 163.

"one member of the company present in person or by proxy shall be deemed to constitute a meeting" (see 1948 Act, ss. 131 (2) and 135 (1)). In view of the recognition, by the courts, in extraordinary circumstances of a "meeting" consisting of one person only it is not surprising that these provisions are made expressly declaratory of the common law; the legislature thus recognises, as is indeed the case, that there may be other unusual cases in which a "meeting" may consist of one member only.

In *Re M. J. Shanley Contracting Ltd.*[8] the directors, having resolved to put the company into liquidation, convened the necessary general meeting. The chairman and his wife owned 95 per cent. of the issued shares and Z owned the rest. Before the meeting Z indicated his assent to the proposed liquidation and did not attend the meeting. The chairman's wife did not attend either but gave her proxy to the chairman who was the only person present at the "meeting." On the question whether the resolution passed at the meeting was valid, Oliver J. held that it could not be said that a meeting had taken place but that an effective extraordinary resolution could be passed without a meeting since all the shareholders entitled to attend and vote had assented. The winding up was therefore effective from the date of the resolution.

Quorum of general meeting

55–03 In order to constitute a general meeting a quorum of members must be present. If there be no provisions as to a quorum in the articles, two members[9] personally present are requisite for a quorum (s. 134 (*c*)).

It is submitted that, if all the members are present, it is immaterial that the quorum required is more than the total number of shareholders.[10]

Where articles provide for a quorum "present in person or by proxy," proxies can be counted. When the articles provide for a quorum "present in person" (see art. 53), proxies cannot be counted[11]: but a company present by its representative under section 139 of the 1948 Act is treated as a member present in person and is counted in the quorum.[12] If the articles require a specified number of "members" to be personally present, one person may be counted as two or more members for this purpose if he holds shares in different capacities, *e.g.* as a trustee and also in his own right.[13] Prima facie "members" means members entitled to vote.[14] Some-

---

[8] (1979) 124 S.J. 239; see also *Cane* v. *Jones* [1980] 1 W.L.R. 1451. These cases are difficult to reconcile with *Grain & Sons* 1947 S.C. 325; 1947 S.L.T. 289.

[9] This has always been the case for private companies, and the reduction from three to two members for public companies is provided by the 1980 Act, Sched. 3, No. 16. But exceptionally the Department of Trade or the court may give directions that one member present in person or by proxy shall constitute a meeting (ss. 131 (2) and 135 (1)).

[10] *Re Express Engineering Works* [1920] 1 Ch. 466; *Re Oxted Motor Co. Ltd.* [1921] 3 K.B. 32.

[11] This includes a person holding a power of attorney: *M. Harris Ltd., Petitioners*, 1956 S.C. 207.

[12] *Re Kelantan Coco-Nut Estates Ltd.* [1920] W.N. 274.

[13] *Neil McLeod & Sons Ltd., Petitioners*, 1967 S.L.T. 46.

[14] *Henderson* v. *Louttit & Co. Ltd.* 1894, 21 R. 674.

times there is a different quorum fixed for general meetings of shareholders and for meetings of particular classes of shareholders (see art. 4).[15]

Where the articles of the company provide—as does article 53 of Table A—that "No business shall be transacted at any general meeting unless a quorum of members is present at the time when the meeting proceeds to business," this requirement is sufficiently complied with if the quorum is present at the beginning of the meeting, that is, when the meeting proceeds to business.[16]

Article 53, as amended by the 1980 Act, provides that two persons present in person or by proxy shall constitute a quorum. If no quorum be present, then there is no meeting and the proceedings are invalid.[17] Sometimes the articles provide that for some particular class of business a smaller quorum shall be sufficient. Usually it is provided that if a quorum is not present the meeting is to stand adjourned, say, for a week, and that at the adjourned meeting those who are present shall be a quorum. A provision to this effect is found in article 54. In the light of *Daimler Co. Ltd.* v. *Continental Tyre and Rubber Co. (Great Britain)*[18] it is sufficient if at the adjourned meeting one member is present in person and one by proxy. It would appear, as a matter of construction, that under such articles two members present by proxy would constitute a meeting, and that even one member may be sufficient for this purpose, since, by virtue of section 6 (c) of the Interpretation Act 1978, the plural "members" includes the singular "member."[19]

The provisions relating to the quorum do not constitute a minority right. They do not enable the minority by absenting themselves from the meetings permanently to frustrate the wishes of the majority. If in these circumstances it is unlikely that a quorum will ever be reached, an application may be made to the court under section 135 of the 1948 Act for an order that a meeting should be convened and one member present in person or by proxy should constitute a quorum.[20]

Chairman of general meeting

55–04 The articles generally provide for the directors electing a chairman of their meetings (see art. 101); and the chairman so chosen is, as a rule, by the articles, to be entitled to preside at a general meeting (see art. 55); or in his absence some other director. If no director is willing to act as chairman, then some person selected by the meeting is to act. In the absence of any

---

[15] See *Hemans* v. *Hotchkiss Ordnance Co.* [1899] 1 Ch. 115.
[16] *Re Hartley Baird Ltd.* [1955] Ch. 143, disapproving, on this point, dicta in *Henderson* v. *Louttit & Co. Ltd., supra.*
[17] *Re Cambrian, etc., Co.* (1875) 31 L.T. 773; *Re Romford Canal Co.* (1883) 24 Ch.D. 85.
[18] [1916] 2 A.C. 307, 325.
[19] *Jarvis Motors (Harrow) Ltd.* v. *Carabott* [1964] 1 W.L.R. 1101.
[20] *Re H. R. Paul & Son Ltd.* (1973) 118 S.J. 166.

such provisions the meeting will itself choose its own chairman from amongst the members present (1948 Act, s. 134 (*d*)). The duty of the chairman is to keep order, to see that the business is properly conducted,[21] and to ensure that the sense of the meeting is properly ascertained in regard to any question before it. His decisions on points of order and upon any incidental questions that arise are to be taken prima facie to be correct.[22] If the articles so provide, the chairman's decision as to the validity of a vote is conclusive.[23] He must give a reasonable chance to the members present to discuss any proposed resolutions, and ensure that all views are adequately aired. But discussion must be kept within reasonable bounds, and he may stop a discussion on a resolution after it has been reasonably debated. The majority present can vote to compel him to stop the discussion, provided that a minority is not thereby stifled or oppressed.[24]

Where the articles say that he "may" adjourn, he has a discretion, and may decline to adjourn,[25] unless, as in article 57, the members present can override this discretion and insist on an adjournment. But if he departs from his duty, *e.g.* by prematurely closing the meeting and purporting to adjourn it, his acts become irregular, and it is open to the meeting to select another chairman and proceed with the business.[26]

55–05 In the case of a special or extraordinary resolution, where no poll is duly demanded, the declaration by a chairman that a resolution has been carried is, by section 141 (3) of the 1948 Act, made "*conclusive* evidence of the fact without proof of the number or proportion of the votes." It is now settled that "conclusive" in this section means what it says, conclusive and not prima facie evidence.[27]

But a chairman's declaration is not, it seems, conclusive where the declaration that the resolution is passed shows on the face of it that it was not passed by the requisite majority. Thus in *Re Caratal (New) Mines Ltd.*[28] special resolutions were put to the meeting, and the chairman declared: "Those in favour, 6; those against, 23; but there are 200 voting by proxy, and I declare the resolutions carried as required by Act of Parliament." The court held that the chairman had no right to count the proxies, and accordingly that on the face of the declaration of the chairman

---

[21] *Re Indian Zoedone Co.* (1884) 26 Ch.D. 70; *John* v. *Rees* [1970] Ch. 345, 382.
[22] *Ibid.*; and see *Wandsworth Gaslight Co.* v. *Wright* (1870) 22 L.T. 404.
[23] *Wall* v. *London and Northern Assets Corporation* [1899] 1 Ch. 550; *Wall* v. *Exchange Investment Corporation* [1926] Ch. 143.
[24] *Wall* v. *London and Northern Assets Corporation* [1898] 2 Ch. 469.
[25] *Salisbury Gold Mining Co.* v. *Hathorn* [1897] A.C. 268.
[26] *National Dwellings Society* v. *Sykes* [1894] 3 Ch. 159. On the limitations of the chairman's discretion to adjourn, see *John* v. *Rees* [1970] Ch. 345, 382. See further, para. 55–15, *post*.
[27] *Re Gold Co.* (1879) 11 Ch.D. 701, 719; *Re Hadleigh Castle Gold Co.* [1900] 2 Ch. 419; followed and approved in *Arnot* v. *United African Lands* [1901] 1 Ch. 518, and, in effect, overruling *Young* v. *South African Syndicate* [1896] 2 Ch. 268; *Graham's Morocco Co.* 1932 S.C. 269; 1932 S.L.T. 210. See further, para. 56–07, *post*.
[28] [1902] 2 Ch. 498; see also *Cowan* v. *Scottish Publishing Co.* 1892, 19 R. 437, and *J. T. Clark & Co. Ltd.* 1911 S.C. 243; 1910 2 S.L.T. 362, and para. 56–07, *post*.

the resolution had not been passed by the majority required by statute. This could not be overridden by an article deeming the chairman's declaration conclusive. If the record shows that a show of hands was not called for, nothing was put to the meeting, and the chairman's declaration is ineffective.[29] It is, however, competent to cure an omission in the minute by proving that a show of hands was in fact taken.[30]

The articles (see art. 58) commonly contain similar provisions making the chairman's declaration conclusive as to the passing or not passing of a resolution by a specified majority, and should be construed accordingly.

The articles usually give the chairman, where the votes are equal, a casting vote, both on a show of hands and at a poll (see art. 60), but in the absence of such provision he has no casting vote.[31]

Resolutions

55–06 Questions for submission to a general meeting are generally expressed in the form of resolutions. A resolution, according to the ordinary practice of companies, may be proposed by the chairman or by some other member, and, in either case, is put by the chairman to the meeting, whereupon it is open to discussion; when the discussion has closed, the chairman puts the resolution formally to the vote by stating what the resolution is, and that it has been proposed by A and seconded by B, and he then calls for a show of hands: "those who are in favour of the resolution . . . ; those who are against the resolution . . . "—and having counted the number for and against he then declares the result, *e.g.* "the resolution is carried," or "the resolution is lost." Thereupon a poll can be demanded if claimed by a sufficient number of members.[32]

A resolution inconsistent with the articles is invalid, unless passed as a special resolution.[33]

Votes at general meeting

55–07 The register is the only evidence of a member's right to vote at a general meeting.[34] So where a bankrupt remained on the register, the bankrupt was held entitled to vote.[35] If the articles so provide, the chairman's decision as to the validity of a vote is, in the absence of fraud, conclusive.[36] A shareholder's vote is a right of property which he may use as he pleases. The propriety or impropriety of his motive is normally immaterial[37]; he is

---

29 *Citizens Theatre* 1946 S.C. 14; 1946 S.L.T. 19.
30 *Fraserburgh Commercial Co.* 1946 S.C. 444; 1946 S.L.T. 370.
31 See, *e.g. Re W. R. Willcocks & Co. Ltd.* [1974] Ch. 163.
32 See para. 55–09, *post*.
33 *Quin and Axtens* v. *Salmon* [1909] A.C. 442.
34 *Pender* v. *Lushington* (1877) 6 Ch.D. 70; *Collins* v. *Donald* 1895, 3 S.L.T. 57.
35 *Wise* v. *Lansdell* [1921] 1 Ch. 420; see para. 39–37, *ante*.
36 *Wall* v. *London and Northern Assets Corporation* [1898] 2 Ch. 469.
37 *Pender* v. *Lushington* (1877) 6 Ch.D. 70.

entirely free to exercise his own judgment as to how he shall vote,[38] even if he votes against a resolution which the court has ordered the company to effect[39]; and may, at any rate in some cases, bind himself by contract, which can be enforced by mandatory injunction,[40] to vote, or not to vote, in a particular way,[41] and the court has no power to go behind the vote and to invalidate it on the ground that the shareholder had a personal interest in the subject matter different from, or opposed to, that of the company, and did not exercise his voting power for the best interests of the company.[42] In the absence of contract a person in whose name shares are registered (*e.g.* a mortgagee) can vote as he pleases.[43] And the company is bound to recognise the vote of the registered holder: if he casts his vote otherwise than in accordance with a contract with some other party, the company nevertheless is bound to accept his vote and the party whose contract is thereby broken has rights only against the shareholder and not against the company. But a majority of the members will not be allowed by vote to commit a fraud on the minority, *e.g.* by sanctioning a sale to themselves of the property of the company at an undervalue.[44] Furthermore, where a shareholder holds ordinary and preference shares he must, when voting at a class meeting of the preference shares, cast his vote in the bona fide belief that he is voting in the interests of the general body of members of that class; otherwise there may be no effective resolution of the class meeting.[45]

There is nothing to prevent a shareholder from transferring some of his shares to nominees to increase, where there is a scale, his voting power.[46] An alien enemy cannot vote.[47] But the Public Trustee can vote, if the shares are vested in him.[48]

A provision in a company's articles that no objection shall be taken to any vote except at the meeting at which it is tendered, or any adjournment thereof, is binding, and votes not then disallowed cannot afterwards be challenged,[49] but such a provision is unusual.

The articles usually contain provisions as to the votes of joint holders. Joint holders are entitled to have their names entered in any order they

---

[38] *North-West Transportation Co.* v. *Beatty* (1887) 12 App.Cas. 589; *Burland* v. *Earle* [1902] A.C. 83; *Northern Counties Securities Ltd.* v. *Jackson & Steeple Ltd.* [1974] 1 W.L.R. 1133; but see *Cook* v. *Deeks* [1916] 1 A.C. 554; *Menier* v. *Hooper's Telegraph Works* (1874) L.R. 9 Ch. 350.

[39] *Northern Counties Securities Ltd.* v. *Jackson & Steeple Ltd., supra.*

[40] *Puddephatt* v. *Leith* [1916] 1 Ch. 200.

[41] *Greenwell* v. *Porter* [1902] 1 Ch. 530.

[42] *East Pant Mining Co.* v. *Merryweather* (1864) 2 H. 6 M. 254; *Burland* v. *Earle, ante.*

[43] *Siemens Bros.* v. *Burns* [1918] 2 Ch. 324, 336; *Musselwhite* v. *C. H. Musselwhite & Son Ltd.* [1962] Ch. 964.

[44] *Menier* v. *Hooper's Telegraph Works* (1874) L.R. 9 Ch. 350; *Atwool* v. *Merryweather* (1868) L.R. 5 Eq. 464n.; see para. 58–13, *post.*

[45] *Holder's Investment Trust Ltd.* [1971] 1 W.L.R. 583.

[46] *Re Stranton Iron, etc., Co.* (1873) L.R. 16 Eq. 559; *Pender* v. *Lushington* (1877) 6 Ch.D. 70.

[47] *Robson* v. *Premier Oil, etc., Co.* [1915] 2 Ch. 124.

[48] *Re R. Pharaon et Fils* [1916] 1 Ch. 1.

[49] *Wall* v. *London and Northern Assets Corporation (No. 2)* [1899] 1 Ch. 550.

like, and may have their holding split into two or more joint holdings, with their names in different orders, and the register must be altered accordingly.[50]

Where the shareholder is a company, that company is by section 139 authorised to vote by its representative. A liquidator can be the "governing body" of the company in winding up for the purposes of section 139 if he has the effective management of the company and its affairs, and as such he is entitled to appoint the representative of the company.[51]

Articles sometimes provide that certain classes of shares shall have no voting rights or restricted voting rights; the latter is often the case as regards, *e.g.* preference shares. Further, at least in private companies[52] and companies limited by guarantee,[53] the articles may provide that certain shares shall have weighted voting rights on certain resolutions.

Show of hands

55–08 Unless the articles otherwise provide, questions arising at a general meeting are to be decided, in the first instance, by a show of hands. This is the common law rule which, unless excluded, applies automatically.[54] In taking a vote by show of hands, the duty of the chairman, unless the articles otherwise provide, is to count the hands held up and to declare the result accordingly, without regard to the number of votes that a member possesses, and without regard to proxies, whether held by members for other members[55] or by non-members for members (1948 Act, s. 136 (1) (*c*)).

Poll

55–09 A vote by show of hands is a rough-and-ready way of taking the sense of a meeting; and it is often a very inadequate means for arriving at the wishes of the whole constituency of the company. To ascertain these, the articles usually provide that a poll may be taken. The right to demand a poll is a common law right, and, according to the law, any one member may demand a poll.[56] The Act provides that any provision in the articles is void which excludes the right to demand a poll on any question other than the election of a chairman or adjournment, or which requires a demand for a poll on such questions to be made by more than five members having the

---

[50] See *Burns* v. *Siemens Bros., etc.* [1919] 1 Ch. 225.

[51] *Hillman* v. *Crystal Bowl Amusements Ltd.* [1973] 1 W.L.R. 162 (C.A.). There may, however, be cases in which, having regard to the interferences by creditors or by court order, the liquidator cannot be regarded as the man in the saddle (*ibid.* on p. 166).

[52] *Bushell* v. *Faith* [1970] A.C. 1099.

[53] *Re N.F.U. Development Trust Ltd.* [1972] 1 W.L.R. 1548.

[54] *Re Horbury, etc., Co.* (1879) 11 Ch.D. 109.

[55] *Ernest* v. *Loma, etc., Co.* [1897] 1 Ch. 1.

[56] Before 1947 the common law rule could be excluded or qualified by express provision in the articles (see *R.* v. *Wimbledon, etc.* (1882) 8 Q.B.D. 459), but not altogether in the case of special and extraordinary resolutions (s. 117 of the Act of 1929). The regulation contained in s. 137 of the Act of 1948 was first introduced by s. 4 of the Act of 1947.

right to vote at the meeting, or by members representing more than one-tenth of the total voting rights of all members entitled to vote at the meeting, or holding shares paid up to the extent of more than one-tenth of the total sum paid up on all the shares conferring a right to vote at the meeting (1948 Act, s. 137 (1)). Articles may effectively provide for a poll to be demanded by less than five persons or less than one-tenth representation, as the case may be. An instrument appointing a proxy confers authority to demand or join in demanding a poll (s. 137 (2)).

The articles generally determine how many votes a member is to have in the event of a poll. Very commonly they provide that a member shall have one vote for every share held by him (see art. 62). Sometimes they provide that the voting shall be in accordance with a scale. In the absence of any regulations as to votes, every member has one vote for every share or each £10 of stock, if the company originally had a share capital; if not, each member has one vote only, whether on a show of hands or at a poll (1948 Act, s. 134 (*e*)).

55–10 On a poll a member holding several shares may vote in one way in respect of some of these shares and in another way in respect of others (1948 Act, s. 138). This enables a nominee for more than one person to cast the votes which he holds in respect of each such person according to their instructions. In construing provisions in the articles as to how many members may demand a poll, two joint holders may count as two.[57] When a poll is duly demanded, it is the chairman's duty to grant it, and to fix the time and place for taking it; for if a poll is duly demanded, the show of hands is nullified.[58] If, by the regulations, the poll is to be taken "in such a manner as the chairman may direct," a poll may be taken then and there.[59] Such a course is often the most convenient where the number of votes to be counted is not unduly great. Otherwise the chairman will generally fix some other time and place for the taking of the poll. If, on the other hand, the articles require that a poll be taken immediately, this means that it must be taken as soon as practicable in all the circumstances.[60] As to the manner of taking a poll, it is usual to require every person who desires to vote to sign a paper headed, as the case may be, "for" or "against" the motion. The votes of each member are then inserted, and, these having been added up, the chairman declares the result. A meeting or the chairman has power to appoint scrutineers to examine and count the votes at a poll and to report the result to the chairman,[61] and this is often done. A member may vote at a poll, though not present when the poll was demanded.[62] If a poll is duly demanded, it must be taken (unless the demand is withdrawn: art. 58, third paragraph), and in such a case the

[57] See *Siemens Bros.* v. *Burns* [1918] 2 Ch. 324, 337.
[58] *Anthony* v. *Seger* (1789) 1 Hagg.Cas.Con. 9, 13.
[59] *Morgan* v. *Gray* [1953] Ch. 83; *Re Chillington Iron Co.* (1885) 29 Ch.D. 159.
[60] *Jackson* v. *Hamlyn* [1953] Ch. 577, 589.
[61] *Wandsworth, etc., Co.* v. *Wright* (1870) 22 L.T. 404.
[62] *Campbell* v. *Maund* (1836) 5 Ad. & El. 865.

meeting subsists in contemplation of law until the poll has been taken; and this is so, even though the chairman refuses to grant the poll and there is no express adjournment of the meeting.[63] If a poll is not completed on the day on which it is commenced, it must be continued subsequently, for the chairman is not entitled to close the poll whilst voters are coming in.[64] To shut out and exclude a voter may invalidate a poll.[65] Upon taking a poll the right to vote and the number of shares is to be determined, if any question arises, by a reference to the register of members.[66] To appoint a subsequent day for the taking of the poll is not an adjournment, although the meeting subsists till the poll is taken.[67] It is not uncommon to adjourn to ascertain the result, and ascertainment of the result is itself part of the poll.[68]

At a poll votes can as a rule only be given by persons present in person or by proxy at a meeting, and there is no power, in the absence of express provision in the articles, to take the poll by voting papers to be deposited at the office of the company.[69]

Proxies

Recognition of proxies

55–11 The common law does not recognise voting by proxy, but the articles generally confer such a right, for it is extremely inconvenient that a member, especially when residing at a distance, should be obliged personally to attend every meeting. Before 1947 a member had no right to vote by proxy except so far as the articles gave him such a right. It was usual to provide that a member could appoint another member of the company as his proxy, but the proxy had as a rule no right to demand a poll or to speak at the meeting; but by section 5 of the Act of 1947, re-enacted in section 136 of the Act of 1948, any member entitled to attend and vote at a meeting (other than a member of a company not having a share capital) is entitled to appoint another person, *whether a member or not*, as his proxy. In a public company a proxy has the right to attend the meeting for which he is appointed, or any adjournment thereof, but has no right to speak at the meeting except to demand or join in demanding a poll, and he can only vote on a poll: the articles can, however, extend the rights of a proxy. The right to appoint a proxy comprises, in a public company, the right to appoint more than one person. Thus a member who is a nominee for several persons can appoint different persons to represent the different interests including, of course, if so desired, the persons who themselves

63 *R.* v. *Wimbledon, etc.* (1882) 8 Q.B.D. 459.
64 *R.* v. *St. Pancras* (1839) 11 Ad. & El. 15; *R.* v. *Graham* (1861) 9 W.R. 738.
65 *R.* v. *Lambeth* (1838) 8 Ad. & El. 356.
66 *Pender* v. *Lushington* (1877) 6 Ch.D. 70.
67 *R.* v. *Chester* (1834) 1 Ad. & El. 342.
68 *Holmes* v. *Keyes* [1959] Ch. 199; see also *Burden* v. *Sinclair* (1961) 105 S.J. 586.
69 *McMillan* v. *Le Roi Mining Co.* [1906] 1 Ch. 331.

have the beneficial interests. A proxy appointed to attend and vote instead of a member of a private company has the same right as the member to speak at the meeting; but, unless the articles otherwise provide, a member of a private company cannot appoint more than one proxy to attend on the same occasion, and a proxy can only vote on a poll. Notices calling a meeting must contain a statement that a member can appoint a proxy and that a proxy need not also be a member. A proxy can demand or join in demanding a poll (1948 Act, s. 137 (2)).

Any provision in the articles is void which requires the instrument appointing a proxy to be received by the company more than 48 hours before the meeting (1948 Act, s. 136 (3)). There is, however, nothing in the Acts which prevents the lodging of a proxy less than 48 hours before the meeting.

When invitations to appoint particular persons as proxies are sent out by the directors at the company's expense, such proxy instruments must be sent to all persons entitled to attend the meeting and vote thereat by proxy, and not to a selected few (s. 136 (4)).

Where articles required instruments of proxy to be "in the usual form" it was held that a misdescription of an extraordinary meeting as an annual general meeting in the instrument did not entitle the company to reject it.[70]

A company may appoint a proxy instead of a section 139 representative even if the company is in winding up.[71] The two concepts should be carefully distinguished.[72]

Ordinary and "two-way" proxies

55–12 The articles generally provide for a form of proxy. Two forms of proxy are in use: the ordinary form and the so-called "two-way proxy form."

The ordinary form commonly runs (see art. 70):

> "I, A B, appoint C D to be my proxy to vote on my behalf at the general meeting of the company to be held on the —— day of ——, and at any adjournment thereof."

The form of two-way proxy, an example of which is given in article 71,[73] directs the proxy before the meeting to vote for, or against, the resolution. Only if the member fails to give the proxy express directions in what manner to vote may the proxy vote according to his discretion. Two-way proxies are required in the case of companies the shares in which are listed on The Stock Exchange for all resolutions intended to be proposed, except for merely procedural resolutions. The company's articles will define what is to be deemed special business (see art. 52).

The articles also as a rule require the instrument of proxy to be signed by

---

[70] *Oliver* v. *Dalgleish* [1963] 1 W.L.R. 1274.
[71] *Hillman Crystal Bowl Amusements* [1973] 1 W.L.R. 162.
[72] *Ibid.*, 165.
[73] *See* Vol. II, Part A.

the appointor, or, in the case of a corporation, to be under its seal or under the hand of an officer duly authorised. In such a case a foreign or colonial corporation which has no seal can nevertheless appoint proxies.[74] Sometimes it is provided that the instrument must be signed in the presence of a witness, and any such provision must be duly complied with.[75] A proxy cannot attest his own appointment.[76] A form of proxy need not be stamped if it relates to a meeting or any adjournment thereof, the adjourned meeting being regarded as the continuation of the previous meeting. Whether a proxy paper requires stamping depends on whether it is capable of being used at more than one meeting and not whether it is likely to be so used.[77]

If a proxy form, which is unstamped, is accepted by the chairman without objection the votes will be validly cast. Such proxies are not void but are capable of being stamped and it is not *ultra vires* for the company to accept them, nor for the chairman to fail to raise objections to them. If the company subsequently wishes to use them in evidence it may have them stamped; such a payment being *intra vires* the company as ascertaining the wishes of the majority of the members entitled to vote. Objections on this point raised after the meeting will not affect the matter whether or not such objections are in general allowed by the articles (*cf.* art. 66, Table A). On the other hand, if the chairman is entitled to and does reject votes cast in reliance on proxies which ought to have been stamped there is in general no duty on him to allow time for them to be stamped.[78]

A proxy paper signed in blank and handed over to someone with authority to fill up the blank is effective if the blank has been properly filled up when the proxy paper is deposited or used.[79] The articles very commonly require instruments of proxy to be deposited with the company a certain number of hours before the meeting. If so (subject to section 136 (3)), further proxies cannot be deposited after the date of the meeting for the purpose of a poll taken subsequently.[80] Nor can such belatedly deposited proxies be used at an adjourned meeting, whether for the purpose of taking a poll or otherwise.[81] But if the articles expressly provide for proxies to be valid if deposited a specified time before an adjourned meeting, this provision validates such proxies although they were not lodged before the original meeting.[82]

The directors, acting in good faith in the interests of the company, may do what they consider requisite to get the members to vote against or in favour of a particular resolution, *e.g.* they may at the expense of the

[74] *Colonial Gold Reefs Ltd.* v. *Free State Rand Ltd.* [1914] 1 Ch. 382.
[75] *Harben* v. *Phillips* (1883) 23 Ch.D. 14, 32.
[76] *Ex p. Cullen* [1891] 2 Q.B. 151.
[77] *Marx* v. *Estates and General Investments Ltd.* [1976] 1 W.L.R. 380.
[78] *Ibid.*
[79] *Sadgrove* v. *Bryden* [1907] 1 Ch. 318; *Ernest* v. *Loma Gold Mines* [1897] 1 Ch. 1.
[80] *Shaw* v. *Tati Concessions* [1913] 1 Ch. 292.
[81] *McLaren* v. *Thomson* [1917] 2 Ch. 261 (C.A.).
[82] *Ibid., per* Swinfen-Eady L.J. at p. 263: see art. 69.

company sent out stamped (postage paid) proxy forms[83]; but if sent to one, they must be sent to all.[84]

Revocation of proxies

55–13 The appointment of a proxy, unless made irrevocable for valuable consideration, can be revoked. The revocation must, however, conform to any provisions in the articles.[85]

If the shareholder, after appointing a proxy, himself attends the meeting, he can vote in person.[86] The right of the shareholder to vote in person is paramount to the right of the proxy. The presence of the shareholder does not avoid the instrument of proxy; but if he votes before his proxy has voted for him, he impliedly revokes the proxy.[87]

The death of a shareholder who has appointed a proxy, in the absence of provisions in the articles, revokes the authority of the proxy,[88] but articles usually provide (art. 73) that a proxy shall be valid notwithstanding the previous death or insanity of, or revocation by, the person giving it, unless the company has received notice of such death, insanity or revocation, as the case may be. Such a provision is obviously necessary in order to ensure that resolutions apparently validly passed at an apparently valid meeting were indeed validly passed.

A corporation which holds shares in a company may by resolution of its directors or governing body[89] appoint any person to act as its representative at a meeting. Such a representative can exercise the same powers on behalf of the corporation which he represents as that corporation could exercise if it were an individual person (s. 139).

Defamatory speeches and reports

55–14 If at a meeting a shareholder makes a speech which is defamatory of the directors, but on a matter affecting the interests of the shareholders, it may be privileged,[90] and the presence of reporters does not in itself destroy the privilege[91]; but the privilege may be lost if the public or the Press are present at the meeting at the express invitation of the shareholder publishing the defamatory matter.[91]

A report sent to the members is prima facie privileged.[92] As regards reports of proceedings of a general meeting by the public Press, the Defamation Act 1952, s. 7, extends the defence of privilege to "fair and

---

[83] *Peel* v. *L. & N.W. Ry.* [1907] 1 Ch. 5.
[84] s. 136 (4); see Vol. II, Part A. This overrules *Wilson* v. *L.M.S. Ry.* [1940] Ch. 393.
[85] *Spiller* v. *Mayo (Rhodesia), etc., Co.* [1926] W.N. 78.
[86] *Cousins* v. *International Brick Co.* [1931] 2 Ch. 90.
[87] *Knight* v. *Bulkeley* (1859) 5 Jur. (N.S.) 817.
[88] *Company Precedents*, Part I (15th ed.), p. 657.
[89] See *Hillman* v. *Crystal Bowl Amusements Ltd.* [1971] 1 W.L.R. 162.
[90] *Parsons* v. *Surgey* (1864) 4 Fost. & Fin.N.P.Cas. 247.
[91] *Pittard* v. *Oliver* [1891] 1 Q.B. 474.
[92] *Laughton* v. *Bishop of Sodor and Man* (1872) L.R. 4 P.C. 495; *Waller* v. *Loch* (1881) 7 Q.B.D. 619.

accurate reports of the proceedings at general meetings of companies registered or certified under any Act of Parliament or incorporated by Royal Charter, not being a private company within the meaning of the Companies Act 1948." In short, fair and accurate reports of meetings of public companies are privileged though defamatory, but those of private companies are not published on a privileged occasion.

It should, however, be realised that in all these cases the privilege is qualified, and malice on the part of the person making the defamatory statement deprives him of the defence of privilege. If several persons make a joint statement of a defamatory character and one acts maliciously but the others act in good faith, the latter are not deprived of their defence of privilege by the malice of the former.[93]

Adjournment of general meetings

55–15 The articles commonly confer on the chairman power, with the consent of the meeting, to adjourn. This gives the chairman a discretion. The meeting may resolve to adjourn, but it is for the chairman to determine whether he will exercise the power vested in him.[94] The articles often provide for a poll being taken—on the spot—on the question of adjournment. If the chairman improperly adjourns or stops the meeting, the meeting can choose another chairman and go on with the business.[95] On the other hand, if the meeting is duly adjourned or dissolved, members who remain behind cannot continue the business.[96] As regards notice, an adjourned meeting is regarded in law as a continuance of the original meeting[97]; accordingly, a fresh notice thereof need not be given[98] unless the articles so provide[99]; resolutions passed at an adjourned meeting have for some purposes been treated as resolutions passed at the original meeting,[1] but a resolution passed at an adjourned meeting is now to be treated as having been passed on the day on which it is in fact passed (1948 Act, s. 144). New proxies, *i.e.* proxies not admitted at the original meeting, cannot be admitted at the adjourned meeting unless the articles so provide (see art. 69).[2] Directors, in the absence of express provisions in the articles, have no power to postpone a meeting which has been duly and properly convened.[3]

---

93 *Longdon-Griffiths* v. *Smith* [1951] 1 K.B. 295; *Egger* v. *Viscount Chelmsford* [1965] 1 Q.B. 248 (C.A.).
94 *Salisbury Gold Mining Co.* v. *Hathorn* [1897] A.C. 268.
95 *National Dwellings Society* v. *Sykes* [1894] 3 Ch. 159.
96 *R.* v. *Gaborian* (1809) 11 East 77.
97 *Scadding* v. *Lorant* (1851) 3 H.L.C. 418.
98 *Wills* v. *Murray* (1850) 4 Ex. 843.
99 See art. 57, which requires fresh notice of an adjourned meeting when the adjournment is for 30 days or more.
1 *Neuschild* v. *British Equatorial Oil Co.* [1925] Ch. 346.
2 *Jackson* v. *Hamlyn* [1953] Ch, 577.
3 *Smith* v. *Paringa Mines* [1902] 2 Ch. 193.

Apart from any powers conferred upon him by the articles, the chairman has an inherent power to adjourn the meeting in the event of disorder; this power can, however, be exercised only as a last resort, if his attempts to restore order and to obtain a resolution of the meeting to adjourn in accordance with the articles have failed. The chairman must act in good faith and must not adjourn the meeting for longer than the necessities appear to dictate.[4]

Irregularities of procedure of general meetings

55–16 The rule in *Foss* v. *Harbottle*[5] is applicable to general meetings, and accordingly the court declines to interfere, at the instance of a minority, in respect of domestic irregularities,[6] the principle being that it is within the power of the persons who have committed the irregularity at once to set the matter right by calling a fresh meeting and dealing with the matter with all due formalities.[7] The rule in *Foss* v. *Harbottle*[8] is, however, subject to considerable qualifications: it does not apply to individual membership rights but applies only to corporate memberships,[9] and even in that province is subject to a number of important exceptions.[10] It further does not apply to qualified minority rights.[11]

The rule in *Foss* v. *Harbottle*[12] and its limitations will be considered later in detail.[13]

Irregularities may also be waived if all those entitled to object assent to the waiver.[14]

[4] *John* v. *Rees* [1970] Ch. 345 (where an adjournment *sine die* was held to be invalid).
[5] (1843) 2 Ha. 461; see para. 58–09, *post*.
[6] *Macdougall* v. *Gardiner* (1875) 1 Ch. D. 13.
[7] *Browne* v. *La Trinidad* (1887) 37 Ch.D. 1.
[8] (1843) 2 Ha. 461.
[9] See para. 58–04, *post*.
[10] See para. 58–11, *post*.
[11] See paras. 59–09, *et seq. post*.
[12] (1843) 2 Ha. 461.
[13] See paras. 58–09 *et seq.*
[14] *Re Bailey, Hay & Co. Ltd.* [1971] 1 W.L.R. 1357. See para. 54–03, *ante*.

CHAPTER 56

RESOLUTIONS OF GENERAL MEETINGS

56–01 DECISIONS of the company are made by resolutions of its members, passed at meetings of the members.[1] The articles of association provide who is entitled to vote and in what circumstances, and they further will normally provide how many votes each such person shall have, either generally or on specific resolutions.[2]

Although the Acts refer to resolutions, any proposal put to the general meeting is not truly a resolution until it has been duly passed by it. But practice is now universal in referring to what the purist would term "motions" or "proposals" as resolutions. The most common types of resolutions—all of which are recognised by the Acts—are:

1. ordinary resolutions;
2. extraordinary resolutions;
3. special resolutions;
4. ordinary resolutions requiring special notice.

To these may be added:

5. resolutions requiring under the company's articles a specific majority.

These types of resolutions are dealt with in this chapter under separate heads, but there are certain common characteristics which will first be considered.

Resolutions in general

56–02 A resolution can only be passed at a meeting which has been duly convened in accordance with the company's articles,[3] and which is duly constituted with the requisite quorum.[4] Upon the resolution being proposed and seconded[5] and put to the meeting, the persons entitled to vote do so in the first place[6] by show of hands (art. 58), *i.e.* by raising their hands either "in favour" or "against" the resolution when the question is put by

---

[1] For the cases where a decision may be expressed otherwise than by a formal resolution see para. 53–12, *ante*.
[2] *Bushell* v. *Faith* [1970] A.C. 1099; *Re N.F.U. Development Trust Ltd.* [1972] 1 W.L.R. 1548.
[3] As to notices, see para. 54–03, *ante*.
[4] *Re Cambrian, etc., Co.* (1875) 31 L.T. 773.
[5] It is not necessary, though usual, for a resolution to be seconded. For the persons who can propose a resolution, see para. 55–06, *ante*.
[6] *Re Horbury Bridge etc. Co.* (1879) 11 Ch.D. 109; *Citizens Theatre*, 1946 S.C. 14; *J. T. Clark & Co.*, 1911 S.C. 243; *Graham's Morocco Co.*, 1932 S.C. 269. A statement by the chairman that a show of hands was taken may be sufficient if no other record exists. *Fraserburgh Commercial Co.*, 1946 S.C. 444.

the chairman.[7] Upon a show of hands, only persons present can vote, and not proxies,[8] unless the articles provide otherwise.

Upon a show of hands the declaration of the chairman is frequently provided by the articles to be conclusive (art. 58 (2)).[9] Before, on or immediately after the chairman's declaration, a poll may be demanded, in the manner and subject to the limitations provided under the articles.[10] The poll is taken as provided in the articles (see art. 61), which frequently give the chairman a discretion whether to take the poll immediately or later.[11]

Amendments

56–03 Where a resolution is proposed, there is prima facie a right to propose any relevant amendment coming within the scope of the notice. Thus, if the notice is "to increase the capital of the company to £20,000," an amendment can be proposed to increase to £10,000 or £15,000, but an amendment to alter the articles or remove the directors would be irregular, and the chairman should not allow such an amendment to be put to the meeting, for it does not come within the scope of the notice. The amendment must be strictly relative to the motion and must be positive and not a mere negation of the main motion. So, too, if the notice is "to increase the capital by £20,000," or "to increase the directors' remuneration by £100," an amendment to increase the capital by £50,000, or the remuneration by £500, would be irregular; for it is not fair to call the members together for an apparently limited and small object, then to spring on them a much larger proposal. Those who are absent may have stayed away because they are content with what is proposed in the notice, and those who are present by proxy are presumed to have given the proxy on the basis of the notice.[12] Similarly, if the notice of meeting is to ratify a particular agreement, it would seem permissible to ratify the agreement subject to modifications or conditions, provided that they do not make the agreement more onerous as regards the company.[13] Where the notice is in general terms, *e.g.* "to increase the directors' remuneration," there is a wide scope for amendment.[14] Where the notice stated that the business was to pass, with such amendments as should be determined, a resolution re-electing three directors, it was held that an amendment to elect two extra directors was

---

7 See para. 55–06, *ante*.
8 *Ernest* v. *Loma, etc., Co.* [1897] 1 Ch. 1.
9 See para. 55–05, *ante*.
10 Art. 58 does not provide that a poll may be demanded "immediately after" the chairman's declaration.
11 Art. 61 requires a poll on the election of the chairman or on an adjournment to be taken "forthwith."
12 *Re Teede & Bishop Ltd.* (1901) 70 L.J.Ch. 409; *Clinch* v. *Financial Corporation* (1868) L.R. 5 Eq. 450, 481; *Wall* v. *London and Northern Assets Corporation (No. 1)* [1898] 2 Ch. 469, 484; *Stroud* v. *Royal Aquarium, etc., Society* (1903) 89 L.T. 243.
13 *Wright's Case* (1871) L.R. 12 Eq. 335n., 341n.
14 *Baillie* v. *Oriental Telephone, etc., Co.* [1915] 1 Ch. 503.

competent.[15] In regard to special or extraordinary resolutions, neither can be validly passed except on the terms or wording in which they were expressed in the notice convening the meeting; in other words, such resolutions cannot be amended, save in the limited way hereinafter mentioned.[16]

A notice of a meeting to pass a resolution to wind up and to appoint a particular person liquidator is sufficient to cover a resolution to appoint as liquidator a person other than the person named; for as soon as a resolution for the voluntary winding up of a company has been passed, a liquidator can be appointed without any previous notice.[17]

If a chairman refuses to allow a proper amendment to a proposed resolution to be put, even under a mistaken idea that the amendment is *ultra vires*, the resolution may be invalid. Failure by the mover of the amendment to challenge the chairman's ruling is not a waiver of his right to impeach the resolution.[18] Unless the regulations otherwise provide, an amendment at a meeting need not be seconded if it is put and voted on.[19]

Ordinary resolutions

56–04 Where it is provided that "the company in general meeting may" do some act, this means that an ordinary resolution is required to be passed. There is no definition in the Acts of "ordinary resolution." It means a resolution which requires a simple majority of the persons who, being present and entitled to vote upon the resolution, do vote. Lord Upjohn in *Bushell* v. *Faith*[20] said: "An ordinary resolution is in the first place passed by a bare majority on a show of hands by the members entitled to vote who are present personally or by proxy and on such a vote each member has one vote regardless of his shareholding. If a poll is demanded then for an ordinary resolution still only a bare majority of votes is required. But whether a share or class of shares has any vote upon the matter and, if so, what is its voting power upon the resolution in question depends entirely upon the voting rights attached to that share or class of shares by the articles of association." Thus, if three members personally present form a quorum, and there are in fact three members, if two of them vote in favour of the resolution this binds all other members of the company, unless a poll is demanded. If the quorum is two, then the chairman himself can bind the rest of the company, provided that the articles give him a casting vote (art. 60), even if the only other member present votes against the resolution. If a poll is duly demanded an ordinary resolution is passed by a simple majority

[15] *Betts & Co.* v. *Macnaghten* [1910] 1 Ch. 430; *Henderson* v. *Bank of Australasia* (1890) 45 Ch.D. 330.
[16] See para. 56–07, *infra*.
[17] *Re Trench Tubeless Tyre Co.* [1900] 1 Ch. 408.
[18] *Henderson* v. *Bank of Australasia* (1890) 45 Ch.D. 330.
[19] *Re Horbury Bridge, etc., Co.* (1879) 11 Ch.D. 109, 118.
[20] [1970] A.C. 1099, 1108.

of the votes given thereat, whether in person or, where proxies are allowed, by proxy.

It is not necessary that there should be in favour of the resolution a majority of all the persons present and entitled to vote, but only a majority of those voting for or against the resolution. If, *e.g.* 15 members are present and two vote in favour, one against, and 12 abstain, the resolution is passed.[21]

It is not necessary in the notice convening a meeting to set out the precise words of a proposed ordinary resolution. If, *e.g.* the business of the meeting is stated to include

(1) the election of a director;

(2) the fixing of the remuneration of the auditors;

such notice is sufficient for all purposes of an ordinary resolution.[22] This indulgence should be contrasted with the precision required for notices of an extraordinary or special resolution.

Extraordinary resolutions

56–05 An extraordinary resolution is one which has been passed by a majority of not less than three-fourths of such members as, being entitled so to do, vote in person or (where proxies are allowed) by proxy at a general meeting of which notice specifying the intention to propose the resolution as an extraordinary resolution has been duly given (1948 Act, s. 141 (1)).[23]

This definition raises three points: first, the specified majority, *i.e.* 75 per cent. of those voting must be in favour of the resolution. Secondly, the resolution in the form in which it is to be passed should be set out in the notice convening the meeting.[24] Thirdly, the notice must state that the resolution is to be proposed as an extraordinary resolution.

The length of notice that must be given of the intention to propose a resolution as an extraordinary resolution depends on the nature of the meeting at which the resolution is to be proposed. If it is to be proposed at an annual general meeting, not less than 21 clear days' notice is required, but if it is to be proposed at an extraordinary general meeting, not less than 14 clear days' notice is all that is required, unless at that extraordinary general meeting a special resolution is also to be proposed, when not less than 21 clear days' notice is necessary.[25] The cases in which the proper length of notice may be dispensed with have been discussed earlier.[26] It has

---

[21] *William Dixon Ltd*. 1948 S.C. 511; 1948 S.L.T. 423.

[22] See under Notice of General Meetings, Chap. 54, *ante*; also under Amendments, para. 56–03, *ante*; and the cases there cited.

[23] In Scotland it may not be necessary to state that it is to be an extraordinary resolution; see para. 54–07, *ante*.

[24] See Palmer, *Company Precedents* (17th ed.), Part I, p. 852.

[25] In Scotland, unless the articles specify "clear" days, *e.g.* art. 50, these periods may be inclusive of the day of the meeting; see para. 54–02, *ante*.

[26] See para. 54–03, *ante*.

been held that where all the shareholders are present, the formalities so required can be dispensed with.[27]

An extraordinary resolution is most frequently used in the winding up of a company.[28] It is also used for putting the company into voluntary liquidation where "it cannot by reason of its liabilities continue its business, and . . . it is advisable to wind up."[29] Articles may provide that an extraordinary resolution shall be used for certain purposes; and frequently require this type of resolution as one of the means of obtaining the sanction of a class of shareholders to a modification of the rights of that class (art. 4).[30]

Special resolutions

56–06 A special resolution requires the same majority as an extraordinary resolution, and, in addition, notice must have been given of the intention to propose it as a special resolution, such notice being of not less than 21 clear days (1948 Act, s. 141 (2)).[31]

Nature of special resolutions

A special resolution is a most useful part of the mechanism of a company. It is by and through the instrumentality of such a "special resolution" that many of the most important things which a company is, by the Companies Acts, empowered to do are ordained to be done. In defining the requisite steps for such a resolution, the aim of the legislature seems to have been to secure that every important change shall be made only after due deliberation, and with the sanction, active or passive, express or tacit, of the greater body of the shareholders of the company.

Acts for which required

The following are some[32] of the various things that a company may do only by special resolution:

(1) Alter its objects, subject to the right of a qualified minority to object (1948 Act, s. 5).
(2) Alter its articles (1948 Act, s. 10).[32a]
(3) Change its name (1981 Act, s. 24).
(4) Reduce its capital, subject to the confirmation of the court (1948 Act, s. 66).
(5) Convert any portion of its capital, uncalled, into reserve capital (1948 Act, s. 60).

---

27 *Re Oxted Motor Co. Ltd.* [1921] 3 K.B. 32. See also *Re Bailey, Hay & Co. Ltd.* [1971] 1 W.L.R. 1357, para. 54–03, *ante*.
28 See ss. 303, 306, 341.
29 s. 278 (1) (*c*).
30 See para. 34–16, *ante*.
31 In Scotland, 20 clear days may suffice (see para. 54–02. *ante*), and it may not be necessary to specify that it is intended to propose it as a special resolution (see para. 54–07, *ante*).
32 See also ss. 23, 65, 165, 203, 204, 222, 278 (1) (*b*), 287.
32a But if all the members of a private company agree and the measure is *intra vires* the company, the articles can be altered without a meeting being held or resolution being passed: *Cane* v. *Jones* [1980] 1 W.L.R. 1451.

(6) If an unlimited company, re-register as limited (1967 Act, s. 44 (1), as amended by the 1980 Act, Sched. 3).

(7) Opt for or change the form of classification of the company as private or public (1980 Act, ss. 5, 7, 8 and 10).

(8) Provide, in the case of a private company, financial assistance for the purchase of its shares (1981 Act, s. 43).

(9) Purchase its own shares (1981 Act, ss. 47 and 49).

Procedure

56–07 The following points should be noted in regard to a special resolution:

(a) Not less than 21 clear days' notice must be given (art. 50, second sentence).[33] A provision in the articles that the date of service of the notice shall be counted does not apply to a special resolution, but a provision that a notice sent by post shall be deemed to be served on the day after posting does apply.[34]

If a majority in number of the members having the right to attend and vote and holding together not less than 95 per cent. of the shares carrying votes agrees, the requirement of 21 clear days' notice may be dispensed with or reduced in time (1948 Act, s. 141 (2), proviso). The consenting members must, however, appreciate that the resolution is being passed without due notice, though such consent may be given at a later date.[35]

(b) The actual resolution—the form in which it is proposed to be passed—must be set out in the notice. In view of the wording of section 141 (2) no amendment can be made, save to the limited extent hereinafter mentioned.

(c) The notice of the meeting must state the intention to propose the resolution "as a special resolution."[36]

(d) The resolution must be passed at the meeting by a three-fourths majority of the votes cast at the meeting (s. 141).

(e) Unless a poll is duly demanded, a declaration of the chairman that the resolution has been carried is to be *conclusive* evidence of the fact, without proof of the number or proportion of the votes recorded in favour of or against the same (s. 141 (3)).

In *Re Moorgate Mercantile Holdings Ltd.*[37] Slade J. summarised the principles relating to notices of, and the subsequent amendment of, special resolutions as follows:

---

[33] Under the Act of 1908 and previous statutes two meetings were required. Since the reform culminating in the Act of 1929 one meeting is sufficient, but 21 clear days' notice is required.

[34] *Re Hector Whaling Ltd.* [1936] Ch. 208; but see, as regards Scotland, *Neil McLeod & Sons Ltd., Petitioners*, 1967 S.L.T. 46. See para. 54–02, *ante*.

[35] *Re Pearce Duff & Co. Ltd.* [1960] 1 W.L.R. 1014; and see *Re Oxted Motor Co. Ltd.* [1921] 3 K.B. 32; *Parker and Cooper Ltd.* v. *Reading* [1926] Ch. 975.

[36] See para. 54–07, *ante*, where the possibility of this not being required in Scotland is mentioned.

[37] [1980] 1 All E.R. 40.

"(1) If the notice of the intention to propose a special resolution is to be a valid notice for the purpose of section 141 (2), it must identify the intended resolution by specifying either the text or the entire substance of the resolution which it is intended to propose. . . .

(2) If a special resolution is to be validly passed in accordance with section 141 (2), the resolution as passed must be the same resolution as that identified in the preceding notice. . . .

(3) A resolution as passed can properly be regarded as 'the resolution' identified in a preceding notice, even though (i) it departs in some respects from the text of a resolution set out in such notice (for example by correcting those grammatical or clerical errors which can be corrected as matter of construction, or by reducing the words to more formal language) or (ii) it is reduced into the form of a new text, which was not included in the notice, provided only that in either case there is no departure whatever from the substance.

(4) However, in deciding whether there is complete identity between the substance of a resolution as passed and the substance of an intended resolution as notified, there is no room for the court to apply the *de minimis* principle as a 'limit of tolerance.' The substance must be identical. . . .

(5) . . . an amendment to the previously circulated text of a special resolution can properly be put to and voted on at a meeting if, but only if, the amendment involves no departure from the substance of the circulated text, in the sense indicated in propositions (3) and (4) above. . . .

(6) References to notices in the above propositions are intended to include references to circulars accompanying notices. . . .

(7) All the above propositions may be subject to modification where all the members, or a class of members, of a company unanimously agree to waive their rights to notice under section 141 (2): see section 143 (4) (*d*) of the 1948 Act, *Re Pearce, Duff & Co. Ltd.* and *Re Duomatic Ltd.*[38]"

Declaration of chairman—conclusiveness

Section 141 (3), it will be observed, says that the declaration of the chairman (if no poll be demanded) "is to be conclusive"; and, in pursuance of this provision, the Court of Appeal, in *Re Gold Co.*,[39] held a declaration by a chairman conclusive, although out of 17 present only 11 voted for and two against, and four abstained from voting. The word "conclusive" seems clear enough, and it is made still clearer when contrasted with the words used in sections 81 and 118, where the legislature has made certain things prima facie evidence only. This decision was followed by Cozens-Hardy J.

---

[38] [1969] 1 All E.R. 161.
[39] (1879) 11 Ch.D. 701, esp. at p. 719; the Act then required three-quarters of the number *present* to vote for the special resolution (s. 69 of the Act of 1908). Under the 1948 Act, which requires three-quarters of the number *voting* (s. 141 (2)), no problem would have arisen.

in *Re Hadleigh Castle Gold Mines*[40] and approved by the Court of Appeal in *Arnot* v. *United African Lands*.[41]

But a chairman's declaration will not be conclusive where in making it he states the figures for and against, and those figures show that he erroneously declares that the resolution has been duly passed.[42]

Ordinary resolutions requiring special notice

56–08 The nature of this type of resolution and the cases in which it is required by the Act have been explained earlier.[43]

Resolutions requiring special majority

56–09 Occasionally the articles of a company provide that something may be done by or with the sanction of a resolution passed by a majority of a special character—for instance, a majority of the members present in person or by proxy and entitled to three-fourths of the votes to which all the members are collectively entitled.

Notice to Registrar of resolutions

56–10 A copy of the following resolutions and agreements must be sent to the Registrar within 15 days (1948 Act, s. 143):

(1) Special resolutions.
(2) Extraordinary resolutions.
(3) Resolutions or agreements passed or agreed to by all the shareholders, which would otherwise have required some special formality.
(4) Resolutions binding upon classes of shareholders.
(5) Resolutions for winding up a company on effluxion of time.
(6) Resolutions of the directors under sections 8 (3) and 37 (2) of the 1980 Act.

Notwithstanding the provisions of section 143 (1) the copy forwarded to the Registrar need not be printed, if instead it is in some other form approved by the Registrar (1967 Act, s. 51 (2)); and the same applies to copies of resolutions authorising an increase of capital forwarded in pursuance of section 63 (2) (*ibid*. s. 51 (1)).[44]

The notice to the Registrar required under section 14 (6) of the 1976 Act of the removal of an auditor before the end of his term of office must however be in the "prescribed form" (see 1976 Act, ss. 35 and 36).

There are penalties for default (1948 Act, s. 143 (6)).

---

[40] [1900] 2 Ch. 419.
[41] [1901] 1 Ch. 518.
[42] *Re Caratal (New) Mines Ltd*. [1902] 2 Ch. 498; see further para. 55–05, *ante*.
[43] See para. 54–06, *ante*.
[44] As to the form of copies which will be accepted by the Registrar, see *Board of Trade Journal*, October 20, 1967, p. 960.

Publicity of alterations in memorandum and articles

56–11 The European Communities Act 1972, s. 9 (5) and (6) contains provisions aimed at making alterations in the constitution of the company more readily accessible to members of the public than before.

The two subsections distinguish between two cases, *viz.* where the alteration is made by or under an Act of Parliament, and where it is made by resolution of the general meeting. In both cases failure to comply with the provisions of the subsections has criminal sanctions.

Statutory alterations

Where the alteration is made by Act of Parliament or in an instrument made under an Act, *e.g.* in a statutory instrument, it is sufficient for the company to file a copy of the Act or the instrument with the Registrar within 15 days after coming into force of the statutory measure. The Registrar will place the copy received by him on record (s. 9 (5)).

If the company was already in existence at the date when the European Communities Act 1972, s. 9, came into force (January 1, 1973) and a copy of the statutory measure had not been filed with the Registrar yet, the company must have done so within a month after the coming into force of the 1972 Act, *i.e.* not later than February 1, 1973 (s. 9 (6)).

Alterations by resolution of the general meeting

Where the memorandum or articles are altered by resolution of the general meeting, the following provisions apply.

First, it should be noted that under the already existing law all such resolutions had to be notified to the Registrar. If they are special resolutions, this duty arises under section 143 (4) (*a*) of the 1948 Act. If such an alteration can be done by ordinary resolution, as in the case of an increase of the nominal capital and the other measures listed in section 61 (1) this is provided by sections 62 and 63 of the 1948 Act.

The European Communities Act 1972 provides in section 9 (5) that, when notice of an alteration in the memorandum or articles is given to the Registrar, "the company shall send with it a printed copy of the memorandum or articles as altered." Subsection (5) exempts an alteration of the objects of the company because in this case the duty to send a reprinted memorandum as altered is already provided for by section 5 (7) of the 1948 Act.

Subsection (6) of the Act of 1972 extends the obligation imposed by subsection (5) to alterations made before the coming into operation of the Act if the reprinted memorandum or articles have not been sent in before. Here the time for sending in the reprinted document was one month from the coming in force of the Act of 1972, *i.e.* the time of grace expired on February 1, 1973.

The object of these provisions is to make available to the public the latest version of the constitution of the company, including the alterations, in one document which is relatively easy to peruse.

"A printed copy" need not necessarily be produced by letterpress. The Registrar is prepared to apply section 51 of the Companies Act 1967 analogously, as the following *Notice of the Department of Trade and Industry* indicates:

What is a printed Document?

56–12 "Section 9 of the Act requires certain printed documents to be sent to the Registrar of Companies in addition to those already stipulated by the Companies Acts. For all these purposes, the registrar will accept as printed documents those produced by the following processes: letterpress, gravure, lithography; 'office' typeset, offset lithography; electrostatic photocopying; 'Photostat' or similar processes properly processed and washed; stencil duplicating using wax stencils and black ink.

No document will be acceptable if in general appearance, format or durability it is unsuitable for publication and use on the company's file. Experience has shown that documents produced by dye-line copying, spirit duplicating or thermo-copying are unsatisfactory.

Memorandum and Articles

Companies may need to comply with the requirement that an up-to-date copy of the memorandum or articles of association must be delivered to the registrar where any alteration has been made. Section 9 requires these documents as altered to be printed. This is already a requirement where the memorandum has been altered by special resolution in accordance with section 5 of the Companies Act 1948. It is a new requirement where the memorandum has been altered in accordance with some other provision or where the articles have been altered.

The registrar will accept copies of the memorandum and articles amended in accordance with the following rules. Where the amendment is small in extent, such as a change of name or change in the nominal capital, a copy of the original document may be amended by rubber stamping, typing or in some other permanent manner (but not a manuscript amendment). An alteration of a few lines or a complete short paragraph may be similarly dealt with if the new version is permanently affixed to a copy of the original in such a way as to obscure the amended words. Where more substantial amendments are involved, the pages amended may be removed from a copy of the original, the amended text inserted and the pages securely collated. The inserted material must be 'printed' as defined above but need not be produced by the same process as the original. In all cases the alterations must be validated by the seal or an official stamp of the company. The registrar reserves the right to change these arrangements if experience should show them to be unsatisfactory."

The duty to reprint and forward to the Registrar extends either to the memorandum or the articles if the alteration affects only one of these documents.

Subsections (5) and (6) do not affect section 51 of the Companies Act 1967 or section 143 of the Companies Act 1948. In particular, subsection (2) or section 143 still applies but where a resolution listed under subsection (4) of that section does not contain an alteration of the memorandum or articles, the company need not forward a reprinted copy of the constitutional document in question to the Registrar.

Under section 35 of the 1976 Act the Secretary of State may by regulations prescribe such requirements as he may consider appropriate to ensure that documents delivered to the Registrar are of a standard size, durable and easily legible. The Registrar may serve a notice on the deliveror if in his opinion the document does not comply with such regulations stating which requirements are not complied with and the document will not be taken to have discharged the duty to deliver such a document. The Registrar may accept material in forms other than a document (1976 Act, s. 36).

CHAPTER 57

MINUTES

57–01 SINCE the 1948 Act deals with the minutes of general meetings of shareholders and those of meetings of boards of directors and managers in one section (s. 145), it is convenient to follow the statutory arrangement and to treat the minutes of these different meetings together in this chapter although, strictly speaking, the minutes of board meetings should be considered later.

Form of minutes

Taking minutes

57–02 The usual plan adopted is for the secretary to make notes at each meeting of what passes, and subsequently to enter the particulars in a proper minute book ready for reading and signature by the chairman after they have been read and approved at the next succeeding meeting (see s. 145 (2)). The minutes may also be kept in a non-legible form (*e.g.* in computers) provided that the recording is capable of being produced in a legible form (Stock Exchange (Completion of Bargains) Act 1976, s. 3).

Keeping records

Section 145 (1) requires minutes to be made and kept of all proceedings of general meetings and of meetings of directors or managers and provides for penalties in case of default (s. 145 (4)). The minutes need not be kept in a bound book but may be recorded in loose-leaf books or in any other manner, provided that adequate precaution is taken for guarding against falsification and facilitating its discovery (s. 436[1]).

It should be noted that section 145 (1) requires the records containing the minutes to be entered into books "kept for that purpose." It would, therefore, appear that a combination of the minutes with other registers or books of the company in one record does not satisfy the statutory requirements.

Minutes as evidence

Prima facie evidence

57–03 The minutes, if purporting to be signed by the chairman of the meeting at which the proceedings took place, or by the chairman of the next succeeding meeting, are evidence of those proceedings (s. 145 (2)). Minutes once made and signed ought never to be altered by striking out or

---

[1] This section overruled *Hearts of Oak Assurance Co.* v. *Flower & Sons* [1936] Ch. 76.

adding anything.[2] Any necessary variation of a minute previously adopted should always be effected by means of a minute passed at a subsequent meeting. Before minutes are signed, minor clerical mistakes made in writing up the minutes can be rectified by crossing out the erroneous words or figures and inserting the correct words or figures. Such alterations should be initialled by the chairman when he signs the minutes. On no account should erroneous words or figures be erased.

Minutes, if signed by the chairman, are to be taken as prima facie correct.[3] They are, however, only prima facie evidence and can be contradicted by other evidence.[4]

In some cases the minutes are made conclusive by the articles, and in such cases the court may look at and consider the regularity of the notice[5]; but the accuracy of the minutes cannot be disputed unless they are shown to have been written up fraudulently,[6] or where the minutes on their face are wrong.[7]

Not the only evidence

57–04 There is no rule which makes minutes the only admissible evidence, and a bargain or transaction may, therefore, be made out and established as against the company though not recorded in the minute book: see *Re Pyle Works (No. 2)*,[8] where a contract to give security by way of indemnity to directors was made out though not entered, and *Re Fireproof Doors Ltd.*,[9] where a resolution of the board of directors fixing the quorum at one was upheld though not entered. So a person may be proved to be a member, although no allotment is entered in the minutes.[10]

Where a notice is taken as read, it must be treated as part of the *res gestae*.[11]

A director who is present at a board meeting, at which the minutes of proceedings at a prior meeting are read and approved as correct, is not thereby made responsible for what was done at the earlier meeting, but he will be deemed to have notice of what was done.[12]

Signing of minutes as regards evidence

Sometimes, *e.g.* in the case of legal proceedings, it may be required to put the minute book in evidence, but the minutes of the last meeting have

---

2 *Re Cawley & Co.* (1889) 42 Ch.D. 209, 226.
3 *Re Indian Zoedone Co.* (1884) 26 Ch.D. 70; and see *Southampton Dock Co.* v. *Richards* (1840) 1 Man. & Gr. 448.
4 *Re Llanharry Hematite Iron Ore Co., Roney's Case* (1864) 4 De G.J. & Sm. 426.
5 *Betts & Co.* v. *Macnaghten* [1910] 1 Ch. 430.
6 *Kerr* v. *Mottram* [1940] Ch. 657.
7 *Re Caratal (New) Mines Ltd.* [1902] 2 Ch. 498; see para. 55–05, *ante*.
8 [1891] 1 Ch. 173, 184.
9 [1916] 2 Ch. 142.
10 *Re Great Northern Salt Co.* (1890) 44 Ch.D. 472, 483.
11 *Betts & Co.* v. *Macnaghten* [1910] 1 Ch. 430.
12 *Re Lands Allotment Co.* [1894] 1 Ch. 616; *Re National Bank of Wales* [1899] 2 Ch. 629; *Burton* v. *Bevan* [1908] 2 Ch. 240. See, however, *Ashurst* v. *Mason* (1875) L.R. 20 Eq. 225.

not been signed. In such a case the chairman can sign, for though it is usual for him to sign at the next succeeding meeting,[13] he is not bound to wait.

Minute book as evidence in writing[14]

The chairman's signature of the minutes stating the terms of a contract may be a sufficient memorandum within section 40 of the Law of Property Act 1925 and section 4 of the Statute of Frauds 1677 (as far as not repealed by the Law Reform (Enforcement of Contracts) Act 1954).[15] See *Gibson* v. *Barton*[16] for an instance in which the minute book was put in evidence.

Omnia rite acta praesumuntur

57–05 Where the minutes have been properly made and signed, a rebuttable presumption arises that the meeting to which they refer, whether a general meeting or a board meeting, has been duly held and convened, all proceedings at it have been duly conducted, and all appointments of directors, managers or liquidators made at the meeting are presumed to be valid (s. 145 (3)). The protection as well as the convenience afforded to a company by these privileges is very great, and the utmost care should be used to keep the minutes in correct form and to make them complete.

Entries in the company's books, which would be irregular unless based on resolutions of the board, afford, on the above principle, prima facie evidence of the resolutions, even though no minute thereof is forthcoming.[17]

Thus, a letter written by the secretary of the company will be assumed prima facie to have been written with the authority of the directors although no minute appears to that effect.[18] The absence of any minute of an alleged transaction is, however, material when the party who alleges the transaction is a director.[19] "Directors," said Kekewich J.,[20] "ought to place on record, either in formal minutes or otherwise, the purport and effect of their deliberations and conclusions; and if they do this insufficiently or inaccurately they cannot reasonably complain of inferences different from those which they allege to be right."

Inspection of minutes

57–06 The records containing the minutes of general meetings[21] have to be kept at the registered office of the company and are open to inspection by

---

[13] See text, *ante*, and *Southampton Dock Co.* v. *Richards* (1840) 1 Man. & Gr. 448.
[14] This paragraph is not applicable in Scotland.
[15] *Jones* v. *Victoria Graving Dock Co.* (1877) 2 Q.B.D. 314.
[16] (1875) L.R. 10 Q.B. 329, 332.
[17] *Knight's Case* (1867) L.R. 2 Ch. 321; *Re Great Northern Salt, etc., Co.* (1890) 44 Ch.D. 472, 483; and see *Lane's Case* (1863) 1 De G.J. & S. 504, 509.
[18] *Johnson* v. *Lyttle's Iron Agency* (1877) 5 Ch.D. 687, 691.
[19] *Re Rotherham, etc., Co.* (1883) 25 Ch.D. 103, 109.
[20] *Re Liverpool Household Stores* (1890) 59 L.J.Ch. 616, 619.
[21] Held on or after November 1, 1929 (s. 146 (1)).

members of the company—but not by creditors or the public—during reasonable office hours without charge (s. 146 (1)). A member is entitled to a copy of the minutes on payment of a small charge (s. 146 (2)). If the company fails to allow inspection or to give copies it can be fined (s. 146 (3)) and the court may order the immediate production of the books or the dispatch of the desired copy (s. 146 (4)). While carrying out an inspection of the minutes under section 146 (1), a member is entitled to be accompanied by an adviser of his own choice.[22]

The minutes of meetings of boards of directors or managers are not open to inspection but it is believed that the auditor of the company has access to them (1967 Act, s. 14 (5)). Although not provided for in the 1948 Act, a director has a common law right to inspect the minutes of proceedings of the directors. He is also entitled to be accompanied by an adviser of his own choice.[23]

Form of minutes

57–07 Specimen minutes for different kinds of meetings and companies are given in *The Chartered Secretaries Manual of Company Secretarial Practice*.

PRACTICE NOTE

Minute books

57–08 Where minutes are not recorded by making entries in a bound book, the nature of the precautions required to be taken by section 436 of the 1948 Act (see para. 57–02, *ante*) needs to be considered. In all cases, the loose-leaf sheets constituting the book should be serially numbered and kept under the control of a responsible officer of the company. If the binder containing the sheets has a locking device, it is usually more convenient that it should be in the spine of the binder rather than in the form of a metal plate between its covers. An added precaution is to number the minutes consecutively throughout the book.

Except in the case of a small private company, where the directors are also the shareholders, a separate book should be kept for minutes of general meetings because of the rights of inspection available to members of the company in respect of minutes of general meetings.

---

22 *McCusker* v. *McRae*, 1966 S.C. 253.
23 *Ibid*.

C. MAJORITY AND MINORITY RIGHTS

CHAPTER 58

RIGHTS OF THE MAJORITY

58–01 A PROPER balance of the rights of majority and minority shareholders is essential for the smooth functioning of the company. Since the passing of the Joint Stock Companies Act 1856, most Acts have extended the protection of the minority. The Companies Acts 1948 to 1981, and the relevant case law, attempt to maintain that balance by admitting, on principle, the rule of the majority but limiting it, at the same time, by a number of well-defined minority rights. Before this system of establishing an equilibrium between the interests of the majority and the minority is considered, it is necessary to define the area in which the rule of the majority operates. It will be seen that that area comprises the corporate membership rights of the owners of the company, but that it does not extend to their individual membership rights which cannot be affected by the will of the majority, whatever its size, except to the extent that statute permits.

Individual and corporate membership rights

58–02 The distinction between individual and corporate membership rights of a shareholder, as evolved by the courts,[1] is founded on the following considerations. By his contract with the company (and the other members: see the 1948 Act, s. 20) the shareholder undertakes with respect to some—and, in fact, most—rights which his membership carries to accept as binding upon him the decisions of the majority of shareholders, if arrived at in accordance with the law and the articles; these membership rights are referred to as corporate membership rights. Other rights of the shareholder, according to his contract with the company, cannot be taken away from him unless he consents or statute expressly permits; if such a right is in question, a single shareholder can, on principle, defy a majority consisting of all the other shareholders. Rights of this type are referred to as individual membership rights.

The procedural aspect of this distinction—and, as will be seen later, the courts often approach this problem from that aspect—is that if a shareholder complains of an unlawful infringement of a right qualifying as a corporate membership right, his remedy is a derivative action in representative form on behalf of himself and the other shareholders,[2] or, in some instances, an action in the name of the company.[3] On the other hand,

---

[1] *Pender* v. *Lushington* (1877) 6 Ch.D. 70; *Pulbrook* v. *Richmond Consolidated Mining Co.* (1878) 9 Ch.D. 610 (as regards directors); *Edwards* v. *Halliwell* [1950] 2 All E.R. 1064; see also *Hayes* v. *Bristol Plant Hire Ltd.* [1957] 1 W.L.R. 499.

[2] See para. 58–24, *post*.

[3] See para. 58–24, *post*.

if the right alleged to be infringed is an individual membership right, no question of suing in the name of the company arises, but the shareholder can sue in his own name and this right of action is unaffected by any decision of the majority.

These categories are not mutually exclusive. Thus, in the cases of *Prudential Assurance Co. Ltd.* v. *Newman Industries Ltd.*[4] the plaintiffs pursued personal, representative and derivative claims. It was held at first instance that derivative claim could be joined with a personal or individual membership claim where the two claims arose out of the same transaction and that the addition of the representative claim to the derivative claim was also justified. However, in the Court of Appeal[4a] it was held that a shareholder cannot allege infringement of an individual membership right simply by reference to a diminution in the profits of the company caused by the infringement of corporate rights.

58–03 To give an example: an increase in capital, followed by an issue of new shares, seriously affects the right to dividend of existing shareholders: that right is, *pro tanto,* diminished if henceforth they have to share the distributable profit with more shareholders. Yet, hitherto an existing shareholder could not normally complain, if the articles authorised such an increase by ordinary resolution and the company passed such a resolution (s. 61 (1) (*a*)); he had contracted to accept the decision of the majority in that respect and the right that had been altered was a corporate membership right.[5] On the other hand, if his share carries a vote but the company refuses to record his vote, an individual membership right is infringed. In the words of Sir George Jessel M.R.[6]:

> "He is a member of the company, and whether he votes with the majority or the minority he is entitled to have his vote recorded—an individual right in respect of which he has a right to sue. That has nothing to do with the question like that raised in *Foss* v. *Harbottle*[7] and that line of cases. He has a right to say, 'Whether I vote in the majority or minority, you shall record my vote, as that is a right of property belonging to my interest in this company, and if you refuse to record my vote I will institute legal proceedings against you to compel you.' "

Similarly Jenkins L.J. observed[8]:

> " . . . the personal and individual rights of membership of each of them have been invaded by a purported, but invalid, alteration. . . . In those circumstances, it seems to me the rule in *Foss* v. *Harbottle*[9]

---

[4] *Prudential Assurance Co. Ltd.* v. *Newman Industries Ltd.* [1979] 3 All E.R. 507; *Prudential Assurance Co. Ltd.* v. *Newman Industries Ltd. (No. 2)* [1980] 2 All E.R. 841.

[4a] [1982] 1 All E.R. 354.

[5] This now has to be read subject to (1) Pt. II of the 1980 Act, and (2) *Clemens* v. *Clemens Bros. Ltd.* [1976] 2 All E.R. 268. See para. 58–04, *post*.

[6] In *Pender* v. *Lushington* (1877) 6 Ch.D. 70, 80; this passage was quoted with approval by Jenkins L.J. in *Edwards* v. *Halliwell* [1950] 2 All E.R. 1064, 1068.

[7] (1843) 2 Hare 461. On the rule in *Foss* v. *Harbottle*, see para. 58–09, *post*.

[8] In *Edwards* v. *Halliwell* [1950] 2 All E.R. 1064, 1067.

[9] (1843) 2 Hare 461.

has no application at all, for the individual members who are suing sue . . . in their own right to protect from invasion their own individual rights as members."

Individual membership rights should not be confused with the rights available to qualified minorities. The characteristic feature of a qualified minority right is that it can be exercised, not at the discretion of a single shareholder, but only by the co-operative act, within the body corporate, of a membership group of statutorily defined size, *e.g.* one-tenth of the paid-up capital carrying voting rights (*cf.* 1948 Act, s. 132). Qualified minority rights are discussed in the following chapter (see para. 59–02, *post*).

Individual membership rights

58–04 It is hardly possible to enumerate all individual membership rights, but the following are the outstanding examples[9a]:

(1) The right "to maintain [himself] in full membership with all the rights and privileges appertaining to that status."[10] This right implies that the individual shareholder can insist on the strict observance of the legal rules, statutory provisions and provisions in the memorandum and articles which cannot be waived by a bare majority of shareholders.[11]

Thus, in *Edwards* v. *Halliwell*[12] the rules of a trade union—which correspond to the articles of a company[13]—provided that alterations of the regular contributions of employed members could only be made by a ballot vote of the members and a two-thirds majority obtained. During the Second World War a delegate meeting of the union, without taking a ballot of members and obtaining a two-thirds majority, passed a resolution increasing the amount of the contributions. The plaintiffs, two members of the union, claimed a declaration that the alteration adopted by the delegate meeting was invalid. The main defence of the union was that an objection to the disregard of the voting procedure laid down in the rules could only be raised by the majority, in short, that the rule in *Foss* v. *Harbottle*[14] applied. The Court of Appeal decided in favour of the plaintiffs; it held that the rights infringed were individual membership rights and that, for that reason, the rule in *Foss* v. *Harbottle*[14] did not apply.

The right of a shareholder to maintain himself in full membership can lead to difficulty if by an increase of capital and/or a fresh issue

---

[9a] The shareholder has no individual membership right to have the annual accounts of the company amended: *Devlin* v. *Slough Estates Ltd.*, *The Times*, June 16, 1982.

[10] *Per* Jenkins L.J. in *Edwards* v. *Halliwell* [1950] 2 All E.R. 1064, 1067.

[11] *Salmon* v. *Quinn & Axtens* [1909] A.C. 442; [1909] 1 Ch. 311 (C.A.).

[12] [1950] 2 All E.R. 1064.

[13] *Cotter* v. *National Union of Seamen* [1929] 2 Ch. 58.

[14] (1843) 2 Hare 461.

of shares there is a tendency to dilute the proportionate shareholding of an existing member. Previously it was appropriate to suggest[15] that, in such circumstances, a minority shareholder could not complain of an infringement of his individual membership rights. However, this suggestion now has to be considered in the light of the decision of Foster J. in *Clemens* v. *Clemens Bros. Ltd.*[16] The plaintiff owned 45 per cent. of the issued share capital of the defendant company and her aunt held the remaining 55 per cent. Although at one time both the plaintiff and her aunt had been directors of the company, at the relevant time the plaintiff was no longer a director. The aunt and her fellow directors proposed to increase the company's share capital by the creation and issue of further shares. The proposal was to issue them as to 200 to the aunt and as to the remaining 850 to a trust for long-serving employees. Resolutions to give effect to these proposals were passed at an extraordinary general meeting notwithstanding the plaintiff's proxy voting against them. The plaintiff was concerned that the proposed share issue would dilute her own holding from 45 per cent. to marginally less than 25 per cent., in other words, she would lose negative control. Accordingly she commenced proceedings against the company and the aunt seeking a declaration that the resolutions were oppressive, and an order setting them aside. Foster J. made such an order having formed the view that the resolutions were "specifically and carefully designed to ensure not only that the plaintiff can never get control of the company but to deprive her of what has been called her negative control," *viz.* the power to prevent the passage of any special resolutions of which she disapproved.

In the past, minority shareholders who have complained to the courts about this type of dilution have tended to be conspicuously unsuccessful. The best-known illustration of failure is probably *Greenhalgh* v. *Arderne Cinemas Ltd.*[17] Moreover, it has generally been considered that when a shareholder, even a director-shareholder, casts his vote at a general meeting, he is entitled to do so in his own interests, free from fiduciary undercurrents, except in the well-known but ill-defined context of "fraud against the minority."[18] Indeed, this is the foundation upon which the principle of majority was constructed. The significance of Foster J.'s decision in the *Clemens* case is that, by drawing freely on the speech of Lord Wilberforce in *Ebrahimi* v. *Westbourne Galleries Ltd.*[19] (which case

[15] See 22nd ed., para. 56–04.
[16] [1976] 2 All E.R. 268.
[17] [1946] 1 All E.R. 512.
[18] See *North-West Transportation Co. Ltd.* v. *Beatty* (1887) 12 App. Cas. 589. See para. 58–13, *post*.
[19] [1973] A.C. 360.

concerned a "just and equitable" winding up)[20] he grafted novel constraints upon the use of the votes of a majority shareholder. Although the learned judge made clear this influence upon his judgment, he did not attempt to synthesise them in the form of a principle; he said[21]—

> "I have come to the conclusion that it would be unwise to try to produce a principle, since the circumstances of each case are infinitely varied. It would not, I think, assist to say more than that in my judgment [the aunt] is not entitled as of right to exercise her votes as an ordinary shareholder in any way she pleases. To use the phrase of Lord Wilberforce, that right is 'subject . . . to equitable considerations . . . which may make it unjust . . . to exercise [it] in a particular way.' "

At this stage it is difficult to estimate the importance of this startling development. The fact that Lord Wilberforce was dealing with a totally different legal principle and that Foster J.'s decision seems irreconcilable with cases such as *Greenhalgh* and *Beatty* (*ante*) makes the tasks of prediction and advice all the more difficult.

It should be added that, by virtue of the 1980 Act the right of pre-emption given to shareholders in certain closely defined circumstances has been placed on a statutory footing.[22]

58–05 As regards expropriation, it will be seen later[23] that a resolution of the general meeting providing that a minority of existing shareholders shall be compelled to sell its shares will often be invalid as being a fraud against the minority, but that in special circumstances, *viz*. if it can be justified as being bona fide for the benefit of the company as a whole and as not discriminating against the minority, it may be valid.

58–06 (2) The right of the shareholder not to be compelled to take or subscribe for more shares or to have his liability increased, without his consent in writing (1948 Act, s. 22).[24]

(3) The right to petition for a compulsory winding up (1948 Act, s. 222).[25]

(4) The right to petition for the remedy for unfairly prejudicial treatment (1980 Act, s. 75).[26]

(5) The right, in a Scottish company, to apply to the court for sequestration of the assets of the company and the appointment of a judicial factor.[27]

---

[20] As to which, see para. 85–09, *post*.
[21] At p. 282.
[22] See s. 17; para. 24–01, *ante*.
[23] When the corporate membership rights are discussed; see para. 58–16, *post*.
[24] See para. 10–03, *ante*.
[25] See para. 85–16, *post*.
[26] See para. 60–08, *post*.
[27] *Patrick Fraser, Petitioner*, 1971 S.L.T. 146. See para. 59–14, *post*.

(6) The right to apply to the Department of Trade for the calling of an annual general meeting if the company defaults in the holding of such meeting, (1948 Act, s. 131 (2)).[28]

(7) In a public company, the right to object to the appointment of two or more directors by a single resolution (1948 Act, s. 183).[29]

(8) At the annual general meeting, the right to object to a shorter notice than the statutory 21 days (1948 Act, s. 133 (3)).[30]

(9) Where an act of the company requires the confirmation or sanction of the court, the right to make representations to the court. Thus, if a special resolution has been passed for reducing the company's capital under section 66 and the company petitions the court to confirm the reduction (s. 67 (1)),[31] a shareholder is entitled to be represented on the petition to oppose the reduction.[32] A similar right exists where the sanction of the court is sought to a scheme of arrangement under section 206 of the 1948 Act.[33] If the court considers that the reduction of capital or the scheme of arrangement is unfair it may refuse to confirm or sanction it.

Further, in schemes of amalgamation under section 287 of the 1948 Act, the shareholder is entitled to arbitration.[34]

58–07 (10) In the case of a "take-over bid," the right to object to a compulsory transfer of his shares (1948 Act, s. 209 (1)).[35]

(11) If his share carries a vote, the right to have his vote recorded.

An illustration of this right is provided by *Pender* v. *Lushington*.[36] In this case a resolution of the general meeting would have been carried had the chairman not disallowed the nominee holdings on behalf of the plaintiff. The plaintiff sued on behalf of himself and the other shareholders who had voted with him, naming the company as co-plaintiff; he asked for an injunction restraining the directors from acting on the assumption that the nominee votes were inadmissible. Jessel M.R. granted the injunction and ordered that the company's name should remain on the record until a general meeting was convened and had decided whether the company wished to sue and act as plaintiff. The court held that, upon the proper construction of the articles, nominee holdings had to be admitted and, further, that the right of a member to record his vote was an individual and not a corporate right of that member.[37]

---

[28] See para. 53–03, *ante*.
[29] See para. 61–04, *post*.
[30] See para. 54–01, *ante*.
[31] See para. 33–11, *ante*.
[32] See *Scottish Insurance Corpn. Ltd.* v. *Wilsons and Clyde Coal Co. Ltd.* [1949] A.C. 462.
[33] See para. 79–08, *post*.
[34] See para. 80–07, *post*.
[35] See para. 81–11, *post*.
[36] (1877) 6 Ch.D. 70.
[37] And, consequently, not subject to the rule in *Foss* v. *Harbottle* (1843) 2 Hare 461. See also para. 58–03, *ante*.

Corporate membership rights

58–08 Corporate membership rights, as has been seen,[38] are membership rights which the member has agreed to submit to the will of the majority, provided that that will is expressed in accordance with the law and the articles. With respect to these membership rights the principle of the supremacy of the majority applies.

The rule in Foss v. *Harbottle*

58–09 This principle is often referred to as the rule in *Foss* v. *Harbottle*,[39] after the leading case in which the facts were as follows: the minority shareholders alleged that the company had a claim in damages against some of the directors by reason of the fraudulent acts of those directors, but at the general meeting the majority resolved that no action should be taken against them. Two of the minority shareholders took legal proceedings against the directors and others to compel them to make good the losses to the company. The court dismissed the action on the ground that, as the acts of the directors were capable of confirmation by the majority of members, the court should not interfere. It was thus left to the majority to decide what was for the benefit of the company.

The rule in *Foss* v. *Harbottle*[39] has been applied in many later cases.[40] In *Macdougall* v. *Gardiner*,[41] on a motion for the adjournment of a general meeting, the chairman had ruled that no poll could be demanded. A single shareholder, suing on behalf of himself and all other shareholders (except the directors), complained of breach of the articles, but the court held that the litigation ought to have been in the name of the company because it was the majority to say whether they wished to complain or not. Mellish L.J. said in that case[42]:

> "In my opinion, if the thing complained of is a thing which in substance the majority of the company are entitled to do, or if something has been done irregularly which the majority of the company are entitled to do regularly, or if something has been done illegally which the majority of the company are entitled to do legally, there can be no use in having a litigation about it, the ultimate end of which is only that a meeting has to be called, and then ultimately the majority gets its wishes."

In *Ving* v. *Robertson & Woodcock Ltd.*[43] a resolution was passed at the general meeting that "in consideration of services rendered" shares should

---

[38] See para. 58–02, *ante*.
[39] (1843) 2 Hare 461.
[40] *Mozley* v. *Alston* (1847) 1 Ph. 790; *Macdougall* v. *Gardiner* (1875) 1 Ch.D. 13; *North-West Transportation Co.* v. *Beatty* (1887) 12 App.Cas. 589; *Burland* v. *Earle* [1902] A.C. 83; *Ving* v. *Robertson & Woodcock* (1912) 56 S.J. 412; *Edwards* v. *Halliwell* [1950] 2 All E.R. 1064; *Greenhalgh* v. *Arderne Cinemas Ltd.* [1950] 2 All E.R. 1120; *Pavlides* v. *Jensen* [1956] Ch. 565; *Heyting* v. *Dupont* [1964] 1 W.L.R 843 (C.A.); *Prudential Assurance Co. Ltd* v. *Newman Industries Ltd. (No. 2)* [1982] 1 All E.R. 354 (C.A.). *Cf. Salmon* v. *Quin & Axtens* [1909] A.C. 442; [1909] 1 Ch. 311 (C.A.).
[41] (1875) 1 Ch.D. 13.
[42] At p. 25.
[43] (1912) 56 S.J. 412.

be issued to the directors at par, although the value of the shares was well above par. The company was in need of new capital. The resolution was carried by the votes of the directors. A minority shareholder brought an action but did not allege fraud, and the court held that the rule in *Foss* v. *Harbottle*[44] applied. Similarly, the rule was applied where it was alleged that the persons who purported to act as directors were not properly appointed.[45] More recent cases have concerned the bona fide issue of shares by directors to supporters so as to prevent an unwanted bidder from obtaining control. The cases have involved breaches of fiduciary duty, but ones held to be curable by the majority in general meeting (excluding votes in respect of the newly issued shares) and therefore ultimately not impugnable by an individual shareholder.[46]

58–10 It should be noted that in English company law, while the substantive aspects of the rule of the majority are not neglected, the emphasis is on the procedural character of that rule. The reasoning on which the rule is founded is that in these cases it is for the company to complain, by suing the alleged wrongdoer; the company is, thus, the proper plaintiff and the company is the majority. This reasoning is equally valid in Scotland.[46a]

The pre-eminently procedural character of the rule in *Foss* v. *Harbottle* was clearly expressed in the following restatement of the rule by Jenkins L.J. in *Edwards* v. *Halliwell*[47]:

> "The rule in *Foss* v. *Harbottle*, as I understand it, comes to no more than this. First, the proper plaintiff in an action in respect of a wrong alleged to be done to a company or association of persons is prima facie the company or the association of persons itself. Secondly, where the alleged wrong is a transaction which might be made binding on the company or association and on all its members by a simple majority of the members, no individual member of the company is allowed to maintain an action in respect of that matter for the simple reason that, if a mere majority of the members of the company or association is in favour of what has been done, then *cadit quaestio*."

Exceptions to the rule in Foss v. *Harbottle*

58–11 The following exceptions to the rule in *Foss* v. *Harbottle*[48] are admitted: the majority cannot confirm

(1) an act which is *ultra vires* the company or illegal;

(2) an act which constitutes a fraud against the minority and the wrongdoers are themselves in control of the company; or

(3) a resolution which requires a qualified majority but has been passed by a simple majority.

---

44 (1843) 2 Hare 461; see also *Pavlides* v. *Jensen* [1956] Ch. 565.

45 *Mozley* v. *Alston* (1847) 1 Ph. 790; *Hattersley* v. *Shelburne (Earl of)* (1862) 10 W.R. 881.

46 *Hogg* v. *Cramphorn Ltd.* [1967] Ch. 254; *Bamford* v. *Bamford* [1970] Ch. 212. See also *Howard Smith Ltd.* v. *Ampol Petroleum Ltd.* [1974] A.C. 821. As regards the nature of the fiduciary obligation, see para. 63–04, *post*.

46a *Orr* v. *Glasgow etc. Rly. Co.* (1860) 3 Macq. 799, 804; *Lee* v. *Crawford* 1890, 17 R. 1094; *Brown* v. *Stewart* 1898, 1 F. 316; 6 S.L.T. 262.

47 [1950] 2 All E.R. 1064, 1066; and see Russell L.J. in *Heyting* v. *Dupont* [1964] 1 W.L.R. 843, 848.

48 The statement in the text is founded on Jenkins L.J. in *Edwards* v. *Halliwell* [1950] 2 All E.R. 1064, 1067.

58–12 ULTRA VIRES AND ILLEGAL ACTS. The rule in *Foss* v. *Harbottle* does not apply where the act complained of is wholly *ultra vires* the company.[49] No majority can sanction such an act. The same is the case where the act in question is illegal.[50]

58–13 FRAUD ON THE MINORITY. The rule in *Foss* v. *Harbottle* likewise cannot be invoked where the act complained of constitutes a fraud on a minority of the shareholders and the company is prevented from taking action against the wrongdoers by the votes controlled by the latter.[51] However, as we shall see,[52] this concept of "wrongdoer control" is now the subject of some judicial controversy.

It is not easy to state when an act qualifies as fraud on the minority and it would be unprofitable to attempt a definition of that term. In *Prudential Assurance Co. Ltd.* v. *Newman Industries Ltd. (No. 2)* Vinelott J. pointed out[53] that fraud on the minority lies in the use of the controllers' voting power rather than in the character of the act or transaction giving rise to the claim. The following are indications of the meaning attached to it:

58–14 "*Bona fide for the benefit of the company as a whole.*" A resolution constitutes a fraud on the minority if it is not passed "bona fide for the benefit of the company as a whole,"[54] or its effect is "to discriminate between the majority shareholders and the minority shareholders so as to give to the former an advantage of which the latter was deprived."[55]

It was at one time doubtful whether the test that the alteration had to be "bona fide for the benefit of the company as a whole" consisted of one component or two. Peterson J.[56] inclined to the view that that test consisted of two components, *viz.* first, that the shareholders adopting the alteration had acted in good faith and, secondly, that *in the opinion of the court* the alteration was for the benefit of the company, but this view was rejected by the Court of Appeal,[57] which held that it was sufficient that the proposed alteration, *in the opinion of the majority of the company*, was bona fide for the benefit of the company as a whole. The Court of Appeal thus decided in favour of the view that the test consisted of one subjective component only.[58]

---

[49] See Jenkins L.J. in *Edwards* v. *Halliwell* [1950] 2 All E.R. 1064, 1067; Danckwerts J. in *Pavlides* v. *Jensen* [1956] Ch. 565, 572. Further, *Burland* v. *Earle* [1902] A.C. 83; *Parke* v. *Daily News Ltd.* [1962] Ch. 927.

[50] *North-West Transportation Co.* v. *Beatty* (1887) 12 App.Cas 589.

[51] *Menier* v. *Hooper's Telegraph Works* (1874) L.R. 9 Ch. 350; *North-West Transportation Co.* v. *Beatty* (1887) 12 App.Cas. 589; *Birch* v. *Sullivan* [1957] 1 W.L.R. 1247.

[52] See para 58–20, *post*.

[53] [1980] 2 All E.R. 841, 862.

[54] Lindley M.R. in *Allen* v. *Gold Reefs of West Africa* [1900] 1 Ch. 656, 671; *Sidebottom* v. *Kershaw, Leese & Co. Ltd.* [1920] 1 Ch. 154; *Shuttleworth* v. *Cox Bros. & Co. (Maidenhead) Ltd.* [1927] 2 K.B. 9, 18 (Bankes L.J.).

[55] Evershed M.R. in *Greenhalgh* v. *Arderne Cinemas Ltd.* [1950] 2 All E.R. 1120, 1126; see also Pennycuick J. in *Rights and Issues Investment Trust Ltd.* v. *Stylo Shoes Ltd.* [1965] Ch. 250, 256.

[56] In *Dafen Tinplate Co. Ltd.* v. *Llanelly Steel Co. (1907) Ltd.* [1920] 2 Ch. 124, 140.

[57] See *Sidebottom* v. *Kershaw, Leese & Co. Ltd.* [1920] 1 Ch. 154; *Brown* v. *British Abrasive Wheel Co.* [1919] 1 Ch. 290.

[58] See Evershed M.R. in *Greenhalgh* v. *Arderne Cinemas Ltd.* [1950] 2 All E.R. 1120, 1126.

It might be difficult in an individual case to state whether the members comprising the majority, in their honest opinion, have been guided by the benefit of the company as a whole. It is therefore more practical in many cases to approach the problem from the other direction and to ask whether the resolution attacked by the minority has the effect of discriminating between the majority and minority shareholders to the detriment of the latter. This formulation was adopted by Evershed M.R.[59] in the following passage:

> "Certain things, I think, can be safely stated as emerging from these authorities.[60] In the first place, it is now plain that 'bona fide for the benefit of the company as a whole' means not two things but one thing. It means that the shareholder must proceed on what, in his honest opinion, is for the benefit of the company as a whole. Secondly, the phrase, 'the company as a whole,' does not (at any rate in such a case as the present) mean the company as a commercial entity as distinct from the corporators. It means the corporators as a general body. That is to say, you may take the case of an individual hypothetical member and ask whether what is proposed is, in the honest opinion of those who voted in its favour, for that person's benefit. I think the thing can, in practice, be more accurately and precisely stated by looking at the converse and by saying that a special resolution of this kind woud be liable to be impeached if the effect of it were to discriminate between the majority shareholders and the minority shareholders so as to give to the former an advantage of which the latter were deprived. When the cases are examined where the resolution has been successfully attacked, it is on that ground that it has fallen down."

Until recently, the tendency was to confine "fraud on the minority" to cases where there was an element of dishonesty or, at least, impropriety. It now appears that the courts will have regard to advantageous consequences to the wrongdoer as much as to his improper intentions. In *Pavlides* v. *Jensen*[61] it was held that a negligent sale at an undervalue could not, without more, amount to fraud on the minority. However, in *Daniels* v. *Daniels*,[62] Templeman J. held that there might be circumstances in which, exceptionally, minority shareholders could bring an action founded on the gross negligence of the controlling directors, at least where the directors themselves benefited from their own negligence (*e.g.* by the sale of corporate assets to one of their number at an undervalue). Moreover, the *Daniels* case receives support from the decision of Sir Robert Megarry V.-C. in *Estmanco (Kilner House) Ltd.* v. *Greater London Council*[63] where the learned Vice-Chancellor stated:

---

[59] In *Greenhalgh* v. *Arderne Cinemas Ltd.* [1950] 2 All E.R. 1120, 1126.
[60] The learned judge has referred to *Sidebottom* v. *Kershaw, Leese & Co. Ltd.* [1920] 1 Ch. 154; *Dafen Tinplate Co. Ltd.* v. *Llanelly Steel Co. (1907) Ltd.* [1920] 2 Ch. 124; *Shuttleworth* v. *Cox Bros. & Co. (Maidenhead) Ltd.* [1927] 2 K.B. 9.
[61] [1956] Ch. 656.
[62] [1978] Ch. 406.
[63] [1982] 1 All E.R. 437, 445.

> " 'Fraud' in the phrase 'fraud on a minority' seems to be being used as comprising not only fraud at common law but also fraud in the wider equitable sense of that term, as in the equitable concept of a fraud on a power."

58–15 *Application of principles of natural justice*. Directors are bound to exercise their powers in the interests of the company as a whole and not in the interests of individual members, even though this may be inconsistent with the observance of natural justice.[64] Megarry J. observed in this case[65]:

> "Where there is corporate personality, the directors or others exercising the powers in question are bound not merely by their duties towards the other members, but also by their duties towards the corporation. These duties may be inconsistent with the observance of natural justice, and accordingly the implication of any term that natural justice should be observed may be excluded."

58–16 *The expropriation cases*. The rules discussed in the preceding paragraphs were largely evolved in the so-called expropriation cases in which the issue was whether a special resolution altering the articles of the company by providing that a minority shareholder holding a small number of shares could be compelled, upon the request of the majority, to sell out his holding at a fair value to the nominees of the majority was valid.

In *Sidebottom* v. *Kershaw, Leese & Co. Ltd.*[66] the company, which carried on the business of cotton spinners, passed a special resolution introducing a clause into the articles whereby a person carrying on "any business which is in direct competition with the business of the company" could be required to sell out his shares to nominees of the directors upon payment of the fair value of the shares at a price to be certified by the auditors. This resolution was plainly directed against the plaintiffs, a partnership carrying on a business competitive to that of the company, but the Court of Appeal held that it was in the interest of the company as a whole to be protected against competition, and upheld the resolution.

Sidebottom's case should be contrasted with the decision of Astbury J. in *Brown* v. *British Abrasive Wheel Co.*[67] In this case, which was decided when the true meaning of the test that the alteration must be "bona fide for the benefit of the company as a whole" was not yet ascertained, the majority held 98 per cent. of the shares and the minority 2 per cent. The company passed a resolution that a shareholder, upon the request of the holders of nine-tenths of the issued shares, should be bound to sell and transfer his shares to the nominees of such holders at a fair value. Astbury J. decided that that alteration was not for the benefit of the company but

---

[64] *Gaiman* v. *National Association for Mental Health* [1971] Ch. 317. *Cf.* the Scottish case of *St. Johnstone F.C. Ltd.* v. *Scottish Football Association Ltd.*, 1965 S.L.T. 171.

[65] *Gaiman* v. *National Association for Mental Health, supra*, at p. 335.

[66] [1920] 1 Ch. 154.

[67] [1919] 1 Ch. 290; see also Peterson J. in *Dafen Tinplate Co. Ltd.* v. *Llanelly Steel Co. (1907) Ltd.* [1920] 2 Ch. 124.

for the benefit of the majority, and granted an injunction against the company prohibiting it from carrying out the resolution.[68]

The true distinction between these two cases is that in *Sidebottom's* case the expropriating article was not discriminatory in character and, in appropriate circumstances, would likewise have operated against the majority, but that in the *British Abrasive Wheel* case the article was plainly and unashamedly discriminatory.

58–17 *Other cases*. In *Cook* v. *Deeks*[69] directors of a railway construction company obtained a contract in their own names to construct a railway. The contract was obtained under circumstances which amounted to a breach of trust by the directors, who then used their voting powers to pass a resolution of the company declaring that the company had no interest in the contract. The Privy Council held that the benefit of the contract belonged in equity to the company, and the directors could not validly use their voting power to vest it in themselves.

On the other hand, at a time when statute did not enable the company to remove a director from office, notwithstanding provisions in the articles or a contract to the contrary,[70] it was held by the Court of Appeal in *Shuttleworth* v. *Cox Bros. & Co. (Maidenhead) Ltd.*[71] that a company which was dissatisfied with the services of a director who, according to the articles, was entitled to hold office for life unless he fell under one of the six disqualifications laid down in the articles could alter its articles by introducing a seventh disqualification under which a life director could be removed "if he be required in writing by all the other directors to resign his office." Here, again, the true test is whether the resolution introducing the alteration of confirming a measure taken by the directors has a discriminatory effect as against the minority, so that the majority obtains—or retains—an advantage denied to the minority.

58–18 *Resolutions obtained by trick*. Similarly, a minority can prevent the company from acting on a special resolution obtained by a trick.[17] It would be a trick, *e.g.* if the notice of the meeting did not give a sufficiently full and frank disclosure to the shareholders of the facts upon which they were asked to vote.[72]

58–19 *Motives of personal benefit*. A resolution cannot be attacked solely on the ground that a shareholder voting for it was motivated by the prospect

---

[68] Astbury J. found, as a fact, that there was no challenge to the bona fides of the directors or the majority; this finding was difficult to reconcile with the subsequent interpretation of the test, and consequently Lord Sterndale M.R. observed in *Sidebottom's* case (at p. 167) that "if that finding be right, and as to that I say nothing, [the alteration] was not bona fide." In short, the *British Abrasive Wheel* case was subsequently interpreted as a case of technical or "legal" fraud in order to bring it into line with Lindley M.R.'s test as construed in the *Sidebottom* and *Shuttleworth* cases.

[69] [1916] 1 A.C. 554; *cf. Regal (Hastings) Ltd.* v. *Gulliver* [1942] 1 All E.R. 378 (H.L.).

[70] See now s. 184, para 61–27, *post*.

[71] [1927] 2 K.B. 9.

[72] *Baillie* v. *Oriental Telephone, etc., Co.* [1915] 1 Ch. 503.

of personal benefit rather than the benefit of the company as a going concern. Evershed M.R. observed[73]:

> "It is . . . not necessary to require that persons voting for a special resolution should, so to speak, dissociate themselves altogether from the prospect of personal benefit and consider whether the proposal is for the benefit of the company as a going concern. If, as commonly happens, an outside person makes an offer to buy all the shares, prima facie, if the corporators think it is a fair offer and vote in favour of the resolution, it is no ground for impeaching the resolution because they are considering the position of themselves as individual persons."

Further, unless it is otherwise provided by the regulations, a shareholder as such is not debarred from voting or using his voting power to carry a resolution by the circumstance of his having a particular interest in the subject-matter of the vote.[74]

The position is different where the resolution carried by the majority purports to confirm a breach of trust or illicit gain on the part of the majority, as is demonstrated by *Cook* v. *Deeks*[75] (see para. 58–17, *ante*).

58–20 *Wrongdoers in control of the company*. Until recently, the orthodox view was that for a minority shareholder to establish "fraud on the minority" he had to show that the wrongdoers were in control of the company.[76] The main significance of the decision of Vinelott J. in *Prudential Assurance Co. Ltd.* v. *Newman Industries Ltd. (No. 2)* was that his lordship decided that the exception to *Foss* v. *Harbottle* is not confined to cases where the wrongdoers have voting control of the company but extends to the situation where, though not holding the majority of the shares in the company, the wrongdoers are able by manipulating their position in the company to ensure that the majority will not allow a claim to be brought by the company for the alleged wrong, in brief, where the wrongdoers are in factual though not necessarily legal control.[77] This conclusion arose from a blurring of the concepts of "wrongdoer control" and the "interests of justice" (as to which see para. 58–22, *post*). It is now clear that the Court of Appeal[78] disapproved of this approach and has separated the "wrongdoer control" requirement. However, it is not wholly clear from the judgment what the criteria are. The learned Lords Justices observed (p. 364) that "control"—

> "embraces a broad spectrum extending from an overall absolute majority of votes at one end to a majority of votes at the other end made up of those likely to be cast by the delinquent himself plus those voting with him as a result of influence or apathy."

---

[73] *Greenhalgh* v. *Arderne Cinemas Ltd.* [1950] 2 All E.R. 1120, 1126; Lord Davey in *Burland* v. *Earle* [1902] A.C. 83, 94.

[74] *Dominion Cotton Mills* v. *Amyot* [1912] A.C. 546; *Foster* v. *Foster* [1916] 1 Ch. 532 (principal shareholder removing managing director and appointing himself in his place). But this now has to be read subject to the condition of Foster J. in *Clemens* v. *Clemens Bros. Ltd.* [1976] 2 All E.R. 268, para. 58–04, *ante*.

[75] [1916] 1 A.C. 554. See also *Birch* v. *Sullivan* [1957] 1 W.L.R. 1247.

[76] See Palmer's *Company Law* (22nd ed.), para. 56–20.

[77] [1980] 2 All E.R. 841, 869 *et seq*.

[78] [1982] 1 All E.R. 354.

The procedural approach of the Court of Appeal is to require a prima facie case of "wrongdoer control" to be established and not merely alleged.

58–21 QUALIFIED MAJORITIES. Where the Acts of the articles require a qualified majority for the passing of a resolution, as, *e.g.* in the case of special or extraordinary resolutions (s. 141 (1) and (2)), the rule in *Foss* v. *Harbottle* cannot be invoked to override these requirements by a resolution passed by a simple majority.[79] If this were not so, provisions requiring qualified majorities would be valueless because a bare majority could always confirm a resolution passed by a majority of less than the required number.

It should, however, be noted that if the vote is taken otherwise than by poll, *e.g.* by show of hands, a declaration of the chairman that the resolution is carried is normally conclusive (s. 141 (3)).

Where the majority by a bare majority resolves a measure not authorised by the Acts or the articles, an individual membership right of the minority shareholder, *viz.* his right to maintain himself in full membership, has been infringed.[80]

58–22 ADMISSIBILITY OF FURTHER EXCEPTIONS. It has been suggested that, apart from the three exceptions to the rule in *Foss* v. *Harbottle* discussed in the preceding paragraphs, a further, general, exception should be admitted in cases in which justice requires that the court should intervene to assist an otherwise helpless minority shareholder.[81]

In *Pavlides* v. *Jensen*,[82] Danckwerts J., after a careful examination of the previous cases, rejected this contention as not being borne out by the authorities. In that case the alleged wrong to the company was done negligently, and not fraudulently.[83] It is, however, respectfully thought that the learned judge did not intend to state more than that, on the facts before him, he would not admit a further exception to the rule in *Foss* v. *Harbottle*, and this view appears to be borne out by the observations on this case made by the Court of Appeal in *Heyting* v. *Dupont*.[84] In the latter case which involved an allegation of misfeasance against the majority shareholder in his capacity as director, Harman L.J. said[85]:

> " . . . there are cases which suggest that the rule [in *Foss* v. *Harbottle*] is not a rigid one and that exception will be made where the justice of the case demands it. I am content . . . to assume that there may be misfeasance in respect of which the exception should be allowed, but I also agree . . . that this is emphatically not a case where the rule should be further stretched."

[79] *Edwards* v. *Halliwell* [1950] 2 All E.R. 1064, 1067.
[80] See para. 58–04, *ante*.
[81] See *Russell* v. *Wakefield Waterworks Co.* (1875) L.R. 20 Eq. 474, 480, 482; *Baillie* v. *Oriental Telephone, etc., Co. Ltd.* [1915] 1 Ch. 503, 518; *Cotter* v. *National Union of Seamen* [1929] 2 Ch. 58, 69; *Edwards* v. *Halliwell* [1950] 2 All E.R. 1064, 1067; *Heyting* v. *Dupont* [1964] 1 W.L.R. 843, 851, 854.
[82] [1956] Ch. 565.
[83] See Harman J. in *Birch* v. *Sullivan* [1957] 1 W.L.R. 1247, 1250.
[84] [1964] 1 W.L.R. 843.
[85] At p. 854; and see Russell L.J. at p. 851.

In an address to the Holdsworth Club, University of Birmingham, Lord Justice Buckley criticised this interpretation of *Heyting* v. *Dupont*. The learned Lord Justice observed that Harman L.J. in the quoted passage, referred to his own judgment which said: "I do not think it necessary for the purposes of this case to review the many authorities on this subject, all or most of which are noted in the report of *Pavlides* v. *Jensen*. I am prepared to assume for the purposes of this case (though I must not be understood as accepting it as a proposition of law) that there may be occasions in which justice requires departure from the rule when all that is asserted is damage to the company arising from misfeasance in withholding an asset of the company without fraud or *ultra vires*. But to my mind it is quite plain that justice does not require it in the present case." In his address to the Club the learned Lord Justice added: "Now I am in a position to assure this Club that neither of these passages was intended to lend any support to the proposition assumed. It was unnecessary to come to a decision upon it, and the simplest and least onerous course for a busy court was to avoid decision." In view of these observations, *Heyting* v. *Dupont* cannot be relied upon in support of the proposition above (which is still adhered to) that the courts have jurisdiction to admit further exceptions to the rule in *Foss* v. *Harbottle*. Indeed, the whole of Vinelott J.'s judgment in *Prudential Assurance Co. Ltd.* v. *Newman Industries Ltd. (No. 2)*[86] can be seen, on one level, as an affirmation of a general principle based on the interests of justice rather than an application of a schematic range of exceptions. However, the Court of Appeal[87] has now restored the schematic approach with the comment (p. 366) that the "interests of justice" exception is not a convincing practical test, "particularly if it involves a full-dress trial before the test is applied."

Minority shareholders' actions in England

58–23 Minority shareholders[88] who contend that a resolution of the general meeting does not bind them because it falls within one of the exceptions to the rule in *Foss* v. *Harbottle* have various ways of taking the matter to court.[89]

The view has often been expressed that the biggest obstacle in the way of a minority shareholder's action is the cost involved, especially in relation to the enforcement of corporate membership rights where any money received is payable to the company itself and not the minority shareholder. In *Wallersteiner* v. *Moir (No. 2)*,[90] however, the Court of Appeal held that it was open to the court in a minority shareholder's action to order that the company should indemnify the plaintiff against the costs incurred in the

---

86 [1980] 2 All E.R. 841.
87 [1982] 1 All E.R. 354.
88 A bankrupt shareholder, as long as he is on the register of members, appears to be entitled to bring a minority shareholders' action: *Birch* v. *Sullivan* [1957] 1 W.L.R. 1247.
89 For the position in Scotland, see para. 58–27, *post*.
90 [1975] Q.B. 373.

action. The test is whether it is reasonable and prudent in the company's interest for the plaintiff to bring the action and it is brought by him in good faith. If so, the court should order the company to pay the plaintiff's costs down to judgment *whether the action succeeds or not*. The costs should be taxed on a common fund basis. Although as a general rule a plaintiff should apply at the commencement of the action for sanction to proceed with it, in *Wallersteiner* v. *Moir (No. 2)* the Court of Appeal authorised the plaintiff to proceed with the prosecution of outstanding issues[91] on a counterclaim down to the close of discovery, after which he should obtain further directions of the court.[92] It was also held that the plaintiff was not entitled to legal aid because, by virtue of the Legal Aid Act 1974, s. 25, the persons entitled to legal aid do not include a body corporate and, if the plaintiff were given legal aid, it would mean that the company on behalf of whom he sued would receive legal aid indirectly; and further (Lord Denning M.R. dissenting), the general rule against contingency fees in English law is not to be departed from for the sake of minority shareholders.

58–24 PROCEDURE. The procedure, founded on R.S.C. 1965, Ord. 15, r. 12, will often be the most suitable one.[93] The minority shareholders sue as plaintiffs on behalf of themselves and the other shareholders (except those constituting the majority); the company will normally be a defendant,[94] and the directors or majority shareholders are likewise often made defendants.[95]

The statement of claim in the minority shareholders' action founded on fraud on the minority is defective unless it contains an allegation that, owing to the wrongdoers being in control of the company, they cannot sue in the name of the company.[96]

In *Heyting* v. *Dupont*,[97] Plowman J. held that if the statement of claim does not allege facts which bring the case within one of the admitted exceptions to the rule in *Foss* v. *Harbottle*, the court has no jurisdiction to hear the action, and must dismiss the action *proprio motu* if the point is not

[91] For previous proceedings, see *Wallersteiner* v. *Moir* [1974] 1 W.L.R. 991 where it was held, *inter alia*, that a full discussion at the general meeting could not be prevented by a director taking out a writ for libel and contending at the general meeting that the matter was *sub judice*; *ibid*. on p. 1005.

[92] For the procedure of obtaining an indemnity, see [1975] Q.B. 373, 392 (*per* Lord Denning M.R.), 404 (*per* Buckely L.J.) and 411 (*per* Scarman L.J.). The general concept is applied analogously from the law of trustees; see *Re Beddoe* [1893] 1 Ch. 547.

[93] See *Pender* v. *Lushington* (1877) 6 Ch.D. 70 (para. 58–07); *Burland* v. *Earle* [1902] A.C. 83; *Towers* v. *African Tug Co*. [1904] 1 Ch. 558; *Pavlides* v. *Jensen* [1956] Ch. 565.

[94] The company must be a party to the suit, either as plaintiff or as defendant; see *Spokes* v. *Grosvenor Hotel Co*. [1897] 2 Q.B. 124, 128; also *Atwool* v. *Merryweather* (1868) L.R. 5 Eq. 464n.; *Menier* v. *Hooper's Telegraph Works Co*. (1874) L.R. 9 Ch. 350; *Mason* v. *Harris* (1879) 11 Ch.D. 97; *Alexander* v. *Automatic Telephone Co*. [1900] 2 Ch. 56; *Anderson* v. *Midland Ry*. [1902] 1 Ch. 369; *Foster* v. *Foster* [1916] 1 Ch. 532, 547; *Pavlides* v. *Jensen* [1956] Ch. 565; *Prudential Assurance Co. Ltd.* v. *Newman Industries Ltd. (No. 2)* [1982] 1 All E.R. 354.

[95] For details, see Palmer's *Precedents*, (17th ed.), Vol. I, p. 1098; and *Supreme Court Practice*.

[96] *Birch* v. *Sullivan* [1957] 1 W.L.R. 1247; and see *Heyting* v. *Dupont* [1964] 1 W.L.R. 843.

[97] *Heyting* v. *Dupont* [1963] 1 W.L.R. 1192.

taken by the defendant. It is respectfully thought that this decision does not take account of all possible circumstances; thus, if the statement of claim includes allegations of misfeasance, the court would appear to have power to consider whether the case is one in which an extension of the existing exceptions to the rule ought to be admitted.[98]

In a representative action an unnamed but represented plaintiff is a "party" as defined by the Supreme Court of Judicature (Consolidation) Act 1925, s. 225, and, if the named plaintiff withdraws, the name of such unnamed party may be added (R.S.C., Ord. 15, r. 6) and the pleadings amended accordingly (R.S.C., Ord. 20, r. 5). If the representative action was commenced in time it does not become statute-barred as against the party who is later named, although the amendment is out of time.[99]

The decision of the Court of Appeal in *Prudential Assurance Co. Ltd.* v. *Newman Industries Ltd. (No. 2)*[1] is now authoritative on the procedural position. Its chief proposition is that when a minority shareholder commences a derivative action, the question whether in fact the company is controlled by the alleged wrongdoers should first be determined before the derivative action itself is allowed to proceed. Moreover, the right to bring a derivative action should not be decided as a preliminary issue on the hypothesis that all allegations in the statement of claim of "fraud" and "control" are facts, as in the trial of a preliminary point of law. The plaintiff should at least be required to establish a prima facie case that (i) the company is entitled to the relief claimed and (ii) the action falls within the proper boundaries of the rule restricting members' actions on behalf of the company. The case is also a salutary warning against expressing what is in reality a corporate matter as an individual wrong merely because the member is indirectly prejudiced by a reduction in the company's profits. However, there is no objection to combining a derivative action with a personal action where the reality justifies such a course.

58–25 PROCEEDINGS IN THE NAME OF THE COMPANY. In earlier days minority shareholders used to sue in the name of the company, particularly when the purpose of the proceedings was to recover damages or illicit gains from directors, founders or other persons.[2] This procedure is still available but in practice it is rarely used in cases which, in the contention of the minority, fall within one of the exceptions to *Foss* v. *Harbottle*.[3] The reason is that its disadvantages outweigh its utility. First, this procedure blurs the issue which, instead of being fought on whether the rule in *Foss* v. *Harbottle*

---

[98] See the decision of the C.A. in the same [1964] 1 W.L.R. 843. On the possibility of the court recognising such further exceptions, see para. 58–22, *ante*.

[99] *Moon* v. *Atherton* [1972] 2 Q.B. 435.

[1] [1982] 1 All E.R. 354.

[2] See *Silber Light Co.* v. *Silber* (1879) 12 Ch.D. 717. On the right of the managing director (who holds the controlling power in the company) to sue in the name of the company, even against the wishes of his co-directors, see *Marshall's Valve Gear Co.* v. *Manning* [1909] 1 Ch. 267.

[3] See Palmer's *Precedents* (17th ed.), Vol. I, p. 1099.

does or does not apply, is fought on whether the plaintiffs are entitled to use the company's name. Lindley M.R. observed in *Alexander* v. *Automatic Telephone Co.*[4]:

> "Under these circumstances an action by some shareholders on behalf of themselves and the others against the defendants is in accordance with the authorities, and is unobjectionable in form: see *Menier* v. *Hooper's Telegraph Works.*[5] An action in this form is far preferable to an action in the name of the company, and then a fight as to the right to use its name."

Secondly, proceedings by a minority in the name of the company will often lead no further than a stay of proceedings, in order to ascertain whether the steps of the minority are approved by the majority or the directors.[6] Thirdly, if the court decides that the minority was not entitled to commence proceedings in the name of the company, the name of the company may be struck out,[7] and the solicitor may be ordered to pay the costs personally.[8]

The case of *Estmanco (Kilner House) Ltd.* v. *Greater London Council*[9] illustrates an unusual example of a minority being permitted to continue proceedings in the company's name after they had been commenced by the board against the wishes of the voting majority.

It follows that only in cases of emergency will a minority shareholder commence proceedings in the name of the company without the support of the majority and ask for the interlocutory relief to ensure that it may be determined whether the proceedings are supported by the majority,[9] but even in that case there must be good reasons for taking this course, otherwise the court will not accede to the request to adjourn proceedings in order to see whether the company will adopt them or not.[10] If this course is unavoidable the minority shareholder should at once himself take steps to have a general meeting convened, *e.g.* by requisitioning an extraordinary meeting under section 132 of the 1948 Act. However, reference should be made to the possibility that an "unfairly prejudiced" shareholder may be able to obtain authorisation from the court under section 75 of the 1980 Act to bring proceedings in the name of the company.[11]

58–26 DECLARATION OF RIGHTS. It will often be a convenient procedure for determining the question whether the minority may maintain an action against the majority to ask for a declaration of rights under R.S.C. 1965,

---

[4] [1900] 2 Ch. 56, 69.
[5] (1874) L.R. 9 Ch. 350.
[6] See *Pender* v. *Lushington* (1877) 6 Ch.D. 70 (para 58–07, *ante*).
[7] An application to this effect may be made by summons or motion under R.S.C. 1965, Ord. 15, r. 6.
[8] *Marshall's Valve Gear Co.* v. *Manning* [1909] 1 Ch. 267; *West End Hotels Syndicate* v. *Bayer* (1912) 29 T.L.R. 92.
[9] *Pender* v. *Lushington* (1877) 6 Ch.D. 70; Palmer's *Precedents* (17th ed.), Vol. I, p. 1099.
[10] *East Pant Du United Lead Mining Co.* v. *Merryweather* (1864) 2 H. & M. 254.
[11] See para. 60–08, *post*.

Ord. 15, r. 16. This procedure was adopted, *e.g.* in *Edwards* v. *Halliwell*[12] and, on an application by the defendants, in *Pavlides* v. *Jensen*.[13]

Procedure in Scotland[14]

58–27 In Scotland a minority shareholder would require to proceed in his own name alone, and there is no suggestion that he acts on behalf of the shareholders as a whole.[15] The courts have entertained actions of interdict,[16] reduction,[17] reduction and interdict[18] and actions ordaining the directors to reimburse the company.[19] Declaratory conclusions have also been admitted.[20] The company as well as the directors alleged to be responsible for the wrong must be called as a defender.[21] The 1980 Act, s. 75, especially s. 75 (4) (*c*) which empowers the court to authorise proceedings to be brought in the name of the company, may reduce the need for a minority shareholder to bring proceedings at common law of the nature discussed in this Chapter.[22]

---

[12] [1950] 2 All E.R. 1064 (see para 58–04, *ante*).
[13] [1956] Ch. 565. But the minority shareholder is not entitled to a declaration that the company's annual accounts should be amended: *Devlin* v. *Slough Estates Ltd, The Times,* June 16, 1982.
[14] See further "The Problem of Enforcement of Directors Duties in Scotland" 1981 S.L.T. (News) 257 and "The Derivative Action in Scotland" 1982 S.L.T. (News) 205.
[15] *Smith* v. *Glasgow etc. Rly. Co.* 1897, 4 S.L.T. 327; *Lochaber District Committee* v. *Invergarry etc. Rly. Co.* 1913, 1 S.L.T. 361.
[16] *Orr* v. *Glasgow etc. Rly. Co.* 1857, 20 D. 327 (Ct. of Sn.); 1860, 3 Macq. 799 (H.L.); *Rixon* v. *Edinburgh Northern Tramways* 1889, 16 R. 353.
[17] *Harris* v. *A. Harris Ltd.*, 1936 S.C. 183; 1936 S.L.T. 227.
[18] *Lee* v. *Crawford* 1890, 17 R. 1094; *Hannay* v. *Muir* 1898, 1 F. 306; *Oliver's Trustees* v. *W. G. Walker & Sons Ltd.* 1948 S.L.T. 140.
[19] *e.g. Harris* v. *A. Harris Ltd., supra.*
[20] *Brown* v. *Stewart* 1898, 1 F. 316, 325.
[21] See Ch. 60, *post.*

CHAPTER 59

QUALIFIED MINORITY RIGHTS; THE SCOTTISH JUDICIAL FACTOR

59–01 THE rule of supremacy of the majority, usually referred to as the rule in *Foss* v. *Harbottle*,[1] is subject to considerable qualifications which can be grouped under three heads:

(1) individual membership rights[2];
(2) qualified minority rights; and
(3) the remedy for unfairly prejudicial treatment.

In addition, in Scots law a further remedy is available, *viz.*

(4) an application for sequestration of the assets of the company and the appointment of a judicial factor.

In this chapter, it is convenient to consider the qualified minority rights and the appointment of a judicial factor in Scots law. The remedy for unfairly prejudicial treatment will be considered in the next chapter.[3]

Qualified minority rights

Their nature

59–02 Qualified minority rights should not be confused with individual membership rights.[4] While the latter can be exercised by an individual shareholder, the former require the co-operation of a minority group of specified size within the corporate body. The statutory requirements as to the composition of the minority vary according to the right which the minority wishes to exercise, and these variations are, perhaps, more arbitrary[5] than is warranted by the nature of the rights in question.

Qualified minority rights should further be distinguished from the requirements of a qualified majority which, in effect, enable the minority to prevent the majority from carrying out its wishes. Thus, extraordinary and special resolutions require a three-quarters majority, the latter resolution having the additional requirement of 21 clear days' notice (1948 Act, s. 141 (1) and (2)),[6] and certain other measures require other qualified majorities.[7] The only justification which can be advanced in favour of this rule of the minority is that it preserves, in important matters, the status quo which is founded on the original contract of the shareholders and the company (or the other corporators).

---

[1] (1843) 2 Hare 461.
[2] See para. 58–04, *ante*.
[3] See para. 60–08, *post*.
[4] See para. 58–04, *ante*.
[5] As the result of the historical development of these rights.
[6] See para. 56–05, *ante*.
[7] See, *e.g.* ss. 133 (3) (*b*), 141 (2), 206 (2), 209 (1).

However, this negative right of the minority to preserve the status quo by vetoing a constitutional or other change requiring a qualified majority is not comprised in the term "qualified minority rights" as employed here. This term refers to rights enabling a minority of specified size to take a particular action. The purpose of qualified minority rights is normally to provide access to a competent forum in which a decision on the disputed measure can be obtained. Thus, if the dispute is with the management, a qualified minority may requisition an extraordinary general meeting of the shareholders (1948 Act, s. 132); if the dispute is between warring groups of shareholders, minority rights give access to the court (*e.g.* 1948 Act, ss. 5, 23, 72) or the Department of Trade (*e.g.* 1948 Act, ss. 164 (1) (*a*), 172 (3)), so that it may be decided or investigated in a more impartial manner than by those who are, or appear to be, parties to the dispute.[8]

The various rights

59–03 REQUISITION OF EXTRAORDINARY GENERAL MEETING. A minority of not less than one-tenth of the paid-up capital carrying voting rights at the date of the deposit of the requisition may requisition the holding of an extraordinary general meeting (1948 Act, s. 132).[9]

REQUISITION OF CIRCULATION OF RESOLUTIONS AND NOTICES. The minority entitled to use this right is: members representing

(1) not less than one-twentieth of the total voting rights of all the members having a right to vote at the meeting to which the requisition relates; or
(2) not less than 100 members holding shares on which there has been paid up an average sum per member of not less than £100 (1948 Act, s. 140 (2)).[10]

59–04 RIGHT TO DEMAND A POLL. The right of the minority specified in section 137 (1) (*b*) of the 1948 Act[11] to demand a poll cannot be excluded by the articles though they may give that right to a smaller minority.

The minority necessary for the demand of a poll is:

(1) not less than five members having the right to vote at the meeting in question; or
(2) not less than one-tenth of the total voting rights entitled to vote at that meeting; or
(3) an aggregate of not less than one-tenth of the total paid-up capital carrying votes at that meeting.

---

[8] Exceptionally, a qualified minority right may be given to debenture holders: see s. 5 (2) (*b*).
[9] See para. 53–08, *ante*.
[10] See para. 55–05, *ante*.
[11] See para. 55–09, *ante*.

59–05 OBJECTION TO ALTERATION OF OBJECTS. The provisions relating to this topic are contained in section 5 of the 1948 Act.[12] The minority entitled to object is:

(1) 15 per cent. of the issued capital of the company;
(2) 15 per cent. of any class thereof;
(3) 15 per cent. of the debentures giving the holders a right to object to the alteration of the objects; or
(4) 15 per cent. of debentures issued before December 1, 1947, and secured by a floating charge.

OBJECTION TO ALTERATION OF CERTAIN NON-OBLIGATORY CLAUSES IN MEMORANDUM. According to section 23 (1) and (3) of the 1948 Act[13] the minority entitled to claim this right is:

(1) 15 per cent. of the issued capital of the company; or
(2) 15 per cent. of any class thereof.

This is the same requirement as that under the first two headings of the previous paragraph; it is also similar to that dicussed in the following paragraph.

OBJECTION TO ALTERATION OF CLASS RIGHTS. If the memorandum or articles provide that the alteration of the rights of a class of shares shall be subject to the consent of a specified proportion of the issued shares of that class or the sanction of a separate class meeting, a minority of the shares of that class has the right to object (1948 Act, s. 72).[14] The minority in this case is 15 per cent. of the class. Section 72 has been enlarged by the 1980 Act to embrace circumstances where the articles do not contain provision with respect to the variation of class rights and an equivalent qualified minority right will obtain (1980 Act, s. 32).

The minority requirement of section 72 (which first came into operation in 1929) was the historical model on which the requirements of sections 5 and 23 of the Companies Act 1948 were framed.

OBJECTION TO SPECIAL RESOLUTIONS RESULTING IN A COMPANY BECOMING A PRIVATE COMPANY. A qualified minority to apply to the court for the cancellation of a special resolution by an old public company not to be re-registered under section 8 of the 1980 Act as a public company or by a public company to be re-registered under section 10 as a private company (1980 Act, s. 11). Such an application may be made:

(a) by the holders of not less in the aggregate than 5 per cent. in nominal value of the company's issued share capital or any class thereof;

---

[12] See para. 9–38, *ante*.
[13] See para. 13–03, *ante*.
[14] See para. 34–16, *ante*.

(b) if the company is not limited by shares, by not less than 5 per cent. of the company's members; or

(c) by not less than 50 of the company's members;

but any such application cannot be made by any person who has consented to or voted in favour of the resolution (1980 Act, s. 11 (2)).[15]

[THE NEXT PARAGRAPH IS 59–13]

59–13 APPLICATION FOR INVESTIGATION INTO AFFAIRS OF COMPANY. A minority of

(1) 200 or more members; or

(2) members holding not less than one-tenth of the shares issued,

may apply to the Department of Trade for the appointment of an inspector to investigate into the affairs of the company; the Department has discretion to grant or refuse the application (1948 Act, s. 164 (1) (*a*)).[16]

APPLICATION FOR INVESTIGATION INTO MEMBERSHIP OF COMPANY. The same minority as stated in the preceding paragraph may apply to the Department of Trade for the appointment of an inspector to investigate into the membership of the company (s. 172 (3)).[17] In this case the Department of Trade is bound to comply with the application unless it is satisfied that the application is vexatious or any of the matters, for which application for investigation is made, is unreasonable.

APPLICATION FOR CANCELLATION OF SPECIAL RESOLUTION BY PRIVATE COMPANY TO PROVIDE FINANCIAL ASSISTANCE FOR THE PURCHASE OF ITS SHARES. An application can be made to the court for the cancellation of a special resolution passed under the provisions of section 43 of the 1981 Act that a private company provide financial assistance for the purchase of its shares. The application can be made:

(a) by the holders of not less in the aggregate than 10 per cent. in nominal value of the company's issued share capital or any class thereof; or

(b) if the company is not limited by shares, by not less than 10 per cent. of the company's members.[18]

Where a private company passes a special resolution under Part III of the 1981 Act approving any payment out of capital for the redemption or purchase of any of its shares, *any* member (other than one who consented to or voted in favour of the resolution) and any creditor can apply to the court for the cancellation of the resolution.[19]

---

[15] See para. 5–10, *ante*.
[16] See para. 78–03, *post*.
[17] See para. 78–18, *post*.
[18] 1981 Act, s.44. See para. 38–17.
[19] 1981 Act, s.57. See para. 33–22.

Appointment of judicial factor and sequestration of assets in a Scottish company

59–14 The Court of Session has power to appoint a judicial factor to administer and manage property to avoid danger of loss or resolve administrative deadlock in certain circumstances by statute, and also at common law by virtue of the *nobile officium*. It has now been held that the court may competently appoint a judicial factor on the estates of a company incorporated under the modern Companies Acts.[20] The appointment of a judicial factor may be sought by anyone having an interest in the property to be preserved and the appointment may be final or *ad interim* and may be recalled when the necessity for the appointment has ended.

In the case of a company, any member or creditor or other person having an interest obviously has sufficient interest to present a petition. It is not necessary that the member is entered on the register or that he controls any particular proportion of the share capital (*Fraser, supra*). A petition may also be presented by the accountant of court.

In addition to appointing a judicial factor, the court may sequestrate the assets of the company. This has the effect of vesting the assets in the judicial factor, although in some respects he may have to take additional steps to complete his title. On sequestration, management of the assets of the company is vested in the factor and he supersedes the directors.

The circumstances in which a judicial factor may be appointed are not limited in theory, although the existence of statutory procedure for winding up obviously limits application to a company. It has now been held,[21] however, that the existence of statutory provisions does not exclude the court's common law power to appoint a judicial factor. It is evident from the decision in *Fraser* that the court will regard this remedy as appropriate only in unusual circumstances where a company is concerned. There does not, however, seem to be any reason in principle why it should not be resorted to by any member, creditor or other interested party if his other remedies are either exhausted or unsuitable.

The petitioner in *Fraser*, together with certain family trusts, claimed to hold 51 per cent. of the shares in Neill & Co. Ltd., but he had apparently been removed from the register of members. He alleged a course of illegal and dishonest conduct by the present directors, and prima facie grounds for objecting to it. There was also a question of urgency, it being doubtful whether the wages due in the week of the application could be paid unless a judicial factor were appointed. The court held that in view of the position of chaos requiring urgently to be dealt with it would sequestrate the assets of the company and appoint a judicial factor *ad interim*.

59–15 A judicial factor is an officer of the court and must submit accounts to the accountant of court. Where he is charged with the administration of

---

[20] *Patrick Fraser, Petitioner,* 1971 S.L.T. 146; see also *Paterson* v. *Best* (1900) 2 F. 1088.
[21] *Patrick Fraser, supra.*

sequestrated assets he must exercise the duty of care to be expected of a trustee at common law and by statute. He has the ordinary powers of a trustee in regard to the administration of the estate and if he requires special powers he must apply to the accountant of court or to the court itself for the necessary authority. In relation to a company his position is in many respects similar to that of a receiver in English law.[22]

It should be noted that the appointment of a judicial factor, even if accompanied by sequestration of the estates of the company, is not a commencement of winding up. Accordingly any floating charge under the Companies (Floating Charges and Receivers) (Scotland) Act 1972 does not crystallise. The assets of the company are vested in the factor subject to any fixed securities, legal preferences or diligences.

[22] For a fuller account of the position of judicial factor and the procedure for appointment, administration, discharge, etc., see David M. Walker, *Principles of Scottish Private Law* (2nd ed.), Chap. 17; and McBryde and Dowie, *Petition Procedure in the Court of Session*, Chap. 7.

CHAPTER 60

THE REMEDY FOR UNFAIRLY PREJUDICIAL TREATMENT

60–01 IT has always been the law that if a majority acts oppressively towards the minority, the latter may petition the court to wind up the company on the ground that it is just and equitable to do so (1948 Act, s. 222 (*f*)). However, very often it is not in the interests of the minority to have the company wound up. The liquidation may result in the sale of the assets at break-up value, without regard to goodwill and the "know-how" of the company. Moreover, winding up by the court is both slow and expensive. Consequently, a minority shareholder who petitions for a winding up may, in effect, play his opponent's game.

In an attempt to meet such cases, statute has for some time given minorities a remedy alternative to winding up. From 1948 until 1980 the so-called alternative remedy was contained in section 210 of the 1948 Act. It was based on the concept of "oppression" and was, in its day, a remarkable statutory innovation. However, partly as a result of the drafting of the section and partly because of the somewhat restrictive interpretation it received in the courts, it became less available and less imaginative than had been intended. As long ago as 1962, the Jenkins Committee[1] was able to point to a number of the inadequacies of section 210 and 10 years later the House of Lords demonstrated in *Ebrahinni* v. *Westbourne Galleries Ltd.*[2] that the alternative remedy was more difficult to obtain than the more cataclysmic one based on "just and equitable" winding up.

Section 75 of the 1980 Act, which came into force on December 22, 1980,[3] has attempted to overcome the difficulties which surrounded section 210. It has repealed section 210 and enacted a new provision based on "unfair prejudice" rather than "oppression." It is probable that, in construing section 75, the courts will look for guidance and for bases of distinction to section 210 of the 1948 Act and the case law that grew out of it. For this reason and for purposes of exposition it is intended in the present edition of this book to precede the consideration of the 1980 reform with a statement of the law under section 210 of the 1948 Act.

Section 210 of the 1948 Act

60–02 The alternative remedy was available upon three conditions:

(1) that the affairs of the company were being conducted in a manner oppressive to some part of the members; and

---

[1] Cmnd. 1749, para. 212.
[2] [1973] A.C. 360. See para. 85–09, *post*.
[3] S.I. 1980 No. 1785.

(2) that the court would have been prepared to make a winding-up order on the "just and equitable" ground (s. 222 (*f*));

(3) but that such winding up would have unfairly prejudiced those members (s. 210 (1) and (2)).

In such a case, upon a petition presented by

(a) any one member of the oppressed minority or the personal representative of such a member who had died[4]; or

(b) the Department of Trade, as the result of an investigation of the company's affairs or an inspection of its books and papers (1967 Act, s. 35 (2));

the court could make such order as it thought fit for ending the matters complained of. The order could regulate the conduct of the company's affairs in the future, or provide for the purchase of the shares of any member of the company by other members, or—an exceptional provision—by the company itself. If the company itself was to be the purchaser the court could, but need not, provide for the reduction of the company's capital (s. 210 (2)); in any event, in the case of an order authorising the company to acquire its own shares, the court would ensure that the interests of the creditors were safeguarded.

The petition had to set out with some particularity the relief sought,[5] if necessary in alternative form.[6] It was always necessary for the affidavit supporting the petition to be of some greater detail than the normal statutory affidavit supporting a winding-up petition.[7]

The court had unfettered discretion to make any order which it considered to be appropriate, *e.g.* for the appointment of additional or other directors; for the removal or the restriction of the powers of a director[8]; for the distribution of dividend or the issue of new shares; or for the prohibition of any of these measures. It could also order or authorise the purchase of the shares of the minority by the majority, the company or others at a price to be fixed by the court.[9] Moreover, since the court could order or authorise the purchase of the shares of *any* member, the majority might have found itself bought out by the minority under the section, a risk which might have considerably affected the attitude of a majority in its negotiations with the minority.

---

4 *Re Jermyn Street Turkish Baths Ltd.* [1970] 1 W.L.R. 1194; reversed on other grounds [1971] 1 W.L.R. 1042. It seems that personal representatives may petition even if they have not themselves been registered as members and whether the oppression relates to the deceased during his lifetime or themselves since his death: *ibid.*

5 *Re Antigen Laboratories* [1951] 1 All E.R. 110.

6 For the contents of the advertisement of the petition (*cf.* Companies (Winding Up) Rules 1949, r. 28), see *Practice Direction* [1957] 1 W.L.R. 915.

7 *Re S. A. Hawken* [1950] 2 All E.R. 408; *Re Davies Investments (East Ham) Ltd.* [1961] 1 W.L.R. 1396; *Re W. R. Willcocks & Co. Ltd.* [1974] Ch. 163.

8 See *Re H. R. Harmer Ltd.* [1959] 1 W.L.R. 62; para. 60–03, *post.*

9 See *Scottish Co-operative Wholesale Society Ltd.* v. *Meyer* [1959] A.C. 324; para. 60–03, *post.*

If the court made an order which it altered any part of the company's memorandum or articles of association, such alteration would itself be unalterable except by the court or in manner indicated in the order (s. 210 (3)).

Scope of the section

60–03 Section 210 did not give the courts unlimited jurisdiction to intervene in the affairs of the company. The court could exercise its jurisdiction only if the requirements of the section were satisfied. As judicially interpreted,[10] these were:

(1) The matters complained of must have affected the petitioner in his character as a member of the company: harsh or unfair treatment in any other capacity, *e.g.* as a director or creditor, could not entitle him to relief under the section.[11]
(2) The matters complained of must have related to the conduct of the affairs of the company.[12]
(3) They must have been such as not only to make the winding up of the company just and equitable, but also to have lead to the conclusion that the affairs of the company were being conducted in a manner which could properly be described as "oppressive" of the petitioner, and, possibly, other members.[13]

Despite the somewhat restricted wording of section 210, the requirements of the section could have been interpreted in a liberal spirit in order to carry out the intention of Parliament, which designed this remedy in order to suppress an acknowledged mischief[14] but unfortunately in the more recent cases the liberal spirit was conspicuously absent.[15]

The liberal interpretation intended by Parliament was applied by the Court of Appeal in *Re H. R. Harmer Ltd.*,[16] where a petition for relief was presented by the two sons of the founder of the business—that of philatelic auctioneers and valuers—who himself controlled the company. The father and the two sons were life directors, and the father was the chairman and governing director, although this gave him no special powers under the articles. The father had continued to regard the business of the company as his own, and had constantly ignored the wishes of his co-directors and resolutions of the board. The Court of Appeal affirmed the order of

---

[10] See *Re Five Minute Car Wash Service Ltd.* [1966] 1 W.L.R. 745, 751, *per* Buckley J.
[11] *Elder* v. *Elder & Watson*, 1952 S.C. 49; *Re H. R. Harmer Ltd., supra*; *Re Bellador Silk Ltd.* [1965] 1 All E.R. 667; *Re Lundie Brothers Ltd.* [1965] 1 W.L.R. 1051; *Re Westbourne Galleries Ltd.* [1970] 1 W.L.R. 1378; *Re Jermyn Street Turkish Baths Ltd.* [1971] 1 W.L.R. 1042.
[12] *Re H. R. Harmer Ltd., supra.*
[13] *Scottish C.W.S. Ltd.* v. *Meyer, supra*; *Re H. R. Harmer Ltd., supra*; *Re Five Minute Car Wash Service Ltd., supra.*
[14] *Per* Lord Denning in *Scottish Co-operative Wholesale Society Ltd.* v. *Meyer* [1959] A.C. 324, 369.
[15] See *infra.*
[16] [1959] 1 W.L.R. 62.

Roxburgh J.[17] that the company should contract for the services of the father as consultant at a stated salary, that he should not interfere in the affairs of the company otherwise than in accordance with the valid decisions of the board of directors, and that he should be appointed president of the company for life, but that this should not impose any duties or confer any rights or powers.

60–04 A more restricted view of the section was, however, taken in later years. In *Re Bellador Silk Ltd.*[18] the petitioner alleged, *inter alia*, that he had been wrongfully excluded from all discussion of the company's affairs. Plowman J. did not accept that this allegation was true, but observed that, even if it were, it would be a complaint of oppression as a director, not as a member, and therefore outside the purview of section 210. The petition also failed because, on the petitioner's own admission, it was not designed primarily to obtain relief under the section, but for the collateral purpose of putting pressure on the company to repay a loan due to another company in which he had a major interest; accordingly, the presentation of the petition was an abuse of the process of the course. The same judge, in *Re Lundie Brothers Ltd.*, [19] reaffirmed the view he had expressed in the earlier case, and rejected a petition for relief under section 210 alleging that the petitioner had been removed from his position as working director and excluded from taking any part in the business of the company, although it was held that the facts justified the making of a winding-up order on the "just and equitable" ground. It is not always easy to draw a clear distinction between the position of a shareholder as such and his position as a director, particularly in the case of small private companies where, as in the case of *Re Lundie Brothers*,[19] the company was formed with the intention that all the members shall participate in running the company, and financial arrangements were made accordingly.

60–05 Unfortunately, the courts continued to interpret section 210 restrictively. In *Re Jermyn Street Turkish Baths Ltd.*[20] the Court of Appeal reversed a well-reasoned judgment of Pennycuick J.[21] who had found oppressive conduct to consist in a chain of events, including an improper issue of shares to a director-shareholder, the taking of excessive remuneration by that director without the approval of the general meeting and the failure to give notice of meetings to the petitioners. The Court of Appeal found that these events were unconnected and that each of them did not constitute oppression. The Court further held that the oppression complained of must be operative at the time when the petition was launched. In *Re Westbourne Galleries Ltd.*[22]; Plowman J. held that, although an isolated act of oppres-

---

[17] [1958] C.L.Y. 424.
[18] [1965] 1 All E.R. 667.
[19] [1965] 1 W.L.R. 1051; see also *Re Westbourne Galleries Ltd.* [1970] 1 W.L.R. 1378; [1973] A.C. 360 (H.L.).
[20] [1971] 1 W.L.R. 1042.
[21] [1970] 1 W.L.R. 1194.
[22] [1970] 1 W.L.R. 1378.

sion had been proved, the facts, taken together, did not establish oppressive conduct.[23] He refused to make an order under section 210 but granted an order for the winding up of the company under section 222 (*f*) on the "just and equitable" ground.[24]

Meaning of "oppression"

60–06 "Oppressive" conduct, for the purposes of section 210, meant that the company had exercised its authority "in a manner burdensome, harsh and wrongful."[25] It had to go beyond what is required to make out a case for a winding-up order and had to indicate some lack of probity or fair dealing towards one or more members of the company.[26] "Oppression under section 210," said Lord Keith in *Scottish Co-operative Wholesale Society Ltd.* v. *Meyer*,[27] "might take various forms. The section introduces a wide power to the court to deal with a situation in an equitable manner." In this case the majority shareholder of a private company who likewise controlled the board of directors of that company lost interest in the company and, after the minority refused to sell its £l shares at par, decided to destroy the private company and threatened to wind it up. The minority petitioned under section 210. The Scottish Court of Session (First Division)[27a] ordered that the majority shareholders should acquire the shares of the minority at £3 15s. each and this decision was affirmed by the House of Lords. The House rejected the argument of the majority that they had only employed legitimate means of commercial warfare, since the majority controlled the board of directors and thereby controlled the private company "from within." The contention of the majority that their nominees on the board were not engaged in active acts of oppression was likewise rejected on the ground that the inaction of the nominee directors who could have saved the company was a breach of their duties as directors and, in the circumstances, amounted to oppressive conduct. Further consideration to the meaning of "oppression" was given in *Re Jermyn Street Turkish Baths Ltd.*[28] The Court of Appeal, while refusing to give a comprehensive definition, said:

> "Oppression occurs when shareholders, having a dominant position in a company, either (1) exercise that power to procure that something is done or not done in the conduct of the company's affairs or (2) procure by an express or implicit threat of an exercise of that power that something is not done in the conduct of the company's affairs; and

---

[23] *Ibid.*, 1390.
[24] No appeal was lodged against Plowman J.'s refusal of an order under s. 210. The order for winding up was reversed by the Court of Appeal ([1971] Ch. 799) but restored by the House of Lords ([1973] A.C. 360). See para. 85–09, *post.*
[25] *Per* Lord Simonds in *Scottish C.W.S. Ltd.* v. *Meyer* [1959] A.C. 324, 342; adopted in *Re H. R. Harmer Ltd.* [1959] 1 W.L.R. 62.
[26] *Per* Plowman J. in *Re Lundie Brothers Ltd.* [1965] 1 W.L.R. 1051, 1058; and see Buckley J. in *Re Five Minute Car Wash Service Ltd.* [1966] 1 W.L.R. 745, 752.
[27] [1959] A.C. 324, 363; 1958 S.L.T. 241; 1958 S.C. 40. (H.L.).
[27a] *Scottish Co-operative Wholesale Society Ltd.* v. *Meyer* 1957 S.L.T. 250; 1957 S.C. 110.
[28] [1971] 1 W.L.R. 1042, 1059–1060.

> when such conduct is unfair or, to use the expression adopted by Viscount Simonds in *Scottish Co-operative Wholesale Society Ltd.* v. *Meyer*,[29] 'burdensome, harsh and wrongful' to the other members of the company or some of them, and lacks that degree of probity which they are entitled to expect in the conduct of the company's affairs: see *Scottish Co-operative Wholesale Society Ltd.* v. *Meyer* and *Re H. R. Harmer Ltd.*[30] . . . Oppression must, we think, import that the oppressed are being constrained to submit to something which is unfair to them as the result of some overriding act or attitude on the part of the oppressor."

Isolated acts of oppression were not normally sufficient to justify relief under the section: the words used in the section, "the affairs of the company are *conducted* in a manner oppressive . . . ," suggested prima facie a continuing process; but they were wide enough to cover oppression by anyone who was taking part in the conduct of the affairs of the company whether *de facto* or *de jure*.[31] It was not essential that the alleged oppressor was oppressing in order to obtain a financial benefit; conduct could be oppressive under the section even if it was due simply to the controlling shareholder's overwhelming desire for power and control.[31] An act of omission might amount to oppressive conduct if it was shown that it had been designed to achieve some unfair advantage over those claiming to be oppressed.[32] Allegations of unwise, inefficient and careless conduct against a director in the performance of his duties could not in themselves give rise to any claim for relief under the section, and a petition limited to such allegations would be dismissed *in limine*.[32]

Insolvency of company

60–07 A further requirement, namely, that the company was solvent at the time of the petition, was sought to be introduced by Plowman J. in *Re Bellador Silk Ltd.*[33] This was based upon the corresponding requirement where a contributory petitions for a winding-up order.[34] In the previous edition of this book it was respectfully submitted that this was not correct. In the case of a winding-up petition the contributory will fail if it is manifestly clear that there are no assets available for distribution among the contributories, since he will then have no tangible interest in the winding up of the company. But in a petition under section 210 no distribution of the assets was contemplated, the petitioner had a concrete interest in the order which the court would make, and the reference in section 210 to the requirements of a winding-up order was purely hypothetical ("*would* justify"). Plowman J.'s view could not be reconciled with the liberal interpretation of the section postulated in the earlier cases.[35]

---

29 [1959] A.C. 324, 342.
30 [1959] 1 W.L.R. 62.
31 *Re H. R. Harmer Ltd., supra.*
32 *Re Five Minute Car Wash Service Ltd., supra.*
33 [1965] 1 All E.R. 667.
34 See para 85–17 and 87–15, *post.*
35 See para. 60–03, *post.*

Section 75 of the 1980 Act

60–08 Section 210 of the 1948 Act has ceased to have effect except in relation to proceedings on a petition presented before December 22, 1980. Section 75 of the 1980 Act, which introduces a remedy for unfairly prejudicial treatment, inherits the structure of section 210 but is different in several material respects.

Requirements of section 75

The remedy for unfairly prejudicial treatment is available upon the following conditions:

(1) that the affairs of the company are being or have been conducted in a manner which is *unfairly prejudicial* to the interests of some part of the members (including at least himself); or

(2) that any actual or proposed act or omission of the company (including an act or omission on its behalf) is or would be so prejudicial (section 75 (1)).

It is immediately noticeable that this time Parliament has severed the link with the "just and equitable" winding up. The petitioner no longer has to show his entitlement to a winding-up order as a precondition to alternative relief. Moreover, he is able to petition for relief not only in relation to the way in which the affairs of the company *are* being conducted but also in relation to the way in which they *have been* conducted. The reference to "any actual or proposed act or omission" is also new. It removes the previous requirement of a continuing course of oppressive conduct.

It will be for the courts to consider the distinction between "oppressive" and "unfairly prejudicial." The intention is clearly to move away from the narrow meaning given to "oppressive." The Jenkins Committee had referred to "actual illegality or invasion of legal rights"[36] and it is clear from cases such as *Re Jermyn Street Turkish Baths Ltd.*[37] that the concept of oppression was being treated thus by the courts. It can therefore be stated that the new provision should divert attention from illegality to unfairness but, beyond that, it remains for the courts to interpret. One of the restrictive aspects of section 210 of the 1948 Act—the need for the petition to relate to the petitioner *qua* shareholder—has probably survived the reform.

Petitioners under section 75

Section 75 of the 1980 Act permits any "unfairly prejudiced" member to present a petition (s. 75 (1)). The Secretary of State may also petition after receiving an inspector's report under section 168 of the 1948 Act or after an inspection of the company's books and papers under Part III of the 1967

[36] Cmnd. 1749, para. 203.
[37] [1971] 1 W.L.R. 1042 (C.A.).

Act or section 36 of the Insurance Companies Act 1974. If, after such investigation or inspection, it appears to the Secretary of State that some part of the members have been unfairly prejudiced, he may petition (s. 75 (2), replacing s. 35 (2) of the 1967 Act). Also, for the first time it is expressly provided that the section ensures for the benefit of a person who is not a member of the company but to whom shares in the company have been transferred or transmitted by operation of law (s. 75 (9)).

Orders under section 75

If the court is satisfied that a petition is well founded it may make such order as it thinks fit for giving relief in respect of the matters complained of (s. 75 (3)). The discretion is very wide indeed and the case of *Re H. R. Harmer Ltd.*[38] remains an object lesson in judicial enterprise. Without prejudice to the generality of the discretion, section 74 (4) provides that an order under section 75 may—

(a) regulate the conduct of the company's affairs in the future;
(b) require the company to refrain from doing or continuing an act complained of by the petitioner or to do an act which the petitioner has complained it has omitted to do;
(c) authorise civil proceedings to be brought in the name and on behalf of the company by such person or persons and on such terms as the court may direct;
(d) provide for the purchase of the shares of any members of the company by other members or by the company itself and, in the case of a purchase by the company itself, the reduction of the company's capital accordingly.

Of this list, (b) and (c) appear in express form for the first time. The type of order envisaged by (b) is akin to a prohibitory or mandatory injection to put an end to the unfair prejudice. Item (c) is a further erosion of the rule in *Foss* v. *Harbottle*[39] in that it makes available a form of derivative action. However, it remains to be seen how many unfairly prejudiced shareholders have the endurance to go through one set of proceedings simply to acquire the right to commence a derivative action in subsequent proceedings. In this regard, as on other issues, much will depend upon the meaning given by the courts to "unfairly prejudicial."

Section 75 of the 1980 Act contains similar provisions to section 210 of the 1948 Act in relation to orders concerning the alteration of the memorandum and articles of association (section 75 (5), (6) and (7)).

---

[38] [1959] 1 W.L.R. 62 (C.A.).
[39] [1843] 2 Hare 461.

Part Six

ADMINISTRATION OF THE COMPANY

A. MANAGEMENT OF THE COMPANY

CHAPTER 61

APPOINTMENT AND RETIREMENT OF DIRECTORS. REMUNERATION

A company must have directors

The directors as governors

61–01 A company can only act by agents, and usually the persons by whom it acts and by whom the business of the company is carried on or superintended are termed directors, but the Acts leave the members free to determine how and by whom the business shall be managed, and accordingly, in some cases, the articles provide that instead of directors there shall be a "council" or a "managing committee," or that the business shall be carried on by "managers." In private companies, it is not uncommon to provide that the business shall be managed by "governing directors" or a sole "governing director," or sometimes by "permanent directors" or "life directors." While in all these matters the articles can be framed as may seem expedient, it should not be overlooked that terms such as "permanent" or "life" directors merely signify that these persons need not retire by rotation, as other directors, by virtue of the relevant articles, are usually bound to do,[1] but that they do not signify permanency of tenure of office since, even in a private company, a "permanent" or "life" director, like any other director, can be removed by the general meeting by ordinary resolution required special notice unless he held office on July 18, 1945 (1948 Act, s. 184 (1), proviso).[2]

The rules which apply to directors apply also to the members of a council or committee, or other persons, who, in substance, stand in the position of directors. The definition of "director" in section 455 of the 1948 Act, "includes any person occupying the position of director by whatever name called."

On principle, a limited company may itself be a director of another company.[3]

Directors are not, as such, employees of company

61–02 Directors are not, as such, employees of the company or employed by the company[4]; nor are they servants of the company, or members of its

---

[1] See para. 61–24, *post*.

[2] But note the possible impact of weighted voting rights: *Bushell* v. *Faith* [1970] A.C. 1099. See para. 61–28, *post*.

[3] *Re Bulawayo Market, etc., Co.* [1907] 2 Ch. 458.

[4] *Normandy* v. *Ind, Coope & Co.* [1908] 1 Ch. 84, 95; *Hampson* v. *Price's Patent Candle Co.* (1876) 45 L.J.Ch. 437; *Kerr* v. *Walker*, 1933 S.C. 458.

"staff."[5] This becomes of importance in three main instances: first, where privileges are granted by the company to employees, or servants or the staff, in particular the granting of pensions or the right to participate in profit sharing schemes; secondly, where in a winding up or receivership preferential debts are to be paid pursuant to sections 319 and 94 of the 1948 Act or section 19 of the Companies (Floating Charges and Receivers) (Scotland) Act 1972; and, thirdly, where a director wishes to claim rights under modern employment protection legislation *e.g.* the right to a redundancy payment or not to be unfairly dismissed under the Employment Protection (Consolidation) Act 1978.

A director can, however, hold a salaried employment or an office[6] in addition to that of his directorship which may, for these purposes, make him an employee or servant,[7] and in such a case he would enjoy any rights given to employees as such: but his directorship and his rights through that directorship are quite separate from his rights as employee, so that he cannot, under section 319 of the 1948 Act, claim priority of directors' fees even if he is also the secretary, or a salaried managing director, or a servant of the company: but he would have preference for remuneration in the other capacity.

These questions arise most frequently in relation to managing or working directors and the matter is considered further below.[8]

An analogous issue may arise as to whether the director is an "employed earner" for the purposes of section 2 of the Social Security Act 1975. This definition of those required to pay Class I contributions, and to receive the benefits thereof, under Part II of the Act is also used to define those covered by the industrial injuries scheme under Part IV of the Act.[9] The definition of "employed earner" covers, however, "a person who is gainfully employed in Great Britain either under a contract of service or in an office (including elective office) with emoluments chargeable to income tax under Schedule E."[10] Thus, a director who is not employed under a contract of service will nevertheless fall within the section if he is in receipt of emoluments, for it has been held that a director of a company, whether public or private, holds a public office and is liable to be charged to tax under Schedule E in respect of the profits of his office.[11]

---

[5] *Hutton* v. *West Cork Ry.* (1883) 23 Ch.D. 654; *Moriarty* v. *Regent's Garage* [1921] 1 K.B. 423, 446; *Burland* v. *Earle* [1902] A.C. 83, 100. A director is, however, a "servant" of the company for the purpose of making the company vicariously liable for his negligence when engaged in company business: *Scobie* v. *Steele & Wilson Ltd.*, 1962 S.L.T. (Notes) 45.

[6] The words "any director holding a salaried employment or office in the company" are used in s. 54 (1) (*b*).

[7] See *Cyclists' Touring Club* v. *Hopkinson* [1910] 1 Ch. 179; *Hutton* v. *West Cork Ry.* (1883) 23 Ch.D. 654; *Stroud* v. *Royal Aquarium Society* (1903) 89 L.T. 243; *Re Lee, Behrens & Co.* [1932] 2 Ch. 46; *Anderson* v. *James Sutherland (Peterhead) Ltd.*, 1941 S.C. 203.

[8] See para. 62–09, *post*.

[9] Social Security Act 1975, s. 50 (1).

[10] *Ibid.* s. 2 (1) (*a*).

[11] *McMillan* v. *Guest* [1942] A.C. 561. See also *Edwards* v. *Clinch* [1981] 3 All E.R. 543.

Maximum and minimum numbers of directors

61–03 While the Acts do not prescribe an upper limit to the number of directors, the 1948 Act lays down minimum numbers as follows:

Every public company registered on or after November 1, 1929, must have at least two directors, and any public company registered before that date, as well as any private company,[12] must have at least one director (s. 176). Further, every company must also have a secretary, and a sole director cannot also be secretary (s. 177 (1)). This provision cannot be evaded by appointing as secretary a company the sole director of which is the sole director of the company, nor by appointing as sole director of the company a company of which the secretary of the company is sole director (s. 178).

The purpose of these provisions is to maintain a dual control in the management of the affairs of the company and to prevent fraudulent machinations by a one-man management. This purpose is regarded by the legislator as a highly important precaution, and, consequently, a statutory or regulatory provision requiring or authorising something to be done by a director and the secretary, *e.g.* the signature of the annual return (1948 Act, s. 126 (1)) and certain documents attached to it (ss. 127 (1) (*a*), 128), is not satisfied if done by (or to) the same person acting both as director and as (or in the place of) the secretary (1948 Act, s. 179)—an important exception from the general principle that any defect in the appointment or qualifications of the directors does not invalidate their acts (s. 180).[13]

The articles usually fix what is to be the maximum and minimum number of the directors. Where a minimum number is fixed, and the number of directors falls below the minimum number, the remaining directors prima facie cannot act,[14] but if there is an article empowering the continuing directors to act notwithstanding any vacancy in their number, this will validate acts of the directors although they are less than the specified minimum.[15] This provision does not make their acts valid if the minimum number never was appointed.[16] Nevertheless their acts may be valid in favour of a person dealing with the company in good faith, within the meaning of the European Communities Act 1972, s. 9 (1).[17] The articles must be considered with care to discover what the powers of continuing directors are: a common form provides that the powers of the continuing

[12] Unless the company is subject to the provisions of Sched. 2, para. 8 of the Banking Act 1979, in which case it must have at least two directors.

[13] See para. 61–19, *post*.

[14] *Re Alma Spinning Co.* (1880) 16 Ch.D. 681.

[15] *Re Scottish Petroleum Co.* (1883) 23 Ch.D. 413; *Re Bank of Syria* [1900] 2 Ch. 272; [1901] 1 Ch. 115.

[16] *Re Sly, Spink & Co.* [1911] 2 Ch. 430; *Re Scottish Petroleum Co.* (1883) 23 Ch.D. 413, 431; *Re Bank of Syria, Owen and Ashworth's Claim, Whitworth's Claim* [1901] 1 Ch. 115.

[17] On the meaning of "good faith," see 9–25, *ante*. Before the coming into operation of the European Communities Act 1972, s. 9 (1) it was held in *British Asbestos Co.* v. *Boyd* [1903] 2 Ch. 439 that acts of directors appointed below the minimum number may be valid in favour of a person who had no notice of the irregularity.

directors are limited to convening a general meeting or appointing further directors to fill the vacancies.[18]

Appointment of directors

First directors

61–04 First directors are usually named in the articles of association, if there are any, but not uncommonly the articles, instead of naming them, contain a power for the subscribers, or the majority of them, by writing, to appoint them (see art. 75).

By section 21 of the 1976 Act there must be provided with any memorandum delivered for registration under section 12 of the 1948 Act a statement of particulars for the first directors of the company, in the absence of which the Registrar may not register the memorandum or any articles delivered with it.[19] The statement must be in the prescribed form and must set out the particulars required by section 200 (2) to be contained in the register of directors.[20] The statement must be signed by or on behalf of the subscribers and must contain a consent signed by each person named in it as a director to act as such.[21] On incorporation the persons named are deemed to have been appointed the first directors; and any appointment of directors by the articles is void unless they are named as such in the statement.[22] Where the statement is delivered by an agent for the subscribers, the statement must specify that fact and the name and address of the agent.[23]

Subsequent directors

61–05 Under the Act of 1929 the method of election was governed entirely by the articles, but it is now provided that, in the case of a public company, a motion for the appointment of two or more persons as directors by a single resolution must not be made at a general meeting of a public company, unless a resolution that it shall be so made has been unanimously agreed to by the meeting (1948 Act, s. 183). The purpose of this prohibition of a composite motion is to enable the shareholders to reject a particular director without compelling them to reject the others. A resolution moved in contravention of section 183 is void; but this does not exclude the operation of section 180, which validates acts where defects are afterwards discovered (s. 183 (2) (*a*)). The appointment of a director by a general meeting at which the result of a poll is ascertained at a day later than the poll itself dates from the ascertainment, and not from the taking, of the poll.[24]

---

[18] See art. 100.
[19] Companies Act 1976, s. 21 (1) and (6).
[20] These particulars are set in at para. 66–02, *post*.
[21] *Ibid*. s. 21 (3).
[22] *Ibid*. s. 21 (5).
[23] *Ibid*. s. 21 (4).
[24] *Holmes* v. *Keyes* [1959] Ch. 199.

The articles may give power to an outsider, *e.g.* the vendor of a business to the company, to appoint one or more directors. If the company then refuses to accept the appointee, the court may enforce acceptance by injunction unless the appointee is unsuitable on personal grounds.[25]

Where the articles delegate to the directors exclusively the power of appointing additional directors, a general meeting has no power to do so,[26] since this would be usurping the directors' powers: but a special resolution can override the provisions of the articles. It is in each case a question of construction of the articles, and if only a limited power is conferred on the directors or if the directors cannot agree or are unable to appoint, the company retains power to appoint new directors.[27] In *Worcester Corsetry Ltd.* v. *Witting*[28] it was held that an article which provided that the directors should have power to appoint additional directors to hold office until the next annual general meeting did not, upon a reading of the articles as a whole, take away the power of the company in general meeting.

Casual vacancy

61–06 Where directors have power to fill a casual vacancy, this appears to include any vacancy other than one caused by effluxion of time or a director retiring by rotation.[29] A vacancy caused by retirement by rotation has normally to be filled by the annual general meeting.[30] Such a vacancy cannot be called a casual one.

Where the articles provide for notice of intention to propose a new director being given at some time before the "day of election," the "day of election" for this purpose, if the meeting is adjourned, is the date of the adjourned meeting.[31]

Assignment of office

61–07 If any director is given power by the articles or by agreement to assign his office to another person, any such assignment is ineffective until approved by special resolution of the company (1948 Act, s. 204). This provision probably does not normally apply to a director of a private company nominating his successor under a power in the articles, since this is not an assignment of an office; but the answer will ultimately depend on the construction of the power.

---

[25] *British Murac Syndicate Ltd.* v. *The Alperton Rubber Co.* [1915] 2 Ch. 186. If the outsider is given a mere right to nominate persons for appointment, he is less likely to be able to secure the appointment of his candidate by injunction or specific performance: *Plantations Trusts* v. *Bila (Sumatra) Rubber Lands* (1916) 85 L.J.Ch. 801.

[26] *Blair Open Hearth Furnace* v. *Reigart* (1913) 108 L.T. 665.

[27] *Barron* v. *Potter* [1914] 1 Ch. 895; *Isaacs* v. *Chapman* [1915] W.N. 28; affirmed [1916] W.N. 28; *Foster* v. *Foster* [1916] 1 Ch. 532; *Worcester Corsetry Ltd.* v. *Witting* [1936] Ch. 640.

[28] [1936] Ch. 640.

[29] *Munster* v. *Cammell Co.* (1882) 21 Ch.D. 187, 188; *York Tramways* v. *Willows* (1882) 8 Q.B.D. 685, 694.

[30] See para. 61–24, *post*.

[31] *Catesby* v. *Burnett* [1916] 2 Ch. 325.

Alternate directors

61–08 There is, on the other hand, no objection to providing that a director, in certain circumstances, may appoint an alternate to act for him in his absence. This power to appoint alternate directors—which is not conferred by Table A—must be contained in the articles, which need to be carefully worded so as to make it clear in what circumstances the alternate director has power to act (this is sometimes confined to acting at board meetings), which director is to be entitled to notices of board meetings, how the alternate director is to be remunerated, whether the alternate requires a share qualification, and other matters. The following is a simple form[32] of an article authorising the appointment of alternate directors:

> *Alternate directors*
>
> Any director may in writing appoint any person, who is approved by the majority of the directors, to be his alternate to act in his place at any meeting of the directors at which he is unable to be present. Every such alternate shall be entitled to notice of meetings of the directors and to attend and vote thereat as a director when the person appointing him is not personally present, and where he is a director to have a separate vote on behalf of the director he is representing in addition to his own vote. A director may at any time in writing revoke the appointment of an alternate appointed by him. Every such alternate shall be an officer of the company and shall not be deemed to be the agent of the director appointing him. The remuneration of such alternate shall be payable out of the remuneration payable to the director appointing him, and the proportion thereof shall be agreed between them. An alternate need not hold any share qualification.

Managing directors

61–09 The position of managing directors is considered at paragraph 62–07 *ff.*, *post*.

Executive, assistant or special directors

61–10 A Practice Note dealing with these persons is appended at paragraph 61–43, *post*.

Age limit

61–11 The legislation culminating in the Act of 1948 provided for the first time the principle of an age limit for directors, but this provision is modified by so many exceptions and saving clauses that it does not appear to have much practical effect, except that in some companies to which the provision applies notice is now necessary to the members of the age of some of the older directors.

---

[32] Taken from Palmer's *Company Precedents*, Vol. 1, (17th ed.), 1956, p. 583, where other forms authorising the appointment of alternate directors are provided.

On principle, in public companies and private companies which are subsidiaries of public companies,[33]

(1) no person is capable of being appointed a director of a company if at the time of his appointment he has attained the age of 70 (s. 185 (1)); and

(2) a director shall vacate his office at the conclusion of the annual general meeting next after he attains that age, and is not to be automatically re-elected as a retiring director (s. 185 (2) and (3)).[34]

The following are the exceptions to these provisions:

(1) the company can abrogate them by its articles (s. 185 (7));

(2) they do not apply if the general meeting appoints the director or approves his appointment with knowledge of his age. This is done by ordinary resolution requiring special notice[35] which has to state the age of the proposed director (s. 185 (5)).

A person appointed, or proposed to be appointed, a director who is affected by the age limit provisions must give notice of his age to the company; but this does not apply to reappointment (s. 186).

Qualification

61–12 No qualification[36] is by law required for a director. In particular, the Acts do not require a director to hold qualification shares.

The articles may provide certain qualifications for the directors. The qualifications are occasionally of personal character, *e.g.* where it is intended to secure British control of a company, as is sometimes the case with shipping companies, the articles may provide that the directors must be British subjects.[37] More frequently the articles provide that the qualification of a director shall be the holding of a specified number of shares in the company.[38]

If the articles of a company contain a provision that the qualification of a director shall be the holding of a specified number of shares in the company, all its directors are bound to acquire and retain such qualification shares. The articles generally permit directors some time in which to acquire the shares: the maximum period permitted by law is two months (1948 Act, s. 182), and this period applies unless a shorter period is stated.[39]

---

33 Or of a company registered as public under the law for the time being in force in Northern Ireland (s. 185 (8)). For the definition of "subsidiary," see s. 154, and para. 71–01, *post*.

34 But the principle of s. 180 applies to acts done by directors continuing in office despite the termination of their appointment pursuant to this provision (s. 185 (2), proviso).

35 See s. 142, para. 54–06, *ante*.

36 For disqualification see para. 61–17, *post*.

37 See *Precedents*, Vol. 1. (17th ed.), 1956, p. 666; and *cf. Governments Stock and Other Securities Investment Co.* v. *Christopher* [1956] 1 W.L.R. 237.

38 The Rules of the Stock Exchange do not require directors to hold qualification shares.

39 The period begins with the date of appointment, on which see *Holmes* v. *Keyes* [1959] Ch. 199, and para. 61–04, *ante*.

The object of requiring directors to hold qualification shares has generally been thought to be to ensure that directors have a personal interest in the company,[40] but since this qualification is not bound to be held beneficially, it is doubtful whether the object is achieved, and, moreover, the qualification holding is usually so small as to make little difference to a director's actions. It is, indeed, often a considerable disadvantage for directors to have a large holding, as their dividend policy and other decisions may well be coloured by the effect upon their own position as shareholders, particularly with regard to their tax position. Moreover, a high qualification may unreasonably restrict the persons able to take up office, and for this reason the modern tendency is even in the articles of large public companies, to exempt from the requirement of qualification shares directors who are employees of the company.

Many questions have arisen in regard to articles requiring qualification shares, and more particularly as to the liability of a director to take up such shares. The normal article does not compel the director to take shares from the company, but the director is under an obligation to acquire the requisite qualification in some way or other, whether from the company or by transfer. If at the end of the period of grace permitted by the articles or statute he has not acquired the necessary shares, he has to vacate his office and is disqualified from acting as a director (s. 182 (3)).[41] The mere acting as a director does not import any agreement to take the shares *from the company*.[42] Nevertheless, if in such circumstances he is put on the register by the officers of the company after the time limited for qualifying has expired and he continues to act as a director, he is estopped by his conduct from repudiating the shares and will be liable for them.[43]

Where the articles provide that if a director does not qualify within, say, one month "he is to be deemed to have agreed to take the shares from the company," it as been held that where, at the end of the month, the director was still in office, and did not hold the requisite qualification, the contract was complete, and the company or its liquidator might place his name on the register for the qualification shares.[44] If, however, the director resigned within the month, he escaped even under such a clause.[45]

If a director by inadvertence acts without possessing his qualification, the court can relieve him from liability for such acts.[46]

Salary paid to an unqualified managing director can be recovered by the company, since there would be no authority to make payments to a person who, because he was not duly qualified, was not and could not be such an

---

[40] *Archer's Case* [1892] 1 Ch. 322.
[41] He is further incapable of being reappointed a director until he is duly qualified (s. 182 (4)).
[42] *Brown's Case* (1873) L.R. 9 Ch. 102.
[43] *Brown's Case, supra*; *Lord Inchiquin's Case* [1891] 3 Ch. 28.
[44] *Isaacs' Case* [1892] 2 Ch. 158.
[45] *Salisbury Jones' Case* [1894] 3 Ch. 356.
[46] *Re Barry and Staines Linoleum* [1934] Ch. 227.

officer[47] but the managing director may be able to claim for the value of services rendered to the company on a *quantum meruit*.[48]

Joint holdings and bearer shares

61–13 A joint holding may qualify a director,[49] but articles frequently provide that the holding must be in his own sole name, in which case a joint holding is insufficient.[50]

The holding of bearer shares by a director does not satisfy a requirement in the articles to hold a share qualification (s. 182 (2)), since a person is not a "qualified person" unless he is the registered holder of shares of the required amount.[51]

Director's holding "in his own right"

Sometimes the articles require that a director's qualification shall be the holding of so many shares "in his own right." These words might seem to mean holding beneficially, and not as a mere trustee for some third party; but it has been decided that this is not so, and that, if the director holds the shares as trustee, he is nonetheless duly qualified.[52] On the other hand it has been held that if a person is entered on the register as holding shares as liquidator of some other company, he does not hold "in his own right"[53]; and in *Sutton* v. *English and Colonial Produce Co.*,[54] where the director was a bankrupt and the trustee in bankruptcy gave notice to the company that he claimed the shares, the words "in his own right" were held to apply only to cases where the company can safely deal with the director as the owner of the shares.

"No person eligible unless holding qualification"

61–14 Articles sometimes say that no person shall be *eligible* as a director unless he holds a specified qualification. This makes the possession of the qualification a condition precedent to election, and if the person elected does not possess the qualification, he does not become a director *de jure*.[55]

Gift of qualification shares from promoter or vendor

61–15 It is thought that an honest and open, *i.e.* duly disclosed, gift of qualification shares to the directors by a promoter or vendor is innocuous.

Different, however, is the position if the object of the gift is to place the director under a moral or legal obligation or to create the false impression

---

[47] *Brown & Green Ltd.* v. *Hays* (1920) 36 T.L.R. 330.
[48] *Craven-Ellis* v. *Canons Ltd.* [1936] 2 K.B. 403; see para. 61–23, *post.*
[49] *Re Glory Paper Mills* [1894] 3 Ch. 473; *Grundy* v. *Briggs* [1910] 1 Ch. 444.
[50] This situation is not covered by *Re Glory Paper Mills, supra.*
[51] *Spencer* v. *Kennedy* [1926] Ch. 125.
[52] *Pulbrook* v. *Richmond, etc., Mining Co.* (1878) 9 Ch.D. 610; *Elliot* v. *Mackie & Sons* 1935 S.C. 91.
[53] *Boschoek Proprietary Co.* v. *Fuke* [1906] 1 Ch. 148.
[54] [1902] 2 Ch. 502.
[55] *Jenner's Case* (1877) 7 Ch.D. 132.

that the director has paid for his qualification shares. Here acceptance by a director from a promoter or vendor of shares to constitute his qualification is likely to constitute a breach of trust on the part of the director. It amounts to accepting a retaining fee from the promoter or vendor, the director is liable to account to the company for any damages sustained by such breach of trust,[56] and there is no right of set-off.[57] The same principle applies if he takes up and pays for his qualification, receiving at the same time an indemnity from the promoter; in such a case the indemnity is a thing of value, and the director must account to the company for it[58]; and likewise if he holds his shares as a bare trustee for the promoters. It has been held that the damages may be the highest value of the shares.[59]

The mere fact that the director of a company holds his qualification shares as trustee for another company does not render him liable to account to that company for the director's fees which he earns.[60]

Raising of share qualification

61–16 A special resolution raising the share qualification does not make the directors "cease" to hold their qualification, or necessarily cause them to vacate their offices under section 182 (3). Where, however, a director of an existing company in which the share qualification was to be raised from 50 to 250 shares signed a prospectus as a director, he was deemed to have agreed to take the additional 200 shares so as to qualify him; and since his name had, without his knowledge but upon the authority of the board, been placed on the register of members in respect of those shares, he was liable for calls made upon them.[61]

Disqualification

61–17 Legislation provides five circumstances in which a person may be disqualified from being a director.

(1) By section 187 of the 1948 Act an undischarged bankrupt may not act as director or liquidator of a company, or be concerned in the promotion, formation or management of any company, except by leave of the court by which he was adjudged bankrupt.

(2) By section 188 (1) (a) of the 1948 Act (as amended by section 93 of the 1981 Act) a court may make a disqualification order against a person who has been convicted of an indictable offence in connection with the promotion, formation, management or liquidation of a company or with the receivership or management of a company's

---

[56] *Hay's Case* (1875) L.R. 10 Ch. 593, 604; *Pearson's Case* (1877) 5 Ch.D. 336; *Re London & S.W. Canal Co.* [1911] 1 Ch. 346.
[57] *Re Carriage Co-operative Supply Association* (1884) 27 Ch.D. 322.
[58] *Archer's Case* [1892] 1 Ch. 322.
[59] *Re London and South Western Canal* [1911] 1 Ch. 346.
[60] *Re Dover Coalfields Extension Ltd.* [1908] 1 Ch. 65.
[61] *Molineaux* v. *London, Birmingham and Manchester Insurance Co.* [1902] 2 K.B. 589.

property. The disqualification order prohibits the person concerned from acting without leave of the court as a director, receiver or liquidator or as a manager of the property of a company or from being concerned, directly or indirectly, in the promotion, formation or management of a company (section 188 (1B)). The disqualification order may be made by the court by which the person was convicted or by any court having jurisdiction to wind up the company in relation to which the offence was committed (section 188 (2D)). If the order is made by a court of summary jurisdiction it may not be made for a period exceeding five years. Otherwise, the order may be for a period not exceeding fifteen years, but, in either case, the period of disqualification runs from the date of conviction, even though a sentence of imprisonment is also imposed.[62] Application for the making of a disqualification order by a court with jurisdiction to wind up may be made by the Secretary of State, the official receiver, the liquidator of the company or any past or present member or creditor of the company in relation to which the offence was committed (section 188 (4)). Leave to promote or form a company may be given to a disqualified person by any court with any jurisdiction to wind up companies; otherwise leave may be given by the court with jurisdiction to wind up the company in relation to which the disqualified person wishes to act (section 188 (2D)). A person who acts in contravention of a disqualification order is liable on conviction on indictment to imprisonment for up to two years, or on summary conviction to imprisonment for up to six months or a fine not exceeding £500 or both (section 188 (6)).[63]

(3) By section 188 (1) (c) of the 1948 Act (as amended by section 93 of the 1981 Act) a court may make a disqualification order against a person if in the course of winding up a company it appears that he has been guilty of an offence under section 332 of the 1948 Act (fraudulent trading)[64] or has been guilty while an officer or liquidator of the company or receiver or manager of the property of the company of any fraud in relation to the company or breach of duty as such officer, liquidator, receiver or manager. The provisions discussed in the previous paragraph relating to disqualification orders under section 188 (1) (a) apply, *mutatis mutandis*, to disqualification orders under section 188 (1) (c).

(4) By section 188 (1) (b) of the 1948 Act (inserted by section 93 of the 1981 Act and replacing section 28 of the 1976 Act) a court having jurisdiction to wind up any company in relation to which the default

---

[62] *R. v. Bradley* [1961] 1 W.L.R. 398. See *Re Civica Investments Ltd., The Times,* June 9, 1982 for a consideration of the principles that should guide the court in fixing, within the maxima, the actual length of the period of disqualification.

[63] Transitional provisions relating to things done before the coming into force of section 93 of the 1981 Act are contained in section 188 (1) (c), (2), (2A) and (2B).

[64] See para. 85–84, *post.*

has been committed may make a disqualification order against a person where it appears that that person has been persistently in default in relation to the provisions of the Companies Act 1948 to 1981 requiring returns, accounts or other documents to be filed with the Registrar or requiring notice to be given to him. Persistent default is conclusively proved by showing that in the five years prior to the application for disqualification the person has been adjudged guilty of three or more defaults in complying with the requirements of the 1948 to 1981 Acts; and a person is adjudged guilty of a default where he has been convicted of an offence by virtue of any failure to comply with the requirements or where a default order has been made against him under sections 337, 375 or 428 of the 1948 Act or section 5(1) of the 1976 Act.[65] But persistent default may also be shown in any other way (section 188 (2C)).

Where a person is convicted of a summary offence by virtue of a failure to comply with the requirements of the 1948 to 1981 Acts and during the previous five years he has been convicted of at least two other such offences or had two default orders made against him (or has been found guilty of one such offence and had one such default order made against him) the court which convicted him may make a disqualification order against him (section 188 (1A)). The provisions relating to disqualification orders made under section 188 (1) (a) apply, *mutatis mutandis*, to disqualification orders made under section 188 (1) (b) and (1) (A).

(5) By section 9 of the Insolvency Act 1976 (as amended by section 94 of the 1981 Act) the court may make a disqualification order against a person where

(a) he is or has at any time been a director of a company which has gone into liquidation and was at that time insolvent; and

(b) he is or has been a director of another such company which has gone into liquidation within five years of the date on which the first-mentioned company went into liquidation; and

(c) his conduct as a director of any of those companies makes him, in the opinion of the court, unfit to be concerned in the management of a company.

The disqualification order has the same scope as a disqualification order made under section 188 of the 1948 Act (section 9 (1)). The order may be made for a period not exceeding fifteen years, except where any of the conduct to which the court had regard occurred before the coming into force of section 94 of the 1981 Act[66] (section

---

[65] See para. 46–11, *ante* and paras. 69–06 and 70–04, *post*. See also *Re Gilgate Properties Ltd.* 131 N.L.J. 579 (decided under the (repealed) s. 28 of the 1976 Act).

[66] In which case the maximum period of disqualification is five years.

9 (1A)), and the period begins with the date of the order. In considering the director's conduct the court may have regard to matters in respect of which the director may be criminally liable, although he has not been convicted (section 9(7A)). At least one of the companies must have gone into liquidation after the coming into force of the section on October 1, 1977, and regard may not be had to conduct as director of a company that went into liquidation before that date.[67] In the case of a company being wound up power to make the order is vested in the court by which the company is being wound up, and application for an order may be made by the official receiver (in Scotland, the Secretary of State). In all other cases application may be made by the Secretary of State to the High Court (Court of Session).[68]

By section 29 of the 1976 Act the Secretary of State shall maintain a register of disqualification orders and of grants of leave made after the coming into operation of the section (June 1, 1977).[69] The register is open to public inspection on payment of a fee.[70]

Apart from the statutory disqualifications the articles commonly specify, certain other cases in which a director is to vacate office by reason of disqualification, *e.g.* if he becomes of unsound mind, or ceases to hold qualification shares, or absents himself or is absent from meetings for a specified length of time; a typical catalogue of grounds for disqualification is contained in article 88.

In such a case the director, upon the event happening, vacates his office automatically,[71] if this is the intent of the article. The effect of the article may, however, be different upon its true construction. Thus, in *Glossop* v. *Glossop*,[72] the articles provided that the office of a director be vacated in certain specified events "provided that . . . the vacation of office shall not take effect unless the directors shall pass a resolution to the effect that the director has vacated his office, *such resolution to be passed within six months from the happening of the event whereby such director has vacated his office.*" Neville J. found that upon the happening of one of the specified events "he has vacated his office, although by the proviso the effect of that vacation is not immediate, but is suspensory, and does not take effect until a resolution has been passed by the directors." Neville J. went on to state that the distinction is a fine one, and it is thought that a similar article without the concluding words *in italics* in the article quoted may well be differently construed.

---

[67] Insolvency Act 1976, s. 9 (9).
[68] *Ibid.* s. 9 (2).
[69] See The Companies (Disqualification Orders) Order 1977 (S.I. 1977 No. 775); Vol. II, para. A–3042, *post*.
[70] Companies Act 1976, s. 29 (4).
[71] *Re Bodega Co. Ltd.* [1904] 1 Ch. 276.
[72] [1907] 2 Ch. 370, 375.

61–18 In the following the judicial interpretation of some usual grounds for disqualification are considered.

Where the articles provided for disqualification if a director held a place of profit under the company, a director who was appointed paid trustee under a debenture holder's trust deed was within the meaning of the articles and disqualified.[73] An "office under the company" has been held not to include a bare appointment as solicitor to the company[74]; but it may do so if he is appointed at a fixed salary and with certain obligations imposed upon him.[75]

"Becomes insolvent" does not necessarily imply any definite act such as compounding with creditors; a person may be "insolvent" for the purpose of such a clause if he is clearly unable to pay his debts as they fall due.[76]

"Cease to hold": a director does not "cease to hold" shares where he has never acquired them.[77] Nor does he "cease to hold" by the qualification being raised from, *e.g.* 50 to 250 shares.[78] "Absenting himself" means being absent voluntarily,[79] so that where a director went abroad for the winter for the sake of his health and on the advice of his doctor, this was nonetheless a voluntary act which disqualified him.[80] A director may be "concerned in any contract with the company," where a firm in which he is interested enters into contracts with the company.[81] A director is "convicted of an indictable offence" when he is convicted and fined by a court of summary jurisdiction for an offence for which he might have been imprisoned if convicted on indictment.[82] Whether the offence is "indictable" depends on the nature and quality of the offence when committed irrespective of the procedural manner in which it might be dealt with; the position might be different where the articles use the phrase "convicted on indictment."

Defective appointments and acting after disqualification

61–19 A person is only a director in the eyes of the law if, first, he has been duly appointed and, secondly, he has not ceased to fill the requirements of the company's articles for being a director by having become disqualified after his appointment. These matters have been dealt with earlier, and it is now necessary to consider the effect of an irregular appointment of a director and of a director acting after he has become disqualified.

---

[73] *Astley* v. *New Tivoli Co.* [1899] 1 Ch. 151.
[74] *Re Harper's Ticket Issuing, etc., Machine Ltd.* [1912] W.N. 263; 29 T.L.R. 63.
[75] *Re Liberator Building Society* (1894) 71 L.T. 406.
[76] *R.* v. *Saddlers Co.* (1863) 10 H.L.C. 404; *Harold Sissons & Co.* v. *S.* (1910) 54 S.J. 802; *James* v. *Rockwood Colliery Co.* (1912) 106 L.T. 128; *London & Counties Assets Co.* v. *Brighton Grand Concert Hall, etc., Ltd.* [1915] 2 K.B. 493.
[77] *Forbes' Case* (1873) 8 Ch.App. 768, 775.
[78] *Molineaux* v. *London, Birmingham and Manchester Insurance Co.* [1902] 2 K.B. 589.
[79] *Mack's Claim* [1900] W.N. 114.
[80] *McConnell's Claim, Re London and Northern Bank* [1901] 1 Ch. 728.
[81] *Star Steam Laundry Co.* v. *Dukas* [1913] W.N. 39; 108 L.T. 367.
[82] *Hastings and Folkestone Glassworks Ltd.* v. *Kalson* [1949] 1 K.B. 214 (C.A.).

De facto directors

61–20 A person who has not been duly appointed a director, or who has become disqualified from being a director, is not *de jure* a director,[83] but since a person in such a position may actually act as a director, he may be a director *de facto*. Two sets of statutory provisions and the rule in *Royal British Bank* v. *Turquand* are relevant to this situation.

European Communities Act 1972, s. 9 and Companies Act 1976, s. 21

By section 9 (3) of the European Communities Act 1972 the Registrar of Companies shall notify officially in the *Gazette* any change in the directors of the company which has been notified to him, and by section 9 (4) the company cannot rely as against other persons, upon any change among the company's directors (*e.g.* as a result of a director's failure to obtain his qualification shares) if the event has not been officially notified and has not been shown by the company to be known to the person concerned.[84] Consequently, the acts of a person, who has ceased to be a director but continues to act as such, may bind the company, if the conditions of section 9 (4) are satisfied. Further, by section 21 (5) of the Companies Act 1976 those named in the statement of particulars are deemed to be the first directors of the company upon its incorporation, even if there is some defect in their appointment.[85]

Companies Act 1948, s. 180[85a]

61–21 Under this section "the acts of a director shall be valid notwithstanding any defect that may afterwards be discovered in his appointment or qualification." Thus a stranger to the company, or a member, is entitled to assume that a person who appears to be a duly appointed and qualified director is so in fact. In *Dawson* v. *African Consolidated Land and Trading Co.*,[86] a director had ceased to hold his qualification shares but had shortly afterwards reacquired them: the parting with his qualification technically caused him to vacate office, and he had not been formally reappointed, but had been accepted as a director by the other directors, who had power to reappoint him. The court held that an article in terms similar to section 180 validated the acts of the directors: Lindley M.R. said[87]:

---

[83] *Jenner's Case* (1877) 7 Ch.D. 132; *Morris* v. *Kanssen* [1946] A.C. 459.

[84] The company cannot rely on even official notification if the material time falls on or before 15 days after the notification if it is shown that the person in question was unavoidably prevented from knowing of the event at that time: s. 9 (4).

[85] See above, para 61–03.

[85a] This section is normally supplemented by an article akin to art. 105, which provides: all acts done by any meeting of the directors or of a committee of directors or by any person acting as a director shall, notwithstanding that it be afterwards discovered that there was some defect in the appointment of any such director or person acting as aforesaid, or that they or any of them were disqualified, be as valid as if every such person had been duly appointed and was qualified to be a director.

[86] [1898] 1 Ch. 6.

[87] At p. 12.

> "If that is not an irregularity in his appointment such as was intended to be cured by [the article], I cannot conceive what irregularities were aimed at by that article."

Accordingly a call made by the directors was held to be valid.[88] Again, in *British Asbestos Co.* v. *Boyd*,[89] the acts of a person who had, innocently, continued to act as director after he had vacated his directorship by becoming secretary to the company (under an article which provided for vacation where any other office was accepted under the company) were valid. When this case was decided no section in the terms of section 180 was in force, but the company's articles contained a similar provision, and the court was also influenced by the existence of a section in terms similar to section 145 (3) of the 1948 Act, which provides, *inter alia*, that where minutes of a meeting have been duly made as required by the Act, the proceedings at the meeting and appointments of directors deemed, until the contrary is proved, to be valid. So, too, in *Mahony* v. *East Holyford Mining Co.*,[90] acts by directors who had not been duly appointed nevertheless bound the company as against outsiders.

It will be seen from the above decisions that two propositions emerge—

(1) acts of *de facto* directors are effective both *vis-à-vis* outsiders and *vis-à-vis* members; and

(2) even if the public documents of the company, and the facts which are apparent, would make it clear that a director was not duly qualified to act, this will not oust the effect of the section. Farewell J. in *British Asbestos Co. Ltd.* v. *Boyd*[91] said:

> "In my opinion, the words 'notwithstanding that it shall afterwards be discovered that there is some defect,' and so on, do not mean . . . that the facts are afterwards discovered, but that the defect is afterwards discovered; the facts in a case like the present necessarily appear on the books of the company. . . . It is not, therefore, that the facts are not known, but that the knowledge of the defect is not present to the mind of any person to whom it is material at the time to know it."

The section has been held to validate the acts of a director appointed at a meeting of which insufficient notice had been given.[92]

61–22 The section will not protect a person who knows of the invalidity,[93] as, for instance, a director making a mala fide transfer of his shares, accepted

---

[88] In the above case the directors would have been reduced in number below the minimum required by the articles had this director not been able to act as such. A second director's qualification was also attacked on the grounds that when he was appointed he was an undischarged bankrupt, and the articles disqualified a director "if he becomes bankrupt." It would appear that that director did not come within the articles since he was already an undischarged bankrupt, but the grounds upon which the court found that the articles did not apply are not clear from the judgments.

[89] [1903] 2 Ch. 439.

[90] (1875) L.R. 7 H.L. 869.

[91] [1903] 2 Ch. 439, 444.

[92] *Briton Medical and General Life Assurance Association* v. *Jones* (1889) 61 L.T. 384.

[93] *Re Staffordshire Gas, etc., Co.* (1892) 66 L.T. 413; *Tyne Mutual Steamship, etc., Association* v. *Brown* (1896) 74 L.T. 283.

collusively by the other directors.[94] Nor can a person take advantage of it if he is on notice of some probable defect or if he knows that the regularity of the appointment has been challenged and takes no steps to ascertain the facts.[95] In *Morris* v. *Kanssen*[96] the facts were as follows: Kanssen and Cromie were the two first directors of the company and held all the shares. Cromie alleged that Strelitz was appointed a director at a board meeting. This meeting never took place and the minute recording it was a forgery. At another meeting Cromie and Strelitz, without Kanssen's knowledge, purported to appoint Morris a director and allotted shares to Morris. Morris knew that Kanssen was contending that Strelitz was not a director and that the issue of shares was invalid; but he made no inquiries. The Court of Appeal held that Morris was put on inquiry and could not rely on the section. Lord Green M.R., in the Court of Appeal,[97] laid down the following propositions as having been established by the authorities:

(1) A party to the transaction may be able to rely on the section, if he does not know of an irregularity, even though other parties know that the appointment was irregular.

(2) The section may apply though the parties concerned know the facts, if the defect is not present in their minds at the time.

(3) Where a person is put on inquiry and makes no inquiries, it is no answer for him to contend that, if he had made inquiries, he would have had false statements made to him.

(4) A person who takes an interest as transferee from one of the parties to the transaction is not protected by the section; and, if the transferor could not rely on the section, the transferee is in no better position.

When this case came before the House of Lords these propositions were neither affirmed nor rejected. The House of Lords held that the appointment of Strelitz and Morris and the allotment of shares to Morris were completely bad, and were not validated by the section. Lord Simonds said[98]:

> "There is, as it appears to me, a vital distinction between (a) an appointment in which there is a defect or, in other words, a defective appointment, and (b) no appointment at all."

A *de facto* director is as much in a fiduciary position as a *de jure* director, and liable accordingly.[99]

61–23 It has further been held that what is now section 180 does not justify the claim of a person against a company for services as liquidator where, because he had not been validly appointed, he never had authority from

[94] *Murray* v. *Bush* (1873) L.R. 6 H.L. 37, 77.
[95] *Morris* v. *Kanssen* [1946] A.C. 459.
[96] [1946] A.C. 459.
[97] *Sub nom. Kanssen* v. *Rialto (West End) Ltd.* [1944] Ch. 346.
[98] [1946] A.C. 459, 471.
[99] *Coventry and Dixon's Case* (1880) 14 Ch.D. 660, 670.

the company to act as liquidator.[1] It would seem that the principle of this decision would also apply to a director who had been invalidly appointed or who acted after becoming disqualified, but in *Craven-Ellis* v. *Canons Ltd.*,[2] a director who acted after having ceased to be qualified as a director was entitled to be paid on a *quantum meruit* for his services of which the company had had the benefit. A person who has not been duly appointed does not give the company any right of action against him by purporting to act as a director unless it can show damage; but the company may bring an action to restrain a *de facto* director from acting as director or representing himself as such.

A director who takes part in irregular proceedings may be estopped from setting up the irregularity.[3] For instance, a *de facto* director who was aware of his invalid appointment or was on notice of the facts which gave rise to that invalidity, and who as a director allotted shares to himself, was not able to avoid the allotment on the technical grounds that since he was aware of the defect in his appointment the allotment was not validated by a clause in terms similar to article 105.[4]

The rule in Royal British Bank v. *Turquand*

This is discussed above in paras. 28–10 to 28–16. The effect of the rule may be to make the company liable for a person's acts even if he has never been properly elected to the office of director, provided that the other requisites of the rule are satisfied.

Retirement by rotation

61–24 The articles of a company usually provide that a proportion of the directors, usually one-third, shall retire by rotation year by year (see art. 89), but in the case of private companies these provisions are often omitted or considerably qualified. Where the articles provide that the number nearest to, but not exceeding, one-third, shall retire, and the number of directors is reduced to two, neither need retire.[5] Where the articles provided that one-third of the whole number of directors should retire, it was held that temporary directors, who had to retire at the next general meeting, should not be counted.[6] In the same case it was held that a provision for determining the director to retire "by ballot" meant by lot.

In some cases articles provide that if the place of a retiring director is not filled, the meeting shall stand adjourned until the same day in the next week. Such a provision was found in Table A to the 1908 Act, but this was held not to prevent the meeting being adjourned to some later date.[7]

---

1 *Re Allison, Johnson & Foster Ltd., ex p. Birkenshaw* [1904] 2 K.B. 327, 329, *per* Kennedy J.
2 [1936] 2 K.B. 403.
3 *Faure, etc.* v. *Phillipart* (1888) 58 L.T. 525, 527.
4 *York Tramways* v. *Willows* (1882) 8 Q.B.D. 685.
5 *Re Moseley & Sons Ltd.* [1939] Ch. 719.
6 *Eyre* v. *Milton Proprietary* [1936] Ch. 244.
7 *Spencer* v. *Kennedy* [1926] Ch. 125.

Modern articles, following article 92, provide frequently that if the retiring director offers himself for re-election, he shall be deemed to be re-elected unless

(a) the general meeting expressly resolves not to fill the vacated office; or

(b) a resolution for the re-election of the director—and it may be recalled that in the case of a public company directors have to submit for re-election individually (s. 183[8])—has been put to the meeting and lost.

The latter provision was introduced by article 92 because, if this provision is omitted,[9] the company may have to retain a director who has been rejected by the general meeting.[10]

61–25 In exceptional circumstances the effect of the articles coupled with failure to hold an annual general meeting may result in the directors vacating office automatically with no one being appointed in their place. Thus, in *Alexander Ward & Co. Ltd.* v. *Samyang Navigation Co. Ltd.*,[11] two individuals, who regarded themselves as directors of the company, instituted proceedings on behalf of the pursuers, which commenced in November 1970. Their articles provided that an "ordinary general meeting" shall be held in each calendar year, and that "at the ordinary general meeting in the year 1968 and at the ordinary general meeting in every subsequent year all the dirctors for the time being shall retire from office." It was proved that no "ordinary general meeting" had been held in 1968 or subsequently. The Lord Ordinary held on construing the articles that by January 1, 1970, at the latest, the pursuers had ceased to have directors and accordingly "there was no person capable of acting or giving instructions on behalf of the company." One may question the soundness of this decision on the ground that there is no compelling logic in the view that failure to hold a meeting means that an event which should have occurred at that meeting must be deemed to have happened in any event. To some extent the decision in *Ward* depends on the special provisions of the articles. Nevertheless all companies are under obligation to hold a general meeting in each calendar year and many adopt articles requiring all the directors to retire at such meeting; even under Table A reg. 89 all must retire at the first annual general meeting. If this decision stands, therefore, it may have unforeseen consequences for a large number of companies. In any event, in the absence of an effective board powers of management

8 See para. 61–05, *ante*.

9 As was the case in the corresponding art. 38 of Table A of the Act of 1929.

10 See *Grundt* v. *Great Boulder Proprietary Gold Mines Ltd.* [1948] Ch. 145 (C.A.), following *Holt* v. *Catterall* (1931) 47 T.L.R. 332, and disapproving of *Robert Batcheller & Sons Ltd.* v. *Batcheller* [1945] Ch. 169.

11 1973 S.L.T. (Notes) 80. Although reversed on other grounds by the Inner House (Second Division) on June 21, 1974 (unreported) this aspect of the decision was not attacked by the appeal court judges, and apparently, was accepted by counsel. The House of Lords dismissed the further appeal: [1975] 1 W.L.R. 673.

revert to the general meeting and in the instant case a subsequently appointed liquidator was able to act as the company to ratify the proceedings instituted by the individuals.[12]

Resignation

61–26 A director can at any time resign his office, and usually the articles make express provision accordingly. If he communicates his resignation to the company, for instance, by a notice upon the company served in the manner provided by section 437 of the 1948 Act, his resignation is effective.[13] A resignation once made cannot be withdrawn, except with the consent of the company.[14]

The same result can, of course, in appropriate cases be achieved by a director parting with his qualification shares, and so vacating office by disqualification.[15]

A verbal resignation accepted at a general meeting is effective, even though the articles provide that a director shall vacate office if by notice in writing he resigns his office.[16] A verbal resignation would not, however, be effective in the light of such an article if made to and accepted by the board, since the board would have no authority to accept, and the resigning director would be unable to end his contract with the company, except in accordance with its terms, express or implied, or with the company's agreement.

Where a director who was both a permanent and an ordinary director resigned, it was held that the resignation applied to both offices.[17]

Removal of directors

Statutory and regulatory provisions

61–27 Section 184 of the 1948 Act provides that the general meeting may by ordinary resolution requiring special notice[18] remove a director before the expiration of his office, notwithstanding anything in its articles or in any agreement between the company and himself. This provision—one of the most important principles of modern company law—applies to all types of companies, public and private (limited or not) with one exception only: it does not apply to a director of a private company who held office for life on July 18, 1945 (s. 184 (1), proviso). This exception is of transitional character; it is designed to safeguard the rights of life directors of private companies who were then in office.[19] A person appointed life director or

---

[12] [1975] 1 W.L.R. 673 *per* Lord Hailsham. On the default powers of the general meeting see *Barron* v. *Potter* [1914] 1 Ch. 895 and *Foster* v. *Foster* [1916] 1 Ch. 532.
[13] See, however, *Municipal Freehold Land Co.* v. *Pollington* (1890) 63 L.T. 238.
[14] *R.* v. *Mayor of Wigan* (1885) 14 Q.B.D. 908; *Glossop* v. *Glossop* [1907] 2 Ch. 370.
[15] *Gilbert's Case* (1870) L.R. 5 Ch. 559, 565.
[16] *Latchford Premier Cinema* v. *Ermion* [1931] 2 Ch. 409.
[17] *Moseley* v. *Koffyfontein Mines Ltd.* [1910] 2 Ch. 382; [1911] A.C. 409.
[18] s. 184 (2); see para. 54–06, *ante*.
[19] *Bersel Manufacturing Co. Ltd.* v. *Berry* [1968] 2 All E.R. 552.

permanent director after that date by the articles or by an outside agreement is nevertheless removable by the general meeting; he cannot be given security of tenure of his office.

At first glance this power appears to be a statutory authority to break a contract on the part of the company. This may be the case, but it merely places the company in the same position as every employer by giving it the discretion of removing a manager and of accepting the consequences of this act by paying compensation or damages to him (s. 184 (6)).

As has already been observed, section 184 is a key provision of modern company law. While the shareholders have no power, apart from that given them by statute or articles—which, in practice, does not amount to much—to intervene in the management of the company's affairs, this section was designed to enable them to control the directors by removing them. In English company law, the balance of power is normally with the directors who by the articles are usually authorised to exercise the general powers of the company,[20] and interference with the managerial activities of the directors is not encouraged by statute or articles. But this section enables the shareholders to assert themselves against the directors, if need be, and makes it clear that the ultimate control is in the hands of the proprietors of the company. The articles usually contain provisions corresponding to those of section 184 (see arts. 96 and 97); where they go further, the section does not derogate from them or from any other power to remove a director, *e.g.* a power arising under a contract (s. 184 (6)).

The resolution for removing the director need not state reasons why he is to be removed.[21]

Weighted voting rights in private companies

61–28 The House of Lords has admitted, in the special circumstances of a private company in the nature of a quasi-partnership company, weighted voting rights of the shares held by a shareholder-director in the case of his threatened removal from office as director. It was held in *Bushell* v. *Faith*[22] that an article of a private company giving a director additional voting rights on his shares in the event of a resolution for his removal being proposed, and thus enabling him to defeat that resolution, was valid and did not infringe section 184. The article was in the following form:

> "In the event of a resolution being proposed at any general meeting of the company for the removal from office of any director, any shares held by that director shall on a poll in respect of any such resolution carry the right to three votes per share. . . ."

---

[20] See para. 64–08, *post*.

[21] Older articles sometimes stated that the power to remove was only for a reasonable cause; the court held that it would not interfere with the decision of the general meeting on what constituted a reasonable cause: *Inderwick* v. *Snell* (1850) 2 M. & G. 216; *Re Gresham Life* (1872) L.R. 8 Ch. 446, 449; *Osgood* v. *Nelson* (1872) L.R. 5 H.L. 636.

[22] [1970] A.C. 1099.

Such an article does not give the shareholder-director absolute protection as it can be deleted by special resolution (s. 10).

Another weighted votes article was used in *Re N.F.U. Development Trust Ltd.*,[23] a company limited by guarantee and not having a share capital. The article provided that at a general meeting every member should have one vote, save that on a resolution to alter the memorandum or articles or to wind up the company or to remove or appoint a director, the N.F.U. Development Co., after seeking the advice of the councils of the three farmers' unions, should have three times the number of votes cast by all the other members who voted. The validity of this article was not in issue before the court. Whatever may be the position in the case of a company limited by guarantee, it is unlikely that an article in the N.F.U. Development Trust Ltd. form would be held to be valid in the case of a private company limited by shares as it contravenes the fundamental right of a company to alter its articles.

The decision in *Bushell* v. *Faith* has been criticised,[24] although it can be justified in the case of private companies of the quasi-partnership type. Its ratio may not extend to public companies.

Circulation of statements by directors

61–29 Section 184 (3) gives a director an opportunity to make representations to the shareholders before he is removed from office. When special notice is given to the company of the intended resolution to remove a director, he may request the company to send his written representations to the members and, unless the representations (which should not exceed a reasonable length) are received too late, the company has to send a copy of them to every member entitled to receive notice and to state the fact that the director has made a representation in the notice. If the representations could not be sent out to the members in time, the director may require them to be read out at the meeting. The court, on application of the company or of another interested party may, however, disallow the director's representations on the ground that these rights are abused to give needless publicity to defamatory matter.

Whether or not the director makes representations under section 184 (3), he is entitled by section 184 (2) to be heard on the resolution to remove at the meeting.

Compensation or damages payable to director

61–30 A director who has been removed from office by the general meeting by virtue of section 184 is not thereby deprived of any claim for compensation or damages which he might have (s. 184 (6)). The calculation of damages

---

[23] [1972] 1 W.L.R. 1548.
[24] See "House of Lords sanctions evasion of Companies Acts," [1970] J.B.L. 1.

for lost income has to take into account his liability to income tax.[25] Directors who are also employed under a contract of service may also have rights under the Employment Protection (Consolidation) Act 1978 as regards redundancy payments, unfair dismissal or minimum periods of notice.

A vacancy created by such removal may be filled as a casual vacancy (s. 184 (4)).

Removal of director as a ground for "just and equitable" winding up

61–31 A company which removes a director in accordance with the procedure laid down in section 184 makes use of its legal rights. Normally the exercise of its legal rights does not constitute a ground for a compulsory winding up of the company. In the case of small private companies founded on a personal relationship between their members (sometimes known as "quasi-partnerships"), however, the exercise of the statutory right to remove a director by virtue of section 184 may constitute a breach of good faith which the members owe each other and may be inequitable. In such a case the courts have power to order the winding up of the company under the "just and equitable" clause of section 222 (*f*) of the 1948 Act.[26] The exercise of the legal rights given to a company by section 184 is thus controlled by equitable considerations imported by the "just and equitable" clause.

No specific performance or injunctions against the company

61–32 The court will not enforce specifically a contract of service either at the instance of employer or employed. Hence, if a director refuses to act, the court will not force him to act, and if, on the other hand, a company, by resolution of a general meeting, refuses to employ a director, the court will not force it to do so.[27] Thus, in *Bentley-Stevens* v. *Jones*[28] the plaintiff had been removed from his directorship by an ordinary resolution passed at an allegedly irregularly convened general meeting. He was refused an injunction by Plowman J. who held that (i) the irregularities were inevitably curable[29]; and (ii) nothing in the *Westbourne Galleries* case suggested that the plaintiff was entitled to an injunction to interfere with the statutory right of the company to remove him from its board; it merely gave ousted directors a right in certain circumstances to petition for a winding up under the "just and equitable" clause. It is a different thing, however, when a

---

[25] *British Transport Commission* v. *Gourley* [1956] A.C. 185; *Beach* v. *Reed Corrugated Cases* [1956] 1 W.L.R. 807; *Phipps* v. *Orthodox Unit Trusts Ltd.* [1958] 1 Q.B. 314; *Parsons* v. *B.N.M. Laboratories Ltd.* [1964] 1 Q.B. 95 (where the Court of Appeal considered the effect on this rule of ss. 37 and 38 of and Sched. 4, para. 13 to the Finance Act 1960).

[26] *Re Westbourne Galleries Ltd.* [1973] A.C. 360. (H.L.). *Cf. Re A. & BC Chewing Gum Ltd.* [1975] 1 W.L.R. 579. For a fuller discussion of "just and equitable" winding up in these and other circumstances, see para. 85–09, *post*.

[27] *Harben* v. *Phillips* (1883) 23 Ch.D. 14; *Bainbridge* v. *Smith* (1889) 41 Ch.D. 462.

[28] [1974] 1 W.L.R. 638.

[29] See *Browne* v. *La Trinidad* (1887) 37 Ch.D. 1, 17.

board of directors excludes one of their body from acting. The court does not regard such exclusion as the act of the company (even though the directors have, under the articles, the general powers of the company), and it will accordingly, on the application of the aggrieved director, grant an injunction restraining the other directors from excluding him from office.[30] It will not, however, restrain the company, and if, after the grant of the injunction, the shareholders, by a resolution in general meeting, declare that they do not wish the particular director to act any longer, the court will discharge the injunction and decline to assist him any further by injunction.[31] For any other redress he may claim he must proceed by an action for damages.

The court will not normally grant an interlocutory injunction restraining a director from acting where a declaration is sought that the director has been validly removed from office, as this would in effect prejudge the trial issue.[32]

Remuneration of directors

Effect of authorisation by articles

61–33 Prima facie, directors of a company cannot claim remuneration,[33] but the articles usually provide expressly for payment of it (see art. 76), and, where this is the case, the provision operates as an authority to the directors to pay remuneration out of the funds of the company; such remuneration is not restricted to payment out of profits.[34]

The amount of remuneration to be paid to directors is a matter of internal management.[35]

A director can sue for remuneration agreed to be paid him by the company,[36] and prove in the winding up like an ordinary creditor,[37] but, as director, he is not entitled to the preference accorded to servants of the company under section 319 (1) (*b*) of the 1948 Act.[38] Time runs against him under the Limitation Act 1939, but a balance sheet stating his remuneration may be an acknowledgment in writing of his debt and constitute a

---

[30] *Pulbrook* v. *Richmond, etc., Co.* (1878) 9 Ch.D. 610; *Hayes* v. *Bristol Plant Hire Ltd.* [1957] 1 W.L.R. 499.

[31] *Bainbridge* v. *Smith* (1889) 41 Ch.D. 462, 475; *Read* v. *Astoria Garage (Streatham) Ltd.* [1952] Ch. 637 (C.A.).

[32] *Burden* v. *Sinclair* (1961) 105 S.J. 586.

[33] *Dunston* v. *Imperial, etc., Co.* (1831) 3 Bar. & Ad. 125; *Hutton* v. *West Cork Ry.* (1883) 23 Ch.D. 654, 672; *Stroud* v. *Royal Aquarium, etc., Society* (1903) 89 L.T. 243.

[34] *Harvey Lewis's Case* (1872) 26 L.T. 673.

[35] *Burland* v. *Earle* [1902] A.C. 83; *Normandy* v. *Ind, Coope & Co.* [1908] 1 Ch. 84.

[36] *Orton* v. *Cleveland, etc., Co.* (1865) 3 H. & C. 868; *Nell* v. *Atlanta, etc., Mines* (1895) 11 T.L.R. 407 (C.A.).

[37] *Ex p. Beckwith* [1898] 1 Ch. 324; *Re Al Biscuit Co.* [1899] W.N. 115; *Re Dale and Plant* (1889) 43 Ch.D. 255; *Re Cinnamond Park & Co.* [1930] N.I. 47. *Re Leicester Club, etc. Co., Cannon's Case* (1885) 30 Ch.D. 629, which was a decision to the contrary, cannot now be relied on.

[38] See para. 14–14, *post*.

new accrual of action.[39] Where a decision of the board as to the mode of division is required, there is no right of action until a resolution of the board dividing the aggregate remuneration between the directors is passed.[40]

The articles as such do not constitute a contract between the directors and the company,[41] so that a director has no contractual claim for remuneration on the grounds that the articles authorise a fixed sum. The same result is, however, achieved indirectly, since the court will often recognise that the director acted in accordance with an implied contract, one of the terms of which was for remuneration at the rate named in the articles.[42] It is open to directors by a resolution to renounce the right to future remuneration under such implied contracts.[43] An agreement by all the directors inter se and with the company to renounce the right to remuneration is binding on each director even at the suit of the company.[44]

Remuneration to be voted in general meeting

61–34 Articles commonly provide that the directors shall be entitled to such remuneration as shall be voted to them in general meeting (see art. 76), in which case there must be a resolution duly passed by the company. If, however, the remuneration is approved by all shareholders entitled to attend and vote at a general meeting, this has the same effect as a resolution duly passed by the company in general meeting.[45] It is not normally sufficient to show the figure taken by directors in the accounts, and the acceptance by the company of the accounts will not in itself authorise remuneration which has not otherwise been authorised. Exceptionally, however, a resolution of the members approving the accounts may be a sufficient authorisation, if all the members are aware that, by being asked to approve the accounts, they are being asked also to approve the remuneration.[46]

Extra remuneration

61–35 The articles will also usually authorise the payment by the directors to one of their number of extra remuneration for special services.[47] Where

---

[39] Except if he has signed the balance sheet himself pursuant to s. 155; *Jones* v. *Bellgrove Properties Ltd.* [1949] 2 K.B. 700 (C.A.); *Re Transplanters (Holding Company) Ltd.* [1958] 1 W.L.R. 822; *cf. Consolidated Agencies Ltd.* v. *Bertram Ltd.* [1965] A.C. 470. See further *Dungate* v. *Dungate* [1965] 1 W.L.R. 1477; *Re Gee & Co. (Woolwich)* [1975] Ch. 52. See also *In re Overmark Smith Warden Ltd, The Times,* March 22, 1982. The 1939 Act does not apply in Scotland, where such a claim would be subject to the general law of prescription.

[40] *Morrell* v. *Oxford Portland Cement Co.* (1910) 26 T.L.R. 682; *Joseph* v. *Sonora (Mexico) Land Co.* (1918) 34 T.L.R. 220.

[41] See para. 14–14, *ante; cf. Re Richmond Gate Property Co. Ltd.* [1965] 1 W.L.R. 33

[42] *Swabey* v. *Port Darwin Gold Mining Co.* (1889) 1 Meg. 385; *Isaacs' Case* [1892] 2 Ch. 158; *Re Peruvian Guano Co.* [1894] 3 Ch. 690; *Re New British Iron Co.* [1898] 1 Ch. 324.

[43] *McConnell's Claim, re London and Northern Bank* [1901] 1 Ch. 728.

[44] *West Yorkshire Darracq Agency* v. *Coleridge* [1911] 2 K.B. 326.

[45] *Re Duomatic Ltd.* [1969] 2 Ch. 365; *Cane* v. *Jones* [1981] 1 All E.R. 533.

[46] *Felix Hadley & Co. Ltd.* v. *Hadley* (1897) 77 L.T. 131.

[47] No such provision is, however, found in Table A.

such provision is made, it is a condition precedent to a director's claim for additional remuneration that the board of directors shall determine the method and amount of the extra payment; it is irrelevant that the director has performed substantial extra services and the payment of additional remuneration would be reasonable.[48]

61–36 *Liabilities incurred in the management of the company.* Directors, as agents, are by law entitled to an indemnity in respect of all liabilities properly incurred by them in the management of the company's business.[49] This extends to costs incurred by an agent in defending a libel action in connection with a report made by him for the company.[50] No express provision for this purpose is necessary; but the articles commonly contain express provision on the subject, and where this is the case a right of indemnity may be and often is given which is more extensive than that implied by law.[51] The right does not extend to indemnity for wrongful or unauthorised acts of the agent.[52]

Travelling expenses. The articles of the company normally contain wide and generous provisions entitling the directors to indemnity for travelling and similar expenses incurred in connection with the business of the company and, if the company has a contract of service with the director,[53] the terms of the contract usually amplify and specify these rights of the directors. In modern days the right to recover his travelling and other expenses is of great practical value to the director because he is entitled to deduct expenses "wholly, exclusively and necessarily" incurred in the performance of his duties from his income for the purposes of assessment to income tax.[54]

An illustration of provisions authorising travelling expenses, as commonly found in the articles, is provided by article 76:

> "The directors may also be paid all travelling, hotel and other expenses properly incurred by them in attending and returning from meetings of the directors or any committee of the directors or general meetings of the company or in connection with the business of the company."

If the articles fail to authorise such travelling expenses, the directors are not entitled to be paid by the company their travelling expenses in attending board meetings.[55] Such expenses are not expenses incurred in the execution of their office within an indemnity clause.[56]

---

[48] *Nelberg* v. *Woking Shipping Co. Ltd.* [1958] 2 Lloyd's Rep. 560.
[49] *Re German Mining Co.* (1853) 4 De G.M. & G. 19; *James* v. *May* (1873) L.R. 6 H.L. 328.
[50] *Re Famatina Development Corporation* [1914] 2 Ch. 271; *cf. Tomlinson* v. *Liquidators of Scottish Amalgamated Silks Ltd.*, 1935 S.C. 1.
[51] *Re Pyle Works (No. 2)* [1891] 1 Ch. 173, 184.
[52] *Smith* v. *Duke of Manchester* (1883) 1 Ch.D. 611.
[53] See para. 61–02, *ante*.
[54] See para. 93–06, *post*.
[55] *Young* v. *Naval and Military, etc., Society* [1905] 1 K.B. 687.
[56] *Marmor Ltd.* v. *Alexander* 1908 S.C. 78 (Ct. of Sess.); *Re Brazilian Rubber, etc.* [1911] 1 Ch. 425.

Unauthorised remuneration

61–37 To take remuneration in excess of what is payable under the regulations is a misfeasance, and directors who are parties to such payments are jointly and severally liable to make good the amount.[57] Extra remuneration may be voted to the directors as a gratuity while the company is a going concern, provided that the vote is consistent with the articles; but if the remuneration is fixed by the articles, and there is no article authorising the voting or payment of extra remunerations, none can be resolved upon without a special resolution.[58] Whether the articles provide that the remuneration of the directors is to be fixed by the company in general meeting, a director has no right of action for remuneration allotted to him by a resolution of the board alone.[59]

By section 189 of the 1948 Act it is not lawful for a company to pay a director remuneration free of income tax except under a contract (outside the articles) which was in force on July 18, 1945, and provides expressly for such payment. Except as to these contracts, any provision for payment of remuneration free of income tax is to take effect as if it provided for payment as a gross sum, subject to income tax, of the net sum for which it actually provides.[60] Where a director was to be paid "£2,500 per annum net of deductions" it was held, applying section 189, that this meant a gross sum of £2,500 per annum, subject to tax.[61]

Remuneration to be shown in accounts

61–38 The company's accounts must show all sums paid to the directors by way of remuneration, and the amount received by the directors by way of emolument whether in the form of cash or other benefit, and pensions of past directors and compensation paid for loss of office.[62]

Apportionment

Where, under the articles, a director is to be paid so much per annum, and he vacates office before the end of a current year, the question has to be considered whether he can maintain a claim for an apportioned part of the remuneration for that year.

If the articles[63] provide, as does article 76, that the remuneration shall accrue "from day to day," there is no doubt that he may maintain such a claim.

The position where the articles do not contain such a provision is more difficult. In *Swabey* v. *Port Darwin Gold Mining Co. Ltd.*[64] this question

[57] *Re Oxford, etc., Society* (1886) 35 Ch.D. 502; *Leeds Estate, etc., Co.* v. *Shepherd* (1887) 36 Ch.D. 787, 809; *Re Whitehall Court* (1887) 56 L.T. 280.
[58] *Boschoek Proprietary Co.* v. *Fuke* [1906] 1 Ch. 148, 163.
[59] *Kerr* v. *Marine Products Ltd.* (1928) 44 T.L.R. 292.
[60] See s. 189 (2) and (3).
[61] *Owens* v. *Multilux Ltd.* 1974 S.L.T. 189.
[62] See para. 70–13, *post*.
[63] Or the contract of the director with the company.
[64] (1889) 1 Meg. 385.

was considered by the Court of Appeal. There the clause in the articles provided that "the directors shall each receive by way of remuneration out of funds of the company in each year the sum of £200, and the chairman in addition £100 per annum." A director resigned in the course of a current year, and he was held entitled to an apportioned part of the remuneration for that year. Lord Halsbury L.C. said:

> "There was . . . a reciprocal right to put an end to the service at an earlier period than the end of the year. It follows from that, as a necessary consequence, that both parties must have contemplated that, as this was a service for hire and reward, a proportionate part of the remuneration agreed upon should be paid if the service was determined at an earlier period than the full year."

61–39 On the other hand, in *Salton* v. *New Beeston Cycle Co.*,[65] Cozens-Hardy J. held that where the article provided that "directors shall be entitled to receive by way of remuneration in each year £5,000," a director who vacated office in a current year was *not* entitled to any apportionment: and this was followed by Wright J. in *McConnell's Claim*,[66] where the words were "each director shall be paid . . . the sum of £300 per annum"; and by the Court of Appeal in *Inman* v. *Ackroyd and Best*,[67] where the words were "the sum of £300 per annum per director."[68] In most of these cases the court proceeded on the erroneous assumption that, in *Swabey* v. *Port Darwin Gold Mining Co. Ltd.*,[69] the Court of Appeal was dealing with a case in which the articles provided that the remuneration to be paid to the directors should be "at the rate of £200 per annum," as stated in the headnote to that case. But on this point the headnote in *Swabey* v. *Port Darwin Gold Mining Co.* is incorrect. The remuneration clause did not contain the words "at the rate." The terms of the clause taken from the registered articles are set out above, and the above decisions, grounded on this inaccuracy, therefore require reconsideration, as noted in the appeal in *Inman* v. *Ackroyd.*[70]

It may, as has been seen, be clear from the agreement that a director is to be entitled *pro rata* if the agreement is terminated before the end of the year, and in that case there will be no difficulty[71]: but the mutual right to terminate the agreement is not, of itself, sufficient to show such intention.[72]

61–40 Furthermore, it is not easy to see why the Apportionment Act 1870 does not apply. This Act expressly provides that all rents, annuities (including salaries and pensions), and other periodical payments in the nature of income shall be apportionable, and provides for the recovery in due course

---

65 [1899] 1 Ch. 775.
66 [1901] 1 Ch. 728.
67 [1901] 1 K.B. 613.
68 See also *Re Central de Kaap Gold Mines* (1899) 69 L.J.Ch. 18.
69 (1889) 1 Meg. 385.
70 [1901] 1 K.B. 613.
71 *Per* Lord Sterndale M.R. in *Moriarty* v. *Regent's Garage Co.* [1921] 2 K.B. 766, 777.
72 See *Diamond* v. *English Sewing Cotton Co.* [1922] W.N. 237.

of an apportioned part of an annuity determined by death or otherwise. In *Salton* v. *New Beeston Cycle Co.*,[73] it was argued that the Act applied, and the case of *Lowndes* v. *Earl Stamford*;[74] (decided on the Apportionment Act 1834, which was very differently expressed) was apparently relied on; but in his judgment, Cozens-Hardy J. made no reference to the Apportionment Act. However, in *Inman* v. *Ackroyd and Best*,[75] Bruce J. considered that the Apportionment Act 1870 must have been taken into consideration by Cozens-Hardy J. and Wright J. and held to be inapplicable. The Apportionment Act was applied by the Divisional Court in *Moriarty* v. *Regent's Garage, etc., Co.*,[76] in which the court in considered judgments reviewed all the authorities, but the decision was overruled on technical grounds in the Court of Appeal[77] which accordingly left the question of apportionment open.

It is submitted that the decision of the Divisional Court on this question is correct and that the words of the Apportionment Act are sufficient to cover directors' fees. If, however, the payment is in the form of a lump sum to the directors as a whole, this would not seem to fall within the Apportionment Act. A claim under the Apportionment Act can be resisted if made before the end of the year in respect of which the claim is made.

Where the plaintiff was entitled to a salary at the rate of £500 per annum, and a percentage of profits, the latter was held to be apportionable[78]; it could not, of course, be claimed until after the end of the year. Where a company went into liquidation a few days before the expiration of a year, and the director's work for the year was completed, he was held to be entitled to remuneration for the year.[79]

61–41 If the remuneration is to be paid "at such a time as the directors determine," a director has no right until such determination.[80] Where a director vacates office by ceasing to hold his qualification, or on failure to be re-elected, remuneration ceases as from the time when he ought to have vacated office under the provisions of the articles,[81] and a person who is a *de facto* director but not a *de jure* director can have no right to remuneration. If, however, the company has made use of his services he may sue on a *quantum meruit.*[82]

Tax treatment of share acquisitions by directors and employees

61–42 The Inland Revenue has published a leaflet on this subject. It is reproduced in Vol. III, paras. K–038 *et seq.*

---

73 [1899] 1 Ch. 775.
74 (1852) 18 Q.B. 425.
75 [1901] 1 K.B. 613.
76 [1921] 1 K.B. 423.
77 [1921] 2 K.B. 766.
78 *Diamond* v. *English Sewing Cotton Co.* [1922] W.N. 237.
79 *Re Shaws, Bryant & Co.* [1901] W.N. 124.
80 *Caridad Copper Mining Co.* v. *Swallow* [1902] 2 K.B. 44 (C.A.); *Inman* v. *Ackroyd and Best* [1901] 1 K.B. 613.
81 *Re Consolidated Nickel Mines* [1914] 1 Ch. 883.
82 *Re Craven-Ellis* v. *Canons Ltd.* [1936] 2 K.B. 403. See para. 61–23, *ante*.

PRACTICE NOTE

Executive, assistant or special directors

61–43 Some companies include in their articles of association an article empowering the directors to appoint a person as a "special," "executive" or "assistant" director and so limiting the rights and liabilities of the person appointed that he is not deemed to be a director within the meaning of s. 455 (1) of the 1948 Act. The article empowering directors to make such appointments will authorise the directors to define and limit the powers, authorities and discretions of the person appointed, provide that an executive director shall not be deemed to be a member of the board or any committee thereof, that he shall not attend board meetings except at the invitation of the board and, when present at a board meeting by invitation, he shall not be entitled to vote.

The purpose of such appointments is to enhance the status of the person appointed in his relationships with other members of the company's staff and customers so that in these relationships he can call himself a director, *e.g.* sales director. Furthermore, the executive director becomes in effect a trainee director for eventual recruitment to full directorial status.

If "executive," "assistant" or "special" directors are not directors within the meaning of s. 455 (1), the requirements of the Acts in regard to register of directors, register of directors' interests, etc., do not apply to these appointments.

CHAPTER 62

PROCEEDINGS OF DIRECTORS

Directors to act as a body

62–01 In this chapter there will be considered the procedure which the directors have to adopt when managing and administering the affairs of the company.

On principle, the management of the company is vested in the board of directors collectively and the directors must, as a general rule, act at board meetings, but the articles, or rules made by the directors under powers vested in them by the articles, may otherwise provide.[1] This principle ensures that the collective wisdom of the board is available to the company on important decisions, and enables discussion to take place before a decision is taken.

It is, however, frequently impracticable for directors to meet to discuss a matter upon which a decision is needed, and, in order to enable the board to consider any such matter without being required to assemble together, articles usually provide that a resolution in writing signed by all the directors entitled to receive notice of a board meeting shall be as effective as if passed at a board meeting (art. 106).

Further, the articles often authorise the directors to delegate any of their powers to committees of directors (arts. 102–105)[2] and to appoint one or more of their body to act as managing directors (arts. 107–109).[3]

Board meetings

62–02 At meetings of directors the proceedings are governed by the company's articles and by any rules made by the directors themselves by virtue of powers given them by the articles.

The articles usually provide that the directors may conduct their proceedings as they think fit. Typical in this respect is article 98, which provides that "the directors may meet together for the dispatch of business, adjourn and otherwise regulate their meetings, as they think fit." The article continues:

> "Questions arising at any meeting shall be decided by a majority of votes. In case of an equality of votes, the chairman shall have a second or casting vote. A director may, and the secretary on the requisition of a director shall, at any time summon a meeting of the directors."

The articles will further normally state what numbers constitute a quorum[4]

---

[1] *Re Haycraft Gold, etc., Co.* [1900] 2 Ch. 230.
[2] See para. 62–06, *post*.
[3] See para. 62–07, *post*.
[4] On the quorum, see para. 62–04, *post*.

and will provide that (subject to a minimum number of directors) the directors may act notwithstanding a vacancy in their number. If, therefore, a company has six directors and four of them cease to hold office, and if articles 99 and 100 apply, the remaining two directors will be able to continue to act as the board. If, however, the number of directors is reduced below the minimum fixed by the articles (under articles 99 and 100 this will be two) the remaining directors may only act for the purposes named in the articles, which will usually be for appointing new directors to satisfy the minimum number, or for summoning a general meeting.[5]

In larger companies it is usual to hold board meetings at regular intervals, *e.g.* monthly or fortnightly; while in small companies board meetings will only be held when there is sufficient business to justify the holding of a meeting. Although, in the absence of other provisions in the articles and in rules made by the directors under the articles, the decisions of the directors are taken at board meetings, a transaction cannot be invalidated as against an outsider who has dealt with the company bona fide merely because the directors acted without meeting.[6]

It is customary for the directors present at a meeting to signify their attendance either by signing an attendance book kept for that purpose (art. 86) or by attaching their signature at the head of the minutes of the meeting in question; the former method is the more usual one. Proxies may be allowed by the articles.

Notice of board meetings

62–03 The articles usually provide that any one director may summon a meeting directly or by requesting the secretary to do so (art. 98).

Prima facie, due notice must be given convening a meeting of directors, and in default the meeting is irregular[7]; but this is not always necessary, for, by the articles, or by the determination of the directors, meetings may be held at fixed times, in which case no notice of each separate meeting need be given.[8] Where notice has to be given, it may be given verbally unless the articles require it to be given in writing, and it must be given a reasonable time before the meeting.[9] Otherwise it will be invalid, unless, indeed, all the directors are present at the meeting. Notice must be given even to a director who has stated that he will be unable to attend.[10] As regards directors for the time being absent from the United Kingdom, the

---

[5] But not always for these purposes only. See *Re Bank of Syria* [1900] 2 Ch. 272, where the power to act notwithstanding vacancies was unrestricted. Compare, however, *York Tramways Co.* v. *Willows* (1882) 8 Q.B.D. 685.

[6] *County of Gloucester Bank* v. *Rudry, etc., Co.* [1895] 1 Ch. 629; *Re Bank of Syria, Owen & Ashworth's Claim* [1901] 1 Ch. 115. As to the effect of the European Communities Act 1972, s. 9 (1), see para. 28–01, *ante*.

[7] *Harben* v. *Phillips* (1883) 23 Ch.D. 14, 34; *Young* v. *Ladies' Imperial Club* [1920] 2 K.B. 523.

[8] Extraordinary meetings and meetings held at a different venue from the usual locality of board meetings require notice even if meetings are held at fixed times.

[9] *Browne* v. *La Trinidad* (1887) 37 Ch.D. 1.

[10] *Re Portuguese Consolidated Copper Mines, Steele's Case* (1889) 42 Ch.D. 160; *cf. Young* v. *Ladies Imperial Club* [1920] 2 K.B. 523.

articles commonly provide that no notice need be given (see art. 98), and even in the absence of such a provision it appears that notice need not be given to a director abroad, unless, indeed, he is within easy reach.[11]

Sometimes, by an accidental omission to give due notice to some one director, a meeting of directors is rendered irregular, but the directors nevertheless transact business on behalf of the company, *e.g.* allot shares, make contracts, etc. In such a case, the rule in *Royal British Bank* v. *Turquand*[12] applies, and outsiders will not, as a general rule, be prejudiced by such irregularities. Moreover, their position has been further secured by the European Communities Act 1972, s. 9 (1).[13] They are not concerned to see to the internal regularity of the company's proceedings—its "indoor management" as Lord Hatherley termed it—and are entitled to assume that everything has been properly done. Where there has been any such irregularity, a subsequent regularly constituted board meeting can always ratify and confirm what was done irregularly, and it will then be valid *ab initio.*[14]

Notice of a board meeting need not, unless the articles otherwise provide, specify the nature of the business to be transacted.[15]

Quorum of directors

62–04 The articles generally fix, or enable the directors to fix, the quorum for a board meeting, that is to say, what number of directors must be present to enable them to act as a board, and exercise the powers vested in the directors collectively (see art. 99). The quorum may be one.[16]

Prima facie, a power to fix a quorum cannot be exercised by less than a majority of the directors at a board meeting. If no quorum is fixed, not less than a majority of the directors can act[17] unless the number to form a quorum is established by the usual practice of the board.[18]

A quorum must be a disinterested quorum, *i.e.* it must be comprised of directors who are entitled to vote on the particular motions before the board[19]; if a director is interested in a transaction which is to be discussed, and is not permitted by the articles to vote thereon, he is not counted for the purposes of the quorum with respect to that particular item of business. The rule is the same if two directors are interested in a combined transaction and each votes on the part of it that concerns the other,[20] and also if

---

[11] *Halifax Sugar, etc., Co.* v. *Francklyn* (1890) 59 L.J.Ch. 593; and see para. 54–03, *ante.*
[12] (1856) 6 E. & B. 327; see para. 28–10, *ante.*
[13] See para. 28–10, *ante.*
[14] *Re Portuguese Consol. Copper Mines Co.* (1890) 45 Ch.D. 16, 26; *Re Land Credit, etc., Co.* (1869) L.R. 4 Ch. 460, 473; *Hooper* v. *Kerr Stuard & Co.* (1900) 83 L.T. 729; *Re State of Wyoming Syndicate* [1901] 2 Ch. 431, 437.
[15] *Compagnie de Mayville* v. *Whitley* [1896] 1 Ch. 788.
[16] *Re Fireproof Doors* [1916] 2 Ch. 142.
[17] *York Tramways Co.* v. *Willows* (1882) 8 Q.B.D. 685.
[18] *Lyster's Case* (1867) L.R. 4 Eq. 233.
[19] *Re Greymouth Point Elizabeth Ry., etc., Co., Yuill* v. *Same* [1904] 1 Ch. 32; *Neal* v. *Quinn* [1916] W.N. 223.
[20] *Re North Eastern Insurance Co.* [1919] 1 Ch. 198.

the quorum is reduced simply for the purpose of enabling an interest in the property of the company to be conferred on one of the directors.[21]

If the requisite quorum is not present, the meeting is irregular and cannot transact business. So, too, if the number of directors of the company is less in the whole than the required quorum, no effective board meeting can be held,[22] unless the articles give power to act notwithstanding vacancies.[23] A provision for a quorum does not dispense with the due convening of a meeting, to which all the directors must be summoned, except those who are outside the United Kingdom.[24]

Resolutions of directors

62–05 At board meetings, the directors exercise their powers by resolutions which are passed in the manner laid down in the articles or agreed upon by them under powers given them by the articles. They decide usually by a majority of votes of those present (see art. 98). Proxies are sometimes admitted. The chairman is usually given a casting vote by or under the articles (see art. 98); at common law he has no such vote.[25]

The following are examples of resolutions of directors[26]:

> *Creation of debenture stock*: That £300,000 7 per cent. First Mortgage Debenture Stock 1997–2007 be created, such stock to be secured by a trust deed in favour of "X" Trustee Corporation Limited as trustees constituting the same a specific first mortgage on the lands, buildings and fixed assets of the company and a floating charge on the undertaking and other assets and that the solicitors of the company be requested to furnish drafts of the debenture stock certificate and trust deed for the approval of the board.
>
> *To offer shares*: That 150,000 unissued shares in the company's capital be offered for subscription at par to the existing shareholders in the proportion in which they hold shares at the date of the offer.
>
> *Situation of registered office*: That the registered office of the company be moved from . . . to . . .[27]
>
> *To offer*: That an offer be made to Mr. —— on behalf of the company to, etc.
>
> *To accept offer*: That Mr. ——'s offer to supply the company with, etc., be hereby accepted, and that the Secretary do give Mr. —— notice of this resolution.

---

21 *Ibid.* at p. 207.

22 *Faure Electric, etc., Co.* v. *Phillipart* (1888) 58 L.T. 525.

23 *Re Scottish Petroleum* (1883) 23 Ch.D. 413; *Re Bank of Syria* [1900] 2 Ch. 272. In this case it was said in argument (at p. 274) that even if the directors are fewer in number than that required to constitute a quorum, they cannot act. The quorum in that case was to be fixed by the directors, but Wright J. held that no quorum was in fact proved to have been fixed. It is submitted that, as regards an outsider, the effect of a board resolution depends upon whether or not he had notice of any irregularity.

24 See para. 62–03, *ante*.

25 *Nell* v. *Longbottom* [1894] 1 Q.B. 767.

26 For further examples, see *Precedents*, Part 1 (17th ed., 1956), pp. 886 *et seq*.

27 The registered office may not be moved from England to Scotland or vice versa as its situation is fixed in the Memorandum (s. 2 (1) (*b*)).

To seal agreement: That the draft agreement with Messrs. —— for the sale of —— be and is hereby approved, and that such agreement be engrossed in duplicate and that the seal of the company be affixed thereto, and that one part of such agreement be handed over to Messrs. —— upon their executing the other part.

To make a call: That a final call of five shillings per share be made on the 200,000 Ordinary Shares of the company numbered 1 to 200,000 inclusive and that such call be payable on or before . . . to the company's bankers . . . at . . .

Forfeiture of shares: That 100 ordinary shares of £l each, 75p. paid up, numbered 1230 to 1329 inclusive, registered in the name of . . . be and the same are hereby forfeited for non-payment of the final call of 25p. per share.[28]

Appointment of committee of directors: That Messrs. —— and —— be and are hereby appointed a committee with power to arrange with Mr. —— the terms on which he shall supply, etc., and make a contract with him accordingly.

Appointment of managing director: That —— be appointed managing director of the company upon the terms of a draft agreement produced to the meeting and for identification signed by the chairman and that such agreement, when engrossed, be signed by a director on behalf of the company.

It is not, however, essential for the validity of a director's resolution that the determination should be embodied in a formal resolution, and the minutes in recording it often, in fact, enter only the substance, *e.g.* "a contract with A B for the supply of . . . was submitted and approved." It is, however, necessary to enter minutes of all directors' proceedings in a book kept for the purpose (s. 145 (1)).[29]

In order to carry a resolution in regard to external matters into effect, it is sometimes necessary to do some further act in the name of the company, *e.g.* where a resolution has been passed to borrow money, it will be necessary to apply to some person or persons to lend the same, or to issue a prospectus, and when a lender has been found and the security agreed on, the directors will pass a resolution approving the terms and directing the seal to be affixed and the contract to be signed by two directors on behalf of the company. Hence, a matter may come before the board several times before it is completed.

Committees of directors

62–06 The directors are not entitled to delegate their powers unless the articles so provide. It is, however, usual for the articles to authorise the directors to delegate their powers to committees, and under article 102 the directors have power to delegate any of their powers to committees; this, it is thought, enables them to delegate *all* their powers to one or more commit-

[28] For a fuller form, see para. 41–09, *ante*.
[29] See *Re Liverpool Household Stores* (1890) 59 L.J.Ch. 616, 619; see para. 57–02, *ante*.

tees, including even the power for the committee itself to delegate. In order to ascertain what powers a committee of directors has, it is thus necessary to examine two questions:

(a) What powers may, according to the articles, be delegated to committees, and upon what conditions; and
(b) What powers have, in fact, been delegated by the board, according to the resolution of the board meeting or other decision of the board?

Where the delegation is permitted by the articles, it will sometimes be presumed to have taken place.[30]

Any delegation of powers by the directors can be revoked by the board at any time, either expressly or by the directors as a board assuming the powers previously delegated, or some of them: such a reassumption of the powers will only be an *ad hoc* revocation unless the intention is that it should be permanent.[31]

The articles frequently provide that a committee of directors may consist of one member of the board (see art. 102). There is no legal objection to a committee consisting of one person only.[32]

Where the articles authorise the delegation of the powers of the board to committees of directors, they usually further provide regulations governing the proceedings of those committees. Unless there are such regulations (see, *e.g.* arts. 103 and 104), all acts of a committee must be done by the whole committee, and a majority cannot act in the absence of any member; but the members need not be unanimous.[33] Minutes of committees' meetings should be kept in the same manner as minutes of board meetings.

Managing directors

Appointment of managing director

62–07 In large companies the day-to-day management and decisions are normally left to one or more managing directors. A managing director as such has no specific powers or duties recognised by the law: what powers and duties he is to have must be derived from the company itself. It is common to find provisions in the articles authorising the appointment by the directors of one or more of their body as managing directors (see arts. 107–109), and in such cases the articles must be looked at to see the terms upon which such appointments may be made by the directors: subject thereto, the actual agreement made between the company and the managing directors has to be considered. Under art. 109 the directors may confer upon the managing director "any of the powers exercisable by them upon such terms

---

[30] *Totterdell* v. *Fareham Blue Brick, etc., Co.* (1866) L.R. 1 C.P. 674; *Lyster's Case* (1867) L.R. 4 Eq. 233; *Mahony* v. *East Holyford Mining Co.* (1875) L.R. 7 H.L. 869; *Dey* v. *Pullinger Engineering Co.* [1921] 1 K.B. 77.
[31] See *Huth* v. *Clarke* (1890) 25 Q.B.D. 391.
[32] *Re Fireproof Doors* [1916] 2 Ch. 142.
[33] *Re Liverpool Household Stores Association* (1890) 59 L.J.Ch. 616.

and conditions and with such restrictions as they may think fit, and either collaterally with or to the exclusion of their own powers and may from time to time revoke, withdraw, alter or vary all or any of such powers."

The directors cannot make an appointment other than in the terms which are permitted by the articles, *e.g.* directors of a company to which article 107 applies cannot appoint any person who is not himself a director, for their power is to appoint "one or more of their body"; nor can they exclude the termination of his appointment if the company were to remove him from his office of director under section 184.[34] Any purported appointment in excess of the powers given to the directors by the articles is of no avail to the person appointed, for he is considered to have constructive notice of the articles.[35]

Subject to the articles, the powers and duties of a managing director are defined by his contract with the company. The provisions of the Acts do not prevent the company from reserving the right to limit the functions of the managing director, and the scope of his appointment depends upon the terms of his contract with the company. In *Harold Holdsworth & Co. (Wakefield) Ltd.* v. *Caddies*,[36] the operative clause in the contract was:

> "Mr. Caddies shall be and he is hereby appointed a managing director of the company and as such managing director he shall perform the duties and exercise the powers in relation to the business of the company and the businesses (howsoever carried on) of its existing subsidiary companies at the date hereof which may from time to time be assigned to or vested in him by the board of directors of the company."

At first, Caddies acted as managing director of both the appellant company and its subsidiary, but later, in consequence of differences of opinion which had arisen between him and the other directors, the board of the appellant company resolved that he should confine his attention to the subsidiary company. In an action by Caddies against the appellant company for breach of contract the House of Lords (Lord Keith dissenting) held that neither the provisions of the Act nor the first part of the operative clause (whereby Caddies was appointed a managing director) prevented the company from limiting his activities to the subsidiary; weight was attributed by the learned judges to the use of the phrase "*a* managing director," instead of "*the* managing director," in the first part of the clause, and to the second part of it. Only Lord Keith held that, since the subsidiary had a different legal entity from the appellant company, the latter had, in fact, forced upon Caddies a new master and thereby broken its contract with him.

Remuneration of managing director

62–08 According to Table A the remuneration of the managing director is to be determined by the board of directors (art. 108). Remuneration for this

[34] See para. 61–27, *ante*, and para. 62–11, *post*.
[35] *Morris* v. *Kanssen* [1946] A.C. 459.
[36] [1955] 1 W.L.R. 352.

purpose includes salary, commission or participation in profits. Article 108 is independent of article 107, and applies whether the managing director is appointed by the articles or by the board under article 107.[37] It has been held that, in consequence, if the company goes into liquidation before his remuneration has been voted by the board of directors, the managing director is not entitled to any remuneration, nor can he claim on a *quantum meruit* if there was an express contract between himself and the company.[37] But if the contract by which he was appointed was invalid a claim on a *quantum meruit* will lie.[38]

Position of managing director

62–09 The position of a managing director was elaborately discussed in the light of English and Scottish decisions in *Anderson* v. *James Sutherland (Peterhead) Ltd.*,[39] where the question for decision was whether a managing director was employed by the company in any capacity.

In that case the managing director claimed that he was not employed by the company, but that his position was an office or function of a director, *i.e.* that he was an ordinary director entrusted with some special powers. It was argued that a series of cases[40] formed "a chain of authority warranting the general proposition that a managing director, apart from context, was not in the employment of the company." The Court of Session refused to accept this view. Each of the decisions was given in cases where the context, *i.e* the meaning of particular statutory or regulatory provisions or of terms of a contract, played a vital part in the conclusions arrived at, and in so far as anything general was said, as in *Dunston's* case[41] and *Hutton's* case,[42] it was with reference to persons in the position of "directors" and not "managing directors." In the cases of *Re Newspaper Syndicate*,[43] *Normandy* v. *Ind, Coope*[44] and *Re Lee, Behrens*,[45] where the position of managing directors was considered, the decisions turned on the special language of welfare clauses, pension or gratuity rights clauses, and the statutory provisions for preferences in bankruptcy. In the last kind of provision the benefit was for "clerks or servants," and a managing director was held not to be within the meaning of the statute.

Lord Carmont pointed out[46] that the proposition that

> ". . . a director can be regarded as having not only the *persona* of director but also the *persona* of employee is plain from the case of *Re*

---

37 *Re Richmond Gate Property Co. Ltd.* [1965] 1 W.L.R. 335.
38 *Craven-Ellis* v. *Cannons Ltd.* [1936] 2 K.B. 403; see para. 61–23, *ante*.
39 1941 S.C. 203. See also *Trussed Steel Concrete Co. Ltd.* v. *Green* [1946] 1 Ch. 115.
40 *Dunston* v. *Imperial Gas Light and Coke Co.* (1831) 3 B. & Ad. 125; *Hutton* v. *West Cork Ry.* (1883) 23 Ch.D. 654; *Re Newspaper Proprietary Syndicate* [1900] 2 Ch. 349; *Normandy* v. *Ind, Coope & Co.* [1908] 1 Ch. 84; *Re Lee, Behrens & Co.* [1932] 2 Ch. 46.
41 (1831) 3 B. & Ad. 125.
42 (1883) 23 Ch.D. 654.
43 [1900] 2 Ch. 349.
44 [1908] 1 Ch. 84.
45 [1932] 2 Ch. 46.
46 1941 S.C. 203, 213.

Beeton & Co.,[47] where a director who had been appointed 'dress editress' of one of the company's publications claimed preferentially for arrears of salary in a winding up and was found entitled to a preference as a 'clerk or servant'; in the case Neville J. said[48]: 'It has been argued with some force that *qua* director she certainly cannot be a servant of the company. Authority to that effect has been cited, and it is a conclusion which is fairly obvious. But it seems to me that in the present case the constitution of the company allows of the employment of directors for special purposes and the fact that she is a director does not prevent her also being a servant within the meaning of the Act.' "

Lord Carmont was fortified in these conclusions by the cases of *Southern Foundries (1926) Ltd.* v. *Shirlaw*[49] and *Fowler* v. *Commercial Timber Co.*[50] The only cases which offered any opposition to the court's view were *Kerr* v. *Walker*,[51] but in this case the various dicta were in conflict *inter se*, and *Re Lee, Behrens*.[52] The latter case (which had been criticised in *Kerr* v. *Walker*)[53] was strongly criticised by Lord Carmont on the ground that "Eve J. made a jump from a dictum as to a director to the position of a managing director which was not justified as an inference from the facts of *Hutton's* case[54] and the other decisions on which he relies." Lord Normand considered that *Re Lee, Behrens*[55] might have rested not upon general propositions but upon the construction of the terms of the articles.

Lord Normand summarised the view of the court as follows:

"In my opinion, therefore, the managing director has two functions and two capacities. *Qua* managing director he is a party to a contract with the company, and this contract is a contract of employment; more specifically I am of opinion that it is a contract of service and not a contract for services. There is nothing anomalous in this; indeed it is a commonplace of law that the same individual may have two or more capacities, each including special rights and duties in relation to the same thing or matter or in relation to the same persons."

It follows from this case that in modern company practice a managing director, in the great majority of cases, combines the position of director and of employee and that, as has been observed earlier, the validity of his appointment and the scope of his duties have to be gathered from the provisions of the articles and the terms of his contract with the company. The view that a director may be an employee of the company is further supported by cases such as *Lee* v. *Lee's Farming Ltd.*[56] and *Boulting* v. *Assn. of Cinematograph, etc., Technicians*.[57]

---

47 [1913] 2 Ch. 279.
48 At p. 285.
49 [1940] A.C. 701: see, in particular, the judgments of Lord Atkin and Lord Wright; see para. 62–12, *post*.
50 [1930] 3 K.B. 1.
51 1938 S.C. 458.
52 [1932] 2 Ch. 46.
53 1938 S.C. 458.
54 (1883) 23 Ch.D. 654.
55 [1932] 2 Ch. 46.
56 [1961] A.C. 12 (P.C.); see para. 18–06, *ante*.
57 [1963] 2 Q.B. 606.

62–10 However, in the case of a family company, if no express contract of service has been entered into, it may be difficult to persuade a court to deduce from the circumstances of the case that the managing or working director is an employee of the company. Here it may be important whether the company has treated the payments to the director as directors' fees rather than as salary for the purposes of section 196 of the 1948 Act and whether the company has complied with the provisions about directors' service contracts (*e.g.* section 26 of the 1967 Act), but the company's treatment of the relationship for the purpose of its own accounts cannot be conclusive.[58] In *Parsons* v. *Albert J. Parsons & Sons Ltd.*[59] the applicant in an unfair dismissal claim had been one of the three brothers who were directors of a family company, the applicant being also managing director of a subsidiary company. He was removed from these offices by the votes of his brothers. There was no express contract of service, remuneration was voted at the end of each year by resolution, and the accounts did not treat the brothers as employees. Although all three brothers worked full-time in the business, the Court of Appeal decided that the industrial tribunal had been entitled to find that the applicant was not an employee. Shaw L.J. said: "They [the industrial tribunal] saw as the reality of the matter that this was a family business and that the members of the family were utilising the companies concerned as agencies to carry on that business rather than the other way round." This decision may be contrasted with the decision in *Folami* v. *Nigerline (U.K.) Ltd.*[60] where the Employment Appeal Tribunal, in express reliance upon the discussion in para. 62–09, refused to consider remuneration paid to the full-time managing director of the United Kingdom subsidiary of a large Nigerian company as remuneration paid in respect of the directorship rather than the employment.

Termination of office. Compensation or damages for loss of office

62–11 There is no doubt that a managing director, like every other director, can be removed at any time from office by the general meeting, by virtue of section 184 of the 1948 Act,[61] whatever terms his contract contains on the length of his tenure of office.[62] But, as has been explained earlier,[63] the section preserves the right of a director to claim compensation or damages if such removal qualifies as a breach of contract, and further preserves the power of the company to terminate his appointment if such power exists

[58] *James* v. *Thomas H. Kent & Co. Ltd.* [1951] 1 K.B. 551. *Cf. Ferguson* v. *John Dawson Ltd.* [1976] 1 W.L.R. 1213.
[59] [1979] I.C.R. 271.
[60] [1978] I.C.R. 277.
[61] See para. 61–27, *ante*.
[62] But *cf.* the possibility of a director of a small private company replying to his removal from office and from participation in management with a petition for the winding up of the company on the "just and equitable" ground: see para. 61–31, *ante*.
[63] See para. 61–30, *ante*.

apart from the section, *i.e.* under the articles or the contract with him (1948 Act, s. 184 (6)).

The question whether the removal of a managing director constitutes a breach of his contract with the company entitling him to claim damages has been before the court from time to time. The position can be understood from a study of the following cases:

In *Nelson* v. *James Nelson & Sons Ltd.*[64] the articles empowered the directors to appoint one or more of their number to be managing director "for such period as they deem fit, and may revoke such appointment." The managing director, who had been appointed by an agreement which stated that he was appointed indefinitely subject to various conditions which were not material to the case, was removed by a board resolution. It was argued that by reason of the concluding words of the article referred to the power of the directors to appoint a managing director was subject to their right to revoke the appointment and that any other appointment would be unauthorised. It was held, however, that the power of the directors to make the appointment "for such period as they deem fit" was unfettered, and their right to revoke the appointment under the concluding words only existed if the contract specifically so provided; and it was clear from the terms of the service agreement that it did not so provide and was entirely inconsistent with such right of revocation. The plaintiff was accordingly entitled to damages. The court, thus, refused to imply from the articles a term as to revocation that was inconsistent with an express term of the contract of service.

Nelson's case should be contrasted with *Read* v. *Astoria Garage (Streatham) Ltd.*[65] where the directors were empowered to appoint a managing director "but his appointment shall be subject to determination *ipso facto* if he ceases for any cause to be a director or if the company in general meeting resolve that his tenure of office of managing director . . . be determined." The plaintiff was removed from office as managing director by a board resolution, and subsequently the company approved the board's action. The plaintiff claimed damages for wrongful dismissal without notice. The Court of Appeal held that where such an article applied, a managing director could not claim to have been wrongfully dismissed unless he could show that an agreement had been entered into between himself and the company, the terms of which were inconsistent with the exercise by the company of the power conferred by that article. In this case the resolution under which the plaintiff was appointed did not specify the conditions under which the contract could be terminated, although it did specify other terms of the contract, and so the plaintiff was taken to have contracted on the terms of the article.

62–12 Thirdly, in *Southern Foundries (1926) Ltd.* v. *Shirlaw*,[66] the managing director was appointed by the board under a service contract for a specified

[64] [1914] 2 K.B. 770 (C.A.).
[65] [1952] Ch. 637 (C.A.).
[66] [1940] A.C. 701.

period. The articles provided that the managing director "shall, subject to the provisions of any contract between him and the company, be subject to the same provisions as to . . . removal as the other directors of the company, and if he cease to hold the office of director, he shall *ipso facto* and immediately cease to be a managing director." Subsequently the company adopted new articles, including one empowering another company ("Federated"), which had acquired the shares of Southern, to remove by written instrument any director of Southern, and another providing that a managing director's appointment should terminate automatically if he ceased to be a director.[67] Federated exercised its power to remove the managing director from his office as director and Southern then treated him as no longer managing director. The House of Lords held by a majority (Lord Maugham and Lord Romer dissenting, as did the Master of the Rolls in the Court of Appeal below[68]) that the dismissal of the managing director pursuant to the new article was wrongful, and awarded him damages.

Shirlaw's case[69] thus establishes the principle that removal of a managing director from his office other than in accordance with the terms of the contract entered into pursuant to the articles then in force would be wrongful dismissal. The House reached this conclusion even though the express provision in the contract was inconsistent with the exercise of the power to remove contained in the subsequently adopted articles. The decision thus goes further than that in *Nelson* v. *James Nelson & Sons Ltd.*,[70] where the court seems to have interpreted the power in the articles to revoke a managing director's appointment as exercisable only when the board had not exercised its discretion to appoint for a specified or indefinite period.

62–13 This principle was followed in *Shindler* v. *Northern Raincoat Co. Ltd.*[71] The plaintiff in this case had sold his shares in the defendant company to another company under a contract of sale which provided that he should be appointed managing director of the defendant company for a period of 10 years. The shares were subsequently resold to a further company which did not wish to retain the services of the plaintiff, and accordingly caused the defendant company to pass a resolution removing the plaintiff from his office as director and terminating his service agreement. The articles of the defendant company included a provision in the same terms as that in *Read's* case.[72] Diplock J. held that the plaintiff was entitled to damages because, notwithstanding the provision in the articles, there was an implied term in the plaintiff's agreement that the defendant company would do

[67] This was art. 68 of the 1929 Table A.
[68] It will be seen that the dissenting judgments were all from Chancery judges.
[69] [1940] A.C. 701.
[70] [1914] 2 K.B. 770 (C.A.).
[71] [1960] 1 W.L.R. 1038.
[72] See note 67, *supra*.

nothing of its own motion to put an end to the state of circumstances which enabled the plaintiff to continue as managing director.

According to Diplock J.,[73] the distinction between this case and *Shirlaw's* case[74] on the one hand, and *Read's* case[75] on the other, is that in the former two cases an agreement had been entered into between the managing director and the company, the terms of which were inconsistent with the exercise of the company's power conferred upon it by the articles, whereas this feature was not present in *Read's* case.

Whether a company can restrict the activities of a managing director to the management of a subsidiary, or possibly to part of the company's business, without committing a breach of contract likewise depends on the terms of its contract with him.[76]

---

[73] At pp. 1046–1047.
[74] [1940] A.C. 701.
[75] [1952] Ch. 637.
[76] *Harold Holdsworth & Co. (Wakefield)* v. *Caddies* [1955] 1 W.L.R. 352; see para. 62–07, *ante*.

CHAPTER 63

GENERAL POSITION OF DIRECTORS VIS-A-VIS THE COMPANY DIRECTORS' DUTIES OF SKILL, CARE AND DILIGENCE

Introduction

63–01 The nature of the legal duties owed by directors to their company depends upon the legal analysis of the relationship between directors and company. The same may be said of the legal duties owed by directors to those dealing with the company. This chapter begins with a consideration of the legal nature of those two relationships. In this and the next chapter the legal duties owed by directors to the company are expounded, and in chapter 65 the duties owed to outsiders.

Directors as agents of company

Contracts on behalf of company

63–02 Directors are, in the eyes of the law, agents of the company for which they act, and the general principles of the law of principal and agent regulate in many respects the relationship of the company and its directors. This position has long been established and in *Ferguson* v. *Wilson*[1] Cairns L.J. said[2]:

> "What is the position of directors of a public company? They are merely agents of a company. The company itself cannot act in its own person, for it has no person; it can only act through directors, and the case is, as regards those directors, merely the ordinary case of principal and agent. Wherever an agent is liable those directors would be liable; where the liability would attach to the principal, and the principal only, the liability is the liability of the company."

Directors, in what sense trustees

Trustees as well as agents

63–03 Directors are not only agents but they are in some sense and to some extent trustees or in the position of trustees; but their position differs considerably from that of ordinary trustees, and the strict rules applicable to such trustees do not apply in all respects to directors.[3]

As early as in 1742, in *Charitable Corporation* v. *Sutton*,[4] Lord Hardwick L.C. held that committeemen or directors of a chartered corporation who had misapplied its funds and committed breaches of its by-laws were liable

---

[1] (1866) L.R. 2 Ch. 77.
[2] At p. 89.
[3] *Smith* v. *Anderson* (1880) 15 Ch.D. 247, 275.
[4] (1742) 2 Atk. 400.

as trustees for "breach of trust." In *York and North Midland Ry.* v. *Hudson*,[5] directors who had improperly dealt with funds of the company were held liable as "trustees." Romilly M.R. there said:

> "The directors are persons selected to manage the affairs of the company for the benefit of the shareholders. It is an office of trust which, if they undertake, it is their duty to perform fully and entirely. A resolution by shareholders therefore, that shares or any other species of property shall be at the disposal of directors, is a resolution that it shall be at the disposal of trustees; in other words, that the persons intrusted with that property shall dispose of it, within the scope of the functions delegated to them, in the manner best suited to benefit their cestuis que trust."

63–04 The dual character of directors is, perhaps, best expressed in Lord Selbourne's words in *G.E. Ry.* v. *Turner*[6] where he said:

> "The directors are the mere trustees or agents of the company—trustees of the company's money and property—agents in the transactions which they enter into on behalf of the company."

Sir George Jessel expressed himself similarly in *Re Forest of Dean, etc., Co.*[7]:

> ". . . directors are called trustees. They are no doubt trustees of assets which have come into their hands, or which are under their control. . . ."

Thus, in *Joint Stock Discount Co.* v. *Brown*,[8] where directors had misapplied funds of the company, it was declared that they had "committed a breach of trust and were jointly and separately liable" accordingly.[9] It was as being trustees that directors were held, before the Trustee Act 1888, disentitled to claim the benefit of the Statutes of Limitation[10]; and it is as trustees that they are entitled to the benefit of the qualified provisions for limitation of actions contained in section 21 of the Limitation Act 1980. This was decided in *Re Lands Allotment Co.*,[11] where Lindley L.J. said:

> "Although directors are not properly speaking trustees, yet they have always been considered and treated as trustees of money which comes to their hands or which is actually under their control, and ever since joint stock companies were invented directors have been held

[5] (1853) 16 Beav. 485; see also Lord Cairns L.C. in *Ferguson* v. *Wilson* (1866) L.R. 2 Ch. 77, 90.

[6] (1872) L.R. 8 Ch. 149, 152.

[7] (1878) 10 Ch.D. 450.

[8] (1869) L.R. 8 Eq. 376, 381.

[9] See also *Flitcroft's Case* (1882) 21 Ch.D. 519; *Re Anglo-French Co-operative Society, ex p. Pelly* (1882) 21 Ch.D. 492; *Re Faure Electric Co.* (1888) 40 Ch.D. 141; *Re Oxford Benefit Building and Investment Society* (1886) 35 Ch.D. 502; *Leeds Estate Building and Investment Company* v. *Shepherd* (1887) 36 Ch.D. 787; *Masonic and General Life Assurance Company* v. *Sharpe* [1892] 1 Ch. 154; *Selangor United Rubber Estates Ltd.* v. *Cradock (No. 3)* [1968] 1 W.L.R. 1555; *Karak Rubber Co. Ltd.* v. *Burden (No. 2)* [1972] 1 W.L.R. 602.

[10] See *Flitcroft's Case* (1882) 21 Ch.D. 519; also *Re Transplanters (Holding Company) Ltd.* [1958] 1 W.L.R. 822.

[11] [1894] 1 Ch. 616. See also *Tintin Exploration Syndicate* v. *Sandys* (1947) 177 L.T. 412. The Limitation Act 1980 does not apply to Scotland.

liable to make good moneys which they have misapplied upon the same footing as if they were trustees. . . ."

Since directors are not trustees in the legal sense, the provisions of the Trustee Act 1925, and, in particular, the relief provision of section 61, do not apply to them, and the Companies Act 1948 has to provide a similarly worded relief provision in section 448.[11a]

True position is that they are in a fiduciary relationship

63–05 For most purposes it is sufficient to say that directors occupy a fiduciary position and all the powers entrusted to them are only exercisable in this fiduciary capacity.

As agents they stand in a fiduciary relationship to the company as principal. The fiduciary relationship imposes upon directors duties of loyalty and good faith, which are akin to those imposed upon trustees properly so called. As agents directors are also under duties of care, diligence and skill, but these duties are very different from the duties to be cautious and not to take risks which are imposed upon many trustees proper. Finally, as agents of the company directors' relationships with third parties need to be considered. Directors' duties of care, diligence and skill are considered in this chapter, their fiduciary duties in the following chapter and their relationships with third parties in Chapter 65.

Directors' duties of care, diligence and skill

63–06 An agent who professes a trade or profession is required to display such care, diligence and skill as would a reasonably competent member of the trade or profession, but other agents are required to exercise only such skill as they possess and such care and diligence as would be displayed by a reasonable man in the circumstances. The tendency of the courts has been to assimilate the duties required of directors to those of a non-professional agent.

General principles

63–07 The general principles governing the duties of a director *vis-à-vis* the company were very fully considered by Romer J. in *Re City Equitable Fire Insurance Co.*,[12] where, after considering the earlier authorities, he said:

> "In order, therefore, to ascertain the duties that a person appointed to the board of an established company undertakes to perform, it is necessary to consider not only the nature of the company's business, but also the manner in which the work of the company is in fact distributed between the directors and the other officials of the company, provided always that this distribution is a reasonable one in the circumstances, and is not inconsistent with any express provisions of

---

[11a] The Trustee Act 1925 does not apply to Scotland but s. 448 does.
[12] [1925] Ch. 407, 427.

the articles of association. In discharging the duties of his position thus ascertained a director must, of course, act honestly, but he must also exercise some degree of both skill and diligence. To the question of what is the particular degree of skill and diligence required of him, the authorities do not, I think, give any very clear answer. It has been laid down that so long as a director acts honestly he cannot be made responsible in damages unless guilty of gross or culpable negligence in a business sense. But as pointed out by Neville J. in *Re Brazilian Rubber Plantations and Estates Ltd.*,[12a] one cannot say whether a man has been guilty of negligence, gross or otherwise, unless one can determine what is the extent of the duty which he is alleged to have neglected. For myself, I confess to feeling some difficulty in understanding the difference between negligence and gross negligence, except in so far as the expressions are used for the purpose of drawing a distinction between the duty that is owed in one case and the duty that is owed in another. . . .

"There are, in addition, one or two other general propositions that seem to be warranted by the reported cases: (1) A director need not exhibit in the performance of his duties a greater degree of skill than may reasonably be expected from a person of his knowledge and experience. A director of a life insurance company, for instance, does not guarantee that he has the skill of an actuary or of a physician. In the words of Lindley M.R.: 'If directors act within their powers, if they act with such care as is reasonably to be expected from them, having regard to their knowledge and experience, and if they act honestly for the benefit of the company they represent, they discharge both their equitable as well as their legal duty to the company.'[13] It is perhaps only another way of stating the same proposition to say that directors are not liable for mere errors of judgment. (2) A director is not bound to give continuous attention to the affairs of his company. His duties are of an intermittent nature to be performed at periodical board meetings; and at meetings of any committee of the board upon which he happens to be placed. He is not, however, bound to attend all such meetings, though he ought to attend whenever, in the circumstances, he is reasonably able to do so. (3) In respect of all duties that, having regard to the exigencies of business, and the articles of association, may properly be left to some other official, a director is, in the absence of grounds for suspicion, justified in trusting that official to perform such duties honestly."

The remarks of Romer J. in the *City Equitable Fire Insurance* case,[14] which are the *locus classicus* on the subject, may be considered under a series of headings.

63–08 1. DIRECTORS NOT EXPECTED TO BE EXPERTS UNLESS APPOINTED AS SUCH. A director is not expected to exercise skill which he does not possess. Thus, for example, a rubber-producing company may have a manager on its estate who is responsible for all the day-to-day work there, but who is responsible to the board of directors; the estate may be in Malaya and the

[12a] [1911] 1 Ch. 425.
[13] *Lagunas Nitrate Co.* v. *Lagunas Syndicate* [1899] 2 Ch. 392, 435.
[14] [1925] Ch. 407, 427.

board in England and the board, or at least certain members of it, may know little or nothing about the management of an estate. In *Re Brazilian Rubber Plantations & Estates Ltd.*[15] it was said:

> "A director's duty has been laid down as requiring him to act with such care as is reasonably to be expected from him, having regard to his knowledge and experience. He is, I think, not bound to bring any special qualifications to his office. He may undertake the management of a rubber company in complete ignorance of everything connected with rubber, without incurring responsibility for the mistakes which may result from such ignorance; while if he is acquainted with the rubber business he must give the company the advantage of his knowledge when transacting the company's business."

Similarly Romer J. said in *Re City Equitable Fire Insurance Co.*[16] that "a director of a life insurance company, for instance, does not guarantee that he has the skill of an actuary or of a physician."[17]

It is clear from these observations that the directors of a specific company are not required to be experts in the type of business which the company promotes unless they are appointed in view of their specialist qualifications. Many boards consist only partly of such experts and, for the rest, of persons who are specialists in business administration or in certain general aspects of business management such as legal, financial, accounting, banking or export trade practice. Upon these principles a director would be entitled to rely upon the advice of his fellow directors in matters in which they are, or should be, experts.

63–09 2. A DIRECTOR MUST EXERCISE REASONABLE CARE AND DILIGENCE BUT IS NOT LIABLE FOR ERRORS OF JUDGMENT. *Care and diligence of ordinary man.* The liability of a director where he takes no part in the company's business is dealt with below.[18] Where he does take part, he must, in the words of Neville J.,[19] display "reasonable care in its despatch. Such reasonable care must . . . be measured by the care an ordinary man might be expected to take in the same circumstances on his own behalf. He is clearly . . . not responsible for damages occasioned by errors of judgment." Lindley M.R. observed[20]:

> "If directors act within their powers, if they act with such care as is reasonably to be expected from them, having regard to their knowledge and experience, and if they act honestly for the benefit of the company they represent, they discharge both their equitable as well as their legal duty to the company."

---

[15] [1911] 1 Ch. 425, 437.
[16] [1925] Ch. 407.
[17] At p. 428.
[18] See para. 63–13.
[19] *Per* Neville J. in *Re Brazilian Rubber Plantations and Estates Ltd.* [1911] 1 Ch. 425, 437; see further *Turquand* v. *Marshall* (1869) 4 Ch.App. 376; *Overend, Gurney & Co.* v. *Gibb* (1872) L.R. 5 H.L. 480.
[20] *Lagunas Nitrate Co.* v. *Lagunas Syndicate* [1899] 2 Ch. 392, 435.

Similarly, Brett L.J. in discussing the ambit of the "misfeasance" section (now 1948 Act, s. 333) said:

> "A director must be guilty of such negligence as would make him liable in an action. Mere imprudence is not negligence: want of judgment is not. It must be such negligence as would make a man liable in point of law."

Opinions of outside experts. From this it follows that in appropriate circumstances a director may rely upon an opinion of an outsider. Where directors had a discretion to refuse to pass a transfer, they were not liable for a transfer after making reasonable inquiries as to the position of the transferee and after obtaining legal advice as to the validity of the transfer.[21] The obtaining of outside advice does not, of course, absolve the directors from the duty of exercising their judgment upon such advice. Where, for instance, they are given a discretion, they must, in fact, exercise that discretion themselves[22]; they would not necessarily be relieved of their responsibility if they obtained outside advice as to whether, in the circumstances, they would be justified in—as in the above case—passing the transfer in connection with which they are given a discretion.

The need for obtaining outside advice in appropriate circumstances was emphasised in *Sheffield and S. York Permanent Building Society* v. *Aizlewood.*[23] In that case there was cited in argument the case of *Fry* v. *Tapson*,[24] where trustees were liable for not having instructed a valuer of property who was independent of the mortgagor with whom they were dealing, but had relied upon their solicitor, who was not qualified to give such advice. It would seem that the same principles will apply to directors.

The position can, thus, be summarised as follows:

(1) directors are entitled to rely upon the advice of an independent outsider; and on some occasions they may be considered negligent if they proceed to a decision without first obtaining expert (*e.g.* legal) advice[25];
(2) such an outsider must appear to be qualified to give such advice; and
(3) upon receipt of such advice the directors must themselves exercise their judgment.

63–10 3. A DIRECTOR MAY REASONABLY RELY ON CO-DIRECTORS AND OFFICERS OF THE COMPANY. In determining a director's duties, consideration must be given to the nature of the company's business, and, provided that the work is distributed in a reasonable way, to the manner in which the work is distributed between the directors themselves and the other officials of the company. As Romer J. said in the passage above: "In respect of all duties

---

21 *Re Faure Electric Accumulator Co.* (1888) 40 Ch.D. 141.
22 *Ibid.*; and see *New Mashonaland, etc., Co.* [1892] 3 Ch. 577; *Leeds, etc., Co.* v. *Shepherd* (1887) 36 Ch.D. 787.
23 (1890) 44 Ch.D. 412, 458–459.
24 (1884) 28 Ch.D. 268.
25 *Re Duomatic Ltd.* [1969] 2 Ch. 365, 377.

that, having regard to the exigencies of business, and the articles of association, may properly be left to some other official, a director is, in the absence of grounds for suspicion, justified in trusting that official to perform such duties honestly." Upon this principle the case of *Dovey* v. *Cory*[26] was decided, in which a bank had sustained heavy losses by the issue of fraudulent balance sheets and the improper advance of money to customers of the bank. The frauds were the work of the manager and the chairman, and the question arose whether a co-director, though, in fact, innocent of any complicity, was liable to the company for negligence in not having discovered the frauds. The House of Lords in the result exonerated him from liability, on the ground that the directors may properly delegate to trusted subordinates the details of management. Lord Halsbury L.C. said[27]:

> "It is obvious if there is such a duty [of detecting frauds] it must render anything like an intelligent devolution of labour impossible . . . . I cannot think it can be expected of a director that he should be watching either the inferior officers of the bank or verifying the calculations of the auditor himself. The business of life could not go on if people could not trust those who are put into a position of trust for the express purpose of attending to details of management."

And Lord Davey added[28]:

> "I think the respondent [Cory] was bound to give his attention to and exercise his judgment as a man of business on the matters which were brought before the board at the meetings which he attended, and it is not proved that he did not do so. But I think he was entitled to rely upon the judgment, information, and advice of the chairman and general manager, as to whose integrity, skill, and competence he had no reason for suspicion."

In determining whether a director has been guilty of negligence, the court will take into account the character of the business, the number of the directors, the provisions of the articles, the ordinary course of management and practice of directors, the extent of their knowledge and experience, and, in short, all the special circumstances of the particular case.

In an early case, *Re Denham & Co.*,[29] a director was, upon this principle, not liable for the fraud of his co-directors for the issue to the shareholders of false and fraudulent reports and balance sheets, in circumstances where the books and accounts of the company had been kept and audited by duly appointed and responsible officers, and where the director had no ground for suspecting fraud: but the articles of the company concerned gave supreme control and all the powers of the directors to the chairman,

---

[26] [1901] A.C. 477. See also *Cargill* v. *Bower* (1878) 10 Ch.D. 502; *Huckerby* v. *Elliott* [1970] 1 All E.R. 189; and *Andrew Oliver & Son Ltd.* v. *Douglas* 1982 S.L.T. 222 (directors not liable to outsider in respect of inaccurate accounts prepared by competent employees and certified by a qualified accountant).

[27] At p. 485.

[28] At p. 492.

[29] (1883) 25 Ch.D. 752.

so that on a summons against one of the directors for misfeasance the court absolved the director although for some four years he had not attended a single meeting of the directors, "being misled as he says, by reason of the extraordinary powers conferred by the articles upon [the chairman]."

The reliance of a director upon his co-directors and the officers of the company should not be unquestioning.[30] Apart from the number of occasions on which directors in whom too much trust has been reposed have defrauded their companies, a director may also find himself liable for some positive action taken in reliance upon a co-director. For instance, a director who signs a cheque cannot claim that he did so as a mere ministerial act: if he neglects inquiry, trusting in his co-directors or one of the company's officers, he will be himself liable to the company if the cheque is not authorised by the board or if it is an improper payment.[31] A director will not, however, be liable if a cheque which has properly signed is used for a purpose for which it was not authorised: nor for not looking into the proposed payment when it has been properly authorised by the board or a duly constituted committee of the board.[32]

Application of general principle

63–11 A director who in practice has to apply the general principle stated above may find no small difficulty in drawing the line. At what point, he may wonder, is he insufficiently diligent if he and the majority of his co-directors put full reliance in, say, the chairman and managing director in connection with the valuation of stocks or the holding of securities, or some other matter in which it will be normal and convenient for those two persons to have day-to-day control? It is obviously impossible here to lay down hard and fast rules. To use the words of Lord Macnaghten in *Dovey* v. *Cory*[33]:

> "I do not think it desirable for any tribunal to do that which Parliament has abstained from doing—that is, to formulate precise rules for the guidance or embarrassment of business men in the conduct of business affairs. There never has been, and I think there never will be, much difficulty in dealing with any particular case on its own facts and circumstances; and, speaking for myself, I rather doubt the wisdom of attempting to do more."

63–12 To a certain extent the cases have established some specific rules arising out of the application of these general principles, but these rules are necessarily little more than guides to conduct, and must be treated as flexible to meet the circumstances of each case; and the overriding principle must be that the director must act honestly and reasonably. Indeed, the

---

[30] It was said in *Land Credit Company of Ireland* v. *Fermoy* (1869) L.R. 8 Eq. 7, 12, that it is a plea of guilty to say that funds of the company were confided to other directors and misapplied by them. That is an extreme view.

[31] *Joint Stock Discount Co.* v. *Brown* (1869) L.R. 8 Eq. 376, 381; *Coats* v. *Crossland* (1904) 20 T.L.R. 800; *Re City Equitable Fire Insurance Co.* [1925] Ch. 407.

[32] *Land Credit Company of Ireland* v. *Fermoy* (1870) L.R. 5 Ch. 763.

[33] [1901] A.C. 477, 488.

importance of these words is emphasised when the relief which the court has power to grant directors under section 448 of the 1948 Act is considered.[34] The following are the specific rules which can be deduced from the decisions of the courts:

(1) It is the duty of each director to see that the company's moneys are from time to time in a proper state of investment, except in so far as the company's articles of association may justify him in delegating that duty to others.[35]

(2) When presenting their annual report and balance sheet directors ought not to be satisfied as to the value of their company's assets merely by the assurances of their chairman nor with the expression of the belief of the auditor.

This point will arise in particular in two instances, first in relation to the company's stock in trade, and secondly in relation to its investments and fixed assets. As regards the latter directors should, if they are not personally skilled in valuing these items, insist on some independent valuation at appropriate intervals; *e.g.* real property may well not require to be revalued for a number of years, whereas the values of stock market or trade investments may require yearly review. At such time as the valuations are made the company's title should also be reported upon by a competent expert.

Stock in trade is a more difficult problem: it may happen that the managing director may be the only person competent to make a full valuation upon the relevant date, but at least the other directors can ensure that stock sheets are accurately compiled, and in accordance with modern accountancy practice, and that physical checks of certain items shown on the stock sheets are carried out by the auditors. The amount of checking that is required will be a question of degree in every case.

(3) A list of cheques to be authorised by the board (whether or not they have already been paid) should be presented at each board meeting showing the amounts and the name of the payee.

This practice, as opposed to an authorisation of cheques to an aggregate amount, will preclude the risk of the managing director obtaining the signature of different co-directors to cheques for the same purpose, as in *Re City Equitable Fire Insurance Co.*[36]

(4) The company's securities should be kept in a safe place.

63–13 4. NEGLIGENCE BY NON-ATTENDANCE AT BOARD MEETINGS. Diligence carries with it the necessity of giving a reasonable amount of attention to the company's affairs. The amount of attention to be given will depend largely

---

[34] See para. 64–33, *post*.
[35] *Per* Romer L.J. in *Re City Equitable Fire Insurance Co.* [1925] Ch. 407, 467.
[36] [1925] Ch. 407.

upon the extent to which devolution of duties has been organised, and upon the number of directors. In *Marquis of Bute's Case*,[37] *e.g.* where there were 50 "trustees" (*i.e.* persons in the position of directors) of a savings bank, a "trustee" who attended no meetings for a number of years was not liable for the misconduct of his "co-trustees."

In general, however, directors are bound, as Jessel M.R. observed[38]:

> " . . . to use reasonable diligence having regard to their position, though probably an ordinary director, who only attends at the board occasionally, cannot be expected to devote as much time and attention to the business as the sole managing partner of an ordinary partnership, but they are bound to use fair and reasonable diligence in the management of their company's affairs, and to act honestly."

Continuous non-attendance at meetings may render a director guilty of the breaches of trust which are committed by others,[39] but it is not necessary for a director to attend every board meeting unless the articles otherwise provide. In *Perry's Case*,[40] Bacon V.-C. said that a director "is not bound to attend every meeting of the directors. It is not part of the duty of a director to take part in every transaction which is considered at a board meeting." It is also thought that, even where a director has been shown to be negligent as a result of non-attendance at board meetings, it may nevertheless be very difficult to demonstrate that any particular loss has accrued to the company as a result of the non-attendance.[41]

The position can be summed up as follows: while the failure to attend board meetings with reasonable regularity is a breach of a director's duty, it depends on the surrounding circumstances and, like the "reasonable time" in the sale of goods,[42] is a question of fact what is to be understood by "reasonable regularity." Thus, in cases such as *Re Denham & Co.*,[43] where the entire control was exercised by a single person, or in *Marquis of Bute's Case*,[44] where the directors were very numerous, the court may find itself able to excuse a director who failed to attend board meetings fairly frequently, but such cases should be considered as exceptional, and other considerations govern a case where, *e.g.* the company has a board of eight directors and a director fails to attend. Speaking generally, the fewer the directors the greater the duty to attend.

The duty of a director is not, however, as strict as that of a trustee because, whereas a trustee is normally liable if he allows trust funds, or the control of such funds, to remain for an unreasonable period in the hands of his co-trustee or co-trustees and loss results therefrom, a director may,

---

37 [1892] 2 Ch. 100.
38 *Re Forest of Dean Co.* (1878) 10 Ch.D. 450, 452.
39 *Per* Lord Hardwicke in *Charitable Corporation* v. *Sutton* (1742) 2 Atk. 400, 405.
40 (1876) 34 L.T. 716.
41 *Barnes* v. *Andrews* (1924) 298 F.614.
42 See Sale of Goods Act 1979, s. 59.
43 (1883) 25 Ch.D. 752.
44 [1892] 2 Ch. 100.

upon the principle stated above,[45] rely upon co-directors or officers of the company, provided that such reliance is reasonable in all the circumstances.

63–14 *Non-feasance.* Since directors are bound to show due diligence, the non-performance of some act which it was their duty to perform may itself amount to a breach of duty. However, the burden of proving that the non-performance of any particular act is equivalent to negligence rests on those who allege such negligence,[46] for directors have a large discretion, and while acting honestly within it, cannot be charged with breach of duty. Thus, directors will not be held liable for breach of duty because, in the exercise of their discretion, they allow calls to remain unpaid,[47] or because they rely on subordinates doing their duty,[48] or do not sue for a debt of the company.[49] It may in some cases be the best policy for the company not to press for payment. Even if it is not, mere errors of judgment and imprudence on the part of directors do not constitute either negligence or breach of duty.[50] The burden of proof is reversed, however, in such cases as *Alexander* v. *Automatic Telephone Co.*,[51] where directors neglected to make calls upon shares which they held themselves.

Where a director was not present at the board meeting when a loan was authorised, and had no part in the making of it, he was under no liability in respect of it.[52] So, too, where an *ultra vires* act was decided at a board meeting, a director who was not present would not be liable thereon, but if he adopted it at a subsequent meeting he would become liable as if he had been an original party.[53] Similarly a director who authorised the issue of a prospectus was liable for a misrepresentation therein because he had authorised the other directors to issue that particular prospectus.[54] On the other hand, a person who had resigned his directorship was not held to be liable for statements in a report on which his name—to his knowledge—appeared, or for funds thereby misapplied.[55]

Directors with full-time service contracts

63–15 The principles discussed above[56] were developed by the courts largely in relation to non-executive directors. It is common today for a proportion of the members of the board of a public company to hold full-time service

---

[45] See para. 63–10, *ante*.
[46] *Re Liverpool Household Stores* (1890) 59 L.J.Ch. 616, 618.
[47] [1925] Ch. 407.
[48] *Dovey* v. *Cory* [1901] A.C. 477; see para. 63–10, *ante*.
[49] *Re Forest of Dean Coal Mining Co.* (1878) 10 Ch.D. 450.
[50] *Marzetti's Case* (1880) 28 W.R. 541.
[51] [1900] 2 Ch. 56.
[52] *Ramskill* v. *Edwards* (1885) 31 Ch.D. 100.
[53] *Re Lands Allotment Co.* [1894] 1 Ch. 616 (C.A.).
[54] *Peek* v. *Gurney* (1873) L.R. 6 H.L. 377, as explained in *Cargill* v. *Bower* (1878) 10 Ch.D. 502, 514.
[55] *Re National Bank of Wales Ltd.* [1899] 2 Ch. 629.
[56] Paras. 63–07 to 63–14.

agreements with the company. The service contract may impose obligations upon the director that go beyond his duties *qua* director. It would seem, for example, that a director with a full-time service contract is obliged by that contract to devote the whole of his working time to the company and that heading 4 above[57] does not apply to him in an unqualified way. Further, it has been said of skilled employees that: "The failure to afford the requisite skill which had been expressly or impliedly promised is a breach of a legal duty, and therefore misconduct."[58] It remains to be seen whether full-time managers will be treated by the courts as skilled employees

Consequences of breach of duty and relief

63–16 The remedies available in respect of breach of directors' duties of care, diligence and skill and the provisions as to relief from such liabilities are discussed below.[59]

[57] Para. 63–13.
[58] *Harmer* v. *Cornelius* (1858) 5 C.B. (N.S.) 236, 247 (*per* Willes J.) (scene painters). See also *Searle* v. *Ridley* (1873) 28 L.T. 411 (general superintendent of building works) and *Van Weyenbergh* v. *British Acetate Ltd.* (1930) 74 S.J. Pt. 1, p. 90 (chemist and works manager).
[59] Paras. 64–27 to 64–41.

CHAPTER 64

DIRECTORS' FIDUCIARY DUTIES

By whom are the duties owed?

64–01 By virtue of their fiduciary position[1] directors owe certain duties to their company and these fiduciary duties form the subject-matter of this chapter. Although supplemented at various points by provisions of the Companies Acts, these duties are largely the product of the courts of equity. The scope of the statutory provisions is determined in each case by the relevant statute, but the equitable principles apply not only to directors but also to officials of the company authorised to act on its behalf, in particular those acting in a managerial capacity.[2]

Relationship is with company

64–02 The fiduciary relationship of a director exists with the company: the director is not usually a trustee for individual shareholders.[3] Thus, a director may accept a shareholder's offer to sell shares in the company although he may have information which is not available to that other, and the contract cannot be upset even if the director knew of some fact which made the offer an attractive proposition. So in *Percival* v. *Wright*[4] a person who had approached a director and sold him shares in the company, afterwards, upon discovering that the director had known at the time of the contract that negotiations were on foot for the purchase by an outsider of all the shares in the company at a higher figure, could not impeach the contract. In his judgment Swinfen-Eady J. said "there is no question of unfair dealing in this case. The directors did not approach the shareholders with the view of obtaining their shares. The shareholders approached the directors and named the price at which they were desirous of selling."[5]

But relationship may also be with the shareholder

64–03 In certain circumstances, however, the directors may by their actions have placed themselves in a relationship with the shareholders by virtue of which they owe fiduciary duties to the shareholders as well as to the company. Thus, in *Allen* v. *Hyatt*[6] the directors had secured from the shareholders options to purchase their shares through representations that this was necessary in order to effect an amalgamation with another company. The directors exercised the options and resold the shares at a profit

[1] See above para. 63–05.
[2] *Canadian Aero Service* v. *O'Malley* (1973) 40 D.L.R. (3d.) 371, 381 (Canadian Supreme Court).
[3] *Percival* v. *Wright* [1902] 2 Ch. 421. But see para. 64–03, *post*.
[4] [1902] 2 Ch. 421.
[5] At pp. 426–7.
[6] (1914) 30 T.L.R. 444.

to the amalgamating company. In holding the directors liable to the shareholders to account for the profit made Viscount Haldane L.C. said that[7]:

> "The appellants appeared to have been under the impression that the directors of a company were entitled in all circumstances to act as though they owed no duty to individual shareholders. No doubt the duty of the directors was primarily one to the company itself. It might be that in circumstances such as those of *Percival* v. *Wright* they could deal at arm's length with a shareholder. But the facts in the present case were widely different from those in *Percival* v. *Wright*, and their Lordships thought that the directors must here be taken to have held themselves out to the individual shareholders as acting for them on the same footing as they were acting for the company itself, that was, as agents. . . ."

So also in *Briess* v. *Woolley*[8] the managing director of the company was held to have been appointed by the general meeting as agent for the shareholders to negotiate the sale of their shares, with the consequence that the shareholders became liable for the fraudulent misrepresentations made by their agent even though they had no knowledge of them.

The leading question is whether directors may owe fiduciary duties to the shareholders in situations where no agency relationship can be established. In the New Zealand case of *Coleman* v. *Myers*[9] the New Zealand Court of Appeal, although regarding *Percival* v. *Wright* as correctly decided on its facts, did not think that case was authority that a fiduciary relationship can never exist between directors and shareholders in the absence of agency. The Court found a fiduciary relationship in the case before it because of the family character of the company in question, the dominant positions of the defendant directors, the defendants' high degree of inside knowledge, and the methods they had used in implementing their scheme. English courts have held directors to be under a duty to act in good faith when giving shareholders advice whether to accept a take-over offer for their shares[10] or whether to sanction a scheme for the purchase of a large block of assets from another company.[11] In *Prudential Assurance Co. Ltd.* v. *Newman Industries Ltd. (No. 2)*[11] this duty was classified at first instance as arising in tort and as being "no more than a particular application, to directors who assume responsibility for giving advice to shareholders, of the general duty to act honestly and with due care."[12] In the Court of Appeal in this case it was emphasised that the damages available to the shareholder in such an action must be limited to the loss suffered personally by the shareholder and that the shareholder cannot "recover damages merely because the

---

[7] At p. 445.
[8] [1954] A.C. 333.
[9] [1977] 2 N.Z.L.R. 298.
[10] *Gething* v. *Kilner* [1972] 1 W.L.R. 337. *Cf. Goldex Mines Ltd.* v. *Revill* (1974) 54 D.L.R. (3d.) 672 (Ontario Court of Appeal).
[11] *Prudential Assurance Co. Ltd.* v. *Newman Industries Ltd. (No. 2)* [1980] 2 All E.R. 841.
[12] At p. 858. The statutory liabilities of directors arising out of insider trading activities are discussed in Chapter 68.

company in which he is interested has suffered damage."[12a] To allow any broader basis of assessment of damages might be to permit double recovery and, more importantly, would subvert the rule in *Foss* v. *Harbottle*[12b] and the principle that the company is a legal entity distinct from its shareholders.

Duty to act bona fide

The definition of the company

64–04 Directors are under a duty to act bona fide in the best interests of the company. Although directors' duties are owed primarily to, and are enforceable by, the company and not to individual shareholders,[13] the company is defined in equity usually by reference to the shareholders as a whole and not by reference to the company as an entity distinct from its members. In a celebrated instance counsel advised that "the expression 'the company' did not mean the sectional interest of some (it may be a majority) of the present members, but of present and future members of the company" and that, on the basis that the company was to continue as a going concern, the directors "should balance a long-term view against short-term interests of present members."[14] A similiar view was taken by Megarry J. in *Gaiman* v. *National Association for Mental Health*[15] when he said:

> "The interests of some particular section or sections of the company cannot be equated with those of the company, and I would accept the interests of both present and future members of the company, as a whole, as being a helpful expression of a human equivalent."

It may be that when the company is no longer solvent the interests of the company include the interests of its creditors.[16]

The interests of the employees

64–05 In the above formulations of the company's interests the interests of the employees are not recognised in their own right as an object of the directors' concerns. So long as the company is a going concern this omission probably has little impact upon company policy since any decision to further the interests of the employees is likely to benefit indirectly the shareholders by creating a more contented workforce.[17] This justification

12a [1982] 1 All E.R. 354, 356 (C.A.).
12b (1843) 2 Hare 461; see paras. 58–08 *et. seq., ante*.
13 See paras. 64–01 to 64–03, *ante*.
14 *Second Savoy Hotel Investigation*, Report of June 14, 1954, by Milner Holland, Q.C.
15 [1971] Ch. 317, 330.
16 *Walker* v. *Wimborne* (1976) 50 A.L.J.R. 446 (High Court of Australia). *Cf. Re Wincham Shipbuilding Boiler and Salt Co.* (1878) 9 Ch.D. 322.
17 *Cf.* the remarks of Bowen L.J. in *Hutton* v. *West Cork Railway Co.* (1883) 23 Ch.D. 654 (an *ultra vires* case) that "the law does not say that there are to be no cakes and ale, but there are to be no cakes and ale except such as are required for the benefit of the company."

is not available if the company is about to be wound up.[18] However, section 46 (1) of the Companies Act 1980 now provides that:

> "The matters to which the directors of the company are to have regard in the performance of their functions shall include the interests of the company's employees in general as well as the interests of its members."[19]

The section thus requires (and does not merely permit) directors to take into account the interests of the employees along with those of the members, but the directors are given no guidance as to how to strike a balance between these two sets of interests, if they conflict. The matter presumably rests within the business judgment of the directors. Section 46 (2) makes it clear that the duty in section 46 (1) is owed by the directors to the company (and not directly to the employees) and is enforceable in the same way as other fiduciary duties owed to a company by its directors.

The extent of the duty

64–06 The duty imposed upon directors to act bona fide in the interests of the company is a subjective one. As Lord Greene M.R. put it in *Re Smith & Fawcett Ltd.*[20] directors must act "bona fide in what they consider—not what a court may consider—is in the interests of the company." So long as the directors have correctly informed themselves as to how the company is defined in law, it is left to the directors in the exercise of their business judgment to decide how the interests of the company may best be promoted. The courts will interfere only if no reasonable director could possibly have concluded that a particular course of action was in the interests of the company.[21] However, directors may act in the interests of themselves or some third party and so fail to act in the interests of the company even though they act without any conscious dishonesty. Thus, in *Re W. & M. Roith Ltd.*[22] a director entered into a service contract with his company in order to provide a pension for his wife in the event of his death and without giving any consideration to the question of whether the contract was for the benefit of the company. The contract was held not to be binding on the company.

Whether entitled to consider interests of group

Where the company is a member of a group of companies, the question may arise whether a director must concern himself solely with the interests of his own company or whether he may take into account the benefit of the

---

[18] *Cf. Parke* v. *Daily News* [1962] Ch. 929.

[19] s. 74 of the 1980 Act makes a more limited amendment to the powers of the company (as opposed to those of the directors) to take account of the interests of the employees. See para. 9–21, *ante*.

[20] [1942] Ch. 304, 306.

[21] *Thompson* v. *J. Barke & Co. (Caterers) Ltd.* 1975 S.L.T. 67; *R.* v. *Sinclair* [1968] 1 W.L.R. 1246.

[22] [1967] 1 W.L.R. 432.

group as a whole. In *Charterbridge Corpn.* v. *Lloyds Bank Ltd.*[23] Pennycuick J. said, *obiter*, that a director must not be guided by the interests of the group as a whole if this might be detrimental to the interests of his own company, particularly if the company has separate creditors. If, however, the intended measure does not conflict with the interest of his company, it is not a breach of duty to his own company that he has taken into account the benefit of the group as a whole.

However, a director cannot be compelled to take into account the interests of the group of companies. Thus, in *Pergamon Press Ltd.* v. *Maxwell*[24] Pennycuick J. refused to grant an injunction to a company, which held 70 per cent. of the shares of its subsidiary, to compel a director of the subsidiary to exercise a discretionary power in the way desired by the parent. In this case the principle that fiduciary duties are owed to the company and not to individual (even majority) shareholders prevailed.

Powers of directors

Acts ultra vires the company and acts intra vires the company but outside the authority of the directors

64–07 The powers of the directors are limited in two ways: first, being agents of the company, the directors can do nothing which the company itself, their principal, cannot do under its memorandum of association, and any purported act by them which is *ultra vires* the company, will be void and of no effect, except to the extent that a transaction may be enforced by an outsider acting in good faith under section 9 (1) of the European Communities Act 1972.[25] Secondly, when acting within the powers of the company, the directors are limited to the powers which the company has delegated to them.[26] If they act outside their own powers but *intra vires* the company, the latter may ratify their acts in general meeting.[27] If, however, acts by directors in excess of their authority are not ratified by the company, they may be liable to those with whom they deal on the footing that they are taken to warrant their authority.[28] Moreover, an outsider acting in good faith may be able to fix the company itself with liability by reason of section 99 (1) of the European Communities Act 1972, notwithstanding constitutional limitations on the authority of the directors.[29] Further

---

23 [1970] Ch. 62.
24 [1970] 1 W.L.R. 1167.
25 See para. 9–25, *ante*.
26 See para. 28–05, *ante*.
27 *Grant* v. *United Kingdom Switchback Ry.* (1888) 40 Ch.D. 135; *Bamford* v. *Bamford* [1970] Ch. 212 (C.A.).
28 *Collen* v. *Wright* (1857) 8 El. & Bl. 647; *Weeks* v. *Property* (1873) L.R. 8 C.P. 427; *Chapleo* v. *Brunswick, etc., Society* (1881) 6 Q.B.D. 696, 715; *Firbank's Executors* v. *Humphreys* (1886) 18 Q.B.D. 54; *Oliver* v. *Bank of England* [1902] 1 Ch. 610, affirmed *sub nom. Starkey* v. *Bank of England* [1903] A.C. 114; see also *Hely-Hutchinson* v. *Brayhead Ltd.* [1968] 1 Q.B. 549 (C.A.).
29 On the meaning of "good faith" in s. 9 (1) of the European Communities Act 1972, see para. 9–25, *ante*.

directors who act in excess of the powers of the company or of the powers conferred upon them are in breach of their duties to the company.

Power given to directors by articles

64–08 The powers delegated to the directors are set out in the company's articles of association. These normally contain a general clause on the lines of article 80 which provides, *inter alia*, that the directors may exercise all the powers of the company not by the articles or by statute required to be exercised by the company in general meeting.

It was at one time common to specify certain powers, but if such a general power is inserted, the insertion of particular specified powers is unnecessary and sometimes gives rise to a doubt in respect of powers not particularly specified. A general vesting of powers in the directors is valid and effective, and all that has to be done, in considering whether any particular transaction is within the powers conferred by such a clause on the directors, is to search the articles and the Acts to see whether there is any express provision requiring, for that transaction, the authority of the company in general meeting, and, if there is no such provision, the directors must be treated as competent to carry out the transaction. "The articles," said Mellish L.J. in *Re Patent File Co.*,[30] "give to the directors the whole powers of the company, subject to the provisions [of the articles and] of the Companies Act . . . and I cannot find anything either in the Act or in the articles to prohibit their making a mortgage by deposit." So, in *Re Anglo-Danubian, etc., Co.*,[31] where the question arose whether directors had power to issue debentures at a discount, Jessel M.R. said: "Looking to the sixty-sixth clause, I cannot have any possible doubt. The directors can do anything the company can do."[32]

The general clause in the articles vesting the management of the company in the directors is of great practical importance: it means that the directors have full powers of management, and are only subject to control by the shareholders in manner laid down by statute and articles. It further means that the shareholders cannot, by ordinary resolution of the general meeting, exercise a power given to the directors by the articles or overrule the directors when exercising such a power. Thus, where the articles contained a clause similar to article 80, a resolution of the company in general meeting for payment of preference dividends in advance by instalments was held to be invalid as interfering with the management, which had been delegated by the articles to the directors.[33] The shareholders are, of course, at liberty by special resolution altering the articles to vest in the

[30] (1870) L.R. 6 Ch. 83, 88.
[31] (1875) L.R. 20 Eq. 339.
[32] See also *Re Pyle Works (No. 2)* [1891] 1 Ch. 173; *Hampson* v. *Price's Patent Candle Co.* (1876) 45 L.J.Ch. 437; *Re a Debtor* [1917] 2 K.B. 808 (authorising presentation of a bankruptcy petition).
[33] *Scott* v. *Scott* [1943] 1 All E.R. 582.

general meeting a power given to the directors, and then to exercise such power.[34] Further, the shareholders have always the statutory power—which gives them ultimate control over the management—of removing a director at any time by ordinary resolution requiring special notice (s. 184),[35] and, if the conditions of section 75 of the 1980 Act are satisfied, to petition for the alternative remedy.[36]

Duty to act for a proper purpose

64–09 Where directors have a discretion and are, bona fide, acting in the exercise of it, the course will not interfere with their acts unless the particular purpose for which the discretion is being exercised is not one of the purposes for which it was conferred. In several cases the court has considered the directors' powers to issue shares, and it has been held that "directors are not entitled to use their power of issuing shares merely for the purpose of maintaining their control or the control of themselves and their friends over the affairs of the company, or merely for the purpose of defeating the wishes of the existing majority of shareholders."[37] The matter was again considered in *Hogg* v. *Cramphorn*,[38] where, in the face of an unwelcome take-over bid, the directors issued 5,707 preference shares to a trust newly established for the benefit of the company's employees, the trustees being provided by the company with an interest-free loan in order to be able to subscribe to the shares. The votes attached to the shares coupled with those of the directors and their friends were sufficient to constitute a majority of the general meeting, and the bid was defeated. A shareholder of the company challenged the validity of the allotment. Buckley J., in holding that the directors had acted for an improper purpose, made it clear that the requirement to act for a proper purpose was distinct from the requirement that directors act bona fide:

> "Accepting, as I do, that the board acted in good faith and that they believed that the establishment of the trust would benefit the company and that avoidance of the acquisition of control by Mr. Baxter would also benefit the company, I must still remember that an essential element of the scheme, and indeed its primary purpose, was to ensure control of the company by the directors. . . . Was such a manipulation of the voting position a legitimate act on the part of the directors? . . . It is not, in my judgment, open to the directors in such a case to say, 'We genuinely believe that what we seek to prevent the majority from doing will harm the company and, therefore our act in arming ourselves or our party with sufficient shares to outvote the majority is a conscientious exercise of our powers under the articles, which should not be interfered with.' Such a belief, even if well founded, would be irrelevant. A majority of shareholders in general meeting is entitled to

[34] *Cf. Greenhalgh* v. *Arderne Cinemas Ltd.* [1951] Ch. 286.
[35] See para. 61–27, *ante*.
[36] See para. 60–08, *ante*.
[37] *Piercy* v. *S. Mills & Co. Ltd.* [1920] 1 Ch. 77, 84; *Fraser* v. *Whalley* (1864) 2 H. & M. 10; *Punt* v. *Symons & Co.* [1903] 2 Ch. 506.
[38] [1967] Ch. 254.

pursue what course it chooses within the company's powers, however wrong-headed it may appear to others, provided the majority do not unfairly oppress other members of the company. These considerations lead me to the conclusion that the issue of the 5,707 shares with the special voting rights which the directors purported to attach to them could not be justified by the view that the directors genuinely believed that it would benefit the company if they could command a majority of the votes in general meetings."[39]

The definition of improper purposes

64–10 A similar situation was considered by the Privy Council in *Howard Smith Ltd.* v. *Ampol Petroleum Ltd.*,[40] where the directors of a company (Millers) issued 4,500,000 shares to the appellant company, which was intending to make a take-over bid for the company, in order to defeat the existing majority position in the company held by the respondent company and another, which had rejected the appellant's offer and which themselves intended to bid for the company. The trial judge found that the allotment had not been made by the Millers' directors for any reason of self interest. The articles of Millers permitted the directors to issue authorised but unissued shares "to such persons on such terms and conditions and with such . . . rights or such restrictions . . . and either at a premium or otherwise and at such time or times as the Directors may think fit. . . ." The court rejected the contention that the allotment was valid simply because the directors had acted bona fide and held that it must be set aside as resulting from the exercise by the directors of their powers under the articles for an improper purpose. The relationship between the wording of articles of the company and the impropriety of the purpose of the exercise of the power was explained in the following manner.

"The constitution of a limited company normally provides for directors, with powers of management, and shareholders, with defined voting powers having power to appoint the directors, and to take, in general meeting, by majority vote, decisions on matters not reserved for management. Just as it is established that directors, within their management powers, may take decisions against the wishes of the majority shareholders, and indeed that the majority of shareholders cannot control them in the exercise of these powers while they remain in office (*Automatic Self Cleansing Filter Syndicate Co. Ltd.* v. *Cunninghame*),[41] so it must be unconstitutional for directors to use their fiduciary powers over the shares in the company purely for the purpose of destroying an existing majority, or creating a new majority

[39] [1967] Ch. 254, 266–268. The view that the requirement of a proper purpose is distinct from that of bona fides has been rejected in certain Commonwealth jurisdictions. See *Teck Corporation Ltd.* v. *Millar* (1973) 33 D.L.R. 3d. 288 (British Columbia Supreme Court). The decision of Buckley J. confirms, however, the view taken by Milner Holland Q.C. in the *Second Savoy Hotel Investigation*, Report of June 14, 1954 (HMSO).

[40] [1974] A.C. 821. In Great Britain the issue may arise less frequently in future in relation to the issuance of shares in view of the provisions of the Companies Act 1980, s. 14 (authority of company required for allotment of certain securities by directors) and s. 17 (pre-emption rights). See paras. 24–01 ff., *ante*.

[41] [1906] 2 Ch. 34 and see para. 64–08, *ante*.

> which did not previously exist. To do so is to interfere with that element of the company's constitution which is separate from and set against their powers."[42]

It thus appears that even broadly worded particular articles conferring powers upon the directors must be construed in the context of the articles as a whole in order to establish whether any limitation should be read into the article conferring an apparently unlimited power.[43] It may be that on a proper construction of the articles no such limitation should be implied, as with a power to refuse to register a transfer of shares in a quasi-partnership company, where it has been held proper for the directors to consider the fact that "the transferee would obtain too great a weight in the councils of the company or might even perhaps obtain control."[44] It has also been held proper for the council of management of a non-profit making company formed to promote certain views to exercise a power to require the resignation of certain members of the association who held antithetical views and who were about to make a bid to secure control of it.[45]

64–11 The object of the court in construing the articles is to determine whether the particular purpose for which the power was exercised in the case before it was an improper one. It is not the right approach to seek to define a single proper purpose for which the power may be exercised and so to conclude that all other purposes are improper, because a power may be legitimately exercisable for any one of a range of purposes. Thus, in *Howard Smith Ltd.* v. *Ampol Petroleum Ltd.* the court concluded that it is "too narrow an approach to say that the only valid purpose for which shares may be issued is to raise capital for the company." The correct approach was described as follows:

> "In their Lordships' opinion it is necessary to start with a consideration of the power whose exercise is in question, in this case a power to issue shares. Having ascertained, on a fair view, the nature of this power, and having defined as can best be done in the light of modern conditions the, or some, limits within which it may be exercised, it is then necessary for the court, if a particular exercise of it is challenged, to examine the substantial purpose for which it was exercised, and to reach a conclusion whether that purpose was proper or not. In doing so it will necessarily give credit to the bona fide opinion of the directors, if such is found to exist, and will respect their judgment as to matters of management; having done this, the ultimate conclusion has to be as to the side of the fairly broad line on which the case falls."[46]

Mixed purposes

It may be that the directors act for more than one purpose and that some of the purpose for which they have acted are proper and others are

---

[42] [1974] A.C. 821, 837.
[43] If the purpose of the directors is unlawful or contrary to public policy their decision will be ineffective for that reason: *Pharmaceutical Society* v. *Dickson* [1970] A.C. 403.
[44] *Re Smith & Fawcett Ltd.* [1942] Ch. 304, 308.
[45] *Gaiman* v. *National Association for Mental Health* [1971] Ch. 317.
[46] [1974] A.C. 821, 835.

improper. In various Commonwealth jurisdictions it has been held that the power was validly exercised if the primary purpose for which it was exercised was a proper one.[47] The quotation from the Privy Council in the *Howard Smith* case, reproduced in the previous paragraph, suggests by its reference to the "substantial purpose for which it was exercised" a similar approach. In *McCanie (London) Ltd.* v. *Cook & Watts Ltd.*[48] it was held that if the primary purpose for which the power was exercised was improper, then a subsidiary proper purpose would not save the directors' decision.

Approval by the general meeting

64–12 In *Hogg* v. *Cramphorn* the judge at the conclusion of his judgment stood the action over for a specified period to enable the directors, if they so wished, to convene a general meeting which would be asked whether it desired to ratify the directors' allotment. The transactions of the directors were in fact ratified[49] and the judge made no order in the case. In *Bamford* v. *Bamford*[50] the Court of Appeal held that the issuance of shares by the directors for an improper purpose could be ratified by the general meeting by ordinary resolution and that a special resolution was not needed to this end. The act of the directors was not an act outside the articles but an act within the articles but in breach of the fiduciary duties laid upon them, and like other breaches of the fiduciary duties their act was ratifiable by ordinary resolution. Thus, although the process of establishing whether there are any restrictions upon the purposes for which the powers of the directors may be exercised involves construing the articles of the company,[51] actions by the directors for an improper purpose do not constitute breaches of the articles but rather abuses by the directors of their powers under the articles.

Conflict of duty and interest

64–13 Like other fiduciaries directors are required not to put themselves in a position where there is a conflict (actual or potential) between their personal interests and their duties to the company. This principle may be applicable in a number of different situations.

Contracts with the company

It has been seen earlier[52] that the position of a director, *vis-à-vis* the company, is that of an agent who may not himself contract with his

---

[47] *Mills* v. *Mills* (1937–8) 60 C.L.R. 150 (High Court of Australia); *Harlowe's Nominees Pty. Ltd.* v. *Woodside (Lake Entrance) Oil Co.* (1968) 121 C.L.R. 483 (High Court of Australia).

[48] (1967) C.L.Y. 482.

[49] [1967] Ch. 254, 272. Counsel for the defendants undertook that the trustees would not vote their 5,707 shares.

[50] [1970] Ch. 212. See also *Winthrop Investments Ltd.* v. *Winns Ltd.* [1975] 2 N.S.W.L.R. 666 (New South Wales Court of Appeal).

[51] See para. 64–10, *ante*.

[52] See para. 63–02, *ante*.

principal, and that it further is similar to that of a trustee who, however fair a proposal may be, is not allowed to let the position arise where his interest and that of the trust may conflict.[53]

It follows from these propositions that a director's powers of contracting with his company are extremely limited. He may take up shares or debentures,[54] including convertible debentures,[55] of the company (though he cannot vote in respect of allotments to himself[56]), and he may buy the right to subscribe for shares or debentures, although he is prohibited from buying options in quoted shares or debentures.[57] In other respects he is, like a trustee, disqualified from contracting with the company[58] and for a good reason: the company is entitled to the collective wisdom of its directors, and if any director is interested in a contract, his interest may conflict with his duty, and the law always strives to prevent such a conflict from arising.[59] The director may enter into a contract only if he makes full disclosure of all material facts to the members of the company, who then approve the contract. Not even if it can be shown that the contract in question is a fair one is the director allowed to enter into it, for the courts will not, in such cases, look into the merits, but adhere strictly to the rule that the possible conflict of interest and duty must not be allowed to arise.[60] "No man," said Lord Cairns L.C., "can in this court, acting as an agent, be allowed to put himself in a position in which his interest and duty will be in conflict."[61]

If, for example, the directors agree to sell to one of themselves part of the property of the company, the company is entitled to have the sale set aside, or, at its option, to sue the directors for breach of duty. So, too, if a director, concealing his interest, sells, through a third party, his property to the company, the company is entitled to reject the property and claim repayment of the purchase money,[62] or to retain the property and claim damages for any loss sustained by the non-disclosure.[63] The same rule applies to contracts in which the director is in any way interested, for example, with any company in which a director holds shares.[64] This rule

---

[53] *Aberdeen Ry.* v. *Blaikie* (1854) 1 Macq. 461; *Re Transplanters (Holding Company) Ltd.* [1958] 1 W.L.R. 822.

[54] *Campbell's Case* (1876) 4 Ch.D. 470; *Re London and Colonial Fin. Corp.* (1897) 77 L.T. 146 (C.A.).

[55] 1967 Act, s. 25 (4).

[56] *Neal* v. *Quinn* [1916] W.N. 223.

[57] 1967 Act, s. 25; see para. 68–15, *post*.

[58] *Albion, etc., Co.* v. *Martin* (1875) 1 Ch.D. 580.

[59] *Imperial Mercantile Credit Association* v. *Coleman* (1871) 6 Ch.App. 558; and see *Costa Rica Ry.* v. *Forwood* [1901] 1 Ch. 746.

[60] *Aberdeen Ry.* v. *Blaikie* (1854) 1 Macq. 461; *Parker* v. *McKenna* (1874) 10 Ch.App. 96, 118; *Bray* v. *Ford* [1896] A.C. 44, 50.

[61] *Parker* v. *McKenna, supra*; see also *Bray* v. *Ford, supra*.

[62] *Re Cape Breton Co.* (1885) 29 Ch.D. 795; *Chesterfield and Boythorpe Colliery* v. *Black* (1877) 26 W.R. 207.

[63] *Re Leeds and Hanley, etc., Co.* [1902] 2 Ch. 809.

[64] *Transvaal Lands Co.* v. *New Belgium, etc., Co.* [1914] 2 Ch. 488. See also *Victors Ltd.* v. *Lingard* [1927] 2 Ch. 323 (contract between company and bank relieved directors of liability under a personal guarantee).

applies whether the shares are held in trust or beneficially. The shareholders can, by resolution of a general meeting, confirm a contract in which the directors or some of them are interested,[65] and upon such a resolution the director is entitled to vote his shares in whatever way he chooses, even if the result will be to assure the passing of the resolution.[66] Such a resolution would not, however, be effective if it amounted to a fraud or oppression of the minority of shareholders.[67]

Relaxation of the above rules

64–14 These are the ordinary equitable rules applicable to transactions in which the directors may have an interest, but a company is at liberty to waive the benefit of such rules and to allow a director to make a contract, or to be interested in a contract, with the company, and modern articles very commonly make some provision accordingly.[68]

A limited relaxation of the strict rules is normally essential in a company. Without them, *e.g.* if a company wished to start a scheme for providing pensions for ex-employees and ex-officers, no director would be able to vote thereon because he may himself be a beneficiary prospectively under the scheme. Similarly it may be impossible to find a completely disinterested quorum if directors are exercising the company's votes in a subsidiary for the appointment of directors of the subsidiary.

At common law the company is at liberty to waive completely the rules protecting it as principal in dealings in which directors have an interest. Such a complete waiver would not be in the interest of the shareholders, and for that reason section 199 of the 1948 Act, which applies to all types of companies and cannot be abrogated by the articles, requires that a director has to disclose to the board of directors any interest, direct or indirect, which he might have in a contract or proposed contract with the company. This statutory minimum requirement, which will be considered in detail later,[69] is now invariably embodied in the articles. Thus, article 84 (1) provides:

> "A director who is in any way, whether directly or indirectly, interested in a contract or proposed contract with the company shall declare the nature of his interest at a meeting of the directors in accordance with section 199 of the Act."

---

[65] *Grant* v. *United Switchback Ry.* (1888) 40 Ch.D. 135; *Kaye* v. *Croydon Tramways Co.* [1898] 1 Ch. 358; *Imperial Mercantile Credit Association* v. *Coleman* (1873) L.R. 6 H.L. 189; *Costa Rica Ry.* v. *Forwood* [1901] 1 Ch. 746 (C.A.); *Bamford* v. *Bamford* [1970] Ch. 212, 238, *per* Harman L.J.

[66] *North West Transportation Co. Ltd.* v. *Beatty* (1887) 12 App.Cas. 589. *Cf. Prudential Assurance Co. Ltd.* v. *Newman Industries Ltd. (No. 2)* [1980] 2 All E.R. 841 (Vinelott J.).

[67] *Cook* v. *Deeks* [1916] 1 A.C. 554; *Menier* v. *Hooper's Telegraph Works* (1874) L.R. 9. Ch. 350.

[68] The company cannot, however, authorise dealing in options prohibited by s. 25 of the 1967 Act.

[69] See para. 64–16, *post*.

Such disclosure puts the other directors on notice to scrutinise the terms of the contract, knowing the interest of one of their body.[70]

The rest of article 84 deals with two separate, but related, questions. Is a director entitled to vote, and be counted in the quorum for a decision, on a contract in which he is interested and, secondly, is a contract in which a director is interested liable to be avoided and is such a director liable to account to the company for any profit made from such a contract? Article 84 (2) lays down a basic principle that a director who is directly or indirectly interested in a contract or arrangement shall not vote or be counted in the quorum, but it then continues to lay down four categories of case where the basic principle is not to apply. These categories are wide and include "any contract or arrangement with any other company in which [the director] is interested only as an officer of the company or as holder of shares or other securities."[71] In *Prudential Assurance Co. Ltd.* v. *Newman Industries Ltd. (No. 2)*[72] this exception was criticised by Vinelott J. at first instance as "far too wide." Article 84 (4) also provides that a director may be counted in the quorum for a meeting at which service contracts between the company and its directors are considered and that he may vote on any service contract other than his own. In a private company with only a few shareholders it is usually essential that the articles should be even freer than this, and in such companies directors are normally given complete freedom to be counted in the quorum of any board meeting at which a contract in which they are interested is to be considered.[73]

64–15 If article 84 (2) and (4) lay down extensive qualifications to the basic rule that an interested director may not vote on or be counted in the quorum for relevant decisions, article 84 (3) comprehensively excludes the equitable principle as to the voidability of contracts and accounting of profits.[74]

> "A director may hold any other office or place of profit under the company (other than the office of auditor) in conjunction with his office of director for such period and on such terms (as to remuneration and otherwise) as the directors may determine and no director or intending director shall be disqualified by his office from contracting with the company either with regard to his tenure of any such other office or place of profit or as vendor, purchaser or otherwise, nor shall any such contract, or any contract or arrangement entered into by or on behalf of the company in which any director is in any way interested, be liable to be avoided, nor shall any director so contracting or being so interested be liable to account to the company for any

---

[70] *Imperial, etc., Association* v. *Coleman* (1873) L.R. 6 H.L. 189; *Southall* v. *British Mutual, etc.* (1871) 6 Ch.App. 614, 619; *Adamson's Case* (1874) L.R. 18 Eq. 670; *Costa Rica Ry.* v. *Forwood* [1901] 1 Ch. 746; and see *Wilson* v. *L.M.S. Ry.* [1940] Ch. 393 (director of a company with which the railway company contracts).

[71] Art. 84 (2) (*d*).

[72] [1980] 2 All E.R. 841, 880.

[73] In respect of companies listed on the Stock Exchange a director is required not to vote on any contract or arrangement in which he has a material interest "subject to such exceptions specified in the articles of association as the Committee [on Quotations] may approve." *Admission of Securities to Listing*, Sched. VII, Pt. A., para. D.2.

[74] See also art. 78.

profit realised by any such contract or arrangement by reason of such director holding that office or of the fiduciary relation thereby established."

The compatibility of this wide exclusion with section 205 of the 1948 Act is considered in para. 64–26. Here it is proposed to consider its relationship with section 199 of the 1948 Act.

Interests to be declared under section 199

64–16 Section 199 (as amended by the 1980 Act, ss. 60, 63 (3), 88 and Sched. 3, para. 25) requires directors of all companies, public and private, and those in accordance with whose directions or instructions the directors of a company are accustomed to act[75] ("shadow directors": s. 63 (3)) to disclose to the board of directors any interest, direct or indirect, which they may have in a contract, proposed contract, transaction or arrangement with the company. This minimum requirement cannot be abrogated by the articles. Unlike the basic equitable principle section 199 requires disclosure only to the board and not to the general meeting. Section 199 (2) and section 63 (3) of the 1980 Act specify the meeting of the board to which disclosure must be made. It has not yet been decided whether the wording of section 199 (2) implies that the duty to disclose the director's interest applies only in relation to contracts, etc., which come before the board.[76]

The director must disclose interests whether they are direct or indirect (s. 199 (1)). The situations in which a director may be said to be interested are not further specified, except that section 60 (2) of the 1980 Act provides that a director is to be interested in certain transactions or arrangements made by a company for a director of the company or a person connected with[77] the director. Where, however, a director is interested, section 199 (1) requires a director to disclose, not merely that he is interested, but the "nature of his interest."[78] However, section 199 (3) (as amended) provides that a director may give a general notice to the effect that he is a member of a specified company or firm and is to be regarded as interested in contracts, etc., made with the company or firm, or that he is interested in any contract, etc., which may be made with a specified person who is connected with him. In either case such a general notice is deemed to be a sufficient declaration of interest in respect of such contracts, provided that it is either given at a meeting of the directors or the director takes reasonable steps to ensure that it is brought up and read at the next meeting of the directors after it is given.

It seems that compliance with section 199 only relieves the director of

---

[75] Other than professional advisers.

[76] The Jenkins Committee thought s. 199 was so restricted but recommended that the law be changed: *Report of the Company Law Committee*, Cmnd. 1749 (1962), para. 99(L).

[77] See para. 64–18, *post*.

[78] *Cf. Imperial Mercantile Credit Association* v. *Coleman* (1873) L.R. 6 H.L. 189, *Gray* v. *New Augarita Porcupine Mines* [1952] 3 D.L.R. 1 (P.C.).

liability to pay a fine[79] and does not amount to compliance with the equitable rules, for section 199 (5) provides that nothing in the section "shall be taken to prejudice the operation of any rule of law restricting directors of a company from having any interest in contracts with the company." Thus, an interested director, in addition to making disclosure to the board, must also disclose his interest to the general meeting or comply with the provisions of any of the articles relaxing the requirement of disclosure to the shareholders.[80] Conversely, non-compliance with section 199 may only render the director liable to a fine and may have in itself no effect upon the validity of the contract in question. This seems to have been the view of Pearson L.J. in *Hely-Hutchinson* v. *Brayhead Ltd.*[81] but Lord Denning M.R. may have been prepared to take a wider view of the civil effect of non-compliance with the section. In many cases, as in *Hely-Hutchinson* v. *Brayhead Ltd.* itself, the question does not arise and non-compliance with section 199 will in any case render the contract voidable, because the validity of the contract and the director's freedom from accounting for profits made are ensured by articles which expressly incorporate the provisions of the section. Article 84 (1)[82] imports the requirements of section 199 into Table A and it seems that the broad exclusion of the basic equitable principle in article 84 (3)[83] must be read as conditional upon the disclosure requirement in article 84 (1).

Statutory restrictions upon directors' freedom to contract

64–17 We have seen that the articles of a company often exclude in a comprehensive way the basic equitable rule that a contract or arrangement with his company in which a director is interested is voidable and that he must account to the company for any profit made from the contract or arrangement.[84] We have also seen that in some cases the director may be counted in the quorum for and voted upon decisions in which he is interested.[85] The exclusion of the equitable rule is qualified by the requirement of disclosure of interests to the board by section 199 of the 1948 Act.[86] Other statutory provisions relating to particular types of contract in which a director may be interested have imposed further restrictions upon directors' freedom to contract. First, there is now a considerable body of rules requiring *ex post facto* disclosure by the company of directors' interests. These requirements are discussed in Chapter 66. Secondly, there are substantive restrictions upon directors' freedom to contract with their company, which may take the form either of prohibitions upon certain

---

79 On summary conviction a fine not exceeding the statutory maximum and on conviction on indictment a fine of unlimited size: 1980 Act, Sched. 2.
80 See para. 64–14, *ante*.
81 [1968] 1 Q.B. 549, 594 (Pearson L.J.) and 585 (Lord Denning M.R.).
82 Quoted *ante* para. 64–14.
83 Quoted *ante* para. 64–15.
84 See para. 64–15, *ante*.
85 See para. 64–15, *ante*.
86 See para. 64–16, *ante*.

types of contract or of requirements that the contract be submitted to the approval of the general meeting. This latter form of substantive restriction thus restores in specific cases the principle of the equitable rule. The substantive restrictions may be classified under the following heads.

1. *Directors' service contracts*

In addition to the requirements that copies of such contracts be made available for the inspection of members[87] and that details of directors' emoluments be disclosed in the annual accounts,[88] section 47 of the Companies Act 1980 requires the approval by the company in general meeting of a term whereby the director's employment with the company is to continue for a period exceeding five years. It will be recalled that the power of the general meeting to dismiss a director at any time by ordinary resolution is expressly made subject to the preservation of the director's right to sue for damages for breach of contract.[89] This section gives the general meeting some control over the amount of damages that may become payable in such a situation. The requirement also applies to those in accordance with whose directions or instructions the directors of a company are accustomed to act ("shadow directors"—1980 Act, s. 63 (1)).

The section applies to all companies within the meaning of the 1948 Act or registered under Part VIII of the Act, unless the company in question is a wholly owned subsidiary (1980 Act, s. 47 (6)). Employment is defined so as to include both contracts of service and contracts for services, for example, consultancy contracts (s. 47 (7) (*a*)). The section applies to service contracts with the company or, in the case of directors of holding companies, service contracts within the group. Where a service contract (as defined) cannot be terminated by the company by notice, or can be so terminated only in specified circumstances, for a period exceeding five years, the requirement of approval by the general meeting applies. The requirement applies whether the contract is a fixed-term contract (not determinable by notice by either party) or whether the contract is extendable at the option only of the director, for a period exceeding five years. In the latter case, it does not matter whether the extension continues the original agreement (s. 47 (2)). Where a director is employed under a contract not terminable by notice or so terminable only in specified circumstances and more than six months before its expiration the company enters into a further agreement of this type with the director,[90] the unexpired portion of the original agreement is added to the period of the further agreement for the purpose of the requirement of approval of the further agreement by the general meeting (s. 47 (3)). Thus, the section cannot be avoided by the director entering into a four-year agreement with the

---

[87] 1967 Act, s. 26 (as amended by the 1980 Act, s. 61). See para. 66–14, *post*.
[88] 1948 Act, s. 196; 1967 Act, ss. 6–7. See para. 70–13, *post*.
[89] 1948 Act, s. 184 (6).
[90] Otherwise than in pursuance of a right conferred upon the director by the original agreement, in which case s. 47 (2) applies.

company and, at the end of the first year of that agreement, concluding a further four-year contract to commence at the expiry of the first contract.[91]

A written memorandum setting out the agreement incorporating the term must be made available for inspection by members both at the company's registered office for a period of 15 days before the meeting and at the meeting itself (s. 47 (4)). A term incorporated in an agreement in contravention of the section is "to the extent that it contravenes the section" void and the agreement (or where s. 47 (3) applies the *original* agreement) are deemed to contain a term entitling the company to terminate it at any time by the giving of reasonable notice.

2. *Loans*[92] *to directors and analogous transactions*

64–18 Loans to directors of companies, and those in accordance with whose directions or instructions the directors of a company are accustomed to act ("shadow directors")[93], are prohibited, as are a range of analogous transactions, by sections 49–53 of the 1980 Act as amended by section 111 of and Sched. 3 to the 1981 Act. The prohibitions can best be analysed as follows.

A. LOANS. No company, public or private, may make a loan to a director of the company or of its holding company nor enter into any guarantee or provide security in connection with a loan from any person to such a director, unless the amount of the loan and of any other such loan does not exceed £2,500 (s. 49 (1) (*a*) and 50 (2A)). No public company nor a company which is part of a group containing a public company (a "relevant company": 1980 Act, s. 65 (1)) may make a loan to a person connected with such a director or provide a guarantee or security in respect of a loan made by another person to a connected person (s. 49 (1) (*b*) (ii) and (iii)). Connected persons are defined by section 64 of the 1980 Act so as to specify:

(a) a director's spouse and infant children and step-children (including illegitimate children);
(b) a company with which the director is associated;
(c) a trustee (except a trustee of a pension scheme or employee share scheme) of a trust the beneficiaries or potential beneficiaries of which include the director, his spouse or infant children or an associated body corporate;
(d) a partner of the director or of any person connected with the director by virtue of paragraphs (a) to (c).

A director is associated with a company if he, and persons connected with him, are interested[94] in at least one-fifth of the equity capital of the

[91] s. 47 imposes stricter requirements than the Stock Exchange which requires approval only for contracts of 10 years' duration or longer: *Admission of Securities to Listing*, Sched. VIII, Pt. A, para 11 (*a*).

[92] Note also s. 189 of the 1948 Act which prohibits a company from paying a director remuneration (whether as director or otherwise) free of income tax and which provides that any agreement to do so has effect as an agreement to pay, subject to tax, the sums stated.

[93] Other than professional advisers: 1980 Act, s. 63 (1).

[94] As defined in s. 28 of the 1967 Act as amended by Sched. 3 to the 1981 Act. See para. 66–06, *post*.

company or exercise or control the exercise of more than one-fifth of the votes at any general meeting. Votes are controlled by a director, *inter alia*, if they are controlled by a company which the director controls.[95]

Although companies with which a director is associated are included within the definition of "connected persons" a company which is a member of a group of companies is not prohibited from making a loan (or providing a guarantee or security) to another member of the group (s. 50 (1), (4) (*a*)), even if in the particular case the director is associated with the recipient of the loan.

The prohibition on loans and the giving of guarantees is also relaxed in respect of companies the ordinary business of which includes the making of loans or the giving of guarantees in connection with loans ("money-lending companies": s. 65 (1)), where the loan or guarantee is effected in the ordinary course of the company's business, is on terms not more favourable than is reasonably to be expected for a person of the same financial standing but unconnected with the company, and does not exceed (together with other relevant transactions) £50,000[96] (unless the loan or guarantee is effected by a recognised bank, where no upper limit is imposed)[97] (s. 50 (4) (*d*), (6)). Money-lending companies may, however, make loans on favourable terms to their directors or directors of their holding companies, provided that the purpose of the loan is to facilitate the purchase or improvement of a dwelling-house for use as the director's only or main residence or is in substitution for a loan made for this purpose, and loans of this type are ordinarily made by the company to its employees on such favourable terms, and the aggregate of the loans made (whether by a recognised bank or not) does not exceed £50,000 (s. 50 (7)).

Finally, the prohibition on loans (and guarantees and securities) is relaxed if the loan is made to provide the director with funds to meet expenditure incurred for the purposes of the company or for the purpose of enabling him properly to perform his duties or to enable the director to avoid incurring such expenditure (s. 50 (4) (*c*)). However, a relevant company may not enter into loans which in aggregate exceed £10,000 by virtue of this exception, and in all cases the loan must either be approved in advance by the general meeting or be made on condition that if approval is not given at the next annual general meeting the loan will be repaid within six months of the meeting (s. 50 (5)).

64–19 B. QUASI-LOANS. A company makes a quasi-loan to a director when it pays a sum for the director to a third person or reimburses expenditure incurred by a third party for the director in such circumstances that the director either agrees or becomes liable to reimburse the company[97a] (s. 65

[95] Control as defined in s. 64 (3) (*b*).
[96] The procedure for aggregating amounts advanced in separate transactions is set out in s. 51.
[97] No limit is imposed on recognised banks.
[97a] Such a transaction does not constitute a loan for the purposes of in the present or previous legislative prohibition on loans to directors: *Champagne Perrier-Jouet S.A.* v. *H. H. Finch Ltd., The Times*, April 29, 1982.

(2)). A relevant company is prohibited from making a quasi-loan to a director of the company or its holding company or to a person connected with such a director and from providing a guarantee or security in connection with a quasi-loan made by any other person to such a director or a person connected with him (s. 49 (1) (*b*)). The same exemptions for quasi-loans to other members of groups of companies apply as in the case of loans (s. 50 (1), (4) (*a*)). The same exemptions also apply as in the case of loans for quasi-loans by money-lending companies on normal terms[98] (s. 50 (4) (*d*), (6)) and quasi-loans by companies to enable directors to discharge their duties (s. 50 (4) (*c*)). In addition, however, a company may make a quasi-loan to one of its directors or to a director of its holding company, provided that the quasi-loan is repayable within two months and the amount of the quasi-loan and of any other quasi-loans still outstanding made under this provision by the company, any subsidiary of the company or (where the director is a director of the company's holding company) any subsidiary of the holding company does not exceed £1,000 (s. 50 (2)).

C. CREDIT TRANSACTIONS. A credit transaction is defined as one in which (i) goods are supplied or land is sold under a hire-purchase or conditional sales agreement, or (ii) land or goods are leased or hired in return for periodical payments, or (iii) goods or services are supplied or land is disposed of on the understanding that payment is to be deferred (whether payment is ultimately to be in the form of periodical payments or not) (s. 65 (3)). A relevant company may not enter into a credit transaction for a director or a director of its holding company or a person connected with such a director. Nor may the company provide a guarantee or security in connection with a credit transaction entered into by another person for such a director or connected person (s. 49 (2)). The same exemption applies as for loans to credit transactions to enable a director to discharge his duties (s. 50 (4) (*c*)). In addition, a company may enter into a credit transaction for its holding company or provide a guarantee or security in respect of a credit transaction made by any other person for the holding company (s. 50 (4) (*b*)). Further, a company may enter into a credit transaction for any person if the aggregate value of the credit and of any outstanding credit under other credit transactions for the same person does not exceed £5,000 (ss. 50 (3) (*a*) and 51). Finally, a company may also enter into a credit transaction for any person if it does so in the ordinary course of its business and the value of the transaction and its terms are those that are reasonably to be expected for a person of the same financial standing but unconnected with the company (s. 50 (3) (*b*)).

D. ASSIGNMENTS AND ARRANGEMENTS. There are finally two "sweeping-up" provisions. A company may not have assigned to it, or assume, rights,

[98] The provisions in s. 59 (7) relating to loans on favourable terms for house purchase do not, however, extend to quasi-loans.

obligations or liabilities under a transaction which, had it been entered into by the company, would have contravened the prohibitions discussed in the previous paragraphs (s. 49 (3)). Further, a company may not enter into any arrangement whereby another person enters into a transaction which would, if entered into by the company, contravene the above prohibitions and under the arrangement that other person obtains a benefit from the company, its holding company or a subsidiary of the company or its holding company (s. 49 (4)). Such arrangements are more commonly called "back to back" transactions.

64–20 Section 53 of the 1980 Act lays down criminal penalties, in respect of relevant companies only, for directors of the company who authorise or permit prohibited transactions, for the company itself and for persons who procure a company to enter into a prohibited transaction. Section 52 provides civil remedies in respect of all types of company (public or private). The section follows the basic equitable principles by providing that a transaction entered into by a company in breach of the prohibitions shall be voidable by the company, but the right to avoid the transaction is lost if restitution of the subject-matter of the transaction is no longer possible, if a third party has acquired rights bona fide for value and without actual notice of the contravention which would be affected by the avoidance, or if the company has been indemnified for its loss (see below) (s. 52 (1)). In addition, the director or connected person for whom the transaction is made and any other director who authorised the transaction are liable to account to the company for any gain made by him directly or indirectly and to indemnify the company for any loss or damage resulting from the transaction (s. 52 (2)). A connected person and an authorising director may escape liability if they can show that they did not know the relevant circumstances constituting the contravention. Also, where a company enters into a prohibited transaction with a person connected with a director, that director is not liable if he can show that he took all reasonable steps to ensure compliance by the company with the law (s. 52 (3)). The section expressly preserves any other liabilities that may arise as a result of the company's entering into the prohibited transaction.

Loans and analogous transactions entered into by companies with directors and connected persons must be disclosed in the annual accounts.[99]

3. *Payments of compensation for loss of office*

Section 191 of the 1948 Act requires payments by a company to a director as compensation for loss of office or in connection with retirement from office to be approved in advance by the company in general meeting. Sections 192 to 194 make similar provisions in relation to payments to a director from any source in connection with the sale of a company's undertaking or a take-over bid for its shares.[1]

---

[99] See para. 70–15, *post*.
[1] See paras. 80–11 and 81–01, *post*.

4. *Substantial property transactions involving directors*

64–21 Section 48 of the 1980 Act (as amended by section 110 of the 1981 Act) requires prior approval or subsequent ratification within a reasonable period (s. 48 (3) (*c*)) by the company in general meeting when a director acquires from or transfers to his company non-cash assets of a certain size (s. 48 (1)). The section also applies to acquisitions and transfers by a director of the company's holding company, and in this case approval or ratification must also be made by the holding company in general meeting. The section further applies to shadow directors (s. 63)[2] and persons connected with[3] a director of the company or of its holding company. The asset is of the relevant size if it is worth more than £50,000 or more than 10 per cent. of the company's net assets,[4] provided that it is worth at least £1,000 (s. 48 (2)).

Approval or ratification are not required for (i) certain intra-group transfers between companies; (ii) arrangements entered into by a company being wound up, unless it is a members' voluntary winding up; or (iii) acquisitions by a director of the company or of its holding company or by a person connected with such a director, where that person is also a member of the company and the arrangement is made with him in his character as a member (s. 48 (7), (8)).

A transaction of the above type entered into by the company without prior authorisation or subsequent ratification is voidable at the option of the company, subject to the same limits as the avoidance of prohibited transactions under section 49 (s. 48 (3) (*a*) and (*b*)).[5] The director, the person connected with him and any other director who authorised the transaction are liable to account for any profit made directly or indirectly from the transaction and to indemnify the company for any loss or damage (s. 58 (4)), again subject to the same defences as apply in the case of prohibited loans (s. 48 (5)).[6]

The provisions of the 1980 Act are supplemented by the requirements of the Stock Exchange in the case of listed companies.[7]

A transaction of the type covered by section 48 must also be disclosed in the company's accounts (s. 54).[8]

Other situations in which the equitable principle may apply

64–22 We have seen[9] that the basic equitable principle, that a director must not put himself in a position where his duty to the company conflicts with his

---

[2] See para. 64–18, *ante*.
[3] *Ibid.*
[4] Calculated in accordance with the company's accounts for the last preceding accounting reference period. In the absence of such accounts the amount of its called-up share capital is the yardstick.
[5] See para. 64–20, *ante*.
[6] *Ibid.*, *cf. Burland* v. *Earle* [1902] A.C. 83, para. 64–24, *post*.
[7] *Admission of Securities to Listing*, Chap. 4, paras. 4 and 8 (Class 4 transactions).
[8] See para. 70–15, *post*.
[9] Above paras. 64–13 to 64–16, *ante*.

personal interests, applies very clearly to directors who contract with their company. In that area the equitable principle has been supplemented by statutory rules which apply to certain types of contract which a director may make with his company. The equitable principle is, however, of general application, and the following circumstances in which it may also apply should be mentioned.

Nominee directors

In *Boulting* v. *A.C.T.T.*[10] Lord Denning M.R. in a powerful dictum said of the appointment of nominee directors: "There is nothing wrong in it. It is done every day. Nothing wrong, that is, so long as the director is left free to exercise his best judgment in the interests of the company which he serves. But if he is put upon terms that he is bound to act in the affairs of the company in accordance with the directions of his patron, it is beyond doubt unlawful." This is a straightforward application of the no-conflict rule. It is unclear, however, whether the dictum was intended to apply only when the nominee director is obliged to act as his patron directs (*i.e.* when the director is mandated to act in a particular way) or whether it was intended to apply whenever a nominee director takes special account of the interests of his appointer and thus does not act in the interests of the company as a whole.[11] Where a director does allow himself to be put in a position where he acts blindly on the instructions of his appointer, he will be fixed with the knowledge of his appointer of the transactions in which he acts.[12]

Fettering of discretion

It is a logical extension of the principle enunciated by Lord Denning M.R. that a director is not permitted to contract with other directors or with third parties in such a way as to fetter his future discretion, though there is a paucity of English authority on the point.[13] It may be necessary, however, to distinguish the situation where the directors have in the bona fide exercise of their discretion entered into a contract which requires them for its effectuation to vote in a certain way at future board meetings.[14]

Directorships of competing companies

The no-conflict rule might also be thought to prohibit a person from being a director of competing companies, but it is unclear whether this is in fact the law. In *London and Mashonaland Exploration Co.* v. *New*

---

[10] [1963] 2 Q.B. 606, 626.

[11] In *Lindgren* v. *L. & P. Estates Co. Ltd.* [1968] 1 Ch. 572, Harman L.J. thought it "irrelevant" that a nominee director might have acted in the interests of his appointer rather than of the company. See also *Charterbridge Corporation Ltd.* v. *Lloyds Bank* [1970] Ch. 62, para. 64–06, *ante*.

[12] *Selanger United Rubber Estates Ltd.* v. *Cradock (No. 3)* [1968] 1 W.L.R. 1555, *Gray* v. *Lewis* (1873) 8 Ch.App. 1035.

[13] See *Clark* v. *Workman* [1920] 1 Ir. R. 107 and *Ringuet* v. *Bergeron* (1960) 24 D.L.R. (2d.) 449 (Supreme Court of Canada).

[14] *Thorbey* v. *Goldberg* (1965) 112 C.L.R. 597 (High Court of Australia).

Mashonaland Corporation Co.[15] Chitty J. refused to restrain a dummy director who had never acted as a director or attended a board meeting of the plaintiff company from acting as director of the competing defendant company. This decision was taken by Lord Blanesburgh L.C. in *Bell* v. *Lever Bros.*[16] as authority for a dictum that a director is generally free to be director of a competing company. In *Scottish Co-operative Wholesale Society Ltd.* v. *Meyer*,[17] however, Lord Denning thought that the directors of the textile company were in breach of duty by continuing their association with the co-operative society when that society set up its own rayon department. This latter view is more in line with the principle applied to employees[18] (including senior managers holding full-time service contracts) and trustees proper.[19]

Delegation of powers

The maxim "*delegatus non potest delegare*" applies to directors, so that prima facie, they cannot delegate their powers[20]; but this rule may be altered by giving the directors express or implied authority to delegate. Usually the articles expressly provide that the directors may appoint servants and agents and determine their duties and powers, and further that the directors may delegate to any one or more of themselves any of their powers (see art. 102). A delegation thus authorised is effective.[21]

Secret profits

64–23 A director of a company may not make a secret profit for himself from the use of corporate assets, information or opportunities. This principle, which has its origins in the no-conflict rule, has probably now attained the status of a separate rule.

Corporate assets, information and opportunities

The use by a director of corporate assets to make a secret profit for himself is clearly a breach of his fiduciary duties.[22] In *Regal (Hastings) Ltd.* v. *Gulliver*[23] the principle was applied by the House of Lords to corporate opportunities. In that case a company, which owned a cinema, wished to take leases on two other cinemas in the same town with a view to the sale of the businesses of all three cinemas as a single concern. To this end the directors formed a subsidiary to lease the two other cinemas, but the owner

---

15 [1891] W.N. 165.
16 [1932] A.C. 161, 195.
17 [1959] A.C. 324, 366. See para. 60–06, *ante*.
18 *Hivac Ltd.* v. *Park Royal Scientific Instruments Ltd.* [1946] Ch. 169; *Thomas Marshall (Exports) Ltd.* v. *Guinle* [1979] Ch. 227.
19 *Re Thomson* [1930] 1 Ch. 203.
20 *Cobb* v. *Becke* (1845) 6 Q.B. 930, 936.
21 *Re Taurine Co.* (1883) 25 Ch.D. 118; *Leeds Estate, etc., Co.* v. *Shepherd* (1887) 36 Ch.D. 787.
22 *Menier* v. *Hooper's Telegraph Works* (1874) 9 Ch.App. 350.
23 [1942] 1 All E.R. 378; [1967] 2 A.C. 134n.

of the two other cinemas would not lease them to the subsidiary without a personal guarantee of the rent by the directors unless the paid-up capital of the subsidiary was at least £5,000. In the directors' view the company could not afford to capitalise the company to the extent of more than £2,000 and so four directors and the company's solicitor agreed to subscribe for 500 £1 shares each, whilst the chairman of the board found two companies and one further person to subscribe between them for a further 500 shares. The sale of the businesses was subsequently effected by a sale of the shares of the company and its subsidiary and a profit of nearly £3 per share was realised on the shares of the subsidiary. The new owners of the company brought an action to recover for the company the profit made and the directors[24] of the company were held liable to account.

It is clear that if the directors act in bad faith or if they use company assets to generate a business opportunity which the company is capable of exploiting commercially but which they then divert to themselves, the directors are liable to account to the company for any profit made.[25] In the *Regal* case, however, it was found that the directors had acted in good faith and in order to facilitate a transaction for the company which the company was unable to finance from its own resources. Their lordships applied, however, strict fiduciary standards and held that the liability of the directors did not depend upon whether the profit would or should otherwise have gone to the company, whether they acted as they did for the benefit of the company, or whether the company was damaged or benefited by the action.[26] The positive principle upon which the decision was based was put by Lord MacMillan in terms that directors are liable to account if "(i) what the directors did was so related to the affairs of the company that it can properly be said to have been done in the course of their management and in utilisation of their opportunities and special knowledge as directors, and (ii) what they did resulted in a profit for themselves."[27]

64–24 In the *Regal* case Lord Russell of Killowen based the liability of the directors upon the fact that the shares had been acquired by the directors "by reason, and only by reason of the fact that they were directors of Regal, and in the course of their execution of that office."[28] Although the acquisition of information and opportunities by reason of the office of

[24] For the position of the solicitor see para. 64–25, n. 35, *post*. The chairman was held not liable to account because he had made no profit; the persons whom the chairman had found to subscribe for shares were not sued. On the liability in general of third parties see para. 64–27, *post*.
[25] *Menier* v. *Hooper's Telegraph Works* (1874) 9 Ch.App. 350; *Cook* v. *Deeks* [1916] 1 A.C. 554; *Canadian Aero Services Ltd.* v. *O'Malley* (1978) 40 D.L.R. (3d.) 371 (Supreme Court of Canada).
[26] [1967] 2 A.C. 134, 144 (*per* Lord Russell of Killowen). See also *Abbey Glen Corporation* v. *Stumborg* (1976) 65 D.L.R. (3d.) 235 (Supreme Court of Alberta) and *Phipps* v. *Boardman* [1967] 2 A.C. 46, where trustees were held liable to account for profits made from information and opportunities acquired as trustees even though the trust was legally unable to exploit the opportunities in question.
[27] *Ibid.* p. 153.
[28] *Ibid.* p. 147.

director may be a sufficient basis for liability, the formulation of Lord MacMillian is rather wider and it has been held subsequently that information and opportunities acquired while a director may give rise to liability, even if they were not acquired by virtue of that office. In such a case, however, the director must be under a duty to offer the information or opportunity to his company. Thus, in *Industrial Development Consultants Ltd.* v. *Cooley*[29] the defendant, who had long worked for a Gas Board as an architect, was appointed managing director of the plaintiff company with the aim of expanding the company's sphere of operations into the public sector. The defendant attempted to obtain contracts for the company with another area Gas Board, but without success because the Board disliked the set-up of the plaintiff company. Sometime later the Board approached the plaintiff with a proposal that he act as architect for a depot for the Board, making it clear that they approached the plaintiff privately, were interested in employing only him, and did not want any trouble from his company. By a fraud the director secured his release from the company and took the contract himself. In holding the defendant liable to account for the profit made Roskill J., in line with previous authority,[30] held it to be irrelevant that it was extremely unlikely that the Gas Board would have agreed to contract with the company, so that as a result of the court's order the plaintiff was obtaining a benefit it would otherwise have failed to obtain. He also held that the duties which attached to the director when he held office did not cease to be applicable upon his release from the directorship in respect of information and opportunities acquired when a director. Finally, the learned judge held that the fact that the offer was made to the director privately and was made in spite of rather than because of the defendant's position as director of the plaintiff company did not relieve the director of the duty to inform his company of the contract which the Board was seeking to place.

Where, as in *Cooley*, the director is appointed for the very purpose of acquiring for the company the sort of opportunity which he in fact takes for himself, it is understandable that he should be regarded as being in breach of his fiduciary duty, even if the opportunity did not come to him in his capacity as director. He should be regarded as under a duty to bring such opportunities to the attention of his company. No English case has yet held that directors are under a general duty to further the interests of their company so as to require them to offer their company opportunities which come to them privately but which the company is in a position to exploit.[31]

[29] [1972] 1 W.L.R. 443. See also *Canadian Aero Services Ltd.* v. *O'Malley* (1973) 40 D.L.R. (3d.) 371 (Supreme Court of Canada).

[30] See note 26, *supra*.

[31] But see the dicta in the *Canaero* case (note 29, *supra*). Such a duty might be more readily accepted in the case of directors with full-time service contracts. The duty discussed in the text refers to a fiduciary duty to offer the opportunity to the company and not to exploit it personally, on pain of being liable to account to the company for the profit made by personal exploitation. A tortious duty to further the interests of the company, which might involve the director in liability in damages for failure to offer the opportunity to his company even in the absence of personal exploitation, would be an even more radical development. See Chap. 63.

Such a development might run counter to the decision in *Burland* v. *Earle*[32] that a director who sells property to his company without disclosing his interest in the property is liable to have the contract set aside by the company, but the company cannot at the same time affirm the contract and claim an accounting of the profit made by the director. At present, this decision can be explained on the basis that the director in that case did not purchase the property on behalf of the company as a result of an instruction or mandate. Had he acted under such an instruction he would have been liable to account for the profit made.[33]

The corporate interest and ratification

64–25 There are two questions that may arise as to when a company may approve a director's personal exploitation of an opportunity so as to relieve him of any duty to account for a profit made. First, may a director in any circumstances rely upon approval by the board of directors? The general principle is that the company has the right to the unbiased advice of every director and so disclosure to and approval by the board is ineffective even if the director in question refrains from voting and is not counted in the quorum.[34] However, full disclosure to and approval by the board will be effective in the case of an agent of the company other than director.[35] However, it may be that, even for directors, a bona fide decision by the board after full disclosure that the company should not avail itself of a particular opportunity would mean that the opportunity is no longer a corporate one and a director's subsequent exploitation of the opportunity personally would not be a breach of duty. There is no English authority on the point, although the Privy Council has held in favour of this view[36] and dicta in the *Regal* case support it.[37]

The second question is whether full disclosure to and approval by the shareholders in general meeting will always relieve the director from liability. In general, this will be so, but in *Cook* v. *Deeks*[38] a purported ratification of the defendants' acts in diverting to themselves a contract which they should have obtained for the company was held to be ineffective. Lord Buckmaster said:

> "If, as their Lordships find on the facts, the contract in question was entered into under such circumstances that the directors could not retain the benefit of it for themselves, then it belonged in equity to the

32 [1902] A.C. 83. See also *Re Cape Breton Co.* (1885) 29 Ch.D. 795.

33 *Peninsular and Oriental Steam Navigation Co.* v. *Johnson* (1938) 60 C.L.R. 189 (High Court of Australia); *Abbey Glen Corporation* v. *Stumborg* (1976) 65 D.L.R. (3d.) 235 (Supreme Court of Alberta).

34 *Imperial Mercantile Credit Association* v. *Coleman* (1871) L.R. 6 Ch.App. 558, 567–568.

35 Hence the conclusion that the solicitor was not liable in the *Regal* case because "he took the shares with the full knowledge and consent of Regal" (at p. 140).

36 *Queensland Mines Ltd.* v. *Hudson* (1978) 18 A.L.R.1 (P.C.). See also *Peso Silver Mines Ltd.* v. *Cropper* (1966) 58 D.L.R. (2d.) 1 (Supreme Court of Canada) and *New Zealand Netherlands Society* v. *Kuys* [1973] 1 W.L.R. 1127 (P.C.).

37 [1967] 2 A.C. 134, 152–153.

38 [1916] 1 A.C. 554. See also *Menier* v. *Hooper's Telegraph Works* (1874) L.R. 9 Ch. App. 350.

company and ought to have been dealt with as an asset of the company. Even supposing it be not ultra vires of a company to make a present to its directors, it appears quite certain that directors holding a majority of votes would not be permitted to make a present to themselves. This would be to allow a majority to oppress the minority."

In *Regal (Hastings) Ltd.* v. *Gulliver*,[39] however, Lord Russell of Killowen thought that the defendant directors "could, had they wished, have protected themselves by a resolution (either antecedent or subsequent) of the Regal shareholders in general meeting."[40] The distinction between the two cases may be that in *Cook* v. *Deeks* the defendants were seen as attempting to appropriate to themselves company property[41] whereas in the *Regal* case the directors were making only an incidental profit. An incidental profit will not be regarded as the property of the company unless it flows from use of the company's property.[42] This view is dependent upon the information acquired by the directors of Regal not being regarded as the property of the company.[43] Or it may be that the distinction between the two cases is that in *Regal* the directors acted in good faith whereas in *Cook* v. *Deeks* they did not; or that in *Cook* v. *Deeks* the transaction was approved by the votes of the wrongdoing directors whereas in *Regal* Lord Russell had in mind approval by an independent majority.[44]

Exclusions from liability in the articles

64–26 We have already seen that article 84[45] purports to relieve a director from the consequences of the equitable rule that a director should not put himself in a position of conflict of interest by contracting with his company or having an interest in contracts by other persons with his company unless he discloses his interest to the company in general meeting. In addition, article 78 is said to have been introduced into Table A in 1948 in order to reverse the effect of the decision in the *Regal* case.[46] However, section 205 of the 1948 Act stipulates that any provision in the articles or in a contract with the company or otherwise that exempts any officer of the company from any liability which by law attaches to him because of "any negligence, default, breach of duty or breach of trust" shall be void.[47] The relationship between section 205 of the 1948 Act and the articles is unclear. It may be that articles in the form of articles 78 and 84 are not to be regarded as contravening section 205 because of the statutory authority conferred upon Table A by section 8, although section 205 is not made expressly subject to

---

39 Para. 64–23, *ante*.
40 [1967] 2 A.C. 134, 150.
41 The contract which the directors were under a duty to acquire for the company.
42 *Lister & Co.* v. *Stubbs* (1890) 45 Ch.D. 1.
43 *Cf. Phipps* v. *Boardman* [1967] 2 A.C. 46.
44 *Prudential Assurance Co. Ltd.* v. *Newman Industries Ltd. (No. 2)* [1980] 2 All E.R. 841, 862.
45 See para. 64–14, *ante*.
46 See para. 64–23, *ante*. Art. 78 is set out at para. A–482. It is not usual for the articles to attempt further to waive a director's duty not to make a secret profit.
47 s. 205 also deals with indemnities for officers. See para. 64–32, *post*.

the provisions of Table A. If a draftsman wishes to go beyond the provisions of Table A, however, section 205 on this view clearly limits to some extent what he may do. It may be that section 205 renders void only exclusions from liability arising from breaches of duty, etc., and does not affect articles that modify the scope of the duty itself. This would be to give the draftsman a very wide power to relieve directors of the duty not to put themselves in a position of conflict of interest. Or it may be that section 205 permits the draftsman to introduce only alternative ways of satisfying the fiduciary duties, *e.g.* by disclosure to the board rather than to the general meeting, although article 78 is difficult to justify on this theory.

Remedies

64–27 For breaches of directors' fiduciary duties and their duties of skill, care and diligence the common law provides a range of remedies. In certain cases these common law remedies have been supplemented by statutory provisions.

Common law remedies

The common law remedies are as follows:

1. Injunction or declaration, for example where the board is threatening to take some action beyond their powers or the powers of the company.
2. Damages or compensation. All directors who participate[48] in the breach are jointly and severally liable, but have rights of contribution *inter se*.[49]
3. Rescission of contracts with the company provided that *restitutio in integrum* is still possible and third-party rights have not intervened.
4. An account of profits. If the profit arises out of a contract with the company, the company can normally[50] claim an account of any profit made by the director whether or not it rescinds the contract.
5. Restoration of company property in the director's hands, including property it was his duty to acquire for the company,[51] which is recoverable by an action *in rem*.
6. Summary termination of any service contract held by the director with his company if his conduct amounts to grave misconduct.[52]

Liabilities of third parties

There is a variety of circumstances in which a third party may become liable to the company as a result of his involvement in a breach of duty by a

[48] *Re Lands Allotment Co.* [1894] 1 Ch. 616.

[49] Either in equity or by virtue of s. 6 of the Law Reform (Married Women and Tortfeasors) Act 1935. See para. 64–35, *post*.

[50] But see para 64–24, *ante*. for the case where the director sells his own property to the company.

[51] *Cook* v. *Deeks* [1916] 1 A.C. 554.

[52] *Boston Deep Sea Fishing & Ice Co.* v. *Ansell* (1888) 39 Ch.D. 339, *Bell* v. *Lever Bros.* [1932] A.C. 161, but see also the impact of the unfair dismissal laws (para. 67–14, *post*.).

director. A third party who agrees with a director to engage in a course of action that involves a breach of duty by the director will be liable to the company for the tort of conspiracy.[53] A third party may also be liable to the company if he induces a director to breach his fiduciary duties to the company.[54] A third party who bribes a director is liable to the company either for the amount of the bribe as money had and received or for damages in tort for the loss sustained by the company, which is irrefutably presumed to be at least equal to the amount of the bribe.[55] The company need not, however, elect between the alternative remedies before the time comes for judgment to be entered.[56] In this context a bribe does not necessarily connote corruption, but the payment by a third party of something in cash or kind to an agent whom the third party knows to be acting as an agent for the principal with whom the third party is dealing in circumstances where the payment is not disclosed to the principal.[57] Alternative claims for money had and received and for damages also lie against the bribed director.[58]

The causes of action described in the previous paragraph are all personal claims.[59] In certain circumstances, however, a third party may be regarded as a constructive trustee for the company. The first is where a third party knowingly participates in a dishonest and fraudulent design on the part of the directors. In such a case the design of the directors must be dishonest (*i.e.* fraudulent) and the third party must have actual knowledge of the design or recklessly fail to make such inquiries as would an honest and reasonable man.[60] Secondly, a third party will be liable as a constructive trustee if he receives corporate property[61] with knowledge (actual or constructive) that the property comes into his hands through a breach of trust.[62] Whether a third party into whose hands corporate property comes can be made liable as a constructive trustee without such knowledge is unclear. On general principles, a bona fide purchaser for value ought to be completely protected, but the company may be able to trace property into

---

[53] *Belmont Finance Corporation* v. *Williams Furniture Ltd. (No. 2)* [1980] 1 All E.R. 393.

[54] *Boulting* v. *A.C.T.T.* [1963] 2 Q.B. 606; *Prudential Assurance* v. *Lorenz* (1971) 11 K.I.R. 78.

[55] *Hovenden & Sons* v. *Milhoff* (1900) 83 L.T. 41; *Industries and General Mortgage Co. Ltd.* v. *Lewis* [1949] 3 All E.R. 573; *Mahesan* v. *Malaysia Government Officers' Co-operative Housing Society Ltd.* [1979] A.C. 374.

[56] *United Australia Ltd.* v. *Barclays Bank Ltd.* [1941] A.C. 1.

[57] *Industries and General Mortgage Co. Ltd.* v. *Lewis* (1949) 3 All E.R. 573; *Taylor* v. *Walker* [1958] 1 Lloyd's Rep. 490.

[58] See the *Mahesan* case (above).

[59] *Metropolitan Bank* v. *Heiron* (1880) 5 Ex.D. 319; *Lister & Co.* v. *Stubbs* (1890) 45 Ch.D. 1. *Cf. Tinton Explorations Syndicate Ltd.* v. *Sandys* (1947) 177 L.T. 412.

[60] *Belmont Finance Corporation* v. *Williams Furniture Ltd.* [1979] Ch. 250, somewhat restricting *Selanger United Rubber Estates Ltd.* v. *Cradock (No. 3)* [1968] 1 W.L.R. 1555 and *Karak Rubber Co. Ltd.* v. *Burden (No. 2)* [1972] 1 W.L.R. 602. See also *Competitive Insurance Co. Ltd.* v. *Davies Investments Ltd.* [1975] 1 W.L.R. 1240 and *Canada Safeway Ltd.* v. *Thompson* [1951] 3 D.L.R. 295 (British Columbia Supreme Court).

[61] The question of how far information may be regarded as property is again relevant here. See para. 64–25, *ante*.

[62] *Belmont Finance Corporation* v. *Williams Furniture Ltd. (No. 2)* [1980] 1 All E.R. 393.

the hands of a volunteer.[63] It has also been suggested that an injunction will go to restrain the use of confidential information by an entirely innocent third party.[64]

Statutory remedies

64–28 If a director has been negligent or has committed some breach of his duty towards the company, he is prima facie liable in an action by the company,[65] or alternatively in a winding up he is liable upon a so-called misfeasance summons under section 333 of the 1948 Act,[66] misfeasance being used as a composite word to cover all matters of breach of duty by a director involving misapplication of assets,[67] but not mere negligence.[68]

Action

As has been stated earlier,[69] under the rule of *Foss* v. *Harbottle*[70] only the company, but not minority shareholders, are entitled to sue the directors for negligence, breach of duty or breach of trust unless the case falls within one of the established exceptions to that rule.[71]

The Department of Trade, on the report of an inspector or in consequence of an inspection of the company's books and papers, may likewise institute proceedings in the name of the company against a director (1967 Act, s. 37).[72]

Misfeasance summons (s. 333)[73]

This section gives a liquidator the right, *inter alia*, to apply to the court to examine the conduct of a director or past director (such examination will include questions of law) and the court may then compel a delinquent director to repay or restore any money which he has misapplied or retained or become liable or accountable for to the company, or to contribute to the company's assets an appropriate sum by way of compensation.[74] Such an application is made by summons which may be taken out by the official receiver, the liquidator, or any contributory or creditor, so that a director who has a controlling interest in the company will not thereby be able to

---

63 *Re Diplock* [1948] Ch. 465; *Baker* v. *Medway Building and Supplies Ltd.* [1958] 1 W.L.R. 1216.

64 *Printers and Finishers Ltd.* v. *Holloway* [1965] 1 W.L.R. 1, *per* Cross J.

65 *Joint Stock Discount Co.* v. *Brown* (1869) L.R. 8 Eq. 376; *Nant-y-glo, etc., Co.* v. *Grave* (1878) 12 Ch.D. 738.

66 The section is, by virtue of s. 307, applicable to a voluntary winding up: s. 333 (1).

67 See *Selangor United Rubber Estates Ltd.* v. *Cradock* [1967] 1 W.L.R. 1168.

68 See *Re B. Johnson & Co. (Builders) Ltd.* [1955] Ch. 634.

69 See para. 58–09, *ante*.

70 (1843) 2 Hare 461.

71 See para. 58–11, *ante*.

72 See para. 78–13, *post*.

73 The expression "misfeasance summons" is exclusively English, but s. 333 applies to Scotland. *Mutatis mutandis* as to court procedure, the text's comments on the section may be taken as valid in Scotland.

74 The section applies to a wider class of persons than directors: the principles upon which it may be employed are here set out in regard to directors, but apply, *mutatis mutandis*, to the other persons against whom the section is directed; see para. 85–89, *post*.

evade an examination of the allegations against him by the court by pleading the rule in *Foss* v. *Harbottle*.[75]

64–29 SECTION 333 DOES NOT CREATE NEW RIGHTS. The section itself does not create any new rights.[76] Accordingly, if the company, or its liquidator, has a right of action against a director, the section can be employed in the winding up as a cheaper and equally effective summary method of enforcing the right. It should, however, be remembered

(1) that the section permits the enforcement of the company's right by any one creditor or contributory (as stated above); and

(2) that the commencement of a winding up itself may create rights for the liquidator which might not have been available to the company itself while a going concern.[77]

WHEN NOT AVAILABLE. This section, on the other hand,

(1) is not available to a creditor or contributory to assert a personal right against a director,[78] *e.g.* for liability towards a shareholder upon a prospectus;

(2) nor does it enable the company to recover from a director a mere monetary claim owed to the company[79];

(3) nor is it available to a creditor or contributory who can have no pecuniary interest in the result[80];

(4) nor is it available if the director's only transgression is negligence.[81]

COURT'S DISCRETION UNDER SECTION 333. The court is given a discretion, both as to whether or not it will grant the relief sought, and as to the amount of relief which it gives. This is in contrast to an action by the company against a director, where the court would be bound to give judgment in accordance with the legal rights established. Thus, in *Re Sunlight Incandescent Gas Lamp Co.*,[82] the court refused relief where the only persons having a pecuniary interest were the shareholders, and where the majority of these were willing to waive a claim in respect of an alleged secret profit by directors.

---

[75] (1843) 2 Hare 461.

[76] *Re Forest of Dean Coal Mining Co.* (1878) 10 Ch.D. 450; *Coventry and Dixon's Case* (1880) 14 Ch.D. 660; *Re Anglo-French Co-operative Society* (1882) 21 Ch.D. 492; *Cavendish-Bentinck* v. *Fenn* (1887) 12 App.Cas. 652; *Re Kingston Cotton Mill (No. 2)* [1896] 1 Ch. 331; affirmed [1896] 2 Ch. 279; *Re Jubilee Cotton Mills* [1923] 1 Ch. 1; reversed [1924] A.C. 958; *Re Windsor Steam Coal Co.* [1929] 1 Ch. 151; *Re City Equitable Fire Insurance Co.* [1925] Ch. 407.

[77] *Re National Funds Assurance Co.* (1878) 10 Ch.D. 118; *Re Whitehouse & Co.* (1878) 9 Ch.D. 595; *Burgess' Case* (1880) 15 Ch.D. 507; and see para. 85–90, *post*.

[78] *Re Hill's Waterfall Estate and Goldmining Co.* [1896] 1 Ch. 947.

[79] *Re Etic Ltd.* [1928] Ch. 861.

[80] *Cavendish-Bentinck* v. *Fenn* (1887) 12 App.Cas. 652.

[81] *Re B. Johnson (Builders) Ltd.* [1955] Ch. 634.

[82] [1900] 2 Ch. 728.

Measure of damages

64–30 If in an action by the company a director is found to be liable for breach of duty, the measure of damages is either the loss suffered by the company or the profit made by him. If, therefore, a director has made a profit for which he is accountable,[83] he will be liable to repay the whole of it to the company, even though the company itself could not have made the profit. If, however, proceedings are taken against the director under section 333 the court may, in its discretion, award less than it would have awarded in an action. In two cases the court awarded only a sum sufficient to pay the company's creditors (excluding any debt of the director himself)[84]; and in another case where a dividend was paid out of moneys obtained by a loan, the liability of the directors was restricted to the amount payable on the company's other debts, *i.e.* the debts exclusive of the loan incurred in order to make the dividend payment.[85]

It should, however, be noted that the provisions of section 333 do not exclude the right of the company to bring an action against the director (in which action the damages recoverable might conceivably be higher), but such an action has to be brought, in the winding up, by the liquidator on behalf of the company, whereas the remedy under section 333 is available not only to the liquidator or the official receiver but likewise to any one contributory or creditor.

No set-off against debt owed by the company

Where a director is found liable, whether upon an action or a misfeasance summons, to contribute to the company's assets, he cannot set-off against that liability any debt owed to him by the company.[86]

Proceedings against de facto and retired directors

64–31 An action or a misfeasance summons can be brought against a *de facto* director in the same way as against a *de jure* director.[87]

It is no defence that the alleged misfeasance was committed after the defendant had ceased to be a director if he is himself a party to it. In the words of Cross J. in *Curtis's Furnishing Stores Ltd.* v. *Freedman*[88]:

> "If a director, who is about to retire and sell his shares, makes a bargain with his intended successors and the purchasers of his shares that when they are in control of the company they will procure it to make a present to him out of its assets and this is done, the recipient is in my judgment as guilty of misfeasance as the directors who actually procure the company to make the gift."

---

[83] See paras. 64–23 and 64–27, *ante*.
[84] *Re Home and Colonial Insurance Co.* [1930] 1 Ch. 102; *Re V. G. M. Holdings* [1942] Ch. 235, where interest at 4 per cent. was also included as part of the provable debts.
[85] *Re Alexandra Palace Company* (1882) 21 Ch.D. 149.
[86] *Re Anglo-French Co-operative Society* (1882) 21 Ch.D. 492; *Re Carriage Supply Association* (1884) 27 Ch.D. 322; *Flitcroft's Case* (1882) 21 Ch.D. 519.
[87] *Coventry and Dixon's Case* (1880) 14 Ch.D. 660; *Gibson* v. *Barton* (1875) L.R. 10 Q.B. 329; see para. 61–20, *ante*.
[88] [1966] 1 W.L.R. 1219, 1224; applying *Head* v. *Gould* [1898] 2 Ch. 250.

Proceedings against estate of deceased director

At common law, under the rule *actio personalis moritur cum persona*, proceedings could not be taken against the state of a deceased director if they were founded on trespass or negligence.[89] The rule applied even to fraud, unless the deceased's estate itself benefited from it.[90] The rule did not, however, bar equitable remedies against the director's estate where he had committed a breach of trust.[91]

In modern law, the old rule is considerably modified by the Law Reform (Miscellaneous Provisions) Act 1934, under which all causes of action which are likely to apply to a director as such[92] survive for and against the estate, provided that no proceedings shall be maintainable in respect of such a cause of action in tort, unless either

(1) proceedings in respect thereof were pending against him (*i.e.* had been commenced) at the date of death, or
(2) the cause of action arose not earlier than six months before the death and proceedings are taken in respect thereof not later than six months after the deceased's personal representative took out representation.[93]

Although a cause of action may survive under these provisions, misfeasance proceedings under section 333 cannot be commenced against a deceased director's personal representative, because on a construction of that section, the court can "compel him" (*i.e.* the director) to repay, restore or contribute, but has no such powers against a personal representative.[94] On the other hand, it is thought that where proceedings under the section have already been commenced before the death, the Act of 1934 enables such proceedings to *survive* against the deceased director's estate.

In Scots law proceedings which have been commenced prior to the death of the defender survive against his estate, whatever their nature. Proceedings may also be taken for reparation against the estate of a deceased director, but his representatives are not liable beyond the value of the estate.

Indemnity for wrongful acts or omissions

64–32 UNDER THE ARTICLES. It is clear from some of the cases already referred to that directors may, through little or no fault of their own, find themselves technically failing in their duty to the company. A dividend may be paid out of capital, owing to defalcations by other directors[95]; or an act may be

[89] *Phillips* v. *Homfray* (1883) 24 Ch.D. 439; *Overend, Gurney & Co.* v. *Gibb* (1872) L.R. 5 H.L. 480.
[90] *Peek* v. *Gurney* (1874) L.R. 6 H.L. 377.
[91] *Erlanger* v. *New Sombrero Phosphate Co.* (1878) 3 App.Cas. 1218; *Ramskill* v. *Edwards* (1885) 31 Ch.D. 100; *Re Sharpe* [1892] 1 Ch. 154.
[92] See s. 1 (1) for the exceptions, and the limitations in s. 1 (2).
[93] s. 1 (3); see also s. 1 (4).
[94] *Feltom's Executors' Case* (1865) L.R. 1 Eq. 219; *Re British Guardian Assurance Co.* (1880) 14 Ch.D. 335.
[95] See Chap. 76, *post*.

done by the directors which is *ultra vires* the company, and for which they are accordingly, prima facie, liable, in circumstances where the directors have good reason to believe that the act is *intra vires*.[96] It accordingly used to be customary to insert a clause in the articles of association protecting the directors and auditors from liability for losses to the company except in the case of their "wilful default," or except in the case of their dishonesty. Directors were held to be protected by such a clause in *Re Brazilian Rubber Estates Ltd.*[97] and the directors and auditors were protected in *Re City Equitable Fire Insurance Co.*[98]

This protection was removed by the 1929 Act, and it is no longer possible to give such a wide indemnity (1948 Act, s. 205). An indemnity in a more limited form is, however, still permitted. Thus, it is still possible to provide in the articles that the directors shall be indemnified against any liability incurred by them in defending any proceedings, whether civil or criminal, in which judgment is given in their favour or in which they are acquitted or in connection with any appplication under section 448[99] of the 1948 Act in which relief is granted to them by the court (s. 205, proviso (*b*)). It is normal practice to include such an indemnity in the articles, and this will ensure that a director is not mulcted in the costs of an action if he wins his case even if the costs are not recoverable, *e.g.* because the court has not awarded him costs or they are not allowed on taxation of costs.

64–33 STATUTORY RELIEF (s.448). Section 448 (which is referred to in s. 205, proviso (*b*)) is a protective section for directors on lines similar to that accorded to trustees.[1] It provides that in any proceedings against, *inter alios*,[2] a director for negligence, default, breach of duty or breach of trust, if a director who is or may be liable has in the opinion of the court acted honestly and reasonably, and if, having regard to all the circumstances of the case, including those connected with his appointment, he ought fairly to be excused, the court may wholly or partly relieve him from his liability; the court has a discretion in the matter, and may impose terms (s. 448 (1)). In spite of the wide words of the section it has been held that the section applies only to actions brought by or on behalf of the company against its directors for breach of duty and to penal proceedings for the enforcement of the Companies Acts.[2a] A director who apprehends such proceedings may apply to the court for such relief (s. 448 (2)).

It is not enough to prove that a director acted reasonably and honestly. It

96 See Chap. 9, *ante*.
97 [1911] 1 Ch. 425.
98 [1925] Ch. 407.
99 See below in the text.
1 Trustee Act 1925, s. 61.
2 The section applies to other officers as well as directors.
2a *Customs and Excise Commrs.* v. *Hedon Alpha Ltd.* [1981] 2 All E.R. 697 (C.A.).

must, in addition, be proved that he ought fairly to be excused.[3] A director is regarded as having acted reasonably if he has acted "in the way in which a man of affairs with reasonable care and circumspection could reasonably be expected to act in such a case."[4]

The section applies to *ultra vires* acts.[5]

Where directors were summoned before court of summary jurisdiction for having served as directors without the requisite qualification shares, the magistrate adjourned the hearing to enable the directors to petition for relief under the predecessor of section 448. It was, however, held that the only court which can give relief is the court before which proceedings are brought, and that the High Court could not, accordingly, give relief against the proceedings already commenced in the magistrates' court; it could, however, and did give relief against all future liability in any court.[6]

Limitation of liability[7]

64–34 The Limitation Act 1980, s. 21, bars any rights against directors for negligence or breach of trust or any breach of duty where the proceedings, whether by way of an action or a misfeasance summons, are commenced more than six years after the alleged wrongful act or omission. If, however, there is a fraud or fraudulent breach of trust, the period of limitation does not apply.[8] The Act does not protect a director who retains the company's property, or who received part of the company's property and converted it to his own use, so far as that property is concerned.[9] Thus, the Act is no defence in an action by the company against the directors for the recovery of money wrongfully paid as dividend to themselves.

Contribution

From co-directors

64–35 Since the liability of directors, who are liable for negligence, breach of trust or duty, is joint and several, the person entitled to damages—whether a third person or the company—may claim the whole amount due to him from one (or a few) of the directors, who have to share in the liability, and may leave it to him (or them) to settle the matter with his (or their) co-directors *inter se* by way of contribution.

---

[3] *Cf. National Trustee Co. of Australasia* v. *General Finance, etc., Co.* [1905] A.C. 373; *Re Smith, Smith* v. *Thompson* (1902) 71 L.J.Ch. 411; *Re Turner, Barker* v. *Ivimey* [1897] 1 Ch. 536; *Re Second Dulwich 745th Starr-Bowkett Building Society* (1899) 68 L.J.Ch. 196; *Re Grindey, Clews* v. *Grindey* [1898] 2 Ch. 593; *Perrins* v. *Bellamy* [1899] 1 Ch. 797; *Re Lord de Clifford* [1902] 2 Ch. 707.

[4] *Re Duomatic Ltd.* [1969] 2 Ch. 365, 377, *per* Buckley J.

[5] *Re Claridges' Patent Asphalte* [1921] 1 Ch. 543 (where directors acted upon an opinion of counsel that the act was *intra vires*).

[6] *Re Gilt Edge Safety Glass Ltd.* [1940] Ch. 495.

[7] The Limitation Act 1980 does not apply to Scotland. Section 21 of the 1980 Act applies to trustees, but this has been held to include directors: *Re Lands Allotment Co.* [1984] 1 Ch. 616; *Tintin Exploration Syndicate Ltd.* v. *Sandys* (1947) 177 L.T. 412.

[8] s. 21 (1).

[9] s. 21 (2).

Under the Civil Liability (Contribution) Act 1978 in principle any person liable to pay compensation in respect of any damage suffered by another person may recover contribution from any other person liable in respect of the same damage.[10] The director entitled to contribution, if sued, may make those obliged to contribute co-defendants by serving on them third-party notices under R.S.C. 1965, Ord. 16. The court has power to fix the ratio of contribution in accordance with the responsibility of the contributors.[11] Where, as will often be the case, the claim against the directors is an equitable one, a right to contribution arises in equity apart from the 1978 Act.[11a] The equitable right is not confined to liability to pay compensation, but is limited to situations where the defendants are liable to the same demand and is in principle a right to equal shares in the liability.

Contribution can be claimed against the executors of a deceased director.[12]

In Scotland, at common law joint dilinquents are liable jointly and severally and have a statutory right of contribution *inter se* (Law Reform (Miscellaneous Provisions) (Scotland) Act 1940, s. 3). This applies to all claims for damages for negligence, breach of trust or duty.

From shareholders or creditors

64–36 In addition, a director may have a right to recover from shareholders or creditors any property of the company wrongly paid to such shareholders or creditors. This right will only arise if the person who received the property had full knowledge of all the facts; *e.g.* if the shareholder knew that there were no profits for payment of dividends, or that the payment made to him was a payment out of the company's capital, he is liable to indemnify the director in respect of any liability which the director may have incurred as a result of such payment.[13]

Statutory and other penalties

Default fines

64–37 Many duties imposed by the Acts upon the company or its directors are fortified in cases of default by penalties which may be applied by the section imposing them upon the company itself or upon the directors, or both. The most common form is a fine imposed upon any "officer who is in default." The maximum amount of the fine is, *for every day of the default*, the amount specified in Schedule 2 to the 1980 Act (s. 80). An officer (which term includes a director) who is in default is one who knowingly and

---

[10] ss. 1 (1) and 6 (1).
[11] s. 2 (1).
[11a] *Ramskill* v. *Edwards* (1886) 31 Ch.D. 100; *Walsh* v. *Bardsley* (1931) 47 T.L.R. 564.
[12] *Shepheard* v. *Bray* [1906] 2 Ch. 235; [1907] 2 Ch. 571.
[13] *Moxham* v. *Grant* [1900] 1 Q.B. 88; *Re Alexandra Palace Company* (1882) 21 Ch.D. 149; *Re National Funds* (1878) 10 Ch.D. 118.

wilfully authorises or permits the default, refusal or contravention mentioned in the relevent section (1948 Act, s. 440 (2)).[14]

Other penalties

64–38 The Acts contain several penal sections. If any officer or contributory of any company being wound up destroys, mutilates, alters, or falsifies any books, papers, or securities, or makes or is privy to the making of any false or fraudulent entry in any register, book of account, or document belonging to the company, with intent to defraud or deceive any person, he is to be guilty of an offence, and liable to two years' imprisonment (1948 Act, s. 329). Under Schedule 2 of the 1980 Act the new mode of trial and penalty are on conviction on indictment a term of imprisonment not exceeding seven years or a fine, or both.

Where any person in any return, report, certificate, balance sheet or other document required by or for the purposes of any of the provisions of the Acts specified in the Fifteenth Schedule wilfully makes a statement false in any material particular knowing it to be false, he is to be guilty of an offence (1948 Act, s. 438).

Further, if on application to a judge in chambers (in England) or one of the Lords Commissioners of Justiciary (in Scotland) there is shown to be reasonable cause to believe that any person has, while an officer of the company, committed an offence in connection with its affairs, an order may be made for the inspection of books or papers (1948 Act, s. 441).[15]

Criminal conspiracy

64–39 Directors who pay dividends out of capital are not only civilly liable but may in appropriate cases be liable for criminal conspiracy.[16] Directors are guilty of a criminal conspiracy to defraud if they agree to use the assets of the company dishonestly, *i.e.* in a manner which they could not honestly have believed to have been in the interests of the company. The test of dishonesty is a subjective one.[17]

Criminal liability for fraud

64–40 Where a director or other company officer, with intent to deceive members of creditors about the affairs of the company, publishes or concurs in publishing a written statement or account which to his knowledge is or may be misleading, false or deceptive in a material particular, he is guilty of an

---

[14] See *Beck* v. *Board of Trade* (1932) 76 S.J. 414; *Burton* v. *Bevan* [1908] 2 Ch. 240; *Dorte* v. *South African Super-Aeration* (1904) 29 T.L.R. 425.

[15] In *Re a Company* [1980] 1 All E.R. 284 (C.A.) it was held that "officer" includes all managers with "supervisory control which reflects the general policy of the company . . . or is related to the general administration of the company" and that "offence" was not restricted to misconduct of which the company was victim. On appeal (*sub. nom. Re Racal Communications Ltd.* [1980] 2 All E.R. 634) the Court of Appeal's decision was upset on the grounds that the decision of the judge in chambers is not appealable.

[16] *Burnes* v. *Pennell* (1849) 2 H.L. 497; *R.* v. *Esdaile* (1858) 1 F. & F. 213. There is no offence of criminal conspiracy in Scotland.

[17] *R.* v. *Sinclair* [1968] 1 W.L.R. 1246 (C.A.).

offence and liable to imprisonment, for a term not exceeding seven years.[18]

A prospectus is a "written statement" within this section. It was held in *R.* v. *Kylsant*[19] that a prospectus may be false in a "material particular" within this section, though it contains no specific false statement, if the prospectus as a whole is misleading.

In a winding up by the court in England the court may direct the liquidator to institute a prosecution against the directors, managers or officers, or members, for criminal offences committed by them, or to refer the matter to the Director of Public Prosecutions, and in a voluntary winding up the liquidator is required to report such matters to the Director of Public Prosecutions with power, if the Director does not take up the matter, to prosecute the delinquents with the sanction of the court (1948 Act, s. 334). The difficulty of working these sections lies in the fact that the costs of the proceedings come out of the assets, in other words, out of the pockets of creditors or shareholders, who are naturally indisposed to have public justice vindicated at their expense. This question was carefully considered by Buckley J. in *Re London and Globe Finance Corpn.*,[20] and the test he there adopted was what would a good citizen feel to be his duty in the matter—if to prosecute, then a prosecution ought to be directed by the court, even against the wishes of the persons entitled to the assets.

In Scotland section 334 empowers the court (in winding up by or subject to supervision by the court) or the liquidator (in a voluntary winding up—but subject to the court's power to issue a direction) to refer such matters to the Lord Advocate. Since criminal proceedings are taken by the Lord Advocate (or his subordinates) in Scotland, and not privately, the problem of costs considered in *Re London and Globe Finance Corpn.*[20] does not arise.

64–41 Where a prospectus includes any untrue statement, any person who issued the prospectus is liable to imprisonment or a fine or both, unless he proves that the statement was immaterial or that he had reasonable ground to believe and did believe the statement (1948 Act, s. 44 and 1980 Act, Sched. 2).[21] A statement in a prospectus or statement in lieu of prospectus is to be deemed untrue if it is misleading in the form and context in which it is included (1948 Act, ss. 46 (*a*) and 30 (5)). This seems to confirm the principles laid down in *R.* v. *Kylsant*[22] and other cases.

In appropriate circumstances, criminal proceedings may be taken against directors under the Prevention of Fraud (Investments) Act 1958, s. 13 or 14.[23]

---

[18] See Theft Act 1968, s. 19. Some of the other, more general, provisions of the Act may also apply; see especially ss. 15–18.
[19] [1932] 1 K.B. 442; see further R. v. *Gurney* (1870) Finlason 254.
[20] [1903] 1 Ch. 728.
[21] See para. 21–59, *ante*.
[22] [1932] 1 K.B. 442.
[23] See paras. 25–01 *et seq.*, *ante*.

Chapter 65

LIABILITY OF DIRECTORS TO OUTSIDERS

Liability to third parties

As to contracts

65–01 CONTRACTS BY DIRECTORS FOR COMPANY. Directors, being agents,[1] are not personally liable on contracts purporting to bind their company. If, having authority, they make a contract professedly for the company, then the company only is liable on it; if they have no authority to make the contract, they are still not personally liable on the contract,[2] although they may be liable in damages for breach of an implied warranty of authority if they can be deemed to have warranted that they had authority to act on behalf of the company.[3] The general rule was thus stated by Lord Cairns in *Ferguson* v. *Wilson*[4]:

> "Wherever an agent is liable those directors would be liable; where the liability would attach to the principal, and the principal only, the liability is the liability of the company."

The directors who have duly acted on behalf of the company are not personally liable to the contracting party even if the company's failure to carry out the contract is due to the fault of the directors, or if the company could not, at the time the contract was made, fulfil it.[5]

65–02 PERSONAL LIABILITY OF DIRECTORS. *Contractual liability.* The directors of a company may, of course, contract so as to make themselves personally liable to third parties.

This may happen expressly; *e.g.* a private company having a small capital and having issued a debenture (secured by a floating charge) to one of its directors asks a supplier for credit; in view of the danger of being an unsecured creditor in the winding up of the company, the supplier may ask the directors to accept personal liability for the goods which he is requested to supply.

More difficult are the cases in which the directors have not made themselves expressly liable to a third party but in which the question is whether,

---

[1] See para. 63–02, *ante*.

[2] *Ferguson* v. *Wilson* (1866) L.R. 2 Ch. 77.

[3] *Collen* v. *Wright* (1857) 7 E. & B. 301; 8 E. & B. 647; *Coventry's Case* [1891] 1 Ch. 202; *Firbank's Executors* v. *Humphreys* (1886) 18 Q.B.D. 54. See, further, *Weeks* v. *Propert* (1873) L.R. 8 C.P. 427 and *Chapleo* v. *Brunswick Permanent Building Society* (1881) 6 Q.B.D. 696.

[4] (1866) L.R. 2 Ch. 77, 89.

[5] *Elkington & Co.* v. *Hürter* [1892] 2 Ch. 452. Nor will directors who at a board meeting cause a breach of contract by the company commit the tort of inducing the breach for they are treated as the *alter ego* of the company (*Scammell & Nephew Ltd.* v. *Hurley* [1929] 1 K.B. 419), but they may commit the tort of conspiracy if before the meeting they agree to induce the board to break the contract (*De Jetley* v. *Marks* [1936] 1 All E.R. 863, 872–873).

having regard to the terms of the contract and the surrounding circumstances, they have to be regarded as being personally liable.

If, for example, they contract in their own names, without disclosing that they are acting for the company, they are, upon the ordinary rules regarding an agent contracting for an undisclosed principal, personally liable; again, if they contract, disclosing the fact that they are directors, but without using words sufficient to bind the company, they may render themselves personally liable on the contract. The test of liability is: does it appear from the terms of the contract that the directors were contracting on behalf of the company? If it does, they are protected.

If the directors contract in their own name, but expressly on behalf of the company or for the company, that is sufficient, and it does not matter whether the words appear in the description of the parties, or in the body of the contract, or are added by way of qualification to the signature.[6] On the other hand, if the directors contract without purporting to bind the company, *e.g.* where they say: "We, the directors of the —— Company Limited, hereby agree," etc., the contract does not bind the company, and the directors are liable.[7]

As to acceptances of bills of exchange in the name of the company, see paragraph 27–22, *ante*.

The personal liability of a director who acts for a company before its incorporation is treated elsewhere.[8]

65–03 *Statutory liability.* In exceptional cases the Act provides that directors who are in default shall be personally liable to persons other than the company. Such liability may arise:

(1) on a misstatement in a prospectus to any subscriber for shares or debentures who has suffered loss or damage (1948 Act, s. 43)[9];
(2) on an irregular allotment, to an allottee (and likewise to the company) if loss or damage is sustained (1948 Act, s. 49 (2))[10];
(3) in the case of failure to repay application money for shares if the minimum subscription has not been subscribed (1948 Act, s. 47 and 1980 Act, s. 16)[11];
(4) in the case of failure to repay application money for shares or debentures if application for these securities to be dealt in on the Stock Exchange is not made or is refused (1948 Act, s. 51)[12];
(5) by order of the court in the winding up of the company, under the "fraudulent trading" section (1948 Act, s. 332).[13]

---

[6] *Gadd* v. *Houghton* (1876) 1 Ex.D. 357.
[7] *Aggs* v. *Nicholson* (1856) 1 H. & N. 165; *McCollin* v. *Gilpin* (1880) 5 Q.B.D. 390; *Dermatine Co.* v. *Ashworth* (1905) 21 T.L.R. 510; *Universal Steam Navigation Co.* v. *James McKelvie & Co.* [1923] A.C. 492; *McLean* v. *Stuart et al.* 1970 S.L.T. (Notes) 77.
[8] See para. 27–02, *ante*.
[9] See para. 21–53, *ante*.
[10] See para. 22–38, *ante*.
[11] See para. 22–25, *ante*.
[12] See para. 22–30, *ante*.
[13] See para. 18–21, *ante*.

(6) on the failure of a company, which has commenced business without a certificate that the company's allotted share capital meets the minimum requirements, to honour a transaction, to any party to the transaction (s. 4 of the 1980 Act)[14];

(7) on the failure of the company to comply with the pre-emption requirements, to any existing shareholder who has suffered loss (s. 17 of the 1980 Act).[15]

65–04 *Liability provided in memorandum.* The memorandum of a company limited by shares (or by guarantee) may provide that the liability of its directors shall be unlimited and the same provisions may be added to the original memorandum by special resolution (1948 Act, ss. 202 and 203).

In practice, such clauses are not used.[16]

As to frauds and other torts

65–05 Any director who is a party to a fraud or to the commission of any other tort is personally liable to the injured party. This is on the principle that whoever commits a wrong is liable for it himself, and nonetheless so that he was acting as an agent or servant on behalf, and for the benefit, of another; for the contract of agency or service cannot impose any obligation on the agent or servant to commit, or assist in the committing of, fraud or any other wrong. The company may also be liable,[17] but that does not exonerate the director. So, too, if, by the order of the directors, a trespass is committed, a patent infringed, or another wrongful act committed, the directors who are parties to it are personally liable. If more than one person is concerned in the commission of a wrong, the person wronged has his remedy against all, or any one or more of them, at his choice; for every wrongdoer is jointly and severally liable for the whole damage, and it does not matter whether they acted as between themselves as equals, or one of them as agent or servant of another.

But a director is not to be held responsible for the fraud of his co-directors, unless he has expressly or impliedly authorised it.[18] "A director," as Lord Hatherley said,[19] "cannot be held liable for being defrauded. To do so would make his position intolerable."

---

[14] See para. 19–04, *ante*. The directors' liability is limited to the amount of paid-up capital the company should have raised.

[15] See para. 24–06, *ante*.

[16] If they were used, the company would be in a position comparable, at least speaking generally, to the French *société en commandite par actions* and the German *Kommandit-Gesellschaft auf Aktien*. The unpopularity of the form of the *commandite* in England can likewise be seen from the insignificant use made in practice of the Limited Partnerships Act 1907.

[17] *Cullen* v. *Thomson's Trustees* (1862) 4 Macq. 424, 432.

[18] *Cargill* v. *Bower* (1878) 10 Ch.D. 502.

[19] *Land Credit Company of Ireland* v. *Lord Fermoy* (1870) L.R. 5 Ch. 763, 772; *Re Denham & Co.* (1883) 25 Ch.D. 752; *Dovey* v. *Cory* [1901] A.C. 477; *Prefontaine* v. *Grenier* [1907] A.C. 101. Exceptionally a director who employs another director as his personal agent may, according to general principles of agency law, be responsible for the fraud of his agent. This, however, has nothing to do with company law but is due to the application of general principles of the law of agency. This proposition is founded on the analogy of *Briess* v. *Wooley* [1954] A.C. 333, where shareholders were liable for the fraud of the managing director whom they had authorised to negotiate for the sale of their shares.

On the principle laid down in *Hedley Byrne & Co. Ltd.* v. *Heller & Partners Ltd.*,[20] a director may incur liability to individual shareholders who act in reliance upon a negligent misstatement made, *e.g.* in the directors' report, since the relationship between a director and the members will normally be such as to impose a duty to take care in making such statements. Whether a similar liability may be incurred to non-members is a question of fact in each case, depending upon the circumstances in which the statement is made.

The court's power to grant relief in appropriate circumstances under section 448 of the 1948 Act apparently applies, so far as civil actions are concerned, only to actions brought by or on behalf of the company.[21]

[20] [1964] A.C. 465; for a fuller discussion of this principle, see para. 73–10, *post*.
[21] See para. 64–33, *ante*.

CHAPTER 66

PUBLICATION OF INFORMATION RELATING TO DIRECTORS

66–01 ACCORDING to the Companies Acts, the following information is required to be made available by a company with regard to its directors:

(1) a register of directors and secretaries must be maintained and available for inspection (s. 200);
(2) a register of directors' share and debenture interests must be maintained and available for inspection (1967 Act, s. 29);
(3) particulars of directors' service contracts must be available for inspection by members (1967 Act, s. 26);
(4) the names of directors must be shown in certain circumstances on business letters on which the company's name appears (1948 Act, s. 201).

In addition, there must be included in the company's accounts details of the directors' emoluments (1948 Act, s. 196) and of substantial contracts with the company in which a director is interested (1980 Act, s. 54). These matters are dealt with in Chapter 70.

Register of directors and secretaries

66–02 Every company has to keep at its registered office a register known as the register of directors and secretaries (1948 Act, s. 200 as amended by section 95 of the 1981 Act).

As far as the directors are concerned, the register has to show:

(1) If the director is an individual:
   (a) his present Christian name and surname, and any former Christian and surnames;
   (b) his usual residential address;
   (c) his nationality (any former nationality need not be shown);
   (d) his business occupation;
   (e) any other directorships currently held by him or which have been held by him at any time during the previous five years.

   Directorships of wholly owned subsidiaries of the company or of the company's holding company or of wholly owned subsidiaries of the company's holding company, if the company is a wholly owned subsidiary, do not, however, have to be shown nor do directorships of dormant[1] companies (s. 200 (2), proviso); and
   (f) in a company to which the age limit of directors applies[1a] his age.

---

[1] A company is dormant during any period in which no significant accounting transaction (as defined by section 12 (b) of the 1981 Act) occurs for that company.
[1a] See para. 61–11, *ante*.

(2) If the director is a corporation:
its corporate name and registered or principal office.

Any person in accordance with those directions the directors are accustomed to act is treated as a director (s. 200 (9) (*a*)).

The register entries relating to the secretary are treated in the next chapter.[2]

Changes in the particulars must be made in the register as and when required. Any change in the particulars must also be notified from time to time to the Registrar; the notification must be sent within 14 days from the occurrence of the change (s. 200 (4)).[2a]

The register must be open to public inspection during business hours[3] for not less than two hours per day; members may see it free of charge and other persons may do so on payment of a charge not exceeding five pence (s. 200 (6)).

It should be noted that a change in the directorships of one of the directors of a company might lead to consequential changes of the register of directors and secretaries in numerous other companies: in English law, no maximum limit is imposed upon the number of directorships which a person may hold. Assuming, *e.g.* that X, a director of A. Ltd. and of 39 other companies, resigns from the board of A. Ltd., this alteration has to be registered not only in the register of that company but likewise in those of the other 39 companies. Further, notification of the alteration would have to be sent to the Registrar by all 40 companies. In practice the exemption in the case of wholly owned subsidiaries, etc., affords some amelioration because multiple directorships are particularly frequent in the case of groups of companies.

On the official notification of any return relating to a company's register of directors or any notification of change among directors, see Chapter 17, *ante*.

Register of directors' share and debenture interests

66–03 The 1967 Act imposes an obligation upon every company to maintain a register[4] of directors' interests in the shares or debentures of the company or a related company,[5] and for this purpose requires directors to notify the company of such interests (ss. 27–29 as amended by Sched. 3 to the 1981

[2] See para. 67–03, *post*.

[2a] Section 95 (4) of the 1981 Act makes transitional provisions in relation to the notification of past directorships.

[3] Subject to such reasonable restrictions as the company may impose in its articles or by resolution of the general meeting, but so that the register is open for inspection during at least two hours per day.

[4] This register replaces the register of directors' holdings formerly required to be kept under s. 195 of the 1948 Act; s. 195 was repealed by the 1967 Act, s. 130 (4) (*c*) and Sched. 8, Part III.

[5] "Related company" is used here as meaning any other body corporate which is a subsidiary or holding company, or a subsidiary of the holding company, of the company of which the person concerned is a director (s. 27 (1) (*a*) and (*b*), other than a body corporate which is the wholly owned subsidiary of another body corporate (s. 27 (13)).

Act). "Director" includes any person in accordance with whose directions or instructions the directors of a company are accustomed to act (s. 27 (11)),[6] and directors' interests include interests of their spouses and infant children (s. 31).

Notification of interests by directors

66–04 NOTIFICATION OF EXISTING INTERESTS. A director must notify the company of any interest in such shares or debentures which exists at the time of his appointment, or, if holding office at the time this provision came into force,[7] of any interest existing at that time (s. 27 (1) (*a*)). The notification must be in writing and must state:

(i) the subsistence of his interests at the time in question; and
(ii) the number or amount of shares or debentures of each class in which each interest subsists (*ibid.*).

NOTIFICATION OF SUBSEQUENT[8] INTERESTS. A director must notify the company of the occurrence of any of the following events:

(1) any event in consequence of which he becomes or ceases to be interested in such shares or debentures;
(2) the making of a contract by him to sell any such shares or debentures;
(3) the assignment by him of a right to subscribe for shares or debentures of the company;
(4) the grant to him by a related company of a right to subscribe for shares or debentures of that company, or the exercise or assignment of such a right (s. 27 (1) (*b*)).

The notification must be in writing and must state the occurrence of the event and the number or amount of shares or debentures involved (*ibid.*), and

(a) in the case of an event under (1) or (2) above, the price[8a] to be paid or received (s. 27 (5));
(b) in the case of an event under (3) above, the consideration for the assignment (s. 27 (6));
(c) in the case of an event under (4) above,
    (i) if a grant of a right to subscribe, the date of the grant, the time within or at which the right is exercisable, the consideration for the grant and the price[8a] to be paid for the shares or debentures (s. 27 (7)), or
    (ii) if an exercise of such a right, the number or amount of shares or debentures involved, and, if registered in his name, that fact, or otherwise the person or persons in whose name they are registered (*ibid.*), or

---

[6] Subject to s. 56 (3) which exempts those giving advice in a professional capacity.
[7] October 27, 1967 (s. 57 (1) (*a*)).
[8] s. 27 (4).
[8a] Including any non-monetary consideration: 1981 Act, Sched. 3, para. 28.

(iii) if an assignment of such a right, the consideration for the assignment (s. 27 (6)).

EXPRESS REFERENCE IN NOTICE TO SECTION 27. The notification must expressly state that it is given in fulfilment of the obligation under section 27 (s. 27 (9)).

66–05 TIME FOR NOTIFICATION. Notification must be given within five[8b] days of the relevant date. The relevant date is:

(1) in the case of existing interests, the day following the director's appointment, or, if he was a director at the time the section came into force,[9] the day prior to that date (s. 27 (3) (*a*));
(2) in the case of subsequent interests, the day following that on which the event giving rise to the obligation occurred (s. 27 (3) (*b*));
(3) in either case, if the director was unaware of the interest or event at the relevant date, the day following that on which he becomes aware of it (s. 27 (3) (*a*) and (*b*)).

In calculating the period for notification, Saturdays, Sundays and bank holidays are excluded (s. 27 (12)).

66–06 INTERESTS TO BE NOTIFIED. In principle, any interest of any kind whatsoever in shares or debentures of the relevant classes must be notified (s. 28 (2)). In addition the following particular provisions lay down that a director is deemed to have a notifiable interest in shares or debentures in the following circumstances:

(1) if he is the beneficiary of a trust the property of which includes any interest in shares or debentures (s. 28 (3));
(2) if a body corporate has such an interest and
    (a) that body corporate or its directors are accustomed to act in accordance with his instructions, or
    (b) he controls one-third or more of the voting power at any general meeting of that body corporate (s. 28 (4A))[9a];
(3) if he enters into a contract for the purchase[10] of such shares or debentures (s. 28 (4) (*a*));
(4) if he has a right, other than under a trust, to call for delivery of such shares or debentures to himself or to his order or has a right to acquire or an obligation to take such an interest (s. 28 (4C)) other

---

[8b] In para. 29 (2) of Sched. 3 to the 1981 Act it is provided that the period shall be ten days in respect of interests requiring notification by virtue only of the coming into force of para. 29 (1) of the Schedule and known to the director on the date of coming into force of para. 29.

[9] See note 7, *supra*.

[9a] Any voting power exercisable by that body corporate at general meetings of another body corporate is deemed for the purpose of the one-third rule to be exercisable by the director (s. 29 (4B)).

[10] A contract for the *sale* of such shares or debentures is treated as an interest under s. 27 (1) (*b*) (ii).

than a right or obligation to subscribe for shares or debentures (s. 28 (4F)).

(5) if, not being the registered holder, he is entitled to control the exercise of any right[10a] conferred by such shares or debentures, other than as a proxy or a representative of a company (s. 28 (4) (*b*) and (4E));

(6) if he has a joint interest in such shares or debentures (s. 28 (5)).

Interests are not excluded merely on the ground that they are subject to some restraint or restriction (s. 28 (2)), or that the shares or debentures in which the interest exists are unidentifiable, as where they are included in trust property (s. 28 (6)).

The following are deemed to be events in consequence of which a director ceases to be interested in shares or debentures:

(i) delivery to his order of shares or debentures under a contract of purchase by him or a contract giving him the right to call for delivery;

(ii) failure to make delivery in accordance with the terms of such a contract or in pursuance of such a right;

(iii) the lapse of his right to call for delivery (s. 28 (11)).

66–07 INTERESTS NOT REQUIRING NOTIFICATION. A director need not notify the company of the occurrence of events within section 27 (1) (*b*) which come to his knowledge after he has ceased to be a director (s. 27 (4)). In addition, the following interests need not be notified:

(1) an interest in reversion or remainder, or (as regards Scotland) in fee, in shares or debentures, where a director has a life interest in the income of trust property comprising the shares or debentures (s. 28 (7));

(2) an interest as a bare trustee or a custodian trustee, or (as regards Scotland) as a simple trustee (s. 28 (8));

(3) an interest subsisting by virtue of an authorised unit trust scheme within the meaning of the Prevention of Fraud (Investments) Act 1958 (s. 28 (9));

(4) certain other interests under statutory schemes (s. 28 (9) and (10)).

The following further exceptions have been added by statutory instruments[11]:

(5) certain interests of persons who are co-trustees of the Public Trustee;

[10a] Control of a right includes situations where the director has such control if he exercises a right which he has or fulfils an obligation he is under (s. 29 (4D)).

[11] The Companies (Disclosure of Directors' Interests) (Exceptions) No. 1 Regulations 1967 (S.I. 1967 No. 1594), made by the then Board of Trade under powers conferred by s. 27 (1) of the 1967 Act; Companies (Disclosure of Directors' Interests) (Exceptions) Nos. 2 and 3 Regulations 1968 (S.I. 1968 Nos. 865 and 1533). For the full texts of these Regulations see Volume 2, Part A.

(6) interests in shares of a private company arising solely out of the existence of a right of pre-emption under the company's memorandum or articles;
(7) interests in shares or debentures of industrial and provident societies;
(8) interests as a trustee of, or a beneficiary under, certain pension schemes;
(9) interests of a director of a wholly owned subsidiary company who is also a director of the holding company and a register of such interests is maintained by the holding company;
(10) interests of a director of a wholly owned subsidiary company in shares or debentures of the holding company or a related company incorporated outside Great Britain.

66–08 NOTIFICATION OF INTERESTS OF SPOUSES AND CHILDREN. A director is under an obligation to notify the company of any interest of his or her spouse or infant children[12] in shares of debentures which would be notifiable if the interest was that of himself or herself (s. 31 (1) (*a*)). Similarly a director must notify the company of the occurrence of an event relating to such persons if the event would be notifiable if it related to himself or herself (s. 31 (1) (*b*) and (2)). Children for this purpose include step-children and adopted children, and the word "infant" in relation to Scotland means pupils or minors (s. 31 (5)). The requirements as to the form of notification and the time for notification are the same as those under section 27,[13] the relevant date being the day following that on which the director became aware of the interest of the spouse or child (s. 31 (2) and (4)).

66–09 PENALTIES FOR NON-NOTIFICATION. A director who fails to give notification of a registrable interest within the prescribed period, or who in purported fulfilment of an obligation to notify, deliberately or recklessly makes a false statement to a company, is guilty of an offence punishable, on summary conviction or on conviction on indictment, by imprisonment or a fine, or both (ss. 27 (8) and 31 (3), as amended by the 1980 Act, s. 80 and Sched. 2). Proceedings in England or Wales may only be instituted by, or with the consent of, the Department of Trade or the Director of Public Prosecutions (ss. 27 (10) and 31 (4)).

Obligations of company to maintain register

66–10 OBLIGATION TO RECORD NOTIFIED INTERESTS. Interests notified to the company by directors in accordance with the requirements of sections 27, 28 and 31, *supra*, must be recorded by the company in a register kept for that purpose (ss. 29 (1) and 31 (6)). The register must contain the name of the

[12] In English law the term "minor" was introduced by s. 18 of the Family Law Reform Act 1969, which also reduced the age of majority from 21 to 18 (s. 1).
[13] See para. 66–05, *ante*.

director giving the information, the information given, and the date of its entry in the register (s. 29 (1)); entries must be made against each name in chronological order (s. 29 (3)). Inscription in the register must be completed within three days from the day following that on which notification of the interest is received by the company, excluding Saturdays, Sundays and bank holidays (s. 29 (4)).

OBLIGATION TO RECORD CERTAIN INTERESTS WITHOUT PRIOR NOIFICATION. Upon the occurrence of the following events, the company is obliged to register the relevant particulars without prior notification:

(1) the grant to a director of a right to subscribe for shares or debentures of the company (s. 29 (2) (*a*));

(2) the exercise of such a right (s. 29 (2) (*b*)).

This obligation of the company does not appear to arise where such a right is given to or exercised by the spouse or infant child of a director.

OBLIGATION TO NOTIFY RECOGNISED STOCK EXCHANGE. Once a listed company has been notified of a director's or other interest under section 27 or section 31 of the 1967 Act, the company must notify the relevant recognised stock exchange of the information (Companies Act 1976, s. 25 (1)). The Stock Exchange may then publish the information in such manner as it may determine. The obligation to notify the Stock Exchange under the section must be discharged by the company before the end of the day after the obligation arises, but the Stock Exchange itself requires immediate notification to be given on receipt of a notice from a director. There is a criminal sanction for default.

66–11 LOCATION OF REGISTER. The register must be kept at the company's registered office, or, if the register of members is kept at a place other than the registered office,[14] at the place where the register of members is kept (s. 29 (7)); in the latter case notice of the location must be given to the Registrar of Companies (s. 29 (8)).

INDEX TO THE REGISTER. Unless the register itself is in the form of an index, the company must keep an index of the names inscribed in the register. Any necessary alterations in the index must be made within 14 days of the inscription of a name in the register (s. 29 (9)). The register or index may be in the form of bound books or in any other form provided that adequate precautions are taken to guard against falsification and to facilitate discovery (s. 56 (6) and Sched. 4, applying s. 436 of the 1948 Act).

---

[14] See s. 110 (2) of the 1948 Act, and para. 50–03, *ante*.

INSPECTION OF REGISTER. The register[15] must be available for inspection by members and other persons[16] to the same extent and subject to the same conditions as in the case of the register of members (s. 29 (7)).[17] The register must be produced at the commencement of every annual general meeting of the company and be available for inspection during the meeting by any person attending (s. 29 (11)). The rules as to the supplying of copies of the register, and the powers of the court to compel inspection and to direct the supplying of copies, are the same as in the case of the register of members (s. 29 (10) and (13)).[18]

66–12 PENALTIES FOR NON-COMPLIANCE. Various penalties are provided for non-compliance with the obligations imposed by section 29, as amended by the 1980 Act, s. 80 and Sched. 2. These penalties may be incurred by the company and by every officer in default (s. 29 (12)).

NOTIFICATION OF INTEREST NOT NOTICE OF TRUST. In order to preserve the position of the company under section 117 of the 1948 Act,[19] it is expressly provided that the company shall not be affected with notice of, or put upon inquiry as to, the rights of any person in relation to any shares or debentures by reason only of the company's carrying out its obligations under section 29 (s. 29 (6)).

Investigation of suspected contraventions of section 27

66–13 The Department of Trade may appoint inspectors to investigate a suspected failure by a director to notify an interest in accordance with section 27 or section 31 (2) (s. 32). The powers and duties of such inspectors are considered in Chapter 78, *post*.

Inspection of directors' service contracts

66–14 The 1967 Act requires every company to make available for the inspection of members the terms of service contracts with its directors (s. 26, as amended by the 1980 Act, s. 61). This obligation does not, however, extend to contracts which have less than 12 months to run or which can be terminated by the company within the following 12 months without payment of compensation (s. 26 (8) (*b*)).

The following must be made available for inspection:

(a) if the service contract is in writing, a copy of the contract;

(b) if the service contract is not in writing, a written memorandum of its terms (s. 26 (l) (*a*) and (*b*)).

---

[15] And presumably the index, though this is not expressly provided by the section: *cf.* s. 34, and s. 113 of the 1948 Act.

[16] In this and other respects the right of inspection is much wider than the corresponding right to inspect the former register of directors' holdings.

[17] See para. 50–11, *ante*. There is, however, no period when the register is to be closed.

[18] *Ibid.*

[19] See para. 50–06, *ante*, and *cf.* s. 73 (4) of the 1981 Act.

Any variations in the contract must be shown in the same manner (s. 26 (7)).

The obligation to make the terms of the contract available for inspection relates, it is thought, to all essential terms and must be fulfilled with fairness, in order to give the members a true and complete indication of the obligations of the company to the director. If all the terms are not contained in the written contract, a memorandum setting out the additional terms must be provided.

The obligation includes service contracts with subsidiaries of the company (s. 26 (1) (*c*)). If the service contract with the company or the subsidiary requires the director to work wholly or mainly outside the United Kingdom, the company need only make available a memorandum stating the name of the director, the provisions of the contract concerning its duration and, where applicable, the name and place of incorporation of the subsidiary (s. 26 (3A)).

Location of documents

66–15 Copies and memoranda of service contracts must be kept by the company at one of the following places:

(i) the registered office, or

(ii) any other place where the register of members is kept,[20] or

(iii) the company's principal place of business, provided that this is situated in that part of the United Kingdom in which the company is registered (s. 26 (2)).

If the documents are not kept at the registered office, notice of the place where they are kept must be given to the Registrar of Companies (s. 26 (3)). All copies and memoranda of directors' service contracts must be kept at the same place (s. 26 (1)).

Inspection of documents

Members of the company, but not other persons, are entitled to inspect the documents during reasonable[21] business hours without charge (s. 26 (4)); in case of refusal of inspection, the court may compel an immediate inspection (s. 26 (6)).

Penalties

Non-compliance by the company with the obligations to make available for inspection, and to allow inspection of, such documents has penal consequences for the company and every officer in default (s. 26 (5), as amended by the 1980 Act, s. 80 and Sched. 2).

Publication of names of directors in business letters

66–16 Section 201 of the 1948 Act formerly required companies to state on a wide range of documents on which the company's name appeared the

[20] See s. 110 (2) of the 1948 Act, and para. 50–03, *ante*.
[21] See para 66–02, *ante*.

names and nationalities (if not British) of all the directors of the company. As amended by Sched. 3 to the 1981 Act, section 201 now applies only to business letters on which the company's name appears and requires simply that, if the name of any director of the company is stated in the letter, then the names (including Christian name or initials) of all the individual directors must be stated and the corporate name of all corporate directors.

Stock Exchange requirements

66–17 The Stock Exchange requires listed companies to give details with respect to their directors. In particular, the Listing Agreement,[22] which every listed company has to sign, requires the company to inform the Stock Exchange of any change in the directorate.[23] In addition, the company must circulate with the annual report of the directors particulars of (i) any significant contract in which the director is or was materially interested[24]; (ii) any arrangement under which a director has waived or agreed to waive any emoluments[25]; and (iii) the interests of each director in the share capital of the company or any subsidiary as disclosed in the register maintained under the 1967 Act.[26]

Take-over bids

66–18 When a take-over bid is made, information with respect to the directors of the bidding company and the company to be taken over has to be given.

The Licensed Dealers (Conduct of Business) Rules 1960[27] require that—

(a) the document containing the offer must disclose whether or not in conjunction with the offer any payment or other benefit shall be made or given to any director of the offeree company for loss of office or retirement, and the particulars of such payment or benefit.[28]

(b) The document containing the offer must likewise state whether there is any other agreement or arrangement made between the bidding company and any of the directors of the offeree company, which is in connection with or conditional of the bid, and, if so, any particulars thereof.[29]

Further, the Rules require the recommendations to be made by the board of directors of the offeree company to its shareholders to contain certain details relating to the interests, agreements and arrangements of the directors of the offeree company.[30]

---

[22] Stock Exchange *Admission of Securities to Listing*, Sched. VIII, Pt. A.
[23] *Ibid.* cl. 5(d).
[24] *Ibid.* cl. 10(l).
[25] *Ibid.* cl. 10(m).
[26] *Ibid.* cl. 10(h).
[27] S.I. 1960 No. 1216.
[28] Sched. 1, Pt. II, cl. 2 (6).
[29] *Ibid.* cl. 2 (7).
[30] Sched. 3.

The City Code on Take-overs and Mergers enlarges on the disclosure requirements relating to directors in case of a bid.[31]

Oversea companies

66–19 An oversea company[32] must deliver to the Registrar for registration, *inter alia*, a list of the directors and secretary of the company.[33] That list must contain the particulars specified in section 407 (2) of the 1948 Act with respect to those persons.

PRACTICE NOTES

Register of directors' share and debenture interests

66–20 The register required by section 29 of the 1967 Act to be kept by every company may be obtained, as a bound book or in loose-leaf form, from leading company stationers. Except in the cases mentioned in section 29 (2), in which the company must act on its own initiative, entries in the register should only be made by reference to notifications given by directors in fulfilment of their obligations under section 27, since the company is not affected with notice of, or put upon inquiry as to, the rights of any person in relation to any shares or debentures.

The rules laid down in section 28 for determining whether or not a person is interested in shares or debentures are complex and, in some cases, will be diffiult to interpret in relation to particular circumstances. Many borderline cases will probably be covered by section 28 (2) and, whenever there is doubt, it is suggested that, in practice, a director should give notice of an interest, however remote it may be.

66–21 When a person is a director of a holding company and also of one or more of its subsidiaries (not being a wholly owned subsidiary), the notice he is required to give to each group company, of which he is a director, other than wholly owned subsidiaries, will contain the same information, since, subject to S.I. 1968 No. 1533,[34] he is required to disclose his interest in "the company or any other body corporate, being the company's subsidiary or holding company or a subsidiary of the company's holding company."

It should be noted that a wholly owned subsidiary is required to maintain a register for the purpose of recording the interests of any of its directors who are not also directors of the holding company. The notices to be given by such directors would relate to their interests in the holding company and in any other group company which is not a wholly owned subsidiary.

A director who has interests under several headings of section 28 and by

---

[31] City Code, General Principle No. 3, Rules 8, 13, 15, 17 (1) (b), (2) (b) (c) and 19; see also Practice Notes Nos. 9 and 10.
[32] See para. 88–02, *post*.
[33] s. 407 (1) (*b*).

virtue of section 31 may aggregate all the various interests for the purpose of his disclosure (subject only to separating each class of shares or debentures) or he may, at his option, disclose each interest separately and require that the nature and extent of an interest be recorded in the register (s. 29 (5)).

Notification is not required:

(a) to a company which is the wholly owned subsidiary of a body corporate incorporated outside Great Britain of interests in shares in, or debentures of, that body corporate or any other body corporate so incorporated, or of any event occurring in relation to any such shares or debentures;

(b) to a company by a director of the company who is also the director of a body corporate of which the company is the wholly owned subsidiary and which is itself required to keep a register under section 29 (1) of the 1967 Act of interests in any shares or debentures or of any event occurring in relation to any shares or debentures.[34]

[34] Companies (Disclosure of Directors' Interests) (Exceptions) No. 3 Regulations 1968 (S.I. 1968 No. 1533). See Vol. II, Part A.

CHAPTER 67

THE SECRETARY

Function of secretary

67–01 Every company, public or private, is required to have a secretary (1948 Act, s. 177 (1)).[1]

Although the Acts do not define the duties of the secretary, it is clear that they conceive them to be ministerial and administrative, and not to be managerial. In the contemplation of the Acts, the secretary is the officer of the company who is charged with the duty of ensuring that the affairs of the company are conducted in accordance with the provisions of the Companies Acts and the company's articles, and generally in accordance with the law. Having regard to the complicated requirements of the Acts and the complex statutory and other provisions applying to business nowadays, this is no mean task.

The position of secretary in a company has altered out of recognition during the past 75 years. From being a humble clerk he has become, in most large companies, an officer of the company having important duties and responsibilities and often with considerable influence. He remains, however, in the eyes of the law what he was originally intended to be, namely, an officer in a ministerial and administrative capacity: he has no managerial functions, and it would, normally, be unwise for an outsider to assume that he has any managerial powers, which are, prima facie, vested in the directors and any managing directors.

In practice the functions of the secretary often exceed those contemplated by the Acts and he is sometimes given considerable managerial responsibility.[2] It should, however, be realised that this is not his primary function: if a company wishes its secretary to have powers of management, these should be derived not from his office of secretary but from some other office, *e.g.* that of director.

Appointment and removal of secretary

67–02 The secretary may be appointed by the articles, but this practice, formerly of frequent occurrence, is now unusual. Such an appointment, without more, gives the secretary no rights against the company, even if he is also a member.[3] Normally the secretary will be appointed, and can be removed,

---

[1] This requirement was introduced by the company law reform culminating in the Act of 1948.

[2] This sentence and the preceding paragraph were quoted with approval by Pennycuick V.-C. in *Re Maidstone Buildings Ltd.* [1971] 1 W.L.R. 1085, 1093. See also *Panorama Developments (Guildford) Ltd.* v. *Fidelis Furnishing Fabrics Ltd.* [1971] 2 Q.B. 711, *per* Lord Denning M.R. and Salmon L.J.

[3] *Eley* v. *Positive Government Security Life Association Co.* (1876) 1 Ex.D. 88, C.A.

by the directors either under an express power in the articles or under the general powers which the articles normally give them. In such a case the company in general meeting cannot effectively appoint a secretary unless either the directors surrender their power to the meeting or the appointment is made by special resolution. Nor can the general meeting remove him from office, for there is no statutory provision which places the secretary in the same position as to removal as directors are placed by section 184: nor, again, is the office of secretary ordinarily dependent on the holder being also a director, as is frequently the case with managing directors.

The secretary may be an individual, a firm, or a body corporate, but a company which has a sole director may not have the same person as secretary nor may it have another company which has itself a sole director if that person is the sole director of the company in question (s. 178 (*a*)). The 1948 Act likewise prohibits a company from having as sole director another company the sole director of which is secretary to the company (s. 178 (*b*)).

Statutory requirements for secretaries in public companies

In relation to public companies section 79 of the 1980 Act imposes a general obligation upon the directors to take all reasonable steps to ensure that the secretary is "a person who appears to them to have the requisite knowledge and experience to discharge the functions of secretary of the company." In addition the directors must take reasonable steps to ensure that the secretary falls into one of the five following categories, *i.e.*

(1) he was on the appointed day (December 22, 1980) a secretary, assistant secretary or deputy secretary of the company;
(2) he has held for three of the five years immediately preceding his appointment the position of secretary of a company (other than a private company);
(3) he is a member of the Institute of Chartered Accountants (for England and Wales, Scotland or Ireland) or of the Association of Certified Accountants or of the Institute of Chartered Secretaries and Administrators or of the Institute of Cost and Management Accountants or of the Chartered Institute of Public Finance and Accountancy;
(4) he is a barrister, advocate or solicitor called or admitted in the United Kingdom;
(5) he is a person who appears to the directors to be capable of discharging the functions of secretary "by virtue of his holding or having held any other position or his being a member of any other body."

It would seem that the directors do not take reasonable steps to secure that the secretary has the requisite knowledge and experience simply by appointing someone who falls within one of the five categories, although there is a considerable overlap between the fifth category and the directors' general obligation.

Number of secretaries

67–03 The Acts require a company to have one secretary only; they refer throughout to "the" secretary. It is, however, clear from section 200 (3) of the 1948 Act that a company may have several secretaries who are the joint secretaries of the company.

A company may further have an assistant or deputy secretary (s. 177 (2)). Large companies also often have a registrar who is in charge of the registration and share transfer department of the company.

Register of secretaries

The provisions of section 21 of the 1976 Act concerning the registration of a statement of a company's first directors[4] apply equally to the first secretary of the company. By section 200 of the 1948 Act (as amended by section 22 of the 1976 Act) a company must maintain a register of its directors[5] and secretaries. In respect of the secretary, or, in the case of joint secretaries, in respect of each of them, the register must contain the name and address, and any former name, of the secretary if he is an individual, and the corporate or firm name and the registered or principal office, if the secretary is a corporation or a Scottish firm. If all the partners of a firm are joint secretaries the name and principal office of the firm may be stated instead (s. 200 (3)). Any change in the particulars must be notified within 14 days and a notification that a person has become a secretary must contain a consent signed by that person to act as such (s. 200 (4)). It is thought that no official notification need be given of returns or notifications relating to the secretary.[6]

Acts to be done or notices to be given by or to the secretary

67–04 If the office of secretary is vacant or if there is for any other reason no secretary capable of acting (*e.g.* if he is ill, or abroad or on holiday), anything which the Acts require or authorise to be done by or to the secretary may be done by or to the assistant or deputy secretary, if capable of so acting, and if not by or to any officer of the company authorised generally or specially in that behalf by the directors (s. 177 (2)). By the definition section (1948 Act, s. 455) "officer" includes a director, manager or secretary but it would seem that this definition does not by implication exclude other persons holding executive office in the company. It appears, however, that a branch manager who has only local functions and does not manage the affairs of the company itself in a governing role cannot be regarded as an "officer" of the company.[7] The directors would not comply

---

4 See para. 61–03, *ante*. 5 See para. 66–02, *ante*. 6 See para. 17–03, *ante*.
7 *Gibson* v. *Barton* (1875) L.R. 10 Q.B. 329, 336; *Registrar of Restrictive Trading Agreements* v. *W. H. Smith & Son Ltd.* [1968] 1 W.L.R. 1541, 1552, *per* Cross J.; [1969] 1 W.L.R. 1460, 1468, *per* Lord Denning M.R.; *cf. Re Vic Groves & Co. Ltd.* [1964] 1 W.L.R. 956, 957.

with the requirements of section 177 (2) if they appointed a person who held no office in the company to carry out the duties of secretary during the secretary's absence.

67–05 If the company has joint secretaries, it is believed that prima facie their authority is joint, and that it is joint and several only if expressly given them as such by the articles or the directors. In the former case they have to do all acts and to give all notices together, and all acts have to be done and notices to be given to both of them. Consequently, statements required by the Acts to be signed by "the secretary" have to be signed by all joint secretaries unless their authority is joint and several.

Where a provision requires or authorises a thing to be done by or to a director and the secretary, the act or notice in question is invalid, and the requirements of the provision are not satisfied, if it is done by or to a person combining the offices of director and secretary in one person (s. 179). This applies, *e.g.* to the annual return (s. 126 (1)) and the documents attached to it.[8]

A secretary is normally authorised by the board of directors to receive and accept notices to the company, but where the same person is secretary of two companies, knowledge acquired by him as secretary of one company will not be treated automatically as knowledge acquired by him as secretary of the other company. However, if there is a duty upon him to communicate the knowledge, the knowledge will be treated as his knowledge as secretary of the second company, and that company will be treated as having it.[9–11]

Powers of secretary

67–06 Since the secretary, by virtue of his office, is the chief administrative officer of the company, he has, as regards matters concerned with administration, ostensible authority to enter into contracts on behalf of the company. His administrative function extends to contracts relating to the employment of staff, the ordering of office machinery and stationery, the hiring of cars to meet customers of the company, and similar matters.[12]

On the other hand, the secretary does not, by virtue of his office, have authority to enter into managerial contracts on behalf of the company, such as contracts for the sale or purchase of goods in which the company deals, but he may have been given express or implied authority by the board of directors to act on behalf of the company in its commercial management. Nor has the secretary authority to make representations as to the company's affairs in order to induce people to take shares in the company.[13]

---

[8] *i.e.* copies of the balance sheet and report of the directors in the case of limited companies (s. 127 (1) (*a*)), and the certificates of private companies (s. 128).

[9–11] *Re Fenwick, Stobart & Co., Deep Sea Fishery Co.'s Claim* [1902] 1 Ch. 507.

[12] *Panorama Developments (Guildford) Ltd.* v. *Fidelis Furnishing Fabrics Ltd.* [1971] 2 Q.B. 711.

[13] *Barnet, Hoares & Co.* v. *South London Tramways Co.* (1887) 18 Q.B.D. 815.

From these statements the following rules can be deduced:

(1) if the secretary is shown to have express authority to perform certain acts, such acts will bind the company;

(2) if it can be shown that he has implied authority, as, for instance, by a course of dealing, the same result follows; and

(3) if the act can be shown to fall within the administrative ambit of the secretary's duties, the secretary has ostensible authority to act on behalf of the company.

The application of these rules may be of great importance to a secretary. Prima facie he is not to be fixed personally with liability for breach of trust or misfeasance by directors, for example, misapplication by them of the company's funds, even though he may have known all about it[14]; but if he had himself, as secretary, assumed the power to deal with the company's funds without supervision, he might himself be liable in such a case.

Without express authority the secretary cannot assume a managerial or corporative power which is vested in the directors: for example, he cannot summon a general meeting himself,[15] though the board can ratify such action before the meeting[16]; nor may he strike a name out of the register[17] or register a transfer before it has been passed by the board.[18]

These rules are merely an application of the well-known principle that a "principal is answerable for the act of his agent in the course of his master's business"[19]; the principle applies to a servant or agent.

Consequently, if within the scope of this authority, the acts of the secretary will bind the company even if done tortiously or fraudulently, and even though they enure not for the company's benefit but for that of the secretary himself.[20] On the other hand, where a director advanced money for the benefit of a company at the request of the secretary, without the authority of a properly constituted board of directors, he was held not to be entitled to recover the money advanced from the company.[21]

It is, accordingly, necessary in any given case to ascertain what authority is given to the secretary, or what is the scope of his duties.

[THE NEXT PARAGRAPH IS 67–08]

Duties of secretary

In general

67–08 The duties of the secretary vary with the size and nature of the company

[14] *Joint Stock Discount Co.* v. *Brown* (1869) L.R. 8 Ex. 376, 396.
[15] *Re State of Wyoming Syndicate* [1901] 2 Ch. 431.
[16] *Hooper* v. *Kerr, Stuart & Co.* (1900) 83 L.T. 729.
[17] *Wheatcroft's Case* (1873) 29 L.T. 324; *Re Indo-China Steam Navigation Co.* [1917] 2 Ch. 100.
[18] *Chida Mines Ltd.* v. *Anderson* (1905) 22 T.L.R. 27.
[19] *Per* Earl of Halsbury in *Lloyd* v. *Grace, Smith & Co.* [1912] A.C. 716, 726.
[20] *Lloyd* v. *Grace, Smith & Co.* [1912] A.C. 716; *Niven* v. *Collins Patent Lever Gear Co.* 1900, 2 S.L.T. 476; see the dicta in *Barwick* v. *English Joint Stock Bank* (1867) L.R. 2 Ex. 259 and *British Mutual Banking Co.* v. *Charnwood Forest Ry.* (1887) 18 Q.B.D. 714 and *Ruben* v. *Great Fingall Consolidated* [1906] A.C. 439, which were overruled by *Lloyd* v. *Grace, Smith & Co.*, *supra*.
[21] *Re Cleadon Trust* [1939] Ch. 286 (C.A.). See also *Edington* v. *Dunbar Steam Laundry Co.* 1903, 11 S.L.T. 117.

and the terms of the arrangement made with him. In the ordinary course he is present at all meetings of the company, and of the directors, and makes proper minutes of proceedings thereat; he issues, under the direction of the board, all necessary notices to members and others; he conducts all correspondence with shareholders in regard to calls, transfers, forfeiture and otherwise; he is in charge of the books of the company, or such of them as relate to the internal business of the company, *e.g.* the register of members, the share ledger, the transfer book, the register of debentures; he certifies transfers; and he performs other administrative functions. He is also responsible for all necessary returns to the Registrar of Companies.

He is usually authorised by the board of directors—rarely by the articles—to receive and accept notices on behalf of the company; these duties have been noted earlier.[22]

Apart from certain statutory duties which will be considered later,[23] the duties of the secretary are not fixed by law: they are those which are assigned to him either by the company under its articles, or under his contract of service with the company, or, as is normally the case, by the directors. In practice a number of duties will be implied by a course of conduct; *e.g.* it is normally one of his duties to certificate transfers, but unless such a duty is expressly placed upon him, or is implied from a course of conduct, certification by the secretary will be ineffective to bind the company (1948 Act, s. 79 (3) (*b*)).[24] This section does not, *ipso jure*, authorise the secretary to certificate.[25]

If the secretary notices that the company has become insolvent or is likely to become insolvent if continuing in business, it is, it is thought, his duty to draw the attention of the directors to this fact and the consequences of allowing the company to continue in business. Failure to give that advice may amount to negligence for which, in appropriate circumstances, the secretary might be liable to the company to which he owes a duty of care. But a mere omission to advise on the insolvency of the company and its consequences does not make the secretary a "party to" carrying on the business of the company in a fraudulent manner within the meaning of section 332 (1) of the 1948 Act.[26] To be a "party to" a fraud requires a positive act and cannot be done by mere inertia. In this case no civil or criminal liability attaches to the secretary under section 332.[27] He is not expected to give legal advice in his capacity as Secretary, even if he is a practising solicitor.[27a]

Statutory duties

7–09 The Acts impose a wide range of duties upon the secretary or upon him as alternative to some other person, including the duty:

---

[22] See para. 67–04, *ante*. [23] See para. 67–09, *post*.
[24] *Cf. Bishops* v. *Balkis Consolidated Co.* (1890) 25 Q.B.D. 512.
[25] See para. 39–27, *ante*.
[26] See para. 85–84, *post*.
[27] *Re Maidstone Buildings Ltd.* [1971] 1 W.L.R. 1085.
[27a] *Niven* v. *Collins Patent Lever Gear Co.*, *supra*.

(1) to sign the annual return and the accompanying documents (1948 Act, ss. 126 (1), 127 (1) (*a*), 128, 129 (1) (*b*))[28];
(2) in the case of winding up of the company by the court, to verify the statement to be submitted to the Official Receiver (1948 Act, s. 235 (2))[29];
(3) in the case of a receiver being appointed by debenture holders whose debentures are secured by a floating charge on substantially the whole of the company's assets, to verify the statement to be submitted to the receiver (1948 Act, s. 373 (2))[30];
(4) where a limited company applies to be re-registered as unlimited, or an unlimited company applies to be re-registered as limited, to sign the prescribed form of application (1967 Act, ss. 43 and 44)[31];
(5) to sign the statutory statement required before the registrar may issue a certificate to a public company so that the company may do business (1980 Act, s. 4(3))[32];
(6) to sign the application for a private company to be re-registered as a public company (1980 Act, s. 5 (1) (*b*))[33]; for an "old public company" to re-register as a public company (s. 8 (3) (6),[34]; for a public company to re-register as a private company (s. 10 (1) (6))[35]; or for a joint stock company[36] to register as a public company (s. 13 (4) (*e*).

67–10 In addition, many of the duties imposed by the Acts upon the company are so clearly within the province of its secretary that default by the company would in appropriate circumstances give rise to liability on the part of the secretary, where the section imposes liability upon officers in default. Such cases include the following:
(7) to deliver a return of allotments (1948 Act, s. 52)[37];
(8) to issue share or debenture certificates (1948 Act, s. 80)[38];
(9) to cause the registration of charges with the Registrar of Companies (1948 Act, ss. 96 and 97); and to keep the company's register of charges and make it available for inspection (1948 Act, ss. 104 and 105)[39];

---

[28] See para. 69–04, *post*.
[29] See para. 85–33, *post*.
[30] See para. 46–11, *ante*. s. 373 (2) applies to English companies only, but the secretary of a Scottish company has a similar duty under the Companies (Floating Charges and Receivers) (Scotland) Act 1972, s. 26 (2). See para. 48–17, *ante*.
[31] See para. 5–17, *et seq.*, *ante*.
[32] See para. 19–02, *ante*.
[33] See para. 5–06, *ante*.
[34] See para. 4–17, *ante*.
[35] See para. 5–09 and 5–15, *ante*.
[36] Defined by s. 383 of the 1948 Act.
[37] See para. 22–42, *ante*.
[38] See para. 36–01, *ante*.
[39] See paras. 45–02–45–03, *ante*. These sections do not apply in Scotland, but corresponding provisions exist in sections 106B, 106C, 106I and 106J, added by the Companies (Floating Charges and Receivers) (Scotland) Act 1972, s. 6 and Sched. See para. 47–17, *ante*.

(10) to publish the company's name outside its places of business, on its seal and on its publications (1948 Act, s. 108)[40];

(11) to permit the inspection of the register of members (1948 Act, s. 113)[41];

(12) to permit the inspection of the register of debenture holders and to forward copies of the trust deed (1948 Act, s. 87)[42];

(13) to keep and to make available for inspection the register of share interests (1981 Act, s. 73)[43];

(14) to keep the register of directors and secretaries (1948 Act, s. 200)[44];

(15) to ensure the publication of names of directors on business letters (1948 Act, s. 201)[45];

(16) to keep and to make available for inspection the register of directors' interests (1967 Act, s. 29)[46];

(17) to permit the inspection by members of copies of directors' contracts (1967 Act, s. 26)[47];

(18) to keep minutes (1948 Act, s. 145) and to make available for inspection the minutes of the general meetings (1948 Act, s. 146)[48];

(19) to send out copies of balance sheets and auditors' reports (s. 158)[49] and directors' reports (1967 Act, s. 24)[50];

(20) to deliver to the Registrar details of the purchase by a company of its own shares (1981 Act, s. 52)[50a];

(21) to cause to be published in the *Gazette* a notice where a company proposes to purchase or redeem its own shares of capital (1981 Act, s. 56).[50b]

In many of these cases the secretary is liable to a fine in case of the default of the company in complying with the requirements of the Acts; but the penalties vary. These are now governed by section 80 and Schedule 2 of the 1980 Act. The Act often provides for a default fine of so much per day for continued contravention after summary conviction (s. 80 (2) and (3)). It should be noted that where under the statutory provision in question a fine is imposed on the secretary as the "officer in default," *mens rea* has to be proved against him because, according to section 440 (2), the phrase means an officer of the company—undoubtedly the secretary falls under that term—"who knowingly and wilfully authorises or permits the default, refusal or contravention mentioned in the enactment."

[THE NEXT PARAGRAPH IS 67–12]

[40] See para. 7–03, *ante*.
[41] See para. 50–11, *ante*.
[42] See para. 43–18, *ante*.
[43] See para. 52–01, *ante*.
[44] See para. 66–02, *ante*.
[45] See para. 66–16, *ante*.
[46] See para. 66–03, *ante*.
[47] See para. 66–14, *ante*.
[48] See para. 57–02 and 57–06, *ante*.
[49] See para. 70–04, *post*.
[50] See para. 70–04, *post*.
[50a] See para. 37–16, *ante*.
[50b] See para. 33–21, *ante*.

Position of secretary vis-à-vis the company

67–12 The rights of the secretary *vis-à-vis* the company depend primarily on his contract with the company, which is governed by the ordinary law relating to contracts of employment. Thus, since his contract is one of personal service, specific performance will not generally be ordered.[51] Where there is a negative stipulation that an employee will not engage elsewhere, the court may grant an injunction to restrain a breach thereof.[52] To found this remedy by injunction, however, the company must put in the contract a clear negative covenant.[53]

Dismissal

67–13 In the absence of express agreement to the contrary, and subject to the provisions of Part IV of the Employment Protection (Consolidation) Act 1978, an employee is entitled to reasonable notice of dismissal, or to damages in lieu thereof[54]; and where power is reserved to the company at its absolute discretion to determine the engagement at an earlier date than that fixed, proper notice of the company's intention to terminate must be given.[55]

There are, however, certain things—going to the root of the contract—for which an employee may be dismissed summarily and without notice; for instance, wilful disobedience of any lawful order of the company,[56] misconduct,[57] incompetence or permanent disability,[58] or even an act of forgetfulness by an employee, if it has, or is calculated to have, serious results, may justify dismissal without notice.[59] In *Pearce* v. *Foster*,[60] where a servant, whose advice was frequently required in the course of his duties upon securities in which money should be invested by the firm, himself speculated to a considerable extent upon the Stock Exchange, "so as to make his interest conflict with his duty,"[61] the employers were justified in dismissing him summarily.

Where a servant is wrongfully dismissed from his employment, the damages for dismissal cannot include compensation for the manner of the dismissal.[62]

An officer who accepts an incompatible office by doing so prima facie

---

51 *Stocker* v. *Brocklebank* (1851) 3 M. & G. 250; *Mair* v. *Himalaya Tea Co.* (1865) L.R. 1 Eq. 411. See also *Bainbridge* v. *Smith* (1889) 41 Ch.D. 462, where specific performance of a contract to employ a managing director was refused.
52 *Lumley* v. *Wagner* (1852) 1 De G.M. & Co. 604.
53 *Whitwood Chemical Co.* v. *Hardman* [1891] 2 Ch. 416.
54 *Creen* v. *Wright* (1876) 1 C.P.D. 592.
55 *Re African Association and Allen* [1910] 1 K.B. 396.
56 *Spain* v. *Arnott* (1817) 2 Stark. 256; *Amor* v. *Fearon* (1839) 9 A. & E. 548.
57 *Pearce* v. *Foster* (1886) 17 Q.B.D. 536; *Boston Deep Sea* v. *Ansell* (1888) 39 Ch.D. 339.
58 *Harmer* v. *Cornelius* (1858) 5 C.B.(N.S.) 236.
59 *Addis* v. *Gramophone Co.* [1909] A.C. 488.
60 (1886) 17 Q.B.D. 536, 541, *per* Lindley L.J.
61 *Baster* v. *London and County Printing Works* [1899] 1 Q.B. 901.
62 *Re African Association and Allen* [1910] 1 K.B. 396. *Addis* v. *Gramaphone Co.* [1909] A.C. 488. *Cf. Cox* v. *Philips Industries Ltd.* [1976] 1 W.L.R. 638.

vacates his original office, but it is doubtful whether any other office, except that of auditor, would be incompatible with that of secretary.

An order for winding up is equivalent to dismissal,[63] and so is the appointment by the court of a receiver and manager in a debenture holders' action[64]; and a voluntary winding up may operate in like manner. The mere fact of voluntary winding up has been held not so to operate,[65] but a voluntary winding up coupled with a sale of the company's business was held to operate as a dismissal.[66]

Where an appointment is made for a fixed period, it becomes a question of construction whether there is a definite agreement by the company to provide employment for the period named; and if there is found to be such an agreement, no term will be implied authorising the company to discontinue its business.[67] If there is no such definite agreement to provide employment, the court will not, as a rule, imply a term that the company will not discontinue its business.[68]

Damages for wrongful dismissal

67–14 Where the secretary is wrongfully dismissed, he is, like any other employee, entitled to damages according to what he would have been entitled to receive had his employment continued, but he has to do his reasonable best to mitigate the damages suffered. Thus, the damages to which the secretary is entitled are reduced by the emoluments which he earned or, had he tried, would have earned[69] in employment of a similar nature.

It would appear that, on the principle of *British Transport Commission* v. *Gourley*,[70] the damages awarded would have to take into account any income tax liability which would have been payable had the servant continued to earn what was due to him under his contract.

If a company by winding up disables itself from carrying out its bargain to continue an employee in its employment, it cannot hold him to his part of the bargain not to compete in business with the company.[71]

Unfair dismissal

Under Part V of the Employment Protection (Consolidation) Act 1978 most employees with more than one year's continuous service with an

---

[63] *Chapman's Case* (1866) L.R. 1 Eq. 346.
[64] *Reid* v. *Explosives Co.* (1887) 19 Q.B.D. 264.
[65] *Midland Counties District Bank* v. *Attwood* [1905] 1 Ch. 357.
[66] *Reigate* v. *Union Manufacturing Co.* [1918] 1 K.B. 592 (C.A.).
[67] *Turner* v. *Goldsmith* [1891] 1 Q.B. 544; *Ogdens* v. *Nelson* [1905] A.C. 109; *Reigate* v. *Union Manufacturing Co.*, *supra*; *Fowler* v. *Commercial Timber Co.* [1930] 2 K.B. 1 (where the plaintiff had himself voted for voluntary liquidation); *Shirlaw* v. *Southern Foundries (1926) Ltd.* [1939] 2 K.B. 206.
[68] *Re T. N. Farrer Ltd.* [1937] 1 Ch. 352; *Rhodes* v. *Forwood* (1876) 1 App.Cas. 256; *Lazarus* v. *Cairn Line* (1921) 106 L.T. 378; *Re Railway and Electric Co.* (1888) 38 Ch.D. 597; *Hamlyn & Co.* v. *Wood* [1891] 2 Q.B. 488.
[69] See *Re Gramophone Records Ltd.* [1930] W.N. 42; *Re W. R. Snow & Co. Ltd.* [1930] W.N. 68.
[70] [1956] A.C. 185; see para. 61–30, *ante*.
[71] *Measures Bros. Ltd.* v. *Measures* [1910] 2 Ch. 248 (C.A.).

employer have the right not to be unfairly dismissed, and dismissal is defined so as to include the expiry without renewal of a fixed-term contract (s. 55).[72] Whether the dismissal was or was not in accordance with the terms of the contract of service is not dispositive of the question of whether it was fair. The question is to be judged according to the statutory criteria.[73] Often the question is whether the industrial tribunal (to which claims lie) is satisfied that the employer "in the circumstances (having regard to equity and the substantial merits of the case) . . . acted reasonably in treating (the reason shown by the employer) as a sufficient reason for dismissing the employee" (s. 57 (3)). The tribunal may order reinstatement or re-engagement of the employee (s. 69), but it is more likely to award compensation, which in the usual case may not exceed £9,850 (ss. 73–75). Where an order to reinstate or re-engage is not complied with by the employer, however, additional compensation must be awarded to the employee (s. 71).

Other employment protection rights

Under Part VI of the 1978 Act an employee with two or more years' continuous service with an employer who is dismissed on grounds of redundancy (as defined in section 81 (2) of the Act) is entitled to a redundancy payment from his employer, calculated according to the employee's length of service, salary level at the date of dismissal and age. The employer is partially reimbursed from the statutory Redundancy Fund. An employee employed under a fixed-term contract of two years or more is not entitled to a redundancy payment arising from the expiry of the contract if, before the term expires, he has agreed in writing to exclude his right to such a payment (s. 142 (2)).

Under section 319 of the 1948 Act any "clerk or servant" has priority in a winding up or receivership[74] in respect of four months' arrears of wages and this has been extended by section 121 of the 1978 Act to include various payments to which employees are entitled under that Act or the Employment Protection Act 1975 (subject to a maximum of £800). It is thought that the question of whether a secretary is a "clerk or servant" will depend upon whether he is employed under a contract of service (the usual case) or a contract for services.[75] Under sections 40, 106 and 122 to 127 of the 1978 Act certain pecuniary entitlements of the employee against his employer may on his employer's insolvency be asserted against the redundancy fund, which will satisfy the claims and then be subrogated to the employee's rights *vis-à-vis* the employer. In this way the employee is

[72] However, under s. 142 (1) of the 1978 Act, as amended by s. 8 (2) of the Employment Act 1980, an employee employed under a fixed-term contract of one year or more may agree in writing to waive his right not to be unfairly dismissed upon the expiry of the contract.

[73] See 1978 Act, ss. 57–63 and 1980 Act, ss. 6–7.

[74] See para. 46–11, *ante*.

[75] *Cf. Cairney* v. *Back* [1906] 2 K.B. 746 where a secretary of a company who supplied the necessary services to the company through a clerk employed by him was held not be a "clerk or servant."

guaranteed, for example, eight weeks' arrears of pay, pay for the statutory minimum period of notice and a redundancy payment, irrespective of the employer's ability to pay.[76]

Trade secrets

67–15 A secretary, like any other employee or ex-employee, may generally be restrained by injunction from revealing trade secrets.[77]

Secret profits

A secretary, like any other servant or agent, must not make a secret profit by virtue of his office. He is in a fiduciary relationship towards the company, and misfeasance proceedings can be instituted against him as against a director (1948 Act, s. 333).[78] It is likewise thought that the principle of *Regal (Hastings)* v. *Gulliver*[79] applies to the secretary, *viz*. that if he is enabled to make a profit by virtue of his office, he will be accountable to the company for that profit. He should not, therefore, deal in shares or commodities on the strength of knowledge acquired by him in the course of his duties.

A secretary sued for breach of trust or misfeasance (including negligence) is entitled to the benefit of the Limitation Act 1980.[80]

---

[76] See Davies and Freedland, "The Effects of Receiverships upon Employees of Companies" (1980) 9 *Industrial Law Journal* 95.
[77] *Merryweather* v. *Moore* [1892] 2 Ch. 518; *Robb* v. *Green* [1895] 2 Q.B. 315.
[78] See para. 64–28, *ante*.
[79] [1942] 1 All E.R. 378 (H.L.); see para. 64–23, *ante*.
[80] *Municipal Freehold Land Co.* v. *Pollington* (1890) 63 L.T. 238, 243. (The Limitation Act 1980 does not apply to Scotland).

Chapter 68

INSIDER DEALING

Introduction

68–01 Under Part V of the Companies Act 1980 insider dealing becomes in certain circumstances a criminal offence. These provisions supplement the equitable rules relating to directors' fiduciary duties, the prohibition on option dealings contained in section 25 of the 1967 Act, and the self-regulatory provisions of the City Code on Take-overs and Mergers and of the Stock Exchange Model Code for Securities Transactions by Directors of Listed Companies.

Prohibition of insider dealing

68–02 Part V of the 1980 Act prohibits insider dealing, as defined, which is effected through a recognised stock exchange or through off-market dealing, by an individual who is connected with the company in question, a Crown servant, a take-over bidder or an individual who has obtained information from them. It also prohibits the counselling or procuring of dealing or the communication of information by these individuals. Bodies corporate as such are excluded from the prohibitions.

Persons connected with a company

68–03 An individual is connected with a company if he is a director of the company. He is also connected if he occupies a position as officer (other than director) or as employee of the company or if there exists a professional or business relationship between himself (or his employer or a company of which he is a director) and the company, and the position or relationship is such that it may reasonably be expected to give him access to unpublished, price-sensitive information which it would be reasonable to expect him not to disclose except in the proper performance of his functions (s. 73 (1)). Finally, an individual is connected with a company if he has any of the above positions or relationships in a "related company," *i.e.* the company's subsidiaries or holding company or in any subsidiary of the holding company (s. 73 (5)). In this case the relevant position or relationship is defined by reference to unpublished, price-sensitive information about either the company or the related company (s. 73 (1) (*b*)). The above definition is exhaustive of connected persons (s. 73 (1)).

Prohibition of stock exchange dealing by connected persons

68–04 An individual who is knowingly connected with a company or has been at any time in the preceding six months knowingly connected with a company is subject to two prohibitions on dealing on a recognised stock exchange. First, he may not deal in the securities of the company if (a) he has information which he knows is unpublished, price-sensitive information, (b) he holds that information by virtue of being connected with the company, and (c) it would be reasonable to expect him, by virtue of the position by which he is connected, not to disclose the information except in the proper performance of the functions of the position (s. 68 (1)). Secondly, an individual so connected with a company may not deal in the securities of any other company if (a) he holds information which he knows is unpublished, price-sensitive information in relation to the securities of the other company, (b) he acquired the information by virtue of being connected with the first company, (c) condition (c) above is satisfied, and (d) the information relates to an actual or contemplated transaction involving both companies or one of the companies and the securities of the other or relates to the fact that such a transaction is no longer contemplated (s. 68 (2)).

Unpublished, price-sensitive information is defined (s. 73 (2)) as information (a) which is not generally known to those accustomed or likely to deal in the securities, (b) which would, if generally known to them, be likely materially to affect the price of the securities, and (c) which relates to specific matters of concern to the company (rather than matters of a general nature). It is thought that the third limb of the definition draws a distinction that may be difficult to apply in practice. Dealing on a recognised stock exchange is defined so as to include dealing through an "investment exchange"[1] (s. 73 (3) and (5)).

Prohibition of off-market dealing by connected persons

68–05 In the same circumstances[2] as a connected individual is prohibited from dealing on a recognised stock exchange he is also prohibited from engaging in off-market dealing in the securities of the company (except where those securities are international bonds). Off-market dealing consists, first, in dealing other than on a recognised stock exchange in the advertised securities of any company through an off-market dealer. Liability is imposed where the off-market dealer is making a market in the securities and the connected person knows that he is an off-market dealer, that he is making a market and that the securities are advertised securities (s. 70 (1) (*a*) (i)). Secondly, the notion of off-market dealing is extended to embrace dealing in advertised securities as an off-market dealer who is making a market in the securities or as an officer, employee or agent of such a dealer acting in the course of the dealer's business (s. 70 (1) (*a*) (ii)).

Off-market dealers are those who are licensed or exempted dealers

[1] An investment exchange "means an organisation maintaining a system whereby an offer to deal in securities made by a subscriber to the organisation is communicated, without his identity being revealed, to other subscribers to the organisation, and whereby any acceptance of that offer by any of those other subscribers is recorded and confirmed" (s. 73 (5)). This presumably covers trading on Ariel.

[2] See para. 68–04, above.

under section 3 of the Prevention of Fraud (Investments) Act 1958 or who are members of a stock exchange or association of dealers in securities recognised under that Act[3] (s. 70 (3)). An individual is taken to deal through an off-market dealer if the latter is a party to the transaction, is an agent for either party to the transaction or acts as an intermediary in connection with the transaction (s. 70 (5)). An off-market dealer is taken to deal not only when he deals in securities by buying or selling or agreeing to buy or sell them (whether as principal or agent) (s. 73 (3)), but also when he acts an an intermediary in connection with deals made by other persons (s. 70 (4)). An off-market dealer makes a market in any securities if in the course of his business as an off-market dealer he holds himself out to both prospective buyers and prospective sellers as willing to deal in them otherwise than on a recognised stock exchange (s. 73 (4)).

Advertised securities are listed securities or those in relation to which, not more than six months before the dealing takes place, information has been published indicating the prices at which people have dealt or were willing to deal, for the purpose of facilitating deals in the securities.

International bonds

68–06 Section 70 (1) (*a*) (ii) imposes a potentially wide liability upon off-market dealers. In particular, it prevents them from making a market when they are connected persons in possession of unpublished, price-sensitive information. This prohibition is relaxed (by section 71 of the 1980 Act as amended by section 112 of the 1981 Act) in the interests of the Eurobond market, where the dealer is an issue manager[4] for an international bond issue who is making a market in the debenture and where the dealing is done in good faith as a person making a market. The relaxation applies to unpublished, price-sensitive information obtained by virtue of his being an issue manager and which it would be reasonable to expect him to have obtained as such (s. 71 (1) (*b*)). A second relaxation, applying to the same information, covers issue managers of international bonds in respect of actions done in good faith in connection with the issue within three months after the issue date or before it is decided not to proceed with the issue (s. 71 (1) (*a*)). This would protect, for example, issue managers when they allot bonds. In both cases the relaxation applies to dealing in the securities and to counselling or procuring others to deal and to communicating information[4a] (section 71 (1A)).

An international bond issue is an issue of debentures (a) all of which are offered by an off-market dealer to persons whose ordinary business includes the buying and selling of debentures, and (b), where the debentures are denominated in sterling, at least 50 per cent. in nominal value of which

[3] The provisions of the 1958 Act are discussed in Chapter 25.
[4] Whether he acts as agent for the issuing company or has the bonds issued to him by the company with the intention that they shall be sold to other persons (s. 72 (2)). S. 71 also exempts officers, employees and agents of the issue manager.
[4a] See para. 68–10, *post*.

are offered to persons who are neither citizens of the United Kingdom and Colonies nor companies formed under the law of any part of the United Kingdom (s. 71 (2)).

The Secretary of State may by regulations bring within the scope of section 71 persons who would not otherwise be issue managers or off-market dealers or issues that would not otherwise be international bond issues; and regulations may also, on the other hand, amend or disapply the two relaxations in favour of true international bond issues (section 71 (3)–(5)).

Prohibited dealing by Crown servants

68–07 Any Crown servant[5] or former Crown servant who knowingly holds unpublished, price-sensitive information relating to the securities of any company, which he has obtained by virtue of his position as a Crown servant and which it would be reasonable to expect him not to disclose except in the proper performance of his functions, may not deal on a recognised exchange (s. 69 (3) (*a*)) nor engage in off-market dealing (s. 70 (1)) in those securities, subject in the latter case to the exception for international bond issues (s. 71).

Prohibited dealing by take-over bidders

68–08 An individual who is contemplating, or has contemplated, making a take-over offer (with or without another person) for a company may not deal on a recognised stock exchange in the securities of that company if he knows that the information that an offer is contemplated, or is no longer contemplated, is unpublished, price-sensitive information in relation to the securities. This prohibition does not apply in dealings on the recognised stock exchange effected by the bidder in the capacity in which he makes the bid but only to dealings effected in another capacity (s. 68 (4)). Thus, market dealings by bidders *qua* bidders are not restricted by this subsection, though they may fall prima facie within section 68 (1) or (2).[6] A take-over bidder prohibited from dealing on a recognised stock exchange is also prohibited from engaging in off-market dealing (s. 70 (1)), subject to the exception for international bond issues. A take-over offer is defined as an offer to the holders of all, or a particular class of, the shares of a company to acquire those shares or a specified proportion of them (s. 73 (5)).

Individuals obtaining information from prohibited dealers also prohibited from dealing

68–09 Any individual who has information (a) which he knowingly obtained (directly or indirectly) from a person connected with a company,[7] (b) which he knows or has reasonable cause to believe was held by the

[5] *i.e.* "an individual who holds office under, or is employed by, the Crown" (s. 73 (5)).
[6] But see the defences discussed in para. 68–12.
[7] See above para. 68–03.

connected person by virtue of being connected, and (c) which he knows or has reasonable cause to believe it would be reasonable for the connected person, by virtue of his connection and position, not to disclose except for the proper performance of his functions, may not deal on a recognised stock exchange in the securities of the company if he knows that the information is unpublished, price-sensitive information in relation to the securities of the company. Nor may the individual deal in the securities of any other company if he knows that the information is unpublished, price-sensitive information in relation to the securities of the other company and it relates to any transaction involving the company with which the connected person is connected and the other company or one of the companies and the securities of the other or it relates to the fact that such a transaction is no longer contemplated (s. 68 (3)). These prohibitions on dealing on a recognised stock exchange by an individual who has obtained information from a connected person parallel those prohibitions imposed on the connected person himself by section 68 (1) and (2).[8] The prohibition extends equally to off-market dealing (s. 70 (1)), subject to the international bond issue exception (s. 71).

There are two further prohibitions of this type. Any individual who knowingly obtains (directly or indirectly) information from a Crown servant or former Crown servant who the individual knows or has reasonable cause to believe held the information by virtue of his position may not deal on a recognised stock exchange in any securities in relation to which the individual knows the information is unpublished, price-sensitive information (s. 69). Further, an individual who knowingly obtains (directly or indirectly) information from a take-over bidder that an offer is being contemplated or no longer contemplated may not deal on a recognised stock exchange in the securities of the company contemplated in the offer if he knows that the information is unpublished, price-sensitive information (s. 68 (5)). Both these prohibitions are extended to off-market dealing (s. 70).

Counselling or procuring dealing

68–10 Any individual who is prohibited from dealing in any securities on a recognised stock exchange or through off-market dealing is also prohibited from counselling or procuring any other person (including a body corporate) to deal in those securities in either of those ways, knowing or having reasonable cause to believe that that person would so deal. This prohibition applies to connected individuals, individuals obtaining information from connected individuals, take-over bidders, individuals obtaining information from take-over bidders (ss. 68 (6) and 70 (1)), Crown servants and individuals obtaining information from Crown servants (ss. 69 (3) (6) and 70 (1) (*b*)).

[8] See above para. 68–04.

Communicating information

The same individuals as in the previous paragraph are also forbidden to communicate the relevant information to any other person (including a body corporate) if they know or have reasonable cause to believe that that person or *some other person* will make use of the information for dealing, or for counselling or procuring another person to deal, on a recognised stock exchange or for engaging in, or for counselling or procuring another to engage in, off-market dealing (ss. 68 (7), 69 (3) (*c*) and 70 (1) (*c*)).

Stock exchanges outside Great Britain

68–11 The individuals listed in para. 68–10 are prohibited from counselling or procuring another person (including a body corporate) to deal in the relevant securities on a stock exchange outside Great Britain (other than a recognised stock exchange[9]) in the knowledge or with reasonable cause to believe that the other person would so deal. They are also prohibited from communicating information to another person in the knowledge or with reasonable cause to believe that that person or some other person will make use of the information for the purpose of dealing, or of counselling or procuring another person to deal, in the relevant securities on such an exchange (s. 70 (2)). Dealing on a stock exchange outside Great Britain (other than a recognised stock exchange) is not as such forbidden.

Defences

68–12 Apart from the specific exception for international bond issues to liability for off-market dealing[10] all the prohibitions listed above are subject to three general defences. These are as follows.

(1) An individual is not liable where he acts otherwise than with a view to the making of a profit or the avoidance of a loss (whether for himself or another person (ss. 68 (8) (*a*), 69 (4) and 70 (2)). A trustee or personal representative is presumed to have acted in this manner when he deals or procures or counsels another to deal in securities, if he acts on the advice of a person who appeared to the trustee or personal representative to be the appropriate person from whom to seek such advice and who did not appear himself to be prohibited from dealing (s. 68 (11)). In such cases the trustee or personal representative is protected even if he himself has unpublished, price-sensitive information.

(2) An individual is not liable if he enters into a transaction in the course of the exercise in good faith of his functions as liquidator, receiver or trustee in bankruptcy (ss. 68 (8) (*c*), 69 (4) and 70 (2)).

(3) An individual is not liable if the information was obtained in the

---

[9] Only the Stock Exchange has been recognised under s. 15 of the Prevention of Fraud (Investments) Act 1958, but the Stock Exchange includes branches which operate in Dublin and Belfast (but *cf.* s. 89 of the 1980 Act).

[10] See above para. 68–06.

course of a business as a jobber[11] and was of a description which it would be reasonable to expect him to obtain in the ordinary course of such a business and he acts in good faith in the course of that business (ss. 68 (8) (*c*), 69 (4) and 70 (2)).

Where an individual would otherwise be liable by virtue of having information about a particular transaction, he will nevertheless not be liable if he acts in order to facilitate the completion or carrying out of the transaction. This is not a general defence because it does not apply to those categories of case where liability arises from unpublished, price-sensitive information which does not concern a transaction (ss. 68 (10), 69 (5) and 70 (2)).

Penalties

68–13 Contravention of the prohibitions is a criminal offence, punishable on indictment by imprisonment for up to two years or an unlimited fine (or both) and on summary conviction by imprisonment for up to six months or a fine of up to £1,000 (or both) (ss. 72 (1) and 87 (1)). Proceedings may be instituted in England and Wales only by the Secretary of State or Director of Public Prosecutions (s. 72 (2)). No provision is made for special investigators or special powers of investigation. No civil remedies are created by the Act and section 72 (3) specifically provides that no transaction shall be void or voidable by reason only of having been entered into in breach of the prohibitions. No specific provision for disgorgement of profits made out of insider dealing is contained in the Act, but under ss. 35 and 39 of the Powers of the Criminal Courts Act 1973[11a] a court by whom a person is convicted may make a compensation order requiring him to pay compensation to any person who has suffered loss resulting from the offence or, in the case of a Crown court, may make a criminal bankruptcy order. A magistrates' court may not make a compensation order in an amount of more than £1,000. Neither type of order can be made if it is not possible to identify a person who has suffered loss as a result of the offence.

Liability in equity

68–14 It is thought that the principles developed in equity concerning the fiduciary duties owed by directors and others are sufficiently wide to make a person subject to the duties accountable to his company for profits realised from insider trading on the basis of information acquired by him in the course of his functions as director or holder of another fiduciary position, although no English case has explicitly recognised such liability.[12]

[11] A jobber is defined as "an individual, partnership or company dealing in securities on a recognised stock exchange and recognised by the Council of the Stock Exchange as carrying on the business of a jobber" (s. 68 (9)).

[11a] The 1973 Act does not apply to Scotland, but Part IV of the Criminal Justice (Scotland) Act 1980 provides for a compensation order against convicted persons.

[12] The fiduciary duties are discussed above at paras. 64–23 to 64–24 and see *Diamond* v. *Oreamuno* 248 N.E. 2d 910 (1968) and *Schein* v. *Chasen* 478 F.2d 817 (1973). Similar principles would apply in Scotland.

In exceptional cases there might also be fiduciary liability to individual shareholders.[12a]

Option dealings

68–15 The Jenkins Committee concluded that "a director of a company should not deal in options in securities of his company or of the group to which the company belongs. A director who speculates in this way with special inside information is clearly acting improperly, and we do not believe that any reputable director would deal in such options in any circumstances."[13] This recommendation was implemented by the 1967 Act.

Penalisation of certain option dealings

The 1967 Act makes it an offence for a director (or the spouse or infant children of a director) to buy options in quoted shares or debentures of the company of which he is a director or of certain related companies.[14] The following option dealings are penalised, *viz*. the buying of

(1) the right to call for delivery of a specified number or amount of such shares or debentures at a specified price and within a specified time ("call" options) (s. 25 (1) (*a*));

(2) the right to make delivery of a specified number or amount of such shares or debentures at a specified price and within a specified time ("put" options) (s. 25 (1) (*b*));

(3) the right (as he may elect) to call for, or make, delivery of a specified number or amount of such shares or debentures at a specified price and within a specified time ("double" options) (s. 25 (1) (*c*)).

Option dealings not penalised

The penalisation of option dealings does not extend to the acquisition of options in securities of private companies or in unquoted securities of a public company (s. 25 (2)).

Further, as regards quoted securities, the following dealings are not penalised:

(1) the purchase of a right to subscribe for shares or debentures directly from the company (in any case unissued shares are not quoted shares);

(2) the purchase of debentures carrying the right to subscribe for shares or to be converted into shares of the company (s. 25 (4)).

Persons whose dealings are penalised

68–16 Penalised option dealings include not only dealings by directors of the company in question or a related company but also dealings by the spouse or infant children, including step-children and adopted children, of a

[12a] See para. 64–03, *ante*.

[13] Report of the Company Law Committee, Cmnd. 1749, 1962, para. 90.

[14] For companies which can be treated as "related" for this purpose, see s. 25 (2).

director, who are not themselves directors (s. 30). It is, however, a defence for such persons to prove that they had no reason to believe that their spouse or parent was a director of the company (s. 30 (1), end).

A person is deemed to be a director for the purposes of sections 25 and 30 of the 1967 Act if the directors of the company are accustomed to act in accordance with his directions or instructions (ss. 25 (3), 30 (2)).[15]

Penalties

A person found guilty of the offence of dealing in penalised options is liable

(1) on summary conviction, to up to six months' imprisonment or to a fine not exceeding £1,000, or both;

(2) on conviction on indictment, to up to two years' imprisonment or to a fine of unlimited amount, or both (s. 25 (1), as amended by the Companies Act 1980, s. 80 and Sched. 2).

Investigation of suspected contraventions of section 25

68–17 The Department of Trade may appoint inspectors to investigate suspected dealings by directors in penalised options (s. 32). The powers and duties of such inspectors are considered at paragraphs 78–25 *et seq., post*.

Validity of penalised option dealings

Section 25 does not state that penalised option dealings are invalid. It is submitted that, unless the third party from whom the option was bought did not act in good faith, prohibited option dealings are not invalid.

The City Code on Take-overs and Mergers[16]

The City Code on Take-overs and Mergers is particularly concerned with the opportunities for insider dealing that may arise during the preliminary stages of a take-over bid. The Code tackles the problem in three ways: by insisting upon secrecy, by prohibiting dealing and by requiring public announcements.

Model Code for Securities Transactions by Directors of Listed Companies

This Code is set out in Volume II at para. C–902, and is discussed at para. 82–26, *post*.

---

[15] Subject to s. 56 (3) which removes from the deeming provision those people in accordance with whose directions or instructions the directors are accustomed to act by reason only that the directors act on advice given by them in a professional capacity.

[16] The City Code is set out at paras. D–001 *et seq.* and is discussed generally at paras. 82–05 to 82–21.

B. ANNUAL RETURN AND ACCOUNTS

Chapter 69

THE ANNUAL RETURN

Requirement to submit annual return

69–01 Every company having a share capital is, apart from exceptional cases which will be considered later, required at least once in every calendar year[1] to make a return to the Registrar setting out specified particulars relating to the company (1948 Act, s. 124). This return is called the annual return.

A similar return has to be made in the case of a company not having a share capital (s. 125).

When not required

69–02 An annual return need not be made in the year of the company's incorporation, nor in the following year if it is exempted under section 131 from being required to hold an annual general meeting in that year (s. 124 (1), proviso (*a*)).

Time for completion of annual return

69–03 There are three requirements as to time which have to be complied with:

(1) the return must be made every calendar year (s. 124);
(2) the return must be made up to the fourteenth day after the annual general meeting; and
(3) it must be sent within 42 days after the annual general meeting (s. 126 (1)).[2]

A Practice Note on the completion and filing of the annual return is appended to this chapter.[3]

Contents and form of annual return

69–04 The matters required to be included in the annual return are set out in Part I of the Sixth Schedule to the Act, and the form of the return must be as near as circumstances permit to that set out in the Companies (Annual Returns) Regulations 1977 (see Vol. II, A3056–3057). The return sent to

---

[1] "Year" for the purposes of these provisions means the period from January 1 to December 31: *Gibson* v. *Barton* (1875) L.R. 10 Q.B. 329; *Edmonds* v. *Foster* (1875) 45 L.J.(M.C.) 41.
[2] Under earlier Acts the return had to be within 28 days of the first general meeting held in any year, whether or not it was the annual general meeting (s. 110 (1) of the Act of 1929).
[3] See para. 69–06, *post*.

the Registrar must be signed by one director and the secretary of the company.[4]

The return puts on public record in summary form facts of import to anyone dealing or concerned with the company. These facts include:

(1) the situation of the register of members and debenture holders;
(2) particulars of the company's share capital;
(3) a list of persons who, on the fourteenth day after the company's annual general meeting, are members of the company and of persons who have ceased to be members since the date of the last return or, in the case of the first return, since the incorporation of the company. A complete list need only be given every third year, and in the intervening two years the changes in the membership have to be stated, *i.e.* particulars of persons who ceased to be, or became, members (s. 124 (1), proviso (*a*), and Sched. VI, Pt. I, para. 5). If the names are not arranged in alphabetical order there must be annexed to the return an index sufficient to enable the name of any particular person to be readily found;
(4) the company's debentures, charges and mortgages; in Scotland charges created before October 27, 1961, were not registered, but will be included in the total in the annual return;
(5) such particulars of the directors and secretary as are required by the Act to be contained in the register of directors and secretaries (para. 66–02, *ante*).

Default in making annual return

69–05 If default is made in making the annual return or annexing requisite documents a default fine may be imposed upon the company and any officers who are responsible.[5] It is no defence that the return could not be made because no annual general meeting was held if the party concerned was himself in default in calling the meeting[6]; nor is it a defence for an individual that he himself was not the person required to make the return if in fact he should have summoned the persons who were so required and he failed to do so.[7] A *de facto* officer is in the same position as one *de jure*.[7]

Alternatively, the Registrar of Companies may serve a notice on the company under section 428 of the 1948 Act, requiring it to file the annual return within 14 days and, in case of default, may apply to the court for an order directing the company and any officer of it to make good the default within the time specified in the court order; if the officers in question, such as the directors or the secretary, fail to comply with the court order, they may be committed to prison for contempt of court.[8]

---

[4] Who must not be the same person (s. 179); see para. 61–03, *ante*.
[5] Proceedings under the Companies Act to recover a fine are a criminal cause or matter: *R.* v. *Tyler and International Commercial Co.* [1891] 2 Q.B. 588.
[6] *Edmonds* v. *Foster* (1875) 45 L.J.(M.C.) 41; *Park* v. *Lawton* [1911] 1 K.B. 588.
[7] *Gibson* v. *Barton* (1875) L.R. 10 Q.B. 329, 339.
[8] *Re George Downman Ltd.*, *The Times*, July 26, 1960.

For the procedure in Scotland, see rule 218B of the Rules of the Court of Session.

PRACTICE NOTES

Completion and filing of annual return

69–06 When changes in the capital structure of a company have occurred from time to time, the annual return should show the position at the date to which it is made up, *i.e.* the fourteenth day after the date of the annual general meeting, since the return is not in itself an historical document and no reconciliation with earlier returns is required.

In part 3 of the return (particulars of indebtedness) only those charges which are required to be registered with the Registrar should be included. The amount outstanding at the date to which the return is made up should be given; this may not always be the full amount covered by the mortgage or charge.

Return of changes only

69–07 Few companies will in modern conditions wish to avail themselves of the concession given in section 124 (1) (*c*) of the 1948 Act, since the operation of mechanical or electronic equipment will usually be geared to the production of complete lists of members.

Amendment of annual return

69–08 If an error in the annual return is discovered after it has been accepted for filing by the Registrar, it is not possible to recover the document for amendment. An amended return should be filed enfaced with a note in the following terms:

> "This return is filed by way of amendment of the return filed on (date) and is rendered necessary by reason of the earlier return . . . [give explanation]."

Shares issued but not registered at date of return

Where shares have been issued with renunciation rights and the renunciation period has not expired at the date of return, it is sufficient if the new shares are included in the summary of the capital in part 2 of the return and in one amount at the end of the list of members in part 4, with a note of the date of issue of the shares and the final date on which renunciations can be registered.

Disclosure of subsidiaries

69–09 When a company has taken advantage of section 3 (4) of the 1967 Act (which permits non-disclosure of certain subsidiaries in the accounts) particulars of all the subsidiaries must be annexed to the annual return (s. 3 (5) (*b*)).

Concessions

69–10 *The Chartered Secretaries Manual of Company Secretarial Practice*, being the Official Manual of the Institute of Chartered Secretaries and Administrators, Joint General Editors, S. J. S. Eley, F.C.I.S. and R. C. Hetherington, F.C.I.S. (Jordan & Sons Ltd., London), contains in paragraph E20 the following statement on concessions allowed by the Registrar of Companies:

> "Modern practices have dictated some relaxation being made in the rigid procedure laid down in the form of annual return. It is understood that the Registrar of Companies will not refuse to accept for registration an annual return which fails to comply with the prescribed form in the undermentioned respects, but it must be emphasised that an amended return could be demanded subsequently if any deficiency were officially brought to the notice of the Registrar by a person inspecting the company's file.
>
> (*a*) The number of stock units being shown instead of the amount of stock.
>
> (*b*) Present and past members being shown in separate alphabetical collations without an index being annexed.
>
> (*c*) Shares transferred by any person being aggregated and the total shown against his name with the word "various" in the column for date of registration, instead of the details of each transfer by that person being shown separately.
>
> (*d*) The omission of past members and the number of shares previously held by them in the case of a class of shares having been cancelled since the last return under the terms of a scheme of arrangement, provided that the return includes a note giving details of the cancellation and the date on which the scheme was approved by the court.
>
> (*e*) The omission of past members whose shares have been acquired as a result of a take-over bid, provided that details of all transfers prior to the bid are shown and the return is accompanied by an explanation signed by a director and the secretary."[9]

[9] Reproduced by kind permission of Jordan & Sons Ltd. and the Institute of Chartered Secretaries and Administrators.

CHAPTER 70

ACCOUNTING RECORDS AND ANNUAL ACCOUNTS

Accounting records

General requirements. Inspection

70–01 Every company is required to keep accounting records sufficient to show and explain the company's transactions (Companies Act 1976, s. 12 (1) and (2)). The accounting records must be such as to enable the directors to ensure that any accounts prepared by them under section 1 of the 1976 Act (see para. 70–04, *post*) comply with the requirements of section 149 of the 1948 Act to give "a true and fair view" (see para. 70–05, *post*). The accounting records shall disclose with reasonable accuracy, at any time, the financial position of the company at that time, and shall contain a record of the assets and liabilities of the company and entries from day to day of all moneys received and paid out and of the matters in respect of which these payments occurred (1976 Act, s. 12 (3) and (4)). In addition, where a company's business involves dealing in goods, the accounting records shall include statements of stock held at the end of each financial year, statements of stock-takings from which such statements of stock are prepared and statements of goods sold and purchased, other than in ordinary retail trade, in sufficient detail to enable the goods and the buyers and sellers to be identified (*ibid.* s. 12 (5)). A summary of counsel's opinion on certain points of difficulty arising in connection with the application of section 12 (3) to (5) has been issued by the accountancy bodies and is reproduced in Vol III, para. F–1826.

The accounting records are to be kept at the registered office of the company or at such other place as the directors think fit and are to be open at all times to inspection by the officers of the company (*ibid.* s. 12 (6)).[1] Although this is not provided for in the Acts, a director has a common law right to apply to the court for an order requiring the company to make its accounting records available to him.[2] If accounting records are kept outside Great Britain, accounts and returns relating to the business dealt with in those records must be sent to and kept at all times available for inspection by officers of the company in Great Britain. These accounts and returns must be such as to enable the directors to ensure that accounts prepared under the requirements of section 1 of the 1976 Act comply with the "true and fair view" provisions of section 149 and to disclose with

---

[1] *Burn* v. *London and South Wales Coal Co.* [1890] W.N. 209.
[2] *McCusker* v. *McRae*, 1966 S.C. 253; *Conway* v. *Petronius Clothing Co. Ltd.* [1978] 1 W.L.R. 72.

reasonable accuracy the financial position of that business at intervals of not longer than six months (*ibid.* s. 12 (7) and (8)).

Except where a direction as to disposal of records is made under winding-up rules, a private company must now preserve any accounting records required under this section for three years after they are made; all other companies must preserve such records for six years after they are made (*ibid.* s. 12 (9)).

Inspection of the records by members of the company who are not directors may be permitted by articles which, like article 125, may provide for the directors to lay down the conditions for such procedure. Sometimes the articles provide that no member is to have a right of inspecting any account, or book, or document, of the company "except as conferred by statute, or authorised by the directors or by a resolution of the company in general meeting." A provision of this kind will not disentitle a shareholder to claim production of copies of the balance sheets and auditors' and directors' reports (see section 158 of the 1948 Act, section 24 of the 1967 Act and section 1 of the 1976 Act), or to inspect the various registers required to be kept under the Acts, such as the register of members, or the register of mortgages; for a member has a statutory right to inspect these. But subject to these qualifications the provision is effective. Occasionally the articles give a wider right of inspection; but even where they provide that the books, wherein proceedings of the company are recorded, may be inspected, a member has no right to inspect the minute book of the proceedings of directors.[3]

The right of inspection includes a right to make extracts[4]; and it is not necessary for the shareholder seeking inspection to assign a reason[5]; but the right to take extracts is impliedly negatived where the Acts give a right to have copies on payment.[6] If need be, the shareholder can obtain an injunction to enforce his rights.

A right of inspection given by the articles ceases on a voluntary winding up.[7]

On a winding up, compulsory or under supervision, the power of the court to order inspection of the statutory registers comes to an end[8]; but the court is invested by section 266 of the 1948 Act with a discretionary power to permit inspection by creditors or contributories.[9]

If the accounting records are kept at a place other than the registered office of the company[10] they may be subject to a lien, *e.g.* a solicitor's

---

[3] *R.* v. *Mariquita, etc., Co.* (1858) 1 E. & E. 289.
[4] *Mutter* v. *Eastern, etc., Co.* (1888) 38 Ch.D. 92; *Nelson* v. *Anglo-American Land, etc., Agency* [1897] 1 Ch. 130.
[5] *Holland* v. *Dickson* (1888) 37 Ch.D. 669.
[6] *Re Balaghat Mining Co.* [1901] 2 K.B. 665, C.A., overruling *Boord* v. *African Consolidated Co.* [1898] 1 Ch. 596.
[7] *Re Yorkshire Fibre Co.* (1870) L.R. 9 Eq. 650; 18 W.R. 541, approved by the C.A. in *Re Kent Coalfields Syndicate* [1898] 1 Q.B. 754.
[8] *Re Kent Coalfields Syndicate, supra*; *Somerset* v. *Land Securities Co.* [1897] W.N. 29.
[9] *Re North Brazilian Sugar Factories* (1887) 37 Ch.D. 83.
[10] *Cf.* 1976 Act, s. 12 (6).

lien.[11] In *Re Rapid Road Transit Co.*,[12] a solicitor's lien was preserved in a winding up.

Duty of directors to keep proper accounting records

70–02 The articles usually provide for the keeping of proper accounting records, and articles 123 and 124 (as amended by the 1976 Act, Sched. 2) substantially repeat the obligations of section 12 of the 1976 Act, but specify that the *directors* shall cause accounting records to be kept. The 1976 Act makes liability for failure to comply with the accounting records provision wider than just the directors and includes "every officer of the company who is in default." An officer "includes a director, manager or secretary" (1948 Act, s. 455); it is not clear just who will count as a manager in this context, and the question of whether the auditor is an officer of the company is relevant here (see para. 73–05, *post*).

Every officer of a company who is in default in respect to accounting records is guilty of an offence unless he acted honestly and his default is excusable in the circumstances; he is also guilty of an offence if he has intentionally caused any default by the company in relation to the provisions for preservation of accounting records (1976 Act, s. 12 (9); see *ante*) or has failed to take all reasonable steps to secure compliance with them (*ibid* s. 12 (10)).

Anyone found guilty of an offence under this section is liable, on summary conviction, to imprisonment for up to six months, or a fine up to £400 or both; on conviction or indictment, he is liable to imprisonment for up to two years, or to a fine or both (*ibid* s. 12 (11)).

Directors are not bound to examine entries in the company's accounting records and are entitled to rely on other officers of the company.[13]

Liability where accounting records not properly kept

70–03 Apart from the liability arising through failure of a director to carry out the statutory obligation indicated above, penalties may arise for offences antecedent to or in the course of winding up the company.

Section 329 of the 1948 Act covers destruction, mutilation, alteration or falsification of any records (which would include accounting records) and an officer or contributory of the company being wound up who is found guilty of a misdemeanour relating to such action is liable to imprisonment.

Outside the Acts, a case may be brought against directors or other officers under the Theft Act 1968, ss. 17–20.[14]

If, in the winding up of the company, it appears that accounting records were not properly kept, the directors and the auditor may be liable for

[11] *Re Capital Fire Association* (1883) 24 Ch.D. 408; as to which see *Re Hawkes, Ackerman* v. *Lockhart* [1898] 2 Ch. 1.

[12] [1909] 1 Ch. 96.

[13] *Dovey and Others* v. *Cory (Re National Bank of Wales)* [1901] A.C. 477.

[14] The Theft Act 1968 does not apply to Scotland.

misfeasance and a misfeasance summons to make good moneys misapplied as the result of that failure may issue against them.[15]

Annual accounts and the Eighth Schedule

Laying, delivering and circulation

70–04 The directors have a duty to prepare accounts in respect of each accounting reference period of the company, and to lay these accounts before the company in general meeting and to deliver a copy to the Registrar of Companies (together with a certified translation if the original is not in English) within a specified time after the end of the accounting reference period (1976 Act, s. 1). This first accounting reference period of a company begins on the day after the date to which was made up the last profit and loss account, if any, laid before the company in general meeting before October 1, 1977, or on the date of incorporation, and must exceed six months but not exceed 18 months in length (1976 Act, s. 2 (4)). The "accounts" referred to shall comprise the following documents:

(1) a profit and loss account (or, in the case of a company not trading for profit, an income and expenditure account) for a period starting on the date to which the previous such account was made up and ending on a date not more than seven days before or more than seven days after the end of the accounting reference period (this allows a company to use 52-week and 53-week financial years with year-ends varying by a few days from year to year);
(2) a balance sheet at the date to which the above account is made up;
(3) an auditors' report as required by section 156 (1) of the 1948 Act;
(4) a directors' report as required by section 157 (1) of the 1948 Act (1976 Act, s. 1 (5)).

The documents comprised in the accounts include any group accounts (s. 150 (1) of the 1948 Act, as amended by s. 8 of the 1976 Act).

The rules in respect of the determination and alteration of the date on which accounting reference periods end (1976 Act, ss. 2 and 3) and in respect of the time allowed for laying accounts before the members and for delivering copies to the Registrar (1976 Act, s. 6) enable the Registrar to be clear at any time whether a company is in default in regard to the requirements for filing accounts with the Registrar. This is in sharp contrast to the confused situation which existed prior to the passing of the 1976 Act.

A company may determine the date on which each of its accounting reference periods shall end by giving notice to the Registrar in the prescribed form before October 1, 1977, or within six months of incorporation. If no such notice is given the date applicable shall be March 31 unless the Registrar determines, within two years of October 1, 1977, with the

---

[15] *Re John Fulton & Co.* [1932] N.I. 35; on the question whether the auditor is an "officer" within the Companies Acts, or within the Theft Act 1968, see para. 73–05, *post*.

consent of the company, that some other date should apply (1976 Act, s. 2 (3)).

A company may, by giving notice to the Registrar in the prescribed form, change the date on which its current and subsequent accounting reference periods are to end, even if this means that the revised period is so shortened that it ends before the date of the notice. The notice must specify whether the current accounting reference period is to be shorter or longer than one year. A notice will not take effect if it would extend the accounting reference period of a company which has previously had an extended accounting reference period within the five years preceding the date of the notice. An exemption from this latter restriction is available to a company which is changing its accounting reference period so that it coincides with that of its holding or subsidiary company. Such a company is also permitted to give notice to change the date of ending of an accounting reference period that has already ended, so as to secure this coincidence, provided that the notice is given before the time allowed for laying and filing the accounts in relation to that period has expired (*ibid.* s. 3).

The time allowed for both laying accounts before a general meeting and for filing copies with the Registrar is 10 months from the end of the accounting reference period for a private company and seven months for other companies. A company which carries on business or has interests overseas may claim a three months' extension of these periods by giving notice to the Registrar in the prescribed form before the normal time allowed has expired. If a company's first accounting reference period after incorporation is a period exceeding 12 months, the time allowed for laying and delivering accounts is reduced by the excess over 12 months. However, in this situation the time allowed for laying and delivering accounts shall not be reduced to less than three months. Similarly where a notice is given under section 3 of the 1976 Act to shorten the current reference period the time allowed for laying and delivering accounts for that shortened period shall not be reduced to less than three months from the date of the notice (*ibid.* s. 6).

If the requirements for laying and/or delivering accounts are not complied with within the time allowed, every person who was a director immediately before the time expired is liable to a fine under the provisions of Schedule 2 to the 1980 Act. It shall be a defence for a director to prove that he took all reasonable steps for securing compliance. The company is also liable to a civil penalty for non-compliance with these requirements, on a sliding scale dependent upon the duration of the default. It shall not be a defence for directors or the company to prove that the documents had not been prepared and could not therefore be laid before the company or delivered to the Registrar (*ibid.* s. 4).

The court may also make an order directing the directors to make good any default in complying with the rules for laying and delivering accounts if they fail to make good the default within 14 days of service of a notice requiring them to do so (*ibid.* s. 5).

A copy of the balance sheet and documents required by law to be annexed thereto and the auditors' and directors' reports must, in general, be sent to all members and debenture holders of the company. There are certain exceptions to this requirement, notably members or debenture holders who are not entitled to receive notices of general meetings, and whose addresses are unknown (1948 Act, s. 158 (1) (*b*)).[16] Despite these exceptions any member or debenture holder is entitled to be furnished on demand with a copy of the accounts and reports (s. 158 (2)). References to the auditors' report in section 158 are to be read as including also references to the directors' report (1967 Act, s. 24).

A Practice Note on laying and delivering accounts is appended to this chapter (see para. 70–18, *post*).

Contents and form

70–05 Every balance sheet of a company shall give a true and fair view of the state of affairs of the company as at the end of its financial year, and every profit and loss account of a company shall give a true and fair view of the profit or loss of the company for the financial year (1948 Act, s. 149 (2)). This general requirement with its emphasis on a "true and fair view" overrides all other requirements of the Acts. This is made much clearer by the new version of section 149 which is inserted by section 1 of the 1981 Act. It recognises that, in order to comply with section 149 (2) it may be necessary in some circumstances to give information additional to that specified by other requirements of the Acts, and/or to depart from one or more of these other requirements (s. 149 (3)).

The meaning of the phrase "a true and fair view" has never been put to direct judicial test. It seems that adherence to normal accounting practice as to the basis of accounting and as to the degree of disclosure would be prima facie evidence of the giving of a true and fair view. Thus the assertion that accounts were misleading because they showed property at original cost and not at current market price was rejected by the court because normal accounting practice had been followed.[17] But particular circumstances may demand additional disclosure or even a different basis of accounting in order to prevent the accounts from being misleading to a reader familiar with normal accounting practice and expecting it to be followed.

This position makes it important for both readers of accounts and for those responsible for issuing and for auditing them that normal accounting practice should be clearly established and documented. From 1942 to 1969 the Institute of Chartered Accountants in England and Wales issued a series of Recommendations on Accounting Principles of which only three

[16] The first of these conditions alone suffices in the case of a company without a share capital: see s. 158 (1) (*a*).

[17] *Re Press Caps Ltd.* [1949] Ch. 434. Further, a minority shareholder is not entitled to demand an amendment of the accounts on the ground that an alleged contingent liability was not recorded: *Devlin* v. *Slough Estates Ltd., The Times,* June 16, 1982.

are still current. These were of persuasive effect only and usually left much discretion to accountants in choosing among several alternative acceptable methods. From 1971 a series of Statements of Standard Accounting Practice[18] has been developed jointly by the Accounting Standards Committee for adoption by the councils of the six major accountancy bodies in the United Kingdom (the Institutes of Chartered Accountants in England and Wales, of Scotland and in Ireland, the Association of Certified Accountants, the Institute of Cost and Management Accountants and the Chartered Institute of Public Finance and Accountancy). Members of these bodies are under a professional obligation to disclose and justify departures from these accounting standards. Exceptional circumstances are however envisaged in which adherence to standard practice fails to produce a true and fair view, or in which accounts have deviated from standard practice so that they show a true and fair view.[19] Thus the true and fair view is a criterion of a higher order than both the requirements of standard accounting practice and the specific requirements of the Companies Acts.

Since 1973 the International Accounting Standards Committee has also been developing a series of International Accounting Standards. The United Kingdom accountancy bodies have issued a revised introduction to International Accounting Standards (reproduced in Vol. III, para. F–900) in which they state it as their policy to implement their support for the international standards by incorporating them into the body of the United Kingdom standards. As far as possible, this will be accomplished by bringing the latter into line with the international standards. But if this cannot be done (*e.g.* because British law forbids it), the United Kingdom Standard should be followed, with disclosure of the fact of non-compliance with the International Accounting Standard.

The status of standard accounting practice has been enhanced by the inclusion in the Listing Agreement, which companies must enter into with the Stock Exchange on admission to listing, of an undertaking (para. 10 (a)) to circulate with the annual report of the directors a statement by the directors as to the reasons for any significant departures from standard accounting practices approved by the accountancy bodies.[20] The Stock Exchange Listing Agreement (paras. 9 and 10) also obliges quoted companies to disclose various items of financial information additional to those required under the Companies Acts.

70–06 Prior to the passing of the 1981 Act the requirements of the Companies Acts in relation to annual accounts were confined almost entirely to the items to be disclosed and to matter of terminology and classification. It was left to professional statements and practice to determine both the bases of measuring assets and profit and the format of presentation of accounts. But

---

[18] See Vol. III, Part F.

[19] See Auditing Standard "Qualifications in Audit Reports," para. 10 (reproduced in Vol. III, Part F).

[20] The Listing Agreement is reproduced in Vol. II, Part C.

these matters are now the subject of legislation in the 1981 Act which implements the requirements of the EEC Fourth Directive on Company Law in relation to annual accounts. This has been achieved by inserting a completely new text for the Eighth Schedule of the 1948 Act (1981 Act, Sched. 1) and by requiring compliance with the Eighth Schedule under the new text of section 149 (1) of the 1948 Act (1981 Act, s. 1).

70–07 FORMAT. Under the 1981 version of the Eighth Schedule, every company balance sheet must follow one of the two formats set out following paragraph 8 of the Schedule (one format being in vertical form and one horizontal) and every company profit and loss account must follow one of the four alternative formats given there (two being in vertical form and two horizontal). Not only must the items listed be disclosed, but they must be shown "in the order and under the headings and sub-headings given in the format adopted" (Sched. 8, para. 1). Directors are given discretion to rearrange or combine sub-headings in certain circumstances (paras. 3 and 4).

70–08 ACCOUNTING PRINCIPLES. Company accounts are normally to be drawn up (i) on the "going concern basis," *i.e.* on the presumption that the company will continue in business for the foreseeable future; (ii) on the basis that accounting policies are applied consistently over time; (iii) on a prudent basis, whereby only profits realised[21] by the balance sheet date should be taken into account but all losses which appear by the date the balance sheet is signed to be likely to arise shall be taken into account; (iv) on the accruals basis under which items are brought into account in the year in which income is earned or charges incurred irrespective of the date in which they are settled in cash (Sched. 8, paras. 9–13). (These principles are almost identical in terms to the four "fundamental accounting concepts" set out in Statement of Standard Accounting Practice No. 2 (para. 14).) If the directors believe that there are special reasons for departing from any of these principles, this is permitted, provided that there is disclosure of the departure, the reasons for it and the effect of it (Sched. 8, para. 15).

The Eighth Schedule lays down "historical cost accounting rules," but also permits "alternative accounting rules." Under historical cost accounting, assets are included at their purchase price or production cost. Any fixed asset which has a limited useful economic life must be reduced systematically by provisions for depreciation such that its purchase price or production cost (less any estimated residual value at the end of its useful economic life) is written off over its useful economic life (Sched. 8, paras. 17, 18, 22). Fixed assets are defined as assets that "are intended for use on a continuing basis in the company's activities"; all other assets are classified as "current assets" (para. 75). A provision for diminution in value must be made where it appears that any fixed asset has suffered a permanent

[21] As defined by Schedule 8, para. 90.

diminution in value (para. 19). There are rules regarding the writing off of any development costs and goodwill that have been treated as assets (paras. 20 and 21). A current asset is to be included at its net realisable value if that is lower than its purchase price or production cost (para. 23). There are rules for the determination of purchase price or production cost (paras. 26–28).

The "alternative accounting rules" (para. 31) allow assets to be included at their current cost, which is not defined but will be presumed to have the meaning given to it in Statement of Standard Accounting Practice No. 16 "Current Cost Accounting." As a further alternative, tangible fixed assets and fixed asset investments may be included at a market value determined as at the date of their last valuation; this permits the continuation of the common practice of revaluing property assets at intervals of several years for inclusion in balance sheets prepared in other respects on a historical cost basis. Where one of these alternative rules has been used, the value so derived is to be "the starting point for determining the amount to be included" in the accounts, *i.e.* depreciation, provisions for diminution in value or reduction to net realisable value may be needed as under the historical cost rules (para. 32). Where the historical cost rules are not followed, the amounts of any asset other than stocks determined according to the historical cost rules must also be shown in the accounts or a note to the accounts (or alternatively there may be shown the difference between the historical cost amount and the amount actually used in the accounts) (para. 33). Any profit or loss arising from the use of rules other than historical cost rules must be put into a separate reserve which must be shown separately on the balance sheet; the Schedule entitles this "the revaluation reserve," but makes clear that it is not required that this name be used for it (para. 34).

70–09 OTHER INFORMATION. Paragraphs 35–58 of the Eighth Schedule require various additional information to be given in the accounts or in the notes to the accounts. It is not necessary to consider these in detail here. They include requirements for disclosure of movements on share, debenture, reserves, provisions, fixed assets and investment accounts during the financial year; for separate disclosure of freehold, long leasehold and short leasehold land and of listed and unlisted investments—whether classified as fixed or current assets. Paragraph 36 requires the disclosure of accounting policies adopted and several of the later paragraphs are expansions of this requirement.

The standard formats of balance sheet and profit and loss account require separate disclosure of information in respect of "related companies." This is a term new to company law which is defined in paragraph 91 and is effectively the same as "associated companies" as defined in Statement of Standard Accounting Practice No. 1. A related company is any body corporate other than a subsidiary or fellow-subsidiary in which the reporting company holds on a long-term basis an interest in its voting equity share capital "for the purpose of securing a contribution to that company's own activities by the exercise of any control or influence arising from that interest" (para. 91 (1)). A company in which 20 per cent. or more of the relevant share capital is held will be presumed to be a related company unless the contrary is shown (para. 91 (3)).

Exemptions

70–10 Companies which qualify to be treated as "small companies" or "medium-sized companies" are entitled to certain exemptions from accounting requirements in relation to accounts delivered to the Registrar of Companies in accordance with section 1 (7) (*a*) of the 1976 Act and so available for public inspection. The exemptions do not apply to the accounts laid before the company in general meeting and circulated to members and debenture holders.

Public companies, banking, insurance and shipping companies and members of any group which includes companies of these types are ineligible to be treated as "small companies" or "medium-sized companies" whatever their size. Other companies and groups are entitled to be treated as "small" if they satisfy, in respect of at least two of the last three financial years at least two of the following conditions:

(i) turnover did not exceed £1,400,000;
(ii) total assets on the year-end balance sheet did not exceed £700,000;
(iii) weekly average number of employees did not exceed 50 (1981 Act, s. 8 (2)).

Eligible companies and groups are entitled to be treated as "medium-sized" if they satisfy, in respect of at least two of the last three financial years, at least two of the following conditions:

(i) turnover did not exceed £5,750,000;
(ii) total assets on the year-end balance sheet did not exceed £2,800,000;
(iii) weekly average number of employees did not exceed 250 (1981 Act, s. 8 (3)).

The Secretary of State may modify any of the accounting exemptions provisions by statutory instrument (1981 Act, s. 5 (7)). It is likely that this power will be used to revise these monetary limits from time to time in line with revisions to the EEC limits which are specified in the Fourth Directive in terms of European Units of Account.

The exemptions to which small companies are entitled are set out in section 6 (2) to (6) of the 1981 Act:

(i) they may deliver to the Registrar an abbreviated balance sheet showing only the main headings—which are given letters or Roman numerals in the standard formats of balance sheet in the Eighth Schedule;
(ii) they are not required to deliver to the Registrar a copy of the profit and loss account;

(iii) they are not required to give the additional information specified in paragraphs 35–58 of the Eighth Schedule (see para. 70–09, *ante*) except for those items listed in section 6 (5) of the 1981 Act;

(iv) they need not give the information in respect of directors' and employees' emoluments required by section 196 of the 1948 Act and sections 6–8 of the 1967 Act (see paras. 70–13 and 70–14, *post*).

(v) they need not deliver to the Registrar a copy of the directors' report as required by section 157 (1) of the 1948 Act (see Chap. 72, *post*).

The accounts delivered to the Registrar by a "medium-sized" company may combine into one item entitled "gross profit" (or "loss") the figures for turnover and cost of sales otherwise required by the standard formats of profit and loss account; they may also omit the analysis of turnover by markets and by classes of business otherwise required by paragraph 55 of the Eighth Schedule (1981 Act, s. 6 (7) and (8)).

Any company which takes advantage of any of the accounting exemptions for small or medium-sized companies must include on its balance sheet as delivered to the Registrar a statement that it has done so on the grounds that it is entitled to do so; the balance sheet must then be signed by the directors in accordance with section 155 (1). The accounts must be accompanied by a special auditors' report reproducing the full text of the auditors' report on the full accounts and stating that in the opinion of the auditors the requirements for the exemptions used are satisfied (1981 Act, s. 7).

Special classes of companies

70–11 Banking, insurance and shipping companies (as defined by 1981 Act, Sched. 2 (8)) may continue to prepare accounts under the pre-1981-Act versions of section 149, section 152 and the Eighth Schedule; now renumbered section 149A, section 152A and Schedule 8A (1981 Act, s. 17 and Sched. 2). The reason for this is a temporary one, that the EEC directives applicable to these classes of company are in preparation and the existing Fourth Directive does not apply to them.

Schedule 8A admits exceptions from the general requirements as to accounts in the case of banking companies recognised as such by the Department of Trade (para. 23), of insurance companies within the meaning of the Insurance Companies Act 1974[22] (para. 24), and of shipping companies as defined by paragraph 25. In the case of companies exempted under paragraph 23, the Department had power to remove all or any of these exemptions (1967 Act, s. 12); it has used this power to remove the exemptions under paragraph 23 from the London Clearing Banks and the

22 See para. 89–37, *post*.

banks represented on the Committee of Scottish Bank General Managers (Banking Companies (Accounts) Regulations 1970).[23]

Requirements for Annual Accounts (excluding the Eighth Schedule)

Annexures

70–12 To effect the main purpose of section 149, *i.e.* to present the true and fair view, it is enacted that any reference to a balance sheet or profit and loss account shall include any notes thereon giving information required by the Acts (s. 149 (8) (*a*)). The profit and loss account, and, if not incorporated in the balance sheet or profit and loss account, any group accounts, are to be annexed to the balance sheet and the auditors' report attached thereto (s. 156 (1)). Any accounts so annexed are to be approved by the board of directors before the balance sheet is signed on their behalf (s. 156 (2)). The balance sheet must be signed on behalf of the board by two of the directors, or by the sole director (s. 155 (1)).

There must be attached to the balance sheet a report by the directors containing a fair review of the development of the business of the company and its subsidiaries during that year and of their position at the end of it and stating the amount which they recommend should be paid by way of dividend, and the amount which they propose to carry to reserves (s. 157 (1)). The directors' report is considered in detail in Chapter 72. Information which is required to be given in the accounts may no longer be given instead in the directors' report, following the repeal of the proviso to section 163 (1981 Act, s. 16).

Directors' emoluments

70–13 Section 196 of the 1948 Act and sections 6 and 7 of the 1967 Act require particulars to be given in a note to the accounts relating to directors' emoluments, pensions and compensation for loss of office.

Section 196 requires the separate disclosure of the aggregate amount under each of these three items, although the section indicates that circumstances may necessitate yet a further subdivision.

Section 6 of the 1967 Act further requires disclosure of:

(1) the actual emoluments of the chairman[24] (subs. (1) (*a*));

(2) the actual emoluments of the highest paid director, if any of the directors received emoluments in excess of those received by the chairman (subs. (2));

(3) a scale dividing directors' emoluments into bands of £5,000[25] and showing the number of directors whose emoluments fell within each band of the scale (subs. (1) (*b*)); and

---

[23] S.I. 1970 No. 327; see Vol II, para. A–3011.

[24] If there was more than one chairman during the year, the emoluments for each chairman during his period of office must be separately shown (1967 Act, s. 6 (1) (*a*)).

[25] S.I. 1979 No. 1618.

(4) the number of directors receiving no emoluments (*ibid.*).

This disclosure is not, however, required in the case of a company whose directors did not receive aggregate emoluments, as shown under section 196, exceeding £40,000, provided that the company is not a holding or subsidiary company (subs. (6), amended by the Companies (Accounts) Regulations 1979).[25] Nor is disclosure required in respect of a chairman or individual director whose duties were wholly or mainly discharged outside the United Kingdom (subss. (1) and (2)).

It should be noted that where disclosure is required under this section, only the number and not the names of the persons in question have to be shown.

Under section 7 of the 1967 Act, if any of the directors have waived their rights to receive emoluments, there must be stated their number and the aggregate amount of emoluments waived.

The expression "emoluments" in the above sections includes any sums paid by way of expense allowance in so far as they are charged to United Kingdom income tax and the estimated money value of benefits received otherwise than in cash (s. 196 (2)). There are sometimes difficulties and delay in agreeing with the Inland Revenue the extent to which an expense allowance is chargeable[26] and therefore permission is given to show the precise amounts charged, or the release from the liability to be charged, in the first accounts in which it is practicable to show them. It is interesting to note that as regards benefits in kind, the section requires the total to be included whether they become chargeable[27] to tax or not.

Employees' emoluments

70–14 In the case of employees who received emoluments in excess of £20,000, other than employees exempted from these requirements (see below), there must be shown in a note to the accounts a scale similar to that required to be shown in the case of directors under section 6 of the 1967 Act, and likewise divided into bands of £5,000, but commencing at £20,000, and the number of employees whose emoluments fell within each band of that scale (1967 Act, s. 8 (1), as amended by the Companies (Accounts) Regulations 1979[28]).

The following employees are exempted from inclusion in the scale:

(1) directors of the company;

(2) persons, other than directors, who worked wholly or mainly outside the United Kingdom (*ibid.*).

The definition of "emoluments," for the purposes of this section, is similar to that under section 196 (2) and (6), *mutatis mutandis* (1967 Act, s. 8 (2) and (3)).

---

[26] For definition of allowable expense, see Income and Corporation Taxes Act 1970, s. 189 (1).

[27] Chargeable under Income and Finance Act 1976, ss. 61–72, but subject to any deduction permitted under s. 189 (1).

[28] S.I. 1979 No. 1618.

Comparative figures for previous year

Where particulars of the emoluments of directors or employees have to be shown, the corresponding amounts for the previous financial year must also be given (1967 Act, s. 11). Penalties for non-compliance with these requirements are specified in the Companies Act 1980, Sched. 2.

Directors' duty of disclosure for above purposes

Every director is under a duty to give notice to the company of all necessary information relating to himself which is required in order to comply with sections 196 of the 1948 Act and sections 6 and 7 of the 1967 Act, subject to a fine in case of default (s. 198, 1967 Act, ss. 6 (5) and 7 (3) and 1980 Act, Sched. 2).

Transactions involving directors

70–15 The Companies Act 1980, ss. 54–65, introduces complex provisions governing the disclosure in annual accounts of particulars relating to transactions and arrangements entered into by the company or by a subsidiary with a person who was a director at any time during the period covered by the accounts.

The transactions covered by the provisions are arrangements or agreements to enter into arrangements whereby the company (or a subsidiary) provides a director of the company or the holding company with a loan, quasi-loan (as defined in the 1980 Act, s. 65 (2)), guarantee or credit; also any other transaction or arrangement with the company (or a subsidiary) in which a director had a material interest (1980 Act, s. 54). A service contract is explicitly exempted from these requirements (though they must be made available for inspection (1967 Act, s. 26—see para. 66–14, *ante*)); but it seems that a consultancy agreement between a company and a director would be within the scope of these provisions.

The principal terms of any such transaction, arrangement or agreement must be shown in notes to the annual accounts, including:

(a) the fact that it was made or subsisted during the period covered by the accounts;

(b) the name of the director concerned and the nature of the "material interest" where relevant;

(c) where a loan is concerned, principal and interest outstanding at the beginning and end of the period, the maximum liability during the period, the amount of any interest due but unpaid, and the amount of any bad debt provision;

(d) where a guarantee is concerned, the amount at the beginning and end of the year, the maximum potential liability and any costs incurred in fulfilling the guarantee;

(e) where any other transaction, arrangement or agreement is concerned, its value (1980 Act, s. 55).

These provisions are extended to connected persons as defined in section 64 of the 1980 Act; to "shadow directors," *i.e.* persons in accordance with whose instructions the directors are accustomed to act (1980 Act, s. 63) and, as regards loans, quasi-loans, guarantees and credit transactions, to officers of the company who are not directors (1980 Act, s. 56 (2)). According to section 455 of the 1948 Act, officer "includes a director, manager or secretary." As to whether an auditor is an officer, see para. 73–05, *post*.

These disclosure provisions do not apply to recognised banks in relation to loans, guarantees or credit transactions (1980 Act, s. 54 (5)). Nor do they apply to credit transactions and guarantees if the aggregate amount relating to a director did not exceed £5,000 at any time during the relevant period, nor to other transactions (excluding loans) if they exceeded neither £5,000 nor 1 per cent. of the net assets of the company at the end of the period (1980 Act, s. 58).

It is the duty of a director to disclose to a meeting of directors any interest he may have (or a person connected with him may have) in any contract, transaction or arrangement made, or proposed to be made, by the company (s. 199 and 1980 Act, s. 60). A shadow director must declare his interest by notice in writing at the appropriate time (1980 Act, s. 63 (3)).

If these disclosure requirements are not complied with in the accounts, it is the duty of the auditors to give the required particulars in their report, as far as they are able to do so (1980 Act, s. 59). Where annual accounts show a debt due from a director, the company cannot sue the director on an account stated.[29]

Particulars of holding, subsidiary and other connected companies

70–16 The 1967 Act requires particulars to be given in a note to the accounts of the company's holding and subsidiary companies, and of certain other companies in which the company has a substantial shareholding.

HOLDING COMPANIES. If the company is a subsidiary of another company, the name of its ultimate holding company must be given and, if known, the country of its incorporation (1967 Act, s. 5 (1)).

SUBSIDIARY COMPANIES. The particulars to be stated are:

(1) the name of each subsidiary;
(2) the country of its incorporation outside Great Britain or, if a British company, the country of its registration, if this is not the same as that of the company giving the information;
(3) the identity of each class of shares held by the company in the subsidiary; and

---

29 *John Shaw & Sons (Salford)* v. *Shaw* [1935] 2 K.B. 113. The mere fact that a director has signed a set of accounts in which a loan to him is shown does not constitute or affect his obligation to the company, although it may be of evidential value (*McMenigall* v. *Central Refrigeration Services Ltd.*, 1963 S.L.T. (Notes) 8).

(4) the proportion of the nominal value of the issued shares in each class held (1967 Act, s. 3 (1)).

(5) the total share capital and reserves at the latest financial year-end and its profit or loss for that financial year (1981 Act, s. 4 (3)).

Any shares held by a nominee for the company or a subsidiary must be stated separately (1967 Act, s. 3 (2)).

OTHER CONNECTED COMPANIES. Similar information to that required at (1) to (4) above concerning subsidiaries must also be given concerning any other company in which, at the end of the financial year, the company giving the information

(1) holds more than one-tenth of the issued shares of any class of equity share capital[30]; or

(2) holds more than one-tenth of the allotted share capital; or

(3) holds shares which represent more than one-tenth of its assets (*ibid.* s. 4 (1) (1A) and (2)).

The information concerning share capital and reserves and profit or loss (at (5) above in list for subsidiaries) must be given in respect of any company in which more than one-fifth of the allotted share capital is held (1981 Act, s. 4 (2)).

EXEMPTIONS FROM ABOVE REQUIREMENTS. Two kinds of exemptions are admitted from the above requirements:

(1) As regards all three cases, if the company about which the information has to be given carries on business, or (except in the case of the holding company) was incorporated, outside Great Britain and, in the opinion of the directors, disclosure would be harmful to any of the companies concerned, the Department of Trade may authorise non-disclosure (1967 Act, ss. 3 (3), 4 (3) and 5 (2)).

(2) As regards subsidiary and other connected companies, if the particulars to be given are of excessive length, these need not be given unless the trading results of those companies principally affect the profit or loss or the amount of the assets of the company giving the information (*ibid.* ss. 3 (4) and 4 (4)). Where advantage is taken of this exemption, a statement to that affect must be included in the accounts, and the exempted particulars must be annexed to the next annual return (*ibid.* ss. 3 (5) and 4 (5)).

GROUP ACCOUNTS. These accounts are required under section 150 of the 1948 Act to be presented to members at the same time as the company's own balance sheet and profit and loss account and are considered in Chapter 71.

---

[30] For definition of "equity share capital" in this context see para. 71–01, *post*.

Power of Department of Trade to alter statutory requirements as to accounts

70–17 The Department of Trade has power by statutory instrument to alter the requirements of the Acts as to the classes of documents to be comprised in the accounts or to be delivered to the Registrar or as to the matters to be stated in any of these documents. This power applies to the sections of the Acts dealing with those subjects as well as to the requirements contained in the Eighth Schedule (1948 Act, s. 454 (1), as substituted by 1981 Act, s. 18).

By virtue of this delegated power the Department may introduce requirements which are more or less onerous than those in operation under the Acts, but a different procedure applies to either case: if the new requirements are more onerous, a draft of the statutory instrument containing the new regulations has to be laid before Parliament and has to be approved by resolution of each House of Parliament (s. 454 (3)), but if the proposed new regulations are less onerous than those in operation under the Acts, the approval of the Houses of Parliament of the statutory instrument introducing the new regulations is not a condition precedent but a condition subsequent, and the statutory instrument is valid subject to annulment in pursuance of a resolution of either House of Parliament (s. 454 (4)).

Regulations made under section 454 which are currently in force are the Companies (Accounts) Regulations 1970,[31] 1973[32] and 1979.[33]

PRACTICE NOTES

Accounts delivered to Registrar

70–18 The balance sheet included in the copy of the accounts delivered to the Registrar of Companies (see para. 70–04) must be signed by two directors of the company or, if there is only one director, by that director (1948 Act, s. 155 (1), as amended by the 1976 Act, Sched. 2). There is no need for the report of the directors or the report of the auditors included in that copy to be signed.

To assist the processing of the documents at Companies House, the Registrar has asked that the company number should be written in bold figures on the first page of the documents or on the cover, if there is one, whether or not the copy of the accounts is accompanied by a covering letter.

---

[31] S.I. 1970 No. 1333.
[32] S.I. 1973 No. 1150.
[33] S.I. 1979 No. 1618.

Companies with interest overseas

70–19 The extension of three months in the time allowed for laying and delivering the accounts in the case of a company carrying on business or having interests overseas (see para. 70–04) must be claimed (on form 5) in respect of each accounting reference period before the end of the period allowed by virtue of section 6 (2) of the 1976 Act, *i.e.* 10 months in the case of a private company and seven months for a company other than a private company.

CHAPTER 71

HOLDING AND SUBSIDIARY COMPANIES.

GROUP ACCOUNTS

Relationship of holding and subsidiary company

71–01 The terms "holding company" and "subsidiary" are defined by section 154 of the 1948 Act, which proceeds initially to establish the circumstances under which a company shall be deemed to be the subsidiary of another. If these circumstances of subsidiary relationship are found to apply, then the other company is deemed to be a holding company. For the purposes of the Acts the principal importance of the existence of this relationship lies in the obligations to submit group accounts (or alternative information) and the extension of the auditors' report to members of any company which is established as a holding company.

In general, a company is deemed to be a subsidiary company of another if

(1) the other is a member of it and controls the composition of its board of directors; or
(2) the other holds more than half in nominal value of its "equity share capital"; or
(3) it is a subsidiary of any company which is in turn a subsidiary of that other company (s. 154 (1)).

It should be noted that the first of these conditions is only satisfied if two requirements are present. As regards membership of the holding in the subsidiary company, presumably the holding of one share, even if it carries no vote, would be sufficient. As regards the control of the composition of the board of directors, this requirement is established only if the member company has the independent power to appoint or remove all or a majority of the directors; and the Act states three circumstances in which the requisite power to *appoint* is considered to exist (s. 154 (2)).

In the case of the second of the conditions stated above, the holding company must hold the majority of the "equity share capital"; in this case it is of no matter who may hold the remainder of the capital of any class. "Equity share capital" has a broader significance than that applied in commercial usage and is defined as meaning the issued share capital, excluding any part thereof which neither as respects dividend nor as respects capital carries any right to participate beyond a specified amount in a distribution (s. 154 (5)). Preference shares entitled to participate without maximum limitation in the distribution of dividend or surplus assets, or both, fall within this definition of "equity share capital"; the extent to which preference shareholders are entitled to participate in such distribution is considered elsewhere.[1]

The foregoing conditions of the relationship between the holding and subsidiary company are all subject to special provisions applying to shares held in a fiduciary capacity, or by nominees, or under a power of appointment exercisable by the potential holding company (s. 154 (3)).

71–02 A subsidiary or its nominee may not be a member of its holding company except as personal representative or as trustee, provided that neither the subsidiary nor the holding company is beneficially interested under the trust, apart from an interest by way of security in the ordinary course of business which includes the lending of money (1948 Act, s. 27 (1), (2), (4)).[2]

This provision does not prevent a subsidiary which was a member of the holding company *at the time of the commencement of the Act* from continuing to be a member, but the right to vote at meetings of the holding company is withheld (s. 27 (3)).

The Act contains no provision for a company which, *after the commencement of the Act*, becomes the subsidiary of a company in which it already held shares before it became a subsidiary of it. The view has already been expressed[2] that, in view of the silence of the legislature, the subsidiary company may vote with these "pre-acquired" shares at the general meeting of its holding company.

The definition of "subsidiary" in section 154 of the Companies Act 1948 is adopted by other enactments, *e.g.* the Restrictive Trade Practices Act 1956, s. 36 (1) (in defining "inter-connected bodies corporate"), and the Redundancy Payments Act 1965, s. 48 (4) (5) (in defining "associated company"); as to the latter, see *Southern Electricity Board* v. *Collins*.[3]

Separate legal character of subsidiary company

In principle, the holding company and its subsidiaries must be treated as separate entities (see, for example, *per* Pennycuick J. in *Charterbridge Corpn.* v. *Lloyds Bank Ltd.*[4]), although the law may provide for the raising of the veil of incorporation in certain specific cases, such as the obligation to present group accounts.

Group accounts

Obligation to present group accounts

71–03 Section 150 of the 1948 Act imposes an obligation on a holding company to present to its members, with its own annual accounts, group accounts relating to the state of affairs and profit or loss of the company and its

---

[1] See Chapter 34, *ante*.
[2] See para. 49–09, *ante*.
[3] [1970] 1 Q.B. 83.
[4] [1970] Ch. 62.

subsidiaries. A holding company which is itself a wholly owned subsidiary is exempt from this requirement. A wholly owned subsidiary company in this connection is one which has no members other than the holding company, the holding company's wholly owned subsidiaries and its or their nominees (s. 150 (4)).

The section provides for some modifications of the requirement which, in effect, recognises that the group accounts would or could not present an overall view that is true and fair of the relationship between a particular subsidiary company and the rest of the group companies. Thus, the accounts need not deal with a subsidiary if the holding company's directors consider it would be impracticable, or of no real value, because of the insignificant amounts involved, or would involve expense or delay out of proportion to the value to the members of the holding company; or the result would be misleading. Further, subject to the approval of the Department of Trade, the same exemption may apply if the directors are of the opinion that inclusion in the group accounts would be harmful to the business of any of the group companies, or, because of differences in the nature of the businesses, treatment as a single undertaking would not be reasonable.

Although a subsidiary is not dealt with in the group accounts, or no group accounts are required with respect to it because exempting circumstances are present, this does not mean that no statutory information is available to members of the holding company regarding such a subsidiary. That this information has to be disclosed in the balance sheet of the holding company, has already been considered.[5] Other important information is required to be given under para. 69 of the Eighth Schedule and is reviewed later in this chapter.[6]

Form and contents

71–04 The form of the group accounts must usually be that of consolidated accounts; but permission is given for other forms to be adopted if the directors of the company are of the opinion that they will better serve the purpose of presenting the same or equivalent information to, or its better appreciation by, members of the holding company. Further, the group accounts may be wholly or partly incorporated in the company's own accounts (1948 Act, s. 151).

However, while the law gives directors wide discretion as to the form of group accounts, the standards of the accounting professional bodies give no discretion at all. Statement of Standard Accounting Practice No. 14 (see Vol. III, Part F) lists four circumstances in which subsidiaries should be excluded from consolidation, and states that group accounts should in all other circumstances be in the form of a single set of consolidated accounts

---

[5] See para. 70–16, *ante*.
[6] See paras. 71–07 *et seq.*, *post*.

including all subsidiaries at home and overseas. The four exceptional circumstances are:

(i) where consolidation would be misleading because the subsidiary's activities are so different from those of the rest of the group;

(ii) where the holding company does not directly or indirectly own shares carrying more than half the votes, or is otherwise restricted or prevented from appointing a majority of the directors;

(iii) where the holding company's control over the assets and operations of the subsidiary is significantly impaired;

(iv) where control over the subsidiary is intended to be temporary.

The Accounting Standard gives separate requirements for dealing in the group accounts with subsidiaries excluded from consolidation for each of these four reasons.

The group accounts (together with any notes to those accounts) must give a true and fair view of the state of affairs and profit or loss of the company and the subsidiaries dealt with thereby as a whole, so far as concerns members of the company (1948 Act, s. 152 (2)). They must comply with the requirements of the Eighth Schedule so far as it applies to them (s. 152 (1)). The Department of Trade may modify these requirements, on the application or with the consent of the directors, for the purpose of adapting them to the circumstances of the company (s. 152 (5)). The requirement to give a true and fair view overrides all the accounting requirements of the Acts, including those of the Eighth Schedule (s. 152 (3), applying *ibid.* s. 149 (3) and (4) to group accounts).

Anyone who is a director of a company when it lays or delivers group accounts which do not comply with the requirements of the Acts as to matters to be included in those accounts is guilty of an offence punishable by fine, unless he can show that he took all reasonable steps for securing compliance (*ibid.* s. 150 (3)).

It is quite clear that the purpose of the consolidated accounts is to present to the members of the holding company a statement of the activity and position of the group companies as if they related to a single undertaking (*cf.* Eighth Sched., para. 62). This overall aim is to be achieved by combining the information given in the separate balance sheets and profit and loss accounts, but allowing for any adjustments thought necessary by the directors of the holding company (Eighth Sched., para. 61). Adjustments which might normally have to be made include the elimination of inter-company indebtedness, the elimination from subsidiary revenue reserves of profits earned by subsidiaries prior to the acquisition of the majority of the equity share capital by the holding company, or allowing for minority interests in subsidiaries, revaluation of assets in subsidiaries, and inter-company transactions whether of capital or revenue nature.

In practice there are differences both in the methods of achieving the consolidated figures and in the extent of the adjustments considered necessary; and, consequently, the final figures presented in the group accounts. Fixed assets may be shown as "at cost to the constituent companies" or as "at cost to the holding company." Again the net excess of the cost of shares in subsidiaries over the appropriate proportion of book values of net assets at the date of acquisition may be described as such at length, or alternatively as "premiums paid on acquisition of shares in subsidiaries, less pre-acquisition reserves (profits)." Shorter terms such as "goodwill arising on consolidation" or "premium on acquisitions" are also used, but it is considered that with this shorter phrasing the significance of the item is not clear unless it is explained in the notes to the accounts.

A method of arriving at consolidated figures known as "merger accounting," which has been in common use in the United States of America, has been used occasionally in Britain where independent companies have combined and much more frequently in internal re-organisations of existing groups of companies. Under this method, which is used only where shares are acquired for shares issued by the other company involved, the two balance sheets are simply added together, the nominal value of the shares being exchanged cancelling each other out as far as possible, any difference being adjusted in reserves. Thus no share premium account is created and the pre-acquisition profits of the subsidiary are accounted for as distributable reserves.

A proposed statement of Standard Accounting Practice including use of merger accounting was not adopted by the accountancy bodies; one of several reasons for this was the possibility that the method contravened section 56 of the 1948 Act which required the excess of value received for shares issued over their nominal value to be transferred to a share premium account. The decision in the tax case of *Shearer (Inspector of Taxes)* v. *Bercain Ltd.*[7] now makes clear that merger accounting has been illegal under British law. But the 1981 Act, sections 36 to 41, give relief for the future and retrospectively from the requirements of Section 56 in certain strictly defined circumstances which cover those in which merger accounting has been used.

Accounting exemptions for holding companies

71–05 A holding company is not entitled to the exemptions for small or medium-sized companies from some of the requirements in respect of information to be delivered to the Registrar of Companies (see para. 70–10, above) unless the group consisting of the holding company and its subsidiaries would, if it were an actual company, qualify for those exemptions (1981 Act, s. 9 (2)). The figures to be used in the necessary calculations are those in the consolidated accounts of the group or the figures that would have been in consolidated accounts if such had been prepared dealing with all companies in the group (1981 Act, s. 9 (4) (5) (6)).

A holding company which qualifies for treatment as a small or medium-sized company in accordance with the above conditions in relation to delivering its own accounts qualifies also for "group exemption." A com-

---

[7] 1980 S.T.C. 359.

pany which qualifies for group exemption may deliver to the Registrar "modified group accounts" taking advantage of the exemptions for small or medium-sized companies in section 6 of the 1981 Act as if the group were an actual company (1981 Act, s. 10).

Financial year of group companies

71–06 It is the duty of the holding company's directors to see that the financial years of the holding and subsidiary companies coincide, unless in their opinion there are good reasons against such an arrangement (1948 Act, s. 153 (1)). It has been noted earlier (see para. 70–04) that there is exemption from some of the restrictions on changing of accounting reference periods for a company which is changing so as to coincide with the accounting reference period of its holding or subsidiary company.

If the financial years do not coincide, then the group accounts must deal with the subsidiaries' accounts for the financial year of each subsidiary ended within that of the holding company, unless the Department of Trade directs otherwise (1948 Act, s. 152 (2)).

The directors are required to disclose their reasons why the subsidiaries' financial years do not end with that of the holding company (Eighth Sched., para. 70).

Absence of group accounts

71–07 The absence of group accounts does not free the holding company from submitting to its members information about its subsidiaries other than that contained in its own accounts. As has been noted previously, group accounts are not necessarily consolidated accounts and could conceivably cover the holding and subsidiary companies' separate accounts submitted jointly. Such group accounts must give the same or equivalent information as that required to be given by consolidated accounts. If, however, no accounting statements are submitted, which could be satisfactorily described as "group accounts," the emphasis for information to be given regarding subsidiaries is on profits and losses rather than assets and liabilities.

There must be given in a note to the holding company's accounts a statement showing:

(1) reasons why the subsidiaries were not dealt with in group accounts;
(2) the aggregate amount of the total investment of the holding company in the shares of the subsidiaries, by way of the equity method of valuation;
(3) any qualifications in auditors' reports on subsidiaries' accounts, or any note or reservation in the accounts, which otherwise would properly have appeared as a qualification, if not dealt with in the holding company's accounts and if material to its members;
(4) if any of the foregoing are not obtainable, a statement to that effect (Eighth Sched., para. 69).

The Department of Trade may direct that any or all of the supplementary information need not be given (Eighth Sched., para. 69 (6)). A company which is itself a wholly owned subsidiary of a company incorporated in Great Britain may omit the information under (2) above, provided that there is annexed to the balance sheet a statement that in the opinion of the directors the shares in and amounts owing from the company's subsidiaries have a total value not less than the total at which they are stated in the balance sheet (Eighth Sched., para. 69 (4)).

Subsidiaries not dealt with by group accounts

71–08 Where a holding company prepares group accounts which do not deal with one or more of its subsidiaries, it must give in a note to its accounts the same information in relation to those subsidiaries as is required where a holding company does not prepare group accounts (see para. 71–07, above). Where the holding company has prepared group accounts in the form of consolidated accounts dealing with its other subsidiaries the required note shall be a note to those consolidated accounts (Eighth Sched., para. 69 (7)).

CHAPTER 72

DIRECTORS' REPORT

General

72–01 A directors' report must be attached to every balance sheet prepared under section 1 of the 1976 Act (see para. 70–04, *ante*) (1948 Act, s. 157 (1)). The information which must be included in the directors' report is specified in the Acts. The 1981 Act moves several items of information from the directors' report to the notes to the accounts. The regulations of the Stock Exchange require additional information to be given by listed companies. The current statutory and Stock Exchange requirements are discussed in more detail in later paragraphs of this chapter.

The provisions of section 158 of the 1948 Act entitling members, debenture holders and certain other persons to receive copies of the balance sheet and the annexures, as well as copies of the auditors' report, not less than 21 days before the general meeting, apply likewise to the directors' report (1967 Act, s. 24).

A director of a company which fails to comply with the relevant provisions of the Acts is liable to a fine. It is, however, a defence if he can prove that he took all reasonable steps for securing compliance with the requirements (1967 Act, s. 23, as substituted by 1976 Act, Sched. 2).

Statutory contents of directors' report

72–02 The 1980 Act (ss. 54–65) has transferred the disclosure of information relating to contracts in which directors have an interest from the directors' report to the notes to the accounts and amended the rules governing the disclosure (see para. 70–15, *ante*). The 1981 Act has removed the requirement to disclose in the directors' report particulars of exports (by repealing section 20 of the 1967 Act) and the principal activities of the company and its subsidiaries (by repealing part of section 16 (1) of the 1967 Act). The 1981 Act has transferred from the directors' report to the notes to the accounts, by inclusion in the new text of the Eighth Schedule, information about new issues of shares and debentures, turnover by class of business and employees' numbers and remuneration. The 1981 Act has also withdrawn the right to give in the directors' report information which would otherwise be required to be given in the accounts (1981 Act, s. 16 (2) (*a*), repealing the proviso to section 163 of the 1948 Act).

Most of these changes introduced by the 1981 Act do not apply to those companies which continue to prepare their accounts in accordance with the pre-1981 version of the Eighth Schedule, now Schedule 8A (see para. 70–11, above).

The current statutory requirements for companies preparing accounts under the new Eighth Schedule are described first below. Then the provisions relating to companies preparing "Schedule 8A accounts" are outlined at para. 72–11.

Development of the company's business

72–03 The directors' report is required to contain "a fair review of the development of the business of the company and its subsidiaries during that year and of their position at the end of it" (s. 157 (1), as substituted by 1981 Act, s. 13 (1)). It is also required to contain particulars of important events affecting the company or any of its subsidiaries which have occurred since the year-end; an indication of likely future developments in the business; and an indication of activities in the field of research and development (1967 Act, s. 16 (1) (*f*), as substituted by 1981 Act, s. 13 (3)).

Dividend and reserve proposals

72–04 The directors' report must state the amount, if any, which the directors recommend should be paid as dividend, and the amount, if any, which they propose to carry to reserves (1948 Act, s. 157 (1)).

Names of directors

72–05 The directors' report must state the names of the persons who were directors of the company at any time during the financial year (1967 Act, s. 16 (1)).

Significant changes in fixed assets

72–06 Significant changes in the fixed assets of the company or of any of its subsidiaries during the financial year have to be explained in the report (1967 Act, s. 16 (1)). While the amount of the fixed assets themselves is stated in the accounts, attention is drawn to any significant changes in their values in the directors' report.

This applies, in particular, if the fixed assets consist of interests in land and their market value has substantially altered in the year of report (s. 16 (1) (*a*)).

If interests in land are not fixed assets, as may be the case in a property company which deals in land, no particulars of substantial changes in the market values need to be given under this heading, but these particulars might have to be given under the general requirements for the directors' report (see para. 72–03, above).

Directors' interests in shares or debentures of the company or related companies

72–07 The directors' report must indicate whether the interests of the directors, their spouses and infant children in the shares or debentures of the company, its holding company or its subsidiaries underwent a change (1967 Act, s. 16 (1) (*e*) and (4)). This information is founded on the register of directors' interests.[1] The report must essentially state, with respect to each director and his dependants, the position at the end and the beginning of the financial year. In both cases particulars have to be given of the number and amount of the shares or debentures, specifying each of the companies in which they are held.

A comparison of these items at the two relevant dates enables the reader to draw his own conclusions.

The required particulars may now be given in notes to the accounts instead of in the directors' report (1967 Act, s. 16 (4A), inserted by the 1981 Act, s. 13 (4)).

Information relating to health, safety and welfare of employees

72–08 The directors' report must also contain such information as may be prescribed by the Secretary of State for securing the health, safety and welfare at work of employees of the company and its subsidiaries and for protecting other persons against risks to health or safety arising out of or in connection with the activities at work of those employees (1967 Act, s. 16 (1) (*g*), added by the Health and Safety at Work, etc., Act 1974, s. 79 (1) and (2)). The regulations which the Secretary of State may make under this provision are specified in section 16 (5) of the 1967 Act (added by the Health and Safety at Work, etc., Act 1974, s. 79 (3)). No statutory instruments have been issued to date.[2]

Political or charitable contributions

72–09 The directors' report has to include particulars of contributions for political or charitable purposes, or both, if the total is in excess of £200 (1967 Act, s. 19 (1)). Where the company has subsidiaries, the directors' report of the holding company must show the contributions made by any company in the group (s. 19 (2)), but, on the other hand, the report of the wholly owned subsidiary[3] of a company incorporated in Great Britain need not show these contributions (s. 19 (1) and (2)).

The following particulars of the contributions have to be stated:

(1) each of the purposes for which the money is given (s. 19 (1)). In other words, the directors' report must differentiate between the political and charitable purposes;
(2) in the case of each of the purposes, the total amount of money given therefor (s. 19 (1));
(3) in the case of political purposes, the name of each person or political party to whom money has been given in excess of £200 and the amount so given (s. 19 (1) (*a*) and (*b*)); a very wide definition of gifts of money for political purposes is provided and it is stated that direct or indirect contributions have to be mentioned (s. 19 (3));

---

[1] See para. 66–03, *ante*.
[2] Position at July 1982.
[3] Within the meaning of s. 150 (4) of the 1948 Act (1967 Act, s. 19 (5)).

(4) in the case of charitable purposes, it is provided that only exclusively charitable purposes fall under this heading, and that in Scotland the term "charitable" shall be construed in the same way as in the Income Tax Acts (s. 19 (5)), but, both as regards England and Scotland, money given for charitable purposes to a person who, when it was given, was ordinarily resident outside the United Kingdom, shall be disregarded (s. 19 (4)).

The names of the charities to which contributions were made need not be given.

Acquisition of company's own shares

72–10 The directors' report must give details of the company's own shares acquired by itself in pursuance of section 35 (2) of the 1980 Act or by someone else in circumstances where sections 37 (1) (*c*) or 37 (1) (*d*) of the 1980 Act applies (1967 Act, s. 16A, inserted by 1981 Act, s. 14). The details required are the number, nominal value and percentage of called-up share capital of such shares (i) acquired during the year; (ii) disposed of or cancelled during the year; (iii) comprised in the maximum holding at any time during the year. The amount or value of the consideration of any shares disposed of for money or money's worth must also be stated in the directors' report (1967 Act, s. 16A (2)).

Companies preparing "Schedule 8A accounts"

72–11 Companies which are entitled under Schedule 2 (1) of the 1981 Act to prepare "Schedule 8A accounts" (see para. 70–11, above) and which exercise that option are subject to rules regarding the directors' report which are in several respects the general pre-1981-Act rules.

Information which would otherwise be required to be given in the accounts may be given instead in the directors' report; comparative figures for the previous year must then be given. The amendments to section 157 (1) and to section 16 of the 1967 Act made by section 13 of the 1981 Act do not apply to companies submitting Schedule 8A accounts, so that the previous wording of these sections applies instead of that given at paragraph 72–03, above. The provision of section 16 (1) (*b*) of the 1967 Act regarding new issues of share and debentures continue to apply to these companies.

Companies which prepare group accounts in accordance with Schedule 8A are required to give in their directors' reports information about the division of turnover and profit between different classes of business (1967 Act, s. 17) and numbers of employees and their aggregate remuneration (1967 Act, s. 18).

Additional requirements of the Stock Exchange

72–12 The Stock Exchange demands that listed companies circulate, with the directors' report, information additional to that required by statute. Listed companies must undertake, by virtue of the listing agreement which they are required to sign, to provide this additional information. The obligation to "circulate with the directors' report" can of course be satisfied by inclusion of the information in the notes to the accounts instead of in the directors' report itself. For full information paragraph 10 of the listing agreement should be consulted[4]; briefly, the requirements relate to the following topics:

(a) a statement as to the reasons for any significant departure from standard accounting practices;
(b) a geographical analysis of turnover and of the contribution to trading results of operations carried out outside the United Kingdom;
(c) the name of the principal country in which each subsidiary operates;
(d) certain particulars of companies in which the group interest in the equity share capital amounts to 20 per cent. or more;
(e) a statement showing the interests of each director in the share capital appearing in the register maintained under the provisions of the Companies Act 1967, distinguishing between beneficial and non-beneficial interests;
(f) a statement showing particulars of an interest of any person, other than a director in any substantial part of the share capital of the company (*i.e.* 5 per cent. or more of the voting capital);
(g) certain statements relating to the Income and Corporation Taxes Act 1970;
(h) particulars of any contract in which a director is or was materially interested and which is or was significant in relation to the company's business;
(i) particulars of any arrangement under which a director has waived or agreed to waive any emoluments;
(j) particulars of any arrangement under which a shareholder has waived or agreed to waive any dividends;
(k) an explanation of any material difference between trading results and any published forecast made by the company;
(l) analyses of bank and of other borrowings according to their repayment dates (within one year, or two years, two to five years, over five years);
(m) a statement of the amount of interest capitalised during the year, with an indication of related tax relief.

PRACTICE NOTE

72–13 The information required to be given in the report of the directors by the Companies Acts 1948 to 1981 and by the Stock Exchange Regulations (in the case of a company any of the securities of which are listed), together

---

[4] See Vol. II, Part C.

with other information usually included by custom, will depend upon the nature of the company's business and whether or not it is a holding company.

The specimen report given below relates to a holding company, the shares of which are listed on the Stock Exchange.

EXE P.L.C.

Report of the directors for the year ended March 31, 19...

Directors:
- A. Bee (Chairman)
- C. Dee
- Y. Zed
- S. Tee (appointed January 15, 19...)
- U. Vee (died December 31, 19...)

Activities and development The company is a holding company and its three subsidiaries operate in Great Britain a chain of hardware stores. Until June 30, 19... one of the subsidiaries carried on the business of a builders' merchant. The business of the group continued to expand during the financial year. Since the end of the year, a second retail shop has been opened in Southtown and plans are being considered for further expansion in the Northtown area. Market research is being conducted to determine the most suitable location for this proposed development.

Accounts	The group accounts for the year disclose a net profit, after taxation, of		£242,107
	Deduct: Minority interest		2,107
			240,000
	Add: Balance brought forward from previous year		20,000
			£260,000
	Less: Transfer to general reserve	£55,000	
	Interim dividend of 1p per share paid December 31, 19...	60,000	
	Proposed final dividend of 2p per share	120,000	
			235,000
	Balance carried forward		£25,000

Assets The sum of £50,000 was expended on capital equipment for the subsidiary which changed the nature of its activities during the year.

The market value of the freehold property of the subsidiaries is, in the opinion of the directors, approximately £100,000 in excess of the amount at which it is included in the consolidated balance sheet.

Contributions for political or charitable purposes

The company and its subsidiaries made the following contributions during the year:—

For political purposes:	
K.L. Limited	£150
For charitable purposes	£465

Directors The death of Mr. U. Vee on December 31, 19..., is reported with deep regret. Mr. S. Tee was appointed a director on January 15, 19..., to fill the vacancy on the board and in accordance with the articles of association, he retires at the annual general meeting and is eligible for re-election. Mr. C. Dee retires by rotation and is eligible for re-election.

Mr. S. Tee has a service contract with the company expiring on March 31, 19... Mr. C. Dee has no service contract.

The interests of the directors in the securities of the company at the beginning and the end of the year were as follows:—

	April 1, 19...		*March 31, 19...*	
	Shares	*Loan Stock*	*Shares*	*Loan Stock*
A. Bee	1,500	—	1,500	£250
C. Dee	400	—	1,000	100
Y. Zed	100	—	100	100
S. Tee	* —	—	200	—

* *at date of appointment*

All the above interests are beneficial interests, except in respect of 100 of the shares recorded for Mr. A. Bee.

No changes in the above interests occurred between March 31, 19..., and .... 19...

The directors have no interests in the minority holding in a subsidiary.

Except for the interest of one director in a contract made by the company, which is disclosed in note 5 of the notes to the accounts, no contracts in relation to the business of the company or its subsidiaries in which directors of the company had a material interest subsisted at the end of the financial year or at any time during the year.

Interest in voting shares At ....19..., an interest of M. N. Limited in 120,000 shares of £1 each, representing ...... per cent. of the issued share capital, had been notified under section 63 of the Companies Act 1981.

Employment of disabled persons The group endeavours to employ disabled persons where the requirements of the job are such that the duties can be effectively performed by a handicapped or disabled person. If existing employees become disabled, every endeavour is made to continue their employment, provided there are duties which they are still able to perform. Suitable training is given in such cases.

Auditors A resolution to reappoint the retiring auditors, Messrs. X & Co., will be proposed at the annual general meeting.

General The company is not a close company, as defined by the Income and Corporation Taxes Act 1970.

By order of the board,
G. H.,
Secretary.

Address)
Date)

NOTE. It has been assumed that any other information required to be disclosed by paragraph 10 of the Stock Exchange listing agreement will have been shown by way of notes to the accounts.

CHAPTER 73

AUDITORS AND AUDIT

Appointment of auditors

73–01 The regulations dealing with the appointment, rights and duties of auditors are contained in section 161 of the 1948 Act, sections 13 and 14 of the 1967 Act and sections 13–19 of the 1976 Act.[1] The articles normally include a reference to these provisions (see art. 130, as amended by Sched. 2 of the 1976 Act).

The first auditors may be appointed by the directors at any time before the first general meeting of the company at which accounts for an accounting reference period are laid before the meeting (1976 Act, s. 14 (3)). If the directors fail to exercise these powers they may be exercised by the company in general meeting (*ibid.* s. 14 (4)).

The general rule is that a company shall at every general meeting before which accounts for an accounting reference period are laid in accordance with section 1 (6) of the 1976 Act appoint an auditor or auditors who shall hold office from the conclusion of that meeting until the conclusion of the next such meeting (*ibid.* s. 14 (1)). The provision for "automatic" reappointment, without a resolution, of an existing auditor who is willing to continue in office has been repealed; if a company does not pass a resolution appointing an auditor, the office of auditor will be vacant. Where at the appropriate general meeting no resolution is passed for the appointment of an auditor, the Secretary of State may appoint a person to fill the vacancy, and the company must notify the Secretary of State within one week of the company's failure to appoint an auditor; otherwise there is liability to a default fine (*ibid.* s. 14 (2), (7)).

Any casual vacancy in the office of auditor may be filled by the directors or the company in general meeting. But while the vacancy continues, the surviving or continuing auditor or auditors may act (*ibid.* s. 14 (5)).

Resolutions for appointment or removal of auditors

73–02 Special notice[2] is required for a resolution—

(1) to fill a casual vacancy in the office of auditor;

(2) to appoint as auditor a retiring auditor who had been appointed by the directors to fill a casual vacancy;

(3) to appoint as auditor a person other than the retiring auditor;

(4) to remove an auditor before the expiration of his term of office (1976 Act, s. 15 (1)).

The company must send forthwith a copy of the notice to the person proposed to be appointed or removed, and, where applicable, to any

[1] ss. 159 and 160 of the 1948 Act were repealed by the 1976 Act s. 14 (11) and s. 15 (7).
[2] See para. 54–06, *ante*.

person who by his resignation caused the casual vacancy in either of the first two situations above, or to the retiring auditor in the third situation above (*ibid.* s. 15 (2)). In the third and fourth situations above, the retiring auditor or auditor proposed to be removed may make representations in writing to the company and request their notification to members of the company. Unless they are received too late, the company must send a copy of the representations to every member of the company to whom notice of the meeting has to be sent. If a copy of the representations is not sent, the auditor who has made them may require that they be read out at the meeting. The court has power to waive these requirements for notifying representations if it is satisfied that the rights conferred have been abused to secure needless publicity for defamatory matter (*ibid.* s. 15 (3), (4), (5)).

An auditor who has been removed is entitled to be notified of, to attend and to be heard, at the general meeting at which his term of office would otherwise have ended and any general meeting at which it is proposed to fill the vacancy caused by his removal (*ibid.* s. 15 (6)).

Within the accountancy profession, it is a requirement of professional ethics, for the person who is approached on behalf of the company to take the place of a retiring auditor, prior to giving assent so to act, to ascertain from the retiring auditor whether there are any reasons why it might not be proper or desirable to accept the appointment.[3]

Resignation of auditors

73–03 Section 16 of the 1976 Act has introduced regulations governing the resignation of auditors which will prevent an auditor from resigning without reporting to the members on a problem situation of which he is aware. To be effective, an auditor's notice of resignation must be sent in writing to the registered office of the company and must *either* state that there are no circumstances connected with his resignation which he considers should be brought to the notice of the members or creditors *or* include a statement of any such circumstances (1976 Act, s. 16 (1), (2)). The company must send a copy of the notice of resignation to the Registrar of Companies within 14 days. If the notice includes a "statement of circumstances connected with the auditors' resignation" the company must also send a copy of the notice of resignation to all persons entitled to receive copies of accounts under section 158 (1). The court may, on application, direct that copies of the notice should not be sent out if it is satisfied that the auditor is using the notice to secure needless publicity for defamatory matter; in this case the company must send out a statement setting out the effect of the order (*ibid.* s. 16 (3), (4), (5), (6)). If a company fails to comply with these requirements for notifying the Registrar and members and debenture holders, it

[3] For instance, in relation to the Institute of Chartered Accountants in England and Wales, see Statement 8 of the "Guide to Professional Ethics" and the Council Statement "Changes in a Professional Appointment"; these are in sections 1.2 and 1.309 respectively of the Members' Handbook and are reproduced in *Accountancy*, August 1975 and December 1969 respectively.

and its officers are liable to a default fine and the provisions of section 428 of the 1948 Act as to enforcement of duty to make returns to the Registrar also apply (*ibid.* s. 16 (7), (8)).

In addition to these duties to report the circumstances of his resignation, the auditor is given the right under section 17 of the 1976 Act to make further statements to the members. If his notice of resignation includes a statement of circumstances to be brought to the notice of members or creditors, it may also be accompanied by a requisition signed by the auditor requiring the directors to convene an extraordinary general meeting for the purpose of considering such explanation of the circumstances connected with his resignation as he may wish to place before the meeting (*ibid.* s. 17 (1)). He may also attend and be heard at the general meeting of the company at which his term of office would have expired if he had not resigned or at any general meeting convened on his requisition or at which it is proposed to fill the casual vacancy caused by his resignation. The auditor who has resigned has the same rights to have statements circulated to members before such meetings as an auditor who is proposed to be removed (see para. 73–02, *ante*) and subject to the same proviso about "needless publicity for defamatory matter" (*ibid.* s. 17 (2), (3), (4), (5)).

For the procedure in Scotland in application to the court see rule 218B of the Rules of the Court of Session.

Qualification for appointment as auditor

73–04 By section 161 (1) and section 13 (1) and (2) of the 1976 Act, a person is qualified to act as auditor only if either:

(1) he is a member of a body of accountants established in the United Kingdom and for the time being recognised for this purpose by the Department of Trade,[4] or

(2) he is for the time being authorised by the Department of Trade to be appointed *either* because he has similar qualifications obtained abroad *or* because he has obtained adequate knowledge and experience in the course of employment by a member of a recognised body. No authorisation will be granted on the latter grounds after April 18, 1978 (1976 Act, s. 13 (4) (*a*) and the Companies Act 1976 (Commencement No. 3) Order 1977). Authorisation on the basis of qualifications obtained abroad may be refused if the overseas country concerned does not grant corresponding privileges to persons holding United Kingdom qualifications (1976 Act, s. 13 (3)).

In the former case, qualification to act proceeds initially from membership of certain professional bodies of accountants; in the latter, from permission given by the Department of Trade to individuals.

None of the following is qualified for appointment as auditor:

---

[4] The following bodies of accountants are recognised:
(1) The Institute of Chartered Accountants in England and Wales;
(2) The Association of Certified Accountants;
(3) The Institute of Chartered Accountants of Scotland;
(4) The Institute of Chartered Accountants in Ireland.

(a) an officer or servant of the company (1948 Act, s. 161 (2) (*a*));
(b) a person who is a partner or in the employment of an officer or servant of the company (s. 161 (2) (*b*));
(c) a body corporate[5] (s. 161 (2) (*c*));
(d) a person disqualified for appointment as auditor of a subsidiary or holding company (s. 161 (3)).

An officer of the company for this purpose includes a director, manager or secretary (1948 Act, s. 455).

An auditor who discovers that he has become disqualified for appointment as auditor shall cease to act as auditor, and shall give notice to the company that he has vacated his office because of disqualification; if he does not comply with these rules he is liable to a fine (1976 Act, s. 13 (5), (6)).[4a]

Additional qualifications under 1967 Act

Under the Act of 1948, the provisions of section 161 (1) and 161 (2) (*b*) did not apply to exempt private companies. As the result of the abolition of exempt private companies by section 2 of the 1967 Act, these requirements now apply in principle to all companies. But, in order to safeguard to some extent the position of persons not qualified under section 161 (1) who acted as auditors of exempt private companies until their abolition, section 13 of the 1967 Act authorises such persons to continue to act as auditors of companies which satisfy the following conditions, *viz.* that

(a) neither the company itself nor its holding company, if any, has obtained a quotation for any of its shares or debentures on a stock exchange (whether in Great Britain or elsewhere) or has offered any of its shares or debentures to the public[6] for subscription or purchase[7] (1967 Act, s. 13 (1)), and
(b) the company is not carrying on business as the promoter of a trading stamp scheme within the meaning of the Trading Stamps Act 1964 (*ibid.* s. 13 (6)).

The Department of Trade will authorise a person who does not satisfy section 161 (1) to be appointed auditor of companies which satisfy the above conditions only if he is a person who was in practice as an accountant throughout the 12 months ending on November 3, 1966, and who was on that date the auditor of an exempt private company. To qualify for appointment to any particular company, a person must also satisfy section 161 (2) to (4). Despite its restrictions, this provision extends considerably the class of persons who may act as auditors in relation to unquoted companies.

4a He cannot be convicted if he has no knowledge of the fact that he was disqualified to act as an auditor because he was a director and secretary: *Secretary of State for Trade and Industry* v. *Hart* [1982] 1 W.L.R. 481.

5 This does not include a Scottish firm, provided that all the partners are qualified for appointment as auditor (s. 161 (4)).

6 "Public" has the same meaning here as it has under s. 55 (1) of the 1948 Act (1967 Act, s. 13 (5)).

7 As to when shares or debentures are offered to the public for this purpose, see para. 21–17, *ante*.

No further authorisations will be granted under these provisions after April 18, 1978 (1976 Act, s. 13 (4) (*b*) and the Companies Act 1976 (Commencement No. 3) Order 1977).

Remuneration of auditor

The remuneration of the auditor of a company is to be fixed by the company in general meeting or in such manner as the company in general meeting may determine. In the case of an auditor appointed by the directors or by the Department of Trade, it may be fixed by the directors or the Department of Trade, as the case may be (1976 Act, s. 14 (8)).

It is a requirement of the Eighth Schedule that the amount of the auditor's remuneration shall be shown in the profit and loss account under a separate heading (para. 53 (7)).

For the purposes of the foregoing subsection and paragraph, any sums paid by the company in respect of the auditors' expenses shall be deemed to be included in the expression "remuneration."

Status of auditor

73–05 The auditors may well be regarded as agents of the members appointed to carry out certain duties as laid down by the Acts and the articles, for the purposes of the audit. The matter was considered in *Spackman* v. *Evans*,[8] where it was held, however, that constructive notice of facts coming to their knowledge cannot be imputed to the shareholders. The auditor is not an agent of the company for the purpose of acknowledging a debt on behalf of the company by signing his statutory report on the balance sheet.[9] But he may be appointed agent by special contract, and by section 167 (5) he is to be regarded as an agent of the company for the purposes of that section.[10]

The question whether an auditor is an officer of the company is not explicitly answered by the Companies Acts. The auditor is not mentioned in the definition of "officer" in section 455, which says merely that an officer "includes a director, manager or secretary." In section 448 there is reference to an "auditor (whether he is or is not an officer of the company)." The matter was fully reviewed in *R.* v. *Shacter*,[11] where it was held that the auditor appointed under section 159 of the 1948 Act (now under section 14 of the 1976 Act) to hold the office of auditor of the company is an officer of the company (with consequent liability under, for instance, Companies Act 1948, ss. 328, 330, 333, 334, Companies Act 1976, s. 12, and Theft Act 1968,[12] s. 19); but a person appointed ad hoc for a limited purpose (*e.g.* by the directors for a private audit) is not an officer.

---

[8] (1868) L.R. 3 H.L. 171.
[9] *Re Transplanters (Holding Company) Ltd.* [1958] 1 W.L.R. 822, 826; see para. 43–26, *ante*.
[10] See para. 78–09, *post*.
[11] [1960] 2 Q.B. 252, C.C.A.; and see para. 73–12, *post*.
[12] The Theft Act 1968 does not apply in Scotland.

Duties of auditors

Auditors' report

73–06 The auditors' principal duty is to make a report to the members on the accounts examined by them and on every balance sheet, profit and loss account and group accounts laid before the company in general meeting during their tenure of office (1967 Act, s. 14 (1)).

Matters to be expressly stated in the auditors' report include—

(1) whether, in their opinion, the company's balance sheet and profit and loss account and (if it is a holding company submitting group accounts) the group accounts have been properly prepared in accordance with the provisions of the Companies Acts 1948 to 1981; and

(2) whether, in their opinion, a true and fair view[13] is given—

(a) in the case of the balance sheet, of the state of the company's affairs as at the end of its financial year;

(b) in the case of the profit and loss account (if not framed as a consolidated profit and loss account), of the company's profit or loss for its financial year;

(c) in the case of group accounts submitted by a holding company, of the state of affairs and profit or loss of the company and its subsidiaries dealt with thereby so far as concerns members of the company (1967 Act, s. 14 (3)).

The statement under (2) above is not required if the company is a banking or insurance company exempted under Part III of Schedule 8A from full compliance with Part I of that Schedule (*ibid.*).

In preparing their report, the auditors are required to carry out such investigations as will enable them to form an opinion as to whether—

(1) proper accounting records have been kept by the company and proper returns adequate for their audit have been received from branches not visited by them; and

(2) the company's balance sheet and (unless it is framed as a consolidated profit and loss account) profit and loss account are in agreement with the accounting records and returns (1967 Act, s. 14 (4)).

It is no longer necessary, as was formerly the case under the Ninth Schedule to the 1948 Act, that the report should state that the auditors have satisfied themselves as to these matters, but if they form a *negative* opinion on any of these matters, that fact must be stated in their report (*ibid.*).

Similarly the auditors must now consider whether the information given in the directors' report is consistent with the company's accounts, but need to include their opinion in their report only if it is that the directors' report is NOT consistent with the accounts (1967 Act, s. 23A, inserted by 1981 Act, s. 15).

---

13 As to the meaning of "a true and fair view" see para. 70–05, *ante*.

Although the auditors must report to the members, they are not bound to send their report to every shareholder.[14] If, however, they know or have reason to believe that their report, when sent to the secretary or the directors, is not laid before the shareholders, it may be doubted whether they can safely rest content without taking some steps to see that it is communicated to the members.

The auditors' report must be read before the company in general meeting and must be open to inspection by any member (1967 Act, s. 14 (2)).

It is clear from the provisions of section 14 of the 1967 Act that the auditors have to base their report to the members both on the accounting records maintained by the company and the accounts laid before the company in general meeting; they have further to report on the relationship between the two—the one containing detailed day-to-day transactions and the other showing the summarised effect of these transactions over a stated period and at a given date. The principal duty of the auditors is to state whether in their opinion, the latter give a true and fair view.

In forming their opinion, the auditors must exercise their own judgment, and if they do, in fact, entertain the opinion they express, they will, in reporting it, have performed their statutory duty. If, in their opinion, the accounts do not represent a true and fair view, or proper accounting records have not been kept, then the auditors must qualify their report to indicate such a position. They may not be satisfied, *e.g.* as to the valuation placed on certain assets or liabilities, and it is their duty to report the matters with which they are not satisfied. Lindley L.J., in the course of his judgment in *Re London and General Bank (No. 2)*,[15] said:

> "A person whose duty it is to convey information to others does not discharge that duty by simply giving them so much information as is calculated to induce them, or some of them, to ask for more. Information and means of information are by no means equivalent terms . . . an auditor who gives shareholders means of information instead of information respecting a company's financial position does so at his peril and runs the very serious risk of being held judicially to have failed to discharge his duty."

In considering whether their report should be qualified, the auditors should assess the nature and importance of the items at issue in relation to the accounts as a whole, so as to determine their significance in judging the truth and fairness of the view presented.[16]

If the auditors have qualified their report on annual accounts which are the only relevant accounts in relation to a proposed distribution (as defined by the 1980 Act, s. 45 (2)) for the determination of the question whether such a distribution would contravene sections 39–41 of the 1980 Act, the auditors must state in writing whether, in their opinion, their qualification

[14] *Re Allen Craig & Co. (London)* [1934] W.N. 68.
[15] [1895] 2 Ch. 673, 684.
[16] See Auditing Standards "The audit report" and "Qualifications in audit reports" (reproduced in Vol. III, Part F).

is material for the purpose of determining that question (1980 Act, s. 43 (3) (*c*)).

Where the directors of a company propose to rely on the "accounting exemptions" for small or medium-sized companies so as to deliver modified accounts to the Registrar of Companies (see para. 70–10, *ante*) the auditors must provide the directors with a report stating whether in their opinion the requirements for the exemptions claimed are satisfied (1981 Act, s. 7 (6)).

General duties in carrying out audit

73–07 Apart from specific duties which emerge from cases considered in this chapter under the heads of "status"[17] and "liability,"[18] the courts have repeatedly stated what should be the approach of the auditor to his duties. The phrase used by Lopes L.J., that an auditor "is a watchdog, not a bloodhound,"[19] goes some way to correct the misleading view that an auditior is a detective or that he should "approach his work with suspicion or with a foregone conclusion that there is something wrong." It was well said by Donovan J. in a Canadian case[20] regarding the watchdog that

> "he will not have performed the functions of his office if after one howl he retreats 'under the barn,' or if he confines his protest to a fellow watchdog."

More recently it has been observed[21]:

> "An auditor is not to be confined to the mechanics of checking vouchers and making arithmetical computations. He is not to be written off as a professional 'adder-upper and subtractor.' His vital task is to take care to see that errors are not made, be they errors of computation, or errors of omission or commission, or downright untruths. To perform this task properly he must come to it with an inquiring mind—not suspicious of dishonesty, I agree—but suspecting that someone may have made a mistake somewhere and that a check must be made to ensure that there has been none."

Further, it is the duty of an auditor to bring to bear on the work he has to perform that skill, care and caution which a reasonably competent, careful and cautious auditor would use. What "is reasonable skill, care and caution must depend on the particular circumstances of each case."[22] This view of reasonable care and skill had previously been emphasised by Lindley L.J.,[23] who made some important observations on the general duties of auditors:

---

17 See para. 73–05, *ante*.
18 See para. 73–10, *post*.
19 *Re Kingston Cotton Mill Co. (No. 2)* [1896] 2 Ch. 279, 288.
20 *International Laboratories Ltd.* v. *Dewar & Others* [1933] 1 D.L.R. 34, 41; reversed [1933] 3 D.L.R. 665.
21 *Per* Lord Denning M.R. in *Fomento (Sterling Area) Ltd.* v. *Selsdon Fountain Pen Co.* [1958] 1 W.L.R. 45, 61, H.L.
22 *Per* Lindley L.J. in *Re Kingston Cotton Mill Co. (No. 2)* [1896] 2 Ch. 279, 284.
23 In *Re London and General Bank (No. 2)* [1895] 2 Ch. 673, 683.

> "An auditor, however, is not bound to do more than exercise reasonable care and skill in making inquiries and investigations. He is not an insurer; he does not guarantee that the books do correctly show the true position of the company's affairs; he does not even guarantee that his balance sheet is accurate according to the books of the company . . . he must be honest—*i.e.* he must not certify what he does not believe to be true, and he must take reasonable care and skill before he believes that what he certifies is true. . . . Where there is nothing to excite suspicion very little inquiry will be reasonably sufficient. . . . Where suspicion is aroused more care is obviously necessary; but, still, an auditor is not bound to exercise more than reasonable care and skill, even in a case of suspicion, and he is perfectly justified in acting on the opinion of an expert where special knowledge is required."

While these general principles remain applicable, the standards of reasonable care and skill are more exacting today than those which prevailed at the time when the above statement was made.[24]

Apart from the matters laid down in section 14 of the 1967 Act, the auditors are also required[25] to include in their report a statement regarding particulars of directors' and employees' emoluments, and transactions involving directors and officers, should the accounts of the company not give the appropriate details as required by section 196 of the 1948 Act, section 6, 7 and 8 of the 1967 Act, and section 54–58 of the 1980 Act.

Rights of auditors

73–08 The rights of auditors regarding their appointment have already been stated.[26]

In order to carry out the duties as laid down with regard to the accounts presented to members, power is given to them to have access at all times to the books and vouchers of the company and to require from the officers of the company such information as the auditors may think necessary for the performance of their duties (1967 Act, s. 14 (5)). Where the auditors were refused access to the books in a case of their alleged negligence, the court refused to make an order for access to be given; but directed that the members should meet to ascertain the wishes of the company.[27] The right of access to the books can be enforced by mandatory injunction, but not where litigation is pending between the company and the auditors.

The position of auditors is strengthened by two new provisions in the 1976 Act. This Act imposes a duty on subsidiary companies and their auditors to give to the auditors of their holding company information and explanations reasonably required by them, and also a duty on the holding company to take all steps open to it to obtain such information and explanations (1976 Act, s. 18). Any officer of a company who, when

---

[24] *Per* Pennycuick J. in *Re Thomas Gerrard & Son Ltd.* [1967] 2 All E.R. 525.

[25] By s. 196 (8) of the 1948 Act, ss. 6 (4), 7 (3) and 8 (4) of the 1967 Act, and s. 59 of the 1980 Act.

[26] See para. 73–01, *ante*.

[27] *Cuff* v. *London and County Land and Building Co.* [1912] 1 Ch. 440.

making any statement which purports to convey information or explanations to the auditors in the course of their audit, knowingly or recklessly makes a statement which is misleading, false or deceptive in a material particular, is now guilty of a statutory offence and liable to a fine, or imprisonment or both (*ibid.* s. 19).

The auditors also have the right to attend any general meeting and to receive any notices or communications relating thereto which members are entitled to receive. They may also be heard on any part of the business of these meetings which concerns them as auditors (1967 Act, s. 14 (7)).

The statutory powers given to auditors are without qualification and are of the greatest importance to them. That these rights cannot be restricted was clearly emphasised by Buckley L.J.[28]:

> "Any regulations which preclude the auditors from availing themselves of all the information to which under the Act they are entitled as material for the report which under the Act they are to make as to the true and correct state of the company's affairs are, I think, inconsistent with the Act."

It is not unusual for the auditors, though not as part of their duties under the Acts, to carry out accountancy work in preparing or assist in preparing the accounts to be presented to the members; and also to carry out other work, such as agreeing the tax liability of the company with the Inland Revenue. The working papers necessary for preparing these accounts are regarded as the property of the auditors, but the correspondence with third parties when they are acting as agents of the company belongs to the company.[29]

Further, while accountants external to the company may have a lien for fees on books of account on which they have been working, it is doubtful how far the lien extends to records on which the sole work has been that of audit.[30] It would appear from *Woodworth* v. *Conroy*[31] that accountants have at least a particular lien on books of account, files and papers given to them for purposes of audit while it is unlikely—though the question is an open one—that they have a general lien on such documents.

Liability of auditors

73–09 The liability of auditors may conveniently be considered under the following heads—

(1) Negligence.
(2) Misfeasance under the Companies Act 1948
(3) Criminal liability under the Theft Act 1968

---

[28] *Newton* v. *Birmingham Small Arms Co.* [1906] 2 Ch. 378, 389.
[29] *Chantry Martin* v. *Martin* [1953] 2 Q.B. 286.
[30] *Burleigh* v. *Ingram Clark Ltd.* (1901) 27 Acct.L.R. 65; *Re Arthur Francis Ltd.* (1911) 44 Acct.L.R. 61.
[31] [1976] Q.B. 834.

Negligence

73–10 LIABILITY TO COMPANY. To hold the auditors to be liable for negligence at common law it is necessary for the company to show that loss has been caused to the company through the failure of the auditors to perform their duties with reasonable care and skill.[32] In *Leeds Estate Building and Investment Co.* v. *Shepherd*[33] the auditor was liable when dividends were paid out of capital, primarily because he had not complied with the provisions of the articles, and that even though he had not been supplied with a copy of them. In *London Oil Storage Co. Ltd.* v. *Seear Hasluck & Co.*[34] the auditor was liable where he had failed to verify one of the assets in the balance sheet, *viz.*, the petty cash. Again, in a counterclaim for damages by the company in *A. E. Green & Co.* v. *Central Advance and Discount Corporation Ltd.*,[35] the auditors were found to be liable through failure to satisfy themselves regarding the adequacy of the provision for bad debts.

Where an individual is appointed as auditor and that individual is a partner in a firm of professional accountants, that firm may be held liable for his negligence in performing the duties as auditor, at least where the audit fee is paid direct to the firm.[36]

The duty of the auditor in the case of private companies was considered in *Pendleburys Ltd.* v. *Ellis Green & Co.*[37] Here the auditors had reported to the directors, who were also the sole shareholders, that the system of book-keeping was inadequate and that there was insufficient internal check upon cash sales. A claim for damages against the auditors failed, Swift J. observing:

> "Where the interests of a small company are confined to a very few persons, and there are no outside people because all the interests in the company are held by the directors themselves, if the auditor has, in fact, reported to the directors, what more could he be expected to do?"

Standards of care and skill change over time; for instance it is highly unlikely that the old decision that, "in the absence of suspicious circumstances, an auditor is entitled to rely entirely upon the certificate of a responsible official as to the value of the stock-in-trade"[38] would be followed today. The only modern reported case on auditors' negligence explicitly left this question open, but held that auditors will be guilty of negligence if they know that the stock records have been altered and fail to make proper inquiries; it is not sufficient in such circumstances to accept

---

[32] As to the general question of what constitutes reasonable care and skill, see para. 73–07, *ante*.
[33] (1887) 36 Ch.D. 787.
[34] (1904) 30 Acct.L.R. 93.
[35] (1920) 63 Acct.L.R. 1.
[36] *Kirkintilloch Equitable Co-operative Society Ltd.* v. *Livingstone*, 1972 S.L.T. 154. Note that this case concerns a Scottish firm and a body registered under the Industrial and Provident Societies Act 1965.
[37] (1936) 80 Acct.L.R. 39.
[38] *Re Kingston Cotton Mill Co. (No. 2)* [1896] 2 Ch. 279.

the explanations of the directors—they must make a complete examination of suppliers' statements and, if necessary as a result of their inquiries, qualify their report.[39]

The auditors of a holding company are entirely responsible for their opinion on the group accounts of that company, even when the accounts of one or more subsidiaries have been reported on by other auditors.[40]

LIABILITY TO THIRD PARTIES. The decision of the House of Lords in *Hedley Byrne & Co. Ltd.* v. *Heller & Partners Ltd.*,[41] that liability for negligent misstatements resulting in financial loss is not limited only to cases where there is an existing contractual or fiduciary relationship, raises the question whether the auditor of a company owes a duty of care to persons other than the members. Such a duty will arise where a person gives information or advice in such circumstances that a reasonable man in his position would know that his skill and judgment was being relied upon, unless he expressly disclaims responsibility for its accuracy,[42] and the auditor is clearly a person who may fall within this category. It is thought, however, that this duty is owed only to those persons for whose particular use or benefit the statement is made, and is limited to the purpose for which the statement is required. Thus, the auditors' report will not normally involve them in liability to outsiders or to individual members who might invest in the company or otherwise act in reliance upon any incorrect statement contained therein, as it has not been legally recognised that annual accounts are prepared with this purpose in view; but, in a situation such as that in *Candler* v. *Crane, Christmas & Co.*,[43] where accounts were prepared specifically for the purpose of inducing the plaintiff to invest in the company, to the knowledge of the defendants, a duty of care will be owed to persons to whom they are shown, and an action in negligence will lie for breach of this duty, unless liability has been expressly disclaimed.[44]

The rule in *Hedley Byrne & Co. Ltd.* v. *Heller & Partners Ltd.*[45] applies only to advisers who carry on the business or profession of giving advice of the kind sought and to advice given by them in the course of that business: *Mutual Life and Citizens' Assurance Ltd.* v. *Evatt.*[46] This requirement is normally satisfied if the auditor acts in his professsional capacity. But the rule in *Hedley Byrne* does not apply to casual advice by a professional man upon a social or informal occasion (*Evatt's* case). An accountant who is the auditor of a private company and is asked by two shareholders one of whom is desirous of selling his shares to the other to value the shares intended to be sold, may be liable if he negligently undervalues those

---

39 *Re Thomas Gerrard & Son Ltd.* [1967] 2 All E.R. 525.
40 See "Group accounts—reliance on other auditors." Institute of Chartered Accountants 1976, reproduced in Vol. III, Part F.
41 [1964] A.C. 465; disapproving *Candler* v. *Crane, Christmas & Co.* [1951] 2 K.B. 164, C.A.
42 See, *e.g. per* Lord Reid at p. 486.
43 [1951] 2 K.B. 164.
44 See "Accountants' liability to third parties—the Hedley Byrne decision," Institute of Chartered Accountants (with approval of counsel) 1965 (reproduced in Vol. III, Part F).
45 [1964] A.C. 465.
46 [1971] A.C. 793.

shares, provided that he acts as a "mutual" valuer; as such he would not enjoy the immunity of judges or arbitrators; but the position is different if the accountant acts as a genuine arbitrator, *e.g.* if a dispute has arisen between the parties as to the value of the shares to be sold and he is asked to decide that dispute, as in the case of *Arenson* v. *Arenson*[47]. This decision is in accord with the decision of the House of Lords in *Sutcliffe* v. *Thakrah*.[48]

A professional adviser who adds a "without responsibility" clause to his advice in order to protect himself against liability under the rule in *Hedley Byrne* cannot rely on that clause if he has acted fraudulently: *Commercial Banking Co. of Sydney Ltd.* v. *R. H. Brown & Co.*[49]

Misfeasance

73–11 Section 333 has already been referred to when considering a misfeasance summons against a director or past director of a company.[50] The section repeats similar provisions in previous Acts,[51] and in his capacity as an officer of the company[52] proceedings may be taken against the auditor under the section. The first case brought under these provisions. *Re London and General Bank (No. 2)*,[53] and also *Re Kingston Cotton Mill Co. (No. 2)*,[54] have been mentioned above in relation to the duties of auditors. In the former, the auditors had failed to report to the members that certain assets in the balance sheet were overvalued and as a result dividends had been paid out of capital; the auditor was found liable and ordered to repay with interest one of the dividends. Both cases had been preceded by earlier summonses in which it had been held in the Court of Appeal that the auditor was an officer of the company, even though in the latter case there was no compulsory audit by statute, only one prescribed by the articles.

Criminal liability

73–12 Criminal liability can arise under sections 17–20 of the Theft Act 1968,[55] which are reproduced in Vol. III, Part L. Section 19 replaces section 84 of the Larceny Act 1861 under which charges could be brought against officers of a company (including auditors), as they were in the case of *R.* v. *Kylsant*.[56] In that case the auditor of the Royal Mail Steam Packet Co. Ltd. was charged with aiding and abetting in the circulation of a written statement of account which he knew to be false in a material particular. In particular, profits for certain years had been stated as being "after adjustment of taxation reserves"; and profits had been increased by the writing

---

47 [1975] 3 W.L.R. 815, H.L.
48 [1974] 2 W.L.R. 295.
49 [1972] 2 Lloyd's Rep. 360.
50 See para. 64–28, *ante*.
51 First introduced in the Companies (Winding-up) Act 1890.
52 See para. 73–05, *ante*.
53 [1895] 2 Ch. 673.
54 [1896] 2 Ch. 279.
55 The Theft Act 1968 does not apply in Scotland.
56 [1932] 1 K.B. 442.

back of these reserves and by inclusion of non-recurring items amounting together to several million pounds. The auditor was acquitted of the charge brought against him, while the chairman of the company, Lord Kylsant, was found guilty on a further charge of publishing a prospectus which he knew to be false in a material particular.

An auditor who has prepared accounts for the purposes of the Companies Acts is not liable to a penalty for preparing false accounts for tax purposes under the Taxes Management Act 1970, s. 99, even if he knows that the company will use his false accounts to make its tax return, so long as he himself takes no part in making the false tax return.[57]

[57] *Lord Advocate* v. *Ruffle* 1979 S.L.T. 212.

Chapter 74

DISCLOSURE OF INFORMATION FOR COLLECTIVE BARGAINING

74–01 In addition to the disclosure requirements of the Companies Acts, modern legislation also requires disclosure of information to trade union representatives for the purposes of collective bargaining. The requirements are set out in the Employment Protection Act 1975.[1]

Employment Protection Act 1975

74–02 The obligation imposed upon employers by the Employment Protection Act 1975 is to disclose information to representatives of independent[2] trade unions for use in collective bargaining. At all stages of such bargaining it is the duty of the employer (subject to the restrictions mentioned in section 18, below) to disclose to such representatives on request all information relating to his undertaking which is in his possession, or that of an associated employer,[3] and is both:

(a) information without which the union representatives would be to a material extent impeded in carrying on with him such collective bargaining, and

(b) information which it would be in accordance with good industrial relations practice that he should disclose to them for the purposes of collective bargaining (s. 17 (1)).

In determining what would be in accordance with good industrial relations practice for this purpose, regard should be had to the provisions of the Code of Practice issued by the Advisory, Conciliation and Arbitration Service under section 6.[4]

Requests for information must be in writing if the employer so requests and the information itself must be in writing or confirmed by writing if the union representatives so request (s. 17 (3) and (5)).

74–03 It is appreciated that there may be circumstances in which an employer should be relieved from the duty to disclose. Disclosure of information is not required in the following circumstances:

(a) where it would be against the interests of national security; or

(b) where the employer could not disclose it without contravening a prohibition imposed by or under an enactment; or

---

[1] In the previous edition of this book reference was also made at this point to disclosure under the provisions of the Industry Act 1975. However, the disclosure provisions of the Industry Act 1975 have now been repealed by s. 19 of the Industry Act 1980.

[2] For the meaning of "independent," see Trade Union and Labour Relations Act 1974, s. 30 (1).

[3] For the meaning of "associated employer," see Trade Union and Labour Relations Act 1974, s. 30 (5).

[4] See Vol. III, para. L-214.

(c) where the information has been communicated to the employer in confidence, or he has otherwise obtained it in consequence of the confidence reposed in him by another person; or
(d) where the information relates specifically to an individual (unless he has consented to its being disclosed); or
(e) where disclosure of the information would cause substantial injury to the employer's undertaking for reasons other than its effect on collective bargaining; or
(f) where the information was obtained by the employer for the purpose of bringing, prosecuting or defending any legal proceedings (s. 18 (1)).[5]

Additional relief is provided for the employer in that he is not required to produce or allow inspection of any document[6] or to make a copy of or extracts from any document. Nor need he compile or assemble any information where the compilation or assembly would involve an amount of work or expenditure out of reasonable proportion to the "value of the information in the conduct of collective bargaining" (s. 18 (2)).

74–04 In the event of a dispute arising as to the performance of this duty to disclose and related matters, the machinery for resolution of the dispute is provided for in sections 19 to 21. This machinery lies exclusively within the control of the Advisory, Conciliation and Arbitration Service and its Central Arbitration Committee. It embraces various stages from attempts at conciliation to binding arbitration awards which take effect as part of the contracts of employment of the employees in question.

[5] It is incumbent upon the Advisory Conciliation and Arbitration Service (ACAS) to have regard to these provisions when formulating a Code of Practice under s. 6.

[6] Except, of course, a document prepared for the purpose of conveying or confirming the information to the union representatives: *ibid*.

C. DIVIDEND AND PROFITS

CHAPTER 75

DIVIDEND

Implied power of company to distribute dividend

75–01 Subject to any restrictions which may be imposed by its memorandum, every company has implied power[1] to apply its profits to the distribution of dividend amongst its members. Exceptionally this power may be restricted in the memorandum or even excluded by it, *e.g.* in the case of a private company which satisfies the requirements of section 25 of the 1981 Act enabling it to dispense with the requirement of "Limited" as the last word in the name of the company.[2] The inherent power of dividing its profits amongst its members, which a company normally possesses, reflects the fact that the company is conceived as a form of organisation of private enterprise and as such is motivated by the profit motive.

The statement that a company normally has implied power to distribute its profits to its shareholders by way of dividend does not imply that the company, while being a going concern, is bound to do so; on the contrary it is entitled, and sometimes even compelled by provisions in its memorandum or articles, to retain part or the whole of its profits. In the absence of such provisions and of provisions in the articles compelling it to divide the profits—and in a public company such provisions would be unusual—it is in the discretion of the directors what part of the profits available for distribution shall be carried to reserve or otherwise set aside or carried forward, and what part shall be made "available for dividend."[3]

Proportion in which dividend is payable

75–02 Normally the articles determine in what proportion dividend is to be made payable as between the members.

It is widely maintained that, if the articles are silent on this point, dividend has to be paid in proportion to the nominal amount of the shares, for members are prima facie entitled to participate in the profits of a company in proportion to their respective interests therein, and the nominal amount of capital held by each is the measure of such interest.[4] The same would be the case if the company had registered its own articles and

---

[1] On implied powers, see para. 9–10, *ante*.
[2] See para. 7–06, *ante*.
[3] *Cf. Re Buenos Ayres Great Southern Ry.* [1947] Ch. 384; *Re Catalinas Warehouses and Mole Co. Ltd.* [1947] 1 All E.R. 51; further, *Long Acre Press Ltd.* v. *Odhams Press Ltd.* [1930] 2 Ch. 196; *Carron Co.* v. *Hunter* 1868 6 M (H.L.) 106.
[4] *Re Bridgwater, etc., Co.* (1889) 14 App. Cas. 525; *Oakbank Oil Co.* v. *Crum* 1882, 10 R (H.L.) 11; (1882) 8 App.Cas. 65.

the latter excluded the application of Table A,[5] and in rare instances the articles themselves may provide that dividend is to be paid "to the members in proportion to their shares," and this means in proportion to the nominal amount of the capital held by them respectively, irrespective of the amount paid up.[6] However, where the articles do not contain such a provision or any other provision compelling this conclusion, the widely held view that dividend is payable in proportion to the nominal amount of the shares cannot be supported. On the contrary, there exists, it is submitted, a strong presumption in favour of the view that dividend shall be paid in proportion to the amount to which the shares are paid up. This view is in accordance with equity, since the shareholder who has not paid up his shares in full has retained the use of his money and can put it to profitable use elsewhere. This view appears to be supported by the decision of the Inner House of the Court of Session in Scotland in *Hoggan* v. *Tharsis Sulphur and Copper Co.*[6a]

Normally, however, the articles state that dividend shall be distributed among the members "according to the amounts paid or credited as paid on the shares," and this is the regulation adopted by Table A (art. 118). In this case dividend is payable on the paid-up, and not on the nominal, capital.

If the company has accepted or credited a payment on a share *in advance of a call*,[7] such an advance is, according to article 118, not regarded as "paid on the shares." The proper yield of the advance is interest (see art. 21) and not dividend, and the two should not be paid on the same portion of the share. The Stock Exchange requires a company, the shares or debentures of which are admitted to dealings, to insert a provision to this effect in its articles.[8]

A provision in a resolution declaring a dividend that enemy shareholders are to be paid out of enemy assets only is void.[9]

Dividend on preference or other special shares

75–03 In distributing a dividend the rights of preference shares and of other special shares have to be observed. Any infringement or attempted infringement of their respective rights will give to the members who are prejudiced the right to apply for an injunction or other relief, and if dividends are paid otherwise than in accordance with the rights of the respective classes of shares, any class which suffers thereby will have a right of action against the company, and the directors who wrongly paid the dividends will be liable to replace the sum so expended.[10]

---

[5] In this case art. 118 cannot be invoked; see s. 8 (2).
[6] *Oakbank Oil Co.* v. *Crum* (1882) 8 App.Cas. 65.
[6a] 1882, 9 R. 1191.
[7] See para. 35–16, *ante*.
[8] Stock Exchange Rules, App. 34, Sched. VII, Pt. A, C, 1, para. 134.
[9] *Aramayo Francke Mines* v. *Public Trustee* [1922] 2 A.C. 406.
[10] See para. 63–09, *ante*.

Payment of dividend out of profits

75–04 It is a cardinal principle of company law that no dividend must be paid otherwise than out of profits legally available for distribution to the shareholders.[11] The definition of such distributable profits is a difficult question and is considered in the next chapter.[12]

Declaration of dividend

Who declares dividend. Final and interim dividends

75–05 The Acts themselves do not provide who shall declare dividend and, in particular, do not require the dividend to be declared by the general meeting. It is possible to lay down in the articles that dividend shall be declared by the directors, and if the company adopts its own articles, excluding the application of Table A, and these articles do not contain provisions relating to the declaration of dividend or clearly exclude the inference that dividend is to be declared in the usual manner, the directors, under their general powers,[13] will be entitled to declare dividend without sanction of the general meeting.

This, however, is not the usual practice. Articles commonly contain provisions on the declaration of dividend, and it is the usual practice to leave it to the general meeting to sanction or declare the final dividend.

In modern practice, a distinction is drawn between the final dividend and interim dividend, *i.e.* dividend paid between two annual meetings.[14] The articles usually provide that

(1) the [final] dividend may be declared by the company in general meeting but no dividend shall exceed the amount recommended by the directors (see art. 114); and

(2) interim dividends may be paid by the directors from time to time (see art. 115).

The declaration of dividend in the manner stated under (1) above is part of the ordinary business of the annual general meeting (art. 52). A provision of the nature of that stated under (1) prevents the general meeting from declaring a higher dividend than that recommended by the directors, but the general meeting, if desirous of declaring a higher dividend, can always remove the directors by virtue of section 184 of the 1948 Act or alter its articles by deleting the provision that its power to declare dividend shall be limited by the recommendation of the directors. The latter course would be very unusual and would not only lead to the resignation of the directors but might be objected to by some shareholders.

The older practice was for the articles to provide that the directors, with

---

[11] See *e.g.* art. 116, as amended by C.A. 1980, Sched. 3, para. 36 (7). *Hawker Siddeley Group Ltd.* v. *Hawker Siddeley Aviation Ltd.* (1981) 125 S.J. 441.
[12] See paras. 76–01, *et seq., post.*
[13] See para. 64–07, *ante.*
[14] *Re Jowitt* [1922] 2 Ch. 442.

the sanction of a general meeting, might declare a dividend. The difference between the modern and the older practice is, thus, that under the former the decisive act of declaration of dividend is done by the general meeting, whereas under the latter it was done by the directors.

75–06 Before declaring an interim dividend, the directors must satisfy themselves that the financial position of the company warrants the payment of such dividend out of profits available for distribution,[15] but, as Lord Alverstone C.J. observed,[16]

> "The declaration of interim dividend depends much more upon estimates and opinions than the declaration of a final dividend, which is made upon the information contained in a formal balance sheet."

The payment of interim dividend is not conditional upon the subsequent declaration of such a dividend by a general meeting. But if the articles empower the directors to pay interim dividends, if justified, a declaration by the directors of an intended dividend to be paid at some future date may be rescinded by a resolution of the directors before that date arrives.[17] This is so even if the cash to cover the proposed dividend has been placed into a separate account.[17] Further, as the learned editors of Palmer's *Precedents*, Vol. I (17th ed.), rightly observe,[18] an article authorising payment of "an interim dividend on account of the next final dividend," or similar wording, might lead to complications: if new shares are issued between the interim dividend and the final dividend, the shareholders of the new dividend may claim to be entitled—retrospectively—to the interim dividend, although it is thought that such a claim would normally be without foundation since they were not shareholders when the interim dividend became payable.

The company has power prima facie to set aside a reserve fund before declaring a dividend,[19] but this power may be negatived by the memorandum or articles.[20]

A dividend forecast by directors in a take-over situation will not generally be treated as a profit forecast for the purposes of the City Code on Take-overs and Mergers.[21]

Stock Exchange requirements

75–07 The Stock Exchange[22] requires a company, the shares or debentures of which are admitted to quotation or dealings, to undertake to notify the Quotations Department of the Stock Exchange of the date of the board

---

[15] See para. 76–01, *post*.
[16] In *Lucas* v. *Fitzgerald* (1903) 20 T.L.R. 16, 18.
[17] *Lagunas Nitrate Co.* v. *Schroeder* (1901) 85 L.T. 22.
[18] On p. 601.
[19] *Re Buenos Ayres Great Southern Ry.* [1947] Ch. 384.
[20] *R. Paterson & Sons Ltd.* v. *Paterson* 1917 S.C. (H.L.) 13; 1916, 2 S.L.T. 227; [1916] W.N. 352; *Evling* v. *Israel and Oppenheimer Ltd.* [1918] 1 Ch. 101.
[21] See para. 82–12, *post*. See also *In re Overmark Smith Warden Ltd., The Times*, March 22, 1982.
[22] Stock Exchange Rules, App. 34, Sched. VIII, Pt. A (General Undertaking), 1 and 2 (*a*), paras. 175 and 176.

meeting at which the declaration or recommendation of a dividend will be considered, and further to notify the Department "by letter (or telex, telegram or telephone[23]) immediately after the relevant board meeting has been held . . . of all dividends and/or cash bonuses recommended or declared or the decision to pass[24] any dividend or interest payment."

Shareholder's claim for declared dividend

75–08 Where a dividend is declared and becomes payable, it is a debt and each shareholder is entitled to sue the company for his proportion.[25] Until the dividend is declared and payable, the shareholder has no right to sue.[26]

If there are arrears of declared dividend in the winding up, the sums due are, by virtue of section 212 (1) (*g*) of the 1948 Act, not deemed to be a debt of the company; this means that a member who competes with a creditor is deferred to the latter until the latter is satisfied. In the final adjustment between the contributories, the sum due on account of a declared dividend may be taken into account (s. 212 (1) (*g*)). These rules likewise apply to arrears due to past members, whether these members can still be placed on the B list of contributories or not.[27]

Limitation of time for suing company

75–09 The time limit to recover dividends in England is six years, as for actions founded on a simple contract debt (Limitation Act 1980, s. 5). This was so decided with reference to an earlier Limitation Act by Slade J. in *Re Compania de Electricidad de la Provincia de Buenos Aires Ltd.*[28] departing from the earlier decision in *Re Artizans' Land and Mortgage Company*[29] that the right was a specialty debt having a time limit of 12 years (Limitation Act 1980, s. 8 (1)). The earlier view was based on the reasoning that the claim arose out of the articles and the share certificate, with the former deemed to be a contract under seal between the company and its members by virtue of section 20, and the latter sealed by the company. Slade J. held that the share certificate being merely evidence of title was not a document under seal creating the obligation to pay but merely acknowledging or evidencing it, and this was insufficient to render the right a specialty debt. Section 20, although deeming the contractual effect of the articles to be under seal, does not state that it is so executed by the company but only that it is deemed to have been sealed by each member. Thus the obligation was not created by the debtor under seal and it was not a specialty debt.

The time limit runs from the declaration of the dividend or the declared date of its payment, whichever is later, unless the shares are in bearer

---

[23] The Department should be consulted respecting the method of transmitting advices to be sent by any of these means.
[24] This means "to omit."
[25] *Re Severn, etc., Ry.* [1896] 1 Ch. 559.
[26] *Bond* v. *Barrow Haematite Steel Co.* [1902] 1 Ch. 353.
[27] *Re Consolidated Goldfields of New Zealand Ltd.* [1953] Ch. 689.
[28] [1978] 3 All E.R. 668.
[29] [1904] 1 Ch. 796.

form. In such a case if the contract by which the company undertakes to pay dividends requires the share warrant to be presented before payment can be made no cause of action arises until such presentation.[30]

A balance sheet showing an entry acknowledging unclaimed arrears of declared dividend may amount to an acknowledgment of the debt by the company which will revive the right of action, after the limitation period has expired (Limitation Act 1980, s. 29 (5)).[31] But an acknowledgment has to be "made to the person or to the agent of the person whose title or claim is being acknowledged" (Limitation Act 1980, s. 30 (2) (*b*)) and therefore only those persons who can prove receipt of the relevant accounts can take advantage of this provision. A person entitled to receive a copy or to whom one is sent but not received will not have had his debt acknowledged.[32] Parol evidence is allowed to show that part of the item is owed to the claimant. In these circumstances the limitation period will run from the date of the last acknowledgment (Limitation Act 1980, s. 29 (5)).

In Scotland unclaimed dividends are subject to the negative prescription of five years under the Prescription and Limitation (Scotland) Act, 1973, s. 6.

Forfeiture of unclaimed dividends

75–10 Sometimes the articles of association (see art. 76 of Table A of the 1862 Act) fix a shorter period, and provide for forfeiture if not claimed within that period; but the Stock Exchange Rules object to an article authorising forfeiture before the claim becomes barred by law,[33] and no forfeiture clause is contained in Table A of the Act of 1948. Relief against forfeiture would probably be given in most cases. It has been held in an Irish case in which no relief appears to have been claimed that such a clause will be strictly construed.[34]

Declared but unpaid dividend passing on transfer

75–11 The person entitled to the dividend is prima facie the person on the register at the time of declaration.

A transfer of shares, after a dividend has been declared, does not, as against the company, carry the dividend, even where the transferee has expressly bought *cum div.*; but, as between a buyer and seller of shares, the buyer is entitled to all dividends declared after the date of the contract for sale, unless otherwise arranged.[35]

---

[30] *Re Compania de Electricidad de la Provincia de Buenos Aires Ltd.*, [1980] Ch. 146.

[31] *Re Gee & Co. Ltd.* [1975] Ch. 52; see para. 43–26, *ante*, and cases there cited. The Limitation Act 1980 does not apply in Scotland.

[32] *Re Compania de Electricidad de la Provincia de Buenos Aires Ltd., supra.*

[33] Stock Exchange Rules, App. 34, Sched. VII, Pt. A, C, 2, para. 135.

[34] *Ward* v. *Dublin North City Milling Co.* [1919] 1 Ir.R. 5.

[35] *Black* v. *Homersham* (1878) 4 Ex.D. 24; *Re Wimbush* [1940] Ch. 92 (a sale by trustees under the provisions of a will to a person to whom they were bound to offer them); and see *Re Kidner* [1929] 2 Ch. 121. On the Stock Exchange Rules applicable to this case, see para. 51–12, *ante*.

Apportionment of dividends

75–12 Wherever there is a transmission of interest in shares during a period in respect of which dividends are subsequently paid, such dividends are apportionable,[36] unless apportionment is excluded by the terms of the settlement or will.[37] This will apply, for instance, in the case of the death of a holder, or where a tenant for life dies and remaindermen thereupon become entitled. Cumulative dividends are dividends for the year in which they are declared, though they may include recoupment of arrears.[38] Where, under a scheme, funded certificates were issued in respect of arrears of preference dividend, the certificates were issued in respect of arrears of preference dividend, the certificates were held to be income of the year in which they were issued[39]; but where the amount of the arrears differed owing to the different dates of issue of the shares, it was held that dividends ought to be declared in proportion to the amount of arrears outstanding.[40] If no dividend is declared by the company in respect of the period of the life of the tenant for life, nothing will be payable to him, even though the company has earned profits during that period.[41] On the other hand, a dividend declared before the death of a stockholder and paid after his death has been, in special circumstances, treated as his capital in existence at the date of his death.[42]

Dividend warrants

75–13 Payment of dividend is normally done in the following manner: the company sends the registered members dividend warrants which usually consist of two parts, *viz.* an advice informing the members of the particulars of the payment, and the warrant proper which is in the form of a cheque and directs the company's bank to pay the sum due to the member.

In the case of a dividend or of interest which is qualifying distribution, the company must provide a warrant to show:

(a) the amount of the dividend or interest paid, and

(b) the amount of the tax credit to which the recipient may be entitled.

With regard to all qualifying distributions,[43] in whatever form, the recipient is entitled to ask the company to provide a statement in writing showing the amount of the payment and the amount of the tax credit to which the recipient might claim entitlement.[44]

This information is usually contained in the advice attached to the warrant, which should be retained by the shareholder and produced by him

---

[36] See ss. 2 and 5 of the Apportionment Act 1870; *Re Oppenheimer* [1907] 1 Ch. 399; *Re Muirhead* [1916] 2 Ch. 181.

[37] *Re Edwards* [1918] 1 Ch. 142.

[38] *Re Wakley* [1920] 2 Ch. 205; *Re Marjoribanks* [1923] 2 Ch. 307.

[39] *Re Sandbach* [1933] Ch. 505.

[40] *First Garden City* v. *Bonham-Carter* [1928] Ch. 53.

[41] *Re Armitage* [1893] 3 Ch. 337; *Re Sale* [1913] 2 Ch. 697.

[42] *Re Winder* [1951] Ch. 916.

[43] See para. 90–12 for definition of "qualifying distribution."

[44] Finance Act 1972, Sched. 24.

to the Inland Revenue authorities in support of any claim for recovery of the tax credit.

Sending a dividend warrant by post will discharge the company, if payment by post is authorised by the articles (see art. 121).[45]

The following is an illustration of a modern dividend warrant:

XYZ COMPANY LIMITED

TAX VOUCHER

75–14 ORDINARY SHARES OF £1 EACH

January 2nd 1980

Account No.

Number of Shares	Tax Credit		Dividend Payable	
1,000	£ 30	p —	£ 70	p —

Dividend 10p.
per share

Year Ending November 30th 1979
To Shareholders registered on September 1st 1979

I certify that Advance Corporation Tax of an amount equal to that shown above as tax credit will be accounted for to the Collector of Taxes. This voucher should be retained as it will be accepted by the Inland Revenue as evidence of tax credit in respect of which you may be entitled to claim payment or relief.

John Doe, Secretary.

Please notify the Secretary of the Company of a change of address. The notification should be signed by the shareholder. An application for a duplicate of this voucher must be accompanied by a fee of 25p.

[45] *Thairlwall* v. *Great Northern Ry.* [1910] 2 K.B. 509.

....(*perforated*)..

XYZ COMPANY LIMITED

January 2nd 1980

ABC Bank Limited

London

Pay to the order of .... | Not negotiable & Co. | ....

the sum of Seventy pounds.

£70.00

For the XYZ Company
Richard Roe,
Chairman of Directors.

Dividend mandates

75–15 It is convenient both for shareholders and for the company that dividends should be paid directly to the shareholders' banks. Shareholders often request the company to make payment directly to their bank, but these requests are sometimes worded in a manner casting duties upon the company which it is unwilling or unable to accept, *e.g.* that the sum due should be credited to a particular account of the shareholder. Public companies having a great number of shareholders normally refuse, therefore, to accept individual requests, but encourage shareholders to sign dividend mandates on forms issued by the company whereby the company is instructed to pay the dividend due to the shareholder to a bank nominated by him.

The practical advantages which accrue to the company from this procedure are that it reduces the amount of unclaimed dividend which has to be carried forward from year to year and one warrant can be used for the payment of dividends due to several shareholders having accounts with the same bank; but the company is not relieved from its duty of sending the bank individual advice notes of dividend warrants relating to the several shareholders in question, which the shareholders have to produce as vouchers to the Inland Revenue authorities in claiming tax credits.

Further observations on the mandate system and a form of dividend mandate will be found in the Practice Notes appended to this chapter.[46]

[46] See para. 75–24, *post*.

Dividends prima facie payable in cash

75–16 In the absence of express authority in the articles, the company must pay dividends in cash and may not, *e.g.* pay them by the distribution of its own shares or shares in another company, or debentures.[47] But articles sometimes contain a clause authorising the company to pay dividends *in specie*, *i.e.* by the distribution of specific assets[48] or by giving the shareholders the choice of electing to take shares in the company in lieu of cash payment; in fact, as will be explained below, in the present time of progressive inflation the latter arrangement has become increasingly popular. Further, the articles normally authorise the capitalisation of profits by applying profits available for dividend in total or partial payment of shares to be allotted to the members (see arts. 128, 128A and 129). This topic will be considered in detail later.[49]

Normally the question in which currency a dividend is payable does not cause difficulty because it is obvious that it is intended to be the currency in which the dividend is declared and payable. Occasionally, however, this question may give rise to difficult problems, as was the case, *e.g.* in the so-called *Australian Pound* cases which arose from the fact that the currencies of the United Kingdom and Australia which were originally the same became eventually two distinct currencies. It may then become necessary to distinguish between the *money of account* by which the substance of the obligation is measured and the *money of payment* by which the obligation is discharged, and it may be necessary to ascertain the proper law of the obligation and the extent to which the proper law governs those two aspects of the undertaking to pay. An examination of these questions is outside the ambit of our subject; it will be found in works on the conflict of laws.[50]

Shares in lieu of cash dividends (scrip dividends)

75–17 In the present period of progressive inflation, an increasing number of listed companies have made arrangements enabling their ordinary shareholders to elect to receive their dividends in the form of additional ordinary shares rather than in cash. The share equivalent is sometimes referred to as scrip dividend or stock dividend and consists of shares fully paid up out of the company's profits. Here the following points have to be borne in mind:

---

[47] *Hoole* v. *Great Western Ry.* (1867) 3 Ch.App. 262; *Wood* v. *Odessa, etc., Co.* (1889) 42 Ch.D. 636.

[48] See *Precedents*, Pt. I (17th ed.), p. 612; and see *Re Sechiari, Argenti* v. *Sechiari* [1950] 1 All E.R. 417; *Re Kleinwort's Settlements* [1951] 2 All E.R. 328; *Re MacLaren's Settlement* [1951] 2 All E.R. 414.

[49] See para. 76–23, *post*.

[50] See Clive M. Schmitthoff, *The English Conflict of Laws* (3rd ed., 1954), where the *Australian Pound* cases are considered on p. 126; apart from the cases referred to there, see *The River Loddon* [1955] 1 Lloyd's Rep. 503, 506 and *National Mutual Life Assurance of Australasia Ltd.* v. *Att.-Gen. of New Zealand* [1956] A.C. 369.

1. The articles must give the directors authority to determine that shareholders shall be entitled to receive in lieu of any dividend (or part thereof), declared or proposed to be declared, an allotment of additional ordinary shares credited as fully paid. This authority should extend to any interim and final dividend.
2. In order to maintain the status of the company's ordinary shares as a trustee investment under the Trustee Investments Act 1961,[51] the directors must provide that any share equivalent made available in any calendar year in which there has not previously been a cash dividend paid to all shareholders shall not extend to the whole of that dividend, but a minimal amount must be paid in cash.
3. As from April 6, 1975, the share equivalent in lieu of cash dividend does not give the shareholders a tax benefit, since it is chargeable, as from that date, to higher rate income tax and to investment income surcharge on the amount or value of the dividend grossed up at the basic rate of tax. (Finance (No. 2) Act 1975, s. 34 and Sched. 8.)
4. The company would, to the extent that ordinary shareholders elected to take the share equivalent, benefit in two ways. First, the company's cash position would be improved; and, secondly, as the result of the issue of shares in lieu of dividends, the company would have an enlarged capital base to support a continuing growth.

Stock Exchange requirements

75–18 If a company listed at the Stock Exchange intends to give its shareholders the right to elect a scrip dividend the value of the shares to be issued must be based on the average of the middle market prices on the five days commencing with the day on which the shares are quoted ex-dividend and such value will be equated to the amount of dividend payable in order to arrive at the ratio of new shares to existing holdings.

The Stock Exchange has issued the following *pro-forma* timetable, which listed companies are expected to observe.

1. Announce dividend and record date	As close as possible to, but not later than, two business days prior to first day of an Account
2. Shares go ex-dividend and ex-capital	First day of Account
3. Base period for calculation of scrip dividend	Five days commencing with the ex-dividend date
4. Record date	Not less than eleven days following the first day of Account
5. Post circular and forms of election to shareholders registered at record date	Within two weeks following record date
6. Election date Date of meeting	Three weeks after despatch of election forms

[51] This Act excludes from the wider-range investments shares of companies which have not in each of the five years immediately preceding the calendar year of the investment paid a dividend on all its shares; see Trustee Investments Act 1961, Sched. 1, Pt. IV, para. 3 (*b*).

7. Payment date and issue of scrip shares	Within two weeks following election date
8. Dealings start in scrip shares	Day following post

The following is an example of calculating the share equivalent. The basis of calculating the number of shares to be allotted in lieu of cash dividend is summarised in the formula $\frac{A \times B}{C}$ where:

A equals the number of ordinary shares in respect of which an election is made;
B equals the dividend, in pence per ordinary share (ignoring the associated tax credit), in respect of which an election can be made; and
C equals the average of the middle-market quotations in pence as shown by the Stock Exchange Daily Official List of an ordinary share for the first five business days on which the ordinary shares are quoted *ex* the relevant dividend.

Specimen article

75–19 The following is an example of an article authorising the directors to issue a share equivalent on election by the shareholders:

"Subject to approval by the company at any annual general meeting the directors may, in respect of any dividend declared or proposed to be declared at that annual general meeting or at any time prior to the next following annual general meeting (and provided that an adequate number of unissued ordinary shares are available for the purpose), determine and announce, prior to or contemporaneously with their announcement of the dividend in question and any related information as to the company's profits for such financial period or part thereof, that ordinary shareholders will be entitled to elect to receive in lieu of such dividend (or part thereof) an allotment of additional ordinary shares credited as fully paid. In any such case the following provisions shall apply:–

(a) The basis of allotment shall be determined by the directors so that, as nearly as may be considered convenient, the value (calculated by reference to the average quotation) of the additional ordinary shares (including any fractional entitlement) to be allotted in lieu of any amount of dividend shall equal such amount. For such purpose the 'average quotation' of an ordinary share shall be the average of the means of quotations on the Stock Exchange, as shown in the Daily Official List, on each of the first five business days on which the ordinary shares are quoted *ex* the relevant dividend.

(b) The directors shall give notice in writing to the ordinary shareholders of the right of election accorded to them and shall send with or following such notice forms of election and specify the procedure to be followed and the place at which the latest date and time by which duly completed forms of election must be lodged in order to be effective.

(c) The dividend (or that part of the dividend in respect of which a right of election has been accorded) shall not be payable on ordinary shares in respect whereof the share election has been duly exercised ('the elected ordinary shares'), and in lieu thereof additional shares shall be allotted to the holders of the elected ordinary shares on the basis of allotment determined as aforesaid and for such purpose the directors shall capitalise, out of such of the sums standing to the credit of reserves (including any share premium account of capital redemption reserve fund) or profit and loss account as the directors may determine a sum equal to the aggregate nominal amount of additional ordinary shares to be allotted on such basis and apply the same in paying up in full the appropriate number of unissued ordinary shares for allotment and distribution to and amongst the holders of the elected ordinary shares on such basis.

(d) The additional ordinary shares so allotted shall rank *pari passu* in all respects with the fully-paid ordinary shares then in issue save only as regards participation in the relevant dividend (or share election in lieu).

(e) The directors may do all acts and things considered necessary or expedient to give effect to any such capitalisation, with full power to the directors to make such provisions as they think fit for the case of shares becoming distributable in fractions (including provisions whereby, in whole or in part, fractional entitlements are disregarded or rounded up or the benefit of fractional entitlements accrues to the company rather than to the members concerned). The directors may authorise any person to enter on behalf of all the members interested into an agreement with the company providing for such capitalisation and matters incidental thereto and any agreement made under such authority shall be effective and binding on all concerned.

(f) The directors may on any occasion determine that rights of election shall not be made available to any ordinary shareholders with registered addresses in any territory where in the absence of a registration statement or other special formalities the circulation of an offer of rights of election would or might be unlawful, and in such event the provisions aforesaid shall be read and construed subject to such determination."

Exchange control regulations

75–20 The exchange control regulations relating to the payment of dividend to shareholders not resident in the United Kingdom were abolished with effect from October 24, 1980 for all countries except Rhodesia, and for all countries with effect from December 13, 1980.[52]

Guaranteed dividend

75–21 As arrangement between a vendor and the company to guarantee certain dividends for a specified period may be valid if it involves merely the personal liability of the vendor.[53]

If the guarantor makes payments under his guarantee, he cannot, even under the express terms of his guarantee, claim to be repaid by the company, except out of profits which ultimately become available for the shareholders.[54]

Payment of interest on shares in construction companies

75–22 Exceptionally certain construction companies were empowered by section 65 to pay interest for a short time out of capital on the paid-up shares. Section 65 was repealed by the 1980 Act.[55]

Counter-inflation measures

75–23 From 1972 until 1979 dividend payments were subject to restrictions under various counter-inflation Acts and orders. There are no current restrictions of this nature.[56]

---

52 Exchange Control (General Exemption) Order 1979 (S.I. 1979 No. 1660).
53 *Ex p. Jegon* (1879) 12 Ch.D. 503; but see *Re Menell et Cie* [1915] 1 Ch. 759.
54 *Re Walters' Deed of Guarantee* [1933] Ch. 321.
55 1980 Act, Sched. 4, para. 1. For the provisions of s. 65 see the 22nd edition of this work, para. 71–22.
56 For the 1972–79 provisions see the 22nd edition, para. 71–23 and supplement.

PRACTICE NOTES

The mandate system of dividend payments[57]

75–24 Apart from other considerations, many companies encourage shareholders to complete dividend mandates in order to facilitate and minimise the work involved on the payment of a dividend. The majority of mandates will be given in favour of one of the "big four" or Scottish banks, and companies are enabled to send one cheque or warrant to the head office of each of the banks concerned in respect of the total dividends due to shareholders whose mandates are in favour of those banks. The cheque is accompanied by a list of persons to be credited at individual branches and the relevant tax certificates. The payment of the dividend to individual shareholders thus becomes a matter of book-keeping entries between the head office of the banks concerned and their respective branches. The tax certificates are made out in respect of each shareholder, showing the amount of the dividend payable and the amount of tax credit relating thereto. A standard form of mandate has been prepared by the Talisman Forms Committee and approved by the Institute of Chartered Secretaries and Administrators.

[57] On dividend mandates generally, see para. 75–15, *ante*.

CHAPTER 76

PROFITS AVAILABLE FOR DISTRIBUTION

Profits, profits available for distribution and profits available for dividend

76–01 These terms have a different meaning and should not be confused. "Profits" is essentially a business term, denoting an amount of gain made during a certain period, as Fletcher Moulton L.J. observed in a classical passage in *Re Spanish Prospecting Co. Ltd.*[1]:

> " 'Profits' implies a comparison between the state of a business at two specific dates usually separated by an interval of a year. The fundamental meaning is the amount of gain made by the business during the year. This can only be ascertained by a comparison of the assets of the business at the two dates. . . . If the total assets of the business at the two dates be compared, the increase which they show at the later date as compared with the earlier date (due allowance of course being made for any capital introduced into or taken out of the business in the meanwhile) represents in strictness the profits of the business during the period in question."

"Profits available for distribution" means the profits which the law allows a company to distribute to the shareholders by way of dividend. Alternative terms are "divisible profits"[2] and "profits in the legal sense."

"Profits available for dividend" has been held to mean the profits which the directors consider should be distributed after making provision for past losses, for reserves or for other purposes.[3]

The principle of payment of dividends out of profits

76–02 It is a cardinal principle of company law that a company must not reduce its capital except by a reduction properly authorised under section 66.[4] The courts have always attempted therefore to limit the payment of dividends to payment out of profits. Their difficulty has been to distinguish between capital and income profits in this context and there has been a divergence between profits in the legal sense and profits as recognised by accountants and businessmen.[5] Until 1980 the legislation avoided any attempts at definition but a new code of profits in the legal sense is contained in sections 39 to 45 of the 1980 Act, as amended by the 1981 Act, together with sections 60, 84 and 85 of the 1981 Act. In general the new rules make

---

[1] [1911] 1 Ch. 92, 98.

[2] Until the 1980 Act this term was used. The new terminology comes from the wording of the 1980 Act.

[3] *Long Acres Press Ltd.* v. *Odhams Press* [1930] 2 Ch. 196; *Re Buenos Ayres Great Southern Ry.* [1947] Ch. 384. See also *Hawker Siddeley Group Ltd.* v. *Hawker Siddeley Aviation Ltd.* (1981) 125 S.J. 441.

[4] See Chap. 32, *ante*.

[5] See the 22nd edition of this work, Chap. 72.

no attempt to distinguish between capital and income profits but concentrate on the difference between realised and unrealised net profits as the guiding line.

Dividend may be paid out of divisible profits though they might not be profits in the business sense

76–03 It is evident from the preceding observations that it is legally permissible for the company to distribute dividend out of assets which do not represent profits made as the result of its trading or business. The connotation of profits in the legal sense is much wider than that of profits in the business sense: the former term includes, *e.g.* reserves accumulated from past profits, from realised net capital profits, and indeed, before the requirement of a share premium account by the 1947–48 legislation,[6] from premiums obtained on the issue of new shares, whereas none of these items is regarded—and rightly so—by the businessman or accountant as trading profits.

In practice, however, companies, as a general rule, ascertain their profits on sound business principles, and do not distribute in dividends the whole of the profits which they may be legally entitled to treat as such, without making at least reasonable provisions for meeting losses on capital. Indeed, unless this is done, the company's auditors may find themselves unable to satisfy themselves in accordance with section 14 of the 1967 Act that the balance sheet gives a true and fair view of the company's affairs or that the profit and loss account gives a true and fair view of the profit or loss.

Generally, where capital has been lost or is unrepresented by available assets, companies take steps to reduce their capital, and the court does not normally refuse to confirm such a reduction.[7]

Profits available for distribution

76–04 Companies are forbidden to make any distribution except out of profits legally available for the purpose (1980 Act, s. 39 (1)).[8] Distributions for these purposes include every type of distribution to shareholders whether in cash or in kind[9] except for the issue of bonus shares,[10] the redemption of redeemable shares or purchase by a company of its own shares in accordance with Part III of the 1981 Act,[11] an authorised reduction of capital

---

[6] The provisions of what is now s. 56 (Chap. 24, *ante*) were introduced into company law by the Companies Act 1947, s. 72. For the position before the introduction of this provision, see *Re Hoare & Co. Ltd.* [1904] 2 Ch. 208, 212, 213; *Drown* v. *Gaumont British Picture Corporation* [1937] Ch. 402.

[7] See the observation of Vaisey J. in *Re Chinese Engineering and Mining Co.* (1956) *The Times*, July 25; [1956] C.L.Y. 1126.

[8] For the consequences of a breach of this rule see para. 76–24, *post*.

[9] 1980 Act, s. 45 (2); *Cf.* the definition for corporation tax purpose in I.C.T.A. 1970, s. 233.

[10] See para. 76–23, *post*.

[11] See paras. 33–13 and 37–08, *ante*.

under section 66,[12] and distribution of assets on a winding up.[13] It is interesting to note that an issue of bonus shares followed by a reduction of capital paying off those shares or vice versa, which is a distribution for corporation tax purposes,[14] does not appear to be a distribution for the purposes of the 1980 Act, unless it is included in the general wording.

The profits available for distribution are defined for all companies by section 39 of the 1980 Act but public companies are subject to an additional restriction in section 40. There are special rules for investment and certain insurance companies. All calculations for such profits must be taken from *the relevant accounts*.[15] These rules are, however, a minimum criteria and stricter provisions may be applied in the company's memorandum or articles.[16]

Basic rule—accumulated realised profits less accumulated realised losses

76–05 To ascertain the profits available for distribution the 1980 Act requires an arithmetical calculation. First, the company's accumulated realised profits must be calculated, then its accumulated realised losses, and the difference, assuming a positive answer, is the fund available for distribution (1980 Act, s. 39 (2)). There is no attempt to distinguish income from capital profits or losses.

Accumulated realised profits

76–06 Prior to the 1980 Act the courts had held that a realised profit from the disposal of a fixed asset at more than book value could be distributed as dividend,[17] provided that the assets were overall in credit above their book value.[18] Since balance sheet values, pending the introduction of current cost accounting, are largely historical such realised gains were not difficult to find. More surprisingly the court had also decided that an unrealised gain arising out of a bona fide revaluation of capital assets made by competent valuers could be distributed provided that the assets involved were not liable to short-term fluctuations.[19] Increases in the value of current assets, being brought into the profit and loss account, were naturally absorbed into the profit figure.[20]

Unrealised profits are no longer available for distribution, nor may they be used to write off any unpaid amount on any of its issued shares.[21] Realised profits are available insofar as they have not previously been utilised by a distribution or capitalised, *i.e.* by the issue of bonus shares[22]

---

[12] See para. 32–01, *ante*.
[13] See para. 90–12, *post*.
[14] I.C.T.A. 1970, ss. 233–235.
[15] See para. 76–17, *post*.
[16] 1980 Act, s. 45 (5).
[17] *Lubbock* v. *The British Bank of South Africa* [1892] 2 Ch. 198.
[18] *Foster* v. *The New Trinidad Lake Asphalte Co. Ltd.* [1901] 1 Ch. 208, 212.
[19] *Dimbula Valley (Ceylon) Tea Co. Ltd.* v. *Laurie* [1961] Ch. 353. For details of these cases see the 22nd edition of this work, paras. 72–11–72–13.
[20] This distinction is still important with regard to other aspects of the rule. See para. 76–10, *post*.
[21] 1980 Act, s. 39 (3).
[22] See para. 76–23, *post*.

or a transfer to the capital redemption reserve,[23] subject to the deduction of realised losses (1980 Act, s. 39 (2)). It should be noted that the principle is a cumulative one, it is not an annual calculation in the sense of realised profits of a year less realised losses of that year, reserves (other than capital reserves) may be built into the accounts for this purpose. Undistributed profits made before the 1980 Act was implemented are therefore to be taken into account in making the calculation (1980 Act, s. 45(4)).

76–07 What then is a realised profit? It is nowhere defined in the Act but an appropriate judicial statement is that of Byrne J. in *Foster* v. *The New Trinidad Lake Asphalte Co. Ltd.*:

> "It is clear, I think, that an appreciation in total value of capital assets, if duly realised by sale or getting in of some portion of such assets, may in a proper case be treated as available for purposes of dividend."

The 1980 Act does, however, deal with four specific problem areas as to the ascertaining of realised profits.

(1) REVALUATION OF A FIXED ASSET FOLLOWED BY A DEPRECIATION ALLOWANCE. Where a fixed asset[24] is revalued upwards so that an unrealised profit has been made and this is followed by the writing off or retention of a sum for depreciation of that asset over a period of time then there will be a deemed realised profit of the amount by which that sum is less than it would have been but for the revaluation (1980 Act, s. 39 (5)).

(2) NO RECORD OF ORIGINAL COST OF AN ASSET. Because of the cumulative nature of the realised profits rule assets acquired before the 1980 Act came into force will be involved in a post-Act calculation. Further, even with recently acquired assets, there may be no record of the original cost of an asset which has been realised. In such a case, or where such a record can only be obtained with unreasonable expense or delay, the cost of the asset to determine whether a profit or loss has been made on the realisation is to be the value ascribed to it in the earliest available record of its value made on or after its acquisition by the company (1980 Act, s. 39 (6)).

(3) PRE-ACT PROFITS. Profits accumulated before the Act are subject to the Act if not distributed by the date of its implementation.[25] Because there was no legal distinction between realised and unrealised profits prior to the implementation of the 1980 Act it may be difficult for the directors *ex post facto* to determine whether a particular undistributed pre-Act profit was realised or unrealised. In such circumstances if the directors after making reasonable inquiries are unable to determine whether a pre-Act

[23] See para. 34–12D, *ante*.
[24] There is no statutory definition, s. 39 (8) of the 1980 Act being repealed by Sched. 4 to the 1981 Act. See para. 76–10, *post*.
[25] 1980 Act, s. 45 (4).

profit is realised or unrealised they may treat the profit as realised (1980 Act, s. 39 (7)).

(4) DISTRIBUTIONS IN KIND. Where a company makes a distribution of, or including, a non-cash asset, part of which represents an element of unrealised profits, the amount of that profit is to be treated as though it were a realised profit for the purposes of section 39 (1980 Act, s. 43A, introduced by 1981 Act, s. 85). This is intended to facilitate the operation of demergers which involve the distribution of real property or shares out of a group.[25a]

Accumulated realised losses

76–08 The debit side of the calculation is the company's accumulated realised losses. Prior to the 1980 Act there was judicial authority for the proposition that a company had no obligation either to take into account debit balances on the profit and loss accounts of previous years before declaring a dividend[26] or to reduce the capital figure by a reduction under section 66 to write off the lost assets. This somewhat myopic view of the nature of funds available for dividend has accordingly been reversed by section 39 (2) of the 1980 Act. Accumulated realised losses must be deducted.

What is a realised loss? It is defined by section 39 (4) of the 1980 Act as any amount written off or retained either as a depreciation, renewal or diminution allowance or by way of providing for any known liability, including disputed or contingent liabilities, which cannot be determined with substantial accuracy.[27] All such provisions are to be regarded as realised losses except for one in respect of any diminution of a fixed asset[28] appearing on a revaluation of all the fixed assets or all such assets except goodwill of the company. Any consideration by the directors of any fixed asset's value will be a sufficient revaluation of that asset for this purpose, but only if, in the absence of an actual revaluation, the directors are satisfied that the aggregate amount of the assets deemed to have been revalued is not less than the aggregate book value of those assets.[28a] A note must also be included in the relevant accounts to that effect.[28b] Thus a full revaluation is not required for the writing down of one asset. Such a writing down will be an unrealised loss. For public companies, however, there is an additional requirement which provides for such losses to be taken into account.[29]

Where development costs are shown as an asset in the accounts (*i.e.* to reflect the final asset to be achieved) they are to be regarded as a realised

---

[25a] Finance Act 1980, s. 117 and Sched. 18. See para. 90–47, *post*.
[26] *Ammonia Soda Co. Ltd.* v. *Chamberlain* [1918] 1 Ch. 266.
[27] This is the definition of a "provision" in the 1948 Act, Sched. 8, paras. 87 and 88, incorporated by 1980 Act, s. 39 (4).
[28] See note 24, *ante*.
[28a] 1980 Act, s. 39 (4A).
[28b] *Ibid.*, s. 43 (7A).
[29] See para. 76–11, *post*.

loss for this purpose, unless it represents an unrealised profit made on a revaluation of those costs. The directors may however ignore this provision provided that there are special circumstances justifying their action and they explain themselves in the note to the accounts.[29a]

It a company writes off its realised losses on a reduction or re-organisation of capital duly made then these will be ignored for future calculations of profits available for distribution (1980 Act, s. 39 (2)).

Where there is no record of the original cost of an asset similar rules to those relating to realised profits apply.[30] Similarly, since pre-1980 Act losses are just as relevant as pre-1980 Act profits,[31] where the directors are unable to ascertain whether such a loss is realised or unrealised after making reasonable inquiries they may treat the loss as unrealised (1980 Act, s. 39 (7)).

Treatment of lost or depreciated assets

76–09 As has been seen earlier,[32] the loss or depreciation of fixed assets was regarded as irrelevent by the pre-1980 Act cases on the profits available for distribution. As a result of section 39 of the 1980 Act a depreciation allowance, if made, will only be a realised loss if it is not made on a revaluation of all fixed assets, as defined by subsection (4A), but as has been stated it does not require one to be made. The pre-1980 case law is therefore still relevant in this respect and applies in full to private companies even after the Act. Public companies are, however, more limited.

Private companies

76–10 FIXED AND CIRCULATING CAPITAL. "Fixed capital" here is used in the sense in which the accountant or businessman uses the expression, and is not confined to property physically fixed. Thus, the ships of a shipping company and the rolling stock of a railway company are fixed capital.[33] "Circulating capital" means all capital which performs its whole office by a single use, *e.g.* the goods which the merchant has for sale, he sells out-and-out and gets the money in exchange; the goods which the tradesman uses up in doing repairs for a customer; the cars of a car dealer. They must be depreciated if they have fallen in value.

The distinctive characteristic is that all assets whose cost is charged in the company's books as capital are fixed assets; assets charged as revenue items in the profit and loss account reduce the balance of that account and are not appropriate for depreciation. The method of treatment for tax purposes is irrelevant.

In view of the distinction between fixed assets and circulating or current

---

[29a] 1980 Act, s. 42A, added by 1981 Act, s. 84.
[30] See para. 76–07, *ante*.
[31] *Ibid.*
[32] See para. 76–06, *ante*.
[33] *Verner* v. *General and Commercial Investment Trust* [1894] 2 Ch. 239, 268.

assets, it is necessary to ascertain what items fall into each category; for it will be appreciated that the test is not whether the company's subscribed capital has been used in acquiring the assets: the capital may be used for acquiring fixed assets or circulating assets, or indeed for purposes such as paying the promotion expenses of the company, which cannot in a commercial sense be treated as assets at all.

Peterson J. pointed out that what is fixed capital in one company may be circulating in another[34]: he decided, with some relief, that it was not necessary in the case before him to decide what was the true view on these vexed questions. Lord Halsbury once doubted whether an abstraction of this kind, however proper in economic treatises, was applicable to the concrete realities of business life.[35] Thus in *Lee* v. *Neuchatel Asphalte Co.*[36] the court treated a concession to work a wasting mine as fixed capital, and in *Bond* v. *Barrow Haematite Steel Co.*[37] leasehold iron ore mines held by a smelting company for the purpose of supplying itself with ore were circulating capital.

DEPRECIATION OF FIXED ASSETS NEED NOT BE PROVIDED. *Stapley* v. *Read Bros. Ltd.*[38] shows that if depreciation has been provided for out of profits upon a fixed asset which has not in fact depreciated in value, the amount so provided for can be treated as profits and used accordingly, but the law goes further than this and provides that even if the asset has depreciated in value, it is not obligatory upon the company to provide out of profits for such depreciation. Thus in *Lee* v. *Neuchatel Asphalte Co.*[39] no sinking fund had been provided for a wasting mine. Stirling J. said:

> ". . . so long as the capital remains intact, and the current receipts exceed the current expenditure, both according to the general law and under the provisions of these particular articles of association, it rests entirely with the shareholders to decide whether the excess shall be divided among them or set apart as a reserve fund for replacing wasting assets, and the court has no power to interfere with their decision however foolish or imprudent it may seem to be."

The principle established by *Lee* v. *Neuchatel Asphalte Co.*,[40] that it is not necessary to provide out of profits for the depreciation of fixed assets, is somewhat weakened by two factors: first, that the capital in that case had been paid up by a transfer to the company of the wasting asset in question; secondly, that in fact the asset was wasting not merely because minerals had been extracted from the mine, so as to reduce its value, but also because the asset was not the mine itself, but a concession to work the mine, and the company had, without issuing further capital, obtained an

---

34 In *Ammonia Soda Co.* v. *Chamberlain* [1918] 1 Ch. 266, 274.
35 In *Dovey* v. *Cory* [1901] A.C. 477, 487.
36 (1889) 42 Ch.D. 1.
37 [1902] 1 Ch. 353.
38 See further on this question, para. 76–08, *ante*.
39 [1924] 2 Ch. 1.
40 (1889) 41 Ch.D. 1.

extension of the concession so that the value had increased rather than decreased. Indeed in *Bond* v. *Barrow Haematite Co.*[41] Farwell J., referring to the decision in *Lee* v. *Neuchatel Co.*, which was cited as an authority for the proposition that no company owning wasting property need ever create a depreciation fund, said:

> "In my opinion, that is not the true result of the decision. . . . The company's assets were larger than at its formation, and the court decided nothing more than the particular proposition that some companies with wasting assets need have no depreciation fund."

However, one proposition is clear: it is not necessary for the surplus assets over liabilities to be sufficient to provide for the whole of the issued capital before a dividend can be paid. As Lindley L.J. said in the *Neuchatel Asphalte* case[42]: "The company is not debtor to capital; the capital is not a debt of the company."

Nevertheless, the proposition that nothing need be provided out of profits to meet depreciations in value of fixed assets is further borne out by *Verner* v. *General and Commercial Investment Trust*,[43] where an investment company was held able to distribute its profit from income although the value of its investments had fallen.[44]

Public companies—net assets value test

76–11 The proposition established by the cases that it is not necessary for the surplus of assets over liabilities to be sufficient to provide for the whole of the issued share capital before a dividend can be paid is not, as noted earlier,[45] affected by section 39 of the 1980 Act. For public companies, however, that proposition is now subject to section 40 of the 1980 Act. Under that section a public company may not make any distribution[46] unless at the time the amount of its net assets is at least equal to the aggregate of its called-up share capital and its undistributable reserves. Further, a public company cannot make a distribution insofar as that distribution would reduce the net assets below that aggregate (1980 Act, s. 40 (1)). In effect therefore public companies must take unrealised losses into account when deciding on distribution profits.

Various parts of this formula require definition:

NET ASSETS. The primary valuation is the amount of the company's net assets. These are defined in the 1980 Act[47] as the aggregate of its assets less the aggregate of its liabilities. Liabilities are those regarded as such for the

---

[41] [1902] 1 Ch. 353.
[42] (1889) 41 Ch.D. 23.
[43] [1894] 2 Ch. 239.
[44] The treatment of depreciated fixed assets in the balance sheet of the company forms the subject-matter of Recommendation 9 of the Recommendations on Acccounting Principles issued by the Institute of Chartered Accountants.
[45] See para. 76–08, *ante*.
[46] The same definition applies as for section 39: 1980 Act, s. 45 (2).
[47] 1980 Act, s. 87 (4) (*c*).

accounts provisions,[48] *e.g.* depreciation allowances, provisions for liabilities whether actual, contingent or disputed, except for those taken into account in valuing the asset. Assets are not defined as such, but uncalled share capital[49] is not be included as an asset in the relevant accounts[50] (1980 Act, s. 40 (5)).

CALLED-UP SHARE CAPITAL. The net assets must be balanced against the called-up share capital figure and the undistributable reserves. The called-up share capital figure is defined generally in the 1980 Act[51] as the aggregate of the amount of calls actually made on a company's shares,[52] whether paid or not, together with any instalments[53] due on a specific date or dates, and any share capital actually paid up without call.

UNDISTRIBUTABLE RESERVES. These are set out in section 40 (2) of the 1980 Act. There are four categories: the share premium account,[54] the capital redemption reserve,[55] the net accumulated unrealised profit, and any other reserve which the company is otherwise prohibited from distributing by statute or by the company's memorandum or articles.[56]

The net accumulated unrealised profits are calculated as follows. The total accumulated unrealised profits must first be ascertained. These are defined by way of contrast to realised profits for the purposes of section 39, set out above.[57] From this gross figure it is then necessary to deduct first those unrealised profits which have been capitalised, *e.g.* by the issue of bonus shares, except for a transfer of profits to the capital redemption reserve fund.[58] All those items will be taken into account under the other categories. The second deduction is of the company's accumulated unrealised losses, *i.e.* those which are not realised for the purposes of section 39,[59] and which have not been written off on a proper reduction or reorganisation of capital.[60]

The methods of calculation of profits and losses are the same as those used in section 39 of the 1980 Act.[61]

---

[48] 1948 Act, Sched. 8, para. 88.
[49] *i.e.* that which is not "called up" share capital—see text below.
[50] See para. 76–17, *post*.
[51] 1980 Act, s. 87 (1).
[52] For calls generally see Chap. 35, *ante*.
[53] See generally Chap. 35, *ante*.
[54] See para. 29–10, *ante*.
[55] See para. 33–13, *ante*.
[56] *e.g.* the quasi-capital fund on nominee shares under s. 38 (10) of the 1980 Act. See para. 29–11, *ante*.
[57] See para. 76–07, *ante*. 1980 Act, s. 40 (4). It includes pre-Act profits where necessary: 1980 Act, s. 45 (4).
[58] 1980 Act, s. 40 (3).
[59] See note 57 above.
[60] *Ibid.* s. 40 (2) (*c*).
[61] *Ibid.* s. 40 (4).

Investment companies

Definition of investment companies

76–12 Special rules apply to "investment companies" in addition to the general provisions of sections 39 and 40 of the 1980 Act noted above (1980 Act, s. 41). There is a complex definition of investment companies for this purpose.

They are public companies which have given the requisite notice to the Registrar of their intention to carry on business as an investment company and have since that time complied with the following four conditions[62]:

(i) the business of the company consists of investing its funds mainly in securities with the aim of spreading investment risk and benefiting its members by the results of the management of its funds (1980 Act, s. 41 (4) (*a*));

(ii) that none of its holdings in other company's securities represent more than 15 per cent. in value of its overall investment. There are exceptions for holdings in other investment companies (1980 Act, s. 41 (4) (*b*)). The 15 per cent. limit does not apply to pre-April 6, 1965 holdings up to a 25 per cent. limit or to holdings which were previously 15 per cent. but have increased either by the issue of bonus shares or simply by an increase in the value of those shares.[63] A holding for this purpose includes all the shares or securities in a specific company or a group of companies (a company and its 51 per cent. subsidiaries)[64];

(iii) the distribution of its capital profits are prohibited by its memorandum or articles (1980 Act, s. 41 (1) (*c*)); and

(iv) the company has not retained, unless required by the legal limits on distributable profits, more than 15 per cent. of its income from securities in any accounting reference period[65] (1980 Act, s. 41 (4) (*d*)).

A company will cease to be an investment company if it gives a prescribed notice to that effect to the Registrar (1980 Act, s. 41 (7)).

Profits available for distribution

76–13 Because investment companies by definition cannot distribute their capital profits[66] the rules in sections 39 and 40 of the 1980 Act are extended by section 41. This allows for additional profits which may be distributed over and above those allowed by the general sections.

An investment company may prima facie make a distribution out of its accumulated realised revenue profits (insofar as not already distributed or capitalised), less its accumulated revenue losses (whether realised or un-

---

[62] *Ibid.* s. 41 (3).
[63] I.C.T.A. 1970, s. 359 (2), (3) (*b*), applied by the 1980 Act, s. 41 (8).
[64] I.C.T.A. 1970, s. 359 (3) (*a*), F.A. 1972, s. 93 (6) (*b*), applied by the 1980 Act, s. 41 (8).
[65] See para. 70–01, *ante*.
[66] 1980 Act, s. 41 (4) (*c*).

realised), except for those already written off on a proper reduction or reorganisation of capital.[67]

This right will be lost, however, unless at the relevant time its assets are at least equal to one and a half times the aggregate of its liabilities, or insofar as the proposed distribution will not reduce its assets below that figure.[68] Uncalled share capital is not to be included in the relevant accounts[69] as an asset.[70] Liabilities has the same meaning as that used in the calculation of net assets in section 40 of the 1980 Act.[71]

This formula creates the problem, avoided by sections 39 and 40 of the 1980 Act, of distinguishing between capital and revenue profits. The distinction between fixed and circulating or current assets has already been discussed, and there is no statutory attempt at such a distinction.[72] The distinction between realised and unrealised revenue profits will be the same as for section 39 of the 1980 Act.[73] The cumulative principle is implied so that pre-1980 Act profits and losses must be taken into account.[74]

Additional requirement for a distribution to be made

76–14 Any investment company, as defined above, which has profits available for distribution under the formula of section 41 of the 1980 Act may only distribute those profits (if not otherwise available under sections 39 or 40) if its shares are listed on a recognised stock exchange and, during the whole of its previous accounting reference periods,[75] it has neither distributed any capital profits nor applied any unrealised profits or capital profits of any kind in paying up debenture or amounts unpaid on its issued shares (1980 Act, s. 41 (5)). If the company is in its first accounting reference period this latter condition must be complied with during the whole of that period up to the date of the distribution.

A further condition is that the requisite notice to the Registrar of the company's intention to be regarded as an investment company must have been given prior to the commencement of the accounting reference period before the accounting period in which the distribution is proposed. For companies incorporated after the Act an alternative is provided whereby the notice may be given as soon as is reasonably practicable after the date of incorporation (1980 Act, s. 41 (6)).

Extension of definition of investment companies

76–15 The 1980 Act contains provisions providing for future extension of the provisions of section 41 to investment companies who invest in securities,

---

[67] *Ibid.* s. 41 (1).
[68] *Ibid.*
[69] See para. 76–17, *post.*
[70] 1980 Act, s. 41 (2), applying *ibid.* s. 40 (5).
[71] 1980 Act, s. 41 (2). See para. 76–11, *ante.*
[72] 1980 Act, s. 41 (11) was repealed by Sched. 4 to the 1981 Act.
[73] See para. 76–07, *ante.*
[74] 1980 Act, 45 (4).
[75] See para. 70–01, *ante.*

land or other assets rather than principally in securities alone.[76] Such extensions together with any necessary modifications must be made by regulations subject to a positive resolution.[77]

Insurance companies with long-term business

76–16 Certain modifications to the general rules relating to the profits available for distribution apply to insurance companies within the Insurance Companies Act 1981. These are contained in section 42 of the 1980 Act and are dealt with in Chapter 89, below.

The relevant accounts

Importance of the relevant accounts

76–17 Any questions as to the legality of a distribution or the amount of a distribution under sections 39 to 41 of the 1980 Act must be solved by reference to the "relevant items" in the "relevant accounts" and, unless those accounts comply with the requirements of the 1980 Act, there will be an automatic breach of those sections on any distribution even if sections 39 to 41 are in fact complied with (1980 Act, s. 43 (1)). Where a distribution is proposed by reference to the same relevant accounts as have already been used for earlier distributions, the proposed distribution is to be regarded as an increase of those earlier distributions for the purposes of ascertaining its legality (1980 Act, s. 43 (7)). Similarly where the relevant accounts have been used to justify a payment out of distributable profits to give financial assistance to a purchaser of the company's shares[78] or such assistance has in fact reduced the company's net assets or increased its liabilities, or to fund either a purchase by a company of its own shares[79] or an option to purchase or variation or release of such contract or option,[80] any such payment must be deducted from the distributable profits as shown in those accounts before a distribution of dividend can be made (1981 Act, s. 60 (1)).

The "relevant items" are the profits, losses, assets, liabilities, share capital, reserves, including undistributable reserves,[81] and provisions[82] as appear in the "relevant accounts."[83]

The "relevant accounts" may be either the last annual accounts of the company together with any interim accounts or a new company's initial accounts (1980 Act, s. 43 (2)).

[76] 1980 Act, s. 41 (9).
[77] *Ibid.* s. 41 (10).
[78] Public companies may use them for the employee share schemes and loans exemption in s. 42 of the 1981 Act, s. 42 (7); private companies may use them to avoid the general prohibition, 1981 Act, s. 43 (2). See Chap. 35, *ante*.
[79] See para 38–07A, *ante*.
[80] *Ibid.* 1981 Act, s. 51.
[81] As defined by the 1980 Act, s. 40 (2), see para. 76–11, *ante*.
[82] As defined by the 1980 Act, Sched. 8, para. 27 (1). See note 27 above.
[83] 1980 Act, s. 40 (8).

76–18 LAST ANNUAL ACCOUNTS. Prima facie the relevent accounts are the company's last annual accounts. These are the annual accounts[84] laid or filed in respect of the last accounting reference period[85] in which such accounts were laid or filed[86] (1980 Act, s. 43 (2) (*a*)).

INTERIM ACCOUNTS. If the distribution would otherwise contravene the relevant criteria certain accounts, the "interim accounts," may be resorted to in addition to the last annual accounts. These additional accounts are those which are necessary to enable a proper judgment to be made as to the amounts of any of the relevant items[87] (1980 Act, s. 43 (2) (*b*)).

INITIAL ACCOUNTS. A new company obviously has no last annual accounts. In such a case until the first accounts are filed or laid[86] for the company's first accounting reference period, the relevant accounts are those which are necessary to enable a proper judgment to be made as to the amounts of any of the relevant items[87] (1980 Act, s. 43 (2) (*c*)).

Requirements for the relevant accounts

76–19 The 1980 Act contains strict requirements relating to the relevant accounts used for the purposes of testing the legality of a distribution of profits. If these requirements are not complied with there is an automatic breach of the relevant section imposing the criteria.[88] Different requirements apply to the last annual accounts, the interim accounts and the initial accounts for this purpose.

76–20 LAST ANNUAL ACCOUNTS. Where the last annual accounts are the only relevant accounts the following four requirements must be complied with (1980 Act, s. 43 (3)).

(i) The accounts or those items relevant for the purpose of determining whether a particular distribution is valid or not, must have been properly prepared in accordance with the provisions of the Companies Act[89];

(ii) There has been an auditor's report under section 14 of the 1967 Act[90]

---

84 Those prepared in accordance with the 1976 Act, s. 1.
85 See para. 70–01, *ante*.
86 Accounts are laid or filed for this purpose only when the directors have complied with their obligations as to the general meeting and the Registrar under s. 1 (6) and (7) of the 1976 Act: 1980 Act, s. 43 (8).
87 See para. 76–17, *ante*.
88 1980 Act, s. 43 (1). See para. 76–01, *ante*.
89 1980 Act, s. 43 (8) (*c*). See Chap. 70, *ante*. If the company has taken advantage of the exemptions available in Pt. II of Sched. 8 to the 1948 Act, it must show sufficient particulars to give a true and fair view of the state of its affairs and its profit or loss: 1980 Act, s. 43 (8) (*c*).
90 See para. 73–01, *ante*.

(iii) If that report is not an unqualified report,[91] the auditors must state in writing[92] whether the qualification is relevant for the purposes of testing the legality of the proposed distribution. This statement may also provide that the qualification is irrelevant for any particular type of distribution even if not yet proposed, and will then suffice for such a future distribution,[93] and

(iv) A copy of any such written statement must have been laid before the general meeting or sent to the Registrar as appropriate.

76–21 INTERIM ACCOUNTS. Where interim accounts are used to decide the legality of a distribution the following three requirements must be complied with by public companies. There are no such requirements for private companies (1980 Act, s. 43 (5)).

(i) The accounts or those items relevant for the purpose of determining whether a particular distribution is valid or not, must have been properly prepared as to comply with the formal requirements of company accounts[94] and the balance sheet must be signed by the directors[95];

(ii) A copy of the accounts must be delivered to the Registrar; and

(iii) An English translation, certified as a correct translation must, if necessary,[96] also be delivered to the Registrar.

76–22 INITIAL ACCOUNTS. The 1980 Act imposes five conditions upon public companies before accounts prepared before the first annual accounts can be used to test the validity of a distribution. There are no such requirements for private company accounts (1980 Act, s. 43 (6)).

(i) The accounts, etc., must have been properly prepared and signed in the same way as is required for the interim accounts;

(ii) The auditors must have made a report stating whether in their opinion the accounts have been so properly prepared;

(iii) If that report is not an unqualified report[97] the auditors must have stated in writing whether the qualification is material to the legality of the distribution[98];

(iv) A copy of the accounts, the report, and any statement must be delivered to the Registrar; and

---

[91] An unqualified report is one which, without any qualifications, states that the auditors are satisfied that the accounts have been properly prepared: 1980 Act, s. 43 (8).

[92] Either at the time of the report or later.

[93] 1980 Act, s. 43 (4).

[94] 1948 Act, s. 149 as applied by the 1980 Act, s. 43 (8) (*b*). These requirements apply except insofar as they relate to accounting reference periods: 1980 Act, s. 43 (9).

[95] 1948 Act, s. 155 as applied by the 1980 Act, s. 43 (8) (*b*). If the company has taken advantage of Pt. III of Sched. 8 to the 1948 Act then s. 43 (8) (*c*) of the 1980 Act will apply: see note 85 above.

[96] This will be so if the accounts are not in English and s. 1 (7) (*b*) of the 1976 Act does not apply.

[97] See note 88 above.

[98] This does not cover future unproposed distribution, *cf.* the requirements for the last annual accounts where s. 43 (4) extends the effect of such a written statement. s. 43 (4) does not apply to initial accounts.

(v) A certified translation of the accounts, the report and any statement must also be sent to the Registrar if necessary.[99]

Capitalisation of profits—bonus shares

76–23 The capitalisation of profits by the issue of shares which are wholly or partly paid up out of profits is only possible if the articles of the company contain provisions authorising this procedure (see arts. 128, 128A and 129).

The capitalisation of profits means that the profits are not divided amongst the shareholders in cash but are allotted further shares—or debentures—which are paid up wholly or in part out of those profits. The amount paid by the company on account of these newly issued shares is known as the bonus, and the shares are referred to as bonus shares.

The 1980 Act expressly provides that the issue of wholly or partly paid bonus shares is not a distribution[1] and so such issues are not subject to the same criteria as cash dividends. The 1980 Act clearly contemplates that profits not available under its provisions for distribution may nevertheless be capitalised. Thus section 45 (1) expressly provides that any pre-Act power in the articles of a company to apply unrealised profits in issuing bonus shares is not affected by the Act, and article 128A, introduced by the 1980 Act,[2] allows the directors to apply such profits in such a manner even though they are not available for distribution. As a result, in addition to the quasi-capital funds,[3] unrealised profts may clearly be capitalised even after the 1980 Act.[4]

Technically the transaction is carried out in the following manner: the bonus is provided out of the credit balance of the profit and loss account or out of reserves—both being items appearing on the liabilities side of the balance sheet, so that the balance sheet thenceforward shows the profit and loss account or reserves at a reduced figure and the issued capital at a correspondingly increased figure. As far as the balance sheet is concerned, the only effect of the transaction is that one item on the liabilities side of the balance sheet and in the company's books becomes replaced (in whole or in part) by another: the assets side of the balance sheet is unaffected. This process reduces the risk of any person gaining control of the company and distributing the liquid resources of the company against a reduction in the profit and loss account; for if the profits have been capitalised, the assets can only be distributed by way of the capital reduction procedure which requires a special resolution and confirmation by the court (see s.

---

[99] See note 93 above.
[1] 1980 Act, 45 (2) (*a*).
[2] 1980 Act, Sched. 3, para. 36 (9).
[3] See below in the text.
[4] *Sed Quaere* whether the other pre-Act cases allowing dividends could be used for capitalisation. See *per* Buckley J. in *Dimbula Valley (Ceylon) Tea Co. Ltd.* v. *Laurie* [1961] Ch. 353, 372.

66).[5] The capitalisation of profits may, thus, in appropriate cases provide an answer to a "take-over bid."

A shareholder to whom the company proposes to allot fully paid bonus shares may renounce his right to the shares, and where these "rights" refer to securities admitted to listing on the Stock Exchange, they can be sold and traded there. Similarly, if the bonus is only partial (*e.g.* shares of a nominal value of £1 are offered for subscription at 50p each, the balance of 50p having been paid up from capitalised profits), the shareholder cannot be compelled to take up the new shares and to pay the balance due on them; apart from general considerations, section 22 would make this course inadmissible. Here again, a shareholder who is unwilling to accept the proposal of the company is normally given facilities to dispose of his "rights" to the new shares on the Stock Exchange or otherwise.

The quasi-capital funds,[6] *i.e.* the share premium account (s. 56 (2))[7] and the capital redemption reserve (1981 Act, s. 53),[8] may be applied in issuing fully paid bonus shares without observance of the capital reduction procedure, although these two quasi-capital funds do not constitute profits in the legal sense.

Where it is intended to offer the shareholders to elect a scrip dividend in lieu of cash dividend, the same considerations apply to the shares issued in lieu of the cash dividend as to other shares paid for out of the divisible profit; the scrip dividend is, as far as the shareholders elect to take the shares, a form of capitalisation of profits. The articles must authorise the directors to offer the shareholders the choice of a scrip dividend.[9]

Liability for making up unlawful distribution

76–24 Any dividend paid in breach of the provisions relating to the profits available for distribution, as defined by the 1980 Act, must be repaid to the company by any shareholder who at the time of the distribution knew or had reasonable grounds for believing such payment to be in breach of those provisions (1980 Act, s. 44 (1)). If the dividend was in kind then the shareholder may pay a sum equal to the value of the distribution. Partly unlawful dividends require a pro rata repayment. This does not apply "in relation to" any unlawful financial assistance given by a company for the acquisition of its own shares[10] or any payment made by a company for the redemption[11] or purchase[12] of its own shares (1981 Act, s. 60(2)).[13] The language of the subsection is ambiguous and could relate either solely to

[5] See para. 33–01, *ante*.
[6] See para. 29–10, *ante*.
[7] See para. 29–11, *ante*.
[8] See para. 34–12D, *ante*.
[9] On the scrip dividend see para. 75–17, *ante*.
[10] 1981 Act, s. 42. See para. 37–17, *ante*.
[11] *Ibid.*, s. 45. See para. 33–12, *ante*.
[12] *Ibid.*, s. 46. See para. 37–08, *ante*.
[13] These are to be calculated in ascertaining distributable profits: 1981 Act, s. 60 (1); see para. 76–17, *ante*.

the liability of the recipient of such payment or to the consequential liability of those who receive dividends which are in breach of the 1980 Act by virtue of such payments having been made.

Prior to the 1980 Act the primary liability for the payment of dividends out of capital fell on the directors. The 1980 Act is silent as to their liability but section 44 expressly preserves any other obligation imposed upon a member of a company to repay a distribution unlawfully made to him.[14] It is thought therefore that the following principles still apply:

1. Directors who are parties to the payment of an unlawful dividend are prima facie jointly and severally liable to repay the amount.[15]
2. Directors who are parties to the payment of a fictitious dividend in order to raise the price of the company's shares may be criminally liable for conspiracy.[16]
3. Shareholders who have, with full knowledge of the facts, received unlawful dividends cannot keep such dividends and at the same time take proceedings against the directors to compel them to replace the amount of the dividend.[17]

   Where, however, dividends are paid on the representation of the directors that they are being paid out of profits, the shareholders are not accountable or precluded from suing.[18]
4. If the directors are compelled to repay the dividends to the company they may recover that amount from all the members who took the dividends with the knowledge of the facts. This indemnity extends against each such member to the extent of the amount each received.[19]

Treatment by trustees of distribution of company's profits

76–25 The question sometimes arises as to whether a distribution by a company is to be treated by trustees as capital or as income. In general, where a dividend is distributed, whether in cash or in assets of the company, such a distribution, by whatever name it is called, is income. This is so even if the dividend is provided for out of capital profits, where, for instance, the company has sold some of its capital assets at a price which gives a profit so that the distribution is not taxable in the hands of the shareholders as income. It will be seen, therefore, that, as far as the trustees under a settlement or a will are concerned, the treatment for tax purposes of the distribution in the hands of the recipients is not the deciding factor and indeed is quite irrelevant.

---

[14] 1980 Act, s. 44 (2).
[15] *Flitcroft's Case* (1882) 21 Ch.D. 519. This is so even if the dividend appears to be sanctioned by the general meeting or the company's article.
[16] See *per* Lord Campbell L.C. in *Burnes* v. *Pennell* (1849) 2 H.L.C. 497, 525, and *R.* v. *Esdaile* (1858) 1 F. & F. 213.
[17] *Towers* v. *African Tug Co.* [1904] 1 Ch. 558.
[18] *Flitcroft's Case, ante.*
[19] *Moxham* v. *Grant* [1900] 1 Q.B. 88 (C.A.).

The principles were stated by Lord Russell of Killowen in *R. A. Hill and Others* v. *Permanent Trustee Company of New South Wales*[20] as follows:

"(1) A limited company when it parts with moneys available for distribution among its shareholders is not concerned with the fate of those moneys in the hands of any shareholder. The company does not know and does not care whether a shareholder is a trustee of his shares or not. It is of no concern to a company which is parting with moneys to a shareholder whether that shareholder (if he be a trustee) will hold them as trustee for A absolutely or as a trustee for A for life only.

(2) A limited company not in liquidation can make no payment by way of return of capital to its shareholders except as a step in an authorised reduction of capital. Any other payment made by it by means of which it parts with moneys to its shareholders must and can only be made by way of dividing profits. Whether the payment is called "dividend" or "bonus," or any other name, it still must remain a payment on division of profits.

(3) Moneys so paid to a shareholder will (if he be a trustee) prima facie belong to the person beneficially entitled to the income of the trust estate. If such moneys or any part thereof are to be treated as part of the corpus of the trust estate there must be some provision in the trust deed which brings about that result. No statement by the company or its officers that moneys which are being paid away to shareholder out of profits are capital, or are to be treated as capital, can have any effect upon the rights of the beneficiaries under a trust instrument which comprises shares in the company.

(4) Other considerations arise when a limited company with power to increase its capital and possessing a fund of undivided profits, so deals with it that no part of it leaves the possession of the company, but the whole is applied in paying up new shares which are issued and allotted proportionately to the shareholders, who would have been entitled to receive the fund had it been, in fact, divided and paid away as dividend.

(5) The result of such a dealing is obviously wholly different from the result of paying away the profits to the shareholders. In the latter case the amount of cash distributed disappears on both sides of the company's balance sheet. It is lost to the company. The fund of undistributed profits which has been divided ceases to figure among the company's liabilities; the cash necessary to provide the dividend is raised and paid away, the company's assets being reduced by that amount. In the former case the assets of the company remain undiminished. . . . "

These principles have been applied in cases where cash has been distributed representing a capital profit,[21] and where specific assets of the company have been distributed.[22]

On the other hand, where a company has capitalised profits and issued

[20] [1930] A.C. 720, 730–732.

[21] *Re Bates* [1928] Ch. 682; *Hill* v. *Permanent Trustee Corpn.* [1930] A.C. 720; *Re Doughty, Burridge* v. *Doughty* [1947] Ch. 263; *Re Whitehead's Will Trusts* [1959] Ch. 579; *Forgie's Trs.* v. *Forgie* 1941 S.C. 188; 1941 S.L.T. 124.

[22] *Re Sechiari, Argenti* v. *Sechiari* [1950] 1 All E.R. 417; *Re Kleinwort's Settlements Westminster Bank* v. *Bennett* [1951] Ch. 860; *Re MacLaren's Settlement* [1951] 2 All E.R. 414.

bonus shares it is more difficult to determine whether the distribution goes to the tenant for life or enures to the benefit of those interested in the capital. In *Bouch* v. *Sproule*,[23] Fry L.J. said:

> "When a testator or settlor directs or permits the subject of his disposition to remain as shares or stock in a company which has the power either of distributing its profits as dividend, or, of converting them into capital, and the company validly exercises this power, such exercise of its power is binding on all persons interested under him, the testator or settlor, in the shares, and consequently what is paid by the company as dividend goes to the tenant for life, and what is paid by the company to the shareholder as capital, or appropriated as an increase of the capital stock in the concern, enures to the benefit of all who are interested in the capital."

Thus, in general where there is capitalisation of profits this will benefit the capital of a trust fund recipient and not the income. But it is always a question of fact whether or not profits have been capitalised, and both the form and substance of the transaction must be looked at[24] in order to discover the true position. The principle is the same if debentures are issues.[25]

Where on the other hand an option is given to the shareholders to take the dividend either in cash or in new shares, such a distribution is income in whichever form it is taken,[26] unless it can be shown that there is not intended to be an option and that shares are intended to be taken.[27] So, too, if a distribution in cash is made and simultaneously a call upon partly paid shares is made, the intention will normally be taken as being one of capitalisation and not a distribution of revenue.[28]

It should be noted that if an option to take cash or shares is given and the option is genuine and if the market value of the shares is greater than the cash distribution, the trustees would normally be bound to take the shares,[29] and in such a case they will be required to treat such shares as income to the extent that the value is equivalent to the cash distribution which would have been taken; the balance they will have to treat as capital.[30]

The court has always power to apportion the distribution on equitable grounds and would do so if any action or omission on the part of the trustees was to the prejudice of either those entitled to income or those entitled to capital.[31]

---

23 (1885) 29 Ch.D. 635, 653 (C.A.); (1887) 12 App.Cas. 385.

24 *Re Malam, Malam* v. *Hitchens* [1894] 3 Ch. 578.

25 *I.R.C.* v. *Fisher's Executors* [1926] A.C. 395; *Re Outen's Will Trusts* [1963] Ch. 291.

26 *Re Despard* (1901) 17 T.L.R. 478; *Blyth's Trs.* v. *Milne* 1905; 7 F. 799; 13 S.L.T. 292. Contrast *Gunnis Trs.* v. *Gunnis* 1903, 6 F. 104; 11 S.L.T. 399.

27 *Re Taylor, Waters* v. *Taylor* [1926] 1 Ch. 923; *Re Evans* [1913] 1 Ch. 23; *Howard's Trs.* v. *Howard* 1907 S.C. 1274, 15 S.L.T. 316 .

28 *Re Hatton, Hockin* v. *Hatton* [1917] Ch. 357.

29 See *Re Pugh* [1887] W.N. 143.

30 *Re Hume, Nisbet's Settlement* (1911) 27 T.L.R. 461; *Re Malam, Malam* v. *Hitchens* [1894] 3 Ch. 578.

31 See the court order in *Re Sechiari, Argenti* v. *Sechiari* [1950] 1 All E.R. 417; *Re Kleinwort's Settlements* [1951] Ch. 860, 863.

The benefit of an option to take up new shares is capital.[32]

Once a winding up commences the matter is entirely different, and, so far as ordinary shares are concerned,[33] the assets have to be regarded entirely as capital.[34] So, too, where a company had sold its business and distributed as dividend the whole balance in excess of its capital and liabilities, this was held to be capital.[35]

Upon a reduction of capital or of the share premium account or capital redemption reserve fund, any return to shareholders will be capital.[36]

[THE NEXT PARAGRAPH IS 76–27]

Remuneration payable out of profits. Profit-sharing schemes

76–27 It happens sometimes that the company undertakes to remunerate its employees by a share in the profits. Two types of arrangements have to be distinguished here: individual contracts of service with the managing director or other employees may provide that the whole or part of the salaries shall be payable out of profits, or that, in addition to a fixed salary, a certain percentage of the profits shall be payable by way of bonus; or a collective scheme of profit sharing may be operated as an incentive for all or a stated class of employees; in modern practice schemes of profit sharing are of growing importance.[37]

In both instances in which a share in the profits is promised to employees the question is: in what profits? This should be provided for expressly by agreement, *i.e.* by the contract of service between the company and the employee, or by the collective scheme of profit sharing. If the agreement is silent, it is a matter of construction of its terms. In profit-sharing schemes the profits which are to be shared are usually those set aside for this purpose by the directors after making due provision for the transfer of part of the net profits to reserves or other items of account.

76–28 If remuneration by way of a share in profits is promised in a service agreement, it should not be overlooked that rights of third parties, *i.e.* the employees to whom such remuneration is promised, are in issue and, in the absence of stipulations to the contrary " 'profits' . . . mean actual profits," and not profits made available for dividend.[38] This was decided in *Re Spanish Prospecting Co. Ltd.*,[39] where the company had stipulated to pay two managers salaries, but only out of profits; the salaries were to be cumulative and arrears were payable out of successive profits. The Court of Appeal held that "profits" within the meaning of these service agreements meant not necessarily profits shown by the company's annual accounts, but included realised accretions in capital.

---

[32] *Re Bromley* (1886) 55 L.T. 145; *Re Anson's Settlement* [1907] Ch. 424.

[33] The same would seem to apply also to arrears of preference dividends: see *Re Armitage* [1893] 3 Ch. 337, 346; *Re Sale* [1913] 2 Ch. 697; *Re Wharfedale Brewery Co.* [1952] Ch. 913.

[34] *Re Armitage* [1893] 3 Ch. 337; *Forgie's Trs.* v. *Forgie, supra.*

[35] *Davison* v. *King* [1927] N.I. 1.

[36] *Duff's Settlement Trusts* [1951] Ch. 923.

[37] See Chap. 94, *post.* For a full account see Morse and Williams, *Profit Sharing Schemes* (Sweet & Maxwell, 1979), Chap. 2.

[38] *Per* Fletcher Moulton L.J. in *Re Spanish Prospecting Co. Ltd.* [1911] 1 Ch. 92, 101.

[39] [1911] 1 Ch. 92.

When construing service agreements providing for remuneration by way of a share in profits, it should be borne in mind that "profits" are limited to the profits made by the company while a going concern.[40] Income (now corporation) tax should not in general be deducted for the purpose of ascertaining the amount of the profits.[41]

[40] *Frames* v. *Bultfontein Mining Co.* [1891] 1 Ch. 140.

[41] *Johnston* v. *Chestergate Hat, etc., Co.* [1915] 2 Ch. 338; *McKay* v. *I. Philp (Holdings) Ltd.*, 1974 S.L.T. (Sh. Ct.) 97. Excess profits duty, when payable, had to be deducted for the purpose of ascertaining "net profits" or "profits available for distribution as dividend." *Collins* v. *Sedgwick* [1917] 1 Ch. 179; *Re Condran* [1917] 1 Ch. 639; *Patent Castings Syndicate* v. *Etherington* [1919] 2 Ch. 254; *Vulcan Motor, etc., Co.* v. *Hampson* [1921] 3 K.B. 597.

D. INSPECTION

CHAPTER 77

INSPECTION OF COMPANY'S BOOKS AND PAPERS

77–01 ALTHOUGH, prior to the 1967 Act, the then Board of Trade had power to call for the production of books and documents by certain special kinds of company[1] for the purposes of inspection, this power was not formerly available in relation to companies generally. Part III of the 1967 Act gives the Department of Trade such powers in relation to all companies regulated by the Companies Acts and certain other bodies. The Department of Trade has now published a guide to its powers of inspection.[2]

Bodies subject to Department of Trade directions

77–02 The Department of Trade may order the production of books and papers by any of the following bodies:

(1) a company formed and registered under the 1948 Act (s. 109 (1) (*a*));

(2) an existing company within the meaning of the 1948 Act (s. 109 (1) (*b*))[3];

(3) a company to which the 1948 Act applies by virtue of section 378 of that Act[4] or which is registered under Part VIII of that Act[5] (s. 109 (1) (*c*));

(4) a body corporate incorporated in, and having a principal place of business in, Great Britain which is subject to any of the provisions of the 1948 Act with respect to prospectuses and allotments by virtue of section 435 of that Act (s. 109 (1) (*d*))[6];

(5) a body corporate incorporated outside Great Britain which is carrying on, or has at any time carried on, business in Great Britain (s. 109 (1) (*e*))[7];

also the Secretary of State may require an insurance company[8] to furnish him with information on matters specified by him or to produce specified books or papers (Insurance Companies Act, s. 36).[9]

---

[1] See Insurance Companies Act 1958, s. 14, and Protection of Depositors Act 1963, s. 18, which powers are now replaced by those considered above (1967 Act, s. 112) and, as far as insurance companies are concerned, by the Insurance Companies Act 1974, s. 36, as amended by the Insurance Companies Act 1981, ss. 22–24.

[2] See *Palmer's Company Law*, Vol. II, Pt. B–1001.

[3] See 1948 Act, s. 455 (1).

[4] See para. 2–19, *ante*.

[5] See para. 89–34, *ante*.

[6] See para. 3–21, *ante*.

[7] See para. 88–08, *post*.

[8] To which Pt. II of the Insurance Companies Act 1974 applies, see s. 28 which refers to s. 12 of the Act.

[9] On the powers of intervention of the Secretary of State generally, see Insurance Companies Act 1974, s. 28–41.

Power of Department of Trade

77–03 In order to carry out an inspection of books and papers under the 1967 Act, the Department, or any duly authorised officer of the Department, may exercise the following powers:

(1) to require the company (or other body) to produce such books or papers as the Department may direct at such time and place as may be specified, or, in the case of a direction by a duly authorised officer of the Department, to produce to him forthwith such books and papers as he may specify (s. 109 (1), end);
(2) to require the production of any such documents by any person who appears to be in possession of them, without prejudice to any lien which that person may claim on those documents (s. 109 (2));
(3) to take copies of, or extracts from, any documents produced to the Department (s. 109 (3) (*a*) (i));
(4) to require the person producing the documents, or any past or present officer or employee of the company, to provide an explanation of them (s. 109 (3) (*a*) (ii));
(5) if the books or papers are not produced, to require the person required to produce them to state, to the best of his knowledge and belief, where they are (s. 109 (3) (*b*));
(6) to obtain from a justice of the peace a warrant for the entry and search of premises on which there are reasonable grounds for suspecting that there are books or documents which the Department have required to be produced under section 109 and which have not been so produced, and for the seizure of such documents (s. 110).

"Books and papers" includes for these purposes all accounts, deeds, writings and documents of the company (1948 Act, s. 455 (1), as applied by s. 117).

The Department may not, however, require the production by a solicitor of any document containing a privileged communication made by or to him (s. 116 (1)), nor the production by a banker of any document relating to the affairs of a customer unless this appears necessary for the purpose of investigating the affairs of the banker or the customer is a person who has been required to produce documents or an explanation thereof under section 109 (s. 116 (2)).

Any company or person failing to comply with a requirement to produce books or papers or to provide explanations thereof is liable to a fine or imprisonment, or both; but it is a defence for a person required to produce any books or papers to prove that they were not in his possession or under his control and it was not reasonably practicable for him to produce them (s. 109 (4)). A statement made by a person in consequence of such a requirement may be used in evidence against him (s. 109 (5)). It seems that the powers of the Department in this respect are considered to be administrative and not encumbered by the rules of natural justice in relation to, for example, advance warning.[10] The notice under section 109 must not be in excessively wide and unreasonable terms and the officers giving the notice must have acted fairly.[11]

Provision for security of information

77–04 It is an offence, punishable by a fine or imprisonment, or both, for any person to publish or disclose any information or document obtained under section 109 or 110 of the 1967 Act, unless:

(1) the publication or disclosure is made to a competent authority (s. 111 (1))[12]; or

(2) it is made with the previous consent in writing of the company or body to which it relates (*ibid.*); or

(3) it is made for one of the following purposes:

  (a) the institution or conduct of criminal proceedings under the Acts, or under the Insurance Companies Act 1974,[13] or under the Protection of Depositors Act 1963,[14] or for any offence involving misconduct in the management of a company's affairs or misapplication or wrongful retainer of its property (s. 111 (1) (*a*));

  (b) the institution or conduct of criminal proceedings under the Exchange Control Act 1947[15] (s. 111 (1) (*b*));

  (c) for the purposes of the examination of any person by an inspector appointed under section 164, 165 or 172 of the 1948 Act or under section 32 of the 1967 Act in the course of his investigation (s. 111 (1) (*c*), as amended by s. 104 (1) of the 1981 Act);

  (d) for the purpose of enabling the Secretary of State to exercise, in relation to that or any other body, any of his functions under the Companies Act 1948 to 1981, the Prevention of Fraud (Investments) Act 1958, the Insurance Companies Act 1974 and the Insolvency Act 1976 (s. 111 (1) (*d*) as amended by s. 104 of the 1981 Act);

  (e) for the purposes of proceedings under section 110 of the 1967 Act (s. 111 (1) (*g*)).

Production of books by court order where offence is suspected

77–05 Where it is shown that there is a reasonable cause to believe that any person, while an officer of the company, has committed an offence in connection with the management of the company's affairs and that evi-

[10] *Norwest Holst Ltd.* v. *Secretary of State for Trade* [1978] Ch. 201 (C.A.).
[11] *R.* v. *Secretary of State for Trade, ex parte Perestrello* [1981] Q.B. 19.
[12] As to the meaning of "competent authority," see s. 111 (3).
[13] See para. 89–39, *post*.
[14] See para. 89–36, *ante*.
[15] See para. 26–24, *ante*.

dence of the commission of the offence may be found in any books or papers of or under the control[16] of the company, the court may order the production of the books or papers (s. 441).

In England and Wales the court is a judge of the High Court in chambers, in Scotland it is one of the Lords Commissioners of Justiciary. In England the application to the court has to be made by the Director of Public Prosecutions, the Department of Trade or a chief officer of police, as defined in section 441 (4). In Scotland it is made by the Lord Advocate.

The decision of the court is not appealable (s. 441 (3)).[17]

Proceedings by Department of Trade in consequence of inspection

77–06 The Department have the same powers to take civil proceedings, or to petition for a winding-up order or for the relief of an oppressed minority of shareholders, in consequence of any information or document obtained under Part III of the 1967 Act as they have in consequence of an inspector's report under the 1948 Act (ss. 35 and 37). These powers are considered at paras. 78–14 *et seq., post.*

Penalties for destruction or concealment of documents

77–07 In addition to the penalties already referred to, it is an offence, punishable by a fine or imprisonment, or both, for an officer of a company to destroy, mutilate, falsify, or dispose of any document relating to the property or affairs of the company, or to be a party thereto, with the intention of concealing the company's state of affairs or of defeating the law (s. 113); or for any person to make a false or reckless statement in purported compliance with an obligation imposed under section 109 (s. 114).

[16] *Lonrho Ltd.* v. *Shell Petroleum Co. Ltd.* [1980] 1 W.L.R. 627 (H.L.).
[17] *Re Racal Communications Ltd.* [1981] A.C. 374.

CHAPTER 78

INVESTIGATION INTO AFFAIRS OF COMPANY, MEMBERSHIP, OR SHARE DEALINGS

78–01 THE Acts provide in appropriate circumstances for the Department of Trade to investigate into a company's affairs (1948 Act, ss. 164, 165, as amended[1]),[2] into the ownership of shares of a company (1948 Act, ss. 172, 173),[3] or into certain dealings in shares or debentures of a company (1967 Act, s. 32).[4] In each case the investigation is carried out by one or several inspectors appointed by the Department of Trade, but the ownership of the shares of the company may be investigated by the Department of Trade without appointing an inspector (s. 173). Special provisions apply to the investigation into the affairs of a unit trust.[5]

Investigation into the affairs of the company

When Department of Trade must appoint inspectors

78–02 The Department of Trade are bound to appoint an inspector (or inspectors) where the court having the appropriate jurisdiction declares that the company's affairs ought to be investigated by an inspector appointed by the Department of Trade (s. 165 (1) (*a*) (ii)). The court having such jurisdiction is the court which, under section 218 or 220, has jurisdiction to wind up the company.[6]

An application for an order is made by originating motion (R.S.C. 1965, Ord. 102, r. 4).[7] Such an order may further be made by the court of its own motion in any proceedings before it.

When Department of Trade may appoint inspectors

78–03 The Department of Trade are empowered but not bound to appoint an inspector (or inspectors) in the following cases:

(1) Upon the application
- (a) of 200 or more members; or
- (b) of members holding not less than one-tenth of the shares issued (s. 164 (1) (*a*)).[8]

Where the application is made by 200 or more members, joint holders count as separate members: that is, a joint holding by A, B and C comprises

---

1 By s. 38 of the 1967 Act, which is to be repealed by the 1980 Act, Sched. 4.
2 See below, in the text.
3 See para. 78–17, *post*.
4 See para. 78–25, *post*.
5 See para. 78–29, *post*.
6 See para. 87–03, *post*.
7 See *Re Miles Aircraft Ltd. (No. 2)*. [1948] W.N. 178. (in Scotland a petition is lodged).
8 The provisions set out in the text apply to companies having a share capital; where the company has no share capital other provisions apply; see s. 164 (1) (*b*).

three members; but a joint holding by D and E, where D and E also hold shares separately, will not add to the number of members.

(2) In any case, if it appears to the Department of Trade that there are circumstances suggesting

(a) that the business of the company is being, or has been,[9] conducted

(i) with intent to defraud its own creditors;

(ii) with intent to defraud the creditors of any other person, *e.g.* of any associated company;

(iii) for another fraudulent purpose;

(iv) for another unlawful purpose;

(v) in a manner which is unfairly prejudicial to some part of its members, or that any act or omission of the company is or would be so prejudicial: (s. 165 (1) (*b*) (i), as amended)[10] for these purposes it would be necessary to show a prima facie case upon the principles relevant to the court's powers under section 75 of the 1980 Act;

(b) that it was formed for any fraudulent or unlawful purpose (s. 165 (1) (*b*) (i));

(c) that promoters or officers of the company have been guilty of fraud, misfeasance or other misconduct towards the company or its members (s. 165 (1) (*b*) (ii));

(d) that the company's members have not been given all the information with respect to its affairs which they might reasonably expect (s. 165 (1) (*b*) (iii)).

78–04 In such cases the Department of Trade have an absolute discretion whether they will appoint an inspector, and in case (1) they can require evidence to accompany the application for the purpose of showing that the applicants have good reason for applying for the investigation; they can further ask the applicants to provide security not exceeding £5,000 or such other sum as the Secretary of State may by order specify for payment of the costs of the investigation (s. 164 (2), as amended by the 1981 Act, s. 86). Thus the mere fact that the statutory number of members applies to the Department of Trade is not sufficient to ensure an investigation, and in practice the Department of Trade are likely to require sufficient evidence to bring the matter within (2) above: the chances of obtaining an investigation are probably somewhat greater where the application is made by the number required by section 164 (case (1), above) than where a small number of members with only small holdings apply under section 165 (*b*) (1) (cases (2) (a) to (d), above). The powers conferred by section 165 (1) (*b*), as amended, are exercisable with respect to a body corporate notwithstanding that it is in the course of being voluntarily wound up; and the reference to "members" in section 165 (1) (*b*) (i) includes persons who are

---

[9] The words "or has been" were added by s. 38 of the 1967 Act.
[10] By the 1980 Act, Sched. 3.

not members but to whom shares have been transferred or transmitted by operation of law (s. 165 (2), as amended by the 1980 Act, Sched. 3).

Companies whose affairs may be investigated under these provisions include past and present oversea companies,[11] subject to any regulations made by the Department of Trade (1967 Act, s. 42).

78–05 THE DEPARTMENT OF TRADE'S DISCRETION. Generally speaking, circumstances will have to be fairly grave before the Department of Trade will exercise its discretion since the attendant publicity and expense may have an adverse effect on the standing of the company and may affect the market in its shares if they are listed. But it is not necessary that there should be an element of unlawfulness before the Department will take action. For example, the provision regarding members not having been given all the information with respect to the company's affairs which they might reasonably expect (*supra*) is, it is thought, not limited to the information which, by virtue of the law, the shareholders are entitled to receive but includes, in excess of the statutory minimum, such information as they may reasonably expect to be given. Thus, it might be possible to invoke a Department of Trade inquiry in the case of a company with shares which are listed if the directors fail to comply with the company's obligations under the listing agreement, *i.e.* if the company persistently fails to give information which, under the listing agreement, it has promised to give.

When deciding whether to institute an inspection of the affairs of the company, the Department will entertain various, and sometimes conflicting, policy considerations; if a complaint is lodged by shareholders, it will be relevant in this context whether the law, the articles or the Stock Exchange regulations already afford a remedy. If the interests of third parties, such as members of the public who have entrusted funds to the company, are involved, other considerations arise. The exercise of the Department's discretion will, in the last resort, be determined by the circumstances of the case with which it is dealing. The Department of Trade cannot be compelled by the court to state reasons why it has ordered an investigation under section 165, absent of any allegation of bad faith. This is illustrated by *Norwest Holst Ltd.* v. *Secretary of State for Trade*,[12] where it was stated that the rules of natural justice do not apply to the exercise of this discretion by the Secretary of State. Provided that he acts in good faith and does not use his discretion improperly, he does not have to disclose the material before him nor the reasons for appointing inspectors.

If the Department of Trade refuse to appoint an inspector, a member may apply to the court for an order under section 165 (1) (*a*) (ii)[13]: this remedy is, it is submitted, available where a company fails for an unreason-

---

[11] See para. 89–40, *post*.
[12] [1978] 3 W.L.R. 73.
[13] See *Re Miles Aircraft* (*No.* 2) [1948] W.N. 178.

able time to send to its members the accounts and reports required by the Acts to be sent.

"Affairs of the company"

78–06 The scope of sections 164 and 165 of the 1948 Act was considered by the Divisional Court in *R.* v. *Board of Trade, ex p. St. Martin Preserving Co. Ltd.*,[14] where the Board of Trade had refused to appoint an inspector under the then section 165 (*a*) (i) on the ground that he proposed investigation related solely to the conduct of a receiver appointed by debenture holders, and the section did not authorise such an investigation. The court unanimously held that the activities of a receiver and manager are the "affair" of the company in respect of which he is appointed, and accordingly allowed an order of mandamus to issue against the Department.

On the general question of what is meant by "the affairs of a company," Phillimore J. said[15] that they included "its goodwill, its profits or losses, its contracts and assets including its shareholding in and ability to control the affairs of a subsidiary, or perhaps in the latter regard a sub-subsidiary . . . "; and Winn J. likewise observed[16] that the expression comprised "all its business affairs, interests or transactions, all its investment or other property interests, all its profits and losses or balance of profits or losses, and its goodwill."

Powers of inspector

78–07 The proceedings conducted by the inspector are not of a judicial or even a quasi-judicial nature but are only administrative. Nevertheless, they must be conducted fairly. As long as the inspector acts fairly, he is not bound by rigid rules of procedure. Fairness demands that, before an inspector criticises a person in his report, that person must be given at least an outline of the allegations against him, so that he has an opportunity of answering them. But he has no right to demand to be shown the statement of the person making the allegation or to cross-examine him, or to be shown a draft of the inspector's report. These are all matters which are entirely in the discretion of the inspector.[17] It is not necessary for the inspector to put the substance of any tentative conclusion of an adverse nature to the witnesses to give them an opportunity of justifying themselves. Natural justice in these circumstances only requires that the inspector should put the relevant points (but not necessarily in great detail) to the witnesses as and when they come. After hearing the evidence, the inspector has to arrive at his conclusions; these need not be tentative but may be final.[18]

When an inspector is appointed under section 164 or 165 he has power,

---

[14] [1965] 1 Q.B. 603.
[15] At p. 613.
[16] At p. 618.
[17] *Re Pergamon Press Ltd.* [1971] Ch. 388 (C.A.).
[18] *Maxwell* v. *Department of Trade and Industry* [1974] 2 All E.R. 122 (C.A.).

so far as he thinks it necessary for the purpose of his investigation, to investigate also the affairs of subsidiaries of the company, its holding company, or co-subsidiaries, and, if relevant, to report thereon.[19]

Duties of company and its officers and agents

78–08 In order to enable the inspector to carry out his investigation, a duty is cast upon the officers and agents of the company, and of any other company which is incidentally investigated as a related company under section 166, to give all assistance which they are reasonably able to give: this duty exists whether or not the inspector specifically approaches an officer or agent, and any such person is bound to offer his assistance without waiting to be asked (s. 167 (1)).

Powers of inspector in relation to company's officers and agents

78–09 The inspector himself has power to require the production by any of the officers or agents of the company (or of any other related company) of books or documents relevant to the investigation: he may also require any of the above persons to attend before him and examine them on oath, and may administer oaths for this purpose (s. 167 (1) and (2), as amended by 1967 Act, s. 39 (*a*)). If any such person refuses to produce any book or document, or to attend before him or answer any question, the inspector (or if more than one, all the inspectors) may certify to the court that there has been such refusal, whereupon the court may, after inquiring into the case, treat the refusal as contempt of court and punish the offender accordingly (s. 167 (3)). If any such person refuses to answer questions on the ground that a shorthand writer instructed by the inspector is present, he is not thereby excused, but is thereby in contempt of court.[20] Likewise, if such a person refuses to answer questions unless he receives undertakings from the inspector as to the conduct of the investigation, which the inspector is not bound to give, he may find himself to be in contempt of court.[21] The inspector himself has no powers to decide whether a refusal to answer questions is justified: this is a matter for the court to decide.[22]

In this context "officers or agents" includes bankers, solicitors and auditors of the company, and covers past as well as present "officers or agents" (s. 167 (5)), but it does not include the company's counsel acting as such (s. 455 (1)), nor does it compel a solicitor to disclose a privileged communication except as to the name and address of the client, nor a company's bankers as such to disclose information as to the affairs of any other customer (s. 175). A receiver and manager may be the agent of the company within the meaning of section 167.[23]

---

[19] See s. 166 for the companies covered by this power.

[20] *Re Gaumont British Picture Corporation Ltd.* [1940] Ch. 506.

[21] *Re Pergamon Press Ltd.* [1971] Ch. 388.

[22] *McClelland, Pope & Langley Ltd.* v. *Howard* [1968] 1 All E.R. 569n.

[23] *Per* Winn J. in *R.* v. *Board of Trade, ex p. St. Martin Preserving Co. Ltd.* [1965] 1 Q.B. 603, 623.

Further powers of inspector

78–10 By section 87 of the 1981 Act inspectors are given powers to secure the attendance of and production of documents by persons other than directors and agents of the company under investigation. Such other persons can be required to assist the investigations and are placed under a statutory duty so to do. Section 87 also confers upon inspectors wide powers to secure information concerning bank accounts operated by directors and others.

Admissibility of statements in evidence

78–11 It was not clear under the 1948 Act whether section 167 made answers given before an inspector by an officer or agent of the company admissible in evidence against him, although by subsection (4) such answers were admissible if given by other persons. Section 50 of the 1967 Act makes it clear that answers by any person, whether an officer or agent of the company or otherwise, are admissible in both civil and criminal proceedings against him. The section is a purely procedural provision having, as such, retrospective effect, with the result that it applies to statements made before the Act came into force.[24] But the only answers admissible in evidence under section 50 of the 1967 Act are those given on oath, in accordance with section 167 (2) of the 1948 Act; unsworn answers to informal questions by the inspectors are outside the ambit of section 50 and inadmissible in evidence, although there is nothing improper in the inspectors questioning a witness informally.[25]

A person prosecuted after and as a result of a Department of Trade investigation is not entitled as a matter of right to copies of transcripts of evidence given during the investigation nor of correspondence produced there. In *R.* v. *Cheltenham Justices, ex p. Secretary of State for Trade*,[26] the Divisional Court quashed a witness summons which had been issued against the Secretary of State requiring him to produce such transcripts and correspondence.

Report by inspector

78–12 At the conclusion of his investigation the inspector makes a written or printed report to the Department of Trade (s. 168 (1)): he may also, of his own initiative or on a direction from the Department of Trade, make interim reports (*ibid.*), and, without making an interim report, he may inform the Department of Trade of any matter coming to his knowledge as a result of the investigation which suggests that a criminal offence has been committed (1967 Act, s. 41).

It would appear that the report of the inspector, or any other official

[24] *Selangor United Rubber Estates Ltd.* v. *Cradock* (*No.* 2) [1968] 1 W.L.R. 319; *R.* v. *Harris* [1970] 1 W.L.R. 1252. On the right of access of a liquidator to evidence produced before the inspector, see *Re Rolls Razor Ltd.* [1968] 3 All E.R. 698. On the admissibility of evidence given to inspectors in civil proceedings see *London & County Securities Ltd.* v. *Nicholson* [1980] 1 W.L.R. 948.

[25] *Karak Rubber Co. Ltd.* v. *Burden* [1971] 1 W.L.R. 1748.

[26] [1977] 1 All E.R. 460.

communication by him to the Department of Trade, is protected by absolute privilege, while statements of witnesses before him are protected only by qualified privilege.[27]

Copies of these reports are dealt with as follows (s. 168 (2)):

(1) one is sent to the company;
(2) if the investigation has been under section 164, one is sent to the applicants if they so request;
(3) if the investigation has been undertaken in pursuance of an order of the court under section 165, the Secretary of State must furnish a copy to the court and may, at his discretion, forward a copy to the company's registered office, to any person whose conduct is referred to in the report, to the auditors, to the applicants for investigation and to any other person whose financial interests appear to be affected (1981 Act, s. 168 (2));
(4) copies may, at the Department of Trade's discretion, be sent, on payment, to any member of any company whose affairs were investigated, or to any creditor of any such company if his interests appear to be affected.

The Department of Trade may, moreover, also cause the report to be printed and published.

The report is not itself a legal decision, nor are the opinions of the inspector expressed therein binding upon any person in the manner that a judgment of the court is. It is merely an expression of the findings and opinions of the inspector.[28] Since there is no right of appeal against such findings or opinions and no effective means of protesting, and since there is no certainty that proceedings will follow, in which a person referred to might defend his name, such investigations are not altogether satisfactory. A copy of the report certified by the Secretary of State to be a true copy is admissible in any legal proceedings as evidence of the opinion of the inspector in relation to any matter contained in the report (s. 171 as amended by the 1981 Act, s. 88 (2)).

Proceedings on report

78–13 CIVIL PROCEEDINGS FOR BREACH OF DUTY. The Department of Trade are empowered to bring civil proceedings in the name of the company in any case where it appears that such proceedings ought in the public interest to be brought (1967 Act, s. 37 (1)).[29] If the Department of Trade commence such proceedings they must idemnify the company against costs and expenses thereby incurred by the company (*ibid.* s. 37 (2)),[29] and such costs

[27] See *Re Pergamon Press Ltd.* [1971] Ch. 388, 400, *per* Lord Denning M.R.

[28] *Re Grosvenor and West-End Railway Terminus Hotel Co. Ltd.* (1897) 76 L.T. 337; *Re S.B.A. Properties Ltd.* [1967] 1 W.L.R. 799, 806, *per* Pennycuick J. See, for example, the (Second) Report on the Savoy Hotel Ltd. and the Berkeley Hotel Co. Ltd., published in an investigation conducted by E. Milner Holland Q.C. and issued June 14, 1954 (H.M.S.O.).

[29] Replacing s. 169 of the 1948 Act which was repealed by the 1967 Act, s. 130 (4) (*c*) and Sched. 8, Pt. III. For the position where proceedings commenced under s. 169 of the 1948 Act are continued after the repeal of that section, see *Selangor United Rubber Estates Ltd.* v. *Cradock* (*No.* 4) [1969] 1 W.L.R. 1773. For a petition under s. 35 of the 1967 Act, see *Re Koscot Interplanetary (U.K.) Ltd.; Re Koscot AG* [1972] 3 All E.R. 829.

and expenses are treated as those of the investigation and so may be recoverable in the manner explained below. These costs and expenses include costs ordered to be paid by the company to other parties, and, if money is paid to the liquidator for this purpose by the Department of Trade, it must be applied in payment of those costs, and not for the benefit of the general body of creditors of the company.[30]

CRIMINAL PROCEEDINGS. If the report appears to disclose any offence in relation to the company for which any person should be prosecuted, the Department of Trade may institute criminal proceedings for this purpose.[31]

78–14 WINDING UP OF A COMPANY. If it appears to the Department of Trade from the inspector's report that it is expedient in the public interest that the company should be wound up, the Department may petition for the compulsory winding up of the company, unless it is already being wound up by the court (*ibid.* s. 35 (1)).[32] The last-mentioned words appear to give the Department power to petition for a winding-up order notwithstanding that the company is already in voluntary liquidation.

The report of the inspector is admissible in evidence, when referred to in the statutory affidavit in support of the petition,[33] but the judge, in the exercise of his discretion, may insist on direct evidence if a charge of fraud or grave misconduct is made,[34] or if the company resists the order.[35] The report of the inspector may also be relied upon by a contributory, if petitioning for a compulsory winding up but the petitioner should select and identify the matters in the report on which he wishes to rely in order to establish that it is just and equitable that the company be wound up.[36]

78–15 REMEDY FOR UNFAIRLY PREJUDICIAL TREATMENT. If it appears to the Department of Trade from the report that the company's business is being conducted in a manner unfairly prejudicial to any part of the members, the Department may, in addition to or instead of presenting a petition for the winding up of the company, present a petition under section 75 of the 1980

---

[30] *Selangor United Rubber Estates Ltd.* v. *Cradock* [1967] 1 W.L.R. 1168. As to the meaning of "costs and expenses," see *Selangor United Rubber Estates* v. (*No.* 4) [1969] 1 W.L.R. 1773, 1785.

[31] It is no longer necessary for such matters to be referred to the Director of Public Prosecutions or, in Scotland, the Lord Advocate (1967 Act. s. 36).

[32] See note 29, *supra.*

[33] *Re Travel & Holiday Clubs Ltd.* [1967] 1 W.L.R. 711; *Re S.B.A. Properties Ltd.* [1967] 1 W.L.R. 799; *Re Allied Produce Ltd.* [1967] 1 W.L.R. 1469; *Re St. Piran Ltd.* [1981] 1 W.L.R. 1300.

[34] *Re A.B.C. Coupler and Engineering Co. Ltd.* (*No.* 2) [1962] 1 W.L.R. 1236; *Re Armvent Ltd.* [1975] 1 W.L.R. 1679.

[35] *Re Travel & Holiday Clubs Ltd.* [1967] 1 W.L.R. 711, 715, *per* Pennycuick J.; *Re Allied Produce Ltd.* [1967] 1 W.L.R. 1469, 1471, *per* Buckley J.; *Re Koscot Interplanetary (U.K.) Ltd.* [1972] 3 All E.R. 829, 833, *per* Megarry J.

[36] *Re St. Piran Ltd.* [1981] 1 W.L.R. 1300.

Act for the relief of the members thereby prejudiced (1980 Act, s. 75 (2)[37]).

Expenses of investigation

78–16 Initially the expenses of an investigation are borne by the Department of Trade but part or all of these may be recovered as follows:

(1) any person who is convicted on a prosecution instituted as a result of the investigation or who is found liable for breach of duty as a result of proceedings by the Department of Trade in the name of the company may be ordered in the same proceedings to pay all or part of the expenses of the investigation;

(2) where in any such proceedings as above any property of the company is recovered, the expenses of the investigation may be recovered out of that property[38];

(3) if no criminal proceedings are brought as a result of the investigation, where the inspector was not appointed by the Department of Trade upon their own motion (*e.g.* investigation under section 164 or upon a special resolution or order of the court under section 165 (*a*)) any company dealt with by the report shall be liable except so far as the Department of Trade directs otherwise (1948 Act, s. 170 (1) (*c*)[39]). If, therefore, an investigation deals with more than one company, each of them will be liable for the whole costs and expenses and it is to be expected that the Department of Trade would limit the liability of each by "directing otherwise" in accordance with the clause, and indeed the inspector may (or may be directed to) recommend how this should be done. If an investigation is made upon the application of members under section 164, these members are liable for the expenses to such extent (if any) as the Department of Trade may direct (s. 170 (1) (*d*)[40]).

If criminal proceedings are commenced as a result of the investigation, neither the companies dealt with nor any applicant members are liable for the costs even if the prosecution is unsuccessful.

Investigation into the membership of the company

78–17 Under section 172 of the 1948 Act (and the two following sections) the Department of Trade are further given powers to investigate and report on the membership of a company, and otherwise for the purpose of determining the true persons who are or have been financially interested in the success or failure, or in the apparent success or failure, of the company, or

---

[37] See note 29, *supra*.

[38] As to the respective liabilities of unsuccessful defendants and of the company for costs and expenses recoverable by the Department of Trade, see *Selangor United Rubber Estates Ltd.* v. *Cradock* (*No.* 4) [1969] 1 W.L.R. 1773.

[39] As amended by s. 40 (2) of the 1967 Act.

[40] Introduced by s. 40 (2) of the 1967 Act.

who are able to control or materially to influence the policy of the company.

These powers, which were new under the 1947–1948 legislation, are in very wide terms.

Normally the Department of Trade exercise the power to investigate into the membership of a company by appointing an inspector, or several inspectors, but the investigation may likewise be arranged by the Department of Trade directly, without appointment of an inspector.

When Department of Trade must appoint inspectors

78–18 The Department of Trade are bound, subject to the qualifications set out in the following paragraph, to appoint an inspector (or inspectors) where an application is made by one of the minorities entitled by section 164 (1)[41] to demand an investigation into the affairs of the company (s. 172 (3)).[42] Here again, it is submitted, the Department of Trade may require evidence that the applicants have good reason for requiring the investigation (s. 164 (2)), but the Department cannot ask them for security as the costs of an investigation under section 172 have to be borne by the Department of Trade (s. 172 (6)).

If the Department of Trade are satisfied that the application is vexatious, they need not appoint an inspector. Similarly if the Department of Trade are satisfied that any of the matters for which application for the investigation is made are unreasonable, they may exclude such matters from the investigation (s. 172 (3)).

When Department of Trade may appoint inspectors

78–19 The Department of Trade are, moreover, empowered but not bound to appoint an inspector (or inspectors) "where it appears to [them] that there is good reason so to so" (s. 172 (1)).

In this case the Department of Trade have full discretion whether or not to make the appointment.

When Department of Trade may investigate membership without appointing inspectors

Where it appears to the Department of Trade that there is good reason to investigate the ownership of shares in or debentures of a company and that it is unnecessary to appoint an inspector for that purpose, they may require any person whom they have reasonable cause to believe to have or to be able to obtain any information as to the present and past interests in those shares and debentures and the names and addresses of the persons interested, to give them any information which he has or can reasonably be expected to obtain as to the present and past interests in those shares or

---

41 See para. 78–03, *ante*.

42 Such an investigation took place in November 1953 upon the application of 224 members of the Savoy Hotel Ltd. The investigation became known as the First Savoy Hotel Investigation. An interim Report was published by the inspector HMSO, S.O. Code No. 51–9999).

debentures and the names and addresses of the persons interested (s. 173 (1) as amended by the 1981 Act, s. 90).

The ambit of this provision is wide: it includes not only persons directly interested in the shares or debentures but likewise persons who have a right to acquire or dispose of the shares or debentures or any interest therein or to vote in respect thereof, or whose consent is necessary for the exercise of any of those rights, and it further extends to cases in which persons other than the *propositus* have to, or are accustomed to, exercise their rights in those shares and debentures in accordance with his instructions (s. 173 (2)).

Non-compliance with these provisions constitutes an offence (s. 173 (3)).

Powers of inspector

78–20 The Department of Trade instruct the inspector as to the scope of his investigation, particularly in regard to the period to which it is to extend (for instance, to cover the persons interested in the shares during the past 10 years), and may specify the particular shares or debentures whose ownership is to be investigated (s. 172 (2)). In the absence of express instructions to the contrary in the terms of reference, the inspector is not restricted in his investigation to the strict facts of his reference. He is empowered to take into account any circumstances suggesting the existence of an arrangement or understanding which, though not legally binding, is or was observed or is or was likely to be observed in practice and which is relevant to the purpose of his investigation (s. 172 (4)), *e.g.* if employees of one person between them hold a large number of shares in a company sufficient to exercise an influence in its affairs if they were to vote consistently together, such circumstances would be relevant to the inspector's investigation.

The powers of the inspector to investigate are not restricted to the company the membership of which he is instructed to examine. Under the general provisions relating to inspection he may extend his investigation to related companies if he considers this necessary for the purposes of his investigation (s. 166, as referred to in s. 172 (5)). In addition, he may extend his investigation to other persons whom he has reasonable cause to believe to be or to have been "financially interested in the success or failure or the apparent success or failure of the company . . . or able to control or materially to influence the policy thereof . . ." (s. 172 (5) (*a*)).

The holding of shares by an agent of any person will be relevant for the purposes.

78–21 "APPARENT SUCCESS OR FAILURE." It will be noticed that an investigation covers not only persons who are interested in the success or failure of a business, that is to say, persons who because they hold beneficial interests in the shares of a company are interested in whether or not it succeeds; but also extends to apparent success or failure. This, it seems, would mean that if any person was likely to benefit from the fact that a company appeared to be flourishing or, vice versa, appeared to be failing so that the value of the shares or debentures of the company would tend to rise or fall, as the case may be, the inspector would be entitled to investigate such matters; thus, if an attempt is made to falsify the market value of shares in contrast to their true value, *e.g.* by concealing facts which should have been made available, an inspector may be appointed and directed to investigate the circumstances.

Further powers, duties and reports of inspector

78–22 The further powers and duties of an inspector appointed under section 172 are the same, *mutatis mutandis*, as those of an inspector appointed for the investigation of the affairs of the company. Section 172 (5) incorporates the provisions dealing with those powers and duties by reference (to ss. 166–168).

The same is true with respect to the inspector's report but here the following variation should be noted: the Department of Trade is not bound to furnish the company or any other person with a copy of a report by an inspector appointed under section 172 or with a complete copy thereof if they are of opinion that there is good reason for not divulging the contents of the report or of parts of it (s. 172 (5) (*b*)).

Powers of Department of Trade where investigation obstructed

78–23 Wherever it appears to the Department of Trade that there is difficulty in finding out the relevant facts about any shares in respect of which they are making an investigation and that the difficulty is due wholly or mainly to the unwillingness of the persons concerned or any of them to assist the investigation, the Department of Trade may by order direct that the shares shall until further order be subject to any or all of the following restrictions (s. 174 as amended by the 1981 Act, s. 91):

(1) they may not be transferred;
(2) no voting rights shall be exercisable in respect of them;
(3) no bonus shares shall be issued in respect of them;
(4) no payments whatsoever in respect of the shares shall be made except in a liquidation.

Any persons aggrieved by such restrictions may apply to the court for the restrictions to be lifted. Such an application is made by originating motion (R.S.C. 1965, Ord. 102, r. 4)[43] and the court has a discretion whether to lift the restrictions or not.

Failure to respect the restrictions or the issue of shares in contravention of them is an offence (s. 174 (5) and (6)), but a prosecution in England—as contrasted with Scotland—requires the consent of the Department of Trade (s. 174 (7)).

---

[43] By petition in Scotland.

Where the Secretary of State has directed that shares should be subject to all restrictions authorised by section 174 and on a later take-over the transferee company is obliged by section 209[44] to acquire the restricted shares (which are held by "dissenting shareholders" within section 209), the transferee company is obliged, by section 209 (3), to pay the sum due on the dissenting shares to the transferor company in order to obtain the transfer of those shares. The transferor company, by virtue of section 209 (4), has to place the sum received into a separate bank account on trust for the dissenting shareholders. This sum is a sum due (from the transferor company) to the dissenting shareholders, within section 174 (2) (*d*).[45] The court can, therefore, order a partial lifting of the restrictions under section 174, with the effect that the transfer of the restricted shares to the transferee company can be carried out by the release of the purchase price held by the transferor company for the benefit of the holders of those shares continues to be restricted.

Similar restrictions may be imposed in a similar manner upon debentures.

Expenses of investigation

8–24 Expenses of investigation are borne by the Department of Trade. This applies likewise in cases in which the Department of Trade is bound to institute an investigation, *viz*. under section 172 (3), a provision which in its generality is hardly defensible.

Investigation of share or debenture dealings

Appointment of inspector

8–25 Where it appears to the Department of Trade that there may have been a contravention of the provisions of the 1967 Act penalising certain option dealings,[46] or requiring disclosure of the interests of directors or their spouses or children in shares or debentures of a company,[47] the Department may appoint inspectors to carry out such investigations as may be necessary to establish whether such contraventions have occurred and to report their findings to the Department (1967 Act, s. 32 (1)). Such an inspector may be appointed for a limited period and his investigation may be confined to a particular class of shares or debentures (*ibid*. s. 32 (2)).

Powers of inspector

8–26 Inspectors appointed for this purpose have the powers conferred upon inspectors under section 167,[48] and the further power to require the assistance of

[44] See Chap. 81, *infra*.
[45] *Re Ashbourne Investments Ltd.* [1978] 1 W.L.R. 1346.
[46] 1967 Act, ss. 25 and 30; see para. 68–15, *ante*.
[47] 1967 Act, ss. 27 and 31; see para. 66–03, *ante*.
[48] See para. 78–09, *ante*.

(1) officers or agents of a subsidiary or holding company of the company in question or a subsidiary of its holding company;
(2) members of a recognised stock exchange[49] or of a recognised association of dealers in securities[49];
(3) dealers in securities licensed under section 3 of the Prevention of Fraud (Investments) Act 1958[50];
(4) exempted dealers for the purposes of that Act[51] (*ibid*. s. 32 (3)).

If the dealer in securities is a corporate body, these powers apply to all past or present officers of that body (*ibid*.). The powers are subject to the saving for solicitors and bankers under section 175[52] (*ibid*. s. 32 (6)).

Report of inspector

78–27 The inspector may make interim reports to the Department of Trade, and must do so if required by the Department, and, on the conclusion of his investigation, must submit a final report to the Department (*ibid*. s. 32 (4)). The report may be written or printed, as the Department direct, and the Department may cause it to be published (*ibid*. s. 32 (5)). No provision is made for the supplying of copies of the report to any person.

Expenses of investigation

78–28 The expenses of the investigation are borne by the Department of Trade (*ibid*. s. 32 (7)).

Investigation into the affairs of a unit trust

78–29 The Department of Trade may appoint one or more inspectors for this purpose if it appears to the Department that the interests of unit holders so require or if the matter is one of public concern (Prevention of Fraud (Investments) Act 1958, s. 12).[53]

---

[49] Within the meaning of the Prevention of Fraud (Investments) Act 1958; see para. 25–04, *ante*.
[50] See para. 25–04, *ante*.
[51] See para. 25–04, *ante*.
[52] See para. 78–09, *ante*.
[53] See para. 89–33, *post*.

Part Seven

ARRANGEMENTS, TAKE-OVERS, MERGERS

A. ARRANGEMENTS AND RECONSTRUCTIONS (OTHER THAN TAKE-OVER BIDS)

CHAPTER 79

ARRANGEMENTS WITH SANCTION OF COURT

Arrangements and reconstructions

79–01 The terms "arrangement" and "reconstruction," although used in the 1948 Act by way of sub-title to sections 206 to 209, are nowhere defined in the Act, and have no precise legal meaning. Generally speaking, however, they may be regarded as describing any form of internal reorganisation of the company or its affairs, as well as schemes for the amalgamation of two or more companies.

Reorganisation of capital structure of company

79–02 Companies frequently require to rearrange their capital structure. Where all the shareholders agree to the proposed course, there is generally no particular difficulty about achieving the result, although even here the process may well be somewhat complex and, in certain circumstances, will require the sanction of the court. In other cases some minority shareholders may oppose the proposals or it may not be possible to trace all the shareholders, and in such cases it is necessary to have a method whereby dissentient or untraced shareholders do not render the arrangement impossible of performance, but become bound by it.

Two methods, each suitable for different circumstances, for effecting the reorganisation of the company's capital structure are provided by the 1948 Act, one in section 206[1] and the other in section 287.[2] The scheme may also involve some other proceeding, such as a reduction of capital[3] or a stay of a winding up.[4] In such a case the procedure for that purpose must be

---

[1] See below in text.

[2] See para. 80–01, *post*. In the case of a creditors' voluntary winding up, s. 287 is made applicable subject to the sanction of the committee of inspection or the court (s. 298).

[3] For the relationship between s. 206 and a reduction of capital, see *Re Robert Stephen Holdings Ltd.* [1968] 1 W.L.R. 522; see para. 79–07, *post*.

[4] For the relationship between s. 206 and a stay of a winding up, see *Re Calgary and Edmonton Land Co. Ltd.* [1975] 1 W.L.R. 355.

followed in conjunction with the procedure of the section under which the scheme is effected.

Arrangements with creditors

Likewise, a company may wish to enter into an arrangement with some or all of its creditors. If the company is in financial difficulties it may wish to make some form of composition agreement or other scheme of arrangement which will be binding on all the creditors. In such cases, the procedure laid down in section 206 may be followed, whether the company is a going concern or in liquidation. In a winding up by the court the liquidator also has power to make a compromise or arrangement with creditors under section 245 (1) (*e*),[5] and where the company is being, or is about to be, would up voluntarily, there is a similar power under section 306.[6] Except in accordance with a scheme under section 206, a company has no power outside liquidation to make a conveyance or assignment of all its property to trustees for the benefit of all its creditors (s. 320 (2)).

Further, a perfectly solvent company may propose a scheme of arrangement, *e.g.* for the purpose of converting debentures into shares or of adjusting the rights of different classes of creditors. Such schemes may also be put into effect under the provisions of section 206.

Amalgamations with other companies

79–03 The methods of reorganisation discussed above are essentially internal arrangements. The provisions of sections 206 and 287 may, however, also be employed to effect an amalgamation with another company. The effect of such an arrangement would be for one of the companies involved to absorb the business and all assets and liabilities of the other, the latter being then dissolved; or, alternatively, both companies might be absorbed into a new company formed for that purpose.[7]

The English court may approve an arrangement under section 206 under which the assets of an English company are transferred to a foreign company, but the procedure under section 208 is not available in this case.[8]

"Take-overs"

The conventional meaning of "take-over" is the acquisition by one company of sufficient shares in another company to give the purchaser control of that other company.[9] A take-over in this sense differs from an

---

[5] As to the circumstances in which the procedure under s. 206 should be used in preference to that under s. 245, see *Re Trix Ltd.* [1970] 1 W.L.R. 1421; see paras. 79–07 and 85–79, *post*.

[6] See para. 86–19, *post*.

[7] See *e.g. Henry Head & Co.* v. *Ropner Holdings Ltd.* [1952] Ch. 124 (para. 24–47, *ante*).

[8] *Re Wilton Royal Carpets Ltd. and Yougal Carpets Holdings Ltd.* (1969, unreported); see Editorial in [1972] J.B.L. 1–3.

[9] *Cf.* the definitions in Weinberg and Blank, *Take-overs and Mergers* (4th ed. (1979), p. 3). See also the observations of Nourse J. in *Re Savoy Hotel Ltd.* [1981] 3 All E.R. 646, 649.

amalgamation in that the company taken over remains in existence. Sections 206 and 287 have no application to such a scheme, which is effected by what is popularly known as a "take-over bid." In particular section 206 requires the consent of the "target" company itself, so that a contested bid cannot utilise a scheme under that section.[9a] The Acts make no special provisions for the regulation of take-over bids,[10] but section 209[11] provides power for the acquisition of shares of shareholders (holding less than a specified percentage of the share or class of shares involved) who dissent from the scheme, if the scheme has been approved by a specified majority. Such take-over bids are regulated by the City Code on Take-overs and Mergers which is considered in Chapter 82, *post*.

Public and private aspects of amalgamations and take-overs

Amalgamations and take-overs are subject to two general forms of control. The private interests to be protected are those of creditors, shareholders and employees[12] and controls of this nature are considered in parts A and B of Part Seven to this work. The public interest in potential monopolies is considered in part C.

Compromises and arrangements under section 206

79–04 This section provides a method whereby a compromise or arrangement may be made between a company and either

(a) its creditors, or any class of its creditors, or
(b) its members or any class of them, or
(c) any combination or permutation of the creditors, the members, or any class or classes of them.

A scheme under this section requires the sanction of the court before it is effective.

Examples where the section applies

The aid of the section may be invoked when it is not otherwise possible to make some arrangement or compromise which would be in the interests of the company and the other party or parties to the arrangement. It can be used whether the company is a going concern or is in the course of winding up. It will not normally be necessary to invoke the section where it is desired to alter rights attached by the articles to a class of shares; but if the rights are defined in the memorandum, they cannot be altered unless either the memorandum itself provides procedure for alteration (s. 23 (2)) or all the members agree to the change (1980 Act, s. 32 (5)). Section 23 of the

---

[9a] *Re Savoy Hotel Ltd.* [1981] 3 All E.R. 646, 656.
[10] As to the statutory and other provisions governing take-over bids, see para. 81–01, *post*.
[11] See para. 81–05, *post*.
[12] *e.g.* City Code on Take-overs and Mergers (February 1981), Rule 15. See Vol. II, Part D.

1948 Act does not, however, preclude an alteration of special rights by means of a scheme under section 206, and such rights can be altered by this means, even if no procedure for alteration is laid down in the memorandum.[13]

The value of the section is even more clearly shown when creditors are concerned. Prima facie no creditor can be bound by the agreement of the company with the other creditors or by an agreement between the latter. A compromise approved by a great majority of creditors might be rendered ineffective if a comparatively small creditor were to object and to stand out against it. It is one of the purposes of section 206 to meet this situation.

The effect of a scheme under this section is[14]:

> "to supply, by recourse to the procedure thereby prescribed, the absence of that individual agreement by every member of the class to be bound by the scheme which would otherwise be necessary to give it validity."

By means of the section a scheme has been effected whereby creditors were required to give up their security and where their debts were replaced by fully paid shares of the company.[15] Similarly, creditors who were not willing to accept as their debtor a company to whom their debtor company's assets were transferred under a scheme were bound to accept a composition.[16] In another case secured creditors agreed to the creation of a prior charge upon the assets of the company.[17]

Meaning of "compromise" and "arrangement"

79–05 The section applies to "compromises" or "arrangements." The word "compromise" offers no particular difficulty with regard to its meaning. In *Sneath* v. *Valley Gold Ltd.*,[18] the question of what is a compromise was discussed. The question arose as a result of the use of the word not in a statute but in a trust deed, but the reasoning is the same. The result of this case and others[19] is that there can be no compromise unless there is some dispute, *e.g.* as to the power to enforce rights, or as to what those rights are.

No such limitation applies to an "arrangement." In *Mercantile Investment and General Trust Co.* v. *International Co. of Mexico (1891)* Fry L.J. said[20]:

---

[13] *City Property Investment Trust Corporation, Petitioners*, 1951 S.L.T. 371; *Balmenach* v. *Glenlivet Distillery* 1916 S.C. 639, 1916 1 S.L.T. 294; *Edinburgh Ry. etc. Co.* v. *Scottish Metropolitan Assurance Co.* 1932 S.C. 2, 1932 S.L.T. 49 and see paras. 13–03 and 33–13, *ante*.

[14] *Per* Younger J. in *Re Guardian Assurance Co.* [1917] 1 Ch. 431, 441.

[15] *Re Empire Mining Co.* (1890) 44 Ch.D. 402.

[16] *Re Browning Guild Pottery Society* [1898] W.N. 80.

[17] *Re Dominion of Canada Freehold Estate and Timber Co.* (1886) 55 L.T. 347.

[18] [1893] 1 Ch. 477. *Mercantile Investment and General Trust Co.* v. *International Co. of Mexico (1891)* [1893] 1 Ch. 484n.; *Mercantile Investment and General Trust Co.* v. *River Plate Trust, Loan and Agency Co.* [1894] 1 Ch. 578.

[19] See preceding note.

[20] [1893] 1 Ch. 484n., 491.

> "In my opinion, the power to compromise does not include the power to give up one chose in action, namely, a secured debenture, in exchange for another chose in action of a totally different kind, namely, a preference share, in the absence of all dispute as to the rights of the creditor, of all difficulty in enforcing those rights, and of any suggestion that the full fruits of these rights could not be obtained. Such a transaction might be described as an exchange, possibly as a barter, or an arrangement."

In 1917 the question arose directly upon the predecessor of the present section 206 in the Companies (Consolidation) Act 1908.[21] The scheme required that each shareholder of the petitioning company should transfer some of his shares to another company and its shareholders. Younger J.[21] refused to sanction the scheme on the ground that there was no dispute or difficulty to be resolved by the compromise or arrangement, but the Court of Appeal reversed his decision on the ground that the word "arrangement" should not be limited to something analogous to a compromise.[22] A scheme providing for the holder of the majority of shares to acquire the minority (on favourable terms) is within the scope of the section.[23]

However, the word "arrangement"—as the word "compromise"—is inappropriate to describe a scheme whereby it is proposed that members should abandon all their rights without any compensating advantage. Such a scheme was proposed in *Re N.F.U. Development Trust Ltd.*[24] where the company was a company limited by guarantee and not having a share capital and the scheme was approved by 85 per cent. of the members. Brightman J. held (1) that, although the members did not hold shares they had to be treated as having an equal stake in the company and consequently the requisite majority of "three-fourths in value" had been obtained, but (2) that he had no jurisdiction to sanction the scheme because it was neither a "compromise" nor an "arrangement" within the meaning of section 206.

In 1981 the question arose as to the meaning of an arrangement "between" the company and its members. In *Re Savoy Hotel Ltd.*[25] a shareholder asked the Court to call a separate meeting of the holders of each of the two classes of shares in order to approve a proposed scheme under which that shareholder would acquire all the shares of the Savoy company. This was opposed by the Savoy directors and one of their arguments[26] was that this could not be described as an arrangment "between" the company and its members so that the section did not apply. Nourse J. held[27] that the word "arrangement" had a wide interpretation, and since the scheme

---

[21] *Re Guardian Assurance Co.* [1917] 1 Ch. 431.

[22] Notwithstanding the words of Buckley L.J. in *Re General Motor Cab Co.* [1913] 1 Ch. 377, 384; and see *Shaw* v. *Royce Ltd.* [1911] 1 Ch. 138, 148.

[23] *Singer Manufacturing Co.* v. *Robinow*, 1971 S.C. 11.

[24] [1971] 1 W.L.R. 1548.

[25] [1981] 3 All E.R. 646.

[26] See also para. 79–08, *post.*

[27] Following *Singer Manufacturing Co.* v. *Rabinow* 1971 S.C. 11; *Re. Guardian Assurance Co.* [1917] 1 Ch. 431.

would affect the contractual relationship subsisting between the company and its members by requiring the company to register the applicant in place of existing members as the holders of the company's shares, the rights and obligations between the company and its members were sufficiently affected for the scheme to be an arrangement between them. All that the *Re N.F.U. Development Trust Ltd.* case decided [28] said the judge, was that there should be some element of give and take.

By section 206 (6) the expression "arrangement" is expressly stated to include a reorganisation of the share capital by the consolidation or division of shares of different classes.[29]

Not applicable where ultra vires

79–06 The section does not extend to arrangements which are *ultra vires* the company.[30] Where—as in the case of a reduction of capital—the Acts provide that a specified procedure must be followed to make a transaction effective, that procedure cannot be evaded by means of a scheme under section 206. Thus, where the reduction of capital procedure was not followed, a scheme involving a reduction was not sanctioned but the petition was stood over to enable the company to comply.[31] If, however, the normal procedure is followed, no difficulty arises: thus in one case a reduction of capital, a subsequent increase, and a stay of a winding up were all dealt with in a scheme.[32] On another occasion a liquidation was to be continued for a specified transaction, and to be stayed as soon as that was completed: the court sanctioned this arrangement.[33] It has been held not to be *ultra vires* to provide that one class of shareholders be paid a sum of money in consideration of their forgoing a possible right under articles which were ambiguous.[34]

Not available where other statutory provisions ignored

79–07 The section cannot be used as a means of avoiding normal requirements of the court. For instance, a scheme framed under section 206 which is in effect a scheme under section 287[35] will not be sanctioned unless the safeguards which section 287 insists upon are made part of the scheme; if such safeguards are retained, sanction will be given.[36] So, too, the court refused to sanction a scheme providing for payment of costs and remuneration except upon terms that these be taxed or allowed by the court.[37]

---

28 See note 23a, *ante*.
29 *Balmenach-Glenlivet Distillers Ltd.* v. *Croall* (1906) 8 F. (Ct. of Sn.) 1135.
30 See *Re Cooper, Cooper* v. *Johnson* [1902] W.N. 199; *Re Stephen Walters & Sons* [1926] W.N. 236; *Re Oceanic Steam Navigation Co.* [1939] Ch. 41.
31 *Re Cooper, Cooper* v. *Johnson* [1902] W.N. 199.
32 *Re Stephen Walters & Sons* [1926] W.N. 236.
33 *Re Western of Canada Oil Lands and Works Co.* [1874] W.N. 148.
34 *Caledonian Insurance Co.* v. *Scottish American Investment Co.*, 1951 S.L.T. 23.
35 See *per* Younger J. in *Re Guardian Assurance Co.* [1917] 1 Ch. 431, 441, and the comments of Astbury J. thereon in *Re Anglo-Continental Supply Co.* [1922] 2 Ch. 723, 731.
36 *Re Mortgage Insurance Corporation* [1896] W.N. 4.
37 See *Re St. James' Court Estate* [1944] Ch. 6.

The section would, however, be available (together with the reduction of capital procedure) for enabling a company to turn non-redeemable shares into redeemable preference shares[38]; the scheme would cancel the issued shares, and create thereby a reserve equivalent to their paid-up value, and as the next step would capitalise the reserve thus created by the issue of redeemable preference shares. It may also be used, notwithstanding section 23 or section 32 of the 1980 Act, to alter special rights attached to shares.[39] If a reduction of capital involves treating one part of a class of equity shareholders in a different manner from another part of the same class, then it is desirable to proceed by way of a scheme of arrangement under section 206 rather than by way of a petition under section 66,[40] as the interests of the minority shareholders are thus better protected.[41]

Furthermore, the procedure under section 206 should be used for a compromise with creditors in a compulsory liquidation in preference to that under section 245, if the assets are to be distributed otherwise than strictly in accordance with the creditors' rights.[42]

It is normally also necessary to use the procedure of section 206 in a voluntary winding up prior to a motion by some—but not *all*—contributories for a stay of the winding up on the ground that there are sufficient assets to satisfy all claims and to distribute the surplus to the contributories; in this case the section 206 procedure is necessary to ascertain how many contributories will assent to the motion and how many will object or remain indifferent; the majority required by that section can be used to bind the dissenting or inert minority.[43] Observance of the procedure prescribed by section 206 is not required in this case if "there is secured to [each contributory] the right to receive all that he would have received had the winding up proceeded to its conclusion."[44] Further, cases out of the normal way call for special treatment and the court has discretion in these exceptional cases to grant a stay although the motion is not preceded by a scheme under section 206.[45]

The fact that the scheme involves the purchase by an outsider of all the issued shares of the company does not necessarily mean that it falls within section 209 so as to require approval by the holders of 90 per cent. in value of the shares.[46]

This would impose a higher numerical limit than the wording of the section requires. Section 206 requires the sanction of the court, section 209

---

[38] *Re Sandwell Park Colliery* [1914] 1 Ch. 589; *Re Canning Jarrah Timber Co. (Western Australia)* [1900] 1 Ch. 708, C.A.; *Re Standard Exploration Co., The Times*, March 21, 1902; *Re Tea Corporation* [1904] 1 Ch. 12 (C.A.).

[39] *City Property Investment Trust Corporation, Petitioners*, 1951 S.L.T. 371. See the remarks of Maugham J. with regard to the form and use of proxies at meetings under the section: *Re Dorman, Long & Co.* [1934] Ch. 635, 662 *et seq*.

[40] See para. 32–07, *ante*.

[41] *Re Robert Stephen Holdings Ltd.* [1968] 1 W.L.R. 522, *per* Plowman J.

[42] *Re Trix Ltd.* [1970] 1 W.L.R. 1421; see para. 85–79, *post*.

[43] *Re Calgary and Edmonton Land Co. Ltd.* [1975] 1 W.L.R. 355.

[44] Megarry J., *ibid.* 360.

[45] Megarry J., *ibid.* 360, and *Re South Barrule State Quarry* (1869) L.R. 8 Eq. 688.

[46] *Re National Bank Ltd.* [1966] 1 W.L.R. 819.

does not and the smaller majority under section 206 can thus be justified. But if the purchaser cannot succeed under section 209 because of opposition from the vendor shareholders there must be a very high standard of proof on the part of the applicant to justify obtaining by section 206 what cannot be obtained under section 209. This will not be satisfied if part of the majority in favour of acceptance is a wholly owned subsidiary of the purchaser.[47] This approach has also been adopted in Canada in relation to the compensation provisions for dissenting shareholders in amalgamations under the Canada Business Corporation Act 1974–75–76.[48]

Not applicable where the company, as a separate entity from its members, does not consent to the scheme

79–08 The court has no jurisdiction to sanction an arrangement which does not have the approval of the company either through the board or, if appropriate, by means of a simple majority of the members in general meeting.[49] This applies equally to an arrangement with its creditors[50] or its members[51] even though either may make an application to the court to convene the necessary meetings, the first step in the procedure under section 206.[52] Thus a shareholder cannot force through a scheme whereby it would acquire a majority of the shares of one class against the wishes of the board and the whole membership in general meeting.[53] This is so even though there is no express provision relating to consent in the section. The contrary argument that because a scheme under section 206 (2) once approved becomes binding "on the company" it must embrace a scheme which does not have the company's approval was rejected by reference to the predecessors of section 206.[54]

Procedure under section 206

79–09 A scheme of arrangement under section 206 is a scheme which requires the sanction of the court. For this reason the court insists on certain formalities being followed so that it can check that the matter is dealt with in a manner which the court approves.

Summons for directions

The first step is a summons[55] to the court asking the court[56] to convene

---

[47] *Re Hellenic & General Trust Ltd.* [1976] 1 W.L.R. 123.
[48] *Neonex International Ltd.* v. *Kolasa* (1978) 84 D.L.R. (3d) 446, 452.
[49] *Re Savoy Hotel Ltd.* [1981] 3 All E.R. 646. See also para. 79–05, *ante*.
[50] *Re International Contract Co., Hankey's Case* (1872) 26 L.T. 358; *Re East of England Banking Co., Pearson's Case* (1872) 7 Ch.App. 309.
[51] *Re Savoy Hotel Ltd., supra.; Re Oceanic Steam Navigation Co. Ltd.* [1938] 3 All E.R. 740.
[52] See para. 79–09, *post.*
[53] Thereby achieving a partial take-over. See para. 79–05, *ante*.
[54] Companies Act 1862, s. 136; Joint Stock Companies Arrangement Act 1870, s. 2.
[55] In Scotland the application is made by petition in the Court of Session or by Initial Writ in the sheriff court if it has concurrent jurisdiction. The rest of this chapter may be taken, *mutatis mutandis*, as valid under Scots law.
[56] For application to the Vacation Court, see *Re Showerings, Vine Products & Whiteways Ltd.* [1968] 1 W.L.R. 1381. See also the Practice Directions of March 3, 1977, reproduced in Vol. II, para. A–5001, and February 23, 1978; Vol. II, para. A–5002; *Dailuaine Talisker Distillery* v. *Mackenzie* 1910 S.C. 913, 1910 2 S.L.T. 57; *Bruce Peebles & Co. Ltd.* v. *Wm. Bain & Co. Ltd.* 1918 S.C. 781, 1918 2 S.L.T. 217.

the necessary meetings. This application is normally made by the company, but any creditor or member may make the application (s. 206 (1)). It would, therefore, seem that a scheme could be started even if the company did not wish it, but the court will, it seems, refuse to convene the meetings if the company, either through its board or a simple majority of its members in a general meeting, has not approved the proposed scheme. This would be an exercise of the court's discretion and not a limit on its powers.[57]

No meeting is required of any class which is not concerned in the arrangement[58]: and such a class cannot successfully object to the arrangement.[59]

What constitutes a class

79–10 The court does not itself consider at this point what classes of creditors or members should be made parties to the scheme. This is for the company to decide, in accordance with what the scheme purports to achieve.[60] If, *e.g.* rights of ordinary shareholders are to be altered, but those of preference shares are not touched, a meeting of ordinary shareholders will be necessary but not of preference shareholders. If there are different groups within a class the interests of which are different from the rest of the class, or which are to be treated differently under the scheme, such groups must be treated as separate classes for the purpose of the scheme.[61] Moreover, when the company has decided what classes are necessary parties to the scheme, it may happen that one class will consist of a small number of persons who will all be willing to be bound by the scheme. In that case it is not the practice to hold a meeting of that class, but to make the class a party to the scheme and to obtain the consent of all its members to be bound. It is, however, necessary for at least one class meeting to be held in order to give the court jurisdiction under the section.

It will be seen from what has been said above that great care must be taken in considering what for the purpose of the scheme constitutes a class. If meetings of the proper classes have not been held, the court may not sanction the scheme.

In *Sovereign Life Assurance Co.* v. *Dodd*,[62] the court had to consider whether certain creditors formed a single class or two different classes. Bowen L.J. said[63]:

> "It seems plain that we must give such a meaning to the term 'class' as will prevent the section being so worked as to result in confiscation

---

[57] *Re Savoy Hotel Ltd.* [1981] 3 All E.R. 646, 657. The submission in the 22nd edition of this work to the contrary, para. 75–08, is thus no longer tenable except by reference to the Court of Appeal. In Scotland it has been held that ratification by the company by special resolution is competent. *Hector & Sons*, 1947 S.C. 641.

[58] *Brownfield Guild Pottery Society* [1898] W.N. 80; *Re Tea Corporation* [1904] 1 Ch. 12; *Re Mortgage Insurance Corporation* [1896] W.N. 4; *Clydesdale Bank*, 1950 S.L.T. 123.

[59] *Re International Contract Co.* (1872) 26 L.T. 358.

[60] See below in the text, and *Practice Note* [1934] W.N. 142.

[61] *Tritonia Ltd.*, 1948, S.L.T. (Notes) 5.

[62] [1892] 2 Q.B. 573.

[63] At p. 583.

and injustice, and that it must be confined to those persons whose rights are not so dissimilar as to make it impossible for them to consult together with a view to their common interest."

In that case the court found that persons whose interests were dissimilar had been treated as a single class, and accordingly it refused to sanction the scheme.[64]

In *Re Hellenic & General Trust Ltd.*[65] Templeman J. stressed that it is the responsibility of the applicants to see that the class meetings are properly constituted. In that case it was held that the majority shareholder, being a wholly owned subsidiary of the outside purchaser for the shares, constituted a separate class from the other shareholders and that accordingly the scheme failed. It was also suggested that a parent company owning 50 per cent. or more of the shares of the subsidiary company can be assumed to have a community of interest for the purposes of section 206. The judge relied on the dictum by Brown L.J. (*ante*) and added: "Vendors consulting together with a view to their common interest in an offer made by a purchaser would look askance at the presence among them of a wholly owned subsidiary of the purchaser."

Classes of creditors

79–11 The question of what constitutes a creditor and what a class of creditors may be much more difficult than that which concerns shareholders. In general any person having a pecuniary claim against the company capable of estimate is a creditor.[66] Creditors can be divided into three categories (which may themselves overlap), of preferential creditors, secured creditors and unsecured creditors.

All preferential creditors who have no security for their debts can be treated as one class, and if, as will frequently be the case, all preferential creditors are to be paid in full, they will be a single class whether or not some are secured and some unsecured.

Similarly, all unsecured creditors will normally form a single class, except where some of them are to be treated in a manner different from the rest and have different interests which might conflict. In such a case fresh classes will be carved out. Thus, in the case of an insurance company the insured persons whose policies have matured form a different class of creditors from those whose policies have not matured.[67]

Secured creditors are, however, in a more complicated position. Those who have a common security, *e.g.* holders of debentures ranking *pari passu*,[68] will comprise a class; but where each of a number of creditors has a similar though not common security the position may not be the same. It

---

[64] [1892] 2 Q.B. 573. See also *Re Hellenic & General Trust Ltd.* [1976] 1 W.L.R. 123, where a wholly owned subsidiary of the purchaser of shares under the scheme was held to constitute a separate class from the independent shareholders.
[65] [1976] 1 W.L.R. 123.
[66] *Re Albert Life Assurance Co.* (1871) 6 Ch. App. 381, 386.
[67] *Sovereign Life Assurance Co.* v. *Dodd* [1892] 2 Q.B. 573.
[68] *Slater* v. *Darlaston Steel and Iron Co.* [1877] W.N. 139.

is, however, submitted that provided that the meaning of the word "class" given by Bowen L.J.[69] is applicable, and the rights of the creditors concerned are not so dissimilar as to make it impossible for them to consult together with a view to their common interest, such creditors can be treated as a single class. It can only be decided in the circumstances of each case whether a group of creditors fall within the meaning of a class as defined by Bowen L.J.

Further, there may be a considerable difference between the position of a creditor whose debt is governed by English law[70] and a creditor whose debt is governed by foreign law. Indeed, it may happen that the mere residence of a creditor abroad in a country where the company has assets will distinguish him from a creditor resident in England. It is not necessary, for the purposes of considering the jurisdiction of the English court under the section, to consider what the effect will be of a scheme which the court sanctions if one of the creditors bound by the scheme attempts to enforce his debt against the company's assets abroad in contravention of the scheme.[71] All that need be considered is whether the classes of creditors are properly constituted. So, in *Re English, Scottish and Australian Chartered Bank*,[72] creditors were treated as a single class whether their debts arose in Australia or in England, and this, it is submitted, is the correct approach.[73]

The court might, however, take into account as a factor to be considered when deciding whether or not to sanction the scheme any risk that creditors resident abroad might be able largely to stultify the effect of the scheme by bringing an action abroad and enforcing their debts against foreign assets of the company.

If any class exists which would have no possible interest in the company, *e.g.* where shareholders of a company have no entitlement because all the assets are exhaustible by creditors, the court may sanction a scheme even if such a class objects.[74]

Form of summons

9–12 The summons seeks the directions of the court for the convening and holding of the class meetings.[75] In due course the notice convening the

[69] Quoted *ante* from *Sovereign Life Assurance Co.* v. *Dodd* [1892] 2 Q.B. 573, 583.

[70] In Scotland the position seems to be the same if for "English law" there is substituted "Scots law."

[71] See *New Zealand Loan and Mercantile Agency Co.* v. *Morrison* [1898] A.C. 349.

[72] [1893] 3 Ch. 385.

[73] See the general remarks in this connection in the case last cited.

[74] *Re International Contract Co.* (1872) 26 L.T. 358.

[75] This is dealt with in detail in Palmer's *Company Precedents* (16th ed.), Pt. I, pp. 1094 *et seq.* The application should include a request for the calling of meetings of special classes of shareholders whose interests are affected by the scheme; but it should not request the calling of a general meeting of all the members, as the company can call such a meeting without any order of the court: *Cayzer Irvine & Co. Ltd., Petitioners*, 1963 S.L.T. 94. For the form of petition in Scotland, see *Encyclopedia of Scottish Legal Styles*, Replacement Vol. 3, pp. 404–420. The petition is to the Inner House unless the sheriff court has jurisdiction, when the action may be initiated, as an alternative by an Initial Writ to that court. See further *Merchiston Castle School*, 1946 S.C. 23; *Wilson Bros.* v. *D. B. Howat & Co.*, 1939 S.L.T. 68.

meetings is sent out, together with a circular and forms of proxy. Notice of the scheme is also given by advertisement in a paper, as directed by the court. At the meetings voting is not on a show of hands but must be by poll, since the statutory majority is concerned with the value of the votes.

After the meetings have been held a petition is presented to the court to sanction the scheme. The petition need not state that the company is carrying on business.[76]

Exercise of the court's discretion

79–13 Before the court sanctions a scheme it will normally need to be satisfied on four matters[77]:

1. *The statutory provisions must have been complied with*

The court must see that the resolutions are passed by the statutory majority in value and number in accordance with the section at a meeting or meetings duly convened and held. Upon this depends the jurisdiction of the court to confirm the scheme.[78]

The court has no power to usurp the right of the class of members or creditors to decide whether they approve the scheme. If, therefore, a class whose interests are affected by a scheme neither assents to the scheme nor approves it at a meeting in accordance with the section, the court cannot confirm the scheme even if it considers that the class concerned is being fairly dealt with, or that it would approve the scheme.[79] The court will not, however, upset a scheme for minor irregularities, as where consent of a class has been subsequently obtained,[80] and where the necessary majority of one class was absent when the petition was presented, the court allowed a fresh petition to be presented subsequently when the necessary majority was later obtained, without requiring the other class meetings to be held again.[81]

2. *The class must have been fairly represented*

79–14 The court must be satisfied that those who attended the meeting are fairly representative of the class and that the statutory majority did not coerce the minority in order to promote interests adverse to those of the class whom they purport to represent.

This requirement is, in part, an offshoot of the first. As regards the majority, there are two requirements: the majority who vote in favour of

---

[76] *Re Great Universal Stores Ltd.* [1960] 1 W.L.R. 78.
[77] *Re Anglo–Continental Supply Co.* [1922] 2 Ch. 723, 733.
[78] *Per* Maugham J. in *Re Dorman, Long & Co.* [1934] Ch. 635, 655. See also *La Lainière de Roubaix* v. *Glen Grove Co.* 1926 S.C. 91, 1926 S.L.T. 5.
[79] See *Re Neath and Brecon Ry.* [1892] 1 Ch. 349, a scheme under the Railway Companies Act 1867; *Re Hellenic & General Trust Ltd.* [1976] 1 W.L.R. 123. But the court in Scotland has dispensed with a class meeting where the members would clearly not be prejudiced. *William Dixon Ltd.*, 1948 S.C. 511.
[80] *Re Dynevor, Duffryn and Neath Abbey Collieries Co.* (1879) 11 Ch.D. 605.
[81] *Re United Provident Assurance Co.* [1911] W.N. 40.

the scheme must be first a majority in number of those members of the class (whether of creditors or shareholders) who are present and voting; and, secondly, it must be three-fourths in value of the holding of such persons.

Thus, if there are 100 members voting of whom (to take an extreme example) one member holds 901 shares and the remainder hold one each, the 99 shareholders holding one share each cannot force a scheme against the vote of the holder of the 901 shares, because they do not muster three-fourths in value. Conversely, that shareholder and 49 of the others could not force a scheme against the votes of the remaining 50 because there would not be a majority in number. The same principle applies to creditors.

It will be seen that the majorities are of those who vote, not of those entitled to vote nor of those who are present.[82] Thus, shareholders who are not present in person or by proxy, or who, although present, do not vote, may be ignored.

79–15 However, this is not the whole requirement, because in addition the court requires to be satisfied that the class is *fairly* represented. If, for instance, there were altogether 1,000 shareholders holding 10,000 shares in all, the court would be unlikely to be satisfied by the statutory majorities at a meeting at which 10 members holding 100 shares in all were present and voted.

If a creditor votes only in respect of part of his claim, he is not precluded from having the benefit of the scheme for the whole of his claim, or for a second claim in respect of which he did not vote.[83]

In the case of shares, each share will carry the same value for this purpose, and, in the case of creditors, the value will depend upon the amount of their debts which come within the class. For this purpose a creditor will only be able to claim in respect of a debt which can have an estimate placed upon it. Thus a lessee from the company, having a right of indemnity against it, has a pecuniary claim and can be bound by the scheme.[84]

A person holding a debenture payable to bearer must produce his debenture before he can be allowed to vote.[85]

The fact that the scheme is approved by the statutory majority is a strong indication that it is a fair one. But this indication is reversed if a substantial proportion of that majority are in a position to gain more from the scheme than other members of the class by reason of their interests in some other capacity; *e.g.* where creditors are to give up something in favour of shareholders, and some of the creditors are also shareholders, the interests of those persons as shareholders may be sufficient to obtain for them a greater

[82] *Re Bessemer Steel and Ordnance Co.* (1875) 1 Ch.D. 251; *California Redwood Co.* 1885 13 R. 335. The requirement was different under the 1908 and earlier Acts.
[83] *Curtis* v. *B.U.R.T. Co.* (1912) 28 T.L.R. 585.
[84] *Re Midland Coal, Coke and Iron Co.* [1895] 1 Ch. 267.
[85] *Re Wedgwood Coal and Iron Co.* (1877) 6 Ch.D. 627. *Columbia Steamship Co.* 1895, 2 S.L.T. 536.

benefit in that capacity than they sacrifice as creditors.[86] In such a case the court will scrutinise the scheme with additional vigilance, and if a minority of the creditors object the court will consider whether or not it is proper to count the votes of the persons with the conflicting interests.

The principle is that expressed in another connection by Lindley M.R. in *Allen* v. *Gold Reefs of West Africa Ltd.*[87]:

> " . . . the power conferred by it must, like all other powers, be exercised subject to those general principles of law and equity which are applicable to all powers conferred on majorities and enabling them to bind minorities. It must be exercised, not only in the manner required by law, but also bona fide for the benefit of the company as a whole, and it must not be exceeded. These conditions are always implied, and are seldom, if ever, expressed."

Bowen L.J. explained[88] the attitude of the court to this principle in cases where there may be a conflict of interest. The case concerned a scheme for binding creditors and, after remarking that some members of the class might have interests of a predominant kind which they held because they belong to some other class, he said:

> "Therefore, although in a meeting which is to be held under this section it is perfectly fair for every man to do that which is best for himself, yet the court, which has to see what is reasonable and just as regards the interests of the whole class, would certainly be very much influenced in its decision, if it turned out that the majority was composed of persons who had not really the interests of that class at stake."

If a holder of a substantial block of the class concerned is offered some inducement to support the scheme, this may well be sufficient to render nugatory the purported approval, unless it is disclosed to the members of the class.[89] If full disclosure is made, the court will, in appropriate circumstances, approve the scheme, and will even allow the votes of the person treated preferentially.[90]

However, in *Re Hellenic & General Trust Ltd.*[91] the scheme for the sale of all the shares to an outside purchaser was not sanctioned even though it was held to be fair "or more than fair" to the ordinary shareholders as a class. The objector did not wish to sell its shares as it would thereby incur a capital gains tax assessment in Greece and Templeman J. held that this individual loss should be borne in mind even though each shareholder "must put himself in the impossible position of deciding what is in the best interests of the class." But the scheme failed on other grounds[92] and these would seem to have been the dominant reasons for refusing approval.

---

[86] See, *e.g. Re Wedgwood Coal and Iron Co.* (1877) 6 Ch.D. 627.
[87] [1900] 1 Ch. 656, 671; see para. 14–19, *ante*.
[88] In *Re Alabama, New Orleans, Texas and Pacific Junction Ry.* [1891] 1 Ch. 213, 244.
[89] *British American Nickel Corporation* v. *M. J. O'Brien Ltd.* [1927] A.C. 369, P.C.
[90] *Goodfellow* v. *Nelson Line (Liverpool)* [1912] 2 Ch. 324.
[91] [1976] 1 W.L.R. 123.
[92] See para. 79–16, *post*.

3. *The arrangement must be such as a man of business would reasonably approve*

79–16 In exercising its discretion whether or not to sanction a scheme, the court, as we have seen, treats it as cardinal that its function does not extend to usurping the view of the members or creditors. This does not mean that, provided that the resolutions are duly passed, and that there is no coercion of a minority by a majority, the court is bound to confirm the scheme and has no discretion.[93] The court is not a mere rubber stamp. It will look at the scheme to see that it is a reasonable one: if it concludes that there is "such an objection to it as that any reasonable man might say that he could not approve it,"[94] then the court may refuse to confirm the scheme.[95]

The court will, however, be strongly influenced by a big majority vote,[96] for, provided that the scheme is fair and equitable, the court will not itself judge upon the commercial merits, which is the function of the class itself. The court will be slow to differ from the conclusion of the majority.[97]

The court will always in the exercise of its discretion refuse an inequitable scheme, as where a creditor had been persuaded not to complete execution of his judgment on the strength of an undertaking given by the company, and the undertaking was frustrated by the scheme.[98]

4. *The arrangement must be compatible with section 209*

If the proposed arrangement is one for the purchase of all the company's shares this may be achieved under section 206 by a three-quarters majority which then becomes binding on a dissenting minority. Under section 209[99] the purchase of shares in a take-over bid only becomes compulsory on the minority if nine-tenths of the shares have been purchased. Thus, a dissenting shareholder with more than one-tenth, but with less than a quarter, of the shares, who can successfully oppose the sale of his shares under section 209, may lose that protection if a scheme is approved under section 206. This situation arose in *Re Hellenic & General Trust Ltd.*[1] where it was accepted, following *Re National Bank Ltd.*[2] that since section 206, unlike

---

[93] As suggested by counsel (Sir Horace Davey) in argument in *Re Alabama, New Orleans, Texas and Pacific Junction Ry.* [1891] 1 Ch. 213, 234.

[94] *Per* Lindley L.J. in *Re Alabama, New Orleans, Texas and Pacific Junction Ry.* [1891] 1 Ch. 213, 239; and see the judgment of Vaughan Williams J. in *Re English, Scottish and Australian Chartered Bank* [1893] 3 Ch. 385, 396 *et seq.*, where he discusses this question and various dicta of the judges upon it. Also *Gillies* v. *Dawson* 1823 20 R. 1119; *Edinburgh etc. Mortgage Co.* v. *Lang's Trustees* 1909 S.C. 488; 1909, 1 S.L.T. 130.

[95] Thus in *Re N.F.U. Development Trust Ltd.* [1972] 1 W.L.R. 1548, Brightman J. rejected as unreasonable a scheme under which it was proposed that the members of a company limited by guarantee and not having a share capital should be expropriated without compensation.

[96] *Re Empire Mining Co.* (1840) 44 Ch.D. 402.

[97] *Re London Chartered Bank of Australia* ([1893] 3 Ch. 540. *Shandon Hydropathic* 1911 S.C. 1153; 1911, 2 S.L.T. 267.

[98] *Re Richards & Co.* (1879) 11 Ch.D. 676. It has even been refused on the grounds of an increase in a dissenting shareholder's personal tax liability. *Re Hellenic & General Trust Ltd.* [1976] 1 W.L.R. 123.

[99] See para. 81–05, *post*.

[1] [1976] 1 W.L.R. 133.

[2] [1966] 1 W.L.R. 819.

section 209, required the court's consent, the smaller majority required for expropriation of the minority's shares could be justified. There is therefore no requirement of a nine-tenths majority for a scheme under section 206 which is akin to a scheme under section 209. But the court refused to sanction the scheme, even though it was fair to the ordinary shareholders as a class, and the dissenter who owned 13.95 per cent. of the shares, objected for personal fiscal reasons. The court would not allow section 206 to be used to deprive the dissenter of his property, which he could lawfully retain under section 209, without a "very high standard of proof" from the applicant. This had not been discharged, principally because the majority accepting shareholder was a wholly owned subsidiary of the purchaser.[3] The relationship between the Canadian equivalents of sections 206 and 209 was discussed in *Neonex International Ltd.* v. *Kolasa*,[4] where a similar approach was adopted.

Effect of court's sanction

79–17 Once the sanction of the court has been given to the scheme, it is binding on all the creditors or the classes of creditors, or on the members or classes of members, who were parties to the scheme, and on the company. If the company is being wound up, the scheme is binding on the liquidator and contributories (s. 206 (2)). The scheme cannot afterwards be altered, even if shareholders and creditors acquiesce in the alteration.[5]

If a company which is a joint and several debtor is discharged by a scheme, the other joint and several debtors are not affected but remain so liable.[6]

The order sanctioning the scheme is not effective (and therefore the scheme is not effective) until an office copy of the order has been delivered to the Registrar of Companies for registration (s. 206 (3)). The order of the court may qualify as a "conveyance or transfer on sale" within the meaning of Schedule I to the Stamp Act 1891 and in that case has to be stamped *ad valorem*, even though the scheme is not operative until the office copy of the order is delivered to the Registrar of Companies; failure to stamp the order makes it inadmissible in evidence by virtue of section 14 (4) of the Act of 1891.[7]

After a scheme has become effective, a copy of the order must be annexed to every copy of the company's memorandum of association issued thereafter, or in the case of a company whose constitution is not found in a memorandum of association, to the document of its constitution (s. 206 (3)).

---

[3] See para. 79–15, *ante*.
[4] (1978) 84 D.L.R. (3d) 447.
[5] *Devi* v. *People's Bank of Northern India* [1938] 4 All E.R. 337.
[6] *Re Garner's Motors Ltd.* [1937] Ch. 594.
[7] *Sun Alliance Insurance Ltd.* v. *I.R.C.* [1971] 1 W.L.R. 432.

Explanatory statement under section 207

79–18 Prior to 1947 there was no statutory requirement for a circular explaining the scheme to be sent out to those concerned. Nevertheless some sort of explanation was normally necessary in order to enable shareholders or creditors to understand the scheme upon which they are asked to vote, and it was a common practice to send out a circular. In one case a great deal of discussion arose as to the adequacy of the circular which was sent, and Maugham J. said that it was "the duty of the court very carefully to scrutinise the circular when the matters involved are matters of considerable difficulty and doubt."[8]

An explanatory circular is now a statutory requirement.[9] Section 207 requires that with every notice summoning a meeting pursuant to a scheme under section 206, there shall be sent a statement explaining the effect of the compromise or arrangement. In particular any material interests of the directors must be stated, whether such interests arise in their capacity as directors or as members or creditors of the company, or otherwise, and if the effect of the compromise or arrangement is different in regard to the interests of the directors from its effect in regard to the interests of other persons, this must be stated (s. 207 (1) (*a*)). Where a statement said "the directors have no interest in the scheme other than as members along with other members of the company," this was not a sufficient compliance with this requirement.[10] If, however, there are no differences, this need not be stated[11]: the section merely requires that any differences be stated. The requirement applies not only to beneficial interests of directors, but also to interests as trustees.[12]

If a meeting is convened by advertisement, the advertisement must state where a copy of the statement may be obtained (s. 207 (1) (*b*)). Even if every member is sent a copy of the statement, the omission to state in the advertisement where a copy is obtainable will invalidate the scheme.[13]

If the rights of debenture holders are involved, the statement must deal with the interests of any trustees of any deed securing the debentures in similar fashion (s. 207 (2)).

Persons whose interests must be disclosed are bound to give any necessary information to the company for the purpose (s. 207 (5)).

Default in compliance with the section gives rise to a fine (s. 207 (4)).

The section appears to be largely concerned with details, but the importance of it lies mainly in making it obligatory to explain the effect of the scheme. This is not satisfied by sending to all shareholders a copy of the

---

[8] *Re Dorman, Long & Co.* [1934] Ch. 635, 665.
[9] But see *Clydesdale Bank* 1950 S.L.T. 123, note (2), *infra*.
[10] *Coltness Iron Co., Petitioners*, 1951 S.L.T. 344.
[11] *City Property Investment Trust Corporation, Petitioners*, 1951 S.L.T. 371; *Scottish Eastern Investment Trust Ltd.*, 1966 S.L.T. 285.
[12] *Second Scottish Investment Trust and Anor., Petitioners*, 1962 S.L.T. 392.
[13] *City Property Investment Trust Corporation, Petitioners*, 1951 S.L.T. 371; *Scottish Eastern Investment Trust Ltd.*, 1966 S.L.T. 285.

petition.[14] The deliberate omission from the statement of information which is exempt information in relation to the company's accounts does not preclude the court from sanctioning the arrangement, if the evidence is sufficient to satisfy the court that the scheme is fair and disclosure of the exempt information might result in damage to shareholders.[15]

Powers of court to facilitate scheme

79–19 The possible types of scheme under section 206 are of a wide variety. It is, therefore, provided under section 208 that the court shall have very wide powers for facilitating a scheme. This section applies in the case of the reconstruction of a company, and of an amalgamation or scheme where one company acquires the undertaking of another provided that the transferee company is itself a company under the Acts (s. 208 (5)). Specific powers are given relating to the following:

(1) The transfer of the property or liabilities of one company to another (s. 208 (1) (*a*)). This does not include a power to enforce the transfer of contracts of service,[16] or of the rights, duties or powers of an executor.[17] Transfers ordered to be made under the section can be made freed (in accordance with the scheme) from any charge (s. 208 (2)).

(2) The allotting of shares, debentures, policies or other like interests (s. 208 (1) (*b*)). This makes it clear that the section applies to insurance companies.

(3) The continuity of legal proceedings (s. 208 (1) (*c*)).

(4) The dissolution of the transferor company without the procedure of winding up (s. 208 (1) (*d*)).

(5) Provision for dissentients (s. 208 (1) (*e*)). Thus, if a scheme was, in effect, similar to one under section 287[18] and some members dissented, the court could impose and enforce a condition providing for such persons.

(6) Finally, general powers are given incidental, consequential or supplemental to the scheme (s. 208 (1) (*f*)).

The order under section 208 may be made by the order sanctioning the scheme or by a subsequent order (s. 208 (1)). If such an order is likely to be required, the order sanctioning the scheme should give liberty to apply. The further application is then made in chambers under R.S.C. 1965, Ord. 102, r. 7 (2) (*b*).[19] This enables

[14] *Rankin & Blackmore, Petitioners*, 1950 S.L.T. 160; see also *Peter Scott & Co., Petitioners*, 1950 S.C. 507, and *Coltness Iron Co., Petitioners*, 1951 S.L.T. 344. When all the shares in the companies proposing the scheme were held by one shareholder, a statement under s. 207 was held to be unnecessary. *Clydesdale Bank*, 1950 S.L.T. 123.

[15] *Re National Bank Ltd.* [1966] 1 W.L.R. 819.

[16] *Nokes* v. *Doncaster Amalgamated Collieries* [1940] A.C. 1014.

[17] *Re Skinner (deceased)* [1958] 1 W.L.R. 1043.

[18] See para. 80–01, *post*.

[19] See *Practice Note* [1939] W.N. 121; *Re Star Tea Co.* [1930] W.N. 4.

the court in due course to bind a company which comes into existence after, and as a result of, the scheme being sanctioned: but the section can also be used, when convenient, if the transferee company already exists.[20] It is not legally necessary to specify all the company's properties.[21] The equivalent procedure in Scotland is governed by the Rules of Court 1965.

[20] *Practice Note* [1939] W.N. 121.
[21] *Re "L" Hotel Co. and Langham Hotel Co.*

CHAPTER 80

RECONSTRUCTIONS BY VOLUNTARY LIQUIDATION

80–01 SECTION 287 of the 1948 Act gives power to a company to reconstruct by means of a voluntary liquidation wherein the liquidator transfers the assets of the company to a new company in exchange for shares or other securities of the new company. These shares or other securities are then distributed amongst the shareholders of the old company and in this way the shareholders of the old company become holders of shares or other securities in the new company.[1] This enables the old company to retain certain of its assets—in particular any cash which it may have—and to distribute these to its shareholders whilst retaining for the shareholders an interest in the business that until then was carried on by the old company.

The section provides for any such arrangement to be binding on all members, provided that the section is complied with. Shareholders who do not approve the arrangement can, however, obtain instead what they would have been entitled to had the company been wound up, its assets realised, and the proceeds distributed amongst the members in accordance with their rights.[2]

The section applies whether or not a company has already gone into liquidation, but it is limited to a members' voluntary liquidation. If the company is in a creditors' voluntary winding up, the powers of the liquidator under the section are only exercisable with the sanction of the court or the committee of inspection (s. 298). If the company is in compulsory liquidation the section cannot itself be used, but the same principles can be adopted by a scheme carried out pursuant to section 245 of the 1948 Act.[3] The rights of members in the case of a scheme under section 245 are the same as if the scheme were under section 287.

The section is also valuable where two companies wish to amalgamate. There are two principal methods by which the amalgamation may be achieved, but the substance is in each case the same. By one method, one company in effect absorbs the other; by the second method both companies are, in effect, absorbed by a new company formed for that purpose.

If the assets which the absorbing company receives in consideration of the shares issued by it exceeds in value the nominal amount of the shares, the excess no longer has to be transferred to a share premium account.[4]

---

[1] As to the power of trustees to accept such a scheme, see Trustee Act 1925, s. 10 (3), and *Re Walker's Settlement* [1935] Ch. 567. The Trustee Act 1925 does not apply to Scotland.
[2] *Re Mysore West Gold Mining Co.* (1889) 42 Ch.D. 535.
[3] See *Re Agra and Masterman's Bank* (1866) L.R. 12 Eq. 509n.; *Re Cambrian Mining Co.* (1882) 48 L.T. 114; *Re Imperial Mercantile Credit Association* (1871) L.R. 12 Eq. 504; *Re London and Exchange Bank* (1867) 16 L.T. 340.
[4] 1981 Act, s.37; see para. 24–47, *ante*, and para. 80–13, *post*.

Transactions to which section 287 applies

80–02 The powers given by section 287 can be used by any company formed and registered under the Acts,[5] or under one of the earlier Companies Acts, provided that it is being wound up altogether voluntarily. It is irrelevant whether the winding up is a members' or creditors' winding up.

It has been held[6] that the section applies to a winding up under supervision, presumably because such a winding up has commenced as a voluntary one. However, subsection (5) provides, *inter alia*, that the special resolution dealt with below shall not be valid if within a year an order is made for the winding up of the company subject to the supervision of the court. This provision suggests that the above construction may be wrong, and this is borne out by section 315, where in subsection (1) such a winding up is distinguished from one which is "altogether" voluntary, and subsection (2) of that section makes such a winding up for all purposes, save those excepted, a winding up by the court. But a scheme on the same lines can then be carried out under section 245.

Where a company is already in voluntary liquidation, the transactions authorised by the section may be carried out at any time.[7] Where it is still a going concern, the first step in such transactions must be to place the company into voluntary liquidation. This liquidation carries all the normal consequences of a liquidation, including such effects as breach of covenants in a lease, or of a service contract, unless the lease or agreement provides otherwise. The company (which in the section and hereafter is called "the transferor company") can then proceed by its liquidator to transfer the whole, or part only, of its business or property, to another company (which in the section and hereafter is called "the transferee company").

To what body assets may be transferred under section 287

80–03 Unlike the transferor company, the transferee company need not be a company formed and registered under the Acts or one of the earlier Acts. The section requires it to be "another company whether a company within the meaning of this Act or not."

Thus, it can be a company incorporated by charter, formed under a different Act, a foreign company,[8] or indeed any association falling within

[5] An unregistered company may become registered and then proceed under the section: *Southall* v. *British Mutual Life Assurance Society* (1870) L.R. 11 Eq. 65; on appeal (1871) 6 Ch.App. 614.

[6] See *Re Imperial Mercantile Credit Association* (1871) L.R. 12 Eq. 504; *cf. Re Cambrian Mining Co.* (1882) 48 L.T. 114. But see *Re Hafod Hotel Co.* (1868) 18 L.T. 144.

[7] The section does not, on the face of it, appear to cover a company already in liquidation, but the same procedure can be adopted, and the same principles apply, where it is already in liquidation.

[8] *Re Irrigation Co. of France, ex p. Fox* (1871) 6 Ch.App.176.

the meaning of the word "company." The dictionary meanings given to the word (so far as applicable to the context of this section) are

> "A body of persons combined or incorporated for some common object, or for the joint execution or performance of anything especially a mediaeval trade guild and hence, a corporation historically representing such, as in the London City Companies" and, in relation to commerce, "an association formed to carry on some commercial or industrial undertaking."[9]

From this it will be seen that it is essential that there should be an association of two or more persons, but there is no need for them to be incorporated or to have a separate juridical personality. It would appear to follow from the above dictionary definition that even a partnership is a "company" in the meaning of this section.[10] In *Commissioners of the Caledonian Canal* v. *Councils of Inverness and Argyll*,[11] it was held that a body of commissioners incorporated by a special Act of Parliament to own and operate a canal in Scotland was a canal company within the meaning of a general Act of Parliament relating to the control of canals. That case was a very special one in which in the context the words "canal company" required to be given a very wide meaning. If, on the other hand, there is no body of persons associated together, the necessary element is not present.

There is no reported case which assists in indicating the limit to be placed on the phrase "another company, whether a company within the meaning of this Act or not." It is clear that the transferee cannot be an individual, even if he is a trustee for another company.[12]

The agreement for transfer

80–04 The next step[13] is for the agreement to be made with the other company. By this it is not intended to be implied that the steps must be in a specific order. It will normally be the case that the whole transaction is worked out before any step is taken.

The directors may already have made the appropriate arrangements, and even if this was outside their powers, the agreement can be ratified by the company in general meeting.[13] The liquidator must be authorised to carry out this agreement and this authority must be conferred upon him by a special resolution.[14] The notice convening the meeting to pass this resolution must state that the resolution is proposed pursuant to section 287.[15] The resolution may either give a general authority, or authority in respect of a specific arrangement, and it must authorise the liquidator to

---

[9] *New English Dictionary,* by J. A. H. Murray, published at the Clarendon Press, Oxford.
[10] *A fortiori* a Scottish partnership which has a separate judicial personality.
[11] (1894) 31 Sc.L.R. 830; 1894, 21 R. 1045; 2 S.L.T. 162.
[12] *Bird* v. *Bird's Patent Deodorising and Utilising Sewage Co.* (1874) 9 Ch.App. 358.
[13] *Clinch* v. *Financial Corporation* (1868) L.R. 5 Eq 450; affd. 4 Ch.App. 117.
[14] *Etheridge* v. *Central Uruguayan Northern Extension Ry.* [1913] 1 Ch. 425; *Re Cambrian Mining Co.* (1882) 48 L.T. 114.
[15] *Imperial Bank of China, India and Japan* v. *Bank of Hindustan, China and Japan* (1868) L.R. 6 Eq. 91; *Re Irrigation Co. of France, ex p. Fox* (1871) 6 Ch.App. 176.

receive as consideration, or as part of the consideration, for the transfer or sale of the business or property, shares, policies or other like interests in the transferee company, for distribution amongst the members of the transferor company.

The subsection is drafted in terms to permit the liquidator to enter into any arrangement whereby the members of the transferor company may participate in the profits of or receive any other benefit from the transferee company, in lieu of receiving cash, shares, policies or other like interests. This further permission is peculiar in two ways: first, since the vendor is the transferor company and not its shareholders, the shareholders would not be entitled to receive anything; and, secondly, the further permission is not expressed to be subject to the consent of the company. However, when the section is read as a whole it is clear that the intention is that the shareholders may authorise the liquidator in very wide terms to make some arrangement whereby the shareholders will eventually have an interest in a new company instead of their interest in the transferor company, or in addition to their interest in the remaining property of the transferor company. This special resolution can be passed before, concurrently with, or after the resolution to wind up.[16] It will apparently be effective, since the power given is statutory, even if the company has not power under its constitution to sell its undertaking.[17] The subsection is sufficiently widely worded to enable an insurance company to take advantage of it, for the power which may be given by the resolution to the liquidator includes not only a power to accept shares or other like interests in the transferee company, for distribution amongst the members, but also a power to accept policies. Thus where policyholders are, *ipso facto*, members of an insurance company, they can become bound under the section to take policies with the transferee company in place of the transferor company (subject always to their rights of dissent and refusal).[18]

Effect of arrangement under section 287

80–05 The effect of an arrangement under section 287 can be seen by considering four simple examples of its use:

(1) Company A sells to a newly formed company all its business and property except a sum in the bank, in exchange for shares in the new company credited as fully paid. The shares in the new company are then distributed, along with the cash retained, to the shareholders of Company A.

(2) Company B sells the whole of its undertaking and property to a new company for shares in the new company credited as partly paid. The

---

[16] s. 287 (5).

[17] *Southall* v. *British Mutual Life Assurance Society* (1870) L.R. 11 Eq. 65; on appeal (1871) 6 Ch.App. 614; *Clinch* v. *Financial Corporation* (1868) L.R. 5 Eq. 450, 472; affd. (1868) 4 Ch.App. 117.

[18] See para. 80–07, *post*.

shares of the new company are then distributed to the shareholders of B, subject to their right of dissent or refusal.[17] If they accept, they will be burdened with a liability which previously did not exist, so that fresh capital can be raised. In such circumstances it is usual to arrange with underwriters to guarantee the provision of the new capital.

(3) Company C sells the whole of its undertaking and property to Company D, which is already a flourishing company. The shareholders of Company C thus become shareholders of Company D, and Company C is dissolved. The business and property of the two companies thus become amalgamated into one company.

(4) Companies E and F want to amalgamate. A new company, E (Holdings), is formed. E (Holdings) issues shares to the shareholders in E and F in exchange for their shares in E and F. The former shareholders in E and F thus become holders of shares (credited as fully paid) in E (Holdings). E and F are then dissolved and E (Holdings) alters its name to E. The amalgamation is complete. This is, in fact, a very popular method of amalgamation.

If the value of assets received by E (Holdings) exceeds the nominal value of the shares issued by that company a sum equal to that excess will no longer have to be transferred to the share premium account.[19]

Effect on creditors

80–06 It will be noticed that nothing has been mentioned about the treatment of creditors, and their position is that they remain creditors of the transferor company, and have all the rights against that company that their debts confer. It will normally be part of the arrangement that the transferee company agrees to meet the liabilities of the transferor company and gives an indemnity to this effect or, alternatively, that the transferor company retains sufficient assets to meet its liabilities.

Creditors are, however, safeguarded by subsection (5), provided that they watch their interests. This subsection provides, *inter alia*, that if within a year of the passing of the special resolution, an order is made for winding up the company by or subject to the supervision of the court, the special resolution shall not be valid unless sanctioned by the court.[20]

Effect on shareholders

The effect on shareholders is that the resolution is valid, but that any shareholder may, in specific circumstances, dissent and require to be bought out and, moreover, no shareholder can be compelled to take his aliquot interest in the new company.

---

[19] 1981 Act, s. 37; see para. 80–13, *post*.
[20] *Re City and County Investment Co.* (1879) 13 Ch.D. 475; see para. 80–10, *post*.

Dissentient shareholders

The right to dissent

80–07 The right of dissent is given by subsection (3). The only members who may dissent and take advantage of this subsection are those who either voted against the special resolution or who did not vote upon it at all: any member who voted in favour of it is bound by it (subject to his right to refuse the acceptance of an interest in the transferee company,[21] which remains unimpaired). Any member who did not vote in favour of the resolution has seven days in which he can express his dissent. Within that time he must leave at the registered office of the transferor company a written dissent, in which he requires the liquidator either to abstain from carrying the resolution into effect or to purchase his interest.[22] It is difficult to see how the liquidator could abstain from carrying the resolution into effect unless it became impossible for him to do so, as, *e.g.* where the transferee company became unable to carry out its part, or if some condition precedent were unfulfilled. If the liquidator proceeds with the arrangement, or intends to do so, he must then purchase the shares or other interests of the dissentient: these interests would only be the interests conferred by, or conferring, membership of the company, and would not apply, *e.g.* to interests in an outside capacity such as a creditor. The liquidator will accordingly have to retain sufficient liquid assets to satisfy dissentients.

The dissentient must serve his dissent at the company's registered office: but if the liquidator waives this requirement and accepts the dissent, this is effective and binds the liquidator.[23] Indeed the provision is for the benefit of dissentients to enable them to prove receipt, and Warrington J. suggested in the case last cited that if, in fact, the liquidator has notice, however it reaches him, that will suffice.

The legal personal representative of a deceased member has the same right of dissent.[24]

If the liquidator and dissentient member agree the purchase price,[25] the dissentient will be bought out at that price. If the liquidator and dissentient member cannot agree, the matter is referred to arbitration in accordance with the Companies Clauses Consolidation Act 1845.[26] The liquidator and dissentient member may agree the arbitration procedure to be adopted; but if not, the above Act provides that each party appoints an arbitrator, and, if these do not agree, they appoint an umpire. If they fail to appoint an umpire, the court may do so, under the Arbitration Act 1950, s. 10. It is

---

[21] See para. 80–08, *post*.
[22] :Re Union Bank of Kingston-upon-Hull (1880) 13 Ch.D. 808; *Re Demarara Rubber Co. Ltd.* [1913] 1 Ch. 331; *Lig. of Melville Coal Co.* v. *Clark* 1904, 6 F. 913; 12 S.L.T. 194.
[23] Brailey v. *Rhodesia Consolidated* [1910] 2 Ch. 95, 100, 101.
[24] *Llewellyn* v. *Kasintoe Rubber Estatesa* [1914] 2 Ch. 670.
[25] Or if the company and the member have already agreed the price: *Baring-Gould* v. *Sharpington Combined Pick and Shovel Syndicate* [1889] 2 Ch. 80.
[26] In the case of a Scottish transferor company, the arbitration is under the Companies Clauses Consolidation (Scotland) Act 1845 and the Arbitration (Scotland) Act 1894.

thought that the basis upon which the purchase price has to be agreed will have regard to the value of the shares before the reconstruction of the company and that any enhanced value of the shares that may arise consequent upon the reconstruction must not be taken into account.

The right to refuse new shares

80–08 Apart from the protection for a dissentient member, there is also a somewhat negative protection for a person who has not duly dissented and required the liquidator to purchase his interest, but who nevertheless does not desire to have any interest in the transferee company. In such a case he cannot be compelled to take the shares, policy or other form of interest in the transferee company[27]; he may refuse to do so; but if he does so refuse he will not be given any compensation. The effect will merely be that he loses all right to the interest. Such a step would appear on the surface to be mere folly, but if the interest in the transferee carries with it present or contingent obligations, such as premiums on an insurance policy or unpaid liability on shares, there may be good reason for declining to accept. If the shares to which he would have been entitled are sold, he is entitled to the proceeds.[28]

This right was expressed by Vice-Chancellor Wood as follows[29]:

> "Unless he dissents within the time and in the manner specified by the Act of Parliament, he is so far bound that he can get nothing else for his own shares, except these new shares, but he is not bound to take such new shares whether he likes them or not. He may have lost all his rights over his own shares by his delay; but he may nevertheless decline to take this consideration for his shares if he thinks that that consideration would prove burdensome rather than beneficial. He may get nothing for his property—that is his loss; but, unless he has compromised himself by some act of his own, he cannot be compelled to incur any further liability."

In another case the same judge said[30]:

> " . . . if a company be desirous of merging themselves in another company, inasmuch as a minority of dissentient shareholders cannot be compelled to take shares in the other company, it may be desirable that the first company shall have a power of closing its concerns and winding up its affairs, and upon so doing of selling its assets to the other company, which may be disposed to purchase those assets, paying for them in shares. Then it would be for the shareholders in the company which was being wound up to say whether they will take shares or not. If they refuse to take shares, they lose all interest in the purchase-money; they are so far bound by the resolution of their own

---

[27] *Re Bank of Hindustan, China and Japan, Higgs' Case* (1865) 2 H. & M. 657; *Cleve* v. *Financial Corporation* (1873) L.R. 16 Eq. 363.

[28] *Re Lake View Extended Gold Mine (Western Australia)* [1900] W.N. 44.

[29] In *Re Bank of Hindustan, China and Japan, Higgs' Case* (1865) 2 H. & M. 657, 665.

[30] In *Clinch* v. *Financial Corporation* (1868) L.R. 5 Eq. 450, 472; approved on appeal, 4 Ch.App. 117; and by Lord Hatherley in *Cleve* v. *Financial Corporation* (1873) L.R. 16 Eq. 363.

company as to lose all right of claiming any portion of it; but the sale may still be a good sale of the concern by one company to the other."

Where a director in effect assented, he was bound.[31] On the other hand, it is not possible for a shareholder to remain passive and see how matters materialise.

Application to court

80–09 In a scheme (not under the section) whereby members of the transferor company were to be entitled to shares in the transferee company upon which there was to be a liability of 10p per share, a shareholder did nothing to accept the shares. A time limit had been set for acceptance. After the expiry of this limit the shareholder, realising that the shares were valuable, attempted to claim those to which he would have been entitled. The court refused his application.[32] Fine distinctions may arise: in a scheme under the articles, where shares were allotted direct to members of the transferor company, a shareholder who acknowledged receipt was a member of the new company, but one who did nothing was not.[33]

A transferee of shares who was not on the register at the time of the resolution was entitled to the benefit of dissenting, and the register was rectified from an earlier date.[34] The court found that no injustice would be worked upon anyone by such rectification.

A dissentient cannot examine the company's officers in an effort to enhance the value of his shares.[35] Nor, at least in the absence of fraud or inaccuracy being shown, will discovery of documents be allowed to a dissentient to enable him to decide whether or not to accept the liquidator's offer.[36] A commission may, however, be granted to enable a dissentient to examine the value of assets abroad by examining witnesses there.[37] If the member refuses the liquidator's offer, arbitration must follow, but if the liquidator did not tender the money offered, costs will be at the court's discretion.[38] If the dissent is reasonable, the court will usually order costs against the company.[39]

Challenge of validity of scheme

80–10 Where a resolution is passed in accordance with section 287, it can be challenged in two ways[40]:

---

31 *Re Empire Assurance Corporation, Leeke's Case* (1870) L.R. 11 Eq. 100.
32 *Zuccani* v. *Nacupai Gold Mining Co.* (1889) 61 L.T. 176, C.A.; 5 T.L.R. 454.
33 *Re Empire Assurance Corporation, Challis's Case, Somerville's Case* (1871) 6 Ch.App. 266.
34 *Re Sussex Brick Co.* [1904] 1 Ch. 598.
35 *Re British Building Stone Co.* [1908] 2 Ch. 450.
36 *Re Glamorganshire Banking Co., Morgan's Case* (1885) 28 Ch.D. 620.
37 *Re Mysore West Gold Mining Co.* (1889) 42 Ch.D. 535.
38 *Re Imperial Mercantile Credit Association* (1871) L.R. 12 Eq. 504.
39 See *Re Mysore West Gold Mining Co.* (1889) 42 Ch.D. 535.
40 *Re Imperial Bank of China, India and Japan* (1866) 1 Ch.App. 339; *Re Financial Corporation* [1866] W.N. 162; *Re International Life Assurance Society* (1868) 20 L.T. 433; *Re Callao Bis Co.* (1889) 42 Ch.D. 169.

first, by shareholders' action against the company; or

secondly, if the company is wound up by the court or under supervision within 12 months of the passing of the resolution, in the course of that winding up.

The amalgamation cannot be challenged upon the winding up petition itself.[41] The action may be brought by any member who dissented, and will be on behalf of himself and all other shareholders, notwithstanding that many of them assented.[42] Where a winding-up or supervision order is made within the statutory 12 months, the agreement will not be valid unless sanctioned by the court (s. 287 (5)).

It will be seen from this provision that the companies concerned, and the liquidator of the transferor company, cannot be certain that the scheme will not be impeached until 12 months have elapsed.[43] This is hardly a satisfactory matter for them, although it may be necessary for the protection of creditors. On the other hand, once the scheme has been sanctioned, it cannot be impeached except on appeal.[44] In one case the transferor company, wishing to be certain, applied to the court, in the course of winding up, for a supervision order. The court sanctioned the scheme.[45]

It is no objection to a scheme that it contains a stipulation that the transferee company shall take a portion only of the assets and liabilities of the transferor company, leaving the rest of the debts to be paid by the liquidator of the transferor company; or that it contains a stipulation that the shares in the transferee company which are to be given as a consideration for the transfer shall be distributed directly among the shareholders of the transferor company, and not given to the liquidator as part of the assets in the winding up.[46]

If an arrangement is void, a member of the transferor company does not become a member of the transferee company.[47]

The court will not sanction a scheme in which the members of the transferor company may be liable to pay calls upon their shares in that company in a certain event, even if the liability is restricted to members who accept.[48] But where a call was first made in the transferor company for its authorised purposes, the scheme was effective, and the case was distinguished from the last cited case.[49] Calls made for the purpose of paying existing debts will be permitted.[50] The court did not sanction a scheme where a premium was payable upon the shares in the transferee

---

[41] *Re Imperial Bank of China, India and Japan* (1866) 1 Ch.App. 339.

[42] *Clinch* v. *Financial Corporation* (1868) L.R. 5 Eq. 450; affd. 4 Ch.App. 117; *Bird* v. *Bird's Patent Deodorising and Utilising Sewage Co.* (1874) 9 Ch.App. 358.

[43] This unsatisfactory position was recognised by the Court of Appeal in *Re Callao Bis Mining Co.* (1889) 42 Ch.D. 169.

[44] *Nicholl* v. *Eberhardt Co.* (1889) 59 L.J.Ch. 103.

[45] *Re New Flagstaff Mining Co.* [1889] W.N. 123; and see the order made by the court.

[46] *Re City and County Investment Company* (1879) 13 Ch.D. 475.

[47] *Re Oriental Commercial Bank, Alabaster's Case* (1868) L.R. 7 Eq. 273.

[48] *Clinch* v. *Financial Corporation* (1868) L.R. 5 Eq. 450; affd. 4 Ch.App. 117.

[49] *New Zealand Gold Extraction Co. (Newberry-Vautin Process)* v. *Peacock* [1894] 1 Q.B. 622, 627, *per* Kennedy J.

[50] *Re Bank of South Australia (No. 2)* [1895] Ch. 578.

company.[51] On the other hand, a scheme was sanctioned in which an option was given to take shares in the transferee company, subject to a payment of 6d. per share.[52]

The court may sanction a scheme upon terms, such as that dissentients be paid out before the assets are transferred.[53] Where the court was satisfied that debenture holders were to be paid their aliquot value at the time of the resolution, the scheme was sanctioned[54]; and again where dissenting shareholders were to be paid out their valuation, the court sanctioned the scheme.[55] The court has approved a scheme in which there was an option to repurchase the shares.[56]

Compensation to directors

80–11 Where compensation is paid to directors under a scheme,[57] this will not render it *ultra vires*; but the resolution must be looked at, together with any explanatory circular, to see if shareholders in fact assented.[58] Sections 191, 192 and 193 make it compulsory for any such compensation to directors not only to be disclosed[59] but also to be approved by the general meeting. It has been held that section 191 requires disclosure to all members whether or not entitled to notice of general meetings, and that disclosure must be made before payment of compensation.[60] The section does not, however, require approval for compensation payments made to directors who are also employees, if the payments are provided for in the relevant service contract. The section relates to "proposed payments" and not contractual obligations incurred before the amalgamation or take-over. Such payments may be included in such contracts if the articles so allow and the directors are acting bona fide and in the interests of the company.[61]

There must be a fair, candid and reasonable explanation of the purpose for which the meeting is summoned.[62] If the bonus to directors is in fact a factor actuating their action, in facilitating the transaction, the majority cannot bind the minority.[63]

It may not, however, be easy, even in cases of fraud,[64] to upset an

---

[51] *Imperial Bank of China, India and Japan* v. *Bank of Hindustan, China and Japan* (1868) L.R. 6 Eq. 91: at this date a premium was distributable as dividend.
[52] *Postlethwaite* v. *Port Phillip and Colonial Gold Mining Co.* (1889) 43 Ch.D. 452.
[53] *Re Hester & Co.* [1875] W.N. 179.
[54] *Re Tunis Rys.* (1878) 10 Ch.D. 270n.; affd. [1874] W.N. 165.
[55] *Re Marine Investment Co., ex p. Poole's Executors* (1873) 8 Ch.App. 702.
[56] *Re Cambrian Mining Co.* (1881) 48 L.T. 114.
[57] *Southall* v. *British Mutual Life Assurance Society* (1870) L.R. 11 Eq. 65; on appeal (1871) 6 Ch.App. 614.
[58] *Kaye* v. *Croydon Tramways Co.* [1898] 1 Ch. 358.
[59] If full and proper disclosure has been made, the court will usually regard the decision of the majority: *Re Imperial Mercantile Credit Association* (1871) L.R. 12 Eq. 504.
[60] *Re Duomatic Ltd.* [1969] 2 Ch. 365.
[61] *Taupo Totara Timber Co.* v. *Rowe* [1977] 3 W.L.R. 466 (P.C.) construing the identical section of the New Zealand Companies Act 1955.
[62] *Kaye* v. *Croydon Tramways Co.* [1898] 1 Ch. 358, 373, *per* Rigby L.J.; *Tiessen* v. *Henderson* [1899] 1 Ch. 861; *Clarkson* v. *Davies* [1923] A.C. 100.
[63] [1898] 1 Ch. 358, 376, 377, *per* Vaughan-Williams L.J.
[64] See *Clarkson* v. *Davies* [1923] A.C. 100, 109.

arrangement afterwards on the ground that there was no full disclosure or a similar defect, since the transferor company may have been dissolved. However, a dissolution may be declared void, under section 352, upon the application to the court of any person who appears to the court to be interested.

Distribution of consideration by liquidator

80–12 So far the process that is gone through pursuant to section 287, the position of creditors, and the effect on members have been discussed.

It is now necessary to examine the next step taken by the liquidator of the transferor company when all (if any) duly dissenting members have been dealt with.[65] He will now have in his hands, *inter alia*, the shares, policies or other like interests in the transferee company which he holds for distribution amongst the members of the transferor company. If these members are of a single class, he will have little difficulty, other than a mathematical one, in making the distributions. If, however, there is more than one class of members, and these classes carry different rights in a winding up, the liquidator may have a problem. His duty is to distribute in accordance with the rights in a winding up: if he holds interests in the transferee company of different types, it may not be easy to make the proper distribution. For example, suppose that the transferor company has 100,000 preference shares of £1 each and 10,000 ordinary shares of 10p each, and that the liquidator receives precisely similar shares in the transferee company. He cannot then adopt the simple direct course of giving one preference share for each one held in the transferor company, and one ordinary share for each one held likewise, even if the general meeting has directed him to do so. He must distribute in accordance with the rights of the two classes. Accordingly, if the preference shares and ordinary shares rank *pari passu* in a winding up, they must receive distributions upon this basis.[66] The section only enables the general meeting to decide on the nature of the consideration, not on the mode of its distribution.[67] If, however, the members of one class agree to accept less than their rights, the other class which benefits thereby cannot complain.[67] If the agreement provides for a distribution which is invalid, this will not necessarily invalidate the whole agreement.[68]

If an arrangement is intended whereby classes will not get their exact rights (as by giving preference and ordinary shares in the new company for

---

[65] It must be borne in mind that the transferor company remains liable for its own debts, and that the liquidator must carry out the liquidation as required by statute. If, therefore, he relies on the transferee company to perform the transferor company's obligations, he should take steps to ensure that this is done: see *Pulsford* v. *Davenish* [1903] 2 Ch. 625; *Argyll's* v. *Coxeter* (1913) 29 T.L.R. 355; *Re Aidall* [1933] 1 Ch. 323; *Re New Zealand Joint Stock Corporation* (1907) 23 T.L.R. 238.

[66] *Simpson* v. *Palace Theatre* [1893] W.N. 91; on appeal, 9 T.L.R. 470; 69 L.T. 70.

[67] *Griffith* v. *Paget* (1877) 5 Ch.D. 894.

[68] *Wall* v. *London & Northern Assets Corporation* [1898] 2 Ch. 469.

like shares in the old), a scheme under section 206, with the safeguards of section 287, is required.[69]

Transfer of excess consideration received by transferee company to share premium account

80–13 In the preceding paragraph the disposal of the consideration received by the transferor company for the transfer of its assets has been explained. It is now necessary to consider how the transferee company has to treat in its books the assets which it received in consideration of the issue of its shares, policies or other interests.

Where the transferee company issues shares in consideration of assets received by it, either from the transferor company directly or from its—or, if there are several transferor companies,[70] their—shareholders, it may happen that the actual value of the assets received by the transferee company exceeds the nominal amount of the shares issued by it. In this case if the transferee company acquires a 90 per cent. holding in the transferor company it no longer has to transfer any sum equal to that excess to the share premium account.[71]

No such obligation exists, either, if the transferee company issues interests other than shares, *e.g.* debentures, in consideration of the assets transferred to it.

Schemes not under section 287 but purporting to achieve the same result

80–14 Many attempts have been made to achieve the effect of section 287 without specifically following the requirements of the section. Sometimes provision is made in the memorandum of association, sometimes in the articles, for this purpose. Such provisions will be effective, provided that they do not attempt to extend the powers of the section, or to deprive dissentient members of their rights.[72]

An article would not be effective which, *e.g.*, attempted to compel a dissentient member to become a member of a new company having extended powers.[73] Nor would a scheme under powers in the memorandum in which no provision was made for the purchase of a dissentient's holding be valid.[74]

---

[69] *Re Sandwell Park Colliery Co.* [1914] 1 Ch. 589; *Re Needhams* [1923] W.N. 289.

[70] See Example 4 in para. 80–05, *ante*.

[71] 1981 Act, s. 37, overruling the decisions in *Henry Head & Co.* v. *Ropner Holdings* [1952] Ch. 124; *Shearer* v. *Bercain* [1980] S.T.C. 359; see para. 24–47, *ante*. For retrospective relief see 1981 Act, s. 39.

[72] *Payne* v. *The Cork Co. Ltd.* [1900] 1 Ch. 308; *Re Irrigation Co. of France, ex p. Fox* (1871) 6 Ch.App. 176; *Baring-Gould* v. *Sharpington Syndicate* [1889] 2 Ch. 80.

[73] *Re Empire Assurance Corporation, ex p. Bagshawe* (1867) L.R. 4 Eq. 341 *Re The Western Life Assurance Society, Driver's Executors' Case* (1871) 15 S.J. 637.

[74] *Bisgood* v. *Henderson's Transvaal Estates* [1908] 1 Ch. 743; *Bisgood* v. *Nile Valley Co.* [1906] 1 Ch. 747; *Manners* v. *St. David's Gold and Copper Mines* [1904] 2 Ch. 593. Earlier cases inconsistent with these were overruled.

An attempted amalgamation under the articles, which was not completed, did not bind a member.[75]

Time limit in scheme

80–15 Provision is frequently made in a scheme for a time limit within which a member of the transferor company must take his interest in the transferee company. The limit may be fixed specifically, or merely left as "within a reasonable time." In either case the stipulation will be valid provided that it is reasonable,[76] and a term that any shares not taken up will be at the disposal of the liquidator or of the transferee company will be valid.[77]

Moreover, since section 208[78] applies to schemes under section 287, the court may itself make any necessary order for dealing with the shares in the transferee company which those entitled to them have failed to take up.

Taxes and stamp duty

80–16 A scheme under section 287 will usually have considerable tax implications, but it is not possible to deal with these here.[79] Indeed, such a scheme may often be carried out in order to obtain tax benefits. There may also be capital transfer tax implications if the transferor company is under the control of a family.

Stamp duty also requires consideration, since in appropriate circumstances it will be possible to obtain relief under the Finance Act 1927, s. 55, as amended by the Finance Act 1928, s. 31 both of which sections were further amended by the Finance Act 1973, Part V under which the law on the raising of capital by companies is brought into line with EEC Directive 69/335; or under the Finance Act 1930, s. 42, as amended by the Finance Act 1967, s. 27.[80] Relief is in essence available where the new shares are issued to replace shares in the transferor company which have already borne duty. Thus if the transferor company is a foreign company no relief is available. Relief is available, however, if it is an unlimited company.[81] This relief is only available, however, if the businesses of the two companies remain in the same hands of the same persons as before the amalgamation, so that if the transferee company ceases to be the beneficial owner of the shares so acquired within two years the duty is payable.[82]

---

[75] *Re Empire Assurance Corporation, Dougan's Case* (1873) 8 Ch.App.540.
[76] *Weston* v. *New Guston Co.* (1889) 1 Meg. 225, 352; *Zuccani* v. *Nacupai Gold Mining Co.* (1889) 61 L.T. 176; *Postlethwaite* v. *Port Phillip and Colonial Gold Mining Co.* (1889) 43 Ch.D. 452.
[77] *Burdett-Coutts* v. *True Blue (Hannan's) Gold Mine* [1899] 2 Ch. 616; *Nicholl* v. *Eberhardt Co.* (1889) 59 L.J. Ch. 103. *Liq. of Melville Coal Co.* v. *Clark* 1904, 6 F. 913; 12 S.L.T. 194.
[78] See para. 79–18, *ante*.
[79] For a consideration of these matters, see Weinberg and Blank, *Take-overs and Mergers*, (4th. ed. 1979), and further texts there cited.
[80] This section abrogates the decision in *Shop and Store Developments, Ltd.* v. *Inland Revenue Commissioners* [1967] 1 A.C. 472 (H.L.).
[81] *Chelsea Land & Investment Co.* v. *I.R.C.* [1978] S.T.C. 221 (C.A.).
[82] *I.R.C.* v. *Ufitec Group Ltd.* [1977] 3 All E.R. 924.

Where shares in the new company are allotted to the shareholders in the transferor company, the original shareholders should be registered as shareholders in the new company. If letters of renunciation of allotment are used, the full stamp duty may become payable.[83]

Moreover, under section 42 of the Finance Act 1930 relief is given from *ad valorem* duty in cases of interconnected companies. This relief is available at any time, and does not require to be connected with an amalgamation or reconstruction.[84]

PRACTICE NOTE

Dissentients under section 287

80–17 It has already been pointed out that no member of a company, provided that his shares are fully paid, can be required to pay any further moneys in respect of those shares (1948 Act, s. 22) or in respect of any shares arising by reason of the reconstruction. Provision is made by section 287 of the 1948 Act for any shareholder who does not agree to a proposed reconstruction formally to dissent therefrom, but it is often found in practice that some shareholders do not formally dissent and simply ignore the offer to take shares in the new company. Where shareholders fail to come into the scheme by not taking up shares in the new company, the amount payable to them in the liquidation is the amount, less expenses, for which the liquidator is able to find a purchaser of their rights to take up shares in the new company. It is usual for the liquidator to sell *en bloc* or in lots the rights of all those shareholders who take no action in regard to the scheme, and to distribute to them, *pro rata* to their holdings, the net amount realised.

If, because of the rights given to dissentients under section 287, there are any doubts as to the reconstruction scheme being carried through, it may be advisable to hold two extraordinary general meetings, the first for the purpose of passing the necessary resolution for the approval of the scheme and the second, at a date not less than seven days later, *i.e.* so that the second meeting is not held until after the time for dissenting under section 287 (3) has expired, for the purpose of putting the company into liquidation. If, in the interval between the two meeting, so many shareholders dissent from the scheme as to make it unworkable, the scheme can be abandoned and the company remains in existence.

---

[83] *Oswald Tillotson Ltd.* v. *I.R.C.* [1933] 1 K.B. 134; and see *Brotex Cellulose Fibres* v. *I.R.C.* [1938] 1 K.B. 158; *Lever Bros.* v. *I.R.C.* [1938] 2 K.B. 518; *Henty & Constable (Brewers) Ltd.* v. *I.R.C.* [1961] 1 W.L.R. 1504, C.A. *Brooklands Selangor Holdings* v. *I.R.C.* [1970] 1 W.L.R. 429; *Canada Safeway* v. *I.R.C.* [1973] Ch. 374; *Clarke Chapman-John Thompson* v. *I.R.C.* [1974] 2 W.L.R. 835.

[84] See *Nestlé Co.* v. *I.R.C.* [1953] Ch. 395.

B. TAKE-OVER BIDS

CHAPTER 81

LEGAL PROVISIONS FOR PROCEDURE AND DISCLOSURE—ACQUISITION OF SHARES FROM DISSENTING SHAREHOLDERS

Application of the Companies Acts

81–01 As has already been observed,[1] the Act of 1948 makes no special provision with regard to the conduct of a take-over bid, and the underlying philosophy of the Act appears to be that, in the interests of efficiency, take-overs should be permitted, and, indeed, facilitated, provided there is no unfair dealing in relation to the existing shareholders.[2]

The facilities afforded by section 209 to an offeror company to acquire the shares of a dissentient minority of shareholders are considered later in this chapter.[3] With regard to the fair treatment of shareholders, section 193 requires that particulars of any payments to be made to directors by way of compensation for loss of office as a result of a take-over bid be sent with any notice of the offer to shareholders, and imposes liability to a fine upon any director who fails to ensure that this is done. The section further requires a meeting to be convened of all the shareholders of the class to which the offer relates for the purpose of approving the payment, and, if these requirements are not complied with, or the payment is not approved, any sums received by a director on account of such a payment are to be held by him on trust for any shareholders who have sold their shares as a result of the offer. Sections 191 and 192 also apply to disclosure to and approval by the general meeting of compensation for loss of office made to directors on a take-over. These will not apply however if the director has a service contract which provides for such payments if the contract was entered into bona fide in accordance with the articles and in the interest of the company.[4] Section 194 (4) expressly preserves the general duties of disclosure imposed on directors apart from these sections, and these and the directors' wider duties of honesty and good faith[5] have a particular relevance when a take-over bid is made, or is known to be imminent.

Further provisions of the Acts which acquire significance in the context

---

1 See para. 79–03, *ante*.
2 As to this "philosophy," and generally with regard to the conduct of take-over bids, see Weinberg and Blank, *Take-overs and Mergers*, (4th ed., 1979).
3 See paras. 81–05, *et seq., post*.
4 *Taupo Totara Timber Co.* v. *Rowe* [1977] 3 W.L.R. 466 (P.C.) See para. 61–27 *et seq., ante*.
5 See paras. 63–03, *et seq., ante*.

of take-over bids are sections 42 to 44 of the 1981 Act[6] which restrict the giving of financial assistance by a company for the purchase of its own shares. The temptation to ignore the former provision, section 54 of the 1948 Act, was often very strong, particularly where a substantial part of the assets of the company to be acquired were easily realisable, and the original statutory penalty for contravention of the section—a fine not exceeding £100—had little deterrent effect when weighed against the rewards which a successful bid can produce. But it became clear that a company contravening section 54 could take proceedings against its directors to recover compensation for their breach of trust in making the company a party to such a transaction,[7] and since this applies to section 42 of the 1981 Act it might provide a more effective deterrent than the increased penalties now imposed by section 42 of the 1981 Act. Further, it is even possible for the company's bank to be liable as a constructive trustee (and in negligence) for assisting, with knowledge of the relevant facts, the directors in a dishonest and fraudulent design aimed at defeating section 42 of the 1981 Act.[8] The financial assistance itself may also be invalid.[9] Any agreement relating to the take-over between the vendors and purchasers of the company, *e.g.* as to dissipation of assets of the company in protection of a security, was held to be binding on them unless it contravened section 54.[10] Further the "purpose" exceptions in the new section[10a] and the general exception for private companies[10b] provide more scope for avoiding the restrictions altogether.

The various criminal offences relating to insider dealing are also of great relevance on take-over bids. These have been dealt with in Chapter 68, *supra*.

Procedure on making a bid

81–02 Although there is no prescribed form of procedure when a take-over bid is made, the offeror company will normally have regard to the provisions of section 209[11] in framing its offer, in order to take advantage of that section in the event of the bid being accepted by a substantial number, but not all, of the persons to whom it is made.

Careful attention must also be given to the provisions, statutory and otherwise, which have been formulated subsequently to the Act of 1948 for the regulation of the conduct of take-over bids, as the result of the increasing economic importance of company mergers, and a degree of public disquiet at the lack of legislative control. These may be divided into public

---

[6] See paras. 38–01, *et seq., ante*.
[7] *Wallersteiner* v. *Moir* [1974] 1 W.L.R. 991. See para. 38–13, *ante*.
[8] *Karak Rubber Co. Ltd.* v. *Burden (No. 2)* [1972] 1 W.L.R. 602.
[9] See para. 38–11, *ante*.
[10] *Swiftervend* v. *Bowman* (Unrep. May 24, 1978, C.A.).
[10a] See para. 38–04, *ante*.
[10b] See para. 38–14, *ante*.
[11] See paras. 81–05 *et seq., post*.

and private controls.[12] The public controls will be considered in Chapters 83 and 84 *post*. The most important private controls are imposed by:

(1) the Prevention of Fraud (Investments) Act 1958 and the rules made thereunder;
(2) the City Code on Take-overs and Mergers;
(3) the Regulations of the Stock Exchange;
(4) the rules of the Council for the Securities Industry.

The first of these is considered here, the other three, being extra-legal, are considered in Chapter 82.

Prevention of Fraud (Investments) Act 1958

81–03 The provisions of this Act have already been considered.[13] The effect of section 13 of the Act is to impose criminal liability upon anyone who knowingly or recklessly makes a statement or promise in connection with a take-over bid with a view to procuring the sale or acquisition of shares which is misleading, false or deceptive or which dishonestly conceals material facts. This section will apply whether the consideration offered for the shares is cash or securities.[14] Under section 14 of the 1958 Act the circularisation of take-over offers is restricted to persons exempted by or under the Act and licensed dealers.[15]

Licensed Dealers (Conduct of Business) Rules 1960[16]

81–04 These Rules were made by the Department of Trade[17] under section 7 (3) of the Prevention of Fraud (Investments) Act 1958. The principal requirements of the Rules may be summarised[18] as follows:

(i) The terms of the offer must be delivered to the offeree company not less than three clear days, excluding holidays, before the offer is dispatched to the offerees.
(ii) A take-over offer must, unless totally withdrawn, remain open for acceptance for at least 21 days.
(iii) Where the offer is conditional, a date must be specified as the latest date on which the offeror can declare the offer unconditional.
(iv) The acquisition of securities to which the offer relates must not be conditional upon the offerees' approving any payment or other benefit to any director of the offeree company.

---

[12] See para. 79–03, *ante*.
[13] See para. 25–01, *ante*.
[14] See *Governments Stock, etc., Investment Co. Ltd.* v. *Christopher* [1956] 1 W.L.R. 237, where it was held that a document offering an exchange of shares for shares is not a "prospectus" (and therefore not exempt from the provisions of the 1958 Act); see para. 21–18, *ante*.
[15] See para. 25–04, *ante*.
[16] Solicitors in Scotland (who are, as a body, licensed dealers) are required to observe the similar provisions of the Solicitors (Prevention of Fraud) (Investments) Rules 1961.
[17] S.I. 1960 No. 1216.
[18] The above summary is based on paras. 274 and 280 of the Report of the Jenkins Committee (Cmnd. 1962 No.1749).

(v) If the offer relates to less than the total amount in issue of any class of securities, the offer must be open to acceptance by all holders, and if too many acceptances are received they must be scaled down *pro rata*.

(vi) Information must be given in the circular containing the offer on certain specified matters, in particular the identity of the bidder and information relating to the securities the offeree is being invited to transfer and, where relevant, the value of the securities he is to receive in exchange for his own securities.

Acquisition of shares from dissenting shareholders

81–05 Section 209 of the 1948 Act provides one of the cases in which the Acts enable the decision of a majority to bind a dissenting minority. In this case the effect, in simple terms, is that where one company makes a take-over bid for all the shares or for the whole of any class of shares of another company, and that offer is accepted by the holders of 90 per cent. of the shares, the offeror can upon the same terms acquire the shares of the members who have not accepted the offer, unless such persons can persuade the court not to permit the acquisition. Special provisions apply for cases where the offeror company already holds more than 10 per cent. in value of the shares concerned.

The machinery for making such compulsory acquisition is specified in some detail by the section and must be strictly complied with. This machinery can be understood readily by means of a time-table.[19]

Stage 1: The offer

81–06 A company (in the section and hereafter called the transferee company) makes an offer to the shareholders of another company (in the section and hereafter called the transferor company) to acquire the shares of the shareholders in the latter company. The procedure of section 209 is available not only in respect of shares of the transferor company already issued at the date of the offer, but also as regards shares then issuable under the terms of convertible loan stock, provided that the holders of the loan stock, by having exercised their right of conversion, have acquired an absolute right to an allotment of shares and that right is covered by the authorised capital of the company.[20]

The transferee company need not be a company within the meaning of the Companies Acts, but it must be a "company" as such. Consideration has already been given to the meaning of "company" in this connection.[21]

On the corresponding section in the New South Wales Companies Act

---

[19] This time-table deals only with the case where the transferee company is not already a holder of 10 per cent. of shares of the class subject to the offer: as to the case where 10 per cent. or more of the shares are already held, see para. 81–10 *post*.

[20] *Re Simo Securities Trust Ltd.* [1971] 1 W.L.R. 1455.

[21] See para. 80–03, *ante*.

1961, it has been held that the offer must be made by a single company and not by several companies jointly, because the underlying philosophy of this provision is one of company structure, *viz.* that the transferee company should not be prevented by a small minority from converting the transferor company into a wholly-owned subsidiary, and not one of concentration of property interests in the hands of the transferee.[22]

The offer may be for all the issued shares of the transferor company, or for all the shares of one or more specified classes; or there may be separate offers for the different classes of shares. It can be a matter of importance which form is adopted, as will be seen later.[23]

The Act does not state which form the consideration offered to the shareholders of the transferor company shall take. This is left entirely to the discretion of the transferee company which will attempt to make its offer so attractive that the directors of the transferor company will recommend its acceptance to their shareholders. The consideration may consist of shares in or debentures of the transferee or another company, of cash to be paid by the transferee company or somebody else, of a combination of these benefits, or some of these benefits may be offered in the alternative at the option of the shareholders of the transferor company. Sometimes an alternative offer of "paper" (shares in the transferee company) or cash is made. In all these cases, however, the fundamental principle of section 209 must be observed that the offer must be on the same terms for the assenting and dissenting shareholders.

When recommending acceptance or rejection of the offer, the directors of the transferor company have a duty to be honest to their shareholders and not to mislead them; dissenting shareholders can complain if, as the result of a breach of that duty, they are wrongfully subjected to the compulsory purchase of their shares.[24]

Stage 2: The acceptance

81–07 Holders of the shares whose transfer is involved accept the offer.

The offer will normally state a date by which the offer must be accepted, but it is also usual and of great importance to the transferee company that a clause should be inserted in the offer enabling the transferee company to extend the date up to which acceptances may be made.

In order to invoke the section, acceptances must be received from the holders of 90 per cent. of the shares concerned[25] and such acceptances must be given within four months of the date of the offer.[26] The offer can be framed so that acceptance must be given within a period of less than

[22] *Blue Metal Industries Ltd.* v. *R. W. Dilley* [1970] A.C. 827 (P.C.).
[23] See para. 81–07, *infra*.
[24] *Gething* v. *Kilner* [1972] 1 W.L.R. 337.
[25] If a 90 per cent. acceptance is impossible to achieve attempts to use section 206 to achieve the same result will be carefully considered by the court: *Re Hellenic & General Trust Ltd.* [1976] 1 W.L.R. 123. See para. 79–16, *ante*.
[26] For the time limits under the City Code see Rules 21–29, outlined at para. 82–13, *ante*.

four months, and this will normally be the case; but if the section is to be invoked, the offer cannot be open for more than the four months' limit.[27] Any shares already held by the transferee company are ignored in calculating the 90 per cent.[28]

Where the transferor company has issued convertible loan stock which, at the option of the stockholder, can be converted into shares when a take-over bid is made for the shares of the company, and the offer of the transferee company extends to the shares issuable on such conversion, the calculation of the 90 per cent. includes the shares of the stockholders who have actually exercised their option to convert but the potential shares of the stockholders who did not convert and preferred to remain creditors of the company are not included in the count.[29] An unwilling acceptance is still an acceptance within section 209.[30] The offer is again normally made conditional in the first place upon the acceptance by the holders of a specified percentage of the shares, or such lesser percentage as the transferee company may decide. Upon the receipt of acceptances in respect of that percentage, the offer becomes unconditional. If a holder of convertible stock entitled to convert the stock into shares on a take-over bid on the shares of the company has not exercised his right to convert but has remained a creditor of the company, he is neither an assenting nor a dissenting shareholder.[31] Once it has become unconditional, the acceptances cannot be revoked. Thus the transferee company can ensure that, even if it fails to acquire the whole of the shares involved, it will have a percentage which it considers satisfactory, for instance, 50 per cent. or 75 per cent., but unless the full 90 per cent. acceptances are made within the four months, the remaining stages do not arise.

It is at this stage that it may be necessary to consider, in cases where the offer is for more than one class of shares, whether there was a single offer for the two classes, or separate offers for each class. There may be a 90 per cent. acceptance, for instance, in the aggregate, but less than 90 per cent. for one class. In such a case if the offer was a single one, the section can be invoked; but, if the offers were separate, the section cannot be invoked in respect of the class where acceptances were under 90 per cent.

Stage 3: Notice to non-acceptors of transferee company's desire to acquire their shares

81–08 Provided that acceptances have been duly received in respect of 90 per cent. of the shares under offer, the transferee company may, within two months after the expiration of the four months mentioned under the

[27] *Re Western Manufacturing (Reading)* [1956] Ch. 436; not following *Rathie* v. *Montreal Trust Co.* [1953] 4 D.L.R. 289; [1954] 2 C.L. 58.

[28] As to the position where the transferee company already holds more than 10 per cent. see para. 81–10, *post*.

[29] *Re Simo Securities Trust Ltd.* [1971] 1 W.L.R. 1455.

[30] *Re Marston Valley Brick Co. Ltd.* (1970) 115 S.J. 10.

[31] *Re Simo Securities Trust Ltd.* [1971] 1 W.L.R. 1455.

preceding heading,[32] give notice to any shareholder who has not accepted the offer that it desires to acquire his shares (s. 209 (1)). The calculation of the time for giving notice to dissentients for this purpose may cause difficulty. Where the time for acceptance of the original offer has been extended, the time for giving notice must be calculated from the date when the original offer was made[33]; but the position may well be different if, instead of extending the time for acceptance, the transferee company makes a completely new offer.

It will be seen that this stage is permissive, not mandatory. The transferee company is not bound to give such notice, but if it wishes to acquire the remaining shares it must do so. It will also be seen that the notice may be given to some only, and not all, of the shareholders who have not accepted the offer.

Form No. 100,[34] the prescribed Department of Trade form of notice to dissenting shareholders, contains only a reference to the majority in value of the assenting shareholders but not a reference to the majority in numbers, and where the transferee company holds already more than 10 per cent. of the shares subject to offer no reference to the majority in numbers need be inserted into the Form.[35]

Subsection (1) uses the expression "dissenting shareholder," but by virtue of subsection (5) this expression includes not only shareholders who refuse the offer, but also those who take no action whatsoever, neither accepting nor refusing, and also any shareholder who, having accepted, fails or refuses to transfer his shares pursuant to the scheme or contract. All these shareholders are hereinafter referred to as "dissenting shareholders,"

The notice must be in the form of Department of Trade Form No. 100.

The dissenting shareholders must be offered the same terms as the assenting shareholders

81–09 This is a fundamental principle of section 209. If the consideration for the shares subject to the offer consists of shares in the transferee company or, in the alternative, in cash to be paid by bankers acting on behalf of the transferee company but the time for the cash alternative has lapsed, the dissenting shareholder whose shares the transferee company wishes to acquire under section 209 (1) may demand that the transferee company must make or procure a comparable cash offer to him, provided that in the circumstances of the case it was impossible for him to opt for the cash alternative in time.[36]

---

[32] Apparently this four to six months' period likewise applies where the acceptances of the offer must be given within a period of less than four months: *Re Western Manufacturing (Reading)* [1956] Ch. 436; not following *Rathie* v. *Montreal Trust Co.* [1953] 4 D.L.R. 289; [1954] 2 C.L. 58.

[33] *Musson* v. *Howard Glasgow Associates Ltd.*, 1961 S.L.T. 87.

[34] See Vol. II, para. A.3135.

[35] *Re Simo Securities Trust Ltd.* [1971] 1 W.L.R. 1455.

[36] *Re Carlton Holdings Ltd.* [1971] 1 W.L.R. 918.

The City Code on Take-over and Mergers contains a similar philosophy embodied in General Principles 8 and 9 and Rules 33 and 34.[37]

Further requirement where transferee company already member of transferor company

81–10 Where the transferee company already holds more than 10 per cent. of the shares subject to the offer, the section does not apply unless

(a) the offer is made to the holders of all the shares other than those held by the transferee company, and
(b) the assenting shareholders not only hold 90 per cent. of the shares involved but are also not less than three-fourths in number of the holders of those shares (s. 209 (1), proviso).

This is illustrated by three simple examples:

(1) Transferor company has 100 shareholders holding in the aggregate 10,000 shares. The transferee company is not a shareholder.
The offer must be accepted by shareholders holding in the aggregate 9,000 shares.
(2) Transferor company has 100 shareholders holding in the aggregate 11,000 shares, of which 1,000 (*i.e.* less than 10 per cent.) are held by the transferee company.
Acceptances must be of shareholders (excluding the transferee company) holding 9,000 shares.
(3) Transferor company has 101 shareholders holding in the aggregate 11,500 shares of which 1,500 (*i.e.* more than 10 per cent.) are held by the transferee company.
Acceptances must be of 75 or more shareholders (excluding the transferee company) holding 9,000 shares.

The provision does not give clear guidance as to the date at which the numerical count has to be made. Therefore the most practical date has to be adopted. This is, in relation to shares already issued, the date of the offer, *i.e.* the shareholders then on the register have to be counted. In the case of loan stock convertible into shares on a take-over bid the three-fourths majority in numbers is calculated by including the shares actually converted during the offer period; the potential shares of the stockholders who have not elected to convert are excluded from the count.[38]

Stage 3a: Dissenting shareholder's application to court

81–11 Within one month of the notice under stage 3, any dissenting shareholder served with the notice may make an application to the court.[39] Only persons served with such notice may apply: other shareholders have their

[37] See para. 82–14, *ante*.
[38] *Re Simo Securities Trust Ltd.* [1971] 1 W.L.R. 1455.
[39] Application is made to the court having jurisdiction to wind up the transferor company: see *Re Samuel Heap & Son Ltd.* [1965] 1 W.L.R. 1458, C.A. An application in the High Court is made by originating summons under R.S.C. 1965, Ord. 102, r. 2.

protection under subsection (2) (*a*), which is dealt with under stage 4 below.

The application asks for a declaration that the transferee company, which is made the respondent to the summons, is not entitled to acquire the shares of the applicant upon the terms of the scheme, notwithstanding that it has been approved by nine-tenths in value of the shareholders, excluding shares held by, or by a nominee for, the transferee company or its subsidiary.[40] It is not necessary to serve the summons upon the transferor company. The court may then make an order as asked or refuse it. The court, in its discretion, might not make an order for costs against an unsuccessful applicant who did not allege fraud or otherwise act unreasonably.[41]

When an application is made to the court by a shareholder who alleges that the terms are not fair, the onus is upon the applicant to establish his allegation, and the court will attach considerable weight to the fact that the large body of shareholders have accepted the offer.[42] An application by a shareholder must allege unfairness: it is not sufficient merely to say that insufficient information was given[43] or to rely on contentions which are speculative.[44] The test of fairness is whether the offer is fair to the offerees as a whole, not to the applicants individually. The offer must be obviously and convincingly unfair, not merely one which is open to criticism or capable of improvement.[45] Discovery will not be allowed, upon such an application, to enable the shareholder to establish his case,[46] but in appropriate circumstances he might be able to take proceedings against the company, which would enable him to compel disclosure of documents or other information which would be regarded by the court as sufficient to satisfy him.[47] On a similar section of the British Columbia Companies Act 1960 it was held that it was not unfair for the acceptors to delete an article prohibiting the transfer of shares to non-members until they had been offered to members who had declined to buy them. The article could have been changed at any time.[48] The court is not empowered to vary the terms of acquisition.[48a]

81–12 The procedure must not, however, be abused. In *Re Bugle Press Ltd.*,[49]

---

[40] *The Supreme Court Practice 1973*, Vol. 1, para. 102/2/21. This does not apply in Scotland.
[41] *Re Trinidad Oil Co. Ltd.*, *The Times*, April 13, 1957.
[42] *Re Hoare & Co.* (1933) 150 L.T. 374; *Re Evertite Locknuts* [1945] Ch. 220; *Re Press Caps* [1949] Ch. 434, C.A.; *Re Sussex Brick Co. Ltd.* [1961] Ch. 289; *Nidditch* v. *Calico Printers' Association*, 1961 S.L.T. 282; *Re Grierson, Oldham and Adams Ltd.* [1967] 1 W.L.R. 385; see also *Re Fras. Hinde & Sons Ltd. The Times*, April 23, 1966.
[43] See *per* Vaisey J. in *Re Evertite Locknuts* [1945] Ch. 220, 224; *Re Press Caps* [1949] Ch. 434, C.A. Although it may be sufficient if a "conspiracy of silence" could be proved.
[44] *Nidditch* v. *Calico Printers' Association Ltd.*, 1961 S.L.T. 282.
[45] *Re Grierson, Oldham and Adams Ltd.* [1967] 1 W.L.R. 385.
[46] *Re Press Caps* [1948] W.N. 351.
[47] See *per* Vaisey J. in *Re Evertite Locknuts* [1945] Ch. 220, 223.
[48] *Re Dad's Cookie Co. (B.C.) Ltd.* (1969) 7 D.L.R. (3d) 243 (Can.).
[48a] *Kinross* v. *Heritable Securities etc. Co.* 1935 S.N. 25.
[49] [1961] Ch. 270; followed in the Canadian case of *Esso Standard (Inter-America) Inc.* v. *J. W. Enterprises Inc.* (1963) 37 D.L.R. 598.

the majority shareholders had formed a new company which, as transferee company, went through the motions of the procedure under section 209 (1) with the aim of acquiring the shares of the minority shareholder. Buckley J. held that in such a case, exceptionally, the onus must lie with the transferee company to prove that the offer is a fair one, which the company was unable to do. The decision was affirmed by the Court of Appeal on the broader ground that the offer was a "barefaced attempt" to evade the fundamental rule forbidding the expropriation of a minority except as sanctioned by the articles.

If the court refuses the application or if no application is made, the transferee company becomes entitled upon the court refusing the application (if any), or (if no application is made) upon the expiration of one month from the notice, to acquire the shares of all persons upon whom notice was served under stage 3, and is, in fact, bound to acquire them. The acquisition is made upon the same terms as in the offer.

In order to make the acquisition the transferee company may appoint a person to execute a transfer of the shares on behalf of the shareholder: it then sends the transfer to the transferor company together with a copy of the notice which was sent to the shareholder, and together also with the consideration. The transferor company is then bound to register the transferee company in respect of the shares (s. 209 (3)). *Ad valorem* stamp duty is payable on the transfer, in the same manner as on the voluntary transfer of the shares of the assenting member.[50]

If the shares are represented by a share warrant, no instrument of transfer is required (s. 209 (3), proviso).

The transferor company pays into a separate bank account any consideration money received by it; and it holds such money and other consideration (*e.g.* shares of the transferee company) on trust for the former shareholders concerned (s. 209 (4)).

Stage 4: Notice to non-acceptors that transferee company holds 90 per cent. of the shares

81–13 If the transferee company acquires under a scheme or contract of this nature 90 per cent. of the shares of the transferor company, or acquires sufficient shares to aggregate, together with those which it already holds (in its own name or that of a nominee), more than 90 per cent., then within one month of the date of the transfer which gives the 90 per cent. it must give a notice to the dissenting shareholders (s. 209 (2)). This notice[51] gives the dissenting shareholders information as to the position and must be given in addition to any notice which may be given under stage 3 above.

[50] *Ridge Nominees Ltd.* v. *I.R.C.* [1962] Ch. 376 (C.A.).
[51] On Department of Trade Form 100A.

Stage 4a: Dissenting shareholders may require that their shares be acquired

81–14 Dissenting shareholders may thereafter within three months of the notice require the transferee company to acquire their shares,[52] and the transferee company is bound to do so. Such acquisition is either upon the same terms as in the offer, or upon terms agreed between the transferee company and the dissenting shareholder, or upon such terms as the court may order. Either the transferee company or the dissenting shareholder may apply to the court[53] for such an order.

Shares subject to Department of Trade restrictions

81–15 Under section 174 the Department of Trade may impose restrictions on the transfer and rights of shares if during the course of an investigation it appears necessary. In *Re Ashbourne Investments Ltd.*,[54] such restrictions had been placed on certain Ashbourne shares purchased by a Swiss bank which would not release the true owners' name. A bid for Ashbourne was made and accepted so that section 209 became operative and the offeror wished to purchase the outstanding shares held by the Swiss bank. To facilitate the bid Templeman J. released the shares from the restriction on transfer imposed under section 174 but upheld the other restrictions as to the receipt of sums due from the company on those shares. Accordingly the purchase money for the shares was to be frozen. In this way sections 174 and 209 could be compatible.

[52] On Department of Trade Form 100B.
[53] The court is that having jurisdiction to wind up the transferor company: application in the High Court is by summons under R.S.C. 1965, Ord. 102, r. 2.
[54] [1978] 1 W.L.R. 1346.

CHAPTER 82

SELF-REGULATION OF TAKE-OVER BIDS AND OF THE SECURITIES INDUSTRY—THE CITY CODE ON TAKE-OVERS AND MERGERS

Development and scope of the City Code on Take-overs and Mergers

2–01 The present, fifth, edition of the City Code was published in February 1981. It is supplemented by Panel Memoranda of Interpretation and Practice contained in the Practice Notes. The City Code, the Practice Notes and other supplementary documents are reproduced in the third volume of this work, Part D. The Panel on Take-overs and Mergers was constituted at the request of the Bank of England. It is representative of the City and has a permanent secretariat, headed by a Director-General. The constitution of the Panel and the supervision which it exercises under the Code are not founded on statutory regulations but represent an attempt by the leading financial interests in the City of London at voluntary self-discipline in the conduct of take-overs and mergers. Since 1978 the City Panel has been an integral part of the wider self-regulatory body, the Council for the Securities Industry,[1] but it is not subordinate to it.

Jurisdiction of the Panel

2–02 'The Code applies to offers for companies resident in the United Kingdom, which include the Isle of Man.[2] Resident for this purpose was defined according to Exchange Control rules, but with their abolition, the definition in the 1981 Code,[3] is based entirely on residence of the offeree company in the United Kingdom (including the Channel Islands) together with any Irish company listed on the Stock Exchange. A company is to be regarded as non-resident if it is incorporated outside the U.K. or if its head office and place of central management and control are situated outside the U.K.

The Code applies in addition to those individuals who "wish to have the facilities of the securities market in the United Kingdom available to them." It also applies to directors of public companies and those who seek to gain control of public companies. Private companies are excluded but not unquoted public companies and in fact it has been applied to such a company even though it no longer had any connection with the Stock Exchange. The matter was "brought to the Panel's attention," a necessarily haphazard process for unquoted companies.[4]

---

[1] See para. 82–21, *post*.
[2] Panel statement on *Manx and Overseas Investments Ltd.* [1978] J.B.L. 184.
[3] See [1981] J.B.L. 205.
[4] Panel statement on *The Anglo-Sumatran Rubber Co. Ltd.* [1980] J.B.L. 126.

A recent difficulty encountered by the Panel is the announcement abroad of a possible offer for a U.K. company, made in breach of the Code.[5] This problem of extra-territoriality in a world of direct communications is one yet to be resolved.

Administration of the Code

82–03 The function of the Panel is not only to supervise the conduct of take-overs and mergers, but also to advise at any stage both before the formal approach to the company and in the course of the actual merger. Accordingly, in any case of doubt, the Panel should be consulted, but naturally it cannot advise on the merits of a particular bid; this is a matter the shareholder must decide for himself. The address of the Panel is: The Stock Exchange Building, 20th Floor, London E.C.2., and communications should be directed to The Secretary of the Panel, P.O. Box No. 226, at that address.

The full Panel consists of a permanent chairman, a permanent deputy chairman, and the chairmen of the nine member bodies of the Panel. The Panel Executive is headed by a Director-General; it is responsible for the day-to-day administration of the Code. The Appeals Committee consists of a permanent chairman and three others drawn from the member bodies; the Appeals Committee is required to hear appeals from the decisions of the full Panel.

The right of appeal lies either where the Panel finds both a breach of the Code and proposes to take disciplinary action or when the dispute is as to the jurisdiction of the Panel. Alternatively, with the leave of the Panel, an appeal will be if a decision inflicts "serious hardship" on an individual or company. There is no appeal, however, on questions of fact or interpretation of the Code. The Panel has no jurisdiction outside the sphere of take-overs and mergers.[6]

Cases have arisen whereby one of the parties to a take-over obtains an injunction preventing the Panel from publishing its findings pending a subsequent hearing.[7] At least such action leaves the Panel with no alternative. More difficult is the situation where the parties are in dispute *inter se* rather than with the Panel, and either become involved in legal proceedings.[8] or merely threaten legal action against each other, *e.g.* over a profit forecast.[9] The attitude of the Panel so far has been to postpone any subsequent investigation until the happening and/or outcome of such proceedings are known. Two points of difficulty arise; first how long will the Panel delay on the threat of proceedings either against itself or between the

---

[5] Panel statement on *Rolls Royce Motors Holdings Ltd.* [1980] J.B.L. 421.

[6] Panel statement on *N.F.U. Development Trust* [1976] J.B.L. 162, and the Panel Report for 1975–76, p. 4. For the difficulties inherent in an extra-legal procedure see the Panel statement on *Seafield Amalgamated Rubber Co. Ltd.* [1976] J.B.L. 351.

[7] Panel statement on *Sandstar Ltd./Graff Diamonds Ltd.* [1979] J.B.L. 274.

[8] See *Dunford & Elliott Ltd.* v. *Johnson & Firth Brown Ltd.*, para. 82–04, *post*.

[9] Panel statement on *Lonrho Ltd./Dunford & Elliott Ltd.* [1979] J.B.L. 159. This particular dispute was resolved by a subsequent statement, [1980] J.B.L. 361.

parties, and secondly what precautions can it take against threats of proceedings by unscrupulous operators made with the sole purpose of delaying such investigation?

A further problem has recently arisen as a result of the Panel's extra-legal status. This concerned a Report, under section 167 of the Companies Act 1948 by two Department of Trade Inspectors, into the 1973 take-over by *C.S.T. Investments Ltd.* of the *Grendon Trust Ltd.* This Report included statements to the effect that the Inspectors were unable to persuade the Panel to hand over documents supplied to them in the course of their own investigations in 1973.[10] It also came to different conclusions from those of the Panel as to the conduct of some of the parties involved in the bid. The Inspectors accordingly recommended extension of their powers under section 167 to rectify their position *vis-à-vis* the Panel. The Panel immediately issued a statement[11] about these two issues. Its refusal to supply the required evidence was justified on the basis of confidentiality. Intending bidders or those involved in a bid would be unwilling to consult the Panel or disclose information if they thought that without this agreement, or under due process of law, this could be passed on to an outside body. Neither factor being present here, (s. 167 does not apply to those not involved with the company), the Panel refused to comply with any request for information which the Inspectors had no legal right to demand. This stance was backed by legal opinion. As to the conflict between the findings of the two investigations the Panel suggests that it would be surprising if an investigation over a number of years with full legal powers could not uncover more than was disclosed to the Panel. That both sides to this dispute have good arguments is obvious—who will win in the end is another matter.

Judicial attitudes to the Code

82–04 Very rarely has a case referred to the Panel also come before the courts but this happened in *Dunford & Elliott Ltd.* v. *Johnson & Firth Brown Ltd.*,[12] where an injunction was sought to prevent the abuse of alleged confidential information in a take-over situation. Both Lord Denning M.R. and Roskill L.J. quoted parts of the Code in their judgments and used it as a guide to good commercial practice in deciding whether to grant the injunction. In particular they were concerned with the giving of confidential information to certain shareholders only because the directors wished them to act as underwriters on a rights issue. Lord Denning M.R., speaking of the Code said: "Although this Code does not have the force of law, nevertheless it does denote good business practice and good business standards."[13]

---

[10] Panel statement on *C.S.T. Investment Trust Ltd./Grendon Trust Ltd.* [1974] J.B.L. 136.
[11] [1980] J.B.L. 364.
[12] [1977] 1 Lloyd's Rep. 505 (C.A.).
[13] *Ibid.* at p. 510.

Roskill L.J., speaking of the specific issue, commented:

> "Without for one moment presuming to criticise—other people are far better able to judge the rights and wrongs of such a situation than any judge can possibly be—I draw attention to the fact that this is perhaps a problem which may hereafter require consideration by the Panel to avoid any possible future conflict of interests, if indeed they are not already considering it."[14]

It would appear that in those areas which depend upon equitable considerations, such as the decision whether to grant an injunction, the Code may play an important role as indicating commercial morality. A panel statement has in fact been accepted as evidence by a Court considering disqualification orders against directors.[15]

In a subsequent case, *Graff* v. *Shawcross, MacDonald and Frazer*,[16] the Panel was held to be protected from any action for defamation in relation to letters it sent to the shareholders of a company under investigation, by the defence of 'qualified privilege.' The judge did not decide on whether such a defence would apply to the general publication of the Panel's findings—which must remain an open question. In fact the judge ordered the Panel not to publish its findings on the whole affair because the plaintiff was currently suing the Daily Telegraph for libel. In vain the Panel argued that by delaying that trial the plaintiff could effectively 'gag' the Panel for up to 3 years. The judge did, however, give the Panel leave to appeal to the court if there was considerable delay in disposing of the trial.[17]

The provisions of the Code fall into two categories: *viz.* the General Principles and the Rules.

General Principles

82–05 These have to be observed in the context of a take-over or merger transaction. There are 14 Principles concerned with the provision of adequate and timely information to the shareholders and the general responsibilities of the boards of both the offeror and offeree companies. The first Principle states that the spirit as well as the precise wording of those Principles and Rules must be observed, and the Panel has decided that this can be a breach of the Code without any specific rule being broken.[18]

Confidentiality of information

82–06 General Principle 3 requires that shareholders must be put in possession of all the facts necessary for the formation of an informed judgment as to the merits or demerits of an offer and shall have sufficient time to make an

---

14 *Ibid.* at p. 515.
15 *Re Gilgate Properties Ltd.* (1981) 131 N.L.J. 579.
16 Unreptd. Q.B.D. October 10, 1981.
17 The position may be different following the Contempt of Court Act 1981.
18 Panel decision and appeal on *Mount Charlotte Investments Ltd./Gale Lister & Co. Ltd.* [1974] J.B.L. 310. See also the Panel statement on *Chadderley Investments Ltd. (No.1)* [1979] J.B. 271, extending the scope of Rule 30 to dealings which were not strictly within its working.

assessment and decision. No relevant information shall be withheld from them. (See also Rule 15). Problems have arisen when information about an offeree company has been given to a restricted group of shareholders albeit in another capacity. One particular issue concerned merchant banks who receive information as advisers on a bid but who also act as shareholders and investment analysts. This was referred to in the Panel's report for 1970 stating that the different departments should act independently and not exchange information. A more complex situation arose in the bid by Johnson & Firth Brown Ltd. for Dunford & Elliott Ltd. which involved both the Panel and the Court of Appeal.[19]

D. & E. was in financial difficulties and decided to make a rights issue. It was thought that most of this would have to be taken up by the underwriters and when the institutional investors in D. & E. indicated that they might act as such, information was released to them on the strict understanding that it should not be used "in any way to influence investment decisions." There was a dispute as to the sufficiency of the proposed underwriters and the largest of them, the Prudential, indicated that further help would be necessary. J.F.B. was approached by the institutions concerned and shown the information. "They took copious notes." J.F.B. were possible bidders for D. & E. and after the underwriting scheme fell through decided to make a full offer for D. & E. D. & E. then applied for an injunction preventing the use of the information received by J.F.B. and restraining the bid. This was refused by the Court of Appeal on the basis that although the information had been given in a confidential manner which would be protected, it was not reasonable in these circumstances to enforce that confidentiality. This was because since the information had been given to the institutional shareholders (43 per cent. of the total) and also used by the directors of D. & E. themselves, the City Code required such information to be given to all shareholders in a bid situation. To withhold the information from the other shareholders would be wrong. The position was stated by Roskill L.J. as follows: "I do not see why this information which 43 per cent. of the shareholders and the directors have already should not . . . be made available to the others. The rules [of the City Code] so far from preventing this would seem to enourage it." Indeed Lord Denning M.R. considered that in asking for the injunction D. & E. was in breach of General Principle 4 which prohibits any attempt to interfere with a bona fide offer.

The bid proceeded and D. & E. appealed to the Panel. The Panel had to consider the wider issues raised—in particular the initial provision of the information to selected shareholders. This situation can of course arise outside a take-over situation but the Panel, despite the reservations of the Court of Appeal which commented on the dangers of giving certain shareholders privileged information, albeit in a different capacity, decided that there had been no breach of commercial ethics. Much reliance was placed

[19] Panel statement [1977] J.B.L. 161; see also [1977] 1 Lloyd's Rep. 505 (C.A.).

on the reputation of the Prudential. The subsequent release of the information to J.F.B. was categorised as an "error of judgment" by the Prudential, although they had been approached earlier by J.F.B. with an offer to purchase their holding in D. & E., a competitor. Finally the Panel allowed the bid to proceed "despite its anxieties" and refused to censure J.F.B. for the use of the information they had received as potential underwriters, apparently because the offer had only been made after the collapse of the underwriting scheme. In this report the observations of the Court of Appeal that D. & E. could also circularise shareholders after the bid and general knowledge of the information would prevent any damage occurring from the breach of confidentiality seem more convincing. Unresolved questions abound. How would a rival bidder fare in this situation? What limits are there to the giving of information to selected shareholders in whatever capacity? Roskill L.J. posed the issue thus:

> "This is a problem which has to be faced. It has to be solved if it possibly can be solved. Above all any solution must surely rest on some principle which secures fairness to all shareholders whether institutional or private so that all are dealing and are dealt with on the same terms."[20]

Creation of a false market in shares.

82–07 General Principle 5 (amplified by Practice Note No. 1) provides that it must be the object of all parties to a take-over or merger transaction to use every endeavour to prevent the creation of a false market in the shares of either an offeror or offeree company. In a statement the Panel has laid down certain criteria to be considered when such a situation arises.[21] The problem concerned the publication of negotiating figures at the pre-offer stage by the offeror's financial advisers because the market price was at that stage substantially above the then potential offer price. In fact this depressed the market but it subsequently recovered and the offeror in fact purchased shares on the market at a price substantially higher than either of the original prices. The Panel regards the concept of a false market as generally involving an element of contrivance by a buyer or seller or by both in collusion but also considers that all parties involved should have regard to the market consequences of their actions, if some step resulted in a market price which was manifestly unrealistic.

On the other hand, offerors should be able to fix their opening offers and revise their offers upwards without any need for justification (except for mandatory bid situations, etc.), and the Panel's declared policy is the encouragement of early announcements by potential offerors. But such announcements should not be made so as to jeopardise useful confidential discussions between a potential offeror and offeree. In particular with regard to the case before it, the Panel considered that if a figure for a

[20] [1977] 1 Lloyd's Rep. 505, 515.

[21] Panel statement on *Rockwell Corporation/Wilmot Breedon (Holdings) Ltd.* [1979] J.B.L. 367.

possible offer is mentioned on a confidential basis, there is no requirement that this figure should be immediately disclosed publicly. Above all the disclosure of the potential offer price was designed to affect the market and great care is needed in such operations.

The Rules

82–08 The 42 Rules[21a] are of a more detailed nature than the General Principles, although some are merely examples of the application of those Principles. In the 1974 version of the Code these Rules were sub-divided into headings but this practice was abandoned in the 1976 version. The headings used below are therefore for guidance only and are not part of the text of the Code. The following points give an indication of the ambit of the Rules—they are not exhaustive but concentrate on those Rules which have given the Panel most trouble in practice and around which an amount of interpretative material has grown up.

(i) *The Approach (Rules 1–4)*

82–09 An offer should be made first to the board of directors of the offeree company or to its advisers. The identity of the principal must be declared at the outset and the board of directors of the offeree company is entitled to be satisfied that the offeror company will be in a position to implement the offer in full. In addition the offeree board must obtain competent independent advice on all offers which must be circulated to the shareholders. This obligation is seen by the Panel[22] as applying not only to potential offers but in all circumstances where the control of the company is likely to be affected. The Panel also draws the attention of boards to ensure that no conflict of interests exist which could cast doubt on the objectivity of the advisers. The Panel has also become concerned at statements made to the media as to the tactical intention of the parties in a contested bid situation. Such statements as the future revision of the offer, profit forecasts, asset revaluations, etc. must not be misleading and any such statements which are misquoted or misleading by virtue of the pressures exerted in such situations must be corrected immediately.

(ii) *Early Stages (Rules 5–10)*

82–10 When a "firm intention" to make an offer is notified to the board of directors from a "serious source" a press notice must be issued immediately, which is followed by a circular to the shareholders. Before the announcement of the board, absolute secrecy must be observed. This should be read in conjunction with the Rules on dealings, *infra*. If there has been an approach which may or may not lead to an offer, Rule 5 used to suggest that an announcement of any talks should be made as soon as the

[21a] The 1981 version of the Code contained 39 rules. Three more were added in April 1982.
[22] Practice Note No. 9, December 1978.

two companies are reasonably confident of a successful outcome to negotiations. But in a joint statement with the Stock Exchange, the Panel instructed that it would expect an announcement either when the target company is reasonably confident that an offer will be made or when negotiations or discussions are about to be extended to embrace more than a small group of people.[23] This was incorporated into rule 5 in the 1981 edition of the Code. A potential offeror is warned as to preventing any such announcement, a frequent problem in the past.

It appears that initially, at least, this procedure was honoured in the breach.[24] In statements subsequent to the joint statement the Panel reiterated the importance of an early disclosure and in general has blamed the offeree company for failure to do so.[25]

In its report for the year ended March 31, 1978, the Panel stated that since the publication of the Joint Statement, 217 firm bid announcements had been made and in only one-third of these was an early announcement made. Against this, however, only in one-sixth of the total number of bids was an early announcement preceded by a price rise in the shares. Further, those early announcements which were made did not give rise to many cases where no actual bid followed—so that the reverse danger of too many speculative announcements has so far been avoided. On a slightly different theme, 70 bid announcements were followed by a temporary halt in dealings—a fact which the Panel regards as encouraging. In its report for the year ended March 31, 1979, the Panel admitted that success was not 100 per cent. and was concerned when a number of people are consulted about the proposed bid without any announcement. It also regards as unacceptable an informal requirement of a stated percentage commitment to an offer before making the offer. Where attempts to acquire this commitment before a public announcement may lead to a sudden rise on the market.

Warehousing, a practice whereby certain people are encouraged to buy shares in the offeree company by the offeror before the bid is announced so that the offeror may obtain their acceptance on such an announcement, is a clear breach of Rule 5. The difficulty is however one of proof and the Panel have been very wary of acting upon circumstantial evidence alone, yet it is difficult to see what other evidence an extra-legal body could adduce.[26]

The formal announcement must include any conditions to which the offer is subject including the "normal" conditions relating to acceptances,

---

[23] Joint statement by the Stock Exchange and the City Panel on the *"Announcement of Price-Sensitive Matters"* [1977] J.B.L. 251. For practical difficulties inherent in this statement see *The Times*, Business News, "Testing the insider trading rules" (12/5/77), "Panel faces problem on inside trading" (11/5/77); see also *Dunford & Elliott Ltd.* v. *Johnson & Firth Brown Ltd.* [1977] 1 Lloyd's Rep. 505 (C.A.). See also the earlier statement in [1977] J.B.L. 161.

[24] *e.g.* Panel statement on *Dickenson Robinson/Royal Sovereign Group Ltd.* [1978] J.B.L. 66.

[25] *e.g.* Panel statement on *Teachers (Distillers) Ltd./Allied Breweries Ltd.* [1978] J.B.L. 67. This does not always seem to be the best course to adopt however, see Panel statement on *Johnson & Firth Brown Ltd./British Rollmakers Corporation* [1978] J.B.L. 65.

[26] See the Panel statement on *Edgar Allen Ltd./Aurora Holdings Ltd.* [1979] J.B.L. 366.

quotation and increase of capital.[27] Further, if there is a possibility of a reference to the Monopolies and Mergers Commission then the offer must be subject to withdrawal on such a reference.[28] The offer document must be posted within 28 days unless the Panel has been consulted. If a definite offer has been announced it cannot be withdrawn without the Panel's consent.[29] If necessary the Panel will take steps to enforce completion of the offer, *e.g.* by freezing the voting rights of shares already obtained.[30]

(iii) *Board consideration of an offer (Rules 10–12; see also General Principles 6 and 11)*

82–11 The directors are required to act in the interests of the shareholders taken as a whole.[31] Special provisions apply to "shut-out" bids, *i.e.* bids under which an acceptance by the directors would give the offeror sufficient shares to render the bid successful. All bona fide potential offerors must be given the same information on request as that given to a preferred suitor. This applies, however, only to specific information given to a potential bidder for the purpose of deciding whether or not to make a bid.[32] The offer document must disclose any arrangements between the offeror and the offeree directors.

(iv) *Formal offers, documents supporting an offer or recommending the acceptance or rejection of an offer, documents evidencing an irrevocable undertaking to accept the offer (Rules 13–20; see also General Principles 3 and 12)*

82–12 These rules elaborate General Principle 12 that all documents, etc., falling within these headings must be treated with the same standard of care as if they were prospectuses within the meaning of the Companies Act 1948. For example, a statement that a company had substantial cash resources, which had in fact been turned into shares, was criticised by the Panel, even though the value of the shares remained the same as the cash figure shown in the offer document. Although the document was technically correct the shareholders were entitled to know the exact nature of the company's holding.[33]

Amongst the minimum content of the information to be disclosed must be the social and employment consequences of the projected take-over

---

[27] These used to be exempted from the Rule but problems arose, when, *e.g.* shareholders refused to sanction the necessary issue of shares because of a change in economic circumstances. See the Panel statements of January 15, 1974, and March 13, 1974 [1974] J.B.L. 135. Also *Northern Counties Securities Ltd.* v. *Jackson & Steeple Ltd.* [1974] 1 W.L.R. 1133.

[28] If any proposed offer requires clearance by, for example, the EEC authorities, the Code used to provide that the offer document must not be despatched without clearance. All such references have been omitted from the 1981 version of the Code.

[29] Panel statement on *Combined English Stores Ltd./David Grieg Ltd.* [1974] J.B.L. 309.

[30] See the Panel statement on *St. Martins Property Ltd./Hays Wharf Ltd.* [1974] J.B.L. 312. But see also the Panel statement on *B.S.Q. Securities Ltd./Court Hotels (London) Ltd.* [1976] J.B.L. 162.

[31] This may also be the legal position. See *Gething* v. *Kilner* [1972] 1 W.L.R. 337.

[32] Panel statement on *Scotia Investments Ltd.* [1975] J.B.L. 303.

[33] Panel statement on *York Trust Ltd./Greenwood and Batley Ltd.* [1978] J.B.L. 68.

(Rule 15). Rule 15 also requires disclosure of the offeror's intention with regard to the continuance of the business. In a statement[34] the Panel took the view that the wording in the offer document constituted only a statement of the offeror's intention at that time and did not impose a binding obligation as to its treatment of the business and considered that shareholders should have alerted themselves to the possibility of a change of policy. Press comment at the time was used by the Panel to justify their conclusion and their interpretation of the wording itself may be difficult to justify, but the real reason for the decision was that the complainant shareholders had purchased their shares subsequent to the offer and after the change of policy in this respect had been announced. This seems an eminently sensible point for the Panel to adopt.

Rule 15 (amplified by Practice Note No. 5) is also an extension of General Principle 3 in the sense that the same information must be given to all shareholders. This was the opinion of the Court of Appeal in *Dunford & Elliott Ltd.* v. *Johnson & Firth Brown Ltd.*[35] Judicial consideration was also given to Rule 16 by Lord Denning M.R. in that case. This rule requires that care must be taken in profit forecasts and assets valuations and that independent valuers should be brought in to certify them. Lord Denning M.R. suggested that if it was urgent to reply to a bid the offeree company could give the forecasts explaining that there had been no time to vouch them. The Panel has been much concerned with profit forecasts. In its Report for 1977–78 the Panel stated that its present practice is to monitor forecasts on a sample basis, chosen at random, unless special factors are present. In judging a failed forecast the Panel will use the standard of what the directors knew and could reasonably have foreseen at the time when it was made. If the company has subsequently been absorbed into a group it is more difficult to judge the accuracy of a forecast made while it was still independent, to results published as a member of the group. The Panel has to decide whether the forecast was valid by estimating the results it would have achieved if the bid had not succeeded, assuming a quotation on the Stock Exchange and a consistent application of the then existing management and accounting policies.[36] If legal action is threatened by one of the parties over the forecast the Panel will postpone its investigations.[37]

Rule 16 is amplified by Practice Note Nos. 4, 6, 7 and 8. This extends the rule to forecasts existing when the bid is made on the grounds that they are likely to be mentioned by financial commentators and thus form an important factor in the shareholder's decisions. They should therefore be included in offer documents even if not expressly referred to in such documents. In its statement on *Vantona Group Ltd./ J. Crompton, Sons & Webb (Holdings) Ltd.*[38] the Panel allowed an exception to this require-

[34] On *British Investment Trust Ltd.* [1979] J.B.L. 161.
[35] [1977] 1 Lloyd's Rep. 505 (C.A.).
[36] See generally the Panel statement on *Crane Fruehauf Ltd.* [1978] J.B.L. 184.
[37] Panel statement on *Dunford & Elliott Ltd.* [1979] J.B.L. 159.
[38] [1979] J.B.L. 160.

ment largely at the request of the other party to the bid, stressing that this was an exceptional case and that it would not regard difficulties in putting such forecasts into a suitable form in the offer document as an excuse. The Panel takes the view that any projection of the type will become subject to the Code if a subsequent bid situation arises and that withdrawal of the forecast at that stage is inappropriate unless replaced by an up-to-date forecast complying with the Code. A full explanation will be required in default.

(v) *Mechanics of the formal offer (Rules 21–29)*

2–13 No offer which if accepted in full, would result in the offeror having voting control can be declared unconditional unless acceptances are received or promised amounting to a total of 50 per cent. of the voting rights of the equity share capital. Time limits are laid down within which each stage of the transaction must be implemented and when public statements as to the result of the bid are to be made.[39] In its Practice Note No.11 the Panel gives guidance to offerors who have included a cash underwritten alternative in their offer and who are faced with having to extend it for 14 days once it has succeeded, by virtue of Rules 22 and 23. In such cases the alternative offer may be limited to the period for which it was negotiated, which will act as a shut-off notice to avoid the 14-day period under Rule 23. On the other hand when there are competing offers no shut-off notice may be given between the time when the competing offer has been announced and the competition situation has ended. If the notice has been given prior to the announcement of a competing offer, there are provisions entitling the offeror to amend or withdraw the notice. A shut-off notice for this purpose includes any public announcement to that effect. There are complex provisions for partial offers (Rule 27) which are, in principle, disapproved. If the offeror intends to invoke section 209[40] and the offer is for more than one class of shares, then the offer should state that section 209 will only be invoked for each class separately.

(vi) *Dealings (Rules 30–37; see also General Principle 9)*

2–14 Rule 30 provides that all persons privy to confidential price-sensitive information must treat that information as secret and must not pass it on to any other person unless it is necessary to do so. Nor should such persons make any recommendations to any other person as to dealing in the relevant securities. Accident leakage of information must be guarded against. In addition, dealings, including options, in the securities of the offeror and offeree company by persons 'privy to such information"[41] are prohibited between the first intimation of the bid and the public

[39] See, *e.g.* the Panel statement on *Babcock & Wilcox Ltd./Woodall-Duckham Group Ltd.* [1973] J.B.L. 235.

[40] See para. 81–05, *ante*.

[41] As defined by the Code. See also the Panel statement on *Johnson & Firth Brown Ltd./ Dunford & Elliott Ltd.* [1977] J.B.L. 161.

announcement. Together with Rule 5 relating to the announcement of a prospective offer, this provision is an attempt to inhibit insider trading by preventing both the leakage of information and dealings by the "informed." Nevertheless, a pattern has been established. There is a substantial price movement in the market price of shares in a company the reason for which becomes apparent when a take-over bid involving the company is subsequently announced. Subsequent investigations rarely bring to light any dealings by actual "insiders."[42]

In a statement the Stock Exchange and the Panel recommended the establishment of security procedures for price-sensitive information both by companies and their advisers which together with the revised Rule 5 noted above and the possibility of a temporary suspension of quotation puts the responsibility for such developments on to the offeree company.[43]

Recent statements by the Panel have extended the application of Rule 30. In *Chaddesley Investments Ltd. (No. 1)*[44] the "spirit" of Rule 30 was held to apply to someone giving advice to another to deal, if he knows that a bid might occur or that at least the share price would rise. The latter seems to be a general definition of insider trading but not necessarily linked to a bid situation. In fact a bid did take place but the "insider" had no certain knowledge of that fact at the time. In *Chaddesley Investments Ltd. (No. 2)*[45] Rule 30 was also applied to an employee who knew of a chain of events, the most probable consequence of which was the creation of a bid situation, and that the company would be reconstituted under new management. This latter event in fact gave rise to the profit, and it was decided that even though the employee could not know the exact shape of the deal which finally emerged the fact that he knew of events which would benefit shareholders was sufficient.

One potential difficulty concerns the position of the directors of a company which has been the potential target company for a substantial period of time and subjected to a series of abortive bid enquiries. In one case,[46]

---

[42] See the Panel statement on *United Drapery Stores Ltd./William Timpson Ltd.* [1973] J.B.L. 37; Panel statement on *G.K.N. Ltd. and Miles Drew & Co. Ltd.* [1974] J.B.L. 309; Panel statement on *Boots Co. Ltd. and House of Fraser Ltd.* [1975] J.B.L. 43; *cf.* the Panel decisions on *P. R. Grimshawe & Co. Ltd. Grimshawe—Windsor Merger* [1973] J.B.L. 46 and *D.F. Lyons & Co. Ltd.* [1973] J.B.L. 451.

[43] Joint statement by the Stock Exchange and the City Panel on the *Announcement of Price Sensitive Matters* [1977] J.B.L. 251. See further the Panel Statements on *Johnson & Firth Brown Ltd./British Rollmakers Corporation* [1978] J.B.L. 65; *Dickenson Robinson Group Ltd./Royal Sovereign Group Ltd.* [1978] J.B.L. 66; *Teachers (Distillers) Ltd./Allied Breweries Ltd.* [1978] J.B.L. 67; *C. H. Johnson and Sons Ltd.* [1978] J.B.L. 183; *J. B. Eastwood Ltd.* [1979] J.B.L. 47. But the problems of defining culpable insider trading remains; see the Panel statement on *Dexion-Comino International Ltd.* [1975] J.B.L. 303. See also the Panel statement on *Racal Electronics Ltd./Electronics Holdings Ltd.* [1978] J.B.L. 67. Problems are compounded when the purchasers are Swiss Banks who legally refuse to disclose their clients' identities: Panel statement on *Dunford & Elliott Ltd.* [1978] J.B.L. 367.

[44] [1979] J.B.L. 271.

[45] [1979] J.B.L. 273.

[46] Panel statement on *Associated Communications Corporations Ltd./Intereuropean Property Holdings Ltd.* [1980] J.B.L. 49.

the Panel had no difficulty in discovering a breach of Rule 30. But in other cases it may prove more difficult.

Rule 30 must now be read subject to the criminal sanctions on insider dealings imposed by the 1980 Companies Act. These are dealt with in Chapter 68, *supra.* All dealings must also be read subject to rules 40 and 41, below, and the C.S.I. Rules governing Substantial Acquisitions of Shares. See para. 82–24, below.

If the offeror or anyone acting in concert with him[47] purchases shares at above the offer price, then that price must be increased to the highest price so paid. If 15 per cent. or more of the shares of a class are acquired for cash, the offer must include a cash alternative, being the highest price paid for such shares. A cash alternative may also be required if the offeror cannot fulfil the paper offer.[48] When a revised offer is announced it should "whenever practicable" disclose the number of securities purchased and the price paid. Where the offer involves a further issue of already listed shares the current value of the offer is the mid-point between the closest prices quoted between jobbers.

Where shares are purchased at above the offer value after the offer has expired the Panel, in its Report for 1977–78, stated that since Rule 32 no longer applies, General Principle 8 (equal treatment of shareholders) requires that even if the offer period has ended, so long as the offer remains open the offeror should not buy shares in the offeree company at above the offer price without prior consultation with the Panel.

The method of calculating whether the requisite 15 per cent. or more of the voting rights have been acquired within the previous 12 months allowed by the Panel so as to invoke the cash alternative obligation, is to use a net figure for that period; *i.e.* purchases less sales. Gross figures are only used when the transactions are actually linked with the offer.[49]

In addition no offerer may, prior to the first closing date, be permitted to announce that his offer price will not be increased.[50]

82–15 MANDATORY BIDS—RULE 34. Since January 1972 the Code has contained rules which require a compulsory bid to be made by a purchaser of shares who has amassed a significant holding of the shares without making a formal offer. This has always presented problems of enforcement, particularly in times of economic depression,[51] and the present position is that

---

[47] See the definitions section of the code, and Panel statements on Midland-Yorkshire Holdings Ltd./Creda International Ltd. [1976] J.B.L. 163; *St. Piran Ltd. (No.1)* [1980] J.B.L. 270.

[48] To avoid the problems such as those raised in the Panel statement on *St. Martins Property Ltd./Hays Wharf Ltd.* [1974] J.B.L. 312.

[49] Panel statement on *Dalgety Ltd./Spillers Ltd.* [1980] J.B.L. 50. For dealings in shares by directors and employees of companies in the shares of those companies on occasions other than a take-over situation see the Stock Exchange Model Code for Securities Transactions by Directors of Limited Companies, see para. 82–26, *post,* and Vol. II, para. C–902.

[50] C.S.I. Statement, 24/9/81.

[51] See, *e.g.* Panel statement on *St. Martin's Property Ltd./Hays Wharf Ltd.* [1974] J.B.L. 312; *Ashbourne Investments Ltd.* [1975] J.B.L. 44; *St. Piran Ltd. (No. 1)* [1980] J.B.L. 270; *St. Piran Ltd. (No. 2).* [1980] J.B.L. 358.

anyone who, together with persons acting in concert,[52] has acquired 30 per cent. or more of the voting rights by a series of transactions or who, owning between 30 and 50 per cent. of such rights within a period of a year shall make an offer. The rule is activated by a relevant purchase by any one member of a group who have previously "come together" to obtain control of a company. There is no need to prove an acquisition by each member after the relevant purchase.[53] The obligation extends to each of the principal members of a consortium if the facts so warrant.

The Panel may waive the enforcement of this rule in special circumstances.[54] The Panel will consider evidence of events after the acquisition to decide whether persons are "actively co-operating" to obtain control of a company within this rule. Ignorance of the Code is no defence but it may affect the interpretation to be given to some aspects of the transaction. In one extreme case ignorance of a Panel ruling that certain persons were acting in concert by one of those persons was held to be sufficient to render a purchase by him triggering off the rule as "inadvertent." Instead of insisting on a mandatory bid the Panel required him to sell the shares so purchased "in the normal way," not to increase his shareholding and to prevent his "partners" from doing the same.[55] The directors of a company are not usually regarded as being "in concert" with their company for this purpose but paragraph 3 of Practice Note No. 15 provides the alternative presumption if a bid has been made.

If the implementation of such an offer would require a resolution, then no purchases which would give rise to the offer shall be made. The offers must be in cash or have a cash alternative. The offer must be conditional on acceptances carrying 50 per cent. of the voting rights and, if it does not become conditional, then no further shares may be purchased.

The rule was strengthened as a result of the prolonged dispute over *Ashbourne Investments Ltd.*[56] In addition to extending liability to all principal members of a consortium, the 1976 Code requires an announcement of an offer "immediately upon an acquisition of shares" giving rise to an obligation under Rule 34, together with confirmation by the financial adviser that resources are available to satisfy full acceptance of the offer. Further, pending the posting of the offer document, no nominees of the potential offerer shall be appointed to the board of the offeree company and the voting strength already acquired by the potential offeror is to be effectively frozen.

Despite the revision of the rule in 1976 it is still causing problems both of proof and enforcement. In its most complex investigation yet the Panel had to rely on strong circumstantial evidence as to the existence of a group who

---

[52] See the Panel statement on *Winchester London Trust Ltd.* [1976] J.B.L. 164.
[53] Panel statement on *St. Piran Ltd. (No. 1)* [1980] J.B.L. 270.
[54] Panel statement on *Manx & Overseas Investments Ltd.* [1978] J.B.L. 184. See also Panel statement on *Rothmans International Ltd.* [1981] J.B.L. 373.
[55] Panel statement on *Orme Developments Ltd./St. Piran Ltd.* [1979] J.B.L. 48.
[56] [1976] J.B.L. 259.

were acting in concert and who had incurred an obligation under this rule. The Panel Statement on *St. Piran (No. 1)*,[57] was concerned with the activities of eight overseas companies, all located in the offices of professional advisers and with no identifiable shareholders. One was described as being owned by "non-beneficial migratory discretionary trusts." None of the principal individuals concerned was disposed to assist the Panel in its investigation and circumstantial evidence of control by one party was accepted as sufficient. The complex nature of the web of control so disclosed has involved the Panel in much time and expense but there remains the enforcement problem, which is as yet unsolved. This is despite a second statement, *St. Piran (No. 2)*,[58] where attempts to extract an undertaking not to vote with acquired shares failed and the blunt weapon of a complete freeze on all dealings in the shares used. The facilities of the market are in addition being withdrawn from those concerned. None of this will help the company's other shareholders.

A similar problem of enforcement arose in the Panel statement on *Gilgate Holdings Ltd.*[59] The three parties acting in concert took elaborate but unavailing steps to conceal their connection. Having been discovered they accepted the obligation to make a general offer under Rule 34 but they then had no money nor could they borrow the necessary funds. Proposals involving the control of or arrangements concerning their companies proved unsatisfactory largely due to the vulnerability of the independent shareholders of those companies. No solution to the problem has yet appeared.

Practice Note No. 15 expanding Rule 34, covers the situation (rare at the moment) whereby control is obtained partly by a purchase of shares giving the purchaser less than 30 per cent. of the offeree shares, and then partly by a subsequent issue to the purchaser of further shares, bringing his holding above 30 per cent. in exchange for assets. If the latter deal is approved by the shareholders no bid would at present need to be made. On the other hand, if the order of the two deals had been reversed, a bid would have had to be made at the highest price paid for the shares. In future the Panel proposes to look at the operation as a whole and intimates that dispensations will not be automatic.

82–16 CITY CODE AND THE C.S.I. RULES. In 1981 the C.S.I. published Rules governing Substantial Acquisitions of Shares.[60] These were originally framed for "dawn raids" of the type experienced in 1980 and were originally intended to apply to acquisitions giving a holding of between 15 and 30 per cent. The limit of 30 per cent. being imposed because Rule 34 of the City Code would then operate. In 1981 events proved that a general offer

57 [1980] J.B.L. 270.
58 [1980] J.B.L. 358.
59 [1980] J.B.L. 269.
60 See para. 82–24, *post*.

would rapidly follow an acquisition of *de facto* control of a company. Accordingly the C.S.I. Rules were amended to leave out the 30 per cent. upper limit. The Rules basically provide a 7 day freeze on all offers to acquire more than a 15 per cent. holding.

In addition the City Code was amended by the introduction of Rules 40, 41 and 42.[61] Rule 40 applies prior to the announcement of a bid. Anyone who owns less than 30 per cent. of the voting rights of a company may not increase his holding above 30 per cent. prior to the announcement of an offer. Anyone who owns 30 per cent. already, but less than 50 per cent., may not acquire more than 2 per cent. prior to the announcement of an offer. There are two exceptions: acquisitions which immediately precede and are conditional on the announcement of an agreed bid and acquisitions from a single shareholder. Similar restrictions apply after the making of an offer (Rules 41 and 42).

82–17 RULE 36. Rule 36 (amplified by Practice Note No. 16) prohibits an offeror from entering into arrangements to make purchases of shares in the offeree company if such arrangements have attached thereto favourable conditions which are not extended to all shareholders. The Panel does however allow an exception if the payments can be justified commercially. This exception was discussed in the statement on *Mooloya Investments Ltd./ Customagic Manufacturing Co. Ltd.*[62] The case involved complex negotiations for the transfer of family shares to the offeror company, during which procurement fees were paid to a shareholder, who did believe the take-over to be essential for the offeree company's survival. On the facts the fees were disallowed. The exception was stated to apply to payments which are commercially justifiable and which would have been made irrespective of whether the recipient owned shares. In this case the payments were seen as inducements for him to sell his own shares. Consultation with the Panel is advised before making any such payments. A legal opinion was not enough—the Code is not a legal document.[63]

82–18 FORMULA BIDS. Recent bids for investment trust companies have been expressed in terms of a formula, *e.g.* an offer of a net precentage of the net asset value per share on the date on which the offer becomes unconditional. This can present problems when shares have been purchased before then for cash on the market. Rule 32 (amplified by Practice Note No. 13) requires the market price of any shares so purchased to be substituted for the offer price if the former is higher. Rules 33 and 34 say in effect that if the offeror buys 15 per cent. of the voting rights of the offeree shares during the offer period or within 12 months before or if he acquires in all 30 per cent. of the voting rights he must make an offer in cash at the highest price paid in the offer period or the 12 months before. How do these relate

61 As from 7/4/82. See [1982] J.B.L. 314.
62 [1979] J.B.L. 49.
63 See also the Panel Report for the year to March 31, 1979, p. 8.

to formula bids? In the Panel Statement on *The National Coal Board Pension Funds/The British Investment Trust*,[64] the Panel surprisingly agreed that for Rule 32 the market price paid for shares should be judged against the formula value on the date of purchase and not the date when the offer becomes unconditional. But for the purposes of Rules 33 and 34 (see also Practice Note Nos. 14 and 15) the requirement of an alternative cash offer meant the highest cash price paid in pence on the market and not the highest percentage under the formula. The Panel accepted the principle of formula bids for investment trust companies "for the purposes of the present case" but left the general question open. In particular they disapproved of a clause in the bid whereby the offeror, but not the offeree, had the right to abandon the bid if there was an alteration in market values. In its report for 1977–78 the Panel expressed concern over the different definitions used of "net asset value" in the various formulae. This may be done on a going concern basis, break-up value basis or a mixture of both. Principals and their advisers are therefore asked by the Panel to clarify which basis is being used, not only in offer documents but also in statements to the Press.

(vii) *Changes in the situation of company during a bid (Rule 38)*

2–19 In the case of an actual or imminent offer, the board must not, without approval of the members, issue shares or grant options or sell or otherwise dispose of material assets, except under a pre-existing contract.[65]

A declaration and payment of interim dividends, outside the ordinary course of business, during the course of a bid, if sufficiently large, could be seen as designed to complicate an offer which, in the usual way, entitles the offeror to the benefit of any dividends subsequently declared and paid. This is seen as a potential breach of Rule 38 which would enable the offeror to withdraw if the offer document has not been posted. Offeree companies are therefore asked to consult the Panel before issuing such a dividend, even during a reference to the Monopolies Commission.

(viii) *Registration of transfers (Rule 39)*

2–20 In order to enable the members to exercise their rights, prompt registration of transfers is required.

(ix) *Sanctions*

2–21 The Introduction to the City Code indicates the sanctions which can be applied if the Panel finds that there has been a breach of the Code. A private reprimand or public censure may be administered and in flagrant cases action may be taken designed to deprive the offender temporarily or

---

[64] [1978] J.B.L. 182.

[65] See, *e.g.* Panel statement on W. Henshall & Sons (Addlestone) Ltd./Bovbourne Ltd. [1979] J.B.L. 46.

permanently of his ability to enjoy the facilities of the security market.[66] The Panel has no power to impose statutory sanctions.

The Panel may also suggest to the Stock Exchange a suspension of dealings in specified shares, a remedy rarely used as it affects the innocent as well as the guilty. The Panel may further make suggestions to the Department of Trade, *e.g.* under the Prevention of Fraud (Investments) Act 1958 or the Licensed Dealers Rules.

The Council for the Securities Industry

82–22 In 1978 the City institutions set up a new self-regulating body, to be known as the Council for the Securities Industry (C.S.I.). The City Panel is an integral part of the C.S.I. but is not subordinate to it. Links are established by the chairman of the C.S.I. becoming a member of the Panel and the deputy chairman of both bodies being the same. The appellate structure of the Panel remains intact. One significant effect on the Panel is that the C.S.I.'s Markets Committee replaces the City Working Party as the body responsible for revising the wording of the Code itself. The ambit of the C.S.I. is the regulation of all aspects of securities regulations. The regulation of take-over bids remains with the City Panel but in practice much of the C.S.I.'s work will impinge upon take-overs, particularly in the grey areas of pre-bid manoeuvres.

The C.S.I. has created a Standing Committee for the investigation of complaints and cases of alleged misconduct within the securities industry. This will consider complaints either from the public or the member associations about decisions made by member associations under their own rules which appear to raise questions of principle for the future. It is not however intended as an appeal body in respect of decisions already taken. The Committee will also deal with any cases of alleged misconduct or breach of a code of conduct which cannot properly be dealt with under the domestic rules of the member associations. Initially complaints will be heard by the Chairman, Deputy Chairman and Secretary of the Council who will initiate any required action.

The C.S.I. is funded by a levy on all contract notes over £5,000. The current levy is 60p. The Council also publishes an annual report and has published several important documents which impinge on the take-over field. The two most important are a code of conduct for all dealers in securities and the Rules governing Substantial Acquisitions of Shares.[67]

Code of conduct for dealers in securities

82–23 With effect from August 1, 1980 all persons in the United Kingdom who, as intermediaries (either as principals or agents) engage in the business of

[66] See Panel statements on *Ashbourne Investments Ltd.* [1975] J.B.L. 44; *St. Piran Ltd. (No. 2)* [1980] J.B.L. 358.

[67] See also the *Statement on Insider Dealing* (C.S.I. No. 5), June 1981; and the *Guidelines for Personal Dealings by Fund Managers* (C.S.I. No. 4), March, 1981.

arranging or undertaking transactions in transferable securities for investors will be subject to a code of conduct published by the C.S.I. in May 1980. Its application will however be the responsibility of the constituent associations of the C.S.I. to whom all complaints of infringement should be directed.

The objective of the new Code is to "establish standards of ethical behaviour so as to promote the effective functioning of the securities markets and to safeguard the public interest." It covers transactions in all transferable securities, whether or not they are listed on the Stock Exchange. There are 25 rules.

Rule 1, like the City Code, requires dealers to observe the spirit as well as the letter of the Code. Rule 2 demands observation of the highest standards of professional conduct and complete integrity, and Rule 3 requires dealers to act 'fairly' in accordance with the Code's objectives even if this means forgoing a personal advantage. Rule 4 embodies the fiduciary principle of avoiding a conflict of interest and duty, particularly where a dealer is operating in several capacities. The duty to the client is paramount but by Rule 5 subject to observing the spirit and letter of the Code.

More specifically Rule 6 prohibits any practice which might lead to a false market. This is defined to include a market in which the movement in the price of a security or the level of the price of a security is created by the publication of information which is false, exaggerated or tendentious or is brought about or sought to be brought about by contrived factors. These include buyers and sellers acting in collaboration calculated to achieve a false market price. When listing is suspended a dealer must not make a market (*i.e.* hold himself out as buying/selling that security), and if he deals in that security he must inform the client of the fact and grounds of suspension (Rules 8 and 9).

Turning to the client-dealer transactions Rule 10 requires transmission to the client of an authenticated duty-stamped contract note or other confirmation for all transactions, and Rule 11 contains a minimum content list for such notes etc. Rule 12 requires compliance with all rulings, etc., of the C.S.I. and Rule 13 with the City Code and City Panel. Rule 14 forbids the encouragement of dealings with the sole object of generating commission. Charges are to make clear to any new client as are generally any arrangements for shared commission (Rules 15 and 16). Commission from the other party to the transaction are to be disclosed except in respect of normal underwriting commission (Rule 17). No commission is to be charged on sales by a dealer as principal to a client except for bona fide placings and separate accounts for each client must be kept (Rules 18 and 19).

The terms and conditions of managing investments for a client should be specified, four compulsory terms are set out, and separate records kept of each such client—Rules 20, 21. Rules 22–24 concern the financial position of the dealer himself. First he must have his accounts properly audited by someone who would satisfy the requirements of the Companies Act. A copy of the latest balance sheet should be available to check, apart from those whose professional body scrutinises them. Insurance against negligence and dishonesty is to be compulsory. Finally, a dealer is to provide, under Rule 25, every possible assistance with enquiries undertaken by the C.S.I.

Rules Governing Substantial Acquisitions of Shares—Market or dawn raids

82–24 A market raid occurs when there is a sudden acquisition of substantial shareholdings in a company in circumstances which, for practical purposes, seen to deny to those whose shares are not held by banker or brokers under discretionary management, the opportunity of selling their shares at the attractive price offered. An example occurred in February 1980 in connection with the shares of *Consolidated Gold Fields Ltd.*[68] On February 11 Gold Fields shares stood at 525p. It appears that the following morning brokers asking for Anglo/De Beers informed clients and/or jobbers that they would be in the market for a substantial number of Gold Fields shares. At the start of trading the price quoted was 615/617p. and by 10.00 a.m. the brokers had acquired 16.5 million shares at 616p. Purchases then ceased and the price eased and fell back to 510p. Because the purchasers had not acquired 30 per cent. of the shares no mandatory bid was required under the City Code. The C.S.I. had to act.

The C.S.I. originally published two statements, the joint effect of which was to ban market raids until some way of regulating them could be discovered.[69] The definitive Rules governing the Substantial Acquisitions of Shares were published in December 1981. They are administered by the City Panel. As originally framed they only applied to acquisitions of shares, within 7 calendar days, carrying voting rights amounting to 5 per cent. or more of those in a company, which would take the purchaser's holding to 15 per cent. or more of that company's shares, up to a maximum of 30 per cent. at which stage Rule 34 of the City Code applies.[70] Such offers could only take place either by means of a full or partial offer under the City Code or by a tender offer under the Rules. However, events in 1981 demonstrated that the dawn or market raid had changed into a number of rapid changes of complete control of public companies by a substantial purchase of a controlling interest of shares, often in a matter of hours. Thus control of a company could pass before the directors of the target company could have an opportunity to consider the bid and give advice. Since the, one price, offer for the controlling number of shares usually amounted to over 30 per cent. the Rules did not apply, and since a full offer for all the remaining shares was made later at the same price the City Code had not been breached.

---

[68] See the Panel Report for 1979–80, [1980] J.B.L. 359.
[69] [1980] J.B.L. 422.
[70] See para. 82–15A, *ante*.

The C.S.I. had to act to slow down the rate at which an offeror is able to acquire a controlling interest. The Rules were amended to cut out the 30 per cent. upper limit so that they apply to any purchase of above 5 per cent. to give the purchaser a total of above a 15 per cent. holding in a company. Such purchases, including options, can now only take effect, first, under a partial or full offer regulated by the City Code and then only after a 7 day waiting period from the announcement of the offer. In other words no offer for shares in a company can be implemented within 7 days of its announcement.[71] Rules 40 and 41 of the City Code further control this situation.[71a] The alternative is to make a tender offer in accordance with the Rules.

TENDER OFFERS. Under this procedure the buyer makes a firm offer to buy a specified number of shares either at a fixed price or up to a maximum price that he is prepared to pay. In the latter case he then invites shareholders to say at what price they tender shares up to that price and he then accepts all shares tendered at or below that price (the striking price) at which his needs are met. *Maximum tender offers* are the only ones allowed to the Stock Exchange at the moment. If insufficient shares are tendered the shareholders will be paid the maximum price unless the aggregate tendered is so low that it becomes void (currently 1% of the voting rights in the company). No other conditions may be enforced. Tendering shareholders will be bound by their tenders. The purchaser and his associates are on the other hand forbidden to deal in the relevant shares during the tender period. There are publicity requirements in addition.

SINGLE PURCHASER. None of the Rules apply if the purchase is from a single seller. This concept includes a group of the same family or companies, or those with a pre-existing common interest.

Stock Exchange Regulations

82–25 The requirements of the Stock Exchange in relation to take-over bids are set out in Chapter 5 of the Stock Exchange publication, *Admission of Securities to Listing*, issued in March 1973 and revised in April 1979 and April 1981. This contains seven rules and the text of the City Code. It is expressly stated that the Council of the Stock Exchange attaches great importance to its observation.[72] The rules for the most part supplement the City Code and are generally applicable where either the offeror or offeree is a listed company.

Model code for securities transactions by directors of listed companies

82–26 On October 25th, 1977, the Stock Exchange published a model code

[71] C.S.I. statement, September 24, 1981.
[71a] See para. 82–16, *ante*.
[72] So that they are prepared to refuse a licence or quotation to anyone in breach of the Code. See, *e.g.* the Panel statements on *St. Martins Property Ltd. and Hays Wharf Ltd.* [1974] J.B.L. 312 and *Ashbourne Investments Ltd.* [1975] J.B.L. 44.
[73] See Vol. II, para. C–902.

under the above-mentioned title.[73] The model code has since been appended to the listing agreement and listed companies are required to adopt a code incorporating no less exacting provisions.

The basic principles of the model code are:

1. Directors shall not deal in their companies' securities on a short term basis.
2. Directors must accept that they are not at all times free to deal in their companies' securities.
3. While there are periods in the year in which the directors are free to deal in their companies' securities, dealing should normally not take place during a minimum period prior to the announcement of recurring information, particularly on profits, dividends and other distributions, or prior to the announcement of exceptional price-sensitive matter.
4. Certain specified topics are presumed to be price-sensitive. As regards others, the directors should use their best judgment.
5. The prohibited period for dealing before the announcement of regularly recurring information is capable of definition, and is so defined in the model rules (see below). The prohibited period prior to the announcement of matters of an exceptional nature is not capable of definition. There should be no delay in making the announcement.

The basic principles are enlarged and rendered more precise in the model rules which follow them in the model code. They are devised to be adopted by listed companies when formulating their own codes. Of particular importance is model Rule 3.1 which provides that during two months prior to the preliminary announcement of the company's annual results and half-yearly results, together with dividends and distributions to be paid or passed, the directors shall not purchase securities of the company, nor shall they sell them unless exceptional circumstances so compel, such as, *e.g.* pressing financial commitments. The attitude of the City Panel to the model code has been to say the least ambivalent. In its statement on *W. Henshall & Sons (Addlestone) Ltd./Bovbourne Ltd.*[74] the Panel dismissed it as irrelevant apparently on the basis that it was not then either part of the listing agreement or the City Code, but in a subsequent statement[75] it was set out in detail but no comment made as to its application. In that case it had been adopted by the company, as in a third statement[76] where the company was censured for not drawing its provisions to the attention of a senior employee. If it is not part of the City Code, should it be mentioned at all? By including the model code in its statements the Panel would appear to be using it as evidence or otherwise of improper conduct whilst purporting not to apply the code itself.

---

[74] [1979] J.B.L. 46.
[75] Panel statement on *J. B. Eastwood Ltd.* [1979] J.B.L. 47.
[76] Panel statement on *Chaddesley Investments Ltd. (No. 2)* [1979] J.B.L. 273.

C. MERGER CONTROL

CHAPTER 83

MERGER CONTROL UNDER UNITED KINGDOM LAW

83–01 CHAPTERS 79–82 dealt with take-overs and mergers purely from the standpoints of investor and creditor protection. In modern times, however, legislation has been enacted to enable large-scale mergers to be investigated and, where necessary, prohibited in the public interest. The concerns of this legislation are industrial structure, competition and consumer protection. Provision for the control of mergers as such was first made in the Monopolies and Mergers Act 1965. That Act has now been repealed and re-enacted, with modifications, in the Fair Trading Act 1973. The general scheme of the provisions on mergers is that the Secretary of State[1] is empowered to refer certain executed and prospective mergers to the Monopolies and Mergers Commission, which will investigate the facts and assess the effects of the merger against public interest criteria. In the event of the Commission concluding that the merger operates or would operate against the public interest, sanctions are available to terminate or prevent the merger. One of the innovations of the 1973 Act was the establishment of the Director-General of Fair Trading, one of whose functions is to keep himself informed about actual and prospective mergers and to make recommendations to the Secretary of State thereon.[2]

In addition to the general provisions concerning mergers, the 1973 Act, like its 1965 predecessor, contains special provisions as regards newspaper mergers.[3] These are subjected to stricter control because of the particular undesirability of press outlets in a democracy becoming concentrated in fewer hands.

In this chapter the emphasis will be on the general merger provisions, newspaper mergers being confined to brief mention at the end.

Ceasing to be distinct enterprises

83–02 The word "merger" attained commercial meaning long before it became a precise legal term. For there to be a merger situation within the meaning of the 1973 Act two or more enterprises, of which at least one was carried on in the United Kingdom or by or under the control of a body corporate incorporated in the United Kingdom, must have *ceased to be distinct*

[1] The powers are now exercised by the Secretary of State for Trade. For more detailed treatment of this topic, together with related monopoly and restrictive practices law, see Cunningham, *The Fair Trading Act 1973: Consumer Protection and Competition Law.*

[2] Fair Trading Act 1973, s. 76. References in this chapter are to that Act unless stated differently.

[3] ss. 57–62.

enterprises (s. 64 (1)). The concept of ceasing to be distinct enterprises is therefore central to merger control and it receives extensive amplification in the Act. Basically enterprises will be regarded as ceasing to be distinct enterprises[4] if either—

(a) they are brought under common ownership or common control, or
(b) one of them ceases to be carried on at all in consequence of an arrangement or transaction entered into to prevent competition between the enterprises (s. 65 (1)).

Common ownership and common control are elaborated by detailed provisions which, *e.g.* treat associated persons as one person[5] and define "control" in flexible terms of economic reality embracing the ability to control or influence policy.[6]

Because of the flexibility of these tests it may be difficult to ascertain a precise moment when two enterprises cease to be distinct. However, it may become necessary to determine the date because there is a six-months' time-limit in respect of the Secretary of State's power to refer a merger after it has taken place.[7] For this reason the Secretary of State is permitted to treat successive events within a two-year period as having all happened on the date of the latest of them (s. 65 (1)).

Anticipatory references

83–03 Although the wording of the Act contemplates the possibility of a reference by the Secretary of State to the Monopolies and Mergers Commission in the period after the consummation of the merger, he is also empowered to make a reference in anticipation of the merger (s. 75). In practice it is this power which the Secretary of State prefers to use, since it is far more practicable to prevent a proposed merger than to unscramble a consummated one. Normally the companies will agree to postpone their merger pending investigation and, in the last resort, the Secretary of State may compel them by order so to do (s. 74). One adverse consequence of the anticipatory procedure is that on several occasions the parties have found it necessary to abandon their merger plans even before the outcome of reference has become known because the delay caused by the reference has upset the sensitive arrangement to which they had come.

Reference criteria

83–04 The Act is not intended to provide machinery for the control of all mergers. Its concern is only with those of substantial economic significance. It therefore provides that, to be referred, a merger must either—

(a) produce a situation in which at least one-quarter of all the goods or services of a particular description which are supplied in the United

---

4 "Enterprise" is defined in s. 63 (2). See also s.137 (2) for meaning of "business."
5 s. 77.
6 s. 65.
7 s. 64 (4).

Kingdom or a substantial part thereof will be supplied by or to the same person; or

(b) involve a transfer of assets exceeding £15 million in value (s. 64 as amended).

As regards (a), the categorisation of different product markets is always a matter for economic disputation, but the Act attempts to avoid legal argument on the subject by providing that the criteria for determining when goods or services can be treated as being of a separate description "shall be such as in any particular case the Secretary of State thinks most suitable in the circumstances of that case" (s. 68 (4)). As regards the £15 million assets criterion, the principles for quantification are set out in section 67.

Reference procedure

83–05 Reference has already been made to the fact that, while the Director-General of Fair Trading is under a duty to keep himself informed about actual and prospective mergers and to make recommendations to the Secretary of State,[8] only the Secretary of State himself has the power to initiate a reference. In fact the Secretary of State is advised by a non-statutory panel which, since 1973, has been presided over by the Director-General. Only a tiny proportion of mergers which could be referred under the above criteria ever come to be referred and the task of predicting whether or not a particular merger is likely to be referred is rendered the more difficult by the fact that prevalent political attitudes towards reference are subject to fluctuation, even within the life of a single government of whatever party. The best guidance to practice on the subject is *Mergers: a Guide to the Procedures under the Fair Trading Act 1973* which was published in 1978 and is reproduced in Volume 3, Part D. Although different Secretaries of State may emphasise different points at different times, the variable range of criteria remains, as described in the *Guide*. Sometimes a merger which could have been subjected to reference is nevertheless allowed to proceed without such reference in the light of assurances given to the Secretary of State by the parties concerned.

The Monopolies and Mergers Commission

83–06 When a merger is referred to the Monopolies and Mergers Commission, the Commission is required to perform two separate functions. Its first task is to ascertain whether in fact the merger falls within the statutory criteria (*i.e.* the one-quarter market share or £15 million assets referred to above). If so, the second task is to consider whether the creation of the merger situation operates, or may be expected to operate, against the public interest (s. 69 (1)). The Act requires the reference to include a time limit for investigation and this limit must not exceed six months. It may be

[8] See para. 83–01, *ante*.

extended, but only once, and then for not more than three months and only on the request of the Commission and upon the Secretary of State being satisfied that special reasons exist (s. 70).

In determining whether a merger operates, or may be expected to operate, against the public interest, the Commission must take into account all matters which appear to them in the particular circumstances to be relevant and, among other things, must have regard to the desirability—

(a) of maintaining and promoting effective competition between persons supplying goods and services in the United Kingdom;
(b) of promoting the interests of consumers, purchasers and other users of goods and services in the United Kingdom in respect of the prices charged for them and in respect of their quality and the variety of goods and services supplied;
(c) of promoting, through competition, the reduction of costs and the development and use of new techniques and new products, and of facilitating the entry of new competitors into existing markets;
(d) of maintaining and promoting the balanced distribution of industry and employment in the United Kingdom; and
(e) of maintaining and promoting competitive activity in markets outside the United Kingdom on the part of producers of goods, and of suppliers of goods and services, in the United Kingdom (s. 84).

83–07 The procedure under which the Commission carries out its investigations is prescribed to a limited extent by the Act[9] but beyond that the Commission is left to devise its own practice. When making its report the Commission is under an obligation to include conclusions on the questions comprised in the reference, together with a sufficient account of their reasons for those conclusions and a survey of the general position with respect to the subject-matter of the reference and to the developments which have led to that position (s. 72 (1)). The Commission must also specify any particular effects, adverse to the public interest, which they consider the merger has or may be expected to have. They must also consider possible ways of remedying such effects and, if they think fit, include in their report recommendations as to such action (s. 72 (2)).

A copy of the Commission's report has to be sent to the Director-General of Fair Trading and the Secretary of State must take account of any advice given to him by the Director-General (s. 86). The report must also be laid before Parliament (s. 83).

Undertakings and orders

83–08 When the report is to the effect that there is no present or foreseeable infraction of the public interest, neither the Director-General nor the Secretary of State has power to terminate or prevent the merger. If, on the

[9] See, in particular, s. 81 and, as regards attendance of witnesses and production of documents, s. 85.

other hand, there is an adverse report, various remedial possibilities arise. First, it is the duty of the Director-General, *if requested by the Secretary of State*, to consult the relevant parties with a view to obtaining from them undertakings to take action specified by the Secretary of State as being requisite for the purpose of remedying or preventing the adverse effects indicated in the report (s. 88). In this way it is sought to remedy the situation on an informal basis. If, however, this proves impossible, the Secretary of State may resort to certain order-making powers provided by the Act (s. 73). The full range of powers is very extensive and is listed in Schedule 8. They are sufficient, *e.g.* to prevent a merger from taking place or to unscramble an existing merger. Alternatively, the Secretary of State may prefer to allow the merger but regulate various aspects of the conduct of the merged unit.

The procedure for making orders is prescribed by the Act. It includes the duty to take into account the advice of the Commission and the Director-General (s. 75 (3)). The ultimate promulgation is by affirmative resolution procedure (s. 90). This necessarily involves a period of delay, but during this time the Secretary of State is empowered to control the situation by interim orders (s. 89).

It must be emphasised that no sanctions of any kind—undertakings or orders—may be applied unless the Commission's report is adverse; and that the ultimate decision whether or not to seek an undertaking or order rests exclusively with the Secretary of State.

Newspaper mergers

3–09 As was mentioned at the beginning of this chapter, newspaper mergers receive separate and special treatment in the Act because of the desirability of controlling any further concentration in respect of such important media in the democratic process. The special provisions are contained in sections 57–62. The essence of these provisions is that a transfer of a newspaper or of newspaper assets to a newspaper proprietor whose newspapers have an average circulation per day of publication amounting, together with that of the newspaper concerned in the transfer, to 500,000 or more is unlawful and void, unless the transfer is made with the written consent of the Secretary of State. In most cases,[10] the Secretary of State cannot give his consent before receiving a report on the matter from the Commission (s. 58).

[10] The exceptions relate to urgency and insignificant size: s. 58 (3) and (4), respectively.

CHAPTER 84

MERGER CONTROL UNDER EEC LAW

84–01 IN addition to the merger control provisions contained in the Fair Trading Act 1973 and considered in the previous chapter, it is also necessary to consider the extent to which mergers may be controlled by certain provisions of European Community law which are directly applicable in this country by virtue of our membership of the EEC. Although Community law is not yet fully developed on this subject, it is anticipated that further development will take place in the near future.[1]

Article 86 of the EEC Treaty

84–02 Unlike the Treaty establishing the European Coal and Steel Community,[2] the EEC Treaty does not expressly provide for a system of merger control. Nevertheless the Commission and, more recently, the Court of Justice have taken the view that Article 86 of the EEC Treaty can be used in certain circumstances as an instrument of merger control. The essence of Article 86 is that it prohibits as incompatible with the common market any abuse by one or more undertakings of a dominant position within the common market or in a substantial part of it in so far as the abuse may affect trade between member states. The article contains four examples of abusive conduct in a non-exhaustive list which makes no mention of mergers. A number of important cases on article 86 have been decided, in particular *Commercial Solvents Corporation* v. *Commission*,[3] *United Brands Co.* v. *Commission*,[4] *Hoffmann-La Roche & Co. A.G.* v. *Commission*,[5] and *Hugin Kassaregister A.B.* v. *Commission*,[6] but only one, the *Continental Can* case, reviewed in the following paragraphs, deals with the abuse of a dominant position by a proposed merger.

In *Europemballage Corpn. and Continental Can Co. Inc.* v. *E.C. Commission*,[7] an American company acting through a subsidiary obtained control of a German company with a share of the German markets for meat tins, fish tins and metal caps. Two years later the American company's subsidiary gained control of a Dutch company that was the largest manufacturer of metal containers in the Benelux countries. The Commission took the view that the acquisition of the Dutch company contravened Article 86. The reasoning behind this view was that the American com-

---

[1] On the subject in general, see Kay, "Company Mergers and the EEC" [1975] J.B.L. 88.
[2] See ECSC Treaty, art. 66, and, for discussion of this sectoral provision and decisions made thereunder, *Encyclopaedia of European Community Law*, ed. Simmonds, Vols. B and C.
[3] [1974] 1 C.M.L.R. 309.
[4] [1978] 1 C.M.L.R. 429.
[5] [1979] 3 C.M.L.R. 211.
[6] [1979] 3 C.M.L.R. 345.
[7] [1972] C.M.L.R. D11 (Commission); [1973] C.M.L.R. 199 (Court of Justice).

pany, by virtue of its acquisition of the Germany company, held a dominant position in the German market and this was a "substantial part of the common market" within the meaning of Article 86. The subsequent acquisition of the Dutch company, the Commission contended, would eliminate the possibility of future competition between the German and Dutch companies (although it was admitted that there was no existing competition between the two companies which operated in different geographical markets). The acquisition of the Dutch company was therefore held to be an abuse of a dominant position which could affect trade between member states. The companies then appealed to the Court of Justice to challenge the Commission's interpretation of Article 86 and its application to mergers. The view of the Court was that the Commission had interpreted Article 86 correctly but, on the facts of the case, the Commission's decision against the companies was annulled because of the Commission's inadequate analysis of the product markets.

Dominant position

84–03 Article 86 has so far only been applied to a merger situation in which one of the parties had already been in a dominant position before the merger in question. It is doubtful whether Article 86 can be invoked if, say, two non-dominant undertakings merge to form a dominant unit. It is submitted that that possibility cannot be ruled out and that the answer depends on the circumstances of the case.

Undertakings are in a dominant position—

> "When they have the power to behave independently, which puts them in a position to act without taking into account their competitors, purchasers or supplies."[8]

In the *Hoffmann-La Roche* case,[9] the following factors were held to be relevant in determining the existence of a dominant position:

(a) the relationship between the market shares of the undertaking and of its competitors, especially those of the next largest;
(b) the technological lead of the undertaking over its competitors;
(c) the existence of a highly developed sales network;
(d) the absence of potential competition,

the first because it enables the competitive strength of the undertaking to be assessed, the second and third because they represent in themselves technical and commercial advantage, and the fourth because it is the consequence of the existence of obstacles preventing new competitors from having access to the market.

Moreover, the dominant position must be "within the common market or a substantial part of it." The *Continental Can* case illustrates that a

[8] [1972] C.M.L.R. D11, D27.
[9] [1979] 3 C.M.L.R. 211, 277.

sizeable national market, *e.g.* the United Kingdom market, will be taken to be a substantial part of the common market.

In the *Hugin Kassaregister* case[10] it was held that, where spare parts can practically only be obtained from the manufacturer of the machines—cash registers—, the relevant market for the purposes of Article 86 may be the market in the spare parts, but if the supply of spare parts is only done by subsidiaries of the manufacturer in the various Member States or the manufacturer himself outside the common market, no inter-state trade in the spare parts takes place and article 86 is not infringed.

Abusive behaviour

84–04 The main point in issue in the *Continental Can* case was whether the extension of a dominant position through merger or acquisition constituted an abuse. After all, such behaviour is not one of the examples of abuse listed in Article 86 and most of those listed seem more directly abusive than a mere merger. Both the Commission and the Court, however, concluded that:

> "There may . . . be abusive behaviour if an enterprise in a dominant position strengthens that dominant position so that the degree of control achieved substantially obstructs competition, *i.e.* so that the only undertakings left in the market are those which are dependent on the dominant undertaking with regard to their market behaviour."[11]

This conclusion was reached by reference to Article 3 (f) of the Treaty which includes among the activities of the Community:

> "the institution of a system ensuring that competition in the common market is not distorted."

Affecting trade between member states

84–05 An abuse is only prohibited by Article 86 to the extent that it "may affect trade between member states." This provision has always been interpreted in a fairly broad way so as to include, for example, conduct within a single member state which might affect the subsequent penetration of that national market by undertakings in other member states.[12]

Procedural problems

84–06 Since it is clear that Article 86 was not created with merger control in mind, it is hardly surprising that certain practical and procedural problems attend its application to mergers. For example, there is no machinery for exempting on efficiency or other public interest grounds a merger which involves the extension of a dominant position. The parties'only safeguard is the rather less secure negative clearance procedure contained in Regula-

---

10 *Hugin Kassaregister A.B.* v. *Commission* [1979] 3 C.M.L.R. 345.
11 [1973] C.M.L.R. 199, 225.
12 See, *e.g. Vereeniging van Cememthanderlaren* v. *Commission* [1973] C.M.L.R. 7.

tion 17/1962.[13] Similarly, there is no provision enabling the Commission to hold up a merger for a limited time pending investigation and decision. Thus the Commission may often have to rely on *ex post facto* control, with all the problems of ultimately having to unscramble a consummated merger, assuming, as now seems probable, that the Commission has power to make an unscrambling order.

The proposed regulation

–07 Given these problems and other uncertainties surrounding the application of Article 86 to mergers, it is hardly surprising that the Community institutions are seeking the promulgation of a more purposeful basis for controlling mergers. A draft regulation on the subject was put forward by the Commission in July 1973[14] and an amended proposal was submitted to the Council of Ministers in December 1981.[15] It may become law in the not too distant future. Its characteristics are a requirement of notification (to the Commission) of certain large-scale mergers, a prohibition of those which are anticompetitive within a specified meaning and a limited possibility of exemption. It is envisaged that a merger could be held up pending investigation but a time limit is provided for the length of the investigation.

---

[13] For the distinction between exemption and negative clearance in the context of article 85, see Bellamy and Child, *Common Market Law of Competition* (2nd ed.), Chaps. 5 to 7.

[14] For text, see Schmitthoff, *European Company Law Texts,* 1974; for comment see Kay, *supra*, n.1.

[15] Com. (81) 773 final.

Part Eight

WINDING UP OF THE COMPANY

A. WINDING UP IN ENGLAND AND WALES

CHAPTER 85

WINDING UP BY THE COURT

Modes of winding up

85–01 The existence of a company incorporated under the Companies Acts cannot be terminated except through the machinery of winding up,[1] or by removal from the register as a defunct company under section 353. Commercially winding up or liquidation—the two terms are used interchangeably—will either take place because of insolvency in which case winding up is a form of company bankruptcy procedure or for reasons which do not connote insolvency, *e.g.* reorganisation or tax. Unfortunately this rational basis of classification is not consistently followed by the Companies Acts.

The different kinds of winding up under the 1948 Act are as follows[2]:

1. Compulsory winding up by the court.
2. Voluntary winding up.
   (1) Purely voluntary.
      (a) Members' voluntary winding up.
      (b) Creditors' voluntary winding up.
   (2) Under the supervision of the court.

In practice there are many more voluntary liquidations than compulsory liquidations. The reasons are obvious. They are generally cheaper and quicker. The procedure of members' voluntary winding up was first introduced by the Joint Stock Companies Act 1856. Creditors' voluntary winding up was introduced by the Companies Act 1929 in order to give creditors effective control of voluntary liquidations where the company was insolvent.[3]

The grounds for compulsory winding up cover situations of insolvency and solvency. A members' voluntary winding up presupposes solvency whereas a creditors' voluntary winding up presupposes insolvency.

Compulsory winding up

85–02 The Acts define certain circumstances in which a creditor or contributory—this latter term refers to the present and certain past members of the

---

[1] *Princess of Reuss* v. *Bos* (1871) L.R. 5 H.L. 176, 193.
[2] See s. 211.
[3] As a result of the Report of the Company Law Amendment Committee (1926) Cmd. 2657, para. 77.

company[4]—is entitled to invoke the intervention of the court and have the assets administered by the court. The provisions relating to a compulsory winding up by the court in England and Wales are contained in Part V of the Act of 1948[5] and the Companies (Winding-up) Rules 1949 as amended.[6]

Courts having jurisdiction to wind up

85–03 The courts having jurisdiction to wind up companies in England and Wales are the High Court, and, as a general rule, all the county courts having bankruptcy jurisdiction.[7] The High Court has jurisdiction to wind up all companies registered in England and Wales (s. 218). If the paid-up capital does not exceed £120,000,[8] the county court has concurrent jurisdiction, unless the registered office of the company is within the metropolis, in which case the jurisdiction is in the High Court.[9] A winding up commenced in the High Court can be transferred to the county court (s. 219), even if the paid-up capital exceeds £120,000.[10] If two petitions, one in the High Court and the other in the county court, are presented, the High Court has to resolve the difficulty.[11] Where the county court has jurisdiction, it can deal with all matters arising in the winding up, *e.g.* setting aside debentures, though the amount involved may be very large.[12] In such cases, however, the jurisdiction of the High Court should now be invoked. The Stannaries jurisdiction for mining companies therein is now vested in a county court of Cornwall although the High Court has concurrent jurisdiction.[13]

Appeals

Appeals from the High Court and the county courts lie to the Court of Appeal.

---

[4] ss. 212 and 213; see para. 85–45, *post.*
[5] See Vol. II, Pt. A., *post.*
[6] See Vol. III, Pt. H., *post.*
[7] See the County Courts (Bankruptcy and Companies Winding-Up Jurisdiction) Order 1971 (S.I. 1971 No. 656), as amended by S.I. 1971 No. 1983, S.I. 1977 No. 151 and S.I. 1977 No. 350 (see Vol. III, paras. H–254 and H–255).
[8] See the Insolvency Act 1976, s. 1. and Sched. 1 and the Insolvency Act (Commencement No. 1) Order 1976 (S.I. 1976 No. 1960).
[9] *Re Southsea Garage Ltd.* (1911) 55 S.J. 314.
[10] *Re Vernon Heaton Co. Ltd.* [1936] Ch. 289.
[11] *Re Filby Bros. (Provender) Ltd.* [1958] 1 W.L.R. 683 (transfer to High Court of county court petition, and winding-up order on both petitions); *cf. Re Audio Systems Ltd.* [1965] 1 W.L.R. 1096 (transfer to High Court, winding-up order on High Court petition, stay of proceedings on county court petition).
[12] *Re F. & E. Stanton Ltd.* [1928] 1 K.B. 464.
[13] See s. 218 (4); *Re Reliance Properties Ltd.* [1951] 2 All E.R. 327n, and paras. 89–14 and 89–34, *post.*

Companies which may be wound up

85–04 The companies subject to this jurisdiction are the following:

(a) Companies formed and registered under Part I or registered under Part VII of the Act of 1948.

(b) Existing companies as defined in section 455, whereby "existing company"means a company formed and registered under the Joint Stock Companies Acts, or under the Companies Acts 1862, 1908 or 1929.

(c) Companies registered but not formed under the Joint Stock Companies Acts, or under the Companies Acts 1862, 1908 or 1929 (1948 Act, s. 378).

(d) Companies registered as limited under the Companies Act 1879 (1948 Act, s. 379).

(e) Unregistered companies, as defined in section 398 of the 1948 Act, that is to say, any partnership, association or company except:

(1) railway companies incorporated by Act of Parliament, except as there mentioned;

(2) registered companies;

(3) a partnership or association consisting of less than eight members and not being a foreign partnership, association or company;

(4) a limited partnership registered in England or Northern Ireland.

Examples of unregistered companies which have been ordered to be wound up are:

1. companies incorporated by special Act[14];
2. companies incorporated by Royal Charter[15];
3. foreign and colonial companies having assets and liabilities in England[16];
4. building societies formed prior to the Building Societies Act 1874[17];
5. trustee savings banks;
6. friendly societies[18];
7. life assurance companies[19];
8. an association for purchase and division of an estate.[20]

---

[14] *Re South London Fish Market* (1888) 39 Ch.D. 324; *Re Barton-upon-Humber Water Co.* (1889) 42 Ch.D. 585.

[15] *Re Oriental Bank Corporation* (1884) 54 L.J.Ch. 481; *Re Bank of South Australia* [1895] 1 Ch. 578.

[16] *Re Mercantile Bank of Australia* [1892] 2 Ch. 204; *North Australian Co.* v. *Goldsborough Co.* (1889) 61 L.T. 716; see para. 88–10, *post*.

[17] *Re Queen's Building Society* (1871) L.R. 6 Ch. 815; *Re Ilfracombe P.M.B. Building Society* [1901] 1 Ch. 102.

[18] *Re Victoria Society, Knottingley* [1913] 1 Ch. 167.

[19] *Re Great Britain Mutual* (1880) 16 Ch.D. 246; *Masonic and General Life Assurance Co.* v. *Sharpe* [1892] 1 Ch. 154.

[20] *Re Osmondthorpe Hall Society* [1913] W.N. 243 (a member who had paid up all instalments due from him being treated as a contributory).

As to the distribution of funds of an unregistered association, see *Re Customs and Excise Officers' Mutual Guarantee Fund*.[21]

Grounds for winding up

85–05 The court may order the winding up of a company if one or several of the following grounds for winding up are present (1948 Act, s. 222 as amended):

(a) the company has by special resolution resolved that the company be wound up by the court;

(b) being a public company which was registered as such on its original incorporation, the company has not been issued with a certificate under section 4 of the Companies Act 1980 and more than a year has expired since it was so registered;

(bb) after the end of the transitional period within the meaning of that Act, the company is an old public company within the meaning of that Act;

(c) the company does not commence its business within a year from its incorporation, or suspends its business for a whole year;

(d) the number of members is reduced below two.

(e) the company is unable to pay its debts;

(f) the court is of opinion that it is just and equitable that the company should be wound up.

In addition to the grounds set out in section 222, the Department of Trade has power: (1) under section 16 (1) of the Protection of Depositors Act 1963 (as amended by s. 83 (1) of the Companies Act 1980) to petition for the winding up of an unexempted deposit-taking company on the grounds set out therein; (2) under section 35 (1) of the Companies Act 1967 to petition where, as a result of an inspectors' report or its powers of investigation under that Act, it appears to the Department that it is in the public interest to wind up the company. The Bank of England has power under section 18 of the Banking Act 1979 to petition for the winding up of a recognised bank or licensed institution.

Let us now look at each of these grounds in more detail.

Special resolution

Such cases are extremely rare[22] because of the availability of voluntary

---

[21] [1917] 2 Ch. 18.

[22] See the unreported case discussed in Palmer, *Company Precedents*, Pt. III, p. 23; see also *Hawkes' Bay Fruit Canning Co. Ltd.* v. *Boardman* (1920) 15 M.C.R. 2 (N.Z.); *Re Buzolich Print Co.* (1884) 10 V.L.R. 276; *Byron Motors Ltd.* v. *Dolphin House Ltd.* [1958] 3 S.A.L.R. 532.

winding up but the existence of this ground has sometimes in the past induced the court to withhold a winding-up order under (*f*).[23]

Failure to obtain a certificate to do business and old public companies

These two grounds which only relate to public companies were introduced by the Companies Act 1980, Sched. 3, para. 27 in substitution for the original section 222 (*b*) which dealt with default in delivering a statutory report or holding a statutory meeting. A petition on the present grounds may be presented by the Secretary of State (Sched. 3, para. 28).

Failure to commence business or suspension of business

The court's jurisdiction is discretionary and the fact that the petitioner can establish this ground does not give him an automatic right to an order.[24] The court has refused to make an order where there are good reasons for the delay and where the great majority of members desire that the company shall continue.[25] An order, however, may be made in appropriate circumstances against the majority's wishes.[26]

Where the business has merely been suspended the court must be satisfied of an abandonment or inability to carry on.[27] In ascertaining such intention the court will have regard to the opinion and wishes of the majority of shareholders whose names appear on the register. Merely abandoning one of several objects is insufficient.[28]

A company which ceases to be active in its field of operations but becomes a holding company holding shares in other companies engaged in the active pursuit of the objects for which the first-named company was incorporated has not suspended its business for a whole year.[29]

Number of members reduced below two

Until recently the Companies Acts stipulated a minimum of seven members for public companies. That requirement was abolished by section 2 (1) of the 1980 Act. All companies now need only have a statutory minimum of two. Past members still contingently liable are not to be counted for these purposes.[30]

---

23 *Re Suburban Hotel Co.* (1867) 2 Ch.App. 737; *Re Langham Skating Rink Co.* (1877) 5 Ch.D. 669.
24 *Re Metropolitan Railway Warehousing Co. (Ltd.)* (1867) 36 L.J. Ch. 827.
25 Bona fides will be considered—*ibid.* p. 830 *per* Cairns L.J.: *Re Capital Fire Insurance Association* (1882) 21 Ch.D. 209, 222; *Re Heatons Steel Co.* [1870] W.N. 85.
26 *Re Tumacacori Mining Co.* (1874) L.R. 17 Eq. 534. This is a peculiar case where there were no creditors and there was doubt as to any solution other than winding up the company.
27 *Re Tomlin Patent Horse Shoe Co.* (1887) 55 L.T. 314.
28 *Re Norwegian Titanic Iron Co.* (1866) 35 Beav. 223.
29 *Re Eastern Telegraph Co.* [1947] 2 All E.R. 104.
30 *Re Bowling & Welby's Contract* [1895] 1 Ch. 663 (C.A.).

Inability to pay debts

85–06 —85–07 This is the usual ground for a petition. Section 223 of the 1948 Act lists a number of situations in which a company shall be deemed to be unable to pay its debts. They are:

(*a*) if a creditor, by assignment or otherwise, to whom the company is indebted in a sum exceeding two hundred pounds[31] then due has served on the company, by leaving it at the registered office of the company, a demand under his hand requiring the company to pay the sum so due and the company has for three weeks thereafter neglected to pay the sum or to secure or compound for it to the reasonable satisfaction of the creditor; or

(*b*) if, in England or Northern Ireland, execution or other process issued on a judgment, decree or order of any court in favour of a creditor of the company is returned unsatisfied in whole or in part; or

(*c*) if, in Scotland, the induciae of a charge for payment on an extract decree, or an extract registered bond, or an extract registered protest have expired without payment being made; or

(*d*) if it is proved to the satisfaction of the court that the company is unable to pay its debts, and, in determining whether a company is unable to pay its debts, the court shall take into account the contingent and prospective liabilities of the company.

To fall within section 223 (*a*), there must be (1) a demand in writing served on the company's registered office for payment of a debt which is due[32] and (2) neglect by the company for three weeks to pay the sum or to secure or compound it to the reasonable satisfaction of the creditor. Under the case law:

(1) the creditor must be one who is capable of giving a valid discharge[33]; and

(2) if the company bona fide disputes the debt then it has not "neglected to pay" within the section.[34]

(3) The creditor's demand must be for a liquidated sum and he cannot serve a demand in respect of a fixed sum less the amount of unliquidated damages claimed by the company in respect of breach of contract.[35]

Where the petition is founded on paragraph (*a*) of section 223 of the 1948 Act, the period of three weeks is computed in accordance with the general rule that, unless there is sufficient indication to the contrary,

---

[31] Originally £50, this was changed to £200 by s. 1 of and Sched. 1 to the Insolvency Act 1976.

[32] "Due" has been said to mean "absolutely due" or "presently payable"—*Re European Life Assurance Society* (1869) L.R. 9 Eq. 122, 127; *The New Travellers' Chambers Ltd.* v. *Messrs. Cheese & Green* (1894) 70 L.T. 271, 272. If a debt is merely contingent it cannot be the subject of a statutory demand under s. 223 (*a*) but may be taken into account in order to establish whether the company is unable to pay its debts within s. 223 (*d*).

[33] *Re Steel Wing Co. Ltd.* [1921] 1 Ch. 349 (equitable assignee of part of a debt needed the assignor or the person presently entitled to the remainder of the debt as a party).

[34] *Re The Island of Anglesea Coal & Coke Co. (Ltd.)* (1861) 4 L.T. 684; *Re Catholic Publishing & Bookselling Co.* (1864) 2 De J. & S. 116; *Re London Wharfing Co.* (1865) 35 Beav. 40; *Re Brighton Club & Norfolk Hotel Co.* (1865) 35 Beav. 204; *Re London & Paris Banking Corp.* (1874) L.R. 19 Eq. 444. See further, *post*.

[35] *Re Humberstone Jersey Ltd.* (1977) 74 L.S. Gaz. 711.

fractions of a day are to be ignored.[36] Consequently the day on which the demand notice is served on the company is excluded and it is insufficient to present the petition on the twenty-first day thereafter; the interval between the day when the notice becomes effective and the presentation of the petition must be 21 full days.[37] Section 223 (*b*) appears to refer principally to a writ of *fieri facias*. Petitioning creditors often rely on the ground that a *nulla bona* has been returned to such a writ.[38] The court may nevertheless investigate the judgment on which the proceedings are based.[39] Section 223 (*c*) relates entirely to Scots law and is discussed in Chapter 87, *post*. Section 223 (*d*) is a residual general category which is not limited by the special provisions of (*a*)–(*b*).[40] A person must, however, be a creditor within section 224 to present a petition under section 222 (*e*) and section 223.[41] If he is not he has no *locus standi* and his petition is bound to fail even though the company is insolvent.

As to inability to pay debts, proof by a creditor that his particular debt has not been paid within a reasonable time is prima facie evidence that the company is insolvent.[42] So too is an admission by the company that it has no assets on which to levy execution.[43] The company may, however, rebut the prima facie evidence by proof that it can in fact pay its debts.[44] Mere evidence that a company has for the time being insufficient liquid assets to pay all its presently owing debts, whether or not repayment of such debts has been demanded, by itself does not prove inability to pay debts within sections 222 and 223.[45]

Creditors' winding up petitions should, as a general rule, be heard promptly. Long or repeated adjournments will not normally be granted even with the consent of all concerned.[45a]

The creditor's prima facie right to an order

A basic question arises, does the court have a discretion under section 222 (*e*) and 223? The general rule is that where a petitioning creditor can prove that his debt is unpaid and the company is insolvent it is the duty of the court to direct a winding up and the creditor is entitled to an order *ex debito justitiae*.[46] On the other hand, it has been said that the latter is a

---

36 *Trow* v. *Ind Coope (West Midlands) Ltd.* [1967] 2 Q.B. 899.
37 *Re Lympne Investments Ltd.* [1972] 1 W.L.R. 523.
38 Palmer, *Company Precedents*, Pt. II, p. 26.
39 *Re Railway Finance Co.* (1866) 14 W.R. 785.
40 *Re Turf Enterprises Pty. Ltd.* [1975] Qd. R. 266; 1 A.C.L.R. 197. See also Palmer, *Company Precedents*, Pt. II, p. 26.
41 *Re H.L. Bolton Engineering Co. Ltd.* [1956] Ch. 577, 583.
42 *Re Globe New Patent Iron and Steel Co.* (1875) L.R. 20 Eq. 337.
43 *Re Flagstaff Silver Mining Co. of Utah* (1875) L.R. 20 Eq. 268.
44 *Re Bradford Tramways Co.* (1876) 4 Ch.D. 18, 22.
45 *Re Capital Annuities Ltd.* [1978] 3 All E.R. 704, 718*e–f*, *per* Slade J. *Cf. Re Agricultural Cattle Insurance Co.* (1849) 1 Mac. & Co. 170, and see R. R. Pennington, *Company Law* (4th ed.), pp. 690–691; *Re European Life Assurance Society* (1869) L.R. 9 Eq. 122.
45a Practice Note [1977] 1 W.L.R. 1066; [1977] 3 All E.R. 64.
46 *Bowes* v. *Hope Life Insurance & Guarantee Society* (1865) 11 H.L.C. 389, 402; *Re West of Canada Oil, Lands, and Works Co.* (1873) L.R. 17 Eq. 1, 4, 7.

phrase which means no more than that in accordance with settled practice the court can only exercise its discretion in one way namely by granting the order.[47] These statements can be reconciled on the basis that although the matter is "a complete and unfettered judicial discretion"[48] the discretion is exercised in accordance with certain established principles, but the principles do not bind the court in an all or nothing way. In accordance with these principles the creditor has a prima facie right[49] to a winding-up order which is subject to certain exceptions. The legal basis of the exceptions[50] is the opening wording of section 222 ("a company may be wound up") and the permissive wording of sections 225 (1) and 346. The exceptions are: (1) where the petitioner's debt is less than £200; (2) the debt is bona fide disputed by the company; (3) the company has paid or tendered payment of the petitioner's debt; (4) the winding up is opposed by other creditors; and (5) the company is in the process of being wound up voluntarily.

Petitioner's debt less than £200

The figure of £200 (formerly £50) only strictly applies to section 223 (*a*). It follows, therefore, that the figure is or should be irrelevant for the purposes of (*b*)–(*d*). Indeed the non-payment of a small sum is in fact better evidence of inability to pay debts than non-payment of a large sum.[51] There are instances of winding-up orders being made on small debts but in a number of cases at the turn of the century the courts indicated that they were unwilling to allow the winding-up court to be turned into a collector of small debts and in the absence of special circumstances making winding up desirable the order was refused.[52]

The present practice in the English courts is not to grant an order on the unsupported petition of a creditor for less than £200 unless; (a) there are special circumstances such as defiance of the creditor[53] or support by other creditors for a considerable amount, (b) the petition is unopposed,[54] or (c) the petition is based on a judgment debt. In Scotland, however, the courts have refused to follow the English practice and will make an order unless there are special circumstances for refusing an order.[55]

---

47 *Re Pritchard* [1963] Ch. 502, 520–521.

48 *Re P. & J. Macrae Ltd.* [1961] 1 W.L.R. 229; *Re Southard & Co. Ltd.* [1979] 1 W.L.R. 1198 (C.A.).

49 *Re Krasnapolsky Restaurant Co.* [1892] 3 Ch. 174, 177.

50 *Re Uruguay Central Railway Co.* (1879) 11 Ch.D. 372; *Re P. & J. Macrae Ltd.* [1961] 1 W.L.R. 229, 238 (C.A.). See also the Australian authorities cited by Dr. B. H. McPherson Q.C., *The Law of Company Liquidation* (2nd ed.), p. 55 whose lucid analysis of the principles is adopted here.

51 Palmer, *Company Precedents*, Pt. II, p. 25.

52 *Re Herbert Standring & Co.* [1895] W.N. 99; *Re Fancy Dress Balls Co.* [1899] W.N. 109; *Re W. H. Hyde Ltd.* (1900) W.N. 245; see also *Re Lympne Investments Ltd.* [1972] 2 All E.R. 385, 389.

53 *Re Leyton Cycle Co. Ltd.* [1901] W.N. 225; *Re World Industrial Bank Ltd.* [1909] W.N. 148; *Re Industrial Insurance Association* [1910] W.N. 245; *Re Alderney Dairy Co.* (1885) 11 V.L.R. 628; *Re Metropolitan Fuel Pty. Ltd.* [1969] V.R. 528, 329.

54 See Palmer, *Company Precedents*, Pt. II, p.26.

55 *J. Speirs & Co.* v. *The Central Building Co.* 1911 S.C. 331.

Bona fide dispute over debt

We have already seen how, where there is a bona fide dispute as to the debt, the company cannot be said to have neglected to pay on a statutory demand.[56] Coupled with this is a related general principle that a petition for winding up with a view to enforcing payment of a disputed debt is an abuse of the process of the court and should be dismissed with costs.[57] Each case ultimately turns on its facts[58] but the following points arise from the cases.

Where a debt is not disputed or the claim is substantial a creditor may present a petition with the object of forcing the company to pay.[59] "Substantial" here means having substance. In such a case pursuit of the claim with personal hostility, even venom and an ulterior motive, does not constitute an abuse of the process of the court.[60] Similarly where the company is proved by other means to be insolvent[61] or where the dispute is as to amount only an order will be made.[62]

To fall within the general principle the dispute must be bona fide in both a subjective and an objective sense. Thus it must be honestly believed to exist and must be based on substantial[63] or reasonable[64] grounds. "Substantial" means having substance and not frivolous and which the court should therefore ignore.[65] There must be so much doubt and question about the liability to pay the debt that the court sees that there is a question to be decided.[66] The onus is on the company "to bring forward a prima facie case which satisfies the court that there is something which ought to be tried either before the court itself or in an action, or by some other proceeding."[67] In considering the matter the court will take into account

---

[56] *Vide, ante.*

[57] See *Imperial Silver Quarries* (1868) 14 W.R. 1220; *Re Kings Cross Industrial Dwellings Co.* (1870) L.R. 11 Eq. 149; *Re London & Paris Banking Corp.* (1875) L.R. 19 Eq. 444, 446; *Cadiz Waterworks Co.* v. *Barnett* (1875) L.R. 19 Eq. 182; *Cercle Restaurant Castiglione Co.* v. *Lavery* (1881) 18 Ch.D. 555; *Re The Imperial Hydropathic Hotel Co.* (1882) 49 L.T. 147; *Re K.L. Tractors Ltd.* (1954) V.L.R. 505; *cf. Bryanston Finance Ltd.* v. *de Vries (No. 2)* [1976] Ch. 63 (C.A) *and Re Claybridge Shipping Co. S.A. The Times*, March 14, 1981 (C.A.); [1981] C.A.T. 143.

[58] Thus in the Russian Bank cases winding up was allowed as it was the only remedy available; see, *e.g. Re Russian & English Bank* [1932] 1 Ch. 663.

[59] *Re St. Thomas' Dock Co.* (1876) 2 Ch.D. 116; see also *Mann* v. *Goldstein* [1968] 1 W.L.R. 1091; *Holt Southey Ltd.* v. *Catnic Components Ltd.* [1978] 1 W.L.R. 630.

[60] *Mann* v. *Goldstein* [1968] 1 W.L.R. 1091, 1095; *Bryanston Finance Ltd.* v. *de Vries (No. 2)* [1976] 2 W.L.R. 41, 50–51 (C.A.): *cf. Cadiz Waterworks Co.* v. *Barnett* (1874) L.R. 19 Eq. 182, 196. Occasionally the courts have rejected a petition which has not been presented in good faith but there has usually been some other ground. *Re Metropolitan Saloon Omnibus Co.* (1859) 28 L.J.Ch. 830; *Re M'Donald Gold Mines* (1898) 14 T.L.R. 204; *Re Amalgamated Properties of Rhodesia (1913) Ltd.* [1917] 2 Ch. 115, 121.

[61] *Niger Merchants Co.* v. *Capper* (1877) 18 Ch.D. 557n; 559, but see the criticisms of that judgment in *Mann* v. *Goldstein* [1968] 1 W.L.R. 1091, 1095, *per* Ungoed-Thomas J.

[62] *Re Steel Wing Co.* [1921] 1 Ch. 349; *Re Tweeds Garages Ltd.* [1962] Ch. 406.

[63] *Re Imperial Silver Quarries Co.* (1868) 16 W.R. 1220; *Re Kings Cross Industrial Dwellings Co.* (1870) 11 Eq. 149, 151; *Re The Imperial Anglo-German Bank* (1872) 25 L.T. 895, 898; *Re Welsh Brick Industries Ltd.* [1946] 2 All E.R. 197, 198 (C.A.); *Re K.L. Tractors Ltd.* [1954] V.L.R. 505; *Mann* v. *Goldstein* [1968] 1 W.L.R. 1091, 1096; *Holt Southey Ltd.* v. *Catnic Components Ltd.* [1978] 2 All E.R. 276, 277–278.

[64] *Re Imperial Hydropathic Hotel Co.* (1882) 49 L.T. 147.

[65] *Mann* v. *Goldstein* [1968] 1 W.L.R. 1091, 1096.

[66] *Re The General Exchange Bank (Ltd.)* (1866) 14 L.T. 582, 583.

[67] *Re Great Britain Mutual Life Assurance Society* (1880) 16 Ch.D. 246, 253, *per* Jessel M.R.

the following factors[68]: (i) the fact that the company has been given leave to defend an action begun by specially indorsed writ[69]; (2) whether there is a set-off or counter-claim based on a substantial ground[70]; (3) whether the company has lodged an appeal against the judgment debt on which the petition is based[71]; and (4) an allegation by the company that the judgment was obtained by fraud.[72] However, none of these factors is conclusive.

Where a debt is disputed on substantial grounds the court may—

(i) dismiss the action outright[73];
(ii) adjourn it conditionally or unconditionally[74];
(iii) grant an injunction to restrain the presentation and advertisement of the petition.[75]

Where the petitioner is forcing payment of a debt which he knows to be in substantial dispute the evidence may support an action by the company against the petitioner for the tort of malicious prosecution. No pecuniary loss or special damage to the company need be proved for the presentation of the petition is, from its very nature, calculated to injure the credit of the company.[76]

Payment or tender

If the company pays the debt before the petition is presented the creditor ceases to be a creditor for the purposes of sections 222 (*e*), 223 and 224.[77] If the debt is paid after presentation the court may allow the substitution of another creditor under rule 37 of the Companies (Winding-up) Rules 1949.[78] If no other creditor comes forward then the petition will be dismissed. A more difficult question arises when the company has tendered payment. This has sometimes led to dismissal of the petition[79] or adjournment[80] but the better view is that tender does not lead to automatic dismissal but is one of the factors to be taken into account by the court.[81]

---

[68] This is based on Dr. B. H. McPherson Q.C., *The Law of Company Liquidation* (2nd ed.), pp. 58 *et seq.*
[69] *Re Welsh Brick Industries Ltd.* [1946] 2 All E.R. 197 (C.A.).
[70] *Re K.L. Tractors Ltd.* [1954] V.L.R. 505; *cf. Re Douglas Griggs Engineering Ltd.* [1963] 1 Ch. 19 (disputed claim in other proceedings); *Re LHF Wools Ltd.* [1970] Ch. 27; *Re Euro-Hotel (Belgravia) Ltd.* [1975] 3 All E.R. 1075.
[71] *Re Amalgamated Properties of Rhodesia (1913) Ltd.* [1917] 2 Ch. 115 (C.A.); *cf. Re Anglo-Bavarian Steel Ball Co.* [1899] W.N. 80.
[72] *Bowes* v. *Hope Life Insurance & Guarantee Society* (1865) 11 H.L.C. 389. The petition will normally be ordered to stand over until the company takes proceedings to impeach the judgment.
[73] *Re Martin Wallis & Co.* (1893) 37 S.J. 822.
[74] s. 225 (1).
[75] *Cadiz Waterworks* v. *Barnett* (1874) L.R. 19 Eq. 182. See the other cases cited by McPherson, *op. cit.* p. 60, n.2.
[76] *Quartz Hill Consolidated Gold Mining Co.* v. *Eyre* (1883) 11 Q.B.D. 674; *Mann* v. *Goldstein* [1968] 1 W.L.R. 1091; *Holt Southey Ltd.* v. *Catnic Components Ltd.* [1978] 1 W.L.R. 630. *Cf. Niger Merchants Co.* v. *Copper* (1881) 18 Ch. 557n.
[77] *Re William Hockley Ltd.* [1962] 1 W.L.R. 555.
[78] *Cf. Fortuna Holdings Pty. Ltd.* v. *FCT* (1976) 2 A.C.L.R. 349.
[79] *Re Times Life Assurance Co.* (1869) L.R. 9 Eq. 382; *Re Amalgamated Properties of Rhodesia Ltd.* [1917] 2 Ch. 115.
[80] *Re Brighton Hotel Co.* (1868) L.R. 6 Eq. 339.
[81] *Re Concrete Pipes & Cement Products Ltd.* [1926] V.L.R. 34.

Company in voluntary liquidation

By section 310 the voluntary winding up of a company is not to be a bar to the right of any creditor to have the company wound up by the court, and a creditor who cannot get paid is entitled to a winding-up order *ex debito justitiae*.[82] The order may, however, be refused if the majority in value of the creditors oppose the petition.[83] An order has been refused where it would not benefit the creditors generally, but only the petitioning creditor.[84] The distinction between these cases and the cases where no winding up is contemplated by the majority was considered in *Re J. D. Swain Ltd.*,[85] where Diplock L.J. said[86]:

> "In the case of a petition for compulsory winding up, if the only circumstances which are available are that the petitioner seeks a compulsory winding up and the majority of the creditors seek that there should be no winding up at all, then prima facie the petitioning creditor is entitled to a winding up unless there are some additional reasons for deciding to the contrary. If, on the other hand, the petitioner seeks a compulsory winding up and the majority of the creditors seek a voluntary winding up, then for the wishes of the petitioner to overrule those of the majority of the creditors there must be some special reason why the wishes of the majority should be overridden. The difference or the distinction seems to me to be an obvious one, namely, in the former case, what is being resisted is any winding up at all, so that the petitioning creditor, if he fails, will be denied the class remedy which he would otherwise have if the winding up took place; whereas, in the latter case, he will obtain the class remedy anyway under the voluntary winding up, and the matter then turns upon his being able to show some reason why the remedy under the voluntary winding up is not an adequate remedy for him."

One reason will be that the liquidator in the voluntary winding up is or is likely to be unfit to perform his duties but in such a case it may be preferable to have him removed and another appointed.[87]

The importance of this factor has declined since the introduction of creditors' voluntary winding up and the assimilation of the powers of liquidators in compulsory and voluntary winding up.[88]

Opposition by other creditors

Under section 346 of the 1948 Act the court may have regard to the wishes of the creditors as proved by sufficient evidence and may for that

---

[82] *Re James Millward & Co. Ltd.* [1940] Ch. 333.

[83] *Re Home Remedies Ltd.* [1943] Ch. 1; *Re B. Karsberg Ltd.* [1956] 1 W.L.R. 57; *Re Riviera Pearls Ltd.* [1962] 1 W.L.R. 722; *Re J.D. Swain Ltd.* [1965] 1 W.L.R. 909, C.A.

[84] *Re Greenwood* [1900] 2 Q.B. 306; *Re Southard & Co. Ltd.* [1979] 3 All E.R. 556 (C.A.).

[85] [1965] 1 W.L.R. 909, C.A.

[86] *Ibid.* p. 915.

[87] *Re Medical Battery Co.* [1894] 1 Ch. 444; *Re E. Bishop & Son Ltd.* [1900] 2 Ch. 254; *Re Caerphilly Colliery Co.* (1875) 32 L.T. 5; *Re Britten & Mullard Ltd.* [1957] 107 L.J. 602; *Re Ryder Installations Ltd.* [1966] 1 W.L.R. 524.

[88] *Re Star & Garter Ltd.* (1873) 42 L.J. Ch. 374; *Re Ryder Installations Ltd.* [1966] 1 W.L.R. 524.

purpose convene meetings. On a creditor's petition this is vitally important because although the petitioner may be said to have a prima facie right to an order it is a right which belongs to the class of creditors to which he belongs.[89] Under section 346 (2) regard is to be had to the value of each creditor's debt. In accordance with this the court will normally give effect to the wishes of the majority.[90] It takes into account numerical majority as well as majority in value but the latter carry greater weight.[91] Opposing creditors should state the reasons for their opposition. The court will investigate whether their reasons are good. A good reason has been held to be that there was a "fair, possible and reasonable chance"[92] of obtaining payment without winding up. Where, however, there are special circumstances rendering a winding up desirable an order will be made in spite of their opposition. An order will be made where the majority view is clearly erroneous[93] or inspired by personal benefit.[94] Where the petitioning and supporting creditors who represent a majority in value belong to the same group of companies as the company in liquidation the court will have regard to the nature of their debts and if these are domestic debts the court may prefer the view of the opposing creditors notwithstanding that they are the minority in value.[95] The absence of assets was formerly regarded as a good reason but now by virtue of section 255 (1) the court is directed not to refuse an order only on that ground. It appears that the use of the word "only" means that it is still capable of being one of the factors taken into account by the court.[96]

Where the opposition comes from creditors of a different class, *e.g.* secured creditors, the court may prefer the wishes of the unsecured creditors since in some cases refusal of the order will rob them of what is virtually their only remedy.[97]

Whether the court will make an order or not does not depend solely on the wishes of the creditors. The court is invested with a wide jurisdiction in the interests of commercial morality; and if the facts disclose a strong prima facie case for investigation into the formation or promotion of the company, or the issue of debentures by it, the court will make a compulsory order irrespective of creditors' opposition.[98] The court will not exercise its discretion to refuse a winding-up order because the closure of the

---

[89] *Re Crigglestone Coal Co.* [1906] 2 Ch. 327.
[90] *Re P. & J. Macrae Ltd.* [1961] 1 W.L.R. 229 (C.A.).
[91] *Re Belmont Land Co. (No. 2)* (1913) 32 N.Z.L.R. 1017; *Re Home Remedies Ltd.* [1943] Ch. 1; *Re B. Karsberg Ltd.* [1956] 1 W.L.R. 57; *Re Riviera Pearls Ltd.* [1962] 1 W.L.R. 722; *Re J.D. Swain Ltd.* [1965] 1 W.L.R. 909, 915 (C.A.).
[92] *Re Western of Canada Oil Co.* (1873) L.R. 17 Eq. 1, 6.
[93] *Re Vuma Ltd.* [1960] 1 W.L.R. 283.
[94] *Re SOS Motors Ltd.* [1934] N.Z.L.R. 129; *Re Greenwood* [1900] 2 Q.B. 306. See also *Re Floors of Bristol (Builders) Ltd.* [1982] Com. L.R. 55.
[96] B. H. McPherson Q.C., *The Law of Company Liquidation* (2nd ed.), p. 68., citing *F & C Building Construction Co.* v. *MacSheil Investments Ltd.* 1959 (3) S.A. 841.
[97] *Re Crigglestone Coal Co.* [1906] 2 Ch. 327; *Re Rubber Improvements Co.* (1962) C.L.Y. 382; *The Times*, June 5, 1962.
[98] *Re Bishop & Sons Ltd.* [1900] 2 Ch. 254; *Re Lichtenstein* (1903) 23 T.L.R. 424; *Re Clandown Colliery Co.* [1915] 1 Ch. 369.

company's business will put its employees out of work or because the general public has an interest in the business being continued.[99]

The petition must not be an abuse of the process of the court. It may be an abuse if, *e.g.* it contains a serious misrepresentation. In such a case the petition is struck out and as there is no longer a subsisting petition, the court has no power to appoint a provisional liquidator under section 238 (1) or to stay proceedings under section 226.[1]

The "just and equitable" clause

85–08 It has sometimes been suggested that there is an exhaustive list of situations that may fall within the scope of the "just and equitable" clause, but it now seems that, although such classification may be convenient for purposes of presentation, the words "just and equitable" require a more flexible interpretation. In the words of Lord Wilberforce: "Illustrations may be used, but general words should remain general and not be reduced to the sum of particular instances."[2] By way of illustration under this clause[3] winding-up orders have been made on the grounds:

that the substratum of the company was gone.[4] The substratum is held to be gone when the main object for which the company was formed has become impracticable[5] (in one case where the substratum had gone, but the company had the widest possible powers, the court allowed the petition to stand over for a scheme to be considered by the shareholders[6]);

that the company was a "bubble"[7];

that the company was formed for the purposes of fraud[8];

that full investigation was necessary[9];

that there was a complete deadlock[10];

---

[99] *Re Craven Insurance Co. Ltd.* [1968] 1 W.L.R. 675.

[1] *Re A Company* [1973] 1 W.L.R. 1566.

[2] *Ebrahimi* v. *Westbourne Galleries* [1973] A.C. 360, 374. See D. D. Prentice (1973) 89 L.Q.R. 107; M. R. Chesterman (1973) 36 M.L.R. 129 and F. H. Callaway, *Winding up on the Just and Equitable Ground.*

[3] These words are not confined to cases *ejusdem generis* with the previous cases of s. 222: *Re Australian Joint Stock Bank* [1897] W.N. 48; *Re Sailing Ship "Kentmere" Co.* [1897] W.N. 58; *Re Yenidje Tobacco Co* [1916] 2 Ch. 426; *Loch* v. *John Blackwood* [1924] A.C. 783 (P.C.); *Ebrahimi* v. *Westbourne Galleries* [1973] A.C. 360 (H.L.).

[4] *Re German Date Coffee Co.* (1882) 20 Ch.D. 169; *Re Haven Gold Co.* (1882) 20 Ch.D. 151; *Re Red Rock Gold Mining Co.* (1888) 61 L.T. 785; *Re Blériot Aircraft Co.* (1916) 32 T.L.R. 253; *Re Eastern Telegraph Co.* [1947] 2 All E.R. 104; *Re Merchant Navy Supply Assn. Ltd.* (1947) 177 L.T. 386; *Galbraith* v. *Merito Shipping Co.*, 1947 S.C. 446; *Re Kitson & Co. Ltd.* [1946] 1 All E.R. 435. See the useful analysis of the cases in *Re Tivoli Freeholds Ltd.* [1972] V.R. 445.

[5] *Re Suburban Hotel Co.* (1867) 2 Ch.App. 737.

[6] *Re Stratton's Independence Ltd.* (1916) 33 T.L.R. 98.

[7] *Re London and County Coal Co.* (1867) L.R. 3 Eq. 355.

[8] *Re T. E. Brinsmead & Sons* [1897] 1 Ch. 45; on appeal [1897] 1 Ch. 406.

[9] *Re Peruvian Amazon Co.* (1913) 29 T.L.R. 384.

[10] *Re Yenidje Tobacco Co.* [1916] 2 Ch. 426. See also *Re American Pioneer Leather Co.* [1918] 1 Ch. 556; *Re Fromm's Extract Co.* 17 T.L.R. 302; *Re Upper Hutt Town Hall* [1920] N.Z.L.R. 125; *Re Nelson Suburban Bus Co.* [1944] G.L.R. 501; *Re National Drive-in Theatres* [1954] 2 D.L.R. 55. *Cf. Re Furriers' Alliance* [1905] 51 S.J. 172; *Re Bambi Restaurants Ltd.* [1965] 1 W.L.R. 750; *Re Expanded Plugs Ltd.* [1965] 1 W.L.R. 514.

that the articles provided for a winding up in the event which had happened[11];

that one of the principal shareholders refused to produce accounts or balance sheets or to pay dividends, he having a majority of the voting power[12];

that the petitioner was excluded from all participation in the business[13];

that, in the case of a small private company, the company was in substance a partnership and the facts would justify the dissolution of a partnership.[14]

85–09 The last two illustrations relate only to small private companies founded on a personal relationship involving mutual confidence between the members. If in such a case a member commits a breach of good faith which the members owe each other as the result of that personal relationship and thereby acts inequitably, equitable considerations, imported into section 222 (*f*) by the words "just and equitable," may apply and enable the court to order the winding up of the company. This was the case in *Ebrahimi* v. *Westbourne Galleries Ltd.*[15] where, without wishing to be exhaustive, Lord Wilberforce described the situations in which such equitable considerations may assert themselves thus[16]:

> "(i) an association formed or continued on the basis of a personal relationship, involving mutual confidence—this element will often be found where a pre-existing partnership has been converted into a limited company; (ii) an agreement, or undertaking, that all, or some (for there may be 'sleeping' members), of the shareholders shall participate in the conduct of the business; (iii) restriction upon the transfer of the member's interest in the company—so that if confidence is lost, or one member is removed from management, he cannot take his stake and go elsewhere."

Such companies are often described as *quasi-partnership companies*. The description has been criticised on the ground that it may be confusing but it has been admitted that it is a conveniently brief description of this type of company.[17]

It is now clear that, in deciding whether a particular company falls within

---

[11] *Re American Pioneer Leather Co.* [1918] 1 Ch. 556.

[12] *Loch* v. *John Blackwood Ltd.* [1924] A.C. 783; and see *Re Newman and Howard Ltd.* [1962] Ch. 257.

[13] *Thomson* v. *Drysdale*, 1925 S.C. 311; *Re Lundie Brothers Ltd.* [1965] 1 W.L.R. 1051; *Ebrahimi* v. *Westbourne Galleries Ltd.* [1973] A.C. 360 (H.L.). As to the relationship between this principle and s. 184 (removal of director by ordinary resolution), see para. 61–27, *ante*; *Re A. and B.C. Chewing Gum Ltd.* [1975] 1 W.L.R. 579.

[14] *Re Yenidje Tobacco Co.* [1916] 2 Ch. 426; *Re Davis & Collett Ltd.* [1935] Ch. 693; *Re Fildes Bros. Ltd.* [1970] 1 W.L.R. 592; *Re Leadenhall General Hardware Stores Ltd.* (1971) 115 S.J. 202; *Ebrahimi* v. *Westbourne Galleries Ltd., supra*; *Re A. and B.C. Chewing Gum Ltd.* [1975] 1 W.L.R. 579.

[15] [1973] A.C. 360 (H.L.). See also *Re A. and B.C. Chewing Gum Ltd.* [1975] 1 All E.R. 1017; *Bentley Stevens* v. *Jones* [1947] 2 All E.R. 653; *Re North End Motels Ltd.* [1976] 1 N.Z.L.R. 446.

[16] *Ibid.* at p. 379.

[17] *Ibid.* at p. 379, *per* Lord Wilberforce.

this description, it is necessary to consider the total relationship of the persons involved. In addition to the articles, the court should have regard to any agreement, express or implied, between the parties, and also to any settled and accepted course of conduct between them, whether or not cast in the mould of a contract.[18]

85–10 In a quasi-partnership company the exercise by the majority in general meeting of their legal right under section 184 of the 1948 Act or the articles to remove a director from office, and consequently to remove him from participation in the business of the company, has been held, in the circumstances of the case, to be inequitable and to form a ground for winding up the company under the just and equitable clause.[19] Further, where in that type of company there is an agreement on management participation which has been broken, the court, in its discretion, may make a winding-up order under the just and equitable clause.[20]

A petitioner who relies on the "just and equitable" clause must come to court with clean hands, and if the breakdown in confidence between him and the other parties to the dispute appears to have been due to his misconduct he cannot insist on the company being wound up if they wish to continue.[21]

In the case of a public company whose shares are quoted on the Stock Exchange, the City Takeover Code sets out a code of conduct which has been laid down by responsible and experienced persons in the City of London as being fair and reasonable conduct. If the directors or principal shareholders of such a company choose to flout that code and to ignore without good reason the consequent directions of the City Takeover Panel and minority shareholders are injured by withdrawal of the Stock Exchange quotation for its shares, then it may be just and equitable to wind up the company. Whether in any case a winding up order should be made will depend on a full investigation of the facts of the particular case.[21a]

In considering whether it is just and equitable to wind up a company, the court must have regard to the facts existing at the time of the hearing of the petition, and not to those existing at the time the petition was presented.[22]

Where directors, holding half the shares, refused to register as members the executors of a deceased shareholder who held the other half, thus giving themselves complete control, a winding-up order was refused.[23] Where the majority shareholder made an offer to buy out the minority at a fair but not generous price and there was no evidence of either lack of

---

[18] *Re Fildes Bros. Ltd.* [1970] 1 W.L.R. 592, 596, *per* Megarry J; *Ebrahimi* v. *Westbourne Galleries Ltd.* [1973] A.C. 360, 379, *per* Lord Wilberforce; *Re A. and B.C. Chewing Gum Ltd.* [1975] 1 W.L.R. 579.

[19] *Ebrahimi* v. *Westbourne Galleries Ltd., supra.*

[20] *Re A. and B.C. Chewing Gum Ltd.* [1975] 1 W.L.R. 579.

[21] *Ebrahimi* v. *Westbourne Galleries Ltd.* [1973] A.C. 360, 387, *per* Lord Cross.

[21a] *Re St. Piran Ltd.* [1981] 1 W.L.R. 1300, 1307 F–G.

[22] *Re Fildes Bros. Ltd.* [1970] 1 W.L.R. 592.

[23] *Rayfield* v. *Hands* [1960] Ch. 1, 9; *Re Lundie Brothers Ltd.* [1965] 1 W.L.R. 1051; *Re Cuthbert Cooper & Sons Ltd.* [1937] Ch. 392; applied in *Charles Forte Investments Ltd.* v. *Amanda* [1964] Ch. 240.

probity or oppression, an order was refused and it was stated that a strong case had to be made out to wind up a successful and prosperous company which was properly managed.[23a]

85–11 Before 1948 the court would not make a winding-up order in cases where the petitioner had, or was thought to have, another remedy. For instance, where the directors were proceeding to do *ultra vires* acts, the proper remedy would be said to be an injunction; or in the case of mismanagement by the directors, it was said that the petitioner should call a meeting.[24] But in some cases this other remedy might be inadequate, as where the manager or managing directors could control a majority of the voting power. This defect was met by section 225 (2), which provides that in the case of a petition by a contributory, if the court considers that the petitioner has some other remedy, but that otherwise it would be just and equitable to order a winding up, the court "shall" make the order unless it considers that the petitioner is acting unreasonably in asking for a winding up instead of pursuing his other remedy.

In cases of this kind it sometimes happens that a winding up would be disastrous to the petitioning members, as where the majority could be in a position to secure most of the goodwill for themselves. This kind of case is provided for by the alternative remedy (1980 Act, s. 75) which has already been considered.[25] In the past, section 210 of the 1948 Act, the forerunner of the present section, was interpreted in an extremely restrictive manner with the ironical and unfortunate result that "just and equitable" winding up was more readily available as a remedy, particularly since it did not require that the petitioner had been oppressed *qua* shareholder.[26] Although the present section refers to unfair prejudice rather than oppression it still appears to be *qua* shareholder. Winding up on the just and equitable ground will, therefore, continue as a possible remedy in such circumstances. Although the winding up of a profitable company is an extreme vehicle for minority protection, its value as a weapon *in terrorem* cannot be overestimated.

Where winding up is not the appropriate remedy the court may restrain the presentation of a petition by injunction under its inherent jurisdiction to stay proceedings which are vexatious or an abuse of the process of the court.[27]

Petition for compulsory winding up

85–12 The application to the court for a compulsory winding-up order is by petition (1948 Act, s. 224). A petition may be presented

---

[23a] *Cumberland Holdings Ltd.* v. *Washington H. Saul Pattinson & Co. Ltd.* (1977) 13 A.L.R. 561 (P.C.).

[24] See *Re Professional, etc., Building Society* (1871) 6 Ch.App. 856, 862, and para. 85–17, *post*.

[25] See Chapter 60, *ante*.

[26] *Ebrahimi* v. *Westbourne Galleries Ltd.* [1973] A.C. 360, 375, *per* Lord Wilberforce.

[27] *Charles Forte (Investments) Ltd.* v. *Amanda* [1964] Ch. 240.

1. by the company;
2. by any creditor;
3. by any contributory;
4. by the official receiver under section 224 (2)[28];
5. by the Secretary of State under section 35 (1) of the 1967 Act[29] and Schedule 3, paragraph 28 to the Companies Act 1980;
6. by the Bank of England under section 18 of the Banking Act 1979;
7. by the Attorney-General, in the case of charitable companies[30];
8. by the Chief Registrar of Friendly Societies, in the case of certain defaults by a building society.[31]

The right to petition, being a statutory right, cannot be excluded by a clause in the articles of association.[32]

Petitions by the company are not very common; for if a company desires to wind up, it has only to pass a special, or an extraordinary, resolution for voluntary winding up (1948 Act, s. 278). However, if the directors find the company to be insolvent owing to matters which ought to be investigated by the court, it may well be that their proper course is to apply at once on behalf of the company to the court by petition for a compulsory order. It has been held in Ireland that the directors cannot present a petition in the name of the company without the sanction of a general meeting,[33] and this has now been accepted as the law in England despite earlier practice to the contrary.[34] It is possible for express authority to be given in the articles but article 80 of Table A does not confer such authority.[34] In any case, a general meeting can ratify the action of the directors.[33] A receiver may have power under a debenture to present a petition in the name of the company where this is "incidental or conducive" to the power to take possession of the company's assets.[34]

Petitions by contributories are likewise not very common, for the scheme of the Acts is that shareholders shall manage their own affairs, and winding up is one of them. However, "just and equitable" winding up as a means of minority protection in small private companies is substantially, if not numerically, important, especially since *Ebrahimi* v. *Westbourne Galleries Ltd.*[35] The great bulk of winding-up petitions is by creditors, a petition for a winding-up order being a proper as well as effective mode of enforcing payment of a debt due from a company.

Sometimes the directors deem it advisable to get a friendly creditor to present a petition in order to gain time to pass a resolution for winding up or to proceed with a scheme of arrangement.

---

28 See para. 85–18, *post*.
29 See para. 78–14, *ante*, and *Re Lubin, Rosen and Associates* [1975] 1 W.L.R. 122.
30 Charities Act 1960, s. 30 (1).
31 Building Societies Act 1962, ss. 22, 50, 55, Sched. I, para. 5.
32 *Re Peveril Gold Mines* [1898] 1 Ch. 122.
33 *Re Galway and Salthill Tramways Co.* [1918] 1 Ir.R. 62.
34 *Re Emmadart Ltd.* [1979] 1 All E.R. 599.
35 [1973] A.C. 360. See para. 85–08, *ante*.

The list of persons who may present a petition under section 224 (1) appears to be exhaustive.[36]

Creditor's petition

85–13 A creditor (including a contingent or prospective creditor) has *locus standi* to present a winding-up petition (1948 Act, s. 224 (1)). The Companies Acts do not define who is a creditor but it appears from the cases that the following will be regarded as creditors:

(1) All persons having any pecuniary claims against the company.[37] This does not include a debt arising out of an illegal transaction[38] and formerly it was held that it did not include an *ultra vires* debt.[39] It now seems that a person who is protected by section 9 of the European Communities Act 1972[40] is a creditor. A person with a statute-barred claim is not a creditor.[41]

(2) An assignee of a debt in law or in equity,[42] including an assignee of part of a debt.[43]

(3) A secured creditor,[44] even after obtaining the appointment of a receiver in an action.[45]

(4) The executor of a deceased life policyholder in respect of an admitted claim.[46]

(5) A person who has obtained a judgment in a claim for unliquidated damages.[47]

(6) A creditor by subrogation.[48]

(7) A local authority in respect of unpaid rates if under a distress warrant no goods are found to be seized.[49]

85–14 The following will not be regarded as creditors:

(1) a person claiming unliquidated damages who has not obtained judgment[50];

---

36 *Re H.L. Bolton Engineering Co. Ltd.* [1956] Ch. 577; *Re William Hockley Ltd.* [1962] 1 W.L.R. 555.

37 *Re Midland Coal, Coke & Iron Co.* [1895] 1 Ch. 267, 277 (C.A.). In *Re North Bucks Furniture Depositories Ltd.* [1939] 2 All E.R. 549, 551 Crossman J. regarded the term as covering every person who had the right to prove in a winding up but the relevant passage was deleted from the report in the Law Reports.

38 *Re South Wales Atlantic Steamship Co.* (1875) 2 Ch.D. 763 (C.A.).

39 *Re National Permanent Benefit Building Society* (1869) L.R. 5 Ch.App. 309.

40 See para. 9–25, *ante*.

41 However it does not matter that the claim is statute-barred at the time of the hearing if it was not so at the time of the presentation of the petition. The latter is the crucial date. (*Motor Terms Pty. Ltd.* v. *Liberty Insurance Ltd.* (1967) 116 C.L.R. 177).

42 *Re Paris Skating Rink Co.* (1877) 5 Ch.D. 959; *Re Montgomery Moore Ship Collision Doors Syndicate* (1903) 72 L.J.Ch. 624.

43 *Re Steel Wing Co.* [1921] 1 Ch. 349.

44 *Moor* v. *Anglo-Italian Bank* (1879) 10 Ch.D. 681.

45 *Re Borough of Portsmouth Tramways Co.* [1892] 2 Ch. 362.

46 *Re Masonic & General Life Assurance Co.* (1885) 32 Ch.D. 373.

47 *Re Pen-y-Van Colliery Co.* (1877) 6 Ch.D. 477, 479, 484.

48 *Re National Permanent Building Society* (1869) 5 Ch.App. 309.

49 *Re North Bucks Furniture Depositories* [1939] Ch. 690.

50 *Re Penn-y-Van Colliery Co.* (1877) 6 Ch.D. 477 but *cf. Re A Company* [1974] 1 All E.R. 256, 260 and *Re M.B. Coogan Ltd.* [1953] N.Z.L.R. 582. In any event once the company is in liquidation provided that the claim is liquidated at the date when the creditor comes into prove he will be able to prove and the court may grant leave under s. 231 to issue a writ in respect of the claim. (*Re Berkeley Securities (Property) Ltd.*, [1980] 3 All E.R. 513.

(2) a guarnishor of a debt who has not obtained an order of the court directing the debt to be paid to him[51];

(3) a debenture stock holder who has no direct covenant with the company[52];

(4) a person whose debt is disputed on substantial grounds[53];

Formerly it was held that the following were not to be regarded as creditors:

(a) a guarantor of a debt owing by the company who had not yet paid[54];

(b) a landlord in respect of future rent[55];

(c) the holder of a bill of exchange not yet payable[56];

(d) the holder of a debenture not yet payable.[57]

85–15 However, section 224 states that creditor includes any contingent or prospective creditor which would appear to cover (a), (b), (c) and (d), and possibly (1) above. Such a creditor has to give security for costs and before a hearing show a prima facie case (s. 224 (1) (*c*)). A contingent creditor means "a person towards whom, under an existing obligation, the company may or will become subject to a present liability on the happening of some future event or at some future date."[58]

Contributory's petition

85–16 Such petitions are comparatively rare; for the Act establishes a domestic tribunal as between the members and the company, and thus enables the members themselves, by passing the requisite resolutions, to determine whether there shall be a voluntary liquidation, or whether the court shall be asked to make a compulsory order (1948 Act, s. 278).[59] Accordingly, a contributory, to obtain an order, must make out a special case,[60] which will usually be founded on the "just and equitable" ground.[61]

No contributory of a company is capable of presenting a petition unless

1 either the number of members is reduced below two; or

2 the shares in respect of which he is a contributory or some of them were

(a) originally allotted to him, or

(b) have been held by him and registered in his name for at least six months during the 18 months before the commencement of the winding up, or

---

[51] *Re Combined Weighing Machine Co.* (1889) 43 Ch.D. 99.

[52] *Re Uruguay Central Ry. Co.* (1879) 11 Ch.D. 372, 380–381; *Re Dunderland Iron Co.* [1909] 1 Ch. 446 but see para. 46–01, *ante*.

[53] *Mann* v. *Goldstein* [1968] 1 W.L.R. 1091. See para. 85–06, *ante*.

[54] *Re Vron Colliery Co.* (1882) 20 Ch.D. 442.

[55] *Re United Club* (1889) 60 L.T. 665.

[56] *Re W. Powell & Sons* [1892] W.N. 94.

[57] *Re Melbourne Brewery Co.* [1901] 1 Ch. 453.

[58] *Re William Hockley Ltd.* [1962] 1 W.L.R. 555, 558 per Pennycuick J.

[59] *Re Langham Skating Rink* (1877) 5 Ch.D. 669, 683.

[60] See *Re Gutta Percha Corporation* [1900] 2 Ch. 665, where resolutions had been passed for voluntary winding up with a view to reconstruction which proved abortive.

[61] See para. 85–08, *ante*.

(c) have devolved upon him through the death of a former holder (s. 224 (1) (*a*) as impliedly amended by the Companies Act 1980, s. 2 (1)).

The object of these provisions is to prevent a person buying shares in order to qualify himself to wreck the company. "Held" means standing in the name of the contributory petitioner.[62] The provisions of section 224 (1) (*a*) must be applied strictly, unless, perhaps, the company itself is in default in allotting shares or registering a transfer.[63]

A purported original allottee whose name is not in the register of members has *locus standi* to petition as a contributory. However, where there is a bona fide dispute concerning the allotment the petitioner must first establish that he is a shareholder before petitioning for the winding up.[64]

The 1948 Act provides in section 216 (*a*) that if a contributory becomes bankrupt, either before or after he has been placed on the list of contributories, his trustee in bankruptcy shall represent him for all purposes of the winding up and shall be a contributory accordingly. Consequently, a shareholder who is adjudicated bankrupt and later discharged (but neither the receiving order nor the adjudication order has been annulled), has no *locus standi* to make an application under section 256 (1) for a stay of the winding-up order against the company in which he held shares because not he, but the official receiver as successor of the shareholder's trustee in bankruptcy, is the contributory. As Goff L.J. observed in *Re Wolverhampton Steel & Iron Co. Ltd.*[65] "the bankruptcy . . . is still subsisting and the shares which he owned beneficially have not revested in him."

A bankrupt shareholder who is still registered as the holder of the shares may petition as a contributory at the instance of his trustee in bankruptcy,[66] but the trustee is not himself a contributory for this purpose.[67] The personal representatives of a deceased shareholder may apparently petition as contributories.[68]

85–17 As a general rule the court will not make a winding-up order on the petition of a contributory whose shares are fully paid unless he shows, on the face of his petition, a prima facie probability that the company is solvent and that there will be a substantial surplus of assets available for distribution among the shareholders; otherwise he has no tangible interest in the winding up.[69] This is so despite the provisions of sections 224 (1) and

62 *Re Wala Wynaad Gold Co.* (1882) 21 Ch.D. 849.
63 *Re Gattopardo Ltd.* [1969] 1 W.L.R. 619 (C.A.). *Cf. Re Patent Steam Engine Co.* (1878) 8 Ch.D. 464.
64 Re JN2 Ltd. [1978] 1 W.L.R. 183.
65 [1977] 1 W.L.R. 860, 863.
66 *Re K/9 Meat Suppliers (Guildford) Ltd.* [1966] 1 W.L.R. 1112. *Cf. Re Wolverhampton Steel & Iron Co. Ltd.* [1977] 1 W.L.R. 860 (C.A.).
67 *Re H.L. Bolton Engineering Co. Ltd.* [1956] Ch. 577.
68 *Re Cuthbert Cooper & Sons Ltd.* [1937] Ch. 392; *Re Bayswater Trading Co. Ltd.* [1970] 1 W.L.R. 343; *Re Chesterfield Catering Co. Ltd.* [1976] 3 W.L.R. 879.
69 *Re Rica Gold Co.* (1879) 11 Ch.D. 36; *Re Kaslo-Slocan, etc., Corpn. Ltd.* [1910] W.N. 13; *Re S. A. Hawken Ltd.* (1950) 66 T.L.R. (Pt. 2) 138; *Re Othery Construction Ltd.* [1966] 1 W.L.R. 69; *Re Expanded Plugs Ltd.* [1966] 1 W.L.R. 514; *Re W. R. Willcocks & Co. Ltd.* [1973] 3 W.L.R. 669, 671 (the allegation of a substantial surplus must be supported by evidence); *Re Chesterfield Catering Co. Ltd.* [1976] 3 W.L.R. 879.

225 (1), and it follows that such a contributory cannot petition for a winding up on the grounds that the company is unable to pay its debts. Where, however, the fully paid shareholder shows that the company's membership has fallen below the statutory minimum he has an interest in an insolvent winding up by reason of his potential liability for the company's debts under section 31 of the 1948 Act. The court may also recognise other interests of such a shareholder provided that they are held *qua* member or former member and not as outsider.[70] Where a petition is founded on section 222 (*f*) and alleges that the company has failed to supply accounts and information, with the consequence that the petitioner is unable to tell whether or not there will be surplus assets, or where the petition alleges that the affairs of the company require investigation in respects which are likely to produce such a surplus, the requirement of proof of a substantial surplus does not apply.[71] But it is no exception to the rule that the company's affairs require investigation in order to protect the interests of the creditors alone,[72] nor that the company is in substance a partnership.[73] The rule does not appear to apply to a petition by the holder of partly paid shares, since his position may be prejudiced if the company continues to trade at a loss.

Mismanagement by directors is prima facie not a ground for a shareholder to petition; he should call a meeting.[74]

A shareholder who is in arrear with calls must make out a very special case to justify his petitioning in such circumstances, and he may be required to pay the calls into court or to give an undertaking for payment of them.[75]

The fact that a voluntary winding up is in progress is prima facie a bar to the winding up on a shareholder's petition,[76] because a shareholder is bound by the wishes of the majority; but the voluntary winding up is not an absolute bar to a contributory's petition, and the court will make the order if satisfied that the rights of the contributory will be prejudiced by the voluntary winding up (1948 Act, s. 310).[77] The court, when exercising its discretion, will examine the composition of the majority passing the resolution and other circumstances to make sure that it was an honest exercise of the wishes of the shareholders.[78]

Formerly a contributory had *locus standi* to present a petition on the ground of default in delivering the statutory report or holding the statutory

---

[70] *Re Chesterfield Catering Co. Ltd.* [1977] Ch. 373.
[71] *Re Newman and Howard Ltd.* [1962] Ch. 257; see also *Re Argentum Reductions (U.K.) Ltd.* [1975] 1 W.L.R. 186 (an indirect interest of the contributory may be sufficient).
[72] *Re Othery Construction Ltd.* [1966] 1 W.L.R. 69.
[73] *Re Expanded Plugs Ltd.* [1966] 1 W.L.R. 514.
[74] *Re Professional, Commercial, etc., Building Society* (1871) 6 Ch.App. 856, 862; but see para. 85–11, *ante*.
[75] *Re Diamond Fuel Co.* (1879) 13 Ch.D. 400; *Re Crystal Reef Co.* [1892] 1 Ch. 408.
[76] *Re Bank of Gibraltar* (1865) 1 Ch.App. 69, 74; *Re Imperial Bank of China* (1866) 1 Ch.App. 339; *Re London and Mercantile Discount Co.* (1865) L.R. 1 Eq. 277; *Re Doré Gallery* [1891] W.N. 98.
[77] *Re National Company for Distribution of Electricity* [1902] 2 Ch. 34.
[78] *Re Varieties* [1893] 2 Ch. 235; *Re Haycraft Gold, etc., Co.* [1900] 2 Ch. 230.

meeting. This ground has now been replaced by failure to obtain a certificate to do business or continuing as an old public company and now only the Secretary of State may petition on these grounds (s. 224 (1) (*b*) as amended by Sched. 3, paras. 27 and 28 to the Companies Act 1980).

Petition by official receiver

85–18 Section 224 (2) of the 1948 Act provides that where a company is being wound up voluntarily or subject to supervision in England, a petition may be presented by the official receiver attached to the court having jurisdiction to wind up the company, as well as by any other person authorised in that behalf under the other provisions of the section, but the court shall not make a winding-up order on the petition unless it is satisfied that the voluntary winding up, or winding up subject to supervision, cannot be continued with due regard to the interests of the creditors or contributories.[79] This is to be determined on a balance of probabilities.[80]

It does not necessarily follow that, because a company was controlled by one shareholder of whom a liquidator in a voluntary winding up might be regarded as the nominee, a voluntary winding up cannot be continued with due regard to the interests of the creditors; whether that is so depends on the facts of each case which have to be considered in the light of the evidence before the court.[81]

Petition by the Secretary of State

85–19 The Secretary of State has power to petition the court for a winding-up order if it appears to him—

(a) from an inspector's report made under section 168 of the 1948 Act; or

(b) from information or a document obtained as the result of the inspection of the company's books or papers under Part III of the 1967 Act; or

(c) from information or a document obtained under section 18 or 19 of the Protection of Depositors Act 1963;

that it is in the public interest that the body should be wound up. If the court thinks it just and equitable for the company to be wound up, it will make a winding-up order (1967 Act, s. 35 (1)).

In addition, under the Companies Act 1980, Sched. 3, para. 28 the Secretary of State may present a petition to wind up a company which was registered as a public company on its original incorporation and which has not been issued with a certificate under section 4 of the 1980 Act if more than a year has expired since it was registered. The Secretary of State may

---

[79] See *Re Jubilee Sites Syndicate* [1899] 2 Ch. 204; *Re Ryder Installations Ltd.* [1966] 1 W.L.R. 524; *Re J. Russell Electronics Ltd.* [1968] 1 W.L.R. 1252.

[80] *Re J. Russell Electronics Ltd.* [1968] 1 W.L.R. 1252.

[81] *Re Medical Battery Co.* [1894] 1 Ch. 444; *Adebayo* v. *Official Receiver of Nigeria* [1954] 1 W.L.R. 681, (P.C.).

also at any time after the end of the transitional period present a petition for the winding up of an old public company. Note there is no express reference to the public interest or to just and equitable grounds in either of these latter two cases.

Where the petition of the Secretary of State under section 35 of the 1967 Act is founded on the allegation that the company is engaged in a disreputable system of trading, the court will not refrain from making a winding-up order against the company on its undertaking to trade in future in an unobjectionable manner because it is not the courts' function to place delinquent companies on probation and to police their undertakings.[82]

Although a petition by the Secretary of State cannot be presented against a company which is already in compulsory winding up it can be presented against a company in voluntary winding up.[83] Such a petition does not require the personal attention of the Secretary of State; it is sufficient that it is presented in his name by one of his officers.[84]

In *Re Lubin, Rosen and Associates Ltd.*[85] Megarry J. indicated the special considerations which apply to a winding-up petition by the Secretary of State in the following passage[86]—

> "It seems to me that a petition presented by the Secretary of State under section 35 of the Act of 1967 is in a somewhat different category from a petition presented by a creditor or contributory. Creditors and contributories petition in their own interests as members of a class; under the section the Secretary of State petitions under a special statutory provision which comes into operation only when it has appeared to him that it is expedient in the public interest that the company should be wound up. The Secretary of State is necessarily acting not in his own interest but in the interests of the public at large. . . . I think that the court, without in the least abdicating any of its judicial and discretionary powers, ought to give special weight to his views."

In proceedings for a winding-up order on the petition of the Secretary of State the inspector's report is admissible as prima facie evidence but if there is evidence before the court which casts doubt on the terms or conclusions of the report, the court would listen attentively and then weigh the evidence before it.[87]

Petition by Bank of England

85–20 The Bank of England may petition for the winding up of a recognised bank or licensed deposit taker and the court may wind it up if it is "unable to pay sums due and payable to its depositors or is unable to pay such sums

[82] *Re Bamford Publishers Ltd.*, *The Times*, June 4, 1977.
[83] *Re Lubin, Rosen & Associates Ltd.*, [1975] 1 W.L.R. 122.
[84] *Re Golden Chemical Products Ltd.* [1976] Ch. 300.
[85] [1975] 1 W.L.R. 122.
[86] *Ibid.* pp. 128–129.
[87] *Re Armvent Ltd.* [1975] 1 W.L.R. 1679 in which the earlier cases are discussed.

only by defaulting on its obligations to its other creditors" or if the value of its assets are less than its liabilities.

Unexempted deposit taking companies continue to be subject to the powers of the Secretary of State for Trade under the Protection of Depositors Act 1963 (s. 83 of the Companies Act 1980).

Form of petition

85–21 A petition[88] for winding up a company states the date of incorporation of the company, the situation of its registered office, the amount of its nominal and paid-up capital, the main objects of the company, and the ground on which the petition is founded, *e.g.* that the company is indebted to the petitioner in a specified sum, that he has made repeated applications for payment, but without success, that the company is unable to pay its debts, and that in the circumstances it is just and equitable that the company should be wound up. The petitioner concludes with the prayer "that the company may be wound up by the court under the provisions of the Companies Act 1948." There is a note at the foot to the effect that it is "intended to serve this petition on the company." In framing a petition, it is essential to allege a case for winding up within the Act (1948 Act, s. 222). If no case is alleged, the petition, unless the court should give liberty to amend, is demurrable, and will be dismissed with costs.[89] If it is intended to plead fraud the facts which give rise to it must be clearly alleged.[90]

Presentation and answering

85–22 A winding-up petition to the High Court is presented at the office of the Registrar of the Companies Court, who appoints the time and place at which the petition is to be heard.[91] After a petition has been presented, the petitioner must, on a day to be appointed by the Registrar, not less than two days before the day appointed for the hearing of the petition, attend before the Registrar and satisfy him that the petition has been duly advertised, that the prescribed affidavit verifying the statements therein and the affidavit of service have been duly filed, and that the provisions of the rules as to winding-up petitions have been duly complied with by the petitioner.[92]

---

88 The general title of the petition should include the words "Chancery Division" and "Group A" but not the name of the judge: Practice Note [1958] 2 All E.R. 124 (drawing attention to the Companies (Winding-up) (Amendment) Rules 1957).

89 *Re Wear Engine Works Co.* (1875) 10 Ch.App. 188.

90 *Re Rica Gold Washing Co.* (1879) 11 Ch.D. 36.

91 Winding-up Rules 1949, r. 27. On the advertisement of the petition, see r. 28 and Practice Note (November 29, 1948) 1 C.L.C. 1405.

92 *Ibid.* r. 33; see *Re Royal Mutual Benefit Bdg. Soc.* [1960] 1 W.L.R. 1143. As to attendance by solicitors, see Practice Notes (1961) 105 S.J. 207; (1975) 119 S.J. 473; [1977] 121 S.J. 708. A Practice Note was issued by Templeman J. on October 10, 1977, drawing attention to the need for compliance with the Rules and stating that "people who did not advertise or who did not appear before the Registrar, as they should, would do so at their own peril and should not be surprised when the necessary consequences followed" (1977) 121 S.J. 708. See also *Re Shusella Ltd.* (1982) 126 S.J. 577.

For a Practice Direction dated October 15, 1979 allowing certain formal business in the chambers of the Companies Court Registrar in London to be transacted by post see Part III, paragraph H–1208. The Practice Direction applies to the winding-up proceedings set out in the Schedule. These are:

(1) The presentation of petitions under Order 102 and the Winding-up Rules.
(2) The issue of summonses under Order 102 and the Winding-up Rules.
(3) The issue of notices of motion under Order 102 and the Winding-up Rules.
(4) The issue of third party notices (where leave to issue such notice has been granted) and notices under Winding-up Rule 68.
(5) The filing and lodging of affidavits, exhibits and other documents required to be filed or lodged.
(6) Entry of appearances.
(7) The issue of notices of appointments for the hearing of originating summonses to which an appearance is required.
(8) Fixing appointments for the restoration of adjourned summonses.
(9) Drawing up orders.
(10) The issue of certificates of taxation.
(11) The adjournment of summonses by consent.
(12) Notification that proceedings have been disposed of.

A further Practice Direction bearing the same date allows the Chief Clerk to assist the Registrar in the hearing of certain applications and the making of orders thereon.

Where several petitions are presented, they rank according to the date of presentation.[93]

Advertisement of petition

85–23 Unless the court otherwise directs, every petition is to be advertised in the Gazette[94] seven clear days (excluding Saturdays, Sundays and public holidays[95]) after it has been served on the company and not less than seven clear days before the day fixed for the hearing. The former requirement of advertisment in a national or local newspaper was abolished by the Companies (Winding-Up) (Amendment) Rules 1979[96] which became operative on April 1, 1979. Every advertisement of a petition is to contain a note at the foot thereof stating that any person who intends to appear on the hearing of the petition, either to oppose or support, must send notice of his

---

[93] *Re Building Societies Trust* (1890) 44 Ch.D. 140, 144; *Re Bamford* [1910] 1 Ir.R. 390.
[94] R. 28 of 1949 as substituted by S.I. 1979 No. 209. As to failure to comply with the new shorter form of advertisement introduced by this rule see *Re Accoustic Transducer Co. Ltd. The Times*, November 12, 1980 but see now the Practice Note, Companies: Advertisement of Petition [1980] 1 W.L.R. 657.
[95] *Re Display Multiples Ltd.* [1967] 1 W.L.R. 571.
[96] S.I. 1979 No. 209.

intention to the petitioner or his solicitor. Notice of intention to appear must be given by any person intending to do so,[97] and must contain his name and address.[98]

Any error in the title, name, day or place for hearing may render the advertisement useless[99]; but a trifling formal defect where no one is misled will not invalidate the petition.[1] In addition, under rule 225 of the 1949 Rules the court is given power to extend or abridge the time for doing any act or taking any proceeding and this includes advertising. Further, under rule 226 it is provided that no proceedings shall be invalidated by any formal defect or irregularity unless the court before which an objection is made is of the opinion that substantial injustice has been caused thereby and that the injustice cannot be remedied by any order of the court. The court in practice will only exercise its discretion under these rules where there are special circumstances.[2]

The advertisement has been held to be notice to the world of the presentation of the petition but only from the time when they may reasonably be supposed to have seen it.[3] This is unaffected by section 9 of the European Communities Act 1972.[4]

The court will restrain the issuing of the advertisements when the petition is an abuse of the process of the court.[5]

If the petition is not duly advertised in accordance with Rule 28 of the 1949 Rules (as amended), the judge may order that it shall be removed from the file.[5a]

85–24 Every petition shall, unless presented by the company itself, be served on the company at its registered office, if any, and if there is none, then at its principal or last known principal place of business, if this can be found, by leaving a copy with any member, officer or servant of the company there. If no one can be found then service can be effected by leaving a copy at the registered office or principal place of business or by serving it on such

---

[97] See r. 34 of 1949. As to the position in relation to appearances notified outside the time limit specified in rule 34, see *Practice Note* [1976] 1 W.L.R. 515, reproduced in Vol. III, para. H–1203.

[98] *Re Descours, Parry & Co.* [1909] W.N. 50.

[99] *Re Army and Navy Hotel* (1886) 31 Ch.D. 644; *Re London and Provincial Pure Ice* [1904] W.N. 136; *Re City & County Bank* (1875) 10 Ch.App. 470; *Re Mont de Piete* [1892] W.N. 166; *Re Hille India Rubber Co.* [1897] W.N. 6; *Re Samuel Birch Co.* [1907] W.N. 31.

[1] *Re l'Industrie Verrière Ltd.* [1914] W.N. 222; *Re J. & P. Sussman Ltd.* [1958] 1 W.L.R. 519; *Re Videofusion* [1974] 1 W.L.R. 1548. For form of advertisement, see *Company Precedents*, Pt. III (16th ed.); *Re Broads Patent Night Light Co.* [1892] W.N. 5. As to errors in spelling see *Re Videofusion Ltd.* [1974] 1 W.L.R. 1548.

[2] *Re London India Rubber Co.* (1866) 14 C.T. 316. A strike in the printing industry would probably suffice.

[3] *Emerson's Case* (1866) 1 Ch. 433; *Re Marlborough Club Co.* (1866) L.R. 1 Eq. 216; *Re New Gas Co.* (1877) 5 Ch.D. 703; *Re Oriental Bank Corpn.* (1885) 28 Ch.D. 634. *Cf. Re Dramstar Ltd.* (1980) 124 S.J. 807.

[4] Presentation of a petition is not subject to official notification within s. 9 (3) and is not within s. 9 (4).

[5] *Re A Company* [1894] 2 Ch. 349; *Re A Company* (May 16, 1950) 1 C.L.C. 1406, 94 S.J. 369; and see *Charles Forte (Investments) Ltd.* v. *Amanda* [1964] Ch. 240.

[5a] Companies (Winding-up) (Amendment) (No. 2) Rules 1981 (S.I. 1981 No. 1309) para. 2(a).

member, officer or servant of the company as the court may direct. Where the company is being wound up voluntarily, the petition shall also be served on the liquidator, if any has been appointed.[6]

Evidence in support of petition

85–25 The Rules provide for the filing of an affidavit by the petitioner in general terms, stating, in effect, that the statements in the petition relating to his own acts and deeds are true, and that he believes the other statements to be true. This is known as the statutory affidavit.[7] It must be sworn and filed within seven days after the presentation of the petition. Notice of the filing need not be given to the company, but if a supplementary affidavit is filed, notice should be given to avoid the necessity for adjournment.[8]

The object of the statutory affidavits is to prevent the abuse of putting upon the file long affidavits in support of the petition which may turn out to be unnecessary.[9] Another purpose is to secure that the petitioner or some person on his behalf goes on oath as to the material matters thus preventing the casual filing of petitions in order to induce payment under threat of advertisement or winding up.[10]

Rule 30 of the 1949 Rules provides that the statutory affidavit "shall be prima facie evidence of the statements in the petition." This means that the affidavit is admissible for the purpose of providing evidence of the truth of the statements in the petition even though such evidence may be hearsay.[11] It is sufficient to require an answer.[12] Additional affidavits are, however, required by some person having personal knowledge of the facts where the petitioner alleges fraud or misconduct,[13] or seeks to have the company wound up by analogy to the dissolution of a partnership,[14] or otherwise where "the case is unusual rather than purely formal."[15] Inspectors' reports[16] have a special status not as evidence in the ordinary sense, but as material on which, if it is not challenged, the court can proceed to make a winding-up order. These are two special categories to which can be added anything else for which some

---

[6] r. 29 of 1949; *Re Edward Chester & Co.* (1903) 52 W.R. 189.
[7] r. 30 of 1949 as substituted by S.I. 1979 No. 209.
[8] *Re New Weighing Machine Co.* [1896] W.N. 48, as explained in *Practice Direction* [1898] W.N. 7; *Re British Cycle Manufacturing Co.* (1898) 77 L.T. 683.
[9] *Per* Lindley L.J., *Re Gold Hill Mines* (1883) 23 Ch.D. 210, 214.
[10] *Re Bond Motors Ltd.* [1976] 1 N.Z.L.R. 368, 370.
[11] *Re Koscot Interplanetary (U.K.) Ltd.* [1972] 3 All E.R. 829.
[12] *Re Gold Hill Mines* (1883) 23 Ch.D. 210, 214 (C.A.); *Re S. A. Hawken Ltd.* [1950] 2 All E.R. 408, 412.
[13] *Re S. A. Hawken Ltd.* [1950] 2 All E.R. 408, *Re A. B. C. Coupler and Engineering Co. Ltd. (No. 2)* [1962] 1 W.L.R. 1236.
[14] *Re Davis Investments (East Ham) Ltd.* [1961] 1 W.L.R. 1396, C.A.; *Re W. R. Willcocks & Co. Ltd.* [1973] 3 W.L.R. 669, 672 (an allegation of deadlock must be particularised, otherwise the petition will be struck out).
[15] *Re Davis Investments (East Ham) Ltd.*, *supra*, at p. 1399, *per* Danckwerts L.J.
[16] See *Re Travel & Holiday Clubs* [1967] 1 W.L.R. 711; *Re SBA Properties Ltd.* [1967] 2 All E.R. 615; *Re Armvent Ltd.* [1975] 3 All E.R. 441; *Re St. Piran Ltd.* [1981] 3 All E.R. 270. See para. 78–12, ante.

statutory sanction can be found. Apart from these special categories there is no open licence to admit hearsay evidence generally on a petition for the winding up of a company. Thus in *Re Koscot Interplanetary (U.K.) Ltd.*; *Re Kosgot A.G.*,[17] Megarry J. rejected as inadmissible evidence an unauthenticated summary of proceedings taken or contemplated in the various states of the United States of America against an American company which was related to the two companies sought to be wound up in proceedings before him.

Where a corporation is petitioner, the affidavit must be made by some person who has been concerned in the matter on behalf of the corporation.[18] In exceptional cases, *e.g.* where the company is not carrying on business in this country, the affidavit may be made by some other person holding a power of attorney for the company.[19]

Affidavits, if put in in opposition to the petition, must be filed within 14 days of the date of the filing of the statutory affidavit.[20] The petitioner may be cross-examined as well as the opposing deponents; but the court has a discretion as to allowing cross-examination in a winding-up petition, and refused, for example, to allow a petitioner to cross-examine the respondent company's witnesses where the petitioner had no direct evidence but the statutory affidavit, and wanted to cross-examine as to the company's business, means and bona fides.[21] If necessary, witnesses who decline to make affidavits can be called and examined at the instance of any party interested.

Hearing of petition

85–26 The petition is heard in open court. Winding-up petitions in the High Court are heard in the Companies Court[22] of the Chancery Division. If the company appears it must be represented by counsel in the Companies Court or by counsel or a solicitor in the county court. If there is a dispute as to the authority of particular directors to instruct a solicitor and his consequent authority to represent the company it cannot be aired on the hearing of the petition but must be the subject of a separate summons or motion.[23]

---

[17] [1972] 3 All E.R. 829.

[18] Companies (Winding-up) (Amendment) Rules 1967 (S.I. 1967 No. 1341), amending r. 30 of the 1949 Rules, which required the affidavit to be made by a director, secretary or "principal officer": see *Re Vic Groves & Co. Ltd.* [1964] 1 W.L.R. 956. *Cf. Registrar of Restrictive Trading Agreements* v. *W. H. Smith & Son Ltd.* [1968] 1 W.L.R. 1541; aff'd by C.A. [1969] 1 W.L.R. 1460.

[19] *Ibid.* at p. 959, *per* Pennycuick J. It is thought that this observation remains applicable under the 1967 Rules.

[20] r. 36 of 1949 as amended by S.I. 1979 No. 209; *Re J. H. Evans & Co.* [1892] W.N. 126.

[21] *Re London Fish Market Co.* (1883) 27 S.J. 600; *Re Emma Silver Mining Co.* (1875) L.R. 10 Ch. 194; *Re West Devon Mine* [1884] W.N. 139.

[22] As to the nature of the Companies Court and its jurisdiction and procedures see *Re Shilena Hosiery Co. Ltd.* [1977] 2 All E.R. 6. As to procedure see further rr. 34–37 (Vol. III, H. 0343–7).

[23] *Richmond* v. *Branson & Son* [1914] 1 Ch. 968; *Russian Commercial Bank* v. *Comptoir d'Escompte de Mulhouse* [1925] A.C. 112.

Only the petitioner and the company are entitled to be heard as of right[24] but in practice the court allows counsel for other parties to address it. If the other parties wish to appear they are required by the Winding-up Rules to give notice to the petitioner in accordance with the Rules (r. 34). Failing this they can only appear by special leave of the court (r. 34 (5)) and will not be entitled to costs.[25] The petitioner must furnish the court with a list in Form 13 of those who have given notice of intention to appear (r. 35).

Upon hearing the petition the court may dismiss it with or without costs, may adjourn the hearing conditionally or unconditionally[26] and may make an interim order or any other order that it deems just (1948 Act, s. 225).[27] But the court will not as a rule order a petition to stand over for a lengthy period: it would not be just to the company.[28]

In all matters relating to the winding up—and winding up includes the petition—the court may have regard to the wishes of creditors and contributories, and may, if expedient, direct meetings to be summoned to ascertain such wishes (1948 Act, s. 346). If the company is solvent, the wishes of contributories, as the persons chiefly interested in the assets, carry most weight; if the company is insolvent, the wishes of creditors.[29]

The element of public policy in regard to commercial morality has likewise to be taken into consideration when the propriety of a winding-up order is examined.[30] A winding-up petition presented by the Secretary of State after an investigation should be given appropriate weight, even though not supported by any creditor and opposed by many creditors with claims of large value, and even though a resolution for voluntary winding up has already been passed.[31] An order is not to be refused on the ground only that the assets of the company have been mortgaged to an amount equal to or in excess of those assets, or that the company has no assets (1948 Act, s. 225).

Where the petitioner consents to the dismissal of his petition or does not press for an order, the court may substitute as petitioner any creditor or contributory who in the opinion of the court would have a right to present a petition.[32]

Commencement of winding up

85–27 In the case of a winding up by the court the winding up dates from the presentation of the petition (1948 Act, s. 229).

---

24 *Re Ibo Investment Trust Ltd.* [1904] 1 Ch. 26.

25 Practice Note [1930] W.N. 78.

26 As regards adjournments to allow defaulting companies to file their annual returns or other requisite documents, see Practice Note [1974] 1 W.L.R. 1459.

27 A dispute as to the beneficial ownership of shares is not an appropriate question for determination on a winding-up petition: *Re Bambi Restaurants Ltd.* [1965] 1 W.L.R. 750.

28 *Re Chapel House Colliery Co.* (1883) 24 Ch.D. 259, 267.

29 See para. 85–06, *ante*.

30 *Re Krasnapolskly Co.* [1892] 3 Ch. 174; *Re New Oriental Bank Corporation* [1892] 3 Ch. 563; *Re Medical Battery Co.* [1894] 1 Ch. 444; *Re Crigglestone Coal Co.* [1906] 2 Ch. 327; *Re Clandown Colliery* [1915] 1 Ch. 369.

31 *Re Lubin, Rosen and Associates* [1975] 1 W.L.R. 122.

32 r. 37 of 1949.

A voluntary winding up dates from the passing of the resolution (1948 Act, s. 280).

Where a winding-up order is made after a voluntary winding up has commenced, the winding up dates from the passing of the resolution (s. 229), and all proceedings taken in the voluntary winding up are deemed to have been validly taken unless the court otherwise orders.

Winding-up order[33]

85–28 The order is to the effect that the company be wound up by the court under the provisions of the Companies Act 1948. Under rule 40 it is not necessary for the Registrar to make an appointment to settle the order, unless in any particular case the special circumstances make an appointment necessary.

The effect of a winding-up order is to avoid all dispositions of the property (including things in action) of the company made between the commencement of the winding up—*i.e.* the presentation of the petition—and the winding-up order, unless the court otherwise orders (s. 227).[34] Likewise any attachment or execution against the property of the company after the commencement of the winding up is void (s. 228).[35] After presentation of the petition the court may stay any proceedings against the company (s. 226); and such proceedings are automatically stayed on the making of the winding-up order, and cannot be continued except by leave of the court (s. 231).[35]

The winding-up order has the further effect of terminating the employment of servants[36] and other agents[37] of the company. The directors are similarly dismissed and their powers to act on behalf of the company cease.[38]

Every invoice, order for goods or business letter issued by or on behalf of the company or the liquidator after the winding-up order must contain a statement that the company is in liquidation (s. 338).

The winding-up order must be registered with the Registrar of Companies and requires official notification.[39]

Rectification and rescission of winding-up order

The court has inherent power to rectify or rescind an order before it is drawn up.[40] Drawing up represents perfection of the order but where the

---

33 As to the procedure see rr. 38–43.
34 See para. 85–75, *post*.
35 See para. 85–70, *post*.
36 *Chapman's Case* (1886) L.R. 1 Eq. 346; *Measures Bros. Ltd.* v. *Measures* [1910] 2 Ch. 248.
37 *e.g.* a receiver: *Gosling* v. *Gaskell* [1897] A.C. 575; see para. 43–29, *ante*.
38 *Fowler* v. *Broad's Patent Night Light Co.* [1893] 1 Ch. 724; *Re Mawcon Ltd.* [1969] 1 W.L.R. 78. On the residuary powers of the board of directors, see *Re Union Accident Insurance Co. Ltd.* [1972] 1 W.L.R. 640.
39 European Communities Act 1972, s. 9 (3)(*f*).
40 *Re Miller's Case* (1876) 3 Ch.D. 661; *Re St. Nazaire Co.* (1879) 12 Ch.D. 88; *Re Crown Bank* (1890) 44 Ch.D. 634. See also Practice Notes (Winding-up Order Rescission) [1971] 1 W.L.R. 4 & 757 (Vol. III–H–1200–1).

justice of the case requires it, it may be regarded as provisionally effective before it is drawn up.[41] The court can correct an order even after it has been drawn up if it does not express its intention.[42] Apart from this an order cannot be rescinded after it has been drawn up even though it was obtained by mistake[43] or is bad on the face of it.[44] The court has no jurisdiction to rehear a case after the order has been perfected.[44a] Any further proceedings to discharge or vary or challenge the order must be by way of appeal[45]—or on application to stay proceedings under section 256 of the 1948 Act.

In exercising its power of rescission, the court will act with great caution and an application will only be entertained if it is made promptly, *i.e.* normally within three or four days after the order is pronounced. The application must be made (a) by a creditor, or (b) by a contributory, or (c) by the company jointly with a creditor or contributory. If the appointment is unsuccessful the costs will normally have to be paid by the creditor or contributory making or joining in the application because, if the company had to pay them, they would unfairly fall on the general body of creditors.[46]

Staying winding-up proceedings

85–29 The court has a discretion, on the application of the liquidator or official receiver, or any creditor or contributory, to stay the proceedings under a winding-up order (s. 256). A shareholder who has been adjudicated bankrupt is not a contributory for the purpose of section 256 even after he is discharged from his bankruptcy and whether he holds the shares as beneficial owner or merely as trustee.[47] In exercising this discretion the court will be guided by the analogy of bankruptcy in rescinding a receiving order—that is to say, it will consider the interests of commercial morality and not merely the wishes of creditors, and will refuse a stay if there is evidence of misfeasance or of irregularities demanding investigation.[48]

A copy of the order staying proceedings must be forwarded by the company to the Registrar of Companies (s. 256 (3)).

Appeal

Appeal against a winding-up order lies to the Court of Appeal. If the order has been made by the High Court appeal is by notice of motion

---

[41] See *Re Harrison's Share* [1955] Ch. 260 (C.A.).
[42] *Tucker* v. *New Brunswick Trading Co.* (1890) 44 Ch.D. 249 (C.A.).
[43] *Re Manchester Economic Building Society* [1883] 24 Ch.D. 488; *Re Lyric Syndicate* (1900) 17 T.L.R. 162.
[44] *Re St. Nazaire Co.* (1879) 12 Ch.D. 88; *Charles Bright & Co.* v. *Sellar* [1904] 1 K.B. 6.
[44a] *Re Orthomere Ltd.* (1981) 125 S.J. 495.
[45] *Re St. Nazaire Co.* (1879) 12 Ch.D. 88.
[46] See Practice Notes [1971] 1 W.L.R. 4; [1971] W.L.R. 757.
[47] *Re Wolverhampton Steel & Iron Co.* [1977] 1 W.L.R. 860.
[48] *Re Telescriptor Syndicate Ltd.* [1903] 2 Ch. 174. See also *Re Calgary & Edmonton Land Co.* [1975] 1 W.L.R. 355.

which must be served within 21 days.[49] The appeal goes into the interlocutory list for reasons of despatch although it is not an interlocutory matter.[50] The court usually orders postponement of the advertisement of the order pending the appeal but the petition will already have been advertised.[51] If the order has been made by the county court appeal is also made by notice of motion which must state the grounds and whether all or part of the order is appealed against. The notice must be served and the appeal entered within 21 days.[52] The notice can be amended and the time limit extended by the High Court.[53]

Creditors and contributories who appeared at the hearing of the petition can appeal[54] but those who did not appear cannot appeal without special leave.[55] Where the appeal is by the company it is made by the directors not the liquidator[56] but the court orders security for costs[57] and in the event of an unsuccessful appeal the directors may be personally liable for the costs.[58]

Costs

85–30 Each case turns on its own facts. The winding-up order usually gives the petitioning creditor and the company their costs, and also one set of costs to creditors, and one set to contributories supporting the petition,[59] but there is no hard and fast rule. Where the contributories and the creditors appear by the same solicitor, one set of costs only will generally be allowed.[60] The costs are paid in the first place (subject to encumbrances) out of the company's assets.[61] If creditors or contributories are served with notice of an appeal, they will be entitled to separate costs if the appeal fails; but a petitioner who does not desire to upset the order as to costs need not serve formal notice of appeal.[62]

Where the original petitioner was paid off by the company, and another creditor was substituted as petitioner and a winding-up order made, the order for costs was made to include the costs of the original petitioner, limited to the fee on presentation of the petition and the costs of advertisement.[63]

In *Re Reprographics Exports (Euromat) Ltd.*[64] the petitioning creditor

[49] R.S.C. Ord. 59, rr. 3, 4, 14.
[50] *Re Reliance Properties Ltd.* [1951] 2 All E.R. 327 (C.A.).
[51] *Re A. & B.C. Chewing Gum Ltd.* [1975] 1 W.L.R. 579.
[52] *Ibid.* r. 19.
[53] *Il id.* rr. 7 and 15.
[54] *Re Silkstone Fall Colliery Co.* (1876) 1 Ch.D. 38 (C.A.).
[55] *Re Securities Insurance Co.* [1894] 2 Ch. 410 (C.A.).
[56] *Re Diamond Fuel Co.* (1879) 13 Ch.D. 400 (C.A.).
[57] *Re Photographic Artists' Co-op. Supply Association* (1883) 23 Ch.D. 370 (C.A.).
[58] *Re Consolidated South Rand Mines (No. 2)* [1909] W.N. 66.
[59] *Re Humber Ironworks Co.* (1866) L.R. 2 Eq. 15; *Re European Banking Co.* (1866) L.R. 2 Eq. 521.
[60] *Re Silberhütte Supply Co. Ltd.* [1910] W.N. 81.
[61] r. 195 of 1949.
[62] *Re Ibo Investment Trust Ltd.* [1903] 2 Ch. 373.
[63] *Re Bostels Ltd.* [1967] Ch. 346; *Re Castle Coulson & MacDonald Ltd.* [1973] Ch. 382.
[64] (1978) 122 S.J. 400.

of a hopelessly insolvent company which was already in receivership applied for the costs to be paid not out of the assets of the company but personally by its sole director. Slade J. held that the court had no jurisdiction to make such an order when the director was not a party. He went on to make an order that the costs of the petitioner should not be paid out of the assets of the company until all the unsecured creditors had been paid in full.

Where a company appeals from a winding-up order, the court may order security for costs.[65] If a contributory has obtained a winding-up order against a solvent company and the company appeals, the court may order that security for costs be provided otherwise than from the company's assets because, if the appeal fails and the costs fall on the company, the share of the successful petitioner in the assets of the company would be reduced proportionately.[66] When ordering security under section 447 of the 1948 Act, the judge has the same general discretion as he has under R.S.C. 1965, Ord. 23, r. 1 (1).[67]

85–31 If a petition by a judgment creditor—who has a right *ex debito justitiae* to a winding-up order[68]—is dismissed because the overwhelming majority of creditors opposes him,[69] no order as to costs will normally be made against him[70]; and the same applies to a creditor who, although not having obtained judgment, has a debt which is not disputed.[71] But an order for costs will be made against a creditor who has acted unreasonably,[72] and likewise if the company is already in voluntary winding up, and the creditor fails to show reasons beyond the mere existence of his debt why the court should make a winding-up order.[73] A creditor who successfully petitions for the compulsory winding up of a company which is in voluntary winding up, must bear the costs attributable to irrelevant matters which he has included into his petition for tactical reasons.[74] It has been held that where the promoters of a company have given it the same name as another company which had recently been struck off, the new company should pay the costs of an unsuccessful but understandably confused creditor whose debt was due to the defunct predecessor.[75] Where a winding-up petition is presented on a judgment debt obtained in default of appearance which is subsequently set aside and the petition is dismissed the petitioning creditor

---

65 s. 447; *Re Consolidated South Rand Mines* [1909] W.N. 66.
66 *Re E. K. Wilson & Sons Ltd.* [1972] 1 W.L.R. 791.
67 *Sir Lindsay Parkinson Ltd.* v. *Triplan Ltd.* [1973] Q.B. 609. The court may exercise its discretion to order security to be given by the company under s. 447 of the 1948 Act even though the company is a co-plaintiff with an individual resident in the jurisdiction; *Pearson* v. *Naydler* [1977] 1 W.L.R. 899.
68 See para. 85–06, *ante*.
69 *Ibid.*
70 *Re R. W. Sharman Ltd.* [1957] 1 W.L.R. 774; *Re A. B. C. Coupler and Engineering Co. Ltd.* [1961] 1 W.L.R. 243.
71 *Re Sklan Ltd.* [1961] 1 W.L.R. 1013.
72 *Re A. E. Hayter & Sons (Porchester) Ltd.* [1961] 1 W.L.R. 1008.
73 *Re Riviera Pearls Ltd.* [1962] 1 W.L.R. 722.
74 *Re A. & N. Thermo Products Ltd.* [1963] 1 W.L.R. 1341.
75 *Re M. McCarthy & Co. (Builders) Ltd. (No. 2)* [1976] 2 All E.R. 339.

may be entitled to have his costs paid by the company. This will be the case where he has proceeded without any fault whatever on his part.[76] Where he has failed to give notice he may be limited to costs after the service of the petition on the company.[76a]

The court has jurisdiction under rule 195 of the 1949 Rules to direct that the company's costs shall not be costs of the petition. The court will look critically at costs incurred by an insolvent company in unsuccessfully opposing a winding-up petition on the ground that the debt was disputed when the advantage in delaying liquidation was a possible surplus for the beneficial owner of the company's capital. In such a case[77] the court ordered part of the costs attributable to the delay not to be paid out of the company's assets until all the unsecured creditors had been paid in full. A solicitor retained on behalf of a potentially insolvent company to oppose a winding-up petition will be well advised to obtain an indemnity from the corporators before incurring costs.[78] The court has no power to order the company's directors to pay the costs personally unless they are parties.[79]

If a contributory petitions for a compulsory winding up but fails to attend at the meeting before the Registrar and does not intend to proceed further with the petition, and the petition is then dismissed, he is liable to pay the costs.[80]

It was held under the Legal Aid (General) Regulations 1950 that unless a legal aid certificate includes the presentation of a winding-up petition the assisted person must pay the costs of an unsuccessful petition on a party and party basis.[81] The wording has now been changed and it has been held under the new wording that a civil legal aid certificate can be granted which relates not only to an action but also to the distinct proceedings for a winding-up order taken to enforce the judgment obtained in the action.[82]

Appointment of provisional liquidators and special managers

85–32 Under section 238 of the 1948 Act the court has power to appoint a liquidator provisionally at any time after the presentation of a winding-up petition (s. 238 (1)). The appointment of a provisional liquidator may be made at any time before the making of a winding-up order and either the official receiver or any other fit person may be appointed (s. 238 (2)). The court may limit and restrict his powers by the order appointing him (s. 238 (4)).

The procedure is set out in rule 32 of the 1949 Rules. Any creditor or contributory of the company may apply and upon proof by affidavit of sufficient ground the court may make the appointment if it thinks fit and on

[76] *Re Lanaghan Bros. Ltd.* [1977] 1 All E.R. 265.
[76a] *Re Edric Audio Visual Ltd.*, *The Times*, May 14, 1981; [1981] C.A.T. 209 (C.A.).
[77] *Re Bathampton Properties Ltd.* [1976] 3 All E.R. 200.
[78] *Ibid. per* Brightman J. *obiter* at p. 206.
[79] *Re Reprographic Exports (Euromat) Ltd.* (1978), 122 S.J. 400.
[80] *Re Royal Mutual Benefit Building Society* [1960] 1 W.L.R. 1143.
[81] *Re Parker, Davies & Hughes Ltd.* [1953] 1 W.L.R. 1349
[82] *Re Peretz Co. Ltd.* [1965] Ch. 200.

such terms as it thinks just and necessary (r. 32 (1)). The order must bear the number of the petition and state the nature and a short description of the property of which the provisional liquidator is ordered to take possession and the duties to be performed by him.

An appointment can only be made if there is an effective subsisting petition pending for otherwise the section would apply to a company in perpetuity merely because there had been an unsuccessful petition to wind it up.[83] If the company makes, consents to, or is shown not to oppose, the application, the appointment is almost a matter of course when it is asked that the official receiver be appointed.[84] The early cases[85] seem to show that the appointment will only be made where the company consents or the petition is unopposed. However where the company opposes or does not appear the order may now be made if there are special circumstances such as danger to the assets[86] or obvious insolvency[87] or the company has admitted that it has no defence to the petition.[88] This is not an exhaustive list of examples. Section 238 confers a general power and depending on the circumstances of each particular case, there may be other matters which may be relevant, such as the public interest.[89] Thus where there is doubt as to the margin of solvency of an insurance company a provisional liquidator can be appointed.[89]

In practice the official receiver is nearly always appointed, but by section 238 the court has power to appoint a fit person as provisional liquidator as an alternative to the official receiver. Thus where a representative of the official receiver had said that the expense of his appointment would lead to the cessation of business, the court would appoint a fit person as provisional liquidator and would require an indemnity and a cash deposit.[90] On the winding-up order being made, the official receiver becomes, *ipso facto*, provisional liquidator until a liquidator is appointed (s. 239).[91]

The official receiver for this purpose is one of the official receivers attached to the Bankruptcy Court appointed by the Department of Trade but the court has power to appoint some other officer to act as official receiver in the winding up of a particular company (s. 234). The provisional liquidator may require a statement of affairs to be made (see below).

The primary object of appointing a provisional liquidator is to maintain the status quo and to prevent anybody from getting priority.[92] The

---

83 *Re A Company* [1974] 1 All E.R. 256, 261.
84 Palmer, *Company Precedents*, Pt. II, p. 101.
85 *Emmerson's Case* (1866) L.R. 2 Eq. 231; *Re Cilfoden Benefit Building Society* (1868) L.R. 3 Ch.App. 462.
86 *Re Marseilles Extension Co.* [1867] W.N. 68.
87 *Re Hammersmith Town Hall Co.* (1877) 6 Ch.D. 112.
88 *Re Railway Finance Co.* (1866) 14 L.T. 567.
89 *Re Union Accident Insurance Co. Ltd.* [1972] 1 All E.R. 1105, 1109.
90 *Re Croftheath, The Times*, February 18, 1975.
91 *Re John Reid & Sons* [1900] 2 Q.B. 634.
92 *Re Dry Docks Corporation of London* (1888) 39 Ch.D. 306, *per* Kay J. at first instance; *Levy* v. *Napier* 1962 S.C. 468, 477; *Re Carapark Industrial Pty. Ltd.* [1967] 1 N.S.W.R. 337, 341.

appointment is not only provisional but contingent in this sense, that it operates to protect the property for an equal distribution only in the event of an order for compulsory liquidation being made; if no such order is made, then the appointment ought not to interfere with the rights of third persons.[93] Thus a provisional liquidator cannot bring proceedings to challenge the validity of a debenture.[94] To contemplate that a provisional liquidator should have authority to wind the company up and distribute its assets appears to be directly inconsistent with the nature of his office.[95]

The powers of a provisional liquidator are usually restricted, more or less, by the court under section 238 (4) and rule 32. But if his powers are not so restricted, it has been said that he has the ordinary powers of a liquidator. The fact that his appointment is "provisional" qualifies the period of his appointment and not the powers conferred on him.[96] This latter proposition must, however, be regarded as doubtful since *Re Dry Docks Corporation of London (supra)* was not cited to the learned judge who did not think himself called on to decide the question. It is suggested that the essence of the appointment of a provisional liquidator is its temporary nature. Although the court is given a discretion as to limits and restrictions it would not seem to be open to it to invest a provisional liquidator with all the powers of an ordinary liquidator. Put in another way, even where the court does not expressly limit his powers they are impliedly limited by the nature of his appointment under section 238. It is important, therefore, that the terms of the provisional liquidator's appointment should be clearly specified in the order and failing this the provisional liquidator, if in doubt, should seek the court's approval for any particular course of action.[96] The court will consider the terms of any particular provision of the Act to determine whether a reference to a liquidator covers a provisional liquidator.[97]

When the official receiver becomes liquidator, whether provisionally or otherwise, he may apply to the court for the appointment of a special manager (s. 263). His application must be supported by a report which states either the amount of remuneration which the official receiver considers ought to be allowed the special manager or that it is desirable that the fixing of such remuneration should be deferred. No affidavit in support of the application is needed. Unless the court otherwise directs the remuneration will be stated in the order but the court may make an order for payment of further remuneration at any subsequent time for "good cause

---

[93] *Re Dry Docks Corporation of London* (1888) 39 Ch.D. 306, 314, *per* Fry J. on appeal.
[94] *Re Chateau Hotels Ltd.* [1977] 1 N.Z.L.R. 381. *Cf. Re Emeritus Pty. Ltd.* [1968] 1 N.S.W.R. 458 which can be explained in terms of the order.
[95] *Re Carapark Industries Pty. Ltd.* [1967] 1 N.S.W.R. 337, 341. See also *Re Dry Docks Corp.* (1888) 39 Ch.D. 306, 314 and *Re Chateau Hotels Ltd.* [1977] 1 N.Z.L.R. 381, 383 but *cf. Re A. B. C. Coupler & Engineering Co. Ltd. (No. 3)* [1970] 1 W.L.R. 702, 715.
[96] *Re A. B. C. Coupler & Engineering Co. Ltd. (No. 3)* [1970] 1 W.L.R. 702, 715, *per* Plowman J.
[97] *Newmont Pty. Ltd.* v. *Laverton Nickel N.L.* (1979) A.C.L.C. 32, 030.

shown." A copy of the order of appointment must be sent by the official receiver to the Department of Trade (r. 50 of the 1949 Rules).

In principle, the directors' powers are terminated on the appointment of a provisional liquidator and cannot be revived while the provisional liquidator remains in office, but they may be appointed special managers by the court under section 263; if in that capacity they exceed the authority given them by the court, the provisional liquidator may ratify and thereby validate their unauthorised acts.[98] In any event, the directors retain the residual power to instruct solicitors and to appeal against the order and also to act in interlocutory proceedings, including a motion to discharge the provisional liquidator.[99] It has been held in Australia that the appointment of a provisional liquidator does not terminate the power of a receiver to carry on the business of the company.[99a] It is undesirable in such a case to give the provisional liquidator power to carry on the company's business.

Official receivers[1]

Under the modern system of compulsory winding up instituted by the Companies (Winding-up) Act 1890 and followed in subsequent Acts the official receiver has a central position. As we have seen above he may be and in fact he invariably is appointed provisional liquidator under section 238 of the 1948 Act. In addition under section 239 (*a*) he becomes the provisional liquidator after a winding-up order has been made until he or another person becomes liquidator and is capable of acting as such. His office has a dual character since he is an official of the Department of Trade (s. 233 and rr. 207 *et seq.*) and an officer of the court (r. 210). In both capacities he is invested with a number of powers and charged with a number of duties under the Companies Acts and the Winding-up Rules. In practice there are now a number of official receivers and assistant official receivers (see rr. 207 *et seq.*).

Transmission and advertisement of winding-up order

85–33 When a winding-up order or an order for the appointment of a special manager has been made:

(a) Three sealed copies must be sent forthwith by post or otherwise by the Registrar to the official receiver.

(b) The official receiver must then: (i) cause one sealed copy to be served on the company; (ii) in the case of a winding-up order, forward another copy to the Registrar of Companies in accordance with section 230; (iii) give notice of the order to the Department of Trade which must then cause the notice to be gazetted; and (iv) send notice of the order to such local papers as the Department may

---

[98] *Re Mawcon Ltd.* [1969] 1 W.L.R. 78.
[99] *Re Union Accident Insurance Co. Ltd.* [1972] 1 W.L.R. 640.
[99a] *Re KVE Homes Pty. Ltd. and the Companies Act* [1979] 4 A.C.L.R. 47.
[1] See Palmer, *Company Precedents*, Pt. II, Chap. 14.

from time to time direct or in default of such direction, as he selects (r. 42 (1)).

Statement of affairs

85–34 Where a winding-up order has been made or a provisional liquidator appointed a statement of affairs must be submitted to the official receiver (s. 235). This must be verified by one or more of the persons who at the relevant date were directors and by the secretary or by such of the following persons as the official receiver subject to the direction of the court may select:

(a) present and past officers of the company;
(b) persons who have taken part in the formation of the company within one year before the relevant date;
(c) employees in the year before or at the relevant date who are capable of giving the information required;
(d) officers and employees of a company which was itself an officer of the company in the year before or at the relevant date (s. 235 (2)).

The statement must give particulars of the assets, debts and liabilities, the names, addresses and occupations of its creditors, their securities and such further information as may be required (s. 235 (1)). In practice the official receiver supplies forms and instructions. The statement must be made out in duplicate and one copy verified by affidavit by the above persons (r. 52). It must be submitted to the official receiver within 14 days of the relevant date or such time as the official receiver or court allows (s. 235 (3) and r. 53). The official receiver then files the statement of affairs with the registrar of the court (r. 52).

The official receiver may hold personal interviews with any of the above persons for the purpose of investigating the company's affairs and it shall be the duty of such persons to attend on the official receiver at such time and place as he appoints and give him all the information which he requires both before and after submission of the statement of affairs (rr. 52 (2) and 54).

Any reasonable costs incurred in the making of the statement will be reimbursed by the official receiver or provisional liquidator out of the assets of the company (s. 235 (4) and r. 56).

Any default in complying with section 235 without reasonable excuse is punishable with a fine (s. 235 (5) as amended by Sched. 2 to the Companies Act 1980). In addition the official receiver can apply to the court for an order directing co-operation and failure to comply will then be contempt of court.

Any person who states in writing that he is a creditor or contributory is entitled to inspect the statement of affairs and to a copy thereof on payment of the prescribed fee (s. 235 (6)) but a false statement for the purposes of section 235 (6) is contempt of court (s. 235 (7)). Comments on a statement of affairs may be contempt of court[2] but the court will be reluctant to commit a person unless an attempt is made to interfere with the proper course of the winding up.[3]

The court has power under section 235 (1) to dispense with the requirement for a statement of affairs. Any application for this purpose must be supported by a report of the official receiver showing the special circumstances which in his opinion renders such a course desirable (r.57 (1)).

As soon as practicable the official receiver must send to creditors and contributories a summary of the statement of affairs including the causes of failure and any observations which he may have (r. 126 (1)).

Preliminary report by official receiver

As soon as practicable after receipt of the statement of affairs or after the date of the order if there is to be no statement of affairs, the official receiver must submit a preliminary report to the court:

(a) as to the issued, subscribed and paid-up capital and the estimated amount of assets and liabilities;

(b) the causes of failure;

(c) whether further inquiry is desirable as to any matter relating to the promotion, formation or failure of the company or the conduct of the business thereof (s. 236 (1)).

In addition he may make a further report or reports about fraud by promoters and officers of the company and any other matters which he thinks it is desirable to bring to the notice of the court (s. 236 (2)). Where there is an allegation of fraud in such a report the court may order a public examination under section 270 (s. 236 (3)) and an application may be made under section 188 to restrain the fraudulent persons from managing companies.[4]

First meetings of creditors and contributories

5–35 Within one month of the winding-up order, or within six weeks if a special manager has been appointed, the official receiver must summon separate meetings[5] of the creditors and contributories for the purpose of determining two preliminary questions:

1. Whether they desire a liquidator of their own choosing in place of the official receiver as liquidator (1948 Act, s. 239), and
2. Whether there shall be a committee of inspection; and, if so, of whom it shall consist[6] (1948 Act, s. 252 (1)).

Notice of the date of the meetings must be forwarded by the official receiver to the Department of Trade for insertion in the *Gazette* (r. 122).

---

[2] *Re New Par Consols* [1898] 1 Q.B. 573 (C.A.).

[3] *Re Hooley* (1899) 79 L.T. 706 (a bankruptcy case). See Palmer, *Company Precedents*, Pt. II, p. 130.

[4] See also the Companies Act 1976, s. 28 and the Insolvency Act 1976, s. 9.

[5] See Winding-up Rules 1949, rr. 121 *et seq.*

[6] See para. 85–41, *post*.

Not less than seven days' notice must be given in the *Gazette* and in a local paper and not less than seven days' notice must be given by post to persons appearing from the company's books to be creditors or appearing in the company's books or otherwise to be contributories (r. 129). Notice must be given in accordance with Forms 71 and 72 in the Appendix to the 1949 Rules and the notice to creditors must state a time within which they must lodge their proofs in order to entitle them to vote at the meeting (rr. 124 and 129).

Where a meeting of creditors or contributories is summoned by notice the proceedings and resolutions thereat shall, unless the court otherwise orders, be valid notwithstanding that some creditors or contributories have not received the notice sent to them (r. 136). As to proof of notice see rule 130.

The official receiver must also give seven days' notice to each of the officers of the company who, in his opinion, ought to attend the meeting. If so required it is the officer's duty to attend and the official receiver must report to the court any failure to comply (r. 125).

No creditor may vote in respect of any liquidated or contingent debt[7] or any debt whose value is not ascertained.[8] No creditor may vote in respect of any debt on or secured by a current bill of exchange or promissory note unless he is willing to treat the liability of every person who is liable thereon antecedently to the company as a security and to deduct the estimated value from his proof for the purposes of voting but not of dividend (r. 140).

A secured creditor, unless he surrenders his security, must state in his proof particulars of his security and the value at which he assesses it, and shall only be entitled to vote in respect of the balance (if any) of the debt owing to him. If he votes in respect of the whole debt he will be deemed to have surrendered his security unless the court is satisfied that the omission to value the security arose from inadvertence (r. 141). Where a creditor mistakenly believed his security to be a collateral one, failed to value it and proved for the full amount it was held that this was inadvertence and the court allowed the amendment on terms as to costs.[9] A mistake as to value, however, does not constitute inadvertence.[10] Where the company has altered its position in reliance on the fact that no security has been claimed, the court will refuse relief.[11]

The official receiver may within 28 days after proof require the creditor to give up the security on payment of the value estimated by the creditor plus 20 per cent. (r. 142).

Where the meeting is summoned by the official receiver or the liquidator

---

[7] This does not include a creditor for untaxed costs or other services rendered; *Ex p. Ruffle* (1873) 8 Ch.App. 997 (C.A.); *Re Canadian Pacific* [1891] W.N. 122.

[8] See *Ex p. Ruffle* (1873) 8 Ch.App. 997 (C.A.).

[9] *Re Henry Lister & Co.* [1892] 2 Ch. 417.

[10] *Re Piers* [1898] 1 Q.B. 627; *Re Safety Explosives Ltd.* [1904] 1 Ch. 226 and *Re Rowe, ex p. W. Coast Goldfields* [1904] 2 K.B. 489.

[11] *Re Safety Explosives Ltd.* [1904] 1 Ch. 226.

he or someone nominated by him is the chairman of the meeting. On subsequent meetings the chairman is such other person as the meeting resolves to appoint (r. 133).

At the meeting the chairman has the power to admit or reject proofs for the purpose of voting but his decision is subject to appeal to the court. If he is in doubt he must mark it "objected to" and allow the creditor to vote subject to the vote being declared invalid in the event of the objection being sustained (r. 143). Proper minutes must be kept of the meeting and a list of creditors and contributories present must be made in accordance with Form 74 in the Appendix to the Rules (r. 145). At a meeting of the creditors a resolution is deemed to be passed when a majority in number and value of the creditors have voted in favour of the resolution. At a meeting of the contributories a resolution is deemed to be passed when a majority in number and value of the contributories present vote in favour of the resolution, the value of the contributories being determined in accordance with the number of votes conferred on them by the regulations of the company (r. 134). The quorum is at least three creditors entitled to vote in the case of a creditors' meeting and at least three contributories in the case of a contributories' meeting. If all the creditors or all the contributories do not exceed three then they shall constitute a quorum (r. 138). A creditor or contributory may vote either personally or by proxy (r. 148). The proxy, which may be general or special, must be in accordance with the forms in the Appendix to the Rules. They must not be witnessed by the person appointed[12] and must be lodged with the official receiver at the time specified in the notice of meeting (r. 154).

Where it appears to the court that there has been any solicitation by or on behalf of a liquidator to obtain proxies or procure his appointment the court may order no remuneration shall be allowed to the person concerned notwithstanding any resolution of a committee of inspection or the creditors or contributories to the contrary (r. 151). In addition, any person who gives or agrees to give any member or creditor of the company any valuable consideration with a view to securing his appointment or securing or preventing the appointment of someone else is liable to a fine (s. 336).

Where a substantial creditor has not been represented at the first meeting[13] or a change of circumstances makes it desirable[14] the court will order the meeting to be reconvened for the purpose of considering whether an application should be made to the court for the appointment of a liquidator.

Appointment of liquidator

85–36 The result of the wishes of the meetings on the points submitted to them is reported to the court, and the court fixes a day for considering these

[12] *Re Parrot* [1891] 2 Q.B. 151.
[13] *Re Radford & Bright* (No. 1) [1901] 1 Ch. 272.
[14] *Re Manmac Farmers Ltd.* [1968] 1 W.L.R. 572.

wishes, and, if it approves, giving effect to them. If there is a difference of opinion, the court is to decide (1948 Act, s. 239 (*c*) and r. 58). Where it is desired to appoint a person other than the official receiver as liquidator the court ultimately makes the appointment (1948 Act, s. 237) and fixes his remuneration (1948 Act, s. 242). He must notify his appointment to the Registrar of Companies, and give security to the satisfaction of the Department of Trade before he can act (1948 Act, s. 240).

A corporation cannot be appointed liquidator (1948 Act, s. 335).

In exercising its discretion the court will have regard to the solvency or otherwise of the company. If the company is solvent then it will pay greater attention to the wishes of the contributories.[14a] If it is insolvent it will pay greater attention to the wishes of the creditors.[15] Ordinarily, as Vaughan Williams J. said in *Re Bank of South Australia (No. 2)*, "the grant ought to follow the interest."[16]

The rule of practice of the Companies Court that only an accountant of not less than five years' standing should be appointed liquidator admits exceptions.[17]

Thereafter, the official receiver must forthwith put the liquidator into possession of all the property of the company of which the official receiver has custody provided that the liquidator has paid all monies owing to him (r. 166 (1)). The official receiver is deemed to have a lien on the company's assets for unpaid monies (r. 166 (2)). "Property of the company" does not include notes and memoranda representing information obtained by the official receiver from officers of the company. However it is the duty of the official receiver, if so requested by the liquidator, to communicate to him "all such information respecting the estate and affairs of the company as may be necessary or conducive to the due discharge of his duties" (r. 166 (3)). It has been held that such notes and memoranda, in the absence of evidence, do not fall within this wording.[18]

Bribery

85–37 Any person who gives or agrees or offers to give any member or creditor of the company any valuable consideration with a view to securing his own appointment, or securing or preventing the appointment of someone else, is liable to a fine (s. 336 as amended by s. 80 of and Sched. 2 to the Companies Act 1980).

The legal status of a liquidator

85–38 The term liquidator was first introduced in the Joint Stock Companies Act 1856.[19] This replaced the system of official managers under the Joint

14a *Re Agricultural Industries Ltd.* [1952] 1 All E.R. 1188.
15 *Re Rubber & Producers Investment Trust Ltd.* [1915] 1 Ch. 382.
16 (1895) 2 Mans. 129, 148.
17 *Re Icknield Development Ltd.* [1973] 1 W.L.R. 537.
18 *Re Lake George Mines Ltd.* [1904] 1 Ch. 803.
19 B. H. McPherson Q.C., *The Law of Company Liquidation* (2nd ed.), p. 180.

Stock Companies Winding-Up Acts 1848–49 (not to be confused with the modern special managers under section 263 of the 1948 Act). Whereas there was a vesting of the property in the official manager there is no automatic *cessio bonorum* to the liquidator, subject to rule 166 discussed above. The court may direct that all or any of the property shall vest in him (1948 Act, s. 244) but otherwise his position is perhaps most analogous to the directors whom he replaces with the qualification that he must display a higher degree of skill and care.[20]

His status is as follows:

(a) He is an officer of the court.[21] This means that the liquidator must act in an honest and impartial manner and is responsible to the court for the performance of his duties.

(b) He is agent for the company.[22] Thus he can bind the company without incurring personal liability.

(c) In certain respects he is a trustee for the creditors as a general body.[23] However as mentioned above the property does not vest in him without an order; he is chosen and remunerated on a commercial basis for his professional skills; he is not protected from liability for breach of trust under section 30 of the Trustee Act 1925[24] and the right of tracing property which passes through his hands is more limited than in the case of an ordinary trustee.[25]

Nevertheless the assets are impressed with a trust in this sense, that they constitute a fund to be administered by the liquidator as officer of the court and agent for the company, under the direction of the court, for the benefit of all persons interested in the winding up.[26] This does not mean that the liquidator is trustee for individual creditors or contributories while the company is still in existence.[27] He owes them a statutory duty for breach of which they can bring an

---

[20] *Re Windsor Steam Coal Co. (1901) Ltd.* [1928] Ch. 609, 612; *Re Home & Colonial Ins. Co. Ltd.* [1920] 1 Ch. 102, 125.

[21] s. 273 and rr. 78 (1) and 86. *Re Contract Corp., Gooch's Case* (1871) 7 Ch.App. 207, 211; *Re Opera Ltd.* [1891] 2 Ch. 154; *Re London & County Commercial Reinsurance Office Ltd.* [1922] 2 Ch. 67, 84. *Cf.* a liquidator in a voluntary winding up who is not an officer of the court.

[22] *Re Anglo-Moravian Hungarian Junction Ry. Co.* (1875) 1 Ch.D. 130 (C.A.); *Knowles* v. *Scott* [1891] 1 Ch. 717; *Butler* v. *Broadhead* [1975] Ch. 97, 108.

[23] *Re Albert Life Assurance Co.* (1871) 15 S.J. 923; *Paraguasu Co., Black & Co.'s Case* (1873) L.R. 8 Ch. 254; *Re Oriental Inland Steam Co.* (1874) L.R. 9 Ch.App. 557, 559, 560; *cf. Pulsford* v. *Devenish* [1903] 2 Ch. 625, 633; *Ayerst* v. *C. & K. (Construction) Ltd.* [1976] A.C. 167; [1975] 2 All E.R. 537, 542–543 (H.L.); *Butler* v. *Broadhead, supra.*

[24] *Re Windsor Steam Coal Co. (1901) Ltd.* [1928] Ch. 609; [1929] 1 Ch. 151 (C.A.); *Re Home & Colonial Ins. Co. Ltd.* [1930] 1 Ch. 102.

[25] *Butler* v. *Broadhead* [1975] Ch. 97; *Re Millingen's Ltd.* [1934] S.A.S.R. 72, 80. See B. H. McPherson Q.C., *The Law of Company Liquidation* (2nd ed.), p. 188.

[26] *Re Oriental Inland Steam Co.* (1874) L.R. 9 Ch.App. 557; *Re Anglo-Moravian Junction Railway Co.* (1875) 1 Ch.D. 130, 133; *Knowles* v. *Scott* [1891] 1 Ch. 717; *Re Hills Waterfall Co.* [1896] 1 Ch. 947. See Palmer, *Company Precedents*, Pt. II, p. 180.

[27] *Knowles* v. *Scott* [1891] 1 Ch. 717; *Re Hills Waterfall Co.* [1896] 1 Ch. 947. *Cf. Re South Australian Petroleum Fields Ltd.* [1894] W.N. 189.

action even after the company has been dissolved.[28] In short, like a director, he is a distinct species of fiduciary whose office is an amalgam of statutory rules and agency and trust principles.[29]

His responsibilities can be divided into general duties and specific functions.

His general duties[30] are as follows:

(1) as fiduciary he must:
  (a) act in good faith[31] and for a proper purpose[32];
  (b) not fetter his discretion[33];
  (c) not allow a conflict of interest and duty[34];
  (d) be impartial[35];

(2) he must exercise a degree of care and skill appropriate to the circumstances[36];

(3) he must exercise his discretion personally[37] or, where appointed jointly, he must act jointly.[38]

His principal specific functions under the Companies Acts are:

(1) to secure control of the company's assets and papers (1948 Act, ss. 243, 258, 273);

(2) to realise the assets (1948 Act, s. 245);

(3) to ascertain its liabilities and discharge them in the proper order (1948 Act, s. 319);

(4) to distribute any surplus amongst the contributories and to adjust their rights (1948 Act, s. 245).

85–39 To carry out these functions the liquidator is given a number of powers by section 245.

---

[28] *Pulsford* v. *Devenish* [1903] 2 Ch. 625; *Re New Zealand Joint Stock Corporation* (1907) 23 T.L.R. 238; *Argyll's Ltd.* v. *Coxeter* (1913) 29 T.L.R. 355; *James Smith & Son (Norwood) Ltd.* v. *Goodman* [1936] 1 Ch. 216; *Re Armstrong Wentworth Securities Ltd.* [1947] Ch. 673.

[29] *Cf. Thomas Franklin & Co.* v. *Cameron* (1935) 36 S.R. (N.S.W.) 286, 296 cited by Dr. B. H. McPherson Q.C., *The Law of Company Liquidation* (2nd ed.), p. 188. In that case Davidson J. said that a liquidator is principally and really an agent for the company but occupies a position which is fiduciary in some respects and is bound by the statutory duties imposed upon him by the Act.

[30] For a more detailed discussion see Dr. B. H. McPherson Q.C., *The Law of Company Liquidation* (2nd ed.), pp. 188 *et seq.* on which this is based.

[31] *Re Silver Valley Mines* (1882) 21 Ch.D. 381, 391 (C.A.); *Knowles* v. *Scott* [1891] 1 Ch. 717; *Silkstone Coal Co.* v. *Edey* [1900] 1 Ch. 167; *Re Regent Finance Corp.* [1930] W.N. 84; *Leon* v. *York-O-Matic Ltd.* [1966] 1 W.L.R. 1450.

[32] *Silkstone Coal Co.* v. *Edey* [1900] 1 Ch. 167; *Re Gertzenstein Ltd.* [1937] Ch. 115; see also rr. 160–162.

[33] *Re Scotch Granite Co.* (1868) 17 L.T. 533; *Ripon Press & Sugar Mill* v. *Gopal Chetti Ltd.* (1931) 58 L.R. Ind.App. 416 (P.C.).

[34] *Re Llynvi & Tondu Co.* (1889) 6 T.L.R. 11; *Silkstone Coal Co.* v. *Edey* [1900] 1 Ch. 167; *Re Charterland Goldfields Ltd.* (1909) 26 T.L.R. 132; *Re Gertzenstein Ltd.* [1937] Ch. 115.

[35] *Re Contract Corporation; Gooch's Case* (1871) 7 Ch.App. 207, 213; *Re Sir John Moore Gold Mining Co.* (1879) 12 Ch.D. 325; *Re Rubber Investment Co.* [1915] 1 Ch. 382.

[36] *Re Home and Colonial Insurance Co.* [1930] 1 Ch. 102, 125, 133. See also *Re Silver Valley Mines* (1882) 21 Ch.D. 381; *Re Windsor Steam Co.* [1929] Ch. 151 and *Re George Bond & Co.* (1932) 32 S.R. (N.S.W.) 301. He is not an insurer but he must show the degree of skill appropriate to the task he has assumed and, by assuming, held himself out as possessing.

[37] *Re Scotch Granite Co.* (1868) 17 L.T. 533; *Rendall* v. *Conroy* (1897) 8 Q.L.J. 89.

[38] *Re London & Mediterranean Bank* (1868) 3 Ch.App. 651; *Ex p. Agra & Masterman's Bank* (1871) 6 Ch.App. 206; *Metropolitan Bank* v. *Jones* (1876) 2 Ch.D. 366.

There are a number of things which the liquidator can do of his own accord but in respect of others he is subject to the control of the court, the committee of inspection or the Department of Trade. Even in respect of the first category he is subject to judicial review (s. 245 (3) and s. 246 (5)) but the court will only intervene if it is shown that he has not exercised his powers in good faith or has acted in a way in which no reasonable liquidator could have acted.[39]

His powers without sanction are as follows:

(a) to sell the real and personal property and things in action of the company by public auction or private contract, with power to transfer the whole thereof to any person or company or to sell the same in parcels;

(b) to do all acts and to execute, in the name and on behalf of the company, all deeds, receipts and other documents, and for that purpose to use, when necessary, the company's seal;

(c) to prove, rank and claim in the bankruptcy, insolvency or sequestration of any contributory for any balance against his estate, and to receive dividends in the bankruptcy, insolvency or sequestration in respect of that balance, as a separate debt due from the bankrupt or insolvent, and rateably with the other separate creditors;

(d) to draw, accept, make and indorse any bill of exchange or promissory note in the name and on behalf of the company, with the same effect with respect to the liability of the company as if the bill or note had been draw, accepted, made or indorsed by or on behalf of the company in the course of its business;

(e) to raise on the security of the assets of the company any money requisite;

(f) to take out in his official name letters of administration to any deceased contributory, and to do in his official name any other act necessary for obtaining payment of any money due from a contributory or his estate which cannot be conveniently done in the name of the company, and in all such cases the money due shall, for the purpose of enabling the liquidator to take out the letters of administration or recover the money, be deemed to be due to the liquidator himself;

(g) to appoint an agent to do any business which the liquidator is unable to do himself;

(h) to do all such other things as may be necessary for winding up the affairs of the company and distributing its assets.

The sale may be for a consideration other than cash.[40] Where the liquidator is personally interested in any purchase the sale may be set aside.[41] A

---

[39] *Leon* v. *York-O-Matic Ltd.* [1966] 1 W.L.R. 1450. See also *Re Wyvern Developments Ltd.* [1974] 1 W.L.R. 1097. "Could" here probably means "should"—see *Re Mineral Securities Aust. Ltd. (in liquidation)* [1973] 2 N.S.W.L.R. 207.

[40] *Re Agra & Masterman's Bank* (1866) L.R. 12 Eq. 509.

[41] *Silkstone Coal Co.* v. *Edey* [1900] 1 Ch. 167.

liquidator cannot without the consent of the landlord sell a lease where there is a covenant against assignment.[42] With regard to raising money the liquidator cannot confer upon the lender any security ranking in priority to existing secured creditors unless they consent or are estopped.[43]

Under section 245 (2) (*g*) a liquidator is given power to appoint an agent to do business which he is unable to do himself. This power is impliedly limited to acts and transactions of a purely ministerial kind and the liquidator is not entitled to delegate his discretion in matters which require the exercise of professional judgment.[44] Thus it has been held in Australia that the appointment of an agent to effect a compromise of a debt owing to the company,[45] and a general authority to the liquidator's firm of accountants as his agents "for the purposes of the liquidation and all accountancy matters"[46] were outside his power.[47]

The sanction of the court or the committee of inspection is necessary before the liquidator can exercise any of the following powers:

(a) to bring or defend any action or other legal proceeding in the name and on behalf of the company;
(b) to carry on the business of the company so far as may be necessary for the beneficial winding up thereof;
(c) to appoint a solicitor to assist him in the performance of his duties;
(d) to pay any classes of creditors in full;
(e) to make any compromise or arrangement with creditors or persons claiming to be creditors, or having or alleging themselves to have any claim, present or future, certain or contingent, ascertained or sounding only in damages against the company, or whereby the company may be rendered liable;
(f) to compromise all calls and liabilities to calls, debts and liabilities capable of resulting in debts, and all claims, present or future, certain or contingent, ascertained or sounding only in damages, subsisting or supposed to subsist between the company and a contributory or alleged contributory or other debtor or person apprehending liability to the company, and all questions in any way relating to or affecting the assets or the winding up of the company, on such terms as may be agreed, and take any security for the discharge of any such call, debt, liability or claim and give a complete discharge in respect thereof.

---

[42] *Re Farrow's Bank* [1921] 2 Ch. 164 (C.A.).
[43] *Re Regent's Canal Ironworks Co.* (1875) 3 Ch.D. 411; *Re Allied Glass Manufacturers Ltd.* (1936) 53 W.N. (N.S.W.) 137.
[44] Dr. B. H. McPherson Q.C., *The Law of Company Liquidaton* (2nd ed.), p. 192.
[45] *Rendall* v. *Conroy* (1897) 8 Q.L.J. 89.
[46] *Re Timberlands Ltd. (in liquidation)* (1979) 4 A.C.L.R. 259.
[47] *Cf.* also *Re Scottish Granite Co.* (1868) 17 L.T. 533; *Re Hatzic Prairie Co.* (1914) 15 D.L.R. 772. A liquidator who is a member of a firm must guard himself against a conflict of interest as a partner and his duty as a liquidator.

An order may be made in general terms giving the liquidator power to act without further sanction[48] but this is rarely made.[49]

If the company's assets have been vested in him under section 244 he can bring an action in his own name. A liquidator should not be over-litigious. He should not resist well-founded claims where there is no real defence[50] and on occasions the court has directed a liquidator not to enforce a legal right where it is unethical to do so.[51]

As to carrying on the company's business, it is sufficient that the liquidator bona fide and reasonably believes that the carrying on of the business is necessary for the beneficial winding up of the company.[52] A liquidator must not carry on the business with a view to its financial reconstruction[53] (but compare 1948 Act, s. 287 discussed in para. 80–01, *ante*). He must not use surplus monies to make short-term loans at a high rate of interest.[54] If no business has in fact been carried on, there is no business to wind up.[55] The onus of proof that a matter is not necessary for the beneficial winding up of the company is on the party objecting to it.[56]

Except in cases of urgency the liquidator should obtain prior sanction for the appointment of a solicitor before the latter takes action. The court may, however, give retrospective sanction in an appropriate case for payment of the solicitor's fees under its inherent powers.[57] Likewise, it may authorise a gratuitous payment where this will help with the realisation of the assets.[58] A solicitor cannot be appointed where his managing clerk is a member of the committee of inspection.[59]

The questions of payment of a class of creditors in full and compromises and arrangements will be discussed later in paragraph 85–60.

Before the liquidator makes any distribution he ought to take every means to satisfy himself that all creditors are paid, not only by advertising, but by writing to those creditors of whose existence he knows, and asking them if they have any claims against the company.[60] A liquidator has been held not to be justified in relying on the ordinary advertisements where he knows of a large number of possible claims against the company under the (since repealed) Workmen's Compensation Act not covered by insurance.[61] He must also be careful to provide, before distribution, for tax

---

[48] *Re Rochdale Property & General Finance Co.* (1879) 12 Ch.D. 775 (Bacon V.-C.).
[49] *Re Britannia Permanent Benefit Building Society* [1890] W.N. 170.
[50] *Re General Share & Trust* v. *Wetley Co.* (1882) 20 Ch.D. 267.
[51] *Re Wyvern Developments Ltd.* [1974] 1 W.L.R. 1097.
[52] *Re Great Eastern Electric Co. Ltd.* [1941] 1 Ch. 241.
[53] *Re Wreck Recovery & Salvage Co.* (1880) 15 Ch.D. 353.
[54] *Re Anon* (1866) 15 L.T. 170 (Lord Romilly commenting on an article in the *Standard* newspaper).
[55] *Wilson Box (Foreign Rights) Ltd. (in liquidation)* v. *Brice* [1936] 3 All E.R. 728, 738 (C.A.).
[56] *The Hire Purchase Furnishing Co. Ltd.* v. *Richens* (1887) 20 Q.B.D. 387 (C.A.).
[57] *Re Associated Travel Leisure & Services Ltd.* [1978] 2 All E.R. 273. Otherwise the liquidator is personally liable for the fees.
[58] *Re Banque des Marchands de Moscou (Koupetschesky)* [1953] 1 All E.R. 278.
[59] *Re Gallard* [1896] 1 Q.B. 68, 71 (C.A.).
[60] *Pulsford* v. *Devenish* [1903] 2 Ch. 625.
[61] *Re Armstrong Whitworth Securities Ltd.* [1947] Ch. 673.

due to the Crown,[62] including any liability for taxation arising in the course of the liquidation.[63]

In *Re Mesco Properties*,[64] a liquidator sold properties in the course of a compulsory winding up. The company was later assessed to corporation tax on chargeable gains arising therefrom. The Court of Appeal held that the tax was not an expense incurred in realising assets but was a charge or expense incurred in the winding up within the meaning of section 267 of the 1948 Act which the court could order to rank after the liquidator's fees. A liquidator who has knowledge of a claim but, due to a mistake of his solicitor, does not deal with it, cannot shelter behind the mistake of the solicitor.[65] But a liquidator who, keeping within the limits of his agency and acting in good faith, inadvertently—though possibly negligently—disposes of trust property is not liable as a constructive trustee.[66] Under the Policyholders Protection Act 1975, s. 13 (3) (*b*) the Policyholders Protection Board has power to give an indemnity to the liquidator not only in his personal capacity but also in his capacity as guardian of the company's assets to protect it against loss.[67]

Disclaimer

85–40 The liquidator has power with the leave of the court to disclaim land burdened with covenants, stocks, shares, unprofitable contracts or other property which is unsaleable because of obligations attached to it (s. 323). The disclaimer extinguishes the rights, interests and liabilities of the company in the property disclaimed but does not except so far as is necessary for the purpose of releasing the company and its property from liability affect the liability of any other person (1948 Act, s. 323 (2)). Thus the original lessee who assigned his interest directly or indirectly to the company will remain liable.[68]

If a person interested in the property makes an application to the liquidator requiring him to decide whether he will disclaim, the liquidator cannot disclaim unless he has within 28 days given notice to the applicant of his intention to apply to the court. The court may make various orders as to the vesting of the property and otherwise, and anyone damaged by the disclaimer may prove in the winding up (s. 323 (7)). This corresponds to the power of a trustee in bankruptcy. The procedure on a disclaimer is set out in Winding-up Rule 75 as amended.

The court will not allow disclaimer to the prejudice of other parties, *e.g.* a landlord entitled to sue another party on a guarantee of the rent.[69]

---

62 *Re New Zealand Joint Stock Corporation* (1907) 23 T.L.R. 238.
63 See para. 90–38, *post*.
64 [1979] S.T.C. 778.
65 *Austin Securities Ltd.* v. *Northgate and English Stores Ltd.* [1969] 1 W.L.R. 529.
66 *Competitive Insurance Co. Ltd.* v. *Davies Investments Ltd.* [1975] 1 W.L.R. 1240.
67 *Policyholders Protection Board* v. *Official Receiver* [1976] 1 W.L.R. 447.
68 *Warnford Investments Ltd.* v. *Duckworth* [1978] 2 All E.R. 517.
69 *Re Katherine et Cie* [1932] 1 Ch. 70.

Administrative supervision by Department of Trade

85–41 Whereas the court exercises judicial supervision over liquidators, the Department of Trade exercises what might be described as administrative regulatory supervision. The following are the most important areas of supervision:

(1) requiring security (1948 Act, s. 241 (*a*));
(2) the liquidator must submit accounts (Insolvency Act 1976, s. 2 (4));
(3) the Department may conduct an inquiry into his conduct (1948 Act, s. 250);
(4) it grants his release (1948 Act, s. 251);
(5) it may audit his accounts (s. 249 as amended by s. 2 of the Insolvency Act 1976);
(6) it exercises overall control over his banking operations (1948 Act, s. 248).

The liquidator's books and accounts

85–42 The liquidator must keep proper books of account and minute books and any creditor or contributory may, subject to the control of the court, inspect them (s. 247). The 1949 Rules specify the books which he must keep. These are:

1. A "record book" in which he must keep all minutes of proceedings and resolutions and a correct record of his administration of the company's affairs (r. 171).
2. A "cash book" in which he must enter particulars of receipts and payments. A liquidator other than an official receiver must submit the record book and cash book to the committee of inspection when required and not less than once every three months (r. 172). It must also be audited by the committee of inspection every three months (r. 174) and duplicate copies sent to the Department of Trade every six months (r. 175).
3. If the liquidator carries on the business of the company he must keep a separate account of trading and must incorporate in the cash book the total weekly amounts of the receipts and payments on the trading account. The trading account must not less than once in every month be verified by affidavit and submitted to the committee of inspection or such member as shall be appointed for the purpose to examine and certify the same (r. 176).

The liquidator must send to the Department of Trade in duplicate an account of his receipts and payments at least twice a year or as often as may be prescribed. One copy is to be retained by the Department and the other is to be available for inspection (Insolvency Act 1976, s. 2 (4)). In addition the liquidator must send the account or a summary to every creditor or contributory. The Department of Trade has, however, a power to dispense with compliance with this requirement (1948 Act, s. 249). The latter section formerly required the Department of Trade to audit the liquidator's accounts. That requirement has now been modified by section 2 of the Insolvency Act 1976. The Department is no longer under an obligation but now has a discretion whether or not to do so.

The Insolvency Act 1976 created a single Insolvency Services Account which replaced the Companies Liquidators' Account and Bankruptcy Estate Account. The liquidator must pay monies received by him into the Insolvency Services Account at the Bank of England unless the committee of inspection persuade the Department of Trade that it will be to the advantage of creditors and contributories for the liquidator to keep an account with another bank (1948 Act, s. 248 as amended). If the liquidator retains more than £100 for upwards of 10 days without the authority of the Department of Trade then unless he can explain the retention to the satisfaction of the Department he must pay interest at the rate of 20 per cent. and will be liable to disallowance of the whole or part of his remuneration. He may also be removed from office and be liable for expenses occasioned by reason of his default (s. 248 (2)).

Garnishee order

85–43 In *Lancaster Motor Co. (London) Ltd.* v. *Bremith Ltd.*[69a] where judgment had been given against a company in liquidation for costs, the judgment creditors issued a garnishee summons against a balance of a banking account standing in the name of the liquidator. The Court of Appeal held that this could not be done, as the bank was not indebted to the company. This decision is, however, contrary to a previous decision of the Court of Appeal,[70] and is difficult to understand. The money in the bank, though legally a debt due from the banker to the customer, was the company's money, the company being beneficially entitled to the debt, which had not been vested in the liquidator under section 244 of the 1948 Act, *infra*.

The liquidator is not prima facie personally liable on contracts made by him while carrying on the company's business with a view to its sale as a going concern.[71]

Disqualification of liquidators

Reference was made in para. 46–10 to the provisions of section 93 of the Companies Act 1981 which deal with disqualification of receivers. Section 93 contains similar provisions for disqualification of liquidators. Disqualification orders may be made in the following circumstances:

(a) where a person is convicted of an indictable offence in connection with the liquidation of a company;

(b) where a person has been persistently in default in filing documents with the Registrar of Companies;

[69a] [1941] 1 K.B. 675.
[70] *Gerard* v. *Worth of Paris Ltd.* (1936) 80 S.J. 633.
[71] *Stead, Hazel & Co.* v. *Cooper* [1933] 1 K.B. 840.

(c) if in the course of the winding up of a company it appears that a person has been guilty of an offence under section 332 of the 1948 Act or has otherwise been guilty while a liquidator of fraud or breach of duty towards the company.

The maximum period of disqualification is fifteen years (1981 Act, s. 94).

Committee of inspection

85–44 The creditors and contributories may, at their first meetings, decide to have a committee of inspection (see 1948 Act, ss. 252, 253). The committee consists of a joint body of creditors and contributories, and its function is to assist the liquidator and supervise his proceedings. It is to meet at such times as the committee from time to time may appoint and is to act by a majority. General meetings of creditors and contributories may be summoned by the liquidator, and if any conflict of opinion arises between such meetings and the committee of inspection, the liquidator is to follow the directions of the meetings in preference to those of the committee. The sanction of the committee, as an alternative to leave of the court, is necessary to the exercise by the liquidator of certain of his powers under section 245. The liquidator should not obtain leave of the court *ex parte* to appoint a solicitor or take any similar step to which he knows the committee object.[72] The court, however, is by no means bound by the decision of the committee.[73]

On a vacancy occurring the liquidator must summon a meeting of creditors or contributories to fill the vacancy, but if he thinks it is unnecessary, he may apply to the court for an order that the vacancy be not filled (s. 253 (7)).[74]

The court may order the liquidator to summon a meeting with a view to reconstituting the committee of inspection so as to represent creditors more fairly.[75]

No member of the committee of inspection can become a purchaser of the company's assets either directly or indirectly, or derive any profit out of winding-up transactions or receive any remuneration without the sanction of the court.[76] This sanction of the court must in all cases be obtained before the business is commenced from which the profit is derived; it cannot be given after.[77]

Where there is no committee of inspection the Department of Trade may, on the application of the liquidator, do any act or give any permission which the Act requires to be done or given by the committee (1948 Act, s. 254). Rule 214 provides that such powers may, subject to the directions of

---

[72] *Re Consolidated Diesel Engine Manufacturers* [1915] 1 Ch. 192.
[73] *Re North Eastern Insurance Co.* [1915] W.N. 210.
[74] This power to apply to the court was first introduced by s. 95 (3) of the Act of 1947.
[75] *Re Radford and Bright Ltd. (No. 1)* [1901] 1 Ch. 272; see also *Re Radford and Bright (No. 2)* [1901] 1 Ch. 735.
[76] *Dowling* v. *Lord Advocate*, 1963 S.L.T. 146. See also rr. 161 and 163.
[77] *Re Gallard* [1896] 1 Q.B. 68.

the Department, be exercised by the official receiver. The breadth of section 254 is, however, cut down by rule 86 (5) which provides that in such a situation the liquidator may not make a call without obtaining the leave of the court.

The court has power to give a retrospective sanction in a proper case to action taken under section 245 (1) without the prior sanction of the committee of inspection or the court.[78]

Contributories

85–45 An important part of a liquidator's duty in getting in the company's assets is to require payment by contributories of the amount, if any, uncalled on their shares in the company.

"Contributory" means every person liable to contribute to the assets of a company under the Act in the event of the company being wound up (1948 Act, s. 213). The liability of a contributory is defined in sections 212 and 214 of the 1948 Act. For the purpose of enforcing this liability the liquidator makes out a list of the persons he claims to treat, or who are entitled to be treated, as contributories, and gives such persons notice that they are included in the list and for what amount, and that he proposes on a stated day to settle the list. On the day in question the liquidator hears any objections by contributories to their being included in the list, and after the hearing settles the list one way or the other finally, and notifies the contributories. Any person who considers himself aggrieved can apply to the court by originating summons to have his name removed from the list.

A fully paid shareholder is a contributory for many purposes and should be put on the list, if there is anything to come to him.[79]

Settlement of list

85–46 In a compulsory winding up the court settles the list of contributories; but it has power to dispense with this where it will not be necessary to make calls or to adjust the rights of contributories (1948 Act, s. 257 (1)). The court should not, however, be too ready to dispense with the list, particularly where a large number of shareholders are involved.[80]

The list of contributories is made out in two parts, A and B, in accordance with section 212 of the 1948 Act. The A list contributories are the present members and are primarily liable. The B list contributories are the past members who have ceased to be members within a year preceding the winding up, and these are only liable to contribute after the A list contributories are exhausted. That is to say, a B list contributory is not liable to contribute in respect of any debt of the company contracted after he ceased to be a member, nor unless the existing members are unable to satisfy the

---

[78] *Re Associated Travel, Leisure and Services Ltd.* [1978] 1 W.L.R. 547.

[79] *Re Anglesea Colliery Co.* (1866) 1 Ch.App. 555; *Re National Savings Bank Assocn.* (1866) 1 Ch.App. 547; *Re Aidall Ltd.* [1933] Ch. 323; *Re Consolidated Goldfields of New Zealand Ltd.* [1953] Ch. 689; *Re Phoenix Oil and Transport Co. Ltd.* [1958] Ch. 560.

[80] *Re Paragon Holdings Ltd.* [1961] Ch. 346.

contributions required to be made by them, and he cannot be called upon to pay more than the amount, if any, which remains unpaid on the shares which he held.[81]

Where the contributions of the contributories on the B list are more than enough to pay the debts incurred before they ceased to be members, the balance must be distributed among the B list contributories.[82] The list distinguishes also between persons who are contributories in their own right and persons who are contributories as representatives of others. After a scheme of arrangement providing for partial payment of creditors and releasing present members of a portion of their liability, it would appear to be impossible to place anyone on the B list.[83]

85–47 Special rules apply where an unlimited company has been re-registered as limited under section 44 of the 1967 Act. In this case the B list is extended to include as contributories all past members of the company who were members at the time of re-registration if the company goes into liquidation within three years thereafter: such persons will be liable to contribute to the company's debts and liabilities incurred before re-registration to the same extent as if the company had not been re-registered as limited and, if there are no A list contributories who have continued to be members since the time of re-registration, all persons who were liable at that time as past or present members will be liable to contribute in the liquidation to debts and liabilities incurred before re-registration, notwithstanding that the A list contributories have paid up the full amount of their liabilities under section 212 (1967 Act, s. 44 (7)).

Calls

85–48 A call can be made on contributories by the liquidator, but only with the sanction of the committee of inspection, if there is one, and if there is not, of the court (1948 Act, ss. 260 and 273 and Winding-up Rule 86). It is not necessary that debts or liabilities should be established against the company before a call can be made. "Debts and liabilities" in section 260 mean estimated debts and liabilities.[84] In sanctioning a call the court may allow payment by instalments.[85] A call made in winding up is in the nature of a specialty debt.[86] Payment of a call is enforced by an order of the court made in chambers on summons by the liquidator. Such an order, called a "balance order," is a summary statutory proceeding for the purpose of enabling the liquidator to get payment from a contributory in lieu of

[81] See s. 242, and *Helbert* v. *Banner* (1871) L.R. 5 H.L. 28; *Webb* v. *Whiffin* (1872) L.R. 5 H.L. 711, 718; *Brett's Case* (1871) 6 Ch.App. 800; L.R. 8 Ch. 800; and *Morris's Case* (1871) 7 Ch.App. 200; 8 Ch.App. 800, 810.

[82] *Re City of London Insurance Co.* [1932] 1 Ch. 226.

[83] So held by Courthope Wilson V.-C. in the Chancery Court of Lancaster in *Re Belgrave Mills*, October 13, 1927.

[84] *Re Contract Corporation* (1866) 2 Ch.App. 95.

[85] *Re Law Guarantee Society* (1910) 26 T.L.R. 565.

[86] s. 214 of the Companies Act 1948; *Buck* v. *Robson* (1870) L.R. 10 Eq. 629; *Re Muggeridge* (1870) L.R. 10 Eq. 443.

proceeding by action.[87] A balance order is not, however, a "final judgment" which will found a bankruptcy notice against the contributory.[87] An action lies by the liquidator in the name of the company against a contributory for calls made before the winding up, notwishstanding that the liquidator has obtained a balance order in the winding up for payment of the same moneys under section 260 of the 1948 Act.[88] Where a director has received, in breach of trust, a present of paid-up shares from the company's vendor, he may be made liable for misfeasance, but he cannot be made liable as a contributory for unpaid shares.[89] The same principle applies to arrears of calls on forfeited shares.[90]

A B list contributory may reduce his prospective liability by purchasing and having extinguished claims against the company *before* a call is made on the B list contributory.[91] It is not settled whether this is still possible for the B list contributory *after* a call is made on him; it is thought that there is no valid reason why the purchase after the call should be treated differently from the purchase before the call, provided that in the former case the company likewise obtains a genuine release from outstanding liabilities.

Adjusting rights of contributories

85–49 Subject to the payment of the creditors and of the costs of winding up, the assets in a winding up are distributable amongst the contributories in accordance with their rights and interests (1948 Act, s. 302). This rule applies even though the memorandum provides that no part of the assets is to be transferred to the members.[92] The uncalled capital is part of the assets.[93] In a compulsory winding up, the distribution of surplus assets amongst contributories entitled thereto always requires an order by the court (s. 265).[94] Assets so distributed are treated as capital for tax purposes.[95]

In the absence of any special provision in the memorandum or articles, the assets available for distribution amongst the members, if sufficient or more than sufficient to pay off the whole of the paid-up capital, are to be applied first in paying off such paid-up capital, and the balance is to be distributed amongst the members or contributories in proportion to the nominal amount of the share capital held by them; but, if insufficient to do this, then such assets are distributable in such manner that the loss of capital which has been sustained may be thrown on the members in

[87] *Re Sanders, ex p. Whinney* (1884) 13 Q.B.D. 476.
[88] *Westmoreland Green, etc., Slate Co.* v. *Feilden* [1891] 3 Ch. 15.
[89] *Carling's Case* (1875) 1 Ch.D. 115; *Re Innes & Co.* [1903] 2 Ch. 254.
[90] *Ladies' Dress Association Ltd.* v. *Pulbrook* [1900] 2 Q.B. 376.
[91] *Re Apex Film Distributors Ltd.* [1960] Ch. 378, C.A.
[92] *Re Merchant Navy Supply Association Ltd.* (1947) 177 L.T. 386.
[93] *Re Bridgwater Navigation Co.* (1889) 14 App.Cas. 525; *Welton* v. *Saffery* [1897] A.C. 299.
[94] *Re Phoenix Oil and Transport Co. Ltd. (No. 2)* [1958] Ch. 565; *Re Paragon Holdings Ltd.* [1961] Ch. 346. (A list showing the contributories and the amounts payable to them has to be appended to the court order unless the court otherwise directs: Companies (Winding-up) Rules 1949, r. 120.)
[95] *Staffordshire Coal and Iron Co. Ltd.* v. *Brogan* [1963] 1 W.L.R. 905 (H.L.).

proportion to the *nominal* capital held by them respectively.[96] Prima facie, preference shares are not entitled to any preference in winding up.[97] Where shares are unequally paid up, an adjustment must be made between the contributories[98]; *i.e.* a call to equalise must, unless the articles otherwise provide, be made,[99] and, on the same principle, where shares have been issued at a discount, the amount credited by way of discount is to be treated as so much uncalled capital, and the rights are to be adjusted accordingly.[1]

Sometimes the memorandum or articles contain express provisions as to the distribution of assets in winding up, *e.g.* it may be provided that the preference shares shall rank first[2]; sometimes that they shall participate in the distribution of the surplus[3]; sometimes arrears of cumulative preference dividend which arose before the winding up have to be paid before the liquidator can proceed to the distribution of assets on the capital.[4]

85–50 The expression "surplus assets" in articles has no technical meaning.[5] It may mean the fund remaining in the hands of the liquidator after all claims of outside creditors and costs of winding up have been met[6]; or it may mean what remains after payment also of the capital paid up on all classes of shares.[7] The meaning must in each case be determined by the context.[8]

Where the articles provide that losses are to be borne in proportion to capital paid up, no call can be made on shares not fully paid for the benefit of the fully paid shares.[9]

If a contributory dies, his personal representatives take his place, and if he becomes bankrupt, his trustee in bankruptcy represents him (1948 Act, ss. 215, 216). Where the liquidator proves for calls in the bankruptcy of a shareholder, that does not make the shares paid up for the purpose of participating in surplus assets.[10]

Capital paid up in advance of calls and interest thereon must, as a rule, be repaid before distribution of capital paid up under calls.[11]

Where present or former shareholders of a company in liquidation have

---

96 *Ex p. Maude* (1870) L.R. 6 Ch. 51; *Re Driffield Gas Light Co.* [1898] 1 Ch. 451; *Re Anglo-Continental Corporation of Western Australia* [1898] 1 Ch. 327.
97 *Re London India Rubber Co.* (1868) L.R. 5 Eq. 519; *Welton* v. *Saffery* [1897] A.C. 299; and see para. 35–08, *ante*.
98 On the meaning of "adjustment," see *Re Phoenix Oil and Transport Co. Ltd.* [1958] Ch. 560.
99 *Ex p. Maude* (1870) L.R. 6 Ch. 51.
1 *Welton* v. *Saffery* [1897] A.C. 299.
2 See para. 35–08, *ante*.
3 See para. 35–08—09, *ante*.
4 *Re E. W. Savory Ltd.* (1951) 2 T.L.R. 1071; see para. 35–09, *ante*.
5 *Re New Transvaal Co.* [1896] 2 Ch. 750.
6 *Re Crichton's Oil Co.* [1902] 2 Ch. 86; *Dimbula Valley (Ceylon) Tea Co. Ltd.* v. *Laurie* [1961] Ch. 353.
7 *Re Ramel Syndicate Ltd.* [1911] 1 Ch. 749; *Re Dunstable Portland Cement Co.* (1932) 48 T.L.R. 223.
8 *Re Bridgwater Navigation Co.* [1891] 2 Ch. 317; *Re Madame Tussaud & Sons Ltd.* [1927] 1 Ch. 657.
9 *Re Kinatan (Borneo) Rubber Ltd.* [1923] 1 Ch. 124.
10 *Re West Coast Goldfields* [1906] 1 Ch. 1.
11 *Re Wakefield Rolling Stock Co.* [1892] 3 Ch. 165.

not claimed their dividends, despite appropriate advertisements having been placed by the liquidators, it is permissible for the liquidators to treat them as creditors rather than as members for the purpose of the liquidation. Moreover, money retained by the company in respect of unclaimed dividends did not become impressed with a trust in favour of the shareholders on the commencement of the liquidation.[12]

Creditors

85–51 The remedy of a creditor is solely against the incorporated company.[13] When the legislature introduced the principle of limited liability, it set up, as Lord Cairns said,[14] the company, and the company alone, as that with which creditors or third persons could contract.

But creditors may have a claim in damages against a liquidator personally for breach of his statutory duty, if he has not used proper diligence to ascertain their claims before the company has been dissolved, and they have thus lost their remedy against it.[15]

The company's debts and liabilities are ascertained as they exist at the date of the winding-up order.[16] "As the tree falls, so must it lie."[17]

Creditors entitled to prove

85–52 The debts for which creditors are entitled to prove are specified in section 316 of the 1948 Act. They include all debts payable on a contingency and all claims present and future, certain or contingent,[18] ascertained or sounding only in damages, and, where necessary, a just estimate is to be made of their value. Where the company is insolvent, this is subject to the rules of bankruptcy as to debts provable (1948 Act, s. 317). Section 317 of the 1948 Act provides that "in the winding up of any insolvent company registered in England the same rules shall prevail and be observed with regard to the respective rights of secured and unsecured creditors and to debts provable and to the valuation of annuities and future and contingent liabilities as are in force for the time being under the law of bankruptcy in England with respect to the estates of persons adjudged bankrupt."

This provision was originally introduced by the Judicature Act 1875 and has been much discussed in the cases. The bankruptcy rules which apply are those which relate to: (1) the rights of secured and unsecured

---

[12] *Re Compania de Electricidad de la Provincia de Buenos Aires* [1978] 3 All E.R. 668.
[13] *Oakes* v. *Turquand* [1867] L.R. 2 H.L. 325, 357.
[14] *Re Reese River Mining Co.* (1867) 2 Ch.App. 604, 616.
[15] *Pulsford* v. *Devenish* [1903] 2 Ch. 625; *Argyll's Ltd.* v. *Coxeter* (1913) 29 T.L.R. 355.
[16] *Re General Rolling Stock Co.* (1872) 7 Ch.App. 646.
[17] *Warrant Finance Co.'s Case* (1869) 4 Ch.App. 643, 647; *Emmerson's Case* (1866) L.R. 2 Eq. 231, 236; *Re W. W. Duncan & Co.* [1905] 1 Ch. 307.
[18] As to the meaning of "contingent creditor," see *Re William Hockley Ltd.* [1962] 1 W.L.R. 555 (para. 85–15, *ante*); *Community Development Pty. Ltd.* v. *Engwirda Construction Co.* (1969) 120 C.L.R. 455. *Cf. Re A Company* [1973] 1 W.L.R. 1566 and *Holt Southey Ltd.* v. *Catnic Components Ltd.* [1978] 1 W.L.R. 630.

creditors[19]; (2) the debts and liabilities provable[20]; (3) set-off of debts[21]; (4) the valuation of annuities and future and contingent liabilities. The bankruptcy rules which do not apply are those which relate to: (1) reputed ownership[22]; (2) avoidance of securities[23]; (3) fraudulent preference; and (4) priorities. The reputed ownership doctrine does not apply to the winding up of companies and the Companies Act 1948 contains special rules about the avoidance of securities, fraudulent preference and priorities.

A company is deemed to be insolvent until it is shown that it is solvent as regards its creditors, but section 317 has no application and the rules of bankruptcy cannot be relied upon, once the liquidation throws up a surplus, whatever may have been the position at the commencement of the winding up.[24]

If the company is insolvent, demands in the nature of unliquidated damages are not provable unless they arise by reason of a contract, promise or breach of trust.[25] Subject to this limitation, every kind of liability, however difficult of valuation, is provable, unless declared by the court incapable of being fairly estimated,[26] the object of the Act being "to put all unsecured creditors upon an equality, and to pay them *pari passu.*"[27] Accordingly, not only creditors to whom the company is indebted in sums presently due can prove, but also creditors whose debts are not yet due, and not only creditors but persons who have any claim or who may have any claim against the company, *e.g.* a person who has a claim for damages for breach of contract,[28] or for the determination of a contract, *e.g.* a policy of insurance, by the company's going into liquidation, or a passenger on a tramcar claiming damages for injuries under the company's contract of carriage.[29] Any liability, in fact, of the company *existing* at the commencement of the winding up may be proved, and not merely debts *due* at the commencement of the winding up.[30] Section 66 (1) of the Bankruptcy Act 1914, which limits interest on debts to 5 per cent. per annum until all

---

[19] *Re Whitaker* [1901] 1 Ch. 9 (C.A.).
[20] *Re Albion Steel & Wire Co.* (1878) 7 Ch.D. 547.
[21] *The Mersey Steel & Iron Co. (Ltd.)* v. *Naylor, Benzon & Co.* (1884) 9 Q.B.D. 648 (C.A.); 9 App.Cas. 434 (H.L.).
[22] *Gorringe* v. *Irwell India Rubber Works* (1887) 34 Ch.D. 128 (C.A.).
[23] *Re Withersea Brick Works* (1881) 16 Ch.D. 337 (C.A.).
[24] *Re Rolls-Royce Co. Ltd.* [1974] 1 W.L.R. 1584, 1591.
[25] s. 317 and Bankruptcy Act 1914, s. 30. However s. 317 does not exclude a claim for damages for tort which has not become liquidated by judgment before the commencement of the winding up but only excludes from proof a claim not so liquidated at the date when the claimant comes in to prove. There are differences in this respect between bankruptcy and insolvent winding up. (*Re Berkeley Securities (Property) Ltd.*, [1980] 3 All E.R. 513, Vinelott J.)
[26] *Hardy* v. *Fothergill* (1888) 13 App.Cas. 351.
[27] *Per* Lindley L.J. in *Re Oak Pitts Colliery Co.* (1882) 21 Ch.D. 322, 329.
[28] *Re Vic Mill Ltd.* [1913] 1 Ch. 456.
[29] *Re Great Orme Tramways* (1934) 50 T.L.R. 450.
[30] See *Macfarlane's Claim* (1880) 17 Ch.D. 337, 339; *Re Printing Co.* (1878) 8 Ch.D. 535, 538; *Re Albion Steel Co.* (1878) 7 Ch.D. 547; *Re Parana Plantations Ltd. (No. 2)* [1948] 1 All E.R. 142.

the bankrupt's debts have been paid in full, applies on the winding up of an insolvent company.[31]

Statute-barred debts

85–53 A statute-barred debt does not constitute a "liability" of the company for the purposes of winding up. The liquidator in a compulsory winding up[32] or an insolvent voluntary winding up is under a duty to reject the proof of a statute-barred debt[33]; in a solvent voluntary winding up he must do so likewise unless the contributories consent.[34]

It may be recalled[35] that an acknowledgment of a debt in the balance sheet of a company may, in exceptional circumstances, take the claim out of the operation of the Limitation Act 1980, if the creditor or his agent received a copy of the balance sheet.[36]

In spite of the rule in *Clayton's Case*,[37] the balance owed on current account is a single and undivided debt, and part payment revives the whole balance outstanding on that account for the purpose of section 29 of the Limitation Act 1980, accordingly, a liquidator who rejected part of a creditor's proof in such circumstances was held to have acted incorrectly.[38]

A winding-up order stops the period of limitation from running in the company's favour so that a debt which is not statute barred at the date of the order can be proved for.[39]

Ultra vires debts

The old rule was that an *ultra vires* debt could not be proved.[40] It would now appear that a debt arising under a transaction protected by section 9 (1) of the European Communities Act 1972 can be proved.[41] The position of damages for anticipatory breach is not settled. In any event money borrowed *ultra vires* but used to pay *intra vires* debts may be proved for to the extent that it has been used for that purpose.[42]

---

[31] *Re Jessel Securities Ltd.* (1979) 129 N.L.J. 171.

[32] *Re General Rolling Stock Co., Joint Stock Discount Co.'s Claim* (1872) 7 Ch.App. 646; *Re River Steamer Co., Mitchell's Claim* (1871) 6 Ch.App. 822.

[33] *Re Fleetwood & District Electric Light & Power Syndicate* [1915] 1 Ch. 486; *Re Art Reproduction Co. Ltd.* [1952] Ch. 89.

[34] *Re Art Reproduction Co. Ltd.* [1952] Ch. 89.

[35] See para. 43–26, *ante*.

[36] *Jones* v. *Bellgrove Properties Ltd.* [1949] 2 K.B. 700, as explained in *Re Transplanters (Holding Company) Ltd.* [1958] 1 W.L.R. 822; *Consolidated Agencies Ltd.* v. *Bertram Ltd.* [1965] A.C. 470; *Ledingham* v. *Bermejo Estancia Co.* [1947] 1 All E.R. 749; *Re Gee & Co. (Woolwich)* [1974] 1 W.L.R. 630; *Re Compania de Electricidad de la Provincia de Buenos Aires Ltd.* [1978] 3 All E.R. 668; *In re Overmark Smith Warden Ltd.*, *The Times*, March 22, 1982.

[37] (1816) 1 Mer. 572.

[38] *Re Footman Bower & Co. Ltd.* [1961] Ch. 443.

[39] *Joint Stock Discount Co.'s Claim* (1872) 7 Ch.App. 646.

[40] *Great North-West Railway* v. *Charlebois* [1899] A.C. 114 (P.C.); *Re Jon Beauforte (London) Ltd.* [1953] Ch. 131.

[41] See para. 9–25, *ante*.

[42] *Re Cork & Youghal Railway Co.* (1869) 4 Ch.App. 748.

Illegal debts

A debt arising out of an illegal transaction and tainted with illegality cannot be proved.[43]

Landlord

85–54 A landlord[44] can prove in a winding up by the court[45] for damages for breach of a covenant not to assign a lease, but not in the case of an unregistered society where the assets vest in the liquidator.[46]

Where a company in liquidation has no defence to a landlord's claim for possession of premises, the court may make an order for possession in winding-up proceedings even though third parties are in possession of the premises. The third parties' rights are protected by R.S.C. 1965, Ord. 45, r. 3, whereby the Registrar cannot give the landlord leave to issue a writ of possession enforcing the order until notice has been given enabling them to apply for relief against forfeiture.[47]

Commission

85–55 As a general rule, no claim can be made for loss of commission due to winding up, unless the failure to earn the commission has been due to the wilful act of the company.[48]

Foreign exchange

85–56 The relevant date for ascertainment of a debt in foreign currency arising under a foreign contract is the notional date of discharge of the debt. That date has to be the same for all creditors and is therefore the date of the winding-up order when all other claims fall to be considered.[49]

Mode of proving

85–57 The court may fix a time or times within which creditors of the company are to prove their debts or claims (s. 264).

However in practice under rule 106 the liquidator fixes a certain day, not less than 14 days after the notice, by which they must prove. Under rule 106 (2) he must: (a) advertise the date in such newspaper as he considers convenient; (b) give notice to every person mentioned in the statement of affairs who has not proved his debt; and (c) give notice to every person

---

43 *Ex p. Dyster* (1815) 1 Meriv. 155; *ex p. Chavasse* (1865) 34 L.J. Bank. 17.

44 See further para. 85–65, *post*.

45 *Re Farrow's Bank Ltd.* [1921] 2 Ch. 164.

46 *Re Birkbeck Building Society* [1913] 2 Ch. 34, 38. As to the general position of a landlord in a winding up, see para. 85–65, *post*.

47 *Re Blue Jeans Sales* [1979] 1 All E.R. 641.

48 *Re R. S. Newman Ltd.* [1916] 2 Ch. 309, 322.

49 So held by Oliver J. in *Re Dynamics Corporation of America* [1976] 1 W.L.R. 757 not following dicta of Lords Wilberforce and Cross in *Miliangos* v. *George Frank (Textiles) Ltd.* [1976] A.C. 443, 467, 497. The report in [1976] 2 All E.R. 682 contains a misprint. *Cf. Re Lines Bros. Ltd.* [1982] 2 W.L.R. 1010 (C.A.). See further the Law Commission's Working Paper No. 80 Private International Law—Foreign Money Liabilities pp. 89 *et seq.*

mentioned therein as a preferential creditor who has not yet established his preference.

Creditor for this purpose includes members in respect of membership matters if the claims have become enforceable by an action in debt against the company before the commencement of the liquidation.[50]

Where a creditor fails to prove his debt within the due time he will be excluded from a benefit in a distribution of assets in the winding up.[51] Debts may be proved by delivering or sending through the post in a pre-paid letter to the liquidator an unsworn claim unless the liquidator requires an affidavit verifying the debt.[52] A creditor may come in and prove at any time before final distribution of the assets, but he cannot disturb any dividend already paid.[53] The liquidator examines every proof tendered, and notifies the person tendering it either that he admits it or rejects the proof in whole or in part, or requires further evidence.[54] The creditor then has 21 days in which to appeal but the time may be extended by leave of the court (r. 108). On an appeal against the rejection of a proof, the court must decide the rights of the claimant, and not merely express a view as to whether the liquidator was right or wrong in rejecting the proof.[55]

A creditor is, by the Winding-up Rules, to bear the cost of proving his debt unless the court otherwise orders. A mortgagee cannot prove for mortgagee's costs on the winding up of the company which guaranteed the mortgage.[56] Where a solicitor proves for costs due before winding up, the costs may be taxed in the winding up.[57]

Set-off

Set-off against company's debts

85–58 In the winding up of an insolvent company the bankruptcy rules apply as regards the rights of secured and unsecured creditors, debts provable, valuation of annuities and future and contingent liabilities (1948 Act, s. 317). This section incorporates into the winding up of companies section 31 of the Bankruptcy Act 1914, which allows set-off where there have been mutual credits, mutual debts or other mutual dealings. Where, therefore, at the commencement of the winding up A has a money claim against the

---

50 *Re House Property & Investment Co.* [1954] Ch. 576, 593; *Re Compania de Electricidad de la Provincia de Buenos Aires Ltd.* [1978] 3 All E.R. 668.

51 *Butler* v. *Broadhead* [1975] Ch. 97.

52 Winding-up Rules 1949, r. 92 (amended by the Companies (Winding-up) (Amendment No. 2) Rules 1977 (S.I. 1977 No. 1395).

53 *Re General Rolling Stock Co.* (1872) 7 Ch.App. 646; *Re Metcalfe, Hicks* v. *May* (1879) 13 Ch.D. 236.

54 Winding-up Rules 1949, rr. 91–118.

55 *Re Kentwood Constructions Ltd.* [1960] 1 W.L.R. 646; *Re Trepca Mines Ltd.* [1960] 1 W.L.R. 1273.

56 *Re Law Guarantee Trust* (1913) 108 L.T. 830.

57 *Re Palace Restaurants Ltd.* [1914] 1 Ch. 492.

company, and the company has a money claim against A, one claim can be set off against the other[58]; an account must be taken and the balance only can be proved for.[59] The right only applies where the cross-claims are "mutual" or "commensurable".[60] Mutual means that the claims must exist between the same parties in the same right although it is sufficient that this is the case in equity and not at common law.[61] Thus a joint claim cannot be set-off against a several claim.[62] Commensurable means that each claim must result in a pecuniary liability. Formerly a claim for the return of goods could not be set-off against a debt.[63] However provided that the claim is provable it need not necessarily be a liquidated sum and even unliquidated damages may be the subject of set-off.[64] So too may future[65] and contingent[66] debts. Difficult questions often arise because of assignment of debts particularly in debt factoring arrangements. Equities arising subsequently cannot be raised unless they arose out of the same contract and are inseparably connected with it.[67] Sometimes, as we have seen in para. 43–23, *ante*, debentures provide that they shall be transferable free of equities. In this case the basic rule is ousted at least before winding up.[68]

The provisions of section 31 are mandatory and cannot be waived.[69] An agreement whereby a bank undertakes to freeze a debit account of a company and to allow it to operate a second account is intended to be operative only while the company is a going concern; if the company is wound up the bank is entitled, apart from section 31, to combine the two accounts.[70]

The Crown Proceedings Act 1947 (s. 35 (2)), as amended for Scotland in section 50, provides, *inter alia*, that the Crown cannot, without leave of the court, avail itself of a right of set-off if the subject-matter relates to a different government department. This applies whether the company is solvent or in liquidation. Where the company's claim was for repayment of premiums under the Selective Employment Payments Act 1966, and the

---

[58] *Sovereign Life Assurance Co.* v. *Dodd* [1892] 2 Q.B. 573, 578; *Re H. E. Thorne & Sons Ltd.* [1914] 2 Ch. 438.

[59] *Mersey Steel Co.* v. *Naylor* (1884) 9 App.Cas. 434.

[60] *Eberle's Hotels, etc., Co.* v. *Jonas* (1887) 18 Q.B.D. 459; *Re Mid-Kent Fruit Factory* [1896] 1 Ch. 567; *Re Auriferous Properties Ltd. (No. 1)* [1898] 1 Ch. 691; *Re Leeds and Hanley Co.* [1904] 2 Ch. 45; *Re City Equitable Fire Insurance Co. (No. 2)* [1930] 2 Ch. 293; *Rolls Razor Ltd.* v. *Cox* [1967] 1 Q.B. 552, C.A.; *National Westminster Bank Ltd.* v. *Halesowen Presswork and Assemblies Ltd.* [1972] A.C. 785 (H.L.).

[61] *Bailey* v. *Finch* (1872) L.R. 7 Q.B. 34.

[62] *Re Pennington & Owen Ltd.* [1925] 1 Ch. 825 (C.A.).

[63] *Eberle's Hotels, etc., Co.* v. *Jonas* (1887) 18 Q.B.D. 459 (C.A.). *Cf.*, however, a claim for damages for conversion which could be set off. The tort of detinue has now been abolished by the Torts (Interference with Goods) Act 1977, s. 2 (1).

[64] *The Mersey Steel & Iron Co.* v. *Naylor, Benzon & Co.* (1884) 9 App.Cas. 434 (H.L.).

[65] *Sovereign Life Assurance Co.* v. *Dodd* [1892] 1 Q.B. 405.

[66] *Re City Life Assurance Co. Ltd. (Grandfield's Case)* [1926] 1 Ch. 199 (C.A.).

[67] *Mangles* v. *Dixon* (1852) 3 H.L.C. 702; *Government of Newfoundland* v. *Newfoundland Railway Co.* (1888) 13 App.Cas. 199, 213 (P.C.) but see para. 46–08, *ante*.

[68] *Goodwin* v. *Robarts* (1876) 1 App.Cas. 476 (H.L.).

[69] *National Westminster Bank Ltd.* v. *Halesowen Presswork and Assemblies Ltd., supra.*

[70] *National Westminster Bank Ltd.* v. *Halesowen Presswork and Assemblies Ltd., supra.* See also *Re E. J. Morell (1934) Ltd.* [1962] Ch. 21.

set-off claimed was for Schedule E taxation, it was held that there was sufficient similarity to make it appropriate to grant leave.[71]

The provision in section 31 of the Bankruptcy Act that a creditor has no right of set-off if, at the time he gave credit, he had notice of an available act of bankruptcy applies by analogy in winding up, so that an assignee of a debt owing by a company who took the assignment knowing that the company had given notice of a meeting of creditors under section 293[72] was not entitled to the benefit of the rules of set-off.[73]

A surety cannot set off his contingent liability unless the principal creditor has waived his right of proof.[74]

Where a bank held money borrowed by the company for a specific purpose, this purpose being known to the bank, the bank was not entitled to set off that sum against the company's other indebtedness, but had to return it to the lender when it ceased to be available for that purpose because of the liquidation of the company.[75]

Set-off under section 31 of the Bankruptcy Act 1914 is not restricted to mutual credit, debts and other dealings arising out of contract but extends, for example, to sums owing to the company by way of refund in respect of "inputs" under the Value Added Tax legislation.[76]

The statutory rules of set-off cannot be excluded by agreement between the parties.[77]

Set-off against calls

85–59 A contributory in a limited company who is also a creditor of the company cannot on a winding up set off his debt against a call made on him by the liquidator[78] until all the creditors have been paid in full (1948 Act, s. 259 (3)); and this is so though in an action by the company, before winding up, to enforce the call the shareholder has obtained unconditional leave to defend under R.S.C. 1965, Ord. 14, r. 4[79]; or though the company has agreed that there shall be such a set-off.[80] And the liquidator cannot set off a debt due to the company from a *deceased* insolvent contributory against the amount due to the contributory in the liquidation.[81] The principle is that where a person entitled to participate in a fund is also bound to make a contribution in aid of that fund, he cannot be allowed to participate until

---

[71] *Laing* v. *Lord Advocate* 1973 S.L.T. (Notes) 81; see also *Re D.H. Curtis (Builders) Ltd.* [1978] 2 All E.R. 183 (sums by way of refund in respect of "inputs" for V.A.T.).
[72] See para. 86–10, *post*.
[73] *Re Eros Films Ltd.* [1963] Ch. 565.
[74] *Re Fenton* [1931] 1 Ch. 85.
[75] *Quistclose Investments* v. *Rolls Razor Ltd.* [1968] 1 All E.R. 613, C.A.; affirmed by H.L. *sub nom. Barclays Bank Ltd.* v. *Quistclose Investments Ltd.* [1970] A.C. 567. See also *Smith* v. *Liquidator of James Bissell Ltd.* 1968 S.L.T. 174.
[76] *Re D. H. Curtis (Builders) Ltd.* [1978] 2 W.L.R. 28.
[77] *Rolls Razor Ltd.* v. *Cox* [1967] 1 Q.B. 552, C.A.; *National Westminster Bank Ltd.* v. *Halesowen Presswork Assemblies Ltd.* [1972] A.C. 785.
[78] *Grissell's Case* (1866) 1 Ch.App. 528; *Gill's Case* (1879) 12 Ch.D. 755.
[79] *Re Hiram Maxim Lamp Co.* [1903] 1 Ch. 70; *Alliance Film Corporation* v. *Knoles* (1927) 43 T.L.R. 678.
[80] *Re Law, Car and General Corporation* [1912] 1 Ch. 405.
[81] *Re Peruvian Railway Construction Co.* [1915] 2 Ch. 144.

he has fulfilled his duty to contribute[82]; and where the question of set-off arises in respect of the estate of a deceased debtor, the "mutual dealings" section does not apply, since there were no mutual dealings between the company and his estate.[83]

The liquidator cannot set off a sum due from a firm in which the contributory was a member against a debt due to the contributory alone.[84]

Where an insolvent company is a contributory in and creditor of another insolvent company there is no set-off and the first company cannot receive dividends until it has paid its calls.[85] Nevertheless the debts will be taken into account in working out the total fund and its distribution. Both the call and the debt are taken at par value for this purpose. If the dividend payable exceeds the call it will be paid. Where two insolvent companies were indebted to one another and were both insolvent and in liquidation, the liquidator of each company was given liberty to distribute its available assets among the other creditors without regard to the claim of the other company.[86]

Payment of unsecured creditors pari passu

85–60 This is expressly laid down for a creditors' voluntary winding up by section 302 of the 1948 Act but a similar rule is imported by section 317 from section 33 (7) of the Bankruptcy Act 1914. Judgment creditors have no priority.[87] The Crown now has no prerogative to be paid first and in full[88] but has certain preferential claims which we shall shortly consider. There can be no contracting out of the *pari passu* rule since this would be against public policy on two counts. The first is that the legislation lays down a mandatory code of procedure to be administered in a proper and orderly way and this is a matter in which the commercial community generally has an interest.[89] In other words it is not simply a matter of private right. Secondly, to allow contracting out would be unfair and possibly a fraud on the general body of ordinary creditors.[90] It seems nevertheless that there are some exceptions to the *pari passu* rule.[91] These

---

[82] *Re Peruvian Railway Construction Co.* [1915] 2 Ch. 144, 150.
[83] *Ibid.*; and see *Re H. E. Thorne & Sons Ltd.* [1914] 2 Ch. 438.
[84] *Re Pennington & Owen Ltd.* [1925] 1 Ch. 825.
[85] *Re Auriferous Properties Ltd. (No. 1)* [1898] 1 Ch. 691; (*No.* 2) [1898] 2 Ch. 428.
[86] *Re National Live Stock Insurance Co.* [1917] 1 Ch. 628.
[87] *Re Leinster Contract Corpn.* [1903] 1 Ir.R. 517.
[88] *Re H. J. Webb & Co.* [1922] 2 Ch. 369; affirmed, *sub nom. Food Controller* v. *Cork* [1923] A.C. 647.
[89] *Per* Lord Simon of Glaisdale and Lord Kilbrandon in *Halesowen Presswork Assemblies Ltd.* v. *National Westminster Bank Ltd.* [1972] A.C. 785, 809, 824 (H.L.). See also *Johnson* v. *Moreton* [1978] 3 All E.R. 37, 55 (H.L.).
[90] *Per* Lord Cross in *British Eagle International Airlines* v. *Compagnie Nationale Air France* [1975] 1 W.L.R. 758, 780–781 (H.L.) but *cf.* the Commonwealth cases cited at notes 95 and 97 below, especially *Re Industrial Welding Co. Pty. Ltd.* (1979) 3 A.C.L.R. 754 which suggests that agreements to *defer* are still valid. *Cf.* also *Elliott* v. *Richardson* (1870) L.R. 5 C.P. 744.
[91] See J. H. Farrar and N. Furey [1977] C.L.J. 27, 30–31; J. H. Farrar [1979] N.Z.L.J. 71; [1980] N.Z.L.J. 100.

are: (a) where the arrangement constitutes a recognised form of security[92]; (b) where goods supplied are the subject of an effective reservation of property clause so that they never become the property of the company[93]; (c) where there is a valid trust[94]; (d) where there has been a scheme of arrangement under section 206 which contains appropriate wording capable of applying after the winding up[95]; (e) if there has been an arrangement under section 306[96]; and (f) (possibly) where there is an informal arrangement between the creditors to vary the rule and to disregard it would be unconscionable and tantamount to equitable fraud.[97] In (f) the court may exercise its powers under section 245 (1) (*d*) or (*e*) to pay any class of creditors in full or allow a compromise since equity will not permit a statute to be used as a method of fraud.

Preferential creditors

85–61 Preferential debts are debts which are unsecured debts but which on the grounds of public policy are given priority. They rank equally among themselves and must be paid in full. If the assets are insufficient to meet them they abate in equal proportions (1948 Act, s. 319 (5) (*a*)). They have priority over the claims of the holders of a floating charge but not over the claims of any other secured creditor (s. 319 (5) (*b*)). In the event of a landlord or other person distraining on any goods or effects of the company within three months next before the date of the winding-up order they are a first charge on the goods or effects so distrained on or the proceeds of sale. In respect of any money paid under any such charge the landlord or other person who has distrained has the same rights of priority as the person to whom the payment is made (s. 319 (7)). This latter provision does not appear to apply to a voluntary winding up. The main preferential debts are:

(1) All local rates due from the company at the relevant date which became due and payable[98] within 12 months next before that date (s. 319 (1) (*a*) (i)). Water rates are excluded unless imposed as part

[92] *British Eagle International Airlines* v. *Compagnie Nationale Air France* [1975] 1 W.L.R. 758, 780–1 *per* Lord Cross.

[93] *Aluminium Industrie Vaassen BV* v. *Romalpa Aluminium Ltd.* [1976] 2 All E.R. 552 (C.A.).

[94] *Re Kayford Ltd.* [1975] 1 All E.R. 604 but *cf. Re London Wine Co. (Shippers) Ltd.* (1976) 26 N.L.J. 977 where the trust failed on the grounds of uncertainty of subject-matter.

[95] s. 206 (2); *Halesowen Presswork Assemblies Ltd.* v. *National Westminster Bank Ltd.* [1972] A.C. 785; *Re Marlborough Concrete Constructions Pty. Ltd. (in liquidation)* (1976) 2 A.C.L.R. 240.

[96] This does not, however, cover a composition.

[97] *Re Walker Construction Co. Ltd. (in liquidation)* [1960] N.Z.L.R. 523 read in the light of *Re Walker Hare Pty. Ltd. (in liquidation)* [1968] V.R. 447. See J. H. Farrar [1979] N.Z.L.J. 71 and [1980] N.Z.L.J. 100 for a discussion of the English, New Zealand and Australian authorities. *Cf. Re Edwin Walker & Co. Ltd.*, *The Times*, October 17, 1962 and *Re Trix Ltd.* [1970] 1 W.L.R. 1421, both decisions of Plowman J., where there does not appear to be any question of unconscionability or fraud. Plowman J. makes no reference to the court's power to require a meeting of creditors to be called to ascertain their wishes (s. 346).

[98] An increase of the rate resulting from an appeal was held to operate retrospectively and increase the amount payable—*Re Airedale Garage Co. Ltd.* [1933] Ch. 64 (C.A.).

of the general rates.[99] The expression relevant date means in the case of a compulsory winding up the appointment of a provisional liquidator or if none was appointed the date of the winding-up order. Where the company is in voluntary winding up it means the date of the resolution to wind up.

(2) All income tax, corporation tax, development land tax or other assessed taxes assessed on the company up to April 5 next before the relevant date and not exceeding in the whole one year's assessment.[1] This provision extends to all taxes so assessed present and future.[2]

Tax deductions for Schedule E under the PAYE system which are due from the employer for the 12 months next before the relevant date are preferential.[3] Value added tax[4] and car tax[5] which became due within 12 months next before the relevant date are also preferential.

Certain other taxes were made preferential debts but are now no longer chargeable.[6] These include land tax, excess profits tax, purchase tax and selective employment tax. Formerly estate duty could be payable on the assets of a company from which a deceased person had received a benefit and such duty was a preferential debt. Estate duty has now been replaced by capital transfer tax.[7]

The Crown's priority is not limited to tax assessed in the year immediately before the winding up. It can claim priority for any one year before that date.[8]

Each tax can be claimed for separately. It should be noted, that the Crown does not have priority apart from these special provisions relating to tax. Compare, however, its right of distress.[10]

(3) All wages or salary of any clerk or servant in respect of services rendered to the company during four months next before the relevant date, not exceeding £800.[11]

The priority applies to wages and salaries whether or not payable wholly or in part by way of commission (Bankruptcy (Amendment) Act 1926, s. 2).

The question whether or not a person is a "clerk or servant" is

---

[99] *Re Baker* [1954] 1 W.L.R. 1144.
[1] s. 319 (1) (*a*) (ii) as amended by the Statute Law (Repeals) Act 1975, Sched., Pt. I and Development Land Tax Act 1976, s. 42.
[2] *Re Winget Ltd.* [1924] 1 Ch. 550.
[3] Income and Corporation Taxes Act 1970, s. 204.
[4] Finance Act 1972, s. 41 (1) (*d*), (2) (*d*) and Finance Act 1976, s. 22.
[5] *Ibid.* s. 52 (11), Sched. 7, para. 18 (1) (*d*), (2) (*d*).
[6] See further *Halsbury's Laws of England* (Hailsham ed.) Vo. 7, para. 1285.
[7] See Finance Act 1975, Pt. III and Sched. 4–13. See especially s. 39 which occasions an apportionment among the participators where a company makes a transfer of value. The company is liable to pay the tax (s. 39 (3)). The tax is a charge on property whose value is transferred (Sched. 4, para. 20).
[8] *Re Pratt* [1951] Ch. 255.
[9] *Food Controller* v. *Cork* [1923] A.C. 647 (H.L.).
[10] See *Herbert Berry Associates Ltd.* v. *I.R.C.* [1977] 1 W.L.R. 1437 (H.L.).
[11] s. 319 (1) (*b*) as amended by the Insolvency Act 1976, Sched. 1.

one of fact.[12] It will depend to some extent on whether he works under the control of the company or at its premises.[13] In most cases a contract of service will be necessary.[14] It has been held that a managing director is not a "clerk or servant"[15] but if a director holds another position in the company he may by virtue of that position be regarded as "a clerk or servant."[16] A company secretary who devotes his whole time to the business of the company may be a "clerk or servant" but not so if he discharges the duties by a clerk appointed and paid by himself[17] or where he is also managing clerk to a firm of solicitors.[18]

A wireless engineer who obtained orders for radios and installed them on commission and a regular newspaper contributor paid at a fixed salary have both been held in the circumstances not to be a "clerk or servant." On the other hand, a chemist employed at a weekly wage to produce a perfume formula who also had a regular engagement with another firm[19] and an opera singer[20] have been held to be covered by the wording. A "labour only" subcontractor is not covered.[21]

Damages in lieu of proper notice in respect of dismissal before the winding up are not wages or salary[22] but payments in respect of proper notice or salary due until the first date upon which the employment became terminable are so regarded.[23] See further, below.

(4) All wages of any labourer or workman not exceeding £800, whether payable for time or for piece-work, in respect of services rendered to the company during four months before the relevant date.[24]

The following are by reason of section 121 of the Employment Protection (Consolidation) Act 1978 to be treated as wages or salary for the purposes of (3) and (4):

(a) a guarantee payment;
(b) remuneration on suspension on medical grounds;
(c) payment for time off;
(d) remuneration under a protective award.

---

12 *Re London Casino Ltd.* [1942] W.N. 138, 139, *per* Uthwatt J.
13 *Re Ashley & Smith Ltd.* [1918] 2 Ch. 378; *Re G. H. Morison & Co. Ltd.* (1912) 106 L.T. 731.
14 *Re General Radio Co. Ltd.* [1929] W.N. 172.
15 *Re Newspaper Proprietary Syndicate Ltd.* [1900] 2 Ch. 349 where Cozens-Hardy J. reviewed the earlier cases.
16 *Re Beeton & Co. Ltd.* [1913] 2 Ch. 279 (dress editress).
17 *Cairney* v. *Back* [1906] 2 K.B. 746 *cf. Scottish Poultry Journal Co.* 1896 4 S.L.T. 167.
18 *Clyde Football Co. Ltd.* 1901 8 S.L.T. 328.
19 *Re G. H. Morison & Co.* (1911) 106 L.T. 731 (fixed hours and weekly wages).
20 *Re Winter Garden German Opera Ltd.* (1907) 23 T.L.R. 662.
21 *Re C. W. & A. L. Hughes Ltd.* [1966] 1 W.L.R. 1369. This is probably unaffected by the introduction of Income Tax deductions at source by s. 29 of the Finance Act 1971 to combat "the lump."
22 *Re VIP Insurances Ltd. and the Companies Act* (1978) 3 A.C.L.R. 751.
23 *Re Leeds Twentieth Century Decorators* (1962) C.L.Y. 365.
24 s. 319 (1) (*d*).

All these are technical terms in the 1978 Act.

(5) Accrued holiday remuneration payable to a clerk, servant, workman or labourer on the termination of his employment before or by the effect of the winding-up order or resolution.[25]

Instead of preferential claims against the company under (3), (4) and (5) an employee may claim payment out of the redundancy fund of any of the following debts under section 122 of the 1978 Act, up to the amount of £135 for any debt in respect of any one week:

(i) any arrears of pay in respect of a period or periods not exceeding eight weeks;

(ii) any amount which the employer is liable to pay to the employee in respect of notice under section 49 (1) or (2) of the 1978 Act;

(iii) any holiday pay in respect of periods of holiday not exceeding six weeks in all, to which the employee became entitled during the 12 months immediately preceding the relevant date;

(iv) any basic award of compensation for unfair dismissal;

(v) any reasonable sum by way of reimbursement of the whole or part of any fee or premium paid by an apprentice or articled clerk.

Under section 123 of the 1978 Act a similar claim may be made by an employee in respect of unpaid relevant contributions to an occupational pension scheme in which case the Secretary of State will pay such contributions into the scheme.

Where any payment has been made out of the Redundancy Fund in respect of any of the above debts, the Secretary of State is subrogated to the rights and remedies (including any preference) of the employee in respect of that debt. This means that the Secretary of State is substituted for the employee (s. 125 of the 1978 Act). A similar subrogation takes place in respect of any rights which the occupational pension scheme may have against the company.

(6) All debts specified in Social Security Act 1975 section 153(2), Social Security Pensions Act 1975 Schedule 3 or any corresponding provision in force in Northern Ireland. These are any sums owed on account of Class 1 contributions (primary or secondary) or Class 2 contributions payable in the period of 12 months immediately preceding the making of the winding up order or the winding up resolution, appointment of a provisional liquidator or appointment of a receiver (if earlier) and any sum owed on account of an earner's contributions to an occupational pension scheme, being contributions deducted from earnings paid in the period.[26] These debts are not preferred if the company is being

---

[25] s. 319 (1) (*e*).

[26] Social Security Act 1975, s. 153 (2); Social Security Pensions Act 1975, Sched. 3; Social Security Pensions Act 1975, Sched. 4.

wound up voluntarily merely for the purposes of reconstruction or amalgamation with another company.

(7) Any amount due by way of general betting duty, gaming licence duty or bingo duty at the relevant date which became due within 12 months next before that date.[27]

These debts must be paid in priority to debts secured by a floating charge over the general body of assets.[28]

Where the only assets available have been obtained by *ultra vires* activities, the court may authorise these to be used to pay the costs and expenses of the liquidation.[29]

The costs of the winding up must be paid in priority to the preferential debts.[30]

Advances for payment of wages

85–62 A person who has advanced money for the purpose of paying wages or salaries of any clerk or servant of the company may, by virtue of section 319 (4), claim to be a preferential creditor[31] to the same extent as the servant would have been. A banker may obtain the maximum benefit under this subsection by opening a separate "wages account" out of which advances are made for the payment of wages, and requiring the company to make regular transfers to that account from current account in discharge of the earliest advances still outstanding on the wages account; if the current account is also overdrawn, this procedure operates to transfer part of the indebtedness from wages account to current account, but does not affect the character of the indebtedness as being an advance for wages. The rule in *Clayton's Case*[32] applies to sums subsequently paid into current account so as to discharge the earliest in date of the debts on that account.[33] Furthermore, if loans made by the bank to the company are secured, the bank may, on realising the security, appropriate the proceeds to paying off first the non-preferential part of the company's indebtedness, so that its preferential rights can be exercised in full in respect of any balance outstanding.[34]

Secured creditors

85–63 A secured creditor is one who has some mortgage, charge or lien on the company's property.

An execution creditor who has seized goods before the commencement

---

27 Betting Gaming Duties Act 1972, ss. 2 (1), 13, 17.

28 *Re Barleycorn Enterprises Ltd.* [1970] Ch. 465 (C.A.). See also *Re Christonette International Ltd.* (1982) 126 S.J. 561.

29 *Re Introductions Ltd. (No. 2)* [1969] 1 W.L.R. 1359. (C.A.).

30 *Corporation of Westminster* v. *Chapman* [1916] 1 Ch. 161.

31 See *Re Primrose (Builders) Ltd.* [1950] Ch. 561; *Re Rampgill Mill Ltd.* [1967] Ch. 1138.

32 (1816) 1 Mer. 529.

33 *Re James R. Rutherford & Sons Ltd.* [1964] 1 W.L.R. 1211; *cf. Re E. J. Morel (1934) Ltd.* [1962] Ch. 21; and see *Re Yeovil Glove Co. Ltd.* [1965] Ch. 148 (C.A.).

34 *Re William Hall (Contractors) Ltd.* [1967] 1 W.L.R. 948.

of a winding up has been held to be a secured creditor[35]; but he may be deprived of his security under section 325 of the 1948 Act,[36] unless the sheriff has sold the goods. He is not a secured creditor if he has merely delivered the writ of *fi. fa.* to the sheriff.[37]

A solicitor who holds a lien on documents of a liquidating company for his costs against the company is a secured creditor, and must mention his lien in his proof.[38]

A creditor who has obtained the appointment of a receiver of land by way of execution is also a secured creditor.[39] Formerly a creditor who obtained a charging order, but had not seized the land or appointed a receiver, was not entitled to rank as a secured creditor, as his claim to the benefit of the charging order was defeated by section 325.[40] This is now altered by the Charging Orders Act 1979 which makes the charging order completion of the execution for the purposes of section 325.

The arrest of a ship in the exercise of a maritime lien is not an "execution" within section 325[41]; consequently the creditor's claim is not subject to that section and he ranks as a secured creditor.[42] Mere issue of a writ *in rem* may give rise to security for this purpose.[43]

Where goods are sold on the basis that property or a right of disposal is retained until the price is paid this is effective to exclude them from the assets of the company and thus creates a right which is even stronger than security.[44] The reservation of property may give rise to a tracing remedy in equity if the goods are mixed with others[45] but great care must be taken to avoid the transaction being regarded as an unregistered charge under section 95.[46] It may be that the rights will be lost if the company sells as a buyer in possession.[47]

Where a building contractor supplied materials on the terms that they should remain his property until paid for, it was held that this condition could only apply while the materials retained their identity, and, since they had become annexed to the land of the company, he must prove as an unsecured creditor for their value.[48]

85–64 A landlord is not a secured creditor merely because he has a power of distress.[49]

---

35 *Re Printing and Numerical Registering Co.* (1878) 8 Ch.D. 535, 538.
36 See para. 85–72, *post*.
37 *Ex p. Nelson* (1880) 14 Ch.D. 41, 45.
38 *Re Safety Explosives Ltd.* [1904] 1 Ch. 226.
39 *Anglo-Italian Bank* v. *Davies* (1878) 9 Ch.D. 275.
40 *Re Overseas Aviation Engineering (G.B.) Ltd.* [1963] Ch. 24, C.A.; see para. 85–72, *post*.
41 See para. 85–72, *post*.
42 *The Zafiro* [1960] P. 1; *cf. The Constellation* [1966] 1 W.L.R. 272.
43 *Re Aro Co. Ltd.* [1980] 2 W.L.R. 453 (C.A.). *Cf. The Monica S.* [1968] P. 741.
44 *Aluminium Industrie Vaassen BV* v. *Romalpa Aluminium Ltd.* [1976] 2 All E.R. 552 (C.A.). For a fuller discussion see para. 46–08, *ante*.
45 *Ibid.*
46 See para. 46–08, *ante*.
47 s. 25 of the Sale of Goods Act 1979; *Re Interview Ltd.* [1975] I.R. 382.
48 *Re Yorkshire Joinery Co. Ltd.* (1967) 111 S.J. 701.
49 *Thomas* v. *Patent Lionite Co.* (1881) 17 Ch.D. 250, 257; *Re Coal Consumers' Association* (1876) 4 Ch.D. 625, 629; and see s. 319, and para. 85–64, *post*.

A secured creditor has several alternatives:

(1) He may rest on his security and not prove.
(2) He may realise his security and prove for the deficiency.
(3) He may value it and prove for the deficiency after deduction of the assessed value, in which case the liquidator may redeem at such assessed value.
(4) He may surrender his security and prove for the whole debt.[50]

If a creditor values his security, he cannot prove for more than the balance, though the security realises less than his valuation.[51] If he wilfully omits to mention his security in his proof, he will not generally be allowed to amend.[52]

Landlord

Re-entry

85–65 If the lease contains a power of re-entry, the landlord may apply for liberty to re-enter, and the court will give him liberty to do so without putting him to the trouble of bringing an action.[53] Where the property is of greater value than the rent due, such an application in effect may compel the payment of the rent in full.

If the landlord re-enters, the liquidator cannot set off any benefit which the landlord obtains by the termination of the lease against the company's liability on the repairing covenants.[54]

The provisions of section 146 of the Law of Property Act 1925 place restrictions on the right of the landlord to exercise his right of re-entry and give the tenant a right to apply for relief within one year from the commencement of the liquidation.[55] Relief may be granted if proceedings are commenced within the year, though the order is not made until after the end of the year.[56]

Distress for rent due before winding up

85–66 A landlord who has levied distress before the commencement of a winding up will only be restrained by the court if there are special circumstances rendering it inequitable that he should be permitted to do so.[57] Such special circumstances may be constituted by unfair conduct, sharp practice and negligent delay.[58]

---

[50] Bankruptcy Act 1914, s. 7 (2), and Sched. II, rr. 10–18, made applicable to winding up by s. 317 of the Act of 1948 (replacing Judicature Act 1875, s. 10); *Re Withernsea Brick Works* (1880) 16 Ch.D. 337.
[51] *Williams* v. *Hopkins* (1881) 18 Ch.D. 370.
[52] *Re Safety Explosives* [1904] 1 Ch. 226.
[53] *General Share and Trust Co.* v. *Wetley Brick Co.* (1882) 20 Ch.D. 260, 266; *Re Blue Jean Sales Ltd.* [1979] 1 All E.R. 641.
[54] *Hanson* v. *Newman* [1934] 1 Ch. 298.
[55] Law of Property Act 1925, s. 146 (10).
[56] *Pearson* v. *Gee and Braceborough Ltd.* [1934] A.C. 272.
[57] *Re Bellaglade Ltd.* [1977] 1 All E.R. 319; *Herbert Berry Associates Ltd.* v. *I.R.C.* [1978] 1 All E.R. 161 (H.L.)—a tax case applying the landlord and tenant principles.
[58] *Herbert Berry Associates Ltd.* v. *I.R.C.* *(supra)* at p. 172.

After the commencement of a winding up by the court, a distress is, by section 228 of the 1948 Act, declared to be void; and, if a landlord threatens to levy or proceeds to levy a distress for rent accrued before the commencement of the winding up, the court will restrain him. He will be left, like other creditors, to his right of proof as an unsecured creditor.[59]

Distress for rent accrued after winding up

As regards rent accrued after the commencement of a compulsory winding up, the landlord claiming a right to distrain should apply for liberty to distrain, and the court will give him such liberty, or direct the payment of the rent if the liquidator has retained possession of the demised premises for the benefit of the winding up.[60]

Where there is no privity between the company and the landlord (*e.g.* where the company is sub–lessee or mortgagee by deposit), and the landlord has therefore no right of proof, he will not be restrained from distraining.[61]

Liberty to distrain will not be given where possession has been retained, with the acquiescence of the landlord, for the benefit of all parties.[62]

Similar rules apply where a mortgagee asks for liberty to distrain for interest[63]; but a mortgagee does not occupy a position so favourable as that of a landlord.[64]

Proof for rent

85–67 The lessor can prove for rent due up to the date of the commencement of the liquidation, and he can also prove for the rent as it accrues due after the commencement of the liquidation.[65] If he seeks to claim that rent accruing after the commencement of the winding up is payable in full, the onus is upon him to show that the liquidator has retained possession of the property "for the convenience of the liquidation," so that the rent is payable as an expense of the liquidation, or that a special equity exists justifying the claim of the landlord.[66]

If the liquidator takes possession or continues in possession of leaseholds for the purpose of the better realisation of the assets, the lessor will be entitled to payment of the rent in full as part of the expenses properly incurred by the liquidator[67]; and in such a case the liquidator becomes responsible for the repairs and must perform all the obligations of the

---

59 See *Re Oak Pitts Colliery Co.* (1882) 21 Ch.D. 322, and the cases there cited.
60 *Re Lundy Granite Co.* (1871) 6 Ch.App. 462; *Re North Yorkshire Iron Co.* (1878) 7 Ch.D. 661; and see proviso to Winding-up Rule 99.
61 *Re Lundy Granite Co.* (1871) 6 Ch.App. 462; *Re Regent United Services Stores* (1878) 8 Ch.D. 616; *Re Carriage Co-operative, etc., Assocn.* (1883) 23 Ch.D. 154.
62 *Re Progress Assurance Co.* (1870) L.R. 9 Eq. 370; *Re Bridgewater Engineering Co.* (1879) 12 Ch.D. 181; *Re Lancashire Cotton Co.* (1887) 35 Ch.D. 656.
63 *Re Brown, Bayley and Dixon Ltd.* (1881) 18 Ch.D. 649.
64 *Re Higginshaw Mills and Spinning Co.* [1896] 2 Ch. 544.
65 *Re Oak Pitts Colliery* (1882) 21 Ch.D. 322; *Re New Oriental Bank Corpn. (No.2)* [1895] 1 Ch. 753.
66 *Re A. B. C. Coupler and Engineering Co. Ltd. (No. 3)* [1970] 1 W.L.R. 702.
67 *Re Oak Pitts Colliery* (1881) 21 Ch.D. 322; *Re Lundy Granite Co.* (1871) 6 Ch.App. 462.

lease.[68] A liquidator is to be treated as having remained in possession of leasehold property with a view to realising it to the best possible advantage from the date of giving estate agents instructions to find a suitable purchaser, and the landlord may claim for rent for that period as an expense in the winding up.[69] Where the liquidator subsequently disclaims the lessor is entitled to the full rent up to the date of service of the notice to disclaim but not up to the date of formal disclaimer.[69a]

A solvent company will not be permitted in winding up to distribute its assets among the shareholders without regard to the landlord's right to future rent.[70]

A sheriff who seizes goods under a *fi. fa.* prior to a winding-up order should proceed with the execution under the Landlord and Tenant Act 1709, and pay to the landlord up to one year's arrears of rent, notwithstanding a subsequent winding-up order.[71]

Disclaimer

85–68 The liquidator may with leave of the court disclaim the lease (1948 Act, s. 323), and the landlord can then prove for the damage he has sustained. As to disclaimer, see paragraph 85–37, *ante*.

The measure of damages is the probable loss to the landlord, *viz.* the difference between the present value of the amount which should have been paid by the company for rent, repairs, etc., and the present value of the rent which the landlord is likely to obtain during the unexpired period of the lease.[72]

Disclaimer by the liquidator will not exonerate an original tenant who has assigned his interest to the company. He will continue to be liable to the landlord.[73]

Interest

85–69 When a company has been ordered to be wound up, the interest upon debts which carry interest ceases to run from the date of the commencement of the winding up, if the company is insolvent.[74] If there are sufficient assets to pay all debts in full, the creditor is entitled to interest on admitted debts down to the date of paying the final dividend.[75]

---

[68] *Re Silkstone and Dodworth Co.* (1881) 17 Ch.D. 158; *Re National Arms, etc., Co.* (1885) 238 Ch.D. 474 (rates); *Re Levi & Co.* [1919] 1 Ch. 416 (repairs).

[69] *Re Downer Enterprises* [1974] 1 W.L.R. 1460.

[69a] *Re H.H. Realisations Ltd.* (1976) 31 P. & C.R. 249.

[70] *Gooch* v. *London Banking Assocn.* (1885) 32 Ch.D. 41; *Lord Elphinstone* v. *Monkland Co.* (1886) 11 App.Cas. 332; *Oppenheimer* v. *British and Foreign Bank* (1877) 6 Ch.D. 744 (where a fund was required to be set apart).

[71] *Re British Salicylates Ltd.* [1919] 2 Ch. 155.

[72] *Ex p. Blake* (1879) 11 Ch.D. 572; *ex p. Llynvi Coal Co.* (1871) 7 Ch.App. 28.

[73] *Warnford Investments Ltd.* v. *Duckworth* [1978] 2 All E.R. 517. For a useful practical discussion of this case see Prof. J. E. Adams [1978] Conv. 256.

[74] *Re Humber Ironworks Co., Warrant Finance Co.'s Case* (1869) 4 Ch.App. 643, 647; *Hughes' Claim* (1872) L.R. 13 Eq. 623; *Re Theo Garvin Ltd.* [1969] 1 Ch. 624; *cf. ex p. Ador* [1891] 2 Q.B. 574.

[75] *Re W. W. Duncan & Co.* [1905] 1 Ch. 307.

Interest may be payable by express agreement or by implication from the course of dealing between the company and the creditor, or on a judgment debt.[76] Rule 100 of the Winding-up Rules 1949 specifies certain further cases in which interest may be proved for, although not provided for in the contract.

In the case of an insolvent company, interest in excess of 5 per cent. is a deferred debt, and cannot be paid until all other creditors have been paid in full.[77] A creditor cannot appropriate any sums already received to the discharge of such excess interest: he must apportion them between interest and capital.[78] However a dividend paid in the winding up in respect of principal and interest is first to be attributed to the interest at the full rate.[79]

Interest may be recovered in full on secured debts up to the date of realisation, provided that the security is sufficient to cover both capital and interest; but proof cannot be admitted for any unsatisfied balance of interest accruing due after the commencement of the winding up.[80]

The statutory interest of 4 per cent. payable on all debts from the date of the receiving order out of surplus assets, under section 33 (8) of the Bankruptcy Act 1914, is not payable in liquidation: if there are surplus assets, the company is not insolvent, and, accordingly, section 317 has no application.[81]

Staying proceedings

85–70 "The object of the winding-up provisions of the Companies Act 1862," said Lindley L.J. in *Re Oak Pitts Colliery Co.*,[82] "is to put all unsecured creditors upon an equality and to pay them *pari passu*." To accomplish this it was indispensable that proceedings against the company by way of action, execution, distress or other process should be suspended; otherwise the winding up would resolve itself into a scramble for the assets. Section 226 of the 1948 Act gives the court power on the application of the company or a creditor or a contributory to restrain proceedings against the

[76] Judgments Act 1838, s. 17, Administration of Justice Act 1970, s. 4411); Judgment Debts (Rate of Interest) Order 1982 (S.I. 1982 No. 696). At present there is no provision for interest on judgment debts in the County Court—see *R.* v. *Essex County Court Judge* (1887) 18 Q.B.D. 704 but see the Proposals of the Lord Chancellor's Department in (1981) 131 N.L.J. 1155.

[77] *Re Theo Garvin Ltd.* [1969] 1 Ch. 624; *Re Jessel Securities Ltd.* (1979) 129 N.L.J. 171, (C.A.); see further, para. 46–18, *ante*.

[78] Bankruptcy Act 1914, s. 66 (2). This section applies in the liquidation of companies by virtue of s. 317: see *Re Theo Garvin Ltd., supra.*

[79] *Re Joint Stock Discount Co. (No. 2)* (1870) L.R. 10 Eq. 11.

[80] *Quartermaine's Case* [1892] 1 Ch. 639; see para. 46–18, *ante*. The position is the same in Scotland: see *National Commercial Bank of Scotland Ltd.* v. *Liquidator of Telford Grier Maday & Co. Ltd.* 1969 S.L.T. 306. The Companies (Floating Charges and Receivers) (Scotland) Act 1972, s. 1 (4), provides that, subject to section 322 of the 1948 Act, interest due on a debt secured by a floating charge shall accrue until payment is made of the sum due under the charge.

[81] *Re Fine Industrial Commodities Ltd.* [1956] Ch. 256; *Re Rolls-Royce Co.* [1974] 1 W.L.R. 1584.

[82] (1882) 21 Ch.D. 322, 329.

company. That power may be exercised at any time in the interval between the presentation of the petition and the making of the order.[83] Section 228 (1) provides that where any company is being wound up by the court any attachment, sequestration, distress or execution put in force against the company after the commencement of the winding up is void. Section 231 provides that when a winding-up order has been made or a provisional liquidator appointed, no action or proceeding shall be proceeded with or commenced against the company except by leave of the court and subject to such terms as the court may impose.[84] In this way creditors and others are compelled to come in and prove their claims in the winding up, and a rateable and just distribution of the company's assets is effected.[85] "Proceedings" under section 231 is given a wide meaning, and includes executions[86] and interpleader summonses.[87] The words "any other action or proceeding" in section 226 (*b*) likewise are general and not limited to actions in England but extend to actions and proceedings in Scotland; Northern Ireland being covered by section 226 (*c*).[88] The court can also, in a voluntary winding up on application under section 307, restrain executions and other proceedings.[89] Where the petition stands over with a view to the adoption of a scheme of arrangement, the court will restrain proceedings unless good reason to the contrary is shown.[90] All that is necessary, where an action is pending against the company in the High Court, is to apply to the particular branch of the court in which it is pending for an order to stay proceedings.[91] As regards inferior courts injunctions can be granted. This is, generally speaking, only necessary where a winding-up petition is pending (1948 Act, s. 226). Where a winding-up order has been made, the combined effect of sections 231 and 228 of the 1948 Act is that such order operates automatically as a stay of all actions, executions,

---

83 In the absence of special circumstances the court will stay proceedings or restrain execution with a view to securing equal distribution of the assets among creditors of the same class: *Bowkett* v. *Fullers United Electric Works Ltd.* [1923] 1 K.B. 161 (C.A.). See also *Hudson's Concrete Products Ltd.* v. *D.B. Evans (Bilston) Ltd.* (1961) 105 S.J. 281; *D. Wilson (Birmingham) Ltd.* v. *Metropolitan Property Developments Ltd.* [1975] 2 All E.R. 814 (C.A.); *Rainbow* v. *Moorgate Properties Ltd.* [1975] 2 All E.R. 821 (C.A.). *Cf.* however, *Re Bellaglade Ltd.* [1977] 1 All E.R. 319—a landlord's distress started before the commencement of the winding up allowed to continue unless there were special circumstances. See also *Herbert Berry Associates Ltd.* v. *I.R.C.* [1978] 1 All E.R. 161 (H.L.).

84 See also s. 325. See these sections discussed in *Herbert Berry Associates Ltd.* v. *I.R.C.* [1978] 1 All E.R. 161 (H.L.).

85 *Re International Pulp Co.* (1876) 3 Ch.D. 594; *Re Dynamics Corporation of America* [1973] 1 W.L.R. 63.

86 *Re Artistic Colour Printing Co.* (1880) 14 Ch.D. 502, 505; and see *The Constellation* [1966] 1 W.L.R. 272.

87 *Eastern Holdings Establishment of Vaduz* v. *Singer and Friedlander Ltd.* [1967] 1 W.L.R. 1017.

88 *Re Dynamics Corporation of America, supra.* As to whether distress is properly regarded as a proceeding within s. 226 see the authorities discussed by Oliver J. in *Re Bellaglade Ltd.* [1977] 1 All E.R. 319 and Lords Simon and Russell in *Herbert Berry Associates Ltd.* v. *I.R.C.* [1978] 1 All E.R. 161. As to s. 226 (b) see also *Re J. Burrows (Leeds) Ltd.* [1982] 2 All E.R. 882.

89 *Anglo-Baltic, etc., Bank* v. *Barber & Co.* [1924] 2 K.B. 410. See also s. 325.

90 *Bowkett* v. *Fuller's United Electric Works* [1923] 1 K.B. 160.

91 *Re Artistic Colour Printing Co.* (1880) 14 Ch.D. 502; *Re General Service Co-operative Stores* [1891] 1 Ch. 496.

distresses, sequestrations, etc., against the company, subject to the discretion of the court to allow such actions, executions, etc., to proceed notwithstanding the winding up.[92] The sale by a landlord of goods on which distress has been levied before winding up will not normally be restrained, even though it be for rent in advance[93]; but a distress may be restrained where the preferential debts will exhaust the assets.[94] The leave of the court is not required, however, in order to set up a counterclaim in an action brought by a company in liquidation, provided that this is in the nature of a set-off for the purpose of reducing or extinguishing the company's claim; but the defendant must obtain leave if he wishes to counterclaim for an amount in excess of the plaintiff company's claim.[95]

85–71 Section 231 does not apply to proceedings in a foreign country,[96] but it does apply to an "action or proceeding" in Scotland (*cf.* s. 276) and Northern Ireland (*cf.* ss. 276 and 461 (2)).[97] The words "in the course of winding up a company" are not limited to what happens after a winding-up order is made but cover everything after the presentation of the winding-up petition.[98]

There is a difference between compulsory and voluntary winding up in this respect. The staying of proceedings is automatic in the case of the former, subject to the power for the court to allow them to be continued. In the case of the latter, there is no automatic staying of proceedings but it is in the court's discretion to order it (see further para. 86–50, *post*).

Execution creditors

85–72 By section 325 of the 1948 Act an execution creditor cannot retain the benefit of his execution against the liquidator unless he has completed the execution before the commencement of the winding up. Completing his execution means obtaining a charging order absolute in the case of all property or seizure *and* sale in the case of goods, receipt of the debt in the case of attachment of a debt, and seizure or the appointment of a receiver in the case of land.[99]

To this basic rule there are the following three provisos:

(a) where any creditor has had notice of a meeting having been called at which a resolution for voluntary winding up is to be proposed, the date on which he had notice shall be substituted for the date of the commencement of the winding up;

(b) a person who purchases in good faith under a sale by a sheriff any

[92] *Re Vron Colliery* (1882) 20 Ch.D. 442; *Armorduct Manufacturing Co.* v. *General Incandescent Co.* [1911] 2 K.B. 143; and see para. 85–76, *post*.
[93] *Venner's Electrical, etc., Appliances* v. *Thorpe* [1915] 2 Ch. 404; and see para. 85–66, *ante*.
[94] *Re South Rhondda Colliery Co.* [1928] W.N. 126.
[95] *Langley Constructions (Brixham) Ltd.* v. *Wells* [1969] 1 W.L.R. 503.
[96] *Re Vocalion (Foreign) Ltd.* [1932] 2 Ch. 196.
[97] *Re Dynamics Corporation of America* [1973] 2 Ch. 196.
[98] *Ibid.*
[99] See s. 325 (2) as amended by Administration of Justice Act 1956, ss. 35 and 36; Charging Orders Act 1979 (para. 85–63, *ante*).

goods on which execution has been levied will acquire a good title against the liquidator[1]; and

(c) the rights conferred by section 325 on the liquidator may be set aside by the court in favour of a creditor to such extent and subject to such terms as the court may think fit.

The "benefit" of the execution means the benefit of the charge which the creditor obtains by the issue of his execution, and does not include money actually received thereunder.[2] But the creditor must account for any money received after he had notice of a proposed resolution to wind up, since that money is only obtained by making use of the charge.[3] Money paid to the sheriff or his officer to avoid sale is not a "benefit of the execution," and can be retained by the creditor.[4]

Where a sheriff has seized goods, he is bound to hand them over to the liquidator, if a notice is served on him of a winding-up order or the appointment of a provisional liquidator or the passing of a resolution to wind up voluntarily (s. 326 (1)). This subsection does not apply to money paid by the company to avoid sale.[4] The costs of execution, which are by the subsection made a first charge on the goods, do not include the creditor's costs of issuing his writ and serving the *fi. fa.*[5]

Where the judgment exceeds £250 the sheriff must retain any money received (subject to deduction of costs) for 14 days and hand it over to the liquidator in case of a winding up (s. 326 (2) as amended by the Insolvency Act 1976, s. 1 and Sched. 1).[6] In *Engineering Industry Training Board* v. *Samuel Talbot (Engineers) Ltd.*[7] Lord Denning M.R. said that section 326 (2) was not to be construed literally but according to its object and intent. The purpose of the subsection was to require notification to the sheriff that a winding up is imminent. It was held that, although the subsection itself contemplated notification by means of notice of a meeting of members to pass a resolution to wind up, it could equally be satisfied by notice of a meeting of creditors convened in connection with the winding up. It has also been held that service of a notice of a meeting to consider a resolution to wind up a company on a sheriff's officer is not service on the sheriff within the meaning of section 326.[8] Where money is paid to the bailiff to avoid sale, the 14-day period runs from the time of receipt by the bailiff, not from the time he hands it over to the sheriff.[8] During this period the creditor has no *locus standi* to present a petition for the winding up of the company.[9]

---

[1] See also Sale of Goods Act 1979, s. 21 (2) (*b*) and s. 26.

[2] *Re Andrew* [1937] Ch. 122, C.A., decided under the corresponding provision in s. 40 of the Bankruptcy Act 1914.

[3] *Re Caribbean Products (Yam Importers) Ltd.* [1966] Ch. 331, C.A., overruling *Re Rainbow Tours Ltd.* [1964] Ch. 66.

[4] *Re Walkden Sheet Metal Co. Ltd.* [1960] Ch. 170.

[5] *Re Woods (Bristol) Ltd.* [1931] 2 Ch. 320.

[6] *Bluston & Bramley* v. *Leigh* [1950] 2 K.B. 548; *cf. Re T.D. Walton Ltd.* [1966] 1 W.L.R. 869.

[7] [1969] 2 Q.B. 270 (C.A.).

[8] *Hellyer* v. *Sheriff of Yorkshire* [1974] 2 W.L.R. 844 (C.A.).

[9] *Re William Hockley Ltd.* [1962] 1 W.L.R. 555; see para. 85–13, *ante*.

85–73 The court has wide powers to set aside the rights which the liquidator has under sections 325 and 326, if it thinks fit (ss. 325 (1) (*c*) and 326 (3)). These provisions give the court "a free hand to do what is right and fair according to the circumstances of each case"[10]; but it seems that the court will require to be satisfied that the creditor has been unfairly treated by the company before it will interfere with the ordinary rule that all unsecured creditors should rank equally in the winding up.[11]

Section 325 does not apply to a distress by a landlord.[12] Sections 325 and 326 do not apply in Scotland, where the effect of a winding up in relation to diligence is governed by section 327.

The effect of section 9 (4) of the European Communities Act 1972

The effect of the European Communities Act 1972, s. 9 (4) on sections 325 and 326 is obscure. Section 9 (4) basically provides that the company shall not be entitled to rely on the making of a winding-up order unless this has been officially notified or the third party has knowledge. Both sections 325 and 326 seem to require actual notice and it would be absurd if a statutory provision designed to disallow a company from relying on certain events until official notification or knowledge should be interpreted in such a way as to prejudice a third party by the gratuitous reintroduction of constructive notice in this context.

Third party insurance

85–74 When a company which is being wound up is insured against liabilities to third parties, and a liability is incurred by the company to such a third party, the company's rights against the insurer are transferred to the third party.[13]

Dispositions and transfers after winding up

85–75 A disposition of the property of the company, including things in action, and a transfer of shares, or alteration in the status of the members of the company, made after the commencement of the winding up, is void unless the court otherwise orders (1948 Act, s. 227); but the practice of the court is to allow such payments or dispositions, pending the petition, if made honestly and in the ordinary course of business.[14] The exercise of the discretion of the court under this section is controlled only by the general

---

[10] *Per* Vaisey J. in *Re Grosvenor Metal Co.* [1950] Ch. 63, 65.

[11] *Re Grosvenor Metal Co.* [1950] Ch. 63; *Re Suidair International Airways* [1951] Ch. 165; *Re Redman (Builders) Ltd.* [1964] 1 W.L.R. 541; *Re Caribbean Products (Yam Importers) Ltd.* [1966] Ch. 331, C.A.

[12] *Re Bellaglade Ltd.* [1977] 1 All E.R. 319.

[13] Third Party (Rights Against Insurers) Act 1930, s. 1, as to which see *Murray* v. *Legal and General Assurance Society Ltd.* [1970] 2 Q.B. 495 (no set-off as regards unpaid premiums); and see Road Traffic Act 1972, s. 149.

[14] *Re Oriental Bank Corporation* (1884) 28 Ch.D. 634; *Gorringe* v. *Irwell India Rubber Works* (1886) 34 Ch.D. 128; *Re Burton & Deakin Ltd.* [1977] 1 All E.R. 631.

principles of justice and fairness.[15] Such an order may be made prior to the hearing of the winding-up order.[16]

If the directors of a solvent company show that they considered a particular disposition to have been necessary or expedient in the interests of the company and the court accepts that the reasons given were such as an intelligent and honest man could reasonably hold, the court will normally sanction the disposition, notwithstanding the opposition of a contributory.[17]

The invalidation of a disposition of the company's property under section 227 and the recovery of the property disposed of are two distinct matters. The section says nothing about recovery but merely avoids the disposition and gives discretionary power to the court to validate the transactions. Its object is that creditors should be paid *pari passu*. On a true construction the term "disposition" includes dispositions of a company's property whether made by the company or by a third party or whether made directly or indirectly. Thus where a director made out a "cash" cheque and bought money orders which were then sent to a creditor with intent to prefer him this was held to be a disposition within the section which must be repaid.[18]

The court has jurisdiction under section 227 to authorise a disposition of the company's property for the benefit of creditors, notwithstanding that a winding-up order has not yet been made.[19] A shareholder of a company in liquidation has sufficient *locus standi* to make an application to the court under section 227 to validate a disposition of the company's property made after the commencement of the winding up.[20]

As to transfers of shares in the winding up, see paragraph 39–28, *ante*.

Where preference shareholders had a right to convert their shares into ordinary shares, a notice given before the winding up was held to take effect after the winding up.[21]

A debenture issued after the presentation of a petition may be valid, if it was for the benefit of the company, as, *e.g.* for payment of wages.[22]

Liberty to proceed

85–76 The power of the court to allow actions and other proceedings to be brought, taken, or proceeded with, notwithstanding a winding-up order

---

15 *Re Steane's (Bournemouth)* [1950] 1 A11 E.R. 21; *Re T. W. Construction Ltd.* [1954] 1 W.L.R. 540; *Re Clifton Place Garage Ltd.* [1970] Ch. 477 (C.A.).
16 *Re Operator Control Cabs Ltd.* [1970] 3 A11 E.R. 657n.
17 *Re Burton & Deakin Ltd.* [1977] 1 W.L.R. 390 (where the opposing contributories were in fact also the petitioners alleging oppression.
18 *Re J. Leslie Engineering Co. Ltd. (in liquidation)* [1976] 1 W.L.R. 292. This case contains a useful analysis by Oliver J. of the way in which the court's discretion will be exercised.
19 *Re A. I. Levy (Holdings) Ltd.* [1964] Ch. 19; see also *Carden* v. *Albert Palace Assocn.* (1886) 56 L.J.Ch. 166; *Re Douglas (Griggs) Engineering Ltd.* [1963] Ch. 19; *cf. Re Miles Aircraft Ltd.* [1948] Ch. 188.
20 *Re Argentum Reductions (U.K.) Ltd.* [1975] 1 W.L.R. 186.
21 *Re Blaina Colliery* [1926] W.N. 30.
22 *Re Park, Ward & Co. Ltd.* [1926] Ch. 828.

(1948 Act, s. 231), is often exercised. Thus secured creditors are, as a matter of course, given liberty to proceed with any action for enforcing their securities.[23] So, too, liberty to proceed is often given where outsiders are involved in some dispute with the company, and it is desirable that the dispute should be decided in an action by the ordinary tribunals: for instance, in the case of an action against the company for damages under Lord Campbell's Act[24]; or for specific performance[25]; or for trespass[26]; or to proceed with an execution, where execution was delayed by a trick[27]; or to bring a new action for the purpose of obtaining the fruits of an earlier action.[28] The leave must not be given on an *ex parte* application.[29] A creditor who issues a writ against a ship owned by a company prior to its liquidation but does not serve the writ or arrest the ship before the commencement of the liquidation may nevertheless obtain leave to continue his action under section 231 since the discretion conferred by the section gives the court freedom to do what is right and fair in the circumstances.[30]

Costs

85–77 The normal basis of taxation of costs of litigious and non–litigious costs of liquidation is the "common fund" basis but the court has a discretion to direct a different basis. The "trustee" basis of taxation will only be ordered in exceptional circumstances. The latter basis was allowed where the preparation of the case was done with expertise and initiative with the emphasis on a speedy solution rather than reducing costs so that there should be minimum delay in distributing a large sum among the numerous claimants in the liquidation of an insurance company.[31] Where a liquidator initiates proceedings he litigates at his own risk. He is personally liable and cannot limit his responsibility for the costs to the assets of the company. Prima facie, however, he can recoup himself out of the assets of the company unless he has been guilty of misconduct. The former general practice in the Companies Registry of assuming that if nothing is said when an order for costs is made against a liquidator that the costs are limited to the assets of the company has been held to be wrong in cases where the liquidator initiates proceedings. It is otherwise where proceedings are brought against him.[32] Proceedings against a company in liquidation[33] may

---

23 *Lloyd* v. *Lloyd & Co.* (1877) 6 Ch.D. 339.
24 *Re Thurso New Gas Co.* (1889) 42 Ch.D. 486, 491.
25 *Thames Plate Glass Co.* v. *Land, etc., Co.* (1870) L.R. 11 Eq. 248.
26 *Wyley* v. *Exhall Coal, etc., Co.* (1864) 33 Beav. 538.
27 *Armorduct Manufacturing Co.* v. *General Incandescent Co.* [1911] 2 K.B. 143 (a voluntary liquidation).
28 *Re National Provincial Insurance, etc., Co.* (1912) 56 S.J. 290. See further *McEwen* v. *London, Bombay and Mediterranean Bank* (1867) 15 W.R. 245; *Re Marine Investment Co.* (1868) 17 L.T. 535; *Re Strand Hotel Co.* [1868] W.N. 2.
29 *Western and Brazilian Telegraph Co.* v. *Bibby* (1880) 42 L.T. 821.
30 *Re Aro Co. Ltd.* [1980] 2 W.L.R. 453 (C.A.).
31 *Re National Life Assurance Co. Ltd. (in liquidation)* [1978] 1 W.L.R. 45.
32 *Re Wilson Lovatt & Sons Ltd.* [1977] 1 All E.R. 274 (where the earlier authorities are reviewed).
33 As to costs of arbitration, see *Van den Hurk* v. *R. Martens & Co.* [1920] 1 K.B. 850.

be transferred to the Chancery Division and assigned to the Company Judge[34] even though other parties are concerned.[35]

Wishes of creditors and contributories

85–78 The court should have regard to these, and may direct meetings for that purpose (1948 Act, s. 346).[36] This rule is not affected by section 310, which enables a creditor to apply for a winding-up order notwithstanding that a voluntary winding up has commenced.[37]

Compromises

85–79 Under section 245 (1) of the 1948 Act the court has a wide power of sanctioning compromises with creditors and contributories, and this power is frequently exercised.[38] As to the alternative method of proceeding under section 206, see paragraph 79–04, *ante*. A scheme under section 245 (1) may be disallowed by the court if it is proposed to distribute the assets otherwise than strictly in accordance with the rights of the creditors in the liquidation; in such a case the proper way to proceed is by a scheme of arrangement under section 206, under which the creditors have a greater opportunity of making known to the court their views on the fairness of the scheme.[39]

A conveyance or assignment by a company of all its property to trustees for the benefit of all its creditors is void, as this would be an evasion of the winding-up procedure, with its strict rules of supervision (s. 320 (2)). This has been held to include a floating charge over all the assets of a company for the benefit of all its creditors.[40]

Fraudulent and undue preferences

85–80 Section 76 of the Joint Stock Companies Act 1856 first introduced the Bankruptcy principles as to fraudulent preferences into the liquidation of insolvent companies. The present provision is contained in section 320 of the Act of 1948.

Under this provision, any act relating to property made or done by or

---

34 Winding-up Rules 1949, r. 44.
35 *Re Pacaya Rubber, etc., Co.* [1913] 1 Ch. 218.
36 *Re Western of Canada Oil Lands and Works Co.* (1873) L.R. 17 Eq. 1, 5; *Re Chapel House Colliery Co.* (1883) 24 Ch.D. 259; *Re West Hartlepool Ironworks Co.* (1875) 10 Ch.App. 618; *Re Great Western (Forest of Dean) Coal Consumers Co.* (1882) 21 Ch.D. 769, 773; *Re Langham Skating Rink Co.* (1877) 5 Ch.D. 669; *Re Suburban Hotel Co.* (1867) 2 Ch.App. 737; *Re Manmac Farmers Ltd.* [1968] 1 W.L.R. 572; and see paras. 85–06 and 85–25, *ante*.
37 *Re Home Remedies Ltd.* [1943] Ch. 1.
38 s. 245 (5) gives a liquidator in Scotland the same powers as a trustee in bankruptcy and under s. 245 (4) the court may authorise the liquidator in Scotland to exercise the powers set out in s. 245 (1).
39 *Re Trix Ltd.* [1970] 1 W.L.R. 1421 but see para. 85–60, *ante*.
40 *London Joint, etc., Bank* v. *Herbert Dickinson* [1922] W.N. 13.

against a company within six months before the commencement of winding up is invalid as a fraudulent preference if it qualified as such in the bankruptcy of an individual. Hereunder fall, in particular, conveyances of property, the grant of mortgages, and the delivery of, or the payment for, goods (s. 320 (1)).

For a transaction to constitute a fraudulent preference, it must appear that the transaction took place within six months[41] of the commencement of the winding up, and that the substantial or effectual or dominant view in the mind of the company, acting by its directors, was to prefer the creditor at a time when the company was unable to pay its debts as they became due.[42] It need not, however, be the sole motive.[43] If these requirements are satisfied, the transaction is deemed to be fraudulent; it is not necessary to prove that any moral blame attaches to the company.[44] If the payment, etc., was made by the directors with a view to shielding themselves from civil or criminal proceedings, or otherwise under pressure from the creditor, this is not a fraudulent preference[45]; and the same principle has been held to apply where the dominant intention of the company is not to confer an advantage on the creditor, but to benefit the company by keeping on good terms with the creditor.[46]

85–81 The court will readily infer that a promise by a company, at the time the loan is made, to execute a charge at the request of the creditor is intended by both parties to give the creditor the right to be preferred on request, and such a charge, if executed, will be void as a fraudulent preference.[47] But it is otherwise where there is a pre-existing equitable charge, created by deposit of title deeds, and the company executes a legal charge in pursuance of an obligation to do so contained in the memorandum of deposit.[48]

Where the company did not oppose an application to the court to extend the time for registration of a charge, this was held by Eve J. to be a judicial proceeding within the section; but the decision was overruled on other grounds.[49] In any event, it is doubtful whether taking or suffering a judicial proceeding can be regarded as a fraudulent preference within section 320

---

[41] On the invalidity of certain floating charges created within 12 months of the commencement of winding up under s. 322, see para. 44–09, *ante*.

[42] *Re Jackson and Bassford* [1906] 2 Ch. 467 (where the company agreed to issue a debenture to Jackson, who had guaranteed the company's overdraft but delayed issuing the debenture until the eve of insolvency); *Re Eric Holmes (Property) Ltd.* [1965] Ch. 1052; *Re F.P. & C.H. Matthews Ltd.* (in liq.) [1982] 2 W.L.R. 495 (C.A.); see s. 44 (1) of the Bankruptcy Act 1914.

[43] *Ex p. Hill* (1883) 23 Ch.D. 695 (C.A.); *Re Cutts* [1956] 1 W.L.R. 728 (C.A.).

[44] *Re Patrick and Lyon Ltd.* [1933] Ch. 786.

[45] *Re Blackpool Motor Car Co.* [1901] 1 Ch. 77; *Re W. Blackburn & Co.* [1899] 2 Ch. 725; *Re Jackson and Bassford* [1906] 2 Ch. 467; *Re F.L.E. Holdings Ltd.* [1967] 1 W.L.R. 1409.

[46] *Re F.L.E. Holdings Ltd.* [1967] 1 W.L.R. 1409; and see Simonds J. in *Re Destone Fabrics Ltd.* [1941] Ch. 319, 324, 325.

[47] *Re Eric Holmes (Property) Ltd.* [1965] Ch. 1052; *Re Allan Fairfield & Sons Ltd.* (1971) 115 S.J. 244.

[48] *Re William Hall (Contractors) Ltd.* [1967] 1 W.L.R 948.

[49] *Re M.I.G. Trust Ltd.* [1933] Ch. 542; affirmed *sub nom. Peat* v. *Gresham Trust Ltd.* [1934] A.C. 252.

(1), having regard to the difference in wording between this section and section 44 (1) of the Bankruptcy Act 1914. The judgment of Eve J. also indicated that a fraudulent preference cannot be inferred from facts which raise a suspicion of fraud, if there is some other explanation of the transaction which indicates some motive other than fraud; but it has since been held by the Court of Appeal that there is no difference in law between the evidence from which an inference may be drawn of an intention to prefer and that supporting an inference of any other fact.[50]

85–82 In *Re Stenotyper Ltd.*[51] it was held that the rule did not apply if the payment was made with a view to giving a surety or a guarantor a preference, but this is now within section 44 (1) of the Bankruptcy Act 1914, and the amount paid can be recovered from the guarantor or surety,[52] but not if the dominant motive was to draw the guarantor into further liability.[53] Where any person becomes liable under this section to repay money paid to him in satisfaction of a debt from the company to him on the grounds that the payment was a fraudulent preference of any surety or guarantor, powers are given to the court to determine questions arising between the person to whom the payment was made and the surety or guarantor and to grant relief in respect thereof (s. 321 (3)).

If a transaction is void as a fraudulent preference of a person whose property is mortgaged or charged to secure the company's debt, that person is put in the same position as if he were a surety for the debt, to the extent of the charge or the value of his interest in it (s. 321 (1)).

85–83 The provision in section 320 as to fraudulent preference by an insolvent company, like the analogous provision in section 44 of the Bankruptcy Act 1914, is for the benefit of *all* the creditors of the company, and cannot be invoked if the result of recovering the property comprised in the fraudulent instrument will not be for the benefit of the creditors at large but only of a mortgagee or debenture holders.[54] Money recovered by the liquidator in respect of a fraudulent preference must be held by him for the benefit of the creditors generally, and is not covered by a floating charge.[55]

Section 31 of the Bankruptcy Act 1914—the mutual debts and credits section—may, if a set-off is bona fide, prevent a transaction from being a fraudulent preference; but not where one of the debts could not be set off in the winding up, *e.g.* a liability for calls.[56]

---

[50] *Re M. Kushler Ltd.* [1943] Ch. 248; and see *Re F.L.E. Holdings Ltd., supra.*
[51] [1901] 1 Ch. 250.
[52] As to direct recovery by the liquidator see *Re G. Stanley & Co. Ltd.* [1925] Ch. 148; *Re A. Singer & Co. (Hat Manufacturers) Ltd.* [1943] Ch. 121 (C.A.); *cf.* the bankruptcy cases of *Re Idenden* [1970] 1 W.L.R. 1015; *Re Lyons* (1934) 51 T.L.R. 24; *Re Conley* [1937] 4 All E.R. 438; [1938] 2 All E.R. 127 (C.A.).
[53] *Re G. Stanley & Co.* [1925] Ch. 148.
[54] *Willmott* v. *London Celluloid Co.* (1886) 34 Ch.D. 147; *Ex p. Cooper* (1875) 10 Ch.App. 510.
[55] *Re Yagerphone Ltd.* [1935] Ch. 392.
[56] *Re Washington Diamond Mining Co.* [1893] 3 Ch. 95, as explained in *Re B. P. Fowler Ltd.* [1938] Ch. 113.

Fraudulent trading

85–84 If in a winding up it appears that any business of the company has been carried on with intent to defraud creditors or for any fraudulent purpose, the court may declare that any of the directors who were knowingly parties to the fraud and any other person who is knowingly a party to carrying on the business in that manner shall be personally responsible for all or any of the debts of the company (s. 332 (1)). The basic question is how extensive an interpretation is to be given to the word "fraud." There are two statements by Maugham J. in cases in the 1930s which are difficult to reconcile with each other. In *Re William C. Leitch Bros. Ltd.*[57] he seemed to give it a liberal construction. The material facts of that case were that L was governing director of the company and held a debenture on the company's property. The company got into difficulties and could not pay £6,500 for goods supplied. After this date L ordered goods to the value of £6,000 and they became subject to the charge in his debenture. L then as chargee appointed a receiver and was appointed manager. He collected debts and removed goods, towards the satisfaction of his debenture. Maugham J. held that "if a company continues to carry on business and to incur debts at a time when there is, to the knowledge of the directors, no reasonable prospect of the creditors ever receiving payment of those debts, it is, in general, a proper inference that the company is carrying on business with intent to defraud." He therefore made a declaration that L should be personally liable for £6,000. Clearly this was a classic case of dishonesty. Indeed, it was the basic paradigm of fraudulent trading which the Greene Committee had in mind when preparing their Report which led to the introduction of the section. It is to be noted that the judge talked about such evidence giving rise to an inference as to the intention to defraud. In other words, he was simply stating a proposition of evidence or proof, not one of substantive law.

In *Re Patrick & Lyon Ltd.*[58] the facts were that an order was sought against a director who had allegedly continued the company's business not genuinely for trading purposes but solely in order that certain debentures which he held would not be invalidated by what is now section 322 of the Act of 1948. Maugham J. held that this conduct was not fraudulent under the section. "No judge," he said, "has ever been willing to define 'fraud' " and he was not going to attempt a definition. He did, however, state what in his opinion must be one of the elements of the word as used in the section. It was not, he thought, used in the extended sense of the fraudulent preference provisions which applied even in the absence of moral blame. Also an infringement of section 322 was not necessarily indicative of fraud. In his view fraud in the context of fraudulent trading connoted "actual dishonesty involving, according to current notions of fair trading

[57] [1932] 2 Ch. 71. For a fuller discussion see J. H. Farrar [1980] J.B.L.336. See also D. W. Fox (1980) 124 S.J. 354.
[58] [1933] Ch. 786.

among commercial men, real moral blame" and that the onus of proof was on those alleging it. This seemed to narrow down the concept from the exposition made by him in *Leitch's* case. Nevertheless, *Leitch's* case would have been decided the same way applying this new test. The cases can perhaps be reconciled on the basis that the later statement reflects the true substantive legal position while the earlier one merely gives practical guidance on the evidence required.

The High Court of Australia expressed doubts with regard to the *Leitch* case in *Hardie* v. *Hanson*[59] but it was nevertheless followed in the unreported case of *Re White and Osmond (Parkstone) Ltd.* on June 30, 1960. In the latter case Buckley J. said he wholeheartedly accepted the interpretation of Maugham J. in the *Leitch* case. His application of it in fact enables one to reconcile the *Leitch* and *Patrick* and *Lyon* cases in the manner suggested above. He said:

> "In my judgment, there is nothing wrong in the fact that directors incur credit at a time when, to their knowledge, the company is not able to meet all its liabilities as they fall due. What is manifestly wrong is if directors allow a company to incur credit at a time when the business is being carried on in such circumstances that it is clear that the company will never be able to satisfy its creditors. However, there is nothing to say that directors who genuinely believe that the clouds will roll away and the sunshine of prosperity will shine upon them again and disperse the fog of their depression are not entitled to incur credit to help them to get over the bad time."

The important thing, therefore, is to consider what was the directors' view of the company's position at the relevant time. The *White and Osmond* case is thus important and should be fully reported to clarify the precedent position. It has been held recently in *Re Sarflax Ltd.*[60] that where the directors knew or had good grounds to suspect that the company would not have sufficient assets to pay all creditors in full, the mere preference of one creditor over another did not amount to an "intention to defraud" within section 332 (1).[61] It may, however, constitute a fraudulent preference within section 320 and there may be circumstances of a peculiar nature involving preferential payments from which the intention required by section 332 may be inferred.[62] Such circumstances might be constituted by the controllers of the company milking it of funds where there was inadequate or illusory consideration on their part.

An application may be made to the court under section 332 by the official receiver or the liquidator or any creditor or contributory. The judgment should be for a fixed sum and, where the application is made by the liquidator, the sum awarded will become part of the general assets.[63] An application by a creditor is made on his own account, and not on behalf

---

[59] [1960] 105 C.L.R. 451.
[60] [1979] 1 All E.R. 529.
[61] *Ibid.* pp. 535, 545.
[62] *Ibid.* p. 545.
[63] *Re Patrick and Lyon Ltd.* [1933] Ch. 786, *(No. 2)* [1933] Ch. 261.

of the creditors generally, and in such a case the court may make a declaration exclusively in favour of that creditor.[64] However it is the Registrar's practice to require the liquidator to be joined.

85–85 To be a "party to" carrying on the business of the company in a fraudulent manner requires a positive step and mere failure on the part of the secretary and financial adviser to draw the attention of the directors to the fact that the company is insolvent and the consequences of continuing in business in these circumstances does not make him civilly or criminally liable under section 332.[65] A single transaction may fall within the section.[66] Where a controlling director caused the company to sell assets warranting them to be in good working order and knew that liability for breach of such warranty could not be met if it resulted in a substantial claim for damages this did not constitute fraudulent trading within section 332.[66a] The carrying on business in section 332 (1) is not synonymous with actively carrying on trade. The collection of assets acquired in the course of business and the distribution of the proceeds of those assets in the discharge of business liabilities can constitute "carrying on of business."[67]

When the court declares that the directors are to be responsible for fraudulent trading, it may charge their liability against any securities which they hold against the company (s. 332 (2)). The court may also disqualify them from acting in the management of companies for a period not exceeding five years (s. 188 (1) (*c*)(i)), and they may be made criminally liable (s. 332 (3)).

A prosecution under section 332 (3) can now be initiated whether or not the company concerned has been put into liquidation.[68] If the accused is convicted of fraudulent trading under section 332 (3), and at the same time of obtaining by deception individual sums contained in the fraudulent trading count, the concurrent sentences for these convictions are not limited to the maximum term laid down in section 332 (3), but may exceed that term.[69]

Fraudulent transfer

85–86 The transfer of the business to a company may have been an act of bankruptcy if the vendor was insolvent at the time of the transfer, and in such a case the transfer may be set aside as against the trustee in bankruptcy of the vendor.[70] Thus, an agreement was set aside in *Gonville's Trustee*

---

64 *Re Cyona Distributors Ltd.* [1967] Ch. 889 (C.A.); but see Russell L.J. at p. 908.

65 *Re Maidstone Builders Ltd.* [1971] 1 W.L.R. 1085 but *cf. Panorama Developments (Guildford) Ltd.* v. *Fidelis Furnishing Fabrics Ltd.* [1971] 2 Q.B. 711 (C.A.). See J. H. Farrar (1972) 122 N.L.J. 13.

66 *Re Gerald Cooper Chemicals Ltd.* [1978] 2 All E.R. 49.

66a *Norcross Ltd.* v. *Amos* (1981) 131 N.L.J. 1213 (C.A.).

67 *Re Sarflax Ltd.* [1979] 1 A11 E.R. 529.

68 s. 96 of the Companies Act 1981 overruling *R.* v. *Schildkamp* [1971] A.C. 1 (H.L.).

69 *R.* v. *Lavender* (1971) 56 Cr.App.R. 355. For the maximum term under s. 332 (3) see now Companies Act 1980 Sched. 2.

70 *Re Slobodinsky, ex p. Moore* [1903] 2 K.B. 517; *Re Goldburg, ex p. Silverstone* [1912] 1 K.B. 384; *Re David and Adlard, ex p. Whinney* [1914] 2 K.B. 694.

v. *Patent Caramel Co.*,[71] where the sale was by two partners, only one of whom was insolvent, but the other partner knew the circumstances; and in *Re Fasey*,[72] a fraudulent agreement for a conveyance to a company was set aside under what is now section 172 of the Law of Property Act 1925.

Generally, third party proceedings are not available in the Companies Court in relation to a claim against a stranger which does not arise in consequence of a winding up. However, in *Re Shilena Hosiery Co.*[73] Brightman J. held that the court does have jurisdiction to grant relief under section 172 of the Law of Property Act 1925 (avoidance of a disposition made with the intention of defrauding creditors) on a summons in a liquidation.

Where a debenture was issued by a company to its managing director and principal shareholder, but was kept back with a view to protecting the credit of the company while preferring the managing director to other creditors, the debenture was held not to be a fraudulent assignment under the Fraudulent Conveyances Act 1571.[74] Section 172 of the Law of Property Act 1925, which replaces the statute of 1571, is expressed in wider terms but still seems to be subject to the old authorities which predicate some personal benefit to the debtor. Mere preference of particular creditors is insufficient.[74a]

Fraudulent transfers or gifts, fraudulent connivances at executions and fraudulent inducements to persons to give credit to a company which is subsequently wound up are now criminal offences (1948 Act, s. 330).

Following trust property

85–87 Property which can be identified as belonging to or held by the company in trust for other persons may be followed and recovered from the liquidator.[75] Purchase-money paid for property which is not delivered may sometimes be recovered.[76]

Money fraudulently obtained may be followed into the banking account of a person who receives it without consideration.[77]

Misfeasance proceedings

85–88 It may happen that promoters, directors, managers, or other officers of a company are liable to the company for money misapplied by them or

---

[71] [1912] 1 K.B. 599.
[72] [1923] 2 Ch. 1.
[73] [1979] 2 All E.R. 6.
[74] *Re Lloyds' Furniture Palace Ltd.* [1925] Ch. 853.
[74a] *Re Sarflax Ltd.* [1979] 1 All E.R. 529.
[75] *Re Lang Propeller Ltd.* [1926] Ch. 585, 595; *Sinclair* v. *Brougham* [1914] A.C. 398, 418; *Re Hallett's Estate* (1880) 13 Ch.D. 696; *Jas. Roscoe Ltd.* v. *Winder* [1915] 1 Ch. 62; *Re Oatway* [1903] 2 Ch. 356; *Re Stenning* [1895] 2 Ch. 433; *Smith* v. *Liquidator of James Birrell Ltd.*, 1968 S.L.T. 174; *cf; Re Kayford Ltd.* [1975] 1 W.L.R. 279; and *Re Chelsea Cloisters Ltd.* [1980] C.A.T. 477; (1981) 131 N.L.J. 482 (C.A.); see further the discussion of reservation of property clauses para. 46–08, *ante*. See also *Chase Manhattan Bank NA* v. *Israel British Bank (London)* [1979] 3 All E.R. 1025.
[76] *Re Regent Finance, etc., Co.* [1930] W.N. 84.
[77] *Banque Belge pour L'Etranger* v. *Hambrouck* [1921] 1 K.B. 321.

wrongfully received, or for which in their fiduciary character they are accountable to the company; or directors may be guilty of some negligence or misfeasance for which they are answerable to the company in damages. In these cases a summary remedy by misfeasance proceedings is provided by section 333.[78]

Definition of "misfeasance"

85–89 Section 333 of the 1948 Act is a procedural section; it does not create a new or distinct wrong. Evershed M.R. said in *Re B. Johnson & Co. (Builders) Ltd.*[79]:

> "I repeat that the section is a procedural section. There is no such distinct wrongful act known to the law as 'misfeasance.' The acts which are covered by the section are acts which are wrongful, according to the established rules of law or equity, done by the person charged in his capacity as 'promoter, director,' etc. But it is clearly established that it is not every kind of wrongful act so done that is comprehended by the section. At one end of the scale it may, I think, be taken as prima facie clear that a wrongful act involving misapplication of property in the hands of the persons charged would be covered by its terms. At the other end of the scale, a claim based exclusively on common law negligence, an ordinary claim for damages simply, would not be covered by the section. Nor is such a claim brought within the section by the mere expedient of adding epithets to the negligence charged, calling it 'gross' or 'deliberate.' Nor, by the same expedient, without more, can what in truth is mere negligence be converted into something else, namely breach of trust. But in between the two extremes that I have mentioned there is obviously a large range of conduct which may (or may not) be within the section."

It is respectfully doubted whether this statement, in its generality, can be regarded as correct. It is undoubtedly correct that, as Lord Evershed observed, section 333 is merely a procedural section and does not establish a new tort but the statement that no misfeasance proceedings lie in any circumstances in the case of negligence is thought to be too wide. In some instances negligence may constitute breach of a fiduciary duty owed by the misfeasor, *e.g.* by a director, and these cases should be treated analogously to a breach of trust.

The procedure under this section is not applicable to every claim which the company may have against any of its officers. It is limited to claims in the nature of misfeasance or breach of trust in the performance of their duties.[80] "Misfeasance" for this purpose does not necessarily involve moral turpitude but comprehends any breach of duty by an officer of the company which involves a misapplication or wrongful retention of the company's monies.[81]

---

[78] See para. 64–29, *ante*.
[79] [1955] Ch. 634, 648.
[80] *Re Etic Ltd.* [1928] Ch. 861.
[81] *Selangor United Rubber Estates Ltd.* v. *Cradock* [1967] 1 W.L.R. 1168, 1173, 1174, *per* Goff J.; and see paras. 64–29 and 64–30, *ante*.

Illustrations of misfeasance

85–90 It is the duty of the liquidator—as part of his general duty of collecting the assets of the company—to proceed under this section against delinquent directors and others when he sees good ground for doing so. The following have been held to be examples of misfeasance under section 333:

(1) the making of a secret profit by a promoter[82] or director[83];
(2) the making of improper payments by directors to a promoter[84];
(3) the application by directors of the company's assets for an *ultra vires*[85] or illegal[86] object;
(4) the payment of dividends out of capital[87];
(5) the making of a payment which is a fraudulent preference[88];
(6) the sale of the company's assets at undervalue[89];
(7) in certain circumstances the sale by promoters[90] or directors of their own property to the company.

In *Reliance Wholesale (Toys, Fancy Goods and Sports) Ltd., Patterson* v. *Mills*,[91] the company owed a director £7,500 on terms that he should be repaid as soon as the company could afford it. The director found at the company office a number of cheques signed in blank by a co-director. He filled one of them in to himself in the sum of £5,500, the sum still owing to him, and countersigned it. In a subsequent telephone conversation the co-director told him not to cash the cheque but he paid the cheque into his account and was paid. Later the company went into voluntary liquidation. On a liquidator's summons under section 333, the judge found that the director was guilty of misfeasance and ordered him to repay the money. The Court of Appeal affirmed this judgment. There was no intention on the part of the company to repay the debt as the co-director had objected. The director would not have been successful on a counterclaim as the company could not afford repayment. Further, a set-off by a director who was in breach of section 333 could not be admitted.

A receiver and manager appointed by debenture holders is not an officer within the section[92]; nor are the company's bankers[93]; nor prima facie is

---

[82] *Gluckstein* v. *Barnes* [1900] A.C. 240 (H.L.).
[83] *Re J. Franklin & Son Ltd.* (1937) 157 L.T. 188.
[84] *Ex p. Pelly* (1882) 21 Ch.D. 492 (C.A.).
[85] *Cullerne* v. *London and Suburban Building Society* (1890) 25 Q.B.D. 485; *Re Liverpool Household Stores* (1890) 59 L.J.Ch. 616; *Joint Stock Discount Co.* v. *Brown* (1869) L.R. 8 Eq. 376; *Hardy* v. *Metropolitan Land Co.* (1872) 7 Ch.App. 427; *Coats* v. *Crossland* (1904) 20 T.L.R. 800.
[86] *Re Faure Electric Accumulator Co.* (1889) 40 Ch.D. 141.
[87] *Re National Funds Assurance Co.* (1872) 10 Ch.D. 118; *Flitcroft's Case* (1882) 21 Ch.D. 519; *Re Sharpe* [1892] 1 Ch. 154; *Moxham* v. *Grant* [1900] 1 Q.B. 88.
[88] *Re Washington Diamond Mining Co.* [1893] 3 Ch. 95 (C.A.).
[89] *Re Travellers' Chambers (Ltd.)* (1895) 12 T.L.R. 529.
[90] *Gluckstein* v. *Barnes* [1900] A.C. 240 (H.L.); *Re Cape Breton Co.* (1885) 29 Ch.D. 795 (C.A.).
[91] (1979) 76 L.S. Gaz. 731 (C.A.).
[92] *Re B. Johnson & Co. (Builders) Ltd.* [1955] Ch. 634.
[93] *Re Imperial Land Co. of Marseilles* (1870) L.R. 10 Eq. 298.

the company's solicitor,[94] but he may be when he does all the work for a fixed salary.[95]

An auditor, if an "officer" of the company, may be proceeded against under this section.[96] But an accountant who is merely called in—*pro hac vice*—to audit the accounts of the company is not an "officer."[97] No set-off is allowed on a proceeding under the section. An order for payment of money under the misfeasance section constitutes a "final judgment" within the meaning of the Bankruptcy Act 1914, s. 1 (1) (*g*), and will found bankruptcy proceedings (by way of bankruptcy notice) against the delinquent director or officer (s. 333 (3)). An order for security for costs will not as a rule be made.[98]

Procedure (Rules 68 et seq.)

85–91 The procedure under section 333 in the High Court is by summons in the winding up, under which an application must now be made to the Registrar for directions as to points of claim and defence, discovery, etc.[99] When ready, the summons is set down in the witness list before the judge of the Companies Court.[1] In any other court the application is by motion. The courts generally prefer the evidence to be given orally in respect of matters in dispute.

In proceedings under a misfeasance summons, the court has power to admit a claim for an indemnity by one respondent to the summons against another,[2] but third party procedure may not be used to bring in a person who is not himself a respondent to the summons.[3]

Dissolution of the company abates misfeasance proceedings; and they are not revived if the dissolution is declared void by virtue of section 352 (1).[4]

Deceased director

85–92 It has been held that misfeasance proceedings under section 333 will not lie against the personal representatives of a deceased director,[5] and that the estate of a deceased director was not liable for his tort, except to the extent that he had appropriated funds or property of the company and his estate had benefited.[6] But by the Law Reform (Miscellaneous Provisions)

---

94 *Re Great Western (Forest of Dean), etc., Co.* (1886) 31 Ch.D. 496.
95 *Re Liberator Building Society* (1894) 71 L.T. 406.
96 *Re Kingston Cotton Mills Co. (No. 2)* [1896] 2 Ch. 279; *Re London and General Bank* [1895] 2 Ch. 166.
97 *Re Western Counties Steam Bakeries* [1897] 1 Ch. 617; and see *R.* v. *Shacter* [1960] 2 Q.B. 252.
98 *Re Strand Wood Co.* [1904] 2 Ch. 1.
99 Winding-up Rules 1949, r. 68. Evidence may be directed to be given on affidavit alone: *Re G. R. Scott & Co. Ltd.* [1948] W.N. 323.
1 Practice Notes [1921] W.N. 356; [1922] W.N. 294.
2 *Re Morecambe Bowling Ltd.* [1969] 1 W.L.R. 133.
3 *Re A. Singer & Co. (Hat Manufacturers) Ltd.* [1943] Ch. 121 (C.A.).
4 *Re Lewis & Smart Ltd.* [1954] 1 W.L.R. 755.
5 *Re British Guardian Assurance Co.* (1880) 14 Ch.D. 335.
6 *Peek* v. *Gurney* (1873) L.R. 6 H.L. 377, 392, 393.

Act 1934, s. 1, on the death of any person all causes of action subsisting against him survive against his estate. This provision would appear to increase the liability of the estate of the deceased director, but it does not, it is submitted, make the procedure under section 333 apply to a deceased director.

Private examinations before the Registrar

85–93 For the purposes of misfeasance proceedings and to ascertain what assets are outstanding, the court may, at the instance of the liquidator under section 268, summon before it any officer of the company or person known or suspected to have in his possession any of the property of the company, or supposed to be indebted to the company, or any person whom the court may deem capable of giving information concerning the promotion, formation, trade, dealings, affairs, or property of the company. This power can be exercised after the appointment of a provisional liquidator or the making of a winding-up order (s. 268), or, in case of a voluntary winding up, on an application under section 307. The application may be made by the liquidator *ex parte* and without affidavit. The jurisdiction of the court to make the order is discretionary[7] and the court will not make the order if it would be oppressive.[8] A person against whom an order is made has only a limited right of appeal. The Court of Appeal will only interfere if the application is oppressive[9] or the making of the order amounts to a serious miscarriage of justice.[10] The court is reluctant to make an order on the application of a creditor or contributory[11] and sometimes refuses to authorise the creditors and contributories to be present or take part in the examination. The official receiver may always attend and take notes (r. 74 (1)). The notes are not available for inspection unless the court so orders (r. 74 (2)).

Since the purpose of section 268 is to enable the court to help the liquidator in the performance of his duties, the court has jurisdiction under the section to order access to all the transcripts of evidence given before inspectors appointed by the Department of Trade and to the documents referred to in that evidence.[12] The Registrar should make it clear whether the order is for the issue of summonses for examination alone or whether there is also a requirement to produce documents.[13]

An order should not be made against a director for production of the company's books, at any rate until after the examination has been held.[14]

---

[7] *Re Joseph Hargreaves Ltd.* [1900] 1 Ch. 347.
[8] *Re Maville Hose* [1939] Ch. 32.
[9] *Heiron's Case* (1880) 15 Ch.D. 139 (C.A.).
[10] *Re Jos. Hargreaves Ltd.* [1900] 1 Ch. 347 (C.A.) *cf. Re Gold Co.* (1879) 12 Ch.D. 77 (C.A.).
[11] *Re Imperial Continental Water Corp.* (1886) 33 Ch.D. 314 (C.A.).
[12] *Re Rolls Razor Ltd.* [1968] 3 A11 E.R. 698.
[13] *Re Rolls Razor Ltd. (No. 2)* [1970] Ch. 576.
[14] *Re Maville Hose* [1939] Ch. 32.

The pendency of an action by the company against an examinee or third party may be a ground for postponing the examination.[15] An examination under section 268 will not be ordered if its real purpose is to enable the company to gain an advantage over and above the ordinary advantages available to parties in pending litigation.[16]

Any person against whom such an order is made may apply to a High Court judge by motion to modify or discharge the order[17]; on such an application the judge has an unfettered discretion in dealing with the matter. He should attach great weight to the views of the liquidator, but should ensure that the section is not used in an oppressive, vexatious or unfair manner.[17]

The fact that questions might be put to the person to be examined, which he could refuse to answer on the ground that his answers might tend to incriminate him, is not a ground for refusing an order.[18]

85–94 The examination is held before the Registrar of the Companies Court or an examiner of the court. It is a strictly private proceeding, and, if a witness is attended by his solicitor, the Registrar or examiner may, as a condition of the solicitor being present, exact an undertaking from him not to use the information acquired for any other purpose than re-examination.[19] Each deponent is, as a rule, entitled to see his own depositions for the purpose of interrogatories, but a special case must be made.[20] The court has an absolute discretion as to whether written interrogatories should be submitted to the examinees before the examination.[21] An examinee cannot refuse to answer any question unless it involves a question of privilege or is incriminating. He must give all the information he is capable of giving.[22] Evidence may be taken down in writing, in which case the court may require it to be signed by the examinee; but he is entitled to read the transcript at his leisure before signing it and correct errors, and sign subject to those corrections.[23] He must attend, even though he has not got the documents specified.[24] The examination may be ordered to be made in open court, but this should not be done except in very exceptional circumstances.[25]

Evidence on examination can be used against the deponent,[26] *e.g.* on cross-examination of the deponent to contradict him, but depositions given

---

[15] *Re London and Northern Bank, ex p. Archer* (1901) 85 L.T. 698; *Re North Australian Territory Co.* (1890) 45 Ch.D. 87.

[16] *Re Bletchley Boat Co. Ltd.* [1974] 1 W.L.R. 630.

[17] *Re Rolls Razor Ltd. (No. 2)*, *supra*; *Re Bletchley Boat Co. Ltd.*, *supra*, where Brightman J. expounded the principles upon which the court should act. See also *Re Castle New Homes Ltd.* [1979] 1 W.L.R. 1075; *Re Spiraflite Ltd.* [1979] 1 W.L.R. 1096.

[18] *Re Repetition Engineering Service Ltd.* (1945) 173 L.T. 75.

[19] *Re London and Northern Bank, Haddock's Case* [1902] 2 Ch. 73.

[20] *Re Merchants' Fire Office* [1899] 1 Ch. 432.

[21] *Re Rolls Razor Ltd. (No. 2)*, *supra*.

[22] *Re Ottoman Co.* [1867] W.N. 164.

[23] *Re Milton Hindle Ltd.* [1963] 1 W.L.R. 1032.

[24] *Re Leitner Electrical Co.* (1916) 32 T.L.R. 474.

[25] *Re Property Insurance Co.* [1914] 1 Ch. 775.

[26] *Re Hercules Insurance Co.* (1872) L.R. 13 Eq. 566; *Ex p. Hall* (1882) 19 Ch.D. 580, 583.

by others cannot be used for this purpose.[27] Notice of intention to read the depositions should be given, but copies should not be served.[27a]

Public examination of directors and others

85–95 In addition to the *report* of the official receiver[28] summarising the statement of affairs and commenting on the history of the company, the official receiver may present a *further report* stating the manner in which the company was formed and whether, in his opinion, any fraud has been committed by any person in the promotion or formation of the company, or by any director or other officer of the company in relation to the company; and the court may, after consideration of any such report, direct the persons implicated, or the directors, to attend before the court and be publicly examined on oath (1948 Act, s. 270). The further report of the official receiver must disclose at least a prima facie case of fraud, but, where several persons are to be examined, it is not necessary to attribute to each of them some particular aspect of the alleged fraud.[29] The order for a public examination is made *ex parte* on the application of the official receiver.[30] A person summoned may move to discharge the order on the grounds that; (1) he is not within the scope of section 270 (1), or (2) that fraud has not been alleged against him.[31] The time for applying to discharge an order for public examination is 14 days from the service of the orders.[32] Under section 270 (9) (as amended by section 56 (4) and Schedule 11, Part IV of the Courts Act 1971) public examinations may be held before a wide range of judges or officers of the court. In practice in the High Court the public examination is heard before the Registrar and in the county courts before a circuit judge.

Section 270 (2) allows the official receiver to take part and where authorised by the Department of Trade, to employ a solicitor and counsel. Section 270 (3) allows the liquidator and any creditor or contributory to take part either personally or by solicitor or counsel. Section 270 (4) empowers the court to put questions to the person being examined. Under section 270 (5) the person examined is examined on oath and must answer all questions that the court puts to him or allows to be put to him. Section 270 (6) provides that the person to be examined may request (at his own cost) a copy of the official receiver's report and may employ a solicitor with or without counsel who may re-examine him to explain or qualify any of his answers. He may also apply to be exculpated from the charges against him in which case the official receiver must attend and call the court's attention to relevant matters. The control of the court over questions to be put at a

---

[27] *North Australian, etc., Co.* v. *Goldsborough Mort & Co.* [1893] 2 Ch. 381.
[27a] *Ex p. Hall* (1882) 19 Ch.D. 580.
[28] See para. 85–31, *ante*.
[29] *Tejani* v. *Official Receiver* [1963] 1 W.L.R. 59, P.C.
[30] *Re Great Kruger Gold Mining Co.* [1892] 3 Ch. 307 (C.A.).
[31] *Re Civil, Naval & Military Outfitters Ltd.* [1899] 1 Ch. 215 (C.A.).
[32] *Re National Stores* [1899] 2 Ch. 773.

public examination was discussed in *Re London and Globe Finance Co.*[33] If a person fails to turn up a warrant may be issued against him (r. 66).

Answers given may be used in misfeasance proceedings against the person examined (s. 270 (7)) and anyone who was present or entitled to be present at and take part in the public examination (see further r. 71).

A liquidator will not be ordered personally to pay the costs of a director-examinee who has exculpated himself, unless the liquidator has accepted the position of a litigant[34]; but the court may order the person procuring the examination to pay the witnesses their costs.[35]

As to the court's powers of examination in Scotland, see section 269. As to the court's powers to disqualify directors see section 188 of the 1948 Act, section 28 of the 1976 Act, section 9 of the Insolvency Act 1976 and section 93 of the Companies Act 1981 discussed at paragraph 61–17, *ante*. See also Winding-up Rules 68 *et seq.*

Prosecution of directors and promoters

85–96 The court has power to direct a prosecution of delinquent directors, managers, officers, or members of the company, and in a proper case will do so.[36] The court also has power to direct the liquidator to prosecute (s. 334). For statutory offences under the Companies Acts see sections 328 *et seq.* of the 1948 Act.

Order of distribution

85–97 The liquidator must distribute, the monies available in the following order:

(1) the costs of the liquidation, including his remuneration[37];
(2) preferred debts;
(3) secured debts under a floating charge only;
(4) ordinary debts;
(5) deferred debts (*i.e.* debts under s. 212 (*g*));
(6) the balance (if any) amongst the contributories.

As regards the costs of an insolvent winding up the court may make an order as to the payment out of the assets of the costs, charges and expenses incurred in the winding up in such order of priority as it thinks just. Assets for this purpose include assets subject to a floating charge.[38] Otherwise, payments in respect of costs and expenses are to be made in the following order of priority[39]:

(1) fees and expenses properly incurred in serving, realising, or getting

[33] (1902) 50 W.R. 253.
[34] *Re Tweddle & Co.* [1910] 2 K.B. 697.
[35] *Re Appleton, French and Scrafton Ltd.* [1905] 1 Ch. 749.
[36] *Re London and Globe Finance Corporation* [1903] 1 Ch. 728.
[37] s. 267.
[38] *Re Barleycorn Enterprises Ltd.* [1970] Ch.465 (C.A.). See also *Re Christonette International Ltd.* (1982) 126 S.J. 561.
[39] Winding-up Rule 195.

in the assets[40] including where the company was already in voluntary liquidation such remuneration, costs and expenses as the court may allow the liquidator in the voluntary winding up[41];

(2) taxed costs of the winding-up petition[42] including the taxed costs of any person appearing on the petition whose costs have been allowed by the court;
(3) remuneration of any special manager;
(4) costs in connection with the statement of affairs[43];
(5) taxed costs of a shorthand writer for any examination[44];
(6) necessary disbursements of the liquidator other than (1);
(7) costs of any person properly employed by the liquidator;
(8) the remuneration of the liquidator;
(9) actual out of pocket expenses of the committee of inspection subject to the approval of the Department of Trade.[45]

The court may vary the order of priority of payment of the liquidation costs but will only do so in exceptional circumstances.[46]

Rule 195 (2) of the 1949 Rules enables certain payments to be made before taxation. These now include payments on account of costs of solicitors.[46a]

Release of liquidator

85–98 This is provided for in section 251, and Winding-up Rule 205.[47]

Unclaimed or undistributed assets

85–99 If such assets are undistributed for more than six months, they have to be paid into the Bank of England to the Insolvency Services Account. The liquidator is bound to furnish accounts to the Department of Trade, and there are stringent provisions for enforcing payment (s. 343).[48] This likewise applies to unclaimed dividends or other money held in trust for shareholders.

As to the position in Scotland, see section 344 of the 1948 Act.

---

40 *Webb* v. *Whiffin* (1872) L.R. 5 H.L. 711, 735 (H.L.). Corporation tax is not such an expense (*Re Beni-Felkai Mining Co. Ltd.* [1934] Ch. 406; *Re Mesco Properties Ltd.* [1979] S.T.C. 778). It is, however, a "necessary disbursement" within r. 195 (1) and an expense "incurred in the winding up" within s. 267.
41 *Re Mortimers (London) Ltd.* [1937] Ch. 289.
42 *Re Bright* [1903] 1 K.B. 735 (a bankruptcy case).
43 s. 235 (4).
44 Winding-up Rule 72.
45 *Ibid.* r. 195.
46 *Re London Metallurgical Co.* [1895] 1 Ch. 758.
46a See the new Rule 195 (2) substituted by the Companies (Winding-Up) (Amendment) Rules 1981 (S.I. 1981 No. 788) para. 2.
47 s. 242 provides for the resignation and removal of a liquidator in Scotland.
48 See *Company Precedents*, Part II, 16th ed., pp. 278 *et seq.*, and *Re Land Mortgage Bank of Florida* [1898] 1 Ch. 444.

Removal of liquidator

A liquidator may be removed by the court "on cause shown" (s. 242 (1)). A liquidator was removed where he insisted on acting in the interests of shareholders only, though there was no reasonable prospect of paying the debts in full.[49]

An order for removal was refused where the applicant had no support from other creditors.[50]

Remuneration of liquidator

The remuneration of the liquidator is fixed by the court (s. 242 (2) but see also Winding-up Rule 159).

Dissolution of the company

85–100 When the affairs of the company have been completely wound up, the court will, if the liquidator makes an application on that behalf, make an order that the company be dissolved from the date of such order, and the company is dissolved accordingly (1948 Act, s. 274 (1)). A copy of the order is to be sent by the liquidator to the Registrar of Companies within 14 days, and the Registrar is to make a minute of the order (s. 274 (2)). Official notification of the order for dissolution is required.[51]

Under the old practice, it was the usual course, when a winding up was completed, to make an order for dissolution and for the destruction of the books, but, in modern times, such orders are rarely made and it is more common, after the compulsory winding up is concluded, to dissolve the company as a defunct company under section 353 of the 1948 Act. Section 353 provides a procedure whereby the Registrar may strike a defunct company off the register at the expiration of three months from the publication of a notice to that effect in the *Gazette*. Under section 353 (2) (*a*) the company is dissolved.

Upon dissolution, all the property of the company vests in the Crown as *bona vacantia*, subject to the power of the Crown to disclaim (ss. 354, 355). This includes an equity of redemption to leasehold property.[52] The Crown may disclaim such property by notice signed by the Treasury Solicitor (s. 355).[53] Apart from disclaimer, where land subject to a rentcharge vests in the Crown by operation of law, no obligation is incurred by the Crown (s. 356).

The principle that unclaimed property vests in the Crown as *bona vacantia* does not affect property held by the company on trust, and, where a company which holds property in trust is dissolved, a vesting order may

---

[49] *Re Rubber and Produce Investment Trust* [1915] 1 Ch. 382.
[50] *Re Amalgamated Properties of Rhodesia Ltd.* (1914) 30 T.L.R. 405.
[51] European Communities Act 1972, s. 9 (3)(*g*),
[52] *Re Wells, Swinburne-Hanham* v. *Howard* [1933] Ch. 29.
[53] For the procedure and other details, see s. 355, Vol. II, Pt. A.

be made.[54] Where the property has become vested in the Crown, the latter continues to hold the property in trust, so that a vesting order can still be made.[55]

Where property has vested in the Crown as *bona vacantia* the person in whom the property is currently vested may dispose of it or an interest in it notwithstanding that an order may be made under section 352 (1) or 353 (6) reviving the dissolved company. Any such order shall not affect such disposition but the Crown shall pay to the company an amount equal to the consideration received or if there was no consideration, equal to the value of the property (1981 Act, s. 108 (1)). The section applies to dispositions on or after the appointed day.

Dissolution declared void

85–101 The dissolution may within two years be declared to have been void (s. 352) on application being made for the purpose by the liquidator or by any other person who appears to the court to be interested. Notice of the application must be given to the Attorney-General through the Treasury Solicitor and no objection must have been taken on behalf of the Crown.[56] In a simple case not requiring any argument on behalf of the Crown it is sufficient for the Attorney-General to show his consent in a letter exhibited to the applicant's evidence.[57] Property which has vested in the Crown as *bona vacantia* on dissolution re-vests or remains vested in the company if the order is made.[58] The purpose of this provision is to make possible the distribution of assets which belonged to the company before the dissolution and were, for some reason, overlooked; accordingly the court refused to make a declaration in favour of the company in order to secure the benefit of a legacy which had never belonged to the company.[59]

An order may be made after the expiration of two years, if the application is made within two years.[60]

An order of the court declaring the dissolution to have been void does not render valid proceedings taken against the company after its dissolution and before the date of the order,[61] nor does it revive a misfeasance summons issued—but not served—on a promoter of the company before its dissolution.[62] A cause of action which is left incomplete or not assigned before dissolution is not held in abeyance. It dies absolutely at the date of

---

[54] *Re General Accident Corpn.* [1904] 1 Ch. 147; *Re Richard Mills & Co., Smith* v. *The Co.* [1905] W.N. 36; *Re No. 9 Bomore Road* [1906] 1 Ch. 359; *Re Dutton's Patent* [1923] W.N. 64.

[55] *Re Strathblaine Estates Ltd.* [1948] Ch. 228.

[56] Practice Notes [1928] W.N. 218 and [1931] W.N. 199.

[57] *Re Belmont & Co. Ltd.* [1952] Ch. 10.

[58] *Re C. W. Dixon Ltd.* [1947] Ch. 251; *Re Henderson's Nigel Ltd.* [1911] W.N. 159 (undistributed assets, the Crown not claiming them as *bona vacantia*).

[59] *Re Servers of the Blind League* [1960] 1 W.L.R. 564.

[60] *Re Scad Ltd.* [1941] Ch. 386.

[61] *Morris* v. *Harris* [1927] A.C. 252.

[62] *Re Lewis & Smart Ltd.* [1954] 1 W.L.R. 755.

the winding up and cannot survive to become effective again by order under section 352.[63]

A company, some of whose shares were held by the dissolved company, was held to be "a person interested" under section 352 (1) for the purpose of enforcing a call on the shares.[64]

A person who, without being appointed liquidator, acts as if he had been a liquidator, is a "person interested" because he might have a claim to a *quantum meruit* for his services or might be liable to the Crown for intermeddling, albeit innocently, with property vested in the Crown as *bona vacantia*.[65] On the other hand, a solicitor, acting on behalf of a client who would be a "person interested" under section 352 (1), is not himself a "person interested" under that section.[66]

Relief will not be automatically granted under section 352 (1). Circumstances can arise, for example where the application is opposed on reasonable grounds by the Official Receiver, Treasury Solicitor or other persons, where the court may feel bound, notwithstanding that the petitioner brings himself within section 352 (1) to refuse to exercise its discretion to declare the dissolution void. Relief should be sought as soon as reasonably practicable where a winding-up order has been made in respect of a dissolved company. In such a case the Official Receiver may have *locus standi* but in all but the most exceptional cases the primary responsibility for making the application falls on the petitioner.[66a]

85–102 The jurisdiction of the court under section 352 (1) to declare void a dissolution is unaffected by section 353, and, in particular, by section 353 (6), which empowers the company or a member or creditor to apply within 20 years for the restoration of the company's name to the register. The former procedure is by motion, the latter by petition.[67] The latter procedure is only available where the company was dissolved as a defunct company under section 353, but the former procedure is available both in the case of section 353 and in other circumstances. Usually the procedure under section 352 (1) will be preferred to that under section 353 (6) because its conditions are less stringent.[68] This statement was, however, criticised by Megarry J. in *Re Test Holdings (Clifton) Ltd.*[69] as a "backdoor" method which, if encouraged by the textbooks, "might engender an undesirable traffic." With respect, it is difficult to see why a person should not make use of a procedure expressly authorised by statute, so long as the

---

[63] *Foster Yates & Thom Ltd.* v. *H. W. Edgehill Equipment Ltd., The Times*, November 30, 1978 (C.A.).

[64] *Re Spottiswoode, Dixon and Hunting Ltd.* [1912] 1 Ch. 410.

[65] *Re Wood and Martin (Bricklaying Contractors) Ltd.* [1971] 1 W.L.R. 293.

[66] *Re Roehampton Swimming Pools Ltd.* [1968] 1 W.L.R. 1693.

[66a] *Re Thompson & Riches Ltd.* [1981] 2 All E.R. 477, 483e–j, 483j–484a.

[67] As regards the form of the petition, see Practice Note [1974] 1 W.L.R. 1459. See further R.S.C., Ord. 102. As to service of a petition, see *Re Vickers & Bott Ltd.* [1968] 2 A11 E.R. 264n.

[68] *Re M. Belmont & Co. Ltd.* [1952] Ch. 10, followed in *Re Test Holdings (Clifton) Ltd.* [1970] Ch. 285.

[69] [1970] Ch. 285, 292.

requirements of the statute are properly complied with. In *Re Wood and Martin (Bricklaying) Ltd.*[70] Megarry J. allowed an originating motion under section 352 to proceed, observing that "if Parliament has given him a choice, he is entitled to avail himself of that choice."

If an application is made under section 352 (1) in respect of a company not in liquidation, the Registrar of Companies should be made a respondent, and he will normally be entitled to his costs against the applicant.[71] This will not normally be necessary where the company concerned is already in liquidation.[71a]

A petition under section 353 must indicate the grounds upon which the name of the company was struck off and the reasons for such grounds. It should also explain the failure to reply to the letters from the Registrar of Companies.[72]

A person who acquires shares in, or takes an assignment of a debt of a company after the date of dissolution is not a "member or creditor" within the meaning of section 353 (6).[73] A person making a claim sounding in damages, and not for a liquidated debt, is a "creditor" for the purposes of section 353 (6), as this section is wide enough to include contingent or prospective creditors.[74] "Member" for the purposes of the section includes the personal representative of a deceased member.[75]

It was held in *Re Cambridge Coffee Room Association*[76] that where a company has been dissolved as defunct under section 353 (5) and, later, property of the company is found which makes it desirable to wind up the company, the prayer of the petition under section 353 (6) should not merely ask for a compulsory winding up of the company but should first ask for the name of the company to be restored to the register and then for a winding-up order, because section 353 does not give the court power to wind up the company and a mere winding-up order would not exclude the operation of section 354; a restoration to the register, on the other hand, would mean that the property of the company never vested in the Crown as *bona vacantia* and that no order for re-vesting is necessary.[77] Where the dissolved company is in liquidation but the order has not been perfected the common practice is to seek (1) to rescind the existing winding-up order (2) to amend the winding-up petition to include an application to restore the name of the company to the register (3) an order for restoration and (4) a new winding-up order. It is, however, possible to apply in the alternative under section 352 (1) for an order declaring the dissolution to be void after the winding-up order has been perfected.[77a]

[70] [1971] 1 W.L.R. 293, 298.
[71] *Re Test Holdings (Clifton) Ltd., supra.*
[71a] *Re Thompson & Riches Ltd.* [1981] 2 All E.R. 477, 483a.
[72] Practice Note [1974] 1 W.L.R. 1459.
[73] *Re New Timbiqui Gold Mines Ltd.* [1961] Ch. 319.
[74] *Re Harvest Lane Motor Bodies Ltd.* [1969] 1 Ch. 457.
[75] *Re Ryls (Walton) Engineering Co.* (1954) (unreported); *Re Bayswater Trading Co. Ltd.* [1970] 1 W.L.R. 343.
[76] [1952] 1 A11 E.R. 112.
[77] *Re C. W. Dixon Ltd.* [1947] Ch. 251.
[77a] *Re Thompson & Riches Ltd.* [1981] 2 All E.R. 477, 481h–j.

85–103 The court has a wide power when making an order under section 352 (1) or 353 (6) to attach such directions to the order as it thinks fit. Thus, where a solvent company, unaware that its name had been removed from the register, purported to create a charge over its assets, the court, in the order restoring its name to the register, directed that the company should be put retrospectively in the same position as if the legal charge had been duly created and the particulars duly delivered for registration.[78]

Section 353 (6) does not, however, authorise the insertion of a clause intended to preserve the remedies which a creditor, who became such after the date of dissolution, would have had against other persons if the company had remained struck off, as this would be to defeat the purpose of the section.[79] The court may, however, make an order that, in the case of creditors not statute-barred at the date of the company's dissolution, the period between that date and the date of the restoration should not be counted for the purpose of any statute of limitation; but it appears that this will only be done where such an order is necessary for the protection of the petitioning creditor, or, possibly, where other creditors might otherwise be unfairly affected.[80]

The court, when making a restoration order under section 353 (6), has no jurisdiction to impose a penalty for the company's default.[81] But on the restoration to the register by virtue of section 353 (6) the court may order the costs to be taxed on a common fund basis (and not a party-to-party basis) if the dissolution of the company was due to breach of statutory obligations and at least one applicant was guilty of some default.[82]

---

[78] *Re Boxco Ltd.* [1970] Ch. 442. See also *Tymans Ltd.* v. *Craven* [1952] 2 Q.B. 101 (C.A.); *Re Donald Kenyon Ltd.* [1956] 1 W.L.R. 1397; *Re Vickers & Bott Ltd.* [1968] 2 All E.R. 264; *Re Huntingdon Poultry Ltd.* [1969] 1 W.L.R. 204; *Re Regent Insulation Co. Ltd.*, *The Times*, November 5, 1981. See also Limitation Act 1980, s. 33 in relation to the court's discretion regarding actions for personal injuries or death.

[79] *Re Lindsay Bowman Ltd.* [1969] 1 W.L.R. 1443, not following *Re Rugby Auto Electric Services Ltd.* (No. 00973 of 1959), December 14, 1959, unreported.

[80] *Re Huntingdon Poultry Ltd.* [1969] 1 W.L.R. 204; distinguishing *Re Donald Kenyon Ltd.* [1956] 1 W.L.R. 1397 and *Re Rugby Auto Electric Services Ltd.*, *supra.*

[81] *Re Brown Bayley's Steel Works Ltd.* (1905) 21 T.L.R. 374; *Re Moses and Cohen Ltd.* [1957] 1 W.L.R. 1007.

[82] *Re Court Lodge Development Co. Ltd.* [1973] 1 W.L.R. 1097.

CHAPTER 86

VOLUNTARY WINDING UP

86–01 OF companies which come to be wound up, by far the larger number are wound up voluntarily; this is in accordance with the intention of the legislature, which contemplates voluntary winding up as the normal mode of liquidation. Unregistered companies cannot wind up voluntarily under the Acts, but they may register under Part VIII of the 1948 Act,[1] and then wind up voluntarily.

Proceedings in a voluntary winding up are not entirely a matter of arrangement by the members of the company, but in certain respects are subject to statutory and official regulations.

The resolution for voluntary winding up

86–02 Voluntary winding up is initiated by a resolution of the shareholders (1948 Act, s. 278). This may be:

(1) a special resolution, as defined by section 141 of the 1948 Act, resolving that the company be wound up voluntarily; or

(2) an extraordinary resolution to the effect that it has been proved to the satisfaction of the shareholders that the company cannot, by reason of its liabilities, continue its business, and that it is advisable to wind up the same; or

(3) an ordinary resolution if the company is restricted in time. This is a case which does not happen frequently in practice.

Of the first two the extraordinary resolution is the more convenient as being quicker, where the company is insolvent and being pressed by creditors; but it is inapplicable where the company desires to wind up for reasons other than inability to carry on its business by reason of its liabilities, *e.g.* with a view to reconstruction; hence, in these cases a special resolution must be resorted to. Proper notices must be given, otherwise the resolution will not be valid. As to what constitutes proper notice of meeting, see Chapter 54, *ante*. Thus a resolution for voluntary winding up is not valid if passed at an extraordinary general meeting convened by the secretary on his own initiative without the authority of the board of directors.[2] However, a defect in the notice or a lack of a quorum at the meeting does not render the resolution for voluntary winding up invalid if the resolution is approved by all the shareholders or if the shareholders have acquiesced in it or if, by virtue of the equitable doctrine of laches it is practically unjust

---

[1] *Southall* v. *British Mutual Life Assurance Society* (1871) L.R 6 Ch. 614.

[2] *Re Haycraft Gold Reduction, etc., Co.* [1900] 2 Ch. 230; *Re State of Wyoming Syndicate* [1901] 2 Ch. 431.

to give relief for the defect.[3] In the case of a creditors' voluntary winding up, notwithstanding any power to exclude or waive the period of notice required, at least 7 days' notice of the extraordinary general meeting must be given (1981 Act, s. 106 (1)). Failure to give such notice shall not affect the validity of any resolution passed or thing done at that meeting which would be valid apart from the subsection (s. 106 (2)). A copy of the resolution must be lodged with the Registrar of Companies within 15 days (1948 Act, s. 143 (1) (4)). The resolution must also be advertised in the *London Gazette* within 14 days; there are penalties on the company and every officer of the company who is in default. For the purposes of section 279 the liquidator is deemed to be an officer of the company.

A resolution to wind up voluntarily is not necessarily invalid because it is followed by other resolutions which are *ultra vires*.[4]

Commencement of voluntary winding up

86–03 A voluntary winding up is deemed to commence at the time of the resolution for voluntary winding up (1948 Act, s. 280). After the commencement the company must cease to carry on its business, except so far as may be required for the beneficial winding up thereof, but the corporate status and corporate powers continue until dissolution (1948 Act, s. 281). A liquidator must be appointed, and with his appointment the directors' powers cease.[5] He can be appointed as soon as the resolution for winding up has been passed, even without notice.[6] Any transfer of shares unless made to or sanctioned by the liquidator and any alteration in the status of the members made after the commencement of the winding up are void (1948 Act, s. 282).

Meeting of creditors

86–04 No such meeting need be held if the winding up is contemplated as a *members' voluntary winding up*; this, as will be seen presently, is only possible if the company is thought to be solvent and a declaration of solvency can be filed accordingly.

In a *creditors' voluntary winding up* such a meeting has to be called for the day or the day next following the day on which the members' meeting at which the resolution for voluntary winding up is proposed. The notices must be sent out simultaneously with the notices of the general meeting (1948 Act, s. 293 (1) as substituted by the 1981 Act, s. 106 (1)).

Where the general meeting is adjourned but the creditors have passed a resolution at the first meeting, their resolution is deemed to be effective

---

[3] *Re Oxted Motor Co. Ltd.* [1921] 3 K.B. 32; *Re Bailey, Hay & Co. Ltd.* [1971] 1 W.L.R. 1357; *Re M. J. Shanley Contracting Ltd.* [1980] 124 S.J. 239.
[4] *Thomson* v. *Henderson's Transvaal Estates* [1908] 1 Ch. 765.
[5] 1948 Act, ss. 285 and 294.
[6] *Bethell* v. *Trench Tubeless Tyre Co.* [1900] 1 Ch. 408.

only after the adjourned meeting of the members which passed the resolution for voluntary winding up (1948 Act, s. 293 (5)).

The 1948 Act contains provisions for advertising the creditors' meeting and for penalties in default (s. 293 (2) and (6)).

Declaration of solvency

86–05 In the case of a solvent company, by section 283 of the 1948 Act, a majority of the directors may make and file a statutory declaration to the effect that they have made a full inquiry into the affairs of the company, and having done so, have formed the opinion that the company will be able to pay its debts in full within a period not exceeding 12 months from the commencement of the winding up. Such a declaration has no effect unless it is made within five weeks preceding the resolution to wind up or on the same day but before the passing of that resolution[7] and must contain a statement of the company's assets and liabilities (s. 283 (2)). It must also be delivered to the Registrar of Companies before the expiration of 15 days immediately following the date on which the resolution to wind up was passed (s. 283 (2A)). The statement of the company's assets and liabilities which has to be embodied in the declaration of solvency is valid as long as it can reasonably and fairly be described as such a statement, even if it subsequently appears that there were errors or omissions in it.[8] Any director making a declaration without having reasonable grounds for the opinion that the company will be able to pay its debts in full within the time specified in the declaration is made liable to a fine or imprisonment or both; the burden of proof that he is innocent is on the director—a very unusual provision in our criminal law (s. 283 (3)). Failure to deliver the declaration within the time specified renders the company and every officer in default guilty of an offence and subject to a fine (s. 283 (4A)).

A declaration of solvency results in a members' voluntary winding up. It does not prevent a winding up by the court, but it may delay the proper protection of the rights of the creditors. By section 288 of the 1948 Act, if in a members' voluntary winding up the liquidator is of the opinion that the company will not be able to pay its debts in full within the period stated, he must summon a meeting of creditors and lay before the meeting a statement of the assets and liabilities of the company, and thereafter certain provisions relating to a creditors' voluntary winding up apply; in particular, meetings of creditors and further final meetings of both members and creditors have to be held (1948 Act, ss. 299 and 300, as declared to be applicable by s. 291).

Definition of members' and creditors' voluntary winding up

86–06 A voluntary winding up with respect to which a declaration of solvency has been made and filed in accordance with the provisions discussed above

---

[7] s. 283 (2) (*a*) as amended by s. 105 (1) of the Companies Act 1981.
[8] *De Courcy* v. *Clement* [1971] Ch. 693.

is known as a "members' voluntary winding up." Every other winding up is a "creditors' voluntary winding up" (s. 283 (4)).

It follows that the test is not whether the company is solvent or not but whether the declaration of solvency has been made before the general meeting passing the resolution for winding up. If this has been overlooked such a declaration cannot be made after that general meeting; in such a case the voluntary winding up will technically be a creditors' voluntary winding up though the company may be solvent. There are now special provisions dealing with the consequences of the strike at the Companies Registry (1981 Act, s. 107). These require a further statutory declaration referring to the posting of the earlier statutory declaration. In such a case the winding up shall be treated as if it had been a members' voluntary winding up.

Members' voluntary winding up

Appointment of liquidator

86–07 The company in general meeting appoints a liquidator and fixes his remuneration. On the appointment all the powers of the directors cease, except so far as the company in general meeting or the liquidator sanction their continuance (1948 Act, s. 285).

If a vacancy occurs, the company in general meeting may fill the vacancy. Any contributory can call the meeting (s. 286) but a single contributory cannot constitute a meeting for this purpose.[9]

Accounts

86–08 If the winding up continues for more than one year, the liquidator must summon a general meeting of the company at the end of the first year and each successive year and lay his accounts before the meeting (1948 Act, s. 289).

Dissolution of company

86–09 When the company's affairs are fully wound up, the liquidator must make up a final account and call a general meeting of the company, which must be advertised in the *Gazette*. Within a week after the meeting the liquidator must send the Registrar of Companies a copy of the accounts and make a return of the holding of the meeting. The Registrar registers the accounts and returns, and at the end of three months from the date of registration the company is dissolved (1948 Act, s. 290). The Registrar must cause a notice of the receipt by him of the return of the final meeting to be published in the *Gazette* (s. 9 (3) (*h*) of European Communities Act 1972). The court may, on the application of the liquidator or of any other person who appears to the court to be interested, make an order deferring the date at which dissolution is to take effect for such time as the court

[9] *Re London Flats Ltd.* [1969] 1 W.L.R. 711.

thinks fit (s. 290 (4)). If such an order is made the applicant must file a copy of the order with the Registrar of Companies (s. 290 (5)).

The requirement that the affairs of the company must be "fully wound up" before the liquidator makes up his final account is sufficiently complied with as soon as the affairs are fully wound up so far as the liquidator is aware, and the company is validly dissolved under section 290 notwithstanding that there are matters outstanding of which the liquidator is not aware at the time.[10]

In addition to the deemed dissolution under section 290 of the 1948 Act, the Registrar may take steps to strike the name of the company off the register under section 353 if the liquidation appears to have been neglected. Section 9 (3) (*g*) of the European Communities Act 1972 which requires publication of an order for dissolution in the *Gazette* would seem to be inapplicable to a deemed dissolution under section 290 and a dissolution under section 353 since in neither case is there an order.

Creditors' voluntary winding up

Meeting of creditors

86–10 In any case where the declaration of solvency has not been made, the company must call a meeting of the creditors for the same day as, or on the next day after, the meeting at which the resolution for voluntary winding up is to be proposed (as to the latter see para. 86–02, *ante*). The meeting must be advertised in the *Gazette* and in at least two local papers, and the directors must lay before the meeting of the creditors a statement of the position of the company with a list of its creditors. There are penalties in default (1948 Act, s. 293). A director must preside at the meeting (s. 293 (4)).

If the meeting of the company at which the resolution for voluntary winding up is to be proposed is adjourned and the resolution is then passed at the adjourned meeting, any resolution passed at the meeting of creditors has effect as if it had been passed immediately after the passing of the resolution for winding up the company (1948 Act, s. 293 (5)).

Rules 127 to 156 of the Winding-up Rules apply to the conduct of such meetings. See para. 85–32, *ante*.

Appointment of liquidator

86–11 The creditors and the company may each nominate a liquidator, but the nomination of the creditors will prevail, subject to an application to the court by any director, member or creditor (1948 Act, s. 294). Thus, in *Re Karamelli and Barnett Ltd.*,[11] a liquidator who was also receiver for the debenture holders was removed at the instance of the creditors. Where a liquidator is nominated by the members, but no meeting of creditors has

[10] *Re Cornish Manures Ltd.* [1967] 1 W.L.R. 807.
[11] [1917] 1 Ch. 203.

The Scottish Mutual Assurance Society

FOUNDED 1883

Notes

CENTENARY

been held, the liquidator has power to act unless and until the creditors bring his appointment to an end.[12]

Where the person nominated as liquidator received the support of a majority in value but not a majority in number of the creditors it has been held that the person nominated by the members was to prevail.[13]

If any vacancy occurs by death, resignation or otherwise, it can be filled by the creditors except that where the liquidator has been appointed by the court any vacancy must be filled by the court (1948 Act, s. 297). Any liquidator apppointed by the court should obtain his release by the court. The court has a general power under section 304 (1) to fill a vacancy. It has also power on cause shown to remove a liquidator and appoint another (s. 304 (2)).

The liquidator must, within 14 days of his appointment, publish in the *Gazette* and deliver to the Registrar of Companies notice of his appointment in the form prescribed by the Department of Trade (s. 305). The publication in the *Gazette* is treated as official notification.[14]

Committee of inspection

86–12 The creditors at their meeting may decide to have a committee of inspection and appoint not more than five persons to be members of the committee. The company may then appoint not more than five persons to be members of the committee, subject to the power of the creditors to disapprove of any persons so appointed (1948 Act, s. 295). If the creditors do disapprove of the persons so appointed the latter may not act unless the court orders otherwise. The court has power to appoint other persons to act in their stead (1949 Act, s. 295 (1)).

The powers of the committee of inspection are:

(1) to fix the renumeration of the liquidator or liquidators (1948 Act, s. 296 (1));
(2) to sanction continuance of the powers of directors (1948 Act, s. 296 (2));
(3) to sanction payment of any class of creditors in full or to make compromises with creditors or contributories in respect of calls (1948 Act, ss. 245 and 303);
(4) to sanction a reconstruction under ss. 287 and 298 of the 1948 Act;
(5) to determine which books should be kept by the liquidator and to require sight of them (r. 172) and to decide upon disposal of the company's books (1948 Act, s. 341);
(6) to make a certificate and request to the Department of Trade in connection with the investment of surplus funds (r. 173).

---

[12] *Re Centrebind Ltd.* [1967] 1 W.L.R. 377.
[13] *Re Caston Cushioning Ltd.* [1955] 1 All E.R. 508.
[14] See Chap. 17, *ante*.

Provisions applicable to every winding up

86–13 The following provisions of the 1948 Act are applicable to every kind of winding up:

s. 316 (proof of debts), s. 317 (application of the bankruptcy rules to insolvent companies), s. 319 (preferential creditors), ss. 320–321 (fraudulent preference), s. 322 (avoidance of certain floating charges), ss. 323–324 (disclaimer of onerous property), s. 325 (restrictions of the rights of execution creditors), s. 326 (duties of sheriff as to goods taken in execution), s. 328 (offences by officers), s. 329 (falsification of books), s. 330 (frauds by officers), s. 331 (no proper accounts), s. 332 (fraudulent trading), s. 333 (misfeasance summons), s. 334 (prosecution of delinquent officers and members), ss. 335–345 (supplementary provisions), ss. 346–351 (supplementary powers of the court), ss. 352–356 (dissolution provisions), ss. 357–359 (special provisions as to stannaries), ss. 360–362 (central accounts), ss. 363–364 (officers) and s. 365 (Rules and Fees).

The most important of these have been discussed in Chapter 85.

Dissolution of company

86–14 If the winding up continues for more than a year, the liquidator must summon a general meeting of the company and a meeting of the creditors at the end of the first year and of each successive year and lay before the meetings an account (1948 Act, s. 299).

When the affairs of the company are fully wound up, the liquidator must make up a final account and call a meeting of the company and the creditors, which must be advertised in the *Gazette*, and lay the account before the meetings. Within a week after the meetings, the liquidator must send to the Registrar a copy of the account and a return which will be registered, and on the expiration of three months from the registration the company is dissolved (1948 Act, s. 300). See also paragraph 86–09, *ante*.

Powers and duties of liquidators in voluntary winding up

86–15 The liquidator is, as has been seen,[15] appointed by the members or creditors. By virtue of section 303 of the 1948 Act a liquidator in a voluntary winding up has all the powers conferred on a liquidator in a compulsory winding up, on which see paragraph 85–35, *ante*. He may exercise any of the powers given by section 245 (1) (*d*) (*e*) and (*f*), in the case of a members' voluntary winding up with the sanction of an extraordinary resolution of the company and in the case of a creditors' voluntary winding up with the sanction of the court or the committee of inspection or (if there is no committee of inspection) a meeting of the creditors. He may exercise any of the other powers without sanction. In addition he may exercise the power of the court of settling a list of contributories (s. 303 (1)

[15] See paras. 86–07 and 86–11, *ante*.

(*c*)), making calls (s. 303 (1) (*d*)), and summoning general meetings of the company (s. 303 (1) (3)). Under section 303 (2) he must pay the debts of the company and adjust the rights of contributories among themselves. Section 302 contains the general provision that subject to the rights of preferential creditors the property of the company must be applied in satisfaction of its liabilities *pari passu* and subject thereto and unless the articles otherwise provide the balance must be distributed among the members according to their rights and interests in the company.

Where several liquidators are appointed any power may be exercised by such one or more of them as may be determined at the time of their appointment or, in default of such determination, by any number not less than two (s. 303 (3)). The liquidators themselves, however, cannot delegate their powers to one of their number[16] and on the death of a liquidator the survivor cannot act until a new liquidator is appointed.

The following is an alphabetical list of the liquidator's powers and duties.

Accounts and books

86–16 A voluntary liquidator must keep proper books of account, showing all receipts and payments made by him in the course of the liquidation. He may take as a guide Winding-up Rules 171 to 181, as to the books to be kept by liquidators in a winding up by the court. He should also keep a diary or minute book, containing notes of all his transactions and negotiations, and books showing the dates at which all notices to creditors and shareholders are sent out and posted, and by whom these were posted. The last-mentioned persons should initial the entries or the summary thereof, so that, if it becomes necessary to make an affidavit as to the service of any notice or circular, the person who directed the notice and posted it may be able to swear to the facts after refreshing his memory by referring to the book. Section 340 of the 1948 Act provides that all books and papers of the company and the liquidators shall as between the contributories of the company be prima facie evidence of the truth of all matters purporting to be therein recorded. This does not appear to affect the rights between company and the contributories nor between the company and the creditors. Even between the contributories themselves the evidence may be rebutted.[17]

Actions

86–17 The liquidator can without any sanction bring or defend any action or other legal proceeding in the name and on behalf of the company (1948 Act, ss. 245 (1) (*a*) and 303 (1) (*b*)).

If, however, there is a committee of inspection, he should, as a rule, obtain their consent. If there is none, it is safer in a case of any doubt to

---

[16] *Re London & Mediterranean Bank* (1871) 6 Ch.App. 206; *Re Metropolitan Bank* v. *Jones* (1876) 2 Ch.D. 366.
[17] *Re Great Northern Salt & Chemical Works* (1890) 44 Ch.D. 472.

apply for liberty to commence proceedings, and, if there is a doubt whether the assets will be sufficient, the liquidator should obtain an indemnity in respect of his costs from the shareholders or creditors.

Appeals from liquidator

86–18 Section 246 (5) of the 1948 Act which enables any person aggrieved by any act or decision of the liquidator to apply to the court and many of the Winding-up Rules allowing particular appeals to the court do not strictly apply to a voluntary winding up. However, section 307 gives a general power to any contributory or creditor to apply to have all such matters determined by the court.

Applications to the court

86–19 When a company is in the course of voluntary winding up, many matters can be dealt with without the need to apply to the court; but an application may become necessary, *e.g.* for the purpose of restraining actions against the company, or fixing the liquidator's remuneration, or for examination of directors, or misfeasance proceedings. Section 307 enables the court to determine "any question" arising in the voluntary winding up, and the powers of the section have been liberally construed, though it is doubtful whether the court has jurisdiction under section 307 to set aside a contract, and if it has such jurisdiction, the jurisdiction is discretionary.[18] It would seem that questions of the right to prove, the rights of contributories and applications for private examinations can be brought under the section. A creditor has under the section the same power of applying to the court as the liquidator or a contributory even where the company is in members' voluntary winding up. The section does not empower the court to authorise the liquidator to carry out transactions which would be *ultra vires* the company.[19] In *R-R Realisations Ltd. (formerly Rolls-Royce Ltd.*[20]*)* an application was made under section 307 to authorise the liquidators in the voluntary liquidation of the former Rolls-Royce Ltd. to distribute the assets among its members notwithstanding a last-minute claim by persons contending they were creditors under the Fatal Accidents Act 1976 for negligence in breach of statutory duty arising out of an accident in India. Sir Robert Megarry V.-C. held that the test to be applied was whether in all the circumstances of the case it was just to make the order. There was no rule that the claimants had to show that they had not been guilty of wilful default or want of due diligence although these were factors and normally important factors in determining what is just. The court could make such order or impose such conditions as it thought just. Where the order sought a distribution among members the court would be more reluctant to grant it than if the distribution was to be made to creditors. He consequently refused the order.

---

[18] *Re Centrifugal Butter Co.* [1913] 1 Ch. 188. As to the scope of s. 307 see *Re J. Burrows (Leeds) Ltd.* [1982] 2 All E.R. 882.
[19] *Re Salisbury Railway and Market House Co. Ltd.* [1969] 1 Ch. 349.
[20] [1980] 1 All E.R. 1019.

Arrangements

86–20 Section 306 of the 1948 Act enables arrangements to be made between a company in voluntary liquidation and its creditors, subject to appeal; but the operation of this section is limited to cases where the voluntary liquidation is to continue,[21] and the power given by section 206[22] can, in most cases, be more readily and effectually exercised for this purpose.

Books

86–21 See *Accounts, supra*, and *Possession of books and assets, infra.*

Borrowing

86–22 Under sections 245 (2) (*e*) and 303 (1) (*b*) of the 1948 Act the liquidator has power to raise upon the security of the assets of the company from time to time any required sum or sums of money, *e.g.* by mortgage of land, or of a call made by the liquidator, or of a debt due to the company, or a claim which the liquidator has for misfeasance against a director. Sometimes it is expedient to obtain the sanction of the court to raising money; but a liquidator cannot raise money in priority to the company's mortgages or other encumbrances even with the sanction of the court.

Calls

86–23 When the liquidator has settled the list of contributories he will proceed forthwith to make a call on the contributories so far as may be necessary. Where there is a considerable amount to be called up, he may think it best to call it up by degrees; but where it is clear that the whole amount will have to be called up, he should, as a general rule, make a call for the full amount unpaid on the shares held by the contributories, and send out notices accordingly.

Sometimes the liquidator, before making a call, sends out notice that he proposes to make a call, and fixes a time and place at which he will consider the matter. He can then within the time mentioned consider any objections made. A call, if and when the liquidator determines to make it, will be made by instrument in writing under his hand, and notice of the making of the call should forthwith be sent to the contributories. Those contributories who do not pay should be given further notice that unless they pay forthwith the liquidator will apply to the court. Subsequently the liquidator should apply by summons to the court for an order against all defaulting contributories, compelling them to pay the amount due with interest.

If the amount recoverable from the contributories settled on the A list will not suffice to pay the debts and costs of winding up, it will be necessary to settle the B list of contributories. This will include those persons who ceased within one year before the commencement of the winding up to be members and their representatives.

---

[21] *Re Contal Radio Ltd.* [1932] 2 Ch. 66.
[22] See para. 79–04, *ante*.

A general meeting, under section 303 (1) (*e*), may appoint directors and sanction their making calls.[23] A call may be made in pursuance of an agreement to amalgamate[24]; or in pursuance of an agreement for the sale of the assets to another company.[25]

Carrying on business

86–24 One of the powers which the liquidator may exercise without the sanction of the court is "to carry on the business of the company so far as may be necessary for the beneficial winding up thereof" (1948 Act, ss. 245 (1) (*b*) and 303 (1) (*b*)). This power must be exercised with caution and under advice; but the carrying on of the business will be held to be justified if the liquidator bona fide and reasonably forms the opinion that the carrying on of the business is necessary for the beneficial winding up of the company, even though he is mistaken.[26] "Beneficial winding up" does not refer necessarily to financial benefit, particularly in the case of a non-profit-making company, but, at least when the winding up is for a reconstruction, includes the carrying on of the business to facilitate a smooth take-over by the new company.[27]

If in a creditors' voluntary winding up no committee of inspection is appointed and the court has not ruled otherwise, the liquidator is in charge of the company's affairs and constitutes the "governing body" of the company within the meaning of section 139 of the 1948 Act (authorisation of representatives at meetings)[28]; he can appoint himself as representative of the company at the general meetings of subsidiary companies and exercise the vote attached to the shares held by the parent company in winding up.[29]

If the liquidator is in doubt as to the advisability of carrying on the business, it is desirable to get the sanction of the court to carry it on. The court in giving leave to carry on business usually imposes some limit, *e.g.* that the business may be carried on for a period, say three or six months, and if the liquidator proposes to carry on the business for longer than that, or even as long, he should seek the sanction of the court or the creditors. Where the liquidator carries on the business, he can do all things reasonably necessary for carrying it on, and accordingly he can buy and sell and make contracts, and draw, accept and indorse bills of exchange. All debts and liabilities incurred in the course of carrying on the business—being in the nature of salvage—will rank for payment in priority to the general debts and liabilities of the company.[30] In carrying on the business the liquidator is not prima facie liable on the contracts which he makes[31]; but

---

[23] *Ladd's Case* [1893] 3 Ch. 450.
[24] *New Zealand Gold, etc., Co.* v. *Peacock* [1894] 1 Q.B. 622.
[25] *Re Bank of South Australia (No. 2)* [1895] 1 Ch. 578.
[26] *Re Great Eastern Electric Co. Ltd.* [1941] Ch. 241.
[27] *Willis* v. *Assocn. of Universities of the British Commonwealth* [1965] 1 Q.B. 140.
[28] See para. 55–13, *ante*.
[29] *Hillman* v. *Crystal Bowl Ltd.* [1973] 1 W.L.R 162 (C.A.).
[30] *Re S. Davis & Co.* [1945] Ch. 402.
[31] *Stead, Hazel & Co.* v. *Cooper* [1933] 1 K.B. 840.

he should be careful to act in the name of the company, and to disclose the fact that the company is in liquidation, so that no one may be misled.

Any application to the court should be made by originating summons under section 307.[32]

Committee of inspection

86–25 There is no committee of inspection in a members' voluntary winding up; but in the case of a creditors' voluntary winding up the creditors at their first meeting (1948 Act, s. 293) or a subsequent meeting may appoint a committee of inspection.

The committee of inspection in a creditors' voluntary meeting is composed differently from that in a compulsory winding up; in the latter it consists of an unlimited number of creditors and contributories or persons holding general powers of attorney from them (1948 Act, s. 253 (1)); in the former it consists of not more than 10 persons, five to be appointed by the creditors and five by the members, but the creditors have power to veto the appointment of all or any of the members' representatives, subject to the power of the court to decide whether any and, if so, which of the members' representatives shall sit on the committee of inspection (1948 Act, s. 295 (1)).

Except for subsection (1), section 253 of the 1948 Act applies to the committee of inspection appointed in a creditors' voluntary winding up (s. 295 (2)). As to the powers of the committee see para. 86–12 ante.

Compromises

86–26 A compromise may be made, with the sanction of the company in a members' voluntary winding up, or in a creditors' voluntary winding up of the court or the committee of inspection under section 303 of the 1948 Act. On the question of the scope of the compromise provisions of section 245 (1) (*e*) and section 303 see paragraphs 85–39 and 85–60, *ante*.

For example, a compromise may be arranged if a contributory cannot pay the full amount of a call made on him, or if a debtor to the company cannot pay the whole of his debt to the company, or if the company has claims against anyone for breach of contract or misfeasance, which it is considered safer to compromise.

Where a compromise is proposed, the liquidator sometimes makes a provisional agreement for compromise, and then calls a meeting or applies to the court to sanction the same. If the court is asked to sanction a compromise, evidence that the compromise is beneficial must be forthcoming.

In the case of a compromise with a contributory, the liquidator, after taking out the summons for liberty to compromise, generally requires the

[32] See para. 86–19, *ante*. For orders giving liberty to carry on business, see Palmer *Company Precedents*, Part II (16th ed.), pp. 302 *et seq*.

contributory to make an affidavit as to his means, and, if necessary, cross-examines him on it.

Contributories

86–27 The liquidator in the voluntary winding up may exercise the power of the court under the Act of settling a list of contributories and of making calls (1948 Act, s. 303 (1) (*c*) and (*d*)).[33] The list of contributories is prima facie evidence of the liability of the persons named therein as contributories (s. 303 (1) (*c*)).

Costs

86–28 All costs, charges and expenses properly incurred in the voluntary winding up, including the remuneration of the liquidator, are payable out of the assets of the company in priority to all other claims (s. 309). This may include costs incurred between the date of a resolution to wind up and the date of a compulsory order.[34]

As the costs of winding up form a first charge, the liquidator can from time to time make payments of these on account. In most cases the liquidator pays the solicitor's bill without taxation, but he may at any time be called on to bring in his account, and, if he has overpaid the solicitor, may be held responsible for the difference. Accordingly, in some cases the solicitor gives the liquidator an undertaking that, if he should at any time be disallowed any part of the bill, the amount will be refunded. Occasionally the parties think it more prudent to have the bill taxed before payment. In order to obtain taxation, a summons should be taken out under section 307 of the 1948 Act. The liquidator is not personally responsible to his solicitor for the costs of the winding up. The solicitor looks to the assets for payment.[35]

The liquidator's costs have no priority over secured creditors of the company except so far as the liquidator's costs are costs of preservation or realisation, of which the secured creditor has had the benefit.[36] A solicitor employed by the company is entitled to his solicitor-and-client costs, if the company is solvent.[37]

The company's solicitor has a lien for costs of recovering a fund by proceedings taken before the voluntary liquidation.[38]

Creditors

86–29 The rights and remedies of the creditors are the same as in a winding up by the court.[39]

---

33 See paras. 85–45 *et seq., ante.*
34 *Re William Adler & Co.* [1935] Ch. 138.
35 *Re Trueman's Estate* (1872) L.R. 14 Eq. 278; *Re Massey* (1870) L.R. 9 Eq. 367; *Re Anglo-Moravian, etc., Ry., ex p. Watkin* (1875) 1 Ch.D. 130, 136.
36 *Re Regent's Canal Ironworks Co., ex p. Grissell* (1875) 3 Ch.D. 411; *cf. Re Anglo-Austrian Printing, etc., Union* [1895] 2 Ch. 891.
37 *Re C. B. & M. (Tailors) Ltd.* [1932] 1 Ch. 17.
38 *Re Meter Cabs Ltd.* [1911] 2 Ch. 557.
39 See paras. 85–51 *et seq., ante.*

Department of Trade

86–30 Unlike the liquidator in a winding up by the court, the voluntary liquidator is not subject to the control of the Department of Trade, except as to such matters as investments (see r. 173) and payment into the Insolvency Services Account of moneys representing unclaimed or undistributed assets (1948 Act, s. 343 as amended by s. 3 (6) of and Sched. 2 to the Insolvency Act 1976). The power of the Department of Trade to issue orders and regulations under Winding-up Rule 224 appears to apply to voluntary winding up. Section 343 does not contain a provision empowering the Department of Trade to settle disputed claims in relation to undistributed monies paid into the Insolvency Services Account, but the court has jurisdiction to resolve such disputes.[40]

Disclaimer

86–31 This right of the liquidator, set out in section 323 of the 1948 Act, applies to a voluntary winding up.[41]

Duty of liquidator to creditors

86–32 This matter is discussed at paragraph 85–38, *ante* and paragraph 86–55, *post*.

Statute-barred debts are not liabilities of the company for the purposes of winding up. The liquidator in a voluntary winding up is, in that respect, in the same position as the liquidator in a compulsory winding up[42] and has to reject the proof of a statute-barred debt, except, it is thought, in a members' voluntary winding up where he may admit such a proof with the consent of the contributories.[43]

Examinations—private and public

86–33 We have seen that in the case of a winding up by the court the liquidator can, under section 268 of the 1948 Act, have directors and contributories and other persons examined as to the affairs of the company. In the case of a voluntary winding up the application is by originating summons under section 307 for liberty to examine, and then the directors or other persons to be examined will be directed by the court to appear and will have to answer on oath.

In the High Court, the examination is to be held in court or chambers, as the court directs.[44]

Apart from the private examination under section 268, the liquidator, or any other of the persons named in section 307 (1), may apply to the court thereunder for the public examination of a director or other officer of the company or a promoter under section 270 of the 1948 Act; a "further

[40] *Birchin Lane Nominees Ltd.* v. *Nicholson* [1969] 1 W.L.R. 1362.
[41] See para. 85–40, *ante*.
[42] See para. 85–53, *ante*.
[43] *Re Art Reproduction Co.* [1952] Ch. 89.
[44] r. 5 (2) of 1949.

report" within the meaning of section 236 (which is a prerequisite for a public examination in a compulsory winding up) is not required in voluntary winding up.[45]

Filing of statement with Registrar

86–34 If the winding up is not concluded within one year after its commencement, the liquidator is under a duty to send to the Registrar of Companies twice a year a statement in the prescribed form concerning the proceedings and position of the liquidation.[46] If, in spite of a court order, the liquidator continuously fails to do so, he commits a grave contempt and, even if he eventually purges the contempt, the court may be inclined, unless there are extenuating circumstances, to impose a fine and, if the liquidator is a chartered accountant, to inform the Institute of Chartered Accountants of his grave dereliction of duty.[47]

Investments

86–35 The liquidator should invest any substantial cash balances in his hands, and in the case of a creditors' voluntary winding up the committee of inspection may sign a "certificate and request" if they think that there are funds requiring investment, and the liquidator must transmit the certificate and request to the Department of Trade.[48]

A similar certificate and request are sent if the committee of inspection think that any securities should be sold. If there is no committee, or in a members' voluntary winding up, the liquidator sends to the Department of Trade a certificate of the facts and a request, where he desires any investment or sale affecting balances in the Insolvency Services Account (see 1948 Act, s. 362, as amended by s. 3 of and Sched. 2 to the Insolvency Act 1976).

Landlords

86–36 The same rules as to the liability of the liquidator to rent, etc., apply as in the case of a winding up by the court.[49] A landlord may prove for damages for breach of a covenant not to assign.[50] As to the landlord's right of distress in voluntary winding up, see paragraph 86–50, *post*.

Litigation

86–37 See *Actions*, paragraph 86–17, *ante*.

Meetings of members and creditors

86–38 As to the meetings of the company or the creditors which must be called by the liquidator, see paragraphs 86–04 and 86–10, *ante*.

---

[45] *Re Campbell Coverings Ltd.* [1953] Ch. 488 and the same *(No. 2)* [1954] Ch. 225; and see *Re Serene Shoes Ltd.* [1958] 1 W.L.R. 1087.

[46] s. 342 and r. 197 of the Companies (Winding-up) Rules 1949.

[47] *Re Grantham Wholesale Fruit, Vegetable and Potato Merchants Ltd.* [1972] 1 W.L.R. 559.

[48] Rule 173 (1) of 1949.

[49] See para. 85–65, *ante*.

[50] *Cohen* v. *Popular Restaurants* [1917] 1 K.B. 480.

The liquidator does not often require to summon meetings to pass special or extraordinary resolutions, but cases sometimes arise, *e.g.* where it is desirable to sell the whole or part of the undertaking in consideration of shares in a new company, in which case a special resolution is required by section 287 of the 1948 Act.[51] Again, where the liquidator requires to make a compromise or arrangement, an extraordinary resolution may be requisite under section 245 (1) of the 1948 Act.

A vacancy in the office of liquidator may, in a members' voluntary winding up, be filled under section 286 by ordinary resolution of a general meeting, and in a creditors' winding up, under section 297, by the creditors.

A meeting called under the section 285 (2) in a members' voluntary winding up may appoint directors and sanction the exercise by them of the power of enforcing calls, and selling, transferring and forfeiting shares under the articles.[52]

When summoning a meeting, the liquidator should send out the notice to the registered addresses of the members or contributories, or to their last-known places of residence, and should state in the notice the object for which the meeting is convened.

The 1948 Act makes express provision for the calling of the first meeting of creditors under section 293, and, under section 299, for the calling of annual meetings to receive his accounts; it is usual to call special meetings when the liquidator desires to consult the creditors as to some important step in the liquidation, *e.g.* a sale or composition or a proposal for reconstruction.

In addition to the above meetings, the court can, by the joint operation of sections 346 and 307 of the 1948 Act, at any time direct meetings of creditors or contributories to be held for the purpose of ascertaining their wishes as to any matter relating to the winding up.

Misfeasance

86–39 One of a voluntary liquidator's most important duties is to look into the affairs of the company and ascertain whether any misfeasance, fraudulent preference, or breach of trust has been committed by any of its officers, and if necessary he must take proceedings in respect thereof. The matter is dealt with in section 333, which is applicable to voluntary as well as to compulsory liquidations.[53]

Official receiver

86–40 The requirements as to information to be given to the official receiver only apply to a winding up by the court. If it is necessary for the liquidator to exercise any powers which cannot be exercised except under a winding

---

[51] See para. 80–01, *ante*.
[52] *Ladd's Case* [1893] 3 Ch. 450.
[53] See para. 85–88, *ante*.

up by the court, or with the intervention of the official receiver, the official receiver can apply to the court for a winding-up order (1948 Act, s. 224 (2)).[54]

Possession of books and assets

86–41 The liquidator in a voluntary winding up is not an officer of the court[55]; but, subject to this, his position as regards taking possession of the assets is the same as in the case of a winding up by the court.

The liquidator should at once take possession of the books, deeds and documents of the company, and ascertain by inquiry the whereabouts of any which are missing and apply for the delivery thereof. He should also with all convenient speed obtain possession of the assets of the company, and, in the case of assets of which physical possession cannot be obtained, *e.g.* book debts owing to the company and property of the company in the possession of mortgagees or a receiver, he should perfect his title as far as possible, by giving notice to the debtors or to the mortgagees or receiver, as the case may be.

Where a solicitor or other person is in possession of books or documents, and claims a lien or charge thereon for money due, the validity of the lien or charge should at once be examined, and if it appears that the lien or charge is valid and effective, and the books or documents are wanted, an arrangement should be made to obtain delivery on some reasonable terms, *e.g.* that the amount of the lien or charge will be paid off out of the first available assets coming into the hands of the liquidator. The liquidator may, however, consider it expedient to raise the requisite funds and discharge the lien. If the lien is by a solicitor for a bill of costs, he should be required to send in the bill, and it may be expedient to have it taxed, and in some cases it may be desirable to obtain delivery before taxation. This can generally be obtained if the liquidator is prepared to pay the amount claimed into court.

86–42 There are some books and documents upon which the company cannot give a lien or charge, *e.g.* the register of members, the register of mortgages, and any documents which the regulations expressly provide are to be kept at the office of the company.[56] Where a lien is claimed on such books, the liquidator should press for delivery.

Where the books or assets are in the possession of a contributory, trustee, receiver, banker, or agent or officer of the company, the liquidator may apply to the court under section 307 for an order under section 258 to deliver up the same.

When the company holds leaseholds and is insolvent, and its interest in the leaseholds is worthless, by reason of their being held at a very high rent, or being subject to onerous covenants or heavy mortgages, there is

[54] *Re 1897 Jubilee Sites Syndicate* [1899] 2 Ch. 204.
[55] See r. 78 of 1949.
[56] *Re Capital Fire Insurance Association* (1883) 24 Ch.D. 408; *Re Rapid Road Transit Co.* [1909] 1 Ch. 96.

danger in taking possession, because the landlord may become entitled to claim payment in full for rent accrued during the liquidation, and recover the full amount required to repair the premises under a covenant to repair, whilst the liquidator may derive little or no benefit from keeping on the premises. Whereas, if the liquidator does not take possession and does not keep on the premises for the purposes of the liquidation, the landlord can only prove and take his dividend *pari passu* with other creditors.[57]

Proof of debts

86–43 It is not necessary for the liquidator in a voluntary winding up to require the creditors to prove their debts. Winding-up Rule 91 does not apply.

But Winding-up Rule 106 applies to every winding up and the liquidator should therefore give notices and advertise as there required.

Prosecution of directors

86–44 A liquidator in the voluntary winding up, with the previous sanction of the court, may prosecute delinquent directors, and all expenses properly incurred in such a prosecution are payable out of the assets of the company in priority to all other liabilities (1948 Act, s. 334).

Purchase of property by liquidator

86–45 A liquidator cannot himself purchase any property of the company except by leave of the court.[58]

Rates and taxes

86–46 The position of the voluntary liquidator is the same as that of the liquidator in a winding up by the court as regards the preferential payment of rates and taxes.[59]

Release

86–47 Section 251 of the 1948 Act, which enables a liquidator to apply to the Department of Trade for his release, only applies to a winding up by the court.[60]

Removal and filling vacancies

86–48 If no liquidator is acting, the court may appoint one (1948 Act, s. 304 (1)).

Further, on cause shown, the court may remove a liquidator and appoint another one (s. 304 (2)).

The court may under that provision make an appointment either on the removal or retirement of a liquidator,[61] and in any other case where due

---

[57] See para. 85–67 *ante*.
[58] r. 161 of 1949.
[59] See paras. 85–61, *et seq.*, *ante*.
[60] *Pulsford* v. *Devenish* [1903] 2 Ch. 625, 633.
[61] *Re Sheppey Portland Co.* [1892] W.N. 184.

cause is shown, *e.g.* when an additional liquidator is required. The appointment may be made on the application of the existing liquidator.[62]

The principles on which the court acts in removing a liquidator were discussed in *Re Sir John Moore Gold Mining Co.*,[63] *Re Adam Eyton Ltd.*,[64] *Re Amalgamated Properties of Rhodesia Ltd.*[65] (where the application was refused; it had been founded on the ground that the liquidator was not independent, but the directors whose conduct was impeached had ceased to be directors and there was no support for the application) and *Re Rubber and Produce Investment Trust*[66] (where the application was granted; in that case a company, thought to be solvent, proved to be insolvent, and the liquidator disregarded the wishes of the creditors). See further paragraph 85–99, *ante*.

Misconduct will justify removal, and so may the existence of interests or connections which may be in conflict, or may be likely to interfere with the performance of his duties. Thus, in *Re Charterland Goldfields*[67] the liquidator had intimate business relations with the directors, and in *Re Karamelli and Barnett Ltd.*[68] it was held that the fact that removal will, in the opinion of the court, be for the benefit of the winding up will amount to "due cause shown"; but immoral conduct is insufficient as a ground for removal.[69]

When the company is insolvent, the court should be asked to fill any vacancy.

If three or more liquidators are appointed, and one dies, it is apprehended that the continuing liquidators (being two or more) may act notwithstanding the vacancy (see 1948 Act, s. 303 (3)).

Remuneration

86–49 In a members' voluntary winding up the remuneration of the liquidator may be fixed by the company in general meeting (1948 Act, s. 285). In a creditors' voluntary winding up it may be fixed by the committee of inspection, or, if there is none, by the creditors (1948 Act, s. 296).

The remuneration is included among the costs payable out of the assets of the company in priority to all other claims (1948 Act, s. 309). Sometimes the remuneration is fixed at the meeting at which the liquidator is appointed. More commonly nothing is said about remuneration at that meeting; the matter is left open, and the remuneration is fixed later by a general meeting or by the court, on the application of the liquidator or some other party interested. Sometimes the liquidator takes such remuneration as he considers proper, and then at the final meeting the accounts

---

62 *Re Sunlight Incandescent Gas Lamp Co.* [1900] 2 Ch. 728.
63 (1879) 12 Ch.D. 325.
64 (1887) 36 Ch.D. 299.
65 (1914) 30 T.L.R. 405.
66 [1915] 1 Ch. 382.
67 (1909) 26 T.L.R. 132.
68 [1917] 1 Ch. 203.
69 *Re Urmston Grange Steamship Co.* (1901) 17 T.L.R. 553.

are passed including the appropriation of this remuneration. There are dangers in leaving the matter in the air since a liquidator may have to accept what he is offered unless he can establish that it is not proper remuneration. A claim by him in quasi-contract for *quantum meruit* may be met by the argument that there was a contract with remuneration to be fixed.[70]

Where an application to the court is made for the purpose of fixing the remuneration, the court considers the circumstances of the particular case and determines what, in those circumstances, is a fair remuneration to pay.[71] The amount of remuneration must be ascertained in relation to the liquidator's services, and not in relation to the means of the remunerating party, or the fortunes of war in the liquidation.[72] The former practice, in the absence of special circumstances, was to be guided by the scale of fees fixed for the remuneration of trustees in bankruptcy.[73] The present practice, in the absence of special circumstances, is to fix the remuneration in accordance with the scale of fees payable to the official receiver in a compulsory winding up.[74] Where the company is insolvent, there is an obvious advantage in getting the court to fix the remuneration, for thereby all questions as to the propriety of the amount are avoided. Occasionally the court has ordered a meeting of creditors to be convened to consider the remuneration of the liquidator. Where there are two or more liquidators the court can determine the proportions in which the remuneration assigned shall be distributed between them (1948 Act, s. 242 (2)); but such an order is not usually made.[75] The court has a discretion as to the priority in which the remuneration will be paid,[76] and may review the remuneration of the liquidator, where the voluntary liquidation is followed by compulsory liquidation.[77]

Restraining actions

86–50 Where a compulsory winding up or supervision order has been made or a provisional liquidator appointed, no action or proceeding can be proceeded with or commenced against the company except with the leave of the court (1948 Act, s. 231). This section does not apply to a purely voluntary winding up; but the court will in general, under sections 226 and 307, restrain actions and proceedings, against the company, the plaintiff being permitted to add his claim to his debt and prove for the amount.[78]

---

[70] *Re Allison, Johnson & Foster Ltd.* [1904] 2 K.B. 327 (Div. Ct); *cf. Craven-Ellis* v. *Canons* [1936] 2 K.B. 403 (C.A.); *Re Richmond Gate Property Co. Ltd.* [1965] 1 W.L.R. 335.

[71] *Re Amalgamated Syndicates Ltd.* [1901] 2 Ch. 181.

[72] *Re Joseph Phillips Ltd.* [1964] 1 W.L.R. 369.

[73] *Re Carton* (1923) 39 T.L.R. 194; *cf. Re Joseph Phillips Ltd.* [1964] 1 W.L.R. 369.

[74] Table B4 (2) and (3) to the Companies (Board of Trade) Fees Order 1969 (S.I. 1969 No. 519) amended by the Companies (Board of Trade) Fees (Amendment) Orders 1970 (S.I. 1970 No. 2008) and 1972 (S.I. 1972 No. 1055).

[75] *Re Langham Hotel Co.* (1869) 17 W.R. 463.

[76] *Re Beni Felkai Mining Co.* [1934] Ch. 406.

[77] *Re Mortimers Ltd.* [1937] 1 Ch. 289.

[78] *Re Thurso New Gas Co.* (1889) 42 Ch.D. 486, 491; *Westbury* v. *Twigg & Co.* [1892] 1 Q.B. 77; *Re Margot Bywaters Ltd.* [1942] Ch. 121 but see the comments thereon by Lord Russell in *Herbert Berry Associates Ltd.* v. *I.R.C.* [1978] 1 All E.R. 161, 172.

The court has a discretion and where the claim is disputed may regard it as more convenient that the action should proceed to resolve the matter. Where the liquidator shows that expense will be saved or that the existence of the liability is substantially admitted the action will be stayed.[79] Where the action is pending in the High Court, the application must be to stay further proceedings, and should be made to the Division in which the action or proceedings is pending.[80]

Section 325 of the 1948 Act disentitles a creditor who has issued execution or attached any debt from retaining the benefit thereof against the liquidator unless he has before the commencement of the winding up completed the execution or the attachment. For the purpose of section 325 a creditors' voluntary winding up is regarded as commencing at the date when the creditor received notice that a meeting had been called at which a resolution to wind up was to be proposed (see further paragraph 85–72, *ante*.) Distress is not a form of execution.[81]

The court acts upon similar principles as to restraining a distress for rent due after winding up as in the case of a compulsory order.[82]

The court will usually give the creditor his costs of action down to the time when he had notice of the winding up.[83] But where the action is brought after notice of the winding up, the plaintiff, except in special circumstances, will not be allowed to add the costs to his debt, and may be ordered to pay the costs of the action.[84]

Sales of property

86–51 The liquidator may, without the sanction of the court, sell the real and personal property and things in action of the company by public auction or private contract (1948 Act, ss. 245 (2) (*a*) and 303 (1) (*b*)).

The liquidator should proceed with all convenient speed to sell the property, either as a going concern or otherwise. If he does not sell the undertaking as a going concern, he must decide what parts to sell and what to realise by collection or otherwise.

For the purposes of any sale the liquidator can employ auctioneers, brokers, and other agents, and may remunerate them for their services. When necessary, a sale must be made subject to special conditions as to title, etc. Great care should be taken in preparing the conditions of sale, and a reserve price should be fixed. Application to the court may be made

---

79 *Currie* v. *Consolidated Kent Collieries Corp. Ltd.* [1906] 1 K.B. 134 (C.A.); *Cook* v. *"X" Chain Patents Co. Ltd.* [1960] 1 W.L.R. 60.

80 *Walker* v. *Banagher Distillery Co.* (1875) 1 Q.B.D. 129; *Re Artistic Colour Printing Co.* (1880) 14 Ch.D. 502.

81 See s. 228 and *Herbert Berry Associates Ltd.* v. *I.R.C.* [1978] 1 All E.R. 161, 171, *per* Lord Russell of Killowen.

82 As to which see paras. 85–66 *et seq., ante*; *Re South Rhondda Colliery Co.* [1928] W.N. 126.

83 *Walker* v. *Banagher Distillery Co.* (1875) 1 Q.B.D. 129; *Re Thurso New Gas Co.* (1889) 42 Ch.D. 486, 492.

84 *Re East Kent Shipping Co.* (1868) 18 L.T. 748; *Rose & Co.* v. *Gardden Lodge, etc., Co.* (1878) 3 Q.B.D. 235.

under section 307 to sanction a sale. If thought desirable an order can be obtained for sale with the approval of the judge, in which case the sale will be carried out by the court. A liquidator should not normally, except under section 287, sell the property for shares in another company; but where it is found desirable to effect such a sale, he should take steps under that section or obtain the direction of the court.[85]

The liquidator can, in the name of the company, make all necessary contracts for the purposes of the winding up, and can execute and sign all necessary conveyances, assignments, surrenders, deeds and documents.

Security

86–52 Section 240 of the 1948 Act, which requires security from a liquidator, does not apply to a voluntary winding up. Hence no security is necessary; but, if the court appoints a liquidator, it usually requires security.

Solicitors and agents

86–53 The liquidator can appoint a solicitor without any sanction (see 1948 Act, ss. 303 and 245 (1) (*c*)).

Statement of accounts

86–54 See *Accounts and books*, paragraph 86–16, *ante*.

Status of liquidator

86–55 The liquidator in a voluntary winding up is not, strictly speaking, a trustee, either for the creditors or the contributories; he is "more rightly described as the agent of the company."[86] Nor is he an officer of the court.[87] Nevertheless, he has statutory duties towards the creditors and contributories, including the administration of a fund—the assets of the company—impressed with a trust for them, and, if he neglects these duties, he may be held personally liable in an action by the party prejudiced,[88] or by misfeasance proceedings under section 333.[89] The liquidator should therefore, in all cases of doubt, make use of the opportunity given to him by section 307 to apply to the court. See further paragraph 86–19, *ante*.

Taxation

86–56 The liquidator is responsible for the payment of corporation tax on profits arising from the carrying on of the company's business or the sale of assets. This is considered in more detail at Chapters 90 *et seq.*

Undistributed assets

86–57 Section 343 of the 1948 Act[90] applies to all liquidations.

In addition to this, all money, besides unclaimed dividends representing

---

[85] See para. 86–19, *ante*.
[86] *Knowles* v. *Scott* [1891] 1 Ch. 717, 723.
[87] *Re Hill's Waterfall, etc., Co.* [1896] 1 Ch. 947, 954.
[88] *Pulsford* v. *Devenish* [1903] 2 Ch. 625, 637 *per* Farwell J.
[89] *Re Windsor Steam Coal Co.* [1929] 1 Ch. 151; see para. 85–88, *ante*.
[90] See para. 85–99, *ante*.

undistributed assets, which the liquidator must pay into the Insolvency Services Account as having been in his hands or under his control, are to be ascertained at the date of his half-yearly statement, and the amount is the minimum balance which has been in his hands during the six months, except so much as the Department of Trade may authorise him to retain for the purpose of the liquidation.[91]

All moneys remaining undistributed at the date of dissolution of the company must be paid into the Insolvency Services Account.[92]

Investments are deemed to be money under his control for the purposes of Winding-up Rule 199 and must be paid or transferred into the Insolvency Services Account.[93]

The Department of Trade may require the liquidator in a voluntary liquidation to submit and verify accounts of undistributed money or assets.[94]

Vesting orders

86–58 Section 244 of the 1948 Act, which enables the court to make an order vesting the company's property in the liquidator, only applies in terms to a winding up by the court; but the liquidator can apply to the court under section 307 to exercise this power in a voluntary liquidation.

Staying winding up

86–59 The court has power under section 307 to stay a voluntary winding up, so that the company may resume business, and the power may be exercised, *e.g.* upon an arrangement with creditors.[95] The court has no power to direct the official receiver to provide a report under section 256 (2) in a voluntary winding up.[96]

Petition by official receiver

86–60 If a voluntary winding up is unduly protracted, or is not being conducted with a due regard to the interest of the creditors or contributories, the official receiver may present a petition to have the company wound up by the court (1948 Act, s. 224 (2)).[97]

Compulsory order after resolution for voluntary liquidation

86–61 By section 310, the voluntary winding up of a company is not to be a bar to the right of any creditor or contributory of such company to have it wound up by the court; but in the case of an application by a contributory

---

[91] ss. 343, 360 to 362, and rr. 199–204 of 1949.
[92] r. 199 of 1949; on the Insolvency Services Account, see para. 85–42, *ante*.
[93] r. 199 (5).
[94] r. 201 of 1949.
[95] *Re S.S. Titian* (1888) 36 W.R. 347; *Re Hafna Mining Co.* (1888) 84 L.T.(O.S.) 403.
[96] *Re Serene Shoes Ltd.* [1958] 1 W.L.R. 1087.
[97] See para. 85–18, *ante*.

the court must be satisfied that the rights of such contributory will be prejudiced by a voluntary winding up. Since 1929 it has been unnecessary to show prejudice in the case of a petition by a creditor.[98] But the wishes of the creditors must still be considered.[99]

Dissolution of company

86–62 As soon as the liquidator has done his work and the affairs of the company are fully wound up, the liquidator makes up an account showing the manner in which the winding up has been conducted and the property of the company disposed of, and calls, by advertisement in the *Gazette*, a general meeting of the company and a meeting of creditors where required[1] for the purpose of laying the account before the meetings and giving them any explanation that may be required. The liquidator within a week after the meeting must send to the Registrar a copy of the account and a return of the meeting having been held and the date thereof, or, if there is no quorum present, a return to that effect. Official notification of the return of the liquidator is required.[2] On the expiration of three months from the registration of the return the company is to be deemed to be dissolved.[3] But the court is given power by section 352, at any time within two years, on the application of the liquidator or any person interested, to declare the dissolution to have been void.

Winding up under supervision

86–63 When a resolution has been passed by a company to wind up voluntarily, the court may make an order directing that the voluntary winding up shall continue, but subject to the supervision of the court, and on such terms and conditions as the court thinks just (1948 Act, s. 311). In making or refusing a supervision order the court has regard, as in the case of a petition for a compulsory order, to the wishes of creditors and contributories (1948 Act, s. 346). Thus, the court will not make the order on a shareholder's petition against the wishes of a majority of the other shareholders; but if a resolution for voluntary winding up is passed by the preponderating influence of a shareholder whose conduct is impeached,[4] or if the petition is supported by creditors, the case is different[5]; so, too, a supervision order may be made where investigation is required and the assets are large.[6]

This was a useful procedure before creditors' voluntary winding up was introduced in 1929 but is now rarely used.

---

[98] See para. 85–06, *ante*.
[99] See para. 85–06, *ante*. For the practice before 1929, see *Palmer's Company Law* (19th ed.), p. 433.
[1] See para. 86–09, *ante*.
[2] See Ch. 17, *ante*.
[3] See para. 86–09, *ante*.
[4] *Re Varieties Ltd.* [1893] 2 Ch. 235; *Re Medical Battery Co.* [1894] 1 Ch. 444.
[5] *Re Lonsdale Vale Ironstone Co.* (1868) 16 W.R. 601.
[6] *Re Barned's Banking Co.* (1866) 14 W.R. 722.

Practical advantage

86–64 There are three grounds on which a supervision order is still useful[7]:

(1) it operates automatically as a stay of actions and other proceedings against the company just as a winding-up order does (1948 Act, ss. 312, 231);

(2) the court on making a supervision order may appoint an additional liquidator or liquidators to act with the existing liquidator (1948 Act, s. 314). This is a valuable power, because in a large number of cases in which a supervision order is asked for, the cause is dissatisfaction on the part of either shareholders or creditors with the appointment or conduct of the acting liquidator; and

(3) in making a supervision order the court commonly inserts as conditions of the order—

(a) that the liquidator shall file with the Registrar of Companies a quarterly[8] report in writing as to the position and progress made with the winding up and with the realisation of the assets, and as to any other matters connected with the winding up, as the court may from time to time direct, and

(b) that no bills of costs, charges or expenses, or special remuneration of any solicitor employed by the liquidator, and no remuneration, charges or expenses of such liquidator, or of any manager, accountant, auctioneer, broker or other person are to be paid out of the assets of the company unless such costs, charges, expenses or remuneration have been taxed or allowed by the Registrar.[9]

86–65 The taxed costs of the solicitor employed by the liquidator incurred during the period down to the date of the supervision order must be paid out of the assets before any remuneration due to the liquidator up to that time. So also must any costs properly incurred after the date of the order in getting in assets of the company or in work done on the instructions of the liquidator.[10]

Separate costs of the company and the liquidators will not be allowed as a rule on the petition.

A supervision order does not affect the commencement of the winding up, which is still the date of the resolution.

The powers of the liquidator in a winding up under supervision are listed in section 315 and Schedule XI to the 1948 Act states the provisions which do not apply to a winding up under the supervision of the court.

In practice supervision orders are made extremely rarely and it is

---

[7] The fact that creditors were enabled by a supervision order to apply to the court was a good reason at one time for making the order; but since the Companies Act 1900, s. 25 (now s. 307 of the Act of 1948), giving creditors power to apply to the court in a purely voluntary winding up, this ground no longer exists.

[8] *Re Horner & Co.* (1898) 5 Manson 355.

[9] *Re Civil Service Brewery Co.* [1893] W.N. 5; 37 S.J. 194; *Re Waterproof Materials Co.* [1893] W.N. 18; 37 S.J. 231; *Re Pritchard, Offar & Co.* [1893] W.N. 153.

[10] *Re Sanitary Burial Association* [1900] 2 Ch. 289.

thought that an abolition of this type of winding-up procedure would not noticeably affect the present practice.[11]

[11] See the Jenkins Report 1962, para. 503 and cl. 87 of the lapsed Companies Bill 1973. But see *Re Manual Work Services (Construction) Ltd.* [1975] 1 W.L.R. 341.

B. WINDING UP IN SCOTLAND

CHAPTER 87

WINDING UP IN SCOTLAND

Modes of winding up

87–01 A company incorporated under the Companies Acts does not cease to exist until formally dissolved. If it has ceased to carry on business, has neither assets nor liabilities and is not heritably vest in any property, the Registrar of Companies may be asked to exercise his powers to strike the company off the register under section 353 of the 1948 Act.[1] This is often used as an alternative to winding up. Apart from section 353, the machinery of winding up (also termed liquidation) is a necessary preliminary to dissolution.[2] It is not competent to sequestrate the estate of a company under the Bankruptcy Acts,[3] but its estate may be sequestrated and a judicial factor appointed at common law,[4] which merely transfers the powers of administration of its estate to the factor and does not have the same effect as the appointment of a trustee in bankruptcy.[5] A company cannot grant a Trust Deed for behoof of its creditors (1948 Act, s. 320 (2)), and this has been held to prohibit a floating charge over all its assets for behoof of all its creditors.[6]

Winding up may take one of the following forms (1948 Act, ss. 211 and 283 (4)):

(1) Winding up by the court ("Compulsory"),
(2) (a) Members' voluntary winding up, or
(b) Creditors' voluntary winding up.

A voluntary winding up of either type may become subject to the supervision of the court. Voluntary winding up is initiated by the shareholders and is accordingly the commonest form. A members' voluntary winding up is one where the directors, at its commencement, have declared that the company will meet its liabilities within 12 months (s. 283; 1981 Act, s. 105). If they do not the liquidation is a creditors' voluntary winding up. This normally, but not necessarily, implies insolvency. There are special provisions for a members' voluntary winding up in which insolvency intervenes (1948 Act, s. 288).

Part V of the Companies Act 1948 contains the statutory provisions applicable to winding up.

---

[1] As to which, see para. 87–103 *infra*.
[2] *Princess of Reuss* v. *Bos* (1871) L.R. 5 H.L. 176, 193.
[3] *Standard Property Investment Co. Ltd.* v. *Dunblane Hydropathic Co. Ltd.* 1884, 12 R. 328.
[4] *Patrick Fraser, Petitioner* 1971 S.L.T. 146.
[5] See further *N.M.L. Walker Judicial Factors* (W. Green & Son, Edinburgh 1974).
[6] *London Joint City and Midland Bank* v. *Herbert Dickinson* (1922) W.N. 13.

Winding up by the court

87–02 In circumstances laid down in the Act, the company, a creditor, a receiver or a contributory (*i.e.* the present and certain past members of the company as defined in ss. 212 and 213 of the 1948 Act) and certain government officials may petition the court for a compulsory winding-up order. Part V (i), (ii) and (v) of the 1948 Act apply to winding up by the court.

Unlike the position in England, there is no comprehensive set of rules of court for the conduct of a compulsory liquidation in Scotland. Such rules as do exist are contained in the Rules of the Court of Session 1965, Chap. IV, s. 3 (referred to in this chapter as "R.C.S.") and (for the Sheriff Court) in the Act of Sederunt of March 20, 1930 (as amended) (referred to in this chapter as "Sh.Ct.R.").[7]

Courts having jurisdiction to wind up

87–03 Where the Companies Acts use the expression "the Court," this means "the court having jurisdiction to wind up the company in question" (1948 Act, s. 455 (1)). The English courts have no jurisdiction to wind up a company registered in Scotland, and vice versa.

The Court of Session has jurisdiction to wind up any company registered in Scotland (1948 Act, s. 220 (1)). During vacation this jurisdiction may be exercised by the vacation judge (s. 220 (2)). Where the paid-up share capital does not exceed £120,000, the Sheriff Court of the Sheriffdom where its registered office is situated has concurrent jurisdiction (s. 220 (3) as amended with effect from December 20, 1976 by the Insolvency Act 1976, s. 1 and Sched. 1).[8] The Court of Session has power (having regard to the assets of the company) to remit a petition for the winding up of a company whose issued capital does not exceed the limit[9] to the sheriff court or to transfer the petition from one sheriff court to another (s. 220 (3) (*a*) and (*b*)). Application for an order under section 220 (3) (*a*) or (*b*) may be made by the liquidator, or any creditor or contributory, or the sheriff (R.C.S. 203 (Sh.Ct.R. 7–12)). The sheriff may also state (or be required by any party to state) a case on any question of law for the opinion of the Court of Session (s. 220 (3) (*c*)).

For the purpose of section 220 "registered office" means the place which has been the company's registered office for the longest time during the six months preceding the presentation of the petition (s. 220 (4)). A company could not, therefore, frustrate a petition in the sheriff court by moving its office outside its jurisdiction at the last moment. A person taking proceed-

---

[7] See Vol. III, Pt. J.
[8] s. 1 of the 1976 Act authorises the variation of this maximum limit to be made by statutory instrument. Prior to December 20, 1976 the limit of sheriff court jurisdiction was £10,000.
[9] *Chayney & Bull Ltd., Petitioners*, 1930 S.C. 759; 1930 S.L.T. 623.

ings against a company is entitled to act on the basis of the registered office as disclosed on the Registrar of Companies' official file.[10]

Appeals

87–04 In general, appeals against court orders in Scotland in respect of liquidation matters follow the same lines as in court actions generally. A sheriff's order may be appealed to the Sheriff-Principal and from him to the Court of Session (Inner House) or direct to the Inner House, and the interlocutor of an outer house judge of the Court of Session (Lord Ordinary) may be appealed to the Inner House (see s. 277 (1) and R.C.S. 217). The Court of Session will not, however, entertain an appeal against the appointment of a particular person as liquidator by the sheriff unless the circumstances are exceptional.[11] Special provision is made in respect of interlocutors pronounced by the vacation judge in liquidations (s. 277 (2) and Sched. 10). Those provisions also apply to orders pronounced by the Lord Ordinary within 14 days of the end of the court session if not reclaimed against during the session (s. 277 (3)). Under these provisions, certain orders by the vacation judge are to be final (Sched. 10, Pt. I) and others are to be treated as final notwithstanding an appeal, until the appeal has been disposed of (Sched. 10, Pt. II). The list in Schedule 10 is not exhaustive, and orders not referred to therein are appealable.[12] Section 277 (2) and (3) require appeals against an interlocutor of the Lord Ordinary or vacation judge to be appealed by reclaiming motion enrolled within 14 days from the date of the order. This limit is imperative and if no reclaiming motion is enrolled within the statutory period the order becomes final.[13]

Where the court had recalled the appointment of a provisional liquidator and this order was the subject of an appeal, it was held that the provisional liquidator remained in office until the reclaiming motion had been disposed of.[14]

Companies which may be wound up

87–05 The Scottish courts have jurisdiction to wind up the following kinds of company:

(a) companies formed and registered under Part I or registered under Part VII of the 1948 Act;

(b) existing companies as defined in section 455 (1), *i.e.* companies formed and registered under the Joint Stock Companies Acts or the Companies Acts of 1862, 1908 or 1929;

---

[10] *Ross* v. *Invergordon Distillers Ltd.*, 1961 S.L.T. 358; 1961 S.C. 286.
[11] *Steel Scaffolding Co.* v. *Buckleys Ltd.* 1935 S.C. 617; 1935 S.L.T. 467.
[12] *Magistrates of Edinburgh* v. *Union Billposting Co. Ltd.* 1912 S.C. 105; 1912, 2 S.L.T. 336.
[13] *Cumpstie* v. *Waterston* 1933 S.C. 1; 1933 S.L.T. 10; *Macarthur* v. *Mackay* 1914, S.C. 547; 1914 1 S.L.T. 336; see also R.C.S. 264 (*g*).
[14] *Levy*, 1963 S.C. 46.

(c) companies registered but not formed under the above pre-1948 Acts (1948 Act, s. 378)[15];
(d) companies registered as limited under the Companies Act 1879 (1948 Act, s. 379);
(e) unregistered companies as defined in section 398,[16] *i.e.* any partnership, association or company except:
   (i) railway companies incorporated by Act of Parliament (with exceptions mentioned therein);
   (ii) registered companies;
   (iii) a partnership or association consisting of less than eight members, not being a foreign partnership or association; and
   (iv) a limited partnership registered in England or Northern Ireland.

In Scotland it has been held that a building society, not registered under the Building Societies Act 1874 or subsequent legislation, could be wound up as an unregistered company.[17] An order for winding-up under the Companies Act was also granted where a friendly society could not comply with winding up procedure under the Friendly Societies Act.[18] An association in which there are no mutual obligations or liabilities among the membership is not, however, capable of being wound up under the Companies Acts.[19]

Further examples of the exercise of this jurisdiction in respect of unregistered companies have occurred in England and are detailed in paragraph 85–04 *ante*. Special rules for the winding up of unregistered and oversea companies are contained in sections 399 to 405 of the 1948 Act (as amended by the Insolvency Act 1976, s. 1 and Sched. 1).

Grounds for winding up

87–06 The court may order a company to be wound up on any one or more of the following grounds:
(a) if the company has by special resolution resolved to be wound up by the court;
(b) if the company does not commence its business within a year of incorporation, or suspends its business for a whole year;
(c) if the number of its members falls below the statutory minimum of two;
(d) inability to pay its debts;

---

[15] *e.g. Liquidators of Western Bank* v. *Douglas, etc.* 1860, 22 D. 447; *Western Bank* v. *Ayrshire Bank* 1860, 22 D. 540.
[16] *e.g. Aberdeen Provision Society* 1863, 2 M. 385.
[17] *Smith's Trustees* v. *Irvine and Fullerton Property and Investment Building Society* 1903, 6 F. 99; 11 S.L.T. 395.
[18] *Canavan and Others, Petitioners*, 1929 S.L.T. 636.
[19] *Caledonian Employees Benevolent Society* 1928 S.C. 633; 1928 S.L.T. 412.

(e) if the court is of the opinion that it is just and equitable that the company should be wound up;
(f) failure to obtain a trading certificate under section 4 of the 1980 Act within 12 months (1948 Act, s. 222 (*b*) as amended by 1980 Act, Sched. 3);
(g) being an old public company and failing to re-register under the 1980 Act (1948 Act, s. 222 (*bb*), added by 1980 Act, Sched. 3); and
(h) if the court is satisfied that the security of the holder of a floating charge over some of the company's property is in jeopardy.

Of these, (a) to (g) apply equally to English companies (1948 Act, s. 222 as amended by the Companies Act 1980, Sched. 4),[20] but (h) applies only to Scottish companies, having been introduced by the Companies (Floating Charges) (Scotland) Act 1961, s. 4, and now contained in the Companies (Floating Charges and Receivers) (Scotland) Act 1972, s. 4.

A bank or institution licensed under the Banking Act 1979 may also be wound up on petition by the Bank of England.[21]

Inability to pay debts

87–07 The normal basis for a compulsory winding up is the company's inability to pay its debts, as defined in section 223 of the 1948 Act.

Under section 223 (*a*) (as amended by the Insolvency Act 1976, s. 1 and Sched. 1) a company is deemed to be unable to pay its debts "if a creditor, by assignment or otherwise, to whom the company is indebted in a sum exceeding £200[22] then due has served on the company, by leaving it at the registered office of the company, a demand under his hand requiring the company to pay the sum so due and the company has for three weeks thereafter neglected to pay the sum or to secure or compound for it to the reasonable satisfaction of the creditor." If the creditor holds security which is marketable and of sufficient value to satisfy his claim section 223 (*a*) is not appropriate.[23] It will be a sufficient answer to a petition founded on section 223 (*a*) if the company finds caution for the amount of the claim[24] or consigns the amount.[25] Section 223 (*a*) is not available to a creditor whose claim is contingent or prospective,[26] or disputed on substantial grounds.[27] The formal procedure under the subsection must be observed, but a demand signed by an agent on behalf of the creditor is to be regarded as "under the hand" of his principal. It has been held in England that the expression "for three weeks thereafter" means a clear period of 21 days

[20] The 1980 Act repealed s. 222 (*b*) (failure to hold the statutory meeting under s. 130) and amended s. 222 (*d*) in respect of the minimum membership provisions, the minimum membership for all companies being now two.
[21] Banking Act 1979, s. 18.
[22] The Insolvency Act 1976, s. 1 empowers the Secretary of State to vary this figure by statutory instrument.
[23] *Commercial Bank of Scotland Ltd.* v. *Lanark Oil Co. Ltd.* 1886, 14 R. 147.
[24] *W. & J. C. Pollok* v. *The Gaeta Pioneer Mining Co. Ltd.* 1907 S.C. 182; 14 S.L.T. 526.
[25] *Cunninghame* v. *Walkinshaw Oil Co.* 1886, 14 R. 87.
[26] *Stonegate Securities Ltd.* v. *Gregory* [1980] 1 All E.R. 241.
[27] *Re Lympne Investments Ltd.* [1972] 1 W.L.R. 523; [1972] 2 All E.R. 385.

excluding the day of service of the demand.[27] In Scotland, however, the period may be held to have expired on the last day of that period.[28]

Under section 223 (*d*) a company is deemed unable to pay its debts "if it is proved to the satisfaction of the court that the company is unable to pay its debts." In determining this, the court is required "to take into account the contingent and prospective liabilities of the company." Evidence of unsuccessful attempts to obtain payment is normally sufficient to satisfy the court.[29]

A winding-up petition is not the proper means of enforcing a debt which is disputed, and accordingly it is a good answer for the company to show that there is a bona fide defence to the debt claimed.[30]

Under section 223 (*c*), a Scottish company is deemed to be unable to pay its debts if "the *induciae* of a charge for payment on an extract decree, or an extract registered bond, or an extract registered protest have expired without payment being made." This applies regardless of the amount of the debt.[31] A parallel provision referring to English companies is contained in section 223 (*b*). These provisions enable a creditor who has obtained a decree against a company to petition for liquidation as an alternative to attempting diligence against its assets.

The Insurance Companies Act 1974, s. 44, provides that an insurance company shall be deemed to be unable to pay its debts if its margin of solvency falls below the statutory minimum. This is in addition to the definitions of "inability to pay its debts" in sections 222 and 223 of the 1948 Act.[32]

Failure to commence business, or suspension of business for a whole year

87–08 This is a most unusual ground for winding up.[33] A company which has ceased to operate directly in its field but has become a company holding shares in others so engaged has not suspended business within the meaning of this provision.[34]

Failure to obtain a trading certificate, etc.

87–09 The Companies Act 1980 contains new grounds for winding up which may only be invoked by the Secretary of State (s. 224 (1) (*b*) as amended by the 1980 Act, Sched 3). The first ground is applicable only to companies formed as new public companies under the 1980 Act. Before such a company may do business or exercise any borrowing powers it must obtain a certificate that it has issued the authorised minimum capital and met the

---

[28] *Neil McLeod & Sons, Ptnrs.* 1967 S.L.T. 46; 1967 S.C. 16, following *Parish Council of Cavers* v. *Parish Council of Smailholm* 1909 S.C. 195.
[29] *Gandy* 1912, 2 S.L.T. 276; *Stephen* v. *Scottish Banking Co.* 1884, 21 S.L.R. 764.
[30] See paras. 87–13 and 87–14, *infra*.
[31] *Speirs & Co.* v. *Central Building Co. Ltd.* 1911 S.C. 330; 1911, 1 S.L.T. 14.
[32] *Re Capital Annuities Ltd.* [1978] 3 All E.R. 704.
[33] See *e.g. Re Middlesbrough Assembly Rooms* (1880) 14 Ch.D. 104—an unsuccessful attempt to invoke this provision.
[34] *Re Eastern Telegraph Co.* [1947] L.J.R. 1247.

other requirements of section 4 of the 1980 Act.[35] Alternatively, it may apply for re-registration as a private company under section 10 of the 1980 Act.[36] If it fails to do so within a year after incorporation it may be wound up under sectin 222 (*b*) (as amended). This is equivalent to a winding up under the original section 222 (*b*) on the grounds of failure to hold the "statutory meeting" required of companies formed as public companies under the 1948 Act. The second ground introduced by the 1980 Act is entirely new. The Act provided for a transitional period of 15 months within which companies which were public companies under the 1948 Act must choose to re-register either as public companies under the 1980 Act or as private companies.[37] If a company fails to do so by the end of the transitional period it is liable to be wound up under section 222 (*bb*).

Floating charge in jeopardy

87–10 As noted above, this ground applies only to a Scottish company which has granted a floating charge, which subsists over property comprised in its property and undertaking.[38] Although it is unlikely that anyone other than the holder of the charge would petition on this ground, the Act does not in terms restrict its use to such a creditor.

For the purposes of section 4 (1) of the 1972 Act, the creditor's security is to be deemed to be in jeopardy "if the court is satisfied that events have occurred or are about to occur which render it unreasonable in the interests of the creditor that the company should retain power to dispose of the property which is subject to the floating charge." This is not an exhaustive definition of "jeopardy," and the court is left with complete discretion as to the events which it may accept as sufficient to entitle the creditor to an order. An order could be granted without the company being insolvent or unable to pay its debts.

This section originally appeared in the Companies (Floating Charges) (Scotland) Act 1961, s. 4. That Act did not enable the holder of a floating charge to appoint a receiver, and accordingly liquidation was his only recourse if his security was endangered. The 1972 Act, however, permits the holder of a floating charge by a Scottish company (including one granted under the 1961 Act) to appoint a receiver, and this facility may make it unnecessary to resort to section 4 as the main grounds for the petition.

The "just and equitable" clause

87–11 Until the passing of the Companies Act 1980 the courts have had to consider the question of whether it would be "just and equitable" to wind up a company in two situations; first, in the context of a winding-up

[35] See para. 19–02, to 19–04, *ante*.
[36] See para 5–09 to 5–11, *ante*.
[37] 1980 Act, s. 9; see para. 4–18, *ante*. The re-registration period expired on March 22, 1981.
[38] Companies (Floating Charges and Receivers) (Scotland) Act 1972, s. 4 (1).

petition under section 222 (*f*), and, second, as an element in determining whether a remedy is available to a member complaining of oppression in the conduct of the company's affairs under section 210. Section 210, introduced by the 1948 Act, has been replaced by section 75 of the Companies Act 1980, which does not require the court to be satisfied that it would be "just and equitable" to wind the company up.[39] Cases decided in the context of section 210 still have relevance in connection with section 222 (*f*).

There is no justification for restricting the circumstances which may be regarded as affording "just and equitable" grounds for winding up, whether by confining the application of this phrase to cases similar to the earlier parts of section 222 or by restricting it to rigid categories such as "loss of substratum" or "deadlock."[40] The courts are at liberty to adopt a liberal approach and previous decisions on whether a winding-up order should be granted on this ground should be treated as illustrations only.[41] The court must nevertheless exercise its discretion judicially on grounds which can be examined and justified.[42] It must proceed on the facts as they are at the date of the hearing, not when the petition was presented.[43] Cases of the application of this rule in England, valid as illustrations for Scotland, are discussed in paragraphs 85–08 to 85–11, *ante*. In Scotland, a winding-up order on this ground has been granted in the following situations:

> Where the business of the company was unsuccessful and a majority of the shareholders, but not sufficient to pass a special resolution for voluntary liquidation, wished it to be wound up.[44]
>
> Where there was a serious failure to comply with the rules of administration of a company laid down by the Companies Acts, such as to deprive the shareholders of the guarantee of commercial probity and efficiency afforded thereby.[45]

There is no reported case in Scotland of a company being wound up on the sole ground that its substratum had been lost. The leading English authority,[46] which has been quoted with approval in Scotland,[47] lays down that before it could be said that the substratum of the company's business has gone and a winding-up order might therefore be justified it is necessary to show that business within its objects had become in a practical sense impossible. A mere discontinuance of business activities, even for a lengthy period, is not enough, so long as this does not show a final and conclusive abandonment of the business, and provided also that the com-

---

[39] See para. 60–08, *ante*.
[40] *Baird* v. *Lees*, 1924 S.C. 83, 90; 1923 S.L.T. 749.
[41] *Ebrahimi* v. *Westbourne Galleries Ltd., per* Lord Wilberforce [1973]; A.C. 360, 374; [1972] 2 All E.R. 292, 296; *Re St. Piran Ltd.* [1981] 3 All E.R. 270; see also paras. 85–08 to 85–11, *ante*.
[42] *Baird* v. *Lees*, 1924 S.C. 83, 90; 1923 S.L.T. 749.
[43] *Re Fildes Bros. Ltd.* [1970] 1 W.L.R. 592; [1970] 1 All E.R. 923.
[44] *Pirie* v. *Stewart*, 1904, 6 F. 847; 12 S.L.T. 129.
[45] *Baird* v. *Lees, supra.*
[46] *Re Suburban Hotel Co.* (1867) 2 Ch.App. 737.
[47] *Galbraith* v. *Merito Shipping Co.*, 1947 S.C. 446, 456.

pany's resources are being conserved so as to make a resumption of business possible.[47a] It may of course be possible to bring such a case within the scope of section 222 (*c*) (suspension of business for a whole year).[48] A petition for winding up was held to be premature where the trading business of the company had come to an end and would not be resumed, but the directors were still engaged in negotiations to bring its affairs to a conclusion.[49]

This ground for winding up has most frequently been invoked by shareholders complaining that the management of the company was being conducted in a manner harmful to their interests. It is not, however, a legitimate means of securing a personal advantage by the premature liquidation of a solvent company.[50]

In approaching the question of whether the complaining shareholders had made out their case, the courts have emphasised the need for the minority to show good cause for the courts to override the wishes of the majority where the question in issue has been simply that of whether to grant a winding-up order on the "just and equitable" ground.[51] The company itself is the proper forum for resolving domestic differences among shareholders, but if these cannot be resolved and a deadlock results a winding-up order will be granted.[52] It is apparent, however, that a strict adherence to the principles of "majority rule" will not always achieve a just and equitable result. Where the holder of the vast majority of the shares was running the company for his personal benefit and with no regard for the interests of the company as a whole, the court granted an order. The case was, however, decided to a large extent on the particular circumstances.[53] If the majority is abusing its position in disregard of statutory obligations, an order may be granted.[54] Cases decided under section 210 reflect this trend.[55] It has recently been held in the House of Lords, in an English case, that if the total relationship of the parties, including agreements outwith the articles of the company, exhibit the characteristics of a partnership the courts may hold a breakdown of mutual confidence among the members to be grounds for regarding a winding-up order as "just and equitable".[56]

[47a] *Galbraith* v. *Merito Shipping Co. supra.*
[48] *Galbraith* v. *Merito Shipping Co. supra, per* Lord Mackay, p. 459.
[49] *Cox* v. *"Gosford" Ship Co.* 1894, 21 R. 334.
[50] *Anglo-American Brush Electric Light Corp. Ltd.* v. *Scottish Brush Electric Light and Power Co. Ltd.* 1882, 9 R. 972.
[51] *Martin* v. *Scottish Savings Investment Society* 1897, 7 R. 352; *Black* v. *United Collieries Ltd.* 1904, 7 F. 18; 12 S.L.T. 373; *Scobie* v. *Atlas Steel Works Ltd.* 1906, 8 F. 1052; 14 S.L.T. 212.
[52] *Symington* v. *Symington Quarries Ltd.* 1905, 8 F. 121; 13 S.L.T. 509.
[53] *Thomson* v. *Drysdale*, 1925 S.C. 311; 1925 S.L.T. 174; see also *Zolkwer* v. *Reid, Carr & Co.*, 1946 S.N. 141.
[54] *Baird* v. *Lees, supra.*
[55] *Elder* v. *Elder & Watson*, 1952 S.C. 49; 1952 S.L.T. 112; *Meyer* v. *S.C.W.S.*, 1954 S.C. 381; 1954 S.L.T. 273; *Meyer* v. *S.C.W.S.*, 1958 S.C. (H.L.) 40; 1958 S.L.T. 241.
[56] *Ebrahimi* v. *Westbourne Galleries Ltd.* [1973] A.C. 360; [1972] 2 All E.R. 292; see paras. 85–09 to 85–10, *ante*.

A contributory may rely on a report by inspectors appointed by the Secretary of State in support of his petition.[56a]

The decisions have to be considered in the context of the statutory provisions of the time. In particular, prior to 1948, there was no "alternative remedy" for an oppressed minority shareholder[57] and if the petitioners had some other remedy, they might be required to exhaust it before proceeding to a winding up.[58] The latter obstacle was removed, or at least substantially reduced, by section 225 (2) under which the existence of another remedy is not to be a reason for refusing to grant a winding-up order on the "just and equitable" ground unless the court is satisfied that the petitioners are acting unreasonably in seeking a winding-up order instead of the alternative remedy. Nevertheless, the replacement of section 210 by the 1980 Act, s. 75 may have increased the likelihood of the court holding that a winding-up petition was unreasonable, since section 75 itself provides a wider range of alternative remedies.

Petition for compulsory winding up

'7–12 Application to the court is by way of petition (1948 Act, s. 224 (1)), which (with the exception of petitions under section 222 (*b*) and (*bb*), which can only be presented by the Secretary of State[59]) may be presented by any or all of:

(a) the company;
(b) any creditor;
(c) any contributory;
(d) a receiver[60];
(e) the Secretary of State.[61]

In addition, the Bank of England has power to petition in certain circumstances for the winding up of a bank or an institution licensed to take deposits[62] and the Department of Trade may petition for the winding up of an insurance company.[63] Insurance companies may also be wound up, in certain circumstances, on a petition by policyholders.[64] The Chief Registrar of Friendly Societies also has power to present a petition for the winding up of a building society in the case of certain defaults by it.[65]

The right to petition cannot be excluded by the articles.[66]

A petition by the company is less usual, since it can more easily commence winding up by resolution (1948 Act, s. 278). A petition may nevertheless be appropriate to obtain the earliest possible date for the com-

---

[56a] *Re St. Piran Ltd.* [1981] 3 All E.R. 270.
[57] Companies Act 1948, s. 210—see paras. 60–02 to 60–07, *ante*.
[58] See para. 85–11, *ante*.
[59] See para. 87–09, *ante*.
[60] Companies (Floating Charges and Receivers) (Scotland) Act 1972, s. 15 (1) (*r*).
[61] 1967 Act, s. 35 (1) see para. 78–14, *ante*.
[62] See para. 85–20, *ante* (Banking Act 1979, s. 18).
[63] See para. 89–38, *post*.
[64] Insurance Companies Act 1974, s. 45.
[65] Building Societies Act 1962, ss. 22, 50, 55 and Sched. I, para. 5.
[66] *Re Peveril Gold Mines* [1898] 1 Ch. 122.

mencement of winding up and thereby cut down diligence and restrain proceedings against the company.[67] With the exception of petitions based on the "just and equitable" clause, shareholders' petitions are also unusual. The majority of petitions are presented by creditors. The list of potential petitioners in section 224 (1) appears to be exhaustive (apart from the statutory additions indicated above).[68] A director cannot present a petition on his own authority.[68a]

Creditor's petition

87–13 WHO IS A CREDITOR? "Creditor" has its ordinary meaning of any person to whom the company is owing money, and by section 224 (1) of the 1948 Act this extends to contingent and prospective creditors. A person to whom a debt has been assigned is as much a "creditor" as the assignor. It appears that the holder of a floating charge may petition for winding up notwithstanding his appointment of a receiver.[69]

A contingent or prospective creditor must find caution for expenses, and must establish a prima facie case to the satisfaction of the court before his petition can be heard (s. 224 (1) (*c*)).

"Contingent creditor" means a creditor in respect of a debt which will only become due in an event which may or may not occur; "prospective creditor" means a creditor in respect of a debt which will certainly become due in the future, either on some date which has already been determined or on some date determinable by reference to future events.[70]

A winding-up petition is not the appropriate process for recovery of a debt which is disputed, and a petition presented in such circumstances may be dismissed with expenses.[71] Although caution was found by the company in both the Scottish cases cited, the court did not regard this as a necessary condition for dismissing the petition. A dispute over part only of a liquid claim is not a ground for refusing to grant an order.[72] The court has, however, the power to sist the petition to enable the petitioner to constitute (by separate court action) a debt which is disputed *in toto*.[73]

A creditor who has failed to establish the basis on which he petitioned cannot oppose an unconditional restraint on further such proceedings on the same basis, nor can the liquidation process be used to resolve a *bona fide* dispute as to whether a claim is presently due, contingent or prospective.[74]

---

[67] See further para. 85–12, *ante*.
[68] *Re William Hockley Ltd.* [1962] 1 W.L.R. 555, 558; 2 All E.R. 111; *Re H. L. Bolton Engineering Co. Ltd.* [1956] Ch. 577.
[68a] *Re Regent Insulation Co.* [1981] C.L.Y. 250.
[69] See para. 48–01, *ante*.
[70] *Stonegate Securities Ltd.* v. *Gregory* [1980] 1 All E.R. 241, 243.
[71] *Cunninghame, etc.* v. *Walkinshaw Oil Co.* 1886, 14 R. 87; *W. & J. C. Pollok* v. *Gaeta Pioneer Mining Co.* 1907 S.C. 182; 14 S.L.T. 526; see also *Re Lympne Investments Ltd.* [1972] 1 W.L.R. 523; [1972] 2 All E.R. 385.
[72] *Cowan* v. *Scottish Publishing Co.* 1892, 19 R. 437; *Re Tweeds Garages* [1962] Ch. 406; [1962] 1 All E.R. 121.
[73] *Landauer & Co.* v. *W. H. Alexander & Co. Ltd.* 1919 S.C. 492; 1919, 2 S.L.T. 2.
[74] *Stonegate Securities Ltd.* v. *Gregory, supra.*

Creditor's right to a winding-up order

87–14 Subject to the discretion of the court to dismiss, adjourn or make any other order in relation to the petition which it thinks fit (1948 Act, s. 225 (1)) a creditor who has established that his debt is due and that the company is unable to pay its debts is *prima facie* entitled to a winding-up order.[75] Such a petition will not in any event be summarily dismissed in the absence of very cogent reasons.[76] An order cannot be refused merely because there are securities equal to or greater than the value of the assets, or because there are no assets available to the liquidator,[77] or because the company is already in voluntary liquidation[78] but the petitioning creditor must demonstrate the likelihood of some advantage accruing to him.[78a] However, a creditor has no inherent right to information about the assets of the company and cannot obtain such information indirectly, *e.g.* by seeking that such disclosure or a Declaration of Solvency be made as a condition of the court restraining further procedure on a winding-up petition whose grounds have not been established.[79]

Section 346 of the 1948 Act provides that the court may have regard to the wishes of the creditors (having regard to the value of their debts) or contributories (having regard to their voting rights), and may convene meetings to ascertain their wishes.[80] In a creditor's petition, apart from cases where there is doubt as to the existence of the creditor's claim, opposition by the company or its members will not result in the petition being refused.[81] Other creditors may, however, oppose the granting of a winding-up order (or any order placing an existing voluntary winding up under the supervision of the court).[82] In such cases the court will normally have regard to the wishes of the majority in value of the creditors.[83] This is not, however, an inflexible rule, and if the court considers there are circumstances justifying its intervention, an order for winding up by the court will be granted notwithstanding the views of the majority of creditors.[84] It may also refuse to grant an order against the wishes of the

[75] *Smyth & Co.* v. *Salem Flour Mills Co. Ltd.* 1887, 14 R. 441; *Gardner & Co.* v. *Link* 1894, 21 R. 967. *Re Tweeds Garages Ltd.* [1962] Ch. 406, 414; *Foxhall & Gyle (Nurseries) Ltd. (Ptnrs.)* 1978 S.L.T.(Notes) 29.
[76] *Foxhall & Gyle (Nurseries) Ltd. (Ptnrs.), supra.*
[77] s. 225.
[78] s. 310.
[78a] *In re Eloc Electro-Optieck* [1981] 3 W.L.R. 176; [1981] 2 All E.R. 1111.
[79] *Stonegate Securities Ltd.* v. *Gregory* [1980] 1 All E.R. 241.
[80] *Wilson* v. *Hadley, etc.* 1897, 7 R. 178.
[81] See para. 87–13, *supra*; *Macdonnell's Trustees* v. *Oregonian Railway Co.* 1884, 11 R. 912 (bondholder with arrears of interest paid since the petition was presented); *Wotherspoons* v. *Brescia Mining and Metallurgical Co. Ltd.* 1896, 24 R. 207; 4 S.L.T. 184.
[82] See para. 87–104, *infra*.
[83] *Elmsie & Son* v. *The Tomatin Spey District Distillery* 1906, 8 F. 434; 13 S.L.T. 722; *Pattisons Ltd.* v. *Kinnear* 1899, 1 F. 551; 6 S.L.T. 304; *Bell's Trs.* v. *The Holmes Oil Co.* 1900, 3 F. 23; *Drysdale & Gilmour* v. *Liquidator of International Exhibition of Electrical Engineering and Inventions* 1890, 18 R. 98.
[84] *Bouboulis* v. *Mann Macneal & Co.*, 1926 S.C. 637; 1926 S.L.T. 417.

majority of creditors if satisfied that it would be more appropriate to allow the wishes of the minority to prevail.[85]

An attempt to suggest some general principles was made in *Re J. D. Swain Ltd.*[86] If the creditors are agreed that the company should be wound up, but a minority (in value) seek a compulsory order, the court will be disposed to refuse the petition since all will in any event receive the class remedy in the voluntary liquidation. On the other hand, if the majority are opposed to winding up in any form, the wishes of the minority should normally prevail and the order be granted, since only thus will the petitioner receive the remedy to which he is prima facie entitled. These general considerations (persuasive only in Scotland) must, of course, be subject to any special factors which may be present in the particular case.[87]

Contributory's petition

87–15 A shareholder's petition for winding up must overcome a number of obstacles:

First, the petitioner must be qualified under section 224 (1) (*a*) which is designed to prevent persons buying shares merely to wreck the company. Unless the petition is on the ground that the number of members has been reduced below the statutory minimum,[88] some at least of his shares must have been originally allotted to him, or have been registered in his name for at least 6 of the 18 months before commencement of the winding up, or have devolved on him through the death of a former holder. Strict compliance with these requirements is necessary, unless perhaps the company is in default in allotting shares or registering a transfer.[89] If there is a genuine dispute whether the petitioner is an allottee he cannot proceed until he has established his rights.[90] A bankrupt shareholder may petition at the instance of his trustee,[91] but not the trustee himself.[92] A discharged bankrupt is not, however, entitled to petition in his own name since the shares remain vested in his trustee in bankruptcy.[93] The personal representatives of a deceased shareholder may petition as contributories.[94]

Second, the petitioner must satisfy the court that constitutional methods of achieving a winding up within the company, such as a resolution for its voluntary liquidation, have been attempted without success or are

[85] *Re Southard & Co. Ltd.* [1979] 1 All E.R. 582. (The minority wished the voluntary liquidation to continue.)
[86] [1965] 1 W.L.R. 909; [1965] 2 All E.R. 761.
[87] See passage quoted from *Swain*, para. 85–06, *ante*. See also *Floors of Bristol (Builders) Ltd.* [1982] 7 C.L. 51a.
[88] Now two in all cases—Companies Act 1980, s. 2 and Sched. 4.
[89] *Re Gattopardo Ltd.* [1969] 1 W.L.R. 619, C.A; [1969] 2 All E.R. 344.
[90] *Re JN 2* [1977] 3 All E.R. 1104.
[91] s. 216 (*a*); *Re K/9 Meat Supplies (Guildford) Ltd.* [1966] 1 W.L.R. 1112; [1966] 3 All E.R. 320.
[92] *Re H. L. Bolton Engineering Co. Ltd.* [1956] Ch. 577; [1956] 1 All E.R. 799.
[93] *Re Wolverhampton Steel & Iron Co. Ltd.* [1977] 1 All E.R. 417 affd. [1977] 3 All E.R. 467. *Cf.* Bankruptcy (Scotland) Act 1913, ss. 144, 152 and 153.
[94] s. 215; *Re Bayswater Trading Co. Ltd.* [1970] 1 W.L.R. 343; [1970] 1 All E.R. 608.

impossible or inappropriate.[95] In *Galbraith* v. *Merito Shipping Co.*[96] it is suggested that such preliminary steps would not be required if the grounds for the petition were "loss of substratum." Normally, this requirement will restrict contributories' petitions to the "just and equitable" clause.[97] There are, however, other circumstances where a shareholder's petition is appropriate, such as an aborted reconstruction scheme.[98]

Third, the petitioner must have a pecuniary interest in the outcome of the winding-up proceedings. Normally, this means that he must show a prima facie probability that a surplus will emerge for distribution to himself and other members.[99] Consequently, a contributory cannot petition on the ground of inability to pay debts. This rule, however, does not apply where the contributory's shares are partly paid, since his interest then may be to minimise his loss which would result from having to contribute in an insolvent liquidation. Where the petitioner bases his application on the "just and equitable" clause (s. 222 (*f*) he may meet this requirement by alleging that information supplied by the company is inadequate to determine whether a surplus will emerge, or that its affairs require investigation which is likely to reveal a surplus.[1] A contributory cannot, however, succeed if the result of investigation would benefit only the creditors,[2] nor if he merely avers that the company is in substance a partnership.[3]

A shareholder who is in arrears with calls must make out an exceptional case to justify his petition, and may be required to pay the arrears into court or give an undertaking in respect of them.[4]

The existence of a voluntary winding up will normally leave no room for a shareholder to justify a compulsory order, but it is not an absolute bar. The court must, however, be satisfied that the rights of contributories would be prejudiced by a voluntary winding up.[5]

Petition by receiver

87–16 The Companies (Floating Charges and Receivers) (Scotland) Act 1972, s. 15, accords to a receiver wide powers of administration, which include power to present a winding-up petition, but which will normally make such a petition unnecessary. If, however, the assets under his control do not suffice to satisfy the claims of the holder of the floating charge, and the

---

[95] *Symington* v. *Symington Quarries Ltd.* 1905, 8 F. 121; 13 S.L.T. 509; *Pirie* v. *Stewart* 1904, 6 F. 847; 12 S.L.T. 179; *Cox* v. *"Gosford" Shipping Co.* 1894, 21 R. 334; 1 S.L.T. 431; *Baird* v. *Lees*, 1924 S.C. 83; 1923 S.L.T. 749; *Scobie* v. *Atlas Steel Works* 1906, 8 F. 1052; 14 S.L.T. 212.

[96] 1947 S.C. 446; 1947 S.L.T. 265.

[97] See para. 87–11, *ante*.

[98] *Re Gutta Percha Corporation* [1900] 2 Ch. 655.

[99] *Ptn Walker* 1894, 2 S.L.T. 230 and 397; *Re W. R. Willcocks & Co. Ltd.* [1974] Ch. 163; *Re Chesterfield Catering Co. Ltd.* [1977] Ch. 373.

[1] *Re Newman and Howard Ltd.* [1962] Ch. 257.

[2] *Re Othery Construction Ltd.* [1966] 1 W.L.R. 69; [1966] 1 All E.R. 145.

[3] *Re Expanded Plugs Ltd.* [1966] 1 W.L.R. 514; [1966] 1 All E.R. 877.

[4] *Re Diamond Fuel Co.* (1879) 13 Ch.D. 400; *Re Crystal Reef Co.* [1892] 1 Ch. 408.

[5] s. 310; *Green & Sons* v. *Frasers (Aberdeen) Ltd.* (1939) 55 Sh.Ct.Rep. 133; *Re National Company for Distribution of Electricity* [1902] 2 Ch. 34.

prior claims which the receiver is required to satisfy, winding up may be the appropriate step.

Petition by Secretary of State

87–17 The Secretary of State for Scotland, representing the Department of Trade, has power to present a petition for the winding up of a company (under s. 35 (1) of the Companies Act 1967) on the grounds that it is in the public interest that the company should be wound up. He may proceed on the basis of an inspector's report under section 168 of the 1948 Act, information derived from an inspection of a company's books and papers under Part III of the 1967 Act, or information or a document obtained under section 18 or 19 of the Protection of Depositors Act 1963. The court has nevertheless the discretion whether or not to grant an order on a petition by the Secretary of State.[6] The Secretary of State may also apply for an order under section 75 of the 1980 Act (replacing s. 35 (2) of the 1967 Act) in addition to or as an alternative to winding up.[7]

Form of petition[8]

87–18 R.C.S. 202 (*a*) and Sh.Ct.R. 2 and 3 require the petition to design the petitioner, and to give the name of the company, its registered office (and any change of address in the last six months known to the petitioner), its nature and objects, details of nominal and issued capital and the amount of its assets so far as known to the petitioner. The facts on which the petitioner relies to establish his prima facie case, and particulars required to instruct his title to petition, must be set out. The petition must include details of the orders sought including intimation and advertisement and any appointment of a liquidator.

Presentation and answering

87–19 Petitions in the Court of Session are presented in the Outer House and are dealt with by the liquidation judge (s. 221 and R.C.S. 202 (*a*)), unless in vacation, when the vacation judge deals with them under section 220 (2). Any documents instructing the petitioner's title or founded on, or instructing the facts relied on, by the petitioner must be lodged with the petition (R.C.S. 202 (*b*) (Sh.Ct.R. 3)).

Any company, shareholder or debenture holder may lodge a *caveat* in the court offices, which has the effect of preventing any order being granted until that party has been given an opportunity to be heard (R.C.S. 202 (*c*) (Sh.Ct.R. 5)). Petitions are heard by the judge as soon as practicable after presentation. The court has complete discretion on how to dispose of a petition (s. 225 (1)), but the normal first order is for intima-

---

6 *Re Lubin, Rosen and Associates Ltd.* [1975] 1 All E.R. 577; see para. 85–19, *ante*.
7 See para. 60–08, *ante*.
8 For a recent discussion of procedural aspects see "Liquidation Procedure in the Court of Session" by William W. McBryde 1977 S.L.T. (News) 237 and *McBryde and Dawie Petition Procedures in the Court of Session* (W. Green & Son, Edinburgh, 1980) p. 19.

tion, service and advertisement. In many cases a provisional liquidator is appointed (see *infra*).

Advertisement of petition

The normal order is for the petition to be advertised once in the *Edinburgh Gazette* and in one or more newspapers circulating in the district of the company's registered office. The advertisement must state the date the petition was presented, particulars of the petitioner and his solicitor, the precise order applied for and the *induciae* within which answers may be lodged (R.C.S. 202 (*d*) (Sh.Ct.R. 5)).

Service of petition

87–20 The petition is directed to be intimated on the walls and in the minute book[8a] and served upon the company and any other person considered to have an interest (*e.g.* an existing voluntary liquidator) in the usual manner, *i.e.* recorded delivery or by registered post or personally. The *induciae* is normally 14 days (R.C.S. 192).

Hearing of petition

87–21 Under section 225 the court may, on hearing the petition, dismiss it, adjourn the hearing conditionally or unconditionally, or make any interim or other order as it thinks fit. It may have regard to the wishes of creditors and contributories, and order meetings to be held to ascertain them (s. 346). If the company is solvent the wishes of the contributories carry more weight than those of the creditors, but the reverse applies in insolvency.[9] A winding-up petition presented by the Secretary of State after an investigation must be given appropriate weight, even if unsupported by any creditor and opposed by many creditors with large claims and in face of a resolution for voluntary winding up.[10]

Substitute petitioner

87–22 When the original petitioner consents to dismissal or does not press for an order, a substitute petitioner may be sisted at the discretion of the court under R.C.S. 204 (Sh.Ct.R. 13). The substitute petitioner must lodge a note before the original petitioner has withdrawn or the petition is refused or dismissed; lodging of a minute of withdrawal by the petitioner is not itself withdrawal, and a note presented afterwards may still be timeous.[11]

Commencement of winding up

87–23 A winding up by the court commences on the date the petition is presented to the court (s. 229 (2)), unless a resolution for voluntary

[8a] Intimation in the minute book is attended to by the court officials. Walling is effected by the petitioner's solicitor (Practice Note November 16, 1961).
[9] See para. 87–14, *ante*.
[10] *Re Lubin, Rosen and Associates* [1975] 1 W.L.R. 122; [1975] 1 All E.R. 577.
[11] *Hepburn & Ross* v. *Tritonia Ltd.*, 1951 S.L.T.(Sh.Ct.) 6. See also *The Tudor Accumulator Co. Ltd.* v. *Scott Stirling & Co. Ltd.*, 1908 S.C. 331.

winding up has already been passed, when it commences on the date of the resolution (s. 299 (1)). Unless the court, on proof of fraud or error, directs otherwise, all proceedings in such a voluntary winding up are deemed valid (s. 229 (1)). Where a petition was first presented founding on a repealed statute (the Companies (Consolidation) Act 1908) and later re-served with amendments showing that it was founded on the current Act (of 1929), the date of commencement of the winding up was held to be the date of the order for re-service.[12]

Provisional liquidator

87–24 The court has power to appoint a provisional liquidator at any time after the presentation of the petition until an official liquidator is appointed (s. 238 (1) and (3); R.C.S. 202 (*e*) (Sh.Ct.R. 6)). The petition should contain an application for such appointment, if desired (R.C.S. 202 (*a*) (iv) (Sh.Ct.R. 2 (iv)), but application may be made by later motion or note (R.C.S. 215 (*a*) (Sh.Ct.R. 47)). It is almost invariable practice to apply for the appointment of a provisional liquidator on presentation of the petition and (assuming the petition is prima facie justified) to grant the application unless the petition is opposed on grounds which appear substantial. In considering whether to make an appointment the court is concerned to maintain the status quo in the affairs of the company and will attempt to avoid prejudice to either party.[13]

The provisional liquidator is normally the duly qualified accountant whom it is proposed should be appointed official liquidator. The court will expect the petitioner to have ascertained that he is willing to act before presenting the petition. If there is dispute as to the proper person to be appointed, the court may nominate an independent person. The appointment may be recalled, but if the interlocutor recalling the appointment is the subject of an appeal the provisional liquidator remains in office until the reclaiming motion has been disposed of.[14]

Under section 238 (4) the court may limit the powers of a provisional liquidator. It is common to restrict his powers to section 245 (1) (*a*), (*b*) or (*c*), at least initially (*i.e.* to bring or defend proceedings, to carry on the company's business, and to appoint a solicitor). The form of interlocutor in use in Scotland is ambiguous as there is no express reference to limits or restrictions on the provisional liquidator's powers. The practice seems to be, however, that his powers are restricted to those specifically mentioned in the interlocutor.[14a] There are reported cases (as well as the unreported case referred to in Mr. McBryde's article[15]) consistent with the view that express powers should be sought.[16] English practice is the reverse.[17] While

[12] *Ballantyne* v. *Train* 1935 S.N. 111.
[13] *Levy* v. *Napier*, 1962 S.L.T. 264.
[14] *Levy*, 1968 S.C. 46.
[14a] See McBryde, "The Powers of Provisional Liquidators," 1977 S.L.T. (News) 145.
[15] *Drummond Wood Ltd.* (December 7, 1971).
[16] *Lochore and Capledraw Cannel Coal Co. Ltd.* 1889, 16 R. 556; *Wilsons (Glasgow & Trinidad) Ltd.*, 1912, 2 S.L.T. 330;
[17] See para. 85–32, *ante*.

a provisional liquidator would obviously be wise to apply for powers in any case of doubt, it may be an open question whether, if he does act as if he had implied powers, his acts could successfully be challenged as unauthorised. The Act makes no distinction between a liquidator and a liquidator appointed provisionally in the matter of powers, except to provide that a provisional liquidator's powers may be *restricted* by the court. If Scottish practice involves an implied restriction, it may be argued that in fact section 238 (4) authorises only an express restriction.

Form of winding-up order

87–25 If no answers are lodged, or after answers have been disposed of, the usual order is to the effect that the company be wound up by the court under the provisions of the Companies Acts. The order will appoint an official liquidator (or liquidators), fix the amount of caution to be found by him and ordain intimation of his appointment. The further procedure required to give effect to this order, and its legal consequences, are noted below.

Expenses

87–26 The normal practice in Scotland is for the successful petitioner to be awarded his expenses against the company, and for any unsuccessful objector to be found liable in the expenses occasioned by his intervention.[18] The court may, however, award expenses or refuse them at its discretion if circumstances warrant this,[19] for example, if the court considers that the expense of a petition was not justified where a company with few assets was already in voluntary liquidation.[20] The expenses of two petitions will not normally be allowed,[21] nor will the expenses of lodging answers merely objecting to the appointment of a particular person as liquidator, the appropriate procedure being to raise such objections at the bar.[22] The courts have used their discretion on expenses to discourage petitioners and objectors from increasing the cost of liquidation by procedures which have no practical value, however justifiable in theory.

A contingent or prospective creditor who petitions may be required to find caution for expenses (s. 244 (1) (*c*)). An appellant company may be required to find caution under section 447.[23]

Proceedings following on winding-up order

87–27 A copy certified by the court of the winding-up order must be delivered (or posted by recorded delivery or registered mail) to the Registrar of

[18] *McGregor* v. *Ballachulish Slate Quarries Ltd.*, 1908 S.C. 1; 15 S.L.T. 397.
[19] For examples see *Pattullo* v. *Caithness Flagstone Co.* 1908 S.C. 25; 15 S.L.T. 398; *The Seafield Preserve Co.*, 1911 S.C. 3; 1910; 2 S.L.T. 199; *Liquidator of the Property Investment Co. of Scotland* v. *Blaik* 1873, 20 R. 1044.
[20] *Matthew Wishart, Ptnr*, 1908 S.C. 690; 15 S.L.T. 953.
[21] *Graham, etc.* v. *Edinburgh Theatre Co.* 1877, 4 R. 1140.
[22] *Hume* v. *Directors of Highland Peat Fuel Co.* 1876, 3 R. 881; *Anderson & Sons* v. *Broughty Ferry Picture House* 1917, S.C. 622; 1917 2 S.L.T. 44.
[23] *Cf. Pearson* v. *Naydler* [1977] 3 All E.R. 531.

Companies within 14 days. The order must also be advertised once in the *Edinburgh Gazette*, within 14 days. Evidence of delivery or posting and a copy of the *Gazette* must be lodged in the process, on pain of forfeiture of the award of expenses (s. 230, R.C.S. 205 (Sh.Ct.R. 14, 15, 16)).

The order also requires official notification by the Registrar of Companies in the *Edinburgh Gazette* under the European Communities Act 1972, s. 9 (3).[24] Only 15 days after such notification is the order fully effective; if it is not notified the company (*i.e.* the liquidator) cannot rely on it against a third party who did not have actual notice of it. If it has been notified but the 15-day period has not expired the order may be relied upon unless a third party shows that he was unavoidably prevented from knowing of it. It is therefore prudent for the liquidator to ascertain whether such notification has in fact been given by the Registrar.

The granting of a winding-up order in Scotland will thus be published twice in the *Edinburgh Gazette* (namely, under R.C.S. 205 and the European Communities Act). The draftsman of the European Communities Act has been careful to avoid this unnecessary duplication elsewhere (*e.g.* voluntary winding up under s. 305 or dissolution under s. 353 of the 1948 Act).

Every invoice, order for goods or business letter issued by or on behalf of the company or the liquidator after the winding-up order must contain a statement that the company is in liquidation (1948 Act, s. 338).

The liquidator

87–28 APPOINTMENT OF LIQUIDATOR. On appointment, and normally within 14 days, a liquidator appointed by the court (including a provisional liquidator) has to find caution, *i.e.* lodge in court an insurance bond with an approved insurance company guaranteeing performance of his duty to protect the assets (s. 241 (*a*), R.C.S. 206 (Sh.Ct.R. 17–21)).[25] The court fixes and may vary the amount of caution (R.C.S. 206 (*a*) (Sh.Ct.R. 17)). The expenses of the bond and of any application to vary the amount of caution are normally allowable as expenses in the liquidation.[26] If a successor is appointed to the original liquidator the court may ordain him to find caution even if his predecessor was not required to do so.[27] Usually the amount of caution is two-thirds of the company's assets.

The liquidator is referred to as "the official liquidator" of the company (s. 241 (*b*)). A body corporate cannot be appointed (s. 335), but this does not prevent a Scottish firm from acting as liquidator. A person may be disqualified by court order from acting as a liquidator under the Insolvency Act 1976, section 9 (1) as amended by the Companies Act 1981, section 94.

---

[24] See para. 17–03, *ante*.
[25] The Sheriff Court Rules specify 15 days for finding caution.
[26] *Alexander Forrester Ltd.*, 1907 S.C. 552; 14 S.L.T. 989; *James Donaldson & Co. Ltd.* 1907, 15 S.L.T. 78.
[27] *Gray*, 1910 S.C. 358; 1910, 1 S.L.T. 156.

Joint liquidators may be appointed (s. 237), but the court will not necessarily agree to a joint appointment if the assets of the company do not justify the additional expense.[28] If joint liquidators are appointed the court shall declare whether any act is to be done by all or any one or more of them (s. 242 (4)).

It is an offence to seek to influence the appointment by corrupt inducement (1948 Act, s. 336). The acts of a liquidator (not being a body corporate) are valid notwithstanding any defects afterwards found in his appointment or qualification (1948 Act, s. 242 (5)).

It is the normal practice to appoint a qualified accountant as liquidator. No rule has been laid down as to how much experience he should have. The name of the proposed first appointee, who must be willing to act,[29] will appear in the petition. The court has unfettered discretion as to the appointment after giving due consideration to the views of contributories and creditors.[30] Any objection to an appointment should be stated at the bar, not by way of answers, and must be "of a tangible and definite nature."[31] The court will assume, in the absence of contrary proof, that a liquidator will properly discharge his statutory duty, mere allegations that he will not be independent being insufficient to sustain objections.[32] As a general rule the wishes of the creditors, or a majority of them, will prevail.[33] If necessary the court will order a meeting to be held to ascertain their wishes, but will not be bound to act in accordance with the result, if it feels that the proper administration of the liquidation requires a different appointment.[34] The liquidator must normally be resident in Scotland although it is not incompetent to appoint a liquidator from outwith the jurisdiction,[35] even as sole liquidator.[36] The court's discretion on the appointment will not readily be disturbed on appeal.[36]

The court also fills vacancies in the office of liquidator (s. 242 (3)).

The court has replaced a liquidator who declined office,[37] appointed a replacement for a joint liquidator who had died or resigned, on the application of creditors or contributories,[38] and appointed a surviving joint liquidator as sole liquidator.[39]

---

[28] *Wishart*, 1908 S.C. 690; 15 S.L.T. 953.
[29] *Charles*, 1963 S.L.T.(Notes) 76.
[30] *Brightwen & Co.* v. *City of Glasgow Bank* 1878, 6 R. 244.
[31] *Anderson & Sons* v. *Broughty Ferry Picture House*, 1917 S.C. 622; 1917, 2 S.L.T. 44; see also *Hume* v. *Directors of Highland Peat Fuel Co.* 1876, 3 R. 881; *Gilmour's Trs.* v. *Kilmarnock Heritable Property Investment Co.* 1883, 10 R. 1221; *Sanderson & Muirhead Ltd.* 1884, 21 S.L.R. 766.
[32] *Anderson & Sons* v. *Broughty Ferry Picture House, supra*; *Ecuadorian Assocn.* v. *Stanmore* 1904, 12 S.L.T. 92.
[33] See note 31, *supra*.
[34] *Argyll's Ltd.* v. *Ritchie & Whiteman*, 1914 S.C. 915; 1914, 2 S.L.T. 136.
[35] *Baberton Development Syndicate Ltd.* 1898, 25 R. 654; *Liquidators of Bruce Peebles & Co.* v. *Shiells*, 1908 S.C. 692; 15 S.L.T. 999.
[36] *Steel Scaffolding Co.* v. *Buckleys Ltd.*, 1935 S.C. 617; 1935 S.L.T. 467.
[37] *Glasgow Commercial Co.* 1913, 1 S.L.T. 117.
[38] *Liquidator of Ecuadorian Assocn.* v. *Fox* 1906, 14 S.L.T. 47.
[39] *P. C. Middleton & Co.* 1903, 11 S.L.T. 450.

Resignation and removal of liquidator

A liquidator may resign or, on cause shown be removed by the court (s. 242 (1), R.C.S. 207 (Sh.Ct.R. 23)). Application for his removal may be by a creditor or a contributory. The court will require cause to be shown even if the majority wish the liquidator's removal.[40] Misconduct does not require to be established, but removal of a liquidator will only be allowed if it is shown to be in the best interests of the liquidation[41] such as the existence of a conflict of interests.[42] The court removed a liquidator (in a voluntary liquidation) who was resident in England and supported a scheme of reconstruction of the company which the shareholders claimed was disadvantageous and unfair.[43]

It is not necessary to apply for the removal of a voluntary liquidator who has refused to act.[44]

Remuneration of liquidator

The remuneration of the official liquidator, and the apportionment of remuneration among joint liquidators, is fixed by the court (s. 242 (2)). The court is not necessarily bound by a prior agreement on apportionment among joint liquidators.[45] The remuneration is determined on the basis of a recommendation by the auditor of court after consultation with the accountant appointed to audit the account of the liquidator's intromissions.[46]

The court will discourage more than one application by the liquidator for the fixing of his remuneration, which should therefore be made only when all work is completed.[47] An application by way of note for interim remuneration (determined in the same way as his final remuneration) is, however, competent[48] and usual in large liquidations.

First meeting of creditors and contributories

87–29 Under section 252 (3) of the 1948 Act the liquidator must summon separate meetings of creditors and contributories, but he need not summon a meeting of contributories if the winding-up order was on the ground of inability to pay debts. If the liquidator fails to summon this meeting he will be refused a discharge.[49] The purpose of this first meeting (or meetings) is to determine whether there is to be a committee of inspection and who are to be its members. The meeting is (normally) to be held not later than one

---

40 *Ker* 1897, 5 S.L.T. 126.
41 *Gaunt's Exrs.* v. *Liquidators of La Mancha Syndicate Ltd.* 1907, 14 S.L.T. 675; *McNight & Co.* v. *Montgomerie* 1892, 19 R. 501.
42 *Monkland Iron Co.* v. *Dun* 1886, 14 R. 242; *Lysons* v. *Liquidator of the Miraflores Gold Syndicate* 1895, 22 R. 605; 3 S.L.T. 5.
43 *Hannan's Development & Finance Corp.* 1899, 6 S.L.T. 388.
44 *Charles* 1963 S.L.T.(Notes) 76.
45 *City of Glasgow Bank Liquidators* 1880, 7 R. 1196.
46 *Reekie* v. *Liquidator of Leith & East Coast Shipping Co.* 1911 S.C. 808; *A. & B. Co. Ltd. (in liquidation)* 1929 S.L.T. 24; see also *W. W. McBryde*, 1977 S.L.T.(News) 237, 240.
47 *Macharg* 1941 S.N. 67.
48 See *McBryde* 1977 S.L.T.(News) 237, 242.
49 *Lovat Mantle Manufacturers Ltd.*, 1960 S.L.T.(Sh.Ct.) 52.

calendar month after the *Edinburgh Gazette* advertisement of the liquidator's appointment (R.C.S. 208 (Sh.Ct.R. 24–32)). The creditors' meeting is convened by *Gazette* and newspaper advertisement giving not less than seven days' notice; the contributories' meeting is convened by post, again on not less than seven days' notice. The details of procedure are laid down in R.C.S. 208 (and Sh.Ct.R. 24–32).[50] A creditor must produce his oath (or claim under the Insolvency Act 1976) to be entitled to vote.[51] Voting may be in person or by mandatory or proxy, and a corporation may appoint a representative under section 139. It is customary, but not essential, to prepare a statement of affairs to present to the meeting and lodge in the court process.

Committee of inspection

87–30 The first meeting of creditors (and contributories if the winding up is not on grounds of insolvency) will determine whether there should be a committee of inspection and its composition (1948 Act, s. 252). The court makes any order necessary to implement such a decision or to resolve a difference of opinion (s. 252 (3)). If the winding up is on the grounds of inability to pay debts, the committee consists only of creditors or their attorneys, otherwise it is a joint committee of creditors and contributories (s. 253 (1)). A "committee" of one cannot be sanctioned.[51a]

The function of the committee is to act with the liquidator and to supervise his proceedings.[52] Its sanction, as an alternative to that of the court, is necessary before the liquidator can exercise any of the powers given to him by section 245 (1) of the 1948 Act.[53] The liquidator should not seek court sanction for a step to which he knows the committee objects. The committee has access to the liquidator's books and accounts, and the committee or any member of it may report to a meeting of creditors or contributories, and may ask the court to order such a meeting (R.C.S. 209 (Sh.Ct.R. 33–34)). The committee has in addition the powers and duties of commissioners on a bankrupt estate so far as applicable (1948 Act, s. 255).

There is no provision in Scotland requiring the liquidator to call meetings of creditors or contributories,[54] and for the views of such meetings to override the committee of inspection (s. 246, which applies in England). Presumably a creditor (or contributory) who wished the liquidator to

[50] R.C.S. 208 (*g*), as amended, precludes the carrying on of business in the absence of a quorum, except to receive oaths, productions or claims in the form mentioned by the Insolvency Act 1976. The corresponding Sh.Ct.R. (31) has not been amended to permit claims under the 1976 Act to be received in such circumstances.

[51] Bankruptcy (Scotland) Act 1913, s. 45, as amended by the Insolvency Act 1976, applied to liquidations by s. 318.

[51a] *Souter*, 1981 S.L.T. (Sh.Ct.) 89.

[52] R.C.S. 209 (Sh.Ct.R. 35); s. 252 (2); *Liquidator of Upper Clyde Shipbuilders Ltd.*, 1975 S.L.T. 39.

[53] See para. 87–55, *infra*. Also *Re Consolidated Diesel Engineering Manufacturers* [1915] 1 Ch. 192.

[54] Other than annual meetings to report under R.C.S. 213, see para. 87–33, *post*.

depart from the instructions of the committee would have to apply to the court under section 346 of the 1948 Act.

No member of the committee of inspection can become a purchaser of the company's assets directly or indirectly, or derive a profit from winding-up transactions or be remunerated without the sanction of the court.[55] Such sanction must be obtained in advance.[56]

87–31 The committee is to meet at such times as it appoints, and failing such appointment, at least once a month, and the liquidator or any member of it may call a meeting (1948 Act, s. 253 (2)). The committee acts by majority of those present, a majority of the total membership being a quorum (s. 253 (3)). A member of the committee may resign in writing to the liquidator (s. 253 (4)), and is retired automatically if he becomes bankrupt or is absent from five consecutive meetings without leave (s. 253 (5)); a member may be removed by ordinary resolution of a meeting of creditors (if he represents creditors) or of contributories (if he represents contributories) called on seven days' notice stating the object of the meeting (s. 253 (6)). On a vacancy occurring on the committee the liquidator is to call a meeting of creditors or contributories (as appropriate) to fill the vacancy, but if the liquidator thinks it is unnecessary to fill it he may apply to the court for a suitable order (s. 253 (7)). The continuing members of the committee, if not less than two, may act notwithstanding any vacancy (s. 253 (8)). The procedure for meetings of creditors and contributories is governed by R.C.S. 208 and 210 (Sh.Ct.R. 25–32 and 36).

The court may order the liquidator to call a meeting with a view to reconstituting the committee so as to represent creditors more fairly.[57]

Wishes of creditors and contributories

87–32 The court should have regard to the wishes of creditors and contributories and may direct meetings to be held to ascertain them (s. 346, R.C.S. 208, 210; Sh.Ct.R. 25–32 and 36); for examples see paragraph 85–78, *ante*. This rule is not affected by section 310 of the 1948 Act which enables a creditor or contributory to apply for compulsory winding up notwithstanding that a voluntary winding up has commenced. The effect of section 310 is only to remove any necessity for the petitioning creditor to show that continuance of the voluntary liquidation would prejudice him.[58]

Information as to pending liquidations; annual meetings of creditors

87–33 Where a company is being wound up and the liquidation is not concluded within a year, the liquidator must lodge with the Registrar of Companies a return (Form 92 (Scot.)) showing his intromissions for the first 12 months and at six-monthly intervals thereafter, and for the final

---

[55] *Dowling* v. *Lord Advocate*, 1963 S.L.T. 146.
[56] *Re Gallard* [1896] 1 Q.B. 68.
[57] *Re Radford & Bright Ltd. (No. 1)* [1901] 1 Ch. 272; *(No. 2)* [1901] 1 Ch. 735.
[58] *Re Home Remedies Ltd.* [1943] Ch. 1.

period until the assets have been fully realised and distributed (1948 Act, s. 342; R.C.S. 213; (Sh.Ct.R.42 and 43)).[58a]

In Court of Session liquidations the liquidator must also send to the creditors an annual statement of his intromissions and call an annual meeting of the creditors and report to them the progress of the winding up (R.C.S. 213 (*c*)). There is no equivalent rule in the sheriff court.

General provisions as to meetings of creditors and contributories

87–34 The procedure for calling and conducting meetings of creditors and contributories in all windings up is governed by R.C.S. 208 as adapted by R.C.S. 210 (Sh.Ct.R. 25–32 and 36). These apply subject to any special provisions in the Act or the Rules (*cf.* R.C.S. 210 (iv)).

The liquidator fixes the time and place of the meeting and gives notice by publication in the *Edinburgh Gazette* and one or more newspapers circulating in the district where the company's registered office is situated at least seven days prior to the meeting; if the meeting is of contributories, notice must be given by post to each contributory and if the meeting is of creditors he must post the notice to the address given in their claims (R.C.S. 208 (*a*), (*b*) and (*c*) (Sh.Ct.R. 25, 26 and 27)).

The liquidator acts as chairman (R.C.S. 208 (*d*) (Sh.Ct.R. 28)), and may with the consent of the meeting adjourn it, but may not change the place of the meeting unless the court allows (R.C.S. 208 (*f*) (Sh.Ct.R. 30)). If he did not call the meeting, the meeting elects its own chairman (R.C.S. 210 (ii) (Sh.Ct.R. 36 (ii)). A resolution passed at an adjourned meeting is deemed to be passed on the date it was in fact passed and not earlier (1948 Act, s. 345).

Three creditors (or contributories) present in person or by mandatory, or all of them if the total is less than three, constitute a quorum. If a quorum is not present within thirty minutes the meeting is to be adjourned for not less than seven nor more than 21 days. Those present at an adjourned meeting constitute a quorum (R.C.S. 208 (*g*) and (*h*) (Sh.Ct.R. 31 and 32)).

At a meeting of contributories a resolution is passed when approved by a majority of those voting on it, according to their voting rights under the constitution of the company (R.S.C. 208 (*e*) (Sh.Ct.R. 29)). Voting at meetings of creditors is governed by the Bankruptcy (Scotland) Act 1913, ss. 55 to 60 and 96.[59]

If a meeting is called by a person other than the liquidator he must deposit with the liquidator security for expenses at the prescribed rate, which may be repayable by order of the court (R.C.S. 210 (i) (Sh.Ct.R. 36 (i)).

[58a] A liquidator who failed to comply with a court order requiring him to submit returns under s. 342 has been imprisoned for contempt of court (*Re The Lane Garage* [1982] 7 C.L. 395).

[59] See para. 87–35, *infra*.

87–35 VOTING. A creditor is not entitled to vote at meetings or draw a dividend in the liquidation until he has proved his claim by lodging an oath or claim and vouchers with the liquidator.[60]

A creditor who holds a security or the obligation of a third party in respect of his claim must, before voting, deduct the value of such security or obligation and can vote only in respect of the balance, but without prejudice to his other rights, *e.g.* to rank for dividend (1913 Act, ss. 55 and 56).[61] An obligant bound along with the company is not released by virtue of the creditor's voting or receiving a dividend.[62]

A creditor may appoint a mandatory to vote for him in his absence (1913 Act, s. 59).

A person who has acquired a debt due by the company after the commencement of liquidation, otherwise than by succession, is not entitled to vote on the election of the liquidator or committee of inspection, but is to rank as a creditor in all other respects (1913 Act, s. 60).

As a general rule all questions at meetings of creditors are to be determined by the majority in value of those present and entitled to vote, but if for any purpose a majority in number is required no creditor whose debt is under £20 is to be counted (1913 Act, s. 96).

Contributories

87–36 In the winding up of the company a "contributory" is every person who is liable (or alleged to be liable) to contribute to its assets for the purposes of meeting its liabilities, the expenses of the liquidation, or for the adjustment of the rights of contributories among themselves (1948 Act, ss. 212 (1) and 213).

Under section 212 contributories consist of:

(1) all[62a] members of the company at the date of the commencement of the winding up;

(2) certain past members[63]; and

(3) a present or former director or manager of a limited company who has incurred unlimited liability under the terms of the Act (s. 212 (2)). (This refers to sections 202 and 203 of the 1948 Act, under which a limited company may impose unlimited liability on such officers in terms of its memorandum of association. This situation is

---

[60] Bankruptcy (Scotland) Act 1913, ss. 45–47 as amended by the Insolvency Act 1976—see para. 87–43, *infra*; *Dickey* v. *Ballantine*, 1939 S.C. 783.

[61] The provision contained in the Companies (Floating Charges) (Scotland) Act 1961, s. 7 (*a*), to the effect that the holder of a debenture secured by floating charge need not deduct the value of his security before voting was repealed by the Companies (Floating Charges and Receivers) (Scotland) Act 1972 s. 30 (1), and the holder of such a security is governed by the general rule.

[62] Bankruptcy (Scotland) Act 1913, s. 52 (1).

[62a] Including holders of fully paid shares, even if no contribution will actually be required from them (*Re Phoenix Oil & Transport Co. Ltd.*, note 66 *infra*).

[63] See para. 87–37, *infra*.

unlikely to arise in practice. If there are persons in this position, section 212 (2) imposes restrictions on their potential liability.)

A contributory (including a past member) is entitled to attend meetings of contributories in the winding up, and to challenge the validity of relevant company proceedings, such as a resolution purporting to place the company in voluntary liquidation.[64]

One of the first duties of the liquidator is to settle the list of contributories, but in many cases this will be unnecessary, and he will instead apply to the court to dispense with this requirement, under section 257 (1) of the 1948 Act, on the ground that he will not need to make calls on or adjust the rights of contributories. The court will dispense with settling the list if the shares are fully paid and there is no likelihood of a surplus, or for any other reason.[65] If the shares of a limited company are all fully paid[66] and it is insolvent (*i.e.* in the majority of liquidations by the court), an early application to dispense with the list is appropriate.

The Act and the Rules of Court require the liquidator to make up the list of contributories (or, presumably, apply for dispensation) "forthwith" after his appointment but do not impose any specific time limit. Failure to do either may prejudice his eventual discharge, but the comment in a recent case[67] that after five years it was "too late" to apply to the court is without authority. Circumstances can be conceived in which the liquidator would be justified in delaying this procedure, and in the leading English case a delay of seven years was accepted.[68]

Although section 213 defines a "contributory" as "every person liable to contribute to the assets of a company in the event of its being wound up," this appears to be restricted to persons whose liability arises by virtue of section 212 and not (for example) to those liable to the company as ordinary debtors of the company, or officers found liable on the ground of fraudulent trading under section 332.

Settling the list of contributories

7–37 If the liquidator requires to settle a list of contributories the procedure is governed by R.C.S. 211 (Sh.Ct.R. 37–39). The list is in two parts, by convention referred to as list A and list B.

List A consists of those persons who are members at the commencement of the winding up. List B consists of past members, restricted in a limited company to those who ceased to be members within one year of the commencement of the winding up, but extended to certain other past members of a limited company which was previously registered as unlimited.[69]

---

[64] *Howling's Trs.* v. *Smith* 1905, 7 F. 390; 12 S.L.T. 628.
[65] R.C.S. 211 (*a*) (Sh.Ct.R. 37).
[66] Holders of such shares are still technically "contributories"—*Re Phoenix Oil & Transport Co. Ltd.* [1958] Ch. 560.
[67] *Lovat Mantle Manufacturers Ltd.*, 1960 S.L.T.(Sh.Ct.) 52.
[68] *Re Phoenix Oil & Transport Co. Ltd., supra.*
[69] Companies Act 1967, s. 44 (7), see para. 87–39, *infra*.

On the death of a contributory his personal representatives (and, in certain circumstances, the heirs and legatees of his heritable estate) take his place (1948 Act, s. 215). If a contributory becomes bankrupt, his trustee in bankruptcy replaces him (1948 Act, s. 216). The discharge of the bankrupt does not reinstate him as a "contributory" so as to entitle him to interfere in the liquidation in that capacity.[70]

The list of contributories must contain their full names and addresses, the number of shares and the interest to be attributed to each, the amount called and paid on each share, and it is divided into the two lists required; so far as practicable, the liquidator must distinguish between those who are contributories in their own name and those listed in a representative capacity (1948 Act, s. 257 (2); R.C.S. 211 (*a*) (Sh.Ct.R. 37)). The list prepared in accordance with the foregoing provisions is submitted by the liquidator to the court by way of note in the petition. The court will normally order intimation to all persons on the list allowing seven days (eight days in the sheriff court) for answers to be lodged. The list is settled by the court after disposing of such objections as may be lodged (R.C.S. 211 (*b*) (Sh.Ct.R. 38)). It is competent to settle "A" and "B" lists separately.[71]

Settlement of the list of contributories, even if the court's interlocutor has become final, will not bar a member's right to petition for his removal under section 116 (rectification of the register of members).[72] It may also be possible to reclaim against or seek suspension of the subsequent decree for calls.[73]

Liability of contributories

87–38 The question of whether a person is a member of a company has been considered.[74] Prima facie membership is determined by the register of members, and a member is not entitled to insist on registration of a transfer presented on the eve of liquidation,[75] but he may escape if it is shown that he never agreed to be a member.[76]

Liability of a contributory in a limited company cannot in any event exceed the amount (if any) unpaid in respect of his shares (and/or his guarantee, where the company is limited by guarantee with or without a share capital) (s. 212 (1) (*d*) and (*e*), s. 212 (3)).[77] The amount unpaid on a share is a question of fact and the liquidator may be personally barred from calling capital where the contributory (being a transferee for value and in good faith) holds a certificate bearing to show that it has been paid up.[78]

---

[70] *Re Wolverhampton Steel & Iron Co. Ltd.* [1977] 1 All E.R. 417 affd.; [1977] 3 All E.R. 467.
[71] *Liquidator of Caledonian Heritable Security Co. Ltd.* 1882, 9 R. 1130.
[72] *Stocker* v. *Liquidator of the Coustonholme Paper Mills Co. Ltd.* 1891, 19 R. 17; *Jackson* v. *Liquidator of Star Fire & Burglary Insurance Co.* 1902, 10 S.L.T. 279.
[73] *Cumpstie* v. *Waterston* 1933 S.C. 1.
[74] Chaps. 49 and 50, *ante*.
[75] *Dodds* v. *Cosmopolitan Insurance Corp. Ltd.* 1915. S.C. 992; 1915 2 S.L.T. 106.
[76] *Liquidator of Florida Mortgage and Investment Co. Ltd.* v. *Bayley* 1890, 17 R. 525.
[77] *Waterhouse* v. *Jamieson* 1870, 8 M. (H.L.) 88.
[78] Para. 36–11 and 36–12, *ante*; *Liquidator of Scottish Heritages Co. Ltd.* 1898, 5 S.L.T. 336.

The liability of B list contributories is further limited by the following:

(1) they are not liable unless the list A contributories are unable to satisfy the amount required of them (s. 212 (1) (*c*));

(2) a past member is not liable in respect of any debt or obligation contracted after he has ceased to be a member (s. 212 (1) (*b*));

(3) a past member's liability is limited to the amount, if any, unpaid on the shares in respect of which he is liable (*i.e.* after crediting any sums paid by the list A contributory in respect of such shares) (s. 212 (1) (*d*)), or in a company limited by guarantee, the amount of his guarantee (s. 212 (1) (*e*)); if the company is limited by guarantee and has a share capital, his liability is limited to the amount due on each of these counts combined (s. 212 (3)).

Where a scheme of arrangement provides for partial payment of creditors and releases present members from a portion of their liability it would appear to be impossible to place anyone on the B list.[79]

Companies re-registered as unlimited

87–39 Special rules apply to an unlimited company which has been re-registered as limited under section 44 of the 1967 Act, and which commences its winding up within three years of re-registration. In this case the B list is extended so as to include as contributories all past members who were members at the time of re-registration, and they are liable to contribute without limit as to amount in respect of debts and liabilities contracted before re-registration (1967 Act, s. 44 (7) (*a*) and (*c*)). If there are no persons on the A list of such a company who were members at the time of re-registration, the B list is further extended so as to include persons who ceased to be members within a year before re-registration, and such past members and all members at the time of registration are liable to contribute without limit as to the amount in respect of debts and liabilities incurred before re-registration, even if all those on the A list have paid in full (1967 Act, s. 44 (7) (*b*) and (*c*)). The liability of those on the extended B list is still limited by section 212 (1) (*b*) of the 1948 Act, under which they are not liable for debts contracted after they ceased to be members.

Calls

87–40 The liability of a contributory is a debt due as from "the time when his liability commenced," but payable only when a call is made. Prescription (if not interrupted) can therefore operate to extinguish liability, five years after the date of the call.[80] It follows that, if a call made by the directors has prescribed, the liquidator cannot call up the same money.

Liability does not arise until a call in proper form has been made, and accordingly a B list contributory may effectively reduce his potential liability by procuring the extinction of debts in respect of which he may be liable

[79] *Re Belgrave Mills*, October 13, 1927 unreported, see para. 85–46, *ante*.

[80] Prescription and Limitation (Scotland) Act 1973, s. 6 and Sched. 1.

between the commencement of the winding up and the making of the call and perhaps even later.[81]

Where shares have been forfeited their former holder is not liable as a contributory (unless under list B) but he may be liable to the company on some other ground, *e.g.* by virtue of the terms of its articles in regard to forfeiture.[82]

In Scotland calls are issued by the court (1948 Act, s. 260). There is no provision, as in England (1948 Act, s. 273), for calls to be made by the liquidator with the sanction of the committee of inspection. The liquidator applies to the court by way of note, stating the proposed amount of call and the reasons for making it (R.C.S. 212 (*a*) (Sh.Ct.R. 40)). The court may order intimation and service (R.C.S. 212 (*b*) (Sh.Ct.R. 41)) and, after consideration of any answers, may order the call to be made in a lump sum or by instalments.[83] The order may take account of the likelihood of some contributories not being able to pay in full (s. 260 (1)). Such an order is conclusive evidence that the amount stated is due, and is also conclusive in all other respects except that it is only prima facie evidence for the purpose of charging the heritable estate of a deceased contributory unless his heirs or legatees of heritage were on the list when the call was made (1948 Act, s. 262). The liquidator can obtain an order which may be enforced by summary diligence by lodging in court a certified list of contributories and particulars of calls due (1948 Act, s. 275).[84]

It is not necessary, before a call is made, that the company's debts and liabilities be fixed; they need only be estimated for the purpose of section 260.[85]

Section 259 (1) of the 1948 Act allows the liquidator to recover from a contributory sums other than calls made "in pursuance of" the Act by court order. Since the Act refers only to calls made in a winding up this section can be invoked by the liquidator to sue for calls made by the directors prior to the commencement of the winding up as well as other debts notwithstanding that he has obtained an order under section 260 for payment of the same sum.[86] If proceeding under section 260 in respect of calls made by the directors the liquidator will be expected to give intimation (not necessarily formal service) to the contributory.[87]

Section 275 of the 1948 Act provides for recovery of calls by the liquidator by summary decree with interest at 5 per cent. If, however, the liquidator is seeking recovery of calls previously made by the directors he is entitled to demand payment of such higher rate as may be provided for in the articles.[87] The wording of section 259 (1) appears to preclude the

---

[81] *Apex Film Distributors Ltd.* [1960] Ch. 378.
[82] *Liquidators of Mount Morgan (West) Gold Mine* v. *McMahon* 1891, 18 R. 772; *Ladies Dress Assoc.* v. *Pulbrook* [1900] 2 Q.B. 376.
[83] *Re Law Guarantee Society* (1910) 26 T.L.R. 565.
[84] See *Cumpstie* v. *Waterston*, 1933 S.C. 1.
[85] *Re Contract Corporation* (1866) L.R. 2 Ch.App. 95.
[86] *Westmoreland Green, etc., Slate Co.* v. *Feilden* [1891] 3 Ch. 15.
[87] *Liquidators of Benhar Coal Co. Ltd.* 1882, 9 R. 763.

liquidator from seeking to recover calls made in the winding up by ordinary action with a view to obtaining interest at a rate higher than is provided for in section 275. If he is proceeding under section 275, however, no notice need be given to the contributories, nor does it appear that a contributory can appear to contest the granting of summary decree for payment.[87a] He may, however, proceed by way of suspension.[88]

Compromises with contributories

87–41 The making of compromises with contributories is one of the powers of the liquidator for which he requires the sanction of the court or the committee of inspection (if any).[89] The liquidator cannot be compelled to accept a compromise with a contributory.[90] A discharge obtained by fraud or concealment of assets may be reduced.[91] If the liquidator decides to disregard a discharge on the basis that it was obtained by concealment of assets and seeks to enforce a decree for payment of a call by summary process under section 275, the contributory may apply for suspension without being required to find caution.[92]

Creditors

87–42 It is fundamental to the concept of corporate personality that a creditor's remedy is solely against the company. This holds equally for a company whose members have unlimited liability.[93] If, however, a creditor has lost his claim against the company owing to the negligence of the liquidator, he may have a claim for damages against the liquidator personally.[94]

If it is found that cash or assets held by the company are subject to a trust in favour of another party and can be identified, they may be recovered from the liquidator (in full) on that basis and not as a ranking in the liquidation.[95] This does not extend to clauses reserving title in sale conditions ("Romalpa Clauses") which are ineffective in Scots law.[95a]

87–43 PROOF OF CLAIMS. The bankruptcy rules contained in sections 45 to 62, 96 and 105 of the Bankruptcy (Scotland) Act 1913[96] are applied to liquidations in general and the general law of bankruptcy so far as relevant is applied to insolvent liquidations (ss. 316, 318). Creditors are entitled to

---

[87a] *Liquidators of Benhar Coal Co. Ltd., supra.*
[88] s. 275 (2); *Cumpstie* v. *Waterston* 1933 S.C. 1. See also *Anderson* v. *Liquidators of City of Glasgow Bank* 1880 8 R. 44.
[89] s. 245 (1).
[90] *Tennent* v. *City of Glasgow Bank* 1879, 6 R. 972.
[91] *Liquidators of City of Glasgow Bank* v. *Assets Co.* 1883, 10 R. 676. *Assets Co.* v. *Tosh's Trs.* 1898 6 S.L.T. 96; *Assets Co.* v. *Shirre's Trs.* 1897, 24 R. 418; 4 S.L.T. 224; *Bain* v. *Assets Co.* 1905, 7 F. (H.L.) 104; [1905] A.C. 317; 13 S.L.T. 147.
[92] *Anderson* v. *Liquidators of City of Glasgow Bank* 1880, 8 R. 44.
[93] See para. 3–13, *ante*.
[94] *Pulsford* v. *Devenish* [1903] 2 Ch. 625; *Argyll's Ltd.* v. *Coxeter* (1913) 29 T.L.R. 355.
[95] *Turnbull* v. *Liquidator of Scottish County Investment Co. Ltd.* 1939 S.C. 5; *Smith, etc.* v. *Liquidators of James Birrell Ltd.*, 1968 S.L.T. 174.
[95a] *Clark Taylor & Co. Ltd.* v. *Quality Site Development (Edinburgh) Ltd.* 1981 S.L.T. 308. See also *Export Credits Guarantee Dept.* v. *Turner* 1981 S.L.T. 286.
[96] See Vol. II, Pt. J.

prove in the liquidation in respect of all debts and claims present, future and contingent, certain or uncertain, liquid or illiquid, including damages, any claims not precisely ascertained being estimated and any sums due at a future date being discounted. Interest may only be claimed up to the date of liquidation. Under sections 49 and 50 of the 1913 Act the creditor in a contingent or unascertained debt or an annuity cannot prove until he has had it valued, on application, by the liquidator or the court. Secured creditors can only claim in respect of the balance due after deducting the value of their security unless they surrender their security.[97]

The liquidator should request the court by way of note to fix the time within which claims should be lodged, which is normally six weeks after the order, and the court will require advertisement of the order for claims.[98] The order will provide that claims lodged after the prescribed date are to be excluded from any distribution made before these debts have been proved. In this context "distribution" includes a distribution to contributories; if the company has been dissolved section 259 ceases to apply and there is no room for the creditor to argue that he is subrogated to any rights the company might have against the contributories under that section.[99] Late lodgement of a claim precludes participation in distributions made before it was lodged even if the liquidator was aware of its existence before making a distribution, but it will be admittted to a ranking in subsequent dividends.[1] It is unsettled whether a creditor lodging a claim after an initial distribution is entitled to an equalising distribution in his favour (by analogy with section 119 of the 1913 Act, which is not expressly applied to liquidations).[2] It is arguable that section 264 of the 1948 Act is procedural and should therefore be subordinated to the general principle of *pari passu* treatment of all creditors (subject to preferential rights) enshrined in section 302 for voluntary liquidations and apparently imported by implication to all insolvent liquidations by section 312. On that view the principle of equalisation in section 119 of the 1913 Act should be applicable in liquidations. Subject to this, however, a creditor may claim at any time and be ranked for any subsequent dividend. A late claimant, unless his delay is "grotesque" and inexcusable, is entitled to protection against loss of effective recourse resulting from a proposed distribution, especially if the distribution is to members rather than creditors.[3] The court may prorogate the time for lodging claims under section 264.[4]

The form of proof of debt is prescribed in section 45 of the 1913 Act, as amended by section 5 (3) of the Insolvency Act 1976. The creditor must produce an account and vouchers sufficient to prove his debt and either a

---

[97] See para. 87–51, *post*.
[98] s. 264; McBryde, "Liquidation Procedure in the Court of Session," 1977 S.L.T.(News) 239.
[99] *Butter* v. *Broadhead* [1975] Ch. 97.
[1] *Dickey* v. *Ballantine*, 1939 S.C. 783.
[2] *Dickey* v. *Ballantine, supra*, p. 785.
[3] *Re R-R Realisations Ltd.* [1980] 1 All E.R. 1019.
[4] *Silvela* v. *Ker* 1900, 8 S.L.T. 194.

claim in the form prescribed by statutory instrument[5] or an oath in the form prescribed by sections 20–24 of the 1913 Act. The liquidator is entitled to require a creditor to provide an oath, even where a claim in the form permitted by the 1976 Act has been lodged.[6]

According to earlier authority[7] a claim in foreign currency should be converted to sterling at the rate of exchange prevailing when payment was due (or the breach of contract or delict occurred), but this rule appears now to be open to question and it is submitted that conversion should be made at the rate applying at the date of the winding-up order.[8]

The lodging of a claim (or presentation of or concurrence in a petition for winding up) interrupts the running of prescription against the claim, even if the liquidation is subsequently recalled.[9]

87–44 DISPUTED CLAIMS. It is the duty of the liquidator to scrutinise all claims and to issue a deliverance (by letter stating his reasons) if he rejects a claim in whole or in part. The deliverance may be appealed to the court before the expiration of seven days from its date (in the Court of Session; in the sheriff court the relevant time limit is eight days) but the court may extend the time for appealing (and may ordain the appellant to find caution).[10] The liquidator is entitled to reject any claim which has not been properly formulated or vouched and until such a claim has been presented and rejected the court will not entertain an appeal.[11] In general, a claim for damage should be constituted by ordinary action and the claimant should not seek to have the merits discussed in the liquidation process.[12] Similar principles should apply to any illiquid claim in respect of which there is a substantial dispute. Claims for damages should be determined as at the date of the winding-up order.[13] Facts relating to a dispute which are within the knowledge of the company must be taken to be within the knowledge of the liquidator also.[13a]

87–45 COMPENSATION; SET-OFF. In contrast to the position in England, the rules governing the question of whether claims due to a person by the company may be compensated by or set off against a claim due by him to it are common law and not statutory. The right of compensation, in respect of

---

[5] S. I. 1977 No. 1495—see Vol. III, para. J–1800.

[6] 1913 Act, s. 45 (1) (*b*) (as amended).

[7] *Macfie's J.F.* v. *Macfie*, 1932 S.L.T. 460; Anton, "Private International Law" (W. Green & Son, Edinburgh, 1967) p. 551.

[8] *Miliangos* v. *George Frank (Textiles) Ltd.* [1975] Q.B. 478; *Re Dynamics Corporation of America* [1976] 2 All E.R. 669, *Re Lines Bros. Ltd.* [1982] 2 All E.R. 183.

[9] Bankruptcy (Scotland) Act 1913, s. 105; Prescription and Limitation (Scotland) Act 1973, s. 9 (1).

[10] R.C.S. 214; Sh.Ct.R. 44–46; *Samuel Noble* 1949 S.L.T.(Notes) 13; *Graham* v. *Macbeath* 1959 S.L.T.(Notes) 25.

[11] *Knoll Spinning Co. Ltd.* v. *Brown* 1977 S.C. 291 (following *Crawford* v. *McCulloch* 1909 S.C. 1063 and distinguishing *Re Kentwood Constructions Ltd.* [1960] 2 All E.R. 655 and *Re Trepca Mines Ltd.* [1960] 1 All E.R. 304).

[12] *Crawford* v. *McCulloch, supra.*

[13] *Re Dynamics Corporation of America* [1976] 2 All E.R. 699.

[13a] *M. Publications (Scotland) Ltd.* v. *Meiland* 1981 S.L.T. (Notes) 72.

pre-liquidation accounts, arises if both parties are debtor and creditor in the same capacity and (in a liquidation) applies equally to liquid and illiquid claims.[14] A claim arising after liquidation has commenced cannot be compensated against a pre-liquidation debt,[15] but if a debt and claim both arose after commencement of the winding up compensation is allowed.[16] A debtor cannot after winding up has commenced, acquire a claim against the company in order to plead compensation.[17] A contributory is in a special position. He cannot plead compensation against a call made in a liquidation[18] whether the call was made by the liquidator or by the directors (prior to the commencement of winding up),[19] even where the company had agreed in writing to hold money deposited with it against calls,[20] unless and until all creditors have been paid in full, when he may claim compensation against subsequent calls (s. 259 (3)).

At common law the Crown is treated as an indivisible entity, and debts due to one department of government can be set off against sums due by another department (and vice versa). The Crown Proceedings Act 1947, s. 35 (2), as amended for Scotland by section 50, provides that; (1) compensation cannot be pled against a claim for taxes, duties or penalties, nor can a claim for repayment of such items be used to compensate a Crown claim of a different nature, and (2) in any other case compensation in respect of claims relating to different government departments is only allowed (to the Crown or to the company) with the leave of the court. This applies whether the company is solvent or insolvent. The requirement to seek leave of the court does not, however, derogate from the common law principle which would allow compensation to apply, but is essentially procedural. Leave will normally be granted (particularly in a liquidation) unless one of the claims is illiquid and would require extensive proceedings to establish.[21]

An English decision, that a surety cannot set off his contingent liability unless the principal creditor has waived his right of proof,[22] appears to be consistent with Scottish principles.

Where a bank held money borrowed by the company for a specific purpose, known to the bank, the bank was not entitled to set off that sum against the company's other indebtedness, but had to return it to the lender when it ceased to be available for that purpose because of the liquidation of the company.[23]

---

[14] *Booth and Anr.* v. *Thomson and Ors.* 1972 S.L.T. 141.
[15] See further Walker, *Scottish Private Law* (2nd ed., 1975, Oxford), p. 668.
[16] *Booth & Anr.* v. *Thomson & Ors. supra*; *Smith* v. *Lord Advocate*, 1979 S.L.T. 233.
[17] *Smith* v. *Lord Advocate (No. 2)* 1981 S.L.T. 19.
[18] *Liquidators of Coustonholme Paper Mills Co. Ltd.* v. *Law* 1891, 18 R. 1076, 1093; see also *Scottish Fishermen's Organisation Ltd.* v. *McLean*, 1980 S.L.T.(Sh.Ct.) 76.
[19] *Cowan* v. *Gowans* 1878, 5 R. 581.
[20] *Liquidator of the Property Investment Co. of Scotland* v. *Aikman* 1891, 28 S.L.R. 955; see also *Liquidators of the Property Investment Co. of Scotland* v. *National Bank of Scotland* 1891, 28 S.L.R. 884.
[21] *Smith* v. *Lord Advocate (No. 2)* 1981 S.L.T. 21; *Laing* v. *Lord Advocate* 1973 S.L.T.(Notes) 81; *Atlantic Engine Co. (1920) Ltd.* v. *Lord Advocate* 1955 S.L.T. 17.
[22] *Re Fenton* [1931] 1 Ch. 85.
[23] *Quistclose Investments* v. *Rolls Razor Ltd.* [1968] Ch. 540; affirmed, *sub nom. Barclays Bank Ltd.* v. *Quistclose Investments Ltd.* [1970] A.C. 567; [1968] 3 All E.R. 651; see also *Smith* v. *Liquidator of James Birrell Ltd.*, 1968 S.L.T. 174.

Where two companies were indebted to one another and were both insolvent and in liquidation, the liquidator of each was given liberty to distribute its assets among the other creditors without regard to the claim of the other company.[24]

87–46 APPLICATION OF ASSETS. Section 257 (1) provides that "the court . . . shall cause the assets of the company to be collected and applied in discharge of its liabilities." Section 319 (5) (*a*) provides for *pari passu* ranking of preferential claims but there is no express statement in the provisions of the Act relating to a winding up by the court (as there is in voluntary liquidations under section 302) that ordinary claims shall also rank *pari passu*. This, however, is consistent with ordinary bankruptcy principles which are imported by section 316. There is no equivalent in company liquidations to postponed claims in bankruptcy.

In principle, the liquidation of the company and the distribution of its assets should be deemed to occur simultaneously, notwithstanding the interval between them occupied by the procedure of winding up.[25] A foreign currency creditor who has suffered loss as a result of exchange rate changes during the liquidation has a postponed claim.[25a]

87–47 EXPENSES. The expenses of liquidation are to be paid in priority to all preferential and unsecured debts (s. 319 (6)). Section 267 provides that if the assets of the company are insufficient to satisfy its liabilities the court may direct the order of payment of the costs, charges and expenses incurred in the winding up as it thinks just. The expenses of realising and ingathering the assets will receive priority but the rules laid down in England as to further ranking of expenses, etc., are not applicable in Scotland, and the courts will exercise their discretion in each case.[26] In general, however, the order of preference will be (1) expenses of realisation (2) liquidator's other expenses (3) liquidator's remuneration and (4) petitioning creditor's expenses.[27] Corporation tax on chargeable gains falls to be treated as a disbursement of the liquidator, not part of the cost of realisation.[28] Where the company has granted a floating charge, the costs, charges and expenses referred to in section 267 (and in section 309, which is the equivalent provision in a voluntary winding up) have priority over the claims of the holder of the charge,[29] provided the charge has not crystallised before the winding-up order.[29a] Where the only assets available

---

[24] *Re National Live Stock Co.* [1917] 1 Ch. 628.
[25] *Re Dynamics Corp. of America* [1976] 2 All E.R. 669.
[25a] *Re Lines Bros. Ltd.* [1982] 2 All E.R. 183.
[26] *The Northern Distilleries (in liquidation)* 1901, 9 S.L.T. 213; *Liquidator of Edinburgh Pavilion Co.* v. *Walker* 1906, 14 S.L.T. 61; *Liquidator of R. & W. Falconer* v. *Drummond* 1908, 15 S.L.T. 1067.
[27] *Liquidator of Edinburgh Pavilion Co* v. *Walker, supra.*
[28] *Re Mesco Properties Ltd.* [1980] 1 All E.R. 117.
[29] *Re Barleycorn Enterprises Ltd.* [1970] Ch. 465.
[29a] *Re Christonette International Ltd.* (1982) 126 S.J. 561.

have been obtained by *ultra vires* activities, the court may authorise these to be used to pay the expenses of liquidation.[30]

The liquidator and any agent employed by him must claim on the company for expenses and not on a creditor who has merely exercised his right in the liquidation (Bankruptcy (Scotland) Act 1913, s. 53).

If there are no assets the liquidator is not entitled to receive any remuneration and he is personally liable for legal expenses incurred in the liquidation; the legal expenses of the petition are the responsibility of those who instructed it. It is not competent to charge the expense of one liquidation against the assets ingathered in another liquidation, even where the first liquidation was undertaken with a view to securing a benefit for the creditors in the second one.[31]

87–48 PREFERENTIAL PAYMENTS. Section 319 of the 1948 Act consolidates various provisions which require certain unsecured debts to be paid in priority to others. These rank *pari passu* (s. 319 (5)). They must also be paid in priority to any debt secured by a floating charge.[32] Claims by the Crown enjoy no preference except to the extent allowed by the Act.[33] Where a liquidator paid a dividend to unsecured creditors in the mistaken belief that certain debts would be recovered to pay preferential claims he was held entitled to recover the dividends under the *condictio indebiti*.[34] Contrast the inability of a liquidator to recover payments made in error to contributories.[35]

The main classes of preferential debts[35a] are:

(1) All local rates due from the company at the "relevant date" (see definition below) and having become due and payable within 12 months next before that date (s. 319 (1) (*a*) (i));

(2) Income tax, corporation tax and other assessed taxes on the company up to April 5 next before the "relevant date" and not exceeding in total one year's assessment (s. 319 (1) (*a*) (ii)). The limitation to one year's assessment applies to each tax separately so that the Revenue are entitled to select a different year of assessment for each tax[36]; it is not necessary for the assessments to have been made before the relevant date, provided that they relate to a fiscal year ending before the previous April 5[37];

(3) Value added tax due at the "relevant date" and having become due within the 12 months next before that date (apportioned where a VAT accounting period falls partly within and partly outwith such

---

[30] *Re Introductions Ltd. (No. 2)* [1969] 1 W.L.R. 1359; [1969] 3 All E.R. 697.

[31] *Taylor (Liquidator of Neil Middleton & Co. Ltd.) Ptnr.* 1977 S.L.T.(Sh.Ct.) 82.

[32] s. 319 (5) (*b*) as amended by the Companies (Floating Charges) (Scotland) Act 1961, s. 7 (*b*); Companies (Floating Charges and Receivers) (Scotland) Act 1972, ss. 1 (2) and 5 (6); and see also ss. 19 and 20 of the 1972 Act.

[33] *Admiralty* v. *Blair's Trs.* 1916 S.C. 247; *Food Controller* v. *Cork* [1923] A.C. 647.

[34] *Purvis Industries Ltd.* v. *J. & W. Henderson Ltd.* (1959) 75 Sh.Ct.Rep. 143.

[35] *Taylor* v. *Wilson's Trs.*, 1974 S.L.T. 298 (affd. 1979 S.L.T. 105).

[35a] See further paras. 85–60 *ante*.

[36] *I.R.C.* v. *Liquidator of Purvis Industries Ltd.*, 1958 S.L.T. 265; 1958 S.C. 338.

[37] *Gowers* v. *Walker* [1930] 1 Ch. 262.

period) (Finance Act 1972, s. 41, replacing s. 319 (1) (*a*) (iii)). Where there is group registration for VAT purposes, one company being registered as the representative member, all the members of the group are jointly and severally liable. The Revenue are therefore entitled to rank for the full amount in the liquidation of any of the members and not merely in that of the representative member[37a];

(4) Wages or salary (including commission) of any "clerk or servant" or "workman or labourer" of the company for four months prior to the "relevant date" up to £800, and all accrued holiday remuneration (s. 319 (1) (*b*) and (2), as amended by the Insolvency Act 1976, s. 1 and Sched. 1). The figure of £800 may be varied by statutory instrument (1976 Act, s. 1).[38] "Guarantee payments," "protective awards" and certain other payments provided for under Employment Protection legislation are treated as "wages" for the purposes of this provision (Employment Protection (Consolidation) Act 1978, s. 121 as amended by the Employment Act 1980 s. 13 and Sched. 1 para. 15);

(5) Amounts payable in respect of social security contributions, etc., under the Social Security Acts of 1973 and 1975 (s. 319 (1) (*e*), as amended by the Social Security Act 1973, Sched. 27 and the Social Security (Consequential Provisions) Act 1975, Sched. 2).

(6) Certain betting duties which became due within 12 months preceding the "relevant date."[38a]

In addition to these, payments due under the Re-instatement in Civil Employment Act 1944 and certain pre-1948 workmen's compensation claims are given preferential status, but are now of little practical importance (s. 319 (*c*), (*f*) and (*g*)).

The "relevant date" is the earliest date of the winding-up order, the appointment of a provisional liquidator or the passing of a resolution for voluntary winding up (s. 319 (8) (*d*)). This is not necessarily the same date as the commencement of the winding up, where the winding up is by the court.

A cautioner (or other party) who meets any preferential claim is entitled to a corresponding preferential ranking.[39]

87–49 APPLICATION OF S. 319 (1) (*b*). To be entitled to a preferential ranking in respect of salary, etc., an employee must fall within either of the two definitions "clerk or servant" and "workman or labourer." The same phrases are used in the equivalent bankruptcy legislation.[40] The secretary of a company was denied a preference on the ground that "clerk or servant" meant "a subordinate servant" "dependent on the company for

[37a] *Nadler Enterprises Ltd*. [1980] 3 All E.R. 350.

[38] See proviso to s. 319 (2) in relation to certain agricultural labourers; as to advances for payment of wages or salaries see *post*.

[38a] Betting and Gaming Duties Act 1972 ss. 2(1), 13, 17.

[39] *Ewart* v. *Latta* (1865) 3 M. (H.L.) 36; *Harvie's Trs.* v. *Bank of Scotland* 1885, 12 R. 1141; *Veitch* v. *National Bank of Scotland*, 1907 S.C. 554.

[40] Bankruptcy (Scotland) Act 1913, s. 118 as amended by the Companies Act 1947, ss. 115 (1) and 91.

his daily bread."[41] A part-time secretary is not within the scope of the section,[42] nor is a director,[43] but if a director is also employed in a capacity which would be regarded as within the section a preferential ranking for salary, etc., earned in that capacity will be allowed.[44] "Labour only" subcontractors cannot benefit from section 319.[45]

87–50 ADVANCES FOR PAYMENT OF WAGES. A person who has advanced money for the purpose of paying wages or salary or accrued holiday money of any clerk or servant of the company is entitled to the same priority in respect thereof as the clerk or servant would have had under section 319 (s. 319 (4)). A bank may obtain maximum benefit from this, on being asked to advance money for such payments, by operating a separate "wages account," requiring the company to make regular transfers from their current account to discharge the earliest advances. If the bank holds security for its advances, it is entitled to apply the proceeds thereof first against its non-preferential advances.[46]

87–51 SECURED CREDITORS. In Scots law a secured creditor is one who holds a valid fixed security over property, a floating charge, a lien, or a hypothec (a limited and exceptional class of security right over corporeal moveables arising without possession). All such securities must be valued and deducted from any claim in the liquidation, and the creditor cannot claim more than the balance (Bankruptcy (Scotland) Act 1913, s. 61; 1948 Act, s. 318). As a deterrent against undervaluing any such security, the creditor may be compelled to sell his security to the liquidator at his valuation plus 20 per cent. but he may "correct" his valuation (Bankruptcy (Scotland) Act 1913, s. 58). A security which is a registrable charge is void against the liquidator unless duly presented for registration under the Companies (Floating Charges and Receivers) (Scotland) Act 1972.[47] If a right of lien arises it may be exercised against the liquidator to the effect of obtaining for the holder a preference for his claim in exchange for release of the subjects of lien.[48] The lien will be lost if the holder parts with the goods without reserving his rights.[49] A company secretary has no right of lien over its books by virtue of his office.[50]

While in England, a landlord is in a special position,[51] in Scotland he is

---

41 *Liquidator of Scottish Poultry Journal Co.* 1896, 4 S.L.T. 167.
42 *Liquidator of Clyde Football Club* 1900, 8 S.L.T. 328; *Cairney* v. *Black* [1906] 2 K.B. 746.
43 *Anderson* v. *James Sutherland (Peterhead) Ltd.*, 1941 S.C. 203.
44 *Re Beeton & Co. Ltd.* [1913] 2 Ch. 279.
45 *Re C. W. & A. L. Hughes Ltd.* [1966] 2 All E.R. 702.
46 *Re William Hall (Contractors) Ltd.* [1967] 1 W.L.R. 948; [1967] 2 All E.R. 1150; and see further, para. 85–62, *ante*.
47 See para. 47–17, *ante*.
48 *Train & McIntyre Ltd.* v. *Forbes*, 1925 S.L.T. 286; *Liquidator of Donaldson & Co.* v. *White & Park*, 1908 S.C. 309; 15 S.L.T. 578; *Rorie* v. *Stevenson*, 1908 S.C. 559; 15 S.L.T. 870; *Liquidator of Bar & Co.* v. *Stevenson & Brownlie* 1901, 10 S.L.T. 456; *Liquidator of Scottish Workmen's Assurance Co.* v. *Waddell*, 1910 S.C. 670; 1910, 1 S.L.T. 315; see also s. 268 (3).
49 *London Scottish Transport Ltd.* v. *Tyres (Scotland) Ltd.* 1957 S.L.T.(Sh.Ct.) 48).
50 *Gladstone* v. *McCallum* 1893, 23 R. 783; 4 S.L.T. 41; *Barnton Hotel Co.* v. *Cook* 1899, 1 F. 1190; 7 S.L.T. 131.
51 See para. 85–65, *ante*.

in the same position as any unsecured creditor except in so far as he is able to claim landlord's hypothec which is a limited security for one year's rent over certain moveables (not necessarily belonging to the tenant) brought onto the leased premises.

The position of creditors who have executed diligence against the company's property is noted below (para. 87–63). A secured creditor may take one of the following courses:

(1) rely on his security and not prove in the liquidation;
(2) realise his security and prove for any deficiency;
(3) value and deduct his security and prove for the balance;
(4) surrender his security and prove for the whole debt.

The holder of a floating charge may, instead of pursuing his rights under the charge, be admitted to an appropriate ranking as a secured creditor in the liquidation.[52]

Section 327 (1) (*c*) applies to all liquidations ("so far as consistent with" the 1948 Act) the provisions of the Bankruptcy (Scotland) Act 1913, ss. 108 to 113 and 116 in respect of the realisaton of heritable estate affected by securities and rights preferable to the liquidator. Section 108 of the 1913 Act preserves the creditor's power of sale (subject to accounting to the liquidator for any surplus); section 109 covers a sale by the liquidator with consent of the creditor having the effect of disburdening the subjects; section 110 empowers the general creditors to authorise a sale by the liquidator without the heritable creditor's consent but for a price not less than sufficient to clear his debt in full; section 111 allows[53] a sale by private bargain by the liquidator with the consent of the heritable creditors, a majority of creditors and the accountant of court; section 112 provides for ranking and division of the price; section 113 allows the court to order interim payments, and section 116 allows a creditor to purchase property exposed for public sale, but not the liquidator or his law agent. It has been held that a member of the committee of inspection, being in a position of trust, requires the sanction of the court before purchasing assets of the company.[54]

87–52 INTEREST. Interest ceases to run on an unsecured debt on the commencement of winding up, unless there is a surplus and interest is due on the original debt.[55] Interest running on a secured debt continues to accrue after winding up until the security is exhausted. Any interest after the date of winding up not covered by the security is irrecoverable if the company is

---

[52] *National Commercial Bank of Scotland Ltd.* v. *Liquidators of Telford Grier Mackay & Co. Ltd.* 1969 S.C. 181; 1969 S.L.T. 306; *Libertas-Kommerz* v. *Johnson* 1977 S.C. 191; 1978 S.L.T. 222.

[53] Unlike the situation in bankruptcy, this section (as applied) is permissive and not mandatory in liquidations because s. 245 (2) (*a*) gives an independent power of sale without such consents (*Liquidators of Style & Mantle* v. *Price's Tailors Ltd.* 1934 S.L.T. 504).

[54] *Dowling* v. *Lord Advocate*, 1963 S.C. 272.

[55] Bankruptcy (Scotland) Act 1913, s. 48. Such interest is preferable to the claim of a foreign currency creditor for exchange rate losses during the liquidation (*Re Lines Bros. Ltd.* [1982] 2 All E.R. 183).

insolvent.[56] The Companies (Floating Charges and Receivers) (Scotland) Act 1972, s. 1 (4) provides ("for the avoidance of doubt") that subject to section 322 of the 1948 Act, interest due on a debt secured by a floating charge accrues until payment of the sum due under the charge.

Duties and Powers of Liquidator

87–53 In general terms the duties of the liquidator are to take control of the assets of the company, to make out lists of creditors and contributories, to resolve disputes, to realise the assets and to apply the proceeds in payment of the company's debts and liabilities in due course of administration; if there is any surplus he will adjust the rights of contributories and distribute the surplus in accordance with them.

Section 243 of the 1948 Act provides that where a winding-up order has been made or a provisional liquidator appointed, the liquidator or provisional liquidator shall assume custody or control of all the assets of the company, and so long as there is no liquidator the company's property is deemed to be in the custody of the court. In order to complete title to any such property, however, the liquidator will require a vesting order under section 244.[56a] While proceedings in the liquidation are normally taken in name of the company,[57] section 244 allows the liquidator (after obtaining a vesting order and, if so required, finding caution) to take proceedings in his own name to recover or protect the property. If the property of the company includes licensed premises he is entitled to delivery of the licence certificate.[58] The liquidator represents the creditors because he represents the company, and the rights and obligations of the company are enforceable only through him.[59] There is no provision for disclaiming onerous property (as in England under section 323).

The liquidator must take all reasonable steps to investigate and discover the company's debts and liabilities. This includes advertising for claims and writing to all known creditors asking for confirmation of their claim[60]; advertising alone is not enough where claims are known to exist but have not been formally made.[61] The liquidator must make due provision for tax, including tax arising during his administration, and if he distributes the surplus without retaining sufficient for this purpose he will be personally liable without right of recovery from the shareholders.[62] A liquidator who has knowledge of a claim but does not deal with it, owing to a mistake by his solicitor, cannot evade responsibility.[63] In a situation where the liquida-

[56] *National Commercial Bank of Scotland Ltd.* v. *Liquidators of Telford Grier Mackay & Co. Ltd.*, 1969 S.L.T. 306.
[56a] This will not normally be required (see para. 87–54 *infra*).
[57] s. 245 (1) (*a*) see para. 87–55, *infra*; *Munro* v. *Hutchison* 1896, 3 S.L.T. 268.
[58] *William Forbes Ltd.* v. *Robertson* 1926 S.L.T. 654; see Licensing (Scotland) Act 1976, s. 25.
[59] *Waterhouse* v. *Jamieson* 1870, 8 M. (H.L.) 88.
[60] *Pulsford* v. *Devenish* [1903] 2 Ch. 803.
[61] *Re Armstrong Whitworth Securities Ltd.* [1947] Ch. 673.
[62] *Taylor* v. *Wilson's Trs.*, 1974 S.L.T. 298, (affd. 1979 S.L.T. 105).
[63] *Austin Securities Ltd.* v. *Northgate and English Stores Ltd.* [1969] 1 W.L.R. 529; [1969] 2 All E.R. 753.

tor has doubt whether he has ascertained all claims, he can ask the court to fix a time limit on claims which are to be considered (1948 Act, s. 264).[64]

87–54 The powers which a liquidator may exercise in fulfilling his duties are listed in section 245 of the 1948 Act. Certain particular powers listed in section 245 (2) may be exercised without the sanction of the court or the committee of inspection, namely:

(a) to sell heritage and moveables by public auction or private contract. A liquidator need not seek the approval of the accountant of court.[65] A disposition of heritage runs in the name of the company with the consent of the liquidator. It is sealed with the company's seal and signed by the liquidator before two witnesses. The company grants absolute warrandice and the liquidator grants warrandice from his own facts and deeds only, although it has been doubted whether the liquidator requires to grant warrandice in any form[66];

(b) to do all acts and to execute deeds and other documents in the name of the company, using its seal where necessary;

(c) to prove, rank, claim and receive dividends from the estate of an insolvent contributory;

(d) to draw, accept, make and indorse bills of exchange and promissory notes in name and on behalf of the company;

(e) to borrow on the security of the company's assets;

(f) to apply for confirmation as executor on the estate of a deceased contributory and to do all acts necessary to obtain sums due from a contributory or his estate;

(g) to appoint an agent to act on his behalf.

Powers requiring sanction

87–55 Certain other specific powers are, under section 245 (1), to be exercised with the sanction of the court or the committee of inspection (if any). Sanction may be granted retrospectively.[67]

These powers are:

(a) To bring or defend proceedings in name of the company. Unless the proceedings are under section 244 (para. 87–53 *supra*) it is incompetent for the liquidator to sue in his own name.[68] Failure to obtain the necessary sanction does not affect the competency of the action.[69] An official liquidator, as an officer of the court, is entitled to be master of the process.[70]

---

[64] See para. 87–43, *ante*.

[65] *Liquidators of Style & Mantle Ltd.* v. *Price's Tailors Ltd.*, 1934 S.C. 548; *Galbraith*, 1964 S.L.T.(Sh.Ct.) 75.

[66] *Liquidators of Style & Mantle Ltd.*, *supra*. This assumes that the liquidator has not completed title in his own name, *via* s. 244 (*supra*).

[67] *Re Associated Travel Leisure and Services Ltd.* [1978] 2 All E.R. 753.

[68] *Munro* v. *Hutchison* 1896, 3 S.L.T. 268.

[69] *Stewart* v. *Gardner, etc.* 1933 S.L.T.(Sh.Ct.) 11; *Dublin City Distilling Ltd.* v. *Doherty* [1914] A.C. 823.

[70] *Millar* 1890, 18 R. 179.

(b) To carry on the business of the company so far as may be necessary for the beneficial winding thereof. This emphasis on the completion of the winding up as the objective of carrying on business is not affected by the introduction of powers to make provision for employees under section 74 of the 1980 Act. The liquidator may obtain sanction to carrying on the business for a limited period in order to seek a sale on a "going concern" basis.[71] It is the company which is carrying on the business, not the liquidator, and employees retain continuity of employment for claims for redundancy and related matters.[72] If he makes it clear that the company is in liquidation he does not incur personal liability.[73]

(c) To appoint a solicitor to assist him. Such an appointment does not relieve the liquidator of personal responsibility for the discharge of his duties.[74]

(d) To pay classes of creditors in full.

(e) To make compromises or arrangements with creditors including prospective, contingent or disputed creditors, to compromise calls and liabilities of contributories and generally all claims or liabilities due to or by the company. Compromises with contributories have already been considered.[75] An arrangement under which a creditor is to receive an agreed sum instead of a ranking is a "compromise" requiring the appropriate sanction.[76] Each proposed compromise with creditors should be sanctioned either individually or in batches, not by unspecific prior authority,[77] but the court may consider a comprehensive or general compromise.[78] If shareholders object they may be permitted to proceed with the claims on granting appropriate indemnities to the liquidator.[78] The liquidator may also avail himself of the procedure for obtaining sanction to a scheme of arrangement binding on all parties under section 206[79] especially where it is proposed to depart from the strict rights of creditors.[80] A compromise which has been sanctioned may be recalled, if matters are still entire, on the emergence of new facts.[81]

If there is no committee of inspection, the court may by order in general terms allow the liquidator to bring or defend proceedings or carry on the business without further sanction (s. 245 (4)).

---

[71] *Liquidator of Burntisland Oil Co. Ltd.* v. *Dawson* 1892, 20 R. 180 (six months refused, six weeks allowed); *Liquidator of Victoria Public Buildings Co.* 1893, 30 S.L.R. 386 (one year sanctioned).

[72] *Smith* v. *Lord Advocate* 1979 S.L.T. 233.

[73] *Stead Hazel & Co.* v. *Cooper* [1933] 1 K.B. 840.

[74] *Austin Securities Ltd.* v. *Northgate and English Stores Ltd.* [1969] 2 All E.R. 753.

[75] See para. 87–41, *ante*.

[76] *Liquidator of R. D. Simpson Ltd.* v. *Beare* 1908, 15 S.L.T. 875.

[77] *Pattisons Ltd.* 1899, 6 S.L.T. 372; *T. H. Bennett & Co.* 1905, 13 S.L.T. 718.

[78] *Ecuadorian Assoc. Ltd., etc.* v. *Fox, etc.* 1907, 14 S.L.T. 699.

[79] See para. 79–02, *ante*.

[80] *Re Trix Ltd.* [1970] 3 All E.R. 397.

[81] *D. & W. Henderson & Co.* v. *Stewart* 1894, 22 R. 154; 2 S.L.T. 367.

87–56 In addition to these particular powers, section 245 gives the liquidator further powers of a general nature:

(a) Without the sanction of the court or committee of inspection, to do all things other than the powers enumerated above which may be necessary for winding up the company and distributing its assets (s. 245 (2) (*h*)).

(b) "Subject to general rules" (*i.e.* of law in general and bankruptcy in particular) to exercise the same powers as a trustee on a bankrupt estate in Scotland (s. 245 (5)).

(c) The liquidator is entitled to apply to the court by motion or note in the liquidation petition (see R.C.S. 215 (Sh.Ct.R. 47–51)) if he is in doubt on any matter. The court may order meetings of creditors or contributories to be held to ascertain their wishes (1948 Act, s. 346).

87–57 CONTROL OF LIQUIDATORS. The liquidator acts under the general control of the court, and any creditor or contributory who is aggrieved may apply to it for an appropriate order on him (s. 245 (3); R.C.S. 214, 215 (Sh.Ct.R. 44–51)). Decisions in England to the effect that the court will only intervene if the liquidator has acted in bad faith or against all reason[82] must be regarded as unsound, in Scotland at least, where an application alleging merely a difference of opinion with the liquidator was heard and granted.[83] As to appeals from the court of first instance, see the 1948 Act, s. 277 and Sched. 10 and R.C.S. 217 (ShCt.R. 54, 55).[84]

Funds ingathered by a liquidator are held by him and not (as in England) in the Companies Liquidation Account of the Bank of England (s. 248). The requirements relating to audit and control by the Department of Trade (ss. 249 and 250) also apply only in England. Supervisory duties of this kind are exercisable by the committee of inspection (R.C.S. 209 (Sh.Ct.R. 33–55)).

Legal effect of a winding-up order

87–58 A winding-up order operates for the benefit of all creditors and contributories (1948 Act, s. 232) and is deemed to be equivalent to completed diligence (1948 Act, s. 327). The property of the company is in the control of the liquidator (or the court if there is no liquidator) (1948 Act, s. 243). Share transfers and dispositions, transfers, etc., of property after the commencement of a winding up by the court are void unless sanctioned by the court (1948 Act, s. 227). If the company has assets in England any attachment, sequestration, distress or execution against such assets after the commencement of the winding up is void (1948 Act, s. 228). After a petition for winding up has been presented the court may sist proceedings

82 See para. 85–39, *ante*. *Cf. Leon* v. *York-o-Matic Ltd.* [1966] 1 W.L.R. 1450; [1966] 3 All E.R. 277. See also *Re Wyvern Developments Ltd.* [1974] 2 All E.R. 535.

83 *Liquidator of Upper Clyde Shipbuilders Ltd.*, 1975 S.L.T. 39.

84 See para. 87–04, *ante.*

against the company (1948 Act, s. 226) and once a winding-up order has been made or a provisional liquidator appointed such proceedings are automatically sisted and cannot be continued except by leave of the court (1948 Act, s. 231).

The directors' powers in relation to the assets and business of the company (and those of any other agent or servant having authority to act in its name) cease on the granting of a winding-up order,[85] but only to the extent that such powers have passed to the liquidator. The powers to act in name of the company which do not pass to the liquidator and remain vested in the directors include the power to appeal against the winding-up order itself, or to seek recall of the liquidator's appointment.[86] The directors will also continue to exercise powers vested in them as trustees of the company's pension scheme.[87]

The appointment of a liquidator does not affect the power of a receiver to enter into contracts in respect of that part of the property and undertaking of the company comprised in the charge by virtue of which he was appointed.[88]

Effect of liquidation on contracts

87–59 (a) CONTRACTS OTHER THAN CONTRACTS OF EMPLOYMENT. Contracts other than contracts of employment are not automatically terminated by liquidation, in the absence of a specific term to that effect. The liquidator has the option to take over any contract with future prestations in favour of the company independently of his decision in respect of any other contract, or to terminate it and concede a ranking for damages.[89] The liquidator must intimate his decision within a reasonable time, having regard to the nature of the contract, failing which he will be deemed to have abandoned the intention to proceed with it.[90] A provision in a lease which purports to exclude liquidators except with the landlord's prior consent does not have the effect of terminating the lease *ipso facto* on the liquidator's appointment, but entitles the landlord to determine it if the liquidator proposes to adopt the lease, or delays unreasonably in intimating his decision.[90]

A pre-liquidation contract to grant security is incapable of being adopted since this would amount to an illegal preference, and likewise the liquidator cannot adopt a contract whose unfulfilled provisions carry no advantage to the company.[91]

The liquidator cannot adopt contracts which, prior to the liquidation,

---

[85] *Re Mawcon Ltd.* [1969] 1 All E.R. 188.
[86] *Re Union Accident Insurance Co. Ltd.* [1972] 1 All E.R. 1105.
[87] *Smith, etc., Ptnrs.* 1969 S.L.T.(Notes) 94.
[88] Companies (Floating Charges and Receivers) (Scotland) Act 1972, s. 15 (1).
[89] *Gray's Trs.* v. *Benhar Coal Co., etc.* 1881, 9 R. 225; *Asphaltic Limestone Concrete Co. Ltd.* v. *Glasgow Corporation* 1907 S.C. 463; 14 S.L.T. 706: *Clyde Marine Insurance Co.* v. *Renwick* 1924 S.C. 113; 1924 S.L.T. 41; *Turnbull* v. *Liquidator of Scottish County Investment Co.* 1939 S.C. 5; 1938 S.L.T. 584.
[90] *Crown Estate Commissioners* v. *Liquidators of Highland Engineering Ltd.* 1975 S.L.T. 58.
[91] *Turnbull* v. *Liquidator of Scottish County Investment Co., supra.*

existed as obligations binding in honour only and not legally enforceable (such as may arise from insurance brokerage practice) however much they formed part of the custom of the trade in which the company was engaged. There is no inherent power in the Scottish courts to overrule legal rights on equitable considerations, as claimed by the English courts.[92] In the event of the liquidator being duly authorised to carry on the business of the company, however, it may be proper to regard the discharge of such obligations as a legitimate aspect of the carrying on of the business.[93] The liquidator may ratify on behalf of the company acts, in themselves invalid, which the company in general meeting could have ratified.[94]

87–60 (b) CONTRACTS OF EMPLOYMENT. A winding-up order or a resolution for voluntary winding up is presumed to constitute constructive notice of termination of all contracts of employment with the company. If the winding up is on the grounds of insolvency, an employee is entitled to leave the services of the company immediately and claim damages. If he continues in the services of the company a separate contract may arise expressly or by implication between the liquidator and the employee.[95]

Prior to the Companies Act 1980, s. 74, a gratuitous payment to employees (or former employees) of a company going into liquidation might be challenged as *ultra vires* on the grounds that it was contrary to the best interests of the company, which no longer had any interest in maintaining good relations with its employees since it had no continuing goodwill to protect, unless there was power to make such payments within the objects of its memorandum.[96] Section 74 of the 1980 Act provides (s. 74 (1)) that the powers of a company shall, if they would not otherwise do so, be deemed to include power to make provision for the benefit of persons employed or formerly employed by the company or any of its subsidiaries in connection with the cessation or the transfer of all or part of its undertaking or that of its subsidiary. The power conferred by this subsection may be exercised (s. 74 (2)) "notwithstanding that its exercise is not in the best interests of the company." Section 74 (3) provides for the manner in which such payments must be sanctioned by the company.

Section 74 (6) provides that any payment under section 74 must be provided, in the case of a payment before the commencement of winding up, out of profits available for distribution as dividend or, in any other case, including in particular a company in liquidation, out of assets available for distribution to the members. Section 74 (4) provides that the liquidator may (but cannot be compelled to) implement any gratuitous provision for employees, etc., which has been validly sanctioned by the

92 *e.g. Clark* v. *Texaco Ltd.* [1975] 1 All E.R. 453.
93 *Clyde Marine Insurance Co.* v. *Renwick & Co., supra.*
94 *Alexander Ward & Co. Ltd.* v. *Samyang Navigation Co. Ltd.* 1975 S.C. (H.L.) 27; 1975 S.L.T. 126.
95 *Day* v. *Tait, etc.* 1900, 8 S.L.T. 40. See further paras. 67–13 and 67–14 *ante*; Miller, *Industrial Law in Scotland* (W. Green & Son, Edinburgh, 1970) p. 391.
96 *Gibson's Executor* v. *Gibson* 1980 S.L.T. 2; *Parke* v. *Daily News Ltd.* [1962] Ch. 927.

company prior to the commencement of winding up. In the case of a winding up by the court a creditor or contributory may apply to the court for an order under section 245 (3) of the 1948 Act to control the liquidator's exercise of this power. Section 74 (5) authorises a liquidator to make such provision, even if it has not been previously sanctioned by the company, provided that all liabilities, expenses, etc., have been met and he obtains the sanction of an ordinary resolution of the company or (if the memorandum or articles so require) a resolution passed by more than a simple majority. While a resolution of the directors may sanction such a payment prior to the winding up (assuming that it is so authorised in its memorandum or articles), in a winding up the sanction of the directors would not be sufficient to fulfil the requirements of section 74 (5). In a winding up by the court the exercise by the liquidator of his power under section 74 (5) is also subject to any order which may be obtained by a creditor or contributory under section 245 (3) (s. 74 (7)). Section 74 (8) provides that the common law and statutory rules providing for the distribution of the property of the company to its members after satisfaction of all liabilities, etc., shall be modified to accommodate any payment validly made under section 74.

The effect of these provisions is to confer upon a gratuitous payment for employees, etc., what is in effect a deferred ranking in the liquidation after ordinary creditors but prior to the claims of members. Section 74 (2) does not prevent a challenge by the liquidator of any such payment which is made by a company prior to the commencement of winding up. In principle, such a payment should be open to challenge as a gratuitous alienation or fraudulent preference, but the liquidator would probably be able to challenge it more readily on the grounds that it had not been made out of profits available for dividend (s. 74 (6) (*a*)). There appears to be no protection afforded to an employee against such a challenge, even if he received it in good faith and without knowledge of the financial position of the company. If, on the other hand, the payment is not made under section 74 but in terms of powers contained in the memorandum or articles, it may be argued that the requirements of section 74 (6) as to the provision of funds from profits available for dividend do not apply.

Personal liability of liquidators

87–61 A liquidator is not personally liable for the obligations of the company, but he is liable to the creditors or contributories for negligence in the performance of his duties. Such a claim cannot be maintained (in the absence of fraud or concealment of material facts) where the court (or committee of inspection) has sanctioned the act complained of.[97]

If a liquidator has failed to obtain the proper sanction for the exercise of

---

[97] *Highland Engineering Ltd., etc.* v. *Anderson, etc.* 1979 S.L.T. 122.

his powers he incurs personal liability but may be relieved of this by the court on cause shown.[98]

A liquidator who enters appearance and defends an action warrants the sufficiency of the company's assets to meet any expenses to which the pursuer may be found entitled, and accordingly incurs personal liability if the assets are insufficient.[99] If the court considers the conduct of the liquidator to be blameworthy, to the extent that he should be deprived of his right of relief against the assets of the company, the decree for expenses must state in terms that the liquidator is found "personally" liable.[1]

A liquidator in a members' voluntary liquidation is not entitled to recover from a liquidator subsequently appointed by the court, from funds required to meet creditors' claims, expenses incurred by him in endeavouring to implement a scheme for reconstruction under section 287.[2]

Proceedings against the company[2a]

87–62 When a winding-up order has been made or a provisional liquidator appointed actions or other proceedings cannot be commenced or continued against the company except by leave of the court and subject to such conditions as the court may impose (1948 Act, s. 231). The expenses of a successful unopposed application for leave are, unless the court otherwise directs, to be added to the applicant's claim (s. 350). The leave of the court is not required for a counter-claim in proceedings brought by the company, if it is pleaded by way of compensation, but leave is required to counter-claim for an amount in excess of the company's claim.[3]

The main purpose of the section is to prevent an accumulation of actions against an insolvent company, and the question of whether to grant or refuse sanction is one of expediency having regard to the interests of creditors generally.[4] Accordingly, while proceedings for which sanction has not been obtained are incompetent,[5] the pursuer should have an opportunity to apply for leave to proceed.[6] If the liquidator does not invoke section 231 it is not for the court to apply it *ex proprio motu.*[7]

Section 231 cannot be invoked so as to validate diligence cut down by section 327.[8]

An order by the court having jurisdiction to wind up the company is

---

98 *Re Associated Travel Leisure & Services Ltd.* [1978] 2 All E.R. 273.

99 *Sinclair* v. *The Thurso Pavement Syndicate Ltd.* 1903, 11 S.L.T. 364; *Liquidator of the Consolidated Coal Co. of Canada* v. *Peddie, etc.* 1877, 5 R. 393, 413; *Anderson's Trs.* v. *Donaldson & Co.* 1908 S.C. 385; 15 S.L.T. 702.

1 *Kilmarnock Theatre Co.* v. *Buchanan* 1911 S.C. 607; 1911, 1 S.L.T. 225.

2 *Liquidator of Scottish Assurance Corp.* v. *Miller* 1881, 18 R. 496.

2a "Proceedings" should be construed widely: *Langley Constructions* (*Brixham*) *Ltd.* v. *Wells* (*infra*, note 3); *Re J. Burrows (Leeds) Ltd.* [1982] 2 All E.R. 882.

3 *Langley Constructions (Brixham) Ltd.* v. *Wells* [1969] 1 W.L.R. 503; [1969] 2 All E.R. 46.

4 *Cf. Re Aro Co. Ltd.* [1980] 1 All E.R. 1067.

5 *Grieve* v. *International Exhibition Assoc.* 1890, 29 S.L.R. 20; *Radford & Bright Ltd.* v. *Stevenson* 1904, 6 F. 429; 11 S.L.T. 695.

6 *D. M. Stevenson & Co.* v. *Radford & Bright* 1902, 10 S.L.T. 82; *Martin* v. *Port of Manchester Insurance Co. Ltd.*, 1934 S.C. 143.

7 *Hill* v. *Black* 1914 S.C. 913; 1914, 2 S.L.T. 123 *Sinclair* v. *Thurso Pavement Syndicate Ltd.* 1903, 11 S.L.T. 364.

8 *Allan* v. *Cowan* 1892, 20 R. 36; *Radford & Bright* v. *Stevenson, supra.*

applicable to proceedings in any court in Great Britain or Northern Ireland.[9] The Scottish court will not question the *ex facie* competent order of the court of jurisdiction in granting or refusing leave.[10] Questions touching on the internal conduct of the liquidation should, as a general rule, be disposed of in the court supervising the liquidation.[11]

Where the proceedings are in a foreign court, outwith Great Britain and Northern Ireland, there appears to be a divergence of opinion between the Scottish and English courts. It has been held in Scotland that, in principle, section 231 is applicable and if the pursuers are subject to the jurisdiction an order restraining the foreign proceedings can be granted.[12] If the order could not be enforced because of want of jurisdiction, however, the court will not grant a restraining order.[13] In England it has been held that section 231 does not apply to proceedings furth of the United Kingdom, although alternative equitable grounds for granting a restraining order exist provided that it can be made effective by virtue of the plaintiff being subject to the jurisdiction.[14]

Since the question of whether leave to proceed should be granted is one of expediency, precedents drawn from English practice[15] should be treated with caution. The court has to determine whether, in the particular circumstances, the balance of convenience lies with allowing an action to proceed in order to establish whether a claim exists against the company or to restrain proceedings at least until the liquidator had adjudicated on the claim. Leave to proceed should normally be granted where the interests of third parties are involved.[16] Leave will be refused if the action seeks to constitute a claim of debt or damages which can be resolved in the liquidation.[17] If the action is to reduce an allotment of shares, leave to proceed may (in the exercise of the court's discretion) be granted if the proceedings are well advanced or an issue is raised which can more readily be determined by a court other than the court of liquidation.[18]

Security holders cannot, of course, be deprived of their legitimate rights, and may take such proceedings against the company as may be required to enforce them without leave of the court.[19]

---

[9] *Re Dynamics Corp. of America* [1972] 3 All E.R. 1046; *Martin* v. *Port of Manchester Insurance Co. Ltd., supra.* See also ss. 276 and 461.

[10] *Queensland Mercantile & Agency Co. Ltd.* v. *Australasian Investment Co. Ltd.* 1888, 15 R. 935.

[11] *Carbon (New) Syndicate Ltd.* v. *Seton* 1904, 12 S.L.T. 191.

[12] *California Redwood Co. Ltd.* v. *Walker* 1886, 13 R. 816; *Redwood Co. Ltd.* v. *Merchant Banking Co. of London* 1886, 13 R. 1202.

[13] *California Redwood Co. Ltd.* v. *Walker, supra.*

[14] *Re Vocaeion (Foreign) Ltd.* [1932] 2 Ch. 196.

[15] See examples at para. 85–76, *ante*.

[16] *Coclas* v. *Bruce Peebles* 1908, 16 S.L.T. 7.

[17] *Coclas* v. *Bruce Peebles, supra*; *Main* v. *Azotine Ltd.* 1916, 2 S.L.T. 252.

[18] *London & Scottish Banking & Discount Corp.* 1895, 3 S.L.T. 21; *James Young & Sons Ltd.* 1900, 7 S.L.T. 301.

[19] *Atholl Hydropathic Co. Ltd.* v. *Scottish Provincial Assurance Co. Ltd.* 1886, 13 R. 818; *Anderson's Trs.* v. *Donaldson & Co. Ltd.*, 1908 S.C. 38; 15 S.L.T. 409. In these cases a heritable creditor and a feudal superior were allowed to proceed with actions of poinding of the ground, which would now be subject to the limitations expressed in s. 327 (1) (*d*) (see *infra*, para. 87–63). See also *Bell's Trs.* v. *The Holmes Oil Co.* 1901, 8 S.L.T. 360.

Section 226 of the 1948 Act governs the position after a winding-up petition has been presented but before section 231 takes effect. The company, any creditor or contributory may apply to the court having jurisdiction to wind up the company for an order restraining further proceedings in any action or proceedings against the company (s. 226 (*b*)); if, however, the action or proceedings is pending in the High Court or Court of Appeal in England or Northern Ireland the application must be made in the court where the action is pending (s. 226 (*a*)). The court may make a conditional order. An order under section 226 (*b*) is effective throughout the United Kingdom.[20]

Section 226 will not be applied to prevent a creditor from proceeding with his claim to the point of decree[21] but it is appropriate to restrain diligence either by a particular creditor,[22] or, after a meeting of creditors directed by the court has expressed its agreement, by creditors generally.[23]

Any attachment, sequestration, distress or execution against the assets of a Scottish company situated in England after the commencement of compulsory winding up is void (s. 228 (2)), but the English court may validate it under section 231.[24]

Effect of liquidation on diligence

87–63 Section 327 (1) provides for the cutting down of diligences executed within 60 days of the commencement of winding up. Rules for cutting down diligence executed within 60 days prior to the commencement of a winding up were introduced into Scots law by the Companies Act 1886, s. 3. This followed criticism of the absence of such rules in a case where creditors who had not executed diligence unsuccessfully applied for the appointment of a trustee in bankruptcy on the assets of a company.[25] The winding up is declared to be equivalent to an arrestment in execution and decree of furthcoming, an executed and completed poinding and a decree of adjudication of heritage subject to preferable heritable rights and securities including sequestration for rent.[26] It is thus made equivalent to completed diligence in respect of incorporeal moveables, corporeal moveables and heritage respectively. All diligences executed by creditors within 60 days of the commencement of liquidation are ineffective.[27]

A creditor holding a *debitum fundi*, such as a feudal superior, the creditor in a contract of ground annual or a heritable creditor (if not *ex facie* the owner) has a limited security over moveables on the ground over which his debt subsists, which he exercises by "poinding of the ground."

---

[20] *Re Dynamics Corporation of America* [1972] 3 All E.R. 1046.
[21] *Benhar Coal Co. Ltd.* v. *Sime* 1878, 6 R. 316.
[22] *New Glenduffhill Coal Co. Ltd.* v. *Muir* 1882, 10 R. 372.
[23] *Benhar Coal Co. Ltd.* 1879, 6 R. 706.
[24] *Re Aro Co. Ltd.*, [1980] 1 All E.R. 1067.
[25] *Standard Property Investment Co. Ltd.* v. *Dunblane Hydropathic Co. Ltd.* 1884, 12 R. 328, 334.
[26] *Scottish Metropolitan Property Co.* v. *Sutherlands Ltd.*, 1934 S.L.T.(Sh.Ct.) 62.
[27] *Allan* v. *Cowan* 1892, 20 R. 36.

Such procedure is not "diligence," nor does it require leave of the court, as it is strictly speaking the enforcement of a security.[28] The position of the holder of such a security has (with a limited exception in favour of a heritable creditor, but not others, entitled to poind the ground) been assimilated to that of a creditor doing diligence. A heritable creditor may obtain security by this process even after liquidation, but only to the extent of the interest due for the current half-year and one year's arrears. Subject to this no poinding of the ground which has not been completed by sale of the effects within 60 days of the liquidation is effective (s. 327 (1) (*d*)).

An inhibition is only a personal diligence which creates no *nexus* over the heritable property of the company,[29] although it may be an effectual preference over the debtor's reversionary interest in a competition with other creditors, in the absence of liquidation.[29a] Since section 327 (1) (*b*) puts the liquidator in the position of the holder of a decree of adjudication he has priority over a creditor who holds an inhibition which has not been followed by adjudication. The liquidator can therefore proceed with a sale notwithstanding the existence of an inhibition, unless he contractually binds himself to provide "clear searches."[30]

Where an arrestment is made within the 60-day period, and the company satisfies the claim, the diligence thereby lapses and the liquidator cannot reclaim the money paid simply on the basis of section 327 (1) (*a*); he may, however, be able to claim on the grounds of fraudulent preference.[31] An arrestment which has not been completed by decree of furthcoming is not effectual.[32] Section 327 also applies to the property of an English company which is situated in Scotland (s. 327 (2)). It appears, however, that the liquidator of a Scottish company cannot avoid executions put in force against its assets in England before the commencement of winding up; section 327 does not extend to England, and sections 325 and 326, which invalidate such executions, do not apply to a Scottish company. Executions in England after commencement of winding up are subject to the restraint of section 228 (2).[33]

A creditor whose arrestment or poinding has been cut down has a preference in respect of his expenses incurred in carrying out such diligence (s. 327 (1) (*a*)).

Third party insurance

87–64 When a company which is being wound up is insured against liabilities to third parties, and a liability is incurred by the company to such a third party, the company's rights against the insurer are transferred to the third

---

[28] See *supra*, para. 87–62.
[29] *McGowan* v. *A. Middlemas & Sons Ltd.* 1977 S.L.T.(Sh.Ct.) 41.
[29a] *Abbey National Building Society* v. *Shaik Azij* 1981 S.L.T. (Sh.Ct.) 29.
[30] *Dryburgh* v. *Gordon* 1896, 24 R. 1.
[31] *Johnston* v. *Cluny Trustees*, 1957 S.C. 184; 1957 S.L.T. 293 (for fraudulent preferences see *infra*, para. 87–66).
[32] *Lord Advocate* v. *Royal Bank of Scotland, etc.* 1977 S.C. 155; 1978 S.L.T. 38.
[33] See para. 87–62, *ante*.

party.[34] The insurer cannot plead set-off in respect of unpaid premiums.[35]

Dispositions and transfers after a winding-up order

87–65 In a winding up by the court, any disposition of the property of the company, including incorporeal moveables, and any transfer of shares or alteration of the status of members after the commencement of winding up is void unless the court orders otherwise (1948 Act, s. 227).[36] The validating order may be made even before winding up commences.[37] After commencement of the winding up a shareholder retains enough locus to apply for or to oppose an order under section 227, even if the application relates to dispositions of property and not to share transfers.[38] For the purposes of section 227 the property of the company is the sum total of its rights and assets, and it is immaterial whether the "disposition" under attack is granted by the company or by a third party, so long as it relates to company property.[39]

Credits paid into the company's bank account and payments to third parties debited against that account are, in principle, "dispositions of property" whether the account is in credit or debit at the time. Such payments are invalid under section 227 unless sanctioned by the court.[40]

In the case of a solvent company, if the court is satisfied that the directors believe a disposition is necessary or expedient in the interest of the company, and that their reasons are tenable, a contributory's opposition will not prevent the disposition being sanctioned unless he adduces compelling evidence to show that it is injurious to the company.[41]

In the case of an insolvent company the applicant for a validation order under section 227 must satisfy the court that the exercise of its discretion in favour of granting the order, whether in respect of transactions that have already taken place or for proposed transactions, would be just and fair in all the circumstances.[42] The creditors are entitled to assume that the court will sanction only such dispositions as are shown to be beneficial to the company.[43] The considerations which should guide the court have been subjected to exhaustive review by the Court of Appeal, in a case[44] which concerned the retrospective validation under section 227 of operations on a company's bank account which the bank allowed to continue in the interval

---

[34] Third Party (Rights Against Insurers) Act 1930, s. 1; see also Road Traffic Act 1972, s. 149.
[35] *Murray* v. *Legal and General Assurance Society* [1970] 2 Q.B. 495.
[36] *Nelson & Mitchell* v. *City of Glasgow Bank*. 1879, 6 R. (H.L.) 66; *Dodds* v. *Cosmopolitan Insurance Co. Ltd.*, 1915 S.C. 992; 1915, 2 S.L.T. 106.
[37] *A. I. Levy (Holdings) Ltd.* [1964] Ch. 19; *Operator Control Cabs Ltd.* [1970] 3 All E.R. 657.
[38] *Argentum Reductions (U.K.) Ltd.* [1975] 1 All E.R. 608; *Burton & Deacon Ltd.* [1977] 1 All E.R. 631.
[39] *J. Leslie Engineers Co. Ltd.* [1976] 2 All E.R. 85.
[40] *Gray's Inn Construction Co. Ltd.* [1980] 1 All E.R. 814.
[41] *Burton & Deacon Ltd., supra.*
[42] *Burton & Deacon Ltd., supra*; *A. I. Levy (Holdings) Ltd., supra.*
[43] *Steane's (Bournemouth) Ltd.* [1950] 1 All E.R. 21; *Clifton Place Garage Ltd.* [1970] Ch. 477.
[44] *Gray's Inn Construction Co. Ltd.* [1980] 1 All E.R. 814.

between presentation of the petition and the granting of the winding-up order.

The duty of the court under section 227 is to protect the unsecured creditors. It should not allow particular transactions, or a series of transactions such as the carrying on of the business of the company, under which one or more pre-liquidation creditors are paid in full at the expense of other such creditors, unless there are special circumstances. If a bank (or a party in a like position) transacts with the company without first obtaining a validation order it does so at the risk of its transactions being invalidated. In exercising its discretion the court will be guided principally by the concern to validate such transactions as would be beneficial for the company and its creditors, which the court suggested would be capable of being placed in one of the following categories:

1. provided that there is no intention to confer a preference on the creditor, transactions carried out in the ordinary course of business and in ignorance of the presentation of the petition would normally be validated;
2. transactions which are entirely post-liquidation would normally be validated;
3. transactions which increase or preserve the value of the assets would normally be validated, even if this meant the payment in full of a pre-liquidation debt, such as the payment of suppliers to permit the company to continue in business.

If the question is whether to allow the company to continue in business, by permitting the bank to maintain its account, the court would expect the bank to freeze the existing account of the company and any subsequent dealings should be carried out on a separate account. The bank should obtain assurances from the directors and such other precautions as it can adopt to ensure that no pre-liquidation debts would be paid out of the fresh account and that all transactions on that account would be in the normal course of business. If the bank chose to allow the company to continue to operate its account without a validation order it exposed itself to the risk of being liable (in addition) for trading losses incurred during that period. The bank should exercise diligence in obtaining adequate information about the affairs of the company and take suitable precautions to ensure that a trading loss is not incurred during that period.

A transfer of fully paid shares in a limited company will be permitted, subject to the consent of the liquidator, since the creditors have no interest in the matter.[45] An assignation of the shareholder's interest in the company does not require sanction under section 227 since the assignor remains a contributory.[46] Where preference shareholders had a right to

---

[45] *Benhar Coal Co. Ltd.* 1897, 6 R. 707; *Surma Valley Saw Mills Ltd.*, 1917 S.C. 105; 1916, 2 S.L.T. 302.

[46] *Jackson* v. *Elphick* 1902, 10 S.L.T. 146.

convert their shares into ordinary shares, a notice given before the commencement of winding up could take effect afterwards.[47]

As a result of powers granted to him by the Conveyancing and Feudal Reform (Scotland) Act 1970, the holder of a standard security is, however, able to grant a valid disposition notwithstanding section 227. In *United Dominions Trust Ltd.*,[48] a creditor had obtained a warrant under section 24 of the 1970 Act from the sheriff court (which was not the court having jurisdiction in the winding up, *i.e.* for the purposes of s. 227) authorising him to sell the heritable property of a company in liquidation. The Court of Session, in the winding-up process, held that no further action was required and to that extent section 227 had by necessary inference from the 1970 Act been amended. The opinion was also expressed that, even without a warrant under section 24, the provisions of the 1970 Act, in particular section 20, authorise the holder of a standard security to sell and grant a disposition of the property subject thereto, without any approval under section 227. The holder of any other form of heritable security, it was suggested, is, however, still subject to section 227.

Gratuitous alienations and fraudulent preferences

87–66 An insolvent company is entitled to continue trading provided that it does not alienate its property gratuitously or without adequate consideration, or grant voluntary ("fraudulent") preferences to a particular creditor or class of creditors.[49] Carrying on business with the intention of defrauding creditors is struck at by section 332, but this requires more than the mere intention to prefer a creditor.[50] A company is not permitted to grant a trust deed for behoof of its creditors[51] or a floating charge in favour of its creditors generally.[52]

A transaction may be challenged at any time short of the relevant prescriptive period, although delay may affect the burden of proof of insolvency.[53] Claims for repayment, restitution or repetition prescribe after five years[54] but actions concluding only for reduction may be brought for up to 10 years in the case of deeds recorded in the Property Register or 20 years in other cases.[56]

Gratuitous alienations

87–67 At common law, any alienation of property is reducible if the challenger can show that the consideration was inadequate and that the company was

[47] *Re Blaina Colliery* [1926] W.N. 30.
[48] 1977 S.L.T.(Notes) 56.
[49] *Nordic Travel Limited* v. *Scotprint Ltd.*, 1980 S.L.T. 189; 1980 S.C. 1.
[50] See para. 87–72, *infra*.
[51] s. 320 (2).
[52] *London Joint City and Midland Bank* v. *Herbert Dickinson* [1922] W.N. 13.
[53] *Goudy on Bankruptcy* (4th ed.), p. 50.
[54] Prescription and Limitation (Scotland) Act 1973, s. 6 and Sched 1.
[55] 1973 Act, s. 1 (as extended by the Land Registration (Scotland) Act 1979 Sched. 3).
[56] 1973 Act, s. 7. See further Walker, *The Law of Prescription and Limitation of Actions in Scotland* (2nd ed., 1976).

insolvent at the time, or became insolvent as a result.[57] Insolvency in this context means "practical insolvency," *i.e.* inability to meet debts as they fall due. In the case of alienations in writing,[58] however, if the challenger can show that the alienation was to a "conjunct or confident person" and that the company is insolvent at the time of challenge, there is a statutory presumption under the Bankruptcy Act 1621, c. 18 of the Scottish Parliament, rebuttable by the defender, that the company was insolvent at the time of the transaction and that the consideration was inadequate. The relationship is "conjunct or confident" if there is a close relationship of business confidentiality with the company, in the case, for example, of a director or manager[59] or a confidential clerk.[60] In the absence of other factors there is no such relationship with a creditor[61] or a shareholder[62] or between an insurance company and policyholder.[63]

Any creditor may challenge a gratuitous alienation regardless of the date of his debt, but the statutory presumptions under the 1621 Act are not available to creditors whose debts post-date the transaction.[64] By virtue of the Bankruptcy (Scotland) Act 1913, s. 9, as applied to companies by section 245 (5) of the 1948 Act, a liquidator may challenge an alienation with the benefit of the 1621 Act regardless of the date of creditors' claims.[65] Liquidation does not prevent a creditor from taking action.[66]

Third parties acquiring property from the grantee in good faith and for onerous consideration are protected, without prejudice to the liability of the grantee to make restitution.[67]

Fraudulent preferences[68]

87–68 At common law, a "fraudulent preference" is any transaction by which a creditor obtains a preference over other creditors either directly from the company or indirectly, as when a cheque received by the company from a debtor is endorsed to the creditor,[69] provided that the challenger can show that the preference was voluntary and that the company was insolvent (*i.e.* "practically insolvent") and aware of its insolvency.

The Bankruptcy Act 1696, c. 5 of the Scottish Parliament, as amended by the Companies Act 1947, s. 115 (3) (and applied to companies by section 320 of the 1948 Act), provides that any voluntary preference

---

57 *Abram Steamship Co. Ltd. (in liquidation), etc.* v. *Abram*, 1925 S.L.T. 243. See further Goudy, *op. cit.*, Chap. III.
58 Goudy, *op. cit.*, p. 44.
59 *Abram Steamship Co. Ltd. (in liquidation), etc.* v. *Abram, supra.*
60 *Bank of Scotland* v. *Gardiner* 1906, 14 S.L.T. 146 (affd. 1907, 15 S.L.T. 229).
61 *Todd* v. *Anglian Insurance Co. Ltd.*, 1933 S.L.T. 274.
62 Goudy, *op. cit.*, p. 46.
63 *Ritchie* v. *Scottish Automobile and General Insurance Co.* 1931 S.N. 83 (quoted in *Todd*, note 61, *supra*).
64 Goudy, *op. cit.*, pp. 33 and 51.
65 *Neil's Trs.* v. *British Linen Co.* 1898, 36 S.L.R. 139; *Abram Steamship Co. Ltd., supra*, p. 246. The decision in *Cleghorn* v. *Fairgrieve* 1982 S.L.T. (Sh.Ct.) 17 that the 1621 Act has no application to companies cannot be reconciled with *Abram*, and s. 245 (5) and appears to be unsound.
66 *Brown and Co.* v. *McCallum* 1890, 18 R. 311.
67 Goudy, *op. cit*, p. 54.
68 See generally, Goudy, *op. cit.*, Chaps. IV and X.
69 *Liquidator of Walkraft Paint Co. Ltd.* v. *James H. Kinsey Ltd.*, 1964 S.L.T. 104.

effected within six months prior to the commencement of winding up is presumed to have been granted at a time when the company was insolvent, unless the defender can show otherwise. The period of six months is to be computed by excluding either the date winding up commences or the date the preference is made effectual.[70]

A floating charge, however, can only be challenged under the provisions of section 322.[71]

A transaction which is involuntary cannot be challenged as a fraudulent preference. An undertaking to grant a security which was entered into in a legally enforceable form at a time of solvency or before commencement of the six-month period can validly be completed, even during the six months before winding up,[72] but not if it is still incomplete when winding up has commenced.[73] Payment by the arrestee to the arresting creditor of sums arrested on the dependence of an action is voluntary and reducible unless and until the creditor has obtained decree in the principal action, after which it becomes involuntary whether decree of furthcoming has been obtained or merely a mandate by the company.[74]

The payment in cash (or by cheque on the company's own account[75]) of debts actually due, *i.e.* not anticipatory payments, and transactions in the ordinary course of business are not fraudulent preferences unless it can be shown that there was collusion between the company and the creditor receiving payment in a scheme to defraud other creditors.[76] A company which knows it is "practically" insolvent is not to be regarded as holding its assets in trust for its creditors, and the mere fact that a creditor receives payment in the knowledge that the company is insolvent, even irretrievably, does not demonstrate the existence of an intention to defraud other creditors.[77] The mere intention to prefer a creditor or to obtain a preference is not fraudulent.[78]

A transaction under which the company grants security in respect of some fair and present consideration (*i.e.* a "*novum debitum*") is not a preference and thus remains valid.[79] This protects both securities for new advances[80] and substituted securities for existing loans.[81] The provision of the consideration and the granting of the security need not be simultaneous, provided that they are *unico contextu*.[82]

---

[70] Goudy, *op. cit*, p. 75; Bankruptcy (Scotland) Act 1913, s. 4.
[71] See para. 87–69, *infra*.
[72] *T.* v. *L.* 1970 S.L.T. 243.
[73] *Turnbull* v. *Liquidator of Scottish County Investment Co. Ltd.*, 1939 S.C. 5.
[74] *Liquidator of Walkraft Paint Co. Ltd.* v. *Lovelock (No.1)*, 1963 S.L.T.(Notes) 6; *Same parties (No. 2)*, 1964 S.L.T. 103. *High-Flex (Scotland) Ltd.* v. *Kentallan Mechanical Services* 1977 S.L.T.(Sh.Ct.) 91.
[75] *Liquidator of Walkraft Paint Co. Ltd.* v. *James H. Kinsey Ltd.*, 1964 S.L.T. 104 (endorsement of a cheque is a preference).
[76] *Whatmough's Trs.* v. *British Linen Bank*, 1932 S.C. 525; 1934 S.C. (H.L.) 51; 1932 S.L.T. 386; 1934 S.L.T. 392; *Nordic Travel Ltd.* v. *Scotprint Ltd.* 1980 S.L.T. 189; 1980 S.C. 1.
[77] *Nordic Travel Ltd.* v. *Scotprint Ltd., supra.* The position in England appears to be the opposite: *Re F.P. & C.H. Matthews Ltd.* [1982] 1 All E.R. 338.
[78] *Re Sarflax Ltd.* [1979] 1 All E.R. 529; see para. 87–72, *infra*.
[79] Goudy, *op. cit.*, p. 90. See also *Thomas Montgomery & Sons* v. *Gallacher* 1982 S.L.T. 138.
[80] *Renton and Gray's Trs.* v. *Dickison* 1880, 7 R. 951.
[81] *Roy's Trs.* v. *Colville and Drysdale* 1903, 5 F. 769.
[82] Goudy, *op. cit.*, pp. 91–98; *T.* v. *L.*, *supra*.

A fraudulent preference may be reduced at the instance of any creditor who can show prejudice, or the liquidator.[83] It is an equitable remedy for the benefit of creditors and therefore cannot be used by a debtor of the company to seek recovery of a sum paid to one of its creditors.[84]

Floating charges

87–69 A floating charge cannot be challenged as a fraudulent preference at common law but only on the grounds specified in section 322.[85] A floating charge (not otherwise invalid, *e.g.* through want of registration) granted within 12 months prior to the commencement of the winding up is presumed to be invalid as a fraudulent preference unless it is proved that, immediately after the creation of the charge, the company was solvent.[86] The creditor does, however, retain a valid security under the charge for cash advanced at the time of or subsequent to the creation of and in consideration for the charge, together with interest at 5 per cent. or such other rate as may be prescribed by statutory instrument. The exception is available only for cash actually paid to the company, and not for payments made to third parties for its benefit, nor is it available to secure existing debts, but it may protect a charge to secure cash advanced to the company on condition that it is used to meet certain debts of the company.[87] In the case of a bank having advanced money to a company on overdraft, however, if it takes a floating charge and subsequently makes further advances it is entitled to apply (on the basis of the rule in *Clayton's* case) sums paid in by the company against the older debts first, and the advances made subsequent to the charge will be secured as cash advanced within the exception.[88] The advancement of "cash" may include the honouring of cheques by a bank.[88]

Fortunately for its subsequent extension to Scotland, it has been established that the phrase "in consideration for the charge" is not to be interpreted as referring to "consideration" in the English law of contract, but as a reference to payments made "in reliance upon and because of the existence (or as appears from other cases listed below, anticipated existence) of the charge."[89] The advance does not require to be made contemporaneously with, in exchange for or at the same moment as the charge to be "at the time of" its creation and each case must be judged on its particular facts.[90] Money paid shortly before the date of the charge may be

[83] See Goudy, *op. cit.*, pp. 42 and 99; Bankruptcy (Scotland) Act 1913, s. 9 applied by s. 245 (5).

[84] *Thompson* v. *J. Barke & Co (Caterers) Ltd.* 1975 S.L.T. 67.

[85] s. 322 (3), added by the Companies (Floating Charges and Receivers) (Scotland) Act 1972, s. 8. Under the Companies (Floating Charges) (Scotland) Act 1961 a challenge at common law remained possible. S. 322 (3) does not expressly exclude a challenge under s. 320.

[86] As to the problem of determining the date of a charge executed by several parties, see para. 47–23, *ante*.

[87] *Libertas-Kommerz* v. *Johnson* 1977 S.C. 191; 1978 S.L.T. 222; *Re Orleans Motor Co. Ltd.* [1911] 2 Ch. 41; *Re Matthew Ellis Ltd.* [1933] Ch. 458; *Re Destone Fabrics Ltd.* [1941] Ch. 319.

[88] *Yeovil Glove Co. Ltd.* [1965] Ch. 148.

[89] *Yeovil Glove Co. Ltd., supra*, at p. 178.

[90] *Columbian Fireproofing Co. Ltd.* [1910] 2 Ch. 120.

regarded as paid at the time of its creation if paid in reliance on an undertaking to grant the charge.[91] If the delay between the advance and the creation of the charge is longer than the period of four or five days accepted as necessary in normal circumstances to create the charge the advance may cease to be regarded as having been made at the time of its creation, although a longer delay, if not caused by the holder of the charge, may still be satisfactorily explained.[92]

The debt secured by a charge which is invalid under section 322 remains an unsecured debt of the company, so that if it is paid off prior to liquidation a challenge can only be made on the basis that the payment was a fraudulent preference.[93]

Examination of books and persons

87–70 At any time after the making of a winding-up order the court may order that books and papers of the company be made available for inspection by creditors or contributories (1948 Act, s. 266). After commencement of a winding up other sections giving the right to obtain an order for inspecting the books of the company, such as sections 113 and 146, cease to be available; accordingly, since section 266 does not apply to persons other than creditors and contributories, a stranger to the company cannot obtain an order to inspect the register of members after commencement of the winding up (whether voluntary or compulsory).[94] The power granted by section 266 should be exercised for the benefit of the liquidation, and not to assist actions by individual shareholders against the directors,[95] nor to assist creditors in obtaining information to pursue a scheme to terminate the liquidation and reconstruct the company.[96]

The court may, at any time after the appointment of a provisional liquidator or the making of a winding-up order, summon before it any person known or suspected to possess property of the company or supposed to be indebted to it, or whom the court deems capable of providing information in respect of the company or its affairs (s. 268 (1)). The court has power to examine such a person on oath (s. 268 (2)), to require production of books and other documents (s. 268 (3)), and to have him brought before it if he refuses to attend (s. 268 (4)).

The court has discretion whether to grant an order under section 268 and the appeal court will not readily interfere, especially where an order has been refused.[97] The section should be used to enable the liquidator to obtain access to material which may assist him in the effective and economic discharge of his duties including Department of Trade inspectors' proceedings.[98] It is legitimate to resort to section 268 to establish whether

[91] *Columbian Fireproofing Co. Ltd., supra; F. & E. Stanton Ltd.* [1929] 1 Ch. 180.
[92] *F. & E. Stanton Ltd., supra.*
[93] *Re Parkes Garage (Swadlincote) Ltd.* [1929] 1 Ch. 139.
[94] *Re Kent Coalfields Syndicate Ltd.* [1898] 1 Q.B. 754.
[95] *Re North Brazilian Sugar Factories* (1887) 37 Ch.D. 84.
[96] *Halden v. Liquidator of Scottish Heritable Security Co. Ltd.* 1887, 14 R. 633.
[97] *Re Joseph Hargreaves Ltd.* (1900) 1 Ch. 347.
[98] *Re Rolls Razor Ltd.* [1963] 3 All E.R. 698.

grounds for proceedings exist, even though the section does give the liquidator an advantage not available to ordinary potential litigants,[99] but it should not be used to enable the liquidator to gain an advantage not available to ordinary litigants in court proceedings which are already under way,[1] nor should it be exercised in a vexatious or offensive manner.[2] An order authorising messengers-at-arms to search for and recover books, and if necessary to open lockfast places, is competent.[3] The question of whether a lien may be claimed, to the effect of requiring the liquidator to concede a preference as a condition of obtaining the books, has already been considered.[4]

Section 268 (4) allows only two excuses for non-attendance, the lack of an offer of reasonable expenses or the existence of a lawful impediment accepted by the court. The existence of civil proceedings between the parties is no excuse, but may justify a postponement.[5] The procedure adopted in Scotland in the event of an examination being called for includes the citation of the individual concerned to appear for examination on oath before the liquidation judge.[6] He may be represented by counsel and re-examined by him to explain his evidence but his counsel is not entitled to be present when other witnesses are examined.[7] An examinee may refuse to answer questions on the grounds that they might incriminate him, but the possibility of such questions being put is no excuse for refusing to attend.[8]

While sections 266 and 268 do not apply to a voluntary winding up, section 307 may be used as the basis for equivalent procedure.

The court may order the examination before the sheriff of any person concerning the winding up of a company, not necessarily a Scottish company, on cause shown, and the sheriff has appropriate powers of examination and report (1948 Act, s. 349). The court may also order the arrest of a contributory who appears to be about to abscond or conceal property or evidence (1948 Act, s. 271).

Public examination of officers

87–71 In a winding up by the court in Scotland, the court is empowered to order the attendance of any officer of the company at any meeting of creditors or contributories or of a committee of inspection for the purpose

---

99 *Re Spiraflite Ltd.* [1979] 2 All E.R. 766; *Re Castle New Homes Ltd.* [1979] 2 All E.R. 775.
1 *Re Bletchley Boat Co. Ltd.* [1974] 1 All E.R. 1225; *Re Malville Hose Ltd.* [1929] Ch. 32.
2 *Re Rolls Razor Ltd. (No. 2)* [1970] Ch. 576, 592.
3 *Ker* v. *Hughes* (1907) S.C. 380.
4 s. 268 (3) see para. 87–51, *supra*.
5 *Re Reliance Taxi-cab Co.* (1912) 28 T.L.R. 529; *Re London and Northern Bank, ex p. Archer* (1901) 85 L.T. 698; *Re North Australian Territory Co.* (1890) 45 Ch.D. 87.
6 *Ker* v. *Hughes* 1907 S.C. 380; *Welch* 1930 S.N. 112. Procedure which may be used if the witness resides in England and is unwilling to attend is illustrated in *Liquidator of the Vegetable Oils Products Co. Ltd.* 1923 S.L.T. 114.
7 *Liquidator of Larkhall Collieries* 1905, 13 S.L.T. 752 (where there is a comprehensive form of interlocutor for such an examination).
8 *Re Repetition Engineering Service Ltd.* (1945) 173 L.T. 75.

of giving information as to the business or property of the company (s. 269). The court may control the questions to be put at a public examination.[9] Because of the powers existing under section 268 it should not normally be necessary to resort to section 269.

Fraudulent trading

87–72 If in the course of a winding up it appears that any of its business has been carried on with intent to defraud creditors of the company or of any other person or for any fraudulent purpose the court may declare that any persons who were knowingly parties to the carrying on of business in such manner are to be personally liable, without limit, for all or any debts or other liabilities of the company (1948 Act, s. 332 (1)). Such persons are also criminally liable under section 332 (3) (as amended by s. 96 of the 1981 Act).

For a successful application under section 332 there must be evidence of actual dishonesty.[10] If the company carries on trading and incurs debts when there is, to the knowledge of the directors, no reasonable prospect of the creditors being paid, it is in general a proper inference that the company is carrying on business with intent to defraud.[11] To be "knowingly a party to" fraudulent trading requires a positive step, and mere failure by the secretary and financial adviser to draw the directors' attention to the position of the company and its consequences is not enough.[12] There must be intent to defraud, not merely intent to prefer, so that the mere granting of a preference does not give grounds for a claim under section 332.[13] If, however, the creditor was aware that the funds which have been used to pay him were obtained from a third party with fraudulent intent, the preferred creditor may be liable to repay the liquidator under section 332.[14] A single transaction may amount to "carrying on business."[14]

Before an application can be made under section 332 the company must actually be in liquidation. A prosecution for fraudulent trading under section 332 (3) may now be initiated whether or not the company has been or is in the course of being wound up (1981 Act, s. 96).[15]

An application under section 332 (1) may be made by the liquidator or any creditor or contributory. The liquidator is bound to disclose to the general body of creditors a report he has obtained on the possibility of an application under the section.[16] Any order against an individual should be for a fixed sum which, where the application was made by the liquidator, will enure to the benefit of the creditors in general.[17] Where a creditor

---

[9] See *Re London and Globe Finance Co.* (1902) 18 T.L.R. 661.
[10] *Re Patrick and Lyon Ltd.* [1933] Ch. 786.
[11] *Re William C. Leitch Bros. Ltd.* [1932] 2 Ch. 71.
[12] *Re Maidstone Buildings Ltd.* [1971] 1 W.L.R. 1085; [1971] 3 All E.R. 363.
[13] *Re Sarflax Ltd.* [1979] 1 All E.R. 529.
[14] *Re Gerald Cooper Chemicals Ltd.* [1978] Ch. 262; [1978] 2 All E.R. 49.
[15] Over-ruling *R.* v. *Schildkamp* [1971] A.C. 1 (H.L.).
[16] *Liquidator of Upper Clyde Shipbuilders*, 1975 S.L.T. 39.
[17] *Re William C. Leitch Bros. Ltd.* [1932] 2 Ch. 71, *ante*; and the same (*No.* 2) [1933] Ch. 261.

applies under the section, the application is on his own account and the court may make a declaration in favour of him exclusively.[18]

The liquidator may give evidence or call witnesses at the hearing of an application (s. 332 (1)).

The court may make orders giving effect to any declaration, for example, charging the liability of directors against any securities they hold against the company (s. 332 (2)).

If in the course of a winding up it appears that a person has incurred liability under section 332, or has otherwise been guilty of fraud or other breach of duty while an officer of the company, the court may disqualify him from being a director or taking part in management of a company for up to five years (1948 Act, s. 188 as amended by 1981 Act, s. 93).

Fraudulent transfers or gifts, fraudulent collusion in diligences, fraudulent inducements to give credit, and similar acts, in relation to a company which is subsequently wound up, committed by an officer of the company, are offences under section 330.

Breach of trust

87–73 If in the course of a winding up it appears that any person who has taken part in the formation or promotion of the company, or any past or present director, manager or liquidator or any officer of the company has misapplied company assets or been guilty of breach of trust in relation to the company, the court may order an investigation into his conduct and may order restoration of the property or other payment to the company by way of compensation (1948 Act, s. 333 (1)). This is without prejudice to any criminal liability (s. 333 (2)). An application to the court under section 333 may be made by the liquidator, or any creditor or contributory.

The debate in England as to the nature of "misfeasance proceedings" under section 333 is of only indirect interest in Scotland. It appears that English law has reached the conclusion that the section refers to breach of fiduciary duty involving a misapplication or wrongful retention of the company's assets.[19] This, it is suggested, is equally true of Scotland where common law principles of breach of trust would apply. An order under section 333 was granted where, after a winding up petition had been presented but before the order had been made, directors procured the payment of certain claims of their own against the company.[20] Illustrations of the application of section 333 in England include directors using funds for objects not sanctioned by the memorandum, paying dividends out of capital, making secret profits and selling their own property to the company.[21]

---

[18] *Re Cyona Distributors Ltd.* [1967] Ch. 889, C.A.; but see Russell L.J. at p. 908.
[19] *Selangor United Rubber Estates Ltd.* v. *Cradock* [1967] 1 W.L.R. 1168, 1173, 1174; [1967] 2 All E.R. 1255; *Re Horsley & Weight Ltd.* [1982] 3 W.L.R. 431 and see paras. 64–28, 73–11 and 85–88, *ante*.
[20] *Liquidator of the Bankers and General Insurance Co. Ltd.* v. *Lithauer* 1924 S.L.T. 775.
[21] See para. 85–90, *ante*.

A receiver is not an "officer" within section 333,[22] nor are the company's bankers,[23] nor prima facie is its solicitor,[24] but he may be if he does all the work for a fixed salary.[25] An auditor if an "officer" of the company, may be proceeded against under section 333,[26] but an accountant merely called in to audit the accounts of the company is not an "officer."[27]

At common law a claim commenced before the death of a person can be maintained against his estate, and a claim can be commenced after death against his representatives up to the value of the estate.

It has been held in England that dissolution of the company terminates proceedings under section 333, and they are not revived if the dissolution is declared void by virtue of section 352.[28]

Criminal liability

87–74 A liquidator who suspects that any past or present officer or any member of the company has been guilty of an offence in relation to the company has a duty to report the matter to the Lord Advocate, and to assist in providing information (s. 334 (2)).[29]

Reciprocal enforcement of court orders

87–75 Section 276 of the 1948 Act provides for the reciprocal enforcement of orders of the courts in the various parts of the United Kingdom which are made "for or in the course of winding up."[30] This applies to any order made after the presentation of the petition, even if a winding-up order has not yet been granted.[31] The application for an enforcement order must be made to that court which would have had jurisdiction over the company if it was registered in the country concerned, and by the procedure laid down in section 276 (3).[32] The section should be confined to matters arising in course of the administration of the liquidation and the court should not make an order which would require to be enforced by a court furth of Scotland if it cannot be made effectual.[33]

Section 276 appears in that part of the Act which is confined to winding up by the court, which by virtue of section 315 (2) and Schedule 11 includes a voluntary winding up subject to the supervision of the court.[34] It may be

---

22 *Re B. Johnson & Co. (Builders) Ltd.* [1955] Ch. 634.
23 *Re Imperial Land Co. of Marseilles* (1870) L.R. 10 Eq. 298.
24 *Re Great Western (Forest of Dean), etc., Co.* (1886) 31 Ch.D. 496.
25 *Re Liberator Building Society* (1894) 71 L.T. 406.
26 *Re Kingston Cotton Mills Co. (No. 2)* [1896] 2 Ch. 279; *Re London and General Bank* [1895] 2 Ch. 166. See para. 73–11 *ante*.
27 *Re Western Counties Steam Bakeries* [1897] 1 Ch. 617; *R.* v. *Shacter* [1960] 2 Q.B. 252.
28 *Re Lewis and Smart Ltd.* [1954] 1 W.L.R. 755; [1954] 2 All E.R. 19.
29 See further s. 334 (as amended by the 1981 Act, s. 96) and s. 328 (as amended by the Insolvency Act 1976, s. 1 and Sched. 1).
30 *E.g. Vegetable Oils Products Co. Ltd.*, 1923 S.L.T. 114.
31 *Re Dynamics Corp. of America* [1972] 3 All E.R. 1046.
32 *Johnstone's Trs.* v. *Roose* 1884, 12 R. 1.
33 *Liquidators of the California Redwood Co. Ltd.* v. *Walker* 1886, 13 R. 810.
34 *Cf. Liquidators of the California Redwood Co Ltd., supra.* The equivalent sections of earlier Acts (ss. 122 and 123 of 1862; s. 180 of 1908 and s. 223 of 1929) are similarly placed.

argued that it is not available in respect of an order made in a voluntary winding up (not being under the supervision of the court).

Sisting winding-up proceedings; recall of winding-up order

87–76 The court has discretion on the application of the liquidator or any creditor or contributory, to stay winding-up proceedings at any time either for a limited period or altogether and on such conditions as it thinks fit (s. 256 (1)). A copy of any such order must be sent by the company, or otherwise as the court may prescribe, to the Registrar of Companies (s. 256 (3)). In exercising it descretion under this section, the court will consider the interests of commercial morality and not merely the wishes of creditors, *e.g.* if there appear to be irregularities requiring investigation to continue.[35]

Books and papers

87–77 All books and papers of the company and the liquidator are prima facie evidence of the matters recorded therein, in questions between the contributories and the company (1948 Act, s. 340).

Where a company has been wound up by or under the supervision of the court and is about to be dissolved, the books and papers of the company and the liquidator are to be disposed of in such way as the court may direct (1948 Act, s. 341 (1) (*a*)). They need not, however, be retained for more than five years (s. 341 (2)).

Stamp duties

87–78 In a winding up by the court, or a creditors' voluntary winding up, all powers of attorney and several other classes of document are exempt from stamp duty, as are conveyances and similar deeds, provided that the subjects remain the property of the company for the benefit of its creditors (1948 Act, s. 339 (2) and (3) as amended by Finance Acts 1949 and 1971).

Adjusting rights of contributories: distribution of surplus

87–79 Subject to the payment of creditors and the expenses of liquidators, and to the adjustment of the rights of contributories *inter se*, any surplus is distributable among the persons entitled thereto by order of the court (1948 Act, s. 265).

Uncalled capital is part of the assets of the company.[36] Where shares are unequally paid up, an adjustment must be made between the contributories by way of call (1948 Act, s. 260),[37] unless the articles provide otherwise.[38] Where articles provided that losses were to be borne in proportion to capital paid up, no call could be made on partly paid shares

---

35 *Re Telescriptor Syndicate Ltd.* [1903] 2 Ch. 174.
36 *Re Bridgewater Navigation Co.* (1889) 14 App.Cas. 525.
37 *Paterson* v. *McFarlane* 1875, 2 R. 490; *Stewart* v. *Liq. of Scottish American Sugar Syndicate Ltd.* 1901, 3 F. 585; 8 S.L.T. 786; *Re Phoenix Oil and Transport Co. Ltd.* [1958] Ch. 560.
38 *Ex p. Maude* (1870) L.R. 6 Ch.App. 51.

for the benefit of those fully paid up.[39] If shares are issued at a discount the amount credited by way of discount is to be treated as so much uncalled capital and the rights adjusted accordingly.[40]

"Surplus assets" has no technical meaning, but must be determined by the context in which the phrase is used.[41] It may mean the fund in the hands of the liquidator after meeting all claims of outside creditors and expenses,[42] or it may mean what remains after payment also of the capital paid up on all classes of shares.[43] Surplus assets distributed are treated as capital for tax purposes, even if they consist to some extent of undistributed profits.[44]

The provisions of sections 215 and 216 of the 1948 Act entitle the representatives of a deceased contributory, and the trustee of a bankrupt one, to participate in any distribution of capital in place of the contributory. Where the liquidator proves for calls in the estate of a bankrupt member, that does not *per se* make the shares paid up for the purpose of participating in surplus assets.[45] Discharge of the bankrupt (or of his trustee) does not re-invest him in the shares, and any subsequent distribution made by the liquidator is available for his creditors.[46]

Capital paid up in advance of calls and interest thereon must, as a rule, be repaid before distribution of capital paid up under calls.[47]

Surplus assets are distributable notwithstanding a provision in the memorandum to the effect that no part of the assets is to be transferred to the members.[48] Where, however, the memorandum not only prohibits distribution of surplus assets to the members but expressly provides for their distribution otherwise (*e.g.* to a charity carrying out similar objects) the court will give effect to these provisions, notwithstanding the absence of parallel provisions in the articles.[49] All shareholders are entitled to equal treatment unless and to the extent that their rights are modified by the contract (as found in the memorandum, articles or terms of issue) under which they hold their shares.[50] Allegations that fraud induced some shareholders to subscribe, but not others, are not grounds for departing

---

39 *Re Kinaton (Borneo) Rubber Ltd.* [1923] 1 Ch. 124.

40 *Welton* v. *Saffrey* [1897] A.C. 299.

41 *Re Bridgewater Navigation Co.* [1891] 2 Ch. 317; *Re New Transvaal Co.* [1896] 2 Ch. 750; *Re Madame Tussaud & Sons Ltd.* [1927] 1 Ch. 657.

42 *Re Crichton's Oil Co.* [1902] 2 Ch. 86; *Dimbula Valley (Ceylon) Tea Co. Ltd.* v. *Laurie* [1961] Ch. 353.

43 *Re Ramel Syndicate Ltd.* [1911] 1 Ch. 749; *Re Dunstable Portland Cement Co.* (1932) 48 T.L.R. 223.

44 *Staffordshire Coal and Iron Co. Ltd.* v. *Brogan*; [1963] 1 W.L.R. 905 (H.L.) [1963] 3 All E.R. 277.

45 *Re West Coast Goldfields* [1906] 1 Ch. 1.

46 Bankruptcy (Scotland) Act 1913, s. 144, and see *Cockburn's Trs.* 1941 S.C. 187; *Trappes* v. *Meredith* 1871, 10 M. 38; *Re Wolverhampton Steel & Iron Co. Ltd.* [1977] 1 All E.R. 417 affd. [1977] 3 All E.R. 467.

47 *Re Wakefield Rolling Stock Co.* [1892] 3 Ch. 165.

48 *Re Merchant Navy Supply Association Ltd.* (1947) 177 L.T. 386.

49 *Liverpool and District Hospital for Diseases of the Heart* v. *Att.-Gen.* [1981] 1 All E.R. 994.

50 *Liquidators of Williamson—Buchanan Steamers Ltd.*, 1936 S.L.T. 106. See also *Town and Gown Assoc. Ltd.* 1948 S.L.T.(Notes) 71; *Scottish Acid and Alkali Co. Ltd.*, 1950 S.L.T.(Notes) 53; *Liquidator of The Humboldt Redwood Co. Ltd.* v. *Coats*, 1908 S.C. 751; 15 S.L.T. 1028; *Monkland Iron and Coal Co.* v. *Henderson* 1883, 10 R. 494.

from the principle of equal treatment.[51] Prima facie, the distribution of surplus assets is to be in proportion to nominal capital (or, in the case of a company limited by guarantee not having a share capital, equally), and any deficiency must be borne on the same basis.[52]

Unclaimed dividends and undistributed assets

87–80 Under section 344 unclaimed dividends and undistributed assets must be deposited in a Scottish bank in name of the accountant of court on deposit receipt. Sums thus deposited are subject to the Bankruptcy (Scotland) Act 1913, s. 153 which provides that if not claimed within seven years they are to be paid over to the Queen's and Lord Treasurer's Remembrancer.

Dissolution of the company

87–81 When the affairs of the company have been fully wound up the liquidator may apply for an order declaring the company to be dissolved, and a copy of the order must be forwarded by the liquidator to the Registrar within 14 days (1948 Act, s. 274). Alternatively, and more usually, the company is struck off the register as defunct under section 353 of the 1948 Act (see s. 353 (4)). An order under section 274 requires official notification under the European Communities Act 1972, s. 9 (3) but a notice of dissolution under section 353 does not.[53]

Upon dissolution, all the property of the company vests in the Crown as *bona vacantia* subject to the power of the Crown to disclaim (ss. 354, 355). This does not affect property held by the company on trust, in respect of which a vesting order may be made, even where the property in question has vested in the Crown.[54] Property vested in the Crown may be disposed of by it notwithstanding any subsequent order declaring the dissolution void or restoring the company to the register, but if such an order is made the Crown is liable to account to the company for the proceeds (1981 Act, s. 108). A dissolved company is not liable to sequestration as a "deceased debtor" under the Bankruptcy (Scotland) Act 1913, s. 11.[55]

87–82 POWER TO DECLARE DISSOLUTION VOID. Where a company has been dissolved, the court may within two years declare the dissolution to have been void (1948 Act, s. 352).[56] The order must be notified to the Registrar of Companies (s. 352 (2)). If the application is made within two years, the order of the court may be made after expiry of that period.[57]

The Court of Session has granted an order under this section 10 years after dissolution, to authorise the liquidator to execute a conveyance of

---

[51] *Edinburgh Employers Liability and General Insurance Co. Ltd.* 1893, 1 S.L.T. 321.
[52] *Re London India Rubber Co.* (1868) L.R. 5 Eq. 519; *Welton* v. *Saffrey* [1897] A.C. 299.
[53] See Chap. 17, *ante*.
[54] *Re Strathblaine Estates Ltd.* [1948] Ch. 228; see also *Smith & Another, Petitioners*, 1969 S.L.T. (Notes) 94 and cases cited at para. 85–100, *ante*.
[55] *Steward & McDonald* v. *Brown* 1898, 225 R. 1042; 6 S.L.T. 85.
[56] *McCall & Stephen Ltd.* 1920, 2 S.L.T. 26.
[57] *Dowling, Petitioner*, 1960 S.L.T.(Notes) 76; *Re Scad Ltd.* [1941] Ch. 386.

foreign property, in the exercise of its *nobile officium*,[58] but this decision has been distinguished as applicable to its peculiar facts only. In general no application under section 352 after the two-year period is competent and application for a grant of title must be made to the Crown.[59] The application under section 352 should not seek further orders authorising the liquidator to take certain steps, since the section itself provides that, on the dissolution being declared void, such proceedings may be taken as if the company had not been dissolved.[60]

An application under section 352 may be made by the liquidator or any person who appears to the court to be interested (s. 352 (1)). "Person" includes a legal person such as a company.[61] A person who has acted as liquidator without being appointed is sufficiently "interested" by virtue of a possible claim for remuneration *quantum meruit* or liability for unauthorised dealing with Crown property.[62] A solicitor acting for a client who would be "a person interested" is not himself so qualified.[63]

The purpose of an order under section 352 is to make possible the distribution of assets which belonged to the company before dissolution and which had for some reason been overlooked; accordingly the court refused to make a declaration in favour of a company to enable it to receive a legacy which had never belonged to it.[64] If the Crown has disposed of property vested in it as *bona vacantia* it must account to the company for the proceeds after the dissolution has been declared void (1981 Act, s. 108).

The granting of an order declaring the dissolution to have been void does not render valid proceedings taken against the company after dissolution but before the date of the order.[65] It has been held in England that a summons under section 332 which had been issued but had not been served prior to dissolution was not revived by an order under section 352.[66]

An application may be made under section 352 in all cases where a company has been "dissolved," including section 353. This is without prejudice to the further power of the court to restore to the register a company which has been struck off under section 353 (s. 353 (6)). The conditions necessary to succeed under section 353 (6) are more onerous than those required by section 352, which may therefore be chosen for preference if both are available.[67] Relief under section 352 or 353 should

---

58 *Collins Brothers & Co. Ltd.* 1916 S.C. 620; 1916, 1 S.L.T. 309.

59 *Lord Macdonald's Curator*, 1924 S.C. 163; 1924 S.L.T. 64; *Forth Shipbreaking Co. Ltd.* 1924 S.C. 489; 1924 S.L.T. 381.

60 *Champdany Jute Co. Ltd.*, 1924 S.C. 209; 1924 S.L.T. 143.

61 *Re Spottiswoode, Dixon and Hunting Ltd.* [1912] 1 Ch. 410.

62 *Re Wood and Martin (Brick Laying Contractors) Ltd.* [1971] 1 W.L.R. 293; [1971] 1 All E.R. 732.

63 *Re Roehampton Swimming Pool Ltd.* [1968] 1 W.L.R. 1963; [1968] 3 All E.R. 661.

64 *Re Servers of the Blind League* [1960] 1 W.L.R. 564; [1960] 2 All E.R. 298.

65 *Morris* v. *Harris* [1927] A.C. 252.

66 *Re Lewis & Smart Ltd.* [1954] 1 W.L.R. 755; [1954] 2 All E.R. 19.

67 *Re M. Belmont & Co. Ltd.* [1952] Ch. 10; *Re Wood and Martin (Brick Laying Contractors) Ltd., ante per* Megarry J. who may be read as impliedly withdrawing his criticisms of this proposition expressed in *Re Test Holdings (Clifton) Ltd.* [1970] Ch. 285, 392; see para. 85–102, *ante*.

be sought as soon as reasonably practicable after discovery of the dissolution.[68]

87–83 RESTORATION TO REGISTER. An application may be made under section 353 (6) within 20 years of the publication in the *Edinburgh Gazette* of the notice of dissolution by the company or any member or creditor who "feels aggrieved" by the company having been struck off. "Creditor" includes "contingent or prospective creditor" or one whose claim is for damages or is otherwise illiquid.[69] "Member" includes the personal representatives of a deceased member.[70] On the other hand, a person who acquired shares in or acquires a debt of the company after dissolution is not qualified to apply under section 353 (6).[71]

The court requires to be satisfied, under section 353 (6), that the company was at the time of striking off in business or otherwise that it is just to restore it to the register.[72] This may be as a preliminary to winding-up proceedings,[73] no order for re-vesting of the property in the company being required.[74] No penalty for default can be made as a condition of granting an application under section 353 (6),[75] but a penalty can in effect be imposed through an order in respect of expenses.[76]

87–84 The court may attach such directions as it thinks fit to an order under section 352 or 353 (6). For example, it may cure retrospectively all defects including want of registration in a charge which a solvent company purported to grant in ignorance of its having been struck off.[77] A creditor who became such after the date of dissolution cannot, however, both have restoration and preserve the remedies against individuals which he had while the company remained struck off.[78] Opposition in name of the company to an application to restore a company to the register must be duly authorised by its directors or members.[79]

If the Crown has disposed of property vested in it as *bona vacantia* it must account to the company for the proceeds after the company has been restored to the register (1981 Act, s. 108).

Voluntary winding up

87–85 The majority of liquidations are voluntary, initiated by resolution of the members. The companies which may be wound up voluntarily are those

---

[68] *Re Thompson & Riches Ltd.*, [1981] 1 W.L.R. 682; [1981] 2 All E.R. 477.
[69] *Re Harvest Lane Motor Bodies Ltd.* [1969] 1 Ch. 457.
[70] *Re Bayswater Trading Co. Ltd.* [1970] 1 W.L.R. 343; [1970] 1 All E.R. 608.
[71] *Re New Timbiqui Gold Mines Ltd.* [1961] Ch. 319.
[72] See *Charles Dale Ltd.*, 1927 S.C. 130; *Beith Unionist Association*, 1950 S.C. 1. A remit to a reporter is normal practice.
[73] *Re Cambridge Coffee Room Association* [1951] 2 T.L.R. 1155; *Beith Unionist Assocn.*, *supra.*
[74] *Re C. W. Dixon Ltd.* [1947] Ch. 251.
[75] *Re Brown Bayley's Steel Works Ltd.* (1905) 21 T.L.R. 374; *Re Moses and Cohen Ltd.* [1957] 1 W.L.R. 1007.
[76] *Re Court Lodge Development Co. Ltd.* [1973] 1 W.L.R. 1097; [1973] 3 All E.R. 425.
[77] *Re Boxco Ltd.* [1970] Ch. 442.
[78] *Re Lindsay Bowman Ltd.* [1969] 1 W.L.R. 1443; [1969] 3 All E.R. 601.
[79] *In re Regent Insulation Co. Ltd.*, *The Times*, November 5, 1981, [1981] C.L.Y. 250.

formed and/or registered under the 1948 and earlier Companies Acts (ss. 278 (1) and 455 (1), 378 and 379). An unregistered company, as defined in section 398, cannot be wound up voluntarily but may register under Part VIII of the Act and then wind up voluntarily (s. 399 (4)).[80]

Part V (i), (iii) and (v) of the Act apply to voluntary liquidations and Part V (iv) to voluntary liquidations subject to the supervision of the court.

In order to avoid unnecessary repetition, it should be noted that the following provisions in particular apply without modification to a voluntary winding up as to a winding up by the court:

SECTIONS 212–217 of the 1948 Act defining a "contributory" and his liability on list A or B, including the extension provided in the 1967 Act, s. 44 (7).

SECTIONS 316 and 318 of the 1948 Act; the Bankruptcy (Scotland) Act 1913, ss. 45 (as amended by the Insolvency Act 1976, s. 5 (3)) to 62, 96 and 105, and R.C.S. 214 (Sh.Ct.R. 44–46), which together regulate proof of claims, ranking and voting, valuation of securities, the interruption of prescription of a claim and appeals from a deliverance by the liquidator.

SECTION 319 of the 1948 Act, defining claims entitled to a preferential ranking.

SECTIONS 320, 322 and 327 of the 1948 Act invalidating fraudulent preferences and certain floating charges and equalising diligences.

SECTIONS 108–113 and 116 of the Bankruptcy (Scotland) Act 1913, as to sale of heritage subject to securities.

SECTIONS 328 to 334 of the 1948 Act as to offences committed in relation to a company which is being wound up, and powers of the court to assess damages against persons (including a liquidator) in breach of trust.

SECTIONS 335 and 336 of the 1948 Act prohibiting the appointment of a body corporate as liquidator and prohibiting bribery to influence an appointment.

SECTION 344 of the 1948 Act as to the lodgement of unclaimed dividends, assets, etc., on deposit receipt in the name of the accountant of court.

These foregoing provisions are examined in detail in the part of this chapter dealing with winding up by the court.

THE NEXT PARAGRAPH IS 87–87

The resolution for voluntary winding up

87–87 Voluntary winding up is initiated by resolution of the company under section 278 of the 1948 Act, either:

(1) a special resolution to wind up voluntarily, no reason being required (s. 278 (1) (*b*)); or

(2) an extraordinary resolution that it cannot by reason of its liabilities continue its business and that it is advisable to wind up (s. 278 (1) (*c*)); or

(3) an ordinary resolution passed in the event or at the time under

---

[80] *Southall* v. *British Mutual Life Assurance Society* (1871) L.R. 6 Ch.App. 614.

which, in terms of its articles, the company is to be dissolved (s. 278 (1) (*a*)).

The proceedings resulting in the passing of a resolution to wind up should conform to the normal requirements for a valid resolution, *e.g.* as to prior authority of the directors[81] and the need to state that it is to be proposed as a special (or extraordinary) resolution,[82] and the necessity for a quorum to be present[83] but a valid resolution may be held to have been passed by the assent of all shareholders, even if the "meeting" was not properly constituted.[84] A resolution having been passed, *ex facie* validly, shareholders and creditors must abide by it until it is shown to be invalid.[85] The minutes recording the resolution remain effective proof of its passing until shown otherwise, *e.g.* by declaratory action.[86] The fact that other, *ultra vires*, resolutions associated with the winding-up resolution were passed at the same time will not necessarily invalidate it.[87] When passed, the resolution must be advertised in the *Edinburgh Gazette* within 14 days, and failure to comply will necessitate a petition to the *nobile officium* for authority to insert the notice out of time.[88]

Commencement of voluntary winding up

87–88 All voluntary liquidations commence on the date of the resolution (1948 Act, s. 280). The company must cease to carry on its business "except so far as may be required for the beneficial winding up thereof," but its corporate existence and powers continue until dissolution (s. 281). There can be no transfer of shares or alteration in the status of membership after winding up has commenced except with the sanction of the liquidator (s. 282).

Members' voluntary winding up

87–89 DECLARATION OF SOLVENCY IN MEMBERS' VOLUNTARY WINDING UP. A winding up is a "members' voluntary winding up" if a declaration of solvency is filed under section 283 of the 1948 Act as amended by section 105 of the 1981 Act. This is a statutory declaration by a majority of the directors to the effect that the company will be able to pay its debts in full within a period not exceeding 12 months after commencement of the winding up (s. 283 (1)). The declaration includes a statement of assets and liabilities,

---

81 *Haycroft Gold Reduction & Mining Co.* [1900] 2 Ch. 230; *State of Wyoming Syndicate* [1901] 2 Ch. 431.

82 s. 141; *Rennie* v. *Crichton's (Strichen) Ltd.* 1927 S.L.T. 459.

83 *Howling's Trs.* v. *Smith* 1905, 7 F. 390; 12 S.L.T. 628.

84 *Re M. J. Shanley Contracting* [1980] C.L.Y. 268.

85 *Lawson Seed and Nursery Co.* v. *Lawson & Son* 1886, 14 R. 154; *Howling's Trs.* v. *Smith*, *supra*; *Re Bailey, Hay & Co. Ltd.* [1971] 3 All E.R. 693.

86 *City of Glasgow Bank Liquidators* 1880, 7 R. 1196; *Grieve* v. *Kilmarnock Motor Co.* 1923 S.C. 491; 1923 S.L.T. 308 (in which an action of declarator in the sheriff court was allowed to proceed).

87 *Thomson* v. *Henderson's Transvaal Estates* [1908] Ch. 765.

88 *Liquidator of Nairn Public Hall Co.*, 1946 S.C. 395; 1946 S.L.T. 326; *Liquidator of A. & J. McCredie & Co. Ltd.* 1946 S.L.T.(Notes) 19.

which need not be absolutely accurate provided that it is capable of being fairly described as such a statement (s. 283 (2) (*b*)).[89]

Under section 283 (2) (*a*) (as amended) the declaration is to have no effect unless it is made within the five weeks immediately preceding the date of the resolution, or on that day but before the passing of the resolution. The absence of such a declaration results in the liquidation being a creditors voluntary winding up, regardless of the financial position of the company (s. 283 (4)).[90] The declaration must be filed with the Registrar within 15 days (1981 Act, s. 105).

87–90 INSOLVENT MEMBERS' VOLUNTARY WINDING UP. Criminal penalties attach to the making of a declaration of solvency without reasonable grounds, and failure to pay or provide for the company's debts in full within the period stated therein is prima facie evidence of an offence (s. 283 (3)).

If the liquidator in a members' voluntary winding up forms the opinion that the company will not be able to pay its debts in full within the stated period he must call a meeting of creditors and submit a statement of assets and liabilities to it (1948 Act, s. 288). Annual meetings of the company and creditors must be held to consider an account of his intromissions (1948 Act, ss. 291 and 299). When the affairs of the company have been fully wound up final meetings of the company and its creditors are held in the same way as in a creditors' voluntary winding up (1948 Act, ss. 291 and 300). R.C.S. 208 and 210 (Sh.Ct.R. 24–32 and 36) govern the procedure for calling and conducting such meetings.[91]

There is nothing in the Act to suggest that, apart from the requirements as to meetings of creditors referred to above, an insolvent members' voluntary winding up is equivalent to a creditors' voluntary winding up. Obviously, however, it will be the duty of the liquidator to attach paramount importance to the interests of the creditors.

87–91 APPOINTMENT OF A LIQUIDATOR. In a members' voluntary winding up the liquidator (or liquidators) is appointed by the company in general meeting (1948 Act, s. 285 (1)). This must be done immediately the winding-up resolution has been passed, and no notice is required.[92]

Any vacancy in the office of liquidator is filled by the company in general meeting, subject to any arrangement with the creditors. Such a meeting may be called by any contributory (1948 Act, s. 286). The court may also fill a vacancy and remove a liquidator (1948 Act, s. 304; R.C.S. 207 (Sh.Ct.R. 23)).[93] A liquidator cannot be a body corporate (1948 Act, s.

---

[89] *De Courcy* v. *Clement* [1971] Ch. 693.
[90] Special provisions apply to a company which made a declaration of solvency between April 7 and August 1, 1981, but failed to deliver it to the Registrar before the resolution to wind up was passed (1981 Act, s. 107).
[91] See paras. 87–34 and 87–35, *ante*.
[92] *Bethell* v. *Trench Tubeless Tyre Co.* [1900] 1 Ch. 408.
[93] On the principles applicable to the removal of a voluntary liquidator, see cases cited in paras. 86–48 and 87–28, *ante*.

335) but in a members' voluntary winding up he is commonly one of the directors. A person may be disqualified by Court order from acting as a liquidator under the Insolvency Act 1976, section 9 (1), as amended by the Companies Act 1981, section 94.

The liquidator's remuneration may be fixed by the company in general meeting (1948 Act, s. 285 (1)).

Creditors' voluntary winding up

87–92 RESOLUTION TO WIND UP AND FIRST MEETING OF CREDITORS. As has been noted, a creditors' voluntary winding up is one in which a declaration of solvency has not been duly filed (s. 283 (4)), usually but not necessarily because of insolvency.

In a creditors' voluntary winding up the company must call a meeting of creditors on the same day as, or on the day following, the meeting of the company at which the resolution to wind up is to be considered. Notwithstanding any power to foreshorten notice, at least seven days' notice of the meeting of the company must be given.[93a] In Scotland, the day the notice is received is excluded but the meeting could be held on the seventh day thereafter.[93b] Notice of the meeting must be given by post to the creditors simultaneously with the notice to members (1948 Act, s. 293 (1) as amended by 1981 Act, s. 106). The meeting must also be advertised once in the *Edinburgh Gazette* and at least once in two newspapers circulating in the district of the company's registered office or principal place of business (1948 Act, s. 293 (2)). The directors must appoint one of their number to attend and preside over this meeting (s. 293 (3) (*b*) and (4)).[94]

If the company meeting is adjourned the effect of any resolution passed by the creditors is suspended until the company duly resolves to wind up (s. 293 (5)). Failure to give notice of the meeting of the company in terms of section 293 (1) (as amended) does not invalidate the proceedings (1981 Act, s. 106 (2)).

The purposes of the meeting of creditors under section 293 are to consider a statement of affairs which the directors are bound to submit, including a list of creditors and their claims (s. 293 (3) (*a*)), to consider whether to nominate a liquidator of the creditors' choice (s. 294) and to appoint (if so desired) a committee of inspection (s. 295).

87–93 APPOINTMENT OF A LIQUIDATOR. The nominee of the company is appointed liquidator if the creditors agree or, as a result of no meeting of creditors having been held, if the creditors make no nomination.[95] If the creditors nominate a different person he is appointed in preference to the members' nominee, subject to the right of any director, member or creditor to apply to the court within seven days to resolve the difference (s. 294).[96]

93a See 1981 Act, s. 106.
93b *Neil McLeod & Sons Ltd.* 1967 S.L.T. 46.
94 The procedure, subject to these provisions, is governed by R.C.S. 208 and 210 (Sh.Ct.R. 24–32 and 36). See paras 87–34 and 87–35, *ante*.
95 *Re Centrebind Ltd.* [1967] 1 W.L.R. 377; [1966] 3 All E.R. 889.
96 *See Karamelli and Barnett Ltd.* [1917] 1 Ch. 203.

Vacancies may be filled by the creditors except in the case of a liquidator appointed by or by direction of the court (1948 Act, s. 297). The court has reserve powers of appointment and removal (1948 Act, s. 304; R.C.S. 207 (Sh.Ct.R. 23)).[97]

Apart from the prohibition on bodies corporate (1948 Act, s. 335) and the possibility of a disqualification order (1981 Act, s. 94), no qualification is required, but in a creditors' voluntary winding up the liquidator will in practice be a qualified accountant.

The committee of inspection or, if there is no such committee, the creditors, may fix the liquidator's remuneration (1948 Act, s. 296 (1)).

87–94 COMMITTEE OF INSPECTION. The creditors in a creditors' voluntary winding-up may at their first or any later meeting decide that there should be a committee of inspection. The creditors may appoint up to five members of the committee and the company may also appoint up to five. Subject to any direction given by the court, however, the creditors may exclude the nominees of the company (s. 295 (1)).

The regulations referring to the proceedings of a committee of inspection in a winding up by the court (1948 Act, s. 253 (2) to (8)) and its general powers (1948 Act, s. 255; R.C.S. 209 (Sh.Ct.R. 33–35)) are applied to the committee in a creditors' voluntary winding up (s. 295 (2)).[98]

87–95 NOTIFICATION OF APPOINTMENT. A voluntary liquidator must, within 14 days, publish notice of his appointment in the *Edinburgh Gazette* (which constitutes official notification under the European Communities Act, s. 9 (3)),[99] and file particulars with the Registrar of Companies (1948 Act, s. 305; R.C.S. 205 (Sh.Ct.R. 14–16)). Every invoice, order or business letter must state that the company is in liquidation (1948 Act, s. 338).

SEVERAL LIQUIDATORS. Where two or more voluntary liquidators are appointed their powers may be exercised by such one or more of them as may be determined at the time of their appointment, failing which, by at least two (1948 Act, s. 303 (3)). This may permit any two surviving liquidators to act notwithstanding a vacancy. The acts of one joint liquidator may be presumed to have the consent of his colleagues, but one of the joint liquidators can be sued for negligence without having to call the others as co-defenders, even where such presumption is not disturbed.[1]

87–96 DUTIES AND POWERS OF A LIQUIDATOR. The general duties of a voluntary liquidator are in principle the same as those in a compulsory liquidation, namely to prepare lists of contributories and creditors, realise assets, discharge liabilities and distribute any surplus among the members in

[97] See paras. 86–48 and 87–28, *ante*.
[98] See paras. 87–30 and 87–31, *ante*.
[99] See Chap. 17, *ante*.
[1] *Highland Engineering Limited, etc.* v. *Anderson*, 1979 S.L.T. 122.

accordance with their rights (*cf.* 1948 Act, ss. 285 (1) and 294, 302 and 303 (2)).[2] On his appointment the powers of the directors cease, except so far as their continuance may be sanctioned, in a members' voluntary winding up by the company in general meeting[3] and in a creditors' voluntary winding up by the committee of inspection or (if there is no committee) by the creditors (ss. 285 (2) and 296 (2)). A voluntary liquidator in Scotland is in no sense "an officer of the court."[4]

The provisions of sections 212 to 217 of the 1948 Act, defining a "contributory" and his liability, apply to a voluntary liquidation as to a winding up by the court.[5] In a voluntary liquidation, however, it is the liquidator and not the court who has power to settle the list of contributories and make calls (1948 Act, s. 303 (1) (*c*) and (*d*)).

As in a compulsory winding up a voluntary liquidator must exercise due diligence in investigating the existence of claims.[6] He must reject all claims which have prescribed or are otherwise barred.

The liquidator must satisfy all preferential claims, and then all other liabilities *pari passu* (1948 Act, s. 302). The expenses of winding up must, however, be paid in priority (1948 Act, s. 309).

A voluntary liquidator has all the powers given to a liquidator in a winding up by the court under section 245 (1948 Act, s. 303 (1) (*a*) and (*b*)). The following powers (s. 245 (1) (*d*), (*e*) and (*f*)) require the sanction, in a members' voluntary winding up, of an extraordinary resolution of the company and, in a creditors' voluntary winding up, of the committee of inspection or (if there is no committee) of a meeting of creditors:

(1) to pay any class of creditors in full;

(2) to make compromises or arrangements.

All the other powers of a compulsory liquidator may be exercised by a voluntary liquidator without any sanction.

87–97 In addition to the foregoing, a number of other powers and facilities are available in a voluntary liquidation:

(1) An arrangement between a company about to be or in course of being wound up and its creditors will bind the company if sanctioned by an extraordinary resolution and the creditors if approved by three-quarters of them in number and value, subject to the right of any contributory or creditor to appeal to the court within three weeks (1948 Act, s. 306). This can only be resorted to if the winding up is to continue.[7] This section is in addition to power to apply to the court for sanction of a scheme of arrangement under section 206 of the 1948 Act.

(2) Where a company is proposed to be, or is in course of being, wound

[2] A fuller account of these appears earlier in this chapter.
[3] The meeting of shareholders may be held at any time after commencement of winding-up (*Re Fairbairn Engineering Co.* [1893] 3 Ch. 450).
[4] *Clyde Marine Insurance Co.* v. *Renwick*, 1924 S.C. 113, 125.
[5] See paras. 87–36 to 87–41, *ante*.
[6] *Pulsford* v. *Devenish* [1903] 2 Ch. 625.
[7] *Re Contal Radio Ltd.* [1932] 2 Ch. 66.

up voluntarily, the liquidator may sell the whole or part of its business or property in consideration for shares, policies or other like interests of another company (1948 Act, s. 287). In a members' voluntary winding up this requires the sanction of a special resolution; in a creditors' voluntary winding up it requires the sanction of the court or the committee of inspection (1948 Act, s. 298). A dissenting member may, within seven days, require the liquidator either to abstain from giving effect to the arrangement or buy his interest at a value to be fixed by arbitration (s. 287 (3), (4) and (6)), but subject to this an arrangement duly approved is binding on the selling company (s. 287 (2)). A special resolution approving a sale on these terms is invalidated if there is a compulsory winding up or supervision order within a year, unless it is specifically confirmed by the court (s. 287 (5)).[8]

(3) The liquidator may summon general meetings of the company to obtain its sanction by special or extraordinary resolution or for any other purpose (1948 Act, s. 303 (1) (*e*)).

(4) The liquidator can apply to the court for an order sisting proceedings against the company and directing that they shall not continue except by leave of the court (1948 Act, s. 308 (1)). There is no automatic sisting of such proceedings as in a compulsory winding up under section 231 of the 1948 Act. The liquidator must show sufficient reason for denying the pursuer the right to proceed, *e.g.* that the claim is admitted and expense will be saved.[9]

(5) The liquidator or any creditor or contributory may apply to the court to determine any question arising in the winding up or to exercise all or any of the powers of the court in a compulsory winding up (1948 Act, s. 307; R.C.S. 215 (Sh.Ct.R. 47–51). R.C.S. 214 (Sh.Ct.R. 44–46) applies where the application seeks to vary or reverse a deliverance on claims).[10] This will enable the court to grant an order under a section which is not automatically applicable to a voluntary winding up, such as for restraint of proceedings (1948 Act, s. 231), a vesting order (1948 Act, s. 244), a sist of the winding up (1948 Act, s. 256) or for delivery of books, etc. (1948 Act, s. 258), enforcing calls (1948 Act, ss. 260 and 262), and the examination of officers and others (1948 Act, ss. 268 and 269). The section is, however, not restricted to these examples and can be used in any appropriate circumstances. It cannot, however, be used to authorise *ultra vires* transactions,[11] nor should it be used to resolve questions more properly determined by an ordinary action, such as claims for damages.[12] The court may order meetings of the contributories or

---

[8] See further Ch. 80, *ante*.

[9] *Cook* v. *"X" Chair Patents Co. Ltd.* [1960] 1 W.L.R. 60; [1959] 3 All E.R. 906.

[10] A copy of such an order must be filed with the Registrar under s. 307 (3).

[11] *Re Salisbury Railway and Market House Co. Ltd.* [1969] 1 Ch. 349.

[12] *Crawford* v. *McCulloch* 1909 S.C. 1063; 1909 1 S.L.T. 536; *Knoll Spinning Co.* v. *Brown* 1977 S.L.T.(Notes) 62; 1977 S.C. 291.

creditors to ascertain their views under section 346. A liquidator who does a specific act after seeking and obtaining the sanction of the court cannot be liable in negligence.[13]

87–98 CARRYING ON BUSINESS. The liquidator should exercise his power to carry on the business with due regard to the qualification that it can only be carried on "so far as may be necessary for the beneficial winding up thereof" (1948 Act, ss. 245 (1) (*b*) and 281). It is not necessary that the motive for carrying on business be exclusively financial, for example, it may be in order to facilitate reconstruction.[14] It is sufficient if the liquidator bona fide and reasonably (in the circumstances in which he has to decide the matter) forms the opinion that the carrying on of the business is necessary for the beneficial winding up of the company.[15] If in doubt he should apply for court sanction under section 307.

If he carries on the business the liquidator will have all the necessary powers, and will not be liable personally provided that he makes it clear that he is acting on behalf of the company and that it is in liquidation.[16] Debts incurred while carrying on the business rank in priority to all claims in the winding up.[17] In carrying on business the liquidator is acting on behalf of the company, and any employees whom he engages for the purposes are entitled to claim continuity of employment for the purpose of their entitlement to redundancy payments, etc.[18]

If there is no committee of inspection and the court has not ruled otherwise the liquidator can appoint himself the company's representative at meetings under section 139.[19]

87–99 POSSESSION OF BOOKS, ETC. The liquidator should take possession of all books, deeds, documents and assets of the company, and take steps to recover same if necessary by asking the court for an order under section 258 of the 1948 Act.

COMPULSORY ORDER. The existence of a voluntary winding up is stated not to bar the right of a contributory or creditor to petition for a winding-up order (1948 Act, s. 310).[20]

87–100 CONTINUING LIQUIDATIONS. Where a voluntary winding up continues for more than a year the liquidator must[21]:

---

[13] *Highland Engineering Ltd.* v. *Anderson*, 1979 S.L.T. 122.
[14] *See Willis* v. *Association of Universities of the British Commonwealth* [1965] 1 Q.B. 140.
[15] *Re Great Eastern Electric Co. Ltd.* [1941] Ch. 241.
[16] *Stead, Hazel & Co.* v. *Cooper* [1933] 1 K.B. 840.
[17] *Re S. Davis & Co.* [1945] Ch. 402.
[18] *Smith* v. *Lord Advocate*, 1979 S.L.T. 233. See also the Transfer of Undertakings (Protection of Employment) Regulations 1981 (S.I. 1981 No. 1794).
[19] *Hillman* v. *Crystal Bowl Amusements Ltd.* [1973] 1 W.L.R. 162; [1973] 1 All E.R. 379 (C.A.).
[20] As to the considerations which will rise in deciding whether to allow such an application see para. 87–14, *ante*.
[21] See *Re Grantham Wholesale Fruit, Vegetable and Potato Merchants* [1972] 1 W.L.R. 559.

(i) file a statement of intromissions[22] then and every six months thereafter, including the final period (1948 Act, s. 342; R.C.S. 213 (Sh.Ct.R. 42, 43);

(ii) call an annual meeting of members and lay before it a statement of his intromissions (1948 Act, ss. 289, 299);

(iii) in a creditors' voluntary winding up, or a members' voluntary winding up in which all debts have not been discharged within 12 months, send a statement to the creditors annually and hold annual meetings of creditors (1948 Act, ss. 291, 299; R.C.S. 213 (*c*)). There is no equivalent in the Sheriff Court Rules to R.C.S. 213 (*c*) which directs the liquidator to call an annual meeting of creditors and send them annually a statement of his intromissions. The requirement to hold a meeting is statutory, however (1948 Act, s. 299 as applied by s. 291), and the statement must be laid before that meeting.

7–101 FINAL MEETINGS AND DISSOLUTION. As soon as the affairs of the company have been fully wound up the liquidator must summon final meetings and submit his final statement. It is immaterial that matters of which the liquidator was unaware may still be outstanding and the emergence of such matters does not invalidate the final procedure.[23] In a members' voluntary winding up only a meeting of the company is required (1948 Act, s. 290 (1)). In a creditors' voluntary winding up, or a members' voluntary winding up which became insolvent, a meeting of creditors must also be held (1948 Act, ss. 291, 300 (1)).

The final meetings are convened simply by notice in the *Edinburgh Gazette* published at least one month before the date thereof (ss. 290 (2) and 300 (2)). R.C.S. 208 and 210 (with the modifications referred to in R.C.S. 210 (iv)) (Sh.Ct.R.24–32 and 36), govern the procedure.

Within one week of the final meetings the liquidator must file a final return with the Registrar, even where no quorum was present (ss. 290 (3) and 300 (3)). Three months after registration of the final return the company is deemed dissolved subject to the power of the court to defer the date of dissolution (ss. 290 (4) and (5) and 300 (4) and (5)). Official notification of the final return under the European Communities Act 1972, s. 9 (3) is required.[24]

The power of the court to declare a dissolution void within 20 years under section 352 of the 1948 Act has been discussed earlier.[25]

7–102 COMPENSATION FOR LOSS OF OFFICE. In a voluntary liquidation, by virtue of the Companies Act 1980, s. 74, the liquidator may pay compensation for loss of employment to persons employed or formerly employed by the

---

[22] Form 92 (Scot.).
[23] *Re Cornish Manures Ltd.* [1967] 1 W.L.R. 807; [1967] 2 All E.R. 875.
[24] See Chap. 17, *ante*.
[25] See paras. 87–82 to 87–84, *ante*.

company or any of its subsidiaries. He does not require the sanction of the committee of inspection (if any).[26]

STAMP DUTIES. A creditors' voluntary winding up enjoys the same stamp duty reliefs as a compulsory liquidation (1948 Act, s. 339).[27]

87–103 STRIKING OFF UNDER SECTION 353. As an alternative to members' voluntary liquidation, and to avoid the expense of this process, it is possible for any officer or the solicitor acting for a company to ask the Registrar to initiate section 353 proceedings. This can be done simply by a letter stating that the company has neither assets nor liabilities, is not trading, and is not heritably vest in any property. The Registrar will then write to the directors for confirmation that this step is desired. After further notification of intention to do so, he will publish a notice in the *Edinburgh Gazette* to the effect that (unless cause is shown to the contrary) the company will be struck off and dissolved three months thereafter.[28] A further notice is published stating that the company has been dissolved but without prejudice to any liability of its directors, managers or members and to the power of the court to wind it up.[29] Similar provisions apply to a company in liquidation.[30] The Registrar may initiate section 353 proceedings, for example, if the company fails to lodge annual returns, etc. The effect of dissolution and the procedure for applying under section 353 (6) to have the company restored to the register have already been considered.[31]

Winding up under supervision

87–104 Where a company is in voluntary liquidation, the court may order the winding up to continue under its supervision, on such terms as it thinks just (1948 Act, s. 311). The court may appoint or remove liquidators (1948 Act, s. 314 (1)).

Any disposition of property after the order is void, as is any execution put in force in England against its property (1948 Act, ss. 313, 227, 228).

The liquidator has the same powers and is in the same position as a liquidator in a winding up by the court (s. 314 (2)), but he may exercise his powers as if he were a voluntary liquidator subject to the court's directions, provided that the powers referred to in section 245 (1) (*d*), (*e*) and (*f*) now require the sanction of the court or (in a creditors' voluntary liquidation) the committee of inspection or (if none) the creditors in general meeting

---

[26] For the conditions for exercising such power see *ante*, para. 87–60.
[27] See para. 87–78, *ante*.
[28] s. 353 (2) and (3).
[29] s. 353 (5). Such notice does not require to be "officially notified" under the European Communities Act 1972, s. 9 (3)—see Chap. 17, *ante*.
[30] s. 353 (4)—see para. 87–81, *ante*.
[31] See paras. 87–82 to 87–84, *ante*.

(1948 Act, s. 315 (1)). The supervision order is to have the same effect as a winding-up order, except for the sections listed in Schedule 11 (s. 315 (2)).

Supervision orders are now rarely sought and this part of the 1948 Act is virtually in desuetude.

Part Nine

SPECIAL KINDS OF COMPANIES AND OTHER FORMS OF BUSINESS ORGANISATION

CHAPTER 88

OVERSEA AND OTHER FOREIGN COMPANIES, THE PROPOSED EUROPEAN COMPANY

In general

88–01 A company incorporated under a law other than that of Great Britain may carry on business in Great Britain with or without having established a place of business in this country.

It should be noted that, in the words of Lord Dunedin in *Lord Advocate* v. *Huron and Erie Loan and Savings Co.*,[1] " 'carrying on business' is one thing and 'establishing a place of business' is another." The latter implies some concrete connection with a locality in Great Britain, *e.g.* having an office in this country, as will be seen presently.

Oversea companies

Definition. Establishing a place of business

88–02 A foreign company, *i.e.* a company incorporated outside Great Britain, which has an established place of business within Great Britain, is called by the Acts an "oversea company" (1948 Act, s. 406). Such a company is subject to the stringent provisions contained in Part X of the 1948 Act (ss. 406–423).[2] Foreign companies not having an established place of business in Great Britain are, apart from exceptional cases,[3] not governed by the Companies Acts. A different definition of "oversea company" is adopted for the purposes of placing the name of such a company on the index of names (1981 Act, s. 23 (2)); this definition is referred to below (para. 88–03, on p. 1316, *post*).

A company has an established place of business in Great Britain if it has a specified or identifiable place at which it carries on business,[4] "a local habitation of its own," *e.g.* an office[5]; there must be some "visible sign or physical indication" that the company has a connection with particular

---

[1] 1911 S.C. 612, 616 (1st Div.).

[2] Excluding s. 410 (accounts of oversea company) which is superseded by the 1976 Act, s. 9 (5) and Sched. 3. Further, excluding s. 408 (power of oversea company to hold lands), which was repealed by the Charities Act 1960, s. 38 (1) and Sched. VII, Pt. II. The powers of a foreign company to hold lands in the United Kingdom have been considered at para. 18–15, *ante*. For the position before 1961, see Palmer's *Company Law* (20th ed.), p. 133.

[3] See on insurance companies para. 89–40, *post*.

[4] Evershed M.R. in *Banque des Marchands de Moscou (Koupetschesky)* v. *Kindersley* [1951] Ch. 112, 126, 132.

[5] Lord Dunedin in *Lord Advocate* v. *Huron and Erie Loan and Savings Co.*, 1911 S.C. 612, 616.

premises.[6] It is not sufficient for the company to carry on business through an agent[7]; nor has a foreign parent company which carries on business in Great Britain through a subsidiary company merely as the result of that fact an established place of business here,[8] nor a foreign company which carries on business from an occasional place of business in Great Britain, such as an hotel at which one of its directors regularly resides on his visits to Great Britain.[9] The requirement of an established place of business is only satisfied if the specified or identifiable habitation of the company is intended to have more than fleeting character.

Statutory requirements

88–03 An oversea company is required to deliver to the Registrar of Companies:

(a) a certified copy of the charter, statutes or memorandum and articles creating the corporation and defining its constitution. If these documents are not in the English language, a certified translation has to be attached;

(b) a list in the prescribed form of the directors and secretary of the company together with the particulars as to directors and secretary required by section 200 of the 1948 Act;

(c) a list in the prescribed form of the names and addresses of some one or more persons resident in the United Kingdom authorised to accept service of process and notices on behalf of the company (1948 Act, s. 407 (1)).

In case of an alteration in any of these, notice of the alteration must be delivered to the Registrar (1948 Act, s. 409).

Accounting requirements

Sections 9 to 11 of the 1976 Act, which have superseded section 410 of the 1948 Act (s. 9 (4)), have assimilated the accounting requirements for oversea companies, with suitable alterations. That applies to the duty to prepare and deliver accounts (s. 9, as amended by s. 19 of the 1981 Act) and to the accounting reference period (s. 10) but if no profit and loss account was delivered to the Registrar before the coming into operation of section 10 of the 1976 Act (October 1, 1977), the first accounting reference period shall begin on a date not later than the date on which a place of business in Great Britain was established by the company (s. 10 (4)). The

[6] Jenkins L.J. in *Deverall* v. *Grant Advertising Inc.* [1954] 3 All E.R. 389, 391 (the part of the decision referred to in the text is not reported in [1955] Ch. 111).
[7] *Re Lloyd Generale-Italiano* (1885) 29 Ch.D. 219.
[8] *Deverall* v. *Grant Advertising Inc.* [1954] All 3 E.R. 389.
[9] *Re Tovarishestvo Manufactur Liudvig Rabenek* [1944] Ch. 404, 409.

oversea company must register charges on property in England (1948 Act, s. 106). If an oversea company has established a place of business both in England and in Scotland it must register the documents required by section 407 and the relevant sections of the 1976 Act both in England and in Scotland (1948 Act, s. 413).

By virtue of section 9 (3A) of the 1976 Act, added by the 1981 Act (s. 19), the Secretary of State has power to modify the ordinary accounting requirements in the case of oversea companies or to exempt them therefrom; he has exercised this power by making the Oversea Companies (Accounts) (Modifications and Exemptions) Order 1982 (S.I. 1982 No. 676) which came into operation on June 15, 1982 and superseded the earlier Oversea Companies (Accounts) (Exceptions) Order 1980.

Prospectuses

The company must, in every prospectus it issues inviting subscriptions for its shares or debentures, state the country in which it was incorporated and it must conspicuously exhibit in every place in the United Kingdom where it carries on business the name of the company and the country where it was incorporated. It must also have the name of the company and of the country of its incorporation mentioned in legible characters in all bill-heads and letter paper, and in all notices—and other official publications of the company (1948 Act, s. 411).

Prospectuses of companies incorporated out of Great Britain—whether oversea or other foreign companies—are subject to the same rules as apply to prospectuses of companies registered in England, with some modifications (1948 Act, ss. 417 and 423).

Limitation of liability

If the liability of members is limited, notice of that fact must be stated, in legible letters, in every prospectus and in all bill-heads, letter paper, notices and other official publications in Great Britain, and must be affixed to every place where it carries on business (s. 411 (d)).

Reconstruction

A sale to a foreign company on a reconstruction can be effected under section 287 of the 1948 Act.[10]

Regulation of names

The name law relating to oversea companies is assimilated to that of companies registered in England and Wales and in Scotland (see Chapter 7, *ante*). Accordingly, the onus of ascertaining whether the use of the corporate name of the oversea company is admissible in Great Britain, falls

[10] See para. 80–03, *ante*. See also para. 79–03, *ante*.

on the company. The special provisions applying to the name of an oversea company will be found in section 31 of the 1976 Act as amended by section 27 of the 1981 Act. They are already noted in paragraph 7–26, *ante*, but some points may be briefly repeated here.

ADMISSIBILITY OF NAME. The prohibition of certain names in section 22 of the 1981 Act likewise applies to the names of oversea companies. These prohibitions, it will be recollected, are either absolute (1981 Act, s. 22 (1)) or conditional on the approval of the Secretary of State (1981 Act, s. 22 (2)).

The names of oversea companies are included into the index of names (1981 Act s. 23 (1) (*b*)) but the definition of an "oversea company" for the purposes of this provision differs from that contained in section 406 of the 1948 Act (1981 Act, s. 23 (2)). In this connection the phrase means a company which has registered with the Registrar in accordance with section 407 of the 1948 Act and appears to the Registrar to have a place of business in Great Britain. An oversea company which has not duly registered its particulars with the Registrar cannot have its name entered on the index of names.

NOTICES OF THE SECRETARY OF STATE. The supervisory jurisdiction of the Secretary of State over the names of oversea companies is exercised by "notices," and not by "directions," as is the case when a company is registered in England or Wales or in Scotland. This change in the terminology is merely a matter of courtesy extended to oversea companies; nothing turns on it.

This subject is fully treated in paragraph 7–26, *ante*. Disregard of a notice served by the Secretary of State on the company may expose it to criminal sanction but does not invalidate any transaction entered into by it (1976 Act, s. 31 (5)).

Service of process or notices

88–04 As has been seen,[11] an oversea company has to register the name and address of at least one person resident in Great Britain who is authorised to accept on behalf of the company service of process or notices. Service on such person is sufficient (1948 Act, s. 412). The European Communities Act 1972, s. 9 (1) does not apply to oversea companies.[12]

If the oversea company has failed to register the name and address of a person authorised to accept service or all these persons are dead or have ceased to reside within the jurisdiction of the courts or refuse to accept service or for other reasons cannot be served, service can be effected by leaving or sending the document by post[13] to any established place of

[11] At para. 88–03, *ante*.
[12] See para. 2–14, *ante*.
[13] The document may be sent by ordinary or registered post: see *T.O. Supplies (London)* v. *Jerry Creighton* [1952] 1 K.B. 42.

business of the company in Great Britain (1948 Act, s. 412, proviso). It is, however, insufficient to serve the company at a former, and at the date of service, vacated, office or other place of business.[14] Service on an oversea company can only be effected in the manner indicated in section 412, it cannot be effected under R.S.C., Ord. 65, r. 3, by serving proceedings on one of the company's officers, who happens to be in the jurisdiction.[15] This rule applies whether the oversea company has or has not registered the name of a person authorised to accept service. If a foreign company does not carry on business in Great Britain at a place within the jurisdiction, *i.e.* if it is not an oversea company, it cannot be served with proceedings by serving them on the company's president who is in the jurisdiction.[16]

An oversea company which has registered the name of a person resident in Great Britain and authorised to accept service on behalf of the company can be restrained by injunction of the English court from aiding and abetting another foreign company to break an injunction issued by the English court against the other company.[17]

Insurance companies

88–05 An insurance company constituted outside the United Kingdom but carrying on insurance business in the United Kingdom or, as the case may be, Northern Ireland, must register as an oversea company even though it has no established place of business here (Insurance Companies Act 1974, s. 75 (2), as amended).[18] Merely carrying on reinsurance business within Great Britain would bring the foreign assurance company within the ambit of this provision.[19]

Part II of the Insurance Companies Act 1974, as amended, likewise applies to insurance companies established outside the United Kingdom, which carry on insurance business within the United Kingdom (s. 12). The authorisation, by the Secretary of State, of an insurance company, whose head office is in another member State of the EEC and which wishes to carry on insurance business in the United Kingdom, is regulated by the Insurance Companies Act 1981, s. 8. As regards an insurance company outside the Community, section 9 of that Act applies.

---

[14] *Deverall* v. *Grant Advertising Inc.* [1955] Ch. 111. In the case of service of the winding-up petition, according to r. 29 of the Companies (Winding-up) Rules 1949, service is possible at the "principal or last known principal place of business of the company" in the jurisdiction. This is possible even if the company had another "principal place of business" in the (foreign) country of incorporation: *Re Naamlooze Vennootschap Handelmaatschappij Wokar* [1946] Ch. 98.

[15] *The Theodohos* [1977] 2 Lloyd's Rep. 428.

[16] *The Theodohos, supra.*

[17] *Acrow (Automation) Ltd.* v. *Rex Chainbelt Inc.* [1971] 1 W.L.R. 1676.

[18] See para. 89–37, *post.* s. 75 (2) of the Insurance Companies Act 1974 (as amended by the Companies Act 1976 Sched. 2 and the Insurance Companies Act 1980, s. 2 and Sched. 1) makes the following provisions applicable to these companies: ss. 407, 409–415 and 425 of the Companies Act 1948, ss. 9–11 of the Companies Act 1976.

[19] *Forsikringsaktieselskabet National (of Copenhagen)* v. *Att.-Gen.* [1925] A.C. 639.

Companies incorporated in the Channel Islands, the Isle of Man and Northern Ireland

88–06 A company incorporated in the Channel Islands or the Isle of Man (known as an "Island company") which has established a place of business in England or Scotland is, as regards the registration of documents under the 1948 Act, treated in Great Britain in the same manner as if it were a company registered in England or Scotland (s. 416 as substituted by the 1981 Act, s. 109). Consequently, such a company, if it would be an unlimited company within the meaning of the Companies Acts, may avail itself, as regards the registration of its accounts, of the exemptions provided in section 1 (8) of the 1976 Act (s. 416 (3) of the 1948 Act, as substituted by s. 109 of the 1981 Act).

A company incorporated in Northern Ireland and having an established place of business in Great Britain is in a less favourable position: it is a proper oversea company and must comply with all the requirements imposed upon such companies.

Penalties

86–07 In the case of non-compliance the oversea company and every officer or agent of the company who knowingly and wilfully authorised the default are liable to a fine (1948 Act, s. 414).[20]

Non-compliance with the statutory requirements for a foreign company to register as an oversea company does not render a contract made by the (unregistered) company illegal and consequently invalid.[21]

Investigation

88–08 Oversea companies, or former oversea companies, may be investigated by the Department of Trade under sections 165 to 171 of the 1948 Act, as amended,[22] subject to such adaptations and modifications as may be specified by regulations made by the Department of Trade (1967 Act, s. 42).

Foreign companies other than oversea companies

88–09 A foreign company which has no established place of business in Great Britain but carries on business here is not an oversea company within section 406 of the 1948 Act. Except as far as the issue of a prospectus relating to its shares or debentures is concerned,[23] it is not governed by the provisions of Part X of the Act unless it is an insurance company,[24] but it may be wound up in Great Britain as an unregistered company (s. 400; see *infra*).

That a foreign company which is not an oversea company is, on principle,

---

[20] See dicta of Winn L.J. in *Martelli* v. *Sulzberger* (1967) 111 S.J. 437.
[21] *Curragh Investments Ltd.* v. *Cook* [1974] 1 W.L.R. 1559. See also 1976 Act, s. 31 (5), end.
[22] See Chap. 78, *ante*.
[23] See para. 21–10, *ante*.
[24] See para. 88–05, *ante*, and para. 89–37, *post*.

not subject to the Companies Acts does not, however, mean that such a company is not governed by English law.[24a] If it is "resident" in the English jurisdiction for the purposes of taxation, service of process or the attribution of enemy character, English law may be applicable to it.[25]

Immunity of State-owned or State-controlled foreign corporations

The position of such corporations is governed by the State Immunity Act 1978 which came into operation on November 22, 1978. The Act provides in section 14 (1) that, in principle, any entity which is distinct from the executive organs of the government of the State and capable of suing or being sued, referred to in the Act as "separate entity," shall not enjoy immunity in proceedings in the English courts. Section 14 (2) of the 1978 Act then provides:

"(2) A separate entity is immune from the jurisdiction of the courts of the United Kingdom if, and only if—
(a) the proceedings relate to anything done by it in the exercise of sovereign authority; and
(b) the circumstances are such that a State (or, in the case of proceedings to which section 10 above applies, a State which is not a party to the Brussels Convention) would have been immune."

The result of these provisions is that a separate entity enjoys immunity if it acts in the exercise of sovereign authority (*acta jure imperii*) but does not enjoy immunity if it has engaged in commercial transactions (*acta jure gestionis*). The 1978 Act has thus adopted the doctrine of restricted immunity, as contrasted with the doctrine of absolute immunity, accepted by older English decisions.[26] It may be mentioned that section 3 (3) of the 1978 Act defines "commercial transactions" very widely; this section provides:

"(3) In this section 'commercial transaction' means—
(a) any contract for the supply of goods or services;
(b) any loan or other transaction for the provision of finance and any guarantee or indemnity in respect of any such transaction or any other financial obligation; and
(c) any other transaction or activity (whether of a commercial, industrial, financial, professional or other similar character) into which a State enters or in which it engages otherwise than in the exercise of sovereign authority;
but either paragraph of subsection (1) above applies to a contract of employment between a State and an individual."

Central banks of foreign and Commonwealth States enjoy a privileged position. Their property shall not be regarded, for the purposes of proceedings in the English courts as defined in section 13 (4), as in use or

[24a] Or, in appropriate cases, Scots law.
[25] See paras. 8–11 *et seq., ante.*
[26] *Mellinger* v. *New Brunswick Development Corporation* [1971] 1 W.L.R 604; *Baccus S.R.L.* v. *Servicio Nacional del Trigo* [1957] 1 Q.B. 438.

intended for use for commercial purposes. This is provided by section 14 (4) which runs as follows:[26a]

> "Property of a State's central bank or other monetary authority shall not be regarded for the purposes of subsection (4) of section 13 above as in use or intended for use for commercial purposes; and where any such bank or authority is a separate entity subsections (1) to (3) of that section shall apply to it as if references to a State were references to the bank or authority."

Before the coming into operation of the State Immunity Act 1978 the Privy Council in *The Philippine Admiral*[27] adopted the doctrine of restricted immunity, and so did the Court of Appeal in *Trendtex Trading Corporation* v. *Central Bank of Nigeria.*[28] The House of Lords has likewise adopted this doctrine in *I Congreso del Partido*[29]; this ruling is important for cases not covered by the Immunity Act 1978.

Winding up of foreign companies[29a]

88–10 A foreign company, whether an oversea company or other foreign company, which has carried on business in Great Britain is an unregistered company within the meaning of section 398 of the 1948 Act and may be wound up by the court as such (s. 399, as amended). The circumstances in which such a company may be wound up are:

(a) if the company is dissolved, or has ceased to carry on business, or is carrying on business only for the purpose of winding up its affairs;
(b) if the company is unable to pay its debts;
(c) if the court is of opinion that it is just and equitable that the company be wound up (s. 399 (5)).[30]

In *Re Compania Merabello San Nicholas S.A.*[31] Megarry J. stated the law relating tc the existence of jurisdiction to make a winding-up order in respect of a foreign company as follows:

> "(1) There is no need to establish that the company ever had a place of business here.
>
> (2) There is no need to establish that the company ever carried on business here, unless perhaps the petition is based upon the company carrying on or having carried on business.
>
> (3) A proper connection with the jurisdiction must be established by sufficient evidence to show (a) that the company has some asset or assets within the jurisdiction, and (b) that there are one or more persons concerned in the proper distribution of the assets over whom jurisdiction is exercisable.
>
> (4) It suffices if the assets of the company within the jurisdiction are

[26a] It is doubtful whether this section has retrospective effect, see *Hispano American Mercantile S.A.* v. *Central Bank of Nigeria* [1979] 2 Lloyd's Rep. 277.
[27] [1977] A.C. 373.
[28] [1977] Q.B. 529.
[29] [1981] 3 W.L.R. 328.
[29a] Although this section refers to winding up in England the position in Scotland is similar.
[30] See *Re Mercantile Bank of Australia* [1892] 2 Ch. 204.
[31] [1973] Ch. 75, 91. *I.R.C.* v. *Highland Engineering Ltd.* etc., 1975 S.L.T. 202.

of any nature; they need not be 'commercial' assets, or assets which indicate that the company formerly carried on business here.

(5) The assets need not be assets which will be distributable to creditors by the liquidator in the winding-up: it suffices if by the making of the winding-up order they will be of benefit to a creditor or creditors in some other way.

(6) If it is shown that there is no reasonable possibility of benefit accruing to creditors from making the winding-up order, the jurisdiction is excluded."

In order to found jurisdiction for a winding-up order in the case of an unregistered foreign company with no assets in the United Kingdom other than a right of action, it is not necessary to show that the action is bound to succeed. It is sufficient for the petitioners to show that it has a reasonable prospect of success.[32] Further, the court has jurisdiction to order the compulsory winding up of a foreign company which had carried on business in this country, where employees of the company allegedly had been unfairly dismissed from their employment and had obtained judgments in respect of unpaid remuneration, and such winding-up order could be made even though the company had ceased trading and had no assets in this country.[33]

A voluntary winding up or winding up subject to the supervision of the court is not admitted for unregistered companies (s. 399 (4)).

As is evident from Megarry J.'s statement, quoted *supra*, a foreign company may be wound up under these provisions even though it did not have an established or, indeed, any place of business in Great Britain; it is sufficient that it carried on business here.[34] Normally, the existence of assets in this country or the presence here of persons claiming as creditors is sufficient indication of a business having been carried on by the dissolved company in Great Britain.[35]

Where the English court has made a winding-up order with respect to a foreign company the English winding up is conducted in accordance with English, and not foreign, winding-up procedure.[36]

A winding-up order relating to a foreign company should not state that the English winding up is limited to the English assets[37]; this, however, is merely a matter of form; normally the winding up will be limited to the English assets of the company as they are the only assets over which the

---

[32] *Re Allobrogia Steamship Corpn.* [1978] 3 All E.R. 423.

[33] *Re Eloc Electro-Optieck and Communicatie BV*, [1981] 3 W.L.R. 176.

[34] *Banque des Marchands de Moscou (Koupetschesky)* v. *Kindersley* [1951] Ch. 112; *Re Azoff-Don Commercial Bank* [1954] Ch. 315; *Re Tovarishestvo Manufactur Liudvig Rabenek* [1944] Ch. 404.

[35] *Banque des Marchands de Moscou (Koupetschesky)* v. *Kindersley* [1951] Ch. 112, 126, 132; *Re Azoff-Don Commercial Bank* [1954] Ch. 315.

[36] *Re Suidair International Airways Ltd.* [1951] Ch. 165, 173 (where in an English winding up of a foreign company English judgment creditors were allowed to retain the benefit of their execution in this country although this conflicted with a prior winding up in the (foreign) country of incorporation).

[37] *Re Hibernian Merchants Ltd.* [1958] Ch. 76.

court has jurisdiction. Foreign creditors are entitled to prove in the winding up in the same manner as English creditors.[38]

Registration of charges on English property by companies incorporated outside England

Section 106 of the 1948 Act extends the registration requirements for charges on property situate in England to "a foreign company (whether a company within the meaning of the Act or not) incorporated outside England which has an established place of business in England," and a similar provision applies to Scotland (s. 106K). Section 106 is a very wide provision. If the foreign company has such a place of business in England, it is irrelevant whether it has been registered under Part X of the 1948 Act as an oversea company or not. It is in any case obliged to comply with the provisions relating to the registration of the charge on English property, as contained in section 95, if the charge is to be valid against the liquidator.

In *N. V. Slavenburg's Bank* v. *Intercontinental Natural Resources Ltd.*[39] Lloyd J. held that a winding-up order by a court of Bermuda relating to a company incorporated there was recognised as a winding-up order for the purposes of section 95 of the 1948 Act and joint liquidators appointed for the company by the Bermuda court were liquidators within the definition of section 95, as applied by section 106. Consequently, an unregistered charge on the company's property situate in England was void as against the liquidators, although the foreign company was not registered under Part X of the 1948 Act and although it was the practice of the Registrar not to register a charge where a foreign company had failed to comply with the requirements of Part X.

Winding up of dissolved foreign companies

88–11 A foreign company which has been carrying on business in Great Britain, but has ceased to do so, may be wound up as an unregistered company even if it has been dissolved according to its own law of incorporation (1948 Act, s. 400).[40] The provisions of the European Communities Act 1972, s. 9 (1) to (7), which apply to companies registered under the Companies Acts 1948 to 1981, likewise apply to unregistered companies, in addition to the provisions of those Acts which apply to these companies in any event. But section 9 (1) to (7) has been slightly modified, in order to adjust these provisions to the case of unregistered companies.[41]

---

[38] *Re Azoff-Don Commercial Bank* [1954] Ch. 315.

[39] [1980] 1 W.L.R. 1076.

[40] The term "unregistered company" includes a foreign company which has been dissolved by its own law of incorporation: Lord Maugham in *Russian and English Bank* v. *Baring Brothers & Co. Ltd.* [1936] A.C. 405, 441; Bennett J. in *Re Russian and English Bank* [1932] 1 Ch. 663, 668; further, *Re Matheson Bros. Ltd.* [1884] 27 Ch.D. 225; *Diaren Kisen Kabushiki Kaisha* v. *Shiang Kee* [1941] A.C. 373 (a decision on the Companies Ordinance of Hongkong).

[41] Companies (Unregistered Companies) Regulations 1975 (S.I. 1975 No. 597); these Regulations are reproduced in Vol. II, Pt. A.

A foreign company which has been dissolved cannot bring an action[42]; but after a winding-up order the liquidator can sue in the name of the company though it has been dissolved[43] and, it is submitted, an order might be made under section 244 of the 1948 Act vesting all the property of the company in the liquidator and he could then, as provided by the section, bring an action in his official name.[44]

In the winding up—as an unregistered company—of a foreign company dissolved under its own law, foreign creditors may prove in the same manner as English creditors,[45] but creditors whose claims are governed by foreign law as the proper law of contract and are discharged by that law at the date of the English winding-up order cannot prove in the English winding up.[46] Further, the partial revivification of the dissolved foreign company by the English winding-up order has no retrospective effect and, consequently, a creditor whose claim came into existence after the foreign dissolution but before the English winding-up order cannot prove in the English winding up, although the court in deserving cases may authorise an *ex gratia* payment.[47] Where the foreign company was a bank and the claim originated in the current account of a customer, the claim was regarded as being due without demand by the customer on the commencement of the English winding-up order, when the relationship of banker and customer ceased.[48]

After payment of the liabilities of the dissolved foreign company, the liquidator of the English winding up has to distribute the surplus assets to the former shareholders of the company in the same proportion as their shares bore to the total issued capital of the company at the date of the dissolution; the Crown is not entitled to the surplus assets as *bona vacantia* in preference to the shareholders who can prove their title,[49] but, it is thought, the Crown is entitled to the portions in the surplus assets of the shareholders who fail to establish their title.

The proposed European Company

88–12 The Commission of the European Communities has published a proposal for the introduction of a new form of business organisation, *viz.* the

---

[42] *Russian and English Bank* v. *Baring Bros. & Co. Ltd.* [1932] 1 Ch. 435.

[43] *Russian and English Bank* v. *Baring Bros.* [1936] A.C. 405.

[44] *Cf.* Bankruptcy Act 1914, s. 76; and see the judgments of Clauson J., *ibid.* [1935] Ch. at p. 125; Slesser L.J. at pp. 133–135; and Lord Russell of Killowen [1936] A.C. at p. 435.

[45] *Re Azoff-Don Commercial Bank* [1954] Ch. 315.

[46] *Re Banque des Marchands de Moscou (Koupetschesky)*; *Royal Exchange Assurance* v. *The Liquidator* [1952] 1 All E.R. 1269; *Re Banque des Marchands de Moscou (No. 2)* [1954] 1 W.L.R. 1108 (where the debt was regarded as locally situate in the foreign country).

[47] *Re Banque des Marchands de Moscou (Koupetschesky)*; *Wilenkin* v. *The Liquidator (No. 1)* [1952] 1 All E.R. 1269; and *Wilenkin* v. *The Liquidator (No. 2)* [1953] 1 W.L.R. 172 (payment to expert on foreign law in advising during the "interregnum"); *cf. Re Russian Commercial and Industrial Bank* (1963) 107 S.J. 415.

[48] *Re Russian Commercial and Industrial Bank* [1955] Ch. 148.

[49] *Re Banque des Marchands de Moscou (Koupetschesky)*; *Re Moscow Merchants' Trading Co. Ltd.* [1958] Ch. 182.

European Company (*societas Europoea*, SE).[50] The statute of the SE will be given effect by a Council Regulation under Article 235 of the EEC Treaty, but so far the Council has not approved the Commission's draft and the proposals on the statute of the SE have not come into effect yet. The following observations are founded on the final draft proposed by the Commission in 1975.[51]

Aims and status

88–13 The aims of the draft Regulation on the formation of the SE are to enable national companies of different member states to create a single business organisation suitable for the conduct of business in the whole common market. The SE will have the status of a national company in every member state. Article 1 (4) of the final draft provides[52]:

> "The SE has legal personality. In each member state and subject to the express provisions of this statute it shall have in all respects the same rights and powers as a company limited by shares incorporated under the national laws."

The draft statute of the SE will thus facilitate the total merger of two or more companies of different EEC nationality across the frontiers by amalgamating them into a new supra-national company (Art. 2 (1)).[53] Secondly, it will also make it possible for two companies or other public or private corporations of different EEC nationality to constitute a joint subsidiary of European character and by that means to engage in a joint venture in the common market (Art. 2 (2)).[54] Thirdly, an SE, together with another SE or a national company, may form a holding or subsidiary company (Art. 3 (1) and (2)). Lastly, a single SE may establish a subsidiary in the form of an SE (Art. 3 (3)).

The form of the SE is not intended to supersede the types of company established under the national laws of the member states. If and when the draft statute is accepted by the Council and put into operation, there will exist[55] in Great Britain British companies incorporated in England and Wales or in Scotland under the Companies Acts, SEs (which are not treated as foreign companies), and oversea companies which are incorporated outside Great Britain and satisfy the requirements of section 406 of

---

[50] The Draft Proposal for a Council Regulation on the Statute for the European Company was submitted by the Commission to the Council on June 30, 1970. The Proposal was amended by the Commission and, in the amended form, re-submitted to the Council on April 1, 1975 (Com. (75) 150 final). Since that date the project has not been given progress. In the text the customary abbreviation SE is used for European Company.

[51] Position: August 1, 1982.

[52] References in this section are to the final draft statute of the SE presented by the Commission to the Council on May 13, 1975 (*Bulletin of the European Communities*, Suppt. 4/75).

[53] An SE can be formed by public or private companies incorporated in the member states.

[54] A joint subsidiary may be formed not only by companies limited by shares but also by co-operative societies and other corporations governed by the private or public law of a member state (Art. 3 (2)).

[55] Apart from special forms of business enterprises; see para. 89–27, *post*.

the Companies Act 1948. British companies are likely to form the great majority of companies operating in Great Britain.

Incorporation and registered office

88–14 An SE will be formed by registration in the European Commercial Register which will be kept by the Court of Justice of the European Communities in Luxembourg (Art. 8 (1)). The SE shall have legal personality from the day following the publication of its registration in the Official Journal of the European Communities (Art. 19). Each member state will maintain a register supplementary to the European Commercial Register in which SEs having the registered office in the territory of that member state shall also be registered (Art. 8 (3)).

The capital of an SE shall amount to not less than:

250,000 units of account in the case of merger or formation of a holding company,[56]

100,000 units of account in the case of formation of a joint subsidiary,

100,000 units of account in the case of formation of a subsidiary by an SE (Art. 4).

The registered office of the SE shall be situate within the EEC but an SE may have several registered offices which may be situate in different member states (Art. 5). The capital of the SE may be expressed in European units of account or in the currency of one of the member states (Art. 40 (1)). The capital of the SE shall be divided into shares which may be bearer or registered shares (Art. 50 (1)). The general meeting may also approve a future increase of capital by altering the statutes of the SE (Art. 42 (1)) but such approval can only be given for a period of not more than five years and the total approved capital shall not exceed one-half of the capital subscribed (Art. 42 (2)).

The structure

88–15 I. The administrative organs of the SE are:

1. the board of management (Arts. 62–72a);
2. the supervisory board (Arts. 73–82);
3. the general meeting (Arts. 83–96).

II. Other organs of the SE are:

4. the auditor (Arts. 203–222);
5. the European works council (Arts. 100–129).

III. Exceptional measures:

6. Appointment of special commissioners by the court[57] in case of suspected maladministration by the board of management or the supervisory board (Arts. 97–99).

---

[56] Or their equivalents in the currency of a member state, see *infra* in text.

[57] The competent court is the court within whose jurisdiction the registered office of the SE is situate, provided that the member state concerned shall not have granted exclusive competence to decide on the appointment of special commissioners to another court (Art. 97 (2)).

Outside shareholder

88–16 The proposed statute of the SE contains important provisions aimed at the protection of minority shareholders, described as outside shareholders. In particular, where the controlling undertaking is an SE or a company limited by shares formed under the law of a member state, the controlling company is under an obligation to acquire the shares of the outside shareholders either for an appropriate cash payment or by issuing shares or convertible debentures in the place of such payment (Art. 228 (1) (*a*)); in addition, the controlling company may offer the outside shareholders the alternative option of annual equalisation payments (Art. 223 (2)). Similar provisions exist if the controlling company is incorporated in a country which is not a member state (Art. 228 (1) (*b*)). This goes further than the regulation provided by section 209 of the 1948 Act.

The board of management

88–17 Its members are appointed and dismissed by the supervisory board (Art. 63 (1) and (7)). Each member shall conclude a contract with the company, acting through the supervisory board, and the appointment shall be for not longer than six years, but they may be re-appointed (Art. 63 (2)). Only natural persons may be appointed members of the board of management (Art. 63 (3)) but there is no nationality requirement. Nobody can be a member of the board of management and the supervisory board at the same time (Art. 69 (1)).

In the following case the board of management requires the prior authorisation by the supervisory board:

(a) closure or transfer of establishments of the company or of appreciable parts thereof;
(b) substantial curtailment, extension or modification of the activities of the undertaking;
(c) substantial organisational changes within the undertaking;
(d) establishment or termination of long-term co-operation with other undertakings (Art. 66 (1)).

The supervisory board

88–18 The number of members of the supervisory board shall be divisible by three and where an SE has establishments in several member states the number shall not be less than nine (Art. 74 (3)). The members of the supervisory board hold office for four years and may be re-elected (Art. 74c (1)). Only natural persons may be members of the supervisory board, and, in principle, no member may sit on the supervisory board of more than 10 companies (Art. 74 (1)).

The supervisory board consists as to one-third of representatives of the shareholders, as to one-third of representatives of the employees, and as to one-third of members co-opted by these two groups (Art. 74a (1)). The proposed statute contains detailed rules about the election and co-option of the members of the supervisory board. As regards the co-opted third, it is provided that "only persons representing general interests, possessing the necessary knowledge and experience, and not directly dependent on the shareholders, the employees or their respective organisations may be nominated" (Art. 75e (3)). But the employees entitled to vote may decide by ordinary majority that they do not wish to be represented on the supervisory board (Art. 138 (1)). In that case the board consists only of representatives of the shareholders. The decision of the employees not to be represented is valid only for the current term of office of the supervisory board (Art. 138 (2)).

The European works council

88–19 A European works council shall be formed in every SE having at least two establishments in different member states, each with at least 50 employees (Art. 100). The members of the European works council are elected by all employees in establishments within the community having at least 50 employees by secret direct ballot (Art. 103 (1)). The number of elected representatives is determined according to the size of the establishment in question by the statute itself (Art. 103 (2)). The members are elected for four years and may be re-elected, and the election to the European works council does not affect the position of an elected member on the local *comité d'entreprise* or a similar body (Art. 107). The statute contains a catalogue of matters which the board of management can only decide with the agreement of the European works council (Art. 123); in other matters listed in the statute the council has to be consulted (Art. 124); these matters concern mainly industrial relations. The members of the council, whether employees of the SE or trade union delegates, are under a duty of secrecy with respect to matters expressly declared to be secret by the board of management, but the council is entitled to refer the question whether the board has correctly designated information as secret to the jurisdiction of the national court in which the SE has its registered office; the court shall hear the matter in chambers and no appeal lies from its decision (Art. 114).

Where the SE is a controlling company within the meaning of Article 223 of the statute and the group comprises at least two undertakings with registered offices in the member states and having at least 50 employees each, a group works council shall be formed (Arts. 130–136).

Groups of companies

88–20 The controlling undertaking of a group shall be liable for the debts and liabilities of dependent group companies (Art. 239). The test constituting a controlling and a dependent undertaking is that of unified management (Art. 223). A dependent undertaking is one over which the controlling company is able, directly or indirectly, to exercise a controlling influence, one of the two being an SE (Art. 6).

Taxation

88–21 The draft statute contains elaborate provisions dealing with the taxation of the SE (Arts. 275–281). The guiding principle is that the adoption of the form of the SE shall not confer special tax advantages.

Offences

88–22 The member states shall introduce into their law appropriate provisions for creating offences in the case of contravention of some of the prohibitions laid down in the statute (Art. 282). Any contravention is prosecuted in the national courts.

CHAPTER 89

LEGAL FORMS OF BUSINESS ORGANISATION IN GREAT BRITAIN

89–01 THE various legal forms of business organisation in use in Great Britain today can be arranged into four major categories:

single traders;
partnerships and other unincorporated associations;
corporations; and
specialised types of business organisation.

Single traders

This term is used, rather inaccurately,[1] to describe natural persons engaged in business on their own, without being associated with others.

Freedom of business

89–02 On principle, every person in England is free to engage in any kind of business activity. The system, adopted in many Continental countries,[2] of registration of merchants or certain other classes of businessmen in a commercial register is, in its generality, unknown to English law, which considers commercial law as part of the general law of the country, and not as the law of a particular class of persons.[3]

Use of a business name

89–03 A single trader, and the same applies, *mutatis mutandis*, to a partnership or a company, may carry on business under a name other than his or its real name. Such other name is known as a business name.

The use of business names was formerly regulated by the Registration of Business Names Act 1916. The Act required the registration of the business name and other particulars in a register of business names. The register was kept in London for single traders, partnerships and companies having their principal place of business in England and Wales, and in Edinburgh for those in Scotland. The Registrar of Business Names had power to refuse the registration of a business name which in his opinion was undesirable, a power co-extensive with that of the Department of

---

[1] Inaccurately because the person in question need not be engaged in "trade" but in any kind of business activity. By "trading" is normally understood the buying and selling of goods: see *Wheatley* v. *Smithers* [1906] 2 K.B. 321; *Higgins* v. *Beauchamp* [1914] 3 K.B. 1192; see also *Re New Finance & Mortgage Co. Ltd.* [1975] Ch. 420.

[2] *e.g.* in France; see the law of March 18, 1919 (as amended).

[3] Occasionally, however, a legal rule or provision applies only to business transactions. See, *e.g.* the doctrine of "reputed ownership" in bankruptcy law (Bankruptcy Act 1914, s. 38 (*c*)).

Trade to refuse the registration of undesirable names of companies under section 17 of the 1948 Act, repealed by the 1981 Act, Sched. 4.

89–04 In accordance with its general policy to transfer the examination of names with respect to their admissibility from the Department of Trade to the persons desirous of using the name in question, the 1981 Act has repealed the Registration of Business Names Act 1916 and has abolished the register of business names. The new regulation came into operation on February 26, 1982.

The law relating to business names, whether used by single traders, partnerships or companies, is now contained in sections 28 to 35 of the 1981 Act. The present legal position was explained earlier when the law relating to company names was treated (paras. 7–30 to 7–33, *ante*). What was stated there with respect to business names used by companies applies with equal force to business names used by single traders and partnerships.

89–05 *Restrictions on business*

PROFESSIONAL RESTRICTIONS. Single traders are further subject to other restrictions of general nature which apply to all persons engaged in a particular trade, profession or calling.

Some businesses can only be carried on by duly qualified persons. It is, *e.g.* an offence for an unqualified person to act as a solicitor in a civil or criminal matter[4] or to prepare for or in expectation of a fee or reward certain legal documents,[5] or to sell poison without being a registered pharmacist complying with the statutory requirements of an "authorised seller of poison."[6]

In other cases licences[7] are required, *e.g.* in the case of justices' licences for the sale of intoxicating liquors.[8] The Director General of Fair Trading administers the licensing system required for persons carrying on a consumer credit business or consumer hire business.[9] Recognised banks and licensed deposit-taking institutions are controlled by the Bank of England.[10]

89–06 ALIENS. Aliens, as such, are not subject to any restrictions relating to business, except that they have to comply with any special restrictions which may be imposed on them under the Immigration Act 1971, as amended by the British Nationality Act 1981.

---

4 Solicitors Act 1974, s. 20.
5 *Ibid.* s. 20.
6 Pharmacy and Poisons Act 1933, s. 18. The Act admits certain exemptions from this prohibition.
7 On licenses generally, see Paterson's *Licensing Acts* and Stone's *Justices' Manual.*
8 Licensing Act 1964.
9 Consumer Credit Act 1974, ss. 1 (1) (a) and 21.
10 Paras. 89–36 *et seq.*

The Companies Acts do not restrict aliens from acquiring or holding shares in companies registered in Great Britain, nor is it provided that the directors or other officers of the company, or any number of them, must be British subjects, or domiciled or resident in the United Kingdom. The company may, however, by its constitution prohibit or restrict the holding of shares or directorships by aliens although such restrictions, as far as affecting nationals of other member states of the EEC, may contravene the EEC Treaty, Art. 52. Such "British control" clauses are sometimes found, *e.g.* in the articles of shipping companies.[11]

Partnerships and other unincorporated associations

89–07 The business associations discussed under this heading have one feature in common: they do not have legal personality,[12] *i.e.* they are not legal entities distinct and separate from the persons of which they consist. Associations which have legal personality are called corporations or bodies corporate.

Ordinary partnerships[13]

89–08 A partnership is defined by the Partnership Act 1890, s. 1, as "the relation existing between two or more persons carrying on a business in common with a view of profit."

In English law,[14] the essential distinction between the partnership and the company is that the former has no legal personality, but the latter is a body corporate. Many important consequences flow from this fundamental distinction, as has been explained earlier.[15]

There are two types of partnership: the ordinary partnership, which is governed by the Partnership Act 1890, and the limited partnership formed under the Limited Partnerships Act 1907. The former is still much used, notably by professional men who, by their rules of etiquette, are prevented from practising as a limited company, *e.g.* solicitors, accountants, company secretaries, stockbrokers and jobbers.[16] and doctors. The limited partnership, on the other hand,[17] is rarely used in practice.

Since an English partnership is not a legal person, the partners themselves are the joint owners of the partnership property and are personally liable for the debts and liabilities of the firm. Unless they are limited partners in a limited partnership,[18] their personal liability is unlimited.

---

[11] See paras. 61–12 (directors) and 39–12 (restrictions on transfer of shares), *ante*.
[12] On legal personality, see para. 18–01, *ante*.
[13] See generally *Lindley on Partnerships*, (14th ed., 1979); *Underhill on Partnerships* (10th ed., 1975); Drake, *Law of Partnerships*, (2nd ed., 1977).
[14] In Scots law, the partnership is treated as having legal personality: Partnership Act 1890, s. 4; see *Douglas* v. *Phoenix Motors*, 1970 S.L.T. (Sh.Ct.) 57.
[15] See para. 18–24, *ante*.
[16] As regards stockbrokers and jobbers the use of the form of unlimited company has been permitted in order to enable these persons to reduce their office costs and to obtain certain tax advantages. Such companies are known as stock exchange service companies; see [1957] J.B.L. 295.
[17] See para. 89–10, *post*.
[18] See below in the text.

Unless they have made other arrangements, their shares in the partnership are not transferable, and each of them is an agent of the others and, on behalf of the partnership, may make contracts, undertake obligations and dispose of partnership property in the ordinary course of the partnership business. As between themselves, the partners may make what private arrangements they please, but as between the partners and the outside world the position is different. As James L.J.[19] observed:

> "As between the partners and the outside world (whatever may be their private arrangements between themselves), each partner is the unlimited agent of every other in every matter connected with the partnership business, or which he represents as partnership business, and not being in its nature beyond the scope of the partnership. A partner who may not have a farthing of capital left may take moneys or assets of this partnership to the value of millions, may bind the partnership by contracts to any amount, may give the partnership acceptances for any amount, and may even—as has been shewn in many painful instances in this court—involve his innocent partners in unlimited amounts for frauds which he has craftily concealed from them."

89–09 RESTRICTED AND UNRESTRICTED SIZE. While the minimum number of partners in a partnership is two, *i.e.* the lowest number logically possible for any type of association, their maximum number is in many cases restricted. The Companies Act 1948 prohibited partnerships and other associations formed for business purposes and consisting of more than 20 persons (s. 434 (1)) but these rules are considerably relaxed by Part IV of the 1967 Act, particularly in the case of professional partnerships. Under the latter Act a partnership may be formed consisting of any number of persons for the purpose of carrying on practice as solicitors or accountants (provided, in the latter case, that each partner is qualified under section 161 (1) (*a*) or (*b*) of the 1948 Act[20]), or of carrying on business as members of a recognised stock exchange (provided that each partner is a member of that stock exchange), and these categories may be extended by regulations made by the Department of Trade (1967 Act, s. 120) which are mentioned below. Further, as regards partnerships carrying on the business of banking, the Companies Act 1948 provided that the maximum number of partners should not exceed 10 (s. 429). The 1967 Act admitted a maximum number of 20, provided that each partner was authorised by the Department of Trade to be a member of such a partnership (s. 119). The Banking Act 1979 has repealed these provisions. They are no longer required as the Banking Act introduced a system of recognition of banks and licences of deposit-taking institutions by the Bank of England.

By the Partnerships (Unrestricted Size) Regulations, the Department of Trade, acting under the powers conferred by section 120 (2) of the 1967

[19] In *Baird's Case* (1870) 5 Ch.App. 725, 733.
[20] See para. 73–04, *ante*.

Act, have authorised partnerships of unrestricted size in the following cases:

(a) firms of registered patent agents carrying on practice as patent agents[21];

(b) firms carrying on any of the following activities:

(1) surveying;
(2) auctioneering;
(3) valuing;
(4) estate agency;
(5) land agency;
(6) estate management;

if at least three-quarters of the partners of the firm in question are members of one or more of the following bodies—

(i) the Royal Institution of Chartered Surveyors;
(ii) the Chartered Land Agents' Society;
(iii) the Chartered Auctioneers' and Estate Agents' Institute;
(iv) the Incorporated Society of Valuers and Auctioneers (*ibid.*);

(c) firms of actuaries each of whom is a fellow of either the Institute of Actuaries or the Faculty of Actuaries[22];

(d) firms of chartered engineers the majority of whom are recognised as such by the Council of Engineering Institutions[23];

(e) firms of building designers of whom not less than three-quarters are registered under the Architects (Registration) Act 1931 or are recognised by the Council of Engineering Institutions as chartered engineers or by the Royal Institution of Chartered Surveyors as chartered surveyors[24];

(f) firms of loss adjusters, if not less than three-quarters of their total number are members of the Chartered Institute of Loss Adjusters.[25]

The consequences of forming a partnership in excess of the prescribed minimum are discussed later.[26]

Limited partnerships

89–10 The limited partnership, as admitted by the Limited Partnerships Act 1907, is an importation from abroad; it is an adaptation of the type of business organisation known in French law as *société en commandité*[26a] and admitted by most Continental legal systems. In Great Britain the limited partnership never took root and, indeed, offered little attraction, because

[21] No. 1 Regulations 1968 (S.I. 1968 No. 1222).
[22] No. 2 Regulations 1970 (S.I. 1970 No. 835).
[23] No. 3 Regulations 1970 (S.I. 1970 No. 992).
[24] No. 4 Regulations 1970 (S.I. 1970 No. 1319).
[25] No. 5 Regulations 1982 (S.I. 1982 No. 530).
[26] See para. 89–16, *post.*
[26a] This developed from the *commenda* which had its origin in the northern Italian trading practice of the 12th century; see Byrne, *Genoese Shipping*, Cambridge, 1930.

in the same year in which it was introduced, businessmen were offered the alternative of forming or joining a private company, with all the advantages and immunities conferred by the law on such companies.

In a limited partnership there must be one or more partners with unlimited liability. These partners are called "general partners"; the other partners are the "limited partners," the latter contributing to the partnership assets a specified amount in money or money's worth, and enjoying immunity from liability beyond the amount so contributed. It is, however, an essential condition of this immunity that a limited partner shall not take part in the management of the business, and he is to have no power to bind the firm. He may inspect the books and may advise, *i.e.* consult with the other partners as to the state and prospects of the business, but he must not go beyond this. If he does, though it be in ignorance of the law, or inadvertently, or at the urgent request of the general partners, he forfeits his immunity from liability, and, in the picturesque phrase of Sir Francis Palmer, "is plunged into the unknown depths of unlimited liability." Thus, the Limited Partnerships Act in effect merely limits the liability of a sleeping partner provided he strictly complies with the statutory requirements.

As the limited partnership is a partnership, the requirements relating to business names[27] and to maximum numbers[28] likewise apply to it. By the Limited Partnerships (Unrestricted Size) No. 1 Regulations 1971[29] a limited partnership is authorised to exceed the maximum number of 20 if the following conditions are satisfied: first, the limited partnership must carry on any of the following activities:

1. surveying.
2. auctioneering.
3. valuing.
4. estate agency.
5. land agency.
6. estate management.

Secondly, not less than three-quarters of the total number of partners must be members of:

1. The Royal Institution of Chartered Surveyors, or
2. The Incorporated Society of Valuers and Auctioneers.

Thirdly, not more than one-quarter of the total number of partners can be limited partners.

Unincorporated companies[30]

89–11 This type of business association made its first appearance in the seventeenth century and was much used in the eighteenth and the first half of the

[27] See para. 89–03, *ante*.
[28] See para. 89–09, *ante*. The exemption of certain partnerships under s. 120 of the 1967 Act is extended to limited partnerships (1967 Act, s. 121).
[29] S.I. 1971 No. 782.
[30] D. Lloyd, *Law of Unincorporated Associations*, 1938.

nineteenth centuries when it developed into the so-called "deed of settlement" company. The promoters of this kind of company attempted, by using the devices of contract and trust, to endow the unincorporated company with many of the privileges and advantages normally reserved to corporations without obtaining the status of a corporation, which in those days could only be obtained by royal charter or special Act of Parliament. In law the unincorporated company has always been regarded as a large partnership with some special features, one of them being the transferability of its shares.

The deed of settlement company was the direct precursor of the modern company and, as such, was considered in the chapter dealing with the historical development of the Companies Acts.[31]

Today the role of the unincorporated company is insignificant. The restriction on the maximum numbers of members of most types of unincorporated business associations imposed by sections 429 and 434 (1) of the 1948 Act has been mitigated by Part IV of the 1967 Act and the formation of this type of association beyond those limits is illegal.[32]

Syndicates and mutual associations

89–12 While the characteristic feature of the partnership and the unincorporated company is that the members carry on business jointly, it may happen that persons combine without accepting joint liability to third parties; they may indicate in their contracts with them that their liability shall be several, not joint, and shall be restricted to a stated amount.

This type of association, which is neither a partnership nor an unincorporated company, is met sometimes in insurance and banking. Syndicates of underwriters at Lloyd's and outside Lloyd's and some mutual assurance associations fall within this category. Further, banks providing finance by means of so-called syndicated loans form syndicates.[33]

In insurance, when underwriters' syndicates issue policies—which they do through managers or agents—it is customary to indicate on them the percentage of the total risk for which each underwriter holds himself responsible. It has been held that neither underwriters' syndicates nor mutual assurance clubs[34] are partnerships and that consequently, a member is not liable to a contracting party for a defaulting member's share.

Mutual assurance clubs—and the same undoubtedly applies to underwriters' syndicates—are, however, associations carrying on business with the object of "acquisition of gain" within section 434 of the 1948 Act[35] so that,

---

[31] See para. 2–03, *ante*.
[32] See para. 89–16, *post*.
[33] See Richard Slater "Syndicated Bank Loans" in [1982] J.B.W. 173.
[34] *Per* Lord Esher M.R. in *Leo Steamship Co. Ltd.* v. *Corderoy and Others* (1896) 1 Com. Cas. 379, 381; *Tyser* v. *The Shipowners' Syndicate* [1896] 1 Q.B. 135.
[35] *Re Arthur Average, etc., Association* (1875) 10 Ch.App. 542; *Re Padstow Total Loss Association* (1882) 20 Ch.D. 137, 149; see Arnould's *Marine Insurance* (16th ed., 1981), Vol. I, para. 129.

if the number of their members exceeds 20 persons, they must incorporate as a company under the Companies Acts.[36] In modern times it is usual for mutual assurance clubs to carry on business as companies limited by shares, by guarantee or as unlimited companies.

Clubs[37]

89–13 A club can be defined as an association of persons combining for purposes other than carrying on a business. The characteristic feature of a business activity is that it has as its object the acquisition of gain.[38] This object is absent in the case of a club. In the proper meaning of that word,[39] a club has as its object social, educational or recreational purposes. As the club is not a form of business organisation, it is outside the ambit of this survey.

A club is founded on the contract between the members. The payments by the members become the property of all members and cease to be their individual property; they cannot, therefore, be the subject of a resulting trust if the club is wound up by order of the court as an unregistered company (1948 Act, s. 399). In that case the surplus assets are distributed to the members for the time being *per capita*, unless the membership contract otherwise provides.[40]

A club may be promoted as a company registered under the Companies Acts. In particular, the form of the private company limited by guarantee,[41] which has obtained exemption from the requirement of "Limited" as the last component of its name (see 1981 Act, s. 25)[42] is often suitable for the constitution of a club.

Prohibition of large unincorporated business associations

89–14 THE PROHIBITION. The Companies Acts, as we have seen,[43] impose a general prohibition upon the formation of an unincorporated association carrying on business that has as its object the acquisition of gain by the association itself or its members, if the number of members exceeds 20 persons, unless exemption is granted from this restriction of size.

The object of this prohibition is to compel business associations in excess of these numbers to organise themselves as registered companies which are

---

[36] An unincorporated association formed by persons in excess of this number is illegal: see para. 89–16, *post*.

[37] D. Lloyd, *op. cit.*; D. Daly, *Club Law and the Law of Unregistered Friendly Societies* (6th ed., 1970); H. A. J. Ford, *Unincorporated Non-Profit Associations* (1959); Josling and Alexander, *The Law of Clubs* (1964).

[38] *Cf. I.R.C.* v. *Eccentric Club Ltd.* [1924] 1 K.B. 390, 414.

[39] Sometimes the expression "club" is applied loosely to associations having as their purpose the acquisition of gain, *e.g.* a mutual assurance club.

[40] *Re Sick and Funeral Society of St. John's Sunday School, Golcar* [1973] Ch. 51.

[41] See para. 3–07, *ante*. On the liability of such a guarantee company for an industrial training levy, see *Warwickshire Masonic Peace Memorial Temple Ltd.* v. *Hotel & Catering Industry Training Board* (1969) 113 S.J. 995.

[42] See para. 7–07, *ante*.

[43] See para. 89–09, *ante*. This prohibition was first introduced into company law by the Joint Stock Companies Act 1844; see para. 2–05, *ante*. where the historical reasons for the prohibition of large unincorporated business associations are explained.

governed by strict statutory provisions and can be supervised and regulated more easily than partnerships which are founded on the autonomous arrangement of the partners' contract. Moreover, it is in the interests of the creditors that the members of the association can be easily ascertained by reference to a register of members, as is the case with the registered company. This was pointed out by James L. J.,[44] who said that the object of the prohibition is " . . . to prevent the mischief arising from large trading undertakings being carried on by large fluctuating bodies, so that persons dealing with them did not know with whom they were contracting, and so might be put to great difficulty and expense, which was a public mischief to be repressed."

The prohibition of unincorporated business associations of unrestricted size, unless expressly permitted, does not apply to:

(1) the cases in which the 1967 Act, s. 120, or regulations made thereunder apply[45];
(2) associations formed in pursuance of some other Act of Parliament, such as friendly societies (1948 Act, s. 434 (1))[46];
(3) associations formed in pursuance of letters patent (*ibid.*)[47];
(4) mining companies within the stannaries of Cornwall and Devon and subject to the jurisdiction of the successors to the ancient Stannaries Court (*ibid.*).[48]

These companies are mainly engaged in tin mining. They may be organised as cost-book[49] companies, as ordinary partnerships, or as companies registered under the Companies Acts.[50]

89–15 "ACQUISITION OF GAIN." Not every unincorporated association having more than the admitted maximum number of members is prohibited; a club, in the proper meaning of this term,[51] may lawfully extend its membership beyond that number. The prohibition is directed against associations "formed for the purpose of carrying on any business . . . that has for its object *the acquisition of gain* by the . . . association . . . or by the individual members thereof" (1948 Act, s. 434 (1)).

These words are very wide. It has been held that a mutual assurance club[52] and a building and loan society[53] (which was not formed under the Building Societies Acts[54]) were associations "for gain," and that it did not make a difference that an association, in its inception, comprised less than

---

[44] In *Smith* v. *Anderson* (1880) 15 Ch.D. 247, 273.
[45] See para. 89–09, *ante*.
[46] See para. 89–30, *post*.
[47] See Chartered Companies Act 1837, s. 2.
[48] The jurisdiction of this court was transferred to the county courts of Cornwall by the Stannaries Court (Abolition) Act 1896.
[49] See para. 89–34, *post*.
[50] Halsbury's *Laws of England* (3rd ed.), Vol. 6, p. 812, para. 1641.
[51] See para. 89–13, *ante*.
[52] *Re Arthur Average, etc., Association* (1875) 10 Ch.App. 542; *Re Padstow Total Loss Association* (1882) 20 Ch.D. 137, 149.
[53] *Shaw* v. *Benson* (1883) 11 Q.B.D. 563; *Greenberg* v. *Cooperstein* [1926] 1 Ch. 657.
[54] See para. 89–28, *post*.

20 persons and subsequently grew beyond that figure[55]; Cave J.,[56] in rejecting this contention, said to hold otherwise "would be making a laughing stock of the Act."[57]

On the other hand, a sickness benefit club ("slate club")[58] and, strangely enough, an early investment trust[58a] were held not to fall under the prohibition although having more than 20 beneficiaries because their business was carried on by the trustees who numbered less than 20. Further, unregistered land companies of more than 20 members have been held[59] not to be prohibited because they had as their objects merely the acquisition and division of land betwen their members, and not the business of land-jobbing or trafficking in land; and a superannuation fund formed by the corporation of Liverpool was held[60] not to be an association formed for the acquisition of gain.

89–16 ILLEGALITY OF PROHIBITED ASSOCIATIONS. An unincorporated business association exceeding the statutory maximum number of members[61] is illegal. Such an association, in the words of Sir Francis Palmer, "is a phantom. It has no legal existence." That, however, does not necessarily mean that all contracts made by and with the persons constituting the association are invalid. Here two cases have to be distinguished:

(1) Contracts between the members and outsiders: the question is here, as Brett M.R. put it,[62] whether the contract in its very nature is illegal, or, as Cave J. said,[63] whether the contract is "made directly for the purpose of carrying on the business of the association."

If the connection between the business and objects of the illegal association is as close as indicated in these judgments, the contract appears to be invalid, but, if it is merely incidental to that business, it is believed to be valid unless the contracting party had actual notice of the illegality. It has, for instance, been held that an illegal loan association could not recover on promissory notes given as securities for a loan.[64] On the other hand, it is thought that a stationer who sold the committee of such an association notepaper without being aware of its illegal character was entitled to the price from those with whom he contracted.[65]

---

55 *Re Thomas* (1884) 14 Q.B.D. 379.
56 At p. 383.
57 See further, as to the meaning of "gain," para. 89–13, *ante*.
58 *Re One and All Sickness and Accident Assurance Association* (1909) 25 T.L.R. 674.
58a *Smith* v. *Anderson* (1880) 15 Ch.D. 247 (it is doubtful whether this decision of the C.A. is correct, overruling, as it did, the decision of Jessel M.R.; see Bagallay L.J. in *Re Siddall* (1885) 29 Ch.D. 1, 6).
59 *Wigfield* v. *Potter* (1881) 45 L.T. 612; *Re Siddall* (1885) 29 Ch.D. 1; *Crowther* v. *Thorley* (1884) 50 L.T. 43.
60 *Armour* v. *Corporation of Liverpool* [1939] Ch. 422.
61 See para. 89–09, *ante*.
62 *Shaw* v. *Benson* (1883) 11 Q.B.D. 563, 571.
63 *Jennings* v. *Hammond* (1882) 9 Q.B.D. 225, 229.
64 *Jennings* v. *Hammond* (1882) 9 Q.B.D. 225; *Shaw* v. *Benson* (1883) 11 Q.B.D. 563.
65 *Re One and All Sickness and Accident Assurance Association* (1909) 25 T.L.R. 674.

(2) Whatever the position as regards the contracts considered under paragraph (1), the court can invariably order an account of the moneys received by the trustees and officers of the illegal association and an inquiry as to who were the members.[66]

Quasi-corporations

89–17 In the case of several types of unincorporated business organisations, the law has recognised that, while the organisation is not a "corporation" within the legal meaning of that term, it can be treated for certain purposes as an entity distinct from its members. This principle is well established in the case of trade unions.[67] More recently it has been extended to other organisations.[68] Thus, in *Willis* v. *Association of Universities of the British Commonwealth*,[69] the Universities Central Council on Admissions—an unincorporated organisation operating in conjunction with the defendant company—was held to be a separate legal entity (a "body unincorporate"[70]) for the purposes of the Landlord and Tenant Act 1954. In *Knight and Searle* v. *Dove*[71] it was held that a trustee savings bank could be sued in tort in its own name by virtue of the Trustee Savings Bank Acts 1954 to 1964. Mocatta J. said in that case[72] that a right to sue or be sued might be conferred by statute either expressly or by implication or by the common law upon legal *personae,* including "quasi-corporations" constituted by Act of Parliament, such as the War Damage Commission,[73] and other parties which were not legal *personae.* In relation to trustee savings banks he observed[74]:

> ". . . I find an institution operating pursuant to statutes, owning considerable property and with numerous staff, possessing a protected name, and carrying on activities which from time to time would, in the nature of things, involve it, were it a natural person or a corporation expressly created by statute, in actions for tort, whether as plaintiff or defendant. These factors in themselves would incline me to the conclusion that it followed by implication from the statutes that the institution could be sued in its own name in tort. That inclination is reinforced by . . . the Act of 1954."

The above criteria may be applied to a wide range of unincorporated associations, and it seems probable that the concept of the quasi-corporation will become of increasing importance, not only in relation to

---

66 *Re London Marine Insurance Association* (1869) L.R. 8 Eq. 176; *Greenberg* v. *Cooperstein* [1926] 1 Ch. 657.
67 See *Palmer's Company Law* (21st ed.), p. 835.
68 See K. W. Wedderburn "Corporate Personality and Social Policy: The Problem of the Quasi-Corporation" (1965) 28 M.L.R. 62.
69 [1965] 1 Q.B. 140 (C.A.).
70 *Per* Lord Denning M.R. at p. 147.
71 [1964] 2 Q.B. 631.
72 At p. 634.
73 See *I.R.C.* v. *Bew Estates Ltd.* [1956] Ch. 407, 415.
74 [1964] 2 Q.B. at p. 644.

procedure, but also, as the *Willis* case shows, in relation to the substantive rights of such bodies.

Corporations

The power to incorporate

89–18 The modern rules on the power to create corporations were first stated by Sir Edward Coke C.J. in the *Case of Sutton's Hospital*,[75] who said that the first essential for a valid corporation is a "lawful authority of incorporation." He explained that a corporation must be created by one of the following four means,[76] *viz*:

(1) by the common law,[77]
(2) by authority of Parliament,
(3) by royal charter, or
(4) by prescription.[78]

The doctrine of incorporation by the voluntary covenant of the members of an association, which played an important role in the development of early American corporation law,[79] is not recognised in English law.

Originally most trading corporations were created by the Crown by royal charter, which often gave the corporations monopolistic trading privileges. Later Parliament increasingly exercised its authority to create corporations,[80] and since 1688, when as the result of the revolution of that year, the royal prerogative became further restricted, most business corporations have been incorporated by, or under, an Act of Parliament.

It should be noted that, apart from the incorporation by the common law itself and by prescription—two cases which today have merely historical interest—the sanction of the state is necessary to confer the status of a corporation on an association.[81]

Corporations sole and corporations aggregate

89–19 It is further necessary to note in passing the distinction between a corporation sole and a corporation aggregate.[82]

The corporation sole[83] is a corporation constituted in a single person who, in right of some office or function, has corporate status.

---

[75] (1612) 10 Co.Rep. 23a, 29b.

[76] Holdsworth, in his *History of English Law*, Vol. IX, p. 46, adds, with reference to (1553) Anon.Dyer 100, that "as in the medieval period, a corporation for a limited purpose could be created by implication."

[77] Some corporations sole, *e.g.* the Sovereign or a parson, are bodies corporate at common law (on corporations sole, see para. 89–19, *post*). Strictly speaking, the prerogative of the Crown to create corporations by royal charter and the creation of corporates by prescription are likewise cases of incorporation by and under the common law.

[78] The Corporation of London is an illustration of a corporation created by prescription. The charters granted to the City (of which that of 1067 is the first known example) merely affirmed the corporate existence of the City.

[79] See Shaw Livermore, *Early American Land Companies*, 1939.

[80] It appears to have exercised this function first in 1606 when the New River Company was incorporated by 3 Jac. 1, c. 18.

[81] The reasons for this are public policy; see Holdsworth, *loc. cit.*, Vol. IX, p. 46.

[82] This distinction does not apply to Scotland.

[83] On corporations sole, see James Grant, *Law of Corporations,* 1st ed., 1850, p. 626.

The object of a corporation sole is to make it possible to distinguish between the holder of an office or function in his official and in his private capacity. By this fiction of law it is possible to attach rights and duties to the holder, for the time being, of the office or function, to convey real or personal property to him in his official capacity, and to sue him and for him to bring an action in his official name and style. When the person holding such corporate office or function relinquishes it, the fiction of the corporation sole makes it unnecessary to convey property held by him in his official capacity to his successor or to amend the pleadings in proceedings to which he is a party in that capacity. In short, a corporation sole has the same characteristics of perpetual succession and separation of rights and duties of the corporate body from those of the corporator as all corporations possess. The earliest examples of corporations sole were ecclesiastical.

Illustrations of corporations sole in existence in modern law are the Sovereign,[84] an archbishop, bishop, parson or vicar,[85] a Minister or officer of the Crown who is given that status, usually by statute, *e.g.* a Minister of the Crown[86] or the Public Trustee.[87]

A corporation aggregate is a corporation consisting of more than one member. The type of corporation aggregate with which this work is most concerned is the company registered under the Companies Acts. A corporation aggregate must consist of at least two members, although one may be the nominee of the other.[88] The French doctrine of *simulation*, according to which a company limited by shares is deemed to be dissolved automatically if all shares are beneficially owned by one person,[89] has no parallel in English law.

Corporations incorporated by royal charter

89–20 The Crown, in the exercise of the royal prerogative, has power to create a corporation by the grant of a charter to persons assenting to be incorporated. This prerogative is founded on the common law.

It is a peculiarity of a chartered corporation created by the royal prerogative that its members are under no liability for the debts of the corporation, the Crown having no power at common law to attach liability to the individual members of the corporation.[90]

The prerogative of the Crown has been supplemented by the Chartered Companies Act 1837, as amended,[91] which authorises the Crown, *inter*

---

[84] *Jennings* v. *Hammmond* (1882) 9 Q.B.D. 225, 229.

[85] And other ecclesiastical dignitaries; see Halsbury's *Laws of England,* 3rd ed., Vol. 9, p. 8, para. 9.

[86] Ministers of the Crown Act 1975, Sched. 1 (5).

[87] Public Trustee Act 1906, s. 1 (2).

[88] In view of s. 117, in an English company a nominee or trustee is treated, in every respect, as the holder of the shares which are registered in his name and is, *e.g.* personally liable for outstanding calls; see para. 50–06, *ante.*

[89] C. M. Schmitthoff, *English Conflict of Laws* (3rd ed., 1954), p. 374, where the effect of this doctrine in the English jurisdiction is discussed.

[90] *Elve* v. *Boyton* [1891] 1 Ch. 501, 507.

[91] By the Chartered Companies Act 1884 (which places it beyond doubt that under the Act of 1837 the Crown has power to renew charters).

alia,[92] to grant charters which it cannot grant by virtue of its prerogative, *viz.* to provide in a charter that the individual members shall be liable to a specified extent in respect of their shares for the liability of the chartered company.[93] The Act of 1837 was a legislative experiment to provide a basis for the general readmission of companies after the repeal of the Bubble Act,[94] but since shortly afterwards, in 1844, the legislator decided in favour of another method, *viz.* that of registration,[95] the Act of 1837 was, in the event, not of great practical effect, although a number of banks and other concerns, formed under that Act, are still in existence.[96]

In earlier times trading companies were often created by royal charter,[97] but after it became possible to create companies by registration this happened only in rare instances, and today charters are mainly granted to non-trading corporations, such as the Institute of Chartered Accountants (1880) or the Institute of Chartered Secretaries and Administrators (1902). The *Stock Exchange Official Year Book* for 1981–1982 notes seven chartered companies, amongst them the Bank of England (1694), Hudson's Bay Company (1670) and the London Assurance (1720). The British Broadcasting Corporation is likewise formed by royal charter which is limited in time; the present charter came into operation on August 1, 1981 and is running for 15 years.

There is a difference of fundamental character between a chartered company and a company formed by or under an Act of Parliament. At common law a corporation created by royal charter has power, as was determined in the *Sutton's Hospital* case,[98] to deal with its property, to bind itself by contracts, and to do all such acts as an ordinary person can do, and so complete is this corporate autonomy that it is unaffected even by a direction contained in the creating charter in limitation of the corporate powers. For the common law has always held that such a direction of the Crown—though it may give the Crown a right to annul the charter if the direction is disregarded—cannot derogate from that plenary capacity with which the common law endows the company, even though the limitation is an essential part of the so-called bargain between the Crown and the corporation.[99] This feature—the unrestricted corporate capacity of the chartered company—is in marked contrast to the strict delimitation to its defined objects which is characteristic of all corporations created by, or

---

[92] The Act further authorises the Crown to grant quasi-corporate rights to associations by letters patent, without actually incorporating them.

[93] Similar authority was conferred upon the Crown by earlier Acts which are now repealed; see, *e.g.* 6 Geo. 1, *c.* 18 (1719), which was in issue in *Elve* v. *Boyton* [1891] 1 Ch. 501. One of the few cases in which the Crown is empowered by statute to regulate the affairs of a company by charter is the Bank of England; see Bank of England Act 1946, s. 3 (3).

[94] See para. 2–01, *ante*.

[95] See para. 2–05, *ante*.

[96] *e.g.* the Chartered Bank (formerly the Chartered Bank of India, Australia and China).

[97] *e.g.* the Russia Company (1555), the East India Company (1600), the South Sea Company (1710).

[98] (1612) 10 Co.Rep. 1a, 23a, 30b.

[99] See Bowen L.J. in *Baroness Wenlock* v. *River Dee Co.* (1883) 36 Ch.D. 675n., 685n. and Blackburn J. in *Riche* v. *The Ashbury Ry.* (1874) L.R. 9 Ex. 224, 255.

under, an Act of Parliament. In short, the *ultra vires* doctrine,[1] which in common law applies to all corporations of the latter type, does not apply to chartered corporations. A chartered corporation cannot by its rules or regulations enlarge the powers conferred upon it by the charter; to do so would require an alteration of the charter.[2]

Certain provisions of the Companies Acts apply to chartered companies formed for the purpose of acquisition of gain, unless the company is exempted by direction of the Department of Trade (1948 Act, s. 435 and Sched. 14; 1967 Act, s. 54). A chartered corporation may register as a company under the Act of 1948 (s. 382).[3]

Corporations incorporated by Act of Parliament

89–21 These corporations have one feature in common: unlike chartered corporations, they exist as corporations only for the particular purposes for which Parliament incorporates them.[4] If they go outside those purposes, if they act *ultra vires* their objects, they cease to act as legal *personae*, and the acts themselves are null and void in common law.[5] In *Eastern Counties Ry.* v. *Hawkes*[6] Lord Cranworth L.C., after reviewing the authorities, said:

> "It must, therefore, be now considered as a well-settled doctrine, that a company incorporated by Act of Parliament for a special purpose cannot devote any part of its funds to objects unauthorised by the terms of its incorporation, however desirable such application may appear to be."

Parliament may incorporate a corporation in one of the following ways:

(1) by a private (or local) Act;
(2) by a (special) public Act, or
(3) under a (general) public Act, by registration in compliance with statutory requirements.

The first method was used particularly frequently for the incorporation of public utility companies, such as canals, railways, gas, water and electricity enterprises, until after the Second World War, when many of these enterprises were nationalised. Companies incorporated by private or local —sometimes called "special"—Acts are known as *statutory companies.* The second method is used for the incorporation of enterprises of national importance, particularly when charged with the management of a nationalised industry or having monopolistic trading rights. Corporations created in this manner are known as *public corporations*.[7] The third method is the usual method of forming business corporations in the private sector of

[1] See para. 9–07, *ante*.
[2] *Soldiers', Sailors', and Airmen's Families Assocn.* v. *Att-Gen.* [1968] 1 W.L.R. 313.
[3] See para. 3–20, *ante*.
[4] See Lord Cranworth L.C. in *Eastern Counties Ry.* v. *Hawkes* (1855) 5 H.L.C. 331, 346; Lord Selborne in *Ashbury Ry. Carriage Co.* v. *Riche* (1875) L.R. 7 H.L. 653, 694; Bowen L.J. in *Baroness Wenlock* v. *River Dee Co.* (1883) 36 Ch.D. 675n., 685n.
[5] On the *ultra vires* doctrine in relation to companies, see para. 9–07, *ante*.
[6] (1855) 5 H.L.C. 331, 348.
[7] These should not be confused with public companies; see para. 4–14, *post*.

business. Parliament has delegated the power to create business corporations to a Registrar of Companies, who, when the statutory requirements are satisfied, will register the company and issue a certificate of incorporation. Corporations created under these Acts are known as *registered companies*.

89–22 COMPANIES INCORPORATED BY PRIVATE ACT (STATUTORY COMPANIES). The formation of companies by private Act of Parliament grew out of the canal construction movement, a movement which followed closely on Brindley's success in the construction of the Bridgewater Canal under the Acts obtained in 1759 and 1760 by the Duke of Bridgewater.

It was soon discovered that the best organisation for the construction of these large undertakings was a company incorporated by private or special Act of Parliament. One of the earliest of these Acts was the Trent Navigation Act 1766. A considerable number of canal companies were so constituted, but it was not until the great movement set in for the construction of railways—inaugurated by the Stockton and Darlington Act of 1821—that companies constituted under special Acts began to multiply. Since then, great numbers of companies, mainly concerned with public utilities, have been so constituted. Following the nationalisation of some of these industries, the major proportion of statutory companies in existence today are waterworks companies; but there are also in existence certain others, such as insurance companies, banks and so on.[8]

89–23 *The "Clauses" Acts.* In the case of most of the companies which were formed for the promotion of railway, dock, water, gas or electricity undertakings, the scheme of constitution and the compulsory powers which they required (see below) were the same or similar, and, therefore, to avoid repetition and save expense, the legislature embodied in certain Acts a code of general regulations or statutory provisions applicable to such companies and incorporated by reference into the special Act creating the company. Among such general Acts, known as "Clauses" Acts, embodying typical provisions were:

The Companies Clauses Consolidation Act 1845;
The Lands Clauses Consolidation Act 1845;
The Railway Clauses Consolidation Act 1845;
The Gas Works Clauses Act 1847;
The Waterworks Clauses Act 1847;
The Harbours, Docks, and Piers Clauses Act 1847;
The Electric Lighting (Clauses) Act 1899.

89–24 *Compulsory powers.* A peculiarity of these statutory undertakings, and one which distinguishes them from ordinary trading companies registered

[8] The *Stock Exchange Official Year Book* for 1981–1982 notes the existence of 51 statutory companies of which 27 are waterworks companies. Not all of these statutory companies are listed at the Stock Exchange.

under the Companies Acts, is that they are, in many cases, invested with compulsory powers, *e.g.* to take land or to commit what, but for these parliamentary powers, would amount to nuisances; otherwise their constitution is closely analogous; the liability of the members, for example, is limited to the amount of their shares, and the company in each case is restricted, as regards its powers, to the purposes of its creation and the terms of its parliamentary mandate.[9]

89–25 CORPORATIONS INCORPORATED BY (SPECIAL) PUBLIC ACT (PUBLIC CORPORATIONS). The public corporation, created by a (special) general Act of Parliament, is the typical form of organisation in the public sector of business. It was already known before the Second World War but became more prominent thereafter when new corporations of that type were created for the purpose of owning and managing the various nationalised industries or new industries promoted, in view of their national importance, by the state. Many of these statutory corporations are affected by the Statutory Corporations (Financial Provisions) Act 1975.

The most important of these public corporations are:

The Port of London Authority (Port of London Authority (Consolidation) Act 1920 and Port of London Act 1968);

The British Airways Board Act 1977[10];

The National Coal Board (Coal Industry Nationalisation Act 1946 to Coal Industry Act 1982);

The Atomic Energy Authority (Atomic Energy Authority Acts 1954 to 1981);

The Transport Holdings Board and a number of transport boards (Transport Act 1962,[11] Transport (Financial Provisions) Act 1977 and Transport Acts 1980 and 1981);

The Central Electricity Generating Board and the area electricity boards (Electricity Acts 1947 and 1957);

The British Gas Corporation (Gas Act 1972);

The Independent Television Authority (Television Act 1954[12]);

The Independent Broadcasting Authority (Broadcasting Act 1981[13]);

The British Steel Corporation (Iron and Steel Acts 1967 to 1981[14]);

The Post Office (Post Office Acts 1969 to 1977);

British Telecommunications (British Telecommunications Act 1981).

---

[9] See *Colman* v. *Eastern Counties Ry.* (1846) 10 Beav. 1; *Mann* v. *Edinburgh Northern Tramways Co.* [1893] A.C. 69.

[10] See Air Corporations (Dissolution) Order 1973 (S.I. 1973 No. 2175), dissolving the British Overseas Airways Corporation and, the British European Airways Corporation.

[11] The Freight Corporation was established by the Transport Act 1968.

[12] See now the Television Act 1964.

[13] Whereas the British Broadcasting Corporation is a chartered corporation; see para. 89–20, *ante*.

[14] The original name was changed by the National Steel Corporation (Change of Name) Order 1967 (S.I. 1967 No. 1107).

The public corporation can be compared to a large public company, but it has no shareholders and its profits are not distributable to private persons; they are "ploughed back" into the enterprise. The public corporation is responsible to the Government and, so far as its policy decisions are concerned, through a "parent" Minister to Parliament.

The characteristics of the public corporation have been described by Denning L.J. in *Tamlin* v. *Hannaford.*[15] The learned judge said, with respect to the British Transport Commission[16]:

> "[This] is a statutory corporation of a kind comparatively new to English law. It has many of the qualities which belong to corporations of other kinds to which we have been accustomed. It has, for instance, defined powers which it cannot exceed; and it is directed by a group of men whose duty it is to see that those powers are properly used. It may own property, carry on business, borrow and lend money, just as any other corporation may do, so long as it keeps within the bounds which Parliament has set. But the significant difference in this corporation is that there are no shareholders to subscribe the capital or to have any voice in its affairs. The money which the corporation needs is not raised by the issue of shares but by borrowing; and its borrowing is not secured by debentures, but is guaranteed by the Treasury. If it cannot repay, the loss falls on the Consolidated Fund of the United Kingdom; that is to say, on the taxpayer. There are no shareholders to elect the directors or fix their remuneration. There are no profits to be made or distributed. The duty of the corporation is to make revenue and expenditure balance one another, taking, of course, one year with another, but not to make profits. If it should make losses and be unable to pay its debts, its property is liable to execution, but it is not liable to be wound up at the suit of any creditor. The taxpayer would, no doubt, be expected to come to its rescue before the creditors stepped in. Indeed, the taxpayer is the universal guarantor of the corporation."

It was held in that case that the British Transport Commission was not a servant or agent of the Crown and the property owned by it was not Crown property.[17]

89–26 CORPORATIONS INCORPORATED UNDER A (GENERAL) PUBLIC ACT (REGISTERED COMPANIES). Since 1844 the creation of commercial corporations — com-

---

[15] [1950] 1 K.B. 18, 22. In criminal proceedings a public corporation is a 'public body' for the purposes of the Prevention of Corruption Acts 1906–1916; see *R.* v. *Manners* [1978] A.C. 43.

[16] Created by the Transport Act 1947, and now superseded by the transport boards set up under the Transport Act 1962.

[17] And as such exempt from the operation of the Rent Acts then in operation. The Court of Appeal held that the property of the British Transport Commission was "as much subject to the Rent Restriction Acts as the property of any other person."
It would, however, be possible for Parliament, when creating a new corporation, to state that it should act on behalf of the Crown, but, in the judgment of the Court of Appeal in *Tamlin* v. *Hannaford* (at p. 25), "in the absence of any . . . express provision, the proper inference, in the case, at any rate, of a commercial corporation, is that it acts on its own behalf, even though it is controlled by a government department."

panies — by registration has been admitted by the Joint Stock Companies Acts and later the Companies Acts.[18]

The present enactment, which authorises the creation of companies by registration, is the Companies Act 1948. It is with that Act, as amended by the Companies Acts 1967, 1976, 1980 and 1981, and the types of companies which may be created under it, with which this work has been pre-eminently concerned.

Specialised types of business organisation

89–27 We have now to consider forms of organisation developed, or adapted, for special business activities. They can be divided into two categories: some differ from the form of company registrable under the Companies Acts, and others are registered companies which, in addition to the general law relating to companies, are governed by special statutory powers.

FORMS OF BUSINESS DIFFERENT FROM COMPANIES

Building societies[19]

89–28 A building society is a society formed for the purpose of raising, by subscription from its members, a fund for making advances to members upon security by way of mortgage of land.[20] The fund is raised by the issue of shares which are either paid up or payable in periodical or other instalments.[21] The object of a building society is to assist its members in the purchase of their houses or other small landed property.

Building societies have corporate status.[22] They are not companies but are governed by their own enactments, which are consolidated in the Building Societies Act 1962.[23] At least ten persons are required to form a building society[24]; they have to register the rules of the society and other particulars with the Registrar of Friendly Societies,[25] who grants a certificate of incorporation and exercises powers of inspecting and dissolving[26] societies.

The liability of the members of an incorporated building society is limited, if they are members who have received an advance upon their share, by the amount payable thereon, or if they are unadvanced members,

---

18 See paras. 2–05 *et seq., ante*.
19 See Wurtzburg and Mills, *Law Relating to Building Societies* (14th ed., 1976 by John Mills).
20 Building Societies Act 1962 (as amended), s.1.
21 *Ibid.* s. 6.
22 *Ibid.* s. 3. Incorporation of building societies was first admitted by the Building Societies Act 1874. Before the Act unincorporated building societies, so-called benefit building societies, were admitted but these are now obsolete because if they have not been incorporated under the Act of 1874 or, since 1962, under the Act of 1962, they fall within the prohibition of s. 434.
23 Formerly the Building Societies Acts 1874, 1875, 1877, 1884, 1894, 1939 and 1960 (certain provisions of the Acts of 1874, 1894 and 1960 are preserved by the Act of 1962). Various sections of the 1962 Act were amended by subsequent legislation.
24 s. 1 (3) of the Act of 1962.
25 For address, see note 36 on p. 1349.
26 See 1962 Act, ss. 99 *et seq.* and 110.

by the amount of their paid-up share or the arrears payable on that share.[27]

It should be noted that the share of a member in a building society has nothing but the name in common with the share in a registered company[28]: the members of a building society receive interest on their paid-up shares, and do not participate in the profits of the society by way of dividend or otherwise; moreover, unadvanced shares in a building society can be withdrawn by the members in accordance with the rules of the society.

If the Registrar of Friendly Societies considers it expedient in the interest of actual or potential investors in a particular society, he may, with the approval of the Treasury, prohibit the publication of invitations by that society to subscribe to its funds or to lend it money (Prevention of Fraud (Investments) Act 1958, s. 11 (1)).

Industrial and provident societies

89–29 These societies can be incorporated under the Industrial and Provident Societies Acts 1965 to 1978.[29] They are not companies, but may convert themselves into companies, and, likewise, companies may convert themselves into such societies.[30]

This form of business organisation can today only be used by co-operative societies which have as their object the improvement of the conditions of members of the working classes or otherwise the benefit of the community.[31] If, in the opinion of the Registrar of Friendly Societies, these conditions are not satisfied—or cease to be satisfied—the association must register as a company or be converted into a company.[32] This is the effect of the Prevention of Fraud (Investments) Act 1958. s. 10 (1).

In practice, the activities of these co-operative societies range over a wide field, covering wholesale and retail trading, loans and insurance, housing, allotments and agricultural production. The societies are intended for small capitalists, and accordingly the interest of a member must not exceed £5,000.[33] Any provision in the rules of such a society endeavouring to increase the liability of members beyond that limit is *ultra vires*.[34]

These societies have to publish half-yearly statements relating to their financial circumstances in the form prescribed by the Companies Act 1948.[35] Their accounting and auditing requirements are much strengthened by the Friendly and Industrial and Provident Societies Act 1968.

---

27 *Ibid.* s. 11.

28 See Lord Dunedin in *Liquidator of Irvine and Fullarton Investment and Building Society* v. *Cuthbertson* (1905) 43 Sc.L.R. 17.

29 The 1965 Act consolidated the Acts of 1893 to 1961. As to the registration of charges created by such societies, see para. 45–06, *ante.*

30 ss. 52 and 53 of the Act of 1965.

31 See s. 1 of the Act of 1965.

32 See *Re First Mortgage Co-operative Investment Trust Ltd.* [1941] 2 All E.R. 529.

33 s. 1 of the Act of 1975.

34 *Dibble* v. *Wilts and Somerset Farmers Ltd.* [1923] 1 Ch. 342.

35 Companies Act 1948, s. 433 and Sched. 13.

Credit unions

The objects of a credit union are defined by the Credit Unions Act 1979, s. 1 (3), as follows:

(a) the promotion of thrift among the members of the society by the accumulation of their savings;

(b) the creation of sources of credit for the benefit of the members of the society at a fair and reasonable rate of interest;

(c) the use and control of the members' savings for their mutual benefit; and

(d) the training and education of the members in the wise use of money and in the management of their financial affairs.

A credit union may, subject to certain conditions, be registered under the Industrial and Provident Societies Act 1965 (s. 1 (1) of the 1979 Act). One of these conditions is that the number of members of a credit union shall not exceed a specified number (s. 6 (2) and (3)). At present that number is fixed at 5,000.

Friendly societies

89–30 These are unincorporated associations having as their object some beneficial aim, such as to provide for life, endowment or sickness insurance to a specified limit, or to establish workmen's clubs for social, educational or recreational purposes, or to promote other benevolent activities, such as old people's homes and so on.

Friendly societies may be registered with the Registrar of Friendly Societies[36] under the Friendly Societies Acts 1974 and 1981[37] which confer various privileges on registered societies. A registered friendly society can convert itself into a company.[38] Apart from registered societies, unregistered societies are admitted, but the maximum number of members must not exceed 20 persons.[39]

A friendly society, whether registered or unregistered, is not a corporation; consequently its property is vested in the trustees of the society.[40]

A friendly society has likewise to publish half-yearly statements relating to its finances.[41] The accounting and auditing requirements of friendly societies are greatly strengthened by the Friendly and Industrial and Provident Societies Act 1968.

An unregistered friendly society may be dissolved on loss of its substratum but the substratum is not lost by mere temporary suspension of its activities or because the officers of the society misinterpret the rules and erroneously think that the society cannot be continued. If the society is

---

[36] The full, but cumbersome, title is "the Central Office of the Registry of Friendly Societies." It consists of the Chief Registrar and Assistant Registrars. Its address is 17 North Audley Street, London, W.1. In Scotland the address is the Registrar of Friendly Societies, 19 Heriot Row, Edinburgh.

[37] The 1974 Act consolidates the Friendly Societies Acts 1896 to 1971. The 1981 Act contains a minor amendment.

[38] s. 84 of the 1974 Act.

[39] See para. 89–09, *ante*.

[40] s. 54 of the Act of 1974.

[41] Companies Act 1948, s. 433 and Sched. 13.

dissolved, the members entitled to participate in the distribution of assets are prima facie the persons who are members at the date of dissolution.[42]

A friendly society, like all unincorporated societies, is founded on contract and there is an implied contract between all its members that their relations *inter se* shall be governed by the rules of the society. On the dissolution of a friendly society, in the absence of other provisions in the rules, any surplus assets have to be distributed among the members then existing in equal parts, to the exclusion of any claim thereto by the Crown as *bona vacantia.*[43]

Trustee savings banks

89–31 These institutions are banks which receive from their customers deposits that they accumulate at compound interest, without deriving any benefit therefrom, apart from deducting any necessary expenses of management.[44] These banks enable small investors to obtain interest on their savings and still to be able to cash them when they need them. The maximum deposit of each customer is limited,[45] and a person is prohibited from making deposits with more than one bank. Trustee saving banks are also able to operate banking services on the conditions authorised by the Trustee Savings Banks Central Board.

Savings banks are regulated by the Trustee Savings Banks Act 1981 and regulations made thereunder. An earlier enactment, the Act of 1976, constituted the *Trustee Savings Banks Central Board* which, *inter alia,* may give directions of a general character to the trustee savings banks and provide banking services for them (1981 Act, ss. 7–10). The Central Board exercises certain functions formerly exercised by the Inspection Committee and the National Debt Commissioners. It has power to levy contributions on trustee savings banks for the purpose of financing its expenditure (1981 Act, s. 9).

Trustee savings banks are not bodies corporate; the property of such a bank is vested in custodian trustees who are appointed from the managers of the bank (the "general trustees"), and who may sue and be sued by the name of "the Custodian Trustees for the . . . Trustee Savings Bank."[46] It has been held that an action in tort may also be brought against the bank in its own name.[47]

A trustee savings bank can be wound up as an unregistered company under the Companies Act 1948, ss. 398 *et seq.* Apart from the persons authorised generally by the Act to petition the court for a winding-up

---

[42] *Re William Denley & Sons Ltd. Sick and Benevolent Fund* [1971] 1 W.L.R. 973.

[43] *Re Bucks Constabulary Widows' and Orphans' Fund Friendly Society (No.* 2) [1979] 1 W.L.R. 936.

[44] Trustee Savings Bank Act 1981. For the National Savings Bank (formerly Post Office Savings Bank), see the Post Office Savings Bank Acts 1954 and 1966, as amended by the Post Office Act 1969. See also the Post Office (Banking Services) Act 1976. For fees payable for certificates of rules and alterations of rules of trustee savings banks, see the Savings Banks (Fees) (Amendment) Warrant 1971 (S.I. 1971 No. 981).

[45] The Limitation at present is £10,000 on ordinary investments (S.I. 1969 No. 939), special investments (S.I. 1969 No. 941) and current accounts (S.I. 1969 No. 942).

[46] Trustee Savings Banks Act 1981, s. 15 (11).

[47] *Knight and Searle* v. *Dove* [1964] 2 Q.B. 631.

order, a petition may be presented by the Trustee Savings Banks Central Board or by a commissioner appointed under section 35 of the Trustee Savings Banks Act 1981.[48]

These banks are within the provisions of section 433 of the Companies Act 1948, and have, accordingly, to publish half-yearly financial statements in the form of Schedule 13.

Unit trusts

89–32 Following the strange decision in *Smith* v. *Anderson*,[49] it was inevitable that the form of the trust should once more[50] be used for business purposes.

The idea of the unit trust[51] is very simple: under a trust deed the managers of the trust[52]—usually a management company—acquire certain more or less rigidly defined securities and transfer them to the trustees named in the trust deed who normally are likewise a company which is distinct from the management company. On the strength of the block of shares so held—sometimes referred to as a unit—the managers issue "sub-units" which in practice are usually also called "units" and which are offered to investors and may be admitted to listing at the Stock Exchange.[53] The investors are the beneficiaries under the trust deed and are entitled to a *pro rata* share of the dividends, interest or other income of the securities comprised in the unit. This arrangement offers the investor—particularly the small one—two advantages: he can spread his risk over more securities than he can otherwise afford to do, and he can sell his sub-units easily, their value being at any day the *pro rata* value of the total value of the securities held in the unit. The statutory definition of a unit trust is[54]:

> "Any arrangements made for the purpose, or having the effect, of providing facilities for the participation by persons, as beneficiaries under a trust, in profits or income arising from the acquisition, holding, management or disposal of securities or any other property whatsoever."

Two types of unit trust schemes are known: the fixed, and the managed or flexible type. Under the former the securities authorised to be held by the trustees are rigidly defined. When all sub-units constituting a unit are

---

[48] s. 399 (8) of the Companies Act 1948, as amended by the Trustee Savings Bank Act 1981, Sched. 6, para. 2.

[49] (1880) 15 Ch.D. 247; see para. 85–15, *ante*.

[50] On the deed of settlement company, para. 2–03, *ante*.

[51] The first investment trust in the United Kingdom was probably the Scottish-American Investment Trust (1865); the modern development began with the First British Fixed Trust (1931).

[52] By the Directive of the Council of the European Community of June 28, 1973, (O.J. 1973 L. 194/1) the United Kingdom Government was directed to amend the provision of the Prevention of Fraud (Investments) Act 1958, s. 17 (1) (*a*) according to which a company which intends to exercise the activity of manager and trustee of a unit trust must be constituted in the United Kingdom. This Directive was given effect by the Authorised Unit Trust Schemes Regulations 1976 (No. 195), reg. 2.

[53] The *Unit Trust Year Book* 1980 states that there were 92 management groups and 450 unit trust funds in 1980.

[54] See Prevention of Fraud (Investments) Act 1958, s. 26.

sold the managers acquire a further portfolio of securities and again issue sub-units against this new unit. Under the latter the managers are given practically unlimited power of investment, but the important principle of diversification of investments is safeguarded by provisions in the trust deed limiting the investments in any one company to a certain percentage of the trust's portfolio, *e.g.* 5 per cent.

89–33 It is today virtually impossible to carry on a unit trust scheme without the authority of the Department of Trade. The Prevention of Fraud (Investments) Act 1958, which, as far as it affects shares and debentures of a company, has been discussed earlier,[55] prohibits in section 14 the distribution of information relating to the investment of money, except in specified exceptional circumstances. One of these exceptions referred to in that section is the issue of documents by an authorised trust scheme.

The conditions under which the Department of Trade may sanction an authorised unit trust scheme are laid down in section 17 of the Act of 1958 and the First Schedule thereto. They are principally designed to protect the beneficiaries and to ensure the honest and proper management of the trust scheme. It is not sufficient that a trust deed contains all the matters specified in these provisions, but they must be so contained "to the satisfaction of the Department of Trade," and if the Department, in their general discretion, are not satisfied, they may refuse to authorise the trust scheme even if the trust deed contains the specified details; for example, the Department may refuse to sanction a scheme because they consider the initial service charge to be too high.[56] However, in December 1979 the unit trust charges were de-restricted.[57]

The Department of Trade have power to order an investigation into the affairs of a unit trust scheme

(a) if it is in the interests of unit holders so to do; and
(b) if the matter is one of public concern.

The investigation is carried out by an inspector appointed by the Department of Trade who has similar powers to those of an inspector investigating the affairs of a company (s. 12 of the Act of 1958).[58]

A provision in the trust deed of a unit trust that any balance of the net income which is not used for distribution to the unit holders shall be added to the capital, and shall thereupon cease to be available for distribution, does not infringe section 164 of the Law of Property Act 1925, which re-enacts the restrictions of the Thellusson Act.[59]

---

[55] See para. 25–01, *ante*. On authorised unit trusts, i.e. unit trusts authorised by the Department of Trade under the Prevention of Fraud (Investments) Act 1958, see para. 25–04, *ante*. Units of a unit trust scheme sanctioned by the Board of Trade under this section are authorised trustee investments of the "wider range" under the Trustee Investments Act 1961.

[56] *Allied Investors Trusts Ltd.* v. *Board of Trade* [1956] Ch. 232.

[57] *The Times*, December 19, 1979.

[58] *i.e.* the powers contained in ss. 167 and 168 (1) and so much of subs. (2) of that section as relates to the sending of the inspector's report to the manager of the trust; see paras. 78–07, *et seq.*, *ante*.

[59] *Re A.E.G. Unit Trust (Managers) Ltd.'s Deed* [1957] Ch. 415.

Cost-book companies[60]

89–34 The cost-book company is an unincorporated type of business organisation founded on commercial usage; it was mainly used in mining, not only in the stannaries of Cornwall and Devon,[61] but also in the High Peak and Wirksworth districts of Derbyshire.[62] This form of business organisation still exists but today its use is rare.

The cost-book company is in the nature of an ordinary partnership; the members of the company are usually known as the adventurers and the principal manager as the purser or secretary; the officer supervising the operation of the mine is known as the captain of the mine.

The cost-book consists of several parts, one containing the rules and conditions of the company, another its accounts, receipts and payments, a third a record of the more important transactions and of the meetings of the company.

The capital of the cost-book company is divided into shares—"doles"—of fixed amount or without par value; these shares can be transferred and relinquished and there is no restriction on the number of adventurers by virtue of section 434 of the 1948 Act,[63] but a register of adventurers has to be kept. An adventurer is liable without limitation for all debts incurred by the company with his actual or apparent authority.[64]

A cost-book company may be wound up as an unregistered company under the provisions of the Companies Act 1948,[65] but the liability of contributories in an unregistered company within the stannaries continues for two years, and not one year as in the case of a company (s. 401 (1)). Further, special provisions exist with respect to the winding up of cost-book companies, *e.g.* as to the preferential payment of wages and salaries of miners and clerks (ss. 357–359).

A cost-book company formed before November 2, 1862, or a company within the stannaries may register as a company under the Act of 1948, provided that it consists of two or more members (s. 382 (1)).

Co-operatives

89–35 The older co-operative societies, which are carrying on production, retail, insurance or loan business, are, as already observed,[66] organised as industrial and provident societies. They are consumer-oriented, *i.e.* the customers of the society are the members who have voting and dividend rights. The newer or larger societies use the form of the company limited

---

[60] Tapping's *Readwin Prize Essay on the Cost Book* (2nd ed.); R. R. Pennington, *Stannary Law*, 1973.
[61] See para. 89–14, *ante*.
[62] Halsbury's *Laws of England* (4th (Hailsham) ed.), Vol. 7, para. 1761.
[63] See para. 89–09, *ante*.
[64] *Tredwen* v. *Bourne* (1840) 6 M. & W. 461.
[65] ss. 398 *et seq.*; see para. 85–04, *ante*. The jurisdiction to wind up exercised by the former Court of the Stannaries is now exercised by the county courts of Cornwall by virtue of the Stannaries Court (Abolition) Act 1896.
[66] See para. 89–29, *ante*.

by shares; an illustration is the Scottish Co-operative Wholesale Society Ltd.[67]

Another type of co-operative enterprise is the co-ownership firm, of which the John Lewis Partnership and Scott Bader are the best known examples. These enterprises are likewise companies limited by shares. In this type of enterprise the employees have some say in the appointment and dismissal of the directors and are also given participating rights in the annual profits. Some of them provide that the bonus is shared amongst the employees per capita, others divide the bonus in proportion to the annual pay. The constitution normally provides for the limitation of top emoluments, by providing a maximum wage differential or by other means.[68]

In recent years a further type of co-operative enterprise has been developed, the so-called worker co-operative. Worker co-operatives may be formed either under the Industrial Common Ownership Act 1976 or as companies.

The Industrial Common Ownership Act 1976[69] defines common ownership enterprises and co-operative enterprises (s. 2); both definitions have in common that "the body is controlled by a majority of the people working for the body and of the people working for the subsidiaries, if any, of the body." The Secretary of State may, with the consent of the Treasury, make grants and loans to a limited extent specified in the Act to any body which appears to him to be constituted for the purpose of encouraging the development of common ownership enterprises or co-operative enterprises (s. 1).

If a worker co-operative adopts the form of a company, the employees have the overwhelming majority of seats on the board of directors or other managing boards.

SPECIAL KINDS OF COMPANIES

Banks

Regulation of banking and deposit-taking

89–36 The regulation of banking and deposit-taking is contained in the Banking Act 1979. This Act gives effect to an EEC Directive relating to credit institutions.[70]

CONTROL. The Act institutes a system of control of deposit-taking. It prohibits, in principle, the taking of deposits but admits a number of exceptions, *e.g.* in case of the provision of a deposit on the purchase of a house (s. 1).

The only institutions which are allowed to take deposits are:

(a) The Bank of England,
(b) a recognised bank,
(c) a licensed institution, and

---

[67] See *Scottish Co–operative Wholesale Society Ltd.* v. *Meyer* [1959] A.C. 324.
[68] See *The Economist,* May 3, 1975, pp. 82–83.
[69] See Vol. III, paras. L–731 to 733.
[70] s. 77/780/EEC.

(d) certain specified institutions or powers, such as the National Savings Bank, the Post Office, a trustee savings bank or penny savings bank, a municipal bank, a building society, a stockbroker or stockjobber, and other institutions listed in Schedule 1 to the Act (s. 2 (1)).

CATEGORIES. The Act distinguishes betwen recognised banks and licensed deposit-taking institutions. The system of recognition and licensing is operated by the Bank of England (ss. 3 to 5).

In order to be recognised as a bank, the institution must satisfy certain criteria defined in Schedule 2, Part I of the Act. They are:

(1) If the institution is already in existence, the business enjoys, and has for a reasonable time enjoyed, a high reputation and standing in the financial community.
(2) The institution provides in the United Kingdom a wide range of banking services or a highly specialised banking service.
The following, taken cumulatively, provide a wide range of banking services:
   (a) current or deposit account facilities in sterling or foreign currency for members of the public or in wholesale money markets.
   (b) finance in the form of overdraft or loan facilities in sterling or foreign currency for members of the public or in wholesale money markets.
   (c) foreign exchange services for domestic and foreign customers.
   (d) finance through the medium of bills of exchange and promissory notes together with finance for foreign trade and documentation in connection with foreign trade.
   (e) financial advice for members of the public and the arranging of purchase and sale of securities.
The Bank of England, when determining, whether a wide range of banking facilities is provided, may disregard three of the types of service, *viz.* those specified under (c) to (e) above.
(3) The business is carried out with integrity, prudence and professional skill.
(4) At least two individuals effectively direct the business.
(5) The institution has minimum assets of—
   (a) £5 million, if it provides a wide range of banking services; and
   (b) £250,000 if it provides a highly specialised banking service.
(6) Apart from these minimum amounts, the institution has financial resources considered appropriate to a bank.

In order to be a licensed institution, according to Schedule 2, Part II of the Act, the business must satisfy the following criteria:

(1) Every person who is a director, controller or manager is a fit and proper person to hold that position.
(2) At least two individuals effectively direct the business.
(3) The net assets must be not less than £250,000.
(4) The institution must—
   (a) apart from the minimum assets, maintain appropriate financial resources,

(b) maintain adequate liquidity; and
(c) make adequate provision for bad, doubtful and contingent debts.

REVOCATION OF RECOGNITION OR LICENCE. The Bank of England may, in certain cases, revoke the recognition of a bank or the licence of a licensed institution. An appeal from the decision of the Bank is admitted to the Chancellor of the Exchequer and from his decision, on a point of law, to the High Court (ss. 7 to 13).

DEPOSIT PROTECTION SCHEME. The Act further constitutes a deposit protection scheme which is administered by a Deposit Protection Board and provides for the formation of a Deposit Protection Fund (ss. 22 to 27). If an institution becomes insolvent, certain deposits are protected and paid out of the Fund. These are deposits to a maximum of £10,000 for every customer (s. 29) and the liability of the Fund is limited to three-quarters of the protected deposit (s. 28 (1)).

OTHER PROVISIONS. The Act further contains provisions on advertisements and banking names (ss. 34 to 37) and miscellaneous and general provisions (ss. 38 to 52), but section 36 (10) is repealed by the Companies Act 1981, Sched. 4. Accounts are prepared by recognised banks and licensed deposit-taking institutions in accordance with Schedule 8A of the 1948 Act.[71] Further, these companies cannot be small or medium-sized companies for the purposes of obtaining the accounting exceptions provided by the 1981 Act.[72]

The former Moneylenders Acts 1900 to 1927

For the purposes of obtaining exemption from the provisions of the Moneylenders Acts 1900 to 1927, which were repealed by the Consumer Credit Act 1974, the company had to carry on a banking business. In this connection, the common law definition of banking was developed. It is described in *United Dominions Trust Ltd.* v. *Kirkwood*[73] as business involving: (1) the collection of cheques for customers; (2) the payment of cheques drawn on the bank by customers; and (3) the keeping of current accounts.[73]

The Bankers' Books Evidence Act 1879

This Act was originally intended to avoid the production of whole ledgers of accounts in court. The Banking Act 1979 extends the application of the Act to licensed institutions (Sched. 6, para. 1).

The Banking Act 1979 further provides, in the same provision, that in

---

[71] This was the original Schedule 8 of the 1948 Act (s. 1 (2) of the 1981 Act). See Sched. 2 of the 1981 Act, paras. 1 (*b*) and 8.

[72] 1981 Act, s. 5 (3) (*b*).

[73] [1966] 1 Q.B. 783 (C.A.); Paget's *Law of Banking*, (8th ed., 1972), pp. 1–19

the Bankers' Books Evidence Act 1879 the expression "bankers' books" shall include records kept in microfilm,[73a] magnetic tape or any other form of mechanical or electronic data retrieval mechanism.

Where a woman charged with theft of money told the police that it was in her husband's bank account, a court order made under section 7 of the Act, authorising the inspection of his bank account was held to be a proper order, even though he was not a party to the proceedings.[74]

Bills of Exchange Act 1882 and other Acts

The Bills of Exchange Act 1882 and some other enactments contain references to banks and bankers. The Bills of Exchange Act provides in section 73 that a cheque is a bill of exchange drawn on a banker and payable on demand, and the Cheques Act 1957 contains in section 4 provisions protecting a banker who collects payment on a cheque in good faith and without negligence. Section 2 of the Bills of Exchange Act defines a banker as including a body of persons, whether incorporated or not, "who carry on the business of banking."

The definition of "banker" and the "business of banking" in the Bills of Exchange Act, the Cheques Act and other enactments not incorporating the terminology of the Banking Act 1979 is the common law definition, as expressed in *United Dominions Trust Ltd.* v. *Kirkwood*.[75] This position is expressly preserved by the Banking Act 1979, s. 36 (2). Consequently a licensed institution which satisfies the requirements of *Kirkwood*, although not a recognised bank within the meaning of the Banking Act 1979, is a banker for the purposes of the Bills of Exchange Act, the Cheques Act and the other enactments referred to earlier.

Insurance companies

89–37 Companies carrying on certain classes of insurance business within the United Kingdom, in addition to being subject to the provisions of the Companies Acts, are also governed by the Insurance Companies Acts 1974 to 1981.[76] The provisions of the Insurance Companies Act 1974 were amended by statutory instruments made under the European Communities Act 1972, s. 2 (2), in order to give effect to Directives issued by the EEC and aimed at the harmonisation of insurance law in the EEC. The most important of these statutory instruments were:

The Insurance Companies (Classes of General Business) Regulations 1977[77];

[73a] *Barker* v. *Wilson* [1980] 1 W.L.R. 884.
[74] *R.* v. *Andover Justices, ex p. Rhodes,* [1980] Crim. L.R. 644 (Div. Ct.).
[75] [1966] 1 Q.B. 783 (C.A.).
[76] The 1974 Act consolidates the Insurance Companies Acts 1958–73 and Pt. II of the Companies Act 1967, as far as unrepealed by the Insurance Companies Amendment Act 1973, except for some specified sections (see 1974 Act, Sched. 2). The following is a summary of some of the main provisions of the Act as they apply to insurance companies generally: it is not intended to be comprehensive, and does not take into account all the exceptions to the general rules which are admitted by the Act.
[77] S.I. 1977 No. 1552.

The Insurance Companies (Solvency: General Business) Regulations 1977[78];

The Insurance Companies (Authorisation and Accounts: General Business) Regulations 1978.[79]

These statutory instruments were then consolidated into the Insurance Companies Act 1981 and repealed. The 1981 Act came into operation, subject to some reservations, on January 1, 1982.[80]

AUTHORISATION. In principle, no person shall carry on any insurance business in the United Kingdom unless authorised by the Secretary of State in accordance with the provisions of the Insurance Companies Act 1981 (ss. 2–4). But this requirement does not apply to insurance business (other than industrial assurance business) carried on:

(a) by a member of Lloyd's; or
(b) by a body registered under the enactments relating to friendly societies; or
(c) by a trade union or employers' association where the insurance business carried on by the union or association is limited to the provision for its members of provident benefits or strike benefits (s. 2 (2)).

Subject to certain conditions, further exceptions from the requirement of authorisation are admitted for registered friendly societies, insurance carried on solely in the course, and for the purposes, of banking business, and for insurers who exclusively or primarily provide benefits in kind (s. 2 (3) to (5)).

The Secretary of State shall not, in principle, authorise a body to carry on both long term and general business unless:

(a) the long term business is restricted to reinsurance; or
(b) the body is at the time the authorisation is issued carrying on in the United Kingdom lawfully both types of insurance (in neither case restricted to reinsurance). (Insurance Companies Act 1981, s. 6).

"Long term business" and "general business" are defined in section 1 of the Act.

The conditions on which the Secretary of State may grant his authorisation differ for applicants whose head office is situate in the United Kingdom (s. 7), in other member States of the EEC (s. 8), and in countries outside the Community (s. 9). In the latter case the Secretary of State may ask that the applicant shall make a deposit. No authority will be granted to a body from outside the Community unless it has a general representative

---

78 S.I. 1977 No. 1553.
79 S.I. 1978 No. 720.
80 The Insurance Companies Act 1981 (Commencement) Order 1981 (S.I. 1981 No. 1657).

resident in the United Kingdom; he must be authorised to accept service on behalf of the applicant.

CLASSIFICATION OF INSURANCE BUSINESS. Regulations which gave effect to the classification of risks contained in the EEC Council Directive No. 73/239 came into operation from January 1, 1978, under a statutory instrument.[81] The classification of business is now set out in Schedule 1 to the Insurance Companies Act 1981.

General business, *i.e.* non-life business, was divided into six classes for the purposes of Part I of the Insurance Companies Act 1974. The new classification replaces the former six classes with 17 classes, set out in the EEC Directive. They are as follows (Sched. 1):

1. *Accident.*—Contracts of insurance providing pecuniary benefits, or benefits in the nature of indemnity (or a combination of both) against
   (*a*) sustaining injury as a result of an accident or of an accident of a specified class;
   (*b*) dying as a result of an accident or of an accident of a specified class;
   (*c*) becoming incapacitated in consequence of a disease or a disease of a specified class.

2. *Sickness.*—Contracts of insurance providing fixed pecuniary benefits or benefits in the nature of an indemnity (or a combination of the two) against risks of loss to the person insured attributable to sickness or infirmity.

3. *Land vehicles.*—Contracts of insurance against loss of or damage to vehicles used on land including motor vehicles, but excluding railway rolling stock.

4. *Railway rolling stock.*—Contracts of insurance against loss or damage to railway rolling stock.

5. *Aircraft.*—Contracts of insurance upon aircraft or upon machinery, tackle, furniture or equipment of an aircraft.

6. *Ships.*—Contracts of insurance upon vessels used on the sea or on inland water, or upon machinery, tackle, furniture or equipment of such vessels.

7. *Goods in transit.*—Contracts of insurance against loss of or damage to merchandise, baggage and all other goods in transit irrespective of the form of transit.

8. *Fire and natural forces.*—Contracts of insurance against loss of or damage to property (other than property to which classes 3 to 7 relate) due to fire, explosion, storm, natural forces other than storm, nuclear energy or land subsidence.

9. *Damage to property.*—Contracts of insurance against loss of or damage to property (other than property to which classes 3 to 7 relate) due to hail or frost, or to any event (such as theft) other than those mentioned in class 8.

10. *Motor vehicle liability.*—Contracts of insurance against damage aris-

[81] S.I. 1977 No. 1552.

ing out of or in connection with the use of motor vehicles on land, including third-party risks and carrier's liability.[82]

11. *Aircraft liability.*—Contracts of insurance against damage arising out of or in connection with the use of aircraft including third-party risks and carrier's liability.

12. *Liability for ships.*—Contracts of insurance against damage arising out of or in connection with the use of vessels on the sea or on inland water, including third-party risks and carrier's liability.

13. *General liability.*—Contracts of insurance against risks of the persons insured incurring liabilities to third parties, the risks in question not being risks to which classes 10, 11 or 12 relate.

14. *Credit.*—Contracts of insurance against risks of loss to the persons insured arising from the insolvency of debtors . . . or from the failure (otherwise than through insolvency) of debtors to pay their debts when due.

15. *Suretyship.*—Contracts of insurance against risks of loss to the persons insured arising from their having to perform contracts of guarantee entered into by them.

16. *Miscellaneous financial loss.*—Contracts of insurance against any of the following risks, *viz.*:

(*a*) loss to the persons insured attributable to interruptions of the carrying on of business carried on by them or to reduction of the scope of business so carried on;

(*b*) loss to the persons insured attributable to their incurring unforeseen expense;

(*c*) risks neither falling within (*a*) or (*b*) above, nor being of a kind such that carrying on of the business of effecting or carrying out contracts of insurance against them, constitutes the carrying on of insurance business of some other class.

17. *Legal expenses.*—Contracts of insurance against risks of loss to the persons insured attributable to their incurring legal expenses (including costs of litigation).

For the purposes of authorisation to transact insurance, these classes are set out into Groups, as follows (Sched. 2):

1. *Accident and health.*—Classes 1 and 2.

2. *Motor.*—Class 1 (to the extent that the relevant risks are risks of the person injured sustaining injury or dying as a result of travelling as a passenger) and Classes 3, 7 and 10.

3. *Marine and transport.*—Class 1 (to the said extent) and Classes 4, 6, 7 and 12.

4. *Aviation.*—Class 1 (to the said extent) and Classes 5, 7 and 11.

[82] A company which formed, owned and managed a proprietary club that, in return for a subscription, undertook to provide a chauffeur service for those members who by disqualification or injury were prevented from driving, was carrying on the business of insurance and accordingly was an insurance company; *Department of Trade and Industry* v. *St. Christopher Motorists' Ltd.* [1974] 1 W.L.R. 99.

5. *Fire and other damage to property*.—Classes 8 and 9.
6. *Liability*.—Classes 10, 11, 12 and 13.
7. *Credit and suretyship*.—Classes 14 and 15.
8. *General*.—All classes.

Transitional arrangements were provided so that companies transacting business under the 1974 Act could arrange for existing authorisations to be transferred to the new classifications and continue to transact the same kind of business as before.

One comment may be permitted. The detailed classification and grouping is a far cry from the rough-and-ready groupings of the Assurance Companies Act 1909 or of any subsequent legislation. But this arrangement, in one step, has brought together all classes of business now transacted, including "legal expenses." The logical development of this detailed classification should be the introduction of standard policies for each class of business transacted by insurance companies in the Community countries.

SOLVENCY OF INSURANCE COMPANIES. The solvency requirements for insurance companies are set out in Regulations made by virtue of the Insurance Companies Act 1974, s. 26A.[83] They are intended to give effect to an EEC Directive.[84]

Section 26A adopts the distinction between insurance companies whose head office is situate in the United Kingdom, those from other member States of the Community, and those from countries outside the Community; this distinction was indicated when the requirements for authorisation by the Department of Trade were discussed.[85] The margins of solvency prescribed by the regulations made under this section vary according to this classification. In particular, a distinction is drawn between the United Kingdom margin of solvency and the Community margin of solvency (s. 26A (5)). The former is computed by reference to the assets and liabilities of the business carried on by the company in the United Kingdom, and the latter by reference to those items in all member States, taken together. Insurance companies from countries outside the Community are often required to provide a deposit in the United Kingdom.

The Insurance Brokers (Registration) Act 1977 is implemented by a number of statutory instruments which are reproduced in Part I in Volume III of this work.

EXTENSION TO NORTHERN IRELAND. By the provisions of the Insurance Companies Act 1980, the application of the Insurance Companies Act 1974 is extended to Northern Ireland and some consequential amendments

---

[83] This section was added by the Insurance Companies Act 1981, s. 21. These solvency requirements were preceded by the Insurance Companies (Solvency—General Business Regulations (S.I. 1977 No. 1553)) which came into operation on July 31, 1978.

[84] 73/239/EEC.

[85] See above in the text.

were made to the 1974 Act. The Insurance Companies Act 1981 likewise extends to Northern Ireland (s. 38 (2)).

INTERVENTION BY SECRETARY OF STATE. In certain circumstances the Secretary of State may direct an insurance company that it shall cease to be authorised to effect contracts of insurance or contracts of a type specified in the direction (1981 Act, s. 11 (1)). The Department must give written notice to this effect, stating their reasons and the company is entitled to make representations to the Department within a month of receiving the order (s. 12). The order, and any subsequent withdrawal, must be gazetted (s. 12 (8)). The Department also has other far-reaching powers of intervention, particularly in the interest of present or future policy holders (1974 Act, s. 28).

The Acts also apply to companies carrying on reinsurance business in the specified classes in the United Kingdom[85a]; in fact, they state so.

89–38 SEPARATION AND APPLICATION OF FUNDS. A separate fund must be kept for either or both classes of long-term business (1974 Act, s. 23).

The assets representing the fund or funds in respect of the long-term business shall be applicable only for the purposes of that business (1974 Act, s. 24).

WINDING UP AND AMALGAMATION. The Insurance Companies Act 1974 contains important special provisions for the winding up of insurance companies.

Thus, an insurance company can be wound up on the petition of not less than 10 policy holders owning policies of an aggregate value of not less than £10,000, but such a petition can only be presented by leave of the court (s. 45).[86]

The Department of Trade may likewise petition for a winding up in certain cases (1974 Act, s. 46).[87]

Special provisions for the transfer of long-term business from one insurance company to another are contained in sections 42 and 43 of the 1974 Act, as amended by sections 25 to 27 of the 1981 Act.

89–39 INVESTIGATION. The Department of Trade has power to inspect the books and papers of an insurance company under Part III of the 1967 Act, and, in consequence of such an inspection, to exercise the same powers as they may exercise upon receiving the report of an inspector made under section

---

85a *Forsikringsaktieselskabet National (of Copenhagen)* v. *Att-Gen.* [1925] A.C. 639.

86 As to the method of proof in respect of policies, see *Re Law Car and General Insurance Co.* [1913] 2 Ch. 103.

87 Where the margin of solvency is likely to be restored within a short time, the court, in its discretion, may refuse to make a winding-up order: *Re Craven Insurance Co. Ltd.*, [1968] 1 W.L.R. 675.

168 of the Companies Act 1948.[88] The Department may further require a company to furnish it with information about specified matters at specified times or intervals (1974 Act, s. 36).

89–40 OVERSEA COMPANIES. An insurance company incorporated outside Great Britain has to register as an oversea company, if carrying on business within Great Britain, even if it has no established place of business within Great Britain, and some of the provisions of the Companies Act 1948 relating to oversea companies (1948 Act, ss. 406 *et seq.*)[89] apply to such an insurance company (s. 75 (2) of 1974 Act). This considerable extension of the provisions of Part X of the 1948 Act might make it convenient for oversea insurance companies to carry on business in Great Britain through a subsidiary company registered here.

89–41 ACCOUNTS. The accounts of insurance companies have to satisfy the requirements of Schedule 8A of the 1948 Act[90] but this schedule, as amended, admits exceptions from the general requirements as to accounts in the case of insurance companies (Schedule 8A, paragraph 24). Further accounting provisions are contained in the Insurance Companies Act 1974, ss. 13 to 22 and the Insurance Companies Act 1981, ss. 17 and 18. Insurance companies cannot be small or medium-sized companies for the purposes of obtaining the accounting exceptions provided by the Companies Act 1981.

Trust corporations

89–42 A corporation may in general be a trustee for any purpose[91] and may be a co-trustee with an individual or another corporation.[92] The growth of corporate trustees in recent years is due to the increasing complexity of the position of a trustee. It was in fact much encouraged in the 1925 property legislation by the creation of trust corporations to fulfil certain statutory functions under the various Acts.[93] A trust corporation for this purpose means the Public Trustee, the Treasury Solicitor, the Official Solicitor and a corporation either appointed by the court in any particular case to be a trustee or entitled by rules made under section 4 (3) of the Public Trustee Act 1906 to act as a custodian trustee. A custodian trustee must be distinguished from a managing trustee. On the appointment of a custodian trustee the trust property must be transferred to him as if he were the sole trustee and all the securities and documents of title relating thereto are to

---

[88] See para. 77–05, *ante*.
[89] See para. 88–05, *ante*. These provisions are: ss. 407 and 409–415 and s. 425.
[90] This was the original Schedule 8 of the 1948 Act (s. 1 (2) of the Companies Act 1981); see Sched. 2 of the 1981 Act, paras. 1 (*b*) and 8.
[91] *Att.-Gen.* v. *St. John's Hospital Bedford* (1865) 2 De G. J. & S. 621, 625; *Re Thompson's S.T.* [1905] 1 Ch. 229.
[92] The bar being removed by the Bodies Corporation (Joint Tenancy) Act 1899.
[93] *e.g.* Trustee Act 1925 s. 68 (18); Law of Property Act 1925, s. 205 (1) (xxviii); Settled Land Act 1925, s. 117 (1) (xxx); Administration of Estates Act 1925, s. 55 (1) (xxvii); Law of Property (Amendment) Act 1925, s. 3.

be in his sole custody. In general all the financial payments concerning the trust must go through him. The management of the trust property and the exercise of any power or discretion relating to the trust remain in the hands of the managing trustees. Any corporation may therefore be appointed as a managing trustee but only a trust corporation as a custodian trustee. In practice the growth of trust corporations has led to an increase in the management trustee function of such bodies.

89–43 Corporations eligible to be custodian trustees and therefore trust corporations are laid down in rule 2 of the Public Trustee (Custodian Trustee) Rules 1975.[94] Apart from (*a*) the Treasury Solicitor the following categories are allowed:

"(*b*) any corporation which:–
(i) is constituted under the law of the United Kingdom or of any part thereof, or under the law of any other member State of the European Economic Community or of any part thereof;
(ii) is empowered by its constitution to undertake trust business (which for the purpose of this rule means the business of acting as trustee under wills and settlements and as executor and administrator) in England and Wales;
(iii) has one or more places of business in the United Kingdom; and
(iv) is—
a company incorporated by special Act of Parliament or Royal Charter, or
a company registered (with or without limited liability) in the United Kingdom under the Companies Act 1948 or under the Companies Act (Northern Ireland) 1960 or in another member State of the European Economic Community and having a capital (in stock or shares) for the time being issued of not less than £250,000 (or its equivalent in the currency of the State where the company is registered), of which not less than £100,000 or its equivalent) has been paid up in cash, or a company which is registered without limited liability in the United Kingdom under the Companies Act 1948 or the Companies Act (Northern Ireland) 1960 or in another member State of the European Economic Community and of which one of the members is a company within any of the classes defined in this sub-paragraph;
(*c*) any corporation which is incorporated by special Act or Royal Charter or under the Charitable Trustees Incorporation Act 1872 which is empowered by its constitution to act as a trustee for any charitable purposes, but only in relation to trusts in which its constitution empowers it to act;
(*d*) any corporation which is constituted under the law of the United Kingdom or of any part thereof and having its place of buiness there, and which is either:–

---

[94] S.I. 1975 No. 1189. Amending the Public Trustee Rules 1912 (S.I. 1912 No. 348).

(i) established for the purpose of undertaking trust business for the benefit of Her Majesty's Navy, Army, Air Force or Civil Service of any unit, department, member or association of members thereof, and having among its directors or members any persons appointed or nominated by the Defence Council or any Department of State or any one or more of those Departments or

(ii) authorised by the Lord Chancellor to act in relation to any charitable, ecclesiastical or public trusts as a trust corporation, but only in connection with any such trust as is so authorised;

(*e*)(i) any Regional Health Authority, Area Health Authority or special health authority, but only in relation to any trust which the authority is authorised to accept or hold by virtue of section 21 of the National Health Service Reorganisation Act 1973;

(ii) any preserved Board as defined by section 15 (6) of that Act, but only in relation to any trust to which the Board is authorised to accept or hold by virtue of an order made under that section;

(*f*) the British Gas Corporation, but only in relation to a pension scheme or pension fund established or maintained by the Corporation by virtue of section 36 of the Gas Act 1972;

(*g*) The London Transport Executive, but only in relation to a pension or pension fund—

(i) which is established or administered by the Executive by virtue of section 6 of the Transport (London) Act 1969, or

(ii) in relation to which rights, liabilities and functions have been transferred to the Executive by an order under section 74 of the Transport Act 1962 as applied by section 18 of the Transport (London) Act 1969;

(*h*) any of the following, namely:

(i) the Greater London Council,

(ii) the corporation of any London borough (acting by the council),

(iii) the Council of the Isles of Scilly,

(iv) the Council of the Isles of Scilly, but only in relation to charitable or public trusts (and not trusts for an ecclesiastical charity or for a charity for the relief of poverty) for the benefit of the inhabitants of the area of the local authority concerned and its neighbourhood, or any part of that area."

Trust corporations as defined have a special role in the law of trusts. Reference should be made to the standard works on the subject for details.[95]

[95] See, *e.g. Underhill's Law of Trusts and Trustees* (12th ed.) ed. Oerton (1970); *Snell's Principles of Equity* (28th ed.) ed. Megarry and Baker (1982).

Part Ten

TAX LAW

Chapter 90

TAXATION OF COMPANIES*

Introduction[1]

90–01 As early as 1893 Kay L.J. had said in the Court of Appeal[2]:

> "In the first place, a corporation is a different thing from the individuals who compose it; and, secondly, the shares and debentures of a corporation are not the same thing as the property which that corporation owns."

Corporation tax was introduced by the Finance Act 1965 which thereby gave effect to this proposition for the purposes of taxation.[3]

The company or "group person" is liable to corporation tax.[4] It is not liable to income tax,[5] although if a close company has an excess of relevant income over distributions income tax at higher rates may be payable by the company if a participator defaults.[6] Conversely, individuals are not assessed to corporation tax. The Finance Act further emphasised the distinction which, for the purpose of limiting legal tax avoidance, has had to be made between the larger public corporations where ownership and control are divorced on the one hand and the family or closely controlled company on the other. Special and onerous taxing provisions apply to the latter, which are called *close companies*.[7]

The second major change in company taxation was made by the Finance Act 1972[8] which, from April, 1973, introduced an imputation system of corporation tax designed to avoid for the basic rate taxpayer the double taxation of distributed profits. It also adds a third general category of company, the small company, which pays corporation tax at reduced "small companies rate."[9]

This exposition must be limited to the main provisions and general scheme of company taxation and can only refer incidentally to tax planning schemes for reducing or avoiding liability. The present chapter deals with corporation tax as applied to all companies, together with an outline of some of the other taxes affecting companies.[10]

---

* This part of the book is written on the law as at February 1, 1982. The Finance Act 1982 will be incorporated in the first supplement.

[1] Unless otherwise stated all statutory references in this and the following chapters are to the Income and Corporation Taxes Act 1970.

[2] *John Foster & Sons* v. *I.R.C.* [1894] 1 Q.B. 516, 530.

[3] Only a general outline of the tax can be given here. Reference may be made to Bramwell, *Taxation of Companies* (2nd ed., 1979).

[4] s. 238 (1). "Company" in this Part of the Act is defined by s. 526 (5).

[5] s. 238 (2) and Finance Act 1971, Sched. 14, Pt. II.

[6] Finance Act 1972, s. 94 and Sched. 16.

[7] s. 282 (1).

[8] Finance Act 1972, Sched. 14, para. 1.

[9] Finance Act 1972, s. 95 (1).

[10] *i.e.* Value Added Tax and Development Land Tax.

The coverage of corporation tax

90–02 Corporation tax is chargeable on the income and a fraction of the chargeable gains,[11] collectively described as the "profits," of companies resident in the United Kingdom.[12] But "company" in this context means "any body corporate or unincorporated association."[13] The latter phrase is somewhat ambiguous but it has been held to include a club,[14] Conservative association[15] and a race-meeting.[16] It does not however include the Conservative Central Office,[16a] because, said the Court of Appeal, that lacked the necessary mutual duties and obligations necessary for an unincorporated association. Lawton L.J. described an unincorporated association in this context as: "two or more persons bound together for one or more common purposes, not being business purposes, by mutual undertakings, each having mutual duties and obligations, in an organisation which had rules which identify who controls it and its funds, upon what terms it can be joined and which can be joined or left at will."[16b] In this and the following chapter the word "company" is given this extended meaning.

Certain associations are specifically excluded from the corporation tax provisions of the Income and Corporation Taxes Act 1970.

This applies to partnerships,[17] but where a company is a member of a partnership it is assessed to corporation tax on its share of the partnership profits.[18] Similarly the Act exempts local authorities and local authority associations from corporation tax, and also from income tax and capital gains tax.[19] Trustees holding property in a fiduciary capacity are not an "unincorporated association" for the purposes of the Act and a company will not be chargeable to corporation tax on profits accruing to it in a fiduciary or representative capacity although, of course, any income received by a company from a trust fund will be included in its taxable profits.[20] Approved superannuation funds and pension annuity trust schemes are thus not subject to the tax and companies are entitled to deduct for corporation tax purposes contributions which they make under deeds of covenant for more than three years in favour of charities.[21]

90–03 Conversely, unit trusts and investment trusts other than certain authorised unit trusts which invest only in governmental and allied securities,[22]

---

[11] *i.e.* those gains which would otherwise be chargeable to capital gains tax.
[12] s.238 (1) and (2) (*a*).
[13] s.526 (5).
[14] *Carlisle and Silloth Golf Club* v. *Smith* [1913] 3 K.B. 75.
[15] *Curtis* v. *Old Monkland Conservative Association* [1906] A.C. 86.
[16] *Smith* v. *York Race Committee* [1934] 1 K.B. 517.
[16a] *Conservative and Unionist Central Office* v. *Burrell.* [1982] S.T.C. 317 (C.A.).
[16b] *Ibid.*
[17] s. 526 (5).
[18] s. 155.
[19] s. 353.
[20] s. 243 (2).
[21] s. 248 (5) (*b*), (8) and (9).
[22] Finance Act 1980, s. 60.

are brought within the charge to corporation tax but subject to certain concessions.[23] In particular such authorised trusts do not pay corporation tax on their capital gains.[24] Life assurance companies, registered industrial and provident societies, approved housing associations, building societies and the nationalised industries are subject to special provisions, and pay corporation tax at the rate of 40 per cent.[25]

The coverage of corporation tax in the case of non-resident companies is limited to those companies which carry on a trade in the United Kingdom through a branch or agency here[26]; and liability is limited, broadly speaking, to income and capital gains attributable to the branch or agency.[27] This accords with the general axiom that residence, and not domicile, is the crucial factor in determining liability to tax.

The charge to corporation tax

90–04 A rate of corporation tax, and the small companies rate, are fixed for each financial year, which runs from April 1 to the following March 31,[28] normally in the Budget statement at the end of the year just passed. A particular financial year means the year beginning on April 1. A company pays corporation tax at a single rate on all its profits, whether distributed or undistributed. The present rates as from April 1, 1980 are 52 per cent.[29] and 40 per cent.[30] respectively. Assessments on companies in respect of the main charge to corporation tax are made on the profits arising in the company's "accounting period"[31]; and where the rates of corporation tax change in successive financial years the profits are apportioned between them on a time basis.[32] If necessary profits arising may be divided into various accounting periods for this purpose.[33] An accounting period cannot exceed 12 months,[34] and special provisions apply where a company changes its accounting period. The first accounting period for corporation tax purposes of a new company begins when it acquires a source of profits which are chargeable to corporation tax[35] The main charge to corporation tax is payable nine months after the end of the accounting period for which it is assessed or, if it is later, within one month from the making of the

---

[23] Pt. XII, Chap. VI, ss. 354–359 as amended.
[24] Finance Act 1980, s. 81.
[25] Finance Act 1972, s. 96 and Finance Act 1974 s. 10 (3).
[26] ss. 238 (2) and 246 (2).
[27] s. 246 (1) and (2).
[28] s. 527 (1).
[29] Finance Act 1981, s. 20.
[30] *Ibid.* s. 22 (1).
[31] s. 243 (3).
[32] s. 527 (4).
[33] s. 129. The Revenue are not however bound by the company's accounts as to whether such an apportionment is necessary: *Marshall Hus & Partners Ltd.* v. *Bolton* [1981] S.T.C. 18.
[34] s. 247 (3).
[35] s. 247 (2) (*a*).

assessment.[36] But in the case of most trading companies which were operating before 1965 the old income tax interval is preserved and the tax is payable on January 1.

The Revenue has power to issue notices requiring a company to make books, documents and accounts available for inspection once it has been required to make a return of income and chargeable gains for corporation tax purposes and has either failed to do so or delivered an unsatisfactory return.[37] There is no time limit to the exercise of this power but the notices must relate to documents covering periods when returns had been required of the company.[38]

Advance corporation tax and the shareholder's tax credit

90–05 "Advance corporation tax"[39] and the shareholder's "tax credit"[40] are the link between the company's corporation tax and the shareholder's own income tax liability. Advance corporation tax is necessary to safeguard the revenue which might otherwise be giving a credit for tax which it would not receive, for instance, because the paying company is not liable to the full rate of United Kingdom corporation tax.

Advance corporation tax liability arises when a company resident in the United Kingdom pays a dividend or other qualifying distribution.[41] The rate of advance corporation tax is expressed as a fraction of the amount of the distributions. It is fixed in advance by the Budget statement at the beginning of the financial year and the relevant rate is that in force for the financial year in which the distribution is made. As from April 6, 1981, the rate of advance corporation tax is 3/7ths of the amount of the dividend or distribution.[42] Liability to advance corporation tax arises solely from the distribution. It is not dependent on the company's final liability to corporation tax and is not affected by any reliefs or outgoings which may reduce the final payment. A company may set off the amount of any advance corporation tax paid in respect of qualifying distributions made by it in an accounting period against the main charge to corporation tax assessed on the profits of the accounting period so as to reduce the amount of tax then payable.[43] But advance corporation tax is set off against corporation tax on income only and not against tax on chargeable gains.

[THE NEXT PARAGRAPH IS 90–07]

90–07 The United Kingdom shareholder on being paid a dividend receives a tax credit for the amount of advance corporation tax which is attributable

---

[36] s. 243 (4).
[37] Taxes Management Act 1970, s. 20.
[38] *B. & S. Displays Ltd.* v. *I.R.C.* [1978] S.T.C. 331.
[39] Finance Act 1972, s. 84 (1).
[40] *Ibid.* s. 86 (1).
[41] *Ibid.* s. 84 (4).
[42] *Ibid.* s. 84 (2); Finance Act 1981, s. 21.
[43] Finance Act 1972, s. 85 (1).

to his dividend.[44] Thus, while companies are liable to corporation tax and individuals to income tax, the tax credit serves to connect the two systems. The qualifying distribution plus the relevant advance corporation tax is described as a "franked payment."[45]

90–08 An example may clarify these provisions.

A Ltd. makes up its accounts annually to September 30 and for its accounting period October 1, 1990, to September 30, 1990, has a corporation tax profit of £60,000 and decides to pay a dividend of £7,000.

Assuming a corporation tax rate of 52 per cent, and an advance corporation tax rate of 3/7ths its tax liability is as follows:

Advance corporation tax £7,000 @ 3/7ths (before declaring a dividend the company must consider its advance corporation tax liability)		£3,000
Total corporation tax liability £60,000 @ 52 per cent.	= £31,200	
Less advance corporation tax paid	3,000	
Final payment of corporation tax at the due date		£28,200
Total corporation tax paid		£31,200

If for the financial year 1991 the rate of corporation tax is increased from 52 per cent. to 60 per cent. the total taxable profits of A Ltd. for this accounting period would be taxed as to one-half (£30,000) at 52 per cent. and as to the other (£30,000) at 60 per cent.

90–09 B is a shareholder in A Ltd. and receives a dividend of £70. This dividend carries a tax credit of £30 (£70 at 3/7). The dividend plus the credit, that is the franked payment, must be included in B's income for tax purposes.[46] Thus at basic rate his liability is 30 per cent. of £100 or £30, but this is exactly offset by his tax credit of £30. Thus the basic rate taxpayer does not pay any further tax on his dividends. A shareholder who is not liable to tax can claim payment of the tax credit. Conversely any liability to the higher rates of tax or to the investment income surcharge is on the franked payment.

For the purpose of collecting advance corporation tax an annual accounting period is divided into four calendar quarters, called "return periods" running from the commencement of the company's accounting period.[47] A company has to make returns within 14 days of the end of a "return period" showing (a) the franked payments made, (b) the franked investment income received, and (c) the amount of advance corporation tax payable in that period.[48] The tax is payable, without any assessment,

---

[44] Finance Act 1972, s. 86 (1).
[45] *Ibid.* s. 84 (3).
[46] *Ibid.* ss. 84 (3) and 86 (4).
[47] *Ibid.* Sched. 14, para. 1.
[48] *Ibid.* Sched. 14, para. 2 (1).

within the said 14 days. Normally a company need not make a return for any return period in which it has made no franked payments.[49]

Other provisions relating to advance corporation tax are designed to protect the Revenue.

90–10 The total corporation tax on a company's profits in an accounting period must be at the full, normal or where appropriate "small companies," rate. To achieve this where a company's distributions plus advance corporation tax in an accounting period exceed its taxable profits the amount of advance corporation tax which can be set off in the accounting period is limited to an amount which, with the distribution to which it relates absorbs the whole of the company's taxable income of the accounting period.[50] This may happen, for instance, on account of capital allowances which for accountancy purposes reduce taxable profits but do not affect the funds available for distribution or because a dividend is paid out of previous profits. Thus the set off of advance corporation tax may never reduce the final liability below 17 per cent., or 7 per cent. in the case of small companies. For the purpose of arriving at this limit, reliefs such as charges, losses and management expenses which take effect against total profits are set first against income and then against chargeable gains.[51] If it were not for this provision a company might, in a particular accounting period, extinguish through set off its final liability altogether, which would mean that it had only paid corporation tax at a rate of 35 per cent. and not 52 per cent. in that accounting period. For example:

90–11 In its following accounting period October 1, 1991, to September 30, 1992, tax rates staying the same, A Ltd. pays the same dividend of £7,000 but its profits have fallen to £5,000.

In the second accounting period its tax liability is computed as follows:

Advance corporation tax £7,000 @ 3/7		£3,000
Total corporation tax liability £5,000 @ 40 per cent. small companies rate	£2,000	
The maximum dividend payable out of its total profits is £3,500 which, together with advance corporation tax thereon (£3,500 @ 3/7) or £1,500 = £5,000.		
The set off of advance corporation tax against final liability is limited to that payable on such maximum dividend: *i.e.*	£1,500	
Final payment of corporation tax at the due date		£ 500
Total corporation tax paid		£3,500

[49] *Ibid.* Sched. 14, para. 3.
[50] *Ibid.* s. 85 (2).
[51] *Ibid.* s. 85 (6).

The surplus advance corporation tax paid, that is, advance corporation tax which because of this restriction cannot be set against the final payment of corporation tax for the accounting period can, subject to the limitation, be carried back for the last two accounting periods[52] (so that profits of the more recent accounting period are used before the more remote one) or carried forward, subject to the limitation, to later accounting periods.[53]

In the example there is a surplus in the second period of £1,500 which can be carried back to the first period where undistributed profits are more than sufficient to absorb it. Thus a repayment of £1,500 can be claimed.

90–12 Normally a company is acting in the best interests of its shareholders by distributing profits in the accounting period in which they arise. If it pays dividends which are larger than its profits will support it is usually better to carry back (if there are then undistributed profits) rather than, or before, carrying forward. If, however, there is a major change in the nature or conduct of the trade or business or its activities have become small or negligible and a change in the ownership of the company takes place, surplus advance corporation tax may not be carried forward to set against corporation tax on income attributable to any period after the change of ownership.[54] The date of payment of a distribution is usually in the year in which it appears in the relevant accounts even though it may actually be paid at a later time.[55]

As the income tax year runs from April 6 to April 5, where a company makes a distribution before April 6 and the rate of advance corporation tax changes, the advance corporation tax payable for a distribution made in the period April 1 to April 5 is calculated at the old rate.[56] If the company's accounting period extends beyond April 5 and another distribution is then made or franked investment income received after that date for these purposes, the remainder of the accounting period as from April 5 is deemed to be a new period.

Qualified distributions comprise dividends and payments akin to dividends, including dividends paid out of the surplus arising on the realisation of capital assets. Thus any provision out of the assets of the company whether in cash or not which is made to a person in respect of shares in the company, is classed as a distribution, except to the extent that it is a repayment of share capital or is made for new consideration, or comes within the definition of a non-qualifying distribution.[57]

Preference shares issued before April 1973 carrying a dividend expressed as a fixed percentage have been assimilated into the new system. The fixed percentage is to be divided into a net receipt and a tax credit based on the rate of advance corporation tax for 1973–74. The net receipt will never vary

---

[52] *Ibid.* s. 85 (3).
[53] *Ibid.* s. 85 (4).
[54] *Ibid.* s. 101.
[55] See *John Peterson (Motors) Ltd.* v. *I.R.C.* [1978] S.T.C. 59.
[56] *Ibid.* s. 103 (5) as amended by Finance Act 1973, s. 34 and Sched. 14.
[57] *Ibid.* s. 84 (4).

but the tax credit will increase or decrease with the change in rates. Thus, the gross dividend may be more, less or the same as the percentage fixed by the company's articles.[58]

90–13 Non-qualifying distributions mean issues of bonus redeemable share capital and bonus securities issued by the company making the distribution; or by another company and received directly or indirectly by the company making the distribution. Advance corporation tax is not payable in respect of a non-qualifying distribution and the recipient does not get a tax credit, but the recipient of such a bonus issue is not liable to income tax at the basic rate thereon.[59] He is, however, liable to tax at the higher rates.[60] When the bonus share capital is redeemed the distribution is a qualifying distribution; and if the recipient of the redemption moneys is the same person to whom the share capital was originally issued, any higher rate tax then paid is credited against liability to such tax in respect of the redemption moneys, thus avoiding double taxation.[61]

Income tax is chargeable in respect of all dividends and other distributions of a company resident in the United Kingdom under Schedule F.[62]

Income tax principles apply

90–14 Corporation tax is charged upon taxable receipts less allowable deductions and expenses; and although interrelated, the credit and debit side of the account will be considered separately. The general plan is that both income and expenditure are determined according to income tax principles. So, for example, payments made to trustees of an employee share scheme were held to be loans and not therefore deductible from profits.[63] All questions as to the amounts which are to be taken into account as income, relating to the computation of income, or as to the time when any such amount is to be treated as arising, are to be decided in accordance with income tax law and practice as if companies' accounting periods were years of assessment.[64] Thus for purposes of corporation tax, assessments are made under the rules applicable to the income tax Schedules and Cases. The amounts so computed for all sources of income, together with any tax liability in respect of capital gains, are aggregated to arrive at the total profits[65] for the relevant accounting period, and are to be deemed to arise in this period.[66]

Accounts prepared for the purpose of the Companies Acts will not always correspond with income tax principles and adjustments may be made. In *Willingale* v. *International Commercial Bank Ltd.*,[67] for example,

[58] Finance Act 1972, Sched. 23, para. 18 (1), Finance Act 1976, s. 46.
[59] *Ibid.* s. 87 (5) (*a*).
[60] *Ibid.* s. 87 (5) (*b*).
[61] *Ibid.* Sched. 22, paras. (5) and (6).
[62] *Ibid.* s. 87 (2) 1.
[63] *Rutter* v. *Sharpe & Co. Ltd.* [1979] 1 W.L.R. 1429.
[64] s. 250 (1). See *e.g. Simmons* v. *I.R.C.* [1980] S.T.C. 350 (H.L.).
[65] ss. 250 (3) and 265 (1).
[66] s. 250 (6).
[67] [1978] 1 All E.R. 754 (H.L.).

discounts were held not to accrue as taxable receipts of a bank until maturity of the bill even though the accounts showed them as accruing during the life of the bill.

Investment income

90–15 Companies have their own share portfolios; and where the recipient of a qualifying distribution is a company resident in the United Kingdom, the amount of the distribution plus the relevant tax credit is not chargeable again to corporation tax and is called "franked investment income"[68] in the hands of the investing company. Where the receiving company is wholly exempt from corporation tax or is only not exempt in respect of trading income, or the distribution is one in relation to which express exemption is given, it may claim payment of the tax credit.[69] This applies to charitable companies and certain provident societies. The vast majority of companies are only entitled to set off their tax credits in two circumstances.

90–16 The first, and usual one, is where the company in effect passes on the credit to its own shareholders. The tax credit can be set off against advance corporation tax liability.[70] Where the franked investment income received in any accounting period is equal to or exceeds the franked payments then made no advance corporation tax is payable. The excess is called a "surplus of franked investment income".[71] It can be carried forward and treated as franked investment income received in the following accounting periods, without limit, for the purpose of calculating the advance corporation tax then payable, but franked payments in earlier periods must first be fully used.[72] The franked investment income is described as being used to frank distributions. Where the franked payments made in any accounting period exceed the franked investment income received (or treated as received) in that period advance corporation tax is payable on an amount which, when the advance corporation tax payable thereon is added to it, is equal to that excess.[73] For example:

90–17 If B Ltd. in an accounting period pays dividends of £14,000 it will make a franked payment of £20,000
and if it receives dividends of £7,000 its franked investment income will be £10,000
advance corporation tax is payable on £7,000 since £7,000 plus 3/7ths of £7,000 = £10,000

The amount payable is £3,000
More simply:
advance corporation tax is payable on £14,000–7,000 = £7,000, *i.e.*, it will be £3,000.

---

[68] Finance Act 1972, s. 88.
[69] *Ibid.* s. 86 (3).
[70] *Ibid.* s. 89 (1) and (2).
[71] *Ibid.* s. 89 (6).
[72] *Ibid.* s. 89 (3).
[73] *Ibid.* s. 89 (2).

90–18 Secondly, there is a residual right to set off certain outgoings against the tax credit. This is considered under the heading "trading losses."

90–19 Whereas these outgoings, but not dividends, are deductible from profits chargeable to corporation tax, it will usually be prudent for a company to try to tide itself over its temporary difficulties by seeking credit in the hope of later being able to absorb its tax credits, which can be carried forward indefinitely, in future profits out of which dividends will be paid. The idea underlying these provisions is that the tax scheme gives an inducement to companies to retain or distribute profits but not to build up share portfolios. Thus they can use their tax credit on their investment income if they pass it on in a form in which their own shareholders will be entitled to tax credits and liable, where appropriate, to income tax at the higher rates.

90–20 Except as aforesaid or as otherwise provided by the Corporation Tax Acts, corporation tax is not chargeable on dividends and other distributions of a company resident in the United Kingdom, nor are any such dividends or distributions taken into account in computing income for corporation tax.[74]

Income from capital gains

90–21 Where a company makes capital gains on the sale of capital assets, such gains are aggregated with the company's other taxable profits for the accounting period in which the gain was realised. The corporation tax charged on capital gains is lower than on income. This is effected by exempting a fraction of the net gains from corporation tax and charging the full corporation tax rate on the remaining fraction. With a fraction of 15/26 (11/26 is exempt from tax[75]) and a corporation tax rate of 52 per cent. the effective rate of tax on chargeable gains is 30 per cent., the same as the full rate applicable to individuals. This tax rate may not be further reduced by any set off of advance corporation tax.

90–22 The amount to be included in respect of chargeable gains in a company's total profits for any accounting period is the total amount of such gains after deducting any allowable losses accruing to the company in the accounting period, together with any allowable losses carried forward from any previous period while the company has been within the charge to corporation tax. Again all questions as to the computing of chargeable gains or allowable losses are governed by the provisions relating to capital gains tax as if accounting periods were years of assessment.[76]

Thus the question of whether there has been a disposal of a chargeable

---

[74] s. 239.
[75] Finance Act 1974, s. 10 (1) (*a*).
[76] s. 265 (2).

asset within section 19 of the Capital Gains Tax Act 1979 depends upon construction of the Capital Gains Tax legislation.[77] The allowable expenditure provisions also apply.[78] In certain circumstances an allowable loss will be made if a company makes a loan to a resident trader, which subsequently becomes irrecoverable. This will also apply if the loan is made to a non-trading company and forwarded to a trading company within the group. It does not apply if the lender and borrower are members of the same group or if the loan is a deductible expense for corporation tax purposes.[79]

Where a company sold the shares of a subsidiary company and also agreed to waive the debt owed to it by that subsidiary the consideration received for the sale of the shares was held to be rateably divisible between the two disposals—the sale of the shares and waiver of the debt. This cannot apply however if the consideration is expressly apportioned in the contract between the two disposals.[80] Waiver of a debt (an asset) will only give rise to an allowable loss or chargeable gain as between the original lender and debtor if it is a "debt on a security."[81] This has no defined meaning and includes more than received debts although the House of Lords has found it impossible to define the concept. It does however include securities which are similar to loan stock.[82]

The major item of expenditure allowed is the acquisition cost of the asset (C.G.T.A. 1979 s. 32 (1)). Where a company purchased shares in another company by means of an issue of its own shares to the vendor it was allowed to deduct the contract value given to its own shares. The consideration provided by the company was the value placed on them in the agreement to allot the shares credited as fully paid, and, in the absence of mala fides, that value should be allowed.[83]

Thus although their capital gains are aggregated with other income, companies are only allowed to set off capital gains losses against capital gains and may not set them off against profits or other income. There is, however, an important provision which relates to companies (and persons) which (or who) are engaged in trade. If business assets which are used exclusively for the purposes of the trade are sold and the proceeds of sale are reinvested in new assets of the same kind, any gain arising on the sale is treated as reducing the price paid for the new assets. In these circumstances no tax will be payable unless and until the new assets are sold.[84]

---

[77] See, *e.g. O'Brien* v. *Benson's Hosiery (Holdings)* [1979] 3 All E.R. 652 (H.L.) (payment by a director to obtain the release of his service contract); *Rank Xerox Ltd.* v. *Lane* [1979] 3 All E.R. 527 (H.L.) (disposal of royalty rights by means of annual payments).

[78] *Emmerson* v. *Computer Time International Ltd.* [1977] 2 All E.R. 545.

[79] C.G.T.A. 1979, s. 136.

[80] *Aberdeen Construction Group Ltd.* v. *I.R.C.* [1978] A.C. 885 (H.L.); *cf. E. V. Booth (Holdings) Ltd.* v. *Buckwell* [1980] S.T.C. 578.

[81] C.G.T.A. 1979, s. 134.

[82] *W. T. Ramsay Ltd.* v. *I.R.C.* [1981] S.T.C. 174 (H.L.).

[83] *Stanton* v. *Drayton Commercial Investment Ltd.* [1982] S.T.C. 585 (H.L.).

[84] C.G.T.A. 1979 s. 115.

90–23

In 1976 such an asset is bought for	£10,000	
in 1986 it is sold for	£12,000	
and replaced by a new asset of the same kind costing		£15,000
No capital gains tax liability arises at this stage.		
The gain of £2,000 reduces the cost of the new asset		£2,000
		£13,000
If later the new asset is sold for	£20,000	
the chargeable gain is £20,000–£13,000=£7,000.		

There are provisions for apportionment where part only of the proceeds of sale are reinvested in this way.[85] This concession relates to land, factory and other buildings of a permanent or semi-permanent nature, fixed plant and machinery, ships, aircraft and goodwill.[86] Its purpose is to facilitate industrial and commercial development and the transfer of businesses out of congested areas. Where the new asset is a "depreciating asset" the right to carry forward the gain on the sale of the asset replaced is restricted. These are known as the "roll-over" provisions.[87]

90–24 The tax treatment of capital gains does contain an element of double taxation. If, as will usually be the case, and to the extent that a capital gain made by a company is reflected in the value of its shares, it will be taxed again in so far as it augments the gain made by its shareholders on the disposal of their assets.

Interest and annual charges

90–25 A company may continue to *receive* certain payments under deduction of income tax, such as interest from other companies or on Government securities. The income represented by such payments is subject to corporation tax in the receiving company's hands, with credit for the income tax suffered by deduction.[88] Alternatively, a company may set the income tax borne on such payments against its own liability to account for income tax on any payments which it itself makes by way of interest annuities or annual charges[89]; but a company cannot off-set such income tax against advance corporation tax nor can it use the tax credit attaching to franked investment income to satisfy any income tax it is liable to account for.

For the purpose of ascertaining trading profits, the valuation of unsold stock must not be carried out on the basis of replacement values; it should be carried out on the basis of cost or market value, whichever is the lower.[90] Work in progress on long term contracts may be valued either on

[85] *Ibid.* s. 116.
[86] *Ibid.* s. 118.
[87] *Temperley (Inspector of Taxes)* v. *Visibel Ltd.* [1974] S.T.C. 64.
[88] s. 240 (5).
[89] Finance Act 1972, Sched. 20, para. 5 (1).
[90] *B.S.C. Footwear Ltd.* v. *Ridgway* [1972] A.C. 544 (H.L.).

an on-cost basis (*i.e.* brought into account only when realised) or an accrued profit basis (*i.e.* bringing into account anticipated profits). If a company elects to change the basis used, it is bound by the consequences, as the same basis must be used at the beginning and end of the account.[91]

Stock relief

To offset the effect of inflation artificially increasing the value of stock and thereby profits, relief is available whenever the closing figure of one accounting period is higher than the opening figure for that period. As originally introduced in 1976 this relief was the difference between the two figures less 15 per cent. of the company's profits without the relief.[92] But this relief also provided for a 'clawback' if the book value of stocks fell in a year, an unfortunate prospect for companies de-stocking in times of recession. Accordingly a new form of relief was introduced by section 35 of and Schedule 9 to the Finance Act 1981. In essence for accounting periods ending on or after 14/11/80 the relief will be calculated on the basis of stocks and work in progress at the opening of an account and will be given by reference to percentage movements in a single "all stocks" index for the period of account. This figure will be published monthly by the Inland Revenue. Unlike the earlier relief there is no profit restriction but the first £2,000 of stock will not be eligible for relief. The only "clawback" will be where a business ceases or the scale of its operations becomes small in comparison with its recent past.

Allowable deductions

90–26 The outgoings which are admissible deductions for the purposes of corporation tax are contained in various sections of the Income and Corporation Taxes Act 1970 as amended, particularly by the Finance Act 1972. Only a brief outline of the main provisions can be attempted.

Charges on income

90–27 Yearly interest, annuities and other annual payments, chargeable to tax under Case III of Schedule D, and interest on a bank overdraft or advance from a person bona fide carrying on a business as a member of a stock exchange or discount house in the United Kingdom, provided in all cases that the payment is made for "a valuable and sufficient consideration" and the other requirements of section 248 are satisfied, can be set against the total profits of the payer.[93] If the payment is one of interest no deduction is allowed if the sole or main benefit accruing for any scheme or arrangement is the deduction itself.[94] The relief for charges on income is given in general as the last of all reliefs other than group relief; and is given against the total

---

[91] *Pearce* v. *Woodall Duckham Ltd.* [1978] 2 All E.R. 793 (C.A.).
[92] Finance Act 1976, s. 37 and Sched. 5; Finance Act 1980 s. 40 and Sched. 7.
[93] Finance Act 1972, s. 75 (1). Interest is so allowable even if it is charged to capital and not income: Finance Act 1981, s. 38.
[94] Finance Act 1976, s. 38.

profits of the period in which the charges are paid. Where in an accounting period the charges on income paid by a company exceed the amount of the profits against which they are deductible and include payments made wholly and exclusively for the purposes of the company's trade, such excess which satisfies the latter requirement[95] can be taken into account in computing a loss to be carried forward against future trading income of the company,[96] or in computing a terminal loss.[97] It has been pointed out that it is cheaper for a company to raise capital by borrowing than by issuing share capital. In the former case, but not the latter payments made in respect of the capital will be corporation tax-free even if the interest is charged to capital.[98] It may be doubted whether it is desirable to encourage companies to minimise their own assets and to trade on borrowed capital. Statutory redundancy payments are exempt from corporation tax and, in the hands of the employee, from income tax under Schedule E.[99] Payments made by way of addition to a redundancy payment will also be deductible from trading profits even if the company has ceased to trade.[1]

Capital allowances

90–28 "Investment by industry in new equipment is one of the keys to industrial expansion" stated the White Paper entitled *Investment Incentives*.[2] This objective can be encouraged by tax allowances and by cash grants. The former have the disadvantage, particularly for a new company, that it is in the early days before the enterprise makes gains that its need for assistance is the greater. Cash grants are available when most needed, but are not dependent upon profitability which is some measure, however imperfect, of efficiency. Capital allowances operating through tax relief is the method currently chosen, but cash grants are used to entice industry into development areas.

Capital allowances are computed with reference to a company's accounting periods by reference to events occurring therein.[3] The right to such an allowance or the liability to a balancing charge and the rate or amount thereof are determined by the law in force for the year of assessment (that is, the income tax year) in which the accounting period ends.[4] A balancing charge arises on the sale price of a capital asset in respect of which a 100 per cent. first year allowance has been given, or where the asset is sold for more than its value as written down by an initial allowance and writing-down allowances. If it is sold for less the deficit, or in the case of plant and

---

95 s. 177 (8).
96 s. 177 (1).
97 s. 174 (1).
98 C. N. Beattie, *Elements of the Law of Income and Capital Gains Taxation* (7th ed.), p. 233. See Finance Act 1981, s. 38.
99 s. 412.
1 Finance Act 1980, s. 41.
2 Finance Act 1972, Sched. 14, para. 1.
3 Capital Allowances Act 1968, s. 73 (2).
4 *Ibid.* s. 72: Finance Act 1971, s. 50 (1).

machinery 25 per cent. of the deficit, is dealt with as a loss and a balancing allowance given.[5]

First-year and writing-down allowances

90–29 In the case of trading companies the main capital allowances for capital expenditure for the purposes of a trade are given for corporation tax purposes as deductions in computing the trade income.[6] Corresponding balancing charges are treated as trade receipts. If the amount to be allowed exceeds the trade income the deficiency will be a trading loss. A 100 per cent. first-year allowance (free depreciation) applies as from March 22, 1972,[7] in respect of both new and second-hand plant and machinery,[8] other than passenger cars.[9]

There are many cases on the definition of plant for this purpose. A structure may fall within the definition of plant if it is something by means of which the business activities of the company are carried, but it will not do so if it is merely the place within which they are carried on. This functional test has been applied in several cases.[10] In any event the expenditure must relate to the acquisition of the plant or machinery and not to interest paid on the finance for such acquisition.[11]

To the extent that a trading loss for an accounting period is attributable to such a 100 per cent. first-year allowance a company may set off the loss against its total profits in the three years preceding the commencement of the accounting period in which the loss is incurred instead of the usual twelve-month period.[12] Alternatively a company can forgo a part of this total allowance and claim writing-down allowances on the unclaimed balance.[13] The writing-down allowance on plant and machinery is 25 per cent.[14]; and where a number of items qualify for it the writing-down allowances are "pooled" and when pooled items are sold a balancing adjustment is made.[15]

The writing-down allowance for a car costing over £8,000 cannot exceed £2,000 in any year and such cars do not go into the taxpayer's pool of allowances.[16] Special provisions apply to cars leased by companies which ensure that only genuinely commercially leased cars are entitled to more than the figures given above.[17]

Initial cost less allowances already given produce the "qualifying

---

[5] Capital Allowances Act 1968, s. 33.
[6] *Ibid.* ss. 46 (1) and 47 (1).
[7] Finance Act 1972, s. 67 (2) (*a*).
[8] Finance Act 1971, s. 41 (1) (*a*).
[9] *Ibid.* s. 43.
[10] *e.g. Benson* v. *Yard Arm Club Ltd.* [1979] 1 W.L.R. 347; *Hampton* v. *Fortes Autogrill Ltd.* [1980] S.T.C. 80; *I.R.C. Scottish & Newcastle Breweries Ltd.* [1981] S.T.C. 50.
[11] *Ben-Odeco* v. *Poulson* [1978] 1 W.L.R. 1093.
[12] s. 177 (3A).
[13] Finance Act 1971, s. 41 (3).
[14] *Ibid.* s. 44 (2) (*a*) (i).
[15] *Ibid.* s. 44; as amended by Finance Act 1976, ss. 39 and 40.
[16] *Ibid.* Sched. 8, paras. 9–12, as amended.
[17] Finance (No. 2) Act 1979, s. 14.

expenditure,"[18] usually referred to as the written-down value of the plant.

The Finance Act 1980 introduced complex provisions relating to first-year allowances for leased assets.[19] There is no allowance where expenditure is incurred on the provision of machinery or plant for leasing unless it appears that it will be used only for certain specified purposes within the first four years from acquisition. The leasor has to certify the validity of any claims to an allowance.

Initial and other allowances

90–30 The construction of an industrial building or structure occupied for the purposes of a trade qualifies, if the expenditure was incurred on or after November 12, 1974, for an initial allowance of 75 per cent.[20] and writing-down allowances of 4 per cent.[21] of the original cost until the residue of expenditure has been reduced by the initial and writing-down allowances to nil. If the building is sold for less than its written-down value the vendor receives a balancing allowance.[22] If the proceeds of sale are the higher figure a balancing charge is made on the difference,[23] but the amount of a balancing charge on any person cannot exceed the amount of the allowances previously made to him in respect of the building. The new residue (that is the sale price as thus decreased or increased by the balancing adjustment) in the hands of the purchaser entitles him to writing-down allowances at such a rate as will, if continuously applied, result in the new residue being written off by the end of the twenty-fifth year after the building was first used.[24] This computation is repeated on subsequent sales until the twenty-five-year period has expired. If the buildings are demolished the balancing allowance is equal to the residue of expenditure.[25]

The same provisions apply if instead of a sale of the building the owner grants a lease of 50 years or more and the lessor and lessee jointly elect to treat the lease as a sale for this purpose and notify the Inspector within two years of the lease taking effect. Any premium paid by the lessee is to be treated as the purchase price. There can be no such election if obtaining a balancing allowance is the "sole or main benefit which may be expected to accrue" from the grant of the lease.[26]

A similar relief is available in relation to qualifying hotels. These are hotels open for at least four months of the summer, with at least 10 bedrooms, and provide dinner, bed and breakfast, and fulfil other conditions.[27] An initial allowance of 20 per cent. is available with a writing-

---

[18] *Ibid.* s. 44 (4).
[19] Finance Act 1980 ss. 64–68.
[20] Capital Allowance Act 1968, s. 1 (2).
[21] Finance Act 1972, s. 67 (2) (*d*). For the definition of an 'industrial building' see Capital Allowances Act 1968, s. 7 (1) (*e*) and *Buckingham* v. *Securities Properties Ltd.* [1980] S.T.C. 166; *Vibroplant Ltd.* v. *Holland* [1982] S.T.C. 164 (C.A.).
[22] Capital Allowances Act 1968, s. 4 (9).
[23] *Ibid.* s. 4 (10).
[24] *Ibid.* s. 2 (3).
[25] *Ibid.* s. 4 (11).
[26] Finance Act 1978, s. 37.
[27] *Ibid.* s. 38.

down allowance of 4 per cent. per annum, and the system of balancing charges and allowances applies as above, even after the building has ceased to be a qualifying hotel, *e.g.* on a sale. But if two years have elapsed after such cessation, and no event giving rise to a balancing charge or allowance has occurred, there is a deemed sale for such purposes at open market value, and a balancing charge or allowance computed accordingly.[28]

90–31 The first-year allowance and the initial allowance differ in two important respects. First the initial allowance and the writing-down allowance are both concurrently available in the accounting period in which the expenditure was incurred; but this does not apply to the first-year allowance. Secondly the writing-down allowance is reduced by the first-year, but not by the initial, allowance.[29]

90–32 An allowance is available to the owner or tenant of agricultural or forestry land in respect of capital expenditure on agricultural or forestry buildings or works.[30]

An initial allowance of 20 per cent. of the qualifying expenditure is available together with a writing-down allowance of 10 per cent. for eight years, but a company may, within two years, either disclaim the initial allowance and take a writing-down allowance of 10 per cent. for 10 years, or have it reduced below 20 per cent. and take the writing-down allowance of 10 per cent. per annum for a correspondingly longer period.[31] There is no provision for a balancing allowance or balancing charge. The allowance is made by way of discharge or repayment of tax and is available primarily against agricultural and forestry income.[32]

90–33 Similarly the other capital allowances given by way of discharge or repayment of tax (for instance, in respect of industrial buildings which are leased by a company) are effected by deducting the amount of the allowance from the income of the appropriate class,[33] in the above instance the income from the letting, and conversely balancing charges increase such income.[34] If the income of the relevant class is insufficient to absorb the allowances, the deficit may be carried forward so as to be allowed against income of that type of succeeding accounting periods without time-limit.[35] Alternatively, at the taxpayers' option, the deficit may be set against any other profits of whatever kind of that accounting period and, so far as it is not absorbed thereby, any balance may be set against profits of whatever description in the immediately preceding accounting period.[36] But allowances in respect of expenditure on patent rights can only be given against income from patents.[37] Capital alowances for expenditure on machinery or

---

[28] *Ibid.* Sched. 6.
[29] Finance Act 1971, s. 44 (4) (*a*).
[30] Capital Allowances Act 1968, s. 68.
[31] *Ibid.* s. 68 (1); Finance Act 1978, s. 39.
[32] *Ibid.* s. 68 (2).
[33] *Ibid.* s. 71 (1) and (3); and s. 74 (1).
[34] *Ibid.* ss. 6 (6), 12 (2), 46 (3) and Sched. 12, paras. 3 (3) and 4 (3).
[35] *Ibid.* s. 74 (2) to (4).
[36] *Ibid.* ss. 71 and 74 (2) and (3).
[37] s. 387 (2).

plant relating to estate management are allowed against profits for the purpose of Schedule A[38] by treating the allowances as an addition to the deductible expenditure; and such allowances for expenditure on machinery or plant used in the management of the business of investment companies are given for corporation tax purposes against any business income of the accounting period. Any deficit is relieved by way of management expenses claims.[39]

Other assets, expenditure on which may qualify for capital allowances, include those used in connection with mines, oil-wells, mineral depletion, dredging[40] and scientific research.[41] The Capital Allowances Act 1968, as amended particularly by the Finance Act 1971, consolidates the law relating to capital allowances.

90–34 The Finance Act 1980 introduced two new developments into the rules for industrial buildings. First expenditure in the first three years on the contribution of a small workshop (2,500 square feet) qualifies for an 100 per cent. initial allowance.[42] The second development is that similar rates of allowance apply to any commercial building or structures, industrial building or hotel built in an enterprise zone during the first 10 years of the zone being so designated.[43]

Expenses

90–35 Only disbursements of expenses "being money wholly and exclusively laid out or expended for the purposes of the trade"[44] are deductible in computing profits, whether for the purposes of the traders' income tax or the trading companies' liability to corporation tax. It seems in practice, however that a more lenient view is often taken of expenses incurred by companies. There are several reasons for this. A company is usually incorporated for the purposes of trade and to allege that its expenditure is not directed to these ends may imply improper conduct of its affairs. Again it can only act through individuals and it is easier to persuade the Revenue that fees paid for a particular purpose are in order than it is for the private trader to justify expenditure incurred in achieving the same result. Moreover, where the auditor is a member of a professional body,[45] then in acting as watch-dog for the shareholders he may be relied upon to perform, incidentally, a similar service for the Revenue. Expenditure incurred in providing business entertainment is not now deductible from profits, except where reasonable hospitality is given to an overseas customer.[46]

---

[38] s. 78.
[39] s. 304 (3).
[40] Capital Allowances Act 1968, Chaps. III and IV.
[41] *Ibid.* s. 91.
[42] Finance Act 1980, s. 75 and Sched. 13.
[43] *Ibid.* s. 74 and Sched. 13.
[44] s. 130 (*a*).
[45] see para. 73–04, *ante*.
[46] s. 411 (1) and (2): *Associated Newspapers Group Ltd.* v. *Fleming (Inspector of Taxes)* [1973] A.C. 628.

Indeed, whether a profit or loss arises from "trading"[47] may, in fringe activities, be largely a question of fact to be determined by reference to all relevant matters including the objects clause of the company's memorandum of association.

Expenses will be disallowed as a deduction from trading profits if they relate to the acquisition of a capital asset or are sums "employed or intended to be employed as capital in such trade . . . ."[48]

This is so even if a future income advantage such as a reduction of rent is obtained by the acquisition or alteration of a capital asset.[49]

Pre-trading expenditure incurred within one year prior to the beginning of a trade is allowable against trading profits once trading commences, provided that it would have been allowable if it had been incurred after the commencement of trading.[50] The incidental costs of raising loan finance for trade or for the purpose of an investment company is allowable in computing profit.[51] There is no such relief for share capital or loan stock convertible into shares within three years, or where the interest payable is dependent to any extent on the profits of the company.

EXPENDITURE FOR SUBSIDIARIES. Where a parent company affords financial or other assistance to a subsidiary company it will be able to deduct such expenditure from its profits only if it is providing such assistance solely in its own interests. If it is to benefit the subsidiary or partly for its own benefit and partly for that of the subsidiary it will not be allowed. The question as to whether the parent company is providing the assistance solely in its own interest is a question of fact in each case. If such a finding of fact is made any incidental benefit to the subsidiary will be ignored.[52]

Trading losses

90–36 The amount of a loss incurred in a trade in an accounting period is computed in the same way as trading income[53]; and the treatment of such losses has an affinity with the provisions relating to capital allowances. A trading loss may be set off for purposes of corporation tax against profits of whatever description of that accounting period. Any loss still outstanding may be carried backwards to the preceding accounting period, or periods,

---

47 "Trade" is defined by the Taxes Management Act 1970, s. 118 (1). "Trading activities" distinguished from insurance transactions: *Wisdom* v. *Chamberlain (Inspector of Taxes)* [1968] 1 W.L.R. 1230; affd. by C.A. [1969] 1 W.L.R. 275; and from property transactions: *Ransom (Inspector of Taxes)* v. *Higgs* [1973] 1 W.L.R. 1180.

48 What is now s. 130 (*f*) was interpreted by the House of Lords in *I.R.C.* v. *Land Securities Investment Trust Ltd.* [1969] 1 W.L.R. 604; see also *Littlewood's Mail Order Stores Ltd.* v. *I.R.C.* [1969] 1 W.L.R. 1241.

49 *Tucker* v. *Granada Motorway Services Ltd.* [1979] 2 All E.R. 801 (H.L.) and cases cited therein. On the appropriation of money to a fund to meet future liabilities see *I.R.C.* v. *Titaghur Jute Factory* [1978] S.T.C. 166. *Cf. British Insulated & Helsby Cables Ltd.* v. *Atherton* [1926] A.C. 205.

50 Finance Act 1980 s. 39.

51 *Ibid.* s. 38

52 *Robinson* v. *Scott Bader Co. Ltd.* [1980] S.T.C. 241, *affd.* [1981] S.T.C. 436 (C.A.).

53 s. 177 (6).

but so that the duration of the preceding period does not exceed that of the accounting period in which the loss is incurred.[54] Usually both will be of a year's duration. They cannot be for longer,[55] but where the immediately preceding period is the shorter, apportionment of the profits of the penultimate period on a time basis will be necessary. Any loss still unrelieved can be carried forward to succeeding accounting periods.[56] Alternatively a trading loss may be carried forward and set against subsequent trading income from the same trade in succeeding accounting periods and so long as the company continues to carry on the trade or until the loss is wholly set off against subsequent profits.[57] This only applies if the company continues to trade, so that if there is a discontinuance either temporary or permanent, the losses cannot be carried forward. Whether there is such a discontinuance is a question of fact.[58] A trading loss cannot at any time be relieved against income derived from a trade carried on wholly abroad and within Case V of Schedule D. Also it must be shown that for any accounting period in which profits are used to absorb losses the trade was being carried on on a commercial basis and with a view to the realisation of gain.[59] With regard to the latter requirement a reasonable expectation of gain is conclusive, and where there is a change in the manner in which a trade is being carried on it is sufficient if it satisfies the "commercial basis" requirement at the end of its accounting period.[60] When, and only when, relief in respect of trading losses, capital allowances given by discharge or repayment of tax, management expenses and charges on income cannot be given against profits within the scope of corporation tax; and the franked investment income received by a company in an accounting period, but not including a surplus of franked investment income brought forward from a previous year, exceeds its franked payments made in that period, the tax credit on the excess may be paid to the company to relieve such losses, allowances and expenses of that accounting period.[61]

90–37 A loss arising under the residual Case V1, which covers casual earnings and annual profits or gains of an income or revenue nature which are not charged under any other Case or Schedule, can only be set off against any Case V1 income for the same or any subsequent accounting period.[62]

Similarly under Schedule A where the income arising from rents and receipts from land is less than the admissible outgoings the deficiency can be absorbed in the same way.

There are complex provisions to curb the right of a purchaser of the shares of a company to get the benefit of (*i.e.* in effect to purchase)

---

54 s. 177 (2) and (3).
55 s. 247 (3) (*a*).
56 s. 177 (1), (2) and (3).
57 s. 177 (1).
58 *Robroyston Brickworks* v. *I.R.C.* [1976] S.T.C. 329; *Rolls Royce Motors* v. *Bamford* [1976] S.T.C. 162.
59 s. 177 (4).
60 s. 177 (5).
61 s. 254, as amended by Finance Act 1972, s. 90 and Sched. 15, Pt. I.
62 s. 179.

accumulated trading losses and then change the nature of the trade or allow it to become small or negligible.[63]

Where any amount of government investment in a company is written off (*e.g.* by cancelling shares or exstinguishing loans) that amount must be deducted from that company's available tax losses (*e.g.* unrelieved capital allowances, trading losses, charges on income, etc.) for the accounting period preceding the write-off date and subsequent ones, if necessary.[64] This can extend to tax losses of another company in the group if required. If the amount written off is replaced by further investment by government then these provisions do not apply.[65]

Winding up

90–38 Where a company is wound up an accounting period ends and a new one begins on the date of the resolution for the winding up or presentation of a winding-up petition, and thereafter accounting periods terminate at the expiration of 12 months or on the completion of the winding up.[66] To facilitate the completion, the Inspector and the liquidator may agree in advance the date when the liquidation is likely to be completed, subject to provisions for appropriate adjustments if the assumption turns out to be incorrect, although even in this case a new accounting period will commence on the agreed date.[67] The commencement of liquidation does not of itself involve the cessation of trade, the transactions of the liquidator being regarded as those of the company. As the rate of corporation tax is fixed in arrear, where a company is wound up corporation tax is charged on its profits arising in the winding up in its final year at the rate of corporation tax fixed for the penultimate year.[68] Its final year is the financial year in which the affairs of the company are completely wound up and the penultimate year is the previous financial year.[69] Thus if the liquidation is completed on June 30, 1990, the profits from April 1 to June 30, 1990, will be charged to corporation tax at the rate fixed for the financial year 1989.

90–39 Capital allowances in respect of a trade, being allowances which fall to be made to the company by way of discharge or repayment of tax, to which a company is entitled during an accounting period falling wholly or partly within the 12 months ending when it ceases to carry on the trade, but not capital allowances from an earlier period, may, so far as they cannot be taken into account to reduce any charge to corporation tax, be added to the loss incurred by the company.[70] A loss incurred by a company in the last 12 months of its life may be carried back and set against trading income in the accounting periods falling wholly or partly within the three years preceding

[63] s. 483.
[64] Finance Act 1981, s. 48.
[65] *Ibid.* s. 47 (10).
[66] s. 247 (7).
[67] ss. 245 (5) and 247 (8).
[68] s. 245 (2) and (3).
[69] s. 245 (1).
[70] s. 178 (3).

those 12 months.[71] The assets of a company which are distributed to the contributories by the liquidator in respect of share capital are not deemed to be "distributions" under Schedule F and no liability to income tax arises thereon.[72] A company will, however, be chargeable to corporation tax on profits, including capital gains, arising in the winding up of the company.[73]

Interrelated and group companies

90–40 Where a company ceases to carry on a trade and another company begins to carry it on, and at any time within two years of the change at least a three-fourths share in the trade belongs to persons who had such an interest at some time within a year before that event, corporation tax assessments will be made as though there had been no such formal transfer of ownership.[74] Capital allowances and trading losses are carried forward for the benefit of the succeeding company; and for the purposes of this continuity an individual together with his or her close relatives is deemed to be "a person."[75] These provisions relating to company reconstructions without change of ownership were not enacted for the benefit of the taxpayer but to prevent him from obtaining the tax advantages accruing from the permanent discontinuance of one trade and the commencement of another.

There are two main types of association between companies which attract special tax treatment. The first type, that of subsidiary and parent, is itself subdivided.

51 per cent. subsidiary

90–41 This parent-subsidiary relationship is defined as one in which the parent owns directly or indirectly more than one-half of the ordinary share capital of the subsidiary *and* is beneficially entitled to more than a half of any profits available for distribution to equity holders of the subsidiary *and* to more than a half of any assets of the subsidiary available for distribution to its equity holders on a winding up.[76]

Where the company paying the dividends is a 51 per cent. subsidiary of the recipient company or both are 51 per cent. subsidiaries of another company both companies may jointly elect that the paying company may pay dividends to the recipient company without any liability to advance corporation tax or creation of a tax credit.[77] When the parent company uses group income to make franked payments to outsiders which exceed its own profits of an accounting period, advance corporation tax in respect of such dividends must first be set against "mainstream" corporation tax on

[71] s. 178 (1).
[72] s. 233 (1).
[73] s. 243 (2).
[74] s. 252 (1) and (2).
[75] s. 253 (4).
[76] s.532 as amended by Finance Act 1973, s. 28 (2). See *Tilcon Ltd.* v. *Holland* [1981] S.T.C. 365.
[77] Finance Act 1972, s. 91 (1).

the parent's own taxable income. The parent company can, if it so elects, surrender advance corporation tax among subsidiaries of which it has a "51 per cent." interest throughout the accounting period.[78] Such surrender is treated as an amount of advance corporation tax paid by any such subsidiary itself in respect of a distribution made by it on the date or dates when the dividends were paid by the parent.[79] But advance corporation tax which has been surrendered may not be set off against profits of the subsidiary in its preceding two accounting periods, and for this purpose advance corporation tax is deemed to off set the subsidiary's mainstream liability in priority to advance corporation tax actually paid by the subsidiary company in respect of its own distributions. Such a claim to surrender may now be made within six years of the end of the accounting period to which it relates. For surrender purposes a company is not a subsidiary if any person or persons together could obtain control of the subsidiary but not of the parent company.[80]

Similarly in respect of charges on income the paying company may be relieved from the requirement to account for income tax.

75 per cent. subsidiary

90–42 Where the parent has at least a three-quarters interest, as above defined, in the subsidiary more far-reaching tax concessions apply.

Relief for trading losses and other amounts eligible for relief from corporation tax may be surrendered by a company (called "the surrendering company"), and claimed by another company (called "the claimant") where the subsidiary relationship exists, by way of a relief from corporation tax called group relief.[81] This relationship must exist throughout the accounting periods of both companies, except that a period before incorporation is ignored for this purpose.[82] If one such company has a trading loss, that loss may be set off for purposes of corporation tax against the total profits of the other company for its corresponding accounting period.[83] Capital allowances which are to be given by discharge or repayment of tax can, subject to certain conditions, be treated in the same way as losses.[84] Management expenses of an investment company, but not management expenses carried forward, and excess charges on income, in so far as not absorbed by profits can be surrendered. Group relief for an accounting period is allowed as a deduction against the claimant company's total profits for the period before reduction by any relief derived from a subsequent accounting period, but as reduced by any other relief from tax,[85] including charges on income. A claim for relief need not be for the

[78] *Ibid.* s. 92 (1) and (8) and Sched. 15, Pt. II, as amended by Finance Act 1973, s. 33 and Sched. 13.
[79] Finance Act 1972, s. 92 (2).
[80] Finance Act 1973, s. 33 and Sched. 13.
[81] s. 258 (1) and (2).
[82] s. 262 (1).
[83] s. 259 (1).
[84] s. 259 (2).
[85] ss. 259 (3)–(8), 248 (1) and 260.

full amount available and requires the consent of the surrendering company. Where the relief surrendered is an excess charge on income consisting of yearly interest relief will be disallowed if the main intended benefit of any scheme or arrangement is obtaining tax relief. The intended benefit must be judged by reference to both the surrendering and claimant companies.[86]

90–43 To prevent other abuse of the group relief provisions two companies are not deemed to be members of the same group of companies if:

(i) one of them or any successor of it could cease to be a member of the same group as the other and could become a member of the same group of companies as a third company; or

(ii) any person or persons could control the one company but not the other; or

(iii) a successor company which is a third company could carry on the whole or any part of the first company's trade.

A similar rule applies if a trading company is owned by a consortium or is a 90 per cent. subsidiary of a holding company which is owned by a consortium.[87]

90–44 There are also provisions to exclude double allowances and to prevent avoidance of the "excess of relevant income over distributions" provisions relating to close companies.[88]

With certain exceptions the disposal of capital assets either by a subsidiary to the parent, amongst subsidiaries, or by the parent to its subsidiary will not be assessed to corporation tax. The disposal will be treated as though no chargeable gain or allowable loss has accrued to either the transferor or the transferee.[89] If the asset is then disposed of to an outside purchaser the gain is calculated by reference to the cost of the asset when, and any expenditure on it since, it was first acquired by a member of the group. Such gain is attributed first to the company disposing of it, but if tax has not been paid in respect of the gain within six months, the parent and other subsidiaries will be jointly and severally liable for any tax outstanding to the Revenue.[90]

90–45 Anti-avoidance provisions limit dividend stripping and the postponement or avoidance of liability to capital gains tax through the creation of artificial losses on shares and certain transactions appertaining to amalgamations and reconstructions. Under section 278 of the Income and Corporation Taxes Act 1970, if a company leaves a group within six years of acquiring a chargeable asset from another member of the group, the company leaving the group is deemed to have disposed of the asset for market value immediately after having acquired it in the then current accounting period, the chargeable gain or loss being the difference be-

---

[86] Finance Act 1976 s. 38 (3).

[87] Finance Act 1973, s. 29 (1). See *Pilkington Brothers Ltd.* v. *I.R.C.* [1981] S.T.C. 219.

[88] ss. 261, 263 and 264.

[89] s. 273 (1). For the use of this section as a means of tax avoidance on the 'sale' of a subsidiary company see *Burman* v. *Hedges & Butler Ltd.* [1979] 1 W.L.R. 160.

[90] s. 277 (1).

tween the original cost of the asset and its value at the date of the inter-group transfer. These provisions do not apply where a company ceases to be a member of a group on being wound-up or dissolved or in consequence of another member of the group being wound-up or dissolved,[91] or where a company ceases to be a member of a group as part of a merger carried out for bona fide commercial reasons and not having tax avoidance as the main or one of the main purposes of the merger.[92]

Consortia

90–46 Dividends may also be paid without any liability to advance corporation tax, or income tax in respect of charges on income, where the paying company is "a trading or holding company owned by a consortium the members of which include the company receiving the dividends."[93] "Trading or holding company" means a trading company or one whose business consists wholly or mainly in the holding of shares or securities of trading companies which are its 90 per cent. subsidiaries.[94] A member's percentage share in a consortium is determined by whichever of the three criteria mentioned above, shareholding profits or assets, gives the lowest figure.[95] A company is "owned by a consortium" if at least three-quarters of its ordinary share capital is beneficially owned between them by five or fewer companies of which none owns less than one-twentieth of that capital.[96] The income of such companies is "group income".

Group relief is available, subject to anti-avoidance provisions,[97] where either the surrendering or claimant company is a trading company which is owned by a consortium and which is not a 75 per cent. subsidiary of any company; or is a trading company which is a 90 per cent. subsidiary of a holding company which is owned by a consortium and which is not a 75 per cent. subsidiary of a company other than the holding company; or is a holding company which is owned by a consortium and which is not a 75 per cent. subsidiary of any company, and the other company is both a member of the consortium in all cases and has an interest in that consortium during the relevant accounting period of the surrendering company.[98]

Demergers

90–47 The Finance Act 1980 introduced new reliefs from ACT and income tax for two kinds of demerger.[99] The aim was to prevent the tax rules from discouraging demergers since the assets of the demerged company could otherwise be charged as distributions. The reliefs apply to a straightforward demerger *i.e.* where a company distributes to its shareholders the

---

91 s. 278 (1).
92 s. 278A (1) (*b*).
93 s. 256 (1) (*b*).
94 s. 256 (6) (*a*).
95 Finance Act 1973, s. 28 (3).
96 s. 256 (6) (*e*).
97 Finance Act 1973, ss. 28 and 29.
98 s. 258 (2), as amended by Finance Act 1981, s. 39.
99 Finance Act 1980, s. 117 and Sched. 18.

shares of a 75 per cent. subsidiary, or a 'three-cornered' demerger—when company A passes the demerged company or trade to company B, and that company issues its shares accordingly to the shareholders of company A, Company B will usually be created for this purpose.[1]

The reliefs will only be available if the companies concerned are U.K. resident trading companies or holding companies of a trading group and the object is to place the demerged company under independent management as distinct from the control of some existing conglomerate company or group.[2] In addition the main purposes must be to benefit the companies concerned and not for the purpose of tax avoidance.[3] There are anti-avoidance provisions[4] and procedures for advance clearance from the Revenue.[5]

The new provisions also provide relief from certain charges to capital gains tax[6] and stamp duty[7] which might otherwise arise.

Double taxation relief

90–48 For the purposes of double taxation relief, corporation tax attributable to any income or gain is determined as if the rate of tax payable thereon is the company's average rate of tax on all its income or gains before credit for foreign tax is given,[8] and as if all deductions for charges on income, expenses of management etc. are first set off against receipts in respect of which credit for foreign tax is not allowed and only as to the remainder against other income or gains in respect of which foreign tax is allowable.[9] Advance corporation tax is apportioned against the corporation tax on domestic income in priority to that on overseas income, and can then be set off, subject to the limit, against foreign sources bearing lower rates of foreign tax before that bearing higher rates, or otherwise as the company may elect.[10] For example:

90–49 C Ltd. receives foreign interest of £10,000 which is taxed abroad at 15 per cent. Assuming a residue of advance corporation tax, after it has been set against domestic income, which is more than sufficient to set against this foreign interest, the tax liability on the foreign interest will be as follows:

Corporation tax liability £10,000 @ 52%	= £5,200	
less advance corporation tax (maximum limit)	= £3,500	
		£1,700
Less credit for foreign tax £10,000 @ 15%		£1,500
Final corporation tax liability		£ 200

Thus companies with foreign income are treated as generously as possible.

[1] *Ibid.* para. 1 & 2.
[2] *Ibid.* paras. 3–6.
[3] *Ibid.* para. 7.
[4] *ibid.* paras. 3–6.
[5] *Ibid.* paras. 15–18.
[6] *Ibid.* paras. 9, 10.
[7] *Ibid.* para. 11.
[8] Finance Act 1972, s. 100 (4).
[9] *Ibid.* s. 100 (5).
[10] *Ibid.* s. 100 (6).

Investment companies and savings banks

90–50 There are special provisions for deduction of management expenses of investment companies. They also apply to savings banks.[11] "Investment company" means "any company whose business consists wholly or mainly in the making of investments and the principal part of whose income is derived therefrom . . . ."[12] Expenses of management, including commissions, are deductible from profits for corporation tax. Such commissions are however only allowable if they are management expenses, *i.e.* an expense to which the company is put in conducting its business. They are not deductible as a separate item.[13] To such management expenses are added, for corporation tax purposes, charges on income paid in the accounting period "wholly and exclusively" for purposes of the company's business.[14] Also thus added are capital allowances for plant and machinery, in so far as they cannot be set off against the income of the business for the accounting period.[15] But expenses, with these additions, relating to investment in real estate are set off against income from rents and receipts chargeable under Schedule A,[16] in accordance with the general principle that disbursements are deducted from the class of income to which they relate.

Where in any accounting period the expenses of management, thus defined, exceed the amount of the profits from which they are deductible the excess can be carried forward to succeeding accounting periods, or can be set off against surplus franked investment income of the same accounting period.[17]

An investment company cannot obtain greater relief from corporation tax than if it were trading.

As from 1981/82 an investment company may set off a loss incurred in an investment of shares in an unrelated unquoted trading company, computed in the usual capital gains tax way, against its income rather than its chargeable gains of that accounting period, or if necessary, because of lack of such income, that of earlier accounting periods.[18] To qualify for this relief the claimant company must have been an investment company for at least six years or since formation.[19] Holding companies and companies which trade in securities, etc., are excluded.[20] The claimant company must in addition have subscribed for the shares, and the disposal must have been either a bona fide commercial sale, a receipt on liquidation or a claim that

---

[11] s. 304 (1).
[12] s. 304 (5).
[13] *Hoechst Finance Ltd.* v. *Gumbrell* [1981] S.T.C. 127.
[14] s. 304 (2). The words "wholly and exclusively" are those used in s. 130 (*a*) and presumably bear the restrictive meaning that has been assigned to them under the said s. 130.
[15] Capital Allowances Act 1968, s. 74 (1) and Sched. 12, para. 4 (2).
[16] s. 304 (1).
[17] s. 254 (2) (*c*).
[18] Finance Act 1981, s. 36 (2).
[19] *Ibid.* s. 36 (1).
[20] *Ibid.* s. 36 (7).

the shares had become of negligible value. There are extensive provisions aimed at preventing abuse by using associated companies. The relief is to be given before any deductions for charges on income management expenses or capital allowances, etc.

The relevant shares will not qualify for relief if the trading company concerned has not been such a company since the date of its incorporation unless it has been one for the previous six years. The trading company must also be resident. Where some of the shares held qualify for relief and others do not a partial disposal is dealt with on a last in first out basis. The loss may alternatively be set off against a surplus of franked investment income in the same way as an unrelieved trading loss or capital allowance.[21] A similar relief for individuals was introduced in 1980 in an attempt to stimulate investment in small companies.[22]

Small companies

90–51 A third general category of corporation, the small company, has been added under the new tax structure. The increase in the rate of corporation tax to 52 per cent. would otherwise be onerous to small companies. They have greater difficulty in raising capital than large concerns and usually have to rely largely on accumulated profits for development and expansion. Small companies pay corporation tax at a lower rate, known as the "small companies rate" which is fixed at the same time as the general rate.[23] For the corporation tax years 1979 and 1980 the rate has been reduced from 42 to 40 per cent.[24]

The lower rate applies to companies, whether or not they are close companies, whose profits, including chargeable gains and with the addition of franked investment income from companies outside its group,[25] for an accounting period on which corporation tax falls finally to be borne, do not exceed £80,000. But the reduced rate of tax does not apply to the corporation tax on chargeable gains of small companies. There is marginal relief for companies whose taxable profits do not exceed £200,000.[26]

90–52 The small company has to pay advance corporation tax in the normal way, *i.e.*, at 3/7ths of the distribution. Dividends carry the normal tax credit for the recipient who is unaffected by whether or not they are paid by a small company. The set-off of advance corporation tax is not permitted to reduce the final corporation tax bill in respect of the distribution below 7 per cent., as opposed to 17 per cent. where the general rate applies.

There are provisions to prevent tax avoidance. For an accounting period of less than 12 months the maximum amounts relating to "small companies

[21] *Ibid.* s. 37.
[22] Finance Act 1980, s. 37. See para. 92–18, *post.*
[23] Finance Act 1972, s. 95 (1).
[24] Finance Act 1980, s. 21 (1); Finance Act 1981 s. 22 (1).
[25] Finance Act 1972, s. 95 (7).
[26] *Ibid.* s. 95 (3) (*a*): Finance Act 1981 s. 22 (2).

rate" are proportionately reduced.[27] Nor can companies be allowed to bring themselves within the lower rate through their subsidiaries. If a company has associated companies, each of the figures is divided by one plus the number of those associated companies.[28] Thus for a company with two associated companies the limit is £26,666 with marginal relief up to £66,666.

As the qualification for "small companies rate" depends solely upon the quantum of annual taxable profits, the company's corporation tax rate may change from the "small companies rate" to the normal rate and vice versa annually; and a company will be able to qualify for the lower rate however large its assets, as opposed to its profits, may be.

In this chapter, unless the contrary is expressly stated, all references to companies imply that the corporation is resident in the United Kingdom.

Value added tax

90–53 The Finance Act 1972, Part I, introduced value added tax with effect from April 1, 1973. V.A.T. is a type of sales tax—a tax on final consumer expenditure in the domestic economy—but is collected in instalments. There are three basic concepts, "taxable person," "taxable transaction" and "accounting period."

Liability to tax arises when goods are imported and at each stage in the chain whenever taxable transactions, irrespective of their profitability or otherwise, are carried out by taxable persons. "Taxable persons" are companies, individuals, partnerships and bodies engaged in trading or professional activities, *i.e.* broadly those chargeable to corporation tax or to income tax under Cases I and II of Schedule D. A group of companies may register for the tax through a representative member. In such cases inter-group transactions are not taxable.[29] Tax due however is due from all the companies in the group.[30] "Taxable transactions" imply all business transactions including the retail trade, with specific exceptions. They include: (a) the supply of goods or services in the home market by a taxable person; (b) the application of goods and services to private and certain business uses[31] by a taxable person; and (c) imports, whether or not by a taxable person.

90–54 Prescribed accounting periods of three months form the basis of assessment. The "invoice" system has been adopted. If taxable person A supplies goods or services (outputs) to another taxable person B, A is accountable to tax on their value and gives B an invoice showing the tax paid as a separate item. If B then sells to another taxable person C, B is accountable

[27] Finance Act 1972, s. 95 (6).
[28] *Ibid.* s. 95 (3) (*b*).
[29] Finance Act 1972, s. 21. See also *Customs & Excise Commissioners* v. *Save & Prosper Group Ltd.* [1979] S.T.C. 205. *Cf. Customs & Excise* v. *Tilling Management Services Ltd.* [1979] S.T.C. 365.
[30] *Re Nadler Enterprises Ltd.* [1980] S.T.C. 457.
[31] Even on a retirement gift to an employee: *R. H. M. Bakeries (Northern) Ltd.* v. *Customs & Excise Commissioners* [1980] S.T.C. 72.

for tax on the full sale price giving an invoice to C but B is credited with the tax that A had paid on goods and services supplied to B (inputs) and so on until the final consumer is reached. The effect of this "credit mechanism" is that the tax "rolls forward" at each stage until the consumer is reached. This can be illustrated by an example. The V.A.T. rate is 15 per cent.[32]

90–55 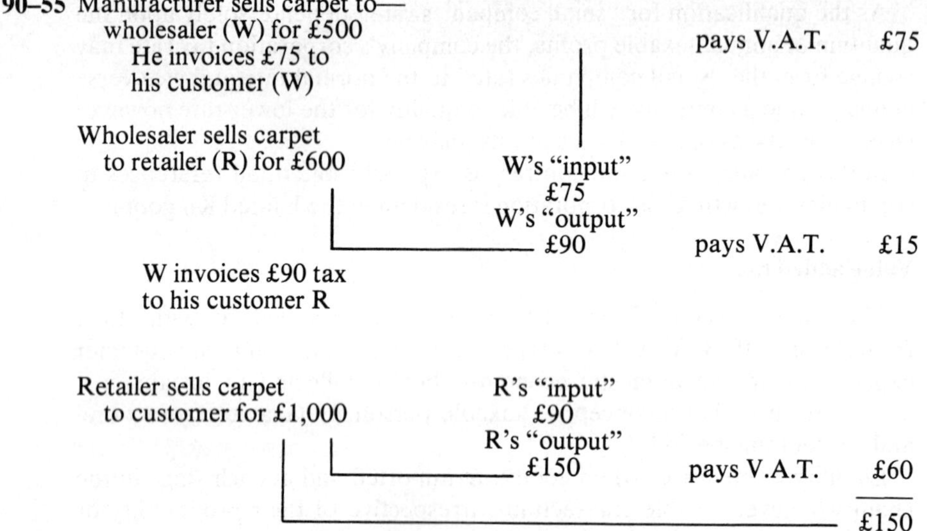

90–56 At the end of each accounting period the taxable person pays tax on his "outputs" less "inputs" during the period; and where the latter exceeds the former he can carry forward a credit or claim a refund. A claim for repayment of output tax may be made in the case of 'bad debts'.[33]

Schedule 5 to the Finance Act 1972 grants certain exemptions. No liability to tax arises when the exempt transaction takes place, but the trader undertaking it is given no credit for tax invoiced to him by his suppliers. The exempt trader, in effect, passes on the tax which has previously been paid to his customer by incorporating it in the price he charges for goods or services. Small traders, those whose taxable supplies do not exceed £5,000 a quarter or £15,000 in a full year are exempt from registration to reduce the number of persons accountable for V.A.T.[34]; but may register, which disguises such fact, if they wish to do so.[35] They then add V.A.T. to their invoices in the normal way but if their customers or clients are taxable persons they will be able to recover any such tax as input tax. Exemption also applies, *inter alia*, to housing and domestic accommodation in respect of sales and rents, and to finance including insurance, dealings in securities and banking.

---

[32] Finance (No. 2) Act 1979, s. 1 (1).
[33] Finance Act 1978, s. 12.
[34] Finance Act 1972, Sched. 1, para. 1; as amended by Finance Act 1981, s. 12.
[35] *Ibid.* para. 11 (*b*).

Schedule 4 lists items which are zero-rated. No tax, or zero tax, is charged on the output but full relief is given for inputs. Exports are relieved of tax by means of this technique. Zero-rating also applies, *inter alia*, to food, to books, periodicals and newspapers, and to the construction of buildings.

90–57 V.A.T. is administered by H.M. Customs and Excise. Control is exercised through registration of taxable persons who have to maintain the accounts necessary to establish their V.A.T. liability, their entitlement to issue invoices to their customers showing tax already paid and their entitlement to credit for tax on inputs. Companies have a certain discretion with regard to registration. A company may apply to have its various divisions registered separately and, conversely, a group of associated companies may register as one trader. Where a receiver has been appointed by a debenture holder and is entitled as between himself and the debenture holder to pay taxes, he has to make V.A.T. returns and pay the V.A.T. due, otherwise he will cause an offence to be committed.[36]

There are the usual provisions relating to inspection to prevent avoidance through artificial transactions, and penalties for evasion.[37]

Development Land Tax

90–58 Development Land Tax (DLT) was introduced by the Development Land Tax Act 1976. It is a separate tax from capital gains tax and applies whether an individual or company holds land as an investment or as stock in trade. The charge to tax arises on a disposal or deemed disposal of an interest in land—a deemed disposal arising on the commencement of a project of material development. DLT is charged on the realised development value accruing as a consequence of the grant of planning permission. £50,000 is exempt and the rate is 60 per cent. DLT will not apply to disposals in "enterprise zones." Reference should be made to the standard works on this subject—there are few special rules for companies although in general intra-group disposals are not chargeable.

---

[36] *Re John Willment (Ashford) Ltd.* [1979] 2 All E.R. 615.
[37] See *Encyclopedia of Value Added Tax*; Willson & Mainprice on *VAT*; De Voil, *Value Added Tax.*

CHAPTER 91

TAXATION OF CLOSE COMPANIES

91–01 "THE life of the law has not been logic; it has been experience."[1] The implications of *Salomon's case*[2] notwithstanding, the public interest in the prevention of tax avoidance necessitates an increasingly wide divergence between the tax treatment of the impersonal corporation and the closely controlled company. Although the former corporations will usually be public and the latter private, the main tax distinction is now between the impersonal and the close company.[3] The purpose of this chapter is to examine the special rules of corporation tax devised for the small "family" company, *i.e.* the close company, together with the capital tax implications of a transfer of such companies by their controllers.

Corporation tax—the close company

91–02 "The immunity of companies from (higher rate tax and investment income surcharge) has . . . led . . . individuals . . . to transform their income into the income of a company and so to escape (such tax)," said Lord Macmillan in *Fattorini Ltd.* v. *Inland Revenue Commissioners.*[4] The close company provisions are designed to restrain such avoidance but also to encourage the efficiency of small companies on which the national economy so largely depends.

Meaning of close company

91–03 "A 'close company' is one which is under the control of five or fewer participators or of participators who are directors."[5] "Control" is exercised by participators who have or can acquire either, first, direct or indirect control over the company's affairs; or, secondly, the greater part of the share capital or issued share capital or voting power in the company; or such part of the issued share capital as would, if all its income were distributed among the participators (excluding rights which he or they have as a loan creditor), entitle him or them to the greater part of such income; or such rights as would, on a winding up or in any other circumstances, give him or them the greater part of the assets of the company.[6] The possible effect of "options" and "rights" must be considered.

A "participator" is one who, alone or with his "associates" has, or can acquire voting rights or any of the wide interests in the income or capital of

---

[1] Mr. Justice Holmes, *The Common Law*, p. 1.
[2] *Salomon* v. *Salomon & Co.* [1897] A.C. 22; see para. 18–03, *ante*.
[3] Chap. III, ss. 282 to 303.
[4] [1942] A.C. 643, 659.
[5] s. 282 (1).
[6] Finance Act 1972, Sched. 17, para. 5.

the company mentioned above under the second or proprietary element of control,[7] or who is a loan creditor, other than a banker acting in the ordinary course of that business, of the company.[8] An "associate" is a spouse, lineal ancestor or descendant, brother, sister, or partner[9]; a trustee of any settlement of which the participator is or any such relative (living or dead) is or was a settlor; and where the participator is interested in any shares or obligations of the company which is subject to any trust, or are part of the estate of a deceased person, any other person interested therein.[10] But this does not apply to approved pensions schemes or trusts exclusively for the benefit of employeees or to unit trusts.[11] Associated companies cannot be used to thwart these provisions.[12] Directors, who as participators are not limited to five or less for control purposes, include those acting as such, by whatever name called, and persons on whose instructions the directors are accustomed to act. Director means, in effect, *de facto* controller as specified in the first part of the definition; and included in the category of participator-directors are paid managers who alone or with their associates own or control 20 per cent. or more of the ordinary share capital of the company.[13] The emphasis is on the separation of ownership and control. Only if this can be achieved can the close company provisions be avoided; and this is what the family company cannot do. Even if, perhaps by bringing in the third generation and possibly wives and excluding parents, it is possible to find a minimum of 10 members of the family none of whom own more than half the assets, the definition of director will be fatal.

91–04 If, however, the company's shares, which, in this context, includes stock carrying not less than 35 per cent. of the voting power in the company, and not being shares entitled to a fixed rate of dividend, whether with or without a further right to participate in profits, are unconditionally and benefically held by the public, are quoted on a recognised stock exchange and have been the subject of dealings within the preceding 12 months, it is not treated as a close company[14]; although this exemption from close company status does not apply where the principal members of the company have more than 85 per cent. of the voting power.[15] Shares are not deemed to be held by the public if they are held by:

(a) any director or associate of a director of the company; or
(b) any company which is controlled by one or more of the directors of the company or their associates; or
(c) any associated company of the company; or

[7] s. 303 (1).
[8] s. 303 (7).
[9] s. 303 (3) (*a*) and (4).
[10] s. 303 (3) (*b*) and (*c*).
[11] s. 303 (3) (i) and (ii).
[12] s. 282 (2).
[13] s. 303 (5); Finance Act 1974, s. 34.
[14] s. 283 (1).
[15] s. 283 (2).

(d) as part of any fund the capital or income of which is applicable to past or present directors or employees or their dependants.[16]

Conversely shares not coming within the above provisions are deemed to be beneficially held by the public if, and only if,

(a) they are beneficially held by a company which is not a close company, or by a non-resident company which would not be a close company if it were resident; or

(b) they are held on trust for certain approved superannuation schemes and retirement benefit schemes; or

(c) they are not comprised in a principal member's holding.[17]

A principal member is one who possesses more than 5 per cent. of the voting power.[18] Thus the effect of the last requirement is to exclude the holding of any minority shareholder having 5 per cent. or less of the voting power, who is not an associate of another where the combined voting rights would exceed this limit.

91–05 But a company is not a close company if it is controlled by one or more non-close companies and it cannot be treated as a close company except by taking as one of the five or fewer participators a company which is not a close company.[19] Both conditions must be satisfied.

The requirement relating to dealings within the previous year is indeed uncertain, but by allotting shares in small quantities and as widely as possible the family may still hope to retain control and a majority proprietary interest.

Nearly all family companies, however, will come within the "close company" category.

Excess of relevant income over distributions

91–06 The Finance Act 1972, Schedule 16, uses new terminology. The conflict between tax avoidance and the ploughing back of profits for necessary development is compromised by designating company income that is deemed to be available for distribution, called "the relevant income." If this exceeds the distributions actually made "powers of apportionment" apply. Broadly such excess is treated as a dividend apportioned to the shareholders for the purposes, where appropriate, of the latter's higher rate tax and investment income surcharge.[20] The tax credit cancels the basic rate liability.[21]

The relevant income is subject to a maximum figure. For trading companies it shall in no case exceed its distributable investment income for the accounting period together with part of its estate income, in both cases net

---

[16] s. 283 (5).
[17] s. 283 (3) and (4).
[18] s. 283 (6) (*a*).
[19] s. 282 (4); Finance Act 1971, s. 25 (6).
[20] Finance Act 1972, Sched. 16, para. 1 (1) and para. 5 (2) (*a*).
[21] *Ibid*. para. 5 (2) (*b*).

of corporation tax. Its trading income is not taken into account.[22] A trading company is defined as one whose primary purpose is the carrying on of a trade and any other company whose income does not consist mainly of investment income.[23] The estate income of a trading company which is used in computing relevant income depends upon the sizes. If the estate income is less than the 'appropriate fractions' of £75,000 it is to be reduced by one-half of the amount required to make it up to £75,000. If it is less than the 'appropriate fraction' of £25,000 it is to be ignored in computing relevant income.[24] The 'appropriate fraction' for this purpose is the ratio of the estate income to the estate and trading income combined.

An example would be:

Estate income: £10,000

Trading income: £40,000

The appropriate fraction therefore is 1/5 (*i.e.* £10,000 to £50,000). To calculate the estate income for relevant income purposes it is necessary divide £75,000 by 1/5 £15,000. The difference between the estate income (£10,000) and that figure is £5,000. Accordingly it is to be reduced by 1/2 of £5,000, *i.e.* £2,500.

The estate income for relevant income purposes is therefore £10,000 – £2,500 = £7,500

Clearly the larger the estate income in proportion to trading income the less the relief.

Trading income means income from a trade which is not investment income, *i.e.* which if it were on individual would be earned income.[25] *Estate income* is that income which is not trading income and is chargeable to tax under Schedule A, B or D but not yearly or other interest, and which arises from the ownership or occupation of land or from furnished lettings.[26]

If a trading company has one or more associated companies in the accounting period the figures of £75,000 and £25,000 above are divided by one plus the number of those associated companies, *i.e.* giving £25,000 and £8,333 if it has two associated companies.[27]

91–07 Non-trading companies have a different calculation. In such situations the relevant income shall in no case exceed its distributable investment income for the accounting period plus 50 per cent. of its estate or trading income, net in both cases of corporation tax.[28] Where such a company has both estate or trading income and distributable investment income, the latter is reduced by 10 per cent. of the estate or trading income, after time, up to a maximum of £3,000.[29] Even a property company which receives

---

[22] *Ibid.* para. 9 (2).
[23] *Ibid.* para. 11 (1).
[24] *Ibid.* paras. 9 (2) and (3) (*a*).
[25] *Ibid.* paras. 10 (4) and (5).
[26] *Ibid.* para. 10 (4) (A).
[27] *Ibid.* para. 9 (3) (b).
[28] *Ibid.* para. 9 (1).
[29] *Ibid.* para. 10 (3).

rents under full repairing lease qualifies for this tax treatment; but an investment company with no estate or trading income is prima facie taxed as though it had distributed the whole of its income.

Charges and expense relating to one category of income are debited against that income; while charges on income, expenses of management or other amounts which are deductible from profits of more than one description are treated as being deducted first for all companies from its chargeable income other than estate or trading income. For a trading company they are then deducted from its estate income, thirdly its trading income and fourthly from chargeable gains. For other companies the subsequent order is estate or trading income, development gains and chargeable gains.[30] No apportionment is made unless the excess of relevant income over distributions of a trading company or a company which is a member of a trading group exceeds £1,000.[31]

No individual is assessed to income tax by virtue of *any* apportionment unless the sum on which he is so assessed amounts at least to £200 or 5 per cent. of the amount apportioned, whichever is the less.[32]

Where a close company is subject to any restriction imposed by law as regards the making of distributions, the excess of relevant income over distributions is disregarded to the extent to which the company could not make distributions up to the amount of its relevant income without contravening that restriction.[33] Thus a transfer of share premiums to the share premium account which is obligatory under section 56 of the 1948 Act is so "imposed by law" for this purpose.[34] Restrictions imposed by the articles of a company alone are not however "imposed by law". The company is only bound by such restrictions as between itself and its members—it may alter its articles at any time.[35]

91–08 The quantum of relevant income is subject to this general qualification. Any company, whether a trading company or not, which has estate or trading income may justify a lower level of "relevant income" by showing that additional income could not be distributed without prejudice to the present and future[36] requirements of the company's business. In addition regard can be had to other requirements necessary or advisable for the acquisition of a trade or of a controlling interest in a trading company.[37] This does not include trades owned within a year by that company or its associated company. The Finance Act 1972[38] states that:

---

[30] *Ibid*. paras. 10 (8) and (9).
[31] *Ibid*. para. 1 (3).
[32] *Ibid*. para. 5 (4).
[33] *Ibid*. para. 14 (1).
[34] *Shearer* v. *Bercain* [1980] S.T.C. 359. This decision is now qualified by statute—see para. 24–01, *ante*.
[35] *Noble* v. *Laygate Investments Ltd*. [1978] 2 A11 E.R. 1067.
[36] *Ibid*. para. 8 (2) (*a*).
[37] *Ibid*. para. 8 (3).
[38] *Ibid*. para. 8 (1).

"the relevant income of a company for an accounting period is—

(a) in the case of . . . a trading company or a member of a trading group, so much of its distributable income other than trading income for that period as can be distributed without prejudice to the requirements of the company's business;

(b) in the case of (any other company) whose distributable income . . . includes estate or trading income—

(i) so much of the estate or trading income as can be distributed without prejudice to the requirements of the company's business so far as concerned with the activities or assets giving rise to estate or trading income; and

(ii) its (other) distributable income; (and)

(c) in the case of any other company, its distributable income for that period."

The onus is on the company to show that the requirements of the business thus justify a lower level of relevant income; and this is primarily a question of fact.[39] The practical application of this somewhat vague test may be an important factor in a company's overall tax position. The Treasury have, however, given assurances that estate or trading income earmarked by close companies for expansion will not be subject to apportionment. Also if the full claim of the company cannot be conceded, a lower level of relevant income than the statutory ceiling may be allowed.

91–09 But companies which are neither trading companies nor members of a trading group, cannot have any income expended, or available to be applied, in or towards the acquisition of an estate or interest in land, or the construction or extension of a building (not constituting an improvement or development of farm or market-garden land) or income applied to repay bank or other loans raised for these purposes regarded as applicable to the requirements of the company's business.[40] Income so used forms part of its relevant income.

91–10 The distributable income for an accounting period, upon which the ascertainment of the relevant income depends, is the amount of the distributable profits exclusive of chargeable gains.[41] Thus chargeable gains arising on the sale of capital assets are not included in computing relevant income and do not attract income tax so long as the gain remains in the company or on its liquidation.

The excess of relevant income over distributions is apportioned among the participators according to their respective interests in the company.[42] The Revenue do have the power to apportion according to the participators' respective interests in the assets of the company available in the event of a winding up or in any other circumstances.[43] An appeal lies to the Special Commissioner but in view of the unfettered powers given any

[39] *MacTaggart Scott & Co. Ltd.* v. *Inland Revenue Commissioners* [1973] 48 T.C. 708; [1973] T.R. 81; *cf. Wilson & Garden Ltd.* v. *I.R.C.* [1981] S.T.C. 301.

[40] Finance Act 1973, Sched. 9, para. 4 (2) and (3).

[41] Finance Act 1972, Sched. 16, para. 10 (2).

[42] *Ibid.* para. 4 (1).

[43] *Ibid.* para. 4 (2).

further appeal to the court is unlikely to succeed.[44] Any sum so apportioned to an individual has to be included in his total income, for tax liability in excess of the basic rate, as though it were income received by him at the end of the accounting period to which the apportionment relates.[45] For this purpose the distributions for an accounting period are:

(a) any dividends which are declared in respect of the period and are paid during the period or within a reasonable time thereafter; and

(b) all distributions made in the period except dividends which, under (a) above, are attributable to a previous period.[46] The provision of benefits for participators[47] may also be deemed to be distributions.

91–11 A close company, unless it is a close investment company having no estate or trading income, can require the Inspector of Taxes to state whether he proposes to make an apportionment for a particular accounting period.[48] This request for a clearance must be accompanied by a copy of the company's accounts for the period as adopted in a general meeting, a copy of the directors' report, if any, and any other information, such as the factors that influenced its dividend policy, which the company wishes to supply. Within three months after receiving these particulars the Inspector may call for any further information he requires. Within three months of receiving it, or within three months of the original application if no further information is required, the Inspector must notify the company whether he proposes to make an apportionment. Unless he replies in the affirmative within this time-limit, he loses the right to do so. Unless the information supplied is defective or the company ceases to carry on its main activity or goes into liquidation within 12 months of the end of the accounting period, the company obtains clearance in respect of the accounts to which the request relates.[49]

Thus if a close company wishes to avoid an apportionment and is uncertain whether the distributions which it makes or proposes to make will be sufficient, it should apply for clearance as soon as possible after the end of the accounting period to ensure that it can, if necessary, increase its distributions within a reasonable time after the end of the accounting period to avoid an apportionment. A subsequent distribution of more than the relevant income may not fully re-imburse the participators for their higher rate tax liability in respect of the apportionment.

91–12 If in a subsequent year the income apportioned, or part of it, is distributed, and if for that year the distributions exceed the relevant income, any person charged to tax on the excess over the basic rate in respect of the apportionment can have his income for the later year reduced, by reference to his share in the apportionment or in the later distributions,

---

[44] *Lothbury Investment Corporation* v. *I.R.C.* [1979] 3 A11 E.R. 860.
[45] Finance Act 1972, Sched. 16, paras. 1 (2) and 5 (2).
[46] *Ibid.* para. 10 (1).
[47] s. 284 (2).
[48] Finance Act 1972, Sched. 16, para. 18.
[49] *Ibid.* para. 18 (4).

whichever is the less.[50] This right to carry forward higher rate tax paid with a view to future set-off should be borne in mind when considering the distribution policy of the company where some of the participators are higher rate tax and/or investment income surcharge payers.

91–13 Where a close company ceases to carry on the trade, or the business of holding investments, or goes into liquidation, the relevant income of a non-trading company for any accounting period in which that event occurs, for any accounting period ending within the preceding 12 months and for periods during the liquidation is the whole, instead of 50 per cent. of its estate or trading income and all its investment income,[51] except capital gains, unless it needs to retain profits in order to satisfy its creditors. For a trading company a similar rule applies except that its trading income is excluded. The broad principle is that it is difficult, in these circumstances, to justify any retention by reference to present and impossible by reference to future requirements. Also, only the ordinary trading debts of its participators may be taken into account to justify any retention. *Salomon's* debentures[52] would not qualify.

91–14 Where there has been an apportionment and the participator subsequently disposes of his shares on a liquidation, relief from any capital gains tax assessment can be obtained.[53]

Directors' fees

91–15 Directors' fees are deductible from profits and thus do not suffer corporation tax; and, although they are liable to income tax in the hands of the recipients, unlike dividends they do not attract the investment income surcharge. In order to determine whether, and the extent to which, directors' remuneration is deductible it is necessary to distinguish between trading companies and investment companies. The law applies generally but is of particular relevance to close companies where the directors are usually the majority shareholders and thus have an unfettered power to fix their own remuneration. From the viewpoint of the company and the recipients it is advantageous from the tax angle to distribute profits as far as possible in the form of fees rather than as dividends.

In the case of a trading company the theoretical requirement is that directors' remuneration, to be deductible, must be "money wholly and exclusively laid out or expended for the purposes of the trade . . . " within the meaning of section 130 (*a*) of the Income and Corporation Taxes Act 1970. The Revenue do not in practice invoke the "wholly and exclusively" rule in relation to the remuneration of directors of a trading company where the directors earn the profits; but in *George J. Smith & Co. Ltd.* v. *Furlong (Inspector of Taxes)*[54] compensation paid to life directors, who

[50] *Ibid.* para. 5 (6).
[51] *Ibid.* para. 13.
[52] *Salomon* v. *Salomon & Co.* [1897] A.C. 22, referred at paras. 91–01 and 18–03, *ante.*
[53] C.G.T.A. 1979, s. 74.
[54] [1969] 2 All E.R. 760.

held a majority shareholding in the company, for loss of office was disallowed in computing the company's profits.

The remuneration of directors of an investment company, however, must qualify as "sums disbursed as expenses of management" under section 304 (1) of the Income and Corporation Taxes Act 1970. Such fees must actually be paid and only a sum which is reasonably proportionate to the work entailed will come within the definition. "It is the duty of the special commissioners," said Plowman J. in *L.G. Berry Investments Ltd.* v. *Attwooll*, "to investigate the question whether sums claimed to have been disbursed as expenses of management not only were disbursed but were in truth and in fact disbursed as expenses of management,"[55] Both in the case of trading and investment companies if directors' fees or a salary is paid to a wife of a director the amount claimed must be paid and if the commissioners do not admit such payments the court will not interfere.[56]

Loans, benefits and restrictive covenants

91–16 Close companies cannot be allowed an unrestricted right to avoid tax by lending money to participators and their associates, instead of paying them dividends, and then allowing the loans to remain outstanding indefinitely or waiving repayment. Where a close company, otherwise than in the ordinary course of a business which includes the lending of money, makes any loan or advances to such an individual the company is charged to tax in respect of the loan at a rate equal to the rate of advance corporation tax in force for the financial year in which the loan is made.[57] Any sum thus paid is not actually advance corporation tax and cannot be set off against mainstream corporation tax liability or be dealt with in any other way applicable to advance corporation tax. The company is also deemed to have made such a loan of an amount equal to the debt where debts to the close company are incurred by participators and their associates either directly or by assignment.[58] This, however, does not apply to debts incurred for the supply of goods or services in the ordinary course of the company's trade unless the credit given exceeds six months or that normally given to the company's customers.[59] When the loan or advance, or any part thereof, is repaid, the whole of the tax, or a proportionate part of it, is discharged or repaid to the company.[60] Liability is imposed upon the company and not on the borrower and unless it is written off no further charge to tax is imposed by reason of the loan. However, if the company releases or writes off the whole or part of the debt, for the purpose of computing the total income[61] of the person to whom the loan was made,

[55] [1964] 1 W.L.R. 693, 699.
[56] *Moschi* v. *Kelly* [1952] 33 T.C. 442.
[57] s. 286 (1).
[58] s. 286 (2).
[59] s. 286 (2) proviso.
[60] s. 286 (5).
[61] s. 528 (1) as amended by Finance Act 1973, Sched. 24, para. 32.

the amount so released is grossed up at the basic rate of income tax and treated as income received by him[62] at the time of the writing off, less any allowable deductions he is charged to tax thereon over and above the basic rate; but no repayment of income tax is made and no charge to basic rate income tax arises in respect of that income.[63] The Revenue is safeguarded where the original borrower has died or where an intermediary comes between the debtor and the company.[64]

Loans made by a non-close company which is controlled or subsequently becomes controlled by a close company, are regarded as being loans made by that close company.[65] Provision is made for the case where two or more close companies control the lending company. There is no such extension if the taxpayer can show that there is no connection between the making of the loan and either the acquisition of control of the lending company or the provision of funds by the close company to facilitate the loan. In deciding the question of whether the loan was made in the ordinary course of business, whether the loan or part of it has been repaid and whether it has been released or written off, the lending company and not the controlling close company is the relevant company.

91–17 Where a close company incurs expense in providing living accommodation, entertainment, domestic or other benefits or facilities of whatever nature for any participator or associate of his,[66] the incurring of such expenditure is a distribution; unless the recipient is a director or employee of the company or the benefit consists of a pension or gratuity given to the spouse or a dependant of a director or employee on his death or retirement.[67] This is the only item ranking as a distribution for close companies alone.[68]

As distributions the payments are not allowed as deductions in computing the company's profits for corporation tax, but are taken into account in determining the excess of relevant income over distributions.

91–18 Payments made in respect of restrictive covenants to individuals who hold, have held or are about to hold directorships or employments in a company, whether or not it is close, are treated as part of their total income after deduction of basic rate income tax.[69] No basic rate income tax assessments are made, but the payments are chargeable to higher rate tax and investment income surcharge in the hands of the recipients. A restrictive covenant is an undertaking not to compete with or accept employment with competitors of the corporation, a course of action which, invariably, the promisor has not the slightest intention of taking.

---

[62] s. 287 (1) (*a*).
[63] s. 287 (1) (*b*).
[64] s. 286 (7) as amended by Finance Act 1972, Sched. 28, Pt. VI.
[65] s. 287 A.
[66] s. 284 (7).
[67] s. 284 (2).
[68] Finance Act 1972, Sched. 17, para. 2.
[69] s. 34 (1).

Capital gains tax—transfer of business

91–19 Problems can arise on the disposal of a business for the proprietor of that business. This is particularly true of the small family company. A disposal of the shares or of the assets of the company will be chargeable to capital gains tax unless the disposal is on death. The usual basis of charge will in general terms be the difference between the proceeds of the disposal and the value of the property at the date of acquisition together with expenditure on the property since that date. Capital gains tax is levied at a flat rate of 30 per cent. on gains over £3,000 in any one year. A sale of the shares or assets is an obvious example of an occasion of charge to the tax but it also applies to *inter vivos* gifts and sales at less than market value.[70] In such cases the disposal proceeds are deemed to be market value at the date of disposal. Such gifts and undervalue sales are also subject to capital transfer tax as are transfers on death. The effect of capital transfer tax is considered below but the incidence of capital gains tax is much reduced by three reliefs from the charge.

General relief for gifts

91–20 Where a person makes a gift or a sale at an undervalue to another U.K. resident they may jointly elect that the consideration for the gift be regarded as whatever figure gives rise to a no gain, no loss situation on the disposal, instead of market value.[71] If the disposal is a sale at an undervalue and the actual consideration received exceeds the transferer's acquisition cost, etc., then that figure will be substituted for market value.

Thus if X buys an asset for £20,000 and gives it to Y when it has a market value of £40,000, if X and Y jointly elect, Y will be deemed to have paid £20,000 for that asset and there will be no chargeable gain on the gift. Y of course will have an acquisition cost of only £20,000 for any subsequent disposal he may make. If X had sold the asset to Y for £30,000 there would have been a chargeable gain of £10,000 and Y would have an acquisition cost of £30,000. In either case if there is no such joint election there would be a chargeable gain to X of £20,000.

Where the donee emigrates before disposing of the relevant asset there is a deemed disposal by him of the amount rolled-over on the gift whereby the original liability becomes payable, initially by the donee, but if he fails to pay, by the donor. This does not apply however if the donee emigrated more than six years after the relief has been claimed.[72]

In addition any capital transfer tax payable on the gift or sale at an undervalue will be allowed to the donee as an additional cost of acquisition. The value of this relief from capital gains tax is enormous and provided that the business is never sold but passed down to the next generation no charge will ever accrue. The relief is however only available

[70] C.G.T.A. s. 29 A.
[71] Finance Act 1980, s. 79, Finance Act 1981, s. 78.
[72] Finance Act 1981, s. 79.

on gifts, etc., from one individual to another or to the trustees of a settlement—it does not apply to gifts to companies.[73]

Transfer of business on retirement

If an individual who has attained the age of 60 disposes by way of sale or gift of a business owned by a trading company which is his family company and of which he is full-time working director, or if he so disposes of shares or securities in such a company, special relief in respect of chargeable gains is given.[74] The conditions required of the company and the individual must have been fulfilled for at least a year prior to the disposal, for the relief to operate, and the longer they have been in existence, the greater the relief up to a maximum of ten years. Where there is an interval between the time when the business is closed down and the time when the business assets are sold or a capital distribution is received by a shareholder the recipient cannot strictly comply with the requirements of ownership of at least one year ending with the disposal. The Inland Revenue have indicated that they will in practice be prepared to apply that test by reference to the period ending with the permanent closure of the business if the actual disposal takes place within three years of the closure, and the business assets are not used or leased for any purpose in the interim period. In such cases the amount of relief will be calculated by reference to the age of the taxpayer at the date of closure.[75] The company will be a family company if either the disposer can exercise 25 per cent. of the voting rights in the company or if 51 per cent. are exercisable by members of his family and 5 per cent. by him.[76] He will be a "full-time working director" if he is required to devote substantially the whole of his time to the service of the company in a managerial or technical capacity; the relief also applies when such an individual receives a capital distribution on the liquidation of a family company.[77]

The relief takes the form of an exemption from the charge to capital gains tax of an amount varying with the age of the individual and the number of years for which the required conditions have been fulfilled. If the individual is aged 65 or over, the maximum amount is £50,000 but only 10 per cent. of that amount is allowable for each of the last 10 years in which the relevant conditions were met. So that if the conditions have been fulfilled for the past four years the amount allowable is £20,000 (4 × £5,000). If the individual is aged between 60 and 65 the maximum amount is £10,000 for every year by which he exceeds 60 (a corresponding allowance being made for part years), with the 10 per cent. rule operating in the same way against that figure. For example, if the disposer is aged

---

[73] Finance Act 1980, s. 79 (5).
[74] C.G.T.A. 1979, s. 124 (1).
[75] Practice Statement 6/79.
[76] C.G.T.A. 1979, s. 124 (8). See *Hepworth* v. *William Smith Group* [1981] S.T.C. 354.
[77] *Ibid.* s. 125 (2).

exactly 63 and the relevant conditions have been fulfilled for the past four years, the amount allowable is 40 per cent. of £30,000, *i.e.* £12,000.[78]

Except in the case of liquidation mentioned above, the gains must relate to chargeable business assets, which are assets including goodwill used for the purpose of the trade but excluding assets held as investments and, in the case of a disposal of shares, assets upon which no chargeable gains would accrue.[79] Where however the chargeable business assets are sold as a preliminary to liquidation, s. 124 (5) may prevent relief on the subsequent disposal of shares in the winding up. The Inland Revenue have, however, indicated that they will be prepared to consider the granting of concessional relief in such circumstances.[80] Even though the relief is calculated in this way there must be a disposal of the whole or part of the business and not simply of some of the business assets leaving the business itself substantially intact. This applies even to disposal of farming land by a farmer.[81]

This relief is of importance as it is applied prior to the general relief for gifts detailed above. If the consideration paid on an undervalue sale exceeds the transferer's acquisition costs etc. any relief available under this heading is deductible from that actual consideration for the purposes of the general relief discussed above.[82]

There are in addition the following extra statutory concessions available to supplement retirement relief:

(i) ASSET OWNED BY A DIRECTOR AND USED BY THE COMPANY: If a director makes a disposal of an asset which he owns and (a) it has throughout his period of ownership been used rent-free for the purpose of a trade carried on by the company; (b) throughout that time he has been a full-time working director of the company and that company has been his family trading company; and (c) the disposal is associated with a disposal of shares in that company which qualifies for relief under C.G.T.A. 1979, s. 124, then the disposal will be regarded as qualifying for the relief. Proportional relief will be available if conditions (a) and (b) were satisfied at the time of the disposal but were not satisfied at some earlier time, or if the company has paid a rent for the asset which is clearly below market rent. Otherwise the payment of rent disqualifies any entitlement to relief.[83]

(ii) BUSINESS PASSING TO SPOUSE: If one spouse's entire interest in a business has passed to the other spouse and they were living together in the year in which the transfer took place, their consecutive periods of ownership may be aggregated for the purposes

---

78 *Ibid.* s. 124 (3).
79 *Ibid.* s. 124 (4) (5).
80 Practice Statement 5/79.
81 *McGregor* v. *Adcock* [1977] 1 W.L.R. 864.
82 Finance Act 1980, s. 79 (3).
83 Press Release, 30/3/79.

of calculating the relief due on the subsequent disposal of the whole or part of the business.

Similarly if one spouse's entire holding of shares in a company has passed to the other spouse, and throughout a period up to the date of transfer it was the transferor's family trading company and he or she was a full-time working director of it, relief will be calculated on the subsequent disposal of those shares as though throughout that period the company had been the transferee's family trading company and he or she had been a full-time working director of it.

In either case where the inter-spouse transfer did not take place on death the amount available for relief under this concession will be determined by reference to the age of the younger of the spouses at the date of the chargeable disposal, and will not be greater than the excess of £50,000 over the amount on which relief under C.G.T.A. 1979 s.124 was given to the transferor in respect of earlier disposals.[84]

Gifts of business assets

91–21 If an individual makes a transfer to a company either of an asset which has been used for the purposes of a trade carried on by his "family company" or of shares or securities in such a company, the chargeable gain which would otherwise accrue can be postponed by a form of roll-over relief.[85] Under these provisions the amount of the gain is deducted from the price which the transferee would otherwise be taken to have paid and which he could therefore have used as an allowable expense on a subsequent disposal. Thus the gain now accruing is postponed until that disposal. The relief does not apply to a bona fide sale to an unconnected purchaser. If actual consideration is received on the disposal only the excess of any chargeable gain over a cash gain is eligible for relief, *e.g.* if market value is substituted for the sale price in the computation. The relief applies therefore only to unrealised gains, where open market value is deemed to be the consideration received. The relief is consequently available to trustees where there is an unrealised gain on such assets according to the deemed disposal rules as they apply to trusts, *e.g.* on the termination *inter vivos* of a life interest where the subject matter of the trust consists of such assets. The relief is reduced if the assets have not been used for the purposes of the trade throughout the transferor's period of ownership or if the subject matter is shares and that company as assets which are not business assets. A family company has the same meaning as in the retirement relief provision noted above.

It is apparent that on most occasions the general relief on gifts will supersede that relating to business assets which now effectively applies

[84] *Ibid.*
[85] C.G.T.A. 1979, s. 126 and Sched. 4.

only to transfers to a company.[86] Retirement relief may overlap with business assets relief. In such cases retirement relief applies first.[87]

Capital transfer tax

91–22 Shareholdings and other interests in companies may be the subjects of lifetime gifts or may be part of a deceased's estate for the purposes of capital transfer tax. The value of a gift for the purposes of capital transfer tax is the loss to the transferor. "A transfer of value is any disposition made by a transferor as a result of which the value of his estate immediately after the disposition is less than it would be but for the disposition; and the amount by which it is less is the value transferred by the transfer."[88] The value of any property is the price which the property might reasonably be expected to fetch if sold in the open market.[89] Tax is chargeable according to two progressive scales, one for lifetime transfers (lower) and one for transfers on death (higher). The value transferred is accumulated with previous transfers of the past 10 years to ascertain the appropriate rate.[90]

The valuation of quoted shares is based on the daily list of the Stock Exchange and is a relatively simple matter. But nearly all family companies are private companies which usually restrict the right to transfer their shares.[91] In these circumstances the House of Lords, when considering a minority shareholding, has held that one assumes a sale in the open market of shares which confer upon the notional purchaser both the rights attaching to them, dividend yield, profit yield, and break-up value of the shares, but also the restrictions on alienation imposed by the articles,[92] the latter restriction in their Lordships' view reducing the value of the shares in question by at least a half.[93] Also relevant are the record of the company, the history of the industry and comparisons with prices quoted on the Stock Exchange. In practice, such valuation of ordinary shares leaves scope for very wide differences of opinion[94]; the valuation of preference shares and debentures proceeding on the same principles is not normally of any great difficulty. The notional purchaser is also assumed to have all the information which a prudent prospective purchaser might reasonably require if he were preparing to purchase them from a willing vendor at arm's length, *e.g.* as to profit trends.[95]

91–23 Where, however, the transfer involves loss of control of the company the open market value of the shares transferred is higher. The statutory "assets

---

86 Finance Act 1980 s. 79 (4).
87 C.G.T.A. 1979, s. 126 (2).
88 Finance Act 1975, s. 20 (2).
89 *Ibid.* s. 38 (1).
90 *Ibid.* s. 37.
91 Companies Act 1948, s. 28 (1) (*a*) no longer applies but most private companies will retain this right.
92 *I.R.C.* v. *Crossman* [1937] A.C. 26.
93 *Ibid. per* Viscount Hailsham L.C. at p. 43.
94 In *Re Holt, decd.* [1953] 1 W.L.R. 1488. The Revenue originally claimed £3 per share, which they reduced to £1.70, then to £1.25; Danckwerts J.'s valuation was 95p.
95 Finance Act 1975, Sched. 10, para. 13, overruling *Re Lynall* [1972] A.C. 680.

basis" of valuation which applied for estate duty broadly to controlling holdings of shares was not continued into the transfer tax but certain holdings of shares are aggregated for valuation purposes. This applies to shares owned by a man and his wife and those comprised in a settlement made by him or his spouse before March 27, 1974, where no interest in possession subsists in that property[96]; together with any shares held by a trust in which either of them has an interest in possession.[97] Thus where husband and wife each hold 40 per cent. of the issued shares of a company, the transfer of the husband's holding is valued as a proportion of the price which an 80 per cent. shareholding would fetch if a higher value is thereby produced.

Aggregation is also required of shares owned by the transferor together with those which he has earlier transferred to a charity, political party or national heritage body and which are still owned by such an organisation or have been within the previous five years. These earlier transfers, as on a transfer to a spouse, are usually exempt and thus the "control element" in the value of the shares could be lost on the earlier exempt transfer, leaving a lower value applicable to the later chargeable transfer.[98]

91–24 Where a close company makes a transfer of value, tax is charged as if each individual to whom an amount is apportioned had made a transfer of value of such amount as after deduction of tax, if any, would be equal to the amount so apportioned, less the amount, if any, by which the value of his estate is more than it would be but for the company's transfer. For this purpose his estate is treated as not including any rights or interests in the company.[99] The value transferred is apportioned among the participators according to their respective rights and interests in the company immediately before the transfer, and any amount so apportioned to a close company is further apportioned among its participators.[1] There is no apportionment of amounts taken into account for income or corporation tax, including franked investment income.[2] Any surrender by a close company of its relief under the group relief provisions, or of its surplus advance corporation tax is also to be disregarded.[3] There are also provisions designed to relieve preference shareholders from an apportionment if the effect of the disposition on the value of their shares is small in comparison with others, and minority participators of a subsidiary company when the disposition is by that subsidiary company and is a group transfer for corporation tax purposes.[4] If the disposition is by a close company to another company, a participator who has had an amount apportioned to him may offset any increase in his estate due to any increase in the value of any interest of his in the transferee company.[5] Any apportionment is

[96] Finance Act 1975, Sched. 10, para. 7.
[97] *Ibid.* Sched. 5, para. 3 (1).
[98] Finance Act 1976, s. 103.
[99] *Ibid.* s. 39 (1).
[1] *Ibid.* s. 39 (2).
[2] *Ibid.* s. 39 (2) (*a*).
[3] *Ibid.* s. 39 (6 A).
[4] *Ibid.* s. 39 (8 A), (8 B), (8 C).
[5] *Ibid.* s. 39 (8 D).

available for exemption under the general exemption for transfers up to £2,000 in any one year.[6] The company is primarily liable for the tax, but if it remains unpaid recourse can be had to the persons to whom any amounts have been apportioned up to the limit of such apportionment to him and excluding an apportionment of not more than 5 per cent. of the value transferred.[7] Where there is an alteration in a close company's unquoted share or loan capital or an alteration in any rights attaching to such shares or debenture the alteration is treated as having been made by a disposition by the participators.[8] If as a result of such a deemed disposition an amount is apportioned to a participator in his capacity as a trustee, resulting in a loss to the trust fund then there will be a charge on that fund either as a partial termination of an interest in possession or as a capital distribution if there is no such interest.[9]

Relief for business property

91–25 The Finance Act 1976 introduced a new relief from capital transfer tax to allay one of the main arguments against the tax—the breaking up of small family businesses to pay the tax. The relief is detailed in Schedule 10, and the general rule is that where a transfer of value attributable to business property is made the value transferred (before any grossing up) is to be reduced by a stated percentage. The relief applies to lifetime, death and settlement transfers.

The relief can be claimed where the property transferred is one of—

(a) a sole proprietor's business or an interest in a business;
(b) a holding of shares giving (either by itself or together with other shares owned by the transferor) control of a company;
(c) land, buildings, plant or machinery owned by a controlling shareholder and used wholly or mainly in the business of the company;
(d) land or buildings subject to a settlement used wholly or mainly for the purpose of a business carried on by the transferor who is a beneficiary under the settlement;
(e) minority holdings of unquoted shares.

The relief for (a) and (b) is 50 per cent. of the value transferred; 30 per cent. for (c) and (d), and 20 per cent. for (e). Businesses carried on otherwise than for gain, and investment and property companies, are excluded unless they are discount houses or holding companies for other business companies. To qualify for the relief the transferor must have owned the relevant business property for at least two years (or, where it has replaced other business property, it and the earlier property must have been owned for a total of at least two out of the last five years). Any change in the business from a sole proprietor to a company controlled by him is to be ignored for this purpose. This time limit is not to apply if there has been

---

[6] Finance Act 1975, Sched. 6, para 2; Finance Act 1976, s. 118 (8).
[7] *Ibid.* s. 39 (3).
[8] *Ibid.* s. 39 (5).
[9] Finance Act 1976, s. 118 (2)–(4).

an earlier transfer of the property exempted under these provisions and either transfer was one on death.

There is no relief for excepted assets. In relation to assets claimed under (a) and (b) above these are assets not used wholly or mainly for the purpose of the business concerned throughout the whole of the relevant two year period, or not so used by another member of a group. In relation to those fixed assets uder (c) and (d) above, the restriction is the same except that relief is available if they are replacements for similar assets which have been used for two out of the last five years in the business.

Trusts for the benefit of employees

91–26 Certain dispositions to trustees for the benefit of employers are exempt from capital transfer tax. The trust must be for a class of employee of a particular trade, profession or undertaking together with their relatives and dependants or for a charity. The exemption applies to such trusts set up by a close company provided that the beneficiaries include all or most of that company's employees or officers, or those of a subsidiary.[10] There is also an exemption for such a trust instituted by a shareholder in a company who transfers shares in that company to the trustees who thereby, or within one year will, hold over half the ordinary shares of the company together with voting control. This state of affairs must be unalterable except with the consent of the trustees. General voting control is not affected if special classes of shares have control over their own rights or on a winding up. In this case the beneficiaries must be all or most of that company's employees or officers, not those of a subsidiary.[11] In either case there is no exemption if the beneficiaries could include participators of the company past, present, or future, or persons connected with them (unless entitled to less than 5 per cent. of the assets of the company on a winding up).[12]

There is also relief from the charges on settlements on such trusts. There is no capital distribution charge if capital is paid to an employee unconnected with the settlor or a participator of a close company if that is the employer. There is no periodic charge until such a chargeable distribution is made or if the trust is terminated. The exemption however applies if one such trust is replaced by another within one month.[13]

Agricultural relief

91–27 Where there is a transfer of shares of an agricultural company and the value of those shares is partly attributable to the value of agricultural property then there may be relief from capital transfer tax by a reduction of 50 or 20 per cent. of the agricultural value of that property.[14] In general

---

[10] Finance Act 1976, s. 90 (1).
[11] Finance Act 1978, s. 67.
[12] Finance Act 1976, s. 90.
[13] Finance Act 1975, Sched. 5 para 17.
[14] Finance Act 1981, Sched. 14.

this relief will operate if the transferor controlled the company and either the company or another company has occupied the property owned by the company for the seven preceding years during which time the property has been occupied for farming, or the company has occupied the land for that purpose for the past two years. The 50 per cent. relief is only available however if the company's interest carries the right to vacant possession or the right to obtain it within the next year. In other cases only the 20 per cent. relief will be available.

In general business relief will be more useful but if only part of the farm is transferred agricultural relief will be the only one available as it is unlikely to amount to a transfer of a business. The 20 per cent. relief applies to landlord companies who need not be carrying on a farming business at all.

Chapter 92

THE INFLUENCE OF COMPANY TAXATION ON THE TAXATION OF SHAREHOLDERS

Income tax

92–01 Dividends and other distributions are chargeable under Schedule F.[1] The tax credit offsets the recipient's basic rate liability. The sum received by the individual shareholder, grossed up to include the tax credit, is assessable to higher rate tax and the investment income surcharge.[2] The tax actually payable is at a rate equal to the difference between the higher rates and the basic rate. Tax is due on July 6 following the tax year for which it is assessed or 30 days after the issue of the notice of assessment whichever is the later.[3] A shareholder in a United Kingdom company is taxed in the same manner whether or not the profits of the company are earned here or abroad.

Income of British residents from shares or debentures in companies resident outside the United Kingdom is taxed under Case V or IV respectively of Schedule D.[4] Where a double taxation agreement is operative, relief is normally given by crediting the foreign tax on the income against income tax payable in the United Kingdom,[5] and where there is no such operative agreement substantially the same result is achieved by unilateral relief.[6] There are income tax reliefs for both investment in and losses on certain equity shares. These are set out below.[7]

Capital gains

92–02 A shareholder may also make a capital gain on changing his share portfolio or on disposing of his shares. Capital gains tax affects disposals made after April 6, 1965 of assets acquired before or after that date.[8] Tax is only chargeable on such disposal, and although in a few cases the transfer may be notional, it is not a capital levy. Where shares are sold in return for a down payment and a right to deferred consideration (*e.g.* a percentage of future profits) there are two separate disposals; one on the sale and another on the subsequent payment of the deferred consideration. This is because the right to the deferred consideration is itself regarded as an asset which can be disposed.[9]

---

1 s. 232 (1) as amended by Finance Act 1972, s. 87.
2 Finance Act 1971, s. 32 (1).
3 *Ibid.*, Sched. 6, para. 3.
4 s. 109.
5 *Bowater Paper Corporation* v. *Murgatroyd* [1970] A.C. 266 (H.L.).
6 s. 498.
7 See para. 92–18, below.
8 C.G.T.A. 1979 s. 28 (2), (3).
9 *Marren* v. *Ingles* [1980] S.T.C. 500 (H.L.), *Marson* v. *Marriage* [1980] S.T.C. 177.

Notional disposals include deriving a capital sum from an asset[10] and if the shares are the subject matter of a trust the beneficiaries becoming absolutely entitled to them otherwise than on a death—in that case there is a notional disposal by the trustees to the beneficiaries[11] provided that the latter are resident in the United Kingdom.[12]

92–03 Transfers for less than full market value, *i.e.* bad bargains or gifts are however unlikely to give rise to a charge for in such circumstances the transferor and transferee may jointly elect that in such a case the transferee will be regarded as having paid an amount exactly equal to the allowable costs of the transferor—so that there will be no gain.[13] Prior to 1980 current market value was used as the disposal value of a gift thus usually giving rise to a charge.[14] The consequence of the new provision is that the transferee will then have a lower acquisition cost to set off against any subsequent disposal although the charge may again be postponed if that is also a gift or bad bargain. Capital transfer tax payable on such a gift is an allowable deduction for capital gains purposes.[15] If the actual consideration received is less than market value but more than the transferor's allowable costs that consideration will be used as the disposal value.[16] Shareholders who transfer their shares to trustees will thus no longer automatically incur a liability to the tax.[17]

92–04 The basic deduction allowed is the acquisition cost of the shares even where they are purchased by non-cash assets.[18] The original purchase price must have been paid "wholly and exclusively" to acquire the shares for it to be allowable.[19] "Incidental costs . . . of the acquisition"[20] and disposal[21] are allowed. To the original purchase price the stamp duties and brokers' commission are added and from the sale price the contract stamp and commission are deductible. Only the difference between the net totals, or profit actually made by the taxpayer, is taxed.

On any attempt by an individual engaged in speculative dealings in shares to establish that he is carrying on a trade as distinct from disposing capital assets, the prima facie assumption is that he is not.[22]

92–05 For capital gains tax purposes the general rule, which applies without modification to purchases and disposals occurring after April 6, 1965, is that any number of shares of the same class held by a person in the same capacity are regarded as indistinguishable parts of a single holding,[23] and

---

[10] C.G.T.A. 1979, s. 20 (1).
[11] *Ibid.* s. 54 (1).
[12] See, *e.g. Chinn* v. *Holchstrasser* [1979] 2 W.L.R. 411 (C.A.).
[13] Finance Act 1980, s. 79. See para. 91–20, *ante*.
[14] C.G.T.A. 1979, s. 19 (3).
[15] Finance Act 1980, s. 79 (5).
[16] *Ibid.* s. 79 (3).
[17] See as to the former position. C.G.T.A. 1979, s. 46 (1); *cf. Berry* v. *Warnett* [1978] 1 W.L.R. 957.
[18] *Stanton* v. *Drayton Commercial Investments Co. Ltd.* [1982] S.T.C. 585 (H.L).
[19] *Eilbeck* v. *Rawling* [1980] S.T.C. 192.
[20] *Ibid.* Sched. 6, para. 4 (1) (*a*).
[21] *Ibid.* para. 4 (1) (*b*).
[22] *Salt* v. *Chamberlain* [1979] S.T.C. 750.
[23] C.G.T.A. 1979 s. 65 (2) (7).

shares are of the same class if they are so treated by the practice of a recognised stock exchange.[24] The cost of the shares is "pooled," and in calculating the gain when any of the shares are disposed of their cost per share is the average cost of acquisition of all the shares in the "pool". An example may illustrate this rule. B. had the following transactions with shares in CD Ltd:

			Cost £
92–06	He bought on June 1, 1980, 1,000 shares @ 115p		1,150
	on September 1, 1980, 1,000 shares @ 100p		1,000
	on December 1, 1980, 1,000 shares @ 120p		1,200
	Total holding 3,000	Total cost	£3,350
	He sold on January 1, 1982, 1,800 shares @ 130p	=	£2,340

The original purchase price of the part-disposal is deemed to be

$$\frac{1,800}{3,000} \times £3,350 = £2,010$$

The chargeable gain is therefore £2,340 less £2,010=£330.

The basis cost of the 1,200 shares which remain undisposed of is £3,350 less £2,010=£1,340.

Note that all acquisitions are *post*-April 6, 1965.

92–07 If shares of securities were acquired before April 6, 1965, the taxpayer takes either their market value on that date, which for this purpose only is midway between the higher and lower of the stock exchange quotations,[25] or their purchase price, whichever is the higher, as the initial cost which may be deducted from the sale price.[26] A similar restriction applies to losses and the Revenue takes the figure which gives the lesser loss. Thus the chargeable gain or loss must not exceed the actual gain or loss over the period of ownership. If there is a loss by reference to the market value of the shares at April 6, 1965, and a gain by reference to their actual cost, or vice versa, for capital gains tax purposes there is deemed to be neither a gain nor a loss.[27] Where an election has not been made the "pooling of shares" provisions do not apply to acquisitions before April 6, 1965; and each disposal is linked with a particular acquisition. The rule is "first in, first out." The first shares acquired are treated as the first shares disposed of.[28]

A shareholder may, however, elect that:

(a) all his fixed-interest securities and preference shares or
(b) all his other quoted securities, or both, held by him on April 6, 1965,

---

[24] *Ibid.* s. 65 (4).
[25] *Ibid.* Sched. 6, para. 3.
[26] *Ibid.* Sched. 5, para. 12 (1)
[27] *Ibid.* para. 12 (2).
[28] *Ibid.* para. 2 (2).

shall be deemed to have been acquired at the price ruling on that date, and the original cost price shall be ignored. The election must be made within two years after the first post-March 19, 1968, disposal (or such further time as the Revenue may allow); and when made is irrevocable. In the case of a group of companies an election by the parent company of the group will bind all other companies in the group and the two-year time-limit runs from the first disposal by any member of the group after March 19, 1968.[29] Where shares held on April 6, 1965 have been exchanged for new shares they may be valued at the date of exchange.[30]

92–08 Assuming in the above example that B's first two acquisitions of shares in CDs Ltd. were 16 years earlier, *i.e.* on June 1, 1964, and September 1, 1964 (thus being pre-April 6, 1965), and the April 6, 1965, value of the shares is 110p, the chargeable gain is computed as follows:

	Cost £
He bought on June 1, 1964, 1,000 shares @ 115p	1,150
on September 1, 1964, 1,000 shares @ 100p	1,000
on December 1, 1964, 1,000 shares @ 120p	1,200
He sold on January 1, 1975, 1,800 shares @ 130p	2,340
The April 6, 1965, value of the shares is 110p.	

The 1,800 shares sold on January 1, 1975 are identified, by the "first in, first out" rule, as to 1,000 with those acquired on June 1, 1964. Their original purchase price was higher than their value on April 6, 1965. Capital gain on 1,000 shares is 1,000 @ 130p less 1,000 @ 115p = £150. This disposes of the June 1, 1964, acquisition. The remaining 800 shares are identified with the acquisition of September 1, 1964, but here the April 6, 1965, valuation (110p) is higher than the cost price (100p). Capital gain on 800 shares is 800 @ 130p less 800 @ 110p = £160.

The total chargeable gain on the sale is £150 + £160 = £310.

The residue is 200 @ 110p and 1,000 @ 120p (the December 1, 1964, acquisition) and on a subsequent disposal the shares will be identified first with the remainder of the September 1, 1964, acquisition.

92–09 If B had elected for the April 6, 1965, valuation the position would have been as follows:

1,800 shares sold @ 130p	=	£2,340
Acquisition value on April 6, 1965 1,800 shares @ 110 p	=	£1,980
Chargeable gain		£ 360

The residue is as above.

As the example shows, election may be disadvantageous.

[29] *Ibid.* paras. 3–7.

[30] *Ibid.* para. 14. See *I.R.C.* v. *Beveridge* [1979] S.T.C. 592 and I.R. Statement of Practice, S.P. 14/79.

The "no gain no loss" provision where the April 6, 1965, value shows a loss and the actual cost a gain, or vice versa, does not apply where an election is made.

92–10 A bonus or a rights issue of shares or debentures is not treated as involving any disposal, and thus does not attract tax; but on a subsequent sale, the original shares and the new holding are treated as the same asset acquired as the original shares were acquired.[31] On a part-disposal where the original and the new shares are of the same class the base cost is apportioned to the shares *pro rata*; where the new shares are of a different class from the original shares the cost of the holding is divided between the old shares and the new by reference to the market value of the two classes on the first day on which they are quoted.[32] The additional consideration given for a rights issue is added to the cost of the original shares in respect of which the rights issue is allocated insofar as it represents the market value increase of the shareholding.[33] If a shareholder receives a provisional allotment of shares or debentures and disposes of his rights the consideration for the disposal is treated as a capital distribution received by him from the company in respect of the original shares, and as if he had, instead of disposing of the rights, disposed of an interest in those shares.[34] But the Inspector of Taxes may direct, if the amount involved is small, normally where such consideration does not exceed 5 per cent. of the value of the shares, that the consideration for the sale of the rights shall instead be deducted from the basis cost attributed to the shares for capital gains tax purposes.

92–11 If the shareholders control the company and exercise their control so that the value of their shares is diminished and passes into other shares in or rights over the company, *e.g.* by refusing a rights issue so passing control, or by issuing new shares to other shareholders, there is a disposal by the controller. In *Floor* v. *Davis*[35] this provision was held to negative an avoidance scheme purporting to transfer the value of the shares to a non-resident company.

Where a shareholder exchanges his shares in a company for shares in another company, *e.g.* on a take-over, there is no disposal on the exchange. Instead the new shares are treated as being the same as the old shares acquired for the same price as the old shares so that no gain will accrue until the new shares are disposed of, *e.g.* X buys 100 shares in Company Y for £100. He exchanges them for shares in Company Z when they are valued at £1,000. There is no gain then. He then sells the Z shares for £1,500. His gain will then be £1,500–£100.[36] Similarly acceptance of shares in a new company under a scheme of reconstruction under section

---

31 *Ibid.* s. 77, 78.
32 *Ibid.* s. 80, 81.
33 *Ibid.* s. 79.
34 *Ibid.* s. 73.
35 [1979] S.T.C. 379 (H.L.)
36 C.G.T.A. 1979, s. 85 (1).

287 of the Companies Act 1948 is not a disposal.[37] Use of these provisions in tax avoidance schemes has been countered by sections 85, 87 and 88 of the Capital Gains Tax Act 1979 and applications for clearance must now be made to the Board of Inland Revenue for the relief to apply. Other avoidance schemes have involved shifting the value out of shares into other shares owned by the same person or a person connected with him. The devalued shares can then be disposed of at a loss to be used against other gains. These schemes have been countered by section 26 of the Capital Gains Tax Act 1979, whereby the value lost can be added back onto the devalued shares.

92–12 British Government securities, which are listed in the Capital Gains Tax Act 1979, Sched. 2, are not subject to capital gains tax unless the disposal of such securities occurs within 12 months after their acquisition. When gilt-edged securities of the same kind are sold, securities disposed of on an earlier date are identified before those disposed of later and with the earliest acquisition or earlier acquisitions within the 12 month period. If it is not possible thus to identify the securities disposed of, or a balance of them, within the 12 month period no capital gains tax will be payable.[38]

92–13 The operation of these rules can be shown by an example:

A had the following transactions with 5 per cent Exchequer Loan 1976–78:

He bought on January 1, 1975, 1,000 units @	80p
on June 1, 1975, a further 1,000 units @	85p
on September 1, 1975, a further 1,000 units @	90p
on December 1, 1975, a further 1,000 units @	95p
He sold on May 1, 1976, 1,500 units @	100p
on October 1, 1976, a further 250 units @	105p

The disposal on May 1, 1976 is taken first; and identified as to 1,000 units with the 1,000 units bought on June 1, 1975—the earlier acquisition WITHIN the 12 month period.

	£
Gain 1,000 @ 15p (100p–85p)	150
As to the remaining 500 units with those bought on September 1, 1975 (leaving 500 in this acquisition)	
Gain 500 @ 10p (100p–90p)	50
The disposal on October 1, 1976 is identified with the acquisition on December 1, 1975 (the 500 units remaining from the September 1, 1975 purchase being now outside the twelve month period).	
Gain 250 @ 10p (105p–95p)	25
The total gain in the tax year 1976–77 is	£225

If on May 1, 1977 A disposes of 1,000 units at 110p the gain made does not attract capital gains tax.

92–14 There are also provisions to curb the exploitation of losses incurred in speculating in Government securities. Where a loss occurs on a disposal of

[37] *Ibid*. ss. 67, 68.
[38] Finance Act 1971, Sched. 10, paras. 4 and 7.

gilt-edged securities and the vendor re-acquires, in the same capacity, the same securities within one month, or six months if this is not done through a stock exchange, the loss can only be set off against a gain arising on the future disposal of the securities re-acquired.[39] Where gilt-edged securities are issued as a replacement for shares, acquired on nationalisation any capital gain is postponed until these securities are disposed of.[40]

92–15 Capital gains tax is charged at a ceiling flat rate of 30 per cent.[41] The first £3,000 of chargeable gains made by each taxpayer in each fixed year is however exempt whatever the total of his gains for the year.[42] This replaced a former exemption of £1,000 which was eliminated by tapering provisions on annual gains of more than £9,500. There is a similar exemption for the first £1,500 gains made by trustees but to discourage everyone from forming large numbers of small settlements to multiply the exemption it is to be shared amongst all settlements created by the same settlor after June 6, 1978.[43]

Assessment is on a current-year basis and the tax is payable three months after the end of the year of assessment or 30 days from the date of assessment, whichever is the later.[44]

92–16 In the case of married persons, unless a claim for separate assessment is made which makes no difference to the total tax payable by both, capital gains tax on gains accruing to a married couple living together is charged on the husband.[45] There is no charge in transactions between husband and wife.[46]

92–17 Options to buy or sell shares in a company, which are quoted on the Stock Exchange, *i.e.* "traded options," are assets which may be disposed of so as to give rise to a charge to capital gains tax. These options are however no longer regarded as wasting assets[47] so that there is no requirement, as prior to 1980, to write down the acquisition cost over the expected life of the option.

Income tax relief for capital losses in unquoted shares

92–18 The Finance Act 1980 introduced a new development in United Kingdom tax law by allowing a relief against one tax for a loss sustained in relation to another.[48] In general where a shareholder makes a loss in shares of an unquoted trading company, computed in the usual capital gains tax way, that loss will be available against his income of the year of loss and/or the subsequent year. This relief only applies if the shareholder subscribed for the shares and the disposal was either a bona fide commercial sale, a

[39] *Ibid.* s. 70.
[40] *Ibid.* s. 84.
[41] *Ibid.* s. 3.
[42] Finance Act 1980, s. 77.
[43] *Ibid.* s. 78.
[44] C.G.T.A. 1979, s. 7
[45] *Ibid.* s. 45.
[46] *Ibid.* s. 44.
[47] Finance Act 1980, s. 84.
[48] *Ibid.* s. 37; *cf.* Finance Act 1981, s. 36.

receipt on a liquidation, or a claim that the shares had become of negligible value. An individual will be regarded as having subscribed for shares if his spouse did so and transferred them to him otherwise than on death.

The shares will not qualify for relief if the company has not been a trading company since the date of its incorporation unless it has been a trading company for the previous six years. A company is also excluded if it has ever been non-resident. Where some of the shares held qualify for relief and others do not a partial disposal is dealt with on a last in first out basis.

Tax relief for investment in new corporate trades—the business start up scheme

The Finance Act 1981 introduced an experimental new relief from income tax by way of deduction from the total income of any individual of any amount, up to £10,000 per annum, invested by him in subscribing for new shares in a *new qualifying company* issued for the purpose of finding a *new qualifying trade* carried on or to be carried on within 12 months by that company.[49] In the first instance this relief will only operate for shares issues in the financial years 1981/82, 1982/83 and 1983/84.[50] The relief can be claimed at any time after the end of the relevant year provided that the company has carried on the trade for at least a year and did commence it within a year of the issue of the shares. The relief may be claimed on amounts between £500 and £10,000 per annum.[51] As may be expected the legislation is concerned to prevent the creation of avoidance schemes and a general anti-avoidance section is included.[52] The salient points of the scheme may be outlined as follows:

(1) The investor must not be connected in any way with the issuing company. Nor must he control more than 30 per cent. of the company's shares, loan capital or voting rights, or be entitled to more than that amount of its assets on a winding up.[53] In other words he must be an independent minority shareholder;

(2) The company must be a United Kingdom resident company which since incorporation or commencement of business has existed solely for the purpose of carrying on one or more new qualifying trades. Its share capital must be of one class of ordinary shares together with any fixed-interest preference shares and all fully paid up, and it must not be a member or a potential member of any group or consortium[54];

(3) The new qualifying trades for which investment is permitted must be "bona fide new ventures" (and not the incorporation of unincorporated businesses) conducted on a commercial basis. Certain

---

49 Finance Act 1981, ss. 52–57.
50 *Ibid.* s. 52.
51 *Ibid.* s. 53.
52 *Ibid.* s. 59.
53 *Ibid.* s. 54.
54 *Ibid.* s. 55.

trades such as dealing in shares, land or futures and the provisions of financial, legal or accounting services are excluded as are service companies[55];

(4) The right to relief is diminished on a disposal by the investor within five years, by the amount he receives. If the disposal is a gift the relief is lost entirely; if otherwise the relief is reduced by the consideration received.[56] The relief is also reduced by any value received by the investor from the company during the relevant five years other than an ordinary commercial return on his investment or the payment of an "ordinary trade debt"[57];

(5) Relief which has been wrongly given may be recovered by a charge to income tax made for the year in question within six years.[58] For this purpose, and others, the claimant and the company are required to furnish information of relevant events[59];

(6) Insofar as relief is given under this scheme it is to be deducted from the allowable expenses for capital gains tax on a subsequent disposal of the shares.[60]

Anti-avoidance provisions

92–19 The Revenue are in running combat with increasingly ingenious tax-avoidance schemes. Anti-avoidance measures take two forms: specific provisions relating to forms of avoidance and, more recently, a wider form of judicial interpretation of the effect of "artificial" avoidance schemes. Anti-avoidance legislation, first dealing with "dividend stripping and bond washing" is now contained in the Income and Corporation Taxes Act 1970, sections 281 and 469 respectively. The former applies where one company holds at least 10 per cent. of the shares of one class in a second company and the second company makes a distribution which reduces the value of the shares. If subsequently on a sale of the shares an allowable loss is claimed which is attributable to the distribution, that loss is reduced by the amount received on the distribution. Section 469, dealing with bond washing, counters the sale by an owner of shares cum-dividend and their repurchase ex-dividend thereby obtaining an accretion of capital by charging the dividend as an income receipt in the hands of the owner.

The main anti-avoidance provisions are, however, contained in section 460, which has been judicially described as having "mounted a massive attack against tax avoidance." The section not only deals with known devices but casts a very wide net to catch increasingly sophisticated future avoidance schemes. Section 460 (1) of the Income and Corporation Taxes Act 1970 states that where in the circumstances mentioned in section 461,

[55] *Ibid.* s. 56.
[56] *Ibid.* s. 57.
[57] *Ibid.* s. 58.
[58] *Ibid.* s. 62.
[59] *Ibid.* s. 63.
[60] *Ibid.* s. 64.

which are *inter alia* that either in connection with the distribution of profits of a company and in consequence of transactions in securities, or their combined effect, or in connection with a transfer of assets from one company to another a person receives non-taxable consideration not in either case being for bona fide commercial purposes, a person can or does obtain a tax advantage, this shall be counteracted by an appropriate assessment.[61] The onus is on the taxpayer to bring himself within the bona fide commercial exemption. "Profits" include "income, reserves or other assets"[62] and the section operates where a person obtains a tax advantage by receiving an abnormal amount by way of dividend.[63]

Section 460 (2) extends the charge to a tax advantage deemed to be obtained in consequence of a transaction in securities or of the combined effect of two or more such transactions if it is obtained in consequence of the combined effect of the transaction or transactions and of the liquidation of a company. In *I.R.C.* v. *Joiner*[64] the House of Lords held that an agreement between the shareholders to liquidate a company, transfer its assets to another controlled company, and distribute its undistributed profits to the majority shareholder was a transaction in securities and came within section 460 (2). Viscount Dilhorne and Lord Diplock held that a liquidation alone could not be a transaction in securities but Lord Wilberforce preferred to leave the matter open. He also suggested the correct approach to be used in interpreting these sections:

> "For whereas it is generally the rule that clear words are required to impose a tax, so that the taxpayer has the benefit of doubt or ambiguities [it is . . .] clear that the scheme of the sections, introducing as they did a wide and general attack on tax avoidance, required that expressions which might otherwise have been cut down in the interest of precision were to be given the wide meaning evidently intended, even though they led to a conclusion short of which judges would normally desire to stop. If we are to follow this path, and I see no other open to us, we must continue to give 'transaction in securities' and 'transaction relating to securities' the widest meaning."

The procedure for implementing the section is for the Commissioners to notify the taxpayer that they have reason to believe that it may apply to him in respect of certain transactions in securities specified therein. The taxpayer can then make a statutory declaration to the effect that he has not obtained any tax advantage from the specified transactions. The Commissioners will then, if they think fit, send a certificate to a tribunal set up undeı section 463 to the effect that further action should be taken together with a counter-statement with reference to the matter. The tribunal will then decide if there is a prima facie case to proceed. In *Balen* v. *I.R.C.* the

---

[61] s. 460 (3).
[62] s. 467 (2) (*a*).
[63] There may well be a tax advantage even though the taxpayers are technically liable under some other provision: *Williams* v. *I.R.C.* [1980] S.T.C. 535 (H.L.).
[64] [1975] 1 W.L.R. 1701 (H.L.).

taxpayer protested that the original notice to him did not specify the Commissioners' reasons for their belief and that he had not been shown the counter-statement which did so specify and which the tribunal had taken into account in determining to proceed. His complaint on both these counts was overruled by the court—the only decision for the tribunal was as to the existence of a prima facie case and not the settlement of a dispute between the parties.[65]

92–20 Examples may further illustrate the ambit of the section. In *I.R.C.* v. *Cleary* two sisters owned in equal shares the whole share capital in two property-holding companies. The assets of one, Gleeson Development Ltd., included £130,000 cash at bank. In 1961 the sisters each sold 22,000 shares out of their holdings in the other, Gleeson Ltd., to Gleeson Development for £60,500 in cash, this being the full value of the shares. The Court of Appeal held that this was a transaction in securities relating to a distribution of profits, being sums which immediately before the transaction were available for payment as dividends, for the purpose of obtaining a tax advantage. The court upheld the Revenue's assessment of the sisters to surtax in the grossed-up amount on £60,500 each.[66]

In determining whether there has been a tax advantage obtained from the transaction the scheme has to be looked at as a whole. In *I.R.C.* v. *Wiggins*[67] a company which owned a valuable picture wished to dispose of it to a purchaser. The company's controller sold all its stock apart from the picture to another of their companies and then sold the shares of the first company to the purchaser. The Special Commissioners held that because the purchase of the shares was a capital payment it could not have been received by the controller in any taxable form and thus no tax advantage could accrue to them. Walton J. held that there had been a transaction in securities and the relevant question as to a tax advantage was whether the controllers could have obtained the profit from the picture in any other way and not whether the purchasers could have made the payment by any other means. The answer to this being in the affirmative the assessment was upheld.

Where, however, in such circumstances, the consideration received by the taxpayer takes the form, not of money, but of non-redeemable share capital, tax will not be chargeable unless and until the share capital is repaid, either in a winding up or otherwise.[68] Any assessment will be made for the year in which the share capital is repaid.[69] This also applies in the case of redeemable capital. In *I.R.C.* v. *Parker Shoes Ltd.*,[70] a controlled company in 1953, capitalised £35,002 of undistributed profits, to meet the contingency of the respondent's estate duty liability by issuing debentures.

---

65 [1978] 2 All E.R. 1033 (C.A.).
66 *I.R.C.* v. *Cleary; I.R.C.* v. *Perren* [1966] Ch. 365. See also *I.R.C.* v. *Kleinwort Benson Ltd.* [1969] 2 Ch. 221 where the taxpayer was able to show that the transaction in question was carried out for bona fide commercial reasons.
67 [1979] 2 A11 E.R. 245.
68 s. 461E (2). But see *Anysz* v. *I.R.C.* [1978] S.T.C. 296, *post*.
69 s. 461E (1) and (2).
70 [1966] A.C. 141.

The debenture issued to the respondent was for £18,002 and repayable at the respondent's death or after seven years. In 1961 the company redeemed the debentures. The House of Lords held that the only object of the operation was to enable the company to distribute £35,002 in such a way as not to attract surtax[71] and upheld, by a majority, the Revenue's claim that the respondent's surtax liability should be adjusted for the year of assessment 1960–61 on the basis that £18,002 was the net amount of a dividend received in the tax year in which it was paid. In both cases tax liability was, of course, greater than it would have been if the profits had been distributed as dividends over the years in accordance with normal procedure.

92–21 If however the consideration received by the taxpayer consists of non-redeemable share capital of another company then it has been held that a tax advantage may be acquired at the date of receipt and not the date of repayment of the shares. The shares must have been received in connection with the distribution of profits of the taxpayer's company (*i.e.* as a constituent part of the scheme) so as to fulfill the requirements of the section (consideration received by way of abnormal dividend) and thus avoid the rules as to the timing of the tax advantage in section 461E.[72] The case involved an exchange of shares coupled with the payment of a dividend by one company to the other which was then lent to a third company controlled by the taxpayer. The majority view in *I.R.C.* v. *Parker (supra)* was distinguished on the question of timing as (i) it related only to one company, and (ii) it had been decided prior to section 461E, which showed that the mere receipt of such share capital or security would constitute a tax advantage were it not for the timing rules in that section.

A contrary view was however taken by the Court of Appeal in *Williams* v. *I.R.C.*[73] who held that where a receipt is within section 461E, *i.e.* as a receipt of share capital, even though it may also fall within another part of the section, the taxpayer was entitled to the deferment of liability within section 461E. The House of Lords upheld the decision on other grounds.[74] In that case loans received by the shareholders of a company without payment of tax and repayable to a company under this control were held to be "transactions in securities."

On the other hand the commercial reason for carrying out a transaction does not have to be connected with the taxpayer's interests in the companies concerned. In *Clark* v. *I.R.C.*,[75] the taxpayer's main reason for selling his shares in a family investment company was to raise money to purchase a farm adjoining his existing one. Fox J. held that in the context of all the circumstances giving rise to the transaction it was carried out for a commercial reason and it did not matter that such a reason was not intrinsic to the transaction itself.

---

[71] *Per* Viscount Dilhorne at p. 157.
[72] *Anysz* v. *I.R.C.* [1978] S.T.C. 296.
[73] [1979] S.T.C. 598 (C.A.).
[74] [1980] S.T.C. 535 (H.L.).
[75] [1979] 1 A11 E.R. 385.

92–22 In *I.R.C.* v. *Goodwin*,[76] where there was a similar capitalisation of profits to attempt to retain maximum family control, the House of Lords held that a reason for a transaction could be both financial and commercial and refused to reverse the decision of the Special Commissioners in favour of the taxpayer that there were bona fide commercial reasons for the transactions, which was a question of fact for the commissioners. Examples of "bona fide commercial reasons" are *Hague* v. *I.R.C.*,[77] involving the return of surplus capital which was genuinely in excess of the company's requirements by means of a bonus issue followed by a reduction of capital. The taxpayers were stockholders in a textile company which received compensation under the Cotton Industry Act 1959 for disposing of two mills. *Bulmer* v. *I.R.C.*[78] shows that attempting to thwart a takeover bid can come within this purpose; particularly where as in *I.R.C.* v. *Brebner*[79] this would have been disastrous to the directors in depriving other companies in which they were interested of cheap credit and bunkering coal. Two points emerge from the latter decision. "Bona fide commercial reason" has to be found in the minds of those who carry out the challenged transaction in securities; and what is in reality all one transaction has to be viewed as a whole. The distinction between a bona fide commercial reason, which incidentally confers tax advantages which may be very substantial and tax avoidance, although it may benefit the company, can be a fine one. It is irrelevant whether the taxpayer actively took part in the transaction if the lack of a "bona fide commercial reason" is proved.[80]

More recently a wider approach to the operation of the section has been used following the approach of Lord Wilberforce in *I.R.C.* v. *Joiner*[81] detailed above. For example in *Emery* v. *I.R.C.*[82] it was held that a scheme under which the taxpayer sold his shares in the company to another company on an instalment basis and then sold the rights to those instalments to a third company, the third company recovering the purchase price by an indirect payment from the taxpayer's company by way of dividend, the taxpayer had received the money both in connection with the dividend and that the whole was a transaction whereby he had gained a tax advantage from the payment of an abnormal dividend to a third party. The judge deciding that a transaction for this purpose covers the whole series of operations leading to the tax advantage. This contrasts with the more restricted view taken in *I.R.C.* v. *Garvin*.[83]

92–23 Of particular relevance to family companies are provisions[84] which apply to sales to or by bodies of persons, which include partnerships[85] and

[76] [1969] 1 Ch. 393.
[77] [1967] Ch. 147.
[78] [1967] 2 A.C. 18.
[79] [1976] 1 W.L.R. 191.
[80] *Addy* v. *I.R.C.* [1975] S.T.C. 601.
[81] [1975] 3 A11 E.R. 1050.
[82] [1981] S.T.C. 150.
[83] [1980] S.T.C. 295, *affd.* [1981] S.T.C. 344 (H.L.).
[84] s. 485.
[85] s. 485 (5).

companies, but not to sales between individual traders,[86] at artificial prices when the parties are not at arm's length. They apply where the seller has control over the buyer or vice versa or both are under the control of a third party.[87] If the price is lower the seller must bring in the "independent" price, unless the buyer is a resident trader and the price is a deduction in his accounts. If the price is higher the buyer must bring in the "independent" price, unless the seller is a resident trader and the price is a trading receipt to him.[88] These requirements also apply to lettings and hirings of property, grants and transfers of rights, interests or licences and the giving of business facilities of any kind.[89] They only apply when the Revenue so direct.

Prevention of avoidance by transferring assets abroad

92-24 The analogy with section 460 will be apparent. Where assets are transferred, other than for bona fide commercial reasons, so that "income becomes payable" to persons outside the United Kingdom and thereby, either alone or with associated operations, the transferor or his or her spouse retains any "benefit,"[90] which includes the receipt of or right to receive any capital sums, the income of the transferee is to be deemed to be the income of the transferor for tax purposes.[91] In principle this relates to the gross income of the transferee, so that investment income received by a company is to be regarded irrespective of any management expenses incurred. There is nothing in the section to authorise any deductions and, *per* Lord Wilberforce, there is no common law of deductions.[92] In *Howard de Walden* v. *I.R.C.*[93] the taxpayer had transferred assets to Canadian companies whose total capital was traceable to this source. The Court of Appeal held that he should be assessed on the whole income of the companies, although he had effectively put most of this income out of his control. The section is a penal one intended to put a stop to practices which the legislature considers to be against the public interest.[94] The question whether a receipt is "income arising from possessions out of the United Kingdom" under Case V of Schedule D is a question to be determined according to English law, but the factual situation (which includes the foreign law) has to be examined in order to apply the English law.[95]

92-25 It is an indictable offence for a company, without the consent of the Treasury, to cease to be resident in the United Kingdom, to transfer the whole or part of its business to a non-resident, to permit a non-resident company which it controls to issue shares or debentures, or, except to

[86] s. 485 (1).
[87] s. 485 (1) (*a*).
[88] s. 485 (1) and (2).
[89] s. 485 (6).
[90] s. 478 (5) (*c*). Now strengthened by Finance Act 1981, ss. 44, 45.
[91] s. 478.
[92] *Lord Chetwoode* v. *I.R.C.* [1977] 1 W.L.R. 248.
[93] [1942] 1 K.B. 389.
[94] See also *Latilla* v. *I.R.C.* [1943] A.C. 377; *Congreve* v. *I.R.C.* [1946] 2 A11 E.R. 170.
[95] *Rae* v. *Lazard Investment Co. Ltd.* [1963] 1 W.L.R. 555.

enable a person to be qualified as a director, to dispose of its shares or debentures in such a non-resident company. The onus is on a director to prove his innocence.[96] In practice the Treasury will normally grant its consent if satisfied that the motivation is economic, and not a desire to escape from United Kingdom taxation.[97]

Artificial tax avoidance schemes

92–26 In a new departure the House of Lords decided, in 1981, that "artificial" tax avoidance schemes will be looked at as a whole to discover the true legal nature of the transaction. The court will no longer be bound to examine each particular act in isolation and give effect to each separate part if the transactions as a whole cancel each other out. This decision came first when the Lords were hearing appeals in two capital gains tax cases.[98] Both involved schemes whereby a series of transactions were undertaken which involved both a gain and a loss to the taxpayer but with the intent that the gain should be exempt and the loss be allowable against other gains incurred. In these circumstances the House decided that it would not be proper to look only at the transactions producing the loss but at the scheme as a whole. Composite transactions of this type which produced neither a gain nor a loss at the end of the day would be regarded as nullities for tax purposes. This approach was reaffirmed by the House of Lords in a later case in 1981, also on capital gains tax, whereby the taxpayer company sought to realise a loss which they had suffered, for tax purposes. Their Lordships decided that the company had suffered no 'real' loss, and held that the 'artificial' aspects of the scheme could be ignored.[99]

The schemes which appear to be subject to this new overall scrutiny are those which are "artificial"; *i.e.* they have aspects which have no commercial purpose apart from tax avoidance. Usually they consist of a number of steps to be carried out, documents to be executed and payments to be made, all according to a timetable, and, at the end of the series of operations, the taxpayer's financial position is usually the same as it was at the beginning, except that he will have paid a fee. Other features may include—an intention to carry through the whole series, the financing of the schemes by a finance house, although that is not essential, and an avowed intention to avoid tax. No longer will such schemes be able to avoid tax on the basis that each step, if legally genuine, must be given full effect. The whole operation, if a composite transaction of this type, will be the subject of interpretation. It appears to be irrelevant whether the scheme was bought "off the peg" or specially designed to cover the taxpayer's needs.

Applying the tests laid down by the House of Lords, Vinelott J. has held[1] that there must be a distinction between transactions where a change in

[96] s. 482 (1) and (5).
[97] Wheatcroft, *British Tax Encyclopedia*, paras. 1–093, 6–321.
[98] *W. T. Ramsay Ltd.* v. *I.R.C*; *Eilbeck* v. *Rawling* [1981] S.T.C. 174 (H.L.).
[99] *I.R.C.* v. *Burmah Oil Co.*, [1982] S.T.C. 30 (H.L.).
[1] *Furniss* v. *Dawson,* [1982] S.T.C. 267.

the legal position of the parties could be regarded as a mere change of form with no enduring legal consequence, which can be ignored for tax purposes, and those, which even as part of a composite scheme, have enduring legal consequences. Length of time seems to be of importance according to this analysis. In his judgment the court may still not substitute a different transaction for the one used by the parties solely because that would have been used by them had tax avoidance not been a factor.

CHAPTER 93

THE INFLUENCE OF COMPANY TAXATION ON THE TAXATION OF DIRECTORS AND EMPLOYEES

93–01 THE object of this chapter is to provide in a short and convenient form an outline of the tax law as it affects a company's officers and employees.

PAYE

93–02 Directors, together with other holders of offices and employments, are taxed on their pay, pensions or other emoluments under Schedule E[1] and to all such persons the "pay as you earn" procedure applies.[2] The PAYE system applies to income tax at the basic and higher rates.[3] Each employee is given a code number. This is determined by the employee's personal circumstances and usually takes into account expenses incurred wholly exclusively and necessarily in performance of the duties,[4–5] certain professional or similar subscriptions, Building Society and other allowable interest, and the various personal reliefs; from which total allowances due are deducted allowances given against other income, and tax unpaid for earlier years. As the code number is based on his total reliefs and allowances, it is essential that the taxpayer should notify the local Inspector of Taxes of all the allowances to which he may be entitled; and also when these change during the year, for instance through marriage so that the code number can be revised. The higher the total of allowances due the higher is the code number.

Cumulative tax tables[6] are sent to employers. These show the tax which is to be deducted or repaid on the occasion of each payment made in the tax year by reference to a total of emoluments paid up to the time of the payment. The amount deducted from fees, salaries and wages, thus calculated, is forwarded by the employer to the Revenue.[7] No formal assessment need be made on the employee.[8] If a company fails to deduct tax when paying an employee it is liable to the Revenue for the tax that it failed to deduct and its only remedy against the employee is by way of deductions frcm future payments,[9] and when a bag in which deducted tax was kept pending payment to the collector was stolen, the loss was held to fall on the employer.[10] The company is only liable to deduct tax on the

---

[1] s. 181.
[2] s. 204.
[3] Finance Act 1971, s. 36. For the current rates see Finance Act 1981, s. 19.
[4–5] s. 189 (1).
[6] s. 205 (1) (*a*).
[7] Income Tax (Employments) (No. 9) Regulations 1979, S.I. 1979 No. 747.
[8] s. 205 (1).
[9] *Bernard and Shaw Ltd.* v. *Shaw and Rubin* [1951] 2 A11 E.R. 267; *cf. R* v. *I.R.C.*, ex. p. *Chisholm* [1981] S.T.C. 253.
[10] *Att.-Gen.* v. *Antoine* [1949] 2 A11 E.R. 1000.

payment of an emolument taxable under Schedule E. This has been held however to include sums credited to directors' accounts with the company where those sums were part of a bonus for the year and had been placed unreservedly at the disposal of the directors and would have been paid on demand.[11]

PAYE is limited to the collection of income tax, but is also used for contributions under the graduated pension scheme. Where the PAYE procedure cannot operate, for instance, because an individual is in foreign employment, the employee is assessed direct.[12]

BENEFITS IN KIND

93–03 Tax under Schedule E is charged in respect of any office or employment on emoluments therefrom[13]; and "emoluments" includes "all . . . perquisites and profits whatsoever."[14] In *Abbott* v. *Philbin*,[15] however, the House of Lords limited the meaning of these words to "something which is by its nature capable of being turned into money." They followed their previous decision in *Heaton* v. *Bell*,[16] where the use of a car was given to employees earning less than, £2,000. The car remained the property of the company and the employee could not let it out on hire. This would not have been a taxable emolument had it not been for a right conferred upon the employee to terminate the agreement and resume a higher salary. Benefits in kind given by employers to employees who earn less than £8,500 per annum and are not directors which cannot be converted into money by the employees are not taxable under Schedule E. In *Wilkins* v. *Rogerson*[17] a company gave its employees a made-to-measure suit as a Christmas present costing, in this case, £14.75. The Court of Appeal held that the employee was only assessable on the immediate second-hand value of the suit which was agreed at £5. Tax is charged on the value of the emolument to the employee.

Reimbursements to such employees are equally not emoluments if there is no element of bounty involved. The question is whether a genuine attempt has been made to provide a reimbursement, not a strict mathematical calculation.[17a]

93–04 With effect from 1976–77, however, the Finance (No. 2) Act 1975 made important changes in respect of this class of employee. In particular vouchers for instance for a made-to-measure suit, are taxed in the hands of the employee on what it costs his employer to provide the goods or services

---

[11] *Garforth* v. *Newsmith Stainless Ltd.* [1979] 1 W.L.R. 409.

[12] An employee working here is not subject to PAYE if his employer is foreign, see *Clark* v. *Oceanic Contractors Inc.*, [1982] S.T.C. 66. (C.A.).

[13] s. 181 (1). This includes the full value of the emoluments, *e.g.* of gold sovereigns: *Jenkins* v. *Horn* [1979] S.T.C. 446.

[14] s. 183 (1).

[15] [1961] A.C. 352.

[16] [1970] A.C. 728. But *cf. Willianson* v. *Dalton,* [1981] S.T.C 753.

[17] [1961] 1 Ch. 133.

[17a] *Donnelly* v. *Williamson,* [1982] S.T.C. 88; *cf. Perrons* v. *Spackman,* [1981] S.T.C. 739.

for which the voucher can be exchanged, less any amount made good by the employee. Vouchers for transport are also taxable on this basis.[18] Vouchers exchangeable for cash are taxed on the amount they are capable of being exchanged for.[19] With effect from 1982/83 the use of company credit or charge cards by employees for their own use will also be taxed. The taxable amount will be the expenses, if any, incurred by the employer in providing the card and the amount paid by him to the credit company for each transaction made by the employee, including any interest, rather than the value of the goods or services received. Only payments which would be deductible from tax if paid by the employees will be exempt. Repayments by the employee will also be deductible.[20]

There are special provisions relating to accommodation provided by the employer either for the employee or his family or household. Such an employee is taxed as if he had been paid an amount equal to the rent he would have had to pay on a yearly tenancy, assuming that the landlord was liable for repairs, etc., less any amount he actually pays for the accommodation. There are exceptions to this charge particularly where it is necessary for the proper performance of his duties for him to reside there or if it is customary to provide such accommodation in order to help him perform his duties. There are further rules if the employer is a company and the employer is a director of that company or an associated company. If the accommodation is "job-related" and exempt from a charge the employee may also obtain interest relief on the purchase of a separate house whether or not he occupies it.[21]

Until 1982/83 the provisions of group medical insurance by an employer was a taxable benefit in kind for all employees. This rule no longer applies.[22]

DIRECTORS AND £8,500 P.A. EMPLOYEES

93–05 Special provisions[23] designed to prevent tax avoidance by means of expense allowances and benefits in kind apply to all directors, which term includes all persons acting as such by whatever name called,[24] and to employees whose emoluments, including the expenses and benefits covered by these provisions, are, or exceed, £8,500 per annum.[25] Where a person is employed in several employments by, or holds a directorship and is employed by, the same corporation, all his emoluments are aggregated.[26] The provisions may be summarised as follows:

---

18 s. 36
19 *Ibid.* s. 37.
20 Finance (No. 2) Act 1975, s. 36A.
21 Finance Act 1977, s. 33.
22 Finance Act 1976, s. 68, Finance Act 1981, s. 72.
23 Finance Act 1976, ss. 60–72, replacing ss. 195–199 of I.C.T.A. 1970 for 1977–78 onwards.
24 Finance Act 1976, s. 72 (8).
25 *Ibid.* s. 69 (2). The figure has increased from £5,000 p.a. in 1977–78 to £7,500 in 1978–79 to £8,500 at the current time.
26 *Ibid.* s. 69 (3).

Payments by way of expenses

93–06 Any sums paid to a director or "higher-paid" employee in respect of expenses, whether as an actual reimbursement or on a flat rate basis are to be regarded as emoluments if paid by reason of the employment.[27] All money paid by an employer to an employee by way of expenses is deemed to be by reason of the employment unless the employee can show that it was made in the normal course of his domestic, family or personal relationships.[28] This is all subject to any claim for a deduction for expenses incurred by the employee "wholly, exclusively and necessarily" in performing the duties of the office or employment, but the onus of proof is on the taxpayer.[29]

Benefits in kind—the general rules

93–07 Apart from the special rules relating to cars, beneficial loans and employee shareholdings, which are dealt with below, and the provisions relating to medical insurance already noted, the following rules apply to the provision of benefits in kind. Section 61 of the Finance Act 1976 provides that the provision of any director or "higher-paid" employee (or his family or household—defined in Finance Act 1976, section 72 (4) to include his guests) of any living or other accommodation, entertainment, domestic or other services and other benefits and facilities of any nature (*e.g.* payment of legal fees to keep employee out of prison, *Rendell* v. *Went (Inspector of Taxes)*[30] are to be included as emoluments if paid by reason of his employment, *i.e.* usually if paid by his employer.[31] The value of this emolument is the cash equivalent of the benefit. This is the cost to the provider if the benefit less any money paid by the director or employee for the benefit.[32] This phraseology does not however tax income which is generally exempt, for example scholarship income.[33] If an asset is placed at the director's or employee's disposal, then its annual value together with the cost of providing it is to be the deemed emolument.[34] To discourage anti-avoidance schemes the benefit on the transfer to the employee of the asset absolutely is assessed on the higher of the market value either at the time of the transfer or *at* the time it was first used by the employer for any employee less the amounts taxed on its use in the meantime.[35] Claims for expenditure allowable generally under Schedule E may be made against any assessment.[36]

---

27 *Ibid.* s. 60.
28 *Ibid.* s. 72 (3).
29 s. 60 (2). See also *Brown* v. *Bullock* [1961] 1 W.L.R. 1095; *Elwood* v. *Utitz* (1966) 42 T.C. 482; *Owen* v. *Pook* [1970] A.C. 244; *Taylor* v. *Provan* [1975] A.C. 194.
30 [1964] 1 W.L.R. 650.
31 Finance Act 1976, s. 61 (3), s. 72 (3).
32 *Ibid.* s. 63 (1).
33 *Wicks* v. *Firth* [1981] S.T.C. 28.
34 *Ibid.* s. 63 (4) (7).
35 *Ibid.* s. 63 (3), (3A).
36 *Ibid.* s. 63 (8).

This general charge is subject to five exceptions:

(i) certain cars and fuel, see para. 93–08, *post*.

(ii) The provisions of any accommodation, supplies or services in the employer's premises and used by the director or employee solely in performing the duties of the office or employment. Finance Act 1976, s. 62 (3).

(iii) The provision of living accommodation for an employee in part of the employer's premises if the employee is required to reside there by the terms of his employment and it is necessary for him to reside there; Finance Act 1976, s. 62 (4), (5).[37]

(iv) Provision of death or retirement benefits; Finance Act 1976, s. 62 (6).

(v) Provision of meals in a staff canteen; Finance Act 1976, s. 62 (7).

(vi) Where there is no charge on the provision of living accommodation under section 33 of the Finance Act 1977[38] because one of the exceptions applies, a director or higher-paid employee is only charged on the provisions by the employer of heating, lighting, cleaning, repairs and maintenance, furniture etc., in relation to the accommodation under section 61, on an amount not exceeding 10 per cent. of his other emoluments for the year.[39]

Company cars and fuel

93–08 If the car is transferred to the director or employee this is a benefit in kind and taxable in full under P.A.Y.E. But in the usual case of a car made available by the employer without any transfer of property the amount of tax payable depends on whether the car is or is not also used for business travel (defined as that necessary for the employment,[40] or, if it is so used, such use is 2,500 miles per annum or less. If the car is used for business then the general rules as to benefits in kind apply only to the provision of a driver and not to the use of the car.[41] Instead the benefit is charged by section 64 of the Finance Act 1976 according to tables contained in Schedule 7 to that Act as set out for 1981–82 onwards in the Income Tax (Cash equivalent of car benefits) Order 1980 (No. 889). These specify a sum according to the age, size and cost of the car. There are reductions for periods when the car is not available for use, if the car is used "substantially" for business purposes (defined as 18,000 miles p.a.) and where the employee makes a contribution. Conversely where the use is 2,500 miles p.a. or less, or a second or further cars are provided the relevant benefit is one and a half times the table figure.[42] If the taxpayer can show that the car is simply part of a car pool (as defined) for the use of employees of one or

---

[37] *Butter* v. *Bennett* [1963] Ch. 185; *Luke* v. *I.R.C.* [1963] A.C. 557.
[38] See para. 93–04, *ante*.
[39] Finance Act 1976, s. 63A.
[40] *Ibid*. s. 72 (5) (*c*).
[41] *Ibid*. s. 62 (1).
[42] *Ibid*. Sched. 7 para. 5.

more employers then the charge is negatived.[43] If there is no private use whatsoever then there is no liability to tax at all.[43a] As from 1982/83 the provision of fuel for an employer or his family will also be regarded as a benefit in kind. Regulations will prescribe how the cash equivalent is to be calculated.[44]

Beneficial loan arrangements

93–09 Loans to directors or "higher paid" employees which are interest free or at less than the "official rate" of interest, are charged under section 66 of the Finance Act 1976. The official rate of interest is prescribed by statutory instrument. There are provisions calculating the cash equivalent of such loans and also certain exemptions—basically loans for purposes which would entitle the borrower to tax relief on any interest paid (*e.g.* mortgage interest); and where the cash equivalent is less than £201. If however, the loan is in respect of expenses necessarily incurred by an employee in performing the duties of his employment and is (a) under £1,000, (b) spent within six months and the employee accounts to the employer at regular intervals for the expenditure of the sum advanced, the Revenue have said that these will not be treated as beneficial loans within section 66.[45]

With the sharp rise in interest rates fixed term loans at fixed interest rates and made within the prescribed rate at that time, are not chargeable by virtue of a subsequent increase in the official rate.[46]

Employee shareholdings

93–10 If a director or higher paid employee acquires shares at an under value in any company in pursuance of a right of opportunity available by reason of the employment, there is deemed to be an interest free loan to the director or employee of the amount of that under value chargeable under section 66 of the Finance Act 1976, noted above.[47] Shares are purchased at an under value if there is either no payment for them or payment of less than their full market value at the date of acquisition. If the director or employee is under an obligation to pay the full value by instalments there will be a charge and each instalment paid will reduce the notional chargeable loan. There is also a separate charge to tax on the disposal of shares acquired by a director, "higher paid" employee or "connected persons" in pursuance of a right available by reason of the employment at a consideration over and above the market value of those shares at the date of acquisition.[48] This does not apply to a disposal after the death of the employee. The amount charged to income tax in this way is an allowable expense for any

[43] *Ibid.* s. 65.
[43a] *Gilbert* v. *Hemsley,* [1981] S.T.C. 703.
[44] *Ibid.* s. 64A.
[45] Statement of Practice S/P 7/79.
[46] Finance Act 1980, s. 50 (2).
[47] Finance Act 1976, s. 67, c/f *Tyrer v Smart* [1979] 1 A11 E.R. 321 (H.L.)
[48] *Ibid.* s. 67 (7).

capital gains tax charge.[49] These provisions do not apply to approved profit sharing or share option schemes. See Chapter 94, *post.*

THE GENERAL LAW RELATING TO THE TAXATION OF ALL BENEFITS

93–11 However it is not sufficient for the Revenue to show that the payment would not have been made had the relationship of employer and employee not existed; assessability depends on the payment being a *reward for services*. Thus in *Hochstrasser* v. *Mayes*[50] certain married employees of the Company (I.C.I) were frequently transferred from one locality to another and the Company established a housing scheme to recompense employees for losses incurred in selling their houses on transfer. The House of Lords held that money paid to an employee in respect of such a loss was not taxable as it was not an emolument from the employment.

The House of Lords has recently framed the test as a question—did the profit arise from the employment? The answer will be "no" if it arose from something else.[51]

Emoluments earned abroad

93–12 If the employee is "ordinarily resident" in the United Kingdom and is actually so resident when the whole of his earnings are chargeable to tax in full even if the work is performed abroad.[52] But deductions are available if he has been absent from the United Kingdom for at least 365 days, apart from short holidays (100 per cent) or if he has performed the work abroad and has been abroad for at least 30 days, including days spent travelling (25 per cent); or if he is employed by a non-resident employer (25 per cent.).[53] If his earnings are foreign emoluments (*i.e.* earnings of a person not domiciled here working for a non-resident employer) a 50 per cent. deduction is allowed. The place where the work is performed is decided in accordance with section 184 (2), (3). Certain expenses incurred by residents who work abroad are allowed as deductions by section 32 of the Finance Act 1977, including travelling abroad and family visits. In addition, by concession, anyone in receipt of foreign emoluments is not assessed on the reimbursement of travelling expenses on the taking up and termination of the employment. Certain family visit expenses are also allowed.[54]

[THE NEXT PARAGRAPH IS 93–14]

The golden handshake

93–14 The general rule is that income tax under Schedule E is payable in respect of any payment made to a person in respect of his retirement. This

[49] *Ibid.* s. 67 (13).
[50] [1960] A.C. 376.
[51] *Brumby* v. *Milner* [1976] 1 W.L.R. 1096.
[52] s. 181 (1).
[53] Finance Act 1977, s. 31 and Sched. 7.
[54] Concession A 25.

applies to such payments although they are made to the employee's spouse, relatives or dependants, and whether or not the employee is still, at the time of the payment, in the employment.[55] But there are exceptions. Payments made on the termination of employment through death, injury or disability are excluded[56] Furthermore, such payments not exceeding £25,000 are exempt from tax under Schedule E in the hands of the recipient,[57] and where this sum is exceeded,[57] the excess is added onto the employee's other taxable income for the year of assessment and the tax charge on the lump sum is then half the difference between (a) the amount of tax payable before taking into account the lump sum, and (b) the amount of tax which would be payable if the whole of the taxable part of the lump sum were treated as additional income for the year.[58] In practice this provision applies mostly to gratuitous termination payments. Whether such payments are deductible from profits in assessing a company's liability to corporation tax depends upon whether they are made wholly and exclusively for the purposes of the trade.[59] In some cases such payments have been disallowed.[60] This concession by which a company can, often largely at the expense of the Revenue, show appreciation for past loyal services should not be overlooked. Compensation for unfair dismissal is caught by these provisions and no deductions are allowed for the legal costs of obtaining such compensation.[61]

---

55 s. 187 (1), (2) and (4).
56 s. 188 (1) (*a*).
57 Finance Act 1981 s. 31 (1).
58 *Ibid.*
59 s. 130 (*a*): *I.R.C.* v. *Brander and Cruickshank* [1971] 1 W.L.R. 212.
60 *George J. Smith & Co. Ltd.* v. *Furlong (Inspector of Taxes)* [1969] 2 A11 E.R. 760.
61 *Warnett* v. *Jones* [1980] S.T.C. 131.

Chapter 94

TAX ADVANTAGES OF APPROVED PROFIT SHARING AND SHARE OPTION SCHEMES

Employee share schemes

94–01 Companies have for a number of years sought to remunerate their officers and employees by the provision of shares in the company. This has given rise to a number of schemes, known as profit sharing schemes or more accurately as employee share schemes.[1] The provision of profits for such schemes will in general be an *intra vires* activity of the company.[2] This chapter is a summary of the major types of scheme in existence and of the general tax position affecting such schemes. In particular there are two schemes specially favoured for tax purposes—the approved profit sharing scheme, operative from 1979 and the approved share option scheme, introduced in the 1980 Finance Act.

The taxation of employee share schemes

94–02 Where an employee or a director is paid in the form of shares in the company the value of the shares received must be treated as emoluments and thus taxable under Schedule E, with tax payable on the value, less any payment made for the shares by the employer.[3] To be taxable the shares must be received *from* the employment and not as a personal gift or as an inducement to enter into employment.[4] For directors and higher-paid employees even these will be taxable as benefits in kind under the special legislation set out in the previous chapter.[5]

An obvious way round these rules was the granting by the company to an employee of an option to buy shares in the company at a given price, either free or for a nominal sum. The option could be exercised at any time when market conditions were favourable. These are known as *share-option schemes*. This device succeeded initially since the House of Lords decided in *Abbot* v. *Philbin*[6] that the only taxable emolument was the monetary value of the option in the hands of the recipient at the time it was obtained. There was no charge to income tax, as distinct from capital gains tax, on the profits arising from the exercise of the option. In 1966 however legisla-

---

[1] For a detailed analysis of employee share schemes, the tax position and the 1979 approved profit sharing scheme see Morse and Williams, *Profit Sharing—Legal aspects of employee share schemes* (Sweet & Maxwell, 1979).

[2] Especially following European Communities Act 1979, s. 9 (1). See Morse and Williams, *op. cit.*, Chap. 2.

[3] I.C.T.A. 1970, s. 181. See Simon's *Taxes* C4. 320, C. 320A.

[4] See, *e.g. Weight* v. *Salmon* (1934) 19 T.C. 174, *Pritchard* v. *Arundale* [1972] 1 Ch. 229 *cf. Tyrer* v. *Smart* [1979] 1 W.L.R. 113.

[5] See para. 93–05, *ante*.

[6] [1961] A.C. 352.

tion was introduced whereby any such gain arising out of the exercise of the option, or its release or by sale or assignment was taxable under Schedule E.[7]

94–03 But this legislation itself was circumvented by this introduction of *share incentive schemes, i.e.* a scheme whereby a director or employee was given an opportunity to buy shares in the company at a set time. Section 186 did not apply to such schemes which were made advantageous either by lending the money to the employer at a lower rate of interest (which would now be taxable for directors and higher paid employees) or by taking measures to distort the market price of the shares at the time of this acquisition. In 1972 legislation was introduced in the Finance Act[8] aimed at encouraging and controlling both share option schemes and share incentive schemes, by allowing tax advantages to schemes which complied with certain conditions and were approved by the Revenue and imposing new charges on them which were not approved. In 1974 the system of approval was dismantled and the 1972 legislation was modified leaving only those parts which imposed tax charges.[9] This hybrid system is the general system of charge today.

94–04 Section 77 of the Finance Act 1972 imposes a charge to Schedule E on the receipt of a share option granted by a company to its employees if it is capable of being exercised more than seven years after it is obtained. The charge is on the market value of the share that could be obtained by exercise of the option, less any consideration to be given on the exercise of that right. This is in addition to any charge under section 186 of the Taxes Act 1970 on the realisation of any gain. Section 79 of the 1972 Act raises a potential charge under Schedule E whenever a director or employee of a company acquires shares in that or any other company by reason of a right conferred on him or an opportunity afforded to him because of his office or employment and not in pursuance of an offer to the problem. The charge is imposed on the amount by which the market value of the shares increases over the period between acquisition of the shares and when the charge is imposed, usually within seven years. In practice however this charge does not apply to shares which are not subject to "special restrictions"[10] or profit sharing schemes as defined for that section.

Shares free from restrictions immediately after acquisition are exempt if a majority of the available shares in the same class were acquired otherwise than by circumstances caught by the section.[11] The exceptions covering profit sharing schemes must not be confused with the approved profit sharing scheme introduced by the 1978 Finance Act. In general such a scheme for this purpose must provide for benefits to employees, as part of his emoluments, by way of shares or interests in shares in the employing

---

[7] See now I.C.T.A. 1970, s. 186.
[8] ss. 77–79.
[9] Finance Act 1974 s. 20.
[10] Finance Act 1972 s. 79 (2A).
[11] *Ibid.* s. 79 (2) (*c*).

company to an extent determined in advance by reference to profits. Any such scheme must be open to everyone aged 25 or more who has been a full-time employee for at least five years. The shares must be quoted or in an independent company and not subject to special restrictions.[12]

94–05 Section 79 also charges, subject to the same exceptions, the value of any benefit received by an employer or director related to shares acquired because of the office or employment, where the benefit is not received by the majority of people holding ordinary shares in the company who did not acquire their shares for that reason.[13]

Types of employee share schemes not specially favoured for tax purposes

94–06 There are four main types of employee share acquisition schemes in use in addition to those which comply with the specially favoured approved profit sharing scheme and share option scheme.

Executive schemes

94–07 These arose around the 1972 legislation and were limited to the higher paid selected employees, usually at the invitation of the board. Details of these schemes varied and are largely of historical interest only except that some were set up under the 1972 framework the repeal of which did not affect shares and options acquired before 1974. A common pattern was to allow participants to receive fully paid up shares from the company through the medium of trustees. The company would lend money to the trustees who would lend it on to the participants to allow them to purchase the company's shares. The participants would then be given a period of years during which, or at the end of which, to pay the loan.

Profit sharing bonus schemes

94–08 These schemes, sometimes called deferred profit sharing schemes, centre around the principle that employees receive a bonus, paid to them in the form of shares, related to the profits of their employer at annual or other regular periods. The key to all such schemes is the way in which the profit-related bonus is distributed amongst employers, which varies widely in practice. Some ban the amount of profits to be distributed on an agreed percentage of the profits of the company, usually subject to a threshold. Others are more sophisticated using the ratio of value added by the company to employee payroll costs or the ratio of payroll costs to productivity (useful during pay holiday periods).

Savings-related share option schemes

94–09 These popular schemes operate by the grant of an option to purchase shares in the employing company where the funds for the purchase of the shares are met by the employers by means of savings contracts, (SAYE),

---

[12] *Ibid.* s. 79 (8) and Sched. 12.
[13] *Ibid.* s. 79 (7).

usually over a four year period. Some schemes use contracts with the Department of National Savings, others with building societies. The bonuses paid through the building society scheme, and the revaluations paid from National Savings are free of both income and capital gains tax. If a seven year contract is used practical problems arise in respect of a potential charge under section 77 of the Finance Act 1972. Where a contract has been completed the rules usually provide that the employee has a certain time in which to exercise his option. If he does exercise the option he will be liable to pay tax under section 186 of the Taxes Act 1970 and a capital gains tax liability may also arise. Under the 1980 Finance Act however a specially approved form of savings-related share option scheme is available to avoid these charges.[14]

Employee shareholding trust

94–10 These are trusts set up to hold shares in a company for the benefit of employees generally and not the specific benefit of individual employees. The finance of such a trust is usually provided by gifts from major shareholders or the company, supplemented by the trust income itself. No income tax privileges relate to such a trust, so the company must make any transfer to the trust out of its profits after tax. Once established the trustees will have a wide direction on spending the income, within the limits allowed by the capital transfer tax legislation.[15]

Approved profit sharing schemes under the Finance Act 1978

94–11 As noted above several types of profit sharing schemes are in existence but all suffer from fiscal problems. In particular the company must be certain that the profits it pays out to employees are deductible from its own taxable profits and that each employee's liabilities to Schedule E tax will be minimised. In response to pressure from the Liberal Party the Labour Government introduced a new concept in 1978—the approved profit sharing scheme, which would enable both these ideals to be obtained in part, provided that the scheme has been approved by the Board of Inland Revenue.

Outline of the scheme

94–12 The provisions relating to approved schemes are contained in sections 53 to 61 of and Schedule 9 to the Finance Act 1978. Minor amendments were made by the Finance Act 1980. In essence the company, or group of companies if a group scheme is envisaged, must make a certain amount of its profits available to trustees, appointed for this purpose, in order for them to purchase that company's shares on behalf of its employees. The trustees must then appropriate those shares to the individual employees

---

[14] See para. 94–40, *post*.
[15] See para. 91–26, *ante*.

(within 18 months of acquiring them) and receive all payments due on those shares on the beneficiaries' behalf, paying them on to the beneficiaries. These shares are to be held by the trustees on the trusts specified in the Schedule for at least two years if any tax benefit is to accrue to the employees.

This period is known as *the period of retention*. After that period the shares may be sold by the trustees for full consideration and the proceeds handed over to the employees but some tax will be payable unless the shares remain in the trust fund for seven years. This time is referred to in the Act as the *release date*. The shares may also be disposed of by a simple transfer to the beneficiary—employee, or by such person assigning his beneficial interest to a third party or by a purchase of the beneficial interest by the trustees at full market value. Again these events must take place after the period of retention if any tax advantage is to accrue.

90–13 If the scheme is approved there is to be no charge to Schedule E on the appropriation of the shares to the employees. There will however, be a charge if there is a sale or deemed disposal of the shares before the release date. If this occurs before the period of retention there is a charge on the employee on the full market value of the shares at that time—no tax advantage at all. If after that time a percentage of the *locked-in value* of the shares is chargeable, depending on the length of time the shares have been in the trust. The locked-in value is usually the initial market value of the shares, *i.e.* at the date of appropriation, but it may be the actual consideration received or the market value at the date of disposal, depending on the circumstances. After the release date the disposal will be free of a charge under Schedule E. Nothing in the Act prevents income tax arising in the normal way on dividends received in respect of the shares or capital gains tax and capital transfer tax on a disposal or transfer of value in relation to the shares.

94–14 The essential features of the scheme required for approval are a limit of £1,000 worth of shares per employee per year; the scheme to be open to all full time United Kingdom employees and directors of the company, although entitlement may vary with length of service, etc.; the shares to be quoted or of an independent private company or of a subsidiary of a quoted company and to be ordinary shares to which no special restrictions attach simply because they are brought under the scheme.

Thus the scheme does not provide for employee shares as a separate class. The provisions in the trust deed are to be backed up by a contract between the company and each participant in the scheme so that they will be bound by its essential provisions. Special provisions have to apply to capital receipts in respect of the shares, rights issues and reconstructions and amalgamations. The Schedule E tax charged under the scheme is to be collected on the PAYE system.

Finally the company will be able to deduct such sums as are allocated to the trustees from their corporation tax assessments, either as a trading expense or management expenses.

Approval of the scheme

The contract

94–15 No scheme may be approved unless the Board are satisfied that every participant (someone to whom shares have been appropriated) is bound by a contract with the company which contains at least the following four clauses:

(a) To allow his shares to remain in the trust for the period of retention, and

(b) not to assign, charge or otherwise dispose of his beneficial interest during that period.[16]

The period of retention is two years from the date of appropriation but it may end earlier if the participant ceases to be an employee or director of the company, or any participating company if it is a group scheme,[17] by reason of injury, disability or redundancy under the Redundancy Payments Act 1965.[18] The period will also end earlier if the participant reaches retirement age or dies before the two years have elapsed.[19] Any breach of these two terms will be harshly treated for income tax purposes as well as being a breach of contract.

(c) an obligation on the employee to pay the tax due under Schedule E if he requires the shares to be transferred to him before the release date.[20] This will be treated as a disposal of the shares and attract a charge. The release date is seven years from the date of appropriation of the shares.[21]

(d) a requirement that the participant will only direct the trustees to dispose of the shares before the release date except by sale for the best cash price reasonably obtainable at the date of sale.[22]

This does not however preclude a repurchase clause in the scheme whereby the trustees may re-acquire the beneficial interest in the shares after the retention period for the same price as on a sale. Such a clause will not be in breach of this condition and will give rise to a charge as on a disposal.[23]

In fact none of these contractual obligations are to prevent the participant from directing the trustees to accept a change in relation to the shares, even during the retention period, if it is the consequence either of an internal re-organisation of the company's share structure under a scheme of arrangement or reconstruction, provided that it applies to all the class of shares in question or to such shares as are identified otherwise than by

---

[16] Finance Act 1978, s. 54 (1) (*a*) (*b*).
[17] See para. 94–21, *post*.
[18] Finance Act 1978, s. 54 (4) (*a*), (5).
[19] *Ibid*. s. 54 (4) (*b*) (*c*).
[20] *Ibid*. s. 54 (1) (*c*).
[21] *Ibid*. s. 54 (6).
[22] *Ibid*. s. 54 (1) (*d*).
[23] *Ibid*. s. 54 (2) (*d*).

reference to their ownership by employees or the scheme, or if the shares are subject to a take-over, at least partly in cash, which is conditional on the offer or obtaining control of the company.[24]

The trust instrument and the trustees

94–16 A scheme will only be approved if it complies with the terms of Schedule 9. The company must make a written application for approval to the Board who must approve the scheme if it contains all the requisite terms and conditions unless it has additional features "which are neither essential nor reasonably incidental to the purpose of providing for employees and directors benefits in the nature of interests in shares."[25]

The scheme must provide for the appointment of trustees resident in the United Kingdom. Nothing else is said in the legislation about their qualifications or replacement—these should however be incorporated into the scheme if it is run smoothly. The trustees must however be bound to acquire certain shares in the company (defined in Pt. II of the Schedule) and appropriate them to eligible participators (defined in Pt. III of the Schedule). The trust itself must be a United Kingdom trust set up by a trust instrument which imposes certain duties and restrictions on the trustees in accordance with Part IV of the Schedule. In brief the trust instrument must require the trustees to inform a participant in writing of the number, description and initial market value of any shares appropriated to him; to pay over any money's worth received by them in respect of those shares after deduction of tax, if any, except for new shares received on a reconstruction; to act only on the instructions of the participant in respect of any bonus or rights issues or other rights attaching to those shares—this will be particularly important in a take-over situation; and to keep records of all transactions and to inform participants of all relevant facts if a Schedule E assessment becomes necessary.[26]

94–17 In addition approval will only be given if the scheme is limited to £1,000 worth of shares per employee per year, and it is open to all full-time employees or directors of the company. A qualification period of up to five years may however be included in the scheme and factors such as length of service and amount of pay may be used to vary the amount of entitlement.[27] In this way a distinction may still be made between directors and employees, although the £1,000 limit will be important in this respect.

Persons eligible to participate

90–18 To participate in an approved scheme a person must have been a director or employee of the company concerned within the 18 months preceding any appropriation of shares to him, and he ceases to be so eligible in any relevant tax year if shares have been appropriated to him in

[24] *Ibid*. s. 54 (2) (*a*) (*b*) (*c*). Control is defined by reference to I.C.T.A. 1970, s. 302.
[25] *Ibid*. Sched. 9, para 1 (1).
[26] *Ibid*. paras. 12–15.
[27] *Ibid*. paras. 1 (4) and 2.

that year under another approved scheme by the same company, its subsidiary or holding company, or by another member of the same group or consortium.[28]

94–19 If the participant is to receive shares in a close company, he is ineligible to participate in the scheme if he has a material interest in that company. A close company for this purpose has the same meaning as for corporation tax except that it includes non-resident companies and those which would not generally be close companies by virtue of a certain amount of public ownership of shares.[29] A material interest is basically ownership of 25 per cent. of the ordinary shares of the company or entitlement to 25 per cent. of its distributable income. Ownership may be through the medium of associates and other companies. Associate for this purpose has the same meaning as for close companies.[30] This general prohibition applies to a scheme in a non-close company if the participant has a material interest in a close company which controls that company or is a member of a consortium which owns it.[31]

Any shares appropriated to an ineligible participator are deemed to be *unauthorised shares* for the purposes of tax liability.

Approved shares

94–20 The shares purchased by the trustees must be part of the company's ordinary share capital, or that of its holding company or a member of consortium owning the participant's company which itself owns 15 per cent. of that company's ordinary shares. In addition the shares must be quoted or of an independent company or of a subsidiary of a quoted company, be fully paid-up and non-redeemable.[32] The whole idea is for the trustees to purchase ordinary equity shares and not to create a special class of employee shares. Thus there are additional requirements for the shares to be approved. There must be no special restrictions on the shares which do not also apply to the rest of that class, thus preventing share incentive schemes, and if there is more than one class of ordinary shares, the majority of the shares of any class purchased by the trustees must be owned by persons who are neither beneficiaries nor trustees of a profit-sharing scheme, whether approved or not. If the company is an unquoted subsidiary of a quoted company the majority of the shares must not be owned by the holding company or its associates.[33]

If non-approved shares are purchased by the trustees there will be a charge to tax on their appropriation under the usual Scheme E rules as no exemption will be given.[34]

---

28 *Ibid.* paras. 9 and 10.
29 I.C.T.A. 1970, ss. 282, 283.
30 *Ibid.* s. 302. Finance Act 1978, Sched. 9, para. 11 (3).
31 Finance Act 1978, Sched. 9, para 11.
32 *Ibid.* paras 5–7.
33 *Ibid.* paras 7 (*c*) and 8.
34 *Ibid.* s. 53 (1).

Group schemes

94–21 Any company which controls another company or companies may apply for approval of a group scheme. Control has its ordinary meaning for tax purposes.[35] A group scheme may be extended to cover employees of all or any of its subsidiaries, such companies being referred to in the legislation as participating companies.[36] The conditions of approval are then extended to cover such participating companies as relevant employers in order to define eligible participators but the shares must be those of the applicant company or its controllers in accordance with Part II of the Schedule.

If an employee or director is participating in a group scheme he is ineligible to participate in another approved scheme of another member of the group.[37]

Withdrawal of approval

94–22 The Board may withdraw approval[38] if a participant is in breach of his contractual obligations (except for an assignment, etc., of his beneficial interest during the retention period) even though all other participants are in order. It may also withdraw approval if the scheme is operated in contravention of sections 53 to 61, the scheme itself or the terms of the trust instrument. In accordance with the general principle of scheme shares being ordinary equity shares, approval can be withdrawn if appropriated shares receive different treatment to other shares of that class in any way and in particular with regard to dividends, repayment of capital, any restrictions attached to the shares or bonus or rights issues connected with those shares. Newly issued shares receiving a dividend payable in respect of a period beginning before the date of issue may be paid less than existing shares of that class without prejudice to this requirement. The word treatment seems deliberately vague.

Approval is automatically withdrawn if the scheme or trust is altered subsequent to the original approval. This operates from the date of the alteration until the alteration itself is approved.

Any appeal against failure to approve a scheme, or an alteration, or the withdrawal of approval must be made in writing to the Board within 30 days of notification of the decision, to be heard by the Special Commissioners.

The appropriation of shares

94–23 When shares have been purchased by the trustees in accordance with the terms of an approved scheme the first stage will be the appropriation of those shares to the individual participants thus fully constituting the trust and giving such individuals a beneficial interest in the shares. Usually this

---

[35] See I.C.T.A. 1970, s. 534.
[36] Finance Act 1978, Sched. 9, para 11 (3).
[37] *Ibid.* para. 10.
[38] *Ibid.* para. 3.

would give rise to a Schedule E charge on the participants but in the case of an appropriation of approved shares under an approved scheme no such charge can arise either under the general rules, or under the specific charges to tax under section 79 of the Finance Act 1972, or on employee shareholdings given at an under value to directors or higher paid employees.[39] Only if the scheme or the shares are non-approved will there be a charge. If the employer is ineligible to participate of the £1,000 limit exceeded such shares will be *unauthorised* or *excess* shares within section 58 but no charge arises at this stage.

94–24 Any income received in respect of those shares between purchase and appropriation will be held according to the terms of the trust if specified. Otherwise it will presumably be held on a resulting trust for the company. The trustees will be liable to income tax at the basic rate on such income but the charge to additional rate tax on certain accumulation or discretionary trusts,[40] which could easily apply is expressly excluded in respect of dividends received during that period.[41] It may still apply however to other distributions received. The appropriation itself will also be a disposal by the trustees for capital gains tax purposes and an acquisition by the participants at the initial market value. Any gain thus accruing to the trustees is however not to be a chargeable gain.[42] Both these reliefs available to the trustees only apply, however, if the appropriation takes effect within 18 months of the acquisition, and earlier shares are deemed for this purpose to be appropriated before later ones. This first in first out rule is a general theme of the legislation and cannot be ousted by a contrary instruction or proof that the order was in fact different.[43]

Disposals of scheme shares within the retention period

94–25 One of the basic conditions of the trust and contract required for approval is that the trustees retain the shares during the retention period. Any transfer of the legal title to the shares will be a breach of contract and trust and lead to a withdrawal of approval. But the trustees cannot control the beneficiary's acts in respect of his beneficial interest in the appropriated shares and he may well assign, charge or in some way dispose of that interest before the end of the period. Such an act will be a breach of contract but it will not lead to withdrawal of approval.[44] Instead the appropriated shares will be regarded as having been appropriated to an ineligible participator and will therefore be treated as unauthorised shares under section 58. The shares will be deemed to have been disposed of by the trustees for their market value at that time[45] and a Schedule E charge

---

39 *Ibid*. s. 53 (3).
40 Finance Act 1973, s. 16.
41 Finance Act 1978, s. 53 (6) (*a*).
42 *Ibid*. s. 53 (6) (*b*).
43 *Ibid*. s. 61 (2).
44 *Ibid*. s. 54 (1) (*b*), Sched 9, para, 3 (1) (*a*).
45 *Ibid*. s. 55 (7), (8) (*c*).

on the full amount levied.[46] There is no such disposal however if a participant's beneficial interest is assigned on his insolvency or by any other operation of law.[47] It seems that an assignment in a composition with creditors might not be covered if there is no judicial insolvency order under English law whereas an assignment to a trustee for the benefit of creditors under Scots law will not give rise to a charge.

Disposals of scheme shares before the release date

94–26 Shares may be disposed of by the trustees after the retention period but if this happens before the release date or the death of the participant, if earlier, a charge to Schedule E will arise under section 55. A disposal for this purpose may take place in one of four ways.

Sales by the trustee

Under the terms of the contract and trust appropriated shares must be sold for the best consideration which may reasonable be obtained at the time.[48] Such a sale will be a disposal and give rise to a charge under section 55 (1). To ascertain the amount of charge it is necessary to find the *appropriate percentage* of the *locked-in value* of those shares. The locked-in value is the initial market value of those shares (*i.e.* at the date of appropriation) less any capital receipts in respect of those shares upon which tax has already been charged under section 56.[49] The theme is therefore to tax the original "emolument" at a later date on realisation. If however the proceeds of sale are less than the locked-in value, that value is to be reduced accordingly. This may lead to abuse and attempts to lower the proceeds of sale and accordingly the Board has power to substitute the market value of the shares if the disposal is not, in their opinion, at arm's length. Having ascertained the taxable amount the actual charge is levied on the participant on a percentage of that amount.[50] This will be 100 per cent. if the event occurs before the end of four years from appropriation, 75 per cent. if it occurs in the fifth year, 50 per cent. in the sixth year and 25 per cent. in the seventh. After seven years there is no charge—the release date applies.[51] In deciding the initial market value and the time limits for the appropriate percentage a disposal of shares is to be regarded as being of those shares appropriated earlier before those appropriated later whatever directions to the contrary are given and whatever the realities of the situation.[52]

46 *Ibid.* s. 56 (1), 58(4) (*a*).
47 *Ibid.* s. 55 (7).
48 *Ibid.* s. 54 (1) (*d*), Sched. 9, para 13.
49 *Ibid.* s. 55 (2). See para. 94–30, *post.*
50 *Ibid.* s. 55 (3), (8) (*b*).
51 *Ibid.* s. 54 (7) as amended.
52 *Ibid.* ss. 55 (6), 61 (2).

Purchase by the trustees

94–27 Any scheme may allow for a sale of the participant's beneficial interest to the trustees for an amount equal to the best consideration which could reasonably have been obtained on a sale of the shares.[53] This will be treated as a sale by the trustees for that amount and the procedure of charge as on a sale under section 55 (1) will operate accordingly.[54]

Assignment of the beneficial interest

94–28 Any assignment of or charge on his beneficial interest by a participant after the period of retention is a deemed disposal of the relevant shares by the trustees. The charge will be calculated in the same way as on a sale by them but the proceeds of sale will be the amount received by the participant. Market value of the shares at the time may however been substituted if the transaction is not at arm's length, and no charge at all will arise if the assignment is on the insolvency of the participant or otherwise by operation of the law.[55]

Transfer of the legal title to the beneficiary

94–29 Under the contract if the scheme allows transfer of the shares to the beneficiary before the release date the participant is obliged to pay to the trustees before transfer the basic tax due on the appropriate percentage of the locked-in value of the shares at that time. This is because a charge will arise on the transfer as being a disposal by the trustees and calculated in accordance with section 55 (1). The only difference will be that the proceeds of sale under section 55 (3) will be the market value of those shares at the time of disposal which may reduce the charge.[56] No charge arises to the beneficiary's personal representatives however.[57]

Capital receipts

94–30 The charge on a disposal of the shares noted above is on the locked-in value of those shares, *i.e.* their initial market value or proceeds of sale or market value at the time of disposal according to the circumstances. This figure may however be reduced if the trustees become entitled to receive any capital receipts in respect of the appropriated shares before the disposal. The reduction is the amount of such capital receipts. The reason for this is that such entitlement to receive capital receipts itself gives rise to a Schedule E charge on the shares for the year in which entitlement arises at any time before the release date.

The charge is the appropriate percentage of the amount or value of the receipt.[58] This means that if a capital receipt arises during the period of

---

[53] *Ibid.* s. 54 (2) (*d*).
[54] *Ibid.* s. 55 (7).
[55] *Ibid.* ss. 55 (7), (8) (*b*).
[56] *Ibid.* s. 55 (8) (*c*).
[57] *Ibid.* s. 54 (1A).
[58] *Ibid.* s. 56 (1).

four years from appropriation 100 per cent. of its value is chargeable although the participant may have little control over such matters especially during the period of retention. The charge is limited to the locked-in value of the shares at that time and does not apply after the participant's death.[59] In effect this charge is not an additional charge to that on a disposal, instead it accelerates that charge on a capital receipt arising prior to a disposal—it does not increase the locked-in value but will increase the appropriate percentage.

What then is a capital receipt? The general definition is any money or money's worth arising in respect of or by reference to a participant's shares, provided that it exceeds £10.[60] Since this would include dividends, proceeds of sale, etc., this general definition is cut down by section 56 (2). Any payment which would be income in the hands of the recipient for income tax purposes is excluded—thus all distributions in respect of the shares are ignored, *e.g.* a bonus issue after a repayment of capital; the usual Schedule F procedure applying. Similarly the proceeds of a disposal are outside this charge and remain within the section 55 charge. Thirdly the receipt of a "new holding" on a reconstruction is not a capital receipt. One example of a capital receipt would be the money received from the disposal of rights under a rights issue.

Rights issues

94–31 If the company makes a rights issue and these rights arise in respect of appropriated shares the participant may either exercise these rights of allotment himself through the trustees or sell the rights, if possible, to a third party. He may of course do both by taking some shares himself and selling the rights on others. If he takes up the rights issue himself he may have to finance the purchase himself and make a payment to the trustees accordingly.

If this happens any such payments are deducted from the ultimate proceeds of any disposal of appropriated shares, including the new ones, thus lowering that figure, which may in turn lower the locked-in value of those shares, and consequently the amount of any charge on such disposal. The amount deducted on a disposal is such a proportion of the money paid to the trustees as the market value of the shares disposed of bears to the market value of all that the participator's shares immediately before the disposal. The same principle applies if there has been more than one such payment, but the amount actually deducted on a disposal is subtracted from the calculation on any subsequent disposals.[61]

If the money paid to the trustees to exercise the rights issue is itself the proceeds of a sale of other such rights it is not available as a deduction against the proceeds of a disposal.[62] Such money is not a capital receipt

[59] *Ibid.* s. 56 (4), (5).
[60] *Ibid.* s. 56 (1), (6).
[61] *Ibid.* s. 55 (4), (5) (*b*).
[62] *Ibid.* s. 55 (5) (*a*).

within section 56 insofar as it is used by the trustees to exercise other rights arising under the issue.[63]

Reconstructions and amalgamations

94–32 Under capital gains tax legislation on a reconstruction, amalgamation or reduction of capital any shares which are received in respect of and in proportion to existing shares are referred to as a "new holding" and there is no disposal or acquisition—instead the new shares are treated as forming one combined asset with such of the former shares as remain.[64] If such a situation arises in respect of appropriated shares special rules apply also in respect to the Schedule E charges discussed above.[65] The situations envisaged include a straightforward issue of bonus shares, any internal reorganisation of the company's capital structure including a reduction of capital, and any exchange of shares on an amalgamation with another company—it cannot include take-over bids where a cash offer is accepted—that will be a disposal. For these purposes however the "new holding" cannot include bonus issues of redeemable shares or securities, þonus issues following a repayment of capital or stock dividends—all of which are treated as distributions for income tax purposes and will therefore be taxable in the trustees' hands under Schedule F in the ordinary way and form no part of a Schedule E charge.[66]

94–33 If a "new holding" arises, referred to in the Act as the "new shares," there is to be no disposal of the original holding, but instead the appropriation date for the new shares is to be that of the old or "corresponding shares," and the approval of those corresponding shares (*i.e.* they are of the right class, etc., within P. II of Sched. 9) is carried forward to the new shares.[67] For the purposes of calculating the charge on any subsequent disposal or capital receipt of the new shares, a complex formula is to be used. To ascertain their locked-in value for disposal purposes their initial market value is to be taken as their locked-in value at the date of the reconstruction. This latter concept is to be found by taking the aggregate amount of each bundle of the original shares having the same locked-in value immediately before the reconstruction and dividing it between such of those shares as remain together with any new shares of which those shares were the corresponding ones. Only capital receipts after the reconstruction can be deducted from the locked-in value on any disposal and for this purpose any such receipts arising on the reconstruction are deemed to accrue before the new shares arise and before their locked-in value falls to be ascertained. They will in effect therefore reduce the locked-in value of the old shares for all purposes.

[63] *Ibid.* s. 56 (3).
[64] C.G.T.A. 1979, ss. 77–80.
[65] Finance Act 1978, s. 57.
[66] I.C.T.A. 1970, s. 233 (2) (*c*), 234 (1); Finance (No. 2) Act 1975, s. 34.
[67] Finance Act 1978, s. 57.

Excess and unauthorised shares

94–34 *Excess shares* are any shares appropriated to a participant over and above the £1,000 per annum limit. If the participant is a member of two or more approved schemes any excess is apportioned rateably according to the number apportioned to him under each scheme.[68]

Unauthorised shares are shares appropriated to a person who is ineligible to participate in the scheme at that time,[69] or shares in respect of which the participant has assigned his beneficial interest during the period of retention.[70] Any new holding of shares under section 57 will be regarded as an excess or unauthorised share if the corresponding shares were such, although if there was more than one corresponding share per new share all of them must have been so tainted.[71] This may provide a way of "rehabilitating" such shares.

94–35 The consequences are identical for both excess and unauthorised shares. The appropriate percentage is always to be 100 per cent. and their locked-in value at any time is to be their current market value and not their initial market value. Thus, any disposal or capital receipt of such shares chargeable under sections 55 and 56 will produce no tax-saving at all. It is no use waiting until the release date for there is to be a deemed disposal at that time at current market value and a charge in full. This also applies on the participant's death, if earlier. Where a participant owns both approved scheme shares and excess or unauthorised ones there is a problem as to the order of disposal. The position is that the first in first out rule applies again but that within each time band, approved scheme shares are deemed to be disposed of before excess or unauthorised ones.[72] Whilst the former rule cannot be ousted by contrary direction or practical reality the latter appears to enjoy no such protection.[73]

Capital gains tax considerations

94–36 The events giving rise to the various charges to Schedule E under the legislation may also be disposals or deemed disposals for capital gains tax purposes. The position is simplified by section 53 (5) which states that nothing in the contract, trust or scheme can prevent the participant being regarded as absolutely entitled to his shares against the trustees for capital gains tax. Thus none of the settlement charges under that tax can arise—instead it will be treated as a bare trust and all acts of the trustees will be those of the beneficiary.

In calculating any charge to capital gains tax three new rules have emerged. First, any charge under Schedule E under this legislation is not in

---

68 *Ibid.* s. 58 (1) (2).
69 *Ibid.* s. 58 (3).
70 *Ibid.* s. 54 (3).
71 *Ibid.* s. 58 (7).
72 *Ibid.* s. 58 (4), (5).
73 *Ibid.* s. 61 (2).

itself an allowable expense against the consideration received. Secondly, the provisions of section 56 charging income tax on a capital receipt are not to affect a capital gains charge based on its being a capital distribution.[74] Thirdly, the various rules as to the order of disposal of appropriate share (first in, first out) have no effect on the capital gains charges either on a whole or part disposal of such shares.[75]

Corporation tax considerations

94–37 Subject to certain conditions any sums paid by a company, or a participating company in a group scheme, to the trustees under an approved scheme are allowable as expenses against trading profits if the company is a trading company. An investment company may deduct such payments as management expenses. For this to happen the sums must either be necessary to meet the "reasonable expenses of managing the scheme" or be used within a certain time limit to purchase shares under the scheme for eligible employees or directors of "the company making the payment."[76] This does not appear to include sums paid by one company under a group scheme for the employees or directors of another company of that group.

The time limit for purchase is nine months after the accounting period for which the relief is claimed. This may however be extended by the Revenue.[77] In deciding the order in which sums have been used the first in, first out rule again applies.[78]

Administration of the scheme

The trustees and the participants

94–38 The trustees must be under an obligation to inform each participant "as soon as practicable" after appropriation of shares to him, of the number, description and initial market value of such shares. In addition they must inform him of any facts relevant to his liability to Schedule E if a charge should arise under the legislation. This seems to be a minimum requirement only.[79]

The trustees and the Revenue

94–39 The trustees, or any other person, can be required, within 30 days, to give any information which the Board considers necessary for the purposes of their functions under the legislation, in particular as to the approval or withdrawal of approval of the scheme and the assessment to tax, including

---

74 C.G.T.A. 1970, Sched. 3., para 3.
75 Finance Act 1978, s. 61 (3).
76 *Ibid*. s. 60 (1), (2).
77 *Ibid*. s. 60 (3).
78 *Ibid*. s. 60 (4).
79 *Ibid*. Sched. 9, paras. 12, 15 (*b*).

capital gains tax, of any participant. Failure to make such information available renders that person liable to sanctions.[80]

But above all the trustees are required to assist in the collection of the Schedule E tax charged under the PAYE system, and must keep all necessary records to enable them to do so.[81] If a charge arises under section 55 or 56 the trustees must pay the taxable amount not to the participant himself but to the company which employs him and whose employees are eligible to participate in the scheme, *at that time*. That company will then hand over the money to the participant after making a PAYE deduction.[82] If there is no such company for any reason or if it is impracticable for it to make such a deduction, the obligation to make PAYE deduction is on the trustees before making the payment as if they were the participant's former employer. Alternatively, the Board may specify another company to whom payment is to be made, who will then make the PAYE deduction and transfer the net amount to the participant. This can only be done if the original company, the substitute company and the trustees all agree. This should apply where an employee has changed employment since the shares were appropriated to him. When a participant acquires his shares from the trustees under section 54 (1) (*c*) the sum he must pay to the trustee is treated as being the necessary PAYE deduction by them. Similarly where he disposes of his beneficial interest to the trustees the amount payable to him by the trustees is regarded as being the disposal proceeds for PAYE purposes. The system applies equally to excess or unauthorised shares.

Approved savings-related share option schemes

94–40 The Finance Act 1980 introduced a second profit sharing scheme specially favoured for tax purposes—based on the savings-related share option schemes already in existence.[83] An approved scheme within the Finance Act 1980 will entitle an employee to acquire and exercise an option to purchase shares in his company without any charge to income tax either under the general charge in the Taxes Act 1970 or under section 79 of the Finance Act 1972.

Outline of the scheme

94–41 In essence under an approved scheme of this nature a company may grant options to its directors and employees to purchase either its ordinary fully-paid up equity shares or those of a member of that company's group of companies, which are to be paid for by the proceeds of a building society or National Savings SAYE contract. The option price must not be "manifestly lower" than 90 per cent. of the value of those shares at the time of granting the option. The exercise of the option must not be allowed before

[80] *Ibid*. s. 53 (7), (8).
[81] *Ibid*. Sched. 9, para. 15 (*a*).
[82] *Ibid*. s. 59.
[83] Finance Act 1980, s. 47 and Sched. 10.

the end of the SAYE contract, referred to in the legislation on the *bonus date*, and must happen within six months of that date. The option must be non-transferable *inter vivos*. Assuming that the scheme is approved, neither the granting nor the exercise of the option will be liable to income tax, unless the option is exercised within three years of its being granted. The scheme must be open to and only to all full-time employees and directors of the company on similar terms, although a five year qualifying period may be improved. It is a much simpler scheme than that introduced by the 1978 Act, but it involves the element of risk in the possible fall in the value of the shares between grant and exercise of the option and require a binding SAYE contract to fund it. But there are no complex SAYE provisions so that it is much simpler to run.

Approval of the scheme

94–42 The Board of Inland Revenue may approve a scheme under the 1980 Finance Act if it fulfils the criteria laid down in Schedule 10 to that Act, unless it appears to them that there are "features of it which are neither essential nor reasonably incidental to the purpose of providing benefit for employees and directors in the nature of rights to acquire shares."[84] Approval is to be sought by application and the Revenue has power to require information from any person if they think it necessary to carry out their functions under the Act, whether it relates to the granting or withdrawal of approval or the determination of any participant's tax liability or for any other proper cause.[85] If the applicant company is the controlling company of a group it may apply for approval of a group scheme which then applies to all the companies in the group.

The Revenue may give either full or conditional approval. The latter will be given if all the conditions are satisfied except for the one relating to the option exercise price being about 90 per cent. of the current value of the relevant shares. With unquoted shares this may take some time to establish—if the requirement is subsequently fulfilled the approval will become absolute, if not, the conditional approval will lapse.[86] Approval may be withdrawn at any time for a subsequent failure to comply with the required conditions or for the non-supply of requested information, although such withdrawal will not affect the tax exemption on the subsequent exercise of options granted before the withdrawal.[87] A right of appeal against a refusal to approve or a withdrawal of approval lies to the special Commissions.[88]

Grant and exercise of the option

94–43 An option must be granted to purchase *scheme shares* and must be available to all those eligible to participate. Both these concepts are de-

[84] *Ibid*. Sched 10, para. 1 (2).
[85] *Ibid*. para. 25.
[86] *Ibid*. para. 2.
[87] *Ibid*. para. 3.
[88] *Ibid*. para. 4.

fined below. The purchase of the shares or exercise of the option must be paid for by the repayments of money invested by the participant in a certified contractual savings scheme approved by the Revenue for this purpose—a SAYE contract.[89] The amount paid in to the SAYE scheme must not exceed £50 per month per person and should be sufficient to provide, together with any interest bonus payable under the scheme, the amount required for the exercise of the option.[90]

The purchase price specified in the option must be stated at the grant of that option and must not be "manifestly less" than 90 per cent. of the market value of shares of that class at that time. Unquoted shares may prove complex in this matter. An alternative valuation may be negotiated with the Revenue and provision may be made for the variation of share capital.[91] The option must not be exercisable before the *bonus date*. That is the day when the SAYE repayment becomes due, which if that involves the maximum bonus under the scheme in the earliest date on which such maximum bonus is payable, or if it involves an ordinary bonus, the earliest date on which that bonus is payable. Whether and what type of bonus is involved in the repayments for this purpose must be specified at the grant of the option.[92] In addition the option must not be exercisable more than six months after the bonus date,[93] and if it is exercised within three years of the grant of the option no tax relief is afforded.[94] The option must be non-transferable.[95]

The rules as to the exercise of the option are however subject to special provisions on the happening of certain events, although this only relates to the approval of the scheme. The three year rules for tax relief still applies. The following six variations of the exercise rules are possible although only the first two are mandatory for the purpose of approval:

(i) DEATH OF PARTICIPANT. The option in this case must be exercised, if at all, within one year of death, unless the death is within six months of the bonus date in which case the exercise must be within one year of that date.[96]

(ii) CESSATION OF OFFICE OR EMPLOYMENT. If the participant ceases to be employed whilst holding scheme options for reasons either of injury, disability, redundancy or retirement (either on reaching the statutory retirement age or that provided for in his contract) the options must be exercised, if at all, within six months of that event. If the participant remains in employment after reaching the statutory retirement age he must in addition have the right to exercise the option within six months of reaching that age. On the

---

89 *Ibid.* para. 5.
90 *Ibid.* para. 13.
91 *Ibid.* para. 14.
92 *Ibid.* para. 6.
93 *Ibid.* para. 11 (*b*).
94 *Ibid.* s. 47 (2).
95 *Ibid.* Sched. 10, para. 11 (*a*).
96 *Ibid.* para. 7.

other hand if the participant ceases to be employed for any reason other than injury, disability, retirement or redundancy within three years of the grant of the option the option must become null and void, and on such a cessation after three years the option must either be cancelled or be exercised within six months of such cessation.[97] To ensure some measure of anti-avoidance no-one will be regarded as having ceased his employment for any of the above rules unless he has ceased to hold any office or employment with the company, its subsidiaries or associated companies.[98]

(iii) TAKEOVER OF RELEVANT COMPANY. If either the whole issued share capital of the company whose shares are the scheme shares, or the shares of that particular class, are the target of a take-over bid which results in the offeror obtaining control of that company, the option may be exercisable within six months of the offeror gaining control provided that the offer is or has become unconditional.[99] Control for this purpose includes control by persons acting in concert.[1]

(iv) SCHEMES OF ARRANGEMENT. Any scheme of arrangement under section 206 of the 1948 Act, whether an amalgamation or not, which affects scheme shares, may have the same effect on the exercise of the scheme options as a take-over; *i.e.* they may be exercised within six months of the court order.[2]

(v) COMPULSORY ACQUISITION. Where anyone becomes either entitled or bound to purchase scheme shares under section 209 of the 1948 Act, the schemes may provide that scheme options will become exercisable for as long as that situation permits.[3]

(vi) VOLUNTARY LIQUIDATION. Where the company whose shares are scheme shares passes a resolution for voluntary winding up the scheme option may be exercisable within six months.[4] This will apply to reconstructions effected under section 287 of the 1948 Act.

Scheme shares

94–44 The scheme shares must either be part of the ordinary capital of the company concerned, or its holding company or a company which is a member of a consortium which controls that company (or its holding company) and which owns at least three twentieths of that company's shares beneficially.[5] Subsidiaries' shares are not allowed.

The requirement that the shares be part of the ordinary capital of a

---

[97] *Ibid.* paras. 8 and 9.
[98] *Ibid.* para. 12. For associated companies see I.C.T.A. 1970, s. 302.
[99] Finance Act 1980, Sched. 10 para 10 (1) (*a*).
[1] *Ibid.* para. 10 (2). For a definition of control, see I.C.T.A. 1970, s. 534.
[2] Finance Act 1980, Sched. 10 para. 10 (1) (*b*).
[3] *Ibid.* para. 10 (1) (*c*).
[4] *Ibid.* para. 10 (1) (*d*).
[5] *Ibid.* para. 15.

company is further amplified in that they must be fully paid up, not redeemable and not subject to any restrictions not applicable to all shares of that class, whether contained in the title to those shares or any other contract, agreement or arrangement which restricts either directly or indirectly the participant's right of disposal of the shares or the proceeds of sale of his ability to exercise any rights attaching to the shares (rights issue).[6] In addition the shares must either be quoted, or of an independent unquoted company, or of a subsidiary of a quoted non-class company.[7] Like the 1978 profit sharing scheme the share must not be of a special class. The majority of the class must be owned by persons other than participants in the scheme and any other profit sharing scheme, trustees of such schemes and, where the shares are of an unquoted subsidiaries of a quoted company, that controlling cmpany or any associated company.[7]

Eligible participants

94–45 The scheme must be open to all full-time employees or directors of the company or group, who are chargeable to Schedule E Case I (*i.e.* residents in the United Kingdom working in the United Kingdom) in respect of that office or employment. This may be made subject to a qualifying period which must not exceed five years. There must be no discrimination between the potential participants other than those relating to the levels of their remuneration, length of service or similar factors.[8] Anyone who is not a director or employee of the company at the relevant time must be excluded.[9] Part time directors may therefore be included if they hold a taxable office.

No person is eligible to participate in more than one approved share option scheme in any given year. This ban extends to approved schemes established by his company, its holding or subsidiary company or any other member of the group, and also to any company which is a member of a consortium which controls his company or is a member of a consortium which owns part of his company.[10]

If the company concerned is a close company, or would be if it were resident here or if none of its shares were quoted,[11] anyone with a material interest in that company must not be eligible to participate in the scheme.[12] Anyone with a material interest in a close company which controls the relevant company or in a close company being a member of a consortium which owns such a company must be similarly ineligible.

Options granted before the approval procedure came into force

94–46 Since implementation of the approved share option scheme legislation

---

[6] *Ibid.* paras. 17 and 18.
[7] *Ibid.* paras 16 and 19.
[8] *Ibid.* para. 20.
[9] *Ibid.* para 21.
[10] *Ibid.* para. 22.
[11] Thus I.C.T.A. 1970 ss. 282 (1) (*a*) and 283 are not to be considered for the definition purposes.
[12] Finance Act 1980, Sched. para. 23.

was initially delayed, Schedule 10 provides that anyone who entered into an approved SAYE scheme before it came into force and is a member of a pre-Act share option scheme using the repayments under the SAYE contract to purchase shares of a company in which he is a director or employee may in effect transfer his SAYE repayments into the purchase of scheme shares under an approved scheme, provided that they do not exceed the repayment amounts which would be allowed under an approved option scheme.[13]

[13] *Ibid*. para. 24.

INDEX TO VOLUME I

[*References are to paragraph numbers*]